CITE THIS BOOK AS:

Business and Commercial Litigation
in Federal Courts § ____ (Robert L. Haig ed.)
(West Group & ABA 1998)

BUSINESS AND COMMERCIAL LITIGATION IN FEDERAL COURTS

Volume 1

ROBERT L. HAIG

Editor-in-Chief

Chapters 1 to 15

AB\ American Bar Association
Section of Litigation

ST. PAUL, MINN.
West Group
1998

BUSINESS AND COMMERCIAL LITIGATION IN FEDERAL COURTS FORMS ON DISK™

The **Forms on Disk**™ which accompany these volumes provide instant access to Corel® WordPerfect® 5.1 versions of the forms and jury instructions included in *Business and Commercial Litigation in Federal Courts*. These electronic forms will save you hours of time drafting legal documents. The electronic forms can be loaded into your word processing software and formatted to match the document style of your law firm. These electronic forms become templates for you to use over and over without having to retype them each time.

The forms and jury instructions in Volumes 1 through 6 that are included on the accompanying disks are marked with the following disk icon for easy identification. 🖫

The views expressed herein are not necessarily those of the
American Bar Association or its Sections.

AUTHORS

AUTHORS

AUTHORS

CHAPTER 28
SETTLEMENTS

by

Charles E. Patterson, Esq.
Bruce A. Ericson, Esq.
Pillsbury Madison & Sutro LLP

CHAPTER 29
JURY SELECTION

by

Hon. David Hittner
United States District Judge
Southern District of Texas
Eric J.R. Nichols, Esq.
Beck, Redden & Secrest

CHAPTER 30
MOTIONS IN LIMINE

by

Anton R. Valukas, Esq.
William A. Von Hoene, Jr., Esq.
Thomas S. O' Neill, Esq.
Jenner & Block

CHAPTER 31
TRIALS

by

John J. Curtin, Jr., Esq.
John R. Snyder, Esq.
Bingham Dana LLP

CHAPTER 32
OPENING STATEMENTS

by

David M. Brodsky, Esq.
Schulte Roth & Zabel LLP

CHAPTER 33
PRESENTATION OF THE CASE IN CHIEF

by

Frank Rothman, Esq.
William P. Frank, Esq.
Jay S. Berke, Esq.
Skadden, Arps, Slate, Meagher
& Flom LLP

CHAPTER 34
CROSS–EXAMINATION

by

Edward L. Foote, Esq.
Winston & Strawn

CHAPTER 35
EXPERT WITNESSES

by

Barry F. McNeil, Esq.
Noel M.B. Hensley, Esq.
Haynes and Boone

CHAPTER 36
EVIDENCE

by

George A. Davidson, Esq.
William R. Maguire, Esq.
Hughes Hubbard & Reed LLP

CHAPTER 37
FINAL ARGUMENTS IN JURY AND
BENCH TRIALS

by

Robert S. Warren, Esq.
Robert E. Cooper, Esq.
Thomas E. Holliday, Esq.
Gibson, Dunn & Crutcher LLP

CHAPTER 38
JURY CONDUCT, INSTRUCTIONS AND
VERDICTS

by

Hon. James G. Carr
United States District Judge
Northern District of Ohio
G. Marc Whitehead, Esq.
McDermott, Will & Emery

CHAPTER 39
COMPENSATORY DAMAGES

by

Benjamin R. Civiletti, Esq.
David W. Goewey, Esq.
Venable, Baetjer and Howard, L.L.P.

CHAPTER 40
PUNITIVE DAMAGES

by

Andrew L. Frey, Esq.
Evan M. Tager, Esq.
Mayer, Brown & Platt

CHAPTER 41
SPECIFIC PERFORMANCE AND
RESCISSION

by

Michael D. Goldman, Esq.
Potter, Anderson & Corroon

AUTHORS

CHAPTER 42
ALTERNATIVE DISPUTE RESOLUTION

by

Hon. Harold Baer, Jr.
United States District Judge
Southern District of New York

CHAPTER 43
TRIAL AND POST–TRIAL MOTIONS

by

Charles H. Dick, Jr., Esq.
Baker & McKenzie

CHAPTER 44
JUDGMENTS

by

Fredric C. Tausend, Esq.
David H. Binney, Esq.
Preston Gates and Ellis, LLP

CHAPTER 45
BANKRUPTCY CODE IMPACT ON CIVIL
LITIGATION IN THE FEDERAL COURTS

by

Lewis Kruger, Esq.
Brian M. Cogan, Esq.
Stroock & Stroock & Lavan LLP

CHAPTER 46
COURT-AWARDED ATTORNEYS' FEES

by

Hon. M. Margaret McKeown
United States Circuit Judge
Ninth Circuit
David J. Burman, Esq.
Perkins Coie

CHAPTER 47
COSTS AND DISBURSEMENTS

by

John H. McElhaney, Esq.
Locke Purnell Rain Harrell, P.C.

CHAPTER 48
SANCTIONS

by

Charles M. Shaffer, Jr., Esq.
Daniel J. King, Esq.
King & Spalding

CHAPTER 49

APPEALS TO THE COURTS OF APPEALS

by

Stephen Rackow Kaye, Esq.
Ronald S. Rauchberg, Esq.
Proskauer Rose LLP

CHAPTER 50
APPEALS TO THE SUPREME COURT

by

Kenneth S. Geller, Esq.
John J. Sullivan, Esq.
Alan E. Untereiner, Esq.
Mayer, Brown & Platt

CHAPTER 51
ENFORCEMENT OF JUDGMENTS

by

Carolyn B. Lamm, Esq.
White & Case

CHAPTER 52
ETHICAL ISSUES IN COMMERCIAL
CASES

by

Harry M. Reasoner, Esq.
Allan Van Fleet, Esq.
Edward A. Carr, Esq.
Vinson & Elkins, L.L.P.

CHAPTER 53
ANTITRUST

by

John H. Shenefield, Esq.
Peter E. Halle, Esq.
William E. Wallace, III, Esq.
Morgan, Lewis & Bockius LLP

CHAPTER 54
SECURITIES

by

Richard M. Phillips, Esq.
Jeffrey B. Maletta, Esq.
Kirkpatrick & Lockhart LLP

CHAPTER 55
PROFESSIONAL LIABILITY

by

Daniel F. Kolb, Esq.
Jerome G. Snider, Esq.
Davis Polk & Wardwell

CHAPTER 56

FOREWORD

Business and Commercial Litigation in Federal Courts is unique in four respects: its extraordinary author team; its focus on business and commercial litigation; its pervasive emphasis on the strategic issues and options that determine success or failure; and its inclusion of federal practice and procedure, substantive law, and litigation tactics and techniques, all in one package.

This set is designed to fill a significant void in the legal literature with a sophisticated work that captures the insights and expertise of the finest litigators in the United States. By utilizing the talents of those noted for their special skills in handling particular kinds of commercial litigation as well as those noted litigators whose practice includes a variety of commercial cases, *Business and Commercial Litigation in Federal Courts* serves as a blueprint for effective litigation.

The Section of Litigation of the American Bar Association has sponsored and inspired this publication. A select group of highly experienced attorneys and judges was invited to author chapters. More than 700 volunteered. As many as 122 offered to write a single chapter and 50-75 volunteered for many of the others. This remarkable willingness to respond when called upon to help reflects the affection and high esteem in which the Section is held by its members.

This publication was written by distinguished federal judges and the cream of the commercial litigation bar, the best lawyers practicing in the federal courts of this nation. They come from all parts of the United States and are diverse in their particular expertise; nevertheless, all were united in their commitment to share with lawyers everywhere the secrets of their craft that distinguish the truly outstanding members of our profession. As a result, this publication is a goldmine of insights and advice about the dynamics of commercial litigation and how to apply expert lawyering skills and techniques to the specific case at hand to achieve client objectives. The size, scope, depth and sophistication of the chapters attest to the generosity of these renowned authors. Despite the press of business and other commitments, the 152 authors of this set completed their chapters on schedule, enabling completion of this monumental six volume, 7,000 page work within one year after the solicitation of authors. The Section of Litigation and commercial litigators everywhere owe them a debt of gratitude. We are grateful as well to their law firms, many of the finest firms in the country, for the extensive support and resources they provided. Thus, this work reflects the efforts and significant contributions of many hundreds of talented lawyers and their staffs.

I particularly thank the federal judges who have graciously shared their valuable time and have given us the invaluable perspective of the bench. They include Judges Harold Baer, Jr., James G. Carr, Warren W. Eginton, David Hittner, William C. Lee, M. Margaret McKeown, Solomon Oliver, Jr., Randall R. Rader and Roger Vinson. I thank as well two particularly distinguished former federal judges, Marvin E. Frankel and Frederick B. Lacey.

The enthusiasm of the American Bar Association and of the Section of Litigation for this project is reflected in the generous participation of its leadership. Authors who are former Presidents of the American Bar Association include N. Lee Cooper, John J. Curtin, Jr., and Robert D. Raven. Authors who are former Chairs of the Section of Litigation include (in addition to Messrs. Cooper and Curtin) Paul J. Bschorr, Benjamin R. Civiletti, Barry F. McNeil, Robert N. Sayler and Barbara M.G. Lynn, the Section's Chair-Elect. We are particularly pleased to have been joined in this venture by those who have rendered distinguished public service to this country including Warren Christopher and Benjamin R. Civiletti.

Business and Commercial Litigation in Federal Courts is a unique contribution to legal literature. There are other books on federal practice and procedure but no other publication focuses on business and commercial litigation. Business litigation is typically more complex than other kinds of litigation. It often involves technical, arcane subjects unfamiliar to many lawyers and most certainly to jurors, complex issues and subtleties as well as ramifications that may extend far beyond any particular lawsuit. It frequently presents complex arrangements of parties and law firms, often in different jurisdictions and requiring application of the law of additional jurisdictions, voluminous documents, sometimes numbering into the millions, large amounts of money and sometimes even the viability of major companies hang in the balance. Furthermore, federal courts are not the place to learn as you go, by trial and error. The magnitude of the cases in dispute causes judges and clients alike to expect from all participants commensurate knowledge and skill. Unlike many other forms of litigation, commercial litigation is largely at the behest of corporate clients. Corporate America increasingly and justifiably demands high quality, strategically focused and cost effective litigation from the lawyers who do battle on its behalf. *Business and Commercial Litigation in Federal Courts* can help meet these needs.

Practitioners have heretofore had to apply general principles of law and practice to the special challenges of commercial litigation. Now readers can be guided by a work that does not oversimplify but which specifically and candidly confronts the opportunities, problems and pitfalls of commercial litigation and supplies strategies and solutions. Authors were continually challenged to share their insights into the issues and problems that worried them most about their cases—that woke them up at night during trials. This work is permeated with these innermost thoughts.

Although many commercial litigators specialize in particular fields, many other commercial litigators handle cases in a variety of substantive areas. Deft handling of diverse litigation requires mastery of substantive law but also understanding of the application of litigation strategies and techniques to those substantive areas. For that reason this publication includes 28 chapters covering the kinds of business and commercial litigation most commonly encountered in federal courts written by litigators chosen to author those chapters because of their special expertise in those fields. Each such chapter guides the reader step by step with a nuts and bolts exposition on the law, procedure and practice in the field including delineation and achievement of objectives; the first considerations in assessing a case and how to proceed; the factors that would influence choice of strategy; steps to advance or secure the positions of both plaintiff and defense; the information necessary to planning trial or settlement strategy; characteristic problems and their solutions; issues to raise with clients; and considerations regarding discovery, motion practice, expert and lay witnesses, trial preparation, trials, and other matters that are unique to the field of law under discussion.

Business and Commercial Litigation in Federal Courts is a self-contained library with everything needed to handle a commercial case. It was painstakingly designed to provide readers with rapid access to this wealth of information. In addition to text on law, procedure and litigation strategies, special features include procedural and practice checklists, checklists of essential allegations and defenses, checklists of sources of proof of essential allegations and defenses, cross references from checklists to text, litigation forms and jury charges. The format makes the information equally accessible and useful for the commercial litigator when he needs an immediate answer as when he has the luxury of several hours to read and learn at leisure. Special finding tools include tables of contents, as well as tables of sections, cases (including the full citations of the 25,000 cases cited), statutes, rules, forms and jury instructions. The forms and jury charges are also contained on computer disks that accompany this set so that they may be easily adapted for particular cases.

This publication is a joint endeavor of the Section of Litigation and West Group. All royalties from this publication go to the Section of Litigation.

Marilyn Minzer of the West Group deserves our special thanks for her extraordinary efforts. She worked closely with me and with the authors in every facet and stage of this project. Her commitment to excellence has been a source of inspiration. It is no exaggeration to say that this worthwhile project could not have been completed without her diligence, expertise and guidance.

I feel privileged to have served as Editor-in-Chief of this publication. In that role I reviewed and commented on the chapters of all of the authors. Throughout I was impressed by the creativity of this magnificent team of volunteer litigators and judges. Their accumulated wisdom made this an educational experience for me far beyond what I could have hoped for. In the best traditions of our profession, our authors have created a significant work which will be a lasting credit to the Section of Litigation. I am grateful for the opportunity to have participated.

ROBERT L. HAIG

June 1998

*

ABOUT THE EDITOR-IN-CHIEF

Robert L. Haig is a partner in the law firm of Kelley Drye & Warren LLP in New York City. His practice includes commercial, products liability, and other types of civil litigation in federal and state trial and appellate courts. He graduated from Yale College and from the Harvard Law School.

Mr. Haig was the President of the New York County Lawyers' Association from 1992 to 1994. He was a member of the New York State Bar Association's Executive Committee from 1991 to 1994. He was the founder and first Chair of that Association's Commercial and Federal Litigation Section and also chaired its Committee on Federal Courts. Mr. Haig was the Chair of the Committee on the Judiciary of the Association of the Bar of the City of New York from 1989 to 1992 and currently chairs that Association's Council on Judicial Administration. He is a member of the House of Delegates of the American Bar Association, a Director of the Committee for Modern Courts, a Fellow of both the American Bar Foundation and the New York Bar Foundation, and a member of the Departmental Disciplinary Committee of the Appellate Division, First Judicial Department.

In February, 1995, Chief Judge of the State of New York Judith S. Kaye and Chief Administrative Judge E. Leo Milonas established a Commercial Courts Task Force to create a Commercial Division of the Supreme Court of the State of New York. The Co-Chairs of that Task Force are Mr. Haig and Judge Milonas.

Mr. Haig has written and lectured extensively on various litigation topics. He is the Editor-in-Chief of a three volume, 3,600 page book, published by the West Publishing Company in 1995, entitled *Commercial Litigation in New York State Courts.* He is the principal author of the *Corporate Counsel's Guide,* published by the New York State Bar Association as well as of numerous articles and book chapters. Mr. Haig is a member of the Board of Editors of Matthew Bender & Co., Inc.'s *Federal Litigation Guide Reporter.* He is also a member of the Board of Advisers to Business Laws, Inc.'s *Law Department Management Adviser.*

In 1991, Mr. Haig became the only New York lawyer to receive the Award For Excellence in Continuing Legal Education from the Association of Continuing Legal Education Administrators. On May 7, 1995, the New York State Bar Association's Commercial and Federal Litigation Section presented Mr. Haig with the Section's first annual Robert L. Haig Award for Distinguished Public Service. The Section has named this Award after Mr. Haig, and presents it in his name each year.

*

ABOUT THE AUTHORS

Robert B. Acomb, Jr. (Chapter 56, *Admiralty*) earned his Bachelor of Business Administration in 1951 and his Doctor of Jurisprudence in 1953, both from Tulane University. He was admitted to the Bar in 1953. He has been elected a Fellow of both the American College of Trial Lawyers and the American Bar Foundation.

While in law school, he was elected to the Board of Editors of the *Tulane Law Review* and the Omicron Delta Kappa National Honorary Society.

Mr. Acomb is a senior partner in the New Orleans firm of Jones, Walker, Waechter, Poitevent, Carrère & Denègre L.L.P. Since 1969 he has been an Adjunct Professor at Tulane School of Law. His professional activities have included membership in the Orleans, Louisiana, and American Bar Associations; the Maritime Law Association of the United States; Chairman of the ABA Standing Committee on Admiralty and Maritime Law, 1978-84; Chairman of the Maritime Committee of the Tort and Insurance Practice Section of the ABA, 1984; the Fifth Circuit Lawyers Advisory Committee; and Chairman of the Average Adjusters Association of the United States in 1993. He has lectured at numerous seminars in the United States and abroad and is the author of the casebook *Maritime Personal Injury and Death* (4th ed. 1997); and the casebook *Collision and Limitation of Liability* (1997).

James R. Adams (Chapter 74, *Sale of Goods*) is a partner at Frost & Jacobs LLP who practices complex business, commercial, accounting malpractice and securities class action litigation. Mr. Adams is also experienced in a number of additional areas including general unfair competition, defense of legal malpractice claims, and general commercial contract disputes.

Mr. Adams received his A.B. from Denison University and his J.D. from Northwestern University School of Law. Mr. Adams has been involved in a number of large, complex multi-party, multi-fora class action cases, including the Beverly Hills Fire Litigation, the Chem-Dyne Litigation, and the Home State Savings Bank Litigation. He was co-trial counsel for Joseph Cardinal Bernardin in the notorious case alleging sexual abuse by the Cardinal. He has served as chief trial counsel for the Cincinnati Reds in various cases, including the defense of the Reds in a "primary facility" antitrust case. Mr. Adams has also represented Big 6 accounting firms in several securities fraud and accounting malpractice cases. He has authored several articles on litigation and has served as Adjunct Professor at Chase College of Law and the University of Cincinnati College of Law. Mr. Adams has served on numerous civic and charitable boards as a member and officer, and resides in the Riverside Drive Historic District in Covington, Kentucky.

ABOUT THE AUTHORS

Samuel Adams (Chapter 14, *Parties*) is a partner with Warner & Stackpole LLP in Boston, where he represents corporations involved in products liability matters and general commercial litigation. He is a graduate of Harvard College (A.B. 1950) and Harvard Law School (LL.B. 1952).

Prior to joining the firm, Mr. Adams served as the chief of the antitrust division of the Massachusetts Attorney General's Office and as a Special Assistant Attorney General for the Commonwealth of Massachusetts. In 1973, the Governor of Massachusetts appointed Mr. Adams a justice of the Superior Court, the state's highest trial court, where he served for nine years before returning to Warner & Stackpole LLP.

A fellow of the American College of Trial Lawyers, Mr. Adams has served as a member of its Board of Regents. He also is a member of the Federation of Insurance and Corporate Counsel. Mr. Adams is admitted to practice in Massachusetts, and before the Supreme Court, the United States Court of Appeals for the First Circuit, and the United States District Court for the District of Massachusetts.

Professor Martin J. Adelman (Chapter 63, *Patents*) has been a Professor of Law at Wayne State University Law School since 1973. Before assuming his present position, Professor Adelman practiced as a patent attorney in the Detroit area for several years. During that period he served as lead counsel in several patent infringement actions. Currently, he is teaching a course on international and comparative patent law and a seminar covering advanced aspects of patent law and practice. He has written many law review articles on patent law and patent-antitrust law. From 1977 to 1988 he was one of the co-authors of the eight volume treatise on patent law entitled *Patent Law Perspectives* published by Matthew Bender. Since 1988 he has been solely responsible for writing the updates as well as the new materials for each of the eight volumes. He has also testified in court or had his deposition taken as an expert in patent law and practice in over 130 patent infringement cases.

Professor Adelman has published many articles and given many speeches on patent related subjects. Professor Adelman will spend the 1998-99 academic year as a Visiting Professor of Law at George Washington University's National Law Center.

Mark H. Alcott (Chapter 73, *Theft or Loss of Business Opportunties*) is a senior partner in the litigation department of Paul, Weiss, Rifkind, Wharton & Garrison in New York City. He has extensive experience handling a wide range of major commercial cases in federal courts throughout the United States.

Mr. Alcott is a Fellow of the American College of Trial Lawyers and served two terms as Chairman of the Downstate New York Committee of the College. He also served as Chair of the New York State Bar Association's Commercial and Federal Litigation Section. He chaired the Section's task force which proposed the creation of a state-wide commercial court, and then served on the committee established by the Chief Judge to implement that proposal. He has chaired and served on numerous other major professional committees and groups. By designation of the Chief Judge of the United States District Court, Southern District of New York, he has served for many years as a federal mediator pursuant to that court's Mandatory Mediation Program. He is also a mediator in the Commercial Division of the New York State Supreme Court, and a member of the Commercial Division's ADR Advisory Council. Mr. Alcott was selected for listing in *The Best Lawyers in America 1997-98* (as well as prior editions) for excellence in business litigation, and in the *Guide to the World's Leading Competition and Antitrust Lawyers,* on the basis of extensive peer review. An honors graduate of Harvard College and Harvard Law School, he has written and lectured extensively, in the United States and abroad, on commercial litigation issues.

William F. Alderman (Chapter 24, *Motion Practice*) is a litigation partner in the San Francisco office of Orrick, Herrington & Sutcliffe LLP. He graduated from Yale Law School in 1970 after receiving an A.B. *summa cum laude* from Miami University. His principal practice area is securities class actions in federal and state courts throughout the country, where he represents issuers, underwriters, professionals and individuals and has won ten initial motions to dismiss in succession. He also resolves technology, intellectual property, insurance coverage, employee benefits and antitrust disputes.

Mr. Alderman regularly writes and speaks on securities law topics and is Co-Editor of the *Securities Reform Act Litigation Reporter.* He is a court-appointed evaluator, mediator and arbitrator in the Northern District of California's ADR Program, and has been a frequent lecturer and moot court judge at Bay Area law schools. His career-long commitment to *pro bono* representation won him the 1996 Robert J. Sproul, Jr. Award presented by the Lawyers Committee for Civil Rights of the San Francisco Bay Area. He is a director of both the Lawyers Committee for Civil Rights and the San Francisco Neighborhood Legal Assistance Foundation and a past President and director of the St. Thomas More Society of San Francisco.

Glen K. Allen (Chapter 5, *The Complaint*) is Of Counsel at Piper & Marbury L.L.P. Mr. Allen's practice consists primarily of surety and insurance defense, complex commercial litigation, representation of media in defamation matters, and securities fraud defense. His practice has had a significant international aspect, including cases involving housing construction in Russia and the enforcement of an international forum selection provision. He has also represented plaintiffs in civil rights litigation and the defendant in a prisoner's right case heard before the United States Supreme Court.

Mr. Allen is admitted to practice before the Court of Appeals of Maryland, the United States District Court for the District of Maryland, the United States Court of Appeals for the Fourth Circuit, and the United States Supreme Court. He received his J.D. from the University of Maryland in 1987, and was a law clerk to Chief Judge Robert C. Murphy of the Court of Appeals of Maryland in 1987-88.

ABOUT THE AUTHORS

John L. Amabile (Chapter 72, *Warranties*) is a commercial and corporate litigator at Putney, Twombly, Hall & Hirson in New York City. He has had over 38 years of experience in state and federal courts throughout the country. Mr. Amabile has also lectured extensively with the Practicing Law Institute and the New York County Lawyers' Association on the art and science of litigation. He is the author of a chapter entitled *"Responses to Complaints"* in *Commercial Litigation in New York State Courts* (Haig ed.) (West 1995 & Supp. 1998).

Mr. Amabile has been active on various committees of the Association of the Bar of the City of New York, chairing its Committees on State Legislation and on Gender Bias in the Federal Courts. He serves as a Mediator for the United States District Court for the Southern District of New York and for the Commercial Division of the New York State Supreme Court, and as an Arbitrator for the United States District Court for the Eastern District of New York. Mr. Amabile had chaired a Hearing Panel for the Disciplinary Committee of New York's Appellate Division for the First Judicial Department, for over 14 years. He is also a member of the American and New York State Bar Associations and of the Federal Bar Council.

Mr. Amabile is a graduate of the College of the Holy Cross and of St. John's University School of Law where he was Articles Editor of the Law Review.

James J. Arguin (Chapter 14, *Parties*) of Warner & Stackpole LLP concentrates his practice in the area of complex commercial litigation, including specifically a broad-based familiarity with the law of business torts. Representative cases include the litigation of commercial contract disputes, commercial lending actions, shareholder derivative suits, corporate freeze outs/buy-outs and breaches of fiduciary duties, particularly as such claims arise in the context of close corporations. Additionally, Mr. Arguin has represented both individual and corporate clients in litigation arising from the termination of the employment relationship, including the defense of employment discrimination and wrongful discharge claims, as well as claims related to the scope and enforceability of restrictions on competition, such as covenants not to compete and confidentiality agreements.

Prior to joining Warner & Stackpole LLP, Mr. Arguin served as a Judicial Clerk with the Honorable Walter Jay Skinner of the United States District Court for the District of Massachusetts, as well as a Special Assistant United States Attorney with the Criminal Division of the Office of the United States Attorney for the Northern District of California. He is a member of the American, Massachusetts and Boston Bar Associations, and is admitted to practice in all state and federal courts within the Commonwealth of Massachusetts.

Arthur H. Aufses, III (Chapter 21, *Interrogatories*) is a partner in Kramer, Levin, Naftalis & Frankel, where he specializes in complex commercial litigation. He has handled securities fraud, RICO, professional malpractice, product warranty, and lender liability claims, as well as real estate and partnership disputes, and bankruptcy litigation. He represents financial advisors on a range of issues, and he has written and lectured on the subject of investment banker liability.

Mr. Aufses is a graduate of Harvard Law School (*cum laude,* 1980), Oxford University (B. Phil., 1975), and Yale University (B.A., *magna cum laude,* 1973). From 1980-81, he clerked for Judge José Cabranes, in the United States District Court for the District of Connecticut. He is a member of the Board of Editors of *Litigation,* the journal of the Litigation Section of the American Bar Association, and is a member of the Executive Committee on the Federal Courts of the New York County Lawyers' Association. He often teaches trial advocacy and litigation practice for the Practicing Law Institute and the National Institute for Trial Advocacy. His articles on legal issues have appeared in *Insights, Litigation, Federal Litigation Guide Reporter, Law and Contemporary Problems, Case & Comment, Legal Times,* and the *Delaware Journal of Corporate Law.*

Wayne E. Babler, Jr. (Chapter 10, *Joinder, Consolidation, and Severance*) is a litigation partner in Quarles & Brady, located in Milwaukee, Wisconsin. He is head of the firm's Intellectual Property Litigation Section. An honors graduate of the University of Wisconsin Law School, J.D. 1967, he was Order of the Coif and Research Editor of the *Wisconsin Law Review.* Mr. Babler is a Fellow of the American College of Trial Lawyers and a Fellow of the American Bar Foundation. He is a past President of the Milwaukee Bar Association and Wisconsin Bar Foundation, he served on the Board of Governors of the State Bar of Wisconsin, and he served in the House of Delegates of the American Bar Association from 1984-96. He currently serves on the Board of Directors of the Legal Aid Society of Milwaukee, Inc. Other professional memberships include the Wisconsin Academy of Trial Lawyers, National Conference of Bar Presidents, and National Institute of Trial Advocacy.

Mr. Babler has concentrated his practice in the area of business litigation for the past 25 years. This has included matters in antitrust, trade regulation, advertising, unfair competition, employment agreements, secrecy and noncompetition covenants, distribution agreements, dealerships, trademarks and trade names, copyrights and patents. He has also served as an expert witness, and he has participated in publications of the Antitrust Section of the ABA including its Monograph 9, *Refusals to Deal and Exclusive Distributorship,* and its *Antitrust Law Developments Second Supplement.*

W. Reece Bader (Chapter 24, *Motion Practice*) is a litigation partner with Orrick, Herrington & Sutcliffe LLP in Menlo Park, California. He received his B.A. in 1963 from Williams College, and his J.D. in 1966 from Duke University School of Law, and clerked for the Honorable Warren E. Burger on the United States Court of Appeals, D.C. Circuit from 1966-68.

Mr. Bader has concentrated his practice in the area of securities and futures litigation since 1970. He has extensive federal and state experience, including jury and non-jury trial work in securities, commodities and public finance litigation. He also handles appellate matters and has represented the Securities Industry Association as amicus curiae in securities litigation. He has acted as lead defense counsel in complex class actions involving initial public offerings and derivative suits, both on behalf of underwriters, companies and officers and directors. He also regularly represents broker-dealers and individuals in both SEC and SRO enforcement actions. As a complement to this practice he assists the firm's Public Finance Department in litigation concerning municipal securities.

He is a former member of the Advisory Committee on Civil Rules, U.S. Judicial Conference, past Co-Chair of the Securities Litigation Committee and current Co-Chair of the ADR Committee of the ABA's Litigation Section, and a frequent author and lecturer on issues pertinent to federal litigation.

The Honorable Harold Baer, Jr. (Chapter 42, *Alternative Dispute Resolution*) is a United States District Court Judge and sits in the Southern District of New York. He resigned from the New York State Supreme Court in 1992 after serving in that capacity for 10 years. For two years before his induction as a District Court Judge, he was the Executive Judicial Officer at JAMS/Endispute where he supervised and did dispute resolution work. Prior to his election to the Supreme Court, he was for a decade in charge of litigation in a Wall Street law firm. He was Assistant United States Attorney and headed the Organized Crime and Racketeering Unit of that office in the 1960s; he returned as First Assistant U.S. Attorney and Chief of the Criminal Division in 1970. Judge Baer served on the Mollen Commission, a Special Unit of the New York State Commission of Investigation and the State Commission on the Governmental Operations of the City of New York. He has been active in the New York State, City and County Bar Associations, chairing committees at each. He was a founder of the Network of Bar Leaders and President of the New York County Lawyers' Association. In addition to hundreds of published opinions, he has written extensively on legal topics, with some 50 books, pamphlets and articles to his credit. He graduated, *magna cum laude* and Phi Beta Kappa, from Hobart College and from the Yale Law School in 1957.

R. Franklin Balotti (Chapter 61, *Collections*) is a member of the Wilmington, Delaware firm of Richards, Layton & Finger, P.A. He earned his B.A. from Hamilton College in 1964 and his LL.B. from Cornell University School of Law in 1967. Mr. Balotti is a member of the American Bar Association Sections of Business Law (and currently a member of its Council), Litigation and International Law & Practice, the Delaware State Bar Association, the Colorado Bar Association, the Board of Directors of the Delaware Bar Foundation, the Cornell Law School Advisory Council, the Board of Overseers of Widener University School of Law and the American Law Institute; Chair of the Delaware Supreme Court Committee on Family Court Internal Operating Procedures; Fellow of the American College of Trial Lawyers; and Fellow of the American Bar Foundation. Mr. Balotti has served as Chair of the Committee on Business and Corporate Litigation and Co-Chair of the Committee on Business Courts of the Business Law Section of the American Bar Association and President, President-Elect, Vice-President, Secretary and Member of the Executive Committee of the Delaware State Bar Association. He has served as Chair of the Delaware State Board of Bar Examiners and Chair of the Board on the Unauthorized Practice of Law of the Supreme Court of Delaware. Mr. Balotti was Adjunct Professor at the Widener University School of Law from 1991-93 and 1995, Distinguished Practitioner-in-Residence at Cornell Law School in the Fall of 1996 and Visiting Distinguished Corporate Professor, University of Miami School of Law for the Spring 1998 semester. Mr. Balotti has co-authored/co-edited numerous publications, including *The Delaware Law of Corporations and Business Organizations* (3d ed. 1998) and *Meetings of Stockholders* (3d ed. 1998).

Garrard R. Beeney (Chapter 16, *Derivative Actions by Stockholders*) is a partner in the New York office of Sullivan & Cromwell. He graduated from Swarthmore College in 1976 and in 1979 *cum laude* from the University of Pennsylvania Law School where he was the winner of the Keedy Cup moot court competition. Mr. Beeney has a general litigation practice, and has litigated and tried state and federal cases throughout the country involving topics such as corporate governance and derivative cases, class actions, antitrust and competition torts, and intellectual property. His practice includes appellate work, including a recent successful argument in the United States Supreme Court.

Mr. Beeney has taught on various aspects of litigation at the University of Pennsylvania Law School, Benjamin N. Cardozo Law School, and is a faculty member of the National Institute for Trial Advocacy. He also has frequently lectured on the topic of derivative actions. He lives with his wife and two daughters in Irvington, New York where he currently serves as Deputy Mayor and a member of the Board of Trustees.

Mark A. Belnick (Chapter 57, *Contracts*) is a senior partner of Paul, Weiss, Rifkind, Wharton & Garrison specializing in litigation. A Fellow of the American College of Trial Lawyers, Mr. Belnick has extensive experience in major federal and state cases involving a broad range of issues. In 1987, Mr. Belnick served as Deputy Chief Counsel to the U.S. Senate Iran-Contra Committee. In 1995, Mr. Belnick served as Chief Counsel to the NASD Select Committee on Structure and Governance, which recommended major reforms (approved by the SEC) to the NASD and Nasdaq stock market. Mr. Belnick graduated *cum laude* from Cornell University (A.B. 1968) and received the J.D. degree from the Columbia University Law School (1971), where he was a Harlan Fiske Stone Scholar. Mr. Belnick has been an Adjunct Professor of Law at the Benjamin N. Cardozo Law School, and has served as Chairman of the Subcommittees on Grand Jury Reform Legislation and Foreign Intelligence Reform Legislation of the Association of the Bar of the City of New York. He is a member of the Board of Visitors of Columbia Law School and of the Advisory Council to Cornell University's College of Arts and Sciences. Mr. Belnick is also a member of the Federal Civil Procedures

Committee and the Downstate Committee of the American College of Trial Lawyers.

Jay S. Berke (Chapter 33, *Presentation of the Case in Chief*) is Special Counsel in the New York office of Skadden, Arps, Slate, Meagher & Flom LLP. Mr. Berke has concentrated on labor and employment law and related litigation; class actions in the areas of civil rights, employment discrimination, and wage and hour; and cases and advice in the areas of occupational safety and health, wrongful termination, defamation, affirmative action and labor standards for government contractors. Prior to joining the firm in 1985, he worked with the Office of the Solicitor of the United States Department of Labor from 1971 to 1985, culminating with his tenure as Regional Solicitor covering the states of New York and New Jersey, the commonwealth of Puerto Rico and the Virgin Islands. As the Labor Department's chief legal officer in the region, Mr. Berke was responsible for the litigation and enforcement of a broad range of labor laws.

Mr. Berke has appeared as a featured panel speaker in conferences on wage and hour issues, employment defamation and workplace privacy, occupational safety and health, and equal opportunity, sponsored by such organizations as Cornell University, The Bureau of National Affairs, The California Business Law Institute and the *San Juan Star*. He has also written several articles in the field of labor and employment law.

David H. Binney (Chapter 44, *Judgments*) a partner at Preston Gates and Ellis, LLP, is a graduate of Harvard College (B.A., 1974) and the University of Michigan Law School (J.D., 1977). He practices general civil litigation with an emphasis on complex cases. His areas of experience include patent, copyright and trademark litigation, antitrust litigation, federal and state securities litigation, and professional liability (architects, engineers, lawyers). Among the cases he has been involved in are *Optiva Corp. v. Teledyne Industries* (W.D. Wash.) (patent infringement and trade secret misappropriation), *Microsoft adv. Apple* (N.D. Cal.) and *In re WPPSS Securities Litigation* (W.D. Wash. and D. Ariz.). Mr. Binney is active in the American Bar Association Section of Litigation, where he is a member of the Intellectual Property and Computer Litigation Committees. He has trial experience in state and federal courts around the country, as well as in numerous arbitrations and mediations.

John J. Broders (Chapter 56, *Admiralty*) is a senior partner in the law firm of Jones, Walker, Waechter, Poitevent, Carrère & Denègre L.L.P. He received his Bachelors of Arts and Juris Doctor from Tulane University. He joined Jones, Walker as an associate in 1971. He became a partner of the firm in 1976. He is a member of The Maritime Law Association of the United States, serving on the Marine Finance Committee since 1980 and the Marine Insurance, General Average and Salvage Committee since 1978. He is also a member of the Association of Average Adjusters of the United States; Association of Transportation Practitioners and the Southeastern Admiralty Law Institute.

He has presented papers at numerous meetings and seminars in the areas of marine financing, enforcement of maritime liens and marine insurance.

Frederick A. Brodie (Chapter 68, *ERISA*) is a partner at Winthrop, Stimson, Putnam & Roberts, where his practice includes ERISA cases and a broad spectrum of other civil litigation. He graduated *magna cum laude* from Brown University, where he was elected to Phi Beta Kappa, and from Yale Law School, where he was Executive Editor of the *Yale Journal on Regulation*. Before joining Winthrop Stimson in 1989, Mr. Brodie clerked for Judge Joseph L. Tauro of the United States District Court of the District of Massachusetts and the Honorable Bruce M. Selya of the United States Court of Appeals for the First Circuit.

Mr. Brodie is Associate Editor of the book *ERISA Fiduciary Law* (BNA Books 1995) and has published articles on ERISA litigation issues in several professional journals. He also co-authored Chapter 59 on *"Theft or Loss of Business Opportunities"* in the treatise *Commercial Litigation in New York State Courts* (Haig ed.) (West 1995 & Supp. 1998).

David M. Brodsky (Chapter 32, *Opening Statements*) is a partner in the law firm of Schulte Roth & Zabel LLP and is Chair of its Litigation Department. An active trial lawyer, he specializes in corporate, securities, white collar criminal, and regulatory disputes. He also conducts corporate internal investigations arising out of alleged fraudulent activity or other significant corporate events. He serves as an arbitrator as well as a court-designated mediator in state and federal court corporate and commercial disputes.

Mr. Brodsky, a graduate of Brown University and Harvard Law School, served as Law Clerk to Federal District Judge Dudley B. Bonsal, and then served as Assistant United States Attorney in the Southern District of New York. He also served as Associate Independent Counsel in the Matter of Michael K. Deaver.

Mr. Brodsky currently serves as Co-Chair of the Annual Meeting of the ABA Section of Litigation and as a Member of the Task Force on the Jury System. He formerly served as Co-Chair of the Committee on Trial Practice and as a Member of the Task Force on Insider Trading Regulation.

Mr. Brodsky is co-author of a one-volume desk treatise entitled *Federal Securities Litigation: Commentary and Forms,* and is the author of *"Judgments"* in *Commercial Litigation in New York State Courts* (Haig ed.) (West 1995 & Supp. 1998).

Mr. Brodsky is a member of the American Law Institute and a Fellow of the American College of Trial Lawyers.

James E. Brown (Chapter 12, *Issue and Claim Preclusion*) is a member of Cozen and O'Connor in its Philadelphia office. Mr. Brown is a graduate of Franklin & Marshall College and Temple University School of Law. He was an Editor on the Law Review. His practice focuses on commercial litigation with particular emphasis on complex insurance coverage disputes. He is admitted to practice in Pennsylvania and New Jersey.

Paul J. Bschorr (Chapter 18, *Discovery Strategy and Privileges*) a partner in the Litigation Department of Dewey Ballantine LLP in New York, is a 1962 graduate of Yale University, where he received a B.A. in Political Science, and a 1965 *cum laude* graduate of the University of Pennsylvania Law School, where he was a Case Editor on the Law Review. Mr. Bschorr's litigation practice is in the area of general commercial litigation, including securities, class and derivative actions, banking, fiduciary, business torts, lender liability, insurance coverage, and sovereign immunity. Mr. Bschorr is a former Chair of the Litigation Section of the American Bar Association and is a Fellow of the American College of Trial Lawyers where he currently serves as a member of the Downstate New York Committee and the International Law Committee. He is also a Fellow of the American Bar Foundation, a member of the American Law Institute, and a member of the New York Panel of the CPR Institute for Dispute Resolution. In addition, he is a member of the New York State and District of Columbia Bar Associations and the Association of the Bar of the City of New York. He continues to be an active member of various ABA, state and local bar association committees and has published a number of articles on, among other things, foreign sovereign immunity, extraterritorial discovery, the attorney-client privilege, and foreign banking secrecy. He is a frequent speaker on various continuing legal education programs and has served as an arbitrator and mediator on a number of matters.

Francis B. Burch, Jr. (Chapter 5, *The Complaint*) is the Chairman of Piper & Marbury L.L.P., where he practices in the areas of securities, corporate and commercial litigation. He received his J.D. from the University of Maryland School of Law (with Honors, Order of the Coif) in 1974 and his B.A. from Georgetown University in 1970. He attended the University of Fribourg, Switzerland, in 1968-69.

Mr. Burch taught Advanced Business Law at The Johns Hopkins University from 1978-83 and has lectured and written extensively on state and federal practice and procedure and on product liability and securities litigation.

Mr. Burch serves on the Boards of Johns Hopkins Medicine, the Greater Baltimore Committee, The Baltimore Museum of Art, Dome Corporation, Western Maryland College, the University of Maryland School of Law, and Calvert School in Baltimore.

Mr. Burch is a Fellow of the American College of Trial Lawyers and of the American and Maryland Bar Foundations, a Member of the American Law Institute a Permanent Member of the Judicial Conference of the United States Court of Appeals for the Fourth Circuit, and is listed in *The Best Lawyers in America, Marquis Who's Who in American Law, Who's Who in America* and *Who's Who in the World*.

David J. Burman (Chapter 46, *Court-Awarded Attorneys' Fees*) is Chair of the Litigation Department of Perkins Coie and has a litigation practice with emphasis on antitrust and trade regulation, intellectual property, constitutional and public law, class actions, and other complex commercial litigation. He graduated from the University of Wyoming (1974) and Georgetown University (1977), where he was Editor-in-Chief of the *Georgetown Law Journal.* He clerked for Judge Spottswood W. Robinson, III, United States Court of Appeals for the District of Columbia Circuit, and the Honorable Byron R. White.

Mr. Burman is listed in *The Best Lawyers in America* (antitrust, business litigation, First Amendment) and *Puget Sound Business Journal, Who's Who of Seattle Lawyers.* He is a frequent author and lecturer on antitrust, intellectual property, and constitutional law issues.

Peter Buscemi (Chapter 15, *Class Actions*) is a partner in the Litigation Section of Morgan, Lewis & Bockius LLP, resident in the Washington, D.C. office. He has had extensive experience in a variety of civil litigation, including litigation in the U.S. Supreme Court. He currently serves as chair of the appellate practice group at Morgan, Lewis.

Immediately after law school, Mr. Buscemi served as a law clerk to Judge Carl McGowan of the U.S. Court of Appeals for the D.C. Circuit. Thereafter, he served for four years as an Assistant to the Solicitor General in the U.S. Department of Justice. For several months during that period, he worked as a Special Assistant U.S. Attorney in the Eastern District of Virginia.

Mr. Buscemi entered private practice in 1981, following his work at the Justice Department. He joined Morgan, Lewis & Bockius LLP in 1986 and became a partner in 1987. While at Morgan, Lewis, Mr. Buscemi has engaged in a wide variety of civil litigation. He has had considerable experience in various aspects of business litigation, including constitutional litigation, antitrust litigation, products liability cases, securities cases, employee benefits litigation, and general commercial disputes.

Mr. Buscemi obtained his undergraduate education at Columbia (B.A. 1969), did graduate work at Princeton (M.A. 1971), and received his law degree from Columbia in 1976. He served as Writing and Research Editor of the *Columbia Law Review* during 1975-76. He was a James Kent Scholar in 1973-74, and a Harlan Fiske Stone Scholar in 1974-75 and 1975-76. During his final year in law school, Mr. Buscemi served as a teaching assistant for then Professor, now Justice, Ruth Bader Ginsburg. Mr. Buscemi currently is a member of the Columbia Law School Board of Visitors and a member of the Board of Directors of the Columbia Law Review Association.

Mr. Buscemi is a member of the American Bar Association's Litigation Section, Administrative Law Section, Antitrust Section, and Criminal Law Section. Since 1995, Mr. Buscemi has served as Co-Chair of the Amicus Curiae Briefs Committee of the ABA Litigation Section. He also is a member of the Litigation Section, the Criminal Law Section, and the Courts, Lawyers and Administration of Justice Section of the District of Columbia Bar Association.

ABOUT THE AUTHORS

John M. Callagy (Chapter 76, *Torts of Competition*) is a Partner and Chairman of Kelley Drye & Warren LLP. He is resident in the New York office. Mr. Callagy is a graduate of Georgetown University and the Root Tilden Program at the New York University School of Law. He is admitted to practice in the States of New York and Connecticut.

Mr. Callagy's extensive litigation background encompasses all aspects of legal issues that affect large international corporate entities: securities, antitrust, unfair competition, indemnity insurance coverage, product liability, intellectual property, contract, employee benefits, labor and personnel, and trade libel.

Edward A. Carr (Chapter 52, *Ethical Issues in Commercial Cases*) is a partner in the Houston Office of Vinson & Elkins L.L.P. His practice emphasizes commercial litigation and legal ethics. He serves as an advisor to Vinson & Elkins' Professional Responsibility Committee, and has authored or co-authored law review articles on legal ethics issues raised by antitrust audits, legal opinions, and multijurisdictional litigation practice. He graduated from Stanford University, B.A., with honors and distinction in 1984, and the University of California at Los Angeles, J.D. in 1987, where he served on the Editorial Board of the *UCLA Law Review*.

The Honorable James G. Carr (Chapter 38, *Jury Conduct, Instructions and Verdicts*) United States District Judge for the Northern District of Ohio, is a graduate of Kenyon College and Harvard Law School. Following his graduation from law school, he was admitted to practice in Illinois, where he practiced law for four years before joining the faculty of the College of Law at the University of Toledo, in 1970. He was appointed as a United States Magistrate Judge in 1979, serving in that position until appointed by President Clinton to his present position in May, 1994. Judge Carr is the author of several books and articles, including a treatise, *The Law of Electronic Surveillance,* published by the West Group, other books on criminal law and procedure and juvenile law, and articles on those topics, and, as well, on civil practice and procedure.

Warren Christopher (Chapter 17, *Litigating International Disputes in Federal Courts*) is the Senior Partner of O'Melveny & Myers LLP. He was the 63rd United States Secretary of State, from 1993 to 1997. Earlier he was Deputy Secretary of State (1977-81), and Deputy Attorney General of the United States (1967-69). Mr. Christopher is a graduate of the University of Southern California (1944) and Stanford Law School (1949), where he was President of the Law Review. Thereafter he was law clerk to Justice William O. Douglas of the United States Supreme Court. Mr. Christopher rejoined O'Melveny & Myers as the firm's Senior Partner on February 1, 1997. His professional activities since his return to the firm in 1997 have involved consultations on a wide variety of international matters, as well as negotiation and advice to clients relating to sensitive disputes.

Frank Cicero, Jr. (Chapter 2, *Personal Jurisdiction and Service*) is a senior partner with the firm of Kirkland & Ellis, Chicago, Illinois. He is a litigation specialist with extensive experience in a wide variety of litigation matters in federal and state trial and appellate courts and in arbitrations. Among the types of cases Frank has tried are: accountants', architects' and attorneys' professional malpractice, admiralty and maritime law, criminal and civil securities law, commercial contracts, construction litigation, libel, slander, and First Amendment cases, tax disputes, antitrust, trade regulation, trade secrets, unfair competition, employment contracts, pollution and toxic substance cases, international arbitrations and litigation, dealer and franchise relationships and terminations, divorce and domestic relations law, product liability and warranty claims. He has tried numerous jury trials, numerous bench trials and arbitrations, and handled numerous appeals.

Benjamin R. Civiletti (Chapter 39, *Compensatory Damages*), Mr. Civiletti is Chairman of Venable, Baetjer and Howard, L.L.P. Before becoming firm Chairman in 1993, he served as Partner-in-Charge of Venable's Washington, D.C. office and then Managing Partner of the firm.

Mr. Civiletti served as Attorney General of the United States from 1979 to 1980.

Mr. Civiletti concentrates in the areas of antitrust, banking, white-collar crime, government regulation, corporate governance, and health law. In addition to trying major cases throughout the country, Mr. Civiletti has developed a significant Alternative Dispute Resolution practice. He has worked successfully as a mediator, facilitator, master and arbitrator in various disputes in order to achieve faster and more cost efficient justice.

Mr. Civiletti received an LL.B. in 1961 from the University of Maryland School of Law, an A.B. from The Johns Hopkins University in 1957 and he has received many honorary awards and degrees.

Brian M. Cogan (Chapter 45, *Bankruptcy Code Impact on Civil Litigation in the Federal Courts*) is a partner in the New York office of the firm of Stroock & Stroock & Lavan LLP. He has a general litigation practice with experience in trials and appeals in state and federal courts. His practice has focused on insolvency litigation, financial fraud, and creditors' rights and remedies, particularly in the international context.

Mr. Cogan has regularly represented both companies and trustees, liquidators, and other fiduciaries in major reorganization and liquidation proceedings. He has served as lead litigation counsel for the Creditors' Committee of Wedtech Corp. in one of the most publicized liquidations of a defense contractor of the 1980s, resulting from a massive fraud upon creditors and the investing public, which turned on complex accounting issues. Mr. Cogan also has represented the Department of Trade and Industry (U.K.). The proceedings he brought resulted in the recovery of millions of dollars, which had been raised in a fraudulent investment scheme in Europe and invested in the United States. Mr. Cogan has also represented a publicly held English company in attempting to recover over $100 million taken from it by the late Robert Maxwell. Most recently, he has been representing the liquidators of an international bank in an action involving hundreds of millions of dollars in damages.

Mr. Cogan is a 1979 graduate of The Cornell Law School, where he was an Editor of the Law Review, and where he received the Gustavus Hill Robinson Moot Court Award, with honorarium, for best third-year argument. He is a frequent author and lecturer on civil and trial practice topics.

James E. Coleman, Jr. (Chapter 22, *Requests for Admissions*) is a partner and founding member of the Dallas, Texas law firm of Carrington, Coleman, Sloman & Blumenthal, L.L.P. Mr. Coleman attended the Georgia Institute of Technology (B.S., 1948) and the University of Virginia (LL.B., 1951). He was Member of the Board of Editors of the *Virginia Law Review* from 1950-51. He presently serves on the Board of Trustees of the University of Virginia Law School Foundation.

Mr. Coleman is actively involved in numerous professional organizations including the National Institute for Trial Advocacy, where he was Chairman of the Board of Trustees from 1991-93, and where he has served on the Board of Directors since 1981. He is also a member of the American Law Institute; the American College of Trial Lawyers; the Southwestern Legal Foundation (Research Fellow, 1976 to present, Board of Trustees, 1979 to present, Chairman, 1995 to present). In the Dallas Bar Association, Mr. Coleman served as Vice President in 1965, and Secretary-Treasurer in 1972. For the American Bar Association, he was a member of the Council of the Litigation Section from 1973-75 and Director of that Section from 1975-81. In the State Bar of Texas, he was Chairman of the Antitrust Section from 1977-78 and served on the Board of Directors from 1988-91. He is a member of the American Board of Trial Advocates (President Dallas Chapter 1976-77), and a Fellow in the American Bar Foundation and the Texas Bar Foundation.

John F. Collins (Chapter 18, *Discovery Strategy and Privileges*) is a partner in the Litigation Department of Dewey Ballantine LLP in New York, received his Juris Doctor degree from The University of Chicago Law School in 1973 and his Bachelor of Arts degree in Political Science, with honors, from Fordham University in 1970, where he was elected to Phi Beta Kappa. Mr. Collins has advised and represented clients in the following practice areas, among others: antitrust, arbitration, class and derivative actions, complex commercial matters, corporate governance, intellectual property, mergers and acquisitions, and securities. Throughout the years, he has also actively lectured on some of these areas at various American Bar Association, ALI-ABA, and Law Journal Seminars programs. He has also served as Assistant Editor of the *Antitrust Law Journal* and *Annual Review of Antitrust Law Developments* published by the Antitrust Section of the American Bar Association. Mr. Collins is a member of the American Bar Association, the New York State Bar Association and the Association of the Bar of the City of New York and has served on committees and on publications for these organizations.

N. Lee Cooper (Chapter 23, *Selection of Experts, Expert Disclosure and the Pretrial Exclusion of Expert Testimony*) is a Founder of Maynard, Cooper & Gale, P.C., in Birmingham, Alabama. Mr. Cooper's primary area of practice is in complex commercial cases. The major emphasis of his practice has been the defense of securities litigation throughout the Southeast for major investment bankers such as Merrill Lynch, Dean Witter, and Salomon Smith Barney, as well as numerous Fortune 100 companies.

Mr. Cooper was President of the American Bar Association from August 1996–August 1997 and was a Founder and Chair of the Litigation Section. He has been Director of the American Bar Endowment since 1984 as well as serving as Chair of the Investment Committee. He is a member of the Board of the Central & Eastern European Law Initiative (CEELI), an organization which aids former Communist block countries to promote the rule of law by developing constitutions appropriate to their status as modern democracies. Mr. Cooper also serves on the Board of the Lawyers Committee on Civil Rights and the Council of the American Law Institute.

Mr. Cooper graduated from the University of Alabama (B.S. 1963) where he was a member of Beta Gamma Sigma. He received his LL.B. in 1964 from the University of Alabama Law School, where he was Articles and Note Editor of the *Alabama Law Review*. Mr. Cooper has appeared on "News Hour with Jim Lehrer" and "NBC Nightly News with Tom Brokaw" and has authored several editorial pieces for *USA Today, Christian Science Monitor, Wall Street Journal* and others. At the appointment of Chief Justice William H. Rehnquist he serves as Vice-Chair of the Congressional Commission on Structural Alternatives for the Federal Courts of Appeals.

Robert E. Cooper (Chapter 37, *Final Arguments in Jury and Bench Trials*) is a partner in Gibson, Dunn & Crutcher's Los Angeles office and a member of the Executive Committee. A member of the firm's Litigation Department, Mr. Cooper joined the firm in 1964, and specializes in antitrust and business tort litigation.

Mr. Cooper received his bachelor of arts degree with distinction from Northwestern University in 1961. He earned his law degree from Yale University in 1964, where he was a member of the Order of the Coif and Article and Book Review Editor of the *Yale Law Journal*. Mr. Cooper is a Fellow of the American College of Trial Lawyers, and is a frequent lecturer on the antitrust laws and trial of complex litigation.

Mr. Cooper has served as trial counsel in many civil jury trials, including a number of major antitrust and patent cases.

Frederick L. Cottrell, III (Chapter 61, *Collections*) is a Director in the Wilmington, Delaware law firm of Richards, Layton & Finger, P.A. where he concentrates his practice in general litigation including intellectual property, products liability, real estate and commercial litigation. He received his B.A. degree in 1985 from the University of Delaware *magna cum laude* and his J.D. degree in 1988 from the Dickinson School of Law *cum laude*. Mr. Cottrell is Chairman of the Execution Process Subcommittee of the Real and Personal Property Section of the Delaware State Bar Association and Chairman of the Intellectual Property Law Section of the Association. He is also a member of the American and

Delaware State Bar Associations' Sections on Real and Personal Property, Intellectual Property and Litigation. Mr. Cottrell has lectured at many seminars on his fields of concentration.

Thomas Cummings (Chapter 75, *Bills and Notes*) is the principal of Thomas Cummings, P.C., a partner in the firm of Armstrong, Teasdale, Schlafly & Davis. He is a resident of the St. Louis office. He holds a B.S.B.A. in Finance from the University of Missouri, Columbia, 1967 and a J.D. from the University of Missouri, Columbia Law School, 1970. He was formerly General Counsel of County Tower Corporation, a multibank holding company. He has considerable litigation experience involving banking, financial institutions, securities, environmental and general commercial matters.

John J. Curtin, Jr. (Chapter 31, *Trials*) is Chairman of the Litigation area of Bingham Dana LLP. Mr. Curtin has served as President of the American Bar Association and Boston Bar Association and was Chairman of the Section of Litigation of the ABA. He has tried criminal and civil cases in many fields of law. He is presently a member of the House of Delegates of the American Bar Association. His government service includes a term as Trial Attorney in the Antitrust Division of the U.S. Department of Justice. He also served as an Assistant U.S. Attorney and Chief of the Civil Division of the U.S. Attorney's Office. He was Special Assistant to the Attorney General of Massachusetts in charge of the "Small Loans" appeals. He is a Fellow in the American College of Trial Lawyers.

Mr. Curtin is Chairman of the American Bar Association Coalition for Justice. He is Chairman of the Boston Bar Association Task Force for Professional Fulfillment. He is Chairman of Boston College Law School Board of Advisors. Mr. Curtin is an Executive Committee member of the Center for Public Resources.

Mr. Curtin has taught trial practice at Boston College Law School for more than 30 years and has taught Federal Courts and Antitrust Law. He has frequently published, lectured and given demonstrations on general litigation, antitrust and intellectual property matters. He is a recipient of the Justice William J. Brennan, Jr. Advocacy Award. In 1994, Mr. Curtin was the recipient of the Learned Hand Human Relations Award for leadership in the fields of advocacy, litigation and human rights on the local, state and national levels.

Mr. Curtin is a graduate of Boston College, Boston College Law School and Georgetown Law School and has many honorary degrees.

George A. Davidson (Chapter 36, *Evidence*), who chairs the Litigation Department at Hughes Hubbard & Reed LLP, has a national trial and appellate practice. He is a graduate of Brown University (1964) and a *magna cum laude* graduate of Columbia University School of Law (1967), where he was an Editor of the Law Review. He served as law clerk to Judge Paul R. Hays of the U.S. Court of Appeals for the Second Circuit. His practice is diverse, extending from securities fraud, accountant's liability, international financial fraud, and trust and indenture trustee law, to First Amendment Freedom of Association law, gender equity, and college and university law. He has written on commodities trading, attorney-client privilege, employment discrimination, and Title IX, and has lectured on international litigation, class actions, recovery of cultural artifacts, and college athletics, in a variety of domestic and international venues, including Switzerland, France, Mexico and South Africa. He is a Fellow of the American College of Trial Lawyers, a member of the American Law Institute, and a past President of the Legal Aid Society.

Gary W. Davis (Chapter 79, *Energy*) is the Chairman of the Board and a director of the law firm of Crowe & Dunlevy in Oklahoma City, Oklahoma, and also serves as the chair of the firm's Oil and Gas Department. His practice emphasizes litigation in the areas of oil and gas, environmental, medical malpractice and commercial law. Mr. Davis has served in numerous leadership roles, including director of the American Petroleum Institute and the National Petroleum Refiners Association. He has also been a member of the Governor's Special Advisory Commission on Oil and Gas and is a member of the Oklahoma Mineral Lawyers' Society. Mr. Davis has authored numerous oil and gas articles and has lectured on trial tactics at the University of Oklahoma College of Law. He is listed in *The Best Lawyers in America* (Business Litigation and Natural Resources Law). Mr. Davis received his Bachelor's and Juris Doctor degrees from the University of Kansas.

Paul H. Dawes (Chapter 13, *Provisional Remedies*) (J.D., University of Wisconsin, 1970; B.A., University of Michigan, 1967), is a partner in the Silicon Valley office of Latham & Watkins. Mr. Dawes is national chairperson of the firm's Litigation Department, which consists of approximately 250 lawyers. His practice focuses upon complex business litigation, including securities litigation, intellectual property disputes and regulatory authority investigations, domestic and international arbitrations and meditations.

Mr. Dawes was a member of the Council of the American Bar Association's Litigation Section, is currently Co-Chair of the Section's Business Torts Committee, and is a member and former Chair of the ABA's Committee on Corporate Counsel. He is a member of the American Law Institute, the Co-Editor of *Corporate Compliance Series,* Clark, Boardman and Callahan (1993), serves on the editorial advisory board of James Publishing, Inc. He also serves on the Federal Courts Committee of the California State Bar Association and the San Francisco Bar Association's Securities Litigation Committee. He has been an active lecturer on litigation programs sponsored by the Practicing Law Institute, the California Continuing Education of the Bar, Prentice Hall-Law and Business, the Association of Business Trial Lawyers, the Directors' Roundtable and the American Bar Association. Mr. Dawes served as a law clerk to Chief Judge David N. Edelstein, United States District Court for the Southern District of New York, in 1970-72.

Charles H. Dick, Jr. (Chapter 43, *Trial and Post-Trial Motions*) is a partner with the San Diego office of Baker & McKenzie. He received his law degree from the University of Iowa, College of Law (J.D., *cum laude,* 1967) where he was Managing Editor of the Iowa Law Review from 1966-67, and a member of Phi Beta Kappa, Omicron Delta Kappa, Order of the Coif, and Phi Delta Phi. He received his undergraduate degree from the State University of Iowa (B.A., *cum laude,* 1964). Mr. Dick was admitted to the bar in Iowa and Illinois in 1967 and the U. S. Supreme Court and California bars in 1977. Mr. Dick is a member of the San Diego County and American (Section on Tort and Insurance Practice, 1979–; Section of Litigation, 1975–) Bar Associations and The State Bar of California.

Mr. Dick is a Fellow, American College of Trial Lawyers, and he serves as a Member of the Southern California governing committee of the College. He is an Associate, American Board of Trial Advocates, and he currently is the Secretary of the San Diego Chapter. Mr. Dick is an elected Diplomate, American Board of Professional Liability Attorneys, and he has been elected a Member, International Association of Defense Counsel. He is a Master, Louis Welsh American Inn of Court; a Founding Director, Association of Business Trial Lawyers, San Diego; a Member of the Defense Research Institute. Mr. Dick has served as a lawyer delegate to the Ninth Circuit Judicial Conference and as a member of the Standing Committee on Lawyer Discipline for the Southern District of California; he currently is the Chair of the Southern District's Merit Selection Committee for Judicial Appointments. A Pro-tem Judge for the San Diego Superior Court and a frequent lecturer on legal issues, Mr. Dick has taught trial techniques for The National Institute of Trial Advocacy.

Carol E. Dinkins (Chapter 80, *Environmental Claims*) is a partner in the firm of Vinson & Elkins L.L.P., where she is head of the environmental practice. She joined Vinson & Elkins in 1973 and was admitted to the partnership in 1980. In 1981 she was appointed United States Assistant Attorney General in charge of the Environment and Natural Resources Division. In 1984 she was appointed Deputy United States Attorney General, the second-ranking official in the Department of Justice. While Assistant Attorney General, Ms. Dinkins supervised the government's litigation in federal environmental, natural resources, and public lands matters. During her tenure, the Division implemented the Comprehensive Environmental Response, Compensation and Liability Act (also known as Superfund) and created the Environmental Crimes Section. She rejoined Vinson & Elkins L.L.P. in April 1985. Ms. Dinkins received her baccalaureate degree in 1968 from The University of Texas at Austin, and her law degree in 1971 from the University of Houston Law Center.

Ms. Dinkins is the Chair of the ABA Section on Natural Resources, Energy, and Environmental Law and a past Chair of the Section on State and Local Government Law, which she currently represents as a delegate to the ABA House of Delegates. She also is a member of the ABA Standing Committee on the Federal Judiciary and was recently elected to the Board of Editors of the ABA Journal. She chairs the board of the Texas

ABOUT THE AUTHORS

Chapter of The Nature Conservancy and is a member of the National Board of Governors of The Nature Conservancy. In 1997, Governor Bush appointed her as a Commissioner on the Texas Parks and Wildlife Commission. In March of 1998, the *National Law Journal* named her one of the Fifty Most Influential Women Lawyers in America.

Mitchell F. Dolin (Chapter 58, *Insurance*) is a partner at Covington & Burling in Washington, D.C., where he heads the firm's Arbitration and ADR Practice Group. He has litigated and arbitrated a wide range of complex civil matters, with a particular emphasis on representing corporate policyholders in disputes over insurance coverage, including coverage for mass tort and environmental liabilities, marine losses, and D&O claims. Mr. Dolin is a member of the American Law Institute, co-chairs the ABA Litigation Section's Task Force on the Judiciary, and serves on the Board of Directors of the Lawyers Committee for Human Rights. He is a graduate of Tufts University (1978) and New York University School of Law (1981) and clerked for Chief Judge Charles Clark of the U.S. Court of Appeals for the Fifth Circuit (1981-82).

John A. Donovan (Chapter 77, *Franchising*) is a partner in the Los Angeles office of Skadden, Arps, Slate, Meagher & Flom LLP. He is the leader of the firm's West Coast Litigation Practice. Mr. Donovan obtained his undergraduate degree from Harvard University and his J.D. from the Fordham University School of Law, where he was Articles Editor of the *Fordham Law Review*. He has written and lectured on franchising subjects, including for the American Bar Association Annual Forum on Franchising.

Mr. Donovan's practice concentrates in franchising, antitrust, entertainment law and securities litigation. He counsels and represents in franchise litigation many national and international franchisors.

Richard E. Donovan (Chapter 76, *Torts of Competition*) is a partner in the New York office of Kelley Drye & Warren LLP, where he heads the Antitrust and Trade Regulation Practice Group. He has practiced in this field for over 20 years. He speaks and writes frequently on antitrust, white collar crime, and trade regulation topics. He authored the chapter on *"Antitrust Litigation"* in *Commercial Litigation in New York State Courts* (Haig ed.) (West 1995 & Supp. 1998). Mr. Donovan is a member of the Section of Antitrust Law and Section of Litigation of the American Bar Association, the Antitrust Law Committee of the New Jersey State Bar Association, the New York State Bar Association (former Secretary of the Commercial and Federal Litigation Section), the Association of the Bar of the City of New York (member of the Committee on Professional and Judicial Ethics), and the Federal Bar Council. He is also a Fellow of the American Bar Foundation.

Mr. Donovan is a graduate of the University of Notre Dame (1974) and the Rutgers University School of Law (1977), where he served on the Law Review Editorial Board.

The Honorable Warren W. Eginton (Chapter 70, *Products Liability*) was appointed United States District Judge for the District of Connecticut on August 1, 1979. He is a graduate of Princeton University, receiving a B.A. degree in 1948, and of Yale Law School, receiving a J.D. degree in 1951.

Judge Eginton, prior to his appointment, was a member of the firm of Cummings & Lockwood of Stamford, Connecticut, where he specialized in products liability litigation. From 1988-93 he was Editor-in-Chief of the *Product Liability Law Journal* published by Butterworth Legal Publishers, and authored several papers dealing with aspects of products liability. Before becoming a judge, he was a founding member of the Product Safety and Liability Prevention Technical Committee of the American Society for Quality Control and a member of the Products Liability Committee of the Defense Research Institute.

Judge Eginton is a member of the American Bar Foundation, the American Bar Association, the American Judicature Society, the Federal Bar Council, the Federal Bar Association, the Judiciary Leadership Development Council, and the Institute of Judicial Administration. As a member of the American Law Institute, he sits on the Members Consultative Group for the *Restatement of Torts (Third), Products Liability*.

Anna P. Engh (Chapter 58, *Insurance*) is a partner at Covington & Burling in Washington, D.C., where she has practiced since 1990. She has litigated a wide range of civil matters, including the representation of corporate policyholders in disputes over insurance coverage. She is a Member of the Task Force on Discovery for the ABA's Litigation Section. She is a graduate of Davidson College (1981) and William and Mary Law School (1989), and clerked for Judge John D. Butzner of the United States Court of Appeals for the Fourth Circuit.

Bruce A. Ericson, (Chapter 28, *Settlements*) is a partner of Pillsbury Madison & Sutro LLP, resident in its San Francisco office. Mr. Ericson specializes in antitrust, banking and securities litigation. Mr. Ericson represented the FHLBB, the FSLIC and the OTS in the investigation of Charles Keating, American Continental Corporation and Lincoln Savings and Loan Association. Along with partner Charles Patterson, Mr. Ericson represented the RTC in an action against the former officers, directors, shareholders and auditors of Southwest Savings (Phoenix, Arizona), including the sitting governor of Arizona, which resulted in settlements totaling $15.3 million. Mr. Ericson also represented the RTC in a mediation against a Big 6 accounting firm, obtaining a seven-figure settlement. Mr. Ericson (along with Charles Patterson and others) represented the RTC in its investigation of potential claims against directors, officers, shareholders, lawyers and others associated with Madison Guaranty S&LA of Arkansas. Mr. Ericson had principal responsibility for the Whitewater and Rose Law Firm portions of the investigation. As part of the investigation, Mr. Ericson interviewed First Lady Hillary Rodham Clinton at the White House and testified before the Senate Special Committee to Investigate Whitewater and Related Matters, chaired by Senator Alfonse D'Amato. Mr. Ericson is a graduate of the University of Pennsylvania (A.B., 1974) and Harvard Law School (J.D., 1977).

ABOUT THE AUTHORS

H. Robert Fiebach (Chapter 12, *Issue and Claim Preclusion*) is a senior member of Cozen and O'Connor in its Philadelphia office, 1900 Market Street, Philadelphia, Pennsylvania, where he co-chairs the Commercial Litigation Department. He is a *cum laude* graduate of the University Pennsylvania Law School, where he served as Research Editor of the Law Review. He is a member of the Order of the Coif.

Mr. Fiebach is a Fellow of the American College of Trial Lawyers, a Life Fellow of the American Bar Foundation, serves on the ABA Board of Governors, and is a past President of the Pennsylvania Bar Association and a past Chair of the ABA Standing Committee on Lawyers Professional Liability. Mr. Fiebach has more than 30 years of experience in the litigation of commercial and business matters in the federal and state courts.

Kathleen V. Fisher (Chapter 9, *Arbitration vs. Litigation: Enforceability and Access to Courts*) is a partner in the San Francisco office of Morrison & Foerster LLP. From 1988 to 1991, Ms. Fisher was the Managing Partner of the firm's San Francisco office and was the national Chair of the firm's Litigation Department from 1993 to 1996. She received her B.A. degree from the University of California, Los Angeles in 1971, *cum laude,* and her J.D. degree from the law school of the University of California, Davis in 1976, Order of the Coif.

Edward L. Foote (Chapter 34, *Cross-Examination*) is a managing partner of Winston & Strawn where he was Head of Litigation from 1968-92. A graduate of Harvard College (1952) and Harvard Law School (1955) Mr. Foote has more than 35 years of trial experience and specializes in jury trials, including commercial, criminal, products liability and patent cases. He is a member of the American College of Trial Lawyers and the International Academy of Trial Lawyers.

William P. Frank (Chapter 33, *Presentation of the Case in Chief*) is a partner in the New York office of Skadden, Arps, Slate, Meagher & Flom LLP where he is the national litigation legal practice leader and a member of the firm's Policy Committee. He represents major corporations, investment banking firms and individuals at both the trial and appellate levels. Mr. Frank has concentrated on commercial, securities, fraud and RICO cases, as well as class actions and derivative suits; takeover cases and proxy contests; and SEC proceedings and investigations.

Mr. Frank is a frequent panelist on seminars regarding securities laws, and federal and state litigation sponsored by the American and New York State Bar Associations and the Practising Law Institute. He is a Trustee of the Federal Bar Council.

The Honorable Marvin E. Frankel (Chapter 21, *Interrogatories*) was admitted to the Bar in 1949. Has covered the gamut of things lawyers do. Assistant to the U.S. Solicitor General (1952-56), briefing and arguing cases in the U.S. Supreme Court; Professor of Law at Columbia (1962-65); U.S. District Judge for the Southern District of New York for 13 years (1965-78); author of several books and numerous articles on law and related subjects. Head of the Litigation Department of Kramer, Levin, Naftalis & Frankel. Has argued over 20 cases in the U.S. Supreme Court, scores of others in various U.S. Courts of Appeals, and a substantial number in the appellate courts of New York and other States. In addition, he has handled a substantial number of cases in the trial courts. He has been involved extensively in alternative forms of dispute resolution, mainly arbitration and mediation, both as an advocate and as arbitrator or mediator.

Andrew L. Frey (Chapter 40, *Punitive Damages*) is a partner in the firm of Mayer, Brown & Platt, specializing in appellate and Supreme Court litigation. He is currently resident in the firm's New York office. Mr. Frey has argued more than 60 cases before the U.S. Supreme Court and numerous cases before state supreme courts and federal courts of appeals. His U.S. Supreme Court appearances include three cases raising constitutional challenges to large punitive damages judgments. Most notable among the latter is *BMW of North Am., Inc. v. Gore,* in which the Supreme Court held for the first time that a punitive damages award was unconstitutionally excessive.

Mr. Frey received his B.A. in 1959 from Swarthmore College and his law degree in 1962 from the Columbia University Law School, where he was first in his class. After clerking for Judge George T. Washington of the D.C. Circuit and serving two years as Special Counsel to the Governor of the U.S. Virgin Islands, Mr. Frey engaged in private law practice in Washington, D.C. until 1972. He then joined the Office of the Solicitor General, which represents the federal government before the Supreme Court. From 1973 to 1986, he served as Deputy Solicitor General, having principal responsibility for the government's criminal cases in the Supreme Court. He joined Mayer, Brown & Platt in 1986. Mr. Frey is a member of the American Law Institute and the American Academy of Appellate Lawyers.

Kenneth S. Geller (Chapter 50, *Appeals to the Supreme Court*) is a partner in the Washington, D.C. office of Mayer, Brown & Platt specializing in Supreme Court and appellate litigation. Mr. Geller, the managing partner of Mayer, Brown's Washington office, is a former Deputy Solicitor General of the United States who has argued approximately 40 cases in the Supreme Court. He is the co-author (along with Robert Stern, Eugene Gressman, and Stephen Shapiro) of the leading treatise on Supreme Court litigation, entitled *Supreme Court Practice* (7th ed. 1993). He received his J.D. *magna cum laude* from Harvard Law School in 1971, where he was an Editor on the *Harvard Law Review.* He also served as an Assistant Special Prosecutor on the Watergate Special Prosecution Force and a law clerk to Judge Walter Mansfield of the U.S. Court of Appeals for the Second Circuit.

Richard M. Goehler (Chapter 74, *Sale of Goods*) is Chairman of the Litigation Department of Frost & Jacobs LLP. His practice is concentrated in the areas of media law and general commercial and business litigation. He represents media clients in prepublication/prebroadcast review matters, defense of defamation and invasion of privacy claims, and in access to public records and meetings disputes. He also regularly represents the firm's corporate and business clients in a wide variety of commercial litigation matters. Mr. Goehler is a charter member of the Special Defense Counsel Section of the Libel Defense Resource Center. He has co-authored the chapter on *"Ohio Libel and Privacy Law"* for the annual *LDRC 50-State Survey* since 1982. He is active as a member of various professional committees, including the American Bar Association's Forum Committee on Communications Law, its Committee on Media Litigation, and the Ohio State Bar Association Media Law & Communications Committee. He has lectured frequently at the OSBA's annual Law & Media Conference and has been an adjunct faculty member at Miami University, teaching business law and mass media law. Mr. Goehler is an active member of the National Institute for Trial Advocacy Associates and he has participated in a number of NITA seminars. He is a member of the Potter Stewart American Inn of Court.

Mr. Goehler received his A.B. from Miami University and his J.D. from the University of Notre Dame Law School. He has been active in a number of local civic and community projects and regularly participates in local scholarship fundraising events for the Miami University and Notre Dame Alumni Associations.

David W. Goewey (Chapter 39, *Compensatory Damages*) is a litigation partner resident in Venable's Washington, D.C. office. Mr. Goewey received his J.D. in 1987 from the College of William and Mary, where he served as an Executive Editor of the *William & Mary Law Review*. He received a B.A. from the University of Virginia in 1984.

Michael D. Goldman (Chapter 41, *Specific Performance and Rescission*) specializes in corporate law and corporate litigation at Potter, Anderson & Carroon, in Wilmington, Delaware. He is Past Chairman, Corporation Law Section, Delaware State Bar Association and the Board of Bar Examiners of The State of Delaware. He is a member of the ABA Committee on Corporate Laws which drafts the Model Act. Mr. Goldman is the author of articles for the *National Law Journal, New York Law Journal* and *Business Lawyer* and a lecturer at seminars on corporation law sponsored by the American Bar Association, Delaware Bar Association, Tulane University School of Law and Widener University School of Law.

Jimmy Goodman (Chapter 79, *Energy*) is a director of the law firm of Crowe & Dunlevy in Oklahoma City, Oklahoma. He focuses his practice in litigation, including banking, business, commercial, real estate, products liability defense and life and health insurance. He served from 1994 through 1997 on the Council of the Section of Litigation of the American Bar Association and as Co-Chair of its Task Force for the Minority Trial Lawyer, and previously served as Chair of its Task Force on Trial by Jury. He is the immediate past-President, current ABA Delegate and a director of the Oklahoma County Bar Association, and a former director of Legal Aid of Western Oklahoma. Mr. Goodman received his Bachelor's degree from the University of Oklahoma and his Juris

Doctor from Stanford Law School, where he was an Editor of the *Stanford Law Review*.

Frank N. Gundlach (Chapter 75, *Bills and Notes*) is the principal of Frank N. Gundlach, P.C., a partner in the firm of Armstrong, Teasdale, Schlafly & Davis. He is a resident of the St. Louis office. He is Co-Chair of the firm's Litigation Department, and is particularly active in product liability, commercial and transportation litigation. He has written and lectured locally and nationally on trial tactics and other litigation subjects. He is listed in the *The Best Lawyers in America* (Business Litigation and Personal Injury Litigation). He holds a B.A., Colgate University, 1960 and a J.D., Washington University Law School, 1963. Mr. Gundlach is a Fellow of the American College of Trial Lawyers and an Advocate of the American Board of Trial Advocates.

Thomas J. Hall (Chapter 60, *Letters of Credit*) is a partner in the New York office of the international law firm Chadbourne & Parke LLP. He specializes in complex commercial litigation, both in the United States and abroad, and has extensive experience in a broad range of commercial litigation matters, including securities, banking, contract, real estate, project finance and letter of credit disputes. He received his law degree from Fordham University School of Law in 1980, where he was Managing Editor of the *Fordham Law Review*.

Mr. Hall is a member of the American Bar Association's Commercial and Banking Litigation Committee and Committee on International Litigation. He is also a member of the New York State Bar Association's Litigation Section, and of the U.K.-based International Litigation Practitioners Forum, and a member of the Federal Bar Council and Real Estate Board of New York. He serves as a court-appointed Neutral Mediator in the Commercial Division of the New York State Supreme Court.

Peter E. Halle (Chapter 53, *Antitrust*) is a partner in the Antitrust and Trade Regulation Section of Morgan, Lewis & Bockius LLP in Washington, D.C. His practice focuses on antitrust counseling and litigation.

Mr. Halle also provides advice and counsel in state and federal criminal antitrust matters; and litigates false advertising claims before the Federal Trade Commission.

After graduating from New York University in 1967, Mr. Halle received his law degree, *cum laude,* from the University of Miami School of Law in 1973, where he was a Member and Associate Editor of the Law Review.

Following graduation, Mr. Halle was hired under the Attorney General's Program for Honor Law Graduates and served as a trial attorney with the Antitrust Division of the U.S. Department of Justice until 1980, when he became the Assistant Chief of the Antitrust Division's Trial Section. He also served as a Special Assistant in the Office of the Deputy Attorney General.

At the Justice Department, he handled both civil and criminal (white collar) litigation. During his tenure in the Antitrust Division he was active in antitrust matters in the telecommunications area, including service on the team that brought the *AT&T* case. He also was lead counsel on the first criminal case to bring maximum corporate penalties after violation of the Sherman Act became a felony. Mr. Halle entered private practice in 1981.

Active in professional organizations, Mr. Halle is a past Chair of the Antitrust Litigation Committee, the Health Law Litigation Committee and the Legislation Committee of the ABA's Litigation Section and a Life Fellow of the American Bar Foundation. He is a past Governor of the Bar Association of the District of Columbia.

Noel M.B. Hensley (Chapter 35, *Expert Witnesses*) is a Partner in the Business Litigation Department at Haynes and Boone, in Dallas, Texas; specializes in civil commercial litigation, securities litigation and corporate control and governance disputes. Graduated 1975 from the University of North Texas, B.S.; 1978 with J.D. *cum laude* at Southern Methodist University, serving as Editor of the *Southwestern Law Journal*. Clerked for the Honorable Robert W. Porter, United States District Judge, Northern District of Texas, Dallas Division from 1978 to 1980.

Member of the Litigation Section, American Bar Association, Derivative and Class Actions Subcommittees; has been a co-leader or instructor of various National Institute of Trial Advocacy-sponsored deposition and trial programs; instructor of trial advocacy at Southern Methodist University's School of Law; research fellow, member of Continuing Legal Education Advisory Board for the Southwestern Legal Foundation; fellow of Texas Bar Foundation; fellow of the Dallas Bar Foundation; member of the College of The State Bar of Texas; author/speaker for various programs sponsored by the State Bar of Texas, University of Houston, Southern Methodist University, SEC Institute, and Southwestern Legal Foundation.

The Honorable David Hittner (Chapter 29, *Jury Selection*) is a United States District Judge for the Southern District of Texas. He received his B.S. from New York University in 1961 and his J.D. from New York University School of Law in 1967 and is a member of the Texas and New York bars. Following law school, he entered the United States Army where he served as an Infantry Captain and Paratrooper. Following military service, he practiced as a trial attorney in Houston for 13 years, and in 1978 was appointed judge of the 133rd District Court by the Governor of Texas. He was subsequently re-elected twice to that bench. He was nominated as a United States District Judge by President Ronald Reagan and assumed the federal bench in July 1986. Among Judge Hittner's many recognitions are the Samuel E. Gates Award of the American College of Trial Lawyers, its highest national recognition for the improvement of the litigation process in the United States, and the Presidents' Award of the State Bar of Texas as the Outstanding Lawyer in Texas. He is a member of the American Law Institute, has published over 75 legal articles, including 10 law review articles, and is the author of a two-volume book, *Federal Civil Procedure Before Trial, Fifth Circuit*

Edition, published by The Rutter Group/West Group, 1997. Judge Hittner is a frequent lecturer throughout the United States and Canada.

Thomas E. Holliday (Chapter 37, *Final Arguments in Jury and Bench Trials*) is a partner in the Litigation Department in Gibson, Dunn & Crutcher LLP's Los Angeles office. He is also Co-Chair of the firm's Business Crimes and Investigations Practice Group. He received his undergraduate degree from Stanford, where he was elected Phi Beta Kappa, and his law degree from the University of Southern California, where he served as an Executive Editor of the Law Review and was elected to the Order of the Coif.

Mr. Holliday is a Fellow of the American College of Trial Lawyers and served as Deputy General Counsel for the Independent Commission on the Los Angeles Police Department (the "Christopher Commission"). In 1997, he received the Criminal Defense Lawyer of the Year Award from the Century City Bar Association. Mr. Holliday specializes in white collar criminal defense work and commercial fraud litigation. He has defended individual and corporate entities in a wide range of criminal and civil business fraud cases.

Stephen F. Humphreys (Chapter 23, *Selection of Experts, Expert Disclosure and the Pretrial Exclusion of Expert Testimony*) practices in the intellectual property section of Kilpatrick Stockton, LLP in Atlanta, Georgia. Humphreys graduated from Princeton University and the University of Georgia School of Law, *summa cum laude.* At Georgia, he was First Honor Graduate, as well as a member of the Order of the Coif and the Editorial Board of the *Georgia Law Review.*

Mr. Humphreys clerked for Chief Judge Sam C. Pointer, Jr. in the U.S. District Court for the Northern District of Alabama, and served as Special Assistant to U.S. Senator Wyche Fowler, Jr. Humphreys' service to the American Bar Association includes terms as Vice-Chair of the YLD Communications Committee, Chair of the YLD International Law Committee and Special Assistant to the President of the American Bar Association.

Robert Jeffrey Jossen (Chapter 64, *Trademark*) is Partner and Chairman of the Litigation Department at Shereff, Friedman, Hoffman & Goodman, LLP, a New York-based law firm with a national reputation in corporate, commercial and financial law. Mr. Jossen's practice includes commercial litigation, trademark litigation, securities and white collar criminal defense and legal ethics. Mr. Jossen is a Fellow of the American College of Trial Lawyers.

Prior to joining Shereff, Friedman in 1979, Mr. Jossen served as Chief Appellate Attorney in the United States Attorney's Office—Southern District of New York. He began working with the United States Attorney's Office in 1975 as an Assistant United States Attorney where he tried numerous cases while an Assistant in the Criminal Division.

Earlier, Mr. Jossen was an associate with the New York law firm Proskauer Rose Goetz & Mendelsohn. He began his career as a law clerk serving with the Honorable Marvin E. Frankel, U.S.D.J., of the Southern District of New York.

Mr. Jossen holds a J.D. from Columbia University School of Law and a B.S. from the New York State School of Industrial & Labor Relations at Cornell University.

Mr. Jossen has been an Adjunct Professor of Law at Columbia University School of Law, where he taught the required ethics course. He is also an Instructor for the National Institute of Trial Advocacy and has taught at Benjamin N. Cardozo Law School and the Rabbinical School of the Jewish Theological Seminary. Mr. Jossen has served as presenter and chairman at numerous programs of the Practicing Law Institute; and has lectured widely throughout the United States on trial practice and ethical issues.

Peter C. Karegeannes (Chapter 10, *Joinder, Consolidation, and Severance*) is a partner with Quarles & Brady in Milwaukee, Wisconsin where he is head of the firm's 70-lawyer Litigation Section. He is a graduate of Harvard University (B.A. 1969) and the University of Michigan (J.D. 1972). Mr. Kargeannes specializes in trying cases on behalf of plaintiffs and defendants on a national basis in a wide variety of complex business and commercial settings.

Stephen Rackow Kaye (Chapter 49, *Appeals to the Courts of Appeals*) is a senior partner and former Chair and Co-Chair of the 150 lawyer Litigation and Dispute Resolution Department of Proskauer Rose LLP. Practicing since his graduation with distinction from the Cornell Law School in 1956, he has been lead trial and appellate counsel in a number of high profile and many other complex commercial cases for corporate and major business clients in federal and state courts in New York and elsewhere in the United States, in administrative agencies and before domestic and international arbitral tribunals. He has argued many times in the Courts of Appeals for the Second Circuit and several other Circuits. Also, he has written extensively on a number of legal subjects and is the author of the nine chapter 500-page segment of the treatise *Commercial Litigation in New York State Courts* (Haig ed.) (West 1995 & Supp. 1998) that concerns the process, presentation, strategy and tactics of conducting jury and non-jury trials of commercial cases. Those chapters have been described by a judicial reviewer as a "complete legal work" which was "perhaps the best" that judge had ever read.

Douglas W. Kenyon (Chapter 65, *Copyright*) is a partner in the Trial Section of Hunton & Williams in Raleigh, North Carolina, where he heads the copyright and trademark components of the Firm's Intellectual Property Group, and also specializes in antitrust litigation. He is past Chair of the North Carolina Bar Association's Antitrust Law Section, and is a member of the American Bar Association's Antitrust, Intellectual Property, and Litigation Sections, The Copyright Society of the U.S.A., the International Trademark Association, and the America Law Institute. Mr. Kenyon has litigation experience in state and federal courts around the country, as well as in numerous arbitrations and mediations.

Mr. Kenyon also has authored many articles in the fields of antitrust and intellectual property. Mr. Kenyon graduated *cum laude* from the University of Notre Dame in 1976, and received his J.D. *cum laude* from Notre Dame Law School in 1979.

Louis B. Kimmelman (Chapter 17, *Litigating International Disputes in Federal Courts*) is a partner in the New York office of O'Melveny & Myers LLP, where he specializes in representing foreign and domestic clients in a broad range of international commercial and construction disputes pending in federal and state courts throughout the United States and in arbitration before the International Chamber of Commerce and the American Arbitration Association. He also serves as an arbitrator in commercial and construction cases and as a mediator in the mediation programs sponsored by the federal and state courts in Manhattan. Mr. Kimmelman is a graduate of Yale College (1972) and Yale Law School (1975) and served as a law clerk to Judge Leonard I. Garth of the U.S. Court of Appeals for the Third Circuit (1975-76).

Daniel J. King (Chapter 48, *Sanctions*) is a partner in King & Spalding's Atlanta and New York offices. He practices in the area of commercial litigation, with extensive experience in bankruptcy and financial litigation.

Prior to joining the Firm in 1985, he was a commercial litigator with the firm of Jenner & Block in Chicago, Illinois.

Mr. King has had significant litigation and trial experience in a wide range of commercial litigation and bankruptcy matters. An active member in the American Bar Association's Section of Litigation, Mr. King is a frequent speaker in areas of bankruptcy law and litigation and is a contributing author to the *ABA Bankruptcy Litigation Manual*.

Daniel F. Kolb (Chapter 55, *Professional Liability*) is a senior partner in the New York firm of Davis Polk & Wardwell, where he serves as practice coordinator for the firm's litigation department. A graduate of the University of Michigan Law School and a Fellow of the American College of Trial Lawyers, Mr. Kolb has extensive experience in major cases involving a broad range of litigation matters including many in which he has represented professional firms. Mr. Kolb has been admitted in both Federal Circuit and District Courts throughout the United States and has served as Chair of the Judiciary Committee of the Association of the Bar of the City of New York.

Lewis Kruger (Chapter 45, *Bankruptcy Code Impact on Civil Litigation in the Federal Courts*), a Senior Partner of Stroock & Stroock & Lavan LLP, is a member of the firm's Executive Committee, and has over 35 years of experience as an insolvency lawyer. He has played a major role in many of the significant reorganization proceedings in this country.

Mr. Kruger has acted as Special Counsel to the U.S. Senate Committee on the Judiciary with respect to reorganizations, as Special Counsel to the Governor of New York and the Urban Development Corporation and as Counsel to the New York State Energy Research and Development Authority. He has been lead counsel representing banks, financial institutions, debtors' and creditors' committees, including: Southmark Corporation, Zale Corporation, The McCall Pattern Company, Columbia Gas Systems, Anchor Glass Corporation, TipHook Finance, Continental Energy Associates, Sanders Technology, NuCorp Energy, Victor Technologies, Penn-Dixie Steel, Phoenix Steel, Neisner Brothers, Hillsborough Holdings, Western Union, Forstmann, Charter Medical, and Cabot, Cabot & Forbes.

Mr. Kruger taught corporate reorganization at Columbia Law School from 1972 to 1988, and is a frequent lecturer on bankruptcy in the United States and overseas. He is a fellow of the American College of Bankruptcy.

Mr. Kruger earned his LL.B. from Columbia Law School in 1959 and was awarded the Jerome Michael Cup. He earned his A.B. *cum laude* from Harvard University in 1956. Mr. Kruger is admitted to practice in New York (1959).

The Honorable Frederick B. Lacey (Chapter 26, *Magistrate Judges and Special Masters*) is a senior litigation partner at LeBoeuf, Lamb, Greene & MacRae, L.L.P., Newark, New Jersey and New York, New York. He served as United States District Court Judge for the District of New Jersey from 1971 to 1986. He was United States Attorney for the District of New Jersey from 1969 to 1971. He graduated from Rutgers University, Phi Beta Kappa and as an Honors Graduate, and from Cornell University Law School where he was a member of the Editorial Board of the Law Review, elected to the Order of the Coif honorary law society, and was an Honors Graduate. He was recommended by the American Bar Association Committee on Judicial Selections in February 1971 with an "exceptionally well-qualified" rating. From 1980-86, he was a Judge on the United States Temporary Emergency Court of Appeals and from 1979-85, he was a Judge on the United States Foreign Intelligence Surveillance Court. He was Chairman of the Supreme Court Advisory Committee on Federal Rules of Criminal Procedure from 1984-86, and a member of the Committee from 1979-88. From 1982-86, he was a member of the Judicial Ethics Committee, Judicial Conference of the United States. He was Chairman of the Executive Committee, National Conference of Federal Trial Judges from 1984-85, and a member of the Executive Committee from 1978-86. He was a Judicial Advisor for the 7th United Nations Congress on Crime in Milan, Italy in August and September 1985. He was an Invitee to the Canadian Judicial Conference in Winnipeg, Manitoba in July 1985. He became a Fellow of the American College of Trial Lawyers in 1991. He was appointed as Independent Administrator by United States District Judge David N. Edelstein to oversee the International Brotherhood of Teamsters matters under the Consent Decree of March 1989. He was a Special Master for a Federal Three-Judge Panel (for the Court of Appeals for the Second Circuit, Chief Judge Pratt and United States District Court Judges Martin and Johnson) on Redistricting of Congressional Districts for the State of

New York, and a Special Master for a Federal Three-Judge Panel (for the Court of Appeals for the Second Circuit, Judges Cardomone, McGurn and Munson) on Redistricting of New York State Legislative Districts in 1992. He was appointed by United States Attorney General Barr as Independent Counsel for the investigation of the Banca Nazionale del Lavoro matter in 1992. He was appointed by United States Attorney General Barr to the Court-appointed Independent Review Board of the International Brotherhood of Teamsters in 1992 for a term expiring in June 1996 and reappointed by United States Attorney General Reno for a second five-year term from 1996-2001. For 1993 and 1994 he was appointed by United States District Court Chief Judge Sam Pointer for the Northern District of Alabama to serve with Judges Higginbotham and Bechtle on the Mediation Panel in the $4.7 billion Breast-Implant Class Action. Judge Lacey has served on the Faculty of the Federal Judicial Center, National Judicial College, American Law Institute, and National Institute for Trial Advocacy.

Carolyn B. Lamm (Chapter 51, *Enforcement of Judgments*) Ms. Lamm is a Partner in the law firm of White & Case, resident in Washington, D.C. She is the head of White & Case's International Trade Practice Group.

She is an experienced litigator specializing in international litigation, international trade and international arbitration matters. Ms. Lamm is primarily involved in the representation on litigation, international trade and arbitration matters of corporate clients and foreign governments such as the Governments of Indonesia, Turkey, Uzbekistan and state owned enterprises from the Russian Federation.

Previously, she served as Assistant Director of the Commercial Litigation Branch, Civil Division, U.S. Department of Justice. She has served previously in the ABA Section of Litigation as Secretary, a member of the Council and currently as Chair of the International Litigation Committee. Ms. Lamm is currently the President of the District of Columbia Bar.

Previously, she served as Chairman of the ABA Young Lawyers Division, Chair of the ABA Standing Committee on the Federal Judiciary and is a member of the House of Delegates. Ms. Lamm is a member of the American Law Institute; serves on the Editorial Advisory Board of *Inside Litigation;* is a Country Editor for the *Journal on International Arbitration;* and is a frequent author and speaker on litigation issues worldwide.

Ms. Lamm was appointed by President Clinton as a member of the U.S. Panel of Arbitrators on the Private Commercial Disputes Committee. She serves as a member of the Board of the American Indonesian Chamber of Commerce; the American Uzbekistan Chamber of Commerce and the American Turkish Council.

The Honorable William C. Lee (Chapter 27, *Scheduling and Pretrial Conferences and Orders*) is Chief Judge of the United States District Court for the Northern District of Indiana, having been appointed to the bench in 1981. Judge Lee is a graduate of Yale University (A.B. 1959)

ABOUT THE AUTHORS

where he was a Griffin Scholar and the University of Chicago Law School (J.D. 1962) where he was a Kirkland Scholar. Prior to his appointment to the bench, Judge Lee was a Deputy (1963-66) then Chief Deputy (1966-69) Prosecuting Attorney for Allen County, Indiana; a partner in the law firm of Parry, Krueckeberg & Lee (1964-70); the United States Attorney for the Northern District of Indiana (1970-73); and a partner in the law firm of Hunt, Suedhoff, Borror, Eilbacher & Lee (1973-81). Judge Lee was elected a Fellow of the American College of Trial Lawyers in 1978 and in 1988 was recognized as the Indiana Trial Judge of the Year. He is a Fellow of the Indiana Bar Foundation and was the Founding President of the Benjamin Harrison American Inn of Court. He has written and spoken often in the areas of trial advocacy, federal practice, employment discrimination, and alternative dispute resolution.

Edward P. Leibensperger (Chapter 7, *Third-Party Practice*) is a partner in Nutter, McClennen & Fish, LLP, where he serves on the Executive Committee and is Co-Chair of the Financial Litigation Practice Group. His practice is the litigation and trial of professional liability, securities, general business and product liability cases. He also receives appointments as a member of the federal Criminal Justice Act panel to defend indigent criminal defendants. Mr. Leibensperger is a Fellow of the American College of Trial Lawyers and is listed in *The Best Lawyers in America*.

Mr. Leibensperger is a former member of the governing Council of the American Bar Association's Section of Litigation. From 1991 to 1994, he was the Co-Chair of the Committee on Corporate Counsel. Mr. Leibensperger has also served as Treasurer of the Boston Bar Association and Chair of the Boston Bar Association's Section of Litigation.

In 1991, Mr. Leibensperger was appointed Special Assistant Attorney General to work with the Massachusetts Attorney General's office in a lawsuit challenging the methodology of the United States Census.

Mr. Leibensperger is also vice president and member of the Board of Directors of a non-profit corporation providing emergency shelter for battered women and education and training services to residents of Roxbury and Dorchester. Mr. Leibensberger is a *summa cum laude* graduate of The Ohio State University College of Law. He is also a certified public accountant.

Jeffrey S. Linder (Chapter 62, *Communications*) is a partner in the Washington, D.C. law firm of Wiley, Rein & Fielding. He received his B.A. degree from Duke University in 1980, and his J.D. from Stanford University Law School in 1983.

Mr. Linder has detailed familiarity with a wide range of telecommunications matters, including regulations applicable to long distance and local exchange carriers, initiatives affecting service quality and network reliability, and developments in emerging wireless technologies. He also has substantial experience negotiating service agreements with AT&T, MCI, Sprint, local telephone companies, and cellular carriers. He also has participated actively in negotiations and arbitrations regarding interconnection agreements between incumbent local exchange carriers and new entrants.

Joan A. Lukey (Chapter 67, *Employment Discrimination*) (Smith College 1971, *magna cum laude;* Boston College School of Law 1974, *cum laude*) is a senior partner in the Litigation Department of Hale and Dorr in Boston. From 1986 until 1990, she served as the first woman partner elected to the Firm's Executive Committee. Since 1990, she has chaired the Employment and Discrimination Practice Group of the Litigation Department.

Ms. Lukey is a co-editor of a treatise entitled *Federal Litigation in the First Circuit,* and the author of the treatise chapter on employment discrimination. Her first novel, *A Fiduciary Duty,* was published in 1994. Her second novel, *Whistleblower,* is in progress.

She is a Fellow of the American College of Trial Lawyers. Since the inception of publication of *The Best Lawyers in America,* she has been listed in the area of Labor and Employment law and has, since the 1993-94 edition, also been included in the area of General Business Litigation.

Patrick Lynch (Chapter 19, *Depositions*), a partner with O'Melveny & Myers, graduated *magna cum laude* from Loyola Law School (LL.B., 1966) and Loyola College (B.A., 1964). Mr. Lynch has extensive litigaiton experience including: Co-lead counsel for Exxon Corporation in multiple actions brought by the United States, the State of Alaska, and classes of private claimants, alleging natural resource damages and private injuries resulting from the Exxon Valdez oil spill; Co-lead counsel for Exxon Corporation in the federal criminal action arising out of the Exxon Valdez oil spill. *United States v. Exxon Corp.* (D. Alaska); Co-lead trial counsel *E. & J. Gallo Winery v. Gallo Cattle Co.,* (E.D. Ct. 1989), an action for trademark infringement and dilution; Lead counsel *IBM v. NCR,* U.S. District Court, Central District, Case No. 82-5946 KN (Mcx), an action for copyright infringement of a computer program written in assembly language; Appellate counsel for Chula Vista Sanitary Service and SCA Services and co-counsel for City of Chula Vista in *Hudson v. City of Chula Vista,* 746 F.2d 1370 (9th Cir. 1984), an action involving the state action doctrine under the antitrust laws; Appellate counsel for National Subscription Television in *ON TV v. S&H TV,* 644 F.2d 820 (9th Cir. 1981), an action involving piracy of private over-the-air television transmissions; Co-lead trial counsel for National Football League in *L.A. Memorial Coliseum Commission v. NFL,* 519 F.Supp. 581 (C.D. Cal. 1981), an action to enjoin the relocation of the Oakland Raiders.

Mr. Lynch is a Fellow of the American College of Trial Lawyers. Mr. Lynch has authored numerous articles which include: *"Voir Dire by Written Questionnaire,"* 1 Fed. Litigation Guide Rptr 129; Chapter 30, *"Trial Consequences of Burden of Proof,"* Antitrust Counseling and Litigation Techniques; *"Silicon Epics & Binary Bards: Determining the Proper Scope of Copyright Protection for Computer Programs,"* 34 UCLA L. Rev. 1943 (August, 1987) and *"The Case for Striking Jury Demands in An-*

titrust Actions Involving Extraordinary Complex Issues," 1 *Review of Litigation* 3 (1980) .

Barbara M.G. Lynn (Chapter 22, *Requests for Admissions*) is a partner with Carrington, Coleman, Sloman & Blumenthal, LLP in Dallas, Texas, where she focuses her practice on complex commercial litigation and the defense of labor and employment claims. She received her B.A., with highest distinction, from the University of Virginia in 1973, and her J.D., *summa cum laude,* from Southern Methodist University in 1976 (first in class). She is currently the Chair-Elect of the 60,000 member Litigation Section of the American Bar Association, and will become its 26th Chair in August of 1998. She is a Fellow of the American College of Trial Lawyers, the American Bar Foundation, and the Dallas Bar Foundation, a Sustaining Life Fellow of the Texas Bar Foundation, and a Research Fellow of the Southwestern Legal Foundation. She has been named in *The Best Lawyers in America* in Business Litigation since 1994. She was named by *The National Law Journal* in 1998 as one of the 50 most influential women lawyers in the United States. She has been a speaker on experts, hearsay, the trial of will contests, and general trial and pretrial practice and evidence at various institutes and before various national, state and local bar and civic groups.

William R. Maguire (Chapter 36, *Evidence*) is a member of Hughes Hubbard & Reed LLP, specializing in business litigation and arbitration, including trials of securities, commodities, business torts and professional liability cases. He is a graduate (first class honors) and Foundation Scholar of the Law School of Trinity College, Dublin, and a graduate of Kings Inns, Dublin, where he was admitted as a Barrister-at-Law before commencing practice as a member of the New York Bar in 1986. He has written and lectured on securities and professional liability litigation, and has participated as visiting faculty at trial advocacy programs of the National Institute of Trial Advocacy, and at Benjamin N. Cardozo and Harvard law schools.

Jeffrey B. Maletta (Chapter 54, *Securities*) is a partner in the Washington, D.C. office of Kirkpatrick & Lockhart LLP. He represents public companies, broker-dealers, investment companies and individuals in private securities litigation and in investigations by the Securities and Exchange Commission and self-regulatory organizations.

Prior to practicing at Kirkpatrick & Lockhart, Mr. Maletta served as law clerk to Barrington D. Parker, United States District Judge for the District of Columbia, and in the Office of General Counsel of the Securities and Exchange Commission. Mr. Maletta is a graduate of Stanford Law School, where he served on the senior editorial staff of the *Stanford Law Review,* and of Harvard College.

James D. Mathias (Chapter 5, *The Complaint*) is a partner at Piper & Marbury L.L.P. in Baltimore, Maryland. Mr. Mathias engages in a general corporate and business litigation practice, with significant experience in litigation concerning securities, class actions, franchises and distributors, closely held corporations, insurance disputes, fraud, internal corporate investigations, trade secrets, unfair competition, and real property disputes. Mr. Mathias has tried cases both in federal and state courts and has argued cases before the Maryland appellate courts and before the United States Court of Appeals for the Fourth Circuit.

Prior to joining Piper & Marbury in 1989, Mr. Mathias clerked for now Chief Judge J. Frederick Motz of the United States District Court of Maryland. Mr. Mathias graduated from the Georgetown University Law Center (*magna cum laude* and Order of the Coif) in 1988. He was an Associate Editor of the *Georgetown Law Journal*. He graduated *magna cum laude* from Amherst College in 1983 with a B.A. in English.

Mr. Mathias is the hiring partner for the Piper & Marbury Baltimore office. He is actively involved in civic and athletic activities in the Baltimore community, including coaching, committee, and fund-raising activities. He is a member of the Serjeants Inn Law Club.

John H. McElhaney (Chapter 47, *Costs and Disbursements*) is a shareholder in the Dallas office of Locke Purnell Rain Harrell (A Professional Corporation). He earned B.B.A. and J.D. degrees from Southern Methodist University and served as Managing Editor of the *Southwestern Law Journal* and is board certified in civil trial law by the Texas Board of Legal Specialization. His civil litigation experience includes a broad range of matters including antitrust, legal and accounting professional liability, libel and defamation, product liability and a variety of tort litigation.

Mr. McElhaney has taught courses in civil procedure and in product liability and air crash litigation at the Southern Methodist University School of Law. Mr. McElhaney has authored law review articles on Texas civil procedure and aviation litigation. He is named in *The Best Lawyers in America* (Business Litigation and First Amendment Law). He is a past President of the Southern Methodist University Law Alumni Association and of the Dallas Association of Defense Counsel, past President of the Dallas Chapter of the American Board of Trial Advocates, a Fellow in the Texas Bar Foundation and a Fellow of the American College of Trial Lawyers.

Thomas McGanney (Chapter 59, *Banking*) is a partner in the firm of White & Case. He graduated from Harvard Law School in 1962. He has been involved in complex commercial litigation, including securities and international banking litigation, in both state and federal courts in New York and around the country.

Mr. McGanney is a member of the American College of Trial Lawyers, and was formerly an Adjunct Professor of Law at New York University Law School where he taught federal civil procedure. He is also the author of several articles on federal jurisdiction and civil procedure.

The Honorable M. Margaret McKeown (Chapter 46, *Court-Awarded Attorneys' Fees*) is a Circuit Judge for the United States Court of Appeals for the Ninth Circuit. She was confirmed in 1998. Judge McKeown attended the University of Madrid, Spain and graduated from the University of Wyoming (B.A., 1972, Phi Beta Kappa) and from Georgetown University Law Center (J.D., 1975). Judge McKeown served as a White House Fellow in 1980-81 and was a Japan Society Leadership Fellow in 1993. Prior to her appointment to the bench, Judge McKeown was a partner in the Seattle and Washington D.C. offices of Perkins Coie. Her practice focused on complex litigation, intellectual property, antitrust and trade regulation. She practiced primarily in federal courts and served as a federal court mediator. She is a member of the bars of Washington and the District of Columbia.

A frequent participant in legal seminars on litigation, computer law and intellectual property, Judge McKeown is widely published in the computer and trade secrets area and is co-author of *"Trial Tactics in Trade Secret Litigation," Intellectual Property Counseling and Litigation* (Matthew Bender) and *"The Promises of a New World Information Order," The Knowledge Economy* (Aspen Institute). A former lawyer representative to the Judicial Conference of the Ninth Circuit, Judge McKeown served as President of the Federal Bar Association of the Western District of Washington, a member of the Ninth Circuit Gender Bias Task Force, and Co-President of Washington Women Lawyers. Judge McKeown is a member of the American Law Institute and a Fellow of the American Bar Foundation. She has been active in community and civic affairs and served for many years on the National Board of Girl Scouts of the U.S.A., and the Executive Committee of the Corporate Council for the Arts. The Seattle-King County Bar Association honored her with its Outstanding Lawyer of the Year Award and she was named by the *National Law Journal* as one of "The 50 Most Influential Women Lawyers" in the United States.

Barry F. McNeil (Chapter 35, *Expert Witnesses*) is a partner in the Specialized Litigation and Government Investigation Section of the Dallas Office of Haynes and Boone and a member of the firm's Executive Committee.

He is a member of the American College of Trial Lawyers and the immediate past Chair of the Litigation Section of the American Bar Association.

Over his 30 year career, first as a federal prosecutor with the Antitrust Division of the Department of Justice and now in private practice, he has appeared before juries throughout the country in cases raising charges of civil and criminal business fraud. Mr. McNeil was recently ranked as one of the 15 top litigators in the trial bar by *International Commercial Litigation,* a European journal.

Mr. McNeil has lectured and written extensively to the legal and business community on issues of law and policy, on professionalism, and on the legality and propriety of business conduct and practices. He was a guest lecturer to the Fifth Circuit Judicial Conference in 1996 where he spoke on "Mass Torts and Class Actions: Facing Increased Scrutiny." The remarks were published in 167 F.R.D. 483 (1996). McNeil was also invited to address the 1997 Conference of Chief United States District

Judges at the Federal Judicial Center and spoke on civil justice and discovery reform. He is Co-Editor of *Internal Investigations: Conducting Them, Protecting Them,* a desk guide of use to investigative counsel in internal corporate investigations.

Mr. McNeil specializes in the defense of corporations and executives in health care and antitrust prosecutions, corporate criminal proceedings and complex business litigation, both civil and criminal.

William J. Meeske (Chapter 13, *Provisional Remedies*) (B.A., University of Michigan, 1969, with honors; J.D., University of Michigan, 1972 *magna cum laude;* Order of the Coif; Associate Editor of the *Michigan Law Review*), is a partner in the Litigation Department of the Los Angeles office of Latham & Watkins and has served as a partner-in-charge of the Los Angeles office Litigation Department. Mr. Meeske specializes in business litigation, with emphasis on antitrust, securities and derivative actions and corporate control litigation.

Mr. Meeske is a member of the Antitrust Law and Litigation Sections of the American Bar Association, the Litigation Section of the California State Bar Association, and the Los Angeles County Bar Association. He has been a speaker for the federal civil practice programs sponsored by the University of Houston and University of California at Davis. He has also been a panelist on antitrust and other issues for the Continuing Education of the Bar's Institute on Competitive Business Practices and has spoken on antitrust law in internal corporate education programs.

Andrew B. Melnick (Chapter 4, *Investigation of the Case*) is a practicing attorney in New York City. He served as the General Counsel of the New York City Department of Investigation, and was an Assistant District Attorney in the New York County District Attorney's Office. Mr. Melnick is a 1973 graduate of Syracuse University (B.A. History) and a 1977 graduate of the New York University School of Law.

James C. Moore (Chapter 78, *Construction*) is a partner in the law firm of Harter, Secrest & Emery in Rochester, New York. He is a 1961 graduate of Cornell University (B.S.) and of the Cornell Law School in 1964.

Mr. Moore has specialized in construction related litigation for more than 25 years, most commonly on behalf of design professionals. He is a member of the American Arbitration Association's Large Complex Case Panel of arbitrators, and is on the Center for Public Resource's panel of distinguished neutrals. Mr. Moore has written and spoken frequently about trial law, construction disputes, and alternative dispute resolution. He is the President of the New York State Bar Association, the nation's largest voluntary state bar. Mr. Moore served as a U.S. Army officer and paratrooper in Vietnam from 1965-66.

Arthur E. Murphy (Chapter 80, *Environmental Claims*) is a partner in the Houston office of Vinson & Elkins L.L.P. His principal area of practice is environmental and toxic tort litigation. He handles a wide variety of cases, including CERCLA, NEPA, Clean Water Act, and Clean Air Act claims, toxic tort cases and class actions involving plant sites, Superfund sites, and underground storage tank sites, in addition to environmental insurance, corporate compliance, and environmental criminal defense work.

Mr. Murphy received his bachelor of arts from Yale University in 1982, and his J.D. from Vanderbilt Law School in 1985. While in law school, he was an Associate Editor of the *Vanderbilt Law Review*. Mr. Murphy is a member of the American Bar Association, the State Bar of Texas, and their environmental, tort, and litigation sections. He was an Adjunct Professor at South Texas College of Law teaching Toxic Tort Litigation from 1993-95. He was Vice-Chair of the Toxic & Environmental Torts Subcommittee of the Section of Natural Resources, Energy, and Environmental Law of the ABA, and has lectured on toxic torts, novel scientific evidence, environmental insurance coverage, environmental enforcement, and the management of complex litigation.

Gary P. Naftalis (Chapter 3, *Venue, Forum Selection and Transfer*) is a partner with Kramer, Levin, Naftalis & Frankel in New York City, where he focuses his practice on securities and complex corporate litigation, as well as white collar criminal defense. He is a Fellow of the American College of Trial Lawyers. Mr. Naftalis served as an Assistant U.S. Attorney for the Southern District of New York for seven years, including two years as Assistant Chief of the Criminal Division. He received his B.A. from Rutgers University in 1963, an M.A. from Brown University in 1965 and his LL.B. from Columbia University School of Law in 1967, where he was an Editor of the *Columbia Law Review*. Mr. Naftalis clerked for the Honorable William B. Herlands of the U.S. District Court for the Southern District of New York in 1967-68. He was the Editor of *White Collar Crimes,* Committee on Continuing Professional Education of the American Law Institute and American Bar Association, 1980. Mr. Naftalis is co-author, with his partner, former federal judge Marvin E. Frankel, of *The Grand Jury: An Institution on Trial and Sentencing: Helping Judges Do Their Jobs.* Mr. Naftalis has served as a member of the Departmental Disciplinary Committee of the First Judicial Department and, among his many bar association activities, has been a member of the White Collar Crime Committee of the American Bar Association Section of Litigation since 1985.

Eric J.R. Nichols (Chapter 29, *Jury Selection*) is a partner with Beck, Redden & Secrest in Houston, Texas, and his practice (and that of the firm) concentrates exclusively on business and other litigation. Prior to joining Beck, Redden & Secrest in 1994, Mr. Nichols was an Assistant United States Attorney for the Southern District of Texas. He received his B.A. with distinction in 1985 from the University of Virginia and his J.D., with honors, in 1989 from the University of Texas at Austin, where he served as the Editor-in-Chief of the *Texas Law Review*. Mr. Nichols has practiced in the federal and state courts of Texas, as well as in federal courts in other parts of the United States in which he has been admitted pro hac vice. Mr. Nichols has written and lectured extensively throughout the United States on the subject of jury selection in federal court. Among his jury selection publications are *Jury Selection in Federal Civil Litigation: General Procedures, New Rules, and the Arrival of Batson,* 23 Texas Tech. L. Rev. 407 (1992), and *The Expansion of Batson in Civil and Criminal Litigation, The Houston Lawyer,* Sept.-Oct. 1991, at 12.

Michael S. Oberman (Chapter 3, *Venue, Forum Selection and Transfer*) has been a partner in Kramer, Levin, Naftalis & Frankel in New York City since 1980. He practices in the areas of complex commercial litigation and copyright and trademark litigation. Mr. Oberman received his A.B., *cum laude,* in 1969 from Columbia College and his J.D., *cum laude,* in 1972 from the Harvard Law School. He was awarded National First Prize in the 1972 Nathan Burkan Memorial Competition. Prior to joining Kramer Levin in 1973, Mr. Oberman served as law clerk to the Honorable Milton Pollack in the United States District Court for the Southern District of New York in 1972-73. Mr. Oberman is on the panel of mediators for the Southern District of New York and is an arbitrator with the American Arbitration Association. He has been a Member of the Executive Committee of the Section on Commercial and Federal Litigation of the New York State Bar Association since 1989, and served in the Association's House of Delegates in 1989-91. Mr. Oberman is now serving a third term as a member of the Committee on Copyright and Literary Property of the Association of the Bar of the City of New York (1981-85, 1988-91, and 1997-). In 1995, he was a member of the Commercial Courts Task Force, which created the Commercial Division of the Supreme Court of the State of New York.

The Honorable Solomon Oliver, Jr. (Chapter 25, *Summary Judgment*) received his B.A. from the College of Wooster and his J.D. from New York University School of Law. He was appointed to the U.S. District Court for the Northern District of Ohio in May, 1994. Prior to Judge Oliver's current appointment, he was Associate Dean and Professor of Law at Cleveland-Marshall College of Law of Cleveland State University. He also served as Chief of the Civil Division and Chief of Appellate Litigation in the U.S. Attorney's Office in Cleveland. He clerked for the late William H. Hastie of the U.S. Third Circuit Court of Appeals. Judge Oliver has taught and written law review articles in the areas of federal jurisdiction, trial practice and civil procedure and has lectured on a wide range of topics at colleges and universities, at continuing legal education seminars and at judicial conferences. He is a member of the ABA Litigation Section's Jury Initiatives Task Force. He is also a member of the Council of the ABA Section of Legal Education and Admissions to the Bar and of that Section's Law School Accreditation Committee.

Thomas S. O'Neill (Chapter 30, *Motions In Limine*) graduated from the University of Illinois in 1985 with a B.A. in English with High Distinction, and from the University of Notre Dame Law School in 1989, where he was a member of the Law Review. He joined Jenner & Block in 1989, became a partner in 1997, and concentrates his practice in the areas of complex civil litigation and criminal defense. He is a member of the firm's Hiring and *Pro Bono* Committees.

Clifford R. Oviatt, Jr. (Chapter 66, *Labor Law*) is Senior Labor Counsel to the firm of McGuire, Woods, Battle & Boothe, LLP. Mr. Oviatt is resident in the firm's Washington D.C. office.

A Member of the National Labor Relations Board from 1989 to 1993 as an appointee of President George Bush, Mr. Oviatt has engaged in the practice of labor law since 1958. He represents management in unionized and non-organized operations throughout the United States.

Born in 1926, Mr. Oviatt was educated at Wesleyan University in Middletown, Connecticut where he received a Bachelor of Arts (History) degree in 1949, and an LL.B from Cornell Law School in 1953. He practiced law in Connecticut with Cummings and Lockwood from 1955 until 1983, and then with McGuire, Woods, Battle and Boothe, LLP until 1989, when he became a Member of the National Labor Relations Board. Mr. Oviatt rejoined McGuire, Woods when he left the Board in 1993. Mr. Oviatt is a Fellow of the College of Labor and Employment Lawyers and a Member of the Developing Labor Law Committee of the Labor Law Section of the American Bar Association. He is listed in *The Best Lawyers in America* for Labor and Employment Law.

James D. Pagliaro (Chapter 15, *Class Actions*) is a partner in the Litigation Section of Morgan, Lewis & Bockius, LLP resident in the Philadelphia office. His practice focuses almost exclusively on product liability and toxic tort litigation. Mr. Pagliaro is the Manager of the Firm's Philadelphia Litigation Section.

Mr. Pagliaro has litigated several cases involving the scientific and medical aspects of tort litigation. In November 1987, he co-wrote an article published in the *Temple Environmental Law and Technology Journal* on the use of expert witnesses in certain categories of "victimless" toxic tort cases.

Additionally, Mr. Pagliaro was lead trial counsel for the defense in a toxic tort case featured by the *National Law Journal* as one of the top Ten Defense Verdicts of 1990.

An active speaker and writer, Mr. Pagliaro co-wrote a chapter on "*Toxic Torts*" in the 1992 Matthew Bender *Deskbook on Environmental Law* and has had several articles published in the *National Law Journal*. He also has written extensively on product liability issues including published articles comparing Japan's and the EC's product liability law with U.S. product liability.

Mr. Pagliaro also has experience handling product liability, environmental liability, class action and OSHA law matters.

From 1979 to 1985, Mr. Pagliaro was an attorney with the Office of the Regional Solicitor, U.S. Department of Labor in Philadelphia, where he handled OSHA prosecutions. Later, he was named senior trial counsel with responsibility for the Labor Department's Black Lung litigation efforts in Region III.

Mr. Pagliaro received the Defense Research Institute's Award for Distinguished Service of a Faculty Member. He is a member of the Third Circuit Historical Society and a lecturer on the "Essentials of Pennsylvania Practice"and "Class Actions" for the Pennsylvania Bar Institute.

He received his bachelor's degree with honors from LaSalle University in 1973, and received his law degree in 1976 from Dickinson School of Law, where he was a member of Dickinson's Woolsack Honors Society for Academic Excellence.

Charles E. Patterson (Chapter 28, *Settlements*) A.B., University of Kansas, 1963, J.D., University of Michigan, 1966, is a partner of Pillsbury Madison & Sutro LLP, resident in its Los Angeles office. Mr. Patterson, who specializes in business litigation, has served as Vice Chairman of Pillsbury and as head of its litigation department. He also has served as President of the State Bar of Missouri. In his 30 years of practice, Mr. Patterson has gained extensive jury trial experience trying everything from murder cases to major business cases (antitrust, securities, fraud) and tort cases (personal injury and products liability). He has tried 100 jury cases to a verdict and, to the best of his recollection, won all but four. He also has tried roughly two dozen bench trials and won all but one. Among his noteworthy settlements was one involving the former officers, directors, shareholders and auditors of Southwest Savings (Phoenix, Arizona), a group that included the sitting governor of Arizona. The settlements totaled $15.3 million.

John F.X. Peloso (Chapter 15, *Class Actions*) is a senior partner of Morgan, Lewis & Bockius LLP resident in the New York office. An experienced trial lawyer, his practice currently focuses on all aspects of securities litigation, including class actions, broker-dealer matters and enforcement and disciplinary proceedings before the Securities and Exchange Commission, the New York Stock Exchange and other self regulatory organizations.

Mr. Peloso has held a number of government positions. In 1960, following graduation from Fordham Law School, where he was Managing Editor of the *Fordham Law Review,* Mr. Peloso served as law clerk to the Honorable John F.X. McGohey in the United States District Court for the Southern District of New York. From 1961 to 1965, he was an assistant United States attorney in the Southern District of New York and, from 1970 to 1975, he was chief trial counsel for the New York Regional Office of the Securities and Exchange Commission.

Active in professional organizations, Mr. Peloso has held several leadership positions in the Business Law Section and the Litigation Section of the American Bar Association. Presently, he is Chair of the Business Law Section Subcommittee on Securities Litigation. In the Litigation Section, he has been a member of the Council, Co-Chair of the Securities Litigation and Trial Evidence Committees, and presently is Co-Chair of the Task Force on the Independent Lawyer. He also has been a member of the National Arbitration Committee of the National Association of Securities Dealers.

Mr. Peloso frequently writes and lectures on securities litigation issues and, for several years, has authored a column on *Securities and Commodities Litigation* for the *New York Law Journal.*

Mr. Peloso is chairman of his firm's Litigation Section, a member of its Executive Committee and Governing Board and managing partner of the New York office.

Richard M. Phillips (Chapter 54, *Securities*) is a partner and head of the securities group in the Washington, D.C. office of Kirkpatrick & Lockhart LLP. He regularly represents clients in private securities litigation, and in enforcement and regulatory matters before the Securities and Exchange Commission and self-regulatory organizations. Mr. Phillips is Past Chair of the Section of Business Law of the American Bar Association. He has previously served as Vice-Chair and Editor of the Section's publication entitled *The Business Lawyer* and Chair of the Committee on Federal Regulation of Securities. He also is the edtior and co-author of a treatise entitled *The Securities Enforcement Manual: Tactics and Strategies* published in 1997 by the Section of Business Law of the American Bar Association. Mr. Phillips has served as Chair of the Executive Council of the Securities Law Committee of the Federal Bar Association. He is a frequent lecturer at securities law conferences and a contributor to legal periodicals on securities law subjects.

Mr. Phillips previously held various positions on the Staff of the Securities and Exchange Commission, including Assistant to the Chairman; Assistant General Counsel; and Staff Director of the agency's Corporate Disclosure and Investment Company Studies. He is a graduate of Yale Law School and Columbia College.

James W. Quinn (Chapter 20, *Document Discovery*) heads the Litigation Department of Weil, Gotshal & Manges LLP. He has experience in all areas of complex litigation and alternative dispute resolution, with particular emphasis in antitrust, products liability, insurance, sports, entertainment, heavy electric equipment and nuclear law.

He has counseled professional football, basketball and hockey player associations for nearly 20 years. Among other cases, he was the lead trial counsel in the NFL players successful antitrust challenge to the player restrictions in the National Football League in the *McNeil v. NFL* (three-month jury trial). Other major trials handled by Mr. Quinn include *Buffalo Broadcasting v. ASCAP* (Southern District of New York), an antitrust suit against the American Society of Composers, Authors and Publishers; and *LILCO v. Imo Industries Inc.,* a jury trial involving a multi-million dollar product liability claim; *Duquesne Co. v. Westinghouse Electric Corp.,* a three-month jury trial resulting in a successful defense verdict on a billion dollar claim; and *Houston Light & Power v. Westinghouse* (settled after six-month jury trial).

Mr. Quinn has substantial experience in proceedings before the International Chamber of Commerce in Paris both as counsel and as an ICC arbitrator. He is currently representing the Arthur Andersen Member Firms in the largest ICC arbitration in history. He has also participated in numerous American Arbitration Association and other commercial arbitrations, again as a litigant and an arbitrator.

Mr. Quinn is an author and lecturer on numerous legal subjects, including management techniques in complex litigation. He was a co-author of both the *Corporate Counsellor's Deskbook* and *Litigating Complex Cases* and has been a contributing editor to various American Bar Association publications, including *The Corporate Litigator*.

Mr. Quinn graduated *cum laude* from the University of Notre Dame and holds an LL.B. from Fordham University School of Law where he was on Law Review. Formerly, he was an Adjunct Professor of Law at Fordham Law School.

The Honorable Randall R. Rader (Chapter 63, *Patents*) is a Circuit Judge on the United States Court of Appeals for the Federal Circuit. He was born on April 21, 1949, in Hastings, Nebraska, son of Raymond A. Rader and Gloria R. Smith. He attended Brigham Young University from 1971-74, graduating with a B.A. in English (*magna cum laude*), Phi Beta Kappa; he obtained his J.D. from George Washington University Law Center in 1978. Prior to his appointment to the bench, Judge Rader was Counsel in the House of Representatives from 1975-80; he was General Counsel, Chief Counsel, Subcommittee on the Constitution from 1981-86; from 1987-88 he was Minority Chief Counsel, Staff Director, on the Subcommittee on Patents, Trademarks, and Copyrights, also on the Senate Committee on the Judiciary. President Ronald Reagan appointed him to be a Judge on the United States Claims Court in 1988. On June 12, 1990, President George Bush nominated Judge Rader for a position on the Court of Appeals for the Federal Circuit. He was confirmed by the Senate on August 3, 1990. Judge Rader teaches Patent Law at the University of Virginia School of Law, Charlottesville, Virginia; Trial Advocacy at the George Washington University Law School, Washington, D.C.; and Comparative Patent Law at Georgetown University Law Center, Washington, D.C. He is a co-author of a casebook, *Patent Law*, West Group, 1998.

Ronald S. Rauchberg (Chapter 49, *Appeals to the Courts of Appeals*) is a leading trial and appellate lawyer in New York City who has handled complex commercial litigation for the Association of American Publishers, Citicorp, Ernst & Young LLP, Metropolitan Life Insurance Co., the National Basketball Association, Rockefeller Group, Inc., Simon & Schuster, Inc. and other clients. He is a partner in Proskauer Rose LLP, where he has been Chair of the Litigation and Dispute Resolution Department and Chair of the Intellectual Property Practice Group. He is also a Fellow of the American College of Trial Lawyers. His appellate work in the federal courts has yielded victories for his clients in the notable decisions of *Simon & Schuster, Inc. v. New York State Crime Victims Board*, 502 U.S. 105 (1991); *Princeton University Press v. Michigan*

Document Services, Inc., 99 F.3d 1381 (6th Cir., *in banc,* 1996), *cert. denied,* 117 S. Ct. 1336 (1997); and *Parker v. Metropolitan Life Ins. Co.,* 121 F.3d 1006 (6th Cir., *in banc,* 1997), *cert. denied,* 118 S.Ct. 871 (1998). He was graduated from Fordham Law School, where he was awarded the Chapin Prize for ranking first academically in his graduating class, and where he was Editor-in-Chief of the *Fordham Law Review.*

Robert D. Raven (Chapter 9, *Arbitration vs. Litigation: Enforceability and Access to Courts*) is Senior Of Counsel in the San Francisco Office of the law firm of Morrison & Foerster LLP. Mr. Raven was President of the American Bar Association in 1988-89. He has also served as Chair of the ABA Section of Dispute Resolution, Chair of The Special Advisory Committee on International Activities, Chair of the Standing Committee on Federal Judiciary, the Standing Committee on Legal Aid and Indigent Defendants, and the Long Range Planning and Management Committee. Outside the ABA, Mr. Raven served as President of the State Bar of California in 1981 and the Bar Association of San Francisco in 1971. Mr. Raven is a graduate of the law school of the University of California, Berkeley (1952), Order of the Coif.

Harry M. Reasoner (Chapter 52, *Ethical Issues in Commercial Cases*) is a partner in the Houston office of Vinson & Elkins. Harry's principal area of practice is complex litigation. Currently, Harry is the firm's Managing Partner.

Harry has chaired the District Court Advisory Group for the U.S. District Court for the Southern District of Texas under the Civil Justice Reform Act, the Texas Higher Education Coordinating Board, and the American Bar Association Section of Antitrust Law. He served on the Texas Supreme Court Advisory Committee. He is a Member of the American Law Institute and the American Board of Trial Advocates. Harry is a Fellow in the American Bar Foundation, the American College of Trial Lawyers, the International Academy of Trial Lawyers, and the International Society of Barristers. He is profiled in *America's Top Trial Lawyers: Who They Are and Why They Win* (1994) and named One of Hundred Most Influential Lawyers in America in 1994 by the *National Law Journal.*

Harry was lead counsel in securing on behalf of ETSI Pipeline a $1.035 billion antitrust verdict. He obtained a $120 million judgment for American General Insurance Co. against Continental Airlines in a Delaware securities litigation. He obtained a take nothing verdict for *The Dallas Morning News* in a $100 million antitrust suit brought by *The Dallas Times Herald* shortly before it went out of business.

As appellate counsel, he obtained reversal and rendition of an $80 million plaintiff's verdict against Unocal. He represented four major utilities in four separate cases before the Supreme Court of Texas, obtaining reversal of orders excluding $2 billion of nuclear power plant construction costs and orders retroactively lowering rates and denying the benefit of tens of millions of dollars in unrelated tax deductions.

ABOUT THE AUTHORS

Harry was born in San Marcos, Texas, on July 15, 1939. He graduated from Rice University, B.A., *summa cum laude* in 1960, and from The University of Texas, J.D. (Chancellors and Order of the Coif) in 1962, ranking first in his law school class. He attended the University of London from 1962-63, and was a law clerk to Judge Charles E. Clark of the United States Court of Appeals for the Second Circuit from 1963-64. Harry was admitted to the Texas Bar in 1962, to the District of Columbia Bar in 1974, and to the New York Bar in 1980.

R. Douglas Rees (Chapter 69, *RICO*) is a partner with the firm of Jenner & Block in Chicago, Illinois, where he practices complex commercial litigation with a focus on telecommunications law, unfair competition, defending class actions, securities litigation, and RICO litigation. He received his B.A. from Brigham Young University in 1985 and his J.D. from Northwestern University School of Law in 1989. He is admitted to practice before the United States Court of Appeals for the Seventh Circuit and is a member of the trial bar of the United States District Court for the Northern District of Illinois. He is a member of the Chicago and American Bar Associations. He serves as a lecturer for the Chicago Bar Association seminar on Chancery and Special Remedies and is the co-author of *Enforcement of Employee Restrictive Covenants: Recent Developments Under Illinois Law* (1998) and *Civil RICO* (1998).

Frank Rothman (Chapter 33, *Presentation of the Case in Chief*) is a partner in the Los Angeles office of Skadden, Arps, Slate, Meagher & Flom LLP. He joined the firm in 1986, after serving four years as chairman and chief executive officer of MGM/UA Entertainment Company. His practice emphasizes entertainment and sports-related litigation, including several high-profile suits involving prominent sports and entertainment figures. Mr. Rothman also is experienced in antitrust, insurance, general business and securities litigation and general criminal matters.

Mr. Rothman was elected by the *National Law Journal* as one of the nation's 100 most influential lawyers, and an article in *California Law Business* named Mr. Rothman as one of two contenders "for the title of most coveted litigator in California." He was also listed in the *Los Angeles Business Journal's "Who's Who in Law."*

D. Alan Rudlin (Chapter 65, *Copyright*) is a partner in the Trial Section of Hunton & Williams in Richmond, Virginia, where he heads the Firm's Alternative Dispute Resolution Group, and specializes in First Amendment, commercial, and toxic tort litigation. He is immediate past Chair of the Virginia State Bar-Virginia Bar Association Joint Committee on Alternative Dispute Resolution, and is a member of the American Arbitration Association Virginia Mediation Panel and CPR Institute for Dispute Resolution Virginia Panel of Distinguished Neutrals. Alan is an active member of the American Bar Association Section of Litigation and currently serves as a member of the Section's Council. He is also the current Chair of the Toxic Torts and Environmental Litigation Committee of the American Bar Association's Section of Natural Resources, Energy, and Environmental Law. Alan has taught as adjunct faculty at the

ABOUT THE AUTHORS

Law Schools of the University of Virginia, University of Richmond, William and Mary, and Washington and Lee, as well as for National Institute for Trial Advocacy courses. Alan has co-authored several textbooks, and published numerous articles. He serves on the Board of Editorial Advisors for *The Environmental Counselor* (Business Laws, Inc.) and the *Toxics Law Reporter* (The Bureau of National Affairs).

Jay G. Safer (Chapter 26, *Magistrate Judges and Special Masters*) is a partner at LeBoeuf, Lamb, Greene & MacRae, L.L.P., New York, New York. He specializes in litigation, including commercial and complex litigation matters. He graduated from Vanderbilt University, *cum laude,* and Columbia Law School as a Harlan Fiske Stone Scholar. He has served as a lecturer on trial practice and faculty member at the Trial Academy on Direct and Cross-Examination Skills jointly sponsored by the New York County Lawyers' Association and the National Institute for Trial Advocacy. He has served as Secretary of the Committee on the Bicentennial of the United States Constitution of the Association of the Bar of the City of New York. He is a member of the Executive Committee of the New York State Bar Association Commercial and Federal Litigation Section. He has served as a member of the Task Force on the Commercial Division of the New York State Supreme Court and of the Task Force on Magistrate Judges in the Southern and Eastern Districts of New York for the New York State Bar Association Commercial and Federal Litigation Section. In those capacities, he participated in the preparation of two articles entitled *A Case Study in Successful Judicial Administration: Commercial Division, New York State Supreme Court* and *Comparing the Use of Magistrate Judges in Civil Cases in the Southern and Eastern Districts of New York* published in the *N.Y. Litigator.* He is co-chairman of the Federal Judiciary Committee and a member of a special task force on federal courts of the New York State Bar Association Commercial and Federal Litigation Section. He is Chairman of the Task Force on Court Restructuring of the New York State Court System of the Association of the Bar of the City of New York. He is co-author of the chapter on *"Contracts"* in the publication entitled, *Commercial Litigation in New York State Courts* (Haig ed.) (West 1995 & Supp. 1998).

Harvey I. Saferstein (Chapter 60, *Letters of Credit*) is a partner in the Los Angeles office of Chadbourne & Parke LLP, a New York law firm of over 300 lawyers. His practice encompasses a wide variety of business, antitrust, and trade regulation counseling and litigation. Since beginning his practice in 1970, he has represented a variety of companies in obtaining the appropriate antitrust clearance for mergers or joint ventures from the Federal Trade Commission and the United States Department of Justice. He has also defended numerous companies in investigations of alleged antitrust and consumer protection violations. Mr. Saferstein has also been lead counsel in a variety of complex business cases, private antitrust treble damage actions, and consumer class actions.

Mr. Saferstein was born in Kansas City, Missouri. He graduated from the University of California at Berkeley, Phi Beta Kappa, in 1965, and from Harvard Law School in 1968, where he served as Executive Editor of the Law Review. He was a law clerk to Chief Judge Bailey Aldrich, U.S. Court of Appeals, First Circuit from 1968-69, and served as attorney advisor to Federal Trade Commissioner Philip Elman from 1969-70. In 1978-80, Mr. Saferstein served as Regional Director of the Federal Trade Commission Los Angeles office. Mr. Saferstein has also taught courses in remedies, antitrust, and consumer protection at the University of Southern California Law Center and Southwestern Law School.

Well known for his public service, Mr. Saferstein served as the President of the State Bar of California in 1993-94, President of the Association of Business Trial Lawyers, Chair of the Ninth Circuit Judicial Conference, and President of the Legal Aid Foundation of Los Angeles. Mr. Saferstein is currently a regular guest on the CNNfn network discussing current mergers and antitrust issues. He is also a frequent lecturer for The Practicing Law Institute on antitrust and consumer issues. Mr. Saferstein's latest articles are *"Romania's New Competition Law,"* published in October, 1997, *Global Competition Review; "The Federal Trade Commission: The History And Future Of This 'Peculiar' Agency,"* published in ABTL, September, 1997; and *"Professor Phillip E. Areeda, Chronicler for the 'Antitrust Masses,'"* published in the Spring, 1996 *Antitrust Law Magazine.*

Robert N. Sayler (Chapter 58, *Insurance*) is a partner at Covington & Burling in Washington, D.C., where he has practiced since his graduation from Stanford University (1962) and Harvard Law School (1965). During the Spring of 1995, he served as the John Ewald Distinguished Professor of Law at the University of Virginia teaching in the areas of advocacy and insurance litigation. In the past decade, his trial experience has focused largely on mega-insurance coverage cases in which he has served as lead counsel for successful policyholders in billion-dollar coverage disputes for asbestos, environmental clean-up, and breast implant liabilities. He is serving a three-year term on the American Bar Association's Standing Committee on the Federal Judiciary and previously served as Chair of the ABA's Litigation Section. Mr. Sayler is a Fellow of both the American College of Trial Lawyers and the American Bar Foundation. He has written and lectured extensively on advocacy, insurance coverage, and professionalism issues and on the need for major changes in the delivery of legal services to the poor. He is a Past President of the Board of Directors of the Legal Aid Society in Washington and Vice-Chair of the Neighborhood Legal Service's program's Board of Directors. In April 1997, the *National Law Journal* named Mr. Sayler one of the nation's 100 most influential lawyers and called him "the nation's pre-eminent insurance coverage lawyer."

James M. Schurz (Chapter 9, *Arbitration vs. Litigation: Enforceability and Access to Courts*) is a litigator in the San Francisco office of Morrison & Foerster LLP. He also serves as Adjunct Professor of Law at the University of California, Hastings College of the Law teaching courses in negotiation and ADR law. He served as President of the Barristers Club of the Bar Association of San Francisco in 1998. Mr. Schurz earned his J.D. degree from the University of California, Berkeley in 1989 and his M.A. and B.A. degrees from Stanford University.

Bart M. Schwartz (Chapter 4, *Investigation of the Case*) is the President and CEO of Decision Strategies/ Fairfax International, a worldwide investigative and consulting firm headquartered in New York City and Washington, D.C. Mr. Schwartz has been a leader in the field of investigative consulting since 1985, and writes and lectures extensively for business and professional audiences. He previously served as the Associate United States Attorney and Chief of the Criminal Division of the United States Attorney's Office for the Southern District of New York. He also was a partner in a New York law firm specializing in federal civil and criminal litigation. Mr. Schwartz is a 1968 graduate of the University of Pittsburgh (B.S. Biology) and a 1971 graduate of the New York University School of Law.

R. Michael Senkowski (Chapter 62, *Communications*) has a B.A. degree from Yale University and a Juris Doctor with honors from George Washington University. He has over 25 years experience in the full range of telecommunications issues at the Federal Communications Commission (1971-77) and in private law practice (1977 to present). His present position is partner with the law firm of Wiley, Rein & Fielding.

At the FCC, Mr. Senkowski initially represented the agency before the U.S. Court of Appeals. Later, he served as chief advisor to the Chairman of the Commission on domestic and international telecommunications policy issues. He also served as a member of President Reagan's Transition Team for Communications with responsibility for domestic common carrier policy matters.

In private practice, Mr. Senkowski has represented a wide variety of telecommunications companies and users in FCC, State and legislative matters involving communications services. On behalf of industry associations, he has represented such diverse interests as Cellular, Broadband PCS, Narrowband PCS, Paging, Unlicensed PCS and computer devices. He has also handled over one hundred telecommunications transfers, including three multi-billion dollar mergers.

Mr. Senkowski has been a frequent lecturer on wireless telecommunications. He has also written numerous reports and handbooks on telecommunications policies.

Charles M. Shaffer, Jr. (Chapter 48, *Sanctions*), joined King & Spalding in 1967. He has served as Chair of the Litigation Department at King & Spalding for the past four years.

Throughout his 29 years of practice, Mr. Shaffer has served as lead counsel in civil jury trials in commercial litigation of all types. He has extensive litigation experience in antitrust, commercial fraud and other complex business matters, and he has also been actively involved in product liability, securities, RICO, healthcare, and real estate litigation. Mr. Shaffer has experience in internal corporate investigations and related

ABOUT THE AUTHORS

shareholder derivative suits and civil litigation involving concurrent grand jury investigations.

Mr. Shaffer is the co-author of the ABA's pamphlet on *Sanctions*.

John H. Shenefield (Chapter 53, *Antitrust*) is chairman of the law firm Morgan, Lewis & Bockius LLP and is chairman of its Antitrust and Trade Regulation Section.

Mr. Shenefield's practice concentrates on antitrust litigation and counseling. He served as lead counsel in a number of national and regional antitrust litigations. He also is involved with international antitrust issues and has handled matters before the European Commission and the United Kingdom's Office of Fair Trading.

Before joining the firm in 1986, Mr. Shenefield held several positions at the Department of Justice. He served as Assistant Attorney General in charge of the Antitrust Division from 1977-79, and as Associate Attorney General of the United States from 1979-81. He also served as Chairman of the National Commission to Review Antitrust Laws and Procedures from 1978-79.

Mr. Shenefield is the co-author of *The Antitrust Laws—A Primer, third edition,* 1998, published by the American Enterprise Institute. He has written several articles on a variety of antitrust topics and speaks frequently on the subject of antitrust law and policy.

He received his undergraduate and law degrees from Harvard in 1960 and 1965, respectively. Mr. Shenefield was in private practice for 12 years before joining the Department of Justice.

Robert S. Smith (Chapter 57, *Contracts*) joined Paul, Weiss, Rifkind, Wharton & Garrison in 1968 and became a litigation partner in 1976. He has extensive trial and appellate experience in a wide variety of civil commercial litigations, particularly contract, securities and bankruptcy-related litigations, and is a Fellow of the American College of Trial Lawyers.

Mr. Smith graduated first in his class from Columbia Law School in 1968, where he was Editor-in-Chief of the *Columbia Law Review*. He is a member of the bars of New York and the District of Columbia, the United States Supreme Court, and several federal courts of appeals. His publications include *"No Forum at All or Any Forum You Choose: Personal Jurisdiction Over Aliens Under the Antitrust and Securities Laws,"* 39 *Business Lawyer* 1685 (1984); *"A Rationale for Paying Blackmail: The Settlement of Securities Class Actions,"* Counsel to Counsel, July/ August 1992 Volume 2, Number 4; and *"Policing the In-House Police: The Gutfreund Report and its Implications for Securities Firm Counsel and Compliance Officers,"* National Law Journal, September 6, 1993.

Mr. Smith served as a full-time Visiting Professor from Practice at Columbia Law School in 1980-81, and as a part-time lecturer in law at Columbia Law School from 1981 to 1990, where he taught a seminar in federal litigation.

ABOUT THE AUTHORS

Jerome G. Snider (Chapter 55, *Professional Liability*) is a litigation partner in the New York office of Davis Polk & Wardwell. Mr. Snider received his undergraduate degree from Rutgers College *summa cum laude* and his law degree from the University of Pennsylvania *cum laude* where he also served as an Instructor in Legal Writing. After law school, Mr. Snider served as a law clerk in the Southern District of New York for then-Chief Judge David Edelstein. At Davis Polk, Mr. Snider litigates complex professional liability cases and other commercial matters in federal and state courts nationally and before regulatory agencies. Mr. Snider is a member of the Committee on Professional Responsibility of the Association of the Bar of the City of New York and the Litigation and Antitrust Sections of the American Bar Association. He has also served as a member of the Executive Committee of the Board of Trustees of the Legal Aid Society of the District of Columbia and the Board of Trustees of the American Friends of the Hebrew University in Washington. He teaches a variety of facets of litigation practice in law school programs and internally at Davis Polk.

John R. Snyder (Chapter 31, *Trials*) is a partner in Bingham Dana LLP. His commercial litigation practice has included class actions and multi-jurisdiction litigation and for several years has focused on securities litigation in federal and state courts, arbitration and regulatory matters. His practice has also included other financial institution litigation and franchise and employment litigation. Mr. Snyder is a graduate of Bucknell University and Harvard Law School. He was a law clerk to the Honorable Robert C. Zampano of the United States District Court for the District of Connecticut.

Louis Michael Solomon (Chapter 64, *Trademark*) is a partner in the Litigation Department at Shereff, Friedman, Hoffman & Goodman, LLP. Mr. Solomon has extensive experience in litigating commercial cases in state and federal courts, including both prosecuting and defending trademark and other intellectual property cases.

Mr. Solomon received his Bachelor of Arts from Cornell University in 1985 (Dean's List) and graduated *cum laude* from the University of Michigan Law School in 1988. He joined Shereff Friedman in 1992, becoming a partner in 1997. Mr. Solomon has participated in the National Institute for Trial Advocacy Program and is a member of the American Bar Association Sections on Litigation and Intellectual Property Law. In conjunction with the Network for Women's Services, Mr. Solomon is also active in providing *pro bono* representation for battered and abused women.

Jerold S. Solovy (Chapter 69, *RICO*) is a partner and Chairman of Jenner & Block, located in Chicago, Illinois. Mr. Solovy was born in Chicago, Illinois on April 10, 1930. He was admitted to bar in Illinois and District of Columbia in 1955 and the United States Supreme Court in 1968. Mr. Solovy graduated from the University of Michigan (B.A. 1952) with high honors and distinction in political science. He obtained his legal education from Harvard Law School (LL.B., *cum laude,* 1955). Mr. Solovy's Honorary Societies include Phi Beta Kappa, Phi Kappa Phi,

Pi Sigma Alpha, and Phi Eta Sigma. Mr. Solovy was a member of the Board of Editors of the *Harvard Law Review* (1953-55), member of the Overseers' Committee to Visit Harvard Law School (1987-91), member of the Harvard Overseers' Committee on University Resources (1993-present), and a member of the Illinois Supreme Court Committee on Jury Instructions in Criminal Cases, (1961-68, 1975-77). Mr. Solovy served as Chairman of the Chicago Bar Association Defense of Indigent Prisoners Committee (1963-64), and Chairman of the Chicago Bar Association Special Committee Studying the Adequacy of Legal Representation Afforded Indigent Defendants (1968-71).

During 1971-75, Mr. Solovy served as Co-Chairman of the Chicago Bar Association Commission to Study Criminal Justice System in Cook County. He served as Chairman of the Chicago Bar Association Continuing Commission on Administration of Criminal Justice in Cook County (1975-76), Chairman of the Discovery Committee of American Bar Association Litigation Section (1982-85), Chairman of the American Bar Association Litigation Section Trial Practice Committee (1985-88), and Co-Chairman of the American Bar Association Litigation Section Federal Procedure Committee (1988-89). Mr. Solovy served as a member of the Special Review Committee on the Federal Civil Rules (1989-92), and as a member of the Task Force on Lawyers' Ancillary Business Activities (1989-91). Mr. Solovy served as Liaison to the ABA Post-conviction Death Penalty Representation Project (1990-92), Chairman of the Special Commission on the Administration of Justice in Cook County (1984-91), Chairman of the Illinois Supreme Court Special Commission on the Administration of Justice (1992-93), and Chairman of the Criminal Justice Project of Cook County (1987-91). Mr. Solovy served as a member of the Judicial Advisory Council of Cook County, Illinois (1975-77, 1982-89), and as Chairman (1989-91). Mr. Solovy served as Chairman of the Cook County Criminal Justice Coordinating Council (1989-91) and served as a member of the Third Circuit Rule 11 Task Force (1987-88).

Mr. Solovy is a member of the Board of Editors, *Federal Litigation Guide Reporter* (Matthew Bender, 1985-present), member and editor of the BNA *RICO Reporter* (1985-present), member of the Editorial Board of *The Practical Litigator* (1989-present), and is currently a member of the Editorial Advisory Board, *Civil RICO Report*. Mr. Solovy has extensively lectured on various subjects, including Complex Litigation, Class Actions, Civil Procedure, Securities Law, Attorneys' Fees, Proxy Fights and Takeover Litigation. He is a member of The American Law Institute, a Fellow of the American College of Trial Lawyers, and a member of the Board of Trustees, United States Supreme Court Historical Society (1993- present) . Mr. Solovy is also the author of *Moore's Federal Practice,* Chapter 11 *"Sanctions"* and Chapter 23 *"Class Actions."*

Mindy J. Spector (Chapter 20, *Document Discovery*) is a partner in the Litigation Department of Weil, Gotshal & Manges LLP. She concentrates her practices in all areas of complex commercial litigation, including product liability, contract and commercial power litigation. Ms. Spector has been involved in many lengthy complex jury trials and also has extensive arbitration experience in AAA and ICC arbitrations. She has been involved in the defense of numerous civil RICO litigations and has a substantive expertise in civil RICO. Ms. Spector has coordinated discovery on a nationwide basis in multiple related litigations.

Ms. Spector has coordinated the defense for Westinghouse Electric Corporation in the nuclear steam generator litigations pending in several district courts around the country. She is also involved on a national basis in defense of market conduct litigation on behalf of insurance company clients.

She has been involved in the defense of commercial nuclear litigation for General Electric Company and Imo Industries. She has also been involved in the defense of antitrust litigation for BMW NA and in the *Matsushita v. Zenith* antitrust litigation in the U.S. Supreme Court and has represented CBS/Fox Video, Fox Inc., Travelers and GE Capital in a variety of matters.

Ms. Spector received her J.D. from The State University of New York at Buffalo. She was law clerk to the Honorable Leonard A. Bernikow, U.S. Magistrate in the Southern District of New York.

John L. Strauch (Chapter 11, *Multidistrict Litigation*) (Phi Beta Kappa, B.A. *summa cum laude* University of Pittsburgh 1960; Editor-in-Chief, Law Review, Order of the Coif, Root-Tilden Scholar, J.D. *magna cum laude* New York University 1963) is a partner with Jones, Day, Reavis & Pogue where he is Firmwide Chairman of the Litigation Group. Mr. Strauch is a Fellow of the American College of Trial Lawyers and a Life Member of the United States Sixth Circuit Judicial Conference. He has been involved in many complex cases concerning product liability, corporate takeovers, class actions, federal securities, government regulation, commercial litigation, and antitrust before a variety of state and federal courts.

Included among matters for which he has been lead counsel are the national coordination and direction of all smoking and health litigation for R.J. Reynolds Tobacco Company throughout the U.S. and representation of Marathon Oil Company from trial through conclusion of appeals in federal court shareholder securities class actions and state court shareholder dissenters' actions in the wake of USX Corporation's tender offer/merger acquisition of Marathon. John also served as co-trial counsel in litigating the successful defense of Marathon against the hostile tender offer of Mobil Corporation. He also represented the commissioner of banking and insurance of the State of Vermont from trial through conclusion of appeals in the contested liquidation of Ambassador Insurance Company, one of the largest excess casualty insurers operating in the late 1980s. John successfully represented British Petroleum in 1996 in preventing an attempt by the Alaska Oil and Gas Conservation Commission to forcibly rearrange the ownership interests of the oil companies that own oil and gas rights in the Prudhoe Bay oil field on Alaska's North Slope, the largest oil field in North America.

ABOUT THE AUTHORS

John J. Sullivan (Chapter 50, *Appeals to the Supreme Court*) is a partner in the Washington, D.C. office of Mayer, Brown & Platt specializing in Supreme Court and appellate litigation. He received his A.B. in 1981 from Brown University and his J.D. in 1985 from Columbia University School of Law, where he was a Harlan Fiske Stone Scholar and Book Reviews Editor of the *Columbia Law Review.* Mr. Sullivan served as a law clerk to Judge John Minor Wisdom of the U.S. Court of Appeals for the Fifth Circuit and Justice David H. Souter of the U.S. Supreme Court. He also served as Counselor to the Assistant Attorney General in the Office of Legal Counsel, U.S. Department of Justice.

Clyde A. Szuch (Chapter 6, *Responses to Complaints*) (B.A., 1952, Rutgers University; LL.B., 1955, Harvard Law School) is a litigation partner at the New Jersey law firm of Pitney, Hardin, Kipp & Szuch and is Chairman of the firm's national litigation practice and is its managing partner. Mr. Szuch served as law clerk to the Honorable William J. Brennan, Jr., Associate Justice of the United States Supreme Court, 1956-57. He was an Assistant United States Attorney from 1957-58 and is a past chairman of the Third Circuit Lawyers Advisory Commitee. Mr. Szuch is a member of the American and New Jersey State Bar Associations and is a Fellow of the American Bar Foundation and of the American Law Institute. He is a member of the New Jersey CPR Panel for ADR and a member of the American Arbitration Association's Greater New York Advisory Committee for Large Complex Cases.

Evan M. Tager (Chapter 40, *Punitive Damages*) is an appellate partner in the Washington, D.C., office of Mayer, Brown & Platt. Mr. Tager specializes in punitive damages litigation. He has been involved in dozens of cases in which punitive damages have been sought or awarded, including *BMW of North Am., Inc. v. Gore,* 116 S. Ct. 1589 (1996). The cases in which he has been involved span the tort gamut from product liability to insurance bad faith to consumer fraud to environmental trespass/nuisance to employment discrimination. In addition, Mr. Tager has written and spoken regularly on the subject of punitive damages.

Mr. Tager received his A.B. *magna cum laude* from Princeton University in 1982 and is a 1985 graduate of the Stanford Law School, where he served as Articles Editor of the *Stanford Law Review.* After clerking for Judge Mary M. Schroeder of the U.S. Court of Appeals for the Ninth Circuit, Mr. Tager became an associate at Weil, Gotshal & Manges. In 1988, he moved to Mayer, Brown & Platt, where he became a partner in 1994.

Blake Tartt (Chapter 1, *Subject Matter Jurisdiction*), a partner with Fulbright & Jaworski L.L.P.'s Houston office since 1970, focuses his practice on general and commercial litigation. Mr. Tartt received a B.B.A. in 1949 and a J.D., *cum laude,* in 1959 from Southern Methodist University. He received the Southern Methodist University Law School Distinguished Alumnus Award in 1996. He was admitted to practice law in Texas in 1959.

ABOUT THE AUTHORS

Active in the American Bar Association, Mr. Tartt serves the ABA's House of Delegates as the Texas State Delegate, and he has served in the past as a State Bar of Texas delegate and as a Houston Bar Association delegate. He has served as the Fifth Circuit Representative on the ABA Standing Committee on the Federal Judiciary and is Chair of the Standing Committee on the Federal Judiciary for 1997 and 1998. He is the only Texas lawyer ever to have served as Chair of the Standing Committee. He is a Life Fellow of the American Bar Foundation, where he has been chair of the fellows and a former state chair in Texas. Mr. Tartt served as a member of the Standing Committee on Public Education; a member of the Special House of Delegates Committee on the Treasurer's Report; and a member of the Sections of Litigation, Tort and Insurance Practice, Antitrust, Public Contract Law, International Law and Individual Rights and Responsibilities.

Mr. Tartt is a Fellow of the American College of Trial Lawyers and is a member of the American Law Institute. He is an Advocate of the American Board of Trial Advocates and a member of the International Association of Defense Counsel. A former member of the Executive Council of the National Conference of Bar Presidents, Mr. Tartt was President of the Southern Conference of Bar Presidents. He has also been a director of the American Judicature Society. In addition, Mr. Tartt has been chair of the Committee on Admissions and Discipline of the United States District Court, Southern District of Texas.

Mr. Tartt has also held many leadership positions in the State Bar of Texas, including serving as President. He has now been appointed by the State Bar of Texas to the 11-member State Commission on Judicial Conduct and is currently serving a six-year term. He is also a life fellow of the Texas Bar Foundation, having served as chair of the Board and chair of the fellows in the past.

Fredric C. Tausend (Chapter 44, *Judgments*) has been a partner at Preston Gates and Ellis, LLP in Seattle, Washington since 1990. Before that he was the senior partner in Schweppe, Krug and Tausend, having practiced with that law firm since 1958. His practice is primarily a litigation and appellate practice concentrating on complex commercial and business litigation, constitutional issues and one-of-a-kind cases. For example, he was lead trial counsel for Seattle's Pike Place Public Market in the successfully concluded litigation to restore full control of the market to the Public Authority chartered by the City of Seattle to own, manage and preserve the market in the public interest. As a member of the Division of Antitrust and Consumer Protection in the State Attorney General's Office in the 1960s, he brought the first enforcement cases under the state antitrust law.

In 1983, he served as special independent counsel for the State of Alaska in an investigation of charges of political corruption. His conduct of the investigation, modeled along the lines of the federal special independent counsel law, was independent of both the governor's office and the state legislature. A portion of his law practice has also consisted of counseling attorneys and law firms on matters affecting disciplinary proceedings, professional conduct and law firm dissolution.

In 1980, Fred took a partial leave of absence from practice to become Dean of the University of Puget Sound Law School (now Seattle University Law School), a position he held for six years. Before becoming Dean, he served as Adjunct Professor of Law teaching courses in antitrust, trademark and copyright, and professional responsibility (legal ethics). In 1991-92 and in 1995, he was appointed Shefelman Distinguished Lecturer at the University of Washington Law School, where he has taught civil procedure and professional responsibility on a part-time basis. While continuing to teach as an Adjunct Professor, Fred is engaged in full-time trial and appellate practice and serves as an arbitrator, mediator and pro tem judge on request. In addition, he has participated in and chaired numerous seminars sponsored by bar associations and other professional groups on such subjects as antitrust law, complex litigation, civil procedure, implementation of federal and state Rule 11, constitutional law, trademark, copyright, federal motion practice, settlement techniques and various aspects of trial practice and alternative dispute resolution.

Fred was named Lawyer of the Year for 1991 by the Seattle-King County Bar Association. Fred chaired the Washington State Bar Association's Task Force on Professionalism and recently served on the Washington State Attorney General's Alternative Dispute Resolution Task Force. He is a Fellow of the American College of Trial Lawyers.

Suzanne Easley Tracy (Chapter 2, *Personal Jurisdiction and Service*) is a partner with the firm of Kirkland & Ellis in Los Angeles, California, where she specializes in corporate, commercial, business, and environmental litigation. She has a wide variety of experience including trial, arbitration and law and motion. She received her J.D. *cum laude* from Southern Methodist University School of Law in 1988 where she was Order of the Coif and served as Coordinating Leading Articles Editor for the *Southwestern Law Journal,* now called *SMU Law Review.*

Harry P. Trueheart, III (Chapter 71, *Agency*) is a partner in the firm of Nixon, Hargrave, Devans & Doyle LLP where he is the Managing Partner. He is principally involved in complex business, commercial, construction, securities and antitrust litigation in state and federal courts and in international and United States arbitration.

Mr. Trueheart received his B.A. and J.D. degrees from Harvard University. He is a Past Chair of the Commercial and Federal Litigation Section of the New York Bar Association. He has served as an arbitrator and mediator for the American Arbitration Association and is a member of the panel of neutrals of the CPR Institute for Dispute Resolution. He is a Fellow with the Chartered Institute of Arbitrators. He has been a regular lecturer for the New York Bar Association programs on federal litigation.

Alan E. Untereiner (Chapter 50, *Appeals to the Supreme Court*) is a partner in the Washington, D.C. office of Mayer, Brown & Platt specializing in Supreme Court and appellate litigation. He received his A.B. *magna cum laude* in 1984 from Harvard College and his J.D. in 1988 from Yale Law School, where was a Notes Editor of the *Yale Law Journal*. He served as a law clerk to Judge J. Clifford Wallace on the U.S. Court of Appeals for the Ninth Circuit. He worked for several years at Onek, Klein & Farr in Washington, D.C. before joining Mayer, Brown in 1991.

Anton R. Valukas (Chapter 30, *Motions In Limine*) graduated from Lawrence University in 1965 and from the Northwestern University School of Law in 1968. He served as Deputy Director of the National Defender Project from 1968 to 1970, and then served as an Assistant United States Attorney for the Northern District of Illinois from 1970 to 1976. In 1976, he became a partner at the law firm of Jenner & Block in Chicago. From 1985 to 1989, Mr. Valukas served as United States Attorney for the Northern District of Illinois, after which time he returned to Jenner & Block. Mr. Valukas has taught at the Northwestern University School of Law and John Marshall School of Law. Mr. Valukas is a Fellow in the American College of Trial Lawyers. Mr. Valukas has tried numerous civil and criminal cases in federal and state courts throughout the country, and is the recipient of numerous awards for his activities in the legal field.

Allan Van Fleet (Chapter 52, *Ethical Issues in Commercial Cases*) is a partner in the Houston office of Vinson & Elkins, L.L.P. His practice focuses on complex litigation, antitrust counseling, and legal ethics. He chairs Vinson & Elkins' Professional Responsibility Committee. He is a member of the Council of the American Bar Association Section of Antitrust Law and is a member of its Committee on Professionalism. His publications include *Federal Civil Procedure Before Trial—Fifth Circuit* (1996) (with George Kazen, et al.); *The Competition Laws of NAFTA, Canada, Mexico, and the United States* (1997) (with Eleanor Fox, et al.); and numerous articles on antitrust, trial practice, and legal ethics. He is former Chairman of the City of Houston Ethics Committee, which investigates alleged violations of the Houston Ethics Code and advises the City Council on ethics ordinances. He is a graduate of Rice University (*summa cum laude*) and the Columbia University School of Law (first in class).

The Honorable Roger Vinson (Chapter 8, *Removal to Federal Court*), Chief United States District Judge for the Northern District of Florida, was appointed to the federal bench in 1983. He is currently serving on the Judicial Conference Advisory Committee on Civil Rules and the Eleventh Circuit Pattern Jury Instructions Committee, and is President of the Eleventh Circuit District Judges Association. Chief Judge Vinson was the charter President of the Pensacola Chapter of the American Inns of Court, is a member of the American Judicature Society, and the Florida Bar. He graduated from the United States Naval Academy in 1962, and in 1971, from Vanderbilt University School of Law where he was a Wilson Merit Scholar and on the *Vanderbilt Law Review*.

He was a U.S. Naval Aviator from 1962 until 1968. From 1971 to 1983, he was in private practice with Beggs & Lane in Pensacola, Florida.

William A. Von Hoene, Jr. (Chapter 30, *Motions In Limine*) graduated from Yale University, *cum laude,* in 1976, and from the University of Chicago Law School, *cum laude,* in 1980, where he served on the Law Review and was elected to the Order of the Coif. Following his graduation from law school, Mr. Von Hoene clerked for the Honorable Milton I. Shadur of the United States District Court for the Northern District of Illinois. Mr. Von Hoene became a partner at Jenner & Block in 1987, where he has tried a wide variety of criminal and civil cases. He is a past President of the Chicago Lawyers' Committee for Civil Rights Under Law, Inc.

William E. Wallace, III (Chapter 53, *Antitrust*) is a partner in the Litigation Section of Morgan, Lewis & Bockius LLP, resident in Washington. His practice focuses on litigation and counseling in a broad range of substantive areas, including trademarks, copyrights, patents, grey market goods, counterfeit goods and trade secrets. He has substantial experience litigating antitrust, product liability, real estate, and commercial and financial disputes. He also counsels extensively on Hart-Scott-Rodino and Robinson-Patman compliance, and represents clients before the Federal Trade Commission, Consumer Product Safety Commission and National Highway Traffic Safety Administration.

Mr. Wallace is a member of the American Bar Association's Litigation, Antitrust and Trademark Sections, Federal Bar Association, Association of Trial Lawyers of America, the Defense Research Institute, International Trademark Association, American Intellectual Property Law Association and U.S. Chamber of Commerce Antitrust Council.

Mr. Wallace received his bachelor's degree, *cum laude,* from Boston College in 1975 and his law degree, *cum laude,* from the University of Miami in 1978. After graduation from law school, he clerked for the Honorable Jose A. Gonzalez of the U.S. District Court, Southern District of Florida. Mr. Wallace is admitted to practice in Washington, D.C. and Florida and before the U.S. Supreme Court, U.S. Courts of Appeals for the District of Columbia, Federal, Second, Third, Fourth, Seventh, Ninth and Eleventh Circuits and numerous U.S. district courts. Mr. Wallace lives in Washington, D.C.

John L. Warden (Chapter 16, *Derivative Actions by Stockholders*) is a partner in the New York office of Sullivan & Cromwell. He graduated from Harvard College in 1962 and from the University of Virginia School of Law, where he was Editor-in-Chief of the *Virginia Law Review,* in 1965.

Mr. Warden has had a trial and appellate practice throughout the United States, emphasizing antitrust, securities and corporate control and governance. He has litigated a number of major hostile takeover cases and has been a speaker at several ABA National Institutes on Corporate Control and Governance.

ABOUT THE AUTHORS

Mr. Warden is a member of the American Law Institute, a Fellow of the American College of Trial Lawyers and a Trustee of the University of Virginia Law School Foundation.

Robert S. Warren (Chapter 37, *Final Arguments in Jury and Bench Trials*) a partner in the Los Angeles office of Gibson, Dunn & Crutcher LLP, joined the firm in 1956. A member of the firm's Litigation Department, Mr. Warren specializes in the practice of trial law and has been a Fellow of the American College of Trial Lawyers since 1974. Mr. Warren received his bachelor of arts degree in economics from the University of Southern California in 1953, was admitted to Phi Beta Kappa, and received his law degree from the University of Southern California in 1956, where he was a member of the Order of the Coif and Associate Editor of the *USC Law Review.*

Mr. Warren's practice has encompassed a broad variety of civil litigation, but with a principal focus upon securities and First Amendment cases. His libel victory for the *Wall Street Journal* was selected in the ABA Journal as one of the top ten defense verdicts of 1988. He is now Chair of the Senior Advisory Board to the Ninth Circuit Judicial Conference.

Awards include: American Jewish Committee, Learned Hand Award, 1988; Los Angeles County Bar Association, Shattuck-Price Award for Outstanding Dedication to the Improvement of the Legal Profession and the Administration of Justice, 1989; the Brennan Center for Justice at N.Y.U., Joseph A. Ball Award for Outstanding Advocacy, 1997; and the Trial Lawyer Hall of Fame Award of the Litigation Section of the California State Bar Association for 1998.

Robert C. Weber (Chapter 11, *Multidistrict Litigation*) (B.A. *cum laude* Yale University 1972; J.D. Editorial Board, Law Journal, Order of the Coif, Duke University 1976) is a partner with Jones, Day, Reavis & Pogue where he chairs the Product Liability and Regulation Practice. He has represented clients in complex product liability matters in state and federal trial and appellate courts throughout the United States. Bob serves as trial and national coordinating counsel in the nationwide defense of R.J. Reynolds Tobacco Company's smoking and health litigation. He served as trial counsel in *Galbraith v. R.J. Reynolds Tobacco Co.* (Cal. Sup. Ct., Santa Barbara County), a highly publicized and lengthy tobacco product liability case tried to a defense verdict in December 1985, and the first such case that had proceeded to jury trial in more than a decade. He has also coordinated and served as lead counsel in multijurisdictional product liability proceedings pending in the U.S., Canada, and Europe for other clients in a wide variety of industries, including the pharmaceutical, heavy equipment, and tire industries.

Bob has extensive experience in defending consumer class actions regarding allegedly defective products and in defending and counseling clients regarding enforcement actions brought by various federal agencies, including the Food and Drug Administration, the National Highway Traffic Safety Administration, and the Occupational Safety and Health

Administration. He has also served as lead counsel for clients in numerous complex commercial matters, including several that were resolved through alternate dispute resolution techniques. In addition, he has also represented the NFL's New England Patriots in litigation over the alleged harassment of female sports reporters. Pursuant to an appointment by the Cleveland Bar Association, Bob also served as trial and appellate counsel for the bar in a complex attorney discipline case brought by the bar under authority of the Ohio Supreme Court.

Professor Harold C. Wegner (Chapter 63, *Patents*) is Director of the Intellectual Property Law Program at the George Washington University Law School and Director of the Dean Dinwoodey Center for Intellectual Property Studies, Washington, D.C. Previously, he was an Adjunct Professor at the Georgetown University Law Center. Prof. Wegner is also a member of the national law firm of Foley & Lardner. Prof. Wegner specializes in global intellectual asset management with a particular focus upon East Asia and patents and other aspects of intellectual property rights. Prof. Wegner deals with technology transfer and the international enforcement of intellectual property rights. Prof. Wegner has received degrees from Northwestern University (B.A.) and the Georgetown University Law Center (J.D.); for three years beginning in 1974 he resided in Munich where he was a Wiss. Mitarbeiter at the Max-Planck-Institut für Ausländisches und Internationales Patent-, Urheber- und Wettbewerbsrecht; thereafter, he was a Kenshuin at the Kyoto University Law Faculty, Kyoto, under Prof. Zentaro Kitagawa. Prof. Wegner served in the United States Department of Commerce as a Patent Examiner before entering the private practice of law in 1969. Professor Wegner is the author of numerous books and articles on intellectual property, most recently as a coauthor of a West casebook on patent law.

Stephen A. Weiner (Chapter 68, *ERISA*) has been a partner of Winthrop, Stimson, Putnam & Roberts since 1968, and served as Vice Chairman of its Management Committee from 1984 to 1997. He graduated *summa cum laude* from Harvard College, where he was elected to Phi Beta Kappa, and *cum laude* from Yale Law School, where he was Comment Editor of the *Yale Law Journal* and was elected to Order of the Coif. Before joining his firm as a partner, he served for three years as Acting Professor of Law at the Boalt Hall School of Law, University of California, Berkeley.

Mr. Weiner practices in the field of state and federal civil litigation, with emphasis in the commercial, securities and banking areas. He is a Fellow of the American College of Trial Lawyers and of the American Bar Foundation, and former Chairman of the Committee on Second Circuit Courts of the Federal Bar Council. He also co-authored Chapter 59 on *"Theft or Loss of Business Opportunities"* in the treatise *Commercial Litigation in New York State Courts* (Haig ed.)(West 1995 & Supp. 1998).

G. Marc Whitehead (Chapter 38, *Jury Conduct, Instructions and Verdicts*) is a partner in the Litigation Department, practicing out of McDermott, Will & Emery's Chicago and New York offices. Prior to joining the firm, Mr. Whitehead was Chair Emeritus of the international law firm of Popham, Haik, Schnobrich & Kaufman, Ltd. He is also the Founding Director of Global Liability Management, an international management consultancy established in 1993, which offers a multi-disciplinary approach to risk analysis and liability prevention.

Mr. Whitehead is a trial lawyer specializing in toxic tort, intellectual property, product liability and commercial litigation. He is a frequent lecturer and author on trial tactics, environmental law, preventative law, and international liability.

Mr. Whitehead has been primarily responsible for the activities of the American Bar Association's Section of Litigation in the area of tort reform and civil litigation reform for the past 15 years and currently serves as Chair of the ABA Litigation Section's Jury Initiatives Task Force. He is co-author of a manual, *Jury Trial Innovations* produced in conjunction with the National Center for State Courts, through a joint grant with the State Justice Institute.

In addition to the ABA's Litigation Section, Mr. Whitehead is a member of the International Bar Association, American Board of Trial Advocates, International Association of Defense Counsel, and a Fellow of the American Bar Foundation. He is the former Chair of the Litigation Section's Task Force on Tort Reform and the former Chair of the Environmental Litigation Committee, as well as a former ABA Council Member and Division Director of the ABA's Litigation Section. He serves on the Editorial Advisory Board for *Inside Litigation,* BNA's *Product Liability Journal* and the *European Environmental Law Review.*

Mr. Whitehead is a graduate of Princeton University (1961) and Yale Law School (1964).

Douglas R. Widin (Chapter 12, *Issue and Claim Preclusion*) is a senior member of the law firm of Cozen and O'Connor in its Philadelphia office. Mr. Widin is a *cum laude* graduate of the Dickinson School of Law, where he served as Projects Editor of the Law Review. He served as law clerk to the Honorable John B. Hannum of the United States District Court for the Eastern District of Pennsylvania from 1983 to 1985.

Mr. Widin has been actively engaged in the litigation of business and commercial disputes in numerous federal courts, as well as the courts of various states. He is licensed to practice in both Pennsylvania and New Jersey and is a member of the American and Philadelphia Bar Associations.

Richard E. Wiley (Chapter 62, *Communications*) is a senior partner at Wiley, Rein & Fielding, a Washington, D.C. law firm with the largest communications practice in the United States. As a former Chairman, Commissioner and General Counsel of the Federal Communications Commission, he was a leading force in the agency's initial efforts to foster increased competition and lessened regulation in the communications field.

Since 1985, Dick Wiley has been regularly recognized as one of the nation's 100 "most influential" lawyers by the *National Law Journal.*

He also has been the subject of a number of recent profiles, including in *The New York Times* ("Telecommunications' Ubiquitous Man of Influence") and *The American Lawyer* ("Brand Name of Communications Law"). He has received both the Electronic Industries Association's Medal of Honor and an "Emmy" from the Academy of Television Arts and Sciences in recognition of his nine year service as Chairman of the FCC's Advisory Committee on Digital Television. He is a member of Broadcasting & Cable magazine's "Hall of Fame" and has served as President of the Federal Bar and Federal Communications Bar Associations.

A native of Illinois, Mr. Wiley graduated with distinction from Northwestern (B.S. and J.D. degrees) and holds a Masters Degree in Law (LL.M.) from Georgetown. He has received a distinguished alumnus award from each University and also is Chair of the Advisory Board of Columbia University's Institute for Tele-Information.

Harry A. Woods, Jr. (Chapter 79, *Energy*) a director of the law firm of Crowe & Dunlevy, P.C. in Oklahoma City, Oklahoma, concentrates his practice in the area of litigation, focusing on products liability, securities, torts and contracts. He currently is serving as the President of the Ruth Bader Ginsburg American Inn of Court. He is an elected member of the American Law Institute and he is listed in *The Best Lawyers in America* (Business Litigation) and *An International Who's Who of Product Liability Defense Lawyers*. He received his bachelor's degree from Oklahoma State University and his juris doctor from New York University, where he was a Root-Tilden Scholar.

W. Carter Younger (Chapter 66, *Labor Law*) is a partner in the Richmond office of McGuire, Woods, Battle & Boothe, LLP, and heads the firm's Labor and Employment Law Group. He represents management in the areas of union-management relations, labor arbitration, employment discrimination, executive employment contracts, and government regulation of the employment relationship. His 25 years of labor and employment law experience includes mediation and employment litigation in federal and state courts and in Virginia and other states throughout the country. He also represents employers before administrative agencies, including the National Labor Relations Board, the Department of Labor's Office of Federal Contract Compliance Programs and Wage and Hour Division, and state and local equal employment opportunity agencies.

Mr. Younger is a 1970 graduate of the University of Virginia School of Law, where he served on the Editorial Board of the *Virginia Law Review* and was a member of Order of the Coif. He was law clerk to Justice Thomas C. Gordon, Jr. of the Supreme Court of Virginia from 1970-71.

Mr. Younger taught labor law at the University of Richmond's T.C. Williams School of Law as an Adjunct Professor from 1984 to 1987. He is a member of the Virginia Bar Association, and from 1987 to 1990 chaired the Association's Section on Labor and Employment Law. He is a member the Labor and Employment Law Section of the American Bar Association and its International Labor Law Committee. He is also a member

ABOUT THE AUTHORS

of the American Bar Association Litigation Section. Mr. Younger is Vice President of the Labor and Employment Commission of the Union Internationale des Advocats. He has been listed in *The Best Lawyers in America* for Labor and Employment Law since 1987.

*

WESTLAW® ELECTRONIC RESEARCH GUIDE

Coordinating Legal Research With WESTLAW

The *Business and Commercial Litigation in Federal Courts* is an essential aid to legal research. WESTLAW provides a vast, online library of over 10,000 collections of documents and services that can supplement research begun in this publication, encompassing:

- Federal and state primary law (statutes, regulations, rules, and case law), including West's editorial enhancements, such as headnotes, Key Number classifications, annotations;

- Secondary law resources (texts and treatises published by West Publishing Company and by other publishers, as well as law reviews);

- Legal news

- Directories of attorneys and experts

- Court records and filings

- Citators

Specialized topical subsets of these resources have been created for more than thirty areas of practice.

In addition to legal information, there are general news and reference databases and a broad array of specialized materials frequently useful in connection with legal matters, covering accounting, business, environment, ethics, finance, medicine, social and physical sciences.

This guide will focus on a few aspects of WESTLAW use to supplement research begun in this publication, and will direct you to additional sources of assistance.

Databases

A database is a collection of documents with some features in common. It may contain statutes, court decisions, administrative materials, commentaries, news or other information. Each database has a unique identifier, used in many WESTLAW commands to select a database of interest. For example, the database containing cases from the 50 states in the area of Commercial Law cases has the identifier MCML-CS.

The WESTLAW Directory is a comprehensive list of databases with information about each database, including the types of documents each contains. The first page of a standard or customized WESTLAW Directory is displayed upon signing on to WESTLAW, except when prior, saved research is resumed. To access the WESTLAW Directory at any time, enter DB.

A special subdirectory, accessible from the main WESTLAW Directory, lists databases applicable to Commercial Law & Contracts research.

Databases of potential interest in connection with your research include:

FCML-CS	Federal Cases - Commercial Law and Contracts
NYCML-CS	New York Commercial Law and Contracts
ULA	Uniform Laws Annotated
CML-TP	Law Reviews, Texts and Journals - Commercial Law and Contracts
WLD-CML	West's Legal Directory - Commercial Law and Contracts
COMLJ	Commercial Law Journal (Commercial Law League of America)
HAWKLAND	Uniform Commercial Code Series (Hawkland)
PLI-COMM	Commercial Law and Practice Course Handbook Series (Practicing Law Institute)
REST-CONTR	Restatement of the Law - Contracts (American Law Institute)
UCC-CS	Uniform Commercial Code Cases (Clark Boardman Callaghan)
UCC-CS+	Uniform Commercial Code Cases Plus (Clark Boardman Callaghan)
UCCGUIDE	Uniform Commercial Code Filing Guide (UCC Guide, Inc.)

For information as to currentness and search tips regarding any WESTLAW database, enter the SCOPE command SC followed by the database identifier (e.g., SC NY-CS). It is not necessary to include the identifier to obtain scope information about the currently selected database.

WESTLAW Highlights

Use of this publication may be supplemented through the WESTLAW Bulletin (WLB), the WESTLAW New York State Bulletin (WSB-NY) and various Topical Highlights, including Finance & Banking Highlights (WTH-FIN). Highlights databases contain summaries of significant judicial, legislative and administrative developments and are updated daily; they are searchable both from an automatic list of recent documents and using general WESTLAW search methods for documents accumulated over time. The full text of any judicial decision may be retrieved by entering FIND.

Consult the WESTLAW Directory (enter DB) for a complete, current listing of highlights databases.

Retrieving a Specific Case

The FIND command can be used to quickly retrieve a case whose citation is known. For example:

FI 616 A.2d 1336

Updating Case Law Research

There are a variety of citator services on WESTLAW for use in updating research.

Insta-Cite® may be used to verify citations, find parallel citations, ascertain the history of a case, and see whether it remains valid law. References are also provided to secondary sources, such as Corpus Juris Secundum®, that cite the case. To view the Insta-Cite history of a displayed case, simply enter the command IC. To view the Insta-Cite history of a selected case, enter a command in this form:

IC 574 A.2d 502

Shepard's® Citations provides a comprehensive list of cases and publications that have cited a particular case, with explanatory analysis to indicate how the citing cases have treated the case, e.g., "followed," "explained." To view the Shepard's Citations about a displayed case, enter the command SH. Add a case citation, if necessary, as in the prior Insta-Cite example.

For the latest citing references, not yet incorporated in Shepard's Citations, use Shepard's PreView® (SP command) and QuickCite™ (QC command), in the same way.

To see a complete list of publications covered by any of the citator services, enter its service abbreviation (IC, SH, SP or QC) followed by PUBS. To ascertain the scope of coverage for any of the services, enter the SCOPE command (SC) followed by the appropriate service abbreviation. For the complete list of commands available in a citator service, enter its service abbreviation (IC, SH, SP or QC) followed by CMDS.

Retrieving Statutes, Court Rules and Regulations

Annotated and unannotated versions of the New York statutes are searchable on WESTLAW (identifiers NY-ST-ANN and NY-ST), as are New York court rules (NY-RULES).

The United States Code and United States Code - Annotated are searchable databases on WESTLAW (identifiers USC and USCA, respectively), as are federal court rules (US-RULES) and regulations (CFR).

In addition, the FIND command may be used to retrieve specific provisions by citation, obviating the need for database selection or search. To FIND a desired document, enter FI, followed by the citation of the desired document, using the full name of the publication, or one of the abbreviated styles recognized by WESTLAW.

If WESTLAW does not recognize the style you enter, you may enter one of the following, using US, NY, or any other state code in place of XX:

FI XX-ST	Displays templates for codified statutes
FI XX-LEGIS	Displays templates for legislation
FI XX-RULES	Displays templates for rules
FI XX-ORDERS	Displays templates for court orders

Alternatively, entering FI followed by the publication's full name or an accepted abbreviation will normally display templates, useful jump possibilities, or helpful information necessary to complete the FIND process. For example:

FI USCA	Displays templates for United States Code - Annotated
FI FRAP	Displays templates for Federal Rules of Appellate Procedure

FI FRCP	Displays templates for Federal Rules of Civil Procedure
FI FRCRP	Displays templates for Federal Rules of Criminal Procedure
FI FRE	Displays templates for Federal Rules of Evidence
FI CFR	Displays templates for Code of Federal Regulations
FI FR	Displays templates for Federal Register

To view the complete list of FINDable documents and associated pre-scribed forms, enter FI PUBS.

Updating Research in re Statutes, Rules and Regulations

When viewing a statute, rule or regulation on WESTLAW after a search or FIND command, it is easy to update your research. A message will appear on the screen if relevant amendments, repeals or other new material are available through the UPDATE feature. Entering the UP-DATE command will display such material.

Documents used to update California statutes are also searchable in California Legislative Service (CA-LEGIS). Those used to update rules are searchable in New York Orders (CA-ORDERS).

Documents used to update federal statutes, rules, and regulations are searchable in the United States Public Laws (US-PL), Federal Orders (US-ORDERS) and Federal Register (FR) databases, respectively.

When documents citing a statute, rule or regulation are of interest, Shepard's Citations on WESTLAW may be of assistance. That service covers federal constitutional provisions, statutes and administrative provisions, and corresponding materials from many states. The command SH PUBS displays a directory of publications which may be Shepardized on WESTLAW. Consult the WESTLAW manual for more information about citator services.

Using WESTLAW as a Citator

For research beyond the coverage of any citator service, go directly to the databases (cases, for example) containing citing documents and use standard WESTLAW search techniques to retrieve documents citing specific constitutional provisions, statutes, standard jury instructions or other authorities.

Fortunately, the specific portion of a citation is often reasonably distinctive, such as 22:636.1, 301.65, 401(k), 12-21-5, 12052. When it is, a search on that specific portion alone may retrieve applicable documents without any substantial number of inapplicable ones (unless the number happens to be coincidentally popular in another context).

Similarly, if the citation involves more than one number, such as 42 U.S.C.A. § 1201, a search containing both numbers (e.g., 42 +5 1201) is likely to produce mostly desired information, even though the component numbers are common.

If necessary, the search may be limited in several ways:

A. Switch from a general database to one containing mostly cases within the subject area of the cite being researched;

B. Use a connector (&, /S, /P, etc.) to narrow the search to documents including terms which are highly likely to accompany the correct citation in the context of the issue being researched;

C. Include other citation information in the query. Because of the variety of citation formats used in documents, this option should be used primarily where other options prove insufficient. Below are illustrative queries for any database containing Commercial Law:

Escott /s Barchris

will retrieve cases citing the seminal case Escott v. Barchris Construction Corporation; and

15 /7 77k 77m /p "class action"

will retrieve cases citing seminal case Escott v. Barchris Construction Corporation.

Alternative Retrieval Methods

WIN® (WESTLAW Is Natural™) allows you to frame your issue in plain English to retrieve documents:

Right to deficiency judgment after sale (selling disposition) of collateral.

Alternatively, retrieval may be focused by use of the Terms and Connectors method:

DI(COLLATERAL /P DEFICIENCY)

In databases with Key Numbers, either of the above examples will identify Secured Transactions ⊂⇒240 as a Key Number collecting head-notes relevant to this issue if there are pertinent cases.

Since the Key Numbers are affixed to points of law by trained specialists based on conceptual understanding of the case, relevant cases that were not retrieved by either of the language-dependent methods will often be found at a Key Number.

Similarly, citations in retrieved documents (to cases, statutes, rules, etc.) may suggest additional, fruitful research using other WESTLAW databases (e.g., annotated statutes, rules) or services (e.g., citator services).

Key Number Search

Frequently, case law research rapidly converges on a few topics, headings and Key Numbers within West's Key Number System that are likely to contain relevant cases. These may be discovered from known, relevant reported cases from any jurisdiction; Library References in West publications; browsing in a digest; or browsing the Key Number System on WESTLAW using the JUMP feature or the KEY command.

Once discovered, topics, subheadings or Key Numbers are useful as search terms (in databases containing reported cases) alone or with other search terms, to focus the search within a narrow range of potentially relevant material.

For example, to retrieve cases with at least one headnote classified to Secured Transactions ⬅︎240, sign on to a caselaw database and enter

349Ak240   [use with other search terms, if desired]

The topic name (Secured Transactions) is replaced by its numerical equivalent (349A) and the ⬅︎ by the letter k. A list of topics and their numerical equivalents is in the WESTLAW Reference Manual and is displayed in WESTLAW when the KEY command is entered.

Other topics of special interest are listed below.

Assignment (38)	Guaranty (195)
Bankruptcy (51)	Interest (219)
Banks and Banking (52)	Judgment (228)
Bills and Notes (56)	Novation (278)
Carriers (70)	Pledges (303)
Chattel Mortgages (76)	Principal and Agent (308)
Consumer Credit (92B)	Reformation of Instruments (328)
Consumer Protection (92H)	Sales (343)
Contracts (95)	Trade Regulation (382)
Damages (115)	Vendor and Purchaser (400)
Debtor and Creditor (117T)	Warehousemen (403)
Fraudulent Conveyances (186)	

Using JUMP

WESTLAW's JUMP feature allows you to move from one document to another or from one part of a document to another, then easily return to your original place, without losing your original result. Opportunities to move in this manner are marked in the text with a JUMP symbol (▶). Whenever you see the JUMP symbol, you may move to the place designated by the adjacent reference by using the Tab, arrow keys or mouse click to position the cursor on the JUMP symbol, then pressing Enter or clicking again with the mouse.

Within the text of a court opinion, JUMP arrows are adjacent to case cites and federal statute cites, and adjacent to parenthesized numbers marking discussions corresponding to headnotes.

On a screen containing the text of a headnote, the JUMP arrows allow movement to the corresponding discussion in the text of the opinion,

▶ (3)

and allow browsing West's Key Number System beginning at various heading levels:

▶ 349A   SECURED TRANSACTIONS
▶ 349AVII   Default and Enforcement
▶ 349Ak240 k. Deficiency and personal liability.

To return from a JUMP, enter GB (except for JUMPs between a headnote and the corresponding discussion in opinion, for which there is a matching number in parenthesis in both headnote and opinion). Returns from successive JUMPs (e.g., from case to cited case to case cited by cited case) without intervening returns may be accomplished by repeated entry of GB or by using the MAP command.

WESTLAW ELECTRONIC RESEARCH GUIDE

General Information

The information provided above illustrates some of the ways WESTLAW can complement research using this publication. However, this brief overview illustrates only some of the power of WESTLAW. The full range of WESTLAW search techniques is available to support your research.

Please consult the WESTLAW Reference Manual for additional information or assistance or call West's Reference Attorneys at 1-800-REF-ATTY (1-800-733-2889).

For information about subscribing to WESTLAW, please call 1-800-328-0109.

*

SUMMARY OF CONTENTS

Volume 1

Volume 2

Volume 3

SUMMARY OF CONTENTS

SUMMARY OF CONTENTS

Table of Jury Instructions
Table of Forms
Table of Statutes
Table of Rules
Table of Cases
Index

*

TABLE OF CONTENTS

Volume 1

CHAPTER 1. SUBJECT MATTER JURISDICTION

TABLE OF CONTENTS

TABLE OF CONTENTS

TABLE OF CONTENTS

TABLE OF CONTENTS

CHAPTER 4. INVESTIGATION OF THE CASE

TABLE OF CONTENTS

TABLE OF CONTENTS

CHAPTER 5. THE COMPLAINT

TABLE OF CONTENTS

TABLE OF CONTENTS

TABLE OF CONTENTS

C

TABLE OF CONTENTS

TABLE OF CONTENTS

CHAPTER 8. REMOVAL TO FEDERAL COURT

TABLE OF CONTENTS

TABLE OF CONTENTS

TABLE OF CONTENTS

TABLE OF CONTENTS

TABLE OF CONTENTS

TABLE OF CONTENTS

CHAPTER 12.   ISSUE AND CLAIM PRECLUSION

TABLE OF CONTENTS

TABLE OF CONTENTS

TABLE OF CONTENTS

TABLE OF CONTENTS

TABLE OF CONTENTS

TABLE OF CONTENTS

TABLE OF CONTENTS

TABLE OF CONTENTS

CHAPTER 1

SUBJECT MATTER JURISDICTION

by
Blake Tartt*

Table of Sections

* The author gratefully acknowledges the assistance of Marcy Hogan Greer of Fulbright & Jaworski L.L.P.'s Austin, Texas, office, in the preparation of this chapter.

WESTLAW Electronic Research

See WESTLAW Electronic Research Guide preceding the Summary of Contents.

---

§ 1.1 Scope Note

Subject matter jurisdiction is the authority of the court to entertain and decide certain types of disputes. A judgment rendered in the absence of subject matter jurisdiction is invalid.[1] The federal courts are courts of limited jurisdiction, and a party seeking adjudication in a federal forum must prove a basis for federal subject matter jurisdiction to be entitled to litigate there.

There are a number of reasons that a litigant may prefer to be in federal court and thus take on the burden of invoking federal subject matter jurisdiction—even though a state court may be equally available. Indeed, the federal courts have proven to be attractive forums for many business and commercial cases. They have a great deal of experience with these types of cases since there are many federal statutes expressly permitting specific types of business and commercial issues to be decided in federal forums.[2] These disputes are generally complex—with numerous parties, difficult issues, and mountains of documents—and the federal courts have been innovative in managing and streamlining litigation of this nature.

The federal courts also generally have a much wider body of law from which to draw precedent and authority than do the state courts, whose role is generally limited to interpreting the law of that particular state.

Another advantage of the federal judicial system is that cases can be transferred between the federal courts throughout the country to a proper or more appropriate federal venue if the original venue is defective or inconvenient. The state courts, by contrast, can order transfer only within their boundaries.

Finally, there may be certain procedural and practical benefits to bringing a case in, or removing it to,[3] federal court—such as more favorable discovery devices, evidentiary standards, or summary disposition possibilities. In some cases, these differences may well be outcome-determinative.

As a cautionary note, however, a risk is taken by litigating in federal court. If jurisdiction is found lacking at any point, the case must be dismissed.[4] That risk is increased when state claims are joined with federal claims that stand an excellent chance of being dismissed at a preliminary, or early, stage of the litigation. If the court dismisses the federal claim, it should also dismiss the state claims in most instances,[5] resulting in delay and expense that would not have been incurred had

---

§ 1.1

1. Caterpillar Inc. v. Lewis, 519 U.S. 61, ___, 117 S.Ct. 467, 477, 136 L.Ed.2d 437 (1996) (holding that a district court must have subject matter jurisdiction by the time it renders a judgment in order for the judgment to be valid).

2. *See, e.g., infra* § 1.6(a)(3).

3. The procedures and special considerations governing removal of a case from state court to federal court are discussed in Chapter 8 "Removal to Federal Court," *infra.*

4. *See infra* § 1.5.

5. *See infra* § 1.8(c)(2).

the state claims been brought initially in state court. For these reasons, all parties to a case brought either in state or federal court should be attuned to the issue of federal subject matter jurisdiction.

This chapter discusses the various standards and procedures for invoking and challenging subject matter jurisdiction in federal court. It also addresses the various issues and limitations affecting the jurisdiction of the federal courts.

Library References:

> West's Key No. Digests, Federal Courts ⬤1–65, 161–247, 261–319, 331–360.
> Wright, Miller, Kane & Cooper, Federal Practice and Procedure: Civil 2d §§ 1061, 1063, 1350, 1414, 1917, 2766, 3505–3507, 3561.

§ 1.2 Strategy, Objectives, and Preliminary Considerations

The federal courts have the authority and duty to insure that federal subject matter jurisdiction exists before affording any relief. Ideally, a federal court should determine subject matter jurisdiction at the outset of the case to prevent the court and parties from expending time and other valuable resources only to find that jurisdiction is lacking. However, a challenge to subject matter jurisdiction may be brought by any party at any time during the litigation proceedings, including appeal.[1] Even the party that originally invoked the court's jurisdiction can change positions and attack it at a later time during the proceedings.[2]

Unlike other procedural challenges, objections to federal jurisdiction cannot be waived, and both the trial and appellate courts can and must examine the issue on their own even if none of the parties attacks the jurisdictional grounds for a dispute.[3] Consent of the parties is not an adequate basis for sustaining federal jurisdiction, and no party can rely upon a stipulation or admission by the opposing party as to the existence of federal subject matter jurisdiction.[4] Even a preliminary finding of jurisdiction, such as the denial of a Rule 12(b) motion to dismiss for want of jurisdiction, is tenuous because if federal jurisdiction is subsequently found to be lacking, the case must be dismissed—regardless of the initial determination.[5] For these reasons, there is no way to guarantee subject matter jurisdiction, and it can provide the ultimate trump card in federal litigation. It is therefore advisable to evaluate seriously and thoroughly the basis of federal jurisdiction at the outset of a case. Even if a party would prefer to be in federal court, it may not be worth the risk of losing

---

§ 1.2

1. *See infra* § 1.5.

2. American Fire & Cas. Co. v. Finn, 341 U.S. 6, 71 S.Ct. 534, 95 L.Ed. 702 (1951) (holding that the party which originally invoked federal jurisdiction may challenge it).

3. *See infra* § 1.5.

4. Sosna v. Iowa, 419 U.S. 393, 398, 95 S.Ct. 553, 556, 42 L.Ed.2d 532 (1975) (agreement of parties held insufficient to cure jurisdictional defects); *cf.* Giannakos v. M/V Bravo Trader, 762 F.2d 1295, 1297 (5th Cir.1985) (holding that parties' conduct, which could amount to waiver or estoppel, did not create federal jurisdiction).

5. FRCP 12(h)(3).

a favorable verdict or judgment on appeal for lack of subject matter jurisdiction.

There is also the risk that, if the parties' dispute involves both issues of state and federal law, the federal court may elect to hear only the federal claims and remand or dismiss the state law claims, leaving the litigants in the difficult and costly position of maintaining parallel suits in two different forums.[6] This threat is heightened when the state law claims are not integrally related to, or dependent upon the resolution of the federal ones.

For these reasons, if federal jurisdiction is questionable or is not sufficiently comprehensive to resolve the entire dispute between litigants, the parties need to factor this problem into their choice of forum and/or their strategy in seeking early adjudication (through dismissal of the case on the pleadings or summary judgment) or attempting settlement of the matter before expending time and other valuable resources litigating the matter in federal court.

§ 1.3   Overview of Federal Subject Matter Jurisdiction

Unlike state courts, which generally have subject matter jurisdiction unless a statute denies them, a federal court may exercise jurisdiction only if it is specifically authorized to do so. Consequently, a party seeking to bring or defend a suit in federal court bears the burden of demonstrating a jurisdictional basis for doing so.[1]

There are three main types of federal subject matter jurisdiction: federal question jurisdiction, diversity jurisdiction, and supplemental jurisdiction. Federal question jurisdiction provides a federal forum for issues or claims derived from, or involving significant issues of, federal law.[2] Diversity is based upon the citizenship of the parties, rather than upon the nature of the claims asserted.[3] Supplemental jurisdiction is available to permit state law claims that are substantially intertwined with a federal dispute to be brought in federal court as well.[4]

Library References:

West's Key No. Digests, Federal Courts ⚖1–65, 161–247, 261–319, 331–360.
Wright & Miller, Federal Practice and Procedure: Civil 2d § 1063.

§ 1.4   Sources of Subject Matter Jurisdiction

Unlike the United States Supreme Court, which derives its authority directly from the Constitution, the lower federal courts must be both constitutionally and statutorily authorized to entertain a given dispute.

---

6. *See infra* § 1.8.

§ 1.3

1. *See, e.g.,* McNutt v. General Motors Acceptance Corp. of Indiana, 298 U.S. 178, 189–90, 56 S.Ct. 780, 785, 80 L.Ed. 1135 (1936) (holding that party invoking federal

jurisdiction bears the burden of proving basis for its existence).

2. *See infra* § 1.6.

3. *See infra* § 1.7.

4. *See infra* § 1.8.

Because this jurisdiction is so jealously guarded, even an agreement between the parties is insufficient to confer jurisdiction on a federal court.[1]

The role of the federal judiciary is limited by the Constitution, statute, and judicially-created doctrines that foster both federalism and separation of powers. By limiting federal court authority and intervention, state courts are assured certain levels of autonomy. Conversely, a more circumscribed federal review preserves issues for federal court jurisdiction that are uniquely within the expertise of the federal courts.

(a) Constitutional Provisions

Article III of the United States Constitution is the starting point for any subject matter jurisdictional analysis. The United States Supreme Court was established by Article III,[2] and its subject matter jurisdiction is defined in the Constitution itself. Articles I and III also confer upon Congress the discretion to create lower federal courts.[3] Because these trial courts originate from statute, their subject matter jurisdiction is also defined by statute. As a result, the district courts and circuit courts of appeals must have both constitutional and statutory authority to sustain their subject matter jurisdiction. The distinction is significant because the Supreme Court has interpreted the scope of federal jurisdiction under Article III and under the general federal jurisdiction statute quite differently, despite virtually identical language.[4]

Article III grants the Supreme Court original jurisdiction in cases affecting ambassadors, other public ministers and consuls, and cases in which a state is a party.[5] Article III additionally defines the kinds of cases the federal courts may hear. The judicial power granted in Article III extends to: (i) all cases, in law and equity, arising under the Constitution, the laws of the United States, and its treaties; (ii) cases affecting ambassadors, other public ministers and consuls; (iii) cases of admiralty and maritime jurisdiction; (iv) controversies to which the United States is a party; (v) controversies between two or more states; (vi) controversies between a state and citizens of another state;[6] (vii) controversies between citizens of different states; (viii) controversies between citizens of the same state claiming lands under grants of different states; and (ix) controversies between a state or its citizens and foreign states, citizens or subjects.[7] Article III does not, however, prescribe any procedures for invoking federal jurisdiction.[8]

§ 1.4

1. Sosna v. Iowa, 419 U.S. 393, 398, 95 S.Ct. 553, 556, 42 L.Ed.2d 532 (1975).

2. *See* U.S. Const. art. III, § 1, cl. 1.

3. *Id.*; *see also* U.S. Const. art. I, § 8, cl. 9.

4. *See infra* § 1.6(a).

5. *Id.*

6. As discussed below at § 1.11(b), the Eleventh Amendment severely limits the authority of a federal court to entertain suits against a state and its agencies and officers.

7. U.S. Const. art. III, § 2.

8. Ankenbrandt v. Richards, 504 U.S. 689, 689–90, 112 S.Ct. 2206, 2207–08, 119 L.Ed.2d 468 (1992).

(b) Statutory Provisions

Article III implicitly grants Congress certain powers with respect to defining federal jurisdiction of the lower federal courts through its grant of the discretion to create these courts—although the extent of its authority in this regard is by no means clear. Congress has implemented its authority through a number of federal question jurisdiction subject matter statutes. Section 1331 of Title 28 is the general federal question statute, which provides for federal question jurisdiction in cases "arising under the Constitution, laws, or treaties of the United States."[9] Section 1332 grants federal courts the authority to hear cases between citizens of different states and/or foreign states.[10] Section 1367 permits supplemental jurisdiction over state law claims that are so related to federal question claims already pending in the action as to constitute "part of the same case or controversy.... "[11] Additionally, there are a number of specific subject matter jurisdiction statutes—relating to areas of federal interest, such as admiralty, intellectual property, and antitrust—that authorize the federal courts to hear these types of cases.[12] These federal statutes confer only a limited amount of the judicial power available under Article III of the Constitution.[13]

(c) Statutory and Prudential Limitations

In addition to creating or expanding subject matter jurisdiction, Congress can also limit the authority of the federal courts. For example, Congress can and has made certain types of claims nonremovable—even though the claim could have originally been brought in federal court.[14] Further, certain types of issues, such as family laws and probate matters, are generally considered to be reserved to the states and their courts, even if a federal forum would otherwise be available.[15] The presumption of concurrent jurisdiction between state and federal courts serves as another limit on federal jurisdiction which permits a plaintiff to choose its forum and defeat a defendant's right to remove the case to federal court unless the federal court has exclusive jurisdiction over the dispute

9. 28 U.S.C.A. § 1331 (West 1993); *see infra* § 1.6(a)(2).

10. 28 U.S.C.A. § 1332 (West 1993 & Supp. 1997); *see infra* § 1.7(a)(2).

11. 28 U.S.C.A. § 1367(a) (West 1993); *see infra* § 1.8(a)(3).

12. *See infra* § 1.6(a)(3).

13. Verlinden B. V. v. Central Bank of Nigeria, 461 U.S. 480, 494–95, 103 S.Ct. 1962, 1971–72, 76 L.Ed.2d 81 (1983).

14. *See, e.g.,* 28 U.S.C.A. § 1445(a) (West Supp. 1997) (deeming certain actions against railroads or their receivers or trustees, to be nonremovable); 28 U.S.C.A. § 1445(b) (West Supp. 1997) (civil actions against carriers for delay, loss or injury of shipments, under certain provisions of title

49); 28 U.S.C.A. § 1445(c) (West 1994) (state workmen's compensation actions); 28 U.S.C.A. § 1445(d) (West Supp. 1997) (civil actions arising under the Violence Against Women Act of 1994).

15. Williams v. North Carolina, 325 U.S. 226, 233, 65 S.Ct. 1092, 1097, 89 L.Ed. 1577 (1945) (observing that federal courts do not entertain family law disputes, which are best left to the state courts and their administrators); *see also* Markham v. Allen, 326 U.S. 490, 66 S.Ct. 296, 90 L.Ed. 256 (1946) (holding that federal courts do not have the jurisdiction to probate wills or administer estates even if federal jurisdiction would otherwise exist).

or the dispute actually involves federal—rather than state—law.[16] Finally, the "well-pleaded complaint" rule generally requires that federal subject matter jurisdiction be evident from the face of the plaintiff's pleadings. Under this rule, even if a federal cause of action could be pled or a federal defense is anticipated, a federal forum will not be available unless the pleadings indicate that the dispute is clearly and exclusively federal in nature.[17]

Library References:

West's Key No. Digests, Federal Courts ⊕1–65.
Wright & Miller, Federal Practice and Procedure: Civil 2d §§ 1067, 1069.

§ 1.5 Challenges to Subject Matter Jurisdiction

Subject matter jurisdiction may be challenged at any time during the pendency of the case, including a direct appeal from the trial court's judgment.[1] A defect in federal jurisdiction can be raised at any time during this process.[2] However, a judgment rendered without subject matter jurisdiction is not subject to collateral attack in another proceeding on that basis if the party had the opportunity to litigate the issue.[3]

(a) Court's Duty to Examine Its Own Jurisdiction

The federal trial courts are duty-bound to examine the basis of their jurisdiction, even if the parties do not advance the issue, and both a trial and appellate court can and must dismiss a case sua sponte at any point if jurisdiction is found to be lacking.[4] A corollary proposition is that the parties cannot, by waiver, agreement, or estoppel, confer federal jurisdiction on a court when it is otherwise lacking.[5] Otherwise, subject matter jurisdiction could be expanded through the conduct of the parties themselves, contrary to the fundamental presumption that federal courts

---

16. See infra § 1.10(b).

17. See infra §§ 1.6(c) & 1.7(c).

§ 1.5

1. Chicot County Drainage Dist. v. Baxter State Bank, 308 U.S. 371, 376–77, 60 S.Ct. 317, 319–20, 84 L.Ed. 329 (1940); see also FRCP 12(h)(3).

2. Louisville & Nashville R.R. v. Mottley, 211 U.S. 149, 29 S.Ct. 42, 53 L.Ed. 126 (1908).

3. McCormick v. Sullivant, 23 U.S. (10 Wheat.) 192, 6 L.Ed. 300 (1825) (refusing to permit a collateral attack on judgment based upon lack of trial court's subject matter jurisdiction); see also Chicot County Drainage District, 308 U.S. at 376–77, 60 S.Ct. at 319–20 (holding that permitting a party to make collateral challenge to final judgment for lack of subject matter jurisdiction would violate principles of res judica-

ta). Although this rule appears to conflict with the principle that subject matter jurisdiction may not be waived, the policy of finality of judgments in this context overrides competing factors of federal jurisdiction.

4. See, e.g., Louisville & Nashville R.R. v. Mottley, 211 U.S. 149, 151–54, 29 S.Ct. 42, 43–44, 53 L.Ed. 126 (1908) (Supreme Court dismissed case on subject matter jurisdiction grounds despite lack of objection by parties or any discussion of issue at trial or court of appeals level.).

5. Sosna v. Iowa, 419 U.S. 393, 398, 95 S.Ct. 553, 556, 42 L.Ed.2d 532 (1975) (agreement of parties held insufficient to cure jurisdictional defects); Giannakos v. M/V Bravo Trader, 762 F.2d 1295, 1297 (5th Cir.1985) (holding that parties' conduct, which could amount to waiver or estoppel, did not create federal jurisdiction).

possess only limited jurisdiction.[6]

(b) Parties' Objections to Defects in Subject Matter Jurisdiction

Any party may challenge federal jurisdiction—even the party which originally brought the case to federal court.[7] In fact, a party can admit the existence of subject matter jurisdiction and later challenge its existence during the same proceeding.[8] Although many federal courts caution that these objections should be made and determined at the outset of the case—and "prior to substantial investment in case preparation,"[9] both the Federal Rules of Civil Procedure and case law make clear that the lack of subject matter jurisdiction cannot be waived.[10]

Library References:

West's Key No. Digests, Federal Courts ⊕29.
Wright & Miller, Federal Practice and Procedure: Civil 2d §§ 1350–1351.

§ 1.6   Federal Question Jurisdiction

Federal question jurisdiction focuses upon the nature of the claim asserted. Although no cohesive bright-line test has been—or probably could be—formulated, a cause of action is deemed to be "arising under" federal law for purpose of federal question jurisdiction either when it derives directly from a federal law or implicates a significant interest of federal law and cannot be resolved without a determination of the federal question.

(a) "Arising Under" Federal Law

Both Article III of the Constitution and 28 U.S.C.A. § 1331, the general federal question statute, employ the same operative language with respect to federal question jurisdiction.[1] Nonetheless, the term "arising under" has been interpreted in a much more restrictive manner with respect to Section 1331. Although the legislative history does not

---

6. Giannakos, 762 F.2d at 1297.

7. American Fire & Cas. Co. v. Finn, 341 U.S. 6, 71 S.Ct. 534, 95 L.Ed. 702 (1951) (holding that the party which originally invoked federal jurisdiction may challenge it).

8. Eisler v. Stritzler, 535 F.2d 148, 151 (1st Cir.1976).

9. Elliott v. Tilton, 62 F.3d 725, 729 (5th Cir.1995) (chastising the parties and lower court for failing to address and decide the jurisdictional defense in the early stages of the case rather than on appeal), *vacated on other grounds*, 69 F.3d 35, 36 (5th Cir.), *vacated on other grounds*, 89 F.3d 260, 262 (5th Cir.1996).

10. *See, e.g.*, FRCP 12(h)(3); Louisville & Nashville R.R. v. Mottley, 211 U.S. 149, 151, 29 S.Ct. 42, 43, 53 L.Ed. 126 (1908).

§ 1.6

1. *Compare* U.S. Const. art. III, § 2 ("The judicial Power shall extend to all Cases, in Law and Equity, arising under this Constitution, the Laws of the United States, and Treaties made, or which shall be made, under their Authority.... ") *with* 28 U.S.C.A. § 1331 (West 1993) ("The district courts shall have original jurisdiction of all civil actions arising under the Constitution, laws, or treaties of the United States.").

necessarily support this result,[2] it has been justified over the years as necessary to prevent federal encroachment on state courts and to limit the number of cases the federal judiciary must actually decide.

(1) Article III

Virtually any claim brought directly under the United States Constitution, except for the Full Faith and Credit Clause of Article IV,[3] provides a basis for federal subject matter jurisdiction. Further, if federal law "forms an ingredient of the original cause," a federal court is authorized to hear the case under Article III.[4] Chief Justice Marshall, writing for the Court in *Osborn v. Bank of United States*, explained that it is "a sufficient foundation for jurisdiction, that the title or right set up by the party, may be defeated by one construction of the constitution or law of the United States, and sustained by the opposite construction."[5] The Court's opinion in *Osborn* was necessarily limited to defining the scope of federal jurisdiction under Article III because the decision predates the enactment of Section 1331, the general federal question statute.

(2) General Federal Question Statute—28 U.S.C.A. § 1331

In the 80 years after the Constitution was ratified, Congress experimented with a number of federal jurisdiction statutes relating to specific subject areas. It was not until 1875 that Congress authorized general federal question jurisdiction.[6] That statute has been codified into 28 U.S.C.A. § 1331, and has remained virtually unchanged since its inception—except to delete the amount in controversy requirement in 1980.[7] Although Section 1331 has the same "arising under" language as Article III, it has never been interpreted to include all matters described in Article III.[8] As the Court explained, "the many limitations which have been placed on jurisdiction under Section 1331 are not limitations on the constitutional power of Congress to confer jurisdiction on the federal courts ...Art. III 'arising under' jurisdiction is broader than federal-question jurisdiction under Section 1331."[9]

2. *See* Erwin Chemerinsky, Federal Jurisdiction § 5.2, at 254–55 (2d ed. 1994) (discussing legislative history of § 1331).

3. U.S. Const. art. IV, § 1 ("Full Faith and Credit shall be given in each State to the public Acts, Records, and judicial Proceedings of every other State. And the Congress may by general Laws prescribe the Manner in which such Acts, Records and Proceedings shall be proved, and the Effect thereof."); *see also* Minnesota v. Northern Sec. Co., 194 U.S. 48, 72, 24 S.Ct. 598, 605, 48 L.Ed. 870 (1904) (holding that the Full Faith and Credit Clause does not provide an independent basis for federal subject matter jurisdiction).

4. Osborn v. Bank of United States, 22 U.S. (9 Wheat.) 738, 6 L.Ed. 204 (1824).

5. *Id.* at 823.

6. *See* Act of Mar. 3, 1875, ch. 137, 18 Stat. 470.

7. Pub. L. 96–486, 94 Stat. 2369 (1980).

8. Verlinden B. V. v. Central Bank of Nigeria, 461 U.S. 480, 494–95, 103 S.Ct. 1962, 1971–72, 76 L.Ed.2d 81 (1983) (noting that the Supreme Court has construed § 1331 much more narrowly than its expansive interpretations of Article III).

9. *Id.* at 495, 103 S.Ct. at 1972; Shoshone Mining Co. v. Rutter, 177 U.S. 505, 508, 20 S.Ct. 726, 727, 44 L.Ed. 864 (1900) (expressly indicating that Article III and § 1331 are to be interpreted differently.)

The opinions limiting the reach of Section 1331 have been justified on the same grounds as federal judicial restraint generally—if Section 1331 were interpreted as expansively as Article III, virtually any case would implicate federal jurisdiction, simply because some ingredient of that case involves federal law and even if the federal law issue is only remotely related to the dispute.

Federal "laws" for purposes of Section 1331 include statutes, federal administrative agency regulations,[10] and the federal common law.[11] International law has also been considered to be part of the laws of the United States for purposes of federal question jurisdiction.[12]

Congressionally-created corporations present a special case. In order to invoke federal question jurisdiction based solely on the ground that Congress incorporated the entity, the corporation must show that the United States owns more than one-half of its capital stock. Further, if the federal charter contains an express provision that the corporation may "sue and be sued" in federal court, a federal forum will be available.[13]

(3) Specific Federal Question Statutes

A number of federal statutes confer original federal jurisdiction upon the district courts relating to particular subject matters. In order to invoke these specific statutory bases for federal jurisdiction, a party must show that the cause of action pled arises under their authority. Examples of these statutes include those relating to admiralty and maritime law,[14] bankruptcy,[15] statutory interpleader,[16] commerce and antitrust,[17] patents and other intellectual property rights,[18] federal taxes and custom duties,[19] civil rights,[20] the United States as a party,[21] the Resolution Trust Corporation and the Federal Deposit Insurance Corporation,[22] the Comprehensive Environmental Response, Compensation and Liability

---

10. Reno v. Catholic Social Servs., Inc., 509 U.S. 43, 56, 113 S.Ct. 2485, 2495, 125 L.Ed.2d 38 (1993).

11. Illinois v. City of Milwaukee, 406 U.S. 91, 100, 92 S.Ct. 1385, 1391, 31 L.Ed.2d 712 (1972) (finding "no reason not to give 'laws' its natural meaning" in concluding that § 1331 includes federal common law claims as well as statutory ones).

12. Torres v. Southern Peru Cooper Corp., 113 F.3d 540, n. 7 (5th Cir.1997); see also Texas Indus., Inc. v. Radcliff Materials, Inc., 451 U.S. 630, 101 S.Ct. 2061, 68 L.Ed.2d 500 (1981) (authorizing the creation of federal common law in the area of foreign relations).

13. American Nat'l Red Cross v. S.G., 505 U.S. 247, 112 S.Ct. 2465, 120 L.Ed.2d 201 (1992).

14. 28 U.S.C.A. § 1333 (West 1993); see also Chapter 56 "Admiralty," infra.

15. 28 U.S.C.A. § 1334 (West 1993 & Supp. 1997); see also Chapter 45 "Bankruptcy Code Impact on Civil Litigation in the Federal Courts," infra.

16. 28 U.S.C.A. § 1335 (West 1993).

17. 28 U.S.C.A. § 1337 (West 1993 & Supp. 1997); see also Chapter 53 "Antitrust," infra.

18. 28 U.S.C.A. § 1338 (West 1993); see also Chapter 63 "Patents," Chapter 64 "Trademark," and Chapter 65 "Copyright," infra.

19. 28 U.S.C.A. § 1340 (West 1993).

20. 28 U.S.C.A. § 1343 (West 1993).

21. 28 U.S.C.A. §§ 1345–1347 (West 1993 & Supp. 1997).

22. 12 U.S.C.A. § 1441a (West 1989 & Supp. 1997); 12 U.S.C.A. § 1819 (West 1989 & Supp. 1997); see also Chapter 59 "Banking," infra.

Act of 1980,[23] and the Racketeer Influenced and Corrupt Organization Act.[24]

(b) Determining "Arising Under" Jurisdiction

Ascertaining whether a claim "arises under" federal law for purposes of Section 1331 continues to be a topic of much debate. For over a hundred years, courts and scholars have wrestled with the determination of whether a claim "arises under" federal law. There is no clear answer today. Federal courts appear to have federal question jurisdiction if it is apparent from the plaintiff's complaint that (i) the cause of action is created by federal law; or (ii) the cause of action is based upon state law but necessarily requires the resolution of a substantial question of federal law involving a significant federal interest.[25] While relatively simple to articulate, this test is quite difficult in application. Although a few rules have been attempted over the years, recent Supreme Court decisions have further muddied these jurisdictional waters.[26] As the Court itself has noted, no one formulation of the "arising under" definition captures all of the nuances involved in determining which cases fall within a federal court's original jurisdiction.[27] Fortunately, as several commentators have remarked, the majority of cases are easily resolved as a practical matter without resorting to the confusing and indeed conflicting lines of "arising under" authorities.[28]

(1) Federal Cause of Action

The first test for "arising under" jurisdiction analyzes whether the cause of action is itself created by federal law. Justice Holmes articulated this so-called "creation" test in *American Well Works Co. v. Layne and Bowler Co.*,[29] holding that a case arises under the law that creates the cause of action. Although the Supreme Court has long since disavowed the notion that a state-created cause of action is insufficient to support the exercise of federal jurisdiction, the converse still appears to be true— *i.e.*, that a cause of action created by a federal law is sufficient.[30]

---

23. 42 U.S.C.A. § 9613 (West 1995); *see also* Chapter 80 "Environmental Claims," *infra*.

24. 18 U.S.C.A. § 1964 (West 1984 & Pamph. 1997); *see also* Chapter 69 "RICO," *infra*.

25. The Fifth Circuit has recently found federal subject matter jurisdiction for a state law cause of action when a prior federal judgment on a federal question completely precluded the state claim. *See* Carpenter v. Wichita Falls Indep. Sch. Dist., 44 F.3d 362 (5th Cir.1995).

26. *See, e.g., infra* § 1.6(b)(2).

27. *See* Merrell Dow Pharmaceuticals, Inc. v. Thompson, 478 U.S. 804, 808, 106 S.Ct. 3229, 3232, 92 L.Ed.2d 650 (1986).

28. *See, e.g.,* 15 James Wm. Moore, Moore's Federal Practice § 103.31[1], at 103–32 to 103–33 (3d ed. 1997); 13B Charles Alan Wright, Edward H. Cooper & Arthur R. Miller, Federal Practice and Procedure § 3562, at 20 (2d ed. 1984).

29. 241 U.S. 257, 258–59, 36 S.Ct. 585, 585–86, 60 L.Ed. 987 (1916).

30. *See* T.B. Harms Co. v. Eliscu, 339 F.2d 823, 827 (2d Cir.1964) (stating that Justice Holmes' jurisdictional formula in *American Well Works* "is more useful for inclusion than for the exclusion for which it was intended").

When a federal statute creates the cause of action, federal question jurisdiction will generally exist. Indeed, it would be ironic if a federally-created remedy or cause of action could not be adjudicated in a federal forum. However, in a few rare instances, federal question jurisdiction has been found to be lacking even though the cause of action was derived solely from federal law. For example, in *Shoshone Mining Co. v. Rutter*, the Supreme Court refused to find "arising under" jurisdiction even though the federal law at issue was specifically designed to resolve conflicting claims of miners to federal lands in the federal courts.[31] Central to its analysis was the fact that the statute incorporated by reference local customs and rules.[32] These instances where the Court has found subject matter jurisdiction lacking when the plaintiff's claim derives directly from federal law, however, are rare. None is a recent decision. Although the Supreme Court has never expressly overruled this line of authority, it has more recently made the unqualified statement that federal question jurisdiction exists if "federal law creates the cause of action."[33]

Federal law can be viewed as the source of a cause of action whether Congress expressly creates the cause of action or whether its intent to do so may be implied through the statutory scheme. Even when federal law does not provide an express cause of action, a federal claim may exist by implication.[34] In these situations, federal law provides a substantive right, and the federal remedy is implied from the statutory framework:

> When Congress enacts new legislation, the question is whether Congress intended to create a private remedy as a supplement to the express enforcement provisions of the statute. When Congress acts in a statutory context in which an implied private remedy has already been recognized by the courts, ... the question is whether Congress intended to preserve the preexisting remedy.[35]

---

31. *See* Shoshone Mining Co. v. Rutter, 177 U.S. 505, 20 S.Ct. 726, 44 L.Ed. 864 (1900); *see also* Shulthis v. McDougal, 225 U.S. 561, 569, 32 S.Ct. 704, 706, 56 L.Ed. 1205 (1912) (holding that a suit to enforce a right which simply "takes its origin in the laws of the United States" does not "aris[e] under" federal law "unless it really and substantially involves a dispute or controversy respecting the validity, construction, or effect of such a law, upon the determination of which the result depends").

32. Shoshone Mining, 177 U.S. at 508–12, 20 S.Ct. at 727–28.

33. Franchise Tax Bd. v. Construction Laborers Vacation Trust, 463 U.S. 1, 27–28, 103 S.Ct. 2841, 2855–56, 77 L.Ed.2d 420 (1983).

34. *See* Cort v. Ash, 422 U.S. 66, 78, 95 S.Ct. 2080, 2087, 45 L.Ed.2d 26 (1975) (de-fining four-part test for determining whether a private right of action may be implied from a federal statute); *see also* Touche Ross & Co. v. Redington, 442 U.S. 560, 569, 575–76, 99 S.Ct. 2479, 2489, 61 L.Ed.2d 82 (1979) (emphasizing that the appropriate inquiry is "whether Congress intended to create a private remedy," by analyzing the language, history, and purpose of the statute). In recent years, however, the Supreme Court has been increasingly hesitant to imply causes of action when Congress has not expressly done so. *See, e.g.,* Thompson v. Thompson, 484 U.S. 174, 188–91, 108 S.Ct. 513, 520–22, 98 L.Ed.2d 512 (1988) (Scalia, J., dissenting).

35. Merrill Lynch, Pierce, Fenner & Smith, Inc. v. Curran, 456 U.S. 353, 378–79, 102 S.Ct. 1825, 1839–40, 72 L.Ed.2d 182 (1982).

So long as an express or implied right of action stems directly from federal law, the federal courts will be available forums to entertain the claim.

(2) Resolution of Federal Law

The mere fact that a cause of action itself does not "arise under" federal law does not necessarily preclude a finding of federal question jurisdiction. In the past, if federal law did not create a cause of action, either expressly or implicitly, federal question jurisdiction would be denied.[36] However, today in some instances, federal jurisdiction can exist even if the cause of action is created by state law, so long as a federal law provides a significant and substantive right. This second type of "arising under" jurisdiction is much more difficult and controversial than the "federal cause of action" test because the controlling cases do not provide much in the way of guidelines or practical application.

One of the significant decisions in this regard is *Smith v. Kansas City Title and Trust Company*,[37] in which the Supreme Court found federal jurisdiction even though federal law did not provide a remedy and the cause of action was entirely state-created. At issue was Kansas City Title & Trust Co.'s attempt to invest company funds in bonds issued by Federal Land Banks pursuant to the Federal Farm Loan Act. The plaintiffs, who were shareholders of the corporation, sued to enjoin the investment and invoked a Missouri law which afforded injunctive relief to prevent illegal investments by corporations.[38] To show illegality, the plaintiffs asserted that the federal Act under which the bonds were issued was unconstitutional.[39]

Although the cause of action was brought under state law, the Court nonetheless found federal question jurisdiction.[40] It justified its ruling by stating that the case arose under federal law because the right to relief "depend[ed] upon the construction or application of the Constitution or laws of the United States."[41]

Since *Smith*, the Court has not been as willing to give expansive interpretations to "arising under" jurisdiction. In *Moore v. Chesapeake & Ohio Railway Co.*,[42] the Court held that federal jurisdiction does not exist if a state has merely incorporated federal law by reference within its own laws. *Moore* involved claims by a railroad employee who was injured while working on an intrastate railroad. He brought suit under a state law which precluded any finding of contributory negligence by the employee if the employer had violated any safety law which contributed to the injury. To satisfy this element of the state tort law, the employee contended that the employer had violated a federal safety statute. He

---

36. *E.g.*, American Well Works Co. v. Layne and Bowler Co., 241 U.S. 257, 258–59, 36 S.Ct. 585, 585–86, 60 L.Ed. 987 (1916) (holding that a cause of action arises under the law of its creation).

37. 255 U.S. 180, 195, 41 S.Ct. 243, 244, 65 L.Ed. 577 (1921).

38. *Id.* at 198, 41 S.Ct. at 244.

39. *Id.* at 195–96, 41 S.Ct. at 244.

40. *Id.* at 209–10, 41 S.Ct. at 248–49.

41. *Id.* at 199, 41 S.Ct. at 245.

42. 291 U.S. 205, 213, 54 S.Ct. 402, 405, 78 L.Ed. 755 (1934).

argued that this federal question provided the basis for federal subject matter jurisdiction over the case. The Supreme Court disagreed. In its view, the mere fact that a violation of a federal standard was an element of state tort recovery was not sufficient to justify the exercise of federal jurisdiction.[43] Although *Moore* did not expressly overrule *Smith*, the two opinions do appear to conflict with one another, resulting in much confusion among the lower courts straining to reconcile them.

Two years after *Moore* was decided, Justice Cardozo formulated what was, for many years, the seminal subject matter jurisdiction test in *Gully v. First National Bank in Meridian*.[44] That case involved the State of Mississippi's attempts to tax a national bank. The bank claimed immunity from the tax on the basis of federal law, which exempted national banks from such taxes except where Congress had specifically provided otherwise. Justice Cardozo, writing for the unanimous Court, found federal jurisdiction to be lacking, reasoning that:

> The tax here in controversy, if valid as a tax at all, was imposed under the authority of a statute of Mississippi. The federal law did not attempt to impose it or confer upon the tax collector authority to sue for it . . . . . *Here the right to be established is one created by the state. If that is so, it is unimportant that federal consent is the source of state authority* . . . . . By unimpeachable authority, a suit brought upon a state statute does not arise under an act of Congress or the Constitution of the United States because prohibited thereby . . . . . With no greater reason can it be said to arise thereunder because permitted thereby.[45]

The Court summarized existing law as requiring that:

> [A] right or immunity created by the Constitution or laws of the United States must be an element, and an essential one, of the plaintiff's cause of action. . . .The right or immunity must be such that it will be supported if the Constitution or laws of the United States are given one construction or effect, and defeated if they receive another.[46]

Justice Cardozo's analysis focused upon the role that federal law played in reaching the result in the case and not the law creating the cause of action.[47] The *Gully* rationale lasted for many years until the Supreme Court decided *Merrell Dow Pharmaceuticals Inc. v. Thompson*[48] in 1986.

In *Merrell Dow*, the Court declined to find jurisdiction over a state law cause of action into which a federal standard was incorporated. The plaintiffs in that case were seeking damages, primarily based upon state

---

43. *Id.* at 217, 54 S.Ct. at 406.

44. 299 U.S. 109, 112, 57 S.Ct. 96, 97, 81 L.Ed. 70 (1936).

45. Gully, 299 U.S. at 115–16, 57 S.Ct. at 99 (emphasis added) (citations omitted).

46. *Id.* at 112, 57 S.Ct. at 97 (citations omitted). *See also* Franchise Tax Board v. Construction Laborers Vacation Trust, 463

U.S. 1, 9, 103 S.Ct. 2841, 2846, 77 L.Ed.2d 420 (1983) (reiterating that a case must "necessarily depend on the resolution of a substantial question of federal law").

47. *Id.*

48. 478 U.S. 804, 813–14, 106 S.Ct. 3229, 3234–35, 92 L.Ed.2d 650 (1986).

negligence and product liability laws and argued that the defendant's alleged violations of the Federal Food, Drug and Cosmetic Act created a rebuttable presumption of negligence.[49] The Court found federal question jurisdiction lacking, reasoning that since Congress did not expressly or impliedly create a federal cause of action in the Federal Food, Drug and Cosmetic Act, it would undermine congressional intent to adjudicate violations of its provisions in a federal forum.[50]

Much confusion has resulted from the analysis in *Merrell Dow* since a compelling argument can be made that the absence of a federal cause of action in the statute does not amount to congressional disapproval of adjudication in a federal forum.[51] Further, *Merrell Dow* seems to overrule *Smith* and its expansive interpretation of "arising under" jurisdiction; however, the Court chose not to overrule *Smith* and in fact distinguished it from *Moore*, stating that the difference was the nature of the federal interest at stake—*i.e.*, *Smith* involved "the constitutionality of an important federal statute," while in *Moore*, it was "the violation of [a] federal standard as an element of state tort recovery [which] did not fundamentally change the state tort nature of the action."[52]

Merrell Dow has failed to provide a cohesive, functional standard for determining federal question jurisdiction in cases involving federal issues and interests.[53] Until the Court gives more guidance in this area, federal courts will have to continue to wrestle with the availability of federal question jurisdiction when federal law is applicable but the cause of action derives from state law.

(3) Federal Question Must Be Substantial

Regardless of whether federal or state law provides the cause of action, in order for federal jurisdiction to exist, the federal issue must be "substantial." In other words, federal courts are prohibited from exercising jurisdiction over claims that would otherwise be within their jurisdiction when the claims are "so attenuated and unsubstantial as to be absolutely devoid of merit."[54] The Court has also interpreted "substantial" as not being "essentially fictitious," "implausible" or "patently without merit."[55] "Substantiality" therefore refers to the legal substance of the plaintiff's position rather than the value of the interest at stake.[56]

49. *Id.* at 805–06, 106 S.Ct. at 3230–3231.

50. *Id.* at 814, 817, 106 S.Ct. at 3235, 3236.

51. *See, e.g., id.* at 825, 106 S.Ct. at 3240 (Brennan, J., dissenting).

52. *Id.* at 814–15 n.12, 106 S.Ct. at 3235–36 n. 12.

53. *Id.* at 821 n.1, 106 S.Ct. at 3239 n.1 (Brennan, J., dissenting) ("[A] test based upon an ad hoc evaluation of the importance of the federal issue is infinitely malleable: at what point does a federal interest become strong enough to create jurisdic-

tion?"); *see generally* Charles Alan Wright, Law of Federal Courts § 17 (5th ed. 1994); *see also* Chemerinsky, *supra* note 2, § 5.2, at 269–73.

54. Newburyport Water Co. v. Newburyport, 193 U.S. 561, 579, 24 S.Ct. 553, 557, 48 L.Ed. 795 (1904).

55. *See* Hagans v. Lavine, 415 U.S. 528, 537, 542–43, 94 S.Ct. 1372, 1381–82, 39 L.Ed.2d 577 (1974).

56. Bell v. Hood, 327 U.S. 678, 66 S.Ct. 773, 90 L.Ed. 939 (1946).

Generally, federal courts will find the federal issue to be "insubstantial" for purposes of federal jurisdiction only when the federal claim has no feasible basis or is absolutely foreclosed by prior Supreme Court precedent and there is no good faith argument for a change in the law.[57] Further, in order to sustain federal question jurisdiction, a party need not prove in advance that it will ultimately prevail on the merits of its federal claims; federal question jurisdiction will not be lacking simply because the court subsequently decides that the federal claim lacks merit.[58]

(c) Scope of Determination

Federal question jurisdiction is determined from the face of the plaintiff's complaint. The "well-pleaded complaint" rule basically directs the court to look to the substance and essential allegations of the complaint to ascertain jurisdiction. The plaintiff is considered the "master to decide what law he will rely upon and therefore does determine whether he will bring a 'suit arising under' the law of the United States."[59] As a result, it is the plaintiff's cause of action that determines federal question jurisdiction; an anticipated defense based upon federal law is generally insufficient to confer jurisdiction.[60]

The actual labels used by the plaintiff in the complaint are not determinative of federal jurisdiction. Rather, the court is to verify the existence of a federal question by examining the substance of the complaint.[61] Thus, even if the plaintiff has inartfully pled what is in reality a federal claim or has failed to mention the relevant federal law, the trial court may look behind the defectively pled allegations to determine whether federal question jurisdiction indeed exists.[62] Indeed, upon removal to federal court from state court, even the plaintiff's affirmative statement that no federal claim exists is not dispositive of the issue; rather, if the claim is necessarily one of federal law, this type of disclaimer will not be controlling.[63] Similarly, upon removal, a federal

57. Parker & Parsley Petroleum Co. v. Dresser Indus., 972 F.2d 580, 586 n. 6 (5th Cir.1992) (holding that "this standard is met only where the plaintiff's claim has no plausible foundation or is clearly foreclosed by a prior Supreme Court decision" (citation omitted)); England v. Louisiana State Bd. of Med. Exam'rs, 259 F.2d 626 (5th Cir.1958) (noting exception to dispositive Supreme Court precedent rule when opinion is outdated and circumstances have changed).

58. Bell v. Hood, 327 U.S. 678, 682, 66 S.Ct. 773, 776, 90 L.Ed. 939 (1946) (stating that a plaintiff may allege a sufficiently substantial claim to give the court subject matter jurisdiction even though that claim is ultimately dismissed on the merits for lack of proof or for failure to state a cognizable cause of action under FRCP 12(b)(6)).

59. Fair v. Kohler Die & Specialty Co., 228 U.S. 22, 25, 33 S.Ct. 410, 411, 57 L.Ed. 716 (1913).

60. Merrell Dow Pharmaceuticals, Inc. v. Thompson, 478 U.S. 804, 808, 106 S.Ct. 3229, 3232, 92 L.Ed.2d 650 (1986); Louisville & Nashville R.R. v. Mottley, 211 U.S. 149, 152, 29 S.Ct. 42, 43, 53 L.Ed. 126 (1908).

61. Aquafaith Shipping, Ltd. v. Jarillas, 963 F.2d 806, 808 (5th Cir.1992).

62. Uncle Ben's, Inc. v. Hapag–Lloyd Aktiengesellschaft, 855 F.2d 215, 217 (5th Cir.1988).

63. Grynberg Prod. Corp. v. British Gas, p.l.c., 817 F.Supp. 1338, 1354 (E.D.Tex.1993).

court is permitted to look past a plaintiff's "artful pleading" when a plaintiff intentionally manipulates his allegations to conceal an obvious federal claim.[64]

Some courts have held that a federal court may "be required to survey the entire record, including the defendant's pleadings, and base its ruling on the complaint, on undisputed facts, and on its resolution of disputed facts."[65] However, the direction to review pleadings and evidence outside of the plaintiff's complaint does not grant a court permission to allow the defendant's pleadings to control; rather, the purpose of the inquiry is to determine whether the "well-pleaded complaint" actually states a federal cause of action.[66]

A corollary to the principle that the plaintiff's, rather than defendant's, pleadings control federal jurisdiction is the rule that a declaratory judgment action, standing alone, will not supply the necessary nexus to federal law. Under the seminal case of *Skelly Oil Co. v. Phillips Petroleum Co.,*[67] the Supreme Court held that the Declaratory Judgment Act[68] does not provide an independent basis for federal subject matter jurisdiction. In its view, to interpret the Declaratory Judgment Act as an independent basis for federal jurisdiction would "distort the limited procedural purpose of the Act" because a party could manipulate jurisdiction solely by seeking a declaration as to an anticipated federal defense.[69] Under the rule in *Skelly Oil,* a party cannot do indirectly what it cannot do directly.

Although the determination of subject matter jurisdiction is to be made based upon the initial federal court pleadings—*i.e.,* the complaint and/or notice of removal—several circuit courts of appeals have recognized an exception to this rule when the plaintiff amends the complaint expressly to state a federal claim and the case is tried on the merits without objection to any prior defect in jurisdiction.[70]

(d) Determining Preemption

An exception to the principle that an anticipated federal defense will not suffice to create federal jurisdiction occurs when a federal court has exclusive jurisdiction, such as when the plaintiff's claim is clearly preempted by federal law. When Congress creates a federal cause of action that so clearly preempts any state law cause of action, a district

---

64. Federated Dep't Stores, Inc. v. Moitie, 452 U.S. 394, 397 n. 2, 101 S.Ct. 2424, 2427 n. 2, 69 L.Ed.2d 103 (1981) (cautioning that a plaintiff cannot "use artful pleading to close off defendant's right to a federal forum").

65. Aquafaith Shipping, 963 F.2d at 808.

66. *Id.*

67. 339 U.S. 667, 70 S.Ct. 876, 94 L.Ed. 1194 (1950).

68. 28 U.S.C.A. §§ 2201, 2202 (West 1994).

69. Skelly Oil Co., 339 U.S. at 673–74, 70 S.Ct. at 880–81; *see also* Franchise Tax Bd. v. Construction Laborers Vacation Trust, 463 U.S. 1, 103 S.Ct. 2841, 77 L.Ed.2d 420 (1983).

70. *E.g.,* Kidd v. Southwest Airlines, Co., 891 F.2d 540, 547 (5th Cir.1990); Bernstein v. Lind–Waldock & Co., 738 F.2d 179, 185 (7th Cir.1984).

court may disregard reference in the pleadings to state law and find a basis for federal jurisdiction.[71] Similarly, when federal law "occupies an entire field, rendering any claim a plaintiff may raise necessarily federal in nature,"[72] federal jurisdiction exists.[73]

However, it is important to note that state courts generally are presumed to have concurrent jurisdiction with the federal courts.[74] Unless a federal statute clearly mandates exclusive federal jurisdiction, a federal court should generally not find preemption.

Library References:

West's Key No. Digests, Federal Courts ⬡161–247.
Wright, Miller & Cooper, Federal Practice and Procedure: Civil 2d §§ 1209, 3562.

§ 1.7   Diversity Jurisdiction

In stark contrast to federal question jurisdiction, which is based upon an issue of federal law, diversity jurisdiction is based upon the locations or "citizenships" of the parties. Although there are numerous schools of thought as to why diversity jurisdiction was created, the traditional theory is that it was intended to protect out of state defendants from any local bias or prejudice in the state courts. As Chief Justice Marshall explained it: "However true the fact may be, that the tribunals of the States will administer justice as impartially as those of the nation, to parties of every description, it is not less true that the constitution itself either entertains apprehensions on this subject, or views with such indulgence the possible fears and apprehensions of suitors, that it has established national tribunals for the decision of controversies between aliens and a citizen, or between citizens of different States."[1]

Other commentators have offered different explanations for the existence of diversity jurisdiction, including fear of populist state legislatures adopting anti-business laws. In Judge Friendly's view, one reason federal constitutional provisions and laws were adopted—and federal court jurisdiction made available—was to protect nonresident creditors and interstate commerce.[2]

---

71. Metropolitan Life Ins. Co. v. Taylor, 481 U.S. 58, 107 S.Ct. 1542, 95 L.Ed.2d 55 (1987).

72. Hubbard v. Blue Cross & Blue Shield Ass'n, 42 F.3d 942, 945 (5th Cir.), *cert. denied*, 515 U.S. 1122, 115 S.Ct. 2276, 132 L.Ed.2d 280 (1995); *see also* Chapter 8 "Removal to Federal Court," *infra*.

73. Metropolitan Life Ins. Co. v. Taylor, 481 U.S. at 63, 107 S.Ct. at 1546.

74. Tafflin v. Levitt, 493 U.S. 455, 459–60, 110 S.Ct. 792, 795, 107 L.Ed.2d 887 (1990) (noting strong presumption in the favor of concurrent state court jurisdiction denied only "by explicit statutory directive, by unmistakable implication from legislative history or by clear incompatibility be-

tween state court jurisdiction and federal interest"); *see also* Yellow Freight Sys., Inc. v. Donnelly, 494 U.S. 820, 110 S.Ct. 1566, 108 L.Ed.2d 834 (1990) (discussing the "presumption of concurrent jurisdiction" that lies at the heart of the federal system); *cf.* The Moses Taylor, 71 U.S. (4 Wall.) 411, 430, 18 L.Ed. 397 (1866) (exclusive federal jurisdiction in admiralty cases).

§ 1.7

1. Bank of United States v. Deveaux, 9 U.S. (5 Cranch) 61, 87, 3 L.Ed. 38 (1809).

2. Friendly, *The Historic Basis of Diversity Jurisdiction*, 41 Harv. L. Rev. 483, 495–97 (1928).

(a) Sources of Authority

As with federal question jurisdiction, federal district courts must have both constitutional and statutory authority to exercise diversity jurisdiction.[3]

(1) Constitutional Authority

Article III is the constitutional source of federal diversity jurisdiction, authorizing federal courts to entertain suits between citizens of different states.[4] Article III also grants the authority for "alienage jurisdiction," *i.e.*, for "cases" or "controversies" between "a State, or the Citizens thereof, and foreign States, Citizens, or Subjects."[5]

(2) Statutory Authority

The statutory authority for diversity jurisdiction is contained in Section 1332 of Title 28. That statute confers upon the district courts "original jurisdiction of all civil actions where the matter in controversy exceeds the sum or value of $75,000, exclusive of interest and costs, and is between—(1) citizens of different States; (2) citizens of a State and citizens or subjects of a foreign state; (3) citizens of different States and in which citizens or subjects of a foreign state are additional parties; and (4) a foreign state, [as defined in the Foreign Sovereign Immunities Act, 28 U.S.C.A. §§ 1602–1611]."[6] The $75,000 amount in controversy requirement is purely a creature of statute, since the Constitution makes no reference to any jurisdictional amount. Nonetheless, an amount in controversy has been required as a part of statutory diversity since its inception.[7]

(3) Jurisprudential Limits

The Supreme Court has set some of its own limitations on diversity jurisdiction, announcing that certain types of cases for which diversity jurisdiction would otherwise be available may not be brought in federal court. For example, the Court has decreed that "the whole subject of the domestic relations of husband and wife, parent and child, belongs to the laws of the States, and not to the laws of the United States."[8] The Court has recently reaffirmed its position that state courts have both the

---

3. *See supra* § 1.4.

4. U.S. Const. art. III, § 2.

5. *Id.*

6. 28 U.S.C.A. § 1332(a) (West Supp. 1997).

7. The amount in controversy floor originally set in the Judiciary Act of 1789, which adopted the first diversity statute, was $500. 1 Stat. 73, 78. Congress recently amended § 1332, the current codification of the diversity statute, to increase the amount in controversy requirement to $75,-

000. Federal Courts Improvement Act of 1996, § 205, Pub. L. 104–317, Title II, § 205(a), 110 Stat. 3847, 3850 (codified at 28 U.S.C.A. § 1332(a)).

8. *In re* Burrus, 136 U.S. 586, 593–94, 10 S.Ct. 850, 852–53, 34 L.Ed. 500 (1890); *see also* Thompson v. Thompson, 484 U.S. 174, 187 & n. 4, 108 S.Ct. 513, 520 & n. 4, 98 L.Ed.2d 512 (1988) (holding that the Parental Kidnapping Prevention Act of 1980 did not create a private cause of action in federal court).

expertise to address the issues and the ability to monitor family cases with the assistance of local social workers.[9] In a similar vein, the Court has determined that probate matters are best left to the state courts.[10]

(b) Requirements for Diversity Jurisdiction

The statute requires diversity of citizenship, a civil action, and an amount in controversy exceeding $75,000 (exclusive of interest and costs). For diversity to exist, each party must be a citizen of a state or a citizen of a foreign country only.[11] To be a "citizen of a state," a party must first be a citizen of the United States.[12] Once the citizenship of each party is established,[13] the federal court must then compare the respective citizenships to determine whether "complete diversity" exists between the plaintiffs and defendants. The United States Supreme Court, presumably in another attempt to circumscribe federal jurisdiction, has read into Section 1332 a requirement that there be complete diversity between all plaintiffs and all defendants[14]—even though there is no statutory or constitutional basis for this interpretation.[15] Consequently, the existence of even one instance of common citizenship between the opposing parties will preclude federal diversity jurisdiction.[16]

In determining whether complete diversity exists, the court is entitled to disregard the actual posture of the case and may realign the parties to reflect the true controversy if need be.[17]

(c) Pleading Diversity

9. Ankenbrandt v. Richards, 504 U.S. 689, 112 S.Ct. 2206, 119 L.Ed.2d 468 (1992).

10. Markham v. Allen, 326 U.S. 490, 494, 66 S.Ct. 296, 298, 90 L.Ed. 256 (1946) (holding that federal courts may not entertain probate cases even if diversity jurisdiction would otherwise exist).

11. A dual citizen of the United States and another country cannot invoke alienage jurisdiction. Sadat v. Mertes, 615 F.2d 1176 (7th Cir.1980).

12. Dred Scott v. Sandford, 60 U.S. (19 How.) 393, 15 L.Ed. 691 (1856).

13. *See infra* § 1.7(c)(1).

14. Strawbridge v. Curtiss, 7 U.S. (3 Cranch) 267, 2 L.Ed. 435 (1806) (first setting forth this view of the diversity statute); *see also* Owen Equip. & Erection Co. v. Kroger, 437 U.S. 365, 373, 98 S.Ct. 2396, 2402, 57 L.Ed.2d 274 (1978) (explaining that "diversity jurisdiction does not exist unless **each** defendant is a citizen of a different State from **each** plaintiff" (emphasis added)).

15. Owen Equip. & Erection Co., 437 U.S. at 373 n.13, 98 S.Ct. at 2403 n.13 ("It is settled that complete diversity is not a constitutional requirement."); *see also* State Farm Fire & Cas. Co. v. Tashire, 386 U.S. 523, 530–31, 87 S.Ct. 1199, 1203–04, 18 L.Ed.2d 270 (1967) (noting that the complete diversity requirement is a product of statutory construction and consequently could be invalidated by Congress).

16. Strawbridge v. Curtiss, 7 U.S. (3 Cranch) 267, 2 L.Ed. 435 (1806).

17. *See* City of Indianapolis v. Chase Nat'l Bank, 314 U.S. 63, 69, 62 S.Ct. 15, 16, 86 L.Ed. 47 (1941) (directing federal courts to realign the parties according to their respective interests in the litigation for purposes of determining diversity jurisdiction); City of Dawson v. Columbia Ave. Sav. Fund, Safe Deposit, Title & Trust Co., 197 U.S. 178, 180, 25 S.Ct. 420, 49 L.Ed. 713 (1905) (stating that a federal court must "look beyond the pleadings and arrange the parties according to their sides in the dispute").

The basis for diversity jurisdiction must be clear either from the face of the plaintiff's complaint or the defendant's removal papers.[18] As with federal question jurisdiction, defects in jurisdictional allegations may be amended, upon leave, in both the trial and appellate courts.[19]

(1) Citizenship Requirement

An individual's "citizenship" is based upon his or her domicile. "Domicile" has been defined as the "place where [the party] has his true, fixed and permanent home and principal establishment, and to which he has the intention of returning whenever he is absent therefrom."[20] Although a person may have a number of residences, he has only one "domicile" and thus is a citizen of only one state for purposes of diversity jurisdiction.[21]

Domicile is generally considered to be a question of intent. A person can change domiciles by taking up residence at the new location with the intent to remain there permanently.[22] The courts rely upon objective evidence as to a person's intended domicile, such as where the person and his family reside, where the person is employed, is registered to vote, owns personal or real property, maintains bank accounts, is a member of churches and organizations, holds a drivers' license, or registers an automobile.[23]

Corporations are deemed to have "dual citizenship"—*i.e.*, they are viewed as being citizens both of the state of their incorporation and of the state where they have their principal place of business.[24] As a result, both states must be consulted to determine whether there is complete diversity between the plaintiffs and defendants. A problem arises when a corporation is incorporated in more than one state. Early Supreme Court precedent indicated that, if a corporation brought suit or was sued in a state of incorporation, it was deemed to be a citizen of that state, and all other states of incorporation were irrelevant.[25] It is unclear whether this rule survived the 1958 amendment to the diversity statute, which codified the dual citizenship rule for corporations, but the "sounder

---

18.   Cameron v. Hodges, 127 U.S. 322, 8 S.Ct. 1154, 32 L.Ed. 132 (1888) (holding that the party invoking diversity jurisdiction bears the burden of pleading the grounds therefor). For detailed discussions as to how to prepare pleadings and removal papers to invoke federal subject matter jurisdiction, *see* Chapter 5 "The Complaint" and Chapter 8 "Removal to Federal Court," respectively.

19.   28 U.S.C.A. § 1653 (West 1994).

20.   Charles Alan Wright, Law of Federal Courts § 26, at 161 (5th ed. 1994).

21.   Reynolds v. Adden, 136 U.S. 348, 10 S.Ct. 843, 34 L.Ed. 360 (1890) (distinguishing between "domicile" and "residence");

see also Williamson v. Osenton, 232 U.S. 619, 34 S.Ct. 442, 58 L.Ed. 758 (1914) (holding that a person can be a "citizen" of only one state at a time).

22.   13B Charles Alan Wright, Arthur R. Miller & Edward H. Cooper, Federal Practice & Procedure § 3612, at 526–33 (2d ed. 1984).

23.   *Id.* at 530–33; *see also* Wright, *supra* note 20, at 163.

24.   28 U.S.C.A. § 1332(c)(1) (West 1993).

25.   Patch v. Wabash R.R. Co., 207 U.S. 277, 28 S.Ct. 80, 52 L.Ed. 204 (1907).

rule" appears to be that the corporation should be considered a citizen of every state of incorporation for diversity purposes.[26]

The alternative "principal place of business" citizenship can be even more troubling. Several courts have adopted a "nerve center" approach to address the question. Under this approach, the focus is on where corporate policies are primarily formulated.[27] Other courts look to where the corporate assets are located.[28] The more modern approach is to evaluate where the bulk of the corporate activity occurs.[29]

At least one circuit court of appeals has held that a domestic corporation that does its principal business abroad is considered to be a "citizen" solely of the state of its incorporation. In *Torres v. Southern Peru Copper Corp.*,[30] the Fifth Circuit noted that, although Section 1332(c)(1) deems a corporation "to be a citizen of any State by which it has been incorporated and of the *State* where it has its principal place of business ...," it was aware of no other authority for classifying a corporation as a citizen of the place of its principal place of business.[31] Conversely, an alien corporation—one which is incorporated abroad— may be found to be a citizen of the state where it has its principal place of business.[32]

A federal corporation is generally considered not to be a citizen of any particular state and consequently cannot be sued in federal court based upon diversity.[33]

As to insurance companies, the diversity statute itself provides that, in a direct action against an insurance company, the company is deemed to be a citizen not only of its state or states of incorporation and principal place of business, but also of the state of its insured's citizenship.[34] As a consequence, complete diversity must exist between the insured and the plaintiff as well.

An unincorporated association is considered to be a citizen of every state in which its members reside.[35] The location of the organization and

---

26. Wright, *supra* note 20, at 166.

27. Topp v. CompAir, Inc., 814 F.2d 830, 834–35 (1st Cir.1987).

28. *E.g.,* Anniston Soil Pipe Co. v. Central Foundry Co., 329 F.2d 313 (5th Cir. 1964); Kelly v. United States Steel Corp., 284 F.2d 850 (3d Cir.1960).

29. Toms v. Country Quality Meats, Inc., 610 F.2d 313, 315 (5th Cir.1980); Lugo–Vina v. Pueblo Int'l, Inc., 574 F.2d 41 (1st Cir.1978).

30. 113 F.3d 540, 543 (5th Cir.1997).

31. *Id.* (quoting 28 U.S.C.A. § 1332(c)(1) (emphasis added)).

32. Panalpina Welttransport GmBh v. Geosource, Inc., 764 F.2d 352, 354 (5th Cir.1985).

33. Bankers' Trust Co. v. Texas & P. Ry. Co., 241 U.S. 295, 36 S.Ct. 569, 60 L.Ed. 1010 (1916).

34. 28 U.S.C.A. § 1332(c)(1) (West 1993). However, when an insurer brings suit "as member" of an unincorporated association "for itself and all other members" of the unincorporated association, some courts consider that neither the association nor its other members are parties to the suit for the purposes of determining diversity jurisdiction. Aetna Cas. & Sur. Co. v. Iso–Tex, Inc., 75 F.3d 216 (5th Cir.1996).

35. Carden v. Arkoma Assocs., 494 U.S. 185, 189, 110 S.Ct. 1015, 1018, 108 L.Ed.2d 157 (1990).

the state law under which it is organized are irrelevant.[36] If a plaintiff fails to allege the citizenship of every member of an unincorporated association in its complaint so that complete diversity can be ascertained, and there is no evidence in the trial record to substantiate the citizenship, diversity jurisdiction may be found lacking.[37] In a similar vein, the citizenship of each limited and each general partner must be considered when determining whether diversity jurisdiction exists in cases involving partnerships.[38]

The United States and its federal agencies are not considered to be "citizens of a state" for purposes of determining diversity jurisdiction.[39]

Neither a state nor an agency that is an alter ego of the state is a "citizen" of a state for purposes of diversity jurisdiction, and federal jurisdiction over these entities is lacking.[40] However, if an agency, officer, or subdivision is separate and distinct from the state, and the other diversity requisites are present, the district court can properly proceed to determine the merits of the case. For example, counties and other independent political subdivisions of a state are generally considered to be "citizens" of a state that can be sued in diversity.[41]

Where the courts draw the line between "state" and "citizen of a state" for agencies and political subdivisions is often less than clear. That inquiry is fact intensive and governed by state law.[42] The enabling legislation that characterizes the agency as a political subdivision of the state is not dispositive of whether the agency is a "citizen" or an alter ego of the state for purposes of diversity jurisdiction.[43] Rather, in grappling with this question, the federal courts have identified a number of inquiries to assist them, including: (i) whether the agency can sue or be sued in its own name; (ii) whether it can implead and be impleaded in any competent court; (iii) whether it can contract in its own name; (iv) whether it can acquire, hold title to, and dispose of property in its own name, and (v) whether it is considered a "body corporate"—*i.e.*, having

---

36. *Id.*

37. Elliott v. Tilton, 69 F.3d 35, 36 (5th Cir.1995).

38. Carden, 494 U.S. at 195, 110 S.Ct. at 1021; *see also* Great Southern Fire Proof Hotel Co. v. Jones, 177 U.S. 449, 20 S.Ct. 690, 44 L.Ed. 842 (1900).

39. Texas v. Interstate Commerce Comm'n, 258 U.S. 158, 160, 42 S.Ct. 261, 262, 66 L.Ed. 531 (1922).

40. Moor v. County of Alameda, 411 U.S. 693, 717–18, 93 S.Ct. 1785, 1799–1800, 36 L.Ed.2d 596 (1973); *see also* Stone v. South Carolina, 117 U.S. 430, 433, 6 S.Ct. 799, 800, 29 L.Ed. 962 (1886) (holding that a suit by a state for damages is not removable on the basis of diversity). The Eleventh Amendment to the Constitution also prohibits a nonconsensual suit against a state in federal court. *See infra* § 1.11(b).

41. Moor, 411 U.S. at 718, 720–21, 93 S.Ct. at 1800–02.

42. Huber, Hunt & Nichols, Inc. v. Architectural Stone Co., 625 F.2d 22, 24 (5th Cir.1980).

43. PYCA Indus., Inc. v. Harrison County Waste Water Mgmt. Dist., 81 F.3d 1412, 1416 (5th Cir.1996). Parties suing a state or state entity must keep in mind that, even if diversity jurisdiction exists, the state agency might still invoke the Eleventh Amendment, *see infra* § 1.11(b), although generally the inquiry as to whether the agency is effectively operating as the state are the same. *Id.* at 1416 n.2 (noting that diversity analysis for state-created entities is "virtually identical" to the Eleventh Amendment analysis for such entities).

the powers normally accorded a corporation.[44] Each of these inquiries goes to the essential and ultimate question—whether the state is the real party in interest in the lawsuit.[45]

Finally, a legal representative of a decedent, infant, or incompetent is deemed to be a citizen of the state where his or her principal is domiciled.[46] Conversely, a trustee determines citizenship for the trust he or she represents.[47]

(2) Amount in Controversy Requirement

In addition to showing complete diversity between the adverse parties, the party invoking diversity jurisdiction must demonstrate that the "matter in controversy" exceeds "the sum or value of $75,000, exclusive of interest and costs."[48] In diversity cases, state law governs the nature and extent of the right to be enforced, but federal law determines the value of the controversy.[49]

When the plaintiff is seeking monetary damages, its "good faith" statement in the complaint regarding the amount of damages is sufficient to establish the amount in controversy.[50] If the amount of damages is unliquidated, the plaintiff need only allege damages in excess of the jurisdictional amount, without specifying a specific sum.[51] Claims for future damages may be considered as part of the amount in controversy.[52] However, speculative damages or purely contingent causes of action which may never accrue are generally not included in determining the jurisdictional floor.[53] If punitive damages are pled for and recoverable

44. Coastal Petroleum v. U.S.S. Agri–Chemicals, Div. of U.S. Steel Corp., 695 F.2d 1314, 1318 (11th Cir.1983).

45. Tradigrain, Inc. v. Mississippi State Port Auth., 701 F.2d 1131, 1132 (5th Cir. 1983).

46. 28 U.S.C.A. § 1332(c)(2) (West 1993).

47. Navarro Sav. Ass'n v. Lee, 446 U.S. 458, 100 S.Ct. 1779, 64 L.Ed.2d 425 (1980) (holding that trust is a citizen of the state of its trustee's citizenship). When there are multiple trustees administering the trust, the citizenship of each trustee must be consulted to determine whether there is complete diversity. See generally id. at 465, 100 S.Ct. at 1784 (referring to rule that jurisdiction may "properly [be] founded upon the diverse citizenship of the individual trustees").

48. 28 U.S.C.A. § 1332(a) (West Supp. 1997).

49. Horton v. Liberty Mut. Ins. Co., 367 U.S. 348, 352–53, 81 S.Ct. 1570, 1573, 6 L.Ed.2d 890 (1961).

50. St. Paul Mercury Indem. Co. v. Red Cab. Co., 303 U.S. 283, 288–89, 58 S.Ct. 586, 589–90, 82 L.Ed. 845 (1938).

51. Bell v. Preferred Life Assurance Soc., 320 U.S. 238, 242–43, 64 S.Ct. 5, 7, 88 L.Ed. 15 (1943).

52. Aetna Cas. & Sur. Co. v. Flowers, 330 U.S. 464, 467, 67 S.Ct. 798, 800, 91 L.Ed. 1024 (1947).

53. E.g. Healy v. Ratta, 292 U.S. 263, 54 S.Ct. 700, 78 L.Ed. 1248 (1934) (Court could not consider the value of business that vacuum salesman might lose if police enforced occupation tax as threatened because that injury was too speculative; rather the amount in controversy was the amount of the disputed tax.); Brotherhood of Locomotive Firemen & Enginemen v. Pinkston, 293 U.S. 96, 55 S.Ct. 1, 79 L.Ed. 219 (1934) (finding amount in controversy to be entire pension fund to be paid out to widow and holding that the mere possibility that she might remarry—and thereby terminate her right to pension benefits—did not render future payments conjectural).

under the facts alleged, they may also be included in the jurisdictional amount.[54]

When the relief sought is declaratory or injunctive, rather than monetary, the federal courts must measure the amount in controversy "by the value of the object of the litigation."[55] Although the decisions interpreting this directive are far from uniform, it appears that the federal courts will uphold diversity jurisdiction if the amount in controversy could exceed the jurisdictional minimum based upon any reasonably estimable value, such as the amount of harm the plaintiff might suffer absent relief or the expense of the defendant's compliance with the injunction.[56] For example, in a challenge to state regulatory action, the amount in controversy is the value of the right to do business free from government interference.[57]

Attorneys' fees may be included in the amount in controversy to arrive at the jurisdictional amount if there is a statutory or contractual basis for their award, so long as they are not more accurately characterized as interest or costs.[58] Even if the state statute designates attorneys' fees as "costs" of litigation, the federal court is entitled to disregard this characterization if the fees form part of the matter in controversy.[59]

As the statute clearly states, interest and costs are not to be included in the "amount in controversy" determination.[60] Although the statute categorically excludes any "interest," the Supreme Court has distinguished between interest "as such" and the use of an interest calculation as part of the principal demand.[61] Interest "as such" means interest that is incidental to the subject of the lawsuit and which cannot be included in the amount in controversy.[62] Conversely, when interest is an integral part of a plaintiff's claim, some federal courts have allowed it to be included in determining the requisite jurisdictional amount.[63] If accrued interest is part of the damages claimed, such as a matured interest in a coupon, it may be included with the principal amount to arrive at the amount in controversy.[64]

---

54. Bell v. Preferred Life Assurance Soc., 320 U.S. 238, 64 S.Ct. 5, 88 L.Ed. 15 (1943).

55. Hunt v. Washington State Apple Adver. Comm'n, 432 U.S. 333, 347–48, 97 S.Ct. 2434, 2443–44, 53 L.Ed.2d 383 (1977).

56. E.g., McCarty v. Amoco Pipeline Co., 595 F.2d 389, 395 (7th Cir.1979) (holding that the amount in controversy should be analyzed from either the viewpoint of the plaintiff or that of the defendant); Kheel v. Port of New York Auth., 457 F.2d 46 (2d Cir.1972) (computing amount in controversy as "the value of the suit's intended benefit or the value of the right being protected or the injury being averted").

57. Kroger Grocery & Baking Co. v. Lutz, 299 U.S. 300, 301, 57 S.Ct. 215, 215, 81 L.Ed. 251 (1936).

58. Id.

59. Id.

60. 28 U.S.C.A. § 1332(a) (West Supp. 1997).

61. See Brown v. Webster, 156 U.S. 328, 15 S.Ct. 377, 39 L.Ed. 440 (1895).

62. Kenholz v. Bache, 184 F.2d 974, 975 (5th Cir.1950).

63. Bailey Employment Sys., Inc. v. Hahn, 655 F.2d 473 (2d Cir.1981).

64. Edwards v. Bates County, 163 U.S. 269, 270–73, 16 S.Ct. 967, 968–69, 41 L.Ed. 155 (1896).

The federal courts have also wrestled with the effect of a counter-claim on the amount in controversy. Can the value of a counterclaim be added to the plaintiff's claim to meet the amount in controversy requirement? For example, consider the situation where a plaintiff's claim is for $40,000, and the defendant has a counterclaim valued at $50,000. Neither claim, standing alone, is sufficient to meet the threshold, but added together, the values exceed $75,000. Although the statute specifically excludes consideration of any right of set-off or counterclaim of the defendant,[65] it would be possible in some instances to aggregate the two claims to arrive at an amount in controversy of $90,000 for purposes of diversity jurisdiction.

An important Supreme Court case on the subject, *Horton v. Liberty Mutual Insurance Co.*, can be read to support the position that a compulsory counterclaim may be considered as part of the amount in controversy.[66] That case does involve a peculiar fact setting[67] and does not necessarily translate into application for all counterclaim situations.

The lower courts appear to be split on the issue, some counting a compulsory counterclaim as part of the amount in controversy when the plaintiff's claim is for less than the jurisdictional minimum, while others have denied diversity-based removal under the same circumstances.[68]

(3) Aggregation of Claims

Generally, a federal court may aggregate all of a plaintiff's claims against a single defendant.[69] As a result, if a plaintiff's individual claims against a single defendant do not exceed $75,000, but the total of its claims added together does, diversity jurisdiction is available.[70] In a similar vein, a plaintiff can aggregate claims against multiple defendants as long as they are jointly liable for the damages.[71] However, claims against separate and individually liable defendants may not be aggregated.[72]

The general rule for determining the amount in controversy is that multiple plaintiffs may not aggregate their claims for damages in order

---

65. 28 U.S.C.A. § 1332(b) (West Supp. 1997).

66. 367 U.S. 348, 354, 81 S.Ct. 1570, 1574, 6 L.Ed.2d 890 (1961); *see also* Wright, *supra* note 20 at 218–19 (opining that per-mitting a compulsory counterclaim to satisfy the amount in controversy requirement so as to permit removal "seems fully in accord" with the principles governing diversity and removal jurisdiction).

67. In *Horton*, an insurer filed a declaratory judgment action in federal court to set aside an award of $1,050 made by the Texas Industrial Accident Board to Horton. The insurer invoked the court's diversity jurisdiction, alleging that Mr. Horton would claim $14,035, as he had before the Board. Horton confirmed this allegation by suing

in state court to set aside the award and recover $14,035. The Supreme Court ultimately held that the matter in controversy exceeded the $10,000 then required and that federal diversity jurisdiction was available. 367 U.S. at 353–54, 81 S.Ct. at 1573–74.

68. Erwin Chemerinsky, Federal Jurisdiction § 5.3, at 293–94 (2d ed. 1994).

69. Marshall v. Holmes, 141 U.S. 589, 12 S.Ct. 62, 35 L.Ed. 870 (1891).

70. Snyder v. Harris, 394 U.S. 332, 89 S.Ct. 1053, 22 L.Ed.2d 319 (1969).

71. Gibson v. Shufeldt, 122 U.S. 27, 29–33, 7 S.Ct. 1066, 1067–68, 30 L.Ed. 1083 (1887).

72. *Id.*

to meet the jurisdictional amount for diversity purposes. Aggregation is sometimes permissible, however, when "two or more plaintiffs unite to enforce a single title or right in which they have a common and undivided interest."[73] For example, courts have aggregated claims by several plaintiffs to a common fund when the plaintiffs have asserted an "integrated" or collective right to that fund.[74]

The amorphous "common and undivided" test has been the subject of great controversy. The mere fact that the claims derived from the same instrument—such as a will or contract—does not support the aggregation of those claims.[75] Further, a "community of interest" among the plaintiffs is insufficient to permit aggregation.[76] As a result, class action plaintiffs must generally demonstrate that each of their individual claims exceeds $75,000 in order to have access to a federal forum.[77]

Some courts have allowed the total amount of punitive damages claimed by multiple plaintiffs to be applied to each plaintiff's amount in controversy in order to satisfy the jurisdictional limit when those plaintiffs share a common and undivided interest in seeking punitive damages.[78]

(4) Failure of the Amount in Controversy

Although the amount in controversy requirement is jurisdictional, the Supreme Court has instructed that a case should not be dismissed for failure of this requirement unless it "appear[s] to a legal certainty that the claim is really for less than the jurisdictional amount...."[79] Generally, this standard can only be met when the plaintiff's alleged damages are capped by statute at an amount below the jurisdictional

---

73. Snyder, 394 U.S. at 336, 89 S.Ct. at 1056.

74. *E.g.*, Berman v. Narragansett Racing Ass'n, 414 F.2d 311, 314–15 (1st Cir. 1969) (holding that the amount in controversy was the entire fund of betting proceeds to be awarded to pursewinners pursuant to a contract with the racetrack, rather than the amount each horseowner would receive if the fund was paid over, because the principal and "integrated" issue was whether the racetracks owed the proceeds under the contract); *see also* Bullard v. City of Cisco, Texas, 290 U.S. 179, 188–89, 54 S.Ct. 177, 180–81, 78 L.Ed. 254 (1933) (permitting aggregation of claims for recovery of bonds and coupons held in trust for collection purposes when integrated issue existed as to the validity of right to recovery).

75. Pinel v. Pinel, 240 U.S. 594, 596, 36 S.Ct. 416, 417, 60 L.Ed. 817 (1916).

76. Thomson v. Gaskill, 315 U.S. 442, 446–47, 62 S.Ct. 673, 675–76, 86 L.Ed. 951 (1942).

77. Zahn v. International Paper Co., 414 U.S. 291, 94 S.Ct. 505, 38 L.Ed.2d 511 (1973). *But see infra* § 1.8(c)(1) for a discussion of cases holding that supplemental jurisdiction statute overruled *Zahn* and permitting the exercise of supplemental jurisdiction over the claims of class action plaintiffs who do not independently satisfy the diversity requirement.

78. Allen v. R & H Oil & Gas Co., 63 F.3d 1326, 1335 (5th Cir.1995) (attributing the total sum of punitive damages claimed to each individual plaintiff to determine whether each satisfied the amount in controversy requirement). *But see* Gilman v. BHC Securities, Inc., 104 F.3d 1418, 1428 (2d Cir.1997) (refusing "to adhere to that principle").

79. St. Paul Mercury Indem. Co. v. Red Cab Co., 303 U.S. 283, 288–89, 58 S.Ct. 586, 590–91, 82 L.Ed. 845 (1938).

minimum or limited by contract, or where extrinsic facts make clear that the amount was pled solely to invoke diversity jurisdiction.[80]

However, if the amount in controversy initially appears to exceed the jurisdictional limit, but the plaintiff is "finally adjudged to be entitled to recover less than the sum or value of $75,000, computed without regard to any set off or counterclaim ..., and exclusive of interest and costs," the court may deny costs to—or award them against—a plaintiff who originally brought the suit in federal court.[81]

(d) Determining Diversity

(1) Complete Diversity Required

Except in cases of statutory interpleader,[82] diversity must be "complete," meaning that all plaintiffs be diverse from all defendants. In making this determination, a federal court must rule out any common instances of citizenship between the opposing parties by evaluating each citizenship of every party to the dispute.

The presence of a "stateless citizen" on either side of the litigation equation precludes diversity jurisdiction.[83] A "stateless" citizen is one who is a citizen of the United States but is domiciled abroad. "Dual citizenship"—*i.e.*, of a person who is a citizen of both the United States and a foreign country—is not recognized by the federal courts for purposes of diversity; rather, the court looks only to the American nationality of the citizen to determine whether diversity jurisdiction exists.[84]

Foreign citizens can invoke "alienage jurisdiction" under Section 1332(a). However, an alien who has been admitted to the United States for permanent residence is deemed a citizen of the state in which he or she is domiciled.[85] Further, if there are alien parties on both the plaintiffs' and defendants' sides of the litigation equation, diversity jurisdiction will be found lacking.[86] Finally, an alien who is not a citizen or subject of a foreign state—*i.e.*, a "man without a country—cannot invoke alienage jurisdiction under Section 1332(a)(2)."[87]

In class actions, it is the citizenship of the named class representatives that controls the diversity question.[88] As a result, complete diversi-

---

80. Pratt Cent. Park Ltd. Partnership v. Dames & Moore, 60 F.3d 350, 353 (7th Cir.1995); Pachinger v. MGM Grand Hotel—Las Vegas, Inc., 802 F.2d 362, 364–65 (9th Cir.1986).

81. 28 U.S.C.A. § 1332(b) (West Supp. 1997).

82. *See infra* § 1.7(d)(3).

83. Sadat v. Mertes, 615 F.2d 1176 (7th Cir.1980); Smith v. Carter, 545 F.2d 909, 911 (5th Cir.1977).

84. Mutuelles Unies v. Kroll & Linstrom, 957 F.2d 707, 711 (9th Cir.1992)

(stating that the American nationality of a law firm with possible dual citizenship was sufficient under § 1332(a)(2) to sustain diversity jurisdiction).

85. 28 U.S.C.A. § 1332(a) (West Supp. 1997).

86. Giannakos v. M/V Bravo Trader, 762 F.2d 1295, 1298 (5th Cir.1985).

87. Hernandez v. Lucas, 254 F.Supp. 901, 902 (S.D.Tex.1966).

88. Supreme Tribe of Ben Hur v. Cauble, 255 U.S. 356, 365–66, 41 S.Ct. 338, 341–42, 65 L.Ed. 673 (1921); Kerney v. Fort

ty is required only between the named plaintiffs and named defendants; the citizenship of other class members is not taken into consideration.[89]

In some cases, fictitious or "Doe" parties may be joined to litigation to preserve confidentiality of the identity of the party, to toll applicable limitations, or for other reasons. These "Doe" parties do not usually destroy diversity jurisdiction. However, if there are sufficient allegations to identify the "Doe" party, the party seeking to establish diversity jurisdiction must show that complete diversity exists, taking into consideration the "Doe" party,[90] or must prove that the "Doe" party has been fraudulently joined by a party seeking to defeat diversity.[91]

(2) Fraudulent Joinder and "Misjoinder"

Under the fraudulent joinder rule, where a nondiverse defendant has been fraudulently joined for the purpose of defeating removal and/or the plaintiff cannot state a claim against the nondiverse defendant as a matter of law, that defendant's citizenship may be disregarded in determining diversity.[92] The defendant bears a rather stringent burden to show fraudulent joinder: The removing party must prove that there is absolutely no possibility that the plaintiff will be able to establish a cause of action against the in-state defendant in state court or that there has been outright fraud in the plaintiff's pleading of jurisdictional facts.[93] All "disputed questions of fact and all ambiguities in the controlling law" must be resolved in favor of the party contesting federal jurisdiction.[94]

Although intent is generally irrelevant to the fraudulent joinder inquiry, fraudulent joinder may also be found if the plaintiff is shown to have no intent to pursue a judgment against the nondiverse defendant.[95]

One circuit court of appeals has recently made a unique—and largely unprecedented—holding that a misjoinder of parties under FRCP 20 can be "so egregious as to constitute fraudulent joinder."[96] Upon finding that one class of claims was wholly unrelated to the other class of claims in the lawsuit—for which diversity jurisdiction would have been available—the Eleventh Circuit upheld the trial court's decision to sever

Griffin Fandangle Ass'n, 624 F.2d 717, 719 (5th Cir.1980); Oskoian v. Canuel, 269 F.2d 311 (1st Cir.1959).

89. Cauble, 255 U.S. at 365–66, 41 S.Ct. at 341–42. *See* Chapter 15 "Class Actions," at § 15.9(a).

90. Pullman Co. v. Jenkins, 305 U.S. 534, 540, 59 S.Ct. 347, 350, 83 L.Ed. 334 (1939).

91. *See infra* § 1.7(d)(2). The removal statute now explicitly provides that "the citizenship of defendants sued under fictitious name shall be disregarded." 28 U.S.C.A. § 1441(a) (West 1994).

92. Cavallini v. State Farm Mut. Auto Ins. Co., 44 F.3d 256, 259 (5th Cir.1995).

93. *Id.*

94. Ford v. Elsbury, 32 F.3d 931, 935 (5th Cir.1994).

95. Chicago R.I. & P. Ry. Co. v. Schwyhart, 227 U.S. 184, 33 S.Ct. 250, 57 L.Ed. 473 (1913); *see also* Rose v. Giamatti, 721 F.Supp. 906, 917 (S.D.Ohio 1989) (holding joinder of Cincinnati Reds baseball team to be fraudulent when the complaint specifically stated that the Reds had engaged in no wrongdoing).

96. Tapscott v. MS Dealer Serv. Corp., 77 F.3d 1353, 1360 (11th Cir.1996).

and remand the nondiverse portion of the action and retain jurisdiction over the portion of the action that could have been properly brought in federal court in the first place.[97]

(3) Statutory Interpleader Exception

The Federal Interpleader Statute, contained in Section 1335 of Title 28, provides an important exception to the "complete diversity" requirement.[98] Under this statute, a federal court is empowered to entertain an interpleader action and decide all claims to a single sum of money if there is "minimal diversity," which the Supreme Court has interpreted to mean at least one plaintiff from a different state from one defendant.[99] The citizenship of defendants who have not yet been served is not considered in making this determination.[100] The interpleader statute also requires that the amount of the interpled funds have the value of $500 or more.[101] Once diversity jurisdiction has been established under this statute, it is not destroyed—even if the stakeholder is discharged, leaving only nondiverse parties.[102]

(4) Timing of Diversity Determination

Diversity jurisdiction is generally determined at the time the original document that commences the case in federal court is filed.[103] When a plaintiff invokes diversity jurisdiction, the inquiry is made as of the time the complaint is filed.[104] However, if a case is removed to federal court from state court, the removing defendant must establish diversity jurisdiction both at the time the case was filed and at the time of removal.[105] Once diversity jurisdiction has attached, subsequent events are usually insufficient to oust it.[106] One important exception to this rule is that the addition of a subsequently-joined nondiverse indispensable party will defeat diversity.[107]

(e) Creation and Destruction of Diversity

Unlike federal question jurisdiction, diversity jurisdiction can be fairly easily manipulated by the parties—especially the plaintiff. For this reason a federal litigant must carefully consider the selection of parties,

---

97. *Id. See also* Chapter 10 "Joinder Consolidation and Severance," at § 10.6, *infra.*

98. 28 U.S.C.A. § 1335 (West 1993). *See also* Chapter 14 "Parties," at § 14.5(d).

99. State Farm Fire & Cas. Co. v. Tashire, 386 U.S. 523, 87 S.Ct. 1199, 18 L.Ed.2d 270 (1967).

100. *Id.; see also* Cripps v. Life Ins. Co. of N. Am., 980 F.2d 1261, 1265–66 (9th Cir.1992).

101. 28 U.S.C.A. § 1335(a) (West 1993).

102. Leimbach v. Allen, 976 F.2d 912, 917 (4th Cir.1992).

103. Newman-Green, Inc. v. Alfonzo–Larrain, 490 U.S. 826, 830, 109 S.Ct. 2218, 2221, 104 L.Ed.2d 893 (1989).

104. Louisville, N.A. & C. Ry. Co. v. Louisville Trust Co., 174 U.S. 552, 19 S.Ct. 817, 43 L.Ed. 1081 (1899) (holding that existence of diversity jurisdiction at the time of judgment is irrelevant so long as there was complete diversity at the time the case was filed).

105. Great N. Ry. Co. v. Alexander, 246 U.S. 276, 38 S.Ct. 237, 62 L.Ed. 713 (1918).

106. *See infra* § 1.7(e)(5).

107. Fortuin v. Milhorat, 683 F.Supp. 1, 4–5 (D.D.C.1988).

the definition of the claims, and the calculation of the amount in controversy in determining whether federal jurisdiction actually exists.

A plaintiff desiring to keep the matter in state court may want to join as defendants parties whose presence would defeat diversity or allege only claims for which the amount in controversy is lower than the $75,000 jurisdictional floor. Moreover, opportunities for creative pleading abound in this arena. A party may assign a claim to another who would either create or destroy diversity. The selection of representatives for a class action, estate, trust, or receivership also has implications upon diversity. Federal or would-be federal litigants are well-advised to consider all of the possibilities before filing their papers.

At some point, however, "creative" pleading or manipulating federal jurisdiction crosses the line into improper litigation practices. The courts recognize that, in some cases, fact should be elevated over fiction and federal jurisdiction recognized where it exists. For example, a trial court can realign the parties to reflect their true relationship to the controversy or ignore fraudulently joined parties in determining whether diversity exists. As a practical matter, and because federal jurisdiction is so jealously guarded, the federal courts seem to reject challenges of this nature and find against diversity unless it is evident from the face of the pleadings or the undisputed facts. Conversely, the courts tend to discredit attempts to manufacture diversity jurisdiction through collusive joinder, assignment, and other means.

(1) Manipulating Diversity

A district court does not have jurisdiction of actions in which any party, by assignment or otherwise, has been improperly or collusively joined to invoke the jurisdiction of such court.[108] As a result, a party cannot manufacture diversity jurisdiction by improperly aligning the parties or omitting indispensable parties whose presence would defeat diversity.[109]

(2) Changing Citizenship

Some attempts to manufacture diversity are valid. For example, a party can move to another state in order to commence a diversity suit without risking a finding of impermissible collusion.[110] Once diversity jurisdiction has been established, a party's change in domicile does not destroy it.[111]

---

108. 28 U.S.C.A. § 1359 (West 1993).

109. Smith v. Sperling, 354 U.S. 91, 97 & n. 4, 77 S.Ct. 1112, 1115 n. 4, 1 L.Ed.2d 1205 (1957).

110. Black & White Taxicab & Transfer Co. v. Brown & Yellow Taxicab & Transfer Co., 276 U.S. 518, 524, 48 S.Ct. 404, 405, 72 L.Ed. 681 (1928) (finding diversity jurisdiction even though plaintiff corporation dissolved its corporate status in defendant's state and reincorporated itself in forum state in order to achieve diversity); Williamson v. Osenton, 232 U.S. 619, 34 S.Ct. 442, 58 L.Ed. 758 (1914) (If person changes domicile with genuine interest to remain permanently, his motive in doing so is irrelevant.).

111. Gaines v. Dixie Carriers, Inc., 434 F.2d 52, 54 (5th Cir.1970).

(3) Appointing Diverse Representatives

Another way that parties manipulate diversity is by appointing a representative who has a different citizenship from the party represented. If these types of appointments are made solely with the intent to manufacture or obstruct diversity jurisdiction, the federal courts will often ignore the citizenship of the representative and look to that of the real party in interest for purposes of determining diversity.[112] As with other attempts to manufacture diversity, the courts look to the relationship between the representative and principal to determine whether the representative appointment is merely a sham for purposes of diversity.[113] Among the factors that the courts consider are the identity of the representative and whether the representative is a real party in interest, the relationship of the representative to the party represented, the scope of authority of the representative, any special expertise of the representative that pertains to the appointment, and whether the representative is the most likely appointment or another nondiverse party would have been more likely to fulfill the role.

(4) Assignment of Claims

Although the federal courts recognize that claims may be assigned for a number of reasons, attempts to use assignments to create diversity are disfavored.[114] For diversity purposes, the validity of the assignment generally turns on whether the transferee or assignee becomes the real party in interest in the claim.[115]

(5) Subsequent Events

The general rule is that jurisdiction vests, if at all, at the time of filing or, in a removed case, at the time of removal. As a result, subsequent events normally do not divest a court of properly acquired jurisdiction. For example, "[a]n amendment to the complaint limiting damages for jurisdictional purposes cannot divest jurisdiction."[116] Similarly, the later addition of a nonessential, nondiverse party will not destroy diversity jurisdiction once it has properly attached.[117] In removed

---

112. Xaros v. U.S. Fidelity & Guar. Co., 820 F.2d 1176, 1181–82 (11th Cir.1987) (finding that ERISA trust funds were voluntary unincorporated associations and evaluating diversity on the basis of the members' citizenships rather than that of the trustees where the pleadings were deficient); McSparran v. Weist, 402 F.2d 867, 871 (3d Cir.1968) (noting that it is proper to disregard the citizenship of nominal fiduciaries appointed to create diversity).

113. Navarro Sav. Ass'n v. Lee, 446 U.S. 458, 464–66, 100 S.Ct. 1779, 1784–85, 64 L.Ed.2d 425 (1980) (characterizing "active" trustees as those who "possess[] certain customary powers to hold, manage and dispose of assets for the benefit of others" and noting that these trustees "may sue in their own right without regard to the citizenship of the trust beneficiaries").

114. See, e.g., Kramer v. Caribbean Mills, Inc., 394 U.S. 823, 89 S.Ct. 1487, 23 L.Ed.2d 9 (1969) (finding lack of diversity jurisdiction when a plaintiff assigned its entire interest in a lawsuit to its attorney in exchange for a nominal amount and promise to repay the corporate plaintiff 95% of the money received in the lawsuit).

115. Id.; see also Nobel v. Morchesky, 697 F.2d 97, 101 (3d Cir.1982).

116. Allen v. R & H Oil & Gas Co., 63 F.3d 1326, 1336 (5th Cir.1995).

117. Freeport-McMoRan, Inc. v. KN Energy, Inc., 498 U.S. 426, 428, 111 S.Ct. 858, 860, 112 L.Ed.2d 951 (1991).

cases, "[w]hen a district judge remands a properly removed case because of subsequent events, [a reviewing] court has both the authority and duty to rescind the remand."[118] However, subsequent papers or events that simply clarify the basis for jurisdiction as it existed at the operative time are to be taken into consideration.[119]

There are a few notable exceptions to the rule that jurisdiction is determined at the time the case is originated or removed. The plaintiff's dismissal of a nondiverse party in a state court action may be sufficient to create diversity jurisdiction so as to permit removal.[120] The relevant inquiry is "whether, at the time of removal, the plaintiffs 'ha[d] taken the resident defendant out of the case, so as to leave a controversy wholly between the plaintiff[s] and the nonresident defendant.' "[121]

Further, once the case is in federal court, a plaintiff can join a nondiverse, indispensable defendant, with the district court's permission, and thus destroy diversity in that manner.[122] However, if the subsequently-joined defendant is not an indispensable party to the lawsuit, its citizenship will not affect diversity.[123]

Library References:
West's Key No. Digests, Federal Courts ⚷261–319.
Wright, Miller & Cooper, Federal Practice and Procedure: Civil 2d §§ 3601–3602, 3605, 3608.

§ 1.8 Supplemental Jurisdiction

Even though federal courts jealously guard their jurisdiction to protect against its unwarranted or unnecessary expansion, as discussed in the preceding sections, once that jurisdiction actually attaches, there is little justification for fragmenting a lawsuit into multiple forums simply because state law claims are also involved—especially when the state issues and claims are integrally related to the issues that are properly within the federal court's jurisdiction. As a result, the federal

118. Matter of Shell Oil Co., 970 F.2d 355, 356 (7th Cir.1992).

119. *E.g.*, Asociacion Nacional de Pescadores v. Dow Quimica de Colombia, S.A., 988 F.2d 559, 565 (5th Cir.1993) (holding that an affidavit submitted after removal that merely clarified the amount in controversy at the time of removal was not a post-removal event and could be considered in determining the propriety of removal).

120. Powers v. Chesapeake & O. Ry. Co., 169 U.S. 92, 101, 18 S.Ct. 264, 267, 42 L.Ed. 673 (1898); *see also* Weems v. Louis Dreyfus Corp., 380 F.2d 545 (5th Cir.1967) (distinguishing between voluntary and involuntary acts of the plaintiff as affecting the defendant's right of removal). If jurisdiction is found lacking for the first time on appeal, the plaintiff can dismiss the nondiverse party at that point, but only in limit-

ed cases. Newman–Green, Inc. v. Alfonzo–Larrain, 490 U.S. 826, 837, 109 S.Ct. 2218, 2225, 104 L.Ed.2d 893 (1989). In making this determination, the court must consider whether the dismissal at the appellate level will prejudice one of the parties and whether the practicalities of the suit weigh heavily in favor of the dismissal. *Id.* at 832–33, 109 S.Ct. at 2222–23.

121. American Car & Foundry Co. v. Kettelhake, 236 U.S. 311, 316, 35 S.Ct. 355, 356, 59 L.Ed. 594 (1915).

122. 28 U.S.C.A. § 1447(e) (West 1994) (directing that, upon plaintiff's request, court may deny joinder of nondiverse defendant or grant and remand).

123. Freeport-McMoRan, Inc. v. K N Energy, 498 U.S. 426, 428, 111 S.Ct. 858, 860, 112 L.Ed.2d 951 (1991).

courts developed several common law approaches to this problem. The most common were called "pendent jurisdiction" and "ancillary jurisdiction." These doctrines have been largely superseded by the adoption of 28 U.S.C.A. § 1367, the supplemental jurisdiction statute, but the opinions that apply pendent and ancillary jurisdiction remain integral to the interpretation and application of Section 1367.

(a) History of Supplemental Jurisdiction

The constitutional basis for all of the species of supplemental jurisdiction is the general endowment of jurisdiction over "cases" and "controversies" in Article III of the Constitution.[1] The United States Supreme Court, in *Osborn v. Bank of United States*, interpreted "cases" and "controversies" to refer to all claims arising from the same set of facts, even though some claims may originate in federal law and some in state law.[2] The common law doctrines discussed in the following sections were largely developed in the wake of *Osborn*. In 1990, Congress essentially codified ancillary and pendent jurisdiction into "supplemental jurisdiction."[3] Although there are many similarities between the common law doctrines and the statute, there are some differences that will be addressed below.

(1) Ancillary Jurisdiction

Nonfederal claims and issues based upon state law that arise from the same set of facts as claims that are properly before the federal court fall within the ambit of a federal court's "ancillary jurisdiction."[4] Classic examples of ancillary jurisdiction are compulsory counterclaims,[5] third-party claims, and intervention as of right.[6] Conversely, permissive counterclaims and permissive intervention have not traditionally supported the exercise of ancillary jurisdiction.

Defining whether the state claims are sufficiently related to the federal claims to support the exercise of ancillary jurisdiction has been the source of some controversy. The Supreme Court has characterized the problem as whether the state law issues arise from the same "common nucleus of operative fact[s]" as the federal ones.[7]

---

§ 1.8

1. U.S. Const. art. III, § 2.

2. Osborn v. Bank of United States, 22 U.S. (9 Wheat.) 738, 823, 6 L.Ed. 204 (1824) ("[W]hen a question to which the judicial power of the Union is extended by the constitution, forms an ingredient of the original cause, it is in the power of congress to give the circuit courts jurisdiction of that cause, although other questions of fact or of law may be involved in it.").

3. *See* 28 U.S.C.A. § 1367 (West 1993).

4. Freeman v. Howe, 65 U.S. (24 How.) 450, 460, 16 L.Ed. 749 (1860).

5. Moore v. New York Cotton Exchange, 270 U.S. 593, 46 S.Ct. 367, 70 L.Ed. 750 (1926) (finding ancillary jurisdiction over defendant's compulsory counterclaim that arose out of the same set of facts as plaintiff's claim).

6. Stewart v. Dunham, 115 U.S. 61, 64, 5 S.Ct. 1163, 1164, 29 L.Ed. 329 (1885) (expanding ancillary jurisdiction to permit intervention by nondiverse parties whose presence destroyed diversity because diversity had already attached as between the original parties).

7. United Mine Workers of Am. v. Gibbs, 383 U.S. 715, 725, 86 S.Ct. 1130, 1138, 16 L.Ed.2d 218 (1966).

(2) Pendent Jurisdiction

Pendent jurisdiction is a type of ancillary jurisdiction. This doctrine permits the exercise of federal jurisdiction over state law claims that are so closely connected to the federal claims properly before the court that their interrelationship "permits the conclusion that the entire action before the court comprises but one constitutional 'case.' "[8] If pendent jurisdiction attaches, the federal court has jurisdiction over the nonfederal claims regardless of whether the federal claims are successful or even reached by the federal courts.[9] One commentator has distinguished pendent jurisdiction from ancillary jurisdiction in the following terms:

> Pendent jurisdiction can be thought of as claims contained in the *plaintiff's complaint* for which there are not independent bases for federal court jurisdiction. In contrast, ancillary jurisdiction can be understood as claims that are asserted *after the filing of the original complaint* that do not independently meet the requirements for federal court jurisdiction.[10]

Another distinction between pendent and ancillary jurisdiction is that pendent jurisdiction is discretionary. As the Supreme Court explained in *United Mine Workers of Am. v. Gibbs*, the "justification [for pendent jurisdiction] lies in considerations of judicial economy, convenience and fairness to litigants; if these are not present a federal court should hesitate to exercise jurisdiction over state claims."[11] Keeping these considerations in mind, the Court has also directed that federal courts should not retain state law claims if the federal ones on which jurisdiction is based are dismissed or if the state issues "predominate."[12]

Pendent jurisdiction was eventually expanded to include claims against other parties that would not otherwise support the exercise of federal jurisdiction, as long as those claims spawned from the same nucleus of operative facts as the claims within the federal court's original jurisdiction. As a result, once federal jurisdiction was established, the original parties could join additional parties that were subject to related state law claims, though not the federal claim on which federal jurisdiction was based. This class of pendent jurisdiction became known as "pendent party jurisdiction," which was widely acknowledged by the lower federal courts until 1989, when the Supreme Court abolished the doctrine.[13]

---

8. *Id.* at 724–25, 86 S.Ct. at 1138–39.

9. Siler v. Louisville & Nashville R.R., 213 U.S. 175, 192, 29 S.Ct. 451, 455, 53 L.Ed. 753 (1909) (deciding case on the basis of ancillary state law claim to avoid constitutional question even though federal jurisdiction was based upon the constitutional issue).

10. Erwin Chemerinsky, Federal Jurisdiction § 5.4, at 314 (2d ed. 1994).

11. United Mine Workers of Am., 383 U.S. at 726, 86 S.Ct. at 1139.

12. *Id.*

13. *See* Finley v. United States, 490 U.S. 545, 109 S.Ct. 2003, 104 L.Ed.2d 593 (1989) (abolishing common law doctrine of pendent party jurisdiction and holding that this jurisdiction was not available absent statutory authorization).

(3) 28 U.S.C.A. § 1367

In 1990, partially in response to the judicial abrogation of pendent party jurisdiction, Congress codified the common law principles of ancillary and pendent jurisdiction.[14]

[I]n any civil action of which the district courts have original jurisdiction, the district courts shall have supplemental jurisdiction over all other claims that are so related to claims in the action within such original jurisdiction that they form part of the same case or controversy under Article III of the United States Constitution.[15]

There are several significant differences between the common law and statutory schemes. The statute creates a presumption that, once a federal court has jurisdiction over a dispute, federal jurisdiction will also be available for interrelated state law claims, subject to a few notable exceptions.

One of the exceptions provides that supplemental jurisdiction is not available when federal jurisdiction is based solely on diversity and the exercise of supplemental jurisdiction would be inconsistent with the requirements of the diversity statute.[16] In this important exception, Congress declined to extend supplemental jurisdiction to most cases barred by the complete diversity rule.[17]

The statute also specifically revives the discredited "pendent party jurisdiction" doctrine: "Such supplemental jurisdiction shall include claims that involve the joinder or intervention of additional parties."[18]

As a result, in federal question cases, supplemental jurisdiction is essentially presumed for interwoven state law claims, including those involving the joinder or intervention of additional parties. However, a federal court can and should decline to exercise jurisdiction under certain enumerated circumstances when it is clear that the dispute is predominately based upon the state issues or if compelling circumstances warrant deference to the state courts.[19]

Finally, the statute provides a tolling provision to mitigate against the threat that a party's state law claim might be dismissed after the applicable statute of limitations has run. Subsection (d) of the statute provides that a party whose state law claim is dismissed may refile in state court within 30 days (or a longer period if state law permits) without risking a limitations bar.[20]

(b) Requirements for Supplemental Jurisdiction

In order for a federal court to exercise supplemental jurisdiction, the following must be present: (1) original federal jurisdiction; (2) the federal

---

14. *See* Judicial Improvements Act of 1990, Pub. L. No. 101–650, 104 Stat. 5089 (codified at 28 U.S.C.A. § 1367 (West 1993)).

15. 28 U.S.C.A. § 1367(a) (West 1993).

16. 28 U.S.C.A. § 1367(b) (West 1993).

17. *See infra* § 1.8(c)(1).

18. 28 U.S.C.A. § 1367(a).

19. 28 U.S.C.A. § 1367(c) (West 1993); *see also infra* § 1.8(c)(2).

20. 28 U.S.C.A. § 1367(d) (West 1993).

and state law claims must arise out of a common nucleus of operative facts; and (3) the federal and state law claims must be sufficiently related that they would ordinarily be expected to be tried in one proceeding.[21]

(1) Existence of a Federal Claim

The fundamental prerequisite for the exercise of supplemental jurisdiction is federal jurisdiction over the original controversy. As supplemental jurisdiction is derivative—rather than original—jurisdiction, there must be a basis for invoking the court's original subject matter jurisdiction so that it can then reach the supplemental claim. Conversely, if original federal jurisdiction is lacking, supplemental jurisdiction becomes a moot inquiry.[22]

(2) Same Case or Controversy

Section 1367 codifies the common law precedent requiring that the state law issue be so effectively intertwined with the federal claim on which jurisdiction is based that the two form the same case or controversy for purposes of Article III. For example, a cross-claim for contribution, indemnity, or reimbursement would necessarily arise from the same facts as the primary claim on which it is based.[23]

(c) Limitations on Supplemental Jurisdiction

There are two important limitations on the exercise of supplemental jurisdiction. First, it does not permit parties to circumvent the rule of complete diversity in most cases. Second, the statute expressly authorizes a federal court not to decide state issues under its supplemental jurisdiction when the state issues are novel, complex, or controlling. A federal court may also decline to exercise supplemental jurisdiction over remaining claims after dismissing the ones on which federal jurisdiction is based or in "exceptional circumstances."

(1) Diversity Jurisdiction Insufficient

Subsection (b) of the statute specifically excludes from its ambit the use of supplemental jurisdiction to append nondiverse parties to actions based upon diversity when the intervention or joinder would frustrate diversity.[24] When federal jurisdiction is based solely on diversity, a federal district court:

---

21. MCI Telecomms. v. Teleconcepts, Inc., 71 F.3d 1086, 1102 (3d Cir.1995), *cert. denied*, ___ U.S. ___, 117 S.Ct. 64, 136 L.Ed.2d 25 (1996).

22. Sarmiento v. Texas Bd. of Veterinary Med. Exam'rs, 939 F.2d 1242, 1245 (5th Cir.1991) (holding that a federal court may decline to exercise both original jurisdiction and supplemental jurisdiction when the federal claim asserted is "frivolous or a mere matter of form").

23. Allen v. City of Los Angeles, 92 F.3d 842, 846 (9th Cir.1996) (upholding the exercise of supplemental jurisdiction over the state law cross-claims of police officer defendants for reimbursement of attorneys' fees in a civil rights action brought by a victim of police beating because the officer's entitlement to reimbursement formed part of the same case or controversy as the victim's claims).

24. 28 U.S.C.A. § 1367(b) (West 1993).

shall not have supplemental jurisdiction ... over claims by plaintiffs against persons made parties under Rule 14, 19, 20, or 24 of the Federal Rules of Civil Procedure, or over claims by persons proposed to be joined as plaintiffs under Rule 19 of such rules, or seeking to intervene as plaintiffs under Rule 24 of such rules, when exercising supplemental jurisdiction over such claims would be inconsistent with the jurisdictional requirements of section 1332.[25]

This exception is designed to prevent a plaintiff from "smuggl[ing] in claims that the plaintiff would not otherwise be able to interpose against certain parties in certain specific contexts for want of subject matter jurisdiction,"[26] while preserving the rights of other parties to bring in additional claims and parties necessary to the dispute. If a plaintiff chooses not to join certain parties in order to invoke federal jurisdiction, the statute precludes the plaintiff from directly asserting claims against those third parties after they intervene or are brought in by others.[27] The final clause of Subsection (b) appears to give the courts some flexibility in determining whether supplemental jurisdiction is available in these contexts, and the commentary suggests that the clause permits courts "some leeway in avoiding an overly rigid construction of" the exception.[28]

An interesting question arises when complete diversity exists between the parties, but the supplemental claim does not independently satisfy the amount in controversy requirement of the diversity statute. It is unclear whether the statute has removed an earlier obstacle to jurisdiction over supplemental claims that do not independently satisfy the amount in controversy requirement. Prior to the adoption of Section 1367, the Supreme Court held in *Zahn v. International Paper Company*[29] that every plaintiff in a federal class action suit based upon diversity must independently satisfy the amount in controversy requirement in order for a federal court to have jurisdiction over the suit. In its view, a federal court could not exercise ancillary jurisdiction over the claims of class members who did not individually and independently meet the amount in controversy requirement.[30] *Zahn* was, however, decided a number of years before Section 1367 became effective, and the federal courts have split over the issue of whether the supplemental jurisdiction statute effectively overrules *Zahn*.[31]

(2) Court's Discretion

The second exception to the jurisdictional presumption is discretionary. Even if supplemental jurisdiction exists, a federal court can refuse to

---

25. *Id.*

26. *Id.* cmt.

27. *Id.*

28. *Id.*

29. 414 U.S. 291, 94 S.Ct. 505, 38 L.Ed.2d 511 (1973).

30. *Id.*

31. *Compare* Free v. Abbott Lab. (*In re* Abbott Lab.), 51 F.3d 524, 529 (5th Cir.

1995) (reasoning that the statute vests general jurisdiction in the federal courts to hear supplemental claims, subject only to the exceptions enumerated in the statute, which exceptions neither address nor exclude class actions) *with* Bernard v. Gerber Food Prods. Co., 938 F.Supp. 218, 223–24 (S.D.N.Y.1996) (rejecting this interpretation and collecting cases).

exercise supplemental jurisdiction over a state law claim under Subsection (c) of the statute if one or more of the following conditions are met:

> (1) the claim raises a novel or complex issue of State law, (2) the claim substantially predominates over the claim or claims over which the district court has original jurisdiction, (3) the district court has dismissed all claims over which it has original jurisdiction, or (4) in exceptional circumstances, there are other compelling reasons for declining jurisdiction.[32]

This section of the statute essentially codifies the rule in *United Mine Workers of Am. v. Gibbs*[33] that a federal court should decline to exercise supplemental jurisdiction when the controversy is actually or predominantly a state law dispute—although it sets specific parameters for the district court's decision not to exercise its supplemental jurisdiction. However, once a federal court determines that supplemental jurisdiction is available for a pendent claim under Section 1367(a), it is not obliged to consider whether it should decline to exercise that jurisdiction under Section 1367(c) unless it is asked to do so by one of the parties.[34] If the court decides not to entertain the nonfederal claim, it can dismiss the claim without prejudice or remand to state court.[35]

The first basis for refusal to hear a supplemental claim—when a "novel or complex issue of State law" is presented—merely codifies the concern that federal jurisdiction should not exist to decide a question that should be answered by the state courts in the first place. Although federal courts are to make *Erie* guesses as to how a state court would decide an issue of state law when the state claim is properly before it,[36] supplemental jurisdiction should not be used to expand federal jurisdiction to decide disputes that are best left to the state courts.[37]

A corollary to this principle is the rule that, when state law claims predominate, a federal court should permit the state court to decide the issues.

---

32. 28 U.S.C.A. § 1367(c) (West 1993).

33. 383 U.S. 715, 725, 86 S.Ct. 1130, 1138, 16 L.Ed.2d 218 (1966).

34. Acri v. Varian Assoc., Inc., 114 F.3d 999 (9th Cir.1997) (en banc); *see also* Myers v. County of Lake, Ind., 30 F.3d 847, 848–50 (7th Cir.1994) (upholding jurisdiction over state law claims since supplemental jurisdiction was available and no party asked the court to exercise its discretionary authority to decline jurisdiction under § 1367(c)); Doe by Fein v. District of Columbia, 93 F.3d 861 (D.C.Cir.1996) (holding that, while Article III jurisdiction must be considered sua sponte, challenge to court's decision to exercise supplemental jurisdiction when one of the § 1367(c) discretionary factors militates against its exercise can be waived).

35. Carnegie-Mellon Univ. v. Cohill, 484 U.S. 343, 351, 108 S.Ct. 614, 619, 98 L.Ed.2d 720 (1988).

36. *E.g.*, Erie R.R. v. Tompkins, 304 U.S. 64, 58 S.Ct. 817, 82 L.Ed. 1188 (1938).

37. Williams v. Van Buren Tp., 925 F.Supp. 1231, 1237–38 (E.D.Mich.1996) (declining to exercise supplemental jurisdiction over claims for violation of Michigan state law, even though claims arose out of same set of facts as federal § 1983 claim for alleged violation of constitutional rights in detaining the plaintiff for 20 hours without arraignment, because state law claims raised novel and complex issues of state law best left to the Michigan state courts).

Federal courts should also decline to retain jurisdiction over a state law dispute once the federal claims on which federal jurisdiction was originally based are dismissed.[38] This concern was also codified in Section 1367(c). Nonetheless, a federal court has the discretion to retain jurisdiction over the remaining state law claims if considerations of judicial economy, convenience, fairness, and comity justify the exercise of supplemental jurisdiction.[39]

Finally, the "exceptional circumstances" catch-all provision preserves a federal court's discretion to decline supplemental jurisdiction over state law claims—even if none of the preceding factors is met— when "compelling reasons" exist for the decision.[40] The commentary to Section 1367(c) suggests that, although it appears to be a "separate category for declining supplemental jurisdiction, distinct from the first three, the language of clause (4) would also appear to indicate that all declinations of supplemental jurisdiction should be reserved for situations in which there are 'compelling reasons.' "[41]

Library References:

West's Key No. Digests, Federal Courts ⚖14–25.
Wright, Miller & Cooper, Federal Practice and Procedure: Civil 2d §§ 3523, 3567, 3567.3.

§ 1.9 Constitutional and Prudential Limitations of Federal Jurisdiction

Article III of the Constitution contains, or has been interpreted to prescribe, a number of limitations as to the matters federal courts can hear in the exercise of their subject matter jurisdiction. The Supreme Court has also developed a number of prudential limits on federal jurisdiction to meet pragmatic concerns about efficient and prudent judicial administration and to insure the requisite balance of autonomy between the federal and state courts. As a result, and even if subject matter jurisdiction would generally exist to entertain a given controversy, these limitations may preclude a party's right to relief in a federal court.

(a) Justiciability

The first of these limitations on federal jurisdiction is the requirement that the matter be justiciable. Justiciability is a threshold determination that the claimant has the burden of establishing before a suit can be heard on its merits. These justiciability principles arise out of Article III's requirement that there exist an actual "case" or "controversy" between adverse parties. They are designed to insure, for example, that the federal courts do not entertain disputes that are premature for

38. Gibbs, 383 U.S. at 726–27, 86 S.Ct. at 1139–40.

39. Cohill, 484 U.S. at 357, 108 S.Ct. at 622.

40. 28 U.S.C.A. § 1367(c)(4) (West 1993).

41. *Id.* cmt.

consideration, those in which any relief the federal court could grant is moot, those in which there is no actual dispute between adverse parties, and cases involving political questions that are best left to other branches of the federal government.

(1) Ripeness

Federal courts have developed two justiciability doctrines that determine when review is appropriate, ripeness and mootness. The ripeness doctrine decides whether a dispute has adequately matured or whether the case is too speculative and thus is premature for review. If the complainant has not yet suffered an injury or is under no immediate threat of injury, a federal court will refuse to hear the case on the basis that it is not ripe.[1]

A common application of the ripeness doctrine is when a plaintiff seeks preenforcement review of a statute or regulation. In this context, the Supreme Court often looks to the hardship associated with denying such preenforcement review in determining whether the controversy is "ripe" for judicial determination.[2] Moreover, the Court has consistently found suits to be ripe where enforcement of a statute is certain but proceedings have yet to commence.[3]

(2) Mootness

At the opposite end of the time spectrum is the mootness doctrine, which prohibits consideration of cases no longer involving an actual dispute. This doctrine demands that a live controversy exist at all stages of review, not merely when the complaint is filed.[4] Thus, if a plaintiff's claim has expired, the federal courts are without power to hear the case because entering a judgment would no longer have an effect on the litigants' rights.

§ 1.9

1. O'Shea v. Littleton, 414 U.S. 488, 94 S.Ct. 669, 38 L.Ed.2d 674 (1974) (denying review of local judge's allegedly discriminatory actions because none of the plaintiffs had been, or were about to be, injured by the judge), *vacated sub nom.* Spomer v. Littleton, 414 U.S. 514, 94 S.Ct. 685, 38 L.Ed.2d 694 (1974).

2. *Compare* Abbott Labs. v. Gardner, 387 U.S. 136, 87 S.Ct. 1507, 18 L.Ed.2d 681 (1967) (holding that 37 drug companies could challenge an FDA regulation imposing costly label alterations without first violating it and facing the applicable civil and criminal sanctions) *with* Toilet Goods Ass'n. v. Gardner, 387 U.S. 158, 87 S.Ct. 1520, 18 L.Ed.2d 697 (1967) (ruling that a cosmetic manufacturer could not challenge an FDA regulation permitting the FDA free access to manufacturing processes because denial

of review would not create a sufficient hardship).

3. Blanchette v. Connecticut Gen. Ins. Corp. (Regional Rail Reorganization Act Cases), 419 U.S. 102, 95 S.Ct. 335, 42 L.Ed.2d 320 (1974) (finding case ripe for decision when eight railroads challenged the transfer of their property to Conrail, even though a special court had not yet ordered the conveyances, because the Court found that there was no doubt the transfers were forthcoming).

4. DeFunis v. Odegaard, 416 U.S. 312, 317–19, 94 S.Ct. 1704, 1706–07, 40 L.Ed.2d 164 (1974) (dismissing a white law student's challenge to Washington State's affirmative action program on the ground that the determination of the legal issues he presented was no longer necessary because the petitioner was in his final year and entitled to his degree).

There are, however, four notable exceptions to the mootness doctrine. First, if the claim on the merits is "capable of repetition, yet evading review"—like those involving events of short duration (*e.g.* pregnancy)—the named plaintiff may continue to litigate the issue despite the loss of his or her individual stake in the lawsuit's outcome.[5] Second, a case is not dismissed as moot if the defendant has voluntarily stopped the offending practice, but is free to resume it.[6] Third, if a collateral injury survives after the primary dispute has been resolved, the case will not be considered moot.[7] Finally, mootness can be avoided through certification of a class prior to expiration of a named plaintiff's personal claim, so long as the claims of others in the class are still viable.[8]

(3) Advisory Opinions

The Supreme Court's interpretation of Article III's "case or controversy" requirement also bars rendition of advisory opinions—*i.e.* opinions not rendered in actual disputes between adverse parties. This doctrine prohibits federal courts from hearing collusive suits brought in the absence of real controversy.[9] It also precludes judicial action in cases in which an opinion would not be binding.[10] In this regard, the Supreme Court has stated that the constitutional courts should render only judgments that are binding and conclusive on the parties and not ones that are subject to later review or alteration by administrative action.[11]

5. Roe v. Wade, 410 U.S. 113, 93 S.Ct. 705, 35 L.Ed.2d 147 (1973) (allowing a plaintiff to continue her challenge to a state law prohibiting abortion after the pregnancy was completed).

6. United States v. W.T. Grant Co., 345 U.S. 629, 632, 73 S.Ct. 894, 897, 97 L.Ed. 1303 (1953) (refusing to invoke the mootness doctrine where the defendants discontinued the allegedly improper practice of using interlocking directorates and promised not to resume it).

7. Sibron v. New York, 392 U.S. 40, 88 S.Ct. 1889, 20 L.Ed.2d 917 (1968) (permitting a challenge to a criminal conviction even after the sentence was complete because the plaintiffs were still suffering the stigmatic collateral harm of the convictions).

8. United States Parole Comm'n v. Geraghty, 445 U.S. 388, 100 S.Ct. 1202, 63 L.Ed.2d 479 (1980) (allowing a named plaintiff, a former federal prisoner, to continue an appeal from a district court's ruling denying class certification for a suit challenging the United States Parole Commission's release guidelines even though he was released from prison while the appeal was pending).

9. Muskrat v. United States, 219 U.S. 346, 31 S.Ct. 250, 55 L.Ed. 246 (1911) (stating that the Supreme Court would not hear a case brought by nonadverse parties in order to facilitate the resolution of a constitutional question); see also United States v. Johnson, 319 U.S. 302, 304–05, 63 S.Ct. 1075, 1076–77, 87 L.Ed. 1413 (1943) (stating that where one party has dominated the conduct of the suit by payment of fees of both, there has not been the honest and actual antagonistic assertion of rights that is indispensable to adjudication of constitutional questions and the suit may be dismissed without judgment).

10. Chicago & Southern Air Lines v. Waterman S.S. Corp., 333 U.S. 103, 68 S.Ct. 431, 92 L.Ed. 568 (1948) (ruling that the federal courts could not review Civil Aeronautics Board decisions if the president could disregard the ruling).

11. *Id.*

(4) Political Questions

The Supreme Court has also ruled that decisions involving certain political disputes should be left to other branches of government, regardless of alleged constitutional violations: "The nonjusticiability of a political question is predominately a function of the separation of powers."[12]

The political question doctrine has been traditionally invoked in cases involving a textually demonstrable constitutional commitment to another branch of government or a lack of discoverable and manageable standards for resolving the controversy.[13] Although the political question doctrine is a somewhat nebulous rule, there are a number of specific areas in which it is frequently applied, such as in the context of foreign relations.[14] The principle has also been consistently employed in cases averring a violation of Article IV's guarantee of a "Republican form of government."[15] The doctrine has also been somewhat sporadically implemented in cases challenging the process by which the Constitution is amended.[16] Finally, the Supreme Court's prohibition on cases involving political questions is often applied to suits challenging the impeachment process.[17]

(b) Standing

Like the doctrines of ripeness and mootness, standing is a threshold determination which limits the types of suits federal courts will hear. However, unlike these two other justiciability doctrines, which concern when litigation may occur, standing focuses on the party entitled to bring suit. Standing is concerned not with whether a particular matter may properly be brought in federal court, but with who is the proper plaintiff to bring the dispute.

(1) Elements of Standing

According to the Supreme Court, a plaintiff must establish three constitutional requirements to prove standing: injury in fact, causation, and redressability. In addition, the Court has recently and effectively added a fourth constitutional obstacle to standing by characterizing a

---

12. Baker v. Carr, 369 U.S. 186, 211, 82 S.Ct. 691, 707, 7 L.Ed.2d 663 (1962).

13. See id. at 211–12, 82 S.Ct. at 706–08.

14. E.g., id.

15. Pacific States Tel. & Tel. Co. v. Oregon, 223 U.S. 118, 32 S.Ct. 224, 56 L.Ed. 377 (1912); Luther v. Borden, 48 U.S. (7 How.) 1, 12 L.Ed. 581 (1849); see also U.S. Const. art. IV, § 4 ("The United States shall guarantee to every State in this Union a Republican form of Government, and shall protect each of them against Invasion . . . .").

16. Coleman v. Miller, 307 U.S. 433, 59 S.Ct. 972, 83 L.Ed. 1385 (1939) (declaring that Congress' control over the amendment process is absolute and thus not subject to judicial review).

17. Nixon v. United States, 506 U.S. 224, 229–30, 113 S.Ct. 732, 736–37, 122 L.Ed.2d 1 (1993) (refusing to rule on propriety of Senate's establishment of a committee to take evidence and testimony prior to the impeachment vote of a federal judge, stating that the Senate's constitutional duty to "try" all impeachments lacked sufficient precision to afford a judicially-manageable standard of review).

previously prudential limitation—the prohibition on generalized grievances—as a constitutional one.

First, the plaintiff must allege that it has suffered or imminently
will suffer an injury in fact. This injury in fact requires a concrete
invasion of a legally protected interest which is actual or imminent.[18]
The Supreme Court has ruled that aesthetic[19] and economic injuries[20]
sufficiently satisfy this requirement, while injuries to marital happiness[21]
and stigma[22] do not. The injury must also be particularized, affecting the
plaintiff in a personal and individualized way.[23] While the requirement
that the complainant be personally injured does eliminate suits founded
on a mere ideological interest, it has proven to be a formal limitation,
easily circumvented by creative pleading.[24] Furthermore, a plaintiff
seeking declaratory or injunctive relief must show a reasonable likelihood that she will be injured by the defendant in the future.[25]

Second, the plaintiff must aver that there is a causal connection
between the injury and the offending conduct.[26] This is inherently a
factual determination of how direct or indirect a particular effect is from
an offending activity. Although the Supreme Court has established some
loose standards in this area,[27] there is still much speculation and

18. See Lujan v. Defenders of Wildlife, 504 U.S. 555, 565, 112 S.Ct. 2130, 2139, 119 L.Ed.2d 351 (1992)

19. *Id.* at 562–63, 112 S.Ct. at 2137–38 (ruling that the desire to view wildlife for purely aesthetic reasons was a cognizable interest for standing purposes).

20. Barlow v. Collins, 397 U.S. 159, 90 S.Ct. 838, 25 L.Ed.2d 192 (1970) (ruling that tenant farmers claiming economic inju-ry from the amended Food and Agriculture Act had established standing).

21. Roe v. Wade, 410 U.S. 113, 127–29, 93 S.Ct. 705, 714–15, 35 L.Ed.2d 147 (1973) (refusing to hear a sister suit brought by a married couple claiming that a prohibition on abortions impaired their marital happi-ness).

22. Allen v. Wright, 468 U.S. 737, 754–56, 104 S.Ct. 3315, 3326–27, 82 L.Ed.2d 556 (1984) (refusing to find standing in a suit involving a private racially restrictive school which claimed it was being stigma-tized by the government's policy of denying tax exemptions to schools that discrimi-nated on race because stigmatic harm only confers standing on those individuals who are denied equal treatment).

23. Valley Forge Christian College v. Americans United for Separation of Church and State, Inc., 454 U.S. 464, 471–72, 102 S.Ct. 752, 757–59, 70 L.Ed.2d 700 (1982) (stating that a party must personally suffer some actual or threatened injury to have standing).

24. United States v. Students Challeng-ing Regulatory Agency Procedures, 412 U.S. 669, 93 S.Ct. 2405, 37 L.Ed.2d 254 (1973) (upholding the standing of a group of stu-dents who claimed that heightened railroad freight rates would reduce the use of recy-cled goods due to the increased shipping costs and thus lead to more natural re-source use causing increased pollution and a subsequent decrease in their enjoyment of specific forests, streams, and mountains).

25. City of Los Angeles v. Lyons, 461 U.S. 95, 103 S.Ct. 1660, 75 L.Ed.2d 675 (1983) (denying standing to a plaintiff who had been injured by a police chokehold and was suing to enjoin the use of such holds in situations where the officer's life was not threatened).

26. Allen, 468 U.S. at 751, 104 S.Ct. at 3324 (ruling that the injury must be "fairly traceable" to the conduct in question); *see also* Lujan v. Defenders of Wildlife, 504 U.S. 555, 112 S.Ct. 2130, 119 L.Ed.2d 351 (1992) (stating that a causal connection is a distinct obstacle to standing).

27. Simon v. Eastern Ky. Welfare Rights Organization, 426 U.S. 26, 96 S.Ct. 1917, 48 L.Ed.2d 450 (1976) (ruling that an injury in fact must be fairly traced to the challenged action).

inconsistency as to how rigorous a causation standard should be applied.[28]

Third, the plaintiff must assert that it is likely the injury will be redressed by a favorable decision. While this determination practically parallels the causal connection prong—because limiting the conduct that caused the injury is presumed to remedy the harm—two recent Supreme Court cases refer to redressability as a distinct obstacle to limiting standing.[29] However, in practice the determination almost never diverges from that of causation.

Finally, the Supreme Court has recently characterized a long standing prudential standing limitation, the ban on generalized grievances, as a constitutional hurdle.[30] For most of this century, the Court has generally not allowed parties to establish standing based solely on citizenship or taxpayer status if their only objection was to allegedly unconstitutional government activity rather than an injury to their personal constitutional rights.[31] This prohibition is normally supported by the reasoning that a harm shared in substantially equal measure by such a large class of citizens is too indefinite and comparatively minute to warrant the exercise of jurisdiction.[32]

The Supreme Court has also developed two prudential standing limitations: limitations on third-party standing and limitations on claims from plaintiffs outside the zone of interest protected by a statute.

First, a party may generally not assert claims of third persons not part of the lawsuit.[33] There are, however, three notable exceptions to this prohibition. The most common exception arises when the interested third party faces substantial obstacles to obtaining relief in an indepen-

---

28. Linda R. S. v. Richard D., 410 U.S. 614, 93 S.Ct. 1146, 35 L.Ed.2d 536 (1973) (ruling that plaintiff's claim regarding state's failure to prosecute father of illegitimate child for failure to pay child support failed for lack of causation because plaintiff had not shown that enforcement of child support law against unwed fathers would have resulted in payment rather than incarceration in her particular situation); Friends of the Earth v. Crown Central Petroleum, 95 F.3d 358 (5th Cir.1996) (stating that an injury suffered downstream is not necessarily fairly traceable to an unlawful discharge upstream in the absence of evidence supporting such a contention).

29. See Northeastern Florida Chapter of Associated Gen. Contractors of Am. v. City of Jacksonville, Fla., 508 U.S. 656, 113 S.Ct. 2297, 124 L.Ed.2d 586 (1993); see also Lujan v. Defenders of Wildlife, 504 U.S. 555, 112 S.Ct. 2130, 119 L.Ed.2d 351 (1992).

30. Lujan, 504 U.S. 555, 112 S.Ct. 2130, 119 L.Ed.2d 351 (diverging from precedent

and treating the bar on citizen standing as constitutional rather than prudential).

31. Commonwealth of Mass. v. Mellon, 262 U.S. 447, 43 S.Ct. 597, 67 L.Ed. 1078 (1923) (denying taxpayer standing to challenge federal expenditures made in conjunction with the Federal Maternity Act of 1921); see also Ex parte Levitt, 302 U.S. 633, 58 S.Ct. 1, 82 L.Ed. 493 (1937) (denying citizenship standing to challenge the appointment of Justice Hugo Black).

32. See Warth v. Seldin, 422 U.S. 490, 499–500, 95 S.Ct. 2197, 2205–06, 45 L.Ed.2d 343 (1975).

33. McGowan v. Maryland, 366 U.S. 420, 81 S.Ct. 1218, 6 L.Ed.2d 393 (1961) (ruling that the plaintiff department stores could not argue that a blue law prohibiting retail sales on Sunday's burdened their religious freedom to observe the Sabbath on Saturday due to the loss of business that would result from closure on both days, because none of the stores averred that their own religious rights were infringed).

dent action.[34] Another exception to the prohibition on third-party standing is seen in situations where there is a very close connection between the third party and the plaintiff.[35] This final exception is known as the overbreadth doctrine because it applies when a statute is overly broad in restricting fundamental rights, but it has thus far only been used in First Amendment cases, where "there is a danger of chilling free speech" that outweighs the prudential presumption against third-party standing.[36] The exception permits a litigant to challenge a statute on the ground that it violates the First Amendment rights of third parties not before the court, even though the law may be constitutional as applied to the particular plaintiff.[37]

Second, a plaintiff suing pursuant to a statutory or constitutional provision must be within the zone of interest (part of the group intended to benefit) of the provision.[38] Although this test has been used by the Court on numerous occasions it is not very demanding and is almost always satisfied.[39] However, the Court has used the test to deny standing in suits seeking review of agency decisions under the Administrative Procedures Act, and thus the requirement should not be overlooked in this context.[40]

(2) Constitutional Versus Prudential Requirements

As previously noted, the six obstacles to standing have been characterized by the Supreme Court as either constitutional or prudential limitations. The four constitutional hurdles (the requirements of injury in fact, causation, and redressability, as well as the limitation on generalized grievances) originate from the Court's explication of Article III,

34. Barrows v. Jackson, 346 U.S. 249, 73 S.Ct. 1031, 97 L.Ed. 1586 (1953) (allowing a white defendant who was a party to a racially restrictive contract to raise a defense based on the rights of blacks because it would be nearly impossible for a black to raise his rights in a similar proceeding).

35. Singleton v. Wulff, 428 U.S. 106, 96 S.Ct. 2868, 49 L.Ed.2d 826 (1976) (allowing a group of physicians to assert the rights of female patients denied Medicaid benefits to pay for nontherapeutic abortions because of the close relationship between physicians and women in the process of making this constitutionally protected decision).

36. Secretary of State v. Joseph H. Munson Co., 467 U.S. 947, 104 S.Ct. 2839, 81 L.Ed.2d 786 (1984) (allowing a professional fundraiser to challenge a law prohibiting charitable organizations from soliciting funds unless at least 75 percent of their revenues were used for charitable purposes, even though the plaintiff did not establish that the charitable organizations could not assert their own rights or that his own rights were being violated).

37. Munson, 467 U.S. at 956, 104 S.Ct. at 2846.

38. Barlow v. Collins, 397 U.S. 159, 90 S.Ct. 838, 25 L.Ed.2d 192 (1970) (ruling that the interest of tenant farmers was within the zone protected by a provision of the Administrative Procedures Act which governed an agency decision allowing such farmers to assign payments from a federal program as security for rented farm land).

39. Clarke v. Securities Indus. Ass'n, 479 U.S. 388, 399, 107 S.Ct. 750, 757, 93 L.Ed.2d 757 (1987) (stating that an association of brokers was in the zone of interest of a federal law and that the test was not meant to be very demanding).

40. Air Courier Conference of Am. v. American Postal Workers Union AFL–CIO, 498 U.S. 517, 111 S.Ct. 913, 112 L.Ed.2d 1125 (1991) (barring a suit by postal workers challenging the suspension of monopoly rights under the Administrative Procedures Act on the grounds that they were not in the provision's zone of interest).

while the two prudential restrictions (limitations on third-party standing and suits from claimants outside the zone of interest protected by a statute) were developed to promote prudent judicial administration. The obvious and primary significance of the Court's distinction between these two groups of restrictions is that the constitutional limitations cannot be overridden by statute, while the prudential ones can.

Library References:

> West's Key No. Digests, Federal Civil Procedure ⬢103.1; Federal Courts ⬢12. Wright, Miller & Cooper, Federal Practice and Procedure: Civil 2d §§ 3529, 3902, 4051.

§ 1.10   Dual Federalism Concerns

(a) Exclusive Jurisdiction of Federal Courts

As discussed in Section 1.4(a), *supra*, under Article III of the Constitution, Congress has the authority to confer jurisdiction, within certain parameters, upon the federal courts. Implicit in Article III's grant of authority is the power to endow the federal courts with exclusive jurisdiction over certain subject matters. In accordance with its authority in this regard, Congress has frequently specified that only federal courts shall preside over specified types of claims, such as those arising under the bankruptcy laws,[1] the federal patent and copyright laws,[2] and in admiralty and maritime cases.[3] Several factors are relevant in the determination that a particular subject area is within the exclusive jurisdiction of the federal courts, including the desirability of uniform interpretation of federal law, the expertise of federal judges in the application of federal law, and the bias in favor of allowing federal forums to entertain certain federal causes of action.[4]

(b) Concurrent Jurisdiction Between Federal and State Courts

Even though Congress has the authority to give the federal court exclusive jurisdiction over specific federal law based claims, this power is sparingly exercised. Both court systems are generally considered to be competent to adjudicate claims originating from federal law.[5] Concurrent jurisdiction between the state and federal courts in cases arising under United States law is therefore presumed unless there is an express reservation of jurisdiction to the federal courts, an intent to do so can

---

§ 1.10

1. 28 U.S.C.A § 1334 (West 1993 & Supp. 1997).

2. 28 U.S.C.A. § 1338(a) (West 1993).

3. 28 U.S.C.A. § 1333(1) (West 1993).

4. 17 James Wm. Moore, Moore's Federal Practice § 120.12[1][c] (3d ed. 1997); *see also* 13 Charles Alan Wright, Arthur R.

Miller & Edward H. Cooper, Federal Practice and Procedure: Jurisdiction 2d § 3527 (2d ed. 1984).

5. *E.g.*, Lockerty v. Phillips, 319 U.S. 182, 187, 63 S.Ct. 1019, 1022, 87 L.Ed. 1339 (1943) (noting that Congress could rely upon state courts to decide issues of federal law).

clearly be inferred from the legislative history, or permitting the state courts to entertain the federal claims would obstruct the federal interests of the statute.[6]

(c) Abstention

There are a number of circumstances in which a federal court may decline to hear a suit or make a ruling even though all jurisdictional and justiciability limitations have been overcome. This deference to state court adjudication and exercise of judicial restraint is known as abstention and is realized through a number of judicially crafted jurisdictional doctrines.

(1) Purpose of Abstention

The number of different abstention doctrines reflect the federal court's vigorous attempt to protect the parallel judicial processes that accompany our federal system. By deferring to state court proceedings in certain situations, the federal courts promote comity and the assumption of parity between the two systems. Furthermore, this policy of noninterference reduces the frequency of inconsistent outcomes, the amount of duplicative litigation, and the strain on federal-state relations that results from federal courts invalidating state laws.

(2) Categories of Abstention

There are four different categories of abstention: (1) *Younger* abstention, which prohibits federal courts from enjoining certain state proceedings; (2) *Pullman* abstention, which allows federal courts to stay constitutional cases when the suit may be disposed of on unresolved questions of state law; (3) *Colorado River* abstention, which is exercised to avoid duplicate state and federal litigation; and (4) *Burford* abstention, which allows federal courts to dismiss actions that extensively interfere with a state's affairs.

The genesis of *Younger* abstention was the Supreme Court's 1971 decision in *Younger v. Harris*,[7] prohibiting federal courts from enjoining pending state criminal proceedings, except under certain limited circumstances. Although *Younger's* holding merely forbids federal court injunctions of pending state criminal proceedings, the Supreme Court has frequently, yet not consistently, extended the case's abstention doctrine to state civil actions,[8] state administrative proceedings,[9] and declaratory

---

6. Gulf Offshore Co. v. Mobil Oil Corp., 453 U.S. 473, 477–78, 101 S.Ct. 2870, 2874–75, 69 L.Ed.2d 784 (1981).

7. 401 U.S. 37, 91 S.Ct. 746, 27 L.Ed.2d 669 (1971).

8. Huffman v. Pursue, Ltd., 420 U.S. 592, 95 S.Ct. 1200, 43 L.Ed.2d 482 (1975) (applying the *Younger* abstention rule to a case involving an Ohio state civil nuisance proceeding against an adult theater because

the state suit was akin to a criminal proceeding); *see also* Trainor v. Hernandez, 431 U.S. 434, 97 S.Ct. 1911, 52 L.Ed.2d 486 (1977) (extending *Younger* into civil litigation involving the state government as a party).

9. Ohio Civil Rights Comm'n v. Dayton Christian Sch., 477 U.S. 619, 106 S.Ct. 2718, 91 L.Ed.2d 512 (1986) (ruling that a federal court should have abstained from

judgments.[10] The Court has also suggested that the *Younger* doctrine should be extended to suits seeking injunctive relief against state and local executive officials.[11] Almost all of the *Younger* progeny require a finding of "important state interest" before abstention is warranted. While these newer applications are not absolute, it is important to be aware that the doctrine has been significantly enlarged and now applies to an extensive number of situations.

Although the Court in *Younger* created a presumption of abstention, it gave three examples of "exceptional circumstances" in which federal courts would be authorized to enjoin parallel state court proceedings. *Younger's* first exception applies to cases involving bad faith state prosecutions and has proven to be very narrow in scope.[12] In fact, it has never been enforced by the Court.[13] The second *Younger* exception is for suits challenging patently unconstitutional state laws.[14] This exception has never even been raised—presumably because federal court proceedings are particularly superfluous in cases where state courts are faced with flagrantly unconstitutional statutes. In contrast, *Younger's* third exception, for litigants who lack an adequate state forum to decide a particular issue,[15] has proven somewhat more functional.[16] Thus, although *Younger* itself contained three particular examples of exceptional circumstances in which abstention would be inappropriate, these exceptions are rarely raised and, when invoked, have often proven to be ineffective.

In *Railroad Commission of Texas v. Pullman Co.*,[17] the Supreme Court articulated a different type of federal abstention doctrine. The Court ruled that a federal district court should have avoided a constitutional challenge to a Texas regulation when a state court's clarification

hearing a suit to enjoin the Ohio Civil Rights Commission when there was a pending state administrative proceeding involving an important state interest and the plaintiff had a full and fair opportunity to litigate its constitutional claim).

10. Samuels v. Mackell, 401 U.S. 66, 91 S.Ct. 764, 27 L.Ed.2d 688 (1971) (holding that declaratory relief should be denied in situations where injunctive relief would be refused, except in some rare cases where injunctive relief would be intrusive whereas declaratory judgments would be acceptable); *see also* Steffel v. Thompson, 415 U.S. 452, 94 S.Ct. 1209, 39 L.Ed.2d 505 (1974) (stating that a federal court could issue declaratory relief to a plaintiff who was threatened with, but not yet subjected to, criminal prosecution).

11. Rizzo v. Goode, 423 U.S. 362, 96 S.Ct. 598, 46 L.Ed.2d 561 (1976) (suggesting, but not requiring, that the principles of *Younger* should apply in a suit seeking injunctive relief against the Philadelphia police department).

12. Younger, 401 U.S. at 53, 91 S.Ct. at 757.

13. Allee v. Medrano, 416 U.S. 802, 94 S.Ct. 2191, 40 L.Ed.2d 566 (1974) (ruling that monthly bad faith prosecutions over an entire year did not warrant this exception).

14. Younger, 401 U.S. at 53, 91 S.Ct. at 747.

15. *Id.*

16. Gibson v. Berryhill, 411 U.S. 564, 93 S.Ct. 1689, 36 L.Ed.2d 488 (1973) (upholding federal intervention into state proceedings under the third *Younger* exception based upon the district court's finding that the Alabama State Board of Optometry, consisting wholly of self-employed optometrists, was a potentially biased and therefore inadequate forum to review the licenses of optometrists who worked for others because the board members stood to profit from the action).

17. 312 U.S. 496, 61 S.Ct. 643, 85 L.Ed. 971 (1941).

of Texas law could have disposed of the case. In doing so, it established an abstention rule that when the clarification of a sufficiently uncertain state law issue[18] can likely dispose of a federal constitutional case, the federal court should abstain from hearing the case and merely retain jurisdiction pending a state determination of those issues.[19] While the Court has repeatedly referred to *Pullman* abstention, it is still unclear whether such stays are mandatory[20] or merely discretionary.[21]

Pullman abstention is meant to promote judicial efficiency, by avoiding unnecessary or premature constitutional pronouncements and to lessen the friction between the state and federal judiciaries by minimizing the frequency with which federal courts invalidate state laws. However, the practical effect of the rule is the unnecessary duplication of effort and expense on the part of litigants and the inevitable delays in obtaining final judgment on a matter. In fact, because a plaintiff is not compelled to accept a state court's ruling on federal issues, cases subject to *Pullman* abstentions are often exposed to a number of different proceedings in both state and federal forums, a factor that can delay final adjudication for years.[22]

Because federal courts apply state law routinely in diversity cases, uncertain state law issues must consistently be resolved at the federal level. While the Supreme Court has generally rejected *Pullman* abstention in such cases,[23] it has accepted that this abstention is acceptable in a limited number of situations. Thus far, these situations have been limited to unsettled questions of state law involving eminent domain[24] and particularly vital natural resources.[25]

18. Thornburgh v. American College of Obstetricians and Gynecologists, 476 U.S. 747, 106 S.Ct. 2169, 90 L.Ed.2d 779 (1986) (ruling that a case involving a clearly unconstitutional Pennsylvania abortion law was not a sufficiently uncertain or unsettled question of state law and thus did not require federal court abstention).

19. Reetz v. Bozanich, 397 U.S. 82, 90 S.Ct. 788, 25 L.Ed.2d 68 (1970) (ruling that for abstention to be appropriate, the state court proceeding must be anticipated to obviate any need to consider the federal constitutional case).

20. City of Meridian v. Southern Bell Tel. Co., 358 U.S. 639, 79 S.Ct. 455, 3 L.Ed.2d 562 (1959) (treating the abstention rule as mandatory in situations where clarification of state law might avoid a federal constitutional ruling).

21. Baggett v. Bullitt, 377 U.S. 360, 84 S.Ct. 1316, 12 L.Ed.2d 377 (1964) (referring to the abstention doctrine as a discretionary tool to be employed after consideration of a number of variables).

22. *See, e.g.*, England v. Louisiana State Bd. of Med. Exam'rs, 375 U.S. 411, 84 S.Ct.

461, 11 L.Ed.2d 440 (1964) (declaring that litigants can maintain their rights to redress in federal courts by withholding certain issues from the judgment of state courts when abstention is ordered).

23. Meredith v. City of Winter Haven, 320 U.S. 228, 64 S.Ct. 7, 88 L.Ed. 9 (1943) (holding abstention was inappropriate in a federal diversity case involving an uncertain issue of Florida law).

24. Louisiana Power and Light Co. v. City of Thibodaux, 360 U.S. 25, 79 S.Ct. 1070, 3 L.Ed.2d 1058 (1959) (establishing an exemption to the *Meredith* rule in eminent domain cases due to the subject's close relationship with Louisiana's sovereign prerogative).

25. Kaiser Steel Corp. v. W. S. Ranch Co., 391 U.S. 593, 88 S.Ct. 1753, 20 L.Ed.2d 835 (1968) (declaring that the federal district court should have abstained in a diversity action involving a New Mexico water use law which possibly violated the state constitution and was of particular concern in a desert state).

In *Colorado River Water Conservation District v. United States*,[26] the Supreme Court addressed abstention for the sole purpose of avoiding duplicative state and federal litigation. The Court ruled that the mere pendency of a state suit concerning the same matter as a federal claim does not warrant the federal court's dismissal of the case absent exceptional circumstances.[27] These extraordinary situations are identified by evaluating the strong obligation of federal courts to exercise their jurisdiction against six countervailing considerations: whether a high probability of piecemeal litigation exists, whether the state court has assumed jurisdiction over property involved in the suit, whether jurisdiction was first obtained by the state forum, whether the federal forum is inconvenient for one or more parties, whether there are any federal issues in the case, and whether the state court proceedings will most likely protect the rights of both parties.[28]

Finally, the Supreme Court has expressed a need for federal courts to abstain from hearing cases which pose the risk of interfering with the state's administration of its own affairs. In *Burford v. Sun Oil Company*,[29] the Court ruled that a federal district court should have dismissed a challenge to a Texas oil field regulatory agency, because the case involved complex and specialized issues of parochial state interest. Although this particular abstention doctrine has consistently been used in cases involving possible disruption of state administrative procedural orders, the Court has suggested it could also be employed in the state judicial context.[30] Unlike other categories of abstention, *Burford* requires an actual dismissal of the action, effectively precluding federal recourse except in the unlikely event that the United States Supreme Court might hear the case in the exercise of its appellate jurisdiction.

Library References:

West's Key No. Digests, Courts ☞489–509; Federal Courts ☞41–65, 1131–1158.
Wright, Miller & Cooper, Federal Practice and Procedure: Civil 2d §§ 3527–3528.

§ 1.11 Sovereign Immunity and Immunity from Federal Jurisdiction

Governmental entities, whether they be federal, state, or foreign, are generally entitled to some form of sovereign immunity or immunity from the jurisdiction of the federal courts. Similarly, agencies and officers of governmental entities are entitled to some immunities when carrying out

---

26. 424 U.S. 800, 96 S.Ct. 1236, 47 L.Ed.2d 483 (1976).

27. *Id.* at 818, 96 S.Ct. at 1247.

28. *Id.*; *see also* Moses H. Cone Mem. Hosp. v. Mercury Constr. Corp., 460 U.S. 1, 103 S.Ct. 927, 74 L.Ed.2d 765 (1983) (applying the four-tiered exceptional circumstances test from *Colorado River* and adding the final two considerations).

29. 319 U.S. 315, 63 S.Ct. 1098, 87 L.Ed. 1424 (1943).

30. New Orleans Pub. Serv., Inc. v. Council of City of New Orleans, 491 U.S. 350, 109 S.Ct. 2506, 105 L.Ed.2d 298 (1989) (suggesting that the *Burford* abstention doctrine would be applicable in cases involving difficult questions of state law which affect important parochial policy concerns even if those questions emanate from judicial proceedings).

official, public functions. The contours of these immunities vary depending upon the individual or entity raising the right.

(a) United States as Defendant

A fundamental axiom of sovereign immunity stems from the ancient proposition that "the king can do no wrong." It remains the rule that the federal government cannot be sued without its consent.[1] The existence of consent is a prerequisite for jurisdiction over the government by a federal court.[2]

(1) Statutory Waivers of Immunity

Only congressional waivers of immunity will permit the federal government to be sued. The government's consent must be absolutely clear from the statute, and the federal courts will construe the statute against waiver if there is any ambiguity as to the extent of the waiver.[3] The terms of the statute will define the court's jurisdiction to hear the suit.[4] Generally, these statutes contain a number of procedural requirements with which a plaintiff must comply in order for jurisdiction to attach, including strictly construed notice provisions.[5]

(2) Federal Agency or Corporation as Defendant

There are similar jurisdictional concerns when the defendant is a federal agency. Claims for damages against a federal agency are typically treated as actions against the United States government itself, and the claimant must show a statutory waiver of immunity in order to proceed.[6]

However, when the United States treasury will not ultimately pay the judgment, suit may be brought against a federal agency or corporation in certain instances.[7] In determining whether the government is the real party in interest for purposes of immunity, the courts generally look to whether there is a sufficient nexus between the government and the challenged action of the regulatory agency that the action may be characterized as that of the government.[8]

---

§ 1.11

1. United States v. Mitchell, 445 U.S. 535, 538, 100 S.Ct. 1349, 1351, 63 L.Ed.2d 607 (1980).

2. Id.

3. Id.

4. United States v. Dalm, 494 U.S. 596, 608, 110 S.Ct. 1361, 1368, 108 L.Ed.2d 548 (1990).

5. E.g. Federal Tort Claims Act, 28 U.S.C.A. § 1346(b) (West 1993 & Supp. 1997); id. at § 2674 (West 1994); Tucker Act, 28 U.S.C.A. §§ 1346(a)(2), 1491 (West 1993); see also Dalm, 494 U.S. at 608–10, 110 S.Ct. at 1368–69 (noting that the claimant's failure to comply with the prerequi-

sites of the statute waiving immunity deprived the district court of jurisdiction).

6. Aviles v. Lutz, 887 F.2d 1046, 1048 (10th Cir.1989).

7. Dugan v. Rank, 372 U.S. 609, 620, 83 S.Ct. 999, 1006, 10 L.Ed.2d 15 (1963) (noting the general rule of immunity for a federal agency or official when the judgment sought would implicate the treasury, interfere with public administration or compel or restrain the federal government).

8. Larson v. Domestic & Foreign Commerce Corp., 337 U.S. 682, 687–89, 703–05, 69 S.Ct. 1457, 1460–61, 1468–69, 93 L.Ed. 1628 (1949) (noting that Congress has entrusted government business to its agencies and officers and that their official actions

(b) The State as Defendant

The Eleventh Amendment is an important limitation upon the jurisdiction of the federal courts. It provides that "[t]he Judicial power of the United States shall not be construed to extend to any suit in law or equity, commenced or prosecuted against one of the United States by Citizens of another State, or by Citizens or Subjects of any Foreign State."[9] Although the provision refers to "Citizens of another State," the Eleventh Amendment has, since its inception, been interpreted to preclude suits against a state by its own citizens as well.[10] The Eleventh Amendment also bars suit against a state agency or official when the state is the real party in interest.[11]

The Eleventh Amendment does not, however, protect a state against suits by the United States government or by other states in federal court because, in joining the union, the states were presumed to have relinquished their immunity to these types of suits.[12] A state can also voluntarily waive its Eleventh Amendment immunity in a suit for which it would otherwise be available, such as by consenting to be sued in a federal forum.[13]

The Eleventh Amendment is the source of much controversy and frustration; according to some of the Supreme Court Justices, it "rests on flawed premises, misguided history, and an untenable vision of the needs of the federal system it purports to protect."[14] There are a number of theories as to the source and purpose of the amendment, and "[t]he theory chosen determines the scope of the ... Amendment and the circumstances under which states may be sued in federal courts."[15] As a result, the opinions interpreting it form a veritable patchwork quilt of inconsistent holdings and conflicting results.

There are several ways to bypass the Eleventh Amendment's absolute bar, the most notable of which has been described as the *Young* fiction, which stemmed from the Supreme Court's decision in *Ex parte Young*.[16] In this seminal case, the Court held that, although a state could

are effectively those of the United States for immunity purposes).

9. U.S. Const. amend. 11.

10. Hans v. Louisiana, 134 U.S. 1, 15–18, 10 S.Ct. 504, 507–08, 33 L.Ed. 842 (1890).

11. Pennhurst State Sch. & Hosp. v. Halderman, 465 U.S. 89, 101, 104 S.Ct. 900, 908, 79 L.Ed.2d 67 (1984).

12. *E.g.*, Maryland v. Louisiana, 451 U.S. 725, 745 n. 21, 101 S.Ct. 2114, 2128 n. 21, 68 L.Ed.2d 576 (1981); United States v. Texas, 143 U.S. 621, 12 S.Ct. 488, 36 L.Ed. 285 (1892).

13. Petty v. Tennessee–Missouri Bridge Comm'n, 359 U.S. 275, 276, 79 S.Ct. 785,

787, 3 L.Ed.2d 804 (1959) (general appearance in federal court amounted to waiver of Eleventh Amendment immunity); *see also* Port Auth. Trans–Hudson Corp. v. Feeney, 495 U.S. 299, 304–09, 110 S.Ct. 1868, 1872–75, 109 L.Ed.2d 264 (1990) (holding that waiver must be express and unequivocal).

14. Atascadero State Hosp. v. Scanlon, 473 U.S. 234, 248, 105 S.Ct. 3142, 3150, 87 L.Ed.2d 171 (1985) (Brennan, J., dissenting); *see also* Erwin Chemerinsky, Federal Jurisdiction §§ 7.1–7.3 (2d ed. 1994).

15. Chemerinsky, *supra* note 14 § 7.3, at 374.

16. 209 U.S. 123, 28 S.Ct. 441, 52 L.Ed. 714 (1908).

not be sued indirectly for damages through its state officers acting in their official capacities,[17] a federal court can enjoin such an officer from taking state action that violates the Constitution—even when the injunction will have the effect of obstructing the implementation of an official state policy.[18] The state officer is considered to be stripped of his state authority for purposes of the Eleventh Amendment when he or she acts in contravention of the Constitution or federal law because no official has the authority to violate the Constitution or laws of the United States.[19] In this context, prospective relief is permissible, even if it will force the state to expend money to comply.[20] However, retroactive relief, such as damages to compensate for past injuries, are not recoverable if the state treasury will be liable.[21]

Further, and although a state official's official functions generally implicate Eleventh Amendment concerns, an official can be sued in his or her *individual* capacity as long as the damages are to be paid by the official, rather than the state treasury.[22] In this context, it is irrelevant that the state may have an indemnification program for state officials; the Court does not consider a voluntary indemnification agreement to implicate state funds directly, and consequently, there is no Eleventh Amendment protection.[23]

Finally, federal suits against agencies or political subdivisions of states are not prohibited if the agency or subdivision operates independently of the state.[24] Conversely, when a state is the true target of the challenged action or the damages will be paid by state funds, the Eleventh Amendment will serve as a jurisdictional bar. For example, in *Pennhurst State Sch. & Hosp. v. Halderman*,[25] a county, which co-operated a school for the mentally retarded that was created and funded by the state, was found to be an arm of the state entitled to Eleventh Amendment protection. The determination of whether the agency or subdivision is the alter ego of the state involves the same considerations

---

17. *See, e.g.*, Pennhurst State Sch. & Hosp. v. Halderman, 465 U.S. 89, 101, 104 S.Ct. 900, 908, 79 L.Ed.2d 67 (1984).

18. Young, 209 U.S. at 159–60, 28 S.Ct. at 454.

19. *Id.*

20. *E.g.*, Graham v. Richardson, 403 U.S. 365, 383, 91 S.Ct. 1848, 1857, 29 L.Ed.2d 534 (1971) (affirming injunction prohibiting Arizona and Pennsylvania officials from denying welfare benefits to aliens).

21. Edelman v. Jordan, 415 U.S. 651, 94 S.Ct. 1347, 39 L.Ed.2d 662 (1974).

22. Kentucky v. Graham, 473 U.S. 159, 105 S.Ct. 3099, 87 L.Ed.2d 114 (1985) (distinguishing between actions against state officials in their official and individual capacities).

23. Blaylock v. Schwinden, 862 F.2d 1352, 1354 (9th Cir.1988) (holding that the Eleventh Amendment barred a plaintiff's attempts to require a state defendant to indemnify state officer defendants under a Montana indemnification statute in order to enhance plaintiff's chances of recovery); Wilson v. Beebe, 770 F.2d 578, 587–88 (6th Cir.1985) (en banc) (holding that a state "cannot create an Eleventh Amendment bar by its voluntary action" of agreeing to indemnify its officials).

24. Mount Healthy City Sch. Dist. Bd. of Educ. v. Doyle, 429 U.S. 274, 279–81, 97 S.Ct. 568, 572–73, 50 L.Ed.2d 471 (1977).

25. 465 U.S. 89, 123–24, 104 S.Ct. 900, 920–21, 79 L.Ed.2d 67 (1984).

as those governing the inquiry for purposes of diversity jurisdiction.[26]

(c) Government Officials as Defendant

As discussed in the preceding section, state officials may be sued in federal court under limited circumstances for violations of federal law. The federal courts also have subject matter jurisdiction over federal officials for redress under federal law.[27] However, this statute does not operate as a waiver of sovereign immunity from tort liability for federal officials in the exercise of their official duties.[28]

Even if there is no jurisdictional bar to a suit against a state or federal official, it is important to note that the official may have certain substantive immunities against suit or against an award of damages under state and/or federal law. Absolute immunity denies a person whose federal rights have been violated by a government official any type of remedy, regardless of conduct. For this reason, the Supreme Court has been "quite sparing" in recognizing absolute immunity.[29] This immunity attaches to the particular official function—not the office.[30] It is recognized in the context of: (i) judges performing judicial acts within their jurisdiction;[31] (ii) prosecutors performing their official functions;[32] or (iii) certain quasi-judicial agency officials performing functions essentially similar to those of judges or prosecutors in a court-type setting.[33]

Qualified immunity applies to bar suit against certain actions of government officials that are not subject to absolute immunity: "[G]overnment officials performing discretionary functions, generally are shielded from liability for civil damages insofar as their conduct does not violate clearly established statutory or constitutional rights of which a reasonable person should have known."[34] This immunity applies, for example, when an officer violates the Fourth Amendment prohibition on illegal searches and seizures unless a reasonable officer would have known that the specific conduct involved was impermissible.[35]

---

26. See supra § 1.7(c)(1); see also PYCA Indus., Inc. v. Harrison County Waste Water Mgmt. Dist., 81 F.3d 1412, 1416 n. 2 (5th Cir.1996) (noting that the factors used for determining alter ego status of a state agency or political subdivision are virtually identical for purposes of diversity and the Eleventh Amendment).

27. See 28 U.S.C.A. § 1442(a)(1) (West Supp. 1997).

28. Areskog v. United States, 396 F.Supp. 834, 838–39 (D.Conn.1975).

29. Forrester v. White, 484 U.S. 219, 224, 108 S.Ct. 538, 542, 98 L.Ed.2d 555 (1988).

30. Id. at 229, 108 S.Ct. at 545.

31. Bradley v. Fisher, 80 U.S. (13 Wall.) 335, 20 L.Ed. 646 (1871).

32. Yaselli v. Goff, 12 F.2d 396 (2d Cir. 1926), aff'd mem., 275 U.S. 503, 48 S.Ct. 155, 72 L.Ed. 395 (1927).

33. Butz v. Economou, 438 U.S. 478, 511–17, 98 S.Ct. 2894, 2913–16, 57 L.Ed.2d 895 (1978).

34. Harlow v. Fitzgerald, 457 U.S. 800, 818, 102 S.Ct. 2727, 2738, 73 L.Ed.2d 396 (1982).

35. E.g., Anderson v. Creighton, 483 U.S. 635, 646, 107 S.Ct. 3034, 3042, 97 L.Ed.2d 523 (1987).

(d) Foreign Sovereign Immunities Act

The Foreign Sovereign Immunities Act ("FSIA"),[36] codifies an important limitation on the federal courts' ability to adjudicate claims against foreign states. Affording sovereign immunity to foreign states is "a matter of grace and comity on the part of the United States and not a jurisdictional limitation imposed by the Constitution."[37] The FSIA is a comprehensive legal scheme governing claims of sovereign immunity by foreign states and their agencies and instrumentalities.

The FSIA essentially "codifies, as a matter of federal law, the restrictive theory of sovereign immunity."[38] This theory shields a foreign sovereign from suits involving its public acts only; it does not protect a foreign state when liability is based solely on its commercial acts,[39] such as the purchase of raw materials from international businesses for the government's use.[40] Otherwise, the foreign state could invoke sovereign immunity as a defense to otherwise binding contractual obligations.[41]

The Act provides generally that a foreign state is not subject to the jurisdiction of the federal and state courts of this country unless one of the enumerated exceptions applies.[42] Congress intended the FSIA to provide the sole basis for the exercise of subject matter jurisdiction by federal courts over foreign sovereigns and their instrumentalities.[43]

(e) Act of State Doctrine

In a similar vein, the "act of state doctrine" is premised upon the principle that the courts of this country should not sit in judgment of political actions taken by a foreign government in its own country.[44] It differs from sovereign immunity in that the sovereign need not be a party to the action for the doctrine to be invoked; as long as the litigation challenges the validity of the foreign state's public actions, the doctrine may apply.[45] This judicially-created doctrine, although rooted in

---

36. 28 U.S.C.A. § 1602 (West 1994).

37. Verlinden B.V. v. Central Bank of Nigeria, 461 U.S. 480, 486, 103 S.Ct. 1962, 1967, 76 L.Ed.2d 81 (1983).

38. *Id.* at 488, 103 S.Ct. at 1968.

39. 28 U.S.C.A. § 1605(a)(2) (West 1994).

40. *E.g.,* Verlinden B.V., 461 U.S. 480, 103 S.Ct. 1962, 76 L.Ed.2d 81 (involving the purchase of cement by the Nigerian government from a Dutch company under a letter of credit established by the Central Bank of Nigeria).

41. Stena Rederi AB v. Comision de Contratos del Comite Ejecutivo General, 923 F.2d 380, 386–87 & n. 9 (5th Cir.1991) (noting that, although the tests for determining commercial activities under the FSIA are somewhat vague, it is relatively clear that "commercial activities" include contractual negotiations and obligations of the foreign sovereign).

42. 28 U.S.C.A. § 1604 (West 1994). The scope and application of the FSIA is discussed in greater detail in Chapter 17 "Litigating International Disputes in Federal Courts," *infra.*

43. Argentine Republic v. Amerada Hess Shipping Corp., 488 U.S. 428, 434, 109 S.Ct. 683, 688, 102 L.Ed.2d 818 (1989).

44. W. S. Kirkpatrick & Co. v. Environmental Tectonics Corp., 493 U.S. 400, 110 S.Ct. 701, 107 L.Ed.2d 816 (1990); Walter Fuller Aircraft Sales, Inc. v. Republic of Philippines, 965 F.2d 1375 (5th Cir.1992).

45. Hunt v. Mobil Oil Corp., 550 F.2d 68 (2d Cir.1977) (holding that a foreign sovereign need not be a defendant to the action for the act of state doctrine to be invoked).

the Constitution, is a prudential, rather than jurisdictional, limitation on federal courts.[46]

§ 1.12 Statutory Limitations

In addition to the statutes granting a federal court subject matter jurisdiction over certain types of disputes, Congress has also exercised its authority to limit the subject matter jurisdiction of the federal courts when important state interests or concerns are implicated. A few of those statutes will be discussed in turn below.

(a) Anti–Injunction Act—28 U.S.C.A. § 2283

Since 1793, there has been a statutory prohibition against the federal courts to prevent them from using their injunctive powers to stay judicial proceedings in the state courts.[1] The Anti–Injunction Act prevents a federal court from enjoining state court proceedings "except as expressly authorized by Act of Congress, or where necessary in aid of its jurisdiction, or to protect or effectuate its judgments."[2] Its purpose is to preserve the autonomy of the state courts by severely circumscribing encroachment by the federal courts. The Act is based upon notions of federalism and the need "to prevent needless friction between [the] state and federal courts" of this nation.[3]

There are four exceptions to the Anti–Injunction Act: (1) injunctions specifically authorized by another Act of Congress, (2) those necessary in aid of a federal court's jurisdiction, (3) injunctions necessary to protect or effectuate a federal court's judgment, and (4) injunctions sought by the United States to protect national interests. Each will be discussed below.

(1) Acts of Congress

Under the first exception to the Anti–Injunction Act, a federal court can enjoin state judicial proceedings when another congressional Act so permits.[4] The exception applies when Congress has created a federally-protected right enforceable in federal court that could be significantly impaired if the federal court were not permitted to enjoin a state court proceeding.[5] Examples of other statutes that expressly come within the

---

46. W.S. Kirkpatrick & Co., 493 U.S. at 409, 110 S.Ct. at 706. *See also* Chapter 17 "Litigating International Disputes in Federal Courts," *infra,* for a more detailed discussion of this doctrine and its applications.

§ 1.12

1. Act of March 2, 1793, c. 22, § 5, 1 Stat. 334.

2. 28 U.S.C.A. § 2283 (West 1994).

3. Oklahoma Packing Co. v. Oklahoma Gas & Elec. Co., 309 U.S. 4, 9, 60 S.Ct. 215, 218, 84 L.Ed. 537 (1940).

4. 28 U.S.C.A. § 2283 (West 1994).

5. Mitchum v. Foster, 407 U.S. 225, 237, 92 S.Ct. 2151, 2159, 32 L.Ed.2d 705 (1972).

ambit of this exception and permit federal injunctions are the Bankruptcy Act[6] and the federal Interpleader Act.[7] The statute need not specifically refer to the Anti–Injunction Act in order to overcome the presumption against federal injunctions.[8] Rather, the provision preserves the right of Congress to determine when an issue is of such importance to federal law that the United States courts should be permitted to enjoin state court proceedings which may adversely affect or impair the federal scheme.

(2) Necessary Aid to Jurisdiction

The "in aid of its jurisdiction" exception to the Anti–Injunction Act, although facially broad, has been interpreted in a limited manner.[9] It is clear that a federal court has the authority to stay state court proceedings in a lawsuit once that case has been removed to federal court.[10] It is also established that a federal court may enjoin parallel state court in rem proceedings if it acquires jurisdiction first.[11] At the other end of the spectrum, the Supreme Court has held that the mere prospect of inconsistent judgments is insufficient to permit a federal court to enjoin concurrent state proceedings.[12] However, the Court, in proclaiming the cardinal rules, has provided little guidance as to how far the "in aid of its jurisdiction" exception is intended to reach:

> First, a federal court does not have inherent power to ignore the limitations of § 2283 and to enjoin state court proceedings merely because those proceedings interfere with a protected federal right or invade an area preempted by federal law, even when the interference is unmistakably clear.... Second, if the District Court does have jurisdiction, it is not enough that the requested injunction is related to that jurisdiction, but it must be "necessary in aid of" that jurisdiction ...to prevent a state court from so interfering with a federal court's consideration or disposition of a case as to seriously impair the federal court's flexibility and authority to decide that case.[13]

Any doubts about the availability of injunctive relief are resolved in favor of deference to the state court proceedings.[14]

---

6. 11 U.S.C.A. § 362 (West 1993 & Supp. 1997) (authorizing automatic stay of related federal and state proceedings by federal bankruptcy court).

7. 28 U.S.C.A. § 2361 (West 1994).

8. Amalgamated Clothing Workers of Am. v. Richman Bros., 348 U.S. 511, 75 S.Ct. 452, 99 L.Ed. 600 (1955).

9. *E.g.,* Atlantic Coast Line R.R. Co. v. Brotherhood of Locomotive Eng'rs., 398 U.S. 281, 288, 90 S.Ct. 1739, 1744, 26 L.Ed.2d 234 (1970).

10. Mitchum, 407 U.S. at 234, 92 S.Ct. at 2157.

11. Donovan v. City of Dallas, 377 U.S. 408, 412, 84 S.Ct. 1579, 1582, 12 L.Ed.2d 409 (1964).

12. Atlantic Coast Line, 398 U.S. at 294–95, 90 S.Ct. at 1747–48; *see also* Texas v. United States, 837 F.2d 184 (5th Cir. 1988).

13. Atlantic Coast Line, 398 U.S. at 294–95, 90 S.Ct. at 1747–48.

14. *Id.* at 296–97, 90 S.Ct. at 1747–48.

(3) To Protect or Effectuate Judgment

The "relitigation exception" permits a federal court to enjoin state court proceedings that interfere with a prior federal judgment and was included to overrule the Supreme Court's decision in *Toucey v. New York Life Ins. Co.*[15] In that case, the Court held that a federal court lacks the power to enjoin the relitigation of cases and controversies it has previously and fully adjudicated.[16] In adding this language, Congress adopted the position of the *Toucey* dissent that federal courts unquestionably have the power to protect and effectuate their judgments.[17]

A trial court is not required to enjoin state court proceedings under this exception, but may do so in its discretion.[18]

The relitigation exception is grounded in traditional principles of res judicata and collateral estoppel. An essential element of both of these doctrines is the requirement that the issues sought to be used preclusively have been actually litigated—as opposed to merely raised in pleadings—in the prior proceeding.[19] As a result, many federal courts will not permit an injunction under this exception unless the issue to be enjoined was actually litigated in the earlier federal proceeding.[20]

(4) Suit by United States

Finally, the Anti–Injunction Act is not applicable to actions by the United States to enjoin state court proceedings that pose a threat of irreparable injury to a national interest.[21]

(b) Tax Injunction Act—28 U.S.C.A. § 1341

The Tax Injunction Act of 1937 prevents a federal district court from "enjoin[ing], suspend[ing] or restrain[ing] the assessment, levy or collection of any tax under State law where a plain, speedy and efficient remedy may be had in the courts of such State."[22] This Act has been interpreted to bar any federal review of state and local taxation, including cases in which the validity of the Act must be determined to afford complete relief to a party.[23] It has also been interpreted to prohibit any equitable remedy in federal court, including declaratory relief in state tax cases.[24] Since it is a limit on the jurisdiction of the federal courts—

---

15. 314 U.S. 118, 62 S.Ct. 139, 86 L.Ed. 100 (1941).

16. *Id.* at 140–41, 62 S.Ct. at 147–48.

17. *See* 28 U.S.C.A. § 2283 reviser's note (West 1994) (citing favorably the *Toucey* dissent and stating that "the revised section restores the basic law as generally understood and interpreted prior to the *Toucey* decision").

18. Merle Norman Cosmetics, Inc. v. Victa, 936 F.2d 466, 468 (9th Cir.1991).

19. *See* Chapter 12 "Issue and Claim Preclusion," *infra*.

20. *See, e.g.,* Farias v. Bexar County Bd. of Trustees, 925 F.2d 866, 879–80 (5th Cir.

1991); Staffer v. Bouchard Transp. Co., 878 F.2d 638 (2d Cir.1989).

21. Leiter Minerals, Inc. v. United States, 352 U.S. 220, 77 S.Ct. 287, 1 L.Ed.2d 267 (1957).

22. 28 U.S.C.A. § 1341 (West 1993).

23. Keleher v. New England Tel. & Tel. Co., 947 F.2d 547 (2d Cir.1991).

24. Edwards v. Transcontinental Gas Pipe Line Corp., 464 F.Supp. 654 (M.D.La. 1979).

rather than an immunity—a state may not waive its application.[25]

The only exception to the jurisdictional bar is when the state fails to provide a "plain, speedy and efficient remedy" in its courts. This limited provision applies when the state has no procedure for review or when the procedure adopted by the state for challenging the tax is uncertain or otherwise unclear.[26] The standard is fairly rigid. For example, the Supreme Court has held that a state procedure requiring a taxpayer to pay the tax and sue for refund—which had the effect of holding the contested tax for two years without interest—was insufficient to invoke the exception.[27]

(c) Johnson Act: Prohibition of Suits Relating to Rate Orders of State Agencies—28 U.S.C.A. § 1342

Another example of a statutory limitation of federal subject matter jurisdiction is the Johnson Act, which prohibits a federal court from enjoining operation of, or compliance with, state rate orders relating to public utilities.[28] The Act provides that a federal district court should not "enjoin, suspend or restrain the operation of, or compliance with, any order affecting rates chargeable by a public utility and made by a State administrative agency or a rate-making body of a State political subdivision" where each of four requirements are met: (1) jurisdiction is based solely on diversity or "repugnance of the order to the Federal Constitution," (2) the order "does not interfere with interstate commerce," (3) reasonable notice and hearing have been provided, and (4) "[a] plain, speedy and efficient remedy may be had in the courts of such State."[29] All four conditions must be met in order to strip a federal court of jurisdiction.[30]

When these four conditions are present, the statute deprives a federal court of the ability to review the propriety of a rate order, including claims for damages and declaratory relief.[31] However, a party can challenge the state statute that authorized the rate order in a federal court, assuming there is a basis for original federal jurisdiction over the claim.[32]

---

25. United Gas Pipe Line Co. v. Whitman, 595 F.2d 323 (5th Cir.1979).

26. Rosewell v. LaSalle Nat'l Bank, 450 U.S. 503, 101 S.Ct. 1221, 67 L.Ed.2d 464 (1981).

27. *Id.*

28. 28 U.S.C.A. § 1342 (West 1993).

29. *Id.*

30. Peoples Nat'l Util. Co. v. City of Houston, 837 F.2d 1366, 1367 (5th Cir. 1988).

31. California v. Grace Brethren Church, 457 U.S. 393, 102 S.Ct. 2498, 73 L.Ed.2d 93 (1982) (finding lack of jurisdiction over declaratory judgment claims even though constitutional challenge was raised to rate order); Tennyson v. Gas Serv. Co., 506 F.2d 1135, 1138–39 (10th Cir.1974) (barring review of claims for damages and declaratory relief joined with claims for injunctive relief).

32. Public Util. Comm'n v. United States, 355 U.S. 534, 78 S.Ct. 446, 2 L.Ed.2d 470 (1958).

Library References:

West's Key No. Digests, Courts ⊕508; Federal Courts ⊕27, 28.
Wright, Miller & Cooper, Federal Practice and Procedure: Civil 2d §§ 3525–3526, 4222.

§ 1.13 Practice Checklist

(a) Original Subject Matter Jurisdiction

A party should first ascertain whether a federal court has original subject matter jurisdiction based upon one of the following:

(1) Federal Question Jurisdiction—28 U.S.C.A. § 1331

To determine the existence of federal question jurisdiction, a party must consider whether:

1. the complaint clearly shows a federal claim "arising under" federal law (*See* § 1.6(a)(2), (3) & (b)(1)); or

2. if the complaint is based upon state law, it nonetheless implicates a federal law creating a cause of action that is an essential element of the plaintiff's claim (*See* § 1.6(b)(2)); and

3. the federal claim or issue is substantial and can be substantiated (*See* § 1.6(b)(3)).

(2) Diversity Jurisdiction—28 U.S.C.A. § 1332

Diversity jurisdiction is available in civil cases if:

1. there is complete diversity between the opposing parties (*See* § 1.7(d)(1)); and

2. the amount in controversy, exclusive of interest and costs, exceeds $75,000 (*See* § 1.7(c)(2)).

To determine whether there is complete diversity, counsel should consider whether:

1. the parties in the complaint are properly aligned according to their interests in the dispute (*See* § 1.7(e));

2. any indispensable, nondiverse parties have been or could be joined (*See* § 1.7(e)(5)); and

3. any nondiverse parties that have been joined are real and proper parties (*See* § 1.7(d)(2) & (e)).

(3) Supplemental Jurisdiction—28 U.S.C.A. § 1367

If there is a basis for original federal jurisdiction, the court will also have jurisdiction over supplemental state law claims:

1. that stem from the same common nucleus of operative facts (*See* § 1.8(b)); unless

    a. the court's original jurisdiction is based upon diversity, and the exercise of supplemental jur-

isdiction would be inconsistent with the requirements of Section 1332 (*See* § 1.8(c)(1)); or

b. the trial court, in its discretion, determines
that the exercise of supplemental jurisdiction
would not be appropriate because the supplemental claims are novel, complex, or dominate
the dispute or if the court determines that
exceptional circumstances require that a state
court decide the claims (*See* § 1.8(c)(2)).

(b) Constitutional, Statutory, and Prudential Concerns

Even if original jurisdiction would otherwise exist, counsel should
consider whether other limitations on the federal court's authority
would impair or preclude a federal forum. Among these considerations are the following:

1. whether the case is ripe for adjudication (*See*
§ 1.9(a)(1));

2. whether the controversy has or could become moot as a
result of intervening circumstances (*See* § 1.9(a)(2));

3. whether there is a valid, existing controversy between
the parties to be adjudicated (*See* § 1.9(a)(3));

4. whether the relief sought interferes with other branches of the federal government (*See* § 1.9(a)(4));

5. whether the plaintiff is the proper party to bring the
action (*See* § 1.9(b));

6. whether there is concurrent jurisdiction in the state
courts (*See* § 1.10(a) & (b));

7. whether there are reasons that the federal court should
defer to state judicial or administrative proceedings (*See*
§§ 1.10(c) & 1.12); and

8. whether the suit implicates immunities of a state, federal, or foreign government, agency, or official (*See*
§ 1.11).

CHAPTER 2

PERSONAL JURISDICTION AND SERVICE

by
Frank Cicero, Jr.
and
Suzanne Easley Tracy

Table of Sections

WESTLAW Electronic Research

See WESTLAW Electronic Research Guide preceding the Summary of Contents.

---

§ 2.1   Scope Note

This chapter addresses personal jurisdiction including the statutory requirements for service of summons primarily set forth in FRCP 4 and due process limitations.[1] Included are strategy considerations regarding service and asserting and contesting personal jurisdiction in the context of business and commercial litigation. The chapter begins with an overview of service of summons and general due process issues, then discusses various personal jurisdiction issues which have arisen in business and commercial cases. Finally, a procedural checklist and a set of basic forms are included.

Library References:

West's Key No. Digests, Constitutional Law ⟜305, 309; Courts ⟜10; Federal Courts ⟜71–97.

Wright & Miller, Federal Practice and Procedure: Civil 2d §§ 1061, 1063.

§ 2.1

1. This chapter does not discuss international service and personal jurisdiction issues in detail as this topic is addressed in Chapter 17 "Litigating International Disputes in Federal Courts," *infra.*

§ 2.2 The Role of the Personal Jurisdiction Requirement

The existence of subject matter jurisdiction is not alone sufficient to subject a defendant to the binding orders of a particular court. The plaintiff must also establish that the particular court has personal jurisdiction over the defendant. A plaintiff can do this by presenting facts establishing (1) proper service (or waiver of service) and (2) that personal jurisdiction over this defendant would comport with constitutional due process requirements. This second point, commonly referred to as minimum contacts, is necessarily fact intensive, varies in application from circuit to circuit and in many instances is unpredictable. In fact, even the Supreme Court has had a difficult time agreeing on standards to apply in analyzing personal jurisdiction due process.[1]

Library References:

> West's Key No. Digests, Courts ⟜10; Federal Courts ⟜71–97.
> Wright & Miller, Federal Practice and Procedure: Civil 2d § 1061.

§ 2.3 Strategy Considerations

(a) Overall Approach to Analyzing Personal Jurisdiction

A lawyer contemplating filing suit against a defendant in a federal forum distant from the defendant's home state or country would do well to review the applicable service statutes (state and federal),[1] research the particular circuit's application of personal jurisdiction due process requirements, and assemble facts supporting the requisite minimum contacts between the defendant, the forum and the litigation prior to filing. He should also review any applicable contracts between the parties for forum selection clauses. At a minimum, he should satisfy himself that he has the ability to serve properly the defendant via a long arm-statute and enough facts to satisfy due process minimum contacts concerns.

A defendant served with process should first determine whether a challenge to service or personal jurisdiction is worth the time, effort and expense even if she can prevail. Second, she should weigh the relative chances of prevailing prior to mounting an aggressive defense. This exercise is best performed with the client completely informed and actively involved in the decision making process so as to avoid any surprise down the line if expense mounts up, discovery into client

---

§ 2.2

1. *See, e.g.,* the discussion of *Asahi Metal Industry Co., Ltd. v. Superior Court of California infra* at § 2.9(b) regarding the stream of commerce theory.

§ 2.3

1. The plaintiff will also need to satisfy himself that state constitutional law does

not prohibit service. *See, e.g.,* RAR, Incorporated v. Turner Diesel, Limited, 107 F.3d 1272, 1276 (7th Cir.1997) (examining Illinois constitutional due process requirements).

contacts with the forum becomes annoying or the challenge is unsuccessful.

(b) Service Strategies

(1) Ramifications of Requesting or Agreeing to Waive Service

It may appear from an initial reading of the FRCP 4(d) voluntary waiver of service of process rule that everyone benefits and no one loses with voluntary waiver of service.[2] The plaintiff avoids the time and expense of chasing a defendant down for service (and in some cases gets paid the costs of service if defendant refuses waiver); the defendant receives extra time to respond. The decision whether to request or agree to waiver is not, however, clear cut.

A plaintiff can benefit from not using the waiver provisions if he wants to move the case along quickly and service is easily accomplished. The costs to serve are usually not great in comparison with the amounts at stake in federal litigation, and service can avoid delay which may occur if a request for waiver is made. For example, under the waiver rule, defendant will receive a copy of the complaint and request to waive on day one. Plaintiff must provide defendant with at least 30 days to respond to the request for waiver. If defense counsel waits until the last day allowed and then agrees to waive, then defendant gets another 30 days to answer. On the other hand if, after waiting 30 days defendant refuses to waive, at least 30 days would have expired. Plaintiff's counsel will then need to arrange for service of process. After plaintiff effects service, the defendant will have an additional 20 days in which to respond. Using the minimum time for the waiver request response period of 30 days, if it took plaintiff's counsel 10 days to effect service, and the defendant is allowed 20 days to answer, the defendant would have obtained 60 days within which to respond—40 more than she would have received if originally served with process instead of receiving a request for waiver. Thus, if plaintiff wants to move the case along it would perhaps be better to serve at the outset or attempt service concurrently with the request for waiver.

A defendant may also benefit in other ways from refusing to waive. For example, the costs of service she would have to pay may be slight compared to the dollars at stake in federal court;[3] if she does not immediately refuse to waive, by the time she is served, she will, more likely than not, have had at least the same amount of time to have reviewed and responded to the complaint as she would have received had

---

2. FRCP 4(d) provides a methodology by which plaintiffs can request that defendants waive technical service of process. If defendants agree they receive 60 days to respond to the complaint. If certain defendants refuse, they can be charged with the costs to serve and attorneys' fees and costs for the motion to recoup these costs.

3. The potential costs include the expense of service (and reasonable attorneys' fees and costs for the motion to recoup them), and perhaps the goodwill of the court should defendant's delaying tactics come into view.

she agreed to waive;[4] and finally, by refusing she will preserve her objections to defective service and summons. These "benefits," are slight, however, if there is little question about the eventual ability of plaintiff to effect service on the defendant and there are no statute of limitations issues.

Regarding statutes of limitations, both parties should research and calendar any applicable deadlines prior to agreeing to or requesting waiver. Failing to do so could result in the loss of a claim or a defense. For example, defendant may lose a good statute of limitations defense if he waives service without considering the applicable time cutoff. Under the waiver rule, if the defendant agrees to waive, service is deemed to occur on the date plaintiff files the signed waiver. Thus, if the statute of limitations requires service before a specific date[5] (for example January 2, 1999) and the plaintiff requests and the defendant agrees to waiver prior to that date, and plaintiff promptly files the waiver (say on December 30, 1998), but plaintiff would have been unable to serve the defendant prior to the cutoff date (*i.e.* prior to January 2, 1999), the defendant who agreed to waiver will be treated as if he had accepted service as of December 29, 1998 and will have lost a statute of limitations defense. Obviously, in such a case a defendant would be wise to refuse to agree to waiver.

The flip side of this factual scenario is that plaintiffs obviously should not rely solely on a request for waiver or delay in filing an executed waiver if a statute of limitations period is about to run. A plaintiff may also lose a good claim if he requests waiver, is unsuccessful and then fails to effect service within the 120 day time period required by FRCP 4(m). Failure to serve within 120 days can result in dismissal without prejudice if good cause cannot be shown and the court does not grant a discretionary extension,[6] and, if the statute of limitations period has run in the interim, the plaintiff's claim will be time barred.[7] Thus, both parties should carefully and promptly research the applicable statutes of limitations, calculate and calendar the applicable dates and carefully analyze service issues.

(2) Obtaining an Extension of Time Within Which to Serve

FRCP 4(m) requires plaintiffs to serve the summons and complaint on defendants within 120 days of filing.[8] If plaintiff encounters problems serving within the time allowed, or suspects the defendant is intentionally dodging service he should be sure to make a good record and let the

---

4. The request for waiver must include a copy of the complaint.

5. While many statutes of limitation are keyed to the filing of a lawsuit, some states in some cases determine time from the date of service.

6. Requesting waiver does not toll the Rule 4(m) provision requiring service within 120 days after filing for service within the U.S.

7. Plaintiffs who request extensions based on the fact that their claim will be time barred are not always successful.

8. Plaintiff is responsible for service, therefore, counsel should assure himself that the person(s) he retains for service are adequately instructed on the rules which apply.

court know as soon as possible. Rule 4(m) provides for mandatory extension of time upon a showing of good cause, and for discretionary extension without such a showing. If plaintiff alerts the court to potential problems early, chances are better that the request for more time will appear justified. If plaintiff waits until the last minute or after a deadline is missed, the request may appear to be an excuse for the failure diligently to attempt service. Failure to show good cause or to convince the court that it should grant a discretionary extension will result in dismissal without prejudice. If the statute of limitations has run on the claim, there may be a time bar to refiling and the dismissal without prejudice will be equivalent to a dismissal with prejudice.

(c) Challenging Personal Jurisdiction

(1) Costs and Benefits of Challenging Personal Jurisdiction

Just because there are good facts with which to challenge personal jurisdiction doesn't mean challenge should be made. The costs of the motion and the attendant discovery are always factors to consider. They include more than attorney time to draft the motion and defend the discovery, such as unwanted disclosure, client annoyance and a diminished opportunity to settle the case early.

A challenge to personal jurisdiction, especially a claim of general personal jurisdiction,[9] may involve discovery of financial or proprietary information the defendant would rather not reveal to the other side, information which would not have been discoverable at this point in the case (or at all) absent the defendant's raising the personal jurisdiction issue. Jurisdictional discovery may also provide plaintiffs with an excuse to depose key employees, officers and directors. Such depositions cost time and money and can often annoy the client.

An acrimonious challenge to personal jurisdiction (including depositions and other discovery) can also create such hostility and cost that early settlement will become impossible. If plaintiffs win, they may gain a sense of momentum which is unrelated to the merits of the substantive case. In such a case they may, therefore, unrealistically evaluate their chance of prevailing in the overall litigation, and again settlement may become more difficult. Thus, prior to asserting a challenge to personal jurisdiction, the defense attorney should carefully weigh the costs and benefits and then clearly explain to her client the potential "costs" involved.

(2) Challenge Jurisdiction and Defects in Process and Service of Process at the First Opportunity, and Explicitly State the Defects

Failure explicitly to raise objections to defects in the summons or service or to personal jurisdiction in either the FRCP 12(b) motion to

---

9. When a plaintiff asserts a particular forum has general personal jurisdiction over a defendant the issue becomes whether the defendant has purposefully established continuous and systematic contacts with the forum state. When a defendant contests the issue, discovery may extend to defendant's contacts with the forum state which are unrelated to this particular plaintiff.

dismiss or the answer (if defendant has not already moved to dismiss),[10] will result in a waiver of the defenses.

If the applicable statute of limitations will expire shortly, a defendant may benefit from pleading lack of personal jurisdiction and service defects in the answer. The court will not immediately resolve the dispute, and, if the defendant prevails on these issues (after the statute date has passed in the appropriate jurisdiction), the plaintiff may be time barred. But there are also risks to asserting the defense only in the answer. Merely stating an affirmative defense of lack of general and/or specific personal jurisdiction in an answer may not be explicit enough to encompass objections to insufficiency of process or insufficiency of service of process. Moreover, the defendant must be careful not to waive, by her conduct in the litigation, the defenses of defects in service, summons or personal jurisdiction.[11]

With respect to waiver, the defendant should carefully analyze the applicable circuit's holdings regarding whether asserting a counterclaim constitutes waiver of a challenge to personal jurisdiction. From a strategy standpoint, it may benefit a defendant who has a counterclaim to bring his Rule 12(b) motion to dismiss based on lack of personal jurisdiction prior to answering and asserting the counterclaim. If he wins, there is obviously no need to proceed further. If he loses at the motion to dismiss stage but still believes he may prevail on the issue at trial,[12] the question of whether counterclaiming constitutes waiver becomes even more important. In such a case, defense counsel should research the state of law within her circuit on this point and satisfy herself regarding waiver prior to asserting a counterclaim.

(3) Couple the Motion to Dismiss for Lack of Personal Jurisdiction with a Motion for Change of Venue

If the primary motivation in challenging personal jurisdiction is the distant location of the forum, the motion to dismiss can be joined with a motion for change of venue. The procedure is common and provides the court a middle ground.[13] If, however, the matter is one of diversity, defendant should make sure to check the relevant statutes of limitations in the new forum prior to requesting a change because they may apply to defeat the claim.[14]

---

10. This is often referred to as raising the issue in the first responsive pleading.

11. See Media Duplication Services, Ltd. v. HDG Software, Inc., 928 F.2d 1228, 1233, n. 2 (1st Cir.1991) (discussing conduct constituting waiver).

12. The showing by plaintiff at the motion to dismiss stage is a prima facie showing with facts interpreted in the plaintiff's favor.

13. Motions for change of venue are discussed in Chapter 3 "Venue, Forum Selection and Transfer," *infra.*

14. See Chaiken v. VV Publishing Corp., 119 F.3d 1018, 1030 (2d Cir.1997) (holding that if a plaintiff moves to transfer an action based on diversity of citizenship from one federal trial court to another so as to cure a defect in personal jurisdiction over the defendant, the state law of the transferee forum governs the action for the purposes of the statute of limitations).

(4) Default and Collateral Attack Options

If a defendant appears, challenges personal jurisdiction and loses, he may not make a collateral attack on the judgment in another forum based upon the lack of personal jurisdiction. If he does not appear and defaults, he may still challenge personal jurisdiction in other forums in which the plaintiff attempts to enforce the judgment. Thus, a defendant must decide, prior to appearing, whether it is worth the risk to default and contest jurisdiction when plaintiffs try to collect on the judgment in another forum or whether it would be more prudent to challenge jurisdiction in the existing forum. The former is an extremely high risk approach, especially given the uncertainty regarding personal jurisdiction rules and the possibility that the defendant may lose the collateral attack and therefore the ability to fight the claim on the merits. Additionally, judgments are often picked up by credit rating services. Therefore defendants who choose to wait and fight another day may find themselves with a recorded judgment which causes other difficulties for the client. This possibility should be discussed should the client be thinking about default and a later challenge.

(d) Asserting Personal Jurisdiction

Plaintiff has the burden to show the facts necessary for the court to find personal jurisdiction. Plaintiff should allege facts supporting both general and specific jurisdiction if possible, as failure to specifically allege general personal jurisdiction can result in waiver.[15] If plaintiff needs discovery, he should promptly serve formal discovery requests and conduct needed depositions. Untimely requests for permission to take discovery which are unwarranted and unreasonable may be denied. If for some reason plaintiff has failed to conduct necessary discovery prior to filing the opposition to a motion to dismiss, he should make note of the need for additional discovery in the opposition papers.[16]

Library References:

West's Key No. Digests, Constitutional Law ⟜305, 309; Courts ⟜1–40; Federal Civil Procedure ⟜531–540; Federal Courts ⟜71–97.

Wright & Miller, Federal Practice and Procedure: Civil 2d §§ 1347, 1349–1351, 1353.

§ 2.4   Personal Jurisdiction Overview

Generally speaking, a federal court obtains personal jurisdiction over a defendant only if the defendant has been properly served with summons (or waived service)[1] and constitutional due process is satisfied.

---

15. *See* RAR, Incorporated v. Turner Diesel, Limited, 107 F.3d 1272, 1277 (7th Cir.1997) (plaintiff who failed to allege continuous and systematic general business contacts with the forum waived any general jurisdiction argument).

16. *See infra* § 2.10(a), for a discussion of discovery issues related to contests of personal jurisdiction in federal court.

§ 2.4

1. *See* United Electrical, Radio and Machine Workers of America v. 163 Pleasant Street Corporation, 960 F.2d 1080, 1085

Service is governed by FRCP 4. The constitutional due process requirements have developed in case law.

Library References:

West's Key No. Digests, Courts ⬚10; Federal Courts ⬚71–97.
Wright & Miller, Federal Practice and Procedure: Civil 2d §§ 1061, 1084.

§ 2.5 FRCP 4

FRCP 4 sets forth the procedures by which a plaintiff may establish personal jurisdiction over a defendant in a federal court, assuming such jurisdiction complies with constitutional due process requirements. The Rule governs basic service issues such as the form[1] and issuance of the summons,[2] the papers to be served,[3] the party responsible for service,[4] the proper person to do it,[5] the time limit,[6] and proof.[7] The Rule also provides methodology to obtain a defendant's waiver of service[8] and, when waiver is not obtained, detailed rules for service on various types of defendants.[9] Finally, it contains territorial limits on effective service in general[10] and specific rules for jurisdiction over property.[11] FRCP 4 has been interpreted as a flexible rule which is to be liberally construed to uphold service so long as the defendant receives sufficient notice of the complaint.[12]

(1st Cir.1992) (a federal court cannot acquire personal jurisdiction over a defendant unless the defendant is properly served with process).

§ 2.5

1. FRCP 4(a). Unlike procedures in some state courts, the summons must be signed by the clerk and bear the seal of the court.

2. FRCP 4(a), (b). If addressed to multiple defendants, a copy of the summons shall be issued for each defendant served.

3. FRCP 4(c). Summons and complaint.

4. FRCP 4(c)(1). The plaintiff is responsible for service of summons and complaint within the time allowed.

5. FRCP 4(c)(2). Any person who is not a party and who is at least 18 years of age. Plaintiff may also request a U.S. Marshal or deputy U.S. Marshal or other person or officer specially appointed by the court for that purpose. Local Rules may, however, restrict the ability to use the Marshals for service of process. *See, e.g.,* Central District of California Local Rule 5.4.

6. FRCP 4(m). If service is not made within 120 days after the filing of the complaint, the court, upon motion or on its own initiative after notice to plaintiff, shall dismiss the action without prejudice as to that defendant or direct that service be effected within a specified time; provided that if plaintiff shows good cause for the failure, the court shall extend the time for service for an appropriate period. The Rule does not apply to service in a foreign country pursuant to FRCP 4(f) or (j)(1). Due to the 1993 revision, Rule 4(m) does not require a showing of good cause for a judge to extend the time within which service must be effected. For a review of court rulings on various excuses for late service *see* 28 U.S.C.A. Rule 4, Supplementary Practice Comments, pp. 103–108.

7. FRCP 4(*l*).

8. FRCP 4(d). If a defendant refuses to agree to waiver, the Rule calls for some defendants to pay the costs of service and the motion to recover costs. Attorney's fees for bringing the motion are also recoverable.

9. Service on individuals (4(e)); individuals in a foreign country (4(f)); infants and incompetent persons (4(g)); corporations, partnerships and other unincorporated associations (4(h)); the United States and its agencies, corporations or officers (4(i)); and foreign, state or local governments (4(j)).

10. FRCP 4(k).

11. FRCP 4(n).

12. *See, e.g.,* Chan v. Society Expeditions, Inc., 39 F.3d 1398, 1404 (9th Cir. 1994).

(a) Form/Issuance

The federal summons will be a federal form in all cases.[13] The 1993 amendment to FRCP 4 eliminated the provision of old FRCP 4(b) which required parties serving pursuant to a state statute or rule of court to use a summons that corresponded as nearly as possible to the state requirements. Thus now, in each case, the form summons will be a federal form and must be signed by the clerk and bear the seal of the court.[14] A summons or a copy of a summons (if addressed to multiple defendants) should be issued for each defendant.[15]

(b) Service

The plaintiff is responsible for service of the summons and complaint,[16] which may be served by any person not a party and at least 18 years old.[17] Although an attorney for plaintiff can serve the summons and complaint, such a tactic may not be wise if the defendant later contests the service as plaintiff's counsel could then become a witness in his own case. If necessary, a plaintiff may ask the court to direct service to be made by a deputy U.S. Marshal or other official specially appointed by the court.[18]

(c) Waiver

FRCP 4(d) provides a procedure whereby a plaintiff may obtain from defendant a waiver of service of a summons. The purpose of the provision is to eliminate the costs of service and foster cooperation among adversaries.[19] Copies of the official forms to be used are included at the end of this chapter.

FRCP 4(d) allows the plaintiff to notify a defendant of the commencement of the action and request that the defendant waive service of the summons and complaint. The notice must be in writing, sent by first class mail or other reliable means,[20] addressed directly to the defendant or in the case of a corporation or business entity to the officer or

---

13. FRCP 4(a).

14. *See* FRCP 4(b) (detail re issuance of summons). Summons which has not been signed and sealed by the clerk of the court, even if properly served, does not confer personal jurisdiction over a defendant. *See* Ayres v. Jacobs & Crumplar, P.A., 99 F.3d 565, 569 (3d Cir.1996). In the Central District of California, the summons is to be prepared by the attorney on forms supplied by the Clerk. *See* U.S. District Court, Central District of California, Local Rule 5.3.

15. FRCP 4(b).

16. FRCP 4(c)(1).

17. FRCP 4(c)(2).

18. *Id.*

19. *See* 28 U.S.C.A. Rule 4, Advisory Committee Notes, Supp. 117–18 (West 1997).

20. It appears sending the notice by fax, Federal Express and other delivery services would comply. The Advisory Committee Notes state that when a party attempts to send notice by fax, he should keep proof of the transmission, and the receiving party has a duty to cooperate. The defendant cannot escape the fee shifting liability provisions by preventing the transmission at the point of receipt. 28 U.S.C.A. Rule 4, Advisory Committee Notes, Supp. 118–19.

managing or general agent or other agent authorized to receive service under FRCP 4(h).[21] As the Advisory Committee Notes point out, the general mailrooms of large corporations cannot be required to identify the appropriate individual recipient for an institutional summons.[22] The notice must include a copy of the complaint, identify the court in which the matter is pending, state a reasonable time in which to respond to the request (at least 30 days from the date sent if sent to an address in the U.S., 60 days if sent to an address outside any judicial district of the U.S.) and inform the defendant, using the language set forth in the official form, of the consequences of complying or failing to comply with the request. The notice must contain an extra copy of the notice and a prepaid means for compliance in writing, *i.e.* envelope and prepaid postage.

FRCP 4(d) provides that in most cases defendants who receive a notice of an action under a waiver request have a duty to avoid unnecessary costs of serving the summons.[23] If the defendant located within the U.S. fails to comply with the request made by a plaintiff located within the U.S., and fails to show good cause[24] for the failure, the court will impose on the defendant the costs plaintiff subsequently incurs to effect service plus the costs of any motion required to collect those costs—including a reasonable attorney's fee for the motion. The costs to be paid are only those incurred to serve after the time period set forth in the notice has passed.[25]

If a defendant timely agrees to waiver she is not required to serve an answer until 60 days after the date on which the request for waiver of service was sent (90 days if sent outside the U.S.). The date the plaintiff sent the request is part of the required form language to be included in the notice. When the plaintiff files the waiver, the action proceeds as if the summons and complaint had been served at the time the waiver was filed and no proof of service is required. In executing a FRCP 4(d) waiver, the defendant does not waive any objection to venue or personal jurisdiction.[26]

---

21. It is not enough to mail a request for waiver to a corporation by name.

22. *See* 28 U.S.C.A. Rule 4, Advisory Committee Notes, Supp. 118.

23. Those with this duty include defendants subject to service under subdivisions (e) (individuals within a judicial district of the United States), (f) (individuals in a foreign country) and (h) (corporations and associations). Infants, incompetents, the United States—its agencies, corporations, or officers, foreign states—their political subdivisions, agencies or instrumentalities, or U.S. states, municipal governments or other governmental organizations do not. Receipt of a notice (to which a defendant does not agree) does not however, give rise to any obligation to answer the lawsuit or provide any basis for taking a default. *See* 28 U.S.C.A. Rule 4, Advisory Committee Notes, Supp. 118.

24. According to the Advisory Committee Notes to FRCP 4(d), sufficient cause for failing to agree to waiver should be rare; it is not good cause that the lawsuit is unjust or the court lacks jurisdiction but good cause could be shown if the defendant did not receive the request or was insufficiently literate in English to understand it. *See* 28 U.S.C.A. Rule 4, Advisory Committee Notes, Supp. 118.

25. FRCP 4(d)(2).

26. The defendant may waive a statute of limitations defense if not careful. *See supra* § 2.2(a).

Request for waiver under FRCP 4(d) does not suspend the statute of limitations in states where the period continues to run until service. It also does not suspend the 120 day time limit for service set by FRCP 4(m).

(d) Service on Individuals Within a Judicial District of the United States

FRCP 4(e) provides that unless otherwise provided by federal law, service upon an individual[27] from whom a waiver has not been obtained and filed may be effected in any judicial district of the United States either (1) pursuant to the law of the state in which the district court is located, or in which service is effected, for the service of summons upon the defendant in an action brought in the courts of general jurisdiction of the state; or (2) by delivering a copy of the summons and complaint to the individual personally or by leaving copies at the individual's dwelling house or usual place of abode[28] with some person of suitable age and discretion[29] then residing therein or by delivering a copy of the summons and complaint to an agent authorized by appointment or by law to receive service of process. Service under Rule 4(e)(2) has been broadly construed.[30] Notably, FRCP 4(e), rather than FRCP 4(f)(service upon individuals in a foreign country), applies to citizens of foreign countries served within the United States.[31]

27. Other than an infant or an incompetent or person located outside a judicial district of the United States. Discussion regarding personal jurisdiction and service involving international issues are contained in Chapter 17 "Litigating International Disputes in Federal Courts," *infra.*

28. For discussion of the term "abode," *see* The Stars' Desert Inn Hotel & Country Club, Inc. v. Hwang, 105 F.3d 521, 523 (9th Cir.1997) (a person can have more than one dwelling house or place of abode; citing National Dev. Co. v. Triad Holding Corp., 930 F.2d 253, 257 (2d Cir.), *cert. denied*, 502 U.S. 968, 112 S.Ct. 440, 116 L.Ed.2d 459 (1991); Rosa v. Cantrell, 705 F.2d 1208, 1214–16 (10th Cir.1982) (discussing definition of place of abode); Nowell v. Nowell, 384 F.2d 951 (5th Cir.1967) (No hard and fast rule re what is or is not an abode, interpreting requirement under former Rule 4(d)(1).); 131 Main Street Associates v. Manko, 897 F.Supp. 1507, 1523–24 (S.D.N.Y.1995) (analyzing usual place of abode).

29. At least one federal court has interpreted the phrase "suitable age and discretion" to include a 13 year old. *See* United Services Automobile Association v. Barger, 910 F.2d 321, 324 (6th Cir.1990) (interpreting an Ohio statutory phrase identical to the Federal Rule 4(e)(2) phrase "person of suitable age and discretion" to be satisfied by the 13 year old son of the defendant, when the defendant testified his son was responsible and gave him messages). Numerous cases have considered whether service upon an apartment or hotel manager or a landlady constitutes valid service on a person of suitable age and discretion then residing therein. *See* 131 Main Street Associates, 897 F.Supp. at 1524–25 (discussing such cases and holding that service upon doorman who did not live at apartment complex was sufficient, interpreting the building as the doorman's business residence, and defining the question of suitable age and discretion as whether the person occupies a position the nature of which ensures that substitute service will result in actual service).

30. *See, e.g.,* Nowell v. Nowell, 384 F.2d 951 (5th Cir.1967) (Rule should be broadly construed where defendant received notice.); Karlsson v. Rabinowitz, 318 F.2d 666, 668–69 (4th Cir.1963) (liberally construed).

31. The Stars' Desert Inn Hotel & Country Club, Inc., 105 F.3d at 523. (Rule 4(f) is triggered by place in which service is effected, not by citizenship of the individual being served.).

(e) Service upon Corporations and Associations

FRCP 4(h) provides that unless otherwise provided by federal statute, service upon a domestic or foreign corporation or upon a partnership or other unincorporated association that is subject to suit under a common name, and from which a waiver has not been obtained and filed, shall be effected (1) pursuant to the law of the state in which the district court is located, or in which service is effected, for service of summons upon the defendant in an action brought in the courts of general jurisdiction, or by delivering a copy of the summons and complaint to an officer, a managing agent, or general agent, or any other agent authorized by appointment or law to receive service of process, and if the agent is one statutorily authorized to receive service, and the statute so requires, by also mailing a copy to the defendant, or (2) in a place not within any judicial district of the United States, in any manner provided under the provision for service upon individuals in a foreign country[32] other than by delivery to the "individual."[33]

To learn the name of the corporation's designated agent for service of process in a given state or the name and address of an officer, one can usually contact the Secretary of State's office. This is commonly done by phone (which often takes a long time to accomplish) or via a computer data base.[34]

(f) Service upon the United States, and its Agencies, Corporations, or Officers

FRCP 4(i)(1) provides that service upon the United States shall be effected by (1) delivering a copy of the summons and complaint to the United States attorney for the district in which the action is brought, or to an assistant United States attorney or clerical employee designated by the United States attorney in a writing filed with the clerk of the court or (2) by sending a copy of the summons and complaint by registered or certified mail addressed to the civil process clerk at the office of the United States attorney, and by also sending a copy of the summons and complaint by registered and certified mail to the Attorney General of the United States at Washington, District of Columbia, and in any action attacking the validity of an order of an officer or agency of the United States not made a party, by also sending a copy of the summons and complaint by registered or certified mail to the officer or agency.

FRCP 4(i)(2) provides that service upon an officer, agency, or corporation of the United States, shall be effected by serving the United

---

32. FRCP 4(f).

33. International service of process issues are discussed in Chapter 17 "Litigating International Disputes in Federal Courts," *infra.*

34. For example, one can access this information via WESTLAW through their Secretary of State databases, ALLCORP (for all states) or the individual state databases which use an abbreviation of the state name followed by CORP, for example CA-CORP for the California corporations data base.

States as described in the prior paragraph, and by also sending a copy of the summons and complaint by registered or certified mail to the officer, agency, or corporation. Defendants in *Bivens* actions, however, must be served as individuals.[35]

Note that if the plaintiff has served either the United States or the Attorney General of United States, the court is to allow a reasonable amount of time for service of process for the purpose of curing the failure to serve multiple officers, agencies, or corporations of the United States.[36]

(g) Service upon a State or Local Government

FRCP 4(j) provides that service upon a state, municipal corporation or other governmental organization subject to suit shall be effected by delivering a copy of the summons and complaint to its chief executive officer or by serving the documents in the manner prescribed by that state's law for the service of summons or other like process upon any such defendant.

(h) Territorial Limits of Service

Rule 4(k)(1) provides that service of summons or filing a waiver is effective to establish personal jurisdiction over a defendant (1) who could be subjected to the jurisdiction of a court of general jurisdiction in the state in which the district court is located, (2) who is joined under FRCP 14 or 19 and is served at a place within a judicial district of the United States and not more than 100 miles from the place from which the summons issues, (3) who is subject to federal interpleader jurisdiction under 28 U.S.C.A. § 1335, or (4) when authorized by federal statute.

In addition, under Rule 4(k)(2), if the exercise of jurisdiction is consistent with the Constitution and the laws of the United States, serving a summons or filing a waiver is also effective, with respect to claims arising under federal law,[37] to establish personal jurisdiction over a defendant who is not subject to the jurisdiction of the courts of general jurisdiction of any state. This provision, newly added in the 1993 amendments, provides for federal long-arm jurisdiction and allows for personal jurisdiction over a foreign defendant who has insufficient contacts with any one state to establish jurisdiction under FRCP 4(k)(1) but

---

35. Simpkins v. District of Columbia Government, 108 F.3d 366, 368–69 (D.C.Cir.1997) ("A Bivens suit is an action against a federal officer seeking damages for violations of the plaintiff's constitutional rights."). *Id.* at 368.

36. *See* FRCP 4(i)(3).

37. *See, e.g.,* United States Securities and Exchange Commission v. Carrillo, 115 F.3d 1540, 1543–44 (11th Cir.1997) (Rule 4(k)(2) applies because personal jurisdiction is invoked based on federal securities laws which provide for worldwide service of process.); and Warn v. M/YMaridome, 961 F.Supp. 1357, 1366 (S.D.Cal.1997) (Rule 4(k)(2) applies to admiralty actions) citing World Tanker Carriers Corp. v. M/V Ya Mawlaya, 99 F.3d 717 (5th Cir.1996); Western Equities, Ltd. v. Hanseatic, Ltd., 956 F.Supp. 1232, 1234–36 (D.V.I.1997); and United Trading Company v. M/V Sakura Reefer, 1996 WL 374154, at *34 (S.D.N.Y. 1996).

may have sufficient contacts with the United States with respect to a claim under federal law such that exercise of jurisdiction would meet constitutional due process requirements.[38]

This rule was added to correct a gap in enforcement of federal law which existed under the former rule when the defendant was a nonresident of the United States, had enough contact with the U.S. to justify applying U.S. law and federal forum selection rules but not enough contact with any one state to support jurisdiction via a state long-arm statute or to comply with the constitutional limits on state court territorial jurisdiction.[39] A precondition of application of this rule is that the defendant cannot be subject to the long-arm jurisdiction of any state.[40]

In analyzing minimum contacts with the U.S., courts have deemed the following contacts relevant; (1) transacting business in the United States, (2) doing an act inside the United States, or (3) doing an act outside the United States which has an effect in the United States.[41] In determining whether a company has transacted business in the U.S., courts look to whether the defendant engaged in purposeful activity in the United States thereby invoking the benefits and protections of U.S. law.[42] Mere sporadic contacts are not enough.[43] In one case, the district court found a defendant insurance company had transacted business in the U.S. when a number of its insureds resided in the U.S., it maintained an agent for service of process in the U. S., it hired a firm in the U.S. to assist in taking care of various legal matters, it maintained two bank accounts in the U.S. from which it disbursed funds to its agents in the U.S., and its representatives visited its insureds and brokers in the U.S. on a regular basis.[44]

In another case, a company was found to be transacting business in the United States when its agent managed a vessel within the U.S., purchased supplies and services for the vessel, arranged for and oversaw repairs, performed budgeting and accounting work, hired crew members, and performed various other activities in the United States. The court noted that the company had purposefully availed itself of goods and services sold by U.S. companies, services offered by U.S. banks, and the

---

38. In order for jurisdiction under Rule 4(k)(2) to be applicable, the defendant (1) must not be subject to the personal jurisdiction of any state or territory, (2) the claims must arise under federal law, and (3) the exercise of jurisdiction must comply with the constraints imposed by the Due Process Clause of the Fifth Amendment. Sevison v. Cruise Ship Tours, Inc., 1997 WL 530267, at *10–12 (D.V.I.1997).

39. Id. at *11. See also World Tanker Carriers Corp., 99 F.3d at 720.

40. Warn, 961 F.Supp. at 1367 citing AT & T v. Campagnie Bruxelles Lambert, 94 F.3d 586, 590 (9th Cir.), supplemented, 95 F.3d 1156 (9th Cir.1996).

41. Sevison, 1997 WL 530267, at *12 citing Western Equities, Ltd., 956 F.Supp.

at 1237. See also Carter v. LaGloria Shipping, 1997 WL 423101, at *2 (E.D.La.1997) (listing the three categories and citing Eskofot A/S v. E.I. Du Pont De Nemours & Co., 872 F.Supp. 81, 87 (S.D.N.Y.1995) and United Trading Company, 1996 WL 374154, at *34.

42. See, e.g., Carter v. LaGloria Shipping, 1997 WL 423101, at *2 (E.D.La.1997).

43. See, e.g., id., citing Warn, 961 F.Supp. at 1357.

44. See Warn, 961 F.Supp. at 1368 (describing the holding of Pacific Employers Insurance Co. v. M/T Iver Champion, 1995 WL 295293, at *5 (E.D.La.1995)).

services of a U.S. citizen as the manager of its yacht. In fact, the agent had, upon instructions from the sole shareholder of the entity which owned the yacht, formed a corporation to transact business in the U.S.[45] Despite the finding that the company had transacted business in the U.S., the court held Rule 4(k)(2) did not apply because the company's activities subjected it to long-arm jurisdiction in another state.

(i) Proof of Service

FRCP 4(*l*) provides that if service is not waived, the person effecting service shall make proof thereof to the court, and if someone other than a U.S. Marshal or deputy U.S. Marshal effects service, the person making the service shall make an affidavit thereof. Failure to make proof of service, does not however, affect the validity of the service. And, the court may allow a proof of service to be amended.

A defendant contesting the validity of a facially valid return of service generated by a private process server, or even opposing counsel, may be required to show clear and convincing evidence in order to prevail.[46]

(j) Time Limit for Service

FRCP 4(m) provides that, except for service in a foreign country on an individual or foreign state,[47] if service of a summons is not made upon a defendant within 120 days after the filing of the complaint, the court, upon motion or on its own initiative after notice to the plaintiff, shall dismiss the action without prejudice as to that defendant or direct that service be effected within a specified time; provided that if the plaintiff shows good cause for the failure, the court shall extend the time for service for an appropriate period of time.

FRCP 4(m) differs from its predecessor FRCP 4(j) in that FRCP 4(m) permits a district court to enlarge the time for service even if there is no good cause shown.[48] Relief is mandatory, however, if a plaintiff can show good cause for failure to serve within 120 days.

---

45. *Id.* at 1368.

46. *See* Trustees of Local Union No. 727 Pension Fund v. Perfect Parking, 126 F.R.D. 48, 52 (N.D.Ill.1989). (Return of service executed under oath by plaintiffs' counsel entitled to same treatment as return of service by U.S. Marshal, therefore defendants bore heavy burden of overcoming the return, by strong and convincing evidence. Defendants' mere filing of an affidavit denying service was not enough where defendants' credibility was diminished by their implausible rendition of events.). Another court has suggested that a rebuttable presumption of correctness might apply to such returns of service. FROF, Inc. v. Har-

ris, 695 F.Supp. 827, 829 (E.D.Pa.1988) (defendant's claim that neither he nor anyone at his residence was ever personally served was not enough to refute private process server's signed return of service filed under penalty of perjury under either the strong and convincing or rebuttable presumption tests).

47. Foreign state in this reference includes foreign state, or a political subdivision, agency or instrumentality thereof.

48. *See* Henderson v. United States, 517 U.S. 654, 116 S.Ct. 1638, 134 L.Ed.2d 880 (1996). (Prior FRCP 4(j) provided for service of the summons and complaint within 120 days after the filing of the complaint, a

Courts have found good cause when defendants have tried to evade service,[49] and also when the parties were conducting settlement negotiations.[50] A district court's determination regarding the presence or absence of good cause will not be disturbed on appeal absent an abuse of discretion.[51] Failure to analyze a discretionary extension has, however, resulted in vacation of the dismissal and remand for consideration of the issue.[52]

Discretionary relief from the 120–day deadline has been granted when (1) there were problems in locating an address, (2) the defendant was evasive or concealed a defect in attempted service,[53] (3) the plaintiff was pro se and service issues were complex, (4) despite good faith attempts to serve, an emergency at plaintiff's counsel's office impeded service, and (5) the statute of limitations expired and would bar refiling.[54] But the fact that a statute of limitations would bar refiling does not guarantee or even assure an extension when the plaintiff has no other excuse than inadvertence for missing the deadline.[55] Similarly, a

time limit subject to extension for good cause. While the substance of FRCP 4(j) is retained in the current Rule, FRCP 4(m) permits a district court to enlarge the time for service even if there is no good cause shown; citing the Advisory Committee Notes on 1993 Amendments to FRCP 4, 28 U.S.C.A., Supp. 654).

49. See Hendry v. Schneider, 116 F.3d 446, 448–49 (10th Cir.1997) (affirming District Court's determination that defendant's evasion of service constituted good cause) citing Cox v. Sandia Corp., 941 F.2d 1124, 1125 (10th Cir.1991); Ruiz Varela v. Sanchez Velez, 814 F.2d 821, 823–24 (1st Cir. 1987); and Wei v. State of Hawaii, 763 F.2d 370, 371 (9th Cir.1985).

50. See Assad v. Liberty Chevrolet, Inc., 124 F.R.D. 31 (D.R.I.1989) (good-faith settlement negotiations with a co-defendant amounted to "good cause," excusing the delay in service of process until 13 days after the end of the 120–day period). For a detailed discussion of cases considering the good cause requirement, see U.S.C.A. FRCP 4, Supplementary Practice Commentary D. Siegel, Supp. (1997) 101–09.

51. Hendry v. Schneider, 116 F.3d 446, 449 (10th Cir.1997), citing Floyd v. United States, 900 F.2d 1045, 1046 (7th Cir.1990). Abuse of discretion is found if the decision is arbitrary, capricious or whimsical.

52. Panaras v. Liquid Carbonic Indus. Corp., 94 F.3d 338, 341 (7th Cir.1996) dismissal vacated and remanded because, district court failed to reach the discretionary analysis having ruled solely on the basis of lack of good cause.

53. See 28 U.S.C.A. Rule 4, Advisory Committee Notes, Supp. 122 (West 1997) (citing Ditkof v. Owens–Illinois, Inc., 114 F.R.D. 104 (E.D.Mich.1987)).

54. See Davis v. National Railroad Passenger Corporation, 1997 WL 527287, at *3 (N.D.Ill.1997) citing MCI Telecomm Corp. v. Teleconcepts, Inc., 71 F.3d 1086, 1097–98 (3d Cir.1995) ("incorrect address and necessity of locating correct address grounds for permissible discretion under Rule 4(m)"), cert. denied, ___ U.S. ___, 117 S.Ct. 64, 136 L.Ed.2d 25 (1996); Espinoza v. United States, 52 F.3d 838, 842 (10th Cir.1995) ("complex requirements of multiple service ... particularly when the plaintiff is pro se, should be a factor in the court's consideration in determining whether a permissive extension of time should be granted"), cert. denied, ___ U.S. ___, 117 S.Ct. 1449, 137 L.Ed.2d 554 (1997); Ellis v. Welch, 1994 WL 87387, at *6 (N.D.Ill.1994) ("pro se plaintiff is entitled to a degree of leniency in regards to service of process"); Donald v. Cook County Sheriff's Dept., 95 F.3d 548, 557 (7th Cir.1996) ("plaintiff who, although unassisted by counsel, made diligent effort to follow rules of process was not defaulted"); In re Ferguson, 204 B.R. 202, 210 (Bankr. N.D.Ill.1997) ("creditor's good faith in repeatedly seeking to serve adversary complaint, coupled with sudden departure of counsel's staff and the flooding of counsel's office, warranted permissive extension of time for service").

55. See Davis v. National Railroad Passenger Corporation, 1997 WL 527287 *2–4 (N.D.Ill.1997) (holding that failure to serve

long delay in service may transform what once may have been good cause for an extension into an unacceptable excuse for either a mandatory or discretionary extension of time to serve.[56]

The message to be taken from the cases addressing Rule 4(m) is that good cause or a basis for discretionary extension is in the eye of the beholder and may vary from court to court. Thus, as more than one court has noted, an attorney who files suit when the statute of limitations is about to expire must take special care to achieve timely service of process because a slip-up can be fatal.[57]

(k) Seizure of Property; Service of Summons Not Feasible

FRCP 4(n) provides rules for in rem and quasi in rem service. Subsection (1) provides the rule applicable to federal seizures, stating that if a statute of the United States provides, the court may assert jurisdiction over property. Notice to claimants of the property must then be sent in the manner provided by the statute, or by service of summons under FRCP 4.

Subsection (2) provides quasi in rem jurisdiction in emergency circumstances. If a plaintiff can show that personal jurisdiction over a defendant cannot, in the district where the action is brought, be obtained with reasonable efforts by service of summons in a manner authorized by FRCP 4, the court is allowed to assert jurisdiction over any of the defendant's assets found within the district by seizing assets under the circumstances and in the manner provided by the law of the state in which the district court is located. Despite this rule, any attempt to exercise personal jurisdiction over a defendant by using as a basis defendant's ownership of property in the forum (in-rem jurisdiction) must also comply with the constitutional due process minimum contact tests discussed in Section 2.6(a), *infra.*[58]

---

within a lengthy statute of limitations without excuse other than inadvertence required dismissal under Rule 4(m), regardless of lack of prejudice to defendant). *But see* Shider v. Communications Workers of America, Local 1105, 1997 WL 470112, at *6–7 (S.D.N.Y.1997) (finding good cause where plaintiff was pro se and service issues complex, and in the alternative providing discretionary relief because statute of limitations would bar the refiled action, stating that the circuit prefers to resolve matters on the merits and it would be unduly harsh to extinguish plaintiff's ability to recover on a meritorious claim). *See also,* Petrucelli v. Bohringer & Ratzinger, 46 F.3d 1298, 1306 (3d Cir.1995) (discretionary dismissal allowed even after considering that refiling of

an action may be time barred); and Adams v. AlliedSignal Gen. Aviation Avionics, 74 F.3d 882, 887–88 (8th Cir.1996) (no discretionary extension even though statute of limitations had run).

56. *See* Webber v. Hammack, 973 F.Supp. 116, 120 (N.D.N.Y.1997) (court granted dismissal where plaintiff was represented by counsel and there was a seven year delay after return of unexecuted service).

57. Davis v. National Railroad Passenger Corporation, 1997 WL 527287, at *4 (N.D.Ill.1997), quoting from Tuke v. United States, 76 F.3d 155, 156 (7th Cir.1996).

58. Shaffer v. Heitner, 433 U.S. 186, 97 S.Ct. 2569, 53 L.Ed.2d 683 (1977).

(l) Supplemental Personal Jurisdiction

Supplemental personal jurisdiction, formerly known as pendent personal jurisdiction, allows a federal court in particular civil actions over which it has original jurisdiction to have supplemental jurisdiction over all other claims which are part of the same case or controversy. Supplemental jurisdiction includes claims that involve the joinder and intervention of additional parties. Thus, pursuant to 28 U.S.C.A. § 1367, in certain cases, a federal court may have jurisdiction over a defendant with respect to a claim which would not otherwise meet personal jurisdictional requirements. The exercise of supplemental jurisdiction is permissive, therefore, courts may decline to exercise supplemental jurisdiction if the claim raises a novel or complex issue of state law, the state law claim substantially predominates over the claim or claims over which the district court has original jurisdiction, the district court has dismissed all claims over which it has original jurisdiction, or there are other compelling reasons for declining jurisdiction.[59]

Library References:

West's Key No. Digests, Federal Civil Procedure ☞401–555.

Wright, Miller & Cooper, Federal Practice and Procedure: Civil 2d §§ 1006, 1084, 1089, 1094, 1100, 1106–1107, 1124, 1137, 1150, 3567.3.

§ 2.6 Constitutional Due Process Requirements

In addition to proper service (or waiver) pursuant to FRCP 4, certain due process requirements must be met in order for a defendant to be subjected to the personal jurisdiction of a particular federal court. The due process analysis is fact intensive, complex and sometimes unpredictable. The U.S. Supreme Court has described the process as necessarily requiring determinations in which few answers will be written in black and white—the grays are dominant and even among them, the shades are innumerable.[1] The First Circuit has used the famous Winston Churchill quote "a riddle wrapped up in a mystery inside an enigma," to describe what it termed the doctrinal vagaries of the concept of personal jurisdiction,[2] and has also described divining personal jurisdiction as more an art than a science.[3]

The rules applied and methods used to analyze due process are grounded in the requirement enunciated in *International Shoe Co. v. Washington*[4] that the defendant have established minimum contacts with the forum such that maintenance of the suit would not offend traditional notions of fair play and substantial justice.[5] For the more

---

59. 28 U.S.C.A. § 1367(c)(1)-(4) (West 19). *See* Chapter 1 "Subject Matter Jurisdiction" at § 1.8, *supra*.

§ 2.6

1. Burger King Corp. v. Rudzewicz, 471 U.S. 462, 486 n. 29, 105 S.Ct. 2174, 2190 n. 29, 85 L.Ed.2d 528 (1985), citing Kulko v. Superior Court of California, 436 U.S. 84,

92, 98 S.Ct. 1690, 1697, 56 L.Ed.2d 132 (1978).

2. Donatelli v. National Hockey League, 893 F.2d 459, 462 (1st Cir.1990).

3. Sawtelle v. Farrell, 70 F.3d 1381, 1388 (1st Cir.1995).

4. 326 U.S. 310, 66 S.Ct. 154, 90 L.Ed. 95 (1945).

5. *Id.* at 316, 66 S.Ct. at 158.

than 50 years since that holding, courts—including the U.S. Supreme Court—have been grappling with the application of the standard.

This grappling has resulted in major inconsistencies in analysis from circuit to circuit and even within Supreme Court decisions. The various circuits have applied different multi-pronged tests in analyzing personal jurisdiction and there are key concepts within the tests which have been treated differently but have yet to be resolved by the Supreme Court.[6] Thus, when analyzing due process in any given case, the attorney should first determine the methodology applied in the applicable circuit (what multi-prong test is used and how is it applied) and then structure arguments accordingly. This is not to say that precedent from other circuits regarding personal jurisdiction concepts will not be relevant, but rather that the attorney should be aware of whether the concept or treatment is consistent with the approach used in the circuit in which the case is pending.

(a) Minimum Contacts

The constitutional personal jurisdiction touchstone is whether the defendant purposefully established minimum contacts with the forum state such that he would reasonably anticipate being haled into the forum court.[7] In judging minimum contacts, the proper focus is on the relationship among the defendant, the forum and the litigation.[8] It is essential in each case that there be some act by which the defendant purposefully availed itself of the privilege of conducting activities within the forum state, thus invoking the benefits and protections of its laws.[9]

The purposeful availment requirement "ensures that a defendant will not be haled into a jurisdiction solely as a result of 'random,'

---

6. For example, the Supreme Court has yet to resolve conflicts regarding the concepts of "arising out of or related to" and the "stream of commerce" theory. *See* discussion of these concepts *infra* at §§ 2.6(a)(2) and 2.9(b).

7. Burger King Corp. v. Rudzewicz, 471 U.S. 462, 474, 105 S.Ct. 2174, 2182, 85 L.Ed.2d 528,(1985) citing International Shoe, 326 U.S. at 316, 66 S.Ct. at 158. *See also,* Shaffer v. Heitner, 433 U.S. 186, 97 S.Ct. 2569, 53 L.Ed.2d 683 (1977) (Minimum contacts standard of *International Shoe* applies even to cases in which personal jurisdiction would have previously been based solely on in rem analysis.).

8. Keeton v. Hustler Magazine, 465 U.S. 770, 775, 104 S.Ct. 1473, 1478, 79 L.Ed.2d 790 (1984), citing Shaffer, 433 U.S. at 204, 97 S.Ct. at 2579. The plaintiff's contacts with the forum are not necessarily irrelevant. *See* Calder v. Jones, 465 U.S. 783, 788, 104 S.Ct. 1482, 1486, 79 L.Ed.2d 804

(1984)(plaintiff's lack of contacts will not defeat otherwise proper jurisdiction but may be so manifold as to permit jurisdiction when it would not exist in their absence. In *Calder,* the plaintiff was the focus of defendants' defamation activities from which the suit arose.).

9. Asahi Metal Industry Co., Ltd. v. Superior Court of California, 480 U.S. 102, 107 S.Ct. 1026, 94 L.Ed.2d 92 (1987); Burger King Corp., 471 U.S. at 475, 105 S.Ct. at 2183. Unilateral activity of another party or a third person is not an appropriate consideration. *See, e.g.,* United States Securities and Exchange Commission v. Carrillo, 115 F.3d 1540, 1542, 1547 (11th Cir.1997); Burlington Industries, Inc. v. Maples Industries, Inc., 97 F.3d 1100, 1103 (8th Cir. 1996); Kuenzle v. HTM Sport–Und Freizeitgerate AG, 102 F.3d 453, 455 (10th Cir. 1996); Sawtelle v. Farrell, 70 F.3d 1381, 1389 (1st Cir.1995); Sher v. Johnson, 911 F.2d 1357, 1361 (9th Cir.1990)

'fortuitous,' or 'attenuated contacts' ... or of the unilateral activity of another party or a third person."[10] Jurisdiction is proper, however, where defendant's contacts proximately result from its actions that create a substantial connection with the forum state.[11] If the defendant has deliberately engaged in significant activities within the state or has created continuing obligations with residents of the forum he will be found to have manifestly availed himself of the privilege of conducting business there, and because his activities are shielded by the benefits and protections of the forum's laws it is presumptively reasonable to require him to submit to the burdens of litigating in the forum.[12]

The unilateral activity of those who claim some relationship with a nonresident defendant cannot satisfy the requirement of contact with the forum.[13] The defendant, however, may not avoid jurisdiction merely because she did not physically enter the forum.[14]

Given these requirements, lawyers have been quite creative in their arguments regarding purposeful availment. In one case, a plaintiff argued that the specific nature of defendant manufacturer's product (tire rims designed for use with sand track tires) made it foreseeable that the corporation would be subject to suit in Puerto Rico, because it is an island containing an abundance of sandy beaches. The court termed the argument creative, but disagreed with the approach to purposeful availment stating that under such a regime, a manufacturer of life preservers would automatically be subject to suit in every jurisdiction whose boundaries included an ocean, a river, a lake, a pond, or a swimming pool, and a manufacturer of air conditioners would be subject to suit worldwide.[15]

In determining whether a nonresident defendant is subject to personal jurisdiction, a federal court exercising diversity jurisdiction must find sufficient contacts between the defendant and the forum to satisfy both the forum state's long-arm statutes and the U.S. Constitution's Due Process Clause.[16] When the claim is one based upon federal law and service is made pursuant to federal statute, the court measures the contacts between the defendant and the United States.[17] If, however, there is no applicable federal service statute and the plaintiff bases

---

10. Burger King Corp., 471 U.S. at 475, 105 S.Ct. at 2183, citing Keeton, 465 U.S. at 74, 104 S.Ct. at 1478; World–Wide Volkswagen Corp. v. Woodson, 444 U.S. 286, 299, 100 S.Ct. 559, 568, 62 L.Ed.2d 490 (1980); Helicopteros Nacionales de Colombia, S.A. v. Hall, 466 U.S. 408, 417, 104 S.Ct. 1868, 1873, 80 L.Ed.2d 404 (1984).

11. Burger King Corp., 471 U.S. at 475, 105 S.Ct. at 2183.

12. *Id*. at 475–76, 105 S.Ct. at 2183–84.

13. World–Wide Volkswagen Corp., 444 U.S. at 298, 100 S.Ct. at 568.

14. Burger King Corp., 471 U.S. at 476, 105 S.Ct. at 2184. (So long as the corporation purposefully directed its activities at the forum state, lack of physical presence will not prevent jurisdiction.).

15. Rodriguez v. Fullerton Tires Corp., 115 F.3d 81, 85 (1st Cir.1997).

16. *See* Sawtelle v. Farrell, 70 F.3d 1381 (1st Cir.1995). The court may also be required to analyze the state constitution should it address due process requirements applicable to service on nonresident defendants. *See, e.g.,* RAR Incorporated v. Turner Diesel, Limited, 107 F.3d 1272, 1276 (7th Cir.1997).

17. *See* United Electrical, Radio and Machine Workers of America v. 163 Pleasant Street Corporation, 960 F.2d 1080, 1085 (1st Cir.1992).

service on Rule 4(k)(1)(persons who could be subjected to the jurisdiction of a court of general jurisdiction in the state in which the district court is located) the relevant contacts will be those between the defendant and the forum state.

Generally speaking in analyzing personal jurisdiction over a nonresident defendant, courts analyze minimum contacts to determine whether they will satisfy either general or specific jurisdiction. General jurisdiction refers to the analysis used when the plaintiff's claim does not arise out of or relate to the defendant's contacts with the forum.[18] Specific jurisdiction refers to the analysis used when the plaintiff's claim does arise out of or relate to those contacts.[19] Satisfying the requirements of either one will provide a proper minimum contacts basis for personal jurisdiction.

(1) General Jurisdiction

Under general jurisdiction analysis, due process requirements may be satisfied when the defendant has purposefully established "continuous and systematic contact" with the forum state.[20] This is a high standard to meet, but once met, the court may exercise personal jurisdiction over the defendant for suits unrelated to or not arising from the defendant's contacts with the forum.

In *Perkins v. Benguet Consolidated Mining*,[21] the U.S. Supreme Court found contacts to be "continuous and systematic" when a corporation's president and general manager maintained an office in the state from which he conducted activities on behalf of the corporation, kept company files and had directors' meetings in the office, carried on correspondence relating to the business, distributed salary checks drawn

---

18. Helicopteros Nacionales de Colombia, S.A. v. Hall, 466 U.S. 408, 414, n. 9, 104 S.Ct. 1868, 1872, n. 9, 80 L.Ed.2d 404 (1984); Burger King Corp., 417 U.S. at 473 n.15, 105 S.Ct. at 2182 n.15.

19. Helicopteros Nacionales de Colombia, S.A., 466 U.S. at 414 n.8; 104 S.Ct. at 1972, n.8.

20. *Id.* at 414, 104 S.Ct. at 1872. (Even when the cause of action does not arise out of or relate to the foreign corporation's activities in the forum state, due process is not offended by a state subjecting a corporation to its in personam jurisdiction when there are sufficient contacts with the state and the foreign corporation.); *See* Perkins v. Benguet Consolidated Mining Company, 342 U.S. 437, 72 S.Ct. 413, 96 L.Ed. 485 (1952) (Foreign corporation had been carrying on in the state a continuous and systematic, but limited part, of its general business and personal jurisdiction was therefore proper.). For a sampling of addi-

tional cases analyzing general jurisdiction, *see, e.g.*, Metropolitan Life Insurance Company v. Robertson–Ceco Corp., 84 F.3d 560 (2d Cir.1996) (systematic and continuing contacts found, however, reasonableness test precluded exercise of personal jurisdiction); Felch v. Transportes Lar–Mex Sa De CV, 92 F.3d 320 (5th Cir.1996) (general jurisdiction not found); Bearry v. Beech Aircraft Corp., 818 F.2d 370 (5th Cir.1987) (appellate court overruled district court finding of general jurisdiction); Glater v. Eli Lilly & Co., 744 F.2d 213 (1st Cir.1984) (general jurisdiction not found); Provident National Bank v. California Federal Savings & Loan, 819 F.2d 434 (3d Cir.1987) (continuous and systematic contacts found); and Sollinger v. Nasco International, Inc., 655 F.Supp. 1385 (D.Vt.1987) (same).

21. 342 U.S. 437, 72 S.Ct. 413, 96 L.Ed. 485 (1952).

on two active state bank accounts, engaged a state bank to act as transfer agent and supervised policies dealing with overseas properties.[22]

In *Helicopteros Nacionales de Colombia S.A. v. Hall*,[23] the Supreme Court did not find general jurisdiction when the defendant did not have a place of business within and was never licensed to do business in the forum, and the only contacts were sending its chief executive officer to the forum for a simple contract negotiation session, accepting into its bank account checks drawn on a forum bank,[24] purchasing helicopter equipment and training services from a forum company for a substantial sum and sending personnel to the forum for training.

The *Helicopteros* Court noted that one negotiation trip was not a continuous and systematic contact. It stated that whether checks were drawn on a forum bank, in the absence of unusual circumstances, was usually the unilateral act of the payor—in this case plaintiff—and unilateral actions of the plaintiff are not a proper consideration in determining whether defendant has sufficient contacts with a forum. The Court also noted that the helicopter purchases and related trips for negotiation and training were not a sufficient basis because purchases alone, even if occurring at regular intervals, are not enough to warrant a state's assertion of general jurisdiction.

In analyzing general jurisdiction, contacts are commonly evaluated over a period of several years prior to the plaintiff's filing of the complaint.[25] The district court is to examine a period that is reasonable under the circumstances to assess whether the contacts satisfy the continuous and systematic standard, with the determination of what period is reasonable in the context of each case left to the court's discretion.[26]

(2) Specific Jurisdiction

As defined by the Supreme Court, specific jurisdiction exists when the plaintiff's claims arise out of or are related to defendant's contacts with the forum state.[27]

---

22. *Id.*

23. 466 U.S. 408, 413–18, 104 S.Ct. 1868, 1871–74, 80 L.Ed.2d 404 (1984).

24. The record did not reflect that defendant had requested the particular bank or that the parties had negotiated regarding the location or identity of the bank on which checks were drawn.

25. *See* Metropolitan Life Insurance Company, 84 F.3d at 569, citing Helicopteros Nacionales de Colombia, S.A., 466 U.S. at 409–11, 104 S.Ct. at 1868–71 (one year held not enough, appellate court analyzed six year time period prior to filing suit); Wilson v. Belin, 20 F.3d 644, 650–51 (5th Cir.1994) (examining defendant's contacts with forum state over a five year period), *cert. denied*, 513 U.S. 930, 115 S.Ct. 322, 130 L.Ed.2d 282 (1994); Bearry, 818 F.2d at 372, 376 (five years); Gates Learjet Corporation v. Jensen, 743 F.2d 1325, 1329, (9th Cir.1984)(three years); and Braman v. Mary Hitchcock Memorial Hospital, 631 F.2d 6, 9 (2d Cir.1980) (five years).

26. Metropolitan Life Insurance Company, 84 F.3d at 569–70. Notably, the Second Circuit, having ruled that the district court improperly limited the inquiry to one year, determined that six years (the time period allowed for discovery) was the applicable period and applied a de novo review to determine whether contacts existing during that period constituted continuous and systematic contacts. *Id.*

27. Helicopteros Nacionales, 466 U.S. at 414, n.8, 104 S.Ct. at 1972 n.8.

The arising out of or relating to requirement, is also referred to as the "relatedness requirement." Its focus is on the nexus between the defendant's contacts and the plaintiff's cause of action.[28] The purpose has been described as two fold, first, to separate general from specific jurisdiction and second to ensure that the element of causation remains in the forefront of the due process investigation.[29]

The circuits differ in their application of the relatedness analysis.[30] Some circuits have applied a "but-for" test, others a proximate cause analysis. For example, the Sixth, and Ninth Circuits have applied "but-for" analyses,[31] and the First, Second and Eighth Circuits have applied proximate cause analyses,[32] (although the First Circuit stated that strict adherence to a proximate cause standard in all circumstances would be overly restrictive.[33]

Although one justice has raised the issue in a dissent,[34] the Supreme Court has yet to settle the issue of whether "related to" is equivalent to "arising out of" or, if they are different, whether specific personal jurisdiction is proper when the cause of action is "related to," but not "arising out of," the defendant's contacts with the forum.[35]

Thus, once again, when analyzing specific jurisdiction, the attorney should be careful to ascertain the applicable interpretation of the relatedness standard using precedent from the circuit in which his case sits as well as from other circuits in which the courts have similarly approached the issue.

28. Nowak v. Tak How Investments, Ltd., 94 F.3d 708, 714 (1st Cir.1996)(describing several circuits' treatments of the issue and citing *Ticketmaster-New York, Inc. v. Alioto*, 26 F.3d 201, 206–07 (1st Cir.1994) for the proposition that the requirement of relatedness is the least developed prong of the due process inquiry).

29. Nowak, 94 F.3d at 713–14.

30. *See id.* at 714–15 (discussing the circuits' varying approaches to this issue).

31. *See* Doe v. American National Red Cross, 112 F.3d 1048, 1051 (9th Cir.1997) citing Shute v. Carnival Cruise Lines, 897 F.2d 377, 385 (9th Cir.1990), *rev'd on other grounds*, 499 U.S. 585, 111 S.Ct. 1522, 113 L.Ed.2d 622 (1991); Creech v. Roberts, 908 F.2d 75, 80 (6th Cir.1990), *cert. denied*, 499 U.S. 975, 111 S.Ct. 1619, 113 L.Ed.2d 717 (1991) (action deemed not arising from the defendant's contacts with the forum state only when they are unrelated to the operative facts of the controversy).

32. *See* Nowak, 94 F.3d 708 (1st Cir. 1996) (citing Pearrow v. National Life & Accident Ins. Co., 703 F.2d 1067, 1069 (8th Cir.1983) and Gelfand v. Tanner Motor Tours, Ltd., 339 F.2d 317, 321–322 (2d Cir. 1964)).

33. *Id.* at 715.

34. *See* Helicopteros Nacionales v. Hall, 466 U.S. 408, 424–428, 104 S.Ct. 1868, 1877–79, 80 L.Ed.2d 404 (1984), (Brennen, J., dissenting, making a distinction between "arising out of" and "related to," and stating that it would be fair and reasonable to subject a defendant to suit in a forum with which it has significant contacts directly related to the underlying cause of action).

35. In *Helicopteros Nacionales, id.* at 415 n. 10, 104 S.Ct. at 1872 n. 10, the Court noted that it had not been presented the following issues and therefore, unlike the dissent of Justice Brennen, would provide no opinion on them: (i) the validity or consequences of a distinction between "arising out of" and "related to," and (ii) whether if the two types of relationships differ, a forum's exercise of jurisdiction in a situation where the cause of action "relates to" but does not "arise out of" the defendant's contacts with the forum state should be analyzed as an assertion of specific jurisdiction.

(b) Reasonableness

Once it has been decided that a defendant purposefully established minimum contacts with the forum state, the contacts may be considered in the light of other factors to determine whether assertion of personal jurisdiction would offend traditional notions of fair play and substantial justice—whether the exercise of jurisdiction in the given case would be reasonable.

In *Burger King Corporation v. Rudzewicz*, the U.S. Supreme Court stated that "[o]nce it has been decided that a defendant purposefully established minimum contacts with the forum State, these contacts may be considered in light of other factors to determine whether the assertion of personal jurisdiction would comport with 'fair play and substantial justice' . . ."[36] Citing *World-Wide Volkswagen Corp. v. Woodson*,[37] the Court also stated that in appropriate cases the courts may evaluate (1) the burden on the defendant, (2) the forum state's interest in adjudicating the dispute, (3) the plaintiff's interest in obtaining convenient and effective relief, (4) the interstate judicial system's interest in obtaining the most efficient resolution of controversies and (5) the shared interests of several states in furthering fundamental substantive policies.[38]

The Supreme Court again used these five reasonableness factors in *Asahi Metal Industry Co., Ltd. v. Superior Court of California*,[39] although this time the Court used the word "must" in reference to factors used in the analysis.

Once again, the circuits have not uniformly applied the reasonableness analysis. Several circuits have applied roughly the same five part test, while others have added additional factors or analyzed less than all five in making a reasonableness determination. For example, the First,[40] Second,[41] Third,[42] Fourth,[43] Fifth,[44] Sixth,[45] Seventh,[46] Tenth[47] and Fed-

---

36. 471 U.S. 462, 476–77, 105 S.Ct. 2174, 2184, 85 L.Ed.2d 528.

37. 444 U.S. 286, 292, 100 S.Ct. 559, 564, 62 L.Ed.2d 490 (1980).

38. Burger King Corp., 471 U.S. at 476–77, 105 S.Ct. at 2174. Application of the substantive policy prong of the analysis has raised the issue of whether First Amendment concerns should be weighed in the balance. Courts, however, have shied away from such an approach. *See, e.g.*, Ticketmaster–New York, Inc. v. Alioto, 26 F.3d 201, 211–12 (1st Cir.1994) (stating that U.S. Supreme Court cases have shied away from allowing First Amendment concerns to enter into the jurisdictional analysis, and therefore refusing to consider those concerns in its own reasonableness analysis).

39. 480 U.S. 102, 107 S.Ct. 1026, 94 L.Ed.2d 92, (1987) (noting that "[w]e have

previously explained that the determination of the reasonableness of the exercise of jurisdiction in each case will depend on an evaluation of several factors. A court must consider [the first three factors]. It must also weigh in its determination [the last two]).''

40. Nowak v. Tak How Investments, Ltd., 94 F.3d 708 (1st Cir.1996). The First Circuit applies the five part test and calls its analysis the "Gestalt Test."

41. Metropolitan Life Insurance Company v. Robertson–Ceco, 84 F.3d 560 (2d Cir. 1996). The Second Circuit applies five factors including (1) the burden that exercise of jurisdiction will impose on the defendant, (2) the interests of the forum state in adjudicating the case, (3) plaintiff's interest in obtaining convenient and effective relief, (4) the interstate judicial systems' interest in

eral[48] Circuits have applied five-part tests. While the Eighth, Ninth and Eleventh have used different approaches.

The Eighth Circuit recently analyzed reasonableness by looking at only two factors—the interest of the forum state in providing a forum for its residents and the convenience of the parties.[49]

The Eleventh Circuit recently applied a three-part test, examining the burden on the defendant, the interests of the forum, and the plaintiff's interest in obtaining relief.[50] The Ninth Circuit has used seven

obtaining the most efficient resolution of the controversy, and (5) the shared interest of the states in furthering substantive social policies. *See also* Chaiken v. VV Publishing Corp., 119 F.3d 1018, 1028 (2d Cir.1997).

42. Grand Entertainment Group, Ltd. v. Star Media Sales, Inc., 988 F.2d 476, 483 (3d Cir.1993). The Third Circuit considers (1) the burden on the defendant, (2) the interests of the forum state, (3) the plaintiff's interest in obtaining relief, (4) the interstate judicial system's interest in obtaining the most efficient resolution of controversies, and (5) the shared interest of the several states in furthering fundamental substantive social policies.

43. Lesnick v. Hollingsworth, 35 F.3d 939, 945–46 (4th Cir.1994). The Fourth Circuit reasonableness test looks at (1) the burden on defendant, (2) the interests of the forum state, (3) the plaintiff's interest in obtaining relief, (4) the efficient resolution of controversies as between states, and (5) the shared interests of the several states in furthering fundamental substantive social policies.

44. Felch v. Transportes Lar–Mex Sa De CV, 92 F.3d 320, 324 n. 9 (5th Cir.1996). The Fifth Circuit fairness inquiry includes (1) the burden upon the nonresident defendant, (2) the interests of the forum state, (3) the plaintiff's interest in securing relief, (4) the interstate judicial system's interest in obtaining the most efficient resolution of controversies, and (5) the shared interests of the several states in furthering fundamental substantive social policies.

45. Theunissen v. Matthews, 935 F.2d 1454, 1460–61 (6th Cir.1991). *But see*, CompuServe, Inc. v. Patterson, 89 F.3d 1257, 1268 (6th Cir.1996). (Analyzing only four factors, leaving out discussion of the shared interests of the states in furthering substantive social policies.)

46. Mid–America Tablewares, Inc. v. Mogi Trading Co., 100 F.3d 1353, 1362 (7th Cir.1996). The Seventh Circuit analyzes

reasonableness with the following factors; (1) burden on the defendant of having to litigate in the forum, (2) the interests of the forum, (3) the plaintiff's interest in obtaining relief, (4) the interstate judicial system's interest in obtaining the most efficient resolution of controversies, and (5) the shared interests of the several states in furthering fundamental substantive social policies.

47. Equifax Services, Inc. v. Hitz, 905 F.2d 1355, 1360 (10th Cir.1990). The Tenth Circuit considers (1) the burden on the defendant, (2) the forum state's interest in adjudicating the dispute, (3) the plaintiff's interest in obtaining convenient and effective relief, (4) the interstate judicial system's interest in obtaining the most efficient resolution of controversies, (5) the shared interest of the several states in furthering fundamental substantive social policies.

48. Viam Corp. v. Iowa Export–Import Trading Co., 84 F.3d 424, 429 (Fed.Cir. 1996). The Federal Circuit looks at (1) the burden on the defendant, (2) the interests of the forum state, (3) the plaintiff's interest in obtaining relief, (4) the interstate judicial system's interest in obtaining the most efficient resolution of controversies, and (5) the interest of the states in furthering their social policies.

49. Digi–Tel Holdings, Inc. v. Proteq Telecommunications (PTE) Ltd., 89 F.3d 519, 522–23 (8th Cir.1996). *See also* Gould v. P.T. Krakatau Steel, 957 F.2d 573, 576 (8th Cir.1992), (Court considered nature and quality of contacts with the forum, quantity of contacts, source and connection of the cause of action with the contacts, and "to a lesser degree," the interest of the forum state in providing a forum for its residents and the convenience of the parties.).

50. United States Securities and Exchange Comm'n. v. Carrillo, 115 F.3d 1540

factors; (1) extent of purposeful interjection (which the court says should be met once a plaintiff has shown the necessary minimum contacts) (2) burden on the defendant to defend the suit in the chosen forum, (3) the extent of conflict with the sovereignty of defendant's state, (4) the forum state's interest in adjudicating the dispute, (5) the most efficient forum for judicial resolution of the dispute, (6) the importance of the plaintiff's chosen forum to the plaintiff's interest in convenient and effective relief, and (7) the existence of an alternate forum, in analyzing reasonableness.[51]

Thus, when an attorney analyzes whether the reasonableness standard will play a part in establishing or negating personal jurisdiction, she would do well to focus on the reasonableness analysis used in the applicable circuit in addition to others applying a similar test.

The reasonableness analysis has been held to apply to general as well as specific jurisdiction analyses.[52] While the burden to show purposeful availment is on the plaintiff, once he has established that point, the forum's exercise of jurisdiction is presumptively reasonable. To rebut the presumption, the defendant must present a compelling case that personal jurisdiction would be unreasonable.[53]

The results of the reasonableness analysis are to be viewed together with defendant's minimum contacts. And, while reasonableness cannot make up for insufficient minimum contacts,[54] it is weighed in context with them.[55] Thus, "these considerations sometimes serve to establish

---

(11th Cir.1997) (citing Vermeulen v. Renault, U.S.A., Inc., 985 F.2d 1534, 1551 (11th Cir.1993).

51. Shute v. Carnival Cruise Lines, 897 F.2d 377 (9th Cir.1990), *rev'd on other grounds*, 499 U.S. 585, 111 S.Ct. 1522, 113 L.Ed.2d 622 (1991).

52. *See* Metropolitan Life Insurance Company v. Robertson–Ceco Corp., 84 F.3d 560, 576 (2d Cir.1996)(finding the five-factor reasonableness inquiry set forth in *Asahi* to be applicable in general jurisdiction cases). In his dissent, Circuit Judge Walker stated that "[t]he sprouting like weeds of multi-pronged tests for the reasonableness inquiry in the circuits in both specific and general jurisdiction cases has left this legal garden in disarray." *Id.* at 577–78 (Circuit Judge Walker dissenting). As examples, Judge Walker cited Amoco Egypt Oil Co. v. Leonis Navigation Co., 1 F.3d 848, 851–53 (9th Cir.1993) (bifurcated test that employs seven-factor reasonableness inquiry); Gould v. P.T. Krakatau Steel, 957 F.2d 573, 576 (8th Cir.1992) (unequally weighted five-factor balancing test), *cert. denied*, 506 U.S. 908, 113 S.Ct. 304, 121 L.Ed.2d 227 (1992); Theunissen v. Matthews, 935 F.2d 1454, 1460–61 (6th Cir.1991) (three-pronged bal-

ancing test in which third factor contains a five-factor sub-balancing test for reasonableness); Donatelli v. National Hockey League, 893 F.2d 459, 465 (1st Cir.1990) (two tiered test in which second tier, which considers "Gestalt" factors measuring reasonableness, is not reached absent minimum contacts); Bearry v. Beech Aircraft Corp., 818 F.2d 370 (5th Cir.1987)(bifurcated test that included four-factor reasonableness evaluation). The Fifth Circuit later applied a five part analysis. *See* Felch v. Transportes Lar–Mex Sa De CV, 92 F.3d 320, 324, n. 9 (5th Cir.1996).

53. Burger King Corp. v. Rudzewicz, 471 U.S. 462, 476, 105 S.Ct. 2174, 2184, 85 L.Ed.2d 528 (1985).

54. *Id.* at 467, 105 S.Ct. at 2184–85; World–Wide Volkswagen v. Woodson, 444 U.S. 286, 294, 100 S.Ct. 559, 565–66 62 L.Ed.2d 490 (1980); Metropolitan Life Insurance Company, 84 F.3d at 568–69; United Electrical Workers v. 163 Pleasant Street Corp., 960 F.2d 1080, 1091 (1st Cir.1992).

55. *See, e.g.,* Metropolitan Life Insurance Company, 84 F.3d at 568–69 (citing Donatelli, 893 F.2d at 465; Nowak v. Tak How Investments, Ltd., 94 F.3d 708 (1st

the reasonableness of jurisdiction upon a lesser showing of minimum contacts than would otherwise be required."[56] Similarly, "minimum requirements inherent in the concept of 'fair play and substantial justice' may defeat the reasonableness of jurisdiction even if the defendant has purposefully engaged in forum activities."[57] However, where a defendant, who has purposefully directed his activities at forum residents, seeks to defeat jurisdiction, he must present a compelling case that the presence of some other consideration would render jurisdiction unreasonable.[58]

Library References:

West's Key No. Digests, Constitutional Law ⊙305, 309.
Wright, Miller & Cooper, Federal Practice and Procedure: Civil 2d §§ 1061, 3801, 3806, 3562.

§ 2.7 Application of Due Process in General

There are few bright-line tests in determining whether personal jurisdiction in a given case will satisfy constitutional requirements. There are, however, certain fact patterns which appear likely to satisfy due process concerns. As discussed below, these include (1) defendant's voluntary physical presence in the state at the time of service, (2) valid consent and/or waiver, (3) domicile and (4) personal jurisdiction based upon a sanction for discovery abuse. Beyond these four scenarios, attorneys will need to review the defendant's contacts with the forum and the litigation, the facts applicable to purposeful availment and reasonableness and then scour the federal precedent in search of cases in which courts have addressed similar fact patterns.

(a) Defendant's Physical Presence in the State at Time of Service

In most cases, actual service on a defendant while he is voluntarily physically present in the forum state meets constitutional due process requirements for personal jurisdiction, even when the suit is unrelated to the defendant's activities within the state and the defendant is present for only a brief period.[1] There are, however, times when service

Cir.1996) (describing the analysis as a sliding scale and noting that the weaker the plaintiff's showing on relatedness and purposeful availment, the less a defendant need show in terms of unreasonableness to defeat jurisdiction, and noting the reverse is true, *i.e.*, an especially strong showing of reasonableness may serve to fortify a borderline showing of relatedness and purposefulness, citing Ticketmaster–New York, Inc. v. Alioto, 26 F.3d 201, 210 (1st Cir.1994)). *See also,* Ellicott Mach. Corp. v. John Holland Party, Ltd., 995 F.2d 474, 479 (4th Cir.1993).

56. Burger King Corp., 471 U.S. at 477, 105 S.Ct. at 2184. *See, e.g.,* Sawtelle v. Farrell, 70 F.3d 1381, 1394 (1st Cir.1995).

57. Burger King Corp., 471 U.S. at 476–77, 105 S.Ct. at 2185.

58. *Id.* at 477, 105 S.Ct. at 2185. *See, e.g.,* Metropolitan Life Insurance Company v. Robertson–Ceco Corp., 84 F.3d 560 (2d Cir.1996) (Despite minimum contacts, exercise of personal jurisdiction would be unreasonable.).

§ 2.7

1. *See* Burnham v. Superior Court of California Marin County, 495 U.S. 604, 110

on a person, physically present in the forum, will be ineffective. For example, parties brought into the state fraudulently or forcibly may not be subject to personal jurisdiction,[2] and parties present in the state for arbitration, litigation or settlement may be immune from service.[3]

(b) Valid Consent/Waiver

Unlike subject matter jurisdiction, the requirement of personal jurisdiction may be waived.[4] A defendant may consent to personal jurisdiction in a forum which may not ordinarily have personal jurisdiction over him.[5] In turn, a plaintiff can lose the ability to show the propriety of general jurisdiction by failing to allege continuous and systematic contacts with the forum.[6] A variety of legal arrangements or actions have been interpreted as defendants' express or implied consent to personal jurisdiction, including waiver by contract,[7] failure to object timely,[8] discovery abuse,[9] domicile[10] and designation of an agent for service of process.[11]

S.Ct. 2105, 109 L.Ed.2d 631 (1990). (Service of defendant while in the state comports with traditional notions of fair play and substantial justice in suit unrelated to activities within the state despite defendant's transitory presence.).

2. *See* James Wm. Moore et al., Moore's Federal Practice, R. Casad, Territorial Jurisdiction: Jurisdiction Over Persons & Property, § 108.141, (3d Ed. 1997) citing Wyman v. Newhouse, 93 F.2d 313, 315 (2d Cir.1937); E/M Lubricants, Inc. v. Microfral, S.A.R.L., 91 F.R.D. 235, 237–38 (N.D.Ill. 1981).

3. For discussion of immunity from service of process while physically present in the forum, and exceptions to the general rule, *see* Cabiri v. Assasie–Gyimah, 921 F.Supp. 1189, 1193–94 (S.D.N.Y.1996) and American Centennial Insurance Company v. Handal, 901 F.Supp. 892, 895–97 (D.N.J. 1995). *See also* Moore's at § 108.142 citing Viking Penguin, Inc. v. Janklow, 98 F.R.D. 763, 766–67 (S.D.N.Y.1983), Higgins v. Garcia, 522 So.2d 95, 96 (Fla.Dist.Ct.App.1988), Pavlo v. James, 437 F.Supp. 125, 126–27 (S.D.N.Y.1977), E/M Lubricants, Inc., 91 F.R.D. at 238 and Lee v. Stevens of Fla., Inc., 578 So. 2d 867, 868 (Fla.App.1991), but also noting limitations on the extent of immunity, citing Sivnksty v. Duffield, 137 W.Va. 112, 71 S.E.2d 113, 114–15 (1952).

4. Insurance Corp. of Ireland, Ltd. v. Compagnie des Bauxites de Guinee, 456 U.S. 694, 703, 102 S.Ct. 2099, 2105, 72 L.Ed.2d 492 (1982). *See also* RAR, Incorpo-

rated v. Turner Diesel, Ltd., 107 F.3d 1272, 1280 (7th Cir.1997). (Personal jurisdiction is waivable, and parties can, through forum selection clauses and the like, easily contract around any rule courts promulgate), citing Burger King Corp. v. Rudzewicz, 471 U.S. 462, 472 n. 14, 105 S.Ct. 2174, 2182 n. 14, 85 L.Ed.2d 528 (1985).

5. Burger King Corp., 471 U.S. at 472 n. 14, 105 S.Ct. at 2182 n. 14. (Defendant may expressly or impliedly consent to jurisdiction of a court which otherwise would not have jurisdiction over it.).

6. *See* RAR, Incorporated 107 F.3d at 1277. (Plaintiff who failed to allege continuous and systematic general business contacts with the forum waived any general jurisdiction argument.).

7. *See* Burger King Corp., 471 U.S. at 473 n. 14, 105 S.Ct. at 2182 n. 14, citing National Equipment Rental, Ltd. v. Szukhent, 375 U.S. 311, 316, 84 S.Ct. 411, 414, 11 L.Ed.2d 354 (1964).

8. FRCP 12(h)(1).

9. Insurance Corp. of Ireland, Ltd. v. Compagnie des Bauxites de Guinee, 456 U.S. 694, 102 S.Ct. 2099, 72 L.Ed.2d 492 (1982).

10. Milliken v. Meyer, 311 U.S. 457, 463–64, 61 S.Ct. 339, 343, 85 L.Ed. 278 (1940).

11. *See* Knowlton v. Allied Van Lines, Inc., 900 F.2d 1196 (8th Cir.1990) (General jurisdiction based on designation of agent.).

(1) Contractual Consent to Jurisdiction in Advance

Parties to a contract may agree in advance to submit to the personal jurisdiction of a particular court.[12] Contractual forum selection clauses are prima facie valid and should be enforced unless grounded on a contract whose terms have been obtained through fraud, undue influence, overweening bargaining power or when application would render litigation so gravely difficult and inconvenient that a party would for all practical purposes be deprived of her day in court.[13]

In order contractually to restrict personal jurisdiction to one forum, however, the contract clause must specifically limit jurisdiction to the particular forum. A forum selection clause which does not explicitly limit jurisdiction to a particular forum may be treated as a permissive rather than mandatory provision and may be held to allow a plaintiff to sue in that or any other forum which might have personal jurisdiction over the defendant in that case.

(2) Failure to Object Timely

Failure to timely object also constitutes consent to personal jurisdiction. Failure to object to personal jurisdiction at the first substantive opportunity, or to amend to include the objection within the time allowed, may constitute waiver of the objection and thus implied consent.[14] FRCP 12(h)(1) provides that a failure to raise objections to insufficiency of summons, insufficiency of service or personal jurisdiction in a FRCP 12(b) motion to dismiss or if no such motion is brought, in the answer (or in the amended answer if permitted) constitutes waiver of these defenses. Thus, defendants must assert their objections early. Further, it may not be enough merely to include a blanket objection to personal jurisdiction in the answer. There is a possibility that the defense of lack of personal jurisdiction might be held not to include objections to defects in the service or the summons. There is also a possibility that all of these defenses could be waived if defendant's conduct in the litigation is inconsistent with these defenses.[15]

---

12. Insurance Corp. of Ireland, Ltd., 456 U.S. at 703–04, 103 S.Ct. at 2105, (citing National Equipment Rental, Ltd., 375 U.S. at 316, 84 S.Ct. at 414).

13. Burger King Corp. v. Rudzewicz, 471 U.S. 462, 473 n. 14, 486, 105 S.Ct. 2174 2182 n. 14, 2189, 85 L.Ed.2d 528 (1985), citing M/S Bremen v. Zapata Off-Shore Company, 407 U.S. 1, 92 S.Ct. 1907, 32 L.Ed.2d 513 (1972); National Equipment Rental, Ltd. v. Szukhent, 375 U.S. 311, 84 S.Ct. 411, 11 L.Ed.2d 354 (1964); McGee v. International Life Insurance Co., 355 U.S. 220, 78 S.Ct. 199, 2 L.Ed.2d 223 (1957). (Inconvenience may at some point become so substantial as to achieve constitutional magnitude.). The *Burger King Corp.* Court specifically stated that jurisdictional rules may not be used against small consumers to cripple their defense. Burger King Corp., 417 U.S. at 486, 105 S.Ct. at 2189. *But see* Carnival Cruise Lines, Inc. v. Shute, 499 U.S. 585, 111 S.Ct. 1522, 113 L.Ed.2d 622 (1991). (Forum selection clause which was not the subject of negotiation between the parties, in small print on back of cruise line's form passage contract ticket requiring litigation of all disputes in distant forum found to be reasonable and enforceable.).

14. Failure to object timely to personal jurisdiction waives the right to object. *See* FRCP 12(h).

15. *See* Media Duplication Services, Ltd. v. HDG Software, Inc., 928 F.2d 1228, 1233 n. 2 (1st Cir.1991) (discussing conduct constituting waiver).

(3) Designation of an Agent for Service of Process Within a State

A split in authority exists as to whether designation of an agent for service of process automatically provides general jurisdiction over the corporate defendant in a particular state. Some circuits have held that designation of an agent is not enough by itself, other circuits have held that it is.[16]

(c) Domicile

Domicile in the forum is a basis for general jurisdiction over a defendant.[17]

(d) Severe Discovery Abuse Related to the Issue of Personal Jurisdiction

Discovery abuse by a defendant may also be interpreted as a waiver of the defendant's right to dispute personal jurisdiction. The United States Supreme Court has held that due process was not violated when a court based its determination of personal jurisdiction on certain facts taken as established as a sanction for a defendant's failure to comply with discovery orders.[18] The Court noted that defendants failed to provide requested material relating to the issue of personal jurisdiction despite repeated agreements by them to comply, repeated orders from the court to do so, and the court's prior warning of imposition of sanctions. The Court also noted the claim of personal jurisdiction was not frivolous.

Library References:

West's Key No. Digests, Constitutional Law ☞305, 309; Federal Civil Procedure ☞401–555; Federal Courts ☞71–97.

Wright, Miller & Cooper, Federal Practice and Procedure: Civil 2d §§ 1100, 1105, 1361, 3571, 3612, 3829.

16. *See* Leonard v. USA Petroleum Corp., 829 F.Supp. 882, 889 (S.D.Tex.1993)(Service on a designated agent alone does not establish minimum contact, rather registration to do business and appointment of an agent for service of process especially when done to fulfill state law requirements are only factors in the jurisdictional equation.), citing inter alia, Perkins v. Benguet Consol. Mining Co., 342 U.S. 437, 72 S.Ct. 413, 96 L.Ed. 485 (1952). *See also,* Ytuarte v. Gruner, 935 F.2d 971, 973 (8th Cir.1991)(Appointment of agent for service of process gives consent to the jurisdiction of the state courts for any cause of action whether or not arising out of activities within the state.), citing Neirbo

Co. v. Bethlehem Shipbuilding, 308 U.S. 165, 170, 174, 60 S.Ct. 153, 155, 157, 84 L.Ed. 167 (1939); *Ex parte* Schollenberger, 96 U.S. (6 Otto) 369, 376–77, 24 L.Ed. 853 (1877).

17. Milliken v. Meyer, 311 U.S. 457, 463–64, 61 S.Ct. 339, 343, 85 L.Ed. 278 (1940).

18. Insurance Corp. of Ireland, Ltd. v. Compagnie des Bauxites de Guinee, 456 U.S. 694, 102 S.Ct. 2099, 72 L.Ed.2d 492 (1982). (A defendant over whom the court would otherwise not have personal jurisdiction may waive its right to dispute personal jurisdiction by violating discovery rules.).

§ 2.8　Application of Due Process to Specific Business/Commercial Persons

(a) Corporations

Proper service on an out of state corporation is not enough to establish personal jurisdiction over that corporate defendant. If challenged, the plaintiff must also show either consent, waiver or that minimum contacts exist between the forum and the defendant such that the exercise of jurisdiction over the defendant does not offend traditional notions of fair play and substantial justice.

If the corporation has established substantial, continuous and systematic contacts with the forum state, general jurisdiction may be found and the district court can exercise personal jurisdiction over the corporation for any suit—regardless of whether the suit arose from or was related to the corporation's contacts with the forum.[1] A corporation has been found to have systematic and continuous contacts with a forum state when its president and general manager maintained an office from which he conducted activities on behalf of the corporation, kept company files and had directors' meetings in the office, carried on correspondence relating to the business, distributed salary checks drawn on two active state bank accounts, engaged a state bank to act as transfer agent and supervised policies dealing with overseas properties—all in the forum state.[2]

If a corporation's contacts are not continuous and systematic, then personal jurisdiction will only attach if the suit arises out of or is related to the corporation's contacts with the state, the corporation has minimum contacts with the jurisdiction and the exercise of jurisdiction in the particular case will not offend traditional notions of substantial justice and fair play. Minimum contacts may be supplied by the activities of officers, directors, employees, and agents acting within the scope of their employment or agency as well as alter egos under certain circumstances.

In *International Shoe*, the Court found personal jurisdiction proper over an out of state corporation. The Delaware shoe corporation, with its principal place of business in Missouri, employed 11 to 13 salesmen who resided in the State of Washington and regularly solicited orders and displayed samples there, sometimes in permanent display rooms paid for by the company. The company paid commissions to them totaling more than $31,000 per year over a four year period. Washington State sued the corporation in Washington to recover unpaid contributions to the state unemployment compensation fund. The U.S. Supreme Court found that the corporation was present and doing business in Washington and therefore amenable to process there.

§ 2.8

1. Perkins v. Benguet Consolidated Mining Company, 342 U.S. 437, 72 S.Ct. 413, 96 L.Ed. 485 (1952). For a discussion of cases analyzing general jurisdiction, *see supra* § 2.6 (a)(1).

2. *Id.*

The *International Shoe* Court noted that, unlike an individual, a corporation's presence within and without the state of its incorporation must be manifested by those authorized to act for it. Corporate presence within the state can therefore be shown by such contacts with the forum as make it reasonable, in the context of the federal system, to require the corporation to defend in the particular suit which is brought there. The bookends for the inquiry place on the one end a corporation continuously and systematically active in the forum which is sued on a claim arising from those in-forum state activities and on the other end a corporation which has no activities in the state and the suit does not relate to the in-forum state activities. Personal jurisdiction is proper in the former, it is not in the latter. Because each case will turn on its own facts, the inquiry in each case involving an assertion of personal jurisdiction over an out of state business entity will look at where between those two bookends a given case belongs.

In *World–Wide Volkswagen Corp. v. Woodson*,[3] the Supreme Court found a lack of personal jurisdiction where a corporation carried on no activity in the state and availed itself of no privileges or benefits of the forum state law. Corporate defendants were an automobile wholesaler and retailer who sold plaintiff an automobile in New York. While driving across the United States, plaintiffs were in an accident in Oklahoma and sued there. Defendants carried on no activity in Oklahoma. The Court ruled that while it was foreseeable that defendant's product (the car) might make it into the forum state, that was not the relevant constitutional inquiry. The due process question to be answered was whether the defendants' conduct and connection with the forum was such that they should reasonably anticipate being haled into court there. The unilateral action of a consumer in bringing a product into a forum state was not enough.

The Court noted that when a corporation purposefully avails itself of the privilege of conducting activities within a forum state, it has clear notice that it is subject to suit there. Due process would not, therefore, be violated if a court were to assert personal jurisdiction over a corporation that delivers its products into the stream of commerce with the expectation that they will be purchased by consumers in the forum state. The Court noted, however, that the defendant's contacts must be such that maintenance of the suit does not offend traditional notions of fair play and substantial justice and that the relationship between the defendant and the forum must be such that it is reasonable to require the corporation to defend the particular suit which is brought there.

In *Helicopteros Nacionales de Colombia, S.A. v. Hall*,[4] the Supreme Court once again found the corporation's contacts insufficient to support either general or specific personal jurisdiction. The corporation's contacts with the forum state consisted of purchases of helicopters and equipment from a Texas manufacturer and related training trips there, one trip to Texas by the corporation's chief executive officer to negotiate

---

3. 444 U.S. 286, 100 S.Ct. 559, 62 L.Ed.2d 490 (1980).

4. 466 U.S. 408, 104 S.Ct. 1868, 80 L.Ed.2d 404 (1984).

a transportation services contract, and acceptance of checks drawn on a Texas bank.[5]

The Court also noted that defendant had never been authorized to do business there, never had an agent for the service of process within the state, and did none of the following in the forum state; performed helicopter operations, solicited business, signed a contract, recruited an employee, owned any real or personal property, maintained an office or establishment, or kept records. Further, the corporate defendant never sold any product that reached the state, had no stockholders there and no employees based there.

The Court held that defendant's acceptance of checks drawn on a forum state bank was insignificant and that purchases in a forum state, even occurring at regular intervals, are not enough to warrant assertion of personal jurisdiction over a nonresident corporation in a cause of action not related to those purchases. The Court also held that the corporation's contacts with the forum were not continuous and systematic and therefore did not create general jurisdiction which would allow personal jurisdiction in suits unrelated to the corporation's activities in the forum.

Thus, generally speaking, with respect to the nonresident corporate defendant, the personal jurisdiction due process analysis includes an inquiry into whether (1) the defendant corporation has established minimum contacts with the forum such that it can be said it purposefully availed itself of the privilege of conducting activities in the forum state and (2) the exercise of jurisdiction is reasonable, applying whatever the particular circuit's iteration of the reasonableness test may be.

With respect to service, generally speaking, a corporation does not submit to jurisdiction merely because one of its officers has voluntarily entered the state.[6] Further, serving a person who happens to own a corporation does not in and of itself establish jurisdiction over a corporate defendant.[7]

(b) Subsidiaries

The activities or contacts of a subsidiary will not usually be attributable to the parent for purposes of the due process minimum contacts analysis.[8] Courts have, however, considered the contacts or activities of

---

5. *Id.* There were no other business contacts between the nonresident defendant corporation and the forum state.

6. Chan v. Society Expeditions, Inc., 39 F.3d 1398, 1404 (9th Cir.1994).

7. *Id.*

8. *See* Cannon Manufacturing Co. v. Cudahy Packing Co., 267 U.S. 333, 336, 45 S.Ct. 250, 251, 69 L.Ed. 634 (1925). (Independence of parent and subsidiary assumed.). *See also* United Electrical Radio

and Machine Workers of America v. 163 Pleasant Street Corporation, 960 F.2d 1080 (1st Cir.1992) (Corporation's passive investor status in subsidiary did not provide sufficient contacts for personal jurisdiction.); Donatelli v. National Hockey League, 893 F.2d 459 (1st Cir.1990) (courts presume separateness, but presumption may be overcome by clear evidence of something beyond subsidiary's mere presence within the bosom of the corporate family); Miller v. Honda Motor Co., 779 F.2d 769, 772 (1st

the subsidiary in analyzing personal jurisdiction of the parent when (1) the subsidiary is the agent of the parent, (2) the parent controls the subsidiary beyond the control normally associated with common ownership and directorship, and (3) the subsidiary is the alter ego of the parent.[9]

(c) Officers/Directors/Stock Owners

Depending on the law of the forum, holding a position as an officer or director of a forum state corporation may subject an out of state defendant to the personal jurisdiction of the forum.[10] An out of state defendant owning stock in a forum corporation standing alone will not provide personal jurisdiction over that defendant for a claim unrelated to that stock ownership.[11]

(d) Partnerships

The Ninth Circuit has addressed the issue of personal jurisdiction as

Cir.1985)(parent and sub assumed separate); Thompson Trading Ltd. v. Allied Lyons PLC., 123 F.R.D. 417 (1989)(Absent a showing that parent-sub relationship is pure fiction, even if it is merely formal, personal jurisdiction over sub does not create jurisdiction over the parent.).

9. *See* Chan v. Society Expeditions, Inc., 39 F.3d 1398 (9th Cir.1994) (whether one company is a general agent for another is a question of fact), *cert. denied*, 514 U.S. 1004, 115 S.Ct. 1314, 131 L.Ed.2d 196 (1995); Donatelli, 893 F.2d at 465–66 (fact of separate incorporation is not determinative rather it creates a presumption of separateness which may be overcome by clear evidence, noting that in cases where personal jurisdiction over the parent has been found, a "plus factor" is invariably present); Wells Fargo & Co. v. Wells Fargo Express Co., 556 F.2d 406, 423–24 (9th Cir.1977)(presence requirement could be satisfied if the subsidiary was acting as the parent's general agent in the state, noting that whether a general agent was a subsidiary of the principal or independently owned was irrelevant); Gallagher v. Mazda Motor of America, Inc., 781 F.Supp. 1079, 1083 (E.D.Pa.1992)(permitting imputation of contacts from subsidiary to parent, where the subsidiary was either established for, or engaged in activities that but for the existence of the subsidiary the parent would have to undertake itself); Hargrave v. Fibreboard Corp., 710 F.2d 1154, 1159 (5th Cir.1983)(stating that generally a foreign corporation is not subject to jurisdiction of a forum state merely because its subsidiary is present or doing business there, but noting that in some circumstances a close relationship between parent and subsidiary (e.g., parent exerts such domination and control over the sub that they are not in reality separate and distinct corporate entities) may justify a finding that the parent does business in a jurisdiction through the local activities of the sub, and specifically that 100% stock ownership and commonality of officers and directors are not alone sufficient to establish an alter ego relationship—that some proof of control by the parent over the internal business operations and affairs of the subsidiary, beyond that normally associated with common ownership and directorship, are necessary), citing inter alia Cannon Manufacturing Co. v. Cudahy Packing Co., 267 U.S. 333, 45 S.Ct. 250, 69 L.Ed. 634 (1925).

10. *See* Shaffer v. Heitner, 433 U.S. 186, 215–16, 97 S.Ct. 2569, 2585–86, 53 L.Ed.2d 683 (1977). (Position as director did not provide sufficient contacts to support personal jurisdiction but noting that result might be different in some states which have enacted statutes which treat acceptance of a directorship as consent to jurisdiction in the state).

11. Shaffer, 433 U.S. at 216, 97 S.Ct. at 2586 (Statutory presence of stock in state does not provide sufficient contacts to support assertion of jurisdiction where stock ownership is unrelated to claim.).

to partners and partnerships, holding that the minimum contacts due process analysis must be shown as to each defendant.[12] The court noted that liability is independent from personal jurisdiction.

The Ninth Circuit stated:

[W]hile each partner is generally an agent of the partnership for the purpose of its business, he is not ordinarily an agent of his partners. Thus, a partner's actions may be imputed to the partnership for the purpose of establishing minimum contacts, but ordinarily may not be imputed to the other partners.[13]

The District of Kansas relied upon the Ninth Circuit's analysis in finding that a limited partner, who plaintiff alleged had converted to a general partner at some point, was not subject to personal jurisdiction due to the activities of the partnership.[14]

Conversely, jurisdiction over the partner in a general partnership has been held to provide jurisdiction over the partnership.[15] This rule is based on the concept that a partner is deemed by law to be the partnership's general agent. The contacts between the partner and the forum state are generally attributed to the partnership. The contacts of the partner are therefore relevant to personal jurisdiction over the partnership regardless of the absence of independent contacts between the partnership as an entity and the forum.[16]

(e) Sales Agents

The term sales agent is not necessarily equivalent to managing or general agent. For example, a sales agent for an insurance company was held not to be a managing agent for purposes of service of process on the company despite the fact that he held a power of attorney for the defendant to issue and deliver bonds, undertakings, recognizance or other written obligations in connection with a particular contract.[17] The court noted that the person served was not the exclusive agent for the defendant in the state, that each agent answered directly to the company in another state, and the power of attorney was not a general power of attorney and did not authorize him to accept service of process for actions arising from disputes concerning the contract.[18]

---

12. Sher v. Johnson, 911 F.2d 1357 (9th Cir.1990), (citing Rush v. Savchuk, 444 U.S. 320, 100 S.Ct. 571, 62 L.Ed.2d 516 (1980)).

13. Id. at 1366.

14. See SBKC Service Corp. v. 1111 Prospect Partners, L.P., 969 F.Supp. 1254 (D.Kan.1997)(noting that the 10th Circuit has not yet addressed the issue, and holding that the partnership's consent to personal jurisdiction via a forum selection clause did not equate to the individual partners consent and therefore did not bind the individ-

ual partners). The Sixth Circuit has analyzed due process contacts with respect to an unincorporated association in Reynolds v. International Amateur Athletic Federation, 23 F.3d 1110 (6th Cir.1994).

15. See, e.g., Donatelli v. National Hockey League, 893 F.2d 459, 467 (1st Cir.1990).

16. Id. at 466–67.

17. Dodco, Inc. v. American Bonding Company, 7 F.3d 1387, 1388 (8th Cir.1993).

18. Id.

(f) Agents/Attorneys

With respect to service, an agent's authority to accept may be either express or implied from the type of relationship between the defendant and the purported agent.[19] It is not enough, however, to show appointment of an agent with broad authority. Rather, it must be shown that the agent had specific express or implied authority to receive service of process.[20] The mere relationship between an attorney and his client does not, without more, provide the authority to accept service.[21]

With respect to the due process analysis, it has been held that the mere existence of an attorney-client relationship with a forum resident, unaccompanied by other sufficient contacts with the forum, does not create sufficient contacts as will confer personal jurisdiction over the nonresident attorney.[22] In addition, comments made by an attorney related to a case during a single phone interview with a journalist initiated by the journalist located in a distant state may not subject the attorney to personal jurisdiction.[23]

(g) Distributors

While the activities of a distributor may provide contacts for a corporation in a specific jurisdiction analysis, in the absence of an agency relationship, the acts of an independent distributor are not ordinarily attributable to a foreign manufacturer for purposes of establishing general jurisdiction.[24] However, not all cases follow this holding.[25]

Library References:

West's Key No. Digests, Constitutional Law ⬥305, 309; Federal Courts ⬥71–97.

Wright, Miller & Cooper, Federal Practice and Procedure: Civil 2d §§ 1066, 1100, 1105, 3571, 3612.

19. United States v. Ziegler Bolt and Parts Company, 111 F.3d 878, 881 (Fed.Cir. 1997) (noting the existence of cases finding authority absent an express grant).

20. Id.

21. See id. (Discussing the limitations on an attorney's authority to accept service.).

22. Sawtelle v. Farrell, 70 F.3d 1381, 1392 (1st Cir.1995) (denying jurisdiction over out of forum attorney whose only connection with the forum state was the plaintiff's residence there).

23. See Ticketmaster–New York, Inc. v. Alioto, 26 F.3d 201 (1st Cir.1994). The court noted, inter alia, that the lawyer's limited contact consisted of a single unsolicited phone call by journalist.

24. See, e.g., Kuenzle v. HTM Sport–Und Freizeitgerate, 102 F.3d 453, 458–59 (10th Cir.1996). See also Conti v. Pneumatic Prods. Corp., 977 F.2d 978, 981 (6th Cir.1992); R.L. Lipton Distrib. Co. v. Dribeck Importers, Inc., 811 F.2d 967, 970 (6th Cir.1987) and Cascade Corp. v. Hiab–Foco AB, 619 F.2d 36, 37 (9th Cir.1980). Wells Fargo & Co. v. Wells Fargo Express Co., 556 F.2d 406, 422 (9th Cir.1977).

25. Michigan National Bank v. Quality Dinette, Inc., 888 F.2d 462, 465 (6th Cir. 1989).

§ 2.9　Application of Due Process Concerns to Certain Business and Commercial Activities

(a) Contracts

An out of state defendant does not create the necessary minimum contacts for personal jurisdiction merely because it enters into a contract with an individual in the forum state.[1] Courts must instead look to the prior negotiations and contemplated future consequences along with the terms of the contract and the parties' actual course of dealing in determining whether a defendant purposefully established minimum contacts with the forum.[2]

More than one circuit has also held that in breach of contract cases, it is only the dealings between the parties in regard to the disputed contract that are relevant to minimum contacts analysis.[3] In those circuits, past contacts involving the forum state, to be relevant for personal jurisdiction, should bear on the substantive legal dispute between the parties or inform the court regarding the economic substance of the contract.[4]

It has been held that "contract negotiations with forum residents can empower a court to exercise personal jurisdiction over a person outside the forum," and that "mail and telephone communications sent by the defendant into the forum may count toward the minimum contacts that support jurisdiction."[5]

§ 2.9

1. Burger King Corp. v. Rudzewicz, 471 U.S. 462, 478, 105 S.Ct. 2174, 2185, 85 L.Ed.2d 528 (1985).

2. Id. at 479, 105 S.Ct. at 2185. See also Vetrotex Certainteed Corporation v. Consolidated Fiber Glass Products Company, 75 F.3d 147 (3d Cir.1996). (Review of several holdings related to personal jurisdiction contract issues.).

3. RAR, Incorporated v. Turner Diesel, Limited, 107 F.3d 1272, 1278 (7th Cir.1997) (quoting the holding from Vetrotex Certainteed v. Consolidated Fiber Glass Products Co., 75 F.3d 147, 153 (3d Cir.1996)).

4. Id. at 1278.

5. Grand Entertainment Group, Ltd. v. Star Media Sales, Inc., 988 F.2d 476, 482 (3d Cir.1993). (Contract negotiations with forum residents can empower a court to exercise personal jurisdiction over persons outside the forum; citing the following: Carteret Savings Bank, FA v. Shushan, 954 F.2d 141, 147–48 (3d Cir.), cert. denied, 506 U.S. 817, 113 S.Ct. 61, 121 L.Ed.2d 29 (1992) (telephone calls and correspondence sent into New Jersey from Louisiana by the representative of a Louisiana real estate developer, coupled with a meeting in New Jersey to facilitate the closing of a loan provided the minimum contacts needed to satisfy due process); Lebel v. Everglades Marina, Inc., 115 N.J. 317, 558 A.2d 1252, 1256 (1989) (personal jurisdiction where only transactional contacts consisted of telephone calls and mailing of sales agreement); Taylor v. Phelan, 912 F.2d 429, 433 n. 4 (10th Cir.1990) ("so long as it creates a substantial connection, even a single telephone call into the forum state can support jurisdiction"), cert. denied, 498 U.S. 1068, 111 S.Ct. 786, 112 L.Ed.2d 849 (1991); Mellon Bank (East) PSFS, National Association v. Farino, 960 F.2d 1217 (3d Cir.1992) (taking a "highly realistic" approach to analyzing minimum contacts that looks to, inter alia, "prior negotiations and contemplated future consequences, along with the terms of the contract . . . . ").

(b) Manufacturing/Sales of Goods and the Stream of Commerce Analysis

The law is unsettled as to what a plaintiff must show in order for a forum to exert personal jurisdiction over an out of state defendant who has produced goods which have caused injury in the forum state. The United States Supreme Court set a standard in *World–Wide Volkswagen v. Woodson*,[6] then muddied the analysis in the plurality opinion of *Asahi Metal Industry Co., Ltd. v. Superior Court*.[7]

In *World–Wide Volkswagen*, the Court stated that the forum state does not exceed its powers under the Due Process Clause if it asserts personal jurisdiction over a corporation that delivers its products into the stream of commerce with the expectation that they will be purchased by consumers of the forum state.[8] However, merely placing products in the stream of commerce was held not to be enough. An expectation of purchase by consumers in the particular forum is required. The Court distinguished an expectation of sale in a forum from the expectation that a product sold outside the forum might unilaterally be taken by a consumer into it. The Court stated that, if the sale arises from the efforts of the manufacturer or distributor to serve directly or indirectly the forum as a market for its products and the allegedly defective merchandise causes injury to its owners or others in the forum, then personal jurisdiction may be proper.

In *Asahi*, the Supreme Court was unable to muster a majority opinion on the personal jurisdiction rules to apply to a stream of commerce fact pattern. The case resulted in three separate opinions. One group of four justices, led by Justice Brennan, opined it was enough to show that defendant knew its final product was being marketed in the forum state. Another group of four justices, led by Justice O'Connor, concluded that some additional conduct beyond a mere awareness must be present. A third group, led by Justice Stevens,[9] refused to join in the portion of the plurality opinion addressing the stream of commerce theory for two reasons; first, it was not necessary to the Court's decision because jurisdiction was ruled unreasonable and unfair so there was no need to reach the minimum contacts/purposeful availment analysis and second, the plurality opinion, authored by Justice O'Conner, misapplied the test to the facts of the case.[10]

The O'Connor group,[11] noting a split in the circuits regarding application of the stream of commerce concept, opined that a defendant's awareness that the placement of a product in the stream of commerce may or will sweep the product into the forum state is not enough. Such awareness does not transform the mere act of placing the product into the stream of commerce into an act purposefully directed toward the

---

6. 444 U.S. 286, 298, 100 S.Ct. 559, 567, 62 L.Ed.2d 490 (1980).

7. 480 U.S. 102, 107 S.Ct. 1026, 94 L.Ed.2d 92 (1987).

8. World–Wide Volkswagen, 444 U.S. at 298, 100 S.Ct. at 567.

9. Justices White and Blackmun joined in Justice Stevens' concurrence in part and concurrence in the judgment.

10. Asahi, 480 U.S. at 122, 107 S.Ct. at 1037.

11. Justice O'Connor, Justice Rehnquist, Justice Powell, and Justice Scalia.

forum state. Without more, according to the O'Conner group, it would not be an act of the defendant purposefully directed to the forum state.

The O'Connor group would require additional conduct of the defendant which would indicate an intent or purpose to serve the market in the forum state. Additional conduct could include (1) designing the product for the market in the forum state, (2) advertising in the forum state, (3) establishing channels for providing regular advice to customers in the forum state, or (4) marketing the product through a distributor who has agreed to serve as the sales agent in the forum state.

The Brennan group[12] opined that no additional conduct was necessary. They noted that stream of commerce refers not to unpredictable eddies and currents, but to the regular and anticipated flow of products from manufacture to distribution to retail sale. Thus, they reasoned, as long as a participant in the process is aware that the final product is being marketed in the forum state, the possibility of a lawsuit there cannot come as a surprise.

The *Asahi* Court clearly did not resolve the issue. And, the circuits are not in agreement on the issue either.[13] Thus, again, when this fact pattern arises, the lawyer will need to focus on the analysis used in the specific circuit in which the suit is pending.

(c) Purchase of Goods

Regular purchases in the forum state and related trips (including training instruction), standing alone, will not support personal jurisdiction over a nonresident corporation for a cause of action not related to those purchase transactions.[14]

(d) Defamation

The Supreme Court has specifically considered personal jurisdiction over nonresidents in the context of defamation and found adequate contacts to support such jurisdiction in *Keeton v. Hustler Magazine, Inc.*[15] and *Calder v. Jones.*[16]

The *Keeton* and *Calder* holdings have been described as follows:[17]

In *Keeton*, the Court found that a magazine publisher's "regular" monthly circulation of 10,000 to 15,000 copies in New Hampshire

---

12. Justice Brennan, Justice White, Justice Marshall and Justice Blackmun.

13. *See, e.g.*, Renner v. Lanard Toys Limited, 33 F.3d 277, (3d Cir.1994) (describing the *Asahi* opinion as well as opinions in which various circuit courts have addressed the stream of commerce theory).

14. Helicopteros Nacionales de Colombia, S.A. v. Hall, 466 U.S. 408, 418, 104 S.Ct. 1868, 1874, 80 L.Ed.2d 404 (1984), *aff'g* Rosenberg Bros. & Co. v. Curtis

Brown Co., 260 U.S. 516, 43 S.Ct. 170, 67 L.Ed. 372 (1923). (Purchases and related trips, standing alone are not sufficient basis for a state's assertion of jurisdiction.).

15. 465 U.S. 770, 775, 104 S.Ct. 1473, 1478, 79 L.Ed.2d 790 (1984).

16. 465 U.S. 783, 104 S.Ct. 1482, 79 L.Ed.2d 804 (1984).

17. *See* Chaiken v. VV Publishing Corp., 119 F.3d 1018, 1028 (2d Cir.1997).

was 'sufficient to support an assertion of jurisdiction in a libel action based on the contents of the magazine.' 465 U.S. at 773–74, 104 S.Ct. at 1478. The Court ruled that 'monthly sales of thousands of magazines' could not be characterized as 'random, isolated, or fortuitous' and therefore provided sufficient 'minimum contacts' between the defendant and the state. *Id.* at 774, 104 S.Ct. at 1478. After examining, among other things, the state's 'interest' in asserting jurisdiction, the interests of the nonresident plaintiff, and the burden on the defendant, the Court found no unfairness in requiring the producer of a 'national publication aimed at a nationwide audience to defend libel actions' wherever a substantial number of copies are regularly sold and distributed.' *Id.* at 781, 104 S.Ct. at 1482 . . .

In *Calder,* the Court held that the due process clause did not prevent California from exercising personal jurisdiction over the writer and editor of an article that allegedly defamed a California resident. The Court emphasized that the story appeared in a weekly newspaper with a California circulation of 600,000 copies, was drawn from California sources, and concerned the California activities of a California resident whose career was 'centered in' that state. Calder, 465 U.S. at 788–89, 104 S.Ct. at 1486. On these facts the Court found that California was the 'focal point both of the story and of the harm suffered,' that defendants knew that the 'brunt' of plaintiff's injury would be felt [in California] and that defendant's actions were expressly aimed at California. *Id.* at 789–90, 104 S.Ct. at 1486–87. For these reasons, the Court ruled that although defendants were Florida residents and had not acted in California, they had directed their activities at that state and could therefore have reasonably anticipated 'being hauled into court there.' *Id.*

The circuit courts have applied the *Keeton* and *Calder* holdings in several defamation cases in which personal jurisdiction over publishers was found proper—even when the circulation in the forum state was described as small.[18]

(e) The Internet

Due to the relative newness of the technology, precedent involving the Internet is evolving. There are enough cases, however, to get a feel as to how courts are applying existing personal jurisdiction concepts to disputes involving this unique medium which can reach into seemingly any jurisdiction around the world.

---

18. *See, e.g.,* Friedman v. Israel Labour Party, 957 F.Supp. 701 (E.D.Pa.1997)(personal jurisdiction over publisher proper because it had published allegedly defamatory article "the effects of which would clearly be felt in the forum," regularly circulated publication in the forum and litigating in forum would not be unreasonable); *and* Gordy v. The Daily News, 95 F.3d 829, 831 (9th Cir.1996)(personal jurisdiction proper, despite small circulation, due to purposeful targeting of plaintiff in the forum state); *but see,* Chaiken, 119 F.3d at 1027–30 (finding lack of sufficient contacts between forum state and defendant newspaper where defendant did not expressly aim its actions at the forum state).

One court has acknowledged the development of the law regarding the scope of personal jurisdiction based on Internet use as "in its infant stages."[19] Nevertheless, the same court concluded that, based upon a review of available authority, "the likelihood that personal jurisdiction can be constitutionally exercised is directly proportionate to the nature and quality of commercial activities that an entity conducts over the Internet."[20] The court described a spectrum, consisting of situations on the one end where a defendant clearly does business over the Internet (and personal jurisdiction would be proper),[21] on the other end where the defendant merely posts information on an Internet Website which is accessible to users in foreign jurisdictions (and personal jurisdiction would be improper)[22] and in the middle where the defendant has an interactive Website and a user can exchange information with the host computer (which requires analysis of the level of interactivity and commercial nature of the exchange that occurs via the Website).[23]

Set forth below are just a few examples of how courts have treated personal jurisdiction in the context of the Internet.

In *Resuscitation Technologies, Inc. v. Continental Health Care Corp. et al.*,[24] the court found personal jurisdiction where defendant's initial contact with plaintiff was the response to an Internet message and the parties, among other things, sent approximately 80 E-mail messages back and forth. The court found that the defendant intended to establish a continuing and long term relationship with the plaintiff forum state company and also noted the state's interest in adjudicating the dispute.

In *Digital Equipment Corp. v. Altavista Technology, Inc.*,[25] the court found jurisdiction where the plaintiff had alleged breach of a trademark license agreement, trademark infringement, unfair competition and trademark dilution against an out of state defendant whose search engine contained an infringing trademark and was accessible in the forum state. The plaintiff had purchased the trademark from defendants. The court focused on the breach of contract with a forum state corporation giving rise to the litigation, confusion which could arise, that potentially thousands of forum residents accessed the site daily, and defendants were soliciting business through the Website and had made actual sales to forum residents.

In *Hearst Corp. v. Goldberger*,[26] the court found no personal jurisdiction in a trademark infringement/dilution case based upon defendant's Website. The defendant's Internet communications were likened to na-

---

19. Zippo Manufacturing Company v. Zippo Dot Com, Inc., 952 F.Supp. 1119, 1123 (W.D.Pa.1997)(also describing the case law as scant).

20. *Id.* at 1124.

21. *Id.* (citing CompuServe, Inc. v. Patterson, 89 F.3d 1257 (6th Cir.1996)).

22. *Id.* (citing Bensusan Restaurant Corp. v. King, 937 F.Supp. 295 (S.D.N.Y. 1996), *aff'd*, 126 F.3d 25 (2dCir.1997).).

23. *Id.* at 1124, (citing Maritz, Inc. v. Cybergold, Inc., 947 F.Supp. 1328 (E.D.Mo. 1996)).

24. 1997 WL 148567 (S.D.Ind.1997).

25. 960 F.Supp. 456 (D.Mass.1997).

26. 1997 WL 97097 (S.D.N.Y.1997).

tional advertisements and telephone calls and mail and therefore held insufficient to establish personal jurisdiction. The court, noting that no passing off had occurred and the defendant had not acted in bad faith, held it would be unreasonable to find jurisdiction where no contract existed.

In *Zippo Manufacturing Co. v. Zippo Dot Com, Inc.*,[27] the court found personal jurisdiction in a case alleging trademark dilution/infringement and false designation where the defendant had contracted with seven Internet access providers in the forum, and sold passwords to approximately 3,000 persons in the forum state. The court distinguished defendant's activities from a general advertising case.[28]

In *State of Minnesota v. Granite Gate Resorts, Inc.*,[29] the court found personal jurisdiction in a deceptive trade practices, false advertising and consumer fraud case against an out-of-state defendant operating a gambling service over the Internet. Key facts included solicitation of consumers in the forum (evidenced by the presence of forum state addresses on the defendant's solicitation list), the constant availability of advertisement in the forum state, and the provision to forum residents of a phone number to call. The court also noted that documents indicated defendants knew forum residents were accessing the service. The court held that defendant's solicitation of forum state residents was purposeful availment of the privilege of conducting business within the forum state.

In *EDIAS Software International v. BASIS International Ltd.*,[30] the court found personal jurisdiction where the alleged defamatory statements were contained in defendant's E–mail, Web page, and form message which were directed at the forum-state.

In *Panavision International v. Toeppen*,[31] the court found personal jurisdiction where the defendant intentionally registered a domain name knowing it belonged to someone else and harm was directed to and felt in the forum state.

In *Bensusan Restaurant Corp. v. King*,[32] the court found no personal jurisdiction over a defendant posting a Website with an allegedly infringing name where the Website was for a local venture outside the forum state, it specifically stated to readers not to confuse the site with the plaintiff's restaurant and there had been no infringement activity directed at nor patronage or revenue derived from the forum state.

In *Maritz, Inc. v. Cybergold, Inc.*,[33] the court found personal jurisdiction over a defendant in a trademark infringement case involving the Internet, noting that harm was felt in the forum and the forum had an interest in determining whether one of its corporation's trademarks was being infringed.

27. 952 F.Supp. 1119 (W.D.Pa.1997).

28. *Id.* at 1126.

29. 1996 WL 767431 (D.Minn.1996), *aff'd* 568 N.W.2d 715 (Minn.App.1997).

30. 947 F.Supp. 413 (D.Ariz.1996).

31. 938 F.Supp. 616 (C.D.Cal.1996).

32. 937 F.Supp. 295 (S.D.N.Y.1996).

33. 947 F.Supp. 1328 (E.D.Mo.1996).

In *CompuServe, Inc. v. Patterson*,[34] personal jurisdiction was found in a trademark infringement/deceptive trade practices case involving the Internet. A nonresident subscriber of a computer network service who developed software and had an ongoing contract with the service to have his software distributed for sale through the service network was found to have purposefully availed himself of benefits of doing business in the state in which the service was based. The court noted that even if the subscriber had few sales in that state, he knowingly entered written agreements with the service and was on notice that they would be governed by the law of that state, the relationship was ongoing, and he advertised the software on the system.

In *Inset Systems, Inc. v. Instruction Set*,[35] personal jurisdiction was found in a case alleging trademark infringement and unfair competition where, among other things, the defendant's advertisement via the Internet was continuous and defendant offered toll free numbers to call.

In *American Network, Inc. v. Access America,* the court found personal jurisdiction in a trademark infringement case involving a Website, where defendant's conduct exceeded merely publishing a page on the Web. The court noted defendant had signed up six forum state subscribers to the services advertised on its home page and inferred that defendant had mailed product and agreements to the forum state subscribers.[36]

Library References:

> West's Key No. Digests, Constitutional Law ⊙=305, 309; Federal Courts ⊙=71–97.
>
> Wright & Miller, Federal Practice and Procedure: Civil 2d § 1125.

§ 2.10   Additional Procedural Concerns

(a) Discovery

Numerous cases have sustained the right of plaintiffs to conduct discovery prior to the district court dismissing their claim for lack of personal jurisdiction.[1] Generally when a defendant challenges personal jurisdiction, courts permit depositions confined to issues raised in the motion to dismiss.[2] Lack of a meaningful opportunity to conduct discovery has been cited in vacating rulings which dismissed actions.[3] Howev-

---

34. 89 F.3d 1257 (6th Cir.1996).

35. 937 F.Supp. 161 (D.Conn.1996).

36. 975 F.Supp. 494 (S.D.N.Y.1997).

§ 2.10

1. Renner v. Lanard Toys Limited, 33 F.3d 277, 283 (3d Cir.1994), citing Edmond v. United States Postal Serv. Gen. Counsel, 949 F.2d 415, 425 (D.C.Cir.1991); Wyatt v. Kaplan, 686 F.2d 276, 283 (5th Cir.1982); and Fraley v. Chesapeake & Ohio Ry. Co., 397 F.2d 1, 3 (3d Cir.1968).

2. Renner, 33 F.3d at 283 (citing Wyatt, 686 F.2d at 283).

3. *Id.* (citing several other cases with similar holdings). In *Renner*, the defendant moved to dismiss within three days from the date the case was removed to federal court, plaintiffs had less than a month to respond to the motion and the case was dismissed within several days of their response. Although they made no formal discovery requests during that time period, they preserved their position that discovery

er, plaintiffs should promptly conduct any needed discovery because an unreasonable delay may result in a loss of the ability to do so.[4]

When plaintiffs allege general jurisdiction, courts have permitted discovery regarding defendant's contacts with the forum extending back several years. In one case, the appellate court upheld the district court's permitting discovery for the six-year period prior to commencement of the suit.[5] The scope of discovery, however, will likely depend on the time period the court determines is relevant to determination of general or specific jurisdiction.[6]

(b) Effect of Asserting a Counterclaim

Whether asserting a counterclaim waives a defense of lack of personal jurisdiction varies by circuit and may be uncertain.[7] It has been stated that as "a general rule," assertion of a permissive counterclaim constitutes waiver of a defense of personal jurisdiction.[8] Some courts have treated compulsory counterclaims differently than permissive counterclaims. Others have not. The variance in treatment has caused courts to term the law regarding this issue as "in disarray."[9]

(c) Challenging Personal Jurisdiction

Defendants may challenge personal jurisdiction either in a motion to dismiss pursuant to Rule 12(b)(2) or by affirmative defense and trial.

If a defendant moves to dismiss pursuant to Rule 12(b)(2), plaintiff bears the burden of proving that jurisdiction lies in the forum state.[10]

was needed in their opposition to the motion to dismiss. Thus, if a plaintiff is facing a motion to dismiss and has not had an opportunity to conduct discovery, he should undertake to do so and should at a minimum make the point in his opposition papers.

4. See, e.g., Rodriguez v. Fullerton Tires Corp., 115 F.3d 81, 86 (1st Cir.1997) (third-party plaintiff moved for reconsideration of ruling and requested permission to conduct discovery on jurisdictional issue, court denied the request noting that request to conduct discovery was untimely because appellant (third-party defendant) appeared in March 1995, brought a third-party complaint in December 1995, third-party defendant moved to dismiss in April 1996 and appellant replied in July 1996); Theunissen v. Matthews, 935 F.2d 1454, 1465 (6th Cir. 1991) (request for additional discovery denied where plaintiff had 5½ months to conduct discovery and knew the issues in dispute 3½ weeks prior to hearing but failed to conduct discovery).

5. Metropolitan Life Insurance Company v. Robertson–Ceco Corp., 84 F.3d 560,

575–76 (2d Cir.1996). (Six years permissible, however, allowing discovery over an unlimited period would have been overly broad and unquestionably burdensome.).

6. For a discussion of the time period to be considered in evaluating the existence of general jurisdiction, see supra § 2.6(a)(1).

7. See, e.g., PDK Labs, Inc. v. Friedlander, 103 F.3d 1105, 1111 n. 4 (2d Cir.1997) citing Cargill, Inc. v. Sabine Trading & Shipping Co., 756 F.2d 224, 229 (2d Cir. 1985).

8. See NDEP Corp. v. Handl-it, Inc., 203 B.R. 905, 910 n. 4 (D.Del. 1996) (describing the "general rule"); General Contracting & Trading v. Interpole, 940 F.2d 20 (1st Cir. 1991).

9. See Cargill, 756 F.2d at 229; PDK Labs, Inc., 103 F.3d at 1111 n. 4.

10. See, e.g., Sher v. Johnson, 911 F.2d 1357, 1361 (9th Cir.1990); Gray v. St. Martin's Press, Inc., 929 F.Supp. 40, 43 (D.N.H. 1996), citing Sawtelle v. Farrell, 70 F.3d 1381, 1387 (1st Cir.1995); Pacific Atlantic

The standard of proof varies depending upon the stage at which jurisdiction is challenged.[11] The prima facie standard is the least taxing from a plaintiff's standpoint and the one most often employed at the early stages of litigation.[12] It requires only that plaintiff assert facts which, if true, would support personal jurisdiction over the defendant.[13] If an evidentiary hearing or trial is held on the issue, the preponderance of evidence standard applies.[14]

Before discovery, a plaintiff may be able to defeat a motion to dismiss for lack of personal jurisdiction by making legally sufficient allegations of jurisdiction.[15] But once the parties have conducted jurisdictional discovery, the plaintiff must allege facts that, if credited would suffice to establish jurisdiction over the defendant.[16] The court is to draw the facts from the pleadings and the parties supplementary filings, including affidavits, taking facts affirmatively alleged by plaintiff as true and construing disputed facts in the light most hospitable to plaintiff.[17] Issues of credibility or disputed fact may, however, require a hearing.[18] The court is not to act as a fact-finder, but instead, is to ascertain only whether the acts duly proffered, fully credited, support the exercise of personal jurisdiction.[19]

Any party may request that the defense of lack of personal jurisdiction be heard and determined before trial.[20] If the matter is determined before trial, and the court denies defendant's motion to dismiss, the court is implicitly ordering that final determination of the propriety of

Trading Co. v. M/V Main Exp., 758 F.2d 1325, 1327 (9th Cir.1985).

11. *See, e.g.,* Rodriguez v. Fullerton Tires Corp., 115 F.3d 81, 83 (1st Cir.1997).

12. *Id.* at 83–84. In fact, the First Circuit has held that all litigants are effectively on notice that motions to dismiss for want of personal jurisdiction will be adjudicated under the prima facie standard unless the court informs them in advance that it will apply a more demanding test. *Id.* at 84.

13. *See* Sher, 911 F.2d at 1361 (In the absence of an evidentiary hearing, plaintiff need only make a prima facie showing of jurisdictional facts.); Data Disc, Inc. v. Systems Tech. Assoc., 557 F.2d 1280, 1285 (9th Cir.1977) (If plaintiff's proof is limited to written materials, it is necessary only for the materials to demonstrate facts that support a finding of jurisdiction in order to avoid dismissal.); Gray, 929 F.Supp. at 43 (Court may utilize prima facie method when the case does not involve incredible affidavits or material issues of credibility.) citing Foster–Miller, Inc. v. Babcock & Wilcox Canada, 46 F.3d 138, 145–46 (1st Cir. 1995) and Boit v. Gar–Tec Prods., Inc., 967 F.2d 671, 675–76 (1st Cir.1992)).

14. *See, e.g.,* Paulucci v. William Morris Agency, Inc., 952 F.Supp. 1335, 1338 (D.Minn.1997).

15. *See* Chaiken v. VV Publishing Corp., 119 F.3d 1018, 1025 (2d Cir.1997).

16. *Id.*

17. *See, e.g.,* Gray, 929 F.Supp. at 43, citing Ticketmaster–New York, Inc. v. Alioto, 26 F.3d 201, 203 (1st Cir.1994); United States Securities and Exchange Commission v. Carrillo, 115 F.3d 1540, 1542 (11th Cir. 1997). (Court to accept the facts alleged in the complaint as true, to the extent they are uncontroverted by the defendant's affidavits, and to the extent the alleged facts conflict, to construe all reasonable inferences in favor of plaintiffs.).

18. Sher, 911 F.2d at 1361, citing Data Disc, 557 F.2d at 1285.

19. Rodriguez v. Fullerton Tires Corp., 115 F.3d 81, 84 (1st Cir.1997).

20. FRCP 12(d) provides that on application of any party, unless the court orders that the hearing and determination thereof be deferred until the trial, the defense of lack of personal jurisdiction shall be heard and determined before trial.

personal jurisdiction be deferred until trial.[21] On appeal, the ultimate question of whether personal jurisdiction was properly exercised is a question of law which is reviewed de novo.[22]

(d) Res Judicata

When a party submits to the jurisdiction of the court for the limited purpose of challenging jurisdiction, the defendant agrees to abide by that court's determination. The decision will be res judicata in any further proceedings.[23] If, however, the party fails to appear and defend, and the court did have personal jurisdiction over him, he loses the right to litigate the substantive issues when the judgment is enforced in another forum.[24]

Library References:

West's Key No. Digests, Federal Civil Procedure ☞1261–1278; Federal Courts ☞71–97.

Wright, Miller & Cooper, Federal Practice and Procedure: Civil 2d §§ 1351, 4405.

§ 2.11 Procedural Checklist

(a) Summons

1. The attorney must present the summons in the proper federal form to the clerk for signature and seal. Failure to obtain the signature or seal will render the summons invalid. (*See* FRCP 4(a); § 2.5(a))

2. If addressed to multiple defendants, a copy of the summons must be issued for each defendant served. (*See* FRCP 4(a), (b); § 2.5(a))

(b) Service

1. Plaintiff is responsible for serving the summons and a copy of the complaint. (*See* FRCP 4(c)(1); § 2.5(b))

2. Any person who is not a party and who is at least 18 years of age may serve the summons and complaint. In some instances, the plaintiff may request the court's permission to have the U.S.

---

21. Gray, 929 F.Supp. at 40 citing Boit v. Gar–Tec Prods., Inc., 967 F.2d 671, 676 (1st Cir.1992).

22. *See, e.g.,* Reebok Int'l, Ltd. v. McLaughlin, 49 F.3d 1387, 1390 (9th Cir.), *cert. denied,* 516 U.S. 908, 116 S.Ct. 276, 133 L.Ed.2d 197 (1995); United States Securities and Exchange Commission v. Carrillo, 115 F.3d 1540, 1542 (11th Cir.1997).

23. Insurance Corp. of Ireland, Ltd. v. Compagnie des Bauxites de Guinee, 456

U.S. 694, 706–07, 102 S.Ct. 2099, 2107, 72 L.Ed.2d 492 (1982).

24. Milliken v. Meyer, 311 U.S. 457, 463–64, 61 S.Ct. 339, 343, 85 L.Ed. 278 (1940). If a party does not appear and defend, and plaintiff seeks to enforce the judgment in another jurisdiction, if the original court did have personal jurisdiction over the defendant, the defendant will be barred from challenging the substantive underlying judgment in the second court.

Marshal serve the summons and complaint. (*See* FRCP 4(c)(2); § 2.5(b))

3. Except for certain defendants, service must be accomplished within 120 days of filing the complaint or the action may be dismissed. (*See* FRCP 4(m); § 2.5(j)) If the deadline is approaching and plaintiff is having difficulty serving the defendant, he should make a good record in support of a request for more time and should alert the court to the problem as early as possible. (*See* § 2.5(j))

4. Service must be made pursuant to the portion of FRCP 4 applicable to the particular defendant or factual scenario. (Service on individuals within a judicial district of the United States—(*See* FRCP 4(e); § 2.5(d)); Corporations and associations—(*See* FRCP 4(h); § 2.5(e)); the United States and its agencies, corporations or officers—(*See* FRCP 4(i)(1), (2); § 2.5(f)); foreign, state or local governments—(*See* FRCP 4(j); § 2.5(g)); Property—seizure of property, service of summons not feasible—(*See* FRCP 4(n); § 2.5(k))

5. Service must be made in compliance with the territorial limits prescribed. (*See* FRCP 4(k)(1); § 2.5(h))

6. The person effecting service must make proof of it and, if not a U.S. Marshal, must make an affidavit. (*See* FRCP 4(*l*); § 2.5(i)) The proof is filed with the court.

(c) Challenging Defects in Process or Service of Process

1. Defendant must challenge defects in process or service of process in the motion to dismiss or answer, if no motion to dismiss, or waive the ability to do so. (*See* FRCP 12(g), (h)(1); § 2.3)

(d) Waiver

1. Plaintiff may request defendant waive formal service. To do so, plaintiff must send two copies of the notice of request for waiver (using the language set forth in the official form), a copy of the complaint and a prepaid means for compliance in writing (prepaid postage and envelope) by first class mail or other reliable means, to the defendant or in the case of a corporation or business entity to the officer or managing, general or other agent authorized to receive service under FRCP 4(h). (*See* FRCP 4(d); §§ 2.5(c), 2.3(b)(1))

2. Defendant has 30 days from the date the request is sent (60 days if the request is sent to an address outside of any judicial district of the United States) within which to respond. Failure to respond within that time period permits the plaintiff to obtain fees and costs for service of certain defendants as well as the attorney's fees for bringing the motion to recover the costs. (*See* FRCP 4(d); §§ 2.5(c), 2.3(b)(1))

3. Plaintiff may concurrently attempt service, although plaintiff may not obtain the fees and costs associated with service activities prior to the time allowed for the defendant to respond to a request for waiver. (*See* FRCP 4(d)(2)(G); § 2.5(c))

4. If defendant agrees to waive, he is not required to serve the answer until 60 days after the request for waiver was sent (90 days if it was sent outside the United States). (*See* FRCP 4(d)(3); § 2.5(c))

5. Upon obtaining a signed waiver, plaintiff files the waiver with the court and the action proceeds as if the summons and complaint had been served at the time the waiver was filed (except for the additional time to answer described above) and no proof of service is required. (*See* FRCP 4(d); § 2.5(c))

(e) Personal Jurisdiction

1. Plaintiff should carefully analyze the applicable circuit's approach to due process personal jurisdiction analysis, assemble the necessary facts regarding compliance with applicable state long-arm statutes, contacts with the forum and reasonableness and accordingly include appropriate allegations regarding both general and specific personal jurisdiction (if possible) in the complaint. (*See* §§ 2.3(a), (c), 2.6–2.9)

2. Plaintiff should begin jurisdictional discovery promptly. (*See* § 2.10(a))

3. Defendant should consider carefully the costs and benefits of challenging jurisdiction prior to doing so and whether it makes sense to default and fight the judgment when plaintiff attempts to enforce it in another jurisdiction rather than fight jurisdiction in the existing case. (*See* § 2.3(c)(1))

4. Defendant must challenge personal jurisdiction in the motion to dismiss or in the answer if no motion to dismiss or waive the defense. (*See* FRCP 12(g), (h)(1); § 2.3(c)(2)) Defendant should consider whether to raise the defense by motion or assert it in the answer. Defendant should also carefully analyze the applicable circuit's approach to the due process analysis and compile facts reflecting lack of compliance with any applicable long-arm statutes, lack of contacts and unreasonableness of exercise of jurisdiction. If desirable, the motion to dismiss should be combined with a motion for change of venue. Prior to including the motion for change of venue, however, defendant should examine what effect the requested forum's law will have on the ability to prevail in the underlying case. (*See* § 2.3(c))

5. Defendant should request discovery be limited to jurisdictional issues until a motion to dismiss can be heard. (*See* § 2.10(a))

6. If considering including the defense of lack of personal jurisdiction in the answer, defendant should carefully consider whether

asserting a counterclaim will constitute waiver of the defense of lack of personal jurisdiction in the applicable circuit, and if in doubt, bring a motion to dismiss prior to answering/counter-claiming. (*See* § 2.10(b)) Defendant should also avoid voluntarily entering the forum state during the time in which plaintiff may serve him. Service in the state while voluntarily present will satisfy constitutional due process. (*See* § 2.7(a))

§ 2.12   Forms

(a) Notice of Lawsuit and Request for Waiver of Service of Summons ▯

TO: (A) [Name of individual defendant (or name of officer or agent of corporate defendant)]

(B) [Title, or other relationship of individual to corporate defendant]

(C) [Name of corporate defendants, if any]

A lawsuit has been commenced against you (or the entity on whose behalf you are addressed). A copy of the complaint is attached to this notice. It has been filed in the United States District Court for the [*District*] and has been assigned docket number [*Docket number of action*].

This is not a formal summons or notification from the court, but rather my request that you sign and return the enclosed waiver of service in order to save the cost of serving you with a judicial summons and an additional copy of the complaint. The cost of service will be avoided if I receive a signed copy of the waiver within [*Addressees must be given at least 30 days (60 days if located in foreign county) in which to return waiver*] days after the date designated below as the date on which this Notice and Request is sent. I enclose a stamped and addressed envelope [*or other means of cost-free return*] for your use. An extra copy of the waiver is also attached for your records.

If you comply with this request and return the signed waiver, it will be filed with the court and no summons will be served on you. The action will then proceed as if you had been served on the date the waiver is filed, except that you will not be obligated to answer the complaint before 60 days from the date designated below as the date on which this notice is sent (or before 90 days from that date if your address is not in any judicial district of the United States).

If you do not return the signed waiver within the time indicated, I will take appropriate steps to effect formal service in a manner authorized by the Federal Rules of Civil Procedure and will then, to the extent authorized by those Rules, ask the court to require you (or the party on whose behalf you are addressed) to pay the full costs of such service. In that connection, please read the statement concerning the duty of parties to waive the service of the summons, which is set forth on the reverse side (or at the foot) of the waiver form.

I affirm that this request is being sent to you on behalf of the plaintiff, [*name of plaintiff*] this _____ day of _____, ___.

_____
Signature of Plaintiff's Attorney
or Unrepresented Plaintiff

(b) Waiver of Service of Summons 💾

TO: [Name of plaintiff's attorney or unrepresented plaintiff]

I acknowledge receipt of your request that I waive service of a summons in the action of [*caption of action*], which is case number [*docket number*] in the United States District Court for the [*district*]. I have also received a copy of the complaint in the action, two copies of this instrument, and a means by which I can return the signed waiver to you without cost to me.

I agree to save the cost of service of a summons and an additional copy of the complaint in this lawsuit by not requiring that I (or the entity on whose behalf I am acting) be served with judicial process in the manner provided by Rule 4.

I (or the entity on whose behalf I am acting) will retain all defenses or objections to the lawsuit or to the jurisdiction or venue of the court except for objections based on a defect in the summons or in the service of the summons.

I understand that a judgment may be entered against me (or the party on whose behalf I am acting) if an answer or motion under Rule 12 is not served upon you within 60 days after [date request was sent], or within 90 days after that date if the request was sent outside the United States.

_____   _____
Date   Signature

                                    Printed/typed name:

                                    _____
                                    [as _____]
                                    [of _____]

To be printed on the reverse side of the waiver form or set forth at the foot of the form:

Duty to Avoid Unnecessary Costs of Service of Summons

Rule 4 of the Federal Rules of Civil Procedure requires certain parties to cooperate in saving unnecessary costs of service of the summons and complaint. A defendant located in the United States who, after being notified of an action and asked by a plaintiff located in the United

States to waive service of a summons, fails to do so will be required to bear the costs of such service unless good cause be shown for its failure to sign and return the waiver.

It is not good cause for a failure to waive service that a party believes that the complaint is unfounded, or that the action has been brought in an improper place or in a court that lacks jurisdiction over the subject matter of the action or over its person or property. A party who waives service of the summons retains all defenses and objections (except any relating to the summons or the service of the summons), and may later object to the jurisdiction of the court or to the place where the action has been brought.

A defendant who waives service must within the time specified on the waiver form serve on the plaintiff's attorney (or unrepresented plaintiff) a response to the complaint and must also file a signed copy of the response with the court. If the answer or motion is not served within this time, a default judgment may be taken against that defendant. By waiving service, a defendant is allowed more time to answer than if the summons had been actually served when the request for waiver of service was received.

CHAPTER 3

VENUE, FORUM SELECTION, AND TRANSFER

by
Gary P. Naftalis
and
Michael S. Oberman*

Table of Sections

* The authors acknowledge with great appreciation the devoted and valuable assistance of our associate Yehudis S. Lewis and our legal assistant Brent Todd in the preparation of this chapter.

WESTLAW Electronic Research

See WESTLAW Electronic Research Guide preceding the Summary of Contents.

---

§ 3.1 Scope Note

This chapter addresses the statutory provisions governing venue for an action together with strategic considerations for the selection of a forum for a commercial case. The principal focus is on the general venue statute as most recently amended. The special venue statutes applicable to particular claims are also discussed. Apart from statutory bases for venue, the chapter addresses the enforceability of forum selection clauses. The chapter concludes with a discussion of litigated contests over venue, including challenges to venue under statute or under the common law doctrine of forum non conveniens; the standards for seeking transfer of an action; and the resolution of races to the courthouse.

Library References:

West's Key No. Digests, Federal Courts ⊂⇒71–157.
Wright, Miller & Cooper, Federal Practice and Procedure: Civil 2d §§ 1825, 3801, 3802.1, 3826, 3828, 3842.

§ 3.2 The Role of the Venue Requirement

The subject of venue is appropriately assigned to Chapter 3 of this treatise. Having determined whether a federal court has subject matter jurisdiction over a claim and, if so, whether it can properly exercise personal jurisdiction over each defendant, plaintiff's counsel should logically next analyze in which district(s) the action may be brought.

The underlying concept of venue is to assure a convenient forum for litigants.[1] The "propriety of the forum is a threshold issue that must be considered before addressing the merits."[2] As presently drawn, the venue statutes provide especially for the convenience of defendants. A plaintiff is not given an express right to select his home court. As stated by the Supreme Court, "the purpose of statutorily specified venue is to protect the *defendant* against the risk that a plaintiff will select an unfair or inconvenient place of trial."[3]

As a corollary to the principle that venue facilitates the convenience of the parties—and especially defendants—parties may consent to a forum that is technically an improper venue under the governing statutes. Consent to a particular forum may be given in at least two ways. First, parties, in advance of litigation, may include in a contract a forum selection clause, which—irrespective of governing statutory provisions—at least initially specifies the locale for suit.[4] Second, a defendant who fails to assert the defense of improper venue in a responsive pleading or motion pursuant to Rule 12(b)(3) will be deemed to have waived that objection.[5] Both of these propositions are subject to the caveat that a party may raise the issue of convenience and seek a transfer at any point in an action;[6] delay in filing a transfer motion, however, will diminish its prospects for success and, as discussed below in Section 3.6, a forum selection clause is hard to overcome.

Because objections to venue may be waived, the failure to satisfy the statutory requirements for venue in a particular action—in the absence of timely objection to improper venue—does not impair the court's power

§ 3.2

1. Neirbo Co. v. Bethlehem Shipbuilding Corp., 308 U.S. 165, 167–68, 60 S.Ct. 153, 154, 84 L.Ed. 167 (1939).

2. Adam v. Jacobs, 950 F.2d 89, 92 (2d Cir.1991).

3. Leroy v. Great W. United Corp., 443 U.S. 173, 183–84, 99 S. Ct. 2710, 2716, 61 L.Ed.2d 464 (1979) (emphasis in original) (decided before the 1990 amendments to the general venue statute; *see also* Cottman Transmission Sys., Inc. v. Martino, 36 F.3d 291, 294 (3d Cir.1994) (holding that current requirement under § 1391(a)(2) that at least "substantial" events or omissions occurred in a district protects defendant against being "haled into a remote district having no real relationship to the dispute").

4. *See infra* § 3.6.

5. FRCP 12(h)(1). By virtue of filing an action, a plaintiff is deemed to have waived any objections to venue. *See infra* § 3.7(e).

6. *See infra* § 3.7(e).

to enter a judgment.[7] The venue requirement is, accordingly, fundamentally distinct from the threshold and unwaivable need for subject matter jurisdiction.[8]

Venue and personal jurisdiction are also distinguishable concepts (although less dramatically different than the comparison of venue to subject matter jurisdiction). Absent consent by a defendant either by prelitigation contract or post-complaint conduct to appear in a given state, the focus of personal jurisdiction is on whether a defendant can be compelled to defend a claim in a particular state consistent with constitutional due process as well as applicable state law.[9] Assuming there is personal jurisdiction, the venue statutes determine the particular district(s) in which an action may be brought. In some instances, the distinction is of limited significance; certain provisions make venue proper in a district in which personal jurisdiction exists over a defendant.[10] Nonetheless, the province of venue remains conceptually distinct from personal jurisdiction in its bedrock principle of convenience since, even where a venue requirement may be satisfied by a showing of personal jurisdiction over the defendant, there remains the possibility of transfer to assure a fair and convenient forum.[11]

Library References:

West's Key No. Digests, Federal Courts ☞71–157.
Wright & Miller, Federal Practice and Procedure: Civil 2d §§ 1061, 1063, 1391.

§ 3.3   Forum Selection—Strategy Considerations

While courts occasionally invoke the phrase "forum shopping" and speak pejoratively of the tactics behind the choice of a particular district,[1] the selection of a forum is a legitimate and fundamental part of the strategy in commencing a suit.[2] The forum for an action will not only affect the convenience of the parties and their counsel but the forum selected might also bear on the governing substantive law, the applicable procedural rules and the psychological "momentum" in an ongoing commercial dispute. For these reasons, the practitioner should evaluate which districts are proper for a contemplated action and then select the

7. 28 U.S.C.A. § 1406(b) (West 1993).

8. *See* Leroy, 443 U.S. at 180, 99 S.Ct. at 2715; *see generally* Chapter 1 "Subject Matter Jurisdiction," *supra.*

9. *See* Chapter 2 "Personal Jurisdiction and Service," *supra.*

10. *See, e.g.,* 28 U.S.C.A. § 1391(a)(3), (c) (West 1993).

11. *See* United States *ex rel.* Thistlethwaite v. Dowty Woodville Polymer, Ltd., 110 F.3d 861, 864 (2d Cir.1997) (distinguishing concepts of subject matter jurisdiction, personal jurisdiction and venue, and observing that venue provisions "assume that the court in question has subject matter jurisdiction, and they simply limit the

locations in which the action may be brought").

§ 3.3

1. *See, e.g.,* Spar, Inc. v. Information Resource, Inc., 956 F.2d 392, 393, 395 (2d Cir.1992) (affirming dismissal, rather than transfer, of action under 28 U.S.C.A. § 1406(a) (West 1993), court declined to permit plaintiff to "forum shop" for a district applying a longer limitations period).

2. *See* Ferens v. John Deere Co., 494 U.S. 516, 527, 110 S.Ct. 1274, 1282, 108 L.Ed.2d 443 (1990) (observing that "a plaintiff already has the option of shopping for a forum with the most favorable law").

one that best advances the client's overall litigation objectives. Nothing in the statutes requires a plaintiff, faced with the option of several proper districts, to select one that favors the adversary; the venue requirements themselves give protection to prospective defendants.[3]

(a) Selection Among Federal Districts

The presence of federal statutes applicable nationally, the existence of a single Judicial Code governing all federal courts, and the adoption of the Federal Rules of Civil Procedure as "the procedure in the United States district courts in all suits of a civil nature"[4] would—in the abstract—suggest that the selection of a particular district is of minor consequence in the adjudication and outcome of an action. Practical realities, however, intercede and the abstraction is not borne out.

In analyzing the available forums, the most significant factor is whether the selection of a particular district will impact the substantive law applied in the action. In preparing a complaint, the practitioner should have determined not only the requisite elements of a claim as set forth in a particular federal statute but also how those elements have been construed by the courts. Differences exist in the construction of statutes by different judges and, most significantly, there are conflicts between the circuits on fundamental issues of law—oftentimes issues that determine whether a motion to dismiss a claim will succeed. Since the Supreme Court does not invariably accept for review and promptly resolve each conflict,[5] the law likely to control upon the filing of a complaint in a given case must be considered. Similarly, in the context of diversity cases consideration should be given to differences in the state law that might be applied and to whether, in a choice of law analysis, the selection of a particular district court might impact the state law ultimately applied.[6]

While less likely to influence the outcome of an action, variations in procedural rules do influence the cost and duration of an action. The pace and progress of discovery vary from district to district not simply due to factors such as caseload but also due to differences in procedural rules. Many districts have exercised the discretion afforded to them to

---

3. *See* Newton v. Thomason, 22 F.3d 1455, 1463–64 (9th Cir.1994) (reversing imposition of sanctions under FRCP 11 for filing in an inconvenient forum, court stated that, absent an improper purpose such as harassment, "[a]ttorneys are not under an affirmative obligation to file an action in the most convenient forum; their only obligation is to file in a proper forum"); *see generally* Note, *Forum Shopping Reconsidered*, 103 Harv. L. Rev. 1677 (1990) (exploring policy arguments underlying criteria of forum shopping together with the ethical and jurisprudential principles supporting forum selection).

4. FRCP 1.

5. *See* Chapter 50 "Appeals to the Supreme Court," *infra*.

6. *See, e.g.*, Manley v. Engram, 755 F.2d 1463, 1471 (11th Cir.1985) (noting "that although venue is largely a principle of litigational convenience, it is inextricably intertwined with choice of law problems and often with the outcome of the case on the merits"); Mission Ins. Co. v. Puritan Fashions Corp., 706 F.2d 599, 602 n. 3 (5th Cir.1983) (discussing possible outcomes if the claims were heard by a California court as opposed to a Texas court).

opt-out of some of the more recent discovery amendments to the Federal Rules of Civil Procedure.[7] Additionally, most districts and many judges have individual rules that influence the way cases are managed.[8] Even if such differences might not drive the selection of a forum, the decision to file in a particular district should not be made oblivious to that district's rules and procedures.

The selection of a forum should include an informal canvass of the factors applied by courts on a transfer motion.[9] Among these factors, the accessibility to witnesses and other evidence and the convenience of the parties, in particular, should be, and most probably are, considered by practitioners. Where permitted under the venue statutes, a client—all other factors being equal—is likely to prefer bringing suit in its home district. This review of the transfer factors will also permit the practitioner to assess whether the plaintiff's choice of venue can likely withstand a motion to transfer.

Sometimes the selection of a forum is influenced by perceptions concerning the juror pool from which fact-finders will be chosen. The location of a district can affect the jury composition, as can a district's rules concerning exemptions from jury service (e.g., exemptions for certain occupations). In cases warranting the assistance of jury consultants, guidance might be sought at the stage of forum selection. The geographic scope and location of a district might also influence a client's decision whether to rely on regularly retained outside counsel or to depend more heavily on local counsel based within the district of suit.

The number of judges in a district can affect the progress of a case in many ways. If a district has vacancies or insufficient authorized judgeships, there is a greater chance of backlog and a diminished chance for close case management. In smaller districts, the identity of the judge might be more easily predicted than in the larger districts with well over a dozen active and senior judges. The manner of assigning cases (i.e., random assignment or some other method) to individual judges and magistrate judges will determine whether there is any room to "judge shop."

The number of variations between districts increases as the anticipated course of a specific litigation is crystallized. For example, some districts, by practice, more readily decide motions for a preliminary injunction on affidavits without evidentiary hearings, whereas in other districts expedited discovery and oral evidence are the norm. Accordingly, the cost and timing (and conceivably likelihood) of injunctive relief can vary district to district. Without attempting to canvass all of the specifics, the general point is simply stated: Deciding which district to select requires an informed analysis.

---

7. See Report of Federal Judicial Center, Implementation of Disclosure in United States District Courts, With Specific Attention to Courts' Responses to Selected Amendments to FRCP 26, March 22, 1996 (update to March 24, 1995 Report).

8. See, e.g., Federal Local Court Rules (2d ed. West 1995); New York State Bar Association, Individual Judges' Rules (2d ed. 1996).

9. See infra § 3.9(a)(1).

(b) Selecting a Federal (Versus State) Forum

Except where Congress has given exclusive jurisdiction over a particular category of claims and assuming that subject matter jurisdiction exists for the particular claim, the practitioner often faces the choice between selecting a federal or state forum. The existence of specialized business courts such as the Commercial Division of the New York State Supreme Court and the Delaware Chancery Court warrants an even closer examination of the available options. Among the factors to be routinely considered would be the respective locations of the federal district court (or divisions of a district) and the alternative state forum; the ease and extent of discovery; the differences in procedural rules (including factors such as the likelihood of ex parte injunctive relief); the availability of interlocutory appeals; the composition of the jury pool; the degree of case backlog; and the sophistication and predictability of decisions governing commercial disputes.[10]

Because Congress has eliminated the plaintiff's residence as an express basis for venue in diversity cases,[11] selecting a state forum might provide the plaintiff's only chance to bring suit close to home and to force an out of state defendant to litigate in the plaintiff's "home court." It is possible that a prospective defendant will have had adequate contacts with the plaintiff's state to support personal jurisdiction over that defendant but there still might not be a basis for laying venue in the plaintiff's home federal district court. In this circumstance, state court might be the best alternative.

There is, to be sure, the chance that the defendant might be able to remove the action from state court to federal court. However, the removed action will go to the federal district in which the state court sits[12]—still giving the plaintiff a forum in its home state. Assuming that there are witnesses and other evidence critical to the case in plaintiff's home district, the defendant might not be able to secure a transfer. In this way, the selection of a state court forum could, at the very least, provide a plaintiff indirectly with its home federal district unavailable to it in a direct filing.

(c) Racing to the Courthouse

Commercial litigation rarely arrives entirely without warning. In the most common situation, a business relationship has deteriorated, and the parties in advance of suit have identified the issues in dispute. In other cases, a party asserting infringement of rights has, as a preliminary step, sent or caused counsel to send a cease and desist letter. Even without prior communications from the other side, a party launching a business activity—such as the release of a new product or the accumulation of stock in a public company—may have anticipated a risk of suit arising from that activity.

---

10. *See generally* Michael S. Oberman, *The Choice of Forum for a Commercial Litigation*, New York State Bar Journal, May/June 1993, at 28.

11. *See infra* § 3.4(b).

12. *See* § 3.5(b)(10) and Chapter 8 "Removal to Federal Court," *infra*.

In any of these or similar scenarios, litigation counsel asked to review the matter should include in their assessment of potential claims an analysis of available forums. Where there are alternative proper venues and where the selection of the forum might affect in a meaningful way either the conduct or outcome of litigation (as described above in Sections 3.3(a), (b)), close attention must be given to the sequence and timing of the commencement of suit(s).

No group of venue cases prompts as much talk of "forum shopping" as do the "race to the courthouse" cases—the cases where parties have filed overlapping actions in different districts. Accepting as a starting premise that these cases involve competing attempts to select the forum for suit, there are nonetheless legitimate strategy considerations to be weighed.

These considerations are necessarily framed by the rules evolved by the courts for resolving the priority of competing actions. As discussed in further detail in Section 3.10, *infra,* as a general rule the first-filed suit has priority unless it is found to be an "improper anticipatory" action (*e.g.,* a declaratory judgment suit seeking a ruling of no infringement brought upon receipt of a specific cease and desist letter charging infringement) or unless the balance of convenience favors a subsequently filed action.[13] The consequences of having to litigate in a particular forum (as described in Section 3.3(a), *supra*) will inform the judgment whether the costs of litigating over the choice of forum can be justified in the specific case.

There are at least three fact patterns that commonly occur. In the first, parties in an on-going business relationship—be it a contract, a joint venture or a loan—have a dispute, with each party asserting potential claims or counterclaims. If a substantial part of the events or omissions giving rise to the dispute occurred in the home districts of each of the parties, there is an opportunity to select the forum and the corresponding risk of losing that selection inherent in how promptly each side acts (subject to transfer for convenience, *see* Sections 3.9 and 3.10, *infra*). Where either party could be the proper plaintiff in its preferred district, the race to the courthouse is of heightened significance. On the other hand, where the events occurred almost exclusively in one party's district, that party—unless it is intent on being the titular plaintiff and unless there is a basis for a state court action in the other side's state—has more latitude to allow events to unfold, since a federal court suit would likely come to its residence (predicated on either subsections (1) or (2) of Sections 1391(a) and (b)).[14]

In a second fact pattern, only one party would ordinarily be the plaintiff (such as the owner of a trademark allegedly being infringed). To assure a selection of the forum, that prospective plaintiff must act with dispatch; while the first-filed rule gives some protection to that party, hesitation by the party asserting the initial claim can permit a successful

---

13. *See infra* § 3.10(b).   **14.** *See infra* § 3.4(c)-(f).

preemptive action by the other side.[15] Cease and desist letters should be specific both in terms of claims asserted and of the litigation that will be brought. If settlement negotiations are initiated, the owner of the trademark, in this example, must promptly file suit following the breakdown of such negotiations.[16] For the other side, a preemptive action might be sustained if that party has independent claims (apart from a mirror image declaratory judgment claim).[17]

In the third fact pattern, an action has been brought, and the defendant in that first-filed action believes that the selected forum is clearly disadvantageous to its position, that it was an unfairly selected forum, and that its own planned suit should have priority. That defendant could, if appropriate, challenge the propriety of venue in the first forum and could often have cause to file a transfer motion. However, that defendant would probably be well advised promptly to file the suit it contemplated in the preferred district. Keeping the competing filings close in time will improve the chances for the defendant in the first-filed action of overcoming the first-filed rule.[18]

Library References:

West's Key No. Digests, Contracts ☞127(4); Federal Courts ☞71–157.

Wright, Miller, Marcus & Cooper, Federal Practice and Procedure: Civil 2d §§ 2003.1, 3801, 3845.

§ 3.4   General Venue Statute

(a) Applicability of the General Venue Statute

The centerpiece of the general venue statutory plan appears in 28 U.S.C.A. § 1391, the general venue statute. Unless there is a special statute on venue for a particular type of claim, the general venue statute applies to actions grounded either on diversity of citizenship or on a federal question. Where a special venue statute is applicable, that statute is technically controlling.[1] However, absent restrictive language in that special statute, the general venue statute may still be relied upon, if needed, to supplement the special statute.[2]

Because the provisions of the general venue statute have been amended and generally broadened over time and after the enactment of many of the special venue statutes, *see* Section 3.5, *infra*, the invocation of the general venue statute in its current form may supply a basis for venue when the requirements of the special statute cannot be met. Indeed, the availability of the amended general venue statute should

---

15. *See infra* § 3.10(c).

16. *See infra* § 3.10(b).

17. *See infra* § 3.10(c).

18. *See id.*

§ 3.4

1. 15 Charles Alan Wright, Arthur R. Miller & Edward H. Cooper, Federal Prac-

tice and Procedure § 3803 n. 2 (2d ed.1984).

2. *See infra* § 3.5(a).

reduce the amount of litigation over the terms of special venue statutes; seeking a ruling on the application of a special statute will have little effect on the action (other than possible delay) if one or more prongs of the current general statute clearly establishes venue. In analyzing the current general venue statute, it should be kept in mind that "Congress does not in general intend to create venue gaps" (*i.e.*, cases for which there is no proper venue) and "in construing venue statutes it is reasonable to prefer the construction that avoids leaving such a gap."[3]

Case law has long held that the general venue statute is not applicable to "local actions"—in general terms, actions in the nature of suits in rem—which must be filed in the district in which the res that is the subject matter of the action is located.[4] However, when the action seeks relief that is personal in nature, such as a contract claim, it will not be treated as a local action even if the contract relates to real property.[5] The phrase "transitory actions" is sometimes used to exclude "local actions" and to define the reach of the general venue statute.

(b) Historical Note

In 1990, Congress rewrote the provisions of the general venue statute,[6] and these provisions (with subsequent technical amendments in 1992 and 1995) currently control venue determinations (except when special statutes are, or must be, invoked). The language now in effect is discussed in Sections 3.4(e)-(i), *infra*. Nonetheless, in addressing this language, the prior law should be briefly recalled. The ways in which Congress expanded and contracted the previously available bases for venue bear on the construction of the current language. Moreover, since so many practitioners grew up on the prior grounds, it is useful to highlight the grounds of venue that no longer apply.

Prior to 1966, if jurisdiction rested only on diversity of citizenship, an action could be brought in the district "where all plaintiffs or all defendants reside."[7] Where a federal question was present, the action could only be brought "where all defendants reside."[8] The disparity between the diversity and federal question provisions, allowing a plaintiff in a diversity action to sue in her own district, dated back to 1887.[9]

---

3. Brunette Mach. Works, Ltd. v. Kockum Indus., Inc. 406 U.S. 706, 710 n. 8, 92 S.Ct. 1936, 1939 n. 8, 32 L.Ed.2d 428 (1972) (decided before the 1990 amendments).

4. 15 Charles Alan Wright, Arthur R. Miller & Edward H. Cooper, Federal Practice and Procedure § 3804, at 28 (2d ed.1986); *id.* § 3822. The definition and scope of local actions is treated in Wright, Miller & Cooper, § 3822.

5. *See* Raphael J. Musicus, Inc. v. Safeway Stores, Inc., 743 F.2d 503, 507 (7th Cir.1984).

6. Judicial Improvements Act of 1990, Pub. L. 101–650, 104 Stat. 5289 (1990); *see*

generally David D. Siegel, *Changes in Federal Jurisdiction and Practice Under the New Judicial Improvements and Access to Justice Act*, 123 F.R.D. 399 (1989).

7. 15 Charles Alan Wright, Arthur R. Miller & Edward H. Cooper, Federal Practice and Procedure §§ 3804, at 30, 3807, at 73–74 (1986).

8. *Id.*

9. *Id.* (and Supp.1997). Between 1887 and 1948, the statutes spoke of individual plaintiffs and defendants; the language specifying "all plaintiffs" and "all defendants" was added in 1948. *Id.* § 3807, at 73–74.

(Under the 1990 amendments to the statute, the residence of the plaintiff(s) was eliminated as a basis for venue even in diversity cases.)[10]

Because the pre–1966 statute conditioned venue on the residence of "all" plaintiffs or defendants, there could be multi-party cases in which venue could not be established.[11] In 1966, Congress added, for both diversity and federal question cases, an alternative ground for venue: the district "in which the claim arose."[12] That provision, as many practitioners will recall, gave rise to a flood of litigation over where a claim arose and over whether a claim could arise in more than one district.[13] Seeking to avoid "the litigation breeding phrase 'in which the claim arose,' "[14] Congress adopted the present standard—the district in which "a substantial part of the events or omissions giving rise to the claim occurred"[15]—in 1990. See Section 3.4(f), infra.

Congress has also added "fallback" venue provisions for both federal question and diversity cases which may be invoked only when neither the residential nor the transactional test establishes venue. The wording of these fallback provisions presents the only remaining difference between the diversity and federal question venue statutes. For diversity cases, venue is proper in a district "in which any defendant is subject to personal jurisdiction."[16] For federal question cases, venue is proper in a district "in which any defendant may be found."[17]

The general venue statute used to contain in Section 1393 a discrete provision addressing the division within a district in which one or more defendants could be sued. That provision was repealed in 1988, eliminating any statutory requirement that an action must be brought in a particular division.[18] Local court rules, however, should be consulted to determine the division or branch of a district in which the action will be heard.

(c) Diversity Cases

Section 1391(a) provides the grounds for venue in an action when

---

10. See infra § 3.4(e). However, in a civil action in which the federal government is the defendant, the residence of the plaintiff remains a basis for venue under § 1391(e) if no real property is an issue in the action. See Seariver Maritime Fin. Holdings, Inc. v. Peña, 952 F.Supp. 455, 457–58 (S.D. Tex.1996).

11. Brunette Mach. Works, Ltd. v. Kockum Indus., Inc., 406 U.S. 706, 710 n. 8, 92 S.Ct. 1936, 1939 n. 8, 32 L.Ed.2d 428 (1972). But see 15 Charles Alan Wright, Arthur R. Miller & Edward H. Cooper, Federal Practice and Procedure § 3806, at 43–44 (1986) (noting the absence of any such reported decisions when venue could not be established).

12. 15 Charles Alan Wright, Arthur R. Miller & Edward H. Cooper, Federal Practice and Procedure § 3806, at 42 (1986).

13. See id. § 3806, at 45–72.

14. H.R. Rep. No. 101–734 (1990), reprinted in 1990 U.S.C.C.A.N. 6860, 6869.

15. 28 U.S.C.A. § 1391 (a)(2), (b)(2) (West Supp.1997). The statute also includes as a basis where "a substantial part of property that is the subject of the action is situated."

16. 28 U.S.C.A. § 1391(a)(2); see infra § 3.4(h).

17. 28 U.S.C.A. § 1391(b)(2); see infra § 3.4(i).

18. Pub. L. 100–702, § 1001, 102 Stat. 4642, 4664 (1988).

the *sole* basis for subject matter jurisdiction is diversity of citizenship.[19] As amended in 1995,[20] that section now reads as follows:

(a) A civil action wherein jurisdiction is founded only on diversity of citizenship may, except as otherwise provided by law, be brought only in (1) a judicial district where any defendant resides, if all defendants reside in the same State, (2) a judicial district in which a substantial part of the events or omissions giving rise to the claim occurred, or a substantial part of property that is the subject of the action is situated, or (3) a judicial district in which any defendant is subject to personal jurisdiction at the time the action is commenced, if there is no district in which the action may otherwise be brought.

Congress has, thus, provided two alternative grounds that may be invoked whenever applicable: 1) that the district is the residence of any defendant (if all defendants reside in the same state), *see* Section 3.4(e), *infra*; or 2) that the district is where a "substantial part of the events or omissions giving rise to the claim" took place (or a "substantial part" of disputed property is located), *see* Sections 3.4(f)-(g), *infra*.[21] If no district is available under either subsection (a)(1) or (a)(2), subsection (a)(3) provides as a fallback that an action may be brought in a district "in which any defendant is subject to personal jurisdiction," *see* Section 3.4(h), *infra*.

(d) Federal Question Cases

Section 1391(b) provides the grounds for venue in an action when subject matter jurisdiction is based in whole or in part on a federal question. That section reads as follows:

(b) A civil action wherein jurisdiction is not founded solely on diversity of citizenship may, except as otherwise provided by law, be brought only in (1) a judicial district where any defendant resides, if all defendants reside in the same State, (2) a judicial district in which a substantial part of the events or omissions giving rise to the claim occurred, or a substantial part of property that is the subject of the action is situated, or (3) a judicial district in which any defendant may be found, if there is no district in which the action may otherwise be brought.

Like Section 1391(a), Section 1391(b) provides two—the same two— alternative grounds that may be invoked whenever applicable: 1) that the district is the residence of any defendant (if all defendants reside in the same state), *see* Section 3.4(e), *infra*; or 2) that the district is where a "substantial part of the events or omissions giving rise to the claim"

---

19. Friedman v. Revenue Management, Inc., 38 F.3d 668, 671 (2d Cir.1994) (when plaintiff alleged claims under both state and federal law, the appropriate venue provision was § 1391(b)).

20. Pub. L. 104–41, § 1, 109 Stat. 293 (1995).

21. *See* Market Transition Facility v. Twena, 941 F.Supp. 462, 464–66 (D.N.J. 1996) (confirming that § 1391(a)(1) and (a)(2) are alternative grounds for venue and rejecting contention that (a)(2) may be invoked only when (a)(1) is inapplicable).

took place (or a "substantial part" of the disputed property is located), *see* Sections 3.4(f)-(g), *infra*. Section 1391(b)(3) also provides a fallback provision if no district is proper under either subsection (b)(1) or (b)(2), but phrased differently from the language in Section 1391(a)(3): a district in which "any defendant may be found," *see* Section 3.4(i), *infra*. (A separate provision, Section 1391(e), governs venue when a defendant is the United States or one of its agencies or employees).

(e) Residence of Defendant Under Sections 1391(a)(1), (b)(1)

Although Congress in the 1990 amendments eliminated the residence of plaintiffs as an express ground for venue in a diversity action,[22] it preserved as a basis for venue in both diversity and federal question actions the residence of "any defendant, if all defendants reside in the same State."[23] The key term in this provision is "residence," a term that had been included and construed in venue statutes from the outset. For individuals and entities other than corporations, case law supplies the definition of the term, *see* Sections 3.4(e)(1), (3), *infra*; for corporations, "residence" is expressly defined for venue purposes in 28 U.S.C.A. § 1391(c), *see* Section 3.4(e)(2), *infra*.

Sections 1391(a)(1) and (b)(1) have a qualification: while the current requirement for venue is the residence of *any* defendant in the district, *all* defendants must reside in the same state. Congress, accordingly, recognized that a state has multiple districts, and provided in Sections 1391(a)(1) and (b)(1) that it is not required that all defendants reside in the same district.[24] Venue cannot be defeated, for example, in the Southern District of New York, sitting in (among other counties) Manhattan, simply because one or more defendants reside in another district in New York. As written, the statute does permit a defendant to be required to appear in a district within its state even if that district is literally in the opposite corner of the state from that defendant's residence. However, all defendants must be residents of at least the same state in which the district selected by the plaintiff is situated.[25]

Under 28 U.S.C.A. § 1391(d), an alien may be sued in any district. As long as personal jurisdiction can be established over the alien, "residence" is not a factor for purposes of venue. In a multi-defendant case, the presence of one or more aliens should not bear on whether all

---

22. *See supra* § 3.4(b).

23. *See* 28 U.S.C.A. § 1391 (a)(1), (b)(1) (West Supp.1997).

24. Sections 1391(a)(1) and (b)(1), however, did not in this particular expand the available forums; Section 1392(a) had already provided that any civil action against defendants residing in different districts of the same state may be brought in any of those districts. Section 1392(a) was subse-

quently repealed as redundant. Pub. L. 104–220, § 1, 110 Stat. 3023 (1996).

25. *See* Gerety v. Sunrise Express, Inc., No. 95 Civ. 2090, 1996 WL 19047, at *2 (S.D.N.Y.1996) (rejecting contention that § 1391(a)(1) may be satisfied when a corporate defendant resided in the Southern District of New York and that corporate defendant also resided in South Carolina, the residence of the individual co-defendant).

defendants live in one state; only the residence of the citizen defendants should determine whether the test of (a)(1) or (b)(1) has been met.[26]

(1) Individuals

"Residence" has been part of the venue statutes since their inception.[27] The general venue statute, however, does not define the term "residence" as it applies to defendants who are natural persons. According to Wright, Miller and Cooper,[28] the weight of authority (including Supreme Court dictum[29]) has treated "residence" as synonymous with "citizenship," as the latter term is used for determining diversity of citizenship.[30] If residence was first added in 1990 as a basis for venue and the term was being approached anew, it could be argued that a person "resides" wherever she maintains a home, be it a primary or second home. Either location should be sufficiently convenient to that defendant. Such an interpretation would expand the available districts for commercial litigations, since many people maintain vacation homes in a district or even in a state different from the location of their legal residence or "domicile." This construction, as noted, is against the weight of authority.

Unlike the test for diversity (citizenship in a particular state), a venue analysis requires focus on a particular district: is the proposed district the legal domicile of any defendant? A person, in this construction, can only reside in one district.[31] Residence is to be determined as of the time the action is commenced.[32]

(2) Corporations

Congress has included in the general venue statute a provision defining the residence of a corporation which is frequently invoked in business litigation. As amended in 1988,[33] Section 1391(c) reads as follows:

(c) For purposes of venue under this chapter, a defendant that is a corporation shall be deemed to reside in any judicial district in

---

26. Moellers N. Am., Inc. v. MSK Covertech, Inc., 870 F.Supp. 187, 193 (W.D.Mich. 1994); 15 Charles Alan Wright, Arthur R. Miller & Edward H. Cooper, Federal Practice and Procedure § 3810, at 95–96 (1986) (interpreting test of where "all defendants" reside prior to 1990 amendment). *But see* Berger Instruments, Inc. v. Northwest Instruments, Inc., No. 96 C 8393, 1997 WL 159377, at *4 (N.D.Ill.1997) (presence of alien precluded use of § 1391(b)(1)).

27. *See supra* § 3.4(b).

28. *See* 15 Charles Alan Wright, Arthur R. Miller & Edward H. Cooper, Federal Practice and Procedure § 3805, at 33–35 (1986). Cited as exceptions to this weight of authority are two circuit court decisions: Arley v. United Pac. Ins. Co., 379 F.2d 183,

185 n. 1 (9th Cir.1967); Townsend v. Bucyrus–Erie Co., 144 F.2d 106, 108 (10th Cir. 1944).

29. Shaw v. Quincy Mining Co. (*Ex Parte* Shaw), 145 U.S. 444, 449, 12 S.Ct. 935, 937, 36 L.Ed. 768 (1892).

30. *See* Chapter 1 "Subject Matter Jurisdiction," *supra.*

31. *See* MacNeil v. Whittemore, 254 F.2d 820 (2d Cir.1958) (venue improper in district of defendant's summer home).

32. 15 Charles Alan Wright, Arthur R. Miller & Edward H. Cooper, Federal Practice and Procedure § 3805, at 40 (1986).

33. Pub. L. 100–702, § 1013, 102 Stat. 4624, 4669 (1988).

which it is subject to personal jurisdiction at the time the action is commenced. In a State which has more than one judicial district and in which a defendant that is a corporation is subject to personal jurisdiction at the time an action is commenced, such corporation shall be deemed to reside in any district in that State within which its contacts would be sufficient to subject it to personal jurisdiction if that district were a separate State, and, if there is no such district, the corporation shall be deemed to reside in the district within which it has the most significant contacts.

This provision unquestionably applies to Sections 1391(a)(1) and (b)(1), which predicate venue on the residence of the defendant. It has also been held that this provision—which begins with the words "For purposes of venue under this chapter"—applies to at least those special venue statutes contained in Chapter 87 of Title 28 (i.e., 28 U.S.C.A. §§ 1391–1413).[34]

Under Section 1391(c), a corporation resides in any district in which, at the time the action is commenced, it is subject to personal jurisdiction. This formulation eliminated an issue that existed under the prior version of this statute: whether the relevant time was the commencement of the action as opposed to the accrual of the claim.[35] The key issue is whether the corporation is subject to personal jurisdiction in the district (assuming that it is subject to personal jurisdiction, and amenable to suit, in the state).

In a single district state, the presence of personal jurisdiction will establish venue over a corporation. In a multi-district state, the court, in contrast, is to analyze the contacts of the defendant corporation within the *district* and determine whether those contacts would establish personal jurisdiction if the district were a separate state. There is growing authority for the principle that, in this analysis, federal (not state) law should apply, requiring only an assessment of constitutional due process.[36] Simply put, under this view the court need only determine

---

34. VE Holding Corp. v. Johnson Gas Appliance Co., 917 F.2d 1574 (Fed.Cir. 1990). Because the definition of corporate residence in § 1391(c) now begins with the phrase "[f]or purposes of venue under this statute," this part of § 1391 arguably does not apply to special venue statutes not in the Judicial Code. The legislative history of the 1988 amendment—recounted in *VE Holding Corp.*, 917 F.2d at 1580–82—does not shed light on the new introductory phrase. As a practical matter, where a special venue statute is found to be supplemented by the general venue statute, § 1391(c) may be invoked in conjunction with § 1391(b)(1). Based on early results, courts are continuing to apply the amended § 1391(c) to special venue statutes outside the Judicial Code to which the predecessor § 1391(c) had been applied. See McCracken

v. Automobile Club, Inc., 891 F.Supp. 559, 561–63 (D.Kan.1995) (analyzing effect of introductory phrase in § 1391(c), observing that courts continue to apply § 1391(c) to supplement special venue statutes, and holding that amended § 1391(c) may be used with ERISA venue provision); Bass v. Energy Transp. Corp., 787 F.Supp. 530, 533 (D.Md.1992) (applying § 1391(c) in Jones Act case).

35. See 15 Charles Alan Wright, Arthur R. Miller & Edward H. Cooper, Federal Practice and Procedure § 3805, at 40 (1986); id. § 3811, at 114.

36. Smehlik v. Athletes & Artists, Inc., 861 F.Supp. 1162, 1169–70 (W.D.N.Y.1994); Bicicletas Windsor, S.A. v. Bicycle Corp. of Am., 783 F.Supp. 781, 786 (S.D.N.Y.1992); Plastic Films, Inc. v. Poly Pak Am., Inc.,

whether the defendant corporation has had "minimum contacts" with the forum and whether that defendant's contacts and connections with the forum "are such that [it] should reasonably anticipate being haled into court there."[37] In districts sitting in states with long-arm statutes that are more restrictive than, and do not reach the outer limits of, constitutional due process, it is unnecessary to determine if the state statute has been satisfied for purposes of determining personal jurisdiction over a defendant corporation in the particular district.[38] Moreover, even if the corporation is not subject to personal jurisdiction in any one district of the state, Section 1391(c) expressly provides that "the corporation shall be deemed to reside in the district within which it has the most significant contacts."

(3) Other Entities

There is no statutory definition for residence of entities other than corporations. The Supreme Court, prior to the 1988 amendments to Section 1391(c) (residence for corporations), had treated the residence of an unincorporated association the same as for a corporation and applied a prong of the then-effective Section 1391(c)—establishing residence wherever the association does business.[39] The current standard of Section 1391(c) has been similarly applied to other entities,[40] making venue proper in a district in which the defendant entity is subject to personal jurisdiction.

(f) Substantial Part of Events or Omissions Under Sections 1391(a)(2), (b)(2)

The new statutory basis for venue added in 1990 as Sections 1391(a)(2) and (b)(2)—the district in which a substantial part of the events or omissions giving rise to the claim occurred—is likely to be of paramount importance in business litigation. With the elimination of the plaintiff's residence as a basis for venue in a diversity case, the availability of the "home court" for a plaintiff will most often turn on whether this new standard can be met.[41] In addition, by their very nature,

---

764 F.Supp. 1238, 1238–40 (W.D.Mich. 1991); Benetton Mfg. Corp. v. Ben–Acadia Ltd., No. Civ. A. 89–1119, 1989 WL 106473 (E.D.La.1989).

37. See Burger King Corp. v. Rudzewicz, 471 U.S. 462, 474, 105 S.Ct. 2174, 2183, 85 L.Ed.2d 528 (1985) (quoting World–Wide Volkswagen Corp. v. Woodson, 444 U.S. 286, 297, 100 S.Ct. 559, 567, 62 L.Ed.2d 490 (1980)); see generally Chapter 2 "Personal Jurisdiction," supra.

38. See Smehlik, 861 F.Supp. at 1169, 1170 n. 7 (holding that § 1391(c) makes no reference to state law and that—once a defendant is subject to personal jurisdiction of the court—venue should be determined by "a simple due process analysis"). Some

courts continue to apply state long-arm statutes to § 1391(c). See, e.g., Micro–Assist, Inc. v. Cherry Communications, Inc., 961 F.Supp. 462 (E.D.N.Y.1997); Rocket Jewelry Box, Inc. v. Noble Gift Packaging, Inc., 869 F.Supp. 152, 155–56 (S.D.N.Y. 1994).

39. Denver & Rio Grande W. R.R. Co. v. Brotherhood of R.R. Trainmen, 387 U.S. 556, 87 S.Ct. 1746, 18 L.Ed.2d 954 (1967).

40. Kingsepp v. Wesleyan Univ., 763 F.Supp. 22, 28 (S.D.N.Y.1991) (college organized as a trust); Graf v. Tastemaker, 907 F.Supp. 1473 (D.Colo.1995) (partnership).

41. Conceivably, the fallback provisions of § 1391(a)(3) and (b)(3) might coincidentally permit a case to be brought in the

business disputes falling within the subject matter jurisdiction of the federal courts frequently have interstate elements, and the "substantial part" test will often make more than one district a proper venue for a particular case.

Courts have, by now, structured the basic principles for this new provision. It is, most importantly, recognized that Congress evinced an "intent that venue may be proper in more than one federal district in a given case."[42] In applying this provision, a court should "no longer ask which district among two or more potential forums is the 'best' venue."[43] Instead, the court should "ask whether the district the plaintiff chose had a substantial connection to the claim, whether or not other forums had greater contacts."[44]

In applying this test, courts do not count deliberate contacts between a defendant and the district.[45] The governing standard requires that a "substantial part of the events or omissions giving rise to the claim" must occur in the district. Thus, the claim should be divided into its essential elements, and the events or omissions supporting these elements should be isolated; in this view, the court must then decide if a "substantial" part of those events or omissions occurred in the chosen forum.[46]

There must be a nexus between what occurred in the district and the requisite elements of the claim asserted.[47] Some courts have conclud-

plaintiff's home district if diversity can still be established or if a federal claim is stated.

42. Sacody Techs., Inc. v. Avant, Inc., 862 F.Supp. 1152, 1157 (S.D.N.Y.1994); *see also* Cottman Transmission Sys., Inc. v. Martino, 36 F.3d 291, 294 (3d Cir.1994) ("The amendment changed preexisting law to the extent that the earlier version had encouraged an approach that a claim could generally arise in only one venue."); Bates v. C & S Adjusters, Inc., 980 F.2d 865, 867 (2d Cir.1992) (new statute disapproved of strong admonition in *Leroy v. Great Western United Corp.*, 443 U.S. 173, 99 S. Ct. 2710, 61 L.Ed.2d 464 (1979) "against recognizing multiple venues").

43. Setco Enters. Corp. v. Robbins, 19 F.3d 1278, 1281 (8th Cir. 1994).

44. *Id.*; *see also* Sheppard v. Jacksonville Marine Supply, Inc., 877 F.Supp. 260, 269 (D.S.C.1995); Vandeveld v. Christoph, 877 F.Supp. 1160, 1166–67 (N.D.Ill.1995); Merchants Nat'l Bank v. SafraBank, 776 F.Supp. 538, 541 (D.Kan.1991); David D. Siegel, Commentary on the 1988 and 1990 Revisions of Section 1391, 28 U.S.C.A. § 1391 (West 1991).

45. *See Bates*, 980 F.2d at 868.

46. *See, e.g.,* State Farm Mut. Auto. Ins. Co. v. Estate of Bussell, 939 F.Supp. 646,

650 (S.D.Ind.1996) (holding that a declaratory judgment claim arising from automobile accident was a tort action under a state guest statute rather than a contract action under an insurance policy, so that venue was proper because accident occurred in the district).

47. *See, e.g.,* Time Prods., plc v. J. Tiras Classic Handbags, Inc., No. 93 Civ. 7856, 1997 WL 139525 (S.D.N.Y.1997) (holding that Southern District of New York was a proper venue, even though a greater proportion of sales of infringing items occurred elsewhere, because the sales in New York were sufficiently substantial to make venue proper in that district); Jordache Enters. Inc. v. Brobeck, Phleger & Harrison, No. 92 Civ. 9002, 1994 WL 74860 (S.D.N.Y.1994) (venue found improper in a malpractice action where plaintiffs failed to show nexus between activities of defendant California law firm conducted in New York and the alleged acts of malpractice); PI, Inc. v. Quality Prods., 907 F.Supp. 752 (S.D.N.Y. 1995) (holding that venue was not established in a contract case where no performance was due in New York and any breach occurred outside of New York); Gruntal & Co. v. Kauachi, No. 92 Civ. 2840, 1993 WL 33345, at *2 (S.D.N.Y.1993) (hold-

ed that "by referring to 'events or omissions giving rise to the claim,' Congress meant to require courts to focus on relevant activities of the defendant, not of the plaintiff."[48] Substantial is, of course, a subjective term, but the Third Circuit has offered a benchmark for approaching it: "Substantiality is intended to preserve the element of fairness so that a defendant is not haled into a remote district having no real relationship to the dispute."[49]

The emerging case law confirms that application of the (a)(2)/(b)(2) basis for venue is fact sensitive and that the plaintiff must establish linkage between what occurred in the district and what is required to establish the claim. For example, in *Bates v. C & S Adjusters, Inc.*,[50] the Second Circuit, reversing the dismissal of a claim brought by a debtor under the Fair Debt Collection Practice Act,[51] held that venue was established in the district in which the plaintiff debtor resided and into which the defendant bill collector's demand for payment was forwarded. Finding that the substantive law reflected congressional concern about the harmful effect of abusive practices on consumers, the court concluded that forwarding dunning letters is an important step in the collection of debts and that receipt of such a letter is a substantial part of the events giving rise to the claim.

In contrast, the Second Circuit affirmed a dismissal of an action for improper venue in *Friedman v. Revenue Management, Inc.*[52] In that action, a shareholder brought an action to obtain dissolution of a New York corporation as well as for damages, inter alia, under RICO. Even though the corporation was organized and actively engaged in business in New York, the acts of impropriety alleged in the complaint and upon which relief was sought occurred in Illinois.[53]

(g) Substantial Part of Property Under Sections 1391(a)(2), (b)(2)

Congress provided for both diversity and federal question cases an alternative branch in Sections 1391(a)(2) and (b)(2): the district in which "a substantial part of property that is the subject of the action is

---

ing venue proper based on telephone calls in which allegedly fraudulent statements were made, where one party to calls was in the district).

48. *See* Woodke v. Dahm, 70 F.3d 983, 985 (8th Cir.1995) (reasoning that, although the revised statute was intended to expand the available forums, the court was "reluctant to impute to Congress an intent to abandon altogether the protection of defendants as a relevant consideration in venue matters"); Seariver Maritime Fin. Holdings, Inc. v. Peña, 952 F.Supp. 455, 460 (S.D.Tex.1996) (following *Woodke*); *see also* Emjayco *ex rel.* Troy v. Morgan Stanley & Co., 901 F.Supp. 1397, 1400–03 (C.D.Ill.

1995) (finding venue improper over a defendant who was not charged with any significant act in the district).

49. Cottman Transmission Sys., Inc. v. Martino, 36 F.3d 291, 294 (3d Cir.1994).

50. 980 F.2d 865 (2d Cir.1992).

51. 15 U.S.C.A. § 1692 (West 1994).

52. 38 F.3d 668 (2d Cir.1994).

53. Venue was not proper in *Friedman* under § 1391(b)(1) because only one of the defendants resided in New York. *See* Friedman v. Revenue Management, Inc., 839 F.Supp. 203, 206 (S.D.N.Y.1993), *aff'd*, 38 F.3d 668 (2d Cir.1994).

situated." This branch does not focus on where actionable conduct occurred; the requirement is met by the location of "tangible, or at least identifiable property" within the district that is in contest.[54] For the ordinary business dispute in which money damages are sought, this provision is apparently inapplicable. Because local actions are not governed by the general venue statutes, see Section 3.4(a), Sections 1391(a)(2) and (b)(2) have limited application—to transitory actions relating to tangible property.

(h) District in which Defendant is Subject to Personal Jurisdiction Under Section 1391(a)(3)

As amended in 1992 and 1995, Section 1391(a)(3) provides a fallback provision in the event there is no district in which a diversity action may be brought under either (a)(1) or (a)(2): "a judicial district in which any defendant is subject to personal jurisdiction at the time the action is commenced."[55]

The scope of this fallback provision is, on its face, broad: it makes venue proper merely because personal jurisdiction can be established. Since no district is proper for suit unless the defendant is subject to, or consents to, personal jurisdiction in the state of the district, this subsection—were it not expressly presented as a fallback—would permit venue to be imposed whenever personal jurisdiction could be obtained in the particular district. The caveat is that the court cannot invoke Section 1391(a)(3) unless it first determines that neither (a)(1) nor (a)(2) is applicable. Thus, a defendant can resist being sued in a particular district in which it is subject to personal jurisdiction if a substantial part of the alleged events or omissions giving rise to the claim took place in a different district.

In commercial cases, the use of Section 1391(a)(3) may be limited. Where the defendant is a U.S.-based corporation, it is deemed under Section 1391(c) to reside in any district in which it is subject to personal jurisdiction. Accordingly, venue against a corporation subject to personal jurisdiction in a district will be based on Section 1391(a)(1). Where the claim is against a foreign individual or corporation, venue is proper in any district under Section 1391(d). Section 1391(a)(3) "is meant to cover the cases in which no substantial part of the events happened in the United States and in which all the defendants do not reside in the same state."[56]

---

54. David D. Siegel, *Changes in Federal Jurisdiction and Practice Under the New Judicial Improvements and Access to Justice Act*, 123 F.R.D. 399 (1989).

55. In 1992, Congress limited the availability of § 1391(a)(3) (as it had already done with respect to § 1391(b)(3) in the 1990 amendments) to those actions, in which but for this provision, there would be no district where the action could be brought. Pub. L. 102–572, Title V, § 504,

106 Stat. 4513 (1992). In 1995, Congress inserted the phrase "any defendant" in place of "defendants," in the plural, making this provision now applicable to the district in which any defendant (as opposed to all defendants) is subject to personal jurisdiction. Pub. L. 104–34, § 1, 109 Stat. 293 (1995).

56. H.R. Rep. No. 101–734 (1990), *reprinted in* 1990 U.S.C.C.A.N. 6869.

Because Section 1391(a)(3) is drafted in terms of individual districts, in a multi-district state venue cannot be established merely because the defendant is amenable to personal jurisdiction in the state in which the district is located. The court must undertake an analysis to determine whether the defendant is subject to personal jurisdiction not only in the state but in the particular district. However, as most recently amended, Section 1391(a)(3) permits venue if one of several defendants is subject to personal jurisdiction in that district and the other defendants are subject to personal jurisdiction in the state. Venue can be established under this sub-section if the defendant was merely served with the summons while physically present in the district.[57] Indeed, even if the defendant is served outside of the district in the same state, venue would be proper since the statute requires only that the defendant is "subject" to jurisdiction in the district.[58] In applying this section, courts have typically relied on state law on personal jurisdiction even though a constitutional due process analysis might suffice.[59]

(i) District in which Any Defendant May Be Found Under Section 1391(b)(3)

For cases not premised exclusively on diversity of citizenship, Section 1391(b)(3) contains as a fallback provision, where venue cannot be established under either (b)(1) or (b)(2), the district in which "any defendant may be found." This phrasing differs from the fallback provision in (a)(3), see Section 3.4(h), supra: whereas for diversity cases the standard is a district "in which any defendant is subject to personal jurisdiction," for federal question cases the standard is the district "in which any defendant may be found." In either case, personal jurisdiction in the state is a prerequisite before the venue analysis is even reached.

---

57. See Burnham v. Superior Court, 495 U.S. 604, 110 S.Ct. 2105, 109 L.Ed.2d 631 (1990) (confirming the constitutionality of jurisdiction based on mere physical presence).

58. See David D. Siegel, Commentary, 28 U.S.C.A. § 1391, at 11 (West 1993).

59. See, e.g., Dunham v. Hotelera Canco S.A., 933 F.Supp. 543, 551 (E.D.Va.1996) (applying Virginia law); Sagmel Inc. v. Firebird Int'l, Inc., No. 93 C 10, 1993 WL 106034 (N.D.Ill.1993) (applying Illinois law); American Motorists Ins. Co. v. Springs Indus., Inc., No. 91 Civ. 2260, 1991 WL 155777 (S.D.N.Y.1991) (applying New York law). However, a number of courts have held that federal law—that is, constitutional minimum contacts—should control determinations of personal jurisdiction for corporations under Section 1391(c). See supra § 3.4(e)(2). Cf. Securities Training Corp. v. Securities Seminar, Inc., 633 F.Supp. 938, 941 n. 5 (S.D.N.Y.1986) (under copyright venue statute, 28 U.S.C.A. § 1400(a) (West 1993), "found" means subject to process under minimum contacts analysis). The reasoning of these cases is applicable to an analysis of the requirements of § 1391(a)(3)—that is, if the court has already determined that there is personal jurisdiction over a defendant in the state, the requirement for venue in a particular district within the state under § 1391(a)(3) should be satisfied by a constitutional minimum contacts analysis. In some cases, the court will determine that it has personal jurisdiction over a defendant and simply carry that determination over to find venue. See, e.g., General Latex & Chem. Corp. v. Phoenix Med. Tech., Inc., 765 F.Supp. 1246 (W.D.N.C.1991) (decided before 1992 amendment to § 1391 (a)(3)). If needed, a state long-arm statute may be invoked through FRCP 4(e) to provide a basis for accomplishing personal jurisdiction through service of process outside the state.

Professor Siegel finds some (but not unequivocal) support in the legislative history for the proposition that Congress intended the word "found" to be equivalent to being "subject to personal jurisdiction."[60] At the least, personal service of the summons within the district should establish that the defendant was "found" there—which would also establish personal jurisdiction within the district.[61] Case law has not yet established whether these two fallback provisions should be identically construed, although guidance for the term "found" might be drawn from its appearance in certain of the special venue statutes.[62] Cases interpreting the word "found" in other venue statutes are not, however, uniform on the question whether it is enough that the defendant be subject to personal jurisdiction in the district.[63]

Library References:

West's Key No. Digests, Federal Courts ☞71–157.
Wright, Miller & Cooper, Federal Practice and Procedure: Civil 2d §§ 3802.1, 3803–3806, 3811.

§ 3.5   Special Venue Statutes

(a) Applicability of Special Venue Statutes

Many commercial litigations rest exclusively on state law claims, such as breach of contract or tortious conduct, and can be brought in federal court only on the basis of diversity jurisdiction. For this group of cases, Section 1391(a) is (with limited exceptions) the sole statutory provision for venue.[1] Where an action contains one or more claims based on a federal statute, venue might be based on Section 1391(b) of the general venue statute *and/or* a special venue statute.

Special venue statutes appear in both the Judicial Code[2] and throughout substantive statutes of the United States Code—literally in the dozens.[3] The pivotal issue for the practitioner at this time is whether an applicable special statute is the exclusive statutory basis of venue for a particular claim. If the special statute is not expressly restrictive, the

---

60. *See* Siegel, Commentary, 28 U.S.C.A. § 1391, at 13–15.

61. *Id.* at 15.

62. *See infra* § 3.5(b)(2), (4), (5), (9) and (11).

63. *See* 15 Charles Alan Wright, Arthur R. Miller & Edward H. Cooper, Federal Practice and Procedure § 3802.1 (Supp. 1997). The word "found" has been equated to personal jurisdiction under the copyright and ERISA statutes. *See infra* § 3.5(b)(4) and (9).

§ 3.5

1. *See supra* § 3.4(c). Among the limited exceptions, claims against aliens may be

brought in any district under § 1391(d) and stockholder derivative actions may be brought in any district "where the corporation might have sued the same defendants." 28 U.S.C.A. § 1401 (West 1993).

2. 28 U.S.C.A. §§ 1400, 1401, 1402, 1403, 1407, 1408, 1409, 1410, 1413 and 1414 (West 1993).

3. *See* 15 Charles Alan Wright, Arthur R. Miller & Edward H. Cooper, Federal Practice and Procedure § 3825 (1986) (collecting the "tremendous proliferation" of provisions); 17 James Wm. Moore, Moore's Federal Practice § 110.60 (3d ed.1997) (table of special venue statutes).

general venue statute may be used to supplement the special statute and—as a practical matter—may permit suit in the forum in which plaintiff would prefer to sue.[4] Congress enacted virtually all of these special statutes prior to the most recent amendments of the general venue statute. While the special statutes were historically viewed as providing broader grounds for venue than appeared in the general venue statute, the general venue statute as most recently amended provides as many—and occasionally more—proper forums than do some of the special statutes.

For many commercial cases, venue can be based on Section 1391(b)(2)—a district where a substantial part of the events or omissions occurred[5]—without extended focus on the jurisprudence of a special statute. A plaintiff might, however, want to invoke one of the special statutes which allow venue in a district where a defendant "may be found"[6] in a case where Section 1391(b)(3) cannot be the basis for venue. Section 1391(b)(3) now does permit suit to be brought in a district in which "any defendant may be found," but Section 1391(b)(3) is a fallback provision, available only if neither Section 1391(b)(1) nor (b)(2) establishes a proper venue. Thus, a special statute allowing suit where the "defendant may be found" adds flexibility if the "may be found" test permits suit in what is seen as a favorable district *and* there are other proper forums under Sections 1391(b)(1) or (2) (thereby negating the fallback provision of Section 1391(b)(3) for that case). Conversely, Section 1391(b)(3) would suffice without resort to a special venue statute in cases when both 1391(b)(1) and (b)(2) are inapplicable.

When an action includes multiple claims, venue must be proper as to each claim.[7] If some, but not all, claims fit within the requirements of a special venue provision, the general venue statute may be invoked to draw in those claims not covered by the special statute. Alternatively, courts have recognized the concept of pendent venue, permitting a court where venue is proper under some claims under a special venue statute to retain other claims having a common nucleus of operative fact.[8]

---

4. *See, e.g.,* Pure Oil Co. v. Suarez, 384 U.S. 202, 86 S.Ct. 1394, 16 L.Ed.2d 474 (1966) (general venue statute can be invoked in addition to special statute for Jones Act claim); Go–Video, Inc. v. Akai Elec. Co., 885 F.2d 1406, 1409 (9th Cir. 1989) (noting that, "as a general matter, courts have interpreted special venue provisions to supplement, rather than preempt, general venue statutes"); Delong Equip. Co. v. Washington Mills Abrasive Co., 840 F.2d 843, 855 (11th Cir.1988) (holding that in antitrust action venue may be established under either special or general statute); Magic Toyota, Inc. v. Southeast Toyota Distribs., Inc., 784 F.Supp. 306, 319 (D.S.C. 1992) (holding that RICO venue provision is supplemental to § 1391); Merchants Nat'l

Bank v. Safrabank, 776 F.Supp. 538, 541 (D.Kan.1991) ("Having concluded that venue is proper here under the general venue statute, we need not consider the defendants' other arguments concerning the propriety of venue under the special venue provisions of RICO and the Securities Exchange Act of 1934."); Shuman v. Computer Assocs., Inc., 762 F.Supp. 114, 116 (E.D.Pa.1991) (holding that RICO venue provision is supplemental to § 1391).

5. *See supra* § 3.4(f).

6. *See, e.g., infra* § 3.5(b)(2).

7. *See infra* § 3.7(d).

8. *See* Rodriguez v. Chandler, 641 F.Supp. 1292 (S.D.N.Y.1986), *aff'd mem.,* 841 F.2d 1117 (2d Cir.1988).

Section 3.5(b), *infra*, briefly states the scope of certain special venue statutes relevant to commercial litigation. Some of the special venue statutes are also discussed in the substantive law chapters of this publication to which the statutes relate.

(b) Particular Claims

(1) Admiralty

Admiralty actions can only be brought under special venue rules and not under the general venue statute.[9] An in rem action may be brought in any district in which the ship can be attached.[10] An in personam action may be brought wherever the ship is or, if not within any district, in any district in which service can be made on the defendant.[11] Although the general venue statute is inapplicable in admiralty actions, the transfer provisions under Section 1404(a) may be invoked.[12]

(2) Antitrust

Venue in an antitrust action is proper in any district "in which the defendant resides or is found or has an agent.... "[13] For a corporate defendant, venue lies not only in the judicial "district in whereof it is an inhabitant," but also "in any district where it may be found or transacts business."[14] Those provisions were enacted as part of the Clayton Act in 1914, at a point when the general venue statute was far narrower in scope than it is now.[15] The 1988 amendment to Section 1391(c), making venue under Section 1391(b)(1) proper over a corporation in any district where it is subject to personal jurisdiction, minimizes the need to revisit the decades of case law applying the special antitrust venue provisions to corporations.

(3) Arbitration

The Federal Arbitration Act contains three separate venue provisions, each of which establishes venue in the district in which the award was made.[16] There is a split of authority among the federal circuits, however, as to whether these provisions are mandatory or permissive. Specifically, some circuits interpret these provisions as limiting venue in actions confirming, vacating, modifying or correcting arbitration awards to the district in which the award was made. By contrast, other circuits

9. *See In re* McDonnell–Douglas Corp., 647 F.2d 515, 516 (5th Cir. Unit A May 1981).

10. *See* The Lydia, 1 F.2d 18 (2d Cir. 1924).

11. *See* Gipromer v. SS Tempo, 487 F.Supp. 631 (S.D.N.Y.1980); Chapter 56 "Admiralty," *infra*.

12. Continental Grain Co. v. Barge FBL–585, 364 U.S. 19, 80 S.Ct. 1470, 4 L.Ed.2d 1540 (1960).

13. 15 U.S.C.A. § 15 (West 1997).

14. 15 U.S.C.A. § 22 (West 1997).

15. *See* 15 Charles Alan Wright, Arthur R. Miller & Edward H. Cooper, Federal Practice and Procedure § 3818, at 173–74 (1986); Chapter 53 "Antitrust," *infra*.

16. 9 U.S.C.A. §§ 9, for confirmation, 10, for vacation, and 11, for correction or modification, of arbitration awards (West 1970). *See* Chapter 42 "Alternative Dispute Resolution," *infra*.

permit such actions to proceed in any federal district court which has jurisdiction over the action and parties.[17]

(4) Copyrights and Patents (But Not Trademarks)

Venue under the Copyright Act is proper in any district where the defendant or his agent resides or may be found.[18] This requirement is met wherever service of process may be made.[19]

Patent infringement actions may be brought in any district in which the defendant resides, or where the defendant has committed infringement and has a regular and established place of business.[20] It is now established that Section 1391(c) can be invoked for showing corporate residence in a patent infringement action.[21] "[R]egular and established place of business" means more than merely doing business; it means a permanent physical location under the defendant's control in the district.[22] Other than infringement actions, patent claims are governed by Section 1391, which can also supplement the special patent statute for infringement claims.[23]

Declaratory judgment actions seeking a determination that there has been no copyright or patent infringement are governed by the general venue statute.[24] In addition, there is no special venue statute for trademark cases.[25]

(5) Derivative Actions

A derivative action may be brought "in any judicial district where the corporation might have sued the same defendants."[26]

17. For a recent survey of cases discussing this issue, see Hubbard v. Prudential Sec. Inc. (In re VMS Sec. Litig.), 21 F.3d 139 (7th Cir.1994); Dombrowski v. Swiftships, Inc., 864 F.Supp. 1242 (S.D. Fla. 1994).

18. 28 U.S.C.A. § 1400(a) (West 1993). See Chapter 65 "Copyright," infra.

19. Columbia Pictures Television v. Krypton Broadcasting, Inc., 106 F.3d 284, 289 (9th Cir.1997) (venue is proper in "any judicial district in which the defendant would be amenable to personal jurisdiction if the district were a separate state"), cert. granted on other questions, ___ U.S. ___, 118 S.Ct. 30, 138 L.Ed.2d 1059 (1997).

20. 28 U.S.C.A. § 1400(b) (West 1993). See Chapter 63 "Patents," infra.

21. See VE Holding Corp. v. Johnson Gas Appliance Co., 917 F.2d 1574, 1578 (Fed.Cir.1990); Rocket Jewelry Box, Inc. v. Noble Gift Packaging, Inc., 869 F.Supp. 152, 155 (S.D.N.Y.1994).

22. See Kinetic Instruments, Inc. v. Lares, 802 F.Supp. 976, 986–87 (S.D.N.Y. 1992); Johnson v. IVAC Corp., 681 F.Supp. 959, 964 (D. Mass. 1987); Lex Tex Ltd. v.

Aileen, Inc., 326 F.Supp. 485, 487 (S.D.Fla. 1971).

23. See United States Aluminum Corp. v. Kawneer Co., 694 F.2d 193, 195 (9th Cir.1982) (stating that "[v]enue in a declaratory judgment action for patent noninfringement and invalidity is governed by the general venue statute and not the special patent infringement venue statute") (citations omitted); Emerson Elec. Co. v. Black & Decker Mfg. Co., 606 F.2d 234, 238 (8th Cir.1979) (same); Barber–Greene Co. v. Blaw–Knox Co., 239 F.2d 774, 776 (6th Cir.1957) (same).

24. See United States Aluminum Corp., 694 F.2d at 195 (patent case); see also Modern Computer Corp. v. Ma, 862 F.Supp. 938, 946–47 (E.D.N.Y.1994) (copyright case).

25. Woodke v. Dahm, 70 F.3d 983, 985 (8th Cir.1995). See Chapter 64 "Trademarks," infra.

26. 28 U.S.C.A. § 1401 (West 1995). See Chapter 16 "Derivative Actions by Stockholders," infra.

(6) Employment Discrimination

Venue for Title VII actions is proper in any district in which the defendant can be found and where the challenged employment practice was committed, where the relevant records are maintained or where the plaintiff would have been employed but for the discrimination.[27] In the alternative, an action may be brought in the district of defendant's principal office.[28] This special statute is one of the few recently to be held as preemptive and exclusive of the general venue statute.[29] Transfer may, nevertheless, be sought under 28 U.S.C.A. § 1404(a).[30]

(7) ERISA

Venue for claims under the Employee Retirement Income Security Act of 1974 may be brought in the district where the pension plan is administered, where the breach of trust took place, or where the defendant resides or may be found.[31] The word "found" has been interpreted liberally to extend not only to the district in which a defendant administers a plan but to any forum in which the defendant is subject to personal jurisdiction under a minimum contacts test.[32]

(8) Interpleader

An interpleader claim may be brought in any district in which one claimant resides.[33]

(9) RICO

Venue is proper under the Racketeer Influenced and Corrupt Organizations Act in any district in which a defendant "resides, is found, has an agent, or transacts his affairs."[34] For a corporation, venue lies in a district in which it is present there, by its officers and agents carrying on its business.[35] The phrase "transacts his affairs" has been construed as requiring that the defendant "regularly transacts business of a substantial and continuous character within the district."[36]

---

27. *See* 42 U.S.C.A. § 2000e–5(f)(3) (West 1995).

28. *Id.*

29. *See* Johnson v. Payless Drug Stores N.W., Inc., 950 F.2d 586, 587–88 (9th Cir. 1992); Garus v. Rose Acre Farms, Inc., 839 F.Supp. 563, 566 (N.D.Ind.1993). Title VII provides: "The provisions of Section 2000e–5(f) through (k) of this title, as applicable, shall govern civil actions brought hereunder.... " 42 U.S.C.A. § 2000e–16(d) (West 1995). *See* Chapter 67 "Employment Discrimination," *infra.*

30. *See* Archuleta v. Sullivan, 725 F.Supp. 602 (D.D.C.1989).

31. 29 U.S.C.A. § 1132(e)(2) (West 1992). For claims relating to withdrawal liability, see 29 U.S.C.A. § 1451(d) (West 1992).

32. *See* Varsic v. United States Dist. Ct., 607 F.2d 245, 248 (9th Cir. 1979); Seitz v. Board of Trustees of the Pension Plan of the N.Y. State Teamsters Conference Pension & Retirement Fund, 953 F.Supp. 100, 102 (S.D.N.Y.1997); Chapter 68 "ERISA," *infra.*

33. 28 U.S.C.A. § 1397 (West 1993). *See* Chapter 14 "Parties," *infra.*

34. 18 U.S.C.A. § 1965(a) (West Supp. 1997). *See* Chapter 69 "RICO," *infra.*

35. *See* Van Schaick v. Church of Scientology, 535 F.Supp. 1125, 1133 (D.Mass. 1982).

36. Magic Toyota, Inc. v. Southeast Toyota Distribs., Inc., 784 F.Supp. 306, 319 (D.S.C.1992).

(10) Removed Actions

Removed actions can only be filed in the district in which the state court action had been pending, subject to a motion to transfer under Section 1404(a).[37]

(11) Securities

Under the Securities Exchange Act of 1934, a claim may be brought in any district in which any act or transaction constituting the securities law violation occurred or the defendant may be found, is an inhabitant or transacts business.[38] Under the Securities Act of 1933, venue is proper in any district "where the offer or sale took place, if the defendant participated therein" or where the defendant may be found, is an inhabitant or transacts business.[39] If an action is brought under more than one securities law statute, venue is proper if the requirements of any of these statutes are met.[40] The co-conspiracy theory of venue—permitting venue over one defendant based on the conduct of an alleged co-conspirator in the district—appears to remain valid in applying the securities laws.[41]

Library References:

West's Key No. Digests, Federal Courts ⊜71–157.
Wright, Miller & Cooper, Federal Practice and Procedure: Civil 2d §§ 3817–3819, 3823–3825.

§ 3.6 Forum Selection Clauses

(a) General Principles

Commercial litigation often springs from a contractual relationship, and the underlying contract can strongly affect—if not determine—the location and forum for adjudication of any dispute under the contract. Arbitration clauses are discussed in Chapter 9, "Arbitration vs. Litigation: Enforceability and Access to Courts," *infra*. This subsection addresses contract clauses that select, or confirm submission to, a specific judicial forum for litigation, most typically by providing for a particular locale and sometimes for a particular court in that locale.

The Supreme Court has, in two cases, calibrated the force of forum selection clauses in the determination of federal venue. In the 1972 case

37. 28 U.S.C.A. § 1441(a) (West 1994). *See* Chapter 8 "Removal to Federal Court," *infra*.

38. 15 U.S.C.A. § 78aa (West 1997).

39. 15 U.S.C.A. § 77v(a) (West 1997). *See* Chapter 54 "Securities," *infra*.

40. SEC v. National Student Mktg., 360 F.Supp. 284, 291 (D.D.C.1973).

41. *See* Securities Investor Protection Corp. v. Vigman, 764 F.2d 1309, 1317 (9th Cir.1985). This theory has been broadly re-jected in other types of cases and is not valid under the general venue statute. *See* Emjayco *ex rel.* Troy v. Morgan Stanley & Co., 901 F.Supp. 1397, 1401 (C.D.Ill.1995); *see also* Jarmuth v. Turetsky, 815 F.Supp. 4, 6 (D.D.C.1993) ("There is substantial authority for the view that there is no conspiratorial theory of venue in civil cases other than those involving violations of the securities acts.").

of *M/S Bremen v. Zapata Off–Shore Co.,*[1] the Court adopted the so-called modern view on forum selection clauses,[2] holding that a "forum [selection] clause should control absent a strong showing that it should be set aside."[3] To overcome the clause, the resisting party must "clearly show that enforcement would be unreasonable and unjust, or that the clause was invalid for such reasons as fraud or overreaching."[4] At least where the inconvenience of litigating in the contract forum was foreseeable, the Court concluded:

> [I]t should be incumbent on the party seeking to escape his contract to show that trial in the contractual forum will be so gravely difficult and inconvenient that he will for all practical purposes be deprived of his day in court. Absent that, there is no basis for concluding that it would be unfair, unjust, or unreasonable to hold that party to his bargain.[5]

While *M/S Bremen* was an admiralty case, its principles have been applied generally in federal court cases, including diversity cases.[6]

Despite this broad acceptance of the "bargain" of the parties as to choice of venue,[7] the Supreme Court subsequently held in *Stewart Organization, Inc. v. Ricoh Corp.*[8] that a forum selection clause is not dispositive of a transfer motion under 28 U.S.C.A. § 1404(a).[9] While the presence of such a clause will be a "significant factor that figures centrally in the district court's calculus" of case-specific transfer factors,[10] the Court added:

> Section 1404(a) directs a district court to take account of factors other than those that bear solely on the parties' private ordering of their affairs. The district court also must weigh in the balance the convenience of the witnesses and those public-interest factors of systemic integrity and fairness that, in addition to private concerns, come under the heading of "the interest of justice."[11]

Thus, inclusion of a clause specifying a particular locale and permitting or providing for a federal court forum in that locale may not be an

---

§ 3.6

1. 407 U.S. 1, 92 S.Ct. 1907, 32 L.Ed.2d 513 (1972).

2. Prior to *M/S Bremen*, it was the traditional view of many American courts that clauses designed to oust the jurisdiction of courts in advance of any dispute were contrary to public policy. 407 U.S. at 6, 9, 92 S.Ct. at 1911–12.

3. *Id.* at 15, 92 S.Ct. at 1916.

4. *Id. See also* Carnival Cruise Lines, Inc. v. Shute, 499 U.S. 585, 111 S.Ct. 1522, 113 L.Ed.2d 622 (1991) (enforcing forum selection clause contained in form passage contracts of cruise line).

5. M/S Bremen, 407 U.S. at 18, 92 S.Ct. at 1917.

6. *See* Stewart Org., Inc. v. Ricoh Corp., 487 U.S. 22, 108 S.Ct. 2239 (1988) (§ 1404(a), and not state laws, controls effect of forum selection clause on a transfer motion in a diversity action).

7. *See M/S Bremen*, 407 U.S. at 18, 92 S.Ct. at 1917.

8. 487 U.S. at 22, 108 S.Ct. at 2239.

9. *Id.* at 31, 108 S.Ct. at 2245.

10. *Id.* at 29, 108 S.Ct. at 2244. Justice Kennedy, concurring, stated that, under § 1404(a), a valid forum selection clause is to be "given controlling weight in all but the most exceptional cases." *Id.* at 33, 108 S.Ct. at 2246. For discussion of the transfer factors, *see infra* § 3.9(a)(1).

11. *Id.* at 30, 108 S.Ct. at 2244.

unmovable anchor for the suit.[12]

Forum selection clauses are, of course, simply contract provisions, subject to rules for construing contracts.[13] The intent of the parties, as reflected in the language employed, is what is being enforced.[14] The wording of the forum selection clause can, and should, affect its scope (*e.g.*, whether it applies to only contract claims) and force (*e.g.*, whether it mandates only one forum). Courts frequently distinguish two types of forum selection clauses: mandatory and permissive. Mandatory clauses designate a particular locale and/or forum to the exclusion of all others; the parties provide, for example, that any claim "shall be brought" in a particular forum or that a particular forum shall be the "exclusive" venue.[15] The clause in *M/S Bremen* was—as the Supreme Court noted— "mandatory and all-encompassing."[16]

Permissive clauses, in contrast, contain a consent to suit in one or more forums; the parties agree to submit to suit in identified forums without excluding otherwise permissible forums.[17] Where parties intend-

12. *See* Red Bull Assocs. v. Best Western Int'l, Inc., 862 F.2d 963, 966–67 (2d Cir.1988) (refusal to transfer to contractual forum was not an abuse of discretion where § 1404(a) analysis pointed to another district).

13. Vasilopoulos v. International Interchange Corp., No. 85 Civ. 9078, 1986 WL 14911, at *2–3 (S.D.N.Y.1986). *See generally* Chapter 57 "Contracts," *infra.*

14. *See* Terra Int'l, Inc. v. Mississippi Chem. Corp., 119 F.3d 688, 692 (8th Cir. 1997) (holding that the phrase "[a]ny dispute or disputes arising between the parties hereunder" was ambiguous as to the application of the forum selection clause to non-contract claims and then following the test in *Lambert v. Kysar*, 983 F.2d 1110, 1121– 22 (1st Cir.1993) that "contract-related tort claims involving the same operative facts as a parallel claim for breach of contract should be heard in the forum selected by the contracting parties"); Manetti–Farrow, Inc. v. Gucci, Am., Inc., 858 F.2d 509, 514 (9th Cir.1988) ("[W]hether a forum selection clause applies to tort claims depends on whether resolution of the claims relates to interpretation of the contract."); S–Fer Int'l, Inc. v. Paladion Partners, Ltd., 906 F.Supp. 211 (S.D.N.Y.1995) (holding that clause covered contract, but not tort, claims); Picken v. Minuteman Press Int'l, Inc., 854 F.Supp. 909, 911 (N.D.Ga.1993) (construing clause to cover any claim arising as a result of contract relationship).

15. *See, e.g.,* Falconwood Fin. Corp. v. Griffin, 838 F.Supp. 836, 838 n. 1 (S.D.N.Y. 1993) ("The parties hereby agree that the exclusive venue for suit with respect to this

Agreement shall be the courts of the State of New York or the federal courts of the Southern District of New York...."); ASM Communications Inc. v. Allen, 656 F.Supp. 838, 839 (S.D.N.Y.1987) ("[J]urisdiction and venue shall be in the state courts located in the City and County of San Francisco, State of California, and in the case of federal jurisdiction, in the Northern District of the State of California." Court finds that the "word 'shall' signifies a command. The word 'may' is permissive."). In *John Boutari & Son, Wines & Spirits, S.A. v. Attiki Importers & Distributors Inc.*, 22 F.3d 51, 52–53 (2d Cir.1994), the Second Circuit stated (citations omitted): "[W]hen only jurisdiction is specified the clause will generally not be enforced without some further language indicating the parties' intent to make jurisdiction exclusive. Of course if mandatory venue language is employed, the clause will be enforced." *See also* Excell, Inc. v. Sterling Boiler & Mechanical, Inc. 106 F.3d 318, 321 (10th Cir.1997) (holding that clause reading "venue shall lie in the County of El Paso, Colorado" was a mandatory clause, because it referred to a specific county and not to a specific federal district).

16. M/S Bremen v. Zapata Off–Shore Co., 407 U.S. 1, 20, 92 S.Ct. 1907, 1918, 32 L.Ed.2d 513 (1972). The clause in *M/S Bremen* stated: "Any dispute arising must be treated before the London Court of Justice." *Id.* at 2, 92 S. Ct. at 1909.

17. *See, e.g.,* Riviera Fin., Inc. v. Trucking Servs., Inc., 904 F.Supp. 837, 839 (N.D.Ill.1995) (consent to the "nonexclusive jurisdiction" of courts in Illinois means that

ed only a permissive forum selection clause, the effect of that clause is diminished: the clause constitutes a consent but not a limitation.[18]

The impact of a forum selection clause under *M/S Bremen* is most pronounced when the parties, in a mandatory clause, agree exclusively on a particular state court forum or on a foreign forum. In this situation, the gloss of *Stewart* is inapplicable for no transfer motion is available.[19] Instead, the federal court action is subject to dismissal (or, if a removed action, remand).[20]

In contrast, the distinction between mandatory and permissive clauses has less impact on a transfer motion. The clause in *Stewart* was a mandatory one.[21] The Court in that case did not address the distinction between mandatory and permissive clauses; instead, the issue before the Court was whether, in a diversity case, Section 1404(a) controlled over state law disfavoring forum selection clauses. In that context, the Court ruled that, under Section 1404(c), a forum selection clause was not dispositive, although it was to be weighed in the analysis.

The lower courts have, in this weighing of the transfer factors, treated the signing of a valid forum selection clause as a waiver of the right to invoke inconvenience to the party opposing the forum selection clause as a factor in support of transfer.[22] Bound by the Supreme Court's admonitions that a forum selection clause is not dispositive but is a significant factor, lower courts appear to give substantial consideration to the presence of a forum selection clause in determining venue among possible federal districts and only rarely decline to enforce a mandatory clause.[23] If the transfer factors are inconclusive, the forum selection

"courts other than those in Illinois may also have 'nonexclusive' jurisdiction"); Vasilopoulos, 1986 WL 14911, at *2 ("Where the language of the forum selection clause is permissive, the parties have consented to jurisdiction in that forum but have not waived their right to bring an action in another forum that has jurisdiction...."); see also SBKC Serv. Corp. v. 1111 Prospect Partners, L.P., 105 F.3d 578, 581–83 (10th Cir.1997) (holding that removal of action to federal court was not barred by clause reading: an action "may be maintained in the State of Kansas and the County of Wyandotte"; court declined to "indulge in a distinction between mandatory and permissive venue selection clauses" and stated that phrase "forum selection clauses" should be used only where an exclusive forum is designated).

18. *See* Blanco v. Banco Indus. de Venezuela, SA, 997 F.2d 974, 980 (2d Cir.1993) (normal rules of forum non conveniens are applicable to challenge venue predicated on a permissive forum selection clause).

19. Jones v. Weibrecht, 901 F.2d 17, 19 (2d Cir.1990)

20. *See* Roberts & Schaefer Co. v. Merit Contracting, Inc., 99 F.3d 248 (7th Cir. 1996) (remanding case where mandatory clause provided for exclusive Illinois state court forum), *cert. denied*, ___ U.S. ___, 117 S.Ct. 1431, 137 L.Ed.2d 539 (1997); International Software Sys., Inc. v. Amplicon, 77 F.3d 112, 114–15 (5th Cir.1996) (and cases cited) (state court specified); Hollander v. K–Lines Hellenic Cruises, SA, 670 F.Supp. 563 (S.D.N.Y. 1987) (foreign forum specified).

21. Stewart Org., Inc. v. Ricoh Corp., 487 U.S. 22, 24 n. 1, 108 S.Ct. 2239, 2241 n. 1, 101 L.Ed.2d 22 (1988).

22. *See* Northwestern Nat'l Ins. Co. v. Donovan, 916 F.2d 372, 378 (7th Cir.1990); Marklyn Controls Supply v. Pall Trinity Micro Corp. By & Through Pall Corp., 862 F.Supp. 140 (W.D.Tex.1994).

23. *See In re* Ricoh Corp., 870 F.2d 570, 573 (11th Cir.1989) (stating that under *Stewart*, "the venue mandated by a choice of forum clause rarely will be outweighed by other 1404(a) factors"); Shaw Group, Inc. v. Natkin & Co., 907 F.Supp. 201, 204

clause can prove to be dispositive.[24]

Whether mandatory or permissive, a forum selection clause should have the effect of establishing venue in a district that would not otherwise be available under the general venue statute or the special venue statutes.[25] For example, i) if parties to a contract had specified that suit may be brought in the Southern District of New York, ii) if the residence of plaintiff is in the Southern District of New York but a substantial part of the events or omissions giving rise to a diversity suit did not occur in that district, and iii) the defendant resides in California and the events giving rise to that suit occurred in the Central District of California, the forum selection clause would enable the plaintiff to file suit in the Southern District of New York—a forum not available under Section 1391(a). That filing might be challenged by a transfer motion,[26] but at least an otherwise unavailable basis to bring suit in New York would have been created.

(b) Challenges to Forum Selection Clauses

Forum selection clauses most frequently operate in commercial litigation without challenge. The *M/S Bremen* rule sets a high burden for challenging a forum selection clause (even while *Stewart* leaves open a transfer motion), and the effect of the clause is to provide the plaintiff with an agreed-upon place for suit which the defendant cannot claim is inconvenient to it. Indeed, the inclusion of a forum selection clause may well reflect that the designated forum is agreeable to both sides, so that a challenge would not be expected.

Challenges addressed by federal courts usually arise in one of three procedural contexts. First, where plaintiff has filed suit in a forum

---

(M.D.La.1995) ("forum selection clause evidences the parties' preference regarding a convenient forum" and is "critical to the Court's section 1404(a) analysis"); Weiss v. Columbia Pictures Television, Inc., 801 F.Supp. 1276, 1278 (S.D.N.Y. 1992) ("[O]nce a mandatory choice of forum clause is deemed valid, the burden shifts to the plaintiff to demonstrate exceptional facts explaining why he should be relieved from his contractual duty."); Rivieri Fin., Inc. v. Trucking Servs., Inc., 904 F.Supp. 837, 839 (N.D.Ill.1995) (with permissive clause, § 1404(a) balancing process undertaken with little reference to clause). In *Terra Int'l, Inc. v. Mississippi Chem. Corp.*, 922 F.Supp. 1334, 1374 (N.D.Iowa 1996), the district court observed that a permissive clause is "indicative of the parties' preference for a particular forum" and, thus, can be weighed in a § 1404(a) analysis. Without labeling the clause as permissive, the Eighth Circuit, on appeal, held that its presence is a "very important" factor in the transfer analysis. Terra Int'l, Inc. v. Mississippi Chem. Corp., 119 F.3d 688, 695 (8th Cir.1997).

24. Brock v. Entre Computer Ctrs., Inc., 933 F.2d 1253, 1258 (4th Cir. 1991).

25. *See* 28 U.S.C.A. § 1406(b) (West 1993) (failure to satisfy venue requirements does not impair the court's power to enter a judgment); Falconwood Fin. Corp. v. Griffin, 838 F.Supp. 836, 839 (S.D.N.Y.1993) ("[T]he forum selection clause guarantees that this action shall not be dismissed for improper venue.").

26. *See* Stewart Org., Inc., 487 U.S. at 31, 108 S.Ct. at 2245 (forum selection clause is not dispositive on a § 1404(a) motion). *But see* American Airlines, Inc. v. Rogerson ATS, 952 F.Supp. 377, 384 n. 11 (N.D.Tex.1996) ("[A] forum-selection clause in a contract, without more, waives a party's right to contest venue under 28 U.S.C.A. § 1404(a).").

different than the contractually specified forum, the defendant might seek to enforce the forum selection clause in a motion to dismiss or stay (in favor of a specified state or foreign forum) or to transfer. Second, where a plaintiff has filed suit in the contractually specified federal forum, the defendant might still move to transfer. Third, where a plaintiff has filed suit in the contractually specified state or foreign forum, the defendant might file in a federal district, prompting a motion in the federal court to dismiss in favor of the first-filed action.

However the challenge arises, the most direct attack on a forum selection clause is to contend that the clause is an unenforceable contract. This is an issue of contract law, turning on questions such as whether a contract was even validly entered into by the parties. Most courts determine the validity of forum selection clauses based on federal common law, not state law.[27] Where a clause is valid, courts tend to reject attempts to plead around the scope of the clause—for example, by asserting tort, rather than contract, claims; tort claims related to the contractual relationship, unless expressly excluded, will generally come within the clause.[28] However, if an action is brought against a party to a forum selection clause as well as one or more other defendants and also asserts claims broader than the scope of the clause, that clause might not be enforced.[29]

A forum selection clause is still subject to challenge on the narrow grounds stated in *M/S Bremen*: a clear showing that "enforcement would be unreasonable and unjust, or that the clause was invalid for such reasons as fraud or overreaching."[30] Reflecting the deference now ac-

---

27. Stereo Gema, Inc. v. Magnadyne Corp., 941 F.Supp. 271, 274 (D.P.R.1996) ("A majority of other courts have ... held that a forum selection clause is a procedural issue governed by federal law."); Frediani & Delgreco S.P.A. v. Gina Imports, Ltd., 870 F.Supp. 217, 219 (N.D.Ill.1994) ("[T]he majority of courts have held that federal common law governs as to enforceability and interpretation of forum selection clauses.... "). *But see* Excell, Inc. v. Sterling Boiler & Mechanical, Inc., 106 F.3d 318, 320–21 (10th Cir.1997) (finding it unnecessary to decide which law governs because there was no difference between federal common law and Colorado law on validity and interpretation of forum selection clauses); Roberts & Schaefer Co. v. Merit Contracting, Inc., 99 F.3d 248, 251–52 (7th Cir.1996) (applying Illinois law in determining both validity and enforceability of forum selection clause in order to give effect to the parties' apparent intent for Illinois law to govern their contract), *cert. denied,* __ U.S. __, 117 S.Ct. 1431, 137 L.Ed.2d 539 (1997); Generale Bank, New York Branch v. Wassel, 779 F.Supp. 310

(S.D.N.Y.1991) (applying state law on issue of fraudulent misrepresentation).

28. *See* Coastal Steel Corp. v. Tilghman Wheelabrator, Ltd., 709 F.2d 190, 203 (3d Cir.1983); *see, e.g.,* S–Fer Int'l, Inc. v. Paladion Partners Inc., 906 F.Supp. 211, 213 (S.D.N.Y.1995) (holding that clause in lease, which contained the phrase "enforcement of any obligation contained herein," was limited to contract actions).

29. *See* Snider v. Lone Star Art Trading Co., 672 F.Supp. 977, 979–80 (E.D.Mich. 1987), *aff'd,* 838 F.2d 1215 (6th Cir.1988).

30. M/S Bremen v. Zapata Off–Shore Co., 407 U.S. 1, 15, 92 S.Ct. 1907, 1916, 32 L.Ed.2d 513 (1972). See Falconwood Fin. Corp., 838 F.Supp. at 836 (recognizing that this was "the very rare case" where a transfer motion trumps a mandatory forum selection clause, court held that interest of justice required transfer of the case to the forum where a key third party could both be joined and compelled to testify); M.G.J. Indus., Inc. v. Greyhound Fin. Corp., Inc., 826 F.Supp. 430 (M.D.Fla.1993) (refusing to enforce forum selection clause which was procured by coercion).

corded to forum selection clauses, courts have sustained the forum selection clause in a contract challenged on the basis of fraud if there is no showing that the forum selection clause was fraudulently induced.[31] Similarly, a clause is not "unreasonable" simply because the designated foreign forum is less favorable to the resisting party than would be a federal forum, even if—as a consequence—a federal statute will not be applied to the dispute by the foreign tribunal.[32] Once again, *M/S Bremen* demands a strong showing: "that ... for all practical purposes [the resisting party will] be deprived of his day in court."[33]

Motions have been brought to transfer actions to the district specified in a forum selection clause as well as, in challenge to a forum selection clause, to transfer actions away from the specified forum. Courts, while considering the transfer factors, tend to give at least special consideration to the presence of a forum selection clause and will enforce the clause absent the presence of unreasonableness.[34] Indeed, in the presence of a forum selection clause, the burden on the transfer motion rests on the party resisting the contractual forum.[35] However, there is authority for contending that a permissive forum selection clause should not heighten the burden of a movant seeking a transfer from the specified forum.[36]

(c) Strategy Considerations

Forum selection clauses provide an opportunity for commercial litigators to influence an action long before a dispute has arisen. Within a law firm, a lawyer drafting a contract might (and probably should) have a litigator review a proposed forum selection clause, asking whether the clause should be included and, if so, what the clause should provide. The general principles concerning forum selection clauses allow some

---

31. Scherk v. Alberto–Culver Co., 417 U.S. 506, 519 n. 14, 94 S.Ct. 2449, 2457 n. 14, 41 L.Ed.2d 270 (1974); Moses v. Business Card Express, Inc., 929 F.2d 1131, 1138 (6th Cir.1991).

32. There is currently a split among the circuits on whether a forum selection clause in an international agreement will be enforced where the effect is to deny the resisting party the availability of the federal securities law. In *Richards v. Lloyd's of London*, 107 F.3d 1422 (9th Cir.1997), the Ninth Circuit held that the federal securities laws, 15 U.S.C.A. §§ 77n, 78cc(a) (West 1997), barred waiver of compliance with any of their provisions and, accordingly, a dispute under a U.S. based transaction should be tried in U.S. courts, despite a forum selection clause providing for litigation in London. The Second, Fourth and Seventh Circuits, relying on *M/S Bremen*, have enforced similar forum selection claus-

es in Lloyd's of London policies. *See* Allen v. Lloyd's of London, 94 F.3d 923 (4th Cir. 1996); Bonny v. Society of Lloyd's, 3 F.3d 156 (7th Cir.1993); Roby v. Corporation of Lloyd's, 996 F.2d 1353 (2d Cir. 1993).

33. 407 U.S. at 18, 92 S.Ct. at 1917.

34. *See supra* § 3.6(a).

35. *See* Jumara v. State Farm Ins. Co., 55 F.3d 873, 880 (3d Cir. 1995); Micro–Assist, Inc. v. Cherry Communications, Inc., 961 F.Supp. 462, 465 (E.D.N.Y.1997) (and cases cited). *But see* Terra Int'l, Inc. v. Mississippi Chem. Corp., 119 F.3d 688, 695–96 (8th Cir.1997) (citing *Jumara* but then declining to rule on whether burden shifts).

36. *Cf.* Blanco v. Banco Indus. de Venezuela, 997 F.2d 974, 980 (2d Cir.1993) (normal rules of forum non conveniens are applicable to challenge venue predicated on a permissive forum selection clause).

informed judgments to be made, taking account of the negotiating leverage of each party to the contract being drafted.

For example, if possible a party would likely want to provide at least for the possibility of suit in its home district (and, by a choice of law clause, for application of the most favorable law, if this can be anticipated). A permissive clause can overcome an absence of a statutory basis to commence suit in that home district. A mandatory clause specifying a state court in a given location would achieve the maximum effect on the choice of venue; absent the limited grounds under *M/S Bremen* for challenging a valid forum selection clause, an effort to remove and transfer the action would likely be defeated.

To the extent that the nature of potential disputes under an agreement being negotiated can be predicted and at least considering the identity of the parties and the characteristics of the transaction, the practitioner should attempt to analyze whether any particular forum is likely to be especially favorable, or unfavorable, for his client. If conclusions can be drawn, a mandatory forum selection clause should be considered. The factors bearing on the selection of a forum for suit, *see* Section 3.3, *supra*, can serve as a checklist. Where a mandatory clause is desired, the language should unambiguously state both the location and the court(s) that are intended.[37] Because the inclusion of even a mandatory forum selection clause does not guarantee that there will be no litigation over the choice of forum, the practitioner might consider including a provision awarding attorneys' fees to be paid if a challenge to the forum selection clause is unsuccessful.

Frequently, however, at the stage of contract formation it is simply too speculative to decide upon a venue, other than to preserve as an option the client's home district. Yet, the practitioner should at least advise on the enforceability of a forum selection clause in general and the effect of a proposed clause—for it is as important to focus on what should be kept out of a contract as on what preferably should be included.

Library References:

West's Key No. Digests, Contracts ⚷127(4), 206.
Wright, Miller & Cooper, Federal Practice and Procedure: Civil 2d § 3841.

§ 3.7   Challenges to Venue

(a) Overview

Sections 3.3 through 3.6, above, have focused on the law and strategy considerations applicable to the selection of a forum for a commercial action primarily from the plaintiff's perspective. Those sections were designed to help answer the question, "In which district should a commercial action be brought?" We now turn to the reciprocal question: faced with a filed commercial action, should the defendant

---

37. For forms of forum selection claus-   es, *see infra* § 3.12(a), (b).

mount a challenge to the plaintiff's choice of forum? We consider, as well, the retort: if venue is challenged by the defendant, how might the plaintiff respond?

This Section begins with a discussion of strategy considerations bearing on a challenge to venue, followed by a summary of fundamental procedural issues: standing to challenge venue; burden of proof; waiver of the right to challenge venue; and appealability of a decision on a venue motion. Section 3.8 then addresses motions to dismiss or transfer an action for improper venue under 28 U.S.C.A. § 1406(a). Section 3.9 presents the most frequently invoked venue challenge, a motion to transfer venue for convenience under 28 U.S.C.A. § 1404(a), concluding with a discussion of the common law doctrine of forum non conveniens.

(b) Strategy Considerations

Just as the selection of a forum is a fundamental part of the strategy in commencing a suit, assessing whether the plaintiff has selected an improper or inconvenient forum must be part of the initial strategic analysis of the defense of a commercial litigation. The analysis of whether to challenge venue, however, has a different starting point from the analysis of which venue to select for an action. When defense counsel appears, there is already a pending action in one identified forum, often assigned to an individual judge. An assessment of that forum and that judge for the defense of the particular action will necessarily be a key component of the venue analysis.

With the existing forum and judge known, defense counsel must undertake a two level analysis: first, to determine whether there is a basis to challenge venue; and, second, if there is a basis, to determine whether a motion should be filed. Initially, defense counsel should examine whether venue in the district is improper. This requires a review of the cited statutory basis of venue (or, if none is pled in the complaint, of the applicable general venue statute and of any special venue statute). Any forum selection clause must be examined as well. An effort should be made to assess the probability that the action will be dismissed for improper venue. In a commercial dispute involving U.S.-based parties, an outright dismissal is rare; where improper venue is found under Section 1406(a), a transfer order is the more likely result.[1] However, with a mandatory forum selection clause designating an exclusive state or foreign forum or with an international transaction primarily based abroad, a motion to dismiss based on the forum selection clause and/or on the doctrine of forum non conveniens might have a significant prospect for success.[2]

Defense counsel should next explore the likelihood of transfer, either where the existing venue may be improper or where that venue is inconvenient. This requires consideration of the transfer factors invoked

---

§ 3.7

1. *See infra* § 3.8.

2. *See supra* § 3.6; *infra* § 3.9(c).

under 28 U.S.C.A. 1404(a).[3] Evaluation of the transfer factors will serve a dual purpose, informing both the questions whether a transfer might be obtained and whether a transfer should be sought. If a transfer motion is filed, the practitioner should remember that venue motions are among the types of motion a judge will encounter most frequently. The transfer factors are well established, and a WESTLAW search is likely to produce a statement of those factors by the judge assigned to the case. Accordingly, the facts of the case being litigated which support transfer should be the primary focus of the motion.[4]

Whether to file a motion challenging venue should ultimately turn on the likelihood of success on the motion, the probable effect of a successful motion on the outcome of the case, and the costs of the motion. When it appears that dismissal of an action might dispose of the case entirely (because, for example, the plaintiff appears unlikely to pursue the claim in a foreign court) and where the basis of the motion appears strong, that motion should probably be brought. Similarly, where the most critical witnesses cannot be compelled to testify in the pending forum and that testimony can advance the defense, a transfer motion is likely warranted. Often, a motion to dismiss for improper venue is accompanied by the request, in the alternative, for a transfer of the action.

The practitioner should review the factors discussed in Section 3.3(a), above, for selecting a forum. In assessing the consequences of a transfer on the governing law, it should be borne in mind that, generally, where a diversity action is transferred for convenience alone under Section 1404(a), the law of the transferor forum will be applied, but where the transfer is made under Section 1406(a) (because of improper venue) the law of the transferee forum will apply.[5] In a federal question case, the law of the transferee forum normally applies.[6] If an action is dismissed, but then refiled in a state or foreign forum, the law applied by that state or foreign forum would determine the dispute.

The cost of a motion must be assessed against the amount at stake and the potential results of the motion (both in terms of outcome and impact). In this calculation, the practitioner should consider whether any motions are being made under Rule 12(b) which would affect the costs of the venue prong. In addition, if any Rule 12(b) motion is being made, the venue challenge must be included or it will be deemed waived.[7] A transfer motion can be made at any time, although undue delay undercuts the potential success of the motion. Under the heading of costs, the practitioner should attempt to determine whether the filing of a venue motion—alone or as part of a broader motion—is likely to cause the court to stay discovery pending determination of the motion.

---

3. See infra § 3.9(a)(1).

4. See infra § 3.12(d) for a form of transfer motion.

5. See infra §§ 3.8 and 3.9(a)(3).

6. See, e.g., Myelle v. American Cyanamid Co., 57 F.3d 411, 413 (4th Cir.1995);

In re Korean Air Lines Disaster, 829 F.2d 1171, 1174 (D.C.Cir.1987), aff'd on other grounds sub nom. Chan v. Korean Air Lines, Ltd., 490 U.S. 122, 109 S.Ct. 1676, 104 L.Ed.2d 113 (1989).

7. See infra § 3.7(e).

When a challenge to venue is filed, the plaintiff is almost always going to oppose the motion. If the forum was initially selected for strategic reasons and if the defendant has concluded it is important to seek a change in venue, it will likely be cost justifiable for the plaintiff to defend the selected forum. If, on the other hand, there was not a strong preference for the original forum or if some unexpected challenge to the selected forum has been made, plaintiff and its counsel might decide not to invest part of a litigation budget on a forum battle. Weighed in the balance for plaintiff will be the signals of strength or weakness it projects in the litigation by the procedural strategy decisions it makes.

A plaintiff may, in limited circumstances,[8] initiate a transfer motion. If successful, this could result in a more convenient forum together with the law applied by the transferor court that may have motivated the original choice of forum.[9] This "win-win" scenario is, indeed, attractive, but successful plaintiff-initiated transfers are too rare to make "file first, seek transfer later" a routine course of strategy.

(c) Standing

(1) Defendant(s)

The venue requirement is intended "to protect the defendant against the risk that a plaintiff will select an unfair or inconvenient place of trial."[10] By definition, a defendant (other than an alien[11]) has standing to challenge the venue selected by the plaintiff.

As a general rule, only the defendant as to whom venue is improper has standing to challenge the propriety of venue because venue is personal to each defendant.[12] However, any defendant in a multi-defendant action has standing to challenge a venue defect, regardless of which defendant's presence in the action causes the defect, to the extent that the defect renders venue improper as to one or more claims alleged against him.[13]

---

8. *See infra* § 3.7(c)(2).

9. *See infra* § 3.9(a)(3).

10. Leroy v. Great W. United Corp., 443 U.S. 173, 183–84, 99 S.Ct. 2710, 2716, 61 L.Ed.2d 464 (1979); *see supra* § 3.2.

11. *See supra* § 3.4(e).

12. *See* Pratt v. Rowland, 769 F.Supp. 1128, 1132 (N.D.Cal.1991); 15 Charles Alan Wright, Arthur R. Miller & Edward H. Cooper, Federal Practice and Procedure § 3829, at 309–10 (1986).

13. Third-party defendants generally have no standing to challenge venue. *See* F & D Inc. v. O'Hara & Kendall Aviation, Inc., 547 F.Supp. 44, 45 (S.D.Tex.1982); Tcherepnin v. Franz, 439 F.Supp. 1340, 1345 (N.D.Ill. 1977); St. Hilaire v. Shapiro, 407 F.Supp. 1029, 1031 (E.D.N.Y.1976);

First Flight Co. v. National Carloading Corp., 209 F.Supp. 730, 732 (E.D.Tenn. 1962). Some exceptions have been recognized. *See, e.g.,* First Fed. Sav. & Loan Ass'n v. Oppenheim, Appel, Dixon & Co., 634 F.Supp. 1341, 1349 (S.D.N.Y.1986) (allowing a third-party defendant to challenge venue under § 27 of Securities Exchange Act, explaining that, "the venue requirements of Section 27 are inextricably intertwined with the statutory grant of personal jurisdiction . . . and any challenge to venue is in a sense a challenge to jurisdiction"); *In re* Continental Sec. Litig., No. 82 C 4712, 1985 WL 3296, at *3 (N.D.Ill.1985) (allowing a third-party defendant to challenge venue under 12 U.S.C.A. § 94 (West 1989), the venue provision for actions against the FDIC as receiver of a national banking association, explaining that the legislative

For example, when venue is based on residence under Sections 1391(a)(1) or (b)(1) and one of the defendants does not reside in the state in which the action was filed, any of the defendants, even those who do reside in the state, should be able to challenge venue because the requirement that all defendants reside in the same state is a necessary prerequisite under those provisions to establish venue as to any defendant.[14] When venue is based on the place where a substantial part of the events or omissions giving rise to a claim occurred, any defendant named in a claim should have standing to challenge whether that basis for venue has been met with respect to it.[15] In a multi-defendant case, it is necessary to isolate the cognizable claim(s) asserted against each defendant, thus defining each claim as to which any defendant may (or need) challenge venue. Any defendant may seek a transfer for convenience.[16]

(2) Plaintiff

A plaintiff is generally deemed to have waived any objection to improper venue by virtue of having chosen the original forum.[17] None-

purpose behind the statute applies to third-party actions as well).

14. See Dyco Petroleum Corp. v. Mesa Operating Co., 935 F.Supp. 1193, 1195 n. 1 (N.D. Okla.1996) (noting that although a defendant cannot assert an objection to venue on behalf of a co-defendant, a defendant can object to venue purportedly established on the basis of residence, even if such defendant itself resides in the forum district, if the co-defendant does not reside in the state). There was considerable authority under the earlier version of § 1391(b), which established jurisdiction in the judicial district "where all defendants reside," that "the defense of improper venue is personal to the party to whom it applies and ... a resident defendant may not avail himself of a dismissal or transfer as to a nonresident unless the latter is an indispensable party." See Goldberg v. Wharf Constructors, Inc., 209 F.Supp. 499, 503–04 (N.D.Ala.1962); 15 Charles Alan Wright, Arthur R. Miller & Edward H. Cooper, Federal Practice and Procedure § 3807, at 78 (1986). The current statute permits venue in a district "where any defendant resides, *if all* defendants reside in the same State." 28 U.S.C.A. § 1391(a)(1), (b)(1) (emphasis added). This language expressly conditions residential venue on the residence of all defendants in the same state.

15. See, e.g., Emjayco ex rel. Troy v. Morgan Stanley & Co., 901 F.Supp. 1397, 1400–01 (C.D.Ill.1995)(finding no basis for venue over a co-defendant which committed no significant act in the district; there was,

thus, no allegation to show that a substantial part of the events giving rise to the claim against that defendant had occurred in the district); Sheppard v. Jacksonville Marine Supply, Inc., 877 F.Supp. 260, 269 (D.S.C.1995) (holding allegations to be sufficient for the court to find that substantial part of events giving rise to all claims against each defendant occurred in the district).

16. The courts are divided on whether a third-party defendant has standing to seek a transfer. See Stringfellow v. S.D. Warren Co., No. 1:91–CV–644, 1991 WL 239993, at *2 (W.D.Mich.1991). For cases stating that a third-party defendant does not have standing, see Acres Int'l Corp. v. Moore Bus. Forms, Inc., No. Civ–85–146E, 1989 WL 158321, at *3 (W.D.N.Y.1989); Pelinski v. Goodyear Tire & Rubber Co., 499 F.Supp. 1092, 1095 (N.D.Ill.1980). For cases stating that a third-party defendant has standing, see Kendall U.S.A., Inc. v. Central Printing Co., 666 F.Supp. 1264, 1266 (N.D.Ind.1987); Krupp Int'l, Inc. v. Yarn Indus., Inc., 615 F.Supp. 1103, 1107 (D.Del. 1985); Daily Express, Inc. v. Northern Neck Transfer Corp., 483 F.Supp. 916, 917 (M.D.Pa.1979).

17. See Olberding v. Illinois Cent. Ry. Co., 346 U.S. 338, 340, 74 S. Ct. 83, 85, 98 L.Ed. 39 (1953) (recognizing in *dictum* that "plaintiff, by bringing the suit in a district other than that authorized by [28 U.S.C.A. § 1391], relinquished his right to object to the venue").

theless, the plaintiff is not barred from moving to transfer an action under Sections 1404(a) or 1406(a).[18] Courts typically require that a plaintiff show a change of circumstances since the filing of the complaint which would warrant a transfer[19] or show that a transfer would be in the interest of justice.[20] However, when a plaintiff selected the original forum without due diligence, courts are less likely to entertain a motion to transfer the action based on supposedly new or unanticipated developments.[21]

(3) The Court

There is limited authority holding that courts may transfer an action sua sponte under either Sections 1404(a) or 1406(a)[22] or dismiss an action under the doctrine of forum non conveniens.[23] Because an objection to venue as improper is personal to each defendant and can be waived if not timely asserted, some courts have held that a sua sponte

18. *See, e.g.*, Manley v. Engram, 755 F.2d 1463 (11th Cir.1985); Anglo Am. Ins. Group, P.L.C. v. CalFed Inc., 916 F.Supp. 1324, 1328 (S.D.N.Y.1996).

19. *See, e.g.*, Manley, 755 F.2d at 1463 (holding that plaintiff had not waived the right to object to venue in the original forum or to seek a transfer under § 1406 in the unusual circumstance where plaintiff diligently filed suit in good faith in the district of the individual defendant's apparent residence, but later discovered that the defendant subjectively considered another state his permanent residence); Anglo Am. Ins. Group, P.L.C., 916 F.Supp. at 1328 ("The threshold question when deciding a § 1404(a) motion by a plaintiff is whether plaintiff has shown that a change in circumstance since the complaint was filed warrants a transfer."). *But see* Cordis Corp. v. Siemens–Pacesetter, Inc., 682 F. Supp. 1200, 1203 (S.D.Fla.1987) (granting plaintiff's motion for transfer in the interest of justice after plaintiff voluntarily dismissed two defendants, but holding that there is no requirement under 28 U.S.C.A. § 1404 that a plaintiff seeking a transfer of venue must show a change of circumstances). In *Washington Public Utilities Group v. United States District Court*, 843 F.2d 319, 327 (9th Cir.1987), the court stated that there is no requirement that a plaintiff who merely joins, as opposed to initiates, a motion to transfer must show a change of circumstances.

20. *See, e.g.*, Fairfax Dental (Ireland) Ltd. v. S.J. Filhol Ltd., 645 F.Supp. 89, 92 (E.D.N.Y.1986), *aff'd mem. on other grounds*, 11 F.3d 1074 (Fed.Cir.1993)

(granting transfer to a district in which a related action was pending); Central Hudson Gas & Elec. Corp. v. Empresa Naviera Santa, S.A., 769 F.Supp. 208, 209 (E.D.La. 1991) (granting plaintiff's motion to transfer action to a district where an identical suit was pending, holding that the convenience of the parties and witnesses and interest of justice required transfer); Young v. Cuddington, 470 F.Supp. 935 (M.D.Pa. 1979) (granting plaintiff's motion to transfer the action under § 1406 to avoid statute of limitations in transferor district); *see also* Anglo Am. Ins. Group, P.L.C., 916 F.Supp. at 1329 (recognizing that a court may transfer an action in the interest of justice upon plaintiff's motion).

21. *See, e.g.*, Spar, Inc. v. Information Resources Inc., 956 F.2d 392, 394 (2d Cir. 1992); Harem–Christensen Corp. v. M.S. Frigo Harmony, 477 F.Supp. 694, 698 (S.D.N.Y.1979).

22. *See* Washington Pub. Util. Group, 843 F.2d at 326 (observing that court could have transferred action under § 1404 sua sponte when it became aware that, due to massive news coverage, a fair trial could not be had in the place where the action was filed); Caldwell v. Palmetto State Sav. Bank, 811 F.2d 916 (5th Cir.1987) (court may transfer action sua sponte under either §§ 1404(a) or 1406(a)); Smith v. City of New York, 950 F.Supp. 55, 59 (E.D.N.Y. 1996) (court may transfer action sua sponte under § 1404(a)).

23. *See* Corporacion Mexicana de Servicios Maritimos, S.A. de C.V. v. M/T Respect, 89 F.3d 650, 656 n. 1 (9th Cir.1996).

transfer or dismissal is not proper in the absence of extraordinary circumstances.[24] It has also been held that a court cannot act sua sponte once a defendant has waived the right to challenge venue.[25] If no motion to transfer has been made under Section 1404(a), the court should provide notice and an opportunity to be heard before acting sua sponte.[26]

(d) Burden of Proof

The plaintiff is not required to plead a basis for venue in the complaint[27] (although, in the detailed complaints common in commercial cases, one or more grounds of venue are most often recited). Once venue is challenged as improper, the plaintiff has the burden of showing that venue is proper[28] or, at least, that further discovery will reveal that venue is proper.[29] Venue must be established as to each claim alleged and as to each defendant named in an action which challenges venue.[30]

24. See, e.g., Davis v. Reagan, 872 F.2d 1025 (6th Cir.1989) (affirming district court's sua sponte dismissal of action for improper venue, where venue had no connection to action and complaint alleged frivolous claims against the president and other federal government officials); Stich v. Rehnquist, 982 F.2d 88, 89 (2d Cir.1992) (sua sponte dismissing for improper venue an action naming a number of judges as defendants, where complaint alleged claims similar to that brought by the plaintiff in another circuit and which resulted there in an order prohibiting the plaintiff from bringing another suit without court approval).

25. See, e.g., Concession Consultants Inc. v. Mirisch, 355 F.2d 369, 371 (2d Cir. 1966).

26. See Feller v. Brock, 802 F.2d 722, 729 n. 7 (4th Cir.1986); Saferstein v. Paul, Mardinly, Durham, James, Flandreau & Rodger, P.C., 927 F.Supp. 731, 737 (S.D.N.Y.1996); Clisham Management, Inc. v. American Steel Bldg. Co., 792 F.Supp. 150 (D.Conn.1992).

27. See SEC v. Ernst & Young, 775 F.Supp. 411, 412 (D.D.C.1991) ("The plaintiff need not plead venue; rather, lack of venue is an affirmative defense."); Ferraioli v. Cantor, 259 F.Supp. 842, 846 (S.D.N.Y. 1966).

28. See, e.g., Micro–Assist, Inc. v. Cherry Communications, Inc., 961 F.Supp. 462, 465 (E.D.N.Y.1997); Emjayco ex rel. Troy v. Morgan Stanley & Co., 901 F.Supp. 1397, 1400 (C.D.Ill.1995); Seariver Maritime Fin. Holdings, Inc. v. Peña, 952 F.Supp. 455, 458 (S.D. Tex.1996). There is, however, contrary authority. See, e.g., Rocket Jewelry Box, Inc. v. Noble Gift Packaging, Inc., 869 F.Supp. 152, 154 (S.D.N.Y.1994) (reasoning that, because plaintiff need not allege a basis for venue, defendant bears the burden of establishing improper venue); 17 James Wm. Moore, Moore's Federal Practice, § 110.01[5][d] (3d ed.1997) (objection to venue should be treated as affirmative defense and a personal privilege, with burden of proof on defendants to establish a basis for dismissing action); see generally 15 Charles Alan Wright, Arthur R. Miller & Edward H. Cooper, Federal Practice and Procedure § 3826, at 259 (1986) (observing that most cases properly place the burden on plaintiff and compiling some contrary authority).

29. Central Sports Army Club v. Arena Assocs., Inc., 952 F.Supp. 181, 188 (S.D.N.Y.1997).

30. See Beattie v. United States, 756 F.2d 91, 100 (D.C.Cir.1984); Berger Instruments, Inc. v. Northwest Instruments, Inc., No. 96 C 8393, 1997 WL 159377, at *3 (N.D.Ill.1997); Emjayco ex rel. Troy, 901 F.Supp. at 1400; Sheppard v. Jacksonville Marine Supply, Inc., 877 F.Supp. 260, 269 (D.S.C.1995). One court had observed that the test of venue under § 1391(b)(2) nullified the rule that venue must be proper as to each defendant inasmuch as the new test changes the "focus from contacts to events." Magic Toyota Inc. v. Southeast Toyota Distribs., Inc., 784 F.Supp. 306, 317 n. 19 (D.S.C.1992). Subsequently, however, in Sheppard (cited earlier in this note) that same court stated and applied the rule that venue must be proper as to each claim against each defendant. 877 F.Supp. at 269.

Because venue is to be determined as of the time the complaint was filed,[31] it is not necessary to separately establish venue over new claims against existing parties (such as counterclaims).[32]

When a motion is made under Section 1404(a) to transfer the action, the movant has the burden of alleging or establishing facts showing that the action should be transferred "[f]or the convenience of parties and witnesses [and] in the interest of justice."[33] Some courts will, where a mandatory forum selection clause is present in a transfer motion, impose the burden on the party resisting enforcement of the clause.[34]

(e) Waiver

An objection to improper venue is waived by a defendant unless raised with specificity in the responsive pleading or a motion to dismiss under Rule 12(b) filed in lieu of an answer.[35] Once the objection is waived, the claim may not be dismissed for improper venue.[36] By contrast, an objection to venue as inconvenient under the doctrine of forum non conveniens is not waived by filing an answer or Rule 12(b) motion without invoking this doctrine, although the objection should be raised within a reasonable amount of time after the facts and circumstances which give rise to the motion have become known or reasonably knowable to the defendant.[37] Similarly, a motion to transfer under Section 1404(a) may be made at any time during the pendency of the case, even after judgment has been entered, although the motion should be brought with reasonable promptness.[38] Timing is important because it

31. See Exxon Corp. v. FTC, 588 F.2d 895, 899 (3d Cir.1978); Sidco Indus. Inc. v. Wimar Tahoe Corp., 768 F.Supp. 1343, 1346 (D.Or.1991).

32. See Lesnik v. Public Indus. Corp., 144 F.2d 968, 977 (2d Cir.1944). Third-party claims have been treated as ancillary to the main suit. See Lone Star Package Car Co. v. Baltimore & O. R. Co., 212 F.2d 147, 152 (5th Cir.1954), superseded by statute on other grounds, Point Landing, Inc. v. Omni Capital Int'l, Ltd., 795 F.2d 415 (5th Cir.1986).

33. 28 U.S.C.A. § 1404(a) (West 1993). See, e.g., Heller Fin., Inc. v. Midwhey Powder Co., 883 F.2d 1286, 1293 (7th Cir.1989); Factors Etc., Inc. v. Pro Arts, Inc., 579 F.2d 215, 218 (2d Cir.1978).

34. See Jumara v. State Farm Ins. Co., 55 F.3d 873, 850 (3d Cir. 1995); Micro–Assist, Inc. v. Cherry Communications, Inc., 961 F.Supp. 462, 465 (E.D.N.Y.1977) (and cases cited). But see Terra Int'l, Inc. v. Mississippi Chem. Corp., 119 F.3d 688, 695–96 (8th Cir.1997) (citing Jumara but then declining to rule on whether burden shifts).

35. See FRCP 12(h)(i); 28 U.S.C.A. § 1406(b) (West 1993) ("Nothing in this chapter shall impair the jurisdiction of a district court of any matter involving a party who does not interpose a timely and sufficient objection to the venue."); King v. Russell, 963 F.2d 1301, 1304 (9th Cir. 1992); St. Hilaire v. Shapiro, 407 F.Supp. 1029, 1031 (E.D.N.Y.1976). For forms of objection, see infra § 3.12 (a).

36. Eastman Kodak Co. v. Goodyear Tire & Rubber Co., 114 F.3d 1547, 1558 (Fed.Cir.1997)(holding that once objection to venue over a state law claim had been waived in a responsive pleading, the trial court erred in dismissing that claim for failure of venue).

37. See In re Air Crash Disaster Near New Orleans, Louisiana on July 9, 1982, 821 F.2d 1147, 1165 (5th Cir.1987), vacated on other grounds sub nom. Pan Am. World Airways v. Lopez, 490 U.S. 1032, 109 S.Ct. 1928, 104 L.Ed.2d 400 (1989).

38. See Chrysler Credit Corp. v. Country Chrysler, Inc., 928 F.2d 1509, 1516 (10th Cir.1991); FTC v. Multinet Mktg., LLC, 959 F.Supp. 394, 395 (N.D. Tex.1997); Lencco Racing Co. v. Arctco, Inc., 953 F.Supp. 69, 70 n. 1 (W.D.N.Y.1997); Catala-

may be properly considered by a court when considering whether to grant a motion to dismiss under the doctrine of forum non conveniens[39] or to transfer an action.[40]

(f) Appealability

As a general rule, only final judgments may be appealed.[41] Since an order dismissing an action for improper venue under the doctrine of forum non conveniens or pursuant to a forum selection clause completely disposes of an action, it is immediately reviewable by an appellate court.[42] Similarly, a remand order based on a forum selection clause is appealable.[43] By contrast, orders either granting or denying a motion to transfer or denying a motion to dismiss are not final judgments and are therefore not immediately appealable as of right.[44] Review of these

no v. BRI, Inc., 724 F.Supp. 1580, 1583 (E.D.Mich.1989) ("The consolidation requirement of Rule 12(g) refers only to motions to dismiss for improper venue.").

39. See Baumgart v. Fairchild Aircraft Corp., 981 F.2d 824, 836 (5th Cir.1993) (instructing that "the court should also consider whether the defendant's motion to dismiss was filed in a timely manner").

40. See, e.g., Peteet v. Dow Chem. Co., 868 F.2d 1428, 1436 (5th Cir.1989) (holding that district court did not abuse its discretion in denying defendant's motion to transfer under § 1404, because it was not filed until eight months after the case was remanded); Multinet Mktg., LLC, 959 F.Supp. at 395 (denying transfer motion where defendant waited nearly seven months after plaintiff filed action, to seek a change of venue). Delay, alone, might not be fatal to a transfer motion absent a showing of prejudice to the plaintiff. See United States Fidelity & Guar. Co. v. Republic Drug Co., 800 F.Supp. 1076, 1082–83 (E.D.N.Y.1992). One court has expressed the view that, absent a showing of prejudice, it is preferable to bring a transfer motion at the later stages of a case so that the trial court "can visualize with more clarity the factors implicit in its determinations." Mobil Oil Corp. v. W.R. Grace & Co., 334 F.Supp. 117, 126 (S.D.Tex.1971).

41. See 28 U.S.C.A. § 1291 (West 1993); Chapter 49, Appeals to the Court of Appeals, infra.

42. See Offshore Sportswear, Inc. v. Vuarnet Int'l B.V., 114 F.3d 848, 850 (9th Cir.1997) (holding that order dismissing an action to enforce a forum selection clause is appealable); Sigalas v. Lido Maritime, Inc., 776 F.2d 1512, 1516 (11th Cir.1985) (holding that order dismissing action on grounds of forum non conveniens, even with certain conditions, constitutes an appealable final order); Cook v. Fox, 537 F.2d 370, 371 (9th Cir.1976).

43. SBKC Serv. Corp. v. 1111 Prospect Partners, L.P., 105 F.3d 578, 581 (10th Cir.1997).

44. For cases discussing the nonappealability of a transfer order, see, for example, Aaacon Auto Transport, Inc. v. Ninfo, 490 F.2d 83, 84 (2d Cir.1974); Ellicott Mach. Corp. v. Modern Welding Co., 502 F.2d 178, 180 (4th Cir.1974); Stelly v. Employers Nat'l Ins. Co., 431 F.2d 1251, 1253 (5th Cir.1970); Kasey v. Molybdenum Corp. of Am., 408 F.2d 16, 18 (9th Cir.1969); Ackert v. Bryan, 299 F.2d 65, 67 (2d Cir.1962); All States Freight v. Modarelli, 196 F.2d 1010, 1011 (3d Cir.1952).

For cases discussing the nonappealability of orders denying a motion to dismiss an action on forum non conveniens grounds, see Van Cauwenberghe v. Biard, 486 U.S. 517, 528, 108 S.Ct. 1945, 1953 (1988); Carlenstolpe v. Merck & Co., 819 F.2d 33, 36 (2d Cir.1987); In re Air Crash Disaster Near New Orleans, Louisiana on July 9, 1982, 821 F.2d 1147, 1167 (5th Cir.1987); Rosenstein v. Merrell Dow Pharmaceuticals, Inc., 769 F.2d 352, 354 (6th Cir.1985).

For cases discussing the nonappealability of orders denying a motion to dismiss for improper venue, see Phaneuf v. Republic of Indonesia, 106 F.3d 302, 309 (9th Cir.1997); Louisiana Ice Cream Distribs., Inc. v. Carvel Corp., 821 F.2d 1031, 1032 (5th Cir. 1987).

interlocutory orders, however, is not entirely precluded. Review may be available upon the district court's certification and the appellate court's acceptance of an interlocutory appeal[45] or through the appellate court's grant of a writ of mandamus.[46] Additionally, these orders are subject to review if the case is ultimately appealed after judgment on the merits,[47] except that a transfer order cannot be reviewed outside the circuit of the transferor court.[48]

Dismissal orders based on venue are rarely disturbed and are usually affirmed in the absence of a clear abuse of discretion.[49] A district court abuses its discretion when it dismisses an action for forum non conveniens and fails to consider the amount of deference due to a foreign plaintiff's choice of forum or fails properly to weigh the private and public interest factors discussed more fully below.[50] It has also been held

For cases discussing the nonappealability of orders denying a motion to dismiss on the basis of a contractual forum selection clause, see Chasser v. Achille Lauro Lines, 844 F.2d 50, 53 (2d Cir.1988), aff'd, 490 U.S. 495, 109 S.Ct. 1976, 104 L.Ed.2d 548 (1989); Louisiana Ice Cream Distribs., 821 F.2d at 1032–34; see also Rohrer, Hibler & Replogle, Inc. v. Perkins, 728 F.2d 860, 862 (7th Cir.1984) (holding that an order denying a motion to remand to state court pursuant to the terms of a forum selection clause was not appealable).

45. See 28 U.S.C.A. § 1292(b) (West 1997); 15 Charles Alan Wright, Arthur R. Miller & Edward H. Cooper, Federal Practice and Procedure § 3855, at 477–79 (1986) (concluding most courts find discretionary rulings to fall outside scope of § 1292(b)). Appellate review, however, might be available if only a question of law is presented and the appeal depends on the power of the district court to enter the order it did. Id. § 3855, at 85 (Supp.1997).

46. See Warrick v. General Elec. Co. (In re Warrick), 70 F.3d 736 (2d Cir.1995) (issuing a writ of mandamus where district court transferred action without considering the convenience of the parties and witnesses); Sunbelt Corp. v. Noble Denton & Assocs., Inc., 5 F.3d 28 (3d Cir.1993) (issuing a writ of mandamus where transferee district was not a district "where the action might have been brought"); 15 Charles Alan Wright, Arthur R. Miller & Edward H. Cooper, Federal Practice and Procedure § 3855, at 479–94 (1986) (examining availability of mandamus on a circuit-by-circuit basis).

47. See Petition of Int'l Precious Metals Corp., 917 F.2d 792, 794 (4th Cir.1990); Robbins v. Pocket Beverage Co., 779 F.2d

351, 355–56 (7th Cir.1985) (reviewing order by transferor court granting summary judgment after it vacated its earlier order transferring the action under § 1404).

48. See TEC Floor Corp. v. Wal–Mart Stores, Inc., 4 F.3d 599, 602–03 (8th Cir. 1993); Moses v. Business Card Express, Inc., 929 F.2d 1131, 1136 (6th Cir.1991); Roofing & Sheet Metal Servs., Inc. v. La Quinta Motor Inns, Inc., 689 F.2d 982, 987 (11th Cir.1982); Illinois Tool Works Inc. v. Sweetheart Plastics, Inc., 436 F.2d 1180, 1188 (7th Cir.1971).

49. For cases discussing the standard of review for actions dismissed on forum non conveniens grounds, see, for example, Piper Aircraft Co. v. Reyno, 454 U.S. 235, 257, 102 S.Ct. 252, 266, 70 L.Ed.2d 419 (1981) (holding that the forum non conveniens determination "may be reversed only when there has been a clear abuse of discretion"); Baumgart, 981 F.2d at 835 (same); Lacey v. Cessna Aircraft Co., 932 F.2d 170, 178 (3d Cir.1991) (same); Howe v. Goldcorp Invs., Ltd., 946 F.2d 944, 951 (1st Cir.1991); In re Air Crash Disaster Near New Orleans, Louisiana on July 9, 1982, 821 F.2d at 1166 (same); Paper Operations Consultants Int'l Ltd. v. SS Hong Kong Amber, 513 F.2d 667, 670 (9th Cir.1975)(same).

For cases discussing the standard of review for actions dismissed under § 1406, see, for example, McFarlane v. Esquire Magazine, 74 F.3d 1296, 1300 (D.C. Cir.), cert. denied, ___ U.S. ___, 117 S.Ct. 53, 136 L.Ed.2d 16 (1996); Oaks of Woodlake Phase III, Ltd. v. Hall, Bayoutree Assocs., Ltd. (In re Hall, Bayoutree Assocs., Ltd.), 939 F.2d 802, 805 (9th Cir.1991).

50. See generally infra § 3.09(c); see also Reid–Walen v. Hansen, 933 F.2d 1390,

to be an abuse of discretion for a district court to dismiss an action for forum non convenience without providing the plaintiff with a right to return to the district court in the event that the plaintiff's efforts to reinstate the action in the foreign forum are obstructed by the defendant.[51] A district court abuses its discretion when it dismisses an action under Section 1406 if it failed to consider the possibility of transfer.[52]

The denial of a motion to dismiss for improper venue is reviewed de novo provided the underlying facts were not in dispute.[53] The district court's findings of fact will be accepted unless clearly erroneous.[54] On review of a transfer decision, the district court's decision will be affirmed absent an abuse of discretion.[55] De novo review has been found to be the appropriate standard on appeal from a district court's interpretation of a forum selection clause.[56]

Library References:

West's Key No. Digests, Federal Courts ⊙71–157.
Wright, Miller & Cooper, Federal Practice and Procedure: Civil 2d §§ 1342, 1355, 1542, 3531, 3841, 3950.2.

§ 3.8   Dismissal or Transfer of an Action Based on Improper Venue

Section 1406(a) reads as follows:

(a) The district court of a district in which is filed a case laying venue in the wrong division or district shall dismiss, or if it be in the interest of justice, transfer such case to any district or division in which it could have been brought.[1]

Upon motion to dismiss for improper venue, a court has authority under Section 1406 to either dismiss the action or transfer it to any district "in which it could have been brought." Courts, however, infre-

1394 (8th Cir.1991) ("An abuse of discretion may occur when the district court fails to consider one or more of the important private or public interest factors, does not hold the defendants to their burden of persuasion on all elements of the forum non conveniens analysis, or has clearly erred in weighing the factors the court must consider."); Lacey, 932 F.2d at 178; In re Air Crash Disaster Near New Orleans, Louisiana on July 8, 1982, 821 F.2d at 1166 ("[A] district court abuses its discretion when it fails to address and balance the relevant principles and factors of the doctrine of forum non conveniens.").

51. See Robinson v. TCI/US West Communications, Inc., 117 F.3d 900, 907 (5th Cir.1997) (holding that failure to include a "return jurisdiction clause" is a per se abuse of discretion).

52. See Jumara v. State Farm Ins. Co., 55 F.3d 873, 878 (3d Cir. 1995).

53. See Columbia Pictures Television v. Krypton Broadcasting, Inc., 106 F.3d 284, 288 (9th Cir.1997), cert. granted on other questions, ___ U.S. ___, 118 S.Ct. 30, 138 L.Ed.2d 1059 (1997).

54. Id. at 288–89.

55. See Friedman v. Revenue Management, Inc., 38 F.3d 668, 672 (2d Cir.1994); see also RFE Indus., Inc. v. SPM Corp., 105 F.3d 923, 925 (4th Cir.) (applying abuse of discretion standard on review of order denying retransfer of an action), cert. denied, ___ U.S. ___, 117 S.Ct. 2512, 138 L.Ed.2d 1015 (1997).

56. Terra Int'l, Inc. v. Mississippi Chem. Corp., 119 F.3d 688, 692 (8th Cir. 1997).

§ 3.8

1. 28 U.S.C.A. § 1406(a) (West 1993).

quently choose to dismiss an action for improper venue, but rather order a transfer instead.[2] The standard for transfer, "if it be in the interest of justice," is easily satisfied[3] and, conversely, the alternative might be severe, especially where, since the action was filed, the statute of limitations has run.[4]

On those occasions in which courts have dismissed an action and held that a transfer would not have been in the interest of justice, the facts most frequently suggest that a plaintiff's original choice of venue evidenced bad faith, harassment or negligence.[5] For example, in *Spar,*

2. *See, e.g.,* Magic Toyota, Inc. v. Southeast Toyota Distribs., Inc., 784 F.Supp. 306 (D.S.C.1992) (transferring an action instituted in an improper venue in the interest of justice because the plaintiff's claims had some merit); Trenwyth Indus. v. Burns & Russell Co., 701 F.Supp. 852 (D.D.C.1988)(transferring an action instituted in an improper venue in the interest of justice because plaintiff's original choice of venue was not unreasonable).

3. *See generally* C.P. Jhong, Annotation, *Construction and Application of Federal Statute (28 U.S.C.A. § 1406) Providing For Dismissal or Transfer of Cases For Improper Venue,* 3 A.L.R. Fed. 467 (1970).

4. *See* Burnett v. New York Cent. R.R. Co., 380 U.S. 424, 430 n. 7, 85 S.Ct. 1050, 1055 n. 7, 13 L.Ed.2d 941 (1965) (observing that numerous courts have found the "interest of justice" to require transfer where the claim would otherwise be, at that point, time barred); *see, e.g.,* Minnette v. Time Warner, 997 F.2d 1023 (2d Cir.1993)(vacating district court's denial of a motion to transfer an action filed in an improper venue because the plaintiff would have been time barred from initiating a new action in the proper forum).

5. *See, e.g.,* McFarlane v. Esquire Magazine, 74 F.3d 1296, 1301 (D.C. Cir.)(affirming denial of a transfer motion and dismissal of the action for lack of personal jurisdiction even though the action would be time-barred if refiled in the proposed transferee district, because the plaintiff was on notice of the defense and failed to file a protective suit before the expiration of the statute of limitations period), *cert. denied,* ___ U.S. ___, 117 S.Ct. 53, 136 L.Ed.2d 16 (1996); Nichols v. G.D. Searle & Co., 991 F.2d 1195, 1200–01 (4th Cir.1993) (following five other circuit courts by affirming lower court's denial of plaintiff's motion to transfer and dismissal of action for lack of personal jurisdiction, explaining

that "the interest of justice is not served by allowing a plaintiff whose attorney committed an obvious error in filing the plaintiff's action in the wrong court, and thereby imposed substantial unnecessary costs on both the defendant and the judicial system, simply to transfer his/her action to the proper court, with no cost to him/herself or his/her attorney"); King v. Russell, 963 F.2d 1301, 1304 (9th Cir.1992)(holding that when an action smacks of harassment and bad faith, it is appropriate for a district court to refuse to transfer the action under § 1406); Oaks of Woodlake Phase III, Ltd. v. Hall, Bayoutree Assocs., Ltd. (*In re* Hall, Bayoutree Assocs., Ltd.), 939 F.2d 802 (9th Cir.1991)(affirming district court's dismissal and denial of a transfer, where action was filed in bad faith in improper venue); Saylor v. Dyniewski, 836 F.2d 341, 345 (7th Cir.1988)(holding that district court did not abuse its discretion in dismissing and not transferring an action for lack of personal jurisdiction because the plaintiffs failed to file a protective suit and instead, "gambled their case on an extremely dubious theory of personal jurisdiction"); Peckio v. Shay, 708 F.Supp. 75, 76 (S.D.N.Y. 1989)(declining to transfer an action for improper venue explaining that the plaintiff's lawyer's continued insistence that venue was proper reflected either an "utter unfamiliarity with the United States Code or a reluctance to be candid with the Court"); Hapaniewski v. City of Chicago Heights, 684 F.Supp. 1011, 1013 (N.D.Ind.1988)(refusing to transfer an action filed in an improper venue and in a state where personal jurisdiction was lacking, stating that "[p]laintiff's improper 'mistaken' venue and possible attempt to usurp the statute of limitations cannot be tolerated"), *aff'd,* 883 F.2d 576 (7th Cir. 1989); *see also* Dubin v. United States, 380 F.2d 813, 816 n. 5 (5th Cir.1967)("It is obviously not 'in the interest of justice' to

Inc. v. Information Resources, Inc.,[6] the Second Circuit affirmed the district court's dismissal of an action as time-barred and its denial of a motion to transfer. The court held that "allowing a transfer in this case would reward plaintiffs for their lack of diligence in choosing a proper forum and thus would not be in the interest of justice," since the plaintiffs knew or should have known that their action was time-barred under the applicable statute of limitations period.[7]

Although generally not articulated in these terms, there appear in practice to be two basic approaches to the application of the "in the interest of justice" standard.[8] Some courts do not require the moving party affirmatively to demonstrate that a transfer of an action under Section 1406(a) is in the interest of justice; these courts find that a transfer is always in the interest of justice, in the absence of evidence to the contrary.[9] Such evidence, by way of example, may include the fact that the case, if transferred, would be time-barred in the transferee district[10] or that the trial of the action in the transferee court would be inconvenient to the litigants and/or the witnesses.[11]

Other courts find that Section 1406(a) authorizes a transfer only upon an affirmative showing by the moving party that a transfer would be in the interest of justice.[12] Thus, transfer has been granted when the

allow [§ 1406] to be used to aid a nondiligent plaintiff who knowingly files a case in the wrong district."); Coffey v. Van Dorn Iron Works, 796 F.2d 217, 221 (7th Cir. 1986) (the interest of justice analysis is "not a vehicle for resurrecting a claim lost because the plaintiff erred in [its] initial choice of forums").

6. 956 F.2d 392 (2d Cir.1992).

7. *Id.* at 394.

8. *See* C.P. Jhong, Annotation, *Construction and Application of Federal Statute (28 U.S.C.A. § 1406) Providing For Dismissal or Transfer of Cases For Improper Venue,* 3 A.L.R. Fed. 467 (1970).

9. *See, e.g.,* Young v. Cuddington, 470 F.Supp. 935, 938 (M.D.Pa.1979) (transferring an action in the interest of justice because the defendant did not allege any prejudice that would result from the transfer); E.H. Sheldon & Co. v. Norbute Corp., 228 F.Supp. 245, 247 (E.D.Pa.1964) (transferring case in the interest of justice because complaint stated a cause of action); AMP Inc. v. Essex Wire Corp., 223 F.Supp. 154, 156 (N.D.Ind.1963) (holding that, "[i]t appearing that plaintiff may be entitled to a determination of its cause of action against the defendant on the merits, the Court deems it to be in the interest of justice to transfer, rather than dismiss, this action").

10. *See, e.g.,* Bolar v. Frank, 938 F.2d 377, 380 (2d Cir.1991); *see generally* Rober-

to Finzi, Note, *The 28 U.S.C.A. § 1406(a) Transfer of Time–Barred Claims,* 79 Cornell L. Rev. 975 (1994).

11. *See, e.g.,* Zumft v. Doney Slate Co., 698 F.Supp. 444, 447 (E.D.N.Y.1988) (transferring an action filed in an improper venue, in part, because it would be more convenient for a majority of the parties); St. Hilaire v. Shapiro, 407 F.Supp. 1029, 1031 (E.D.N.Y.1976) (denying a transfer under § 1406 stating that even if the movant had standing to object to venue, the motion would be denied because the proposed transferee court would be inconvenient to all parties). *But see* Martin v. Stokes, 623 F.2d 469, 472 (6th Cir.1980)("A transfer under § 1406(a) is based not on the inconvenience of the transferor forum but on the impropriety of that forum.").

12. *See, e.g.,* Costlow v. Weeks, 790 F.2d 1488, 1488 (9th Cir.1986) (stating that § 1406(a) requires a transfer "only in cases where it is in 'the interest of justice' "); Big Island Yacht Sales v. Dowty, 848 F.Supp. 131, 134–35 (D.Haw.1993); Coleman v. Crisp, 444 F.Supp. 31, 33 (W.D.Okla.1977); Mulcahy v. Guertler, 416 F.Supp. 1083, 1086 (D. Mass.1976); Farkas v. Texas Instruments, Inc., 50 F.R.D. 484, 487 (D. Mass.1969), *aff'd in part and rev'd in part on other grounds,* 429 F.2d 849 (1st Cir. 1970).

moving party has shown that the statute of limitation would bar a new action in the proper forum if the original action were dismissed,[13] when the action was brought in the wrong district in good faith,[14] when a transfer would keep related claims together in one forum,[15] or when a related action is pending in the transferee court.[16] On a transfer in the interest of justice under Section 1406(a), the plaintiff's preference among proper transferee forums will be given little weight.[17]

Section 1406(a), by its terms, could be read to be a procedural device authorizing dismissal or transfer of an action where the sole infirmity is improper venue. However, in *Goldlawr Inc. v. Heiman*,[18] the Supreme Court held that Section 1406(a) authorizes the transfer of an action where venue was improper and the court also lacked personal jurisdiction over the defendant.[19] This application of Section 1406(a), the Court reasoned, was in accord with the general purpose of the statute to remove "whatever obstacles may impede an expeditious and orderly adjudication of cases and controversies on their merits.[20] Although *Goldlawr* involved improper venue under Section 1406, subsequent cases have extended its rationale to allow transfers under either Section 1406(a) or Section 1404 where venue is proper but where the transferring court lacks personal jurisdiction over the defendants[21] (a situation

---

13. *See, e.g.*, Sinclair v. Kleindienst, 711 F.2d 291, 294 (D.C.Cir. 1983); Corke v. Sameiet M.S. Song of Norway, 572 F.2d 77, 80 (2d Cir.1978); LaRose v. Sponco Mfg., Inc., 712 F.Supp. 455, 461 (D.N.J.1989); Asociacion de Pescadores de Vieques, Inc. v. United States, 497 F.Supp. 54, 56 (D.P.R.1979); Tillman v. Eattock III, 385 F.Supp. 625, 627 (D.Kan.1974).

14. *See, e.g.*, Zumft, 698 F.Supp. at 447 (transferring an action filed in an improper venue, in part, because the plaintiff did not knowingly file the action in the wrong district); Nanz Trustee Inc. v. American Nat'l Bank & Trust Co., 423 F.Supp. 930, 931–32 (E.D.Wis.1977) (transferring an action filed in an improper venue where "[t]he plaintiff's action does not appear to constitute harassment or to be brought in bad faith, and defendant does not contend that it is").

15. *See* Cottman Transmission Sys., Inc. v. Martino, 36 F.3d 291, 296 (3d Cir.1994); Emjayco *ex rel.* Troy v. Morgan Stanley & Co., 901 F.Supp. 1397, 1403 (C.D.Ill.1995).

16. *See, e.g.*, Professional Ass'n Travel Serv., Inc. v. Arrow Air, Inc., 597 F.Supp. 475, 476 (D.D.C.1984); General Elec. Co. v. FTC, 411 F.Supp. 1004, 1012 (N.D.N.Y. 1976); Allis–Chalmers Mfg. v. Gulf & W. Indus., Inc., 309 F.Supp. 75, 81 (E.D.Wis. 1970).

17. *See* Seitz v. Board of Trustees of the Pension Plan of the N.Y. State Teamsters

Conference Pension & Retirement Fund, 953 F.Supp. 100, 103 (S.D.N.Y.1997) (stating that "[p]laintiffs will not be afforded a second chance at choosing an appropriate venue").

18. 369 U.S. 463, 82 S.Ct. 913, 8 L.Ed.2d 39 (1962).

19. Section 1406(a) may not be applied by a court lacking subject matter jurisdiction. *See* Corke v. Sameiet M.S. Song of Norway, 572 F.2d 77, 79 n. 6 (2d Cir.1978). With respect to an absence of subject matter jurisdiction in a district, see 28 U.S.C.A. § 1631 (West 1994).

20. 369 U.S. at 466–67, 82 S.Ct. at 916.

21. *See, e.g.*, Dubin v. United States, 380 F.2d 813 (5th Cir. 1967) (applying *Goldlawr* where venue was proper under § 1406(a) but case was pending in "wrong district" due to lack of personal jurisdiction); United States v. Berkowitz, 328 F.2d 358, 361 (3d Cir.1964) (holding that the rationale in *Goldlawr* applies equally to § 1404); Koehring Co. v. Hyde Constr. Co., 324 F.2d 295, 297–98 (5th Cir.1963) (holding that "there is no basis for distinguishing between [§§ 1404 and 1406] insofar as the rule enunciated in *Goldlawr* is concerned"); Jaffe v. Julien, 754 F.Supp. 49, 53 (E.D.Pa.1991) (noting in dicta, that action could also be transferred under § 1404 even though the court lacked personal jurisdic-

less likely to occur with the 1990 amendments to the general venue statute).[22] There is also some authority for extending *Goldlawr* to permit a court to use a Section 1406(a) transfer in order to overcome any procedural impediment to a decision on the merits, such as a statute of limitations bar in the transferor forum.[23]

Upon transfer of an action under Section 1406(a) for improper venue, the transferee court will apply the law that would have controlled had the case been brought originally in that court.[24] Similarly, the law of the transferee court will apply to an action transferred for lack of personal jurisdiction in the transferor court.[25] Consistent with these principles, the statute of limitations period applied to the action is governed by the relevant period prescribed under the transferee court's choice of law principles. However, the question of whether the action was timely commenced is determined with reference to the time the action was filed in the transferor court. This result is the product of two post-transfer effects of Section 1406(a): as noted, the choice of law rules of the transferee court's jurisdiction govern the action but the filing of the action in the transferor district operates as a toll on the running of the statute of limitations period in the transferee district.[26]

Library References:

West's Key No. Digests, Federal Civil Procedure ☞1742(5); Federal Courts ☞101–157.

Wright, Miller & Cooper, Federal Practice and Procedure: Civil 2d § 3827.

tion over the defendant). *But see* Rhea v. Muskogee Gen. Hosp., 454 F.Supp. 40, 43 (E.D.Okla.1978).

22. Personal jurisdiction is likely to exist when all defendants reside in the state (a prerequisite for venue to be proper under § 1391(a)(1) or (b)(1)) or when a substantial part of the events or omissions giving rise to the claim occurred in the district (making special jurisdiction likely). Under the fallback provisions, venue could be proper where personal jurisdiction exists in the district over one, but not all, of the defendants.

23. *See* Porter v. Groat, 840 F.2d 255, 258 (4th Cir.1988) (holding that § 1406 (a) "authorizes the transfer of a case to any district, which would have had venue if the case were originally brought there, for any reason which constitutes an impediment to a decision on the merits in the transferor district but would not be an impediment in the transferee district" and applying this principle to permit a transfer from a district with a limitations bar to a district where the action would still be timely). In *Spar, Inc. v. Information Resources, Inc.*, 956 F.2d 392, 394 (2d Cir.1992), the Second Circuit,

disagreeing with the analysis of *Porter*, declined to use § 1406(a) as a way to overcome any procedural bar without any assessment of the interest of justice.

24. *See* Myelle v. American Cyanamid Co., 57 F.3d 411, 413 (4th Cir.1995); Tel–Phonic Servs., Inc. v. TBS Int'l, Inc., 975 F.2d 1134, 1141 (5th Cir.1992); Martin v. Stokes, 623 F.2d 469, 472 (6th Cir.1980); Murphy v. Klein Tools, Inc., 693 F.Supp. 982, 986 (D.Kan.1988); *see also* Geehan v. Monahan, 382 F.2d 111 (7th Cir.1967).

25. *See* Schaeffer v. Village of Ossining, 58 F.3d 48, 53 (2d Cir. 1995); Ellis v. Great Southwestern Corp., 646 F.2d 1099, 1111 (5th Cir. Unit A June 1981)(holding that following a transfer from a district in which personal jurisdiction over the defendant could not be obtained in a diversity suit, the transferee court is required to apply its own choice of law principles, regardless of which party requested the transfer).

26. *See* Goldlawr Inc. v. Heiman, 369 U.S. 463, 465–67, 82 S.Ct. 913, 915–16, 8 L.Ed.2d 39 (1962); Corke v. Sameiet M.S. Song of Norway, 572 F.2d 77, 80 (2d Cir. 1978); Mayo Clinic v. Kaiser, 383 F.2d 653, 656 (8th Cir.1967).

§ 3.9 Transfer or Dismissal of an Action for Convenience of Venue

(a) Convenience and Section 1404(a)

(1) Transfer Factors

Section 1404(a) reads as follows:

(a) For the convenience of parties and witnesses, in the interest of justice, a district court may transfer any civil action to any other district or division where it might have been brought.[1]

There are literally thousands of reported or retrievable transfer decisions. Apparently prompted by appellate court admonitions to state reasons for granting or denying transfer motions,[2] district courts routinely state and apply factors to be considered on a transfer motion. These factors were originally derived from the private and public interest factors considered under the common law doctrine of forum non conveniens,[3] but the standard for a transfer under Section 1404 is now recognized as distinct from the standard for a forum non conveniens dismissal.[4] As a result, there is a plethora of similar, but subtly different, formulations on which to draw when briefing a transfer motion in a commercial case. It is both practical and prudent to retrieve through WESTLAW one or more decisions by the assigned judge to adopt as the framework for the motion.

In evaluating whether a proposed transfer "serve[s] the convenience of the parties and witnesses and the interest of justice," courts over time have, with varying phrasing, generally applied a list of factors including: (1) the convenience of the litigants; (2) the convenience of the witnesses; (3) the location of relevant documents and the relative ease of access to sources of proof; (4) the locus of the operative facts; (5) the availability of compulsory process for attendance of unwilling, and the cost of obtaining attendance of willing, witnesses; (6) the weight to be accorded the plaintiff's choice of forum; (7) the presence and terms of a forum selection clause; (8) the economic disparity between the parties; and (9)

§ 3.9

1. See 28 U.S.C.A. § 1404(a) (West 1993); see generally Stowell R.R. Kelner, Note, "Adrift on an Unchartered Sea"; A Survey of Section 1404(a) Transfer in the Federal System, 67 N.Y.U. L. Rev. 612 (1992); David E. Steinberg, The Motion to Transfer and the Interests of Justice, 66 Notre Dame L. Rev. 443 (1990).

2. Charles Alan Wright, Federal Courts § 44, at 279 n. 26 (1994).

3. See infra § 3.9(c); see also Norwood v. Kirkpatrick, 349 U.S. 29, 32, 75 S.Ct. 544, 546, 99 L.Ed.2d 789 (1955) (stating that the factors which are relevant in a forum non conveniens analysis are also relevant when considering a transfer motion);

Koehring Co. v. Hyde Constr. Co., 324 F.2d 295, 296 (5th Cir.1963); United States Fidelity & Guar. Co. v. Republic Drug Co., 800 F.Supp. 1076, 1080 (E.D.N.Y.1992) (stating that factors considered on a motion to transfer are "essentially the same" as those considered in determining whether an action should be dismissed for forum non conveniens).

4. See Piper Aircraft Co. v. Reyno, 454 U.S. 235, 253, 102 S.Ct. 252, 265, 70 L.Ed.2d 419 (1981) ("District courts were given more discretion to transfer under § 1404(a) than they had to dismiss on grounds of forum non conveniens.").

trial efficiency and the interests of justice, based on the totality of the circumstances.[5]

Although all factors should be canvassed, the weight to be given to each of the factors is entrusted to the sound discretion of the court.[6] Courts have frequently accorded greater weight to some factors over others. For example, many courts view the convenience of material witnesses as the single most important factor.[7] While the budgets for commercial litigations can often allow videotaping of depositions taken outside the district and teleconferencing of trial testimony of out-of-district witnesses, some courts continue to weigh the ability to present live testimony of the key witnesses at trial as an important factor to be considered on a transfer motion.[8]

In order to show that a transfer would serve the convenience of the witnesses, the movant should by affidavit specifically set forth the material witnesses for whom the transferee district would be more convenient (and/or on whom a subpoena could be served in the transferee district) together with a statement of the topics of each witness' testimony.[9] Some courts have held that a movant's failure to specify the

5. See generally Annotation, Questions as to Convenience and Justice of Transfer Under Forum Non Conveniens Provision of Judicial Code (28 U.S.C.A. § 1404(a)), 1 A.L.R. Fed. 15 (1969). For representative examples of district court formulations of the transfer factors, see, e.g., Duncan v. International Bus. Mach., Corp., No. 95 Civ. 1785, 1996 WL 720106, at *2 (S.D.N.Y. 1996); Terra Int'l, Inc. v. Mississippi Chem. Corp., 922 F.Supp. 1334, 1357–65 (N.D. Iowa 1996), aff'd, 119 F.3d 688 (8th Cir. 1997); Pilates, Inc. v. Pilates Inst., Inc., 891 F.Supp. 175, 183 (S.D.N.Y.1995); Miller v. Meadowlands Car Imports, Inc., 822 F.Supp. 61, 66 (D. Conn.1993); International Show Car Ass'n v. American Soc'y of Composers, Authors & Publishers, 806 F.Supp. 1308, 1310 (E.D.Mich.1992); United States Fidelity & Guar. Co., 800 F.Supp. at 1080; Cordis Corp v. Siemens–Pacesetter, Inc., 682 F.Supp. 1200, 1202 (S.D.Fla.1987); Hite v. Norwegian Caribbean Lines, 551 F.Supp. 390, 394 (E.D.Mich.1982).

6. See Coffey v. Van Dorn Iron Works, 796 F.2d 217, 219 (7th Cir.1986); Georgouses v. Natec Resources, Inc., 963 F.Supp. 728, 730 (N.D.Ill.1997).

7. See, e.g., Duncan, 1996 WL 720106, at *4; Pilates, Inc., 891 F.Supp. at 183; French Transit, Ltd. v. Modern Coupon Sys., Inc., 858 F.Supp. 22, 27 (S.D.N.Y. 1994); Houk v. Kimberly–Clark Corp., 613 F.Supp. 923, 928 (W.D.Mo.1985); Cambridge Filter Corp. v. International Filter Co., 548 F.Supp. 1308, 1311 (D.Nev.1982).

8. See Rohde v. Central R.R., 951 F.Supp. 746, 748 (N.D. Ill.1997) (holding that the convenience of the witnesses factor did not favor transfer since the testimony of key witnesses could be obtained in the transferee district only through deposition); Anderson v. Century Prods. Co., 943 F.Supp. 137, 149 (D.N.H.1996) (stating that "justice is better served when the testimony of witnesses is live, rather than by deposition"); see also Notes of Advisory Committee on 1996 Amendments to FRCP 43(a) (permitting teleconferenced testimony in lieu of live testimony only upon a showing of good cause). Other courts, however, have accorded increasingly less weight to the convenience of witnesses factor because of the availability of deposition testimony. See Duncan, 1996 WL 720106, at *5 (stating any inconvenience to witnesses can be remedied by presenting videotaped depositions of out of state witnesses); Caribbean Wholesales & Serv. Corp. v. US JVC Corp., No. 93 Civ. 8197, 1996 WL 140251, at *6 (S.D.N.Y.1996); ROC, Inc. v. Progress Drillers, Inc., 481 F.Supp. 147, 152 (W.D.Okla. 1979); Bussey v. Safeway Stores, Inc., 437 F.Supp. 41, 44 (E.D.Okla.1977); In re Eastern Dist. Repetitive Stress Injury Litig., 850 F.Supp. 188, 194 (E.D.N.Y.1994).

9. See Pilates, Inc., 891 F.Supp. at 183; United States Fidelity & Guar. Co., 800 F.Supp. at 1081; Central Hudson Gas & Elec. Corp v. Empresa Naviera Santa, S.A., 769 F.Supp. 208, 209 (E.D.La.1991); Houk,

names, locations and expected testimony of important witnesses is sufficient to deny a motion to transfer.[10] If discovery is required to enable this specification, a transfer motion may be denied pending discovery.[11] Conversely, when opposing a transfer motion, it would be prudent to specify the names, locations and expected testimony of important witnesses who reside within the pending district.[12] It is ultimately the substance, uniqueness and unavailability in the pending forum of the testimony of the various witnesses, rather than the mere number of witnesses identified by each side, that is to be weighed.[13] Thus, nonparty witnesses outside the control of the movant are more heavily considered.[14] If the case is likely to be decided without trial (such as an insurance coverage dispute depending on the interpretation of the insurance policies), the availability of witnesses in the forum is of little importance.[15]

Expert witnesses are often engaged in commercial cases.[16] However, the convenience of expert witnesses is often accorded little or no weight on a motion to transfer.[17] Most courts have concluded that expert

613 F.Supp. at 928; ROC, Inc., 481 F.Supp. at 152; Bussey, 437 F.Supp. at 44; Myers v. Pan Am. World Airways, Inc., 388 F.Supp. 1024, 1025–26 (D.P.R.1974).

10. *See, e.g.*, Factors Etc., Inc. v. Pro Arts, Inc., 579 F.2d 215, 218 (2d Cir.1978), *superseded on other grounds by* Pirone v. MacMillan, Inc., 894 F.2d 579 (2d Cir.1990); Pilates Inc., 891 F.Supp. at 183; Aamco Automatic Transmissions, Inc. v. Hagenbarth, 296 F.Supp. 1142, 1143 (E.D.Pa. 1968); Struthers Scientific & Int'l Corp. v. General Foods Corp., 290 F.Supp. 122, 126–27 (S.D.Tex.1968); *see also* Carlile v. Continental Airlines, Inc., 953 F.Supp. 169, 171 (S.D.Tex.1997) ("Generalized allegations concerning the inconvenience of witnesses are insufficient to justify a transfer of venue."); ROC Inc., 481 F.Supp. at 152.

11. *See* Kron Med. Corp. v. Groth, 119 F.R.D. 636, 638 (M.D.N.C.1988) (recognizing that prior to ruling on a motion to transfer, "discovery may be required in order to identify and refine the issues pertinent to the transfer issue"). *Cf.* McQueeny v. J.W. Fergusson & Sons, Inc., 527 F.Supp. 728, 732 (D.N.J.1981) (denying motion to transfer without prejudice to renew after discovery, because discovery was more convenient in pending venue). In *Heyco, Inc. v. Heyman*, 636 F.Supp. 1545, 1550–51 (S.D.N.Y.1986), the court excused movant's failure to list out of state witnesses with particularity because discovery had been stayed.

12. *See, e.g.,* Greenberg v. Greenberg, 954 F.Supp. 213 (D. Colo.1997) (denying

motion to transfer, where moving party failed to provide, but nonmoving party provided, a detailed list of witnesses).

13. *See* O'Neil v. Gencorp, Inc., No. 88 Civ. 8498, 1991 WL 41631, at *3 (S.D.N.Y. 1991); *see also* Howell v. Shaw Indus., Nos. Civ. 93–2068, Civ. 93–2638, 1993 WL 387901, at *5 (E.D.Pa.1993) ("When examining the convenience to witnesses factor, greater weight should be given to the convenience of witnesses on liability than to witnesses on damages.").

14. *See* State St. Capital Corp. v. Dente, 855 F.Supp. 192, 197 (S.D.Tex.1994); Aquatic Amusement Assocs., Ltd. v. Walt Disney World Co., 734 F.Supp. 54, 57 (N.D.N.Y.1990).

15. *See* Evangelical Lutheran Church in Am. v. Atlantic Mut. Ins. Co., 973 F.Supp. 820, 823 (N.D.Ill.1997).

16. *See* Chapter 23 "Selection of Experts, Expert Disclosure and the Pretrial Exclusion of Expert Testimony" and Chapter 35 "Expert Witnesses," *infra.*

17. *See* Houck v. Trans World Airlines, Inc., 947 F.Supp. 373, 376 n. 5 (N.D.Ill. 1996) (noting that the location of expert witnesses is not relevant); Brown v. Dow Corning Corp., No. 93 Civ. 5510, 1996 WL 257614, at *2 (S.D.N.Y.1996) (stating that "since an expert witness is paid for his or her time, 'the convenience of expert witnesses is of little or no significance on a motion to transfer'") (citations omitted); Fluor Corp. v. Pullman, Inc., 446 F.Supp.

testimony can be received through depositions, or that a new expert can be retained in the forum district. Also, experts in commercial cases are typically accustomed to traveling for deposition and trial.

Other courts view the "interest of justice" as the single most important factor.[18] The interest of justice factor generally relates to issues concerning the convenience of the court[19] and the integrity of the judicial process.[20] Courts under this factor consider the pendency of related actions in the transferee court,[21] economic and efficient utilization of judicial resources,[22] the ability to implead third parties,[23] and, to a

777, 779 (W.D. Okla.1977) (giving little weight to the convenience of expert witnesses "for whom travel and expense are customary"); *see also Howell*, 1993 WL 387901, at *5; Paul v. International Precious Metals Corp., 613 F.Supp. 174, 179 (S.D.Miss.1985) ("Traditionally, the convenience of expert witnesses is entitled to little consideration on a motion to transfer venue...."). *But see* Stolz v. Barker, 466 F.Supp. 24, 28 (M.D.N.C.1978) (giving some weight to the convenience of expert witnesses on motion to transfer a shareholder's derivative suit alleging securities fraud); *see also* Oscar Meyer Foods Corp. v. Bryan Foods, Inc., No. 1:89–CV–364–RHH, 1989 WL 164358, at *1 (N.D.Ga.1989) ("In determining whether a change of venue serves the interests of justice, the court is to consider several factors, among them are: the convenience of the witnesses—expert and nonexpert.... "); Duman v. Crown Zellerbach Corp., 107 F.R.D. 761, 766 (N.D.Ill.1985) (considering convenience of expert witnesses on a motion to transfer explaining that, "the present case may well present the rare occasion where the convenience of expert witnesses, or more properly, the considerable expense of paying for their time, is entitled to some weight").

18. *See* Regents of Univ. v. Eli Lilly & Co., 119 F.3d 1559, 1565 (Fed.Cir.1997) ("Consideration of the interest of justice, which includes judicial economy, 'may be determinative to a particular transfer motion, even if the convenience of the parties and witnesses might call for a different result.' ") (citation omitted); Frazier v. Commercial Credit Equip. Corp., 755 F.Supp. 163, 167 (S.D.Miss.1991); *see, e.g.,* Lemke v. St. Margaret Hosp., 594 F.Supp. 25, 28 (N.D.Ill.1983).

19. *See* Coffey v. Van Dorn Iron Works, 796 F.2d 217, 221 (7th Cir.1986) ("Factors traditionally considered in an 'interest of justice' analysis relate to the efficient administration of the court system."); SRAM

Corp. v. SunRace Roots Enter. Co., 953 F.Supp. 257, 260 (N.D.Ill.1997) (stating that "the interests of justice" component includes "the speed at which case will proceed to trial, the feasibility of consolidation, the court's familiarity with applicable law, and the public interest in having a case resolved in a particular forum"); Frazier, 755 F.Supp. at 167.

20. *See* Aviles v. Cantieri de Baia–Mericraft S.P.A., 943 F.Supp. 154, 155 (D.P.R. 1996) (stating that court must consider "those public interest factors of systematic integrity and fairness, that in addition to private concerns come under the heading of 'the interest of justice' ") (citation omitted); Terra Int'l, Inc. v. Mississippi Chem. Corp., 922 F.Supp. 1334, 1363 (N.D.Iowa 1996) (listing the ability to enforce a judgment and the relative advantages and obstacles to a fair trial, as relevant factors in considering the whether a transfer would be in the interest of justice), *aff'd on other grounds*, 119 F.3d 688 (8th Cir.1997).

21. *See* A.J. Indus., Inc. v. United States Dist. Ct., 503 F.2d 384, 389 (9th Cir.1974); Wyndham Assocs. v. Bintliff, 398 F.2d 614, 619 (2d Cir.1968); Vasconcellos v. Cybex Int'l, Inc., 962 F.Supp. 701, 707 (D.Md. 1997); Nieves v. American Airlines, 700 F.Supp. 769, 773 (S.D.N.Y. 1988); Fossett Corp. v. Gearhart, 694 F.Supp. 1325, 1327 (N.D. Ill.1988); Cordis Corp v. Siemens–Pacesetter, Inc., 682 F.Supp. 1200, 1202 (S.D.Fla.1987).

22. *See* Howell v. Tanner, 650 F.2d 610, 616 (5th Cir. Unit B July 1981); Frazier, 755 F.Supp. at 167 (holding that "the interests of justice cannot be served by the transfer of a case to another forum where the motion to transfer is placed before the court at a point where the forum court has already expended substantial resources on consideration and management of the case"); Lencco Racing Co. v. Arctco, Inc.,

lesser degree, the state law to be applied (if a diversity action)[24] and congestion of the respective court dockets.[25]

In evaluating the convenience of the parties, it is often said that the plaintiff's choice of forum is usually accorded great weight and should not be disturbed unless the balance of factors tips heavily in favor of transfer.[26] Thus, a transfer will not be granted if it merely shifts the inconvenience from one party to another.[27] Nor will a transfer be granted upon motion by defendant simply on the strength that the pending forum is supposedly inconvenient to the plaintiff.[28]

In order to demonstrate that the convenience of the parties favors transfer, a defendant in a commercial action should, where relevant, present evidence demonstrating that litigating the action in the pending forum would substantially and unavoidably disrupt its business operations.[29] In addition, a defendant can greatly reduce the substantial

953 F.Supp. 69, 73 (W.D.N.Y.1997) (granting transfer, in part, to permit related claims to proceed together where there were jurisdictional and venue objections raised by co-defendants); Willemijn Houdstermaatschaapij BV v. Apollo Computer Inc., 707 F.Supp. 1429, 1438 (D.Del.1989) ("Judicial economy favors the retention of the present case since this Court has already become involved with substantive aspects of the matter.").

23. *See* Murphy v. Allen County Claims & Adjustments, Inc., 550 F.Supp. 128, 132–33 (S.D. Ohio 1982) ("Where convenience and other facts are inconclusive, the pendency of related litigation may be dispositive; however, it does not outweigh facts militating against transfer."); Prentice–Hall Corp. Sys. v. Insurance Co. of N. Am., 81 F.R.D. 477, 481 (S.D.N.Y.1979).

24. *See* Merritt v. Jay Pontiac–GMC Truck, Inc., 952 F.Supp. 754, 756–57 (M.D.Ala.1996); Duncan v. International Bus. Mach., Corp., No. 95 Civ. 1785, 1996 WL 720106, at *7 (S.D.N.Y.1996); Frazier, 755 F.Supp. at 168; Terra Int'l Inc., 922 F.Supp. at 1363.

25. *See* Trout Unlimited v. United States Dep't of Agric., 944 F.Supp. 13, 19 (D.D.C.1996); Lencco Racing Co., Inc. v. Artco, Inc., 953 F.Supp. 69, 73 (W.D.N.Y. 1997); Houk v. Kimberly–Clark Corp., 613 F.Supp. 923, 932 (W.D.Mo.1985); United States Fidelity & Guar. Co. v. Republic Drug Co., 800 F.Supp. 1076, 1082 (E.D.N.Y. 1992); International Show Car Ass'n v. American Soc'y of Composers, Authors & Publishers, 806 F.Supp. 1308, 1315 (E.D.Mich.1992). Data is usually obtained from Federal Court Management Statistics.

26. *See* Duncan, 1996 WL 720106, at *2; United States Fidelity & Guar. Co., 800 F.Supp. at 1082; Willemijn Houdstermaatschaapij BV, 707 F.Supp. at 1436; Heyco, Inc. v. Heyman, 636 F.Supp. 1545, 1550 (S.D.N.Y.1986); Houk, 613 F.Supp. at 927. However, plaintiff's choice of forum is accorded little or no weight when the plaintiff sues in a representative capacity. *See* Georgouses v. Natec Resources, Inc., 963 F.Supp. 728, 730 (N.D.Ill.1997); Howell, 1993 WL 387901, at *3 (and cases cited therein); Burstein v. Applied Extrusion Techs., Inc., 829 F.Supp. 106, 111 (D.Del. 1992); Stolz v. Barker, 466 F.Supp. 24, 27 (M.D.N.C.1978) (stating that plaintiffs' choice of forum was entitled to almost no deference in a shareholder's derivative action).

27. Greenberg v. Greenberg, 954 F.Supp. 213, 217 (D.Colo.1997); Symons Corp. v. Southern Forming & Supply, Inc., 954 F.Supp. 184, 186 (N.D.Ill. 1997); Central Sports Army Club v. Arena Assocs., Inc., 952 F.Supp. 181, 189 (S.D.N.Y.1997); Howell, 1993 WL 387901, at *3.

28. *See* Hayes v. Chesapeake & Ohio Ry., 374 F.Supp. 1068 (S.D. Ohio 1973); American Can Co. v. Crown Cork & Seal Co., 433 F.Supp. 333 (E.D.Wis.1977).

29. *See, e.g.,* SRAM Corp. v. SunRace Roots Enter. Co., 953 F.Supp. 257, 260 (N.D.Ill.1997) (holding that convenience of parties weighed in favor of transfer where the plaintiff was a large international corporation and the defendant was a small corporation, because the "disruption of business affairs due to the time and cost of distant litigation is far more severe and

deference normally accorded plaintiff's choice of venue by demonstrating that the pending venue is neither the plaintiff's place of residence, or in a commercial action, principal place of business, nor has a material relation or significant connection to the transaction giving rise to the action.[30] Also, as discussed in Section 3.6 of this chapter, a defendant might supersede the plaintiff's choice of venue by presenting to the court proof of a controlling valid forum selection clause designating venue in a district other than the venue chosen by the plaintiff.

Commercial cases are often characterized by substantial volumes of documents related to the dispute. Movants often invoke the location of their records outside the district as a factor supporting transfer. Frequently, courts respond that, through photocopying and other means, the necessary documents from outside the pending district can be made available for trial and—absent a great disparity between the parties' volume of documents—this is not a persuasive factor.[31] This factor is likely to become even less important with technological advances such as document imaging.[32] The location of documents is sometimes cited as an

detrimental to a small corporation than it is to a much large corporation"); Burstein, 829 F.Supp. at 112 (on a motion to transfer, considering the potential disruption to defendant's business); Paul v. International Precious Metals Corp., 613 F.Supp. 174, 179 (S.D.Miss.1985) (stating that "the disruption to the Defendant's business operations by requiring seven or eight key employees to appear for trial in the Southern District of Mississippi is a significant factor counselling in favor of transfer"); see also Stolz, 466 F.Supp. at 28.

30. See, e.g., Rock Bit Int'l, Inc. v. Smith Int'l, Inc., 957 F.Supp. 843, 844 (E.D.Tex.1997); Viacom Int'l, Inc. v. Melvin Simon Prods., Inc., 774 F.Supp. 858, 868 (S.D.N.Y.1991) (holding that "center of gravity of the litigation" is a "core determination" under § 1404 and concluding that absence of connection with district in this case weakens weight due to plaintiff's choice of forum); United States Fidelity & Guar. Co., 800 F.Supp. at 1082; Heyco, Inc., 636 F.Supp. at 1550; Jordan v. Delaware & Hudson Ry. Co., 590 F.Supp. 997, 998 (E.D.Pa.1984); see also State Farm Mut. Auto. Ins. Co. v. Estate of Bussell, 939 F.Supp. 646, 651 (S.D.Ind.1996) (stating that where "the chosen forum is not the plaintiff's residence, the defendants' place of residence becomes more important in determining the convenience of the parties"); Willemijn Houdstermaatschaapij BV, 707 F.Supp. at 1436 (explaining that the "home turf" exception to the deference afforded a plaintiff's choice of forum applies when the selected venue is connected to the

subject matter of the action); ROC, Inc. v. Progress Drillers, Inc., 481 F.Supp. 147, 151 (W.D.Okla.1979) (holding that less deference is accorded to plaintiff's choice of venue where there is no significant connection between the forum state and the conduct underlying the action).

31. See, e.g., Southland Terrace Assocs. v. Mellon Bank, N.A. 874 F.Supp. 69, 71 (S.D.N.Y.1995) (observing that "defendant's reliance on the location of documents overlooks the fact that copying technology has made the use of original documents in litigation about as common as the dodo bird except in unusual circumstances involving issues of authenticity and legibility"); Howell, 1993 WL 387901, at *4 ("Today, with the advent of photocopying and the easy accessibility to copies, the location of documents is entitled to little weight when considering a motion to transfer venue."). In *Falconwood Financial Corp. v. Griffin*, 838 F.Supp. 836, 841 (S.D.N.Y.1993), the court considered the location of documents of a nonparty, where that nonparty was a party in an action in the proposed transferee forum.

32. Sunshine Cellular v. Vanguard Cellular Sys., Inc., 810 F.Supp. 486, 500 (S.D.N.Y.1992) (holding that "[a]ccess to documents and other proof is not a persuasive factor in favor of transfer without proof that documents are particularly bulky or difficult to transport, or proof that it is somehow a greater imposition for defendant to bring its evidence to New York than for

additional item when a court finds that the proof and operative facts related to the dispute are linked to the transferee forum.[33]

(2) Limitations on Transfer

Section 1404(a) authorizes only the transfer of an entire action, not individual claims,[34] unless the claims are properly severed under Rule 21 before a transfer is effectuated.[35] In addition, Section 1404(a) permits the transfer of an action only from a district where venue is proper to a different district "where the action might have been brought." In interpreting this statutory language, the Supreme Court in *Hoffman v. Blaski*[36] held that a court may not transfer an action to a district which would have been improper if the plaintiff had originally filed the action there, even if the motion under consideration is filed by a defendant who now waives any objection to improper venue. The limitation of *Hoffman* also precludes transfer to a district in which process could not have been served on defendant.[37]

Some limited exceptions have been fashioned by the lower courts to the restrictive rule announced in *Hoffman*.[38] Moreover, the effect of this

plaintiff to bring its evidence to [the moving party's proposed forum]").

33. *See, e.g.,* Lencco Racing Co. v. Arctco, Inc., 953 F.Supp. 69, 71 (W.D.N.Y.1997); Hardee's Food Sys., Inc. v. Beardmore, 169 F.R.D. 311, 317 (E.D.N.C.1996) (rejecting argument that transfer was warranted because evidence consisted of voluminous records, where movant failed to identify the location of the documents or explain the difficulty in transporting them).

34. *See, e.g.,* Chrysler Credit Corp. v. Country Chrysler, Inc., 928 F.2d 1509, 1518 (10th Cir.1991); Wyndham Assocs. v. Bintliff, 398 F.2d 614, 618 (2d Cir.1968); Cain v. New York State Bd. of Elections, 630 F.Supp. 221, 226 (E.D.N.Y.1986).

35. *See* Gold v. Burton Corp., 949 F.Supp. 208, 210 (S.D.N.Y.1996); Mobil Oil Corp. v. W.R. Grace & Co., 334 F.Supp. 117, 121–24 (S.D. Tex.1971); Leesona Corp. v. Cotwool Mfg., 204 F.Supp. 139, 140–41 (W.D.S.C. 1962). *But see* Williams v. National Hous. Exch., Inc., 898 F.Supp. 157 (S.D.N.Y.1995) (transferring under § 1404(a) only some of the claims in a multi-claim action and retaining the rest). *See also* Saferstein v. Paul, Mardinly, Durham, James, Flandreau & Rodger, P.C., 927 F.Supp. 731, 737 (S.D.N.Y.1996)(transferring a multi-claim action under both §§ 1404(a) and 1406(a), because venue as to some of the claims were proper while venue as to the remaining claims was improper).

36. 363 U.S. 335, 80 S.Ct. 1084, 4 L.Ed.2d 1254 (1960).

37. *See* Lamont v. Haig, 590 F.2d 1124 (8th Cir.1978); Karriem v. American Kennel Club, 949 F.Supp. 220, 222 (S.D.N.Y.1996) (stating that in a multi-defendant case, "an action 'might have been brought' only in a district in which all defendants are amenable to process and in which venue would be proper for all of them").

38. *See, e.g.,* Liaw Su Teng v. Skaarup Shipping Corp., 743 F.2d 1140 (5th Cir. 1984), *overruled on other grounds by In re Air Crash Disaster Near New Orleans, Louisiana On July 8, 1982,* 821 F.2d 1147 (5th Cir.1987) (holding that a court may transfer an action to a venue that was improper at the time the action was commenced, if the plaintiff and not the defendant is the one seeking the transfer and the objecting defendant had itself previously sought the same transfer); *In re* Fine Paper Antitrust Litig., 685 F.2d 810 (3d Cir.1982) (holding that a court may transfer an action on a defendant's motion to a district that was improper at the time the action was commenced, if the defendant whose presence in the action made that district improper is no longer a party to the action at the time the motion was made); A.J. Indus., Inc. v. United States Dist. Ct., 503 F.2d 384, 389 (9th Cir.1974) (holding that a court may transfer an action to a district where procedural difficulties, such as lack of personal jurisdiction, prevented the action from being

restriction has been lessened since *Hoffman* was decided in 1960 by the broadening amendments to the general venue statute, which provide for venue in a district in which (i) any defendant resides if all of the defendants reside in the same state; (ii) a substantial part of the events or omissions giving rise to the claim occurred; or (iii) any defendant is found or subject to personal jurisdiction at the time the action is commenced (provided neither ground (i) nor (ii) is available).[39]

(3) Governing Law After Transfer

The Supreme Court has made clear in two separate decisions that when a diversity action is transferred pursuant to Section 1404(a), the law of the transferor court controls the action, regardless of which party initiated the transfer.[40] A defendant who successfully transfers an action under Section 1404(a) acquires a convenient forum without effecting a change of the governing law. Conversely, a diversity plaintiff who secures a transfer under Section 1404 can enjoy the best of both worlds: a more convenient forum and a favorable governing law.[41]

The Supreme Court, however, has yet to rule on which district's law governs a federal question action transferred under Section 1404.[42] Theoretically, federal law should be uniform in all federal districts; in practice, however, that is not always the case.[43] Despite the lack of

brought there originally, if the moving party had the ability to raise the subject matter of the action in the transferor district by counterclaim in the transferee district); *see generally* 15 Charles Alan Wright, Arthur R. Miller & Edward H. Cooper, Federal Practice and Procedure § 3845, at 345–56 (1986).

39. *See supra* § 3.4(b).

40. *See* Ferens v. John Deere Co., 494 U.S. 516, 110 S.Ct. 1274, 108 L.Ed.2d 443 (1990) (holding that in a diversity action, the law of the transferor court applies even when the transfer was initiated by the plaintiff); Van Dusen v. Barrack, 376 U.S. 612, 84 S.Ct. 805, 111 L.Ed.2d 945 (1964) (holding that in a diversity action, the law of the transferor court controls when the defendant secures a transfer); Thorn v. International Bus. Machs., Inc., 101 F.3d 70, 73 (8th Cir.1996) (holding that the statute of limitations from the transferor forum governs diversity cases after transfer). However, a number of circuit courts have stated that the law of the transferee court should apply when an action is transferred under § 1404(a) for lack of personal jurisdiction. *See* Muldoon v. Tropitone Furniture Co., 1 F.3d 964, 967 (9th Cir.1993); Levy v. Pyramid Co., 871 F.2d 9, 10 (2d Cir.1989); Ellis v. Great Southwestern Corp., 646 F.2d 1099, 1110 (5th Cir.1981)

(holding that following a transfer from a district in which personal jurisdiction over the defendant could not be obtained in a diversity suit, the transferee court is required to apply its own choice of law principles, regardless of which party requested the transfer and regardless of whether the action was transferred under § 1406(a) or § 1404(a)). *But see* Myelle v. American Cyanamid Co., 57 F.3d 411, 412–13 (4th Cir.1995).

41. *See* Ferens, 494 U.S. at 531, 110 S.Ct. at 1284 ("Our rule may seem too generous because it allows [plaintiffs] to have both their choice of law and their choice of forum.... "); *see generally* Kimberly Jade Norwood, *Double Forum Shopping and the Extension of Ferens to Federal Claims that Borrow State Limitation Periods*, 44 Emory L.J. 501 (1995).

42. *See generally* Maryellen Corna, Note, *Confusion and Dissension Surrounding the Venue Transfer Statutes*, 53 Ohio St. L.J. 319 (1992).

43. *See In re* Korean Air Lines Disaster, 829 F.2d 1171, 1174 (D.C. Cir.1987)(recognizing conflicts among the circuits on the proper interpretation of federal law), *aff'd on other grounds sub nom.* Chan v. Korean Air Lines, Ltd., 490 U.S. 122, 109 S.Ct. 1676, 104 L.Ed.2d 113 (1989).

Supreme Court authority on this issue, the federal courts, following the District of Columbia Circuit's decision in *In re Korean Air Lines Disaster*,[44] almost uniformly agree that the law of the transferee district should control purely federal question actions transferred under Section 1404(a).[45]

However, there is some disagreement among the courts as to which district's law governs a federal question action transferred under Section 1404(a) when the court must consult state law to resolve a federal claim.[46] This issue is most commonly presented in commercial litigation when federal courts apply the most analogous state statute of limitations period to a federal claim for which Congress did not prescribe a limitations period.[47]

(b) Retransfer

Since transfer orders are interlocutory and not final judgments, principles of res judicata do not apply[48] and accordingly, transferee courts are technically empowered to retransfer an action. However, transferee courts should only retransfer an action under the "most impelling and unusual circumstances" or when the transfer is "manifestly erroneous."[49] The "impelling and unusual circumstances standard" has been defined as "unanticipatable post-transfer events [that would] frustrate the original purpose for transfer."[50] The "manifestly

---

44. *Id.* This motion was under § 1407. In fact, the court stated at the conclusion of its analysis that, "we deal here not with an 'all purpose' transfer under 28 U.S.C.A. § 1404(a), but a transfer under 28 U.S.C.A. § 1407 'for coordinated or consolidated pretrial proceedings.' " *Id.* at 1176. Other courts have adopted the analysis for § 1404 transfers. *See, e.g., In re* United Mine Workers of Am. Employee Benefit Plans Litig., 854 F.Supp. 914 (D.D.C.1994)(noting that the District of Columbia Circuit's decision in *In re* Korean Air Lines Disaster, was premised on the assumption that the same choice of law principles apply to cases transferred under §§ 1404(a) and 1407).

45. *See, e.g.,* Wilborn v. Department of Health & Human Servs., 49 F.3d 597, 600 n. 2 (9th Cir.1995); Newton v. Thomason, 22 F.3d 1455, 1460 (9th Cir.1994); Eckstein v. Balcor Film Investors, 8 F.3d 1121, 1126 (7th Cir.1993); *In re* Air Disaster, 819 F.Supp. 1352, 1370–71 (E.D. Mich.1993).

46. For cases applying the law of the transferee district, see, for example, Menowitz v. Brown, 991 F.2d 36, 40–41 (2d Cir.1993)(action consolidated under § 1407); *In re* Taxable Mun. Bond Sec. Litig., 796 F.Supp. 954, 963 (E.D.La.1992) (action consolidated under § 1407); *In re*

Litigation Involving Alleged Loss of Cargo, 772 F.Supp. 707, 711 (D.P.R.1991).

For cases applying the law of the transferor district, see, for example, Eckstein v. Balcor Film Investors, 8 F.3d 1121, 1126 (7th Cir.1993); *In re* United Mine Workers of Am. Employee Benefit Plans Litig., 854 F.Supp. at 919 (action consolidated under § 1407); *In re* Rospatch Sec. Litig., 760 F.Supp. 1239, 1256–57 (W.D. Mich.1991).

47. *See, e.g.,* Eckstein, 8 F.3d at 1126; *In re* Taxable Mun. Bond Sec. Litig., 796 F.Supp. at 963 (action consolidated under § 1407); *In re* Rospatch Sec. Litig., 760 F.Supp. at 1256–57.

48. *See* Hoffman v. Blaski, 363 U.S. 335, 340 n. 9, 80 S.Ct. 1084, 1088 n. 9, 4 L.Ed.2d 1254 (1960); Buhl v. Jeffes, 435 F.Supp. 1149, 1151–52 (M.D.Pa.1977).

49. *See In re* Cragar Indus., Inc., 706 F.2d 503, 505 (5th Cir.1983) (citation omitted); *see also* Caribbean Wholesales & Serv. Corp. v. US JVC Corp., No. 93 Civ. 8197, 1996 WL 140251, at *4 (S.D.N.Y.1996) (citing *In re* Cragar Indus., Inc., 706 F.2d at 505); Russell v. IU Int'l Corp., 685 F.Supp. 172, 176 (N.D.Ill.1988) (same).

50. *See In re* Cragar Indus., Inc., 706 F.2d at 505; *see also* Caribbean Wholesales & Serv. Corp., 1996 WL 140251, at *4.

erroneous" standard has been invoked to retransfer actions which were transferred under Section 1406 where venue was proper in the transferor district;[51] where the transferee court was not a district where the action may have been brought, *e.g.*, because venue and/or personal jurisdiction did not exist in the transferee district;[52] or where the transferring judge was misinformed as to crucial facts affecting the propriety of the transfer.[53]

Despite having the authority to do so, there are two principal reasons why transferee courts are reluctant to retransfer actions. First, there is a concern that by reviewing a transfer order, the transferee court is in effect acting as an appellate court.[54] Second, there is a concern that an action could "conceivably shuttle back and forth interminably" between the transferor and transferee districts, without any adjudication of the action on the merits.[55]

(c) Forum Non Conveniens

Prior to the enactment of Section 1404(a), an action could only be dismissed upon a showing of inconvenience under the doctrine of forum non conveniens. However, since the enactment of Section 1404(a), which affords courts with the discretion to transfer actions among federal districts, the doctrine of forum non conveniens has almost exclusively been applied to actions which should have been brought in a foreign country[56] and, in very rare circumstances, to actions which should have

---

51. *See, e.g.*, Buhl, 435 F.Supp. at 1151–52.

52. *See, e.g.*, Ferri v. United Aircraft Corp., 357 F.Supp. 814 (D.Conn.1973).

53. *See, e.g.*, Hite v. Norwegian Caribbean Lines, 551 F.Supp. 390 (E.D.Mich.1982); *see also* Plywood Panels, Inc. v. M/V Thalia, 141 F.R.D. 689 (E.D.La.1992).

54. *See* Gulf Research & Dev. Co. v. Schlumberger Well Surveying Corp., 98 F.Supp.198, 201 (D.Del.1951); *see also* Technitrol, Inc. v. McManus, 405 F.2d 84, 89 (8th Cir.1968).

55. *See* Gulf Research & Dev. Co., 98 F.Supp. at 201; *see also In re* Cragar Indus., Inc., 706 F.2d at 505. The basis for this cited concern is vividly illustrated in *Hite v. Norwegian Caribbean Lines*, 551 F.Supp. 390 (E.D.Mich.1982). In that case, the plaintiff originally filed her action in a Michigan state court, and the defendant removed the action to the Eastern District of Michigan. The Eastern District sua sponte transferred the action to the Western District of Michigan because the plaintiff and all of the witnesses resided in the Western District; the plaintiff, who was injured on a boat, had bought her cruise

ticket in the Western District from a travel agent representing the defendant there; and any business the defendant conducted in Michigan was conducted in the Western District. The Western District, on defendant's motion to transfer the action to the Southern District of Florida, retransferred the action to the Eastern District, without holding a hearing on the matter. The Eastern District retransferred the action to the Western District pursuant to the "manifestly erroneous" standard, citing the fact that the Western District based its transfer decision on the erroneous belief, among other things, that venue could not be established in the Western District because the plaintiff did not reside there (prior to the 1990 amendment to § 1391(a)).

56. *See* Howe v. Goldcorp. Invs., Ltd., 946 F.2d 944, 947–48 (1st Cir.1991); Paper Operations Consultants Int'l, Ltd. v. SS Hong Kong Amber, 513 F.2d 667, 670 (9th Cir.1975) ("The continued vitality of the doctrine in federal courts was severely limited with the passage of 28 U.S.C.A. § 1404(a)...."); *see generally* Marc O. Wolinsky Note, *Forum Non Conveniens and American Plaintiffs in the Federal Court*, 47

been brought in state court.[57] Forum non conveniens, thus, remains a powerful procedural device at least in litigating international commercial disputes, where the alternative forum is outside the jurisdictional reach of the federal courts.[58]

The doctrine of forum non conveniens permits a federal court to dismiss a properly filed action where the convenience of the parties and the ends of justice weigh heavily against the exercise of jurisdiction.[59] As prerequisites to reaching a forum non conveniens motion, the district court must have subject matter and personal jurisdiction, and venue must be proper.[60] The burden of persuasion remains on the defendant at all stages of inquiry in a forum non conveniens analysis.[61]

The threshold inquiry is whether an "adequate alternative" forum is "available."[62] Generally, a forum is "available" when all of the defendants are amenable to process in the competing jurisdiction.[63] A

U.Chic.L.Rev. 373 (1980). *But see* Hall v. National Serv. Indus., Inc., 172 F.R.D. 157 (E.D.Pa.1997) (considering inconvenience of forum on defendant's motion to dismiss or otherwise transfer, under both doctrine of *forum non conveniens* and § 1404(a), where the competing venue was another federal court).

57. *See* Ott v. Kaiser–Georgetown Community Health Plan, Inc., 689 F.Supp. 9 (D.D.C.1988) (dismissing action on forum non conveniens grounds where plaintiffs already had an action pending in state court); Kettenbach v. Demoulas, 822 F.Supp. 43, 45 (D.Mass.1993)(recognizing that doctrine of forum non conveniens is available when alternative forum is a state court, but denied defendant's motion to dismiss on those grounds where state court was only a few miles from federal court); Poe v. Marquette Cement Mfg. Co., 376 F.Supp. 1054, 1060 (D.Md.1974) (recognizing that "[o]nly in rare instances where the alternative forum is a state court may a federal court now dismiss on the grounds of *forum non conveniens*"); Rogge v. Menard County Mut. Fire Ins. Co., 184 F.Supp. 289, 291 (S.D.Ill.1960) (same); *see also* 15 Charles Alan Wright, Arthur R. Miller & Edward H. Cooper, Federal Practice and Procedure § 3828, at 279–80 (2d ed.1986) ("It is only when the more convenient forum is in a foreign county—or perhaps, under rare circumstances, in a state court or a territorial court—that a suit brought in a proper federal venue can be dismissed on grounds of forum non conveniens.")

58. *See, e.g.,* Howe, 946 F.2d at 944 (holding that action should have been instituted in Canada); Contact Lumber Co. v.

P.T. Moges Shipping Co., 918 F.2d 1446 (9th Cir.1990) (holding that action should have been instituted in the Philippines); Paper Operations Consultants Int'l, Ltd., 513 F.2d at 667 (holding that action should have been instituted in Canada); Blimpie Int'l, Inc. v. ICA Menyforetagen AB, No. 96 Civ. 3082, 1997 WL 143907 (S.D.N.Y.1997) (holding that action should have been instituted in Sweden).

59. *See* Fitzgerald v. Texaco, Inc., 521 F.2d 448, 450 (2d Cir.1975); *see also In re* Air Crash Disaster Near New Orleans, Louisiana on July 9, 1982, 821 F.2d 1147, 1154 (5th Cir.1987); Paper Operations Consultants Int'l, Ltd., 513 F.2d at 670.

60. *See* Driscoll v. New Orleans Steamboat Co., 633 F.2d 1158, 1159 n. 1 (5th Cir.1981).

61. *See* Robinson v. TCI/US West Communications, Inc., 117 F.3d 900, 907 (5th Cir.1997); Lacey v. Cessna Aircraft Co., 932 F.2d 170, 180 (3d Cir.1991); *In re* Air Crash Disaster Near New Orleans, Louisiana on July 9, 1982, 821 F.2d at 1163–64; Supra Med. Corp. v. McGonigle, 955 F.Supp. 374, 384 (E.D.Pa.1997).

62. *See* Piper Aircraft Co. v. Reyno, 454 U.S. 235, 254 n. 22, 102 S. Ct. 252, 265 n. 22, 70 L.Ed.2d 419 (1981); Baumgart v. Fairchild Aircraft Corp., 981 F.2d 824, 835 (5th Cir.1983); Lacey, 932 F.2d at 180; *In re* Lloyd's Am. Trust Fund Litig., 954 F.Supp. 656, 673 (S.D.N.Y.1997); Blimpie Int'l, Inc., 1997 WL 143907, at *4.

63. *See* Piper Aircraft Co., 454 U.S. at 254 n. 22, 102 S.Ct. at 265 n. 22; Gulf Oil Corp. v. Gilbert, 330 U.S. 501, 506–07, 67

forum is "adequate" as long as the court is satisfied that the parties will not be completely deprived of a remedy and will be treated fairly, even if the law applied in the other jurisdiction is not as favorable as the law that would have been applied had the action remained in the United States.[64]

If the defendant satisfies the court that an adequate alternative forum is available, then the court must consider certain private and public interest factors.[65] When engaging in this inquiry, a court is to consider the facts as they exist at the time of the motion and not at the time the action was commenced.[66] There is a presumption in favor of a plaintiff's choice of forum,[67] particularly when the plaintiff is a United States citizen.[68] If the factors in favor and against retaining jurisdiction are in equipoise or the factors against retaining jurisdiction are only slightly greater, a court may not disturb the plaintiff's choice of forum.[69]

The Supreme Court in *Gulf Oil Corp. v. Gilbert* provided a list of relevant private and public interest factors for courts to consider when faced with a motion to dismiss.[70] This list is not exhaustive[71] and no one

---

S.Ct. 839, 842, 91 L.Ed. 1055 (1947); Baumgart, 981 F.2d at 835; Lacey, 932 F.2d at 180; *In re* Air Crash Disaster Near New Orleans, Louisiana on July 9, 1982, 821 F.2d at 1165; *In re* Lloyd's Am. Trust Fund Litig., 954 F.Supp. at 672; Blimpie Int'l Inc., 1997 WL 143907, at *4.

64. *See* Piper Aircraft Co., 454 U.S. at 255, 102 S.Ct. at 265; Baumgart, 981 F.2d at 835; Republic of Panama v. BCCI Holdings (Luxembourg) S.A., 119 F.3d 935, 951–52 (11th Cir.1997); *Lacey*, 932 F.2d at 180; *In re* Air Crash Disaster Near New Orleans, Louisiana on July 9, 1982, 821 F.2d at 1165; Fitzgerald, 521 F.2d at 453; *In re* Lloyd's Am. Trust Fund Litig., 954 F.Supp. at 672.

65. *See* Lacey, 932 F.2d at 180; *In re* Air Crash Disaster Near New Orleans, Louisiana on July 9, 1982, 821 F.2d at 1165; *In re* Lloyd's Am. Trust Fund Litig., 954 F.Supp. at 672; Blimpie Int'l Inc., 1997 WL 143907, at *4.

66. *See In re* Air Crash Disaster Near New Orleans, Louisiana on July 9, 1982, 821 F.2d at 1166.

67. *See* Koster v. (American) Lumbermens Mut. Casualty Co., 330 U.S. 518, 524, 67 S.Ct. 828, 831, 91 L.Ed.2d 1067 (1947); *In re* Air Crash Disaster Near New Orleans, Louisiana on July 9, 1982, 821 F.2d at 1165; Marsin Med. Int'l, Inc. v. Bauhinia Ltd., 948 F.Supp. 180, 190 (E.D.N.Y.1996) (requiring that the defendant offer "evidence of 'unusually extreme circumstances' demonstrating that 'material injustice is manifest' to justify overturning plaintiff's

choice in favor of a foreign forum") (citations omitted).

68. *See* Piper Aircraft Co., 454 U.S. at 235, 102 S.Ct. at 252 (holding that "the presumption in favor of [plaintiff's choice of forum applies] with less than maximum force when the plaintiff or (as here) real parties in interest are foreign," but also noting that "[a] citizen's forum should not be given dispositive weight," 454 U.S. at 256 n. 3, 102 S.Ct. at 266 n. 3; Republic of Panama, 119 F.3d at 952; *see also* Reid–Walen v. Hansen, 933 F.2d 1390, 1394 (8th Cir.1991) (explaining that "the 'home' forum for the plaintiff is any federal district in the United States, not the particular district where the plaintiff lives"); *In re* Air Crash Disaster Near New Orleans, Louisiana on July 9, 1982, 821 F.2d at 1164; Blimpie Int'l Inc., 1997 WL 143907, at *4.

69. *See* Gulf Oil Corp. v. Gilbert, 330 U.S. 501, 508, 67 S.Ct. 839, 843, 91 L.Ed. 1055 (1947) (plaintiff's choice of forum should "rarely be disturbed" unless the balance is "strongly in favor" of adjudicating the matter in another forum"); Lacey, 932 F.2d at 180 ("If, when added together, the relevant private and public interest factors are in equipoise, or even if they lean only slightly toward dismissal, the motion to dismiss must be denied."); Paper Operations Consultants Int'l, Ltd. v. SS Hong Kong Amber, 513 F.2d 667, 671 (9th Cir.1975).

70. 330 U.S. at 508–09, 67 S.Ct. at 843; *see generally* Annotation, *Questions as to Convenience and Justice of Transfer Under*

factor is determinative;[72] it is the quality and not the quantity of the factors that controls this highly factual inquiry.[73]

The private interest factors include:

the private interests of the litigants; the relative ease of access to sources of proof; availability of compulsory process for attendance of unwilling, and the cost of obtaining attendance of willing, witnesses; the enforceability of a judgment; and "all other practical problems that make a trial of a case easy, expeditious and inexpensive."[74]

The public interest factors include:

the interest in avoiding administrative difficulties arising from court congestion; the interest in avoiding the unfair imposition of jury duty on citizens of an unrelated forum; the "local interest in having localized controversies decided at home;" the interest in having a diversity case tried in a forum that is at home with the law governing the case; the interest in avoiding unnecessary problems with the conflict of law, or the application of foreign laws; and the interest "[i]n cases which touch the affairs of many persons" in insuring that such individuals will have access to the trial.[75]

If a court concludes that the balance of private and public interest factors weighs heavily in favor of dismissing an action, the court will generally provide that the plaintiff will be able to reinstitute the action in the foreign forum by preventing the defendant from raising certain defenses which would defeat the plaintiff's action.[76] For example, courts

---

Forum Non Conveniens Provision of Judicial Code (28 U.S.C.A. § 1404(a)), 1 A.L.R. Fed. 15 (1969) (discusses the public and private interest factors).

71. *See* Van Cauwenberghe v. Biard, 486 U.S, 517, 529–30, 108 S.Ct. 1945, 1953, 100 L.Ed.2d 517 (1988) (recognizing that the "list of considerations to be balanced is by no means exhaustive"); Gulf Oil Corp., 330 U.S. at 508, 67 S.Ct. at 843 ("Wisely, it has not been attempted to catalogue the circumstances which will justify or require either grant or denial of [a dismissal based on forum non conveniens].*"*); Blimpie Int'l Inc., 1997 WL 143907, at *4 (referring to the list of private and public interest factors in *Gilbert* as "nonexclusive").

72. *See In re* Air Crash Disaster Near New Orleans, Louisiana on July 9, 1982, 821 F.2d at 1162; *see also* Lacey, 932 F.2d at 189 ("As a general rule, a trial court may not predicate a forum non conveniens dismissal on a single factor.").

73. *See* Lacey, 932 F.2d at 182.

74. *See In re* Lloyd's Am. Trust Fund Litig., 954 F.Supp. 656, 673 (S.D.N.Y.1997) (quoting in part, Gulf Oil Corp., 330 U.S. at 508, 67 S. Ct. at 843; *see also infra*

§ 3.9(a)(1); Baumgart v. Fairchild Aircraft Corp., 981 F.2d 824, 835–36 (5th Cir.1983); Lacey, 932 F.2d at 180; *In re* Air Crash Disaster Near New Orleans, Louisiana on July 9, 1982, 821 F.2d at 1162; Paper Operations Consultants Int'l, Ltd., 513 F.2d at 671.

75. *See In re* Lloyd's Am. Trust Fund Litig., 954 F.Supp. at 673 (quoting in part, Gulf Oil Corp., 330 U.S. at 508, 67 S.Ct. at 843; *see also infra* § 3.9(a)(1); Baumgart, 981 F.2d at 837 n. 14; Lacey, 932 F.2d at 180; *In re* Air Crash Disaster Near New Orleans, Louisiana on July 9, 1982, 821 F.2d at 1162–63; Paper Operations Consultants Int'l, Ltd., 513 F.2d at 671.

76. *See In re* Air Crash Disaster Near New Orleans, Louisiana on July 9, 1982, 821 F.2d at 1166. In a later and more recent decision, the Fifth Circuit, in *Robinson v. TCI/US West Communications Inc.*, 117 F.3d 900, 907 (5th Cir.1997), held that a district court's failure to include a return jurisdiction clause in an order dismissing an action on the grounds of forum non conveniens constitutes a per se abuse of discretion.

commonly condition dismissals based on forum non conveniens on defendants' waiver of all jurisdictional defenses[77] and any defense of statute of limitations which would otherwise have been available to them in the foreign court,[78] and a formal agreement by a defendant to satisfy any final judgment.[79]

Library References:

West's Key No. Digests, Federal Courts ⟜101–157.
Wright, Miller & Cooper, Federal Practice and Procedure: Civil 2d §§ 3827–3828, 3841, 3847.

§ 3.10　Priority of Actions

(a) Competing Actions

In the most common pattern of commercial litigation, a business relationship has been allegedly breached or a legal right allegedly violated, and the party asserting that breach or violation selects the forum. The propriety of that selection might be challenged, *see* Section 3.8, *supra*, or a change in forum might be sought for convenience, *see* Section 3.9, *supra*. Subject to challenges to venue, the typical case proceeds with all claims and counterclaims presented in the original forum or, less commonly, in a transferee forum.

Sometimes, however, as a business relationship deteriorates, each side in the dispute perceives strategic advantage in the selection of the forum and races to its preferred courthouse to file suit. In a variation, sometimes a party in receipt of a cease and desist letter or other message that litigation is imminent will preempt the selection of a forum and file an action for a declaratory judgment that such party has no legal liability.

With the expansion of available forums accomplished by the 1990 amendments to the general venue statutes, the possibility for competing actions increases. This Section examines the rules that the federal courts have developed for addressing competing federal court actions and, more particularly, for determining which action should have priority.[1]

---

77. *See, e.g.,* Magnin v. Teledyne Continental Motors, 91 F.3d 1424, 1430–31 (11th Cir.1996); Paper Operations Consultants Int'l, Ltd., 513 F.2d at 672–73; Contact Lumber Co. v. P.T. Moges Shipping Co., 918 F.2d 1446, 1450 (9th Cir.1990).

78. *See, e.g.,* Magnin, 91 F.3d at 1430–31 (11th Cir.1996); Contact Lumber Co., 918 F.2d at 1450; Ahmed v. Boeing Co., 720 F.2d 224, 225 (1st Cir.1983); Paper Operations Consultants Int'l, Ltd., 513 F.2d at 672–73.

79. *See, e.g.,* Diaz v. Humboldt, 722 F.2d 1216, 1219 (5th Cir.1984) (vacating order dismissing action on forum non conveniens grounds and remanding the case so

that the lower court could attach appropriate conditions to the dismissal, such as, that the defendant formally agree to satisfy any final judgment rendered by the foreign court), *overturned in part by In re* Air Crash Disaster Near New Orleans, Louisiana on July 9, 1982, 821 F.2d at 1163, n. 25; *see also* Warn v. M/Y Maridome, 961 F.Supp. 1357, 1380 (S.D.Cal.1997) (conditioning dismissal on defendant's posting security).

§ 3.10

1. This chapter does not examine how the federal courts respond to multiple actions with overlapping claims brought in numerous districts; for that array of issues,

(b) First–Filed Rule

In response to duplicate suits involving the same parties and issues, the federal courts typically invoke the first-filed rule.[2] As its name suggests, this rule accords priority to the action that is commenced first in time. By doing so, the rule at once eliminates duplicative litigation and adheres "to the inherently fair concept that the party who commenced the first suit should generally be the party to attain its choice of venue."[3] As an alternative basis, the same result might be reached if the claims pleaded in the second action are treated as compulsory counter-claims that should have been interposed in the first-filed action; courts, however, generally apply the first-filed rule (with its exceptions) instead of applying the compulsory counterclaim rule.[4]

The rule, while generally favoring the first-filed action, is not expressed in absolute terms. For example, the Second Circuit formulation provides that "the first suit should have priority, absent the showing of balance of convenience in favor of the second action, or unless there are special circumstances which justify giving priority to the second."[5] The "special circumstances" are exceptions to the rule, *see* Section 3.10(c), *infra*; convenience refers to a type of transfer analysis, *see* Section 3.10(d), *infra*.

(c) Exceptions to First–Filed Rule

Mechanical application of the first-filed rule could potentially conflict with the stated policy rationale for the rule. The inherent fairness in generally giving the first to file the selection of forum diminishes if the purpose of that first filing is simply to preempt the choice of venue.

see Chapter 11 "Multidistrict Litigation," *infra.* Nor does this chapter address whether a federal district court may, or should, abstain, in favor of a pending state court action. *See generally* John F. Cambria, *Parallel Litigations: Declaratory Judgment Actions*, N.Y.L.J., May 14, 1997, at 1; 17A Charles Alan Wright, Arthur R. Miller & Edward H. Cooper, Federal Practice and Procedure §§ 4241, 4247 (1988).

2. *See, e.g.,* First City Nat'l Bank & Trust Co. v. Simmons, 878 F.2d 76, 79 (2d Cir.1989).

3. *See* Ontel Prods., Inc. v. Project Strategies Corp., 899 F.Supp. 1144, 1150 (S.D.N.Y.1995); *see also* Church of Scientology v. United States Dep't of Army, 611 F.2d 738, 750 (9th Cir.1979) (first to file rule was developed to "serve[] the purpose of promoting efficiency well and should not be disregarded lightly").

4. *See* Adam v. Jacobs, 950 F.2d 89, 93 (2d Cir.1991) (noting that "nothing in Rule 13 prevents the filing of a duplicative action instead of a compulsory counterclaim" and then applying first-filed rule); Warshawsky & Co. v. Arcata Nat'l Corp., 552 F.2d 1257, 1263 (7th Cir. 1977) (claims asserted in second action characterized as compulsory counterclaims in first action; court then proceeds to first-filed rule analysis); J. Lyons & Co. v. Republic of Tea, Inc., 892 F.Supp. 486, 490 (S.D.N.Y.1995) (same); *see generally* Chapter 6 "Responses to Complaints," *infra.*

5. Motion Picture Lab. Technicians Local 780, I.A.T.S.E. v. McGregor & Werner, Inc., 804 F.2d 16, 19 (2d Cir.1986) (citation omitted); *see also* West Gulf Maritime Ass'n v. ILA Deep Sea Local 24, 751 F.2d 721, 729 (5th Cir.1985) (absent "compelling circumstances," first filed action has priority); Warshawsky & Co., 552 F.2d at 1263 (7th Cir.1977) ("[U]nless unusual circumstances warrant, the party filing later in time should be enjoined from further prosecution of his suit.").

Thus, an exception to the first-filed rule is widely recognized; priority in time will not be enforced where the first-filed action is seen as an "improper anticipatory filing"—that is, a filing made under threat of an imminent suit and asserting the mirror image of that suit in another district.[6]

A declaratory judgment action brought in the face of a clear threat of suit and seeking a determination that no liability exists will be closely scrutinized as a potentially "improper anticipatory filing" where the other party (for example, the party sending the cease and desist letter) then proceeds to file an action alleging a breach or infringement of rights.[7] Whether the first-filed rule or its exception is applied generally depends on three clusters of facts.

First, the circumstances of the first filing are examined. If the party that ordinarily would be the plaintiff is prepared to sue but delays filing in an effort to achieve a settlement, a preemptive filing of a mirror image claim will likely be treated as an improper anticipatory suit. This result facilitates the settlement process, by assuring parties that a good faith attempt to settle will not compromise the opportunity to select the forum.[8] However, this exception does not invariably protect whichever party first expresses an interest in negotiating a settlement; to recognize the first to suggest settlement "would simply change the proverbial 'race to the courthouse' into the race to the post office, facsimile machine, or telephone, in which parties would, at the first sign of conflict, communicate their desire to resolve the conflict without involving the courts."[9] Among the other circumstances considered, courts will look for concreteness in the threat of litigation; the more specific the threat of litigation, the more likely a preemptive suit by the recipient of the threat will be deemed an "anticipatory" filing.[10] Courts will also weigh evidence of bad

---

6. While courts occasionally invoke the terms "forum shopping" or "bad faith," in application the central exception to the first-filed rule appears to be the finding of an improper anticipatory filing. *See, e.g.,* Alltrade, Inc. v. Uniweld Prods., Inc., 946 F.2d 622, 628 (9th Cir.1991); Mission Ins. Co. v. Puritan Fashions Corp., 706 F.2d 599, 602 n. 3 (5th Cir.1983).

7. In *Boatmen's First National Bank v. Kansas Public Employees Retirement System,* 57 F.3d 638, 641 (8th Cir.1995), the Eighth Circuit has identified certain "red flags" which suggest an improper anticipatory filing:

[F]irst, that the "first" suit was filed after the other party gave notice of its intention to sue; and, second, that the action was for declaratory judgment rather than for damages or equitable relief.

8. *See* Riviera Trading Corp. v. Oakley, Inc., 944 F.Supp. 1150, 1158–59 (S.D.N.Y. 1996) (transferring first-filed action to dis-

trict of second-filed action, where plaintiff in second-filed action had been engaged in good faith settlement effort and first-filed action was motivated in part by forum shopping).

9. Ontel Prods., Inc. v. Project Strategies Corp., 899 F.Supp. 1144, 1151 (S.D.N.Y.1995).

10. *See* J. Lyons & Co. v. Republic of Tea, Inc., 892 F.Supp. 486, 491 (S.D.N.Y. 1995) ("When a notice letter informs a defendant of the intention to file suit, a filing date, and/or a specific forum for the filing of the suit, the courts have found, in the exercise of discretion, in favor of the second-filed action."); Employers Ins. of Wausau v. Prudential Ins. Co. of Am., 763 F.Supp. 46, 49 (S.D.N.Y.1991) (action commenced in response to a letter expressing "hope[] to avoid litigation" not treated as anticipatory filing; letter deemed an attempt to initiate settlement negotiations rather than as a notice of suit).

faith; the first-filed rule is likely inapplicable "where the plaintiff in the first-filed action was able to file first only because it had misled the filer of the second-filed action as to its intentions regarding filing suit in order to gain the advantages of filing first."[11]

Second, the scope of the first filing is examined. Where an action is merely the mirror image of an anticipated suit—for example, an action for a declaration that there is no copyright violation when an infringement action has been threatened—it is likely to be deemed an "improper anticipatory" suit.[12] If the first-filed action, however, contains distinct claims which appear to be reasonably asserted, that action is more likely to be accorded priority. In the latter case, the first filer is viewed as a potential plaintiff who had claims to assert and, with them, the initial control over the choice of forum.[13] Where the first-filed action presents a narrow substantive law claim and a later, broader action is brought, priority has been accorded to the first action if full relief could be obtained there.[14] Complete identity of parties in the two actions is not required for a dismissal or transfer of the second action.[15]

Third, the timing of the two actions will be examined. If the putative plaintiff is found to be hesitant in suing—by delaying after settlement talks have failed or by evidencing ambivalence about litigating—a preemptive suit by the other side is more likely to be given priority.[16] A "photo-finish," on the other hand, might suggest that the initial claimant was intent on suit and that a preemptive action came first. However, some courts have concluded that the policy of recognizing the first to file is less apparent when two actions are filed close in time and have not

---

11. Brower v. Flint Ink Corp., 865 F.Supp. 564, 569 (N.D.Iowa 1994).

12. *See* Factors Etc., Inc. v. Pro Arts, Inc., 579 F.2d 215, 219 (2d Cir.1978) ("[T]he federal declaratory judgment is not a prize to the winner of race to the courthouses.") (citation omitted), *superseded on other grounds by* Pirone v. MacMillan, 894 F.2d 579 (2d Cir.1990); American Auto. Ins. Co. v. Freundt, 103 F.2d 613, 617 (7th Cir.1939) ("The wholesome purposes of declaratory acts would be aborted by its use as an instrument of procedural fencing either to secure delay or to choose a forum.").

13. *Compare* 800–Flowers, Inc. v. Intercontinental Florist, Inc., 860 F.Supp. 128 (S.D.N.Y.1994) (first-filed action sustained where, apart from declaratory judgment of no trademark infringement, it sought relief for alleged trade disparagement) *with* Service Corp. Int'l v. Loewin Group Inc., No. Civ. A. H–96–3269, 1996 WL 756808 (S.D.Tex.1996) (dismissing first-filed action which consisted of a declaratory judgment action and intimately connected claims).

14. *See, e.g.,* Channel Four Television Co. v. Wildmon, No. 92 Civ. 2555, 1992 WL 114516 (S.D.N.Y.1992); Hollinee Corp. v. Weyher, No. 91 Civ. 6855, 1992 WL 110989 (S.D.N.Y.1992).

15. *See* Save Power Ltd. v. Syntek Fin. Corp., 121 F.3d 947, 951 (5th Cir.1997).

16. *See, e.g.,* Hanson PLC v. Metro–Goldwyn–Mayer Inc., 932 F.Supp. 104, 107 (S.D.N.Y.1996) (declaratory judgment suit filed just three days after cease and desist letter found to be an anticipatory suit); British Telecommunications v. McDonnell Douglas Corp., No. C–93–0677, 1993 WL 149860 (N.D.Cal.1993) (anticipatory suit exception not applied when defendant in the first action waited two months to file second action). *But see* Continental Ins. Cos. v. Wickes Co., No. 90 Civ. 8215, 1991 WL 183771 (S.D.N.Y.1991) (anticipatory action exception applied even when second action filed two months later than first action).

applied the first-filed rule as vigorously, if at all, when there are near simultaneous filings.[17]

(d) Resolving the Priority of Actions

The determination of priority might arise through different procedural routes. For example, the defendant in the first-filed action can, if appropriate, move to dismiss for improper venue or can move to transfer; alternatively, it can move to stay the action as an improper anticipatory action. That same party, as plaintiff in the second-filed action, can move to enjoin prosecution of the first-filed action. Conversely, the plaintiff in the first-filed action can move to enjoin prosecution of the second-filed action or can challenge venue in the second-filed action. However, to avoid potentially conflicting rulings on the issue of priority, it has been held that the decision whether to apply the first-filed rule is best left to the district of the first-filed action.[18]

Because courts treat the sequence of filing as only a factor to consider in ruling on the priority of competing actions, courts typically engage in a convenience analysis as applied on a transfer motion, *see* Section 3.9(a)(1), *supra*.[19] If a transfer-type analysis is utilized, weight will be accorded to the plaintiff's choice of forum in the absence of an "improper anticipatory" suit. If priority is given to the first-filed action, the court will likely enjoin prosecution of the second action. If priority is not given to the first-filed action, it can be dismissed or stayed in deference to the second-filed action or transferred to the district of the second-filed action. Typically, a ruling disposes of the entire case, although at least one court transferred part of an action found to mirror a prior pending action while retaining additional claims not foreshadowed in the prior suit.[20]

17. *See, e.g.*, Terra Int'l, Inc. v. Mississippi Chem. Corp., 922 F.Supp. 1334, 1350–53 (N.D. Iowa 1996) (citation omitted) (concluding, after exhaustive review of prior cases, that there is no "dead heat" exception which stands alone "unless the finish to the race was really just too close to call," but holding that presence of "dead heat" should "counsel the court to avoid a 'slavish adherence' to the first-filed rule"), *aff'd*, 119 F.3d 688 (8th Cir.1997); Ontel Prods., Inc. v. Project Strategies Corp., 899 F.Supp. 1144, 1153 (S.D.N.Y.1995) ("[B]ecause the lawsuits were both filed on the same day, the first-filed rule is inapplicable."); Capitol Records, Inc. v. Optical Recording Corp., 810 F.Supp. 1350, 1355 (S.D.N.Y.1992) (noting that actions filed only 20 days apart, during which time no pretrial proceedings occurred in the first forum).

18. *See* Save Power Ltd., 121 F.3d at 950; British Telecommunications v. McDonnell Douglas Corp., No. C–93–0677, 1993 WL 149860, at *4 (N.D.Cal.1993); Donald-

son, Lufkin & Jenrette v. Los Angeles County, 542 F.Supp. 1317, 1321 (S.D.N.Y. 1982).

19. *See, e.g.*, Terra Int'l, Inc., 922 F.Supp. at 1348–49 (collecting cases where § 1404(a)-type analysis applied and concluding that, "where a § 1404(a) analysis dictates transfer, the first-filed rule should be abrogated"); Ontel Prods., Inc., 899 F.Supp. at 1153 (applying § 1404(a) transfer analysis).

20. *See* Williams v. National Hous. Exch., Inc., 898 F.Supp. 157 (S.D.N.Y.1995). The authors' firm represented the co-plaintiff, Donna Lee Williams, Insurance Commissioner of Delaware, in this action. While the Southern District of New York deferred to the Northern District of Illinois in transferring part of the action, the Northern District of Illinois judge assigned to the first-filed action subsequently dismissed that action, finding that the more comprehensive New York complaint included the

Library References:

West's Key No. Digests, Federal Courts ⊕71–157, 1131–1158.
Wright, Miller & Cooper, Federal Practice and Procedure: Civil 2d § 3802.1.

§ 3.11   Practice Checklist

(a) Selecting a Forum

1. If consulted on an agreement being negotiated, consider inclusion of a forum selection clause if your client has negotiating leverage to designate a preferred court or locale. Review any proposed clause to determine its type (mandatory or permissive), scope (type of claims covered) and enforceability, as well as the substantive and procedural implications of including it. (*See* § 3.6)

2. When a dispute arises, determine which forums might be proper under the general venue statute. Check the current statute; there have been major amendments in 1988 and 1990 and significant technical amendments in 1992 and 1995. (*See* § 3.4; 28 U.S.C.A § 1391(a) (where subject matter jurisdiction is to be based solely on diversity); 28 U.S.C.A. § 1391(b) (where subject matter jurisdiction for one or more claims is to be based on a federal question).

3. If one or more claims arises under a federal statute, determine whether a special venue statute applies and, if so, whether that statute supplements or is exclusive of the general venue statute. (*See* § 3.5)

4. If the dispute arises from a contractual relationship, determine whether there is a forum selection clause in the contract and, if so, analyze its type, scope and enforceability. (*See* § 3.6)

5. Once it is determined which forums might be proper, analyze which forum is preferred for the adjudication of the dispute. Consider especially the governing law likely to be applied by each proper forum and the relative convenience of each forum to your client and to material witnesses. Assess the probability that the selected forum can survive a motion challenging venue or seeking transfer of the action. It is both proper and prudent to select the most advantageous forum for your client. (*See* §§ 3.3(a) 3.8, 3.9)

6. In evaluating possible forums, consider the relative advantages between a state versus federal forum. Recall that, if the action

necessary issues and parties required for full resolution of the dispute; the transferred claims had been assigned on transfer to a different judge in that district and that transferred action survived. *See* Resource Asset Management, Inc. v. Continental Stock Transfer & Trust Co., 896 F.Supp. 782 (N.D.Ill.1995).

The Tenth Circuit has stated that "[s]ection 1404(a) only authorizes the transfer of an entire action, not individual claims ... ;

the section 'contemplates a plenary transfer' of an entire case." Chrysler Credit Corp. v. Country Chrysler, Inc., 928 F.2d 1509, 1518 (10th Cir.1991) (citation omitted). However, "where certain claims in an action are properly severed under [FRCP] 21, two separate actions result; a district court may transfer one action while retaining jurisdiction over the other." *Id.* (footnote omitted).

is brought in your client's home state court, the action can only be removed to the federal district where that state court is based (perhaps providing the only means of obtaining the federal forum in which your client resides). (*See* 28 U.S.C.A. § 1441(a); §§ 3.3(b), 3.5(b) (10))

7.   While the complaint need not allege a basis for venue, upon challenge, the plaintiff must be able to show that venue is proper as to each claim and each defendant. (*See* § 3.7(b)).

(b) Challenging Venue

1.   Upon initial review of the complaint, analyze whether venue is proper and whether the chosen forum is convenient. (*See* §§ 3.7(b), 3.8, 3.9).

2.   Examine the provisions of any forum selection clause. If an action has been brought in violation of the clause, there might be grounds to challenge the action. Recall that a motion may be made to transfer the action under § 1404(a) when the clause permits a federal forum; dismissal of the action is most likely where there is a mandatory forum selection clause specifying a state or foreign forum. (See § 3.6)

3.   If venue is improper, a defendant must object to venue either in the responsive pleading or in a motion to dismiss filed in lieu of an answer. Failure to assert the objection will result in a waiver of it. (*See* FRCP 12(h)(1); 28 U.S.C.A. § 1406; § 3.7(e))

4.   Motions to dismiss for forum non conveniens or to transfer for convenience may be made at any time, although delay in bringing such a motion is likely to diminish its chance of success. (*See* § 3.7(e)).

5.   An action can only be transferred to a district in which it might have been brought. Accordingly, it is necessary to analyze which other forums are proper, if any. (*See* 28 U.S.C.A. § 1404; § 3.9(a)(2))

6.   If there is a basis to challenge venue, assess whether it is strategically advantageous and cost justifiable to bring the motion. Consider closely the likely effect of a successful motion on the law to be applied and on the relative convenience of the parties and material witnesses. Be certain on a transfer motion to list specifically the material nonparty witnesses for whom transfer would be convenient and the subject areas of their testimony. (*See* §§ 3.7(b), 3.8, 3.9(a) (1),(a)(3)).

7.   Where multiple suits have been filed, assess whether the first-filed rule will likely control and, if a stay or transfer is to be sought, determine in which court to seek relief. (*See* § 3.10).

8.   While a plaintiff cannot challenge the venue selected as improper, it may, in unusual circumstances, seek a transfer under Sections 1406(a) or 1404. (*See* § 3.7(c)(2)).

9. An order dismissing an action for improper venue (including dismissal based on forum non conveniens or a forum selection clause) is immediately appealable. Upon determination of a transfer motion or a denial of a motion to dismiss for improper venue, consider whether the determination warrants seeking the rarely granted appellate review. (*See* § 3.7(f); 28 U.S.C.A. §§ 1291, 1292(b)).

§ 3.12 Forms ⊞

(a) Mandatory Forum Selection Clause ⊞

The parties agree that (i) any claim of whatever character arising under this Agreement or relating in any way, directly or indirectly, to the dealings between them during the term of this Agreement shall be brought exclusively in a federal or state court of competent jurisdiction in [New York][1] County in the State of [New York] and (ii) that any claim described in the foregoing clause that is filed in any other court shall be conclusively deemed as violating the expressed intent of the parties in this mandatory forum selection clause.

(b) Permissive Forum Selection Clause ⊞

The parties agree that any claim arising under, or relating in any way to, this Agreement may be brought in any federal or state court of competent jurisdiction in [New York] County in the State of [New York], which court shall be deemed a nonexclusive but permissible forum for resolution of such claim.

(c) Affirmative Defense—Improper Venue ⊞

(1) First Alternative: Venue is improper in this District.

(2) Second Alternative: The complaint should be dismissed for improper venue.

(d) Motion to Transfer Action

(1) Notice of Motion ⊞

UNITED STATES DISTRICT COURT
_____ DISTRICT OF _____

§ 3.12

1. Because a motion to transfer an action may be brought and might be granted (albeit rarely) under § 1404(a) even where a mandatory forum selection clause designates one federal district only, *see supra* § 3.6, the practitioner might prefer to designate only a state forum; such a clause should result in the dismissal of any federal court action based on a claim within the scope of the clause. *See supra* § 3.6. If a federal forum is preferred and the risk of a transfer motion is acceptable, the practitioner should designate, or include in the designation, a specific federal district.

```
[Names],                        )
                                )
                                )   NOTICE OF
                                )   MOTION TO
              Plaintiffs,       )   TRANSFER ACTION
                                )
     -against-                  )
                                )
[Names],                        )
                                )
              Defendants.  )
                                )
```

PLEASE TAKE NOTICE that, upon the annexed declaration of [Defendant's officer], with exhibit, and the accompanying Memorandum of Law, defendant [Name] will move this Court before the Honorable [Judge's Name] at the United States Courthouse [address] on _____ __, 1998 at _____ a.m., or as soon thereafter as counsel may be heard, for an order, pursuant to 28 U.S.C.A. § 1404(a), transferring this action from Transferor District to Proposed Transferee District, and for such other and further relief as the Court deems just.

Date: [City, State]   [Firm Name]
       [Date]

                         By: _____
                              [Counsel of Record]

                              [Firm Address]
                              [Firm Phone Number]

                              Attorneys for Defendant [Name]

To: [List all other Counsel of Record to be Served]

(2) Declaration of Moving Defendant's Officer 💾

UNITED STATES DISTRICT COURT
_____ DISTRICT OF _____

```
[Names],                        )
                                )
                                )
              Plaintiffs,       )   Declaration of
                                )
     -against-                  )   [Officer's Name]
                                )
[Names],                        )
                                )
              Defendants.  )
                                )
```

[Name]   declares as follows[2]:

1.   I am the [Title] of defendant [Name]. I submit this declaration in support of defendant's motion to transfer this action from the Transferor District to the Proposed Transferee District. I have personal knowledge of the matters set forth below. A copy of the complaint is attached as Exhibit A to this Declaration.

2.   [Briefly state nature, and principal place, of business of defendant]

3.   The accompanying memorandum of law sets forth the factors which I understand are considered by a court on a motion to transfer. In this declaration, I will present the facts relevant to those factors.[3]

4.   Most of the principal events alleged in the complaint—to the extent they took place in fact—and most of the dealings between the parties occurred in [city]. The remainder took place in [other locales]. Almost none of the key events occurred in this District. [Provide summary statement of background facts, claims and location of key events, emphasizing contacts with Proposed Transferee District. If there is a forum selection clause specifying Proposed Transferee District, highlight this clause.] Not surprisingly, most of the witnesses and key evidence are in the Proposed Transferee District.

5.   I reside in [city]. I expect that my testimony will be needed at trial, because of my close involvement in the underlying transaction. In particular, I can testify about [_____]. Other key witnesses who live in [or closer to] the Proposed Transferee District include: [Name and Positions]. While [list] are employed by defendant, [list] are not employed by us and, I understand, would only testify if served with a subpoena or would find the Proposed Transferee District far more convenient.[4] The anticipated subjects of the testimony of these key witnesses is as follows:

[List in tabular form names of witnesses and anticipated areas of testimony to show materiality of testimony).

6.   In contrast, there appear to be only _____ potential witnesses who could be compelled to testify in the Transferor District. [List; do not create opportunity for adversary to say "movant ignores key witnesses in this District."]

7.   The Proposed Transferee District would be more convenient not just for defendant but also for defendants [Name Co-defendants]. [Explain, focusing on disruption to business if litigation continues in Trans-

---

2. For form and authority for use of declaration in lieu of an affidavit, *see* 28 U.S.C.A. § 1746 (West 1994).

3. The rules and practices of federal districts vary as to the amount of argument that is permitted in an affidavit or declaration. Some attorneys prefer to discuss mate-

rial witnesses and relative court congestion in an attorney's declaration.

4. If possible, obtain declarations of one or more nonparty witnesses who would appear without subpoena as to express preference for Proposed Transferee District.

feror District; party witnesses in Proposed Transferee District; and other proof in Proposed Transferee District.[5]]

8. In this case, plaintiff's selection of this District is to be accorded little weight. [Specify any applicable factors, such as locus of events in Proposed Transferee District; contacts of plaintiff with Proposed Transferee District; small amount of proof in Transferor District; absence of residence of Plaintiff in Transferor District.]

9. [Discuss reasons why transfer would be in interest of justice, such as related litigation in Proposed Transferee District; need/ability to implead third parties; controlling state law [note if any contract specified governing law]; and congestion of respective court dockets.]

10. It is respectfully requested that the action be transferred to the Proposed Transferee District.

I declare, under penalty of perjury, that the foregoing is true and correct.

Date:
[City/State]
[date]

s/ _____
[name]

---

5. If possible, obtain supporting declarations from co-defendants, or see if they will join in motion.

Chapter 4

INVESTIGATION OF THE CASE

by
Bart M. Schwartz
and
Andrew B. Melnick

Table of Sections

WESTLAW Electronic Research

See WESTLAW Electronic Research Guide preceding the Summary of Contents.

----

§ 4.1 Scope Note

During the last decade, the legal profession has experienced a sea change in the acceptance and use of investigations. Where attorneys once hired investigators for the limited purposes of finding and interviewing witnesses, law firms today regularly engage investigators to conduct broad scale searches of publicly filed documents, computerized databases and other specialized information repositories, in order to unearth vital information about the corporate entities, officers and employees with whom their clients are engaged in litigation. Cases today also are benefitted from many of the sophisticated investigative strategies and techniques often associated with law enforcement efforts, such as undercover operations and forensic examinations by experts.

In this chapter, we discuss how such investigations may be used during all phases of litigation. In particular, we highlight the benefits that may be derived from properly conducted investigations and provide practical guidance regarding the planning and conduct of investigations. The chapter further suggests approaches for coordinating investigative activities with traditional discovery techniques and highlights the pertinent legal issues that should be evaluated when utilizing particular investigative strategies. The steps to be taken in conducting an asset search—an investigative technique useful in many types of cases—also are discussed in detail. Finally, forms for a model retainer agreement and for model guidelines to be given investigators are included as helpful guides to practitioners.

§ 4.2 Why Conduct Investigations?

The development of a complete factual record is often critical to the outcome of a lawsuit. Although the Federal Rules of Civil Procedure provide counsel with several important discovery methods to uncover and develop the facts,[1] the use of investigations outside the customary discovery practice often is a fast and cost effective means of obtaining important information, evidence and leads. Moreover, the use of skilled investigators may uncover facts and information that ordinarily would not be developed through the formalities of the discovery process, including the disclosure of such matters as an adverse witness' use of aliases and prior criminal convictions, a party's history of commencing baseless litigation, the location of key witnesses sought for deposition or trial, or the record of professional discipline imposed on an expert proffered by a party. When used in tandem, the two separate discovery approaches should complement each other and result in the accumulation of considerably more useful information and evidence than if either technique had been employed alone.

§ 4.3 The Decision to Hire an Investigator

When deciding if an investigator should be retained, counsel must examine the facts and circumstances of each case. While each determination requires a separate analysis, there are a number of common questions that can guide counsel in making his or her decision. First, counsel should ask which investigative techniques can be used most effectively in the case. Counsel litigating a complex financial fraud case, for example, might require the use of one or more forensic accountants to unravel the scheme and trace the stolen or misappropriated assets to the suspected wrongdoers. On the other hand, an attorney seeking to obtain a court

---

§ 4.2

1. *See* Chapter 19 "Depositions," Chapter 20 "Document Discovery," Chapter 21 "Interrogatories," and Chapter 22 "Re-

quests for Admissions," *infra*, for a detailed discussion of the particular discovery devices available to counsel under the FRCP.

order authorizing the seizure of bootleg video tapes or other pirated merchandise might want to identify the persons responsible for producing and manufacturing the fake goods after locating the places of sales and distribution. In these circumstances, counsel might well consider retaining an investigative team with demonstrated experience conducting surveillances and other covert field operations, such as stings.

After considering the investigative techniques to be used in a case, counsel next should decide who would most effectively perform these functions. As trained and experienced advocates, lawyers by definition do their best work in courtrooms and other controlled environments where the procedural and substantive rules of law apply. They generally have little experience using the many commercial and online databases that investigators regularly probe to uncover assets, locate persons and discover other important types and sources of information; nor do attorneys, as a rule, subscribe to these services. When they do, they do not subscribe as extensively as investigators.

Further, as a general matter, most attorneys lack the experience or inclination to conduct effective field interviews. Counsel must candidly and critically assess whether other trained professionals, such as investigators, would conduct these types of interviews more effectively. In making this determination, counsel must also consider the reality today that many people do not like attorneys and are not particularly willing to cooperate with them. Investigators, in contrast, often have enjoyed long careers in law enforcement and are particularly experienced at interviewing witnesses and obtaining their cooperation in a variety of circumstances and locations.

Another factor to be considered is the possibility of counsel inadvertently becoming a fact witness in an investigation he or she is conducting. Should this occur, the attorney risks being precluded from continuing as trial counsel in the matter. Government prosecutors avoid this problem by ensuring that an agent or investigator is present during all interviews, and by having these individuals conduct arrests, execute search warrants, and perform other field work where the likelihood of testifying in a subsequent hearing or trial is apparent. Moreover, recent efforts by government prosecutors to disqualify defense counsel by calling them as witnesses illustrate the real and nonhypothetical nature of this risk.[1]

Finally, in weighing the need for investigative assistance, counsel should consider the number of interviews to be conducted, the location of the witnesses, and the speed with which the interviews must be completed. Depending on the circumstances of the case, counsel may be faced with the need to conduct simultaneous interviews over a broad geographic area or to conduct multiple inquiries on a moment's notice, in order to counter an adversary's unexpected evidence at trial. An investi-

---

§ 4.3

1. *See, e.g.*, United States v. Locascio, 6 F.3d 924, 933 (2d Cir.1993) (defense attorney's potential role as unsworn witness with first hand knowledge of events to be presented at trial warranted attorney's disqualification).

gative firm with a national practice can complete these tasks within the time frames dictated by the litigation, either by utilizing its own staff or by drawing on the firm's relationships with reliable investigators in other locations throughout the country or abroad.

§ 4.4   Prefiling Investigations

Investigations can aid counsel at all stages of the case: prefiling; during the pendency of the litigation; and post verdict. With regard to the prefiling stage of an action, where only limited formal discovery may be available to develop or test the material facts on which a proposed litigation will rely, attorney-directed investigations are often the primary source of gathering and confirming information before instituting a lawsuit. By directing investigators to search commercial databases, on-line services, public records or media sources, an attorney contemplating filing a complaint can obtain evidence of business relationships, agreements, stock ownership holdings, or other financial or legal interests involving the prospective defendant(s) which may support or give rise to actionable claims. In addition, by reviewing the results of these searches, counsel often can determine before filing a lawsuit whether a putative defendant has sufficient assets to justify commencing the action. In light of *Gillin v. Patterson, Belknap, Webb & Tyler*,[1] a recent New York case in which a prominent law firm was sued for malpractice by its client for failing to make a prefiling determination of a party's assets, the performance of these investigative steps *before* starting a lawsuit would appear not only to be a prudent act, but also a necessary measure to protect both the attorney's and the client's particular interests.

Further, before commencing an action, counsel may be unaware of what potential witnesses—particularly those aligned with an adverse party—may know or say about the matters in dispute.[2] By having investigators interview these persons before the lawsuit is started, counsel can learn what they know and "freeze" their stories, obtaining statements and candid observations from these individuals that might differ from what they would say if they believed they were operating in a

---

§ 4.4

1. Webb & Tyler, No. 93–104543 (Sup. Ct. New York County, filed Feb. 23, 1993), N.Y.L.J., Sept. 2, 1994, at 1, *aff'd*, 225 A.D.2d 1113, 639 N.Y.S.2d 877 (1st Dep't 1996). In *Gillin*, on advice of her attorneys (Patterson Belknap), Agneta Gillin accepted her husband's offer of $8 million plus the interest from a $17 million trust to settle their matrimonial action. After later learning that her husband (Martin Gruss) was worth a reported $250 million at the time of the settlement, Gillin twice unsuccessfully moved to set the settlement aside as inadequate. She then sued Patterson Belknap for $100 million, basing her malpractice action on the firm's failure to independently check

her husband's assets at the time they encouraged her to accept the settlement. In rejecting Patterson Belknap's motion to dismiss Gillin's complaint, the court stated: "PBW & T knew or should have made themselves aware of Gruss' financial status [and] they could not rely on Gillin; they were hired to represent her in the marital separation and it was their duty to . . . make themselves aware of Gruss' financial status." N.Y.L.J., Sept. 2, 1994 at 1.

2. *See infra*, § 4.13(e)(1), for a discussion of when, and under what circumstances, interviews of represented parties or current and former employees of a party may be conducted.

litigation environment. Equally important, if their stories change later on, they can be impeached with their prior inconsistent statements.

Prefiling investigations offer counsel a number of other important benefits. A properly directed investigation will inform counsel of any weaknesses in the proposed case. Former employees of a putative defendant, for example, may provide investigators with credible statements which directly undermine the proposed theory of the plaintiff's case, or which cast doubt on the veracity of the client's claims. Database and public records searches also may reveal facts which, if disclosed, would damage the case. Alternatively, as noted above, the investigation may develop or verify facts which enable the lawsuit to be filed. In either case, the investigation will have provided counsel with a sufficient factual basis to make recommendations to his or her client concerning the appropriateness of commencing an action, as required by Rule 11's prefiling due diligence requirements.[3]

The development of a full factual basis for the lawsuit before commencing the action also may furnish counsel with sufficient leverage to enter into successful settlement negotiations. By disclosing to the proposed defendant (or counsel) some or all of the evidence that will establish the contemplated claims, settlements may be achieved quickly and without the expense of a full blown litigation.

Parties who are aware that they are about to be sued also can benefit from effective prefiling investigations. Using the same investigative techniques described above, counsel for a putative defendant can develop evidence and other information to defend the action, to assert counterclaims, or to settle the dispute on terms favorable to the defendant.

§ 4.5 Investigations of Pending Cases

Most of the investigative work in a case is usually done after the lawsuit has been filed and at least some of the key issues and witnesses have been identified. At this point, the investigation can focus on developing specific facts which will aid counsel in proving or defending the case, or which will establish the liability of a third party. Examples of how counsel can effectively use investigators to accomplish these goals follow:

- During discovery, plaintiff's counsel learns the names but not the locations of several third-party witnesses who were present at a pivotal meeting with defendant's representatives. Because these nonparty witnesses may recall statements or possess documents that can help prove plaintiff's version of what occurred at the meeting, investigators are retained to locate and interview these persons. Using commercial databases and other investigative techniques, the investigators find and interview a witness whose

---

3. *See* Chapter 48 "Sanctions," *infra,* for a complete discussion of the obligations imposed on parties and counsel under FRCP 11.

recollection and contemporaneous notes of the meeting fully support plaintiff's position.

● Many years after a major apparel company purchases a former industrial site to expand its warehouse and distribution capacity, the EPA sues the company under CERCLA,[1] seeking to have it remediate environmental contamination caused by one or more prior owners or users of the property. The company's attorney promptly engages an investigative firm with experience conducting environmental investigations to locate and identify additional "responsible parties" who can be sued for contribution. By determining the property's chain of title, examining aerial photographs of the site, reviewing files maintained by the applicable local, state and federal environmental agencies, and by interviewing persons who may have knowledge of the events that contributed to the site's contamination, the investigative firm provides counsel with the necessary information to shift all or part of the cleanup costs to other responsible parties.

During the pendency of an action, investigators also may be used to develop information about the credibility of parties and witnesses. Commercial database checks and other public records searches, for example, can disclose a witness' prior criminal convictions, lawsuits in which the person was accused of making false or deceitful statements bearing on the witness' credibility, or other pertinent impeachment material. Interviews of a witness' neighbors and former employers, moreover, also are excellent sources of such information. In addition, former employees of a party—particularly those discharged or laid off after years of service to the company—often are invaluable sources of information detailing the wrongful acts of their ex-employers.

Investigative firms also can be used in connection with the selection of juries. Experienced investigators are adept at obtaining demographic, financial, and other vital information relating to the geographic areas from which potential jurors will be drawn; moreover, complementing the work of jury selection specialists, investigators can perform other services to assist counsel conduct jury pool investigations, including developing questionnaires to be submitted to the court for completion by all prospective jurors.

During the trial, investigators can assist counsel to rebut an adverse witness' surprise testimony by carefully checking out the statements the witness made on direct examination. If the investigators uncover prior inconsistent statements attributable to the witness or other discrepancies in the person's story, counsel can effectively use this information on cross-examination. Finally, investigators can assist counsel with any number of last minute issues and questions that arise during the trial.

§ 4.5

1. Comprehensive Environmental Response, Compensation, and Liability Act of 1980 ("CERCLA"), 42 U.S.C.A. § 9601, as amended by the Superfund Amendments and Re-authorization Act of 1986 ("SARA"), 42 U.S.C.A. §§ 9601–9675 (West 1995).

§ 4.6 Post Verdict/Judgment Investigations

Investigators can search commercial databases and public records to help counsel locate assets with which to satisfy judgments. Additionally, after a verdict has been rendered, investigators can assist counsel to examine allegations of juror misconduct which may serve to set aside the jury's determination.[1] However, because courts have set different rules and guidelines for conducting post-verdict investigations, extreme care must be exercised to ensure that an investigation does not run afoul of the operative rules of the particular jurisdiction in question.

§ 4.7 Court Orders and Consent Degrees

Although many lawsuits conclude with obtaining a monetary judgment, some disputes are resolved by the entry of consent decrees or court orders. Investigators can be used to test compliance with these mandates in a variety of ways. Effective surveillance, for example, can disclose whether a party is complying with an agreement to conduct business operations only during specified hours and at designated locations. Coordinated "sweeps" of preselected streets and other public areas, moreover, will promptly determine whether an adjudicated trademark infringer is continuing to sell knock-offs and other counterfeit items in contravention of a court order. Together with counsel, investigators can readily devise any number of effective strategies to test compliance with whatever court orders or consent decrees require evaluation. Equally important, if an investigation uncovers a party's intentional or material noncompliance, counsel will be armed with sufficient proof to obtain injunctive relief or a contempt order from the court.

Additionally, counsel can use investigations affirmatively to establish a client's compliance with a given court order or consent decree, thereby seeking relief from the mandate as no longer necessary. For example, an attorney representing a franchisor under court order to follow particular rules and regulations in connection with the solicitation of new franchisees, can engage an investigative firm to test the client's compliance with the regulations. Posing as prospective franchisees, investigators can record the sales pitch of company representatives and report to counsel the results of these tests. Armed with a sufficient number of recordings showing the company's observance of the rules, the attorney can return to court urging dissolution of the order or decree.

Library References:

West's Key No. Digests, Federal Civil Procedure ☞2397.

Wright, Miller & Cooper, Federal Practice and Procedure: Civil 2d § 4443.

§ 4.8 Alternate Dispute Resolution

In view of the number and kinds of commercial disputes that are being decided by alternate dispute resolution procedures ("ADR") today,

---

§ 4.6

1. *See* Chapter 38 "Jury Conduct, Instructions and Verdicts" at § 38.6, *infra*, for a complete discussion of the legal issues pertaining to post-trial contact with jurors.

counsel should consider engaging investigators in these matters. Because discovery is often extremely circumscribed in ADR proceedings, the use of investigators may be the only effective means available to counsel to gather the facts and help prepare the case. Moreover, investigators can develop detailed professional histories of the proposed panelists, including their philosophies, inclinations, likes and dislikes, all of which will be important if they are selected as arbitrators. In this manner, investigators can effectively assist counsel in making informed decisions in selecting the arbitrators to hear the matter.

Library References:

West's Key No. Digests, Arbitration ☞1–4.1.
Wright, Miller & Cooper, Federal Practice and Procedure: Civil 2d § 4246.

§ 4.9 Retaining Investigative Professionals

Counsel should select an investigator in the same manner as choosing any other professional. While recommendations from other attorneys remain one of the best ways to find the right investigative firm for the job, counsel nevertheless should carefully scrutinize the prospective firm's ethics, conflicts, background, reporting lines of authority, personnel, relevant experience, access to sources, fee structure, and other pertinent factors in making an informed decision. Each of these considerations is addressed in some detail below.

(a) Conflicts

Actual or potential conflicts should be checked immediately with the proposed firm. The best and most direct way to do this is to provide the firm with the names of the parties and any interested witnesses. Regardless of the sophistication or experience of the prospective investigative firm, counsel should never assume that the firm's investigators fully appreciate all of their ethical responsibilities. Instead, because counsel will more fully understand the case's factual and legal issues and nuances at this particular stage of the litigation, he or she should carefully explain to the investigative firm the various ways in which a conflict could arise.

(b) Ethics

Although the use of an investigator can add considerable value to the case, these benefits do not come risk free. Because an investigator serves as the agent of an attorney, counsel must take great care in selecting an ethical investigative firm. In this regard, counsel may not use an investigator to circumvent the canons of ethics, as courts' and lawyers' disciplinary panels treat the investigator as the lawyer's alter ego, holding the attorney fully accountable for the investigator's conduct performed on the attorney's behalf.[1] Thus, by carefully interviewing

§ 4.9   1. *See* Model Rules of Professional Con-

prospective investigators, checking their references and testing their understanding of their legal and ethical obligations, counsel can help ensure that the firm obtains information lawfully and at all times conducts itself within the bounds of the law and any applicable codes of ethics.

Accordingly, in order to ensure that an attorney does not become subject to disciplinary action or personal liability arising from the unlawful acts of an investigator, counsel must be prepared to exercise control over the investigation and work closely with the investigative firm hired to work on the case.

(c) Accountability and Responsibility

Counsel must determine who at the investigative firm will be accountable and responsible for the inquiry. At the outset, counsel must have complete confidence in the person designated to run the investigation. Counsel must be certain, for example, that the lead investigator will take instructions and direction easily. Besides checking the investigator's credentials and testing him/her in a face-to-face meeting, counsel should ask for a written proposal for the investigation, which should provide further guidance regarding the investigator's skills and abilities. Counsel should insist on a different lead investigator if the person initially selected by the firm does not appear right for the case.

Reporting relationships within the investigative firm should be fully explored so that counsel understands to whom investigators will report and from whom they will receive their assignments and direction. Clear and well defined lines of authority and accountability, although important in all investigations, are vital to national investigations, where work is performed in many jurisdictions. In these cases, counsel must be assured that the lead investigator will effectively coordinate communications between the attorneys working on the matter and the investigators, so that a call to the lead investigator will be as good as speaking to any investigator assigned to the case.

Further, the lead investigator must be capable of coordinating all investigative activities nationwide. This ensures that counsel will be promptly and accurately informed of all important investigative developments in the case—regardless of where they occur—and that investigators in each jurisdiction will follow the case's investigative plan and not perform independent investigations that may actually interfere with the case's litigation and investigative strategies and goals.

(d) The Retainer Agreement

A written retainer agreement between counsel and the investigative firm ultimately selected for the case is essential. The retainer agreement should set out only in the most general terms the scope of the assignment and include representations from the investigators regarding the

duct Rule 8.4(a) (1983).

methodology they will use (*e.g.*, that they will obey the law) and any other matters of importance to counsel.[2]

Most importantly, however, the retainer agreement should expressly provide that the notes and reports of the investigators are protected as attorney work-product and are covered by the attorney-client privilege. This type of agreement is commonly known as a *Kovel* letter, taking its name from *United States v. Kovel*, a 1961 decision of the U.S. Court of Appeals for the Second Circuit.[3] *Kovel* extended the protections of the attorney-client privilege and the work-product doctrine to communications between a lawyer and his or her agents hired to assist in the rendition of legal services; however, in order for the privilege to be effective, the attorney—and not the client—must hire the investigator or other expert. The protections afforded investigators and other experts under *Kovel* and its progeny remain subject to all of the customary limitations on the attorney-client privilege.[4]

In order to protect the confidential relationship, all written communications between counsel and the investigative firm, including documents created before the firm was formally retained, should contain a legend indicating that the materials are protected from disclosure under the attorney-client privilege and the work-product doctrine. For example, at least the first page of each document should contain the following legend:

PRIVILEGED ATTORNEY–CLIENT AND
CONFIDENTIAL WORK–PRODUCT COMMUNICATION

or

PRIVILEGED JOINT DEFENSE ATTORNEY–CLIENT AND
CONFIDENTIAL WORK–PRODUCT COMMUNICATION

Marking all pages of the documents in this manner may help guard against the inadvertent production of privileged materials, and should make it easier to identify privileged documents at a later date. The consistent use of these legends, moreover, may help convince a court that the materials are indeed privileged from disclosure.[5]

Counsel should make sure that all members of the investigative team understand the privilege's confidentiality requirements and do not inadvertently waive or disclose privileged information.

(e) Professional Licenses

Counsel must be sure that the prospective investigative firm is properly licensed. Almost all states require that investigators be licensed,

---

2. A copy of a model retainer agreement is included in § 4.19(a), *infra*.

3. 296 F.2d 918 (2d Cir.1961).

4. *See, e.g.*, Chapter 18 "Discovery Strategy and Privileges" at § 18.6, *infra*; 2 Jack B. Weinstein & Margaret A. Berger, Weinstein's Evidence 503(a)(3)[01] (1993); United States Postal Service v. Phelps

Dodge Refining Corp., 852 F.Supp. 156, 161 (E.D.N.Y.1994).

5. *See* Vincent C. Alexander, *The Corporate Attorney–Client Privilege: A Study of the Participants*, 63 St. John's L. Rev. 191, 333 (1989).

but the standards for obtaining a license vary from state to state. Some states require an investigator to pass a written examination, demonstrate prior investigative experience either as a law enforcement officer or an employee of a licensed investigative firm, possess good moral character, and post a bond.[6] Other states issue licenses upon registration and payment of the appropriate fees. Regardless of a particular jurisdiction's licensing requirements, counsel should retain only licensed investigators for the case, since the performing of investigations without a license is a crime in some states.[7]

(f) Firm Size and Personnel

The size of an investigative firm is an important factor to consider in choosing an investigative agency. Some investigative firms consist of a single investigator or a group of investigators who share the same general background and experience (*e.g.*, former federal agents or police officers). Other investigative firms have national and international practices, drawing their members from a broad range of professional disciplines, including former police detectives and federal agents, ex-prosecutors, database researchers, forensic accountants, industry specific specialists, and other experts.

The scope of the investigation, the complexity of the issues, and speed with which the inquiry must be completed directly bear on the size of the investigative firm to be awarded the job, and the particular skills it must have to successfully complete the assignment. Because of their greater size, in-house expertise, and access to local investigators throughout the country, national firms are often better suited to conduct certain types of complex and multi-district investigations than their smaller counterparts.

Depending on the particular needs of the case, counsel may require that an investigative firm have adequate computer resources and computer literate personnel who are capable of establishing or working with an investigative database. When there is particular urgency to the inquiry, the firm should be capable of preparing and downloading investigative reports in the field, and sending them directly to counsel. Nevertheless, counsel should bear in mind that the case always will be better served by investigators who perform excellent work—even if in a noncompatible computer format—than by a firm which delivers a compatible but mediocre work product.

Like other professionals, some investigators are more adept than others at performing particular tasks. Investigators especially skilled at conducting surveillances, for instance, may lack the experience or ability to conduct effective field interviews. Other investigators who excel at performing records searches and database research may perform poorly as witnesses in court. In making the selection decision, therefore, counsel may wish to meet with the prospective firm's field agents and other

---

6. *See, e.g.*, N.Y. General Business Law §§ 70–89–a (McKinney 1988).

7. *See id.* (performance of unlicensed investigations constitutes a misdemeanor).

personnel assigned to the case, in order to ensure that they are sufficiently skilled as investigators and witnesses, understand the proposed assignments, and can work comfortably with counsel. In short, counsel should make every effort to choose an investigative firm whose personnel and skills best match the investigative requirements of the case.

(g) Experience and References

Perhaps the most valuable quality an investigative firm can possess is prior experience with the type of matter counsel is handling. The more experience the firm has, the better it will understand and anticipate the needs of counsel and the case. Moreover, a firm with relevant experience can quickly adapt successful investigative strategies from prior matters to the current project, immediately eliminating less productive techniques without loss of time or expense to the client.

Firms seeking to be retained should be willing to identify similar projects they have completed. Counsel should check the firm's references to ensure that the work was satisfactorily performed within budget and on time.

(h) Availability and Subcontractors

In seeking an assignment, investigative firms generally promise to dedicate a given number of investigators and other resources to the investigation. Counsel should obtain a clear commitment from the investigator that these resources will in fact be available, when needed, throughout the duration of the case.

Depending on the circumstances of the case (e.g., number and location of interviews, existence of documents in a distant location, etc.), investigative firms may retain local investigators (i.e., subcontractors) to satisfy their staffing needs. Generally, local investigators are hired when they can perform important investigative services more efficiently and at a lower cost than if the lead investigative firm were to fly its personnel to some distant location to do the work. Investigative firms also retain subcontractors to meet local licensing requirements, when they require specialized expertise (that the firms do not possess), or when they need additional investigators to properly staff their cases.

Whatever the reason for hiring subcontractors, counsel should ensure that the local investigators are licensed, bonded and insured. Counsel also should ensure that the local investigators maintain the confidentiality of all information pertaining to the investigation, requiring them to sign confidentiality agreements when appropriate. In certain cases, counsel must be alert to the possibility of subcontractors trading on inside information they may have learned from the investigation or assisting others to do so. To lessen this risk, counsel should warn all subcontractors of the serious civil and criminal consequences that can befall persons caught engaging in insider trading. Most experienced investigative firms have their employees and subcontractors execute "Insider Trading Compliance" statements.

(i) Assembling a Team

It is important that counsel assemble an investigative team as soon as practically possible. Generally, counsel will rely on the investigative firm's contacts and expertise in putting the team together, although the attorney may wish to meet with and approve any member who is expected to testify. Once the team has been mustered, important ground rules for the conduct of the investigation should be established for the duration of the case, including the relationship between counsel and the investigators, and the manner in which the latter will communicate and report investigative results. At the outset of the case, for example, counsel should adopt a team approach to the investigation. One useful model is the approach used by federal prosecutors and agents, who conduct criminal investigations together as a team from the inception of the case through the prosecution. Employing this model, counsel's investigators, although working under an attorney's direction, should be included as essential members of the team right from the start.

Questions involving access to the client should be quickly decided. In most instances, there is no reason to restrict the investigators from having direct access provided that counsel is a party to the communications and the attorney-client and work-product privileges are observed.

Counsel also should make clear the types and frequency of reports he or she expects to receive from the investigative team. Written reports should be uniform, well written, and, as discussed in Section 4.9(c), *supra*, contain appropriate legends protecting the confidentiality and privileged nature of the materials. In order to prevent counsel's time from being wasted on issues and details better handled by others, the lead investigator should first review all written reports for accuracy and completeness.

In addition, investigators should be instructed that interview reports should not contain opinions concerning the veracity of witnesses and other persons. Instead, the team should be encouraged to deliver their opinions verbally to counsel for at least two reasons. First, by speaking with the investigator, counsel can explore the matters on which the opinion is based, thereby assessing the accuracy and reliability of the investigator's point of view. Second, because uninformed opinions or opinions based on limited information can unnecessarily impeach the credibility of witnesses, the elimination of these matters from written investigative reports will prevent needless complications in the case.

(j) Billing and Costs

The costs of the investigation should be discussed and agreed upon at the start of the case. Most investigators bill their time on an hourly basis plus disbursements for customary expenses such as travel and database costs. Depending on the type of matter involved, billing arrangements setting a flat fee for an entire project also may be offered. Finally, although attorneys and other professionals may accept certain types of matters on a contingent fee basis, it is illegal for investigators to charge contingent fees in some jurisdictions.

Some investigative firms use a blended rate to bill all of their personnel at the same hourly fee regardless of experience or particular expertise. Firms which use this method may have an incentive to assign their least experienced investigators to the case since they cost the firm less than the more experienced workers. Accordingly, if counsel agrees to a blended rate structure, he or she should insist on reviewing the résumés of the persons to be assigned to the matter and use other controls for ensuring that those persons have adequate experience. For example, counsel may require that experienced personnel devote to the matter a specific percentage of the total number of hours budgeted.

Counsel can anticipate and control the costs of the investigation by agreeing with the investigator on a written budget for all phases of the assignment. Once counsel defines all of the items of work to be performed, the budget can be calculated based on the estimated tasks and disbursements for each phase of the inquiry. For example, if the initial phase of the investigation involves witness interviews and computerized database searches, counsel and the investigator can estimate the number of hours for the interviews and the costs of the database research. Other costs to be added are the time for coordination and the hours already spent learning the case. As an additional cost control measure, the budget may include an agreement that no unusual out-of-pocket expenses (usually defined as costs above a certain dollar amount) or hourly fees in excess of the budgeted amounts will be incurred without counsel's prior approval.

If no overall budget is set, interim "stopping off" points should be set above which no additional fees will be billed without counsel's approval. These plateaus provide counsel with excellent opportunities to measure the costs of the investigation against the results achieved to date.

When a group of counsel representing different parties retains an investigator to perform services, the costs of the investigation are shared by each member of the group. Under such cost-sharing arrangements, the group is responsible for paying the investigator's fees and expenses, and the investigator should not be expected to seek payment separately from each group member. As a practical matter, the group should designate one of its members to review and approve the investigator's bills and to arrange for payment.

Investigator's bills should be sent directly to counsel and not the ultimate client. This arrangement helps preserve the confidential relationship between the investigators and counsel under *Kovel*,[8] and should be clearly spelled out in the retainer agreement. In addition, the bills should not include a narrative description of the work the investigators performed. In some jurisdictions, attorneys' and other experts' bills are discoverable. If produced during discovery, an investigator's detailed bill will disclose the steps and goals of the investigation, which in turn may provide a road map of the case's litigation strategy. Should counsel want

8. *See supra* § 4.9(c).

or need the details, they can be provided in a separate confidential document.

§ 4.10   Planning the Investigation

(a) The Investigative Plan

Successful investigations are based on careful planning, a full understanding of the factual and legal issues of the case, and constant teamwork between counsel and the investigative firm. In getting started, counsel and the investigator first should develop a comprehensive investigative plan identifying the goals and objectives of the investigation. The plan should identify and prioritize the investigative steps to be taken, setting timetables for accomplishing each of the tasks in question. In fashioning the plan, counsel also must decide whether the investigation should begin covertly, thereby keeping the inquiry secret for all or a portion of the relevant time period, or whether the goals of the case would be better served from the start by an overt and visible probe.[1]

After the objectives of the investigation have been set, the investigative team can choose the appropriate strategies and techniques to use (*e.g.*, field interviews, database research, surveillance, etc.).

(b) Educating the Team

Counsel should set aside sufficient time to review the important legal and factual issues with the investigative team. Background information should be shared with the investigators so as to increase the likelihood that they will recognize relevant materials discovered in the field. For example, if an object of the case is to prove that the transfer of certain assets constitutes a fraudulent conveyance, the investigators should be told the factors courts consider in deciding that kind of issue. The more time counsel spends educating the investigators at the beginning of the case, the less time they will likely spend pursuing false leads or taking other unproductive steps.

A careful briefing at the beginning of the investigation helps investigators avoid common pitfalls and traps, such as inadvertently interviewing represented parties or witnesses,[2] and also establishes counsel's good faith efforts to conduct a disciplined and ethical investigation. As part of the briefing, therefore, counsel should provide the investigative team with a list of persons and entities that are not to be contacted. Additionally, the investigators should be given written guidelines to use during all interviews. Such instructions force investigators at the start of an interview to inquire about the witness' affiliation and employment, and

---

§ 4.10

1. *See infra* § 4.12, for a discussion of the different investigative approaches that can be used (*e.g.*, "quiet" or "visible" inquiries or a combination of both).

2. *See infra* § 4.13(e)(1), for a discussion of the issues pertaining to interviewing represented parties.

to ask other pertinent questions the answers to which may lead to the immediate termination of the interview. Further, because the instructions accurately identify the investigators' purpose and affiliation, the risk of these matters being misrepresented to witnesses and others in the field is significantly reduced. *See* Section 4.19(b), *infra* for Model Guidelines for Investigators.

Finally, consideration should be given to videotaping the instructions so that they can be shown to investigators in the field who are unavailable for a face-to-face discussion.

(c) Lines of Authority and Reporting

The lines of authority and reporting must be understood by everyone on the team and function effectively. As goals and strategies shift, directions from counsel or the lead investigator must be promptly and accurately communicated and followed, as delays and mistakes can harm the case. For example, if a witness inadvertently is interviewed by separate investigators who prepare separate statements subject to discovery, inconsistencies in the two statements may be used by opposing counsel to undermine the witness' testimony. Duplicative assignments also may add unnecessary costs to the investigation and damage relationships with witnesses, who resent the inconvenience and intrusiveness of multiple interviews. Further, in order to ensure that information developed during the investigation is protected by the attorney-client and work-product privileges, investigators' reports should be directed to counsel and not the client.[3]

(d) Joint Defense Agreements

Joint defense agreements should be executed when there is a need for multiple parties, whether represented by the same or separate counsel, to share information in a litigation without waiving the attorney-client or work-product privileges.[4] In order to avail themselves of the joint defense privilege, parties must comply with the following three requirements: (1) the communications must be made in the course of a joint defense effort, (2) the statements must be designed to further the effort, and (3) the joint defense privilege must not have been waived.[5] Assuming all of the other traditional elements of the attorney-client privilege have been met, the joint defense privilege protects "communications passing from one party to the attorney for another party where a joint defense effort has been decided upon and undertaken by the parties and their respective counsel."[6] The privilege also protects communica-

---

3. *See supra* § 4.9(d).

4. *See* Webb Tarun Molo, Corporate Internal Investigations § 5.05[1] (1994).

5. *Id.*

6. United States v. Schwimmer, 892 F.2d 237, 243–44 (2d Cir.1989) (protection afforded by the privilege extended to communications made in confidence to an accountant assisting attorneys who were conducting a joint defense on behalf of communicating clients).

tions made to accountants and other experts, such as investigators, who are assisting counsel conduct a joint defense.[7]

(e) Communication and Teamwork

The best results are obtained when counsel and the investigators communicate frequently and regularly. Weekly meetings or telephone calls should be scheduled to set the following week's agenda, summarize the past week's developments, and resolve any anticipated issues or problems.

Although written reports are essential and should be prepared as soon as possible after witness interviews are completed, they may slow down the process and prevent counsel from being kept up to date. Thus, important information elicited in the field or lines of questioning proven to be effective with witnesses (*e.g.*, a witness offered money by an adversary in exchange for testimony) should be communicated immediately to counsel. Once the information or strategies have been assessed, they can be passed along to all other members of the team.

As the investigation unfolds in the field, counsel must be available on short notice and the investigators must know how and where to reach him or her. This is particularly important during the interviewing phase of the case, when investigators may need to reach counsel to answer a witness' question (*e.g.*, Am I exposing myself to criminal liability?), or to alert the attorney that a witness is providing such important information that counsel may wish to join the interview.

Finally, the investigative plan must always remain consistent with counsel's litigation goals. Thus, as the landscape of the case changes with the discovery of new information or the emergence of additional issues, the investigative plan should be modified to meet the shifting needs of the litigation. For example, in a securities fraud litigation, initial interviews of a number of brokers may disclose that a problem which counsel originally believed to be local in nature (*e.g.*, improper sales instructions from a single field office) actually can be traced to directions issued from the company's headquarters. Armed with this information, the investigative plan can be expanded to include a review of the company's organization chart and lines of authority, as well as an examination of the company's compensation system to see whether it encourages illegal behavior.

With proper lines of communication in place, the investigation's refashioned objectives can be communicated promptly and effectively to all members of the team.

§ 4.11   Investigative Goals

The investigative goals of a case usually can be divided into two categories: Developing leads, facts and general information:

---

7. *See id*; *see also* Reid Weingarten,   107 (1992).
Maintaining Privileges, 763 PLI/Corp. 106,

- about the issues in dispute, or

- going to the credibility of witnesses and potential witnesses.

With regard to the first set of goals, the investigative team generally seeks to obtain evidence that can help prove the case or, alternatively, disprove an adverse party's litigation position. The following examples illustrate investigative strategies that may be helpful in establishing a case or disproving an adversary's assertion.

- Counsel's client, a well-known producer of financial software for individuals and small businesses, hires a freelance software designer to produce a new program to be sold in combination with the Company's other software packages. In performing the work, the programmer is given unrestricted access to all of the Company's other financial software packages, including the source codes for the programs. Without the Company's knowledge or consent, the programmer downloads and copies these materials. A number of months after the programmer's work is completed, the Company's marketing director notices that a new competitor is advertising and selling financial programs virtually identical to the Company's. In gathering the facts to commence a possible lawsuit for infringement and other claims, investigators retained by the Company's litigation firm review commercial databases. They rapidly discover a newly-formed joint-venture between the competitor and the programmer.

- A distributor of consumer electronic equipment sells VCRs and other equipment on credit to a small retail chain in another state. After payment for a particular shipment is substantially overdue, the retailer advises the distributor that most of the equipment in the order, after being removed from the packing cartons and examined, was damaged beyond repair and junked. Civil litigation records, examined by an investigator in the retailer's home state, reveal that a judgment has been entered against the retailer in an earlier nonpayment action involving the same ploy.

Similarly, investigators can develop impeachment materials from a variety of sources to undermine the credibility of witnesses. Inspection of court records and commercial databases, for example, may reveal that a key witness has a prior criminal record, uses aliases or multiple social security numbers, or has been sued for conduct involving deceit or false statements. Additionally, careful scrutiny of documents and tape recordings by forensic experts may undermine the authenticity of the materials, or establish evidence of tampering; conversely, forensic work can help prove that the disputed items are genuine and admissible.[1]

§ 4.11

1. *See infra* § 4.13(g), for a complete discussion of the use of forensics in investigations.

§ 4.12 Investigative Approaches

There are two approaches to investigations: "quiet" (covert) or "visible" (overt) inquiries. A number of investigations also have a transition phase, when the inquiry moves from using covert to overt investigative techniques. Each of these phases is discussed below.

(a) Quiet Inquiries

The quiet or covert phase of an investigation consists of the investigative steps that can be taken with reasonable assurance that an adversary will not learn of the inquiry. In almost all cases, this is the first stage of an investigation, which should be performed as quietly and secretly as possible.

Quiet investigations are usually conducted when counsel is particularly sensitive about the adversary learning of the inquiry. These situations arise during the prefiling stage of a case, when counsel and the investigative firm are gathering and assessing the factual underpinnings of the client's potential claims or defenses, or when the matter in question involves sensitive issues.

In order to maintain the secrecy of the inquiry, investigators are careful not to contact any persons during this phase of the probe who are likely to disclose its existence. Instead, the techniques investigators usually employ at this juncture include: commercial database and public records searches; reviews of online media articles and local newspapers; criminal records checks; loose surveillances (e.g., investigators are instructed to avoid being seen or caught because maintaining secrecy at this stage is more important than obtaining particular information); undercover ("sting") operations; forensic examination of handwriting, tape and audio recordings, or other items in the client's possession or control; review of client documents and materials; limited interviews of the client's top management; and perhaps contacts with confidential sources of known reliability.

(b) Visible Inquiries

Visible inquiries are conducted at two separate levels. On one level, counsel may not care if an adversary finds out about the investigation; nevertheless, the attorney's investigators are not urged to go out of their way to advertise the inquiry.

On the second level, as an extra dimension of the investigation counsel may instruct the investigative team to take overt actions which ensure that the adversary knows about the inquiry. Such visible tactics often are used to demonstrate the seriousness with which counsel's client considers the matter and the client's willingness to commit substantial resources to the case. Mass interviews of witnesses, for example, are an effective means of alerting an adversary to the seriousness of the situation. Visible investigations also are helpful in attracting potential witnesses who may be willing to talk if they believe there is someone interested in hearing what they know.

The overt stage of an investigation is typically the most extensive phase of the inquiry, involving the traditional investigative techniques of witness interviews and audits.

(c) Transition from Quiet to Visible Inquiries

The transition from a quiet to visible inquiry usually occurs just before an adversary learns of the investigation or contemporaneous with the discovery. The timing and method of moving from a covert to an overt investigation should be planned so as to gain advantage, since the circumstances and timing of the change are usually matters within counsel's control. Thus, surprise interviews of witnesses, for example, can be conducted at counsel's direction before an adversary has time to react and, perhaps, urge the witnesses not to cooperate.

The transition phase of an investigation often begins with the interviewing of witnesses. Even at this stage, interviews usually start with persons who are likely to keep the existence of the investigation confidential. As the investigation broadens, the investigators are more likely to interview people who will reveal the existence of the inquiry. Accordingly, identifying the order and timing of witness interviews is an important decision counsel should make jointly with the lead investigator, weighing what may be gained from interviewing a particular person against what may be lost if the witness discloses the existence of the investigation to the adversary.

§ 4.13 Tools Available in an Investigation

There are many tools from which an investigative team may choose. If used effectively and creatively, the investigative options described below can be used to obtain information that will substantially benefit the case.

(a) The Client

Not surprisingly, clients are often the source of significant information. Based on their experience in their industry or with a particular adversary, clients may have anecdotal information that is of great value to the investigation. They also may have trade journals and magazines, industry studies, databases, and confidential sources that are laden with information. In addition, former employees of the adversary may work for the client and may be the source of leads and evidence. In any event, carefully debriefing the client is a secure starting point for the investigation because the fact of the inquiry is unlikely to be disclosed by the client's own personnel.

(b) The Law Firm

Law firms often have substantial in-house expertise and information regarding their clients' industries, suppliers, customers, competitors and regulatory environment. Thus, as another initial starting point in the investigation, the investigative team should debrief any of the firm's attorneys with knowledge of these matters and, with consent of the client, review the client's pertinent legal files and other relevant documents maintained by the firm.

(c) Public Information

There is a wealth of useful public information available from sophisticated commercial databases, public records repositories and the Internet. Depending on the nature of the data, this information can be used as evidence, to discredit witnesses, and as leads. Each of these sources of public information is discussed in detail below.

(1) Commercial Databases

Competent investigative firms have experienced computer researchers skilled at navigating through the many sophisticated commercial databases available today and retrieving information in a fast and cost-effective manner. While the information obtained from these databases often provides leads rather than evidence of the ultimate facts needed to be established in a case, they are, nevertheless, superb tools for finding people, identifying witnesses to events, and performing other important functions.

Commercial databases, for instance, can provide the following types of information among other useful data:

social security numbers; dates of birth; address histories; names, addresses and telephone numbers of neighbors; assumed and fictitious names; criminal records; names and addresses of spouses and other family members; corporate and limited partnership interests; real property ownership and mortgages; bankruptcy filings; judgments, liens and other civil litigation records; national and local media exposure; vehicle ownership and driving records; and professional licenses.

These databases also can disclose highly technical information such as the ownership of patents and copyrights.

Databases are excellent sources of impeachment material to undermine the credibility of an adversary's witnesses. They may disclose, for example, that a witness has a criminal record or has been sued for fraud or other deceitful conduct bearing on the person's credibility. Searches of print media databases also may reveal newspaper articles containing negative information about a witness or other important leads. In addition, commercial databases can be used to test the background of counsel's own witnesses and thus avoid potential surprise and embarrassment when a tarnished witness testifies at trial.

What follows is a chart identifying several available commercial databases and the types of information they contain.

Name of Database	Available Information
CDB INFOTEK	This computer accessible database contains a broad range of information permitting the user to perform national, state, and regional searches regarding individuals, corporations, partnerships and other business entities. Available information includes, but is not limited to: current and former addresses; social security numbers; dates of birth; business relationships; civil and criminal litigation history; property ownership; bankruptcy filings and liens; professional licenses; and motor vehicle records.
LEXIS–NEXIS PUBLIC RECORDS	Searches of this database disclose, among other things: real estate ownership and transfers; the locations of individuals and businesses; civil and criminal court indices of the parties in various local and federal jurisdictions; corporate, limited partnership, and fictitious business name filings; and judgments and liens.
LEXIS–NEXIS ON–LINE SERVICES	This database contains a broad range of news and information services, including: world, national and regional news and media; business analyses, profiles, and directories; and company financial statements and information. These files can be searched for information concerning individuals and businesses.
DUN & BRADSTREET	Access to this database enables the user to obtain financial and other key information pertaining to many national and international businesses, including annual sales, reported earnings, payment histories, corporate hierarchies, profiles of officers, and number of employees.
DATABASE TECHNOLOGIES, INC.	Distinctive features of the DBT system, also known as AUTOTRACK, include individuals' dates of birth and names of relatives. Also available are current and former addresses and neighbor lists, driver's license and vehicle registration information, liens, judgments and bankruptcies, and information on corporations and limited partnerships.
INFORMATION AMERICA	Information America is one of the largest public records vendors in the United States, offering many proprietary databases and searches. Information contained in this database can be

	searched when performing due diligence investigations, evaluating general business background information, identifying assets for recovery and involved parties, locating and tracking Uniform Commercial Code ("UCC") filings, and locating people and businesses.

(2) Public Records

Many public records are not yet online or in CD–ROM databases. Thus, these records can only be obtained by sending members of the investigative team to court houses and other document repositories, such as local building departments and county clerk's offices. Similarly, local news articles, which are not online, can be reviewed in public libraries.

Public records searches can provide important evidence and leads. Searches of civil litigation files, for example, may reveal the names of prior adversaries who may be willing to provide information about the adverse party or its witnesses in the current case. In addition, the records may contain helpful admissions by an adversary which are inconsistent with its current litigation position (*e.g.*, in an earlier lawsuit, an adversary admits or even asserts that a particular person is an officer and shareholder of the company; in the current case, the adversary claims that the same person is merely an employee without authority to bind the company). Further, public records and database searches may reveal the names and locations of former business partners and employers of witnesses. These persons often are excellent sources of impeachment material and leads.

The following list provides examples of the types of files and records that can be checked when conducting public records searches:

- Civil and criminal litigation records
- Civil judgments and liens
- Federal tax litigation files in the district and tax courts
- Federal, state and local tax liens and warrants
- Bankruptcy court filings
- Uniform Commercial Code filings
- Business certificates, partnership agreements, and other corporate filings
- Real property ownership and mortgage records
- Violations of state or local building, health and environmental codes
- Zoning and renovation building permits (these are particularly valuable in asset searches because they may disclose properties owned by businesses and other parties)

- Records of federal magistrate judge proceedings (*e.g.*, arrest warrants)
- Fictitious business name and/or assumed name indices
- Motor vehicle, marine vessel and aircraft records

(3) The Internet

The Internet is emerging today as an important investigative tool. Many federal, state and local agencies have placed their regulatory databases and other information online. The federal government, for example, has constructed World Wide Websites that enable users to identify individuals and businesses that have been convicted of health care fraud offenses, or who have been excluded from participation in the government funded Medicare and Medicaid programs because of health care convictions or serious patient care deficiencies.[1] In addition, a skilled Internet user can rapidly retrieve reports that publicly held companies are required to file electronically with the Securities and Exchange Commission's EDGAR database system.

Internet searches also can disclose records reflecting administrative disciplinary penalties that states have imposed on a broad range of professionals and experts. This can be particularly useful in obtaining impeachment material for cross-examination of an adversary's expert. Further, the Internet's people finder programs, business libraries, and news and media sources are additional sources of information and intelligence gathering.

A chart identifying a number of useful Internet sources, including the databases and other information accessible through them, is set forth below.

DIALOG http://dialog.krinfo.com.	DIALOG, a unit of Knight Ridder, offers over 450 individual databases containing over 100,000 publications covering virtually all subject areas. Available files include SEC records, information on U.S. copyrights and patents, and imports and exports to and from U.S. seaports. An index search permits the user to scan all DIALOG files for references to an investigative subject.
DATATIMES http://www.datatimes.com	Database of regional and international newspapers and news wires, more than 5,000 sources in all.
INFORMATION AMERICA 800/235–4008 http://www.infoam.com	An affiliate of West Group, Information America provides access to lawsuits, corporate and limited partnership records, county records, and real

§ 4.13

1. *See,* *e.g.,* http://www.sbaonline.sba.gov/ignet/internal/hhs/hhs.html (the home page of the Health and Human Services Office of the Inspector General).

	property liens and judgments. Database covers state court litigation in selected counties in 43 states and Puerto Rico. Its Executive Affiliation® search probes state corporate and limited partnership information, fictitious names and other data sources to link individuals to business entities.
DOW JONES 800/522–3567 http://www.wsj.com	Database offers full-text Wall Street Journal, Dow Jones news wires, and other full-text newspapers. News wires cover breaking national, international and business news. Other services offer financial markets information.
Switchboard http://www.switch-board.com	This database, the equivalent of an electronic white pages, permits users to locate the addresses and telephone numbers of individuals and businesses that have listed telephone numbers. Searches are performed by inputting the name of the person or business in question, which is then associated with any listed telephone number and address.
Yahoo People Finder http://www.yahoo.com/search/people	By inputting a person's name, this search engine also will find the individual's telephone number (if listed) and any corresponding address.
SEC—EDGAR http://www.sec.gov	This database contains all SEC corporate public filings, but only from 1995 through the present.
Superintendent of Documents, Government Printing Office http://www.access.gpo.gov/su_docs	This link provides online access to congressional bills, Congressional Record, Federal Register and other government documents.
Federal Agency Inspectors General http://www.sbaonline.sba.gov/ignet/ig.html#about	This database contains reports of investigations and audits of federal agency departments and programs.
General Accounting Office http://www.gao.gov	U.S. government reports are available on this link within days of their release.
Hoovers Directory http://www.hoovers.com	This business directory, which lists thousands of companies, provides the names of company executives, business addresses, number of employees, etc.
IPO Central http://www.ipocentral.com	This database, using information from Hoovers Directory and SEC EDGAR filings, provides information on U.S.

	companies that recently have gone public or have filed to do so.
Massachusetts Physician Profiles http://www.doc-board.org/ma/ma_home.htm	Although there are a number of Internet databases to track physicians throughout the county, this searchable file contains information on all 27,000 licensed physicians in Massachusetts, including their education and training, disciplinary history and paid malpractice claims.

(d) People as Sources

Identifying and interviewing people who have relevant knowledge about the issues, parties or witnesses in a case remains one of the key techniques of an effective investigation. Although public records investigations may lead to these sources, interviews of industry personnel and "networking" usually develop this kind of information. These activities, moreover, often can be done during the covert stage of an investigation if the interviews are limited to people who have no relationship to the adversary.

Grand jury investigations concerning an adversary or the subject matter of the litigation (*e.g.*, price fixing) may provide a fruitful source of leads and witnesses to pursue. By actively shadowing such an investigation, the investigative team can interview persons contacted by the government and evaluate documents and other materials turned over to the prosecution. These individuals can be identified in a number of ways, including reviewing newspaper reports of grand jury investigations, examining unsealed records of litigation brought by subjects and nonparties (*e.g.*, motions to suppress evidence, quash subpoenas, controvert search warrants, etc.), and speaking with the attorneys representing any of the targets, subjects or other persons or entities involved in the probe. Additionally, since witnesses are free to talk to the investigators, other persons with knowledge often can be identified directly from these conversations or indirectly from the information these individuals provide. Such efforts, moreover, do not run afoul of the grand jury obligation of secrecy, which does not cover witnesses, subjects, targets or their counsel.[2]

(e) Interviews of Witnesses

(1) Who May Be Interviewed?

One of the thorniest issues counsel may face in conducting an investigation is whether current or former employees of an adversary

---

2. *See, e.g.*, Fed.R.Crim.P. 6(e), which provides in relevant part:

A grand juror, an interpreter, a stenographer, an operator of a recording device, a typist who transcribes recorded testimony, an attorney for the government, or any person to whom disclosure is made

under paragraph (3)(A)(ii) of this subdivision shall not disclose matters occurring before the grand jury, except as otherwise provided for in these rules. No obligation of secrecy may be imposed on any person except in accordance with this rule.

may be interviewed ex parte. Because ethical rules governing the conduct of attorneys and varying decisional authority may prohibit or otherwise place restrictions on contacting current and former employees of a party, counsel must take extreme care in initiating such contacts and should be completely familiar with the law in each jurisdiction where ex parte interviews are planned.[3]

Counsel first should ensure that ex parte interviews are permitted in the particular jurisdictions where the current or former employees are currently located. Counsel then should make sure that the investigators fully understand that they may not seek or obtain privileged information from any current or former employee, and that they may not interview any such person who is represented by an attorney. Counsel also should cover with the investigators any other limitations particular jurisdictions may impose on such interviews.

To further guard against the possibility of investigators conducting prohibited interviews, they should be given model guidelines to take with them in the field. The instructions should contain introductory questions which seek to identify the witness' employer and affiliation, and whether the person is represented by counsel. Armed with answers to these questions, an investigator can immediately terminate any meeting with a witness who should not be interviewed.[4] The use of such instructions also protects counsel against an adversary's claim that an attempt was made to circumvent the rules.

(2) Practical Considerations

Once an investigation moves to the field and interviews are to begin, three questions are immediately presented: (1) where should the interview be conducted? (2) who should conduct the interview? and (3) how many interviewers should be present? As a general rule, the interview should be conducted wherever the witness is most comfortable—usually the witness' home. However, the investigative team must be flexible about the location of interviews, since witnesses occasionally will agree to be interviewed only at places away from their homes or businesses, such as at restaurants.

Strategic considerations also may dictate the site of an interview. If the investigative plan calls for surprise interviews, showing up unannounced at an interviewee's home or place of business is more likely to result in an interview than calling for an appointment.

Generally, the interviews should be handled by investigators, who are experienced at gathering information from people. If counsel chooses to participate in an interview, at least one investigator should be present to take notes of the meeting. Thus, if a factual dispute arises over what

---

3. Please refer to Chapter 18 "Discovery Strategy and Privileges," at § 18.11(c), and Chapter 52 "Ethical Issues in Commercial Cases," at § 52.6(f)(2), for discussion of the legal and ethical issues pertaining to interviews of current and former employees of a party.

4. Model Guidelines for Investigators are included in § 4.19(b), infra.

was said during the interview, the investigator and not counsel can be called as a witness.

Ideally, two investigators should be present at each interview. This becomes particularly important when a witness subsequently recants his story or claims the investigator simply got it wrong. In these circumstances, the second investigator's recollection and notes of the meeting help buttress the other investigator's testimony. Nevertheless, there are times when a budget does not allow for two investigators, or the presence of more than one interrogator may seem intimidating to a witness.

Careful notes should be taken unless this intimidates or puts-off a witness. Detailed notes help ensure that written reports are complete and accurate. The investigator should reduce his or her notes to a written report as soon as possible after the interview has been completed. Although there is no requirement that the notes be retained once a written report has been completed, there are good arguments both for retaining and destroying the notes. One reason for retaining the notes is that an investigator's contemporaneous notes sometimes are more accurate than the resulting interview report. Thus, if an important statement has been left out of the report but appears in the investigator's notes, the presence of the statement in the notes will make the witness' subsequent testimony on the matter more believable.

There are equally compelling reasons for discarding the notes after an interview report has been completed. First, because investigators' note taking skills and techniques may be quite idiosyncratic and vary from person to person, an adversary's review of the notes may raise false issues which unnecessarily complicate a case. Second, when notes are not retained, investigators may exercise greater care in preparing their written reports. Most federal agencies, for example, require their agents to destroy their interview notes after their written reports have been completed. Whatever choice is made concerning the interview notes, it is important that the practice be consistently observed throughout the case so that an adversary cannot claim that counsel is selectively retaining or destroying the investigators' notes.

On occasion, a witness may demand to receive a final copy of the interview report as a precondition to being interviewed. In almost all cases, providing the person with a copy of the report is a small price to pay in order to hear what the witness has to say, but investigators should discuss this first with counsel before agreeing. In exchange for giving a witness a copy of a statement, it is often a good idea to ask the witness to sign it.

Counsel and the investigators often need to decide whether to obtain sworn statements or affidavits from witnesses. These decisions turn on several factors, including the particular stage of the investigation or litigation, the importance of the witness' statement, and the desirability of "freezing" the witness' story. For example, where counsel anticipates having a witness testify at a court proceeding or deposition, there would be little purpose in memorializing the person's statement in an affidavit.

However, if the parties are participating in ADR proceedings, counsel may seek to obtain an affidavit from the witness, which may be admissible in that particular forum.

(3) Different Approaches for Interviews

There are several approaches for interviewing witnesses. Choosing the best approach depends on the unique circumstances of each interview, including the witness' attitude, demeanor and role, if any, in the matter under investigation; the timing and location of the meeting; whether the witness has prior knowledge of the investigation; whether the person has spoken to others about the case; and the investigator's ability to intuit the most effective technique to use.

One approach investigators use—appearing assertive and knowledgeable—may work well with some witnesses but have no effect on others. The opposite strategy—appearing uninformed and seeking assistance—may be effective with particular witnesses who like to help people or who feel empowered when they think they know more than others. Simply letting the witness tell his or her story and memorializing the statements is yet another effective approach for gathering the facts. Moreover, investigators can use a combination of the three strategies in seeking to maximize the amount of information and leads emanating from the interviews.

Whatever approaches are taken, properly conducted interviews create important opportunities for investigators to develop ongoing relationships with witnesses. Over time, carefully cultivated witnesses may remember information they had forgotten during their initial interviews or come across new information to provide the investigators, thereby leading them to additional sources, documents and witnesses.

(4) Tape Recording Interviews

Whether to tape record the interview of a witness raises separate ethical, legal and practical issues for counsel to consider. As a practical matter, open tape recording of an interview will assure that the investigator's account of the conversation is accurate and complete. But experience has shown that witnesses often are inhibited when tape recorders are used, particularly at the start of the session. After the investigator has developed a relationship with a witness, tape recording complex matters can be helpful if the witness is comfortable with the idea of providing a recorded statement.

Most interactions between witnesses and investigators, however, do not allow for open tape recording. In these situations, which include undercover operations and telephone calls and meetings with particular witnesses, counsel and the investigative firm should fully understand both federal and state laws concerning electronic surveillance before even considering the possibility of surreptitiously recording a witness' statement.

The federal wiretap statute permits aural recordings when one party to the conversation—whether in a face-to-face discussion or during a telephone call—consents to the taping.[5] This is rarely an issue in undercover operations, since an undercover operative is always a party to the conversation and can consent to the recording. Similarly, field investigators can consent to the taping of their telephone conversations and face-to-face conversations with witnesses. When these procedures are used, it is prudent to have the investigator explicitly consent to the recording at the beginning of the tape. Both during undercover situations and in all other circumstances where the other party to the conversation is to remain unaware of the taping, the undercover operative (or field investigator) should record his or her consent before the taped conversation begins and outside the presence or hearing of the other party.

As an additional precautionary step to ensure the completeness and integrity of an undercover recording, after an operative records his or her consent to the recording (including the date, time and place of the recording at the beginning of the tape), another investigator helping to "wire up" the undercover operative with a concealed recording device should use adhesive or other durable tape to secure the tape recorder's "record" switch or button in the record position. After the undercover meeting is concluded, the same investigator who wired up the undercover operative should remove the recording device, checking to make sure that the record button remained securely taped in the record position. These procedures not only demonstrate the care with which the investigative team obtained the tape recorded statements, but they also help rebut any subsequent accusation that the undercover operative either purposefully or unintentionally turned off the tape recorder and thus selectively recorded only portions of the conversation in question.

Once federal requirements have been met, counsel next must examine whether state law permits one-party consensual recording. Although 36 states currently follow federal law and allow recordings with the consent of only one party,[6] 15 jurisdictions require *all* parties to the conversation to consent to the taping.[7] Further, where state consent requirements are more exacting than the federal standards, tape recordings must comply with the higher state standards in order to be lawful under both state and federal law. Accordingly, because recording a conversation without proper consent in so called "dual consent" states is

5. *See* 18 U.S.C.A. §§ 2510–2522 (West 1997 & Supp. 1997).

6. *See* James G. Carr, The Law of Electronic Surveillance § 3.5(b) (2d ed. 1995).

7. *See, e.g.,* Alaska Stat. § 42.20.310 (Michie 1996); Cal. Pen. Code § 631 (West Supp. 1997); Del.Code Ann. tit. 11, § 1336(c)(2) (Michie 1995); Fla. Stat. Ann. ch. 934.03(2)(d) (West 1996); Ga. Code Ann. § 16–11–62 (Michie 1996); Ill. Ann. Stat. ch. 720, para. 5/14–2 (Smith–Hurd 1993); Md. Cts. & Jud. Proc. Code Ann. §§ 10–402 (a)(1) & (c)(3) (Michie 1995); Mass. Gen. Laws Ann. ch. 272, §§ 99B(4) & C(1) (West 1990); Mich. Comp. Laws Ann. § 750.539(c) (West 1991); Mont. Code Ann. § 45–8–213(1)(c) (1997); Nev. Rev. Stat. Ann. § 200.620 (Michie 1997) (telephone only); N.H. Rev. Stat. Ann. § 570–A:2(I) (Supp. 1995); Pa. Cons. Stat. Ann. § 5704(4) (Supp. 1997); P.R. Laws Ann. tit. 33, § 2160 (1984); Wash. Rev. Code Ann. § 9.73.030 (West 1988).

a crime, it is imperative that counsel clearly understand the relevant law before authorizing any taping procedures.[8]

Even when lawful, covert tape recording should be reserved for the most unusual of circumstances and performed only after counsel has specifically authorized the procedure and instructed the investigators regarding their legal obligations. Counsel should carefully weigh the benefits that may be obtained from the taping (e.g., admissions; freezing a witness' statement; false exculpatory statements; etc.) against the strategic risks the recording may pose to the case (e.g., a jury viewing with disfavor the tactic of surreptitiously recording a witness' statement; an investigator making false or misleading statements to a witness that are captured on tape) before approving any such recordings.

Further, even where one-party consensual recording is permitted under both federal and state law, attorneys also must consider whether authorizing such procedures violates the ethical rules of their states. While courts are generally in agreement that it is not unethical for attorneys to overtly tape record conversations, there is considerable disagreement among the states whether lawyers should be permitted to record conversations surreptitiously. This issue was first raised in 1974, when the ABA's Committee on Ethics and Professional Responsibility issued Opinion 337. The Opinion asserted that, with few exceptions, it is unethical for an attorney to record conversations of any persons without the prior knowledge and consent of all parties to the conversation.[9]

Since the release of Opinion 337, a number of state courts and bar associations have followed the ABA standard, requiring the consent of all parties to a conversation recorded by an attorney.[10] In 1991, for example, the South Carolina Supreme Court, in upholding the state's ethics rules regarding attorney initiated tape recording, declared it unethical for an attorney to record a conversation without the consent of all parties regardless of

> the purpose(s) for which such recordings were made, the intent of the parties' conversation, whether anything of a confidential nature was discussed and whether any party gained an unfair advantage from the recordings.[11]

---

8. See generally James G. Carr, supra note 6.

9. ABA Comm. on Ethics and Professional Responsibility, Formal Op. 337 (1974). The exceptions noted in the ABA opinion were limited to "extraordinary circumstances" in which prosecutors or law enforcement officers acting under their direction "might ethically make and use secret recordings if acting within strict statutory limitations conforming to constitutional requirements." Id.

10. See, e.g., Dallas Bar Ass'n, Op. No.1981–5; Hawaii Disc. Bd., Op. No. 30

(1988); Minnesota Prof. Resp. Bd., Op. No. 3 (1986); Texas Bar Ass'n, Op. No. 392 (1978).

11. In re Anonymous II, 304 S.C. 342, 404 S.E.2d 513 (1991), modified sub nom. In the Matter of the Attorney General's Petition, 308 S.C. 114, 417 S.E.2d 526 (1992)(not unethical for attorney to record conversation surreptitiously with prior consent of, or at request of, appropriate law enforcement agency in the course of a legitimate criminal investigation).

Moreover, in jurisdictions which prohibit attorneys from making surreptitious recordings, the use of an investigator to conduct the taping will not insulate counsel from ethics charges, since the investigator will be performing this function as the agent of the attorney, acting at his or her direction.

Other states categorically reject the ABA Opinion and permit attorneys to make surreptitious recordings in a variety of circumstances. Arizona, for example, allows the covert recording of statements from potential witnesses if the attorney's intent is to prevent perjury or develop impeachment evidence.[12] Mississippi, following a similar rule, permits an attorney to protect himself or his client from the effects of future perjured testimony by surreptitiously recording a conversation.[13] Tennessee allows secret recordings by defense attorneys for use in criminal investigations, including the recording of the statements of potentially adverse witnesses for use as impeachment material.[14] Moreover, the Utah state bar allows lawyers to make surreptitious recordings of conversations with clients, witnesses or other attorneys.[15]

In New York, state and city bar associations have rendered conflicting opinions on the propriety of attorney initiated surreptitious recordings.[16]

Often, a kind of "crime/fraud" exception may permit the secret tape recording of conversations when counsel suspects potential criminal conduct including obstruction or perjury in the civil case.

In view of the sharply conflicting ethical standards that state courts and various state and local bar associations have applied to the question of surreptitious tape recordings by attorneys, counsel is again reminded to review carefully state wiretapping laws and ethics decisions before undertaking or authorizing any covert taping.

(5) Eavesdropping and Bugging

As a further cautionary note to practitioners, with the exception of consensual tape recordings discussed above and an employer's limited right to monitor employee telephone calls,[17] federal and state wiretap

---

12. Arizona State Bar, Op. No. 90–2.

13. Attorney M. v. Mississippi Bar, 621 So.2d 220, 223, 32 A.L.R. 5th 891 (Miss. 1992).

14. Tennessee Prof. Resp. Bd., Op. No. 81–F–14 (1986).

15. Utah State Bar, Op. No. 90.

16. The New York State Bar Association, for example, views as unethical the recording by attorneys of all conversations without the consent of all parties. New York State Bar, Op. No. 328 (1974). The Association of the Bar of the City of New York, although permitting a defense lawyer in a criminal case to secretly record conversations with witnesses, "continue[s] to view as unethical secret recording of lawyers or clients in any context, and secret recordings of any persons in civil or commercial contexts." NYC Formal Op. No. 80–95 (1981). See also NYC Formal Op. No. 1995–10 (1995). In contrast to these opinions, the New York County Lawyers' Association contends that "a lawyer may secretly record telephone conversations with third parties, including other lawyers, provided one party to the conversation has consented and provided that such recording does not violate any applicable law or a specific ethical rule." NYCLA Comm. on Prof. Ethics, Op. No. 697 (1993), 1993 WL 837937, at *1–3.

17. See Electronic Communications Privacy Act of 1986 ("ECPA"), 18 U.S.C.A. §§ 2510–2522 (West 1997). In general, under the ECPA, an employer may monitor

laws prohibit all other kinds of aural recordings of conversations. All other intercepts of conversations require the government first to obtain a court order based on a detailed showing, among other things, that it is investigating certain enumerated felony offenses designated in the wiretap statute (*e.g.*, bribery of public officials, money laundering, bank fraud, etc.), and that all other investigative methods have proven unavailing, are unlikely to succeed, or are too dangerous to use.[18]

Typically, eavesdropping orders are obtained to enable government investigators to overhear and record telephone calls and in-person conversations without obtaining the consent of any party. The orders are effectuated by installing electronic "bugging" devices in rooms, telephones, cars and other places. The devices record and/or transmit the intercepted conversations without the knowledge or consent of any of the speakers. Violations of the federal wiretap statute expose the offender to criminal sanctions,[19] provide for a private right of action for invasion of privacy,[20] and generally require the exclusion of any illegally seized evidence in both federal and state criminal and civil proceedings.[21]

Against this backdrop, virtually all of the wiretapping and bugging equipment sold today is illegal under state and federal law, since these devices can be used by private individuals to engage in unlawful nonconsensual eavesdropping. Thus, under no circumstances should counsel or an investigator even consider installing a bugging device in a room, car, telephone or other location. In short, engaging in unlawful eavesdropping—even if mistakenly or unintentionally done—is a prescription for disaster both for counsel and the investigation.

(6) Demands for Payment and Other Requests

Witnesses may demand compensation as the price for an interview or their subsequent testimony. In most cases there are no legal prohibitions barring these payments. Under the ABA Code of Professional Conduct, expert witnesses may receive compensation provided the amount is reasonable and is not contingent on the outcome of the trial.[22] As to nonexpert witnesses, the ABA Code permits these individuals to be paid for their reasonable travel and lodging expenses, but not for their testimony.[23] Moreover, under the applicable federal rules, attorneys may

---

the telephone calls of employees with their informed consent or when the calls originate or are received on the employer's business extension and are relevant to the employer's business. *See also* Kirk W. Munroe, *Commercial Eavesdropping, A Catch 22*, Fla. B.J., Mar. 1989, at 13.

18. 18 U.S.C.A. §§ 2516 & 2518 (1)(a-f) (West 1970 & Supp. 1997).

19. 18 U.S.C.A. § 2511(4)(a) (West Supp. 1997).

20. 18 U.S.C.A. § 2520 (West 1970 & Supp. 1997).

21. 18 U.S.C.A. § 2515 (West 1970). *See also* Susan L. Kopecky, *Dealing With Intercepted Communications: Title III of the Omnibus Crime Control and Safe Streets Act in Civil Litigation*, 12 Rev. Litig. 441, 454. Under certain limited circumstances, illegally recorded evidence may be admissible, such as when the evidence was used to coerce a settlement. *Id.* at 456.

22. *See* Model Rules of Professional Conduct Rule 3.4 cmt. 3 (1994).

23. *Id.*

compensate nonexpert witnesses for lost income or the opportunity cost of testifying.[24]

Although paying a witness is generally permissible, counsel must consider the near certainty that an adversary will seek to discredit a compensated witness as a person whose testimony has been bought. Thus, before agreeing to compensate a witness, counsel should weigh the expected benefits of the testimony against the anticipated damage to the witness' credibility when the matter of payment is revealed. After weighing the pluses and minuses, if counsel nevertheless chooses to compensate a witness, careful attention should be given to ensuring that the payment is reasonable and in line with the witness' actual out-of-pocket expenses or other economic losses. By following this approach, counsel may be able to obtain useful testimony for the case while at the same time blunting the impeachment value of the witness' payment.

Besides seeking money, witnesses also may ask for assistance in avoiding any civil or criminal penalties which may result from their cooperation or admissions, or which may flow from the investigation itself. Obviously, counsel is in no position to offer "immunity" from criminal prosecution or to make any other promise that cannot be kept. However, counsel may be able to offer a witness immunity from any civil claims counsel's client may have against the individual, as well as some form of indemnity against any civil claims an adversary or others may assert against the witness. Because such agreements are discoverable and can be used by an adversary to impeach the credibility of a witness receiving these benefits, counsel should carefully weigh the benefits and risks of the arrangement before agreeing to the deal.

Promises of indemnity or immunity from civil liability should never be made by an investigator without explicit authority from counsel and, in most cases, should be left for discussions between counsel and the witness. If such an agreement is reached, it should be reflected in the notes or final report of the interview.

(7) Hiring Former Employees of an Adversary

The concept of hiring former employees of an adversary, although seemingly attractive as an unparalleled source of information and leads, is fraught with danger for counsel and the client. First, many employers require their key personnel to sign confidentiality agreements prohibiting the disclosure of the employer's proprietary information. Hiring persons subject to these restrictions invites an adversary's motions for protective orders, injunctions, and disqualification of counsel.[25]

24. 18 U.S.C.A. § 201(d) (West 1969 & Supp. 1997).

25. See Brad Bole, *The Practical and Ethical Implications of Retaining a Turncoat Employee*, Litigation News, Mar. 1997, at 3, 11. In *Baker v. General Motors*, 86 F.3d 811 (8th Cir.1996), a case cited in the foregoing article, plaintiff's attorney retained a former employee of defendant General Motors to serve as an expert witness in a products liability case. Because the former employee had signed a confidentiality agreement with the defendant, the court enjoined the employee's testimony as an expert witness.

Second, ethical rules and decisional authority in many states prohibit ex parte contacts with former employees.[26] Even in jurisdictions which do not flatly ban such contacts, disqualification of counsel's law firm may result if the former employee was exposed to privileged information relevant to the pending case.[27] Additionally, as a practical matter, the hiring of an adversary's former employee may suggest to the judge and the jury that any testimony from that person has been bought and paid for with the salary the former employee is now receiving from counsel's client. It may also suggest that the client and counsel are up to something they should not be doing.

Notwithstanding the foregoing practical and ethical concerns, if counsel nevertheless engages in employment discussions with a former employee of an adversary, considerable care should be exercised to find out whether the employee was involved in any prior litigation on behalf of the adversary which concerned issues similar to those currently under investigation, or whether the employee was exposed to any of his prior employer's privileged information. Should counsel receive an affirmative answer to either question, no further ex parte contact should be pursued because of the risk that the witness and counsel may be disqualified from participating in the pending litigation; however, as an available and ethically permissible option, counsel should consider deposing the former employee as a fact witness.[28]

(f) Surveillance

Surveillance is a powerful investigative tool, albeit one that should be exercised carefully and with appropriate planning. When properly performed, covert observations of people, motor vehicles, and locations provide one of the most effective means of developing information, evidence and leads. For example, in infringement cases involving the street level sale of knock-off merchandise, surveillance is usually the best investigative technique to identify the sellers and distributors of the goods, and to locate the places where the counterfeit items are being made. Similarly, surveillance is particularly useful in monitoring compliance with court orders and consent decrees. Appropriately placed investigators can readily determine, for example, if a company ordered to shut down its waste hauling operations in a particular geographic area is continuing to operate in violation of the decree.

Surveillance is best employed during the initial phase of an investigation before an adversary learns of the inquiry. Once the fact of an investigation is widely known, experience teaches that the targets of surveillance often act more cautiously, deviate from their usual routines, and look for anyone who may be watching them.

---

26. See supra § 4.13(e)(1).

27. See Brad Bole, supra note 25 at 3, 11; Rentclub v. Transamerica Rental Fin. Corp., 811 F.Supp. 651 (M.D.Fla.1992), aff'd, 43 F.3d 1439 (11th Cir.1995) (law firm disqualified because of appearances that it induced a former employee of an adverse party to disclose confidential information, and that it was paying the employee for his factual testimony and not as a trial consultant).

28. Brad Bole, supra note 25 at 11.

In almost all cases, surveillances should be conducted covertly by one or more teams of experienced investigators. When a subject leaves a location under surveillance, for example, the investigative teams must have the flexibility and available resources to follow the person either on foot, by car, on public transportation, or by using a combination of these methods.

There are dangers inherent in the use of this technique. Simply put, if a surveillance is blown because of inexpert performance or simple bad luck, the investigation in question will likely be exposed. Should this happen, other covert strategies included in the investigative plan may no longer be appropriate or effective. For example, when investigators place an individual under surveillance in order to identify the foreign banks he uses to deposit funds, it is imperative that the person not be alerted to the surveillance before the banks have been identified and efforts made to seize the accounts in question. If the person becomes aware of the surveillance either before the banks have been identified or before the accounts have been seized, he will undoubtedly cause the monies to be transferred and hidden elsewhere. In addition, witness interviews may need to be accelerated so that the investigators can speak with these people before an adversary, now aware of the investigation, contacts them.

(g) Forensics

The use of forensic experts to examine handwriting and documents, enhance video and audio tapes, recover deleted computer files, and perform a variety of other technical services can be of substantial value to many investigations. A discussion of the uses and merits of several frequently employed types of forensic examinations now follows.

(1) Handwriting and Document Analysis

Forensic examination of questioned documents and handwriting can be pivotal to the outcome of cases. Issues regarding when a document was created or whether it was written by a particular person, for example, often require resolution in a variety of civil and criminal cases. Forensic examination and testing often can answer these questions, provided the experts are given the appropriate materials to examine.

Most if not all examiners of questioned documents only will test or examine original documents. In the case of handwriting analysis, this requires providing the expert with a "known" sample of an adversary's (or other person's) handwriting and comparing it with the "questioned" document. Although locating a "known" sample sometimes can be problematic, suggested places to look include: correspondence, contract and personnel files (assuming the adversary had prior business dealings with, or was a former employee of, counsel's client); canceled checks; election district voting records; litigation files—an adversary may have signed or written documents that are contained in the court files; and the records of an adversary's former adversaries (they may have documents bearing the sought after handwriting). The more known samples an examiner receives, the more likely he or she will be able to provide an unqualified opinion regarding the questioned document.

Some chemical tests used to date a questioned document's paper stock or ink supply can destroy these materials and thus lessen the document's usefulness in subsequent proceedings. Before permitting a document to be tested in this manner, therefore, counsel should ensure that clear and accurate copies of the document are made, that only a small, nonmaterial portion of the original document will be treated, and that the remainder of the document will be unaffected by the testing.

(2) Enhancing Video and Audio Tapes

The quality of video and audio tapes relevant to a matter often can be enhanced by experts using sophisticated equipment. By identifying the frequencies of distracting background noises, for example, experts can eliminate these sounds from the tapes and thus significantly enhance their audibility. Other recording errors, such as tape speed, also can be fixed. Similarly, experts can enhance fuzzy video images, create still photographs from particular frames, or make other repairs that will improve the usefulness of the tape. In addition, forensic experts can determine whether a video or audio tape has been erased, cobbled together from several different sources, or altered in other ways.

When retaining tape enhancement experts, counsel must supply them with the original audio or video tapes. Before enhancing or analyzing the tapes, the forensic specialists first will produce exact copies of the materials to guard against the inadvertent erasure or destruction of the items. Thereafter, any enhancements will be made on the copies and not on the original tapes.

(3) Tape Recordings and Transcripts

Tape recorded statements often carry enormous evidentiary weight with fact-finders. But when tape recordings are virtually inaudible or sloppily done, they can actually harm a case by permitting a witness to change his story without fear of being impeached by his own spoken words, and by arousing suspicion among the jurors about the party who made the tapes.

Although tape recorders and tapes occasionally fail because of manufacturing defects or other unanticipated mechanical failures, there are a number of steps that can be taken before making a recording that will almost always improve the results. First, the adequacy of the tape recorder's power source—batteries or electric cord—should always be checked before starting the recording. Second, in almost all cases, a new or unused tape should be used. Third, a short statement should be recorded and played back to test whether the recorder and tape are working properly. Next, before recording a witness' statement, the investigator or other operator should record an introductory statement or "header" on the tape, identifying the date, time and place of the recording, the names of the participants, and the consent of one or both of the parties to the taping. As noted previously (see supra Section

4.13(e)(4)), when a concealed recording device is being used, the record switch should be taped in the "on" position so that the undercover operative (or cooperating witness wearing the recorder) cannot control what is and is not recorded. Finally, after the recording has been completed, the two plastic tabs on the spine of the tape cassette should be pushed out to prevent any accidental or intentional alterations or erasures, and the tape should be marked with the date of the recording and the names of the participants.

Verbatim transcripts, if properly prepared, will enhance the value of most tape recordings. Probably the best way to create an accurate transcript is to listen to the tape using headphones and high quality audio equipment. Once the investigator or other transcriber has deciphered the statements on the tape, he or she should prepare a typewritten transcript, identifying each speaker by name on the left side of the page, followed by the text of his or her statement. Inaudible statements should be noted parenthetically on the transcript (*e.g.*, [inaudible]).

An accurate transcript prepared by counsel, which also shows the length of inaudible sections and talk overs (*i.e.*, indecipherable portions caused by two or more persons speaking at the same time), is one of the best opportunities available to counsel to show a jury the care with which his or her case has been prepared and to gain the confidence of the panel. At trial, the transcript should be authenticated by a participant to the tape recorded conversation and made available to the jury when the tape itself is played.

(4) Computers

Computers are a potentially invaluable source of information when a skilled professional recovers "deleted" information and conducts other forensic inquiries. For example, using one or more commercially available programs, a computer consultant can recover deleted files. An expert also can examine a computer's hard drive, sector by sector, and recover old versions of documents and fragments of files which may have been deleted years ago. With concentrated effort, the file fragments often can be pieced together, thereby revealing whole documents or significant chunks of information that a witness or an adversary may have believed was permanently obliterated. Further, an expert can examine a Local Area Network's ("LAN") access logs and determine when any users of particular work stations logged on and off the system.

In addition, by examining a computer's backup and other software programs, a computer expert can reconstruct a user's historical activities, including whether the person downloaded and copied any of the company's files. This is particularly useful in cases where current or former employees of a business are believed to have misappropriated the company's confidential or proprietary information. For example:

- Certain backup programs installed in laptops and other computers allow a user to copy files that have been downloaded and stored in the computer's hard drive on to a floppy disc or an external tape. These files later can be restored and used on another computer with the appropriate software. Because backup programs are configured automatically to create a "backup" report each time the program is used, a computer expert can examine the backup report and determine, among other things: (a) the time and date any copying from the hard drive was started; (b) the type of device on which the information was copied; (c) the time and date the copying was completed; and (d) the number of files and megabytes of information that were copied from the hard drive's memory.

• Further, each time a backup program is used to copy files, the program automatically creates a catalog file, which identifies the files that were copied and the directories in which they were stored. Armed with this list, an expert can locate the files on the computer's hard drive and determine the nature of the information they contained. Even when the copied files have been deleted from the hard drive, a computer consultant, using a hard drive maintenance utility program, may be able to restore them under certain circumstances. Moreover, even if this procedure is unsuccessful, the company should be able to locate and review the misappropriated information by retrieving all of the data listed on the catalog file from the company's network or another computer's hard drive.

(5) E-mail

Computer experts can locate and retrieve E-mail from both LAN systems and the Internet. Regardless of the medium by which it is sent, all E-mail is stored locally on a computer's hard drive. By running the computer's E-mail program, a consultant can easily locate, read and print any E-mail sent or received by the computer's user.

A consultant also can track a user's Internet activity. By examining the Internet browser's cache files, the expert can obtain a list of all Internet locations a user has visited.

(6) Accounting

Forensic accountants, unlike traditional accountants, are investigators who are particularly skilled at reviewing financial records for evidence of fraud, criminal activity or other wrongdoing. In many cases, forensic accountants can help counsel understand complex financial transactions, trace money and other assets that have been diverted or hidden, and assemble financial information in an effective format.

While the types of records that may be useful to a forensic accountant will vary from case to case, access to an adversary's tax returns, canceled checks, internal audit files, general ledger, purchase and sales journals, cash receipt and disbursement journals, and other books of account may often provide the accountant with valuable evidence and leads. Accordingly, in order to assist the forensic accountant's analysis, counsel should seek production of an adversary's pertinent financial records through discovery.

In addition to the functions described above, during a broad scale investigation, a forensic accountant can help counsel assess the strengths and weaknesses of an adversary's financial proof, predict an adversary's defenses and affirmative claims, and analyze the client's potential exposure to an adverse judgment based on information which the client will have to produce during discovery (*e.g.*, the likelihood of the client being prosecuted for tax fraud). At trial, forensic accountants can be used effectively to attack an adversary's financial analyses, damage claims, and other pertinent elements of its case.

(h) Stings

Sting operations, although often associated with celebrated criminal cases, can be used as powerful tools in any investigation. "Stings" can elicit exculpatory evidence about counsel's client, obtain impeachment material regarding an adversary or its witnesses, garner admissions of past misconduct, and develop direct evidence of an adversary's ongoing wrongdoing.

Although powerful weapons in a case, undercover operations are fraught with danger and should be conducted only by experienced investigators and only after counsel is satisfied that this procedure is legal and ethical in the jurisdiction. Because stings are most effective when the recorded statements of an adversary or witness are played to a jury, it is imperative that counsel and the investigative team be fully aware of the state and federal electronic surveillance laws pertinent to their operation. While an undercover operative can supply the needed consent in most states to tape record conversations, 15 jurisdictions require the consent of all parties to a conversation in order for audio recordings to be lawful.[29] These states, moreover, treat violations of their wiretap statutes as criminal offenses.[30] In these dual consent jurisdictions, video tapes without sound generally can be used, but these are of limited value to a jury unable to hear the words of the participants.

In addition, counsel and the investigators must be mindful of the ethical rules which prohibit ex parte contacts with represented parties, including the current and former employees of an adversary.[31] Further, while the investigative team does not have to be concerned with the legal defense of entrapment since that doctrine does not apply to private civil litigation or investigations, considerable care, nevertheless, should be taken to ensure that the undercover operation does not appear unfair or overbearing to a jury.

As a final cautionary note regarding the use of sting operations, practitioners should be aware of the case of *Food Lion, Inc. v. Capital Cities/ABC, Inc.*,[32] a 1997 federal jury trial in which the subject of a sting operation conducted by a television news magazine successfully sued the broadcasting network for fraud and other tortious conduct. In *Food*

---

29. *See supra* § 4.13(e)(4)n. 7.

30. *See supra* § 4.13(e)(4) & (5).

31. *See supra* § 4.13(e)(1).

32. 984 F.Supp. 923 (M.D.N.C.1997).

Lion, two producers of the ABC news magazine *Prime Time Live* obtained jobs with Food Lion, a regional supermarket chain, by submitting false references and personal information. While working as supermarket employees, the undercover producers wore hidden cameras and obtained highly critical footage depicting Food Lion's food handling and labor practices.[33]

In November 1992, *Prime Time Live* aired an exposé unfavorably depicting Food Lion's operations. The broadcast included footage shot by the producers during their undercover jobs as supermarket employees. Although never challenging the truthfulness of the investigative report, Food Lion subsequently sued Capital Cities/ABC, Inc., the broadcast network which aired the show, for fraud, trespass, and breach of loyalty.

In December 1996, a federal jury in North Carolina returned a verdict in favor of Food Lion and, in January 1997, awarded the company $5.5 million in punitive damages. The district court judge set aside the jury's award of compensatory damages, holding that Food Lion's loss of profits was caused by its own practices and the public's loss of faith in the stores' operations.[34] On August 29, 1997, the district court judge also reduced the jury's award of punitive damages to Food Lion to $315,000.[35]

In view of *Food Lion's* assessment of punitive damages against the corporate sponsor of an undercover operation, counsel may wish to consider whether a contemplated sting implicates any legal rights or duties owed to a subject under a state's statutory and common law.

(i) Polygraphs

The use of polygraphs to test the truthfulness of a person's statements is subject to strict controls under federal and state law. Under the federal Employee Polygraph Protection Act of 1988 ("EPPA"),[36] employers generally may not use polygraphs or "lie detector tests" to screen applicants for employment or to test current employees except when the following four conditions have been met:[37]

(1) the test is administered as part of an ongoing investigation involving economic injury to the employer's business, such as theft, embezzlement or industrial espionage;[38]

(2) the employee had access to the property that is the subject of the investigation;[39]

(3) the employer has "reasonable suspicion" that the particular employee to be examined was involved in the activity being investigated;[40] and

---

33. *Id.*

34. *Id.*

35. *Id.*

36. 29 U.S.C.A. §§ 2001–2009 (West 1997).

37. The EPPA does provide certain narrow exceptions permitting preemployment screening of employees by the U.S. government, defense contractors, drug manufacturers, and security firms. 29 U.S.C.A. § 2006.

38. 29 U.S.C.A. § 2006 (d)(1).

39. 29 U.S.C.A. § 2006 (d)(2).

40. 29 U.S.C.A. § 2006 (d)(3).

(4) the employer executes a statement of the specific economic injury, the employee's access, and the basis for the reasonable suspicion that the employee was involved in the illegal activity.[41]

Employers who violate the EPPA face the prospect of civil penalties of up to $10,000 assessed by the U.S. Department of Labor, and private actions for damages brought by their employees.[42]

Additionally, nearly half of the states prohibit employers from directly or indirectly requesting or requiring an employee or prospective employee to take or submit to a lie detector test as a condition of employment or continued employment.[43]

Notwithstanding their limited use with respect to current and prospective employees, polygraph examinations can have a number of important uses in investigations and litigation. First, in discussions or negotiations with an adversary, counsel can use the results of a successful examination to buttress the claims of a party or other key witnesses. For example, where handwriting analysis concerning the authorship of a key document is inconclusive (e.g., notes taken at a meeting where events central to the litigation are alleged to have occurred), the results of a polygraph examination could be used to exclude a person suspected of being the document's creator. Conversely, with the consent of an adversary, the account of an adverse party can be checked out. Finally, counsel and the investigative team can use polygraphs to vet their own witnesses' stories, provided the requirements of EPPA and pertinent state law do not prohibit the tests.

Although once per se inadmissible in federal courts, the results of polygraph examinations, like other scientific evidence or testimony, are now tested on a case by case basis for relevancy and reliability.[44] In weighing the admissibility of polygraph test results, federal courts also determine whether the probative value of the test is substantially

---

41. 29 U.S.C.A. § 2006 (d)(4); BNA/ACCA Compliance Manual, Prevention of Corporate Liability, Chapter 4, § B–4a (1996).

42. 29 U.S.C.A. § 2005 (West Supp. 1997); BNA/ACCA Compliance Manual, Chapter 4, § B–4a.

43. BNA/ACCA Compliance Manual, Chapter 4, § B–4a. See, e.g., N.J. Stat. Ann. § 2C:40A–1 (West 1995) (disorderly conduct offense to influence, request or require an employee or prospective employee to take a lie detector test as condition of employment or continued employment); Cal. Lab. Code § 432.2(a) (West 1989) ("no employer shall demand or require any applicant for employment or prospective employment or any employee to submit to or take a polygraph,

lie detector or similar test or examination as a condition of employment or continued employment").

44. Daubert v. Merrell Dow Pharmaceuticals, Inc., 509 U.S. 579, 589, 113 S.Ct. 2786, 2794, 125 L.Ed.2d 469 (1993). In Daubert, the Supreme Court suggested that in assessing the admissibility of reportedly scientific evidence, federal courts should assess: (a) whether the evidence is scientific in nature, (b) whether the theory or technique in question can be tested, (c) whether it has been subjected to peer review and publication, (d) whether it has become accepted in the scientific community, and (e) the rate of error of the proffered technique or procedure. See Chapter 35, "Expert Witnesses," at § 35.3(a), infra for further discussion of Daubert.

outweighed by the danger of unfair prejudice, confusion of issues, or misleading the jury.[45] Applying these standards, most federal courts remain unconvinced of the reliability of polygraph examinations.[46] In the rare instance where it is utilized, courts require a careful foundation such as a qualified polygraph expert and appropriate questioning.[47]

Notwithstanding their potential value to a case, counsel should keep in mind that there is considerable legal and scientific debate over the validity and reliability of polygraph testing.[48] Indeed, several commentators have suggested that the results of polygraph examinations can be altered or affected by a subject's skill at lying, emotional state at the time of the exam (*e.g.*, anger, embarrassment, fear, etc.), preexisting mental condition (*e.g.*, neurosis), or ingestion of tranquilizers or alcohol before the test.[49] Thus, practitioners must exercise extreme caution when relying on the results of these tests.

(j) Examinations of Trash

Discarded trash can provide a treasure trove of evidence and leads. For many years, government investigators have covertly removed the abandoned trash of businesses and private individuals, later examining the items at a secure location. These searches, often described as "trash covers," can be used with equal effect in private investigations, and more and more counsel seek advice on conducting such operations.

Before conducting a "trash cover," there are several critical issues for counsel to consider. First, although searching through an adversary's or a witness' trash may produce helpful evidence or leads, counsel must determine whether this investigative technique is something his or her client is willing to authorize and be associated with, particularly when the circumstances of the search are likely to be disclosed at trial and to

---

45. Fed.R.Evid. 403. *See, e.g.*, United States v. Toth, 91 F.3d 136 (4th Cir.1996) (refusing to find error in trial court's exclusion of polygraph evidence where potential for confusion and prolonging the trial outweighed probative value of test results).

46. *See, e.g.*, United States v. Cordoba, 104 F.3d 225 (9th Cir.1997) (in remanding case to the district court for a particularized inquiry regarding the admissibility of polygraph results, the circuit court noted the "grave potential for interfering with the deliberative process" and "problematic nature" of polygraph evidence); United States v. Williams, 95 F.3d 723, 728–30 (8th Cir. 1996) (upholding lower court's exclusion of polygraph evidence because of the defendant's failure to lay a proper foundation regarding the test's reliability). *But see* United States v. Weekly, 118 F.3d 576 (8th Cir.1997) (Eighth Circuit affirmed district court's reliance on polygraph test of one

defendant to deny co-defendant's application for a reduced sentence under the U.S. Sentencing Guidelines' safety valve provision).

47. *See, e.g.*, United States v. Kwong, 69 F.3d 663, 668 (2d Cir.1995), *cert. denied*, 517 U.S. 1115, 116 S.Ct. 1343, 134 L.Ed.2d 491 (1996) (polygraph results inadmissible because "the questions posed to Kwong were inherently ambiguous no matter how they were answered").

48. *See, e.g.*, United States v. Beyer, 106 F.3d 175, 178 (7th Cir.1997) (declining to find error in district court's exclusion of evidence that defendant had offered to take a lie detector test).

49. *See, e.g.*, P. Ekman, Telling Lies 217 (1985); Michael Tiner & Daniel J. O'Grady, *Lie Detectors in Employment*, 23 Harv. C.R.-C.L. L. Rev. 85, 102 (1988).

the media. Next, counsel must determine whether conducting a trash cover is legal in the jurisdiction in which the rubbish is located. In making this assessment, counsel initially must evaluate whether the contemplated search violates the jurisdiction's trespassing laws, since private individuals who trespass when conducting such searches may be arrested or face civil liability for their torts. Additionally, if, for example, the effort is likely to collect discarded attorney-client documents, counsel must consider the implications of such a seizure as well.

Counsel then must consider whether searching through and seizing the targeted trash violates anyone's privacy rights under applicable federal and state law. Although the Supreme Court has held that the Fourth Amendment's privacy limitations do not extend to government searches and seizures of trash discarded outside a person's residence,[50] some states have concluded that their citizens' privacy rights are violated by such conduct.[51] Thus, no searches and seizures of trash should be contemplated if there exists any question regarding the lawfulness of these actions.

Finally, if all of the foregoing hurdles have been passed, counsel should have the investigative team conduct a preliminary observation of the location, reporting back to him or her whether the rubbish is stored in a publicly accessible area, whether any special efforts have been taken to enclose the area or protect it from public view, and whether the team will be trespassing on private property in order to effectuate the search. Only when counsel receives clear and unequivocal answers to these questions (*i.e.*, that the trash is accessible to the public; that no special efforts have been made to enclose or protect it; and that the rubbish can be seized without trespassing), should the contemplated search be pursued.

---

50. California v. Greenwood, 486 U.S. 35, 39, 108 S.Ct. 1625, 1628, 100 L.Ed.2d 30 (1988) (Supreme Court refused to exclude the results of a government conducted warrantless search and seizure of trash taken from outside a residential home, holding that any expectation of privacy the residents may have had in their trash was unreasonable and thus not protected under the Fourth Amendment). *See also* United States v. Hall, 47 F.3d 1091, 1097 (11th Cir.1995) (holding that a business' expectation of privacy was not objectively reasonable where its rubbish, left for collection by a private sanitation service, was placed within the "commercial curtilage" of the building in trash bins accessible to the public).

51. *See, e.g.,* People v. Edwards, 71 Cal.2d 1096, 80 Cal.Rptr. 633, 458 P.2d 713 (1969) (pre–*Greenwood* decision holding that police search of trash cans in the back

of defendant's residence was unlawful because defendant had a justified expectation of privacy in his garbage); State v. Hempele, 120 N.J. 182, 576 A.2d 793 (1990) (rejecting *Greenwood* under New Jersey state constitutional law, the court held that "the State must secure a warrant based on probable cause in order to search garbage bags left on the curb for collection"); State v. Boland, 115 Wash.2d 571, 800 P.2d 1112 (1990) (also rejecting *Greenwood* under Washington State Constitution, the court focused its analysis on whether the private affairs of an individual have been unreasonably violated). *But see* People v. Hillman, 834 P.2d 1271 (Colo.1992) (collecting cases indicating that the majority of states generally have found no reasonable expectation of privacy in garbage left for collection either under state or federal constitutional law).

Accordingly, as the foregoing discussion makes clear, the use of a trash cover as an investigative tool should not be engaged in lightly.

§ 4.14 Coordinating Investigative Approaches with Traditional Discovery Efforts

Once an action has been commenced, counsel can use traditional discovery devices in tandem with the smorgasbord of available investigative options to benefit the case as a whole. For example, by coordinating document demands with the needs of the investigative team, counsel can obtain financial records and tax returns required for a forensic audit of an adversary. Other discoverable records helpful to the investigation may include: personnel files to facilitate background investigations; payroll records to identify current and former employees for possible interviews; local and toll call records to identify the dates and times of particular conversations and other leads; and contract files to identify suppliers and vendors who may have information pertinent to the case.

Additionally, through regular discussions and consultations with counsel, the investigative team can suggest ways to use depositions to answer investigative questions or develop new leads. The investigators also can help counsel identify persons who should be deposed and documents that should be sought. In order to maximize the benefits of these complementary approaches to discovery, it is critical that counsel keep the investigative team apprised of all deposition schedules and deadlines. In this manner, investigative efforts can be prioritized to meet counsel's immediate needs.

Library References:

West's Key No. Digests, Federal Civil Procedure ⬥1261–1686.
Wright & Miller, Federal Practice and Procedure: Civil 2d §§ 1528, 2004, 2005.1, 2030, 5393.1, 5681.

§ 4.15 Additional Legal Considerations

(a) The Bank Secrecy Act

The Bank Secrecy Act of 1970, enacted by Congress in recognition of the usefulness of bank records in criminal, tax and regulatory investigations and proceedings, requires financial institutions to maintain records of their customers' identities, and to make microfilm copies of their checks and similar instruments.[1] Under the Bank Secrecy Act and the Right to Financial Privacy Act,[2] a depositor's records may not be disclosed to the government voluntarily but instead the use of legal process is required.[3]

§ 4.15

1. See Title I of the Bank Secrecy Act, 12 U.S.C.A. § 1829b(a)(1) (West 1989). See also United States v. Miller, 425 U.S. 435, 441–42, 96 S.Ct. 1619, 1623–24, 48 L.Ed.2d 71 (1976).

2. 12 U.S.C.A. § 3401–3421 (West 1989 & Supp. 1997).

3. See 12 U.S.C.A. § 3402. See also California Bankers Association v. Shultz, 416 U.S. 21, 94 S.Ct. 1494, 39 L.Ed.2d 812

Similarly, private litigants can subpoena the bank records of adversaries and witnesses directly from financial institutions. While these records may be extremely useful in satisfying judgments, establishing the submission of false financial information to clients, and for other important litigation purposes, counsel should be aware that financial institutions generally alert their customers when their accounts have been subpoenaed. Given such notice, the account holders may transfer and hide their assets even before the banks have identified the relevant accounts to the issuers of the subpoenas; equally important, the account holders may move to quash the subpoenas or seek other relief from the courts (*e.g.*, protective orders), capitalizing on these gratuitous opportunities to learn about their adversaries' cases and litigation strategies. In view of these risks, counsel should exercise due care when contemplating the use of bank subpoenas to obtain customer account information directly from financial institutions.

(b) The Fair Credit Reporting Act

Consumer credit reports contain considerable information concerning a person's financial history, credit, employment, and current whereabouts. A typical consumer credit report, for example, may disclose information regarding an individual's loans, mortgages, lines of credit, credit cards, credit card balances, credit card limits and payment histories, bankruptcy filings, adverse judgments, employers, addresses, and telephone numbers. An "investigative consumer report" may provide information relating to a person's character, general reputation, personal characteristics or mode of living.[4]

Although limited to individuals, both investigative and consumer credit reports provide important information about the activities, assets and finances of the people who play key roles in commercial disputes—*e.g.*, the employees, managers, officers and directors of the opposing parties, as well as other persons who come into contact with these individuals and businesses. Moreover, because commercial litigation often requires a substantial review of these matters, consumer reports are clearly relevant investigative tools to be considered and, where appropriate, used in connection with such disputes.[5]

(1974) (Bank Secrecy Act's record keeping requirements do not violate the Fourth Amendment as the mere maintenance of records without requiring disclosure to the government absent legal process does not constitute an illegal search and seizure); Neece v. Internal Revenue Service, 96 F.3d 460 (10th Cir.1996) (records government procured voluntarily from a bank held inadmissible).

4. *See* Fair Credit Reporting Act ("FCRA"), 15 U.S.C.A. § 1681a(e) (West 1982).

5. Consumer credit reports should not be confused with the various types of business information reports about companies that can be obtained from investment banks, financial institutions and commercial vendors, such as Dun & Bradstreet. These reports, which are not subject to the stringent controls and limitations of the FCRA (discussed *infra*), are extremely useful sources of credit information and intelligence about businesses, and should be obtained whenever appropriate in an investigation.

As valuable as these reports may be, most attorneys are completely uninformed of the very limited circumstances under which credit reports can be lawfully obtained, and the serious trouble they and their agents can face by improperly obtaining these documents. The FCRA, enacted in 1970, sets strict controls on the dissemination and use of consumer credit reports, imposing duties on both credit report generators and recipients.[6] Credit bureaus must take "reasonable measures" to ensure the confidentiality of consumer information and to guard against the misuse of the data.[7] Requestors of reports must be equally careful, as the knowing or wilful obtaining of a report under false pretenses is a crime under the FCRA[8] and can expose the violator to civil liability.[9]

Under the FCRA, a consumer reporting agency may furnish a report to a private (nongovernmental) requestor only under the following circumstances:

1. pursuant to a court order;

2. with the written consent of the consumer; or

3. where the agency reasonably believes that the recipient will use the information:

    (a) in connection with a credit transaction or extension of credit involving the consumer, or regarding the review or collection of a consumer account;

    (b) for employment purposes;[10]

    (c) in connection with underwriting insurance;

    (d) to evaluate or assess the credit or prepayment risks associated with an existing credit obligation; or

    (e) for a legitimate business need in connection with a business transaction initiated by the consumer, or to determine whether a consumer continues to meet the conditions of an account.[11]

Under the FCRA, private attorneys and investigators properly may obtain credit reports for use in connection with the collection of a

---

6. 15 U.S.C.A. § 1681 (West 1982). The Consumer Credit Reporting Reform Act of 1996 (the "Reform Act"), which became effective September 30, 1997, made substantial modifications to the FCRA, particularly in the area of imposing greater requirements on employers who use consumer reports in their employment decisions. Consumer Credit Reporting Reform Act of 1996, Pub. L. No. 104–208. See infra note 11.

7. 15 U.S.C.A. § 1681b.

8. 15 U.S.C.A. § 1681q. Violators can be fined and imprisoned for up to two years.

9. 15 U.S.C.A. § 1681n. Under this provision, consumers and credit reporting agencies can obtain actual damages of not less than $1000 from persons who wilfully violate the statute; consumers also can obtain punitive damages.

10. Under the Reform Act, an employer may obtain an applicant's or an employee's consumer credit report only when it satisfies the following two requirements: (1) it provides the applicant or employee with a clear written statement, contained in a separate document consisting solely of the disclosure, notifying the person that a consumer report may be obtained; and (2) it obtains a written authorization from the applicant or employee. See 15 U.S.C.A. § 1681b(b)(2).

11. 15 U.S.C.A. § 1681b.

judgment or a debt owed by a consumer.[12] Of the remaining permissible purposes available to obtain credit reports under the FCRA, only two have application to investigations—i.e., court orders and written consents. These approaches, however, are of limited utility since hostile subjects are unlikely to cooperate with an investigation and court orders, if obtainable, will generally alert an adversary to counsel's investigative and/or litigation strategy. For these reasons, practitioners should be extremely wary of procuring or obtaining credit reports for investigative or litigation purposes except in connection with the collection of a judgment or a consumer debt.

(c) Telephone Records

Telephone records can be an important source of information and evidence in an investigation. Telephone companies maintain computerized records of all outgoing calls generated from a user's telephone, including records identifying the telephone numbers of all local and long distance calls made during a particular billing period. Besides capturing the telephone number of each party called, these records log the date, time and duration of each conversation. Much but not all of this information is included in a customer's monthly bill.[13] In addition, the telephone systems of many businesses generate detailed internal records of their own outgoing calls.

The Electronic Communications and Privacy Act of 1986 governs access to and disclosure of telephone company records and bills.[14] In particular, the statute requires that a subpoena be issued in order to obtain telephone records directly from a telephone company without the consent of a subscriber.[15]

In appropriate cases, counsel should issue telephone company subpoenas to obtain the relevant phone records and bills of an adversary or key witness.[16] Counsel also should obtain these materials directly from

---

12. *See, e.g.,* Baker v. Bronx–Westchester Investigations, 850 F.Supp. 260, 262 (S.D.N.Y.1994) (judgment creditor and private investigators working on her behalf had permissible purpose to obtain credit report on judgment debtor as collection of her judgment constituted a "collection of an account" under FCRA § 1681b (3)(A)). *See also* 16 C.F.R. Pt. 600, App. at 358 (1993). According to the Federal Trade Commission's interpretation of FCRA § 1681b (3)(A), "a detective agency or private investigator, attempting to collect a debt owed by a consumer, would have a permissible purpose to obtain a consumer report on that individual for use in collecting that debt." Further, the FTC's interpretation of this section explicitly approves the use of a consumer report to locate such a debtor. *Id.*

13. The monthly records telephone companies send to their customers may not provide the same level of detail regarding a subscriber's local telephone calls as the phone company's computerized records show. For example, the monthly bills may not disclose the telephone numbers of all local calls made.

14. 18 U.S.C.A. §§ 2701–2711 (West 1997).

15. 18 U.S.C.A. § 2703(c)(1)(B). *See* William R. McLucas & Thomas D. Hamill, *An Overview of Various Procedural Considerations Associated with the Securities & Exchange Commission's Investigative Process*, 692 PLI/Corp. 7, 43 (1990).

16. *See* Broadcort Capital Corporation v. Flagler Securities, Inc., 149 F.R.D. 626 (D.Colo.1993) (court finds no legal basis to

the individuals or businesses through discovery. Careful review of these records, often using reverse telephone directories, may enable investigators to identify the persons or companies a subject called, establish connections between the subject and the other parties to the conversations, and develop additional sources and leads.

§ 4.16 The Attorney–Client and Work–Product Privileges

(a) Creating Databases

In creating databases for use in connection with investigations and litigation, there are several practical steps counsel and the investigative team should take in order to enhance the prospect of the material being afforded attorney work-product protection.[1] First, all materials should be marked with a legend, such as the following, which indicates the privileged and confidential nature of the items:

PRIVILEGED ATTORNEY–CLIENT AND CONFIDENTIAL
WORK–PRODUCT COMMUNICATION

Next, counsel should tightly limit access to and distribution of the database materials only to those persons whose viewing of the items would be covered by the attorney-client and work-product privileges— *i.e.*, personnel of the client whose use or review of the materials will assist counsel in connection with the investigation or lawsuit, members of the investigative team with a need to see the items, and other experts retained by counsel. Third, counsel should ensure that all out-of-date computer disks and CD–ROMS are promptly destroyed. By implementing these controls, counsel not only will have taken measures to help guard against the inadvertent waiver of the attorney work-product privilege, but he or she also will have established a tangible record of maintaining the confidentiality of the database.

(b) The Self–Evaluative Privilege

The "self-evaluative" or "self-critical analysis" privilege has been used in recent years to protect from disclosure the records and reports of internal reviews and investigations conducted by corporations and other organizations.[2] Although judicial acceptance of the self-evaluative privi-

---

quash subpoena for telephone records relating to nonparty in securities action where records were potentially relevant to the case).

§ 4.16

1. Counsel should note that the courts are far from uniform in deciding whether and to what extent databases are protected work-product. Accordingly, for a full discus-

sion of the legal issues concerning the application of the attorney work-product privilege to databases, please *see infra* Chapter 18, "Discovery Strategy and Privileges," at § 18.8.

2. *See* Black & Pozin, Internal Corporate Investigations (Business Law Monograph #20), Chapter 6, § 6.01 (1991).

lege is anything but uniform,[3] counsel nevertheless should consider asserting the self-evaluative privilege, where appropriate, to protect from disclosure investigative work-product and reports developed in connection with a client's internal investigation or self-critical review.

As with the creation of databases, counsel should take precautions to ensure that all investigative work-product and reports created in connection with these self-critical analyses are cloaked with the indicia of privilege. These measures should include marking all documents and reports with legends indicating the privileged and confidential nature of the materials, and carefully controlling access to and dissemination of the items.

Library References:

West's Key No. Digests, Federal Civil Procedure ☞1600(3); Witnesses ☞197.
Wright, Miller & Marcus, Federal Practice and Procedure: Civil 2d §§ 2017, 2021, 2024, 2025.

§ 4.17   Conducting an Asset Search

Asset searches have many practical uses in litigation. They can help clients satisfy judgments, assess the financial resources of actual and putative adversaries and, armed with this knowledge, negotiate or litigate from a position of strength. For example, with regard to a corporation or other business entity, the organization's receivables may be its most significant and liquid asset. Thus, by developing the names of the business' customers and projects, payments owed to the business can be identified and then attached to satisfy a judgment.

What follows is a description of the tools and techniques ordinarily used in a typical asset search.

(a) Types of Assets

An "asset" for purposes of this discussion is any property or interest that can be reduced to cash. Assets can be individually owned or held in the name of a corporation or other business entity, and may include any of the following:

- **Real Property**

    (land; buildings and improvements; oil, gas and mineral leases)

- **Motor Vehicles**

    (automobiles, motorcycles and trucks; mobile homes and campers; marine vessels; aircraft)

- **Other Material Assets**

    (racehorses and livestock; art; antiques; jewelry; collectibles—stamps, coins, etc.; equipment and machinery)

---

3. For treatment of the legal issues applicable to the self-evaluative privilege, *see* *infra* Chapter 18, "Discovery Strategy and Privileges," at § 18.10(b)(9) & (c).

- **Financial & Business Assets**

    (wages; bank accounts; brokerage accounts; stocks and bonds; ownership interests in businesses, including limited partnerships, general partnerships, and businesses operated under trade and fictitious business names; accounts receivable, including mortgages and leases; royalties, patents and copyrights)

- **Indirect Assets**

    (assets of a spouse and other family members; assets of corporations or partnerships controlled by the subject)

(b) Steps to Be Taken in an Asset Search

A typical asset search involves the following steps and procedures:

(1) Client Interviews

The client should be carefully interviewed at the start of an asset search. Not only is it important to understand what the client wishes to accomplish, but it is equally important to find out what the client knows about the assets, liabilities and business relationships of the subject. During the interview, the client should be asked to provide as much pedigree information about the subject as he or she knows. The subject's current and former addresses, telephone numbers, full name (and any aliases), date of birth, social security number, and business identification number should be fully explored.

The client should be asked where the subject's assets are most likely to be found, and whether he or she has heard any rumors about the subject's finances, businesses, properties and the like. For example, clients may be aware that a subject flies an airplane, owns a summer home, or owns shares in a particular company. In addition, clients often can provide investigators with copies of canceled checks and other financial instruments of the subject. These immediately identify important sources of assets (*e.g.*, the subject's bank accounts, certificates of deposit, etc.). Clients also may have important information gleaned from required corporate filings, trade journals and other industry sources concerning a business' receivables, inventory, real property and other significant assets.

(2) Other Field Interviews

Other sources of information should be explored at the beginning of the search. Disgruntled former and present employees, for example, may be able to identify assets or provide important leads. If the investigation does not need to be "quiet," neighbors of the subject as well as competitors, suppliers, clients, adversaries in lawsuits, former spouses, and trade union officials also can be interviewed.

(3) Media Searches

Media sources should be checked through on-line searches and visits to public libraries to review local papers. Newspapers, magazines and other media can be a source of significant information regarding a subject's acquaintances, acquisitions, properties, and ownership interests in businesses, among other things.

(4) Database Research

Armed with the information gathered from interviews and media searches, the investigation should proceed to the database inquiry stage. Computerized commercial databases should be fully plumbed to develop complete background information for all individual subjects and related business entities. As to any individual, after providing (or verifying) the person's name, the search results should identify the person's date of birth; social security number; business identification number; residential and business addresses; telephone numbers; family members; place of employment; business interests, including corporations, partnerships and businesses operated under fictitious names; real property; mortgages; liens; UCC filings; motor vehicles, water craft and aircraft; adverse judgments; bankruptcies; and past and pending litigation. Database searches also should disclose the subject's ownership of any patents or copyrights.

Similar searches should be performed for all pertinent corporate and business entities. These probes should seek to identify the correct name of the corporation or other business operating under a fictitious designation; all addresses used by the business, including business, mailing and registered agent addresses; the business' date and place of incorporation; the entity's corporate tax identification number; the officers, directors, partners and shareholders of the business entity in question; any subsidiaries or affiliated companies owned or controlled by the business; and all real property and motor vehicles owned by the business.

Additionally, searches should be performed to disclose all litigation, liens, judgments and UCC filings involving any of the corporations or business organizations in question. Moreover, all required public filings these businesses have made with the SEC and other regulatory bodies, and all applications they have filed to obtain or renew licenses, should be carefully reviewed. Besides ferreting out hidden corporate assets, these searches may disclose the existence of people who can identify other assets or provide additional information relevant to the case.

(5) Public Records Searches

Central to an effective asset search is a comprehensive, on-site review of available public records. Earlier interviews as well as database and media probes may have provided indications of assets belonging to a subject. The existence of these and other assets can be established from the official (and publicly available) records maintained in various government offices.

Usually indexed under the owner's name, pertinent public records can be found in municipal, county, and state offices which are known by a variety of names in different jurisdictions, including "Recorder's Office," "Office of Official Records," "County Clerk's Office," "Tax Assessor's Office," "Office of the Secretary of State," and many more. By reviewing Grantor/Grantee indices, zoning and renovation permits, fictitious name indices (*e.g.*, listings which identify companies being operated under fictitious business names, and which provide the names and business addresses of the actual owners), and similar registers maintained in these offices, investigators can locate and obtain copies of recorded deeds, mortgages, leases and other official instruments evidencing an individual or corporate subject's ownership of real property (*e.g.*, land, buildings, and residential and commercial leases); oil, gas, and mineral leases; motor vehicles (*e.g.*, automobiles,[1] marine vessels,[2] and aircraft[3]); collateral pledged to secure an indebtedness (*e.g.*, UCC financing statements); and interests in corporations, limited and general partnerships, and other businesses.

With regard to publicly traded companies, required corporate filings with the SEC and other federal and state regulatory bodies also are important sources of financial information about the companies and their management.

(6) Litigation Searches

Field investigators should always review the plaintiff/defendant indices in the state and federal courthouses in all jurisdictions where a subject resides and works. Past and current litigation files involving a subject may identify adversaries with pertinent knowledge, officers and directors of a relevant business entity, real and personal property owned by a subject, and other information and leads. It may be that other adversaries and creditors have previously devoted extensive efforts to search for the subject's assets. Thus, counsel should seek to take advantage of any such prior efforts whenever possible.

§ 4.18   Conclusion

No treatise can possibly predict all of the opportunities and potential pitfalls of an investigation. Nevertheless, the choice of the right investigative team at the beginning of a case, together with counsel's ongoing communication with the investigators, will go a long way toward maximizing the benefits of an investigation and minimizing any problems. With appropriate planning, teamwork, and imagination, the results of an investigation can benefit virtually every case.

§ 4.17

1. These records can be obtained on-line from many state department of motor vehicle offices or from commercial databases which purchase the information from the states.

2. These records can be accessed through state registry offices or the U.S. Coast Guard registry for vessels not recorded with a state.

3. Evidence of aircraft ownership can be obtained from FAA microfiche records or commercial services.

§ 4.19   Forms

(a) Model Retainer Agreement   🖫

**PRIVILEGED AND CONFIDENTIAL
ATTORNEY-CLIENT COMMUNICATION AND
ATTORNEY WORK–PRODUCT**

Date:

**VIA FACSIMILE
VIA FEDERAL EXPRESS
BY HAND**

_____

_____

Re: _____

Dear Mr. _____:

    1.0   *Engagement*

    1.1   This letter confirms your agreement to retain _____ and its employees and agents to perform investigative and research services in connection with (potential) litigation ("The Engagement").

    2.0   *Purpose*

    2.1   The Engagement is for the purpose of assisting you and consulting with you in aid of your formulating your legal strategy and advising your client _____ ("Client").

    2.2   All work performed and materials and work-product of any kind generated in furtherance of The Engagement will be deemed to be confidential work-product prepared in connection with the (potential) litigation which is the subject of The Engagement.

    3.0   *Subpoena or Third–Party Efforts to Thwart the Investigation*

    3.1   Should any effort be made (a) either by subpoena or otherwise to gain access to materials or documents or information of any kind in the possession of _____ which is generated or obtained or learned as a result of the work performed by _____ under The Engagement, or (b) to otherwise stop, interrupt or interfere with the performance of _____ 's work pursuant to The Engagement, whether by judicial action or other means, _____ shall promptly notify you.

    3.2   Your Client agrees to indemnify and hold harmless _____ for all costs, attorney's fees and disbursements, as may be incurred, associated with resisting or complying with any efforts as described in paragraph "3.1."

    3.3   Your Client also agrees to indemnify _____ for any judgments or claims against _____ arising out of The Engagement, unless it were to be finally adjudicated that _____'s actions were negligent or tortious or beyond the scope of The Engagement.

    4.0   *Fees*

4.1 _____ will bill you monthly, or more frequently, if you request.

4.2 Our rates range from $_____ to $_____ per hour in the United States. Disbursements and taxes, if applicable, are billed in addition to fees.

4.3 If bills remain outstanding for more than 60 days, _____ reserves the right to stop all work.

4.4 If _____ must engage counsel or otherwise expend funds to collect bills over 60 days old, your client will be responsible for reimbursing _____ for all such costs, plus interest on the outstanding balance.

4.5 We have set an initial budget of $_____, plus disbursements. _____ requests a retainer in the amount of $_____. We will bill against this retainer at our customary rates (paragraph 4.2) depending on the personnel assigned to this matter.

5.0 *Termination*

5.1 The terms and understandings set forth in this letter shall survive the termination of any and all work performed pursuant to The Engagement.

6.0 *Effective Date*

6.1 The Engagement and the terms of the letter shall be deemed to be effective as of _____.

7.0 *Signature*

7.1 Your signature below on the enclosed copy of this letter is your representation that you are authorized to enter into The Engagement and to agree to the terms of this letter on behalf of your Client.

Please execute and return the enclosed copy of this letter to us.

We look forward to working with you toward a successful completion of The Engagement.

Very truly yours,

By: _____

The above sets forth the terms of The Engagement and is Agreed to on behalf of the Client:

Addressee Firm Name

By: _____

Name
Title

Dated: _____

(b) Model Guidelines for Investigators 💾

PRIVILEGED AND CONFIDENTIAL
ATTORNEY-CLIENT WORK–PRODUCT
NOT TO BE DISSEMINATED

INVESTIGATIVE GUIDELINES CONTROLLING INTERVIEWS

All _____ investigators are required to thoroughly acquaint themselves with the following guidelines and procedures for the conduct of interviews of witnesses in this case and shall comport themselves in accordance with these guidelines:

1. _____ investigators shall clearly identify themselves and the interest they represent to any potential interviewee.

2. No _____ investigators shall contact or communicate with any person:

    (a) Who is known to be represented by an attorney in connection with this matter;

    (b) Who is known to be a party of record or an attorney for a party of record adverse to the interest represented by _____ in the pending lawsuit, without prior approval from the client;

    (c) Who is known or has represented himself or herself to be a current employee of a party to the pending lawsuit;

    (d) Who was not previously known to fall within one of the above categories, but during the course of the interview it becomes apparent does fall within one of the above categories. In such event, the investigators shall terminate the interview and notify the client of the occurrence and request directions on how to proceed.

3. When conducting interviews with individuals for whom contact is not prohibited, the following procedures apply:

    (a) At the outset of contact with a potential witness, the interviewee shall be provided with a business card or other form of identification from the investigators. The interviewee shall be asked whether he or she is an employee of _____ or any subsidiary thereof. If not, the interview may proceed. Investigators shall always clearly identify themselves as investigators retained by a party's counsel in the pending litigation to obtain facts with regard to this matter;

    (b) No statement shall be made to any potential interviewee which intentionally misleads that person with regard to the identity either of the investigators or of the entity which has retained the investigators;

    (c) All reasonable measures shall be taken to establish that the individual being contacted clearly understands and continues to understand whom the investigators are and whom they represent;

    (d) At the outset of any interview, investigators shall determine whether the prospective interviewee is represented by an attorney in connection with the pending litigation or related litigation. If the potential interviewee is represented by an attorney, the investigators shall ask for the name and telephone number of that attorney. The investigators shall then discontinue contact with the interviewee.

The client shall be notified whenever a contact with an individual has occurred in which the individual has advised that he or she is represented by an attorney in connection with this case.

4. Investigators shall maintain a chronological written record, in detail, of the following:

(a) Names, addresses, and telephone numbers of all persons contacted during the investigation, whether or not interviewed, concerning the facts of this case;

(b) Any and all information received from any source which may be considered as confidential information concerning an adverse party;

(c) A list of all persons known to have access to said confidential information or to whom such information may have been disseminated. Such list will enable the client to provide copies of any confidentiality agreement or court order pertaining to the use and dissemination of confidential information to all covered individuals.

Under no circumstances shall any _____ investigators disseminate any information about this case or about any persons related to this case except in written and verbal reports to _____ supervisors. Nor shall any _____ investigators show copies of this document or any other documents to any person without the prior approval of _____ supervisors.

PLEASE SIGNIFY YOUR UNDERSTANDING and acceptance of these guidelines by initialing each page and executing both copies of this document, returning one copy to _____ and keeping one for your records.

I understand and agree to comport myself according to the terms of these guidelines.

_____

Signature

_____

Dated

CHAPTER 5

THE COMPLAINT

by
Francis Burch, Jr.,
James D. Mathias,
and
Glen K. Allen

Table of Sections

WESTLAW Electronic Research

See WESTLAW Electronic Research Guide preceding the Summary of Contents.

---

§ 5.1   Scope Note

The art of drafting complaints encompasses both a knowledge of pleading rules and an attention to litigation strategy. Without a knowledge of rules, the best of strategic decisions may go awry; without the right strategic decisions, the most perfectly rule-compliant of complaints may accomplish little or nothing. This chapter discusses both rules and strategy, with an emphasis on strategy.

With regard to strategy, the chapter first discusses the importance of determining the complaint's target audience or audiences. There are, of course, many different potential audiences for any complaint, including the adversary, the client, the court, the adversary's insurer, the public and the media, and possibly the jury. A complaint is no more a one-size-fits-all document than is a letter or a literary composition, so a focus on who will most attentively be reading the complaint is a prerequisite to preparing an effective complaint. The chapter then discusses the tactical considerations that favor either a factually developed or, on the other hand, a fact-bare complaint. Here the chapter makes the point that although factual detail in a complaint is often necessary and appropriate, not every complaint needs such detail to accomplish its strategic aims.

Next, after reviewing the most important pleading rules and principles, the chapter addresses issues of style and organization. Here it first sets forth the authors' bias towards a "lean and mean" writing style. It then discusses the structure the authors typically use in drafting complaints.

The chapter concludes with shorter sections on amendments to complaints, complaints for injunctive relief and for declaratory judgment, and issues relating to filing.

Library References:

West's Key No. Digests, Federal Civil Procedure ☜621–1150.
Wright, Miller & Kane, Federal Practice and Procedure: Civil 2d § 1827.

§ 5.2   Strategies and Objectives in Drafting the Complaint

Many, often conflicting, strategic priorities and drafting objectives must be weighed when deciding on the appropriate tone, content, structure, and length of the complaint in a particular case. This section addresses these concerns. Underlying these specific issues is the Golden Rule that any pleading, and especially the complaint, should be written in crisp, concise, and plain English that conveys the client's message in a persuasive fashion, without unnecessary legalese, distracting elaboration of inessential or collateral matters, or artificial formality. The style and appearance of the complaint, of course, should not offend local rules or practice, even when conformity requires a nod to what may seem antiquated conventions. Beyond these practical concessions to time-honored formalities, however, the complaint has but one goal—to tell the client's story in the manner that will most effectively serve the client's interests.

To do so, before putting pen to paper or fingers to keyboard, you must adopt a disciplined approach to identifying the specific strategic priorities and drafting objectives that are appropriate to your client's claims. Once the priorities and objectives have been identified, the inclusion, or exclusion, of every word and sentence of the complaint should be guided by whether it supports the goal of telling the most effective story possible on your client's behalf. While the priorities and objectives that control the attorney's task will vary depending on the circumstances of each case, the goal of this section is to provide a framework and a discipline to ensure that the drafter considers carefully all of the most important aspects of the task and adopts the strategies and objectives most appropriate to the case. The final product will be good in proportion to the quality of the preparation that creates it. Good complaints don't "just happen" any more than a good novel, poem, speech, or client presentation just happens. Decide what story you want and need to tell, and then tell it. Stripped to its essentials, that is the job of drafting a good complaint.

(a) Different Audiences, Different Tactics

The initial step in drafting a good complaint differs little from preparing a good opening statement or speech, an article, a letter to a friend, or even a skit for the firm party. You must first determine who your target audience is and then focus on what approach will deliver your desired message with the greatest intended impact. Any effective presentation must take into account, among other things, who the audience is, the audience's knowledge of the subject matter, and the audience's anticipated receptivity to the message to be delivered. To be compelling, any presentation must capture the audience's interest and address the audience's special concerns. A discussion of shareholders' rights to challenge decisions of the board of directors of a publicly traded company, for instance, if delivered to shareholders who are quite interested in maximizing the value of their investments but who may be unsophisticated in legal matters, would not employ unfamiliar legal phrases or discuss a board's *Revlon* duties without first explaining the import of the *Revlon* case holding and subsequent interpretations of it in terms the audience could understand and appreciate. The shareholders likely would be more interested in *whether* controversial board actions can be challenged than in the esoterica of how and why the law does or does not allow the challenge. A speech on the same subject presented to attorneys at a securities law seminar obviously should operate at a very different level and reasonably might employ a more specialized vocabulary and venture into subtleties of the subject matter that would only confuse and bore a less informed audience with different interests.

Likewise, a complaint must derive its theme and appropriate level of detail and sophistication from the drafter's decision on who is to be affected and in what manner by reading the complaint. Consideration of the audience—or, more realistically, audiences, as there always will be more than one—will guide the drafter's decision on the amount and nature of detail and advocacy to include in the complaint. Audiences for the complaint that must be considered include the client, the defendants, related third parties such as insurers or potential indemnitors of the defendants, the court, and, in some instances, the public, the media, and the jury.

A client whose interests the complaint represents may desire, or even insist upon, a forceful and detailed articulation of all the respects in which the client has been wronged and deserves redress. In another instance, a very cost-conscious plaintiff may want nothing more than a bare-bones complaint that satisfies the necessary pleading elements and accomplishes little more than instituting the legal process. From the opposite perspective, how will the adversary, the defendant, react to the story told by the complaint? Is detail helpful to convince the opposition, and opposing counsel, that they have a serious problem that must be addressed promptly? Or are they sufficiently conversant with the facts that extensive detail is unnecessary or, worse, rings hollow because it is not supported by the opponent's understanding of the facts? Does a factually developed pleading advance the plaintiff's cause, or does it simply provide the defendants a road map for improving their defense and discovery strategies?

From a third vantage point—the perspective of the court—it is always useful to contemplate how reading the complaint might influence the judge's overall approach to the litigation. This task is made more difficult because, while you know who your client and adversaries are when you draft the complaint, you typically do not know who the judge will be. In those instances where the judge is known, such as where you expect your complaint to be consolidated with a related case or where you are drafting a counterclaim, careful attention should be given to the perceived predilections of the human being who will control the course of discovery, scheduling, motions, and trial.

More remote potential audiences also exist and deserve at least some contemplation when you are preparing the complaint. Juries may hear portions of the complaint in the context of, for example, cross-examination for impeachment purposes. How will your words sound in the courtroom? A complaint should be aggressive advocacy, but overreaching can haunt you later. If your complaint deals with matters of public concern or interest, will members of the media or the public who are likely to read it understand the claims in a manner that will evoke sympathy for your client's cause and generate a positive public reaction? Although our legal system is designed to minimize the influence public perceptions and pressures have on court proceedings and often performs well in this regard, it would be naive to ignore the fact that public commentary and reporting in certain circumstances can and do exert influence on such matters as the parties' decisions on whether to litigate or pursue settlement, a court's handling of discovery and trial, and even a jury's consideration of the case.

Beyond identification of the possible audiences for the complaint, drafting decisions always should account for the sophistication of the litigation involved and the procedural posture in which the case may be considered by the audiences. To illustrate with an easy example, a routine breach of contract case where a motion to dismiss is not anticipated obviously merits less specificity and detail than a securities class action complaint alleging fraudulent disclosures and statutory control person liability under the 1934 Securities Exchange Act, where pleading requirements are specific and complicated, factual support often is circumstantial and subject to competing interpretations, and a forcefully presented motion to dismiss by experienced and creative defense counsel can be expected as almost standard procedure.

How issues of audience, objective, and complexity might influence drafting decisions in any particular case involves sufficiently individual combinations of considerations that generalizations should be advanced cautiously. The subsections that follow seek to identify the primary considerations that would favor either a factually developed complaint, on the one hand, or a brief and general complaint, on the other hand. The lawyer then can apply these considerations to the particular circumstances of the case at hand to make a fully informed decision on drafting the best complaint for the audiences and purposes to be addressed.

(b) Tactical Considerations Favoring a Factually Developed Complaint

This section identifies several tactical purposes that may be achieved by filing and serving a factually detailed and comprehensive complaint.

(1) Establishing the Equities of the Dispute

The complaint usually is the plaintiff's first organized, written articulation of the factual and legal basis for the claims advanced. If crafted in a supportable and thoughtful manner, the complaint can serve many of the same purposes as the well-delivered opening statement, predisposing the audience to find merit in the client's claims and establishing the point of departure for future discussions of the equities of the dispute. Under the Federal Rules, a factually detailed complaint literally puts the opposition on the defensive immediately, forcing them to marshal specific facts in quick fashion in order to file an adequate answer or other responsive pleading. With an eye to the court as audience, a well-developed complaint may provide the judge with a beneficial initial understanding of the nature of the claims that could assist the plaintiff in connection with later discovery disputes, scheduling decisions, and other matters that may directly involve the court, such as preliminary motions, settlement conferences, pretrial motions, motions in limine, voir dire, and jury instructions. The complaint may be the only organized articulation of the plaintiff's claims that the judge reads prior to the pretrial statement. If a motion to dismiss or a motion for summary judgment is filed, the judge will surely re-read the complaint. The complaint can signal to the court that the plaintiff and the plaintiff's counsel have done their homework before filing, will approach the litigation in a thorough and professional manner, and are committed to seeing the case through to a successful conclusion. A poorly drafted complaint—one containing stray and inessential facts, inconsistencies and errors, unsupported conclusions, gratuitous invective, or a lack of internal organization—very well may have the opposite effect.

Expressed as a cliché, whether the reader will be your own client, the defendants, other attorneys, or the judge assigned to the case, you never get a second chance to make a first impression.

(2) Settlement Value

Related to the equities of the dispute, the complaint can help establish the initial settlement value of the plaintiff's claims. A factually developed complaint may force the defense to confront many questions that will require answers if they hope to prevail; the more of these questions that give the defense pause, the more likely they will be receptive to considering early settlement discussions or mediation on terms favorable to your client. Effective factual development should establish the case for the defendants' liability and at the same time build the case for substantial damages, including, where possible, punitive damages, statutory damages, such as treble damages, and injunctive or equitable remedies, in addition to compensatory damages. Likewise, the complaint should never miss an opportunity to develop a plausible argument for the recovery of contractual or statutory attorneys' fees and costs. Nothing attracts an adversary's attention quicker than the possibility that they ultimately will have to pay for all your fine work in pursuing claims *against* them.

A well-written, detailed complaint also announces that the plaintiff is serious about the claims and will be a formidable opponent. By contrast, a hastily prepared complaint may suggest that the plaintiff is not yet committed to litigating the dispute to a conclusion. A defendant who hears the latter message will not as readily take a chair at the settlement negotiation table. With regard to settlement value, a well-drafted complaint frequently plays a significant role in the decisions of a defendant or an insurer on whether a claim is defensible and on an appropriate reserve amount to cover a future judgment or settlement. The establishment of a high reserve, even though not known by the plaintiff or plaintiff's counsel, makes a favorable settlement easier to attain because the defense already has accounted for it on the books.

(3) Public Relations Value

Related to settlement value, in certain types of cases, is the public relations or media value of the complaint. If you determine that the lawsuit at hand is likely to capture attention from the media and public, the complaint should be written in a manner that explains the dispute in an understandable and sympathetic manner. Whereas an adversary or judge may be expected to read a long complaint with reasonable care, the media and public may show less interest in minute detail, even where pertinent to the plaintiff's claims. An effective way to address this concern—and one that may help with more sophisticated readers as well—is to begin the complaint with a concise overview of the detail that follows, capturing the heart of the dispute in a short paragraph or two. This introductory section should be reasonable, factual, and supported by the remainder of the complaint, but it also should have good "sound bite" value. Even when public attention is not expected, the introduction can be an effective device because it immediately identifies for the reader the import and intent of the complaint; in its absence, many paragraphs of a complaint might be read before sufficient context has been developed to indicate to the reader why the information presented is important. Happily, this advice on consideration of public relations concerns probably is applicable to every case, because judges, lawyers, clients, and adversaries, despite their possible sophistication, are members of the general populace as well; however, a drafter sails into dangerous waters if the primary focus of a pleading ever becomes the media or public at the expense of the concerns of the audiences directly involved in the litigation. A sensitivity to public relations concerns should complement and supplement your more direct audience concerns, not supplant them.

(4) Injunctive Actions and Short–Lived Litigation

A factually developed complaint often is critically important in lawsuits that either are expected to be short-lived or that will crescendo early in the litigation process. Common examples of such cases include temporary restraining order or other injunctive actions, certain declaratory judgment actions, trade secret theft and noncompetition claims, and challenges to corporate mergers, acquisitions, or other pending board actions. These cases often find the parties before a judge almost immediately, seeking relief on the merits of the dispute. Under this sort of time pressure, with judgments being made without the benefit of full discovery or a gradual maturation of the factual record, the arguments favoring factual development in the complaint apply with even greater force.

An injunctive action requires factual development in order to establish entitlement to the equitable remedy sought. For instance, the drafter must plead not only facts supporting the violation of a covenant not to compete but also facts demonstrating that the test for issuing an injunction can be satisfied. If the complaint advances a cause of action but does not give facts supporting the conclusion, for example, that irreparable injury is occurring or likely to occur without the court's intervention, the injunctive remedy may not have been pleaded satisfactorily. Any time an equitable remedy is sought, the drafter should include all helpful factual information in order to establish the equities; a mere recitation of the notice pleading standards for the cause of action with a conclusory statement that each element has been satisfied is poor advocacy and may be deemed technically deficient, if challenged. Such flaws in the complaint can lead to costly delays, as where amended pleadings are required, or an early loss in the litigation from which it can be difficult to recover. *See* Section 5.6, *infra* (discussing injunctive actions in greater detail).

(5) Anticipating an Inevitable Motion to Dismiss

Certain causes of action seem to invite a motion to dismiss by their very nature. Prime examples are claims that must meet the specificity requirements of Rule 9(b), such as fraud claims, or claims that require a showing that prerequisites have been satisfied, such as exhaustion of administrative remedies or an opportunity to cure. When drafting a complaint where a motion to dismiss may be expected, factual development is an absolute necessity. Helpful information will be of no assistance if it has not been included in the pleading. Using fraud as an example, the drafter needs to examine each element of the claim and insert factual detail capable of sustaining that element. It is not enough to say that the CEO of the corporation made statements that, in retrospect, turned out not to be true. Nor is it sufficient to allege without factual support that the CEO knew the statements were false when made. Facts must be specifically pled that support an inference of such contemporaneous knowledge of falsity. Without this support, the complaint becomes an easy target for the defense's motion to dismiss.

(6) Ferreting out the Defense Through the Answer

The more factually developed the complaint, the more factually developed the answer must be. Rule 8(b) requires that "[d]enials shall fairly meet the substance of the averments denied." Thus, if a tactical advantage may be gained by learning very quickly the details of the defense's theory of the case, a specific and detailed complaint can ferret out the defenses. Short, plain sentences containing one thought or idea are preferable to compound sentences that contain many factual premises; the latter type of pleading makes it easier for the defense to simply deny the truth of the sentence when one of the premises is subject to denial. (It should be noted, however, that this defense tactic arguably is improper under Rule 8(b), which provides that "[w]hen a pleader intends in good faith to deny only a part or a qualification of an averment, the pleader shall specify so much of it as is true and material and shall deny only the remainder.") Another advantage of a detailed series of concise factual statements in the complaint is that if the answer fails to respond comprehensively to the factual allegations of the complaint, those factual assertions not denied are deemed admitted, pursuant to Rule 8(d).

(c) Tactical Considerations Favoring a Brief and General Complaint

This section identifies tactical considerations that may make the filing of a less detailed factual account in the complaint appropriate.

(1) Cost and Efficiency

A short, general complaint costs less to prepare. In some instances, particularly when pleading generic causes of action such as simple breach of contract, this may represent a true savings. In other instances, however, such savings may be illusory, such as when the failure to plead in a more detailed fashion leads to a motion to dismiss and to the costs of opposing the motion, costs that otherwise may have been avoided. It goes without saying, of course, that an attorney cannot permit cost considerations to serve as a justification for filing a complaint without first performing a reasonable factual and legal investigation to determine whether a good faith basis exists for pleading the causes of action.

(2) A Broad Complaint May Encourage Broad Discovery

A fully developed factual account in the complaint may offer the defense many specific ideas on avenues of discovery to pursue that they would not have considered so comprehensively without the complaint as a guide. This may affect document requests, interrogatories, and depositions. Some lawyers use a detailed complaint as their outline for questioning the plaintiff's deposition witnesses. A broad complaint also may persuade a judge to allow broader discovery than is routine in that particular jurisdiction. In certain federal courts, limits on the permissible amount of discovery by each party are set. For example, if the plaintiff hopes to confine the number or length of depositions narrowly, a general complaint may not appear to signify as complex a dispute as a more detailed pleading would. Thus the court might be more reluctant to allow upward departures from the standard restrictions on depositions, interrogatories, and document requests.

(3) An Overly Specific Complaint May Tip the Plaintiff's Hand

While a specific complaint has many advantages, it must be recognized that, in effect, it frequently serves as the defense's initial frame of reference for investigation. Making comprehensive information on the claims immediately available facilitates the defense's inquiry. In an instance where, for example, you have reason to believe that the defense may not thoroughly investigate on its own, or may not recognize specific areas that are worthy of inquiry, you may decide not to highlight those areas in your complaint except to the extent absolutely necessary to support your claims.

(4) Certain Information May Be Unavailable

Reality dictates that even the most conscientious lawyer may not have complete information available on all relevant details of the claims when the complaint is drafted. As everyone who has ever conducted a litigation investigation knows, stories unfold and mature gradually as additional documents and accounts surface and the primary actors react to that information and refresh their recollections. The result is that the story told in the complaint rarely is the same in every material detail as the story that you as plaintiff's counsel would deliver to the judge or jury at trial. Sensitivity to this reality will help the drafter avoid making tenuous statements in the complaint that later may turn out to be verifiably false and thus undermine the plaintiff's and counsel's credibility with the court and the jury. In some instances, discretion will suggest that uncertain details or allegations be omitted. Better to amend after later investigation to include additional positive facts or claims than to amend to retract unsupportable claims you already have advanced. If a fact is essential but uncertain, use of the "upon information and belief" convention provides some cover, though this tactic should not be overused, as it tends to dilute the effectiveness of the complaint as advocacy.

(5) Rule 11: Enhanced Burden with Specific Allegations

Where a detailed factual account is advanced, the burden of ensuring compliance with Rule 11 may be enhanced. All allegations and other factual contentions must have evidentiary support or, where so identified, be likely to have evidentiary support upon further investigation (i.e., "upon information and belief . . ."). Logic suggests that the more facts pled, the greater potential for an unsupported allegation. If this is true, however, it is true only in the narrow sense, as it also stands to reason that a detailed complaint should result from a detailed investigation, and the better the investigation, the less likelihood for a Rule 11 issue. This concern should not create significant difficulties for the experienced litigator, because more often than not, the uncertain or likely unsupportable fact will be omitted for strategic reasons before one even reaches concerns about procedural correctness. Credibility and forcefulness ultimately are achieved by *showing* that claims have merit, not merely by *saying* so.

(6) Impact of Relation Back Rule

Rule 15(c) governs the relation back of amended pleadings to the time of the original pleading for statute of limitations purposes. While it is not the province of this subsection to discuss the relation back rule comprehensively, it should be taken into consideration when making drafting decisions. Obviously, if a fact or claim that seems somewhat tenuous based on the state of your investigation at the time of drafting the complaint can be added in an amended complaint filed later, without concern for a time bar, then you can more comfortably leave out the fact or claim until further investigation establishes its support. This concern frequently arises when plaintiff's counsel is uncertain as to the proper name or identity of the prospective defendants, such as where there are several corporate bodies with similar names. *See* Form 10, Federal Rules of Civil Procedure (dealing with a form complaint where the identity of proper defendant is uncertain). Where limitations is a problem, error probably should be on the side of inclusion.

(7) Collateral Estoppel Issues

Particularly where a lawsuit is intended to address only a portion of a more complicated relationship between or among the parties, the plaintiff's counsel may want to confine the factual account in the complaint narrowly so as to navigate away from potential collateral estoppel pitfalls created by unnecessarily addressing factual disputes that may have unintended or adverse implications in other potential disputes involving these same or similar parties.

(d) Tactical Considerations Concerning Civil Cover Sheets—"Related Cases"

Civil cover sheets used in conjunction with the filing of a complaint at times can be used to good advantage by the plaintiff to reduce some of the uncertainty associated with the process. For example, as discussed in Section 5.2(a), *supra*, a major uncertainty in filing any complaint is that you do not know a major component of your eventual audience, namely, the identity of the judge. In some circumstances, however, you may employ the civil cover sheet to increase the likelihood that a case will go to a particular judge, and then the complaint can be tailored according to any specific predilections of the judge who will receive the case. The complaint may be tailored as well as to any prior statements or rulings by the court that may impact the new claims.

One way this situation arises is when the complaint you intend to file arguably is a "related case" to a case already pending before a judge in the same court. Highlighting this fact on the civil cover sheet and otherwise bringing it to the attention of the clerk's office and court, as in a cover letter accompanying the filed copy or a courtesy copy of the complaint, will increase the probability that you will know your audience in advance.

(e) Filing Duplicative Complaints in State and Federal Court

Where the statute of limitations is a potential issue and you have a concern about whether your federal complaint will be sustained, be it for jurisdictional or other reasons, generally nothing prevents the filing of a contemporaneous state court action. You should then take steps to stay the state court action, without allowing it to be dismissed until any possibility of the federal action being dismissed has passed. You can expect the defense to seek to have the state court action dismissed as duplicative immediately upon its filing or seek to dismiss the federal action and force the case into state court. As plaintiff's counsel, however, you should do whatever is possible to make sure that your client is not left without any relief because of procedural maneuvering.

Library References:

West's Key No. Digests, Federal Civil Procedure ☞671–717.
Wright, Miller & Marcus, Federal Practice and Procedure: Civil 2d § 3044.

§ 5.3 Pleading Rules and Drafting Considerations for Initial complaints

Tactical decisions regarding the drafting of the complaint must, of course, be executed in accordance with established rules and principles of federal pleading. The following subparagraphs address the most important of these rules and principles.

(a) Honesty and Reasonable Investigation

Honesty and a reasonable factual and legal investigation are First Principles in pleading an effective and proper complaint in accordance with the Federal Rules. These requirements are set forth in and are enforceable under Rule 11, a Rule discussed in depth in Chapter 48, "Sanctions," *infra*.

These requirements do not demand of a pleader full certainty regarding legal theories and their evidentiary support before filing a complaint. As will be further discussed in this Section 5.3, the Federal Rules allow alternative and hypothetical pleading (Section 5.3(g)), inconsistent claims (Section 5.3(g)), and, in some circumstances, pleading on information and belief (Section 5.3(e)). The Federal Rules' liberality in this respect, however, is not a license for lax legal and factual investigation or weakly supported or confusing complaints. A creative and effective complaint requires thorough factual investigation and legal analysis. A day of research and investigation during the drafting of the complaint may save weeks of anxious labor later, as you struggle to cope with a defendant's defenses or a court's doubts.

It goes without saying that knowingly false allegations have no place in a complaint. Such allegations are unethical and a violation of Rule 11; in addition, they are tactically unwise. A skillful adversary can turn departures from the truth, even on relatively minor points, into weapons to damage your credibility seriously.

(b) The Option of Brevity: Rule 8; Notice Pleading; The Appendix of Official Forms

If for tactical reasons you have chosen to file a "bare bones" complaint, the question may arise: How bare of facts can it be? The answer is that there is substantial support in the Federal Rules, the background and commentary to the Federal Rules, and case law— especially United States Supreme Court case law—for the proposition that a complaint need not be lengthy or recite extensive facts to survive a motion to dismiss. Even so, a degree of caution is appropriate before filing a complaint that states few facts.

The text of the Federal Rules provides solid authority protecting a factually lean complaint from dismissal. Rule 8(a)(2) requires only that a claim contain "a short and plain statement of the claim showing that the pleader is entitled to relief"; Rule 8(e)(1) states that "[e]ach averment of a pleading shall be simple, concise, and direct. No technical forms of pleading . . . are required"; and Rule 8(f) provides that "[a]ll pleadings shall be so construed as to do substantial justice." These textual bases for notice pleading were created to escape the complexities of fact pleading that existed under the prior codes.[1]

The official forms attached to the Federal Rules illustrate this point. Rule 84 explicitly states that the forms contained in the Appendix of Forms "are sufficient under the rules and are intended to indicate the simplicity and brevity of statement which the rules contemplate." The complaints in the Appendix of Forms are dramatically short and simple. Form 9, for example, which is the standard negligence complaint, consists of three brief paragraphs.

Although few complaints actually follow the forms in the Appendix of Forms,[2] a drafter who does wish to file so skeletal a complaint can invoke the authority of Rule 84 to avoid dismissal.[3] Use of a form may be

---

1. Richard L. Marcus, *The Revival of Fact Pleading Under the Federal Rules of Civil Procedure*, 86 Col. L. Rev. 433, 433 (1986); American Nurses' Ass'n v. State of Illinois, 783 F.2d 716, 723 (7th Cir.1986).

2. American Nurses Ass'n, 783 F.2d at 723.

3. *See, e.g.,* Crull v. GEM Ins. Co., 58 F.3d 1386, 1391 (9th Cir.1995); Trevino v. Union Pacific Railroad Co., 916 F.2d 1230, 1234 (7th Cir.1990); District of Columbia v. Transamerica Ins. Co., 797 F.2d 1041, 1044 (D.C.Cir.1986); Iadanza v. Mather, 820 F.Supp. 1371, 1383 n. 19 (D.Utah 1993): Beery v. Hitachi Home Electronics (America), Inc., 157 F.R.D. 477, 480 (C.D.Cal. 1993) (Form 16 for patent infringement).

especially helpful if the form states language necessary to comply with a federal statute, such as 28 U.S.C.A. § 1332(a) (diversity jurisdiction).[4]

Supreme Court precedents provide an additional bulwark protecting laconic complaints from dismissal. The seminal case in this regard, of course, is the much-cited *Conley v. Gibson*[5] decision, in which the Supreme Court held that the Federal Rules "do not require a claimant to set out in detail the facts upon which he bases his claim. To the contrary, all the Rules require is a 'short and plain statement of the claim' that will give the defendant fair notice of what the plaintiff's claim is and the grounds upon which it rests." The Supreme Court more recently reaffirmed the vitality of *Conley* in *Leatherman v. Tarrant County Narcotics Intelligence and Coordination Unit.*[6] In *Leatherman*, the Court addressed whether a heightened pleading standard could be applied in civil rights cases alleging municipal liability under 42 U.S.C.A. § 1983. Nearly every circuit court had held such a heightened pleading requirement appropriate, but the Supreme Court rejected it, stating that "it is impossible to square the 'heightened pleading standards' applied . . . in this case with the liberal system of 'notice pleading' set up by the Federal Rules."[7]

A plaintiff filing a factually lean, even skeletal complaint, can thus invoke powerful authority to defend the pleading. Yet circumspection is necessary. The notice pleading provisions of Rule 8 were drafted in 1938 and *Conley v. Gibson* decided in 1957, both before the pressure of heavy caseloads in district courts that have arisen in more recent decades. As Judge Posner observed in *Jackson v. Marion County*,[8] "[m]ost judges are pragmatists, and will allow rules to be bent when the pressure is great." As a result of this pressure toward fact pleading, in virtually every circuit there are precedents qualifying the liberal ethos of notice pleading. The courts have given themselves leeway to refuse to accept "legal conclusions," "unwarranted inferences," and "conclusory allegations" and to require "well-pleaded facts" and "well-pleaded allegations." Indeed, although the *Leatherman* decision can reasonably be understood as a revitalization of notice pleading, the Supreme Court has also at least hinted elsewhere that sometimes, such as in litigation involving "a potentially massive factual controversy," more particularity in pleading may be required.[9] It is instructive in this regard that several courts have

---

4. *See, e.g.,* Molett v. Penrod Drilling Co., 872 F.2d 1221, 1227 (5th Cir.1989).

5. 355 U.S. 41, 47, 78 S.Ct. 99, 103, 2 L.Ed.2d 80 (1957).

6. 507 U.S. 163, 113 S.Ct. 1160, 122 L.Ed.2d 517 (1993).

7. *Id.* at 168, 113 S.Ct. at 1163.

8. 66 F.3d 151, 153 (7th Cir.1995).

9. *See, e.g.,* Associated General Contractors of California, Inc. v. California State Council of Carpenters, 459 U.S. 519, 528 n. 17, 103 S.Ct. 897, 903, 74 L.Ed.2d 723 (1983) (dictum) ("[I]n a case of this magni-

tude, a district court must retain the power to insist upon some specificity in pleading before allowing a potentially massive factual controversy to proceed."); Butz v. Economou, 438 U.S. 478, 507–08, 98 S.Ct. 2894, 2911–12, 57 L.Ed.2d 895 (1978) (dictum) (suggesting that "insubstantial" cases can be dismissed despite "artful pleading"); *cf.* Warth v. Seldin, 422 U.S. 490, 503, 509, 95 S.Ct. 2197, 2207, 2210, 45 L.Ed.2d 343 (1975) (in denying standing, rejecting plaintiffs' allegations as "conclusory" and "conjectural"). *See generally* Richard L. Marcus, *supra* note 1, at 433–37, 446–47 (identifying

limited the *Leatherman* decision to its facts.[10]

The instances in which courts have invoked the above-noted qualifications to notice pleading are legion, and it is difficult to summarize neatly the character of the complaints that have caused the courts to invoke the qualifications. A discussion of several representative cases, however, may impart some sense of the factors that have triggered courts' discomfort with strict notice pleading.

Labram v. Havel[11] is representative of courts' refusal to allow parties to plead "legal conclusions." In that case, the plaintiff alleged certain facts and then stated the conclusion that the facts stated a claim of breach of fiduciary duty. The court, however, held that although it was required to accept the plaintiff's factual allegations as true, it was not bound to accept the plaintiff's conclusion that these facts added up to a breach of fiduciary duty.[12] *Labram* contrasts, perhaps, with Form 9 of the Appendix of Forms, which, in alleging a negligence claim in three paragraphs, arguably also states a legal conclusion. Form 9, however, states no facts inconsistent with the legal conclusion of negligence. The moral here is to be sensitive to the import of your factual allegations. If they add up to conclusion X, you cannot expect a court to accept that they add up to conclusion Y simply because you allege that they add up to conclusion Y.

A similar type of mispleading is the description of the effect of a legal document, such as a contract or treaty, as though it were a fact. In *United States ex rel. Chunie v. Ringosa*,[13] for example, the plaintiff Indian tribe alleged as part of its factual allegations that the Santa Barbara Islands were not within the territory ceded by Mexico to the United States under the Treaty of Guadalupe Hidalgo.[14] The court refused to accept this allegation as true even on a motion to dismiss, holding that "[w]hile the court generally must assume factual allegations to be true, it need not assume the truth of legal conclusions cast in the form of factual allegations.... The interpretation of a treaty is a question of law and not a matter of fact."[15]

Another insight under this topic was provided by the First Circuit in *The Dartmouth Review v. Dartmouth College*.[16] In that case, the court, noting that "the threshold [for stating a claim] may be low, but it is real," stated that "gauzy generalities, unsupported conclusions, subjective characterizations, and problematic suppositions can sprout as easily as crabgrass in an imaginative litigant's (or lawyer's) word processor."[17] The lesson suggested by this admonition is that a complaint that is short on facts and long on legal conclusions may make the court suspicious

---

trend toward requiring greater specificity in pleadings in federal court).

10. *See, e.g.*, Ross v. State of Alabama, 893 F.Supp. 1545, 1552 (M.D.Ala.1995); Payne v. Axelrod, 871 F.Supp. 1551, 1556 n. 7 (N.D.N.Y.1995); Orange v. County of Suffolk, 830 F.Supp. 701, 707 (E.D.N.Y.1993).

11. 43 F.3d 918 (4th Cir.1995).

12. *Id.* at 921.

13. 788 F.2d 638 (9th Cir.1986).

14. *Id.* at 643 n.2.

15. *Id.*

16. 889 F.2d 13 (1st Cir.1989).

17. *Id.* at 16.

that the complaint is more the result of imagination than factual investigation. Having such a view, the court may find a way to cause the complaint to suffer an early death.

In summary, whatever the letter of the law regarding notice pleading, no attorney proposing to file a skeletal complaint should rely too heavily on legal conclusions, treat the import of legal documents as a question of fact, or ignore the fact-pleading tendencies that may exist in that particular circuit. The pleader should also be sensitive to the docket pressures on, and predilections of, the judge likely to read the complaint. A tin ear here may have fatal consequences.

(c) The Dangers of Prolixity

The prior section addressed the question of how fact-bare a complaint can be. This section addresses the reverse: if your chosen strategy involves filing a lengthy and detailed complaint, how lengthy and detailed can it be?

Although the Federal Rules envision brevity, they do not require it.[18] There are, however, aspects of extensive factual development that require caution. A plaintiff who files a long and detailed complaint may plead itself out of court.[19] Unless you are careful, the more facts you state, the more ammunition you may provide your adversary for a motion to dismiss. Moreover, you should develop only relevant facts. Although the complaint should tell a story, if you plead too much immaterial background information, you may ultimately try only the court's patience and not your case.[20] Finally, there must be a logical flow to the story told in the complaint: like any good story, it should have a beginning, a development, and an end. A confusing complaint will, at a minimum, irritate the judge. If the confusion seems irremediable, the complaint may be dismissed as violating Rule 8(e)'s requirement that averments be concise and direct. As the Ninth Circuit noted in *McHenry v. Renne*:[21] "Something labeled a complaint but written more as a press release, prolix in evidentiary detail, yet without simplicity, conciseness and clarity as to whom plaintiffs are suing for what wrongs, fails to perform the essential function of a complaint."

Complaints showing limitations have run on the claims alleged are perhaps the most common instances of pleaders pleading themselves out of court.[22] Complaints can also self-destruct, however, from the pleading of other matters helpful to defendants, such as allegations showing the

---

18. American Nurses' Ass'n v. State of Illinois, 783 F.2d 716, 723 (7th Cir.1986).

19. *E.g.*, Trevino v. Union Pacific Railroad Co., 916 F.2d 1230, 1234 (7th Cir. 1990).

20. McHenry v. Renne, 84 F.3d 1172, 1179 (9th Cir.1996) (stating that prolix, confusing complaints impose unfair burdens on litigants and on judges).

21. *Id.*

22. *E.g.*, Brooks v. City of Winston-Salem, North Carolina, 85 F.3d 178, 181 (4th Cir.1996); Hi–Lite Products Co. v. American Home Products Corp., 11 F.3d 1402, 1406–07 (7th Cir.1993).

existence of privileges or immunities[23] or statute of frauds defenses.[24]

There is substantial authority, with a few discordant decisions, for the proposition that plaintiffs need not anticipate the defendant's affirmative defenses in their complaints.[25] The discordant cases relate primarily to the statute of limitations defense in securities fraud cases.[26] In light of this general rule, and assuming that you have at least an arguable basis for defeating the defendant's affirmative defenses—if you do not, you should not be filing a complaint in the first place—you should reflect on whether there are any substantial reasons to plead facts in anticipation of the defendant's affirmative defenses. There may, to be sure, be such reasons. Perhaps it is impossible to tell your story coherently without setting forth facts that raise an issue of limitations or statute of frauds; perhaps you realize that the defendant's affirmative defense is a decisive one that must inevitably be addressed, and you conclude that you may as well address it at the outset of the case; or perhaps you want to "pull the sting" from the affirmative defense by presenting the critical issues relating to it from the aspect most favorable to you.

As a general rule, however, there are more and better reasons for not pleading facts in anticipation of affirmative defenses than for pleading them. First, there is the diseconomy of time and resources of provoking a motion to dismiss that might otherwise never have been filed. Second, you may tell part of the defendant's story—or give it an opportunity to tell its story in a motion to dismiss—at the outset of the case, sooner than this would otherwise have occurred, thus giving the defendant a head start in influencing the judge and setting the agenda of issues that will be dispositive in the litigation. Third, the defendant may not realize that it has such an affirmative defense. There is no need to assist the defendant in its defense. Your role is to tell *your* story.

(d) Heightened Pleading Standards

In certain circumstances, of course, the notice pleading standards of the Federal Rules give way to heightened pleading requirements. Rule 9(b) sets forth two such circumstances, namely, pleading fraud and pleading mistake. Rule 9(g) sets forth another: pleading special damages. Case law has also imposed heightened pleading requirements in other areas of the law.

The heightened pleading standard for fraud applies in several different contexts. It applies, of course, to pleading fraudulent misrepresenta-

---

23. *E.g.*, Atlantic Paper Box Co. v. Whitman's Chocolates, 844 F.Supp. 1038, 1043 (E.D.Pa.1994).

24. *E.g.*, Carter by Carter v. Cornwell, 983 F.2d 52, 54–55 (6th Cir.1993).

25. *E.g.*, Gomez v. Toledo, 446 U.S. 635, 640–41, 100 S.Ct. 1920, 1923–24, 64 L.Ed.2d, 572 (1980); Tregenza v. Great American Communications Co., 12 F.3d

717, 718–19 (7th Cir.1993); *see also* Form 9 of Appendix of Forms (noting that "[s]ince contributory negligence is an affirmative defense, the complaint need contain no allegation of due care by the plaintiff").

26. *E.g.*, Davidson v. Wilson, 973 F.2d 1391, 1402 n. 8 (8th Cir.1992).

tion as a cause of action. It also applies, however, where fraudulent concealment is pled in anticipation of the affirmative defense of the statute of limitations.[27] Moreover, more broadly, there is substantial authority for the proposition that the requirements of Rule 9(b) apply wherever the gravamen of the claim is misrepresentation even though the theory supporting the claim is not termed fraud. Thus, many courts have held that Rule 9(b)'s requirements apply to claims of negligent misrepresentation,[28] conspiracy to defraud,[29] and suits based on the False Claims Act, 31 U.S.C.A. §§ 3729–3731.[30] Rule 9(b) also applies to claims under RICO alleging mail or wire transfer as predicate acts[31] and the federal securities fraud acts. In light of this, whenever your claim involves allegations of misrepresentation you are probably safest in assuming that Rule 9(b) governs, unless you know of definitive case law holding to the contrary.

To comply with the pleading requirements of Rule 9(b), a plaintiff will usually be required to allege with reasonable particularity the statements alleged to be fraudulent, the identity of the speaker, where and when the statements were made, and why they were fraudulent.[32] Additionally, where multiple defendants are alleged to have participated in the fraud, the complaint should allege with reasonable particularity the specific role played by each defendant.[33]

Allegations of fraud generally cannot be made on "information and belief" unless (1) the matters are particularly within the defendant's knowledge and (2) facts are stated upon which the belief is founded.[34] If you must plead fraud on information and belief, you should also delineate the nature and scope of the plaintiff's efforts to obtain the information needed to plead with particularity.[35]

Pleading a defendant's mental state for purposes of a fraud claim requires considerable care. Rule 9(b) permits malice, intent, knowledge, and other conditions of mind to be averred generally. Nonetheless, many circuits require that the plaintiff, at a minimum, plead facts that give rise to a strong inference of fraudulent intent.[36] Thus, a plaintiff will be required to allege facts that establish a motive to commit fraud and an

27. *E.g.*, J. Geils Band Employee Benefit Plan v. Smith Barney Shearson, Inc., 76 F.3d 1245, 1255 (1st Cir.1996).

28. Breeden v. Richmond Community College, 171 F.R.D. 189, 199 (M.D.N.C. 1997).

29. *E.g.*, Hayduk v. Lanna, 775 F.2d 441, 443 (1st Cir.1985).

30. *E.g.*, United States *ex rel.* Stinson, Lyons, Gerlin & Bustamante, P.A. v. Blue Cross Blue Shield of Georgia, Inc., 755 F.Supp. 1055, 1058 (S.D.Ga.1990).

31. *E.g.*, Murr Plumbing, Inc. v. Scherer Brothers Financial Services Co., 48 F.3d

1066, 1069 (8th Cir.1995). *See* Chapter 69 "RICO," *infra*.

32. Acito v. IMCERA Group, Inc., 47 F.3d 47, 51 (2d Cir.1995).

33. Simon v. Castello, 172 F.R.D. 103, 106 (S.D.N.Y.1997).

34. *E.g.*, Luce v. Edelstein, 802 F.2d 49, 54 n. 1 (2d Cir.1986); Andrews v. Fitzgerald, 823 F.Supp. 356, 375 (M.D.N.C.1993).

35. Shapiro v. UJB Financial Corp., 964 F.2d 272, 285 (3d Cir.1992).

36. *E.g.*, Acito, 47 F.3d at 53.

opportunity to do so or facts constituting circumstantial evidence of either conscious or reckless misbehavior.[37]

Pleading a claim subject to Rule 9(b) can be considerably more challenging than pleading a claim subject only to Rule 8. You must expect greater judicial scrutiny of your claim subject to Rule 9(b). In this regard you should be wary of attempting to create the semblance of particularity by adding immaterial facts. Rule 9(b)'s heightened pleading standard is not an invitation to disregard Rule 8's requirements of clear and concise averments.[38] You will do well to ask yourself *why* you believe the defendant has acted fraudulently, and then to particularize in your pleading every circumstance that led you to your belief.

In addition to claims that involve or resemble fraud, other types of claims have been held subject to heightened pleading standards, either under Rule 9(b) or independently of it. Thus, several cases have required that averments of defamation be pled with particularity.[39] In accordance with these precedents, a plaintiff must plead the time, place, content, speaker, and listener of the alleged defamation.[40] Other areas of law that have been held subject to heightened pleading include antitrust, at least with respect to pleading exceptions to the *Noerr-Pennington* doctrine,[41] environmental litigation,[42] and the Federal Tort Claims Act. The impact of the *Leatherman*[43] decision, which involved a civil rights claim against a municipality but arguably has a broader import, on pleading standards in these areas of the law is not yet entirely clear. If you are pleading a claim in one of these areas you should carefully inform yourself of the latest developments.

Rule 9(g)'s requirement that "[w]hen items of special damage are claimed, they shall be specifically stated" raises the question of what is meant by "special damages." There are in fact two distinct categories of damages that have been found "special damages" subject to Rule 9(g): (1) damages that are unusual for the particular cause of action, and (2) damages that, as a matter of substantive law, are required to be pleaded as an essential element of a cause of action.

The Seventh Circuit addressed the question of "unusual damages" as "special damages" in *Avitia v. Metropolitan Club of Chicago, Inc.*:[44]

> [Special damages] are damages that are unusual for the type of claim in question–that are not the natural damages associated with such a claim.... Damages for personal injury are unusual in com-

---

37. *In re* Time Warner, Inc. Securities Litig., 9 F.3d 259, 268–69 (2d Cir.1993).

38. McHenry v. Renne, 84 F.3d 1172, 1178 (9th Cir.1996).

39. *E.g.,* Asay v. Hallmark Cards, Inc., 594 F.2d 692, 699 (8th Cir.1979); Wiggins v. Philip Morris, Inc., 853 F.Supp. 458, 465 (D.D.C.1994); Jones v. Capital Cities/ABC, Inc., 874 F.Supp. 626, 629 (S.D.N.Y.1995).

40. *E.g.,* Wiggins, 853 F.Supp. at 465.

41. Oregon Natural Resources Council v. Mohla, 944 F.2d 531, 533 (9th Cir.1991). *See* Chapter 53 "Antitrust," at § 53.7(c)(9) *infra.*

42. *See* Carl W. Tobias, *Elevated Pleading in Environmental Litigation,* 27 U.C. at Davis L. Rev. 357 (1994).

43. Discussed earlier beginning at § 5.3(b).

44. 49 F.3d 1219 (7th Cir.1995).

mercial cases, normal in tort cases; lost profits are normal in contract cases, unusual in personal injury tort cases. Perhaps emotional distress is a sufficiently unusual concomitant of wrongful discharge to bring Rule 9(g) into play.[45]

Defamation (unless the defamatory statement is defamatory per se, in which case damages are presumed) and product disparagement are examples of causes of action for which, as a matter of substantive law, damages are an essential element. This substantive law requirement is also enforced under Rule 9(g). Thus, in *Woodmont Corp. v. Rockwood Center Partnership*,[46] a defamation case, the court, invoking Rule 9(g), found a general allegation that the plaintiff's reputation had been injured insufficient and required that the plaintiff name at least one customer whose business it had lost and the amount of such loss.

The consequence of a failure to plead special damages—of either type—with specificity is that the plaintiff may be precluded from recovering such damages. Attorney's fees are a common example. Several courts have held that a failure to specifically request attorney's fees in the complaint precludes their recovery.[47]

(e) Pleading on Information and Belief

Rule 11(b)(3) alludes to the practice of pleading upon information and belief, although without using the words "information and belief"; and the Advisory Committee Notes to the 1993 amendment to Rule 11 specifically discuss such pleading, stating:

> The certification with respect to allegations and other factual contentions is revised in recognition that sometimes a litigant may have good reason to believe that a fact is true or false but may need discovery, formal or informal, from opposing parties or third persons to gather and confirm the evidentiary basis for the allegation. Tolerance of factual contentions in initial pleadings by plaintiffs or defendants when specifically identified as made on information and belief does not relieve litigants from the obligation to conduct an appropriate investigation into the facts that is reasonable under the circumstances; it is not a license to join parties, make claims, or present defenses without any factual basis or justification.

The Rules thus give qualified approval to the practice of pleading upon information and belief.

Two points merit mention with regard to this type of pleading. First, as discussed in Section 5.3(d), *supra*, many courts are reluctant to allow matters subject to heightened pleading requirements, such as allegations of fraud, to be alleged upon information and belief unless the matters are peculiarly within the defendant's knowledge and the pleader states facts upon which its belief is founded. Second, more generally, even

---

45. *Id.* at 1226.

46. 811 F.Supp. 1478, 1484 (D.Kan. 1993).

47. *E.g.* United Industries, Inc. v. Simon–Hartley, Ltd., 91 F.3d 762, 764–65 (5th Cir.1996).

under Rule 8 standards, it is improper to plead on information and belief as to matters that are within the personal knowledge of the pleader, or would be if the pleader conducted a reasonable investigation. Rule 11(b)(3) is not "a general license to plead a claim first and then ... conduct the necessary investigation in support of it."[48]

(f) Exhibits to the Complaint

Rule 10(c) provides, in its second sentence, that "[a] copy of any written instrument which is an exhibit to a pleading is a part thereof for all purposes." Although this sentence refers to "any written instrument," Rule 10(c) has been interpreted to apply more broadly to many other types of document appended as exhibits to complaints.[49]

Despite its brevity, Rule 10(c) is an important rule, for exhibits can make a complaint dramatically more effective than it might otherwise be. Under certain circumstances appending a photograph, videotape, map, or diagram to a complaint, for example, will be a good pleading tactic. The adage that a picture is worth a thousand words may be hackneyed, but it is peculiarly apt here.

While there frequently are good reasons to attach a document to a complaint, the dangers of pleading oneself out of court by doing so must also be evaluated. Instances of such self-demolition are not uncommon. In *Chester County Intermediate Unit v. Pennsylvania Blue Shield*,[50] for example, the major medical benefits policy that plaintiffs attached to the complaint was reviewed by the court and used as a basis for granting the defendant's motion to dismiss.[51] The Seventh Circuit's recent decision in *Howell v. Tribune Entertainment Co.*[52] is another interesting example. In that case, a young woman had appeared with her stepmother on a television talk show dedicated to the topic of the relationship between stepchildren and stepparents. The young woman later sued the television producer for invasion of privacy after the stepmother, during the talk show, disclosed that the young woman had been characterized in a police report as having engaged in "violent, abusive, indecent, profane, boisterous, unreasonably loud behavior." The Seventh Circuit, however, after reviewing a videotape of the program that it deemed attached to the complaint under Rule 10(c), concluded that the young woman had invited and consented to any invasion of her privacy by making certain pointed remarks about the stepmother on the talk show.

---

48. Geisinger Medical Center v. Gough, 160 F.R.D. 467, 469 (M.D.Pa.1994); *see also* Sprague Farms, Inc. v. Providian Corp., 929 F.Supp. 1125, 1130–31 (C.D.Ill.1996); Oil Express Nat'l, Inc. v. Burgstone, No. 96 C 4816, 1996 WL 666698 (N.D.Ill.1996) (Not accepting information and belief allegations for tortious interference with contract claim.).

49. *E.g.*, Howell v. Tribune Entertainment Co., et al., 106 F.3d 215, 219–20 (7th Cir.1997) (videotape); Gant v. Wallingford Board of Education, 69 F.3d 669, 671 (2d Cir.1995) (copy of investigatory report).

50. 896 F.2d 808, 812 (3d Cir.1990).

51. *See also, e.g.*, Microtel Franchise & Development Corp. v. Country Inn Hotel, 923 F.Supp. 415, 418–19 (W.D.N.Y.1996) (dismissing claim based on court's interpretation of contract attached to complaint).

52. 106 F.3d 215 (7th Cir.1997).

Whether appending an exhibit to a complaint is a good or bad tactic depends on a number of factors. One important factor is the law of your jurisdiction on whether the court may consider in connection with a motion to dismiss any document, such as a contract, prospectus, or allegedly defamatory article, on which the plaintiff's claim is based, even if the plaintiff fails to attach it to the complaint. Many, but not all, circuits permit this.[53] If you are in a jurisdiction that permits the court to consider such documents, and if the document discloses a weakness in your case, the defendant is likely to ask the court to consider it in connection with a motion to dismiss and it may make sense to attach it yourself and to attempt to deal with it preemptively. This would be especially sensible if the judge before whom you are likely to appear does not like surprises. On the other hand, if you are in a jurisdiction that does not permit the court to consider the document in ruling on a motion to dismiss and your aim is to obtain discovery before having to deal with a legal challenge to your complaint, the balance of factors probably tips toward not attaching the document.

Another consideration is surprises. Consider a scenario where you have a videotape of an incident which is the subject of the complaint, such as a complaint alleging police brutality. Do you attach the videotape to the complaint? You might, if you are concerned that the judge, jaded by exaggerated allegations in police brutality complaints, may stereotype your case. On the other hand, a better strategy might be to plead the complaint in great detail and bait the defendants into denials before they know of the existence of the videotape.

Although Rule 10(c) has been interpreted broadly to encompass documents of many types, writings such as contracts, leases, and prospectuses are undoubtedly among the most common exhibits appended to complaints under the aegis of the Rule.[54] If there is no issue of pleading oneself out of court, attaching such documents may make sense. Doing so will simplify the complaint; will get to the heart of the matter promptly; and will likely be welcomed by the judge, who will not be forced, for example, to read a claim based on a contract without having the contract itself to review.

A thought-provoking and not yet fully resolved question relating to exhibits attached to complaints concerns the degree to which they should be deemed "true" for purposes of a motion to dismiss. Given Rule 10(c)'s statement that such exhibits are part of a pleading "for all purposes," it is logical that the exhibits, like the averments in the complaint, should enjoy a presumption of truth on a motion to dismiss. Suppose, however, that the exhibit is a report that you have attached to the complaint for purposes of your own but which contains statements that exculpate the defendant. Should *all* the statements in the exhibit be deemed true? The

---

53. *E.g.*, Branch v. Tunnell, 14 F.3d 449, 453–54 (9th Cir.1994); Pension Benefit Guaranty Corp. v. White Consolidated Industries, Inc., 998 F.2d 1192, 1196 (3d Cir. 1993); Cortec Industries, Inc. v. Sum Holding L.P., 949 F.2d 42, 48 (2d Cir.1991).

54. *E.g.*, Appendix of Forms, Form 3 (attaching promissory note) and Form 12 (attaching contract to convey land).

Second Circuit recently addressed this issue in *Gant v. Wallingford Board of Education*.[55] In that case the parents of a first grade student filed suit against school officials alleging racial discrimination. The parents attached to their complaint a report by the school's superintendent, Dr. Cirasuolo, regarding the child, stating in their complaint: "The defendant, Dr. Joseph Cirasuolo, in his administrative capacity, adopted, approved, and/or ratified the actions and/or omissions of [the child's teachers]." The superintendent's report, however, concluded that the teachers had not acted improperly. The district court dismissed the parents' complaint, holding that the parents, by affirmatively pleading and adopting the conclusions of the superintendent's report, had contradicted and defeated their own claim. On appeal, however, the Second Circuit reversed, with one judge dissenting, stating:

> An appended document will be read to evidence what it incontestably shows once one assumes that it is what the complaint says it is (or, in the absence of a descriptive allegation, that it is what it appears to be). For example, a written contract appended to the complaint will defeat invocation of the Statute of Frauds, and a document that discloses what the complaint alleges it concealed will defeat the allegation of concealment. By the same token, however, a libel plaintiff may attach the writing alleged in the complaint to be libelous without risk that the court will deem true all libels in it.

> Given the allegations of the complaint that we must accept as true, the [parents] have invited us to read [the Superintendent's Report] as a self-serving document rather than a particularization of their claim. It was therefore error for the district court to assume that plaintiffs' complaint adopted the Superintendent's exculpatory conclusions.[56]

The *Gant* decision appears analytically sound. The facts that the trial court in that case dismissed the plaintiffs' claims based on the exculpatory statements in the report and that one judge on appeal would have affirmed on this ground, however, point out the dangers to plaintiffs of appending documents that contain statements helpful to the defendants.[57] You should also bear in mind in this connection that, to the degree the appended document is inconsistent with the allegations in your complaint, the document controls.[58] In *Scott v. Performance Contractors, Inc.*,[59] for example, the plaintiff in a sexual discrimination suit attached as an exhibit an EEOC document that contradicted the plaintiff's allegation that she had filed her complaint within 180 days of the alleged discriminatory practice, as 42 U.S.C.A. § 2000e–5(e) requires.

55. 69 F.3d 669 (2d Cir.1995).

56. *Id.* at 674.

57. *See also* Banco del Estado v. Navistar Int'l Transportation Corp., 942 F.Supp. 1176, 1178–80 (N.D.Ill.1996) (holding that any factual assertion in a written instrument attached to a complaint is a "judicial admission" and can be used against the plaintiff).

58. *E.g.*, Fayetteville Investors v. Commercial Builders, Inc., 936 F.2d 1462, 1465 (4th Cir.1991); Scott v. Performance Contractors, Inc., 166 F.R.D. 372, 374 (M.D.La. 1996).

59. 166 F.R.D. 372, 374 (M.D.La.1996).

The court held that the document controlled and dismissed the complaint.

One last point regarding Rule 10(c) merits mention. Although courts have permitted many types of documents to be appended under that Rule, one important exception involves affidavits. In *Rose v. Bartle*,[60] certain county employees brought civil rights and RICO actions against various county and political party officials. Two of the plaintiffs, Hill and Reed, appended to their complaint a 31–page affidavit prepared by one of the other plaintiffs, Rose. Rose had previously submitted his affidavit in support of his opposition to the defendant's motion for summary judgment. The Third Circuit refused to accept the Rose affidavit in the Hill and Reed cases as a written instrument under Rule 10(c), concluding that to do so would "blur the distinction between summary judgment and dismissal for failure to state a claim upon which relief can be granted."[61]

(g) Alternative, Hypothetical, and Inconsistent Pleading

Rule 8(e)(2) provides:

A party may set forth two or more statements of a claim or defense alternately or hypothetically, either in one count or defense or in separate counts or defenses. When two or more statements are made in the alternative and one of them if made independently would be sufficient, the pleading is not made insufficient by the insufficiency of one or more of the alternative statements. A party may also state as many separate claims or defenses as the party has regardless of consistency and whether based on legal, equitable, or maritime grounds. All statements shall be made subject to the obligations set forth in Rule 11.

A prototypical instance of pleading in the alternative is a complaint that pleads both a claim for breach of contract and a claim for unjust enrichment based on the same core facts. A plaintiff cannot, of course, recover under both theories; if there *is* an express contract, as a matter of substantive law the unjust enrichment theory is unavailable.[62] Under these circumstances a plaintiff is authorized to plead in the alternative, and inconsistently, both that there is an express contract and that, if there is not, plaintiff is entitled to recover under restitutionary principles.

A prototypical instance of pleading hypothetically is an indemnity or contribution claim: a plaintiff pleads that *if* it incurs a loss or liability, *then* the defendant is liable to it for indemnity or contribution. The plaintiff in such a hypothetical pleading must, of course, plead enough facts to show that its claim is not entirely hypothetical—*i.e.*, it must show that there is some reason to believe it will have a claim, such as a third party's assertion of a claim against the plaintiff. In *Sprague Farms,*

---

60. 871 F.2d 331, 339 n. 3 (3d Cir.1989).

61. *Id*. at 340 n. 3.

62. *E.g.*, Pilarczyk v. Morrison Knudsen Corp., 965 F.Supp. 311, 323 (N.D.N.Y. 1997).

Inc. v. Providian Corp.,[63] for example, the plaintiff alleged, with respect to a parcel of property that it owned, that *if* the property was contaminated by gasoline, *then* the defendants were responsible. The court found this hypothetical pleading insufficient, noting that "[the plaintiff] offers no reason why it could not first determine whether Parcel 3 was polluted. Third parties and opponents did not control this information—[the plaintiff] did."[64]

Despite the authority given by Rule 8(e)(2) for pleading inconsistently, you should be cautious in doing so. Some courts explicitly limit the pleading of contradictory statements of fact to instances in which the pleader is "legitimately in doubt about the facts in question."[65] Whether explicitly stated or not, such a requirement seems to follow logically from the interplay between Rule 8 and Rule 11's requirement of a reasonable investigation. Moreover, the further removed you are from the typical instances of alternative or hypothetical pleading, the more dubiously a court may look upon inconsistent factual allegations. The safest tactic, when pleading in the alternative and inconsistently in cases involving unusual claims—and perhaps all types of claims—is to invoke Rule 8(e)(2) explicitly. Thus, after pleading the first of your alternative claims in one count, consider including under your alternative count a separate paragraph that states: "This Count is pleaded in the alternative to Count ___ as permitted by FRCP 8(e)(2)." Such a paragraph may impart clarity to the pleading and prevent your adversary, or the court, from starting down the wrong path.

You should not, of course, plead inconsistent factual allegations if you are not pleading alternative claims. If your *only* claim is for unjust enrichment, an allegation that an express contract exists will be fatal to your claim. Indeed, in one case a court dismissed a plaintiff's unjust enrichment claim, which the plaintiff apparently intended as an alternative to its contract claim, because the pleader alleged the existence of the contract within the same count alleging unjust enrichment.[66] You should also be aware that inconsistent factual allegations that are not linked to alternative claims can be used as admissions against interest and for impeachment purposes.[67] By contrast, "a pleading should not be construed as an admission against another alternative or inconsistent pleading in the same case."[68]

Moreover, irrespective of what the Rules allow, inconsistent pleading exposes the pleading to misuse by opposing counsel, who will take every opportunity to suggest that the plaintiff is unsure about his case. Accordingly, inconsistent allegations should be carefully drafted.

63. 929 F.Supp. 1125 (C.D.Ill.1996).

64. *Id.* at 1131.

65. *E.g.*, American International Adjustment Co. v. Galvin, 86 F.3d 1455, 1461 (7th Cir.1996).

66. Allied Vision Group, Inc. v. RLI Professional Technologies, Inc., 916 F.Supp. 778, 782 (N.D.Ill.1996).

67. *E.g.*, Contractor Utility Sales Co. v. Certain–teed Products Corp., 638 F.2d 1061, 1084 (7th Cir.1981).

68. *E.g.*, Henry v. Daytop Village, Inc., 42 F.3d 89, 95 (2d Cir.1994).

(h) Pleading the Elements of Your Causes of Action

Nothing in the Federal Rules requires a pleader to plead all the elements of his causes of action. Moreover, such a requirement seems at odds with the liberal notice-pleading standard set forth in *Conley v. Gibson*. Nonetheless, in practice, courts do require that a complaint contain either direct or inferential allegations respecting all the material elements necessary to sustain a recovery under some viable legal theory. It is true that a pleader need not specifically identify the legal theory justifying the relief sought; identifying no legal theory or an incorrect legal theory is not fatal.[69] A federal statutory claim, for example, may be pleaded without citing the specific statute.[70] Nonetheless, a plenitude of courts have echoed the views of later Chief Justice Burger in *Daves v. Hawaiian Dredging Co.*,[71] when he stated that "if a pleader cannot allege definitely and in good faith the existence of an essential element of his claim, it is difficult to see why this basic deficiency should not be exposed at the point of minimum expenditure of time and money by the parties and the court."

In light of this, you should take pains to identify all the elements of your causes of action and to plead facts in support of each element or satisfy the element by information and belief pleading, if necessary. Such an analytical exercise is helpful in any event, even if it were not required by pleading rules. At some point you must prove all the elements of your causes of action, and the sooner you become aware of any weak links in your claim, the better.

Library References:

West's Key No. Digests, Federal Civil Procedure ☞671–717.
Wright & Miller, Federal Practice and Procedure: Civil 2d §§ 1202, 1203, 1206.

§ 5.4   Style and Organization

(a) Style

Rigid rules are probably not appropriate in matters of style, for no sooner are they formulated then some creative rebel bends or breaks them to good effect. With that preface, however, here are a few words on the topic.

More often than not, a "lean and mean" writing style, for complaints as well as motions and memoranda, is most effective. Such a style is consistent with Rule 8(e)(1)'s directive that averments be concise and direct, but would be the proper style even without the Rule. Avoid the use of unnecessary adjectives and adverbs. They may well be accurate, but if they are unduly pejorative or exaggerated they are often counterproductive. Stick with the unvarnished facts; use nouns and verbs; and

---

69. *E.g.*, Bartholet v. Reishauer A. G (Zurich), 953 F.2d 1073, 1078 (7th Cir. 1992).

70. *E.g.*, Martin v. Deiriggi, 985 F.2d 129, 135 (4th Cir.1992).

71. 114 F.Supp. 643, 645 (D.Haw.1953).

let the reader draw the characterizations. Avoid the word "clearly" as you would poison. If you have not made your point, adding the word "clearly" will not achieve clarity.

Watch out for passive voice and legalisms like "heretofore." The complaint is, of course, a formal document, but need not be stiff and decorous. It can be lean but fresh and agile. If you make every word count, you will throw out legalisms.

If your filing deadline allows time, set aside your complaint for a few days after you have drafted it. A little distance from your complaint may bring unnoticed flaws into view. For the same reason, if time permits, show your complaint to a person unfamiliar with the matters in the complaint. After that person has read it, ask a few questions to see how well he or she understood the complaint or what impression it made. If your reviewer finds it boring, confusing, or unconvincing, you may have some work to do.

(b) Organization

One structure that is usually effective in the organization of a complaint has nine components, in addition to a signature page: Caption, Parties, Venue, Jurisdiction, Introduction, Facts Common to All Counts, Counts, Demand for Judgment and Request for Relief, and Demand for Jury Trial (if one is demanded). Each of these components is discussed below.

(1) Caption and Title

Rule 10(a) requires that the caption set forth the name of the court, title of the action, file number, and nature of the pleading. There are different ways that this information can be organized in the caption; the captions in the official forms show the way it is commonly done. Unlike subsequent papers, in the complaint all the parties must be named; "et al." cannot be used. In addition, many local rules require that the addresses of all parties be stated in the complaint's caption.

(2) Jurisdiction

Rule 8(a)(1) requires the complaint to contain allegations setting forth the grounds upon which the court's jurisdiction depends. To the extent a court's jurisdiction depends on the existence of certain facts, you should plead those facts. A complaint without these allegations is subject to dismissal. The topic of jurisdiction is discussed in depth in Chapter 1 "Subject Matter Jurisdiction," *supra*.

(3) Venue

Since improper venue is an affirmative defense, it is not necessary for the plaintiff to include allegations showing venue to be proper.[1] It is

---

§ 5.4   F.Supp. 411, 412 (D.D.C.1991).

1. *See* Notes to Form 2 of Appendix of Forms; S.E.C. v. Ernst & Young, 775

nonetheless a good practice to do so. Venue, like jurisdiction, is a question the parties and the court will want definitely ascertained at the outset of the litigation to avoid the needless waste of time and resources resulting from bringing a case in the wrong court.

(4) Parties

If your complaint is based on diversity jurisdiction, you will need to identify the state of residence of all individual parties and the place of incorporation and principal place of business of all corporate defendants. For this reason, most circuits do not permit the inclusion of "John Doe"—*i.e.*, unknown—defendants in diversity actions.[2]

Plaintiffs are allowed to use fictional names under limited circumstances. The test is whether the plaintiff has a substantial privacy right, such as that of a child protesting compulsory religious observances at the child's public school, that outweighs the presumption of openness in judicial proceedings.[3]

Issues concerning parties are addressed in depth in Chapter 14, "Parties," *infra*.

(5) Introduction

A short introduction can greatly assist your audience in understanding the complaint. Like an abbreviated version of the opening statement in a trial, an introduction can state a theme or structure for organizing the information that follows. It gives you an opportunity to begin educating your reader to your point of view from the outset, when the reader's attention is probably well-focused.

(6) Facts Common to All Counts

This section of the complaint tells the plaintiff's story. If there are many different claims and parties, facts specific to a particular claim or defendant may appropriately be discussed within the count relating to that claim or defendant. In general, however, it is a good idea to include as many of the facts as possible in this common facts section, if those facts are common to all counts.

If the facts set forth in this section are lengthy, involve many persons, or involve events distinct in time and place, the use of subheadings is appropriate. Like chapters in a book or acts in a play, these subheadings enhance the coherence and readability of the complaint.

(7) Counts

Rule 10(b), in its second sentence, provides that "[e]ach claim founded upon a separate transaction or occurrence . . . shall be stated in a separate count . . . whenever a separation facilitates the clear presentation of the matter set forth." Although this Rule requires separate counts for claims based on separate transactions or occurrences, it does

---

2. *E.g.*, Howell v. Tribune Entertainment Co., 106 F.3d 215, 218 (7th Cir.1997).

3. *E.g.*, Doe v. Stegall, 653 F.2d 180, 186 (5th Cir. Unit A 1981).

not require separate counts for different theories based on the same transaction or occurrence. Nonetheless, it is a good practice to plead different theories based on the same facts in different counts.

For clarity, it is helpful to put in parentheses under the count caption a brief description of the claim and, if there are multiple defendants, a designation of which defendant the claim is directed against. For example:

COUNT I

(BREACH OF CONTRACT CLAIM AGAINST DEFENDANT ALPHA CORPORATION)

The allegations under the particular count set forth the elements of the claim. Given that the first paragraph under each count will incorporate by reference all (or a designated portion) of the Facts Common to All Counts, this pleading of the elements can be done briefly—assuming, of course, that in the Facts Common to All Counts the necessary facts have been set forth in support of each element. In addition, facts that may be specific to that particular claim or defendant may be set forth within the count, as opposed to in the Facts Common to All Counts section.

(8) *Demand for Judgment and Request for Relief*

A complaint is incomplete and subject to dismissal if it does not demand judgment and request relief. This can be done after each count, or at the end of the complaint in a single section as to all counts. Both ways of demanding judgment and requesting relief are common.

There is no requirement that a specific amount be requested when seeking damages, but if the basis of jurisdiction is diversity, you will want to state that you are seeking more than $75,000, exclusive of interest and costs, or state facts that support such an inference. Moreover, bear in mind that if you are fortunate enough to obtain a default judgment, your damages will be limited to what you plead. Under Rule 54(c), "[a] judgment by default shall not be different in kind from or exceed in amount that prayed for in the demand for judgment."

(9) *Demand for Jury Trial*

Under Rule 38(b), a jury trial demand need not be part of the complaint; it need only be served upon the other party in writing not later than 10 days after the service of the "last pleading directed to such issue." If you know while drafting your complaint that you want a jury trial, however, an appropriate place to put your demand is after the body of your complaint and before the signature line.

Library References:

West's Key No. Digests, Federal Civil Procedure ⊙=621–665, 671–717.
Wright & Miller, Federal Practice and Procedure: Civil 2d § 1202.

§ 5.5 Amendments to Complaints

(a) Reasons for Amending Complaints

Complaints are amended for many reasons. Some of these reasons are consistent with good litigation strategy; some, by contrast, impair credibility or do greater harm. Some of the more significant reasons, good and bad, for amending a complaint are discussed below.

A sound tactical reason for amending a complaint might arise where you believe that it may be possible to settle the case early in the litigation. On these facts and assuming no limitations issue, filing a complaint that does not contain all the claims available to the plaintiff— leaving out the civil RICO claim, for example—may make sense. Adding such claims could terminate any settlement dialogue. If the settlement discussions go nowhere, the complaint may be amended to add the other available claims. A similar tactic may be appropriate with respect to claims against multiple parties; you may want to file the initial complaint against only one wrongdoer, serving copies on the others and amending if settlement discussions are unproductive. This tactic of phased escalation, however, makes most sense when the amended complaint containing all available claims or parties can be filed before the defendant's responsive pleading is served, for until then, under Rule 15(a), the plaintiff need not seek leave of court to amend. If a plaintiff at a later phase of the litigation, such as after discovery has been completed, seeks to add claims or parties that were available from the outset, the court may deny leave to amend.

Another reason for amending a complaint may be to respond to a defendant's motion to dismiss. Usually a memorandum in opposition is the appropriate response. If, however, the motion to dismiss is based on a defect in the complaint that cannot be argued away but can easily be corrected, the best response may be to amend the complaint. Do not try this tactic too often, however, in the same case. If the defendant moves to dismiss three times and you respond each time with a new amended complaint, the court not surprisingly may suspect that you failed to take proper care in investigating and pleading the complaint initially and that you have unfairly given the defendant a constantly moving target for its motions.

Another reason for amending your complaint may be to add matters that occurred after the complaint was filed. Strictly speaking, this is not amendment but supplementation of a complaint in accordance with Rule 15(d). The courts, however, have not regarded this distinction as important, and the standards are essentially the same for supplementation and amendment.[1]

---

§ 5.5

1. *E.g.*, Ford Motor Co. v. United States, 896 F.Supp. 1224, 1230–31 n. 3 (Ct.   Int'l Trade 1995).

The most common reason for amending a complaint, of course, is simply that, through discovery or by other means, you have learned important facts not known when the complaint was filed. Perhaps discovery has uncovered facts showing that what you believed to be the defendant's negligence was actually an intentional act, justifying the pleading of an intentional tort and a request for punitive damages. Perhaps newly discovered facts disclose the identity of an entity equally responsible with the defendant for the wrongdoing alleged in the complaint. On the other hand, newly learned facts may lead you to conclude that some of your claims cannot be supported and you may wish to dismiss them.

An inappropriate reason for amending the complaint is also probably a common one: a failure to conduct an adequate legal and factual investigation before filing the complaint. It is unwise to assume that the Federal Rules' liberality in allowing amendments to complaints can save a lack of diligent investigation before filing a complaint. Amending a complaint once or twice is not uncommon and not many judges will be irritated by doing so. After a fourth or fifth amended complaint, however, the court's patience may be at an end. Moreover, each superseded complaint can be used for impeachment purposes to the extent it contains factual averments inconsistent with the operative complaint.

(b) Pleading Rules

The matters discussed in Sections 5.3 and 5.4, *supra*, generally apply as well to amended complaints, with minor differences. The caption of the amended complaint, of course, should identify it as an amended complaint by number (*e.g.*, "First Amended Complaint"). Under many local rules, a redlined copy of the original complaint, marked up to show the changes made, must accompany the amended complaint.

A shortcut to pleading an amended complaint is to incorporate by reference all of the prior complaint that has not been amended. Such incorporation by reference is authorized by Rule 10(c). The temptation to take this shortcut, however, should be resisted. It is much more convenient for everyone to have one operative document, rather than two documents that must be collated.

(c) Procedure for Obtaining Leave to Amend

Under Rule 15(a), a plaintiff may file an amended complaint: (1) before a responsive pleading has been served; (2) with the written consent of the adverse party; or (3) with leave of court. The Rule does not prescribe a time limit for the filing of amendments. Consequently, motions for leave to amend have been granted at various stages of litigation, including after the entry of judgment.[2]

---

2. *E.g.*, Newark Branch, NAACP v. Harrison, New Jersey, 907 F.2d 1408, 1417 (3d Cir.1990).

The first basis for filing of an amended complaint—that it is filed prior to the defendant's filing of a responsive pleading—is considered amendment as a matter of right. Only one such amendment is permitted. Note that there is substantial authority for the proposition that a motion to dismiss is not considered a responsive pleading for purposes of Rule 15(a).[3] The second basis requires consent by the other party in writing. In certain situations, however, consent may be implied—as, for instance, when the defendant files a responsive pleading that does not object to the amendment.[4]

Leave of court is the third basis for filing an amended complaint. When requesting leave of court, a motion should be filed that explains with particularity the reasons for the amendment and the proposed amended complaint itself should be attached. Although oral motions for leave to amend are sometimes permitted, the usual course is to file a written motion. The Supreme Court has enumerated several factors that are given weight by the court in the exercise of their discretion on a motion for leave to amend: (1) undue delay; (2) bad faith; (3) dilatory motive; (4) repeated failure to remedy problems in the complaint; (5) undue prejudice; and (6) futility.[5] Courts also consider the effect denial of leave to amend would have on the plaintiff, the reasons for plaintiff's failure to include or delete information earlier, and possible injustice to third parties. There is a strong bias toward granting motions for leave to amend.[6] Rule 15(a) itself directs that leave to amend "shall be freely given when justice so requires."

Bear in mind that there is authority for the proposition that the court has the power to accept all or only part of the proposed amendment and, if warranted, may impose conditions to ensure that any deleterious effects of the amendment are mitigated. These conditions may include assessing fees, allocating costs, allowing additional discovery, and delaying trial dates.[7] Note also that the filing of an amended complaint including more than technical changes provides the defendant with the opportunity to withdraw its original answer and replead.

Library References:

West's Key No. Digests, Federal Civil Procedure ⊂→821–853.
Wright & Miller, Federal Practice and Procedure: Civil 2d § 1207.

§ 5.6   Complaints for Injunctive Relief

This section discusses the requirements and strategies associated with filing a complaint seeking injunctive relief in federal court.

3. *E.g.*, Doe v. United States, 58 F.3d 494, 497 (9th Cir.1995); Fortner v. Thomas, 983 F.2d 1024, 1032 (11th Cir.1993).

4. *See* FRCP 15(b).

5. *See* Foman v. Davis, 371 U.S. 178, 182, 83 S.Ct. 227, 230, 9 L.Ed.2d 222 (1962).

6. *Id.*

7. *E.g.*, Hayden v. Feldman, 159 F.R.D. 452, 454 (D.C.N.Y.1995); Chicago Pneumatic Tool Co. v. Hughes Tool Co., 192 F.2d 620, 631 (10th Cir.1951).

(a) Tactical Considerations

The essence of the decision on whether to seek injunctive relief perhaps is best summed up in the following rough wisdom: "if you are going to fire the shot, make sure it strikes the target." An injunctive action, be it both a temporary restraining order and preliminary injunction request or just a preliminary injunction request, is an aggressive step. If injunctive relief is granted, a quick and often important victory is won. If this initial strike fails, however, it can be damaging, and recovery can be difficult. The notion that the complaint, like an opening statement, creates either a positive or negative first impression and establishes a sense of the equities of a dispute in the eyes of attorneys, parties, and the court applies with even greater force when the complaint is accompanied by a demand for swift restrictive action against the defendants. On at least the level of "likelihood of success on the merits," the final outcome of the dispute is debated in a preliminary, somewhat general fashion at the very outset of the process—even before any discovery has been conducted in the case of a temporary restraining order. Little seems to be accomplished by firing the injunction shot if it won't hit the target. Telling the court injunctive action is necessary and having the court disagree can become the legal equivalent of "crying wolf."

Given the heightened consequences attaching to a complaint for injunctive relief, alternatives merit consideration. The primary purpose of a temporary restraining order or preliminary injunction action is to maintain the status quo and to avoid further potential injury while the ultimate merits of the dispute are addressed. As the plaintiff's counsel your first question should be whether maintenance of the status quo or some acceptable alternative arrangement can be accomplished by agreement through negotiations with the potential defendants so that the risks inherent in seeking an injunction can be avoided. This requires a judgment call. In some instances, a plaintiff may spend a tremendous amount of time and money marshaling evidence to rush into court and demand an injunction when a telephone call to defense counsel may have accomplished much the same thing. Moreover, if the telephone call is made and is unsuccessful, the plaintiff at times can use the fact that overtures of compromise were rebuffed to advantage before the court by showing that reasonable alternatives were pursued before troubling the court with an emergency request. In other instances, a telephone call in advance likely would be futile and thus serves only to give the opposition advance notice and a greater opportunity to prepare. Timing issues, strategic considerations, or the sensitive nature of the dispute may be such that better judgment suggests that an injunction from the court, and its attendant deterrent effect, is essential.

The nature of the injunction sought also deserves some thought. The more reasonable the relief sought, the more likely it will succeed. For instance, injunctive actions frequently involve efforts to enforce covenants not to compete or to prevent trade secret violations. Often, such cases require the plaintiff to request that the defendant be prevented from working at a new employment. If that is what is necessary to protect the trade secrets or noncompete, then it must be sought. In other instances, however, the plaintiff's rights might be protectible without depriving the defendant completely of a right to work while the merits are addressed. Such alternative restrictions should be considered, even if only as "Plan B," as being distinctly preferable to no injunctive relief at all.

(b) Pleading Rules

Injunctions are governed by Rule 65 and the applicable case law. Injunctions generally are the subject of Chapter 14, "Provisional Remedies," *infra*. The focus of this section is confined to the special considerations that influence how an injunctive action should be pled in the complaint. Notice to the adverse party of a temporary restraining order hearing is a matter that may need to be addressed in the complaint. Rule 65(b) provides that "[a] temporary restraining order may be granted without written or oral notice to the adverse party or that party's attorney only if (1) it clearly appears from specific facts shown by affidavit or by the verified complaint that immediate and irreparable injury, loss, or damage will result to the applicant before the adverse party or that party's attorney can be heard in opposition, and (2) the applicant's attorney certifies to the court in writing the efforts, if any, which have been made to give the notice and the reasons supporting the claim that notice should not be required." Given the time pressures in filing a complaint and motion for temporary restraining order and preliminary injunction, a supporting affidavit in some instances may seem duplicative and just extra paper where the same purpose can be accomplished by filing a verified complaint. When this is done, if time for notice does not exist, Rule 65(b) must be satisfied by the pleading. Having said this, where the supporting affidavit can be much shorter and more straightforward than the complaint itself, a separate affidavit probably is warranted for clarity's sake.

The complaint seeking injunctive relief should include sufficient factual detail to impress upon the court on quick reading that intervention is warranted. Bare conclusory allegations that the plaintiff is likely to prevail on the merits, that the balance of inconveniences to the parties supports entry of the injunction, that irreparable harm likely will result if an injunction is not entered, that damages will be difficult to ascertain with reasonable certainty, and that the public interest is best served by injunctive action do not accomplish the plaintiff's pleading requirements. Facts supporting these inferences should be included both in the complaint and in the memorandum in support of the motion for injunction and should be supported by verification of the complaint or by affidavit.

(c) Organization

The internal organization or format of a complaint for injunctive relief should follow the pattern described in Section 5.3, *supra*, with a few possible exceptions. The setting forth of the prayer for relief in an injunctive action often can become complicated and contain several different requested forms of relief, some containing sub-parts. Separate enumeration of the distinct requests for relief thus is recommended, as discussed further below in Section 5.6(d). As discussed in Section 5.6(d), *infra*, a complaint for injunctive relief often will be verified; a separate verification at the end of the complaint thus must be included.

(d) Drafting Considerations

The same drafting considerations applicable to any complaint apply to an injunctive claim, but perhaps with greater urgency. For instance, a short introductory section summing up the essence of the complaint is highly recommended, as the judge considering the dispute may not have much time to review the papers before hearing argument and deciding whether an injunction should be entered. Establishing the proper context for that decision-making process is crucial.

As to the appropriate amount of factual detail to include in the complaint seeking injunctive relief, a tension exists between competing interests. Brevity has its value given the hurried conditions under which the complaint may initially be considered. Moreover, given that the complaint often must be prepared in rushed circumstances, the potential for including incorrect or unsupportable information increases as the level of detail increases. By contrast, however, if facts support the claim and need for immediate court intervention, they should not be ignored, because it is essential that the injunction be won. The best compromise probably is to include all helpful facts, but with a premium on concise wording and directness.

The prayer for relief in an injunctive complaint raises special concerns. Frequently, the "wherefore" clause of each claim will seek many different forms of relief, be it compensatory damages, specific performance, declaratory judgment, or injunctive restrictions. The last of these often will involve several subsections. In the interest of clarity and distinctness, it is recommended that the prayer for relief separately set forth in block form, using separate sections and subsections, the relief requested. An example is set forth below:

WHEREFORE, plaintiff ABC Corporation respectfully requests that this Court:

    A.   Enter a judgment in favor of ABC Corporation and against defendants XYZ Corporation and Mr. Z in an amount to be determined at trial, but in excess of $75,000, to compensate ABC Corporation for any losses proximately caused by the defendants' breaches, to the extent such losses are reasonably capable of calculation;

B. Specifically enforce the defendant Mr. Z's obligations under the terms of his noncompetition agreement and order Mr. Z to cease and desist from any and all efforts to solicit ABC Corporation employees, use ABC Corporation trade secrets or confidential information, or otherwise compete with ABC Corporation in violation of his agreement;

C. Enter an injunction, preliminary until a hearing on the merits and then permanent, that:

1. Enjoins defendant Mr. Z and his new company, XYZ Corporation, from soliciting or contacting for business purposes ABC employees;

2. Enjoins defendants Mr. Z and his company, XYZ Corporation, from revealing or otherwise using ABC Corporation trade secrets or confidential information, including, but not limited to, ABC training materials, ABC documents, ABC software or computer records, ABC pricing information, ABC client lists, or ABC programs and processes;

3. Enjoins defendant Mr. Z from competing with ABC Corporation through his employment with XYZ Corporation or otherwise during the pendency of his one-year period of noncompetition, to be calculated from the date of injunction;

D. Grant ABC Corporation the costs of this action, including reasonable attorneys' fees, and such other and further relief as this Court deems just and appropriate.

This format, with a few wording changes, then can be incorporated directly into the proposed Order granting the requested injunction. This consistency of form avoids confusion. It also allows the court to grant some of the proposed relief and excise those few passages that are not to be granted. You may note that subsection A, dealing with the request for compensatory damages, does not seek a particular amount and adds a qualifier: " . . . to the extent such losses are reasonably capable of calculation." This is in recognition of the tension between proving damages and arguing, for injunctive purposes, that an injunction is necessary because money damages ultimately will not be an adequate remedy since damages are not reasonably capable of calculation. This qualifier does not indicate damages are not quantifiable to any extent, only that "damages" as a classification will have some uncertainty; in most injunctive cases, there are some damages that are calculable and others that are not.

Library References:

West's Key No. Digests, Injunction ⚷116.
Wright, Miller & Kane, Federal Practice and Procedure: Civil 2d §§ 2942, 2962.

§ 5.7 Complaints for Declaratory Judgment

(a) Reasons for Seeking Declaratory Judgments

Speed and economy are two excellent reasons for seeking a declaratory judgment, if the elements for such an action are present. As the Advisory Committee Notes to Rule 57 state, "[i]nasmuch as [a declaratory judgment action] often involves only an issue of law on undisputed or relatively undisputed facts, it operates frequently as a summary proceeding." Moreover, Rule 57 expressly authorizes a court to order a speedy hearing of an action for declaratory judgment and to advance it on the calendar. In light of this, you will do well in drafting your complaint to examine your dispute with a view to determining whether you can isolate a decisive issue of law that needs few or no factual determinations for its resolution. If you can do so, use of the declaratory judgment procedure could lead to a quick and relatively inexpensive resolution of the dispute.

The declaratory judgment procedure is also a means by which, under some circumstances, a party in a defensive posture can take the offensive. This may be advantageous for many reasons, including, public relations, and framing of the issues. In this regard, however, you must be sensitive to the wealth of authority prohibiting the use of declaratory judgment procedure to anticipate defenses and to deprive the real plaintiff of its traditional choice of forum and timing.[1] The court in *State Farm Fire & Casualty Company v. Taylor* struck the balance on this question as follows:

> On the one hand, the person who may be entitled to coercive relief has traditional interest in choice of forum, timing, and avoiding a race to the courthouse. On the other hand, if the person who may be entitled to coercive relief does not bring an action, the other party has an interest in being relieved from uncertainty and insecurity arising from the controversy.[2]

(b) Pleading Rules

Rule 57 expressly provides that the procedure for obtaining a declaratory judgment shall be in accordance with the rules of civil procedure. The pleading requirements for complaints seeking declaratory relief, therefore, are the same as those for civil actions. Against that background, however, the following points merit emphasis.

(1) Pleading Jurisdiction

The Declaratory Judgment Act and Rule 57 are procedural only and are not grants of jurisdiction. A complaint seeking a declaratory judg-

1. *E.g.*, Hanes Corp. v. Millard, 531 F.2d 585, 592–93 (D.C.Cir.1976); State Farm Fire & Casualty Co. v. Taylor, 118 F.R.D. 426, 430 (M.D.N.C.1988). *See supra* Chapter 3 "Venue, Forum Selection and Transfer," at § 3.10(c).

2. Taylor, 118 F.R.D. at 430.

ment in federal court, therefore, must plead a basis for federal jurisdiction—diversity or federal question—just as any other civil action. In declaratory judgment cases, the well-pleaded complaint rule dictates that federal question jurisdiction is determined by whether federal question jurisdiction would exist over the presumed suit by the declaratory judgment defendant.[3] Thus, in federal question cases, the declaratory judgment plaintiff's complaint must provide sufficient information for a court to determine what claims would have been brought by the declaratory judgment defendant if it had brought suit as a plaintiff.

(2) Notice Pleading

Pleadings in declaratory judgment actions are subject to the same rules of notice pleading as all other actions.[4]

(3) Actual Controversy

In all cases arising under the Declaratory Judgment Act, the threshold question is whether there exists an "actual controversy" sufficient to satisfy constitutional "case and controversy" requirements.[5] Whether such a controversy exists must be determined on a case-by-case basis.[6] It is beyond the scope of this chapter to explore all the factual variations that lead to one conclusion or the other on the existence of an actual controversy. The Seventh Circuit's decision in *Highsmith v. Chrysler Credit Corp.*,[7] however, bears mention as an illustration of allegations that do not support a conclusion of actual controversy. In that case the plaintiff sought a declaratory judgment that an early termination provision in his car lease with Chrysler Credit Corporation violated the Consumer Leasing Act and other statutes. The plaintiff, however, alleged neither that he had terminated the lease nor that he intended to terminate it. On such allegations the Seventh Circuit held that no actual controversy existed.

(4) The Borchard Criteria

A multitude of cases have quoted with approval the criteria set forth by Professor Edward Borchard at page 299 of his classic treatise *Declaratory Judgments* 299 (2d ed. 1941) as justifying a declaratory judgment: (1) that the judgment will serve a useful purpose in clarifying and settling the legal relations at issue; and (2) that the judgment will terminate and afford relief from the uncertainty, insecurity, and controversy giving rise to the proceeding.[8] In pleading a declaratory judgment complaint, therefore, you should take pains to plead facts showing that these criteria will be satisfied by the declaratory judgment that you seek.

3. *E.g.*, GNB Battery Technologies, Inc. v. Gould, Inc., 65 F.3d 615, 619 (7th Cir. 1995).

4. *Id.* at 620.

5. *E.g.*, Atlanta Gas Light Co. v. Aetna Casualty & Surety Co., 68 F.3d 409, 414 (11th Cir.1995).

6. *E.g.*, Maryland Casualty Co. v. Pacific Coal & Oil Co., 312 U.S. 270, 273, 61 S.Ct. 510, 512, 85 L.Ed. 826 (1941).

7. 18 F.3d 434 (7th Cir.1994).

8. *E.g.*, State Farm Fire & Casualty Co. v. Mhoon, 31 F.3d 979, 983 n. 5 (10th Cir.1994).

Library References:

West's Key No. Digests, Declaratory Judgment ☞311–329.
Wright, Miller, Kane & Cooper, Federal Practice and Procedure: Civil 2d §§ 1238, 1406, 1616, 2313, 2751, 4446.

§ 5.8   Filing Issues

(a) Filing of Complaint Commences Civil Action

Rule 3 establishes one uniform manner of commencing a civil action in federal court: filing a complaint with the court. An action is not commenced by service of process under Rule 4.[1] Similarly, an amended complaint becomes effective on the date it is filed with the court.[2]

(b) What Constitutes Filing

Rule 5(e) defines filing with the court. The most common method of filing a complaint pursuant to Rule 5 is delivery to the clerk of the court. A complaint, however, may be filed with the judge if the judge allows, and may be filed by electronic means if local rules allow.

(c) After–Hours Filing

Be aware that local rules and practices regarding after-hours filing— *i.e.*, filing after the clerk's office closes, usually at 5:00 p.m.—differ significantly. Many district court clerk's offices have drop boxes for after-hours filing. Some clerk's offices, however, do not have such drop boxes or any other provision for after-hours filing. If you find yourself needing to file your complaint in a district with no provision for after-hours filing, and it's 8:00 p.m. on the day before the statute of limitations expires, you may be forced to such desperate measures as trying to find the personal residence of the clerk. Although such measures might succeed,[3] they are not good practice, and undoubtedly are not welcomed by clerks.

Moreover, even among districts that do provide after-hours drop boxes, practices differ as to what date will be stamped on the pleading deposited in the box. In some districts, if you place your complaint in the drop box at, for example, 1:00 a.m. on January 10, the complaint will still be date-stamped the prior day, January 9. By contrast, in some other districts, if you place your complaint in the drop box at 5:30 p.m. on January 9, it will be date-stamped the next day, January 10. There is authority for the proposition that this latter practice is improper,[4] but

---

§ 5.8

1. Howell v. Tribune Entertainment Co., 106 F.3d 215, 217 (7th Cir.1997).

2. Donner v. Sulcus Computer Corp., 103 F.R.D. 548, 549 (N.D.Ga.1984).

3. *See* Greeson v. Sherman, 265 F.Supp. 340 (D.Va.1967) (allowing filing of com-

plaint with clerk at clerk's residence at night).

4. Greenwood v. State of New York Office of Mental Health, 842 F.2d 636, 639–39 (2d Cir.1988).

the last thing you want to do is create an appellate issue at the very commencement of your suit. The lesson here is to know your local rules and practice, and if you are filing in a district with which you are unfamiliar, engage local counsel.

(d) Payment of Filing Fees

The circuits are split on whether a complaint filed without payment of the filing fee commences the action. Moreover, there is no conformity among the district courts as to the amount of the filing fee. These two circumstances may create a trap for the unwary: in some districts, you may find your complaint not accepted for filing simply because you accompanied your complaint with a check in the wrong amount.[5] Such things should not happen to attentive attorneys, and will not happen to you if you know your local rules and practice and, when necessary, engage local counsel.

(e) Relationship of Filing to Tolling of Statutes of Limitation.

You should not uncritically assume that the filing of your complaint will toll the applicable statutes of limitation on your causes of action, for there are two sets of circumstances in which this may not occur. The first is where you have alleged a claim under a statute that has specific provisions regarding what actions, in addition to filing, must be taken to stop limitations.[6] The second is where you have alleged state law claims and federal diversity jurisdiction. In this case state, not federal law, determines what constitutes commencement of an action for purposes of tolling the statute of limitations,[7] and under the law of some states, unlike federal law under Rule 3, a complaint is not deemed filed until it is both delivered to the clerk's office and served on the defendant.[8]

Library References:

West's Key No. Digests, Federal Civil Procedure ⏇664.
Wright, Miller, Kane, Marcus & Cooper, Federal Practice and Procedure: Civil 2d
     §§ 1055, 1141–1153, 1346, 1509, 2119, 2611, 3079.3, 3949.1, 3963, 3971.1,
     3976.1, 3977.

§ 5.9   Impact of Local Rules

As has been mentioned at various stages throughout this chapter, local rules and conventions must be heeded in drafting any complaint. Failure to follow the course mandated or expected by the local rules runs

---

5. *Compare* Wanamaker v. Columbian Rope Co., 713 F.Supp. 533, 538 (N.D.N.Y. 1989) (action not commenced without payment of fee) *with* Johnson v. Brown, 803 F.Supp. 1414, 1418–19 (N.D.Ind.1992) (action commenced despite no payment).

6. *E.g.*, 8 U.S.C.A. § 1451(a) (Immigration and Nationality Act; affidavit showing good cause necessary in revocation proceeding).

7. Henderson v. United States, 517 U.S. 654, 657 n. 2, 116 S.Ct. 1638, 1641 n. 2, 134 L.Ed.2d 880, 886 n. 2 (1996).

8. *Id.*

the risk of being perceived as lack of care or respect for the tribunal and its standards. It also can label the attorney, and by implication, the client, an "outsider." These considerations reinforce the importance of selecting local counsel who is competent, well-versed in the local rules and practices, and familiar with the clerk's office and the judges on the bench.

It is not the province of this chapter to identify every local rule that might impact the drafter of the complaint. The core message is that local rules can set traps for the unwary. Before filing the complaint, whenever possible, obtain a copy of the local rules and review them thoroughly to make certain anything that might impact the drafting and filing of the complaint has been given full consideration. And, yes, this advice applies even if you are an experienced practitioner dealing with your local federal bench. It is always surprising how frequently a review of the Federal Rules and local rules before filing a new complaint brings to attention some provision that had not been pertinent in past cases.

Library References:

West's Key No. Digests, Federal Civil Procedure ⊂⟩621–1150.
Wright, Miller, Marcus & Cooper, Federal Practice and Procedure: Civil 2d §§ 3151, 3153–3155, 3993.

§ 5.10 Practice Checklist

1. Have you determined the target audience or audiences for your complaint?
   - client
   - defendants
   - judge
   - third parties such as insurers or indemnitors of the defendants
   - media and the public
   - jury

   (*See* § 5.2(a))

2. Have you reviewed the factors that favor a factually developed complaint?
   - establishes equities of the dispute
   - enhances settlement value
   - has public relations value
   - anticipates an inevitable motion to dismiss
   - ferrets out the defense through the answer

   (*See* § 5.2(b))

3. Have you reviewed the factors that favor a brief and general complaint?
   - cost and efficiency

- avoids broad discovery
- avoids tipping your hand
- certain information may be unavailable
- avoids certain Rule 11 burdens
- impact of relation back rule
- avoids potential collateral estoppel pitfalls

(*See* § 5.2(c))

4. Have you considered checking the "related case" box on the civil cover sheet? (*See* § 5.2(d))

5. Have you considered filing similar complaints in state and federal court to avoid limitations concerns? (*See* § 5.2(e))

6. Have you complied with Rule 11's requirement of a factual investigation reasonable under the circumstances? (*See* § 5.3(a) and Chapter 48)

7. Are your legal contentions warranted by existing law or a nonfrivolous argument for extension, modification, or reversal of existing law? (*See* § 5.3(a) and Chapter 48)

8. Have you avoided all knowingly false allegations in your complaint? (*See* § 5.3(a) and Chapter 48)

9. If you are pleading a "bare bones" complaint, have you checked the Appendix of Official Forms for examples of short and simple complaints? (*See* § 5.3(b))

10. Have you checked your circuit's case law to see to what degree strict notice pleading has been qualified by requirements of "well-pleaded facts?" (*See* § 5.3(b))

11. To the degree possible, have you determined any fact-pleading predilections of the judge who may read your complaint? (*See* § 5.3(b))

12. Do the facts you plead support the legal conclusions—*e.g.*, negligence, breach of fiduciary duty—that you plead? (*See* § 5.3(b))

13. Have you avoided pleading the effect of a legal document as though it were a fact? (*See* § 5.3(b))

14. If you are pleading a factually developed complaint, have you alleged facts that "plead yourself out of court" by showing:
    - a statute of limitation defense?
    - that the defendant has a privilege or immunity?
    - a statute of frauds defense?
    - waiver or consent by the plaintiff?
    - other affirmative defenses? (*See* § 5.3(c))

15. Have you checked whether your case is one of the rare cases in which you should plead facts in anticipation of the defendant's affirmative defenses? (*See* § 5.3(c))

16. Do heightened pleading standards apply to any of the causes of action in your complaint? Specifically, do any of your claims involve allegations of misrepresentation, mistake, or special damages? (*See* § 5.3(d))

17. If you are pleading claims in defamation, antitrust, environmental litigation, or under the Federal Tort Claims Act, have you checked whether the case law in your circuit requires heightened pleading? (*See* § 5.3(d))

18. If your complaint involves allegations of misrepresentation, have you pleaded with particularity the statements alleged to be fraudulent, the identity of the speaker, where and when the statements were made, and why they were fraudulent? (*See* § 5.3(d))

19. If you have alleged that multiple defendants participated in a fraud, have you alleged the role played by each defendant? (*See* § 5.3(d))

20. Have you alleged damages that are unusual for the type of claim in question—*e.g.*, personal injury in a commercial case? If so, these may constitute "special damages" and require heightened pleading under Rule 9(g). (*See* § 5.3(d))

21. Have you pleaded a cause of action such as defamation or product disparagement that requires some level or type of damages as an essential element of the claim? If so, Rule 9(g)'s heightened pleading requirements may apply. (*See* § 5.3(d))

22. If you have pleaded matters in a fraud claim on information and belief, have you alleged that the matters are peculiarly within the defendant's knowledge, and have you stated facts upon which your "information and belief" allegation is based? (*See* § 5.3(d), (e))

23. More generally, have you avoided pleading on information and belief any matters within your personal knowledge or that would be within your personal knowledge if you conducted a reasonable investigation? (*See* § 5.3(e))

24. Have you considered adding an exhibit to your complaint? (*See* § 5.3 (f))

25. Are you in a circuit that allows the defendant to attach to its motion to dismiss any document upon which your claim is based? If so, you may wish to attach the document yourself and deal preemptively with any weaknesses in your case disclosed by the document. (*See* § 5.3(f))

26. If you have pleaded inconsistent facts in support of alternative claims, have you done so because the facts are legitimately in doubt? (*See* § 5.3(g))

27. If you have pleaded inconsistent facts in support of alternative claims, have you explicitly invoked Rule 8(e)(2)? (*See* § 5.3(g))

28. Have you pleaded all elements of your cause of action? (*See* § 5.3(h))

29. Have you checked your complaint for unnecessary adjectives and adverbs? (*See* § 5.4(a))

30. Have you avoided passive voice and legalisms? (*See* § 5.4(a))

31. If time permits, have you shown your complaint to a person unfamiliar with the matters in the complaint and asked his or her impressions? (*See* § 5.4(a))

32. Does the caption of your complaint comply with Rule 10(e)? (*See* § 5.4(b))

33. Have you named all parties in your caption, avoiding the use of "et al."? (*See* § 5.4(b)(1))

34. Does your complaint have an introduction? (*See* § 5.4(b)(5))

35. Does your complaint contain allegations setting forth the grounds upon which the court's jurisdiction depends? (*See* § 5.4(b)(2); Chapter 1)

36. Have you included allegations showing proper venue? (*See* § 5.4(b)(3); Chapter 3)

37. Does your complaint contain a demand for judgment and request for relief? (*See* § 5.4(b)(8))

38. Does your complaint contain a demand for jury trial if you are seeking one? (*See* § 5.4(b)(9))

39. If you are filing an amended complaint after the defendant has filed a responsive pleading, have you either obtained the defendant's consent or filed a motion for leave to amend with the court? (*See* § 5.5(c))

40. If required by local rules, does a redlined copy of the original complaint, marked up to show the changes made, accompany the proposed amended complaint? (*See* § 5.5(b)).

41. Does the caption of your amended complaint identify it as an amended complaint by number, *e.g.*, "First Amended Complaint?" (*See* § 5.5(b)).

42. What is your goal in seeking an injunction, how can that objective be advanced by the injunctive action you are considering, and what alternatives exist? (*See* § 5.6(a))

43. Have you adequately satisfied the notice requirements of Rule 65(b)? (*See* § 5.6(b))

44. Have you articulated your primary concerns and objectives in an introductory fashion and clearly organized your requests for relief in your injunctive complaint? (*See* § 5.6(c))

45. Does your complaint for a declaratory judgment provide sufficient information for a court to determine, for purposes of federal jurisdiction, what claims would have been brought by the declaratory judgment defendant if it had brought suit as a plaintiff? (*See* § 5.7(b)(1))

46. Does your complaint for a declaratory judgment allege facts sufficient to show the existence of an "actual controversy"? (*See* § 5.7(b)(3))

47. Does your complaint for a declaratory judgment allege facts showing that the Borchard criteria have been satisfied? (*See* § 5.7(b)(4))

48. Have you examined the pertinent local rules with respect to requirements for filing complaints? (*See* § 5.8)

49. Have you accompanied your complaint with the correct filing fee? (*See* § 5.8(d))

50. Have you checked to see if your statutory claim (if you have filed one) has specific provisions regarding what action is necessary to commence an action for limitations purposes? (*See* § 5.8(e))

51. Have you checked to see what state law requires with respect to your state law claims (if you have filed any) for commencement of an action for limitation purposes? (*See* § 5.8(e))

§ 5.11   Forms

(a) Complaint and Demand for Jury Trial

UNITED STATES DISTRICT COURT
FOR THE DISTRICT OF MARYLAND

```
ALPHA CORPORATION          )
3333 Sunshine Place        )   COMPLAINT
Lincoln, Maryland 11111    )
             Plaintiff     )
                           )
    vs.                    )
BETA INC.                  )
321 Lake Avenue            )
Seabrook, Ohio 22222       )
    Serve On:              )
    [Insert name and address of  )
      resident agent, if defendant  )
      has one, e.g.        )
                           )
    The Corporation Trust  )
    16 North Street        )
    Lincoln, Maryland 21212]  )
             Defendant     )
```

* * * * * * * * * * * *

COMPLAINT AND DEMAND FOR JURY TRIAL

Plaintiff Alpha Corporation ("Alpha"), by its attorneys, sues the defendant Beta Inc. ("Beta"). As grounds for its complaint, Alpha states as follows:

JURISDICTION AND VENUE

1. This Court has jurisdiction pursuant to 28 U.S.C.A. § 1332. The amount in controversy exceeds $75,000, exclusive of interests and costs.

2. Venue is appropriate in this judicial district under 28 U.S.C.A. § 1391(a).

PARTIES

3. Plaintiff Alpha is a corporation formed under Maryland law. Its principal place of business is in Maryland. Alpha designs, manufactures, and operates products in technologies including aerospace, electronics, information management, materials, and energy.

4. Defendant Beta is a corporation formed under Delaware law. Its principal place of business is in Ohio. It has done and continues to do business in Maryland. Beta designs and manufactures electronic products.

INTRODUCTION

5. Alpha brings this action to recover the losses it has incurred in connection with Alpha's 1991 purchase of Beta's Ocean Systems Division—Whitehall, Delaware segment ("BOSD–WD"), as a result of Beta's breaches of the contract of purchase and otherwise. These losses exceed 30 million dollars.

FACTS COMMON TO ALL COUNTS

6. In 1990 Alpha was seeking to develop its anti-submarine warfare capabilities by gaining a strong market position in the development and production of undersea surveillance systems known as "towed arrays." Towed arrays are lightweight, flexible tubes containing sensitive sound detection equipment. Typically several inches in diameter and up to a mile in length, they are towed behind surface ships and submarines to detect enemy submarines.

7. Alpha had no experience in the development or production of towed arrays and was considering the possibility of acquiring a company that had such experience and capabilities.

8. In 1990 Beta decided to reduce its presence in the defense industry and retained the Epsilon Capital Corporation ("Epsilon Capital") to assist in selling certain divisions including BOSD–WD. Thereafter, Alpha was provided an offering memorandum prepared by Beta and Epsilon Capital and the possible acquisition of BOSD–WD by Alpha was discussed. Beta represented that BOSD–WD had nearly 30 years of experience in the design, development, production, and support of towed arrays and enjoyed approximately 70% of the towed array market.

9. During the spring and summer of 1991, Alpha continued to discuss with Beta the possible acquisition of BOSD–WD. Among other representations, Beta provided Alpha a second offering memorandum, made an oral management presentation to Alpha, and provided detailed financial projections regarding BOSD–WD.

10. While the discussions regarding the acquisition were taking place, on June 29, 1991, BOSD–WD received from the Naval Sea Command ("NAVSEA") a Request for Proposal D00131–77M–4321(F)

("RFP") for the production at a fixed price of towed arrays pursuant to a program known as the QZ–59A.

11. Beta had long anticipated the QZ–59A RFP. In 1982 Beta, Omega Corporation ("Omega"), and Sigma Corporation ("Sigma") each had received contracts from NAVSEA for studies addressing the feasibility of producing the QZ–59 towed array, the predecessor to the QZ–59A. Those three competitors submitted proposals for development and production of the QZ–59. Beta, unlike Omega and Sigma, told NAVSEA that the contract specifications were too difficult to meet. As a result, Beta was eliminated from the competition and in 1987 Omega was given a limited production contract for the QZ–59.

12. Omega thereafter encountered problems in complying with NAVSEA's specifications in the production contract for the QZ–59. It was known among the interested companies involved in manufacturing towed arrays that in the summer of 1991 NAVSEA would issue RFPs for a new, improved version of the QZ–59, namely, the QZ–59A.

13. When Beta received the QZ–59A RFP in June 1991 it determined that the specifications would be difficult to satisfy. The QZ–59A RFP called for a 1″ diameter array. This was substantially thinner than arrays then in production, and represented a new generation of technology. The RFP set out strict "self-noise" requirements, i.e., requirements regarding the amount of mechanically and acoustically generated noise that the array itself could generate as it was towed through the water, as well as strict "reeling" requirements, i.e., the durability of the array for extending into the water and returning to the submarine. The QZ–59A RFP requested a proposal by August 23, 1991, a date later extended to September 12, 1991.

14. The QZ–59A project was important to Beta for a number of reasons. First, it was a project of great magnitude, involving tens of millions of dollars in potential sales and millions of dollars in potential profits. Second, Beta knew that in future years there would be subsequent orders from NAVSEA for 1″ towed arrays, including an anticipated QZ–15M towed array project. Third, Beta could not endanger its dominant position in the towed array market by losing the QZ–59A project to a competitor, because it would not be a manufacturer of the next generation of towed array technology. Fourth, winning the QZ–59A would fill a production void for Beta and make BOSD–WD more attractive to potential purchasers. Accordingly, BOSD–WD assembled a QZ–59A proposal capture team which undertook to prepare a proposal to win the QZ–59A contract.

15. Meanwhile, by July 1991 discussions regarding Alpha's acquisition of BOSD–WD had progressed to the point that the parties entered into negotiations toward a definitive asset purchase agreement. During the negotiations, Beta informed Alpha that it was preparing a proposal to submit to the U.S. Navy for the QZ–59A contract. Beta represented that the QZ–59A design was essentially complete, that no significant development effort was required, that the contract basically required only a production program, and that the proposal would not present any

substantial risk. Beta also represented that the design and development of a hybrid telemetry system to be incorporated into its QZ–59A design were sufficiently advanced so as to satisfy the QZ–59A specification and to be used in other programs. Financial projections provided by Beta to Alpha during the negotiations forecast revenues and profits based upon successfully obtaining and completing the QZ–59A contract.

16.   On August 26, 1991, Beta and Alpha agreed to the terms of the acquisition and executed an Asset Purchase and Sale Agreement (the "Agreement"). A copy of this Agreement is attached to this complaint as Exhibit 1 and incorporated herein. Alpha did not possess expertise in the design and development of towed arrays in August 1991. Furthermore, the QZ–59A proposal was in the process of being prepared by Beta during the negotiations and drafting of the Agreement. For these and other reasons, Alpha determined—and Beta agreed—that the Agreement would require Beta to provide Alpha broad indemnification protection.

17.   The Agreement consists of ten articles. The third article sets forth 26 warranty provisions given by Beta to Alpha. Included among the warranties are those in § 3.05, in which Beta warranted that all forward-looking statements by Beta in writing were based on reasonable grounds and were made in good faith; and those in § 3.26, in which Beta warranted that no statement or representation made by Beta in the Agreement, or in any Exhibit, Schedule, or other document delivered or furnished to Alpha under the Agreement, contained any untrue statement of material fact or failed to state a material fact necessary to make the statements that were made not misleading.

18.   The fifth article of the Agreement consisted of covenants. In § 5.01, Beta covenanted that from the date of the Agreement until the Closing Date Beta would conduct BOSD–WD's business diligently and substantially as it had in the past.

19.   The eighth article consisted of indemnification provisions. In § 8.02, Beta agreed to indemnify Alpha on a dollar-for-dollar basis for all losses, including consequential damages, that, directly or indirectly, arose out of or resulted from (1) any inaccuracy or misrepresentation in, or any breach or nonfulfillment of, any of Beta's warranties or covenants, or (2) even more broadly, "any and all events, circumstances, actions or omissions of [Beta], or any and all conditions existing, on or prior to the Closing Date, (whether or not disclosed to [Alpha]) with respect to the Assets." The term "Assets" was defined in the Agreement to include bids and proposals.

20.   Schedules were a part of the Agreement. Schedule 3.05, the disclosure schedule corresponding to Beta's warranties regarding forecasts, contained a March 3, 1991 Confidential Offering Memorandum prepared by Beta. That Offering Memorandum, and updates thereto, contained financial statements forecasting substantially increasing revenues and operating profits for BOSD–WD for the years 1992 and beyond. Those forecasts stated that BOSD–WD would receive the QZ–59A contract and perform it profitably. Schedule 3.08.03, the disclosure schedule regarding bids and proposals, described the QZ–59A project. It stated

that its revenue value was $32,117,152, that its cost would be $29,250,-160, and that its profit at completion would be $2,866,992.

21. The Agreement provided for a purchase price for BOSD–WD of approximately $117,500,000. That purchase price consisted of "Transferable Equity"—book value—as of July 31, 1991, of approximately $47,-500,000, plus an "Excess Amount"—essentially a premium over book value—of $70,000,000. The Agreement provided for a Post–Closing Adjustment of the purchase price to reflect changes in the Transferable Equity between July 31, 1991 and the Closing Date.

22. On August 30, 1991, representatives of Alpha and Beta met for a price review regarding the QZ–59A RFP and Beta's proposal. At that meeting, as before, Beta employees represented orally and in writing that Beta's QZ–59A design was essentially complete, that no significant development effort was required, that the contract basically required only a production program, that the probability of the success of the program was extremely high, that the risk that Beta's QZ–59A design would not meet NAVSEA's specifications was slight, that the dollar impact of any noncompliance, should it occur, would not exceed $500,-000, and that any noncompliance could be mitigated easily. Beta also represented to Alpha that the design and development of the hybrid telemetry system were sufficiently advanced so as to satisfy the QZ–59A specifications, as well as to be used in other programs. In sum, Beta assured Alpha that the QZ–59A contract would be performed successfully and that it posed no material economic risk to Beta, or to Alpha should the acquisition occur.

23. On September 12, 1991, Beta submitted its QZ–59A proposal to NAVSEA. In the proposal, which was incorporated in schedules to the Agreement, Beta stated that:

(a) "Our QZ–59A/CR design ... achieves specification compliant self-noise performance over the full temperature range.... " Beta based this assertion on "validated models and extensive sea trial data base ... used to predict self-noise levels below the specification."

(b) "In fact, we are confident in proposing an accelerated program schedule ... that shortens the production run by 12 months."

(c) "The maturity of our QZ–59A/CR design coupled with our capabilities, experience, investment and commitment to towed array development and production assures the Navy of a successful program."

(d) "Successful execution of the QZ–59A/CR program requires use of low risk technology and components competently designed, fabricated, and integrated by engineering and production personnel with extensive towed array sonar and handling system experience."

(e) "In fact, the array design is already 90% complete."

(f) *"Our fully compliant QZ–59A/CR is the culmination of 30 years of related experience and an IRAD program specifically aimed* at solving critical thin line towed array design programs." (Emphasis supplied.)

(g) "Specification compliant self-noise performance over the full temperature range is achieved.... "

(h) "Our preaward design initiative coupled with early R & M, manufacturing and product assurance involvement resulted in a fully specification compliant QZ–59A/CR design."

(i) "Employment of fully populated array concepts with high loss hose materials resulted in an array capable of meeting the self-noise specification over the full temperature range."

(j) "The Beta 0SD QZ–59A/CR towed array design meets all acoustic performance specifications at all towspeeds, frequencies and temperatures."

(k) "Validated analytical ... and finite element ... models along with scaled sea test data were used to predict specification compliant performance."

(*l*) "The specification compliant self-noise performance predictions for our QZ–59A/CR towed array designs are based upon validated models, the scaling of sea test data and design concepts used successfully in programs such as the QZ–22B/CR, QZ–22D/CR and BR/NSQ–26."

(m) "The combination of scaled and model predictions (*all of which were specification compliant*) represents a conservative approach to performance estimation." (Emphasis supplied.)

(n) "We are proposing to use our standard telemetry system, already accepted by the Navy on the Reconfigurable Multiline Evaluation System ("RMES") and the Surface Ship Torpedo Defense ("BR/PZR–29") program. This telemetry has been reduced to hardware with over 600 channels produced to support the RMES program. Our approach of developing a common telemetry system applicable to a number of programs reduces QZ–59A/CR program cost through economies of scale."

(*o*) "We have conducted a system analysis and critical item testing to ensure that [our hybrid telemetry system] does meet all QZ–59A/CR requirements."

24.   Closing on the BOSD–WD acquisition by Alpha took place on September 30, 1991. At that time Beta certified that all of its representations and warranties were "true and correct with the same force and effect as if made on and as of this date, which is the date of Closing, subject only to changes contemplated by the Agreement."

25.   On January 11, 1992, NAVSEA awarded a QZ–59A production contract based upon Beta's proposal for the fixed contract price of $32,134,482 which was the price proposed to NAVSEA by Beta prior to the Closing.

26.   On February 23, 1992, Alpha and Beta agreed to a post-closing adjustment of the purchase price as provided for in the Agreement.

Alpha paid Beta $2,592,361 out of escrow and Beta agreed that the rights and obligations of the parties would continue as provided under the Agreement.

27. On March 13, 1992, the Navy conducted a preliminary design review of Beta's QZ–59A proposal. The review identified numerous problems with Beta's design. It found, for example, that the self-noise models used by Beta to predict performance did not account for vibrational noise mechanisms, thus making Beta's low-speed performance predictions inaccurate. It found further that the hose materials Beta selected would generate the same self-noise problems in cold water as those experienced by the Omega QZ–59 design. The review also expressed concern regarding a "serious risk" relating to the proposed hybrid telemetry production.

28. On November 20–21, 1992, the Navy conducted a Critical Design Review. The Navy found many substantial faults in Beta's QZ–59A design.

29. In August 1993 Beta's QZ–59A design failed a sea test, demonstrating that it could not meet NAVSEA's contractual specifications.

30. Alpha diligently and reasonably attempted to meet the QZ–59A contractual specifications but was not able to do so as a result of deficiencies in Beta's QZ–59A design and the difficulties of the NAVSEA contractual specifications.

31. On January 6, 1995, the Navy notified Alpha that the QZ–59A contract was terminated for default in its entirety. The principal basis for the termination for default was the failure of the array to comply with contract specifications. As a result of the termination for default, Alpha faced potential liability to the Navy for consequential damages including excess costs and reprocurement costs incurred by the Navy, and the Navy stated an intention to pursue those remedies.

32. Alpha immediately notified Beta of the termination for default and, in light of the substantial financial exposure created by the termination for default, began attempting to negotiate a settlement with the Navy. Alpha notified Beta of these discussions and invited Beta to participate in the administration and defense of the termination proceedings with the Navy and to propose any reasonable financial settlement with the Navy.

33. On April 2, 1995, Alpha successfully concluded the negotiations with the Navy with a modification of the QZ–59A contract. The contract modification withdrew the termination for default and significantly reduced the financial exposure of Alpha to the Navy arising out of the QZ–59A contract. Pursuant to that settlement, the Navy's payment obligation to Alpha was fixed at $14.1 million; however, at that time Alpha had already spent in excess of $30.8 million in an effort to perform the contract.

34. In the course of its attempts to perform the QZ–59A contract and in the course of investigating the causes of the losses on the QZ–59A

contract Alpha learned that when Beta submitted the QZ–59A proposal on September 12, 1991, among other things:

(a) Beta knew—and failed to disclose to Alpha—that the QZ–59A design could not reasonably be expected to meet the QZ–59A specifications.

(b) Beta knew—and failed to disclose to Alpha—that its claims of specification compliance were based upon highly selected data that did not reasonably support a prediction of compliance with the specifications. Indeed, much of Beta's computer modelling of the QZ–59A design predicted a failure to comply with NAVSEA's specifications but the results of this modelling were not disclosed to either Alpha or the Navy. During the development of the proposal, the rejection of noncompliant projections generated by the computer modelling effort became so prevalent that a "joke" circulated that the Beta employee responsible for running the models had a "spec compliance button" on his computer.

(c) Beta knew—and failed to disclose to Alpha—that the Beta models for predicting the performance of vibration isolation modules ("VIMs"), an essential component of the Beta QZ–59A design, did not work and that Beta was "building VIMs by experience and 'feel' alone, without a solid analytical base."

(d) Beta knew—and failed to disclose to Alpha—that Beta management instructed the QZ–59A proposal team as follows: "Do not state that we *can't meet the spec*. Where our data/evidence does not meet spec, evolve a solution based on generally accepted theory. Describe the solution and *state we will meet the spec*." (Emphasis in original.)

(e) Beta knew—and failed to disclose to Alpha—that specification compliance could be achieved—if at all—only with a substantial development effort, the cost of which was not included in the pricing of the QZ–59A proposal and contract. Indeed, Beta had concluded that, even assuming optimum performance when all existing state of the art materials were assembled into a fully integrated array, NAVSEA's specifications would not be met. Beta had determined to gamble that it would later be able to negotiate specification relief from NAVSEA.

(f) Beta knew—and failed to disclose to Alpha—that the Beta design for the QZ–59A was not 90% complete. In fact, the Beta employees responsible for the proposal actually had estimated that the design was no more than 40% to 70% complete. Even these estimates appear to have been unreasonably optimistic.

(g) Beta knew—and failed to disclose to Alpha—that it had designed the QZ–59A in the hope of obtaining specification compliance at high speed, high frequency, since it had more measured data for these conditions, and to "take what we can get" at low speed, low frequency, low temperature, which was the anticipated operating environment for the QZ–59A.

(h) Beta knew—and failed to disclose to Alpha—that Beta did not conduct the same type and level of internal review of the QZ–59A proposal as Beta had previously conducted in the ordinary course of business and consistent with Beta's past practices.

35. As a result of the foregoing failures and misrepresentations by Beta, Alpha has sustained large losses in its efforts to perform the QZ–59A contract as well as consequential and other damages. Alpha also incurred other reasonably foreseeable losses as a result of the omissions and statements of Beta.

36. In accordance with the provisions of the Agreement, Alpha provided Beta timely, written notification of the claims set forth in this complaint and provided Beta with extensive access to the information necessary to assess the claims. In return Beta agreed that the applicable statutes of limitations were tolled from December 9, 1994 through June 22, 1995. Beta has thus far failed to acknowledge or satisfy its obligations under the Agreement and as set forth in this complaint.

37. Alpha now seeks to recover its losses and damages, including all costs, expenses, lost profits and attorneys' fees, in accordance with the contract representations and promises made by Beta in the Agreement.

COUNT I

(Indemnity for Breach of § 8.02.01(d) of the Agreement)

38. Alpha incorporates the allegations in paragraphs 1 through 37 above.

39. Under § 8.02.01(d) of the Agreement, Beta agreed to

indemnify and hold [Alpha] harmless on a dollar-for-dollar basis from and against all losses, damages, reasonably foreseeable consequential damages, liabilities, claims, demands, obligations, deficiencies, payments, judgments, settlements, costs and expenses of any nature whatsoever ... resulting from, arising out of, or due to directly or indirectly from the following:

* * *

(d) Any and all events, circumstances, actions or omissions of [Beta], its agents or affiliates, or any and all conditions existing, on or prior to the Closing Date, (whether or not disclosed to [Alpha]) with respect to the Assets.

40. Section 1.01.07 of the Agreement defines "Assets" to include "all ... proposals [and] bids."

41. As described above, the QZ–59A proposal submitted by Beta to NAVSEA on September 12, 1991 was fundamentally inaccurate in describing the maturity of the QZ–59A design and in stating that the QZ–59A design achieved specification compliance. In reality, as Beta knew, the claims of specification compliance were based upon highly selected data and a design that was only partially developed.

42. Beta's submission of the fundamentally inaccurate QZ–59A proposal was an "action or omission ... with respect to the Assets" as set forth in § 8.02.01(d) of the Agreement. It was also a "condition existing, on or prior to the Closing Date ... with respect to the Assets" as set forth in § 8.02.01(d).

43. Further, Beta's failure to inform Alpha that the QZ–59A proposal was fundamentally inaccurate was an "action or omission ... with respect to the Assets" as set forth in § 8.02.01(d) of the Agreement.

44. Further, Beta's representation to Alpha that the risk from noncompliance with NAVSEA's QZ–59A self-noise specifications was only $500,000 and could be easily mitigated, when in reality the risk of noncompliance was significantly greater and significantly more difficult to mitigate, was an "action or omission ... with respect to the Assets" as set forth in § 8.02.01(d) of the Agreement.

45. As a result of these and other actions and omissions by Beta, and of these and other conditions existing with respect to the Assets, Alpha has sustained large losses in its efforts to perform the QZ–59A contract as well as consequential and other damages. Alpha also incurred other reasonably foreseeable losses as a result of the omissions and statements of Beta.

WHEREFORE, plaintiff Alpha demands judgment against defendant Beta in an amount to be determined at trial but which is currently in excess of $30,000,000, plus costs and expenses, including attorneys' fees.

COUNT II
(Indemnity for Breach of § 3.05 of the Agreement)

46. Alpha incorporates the allegations in paragraphs 1 through 37 above.

47. Under § 8.02.01(a) of the Agreement, Beta agreed to

indemnify and hold [Alpha] harmless on a dollar-for-dollar basis from and against all losses, damages, reasonably foreseeable consequential damages, liabilities, claims, demands, obligations, deficiencies, payments, judgments, settlements, costs and expenses of any nature whatsoever ... resulting from, arising out of, or due to directly or indirectly from the following:

(a) Any inaccuracy or misrepresentation in, or breach or nonfulfillment of, any representation or warranty of [Beta], or any breach or nonfulfillment of any covenant of [Beta], contained in this Agreement, in any Schedule delivered hereunder by [Beta], or in any certificates or documents delivered by [Beta] pursuant to this Agreement.

48. Section 3.05 of the Agreement is a "representation or warranty of [Beta] contained in th[e] Agreement" as set forth in § 8.02.01(a). Section 3.05 provides:

Section 3.05. *Forecasts.* Notwithstanding any disclaimers to the contrary (whether oral or in writing) made by or on behalf of [Beta], all forward looking statements made in writing (including but not limited to forecasts and projections of revenues, income or losses, capital expenditures, or other financial items, management plans and objectives for future operations, statements of future economic performance, the Offering Memorandum dated on or about March 3, 1991 set forth in Schedule 3.05 delivered hereunder, the Management Presentation given on or about April 26, 1991 set forth in Schedule 3.05, the letter dated May 19, 1991 from Mr. Simms of [Beta] to Mr. Rock of [Alpha] set forth in Schedule 3.05, and statements of the assumptions underlying or relating to any of the foregoing), by [Beta] to [Alpha] were made based upon reasonable grounds and disclosed in good faith. Such forward looking statements are hereby reaffirmed in all material respects based upon reasonable grounds and disclosed in good faith except for changes in the ordinary course of business or except as separately and specifically delineated in Schedule 3.05.

49. Beta's forward looking statements contained in Schedule 3.08.03 with respect to the anticipated value, costs, and profits of the QZ–59A proposal were not based upon reasonable grounds and disclosed in good faith.

50. Further, Beta's forward looking statements contained in the Confidential Offering Memorandum (part of Schedule 3.05), and updates thereto, with respect to BOSD–WD's revenues and profits for 1992 and future years were not based upon reasonable grounds and disclosed in good faith.

51. Further, Beta's forward looking statements made in writing at the August 30, 1991 price review meeting regarding the economic risks of the QZ–59A design's noncompliance with self-noise specifications and other contractual requirements were not based upon reasonable grounds and disclosed in good faith.

52. Beta, by these and other statements and omissions, breached § 3.05 of the Agreement. As a result of this breach, Alpha has sustained large losses in its efforts to perform the QZ–59A contract as well as consequential and other damages. Alpha also incurred other reasonably foreseeable losses as a result of the omissions and statements of Beta.

WHEREFORE, plaintiff Alpha demands judgment against defendant Beta in an amount to be determined at trial but which is currently in excess of $30,000,000, plus costs and expenses, including attorneys' fees.

COUNT III

(Indemnity for Breach of § 3.26 of the Agreement)

53. Alpha incorporates the allegations in paragraphs 1 through 37 and 47 above.

54. Section 3.26 of the Agreement is a "representation or warranty of [Beta] contained in th[e] Agreement" as set forth in § 8.02.01(a). Section 3.26 provides:

Section 3.26. *Material Disclosures*. No statement, representation or warranty made by [Beta] in this Agreement, in any Exhibit hereto or Schedule delivered hereunder, or in any certificate, statement, list, schedule or other document furnished or to be furnished to [Alpha] hereunder, contains any untrue statement of a material fact, or fails to state a material fact necessary to make the statements contained herein or therein, in light of the circumstances in which they are made, not misleading.

55. Beta made untrue statements of material facts as set forth above including but not limited to the following:

a) that the "anticipated cost" of the QZ–59A proposal was $29,250,160 and that the anticipated profit at completion was $2,866,992 as set forth in Schedule 3.08.03;

b) that BOSD–WD expected future profits of $10 million in 1992 and more in subsequent years, as set forth in the March 3, 1991 Confidential Offering Memorandum (part of Schedule 3.05) and updates thereto;

c) that Beta expected future profits on the QZ–59A system of $7,749,000 (including the $2,866,992 described in (a) above) through 2000, as set forth in the March 3, 1991 Offering Memorandum; and

d) that the risk of the QZ–59A design's noncompliance with self-noise specifications was $500,000 and that this risk could be easily mitigated, as set forth in writing at the August 30, 1991 price review meeting.

Further, in failing to state the facts set forth above, including those in paragraph 34, Beta failed to state material facts necessary to make the statements made not misleading.

56. By these and other statements and omissions, Beta breached § 3.26 of the Agreement. As a result of this breach, Alpha has sustained large losses in its efforts to perform the QZ–59A contract as well as consequential and other damages. Alpha also incurred other reasonably foreseeable losses as a result of the omissions and statements of Beta.

WHEREFORE, plaintiff Alpha demands judgment against defendant Beta in an amount to be determined at trial but which is currently in excess of $30,000,000, plus costs and expenses, including attorneys' fees.

COUNT IV
(Indemnity for Breach of § 5.01 of the Agreement)

57. Alpha incorporates the allegations in paragraphs 1 through 37 and 47 above.

58. Section 5.01 of the Agreement is a "covenant of [Beta] contained in th[e] Agreement" as set forth in § 8.02.01(a). Section 5.01 provides:

Section 5.01. *Conduct of the Business*. Except as contemplated by this Agreement or as otherwise agreed to in writing by [Alpha], during the period from the date of this Agreement to the close of business on the Closing Date, [Beta] will conduct the business of [BOSD–WD] diligently and substantially in the same manner as heretofore conducted and will maintain the Assets in the ordinary course of business and consistent with [Beta's] past practices.

59. In submitting on September 12, 1991 to NAVSEA a proposal, namely the QZ–59A proposal, that was fundamentally inaccurate, that had not been subjected to an appropriate internal review and that exposed Beta or its corporate successors to losses and damages exceeding $30 million, Beta did not conduct its business diligently or substantially in the same manner as it had in the past.

60. Beta thus breached § 5.01 of the Agreement. As a result of this breach, Alpha has sustained large losses in its efforts to perform the QZ–59A contract as well as consequential and other damages. Alpha also incurred other reasonably foreseeable losses as a result of the omissions and statements of Beta.

WHEREFORE, plaintiff Alpha demands judgment against defendant Beta in an amount to be determined at trial but which is currently in excess of $30,000,000, plus costs and expenses, including attorneys' fees.

COUNT V
(Negligent Misrepresentation)

61. Alpha incorporates the allegations in paragraphs 1 through 37 above.

62. The representations by Beta to Alpha, including those described above, and the representations by Beta to the Navy, including those described above, were false.

63. Beta owed Alpha a duty of due care not to be negligent in making these representations.

64. Beta was negligent in making the representations.

65. Beta intended that Alpha take action based upon the representations.

66. Beta knew that Alpha would probably rely upon the representations which, if false, would cause Alpha loss.

67. Alpha justifiably took action based upon the representations.

68. As a result of Beta's negligence in making the representations, Alpha has sustained large losses in its efforts to perform the QZ–59A contract as well as consequential and other damages. Alpha also incurred other reasonably foreseeable losses as a result of the omissions and statements of Beta.

WHEREFORE, plaintiff Alpha demands judgment against defendant Beta in an amount to be determined at trial but which is currently in excess of $30,000,000, plus costs and expenses, including attorneys' fees.

COUNT VI
(Breach of Fiduciary Duty)

69. Alpha incorporates the allegations in paragraphs 1 through 37 above.

70. Under the circumstances of this case, Alpha was justified in believing that Beta, in submitting the QZ–59A proposal to NAVSEA, would not act in a manner adverse to Alpha's interest. Alpha reposed trust and confidence in Beta. Beta was in a dominant position respecting the QZ–59A proposal, as it possessed knowledge and expertise that Alpha lacked regarding towed arrays and the QZ–59A proposal, yet Beta's QZ–59A proposal could lead to a contract binding Alpha.

71. Because of the relationship of trust and confidence existing between Alpha and Beta respecting the QZ–59A proposal, Beta had a fiduciary duty to disclose to Alpha all material facts regarding the proposal.

72. Beta breached this duty of disclosure, by failing to disclose to Alpha the matters described in paragraph 34 above.

73. As a result of Beta's breach of its duty of disclosure, Alpha has sustained large losses in its efforts to perform the QZ–59A contract as well as consequential and other damages. Alpha also incurred other reasonably foreseeable losses as a result of the omissions and statements of Beta.

WHEREFORE, plaintiff Alpha demands judgment against defendant Beta in an amount to be determined at trial but which is currently in excess of $30,000,000, plus costs and expenses, including attorneys' fees.

DEMAND FOR JURY TRIAL

Plaintiff demands trial by jury on all issues so triable.

Respectfully submitted,

_____

John J. Doe
James G. Doe
Jane F. Doe

15 West Pratt Street
Baltimore, Maryland 21202
(410) 555–1665

CHAPTER 6

RESPONSES TO COMPLAINTS

by
Clyde A. Szuch*

* This chapter represents the substantial contributions of my colleague, Ronald D. Coleman. Mr. Coleman is a graduate of Princeton University and Northwestern University School of Law and has authored and contributed to numerous law-related works. He is engaged in the practice of commercial litigation with an emphasis on resolution and litigation of technology and intellectual property disputes.

WESTLAW Electronic Research

WESTLAW Electronic Research Guide preceding the Summary of Contents.

---

§ 6.1 Scope Note

Chapter 6 addresses the various approaches available to a defendant upon being served with a complaint. After fundamental internal procedures are briefly addressed in Section 6.2, Section 6.3 introduces FRCP 12, the Rule that sets out the defenses and objections available to a defendant. Section 6.4 discusses the "mechanics of response," specifically the calculation and extension of deadlines applicable to responses to complaints, and the methods by which service of a response to the complaint is effected. The next section, 6.5, discusses motions to dismiss generally. Section 6.6 focuses on motions to dismiss under FRCP 12, one of the provisions of which, FRCP 12(b)(6)—the motion to dismiss for failure to state a claim for which relief can be granted—is the topic of Section 6.7. Section 6.8 deals with the availability of other motions under FRCP 12. Preparation of the answer is discussed in Section 6.9. Section 6.10 is an introduction to affirmative defenses, which are considered in closer detail in the following section, 6.11. The next two sections address counterclaims and cross-claims, respectively, and the last two sections provide a practice checklist and sample forms.

Library References:

West's Key No. Digests, Federal Civil Procedure ☞621–1150.
Wright, Miller & Marcus, Federal Practice and Procedure: Civil 2d § 2170.

§ 6.2 Preliminary Considerations: Internal Procedures

Under most circumstances, a complaint[1] will be served on a client directly and not through an attorney's office. (*See* Section 6.4, *infra*.) Once a summons and complaint are turned over to the office of an attorney who will likely represent the defendant, the complaint should receive immediate attention because the time to respond is passing. There are two main areas of immediate concern when a complaint is received: conflicts of interests and docket control.

(a) Conflicts of Interest

The need to identify and, if necessary, resolve conflicts of interest between the client and other present or former clients is especially acute where a client asks an attorney to represent it in a lawsuit that has just begun. Neither the client nor the lawyer have had the leisurely opportunity that the plaintiff has had to survey the players, search for conflicts and perhaps resolve them in advance of filing. The press of time may sometimes make proper scrutiny of the conflicts issues difficult or almost impossible. Yet the failure to evaluate the conflicts situation properly may result in the loss of the present client, of another client or, more seriously, may result in ethics or malpractice problems.

For all these reasons, conflicts must be cleared promptly. This ideally should take place before doing anything other than reading the complaint and determining the date of service (*see* Section 6.4, *infra*). For example, it is not uncommon for the client to transmit to its lawyer,

---

§ 6.2

1. For ease of presentation, the discussion will speak generally of answers to complaints, though normally the rules and principles apply as well to answers to counterclaims and cross-claims. Similarly, all parties that may be in the position of drafting responsive pleadings, such as counterclaim or cross-claim defendants, are included generally in the category of "defendants."

along with the complaint, internal documents relating to the subject matter of the case. Nonetheless outside counsel should refrain from reading such documents until the conflicts issue is resolved. Once client confidences relating to a response to the complaint are exchanged, the horse has left the barn. Even if the representation is eventually declined, an extant client relationship may be undermined or even forfeited by the information gathered from documents or discussions concerning the potential new matter.

(b) Docket Control

Docket control simply means making sure that (1) attorney responsibility for legal matters is clearly delineated and (2) those with responsibility are notified of all critical dates. In a small practice, the most basic docket control may be a law diary where all scheduling information is kept. Larger organizations, and many smaller ones as well, use computerized scheduling, "tickler" or docketing programs that offer great flexibility. No matter the size of the practice, it is critical that there be one centralized place where the responsible lawyer always knows that litigation deadlines can be found.

Regardless of the system used, each lawyer with case responsibility must regard himself as *personally* responsible for monitoring (and being prepared for) all crucial dates. And, like all systems, even the best docketing system is no better than the information put into it. For example, once an answer date has been extended by stipulation or otherwise, that change must be reflected by updating the docket. A good docketing system should allow for automatic 10–, 5–, and 1–day advance notice of impending deadlines. With such a system in place there should be no unpleasant surprises.

Library References:

West's Key No. Digests, Federal Civil Procedure ⚯621–1150.
Wright, Miller, Kane & Cooper, Federal Practice and Procedure: Civil 2d §§ 1768, 4515.

§ 6.3 Defenses and Objections: FRCP 12

The fundamentals of response, whether by answer or motion (*see* Section 6.6, *infra*), are addressed in FRCP 12, which is divided into eight sections. The themes of each section are as follows:

FRCP 12(a): The responsive pleading (whether an answer or a motion to dismiss) must be served within *20 days* after service upon the defendant of the summons and complaint (unless service is waived; *see* Section 6.4(d), (f)(1), *infra*).

FRCP 12(b): Most defenses, whether in "law or fact," must be asserted in the answer. The exceptions are certain enumerated defenses which may, at the party's option, be made by motion alone. Such a motion must be made before filing the answer and must be resolved before trial (*See* Section 6.6, *infra*).

FRCP 12(c): Prior to answering, the defendant may make a motion for judgment on the pleadings. As discussed in Section 6.8(b), *infra*, this provision is largely an anachronism since such motions are rarely granted.

FRCP 12(d): Certain motions made in response to a complaint (*see* FRCP 12(b) above) must be resolved in a preliminary hearing and not later during the course of litigation. (*See* Section 6.6(b), *infra*.)

FRCP 12(e): The defendant may make a motion for a more definite statement of the claims in the complaint. (*See* Section 6.8(c), *infra*.)

FRCP 12(f): The defendant may make a motion to strike material from the complaint. (*See* Section 6.8(d), *infra*.)

FRCP 12(g): Motions made in response to a complaint must be consolidated (joined together), failing which they may be deemed to have been waived. (*See* Section 6.8(a), *infra*.)

FRCP 12(h): Certain enumerated defenses are *waived* if not asserted at all in the answer or in a motion made under this Rule. Others may be asserted in subsequent motions. (*See* Section 6.8(a), *infra*.)

Of the principles established by these sections of FRCP 12, the most essential points are that: (i) The defendant has a 20–day deadline to *serve* (not file; *see* Section 6.4, *infra*) the responsive pleading (*see* Section 6.4, *infra*), and (ii) certain defenses must be asserted at this point of the proceedings or are waived. Both of these points are of particular importance and, if missed, there may never be an opportunity to cure.

Library References:

West's Key No. Digests, Federal Civil Procedure ⊗751–759, 901–907, 1041–1068, 1721–1842.
Wright & Miller, Federal Practice and Procedure: Civil 2d §§ 1341–1344, 1356, 1357, 1360, 1361, 1364, 1366, 1368, 1371, 1372, 1376–1378, 1383–1397.

§ 6.4 The Mechanics of Response

As previously mentioned, FRCP 12(a) mandates that an answer or other response be served 20 days after service of the complaint. It must be re-emphasized that this deadline is a *service* deadline, not a filing deadline. Therefore, if the practitioner were to err and *file* the answer at the end of the 20–day period and then wait to serve a file-stamped copy (as is done with a complaint), service of the answer would be untimely and the defendant subject to a default.

The one exception to this rule requiring service, not filing, is where the plaintiff's address and that of its lawyer are unknown (despite the defendant's due diligence in attempting to find them). In that case FRCP 5(b) provides that the answer be "left" with the clerk, which is little different in practice from filing it. (A "received" stamp, rather than a "filed" stamp, may be used in such a case.) This is not, however, a scenario most defense counsel will ever encounter.

(a) Mechanics of Service

Service of the answer is relatively simple, especially compared to effecting proper service of a summons and complaint. The main reason for this is that the name of the person on whom to serve the answer and that person's address are typed plainly on the complaint. That person, of course, is the plaintiff's lawyer (or, in the rare instance of a pro se complaint, the plaintiff himself[1]), who becomes amenable to service on its client's behalf once the lawsuit is begun.

FRCP 5(b) sets out the rules for how service is accomplished on a party already in the action. There are two basic modes of service: What the Rule plainly calls "delivery" (*i.e.*, personal delivery), and mail. Service may be made by personal delivery on the plaintiff's counsel by the end of the 20th day after service of the complaint. Or service may be made by mail on the 20th day, effective the date of mailing.

(1) Methods of Service: Practice Pointers

The preferred method of serving the answer is by mail to the plaintiff's attorney. The advantages of service by mail are manifold. For one, mail service is much simpler for defense counsel than personal service; the mail carrier already knows the way to the adversary's office. The office procedures of plaintiff's counsel are irrelevant when service is made by mail. Service by mail is inexpensive. And finally, the last sentence of FRCP 5(b) reads, "Service by mail is complete upon mailing." This is the most compelling reason of all.

Having said all that, some lawyers do not trust something as important as a pleading to naked mailing, first-class or otherwise. It is true, as discussed in Section 6.4(c) below, that the certificate of service is presumptive proof of the date of service. But in some situations service

---

§ 6.4

1. Not "itself," however; only a natural person can represent himself, without counsel, in court. A corporation cannot represent itself pro se because it is only "an abstraction." Scandia Down Corp. v. Euroquilt, Inc., 772 F.2d 1423, 1427 (7th Cir. 1985). Thus a corporation, partnership or association "may appear in the federal courts only through licensed counsel." Rowland v. California Men's Colony, Unit II Men's Advisory Council, 506 U.S. 194, 202, 113 S.Ct. 716, 721, 121 L.Ed.2d 656 (1993). Based on this rule, it is possible for a defendant to succeed on a motion to dismiss based on a corporate plaintiff's failure to be properly represented by counsel. *See, e.g.*, Capital Group, Inc. v. Gaston & Snow, 768 F.Supp. 264, 265 (E.D.Wis.1991) (appealing purported pro se complaint by corporate plaintiff without prejudice); Schoonmaker v. Hubner, 1993 WL 311776 (E.D.Pa.1993) (claims by corporation styled as pro se claimant dismissed for lack of representation). *See also*, Triangle Fabricators, Inc. v. Forward Industries, Inc., 866 F.Supp. 467, 473 (D.Or.1994) (plaintiff corporation given 30 days to obtain counsel on pain of dismissal); Red Roof Storage, Inc. v. Red Roof Inns, Inc., 897 F.2d 529 (table), 1990 WL 25080 (6th Cir.1990) (dismissing appeal for want of prosecution where brief was filed by nonattorney president of appellant); US JVC Corp. v. Caribbean Wholesales & Service Corp., 1993 WL 307803 (S.D.N.Y.1993) (defendant corporation given 30 days to obtain counsel, failing which default judgment would be entered). Therefore another matter for defense counsel to "scan" for upon receipt of the complaint in a commercial case is whether the plaintiff, if not a natural person, is properly represented.

of pleadings may be an appropriate occasion for the donning of both belts and suspenders.

Therefore, if the Postal Service is to be utilized, many attorneys use certified mail with return-receipt requested and include a cover letter indicating this method of mailing above the addressee's name. Thus a complete record of mailing, service and receipt is created for the file. Other attorneys take a more relaxed approach, however, relying entirely on regular mailing and on the fact that there are few instances of a default being taken on the basis of a few days' tardiness in the answer.

Personal delivery has the advantage of being under the control of the defense attorney, who can hand-deliver the answer himself if he wishes. If successful, personal service usually will result in a stamp or other written acknowledgment of receipt of the answer by plaintiff's attorney. The acknowledgment is customarily placed on the defendant's attorney's "office copy" of the answer as well as on the original. Thus, there will be no question that plaintiff's attorney actually received the answer and that any time periods which may be triggered by service of the answer have begun to run.

But personal delivery also has a number of pitfalls. The defendant has to concern itself with the office procedures of the plaintiff's attorney. For all the defendant knows the office will close early, or perhaps not open at all, on Day 20. The server may get lost or come to some other mishap. A plaintiff can take as much time as it wishes to file a complaint and start the clock on time to effect service,[2] unless it is facing a statute of limitations bar; the defendant does not have that luxury.

The Rules do allow for a certain amount of help in overcoming delivery problems. FRCP 5(b) states that personal delivery is effective on handing the paper to the attorney, assuming there is one, or by leaving it at the attorney's office with "a clerk or other person in charge thereof," and, failing that, "leaving it in a conspicuous place" at that office or even at the home of the person in charge of the office. On the whole, these requirements are much easier to satisfy that those surrounding service of a summons and complaint. But the whole idea of personal service usually suggests a degree of randomness and unpredictability that should leave defense counsel in a commercial case cold. For all these reasons personal service of the answer is not typically utilized in commercial litigation.

(2) Practice Pointer: Overnight Delivery

Many law offices make routine use of overnight couriers such as Federal Express, United Parcel Service and the like instead of the Postal Service. These services have some advantages over mail, even certified mail with a return receipt. An "airbill" is routinely generated for each piece sent. Overnight courier services usually offer sophisticated, real-time tracking of packages. There is a perceived dependability offered by

---

2. FRCP 4(m).

these services superior to that offered by the Postal Service. Overnight couriers are also fairly economical compared to hand-delivery services.

A question arises, however, as to whether one gets the benefit of the "effective upon mailing" rule by use of such a service or whether the overnight courier is simply a fancy messenger. The difference is more than academic. Where service is effective upon mailing, the lawyer or an assistant can walk to a mailbox at a minute to midnight on the 20th day after service of the summons and complaint and by dropping the responsive papers in the chute effect timely service. This would be true even if the mailing took place on a Friday night and that mailbox were not to be serviced until the end of an approaching three-day weekend. It matters not that it could be a week or more before the plaintiff gets the papers. In contrast, service by personal delivery means the papers must be *at* the office of the plaintiff *on* the 20th day.

Two federal courts have come to opposite conclusions about the status of overnight couriers, meaning that practitioners should beware. One 1992 district court case held that the use of an overnight service was the same as mailing and that the "effective on mailing" rule applied.[3] More recently the Ninth Circuit has ruled to the contrary.[4] The effect of the latter ruling is demonstrated by the following example: On Day 20, defendant's counsel transmits the answer to the courier for delivery the next day by 10 a.m. Under the Ninth Circuit rule the plaintiff may appreciate getting the tardy service faster, but would still technically be able to seek a default since personal delivery was received on Day 21—a day late.

As was mentioned above, it is unusual an occurrence for a plaintiff to actually seek, much less get, a default in routine commercial litigation for this slight delay. Technically speaking, however, it is better to get the advantage of "effective on mailing" by transmitting the answer to the Postal Service at some time on or before the 20th day, using certified mail and getting a receipt. If cooperation with and courtesy to plaintiff's counsel are desired, there are two possible approaches: Use mail for the official service but fax or "overnight" a courtesy copy. Or, better still, ask for courtesy in return and "trade" a one-day extension from the plaintiff (to be safe, include a formal written stipulation; *see* Section 6.4(f), *infra*) in exchange for faster delivery of the answer by defendant— an eminently reasonable bargain.

(b) Multiple Defendants

Pursuant to FRCP 5(a) the answer (and all other papers to be served besides the complaint, summons or subpoena) must be served on all parties to an action. This includes not only co-plaintiffs but also co-defendants. Similarly, if the client is served with a cross-claim, the

---

3. United States v. Certain Real Property and Premises Known as 63–29 Trimble Road, Woodside, New York, 812 F.Supp. 332 (E.D.N.Y.1992).

4. Magnuson v. Video Yesteryear, 85 F.3d 1424 (9th Cir.1996).

responsive papers must be served on the original plaintiff and other defendants, including those not making a cross-claim.[5]

Defense counsel should also pay close attention to service of cross-claims against co-defendants. Cross-claims are essentially complaints against co-defendants (*see* Section 6.13, *infra*). If another other defendant was served earlier or for some other reason has appeared earlier in the case, it can be served with cross-claims along with service of the answer (*i.e.*, by mail). If, however, it has not yet appeared in the case, the cross-claims must be served on the co-defendant in the same manner as a complaint.[6] Failure to recognize this obligation can result in unpleasant surprises. For example, it may turn out that a co-defendant that should properly bear your client's liability never responds to the complaint. If the defendant has not brought that co-defendant into the case by service of its cross-claim, that cross-claim will be lost.

(c) The Certificate of Service

Service of the answer, including service by mail, is essentially self-proving because of the institution of the certificate of service, mandated by FRCP 5(d). More accurately, what the Rules call the "certificate" is a *certification* by the defendant's counsel that he has complied with the Rules in executing service, whether by mail or personal delivery. The certificate sets out the method of service used and the date of service. (*See* Section 6.15(c), *infra*.) Typically the certifying person cannot certify to the actual date of receipt, but since service is effective upon mailing it is sufficient to state the date on which the document was transmitted to the carrier, *e.g.*, delivered to the post office or placed in a mailbox (*see* Section 6.4(a)(1), *supra*).

The typical certificate of service formulation states that the paper was "caused by [the certifier] to be sent by" first class mail, overnight courier, or whatever method was used. This locution is appropriate where the person certifying did not personally place the paper in the mailbox or take it to the post office, as the case may be. In the unlikely event of a dispute, the usefulness of this language in a certification of service would likely depend on the regularity of the office procedures that are implied by "caused to be sent." The certification is virtually unshakable proof of the date of service.[7]

---

5. In some rare cases, however, where there is an unusual number of parties, the court may order that some pleadings or other papers need not be served on all parties, and that filing is sufficient. *See* FRCP 5(c).

6. American Telephone & Telegraph Co. v. Merry, 592 F.2d 118 (2d Cir.1979); Apple v. Jewish Hosp. and Medical Center, 829 F.2d 326, 332 (2d Cir.1987) ("Original service of process is ... a sine qua non requirement for a court to acquire jurisdiction over an additional party"); Barnett v. City of Yonkers, 731 F.Supp. 594, 601–02 (S.D.N.Y.1990) (when summons and cross-claims were mailed to counsel for co-defendant, court did not have jurisdiction over party against whom cross-claim was allegedly asserted, since that party did not receive proper service).

7. *See, e.g.,* United States v. Duke, 50 F.3d 571, 575 (8th Cir.) (using typewritten date on certification of service to determine whether motion for reconsideration was timely served), *cert. denied,* 516 U.S. 885, 116 S.Ct. 224, 133 L.Ed.2d 154 (1995); Em-

The certificate is filed with the court along with the answer, both in a "reasonable" amount of time following service.[8] It is good practice not to delay in the filing of the answer. One reason to file promptly is so third parties such as customers, suppliers, creditors or the press can know that the defendant has answered and what its defenses are. In any event, there is seldom any reason the answer cannot be filed at the same time as it is mailed to the plaintiff, or certainly on the next business day.

(d) Calculating the Time to Respond

There are two things the practitioner must do upon receiving the summons and complaint served upon its client. As discussed above, he must immediately begin the process of investigating potential conflicts. At the same time, he must ascertain the date service was effected on the client in order to determine when a response is due.[9]

Once the date of service is determined, the due date for responsive papers must be docketed immediately. As stated earlier, a response to a complaint is due 20 days after service of the summons. Under FRCP 6(a), when computing any period of time prescribed under the Rules which is more than 11 days, Saturdays, Sundays and legal holidays[10] *are* counted in the computation of deadlines. If, however, the *last* day of the period (the due date) falls on a Saturday, Sunday or legal holiday, the due date is the next regular weekday (typically, though not always, the next Monday). Also note that under FRCP 6(a), the first day of the period, which in this case would be the day of service, is *not* included in the computation. For purposes of completing the discussion of this Rule, note that it also provides an extra three days on top of any deadline triggered by service that is mailed.

(e) Enlargement of Time in the Rules

Under FRCP 6(b), the court has the power to grant an extension or enlargement of time "for cause shown." The local rules of many federal

---

ory v. Secretary of Navy, 819 F.2d 291, 293 (D.C.Cir.1987) (date of service is date appearing on certificate itself rather than in its text).

8. *See, e.g.,* D.N.J. Local Rule 5.1 (failure to make proof of service does not affect validity of service).

9. As with reading the complaint, there is no chance of compromising a client relationship by simply determining when service took place. *See* Bobal v. Rensselaer Polytechnic Institute, 916 F.2d 759, 765 (2d Cir.1990) (review of complaint by legal services agency which subsequently refused to accept case due to conflict does not give rise to basis for disqualification motion). Even if representation is declined because of a conflict, the attorney may still be obligated to

at least take actions to prevent a default. *See* Jackson v. Mares, 802 S.W.2d 48, 50 (Tex.App.1990) (dictum stating that on receipt of papers, attorney should promptly see to filing of answer or advise client that he declines the representation); South Carolina Adv. Op. 89–19, 1989 WL 608457 (S.C. Bar Eth. Adv. Comm. 1989) (attorney in receipt of complaint from client may have had sufficient confidential communication with client to give rise to attorney-client relationship).

10. These are defined by a list of holidays set forth in the Rule, or any other federal holiday or any legal holiday in the state where the district court sits. FRCP 6(a).

districts contain "breathing room" provisions that allow one "free" automatic extension of time, such as for 15 days, to answer, to any party that requests it in writing from the clerk.[11] Where such a provision exists, defense counsel should invoke its use well before the deadline. Even if it would not take more than 20 days to draft, approve, execute and serve the answer, there is no reason not to allow oneself the luxury of not having to worry about a last-minute deadline.

If, on the other hand, defense counsel anticipates meaningful difficulty in getting the answer out in the total time allowed in many districts (*e.g.*, 35 days), *i.e.*, there is a good, known, concrete reason the extra days will not suffice, it may be worth bringing the problem to the judge's attention before filing for the automatic extension and thereby preserving credibility on the issue. A party may also move for an extension for "cause" under FRCP 6(b).

Keep in mind that not every clock stops when an extension of time to answer or otherwise respond is obtained. It is necessary also to determine if the applicable local rules provide for the commencement of discovery during the extended period and where this fits in with the mandatory discovery-planning conference held early in the case. Since discovery under the Federal Rules in most districts is essentially self-generated now, this may be less of an issue; but the wide variety of systems presently in place in the various districts requires diligence.

(f) Stipulations of Extension

Usually the parties will agree to an extension of time, and in most cases it is common practice for plaintiff's counsel, with the client's consent, to agree to at least one reasonable extension. The use of one or more stipulations (proposed order agreed to by the parties) extending time to answer, move or otherwise respond is a common and important practice to allow sufficient time to prepare the answer or responsive motion and when settlement discussions follow service of the complaint.

Note that some districts' local rules and some judges' rules address the extent of permissible stipulations of this nature. Some local rules even require a pro forma submission (motion) to the court for consideration of the mutual application for an extension "on the merits,"[12] though one "free" stipulation may be granted as of right.[13] In any event,

---

11. *See, e.g.*, D.N.J. Local Civil Rule 6.1 (allowing automatic 15 day extension where motion is served prior to expiration of deadline, and requiring disclosure in application of date service of process effected and all previous extensions); D. Neb. Local Rule 6.1 (permitting one enlargement of time not to exceed 30 days granted by order signed by clerk, provided the party seeking the enlargement moves to obtain it before the expiration of time originally allotted).

12. *See, e.g.*, D.S.D. Local Rule 29.1; N.D. Fla. Local Rule 6.1 (stipulations between counsel with respect to extensions of time for serving or filing not effective until approved by court "for good cause shown").

13. *See, e.g.*, D.R.I. Local Rule 22(a) (providing for one extension as of right but requiring formal motion); W.D. Ark. Local Rule C-5 (if within originally prescribed time frame and with consent of all counsel, clerk may enter order for extension of not more than 15 days; other extensions require

the court must approve the stipulation, so it should be submitted for approval promptly upon execution.

(1) Extensions of Time: Waiver of Service

There is no need to answer or otherwise respond to a complaint that is not properly served. The exception is where service is waived pursuant to the procedures set forth in FRCP 4(d), discussed in Chapter 2 "Personal Jurisdiction and Service," *supra*. When plaintiff and defendant agree to waive service under FRCP 4(d), they have traded the waiver for a 60–day extension of time specified in the Rule. Practically speaking, this procedure is rarely used.

Few plaintiffs have reason to delay the progress of their lawsuit for 60 days merely to avoid service on a party that is ultimately amenable to the court's jurisdiction. But defendants should take advantage of FRCP 4(d) whenever they can; there is never a disadvantage for the defendant in a 60–day extension. One advantage in agreeing to the extension is that preparation of a motion may take longer than expected. This is a common occurrence where first-hand affidavits, needed for a 12(b)(2) or other motion, must be prepared, revised, executed and authenticated along with the relevant exhibits. Another advantage is that the 60 days sets a deadline but does not bar an earlier filing; in fact, acceptance of the extension could enhance the surprise of a prompt dismissal motion. Therefore the defendant presented with the option to waive service under FRCP 4(d) should seldom turn it down.

(2) Extensions of Time: Practical Considerations

Once a stipulation is agreed to, the practice in all federal courts is that the stipulation be in writing. Section 6.15(b) *infra* contains a typical form of stipulation. It is very important that both the title of the order and the mandatory language indicate that the extension of time applies to answering, moving or otherwise responding, and not just answering. This may be more than a technical problem if not adequately drafted. The plaintiff may credibly argue, for example, that its extension of the time to answer was only in consideration for the implied promise not to make a motion to dismiss.

It is also good practice—and this is relevant whether using a clerk's order or a joint application for stipulation—to use the phrase, "until and including [the new deadline]" in the order submitted to the court. This makes it clear what the last day of the new deadline is, as well as the fact that if served *on* that day, the answer is timely.

Also note that the stipulation in Section 6.15(b), *infra* also stays discovery for the period of the extension. If the parties do not stipulate to stay discovery this clause should be omitted.

approval of court); W.D. Pa. Local Rule 7.4 (counsel may file stipulation once, without   approval of court, extending due date for the filing of an answer or motion).

(g) When Preliminary Relief Is Sought: Strategic Considerations

The topic of preliminary injunctions and orders to show cause are treated extensively in Chapter 14, "Provisional Remedies," *infra*. Though a prayer for provisional remedies may seem to give the upper hand to the plaintiff, in reality many benefits inure to the defendant where preliminary relief is sought. The plaintiff must lay out its whole case on a motion for preliminary relief. If the plaintiff's application fails, the loss can be used by the defendant for the rest of the case, if there is one. The exact terms spelling out when and if an answer or other response is required will be set out in the order sought by the plaintiff.

Generally speaking, when faced with a complaint accompanied by an application for preliminary relief, the defendant's main concern should be resisting the preliminary relief sought by the plaintiff. Thus it is often possible to build a stay of the time to answer into the proposed order for preliminary proceedings. (Where the plaintiff's application is made ex parte this issue should be brought to the judge's attention at the very first appearance on the order to show cause.) For this reason some cases have gone for months in preliminary proceedings without an answer ever being filed. Thus, in Lanham Act cases and other areas where preliminary injunction practice is common, it is said that the injunction is all and the final judgment is rarely an issue.

(1) The Verified Answer: Practical Considerations

In a case where the complaint has been accompanied by an application for a provisional remedy, it may be worth considering the use of a verified answer instead of answering affidavits in response to the motion. Verification, while unusual in answers it is certainly permissible.

There are several disadvantages to a verified answer. One is that it is difficult—especially on an expedited schedule, as is common when preliminary restraints are sought—to answer a wide-ranging complaint adequately. It is a much simpler task to resist a single criterion among those the plaintiff must meet to qualify for a preliminary injunction, such as irreparable harm. The answer may require pleading matter not necessary to resist the motion and to which verification may not be necessary or desirable. And while there are advantages to the fact that a verified pleading is a more compelling representation of the defendant's overall position than a nonverified one, subsequent requests to amend the answer for nontechnical reasons will be viewed with more skepticism than usual because of the verification.[14] The verifying person is also exposed to early deposition and other discovery as well as damaging impeachment if facts contrary to the verification emerge. Finally, verified pleadings often contain more evidentiary detail than may be appreciated by the judge.

In general, then, use of a verified answer adds a certain power to the response, but it raises the stakes for both sides. Therefore all the

---

14. Bernard v. U.S. Aircoach, 117 F.Supp. 134 (S.D.Cal.1953) (refusal of motion to amend verified answer on grounds, inter alia, that verifying officer must have known of defense at outset).

implications of such an approach must be discussed with the defendant itself.

Library References:

West's Key No. Digests, Federal Civil Procedure ☞621–1150.
Wright, Miller & Marcus, Federal Practice and Procedure: Civil 2d §§ 2048–2050, 2170, 2179–2181.

§ 6.5 Motions to Dismiss Generally

(a) Motions to Dismiss: Strategy

Why is discussion of motions to dismiss placed before the section on answering the complaint? The reason is that every complaint must at one point be evaluated to determine whether or not dismissal would be appropriate, even though many such motions fail. If a strong motion to dismiss can be made, it should be seriously considered. This is especially true where the motion is to be based on a fundamental insufficiency in the complaint, such that little factual investigation is required by the defense, and where answering the complaint and preparing affirmative defenses, counterclaims, cross-claims or third-party complaints would be a substantial undertaking.

There is also a conceptual reason: the idea of a motion to dismiss is that the complaint—or more specifically, the claim—is so lacking in merit that no answer is necessary. Certainly if that is the case, and it seems likely that the judge can be made to agree that dismissal is appropriate, there is no reason to start drafting an answer.[1]

(b) Practical Considerations

Successful motions to dismiss a complaint are a rarity, more the subject of law school civil procedure classes than actual practice. There are several reasons for this. One is the modern doctrine mandating liberal pleadings standards. In effect this means that courts will look not so much at the artfulness in the drafting of the complaint as much as the substance of the purported claim. There is also a corollary to this doctrine: The courts have a general policy of determining actions on the merits.

The effect of these approaches must be fully appreciated when considering the seeming promise of motions to dismiss, especially motions for failure to state a claim under FRCP 12(b)(6). Too often a brilliant motion to dismiss the complaint that ruthlessly exposes holes and inconsistencies in the pleadings results only in the plaintiff's filing, at the court's invitation, an amended complaint now free of all the

§ 6.5

1. For discussion of motion practice, procedure and strategy generally, *see* Chap-ter 24, "Motion Practice," *infra.*

deficiencies pointed out in the motion. All that is accomplished substantively is that the plaintiff has been forced to focus on its case and, with the assistance of the court's decision on the dismissal motion, recast areas in which its complaint was weak. In the process the defendant has helped the plaintiff eliminate sinkholes and traps in the complaint that may have been useful to the defense on a later summary judgment motion or at trial. Furthermore, judges sometimes become de facto "advocates" of claims "revived" in their opinions denying motions to dismiss.

For these reasons a motion to dismiss a fundamentally meritorious claim based on technical deficiencies may not be worth the price of the motion and of the defense's credibility with the judge. Faced with obvious weaknesses in the plaintiff's case, it may be worth considering whether a stronger motion may be brought as a summary judgment application following a limited amount of discovery. In this instance keep in mind that many judges will not permit summary judgment motions prior to the close of discovery because of their wariness of "dueling affidavits" as a basis for making substantive rulings.

None of this is to say that there is no place for Rule 12(b) motions. There are times when the defendant simply should not have to appear in federal court, or at least not in the venue where suit has been brought. Perhaps there is an arbitration clause, bargained for at some cost, on which the defendant is entitled to rely. Some complaints are just too lacking in merit to be worthy of the defendant's time and money.[2] And though the phrase has become a cliché, in the right circumstance there is something to be said for "educating the judge" about a case by bringing a Rule 12 motion early on, even if, while meritorious, the motion may not be enough to end the proceedings.

Library References:
    West's Key No. Digests, Federal Civil Procedure ⊕1721–1842.
    Wright & Miller, Federal Practice and Procedure: Civil 2d §§ 1349, 1350.

§ 6.6 FRCP 12(b) Motions to Dismiss

(a) Time to Move

Just as with any other response to a complaint, a motion to dismiss under FRCP 12(b) must be made within 20 days of receipt of the summons and complaint. Making the motion stops the clock on the answer itself, pursuant to FRCP 12(a)(4). This applies to the whole of the pleadings, regardless of what part of the complaint is the subject of the motion to dismiss. Therefore, it has been held that a motion to dismiss one count of a 10–count complaint stays the time to answer the entire complaint.[1] Note, however, that this fact should not give rise to

----

2. Counsel should also consider a motion to dismiss if a nonnatural person—*i.e.,* a corporation, partnership or association— is the plaintiff, and is not properly represented by counsel. *See supra* § 6.4, note 1.

§ 6.6

1. 5A Charles Alan Wright & Arthur R. Miller, Federal Practice and Procedure § 1346 at 181 (2d ed.1990); Brocksopp

"creative" approaches to obtaining more time to answer the complaint. Courts have defaulted parties for filing frivolous FRCP 12 motions solely to extend time.[2] If the motion is denied or postponed, the answer is due within 10 days of receiving notice of the court's action.

As usual, an eye must be kept on discovery. Here local rules may govern whether discovery is stayed; or the judge may have a policy that is embodied in a standing order or that is simply stated to the parties when the motion is filed. The parties also may seek from the court either a stay of discovery or permission to proceed.

(b) Strategy: Defenses vs. Motions to Dismiss

FRCP 12(b) requires all defenses to be asserted in the answer, but directs that the following seven of them may be resolved by motion or merely left as defenses:

1. Lack of subject matter jurisdiction

2. Lack of personal jurisdiction

3. Improper venue

4. Insufficiency of process

5. Insufficiency of service of process

6. Failure to state a claim on which relief can be granted

7. Failure to join a party under Rule 19.

These seven are the Rule 12 bases for motions to dismiss. The question arises whether they should be invoked in such a motion, asserted as a defense, or both.

These grounds for dismissal should always be asserted as defenses if available in good faith, regardless of whether motion practice is intended when the answer is filed or even if motions have been brought and have failed on these bases. Ultimately, however, FRCP 12(d) requires that the merits of FRCP 12 defenses must be decided at some point before trial, unless the court decides otherwise. The exception to this is where the court lacks subject matter jurisdiction, discussed in the next section.

(c) Subject Matter Jurisdiction, FRCP 12(b)(1)

As discussed in Chapter 1 "Subject Matter Jurisdiction" *supra,* federal courts are courts of limited jurisdiction.[3] The complaint must

Eng'g, Inc. v. Bach–Simpson Ltd., 136 F.R.D. 485 (E.D.Wis.1991) (separation of counts leads to confusion and duplication). *But see,* Gerlach v. Michigan Bell Tel. Co., 448 F.Supp. 1168, 1174 (E.D.Mich.1978) (separate counts separated bases for lawsuit; no change in deadline to respond to counts not challenged).

2. *See, e.g.,* Ricke v. Armco, Inc., 158 F.R.D. 149 (D.Minn.1994) (denying motion

styled as one to dismiss but containing extensive extraneous material filed "simply to avoid filing an answer").

3. *See also* Chapter 8 "Removal to Federal Court," *infra,* for discussion of remanding an improperly removed case back to state court.

state that the requirements of subject matter jurisdiction are met in the matter. More importantly, they must actually be met. If a court lacks subject matter jurisdiction, it simply has no authority to decide the case—even if the parties are willing to waive objection or stipulate to the federal court's jurisdiction.[4]

For this reason, a challenge to the court's subject matter jurisdiction may be brought at any time,[5] even after final judgment is entered[6] and regardless of the prejudice that would result by dismissing the action after proceedings have been under way.[7] On a motion challenging jurisdiction, the court tests the existence of subject matter jurisdiction as of the date the lawsuit was filed, not later.[8] It is not a useful strategy, therefore, to attempt to deprive the court of jurisdiction in a diversity case after the suit is filed by having the defendant move its domicile to the same state as the plaintiff.

As the party invoking the federal court's jurisdiction, the plaintiff must show that it has the right to do so.[9] Therefore, once the defendant attacks the basis of the court's subject matter jurisdiction, it has shifted the burden of coming forward to the plaintiff.

(1) Attack on Jurisdiction

One critical area of attack on the plaintiff's assertion of federal jurisdiction is where the plaintiff has asserted the existence of a federal question. It is not uncommon for a civil RICO or antitrust count to be asserted in commercial litigation, thus bringing the case under the aegis of federal law. Similarly, disputes that include alleged copyright or trademark violations are federal question cases. These causes of action, however, are sometimes just "tagged" onto standard, nondiverse contractual disputes in order to get into federal court. If the defendant can

---

4. State of Missouri ex rel. Missouri Highway and Transp. Com'n v. Cuffley, 112 F.3d 1332, 1334 (8th Cir.1997) (waiver); Holman v. Laulo–Rowe Agency, 994 F.2d 666, 668 n. 1 (9th Cir.1993) (stipulation).

5. FRCP 12(h) (3).

6. FRCP 60(b) (4).

7. Wilson v. Glenwood Intermountain Properties, 98 F.3d 590, 593 (10th Cir. 1996); Augustine v. United States, 704 F.2d 1074, 1077 (9th Cir.1983) (court is under continuing duty to dismiss action "whenever it appears the court lacks jurisdiction"); Fitzgerald v. Seaboard System R.R., Inc., 647 F.Supp. 205, 206–07 (S.D.Ga.1985) (delay in raising defense of lack of subject matter jurisdiction does not estop defendant to assert such defense, since no action by parties can confer subject matter jurisdiction upon federal court).

8. Damiano v. Federal Deposit Ins. Corp., 104 F.3d 328, 333 (11th Cir.1997).

9. Toste Farm Corp. v. Hadbury, Inc., 70 F.3d 640, 645 (1st Cir.1995) (rejecting diversity jurisdiction claim based on "concocted" diversity resulting from plaintiff's assignment of claim to out of state entity for sole purpose of litigation); Media Duplication Services, Ltd. v. HDG Software, 928 F.2d 1228, 1235–36 (1st Cir.1991) (facts insufficient to support diversity jurisdiction where no evidence in record indicated party corporation's principal place of business on date complaint filed); United States ex rel. LeBlanc v. Raytheon Co., 874 F.Supp. 35, 37 (D.Mass.1995) (in qui tam action under federal False Claims Act, plaintiff has burden of establishing subject matter jurisdiction exists once defendant raises issue), aff'd, 62 F.3d 1411 (1st Cir.), cert. denied, 516 U.S. 1140, 116 S.Ct. 973, 133 L.Ed.2d 893 (1996).

dismiss these counts, it may be able to end the federal litigation then and there.[10]

The other avenue of attack is on the plaintiff's claim that there is "complete" diversity and that the $75,000 jurisdictional amount is met. These requirements are addressed in Chapter 1 "Subject Matter Jurisdiction," *supra.*

(d) Personal Jurisdiction, FRCP 12(b)(2)

This topic is discussed extensively in Chapter 2 "Personal Jurisdiction and Service," *supra.* It is no longer the case that a defendant, by appearing in court to argue a defense of lack of personal jurisdiction, waives the right to that defense by coming within that jurisdiction.[11] On the other hand, under FRCP 12(h)(1), the defense is waived if not asserted in the answer or raised in the motion.[12]

In commercial litigation, personal jurisdiction is rarely dependent on an individual's physical presence in a district. Rather the focus is on the minimum contacts discussed in Chapter 2. One important point to remember is that the assertion of jurisdiction over out of state defendants is based on state law.[13] Though the long-arm statutes in most states extend jurisdiction to the full extent constitutionally permissible, not all do.[14] Defense counsel should therefore investigate closely whether the defendant's activities satisfy the applicable long-arm statute.

10. *See, e.g.,* Edmondson & Gallagher v. Alban Towers Tenants Ass'n, 48 F.3d 1260, 1266 (D.C.Cir.1995) (district court properly exercised discretion in refusing to hear supplemental state claims following dismissal of civil RICO count); Merlino v. Getty Petroleum Corp., 916 F.2d 52, 53 (2d Cir. 1990) (state law claims dismissed following dismissal of claims under Petroleum Marketing Practices Act); Alfred Dunhill Ltd. v. Interstate Cigar Co., Inc., 499 F.2d 232, 237 (2d Cir.1974) (dismissing state claims following dismissal of Lanham Act claims).

11. Bayou Steel Corp. v. M/V Amstelvoorn, 809 F.2d 1147, 1149 n. 6 (5th Cir. 1987); Marcial Ucin v. SS Galicia, 723 F.2d 994, 997 (1st Cir.1983) ("well settled" that general appearance no waiver of defense of lack of personal jurisdiction). *But see* Trans World Airlines, Inc. v. Mattox, 897 F.2d 773, 786–87 (5th Cir.) (personal jurisdiction waived and de facto intervenor status established when nonparties described themselves as "specially appearing," but sought affirmative relief from the court by asking it to deny injunction against the defendant), *cert. denied,* 498 U.S. 926, 111 S.Ct. 307, 112 L.Ed.2d 261 (1990).

12. S. Baicker–McKee, W. Janssen and J. Corr, Federal Civil Rules Handbook (West 1997), at 197.

13. *See, e.g.,* Omni Capital Int'l v. Rudolf Wolff & Co., 484 U.S. 97, 108–10, 108 S.Ct. 404, 411–13, 98 L.Ed.2d 415 (1987) (applying long-arm statute of Louisiana, the state in which the district court sits); Federal Deposit Ins. Corp. v. British–American Ins. Co., Ltd., 828 F.2d 1439, 1441 (9th Cir.1987) (applying forum state's jurisdictional statute to determine that court had no personal jurisdiction over nonresident defendant despite attenuated contacts).

14. The Topps Co., Inc. v. Gerrit J. Verburg Co., 961 F.Supp. 88, 90 (S.D.N.Y.1997) (New York law does not extend long-arm jurisdiction as far as constitution permits). *Compare* Federal Deposit Ins. Corp., 828 F.2d at 1441 ("California statute extends jurisdiction to the maximum extent permitted by due process.").

In federal question cases, FRCP 4(k)(2) purports to provide federal courts with jurisdictional reach to the full extent of the Due Process Clause of the Constitution, regardless of the forum state's own policy. Note, however, that in diversity cases, state law limitations would still apply. Further-

(1) Burden of Proof and Procedure

As with subject matter jurisdiction, once an objection is raised to the plaintiff's assertion of personal jurisdiction over the defendant, the burden shifts to the plaintiff to establish that it exists.[15] How this burden is met, however, depends on the circumstances; this shift may be more technical than actual.[16] Where the court is considering only the pleadings or affidavits in support of a motion to dismiss on this basis, the plaintiff may meet its burden by making a prima facie showing of facts to support its claim of jurisdiction.[17] In other cases the court may conduct an evidentiary hearing and require the plaintiff to establish personal jurisdiction by the preponderance of the evidence,[18] or it may take an intermediate position requiring the plaintiff to show the "likelihood" of personal jurisdiction.[19]

It is beyond the scope of this chapter to go into more extensive detail concerning the standards to be applied in a motion to dismiss for lack of personal jurisdiction. But the diversity of legal standards and factual situations that may trigger this motion requires close investigation by defense counsel to project how a motion would actually be decided in a given situation.

(e) Venue, FRCP 12(b)(3)

The topic of venue, including application of forum selection clauses, is treated in Chapter 3 "Venue, Forum Selection and Transfer," *supra.*

---

more, practically speaking there is no escape from the limitations of state law, at least some state's law. The Rule's language limits its application to defendants who are not subject to the jurisdiction of the courts of general jurisdiction of any state. Thus it has been held that Rule 4(k)(2) cannot be used to force a defendant into the plaintiff's choice of federal venue which otherwise lacks state long-arm authority, where long-arm jurisdiction over that defendant can be shown to exist in any state of the Union. *See, e.g.,* AT & T Co. v. Compagnie Bruxelles Lambert, 94 F.3d 586, 590 (9th Cir. 1996); Warn v. M/Y Maridome, 961 F.Supp. 1357, 1368 (S.D.Cal.1997). Defendants, therefore, can avoid the application of 4(k)(2) in unfavorable venues by establishing long-arm jurisdiction in any other state.

15. Rodriguez v. Fullerton Tires Corp., 115 F.3d 81, 83 (1st Cir.1997); D.J. Investments, Inc. v. Metzeler Motorcycle Tire Agent Gregg, Inc., 754 F.2d 542, 545 (5th Cir.1985) (once objection to personal jurisdiction is raised, party seeking to invoke court's jurisdiction has burden of establishing jurisdiction over nonresident defendant); Combs v. Bakker, 886 F.2d 673, 676

(4th Cir.1989) (issue of personal jurisdiction is for judge, but plaintiff must show jurisdiction by preponderance of evidence).

16. S. Baicker–McKee, W. Janssen and J. Corr., *supra* note 12, at 199.

17. PDK Labs, Inc. v. Friedlander, 103 F.3d 1105, 1108 (2d Cir.1997) (only prima facie showing required); D.J. Investments, Inc., 754 F.2d at 545–46 (plaintiff bears burden of establishing jurisdiction over nonresident defendant, but court faced with conflicting affidavits may find burden met by prima facie evidentiary showing short of preponderance of evidence).

18. National School Reporting Servs., Inc. v. National Schools of C.A., Ltd., 924 F.Supp. 21, 23 (S.D.N.Y.1996). See also, Combs v. Bakker, 886 F.2d 673, 676 (4th Cir.1989) (plaintiff has burden to prove jurisdiction by preponderance of evidence once jurisdiction challenged); Mylan Lab., Inc. v. Akzo, N.V., 2 F.3d 56, 59–60 (4th Cir.1993) (burden on plaintiff to prove ground for jurisdiction exists).

19. Barry v. Mortgage Servicing Acquisition Corp., 909 F.Supp. 65, 67 (D.R.I. 1995) (compromise standard).

It should be noted, however, that a venue objection must be included in any omnibus motion under FRCP 12 or as an affirmative defense. Otherwise, according to some authorities, it is waived.[20] The related topic of arbitration clauses is addressed in Chapter 9 "Arbitration vs. Litigation: Enforceability and Access to Courts," *infra*.

(f) "Process Motions" Under FRCP 12(b)(4)-(5)

Motions to dismiss on the basis of insufficient process (FRCP 12(b)(4)), and insufficient service of process (FRCP 12(b)(5)), are often incorrectly brought under the guise of a Rule 12(b)(6) motion to dismiss. The courts, however, may and do construe them as if they were brought under the proper Rule.[21] In any event, like personal jurisdiction and venue, they are waived if not asserted in a motion or as an affirmative defense.[22]

(1) Practical Considerations

The procedural misdesignation of process motions is not typically their biggest hurdle. The federal courts are not inclined to engage in coy games surrounding service of process. Federal judges faced with motions based on technical deficiencies in service typically will ask if re-service is possible and, if it is, will often merely require re-service without dismissing the action[23]—effectively "quashing" service[24]—or will simply reject the motion to dismiss.

Ultimately, the test is whether the failure of process or service prejudices the defendant.[25] Yet if there is something more than a niggling deficiency, the motion should be made, or at least included with other FRCP 12 motions that may be brought. (*See* Sections 6.7–6.8, *infra*). The process motion does not always fail, especially where the court can be persuaded that the deficiency in process or service is more than technical.[26] It is not a coincidence that such motions often succeed where the statute of limitations is on the verge of running out, because it

---

20. *See, e.g.*, Misch v. Zee Enters., Inc., 879 F.2d 628, 632 (9th Cir.1989) (citing cases).

21. Travel All Over the World, Inc. v. Kingdom of Saudi Arabia, 73 F.3d 1423, 1429 (7th Cir.1996) (nomenclature ignored; court's duty is to construe submissions so as to promote justice).

22. FRCP 12(h)(1). *See supra* § 6.5(a).

23. *See* Umbenhauer v. Woog, 969 F.2d 25, 30 (3d Cir.1992). *Compare* Montalbano v. Easco Hand Tools, Inc., 766 F.2d 737, 740 (2d Cir.1985) (affirming trial court's dismissal with respect to one defendant because of improper service of process, absent reasonable possibility that service could ever be properly made on that defendant).

24. S. Baicker–McKee, W. Janssen & J. Corr, *supra* note 12, at 203, citing R. Griggs Group Ltd. v. Filanto Spa, 920 F.Supp. 1100 (D.Nev.1996); Montalbano, 766 F.2d at 740 (service ordinarily quashed and action preserved when service of process is improper).

25. Libertad v. Welch, 53 F.3d 428, 440 (1st Cir.1995). *See also*, Lenoir v. Federal Deposit Ins. Corp., 709 F.Supp. 830, 832 (N.D.Ill.1989) (improper service not grounds for dismissal, since defendant received actual notice and did not suffer any prejudice from the defect).

26. *See, e.g.*, Tuke v. United States, 76 F.3d 155, 157 (7th Cir.1996) (deadlines set by Rules not amenable to judicial second-guessing).

is then that mistakes in last-minute preparation or service of process are apt to be made and where re-service is no longer possible.

(g) Failure to State a Claim upon Which Relief Can Be Granted, FRCP 12(b)(6)

See Section 6.7, below.

(h) Failure to Join Indispensable Parties, FRCP 12(b)(7)

This topic is discussed in detail in Chapter 10 "Joinder, Consolidation and Severance."

Library References:

West's Key No. Digests, Federal Civil Procedure ⊕1721–1842.
Wright & Miller, Federal Practice and Procedure: Civil 2d §§ 1361, 1363, 1389.

§ 6.7 Motions to Dismiss Under FRCP 12(b)(6)

(a) Introduction

The successful FRCP 12(b)(6) application is the home run of motions. It is a challenge made at the very beginning of a case[1] and strikes at the very heart of the lawsuit. It is a statement that even if the plaintiff were given every benefit of the doubt and everything it claimed were true, the plaintiff's claim should be dismissed—either because it is not legally cognizable or because sufficient facts have not been alleged to make out a cognizable claim.[2]

When considering a 12(b)(6) motion, the court presumes that all the allegations of the complaint are true; it resolves all doubts or inferences in the plaintiff's favor; and it reads the complaint in the light most favorable to the plaintiff.[3] Needless to say, the burden of proof on such a motion is on the party making it.[4] No material from outside the plead-

---

§ 6.7

1. If a motion to dismiss is brought after responsive pleadings are filed, it will be designated as a motion to dismiss on the pleadings under FRCP 12(c); *see infra* § 6.8(b)

2. *See, e.g.,* Brown v. Hot, Sexy, and Safer Productions Inc., 68 F.3d 525 (1st Cir.1995), *cert. denied,* 516 U.S. 1159, 116 S.Ct. 1044, 134 L.Ed.2d 191 (1996) (parent's and students' complaint alleging various causes of action rising from attendance at mandatory AIDS awareness program at school dismissed as meritless).

3. Albright v. Oliver, 510 U.S. 266, 114 S.Ct. 807, 127 L.Ed.2d 114 (1994). *See also,* Pompano–Windy City Partners, Ltd. v. Bear

Stearns & Co., Inc., 794 F.Supp. 1265, 1280–81 (S.D.N.Y.1992) (motion to dismiss must be denied "unless it appears beyond a doubt that the plaintiff can prove no set of facts in support of its claim which would entitle him to relief"), citing Scheuer v. Rhodes, 416 U.S. 232, 236, 94 S.Ct. 1683, 1686, 40 L.Ed.2d 90 (1974); General Electric Co. v. Lyon, 894 F.Supp. 544, 548 (D.Mass.1995) (all inferences must be drawn in favor of nonmoving party).

4. *See, e.g.,* Sabow v. United States, 93 F.3d 1445 (9th Cir.1996); General Electric Co. v. Lyon, 894 F.Supp. at 548 (burden is heavy on party moving to dismiss); Kearney v. Jandernoa, 957 F.Supp. 116, 118 (W.D.Mich.1997) (burden on moving party to prove that no claim exists).

ings may be considered or the motion will be considered one for summary judgment (*see* Section 6.7(d), *infra*).

Given all these benefits and the liberal pleading requirements of the Rules, all the plaintiff has to do to survive the motion is make out *some* sort of claim for which a court might provide relief. For every home run, therefore, there are innumerably more strikeouts or at best routine hits (*i.e.*, when partial dismissal is granted as to some claims). The purpose of this section is to assist in picking the right pitches, and to consider when a "long out" (*see* Section 6.7(c)(3), "Educating the Judge," *infra*) can have the desired effect, even though the ball stays in the park.

(b) Issues to Raise with Clients

There is little that is more satisfying in commercial litigation defense than winning a dramatic 12(b)(6) motion on behalf of a defendant eager to end a potentially expensive and vexatious court case. Conversely, the attorney should visualize the expression on the client representative's face as he realizes the implications of an unsuccessful 12(b)(6) motion in a commercial case—unless he has been adequately counseled about the potential costs, risks and rewards involved in the undertaking.

Because the plaintiff is given every benefit of the doubt in both law and fact, the 12(b)(6) motion theoretically requires the movant to "play out" every factual scenario that could be contained in the four corners of the complaint, and then apply the applicable legal standards. Similarly, every plausible legal theory that might provide relief to the plaintiff, based on the facts pleaded, must be considered.

For this reason the 12(b)(6) motion can, in some instances, be more costly and difficult than a summary judgment motion, though the motion to dismiss does not usually involve extensive affidavits as does a summary judgment application. In the latter proceeding, however, it is easier to limit the factual scenario that must be considered by submission of competent evidence that circumscribes the possibilities sketched out by the pleadings. That is harder to do under 12(b)(6), though much depends on the judge's inclinations.

Indeed, as a final caveat to the 12(b)(6) approach, practitioners should advise their clients that granting the motion takes a certain level of judicial confidence that not every court can muster. The number of cases overturning 12(b)(6) dismissals surely dwarfs those that affirm such rulings, and it is the path of least resistance simply to decree that it would be more appropriate to decide the issues after "some discovery" has been taken. This seems to the judge like not deciding the motion, and in a sense it is; yet it is a denial of the motion, for the effects of which the defendant must be prepared.

Still and all there is a place for the judicious use of a 12(b)(6) motion. That place is not only the obvious case where the complaint puts forth a cause of action that is plainly not justifiable (*e.g.*, seeking damages for invasion of privacy arising from the defendant's alleged use of microwave beams to read the plaintiff's mind[5]). The scenarios in which a 12(b)(6) motion is appropriate will be discussed below in Section 6.7(c). The critical point is to lay out the risks, rewards and benefits clearly for the client to allow a maximally-informed choice about whether to proceed.

(c) Reasons to Bring a 12(b)(6) Motion

Despite the long odds, there are several reasons why a defendant might bring a 12(b)(6) motion, only one of which is that it might succeed in full:

(1) Elimination of Plainly Nonjusticiable Cases

It should go without saying that a 12(b)(6) motion is the appropriate vehicle for certain lawsuits that, on simple inspection, do not make out claims for legal relief. There is some point where even the minimal pleading requirements are not met,[6] where even given every benefit of the doubt, the facts alleged cannot in any way be scrambled to create a cause of action.[7] Identifying the line between the obvious and the less obvious candidates for inclusion in this category requires a certain amount of experience, but it can fairly be said that some complaints fall into the category of "I [the judge] know it when I see it."

This must be contrasted, however, with the situation where the plaintiff has pleaded facts that in themselves may add up to a valid legal claim but has set forth inappropriate legal theories as the basis for recovery. Dismissal will not be granted when this is the case,[8] though if

---

5. Shibuya v. George Washington University, 1987 WL 14638 (D.D.C.1987) (also alleging that defendant used "advanced technology" to create artificial noises and smells and to scramble plaintiff's intellectual processes at the time she sat for New York and District of Columbia bar examinations; dismissing complaint as frivolous and for failure to state claim). *See also,* United States *ex rel.* Mayo v. Satan and His Staff, 54 F.R.D. 282, 283 (W.D.Pa.1971) (civil rights complaint brought on grounds defendants placed obstacles in plaintiff's path and caused plaintiff's downfall; in denying motion to proceed *in pauperis,* court also noted that complaint failed to state claim for which relief could be granted and may more properly have been brought as class action; court also expressed doubt about efficacy of plaintiff's ability properly to serve defendants with process).

6. *See, e.g.,* Doyle v. Hasbro, 103 F.3d 186, 191 (1st Cir.1996) (civil plaintiff's failure to identify enterprise fatal under RICO); Rumford Pharmacy, Inc. v. City of East Providence, 970 F.2d 996, 998 (1st

Cir.1992) ("The pleading requirements, though 'minimal,' are not nonexistent."), quoting Gooley v. Mobil Oil Corp., 851 F.2d 513, 514 (1st Cir.1988).

7. Rumford Pharmacy, Inc., 970 F.2d at 999 (allegations in complaint failed to state elements of claim that plaintiff's constitutional rights were violated); Brayton v. Monson Pub. Sch., 950 F.Supp. 33, 36–38 (D.Mass.1997) (failure of complaint for wrongful termination arises not from inspecificity of allegations but insufficiency of allegations themselves).

8. Vidimos, Inc. v. Laser Lab Ltd., 99 F.3d 217 (7th Cir.1996); Doss v. South Cent. Bell Tel. Co., 834 F.2d 421 (5th Cir. 1987) (vacating order of dismissal where complaint alleged facts which, if true, would have entitled plaintiff to relief under a different legal theory than that alleged); Bartholet v. Reishauer A.G., 953 F.2d 1073, 1078 (7th Cir.1992) ("the complaint need not identify a legal theory, and specifying an incorrect theory is not fatal").

the complaint is truly incomprehensible, the defendant may be entitled to relief under FRCP 12(e), a motion for a more definite statement (*see* Section 6.8(c), *infra*).

(2) *Cutting off Novel Legal Theories*

Faced with a complaint, some commercial clients may have an interest, eminently reasonable, in "snuffing out" novel legal theories put forth or even suggested by the complaint. Such theories of recovery may pose a larger threat to some defendants' interests than the immediate pending litigation. In such cases clients might put a very high premium on delivering a crashing blow to the plaintiff and discouraging similar litigation by those similarly situated.

These are the situations, however, where fully apprising the client of the range of possibilities under 12(b)(6) is essential. The unsuccessful 12(b)(6) motion in this situation may be far worse than no motion at all and will, in all likelihood, have precisely the opposite effect from the one intended because the judge may help the plaintiff articulate the theory better. Since most 12(b)(6) motions are unsuccessful, taking this approach is one of the more daring maneuvers in commercial litigation.

The risk of this preemptive strike strategy, great as it is inherently, is heightened by a line of authority stating that it is precisely where novel legal theories are proffered that dismissal is inappropriate, on the theory that development in discovery—the bugaboo of motions to dismiss—can help the court assess the propriety of the claim.[9]

(3) *"Educating the Judge"*

There may be some situations, as discussed in Section 6.5(b), *supra,* where a 12(b)(6) motion is an appropriate vehicle to put the defendant's prima facie case in front of the judge, even though it is not likely to prevail. (Of course, it must still be brought in good faith, *i.e.*, counsel must believe that it *could* prevail.) For example, a motion driven by the "educating the judge" goal could be useful if a fairly short track until trial is anticipated and collateral issues, or some "straw man" in the complaint, could unduly sway the court to the plaintiff's point of view, affecting interlocutory decisions or even the trial. Similarly, the 12(b)(6) motion could clarify for the court early on just how high a burden of proof the plaintiff will have to meet to make its case. Here the 12(b)(6) motion is a way of amplifying and framing the defense in a way that the answer, even with properly crafted affirmative defenses, cannot do.

There are risks in this strategy. One is that judges can usually recognize it from afar and may not appreciate what may seem like manipulation. Another is the likelihood that in complex litigation a long discovery and motion schedule, and the attendant involvement of a magistrate, stand between the pleadings stage and trial. In that case the judge's preliminary opinion on the merits of the respective parties will

---

9. Baker v. Cuomo, 58 F.3d 814 (2d Cir.) *vacated on other grounds*, 85 F.3d 919 (2d Cir.1996). *Compare*, Kugel v. United States, 947 F.2d 1504 (D.C.Cir.1991) (novelty of theory does not excuse plaintiff from obligations under pleading rules).

matter less than the magistrate's view of the proper scope of interrogatories.

(4) Educating the Adversary

When facing a plaintiff whose litigation posture is vulnerable, a forceful motion may be the right tactic. Even a less assailable plaintiff may greet a motion to dismiss, and the attendant effort required to defend against it, with a new sense of realism about the ultimate sustainability of its claim or its desire to proceed as well as about the defendant's resources and abilities.

(5) Partial Dismissal

Finally, the utility of a motion to dismiss under 12(b)(6) should be considered in light of the availability of *partial* dismissal, *i.e.*, dismissal of only part of a complaint or of some but not all counts of a complaint.[10]

This tool can be very powerful in the defense of commercial cases. Many cases involving multiple counts, often including fraud, conspiracy or RICO claims, merely come down to a basic dispute over a contract.[11] Besides providing spurious bases for federal jurisdiction, illegitimate counts such as those are added because they make available punitive, treble or other enhanced damages as well as attorneys' fees, none of which are normally available in contract actions. Often these "add-ons" can be eliminated early, even before discovery, because many such claims have specific pleading requirements that act as gatekeepers at the earliest stage of the litigation. If it is successful with a partial dismissal motion, the defendant can:

- close off potentially dangerous or unreasonably burdensome areas of discovery;

- knock the wind out of a complaint's sails and perhaps cause the plaintiff to question its counsel's judgment; and

- fulfill the "education of the judge" function by undermining the credibility of the plaintiff's claims as well as its way of presenting them to the court.

(d) Conversion into Summary Judgment Motion

If materials extrinsic to the pleadings are submitted to the court in support of or in opposition to a 12(b)(6) motion, the court does not have to consider them.[12] Under FRCP 12(b), however, once the court does

---

10. *See, e.g.*, Edwards v. City of Houston, 78 F.3d 983, 995 (dismissal of long-dormant counts granted in consolidated action); Quinones v. Howard, 948 F.Supp. 251 (W.D.N.Y.1996) (motion to dismiss as to one defendant on grounds of immunity granted but dismissal based on other defendants' asserted grounds denied).

11. *See infra* § 6.8(c)(1).

12. Finley Lines Joint Protective Bd. Unit 200 Brotherhood Ry. Carmen, a Div. of Transp. Communications Union v. Norfolk Southern Corp., 109 F.3d 993, 995–96 (4th Cir.1997) (court has discretion whether to consider extrinsic materials); Schaffer v. Timberland Co., 924 F.Supp. 1298, 1305–06 (D.N.H.1996) (court declined to consider ex-

consider such matter the motion is automatically "converted" to a motion for summary judgment pursuant to FRCP 56.

Material does not literally have to be bound into the complaint to be considered "intrinsic" to it and a proper part of the consideration of a 12(b)(6) motion, without a "conversion" taking place. Courts have considered, on motions under 12(b)(6), SEC filings and other public records, legislative histories, concurrently or earlier-filed pleadings and papers not part of the motion, and any documents incorporated by reference in the pleadings.[13] It can fairly be said that any oral or written evidence not already "in the record"—public or court, physically or by reference—is regarded as "extrinsic" and will spur a conversion.[14]

If the court does convert the 12(b)(6) motion to a summary judgment motion, it opens the door for all parties to submit their own evidence in support of the motion[15] Rather than entertain a full-blown summary judgment motion at this stage, most judges will simply deny the motion until "the record is developed."

(e) Procedure

Motion practice in general is discussed in Chapter 24 "Motion Practice," *infra*. Regarding the 12(b)(6) motion in particular, take note of FRCP 12(d) which authorizes, subject to the court's discretion, the motion hearing that is the essence of 12(b)(6) practice.

(f) Conclusion

Much attention is paid to FRCP 12(b)(6) in law school civil procedure classes because it is an excellent device for focusing legal neophytes on the concepts of "cause of action" and "justiciability." Unfortunately this emphasis may leave some lawyers with a disproportionate sense of the importance of the Rule in real-life practice. In fact, motions under this Rule are granted sparingly, and invocation of the provision carries a

traneous materials when ruling on motion to dismiss).

13. *See, e.g.*, Lovelace v. Software Spectrum Inc., 78 F.3d 1015, 1018–19 (5th Cir. 1996) (consideration of SEC-filed materials for purposes of documents' contents, not truth, on motion to dismiss); S. Baicker–McKee, W. Janssen & J. Corr, Federal Civil Rules Handbook (West 1997), at 208, n. 99 (collecting cases).

14. Anderson v. Angelone, 86 F.3d 932, 934 (9th Cir.1996) (district court considered prison regulations attached to affidavit while considering motion to dismiss and therefore should have notified adversary that motion would be considered one for summary judgment and that submissions could be made). *See also*, Despain v. Chapman, 507 F.Supp. 70, 71 (S.D.Tex.1981)

(factual materials in proceedings below, subject of constitutional challenge, considered on motion); Barrett v. United Hospital, 376 F.Supp. 791, 795 (S.D.N.Y.) (affidavits are not merely "argument" but are factual submissions which trigger conversion to summary judgment), *aff'd without op.*, 506 F.2d 1395 (2d Cir.1974).

15. David v. City and County of Denver, 101 F.3d 1344, 1351 (10th Cir.1996). *Compare* Brown v. Zavaras, 63 F.3d 967 (10th Cir.1995) (court erred in ruling on summary judgment motion absent notification to plaintiff that motion to dismiss was converted to motion for summary judgment and that therefore plaintiff could submit evidence to court); Anderson, 86 F.3d at 934–35.

high degree of cost and risk in almost every circumstance. It must be remembered that there is not a home run in every game, and that swinging for the fences is usually a ticket back to the dugout.

Library References:

West's Key No. Digests, Federal Civil Procedure ⊙═1771–1775.
Wright & Miller, Federal Practice and Procedure: Civil 2d §§ 1355–1358, 1366.

§ 6.8   Other Provisions of FRCP 12

FRCP 12(b), discussed in the previous two sections, sets out a specific list of defenses that may be asserted by motion. There are numerous other motions that may be made in response to a complaint and many of them are discussed in this section. As these provisions are examined, it will be evident that a surprisingly large number of them are virtually obsolete, vestiges of the era of technical pleading.

(a) Effect of FRCP 12(g) Requiring Consolidation

If the defendant were allowed to make serial Rule 12 motions based on different provisions of the Rule, doing so would be a marvelous way, from the defendant's perspective, to extend the time to answer and tie up the plaintiff almost indefinitely. Wisely, the Federal Rules of Civil Procedure do not allow this: The defendant gets only one bite at the Rule 12 apple. FRCP 12(g) states that a party making a motion under Rule 12 "may" join it with other motions under the Rule, but do not be fooled by this permissive-sounding language. The very next sentence makes it clear that any party that does not join all its Rule 12 motions into one motion loses the chance to bring another motion under the Rule. In other words, it is waived.[1]

There are two important caveats to the 12(g) consolidation requirement:

- FRCP 12(g) quickly gives back some of what it seemed to take away by cross-referring to FRCP 12(h)(2). This provision states that there is no waiver of motions for (i) failure to state a claim upon which relief can be granted (*i.e.*, the basis of a FRCP 12(b)(6) motion), (ii) failure to join an indispensable party (per FRCP 12(b)(7); *see* below and Chapter 10 "Joinder, Consolidation and Severance," *infra*), and (iii) failure to state a legal defense (a little-used aspect of FRCP 12(f), discussed below). These defenses may be brought at any time through (though not after[2]) trial.[3]

§ 6.8

1. There is no waiver of defenses not available at the time a Rule 12 motion is brought but which become available as a result of a change in the law, circumstances or litigation. *See* Holzsager v. Valley Hosp., 646 F.2d 792 (2d Cir.1981) (changes in law wrought by U.S. Supreme Court ruling permitted late addition of defense previously

not available). *Accord*, Chatman–Bey v. Thornburgh, 864 F.2d 804 (D.C.Cir.1988) citing Holzsager.

2. Brown v. Trustees of Boston Univ., 891 F.2d 337, 357 (1st Cir.1989) (motion to dismiss made for first time on appeal not generally entertained); Miller v. Cudahy Co., 656 F.Supp. 316, 323–24 (D.Kan.1987) (post-trial motion to dismiss for failure to

Once, however, responsive pleadings have been filed, a motion on any of these bases is styled a motion on the pleadings under FRCP 12(c) (*see* Section 6.8(b), *infra*).

- There is no waiver of an actual defense—as opposed to waiver of the opportunity to make a preliminary motion based on the defense—as long as the answer asserts the defense. Certainly, any defense important enough to be the subject of a motion deserves a paragraph at the end of the answer as well. All defenses should be pleaded affirmatively, regardless of the motion plan. *See* Section 6.11, *infra*.

(b) Motion for Judgment on the Pleadings, FRCP 12(c)

Conceptually, judgment on the pleadings is the equivalent of a 12(b)(6) motion made after the pleadings have been closed. It asks the court to look at the face of the pleadings and materials "intrinsically" in the record (*see* Section 6.7(d), *supra*) and determine that the adversary cannot maintain a cognizable claim. As with a 12(b)(6) motion, if the court considers "extrinsic" material, it must convert the motion to one for summary judgment and notify the parties of the change.[4]

The standards of decision are the same as on a motion under FRCP 12(b)(6).[5] The party against whom the relief is sought is given every inference and benefit of the doubt,[6] and if any factual issue remains in dispute that would have an effect on the claim at issue, the motion will be denied.[7]

state a claim upon which relief may be granted was untimely); *compare,* Alford v. Nat'l Post Office Mail Handlers, 576 F.Supp. 278, 280–81 (E.D.Mo.1983) (motion to dismiss for failure to state a claim upon which relief can be granted may be raised at any time).

3. In contrast, a motion to dismiss on the basis of a lack of subject matter jurisdiction may be brought at any time, even after judgment. FRCP 12(h)(3). *See supra* § 6.6(c) and Chapter 1 "Subject Matter Jurisdiction," *supra*.

4. *See, e.g.,* Noble v. Schmitt, 87 F.3d 157, 160 (6th Cir.1996) (district court decided 12(c) motion on factual submissions outside pleadings, rendering it a motion for summary judgment); Church v. General Motors Corp., 74 F.3d 795 (7th Cir.1996) (submission of exhibits and deposition transcripts on 12(c) motion makes summary judgment treatment appropriate); Sheppard v. Beerman, 18 F.3d 147, 151 (2d Cir.1994) (reversing district court's grant of defendant's motion for judgment on the pleadings of plaintiff's claim that plaintiff's discharge from employment violated plaintiff's

First Amendment rights, partly on the ground that court's factual determination that plaintiff was discharged for insubordination was improper on such motion).

5. Frey v. Bank One, 91 F.3d 45 (7th Cir.1996); Lanigan v. Village of E. Hazel Crest, 110 F.3d 467, 470 (7th Cir.1997) (distinction between 12(b)(6) and 12(c) motion immaterial since both are evaluated under same standard of review); United States v. Wood, 925 F.2d 1580, 1581 (7th Cir.1991) (applying same standard to Rule 12(c) motion for judgment on the pleadings as that of a Rule 12(b)(6) motion to dismiss).

6. *See, e.g.,* McKamey v. Roach, 55 F.3d 1236 (6th Cir.1995); United States v. Wood, 925 F.2d 1580, 1581 (7th Cir.1991); City of New York v. United States, 971 F.Supp. 789 (S.D.N.Y.1997).

7. *See, e.g.,* ThunderWave, Inc. v. Carnival Corp., 954 F.Supp. 1562 (S.D.Fla.1997) (granting defendant's motion to dismiss tortious interference and false representation claims and denying motion as to unjust enrichment claim).

This is the concept. In reality, successful motions for judgment on the pleadings are even more rare than winning applications under FRCP 12(b)(6). The truth of this is illustrated by the following: One very experienced practitioner was told that one purpose of this chapter was to discuss the Rules and elucidate the practical application of the various provisions. He instantly indicated its understanding by exclaiming, "You mean things like, 'Don't bother with motions for judgment on the pleadings'?"

Simply stated, motions under this Rule are highly unusual and not part of the typical commercial litigation plan.

(c) Motion for a More Definite Statement, FRCP 12(e)

This motion is a vestige of the old bill of particulars. The range of relief available under a motion for a more definite statement, in this era of notice pleading, is minimal. The test is whether the pleading is sufficiently intelligible to allow for a responsive pleading,[8] and the burden of showing that the pleadings are too incoherent for response is on the moving party.[9] Inconsistent pleadings, which are permitted by FRCP 8(e), are not a proper subject of this motion.

Case after case has stated that the grant of relief under this provision is "disfavored."[10] But courts have from time to time used 12(e) as a cudgel to enforce the minimal standards of pleading against incompetently drafted claims. One court has recently stated that though it is a commonplace that a motion for a more definite statement is not a substitute for discovery, parties should not rely on costly and time-consuming discovery as a substitute for meeting the basic requirements of pleading.[11]

(1) Special Pleading Requirements

A motion for a more definite statement may be the right device to force plaintiffs to meet the requirements of provisions such as FRCP

---

8. Young v. Warner–Jenkinson, 170 F.R.D. 164 (E.D.Mo.1996); Sagan v. Apple Computer, Inc., 874 F.Supp. 1072, 1077 (C.D.Cal.1994); Lodge 1916 v. General Elec. Co., 49 F.R.D. 72, 73–74 (E.D.Wis.1970) (denying motion for more definite statement where information sought was provided in general form sufficient to provide defendant with opportunity to frame answer).

9. See, e.g., Parsons v. Burns, 846 F.Supp. 1372, 1382 (W.D.Ark.1993) (motion infrequently granted); Sagan, 874 F.Supp. at 1077 (motion proper only where complaint so indefinite that defendant cannot ascertain nature of claim being asserted); In re Hanford Nuclear Reservation Litig., 780 F.Supp. 1551, 1582–84 (E.D.Wash.1991)

(denying motion even where complaint is "technically deficient in many of the ways cited by the defendants" since complaint provides adequate framework for answer, the defendants appear to understand nature of action, and it is questionable whether greater pleading precision could be reached).

10. See S. Baicker–McKee, W. Janssen & J. Corr, Federal Civil Rules Handbook (West 1997), at 216, n. 134.

11. Eisenach v. Miller–Dwan Medical Ctr., 162 F.R.D. 346 (1995). See also McHenry v. Renne, 84 F.3d 1172 (9th Cir. 1996) (decrying incomprehensible complaint).

9(b), which sets out specific standards for pleading capacity, fraud, mistake, and a number of other claims or elements of claims.

(2) Strategic Considerations

A motion for a more definite statement is no substitute for discovery, but it can be close. At the very least, if granted it can give the defendant additional insight into the plaintiff's case, provide additional time for preparation of the answer (which, axiomatically, is not required to be filed until the motion is resolved[12]) and, like a 12(b)(6) motion, can "educate" both judge and plaintiff about the case, parties and counsel.

The motion is also a useful tool for coaxing material facts out of the plaintiff that, once pleaded, could be a basis for a motion to dismiss, such as the applicability of the statutes of limitations or frauds.[13] Though this could be accomplished with a motion to dismiss under FRCP 12(b)(6), a motion for a more definite statement may be taken more seriously by a judge who can perceive, as well as the defendant, that a cognizable claim is "in there somewhere."

Finally, a motion under this provision can be considered a sort of pop-gun assault on the complaint compared to the battle-to-the-death offensive of 12(b)(6). Technically a pleading that is incoherent or which fails under FRCP 9(b) does not state a claim, but a motion under this Rule may be more appropriate when it is obvious that the defendant is getting at *something* justiciable and that it will in due time get the chance to adjudicate that something on the merits. The caveats raised regarding the 12(b)(6) motion in Section 6.7(b), *supra,* apply, therefore— especially the point that sometimes it may be of no benefit to the defendant to get a clearer statement or a more artful pleading from the plaintiff.

(3) Relief and Sanctions

The purpose of the 12(e) motion for a more definite statement is to obtain a better pleading, and if the motion is successful the court will order the plaintiff to provide one. If it is provided on the timeline set by the court, the defendant has 10 days under the Rule to serve its response. The court may, however, allow the defendant more time, and often does.[14] If the motion is denied, the court will direct the date when the defendant must respond.

What if the new pleading is also insufficient? Note that at this juncture the typical practice is to require something more than intelligibility in the pleading, since the court usually includes in its order specific

---

12. 5A Charles Alan Wright & Arthur R. Miller, Federal Practice and Procedure § 1378, at 629 (2d ed. 1990).

13. S. Baicker–McKee, W. Janssen & J. Corr, *supra* note 10, at 217, citing Rose v. Kinevan, 115 F.R.D. 250 (D.Colo.1987). *But see*, 5A Charles Alan Wright & Arthur R. Miller § 1376 (2d ed. 1990), citing Pritch- ard v. Liggett & Myers Tobacco Co., 134 F.Supp. 829 (W.D.Pa.1955) (such an approach is antithetical to notice pleading).

14. 5A Charles Alan Wright & Arthur R. Miller, Federal Practice and Procedure § 1379 at 636 (2d ed. 1990) (collecting exemplary cases).

information required in the new pleading.[15] If the new complaint lacks this information, the defendant can bring the deficiencies to the court's attention. If the court agrees, the plaintiff has failed to comply with the order. Under the Rule, the court may then strike the pleading or take whatever action it deems appropriate, which may include giving the plaintiff yet "one more chance."[16]

(d) Motion to Strike, FRCP 12(f)

Another vestige of antiquity, the motion to strike is basically an irrelevancy in federal commercial litigation. The Rule permits an application to strike, or remove, from the pleadings "any insufficient defense or any redundant, immaterial, impertinent, or scandalous matter." A simple review of the level of modern discourse should make it clear that it would be difficult indeed to impress any judge with the impertinence or scandalousness of a pleading. And if redundancy were truly subject to attack by motion, judges would be spending their days granting motions to strike—a needed tonic, but one that will not occur any time soon.

Where it is considered, the movant must show that the matter it seeks to have struck is (i) not material to the claim and (ii) prejudicial to the movant.[17] But the motion is "disfavored" and is often regarded as a delaying tactic and as a rather impertinent submission in and of itself.[18]

> **Library References:**
> West's Key No. Digests, Federal Civil Procedure ⟊941–1020, 1041–1068, 1101–1150.
> Wright & Miller, Federal Practice and Procedure: Civil 2d §§ 1371, 1376, 1377, 1383.

§ 6.9   Drafting the Answer

(a) Introduction

Though much ink is spilled, and has been here, on the topic of motions in response to complaints, the majority of cases involve the preparation and filing of an answer. Even if settlement is likely (*see* Chapter 28 "Settlements," *infra*), there are few situations where the defendant will not be required to stake out its opening position.

Upon receipt of the complaint, it is essential that investigation of the allegations begin. (*See* Chapter 4 "Investigation of the Case," *supra*.)

---

15. *Id.* at 638.

16. *See* Raylite Elec. Corp. v. Noma Elec. Corp., 7 F.R.D. 239, 240 (S.D.N.Y. 1946) (plaintiff granted one more chance to provide particulars).

17. *See, e.g.,* Government Guarantee Fund v. Hyatt Corp., 166 F.R.D. 321, 324–25 (D.V.I.1996) (motion denied where no prejudice shown); Environ Prods., Inc. v. Total Containment, Inc., 951 F.Supp. 57, 59–60 (E.D.Pa.1996) (motions usually de-nied unless allegations have "no possible relation" to controversy and may prejudice party), quoting Charles Alan Wright & Arthur R. Miller, Federal Practice and Procedure § 1382 at 685–90 (2d ed. 1990).

18. *See, e.g.,* Boreri v. Fiat S.p.A., 763 F.2d 17, 23 (1st Cir.1985) (such motions "not calculated readily to invoke the court's discretion"); S. Baicker–McKee, W. Janssen & J. Corr, *supra* note 10, at 219, n. 147 (collecting cases).

It is likely that the answer will have to be filed before all the relevant facts come in, especially in complex cases where discovery in the true sense of the word goes on for months or years. No stipulation extending time will extend that far. In all probability, the answer must be drafted sooner than desired. Because of the relative scarcity of information, the defense counsel's job is to minimize the extent to which it ethically must acknowledge the truth of the allegations in the complaint while maximizing its future flexibility as facts, legal theories and the dynamics of litigation develop.

(b) The Critical FRCP Provisions: FRCP 12 and 8

Answering a complaint seems deceptively simple in commercial litigation. Because of the seeming simplicity of "admit" and "deny," many attorneys have answered innumerable complaints without giving their responses the careful thought they deserve. The superficial simplicity of an answer may obscure the fact that oftentimes the answer is the defendant's first defining moment in litigation.

Two FRCP provisions deserve immediate attention. FRCP 12, discussed in Section 6.3, *supra*, sets out the rules regarding pleading or moving on the basis of defenses and objections. FRCP 8 governs the general rules of pleading. Both rules must be understood before the practitioner can properly decide both *what* its client's response to a complaint should be and *how* to craft the response to achieve the desired goal.

(1) FRCP 8: General Rules of Pleading

Five of the six sections of FRCP 8 are directly relevant to the topic of answering complaints, though two—section (e) on the general standards of pleading and the "catchall" provision of section (f)—apply to all pleadings.[19] The other sections define what constitutes an answer (section (b)), how defenses are asserted (sections (b) and (c)) and the parameters of admission and denial (section (c)).

The essence of the rules for answering a complaint, based on FRCP 8(b), is as follows:

- The basic responses to averments (allegations) are *admission, denial*, and a functional denial based on a *lack of knowledge or information* sufficient to form a belief as to the truth of the allegations.

- Responses to particular allegations can be partial or whole; but a partial response must specify what part of the allegation is being denied and what admitted.

(2) The Denial

As alluded to above, there are certain allegations which simply must be denied in all instances if the answer is to qualify as a "defense." They include the following:

---

19. Subsection (a) of FRCP 8, "Claims for Relief," is addressed in Chapter 5 "The Complaint," *supra*, as is Rule 8(e); the latter is also discussed below.

- Liability of the defendant (including its agents, employees and assigns);

- Misfeasance or negligence of the defendant, or any conclusory characterization of an act as a failure to perform a duty to others;

- Malfeasance, *i.e.* any form of wrongdoing of the defendant even if not legally cognizable; and

- Illegal conduct by the defendant (even if not morally wrong, such as certain legal wrongs defined by strict liability statutes).

This list is not exhaustive, but the idea it imparts is essential. To admit allegations of this nature is literally to give away the game.

The question may arise whether it is ethically possible to deny these allegations in every case. To answer this question, the attorney must recall that these types of allegations are *legal* (or moral) *conclusions* or their conceptual building blocks—not facts. This would be the case even if every fact artfully pleaded were true—especially considering the effect of affirmative defenses in that determination. (*See* Section 6.11, *infra*.) In the absence of an adjudication of the claim, the defendant is under no obligation to admit to its liability.

(3) General and Specific Denials

FRCP 8(b) provides for something called a "general denial," a method that is still fairly common in some state practices, as in New York. This consists of a short statement denying all the allegations of the complaint. A qualified general denial sets out exceptions to the denial. Many practitioners believe that there is simply no call for the use of the shotgun approach of general denial in federal commercial litigation since it deprives the defendant of the ability to craft an answer that at least begins the job of telling the defense story. Others maintain, however, that the general denial preserves a measure of flexibility that may prove useful later. The prevalent approach is to set out denials for each specific averment.

(c) Denial of Knowledge or Information

Pleading a lack of knowledge or information sufficient to admit or deny an allegation has the effect of a denial.[20] This is the most common-ly-asserted response to allegations in a pleading involving complicated facts that, in good faith, the defendant does not or cannot know.

This category includes allegations concerning third parties. Note that such allegations may not always be explicit but may come about, for example, when the defendant is lumped in with some group to which the plaintiff is antagonistic, be it co-defendants or an entire industry. The proper response in such a case is that "The defendant denies knowledge or information sufficient to form a belief as to truth of the allegations insofar as they refer to the action of parties [entities, persons, defen-

20.　FRCP 8(b).

dants] other than itself, but as to [this defendant], the allegation is denied."

(d) Admissions

Some pleaded facts will be admitted either because there is no getting around them or because they are helpful to the defendant. In some instances it is appropriate to recast admitted facts under the "partial denial" rule (*see* below). Other times there is simply no reason or basis to deny them. Thus, if correctly pleaded, it is entirely appropriate to admit facts such as the name of the defendant or the address alleged, and the like. Conversely, if the entity named in the complaint is not the defendant served or no longer exists in the form it was named, admission is inappropriate.

(1) *Numbering and Correspondence of Paragraphs*

Although it is not required by any Rule, the custom is to number the answering paragraphs to correspond to the complaining paragraphs, even if the text of the answering paragraph reads, "The allegations of paragraph 1 [etc.] are denied." It is also acceptable to state in a preface that the paragraphs set forth below correspond to the paragraphs of the complaint, and merely to state "Admit" or "Deny," etc., as appropriate. Some defendants take an entirely different tack and lump all their denials and "DKI's" (denials of knowledge or information; *see* Section 6.9(c), *supra*) into two paragraphs, one for denials and one for "DKIs." Numbering the paragraphs in accordance with the ones they are answering, however, fosters ease of cross-reference for all parties and minimizes the chance of accidentally omitting a response to an allegation.

(e) Answering the Allegations: Objectives

The art of the answer is to avoid admitting liability without submitting a false response. This task is made easier if defense counsel keeps the following five guidelines in mind when answering a complaint:

1. To *admit* as few factual allegations as possible that are material to the plaintiff's cause of action;
2. To *avoid admission* of factual allegations that are *elements* of the plaintiff's purported cause of action;
3. To *deny* all conclusory legal allegations of liability, misfeasance, malfeasance or illegality;
4. To *recast* any allegation that is compound, conclusory, general, or that implicates the defendant's wider interests; and
5. To *deny knowledge or information* of all factual allegations whose truth the defendant does not or cannot know.

The practical application of these guidelines is examined below.

(1) *Making the Answer Work: Practice Pointers*

A well-drafted complaint should give the defendant a minimum amount of leeway to avoid the allegations, thereby leaving the defendant to its affirmative defenses (*see* Sections 6.10–6.11, *infra*) to state its side of the story. But most complaints are not well drafted. They are typically verbose and rambling, packing too many facts, conclusions and assumptions into too few numbered paragraphs.

Even well-drafted complaints based largely on undeniable facts have their vulnerabilities (unless the allegations are so accurate that the defendant has a very serious problem). Many complaints reach a point where they attempt to tie up all the elements of the complaint into one grand, largely conclusory paragraph. Faced with such a typical complaint, the defense lawyer's job is simple, and that job is the essence of his craft: To find and tear apart the seams that hold these seemingly smooth allegations together, denying the thrust of the allegations and admitting only undeniable but isolated segments.

This is done by parsing, or breaking down, each individual allegation-paragraph into its component parts and focusing on the interstices. The devices that makes this possible are Rule 8's provision for partial admission and denial and for denial on the basis of insufficient knowledge or information. Thus the defendant may be able to break up an otherwise damning allegation into relatively harmless pieces.

What follows are two examples of this technique, adapted from an actual complaint and answer in a class action suit alleging that the defendant deceptively placed an unsafe product into the stream of commerce:

COMPLAINT:

14. Autoco has spent millions of dollars in advertising its product line, including its X45 model line of automobiles. These advertisements have carefully cultivated the image of safety, reliability and longevity of Autoco automobiles to such an extent that Autoco automobiles are publicly perceived to be among the safest vehicles available. Autoco, being fully aware of its customers' safety expectations for their vehicles, has concealed the fact that the Autoco X45 equipped with Venetian Vibrafome suspension is not safe and durable as advertised.

ANSWER

14. Autoco denies the allegations contained in paragraph 14, except admits that Autoco has invested in promoting the safety, reliability and longevity of its vehicles, and that Autoco automobiles are publicly perceived to be among the safest vehicles available.

Another example:

COMPLAINT

19. Consumers of automobiles such as the Autoco X45 model are particularly vulnerable to such deceptive and fraudulent practices. Most consumers, plaintiff included, possess a very limited knowledge of the complex operating systems of motor vehicles. Plaintiff and other members of the Class, reasonably believing that

Autoco and its employees and agents possess, as they claim to, special expertise in the design and manufacture of automobiles, and would not place profits over the safety of their customers, reasonably relied on the representations and omissions of Autoco and its employees and agents.

ANSWER

19. Autoco denies the allegations contained in paragraph 19, except admits that Autoco and its employees and agents possess special expertise in the design and manufacture of automobiles and do not place profits over the safety of their customers; and is without knowledge or information sufficient to form a belief as to the truth of the allegations concerning the alleged extent of automotive knowledge possessed by "most consumers."

(2) Answering Incompletely Presented Facts: Practice Pointer

Consider the following allegations made in an action filed in May of a given year against a defendant which licensed from the plaintiff the right to sell clothing bearing the likeness of a children's cartoon character, "Happy Surprise," in a territory defined as encompassing Clifton, New Jersey:

COMPLAINT

4. Section 82(c) of the Happy Surprise Contract entered into between plaintiff Happy Surprise and defendant licensee specifically required the defendant to remit to the plaintiff all licensing fees by the 30th day of January of each year.

5. Plaintiff has not remitted the aforementioned licensing fees as of April 1 of this year.

6. Plaintiff is in breach of the Happy Surprise Contract.

Evaluation of this allegation indicates that Section 82(c) of the Happy Surprise contract provides as follows:

82(c): The licensee shall remit to Happy Surprise Company all licensing fees by the 30th day of January of each year, unless the licensee's territory shall include Clifton, New Jersey, in which case such fees shall be remitted to Happy Surprise Company on the 30th day of June each year.

The response should be as follows:

ANSWER

4. Defendant denies the allegations of Paragraph 4, except admits that the Happy Surprise Contract contains a provision designated as Section 82(c), and refers to the document itself for its contents.

OR

4. Defendant denies the allegations of Paragraph 4, except states that the full text of the provision is as follows: [*quoting the provision*]

Paragraph 5 can be denied, since the "aforementioned" licensing fees were not due to be remitted; a more cautious approach may be, again, affirmatively to cast the denial in terms of the fact that there was no obligation to remit the fees. Paragraph 6 should be denied in any event.

This same technique should be used when the plaintiff has attached an incomplete document or other piece of evidence to the complaint. Technically speaking, a mere denial might be sufficient in either of these cases, for the allegations are not "the whole truth." It may be more effective, though more revealing of the defendant's ultimate strategy, either to quote the actual language or attach the document containing the provision to the pleadings, stating in the answer that a "true copy" of the document is attached. By this method the defendant demonstrates to the court the type of game the plaintiff is attempting to play.

(f) Demand for Judgment, Jury Demand

The answer should conclude with a demand for judgment in favor of the defendant.[21] If a jury is desired, it should be demanded at the end of the answer as well.[22] This is true even if the plaintiff has demanded one already, since if the plaintiff settles but the defendant remains in the case with other parties, that jury demand will be gone.[23] If a jury demand is not made by a party, that party's right to a jury is waived.[24]

(g) Conclusion

There is a limit to what the defendant can do in its answer. At best it can exploit soft spots in the complaint, but because it is literally "on the defensive" the defendant will never do better than a draw in admitting and denying the other side's allegations. There is a way, however, that the defendant can take control of its responsive pleading, besides by making a motion. That is by the assertion of affirmative defenses, discussed in the following section.

Library References:

West's Key No. Digests, Federal Civil Procedure ⟺731–786.
Wright & Miller, Federal Practice and Procedure: Civil 2d §§ 1201–1204, 1384–1386.

21. FRCP 8(a)(3).

22. FRCP 38(b).

23. The plaintiff cannot simply amend its complaint and take out the jury demand,

however, without the consent of all parties. FRCP 38(d).

24. FRCP 38(d).

§ 6.10   Affirmative Defenses: Introduction

(a) Affirmative Defenses Defined

Affirmative defenses are the way the defendant sets forth defenses that would, if proved, avoid or reduce liability but that cannot be conveyed by simple admission or denial of the factual allegations in a complaint. Note the difference between an affirmative defense and a presumption, which is a legal principle that may provide a complete defense but does not raise new matter.[1] Similarly, bare statements of legal principles, in and of themselves (*e.g.*, "Contracts require consideration"), are not appropriately pleaded as affirmative defenses. Generally speaking affirmative defenses must meet notice-pleading standards but state the legal and, according to some courts, *factual* basis of the defense.

The necessary standards for pleading affirmative defenses are not obvious from the decisions. In one recent case,[2] the Second Circuit ruled that the defendants failed to establish their entitlement to qualified immunity by asserting, as an affirmative defense, that they "were, at all times relevant to the amended complaint, government officials immune from suit under both the doctrines of absolute and qualified immunity." The court ruled that such a "bald assertion" failed to preserve the defense since it failed to allege "that the *specific acts at issue* were performed within the scope of their official duties."[3] Thus, from a "notice pleading" perspective, an essential element of the defense—that the complained-of acts themselves be performed as part of the defen-

---

§ 6.10

1. Ferris Elevator Co. v. Neffco, Inc., 285 Ill.App.3d 350, 220 Ill.Dec. 906, 674 N.E.2d 449 (Ill.App.1996) (test for whether defense is technically affirmative defense is whether it "gives color to the opposing party's claim and then asserts new matter by which the apparent right is defeated"); *In re* Rawson Food Service, Inc., 846 F.2d 1343, 1348–49 (11th Cir.1988) ("a defense pointing out a defect in plaintiff's prima facie case is not an affirmative defense; rather, an affirmative defense raises matters extraneous to plaintiff's prima facie case ..."), quoting 5 Charles Alan Wright and Arthur R. Miller, Federal Practice and Procedure § 1270 at 289 (2d ed. 1990).

2. Shechter v. Comptroller of New York, 79 F.3d 265, 269–70 (2d Cir.1996) *See also*, Heller Fin., Inc. v. Midwhey Powder Co., Inc., 883 F.2d 1286, 1294–95 (7th Cir.1989) (affirming trial court striking affirmative defenses as lacking merit and "are nothing but bare bones conclusory allegations").

3. Shechter, 79 F.3d at 270 (emphasis in original). *See also,* Edmonds v. United States, 148 F.Supp. 185, 186 (E.D.Wis.1957) (defense stating that claim was "barred" and "settled and compromised" did not preserve affirmative defense of estoppel); Video Views, Inc. v. Studio 21, Ltd., 1986 WL 12052 (N.D.Ill.1986) (affirmative defense "not pled in sufficient detail for [plaintiff] and the court to obtain a fair idea of what defendant is asserting and to see that there is some legal basis for the defense"). *But see,* Conjugal Partnership Comprised by Joseph Jones and Verneta G. Jones v. Conjugal Partnership Comprised of Arthur Pineda and Toni Pineda, 22 F.3d 391 (1st Cir. 1994) (affirmative defense not explicitly pled but tried by implied consent of parties treated as if raised in pleadings); Mobley v. Kelly Kean Nissan, Inc., 864 F.Supp. 726, 732 (N.D.Ill.1993) (refusing to strike affirmative defense asserting only that plaintiffs failed to mitigate their damages, since the affirmative defense provided notice that the defense would be raised); Coleman v. Ramada Hotel Operating Co., 933 F.2d 470, 475 (7th Cir.1991) (assumption of risk defense subsumed by pleading of contributory negligence).

dants' duties—was not part of the pleading. At the other extreme, evidentiary facts, such as the names of witnesses or the identity of collateral documents that contradict plaintiff's claim, are not typically the proper subject of affirmative defenses.[4]

In reality, the cases cited below are representative of the few reported decisions on this topic. These decisions are sufficiently divergent in their approaches that the disparity may well be attributable to the unrecorded ebb and flow of a case or other subjective factors not obvious from the reported decisions. How much, then, does the practitioner have to concern himself with the opinions that seem to imply strict explication of the factual bases of affirmative defenses? In earlier years affirmative defenses were routinely pleaded with relatively detailed factual averments, *e.g.*:

1.   The plaintiff had full knowledge of the facts, events and transactions on which its claim herein is based nine years prior to the filing of this action.

2.   The plaintiff failed to act on its claim despite having no reason to delay and having ample opportunity to do so.

3.   The plaintiff's claims are barred by the doctrine of laches.

Today the nearly universal approach is to utilize the simple statement, "Plaintiff's claim is barred on the grounds of laches." Few practitioners go beyond this and, given the plaintiff's opportunity to serve interrogatories inquiring as to the basis of the defense, even fewer judges would regard this as insufficient. Ultimately, under the standard of FRCP 8(c), the requirement is to plead as an affirmative defense any fact that would, if not pleaded, surprise the plaintiff at trial[5]—and not more.

(b) How Asserted: Practice Pointer

Affirmative defenses are set forth in the responsive pleading usually after the responses to the specific allegations of the complaint. Each affirmative defense should be set forth in a separate paragraph or group of paragraphs under the same heading and labeled as an affirmative defense. It is not necessary to label each defense specifically (*e.g.*, "waiver," "failure of consideration") but doing so often helps defense counsel ensure that the defense is cogently drafted and appropriately asserted. Some offices have the custom of designating the successive affirmative defenses as "First Affirmative Defense," "Second Affirmative Defense" and so on, but this is not required.

(1) FRCP 8(c) and "Substantive Law" Affirmative Defenses

FRCP 8(c) enumerates certain matters that must be affirmatively pleaded in response to a complaint (*see* Section 6.11, *infra*). In addition

---

4. Securities and Exchange Comm'n v. Platt, 565 F.Supp. 1244 (W.D.Okla.1983).

5. *In re* Madle, 87 F.3d 1320 (9th Cir. 1996); Swasey & Co. v. Bortolotti, 825 F.2d 412, 412 (6th Cir.1987) (affirmative defenses must be set forth in the pleadings or be raised by express or implied consent to prevent unfair surprise); Ingraham v. United States, 808 F.2d 1075, 1079 (5th Cir.1987) ("Central to requiring the pleading of affirmative defenses is the prevention of unfair surprise.").

to these, the Rule requires that "any matter constituting an avoidance or affirmative defense" based on the substantive cause of action be pleaded in the response. Examples of these include:

- The statute of limitations (*see* Section 6.11(t), *infra*);

- Failure of the plaintiff to mitigate damages;[6]

- Causation of the complained-of injury by a party not under the control of the defendant.[7]

(2) Traditional Equitable Defenses

FRCP 8(e)(2) provides that defenses may be based on "legal, equitable, or maritime grounds." Thus the defendant should avail itself of the appropriate traditional equitable defenses, such as unclean hands[8] and in pari delicto[9] besides those such as laches and waiver which are enumerated in FRCP 8 (*see* Section 6.11, *infra*).

Not all courts are in agreement that these traditional equitable defenses need to be pleaded. It has been asserted that because the classic equitable defenses such as unclean hands are fundamental to the judicial process, they are not even defenses as such, but axioms of the system.[10] Nonetheless it is clearly the better practice to plead equitable defenses affirmatively than to rely on hazy pronouncements that the courts will not countenance unfairness and inequity, especially if it is part of the defense strategy to make active, affirmative use of an equitable defense.

(3) FRCP 9(b)–Based Defenses

There are also a number of additional affirmative defenses which FRCP 9 requires be pleaded with specificity. These are:

- Capacity to sue or be sued or the authority of a party to sue or be sued in a representative capacity;

- Fraud (discussed in Section 6.11(k), *infra*), mistake or "condition of mind"; and

- Failure of a condition precedent.

---

6. *See, e.g.*, United Coin Meter Co., Inc. v. Seaboard Coastline R.R., 705 F.2d 839 (6th Cir.1983); Mobley, 864 F.Supp. at 732.

7. Metro Traffic Control, Inc. v. Shadow Network, Inc., 104 F.3d 336 (Fed.Cir.1997).

8. *See, e.g.*, Fina Oil and Chemical Co. v. Pester Marketing Co., 1997 WL 225900, at *35 (D.Kan.1997) (applying doctrine of unclean hands under Kansas law in contract action for damages); *In re* Tamen, 22 F.3d 199, 205 (9th Cir.1994) (declining to consider defense of unclean hands on appeal because not asserted at trial).

9. This defense, related to unclean hands, is based on the premise "that courts should not lend their good offices to mediating disputes among wrongdoers; and . . . that denying judicial relief to an admitted wrongdoer is an effective means of deterring illegality." Bateman Eichler, Hill Richards, Inc. v. Berner, 472 U.S. 299, 105 S.Ct. 2622, 86 L.Ed.2d 215 (1985). *See also,* South–East Coal Co. v. Consolidation Coal Co., 434 F.2d 767, 783–84 (6th Cir.1970) (affirming trial court's jury instruction on in pari delicto defense), *cert. denied,* 402 U.S. 983, 91 S.Ct. 1662, 29 L.Ed.2d 149 (1971).

10. Camarillo v. McCarthy, 998 F.2d 638 (9th Cir.1993).

(4) Federal Rule–Deficiency Defenses

It is also a common practice to plead as affirmative defenses any failure by the plaintiff to comply with mandatory provisions of the Federal Rules, such as:

- Failure to join an indispensable party (see Chapter 10 "Joinder Consolidation and Severance," infra);

- Lack of subject matter jurisdiction (see Section 6.6(c), supra); and

- Existence of a forum selection or arbitration clause that would bar the action (see Chapters 3 "Venue, Forum Selection and Transfer," and 9 "Arbitration vs. Litigation: Enforceability and Access to Courts").

This category of affirmative defenses includes ones that are potential bases for motions to dismiss. Note that under FRCP 12(h)(1), lack of personal jurisdiction, improper venue, or insufficiency of process are waived unless either asserted in a motion or as an affirmative defense; if any of these defenses is germane it should certainly be included as an affirmative defense.

Besides those defenses enumerated in FRCP 12, though, affirmative defenses may not normally be the basis of a motion to dismiss;[11] classically they are the stuff of which summary judgments are made.[12] A motion to dismiss, however, may succeed where the defense can be made out from the "face" of the complaint itself. This is not uncommon on motions to dismiss based on the statute of limitations,[13] i.e., where the complaint states, as the bases of the claim, events that took place so long ago as to no longer be actionable.

(5) Affirmative Defenses to Federal Statutory Claims

Equitable defenses are not limited to equitable claims.[14] Since federal district courts sit as courts of equity, they may apply any affirmative defense that equity would allow, though typically not in cases in which a doctrine of strict legal liability is applicable.[15] Certainly, then, in matters of civil commercial litigation, any defense that could be asserted in a state court action should be asserted in federal court as well—even if the defense is asserted to a federal cause of action such as trademark infringement,[16] RICO[17] or the like.[18]

11. BTI Computer Sys. v. Reynolds and Reynolds Co., 875 F.2d 870 (table) (9th Cir.1989) (sua sponte motion for summary judgment based on defendant's affirmative defenses reversed).

12. Velez v. City of New London, 903 F.Supp. 286 (D.Conn.1995).

13. See, e.g., Hoover v. Langston Equipment Associates, Inc., 958 F.2d 742 (6th Cir.1992)

14. In re Lapiana, 909 F.2d 221 (7th Cir.1990) (applying estoppel to claims brought under Bankruptcy Code); A.C.

Aukerman Co. v. R.L. Chaides Constr. Co., 960 F.2d 1020, 1031 (Fed.Cir.1992) (parties allowed to plead equitable defenses at law without resort to bills in equity.).

15. Mathis v. Velsicol Chemical Corp., 786 F.Supp. 971, 976 (N.D.Ga.1991) (CERCLA liability not subject to equitable defenses; citing cases).

16. Westinghouse Elec. Corp. v. Gen. Circuit Breaker and Elec. Supply, Inc., 106 F.3d 894, 899 (9th Cir.1997) (applying equitable defense to Lanham Act claim).

(c) Practical Considerations

Since FRCP 8(c) requires a party to plead affirmative defenses to prevent surprise at trial,[19] it has been held that affirmative defenses may be waived if not asserted,[20] though some courts hew to a standard requiring prejudice to the plaintiff before ruling that an affirmative defense has been waived.[21]

Technically speaking, the absence of an element of the cause of action asserted by the plaintiff need not be pleaded as an affirmative defense since such an element is not waivable.[22] Yet, as demonstrated in Section 6.11 *infra,* some recognized and waivable defenses, such as failure of consideration in defense to a contract claim,[23] seem to violate that neat conception. Therefore, in framing affirmative defenses to claims brought under state law, it is necessary to examine the case law in the relevant jurisdiction and, by "reverse engineering" the elements of the cause of action, determine what legal affirmative defenses may be available. Care should also be taken to examine what traditional equitable defenses may be available. Section 6.15(d), *infra,* contains exemplary versions of many affirmative defenses.

Affirmative defenses can present fruitful opportunities for creative defense lawyering. And the process of identifying defenses also points the way to the proof that must be developed in discovery for a successful defense.

(d) Expansiveness in Pleading: Strategy

The Rules set a liberal standard—subject to the standards of FRCP 11—for what is permissible in pleadings. This goes for affirmative defenses as well. Thus, affirmative defenses may be hypothetical as long as they are made in good faith. They should usually include every colorable approach to avoidance of liability, even if mutually inconsis-

---

17. Levin-Richmond Terminal Corp. v. International Longshoremen's and Warehousemen's Union Local 10, 751 F.Supp. 1373 (N.D.Cal.1990) (applying estoppel to civil RICO claim).

18. *See, e.g.,* Austin v. Shalala, 994 F.2d 1170, 1177–78 (5th Cir.1993) (federal statute confers equitable defense of waiver to legal cause of action to recover overpaid Social Security benefits).

19. *See supra* § 6.10(a).

20. Charpentier v. Godsil, 937 F.2d 859 (3d Cir.1991); Morgan Guaranty Trust Co. of New York v. Blum, 649 F.2d 342, 343–45 (5th Cir.1981) (affirming district court's denial of defendant's motion for leave to amend answer in order to assert new defenses on the ground that they were deemed waived).

21. Woodson v. Scott Paper Co., 109 F.3d 913 (3d Cir.1997), Rivera v. Anaya, 726 F.2d 564, 566 (9th Cir.1984) (absent prejudice to plaintiff, defendant may raise affirmative defense in summary judgment motion); Coleman v. Ramada Hotel Operating Co., 933 F.2d 470, 475 (7th Cir.1991) (defendant's failure to specifically plead assumption of risk did not result in waiver because pleading contributory negligence sufficient to prevent prejudice).

22. *In re* Mayo, 112 B.R. 607 (Bankr. D.Vt.1990).

23. *See infra* § 6.11(j).

tent.[24] Taking advantage of the liberality permitted in pleading affirmative defenses allows for a greater scope of discovery from the plaintiff (though it also expands the scope of discovery the plaintiff may take from the defendant). Similarly, the assertion of an affirmative defense may pay off at trial by rendering important matters otherwise not covered by the pleading admissible in evidence. An example of this, regarding the defense of contributory negligence, is discussed in depth at Section 6.11(f)(1) below.

(e) Practice Pointer

As has been stressed in the last section, defense counsel should be generous in including affirmative defenses that may apply to the defendant's position. Yet a lawyer should no more apply the boilerplate approach to affirmative defenses than to any other area of practice. This is not solely a matter of complying with FRCP 11; though that is a factor that must always be considered. But meritless affirmative defenses are usually ignored by plaintiff and judge alike.

And therein lies the problem: If obviously bogus defenses are included along with meritorious ones, the good ones may be tainted by the bad. A properly pleaded answer with carefully-crafted affirmative defenses could be the difference between early settlement and yet another war of attrition.

For example, "injury by fellow servant" has no place as an affirmative defense in a dispute over a breach of contract. Similarly, there is no reason to assert the bar of the statute of limitations in a declaratory judgment action over a contract that is still executory. To the extent that throwing in "the kitchen sink" will preserve every possible option for the future, the boilerplate strategy has some logic (assuming no sanctions follow). But keeping in mind the importance of not waiving potentially useful defenses, a better-prepared answer should plead only those affirmative defenses that may actually make a difference in the case. If one or two of those is a novel or unusual affirmative defense, the credibility of that defense will be enhanced by the selectivity shown in the pleading. But if the best-researched, most original and most devastating affirmative defense is included like just another spud in a potato sack, it is unlikely to have a meaningful impact at this early stage of the case.

There is another reason not to include every conceivable affirmative defense, namely that each defense opens up doors of discovery. As often as not these doors lead more to embarrassment for the defendant than defeat, but neither is a particularly desirable destination. Each affirmative defense asserted is an invitation to an interrogatory requesting the factual basis of the defense. Interrogatories are addressed to and ultimately answered by the client, and if for no other reason, such interrogatories should have good answers waiting for them.

---

24. FRCP 8(e) (2).

Library References:

West's Key No. Digests, Federal Civil Procedure ⬤➾751–759.
Wright & Miller, Federal Practice and Procedure: Civil 2d §§ 1270–1278.

§ 6.11   Specific Affirmative Defenses

(a) Introduction

The following are the affirmative defenses specifically set forth in FRCP 8(c). Most of these are common law type defenses that are available as defenses against traditional causes of action typically asserted in diversity actions or as pendent claims under supplemental jurisdiction. Therefore, the specific elements of the defenses discussed below depend on the state law being applied in the litigation.[1] Nonetheless, many of these affirmative defenses have elements that are consistent across most jurisdictions or are applied consistently by the federal courts, so their traditional elements have been set forth below.

These are not the only affirmative defenses available in federal court. As discussed in the previous section, any common law or state law affirmative defense can be asserted in defense of a state law claim. The use of common law defenses for federal statutory claims is also discussed in the previous section.

(b) Analysis

Many of the affirmative defenses, having their roots in the common law, are more typically applied to traditional torts than to commercial litigation. Commercial litigation, however, frequently draws on historical common law causes of action, evolved in much simpler circumstances, to meet the needs of modern business clients.

Similarly, the defense litigator should know and understand even those affirmative defenses that, in their essence, are based in personal injury and other tort causes of action. They are the building blocks of all law, including commercial litigation. And they are, of course, relevant in the defense of that species of commercial litigation known as products liability, discussed in detail in Chapter 70 "Products Liability."

(c) Accord and Satisfaction

Accord and satisfaction is a common law doctrine sometimes called a "judicial blessing" on those who attempt to settle their own disputes since it empowers a court to prohibit litigation of a settled dispute. The essential elements of accord and satisfaction are a bona fide dispute as to the amount or performance owed; a clear manifestation of intent by the debtor to the creditor that a payment or performance is in full satisfac-

---

§ 6.11

1. Erie R.R. v. Tompkins, 304 U.S. 64, 58 S.Ct. 817, 82 L.Ed. 1188 (1938) (in diver-sity jurisdiction cases law to be applied is law of state).

tion of the disputed agreement; and acceptance of satisfaction by the creditor.[2]

(d) Arbitration and Award

The defense of arbitration and award is a statement by the defendant that the plaintiff's claim has already been adjudicated in arbitration. This topic is discussed extensively in Chapter 9 "Arbitration vs. Litigation: Enforceability and Access to Courts," *infra*. As a defense, arbitration and award has attributes of accord and satisfaction, a substantive contract defense and res judicata (*see* Section 6.11(r) *infra*). The elements of arbitration and award are the existence of a decision by an extra-judicial tribunal, which the parties themselves have designated and by whose judgment they have mutually agreed to abide.[3]

(e) Assumption of Risk

Under the doctrine of assumption of risk, a party is barred from recovery for injuries sustained after proceeding into an open and obvious danger. The elements of assumption of risk generally are: a voluntary exposure of oneself or one's property to a subjectively known and appreciated danger arising from the actions of or a relationship with another.[4] The defense of assumption of risk has largely been subsumed by the principles of contributory and comparative negligence (*see* Section 6.11(f) *infra*).[5]

(f) Contributory and Comparative Negligence

Under the classic defense of contributory negligence, any negligence on the part of the plaintiff that contributed to its injuries completely

---

2. F.D.I.C. v. Inhofe, 16 F.3d 371 (10th Cir.1994) (Oklahoma law; purported settlement only functioned to change source of underlying obligations from underlying contracts to agreement itself, hence full discharge of obligations not included); Community Heating and Plumbing Co., Inc. v. Kelso, 987 F.2d 1575 (Fed.Cir.1993) (discharge of claim by accord and satisfaction occurs when a performance, different from that which is due, is rendered, and this substituted performance is accepted by claimant as full satisfaction of claim; applying Court of Claims precedent, defense rejected where parties' course of conduct showed lack of intention to abandon or discharge claim); Parker v. Prudential Ins. Co. of America, 900 F.2d 772 (4th Cir.1990) (Maryland law requires a showing that a bona fide dispute exists, that there is an agreement reflecting a compromise for an amount in excess of that which the debtor admittedly owes, and that such agreement has been performed; acceptance of insurer's check refunding premium, without more, is not release by policyholder of all claims based on policy).

3. AT & T Technologies, Inc. v. Communications Workers of America, 475 U.S. 643, 106 S.Ct. 1415, 89 L.Ed.2d 648 (1986) (district court is obligated, despite this doctrine, to analyze terms of arbitration agreement in dispute over what is arbitrable).

4. Smith v. Seven Springs Farm, Inc., 716 F.2d 1002 (3d Cir.1983) (Pennsylvania law; state comparative negligence statute preserves defense of assumption of risk).

5. Moreno v. Stahmann Farms, Inc., 693 F.2d 106 (10th Cir.1982) (assumption of risk defense treated as contributory negligence defense, since New Mexico no longer recognizes the former); *but see* note 4, *supra*.

barred a plaintiff's recovery from a negligent and otherwise liable defendant.[6] This doctrine was widely criticized as harsh and inconsistent with notions of fairness. Most jurisdictions have either statutorily or judicially replaced the doctrine with some type of comparative negligence scheme.

In pure contributory negligence jurisdictions, the elements generally were a failure by plaintiff to exercise ordinary reasonable care, concurring and cooperating with the actionable negligence of defendant, contributing as a proximate cause to the injury alleged in the complaint.[7] Under comparative negligence, the plaintiff's negligence is a factor in reducing the amount of recovery available to him. The finder of fact is asked to assign a percentage of fault to each party; thus, for example, if the plaintiff were found to be 25% responsible for its injuries, the total damages awarded to it would be reduced by 25%. Few jurisdictions use the "pure" comparative negligence system whereby a plaintiff can recover even if the plaintiff is 99% responsible for the injuries suffered. Most use a hybrid that bars recovery to any plaintiff found more than 50% negligent.[8] This approach nods to the policy represented by old-fashioned contributory negligence.

(1) Practice Pointers

Negligence claims are an increasingly common part of complex commercial litigation. *See infra* Chapters 55 "Professional Liability," 70 "Products Liability," 73 "Theft or Loss of Business Opportunities" and 76 "Torts of Competition." Where a negligence claim is asserted in a complaint, therefore, defense counsel must understand the contributory/comparative negligence rules in the state whose law is to be applied to the dispute.

When negligence is an element of the complaint, there is virtually no situation in which contributory/comparative negligence should not be asserted as a defense. Only discovery can determine the applicability of the defense, but there are few cases where a plaintiff has not done *something* that could have contributed to its present problems. Whether that "something" is blameworthy in a legal sense—*i.e.*, negligence—is for the fact-finder to decide. Until it makes that decision, discovery may proceed in the direction of *any* action by the plaintiff that could result in evidence of contributory/comparative negligence.

Similarly, unless the contributory negligence defense is eliminated by a successful pretrial motion, evidence of contributory negligence is admissible at trial. This evidence of "the plaintiff's fault" would often otherwise be inadmissible as irrelevant or prejudicial. But as long as contributory/comparative negligence is part of the case, this proof has a much better chance of being part of the picture the defense paints of the plaintiff. Since proving contributory negligence might defeat or reduce

---

6. *See, e.g.*, Peacock v. Wal–Mart Stores, Inc., 50 F.3d 7 (table) (4th Cir.1995).

7. Keegan v. Anchor Inns, Inc., 606 F.2d 35 (3d Cir.1979).

8. *See, e.g.*, Edwards v. Sears, Roebuck & Co., 512 F.2d 276 (5th Cir.1975) (regarding Mississippi's pure comparative negligence regime).

the recovery, the importance of asserting the affirmative defense of contributory or comparative negligence cannot be overstated.

(g) Discharge in Bankruptcy

The effect of bankruptcy on a commercial claim is discussed in detail in Chapter 45 "Bankruptcy Code Impact on Civil Litigation in Federal Courts." Generally, a discharge in bankruptcy releases a bankrupt from all of its or its provable debts subject to statutory and common law exceptions. The elements of a discharge in bankruptcy are a claim against a bankrupt, for a debt which originated prior to the declaration of bankruptcy, which debt has been discharged under the bankruptcy law.[9]

(h) Duress

A defendant claiming duress as a defense is claiming that the contract or obligation the plaintiff is asserting as a basis of recovery was assumed under the threat of some kind of force. The elements, generally, are that one side involuntarily accepted terms imposed by another, that circumstances permitted no other alternative, and that the circumstances were the result of the coercive acts of the opposite party.[10]

Theoretically, duress does not have to come about as a result of a physical threat, and indeed in commercial litigation defendants often assert economic duress. Generally speaking, economic duress is present where a party is induced by another's wrongful act to make a contract under circumstances which deprive it of the exercise of free will. A contract executed under duress is voidable. But the mere fact that a party is in a difficult bargaining position due to desperate financial circumstances does not mean its actions were the result of economic duress.[11] (*See* Chapter 57 "Contracts," *infra*.)

(i) Estoppel

There are several different species of estoppel. The defendant with a strong case for the assertion of estoppel should specify the type of estoppel it is asserting in its affirmative defenses.

Equitable estoppel, perhaps the essential equitable doctrine, is the principle that where it is reasonable to do so, a party is entitled to rely

---

9. Kelly v. Robinson, 479 U.S. 36, 107 S.Ct. 353, 93 L.Ed.2d 216 (1986).

10. Augat, Inc. v. Collier, 1996 WL 110076 (D.Mass.1996) (rejecting summary judgment and dismissing duress claim where defendant's conduct contributed to plaintiff's difficulties). *Compare*, Employers Ins. of Wausau v. United States, 764 F.2d 1572, 1576 (Fed.Cir.1985) (setting forth elements; defense rejected where defendant had alternative course of action); Vasapolli v. Rostoff, 39 F.3d 27, 34 (1st Cir.1994)

(presence of profit motive negates claim of duress); JPM, Inc. v. John Deere Indus. Equip. Co., 94 F.3d 270, 272 (7th Cir.1996) (rejecting franchisee's claim of economic duress on summary judgment).

11. Resolution Trust Corp. v. Ruggiero, 977 F.2d 309, 313 (7th Cir.1992) (no economic duress absent wrongful act; lender's insistence on its terms to extend credit merely hard bargaining).

on another party's representations; and that if that reliance results in the relying party's changing its position to its detriment, it should be able to enforce the representation made by the first party. It is necessary that the party making the representation *know* that its statements would cause the second party to rely on it, and that the party claiming the estoppel did not know nor should it have known its adversary's conduct was misleading.[12]

Reasonableness and good faith are critical to an estoppel defense. Thus, estoppel claims have been rejected where, rather than reasonable reliance on an act or statement, the party claiming estoppel proceeded cynically and took its "relying" actions in an attempt to manufacture an estoppel defense.[13]

The elements of equitable estoppel, then, are that the party to be estopped must have known the facts and must have intended that its conduct would be acted upon or must so act that the party asserting the estoppel has the right to believe it was so intended; that the party asserting estoppel must have been ignorant of the true facts, and that the party asserting estoppel must have relied on the other party's conduct to its injury.[14]

(1) Equitable Estoppel as a Defense

One typical use of estoppel is as a theory of affirmative recovery in contract actions. (*see* Chapter 57 "Contracts," *infra*). As a defense, estoppel says that the defendant's alleged actions, which would otherwise be a basis of liability, were done in reasonable reliance on misrepresentations knowingly made by the plaintiff.[15] Some attorneys take the approach of generally asserting some formulation based on "reliance" as an affirmative defense, but however phrased, there are few reported cases where estoppel has won the day for a defendant.

12. Heckler v. Community Health Servs. of Crawford County Inc., 467 U.S. 51, 59, 104 S.Ct. 2218, 2223, 81 L.Ed.2d 42 (1984); Phillips v. Borough of Keyport, 107 F.3d 164 (3d Cir.1997) (New Jersey law; alleged conduct must have been engaged in with understanding that it would likely induce action, such conduct must be relied on, and the other party must act, in reliance, to change its position to its detriment); International Minerals and Resources, S.A. v. Pappas, 96 F.3d 586 (2d Cir.1996) (factual elements purportedly amounting to estoppel are jury questions).

13. Phillips, 107 F.3d at 183 (applicants for zoning permits may not hastily begin construction to short-circuit review of zoning rulings).

14. *In re* Jones, 181 B.R. 538 (D.Kan. 1995) (IRS estopped to apply bankrupt taxpayer's voluntary prepetition payment to personal tax liability where IRS agent had agreed to apply it to payroll withholding tax liability due to taxpayer's reasonable reliance on agent's statements and fact that plaintiff's voluntary payment resulted in greater taxpayer liability).

15. K. Bell & Assoc., Inc. v. Lloyd's Underwriters, 827 F.Supp. 985 (S.D.N.Y.1993) (insurer equitably estopped to invoke policy exclusion where policyholder relied on insurer's delay in denying coverage and therefore did not settle underlying claim;) Broussard v. Phillips Petroleum Co., 160 F.Supp. 905 (W.D.La.1958) (claim of estoppel against plaintiff's claim that mineral lease was forfeited where plaintiff accepted royalty checks from lessee; no estoppel where checks not cashed, even if defense were applicable to such contracts).

(2) Judicial Estoppel

Judicial estoppel prevents a party from asserting a legal position that is contrary to a position previously taken by it in a legal proceeding. Its elements, according to the majority view, are that the party against whom the estoppel is asserted must have argued an inconsistent position in a prior proceeding; and the prior inconsistent position must have been adopted by the court.[16] The minority view is that it does not matter whether the court adopted the position urged in the previous litigation; judicial estoppel may be invoked whenever the court determines that the allegedly offending party has played "fast and loose" with the judicial process.[17] See Chapter 12 "Issue and Claim Preclusion," infra.

Judicial estoppel is not a common defense, nor is it generally one that should be actively pursued because it is seldom received with enthusiasm by judges. As lawyers, judges appreciate the flexibility parties must have to succeed in litigation as well as the differences between different cases. On the other hand, bringing truly radical departures in the adversary's positions to the court's attention could affect the judge's sympathy for that party's cause.

(3) Collateral Estoppel/Claim Preclusion

Collateral estoppel bars relitigation of any factual issue that actually was decided in previous litigation between the same parties, whether the previous litigation concerned the same or a different claim. Its elements are that the issue sought to be precluded must be the same as that involved in the prior action; that the issue must have been actually litigated; that the issue must have been determined by a valid and binding final judgment; and that the determination of the issue must have been essential to the judgment.[18]

Claim preclusion is discussed extensively in Chapter 12 "Issue and Claim Preclusion," infra.

(j) Failure of Consideration

Failure of consideration is a defense to contract actions. It arises when a valid contract, including valid consideration terms, is made but the promised performance fails because of some supervening cause. It goes to the heart of any claim based on an agreement and is thus always available as a defense to that claim.[19]

This defense is essentially an allegation that the plaintiff has not met its contractual obligation to the defendant.[20] It might seem that

---

16. Bates v. Long Island R.R. Co., 997 F.2d 1028 (2d Cir.1993).

17. Stevens Technical Servs., Inc. v. S.S. Brooklyn, 885 F.2d 584, 588 (9th Cir.1989).

18. Keystone Shipping Co. v. New England Power Co., 109 F.3d 46, 50 (1st Cir. 1997).

19. Resolution Trust Corp. v. Forest Grove Inc., 33 F.3d 284, 292 (3d Cir.1994) (defense rejected where plaintiff's promise

to lend money to plaintiff corporation provided ample consideration under Pennsylvania law); In re Topco, Inc., 894 F.2d 727 (5th Cir.1990) (Texas law; though district court found failure of consideration in transfer of nonexistent oil and gas interests, circuit court found partial, and legally sufficient, consideration since transfer included some valuable property).

20. Seaboard Sur. Co. v. Harbison, 304 F.2d 247, 250 (7th Cir.1962) (affirmative

merely denying the averments of the complaint alleging a contractual obligation would be sufficient, but it has been held that failure to plead lack of consideration as an affirmative defense can work a waiver of the defense.[21] Past consideration based on events preceding the contractual relationship does not count as consideration.[22]

(k) Fraud

Fraud is an affirmative defense that is not pleaded casually or as part of a boilerplate response. In fact, just as an affirmative claim for fraud must meet the particularity requirements of FRCP 9(b), so too must an assertion of fraud as an affirmative defense under FRCP 8(c).[23] *See* Section 6.8(c)(1), *supra.*

The elements of a fraud defense—typically one for "fraud in the inducement" of a contract—are that the plaintiff made a false representation or omission of fact, which plaintiff either knew to be untrue or made recklessly, which was made to deceive the defendant, and which was made to induce the defendant to act on the misrepresentation, thereby causing injury (the defendants' entering into the contract under false pretenses).[24]

(*l*) Illegality

As a matter of public policy, an illegal contract cannot be enforced; it is void ab initio.[25] Illegal contracts include, most obviously, contracts to

defense of failure of consideration casts upon plaintiff burden of making prima facie case on element of consideration); Serpe v. Williams, 776 F.Supp. 1285, 1287 (N.D.Ill. 1991) (failure of consideration is failure of contract; rejecting claims by wives of employees for breach of employment contract with husbands where wives were not obligated to do anything under contracts, despite their having signed documents).

21. Hanover Ins. Co. v. Cameron Country Mut. Ins. Co., 730 F.Supp. 998, 1000 (E.D.Mo.1990).

22. Van Brunt v. Rauschenberg, 799 F.Supp. 1467, 1471 (S.D.N.Y.1992) (under New York law, past services do not constitute consideration); *compare*, Kelly–Springfield Tire Co. v. Action Automotive Distributors, Inc., 648 F.Supp. 731, 733–34 (N.D.Ill.1986) (Maryland law; though past consideration may not be "recycled" to support new contracts, new guaranties of past indebtedness in return for new extensions of credit do constitute consideration).

23. Carr v. Wisecup, 263 F.2d 157, 159 (3d Cir.1959); Federal Deposit Ins. Corp. v. Fireman's Fund Ins. Co., 271 F.Supp. 689 (S.D.Fla.1967) (defensive plea of fraud requires pleading with particularity).

24. Banque Franco–Hellenique de Commerce Int'l v. Christophides, 106 F.3d 22, 25 (2d Cir.1997) (defendant guarantor of loan claimed fraud in inducement in action brought by bank, on grounds that bank knowingly misrepresented that loan had not been secured in violation of law, specifically by use of bribe; case remanded for findings as to whether bank was responsible for misrepresentation).

25. Development Finance Corp. v. Alpha Housing & Health Care Inc., 54 F.3d 156, 158 (3d Cir.1995) (contract alleged by defendant to violate nursing home regulations); Total Medical Management, Inc. v. United States, 104 F.3d 1314, 1320 (Fed. Cir.1997) (contract void ab initio under Civilian Health and Medical Program of the Uniformed Services provisions, and plaintiff health care provider thus failed to state claim on which relief would be granted).

do acts prohibited by criminal law or environmental regulations. But they also include contracts violative of less obvious laws and regulations such as the arcane rules regulating employee benefits.[26] Thus, the technical legality of transactions that, in another context, might not be evaluated as such should be considered when framing a defense.

May a defendant reap the benefits of an illegal contract and then evade its contractual obligations by claiming illegality as a defense? Some cases have so held, ruling, for instance, that an unlicensed professional may not sue to collect his fee, regardless of the quality of services provided.[27] But some courts have looked at such rulings in terms of whether the legal violation is "technical" or is instead meant to protect the public. Thus contracts involving the former have been enforced.[28] Thus the oft-cited maxim that this defense exists "not for the sake of the defendant, but because [the law] will not aid such a plaintiff,"[29] should be kept in mind. It has been held that this defense, as a matter of state law, may not be waived.[30]

(m) Injury by Fellow Servant

The "fellow servant" rule exempted an employer from liability for injuries to one of its employees when those injuries were caused by the negligence of a fellow employee.[31] The employer's exemption was destroyed if its own negligence contributed to the servant's injury, or when the servant who caused the injury occupied such a relation to the injured party or to his employment as to make the negligence of such servant the negligence of the employer.[32] Although still referred to in FRCP 8(c), this common law doctrine has largely been abrogated by workers' compensation acts and the Federal Employer's Liability Act ("FELA").[33]

26. Stuart Park Associates Ltd. v. Ameritech Pension Trust, 51 F.3d 1319, 1324 (7th Cir.1995) (trial court's instructions to jury concerning possible illegality of scheme under ERISA not improper) *but see*, Licciardi v. Kropp Forge Div. Employees' Retirement Plan, 990 F.2d 979, 984 (7th Cir.1993) (possibility of illegality in complex contracts cases involving regulatory sophistication should not be made "fulcrum" for resolving contract litigation).

27. Rush-Presbyterian–St. Luke's Medical Center v. Hellenic Republic, 980 F.2d 449, 454 (7th Cir.1992)

28. *Id.* at 455; Marketing Specialists, Inc. v. Bruni, 129 F.R.D. 35, 44–47 (W.D.N.Y.1989) (agreement not illegal but contemplating illegal conduct was enforced, where class sought to be protected by regulation not threatened by conduct).

29. Fitzsimons v. Eagle Brewing Co., 107 F.2d 712 (3d Cir.1939) (quoting Restatement (Second) of Contracts § 598)

30. Stuart Park Associates, 51 F.3d 1319.

31. Central R.R. Co. of New Jersey v. Keegan, 160 U.S. 259, 264, 16 S.Ct. 269, 270, 40 L.Ed. 418 (1895); New England R.R. Co. v. Conroy, 175 U.S. 323, 20 S.Ct. 85, 44 L.Ed. 181 (1899) (conductor, engineer, and brakeman were fellow servants and therefore their employer, the railroad company, was exempt from liability for injuries caused to one employee by negligence of another).

32. New England R.R. Co. , 175 U.S. at 336, 20 S.Ct. at 90; Northern Pacific R.R. Co. v. Peterson, 162 U.S. 346, 16 S.Ct. 843, 40 L.Ed. 994 (1896) (when employer fails in duty owed to employee to provide a reasonably safe place to work, it may be held liable for injuries arising from its negligence).

33. Consolidated Rail Corp. v. Gottshall, 512 U.S. 532, 114 S.Ct. 2396, 129 L.Ed.2d 427 (1994); McDermott Int'l v. Wilander, 498 U.S. 337, 111 S.Ct. 807, 112 L.Ed.2d 866 (1991) (Jones Act provides cause of action in negligence for any seaman injured

(n) Laches

Laches is an equitable defense based on the well-known maxim that "equity aids the vigilant, not those who sleep on their rights."[34]

Laches is closely related to waiver. Waiver is based on an actual or legally implied surrender of a right or privilege, while laches is based on the fundamental equitable principle of reliance—that other parties have been disadvantaged by the late assertion of a legal claim. In this respect laches approximates estoppel. The difference is that in estoppel, there is action by one party that misleads another, whereas in laches the prejudice is caused by inaction.[35] Thus laches has been found where a patentholder delayed five years in bringing an infringement action, despite the defendants' explicit communication inviting the patentee to indicate its intentions or concerns. Though it originally threatened "prompt and vigorous" enforcement of the patent, the patentee's failure to follow up, during which time a crucial defense witness died, prejudiced the defendant.

The elements of laches, therefore, are lack of diligence by the party against whom the defense is asserted and prejudice to the party asserting the defense. A lack of diligence is shown by proof that either (1) the action was not commenced within the period provided by the applicable statute of limitations or (2) by facts otherwise indicating a lack of vigilance.[36] The mere fact of delay may establish a presumption of prejudice.[37] Where the issue is litigated, the "reasonableness" of the delay may be the heart of the issue.[38] The second element, prejudice to the defendant asserting laches, is demonstrated by showing disadvantage on the part of the defendant in asserting or establishing a claimed right or some other harm caused by detrimental reliance on the plaintiff's conduct.[39]

---

in the course of employment, thus removing any traces of the fellow servant rule).

34. Ivani Contracting Corp. v. City of New York, 103 F.3d 257, 259 (2d Cir.), *cert. denied,* ___ U.S. ___, 117 S.Ct. 1695, 137 L.Ed.2d 821 (1997) (discussing history of doctrine; defense rejected as inapplicable to claims brought under federal civil rights statutes).

35. Advanced Hydraulics, Inc. v. Otis Elevator Co., 525 F.2d 477 (7th Cir.), *cert. denied,* 423 U.S. 869, 96 S.Ct. 132, 46 L.Ed.2d 99 (1975) (quoting Lebold v. Inland Steel Co., 125 F.2d 369, 375 (7th Cir.1941)). *See also,* White v. Daniel, 909 F.2d 99, 102 (4th Cir.1990) (presumption of prejudice stems from plaintiff's delay where voters brought action under Voting Rights Act 17 years after redistricting at issue). *Compare,* United States v. Koreh, 59 F.3d 431 (3d Cir.1995) (setting out elements; defense re-

jected in denaturalization proceeding where defendant war criminal claimed that five-year delay between beginning of investigation and filing of action resulted in laches; court found neither prejudice nor possibility of prejudice).

36. White, 909 F.2d at 102.

37. *Id.*

38. Exxon Corp. v. Oxxford Clothes, Inc., 109 F.3d 1070, 1082–83 (5th Cir.1997) (setting out various chronological stages where clothes maker could and should have brought trademark dilution claim).

39. White, 909 F.2d at 102. *See also,* Cornetta v. United States, 851 F.2d 1372 (Fed.Cir.1988) (criticizing "presumption of prejudice" concept in wrongful discharge claim; rejecting proffered grounds of prejudice to employer such as possibility of back pay or benefits due to former soldier).

(1) Analysis

Laches may be seen as the common law version of the policies embodied in statutes of limitation, which are discussed below. The laches defense is used frequently in conjunction with a statute of limitations defense.[40] There are distinctions between the two: No showing of prejudice by the defendant is necessary to assert the statute of limitations, while laches, at least theoretically, may succeed on an equitable basis where the statute of limitations has not run.

(2) Practice Pointer

Laches is part of every boilerplate set of affirmative defenses, often regardless of whether it is justified. Laches is seldom a successful defense standing by itself, however, because many areas of law are governed by statutes of limitation.[41]

(o) License

In its simplest form, a license grants a party leave to do something that the licensor would otherwise have a right to prevent—in other words, it is legal "permission" or "leave to do a thing which the licensor would otherwise have the right to prevent."[42]

(1) Implied Licenses

A license may be explicit, as it frequently is in the intellectual property area (see Chapters 63–65). It also may be implicit. An implied license is one that is presumed to have been given from the acts of the party authorized to give it. The elements of an implied license are that there was an existing relationship between the two parties; within that relationship, the plaintiff transferred a right to the defendant; the right was transferred for valuable consideration; despite presently denying the existence of the license, the plaintiff's statements and conduct created the impression that it consented to defendant's use of the property in question.[43]

---

40. *But see,* Ivani Contracting Corp. v. City of New York, 103 F.3d 257, 259 (2d Cir.) *cert. denied,* ___ U.S. ___, 117 S.Ct. 1695, 137 L.Ed.2d 821 (1997) (quoting Morgan v. Koch, 419 F.2d 993, 996 (7th Cir. 1969)).

41. *See* Park County Resource Council, Inc. v. U.S. Dept. of Agriculture, 817 F.2d 609, 617 (10th Cir.1987) (since National Environmental Policy Act ("NEPA") contains no statute of limitations, defense that NEPA claim is time-barred must be based on laches), *overruled on other grounds by,* 956 F.2d 970 (10th Cir.1992).

42. Western Elec. Co. v. Pacent Reproducer Corp., 42 F.2d 116, 118 (2d Cir.), *cert.*

denied, 282 U.S. 873, 51 S.Ct. 78, 75 L.Ed. 771 (1930) (patent license).

43. Hewlett-Packard Co. v. Repeat-O-Type Stencil Mfg. Corp., Inc., 123 F.3d 1445 (Fed.Cir.1997) (license for use of patented ink jet cartridges implied by patentee's sale of cartridges without restriction to company that modified, refilled and resold them); Wang Laboratories v. Mitsubishi Elec. America, Inc., 103 F.3d 1571, 1580–82 (Fed. Cir.), *cert. denied* ___ U.S ___, 118 S.Ct. 69, 139 L.Ed.2d 30 (1997) (patentee waived its statutory right to exclusive manufacture, use or sale of invention by close commercial and technical cooperation with defendant).

Thus, for example, in one recent patent case an implied license was found because the "course of conduct" between the parties implied permission to manufacture and sell the patented products. That conduct included close technical and commercial cooperation, and the extraction by the plaintiff of payment for the implied license granted to the defendant, plus other benefits.[44]

(2) Defense to Trespass

License can also be a defense to a trespass claim.[45] Though few commercial cases involve actions for trespass, the theory of trespass is at the heart of certain business torts (*see* Chapters 73 and 76) and common law environmental claims (*see* Chapter 80).

(p) Payment

The payment defense is what it sounds like: The performance of a duty, promise or obligation, or the discharge of a debt or liability, by the delivery of money or other value by a debtor to a creditor, where the money or other valuable thing is tendered and accepted as extinguishing the debt or obligation in whole or in part.[46] It differs from accord and satisfaction in that the payment defense alleges that the promise being sued upon was kept as opposed to being compromised.

The payment defense therefore can be seen as the mirror-image of the defense of failure of consideration. And as with that defense, although it speaks to a fundamental element of the plaintiff's claim, it can be waived if not pleaded.[47] The burden of proving payment lies with the party asserting the defense.

(q) Release

A release is an enforceable promise by a party that it is discharging a duty owed to it either immediately or upon the occurrence of a condition. Thus it is a specialized type of accord and satisfaction. A release can be in the form of an oral statement but usually is contained in a writing. The majority rule today is that a release is binding even in the absence of consideration.[48]

The interpretation of releases is governed by principles of contract

---

44. *Id.*

45. Machleder v. Diaz, 801 F.2d 46, 59 (2d Cir.1986) (reporter who was invited onto premises not liable for trespass); Butler v. Pollard, 800 F.2d 223, 226 (10th Cir. 1986) (county invited to improve ditch on plaintiff's land, barring trespass claim); *compare*, Food Lion, Inc. v. Capital Cities/ABC, Inc., 951 F.Supp. 1217, 1220 (denying license defense to trespass claim due to defendant's misrepresentation in obtaining consent, and on grounds that plaintiff

television news producers and personnel exceeded scope of any consent).

46. Black's Law Dictionary at 1129 (6th ed. 1990); U.C.C. §§ 2–511, 3–604.

47. Bank Leumi Le–Israel B.M. v. Lee, 928 F.2d 232 (7th Cir.1991) (failure to plead FRCP 8(c) affirmative defense results in waiver).

48. Restatement (Second) of Contracts § 284 (1981).

law.[49]

(r) Res Judicata

A final judgment on the merits of an action precludes the parties or their successors from relitigating issues that were or could have been raised in that action.[50] The decision made (i) must be a final judgment on the merits and (ii) have involved the same parties as the new action.

Res judicata is discussed at length in Chapter 12 "Issue and Claim Preclusion," *infra*.

(s) Statute of Frauds

The statutes of frauds in effect in the various states bar enforcement of certain oral contracts. (*See* Chapter 57 "Contracts," *infra*.) While a majority of the states have adopted the Uniform Commercial Code's ("U.C.C.") statute of fraud provisions regarding commercial contracts, there are many state variations of the categories of oral contracts that fall under the statute of frauds.[51] The general categories of contracts requiring a writing are as follows:

(1) Sales of Goods

Except as otherwise provided, a contract for sale of goods for the price of $ 500 or more is not enforceable unless there is (i) a writing sufficient to indicate that a contract for sale has been made between the parties and (ii) a signature by the defendant or its agent. A writing is not insufficient because it omits or incorrectly states a term agreed upon, but the contract is only enforceable up to the quantity of goods shown in the writing.[52]

(2) Personal Property

The U.C.C. also requires that to enforce a contract for sale of personal property above $ 500, a plaintiff must produce (i) a writing sufficient to indicate that a contract for sale has been made between the parties and (ii) a signature by the defendant or its agent.[53]

(3) Securities

Historically the statute of frauds applied to securities transactions. If the securities transactions were not in writing, the transaction was

---

49. Ismert and Assoc. Inc. v. New England Mutual Life Ins. Co., 801 F.2d 536 (1st Cir.1986) (applying contract principles to purported release of claims by property tax consultant against life insurance company arising out of joint venture).

50. Federated Dept. Stores v. Moitie, 452 U.S. 394, 398, 101 S.Ct. 2424, 2427, 69 L.Ed.2d 103 (1981).

51. *See* LaBarre v. Shepard, 84 F.3d 496 (1st Cir.1996); Jensen v. Taco John's Int'l, Inc., 110 F.3d 525 (8th Cir.1997) (under Minnesota law, oral franchise contract barred by statute of frauds).

52. U.C.C. § 2–201. *But see* Flight Systems, Inc. v. Electronic Data Systems Corp., 112 F.3d 124 (3d Cir.1997) (where defendant admitted under oath that contract was formed, purposes of statute of frauds served, so contract, although limited, not barred because made orally).

53. U.C.C. § 2–201.

unenforceable, with some exceptions. In 1994, however, the U.C.C. was amended by the addition of Section 8–113, stating that a contract or contract modification for the sale of securities is enforceable regardless of whether there is a written contract. Therefore it is necessary to look at the local law to see if this provision has been added.

(4) Interests in Real Estate

Not covered by the U.C.C., it is nonetheless universal that transactions involving interests in real estate must be in writing and signed by the party to be charged to be enforceable.[54] Different states have different statutes of frauds requirements depending on the interest involved, such as leases, deeds, mortgages and easements.

(5) Practice Pointer

The defense of the statute of frauds is often met with a claim by the plaintiff of a contract formed by promissory estoppel or some other reliance theory. Thus it is important to develop evidence that the parties intended their ultimate agreement to be memorialized in writing. (*See* Chapter 57 "Contracts," *infra*.)

(t) Statute of Limitations

The federal courts look to state law for the applicable statutes of limitation for state law claims[55] and to the relevant federal statute for federal claims. Where state law is applied, however, federal procedural standards apply to their application, such as whether the defense has been timely raised.[56] The federal courts generally rule that both state and federal statutes of limitation begin to run when the claimant discovers or should discover, through the exercise of reasonable care, acts constituting the alleged violation.[57]

(u) Waiver

Waiver is the intentional relinquishment or abandonment of a known right.[58] It may arise in a civil litigation context as a defense

---

54. *See, e.g.,* N.Y. Real Prop. Law § 243 (McKinney 1997); Tex. Bus. & Com. Code Ann. § 26.01 (West 1997); N.H. Rev. Stat. Ann. § 506:1 (1995); Mich. Comp. Laws Ann. § 566.106 (West 1997); Minn. Stat. Ann. § 513.04 (West 1997); Or. Rev. Stat. § 41.580 (1996).

55. *See, e.g.,* Gnazzo v. G.D. Searle & Co., 973 F.2d 136, 138 (2d Cir.1992) (applying Connecticut law to analysis of when statute of limitations began to run in product liability action).

56. Santos v. District Council of New York City Vicinity of United Broth. of Carpenters and Joiners of America, AFL–CIO,

619 F.2d 963, 968 (2d Cir.1980) (accrual of cause of action based on federal law); Perry v. O'Donnell, 749 F.2d 1346, 1350 (9th Cir. 1984) (applying state statute of limitations, but Rule 8(c) governs manner of raising defense).

57. N.L.R.B. v. Don Burgess Const. Corp., 596 F.2d 378, 382 (9th Cir.1979) (fraudulent concealment tolls running of statute).

58. United States v. Olano, 507 U.S. 725, 733, 113 S.Ct. 1770, 1777, 123 L.Ed.2d 508 (1993). *See also* Essex Ins. Co. v. Stage 2, Inc., 14 F.3d 1178 (7th Cir.1994) (waiver arises from "an affirmative act and not by

where the defendant maintains that the plaintiff has waived, or given up, the right on which it is suing—*e.g.*, the right of an insurer to reserve its right to disclaim coverage while defending a policyholder in litigation,[59] the right to assert a defense in litigation over the subject agreement,[60] or the right to sue for injuries for which, absent the waiver, the defendant might be liable.[61] The essential elements of waiver are an existing right, benefit, or advantage; knowledge, actual or constructive, of its existence; and actual intent to relinquish the right, which can be inferred.[62] Waiver thus may be express or implied from "clear and unequivocal" conduct.[63]

Library References:

West's Key No. Digests, Federal Civil Procedure ⚙️751–759.
Wright, Miller & Cooper, Federal Practice and Procedure: Civil 2d §§ 1249, 1456, 1500, 1715, 3569, 3706.

§ 6.12   Counterclaims

The best defense is a good offense, and in litigation this maxim is realized via the counterclaim. The counterclaim is the assertion of a claim that could be a suit in itself against the plaintiff,[1] if not for the fact that the plaintiff sued first. Unlike a defense, which says that the defendant owes the plaintiff nothing, the counterclaim is an affirmative demand for something *from* the plaintiff—even if that something amounts to more than what the plaintiff originally sought from the defendant.[2] Thus a borrower, sued for default on a loan, may counter-

---

operation of law"). *See* Chapter 15 "Class Actions," *infra* for discussion of the applicability of these principles to class action plaintiffs.

59. *See, e.g.*, Continental Cas. Co. v. Hartford Fire Ins. Co., 116 F.3d 932, 938 n. 8 (D.C.Cir.1997) (insurer proceeded with defense without reserving rights).

60. *See, e.g.*, Snyder v. Bank One, Kentucky, N.A., 113 F.3d 774 (7th Cir.1997) (guarantor's waiver of "impairment of collateral" defense in guaranty agreement valid under Kentucky law).

61. *See, e.g.*, Anderson v. Eby, 83 F.3d 342, 345 (10th Cir.1996) (enforcing release of liability signed by injured snowmobile rider in action against park service).

62. *See, e.g.*, First Nat. Bank v. Allen, 118 F.3d 1289, 1294 (8th Cir.1997) (collecting cases; waiver of unsecured claims by creditors found based on silence that benefited them at earlier point in bankruptcy proceedings); Bank v. Truck Ins. Exchange, 51 F.3d 736, 739 (7th Cir.1995) (though waiver is simply relinquishment of contractual rights, courts must be skeptical of self-serving claims of other party's waiver).

63. Garfield v. J.C. Nichols Real Estate, 57 F.3d 662, 667 (8th Cir.1995). *See also* National Liberty Corp. v. Wal–Mart Stores, Inc., 120 F.3d 913, 915 (8th Cir.1997) (Missouri law; where insurer expressed no objection to assignment of agency for sale of its insurance, waiver of its contractual right to prevent assignment was implied); *cf.*, Sybron Transition Corp. v. Security Ins. Co. of Hartford, 107 F.3d 1250 (7th Cir.1997) (under New York law, insurer does not impliedly waive right to disclaim coverage of insured by "following" developments in underlying litigation).

§ 6.12

1. The counterclaim must be asserted against the plaintiff in the same capacity in which it sued, *e.g.*, if the plaintiff is a trustee suing on behalf of the trust beneficiaries, a counterclaim will not lie as against the plaintiff individually. *See, e.g.*, Banco Nacional de Cuba v. Chase Manhattan Bank, 658 F.2d 875 (2d Cir.1981).

2. FRCP 13(c).

claim for breach of contract by the lender for the alleged failure to extend credit as required under the loan instrument. A franchisor seeking to terminate a franchise may receive a counterclaim for unlawful termination or another business tort. One driver suing another for injuries sustained in a collision may be served with a virtually identical counterclaim for damages suffered by the defendant. The rules for pleading a counterclaim—a defendant's complaint—therefore, are best understood by reference to Chapter 5's discussion on complaints.

(a) Compulsory Counterclaims: FRCP 13(a)

FRCP 13(a) requires that a counterclaim must be brought if:

- it exists at the time the answer is filed and is not presently being litigated in another court;

- it arises from the same "transaction or occurrence" as the complaint; and

- its adjudication does not require the involvement of third parties over whom the court cannot acquire jurisdiction.

If a compulsory counterclaim is not pleaded, it is waived.[3] The crux of compulsory counterclaims is judicial economy, *i.e.*, that matters in dispute should be decided in one proceeding and not in piecemeal fashion.

(1) Transaction or Occurrence

The question often arises whether a potential compulsory counterclaim does indeed arise out of the same transaction or occurrence as the claims of the plaintiff. Because this is a fact-sensitive determination, hard and fast guidelines as to meeting this standard are difficult to set. Many decisions use the standard requiring that there be a "logical relationship"[4] between the two claims, but all this formulation does is restate the question. Perhaps the most useful formula is the one that analyzes whether a subsequent suit on what would have been the counterclaim would be barred by res judicata if not brought in the pending action.[5]

---

3. Driver Music Co., Inc. v. Commercial Union Ins. Co., 94 F.3d 1428 (10th Cir. 1996). *But see* Union Paving Co. v. Downer Corp., 276 F.2d 468 (9th Cir.1960) (no waiver occurs when the cause of action which would otherwise be necessary to assert as a compulsory counterclaim is also the subject of pending litigation in another court).

4. *See, e.g.,* In re Pinkstaff, 974 F.2d 113 (9th Cir.1992); Aguilar v. Southeast Bank, N.A., 117 F.3d 1368 (11th Cir.1997) (under Florida law, a counterclaim is compulsory if it meets the logical relationship test); Tank Insulation Int'l, Inc. v. Insultherm, Inc., 104 F.3d 83, 85–86 (5th Cir.) (antitrust claim based on an alleged con-

spiracy to file a wrongful patent infringement lawsuit held barred as a result of the failure to raise such allegation as a counterclaim in the infringement action, partly based on the logical relationship between the infringement action and antitrust claim) *cert. denied,* ___ U.S. ___, 118 S.Ct. 265, 139 L.Ed.2d 191 (1997).

5. Tank Insulation, 104 F.3d at 83. *But see* Painter v. Harvey, 863 F.2d 329, 331–33 (4th Cir.1988) (criticizing the use of a res judicata test to determine whether a compulsory counterclaim exists; "[i]f the limits of the compulsory counterclaim are no broader than res judicata, then Fed.R.Civ.P. 13(a) would be superfluous").

Although the tests for determining compulsory counterclaims may be somewhat ephemeral, actually identifying them is not so difficult. Practically speaking, defense counsel should consider pleading a counterclaim if the potential claim "looks like one." In commercial litigation counterclaims are most commonly asserted in actions where an identifiable, discrete business relationship or transaction has broken up and each side claims the other one is responsible for the resulting damage. This situation epitomizes the compulsory counterclaim. More difficult is the case where the plaintiff and defendant have been involved in a series of "related" transactions, such as the granting of a number of franchises in different locations. There the question will likely turn on whether the dispute is indeed over the same transaction, and not just between the same parties.[6]

(2) Permissive Counterclaims and Local Substantive Law

Claims by the defendant against the plaintiff that do not satisfy the "same transaction or occurrence" test are permissive counterclaims when they are nonetheless amenable to adjudication in the pending federal case.[7] Such counterclaims do not have to be brought at all, and the defendant must determine whether it wishes to proceed in the time and place selected by the plaintiff before these are added to the pleadings.

Not all permissive counterclaims, however, are as optional as they may appear. Strange as it may seem, the Federal Rules regarding compulsory counterclaims may not be the end of the story in terms of which claims should be asserted as such. Federal courts adjudicating state law claims are obligated to consider all state law doctrines that may govern those claims. For example, New Jersey has an extraordinarily wide-ranging requirement regarding what amounts to compulsory counterclaims.[8] This "entire controversy doctrine" has consistently been interpreted as *substantive* law by the federal courts.[9] Thus practitioners must look at local law in determining whether a counterclaim that may not be required under the "transaction or occurrence" test is nonetheless, practically speaking, "compulsory."

(b) Late–Maturing Counterclaims: FRCP 13(e)

If a counterclaim matures or is "acquired," *e.g.*, by assignment resulting from a merger or acquisition, after the answer has been filed, FRCP 13(e) permits an application for the filing of a supplemental pleading including that counterclaim. A motion with supporting materi-

---

6. *See, e.g.*, Alesayi Beverage Corp. v. Canada Dry Corp., 797 F.Supp. 320, 322 (S.D.N.Y.1992) (in case for wrongful termination of soft drink distributorship, tort-based intellectual property claims arising from foreign activities not appropriate subject of counterclaim).

7. FRCP 13(b)

8. Cogdell v. Hospital Center At Orange, 116 N.J. 7, 560 A.2d 1169 (1989); N.J. Rules of Ct. 5:30A.

9. Kozyra v. Allen, 973 F.2d 1110 (3d Cir.1992). *See infra* § 12.12(c) for discussion of the doctrine.

als explaining how the counterclaim has become available must be filed with the court.[10] Supplemental counterclaims, especially if they are compulsory, will usually be permitted if prejudice is not threatened.[11]

(c) Jurisdiction

A third party needed for adjudication of a counterclaim is not necessarily a third-party defendant or cross-claim defendant.[12] The counterclaim provisions, however, do not extend the court's jurisdiction. They explicitly state that if adjudication of the counterclaim would require the joinder of an additional party over whom the court cannot assert jurisdiction, the counterclaim is not mandatory. For the same reason, it cannot be brought as a permissive counterclaim either. Note also that it is often difficult to get supplemental jurisdiction over a permissive counterclaim because by definition it does not arise from the same case or controversy as the underlying federal complaint.[13]

(d) Strategy

As a matter of strategy, a potential compulsory counterclaim must be pleaded to avoid a subsequent bar. It is true that a court will usually allow a counterclaim to be added late by amendment as long as no prejudice results to the opposing party.[14] Considering the liberality permitted in pleading a late counterclaim, the defendant may be able to bide its time—in terms of a few weeks' delay, for instance—in considering whether to pull the lever of what amounts to initiating a lawsuit; and this is even more true as regards a permissive counterclaim. It must be remembered, however, that with the passage of time, both the court's discretionary power and the risk of prejudice loom larger.

10. Fidelity Fed. Svgs. & Loan Assoc. v. Felicetti, 149 F.R.D. 83 (E.D.Pa.1993).

11. Four Seasons Solar Products Corp. v. Sun System Prefabricated Solar Greenhouses, Inc., 101 F.R.D. 292 (E.D.N.Y. 1983); Spencer v. Newton, 79 F.R.D. 367, 373 (D.Mass.1978) (granting motion to amend answer to include after-acquired counterclaims that would "neither confuse nor unduly protract" the litigation). *Compare* Insurance Concepts, Inc. v. Western Life Ins. Co., 639 F.2d 1108, 1114 (5th Cir.1981) (holding district court did not abuse its discretion in denying motion for leave to assert after-acquired counterclaim, since proposed counterclaim was "not peculiarly relevant" to original action).

12. FRCP 13(h). For discussion of the situation where addition of the third party necessary for the counterclaim would destroy diversity jurisdiction, see Chapter 10 "Joinder Consolidation and Severance," at § 10.3(b) *infra*.

13. Skaro v. Eastern Sav. Bank, 866 F.Supp. 229 (W.D.Pa.1994); Clark v. Universal Builders, Inc., 501 F.2d 324, 341 (7th Cir.) (holding trial court erred in grant of conditional dismissal of permissive counterclaim; such counterclaim should have been dismissed with prejudice since it was permissive and not supported by federal subject matter jurisdiction independent of that supporting the plaintiff's complaint), *cert. denied*, 419 U.S. 1070, 95 S.Ct. 657, 42 L.Ed.2d 666 (1974); Unique Concepts, Inc. v. Manuel, 930 F.2d 573, 574 (7th Cir.1991) ("A federal court has supplemental jurisdiction over compulsory counterclaims.... Permissive counterclaims, however, require their own jurisdictional basis.") (citations omitted).

14. FRCP 13(f); *see, e.g.*, Budd Co. v. Travelers Indem. Co., 820 F.2d 787 (6th Cir.1987).

As to permissive counterclaims, judicial economy notwithstanding, the client may not be ready to assert its claim against the plaintiff. If the first claim can be settled quickly without prejudicing the potential counterclaim, it may be better to hold off so the client can assert its own claim when—and where—it chooses.

(e) Pleading Counterclaims

The counterclaim is included along with the answer and placed after the affirmative defenses. The counterclaim should be labeled as such in the pleadings, though the court will ultimately consider the substance and not the form of a pleading.[15] It is not necessary to plead venue in the counterclaim.[16]

Library References:
> West's Key No. Digests, Federal Civil Procedure ☞771–786.
> Wright, Miller, Kane & Cooper, Federal Practice and Procedure: Civil 2d §§ 1431–1433, 1456, 1715, 3706.

§ 6.13   Cross–Claims: FRCP 13(g)

Cross-claims are claims made against co-defendants in the same action. Unlike counterclaims, it has been held that all cross-claims are, technically, permissive.[1] Unlike permissive counterclaims, however, a cross-claim is only allowed if it arises from the same transaction or occurrence—the same standard as applies to compulsory counterclaims.[2] Jurisdiction over the cross-claim defendant is no better for the cross-claim plaintiff than for the original plaintiff, and if this is defective the cross-claim will fail too.

(a) Indemnification and Contribution

In commercial litigation the most common occasion to assert a cross-claim is when one defendant owes a duty of indemnification or contribution to the other for any damages that may be due to plaintiff. This is explicitly permitted under FRCP 13(g) and is one of the most important uses of the provision. Note that failure to assert a cross-claim for indemnity or contribution could result in waiver.[3]

---

15. *In re* Jones Truck Lines, Inc., 860 F.Supp. 1360 (E.D.Wis.1994); Reiter v. Cooper, 507 U.S. 258, 263, 113 S.Ct. 1213, 1217, 122 L.Ed.2d 604 (1993) ("[I]t makes no difference that petitioners may have mistakenly designated their counterclaims as defenses, since Federal Rule of Civil Procedure 8(c) provides that 'the court on terms, if justice so requires, shall treat the pleading as if there had been a proper designation.' ").

16. Schoot v. United States, 664 F.Supp. 293 (N.D.Ill.1987).

§ 6.13

1. United States v. Confederate Acres Sanitary Sewage and Drainage System, Inc., 935 F.2d 796, 799 (6th Cir.1991) (court has no authority to infer or compel adjudicating of cross-claim).

2. Kane v. Magna Mixer Co., 71 F.3d 555, 562 (6th Cir.1995) (analyzing cross-claim under "same transaction or occurrence" test).

3. *See* FRCP 13(g).

(b) Strategy

The issues discussed in Sections 6.12(e), *supra* apply to cross-claims as well as counterclaims. The only additional caveat is that since cross-claims are usually permissive, the client should be advised carefully as to whether a suit brought by a third party is the proper occasion to "start up" with a co-defendant. This is especially true when co-defendants have more to gain by cooperating against the plaintiff through a joint defense agreement than by allowing the plaintiff to succeed in a "divide and conquer" strategy. Elaborate mechanisms and strategies are available and are frequently used in commercial litigation to allocate responsibility and damages among defendants by alternative dispute resolution after the main court case is completed.

Library References:

West's Key No. Digests, Federal Civil Procedure ☞786.
Wright, Miller, Kane & Cooper, Federal Practice and Procedure: Civil 2d §§ 1431–1433, 1456, 1715, 3706.

§ 6.14 Practice Checklist

(a) Receipt of the Summons and Complaint

(1) You must immediately ascertain when the complaint was received by the defendant, add 20 days to determine the due date of the response, and docket that date. (*See* FRCP 12(a); §§ 6.2, 6.4(d))

(2) While the facts surrounding receipt of the summons and complaint are fresh, investigate whether service was properly effected. (*See* FRCP 12(b)(4), (5); § 6.5(f))

(3) Determine whether there is a conflict of interest in your representation of the defendant before beginning substantive discussion of the lawsuit or any investigation. (*See* § 6.2(1))

(4) If a provisional remedy is sought, focus on resisting it while remembering to keep an eye on the due date for the response to the complaint itself. (*See* § 6.4(g))

(b) Extensions of Time

(1) Once conflicts are cleared and the date of initial response set, determine if an extension of time to answer or otherwise respond will be needed. If so, see if the local rules of the district where the suit is pending allow for an automatic extension of time and additionally determine the local requirements for obtaining extensions of time by stipulation.

(2) Extensions of time to answer or otherwise respond are often agreed to orally, so remember to prepare a written stipulation and have it executed as soon as possible in order to meet the appropriate FRCP and local rule requirements. (*See* FRCP 6(b) and local rules ; § 6.4(e), (f))

(3) The stipulation or order extending time should clearly state that it is an extension of time "to answer, move or otherwise respond" so it cannot be construed as an extension of time to answer only and a bargained-for waiver of the right to move or otherwise respond. (*See* § 6.4(f)(2))

(c) Investigation of the Case and Choice of Initial Strategy

(1) Once conflicts are cleared and the date of initial response is set or has been extended, learn the facts of the case, at least at the level necessary to respond to the complaint. An understanding of the basic facts and a close reading of the complaint, with legal research if necessary, will suggest whether there are grounds for a motion to dismiss or whether an answer is to be filed.

(d) Assessment of Technical Motions to Dismiss

(1) Inspect the summons and insure that it is in proper form. Follow up on the investigation of whether service was properly effected. If there is a substantive deficiency in service of process that is not readily curable, consider a motion to dismiss on this basis. But do not base a "process motion" solely on trivial technical deficiencies. (*See* FRCP 12(b)(4), (5); § 6.5(f))

2) Read the complaint to determine if, on its face, it meets any of these criteria, each of which could provide a ground for a motion to dismiss:

- It is based on an incorrect assertion of the court's personal or subject matter jurisdiction

- It was brought in an improper venue, including whether the parties are under a contractual obligation to sue in a certain venue or to use arbitration

- Adjudication of the dispute will require joinder of a third party over whom the court cannot assert jurisdiction

If any of these grounds are present, the motion to dismiss should be prepared. (*See* FRCP 12(b)(1), (2), (3) and (7); § 6.6)

(3) If *any* motion is made on one of the above grounds, include *all* possible good faith FRCP 12(b) defenses in that motion or they may be waived. (*See* FRCP 12(g); § 6.8(a))

(4) If you determine that one of the defenses enumerated above is available to your client but choose not to make a motion, remember to assert it as an affirmative defense in the answer. (*See* FRCP 12(b); § 6.6(b))

(e) Assessment of Motions to Dismiss for Failure to State a Claim

(1) Read the complaint to assess the potential for a motion to dismiss for failure to state a claim for relief. Such a motion should be *considered* when:

> • The complaint is based on a frivolous or plainly nonjusticiable claim

> • The plaintiff is asserting a legal theory which, while not frivolous, is without precedent

> • It is advisable to "educate the judge" about what is really at issue in the case or to frame the case very differently from how it is presented in the complaint

> • Filing such a motion has the capacity to send a strong message to the plaintiff about the defendant's readiness to litigate or the weakness of the plaintiff's case.

> • The plaintiff has failed to plead some necessary element of the purported claim or has failed to meet special pleading requirements for certain types of claims as provided by the Federal Rules of Civil Procedure.

(*See* FRCP 9(b), 12(b)(6), (e); §§ 6.7(c), 6.8(c))

(2) Break the complaint down into its constituent parts and analyze whether any individual count, claim or theory of recovery is amenable to a motion for partial dismissal. Pay special attention to counts that may provide the sole basis of federal jurisdiction and may have been added for that sole purpose. Also look for counts that are attempts to make more of a simple commercial dispute or that have been added to provide for enhanced damages or attorneys' fees. (*See* § 6.7(c)(5))

(3) Before making any motion to dismiss for failure to state a claim for which relief can be granted, consider all the strategic implications of the above factors, including the fact that such motions are granted "sparingly" and can be costly to prepare and argue and may simply educate the plaintiff. (*See* § 6.7(b))

(4) If *any* motion is made on the grounds of failure to state a claim, include *all* possible good faith FRCP 12(b) defenses in that motion or they may be waived. (*See* FRCP 12(g); § 6.8(a))

(5) If you determine that the plaintiff has failed to state a claim on which relief can be granted or has some other fatal flaw in its legal theory but choose not to make a motion, remember to assert it as an affirmative defense in the answer. (*See* FRCP 12(b); § 6.6(b))

(f) Motions for a More Definite Statement

(1) A motion for a more definite statement may be appropriate where the complaint seems to set out some claim for relief, but because the complaint is poorly drafted it is not possible to frame a responsive pleading. It should be made within 20 days of service of the summons and complaint, unless extended. (*See* FRCP 12(e); § 6.8(c))

(g) Motion Procedure

(1) Read the applicable local rules and, if applicable, the judge's own rules regarding motion practice and adhere to them.

(2) Motion practice is discussed generally in Chapter 24.

(3) A motion to dismiss for failure to state a claim should *not* include any affidavits or materials extraneous to the pleadings or it will be converted to a summary judgment motion. (*See* FRCP 12(b)(6); § 6.7(d))

(4) The motion must be served within 20 days of receipt of the summons and complaint, unless that time has been extended. Service is effective upon mailing. The papers should then be filed with the court clerk. (*See* FRCP 5(b), 12(a); § 6.4(a))

(h) The Answer

(1) Read the complaint carefully and break each paragraph and allegation into constituent parts. Plead responses to each part individually. Prepare a response to each and every paragraph of the complaint. (*See* FRCP 8(b); § 6.9(b)(3))

(2) Recall that there are only three basic responses to an allegation: Admission, denial, or denial on the basis of a lack of knowledge or information. Remember that a denial can be partial, specifying what part of the allegation is being denied and what admitted. (*See* FRCP 8(b); § 6.9(b))

(3) *See* Chapter 5, "The Complaint" on the general rules and forms of pleading.

(4) Admit as few material factual allegations as possible. (*See* § 6.9(e))

(5) Avoid admission, if possible to do so truthfully, of factual allegations that are elements of the plaintiff's purported cause of action. (*See* § 6.9(e))

(6) Deny all conclusory legal allegations of liability, misfeasance, malfeasance or illegality. (*See* § 6.9(e))

(7) Recast, by use of the partial denial response, any allegation that is compound, conclusory, general or that implicates the defendant's wider interests. (*See* § 6.9(e))

(8) Answer facts presented incompletely in the complaint by denial or by partial denial, setting forth or attaching the complete relevant statement or document and stating in the pleadings that the attached version is a "true copy" of the document. (*See* § 6.9(e)(2))

(9) Deny knowledge or information sufficient to respond to a given allegation where the defendant cannot definitively answer the allegation, whether subsequent investigation (beyond that available before answering) would allow the defendant to answer or whether it could never know the answer. The latter category includes allegations about the state of minds of third parties or about their actions.

(10) Each response in the answer should be contained in a numbered paragraph that corresponds to the numbered paragraph of the allegation to which it is response. (*See* § 6.9(d)(1))

(11) The answer should end with a demand for judgment in the defendant's favor. (*See* § 6.9(f))

(12) Include a jury demand if appropriate and desired. Do not rely on the plaintiff's jury demand, if there is one, if you want a jury. (*See* § 6.9(f))

(13) The answer must be signed by the attorney of record and include the address of the law office and its telephone number. Other information may be required by local rule. (*See* FRCP 11)

(14) A certificate of service must be prepared. It does not have to be served with the answer, only in a "reasonable time" following service; but the usual practice is to prepare, serve and file the answer and the certificate all at once. (*See* FRCP 5(d); § 6.4(c))

(i) Affirmative defenses

(1) All defenses should be asserted as affirmative defenses. These include:

- The affirmative defenses listed in FRCP 8(c)
- Other traditional equitable defenses
- Deficiencies in the complaint based on substantive or procedural law

(*See* § 6.10)

(2) Research the substantive state or federal law for each cause of action in order to determine what affirmative defenses are available.

(3) Affirmative defenses need not be mutually consistent, nor is it necessary when pleading them that you know them to be true. (*See* FRCP 8(e)(2); § 6.10(d))

(4) Do not assert affirmative defenses that have no basis whatsoever in possibility or that are irrelevant to the defendant's case. (*See* § 6.10(e))

(5) Affirmative defenses should be set forth in separately numbered paragraphs following the responses to the complaint in the answer, and should be designated as affirmative defenses. (*See* § 6.10(b))

(j) Counterclaims

(1) While you prepare the defense, your factual investigation should determine whether the defendant has any claims against the plaintiff arising out of the same transaction or occurrence as the complaint. If it does, these claims are compulsory counterclaims, and generally must be asserted during the early stages of the litigation or may be barred from future litigation. The main exception to this is when joinder of a third party would be necessary to resolve the counterclaim but the court cannot acquire jurisdiction over that party. (*See* FRCP 13(a); § 6.12(a))

(2) Keep an eye out for counterclaims that arise or develop after the filing of the answer. These can be asserted later in the proceedings on motion to the court. (*See* FRCP 13(e); § 6.12(b))

(3) Permissive counterclaims, *i.e.* those that do not arise from the same transaction or occurrence as the complaint, may be asserted in some situations. But before filing permissive counterclaims, examine whether this action, in this venue and at this time present the appropriate occasion for the defendant to assert its claims against the plaintiff. (*See* FRCP 13(b); § 6.12(a)(2))

(4) Plead counterclaims after the affirmative defenses. Label the counterclaims as such. (*See* § 6.12(e))

(k) Cross–Claims

(1) Cross-claims are claims made against fellow defendants. They are technically permissive, but indemnity and contribution claims should be brought where available to avoid waiver. (*See* FRCP 13(g); § 6.13)

(2) Cross-claims must be served on a co-defendant in the same manner that a complaint is served on a party not already in the action, if that defendant has been named in the action but has not yet made an appearance in the case. (*See* § 6.4(b))

§ 6.15 Forms

(a) Application for Automatic Extension of Time to Respond Pursuant to Local Rule 🖫

UNITED STATES DISTRICT COURT
DISTRICT OF _____

_____,   HONORABLE _____

Plaintiff,   Civil Action No. _____

v.   APPLICATION FOR AN EXTENSION
                                          OF TIME TO ANSWER, MOVE OR
_____,   OTHERWISE REPLY PURSUANT TO
                                          LOCAL CIVIL RULE 6.1
Defendant.

Application is hereby made pursuant to Local Civil Rule 6.1 for a Clerk's Order extending the time within which defendant _____ may answer, move or otherwise reply to the Complaint for a period of fifteen days, up to and including [*insert date 15 days from the day the Answer was originally due*]; and it is represented that:

Service of process was effected on _____, 199__ [*if required under local rules; see D.N.J. L. Civ. R 6.1, requiring such statement*];

The time to answer, move or otherwise reply expires on _____, 199__; and

No previous extension has been obtained.

_____

Attorneys for Defendant _____

By: _____

ORDER

The above application is ORDERED GRANTED and the time within which defendant_____ shall answer or otherwise move is extended through and including _____.

ORDER DATED _____, 199__.

_____, Clerk

By: _____
Deputy Clerk

(b) Stipulation and Order Extending Time to Respond 🖫

UNITED STATES DISTRICT COURT
DISTRICT OF _____

```
_____,              )   HONORABLE _____
                  Plaintiff,  )   Civil Action No. _____
v.                            )
                              )
                              )   APPLICATION FOR AN EXTENSION
_____,              )     OF TIME TO ANSWER, MOVE OR
                  Defendant.  )   OTHERWISE REPLY PURSUANT TO
                              )   [Local Rule]
                              )
                              )
                              )
```

Application is hereby made pursuant to [*insert Local Rule*] for a Clerk's Order extending the time within which defendant_____
_____ may answer, move or otherwise reply to the Complaint for a period of fifteen days, up to and including [*insert date 15 days from the day the Answer was originally due*]; and it is represented that:

1. Service of process was effected on _____, 199__;

2. The time to answer, move or otherwise reply expires on _____, 199__; and

3. No previous extension has been obtained.

                              _____
                              Attorneys for Defendant _____

                              By: _____

ORDER

The above application is ORDERED GRANTED and the time within which defendant_____ shall answer or otherwise move is extended through and including _____.

ORDER DATED, _____ 199__.

                              _____, Clerk

                              By: _____
                              Deputy Clerk

(c) Certificate of Service

UNITED STATES DISTRICT COURT
DISTRICT OF _____

```
_____,              )   HONORABLE _____
                              )   Civil Action No. _____
                  Plaintiff,  )
                              )
v.                            )   PROOF OF SERVICE
                              )
_____,              )
                              )
                  Defendant.  )
                              )
                              )
```

The undersigned hereby certifies that on this date, a true copy of _____'s [*identify all documents served*] was served by [*mail/hand delivery/Federal Express/United Parcel Service overnight delivery*] addressed to the following:

_____

_____

_____

I hereby certify that the foregoing statements made by me are true. I am aware that if any of the foregoing statements are willfully false, I am subject to punishment.

_____
[*Attorney or assistant certifying to service*]

DATED: _____, 19__

(d) Answer with Affirmative Defenses

UNITED STATES DISTRICT COURT
DISTRICT OF _____

_____,	)	HONORABLE _____
	)	Civil Action No. _____
Plaintiff_____,	)	
	)	
v.	)	ANSWER ON BEHALF OF
	)	_____
_____,	)	
	)	
Defendant_____.	)	
	)	

Defendant _____ ("_____"), by way of an Answer to the Complaint of plaintiff _____, says:

FIRST COUNT

It denies the allegations contained in paragraph ___.

[or]

It admits the allegations contained in paragraph ___.

[or]

Is without knowledge or information sufficient to form a belief as to the truth of the allegations contained in paragraph ___.

FIRST AFFIRMATIVE DEFENSE

The Complaint, in whole or in part, fails to state a claim upon which relief may be granted.

SECOND AFFIRMATIVE DEFENSE

Plaintiff's claims are barred due to insufficiency of service of process.

[successive affirmative defenses]

The Court lacks personal jurisdiction over this defendant.

The Court lacks subject matter jurisdiction over this action.

Plaintiff's claims are subject to dismissal because venue is improperly laid in this Court

Plaintiff's claims should be dismissed on the grounds of *forum non conveniens.*

Any loss sustained by plaintiff was due to the negligence of plaintiff or some other third party over whom the defendant exercised no control.

Plaintiff's claims are barred by the failure to join an indispensable party.

Plaintiff's claims are barred by the doctrine of estoppel.

Plaintiff's claims are barred by the doctrine of laches.

Plaintiff's claims are barred by the doctrine of waiver.

Plaintiff's claims are barred by [claims are reduced by] the doctrine of set-off.

Plaintiff's claims are barred by the applicable statute of limitations.

Plaintiff's claims are barred by the doctrine of unclean hands.

At all times relevant herein, the defendant conducted _____ in a commercially reasonable manner, consistent with the requisites of the Uniform Commercial Code.

Plaintiff's claims are barred by the doctrine of accord and satisfaction.

Plaintiff's claims are barred due to failure of consideration.

Plaintiff's claims are barred due to fraud by the plaintiff.

Plaintiff's claims are barred due to the illegality of the contract.

[*New Jersey:*] Plaintiff's claims are barred by the entire controversy doctrine.

Plaintiff's claims are barred by the doctrine of res judicata.

Plaintiff's claims are barred by the doctrine of collateral estoppel.

Plaintiff's claims are barred by the statute of frauds.

WHEREFORE, defendant _____ demands _____ judgment in its favor and against plaintiff _____ dismissing the Complaint with prejudice, together with costs.

———————————————

Attorneys for Defendant _____

———————————————

By: _____
A Member of the Firm

DATED: _____, 19__

JURY DEMAND

DEFENDANT HEREBY DEMANDS _____ *A TRIAL BY JURY OF ALL ISSUES SO TRIABLE HEREIN.*

_____

Attorneys for Defendant _____
_____

By: _____
A Member of the Firm

DATED: _____, 19__

CHAPTER 7

THIRD–PARTY PRACTICE

by

Edward P. Leibensperger*

Table of Sections

* The author gratefully acknowledges the substantial assistance provided by Kathryn K. Conde and David L. Ferrera, litigation attorneys in the firm of Nutter, McClennen & Fish, LLP.

WESTLAW Electronic Research
See WESTLAW Electronic Research Guide preceding the Summary of Contents.

---

§ 7.1 Scope Note

This chapter discusses the procedure for impleading a third-party defendant under FRCP 14 and the rights and obligations of the parties with regard to a party joined under this Rule. Third-party practice is intended to promote judicial efficiency and to avoid circuity of actions and inconsistent judgments.[1] Although a defendant's right to assert a third-party complaint is subject to the court's discretion,[2] third-party complaints are liberally allowed because they enhance efficiency and allow related claims to be disposed of in one action.[3]

This chapter begins with a discussion of the requirements for a proper third-party claim under FRCP 14. Additional requirements for venue and jurisdiction are also reviewed. Because impleader is ultimately a question for the court's discretion, this chapter will discuss the factors which courts consider when deciding whether to allow impleader. Strategic considerations which should be evaluated by a party regarding whether to implead a third-party defendant are addressed. Finally, the procedural aspects of third-party practice will be discussed, including the timing and proper form of the motion and third-party complaint, as well as the procedural options which the plaintiff and the third-party defendant have in opposing impleader or responding once a third-party defendant has been joined.

Library References:
West's Key No. Digests, Federal Civil Procedure ⊕281–297.
Wright, Miller & Kane, Federal Practice and Procedure: Civil 2d §§ 1187, 1141–
    1465, 1549, 1708, 2374.

§ 7.2 Preliminary Considerations and Strategic Objectives

Under FRCP 14, a "defending party" may bring into the lawsuit a person not already joined who "is or may be liable" to the defending party for all or part of plaintiff's claim against the defending party. This procedure, referred to as impleader or third-party practice, is available to any party defending against a claim whether it be the original action, a counterclaim, cross-claim, or a third-party claim. For convenience, this chapter will refer to the defending party as the defendant, even though a

---

§ 7.1

1. Certain Interested Underwriters at Lloyds v. Gulf Nat'l Ins. Co., 898 F.Supp. 381, 384 (N.D.Miss.1995) ("The rule's general purpose is to adjudicate interrelated matters in one litigation, so as to obtain consistent and fair results for the parties and avoid duplication of effort for the court."), aff'd, 95 F.3d 48 (5th Cir.1996).

2. Highlands Ins. Co. v. Lewis Rail Service Co., 10 F.3d 1247, 1251 (7th Cir.1993) ("The decision to permit a third party complaint is within the sound discretion of the trial court.").

3. Monarch Life Ins. Co. v. Donahue, 702 F.Supp. 1195, 1197 (E.D.Pa.1989).

plaintiff or a third-party defendant may also use this procedure.[1] The party asserting the third-party claim is called the "third-party plaintiff" and the party joined in the action is called the "third-party defendant."

Impleader offers a number of benefits to the defending party. Principal among them is the fact that a third-party defendant will be bound by the judgment in the underlying case. Without the impleader process, the original defendant would have to sue the party liable to it in a separate action in order to recover. The impleader process eliminates the risk attendant with a separate action that the defendant will be unable to prove in the second action the facts establishing liability. By consolidating the two actions into one, impleader also reduces litigation costs. Impleader offers an additional benefit by reducing the costs associated with the lag between the accrual of a right of contribution or indemnity and its satisfaction.[2] This benefit is particularly important where, under a state's substantive law, the right of contribution arises only after the party seeking contribution has satisfied a judgment to the plaintiff. FRCP 14 allows for immediate impleader despite the substantive law that would require the third-party plaintiff to commence a separate action.

Since FRCP 14 is not a mandatory procedure, the defending party may choose whether to exercise this procedural right,[3] and the jury is not entitled to know that the defendant chose not to implead another party.[4] On the other hand, because impleader is voluntary, a defendant who exercises this right may be viewed as consenting to the court's jurisdiction. Courts have held that the defendant waives the right to remove a case to federal court by impleading a third party in state court.[5]

§ 7.2

1. A "defending party" must be a party to the suit in order to assert and litigate a third party claim. If the claim against the defending party has been dismissed or judgment has been entered on it, the party is no longer considered a defending party and may not assert a third party claim. Faser v. Sears, Roebuck & Co., 674 F.2d 856, 860 (11th Cir.1982) (defendant's claims against third party held moot because court granted summary judgment for defendant).

2. Blais Construction Co. v. Hanover Square Associates–I, 733 F.Supp. 149, 152 (N.D.N.Y.1990) (impleader limits the prejudice incurred by defendant due to the time lag between a judgment against the defendant and a judgment over against a third party defendant).

3. Janney Montgomery Scott, Inc. v. Shepard Niles, Inc., 11 F.3d 399, 412 (3d Cir.1993) (the decision not to bring a third party action does not affect a party's right to bring a separate action for contribution or indemnity).

4. Fernandez v. Corporacion Insular De Seguros, 79 F.3d 207, 210 (1st Cir.1996) (affirming trial court's refusal to instruct jury in medical malpractice case that the defendant had the right to implead plaintiff's personal physician, if the defendant thought that physician was negligent, because impleader is not mandatory).

5. Knudsen v. Samuels, 715 F.Supp. 1505, 1506 (D.Kan.1989) ("The rationale for this rule is that a defendant who asserts a permissive pleading seeking affirmative relief in state court invokes and submits to the jurisdiction of the state court."); California Republican Party v. Mercier, 652 F.Supp. 928, 931 (C.D.Cal.1986) (filing a permissive counterclaim or a third party complaint constitutes waiver of the right to remove).

In most cases, the alternative to impleader is to bring a separate suit. In some instances, however, the defending party may be able to utilize the common law practice of vouching-in.[6] There are numerous strategic factors which should be considered before asserting a third-party complaint which are reviewed in Section 7.2(f),(g), *infra*. However, the first question which a potential third-party plaintiff must consider is whether it can assert a third-party claim.

(a) Claims Which May Be Brought as Third–Party Actions

A third-party claim can be brought only against a party whose liability is derivative of the original defendant's liability.[7] FRCP 14(a) provides that the defending party may serve a summons and complaint on a "person not a party to the action who is or may be liable to the third-party plaintiff for all or part of the plaintiff's claim against the third-party plaintiff."[8] FRCP 14 does not grant a defending party the ability to implead any party who might be liable to the defendant, even if the claim arises from the same transaction or occurrence.[9] In this sense, the scope of impleader is much more limited than the scope of cross-claims or counterclaims. Furthermore, with the exception of certain admiralty claims, a defendant cannot implead a person merely because that person is or may be primarily liable to the original plaintiff.[10] Most commonly, a proper third-party claim is asserted on a theory of indemnity, subrogation, contribution, or warranty, although any other theory of secondary liability is sufficient.

As long as the third-party defendant's liability is derivative of the defendant's, the third-party claim need not be based on the same theory as the main claim by the plaintiff.[11] For example, a third-party plaintiff

---

6. *See infra* § 7.2(e).

7. Stewart v. American Int'l Oil & Gas Co., 845 F.2d 196, 199 (9th Cir.1988) (a third party claim may be asserted only when the third party's liability is dependent on the outcome of the main claim and is secondary or derivative thereto); Ocasek v. Hegglund, 673 F.Supp. 1084, 1087–88 (D.Wyo.1987) (dismissing third party complaint brought by defendant in copyright infringement suit against a licensing agency for torts because third party's liability was not derivative).

8. FRCP 14(a).

9. Ocasek, 673 F.Supp. at 1088 ("A common nucleus of facts is not a proper foundation of a third party complaint."); Saine v. A.I.A., Inc., 582 F.Supp. 1299, 1309–10 (D.Colo.1984) (dismissing third party complaint against company that hired insurance agent in suit by agent to recover commission from former employer).

10. Galt G/S v. Hapag–Lloyd A.G., 60 F.3d 1370, 1373–74 n. 2 (9th Cir.1995)

("Rule 14(a), unlike Rule 14(c), does not allow a third party plaintiff to tender the third party defendant with the defense of a claim by the principal plaintiff."); Feinaugle v. Pittsburgh and Lake Erie R.R. Co., 595 F.Supp. 316, 317 (W.D.Pa.1983) (dismissing third party complaint against Union in FELA action where complaint merely alleged that union was partly or fully responsible for harassing plaintiff employee). In the original version of FRCP 14, a third party plaintiff could implead any party who might be liable to the plaintiff. This provision in the Rule was repealed by the 1946 amendment.

11. Crude Crew v. McGinnis & Associates, Inc., 572 F.Supp. 103, 109 (E.D.Wis. 1983) ("[I]t is not necessary that the claim alleged in the third party complaint be based on the same theory or on the same contract."); Givoh Associates v. American Druggists Insurance Co., 562 F.Supp. 1346, 1350 (E.D.N.Y.1983) (allowing impleader of defendant sureties on breach of loan agree-

in a products liability suit may implead a party for negligence in a suit where the third-party plaintiff is being sued on a theory of strict liability.[12] The third-party plaintiff may also seek a different type of relief than the relief sought in the underlying action. Thus, a defendant sued for a declaratory judgment may implead a third party for monetary damages.[13] This situation often arises in the insurance context where an insurer seeks a declaration of noncoverage against the insured. Most courts have allowed the insured in these cases to implead an insurance agent or other party for money damages where the third-party defendant will be liable for the insured's loss if the insurer prevails.[14]

In order to assert a third-party claim, the third-party plaintiff must actually have a right to relief under the substantive law.[15] In most cases, the right of contribution, indemnity or other derivative liability is governed by state law,[16] although federal statutory or common law will govern in some instances.[17] If the court determines that the claim asserted by the third-party plaintiff is not meritorious, it will be dismissed.[18]

Whether the original plaintiff also has a claim against the third-party defendant is irrelevant to the propriety of the third-party claim.[19]

---

ment where main action was for breach of performance bond).

12. Pitcavage v. Mastercraft Boat Co., 632 F.Supp. 842, 846–47 (M.D.Pa.1985).

13. Eastern Enterprises v. Shalala, 942 F.Supp. 684, 689 (D.Mass.1996) (allowing third party action for damages in underlying declaratory judgment action because Rule 14 does not expressly require that the main claim be for damages), aff'd sub nom. Eastern Enterprises v. Chater, 110 F.3d 150 (1st Cir.1997).

14. E.g., Monarch Life Ins. Co. v. Donahue, 702 F.Supp. 1195, 1197 (E.D.Pa.1989) (impleader of investment broker by insured allowed); United of Omaha Life Ins. Co. v. Reed, 649 F.Supp. 837, 841–42 (D.Kan. 1986) (insured could implead insurance agent for misrepresentation because agent would be liable for losses incurred by insured if not covered by policy). But see United States Fire Insurance Co. v. Reading Municipal Airport Authority, 130 F.R.D. 38, 39 (E.D.Pa.1990) (dismissing third party claim by insured against insurance agent because insurer would not be liable to the plaintiff if plaintiff prevailed on declaratory judgment action).

15. Southern Mortgage Co. v. O'Dom, 699 F.Supp. 1223, 1226 (S.D.Miss.1987) (dismissing third party complaint for fraud in action to collect on promissory note because the third party complaint failed to state a claim for fraud).

16. Montgomery County, Md. v. Jaffe, Raitt, Heuer & Weiss, 897 F. Supp. 233, 238 (D.Md.1995) (applying the law of Maryland to third party claim for contribution based on diversity jurisdiction).

17. Kim v. Fujikawa, 871 F.2d 1427, 1434 (9th Cir.1989) (dismissing third party claim in ERISA action because ERISA does not recognize a right of contribution or indemnity); In re Dep't of Energy Stripper Well Exemption Litigation, 752 F.Supp. 1534, 1536 (D.Kan.1990) (dismissing third party complaint for restitution of tax rebate in action involving federal petroleum price controls because federal common law does not provide a right to reimbursement where a party has failed to obtain a tax refund).

18. FRCP 14, Advisory Committee Note on 1963 amendment ("[T]he court has discretion to strike a third party claim if it is obviously unmeritorious and can only delay or prejudice the disposition of plaintiff's claim.").

19. Smithkline Beckman Corp. v. Pennex Products Co., Inc., 103 F.R.D. 539, 540–41 (E.D.Pa.1984) (allowing defendant in trade infringement action to implead retailers of product as joint tortfeasors despite plaintiff's contention that plaintiffs did not want to sue retailers because they were plaintiff's customers); see also Andrulonis v. United States, 26 F.3d 1224, 1228 (2d Cir. 1994) (third party plaintiff could implead

In fact, in many cases the plaintiff may have no right to sue the third-party defendant. For example, the statute of limitations may have run on plaintiff's claim against the third-party defendant, but not on the third-party plaintiff's claim.[20] This commonly happens because the statute of limitations typically does not start running on a claim for secondary liability until there is a judgment against the party seeking reimbursement.[21]

Although the third-party plaintiff must have a substantive right to sue, the claim need not be mature, since one of the principal purposes of third-party practice is to accelerate the adjudication of third-party claims.[22] FRCP 14 explicitly allows for the acceleration of claims by authorizing third-party claims against persons who "may be" liable to the third-party plaintiff. Of course, in many cases, it may not be obvious at the outset whether the third-party defendant may be liable. It is sufficient if the third-party plaintiff is able to show that it could recover on some version of the facts.[23]

The law of contribution for joint tortfeasors illustrates the difference between a permissible acceleration of a claim and a third-party claim which has no basis in substantive law.[24] The ability of a tortfeasor to implead a joint tortfeasor depends upon how the right of contribution accrues. Impleader is permissible where state law provides that the right of contribution from a joint tortfeasor accrues when there is a judgment against the party seeking contribution or where a party pays more than a fair share of its liability.[25] In these states, it is a permissible acceleration of the claim for the party seeking contribution to implead the joint tortfeasor as a third-party defendant. The effect of impleader is to accelerate the adjudication of the claim for contribution, but not to accelerate payment by the third-party defendant. Impleader will not affect the substantive rights of the third-party defendant who will not

---

plaintiff's employer even though New York's Workers' Compensation Act prohibited the plaintiff from suing his employer).

20. Wandrey v. McCarthy, 804 F.Supp. 1384, 1386–87 (D.Kan.1992) (allowing third party complaint against principals by agent where plaintiffs' complaint against principals had been dismissed due to statute of limitations).

21. *Id.* (an action for indemnity does not accrue until the party seeking payment becomes obligated to pay the original plaintiff).

22. National Union Fire Ins. Co. of Pittsburgh, Pa. v. F.D.I.C., 887 F.Supp. 262, 264 (D.Kan.1995) (allowing plaintiff insurer to assert third party claim based on subrogation against third party defendants even though Kansas law provided that an insurer has no right of subrogation until claim has been paid); Fidelity and Deposit Co. of Maryland v. C and A Currency Exchange, Inc.,

738 F.Supp. 302, 305 (N.D.Ill.1990) (allowing third party complaint by defendant bank against guarantors in action for wrongful collection on certain checks although the bank's liability had not yet been established).

23. Pitcavage v. Mastercraft Boat Co., 632 F.Supp. 842, 845 (M.D.Pa.1985) (In order to assert a third party complaint, the third party plaintiff "must demonstrate some substantive basis for its claim."); Diar v. Genesco, Inc., 102 F.R.D. 288, 290 (N.D.Ohio 1984) (third party plaintiff must make showing that third party defendant may be liable, but need not show that recovery is a certainty).

24. For an excellent summary of the law in this area see Connors v. Suburban Propane Co., 916 F.Supp. 73, 80–81 (D.N.H. 1996).

25. Andrulonis v. United States, 26 F.3d 1224, 1233 (2d Cir.1994).

become liable until there is a judgment against the original defendant. In these cases, the court typically will stay execution of the judgment against the third-party joint tortfeasor[26] or issue a conditional judgment. In addition, in states where the right of contribution accrues only after a tortfeasor *satisfies* a judgment, the court will calculate prejudgment interest against the third-party defendant only from the time that the third-party plaintiff satisfies the judgment, rather than from the date that the judgment is entered.[27]

A different result is reached where the substantive law provides that a right of contribution accrues only if there is a joint judgment against the tortfeasors. In this situation, impleader of a third-party defendant as a joint tortfeasor is impermissible.[28] Under the substantive law, the third-party plaintiff has no cause of action unless the original plaintiff sues all joint tortfeasors in one action. Courts have read these statutes as a grant to the plaintiff of the substantive right of choosing which tortfeasors to hold liable, and have held that impleader is impermissible in this situation.[29]

One court recently considered this question reaching the same result with regard to the New Hampshire statute on contribution.[30] The New Hampshire statute provides that a party may sue a joint tortfeasor in an independent action once the party has satisfied a judgment or a settlement on a claim. The statute also provides that a party may implead a joint tortfeasor if the plaintiff in the principal action agrees.[31] Interpreting the statute as granting the plaintiff the substantive right to control which parties participate in the litigation, the court held that impleader under FRCP 14 was not permissible.[32]

(1) Products Liability: Claims Against Joint Tortfeasors and Warrantors

Products liability cases are a fertile source for discussion of third-party claims. Defendants have attempted with varying success to implead for contribution such parties as the employer and/or co-employee of the plaintiff (where the injury occurs within the scope of employment) to third-party automobile drivers in highway accidents.[33] Under the right

---

26. *Id.* at 1234 (court can enter judgment against third party defendant but stay execution until the third party plaintiff demonstrates that contingency has been satisfied); Burris v. American Chicle Co., 120 F.2d 218, 223 (2d Cir.1941) (indemnity judgment entered but execution stayed until defendant satisfied judgment; Klinger v. Dudley, 41 N.Y.2d 362, 393 N.Y.S.2d 323, 326, 327, 329, 361 N.E.2d 974, 977, 978, 980 (1977) (entering conditional judgment for third party plaintiff).

27. Andrulonis, 26 F.3d at 1233–35 (allowing post-judgment interest on third party action for contribution only from the date that the third party plaintiff satisfied the judgment).

28. *E.g.*, Travelers Ins. Co. v. Busy Elec. Co., 294 F.2d 139, 145–46 (5th Cir.1961).

29. *Id.*; D'Onofrio Constr. Co. v. Recon. Co., 255 F.2d 904, 906 (1st Cir.1958) (allowing impleader in this case would "enhance the substantive rights of the original defendant over what is given by state law").

30. Connors v. Suburban Propane Co., 916 F.Supp. 73 (D.N.H.1996).

31. *Id.* at 81.

32. *Id.*

33. Bike v. American Motors Corp., 101 F.R.D. 77, 78 (E.D.Pa.1984) (in action by plaintiff injured in jeep accident, court denied jeep manufacturer's motion to file

of contribution, a tortfeasor who has been found liable may recover a proportional share from other persons jointly or severally liable for the same injury to a person or property. Most states allow some right of contribution from joint tortfeasors, although some states still follow the common law rule that there is no right of contribution among joint tortfeasors. In order to join a joint tortfeasor as a third-party defendant, a potential third-party plaintiff will have to establish both that the state law does provide a right of contribution and that the third-party defendant is a joint tortfeasor.[34]

Independent tortfeasors cannot be joined as third-party defendants because their liability runs to the original plaintiff rather than to the third-party plaintiff.[35] For example, in an action against a physician for aggravation of injuries, the physician could not implead the individuals who caused the accident because they were not joint tortfeasors.[36] A potential third-party plaintiff need not establish conclusively that the third-party defendant is a joint tortfeasor. It is enough if the facts indicate that the third-party defendant may be a joint tortfeasor.[37]

Where there is no right of contribution from a joint tortfeasor, a claim for breach of warranty may offer a valid derivative claim against a third-party defendant. In this scenario, the liability of the defendant to the plaintiff must be as a result of breach of warranty by potential third-party defendants.[38] In addition, however, there must be a causal relationship between third-party defendant's breach and the injury or loss to the plaintiff. A third-party plaintiff's claim that "you owe me because your breach of our contract caused me to breach my contract with plaintiff" will not be allowed because such claim is not dependent on the initial claim against defendant.[39] Thus, the liability to justify impleader must

---

third party complaint against estate of deceased driver because manufacturer sought to impose sole responsibility for the accident on the driver and did not assert derivative liability as required by Rule 14); Bullock v. Black & Decker, Inc., 502 F.Supp. 580, 583 (E.D.Mich.1980) (in complaint by injured worker against manufacturer of radial arm saw, court dismissed third party complaint against worker's employer because manufacturer had duty to guard against foreseeable misuse by employer).

34. Weil v. Dreher Pickle Co., 76 F.R.D. 63, 65 (W.D.Okla.1977) (denying motion for leave to file third party complaint by defendant food packager against restaurant which served allegedly defective sweet cherry peppers on ground that under Oklahoma law there is no right of contribution or indemnity between joint tortfeasors).

35. Mills v. Ford Motor Co., 142 F.R.D. 271, 272–73 (M.D.Pa.1990) (dismissing third party complaint against driver of automobile in products liability suit against

auto manufacturer because plaintiff was suing only for additional injuries and death on a theory that the vehicle was not crashworthy so third party was not joint tortfeasor).

36. Voyles v. Corwin, 295 Pa.Super. 126, 441 A.2d 381, 383 (1982).

37. Paur v. Crookston Marine, Inc., 83 F.R.D. 466, 470 (D.N.D.1979) (allowing defendant retailer's third party complaint against boat manufacturer as giving fair notice of claim resulting from boat going out of control and spilling occupants into lake).

38. Mitchell v. Duquesne Brewing Co. of Pittsburgh, 34 F.R.D. 145, 146 (W.D.Pa. 1963) (permitting claim of defendant bottler against third party defendant glass companies alleging that any liability for the results of an accident to plaintiff was due to a breach of certain implied warranties by third party defendants).

39. Leasetec Corp. v. Inhabitants of County of Cumberland, 896 F.Supp. 35, 41 (D.Me.1995).

arise out of the *plaintiff's* claim against the defendant and not out of an asserted defense or counterclaim of the defendant.[40]

(2) Claim by and Against Insurers

Impleader is used in insurance disputes in a variety of ways.[41] For example, an insured may join an insurer as a third-party defendant where the insurer has disclaimed liability on the policy[42] or where multiple insurers cover a single risk.[43] An insured or an insurer may likewise implead an insurance agent for misrepresentation or for failure to correctly process a claim or insurance application.[44] An insurer also may utilize the impleader process to exercise its subrogation rights against parties who are responsible for damage to the insured. For example, an insurer sued for coverage on a ship involved in an accident could implead the owners of other ships responsible for the accident.

If the insurer disclaims liability and refuses to defend a suit against the insured, the insured party may implead its insurer. The insurance policy usually does not present an obstacle to impleader in these cases. A provision commonly found in insurance policies providing that the insured will not sue the insurer unless the insured has already paid a judgment does not prevent impleader since impleader merely accelerates the adjudication of this claim.[45] Moreover, courts have concluded that it would undermine the purpose of FRCP 14 to allow insurers to use these "no action" clauses to avoid joinder where the insurer has refused to defend the claim.[46]

Although an insurance policy typically will not bar impleader of an insurer by an insured, the court in its discretion may deny impleader if it is concerned that the third-party defendant will be prejudiced or that the case will be unduly complicated.[47] Frequently, a third-party defendant will oppose impleader by arguing that the jury will be more likely to render a verdict in favor of the plaintiff if informed of the existence of insurance.[48] Alternatively, a plaintiff may argue that the jury's award of

40. Greene Line Mfg. Corp. v. Fibreboard Corp., 130 F.R.D. 397, 400 (N.D.Ind. 1990) (in an action by a manufacturer against a buyer to make full payment for industrial equipment, denying motion by defendant buyer to implead seller based on buyer's counterclaim against manufacturer for alleged breach of warranty, negligence, and indemnity).

41. *See* Chapter 58 "Insurance," *infra*.

42. United States v. A & N Cleaners & Launderers, Inc., 747 F.Supp. 1014, 1017, 1020 (S.D.N.Y.1990) (allowing impleader of insurers by defendant sued for environmental clean-up under CERCLA).

43. Certain Interested Underwriters at Lloyds v. Gulf Nat'l Ins. Co., 898 F.Supp. 381, 384 (N.D.Miss.1995).

44. Monarch Life Ins. Co. v. Donahue, 702 F.Supp. 1195, 1198 (E.D.Pa.1989).

45. Colton v. Swain, 527 F.2d 296, 299 (7th Cir.1975) (refusal to defend estops the insurer's right to enforce a "nonjoinder" provision); LaSalle Nat'l Trust v. Schaffner, 818 F.Supp. 1161, 1166 (N.D.Ill.1993) (a "no joinder" clause in an insurance contract does not prohibit a third party action because it is contrary to the purposes of Rule 14).

46. LaSalle Nat'l Trust, 818 F.Supp. at 1166.

47. Green v. Shepherd Constr. Co., 46 F.R.D. 434, 437–38 (N.D.Ga.1969).

48. Rosalis v. Universal Distrib., Inc., 21 F.R.D. 169, 172 (D.Conn.1957).

damages may be adversely affected (limited) by the jury's knowledge of insurance coverage. Most courts allow impleader of an insurer, however, particularly where the existence of insurance is common knowledge and there is little risk of prejudice.[49]

Impleader may also be utilized to join an insurance agent to the suit.[50] Both insurers and insured parties have impled insurance agents on theories of negligence, fraud, and breach of contract. In a typical scenario, an insurer brings a declaratory action against an insured party alleging that the insured made misrepresentations on the insurance application and is, therefore, not entitled to coverage. The insured party then brings a third-party claim against an insurance agent for failing to correctly complete the application or for making misrepresentations to the insured.[51] As is discussed in Section 7.1(a), *supra*, the fact that the claim against the agent is for money damages while the underlying action is only for declaratory relief does not ordinarily bar impleader.[52] The predominate,[53] although not universal view,[54] is that the claim against the agent is derivative of the underlying claim even though the defendant will not be "liable" to the plaintiff on the declaratory action.

Although the requirement of derivative liability will not in most instances bar the impleader of a negligent insurance agent, it may bar a third-party suit by an insurer against a law firm for its professional negligence in defending an insured. In *City of Orange Beach v. Scottsdale Insurance Co.*,[55] Orange Beach sued its insurer for breach of the duty to settle in good faith. In a previous suit brought by private developers against the city in which the insurer defended the city, the insurer refused the city's demands that it settle the claim for the amount covered under the policy. When the jury returned a verdict in an amount greater than the policy limit, the city commenced a new action against its insurer. The insurer sought to implead the law firm it had hired to defend the city in the previous suit on a malpractice claim, alleging that the firm had breached its duty to keep the insurer informed about the progress of the litigation and had represented the city despite a conflict of interest.[56] The court denied the insurer the right to implead, holding that the insurer's claim against the law firm was not derivative of its liability to the plaintiff because the insurance company had an independent duty to settle in good faith.[57] The court reasoned that the law firm's

---

49. *Id.*

50. An insurance agent who is sued directly by an insured may likewise utilize the impleader process to implead the insurer. *E.g.,* United States Surgical Corp. v. John K. Pulsifer & Co., 119 F.R.D. 18 (D.Md.1988).

51. Monarch Life Ins. Co. v. Donahue, 702 F.Supp. 1195, 1198 (E.D.Pa.1989).

52. United of Omaha Life Ins. Co. v. Reed, 649 F.Supp. 837, 841 (D.Kan.1986).

53. *Id.* at 841–42.

54. United States Fire Ins. Co. v. Reading Municipal Airport Authority, 130 F.R.D. 38, 39 (E.D.Pa.1990) (in action by insurer for declaration of noncoverage, third party claim by insured against agent for negligence and breach of contract dismissed because third party claim sought damages and was not derivative).

55. 166 F.R.D. 506 (S.D.Ala.1996), *aff'd*, 113 F.3d 1251 (11th Cir.1997).

56. *Id.* at 511.

57. *Id.* at 511–12.

liability was not derivative because the law firm could be held liable even if the insurer were not, and vice versa.[58]

Another party commonly impled in insurance disputes by insurers is an excess insurer or a reinsurer.[59] A reinsurer or excess insurer has a corresponding right to implead the original insurer.[60] Despite the benefits of resolving claims against multiple insurers in one suit, the complexity of the relationships between primary, excess, and reinsurers may preclude impleader. For example, if the introduction of an excess or reinsurer would add too many new issues or if the relationships between the insurers would be confusing to the jury, a court may exercise its discretion to deny impleader.[61]

The party seeking to implead an excess or reinsurer must also establish that it has a substantive claim against the excess or reinsurer.[62] If the duty owed by the insurer sought to be impled runs to another insurer rather than to the defendant, impleader will be denied.[63] For example, a co-reinsurer cannot implead another reinsurer since the reinsurers owe a duty to the primary insurer and not to one another.

An insurer's subrogation rights provide another basis for impleading third parties. An insurer who pays a claim steps into the shoes of the insured and may assert any claims which the insured could have asserted. Frequently, an insurer sued for coverage by an insured will implead the individuals responsible for the insured's loss.[64] Even though the insurer's right to assert subrogation rights does not accrue until it satisfies a claim against the insured, the insurer may assert the subrogation claim because FRCP 14 allows acceleration of the claim.[65] Although impleader of the individuals responsible for the insured's loss is generally permissible,[66] a court may dismiss a third-party complaint against the individuals at fault if impleader will complicate the case.[67]

The acceleration of subrogation claims allowed by impleader may provide an advantage to the insurer in terms of the statute of limitations. As subrogee, an insurer's rights against third parties extend only as far as those of the insured. Thus, if the statute of limitations has run on the insured's claim against a tortfeasor, the insurer may not bring a third-party claim (as subrogee) against that tortfeasor. As a result, the insurer's ability to enforce its subrogation rights depends on the timeli-

---

58. *Id.* at 511.

59. Certain Interested Underwriters at Lloyds v. Gulf Nat'l Ins. Co., 898 F.Supp. 381, 384 (N.D.Miss.1995) (in action by reinsurer of insured's excess insurer seeking declaration of nonliability against insured, reinsurer could implead excess insurer).

60. Karon Business Forms, Inc. v. Skandia Ins. Co., 80 F.R.D. 501, 505 (D.P.R. 1978).

61. *Id.* at 504–05.

62. *Id.*

63. *Id.*

64. Fuel Transp. Co., Inc. v. Fireman's Fund Ins. Co., 108 F.R.D. 156, 158 (E.D.Pa. 1985) (impleader of owner of tractor and owner's insurer involved in auto accident).

65. Nat'l Union Fire Ins. Co. v. F.D.I.C., 887 F.Supp. 262, 264 (D.Kan.1995) (impleader of parties who conspired with insured's director).

66. Banks Tower Communications, Ltd. v. The Home Ins. Co., 590 F.Supp. 1038, 1041 (E.D.Pa.1984).

67. Fuel Transp. Co., 108 F.R.D. at 158.

ness of the insured's suit against the insurer. If the insured sues its insurer (but not the third-party tortfeasor) the statute of limitations may expire with respect to the insured's claims against the third party. As a result, the insurer will not be able to assert a third-party claim.

Impleader allows an insurer to file a third-party claim within the statute of limitations because the insurer may bring the claim before it has paid the insured. This aspect of impleader is illustrated by *National Union Fire Insurance Co. of Pittsburgh v. FDIC*.[68]

The claims in *National Union* involved a bond issued by National Union to several banks, which insured the banks against losses caused by the fraudulent or dishonest acts of bank employees. When one of the banks submitted a claim on the bond, National Union sued the bank seeking rescission of the bond on the ground that the bank made material misrepresentations. The bank counterclaimed against National Union seeking a declaration that its losses were covered. The bank, however, did not sue the individuals responsible for the fraud. National Union sought to exercise its subrogation rights by impleading the individuals responsible for the fraud.

At the time National Union asserted its third-party claims, the statute of limitations for claims by the bank against the responsible individuals had not run.[69] Shortly after its motion for leave to implead was filed, however, the statute of limitations expired on the bank's claims against the third-party defendants.[70] The third-party defendants moved to dismiss the insurer's claim arguing that since the insurer's subrogation claim would not accrue until there was a judgment against the insurer, the insurer could not bring a claim within the statute of limitations.[71] Although the court acknowledged that the statute of limitations would bar the insurer's claim in an independent action, the court found that the third-party complaint was a permissible acceleration of the claim and was within the statute of limitations.[72]

(3) Labor, Employment and ERISA

While employers and unions may seem easy prey for impleader, practitioners should be mindful of the need for derivative liability of the third-party defendant. Third-party practice cannot be used to bring into a controversy other matters which only happen to have some relation to the original matter.[73] This raises substantive legal issues under the

68. 887 F.Supp. 262 (D.Kan.1995).

69. *Id.* at 264.

70. *Id.*

71. *Id.*

72. *Id.* at 264–65.

73. Saine v. A.I.A., Inc., 582 F.Supp. 1299, 1310 (D.Colo.1984) (in action by former salesman to recover commissions allegedly due, defendant insurance company could not implead rival insurance company who hired salesman away because the underlying claim was for breach of contract, regardless of the counterclaim for fraud and interference with contractual relations); Feinaugle v. Pittsburgh and Lake Erie R.R. Co., 595 F.Supp. 316, 318 (W.D.Pa.1983) (in action by worker against employer for harassment in conjunction with testifying at co-worker's lawsuit, defendant employer could not implead union who told employee not to testify, against the wishes of the employer).

Employment Retirement Income Security Act ("ERISA"), an act governing the funding, vesting, administration, and termination of private pension plans. For purposes of finding a right of impleader in claims involving these topics, one must decide if there is a right to contribution under ERISA. Some courts have held there is such a right,[74] while others have held the contrary.[75] One court has opined that keeping close watch on third-party ERISA claims is consistent with the purpose of a streamlined and simplified procedure for employee benefit funds to correct delinquent contributions.[76] A more detailed discussion of ERISA can be found in Chapter 68 "ERISA," *infra*, and practitioners considering third-party ERISA claims must determine the availability of a substantive theory for holding a party liable as a third-party defendant. However, even if there is no substantive right of impleader under ERISA, a defendant may have substantive state law claims that permit impleader of potentially liable parties.[77]

(4) Professional Liability

Professional liability may form the basis of a third-party complaint.[78] Impleader as a third-party defendant has been sought against lawyers and accountants on a variety of theories, including contribution as a joint tortfeasor,[79] breach of contract,[80] misrepresentation,[81] malpractice,[82] and various statutory claims.[83] Similarly, professionals being sued for malpractice may seek to join a third-party defendant.[84]

74. Chemung Canal Trust Co. v. Sovran Bank/Maryland, 939 F.2d 12, 16 (2d Cir. 1991) ("[T]he traditional trust law right to contribution must also be recognized as a part of ERISA."), *cert. denied*, 505 U.S. 1212, 112 S.Ct. 3014, 120 L.Ed.2d 887 (1992); Duncan v. Santaniello, 900 F.Supp. 547, 551 (D.Mass.1995) (upholding third party plaintiff's standing to bring ERISA claim under implied right of contribution). *See* Chapter 68 "ERISA," *infra*.

75. Daniels v. Nat'l Employee Benefit Serv., Inc., 877 F.Supp. 1067, 1074 (N.D.Ohio 1995) ("ERISA does not provide a right of contribution among fiduciaries.").

76. Southwest Administrators, Inc. v. Rozay's Transfer, 791 F.2d 769, 777 (9th Cir.1986) (holding that district court reasonably concluded that impleading the union would be inconsistent with the purposes of ERISA), *cert. denied*, 479 U.S. 1065, 107 S.Ct. 951, 93 L.Ed.2d 999 (1987).

77. McLaughlin v. Biasucci, 688 F.Supp. 965, 967–68 (S.D.N.Y.1988) (in action by Secretary of Labor for alleged violations of fiduciary duties under ERISA, third party complaint against attorney advisor failed to state a claim under ERISA but did contain possible state law claims for malpractice and negligence).

78. *See* Chapter 55 "Professional Liability," *infra*.

79. Jordan v. Madison Leasing Co., 596 F.Supp. 707, 711 (S.D.N.Y.1984).

80. Taylor v. G I Export Corp., 78 F.R.D. 494, 496 (E.D.N.Y.1978) (denying motion to dismiss third party claim by client against its accounting firm based on breach of contract for auditing engagement).

81. Standard Wire & Cable Co. v. AmeriTrust Corp., 697 F.Supp. 368, 375–76 (C.D.Cal.1988) (allowing impleader of plaintiff's accountants by the defendant for alleged fraudulent misrepresentations made in the course of negotiations for plaintiff's secured line of credit from defendant).

82. Hartford Accident and Indem. Co. v. Parente, Randolph, Orlando, Carey and Associates, 642 F.Supp. 38, 39 (M.D.Pa.1985) (dismissing third party complaint against auditors for failure to discover misappropriation by bank employees because the defendant was not in privity with the auditors and did not allege secondary or derivative liability).

83. Resolution Trust Corp. v. Farmer, 836 F.Supp. 1123, 1132–33 (E.D.Pa.1993) (third party plaintiff sought to implead law-

For example, a company sued for misrepresentations made in connection with the sale of tax shelters impleaded the accountants who audited its financial statements. The third-party claim was allowed on the theory that the accountants might be joint tortfeasors and, thus, possibly liable to the company (the third-party plaintiff).[85] On the other hand, where accountants were sued by shareholders of a company audited by the accountants, the accountants were allowed to assert third-party claims for contribution against the officers and directors of the company.[86] The availability of contribution, however, which provides the basis for such third-party claims, is a matter of substantive law.

One of the more common reasons for dismissal of a third-party complaint against a professional is that the professional's liability is not derivative of the defendant's liability to the plaintiff.[87] This might occur where the original defendant's liability to plaintiff is based on its independent conduct, *regardless* of services provided by the professional.[88]

Impleader of a professional on a negligence theory (as opposed to a contribution theory) may be dismissed if state law requires that the third-party plaintiff be in privity with the professional. For example, a director or officer sued for securities law violations may seek to implead the corporation's counsel for malpractice. If state law requires privity as an element of a professional malpractice claim, the third-party claim will be dismissed because counsel is engaged by the corporation, not the directors and officers.[89] On the other hand, a third-party plaintiff will have a greater ability to implead a professional if state law provides that professionals may be liable to a broader class of persons (not in privity) such as those who foreseeably rely on their representations.[90] For instance, where this broader view of professional liability exists, officers or directors may commence a third-party claim against the corporation's auditors even though the auditor was in privity only with the corporation.[91]

Third-party complaints against professionals are frequently challenged on the basis that the professional is liable directly to the plaintiff rather than to the third-party plaintiff. A third-party plaintiff seeking to

yers on RICO claim); Stratton Group, Ltd. v. Sprayregen, 466 F.Supp. 1180, 1188 (S.D.N.Y.1979) (impleader based on securities laws violations).

84. St. Thomas v. Harrisburg Hosp., 108 F.R.D. 2, 3 (M.D.Pa.1985).

85. Jordan v. Madison Leasing Co., 596 F.Supp. 707, 711 (S.D.N.Y.1984).

86. *In re* Leslie Fay Companies, Inc. Securities Litigation, 918 F.Supp. 749, 755 (S.D.N.Y.1996).

87. City of Orange Beach v. Scottsdale Ins. Co., 166 F.R.D. 506, 511–12 (S.D.Ala. 1996).

88. *Id.*

89. Stratton Group, Ltd. v. Sprayregen, 466 F.Supp. 1180, 1184–85 (S.D.N.Y.1979) (directors and officers had no claim for negligence against corporate lawyers who owed duty only to corporation).

90. Federal Deposit Insurance Corp. v. Loube, 134 F.R.D. 270, 273 (N.D.Cal.1991) (allowing third party claim against auditors by bank officer alleging indemnity theory).

91. *Id.* at 272.

join a professional on a theory of contribution must be careful to allege sufficient facts to establish that the professional was a joint tortfeasor with the third-party plaintiff.[92] It is not sufficient to allege merely that the professional's negligence caused injury to the plaintiff.[93] For example, a director or officer sued for violations of Section 10(b) of the Securities Act cannot implead the corporation's law firm merely because the law firm prepared documents for the sale of the securities.[94] Rather, the third-party complaint must allege that the law firm's conduct jointly caused the plaintiff's injury.

In some cases, a third-party claim against a professional may be barred as a matter of law. For example, in *St. Thomas v. Harrisburg Hospital*,[95] physicians who were sued for malpractice in the treatment of a patient following a car accident sought to implead the driver of the vehicle who caused the accident. The physicians argued that impleader was necessary because the cause of the patient's injury was not identifiable.[96] The court dismissed the third-party complaint, holding that the negligence of the doctors and the driver were independent in time and nature and therefore the parties were not jointly liable for the patient's injuries.[97] However, the court emphasized that the physicians could assert the negligence of the driver as an affirmative defense in the action against them.[98] Similarly, in *City of Orange Beach v. Scottsdale Insurance Company*,[99] an insurance company which was sued for bad faith failure to settle was not allowed to implead its attorneys because the attorneys could not be joint tortfeasors with the insurer. The insurance company owed an independent duty to its insured to settle in good faith.[100] Any claim by the insurer against the attorneys would have to be asserted as an independent professional malpractice action.

(5) Securities

In securities cases, typical defendants are the issuing company, officers and directors of the issuer, underwriters, and professionals involved in the securities offering or required filings with regulators. When one or more of these potential defendants is left out of plaintiffs' initial action, the sued defendant may consider impleader. Third-party claims for indemnity are not available under federal securities laws.[101] However, claims for contribution are permissible third-party claims.[102]

---

92. Stratton Group, Ltd., 466 F.Supp. at 1185 (dismissing third party complaint against law firm for contribution because the complaint did not allege that the law firm was a joint participant in the alleged fraud).

93. Hartford Accident and Indem. Co. v. Parente, Randolph, Orlando, Carey and Associates, 642 F.Supp. 38, 41 (M.D.Pa.1985).

94. *Id.*

95. 108 F.R.D. 2 (M.D.Pa.1985).

96. *Id.* at 3.

97. *Id.* at 4.

98. *Id.*

99. 166 F.R.D. 506 (S.D.Ala.1996).

100. *Id.* at 510–12. For a more extensive discussion of this case, *see supra* § 7.2(a)(2).

101. Stewart v. American Int'l Oil & Gas Co., 845 F.2d 196, 199–200 (9th Cir. 1988) (disallowing third party complaint because indemnity is unavailable under Section 10–b of the Securities Exchange Act of 1934 and SEC Commission Rule 10b–5). *See* Chapter 54 "Securities," *infra.*

102. Musick, Peeler & Garrett v. Employers Ins. of Wausau, 508 U.S. 286, 292–98, 113 S.Ct. 2085, 2088–92, 124 L.Ed.2d

Thus, practitioners looking to spread potential liability for violations of securities laws will examine claims for contribution against other defendants, such as underwriters of public offerings.[103] Given the often high exposure of securities cases, courts may look at whether the potential third-party defendant has sufficient financial resources to contribute to a judgment against the original defendant, and may dismiss third parties who lack significant resources.[104]

(6) Claims by or Against the United States

The general rules of third-party practice apply to the United States government. The federal government may sue[105] or be sued[106] as a third party the same as any private party. The primary limitation upon suits against the United States as a third-party defendant is sovereign immunity. Like any claim against the United States, a third-party claim against the federal government must fall under one of the exceptions to sovereign immunity provided in the Federal Tort Claims Act ("FTCA"),[107] the Tucker Act,[108] or for Suits in Admiralty.[109] These statutes may place additional constraints on a third-party complaint against the United States. For example, third-party claims under the

194 (1993) (holding that defendants in action under Rule 10b–5 of Securities and Exchange Act had a right to seek contribution as a matter of federal law); Kilmartin v. H.C. Wainwright & Co., 637 F.Supp. 938, 940–41 (D.Mass.1986) (holding that contribution is available under federal securities law for joint tortfeasors, but dismissing third party complaint for failure to allege facts with particularity).

103. Robin v. Doctors Officenters Corp., 686 F.Supp. 199, 202 (N.D.Ill.1988) (granting defendant's motion for leave to serve third party complaint against managing underwriter for public offering as not causing prejudice to plaintiffs nor disadvantage to the proceedings).

104. Bernstein v. Crazy Eddie, Inc., 702 F.Supp. 962, 986–88 (E.D.N.Y.1988) (in a claim involving sales of securities through false registration statements and prospectuses, disallowing third party claim against former employees for civil conspiracy because the fact that employees would lack sufficient financial resources to diffuse defendant's potential liability to plaintiffs indicated lack of good faith in bringing third party claim), *vacated in part on other grounds*, 714 F.Supp. 1285 (E.D.N.Y.1989).

105. Collins v. General Motors Corp., 101 F.R.D. 4, 7 (W.D.Pa.1983) (government sued for accident of government employee could implead manufacturer of automobile).

106. Hassan v. Louisiana Dep't of Transp. & Dev., 923 F.Supp. 890, 893 (W.D.La.1996) (allowing government contractor defending a trespass claim to bring a third party claim against the U.S. Army Corp. of Engineers for negligence).

107. Complaint of Valley Towing Serv., 609 F.Supp. 298, 302 (D.C.Mo.1985) (dismissing third party complaint against the United States because government's action fell within discretionary function exception to the waiver of sovereign immunity); DuPont Glore Forgan, Inc. v. American Telephone & Telegraph, 428 F.Supp. 1297, 1308 (S.D.N.Y.1977) (third party claim against United States dismissed because claim for collection of taxes does not fall under exception to sovereign immunity under the FTCA), *aff'd*, 578 F.2d 1367 (2d Cir.), *cert. denied*, 439 U.S. 970, 99 S.Ct. 465, 58 L.Ed.2d 431 (1978).

108. Colombo v. Johns–Manville Corp., 601 F.Supp. 1119, 1139–40 (E.D.Pa.1984) (third party claim could not be maintained against government for breach of warranty because Tucker Act only applies to express contracts or contracts involved in fact, not contracts imputed by operation of law).

109. Cassens v. St. Louis River Cruise Lines, 44 F.3d 508, 514–15 (7th Cir.1995) (affirming dismissal of third party complaint against the United States because conduct fell within discretionary function

Tucker Act will be limited in amount since the statute provides that the United States may be sued in federal district court only for claims less than $10,000.[110] The third-party plaintiff with a larger claim will have to waive the excess in damages[111] or bring a separate suit in the United States Claims Court.

The FTCA requirement that claimants exhaust administrative remedies will not ordinarily limit third-party claims. Under the FTCA, parties suing the United States must first bring a timely administrative claim.[112] The Act specifically exempts third-party claims against the United States from this exhaustion requirement.[113] However, the exemption does not apply to claims brought under FRCP 14(a) by a plaintiff directly against a third-party defendant already impled by the defendant.[114] Courts have held that the FTCA exemption for third-party claims does not apply to claims brought by the plaintiff because the claim is a direct claim not a third-party claim.[115] Under the rationale of these cases, a claim by a third-party defendant directly against the plaintiff would also be subject to the exhaustion requirement.

The FTCA's prohibition on jury trials will also apply to third-party claims. If the United States is impled as a third-party defendant under the FTCA, the third-party plaintiff will have no right to a jury trial on its third-party claim.[116] In contrast, the FTCA prohibition on jury trials does not apply when the United States brings a third-party action. When the government as a defendant in a FTCA suit impleads a third party, that party is still entitled to a jury trial since the FTCA bars a jury trial only for claims brought against the United States.[117] In these cases, the underlying action will be tried to the court, while the third-party claim may be tried to a jury.

In most cases, courts look to state law to determine whether there is a right of contribution, indemnity or other theory of secondary liability for a third-party claim against the United States.[118] In fact, some

exception to the waiver of sovereign immunity under the Suits in Admiralty Act).

110. 28 U.S.C.A. § 1346(a)(2) (West 1993).

111. Fox v. City of Chicago, 401 F.Supp. 515, 518 (N.D.Ill.1975) (third party plaintiff's persistence in asserting court's jurisdiction can be construed as a waiver of claims in excess of statutory limit).

112. 28 U.S.C.A. § 2675(a) (West 1993).

113. Hassan v. Louisiana Dep't. of Transp. & Dev., 923 F.Supp. 890, 893 (W.D.La.1996).

114. West v. United States, 592 F.2d 487, 491 (8th Cir.1979).

115. Id.; Rosario v. American Export–Isbrandtsen Lines, Inc., 531 F.2d 1227, 1233–34 (3d Cir.) (claim by plaintiff seaman against United States as third party defen-

dant dismissed because seaman did not bring timely administrative action), cert. denied, 429 U.S. 857, 97 S.Ct. 156, 50 L.Ed.2d 135 (1976).

116. 28 U.S.C.A. § 2402 (West 1994).

117. Barron v. United States, 654 F.2d 644, 650 (9th Cir.1981) (contractor impled by government on theory of indemnity had right to jury trial on all issues of fact); Collins v. General Motors Corp., 101 F.R.D. 4, 7–8 (W.D.Pa.1983) (auto manufacturer impled by government in FTCA action arising from car accident had right to jury trial).

118. Lopez v. Johns Manville, 649 F.Supp. 149, 153–56 (W.D.Wash.1986) (dismissing third party complaint against the United States under the FTCA because state law did not create a right of contribution or indemnity), aff'd, 858 F.2d 712 (Fed.

statutes, like the FTCA, require that state law be applied.[119] In some cases, however, federal common law will be applied. For example, when the third-party claim is based on a federal contract[120] or when federal interests, such as national defense, are implicated,[121] federal common law may govern the question of whether the government is secondarily liable to the third-party plaintiff. In many instances, whether the United States has a duty to contribute or indemnify the third-party plaintiff is a mixed question of both federal and state law.[122]

(7) Admiralty Claims

Admiralty claims arise in the impleader context in one of two ways and are governed by separate provisions of FRCP 14.[123] An admiralty claim may be asserted against a third-party defendant where the original claim is civil in nature. For example, a manufacturer sued for breach of contract based on the delivery of damaged goods may implead the shipper of the goods claiming that they were damaged in transit by the shipper's negligence. The procedure for impleading the third-party defendant in this case is governed by FRCP 14(a).

The second way in which an admiralty claim arises under FRCP 14 is when the *underlying* claim is based in admiralty law. For instance, a vessel owner sued for negligence in causing a collision with another ship may implead a third vessel involved in the accident. Alternatively, the ship owner defendant may implead the manufacturer of its ship claiming that the ship was defective. Thus, it does not matter whether the claim asserted by the third-party plaintiff is based in admiralty law or in civil law. When the underlying action is brought as an admiralty or maritime claim, FRCP 14(c) governs all third-party claims regardless of whether they fall under admiralty jurisdiction.[124]

Prior to 1966, civil claims and admiralty claims were governed by separate rules of procedure. Traditionally, the impleader procedure for admiralty claims was very liberal. Under Admiralty Rule 56, a third-party plaintiff could implead a person who might be liable to the third-

---

Cir.1988), *cert. denied sub nom.* Eagle–Picher Industries, Inc. v. United States, 491 U.S. 904, 109 S.Ct. 3185, 105 L.Ed.2d 694 (1989).

119. *Id.* at 153.

120. *E.g.*, Irvin v. United States, 148 F.Supp. 25, 30–32 (D.S.D.1957) (government had right of indemnification under insurance policy even though policy named government employee as insured and government has no right of indemnification from its employees).

121. United States v. Standard Oil of California, 332 U.S. 301, 305–11, 67 S.Ct. 1604, 1607–10, 91 L.Ed. 2067 (1947) (federal government's right to indemnification of injury to a soldier is a question of federal common law), *superseded by*, Federal Medi-

cal Care Recovery Act, 42 U.S.C.A. §§ 2651–2653 (West 1994 & Supp. 1997).

122. Colombo v. Johns–Manville Corp., 601 F.Supp. 1119, 1132–39 (E.D.Pa.1984) (applying Federal Tort Claims Act and Pennsylvania law to determine whether third party plaintiff had substantive claim).

123. For discussion of the procedural issues governing admiralty claims see Chapter 56 "Admiralty," *infra.*

124. *E.g.*, Robert E. Blake, Inc. v. Excel Environmental, 104 F.3d 1158, 1162 (9th Cir.1997) (impleader of nonmaritime contract claim in underlying admiralty tort claim); Ins. Co. of North America v. S/S Cape Charles, 843 F.Supp. 893, 895 (S.D.N.Y.1994) (impleader of nonmaritime tort claim in underlying admiralty suit).

party plaintiff *or* a person who might be liable directly to the plaintiff. The liberal impleader standard under admiralty law was justified by the need to resolve admiralty disputes in one action due to the highly mobile nature of the parties and the assets.[125] As is discussed more fully in this section, the liberal rules of admiralty impleader have been preserved in FRCP 14(c). It is important to keep in mind, however, that where the underlying action is civil in nature and an admiralty claim is brought against a third-party defendant, the less permissive standards of FRCP 14(a) will apply.

Under FRCP 14(a), a third-party plaintiff may assert an admiralty claim against a third-party defendant. The last sentence of FRCP 14(a) states that a third-party complaint within admiralty or maritime jurisdiction "may be in rem against a vessel, cargo, or other property subject to admiralty or maritime process in rem." This provision does not limit a defendant's right to assert an admiralty claim against a third-party defendant but rather emphasizes that the right to implead based on admiralty law extends to in rem claims. For third-party admiralty claims brought in rem, FRCP 14(a) requires that references in the Rule to the summons must be read to include the warrant of arrest, and references to the third-party plaintiff or defendant must apply to the in rem claimant where appropriate.

In general, all the requirements for a valid third-party claim apply to admiralty claims brought under FRCP 14(a). In addition, however, third-party admiralty claims are governed by rules pertaining to admiralty and maritime including the Supplemental Rules for Certain Admiralty and Maritime Claims and special provisions in the FRCP and the United States Code. Where the Supplemental Rules and the FRCP conflict, the Supplemental Rules govern.[126] Particularly relevant to a third-party admiralty claim are the territorial limits for service of process applicable to maritime actions,[127] the rule governing service of interrogatories,[128] the Federal Rule providing that admiralty claims are to be tried to a judge,[129] and the Federal Rule governing interlocutory appeal of orders in admiralty and maritime cases.[130]

FRCP 14(c) governs impleader in cases where the original suit was brought under admiralty or maritime law. This provision was added to the Rule when admiralty practice was brought under the FRCP in 1966.

---

125. As was discussed in § 7.2(a), *supra*, the rules governing impleader in civil actions, following the tradition of admiralty law, allowed impleader of a person directly liable to the plaintiff until 1946 when the Rule was amended.

126. Supplemental Rule A.

127. Supplemental Rule E(3)(a) requires that process be served within the judicial district and does not allow service of process statewide or under the 100 mile bulge rule.

128. Supplemental Rule C(6) requires/allows the service of interrogatories with the complaint and requires that the answers to both be returned at the same time.

129. FRCP 38(e) provides that the federal rules do not create a right to trial for admiralty or maritime claims.

130. FRCP 9(h) incorporates the right under 28 U.S.C.A. § 1292(a)(3) to take an interlocutory appeal of decrees determining the rights and liabilities of the parties in an admiralty or maritime action.

Following long-standing admiralty practice,[131] FRCP 14(c) allows a defendant to implead a party who may be directly liable to the plaintiff,[132] as well as a party whose liability is derivative of the defendant's. Thus, a vessel owner sued in a maritime collision may implead the owner of another vessel involved in the accident, alleging that the second ship was jointly responsible for the damage to the plaintiff or that the second vessel was independently responsible for plaintiff's entire loss.

Where the third-party plaintiff alleges that the third-party defendant is directly liable to the plaintiff, "the third-party plaintiff may also demand judgment against the third-party defendant in favor of the plaintiff."[133] This procedure is utilized in cases where the third-party defendant may be independently liable for the plaintiff's loss. The effect of the procedure is to bring the third-party defendant into the suit as a co-defendant. Thus, the court will treat the parties as if the plaintiff had sued both the third-party defendant and the third-party plaintiff,[134] and the third-party defendant will be required to assert any defenses it has against the plaintiff as well as any defenses it has against the third-party plaintiff. By demanding judgment against the third-party defendant, the third-party plaintiff will shift the focus of the suit toward the third-party defendant. While this aspect of the procedure may help the third-party plaintiff, it will also increase the amount of finger-pointing between the defendants at trial and reduce any incentive they may have to cooperate against the plaintiff.

The more permissive impleader standards of FRCP 14(c) will not apply unless the plaintiff has asserted an admiralty or maritime claim in the original action as provided by FRCP 9(h).[135] There are two ways under FRCP 9(h) that an action will be considered an admiralty or maritime claim. First, a plaintiff may include a statement in the complaint identifying the claim as an admiralty or maritime claim. Alternatively, if the plaintiff does not designate the claim in the complaint, the claim will be treated as arising under admiralty or maritime law if the

131. Impleader in admiralty actions was previously governed by Admiralty Rule 56.

132. Montauk Oil Transp. Corp. v. Steamship Mutual Underwriting Ass'n (Bermuda) Ltd., 859 F.Supp. 669, 675–76, 678 (S.D.N.Y.1994) (allowing impleader of the United States because the government was directly liable to plaintiff under the Federal Water Pollution Control Act); Ins. Co. of North America v. S/S Cape Charles, 843 F.Supp. 893, 894 (S.D.N.Y.1994) (allowing impleader of trucking company by third party plaintiff ocean carrier alleging that goods were damaged by trucking company and not during shipment).

133. Harcrest Int'l, Ltd. v. M/V Zim Keelung, 681 F.Supp. 354, 355 (E.D.La. 1988) (third party requested judgment in favor of original plaintiff against third party

defendant); Ohio River Co. v. Continental Grain Co., 352 F.Supp. 505, 511–12 (N.D.Ill.1972) (entering judgment for plaintiff against third party defendant).

134. *See, e.g.,* General Marine Const. Co. v. United States, 738 F.Supp. 586, 589–90 (D.Mass.1990) (government's third party claim against contractor would not be governed by Contract Disputes Act because third party must be treated as if plaintiff sued directly and CDA would not apply on claim between plaintiff and third party); United States v. Isco, Inc., 463 F.Supp. 1293, 1294–95 (E.D.Wis.1979) (third party defendant impled on basis of liability directly to plaintiff could not be dismissed voluntarily without the plaintiff's consent).

135. Harrison v. Glendel Drilling Co., 679 F.Supp. 1413, 1417–19 (W.D.La.1988).

court has no basis for jurisdiction other than admiralty or maritime law. If the complaint does not satisfy the requirements of FRCP 9(h), the defendant will not be able to implead under the broader provisions of FRCP 14(c) and will have to implead under the general provisions in FRCP 14(a).[136]

An additional requirement of FRCP 14(c) is that the third-party claim arise from the same "transaction or occurrence." This requirement is necessary to limit the scope of impleader with respect to persons who may be directly liable to the plaintiff. Without this limitation, a third-party plaintiff could implead a person who is liable to the plaintiff on an entirely separate claim. Allowing impleader of an unrelated claim would undermine the efficiency rationale of impleader. Despite the limiting function of this requirement, courts have interpreted this language broadly, in keeping with the former provision in Admiralty Rule 56. Third-party plaintiffs in admiralty actions have been allowed to implead on a variety of claims including claims for contractual indemnification,[137] claims for product liability,[138] and claims arising under the Contract Disputes Acts.[139] However, the requirement that the third-party claim arise from the same transaction or occurrence may be the basis for dismissal under FRCP 14(c).[140]

As is discussed in more detail in Section 7.2(c), *infra,* the court must have subject matter jurisdiction over a third-party claim. Although in most instances a third-party claim will be covered under supplemental jurisdiction, the applicability of supplemental jurisdiction to third-party claims under FRCP 14(c) is unsettled. Prior to the passage of the supplemental jurisdiction statute in 1990, courts were split on whether a third-party claim under FRCP 14(c) fell within the court's ancillary jurisdiction. In *McCann v. Falgout Boat Company,*[141] the owners of a vessel defending a claim by an injured seaman attempted to implead the seaman's doctor for malpractice in treating the seaman's injury when he returned home. The court dismissed the third-party claim holding that there was no independent basis of subject matter jurisdiction for the claim and that ancillary jurisdiction was not applicable.[142] The *McCann* court reasoned that FRCP 14(c) did not alter impleader under the predecessor rule, Admiralty Rule 56, which required an independent basis of subject matter jurisdiction.[143] Although some courts followed the

---

136. *Id.* at 1422.

137. Robert E. Blake, Inc. v. Excel Environmental, 104 F.3d 1158, 1159 (9th Cir. 1997).

138. Vaughn v. Farrell Lines, Inc., 937 F.2d 953, 955 (4th Cir.1991).

139. General Marine Constr., 738 F.Supp. at 589–90 (holding that Rule 14(c) rather than the Contract Dispute Act governed third party claim based on government contract in underlying admiralty action because claims arose from the same transaction or occurrence).

140. Vaughn, 937 F.2d at 955 n. 1 (third party claim against asbestos manufacturers and suppliers in suit by seaman against ship owner for injuries caused by asbestos in ship's boiler and engine room).

141. 44 F.R.D. 34 (S.D.Tex.1968).

142. *Id.* at 37. It is important to note, however, as the *McCann* court acknowledged, that supplemental jurisdiction applies to an admiralty claim brought under FRCP 14(a).

143. *Id.* at 41.

McCann holding,[144] the opinion was widely criticized and other courts declined to follow it.[145]

The passage of the supplemental jurisdiction statute has done little to clarify the issue. The statute does not provide an exception to supplemental jurisdiction for admiralty, and numerous courts have held that ancillary jurisdiction applies to claims brought under FRCP 14(c).[146] However, some courts have continued to apply the *McCann* rule,[147] particularly where the third-party claim is based on the third party's liability directly to the plaintiff.[148]

A final peculiarity of impleader under FRCP 14(c) is the question of whether a third-party claim not based in admiralty may be tried to a jury. A claim which has been designated under FRCP 9(h) as an admiralty or maritime claim is not tried to a jury. In applying this rule to a claim under FRCP 14(c), some courts have found that a third-party defendant impled on a civil claim is not entitled to a jury trial where the original claim is based in admiralty.[149] On the other hand, the Supreme Court's holding in *Fitzgerald v. United States Lines Co.*,[150] requires that factual questions must be submitted to a jury where issues involved in an admiralty and civil action are related. [151]

At least one court has found that a third-party defendant retains the right to a jury trial on nonmaritime claims against it even though the underlying action is governed by admiralty law. In *Insurance Company of North America v. S/S Cape Charles*,[152] an ocean carrier, sued for damage to cargo, filed a third-party complaint against the trucking company which transported the cargo on the last leg of the trip. The

---

144. *E.g., In re* Oil Spill by the Amoco Cadiz off the Coast of France, 699 F.2d 909, 913 (7th Cir.) (there is a question whether admiralty impleader requires an independent jurisdictional basis), *cert. denied sub nom.* Astilleros Espanoles v. Standard Oil Co., 464 U.S. 864, 104 S.Ct. 196, 78 L.Ed.2d 172 (1983).

145. *E.g.,* Joiner v. Diamond M. Drilling Co., 677 F.2d 1035, 1040–41 (5th Cir.1982) (early decisions denying ancillary jurisdiction to third party claims brought by admiralty defendants were "consistently rejected by both the courts and the commentators"); Leather's Best, Inc. v. S.S. Mormaclynx, 451 F.2d 800, 810 n. 12 (2d Cir.1971) ("[T]he practical considerations which support the doctrine of ancillary jurisdiction in the context of civil impleader are equally persuasive on the admiralty side.").

146. Robert E. Blake, Inc. v. Excel Environmental, 104 F.3d 1158, 1162 (9th Cir. 1997) (supplemental jurisdiction governs nonadmiralty action arising from same transaction or occurrence); Ins. Co. of North America v. S/S Cape Charles, 843

F.Supp. 893, 895 (S.D.N.Y.1994) (nonmaritime third party claim by ocean carrier against trucking company for damage to cargo covered under supplemental jurisdiction statute).

147. Lewis v. United States, 816 F.Supp. 1097, 1102 (E.D.Va.1993) (dismissing third party claim under FRCP 14(c) where claim was brought based upon liability directly to plaintiff).

148. *Id.* at 1100.

149. McCann v. Falgout Boat Company, 44 F.R.D. 34, 44 (S.D.Tex.1968); Harrison v. Flota Mercante Grancolombiana, 577 F.2d 968, 987 (5th Cir.1978) ("[W]e refuse to permit a third party defendant to emasculate the election given to the plaintiff by Rule 9(h) by exercising the simple expedient of bringing in a fourth-party defendant.").

150. 374 U.S. 16, 83 S.Ct. 1646, 10 L.Ed.2d 720 (1963).

151. *Id.* at 21.

152. 843 F.Supp. 893 (S.D.N.Y.1994).

trucking company demanded a jury trial, and the third-party plaintiff moved to strike the demand. The court held that the third-party defendant could not be deprived of its right to a jury trial merely because the underlying action was brought under admiralty law.[153]

(b) Personal Jurisdiction and Venue

Once the third-party plaintiff has determined that a claim can be asserted against a third-party defendant according to FRCP 14, the third-party plaintiff must determine whether the court can exercise jurisdiction. In order to assert a third-party claim, the court must have personal jurisdiction over the third-party defendant.[154] The third-party defendant must have sufficient contacts with the forum state to satisfy constitutional requirements,[155] and the third-party plaintiff must be able to effect service of process on the third-party defendant.[156]

Although the constitutional requirement that the third-party defendant have "minimum contacts" with the forum state must be satisfied, some courts have applied this requirement more loosely when evaluating jurisdiction over third-party defendants. Courts sometimes consider the third-party defendant's contacts with the original plaintiff as well as with the third-party plaintiff when deciding whether there are minimum contacts.[157]

In order to exercise personal jurisdiction over a third-party defendant, process must have been properly served. The same general principles of service of process discussed in Chapter 2 "Personal Jurisdiction and Service," *supra,* apply to third-party defendants. In addition to effecting service according to the law of the forum state, however, a third-party plaintiff may also effect service of process on a third-party defendant under the "bulge" rule provided in FRCP 4(k)(1)(B). Under the "bulge" rule, service of process may be effected on a third-party

153. *Id.* at 895.

154. Plywood Panels, Inc. v. M/V Thalia, 141 F.R.D. 689, 692 (E.D.La.1992) (dismissing third party complaint by vessel owner in admiralty action because the court did not have personal jurisdiction over most of the defendants); Nat'l Gypsum Co. v. Dalemark Industries, Inc., 779 F.Supp. 147, 148 (D.Kan.1991) (denying leave to file third party complaint because third party defendant could not be reached under state long-arm statute).

155. Froning & Deppe, Inc. v. Continental Illinois Nat'l Bank & Trust Co., 695 F.2d 289, 292–95 (7th Cir.1982) (dismissing third party complaint because third party defendant did not have sufficient contacts with forum state).

156. Hill v. United States, 815 F.Supp. 373, 375–77 (D.Colo.1993) (dismissing third party complaint because court lacked jurisdiction over third party defendant under state's long-arm statute).

157. Synder Int'l, Inc. v. Tap Equip. Co., 770 F.Supp. 279, 282 (W.D.Pa.1991) (delivery of vehicle by third party defendant to plaintiff under contract with third party plaintiff executed out of state was sufficient to satisfy minimum contacts); Southern Iowa Mfg. Co. v. Whittaker Corp., 404 F.Supp. 630, 632 (D.C.Iowa 1975) (court could consider contacts between third party defendant and all other parties in evaluating minimum contacts). *But see* National Precast Crypt Co. v. Dy–Core of Pennsylvania, Inc., 785 F.Supp. 1186, 1193 n. 4 (W.D.Pa.1992) (third party plaintiff asserting a third party complaint against the president of plaintiff's company could not rely on president's contact with company in forum to show jurisdiction).

defendant if it is done within the judicial district where the action is pending and, in addition, not more than 100 miles from the court. Service under the "bulge" rule is proper even if the third-party defendant could not be served under the long-arm statute of the state where the action is pending or of the state of service.

The "bulge" rule affects not only the procedural requirements for service of process but also the due process requirement of minimum contacts. The rule has been interpreted to broaden the jurisdiction of the federal courts by expanding the area in which the third-party plaintiff can establish that the third-party defendant has minimum contacts. The predominant view is that a party served under the bulge rule need not have minimum contacts with the forum state.[158] Instead, courts require either that the third-party defendant have minimum contacts with the bulge area[159] or that it have minimum contacts with the state in which bulge service is made.[160]

Venue does not generally pose an obstacle to a third-party claim. Courts have applied a concept of ancillary venue to third-party defendants, finding that if venue is satisfied in the underlying action, then venue as to the third-party defendant is also satisfied.[161] Because venue is a personal defense, third-party defendants cannot circumvent this analysis by challenging the venue of the underlying claim. Similarly, a plaintiff cannot challenge a third-party claim on the basis that venue requirements are not satisfied.[162] Although a third-party defendant may not object to improper venue, a third-party defendant joined in an action

---

158. Gamble v. Lyons Precast Erectors, Inc., 825 F.Supp. 92, 94 (E.D.Pa.1993) (every circuit court to have considered the issue has held that the rule extends the territorial jurisdiction of the courts); Associates Commercial Corp. v. Lincoln General Ins. Co., 702 F.Supp. 104, 106 (W.D.Pa. 1988) (while an argument can be made that the bulge rule affects only service of process, the weight of authority is to the contrary). See Chapter 2 "Personal Jurisdiction and Service" at § 2.5(h), *supra*.

159. Quinones v. Pennsylvania General Ins. Co., 804 F.2d 1167, 1178 (10th Cir. 1986) (New Mexico court had personal jurisdiction over third party defendant Texas resident who was served within and resided in bulge area); Sprow v. Hartford Ins. Co., 594 F.2d 412, 416 (5th Cir.1979) (Louisiana had personal jurisdiction over insurance agent located in Mississippi even though agent did not have minimum contacts with the State of Louisiana because agent had sufficient contacts with bulge area).

160. Coleman v. American Export Isbrandtsen Lines, Inc., 405 F.2d 250, 253 (2d Cir.1968).

161. Gundle Lining Const. Co. v. Adams County Asphalt, Inc., 85 F.3d 201, 209 (5th Cir.1996) ("[s]tatutory venue limitations have no application to Rule 14 claims.") (quoting 6 Charles Alan Wright, Arthur R. Miller & Mary Kay Kane, Federal Practice & Procedure § 1445 (2d ed. 1990)); ABCKO Music, Inc. v. Beverly Glen Music, Inc., 554 F.Supp. 410, 412 (S.D.N.Y.1983) ("If venue is proper in the main action, then venue is also proper as to third party claim which is predicated under the court's ancillary jurisdiction."). Note, however, that if venue is a prerequisite to proper personal jurisdiction, the third party defendant may object to venue on the grounds of improper personal jurisdiction. First Federal Savings & Loan Ass'n of Pittsburgh v. Oppenheim, Appel, Dixon & Co., 634 F.Supp. 1341, 1349 (S.D.N.Y.1986) (where personal jurisdiction is based on a statute which designates proper forum, the third party may object to venue).

162. Seemer v. Ritter, 25 F.Supp. 688, 688–89 (M.D.Pa.1938).

can move to transfer venue to a more convenient forum.[163] A third-party defendant moving to transfer venue must show that the preferred forum is more convenient in terms of the entire action, not just with regard to the third-party claim.[164]

(c) Subject Matter Jurisdiction

As with any claim adjudicated in federal court, the court must have subject matter jurisdiction over the third-party claim. FRCP 14 does not provide an exception to this general rule. A court can exercise jurisdiction over a third-party claim, either on an independent basis or through supplemental jurisdiction. These topics are discussed in greater detail in Chapter 1 "Subject Matter Jurisdiction," *supra*, but they will be briefly reviewed here as they pertain to third-party practice.

A third-party claim may satisfy subject matter jurisdictional requirements independent of the underlying claim. The two primary bases of subject matter jurisdiction are federal question jurisdiction and diversity jurisdiction. An interesting question is raised by the complete diversity requirement in the context of third-party practice. Take the situation where the original plaintiff is from state X, and the original defendant is from state Y. The defendant chooses to implead its indemnitor from state X. Although the parties on the third-party claim are diverse, all parties are not diverse. While it is possible that the diversity statute might be interpreted to deny jurisdiction on these facts, courts uniformly have found that the citizenship of the original plaintiff is not relevant to the question of whether the claim between the third-party plaintiff and the third-party defendant qualifies for diversity jurisdiction because the third-party defendant and the plaintiff are not adverse.[165] In most cases, the question is purely academic since most third-party claims are covered under supplemental jurisdiction.[166]

The supplemental jurisdiction statute passed in 1990 makes clear what federal courts had already concluded[167]—that third-party claims

---

163. *E.g.*, Kendall U.S.A., Inc. v. Central Printing Co., 666 F.Supp. 1264, 1269 (N.D.Ind.1987). *See* Chapter 3, "Venue, Forum Selection, and Transfer," *supra*.

164. *See* Richter v. Analex Corp., 940 F.Supp. 353, 360 (D.D.C.1996) (denying motion to transfer venue because all relevant documents and witnesses on main claim were located in forum state); Kendall U.S.A., 666 F.Supp. at 1267 (court must consider convenience of all parties to suit).

165. Caterpillar, Inc. v. Lewis, 519 U.S. 61, ___ – ___ n. 1, 117 S.Ct. 467, 472–73 n. 1, 136 L.Ed.2d 437 (1996) (once federal subject matter jurisdiction is established in underlying case, the propriety of allowing defendant to implead a third party under diversity jurisdiction is determined independently of the plaintiff)(dicta); Landmark Bank v. Machera, 736 F.Supp. 375, 378 (D.Mass.1990) (plaintiff and third party defendant are not opposing parties for purposes of diversity jurisdiction).

166. Landmark Bank, 736 F.Supp. at 379 n.5 (even if diversity jurisdiction were lacking, court could exercise jurisdiction under doctrine of ancillary jurisdiction).

167. *E.g.*, United States v. Pioneer Lumber Treating Co., 496 F.Supp. 199, 201 (E.D.Wash.1980) ("Impleader of a third party defendant under Rule 14 falls within ancillary jurisdiction."); Gauthier v. Crosby Marine Serv., Inc., 87 F.R.D. 353, 354–55 (E.D.La.1980) (third party complaint arising out of the same claim as the main action is covered by ancillary jurisdiction).

fall under supplemental jurisdiction.[168] There is one significant exception, however, which limits the ability of the original plaintiff to assert a claim against a third-party defendant. The supplemental jurisdiction statute provides that where the court's jurisdiction over the main claim is based on diversity of citizenship, the court may not exercise supplemental jurisdiction over claims brought by "plaintiffs against persons made parties under Rule 14."[169] This provision in the statute codifies the Supreme Court's holding in *Owen Equipment & Erection Co. v. Kroger*,[170] where the Court held that ancillary jurisdiction did not apply to a plaintiff's state law claim against a nondiverse third-party defendant who had been impled by the defendant. The rationale of the *Owen* decision was that a plaintiff should not be able to circumvent the requirement of complete diversity by "suing only those defendants who were of diverse citizenship and waiting from them to implead nondiverse defendants."[171]

There are three situations in which a plaintiff's claim against a third-party defendant will be barred by the supplemental jurisdiction statute. Supplemental jurisdiction is unavailable if the plaintiff, like the plaintiff in *Owen*, brings a state law claim against a nondiverse third-party defendant who has been impled by the defendant in a diversity action. Supplemental jurisdiction is also unavailable under the statute where the plaintiff brings a counterclaim based in state law against a third-party defendant joined in a diversity action who asserts a claim directly against the plaintiff. The Supreme Court did not address this scenario in *Owen,* and lower courts considering the issue prior to the passage of the new statute had held that supplemental jurisdiction applied in this scenario.[172] The oddity of the result under the statute is that the third-party defendant's claim against the plaintiff will be covered by supplemental jurisdiction, but the plaintiff's counterclaim, which is by definition a compulsory counterclaim, will not be covered under supplemental jurisdiction. Most likely, this aspect of the statute was an unintended consequence of poor drafting.

The final scenario in which the statute prohibits supplemental jurisdiction is where the plaintiff seeks to implead another nondiverse third-party defendant on a counterclaim by the defendant or a claim by the third-party defendant against the plaintiff.[173] This is the most controversial aspect of the supplemental jurisdiction statute. Lower courts that had considered this question prior to the passage of the supplemental jurisdiction statute had allowed the claim under supplemental jurisdiction. Courts[174] and commentators[175] have criticized this

---

168. Chase Manhattan Bank v. Aldridge, 906 F.Supp. 866, 868 (S.D.N.Y. 1995).

169. 28 U.S.C.A. § 1367(b) (West 1993).

170. 437 U.S. 365, 98 S.Ct. 2396, 57 L.Ed.2d 274 (1978).

171. *Id.* at 374, 98 S.Ct. at 2403.

172. Finkle v. Gulf & Western Mfg. Co., 744 F.2d 1015, 1018, 1019 (3d Cir.1984).

173. Chase Manhattan Bank, 906 F.Supp. at 868, 869.

174. Guaranteed Systems, Inc. v. American Nat'l Can Co., 842 F.Supp. 855, 857–58 (M.D.N.C.1994) (denying jurisdiction but noting that the rationale of *Owen* and Section 1367(b) of preventing the plaintiff from evading diversity requirements does not apply in this situation).

175. 14 James Wm. Moore, et al., Moore's Federal Practice § 14.41[4][d] (3d

aspect of the statute and have suggested that Congress did not intend to limit the plaintiff's ability to implead in this manner.[176]

(d) Discretion of the Court

Even though all the prerequisites for a valid third-party claim are met, the court may still refuse to join a third-party defendant. The decision to exercise jurisdiction over a valid third-party complaint is within the sound discretion of the trial court.[177] However, impleader is to be liberally allowed because it facilitates the adjudication of related claims in one suit.[178] As a general rule, impleader should be allowed unless it unfairly prejudices the parties.[179]

Courts consider a variety of factors in determining whether to allow a third-party complaint. Included among these factors is whether the third-party claim will unduly complicate issues for trial.[180] A third-party complaint may complicate the suit by presenting novel or difficult questions of law[181] or by presenting additional legal or factual issues unrelated to the original claim.[182] In addition, the third-party complaint may unnecessarily complicate the trial by requiring the presentation of additional evidence or witnesses which are not relevant to the underlying action.[183] Although some of these difficulties may be overcome by

ed. 1997) ("[T]he unfortunate result seems dictated by the poor drafting of the statute, which, by using the term "plaintiffs" in the second subsection ignores the fact that plaintiffs often assert claims in a defensive posture."); *see also* 6 Charles Alan Wright, Arthur R. Miller & Mary Kay Kane, Federal Practice & Procedure § 1444 (2d ed. 1990).

176. Guaranteed Systems, 842 F.Supp. at 857–58; Moore, *supra* note 175, § 14.41[4][d].

177. Southwest Administrators, Inc. v. Rozay's Transfer, 791 F.2d 769, 777 (9th Cir.1986) (affirming decision of trial court not to allow impleader of union in ERISA case because it would have complicated trial and introduced extraneous issues).

178. United States v. Acord, 209 F.2d 709, 712 (10th Cir.), *cert. denied*, 347 U.S. 975, 74 S.Ct. 786, 98 L.Ed. 1115 (1954).

179. Clark v. Associates Commercial Corp., 149 F.R.D. 629, 635 (D.Kan.1993) (allowing impleader of creditor's agent where creditor sued by debtor for breach of peace on basis of creditor's agent's repossession of tractor-trailer unit); Hicks v. Long Island R.R., 165 F.R.D. 377, 379 (E.D.N.Y.1996) (a motion to implead a third party defendant should be freely granted unless it would prejudice the plaintiff).

180. Con–Tech Sales Defined Benefit Trust v. Cockerham, 715 F.Supp. 701, 703 (E.D.Pa.1989).

181. Blais Construction Co. v. Hanover Square Associates–I, 733 F.Supp. 149, 156–57, 159 (N.D.N.Y.1990) (declining to allow impleader of FDIC, in part, because third party claim would add complicated federal legal issues and choice of law questions to a simple breach of contract claim).

182. Southwest Administrators, 791 F.2d at 777 (affirming trial court's denial of leave to file third party complaint against union in ERISA action because ERISA provides for streamlined procedure to collect delinquent contributions and impleader of union would introduce extraneous issues about validity of collective bargaining agreement).

183. Fuel Transp. Co., Inc. v. Fireman's Fund Ins. Co., 108 F.R.D. 156, 159 (E.D.Pa. 1985) (dismissing third party claim by defendant insurer against party allegedly responsible for accident because third party claim would complicate suit with issues of fault where the original complaint concerned only straight-forward issues of contract interpretation); Collins v. General Motors Corp., 101 F.R.D. 4, 7 (W.D.Pa.1983) (considering whether third party claims involve the same evidence and witnesses).

simply severing the claims at trial rather than denying impleader, courts may still exercise their discretion to deny impleader on this basis.

Another factor which courts consider is the timeliness of the motion to implead.[184] Delay in seeking to implead a third-party defendant can be a reason for denial of leave to file a third-party claim.[185] FRCP 14 does not provide a specific time limit for bringing a third-party claim, and courts have not imposed a bright-line rule governing how long a third-party plaintiff has to file a third-party complaint. Nevertheless, delay is weighed heavily in a court's decision about whether to allow impleader, although courts have allowed third-party complaints filed years after service of the answer.[186]

Some district courts have promulgated local rules which place a limit on when third-party claims must be filed.[187] In keeping with the flexible approach taken with impleader claims, these rules are not applied strictly and instead are relied upon by courts merely as a guideline.[188] Effectively, however, these local rules shift the burden of proof to the third-party plaintiff to explain why delay beyond the deadline set in the local rules was reasonable.[189]

In determining whether to allow impleader, courts will consider how long the third-party plaintiff was aware of the facts and the parties relevant to the third-party claim.[190] Courts also will consider the reasons

184. Con–Tech Sales Defined Benefit Trust, 715 F.Supp. at 703.

185. Insurance Co. of North America v. Morrison, 148 F.R.D. 295, 297 (M.D.Fla. 1993) (dismissing third party complaint filed more than a year after answer was served); Blais Construction, 733 F.Supp. at 158 (dismissing third party complaint which was served more than two years after service of the answer).

186. United States v. New Castle County, 111 F.R.D. 628, 636 (D.Del.1986) (allowing leave to implead more than two and a half years after complaint filed); State of New York v. Solvent Chemical Co., Inc., 875 F.Supp. 1015, 1021 (W.D.N.Y.1995) (allowing leave to implead more than 10 years after filing of original suit).

187. Morrison, 148 F.R.D. at 295, 296 (6 months after serving answer); Local 144, Hotel, Hosp., Nursing Home and Allied Services Union v. C.N.H. Management Associates, Inc., 741 F.Supp. 415, 419 (S.D.N.Y. 1990) (6 months after filing answer); Con–Tech Sales Defined Benefit Trust, 715 F.Supp. at 703 n. 2 (90 days after service of answer).

188. Con–Tech Sales Defined Benefit Trust, 715 F.Supp. at 704 ("This court has

treated the time limits for filing a motion for leave to file a third party complaint as mere guidelines, allowing substantial room for exercise of discretion.").

189. Morrison, 148 F.R.D. at 296 (defendants "bear the burden of establishing the excusability of their own delay" beyond the time allowed by local rule; Local 144, Hotel, Hosp., Nursing Home and Allied Services Union, 741 F.Supp. at 420 (local rule requiring motion to be filed within six months of answer "is designed to place the burden on the defendant to show special circumstances that would outweigh the prejudice to the parties"); Bambu Sales, Inc. v. Sultana Crackers, Inc., 683 F.Supp. 899, 916 (E.D.N.Y.1988) (when party files third party complaint beyond the time required by local rule, the party must establish "special circumstances").

190. Consolidated Rail Corp. v. Metz, 115 F.R.D. 216, 219 (S.D.N.Y.1987) (denying motion to implead where third party plaintiff knew necessary facts for more than a year before filing); Blais Construction Co., 733 F.Supp. at 158 (denying motion to implead where third party plaintiff had laid out the facts relevant to the third party claim more than a year earlier in its answer).

for the delay.[191] If the third-party plaintiff has deliberately delayed filing its third-party complaint[192] or cannot offer a reasonable justification for its delay,[193] a court may deny leave to implead. The nature of the claims may also be a factor relied on by the court to evaluate the prejudice created by delay. In complex civil litigation, courts may be more likely to give a third-party plaintiff additional leeway.[194] One of the principal considerations in evaluating delay is the effect on trial and discovery. If the third-party claim is likely to delay trial due to additional discovery or if discovery is already substantially completed, the court may deny leave to implead a third-party defendant.[195]

A final factor considered by courts is the prejudice to the other parties.[196] A third-party complaint may prejudice a plaintiff in a variety of ways. For instance, impleader has been denied because the plaintiff will suffer economic hardship due to the delay of adding a third-party defendant.[197]

A third-party complaint may also be dismissed because it prejudices a third-party defendant. For example, if the third-party defendants were formerly principal defendants in the case and the claims against them were dismissed or settled out of court long before third-party claims were asserted against them, a court may deny impleader to avoid prejudice.[198] In order to establish prejudice, a third-party defendant must show something more than the fact that it will expend more resources defending rather than not defending the third-party suit.[199] The third-party defendant must demonstrate that it will incur greater expense or be at a greater disadvantage in defending a third-party suit in comparison with an independent suit.[200]

---

191. Solvent Chemical Co. Inc., 875 F.Supp. at 1021 (a court may "consider whether the party deliberately delayed or was derelict in filing the motion.").

192. Consolidated Rail Corp., 115 F.R.D. at 219.

193. Id. at 219–20 (denying motion to implead third party where third party plaintiff offered no reasonable explanation for delay); Highlands Ins. Co. v. Lewis Rail Serv. Co., 10 F.3d 1247, 1251 (7th Cir.1993) (affirming denial of leave to file third party complaint where only excuse for delay was that counsel was trying to save money for the client); Hicks v. Long Island R.R., 165 F.R.D. 377, 380 (E.D.N.Y.1996) (finding third party's explanation that other priorities required attention "wholly unpersuasive").

194. United States v. New Castle County, 111 F.R.D. 628, 634, 636 (D.Del.1986) (allowing a third party complaint to be filed 2 1/2 years after the answer because of the "enormous factual and technical complexity of CERCLA actions.").

195. Hicks, 165 F.R.D. at 380 (denying leave to file third party claim where discovery is almost complete and adding a third party will delay trial); First Nat'l Bank of Nocona v. Duncan Savings and Loan Ass'n, 957 F.2d 775, 777–78 (10th Cir.1992) (affirming trial court's denial of motion to implead third party where defendant filed motion almost a week after its motion for summary judgment and less than a month before trial was scheduled).

196. New Castle County, 111 F.R.D. at 632.

197. Hicks, 165 F.R.D. at 380 (denying leave to implead where plaintiff asserted economic hardship because he had used all his paid sick days and was depleting the remainder of his partially paid sick days).

198. Oliner v. McBride's Industries, Inc., 106 F.R.D. 14, 21 (S.D.N.Y.1985) (denying leave to implead where six years had passed from time that third party defendants settled out of the case).

199. New Castle County, 111 F.R.D. at 633.

In order to avoid dismissal of a valid third-party claim, the third-party plaintiff should seek to present its claim in a timely manner, preferably as soon as is practical after becoming aware of such a claim. The third-party complaint should also be kept as simple as possible. The addition of too many third-party defendants or complex evidentiary issues will reduce the chance that impleader will be allowed. For the same reason, the third-party plaintiff should carefully consider whether to join additional claims against the third-party defendant in the third-party complaint. The joinder of claims against the third-party defendant which are unrelated to the underlying claim will increase the complexity of the suit and the chances that impleader will be denied.

A plaintiff or third-party defendant opposing a valid third-party claim will have to demonstrate that impleader is prejudicial. A plaintiff opposing impleader may do so by arguing that impleader will delay trial. This argument will be particularly persuasive if the parties are close to completing discovery and to trial, or if the plaintiff will suffer a particular hardship (*e.g.*, such as loss of a job or insurance benefits) if trial is delayed. A third-party defendant will not be able to rely on delay as a reason for opposing impleader since delay harms the plaintiff not the third-party defendant. However, both the plaintiff and the third-party defendant may argue that joining the third-party claim will confuse the jury and add unnecessary complexity to the trial.

Parties seeking dismissal of a proper third-party complaint on the basis of delay, complexity or confusion should be aware that the court may address these objections by simply ordering severance or a separate trial instead of dismissal. Although third-party claims are frequently dismissed for these reasons, a party seeking dismissal has a stronger case if it can show that the claim is not a valid third-party claim. A party may challenge the validity of the claim by arguing that there is no substantive basis for the claim, or that the third-party defendant's liability is not derivative of the third-party plaintiff's liability to the plaintiff.

(e) Weighing the Alternatives—Separate Suit and Vouching In

The obvious alternative to impleader is a separate suit between the defendant and the third-party defendant. A not-so-obvious alternative is the common law practice of "vouching in."[201] Under principles of voucher, the defendant serves notice on a potential third-party indemnitor. Such notice informs the third party of the action and offers the opportu-

---

200. *Id.* at 633–34 (allowing impleader of third parties even though principal parties had engaged in discovery for over four years because third party defendant would have to review all this discovery and conduct its own even if the action was brought separately).

201. SCAC Transport (USA) Inc. v. S. S. Danaos, 845 F.2d 1157, 1161–62 (2d Cir. 1988) (holding that stevedore could be vouched into arbitration proceeding by the vessel owner without stevedore's consent and was bound by arbitrator's finding that its negligence caused the accident during loading of cargo on a vessel).

nity to the third party to appear and defend the action. If the third party so elects, it becomes a party to the action and takes over the defense. If the third party decides not to defend, it will be bound in any subsequent litigation between them by the factual determinations necessary to the original judgment. Thus, if the defendant chooses to bring a separate action for indemnification against the third party, the third party would be able to dispute only its obligation to indemnify.[202] The extent to which the third party who declines to assume the defense of an action is bound will be governed by traditional notions of estoppel.[203] A third party may also dispute whether the notice to defend was adequate.[204]

Vouching has been largely supplanted by the modern Federal Rules governing impleader. When available, impleader is a superior method of practice because it forces the indemnitor to participate in the original action. As a result, vouching is best used in cases where a lack of personal jurisdiction prevents process on the indemnitor from being obtained.[205] Note that the Uniform Commercial Code also provides an independent basis for voucher of warranty claims.[206]

(f) Evaluating the Impact on Settlement

Impleader offers the practical advantage of bringing all the parties together to negotiate a comprehensive settlement. If settlement negotiations are successful, the parties will all be bound by the court's consent order. If, on the other hand, only some of the parties reach settlement, the remaining claim may still be tried.[207] Most importantly, impleader brings to the settlement table additional resources to satisfy the plaintiff.

Impleader can affect the chances of settlement of both the main claim and the third-party claim. The impact of impleader on settlement will depend upon the strength of the evidence, the alignment of interests between the parties, and the objectives of the defendant. Although impleader may affect settlement opportunities differently in each case, some general observations can be made.

---

202. Humble Oil & Refining Co. v. Philadelphia Ship Maintenance Co., 444 F.2d 727, 735 (3d Cir.1971) (refusing to bind stevedore to shipowner where the scope of the stevedore's indemnity for injury was less than that of shipowner).

203. Restatement (Second) of Judgments § 57 (1982) ("Effect on Indemnitor of Judgment Against Indemnitee").

204. SCAC Transport (USA) Inc., 845 F.2d at 1162.

205. Hessler v. Hillwood Mfg. Co., 302 F.2d 61, 62 (6th Cir.1962) (in action by New York hardware retailer against Ohio nail manufacturer to recover amount of judgment paid to buyer who was injured by defective nail, "vouched in" manufacturer

precluded in indemnification action by earlier judgment for buyer against retailer).

206. U.C.C. § 2–607(5) ("Where the buyer is sued for breach of a warranty or other obligation for which his seller is answerable over (a) he may give his seller written notice of the litigation. If the notice states that the seller may come in and defend and that if the seller does not do so he will be bound in any action against him by his buyer by any determination of fact common to the two litigations, then unless the seller after seasonable receipt of the notice does not come in and defend he is so bound ....").

207. Vaughn v. Farrell Lines, Inc., 937 F.2d 953, 955–56 (4th Cir.1991).

Impleading a third party may improve the defendant's chances for settling the main claim by increasing the defendant's leverage in settlement negotiations. Joining the third party will result in higher litigation costs for the plaintiff who will have to respond to discovery requests from both parties. Furthermore, if the third-party defendant asserts claims directly against the plaintiff, the risk to the plaintiff of litigating increases. There may also be instances where, because of their relationship to the plaintiff, third-party defendants serve to benefit the third-party plaintiff strategically (*e.g.*, auditor sued by client corporation for failure to detect fraud asserts third-party claim against corporation's officers who made representations to auditor). In addition, in cases where the interests of the third-party defendant and the defendant coincide, impleader may enhance the defendant's bargaining position by improving the quality of its defense. For example, where an insured impleads its insurer, the insurer generally will want to defend the insured against liability to the plaintiff.

On the other hand, if the interests of the defendant and the third-party defendant diverge, impleader may undermine the defendant's chances of success in settlement. This may be the case where a joint tortfeasor impled as a third party may seek to prove that the defendant was solely liable for the plaintiff's injury.

Impleader may also affect the defendant's chances of settling its claim against the third-party defendant. By joining the third party to the suit, the defendant may be able to convince the third-party defendant of the strength of the case against it and the extent of the third party's potential liability. By the same token, if the case against the defendant is weak, impleader may reduce the defendant's chance of settling with the third party. In any event, impleader causes the third-party defendant to pay attention to the initial action, engage counsel, and evaluate its potential liability to the third-party plaintiff. Thus, where settlement (as opposed to trial) is highly likely, there are good reasons for the defendant to consider impleader.

(g) Evaluating the Impact on Trial

As a general statement, the existence of third-party claims at the time of trial tends to benefit the plaintiff and disadvantage the defendants. At minimum, there is uncertainty created for each defendant by the participation of another defending party. The worse, and not unusual, case is when defendants point fingers at each other leaving the jury to conclude that liability to the plaintiff is established and that the trial is about who pays.

In contrast to settlement negotiations where the third-party defendant may be crucial to accumulating sufficient funds to reach a result, a case going to trial has a different focus. At trial, the original defendant is bent on presenting the best possible case to defeat plaintiff's claims. Defendant's concern is not with sharing a loss with a third-party defendant who is or may be liable to the third-party plaintiff, but, instead, to suffer no loss at all. Thus, in a case with a very high likelihood of going to trial, the original defendant will often prefer to defer any third-party claims to the time, if ever, when it has been found liable. In fact, a successful tactic during the trial will likely be to assert that the putative third-party defendant is responsible for any loss suffered by plaintiff. This "blame the empty chair" defense is effective precisely because the third-party claim has not actually been asserted and, thus, the third-party defendant is not present.

Where the third-party defendant is present at trial, counsel for defendants should cooperate so as to avoid finger pointing and inconsistencies in an effort to defeat plaintiff's claim. As a practical matter, however, the cooperation can only extend so far as not to prejudice the interests of counsel's client. Risks to the defense theory of each defendant abound. The third-party defendant may assert defenses, call witnesses, or engage in examination of witnesses, that do not fit the trial presentation of the original defendant. The instructions for determination of the third-party claim run the risk of confusing the jury. The most pernicious risk is that a weak liability case is made stronger by defendants adducing evidence and arguing that, if there is liability, it is the responsibility of the other defendant.

There may be some situations where, despite the trial risks, an original defendant is advantaged by having a third-party defendant at trial. For example, if the original defendant has limited resources it may rely on the trial preparation of the third-party defendant. Also, the original defendant might accept the trial risks in exchange for having federal court jurisdiction over its claim against the third-party defendant. Finally, if the nature of the third-party claim or the nature and relationship of the third-party defendant suggest a unified, consistent trial presentation focused on defeating plaintiff's claim, the existence of the third-party defendant gives the defense multiple cross-examinations of plaintiff's witnesses and arguments to the jury.

Library References:

West's Key No. Digests, Federal Civil Procedure ⚷281–297.

Wright, Miller & Kane, Federal Practice and Procedure: Civil 2d §§ 1448–1450, 1462, 1465.

§ 7.3 Procedure for Third–Party Actions

(a) Timing of Claim and Filing of Motion

A defendant may serve a third-party complaint without leave of court if it is done within 10 days after serving the answer in the underlying action.[1] After that time, the defendant must seek leave of court to file a third-party claim.[2] In order to seek leave of court, the

§ 7.3

1. FRCP 14(a).

2. Maineline Industries, Inc. v. Palco Linings, Inc., 113 F.R.D. 148, 150 (D.Nev. 1986) (dismissing third party action filed

third-party plaintiff must file a motion which includes a notice of motion to the plaintiff and must serve a copy of the motion on the plaintiff. A copy of the third-party complaint and the summons should be attached as exhibits to the motion so that the court can consider whether the claim is supported by substantive law.[3] A copy of the motion is not served on the third-party defendant who has no right to notice at this stage and no automatic right to appear at the hearing.[4] If the third-party defendant learns of the motion, however, the court has discretion to allow the third-party defendant to participate in the hearing.[5] Although FRCP 14 does not place an explicit time limit on the filing of a third-party complaint,[6] it is advisable for the defendant to file the third-party complaint as soon as possible after learning that another party may be liable on the underlying claim.[7]

(b) The Third–Party Complaint

Once leave is granted or if it is within 10 days of the time that the defendant filed an answer, the third-party complaint must be filed with the court and a copy of the third-party complaint and summons served on the third-party defendant.[8] All these pleadings must also be served on the plaintiff according to FRCP 5(a).

A proper third-party complaint should be framed as an original complaint. In addition, however, the complaint must indicate that the third-party defendant is or may be liable to the third-party plaintiff for all or part of the original plaintiff's claim.[9] Form 22–A included in the

more than 10 days from service of answer without leave of court). The 10 day period is measured from the date that the first answer is served. Nelson v. Quimby Island Reclamation District Facilities Corp., 491 F.Supp. 1364, 1387 (N.D.Cal.1980). Filing an amended answer does not extend the 10 day time period. *Id.*

3. Maineline Industries, 113 F.R.D. at 150 (proper method if filing third party complaint is to file motion along with copy of third party complaint); Liberty Folder v. Curtiss Anthony Corp., 90 F.R.D. 80, 84 (S.D.Ohio 1981) (the "better practice" is for third party plaintiff to attach summons and complaint to motion).

4. Pantano v. Clark Equip. Co., 139 F.R.D. 40, 42 (S.D.N.Y.1991) (Rule 14 requires notice only to plaintiff not to the third party defendant); Nelson, 491 F.Supp. at 1387 n.48 (leave of court must be obtained in order to protect the right of parties to the main action to a timely disposition of the action, not to protect third parties).

5. Dunning v. Mutual Broadcasting Systems, Inc., 16 Fed. R. Serv. 156, 157

(S.D.N.Y. 1952) (allowing third party defendant to participate in motion for leave to implead). *But see* Pantano, 139 F.R.D. at 42 (disregarding the opposition filed by prospective third party defendant in deciding third party plaintiff's motion for leave to file third party complaint).

6. *See* Dysart v. Marriott Corp., 103 F.R.D. 15, 19 (E.D.Pa.1984) (defendant can file third party complaint until the statute of limitations runs on the claim); *see supra* § 7.2(d).

7. Bambu Sales, Inc. v. Sultana Crackers, Inc., 683 F.Supp. 899, 916 (E.D.N.Y. 1988) (defendant in trademark infringement suit could not implead suppliers of allegedly infringing product more than 9 months after commencement of action where defendants knew the identity of the suppliers at the time the original suit was filed).

8. Maineline Industries, Inc., 113 F.R.D. at 150.

9. Lopez de Robinson v. United States, 162 F.R.D. 256, 258–59 (D.P.R.1995) (discussing pleading requirements under Rule

Appendix to the FRCP provides guidance for the form of a third-party complaint.[10] Although the sample third-party complaint does not include allegations of jurisdictional grounds, it is sound practice to include an allegation of jurisdiction under supplemental, diversity or federal question jurisdiction. A copy of the complaint from the underlying claim should be attached as an exhibit to the third-party complaint, particularly if the third-party complaint incorporates the original complaint.[11]

The general rules of pleading are applicable to third-party complaints. Alternative pleading is allowed, and therefore, a third-party plaintiff may plead inconsistently with the answer it has filed.[12] For example, the third-party plaintiff may deny all liability to the plaintiff in its answer and at the same time allege in its third-party complaint that if it is liable to the plaintiff, the third-party defendant is also liable as a joint tortfeasor.

(c) Joinder of Additional Claims

As long as the third-party plaintiff has asserted a valid third-party complaint, the third-party plaintiff may join any claim against the third-party defendant, as long as it has a jurisdictional basis.[13] These additional claims must be supported either by an independent basis for subject matter jurisdiction or by supplemental jurisdiction.[14] Once a third-party claim has been asserted, all claims arising from the same transaction and occurrence must be joined since these claims will be precluded in a separate action. Potential third-party plaintiffs should consider what additional claims will have to be brought together with the third-party claim since it may be more advantageous to bring all the claims in a separate suit to avoid confusion, or diversion of resources from defense of the underlying claim.

14 in general); Toberman v. Copas, 800 F.Supp. 1239, 1243 (M.D.Pa.1992) (dismissing third party complaint because there were no factual allegations to support claim); Stewart v. American Int'l Oil & Gas Co., 845 F.2d 196, 200–02 (9th Cir.1988) (imposing Rule 11 sanctions where third party complaint did not allege derivative liability, was patently groundless, and was asserted for an improper purpose); Pitcavage v. Mastercraft Boat Co., 632 F.Supp. 842, 845 (M.D.Pa.1985) ("Impleader is not proper when the third party plaintiff alleges only that the third party defendant is solely liable to the plaintiff."); Pennine Resources, Inc. v. Dorwart, Andrew & Co., 639 F.Supp. 1071, 1072–76 (E.D.Pa.1986) (discussing pleading requirements for third party claims for indemnity and contribution under Pennsylvania law).

10. See infra § 7.7(b).

11. Toberman, 800 F.Supp. at 1243 (merely attaching original complaint to third party complaint is not insufficient to incorporate it; third party complaint must reference original complaint by paragraph number).

12. Clark v. Associates Commercial Corp., 149 F.R.D. 629, 634 (D.Kan.1993).

13. United of Omaha Life Ins. Co. v. Reed, 649 F.Supp. 837, 842 (D.Kan.1986) (allowing joinder of claim for misrepresentation with claim for indemnity since additional claim was covered by ancillary jurisdiction); Executive Financial Services v. Heart Chec, Inc., 95 F.R.D. 383, 384 (D.Colo.1982) (allowing third party plaintiff to join claim for negligence with claim for indemnity because negligence claim fell under court's ancillary jurisdiction).

14. United of Omaha Life Ins. Co., 649 F.Supp. at 842 (the court must have subject matter jurisdiction over additional claims).

(d) Appealing an Adverse Decision

In general, rulings on motions concerning impleader are not appealable, because such rulings do not constitute a "final judgment."[15] There are two important exceptions to the final judgment rule: specially certified issues under 28 U.S.C.A. § 1292(b) and entry of a final judgment on fewer than all claims pursuant to FRCP 54(b). Certain admiralty decrees are also appealable under 28 U.S.C.A. § 1292(a)(3).[16] A more detailed discussion of interlocutory appeals and the final judgment rule can be found in Chapter 49 "Appeals to the Court of Appeals," *infra.*

Because there is no immediate appeal from rulings on impleader, all efforts must be directed to persuading the district court of a party's position. For instance, a plaintiff cannot appeal an adverse ruling allowing a third-party defendant to be impled. Similarly, the third-party defendant cannot appeal an order impleading it or denying its motion to dismiss. Furthermore, if the main claim or the third-party claim is dismissed or resolved while the other is still pending, there is no final judgment to appeal until the entire case is disposed of or a FRCP 54(b) certification is made.[17]

Library References:

West's Key No. Digests, Federal Civil Procedure ⚮281–297.
Wright, Miller & Kane, Federal Practice and Procedure: Civil 2d §§ 1453–1458, 1463.

§ 7.4   Options and Rights of Third–Party Defendant

(a) Opposing the Motion

A third-party defendant does not have a right to notice of or to participate in the hearing regarding the third-party plaintiff's motion for leave to assert a third-party claim.[1] However, once the third-party complaint has been served, the third-party defendant has a number of options for opposing the third-party complaint. The third-party defendant may move to strike the complaint, to vacate the order granting

---

15. State of Minn. v. Pickands Mather & Co., 636 F.2d 251, 252–255 (8th Cir.1980) (holding that appeals court had no jurisdiction to entertain an appeal from an order of the district court denying a party leave to file a third party complaint); Thompson v. American Airlines, Inc., 422 F.2d 350, 351 (5th Cir.1970) (while trial court has it within its power to reconsider dismissal of impleader until whole case is disposed of, appeals court is without jurisdiction for want of an appealable order).

16. "[T]he courts of appeals shall have jurisdiction of appeals from ... (3) Interlocutory decrees of such district courts or the judges thereof determining the rights and liabilities of the parties to admiralty cases

in which appeals from final decrees are allowed." 28 U.S.C.A. § 1292(a)(3) (West 1993).

17. *In re* Yarn Processing Patent Validity Litig., 680 F.2d 1338, 1340 (11th Cir. 1982) (finding lack of jurisdiction to consider appeal where district court dismissed third party complaints with prejudice but failed to enter a Rule 54(b) certification making an express determination that there was no just reason to delay).

§ 7.4

1. Pantano v. Clark Equipment Co., 139 F.R.D. 40, 42 (S.D.N.Y.1991).

leave to file the complaint, or to dismiss the complaint under FRCP 12(b)(6). A motion to strike is most appropriately used to object to a third-party complaint which has been filed without leave of court after the 10 day period has expired. A motion to vacate the order typically is used to object to the exercise of the court's discretion in granting leave to implead.[2] For example, the party bringing a motion to vacate might argue that adding the third-party defendant would unduly complicate the suit, or unfairly prejudice the third-party defendant (*e.g.*, insufficient time to prepare for trial; nonparticipation in completed discovery; etc.). A motion to dismiss is the most appropriate type of motion to challenge the substance of the claim. For example, a party opposing impleader might argue in a motion to dismiss that the claim was not a proper third-party claim because the third-party defendant's liability was not derivative of the third-party plaintiff's liability.[3] Nevertheless, the form of the motion is not determinative[4] and using one form over another does not necessarily provide a strategic advantage. Courts will treat such motions according to their substance rather than their form.

More important than the form of the motion is the timeliness of the motion. Rule 14 does not provide a time limit for filing a motion to strike or to vacate, but third-party defendants should make this motion as soon as possible. For example, in *United States v. Costa*, the court found that a motion to vacate was untimely where it was filed after the third-party defendant had filed an answer and requests for admissions.[5]

As an alternative to the motions to strike, vacate, or dismiss, the third-party defendant may also move to sever its claim from the underlying action for a separate trial under FRCP 42(b). The effect of a motion to sever or for a separate trial will be to continue discovery of all claims jointly but to separate the trials of the underlying and third-party claim. This option may be beneficial to a third-party defendant who wishes to preserve the economy of joint discovery but to avoid finger pointing between the defendant and the third-party defendant at trial.

(b) Filing an Answer

A third-party defendant must answer the third-party complaint like any other defendant. FRCP 14 makes it explicit that the third-party defendant shall assert all counterclaims and cross-claims according to FRCP 13.[6] Thus, the third-party defendant must assert all compulsory counterclaims in the answer, as well as any affirmative defenses.

2. 6 Charles Alan Wright, Arthur R. Miller & Mary Kay Kane, Federal Practice and Procedure § 1460 (2d ed. 1990).

3. *See supra* § 7.2(d) (factors guiding the court's decision regarding leave to implead).

4. *See, e.g.*, Rosalis v. Universal Distributors, Inc., 21 F.R.D. 169, 172 (D.Conn. 1957) (treating motion to dismiss as a motion to vacate order); United States v. Costa, 11 F.R.D. 492, 494 (W.D.Pa.1951) (treating motion for summary judgment as motion to vacate and to strike).

5. Costa, 11 F.R.D. 492, 495 (motion to strike was untimely where it was filed after third party defendant had filed answers and requests for admissions).

6. Nordale, Inc. v. Samsco, Inc., 154 F.R.D. 232, 233 (D.Minn.1994) (allowing third party defendants, as principals of cor-

A third-party defendant may also assert any defenses the third-party plaintiff has to the underlying action but did not assert.[7] This may be done either in the third-party defendant's answer[8] or in a separate answer to the original plaintiff.[9] Allowing the third-party defendant to assert these defenses protects the third-party defendant from the risk that the third-party plaintiff will not competently defend on the underlying claim.[10] Constitutional requirements of due process necessitate this rule since the third-party defendant is bound by the judgment in the underlying action.[11] The rule also reduces the ability of a third-party plaintiff to collude with the original plaintiff against the third-party defendant.[12] Once the third-party defendant asserts the third-party plaintiff's defenses, the third-party defendant is considered an adverse party to the plaintiff and may serve discovery requests on the plaintiff with respect to those defenses.[13] Because the third-party defendant will be bound by the outcome of the suit between the plaintiff and the third-party plaintiff, the third-party defendant should assert any defenses that the third-party plaintiff has neglected to assert.

The right to assert the third-party plaintiff's defenses includes the right to move for dismissal or for summary judgment on plaintiff's claim against the defendant.[14] There are some limitations, however, on which defenses the third-party defendant can assert. A third-party defendant cannot assert the third-party plaintiff's personal defenses such as personal jurisdiction, service of process or venue.[15] Nor can a third-party defendant assert any defense which has been litigated and lost by the third-party plaintiff.[16]

poration, to bring counterclaim against third party plaintiff even though they could not bring the claim as plaintiffs and shareholders of the corporation).

7. Oyster v. Bell Asbestos Mines, 568 F.Supp. 80, 82 (E.D.Pa.1983) (allowing third party defendant's motion to disqualify plaintiff's attorney for conflict of interest); Commercial Credit Dev. Corp. v. Scottish Inns of America, Inc., 69 F.R.D. 110, 113 (E.D.Tenn.1975) (third party defendants may assert against plaintiff any defenses which third party plaintiff has on underlying claim).

8. Carey v. Schuldt, 42 F.R.D. 390, 394 (E.D.La.1967) ("The answer to the third party complaint is the most logical place in which to raise the defenses.").

9. M.V.M. v. St. Paul Fire & Marine Ins. Co., 20 F.R.D. 296, 297 (S.D.N.Y.1957) (requiring defenses to be asserted).

10. Kansas Public Employees Retirement System v. Reimer & Koger Associates, Inc., 4 F.3d 614, 619 (8th Cir.1993), *cert. denied*, 511 U.S. 1126, 114 S.Ct. 2132, 128 L.Ed.2d 862 (1994).

11. 14 James W. Moore et al., Moore's Federal Practice § 14.25 (3d ed. 1997); 6 Charles Alan Wright, Arthur R. Miller & Mary Kay Kane, Federal Practice and Procedure § 1457 (2d ed. 1990).

12. Kansas Public Employees Retirement System, 4 F.3d at 619.

13. Schonberger v. Blumenkranz of Lakewood, New Jersey, Inc., 23 F.R.D. 16, 16 (D.N.J.1958) (manufacturer and distributor impled as third party defendants could propound interrogatories to plaintiff where third party defendants asserted defenses of contributory negligence and assumption of the risk against plaintiff); Pettus v. Grace Line, Inc., 166 F.Supp. 463, 464–65 (E.D.N.Y.1958) (a third party defendant may propound interrogatories to plaintiff if the third party defendant has asserted the third party plaintiff's defenses against the original plaintiff).

14. *In re* Phar–Mor, Inc. Securities Litigation, 900 F.Supp. 784, 785 n. 1 (W.D.Pa. 1995).

15. *E.g.*, Brandt v. Olson, 179 F.Supp. 363, 372–73 (N.D.Iowa).

(c) Claims Against Plaintiff

In addition to asserting any cross-claims against co-defendants and counterclaims against the third-party plaintiff, a third-party defendant may also assert a claim against the original plaintiff.[17] FRCP 14(a) allows the third-party defendant to assert "any claim against the plaintiff arising out of the transaction or occurrence that is the subject matter of the plaintiff's claim." Since the claim must arise from the same transaction or occurrence, it falls under supplemental jurisdiction and will not require an independent basis of subject matter jurisdiction. As is discussed in Section 7.5(b), *infra*, the original plaintiff has a corresponding right to assert a claim against the third-party defendant.

An important difference between a third-party claim and a claim asserted by the third-party defendant against a plaintiff is that the claim asserted by the third-party defendant must be a mature claim. Unlike the provision of FRCP 14(a) for third-party claims, the provision of FRCP 14(a) governing claims against the plaintiff does not allow the third-party defendant to assert a claim if the plaintiff "may be liable" to the third-party defendant.[18] As at least one circuit court has held, a claim against the plaintiff asserted by the third-party defendant, unlike a third-party claim, must have accrued.[19]

FRCP 14 does not provide a time limit for the assertion of these claims and does not require leave of court before filing such a claim. Once a third-party defendant has asserted a claim against the plaintiff, the third-party defendant may join any other claims against the plaintiff which have a jurisdictional basis.

(d) Asserting a Fourth–Party Claim

FRCP 14(a) provides that a third-party defendant may implead another person not a party to the action who is or may be liable to it for some or all of the claims asserted against the third-party defendant. This party is called a fourth-party defendant.[20] The fourth-party similarly may implead a fifth-party defendant.[21]

(e) Trial and Discovery

In general, a third-party defendant has the same right to discovery as any other party.[22] Third-party defendants may participate in the trial

---

16. Casey v. United States, 635 F.Supp. 221, 225 (D.Mass.1986).

17. Finkle v. Gulf & Western Manufacturing Co., 744 F.2d 1015, 1017 (3d Cir. 1984).

18. FRCP 14(a).

19. Stahl v. Ohio River Co., 424 F.2d 52, 55–56 (3d Cir.1970).

20. Dysart v. Marriott Corp., 103 F.R.D. 15, 17 (E.D.Pa.1984) (third party defendant allowed to implead a fourth party).

21. Bevemet Metais, Ltd. v. Gallie Corp., 3 F.R.D. 352, 353 (S.D.N.Y.1942) (allowing impleader of fifth and sixth-party defendants).

by examining witnesses with as broad a scope of cross-examination as is sanctioned by the rules of evidence.[23] Such broad rights do not come without cost, however; parties should be aware of the potential for a preclusive effect in future actions. Indeed, one court has precluded a third-party defendant from disputing the authenticity of exhibits accepted by the defendant.[24]

Occasionally, courts have limited a third-party defendant's right to discovery where the delay would be prejudicial to the original plaintiff.[25] However this scenario is rare due to the prejudice it would cause to third parties. In most cases, if discovery by the third-party defendant will render the case unmanageable, the court will simply deny the motion to implead.[26]

Library References:

West's Key No. Digests, Federal Civil Procedure ⊙281–297.
Wright, Miller & Kane, Federal Practice and Procedure: Civil 2d §§ 1455–1458, 1461, 1463.

§ 7.5   Options for Original Plaintiff

(a) Opposing the Motion

The original plaintiff may oppose the third-party plaintiff's motion for leave to file a third-party complaint or, if a third-party complaint has been filed, may move to strike or to dismiss the third-party complaint or to vacate the order granting leave to implead.[1] Alternatively, the original plaintiff may move for a separate trial or for severance under FRCP 42(b). In opposing the third-party complaint, the plaintiff may argue that the third-party complaint will prejudice the plaintiff or unduly complicate the suit. Alternatively, the plaintiff may challenge the substantive basis for the third-party claim.[2]

22. Oyster v. Bell Asbestos Mines, 568 F.Supp. 80, 82 (E.D.Pa.1983) ("Third party defendants are entitled to fully participate in, and defend themselves during, the trial of plaintiff's claims.").

23. Wiggins v. City of Philadelphia, 331 F.2d 521, 529 (3d Cir.1964) (affirming trial court permitting third party defendant Philadelphia Transportation Company to cross-examine plaintiff accident victim's witness).

24. Glick v. White Motor Co., 458 F.2d 1287, 1291–93 (3d Cir.1972) (holding that where defendant truck manufacturer in a personal injury suit accepted authenticity of exhibits allegedly cut from defective truck spring manufactured by third party defendant, third party defendant could not dispute the exhibit's authenticity on an appeal prosecuted on behalf of defendant).

25. Jean–Marie v. Wheels Inc., 1992 WL 358794, at *1 (S.D.N.Y.1992) (where discovery was near completion in principal case, requiring third party plaintiff automobile driver to expedite and limit discovery from third party defendant's car owner and driver in the interest of fairness).

26. Gross v. Hanover Ins. Co., 138 F.R.D. 53, 56 (S.D.N.Y.1991) (allowing third party plaintiff insurer to implead jewelry store owner and employee without any discovery restrictions in part because it was plaintiff who recently served an amended complaint thus expanding the scope of the action and discovery process).

§ 7.5

1. *See supra* § 7.4(a) (discussing the differences between the motions).

Although a third-party complaint may be dismissed for any of the reasons discussed in Section 7.2(a)-(d), *supra*, some arguments are more persuasive than others. If the court finds that the plaintiff's objections to the third-party claim can be overcome by severing the claim or by ordering a separate trial, the court may do so instead of ordering dismissal of the claim. This may happen where the plaintiff objects that the third-party claim will complicate the trial or confuse the jury. A separate trial may also be ordered where the plaintiff objects that the tardiness of the third-party complaint will delay trial in the original action. If the plaintiff can demonstrate that the third-party claim is not meritorious or that the third-party defendant's liability is not derivative of the third-party plaintiff's liability, the court will be more likely to dismiss the third-party claim rather than to sever it. Nevertheless, severance or a separate trial may still be advantageous to a plaintiff because it will prevent the defendants from mounting a united defense against the plaintiff at trial.

(b) Asserting a Claim Against the Third–Party Defendant

The original plaintiff may assert against the third-party defendant a claim arising from the same transaction or occurrence as the underlying action. The plaintiff may assert this claim regardless of whether the third-party defendant asserts a claim against the plaintiff.[3] The claim may be asserted by either serving a complaint on the third-party defendant[4] or by filing an amended complaint.[5] FRCP 14 does not require that the plaintiff seek leave of court to file the claim against the third-party defendant,[6] although if the plaintiff asserts the claim through an amended complaint it will need to seek leave of court pursuant to FRCP 15(a).[7] There is no time limit for filing this claim,[8] but it is advisable to file this claim as soon as possible to avoid dismissal for violation of deadlines for completion of pleadings and to avoid arguments that the claim is untimely or is barred by laches. The plaintiff may even choose to file the claim before the third-party defendant has served an answer to the third-party complaint.[9]

---

2. *See supra* § 7.2(d) (discussing the basis for the court's decision to allow impleader).

3. *E.g.*, State Mutual Life Assurance Company of America v. Arthur Andersen & Co., 581 F.2d 1045, 1047 (2d Cir.1978).

4. Straub v. Desa Industries, Inc., 88 F.R.D. 6, 9 (M.D.Pa.1980) (allowing claim to be asserted in separate complaint but suggesting that amended complaint is preferred).

5. Martin v. Lociccero, 917 F.Supp. 178, 183 (W.D.N.Y.1995) (Rule 14 does not discuss the procedure for a plaintiff to bring a claim against a third party defendant, but

usually it is accomplished by amending the original complaint).

6. Dysart v. Marriott Corp., 103 F.R.D. 15, 17 (E.D.Pa.1984).

7. *E.g.*, Martin, 917 F.Supp. at 183. *See* discussion of amendment of complaint in Chapter 5 "The Complaint," at § 5.5, *supra.*

8. Dysart, 103 F.R.D. at 18 (Rule 14 does not provide a time limit for plaintiff to file a claim against a third party defendant; plaintiff may file a claim anytime before statute of limitations runs).

9. Sklar v. Hayes, 1 F.R.D. 594, 596 (E.D.Pa.1941).

Unlike claims by a third-party defendant against a plaintiff which are covered by supplemental jurisdiction, claims by the plaintiff against the third-party defendant are not necessarily covered by supplemental jurisdiction. As was discussed in Section 7.2(c), *supra,* supplemental jurisdiction does not apply to claims by the plaintiff against the third-party defendant when the underlying action is based on diversity of citizenship. In these cases, the plaintiff will not be able to assert a claim against a third-party defendant unless there is an independent basis for jurisdiction.

Once the plaintiff asserts a claim against the third-party defendant, the third-party defendant is aligned with the third-party plaintiff as a co-defendant. The third-party defendant may then assert cross-claims against the third-party plaintiff.[10]

(c) Asserting a Third–Party Claim on a Counterclaim or on a Claim by the Third–Party Defendant

Rule 14(b) explicitly allows a plaintiff to assert a third-party claim on a counterclaim asserted against the plaintiff. Either the original defendant or a third-party defendant may assert a counterclaim against the plaintiff. By its terms, FRCP 14(b) applies only to third-party claims asserted on *counterclaims* against the plaintiff, and does not apply to the situation when the third-party defendant asserts a claim directly against the plaintiff. The more general language of FRCP 14(a) covers this situation because it authorizes "any defending party" to assert a third-party claim. As a party defending against a claim by the third-party defendant, the plaintiff qualifies to assert a third-party claim in this situation as well.

Library References:

West's Key No. Digests, Federal Civil Procedure ☞281–297.
Wright, Miller & Kane, Federal Practice and Procedure: Civil 2d §§ 1459, 1464.

§ 7.6 Procedural Checklist

(a) Asserting a Third–Party Complaint

(1) In order to assert a third-party claim more than 10 days after the time that an answer is served, the third-party plaintiff must file a motion for leave to implead. For the court's convenience the third-party complaint and summons should be attached as exhibits. The third-party plaintiff must serve the motion along with notice of the motion on the plaintiff. (FRCP 14(a); *See* § 7.3).

(2) If the motion for leave to file the third-party complaint is granted or if it is within 10 days from the day that the answer was served, the third-party plaintiff must file the third-party complaint with the clerk who then issues a third-party summons. Unless the

---

10. FRCP 14(a).

underlying claim is based in admiralty law, the third-party complaint must aver that the third-party defendant is or may be liable to the third-party plaintiff for some or all of the third-party plaintiff's liability to the original plaintiff. If the original claim is an admiralty claim, the complaint must allege the third-party defendant's derivative liability to the third-party plaintiff *or* the third-party defendant's liability directly to the plaintiff. Jurisdictional grounds need not be alleged, although it is good practice to do so. A copy of the original complaint should be attached as an exhibit to the third-party complaint. (*See* § 7.3).

(3) The third-party complaint must be served on the third-party defendant according to the law of the forum state, the law of the state of service, or under the bulge rule. Under the bulge rule, the third-party defendant may be served within 100 miles of the court where the summons was issued, as long as it is within the same judicial district. A copy of the third-party complaint must also be served on the original plaintiff according to FRCP 5(a). (*See* FRCP 4(k), 5(a); §§ 7.2(b), 7.3).

(b) Third–Party Defendant's Response

(1) The third-party defendant must file and serve on the third-party plaintiff and the original plaintiff an answer, a motion to dismiss under FRCP 12(b), a motion to strike the third-party complaint or to vacate the order granting leave to implead, or a motion for a more definite statement within 20 days of service, unless service was waived and the longer time limits apply according to FRCP 12(a)(1)(B). When service has been waived, the third-party defendant will have 60 days to respond or 90 days if the third-party defendant received the request for waiver outside of a judicial district of the United States. If the third-party defendant's motion is denied, the third-party defendant has 10 days in which to file an answer. (*See* FRCP 12, 14(a); § 7.4).

(2) The third-party defendant must assert all compulsory counterclaims and cross-claims and all defenses in its answer. The third-party defendant may also assert any defense which the third-party plaintiff has against the original plaintiff, except that the third-party defendant may not assert the defenses of lack of personal jurisdiction, improper process, or improper service of process on the third-party plaintiff's behalf. The third-party defendant may assert the third-party plaintiff's defenses either in its answer to the third-party complaint or in a separate answer to the plaintiff's complaint. (*See* FRCP 14(a); § 7.4).

(3) To assert a claim against the plaintiff, the third-party defendant must serve a complaint and summons on the plaintiff and serve a copy on the third-party plaintiff. The claim must arise from the same transaction or occurrence as the underlying claim. Additional claims against the plaintiff may be joined as long as the court has

subject matter jurisdiction over them. (*See* FRCP 5(a), 14(a) 18(a); §§ 7.4(c), 7.3(c)).

(c) Plaintiff's Response

(1) The plaintiff may oppose the third-party plaintiff's motion for leave to file a third-party complaint. The plaintiff may also file a motion to strike or to dismiss the third-party complaint or to sever the third-party claim. These motions should explain how impleader will prejudice the plaintiff or why the third-party complaint lacks merit. For example, plaintiff may argue that the third-party plaintiff was dilatory in asserting the third-party claim and that the delay will prejudice the plaintiff. (*See* FRCP 14(a); § 7.5(a)).

(2) The plaintiff may assert a claim directly against the third-party defendant, regardless of whether the third-party defendant asserts a claim against the plaintiff. The Rule does not provide a time limit for filing such a claim, but the plaintiff should assert the claim as soon as possible to avoid dismissal of the claim as untimely or barred by laches. The plaintiff may assert this claim by serving a new complaint on the third-party defendant. If, however, the court in its discretion has imposed a time limit for the filing of such a claim, the plaintiff will have to seek leave of court to file an amended complaint which includes the claim against the third-party defendant. (*See* FRCP 14(a), 15(a); § 7.5(b)).

§ 7.7 Forms

The Federal Rules of Civil Procedure provide example forms in the Appendix.[1] These forms are reprinted below.

(a) Motion—Form 22–B

UNITED STATES DISTRICT COURT FOR THE
SOUTHERN DISTRICT OF NEW YORK

Civil Action, File Number _____

A. B., Plaintiff,)	
)	
v.)	
)	MOTION TO BRING IN
C. D., Defendant and)	THIRD–PARTY DEFENDANT
Third–Party Plaintiff,)	
)	
v.)	
)	
E. F., Third–Party Defendant.)	

§ 7.7

1. Federal Civil Judicial Procedure and Rules 277–78 (1997 ed.).

Defendant moves for leave, as third-party plaintiff, to cause to be served upon E. F. a summons and third-party complaint, copies of which are hereto attached as Exhibit X.

Signed: _____
Attorney for Defendant C. D.

Address: _____

NOTICE OF MOTION

To: _____
(Attorney for Plaintiff)

Address: _____

_____

Please take notice that the undersigned will bring the above motion on hearing before this Court at Room _____, United States Court House, Foley Square, City of New York, on the ___ day of _____, 19__, at 10:00 o'clock in the forenoon of that day or as soon thereafter as counsel can be heard.

Signed: _____
(Attorney for Defendant)

Address: _____

_____

(b) Complaint—Form 22–A

UNITED STATES DISTRICT COURT FOR THE
SOUTHERN DISTRICT OF NEW YORK

Civil Action, File Number _____

A. B., Plaintiff,	)	
	)	
v.	)	
	)	THIRD–PARTY COMPLAINT
C. D., Defendant and	)	
Third–Party Plaintiff,	)	
	)	
v.	)	
	)	
E. F., Third–Party Defendant.	)	

1. Plaintiff A. B. has filed against defendant C. D. a complaint, a copy of which is hereto attached as "Exhibit A."

2. [Here state the grounds upon which C. D. is entitled to recover from E. F., all or part of what A. B. may recover from C. D. The statement should be framed as in an original complaint.]

WHEREFORE C.D. demands judgment against third-party defendant E. F. for all sums[2] that may be adjudged against defendant C. D. in favor of plaintiff A. B.

Signed:_____

Attorney for C. D., Third–Party Plaintiff

Address:_____

_____

(c) Summons—Form 22–A

UNITED STATES DISTRICT COURT FOR THE
SOUTHERN DISTRICT OF NEW YORK

Civil Action, File Number _____

A. B., Plaintiff,	)	
	)	
v.	)	
	)	SUMMONS
C. D., Defendant and	)	
Third–Party Plaintiff,	)	
	)	
v.	)	
	)	
E. F., Third–Party Defendant.	)	

To the above-named third-party Defendant:

You are hereby summoned and required to serve upon _____, plaintiff's attorney whose address is _____, and upon _____, who is attorney for C. D., defendant and third-party plaintiff, and whose address is _____, an answer to the third-party complaint which is herewith served upon you within 20 days after the service of this summons upon you exclusive of the day of service. If you fail to do so, judgment by default will be taken against you for the relief demanded in the third-party complaint. There is also served upon you herewith a copy of the complaint of the plaintiff which you may but are not required to answer.

_____

Clerk of Court

[Seal of District Court]
Dated: _____

2. Make appropriate change where C. D. is entitled to only partial recovery-over against E. F.

CHAPTER 8

REMOVAL TO FEDERAL COURT

by

The Honorable Roger Vinson*

Table of Sections

* The author would like to express his appreciation to his law clerks, Roland Hall and David King for their assistance in the preparation of this chapter.

---

§ 8.1 Scope Note

The removal of a state court action to federal court and the remand of an action already removed are matters that normally arise early in the litigation of a case. This chapter addresses the requirements for removal jurisdiction and the procedures for removing an action from state court, as well as the grounds and procedures for seeking remand of a removed case. It also deals with issues relating to appellate review of orders involving removal and remand.[1]

Since plaintiffs choose where to file the complaint, the defendants are the parties seeking removal in most situations. Likewise, plaintiffs are the parties who generally are seeking to have a removed case remanded back to state court. This chapter examines the removal issues first, and then the remand issues, since this will be the natural progression of the litigation.

Library References:

West's Key No. Digests, Removal of Cases ⚖1–120.
Wright, Miller, Kane & Cooper, Federal Practice and Procedure: Civil 2d §§ 1149, 1824, 3674, 3721–3740, 3914.11.

§ 8.2 Strategy, Objectives, and Preliminary Considerations

An understanding of the requirements and procedures for removal of a state court action to federal court is essential for the commercial litigator. Likewise, the grounds and procedural requirements for remand back to state court are very important in commercial litigation.

As a first step, the defense attorney contemplating removal must decide whether removal to federal court is in the best interests of the client. The decision must be based not only on the fundamental differences between federal and state court, but on a consideration of the nature of the case and on the individual characteristics of the courts in question. General factors favoring removal to federal court include:

§ 8.1

1. Since the federal court must have original jurisdiction over the action in order for a defendant to be entitled to remove it from state court, issues of subject matter jurisdiction invariably arise in the removal context. For example, removal based on diversity of citizenship under 28 U.S.C.A. § 1332 (West 1993 & Supp. 1997) requires that the parties be of diverse citizenship and that the amount in controversy exceed $75,000 exclusive of interest and costs. The determination of the parties' citizenship, as well as other issues of subject matter jurisdiction, are covered at length in Chapter 1 "Subject Matter Jurisdiction," *supra*. Therefore, such jurisdictional issues will be addressed in this chapter only when doing so is relevant to the discussion of removal and remand.

(1) Federal judges are generally considered to be more knowledgeable concerning complex cases, or cases in which federal issues predominate;

(2) Federal judges are generally less subject to local political considerations;

(3) Federal judges have excellent law clerks and support staff to assist in complex or lengthy litigation;

(4) Federal juries may be more desirable in your geographic location;

(5) The possibility exists in federal court of subsequently moving the case to the district court of a different state through a motion to transfer venue, or a transfer to a multidistrict litigation ("MDL") court;

(6) Removal itself may have a tactical value in inducing a settlement; especially with some types of cases or when the plaintiff's lawyer is not as familiar with federal practice;

(7) Summary judgments or other pretrial dispositions may be more likely in federal courts; and

(8) There may be practices or procedures utilized by the federal court which may benefit your client in a particular case.

Factors favoring the use of state court include:

(1) State courts may have fewer procedural requirements prior to trial;

(2) State courts may be more knowledgeable where the controlling question in the case is one of state law;

(3) State court juries are generally viewed as more favorable to plaintiffs in many locations;

(4) Attorneys are generally allowed to voir dire the jury panel in state court, which may help your trial tactics;

(5) Transfer of the case to another state is much less likely; and

(6) Local policies and practices in the state court may benefit your client in a particular case.

Other factors depend on the nature of the case and the locality of the courts in question, and include:

(1) The relative congestion of the civil trial dockets of state and federal courts;

(2) The differing use by state and federal courts of mandatory or optional alternative dispute resolution procedures;

(3) The scope of discovery procedures available in each court;

(4) Differences between federal and state rules of evidence;

(5) The difference in verdicts awarded by each court;

(6) The available jury pool and differences in procedures for voir dire, or the differences in the size of the jury normally selected in civil trials;

(7) The desirability of being in the state or federal appellate court if the case is a likely candidate for appeal;

(8) The availability in some state courts of interlocutory appeals not available in federal courts; and

(9) Possible differences in standards of review between federal and state appellate courts.

Because the plaintiff is the master of the complaint, the plaintiff may attempt to avoid removal by seeking damages less than the jurisdictional amount in cases potentially removable on grounds of diversity, or by exclusively pleading state law claims in cases where diversity jurisdiction does not appear to be a possibility. The plaintiff has further options once the case is removed. In cases removed on the basis of diversity jurisdiction, the plaintiff can join nondiverse defendants and seek remand. While fraudulent joinder solely for the purpose of remand will not defeat removal jurisdiction, the burden of establishing fraudulent joinder is on the defendant. If the plaintiff has not sought a specific amount of damages in the initial complaint, the plaintiff can attempt to amend the complaint to limit damages to below the jurisdictional amount. The plaintiff could also assign a portion of the recovery to a nondiverse person; however, the court will inquire whether the purpose of the assignment is solely to defeat removal jurisdiction.

Because diversity cases cannot be removed to federal court more than one year after the commencement of action in state court, the plaintiff could use tactics such as joining a nondiverse defendant and dismissing the defendant after the expiration of the year period, or pleading less than the jurisdictional amount and later amending the complaint to seek higher damages. However, judges have grown skeptical of such manipulative tactics in connection with the one-year requirement, and several courts have applied equitable considerations in such cases to estop a plaintiff contesting removal from arguing that removal is untimely.

The defendant seeking grounds for removal must pay careful attention to statutory time limits, since the removal notice must be filed within 30 days of the notice of the lawsuit through service or otherwise or within 30 days of notice of an amended pleading or discovery that provides a basis for removal. Failure to timely remove will result in waiver of the removal right. Where multiple defendants are involved, the defendant seeking removal must ensure that consent is obtained from all defendants within the time limit and that the required notices are given.

Defendants should be on the alert for state law causes of action that are completely preempted by federal statutory schemes, since in some

426

cases, federal preemption provides a ground for removal despite the apparent absence of a federal question in the complaint. In multiple defendant cases where complete diversity does not exist, the diverse defendant seeking removal should carefully examine all claims against nondiverse defendants, since, for purposes of determining diversity, the existence of nominal, sham, and fraudulently joined defendants is disregarded. If nondiverse defendants are actually adverse to the defendant, rather than to the plaintiff, the defendant could remove the case and seek re-alignment of the parties to achieve complete diversity.

Defendants should also carefully examine demand letters or other correspondence or documents to see if such materials provide a basis for the amount in controversy in federal jurisdiction. Also, correspondence, answers to interrogatories, or admissions may trigger the 30–day time period for filing the notice of removal. Where the plaintiff seeks unspecified damages, or damages below the jurisdictional amount, the defendant may seek removal upon a good faith belief that damages actually meet the jurisdictional requirement; however, since the burden of proof is on the defendant, the defendant must be prepared to present evidence of the plaintiff's damages. Where the defendant is required to establish that the plaintiff's damages claim is greater than $75,000, the defendant must consider the risks involved in attempting to show that the plaintiff suffered damages in excess of the amount requested. If the defendant elects to do so, the defendant can present evidence as to the severity of the plaintiff's injury or loss, and can refer to damages awards in other similar cases. Where multiple plaintiffs are involved, the defendant may be able to aggregate the plaintiffs' damages for purposes of meeting the jurisdictional amount, depending upon the claims involved.

Once the defendant files a notice of removal, the plaintiff seeking remand must be careful to follow all procedural requirements, since failure to file the motion to remand within the 30–day time period can result in the waiver of procedural defects in the notice of removal. Where the action is based on a contract between the parties, the plaintiff should determine whether the defendant has contractually waived its right to remove the case. In addition, the plaintiff might have good grounds for remand where the defendant took substantial action in state court, such as filing a motion to dismiss or a permissive counterclaim. The plaintiff should also determine whether the notice of removal alleges with particularity the necessary facts to support federal jurisdiction, and whether the notice provides factual support for claims that defendants were fraudulently joined or damages are in excess of the jurisdictional amount.

Library References:

West's Key No. Digests, Removal of Cases ⟸1–120.
Wright, Miller & Cooper, Federal Practice and Procedure: Civil 2d §§ 1149, 3674.

§ 8.3 Removal Jurisdiction

(a) In General

(1) Historical Background and Reasons for Removal Jurisdiction

The removal of cases from state to federal courts is not referenced in the Constitution of the United States, and is purely statutory in nature. Removal jurisdiction was first established by the Judiciary Act of 1789,[1] and the authority of Congress to authorize removal has been recognized repeatedly by the Supreme Court of the United States.[2] Because the first removal statute gave limited rights of removal to aliens and nonresident defendants, it appears certain that the original purpose of the right of removal in diversity cases was to protect out of state residents from local prejudices of state courts. As to removal in federal question cases, it is also obvious that the purpose was to have questions of federal law presented to the system of courts more familiar with such issues.

The original removal statute was gradually expanded until, by 1875, virtually all cases within the constitutional jurisdiction of federal courts could be removed by either party.[3] The power of removal was narrowed by the Judiciary Act of 1887, which raised the jurisdictional amount and limited the right of removal to defendants.[4] The 1887 statute is the basis for the present removal statute.[5]

(2) Differences Between Original and Removal Jurisdiction

Removal jurisdiction is fundamentally different from original federal jurisdiction. While removal jurisdiction is created by statute, original federal jurisdiction derives from Section 2 of Article III of the United States Constitution. As a result, federal courts have determined that removal procedures, as creatures of statute, are to be strictly construed, with uncertainties generally resolved in favor of remand to state court.[6]

Removal jurisdiction differs from original federal jurisdiction in other, more specific, ways, which include:

(1) The removal of diversity cases is subject to a one-year time limit;[7]

(2) Unlike original federal jurisdiction, a diversity case cannot be removed if a defendant is a citizen of the state in which the action is brought;[8] and

---

§ 8.3

1. 1 Stat. 73, § 12.

2. *See, e.g.*, Home Life Insurance Co. v. Dunn, 86 U.S. (19 Wall.) 214, 22 L.Ed. 68 (1874); The Mayor of Nashville v. Cooper, 73 U.S. (6 Wall.) 247, 18 L.Ed. 851 (1868).

3. 18 Stat. 470, § 2.

4. 24 Stat. 552, §§ 1 and 2.

5. *See* 14A Charles Alan Wright, Arthur R. Miller & Edward H. Cooper, Federal Practice & Procedure § 3721, at 188 (2d ed. 1985).

6. Shamrock Oil & Gas Corp. v. Sheets, 313 U.S. 100, 108, 61 S.Ct. 868, 872, 85 L.Ed. 1214 (1941); Hurt v. Dow Chem. Co., 963 F.2d 1142, 1144 (8th Cir.1992); Coker v. Amoco Oil Co., 709 F.2d 1433, 1440–41 (11th Cir.1983).

7. 28 U.S.C.A. § 1446(b) (West 1994).

8. 28 U.S.C.A. § 1441(b) (West 1994).

(3) Removal is authorized by statute for specific kinds of actions, some of which would not be within the federal district court's original federal jurisdiction.

(b) Federal Question Jurisdiction

(1) "Federal Question" Defined

By statute, 28 U.S.C.A. § 1441(b) provides the basis for removal jurisdiction over cases involving a federal question. That section provides in relevant part that:

> Any civil action of which the district courts have original jurisdiction founded on a claim or right arising under the Constitution, treaties or laws of the United States shall be removable without regard to the citizenship or residence of the parties.

Whether removal is proper depends upon whether the court has jurisdiction under 28 U.S.C.A. § 1331, which gives federal courts jurisdiction over cases that "arise under the Constitution, laws, or treaties of the United States." Any action in which an issue of federal law is an essential element of the plaintiff's cause of action is a case arising under federal law, even if other questions of law are involved in the case.[9] An action may also arise under federal law if "the vindication of a right under state law necessarily turn[s] on some construction of federal law."[10] In this latter situation, the mere presence of a federal issue in a state cause of action does not automatically confer federal question jurisdiction.[11] For example, while federal jurisdiction exists over a state breach of contract action that requires the interpretation of federal laws and regulations,[12] the mere fact that a state statutory scheme provides that federal law should be used for purposes of interpretation is insufficient to confer jurisdiction.[13] If the action arises under federal law, the case is removable without regard to the citizenship of the parties.[14]

(2) Centrality of Federal Question to Main Claim

To determine whether a claim arises under federal law, courts begin with the "well-pleaded complaint rule." Under that rule, a judicial creation, a cause of action arises under federal law, and removal is proper only if a federal question is presented on the face of the plaintiff's properly pleaded complaint.[15] The presence of a federal question in a

---

9. Franchise Tax Bd. v. Constr. Laborers Vacation Trust, 463 U.S. 1, 8, 103 S.Ct. 2841, 2845, 77 L.Ed.2d 420 (1983); First Nat. Bank of Aberdeen v. Aberdeen Nat. Bank, 627 F.2d 843 (8th Cir.1980).

10. Franchise Tax Bd., 463 U.S. at 8, 103 S.Ct. at 2845.

11. Merrell Dow Pharmaceuticals Inc. v. Thompson, 478 U.S. 804, 813, 106 S.Ct. 3229, 3235, 92 L.Ed.2d 650 (1986).

12. Katz v. Cisneros, 16 F.3d 1204, 1207 (Fed.Cir.1994).

13. Hunneman Real Estate Corp. v. Eastern Middlesex Ass'n of Realtors, Inc., 860 F.Supp. 906, 910 (D.Mass.1994).

14. 28 U.S.C.A. § 1441(b) (West 1994).

15. Metropolitan Life Ins. Co. v. Taylor, 481 U.S. 58, 63, 107 S.Ct. 1542, 1546, 95 L.Ed.2d 55 (1987); Dukes v. U.S. Healthcare, Inc., 57 F.3d 350, 353 (3d Cir.), cert. denied, 516 U.S. 1009, 116 S.Ct. 564, 133 L.Ed.2d 489 (1995).

defendant's responsive pleading is insufficient to warrant removal.[16] Removal is generally improper even if a federal defense, such as preemption, is anticipated in the complaint, and both parties concede that it is the only question truly at issue.[17] Similarly, a federal question in the defendant's counterclaim is insufficient to support removal.[18] These results follow from the policies behind the well-pleaded complaint rule "that the plaintiff is the master of the complaint, that a federal question must appear on the face of the complaint, and that the plaintiff may, by eschewing claims based on federal law, choose to have the cause heard in state court."[19] Of course, the federal law under which a claim arises must be a direct and essential element of the plaintiff's cause of action for a federal question to exist.[20] But there does exist, however, an "independent corollary" to the well-pleaded complaint rule, known as the "complete preemption" doctrine.

(3) Preemption

Where both federal and state remedies are available, the plaintiff's election to proceed exclusively under state law does not give rise to federal jurisdiction.[21] However, the Supreme Court of the United States has recognized an exception to the well-pleaded complaint rule—the so-called "complete preemption" exception—under which Congress "may so completely preempt a particular area that any civil complaint raising this select group of claims is necessarily federal in character."[22] As a result, if the plaintiff's claim falls in the category of cases where federal law has so occupied the field as to extinguish any remedy under state law for the injury alleged by the plaintiff, jurisdiction exists for removal purposes.[23]

Where the plaintiff necessarily has available no legitimate state cause of action, but only a federal claim, the case is removable—even though the complaint does not appear to allege a federal question.[24] Courts have held that the complete preemption doctrine applies only if the federal statute contains civil enforcement provisions whose scope

---

16. Caterpillar Inc. v. Williams, 482 U.S. 386, 398–99, 107 S.Ct. 2425, 2433, 96 L.Ed.2d 318 (1987); Great Northern Ry. Co. v. Alexander, 246 U.S. 276, 281, 38 S.Ct. 237, 239, 62 L.Ed. 713 (1918); Rice v. Panchal, 65 F.3d 637, 639 (7th Cir.1995); Dukes, 57 F.3d at 353.

17. *Id. See also* Lazuka v. Federal Deposit Ins. Corp., 931 F.2d 1530, 1534 (11th Cir.1991); Pena v. Downey Sav. & Loan Ass'n, 929 F.Supp. 1308 (C.D.Cal.1996); Anderson v. Household Finance Corp. of Alabama, 900 F.Supp. 386 (M.D.Ala.1995).

18. Karambelas v. Hughes Aircraft Co., 992 F.2d 971, 974–75 (9th Cir.1993).

19. Caterpillar Inc., 482 U.S. at 398–99, 107 S.Ct. at 2433. *See* Chapter 1 "Subject Matter Jurisdiction" at § 1.6(c), *supra*.

20. *See* Carpenter v. Wichita Falls Ind. Sch. Dist., 44 F.3d 362, 366 (5th Cir.1995); Smith v. Industrial Valley Title Ins. Co., 957 F.2d 90, 92 (3d Cir.), *cert. denied*, 505 U.S. 1221, 112 S.Ct. 3034, 120 L.Ed.2d 903 (1992).

21. *See, e.g.*, Avitts v. Amoco Production Co., 53 F.3d 690, 693 (5th Cir.1995).

22. Metropolitan Life Ins. Co. v. Taylor, 481 U.S. 58, 63–64, 107 S.Ct. 1542, 1546, 95 L.Ed.2d 55 (1987).

23. Glisson v. United States Forest Serv., 55 F.3d 1325, 1328 (7th Cir.1995).

24. Carpenter v. Wichita Falls Ind. School Dist., 44 F.3d 362, 366 (5th Cir. 1995).

includes the plaintiff's state law claim, and a clear indication exists of congressional intent to permit removal, despite the plaintiff's reliance on state law.[25]

Two examples of claims subject to the complete preemption doctrine are certain state causes of action preempted by the Employee Retirement Income Security Act ("ERISA")[26] and the Labor–Management Relations Act ("LMRA").[27] State causes of action for improper handling of employee benefits are preempted by ERISA and are subject to removal, even where the complaint is pleaded as a state breach of contract claim.[28] State law claims based directly on collective bargaining agreements, or that require interpretation of such agreements, are preempted under Section 301 of the Labor Management Relations Act, which gives federal district courts jurisdiction of collective-bargaining contract litigation between employers and labor organizations in industries affecting interstate commerce.[29] Defendants have raised claims of preemption on the basis of numerous other federal statutory schemes.[30]

(4) The Artful Pleading Doctrine

Under the so-called "artful pleading" exception to the well-pleaded complaint rule, where the plaintiff has no legitimate or viable state cause of action, but only a federal claim, the plaintiff may not avoid removal by framing the suit as one arising exclusively under state law.[31] Accordingly, in some situations a federal court may look beyond the face of the complaint to determine whether the plaintiff has disguised a federal claim in terms of state law.[32] Courts have also utilized the doctrine where a plaintiff files his state law claims in state court in an attempt to

25. *See, e.g.,* Schmeling v. NORDAM, 97 F.3d 1336, 1341–42 (10th Cir.1996); Goepel v. Nat'l Postal Mail Handlers Union, 36 F.3d 306, 311–12 (3d Cir.1994), *cert. denied,* 514 U.S. 1063, 115 S.Ct. 1691, 131 L.Ed.2d 555 (1995).

26. 29 U.S.C.A. §§ 1001–1461 (West 1985 Supp.1997).

27. 29 U.S.C.A. §§ 151–157 (West 1973 Supp.1997).

28. Clorox Co. v. U.S. Dist. Ct. For N.D. of California, 779 F.2d 517, 519–21 (9th Cir.1985) (state actions for improper handling of employee benefits completely preempted by ERISA). *See* Chapter 68 "ERISA," *infra.*

29. Caterpillar Inc. v. Williams, 482 U.S. 386, 394–95, 107 S.Ct. 2425, 2430–31, 96 L.Ed.2d 318 (1987); Atchley v. Heritage Cable Vision Assocs., 101 F.3d 495, 498 (7th Cir.1996).

30. *See* Rosciszewski v. Arete Associates, Inc., 1 F.3d 225 (4th Cir.1993) (state law claims preempted by federal Copyright Act would be deemed as having arisen under federal law for purposes of removal); Caudill v. Blue Cross and Blue Shield of North Carolina, 999 F.2d 74 (4th Cir.1993) (plaintiff's suit against administrator of Federal Employees Health Benefits Act health plan seeking coverage was governed by federal common law that displaced state law; federal jurisdiction existed over claim and removal was proper); *compare* Railway Labor Executive Ass'n v. Pittsburgh & Lake Erie R.R. Co., 858 F.2d 936 (3d Cir.1988) (holding that neither the Railway Labor Act nor the Interstate Commerce Act completely preempted plaintiffs' state law fraudulent conveyance claims against railroads and railroad officials).

31. *See, e.g.,* Rains v. Criterion Systems, Inc., 80 F.3d 339 (9th Cir.1996).

32. Burda v. M. Ecker Co., 954 F.2d 434, 438 (7th Cir.1992) (plaintiff's challenge to defendant's withholding of 20 percent of attorney's fees when plaintiff's attorney refused to provide taxpayer identification number was in fact a challenge to federal income tax laws; plaintiff's complaint was removable).

avoid the res judicata effect of a prior federal claim that has been reduced to judgment.[33] However, several courts have held that because the artful pleading doctrine raises difficult issues of state and federal relationships, it should apply only in exceptional circumstances.[34] "[A]n expansive application of this doctrine would allow the artful pleading 'exception' to swallow the well-pleaded complaint rule."[35]

(c) Diversity of Citizenship Jurisdiction

(1) "Diversity" Defined

Section 1441(b) defines the right to remove actions arising under the Constitution, treaties, or laws of the United States, and goes on to provide that "any other such action [of which the district courts have original jurisdiction] shall be removable only if none of the parties in interest properly joined and served as defendants is a citizen of the State in which such action is brought." In general, diversity jurisdiction exists over any civil action in which the amount in controversy exceeds the sum or value of $75,000, exclusive of costs and interest, and the action is between citizens of different states.[36] Diversity jurisdiction exists only where there is complete diversity, which occurs when none of the defendants is a citizen of the same state as any of the plaintiffs.[37]

(2) Determination of Diversity

The basic principles of diversity jurisdiction apply under Section 1441(b), such as the requirement of complete diversity between plaintiffs and defendants and the amount in controversy requirement. Removal jurisdiction over diversity cases is more limited than jurisdiction over diversity cases originally brought in federal court, since removal is permissible only if none of the parties in interest properly joined and served as defendants is a citizen of the state in which the action is filed.[38] The right to remove a state court action to federal court on diversity grounds is statutory in nature, and courts have required strict conformance with the statutory requirements.[39]

For purposes of determining diversity, the existence of nominal, sham, and fraudulently joined defendants is disregarded. Federal courts have not allowed removal to be defeated by the collusive or fraudulent

---

33. *See* Salveson v. Western States Bankcard Ass'n, 731 F.2d 1423, 1429 (9th Cir.1984).

34. *See* Carpenter v. Wichita Falls Ind. Sch. Dist., 44 F.3d 362, 367 n. 3 (5th Cir. 1995); *In re* Agent Orange Product Liability Litig., 996 F.2d 1425, 1430–31 (2d Cir. 1993), *cert. denied*, 510 U.S. 1140, 114 S.Ct. 1125, 127 L.Ed.2d 434 (1994); Salveson v. Western States Bankcard Ass'n, 731 F.2d 1423, 1427 (9th Cir.1984).

35. *In re* County Collector of Winnebago, 96 F.3d 890, 896 (7th Cir.1996).

36. 28 U.S.C.A. § 1332(a) (West 1994).

37. *Id.*; Midlantic Nat'l Bank v. Hansen, 48 F.3d 693, 696 (3d Cir.1995); Fritz v. American Home Shield Corp., 751 F.2d 1152, 1153 (11th Cir.1985).

38. 28 U.S.C.A. § 1441(b) (West 1994); Hurt v. Dow Chem. Co., 963 F.2d 1142, 1144–45 (8th Cir.1992).

39. Somlyo v. J. Lu–Rob Enterprises, Inc., 932 F.2d 1043 (2d Cir.1991); National Indem. Co. v. Hanna, 778 F.Supp. 13 (N.D.Ohio 1991).

joinder of a resident defendant.[40] If no reasonable basis in fact or law supports the claim against the resident defendant, or if the reviewing court finds that the plaintiff has no real intention of prosecuting the action against the resident defendant, joinder is fraudulent and removal is proper.[41] Joinder is fraudulent if, on the face of the state court complaint, no cause of action lies against the resident defendant.[42] For example, in *Anderson v. Home Insurance Company*, the Eighth Circuit Court of Appeals held that where the plaintiff and the defendant insurer were the only parties to the insurance contract, and the complaint stated no claim against the resident defendant insurance agent, the agent was fraudulently joined, and removal was proper.[43]

(3) Time for Making Diversity Determination

For purposes of determining original jurisdiction, diversity is determined on the basis of the parties' citizenship at the time the suit is commenced, but for purposes of removal, diversity must have existed both when the complaint was originally filed and at the time of removal.[44] Because the addition of a nondiverse party after removal may require remand, diversity essentially must be maintained throughout the case.

In an exception to the above principle, a case can become removable where a voluntary act of the plaintiff creates diversity after the filing of the complaint. Such acts may include dismissing the state action against a nondiverse defendant,[45] or moving to another state after the complaint is filed and creating diversity.[46] "The rationale for this rule is that although a defendant should not be allowed to change his domicile after the complaint is filed for the sole purpose of effectuating removal, there is no reason to protect the plaintiff against the adverse consequences of his own voluntary acts."[47] However, a case cannot be removed where the nondiverse defendant is dismissed by order of the state court, since such an act is not a voluntary act by the plaintiff.[48] Similarly, a defendant

---

40. Tapscott v. MS Dealer Service Corp., 77 F.3d 1353 (11th Cir.1996); Tedder v. FMC Corp., 590 F.2d 115, 117 (5th Cir. 1979).

41. Tapscott, 77 F.3d at 1360; Boyer v. Snap–On Tools Corp., 913 F.2d 108, 111 (3d Cir.1990), *cert. denied*, 498 U.S. 1085, 111 S.Ct. 959, 112 L.Ed.2d 1046 (1991); American Dredging Co. v. Atlantic Sea Con, Ltd., 637 F.Supp. 179, 183 (D.N.J.1986).

42. Anderson v. Home Ins. Co., 724 F.2d 82, 84 (8th Cir.1983); Lobato v. Pay Less Drug Stores, 261 F.2d 406, 408–09 (10th Cir.1958) (removal was not defeated when the state court complaint failed to allege facts sufficient to state a claim against the resident defendants).

43. Anderson, 724 F.2d at 84.

44. *See, e.g.,* Knop v. McMahan, 872 F.2d 1132, 1138 (3d Cir.1989).

45. *See* Poulos v. Naas Foods, Inc., 959 F.2d 69 (7th Cir. 1992); Higgins v. E.I. DuPont de Nemours & Co., 863 F.2d 1162, 1166 (4th Cir.1988); Self v. General Motors Corp., 588 F.2d 655 (9th Cir.1978).

46. DeBry v. Transamerica Corp., 601 F.2d 480, 488 (10th Cir.1979).

47. Yarnevic v. Brink's, Inc., 102 F.3d 753 (4th Cir.1996); *see* DeBry v. Transamerica Corp., 601 F.2d 480, 486–87 (10th Cir.1979).

48. *See* Higgins v. E.I. DuPont de Nemours & Co., 863 F.2d 1162, 1166 (4th Cir. 1988).

cannot create diversity for removal purposes by moving to another state after the plaintiff files the original complaint.[49]

(4) Realignment of Parties According to Interest

The plaintiff's alignment of the parties in the complaint is not binding on the federal court considering the defendant's removal petition. The court, if necessary, may realign the parties as plaintiffs and defendants according to their real interests.[50] Different tests have evolved for determining the necessity for realignment. Some courts look to the single, primary purpose of the lawsuit, and then align the parties "in accordance with the primary dispute in the controversy, even where a different, legitimate dispute between the parties supports the original alignment."[51] Other courts have adopted a broader "collision of the interests" test, where courts look for an actual, substantial controversy, or a collision of the interests, "but the conflict may in some cases concern an issue other than the so-called primary issue in dispute."[52] Under the collision of the interests test, courts consider the multiple interests and issues involved in the litigation in deciding whether diversity exists. For example, in *Maryland Casualty Company v. W.R. Grace and Company*, where the plaintiff insurer brought a declaratory judgment action against an asbestos manufacture and its other insurers, and the defendant manufacturer sought realignment of the parties on the ground that all the insurers were adverse to it, the Second Circuit Court of Appeals held that under the collision of the interests test, actual and substantial controversies existed among the insurers preventing realignment.[53] Under either the primary purpose test or the collision of the interests test, courts look beyond the pleadings and arrange the parties according to their positions in the dispute.[54]

(d) Separate and Independent Claims or Causes of Action

(1) In General

Section 1441(c) of Title 28 provides:

Whenever a separate and independent claim or cause of action within the jurisdiction conferred by section 1331 of this title is

---

49. *See, e.g.,* Kilpatrick v. Arrow Co., 425 F.Supp. 1378 (W.D.La.1977).

50. City of Indianapolis v. Chase Nat'l Bank, 314 U.S. 63, 62 S.Ct. 15, 86 L.Ed. 47 (1941); Maryland Cas. Co. v. W.R. Grace and Co., 23 F.3d 617, 622–23 (2d Cir.1993), *cert. denied,* 513 U.S. 1052, 115 S.Ct. 655, 130 L.Ed.2d 559 (1994).

51. United States Fidelity & Guaranty Co. v. Thomas Solvent Co., 955 F.2d 1085, 1089 (6th Cir.1992); Employers Ins. of Wausau v. Crown Cork & Seal Co., 942 F.2d 862, 864 (3d Cir.1991); Continental Airlines, Inc. v. Goodyear Tire & Rubber Co., 819 F.2d 1519, 1523 & n. 2 (9th Cir.1987).

52. Maryland Cas. Co., 23 F.3d at 622; U.S.I. Properties Corp. v. M.D. Constr. Co., 860 F.2d 1, 4–5 (1st Cir.1988), *cert. denied,* 490 U.S. 1065, 109 S.Ct. 2064, 104 L.Ed.2d 629 (1989); Zurn Indus., Inc. v. Acton Constr. Co., 847 F.2d 234 (5th Cir.1988); American Motorists Ins. Co. v. Trane Co., 657 F.2d 146 (7th Cir.1981).

53. Maryland Cas. Co., 23 F.3d at 615–16.

54. City of Indianapolis, 314 U.S. at 69, 62 S.Ct. at 16.

joined with one or more otherwise nonremovable claims or causes of action, the entire case may be removed and the district court may determine all issues therein, or, in its discretion, may remand all matters in which State law predominates.

The authority for removal in Section 1441(c) applies only in federal question cases.[55]

Suits involving supplemental state claims that derive from a common nucleus of operative fact do not fall within the scope of Section 1441(c), since supplemental claims are not "separate and independent."[56] Even where the complaint contains different counts pleading multiple theories of recovery or different legal theories, such counts are not "separate and independent" when based on the same set of facts.[57] "Where there is a single wrong to plaintiff for which relief is sought, arising from an interlocked series of transactions, there is no separate and independent claim or cause of action under Section 1441(c)."[58] For example, in *Kabealo v. Davis*,[59] where the complaint alleged a federal claim under the Racketeer Influenced and Corrupt Organizations Act ("RICO") and state law claims of breach of fiduciary duty, breach of contract, and fraud, but all claims arose from the same series of events and were closely related, the district court held that the case did not fall within the scope of Section 1441(c).[60]

Because the statute provides that district courts have discretion to "remand all matters in which State law predominates," the majority of courts to consider the issue have held that Section 1441(c) authorizes the remand of the entire case, including the federal law claim.[61] Courts adopting this position have also held that Section 1441(c) still allows the district court to remand separate and independent state claims if state law predominates as to the individual claim.[62] Other courts have held that the discretion given under Section 1441(c) does not permit the district court to remand an entire case containing a properly removed federal claim.[63]

55. *See, e.g.,* Bady v. Estate of Woodrow, 941 F.Supp. 71, 71 (N.D.Miss.1996).

56. *In re* City of Mobile, 75 F.3d 605, 608 (11th Cir.1996); Borough of West Mifflin v. Lancaster, 45 F.3d 780, 786 (3d Cir. 1995); Marshall v. Manville Sales Corp., 6 F.3d 229, 232 (4th Cir.1993).

57. Mayo v. Christian Hospital Northeast–Northwest, No. 4:97CV28SNL, 1997 WL 220249 (E.D.Mo.1997); Dunn v. Ayre, 943 F.Supp. 812 (E.D.Mich.1996); Kabealo v. Davis, 829 F.Supp. 923 (S.D.Ohio 1993), *aff'd,* 72 F.3d 129 (6th Cir.1995).

58. American Fire & Casualty Co. v. Finn, 341 U.S. 6, 14, 71 S.Ct. 534, 540, 95 L.Ed. 702 (1951) (interpreting prior version of § 1441); *see* Brockman v. Merabank, 40 F.3d 1013, 1017 (9th Cir.1994).

59. 829 F.Supp. 923 (S.D.Ohio 1993), *aff'd,* 72 F.3d 129 (6th Cir.1995).

60. *Id.* at 926–27.

61. Eastus v. Blue Bell Creameries, L.P., 97 F.3d 100, 106 (5th Cir.1996); Spaulding v. Mingo Cty. Bd. of Educ., 897 F.Supp. 284, 288 (S.D.W.Va.1995); Bodenner v. Graves, 828 F.Supp. 516, 519 (W.D.Mich.1993); Moore v. DeBiase, 766 F.Supp. 1311 (D.N.J.1991); Moralez v. Meat Cutters Local 539, 778 F.Supp. 368, 370 (E.D.Mich.1991).

62. *See, e.g.,* Eastus, 97 F.3d at 106.

63. *See* Hickerson v. City of New York, 932 F.Supp. 550, 558 (S.D.N.Y.1996).

A division of authority also exists as to whether Section 1441(c) applies to statutorily nonremovable claims. By statute, several types of claims have been made nonremovable, such as civil actions against common carriers,[64] and actions arising under state workers' compensation laws.[65] Some courts have held that Section 1441(c) may not be used to remove such claims, since to do so would undermine Congress' intent in making such claims nonremovable.[66] However, the majority of courts to consider the issue have held that Section 1441(c) does apply to claims made nonremovable by statute and that such claims are therefore removable.[67] These courts have reasoned that, unlike Section 1441(a), which contains an exception to removability where "expressly provided by Act of Congress," Section 1441(c) contains no such restriction.[68]

(2) Consideration of Third–Party Claims, Cross–Claims and Counterclaims

The Fifth Circuit Court of Appeals has held that third-party defendants may remove an action where the third-party complaint states a separate and independent claim which, if sued upon alone, could have been properly brought in federal court.[69] However, most courts have held that a third-party cause of action is not removable where removal is based solely on the third-party claim, and the main claim could not have been originally filed in federal court.[70] The same principles apply to cross-claims asserted by defendants.[71]

(e) Special Considerations for Class Actions

As with any other action, for a class action to be removed from state to federal court, the jurisdictional requirements must be met. When federal question jurisdiction is invoked, each plaintiff generally must meet all jurisdictional requirements for the particular statutory cause of action, such as exhaustion of administrative remedies.[72] In class actions

---

64. 28 U.S.C.A. § 1445(b) (West 1994).

65. 28 U.S.C.A. § 1445(c) (West 1994).

66. See, e.g., Green v. Hajoca, 573 F.Supp. 1120 (E.D.Va.1983).

67. Emrich v. Touche Ross & Co., 846 F.2d 1190 (9th Cir.1988); Gonsalves v. Amoco Shipping Co., 733 F.2d 1020 (2d Cir.1984); Newton v. Coca–Cola Bottling Co. Consolidated, 958 F.Supp. 248 (W.D.N.C.1997); Palser v. Burlington Northern R.R. Co., 698 F.Supp. 793 (E.D.Mo.1988).

68. See, e.g., Newton, 958 F.Supp. at 251.

69. Carl Heck Engineers, Inc. v. Lafourche Parish Police Jury, 622 F.2d 133 (5th Cir.1980). See Hayduk v. United Parcel Service, Inc., 930 F.Supp. 584, 593–94 (S.D.Fla.1996); Price v. Alfa Mut. Ins. Co., 877 F.Supp. 597, 601 (M.D.Ala.1995).

70. See Lewis v. Windsor Door Co., 926 F.2d 729 (8th Cir.1991); Thomas v. Shelton, 740 F.2d 478 (7th Cir.1984); Starr v. Prairie Harbor Development Co., 900 F.Supp. 230, 232 (E.D.Wis.1995); Baylor v. District of Columbia, 838 F.Supp. 7, 9 (D.D.C.1993).

71. Compare Acme Brick Co. v. Agrupacion Exportadora de Maquinaria Ceramica, 855 F.Supp. 163 (N.D.Tex.1994) (co-defendant could remove action where defendant's cross-claim for indemnity constituted a separate and independent claim), with M.D.C. Wallcoverings v. State Bank of Woodstock, No. 90 C 20089, 1990 WL 304189 (N.D.Ill. 1990) (action not removable on basis of cross-claim, even if cross-claim was separate and independent).

72. See, e.g., Lunsford v. United States, 570 F.2d 221 (8th Cir.1977) (each class member required to exhaust administrative remedies in suit under Federal Tort Claims

removed on the basis of diversity jurisdiction, the determination of whether diversity jurisdiction exists is based only on the citizenship of the named parties in the action.[73]

(f) Waiver of the Right to Removal

(1) Express Waiver

A defendant may contractually waive the right to remove a case from state to federal court through the use of a forum selection clause.[74] However, any such waiver must be clear and unequivocal.[75] Courts have generally held that forum selection clauses are prima facie valid, and that where the language of such a clause is found to be unambiguous, the burden is on the opposing party to show that enforcement would be unreasonable.[76] Courts have held that such clauses are "unreasonable" where the clause was the result of fraud, undue influence, or lack of bargaining power, or where trial in the selected forum would be so difficult and inconvenient that the party would effectively be denied a meaningful day in court.[77] While clauses that merely specify the applicability of state law have been held ambiguous,[78] clauses that provide for venue in state court have been upheld as waiving the right to removal.[79]

(2) Otherwise Removable Cases That Have Substantially Progressed in State Court

Waiver of the right to remove can also occur if a defendant takes action in state court after it is apparent that the case is removable. Such action must manifest the defendant's intent to have the matter adjudicated in state court and to abandon the right to a federal forum.[80] A

Act). *But see* Briggs v. Anderson, 796 F.2d 1009 (8th Cir.1986) (only class representative required to file EEOC charge in employment discrimination action).

73. Supreme Tribe of Ben–Hur v. Cauble, 255 U.S. 356, 41 S.Ct. 338, 65 L.Ed. 673 (1921). *See* Chapter 15 "Class Actions," at § 15.9(a), *infra.*

74. *See* Pelleport Investors, Inc. v. Budco Quality Theatres, Inc., 741 F.2d 273, 279–80 (9th Cir.1984).

75. *See, e.g.,* Milk 'N' More, Inc. v. Beavert, 963 F.2d 1342, 1346 (10th Cir.1992); Regis Associates v. Rank Hotels (Management) Ltd., 894 F.2d 193, 195 (6th Cir. 1990) (clause requiring parties to submit to the jurisdiction "of the Michigan Courts" not sufficient to show intent to waive right of removal).

76. Kevlin Services, Inc. v. Lexington State Bank, 46 F.3d 13, 15 (5th Cir.1995) (plaintiff failed to prove provision unreasonable because of fraud or overreaching; re-

mand required); *see* M/S Bremen v. Zapata Off–Shore Co., 407 U.S. 1, 10, 92 S.Ct. 1907, 1913, 32 L.Ed.2d 513 (1972).

77. M/S Bremen, 407 U.S. at 12–13, 92 S.Ct. at 1913; Argueta v. Banco Mexicano, S.A., 87 F.3d 320, 325 (9th Cir.1996); Bense v. Interstate Battery Sys. of America, 683 F.2d 718, 720 (2d Cir.1982) (inconvenience and expense of travelling not sufficient basis for not enforcing contractual forum selection clause). *See* Chapter 3 "Venue, Forum Selection and Transfer," at § 3.6(a), *supra.*

78. *See* Regis Associates, 894 F.2d 193.

79. *See* Milk 'n' More, 963 F.2d 1342; Intermountain Sys., Inc. v. Edsall Constr. Co., 575 F.Supp. 1195 (D.Colo.1983). *See* Chapter 3 "Venue, Forum Selection and Transfer," *supra.*

80. *See* Resolution Trust Corp. v. Bayside Developers, 43 F.3d 1230, 1240 (9th Cir.1994); Grubb v. Donegal Mut. Ins. Co., 935 F.2d 57, 58–59 (4th Cir.1991).

waiver of the right must be clear and unequivocal.[81]

Where a defendant takes necessary defensive action to avoid a judgment being entered automatically against him at an early stage of the proceedings, such action does not waive the right to remove, since it does not indicate an intent to litigate in state court.[82] As a result, such acts as filing an answer, opposing a motion for a preliminary injunction, or filing a motion to vacate a temporary restraining order have been held insufficient to constitute a waiver.[83] In contrast, taking affirmative action, such as filing a motion to dismiss or filing a permissive counterclaim, has been held sufficient to demonstrate an unequivocal intent to proceed in state court.[84] The basis for this rule is that it is unfair to permit the defendant to attempt to gain a favorable result in state court, and then allow the defendant another try in federal court.[85] In general, courts have held that the right to remove is maintained where there has been no litigation on the merits and no prejudice to any of the parties.[86]

Library References:

West's Key No. Digests, Removal of Cases ⊕1–61.
Wright, Miller & Cooper, Federal Practice and Procedure: Civil 2d §§ 1209, 1210, 1556, 1685, 3721–3740, 3914.11.

§ 8.4 Calculation of the Amount in Controversy

(a) When Calculation is Made

For removal purposes, the amount in controversy is determined on the basis of the record existing at the time the petition for removal is filed.[1] As a result, where a plaintiff amends the complaint after removal and attempts to reduce the amount of damages claimed, such amendment has no effect on the removal determination.[2]

81. *See, e.g.,* Beighley v. FDIC, 868 F.2d 776, 782 (5th Cir.1989).

82. Resolution Trust Corp., 43 F.3d at 1240.

83. Warner v. Crum & Forster Commercial Ins. Co., 839 F.Supp. 436, 439 (N.D.Tex.1993) (filing answer); Rose v. Giamatti, 721 F.Supp. 906, 922 (S.D.Ohio 1989) (opposing temporary restraining order); Bedell v. H.R.C. Ltd., 522 F.Supp. 732, 738–39 (E.D.Ky.1981) (seeking to dissolve preliminary injunction).

84. *See* Kam Hon, Inc. v. Cigna Fire Underwriters Ins. Co., 933 F.Supp. 1060, 1061–62 (M.D.Fla.1996) (filing motion to dismiss in state court waived right to removal); Isaacs v. Group Health, Inc., 668 F.Supp. 306, 308–09 (S.D.N.Y.1987) (filing permissive counterclaim resulted in waiver).

85. *See* McKinnon v. Doctor's Associates, Inc., 769 F.Supp. 216, 217 (E.D.Mich. 1991); Rose, 721 F. Supp. at 922.

86. *See* Selvaggi v. Prudential Property and Cas. Ins. Co., 871 F.Supp. 815, 817–18 (E.D.Pa.1995).

§ 8.4

1. Allen v. R & H Oil & Gas Co., 63 F.3d 1326 (5th Cir.1995); United Food & Commercial Workers Union v. CenterMark Properties Meriden Square, Inc., 30 F.3d 298 (2d Cir.1994).

2. *See, e.g.,* Angus v. Shiley, Inc., 989 F.2d 142 (3d Cir.1993); McCorkindale v. American Home Assurance Co., 909 F.Supp. 646 (N.D.Iowa 1995).

(b) Factors to be Considered

(1) Multiple Claims for Relief

Where a single plaintiff has multiple claims against a single defendant, all claims, whether related or unrelated, may be aggregated for purposes of determining the amount in controversy.[3] However, a plaintiff's claims against multiple defendants may not be aggregated to satisfy the amount in controversy unless the defendants may be held jointly liable to the plaintiff on each claim.[4]

In cases involving multiple plaintiffs, if no plaintiff is able to meet the amount in controversy requirement, the general rule is that separate and distinct claims of plaintiffs may not be aggregated to meet the jurisdictional amount.[5] An exception to the rule against aggregation occurs when plaintiffs are bringing suit based on "a single title or right in which they have a common and undivided interest."[6]

No clear dividing line exists between separate and distinct claims and common and undivided claims. However, courts have typically found common and undivided claims where one plaintiff's failure to collect would increase the recovery of the remaining plaintiffs, such as in cases involving a common fund in which members share an interest.[7] It has been held that to derive from "a single title or right," the plaintiffs' "claims of right must be 'integrated' meaning that their respective rights to damages arise from the same legal source."[8] "Plaintiffs in paradigm 'common fund' cases assert claims to a piece of land, a trust fund, an estate, an insurance policy, a lien, or an item of collateral, which they claim as common owners or in which they share a common interest arising under a single title or right."[9] In contrast, the typical case containing separate and distinct interests involves a class of plaintiffs, each of whom has individual claims against the defendant, such as a case in which each class member has a separate contract with the defendant.[10]

The law is less settled where at least one plaintiff can meet the amount in controversy requirement. Prior to 1990, it was well estab-

---

3. See Shanaghan v. Cahill, 58 F.3d 106, 109 (4th Cir.1995); Adams v. State Farm Mut. Auto. Ins. Co., 313 F.Supp. 1349 (N.D.Miss.1970).

4. Sovereign Camp Woodmen of the World v. O'Neill, 266 U.S. 292, 295–96, 45 S.Ct. 49, 50, 69 L.Ed. 293 (1924); Reason v. General Motors Corp., 896 F.Supp. 829 (S.D.Ind.1995).

5. Snyder v. Harris, 394 U.S. 332, 89 S.Ct. 1053, 22 L.Ed.2d 319 (1969).

6. Id. at 335, 89 S.Ct. at 1056.

7. See Eagle v. American Tel. & Tel. Co., 769 F.2d 541 (9th Cir.1985) (class of minority shareholders claimed wrongful depletion of corporate assets; claims held to be common and undivided), cert. denied, 475 U.S. 1084, 106 S.Ct. 1465, 89 L.Ed.2d 721 (1986); Dollar v. General Motors Corp., 814 F.Supp. 538, 544 (E.D.Tex.1993).

8. Allen v. R & H Oil & Gas Co., 63 F.3d 1326, 1331 (5th Cir.1995); see Potrero Hill Community Action Committee v. Housing Auth. and City of San Franciso, 410 F.2d 974 (9th Cir.1969) (claims are properly aggregated when they derive from rights which plaintiffs hold in group status).

9. Gilman v. BHC Securities, Inc., 104 F.3d 1418, 1424 (2d Cir.1997).

10. See Herlihy v. Ply–Gem Indust., Inc., 752 F.Supp. 1282 (D.Md.1990).

lished that each individual plaintiff had to satisfy the amount in controversy requirement, and that pendent-party jurisdiction could not be used to obtain federal jurisdiction over plaintiffs with claims for less than the jurisdictional amount.[11] This principle was called into question in 1990 by the passage of the supplemental jurisdiction statute, codified at 28 U.S.C.A. § 1367. Section 1367(b) provides that federal courts are granted supplemental jurisdiction over all claims that are part of the same case or controversy as the matter over which the court has original jurisdiction. Several courts, including the Seventh Circuit Court of Appeals, have held in the context of nonclass actions that Section 1367 authorizes the district court to exercise supplemental jurisdiction over plaintiffs whose claims do not separately meet the amount in controversy requirement.[12] However, many district courts have concluded (on the basis of their interpretation of the statute's legislative history) that Section 1367 was not intended to change prior law.[13] Of course, even in those circuits that apply Section 1367 supplemental jurisdiction to plaintiffs in the removal context, at least one plaintiff must meet the jurisdictional minimum.

(2) Unspecified Damages

Since many states do not require (or allow) a demand for a specific monetary amount in the complaint, federal courts often face the difficulty of determining the amount in controversy for purposes of removal when the amount of damages is not specified in the complaint. The courts have not arrived at a single approach for such situations, and have applied varying techniques and burdens of proof.[14] The burden is generally placed on the defendant of establishing that the amount in controversy exceeds the statutory amount.[15]

At least four different approaches have been taken as to what burden is required. One approach is to require defendants to prove that it does not appear to a legal certainty that the plaintiff's claim is actually for less than the requisite jurisdictional amount.[16] This so-called "converse legal certainty test" has been criticized as resulting in an unwarranted expansion of federal diversity jurisdiction, since federal courts

11. Clark v. Paul Gray, Inc., 306 U.S. 583, 59 S.Ct. 744, 83 L.Ed. 1001 (1939).

12. See, e.g., Stromberg Metal Works v. Press Mechanical, Inc., 77 F.3d 928, 930–32 (7th Cir.1996).

13. Borgeson v. Archer–Daniels Midland Co., 909 F.Supp. 709 (C.D.Cal.1995); Waters v. Grosfeld, 904 F.Supp. 616 (E.D.Mich. 1995); In re Potash Antitrust Litigation, 866 F.Supp. 406 (D.Minn.1994); Riverside Transp., Inc. v. Bellsouth Telecommunications, Inc., 847 F.Supp. 453 (M.D.La.1994); Pierson v. Source Perrier, S.A., 848 F.Supp. 1186 (E.D.Pa.1994); North American Mechanical Servs. Corp. v. Hubert, 859 F.Supp. 1186 (C.D.Ill.1994); Mayo v. Key Fin. Serv., Inc., 812 F.Supp. 277, 278 (D.Mass.1993); Averdick v. Republic Fin. Serv., Inc., 803 F.Supp. 37 (E.D.Ky.1992).

14. See Gafford v. General Elec. Co., 997 F.2d 150 (6th Cir.1993) (discussing different approaches taken by federal courts).

15. See Tapscott v. MS Dealer Service Corp., 77 F.3d 1353, 1356–57 (11th Cir. 1996); De Aguilar v. Boeing Co., 11 F.3d 55 (5th Cir.1993).

16. See Atkins v. Harcros Chemicals, Inc., 761 F.Supp. 444 (E.D.La.1991); Locklear v. State Farm Mut. Auto. Ins. Co., 742 F.Supp. 679 (S.D.Ga.1989); Partlow v. Jones Motor Co., 736 F.Supp. 744 (E.D.Mich.1990).

might in some instances be required to exercise jurisdiction even if there was only a legal possibility that the amount in controversy exceeded $75,000.[17] A second approach is to require the defendant to show some reasonable probability that the amount in controversy exceeds the required amount.[18] Under the third approach, the defendant is required to show to a legal certainty that the amount exceeds the jurisdictional amount.[19] This approach has been criticized as placing the defendant in the position of proving the plaintiff's case.[20] Under the fourth approach, adopted by the majority of courts to consider the issue, where a plaintiff's state court complaint does not specify a particular amount of damages, the removing defendant must establish by a preponderance of the evidence that the amount in controversy exceeds $75,000.[21]

In contrast, where the complaint pleads damages in a specific amount that is less than the jurisdictional amount, removal is improper unless the defendant can prove to a legal certainty that the plaintiff's claim exceeds the jurisdictional amount.[22] Because this places the defendant in the unusual position of attempting to show that the plaintiff suffered damages in excess of the amount requested, the defendant must be cautious in meeting its burden of proof.

(3) Punitive Damages

The claims of a single plaintiff for compensatory and punitive damages may be aggregated to meet the jurisdictional amount.[23] However, courts typically examine whether punitive damages are available under state law for the claims presented in the complaint.[24] Facts supporting the defendant's estimate of the amount of punitive damages must be presented in the notice of removal.[25]

The state of the law is more complex as to the aggregation of punitive damages in suits involving multiple plaintiffs or class action claims. Recent decisions by the Fifth and Eleventh Circuit Courts of Appeals have examined the purpose of punitive damages under state law

---

17. *See, e.g.*, Sanchez v. Monumental Life Ins. Co., 102 F.3d 398, 403 (9th Cir. 1996); De Aguilar v. Boeing Co., 47 F.3d 1404, 1411 (5th Cir.), *cert. denied*, 516 U.S. 865, 116 S.Ct. 180, 133 L.Ed.2d 119 (1995); Gafford v. General Elec. Co., 997 F.2d 150, 158–59 (6th Cir.1993).

18. *See* Kennard v. Harris Corp., 728 F.Supp. 453 (E.D.Mich.1989).

19. *See* Shelly v. Southern Bell Tel. & Tel. Co., 873 F.Supp. 613 (M.D.Ala.1995); White v. J.C. Penney Life Ins. Co., 861 F.Supp. 25 (S.D.W.Va.1994).

20. Garza v. Bettcher Industries, Inc., 752 F.Supp. 753, 756 (E.D.Mich.1990).

21. Sanchez, 102 F.3d at 404; Tapscott v. MS Dealer Service Corp., 77 F.3d 1353, 1357 (11th Cir.1996); De Aguilar v. Boeing Co., 11 F.3d 55, 58 (5th Cir.1993); Shaw v. Dow Brands Inc., 994 F.2d 364, 366 n. 2 (7th Cir.1993); Gafford v. General Elec. Co., 997 F.2d 150, 158 (6th Cir.1993)

22. Burns v. Windsor Ins. Co., 31 F.3d 1092, 1095 (11th Cir.1994); Gilmer v. Walt Disney Co., 915 F.Supp. 1001, 1005 (W.D.Ark.1996); Visintine v. Saab Auto., A.B., 891 F.Supp. 496 (E.D.Mo.1995).

23. Smith v. Bally's Holiday, 843 F.Supp. 1451 (N.D.Ga.1994); Griffin v. Holmes, 843 F.Supp. 81 (E.D.N.C.1993).

24. *In re* Corestates Trust Fee Litigation, 39 F.3d 61 (3d Cir.1994); Klepper v. First American Bank, 916 F.2d 337, 341 (6th Cir.1990).

25. *See* Gilman v. BHC Securities, Inc., 104 F.3d 1418, 1428 (2d Cir.1997).

to determine whether punitive damages claims can be considered as comparable to claims for a common and undivided interest.[26]

In *Tapscott v. MS Dealer Service Corp.*, the Eleventh Circuit Court of Appeals held, in the context of a class action suit, that since the purpose of punitive damages under Alabama law was to deter wrongful conduct, and such damages were awarded for the public benefit, punitive damages reflected the defendant's course of conduct towards all of the putative class members, and could properly be considered in the aggregate.[27] In *Allen v. R & H Oil & Gas Co.*,[28] a mass tort case that was not a class action, the Fifth Circuit Court of Appeals concluded that because punitive damages were fundamentally collective in nature under Mississippi law, punitive damages could be treated as belonging to each plaintiff for jurisdictional purposes.[29]

Under these decisions, even if the claims for actual damages are separate and distinct and cannot be aggregated, punitive damages claims can be aggregated if such claims are considered to be collective in nature under state law. Several district courts have reached similar conclusions on the basis of *Allen* and *Tapscott*.[30]

In contrast, other courts have held that the claims of class members or multiple plaintiffs for punitive damages are as separate and distinct as their claims for actual damages, and cannot be aggregated.[31] In *Gilman v. BHC Securities*, Inc.,[32] the Second Circuit Court of Appeals held that punitive damages could not be aggregated where the underlying cause of action did not assert a single title or right.[33] Some courts have refused to follow *Tapscott* and *Allen* on the grounds that requiring plaintiffs to independently satisfy the amount in controversy requirement while allowing aggregation of punitive damages is illogical, and defeats the purpose of the aggregation rules.[34]

(4) Attorney's Fees

Generally, attorney's fees are not considered a part of the amount in controversy because the successful party does not typically collect a

---

26. Tapscott v. MS Dealer Serv. Corp., 77 F.3d 1353 (11th Cir.1996); Allen v. R & H Oil & Gas Corp., 63 F.3d 1326 (5th Cir.1995).

27. Tapscott, 77 F.3d at 1358–59.

28. 63 F.3d 1326 (5th Cir.1995).

29. *Id.* at 1333–34.

30. *See* Brooks v. Georgia Gulf Corp., 924 F.Supp. 739 (M.D.La.1996) (Louisiana law); Gilmer v. Walt Disney Co., 915 F.Supp. 1001 (W.D.Ark.1996) (Arkansas law); *In re* Norplant Contraceptive Prods. Liabl. Litig., 907 F.Supp. 244 (E.D.Tex. 1995) (Texas law).

31. Visintine v. Saab Automobile A.B., 891 F.Supp. 496, 498 (E.D.Mo.1995); Smiley

v. Citibank, 863 F.Supp. 1156 (C.D.Cal. 1993).

32. 104 F.3d 1418 (2d Cir.1997).

33. *Id.* at 1430–31.

34. *See* Bernard v. Gerber Food Products Co., 938 F.Supp. 218, 223 (S.D.N.Y. 1996); Haisch v. Allstate Ins. Co., 942 F.Supp. 1245 (D.Ariz.1996); Hasek v. Chrysler Corp., No. 95 C 579, 1996 WL 48602 (N.D.Ill.1996); Bishop v. General Motors Corp., 925 F.Supp. 294, 298 (D.N.J. 1996) ("Tapscott represents an unwarranted and ill-considered extension of the doctrine of 'common and undivided interest' to highly speculative punitive damages claims."); Visintine, 891 F.Supp. 496.

separate attorney's fee.[35] However, where separate attorney's fees are provided by contract or allowed by statute, attorney's fees are considered part of the amount in controversy for jurisdictional purposes.[36] Only a reasonable estimate of attorney's fees may be included in determining whether the jurisdictional amount has been met.[37]

Where separate and distinct claims are raised in class actions and cases involving multiple plaintiffs, courts have generally refused to aggregate attorney's fees for purposes of the amount in controversy requirement.[38] Instead, courts usually attribute the total amount of potential attorneys' fees pro rata among the individual class members.[39] However, in the context of class actions, it has been held that where state law allocates all attorneys' fees to the class representative, attorney's fees can be aggregated to meet the requirement. In *In re Abbott Laboratories*,[40] the Fifth Circuit Court of Appeals attributed the entire pool of attorneys' fees to the named representatives, based on the court's finding that state statutes required such attribution.

Taking into account the true nature of the attorney's representation in class actions, there is a rational reason to allow the aggregation of attorney's fees without proration. Today, "attorneys function essentially as entrepreneurs who bear a substantial amount of the litigation risk and exercise nearly plenary control over all important decisions in the lawsuit."[41] Therefore, the outmoded concept of viewing the attorney as the agent for each plaintiff and allocating a pro rata share of the attorneys' fee to each plaintiff no longer seems either reasonable or appropriate. Certainly, the unnamed members of the class do not consider the class attorney as their own individual attorney. They made no agreement to retain or compensate the lawyer. There is no obligation on their part to compensate the lawyer, or even reimburse the litigation costs, in the event that the lawsuit proves to be unsuccessful. Even the named plaintiffs are unlikely to have made such an agreement. The fee for the class attorneys usually goes directly to the lawyers—not to the plaintiffs for further payment of their fees. In almost every respect, the award of an attorney's fee against a defendant in a class action is more comparable to a punitive damage award than to an award of compensatory damages or any other specific benefit to an individual plaintiff. While

---

35. Department of Recreation v. World Boxing Ass'n, 942 F.2d 84, 89 (1st Cir. 1991); Quebe v. Ford Motor Co., 908 F.Supp. 446, 449 (W.D.Tex.1995).

36. Missouri State Life Ins. Co. v. Jones, 290 U.S. 199, 54 S.Ct. 133, 78 L.Ed. 267 (1933); Clark v. Nat'l Travelers Life Ins. Co., 518 F.2d 1167, 1169 (6th Cir. 1975).

37. *See, e.g.,* Sarnoff v. American Home Products Corp., 798 F.2d 1075, 1078 (7th Cir.1986).

38. Goldberg v. CPC Int'l, Inc., 678 F.2d 1365 (9th Cir.), *cert. denied,* 459 U.S. 945,

103 S.Ct. 259, 74 L.Ed.2d 202 (1982); Johnson v. Gerber Products Co., 949 F.Supp. 327 (E.D.Pa.1996).

39. Gilmer v. Walt Disney Co., 915 F.Supp. 1001, 1014 (W.D.Ark.1996) (total amount of attorneys' fees attributed pro rata among individual class members); Quebe, 908 F.Supp. at 451–52.

40. 51 F.3d 524 (5th Cir.1995).

41. Jonathan R. Macey & Geoffrey P. Miller, *The Plaintiff's Attorney's Role in Class Action and Derivative Litigation: Economic Analysis and Recommendations for Reform,* 58 U. Chi. L. Rev. 1, 3 (1991).

each individual plaintiff could sue on his own behalf, in separate cases, the right to seek attorney's fees is "based on public policy as expressed through state statutes," not some right that is separate and individual to each plaintiff.[42] Thus, in certain types of class actions for claims having a statutory right to attorney's fees, those fees may be viewed in the aggregate.[43]

(5) Declaratory and Injunctive Relief

Actions seeking equitable relief such as an injunction or a declaratory judgment, instead of monetary damages create difficulties in evaluating whether the amount in controversy requirement has been met for removal purposes. Most courts have held that the amount is determined from the plaintiff's point of view. As a result, the court examines the amount the plaintiff would recover or avoid losing if the plaintiff succeeded.[44] However, a few courts have determined the amount in controversy according to the cost to the defendant of complying with the order sought by the plaintiff.[45] For example, in *Grotzke v. Kurz*, where the plaintiff brought a breach of contract action against the defendants, who were purchasers of the plaintiff's business, the district court held that because the effect of the injunction sought by the plaintiff would be to shut down the defendant's operations, the amount in controversy requirement was met.[46]

Under another approach, the interests of either party with respect to the equitable claim may be looked to in determining the amount in controversy for purposes of removal.[47] In two-party litigation, establishing the amount in controversy of injunctive relief by either party's perspective seems to have a rational basis.[48]

Where multiple plaintiffs are involved, the question becomes whether the value of injunctive relief may be aggregated for purposes of meeting the amount in controversy requirement. As with compensatory damage claims, whether the value of injunctive relief may be aggregated depends on whether the claims of the plaintiffs are separate and distinct or common and undivided.[49] If the claims are separate and distinct, then injunctive relief would satisfy each plaintiff's claims, rather than the claims of the class as a whole, and the value of injunctive relief cannot be

---

42. *See* Allen v. R & H Oil & Gas Co., 63 F.3d 1326, 1333 (5th Cir.1995).

43. *See* Tapscott v. MS Dealer Serv. Corp., 77 F.3d 1353, 1356 (11th Cir.1996).

44. *See, e.g.,* Freeman v. Sports Car Club of America, Inc., 51 F.3d 1358, 1362 (7th Cir.1995); Burns v. Massachusetts Mut. Life Ins. Co., 820 F.2d 246, 248 (8th Cir.1987); Cowan v. Windeyer, 795 F.Supp. 535, 538 (N.D.N.Y.1992); Ferris v. General Dynamics Corp., 645 F.Supp. 1354, 1362 (D.R.I.1986); Miller–Bradford & Risberg, Inc. v. FMC Corp., 414 F.Supp. 1147, 1149 (E.D.Wis.1976).

45. Grotzke v. Kurz, 887 F.Supp. 53, 55–57 (D.R.I.1995) (applying defendant's viewpoint approach); Bedell v. H.R.C. Ltd., 522 F.Supp. 732, 735 (E.D.Ky.1981).

46. Grotzke, 887 F.Supp. at 55–57.

47. *See* Oklahoma Retail Grocers v. Wal–Mart Stores, 605 F.2d 1155, 1159 (10th Cir.1979); Hambell v. Alphagraphics Franchising, Inc., 779 F.Supp. 910, 912 (E.D.Mich.1991).

48. As to class actions, *see infra* § 8.4(b)(6).

49. *See* Snow v. Ford Motor Co., 561 F.2d 787 (9th Cir.1977).

aggregated.[50] Where separate and distinct claims are involved, courts have divided the cost of injunctive relief pro rata among the plaintiffs, or, in class actions, among all members of the class.[51]

(6) Special Considerations for Class Actions

A recurring issue in class actions based on diversity jurisdiction is whether the claims of the putative class members may be aggregated to meet the amount in controversy requirement. As with nonclass actions, the general rule is that while separate and distinct claims of class members may not be aggregated to meet the amount in controversy requirement, claims enforcing a single title or right in which the plaintiffs have a common and undivided interest can be aggregated.[52]

In 1973, the Supreme Court of the United States held in *Zahn v. International Paper Corporation* that each individual class plaintiff had to satisfy the amount in controversy requirement, or be dismissed from the class action.[53] The continuing viability of this *Zahn* requirement has been called into question by the passage of the supplemental jurisdiction statute [28 U.S.C.A. § 1367]. Section 1367(b) now provides that federal courts are granted supplemental jurisdiction over all claims that are part of the same case or controversy as the matter over which the court has original jurisdiction. Several courts, including the Fifth Circuit Court of Appeals, have held that because Section 1367 does not specifically exclude class actions, class members may sue together as a class in federal court as long as at least one class member meets the amount in controversy requirement.[54] In contrast, many district courts have concluded that Section 1367 was not intended to change the result in *Zahn*.[55]

(c) Effect of Amendments to Complaint

If the plaintiff amends the complaint before removal and increases

---

50. Asten v. Southwestern Bell Tel. Co., 914 F.Supp. 430, 433–34 (D.Kan.1996) (class action); Hall v. ITT Financial Services, 891 F.Supp. 580 (M.D.Ala.1994) (contractual claims based on sale of credit life insurance were separate and distinct); Copeland v. MBNA America, N.A., 820 F.Supp. 537 (D.Colo.1993) (cost of complying with injunctive relief may not be aggregated for putative class members).

51. Packard v. Provident Nat'l Bank, 994 F.2d 1039 (3d Cir.1993); Asten v. Southwestern Bell Tel. Co., 914 F.Supp. 430, 433–34 (D.Kan.1996).

52. Snyder v. Harris, 394 U.S. 332, 89 S.Ct. 1053, 22 L.Ed.2d 319 (1969). *See* Chapter 15 "Class Actions," at § 15.9(a), *infra*.

53. 414 U.S. 291, 94 S.Ct. 505, 38 L.Ed.2d 511 (1973).

54. *In re* Abbott Laboratories, 51 F.3d 524, 529 (5th Cir.1995); Gilmer v. Walt Disney Co., 915 F.Supp. 1001, 1010 (W.D.Ark.1996); Patterson Enterprises, Inc. v. Bridgestone/Firestone, Inc., 812 F.Supp. 1152 (D.Kan.1993).

55. Borgeson v. Archer–Daniels Midland Co., 909 F.Supp. 709 (C.D.Cal.1995); Waters v. Grosfeld, 904 F.Supp. 616 (E.D.Mich. 1995); *In re* Potash Antitrust Litig., 866 F.Supp. 406 (D.Minn.1994); Riverside Transp., Inc. v. Bellsouth Telecommunications, Inc., 847 F.Supp. 453 (M.D.La.1994); Pierson v. Source Perrier, 848 F.Supp. 1186 (E.D.Pa.1994); North American Mechanical Servs. Corp. v. Hubert, 859 F.Supp. 1186 (C.D.Ill.1994); Mayo v. Key Fin. Serv., Inc., 812 F.Supp. 277, 278 (D.Mass.1993); Averdick v. Republic Fin. Serv., Inc., 803 F.Supp. 37 (E.D.Ky.1992).

the amount of damages above the jurisdictional amount, the case can be removed by the defendant, provided that the one-year time limit applicable to diversity cases has not expired.[56] In contrast, a plaintiff may not defeat diversity jurisdiction by filing a post-removal amendment which reduces the amount of damages below the jurisdictional amount.[57] However, if the complaint is ambiguous as to the damages asserted, a plaintiff may stipulate to an amount of damages below the jurisdictional amount after removal.[58] Such a stipulation is treated as a clarification of the amount in controversy at the time of removal, rather than as an amendment.[59]

(d) Effect of Permissive and Compulsory Cross–Claims and Counterclaims

Most courts follow the rule that the amount in controversy is determined by the plaintiff's complaint, and that the defendant's counterclaim, whether permissive or compulsory, may not be considered by the district court.[60] However, at least one court has held that when the counterclaim is a compulsory counterclaim, it should be considered in determining the amount in controversy.[61] As to cross-claims, most courts have held that a defendant cannot remove on the basis of a cross-claim asserted against him for more than the jurisdictional amount.[62]

Library References:

West's Key No. Digests, Removal of Cases ⚷71–76.
Wright, Miller, Kane & Cooper, Federal Practice and Procedure: Civil 2d §§ 1823, 3702, 3703, 3707, 3725.

56. See Power v. Norfolk & Western Ry. Co., 778 F.Supp. 468, 469 (E.D.Mo.1991); Gibson v. Atlantic Coast Line R. Co., 299 F.Supp. 268, 269 (S.D.N.Y.1969). For discussion of the one-year time limit, see infra § 8.7(b)(1).

57. Griffin v. Holmes, 843 F.Supp. 81, 86 (E.D.N.C.1993).

58. See Asociacion Nacional v. Dow Quimica, 988 F.2d 559, 565 (5th Cir.1993), cert. denied, 510 U.S. 1041, 114 S.Ct. 685, 126 L.Ed.2d 653 (1994); Griffin, 843 F.Supp. 81; Workman v. Kawasaki Motors Corp., 749 F.Supp. 1010 (W.D.Mo.1990); Cole v. Great Atlantic & Pacific Tea Co., 728 F.Supp. 1305 (E.D.Ky.1990). But see In re Shell Oil Co., 970 F.2d 355, 356 (7th Cir.1992) ("Because jurisdiction is determined as of the instant of removal, a post-removal affidavit or stipulation is no more effective than a post-removal amendment of the complaint.").

59. See, e.g., Printworks, Inc. v. Dorn Co., 869 F.Supp. 436 (E.D.La.1994).

60. See Continental Ozark, Inc. v. Fleet Supplies, Inc., 908 F.Supp. 668, 672 (W.D.Ark.1995); Meridian Aviation Serv. v. Sun Jet Int'l, 886 F.Supp. 613, 615 (S.D.Tex.1995); Iowa Lamb Corp. v. Kalene Industries, Inc., 871 F.Supp. 1149, 1157 (N.D.Iowa 1994); Oliver v. Haas, 777 F.Supp. 1040, 1042 (D.Puerto Rico 1991). However, one treatise suggests that compulsory counterclaims should be considered in determining whether the amount in controversy has been met in removal cases, on the basis that removal statutes are silent as to the amount in controversy. See 14A Charles Alan Wright, Arthur R. Miller & Edward H. Cooper, Federal Practice & Procedure § 3725, at 430 (2d ed. 1985).

61. See Swallow & Assoc. v. Henry Molded Products, Inc., 794 F.Supp. 660, 661 (E.D.Mich.1992).

62. See, e.g., Dowell Div. of Dow Chem. Co. v. Ormsby, 204 F.Supp. 38 (W.D.Ky. 1962).

§ 8.5   Venue and Transfer

(a) Difference Between Original and Removal Jurisdiction

The general venue statutes do not apply to cases brought in state court and removed to federal court.[1] Instead, venue for such actions is provided in Section 1441, which provides that the venue of a removed case is the "district and division embracing the place where such action is pending."[2] As a result, the fact that venue would have been improper if the action had been originally brought in the district court is immaterial, where venue is proper under Section 1441.[3] Most courts have held that an action may be removed to federal court even though the state court did not properly have jurisdiction.[4] For example, in *Johnston v. Foster–Wheeler Constructors, Inc.*, the district court held that federal jurisdiction existed over a case removed on the basis of diversity jurisdiction, even though the state court had no subject matter jurisdiction over a case arising under the workers' compensation laws of another state.[5]

(b) Potential for Transfer

Transfer of venue is available in federal court in two circumstances—on grounds of convenience, as provided in 28 U.S.C.A. § 1404,[6] and on grounds that venue is improper in the transferor court, as provided in 28 U.S.C.A. § 1406.[7] Most courts considering the issue have held that an action removed to the improper district or division of a district should be transferred to the proper district or division under Section 1406, rather than remanded or dismissed.[8] Even where a case is removed to the proper court, either party may seek transfer under Section 1404(a) on grounds of convenience.[9] Under Section 1404, the

---

§ 8.5

1. The venue statutes applicable to cases initiated in federal court are located at 28 U.S.C.A. §§ 1391–1393 (West 1993 & Supp.1997).

2. 28 U.S.C.A. § 1441(a) (West 1994); *see* Hartford Fire Ins. Co. v. Westinghouse Elec. Corp., 725 F.Supp. 317, 320 (S.D.Miss. 1989).

3. Bacik v. Peek, 888 F.Supp. 1405, 1413 (N.D.Ohio 1993); Hartford Fire Ins. Co., 725 F.Supp. at 320.

4. 28 U.S.C.A. § 1441(e) (West 1994); *see, e.g.,* Johnston v. Foster–Wheeler Constructors, Inc., 158 F.R.D. 496 (M.D.Ala. 1994). *But see* Brown v. Texarkana Nat. Bank, 889 F.Supp. 351 (E.D.Ark.1995) (where state court lacked jurisdiction because of improper venue, no jurisdiction existed for purposes of removal).

5. Johnston, 158 F.R.D. at 499–500.

6. Section 1404(a) provides that "[f]or the convenience of parties and witnesses, in the interest of justice, a district court may transfer any civil action to any other district or division where it might have been brought."

7. Section 1406(a) provides that "[t]he district court of a district in which is filed a case laying venue in the wrong division or district shall dismiss, or if it be in the interest of justice, transfer such case to any district or division in which it could have been brought."

8. *See, e.g.,* Kreimerman v. Casa Veerkamp, S.A. de C.V., 22 F.3d 634 (5th Cir.), *cert. denied*, 513 U.S. 1016, 115 S.Ct. 577, 130 L.Ed.2d 492 (1994).

9. *See* Hatch v. Reliance Ins. Co., 758 F.2d 409 (9th Cir.), *cert. denied*, 474 U.S. 1021, 106 S.Ct. 571, 88 L.Ed.2d 555 (1985); Midwest Motor Supply Co. v. Kimball, 761 F.Supp. 1316 (S.D.Ohio 1991).

court can transfer the action to another district court if the court determines that transfer will enhance the convenience of the parties and witnesses and is in the interest of justice, and that the proposed transferee district is one in which the action might originally have been brought.[10]

The party seeking transfer has the burden of establishing that transfer is warranted.[11] In general, factors used in determining convenience include the plaintiff's initial choice of forum, the relative ease of access to sources of proof, the availability of compulsory process for the attendance of unwilling witnesses, the costs of obtaining the attendance of witnesses, and the situs of material events.[12]

Library References:

West's Key No. Digests, Federal Courts ⚷101–157; Removal of Cases ⚷13, 14, 111.

Wright, Miller, Kane & Cooper, Federal Practice and Procedure: Civil 2d §§ 1825, 1928, 3141, 3253, 3801–3802, 3826–3828, 3842, 3844–3846, 3914.12, 3935.4.

§ 8.6 Removal of Particular Cases

Special removal procedures exist for specific types of defendants and actions. While complete coverage of such procedures is beyond the scope of this chapter, defendants to whom special procedures apply include the Federal Deposit Insurance Corporation ("FDIC")[13] and the Resolution Trust Corporation ("RTC").[14] Special removal procedures also exist for claims supported by bankruptcy jurisdiction,[15] foreclosure actions against the United States,[16] civil actions against foreign states,[17] and civil actions or criminal prosecutions brought against the United States, any federal agency, and any officer of the United States or a federal agency.[18]

In addition, some types of actions are specifically nonremovable. Civil actions in any state court arising under workers' compensation laws are not removable to federal court.[19] Civil actions filed in state court based on claims arising under the Securities Act of 1933 are not removable.[20] Civil actions in state court arising under federal statutes regulating common carriers brought against a carrier or its receivers or trustees to recover damages for delay, loss, or injury of shipments may not be removed unless the amount in controversy exceeds $10,000, exclusive of costs and interest.[21]

10. *See* Van Dusen v. Barrack, 376 U.S. 612, 84 S.Ct. 805, 11 L.Ed.2d 945 (1964).

11. *See, e.g.,* Coffey v. Van Dorn Iron Works, 796 F.2d 217, 219–20 (7th Cir.1986).

12. *See* Van Dusen, 376 U.S. 612; Federal Trade Comm'n v. MacArthur, 532 F.2d 1135 (7th Cir.1976); Koehring Co. v. Hyde Constr. Co., 324 F.2d 295 (5th Cir.1963). *See generally* Chapter 3 "Venue, Forum Selection and Transfer," *supra.*

13. 12 U.S.C.A. § 1819(b)(2) (West 1989).

14. 12 U.S.C.A. § 1441a(*l*)(3) (West 1989).

15. 28 U.S.C.A. § 1452 (West 1994).

16. 28 U.S.C.A. § 1444 (West 1994).

17. 28 U.S.C.A. § 1441(d) (West 1994).

18. 28 U.S.C.A. § 1442 (West 1994 & Supp.1997).

19. 28 U.S.C.A. § 1445(c) (West 1994).

20. 15 U.S.C.A. § 77(v)(a) (West 1997).

21. 28 U.S.C.A. § 1445(b) (West 1994 & Supp.1997).

Library References:

West's Key No. Digests, Removal of Cases ⊕1–99.
Wright, Miller, Kane & Cooper, Federal Practice and Procedure: Civil 2d §§ 1149, 1824, 3674, 3727.

§ 8.7   Procedure for Removal—In General

(a) Who May Seek Removal

(1) All Defendants to Original Action Against Them

Because Section 1441 provides for removal by "the defendant or the defendants," only defendants are permitted to remove a civil action from state to federal court.[1] Ordinarily, all defendants in the state action must join in the petition for removal, except for nominal, unknown, or fraudulently joined parties.[2] As a result of this unanimity requirement, in the typical case any defendant can dictate that the action remain in state court by refusing to join in the notice of removal.[3] However, a defendant with an independent right of removal, such as a federal agency, is not required to obtain the consent of other defendants to remove.[4] In addition, where removal occurs under 28 U.S.C.A. § 1441(c),[5] only the defendant to the separate and independent federal claim is required to seek removal.[6] In all cases, the defendant has the burden of establishing federal jurisdiction over a suit filed in state court.[7] The defendant also has the burden of establishing that it has complied with the removal procedures.[8]

(2) Removal on Counterclaim Not Permitted

Under the general removal statute, plaintiffs may not remove on the basis of counterclaims filed against them.[9] However, a different result may occur in the context of special removal statutes applicable to particular entities. Thus, it has been held, on the basis of special removal statutes applicable to the Federal Deposit Insurance Corporation and the

§ 8.7

1. *See, e.g.,* American Int'l Underwriters, Inc. v. Continental Ins. Co., 843 F.2d 1253 (9th Cir.1988); Geiger v. Arctco Enterprises, Inc., 910 F.Supp. 130 (S.D.N.Y. 1996).

2. Balazik v. County of Dauphin, 44 F.3d 209, 213 n. 4 (3d Cir.1995); Emrich v. Touche Ross & Co., 846 F.2d 1190 (9th Cir.1988); Brown v. Demco, Inc., 792 F.2d 478 (5th Cir.1986).

3. *See, e.g.,* Ford v. New United Motors Mfg., Inc., 857 F.Supp. 707 (N.D.Cal.1994).

4. *See, e.g.,* Davis v. FSLIC, 879 F.2d 1288 (5th Cir.1989).

5. *See supra* § 8.3(d) (discussing removal under § 1441(c)).

6. Costantini v. Guardian Life Ins. Co. of America, 859 F.Supp. 89 (S.D.N.Y.1994); Alexander by Alexander v. Goldome Credit Corp., 772 F.Supp. 1217, 1222 (M.D.Ala. 1991).

7. United Food and Commercial Workers Union, Local 919 v. CenterMark Properties, 30 F.3d 298 (2d Cir.1994); Emrich, 846 F.2d 1190.

8. Burns v. Windsor Ins. Co., 31 F.3d 1092 (11th Cir.1994).

9. Shamrock Oil & Gas Corp. v. Sheets, 313 U.S. 100, 108–09, 61 S.Ct. 868, 872, 85 L.Ed. 1214 (1941); Federal Deposit Ins. Corp. v. S & I 85–1, Ltd., 22 F.3d 1070, 1072 (11th Cir.1994); Starr v. Prairie Harbor Development Co., 900 F.Supp. 230 (E.D.Wis.1995).

Resolution Trust Corporation, that those entitles may remove actions when counterclaims are filed against them.[10]

(3) Third-Party Defendants

The courts are divided on the issue of whether third-party defendants may remove. A substantial number of courts have held that a third-party defendant is not a "defendant" within the meaning of the removal statute, and is accordingly not able to remove a state action to federal court.[11] In contrast, some courts have held that third-party defendants should be treated as defendants for purposes of removal.[12] Where special removal statutes are involved, such as those governing foreign states or federal agencies, such statutes may provide an independent basis for removal by certain third-party defendants.[13] In addition, any party may remove a bankruptcy claim or cause of action, provided the district court has jurisdiction.[14]

(4) Disregard of Nominal, Unserved, or Fraudulently Joined Parties Permitted

In an exception to the unanimity rule, unserved defendants are not required to join in the notice of removal.[15] However, in cases removed on the basis of diversity of citizenship, even though the unanimity rule does not apply to unserved defendants, the federal court examining the citizenship of the parties must consider all named defendants, regardless of service.[16] "[T]he fact that the resident defendant has not been served with process does not justify removal by the nonresident defendants."[17]

The unanimity rule may also be disregarded where a nonjoining defendant is an unknown or nominal party, or where a defendant has been fraudulently joined.[18] Courts have held defendants to be nominal where no reasonable basis exists for predicting that the defendant will be

10. *See* Federal Deposit Ins. Corp., 22 F.3d at 1072 (FDIC); FSLIC v. Quinn, 419 F.2d 1014, 1018 n. 4 (7th Cir.1969) (FSLIC); Federal Deposit Ins. Corp. v. Greenhouse Realty Assocs., 829 F.Supp. 507, 510 (D.N.H.1993) (FDIC).

11. *See, e.g.*, Starr v. Prairie Harbor Development Co., 900 F.Supp. 230 (E.D.Wis.1995); Fleet Bank–New Hampshire v. Engeleiter, 753 F.Supp. 417 (D.N.H.1991); Morris v. Marshall County Bd. of Educ., 560 F.Supp. 43 (N.D.W.Va. 1983).

12. *See, e.g.*, Motor Vehicle Cas. Co. v. Russian River Cty. Sanitation Dist., 538 F.Supp. 488, 491–92 (N.D.Cal.1981).

13. *See* Nolan v. Boeing Co., 919 F.2d 1058 (5th Cir.1990) (foreign state), *cert. denied*, 499 U.S. 962, 111 S.Ct. 1587, 113 L.Ed.2d 651 (1991); California v. Keating,

986 F.2d 346 (9th Cir.1993) (Resolution Trust Corporation).

14. 28 U.S.C.A. § 1452 (West 1994).

15. Getty Oil v. Ins. Co. of North America, 841 F.2d 1254, 1261 (5th Cir.1988); Lewis v. Rego, 757 F.2d 66, 68–69 (3d Cir. 1985).

16. *See* Pullman Co. v. Jenkins, 305 U.S. 534, 541, 59 S.Ct. 347, 350–51, 83 L.Ed. 334 (1939); Everett v. MTD Products, Inc., 947 F.Supp. 441, 443–44 (N.D.Ala. 1996); Zaini v. Shell Oil Co., 853 F.Supp. 960, 963–64 (S.D.Tex.1994).

17. Pullman Co., 305 U.S. at 540–41, 59 S.Ct. at 350–51.

18. Balazik v. County of Dauphin, 44 F.3d 209, 213 n. 4 (3d Cir.1995); Emrich v. Touche Ross & Co., 846 F.2d 1190 (9th Cir.1988); Brown v. Demco, Inc., 792 F.2d 478 (5th Cir.1986).

held liable in the action.[19] The removing party may establish fraudulent joinder by showing that "there is no possibility that the plaintiff would be able to establish a cause of action against the resident defendant in state court or that there has been outright fraud in the plaintiff's pleading of jurisdiction facts."[20]

(5) Special Rule for Foreign Defendants

Section 1441(d) provides that a foreign state may remove any civil action brought against it in state court to the district court in the place where the action is pending. A foreign state may remove a case from state court even if all defendants do not desire removal.[21] Foreign states can remove as third-party defendants, with removal jurisdiction extending to the whole action, and not merely the third-party claim.[22]

(b) Time for Seeking Removal

(1) General Time Limits

The time limits for removal are given in 28 U.S.C.A. § 1446, which provides the procedures for removal. In cases where the action is removable based on the initial pleading, the defendant must file the notice of removal within 30 days after the earlier of the date that: (1) the defendant receives a copy of the initial pleading setting forth the claim for relief upon which the action is based; or (2) that the defendant is served with a summons if the initial pleading has been filed in court and is not required to be served on the defendant.[23] Where the action is not removable upon the basis of an initial pleading, but becomes removable at a later date, the defendant must file the notice of removal within 30 days "after receipt by the defendant, through service or otherwise, of a copy of an amended pleading, motion, order or other paper from which it may first be ascertained that the case is one which is or has become removable."[24] Diversity cases cannot be removed to federal court "more than one year after the commencement of the action" in state court, regardless of when the case becomes removable.[25] Courts are divided on whether "commencement" is to be determined by reference to federal or state law.[26]

---

19. *See, e.g.,* Shaw v. Dow Brands, Inc., 994 F.2d 364 (7th Cir.1993); Selfix, Inc. v. Bisk, 867 F.Supp. 1333 (N.D.Ill.1994) (bank that issued letters of credit for sale of company was nominal party in action brought by buyer against seller and bank regarding agreement to sell company); Norman v. Cuomo, 796 F.Supp. 654 (N.D.N.Y.1992).

20. Coker v. Amoco Oil Co., 709 F.2d 1433, 1440 (11th Cir.1983).

21. 28 U.S.C.A. § 1441(d) (West 1994). *See* Fabe v. Aneco Reinsurance Underwriting Ltd., 784 F.Supp. 448 (S.D.Ohio 1991).

22. *See* Delgado v. Shell Oil Co., 890 F.Supp. 1324 (S.D.Tex.1995); Lopez del

Valle v. Gobierno de la Capital, 855 F.Supp. 34 (D.Puerto Rico 1994).

23. 28 U.S.C.A. § 1446(b) (West 1994).

24. *Id.*

25. *Id.*

26. *Compare* Norman v. Sundance Spas, 844 F.Supp. 355 (W.D.Ky.1994) (federal law); O'Brien v. Powerforce, Inc., 939 F.Supp. 774 (D.Haw.1996), *with* Robinson v. J.F. Cleckley & Co., 751 F.Supp. 100 (D.S.C.1990) (state law); Kite v. Richard Wolf Med. Instruments Corp., 761 F.Supp. 597 (S.D.Ind.1989).

An issue that frequently arises concerns the effect of the 30–day time period on later-joined defendants. Where the initial defendant waives his right to remove by failing to file the notice of removal within the 30–day time period, defendants joined after the expiration of the period will necessarily argue that the time period should not be applicable to them. The Fifth Circuit and several district courts have concluded that a later-joined defendant is barred from removing the case to federal court when the original defendant does not remove within 30 days of service.[27] These courts base this conclusion on the unanimity rule.[28] However, the Fourth Circuit and other courts have concluded that because allowing later-joined defendants an opportunity to remove still requires all defendants to consent to the petition for removal, allowing later-added defendants to remove does not violate the unanimity rule.[29] These courts have held that a later-joined defendant may remove to federal court, as long as all the other defendants consent to removal and the notice of removal is filed within 30 days of service on the later-joined defendant.[30]

The one-year limitation on the removal of diversity cases raises several important issues. Congress intended the one-year limitation to prevent removal after substantial progress has been made in state court.[31] This one-year limitation lends itself to strategic planning by the plaintiff. To avoid removal, plaintiffs may attempt to use tactics such as joining a nondiverse defendant and dismissing the defendant after the expiration of the year period, or pleading less than the jurisdictional amount and then amending the complaint to seek higher damages after the expiration of the period. While the defendant can remove the action and attempt to prove that the nondiverse defendant was fraudulently joined, or that the amount in controversy is actually higher than the jurisdictional amount, the defendant must meet a heavy burden of proof in doing so.[32] Most courts have held that the one-year limitation should be strictly enforced where removal is objected to by the plaintiff, and that the plaintiff's use of manipulative tactics should not be considered.[33]

27. Brown v. Demco Inc., 792 F.2d 478, 482 (5th Cir.1986); Kuhn v. Brunswick Corp., 871 F.Supp. 1444, 1447 (N.D.Ga. 1994); Murjani v. Allstate Ins. Co., 679 F.Supp. 601, 603 n. 3 (M.D.La.1988).

28. See, e.g., Brown, 792 F.2d at 481.

29. See, e.g., McKinney v. Board of Trustees of Mayland Community College, 955 F.2d 924 (4th Cir.1992); Collings v. E–Z Serve Convenience Stores, Inc., 936 F.Supp. 892, 893–94 (N.D.Fla.1996).

30. Collings, 936 F.Supp. at 894–95; Eltman v. Pioneer Communications of America, Inc., 151 F.R.D. 311, 318 (N.D.Ill.1993); Ford v. New United Motors Mfg., Inc., 857 F.Supp. 707, 710 (N.D.Cal.1994); Garside by Garside v. Osco Drug, Inc., 702 F.Supp. 19, 21–22 (D.Mass.1988).

31. Singh v. Daimler–Benz AG, 9 F.3d 303, 309 (3d Cir.1993).

32. See Kliebert v. Upjohn Co., 915 F.2d 142 (5th Cir.1990) (although the court recognized the tactical nature of plaintiff's damage request, defendants produced no evidence that award of less than jurisdictional amount would be below range of awards expected).

33. See Burns v. Windsor Ins. Co., 31 F.3d 1092, 1097 n. 12 (11th Cir.1994) (Congress has recognized and accepted that, in some circumstances, plaintiff can and will intentionally avoid federal jurisdiction); Jenkins v. Sandoz Pharmaceuticals Corp., No. 1:97CV62–D–A, 1997 WL 271707 (N.D.Miss.1997); Cofer v. Horsehead Research and Development Co., 805 F.Supp. 541 (E.D.Tenn.1991) (one-year limit en-

However, judges should be skeptical of manipulative tactics and some have applied equitable considerations to estop a plaintiff from arguing that removal is untimely.[34] In *Morrison v. National Benefit Life Insurance Company*,[35] for example, the plaintiffs filed a motion to amend the complaint to increase damage demands from $49,000 to $2 million one-year and seven days after the action was commenced. The court held that the plaintiffs were equitably estopped from asserting the one-year limit because of their obvious attempt to manipulate the forum.[36]

The courts are divided on whether a plaintiff can waive an objection on the basis of the one-year limit by failing to timely move for remand. The Fifth and Ninth Circuits have held that removal outside the one-year limitation is a procedural defect which is waived if not raised in a timely motion for remand.[37] In contrast, several district courts have held that the one-year time limit is a jurisdictional limitation that may be raised at any time before final judgment.[38]

(2) Notice Given by Initial Pleading

The time limit for filing the notice of removal in district court is triggered when the writ of summons or complaint provides adequate notice to the defendant of federal jurisdiction.[39] While most courts have held that as long as the complaint has been filed, receipt of the complaint through formal or informal means triggers the 30–day period,[40] some courts have held that the period does not begin to run until proper service of process is made of the complaint.[41] Because the purpose of the

---

forced even though plaintiffs amended complaint to request damages in excess of jurisdictional amount after one-year period had elapsed).

34. Kinabrew v. Emco–Wheaton, Inc., 936 F.Supp. 351 (M.D.La.1996); Morrison v. National Benefit Life Ins. Co., 889 F.Supp. 945 (S.D.Miss.1995).

35. 889 F.Supp. 945 (S.D.Miss.1995).

36. *Id.* at 951.

37. Maniar v. F.D.I.C., 979 F.2d 782, 785 (9th Cir.1992); Baris v. Sulpicio Lines, Inc., 932 F.2d 1540, 1544 (5th Cir.), *cert. denied*, 502 U.S. 963, 112 S.Ct. 430, 116 L.Ed.2d 449 (1991); *see also* Leidolf by Warshafsky v. Eli Lilly & Co., 728 F.Supp. 1383, 1388 (E.D.Wis.1990); Gray v. Moore Business Forms, Inc., 711 F.Supp. 543 (N.D.Cal. 1989).

38. *See* Rashid v. Schenck Const. Co., 843 F.Supp. 1081 (S.D.W.Va.1993); Brock by Brock v. Syntex Lab, Inc., 791 F.Supp. 721 (E.D.Tenn.1992), *aff'd*, 7 F.3d 232 (6th Cir.1993); Perez v. General Packer, Inc., 790 F.Supp. 1464 (C.D.Cal.1992); Foiles by Foiles v. Merrell Nat'l Lab., 730 F.Supp. 108 (N.D.Ill.1989). The Sixth Circuit Court of Appeals has agreed with this conclusion in an unpublished opinion. *See* Brock v. Syntex Lab, Inc., 7 F.3d 232 (6th Cir.1993).

39. Leffall v. Dallas Ind. School Dist., 28 F.3d 521 (5th Cir.1994); Foster v. Mutual Fire, Marine & Inland Ins. Co., 986 F.2d 48 (3d Cir.1993).

40. *See* Tech Hills II v. Phoenix Home Life Mut. Ins. Co., 5 F.3d 963, 968 (6th Cir.1993) (adopting receipt rule); Ponce v. Alitalia Linee Airee, 840 F.Supp. 552 (N.D.Ill.1994) (receiving courtesy copy of complaint properly filed in state court triggered period); Lofstrom v. Dennis, 829 F.Supp. 1194 (N.D.Cal.1993); Greensmith Co. v. Com Systems, Inc., 796 F.Supp. 812 (D.N.J.1992); Kerr v. Holland America–Line Westours, Inc., 794 F.Supp. 207 (E.D.Mich. 1992); *see generally* Robert Koets, *What Constitutes "Initial Pleading" for Purposes of Computing Time for Removal of Civil Action from State to Federal Court Under 28 U.S.C.A. § 1446(b)*, 130 A.L.R. Fed. 581 (1996).

41. Schollenberger v. Sears, Roebuck & Co., 876 F.Supp. 153 (E.D.Mich.1995) (courtesy copy of complaint insufficient; actual service required); Estate of Baratt v. Phoe-

notice provision is to ensure that the defendant is given adequate information upon which to base the decision to remove, a summons that does not indicate the nature of the claim for relief is insufficient to trigger the 30–day period.[42] In cases where the complaint raises state law claims that are subject to complete preemption, the complaint is considered to provide adequate notice of federal jurisdiction for purposes of the time limit.[43]

(3) Notice Given by Amended Pleading, Motion, Order or Other Paper

When the right to remove becomes available for the first time during the pendency of state court litigation, the defendant must file the notice of removal "within thirty days after receipt by the defendant, through service or otherwise, of a copy of an amended pleading, motion, order or other paper from which it may first be ascertained that the case is one which is or has become removable."[44] The time limit is strictly construed, and is not subject to extension by the consent of the parties or by order of the court.[45]

Removal is appropriate only where the change that makes the action removable occurs as the result of a voluntary act by the plaintiff.[46] Thus, the amended pleading, motion, order or other paper upon which removal is based must be a product of the plaintiff's voluntary act. Where the amended complaint gives notice of the plaintiff's change of residence,[47] asserts a claim within the jurisdiction of the federal courts,[48] or increases the amount in controversy, the defendant may remove the case to federal court. Dismissal by the plaintiff of a nondiverse defendant may also create a right to removal.[49] However, removal is not appropriate where the nondiverse defendant is dismissed by the action of the defendant or the court against the wishes of the plaintiff.[50] This has been applied even where the motion to dismiss by the nondiverse defendant is not opposed by the plaintiff.[51] When the defendant seeking removal demonstrates

nix Mut. Life Ins. Co., 787 F.Supp. 333 (W.D.N.Y.1992); Marion Corp. v. Lloyds Bank, PLC, 738 F.Supp. 1377 (S.D.Ala. 1990); Thomason v. Republic Ins. Co., 630 F.Supp. 331 (E.D.Cal.1986).

42. See, e.g., Gervel v. L & J Talent, 805 F.Supp. 308 (E.D.Pa.1992).

43. See Cantrell v. Great Republic Ins. Co., 873 F.2d 1249 (9th Cir.1989).

44. 28 U.S.C.A. § 1446(b) (West 1994).

45. See Barton v. Lloyd's of London, 883 F.Supp. 641 (M.D.Ala.1995).

46. Yarnevic v. Brink's, Inc., 102 F.3d 753, 754 (4th Cir.1996); S.W.S. Erectors, Inc. v. Infax, Inc., 72 F.3d 489, 494 (5th Cir.1996); Poulos v. Naas Foods, Inc., 959 F.2d 69 (7th Cir.1992); Rodgers v. North-

western Mut. Life Ins. Co., 952 F.Supp. 325 (W.D.Va.1997).

47. DeBry v. Transamerica Corp., 601 F.2d 480 (10th Cir.1979).

48. See, e.g., Federal Deposit Ins. Corp. v. Otero, 598 F.2d 627 (1st Cir.1979) (claim involving federal question raised in complaint; removal appropriate).

49. See McAllister Bros., Inc. v. Ocean Marine Indem. Co., 742 F.Supp. 70 (S.D.N.Y.1989).

50. Poulos, 959 F.2d 69; Spann v. Northwestern Mut. Life Ins. Co., 795 F.Supp. 386 (M.D.Ala.1992).

51. Machinsky v. Johnson & Johnson Medical, Inc., 868 F.Supp. 269 (E.D.Mo. 1994).

that the nondiverse defendant was fraudulently joined by the plaintiff, removal is allowed without a voluntary act on the plaintiff's part.[52]

Because the statute specifies that a case may be removed during the pendency of a state court proceeding only "[i]f the case stated by the initial pleading is not removable,"[53] an amendment of the complaint will not revive the period for removal where the case was removable on the basis of the initial pleading, but the defendant failed to exercise the right to removal.[54] An exception sometimes exists where the plaintiff files an amended complaint that so changes the nature of the action "as to constitute 'substantially a new suit begun that day.' "[55] In that event, the defendant is permitted to remove within the 30–day period, despite his failure to timely remove on the basis of the original complaint. Although this situation is common, the exception has rarely been applied.[56]

As noted above, Section 1446(b) provides that the defendant must file the notice of removal "within thirty days after receipt by the defendant, through service or otherwise, of a copy of an amended pleading, motion, order or *other paper* from which it may first be ascertained that the case is one which is or has become removable."[57] A recurring issue under this part of Section 1446(b) concerns what materials constitute "other paper" for notice purposes. In general, the "motion, order or other paper" requirement "is broad enough to include any information received by the defendant, 'whether communicated in a formal or informal manner.' "[58] However, it has been required that the communication be reduced to writing—a "paper."[59]

The courts have disagreed as to what specific items are sufficient as an "other paper" to begin the running of the period. One line of cases holds that the "other paper" provision applies only to papers filed in the state court proceeding.[60] Other courts have applied the provision to

---

52. Poulos, 959 F.2d at 73; Lane v. Champion Int'l Corp., 844 F.Supp. 724 (S.D.Ala.1994); Todd Holding Company, Inc. v. Super Valu Stores, 744 F.Supp. 1025, 1027 (D.Colo.1990).

53. 28 U.S.C.A. § 1446(b) (West 1994).

54. Cantrell v. Great Republic Ins. Co., 873 F.2d 1249 (9th Cir.1989); Samura v. Kaiser Foundation Health Plan, Inc., 715 F.Supp. 970 (N.D.Cal.1989); Hubbard v. Union Oil Co., 601 F.Supp. 790 (S.D.W.Va. 1985).

55. Wilson v. Intercollegiate (Big Ten) Conference Athletic Ass'n, 668 F.2d 962, 965 (7th Cir.1982).

56. *See* Potty Pals, Inc. v. Carson Financial Group, Inc., 887 F.Supp. 208 (E.D.Ark.1995) (amendment requesting injunctive relief did not warrant extension of 30–day limit); Samura v. Kaiser Foundation Health Plan, Inc., 715 F.Supp. 970 (N.D.Cal.1989) (amendment of complaint

adding additional parties and federal claim did not materially change nature of case); Douglass v. Weyerhaeuser, 662 F.Supp. 147 (C.D.Cal.1987) (defendant could have initially removed complaint on federal question ground; right of removal not revived when nondiverse defendants were dismissed).

57. 28 U.S.C.A. § 1446(b) (West 1994) (emphasis added).

58. Yarnevic v. Brink's, Inc., 102 F.3d 753, 755 (4th Cir.1996) (citations omitted) (memorandum indicating plaintiff's change of domicile constituted "other paper").

59. Smith v. Bally's Holiday, 843 F.Supp. 1451 (N.D.Ga.1994) (oral statement by attorney was not "other paper").

60. *See* Phillips v. Allstate Ins. Co., 702 F.Supp. 1466 (C.D.Cal.1989) ("paper" does not include intervening statutory or case law changes); Johansen v. Employee Bene-

"papers" generally.[61] The status as "other paper" of such items as demand letters, depositions, and correspondence between the parties depends on the interpretation given to Section 1446(b) by the individual court.[62]

Several courts, including the Fifth Circuit Court of Appeals, have concluded that since the second paragraph of Section 1446(b) only applies when the case stated by the initial pleading is not removable, the defendant must receive the "other paper" only after it receives the initial pleading in order for the 30–day period to be triggered.[63] Under this holding, a presuit demand letter providing a basis for removal would not result in the 30–day period being triggered upon the filing of the complaint, although the information in the letter could be utilized by the defendant to support removal.[64] It has also been required that the "other paper" be generated by a voluntary act of the plaintiff, rather than by the defendant.[65] An affidavit created by the defendant that memorialized a telephone conversation with the plaintiff did not constitute "other paper."[66]

Even where correspondence such as a demand letter is held to be an "other paper," the court must still determine whether the "other paper" is sufficient to show that removal is appropriate. In *Sunburst Bank v. Summit Acceptance Company*,[67] the plaintiff brought an action for breach of contract for the assignment of security agreements in state court. The plaintiff sent a letter notifying the defendant that the total amount of claims pending equaled approximately $52,000. The district court held that while the letter constituted "other paper" for purposes of Section 1446(b), the defendant failed to prove that the contents of the letter established that the amount in controversy requirement was met.[68]

fit Claims, Inc., 668 F.Supp. 1294 (D.Minn. 1987) ("other paper" refers solely to documents generated within state court litigation).

61. See, e.g., Sunburst Bank v. Summit Acceptance Corp., 878 F.Supp. 77 (S.D.Miss.1995) (demand letter was "other paper" triggering right of removal); Central Iowa Agri–Systems v. Old Heritage Advertising & Publishers, 727 F.Supp. 1304 (S.D.Iowa 1989).

62. Compare Rahwar v. Nootz, 863 F.Supp. 191 (D.N.J.1994) (correspondence between parties including statement of damages was "other paper"); Central Iowa Agri–Systems, 727 F.Supp. 1304 (demand letter constituted "other paper"); Van Gosen v. Arcadian Motor Carriers, 825 F.Supp. 981 (D.Kan.1993) (answers to interrogatories and depositions may be "other papers"), with Woodward v. Employers Cas.

Co., 785 F.Supp. 90 (S.D.Tex.1992) (correspondence was not "other paper"); Campos v. Housland, Inc., 824 F.Supp. 100 (S.D.Tex.1993) (deposition of plaintiff was not "other paper").

63. Chapman v. Powermatic, Inc., 969 F.2d 160 (5th Cir.1992), cert. denied, 507 U.S. 967, 113 S.Ct. 1402, 122 L.Ed.2d 774 (1993); Jade East Towers Developers v. Nationwide Mutual Ins. Co., 936 F.Supp. 890, 891–92 (N.D.Fla.1996).

64. Jade East Towers Developers, 936 F.Supp. at 892.

65. See S.W.S. Erectors, Inc. v. Infax, Inc., 72 F.3d 489, 494 (5th Cir.1996).

66. Id.

67. 878 F.Supp. 77 (S.D.Miss.1995).

68. Id. at 82. [Amount in controversy must now be $ 75,000].

(4) Premature Removal

Where an action is removed prematurely, the district court lacks subject matter jurisdiction over the action, and is required to remand the case to state court.[69] Premature removal may occur where defendant relies on statements or documents concerning the jurisdictional amount that are later found not to be an "other paper" within the meaning of the statute,[70] or where the summons or complaint has not yet been served on the defendant.[71]

(5) Fraudulent Joinder

The doctrine of fraudulent joinder comes into play in cases removed on the basis of diversity jurisdiction. Where removal would normally be prevented by the presence of a nondiverse defendant, the defendant can remove the case to federal court by demonstrating that the nondiverse defendant was fraudulently joined by the plaintiff.[72] Since the case would not have been removable on the basis of the initial pleading, the second paragraph of Section 1446(b) applies, and the defendant is required to file the notice of removal within 30 days of receiving an amended pleading, motion, order, or other paper from which the defendant can ascertain that the nondiverse defendant has been fraudulently joined. To establish fraudulent joinder, the removing party must show either that there is no possibility that the plaintiff would be able to establish a cause of action against the nondiverse defendant, or that there has been outright fraud in the plaintiff's pleadings of jurisdictional facts.[73]

It has been held that claims of fraudulent joinder must be pleaded with particularity and supported by clear and convincing evidence.[74] In examining claims of fraudulent joinder, the district court must resolve all contested issues of fact in favor of the plaintiff and resolve any uncertainties in the current state of the controlling substantive law in favor of the plaintiff.[75]

(6) Statutory Exceptions to Time Limits

Different time limits apply if the Resolution Trust Corporation ("RTC") or the Federal Deposit Insurance Corporation ("FDIC") is a

---

69. See, e.g., Navarro v. LTV Steel Co., 750 F.Supp. 928 (N.D.Ill.1990).

70. Coleman v. Southern Norfolk, 734 F.Supp. 719 (E.D.La.1990).

71. London v. Accufix Research Institute, Inc., 953 F.Supp. 255 (N.D.Ill.1997) (plaintiff's motion for order of protection and disclosure was not initial pleading on which removal could be based).

72. Poulos v. Naas Foods, Inc., 959 F.2d 69, 73 (7th Cir.1992); Lane v. Champion Int'l Corp., 844 F.Supp. 724 (S.D.Ala.1994); Todd Holding Company, Inc. v. Super Valu Stores, 744 F.Supp. 1025, 1027 (D.Colo. 1990).

73. See Boyer v. Snap–On Tools Corp., 913 F.2d 108 (3d Cir.1990); B., Inc. v. Miller Brewing Co., 663 F.2d 545 (5th Cir.1981); Katonah v. USAir, Inc., 876 F.Supp. 984 (N.D.Ill.1995); Horton v. Scripto–Tokai Corp., 878 F.Supp. 902 (S.D.Miss.1995).

74. B., Inc., 663 F.2d at 550; Everett v. MTD Products, Inc., 947 F.Supp. 441, 445 (N.D.Ala.1996); Parker v. Crete Carrier Corp., 914 F.Supp. 156 (E.D.Ky.1996).

75. Boyer, 913 F.2d at 111; Carriere v. Sears, Roebuck & Co., 893 F.2d 98, 100 (5th Cir.1990).

457

party to the action. The RTC may remove a case within 90 days after it is substituted as a party.[76] For RTC removal purposes, the RTC is substituted as a party when someone files a copy of the order appointing the RTC as conservator or receiver for that party.[77] Under the FDIC removal statute, the FDIC also has 90 days within which to remove a case after it is substituted as a party.[78] However, the FDIC is not substituted as a party until it actually intervenes in the state court proceeding.[79] Many courts have held that the RTC and the FDIC can remove cases from state court even after a state court has entered judgment and the case is pending on appeal.[80]

(c) Content and Amendment of the Notice of Removal

Section 1446(a) requires the defendant seeking removal to file a notice of removal "containing a short and plain statement of the grounds for removal, together with a copy of all process, pleadings, and orders served upon such defendant or defendants in such action." A copy of the notice must also be filed with the clerk of the state court.[81]

(1) Concurrence of All Defendants Required, with Limited Exceptions

Ordinarily, all defendants in the state action must join in the petition for removal, with the exception of nominal, unknown, or fraudulently joined parties.[82] As a result of the unanimity requirement, in the typical case, any defendant can dictate that the action remain in state court by refusing to join in the notice of removal.[83] However, a defendant with an independent right of removal, such as a federal agency, is not required to obtain the consent of other defendants to remove.[84] In addition, where removal occurs under 28 U.S.C.A. § 1441(c),[85] only the defendant to the separate and independent federal claim is required to seek removal.[86]

76. 12 U.S.C.A. § 1441a(l)(3) (West 1989).

77. *Id.; see* Ventana Investments v. 909 Corp., 71 F.3d 168 (5th Cir.1995).

78. 12 U.S.C.A. § 1819(b)(2)(B) (West 1989).

79. Ventana Investments, 71 F.3d at 170.

80. *See* Ward v. Resolution Trust Corp., 901 F.2d 694 (8th Cir.1990) (RTC); *In re* 5300 Memorial Investors, Ltd., 973 F.2d 1160 (5th Cir.1992) (RTC); Lester v. Resolution Trust Corp., 994 F.2d 1247 (7th Cir. 1993); Federal Dep. Ins. Corp. v. Keating, 12 F.3d 314 (1st Cir.1993) (FDIC); *In re* Savers Federal Sav. & Loan Ass'n, 872 F.2d 963 (11th Cir.1989) (interpreting § 1730(k)(1), the predecessor to § 1819).

81. 28 U.S.C.A. § 1446(b) (West 1994).

82. Balazik v. County of Dauphin, 44 F.3d 209, 213 n. 4 (3d Cir.1995); Emrich v. Touche Ross & Co., 846 F.2d 1190 (9th Cir.1988); Brown v. Demco, Inc., 792 F.2d 478 (5th Cir.1986).

83. *See, e.g.,* Ford v. New United Motors Mfg., Inc., 857 F.Supp. 707 (N.D.Cal. 1994).

84. *See, e.g.,* Davis v. FSLIC, 879 F.2d 1288 (5th Cir.1989).

85. *See supra* § 8.3(d) (discussing removal under § 1441(c)).

86. Constantini v. Guardian Life Ins. Co. of America, 859 F.Supp. 89 (S.D.N.Y.1994); Alexander by Alexander v. Goldome Credit Corp., 772 F.Supp. 1217, 1222 (M.D.Ala. 1991).

(2) Explanation of Grounds for Removal

The notice of removal must plainly indicate the grounds for removal, and must show that the federal jurisdictional requirements are met.[87] Courts have required that the notice of removal allege facts giving rise to federal jurisdiction with particularity.[88] A notice of removal based on the existence of a federal question must allege all facts essential to the existence of the federal question.[89] As to actions removed on the basis of diversity jurisdiction, the notice must allege complete diversity of citizenship, and must allege facts showing that the amount in controversy requirement is satisfied.[90] Where less than all defendants have joined in the notice of removal, the notice must contain an explanation for the absence of any co-defendants.[91] It is insufficient for the removing party to represent in the notice that other defendants consent or do not object to removal.[92] However, the failure to explain the absence of co-defendants in the petition has been held to be a nonjurisdictional defect which is waivable by the plaintiff.[93]

Where the defendant seeks to remove on the basis that a nondiverse co-defendant was fraudulently joined by the plaintiff, the defendant must plead with particularity the facts supporting the defendant's allegation of fraudulent joinder.[94] Mere conclusory allegations of fraudulent joinder are insufficient.[95]

(3) No Limitation to Facts of Complaint

District courts do not limit their inquiry as to the propriety of removal to the plaintiff's complaint, but also consider the removal petition and the record as a whole.[96] The district court can thus look to the notice of removal to determine the amount in controversy when the complaint contains no specific demand.[97] In addition, courts may perform an independent valuation of the amount in controversy by such methods

---

87. 28 U.S.C.A. § 1441(a) (West 1994); Laughlin v. Kmart Corp., 50 F.3d 871 (10th Cir.1995), *cert. denied,* 516 U.S. 863, 116 S.Ct. 174, 133 L.Ed.2d 114 (1995).

88. *See* State of Ohio v. Denman, 462 F.2d 1292 (6th Cir.1972); Stanley Elec. Contractors, Inc. v. Darin & Armstrong Co., 486 F.Supp. 769 (E.D.Ky.1980).

89. *See, e.g.,* Thomas v. Burlington Industries, Inc., 763 F.Supp. 1570 (S.D.Fla. 1991) (bare-bones contention that action was governed by ERISA was subject to remand).

90. Gaus v. Miles, Inc., 980 F.2d 564 (9th Cir.1992) (conclusory allegation that amount in controversy requirement was met did not satisfy requirement of setting forth facts supporting claim amount).

91. Northern Illinois Gas Co. v. Airco Indus. Gases, 676 F.2d 270 (7th Cir.1982); Scheall v. Ingram, 930 F.Supp. 1448

(D.Colo.1996); P–Nut Carter's Fireworks, Inc. v. Carey, 685 F.Supp. 952 (D.S.C.1988).

92. Henderson v. Holmes, 920 F.Supp. 1184 (D.Kan.1996).

93. Marshall v. Skydive America South, 903 F.Supp. 1067 (E.D.Tex.1995); Rashid v. Schenck Constr. Co., 843 F.Supp. 1081 (S.D.W.Va.1993).

94. American Mutual Liability Ins. Co. v. Flintkote Co., 565 F.Supp. 843 (S.D.N.Y. 1983); Saylor v. General Motors Corp., 416 F.Supp. 1173 (E.D.Ky.1976).

95. *See, e.g.,* Shane v. Kansas City Southern Ry. Co., 121 F.Supp. 426 (W.D.Ark.1954).

96. *See* Baccus v. Parrish, 45 F.3d 958, 960 (5th Cir.1995).

97. *See, e.g.,* Corwin Jeep Sales & Serv., Inc. v. American Motors Sales Corp., 670 F.Supp. 591 (M.D.Pa.1986).

as looking to damage awards in similar cases.[98] Where the case is removed on the basis of an amended pleading, motion, order or other paper, such documents may be considered by the court in determining the amount in controversy.[99] In cases removed on the basis of federal question jurisdiction, the "well-pleaded complaint" rule usually controls, and the court is limited to determining whether a federal question is presented on the face of the plaintiff's properly pleaded complaint.[100] However, the court may look beyond the face of the complaint to determine if a state law claim is subject to complete preemption on the basis of a federal statute.[101]

(4) Amending the Notice of Removal

The defendant can freely amend the notice of removal to correct deficiencies within the 30–day time period for seeking removal provided in Section 1446(b).[102] After the end of the period, any amendments to the removal notice must be made in accordance with 28 U.S.C.A. § 1653, which provides that "[d]efective allegations of jurisdiction may be amended, upon terms, in the trial or appellate courts." Courts interpreting Section 1653 in the context of removal have held that it cannot be invoked to claim an entirely new and distinct jurisdictional basis, and is limited to the curing of technical defects in the notice of removal.[103] Courts have also distinguished between an imperfect or defective allegation as to jurisdiction, which can be amended after the expiration of the 30–day period, and missing allegations of jurisdiction, which cannot be added by amendment. In general, the notice may be amended only to set out more specifically grounds for removal that have been imperfectly stated in the original notice.[104] Thus, where only federal question jurisdiction is alleged as a basis for removal, diversity jurisdiction cannot be added as a basis for removal after the expiration of the 30–day period.[105]

(5) Service on All Parties and State Court

Section 1446(d) requires that "[p]romptly after the filing of [the] notice of removal of a civil action [with the federal court] the defendant

98. See, e.g., Harding v. U.S. Figure Skating Ass'n, 851 F.Supp. 1476 (D.Or. 1994); Smith v. Executive Fund Life Ins. Co., 651 F.Supp. 269 (M.D.La.1986).

99. Rahwar v. Nootz, 863 F.Supp. 191 (D.N.J.1994).

100. See McQuerry v. American Medical Systems, Inc., 899 F.Supp. 366 (N.D.Ill. 1995); Campos v. Sociedad Aeronautica de Medellin Consolidada, 882 F.Supp. 1056 (S.D.Fla.1994); Zandi–Dulabi v. Pacific Retirement Plans, Inc., 828 F.Supp. 760 (N.D.Cal.1993).

101. See, e.g., Oglesby v. RCA Corp., 752 F.2d 272, 278 (7th Cir.1985); Blair v. Source One Mortg. Services Corp., 925 F.Supp. 617 (D.Minn.1996).

102. Bradwell v. Silk Greenhouse, Inc., 828 F.Supp. 940 (M.D.Fla.1993); Iwag v. Geisel Compania Maritima, S.A., 882 F.Supp. 597 (S.D.Tex.1995).

103. See Boelens v. Redman Homes, Inc., 759 F.2d 504 (5th Cir.1985); Energy Catering Services, Inc. v. Burrow, 911 F.Supp. 221 (E.D.La.1995); Bradwell, 828 F.Supp. 940.

104. Zaini v. Shell Oil Co., 853 F.Supp. 960 (S.D.Tex.1994); Bahrs v. Hughes Aircraft Co., 795 F.Supp. 965 (D.Ariz.1992).

105. Roeder v. ChemRex, Inc., 863 F.Supp. 817 (E.D.Wis.1994).

or defendants shall give written notice thereof to all adverse parties and shall file a copy of the notice with the clerk of such State court." The courts have held that since no particular time is specified in the statute, what constitutes undue delay on the part of the defendant depends on the circumstances of the case.[106] Several courts have held that where the defendant makes a good faith effort to give notice, and the plaintiff suffers no prejudice as a result of the delay, remand is not required.[107]

Library References:

West's Key No. Digests, Removal of Cases ⟐77–99.
Wright, Miller & Cooper, Federal Practice and Procedure: Civil 2d §§ 3730–3737.

§ 8.8   Procedure After Removal

(a) When Does Removal Become Effective

Although 28 U.S.C.A. § 1446(d) clearly states that removal is effected when the defendant has: (1) filed its notice of removal in federal court; (2) "promptly" given written notice to all adverse parties; and (3) filed a copy of the notice with the clerk of the state court, federal courts have adopted three different rules for determining when removal is effected.[1] The first rule is based on the plain meaning of Section 1446(d). The majority of federal courts follow this rule. These courts hold that removal is effected at the time that the defendant satisfies Section 1446's last requirement by filing a copy of the notice of removal in the state court.[2] However, these courts also sometimes hold that constructive knowledge on the part of the state court is sufficient, even though the notice has not actually been filed.[3] The federal courts that follow the second rule find that removal is effected simply by filing the notice of removal in federal court.[4] The third rule is somewhat of a compromise between the first and second rules. The federal courts following this rule find that the federal and state courts have concurrent jurisdiction after the notice is filed in federal court but before the defendant notifies the state court.[5]

---

106. Brister v. Jolly, 1997 WL 16633 (E.D.La.1997).

107. See, e.g., L & O Partnership No. 2 v. Aetna Cas. & Surety Co., 761 F.Supp. 549 (N.D.Ill.1991).

§ 8.8

1. See supra § 8.7; 28 U.S.C.A. § 1446(d) (West 1994); see also Anthony v. Runyon, 76 F.3d 210, 213 (8th Cir.1996)(removal is not complete and jurisdiction does not "shift" to the federal court until the defendant files its notice of removal in state court); Dukes v. South Carolina Insurance Company, 770 F.2d 545 (5th Cir.1985).

2. See 14A Charles Alan Wright, Arthur R. Miller & Edward H. Cooper, Federal Practice and Procedure § 3737 at 550 (2d

ed. 1985)(The authors state that this rule is the one which is most consistent with the language of the statute and is, therefore, the "sounder rule."); see also Usatorres v. Marina Mercante Nicaraguenses, 768 F.2d 1285, 1286–87 (11th Cir.1985) (per curiam).

3. See Dukes, 770 F.2d at 547; United States v. Silberglitt, 441 F.2d 225, 227 (2d Cir.1971).

4. See Anthony v. Runyon, 76 F.3d 210, 213 (8th Cir.1996)(citing First Nat'l Bank v. Johnson & Johnson, 455 F.Supp. 361, 363 (E.D.Ark.1978)).

5. See Resolution Trust Corp. v. Nernberg, 3 F.3d 62, 69 (3d Cir.1993), modified 16 F.3d 568 (4th Cir.1994); Stephens v. Portal Boat Company, 781 F.2d 481 (5th

Regardless of which rule the federal court follows, once removal is effected, the federal court has exclusive jurisdiction over the action and "the State court shall proceed no further unless and until the case is remanded."[6] This means that actions taken by the state court after removal is properly completed are null and void.[7] However, if the defendant fails to follow the steps set forth in the statute (*e.g.*, the defendant fails to give notice to the plaintiff), removal is not effected and state court orders subsequent to the ineffective removal attempt remain valid.[8]

Actions taken or orders entered by the state court before removal is completed normally remain in effect after the case is removed.[9] However, the federal court has the power to modify or dissolve any state court order or action taken before the case was removed.[10] If the state court order is of a temporary nature (*e.g.*, a temporary restraining order), it will be valid in federal court only as long as it would have remained in effect in state court unless the federal rules of procedure state otherwise.[11]

(b) Compliance with the Federal Rules of Civil Procedure

After the case is properly removed, the federal court may issue "all necessary orders and process to bring before it all proper parties whether served by process issued by the state court or otherwise."[12] The federal court may also allow the plaintiff to complete service of process or issue new process, in the same manner as it would in cases that were originally filed in federal court, when service was not completed before removal or there was some defect in the process issued in the state court.[13]

Once the notice of removal is filed with the state court clerk, the case proceeds as though it had been originally filed in federal court.[14]

Cir.1986); Berberian v. Gibney, 514 F.2d 790 (1st Cir.1975).

6. 28 U.S.C.A. § 1446(d) (West 1994).

7. *See* National S.S. Co. v. Tugman, 106 U.S. 118, 1 S.Ct. 58, 27 L.Ed. 87 (1882); E.D. Systems Corp. v. Southwestern Bell Tel., 674 F.2d 453, 457–58 (5th Cir.1982); *see also* 14A Charles Alan Wright, Arthur R. Miller & Edward H. Cooper, Federal Practice and Procedure § 3737 at 551 (2d ed. 1985).

8. *See* Anthony, 76 F.3d 210; Pacor v. Higgins, 743 F.2d 984, 989 n. 8 (3d Cir. 1984).

9. 28 U.S.C.A. § 1450 (West 1994) (injunctions, attachments, sequestrations, and associated security filed as bonds remain in effect pursuant to federal law); *see also* Rorick v. Devon Syndicate, 307 U.S. 299, 59 S.Ct. 877, 83 L.Ed. 1303 (1939).

10. 28 U.S.C.A. § 1450 provides, inter alia, that all injunctions, orders, and other proceedings occurring prior to removal shall remain in full force and effect until dissolved or modified by the district court.

11. Granny Goose Foods, Inc. v. Brotherhood of Teamsters, 415 U.S. 423, 94 S.Ct. 1113, 39 L.Ed.2d 435 (1974); Nissho–Iwai American Corp. v. Kline, 845 F.2d 1300, 1307 (5th Cir.1988).

12. 28 U.S.C.A. § 1447(a) (West 1994).

13. *See* 28 U.S.C.A. § 1448 (West 1994); Allen v. Ferguson, 791 F.2d 611, 616 (7th Cir.1986).

14. *See* FRCP 81(c)("These rules apply to civil actions removed to the United States district courts from the state courts and govern procedure after removal.").

The Federal Rules of Civil Procedure and each district's local rules control the action. In most districts that means that the parties will be required to submit written memoranda for any pending motions filed in state court before removal became effective. The plaintiff is generally not required to replead to meet federal standards and is not subject to FRCP 11 sanctions for pleadings or motions filed in state court before removal.[15] However, the federal court can require the plaintiff to replead if it deems such action necessary.[16]

Amendments may be made to pleadings filed before the case was removed.[17] The plaintiff may also amend to assert a cause of action over which the state court would not have had jurisdiction.[18] However, the federal court will not normally allow an amendment that has the effect of taking away its jurisdiction.[19] Also, if either party made a demand for a jury trial in state court before removal, that demand does not have to be repeated in federal court.[20] If the case is removed from a state court that does not require the parties to make an express jury demand, no demand is required in federal court unless the federal court directs otherwise.[21] If the state court requires the parties to make an express jury demand at some subsequent point in the litigation and neither party made a demand for a jury trial in state court before removal, they must comply with the Federal Rules of Civil Procedure in order to be entitled to a jury trial in the removed action.[22]

When the defendant removes without answering the state court complaint, the defendant must answer or present its defenses or objections within 20 days after receipt, through service or otherwise, of a copy of the initial pleading setting forth the claim for relief upon which the action or proceeding is based, or within 20 days after the service of summons upon such initial pleading, or within five days after the filing of the petition for removal, whichever period is longest.[23]

Library References:

West's Key No. Digests, Removal of Cases ☞111–120.

Wright, Miller & Cooper, Federal Practice and Procedure: Civil 2d §§ 3738, 3914.11.

15. *Id.*; *see* Griffen v. Oklahoma City, 3 F.3d 336, 340 (10th Cir.1993) ("no sanctions can be imposed under Rule 11 in an action that is removed to federal court, unless a party files sanctionable papers in federal court"); Schoenberger v. Oselka, 909 F.2d 1086 (7th Cir.1990)(Rule 11 only provides sanctions for papers signed and filed in the federal court.).

16. *Id.*

17. *See* Kidd v. Southwest Airlines, Co., 891 F.2d 540, 547 (5th Cir.1990).

18. *See* Freeman v. Bee Machine Co., 319 U.S. 448, 63 S.Ct. 1146, 87 L.Ed. 1509 (1943).

19. *See* Winner's Circle of Las Vegas Inc. v. AMI Franchising Inc., 916 F.Supp. 1024 (D.Nev.1996); *see also* 6 Charles Alan Wright, Arthur R. Miller & Mary Kay Kane, Federal Practice & Procedure § 1477 at 562 (2d ed. 1990) ("'[A] party may not employ Rule 15(a) to interpose an amendment that would deprive the district court of jurisdiction over a removed action.'").

20. FRCP 81(c); *see also* Mondor v. United States Dist. Court for the Cent. Dist. of Cal., 910 F.2d 585, 586 (9th Cir. 1990).

21. FRCP 81(c).

22. FRCP 38.

23. FRCP 81(c).

§ 8.9 Remand

(a) Who May Seek Remand

Either the plaintiff or the defendant may seek to remand the case where the federal court lacks subject matter jurisdiction. 28 U.S.C.A. § 1447(c) provides that "[i]f at any time before final judgment it appears that the district court lacks subject matter jurisdiction, the case shall be remanded." Section 1447(c) allows the plaintiff 30 days after the filing of the notice of removal to seek remand on the basis of any defect in removal procedure. The defendant, as the party seeking to remove the case, bears the burden upon the motion for remand of establishing that the case is within the federal court's removal jurisdiction, and that the procedural requirements for removal have been met.[1]

(b) Time for Seeking Remand

(1) Based on Procedural Defects

A motion to remand a case based on a procedural defect in removal procedure must be filed within 30 days after the filing of the notice of removal with the federal court.[2] A plaintiff that fails to object to a procedural defect within the time period waives his right to object.[3] Where the plaintiff files a timely motion to remand, but does not raise a procedural defect until after the time period, the objection to such defect is waived.[4] Generally, the phrase "defect in removal procedure" is not limited to mistakes concerning timing, form, and content of removal, but includes any impropriety excepting those based on lack of subject matter jurisdiction.[5]

(2) Based on Jurisdictional Defects

Under Section 1447(c), "[i]f at any time before final judgment it appears that the district court lacks subject matter jurisdiction, the case shall be remanded." Lack of subject matter jurisdiction thus may be raised at any time, and is not governed by the 30-day limit.[6]

(3) Remand After Final Judgment

Ordinarily, if the district court could never have exercised original jurisdiction over the case, remand to the state court is required—even

---

§ 8.9

1. *In re* NASDAQ Market Makers Antitrust Litig., 929 F.Supp. 174 (S.D.N.Y. 1996); Bishop v. General Motors Corp., 925 F.Supp. 294 (D.N.J.1996); Lamb v. Laird, 907 F.Supp. 1033 (S.D.Tex.1995).

2. 28 U.S.C.A. § 1447(c) (West 1994).

3. *See In re* Shell Oil Co., 932 F.2d 1523 (5th Cir.1991), *cert. denied*, 502 U.S. 1049, 112 S.Ct. 914, 116 L.Ed.2d 814 (1992); Sel-

vaggi v. Prudential Property & Cas. Ins. Co., 871 F.Supp. 815 (E.D.Pa.1995).

4. *See, e.g.,* Northern Calif. Dist. Council of Laborers v. Pittsburg–Des Moines Steel Co., 69 F.3d 1034 (9th Cir.1995).

5. Pierpoint v. Barnes, 94 F.3d 813 (2d Cir.1996).

6. Horton v. Scripto–Tokai Corp., 878 F.Supp. 902 (S.D.Miss.1995).

after the entry of final judgment.[7] In such circumstances, the federal appellate court can order remand of the case.

However, a federal appellate court will not remand a case to state court if the federal district court had subject matter jurisdiction over the action at the time it entered final judgment.[8] Thus, if a district court erroneously exercises removal jurisdiction over an action, and the plaintiff voluntarily amends the original complaint to allege federal claims, the plaintiff waives the ability to challenge removal jurisdiction.[9]

(c) Grounds for Remand

(1) Removal Statute Strictly Applied

The courts are in agreement that the removal statute is to be strictly construed against removal, with all doubts resolved in favor of remand.[10] Courts base this conclusion on the fact that federal courts are courts of limited jurisdiction and removal implicates significant federalism concerns.[11]

(2) Reference Is Made to Complaint at Time of Removal

The district court looks to the state complaint to determine whether removal to federal court was proper.[12] As a result, even where the plaintiff files an amended complaint in federal court that clarifies the remedies sought, the state complaint provides the reference point for purposes of removal.[13]

(3) Evidentiary Hearing

Where the notice of removal plainly indicates a basis for removal, a factual hearing is not necessary.[14] However, where the plaintiff moves for remand and the notice does not clearly state jurisdictional grounds for removal, the district court may take arguments and written materials into account in determining the issue.[15] The district court, in its discretion, may hold an evidentiary hearing.[16] The party seeking removal has

7. Barbara v. New York Stock Exchange, Inc., 99 F.3d 49, 55 (2d Cir.1996); see American Fire & Cas. Co. v. Finn, 341 U.S. 6, 71 S.Ct. 534, 95 L.Ed. 702 (1951).

8. Barbara, 99 F.3d at 56; see Kidd v. Southwest Airlines, 891 F.2d 540 (5th Cir. 1990).

9. Kidd, 891 F.2d 540; Bernstein v. Lind–Waldock & Co., 738 F.2d 179 (7th Cir.1984). But see Kelly v. Carr, 691 F.2d 800, 805–06 (6th Cir.1980) (amendment does not cure defects in removal jurisdiction).

10. See State of Nevada v. Culverwell, 890 F.Supp. 933 (D.Nev.1995); Boyle v. MTV Networks, Inc., 766 F.Supp. 809 (N.D.Cal.1991).

11. In re NASDAQ Market Makers Antitrust Litig., 929 F.Supp. 174 (S.D.N.Y. 1996).

12. Miller v. Grgurich, 763 F.2d 372 (9th Cir.1985); McElroy v. SOS Int'l, Inc., 730 F.Supp. 803 (N.D.Ill.1989).

13. See, e.g., McElroy, 730 F.Supp. 803.

14. News–Texan, Inc. v. City of Garland, Texas, 814 F.2d 216 (5th Cir.1987).

15. See Institute of Penn. Hosp. v. Travelers Ins. Co., 817 F.Supp. 24 (E.D.Pa. 1993); Dent v. Packerland Packing Co., 144 F.R.D. 673 (D.Neb.1992); Kerbow v. Kerbow, 421 F.Supp. 1253 (N.D.Tex.1976).

16. See In re Business Men's Assurance Co. of America, 992 F.2d 181, 183 (8th Cir.1993); Institute of Penn. Hosp., 817

the burden of proving the grounds necessary to support removal, including compliance with procedural requirements.[17] The district court is required to resolve all doubts about federal jurisdiction in favor of remand.[18]

(4) Lack of Subject Matter Jurisdiction

Either party may seek to remand a case, or the court may remand sua sponte, where the federal court lacks subject matter jurisdiction.[19]

(5) Procedural Defects

A case may be remanded for any defect in removal procedure.[20] Some courts have held that a defect in removal procedure refers to any defect that does not concern whether the case could have originally been filed in federal court, and thus includes all nonjurisdictional defects existing as of the time of removal.[21] In contrast, other courts have limited the term to defects in the actual procedure used to remove the case to federal court.[22] Examples of defects held to be procedural include: (1) removal of a case where removal is prohibited by statute;[23] (2) filing a notice of removal after the 30–day period;[24] (3) failing to explain a defendant's failure to join in the notice of removal;[25] and (4) filing a notice of removal where less than all defendants join in the removal notice.[26] The courts are divided as to whether the fact that a defendant is a citizen of the forum state in a diversity action is a procedural or a jurisdictional defect.[27] Another split of authority exists as to whether the failure to remove a case based on diversity jurisdiction within the one-year time limit is jurisdictional or procedural.[28]

(6) Joinder of Additional Defendants

28 U.S.C.A. § 1447(e) provides that "[i]f after removal the plaintiff seeks to join additional defendants whose joinder would destroy subject

F.Supp. 24. *But see* Burden v. General Dynamics Corp., 60 F.3d 213, 217 (5th Cir. 1995) (in determining fraudulent joinder claim, district court should not conduct evidentiary hearing, but may look to evidence outside of pleadings).

17. *See, e.g.,* Laughlin v. Prudential Ins. Co., 882 F.2d 187 (5th Cir.1989); Parker v. Brown, 570 F.Supp. 640 (S.D.Ohio 1983).

18. Steel Valley Auth. v. Union Switch & Signal Div., 809 F.2d 1006 (3d Cir.1987).

19. *See* American Fire & Cas. Co. v. Finn, 341 U.S. 6, 71 S.Ct. 534, 95 L.Ed. 702 (1951).

20. 28 U.S.C.A. § 1447(c) (West 1994).

21. *See, e.g., In re* Allstate Ins. Co., 8 F.3d 219, 221 (5th Cir.1993).

22. *See* Foster v. Chesapeake Ins. Co., 933 F.2d 1207 (3d Cir.1991).

23. Pierpoint v. Barnes, 94 F.3d 813 (2d Cir.1996).

24. Wilson v. General Motors Corp., 888 F.2d 779 (11th Cir.1989).

25. Home Owners Funding Corp. of America v. Allison, 756 F.Supp. 290 (N.D.Tex.1991).

26. Roe v. O'Donohue, 38 F.3d 298 (7th Cir.1994).

27. *Compare In re* Shell Oil Co., 932 F.2d 1518 (5th Cir.1991) (presence of local defendant is procedural defect), *with* Hurt v. Dow Chem. Co., 963 F.2d 1142 (8th Cir. 1992).

28. *Compare* Brock by Brock v. Syntex Labs., Inc., 791 F.Supp. 721 (E.D.Tenn. 1992), *aff'd,* 7 F.3d 232 (6th Cir.1993) (failure to meet one-year limit is jurisdictional), *with* Barnes v. Westinghouse Elec. Corp., 962 F.2d 513, 516 (5th Cir.1992) (failure to meet one-year limit is procedural).

matter jurisdiction, the court may deny joinder, or permit joinder and remand the action to the State court." In determining whether to deny joinder or to permit joinder and remand, courts consider FRCP 19, which governs the joinder of necessary parties. Courts also consider factors which include: (1) whether the statute of limitations would bar the action against the new defendant in state court if joinder is denied; (2) the explanation for the delay in seeking joinder; and (3) the plaintiff's reasons for seeking joinder.[29] Where the party sought to be joined is indispensable, and the party is nondiverse, the case will be remanded to state court.[30] If the party is not indispensable, the court may either continue jurisdiction without joining the party, or allow joinder and remand the case to state court.[31]

(7) Sua Sponte Determination by the Federal Courts

Where the district court determines before final judgment that it lacks subject matter jurisdiction over the case, the court must remand the case.[32] As to procedural defects, most courts have held that a district court may not remand a removed case sua sponte based on defects in removal procedure.[33] Under this view, only the parties may seek remand based on defects in the removal procedure. Additionally, prohibition against sua sponte remand allows for the plaintiff to waive any objections to procedural defects by failing to raise such objections in a timely motion for remand.[34] The district court may not remand a case on the basis of administrative considerations, such as the court's heavy workload or the likelihood of a lengthy delay following removal.[35]

Some courts permit remand sua sponte as long as remand occurs within the 30–day period for remand motions based on procedural defects.[36]

(d) Waiver of Right to Remand

The plaintiff is required to move for remand of a case based on a defect in removal procedure within 30 days after the filing of the notice of removal in federal court.[37] If the plaintiff fails to object to a procedural

---

29. Yniques v. Cabral, 985 F.2d 1031 (9th Cir.1993); Goodman v. Travelers Ins. Co., 561 F.Supp. 1111 (N.D.Cal.1983). *See* Chapter 10 "Joinder, Consolidation and Severance," *infra.*

30. *See, e.g.,* Yniques, 985 F.2d 1031.

31. *Id.*

32. 28 U.S.C.A. § 1447(c) (West 1994).

33. *See, e.g.,* Page v. City of Southfield, 45 F.3d 128 (6th Cir.1995); *In re* Continental Cas. Co., 29 F.3d 292 (7th Cir.1994); *In re* Allstate Ins. Co., 8 F.3d 219, 223 (5th Cir.1993) ("[W]here subject matter jurisdic-

tion exists and any procedural shortcomings may be cured by resort to § 1653, we can surmise no valid reason for the court to decline the exercise of jurisdiction.").

34. *See In re* Allstate Ins. Co., 8 F.3d at 223.

35. Thermtron Products, Inc. v. Hermansdorfer, 423 U.S. 336, 96 S.Ct. 584, 46 L.Ed.2d 542 (1976); Levy v. Weissman, 671 F.2d 766 (3d Cir.1982).

36. Maniar v. FDIC, 979 F.2d 782 (9th Cir.1992); Air–Shields, Inc. v. Fullam, 891 F.2d 63 (3d Cir.1989).

37. 28 U.S.C.A. § 1447(c).

defect within the 30–day limit, the plaintiff waives its right to object.[38] However, if the plaintiff moves to remand after the time limit and the defendant does not raise the issue of the plaintiff's untimeliness, the defendant waives any objection and the case may be remanded.[39]

As to motions for remand based on lack of jurisdiction, Section 1447(c) states that the case shall be remanded "[i]f at any time before final judgment it appears that the district court lacks subject matter jurisdiction." Thus, it has been held that a plaintiff does not waive the right to contest the sufficiency of the amount in controversy where the plaintiff fails to timely raise the issue in a motion for remand.[40] In *United Food & Commercial Workers Union, Local 919 v. CenterMark Properties Meriden Square, Inc.*,[41] the plaintiff challenged the defendants' assertion in the removal petition that the amount in controversy exceeded $50,000. Although the defendants argued that the amount in controversy issue was factual in nature, and was conceded by the plaintiff when the plaintiff failed to challenge the issue in a motion for remand, the Second Circuit Court of Appeals held that subject matter jurisdiction could not be waived by the plaintiff.[42] However, in cases where jurisdiction exists at the time of removal, some courts have held that the defendant's failure to properly allege jurisdictional facts, such as the plaintiff's citizenship in a diversity case, constitutes a procedural, rather than a jurisdictional, defect, and may be waived by the plaintiff.[43]

(e) Partial Remand

Where the federal claims forming the basis for removal jurisdiction are dismissed before trial, the federal district court has discretion under 28 U.S.C.A. § 1367(c) as to whether to adjudicate remaining pendent state claims, remand the claims to state court, or dismiss the claims without prejudice.[44] Section 1367(c) is applicable where federal jurisdiction exists at the time of removal.[45] The decision to retain jurisdiction or remand depends upon the factors of judicial economy, convenience, fairness, and comity.[46] Generally, courts will remand state law claims where the federal claim is dismissed shortly after removal.[47] However,

---

38. *In re* Continental Cas. Co., 29 F.3d 292; *In re* Shell Oil Co., 932 F.2d 1523 (5th Cir.1991); Patin v. Allied Signal, Inc., 865 F.Supp. 370 (E.D.Tex.1994).

39. Student A v. Metcho, 710 F.Supp. 267 (N.D.Cal.1989).

40. *See, e.g.*, United Food & Commercial Workers Union, Local 919 v. CenterMark Properties Meriden Square, Inc., 30 F.3d 298, 303–04 (2d Cir.1994); Saunders v. Rider, 805 F.Supp. 17, 19 (E.D.La.1992).

41. 30 F.3d 298 (2d Cir.1994).

42. *Id.* at 303.

43. *See In re* Allstate Ins. Co., 8 F.3d 219 (5th Cir.1993); Harmon v. OKI Sys-

tems, 902 F.Supp. 176 (S.D.Ind.1995), *aff'd*, 115 F.3d 477 (7th Cir.1997).

44. *See* Carnegie–Mellon University v. Cohill, 484 U.S. 343, 108 S.Ct. 614, 98 L.Ed.2d 720 (1988); Lee v. City of Beaumont, 12 F.3d 933, 937 (9th Cir.1993); PAS v. Travelers Ins. Co., 7 F.3d 349 (3d Cir. 1993).

45. *See* Bogle v. Phillips Petroleum Co., 24 F.3d 758 (5th Cir.1994).

46. Engstrom v. First Nat. Bank of Eagle Lake, 47 F.3d 1459 (5th Cir.1995).

47. *See, e.g.*, Trans Penn Wax Corp. v. McCandless, 50 F.3d 217 (3d Cir.1995); Taylor v. First of America Bank—Wayne,

district courts have discretion to dismiss or remand state law claims even where the case has been pending in federal court for quite some time.[48] Section 1367(c) does not give the district court the authority to remand the entire case, including a properly removed federal claim, merely because state law issues predominate in the case.[49] Even where the federal claims are not dismissed, the district court may exercise its discretion under Section 1367(c) to decline supplemental jurisdiction and dismiss or remand state law claims.[50]

Courts have distinguished remand on the basis of Section 1367(c) from the remand of claims under Section 1441(c), which provides that whenever "a separate and independent claim or cause of action within the jurisdiction conferred by section 1331 of this title is joined with one or more otherwise nonremovable claims or causes of action, the entire case may be removed and the district court may determine all issues therein, or, in its discretion, may remand all matters in which State law predominates."[51] While Section 1367(c) is applicable where federal jurisdiction existed at the time of removal, but all federal claims are dismissed after removal, Section 1441(c) is applicable where federal question claims removed by the defendant are separate and independent from the state law claims.[52]

Because the statute provides that district courts have discretion to "remand all matters in which State law predominates," most courts have held that Section 1441(c) authorizes the remand of the entire case, including the federal law claim.[53] Courts adopting this position have also held that Section 1441(c) still allows the district court to remand separate and independent state claims, if state law predominates as to the individual claim.[54] However, other courts have held that the discretion given under Section 1441(c) does not permit the district court to remand an entire case containing a properly removed federal claim.[55]

(f) Imposing Costs

Section 1447(c) provides that "[a]n order remanding the case may

---

973 F.2d 1284, 1287 (6th Cir.1992) (when all federal claims are eliminated before trial, balance of factors usually points toward declining to exercise jurisdiction).

48. See, e.g., Engstrom, 47 F.3d at 1465 (district court did not abuse discretion in remanding remaining state law claims where case had been pending for three years).

49. In re City of Mobile, 75 F.3d 605 (11th Cir.1996).

50. Transcontinental Leasing, Inc. v. Michigan Nat'l Bank of Detroit, 738 F.2d 163, 166 (6th Cir.1984); Padilla v. City of Saginaw, 867 F.Supp. 1309 (E.D.Mich. 1994).

51. 28 U.S.C.A. § 1441(c) (West 1994); see supra § 8.3(d) (discussing removal under § 1441(c)).

52. See, e.g., Borough of West Mifflin v. Lancaster, 45 F.3d 780 (3d Cir.1995).

53. Eastus v. Blue Bell Creameries, L.P., 97 F.3d 100, 106 (5th Cir.1996); Spaulding v. Mingo Cty. Bd. of Educ., 897 F.Supp. 284, 288 (S.D.W.Va.1995); Bodenner v. Graves, 828 F.Supp. 516, 519 (W.D.Mich.1993); Moore v. DeBiase, 766 F.Supp. 1311 (D.N.J.1991); Moralez v. Meat Cutters Local 539, 778 F.Supp. 368, 370 (E.D.Mich.1991).

54. See, e.g., Eastus, 97 F.3d at 106.

55. See Hickerson v. City of New York, 932 F.Supp. 550, 558 (S.D.N.Y.1996).

require payment of just costs and any actual expenses, including attorney fees, incurred as a result of removal." However, costs may not be awarded when the court remanded the case on grounds other than those listed in Section 1447(c) (procedural defects and lack of subject matter jurisdiction).[56]

The imposition of costs and attorney's fees is at the discretion of the district court.[57] Some courts refuse to award costs and fees unless the removal petition is brought by the defendant in bad faith.[58] Other courts have held that the standard is not whether the action was removed in bad faith, but whether the nonremovability of the action was obvious.[59] At least one court has held on the basis of Section 1447(c) that a defendant may be entitled to costs and attorney's fees for defending a justified removal against a frivolous motion for remand.[60] An award of costs and fees is inappropriate where the ground for removal presents an unsettled area of law.[61] However, costs and fees may be awarded if the defendant files a second notice of removal based on the same grounds as a prior unsuccessful notice of removal.[62]

Library References:

West's Key No. Digests, Removal of Cases ⊕100–110.
Wright, Miller & Cooper, Federal Practice and Procedure: Civil 2d §§ 3739, 3914.11.

§ 8.10 Review of Orders Relating to Removal

(a) Review of Orders Granting Remand Is Generally Prohibited

Orders granting remand entered pursuant to the grounds listed in Section 1447(c) (lack of subject matter jurisdiction or procedural defects in the removal procedure) are generally immune from appellate review.[1] Additionally, once the district court notifies the state court of its decision

56. Ferrari, Alvarez, Olsen & Ottoboni v. Home Ins. Co., 940 F.2d 550 (9th Cir. 1991).

57. Lathigra v. British Airways PLC, 41 F.3d 535 (9th Cir.1994).

58. See, e.g., Gefen by Gefen v. Upjohn Co., 893 F.Supp. 471 (E.D.Pa.1995); Nichols v. Southeast Health Plan of Alabama, Inc., 859 F.Supp. 553 (S.D.Ala.1993); Farm Bureau Mut. Ins. Co. v. Eighmy, 849 F.Supp. 40 (D.Kan.1994).

59. See, e.g., Katonah v. USAir, Inc., 876 F.Supp. 984 (N.D.Ill.1995); Nill v. Essex Group, Inc., 844 F.Supp. 1313 (N.D.Ind. 1994); H.F. Vegter Excavation Co. v. Village of Oak Brook, 790 F.Supp. 184 (N.D.Ill. 1992) (costs awarded when minimal research could have prevented removal notice).

60. Shrader v. Legg Mason Wood Walker, Inc., 880 F.Supp. 366 (E.D.Pa.1995).

61. In re Potash Antitrust Litig., 866 F.Supp. 406 (D.Minn.1994).

62. Smith v. Student Non–Violent Coordinating Committee, 421 F.2d 522 (5th Cir. 1969).

§ 8.10

1. See 28 U.S.C.A. § 1447 (c) & (d) (West 1994); Things Remembered, Inc. v. Petrarca, 516 U.S. 124, 125, 116 S.Ct. 494, 495, 133 L.Ed.2d 461 (1995) (Section 1447(d) "must be read in pari materia with § 1447(c), so that only remands based on grounds specified in § 1447(c) are immune from review under § 1447(d)."); Thermtron Products, Inc. v. Hermansdorfer, 423 U.S. 336, 96 S.Ct. 584, 46 L.Ed.2d 542 (1976).

to remand it loses jurisdiction to reconsider its remand order. Therefore, defendants who believe that removal jurisdiction exists should file a motion to stay the filing of the remand in state court and ask the district court for permission to file additional memoranda on the issue.

District courts are not required to expressly state their reliance on Section 1447(c) to preclude appellate review.[2] Similarly, remand orders entered pursuant to Section 1447(e), because the plaintiff joined additional defendants whose presence destroyed diversity, are also unreviewable.[3] However, a district court's decision to remand can be reviewed by the appellate court if the district court remanded the case, sua sponte, for procedural defects,[4] or if the district court remanded despite the fact that the plaintiff's motion to remand was untimely filed.[5] There are also other statutory and nonstatutory exceptions to the general rule (discussed below), which leave some remand orders subject to review.

(1) Statutory Exceptions to the General Rule

There are two main statutory exceptions to Section 1447(c)'s prohibition against reviewing remand orders. Section 1447(d) permits review of a district court order granting remand when the defendant removed the case pursuant to 28 U.S.C.A. § 1443 (Civil rights cases), while the Financial Institutions Reform, Recovery, and Enforcement Act of 1989 ("FIRREA"),[6] provides both the Resolution Trust Corporation[7] and the Federal Deposit Insurance Corporation,[8] with the statutory authority to appeal any adverse remand order.

(2) Nonstatutory Exceptions to the General Rule

Remand orders are subject to review if they were based on any of the following nonstatutory grounds.

- The district court remanded the case based on a substantive decision it made on a collateral issue, rather than on the basis that it lacked subject matter jurisdiction over the action.[9] For

2. See New v. Sports & Recreation, Inc., 114 F.3d 1092 (11th Cir.1997) ("While the district court failed to specify that it remanded the case pursuant to section 1447(c), and only referred to section 1445(c) in its order, the court premised its order on a deficiency in federal jurisdiction."); Fowler v. Safeco Ins. Co., 915 F.2d 616, 617 n. 3 (11th Cir.1990).

3. See supra § 8.9(c)(6); In re Florida Wire & Cable Co., 102 F.3d 866 (7th Cir. 1996); Washington Suburban Sanitary Comm'n v. CRS/Sirrine, Inc., 917 F.2d 834 (4th Cir.1990).

4. Page v. City of Southfield, 45 F.3d 128, 134 (6th Cir.1995); In re Continental Casualty Co., 29 F.3d 292 (7th Cir.1994); Ziegler v. Champion Mortgage Co., 913 F.2d 228, 230 (5th Cir.1990).

5. Korea Exch. Bank v. Trackwise Sales Corp., 66 F.3d 46, 50 (3d Cir.1995); In re Ocean Marine Mutual Protection & Indemnity Ass'n, 3 F.3d 353, 355 n. 3 (11th Cir. 1993); In re Allstate Ins. Co., 8 F.3d 219 (5th Cir.1993).

6. Financial Institutions Reform, Recovery and Enforcement Act of 1989, Pub. L. No. 101–73, 103 Stat. 183, 187 (1989).

7. 12 U.S.C.A. § 1441a(l)(3)(C) (West 1994).

8. 12 U.S.C.A. § 1819(b)(2)(C) (West 1989).

9. See Waco v. United States Fidelity & Guaranty Co., 293 U.S. 140, 143, 55 S.Ct. 6, 7, 79 L.Ed. 244 (1934); Kozera v. Spirito, 723 F.2d 1003, 1005 n. 1 (1st Cir.1983); See also 16 James Wm. Moore et al., Moore's

example, if the district court remands after dismissing the only claim that provided it with federal question jurisdiction, the remand is reviewable because it made a substantive determination (dismissal) on the merits of an issue over which it had jurisdiction.[10] However, when the court makes a decision that is necessary in order for it to determine whether it has subject matter jurisdiction over the action, that decision and any subsequent remand order based on that decision are not subject to review.[11]

- The district court remanded the case based on one of the abstention doctrines.[12] For example, the Supreme Court decided in *Quackenbush v. Allstate Insurance Company*, that *Burford* abstention is limited to equitable actions, and that federal courts may stay actions for damages based on abstention principles, but that those principles do not support the outright dismissal or remand of an action for damages.[13] A remand order based on one of the abstention doctrines is immediately appealable under 28 U.S.C.A. § 1291 because it conclusively determines a disputed question that is completely separate from the merits of the action and effectively unreviewable on appeal from a final judgment.[14] Abstention based remand orders effectively put the parties out of court.[15]

- The district court remanded a case over which it had subject matter jurisdiction because its docket was too crowded.[16]

- The district court remanded the case based on a determination that a forum or venue selection clause barred removal,[17] or that

Federal Practice, ¶ 107.44[2][a][i] (3d ed. 1997).

10. See Waco, 293 U.S. at 143, 55 S.Ct. at 7; see generally, Beauclerc Lakes Condominium Ass'n v. City of Jacksonville, 115 F.3d 934 (11th Cir.1997); Anusbigian v. Trugreen/Chemlawn, Inc., 72 F.3d 1253, 1256 (6th Cir.1996).

11. Anusbigian, 72 F.3d at 1256 ("If a district court determines, rightly or wrongly, that it lacks subject matter jurisdiction over a removed case, and for that reason remands it to the court from which it was removed, the court of appeals lacks jurisdiction to review the district court's decision.").

12. Quackenbush v. Allstate Ins. Co., 517 U.S. 706, ___, 116 S.Ct. 1712, 1721–22, 135 L.Ed.2d 1 (1996).

13. Id.; see also Louisiana Power & Light Co. v. Thibodaux, 360 U.S. 25, 28, 79 S.Ct. 1070, 1072–1073, 3 L.Ed.2d 1058 (1959). See Chapter 1 "Subject Matter Jurisdiction," at § 1.10(c)(2), supra.

14. Quackenbush, 517 U.S. at ___, 116 S.Ct. at 1721–22; Richardson–Merrell Inc.

v. Koller, 472 U.S. 424, 431, 105 S.Ct. 2757, 2761, 86 L.Ed.2d 340 (1985); Coopers & Lybrand v. Livesay, 437 U.S. 463, 468, 98 S.Ct. 2454, 2458, 57 L.Ed.2d 351 (1978).

15. Moses H. Cone Memorial Hosp. v. Mercury Constr. Corp., 460 U.S. 1, 9, 103 S.Ct. 927, 933, 74 L.Ed.2d 765 (1983).

16. Thermtron Products, Inc. v. Hermansdorfer, 423 U.S. 336, 96 S.Ct. 584, 46 L.Ed.2d 542 (1976)(district court remanded action because of its crowded federal docket); see also In re Surinam Airways Holding Co., 974 F.2d 1255, 1257 (11th Cir. 1992)(the district court determined that it had supplemental jurisdiction over some of the plaintiff's claims, but remanded them anyway because they raised a novel or complex issue of state law); Kolibash v. Committee on Legal Ethics, 872 F.2d 571, 575 (4th Cir.1989)(district court remanded based on public policy considerations).

17. Karl Koch Erecting Co. v. New York Convention Center Development Corp., 838 F.2d 656 (2d Cir.1988)(Section 1447(d) does not bar a direct appeal where remand is based upon court's interpretation of a fo-

the defendant waived its right to remove.[18]

- The district court remanded the case based on developments in the case that occurred after it was properly removed.[19]

- The district court remanded the case after finding that the federal statute that provided it with subject matter jurisdiction was unconstitutional.[20]

(b) Review of Orders Denying Remand

Since an order denying remand is not a final order,[21] it is generally not subject to immediate appellate review and can only be challenged in an appeal from a final judgment in the case.[22] However, there are three instances where the district court's denial of a motion to remand is subject to immediate review.[23] The first instance is where the district court certifies that the circumstances of the case make it an appropriate candidate for an interlocutory appeal.[24] The second instance is where the appeal of the remand is joined with an appeal of another order that is subject to immediate appeal, such as a denial of a preliminary injunction[25] or a motion to dismiss.[26] The third instance is where the circumstances of the case justify a grant of mandamus.[27]

rum selection clause); Ferrari, Alvarez, Olsen & Ottoboni v. Home Ins. Co., 940 F.2d 550, 553 (9th Cir.1991)(Section 1447(d) does not bar a direct appeal where remand is based upon application of a venue selection clause). See Chapter 3 "Venue, Forum Selection, and Transfer," supra.

18. Rothner v. City of Chicago, 879 F.2d 1402, 1411–12 (7th Cir.1989).

19. St. Paul Mercury Indemnity Co. v. Red Cab Co., 303 U.S. 283, 58 S.Ct. 586, 82 L.Ed. 845 (1938); In re Amoco Petroleum Additives Co., 964 F.2d 706, 708–09 (7th Cir.1992).

20. In re TMI Litigation Cases, 940 F.2d 832, 844–47 (3d Cir.1991)("We are confident that the jurisdictional determination of the district court, resting as it did upon the conclusion that the entire statutory scheme authorizing removal is unconstitutional, was not the type of federal subject matter jurisdictional decision intended to be governed by the terms of or the policy underlying Section 1447(c).... [I]n enacting section 1447(d), Congress did not intend to vest the district courts with the authority to make final determinations regarding the constitutionality of federal statutes."), cert. denied sub nom. Gumby v. General Pub. Utils. Corp., 503 U.S. 906, 112 S.Ct. 1262, 117 L.Ed.2d 491 (1992); see also Baldridge v. Kentucky–Ohio Transp., Inc., 983 F.2d

1341, 1347–50 (6th Cir.1993)(citing In re TMI Litigation Cases).

21. Burden v. General Dynamics Corp., 60 F.3d 213, 216 (5th Cir.1995); Neal v. Brown, 980 F.2d 747, 748 (D.C.Cir.1992), cert. denied, 507 U.S. 1051, 113 S.Ct. 1945, 123 L.Ed.2d 650 (1993); Estate of Bishop v. Bechtel Power Corp., 905 F.2d 1272, 1274 (9th Cir.1990).

22. Carpenters Health and Welfare Trust Fund for Cal. v. Tri Capital Corp., 25 F.3d 849 (9th Cir.), cert. denied, 513 U.S. 1018, 115 S.Ct. 580, 130 L.Ed.2d 495 (1994).

23. See 16 Moore, supra note 9, § 107.44[1][b][i-iii].

24. See 28 U.S.C.A. § 1292(b) (West 1993); see also In re Chimenti, 79 F.3d 534 (6th Cir.1996); Neal, 980 F.2d at 748; Gould v. Mutual Life Insurance Co., 790 F.2d 769, 773 (9th Cir.1986).

25. Tri–State Generation and Transmission Assn., Inc. v. Shoshone River Power, Inc., 874 F.2d 1346, 1351 (10th Cir.1989); Lou v. Belzberg, 834 F.2d 730, 738–39 (9th Cir.1987), cert. denied, 485 U.S. 993, 108 S.Ct. 1302, 99 L.Ed.2d 512 (1988).

26. Chicago, R.I. & Pac. R. Co. v. Stude, 204 F.2d 116, 119 (8th Cir.1953), aff'd, 346 U.S. 574, 578–79, 74 S.Ct. 290, 293–94, 98 L.Ed. 317 (1954).

27. 28 U.S.C.A. § 1651 (West 1994).

However, mandamus is only granted in exceptional circumstances.[28] The party seeking review by mandamus must demonstrate a clear and indisputable right to such relief.[29] This usually amounts to a showing that the district court committed clear error, approaching the magnitude of an unauthorized exercise of judicial power, when it retained the case.[30]

(c) Waiver of Right to Contest Removal Jurisdiction

Unless the party seeking remand is successful in obtaining one of these three avenues of immediate review, the first opportunity to appeal the remand denial will be on an appeal from the final judgment. Failure to seek immediate review does not waive the right to challenge the issue on an appeal from the final judgment.[31] However, it is to that party's benefit to attempt to obtain an interlocutory review of the remand issue for the following reason. If the district court decides the case on its merits and the party seeking remand does not obtain an interlocutory review of the order denying remand, the appellate court will decide the issue of removal jurisdiction by determining whether the district court would have had jurisdiction at the time of the trial or judgment, instead of at the time the complaint was filed or the case was removed.[32] Therefore, if the party seeking remand does not attempt to obtain an interlocutory review, it runs the risk that any removal defects will be cured by the time a final judgment is entered in the case.[33] Furthermore, if the party has filed an appeal on an issue that is subject to immediate appeal, caution would dictate that it also raise the remand issue at the same time.[34]

28. Bankers Life & Casualty Co. v. Holland, 346 U.S. 379, 382–83, 74 S.Ct. 145, 147–48, 98 L.Ed. 106 (1953); J.H. Cohn & Co. v. American Appraisal Associates, Inc., 628 F.2d 994, 997 (7th Cir.1980).

29. Gulfstream Aerospace Corp. v. Mayacamas Corp., 485 U.S. 271, 289, 108 S.Ct. 1133, 1143, 99 L.Ed.2d 296 (1988); Bankers Life & Casualty Co., 346 U.S. at 384, 74 S.Ct. at 148; Carteret Sav. Bank, FA v. Shushan, 919 F.2d 225, 232 (3d Cir.1990), *cert. denied*, 506 U.S. 817, 113 S.Ct. 61, 121 L.Ed.2d 29 (1992).

30. Will v. Calvert Fire Ins. Co., 437 U.S. 655, 661, 98 S.Ct. 2552, 2556, 57 L.Ed.2d 504 (1978); Lusardi v. Lechner, 855 F.2d 1062, 1069 (3d Cir.1988).

31. *See* Caterpillar Inc. v. Lewis, 519 U.S. 61, ___, n. 11, 117 S.Ct. 467, 472, 476 n. 11, 136 L.Ed.2d 437 (1996)(Failure to seek interlocutory appeal does not waive objections to removal.); La Chemise Lacoste v. Alligator Co., 506 F.2d 339, 341 (3d Cir.

1974) (per curiam), *cert. denied*, 421 U.S. 937, 95 S.Ct. 1666, 44 L.Ed.2d 94 (1975).

32. *See* Grubbs v. General Electric Credit Corp., 405 U.S. 699, 705, 92 S.Ct. 1344, 1349, 31 L.Ed.2d 612 (1972).

33. *See* Caterpillar Inc., 519 U.S. at ___ n. 11, 117 S.Ct. at 472, 476 n. 11 (When the case proceeds to judgment, considerations of finality, efficiency, and economy become overwhelming and judgment would not be disturbed as long as the court had jurisdiction over the parties when it entered judgment.); American Fire & Casualty Co. v. Finn, 341 U.S. 6, 16, 71 S.Ct. 534, 541, 95 L.Ed. 702 (1951).

34. *See* Alligator Co. v. La Chemise Lacoste, 421 U.S. 937, 938, 95 S.Ct. 1666, 1666, 44 L.Ed.2d 94 (1975) (White, J., dissenting) ("[I]t would appear that jurisdictional questions should be reviewed at the first available opportunity, and I perceive no good reason for not permitting the removal issue to be raised in connection with an appeal from the denial of a preliminary

(d) Mandamus or Appeal

If the order denying or granting remand is reviewable before a final judgment is reached in the case, the avenue for review may be mandamus or appeal. The main difference between these two is the standard of review.[35] However, an appellate court will not issue a writ of mandamus if relief may be granted by way of an ordinary appeal.[36]

Recently, the Supreme Court of the United States, in *Quackenbush v. Allstate Insurance Co.*,[37] disavowed its earlier holding in *Thermtron Prods., Inc. v. Hermansdorfer* that "an order remanding a removed action does not represent a final judgment reviewable by appeal." The *Quackenbush* Court held that to the extent that *Thermtron* conflicts with the rule that allows parties to appeal remand orders that are final judgements or collateral orders, *Thermtron* is no longer good law.[38] The decision in *Quackenbush* was based, in part, on the 1983 decision in *Moses H. Cone Memorial Hospital v. Mercury Construction Corporation*,[39] where the Court determined that an abstention based stay order that "put[s] the litigants effectively out of court" and produces the "surrender" of federal jurisdiction is appealable as either a final decision or a collateral order. Thus, orders granting remand on a nonstatutory basis (other than lack of subject matter jurisdiction or procedural defects in the removal procedure) are now subject to review by appeal if they are final judgments or collateral orders.[40]

Library References:

West's Key No. Digests, Removal of Cases ⊗107, 119.
Wright, Miller & Cooper, Federal Practice and Procedure: Civil 2d § 3740.

§ 8.11   Procedural Checklist

(a) Removal

(1) To remove a case from state court to federal court, prepare a notice of removal to be filed in federal court and served on all

injunction."). *Compare* 16 Moore's Federal Practice, *supra* note 9, § 107.44[1][b][ii](Motion to remand may be appealed when the court has issued another order that is subject to immediate appeal.), *with* 14A Charles Alan Wright, Arthur R. Miller & Edward H. Cooper, Federal Practice and Procedure § 3740 at 598–99 (2d ed. 1985) (The courts of appeals are divided on whether the motion to remand may be appealed along with another immediately appealable order, but "concluding that a refusal to remand can be reviewed on an interlocutory appeal would be tantamount to a requirement that the issue be raised at that time.").

35. Garamendi v. Allstate Ins. Co., 47 F.3d 350, 352 n. 6 (9th Cir.1995).

36. *See* 28 U.S.C.A. § 1651 (West 1994); Moses H. Cone Memorial Hosp. v. Mercury Constr. Corp., 460 U.S. 1, 8 n. 6, 103 S.Ct. 927, 933 n. 6, 74 L.Ed.2d 765 (1983); Hahnemann Univ. Hosp. v. Edgar, 74 F.3d 456, 461 (3d Cir.1996).

37. 517 U.S. 706, ___, 116 S.Ct. 1712, 1721–22, 135 L.Ed.2d 1 (1996).

38. Quackenbush, 517 U.S. at ___, 116 S.Ct. at 1720; Thermtron Prods., Inc. v. Hermansdorfer, 423 U.S. 336, 96 S.Ct. 584, 46 L.Ed.2d 542 (1976).

39. 460 U.S. 1, 8, 103 S.Ct. 927, 933, 74 L.Ed.2d 765 (1983).

40. Quackenbush, 517 U.S. at ___, 116 S.Ct. at 1720.

adverse parties. The notice of removal must be signed pursuant to FRCP 11, and must contain a short and plain statement of the grounds for removal (basis for federal jurisdiction), together with a copy of all process, pleadings, and orders served upon the defendant or defendants in the state court. (*See* 28 U.S.C.A. § 1446(a); FRCP 11; § 8.7)

If diversity of citizenship is the basis for federal court jurisdiction, you must include the following in your notice of removal:

- the citizenship of the parties when the complaint was filed as well as at the time of removal;

- the date you were served with the complaint or the date you were on notice that the action was removable; and

- the amount in controversy, which now must be in excess of $75,000 excluding costs. (*See* 28 U.S.C.A. § 1446(a); 28 U.S.C.A. § 1441(b); 28 U.S.C.A. § 1332(a); § 8.7)

However, the case cannot be removed on the basis of diversity of citizenship if any of the properly joined and served defendants is a citizen of the state in which the action was originally brought. (*See* 28 U.S.C.A. § 1446(a); 28 U.S.C.A. § 1441(b); § 8.7)

(2) File the notice of removal with the attached copies of the pleadings in the district court of the United States for the district and division within which the action is pending. (*See* 28 U.S.C.A. § 1446(a); § 8.7) This means that you will have to pay the federal court's filing fee and complete a civil cover sheet for the case.

You must file the notice of removal within 30 days after the receipt, through service or otherwise, of a copy of the initial pleading setting forth the claim for relief upon which such action or proceeding is based, or within 30 days after the service of summons, if such initial pleading has then been filed in court and is not required to be served on the defendant, whichever period is shorter. (*See* 28 U.S.C.A. § 1446(b); § 8.7(b))

If the case stated by the initial pleading is not removable, the notice of removal must be filed within 30 days after receipt, through service or otherwise, of a copy of an amended pleading, motion, order or other paper from which it may first be ascertained that the case is one which is or has become removable. However, the case may not be removed on the basis of diversity jurisdiction more than one year after commencement of the action. (*See* 28 U.S.C.A. § 1446(b); § 8.7(b))

(3) Generally, when there are multiple defendants, they must all join in the notice of removal or file a written consent to removal with the federal court. This must be done within the statutory time for filing the notice of removal. (*See* 28 U.S.C.A. § 1446(b); § 8.7(c)(1))

(4) Promptly after filing the notice of removal, you must give written notice thereof to all adverse parties and file a copy of the

notice with the clerk of the state court from which the case was removed. (*See* 28 U.S.C.A. § 1446(d); § 8.7(c)(5))

(5) If you did not answer the state court complaint before you removed, you must answer or present your defenses or objections within 20 days after the receipt, through service or otherwise, of a copy of the initial pleading setting forth the claim for relief upon which the action or proceeding is based, or within 20 days after the service of summons upon such initial pleading, or within five days after the filing of the petition for removal, whichever period is longest. (*See* FRCP 81(c); § 8.8(b))

(6) After you remove the case, you must comply with the Federal Rules of Civil Procedure as well as the local rules for each district. The local rules in most districts require the moving party to support its motions with legal memoranda. Accordingly, if there were pending motions in state court before removal, the moving party will now be required to file memoranda in support of those motions in federal court. The party opposing the motions will then be required to file responsive memoranda.

(7) It is possible to lose your right to remove by taking actions in the state court that manifest your intent to either (1) abandon your right to a federal forum, or (2) to have the case adjudicated in state court. (*See* § 8.3)

(b) Remand

(1) To remand a case to state court you will need to file a motion to remand, with a memorandum in support, in federal court. Motions to remand may be based on jurisdictional defects (lack of subject matter jurisdiction), procedural defects (in the removal procedure), or exceptional circumstances (abstention in equitable cases). (*See* 28 U.S.C.A. 1447(c); § 8.9(c))

A motion to remand the case to state court on the basis of any defect other than lack of subject matter jurisdiction must be made within 30 days after the defendant files its notice of removal. A motion to remand the case on the basis of a lack of jurisdiction can be made at any time prior to final judgment. (*See* 28 U.S.C.A. § 1447(c); § 8.9(b))

(2) A defendant upon whom process is served after removal still has the right to seek remand of the case. (*See* 28 U.S.C.A. § 1448; § 8.9)

(3) If, after removal, the plaintiff seeks to join additional defendants whose joinder would destroy subject matter jurisdiction, the court may deny joinder, or permit joinder and remand the action to the state court. (*See* 28 U.S.C.A. § 1447(e); § 8.9(c)(6))

(4) If the motion to remand is granted, the plaintiff may move for payment of just costs and any actual expenses, including attorney's fees, incurred as a result of the defendant's failed removal attempt. (*See* 28 U.S.C.A. § 1447(c); § 8.9(f)) If the defendant believes that the remand order is erroneous, then the defendant should file a

motion to stay the remand order in federal court and request permission to file additional memoranda on the issue. The federal court loses jurisdiction to reconsider its remand order once it has been remanded to the state court. (*See* 28 U.S.C.A. § 1447(c); § 8.10)

§ 8.12   Forms

(a) Notice of Removal

United States District Court
_____ District of _____,
_____ Division.

[_____],) Plaintiff)	)	Case No. _____
-against-	)	
[_____],) Defendant.)	)	

Notice of Removal

TO THE CLERK OF THE ABOVE ENTITLED COURT:

Please take notice that the defendant, _____ [or defendants] hereby serves this Notice of Removal of Case No. _____ currently pending in the _____ Court of _____ County, in the State of _____, which is described below.

1. On [date], the plaintiff commenced an action in the _____ Court of _____ County, in the State of _____. The action is entitled _____ [caption]. A copy of the complaint is attached and marked as Exhibit "A".

2. This action is a civil action over which this Court has original jurisdiction, in that it is one to recover _____ [state nature of claim or claims].

3. The defendant (or defendants) seek removal of this action to this Court upon the ground and for the reason that _____. [*See* §§ 8.3 & 8.7 for a discussion of the grounds and requirements for removal.]

4. Process in action No. _____ was served on the defendant [or defendants] on [date]; and a copy of the complaint was received by the defendant [or defendants] on [date]. This removal is timely.

5. A copy of all pleadings, process, orders, and other papers filed in the state court action are attached and marked as Exhibit "B".

WHEREFORE, the defendant prays that this action will be removed.

Dated _____.

_____,
Attorney for the Defendant
_____, Address.

(b) Motion to Remand 🖫

United States District Court
_____ District of _____,
_____ Division.

[_____],) Plaintiff)	Case No. _____
-against-)	
[_____],) Defendant.)	

Motion to Remand to the State Court

The plaintiff moves this court to remand this cause to the _____ Court of the State of _____, in and for _____ County, from which court it was attempted to be removed to this Court. In support of this Motion, the plaintiff states as follows: [*See* § 8.9 for a discussion of the grounds and requirements for remand.]

1. _____.

2. _____.

3. _____.

WHEREFORE, the plaintiff respectfully requests that this Court remand this action to the _____ Court of _____ County, _____.

Dated _____.

_____,
Attorney for the Plaintiff
_____, Address.

CHAPTER 9

ARBITRATION VS. LITIGATION: ENFORCEABILITY AND ACCESS TO COURTS

by

Robert D. Raven
Kathleen V. Fisher
and
James M. Schurz

Table of Sections

(1) American Arbitration Association. 🖫
(2) CPR Institute for Dispute Resolution. 🖫
(3) JAMS/Endispute. 🖫
(b) Standard Clauses of International Providers. 🖫
    (1) International Chamber of Commerce.
    (2) United Nations Commission on International Trade Law.
    (3) Stockholm Chamber of Commerce.
    (4) London Court of International Arbitration.
(c) Special Considerations.
    (1) Appointment of Arbitrator. 🖫
    (2) Confidentiality. 🖫
    (3) Discovery and Evidentiary Rules. 🖫
    (4) Power of Arbitrators: Provisional Relief. 🖫
    (5) Power of Arbitrators: Remedies. 🖫
    (6) Access to the Courts for Interim Relief. 🖫
    (7) Stenographic Records. 🖫
    (8) Time Limits for Decisions and Relief. 🖫
    (9) Written Opinion. 🖫
    (10) Interest. 🖫
    (11) Notice. 🖫
    (12) Fees and Expenses. 🖫
    (13) Right to Appeal by Appellate Arbitration Panel. 🖫
    (14) Right to Judicial Review. 🖫
(d) Special Considerations Regarding International Arbitration Agreements.
    (1) Language. 🖫
    (2) Governing Law. 🖫
    (3) Location. 🖫
    (4) Sovereign Immunity Waiver, etc. 🖫
    (5) Enforceability of Award. 🖫

WESTLAW Electronic Research

See WESTLAW Electronic Research Guide preceding the Summary of Contents.

---

§ 9.1 Scope Note

This chapter discusses federal civil practice involving the enforceability of arbitration agreements and the procedures for vacating, modifying, and confirming arbitration awards in domestic and international arbitrations. Specifically, this chapter examines the Federal Arbitration Act (the "FAA" or "Act") and explores the construction of the Act as well as its evolution into a substantive body of federal arbitration law that applies in most federal cases and in many state cases. This chapter does not address court-annexed and private dispute resolution processes which are discussed in Chapter 42 "Alternative Dispute Resolution", *infra*.

Domestic Arbitration. Frequently, the first question to be resolved in litigating matters relating to an arbitration involving domestic parties is which law applies to the construction and enforcement of an arbitration agreement and/or award. For this reason, we begin with an overview of the applicability of the Federal Arbitration Act. The analytical framework applied by federal courts asks (1) does the underlying contract "involve" interstate commerce (broadly defined to encompass Congress' power under the Commerce Clause); and (2) if the answer is yes, is the applicable state law in conflict with, and thereby preempted by, federal law? Section 9.2 addresses both of these issues and provides insight and advice regarding litigating this issue in federal court.

Section 9.3 analyzes the second threshold situation of whether the agreement to arbitrate is enforceable. Defenses to the enforcement of an arbitration agreement are also discussed. The question of the enforceability of an arbitration agreement comes up most frequently in the context of a motion (or petition) to compel arbitration. The issue of enforcing, confirming and vacating arbitration awards is addressed in Sections 9.4 through 9.19. The procedural context in which an award may be challenged or confirmed is premised on the agreement to arbitrate. There are, however, a set of well-defined procedures for confirming, modifying and vacating an award. Finally, the substantive grounds for vacating or modifying an award are analyzed and discussed.

International Arbitration. Beginning at Section 9.10, the problems peculiar to federal litigation relating to international arbitration are discussed. Specifically, this chapter addresses the procedures under the New York Convention and the Inter–American Convention. Both of these acts are part of the statutory scheme of the Federal Arbitration Act. The Act, like many of its state law counterparts, includes separate provisions that govern the procedures for litigating matters relating to international arbitration. These provisions are independent of, though related to, the "domestic" provisions of the Federal Arbitration Act.

Section 9.14 provides examples of model language used by some of the large providers of dispute resolution services.

Library References:

West's Key No. Digests, Arbitration ⟨⟨⟩⟩1–4.1.
Wright & Miller, Federal Practice and Procedure: Civil 2d § 1015.

§ 9.2 Preliminary Considerations

Arbitration frequently conjures up perceptions of parties resolving their dispute with the assistance of a skilled neutral in a relatively informal, confidential environment free of the procedural requirements that accompany commercial litigation. While this characterization may be accurate in many instances, it is not always the case. In cases where one party is resisting arbitration or unlikely to perform pursuant to an arbitrator's award, resort to federal courts is unavoidable. While compelling arbitration and enforcing/modifying/vacating an award are the most frequently cited reasons for resorting to the federal courts, parties may avail themselves of the assistance of the court to appoint a neutral arbitrator, to obtain provisional relief, and to obtain a number of procedural benefits during the course of an arbitration.

At the outset, however, it is necessary to identify the core group of principles which define the scope of commercial litigation in federal courts regarding domestic and international arbitrations.

The Arbitration Agreement. The starting point of any discussion relating to arbitration is the agreement itself. It is frequently stated that arbitration is a creature of contract and that the parties' rights and obligations are defined and determined within the four corners of the arbitration agreement. This premise is equally applicable to the treatment the parties will receive in federal court. Any litigation in federal court involving an arbitration agreement begins with the agreement itself. The Supreme Court has repeatedly held that under the Federal Arbitration Act, federal courts will enforce arbitration agreements "according to their terms." This requires careful consideration at the drafting stage of the type of procedure the parties believe will best suit their interests. For this reason, throughout this chapter, model language is provided addressing specific issues.

Predispute Agreements Versus Submission Agreements. The large majority of arbitration agreements are entered into before any dispute has arisen between the parties. This is frequently because parties in the midst of a litigated dispute are unlikely to agree on a matter such as submitting the case to a binding procedure. The American Arbitration Association reports that over 95% of the cases it administers in a given year are the result of a predispute arbitration agreement. By contrast, submission agreements arise in instances where the parties decide either before or after a piece of litigation has been initiated, to submit their dispute to arbitration. The dangers of using predispute clauses are well-known. To name just a few, how can a party anticipate before a dispute arises what scope of discovery rights it will want? whether it will need to seek provisional relief? what law should apply (if any)? and what remedies the arbitrator should be empowered to employ? For this reason, in recent years parties engaged in complex commercial transactions have provided more detail in structuring arbitration agreements.

Scope of Agreement. A draftsperson must determine which, if any, disputes the parties wish to resolve by ADR. It is frequently the case that parties to an agreement may differ on which types of disputes they believe should be resolved through some form of ADR. Some parties may wish to resolve disputes under a certain dollar figure through mediation or arbitration and leave larger disputes within the public court system. In the case of arbitration, the arbitrator's jurisdiction is based upon the agreement of the parties. The draftsperson, therefore, must carefully define the arbitrable subject matter. The clause must be tied specifically to the contract, otherwise one party may find itself required to arbitrate an aspect of its relationship wholly unrelated to the contract. Conversely, because courts in various countries construe descriptive terms in different ways (*e.g.,* "dispute" vs. "controversy" or "arising out of" vs. "relating to"), the clause should fully describe the arbitrable subject matter. If the parties do not wish particular claims to be subject to the ADR clause, such as antitrust-or securities-related disputes (which are within the ambit of a basic arbitration agreement, these areas must be expressly omitted.[1]

However, if speed is a high priority, carving out certain issues is not recommended, as doing so increases the likelihood of prolonging the arbitration due to disagreements regarding the characterization of disputes.

Selecting a Provider. Negotiations for selecting a particular regime and set of procedures typically reflect the nationalities of the parties (Americans tend to prefer American Arbitration Association arbitration, continental Europeans are more comfortable with the International Chamber of Commerce, and Japanese tend to prefer the Japan Commercial Arbitration Association). In selecting the regime, it is important to note that there are some major differences between the regimes which may affect time, cost, procedures, location, etc. For example, under the Japan Commercial Arbitration Association, arbitration may occur only in a limited number of Japanese cities, whereas the American Arbitration Association will administer arbitration in many international as well as domestic locations. The International Chamber of Commerce is a for-profit entity, and its court strictly controls the arbitral tribunals, whereas the American Arbitration Association is a not-for-profit organization, and it vests its arbitrators with broad discretionary powers. Furthermore, the American Arbitration Association administers arbitrations under a broad spectrum of rules, whereas the Japan Commercial Arbitration Association and the International Chamber of Commerce administer only their own rules. There are several hundred domestic and over 80 international institutions that provide mediation and arbitration services; some may be better suited to a party or a given dispute than others. In addition, the parties may refer to a country or state arbitral codification scheme or construct an ad hoc arbitration clause pursuant to the parties' own desires. An example of this latter model is the UNCITRAL regime, which was put in place comparatively recently and has been gathering momentum and increasing acceptance.

Whichever regime is selected, the parties should understand that by designating a particular regime's rules, the parties incorporate a broad set of provisions that will apply to their arbitration (*e.g.*, if the parties simply select the International Chamber of Commerce's rules and do not establish any other requirements to govern their arbitration, they may well find themselves in a foreign country with a proceeding conducted in a foreign language).

If parties are amenable to "legal planning," it may be prudent to add the following language to the basic clauses set forth in Section 9.14, *infra,* if you are identifying a smaller provider:

Model Language: If the [arbitral organization] or its successor is not then in existence or for any reason fails or refuses

§ 9.2

1. *See* Mitsubishi Motors Corp. v. Soler Chrysler Plymouth, 473 U.S. 614, 105 S.Ct. 3346, 87 L.Ed.2d 444 (1985), and Shearson/American Express, Inc. v. McMahon, 482 U.S. 220, 107 S.Ct. 2332, 96 L.Ed.2d 185 (1987)

to act, the arbitration shall proceed in conformity with and subject to the laws of [State or Country] relating to arbitration at the time of the notice.

Interplay with Other Laws. Several regimes may potentially govern an arbitration. It is important to be aware of these regimes and the potential for conflict with the chosen law of the dispute resolution clause. Congress enacted the Federal Arbitration Act in 1925 to provide for the enforcement of arbitration agreements and to supply various rules for arbitration proceedings. Similar provisions were enacted by state legislatures, many of which (though not New York or California) adopted the Uniform Arbitration Act. In addition, foreign legislatures have enacted numerous laws relating directly and indirectly to arbitration, and various conventions and treaties may have applicability to a particular international arbitration. These legal regimes may become applicable to an arbitration due to their express incorporation into the agreement, the location of the arbitration, the location of the court where enforcement of the award is sought, or the residence of the parties or location of their assets.

As discussed below, different jurisdictions and courts may treat identical language in an arbitration clause differently. For example, where the arbitration clause is silent on the issue, some jurisdictions will consolidate related arbitrations over the objections of some of the parties, or allow for broad discovery rights and interim relief. Moreover, unless expressly waived by the parties in the agreement, some courts require written explanations by the arbitrator of the award, or the appearance of the parties as witnesses, as a prerequisite for enforceability.

The draftsperson must review the law of the contract, of the place of the arbitration and of the jurisdictions of intended enforcement of the award, if different, to determine whether such law(s) conflict with, or add to, the parties' expressed intention in the arbitration provision and whether specific waivers should be agreed to in advance to allow for the effective and prompt enforcement of the award.

Library References:

West's Key No. Digests, Arbitration ⊕1–4.1.
Wright, Miller & Cooper, Federal Practice and Procedure: Civil 2d § 3569.

§ 9.3   The Federal Arbitration Act: Scope and Application

FAA § 2 provides that "[a] written provision in any maritime transaction or a contract evidencing a transaction involving commerce" that calls for arbitration of disputes "shall be valid, irrevocable, and enforceable, save upon such grounds as exist at law or in equity for the revocation of any contract."

"Maritime transactions" and "commerce" as used in the Act are defined in Section 1. Of most significance to the operation of the FAA is the definition of commerce, which encompasses "commerce among the several States or with foreign nations, or in any Territory of the United States or in the District of Columbia, or between any such Territory and any State or foreign nation, or between the District of Columbia and any State or Territory or foreign nation."

Section 1 also contains an exception to the operation of the Act: "nothing herein contained shall apply to contracts of employment of seamen, railroad employees, or any other class of workers engaged in foreign or interstate commerce."

For purposes of enforcement of arbitration agreements, the two most important sections of the Act are Section 3, which requires a court to stay an action pending arbitration once it is satisfied that the issue is arbitrable under an arbitration agreement, and Section 4, which requires a court to order arbitration if it is satisfied that an agreement to arbitrate has been made and has not been honored.

For many years, there was uncertainty about the reach of the FAA over commerce. The Supreme Court resolved this issue in *Allied-Bruce Terminix Cos., Inc. v. Dobson*,[1] holding that the FAA reaches to the fullest extent of Congress' power over commerce. Consistent with the expansive interpretation of the FAA's reach, the exceptions to the Act have been interpreted narrowly.

(a) Agreements Involving Commerce

Historically, Congress' use of the term "involving commerce" in Section 2 had created uncertainty about the extent of the reach of the FAA. In particular, it was unclear whether Congress intended the statute to reach to the limits of Congress' Commerce Clause powers, or whether its failure to use the term "affecting commerce" signaled an intent to limit the reach of the statute at some point short of those powers.

In addition, the phrase "evidencing a transaction" led some state courts to hold that the FAA did not apply to a contract unless the contract's connection to commerce was plain from the nature of the transaction. Thus, some states limited the Act's application to transactions in which the parties "contemplated" a connection with interstate commerce at the time of making the contract.[2]

The Supreme Court resolved these issues in *Allied-Bruce Terminix Cos., Inc. v. Dobson*,[3] holding that the FAA reaches to the fullest extent of Congress' power over commerce. To reach this conclusion, the Court interpreted the term "involving commerce" to be the equivalent of the term "affecting commerce." The Court based this interpretation on the common meaning of the words; the legislative history of the FAA, which

§ 9.3

1. 513 U.S. 265, 115 S.Ct. 834, 130 L.Ed.2d 753 (1995).

2. *See, e.g.,* Allied–Bruce Terminix Cos., Inc. v. Dobson, 628 So.2d 354 (Ala.1993),

rev'd, 513 U.S. 265, 115 S.Ct. 834, 130 L.Ed.2d 753 (1995).

3. 513 U.S. 265, 115 S.Ct. 834, 130 L.Ed.2d 753 (1995).

it found to indicate "expansive congressional intent"; and the confluence between a broad interpretation of the term and the FAA's basic purpose of putting arbitration agreements "on the same footing" with a contract's other terms.[4] Similarly, the Court held that Section 2's reference to a contract "evidencing a transaction" involving commerce means only that the transaction evidenced by the contract must involve interstate commerce, regardless of whether the parties contemplated a connection with interstate commerce at the time of the transaction.[5]

(b) Maritime Transactions

Maritime transactions are defined in the FAA to mean "charter parties, bills of lading of water carriers, agreements relating to wharfage, supplies furnished vessels or repairs to vessels, collisions, or any other matters in foreign commerce which, if the subject of controversy, would be embraced within admiralty jurisdiction."[6] Not surprisingly, the provision of the FAA extending its reach to maritime transactions has received far less attention from the courts than the provision regarding interstate commerce. While there is comparatively little controversy concerning the applicability of the FAA to specific maritime transactions, the effect of the FAA's application is the same regardless of whether the statute applies because of commerce or maritime transactions. Thus, while the analysis herein focuses on commerce cases, the principles and results are the same in maritime cases.

(c) Exceptions

The FAA specifically excepts from its reach "contracts of employment of seamen, railroad employees, or any other class of workers engaged in foreign or interstate commerce."[7] The exception has been applied to workers in the transportation industries, such as postal workers[8] and bus drivers.[9]

Ironically, while the Court in *Terminix* interpreted the term "involving commerce" broadly, in order to achieve Congress' intent of widely enforcing arbitration agreements, the achievement of the same goal requires that the term "engaged in ... commerce" in Section 1 be interpreted narrowly, so that fewer agreements are excluded from the reach of the FAA. Courts, in a number of states, including California, have done just that, limiting the exception to "employees involved in the actual movement of goods in interstate commerce."[10] Thus, in *Spellman v. Securities, Annuities & Ins. Services, Inc.,* despite the fact that

---

4. *Id.* at 274, 115 S.Ct. at 840.

5. *Id.* at 269, 115 S.Ct. at 837.

6. 9 U.S.C.A. § 1 (West 1970).

7. *Id.*

8. Bacashihua v. United States Postal Service, 859 F.2d 402 (6th Cir.1988).

9. Pennsylvania Greyhound Lines v. Amalgamated Ass'n, 193 F.2d 327 (3d Cir. 1952).

10. Spellman v. Securities, Annuities & Ins. Services, Inc., 8 Cal.App.4th 452, 459–60, 10 Cal.Rptr.2d 427, 431–32 (1992); *see* Tonetti v. Shirley, 173 Cal.App.3d 1144, 1148–49, 219 Cal.Rptr. 616, 618–19 (1985).

securities representatives engage in interstate commerce, the court applied the narrow interpretation of the Section 1 exception and held that employment contracts for securities representatives did *not* fall within the exception.

The majority of circuit courts that have considered the issue have also adopted this narrow interpretation of the exclusion.[11]

Also excepted from the reach of the FAA are collective bargaining agreements.

The exclusion was first noted in *Textile Workers Union of America v. Lincoln Mills.*[12] In *Lincoln Mills*, the Court held that Section 301(a) of the Labor Management Relations Act ("LMRA") required enforcement of arbitration agreements in collective bargaining agreements. The Court looked to Section 301(a) of LMRA, rather than to the FAA, as the source of law governing the arbitrability of collective bargaining agreements. Justice Frankfurter's dissent recognized the Court's implicit rejection of the applicability of the FAA with respect to such agreements, and urged that their exclusion under Section 1 be made explicit.[13]

More recently, in *United Paperworkers Int'l Union v. Misco, Inc.,*[14] the Supreme Court stated:

> The Arbitration Act does not apply to "contracts of employment of ... workers engaged in foreign or interstate commerce," 9 U.S.C.A. § 1, but the federal courts have often looked to the Act for guidance in labor arbitration cases, especially in the wake of the holding that § 301 of the Labor Management Relations Act of 1947, empowers the federal courts to fashion rules of federal common law to govern "[s]uits for violation of contracts between an employer and a labor organization" under the federal labor laws.[15]

The Supreme Court has failed to state explicitly whether the basis of the exclusion of collective bargaining agreements is due to the LMRA's having superseded the FAA (as is suggested by the result of *Lincoln Mills*) or instead arises from application of the Section 1 exclusion for contracts of employment. Under either theory, the FAA does not govern

---

11. *See, e.g.,* Rojas v. TK Communications, Inc., 87 F.3d 745 (5th Cir.1996) (radio station disc jockey not subject to § 1 exclusions); Asplundh Tree Expert Co. v. Bates, 71 F.3d 592, 596–602 (6th Cir.1995) (reviewing legislative history of § 1 exclusion as well as circuit court opinions regarding this issue); Miller Brewing Co. v. Brewery Workers Local Union No. 9, 739 F.2d 1159, 1162 (7th Cir.1984) *cert. denied* 469 U.S. 1160, 105 S.Ct. 912, 83 L.Ed.2d 926 (1985)(§ 1 exclusion is limited to transportation workers engaged in the movement of goods); Dickstein v. duPont, 443 F.2d 783, 785 (1st Cir.1971); Erving v. Virginia Squires Basketball Club, 468 F.2d 1064, 1069 (2d Cir.1972) (basketball player's employment contract not subject to § 1 exclu-

sion because not involved in transportation industry); Tenney Engineering v. United Electrical Radio & Machine Workers, 207 F.2d 450, 453 (3d Cir.1953) (employees engaged in production of goods for subsequent sale in interstate commerce do not fall within § 1 exclusion).

12. 353 U.S. 448, 77 S.Ct. 912, 1 L.Ed.2d 972 (1957).

13. *Id.* at 466–67 (Frankfurter, J., dissenting).

14. 484 U.S. 29, 108 S.Ct. 364, 98 L.Ed.2d 286 (1987).

15. *Id.* at 40 n.9, 108 S.Ct. at 372 n.9 (alterations in original) (citations omitted).

such agreements, but may be looked to as a source of guidance on the subject, as was done in *Misco*.

Library References:

West's Key No. Digests, Arbitration ⚯2.
Wright, Miller, Marcus & Cooper, Federal Practice and Procedure: Civil 2d §§ 3142, 3574, 3675, 3676.

§ 9.4   Procedures for Enforcing Arbitration Agreements

This section addresses the procedures for moving to compel arbitration in federal district court as well as the federal law regarding the presumption of arbitrability.

(a) Compelling Arbitration

A petition (or motion) to compel arbitration may be necessary where one party to an arbitration agreement is resisting arbitration. If no lawsuit is pending, a petition as opposed to a motion should be filed to commence the proceeding. Where there is voluntary compliance, a court order is not necessary and may not be desirable. However, in many instances it may be necessary to invoke Section 4 of the Federal Arbitration Act which provides in pertinent part that a party aggrieved by the "alleged failure, neglect or refusal of another to arbitrate under a written agreement for arbitration may petition . . . for an order directing that such arbitration proceed in the manner provided for in such agreement."

A petition to compel arbitration under Section 4 must include at least the following:

- Jurisdictional Allegations. 9 U.S.C.A. § 4 provides that the proceeding may be brought in any United States district court which, save for such agreement would have jurisdiction under Title 28, in a civil action or in admiralty of the subject matter of a suit arising out of the controversy between the parties. . . . "Therefore, the forms of jurisdictional allegations in civil actions generally, set out in Federal Rule 8(1) are appropriate."

- Venue. A petition should also include relevant allegations establishing that venue is proper. For a complete discussion of allegations necessary to establish venue see Chapter 3 "Venue, Forum Selection and Transfer," *supra*.

- Existence of Agreement to Arbitrate. 9 U.S.C.A. applies only to written agreements to arbitrate involving maritime transactions or interstate commerce. It is necessary, therefore, to include allegations of the written agreement to arbitrate, including the execution date of the underlying agreement, the parties, and the terms of the arbitration clause. In fact, it is advisable to quote the entire arbitration clause in the petition whenever possible.

- Existence of a Controversy Relating to Arbitration. The petition must also contain some allegations that respondent has failed and refused to consent to the arbitration.

- Underlying Dispute Is Within Scope of Agreement to Arbitrate. The petition should also include allegations that the underlying dispute and each claim for relief is within the scope of the arbitration agreement. In most cases, it is sufficient to identify the separate causes of action and a brief description of why each cause of action is within the scope of the arbitration agreement.

The petition to compel arbitration is frequently quite short. Depending on the scope of the proceeding, the above allegations can be adequately set forth in most cases in 12 to 18 separate allegations. The tendency in some cases is to describe the scope of the dispute in great detail. This temptation should be resisted. In most cases, the arbitration agreement provides that "any and all disputes arising under this agreement shall be resolved by arbitration." It is sufficient in that case, therefore, to identify the dispute and allege that it arises under the agreement.

In addition to the petition, the moving party should provide the court with an affidavit (or multiple affidavits if necessary) supplying a copy of the arbitration agreement, verifying the execution date of the underlying agreement, and providing competent evidence that respondent has failed to consent to arbitration. Together with the notice of hearing and petition, these constitute your petition.

(b) Determining the Scope of an Arbitration Agreement

The Supreme Court has recognized a series of policies underlying the FAA.[1] As a result, the scope of an arbitration agreement is a question of federal law, and any doubts about the arbitrability of an issue are to be resolved in favor of arbitration.[2] Second, where an arbitration agreement satisfies the requirements of Section 2, arbitration is mandatory, and the courts have no discretion regarding its enforcement.[3] Third, where an attack is made on an arbitration agreement, the courts will determine the merits of the challenge and decide whether there is an agreement to arbitrate and whether it should be enforced. However, where there is an attack on the overall contract containing the agreement, the matter will be referred to arbitration.[4]

There is some degree of tension in the Supreme Court's interpretation of the FAA and its underlying policies. On one hand, the Court has discerned in the FAA an overriding goal of enforcing arbitration agree-

§ 9.4

1. Moses H. Cone Memorial Hospital v. Mercury Constr. Corp., 460 U.S. 1, 24–25, 103 S.Ct. 927, 941–42, 74 L.Ed.2d 765 (1983).

2. Id.

3. Dean Witter Reynolds, Inc. v. Byrd, 470 U.S. 213, 218, 105 S.Ct. 1238, 1241, 84 L.Ed.2d 158 (1985).

4. Prima Paint Corp. v. Flood & Conklin Mfg. Co., 388 U.S. 395, 87 S.Ct. 1801, 18 L.Ed.2d 1270 (1967).

ments to the fullest extent possible. Thus, the Court has discerned from the FAA a liberal policy in favor of arbitration that requires that all doubts concerning the arbitrability of issues in contracts governed by the Act be resolved in favor of arbitration.[5] As stated by the Court: "Section 2 is a congressional declaration of a liberal federal policy favoring arbitration agreements, notwithstanding any state substantive or procedural policies to the contrary."[6]

The Court's tendency to read the Act expansively has been limited by its recognition of another side of the legislative history, from which the Court has discerned that "the basic purpose of the [FAA] is to overcome courts' refusals to enforce agreements to arbitrate."[7] In accordance with this purpose, the Court has found that Congress intended arbitration agreements to be enforceable to the same extent as other contracts, but not more so.[8] Accordingly, in *Dean Witter Reynolds Inc. v. Byrd*,[9] the Court found that the enforcement of agreements was a more important goal of the FAA than the goal of speedy resolution of claims:

> The legislative history of the Act establishes that the purpose behind its passage was to ensure judicial enforcement of privately made agreements to arbitrate. We therefore reject the suggestion that the overriding goal of the Arbitration Act was to promote the expeditious resolution of claims. The Act, after all, does not mandate the arbitration of all claims, but merely the enforcement—upon the motion of one of the parties—of privately negotiated arbitration agreements.... [P]assage of the Act was motivated, first and foremost, by a congressional desire to enforce agreements into which parties had entered, and we must not overlook this principal objective when construing the statute, or allow the fortuitous impact of the Act on efficient dispute resolution to overshadow the underlying motivation.[10]

The Court attempted to balance the competing goals of the FAA in *Mitsubishi Motors Corp. v. Soler Chrysler–Plymouth, Inc.*,[11] stating: "as with any other contract, the parties' intentions control, but those intentions are generously construed as to issues of arbitrability." While the Court's tendency to interpret the Act broadly has played the greatest role in shaping the federal common law of arbitration, its recognition that the parties cannot be forced to arbitrate where they have not agreed to do so serves as an important limit on the expansion of the evolving law. The Supreme Court wrote in *First Options of Chicago, Inc. v. Kaplan, et Ux. and MK Investments, Inc.*,[12] that "[c]ourts should not

5. Moses H. Cone, 460 U.S. at 24–25, 103 S.Ct. at 941–42.

6. *Id.* at 24, 103 S.Ct. at 941.

7. Allied-Bruce Terminix Cos., Inc. v. Dobson, 513 U.S. 265, 115 S.Ct. 834, 130 L.Ed.2d 753 (1995).

8. *See, e.g.,* Volt Information Sciences v. Board of Trustees of Leland Stanford Jr. University, 489 U.S. 468, 474–75, 109 S.Ct. 1248, 1253, 103 L.Ed.2d 488 (1989).

9. 470 U.S. 213, 105 S.Ct. 1238, 84 L.Ed.2d 158 (1985).

10. *Id.* at 219–20, 105 S.Ct. at 1241–42.

11. 473 U.S. 614, 626, 105 S.Ct. 3346, 3353, 87 L.Ed.2d 444 (1985).

12. 514 U.S. 938, 115 S.Ct. 1920, 131 L.Ed.2d 985 (1995).

assume that the parties agreed to arbitrate arbitrability unless there is 'clear and unmistakable' evidence that they did so."[13] *First Options* was a case arising out of disputes centered on agreements to "work out" debts by Kaplan, his wife, and his wholly owned investment company. While the company had signed an agreement containing the arbitration clause, Kaplan and his wife had not. In finding that the court of appeals was correct in its conclusion that the issue of arbitrability was subject to independent review by the courts, the Supreme Court emphasized that "a party who has not agreed to arbitrate will normally have a right to a court's decisions about the merits of its dispute."[14] The Court further indicated that in deciding whether parties agreed to arbitrate an issue, courts generally should apply ordinary state law principles that govern the formation of contracts.[15] As for who has jurisdiction to determine whether a party entered into an arbitration agreement, courts, not arbitrators, may make the finding.[16]

(c) Federal Law Governs Scope of Arbitration

In *Moses H. Cone Memorial Hospital v. Mercury Constr. Corp.*,[17] the first case in which the Court articulated the liberal federal policy favoring arbitration, the Court held that the district court had erred by staying a federal action that had sought an order compelling arbitration pursuant to Section 4, in favor of state court proceedings concerning the arbitrability of the same issues. As stated by the Court: "Section 2 is a congressional declaration of a liberal federal policy favoring arbitration agreements, notwithstanding any state substantive or procedural policies to the contrary.... [A]s a matter of federal law, any doubts concerning the scope of arbitrable issues should be resolved in favor of arbitration, whether the problem at hand is the construction of the contract language itself or an allegation of waiver, delay, or a like defense to arbitrability."[18]

As a result of *Moses H. Cone*, the determination of the scope of an arbitration agreement governed by the FAA is an issue of federal law, which is determined with reference to the federal policy favoring arbitration.[19] In accordance with this federal law, all doubts and ambiguities concerning the scope of arbitrable issues are to be resolved in favor of arbitration.[20]

It is apparent that the actual interpretation of any arbitration agreement subject to the FAA will be made with reference to state law,

---

13. *Id.* at 938, 115 S.Ct. at 1921.

14. *Id.* at 942, 115 S.Ct. at 1923.

15. *Id.* at 943, 115 S.Ct. at 1924.

16. *Id.* at *6.

17. 460 U.S. 1, 103 S.Ct. 927, 74 L.Ed.2d 765 (1983).

18. *Id.* at 24–25, 103 S.Ct. at 941–42.

19. *See, e.g.*, Tracer Research Corp. v. National Environmental Services Co., 42 F.3d 1292 (9th Cir.1994).

20. Moses H. Cone, 460 U.S. at 24, 103 S.Ct. at 941 ("questions of arbitrability must be addressed with a healthy regard for the federal policy favoring arbitration"); Mitsubishi Motors Corp. v. Soler Chrysler–Plymouth, Inc., 473 U.S. 614, 626, 105 S.Ct. 3346, 3353, 87 L.Ed.2d 444 (1985) (parties' intentions "are generously construed as to issues of arbitrability").

given that there is no federal law of contract. However, those state law policies will be modified by the federal policy favoring arbitration. As stated by the Supreme Court in *Volt Info. Sciences, Inc. v. Board of Trustees of Leland Stanford Jr. University:*[21] "in applying general state-law principles of contract interpretation to the interpretation of an arbitration agreement within the scope of the Act, due regard must be given to the federal policy favoring arbitration, and ambiguities as to the scope of the arbitration clause itself resolved in favor of arbitration."

The federal policy requiring resolution of doubts in favor of arbitration applies notwithstanding contrary state law, which may, for example, require a contract to be construed against its drafter.[22]

(d) Separability of Arbitration Clauses

The liberal federal policy favoring arbitration has led the Supreme Court to hold that an arbitration agreement contained in a contract is a separate, independent agreement. Under the doctrine of separability, only challenges to the separate arbitration agreement are decided by the courts; challenges to the overall contract are referred to arbitration. The effect of this doctrine is to enlarge the number of disputes that are decided in arbitration rather than in courts.

The doctrine of separability was first recognized by the Court in *Prima Paint Corp. v. Flood & Conklin.*[23] In *Prima Paint*, the buyer and seller of a paint business were parties to a contract that required the seller to perform consulting and other services relating to the operation of the transferred business. The buyer asserted claims against the seller for fraudulent representations of its solvency to induce the buyer to enter into the consulting agreement, and the seller served a notice of intention to arbitrate pursuant to an arbitration clause contained in the agreement. The buyer then filed a diversity action in the district court to rescind the consulting agreement on the basis of fraud in the inducement, and sought to enjoin the seller from proceeding with arbitration. The district court granted a motion by the seller to stay the action pending arbitration pursuant to Section 3 of the Act, and the court of appeals dismissed the buyer's appeal.

The Supreme Court held that the arbitration agreement was governed by the FAA, and proceeded to decide the issue of whether a claim of fraud in the inducement of the contract was to be resolved by the federal court or the arbitrators. The Court resolved a split in the circuits between courts such as the Second Circuit, that held arbitration agreements to be "separable" from the contracts in which they are contained as a matter of federal law, and those, such as the First Circuit, that held

---

21. 489 U.S. 468, 475–76, 109 S.Ct. 1248, 1253–54, 103 L.Ed.2d 488 (1989) (citations omitted).

22. *See* Chan v. Drexel Burnham Lambert, Inc., 178 Cal.App.3d 632, 639, 223 Cal.Rptr. 838 (1986).

23. 388 U.S. 395, 87 S.Ct. 1801, 18 L.Ed.2d 1270 (1967).

the issue to be one of state law, requiring federal courts to decide issues of fraud where the state law viewed the arbitration clause to be inseparable from the contract.[24]

The Court found the answer in Section 4 of the Act,[25] which requires that, when a party seeks to compel compliance with a written agreement for arbitration: "The court shall hear the parties, and upon being satisfied that the making of the agreement for arbitration or the failure to comply therewith is not in issue, the court shall make an order directing the parties to proceed to arbitration in accordance with the terms of the agreement." As the Court read Section 4, "if the claim is fraud in the inducement of the arbitration clause itself—an issue which goes to the 'making' of the agreement to arbitrate—the federal court may proceed to adjudicate it. But the statutory language does not permit the federal court to consider claims of fraud in the inducement of the contract generally."[26]

The Court then held that the same standard applied to Section 3 of the Act, so that a court could only consider issues related to the making and performance of the agreement to arbitrate, rather than the contract as a whole, in deciding whether to grant a stay of proceedings pending arbitration. The Court concluded that this interpretation "not only honor[s] the plain meaning of the statute but also the unmistakably clear congressional purpose that the arbitration procedure, when selected by the parties to a contract, be speedy and not subject to delay and obstruction in the courts."[27]

The concept of separability has been applied to defenses beyond fraudulent inducement to encompass any challenge to the making of the contract. For example, in *Unionmutual Stock Life Ins. Co. v. Beneficial Life Ins. Co.*,[28] the court applied the separability doctrine to claims of rescission based on mutual mistake and frustration of purpose. As the court explained: "The teaching of *Prima Paint* is that a federal court must not remove from the arbitrators consideration of a substantive challenge to a contract unless there has been an independent challenge to the making of the arbitration clause itself. The basis of the underlying challenge to the contract does not alter the severability principle."[29]

Library References:

   West's Key No. Digests, Arbitration ⚯22–25.

   Wright, Miller & Cooper, Federal Practice and Procedure: Civil 2d §§ 3569, 3914.17, 3923.

§ 9.5   Defenses to Enforceability of Arbitration Agreements

Section 2 of the FAA mandates that arbitration agreements governed by the Act are "valid, irrevocable, and enforceable" unless the

---

24. *Id.* at 402–03, 87 S.Ct. at 1805–06.

25. 9 U.S.C.A. § 4 (West 1970).

26. Prima Paint, 388 U.S. at 403–04, 87 S.Ct. at 1805–06.

27. *Id.* at 404, 87 S.Ct. at 1806.

28. 774 F.2d 524, 528–29 (1st Cir.1985).

29. *Id.* at 529.

agreement can be avoided "upon such grounds as exist at law or in equity for the revocation of any contract." Section 4 provides that if the court is "satisfied that the making of the agreement for arbitration or the failure to comply therewith is not in issue, the court *shall* make an order directing the parties to proceed to arbitration in accordance with the terms of the agreement."[1] These provisions make clear that the enforcement of arbitration agreements under the Act is mandatory: "By its terms, the Act leaves no place for the exercise of discretion by a district court, but instead mandates that district courts *shall* direct the parties to proceed to arbitration on issues as to which an arbitration agreement has been signed."[2]

In accordance with the mandatory nature of the Act, the Supreme Court has held that the courts must compel arbitration of state law claims regardless of any inefficiencies caused by the fact that federal claims on the same issues may be litigated in separate federal proceedings.[3] In *Dean Witter Reynolds, Inc. v. Byrd*, a securities investor asserted federal securities claims and pendent state law claims in an action in federal court against his securities broker-dealer. While the parties had an arbitration agreement, it was believed at that time that the federal securities claims were not subject to arbitration. Accordingly, the broker sought to compel arbitration only of the state law claims. Thus, if the order was granted, the federal action would go forward at the same time as an arbitration on similar claims. The Court held that the Act did not permit the exercise of discretion, but instead mandated that the district court compel arbitration upon filing of an appropriate motion, regardless of any inefficiencies.

The Court has also required arbitration to go forward, notwithstanding that the disputes encompassed claims against a third party who had not agreed to arbitration.[4] The underlying dispute in *Moses H. Cone Memorial Hospital v. Mercury Contr. Corp.* arose from construction of additions to a hospital. The contractor had asserted claims against the hospital, which in turn had asserted claims for indemnity against the architect. The hospital had resisted the motion to compel arbitration, in part, on the ground that only the claims with the contractor were subject to the arbitration agreement, and it would be forced to pursue its related claim against the architect in a separate forum. The Court held that the FAA nevertheless required the court to grant the order compelling arbitration: "The relevant federal law *requires* piecemeal resolution when necessary to give effect to an arbitration agreement. Under the Arbitration Act, an arbitration agreement must be enforced notwithstanding the presence of other persons who are parties to the underlying dispute but not to the arbitration agreement."[5]

---

§ 9.5

1. 9 U.S.C.A. § 4 (West 1970) (emphasis supplied).

2. Dean Witter Reynolds Inc. v. Byrd, 470 U.S. 213, 218, 105 S.Ct. 1238, 1241, 84 L.Ed.2d 158 (1985) (emphasis in original).

3. *See id.* at 217, 105 S.Ct. at 1240.

4. Moses H. Cone Memorial Hospital v. Mercury Constr. Corp., 460 U.S. 1, 20, 103 S.Ct. 927, 939, 74 L.Ed.2d 765 (1983).

5. *Id.* at 20, 103 S.Ct. at 939.

Under this provision, an arbitration agreement is enforceable if (1) it is in writing, and (2) there are no grounds for the revocation of such an agreement. This section addresses the specific defenses to enforcement of arbitration agreements. At the outset, it is important to point out the recognized public policy favoring arbitration.[6]

(a) Lack of Agreement

The existence of an agreement to arbitrate is the predicate for enforcement of any arbitration agreement: "Arbitration is a matter of contract and a party cannot be required to submit to arbitration any dispute which he has not agreed so to submit."[7] Importantly, the presence of a written arbitration agreement does not by itself determine "whether the minds of the parties ever met so as to bring about the very contract of which that arbitration clause is part."[8] In determining whether there is an agreement to arbitrate, courts will look to the arbitration clause itself rather than the contract as a whole.[9]

Under Section 4 of the FAA it is the court's responsibility to determine whether the parties agreed to arbitrate the dispute. "If the making of the Arbitration Agreement ... be in issue, the Court shall proceed summarily to the trial thereof...."[10] State contract law will govern whether a valid agreement to arbitrate exists. Application of state contract law requires special attention from the litigator as the following example illustrates. In *Chan v. Drexel Burnham Lambert, Inc.,*[11] a stockbroker's employment agreement with a national securities firm obligated him to "to abide by ... the rules and by-laws of" the New York Stock Exchange ("NYSE") "as amended from time to time hereafter." NYSE rules provide for arbitration of disputes between employees and securities firms. Whether this rule was incorporated by reference, however, was to be determined under California contract law. The court of appeals ruled that under California law, the reference was inadequate to bind the party to arbitration because arbitration was not mentioned in the employment agreement.[12]

A party can resist arbitration on the ground that he or she never agreed to the arbitration clause. Failure to read or understand the arbitration clause, however, is not a defense.[13]

6. *Id.* at 24, 103 S.Ct. at 941.

7. United Steelworkers of America v. Warrior and Gulf Navigation Company, 363 U.S. 574, 582, 80 S.Ct. 1347, 1353, 4 L.Ed.2d 1409 (1960).

8. Kulukundis Shipping Co. v. Amtorg Trading Corp., 126 F.2d 978 (2d Cir.1942).

9. Prima Paint Corp. v. Flood & Conklin Mfg. Co., 388 U.S. 395, 403–04, 87 S.Ct. 1801, 1805–06, 18 L.Ed.2d 1270 (1967).

10. Perry v. Thomas, 482 U.S. 483, 492, n. 9, 107 S.Ct. 2520, 2527 n. 9, 96 L.Ed.2d 426 (1987).

11. 178 Cal.App.3d 632, 223 Cal.Rptr. 838 (1986).

12. *Id.* at 643, 223 Cal.Rptr. at 844.

13. *See, e.g.,* Madden v. Kaiser Foundation Hospitals, 17 Cal.3d 699, 710, 131 Cal. Rptr. 882, 889, 552 P.2d 1178 (1976).

(b) Fraud

Fraud is a recognized basis for not enforcing an agreement to arbitrate. In order to satisfy this standard, a party must establish the elements of fraudulent misrepresentation.[14] The leading case addressing the application of the fraud standard is *Cohen v. Wedbush, Noble, Cooke, Inc.*[15] In *Cohen*, customers in a broker agreement alleged that they signed the agreement without reading the arbitration clause. The customers further alleged that the broker represented that the agreement would not "compromise" any of their rights. The court rejected the customers' claim, holding that "reliance on a misrepresentation is not reasonable when the plaintiff could have, through the exercise of reasonable diligence, ascertained the truth of the matter."[16] The court further stated that "allegations of misrepresentations directly contrary to the specific and unambiguous terms of a written arbitration agreement do not, as a matter of law, state a claim for fraud."[17]

Fraud may be a defense to the enforceability of an arbitration agreement where the fraud is directed to the arbitration clause itself. Claims that the underlying contract was procured by fraud are subject to arbitration.[18] Claims of fraud directed to the arbitration clause itself are to be resolved by the court, not the arbitrator, under federal law.[19]

Importantly, parties do not have a duty to explain the terms of an arbitration agreement or the meaning and effect of such an agreement.[20] Where a fiduciary relationship exists, however, the parties seeking to enforce arbitration may be held to a higher standard. For example, in *Main v. Merrill Lynch, Pierce, Fenner & Smith, Inc.*,[21] an unsophisticated client alleged that a confidential relationship existed between her and her stockbroker. The client further alleged that she was accustomed to signing documents at her stockbroker's request, and that her stockbroker induced her to sign documents based on his representations. A California court of appeal found these allegations were sufficient to allege that fraud and undue influence permeated the entire agreement, including the arbitration agreement.[22]

---

14. *See* Ingbar v. Drexel Burnham Lambert, Inc., 683 F.2d 603, 607 (1st Cir.1982).

15. 841 F.2d 282 (9th Cir.1988).

16. *Id.* at 287.

17. *Id.* at 288.

18. Prima Paint Corp. v. Flood & Conklin Manufacturing Co., 388 U.S. 395, 87 S.Ct. 1801, 18 L.Ed.2d 1270 (1967).

19. Moseley v. Electronic & Missile Facilities, Inc., 374 U.S. 167, 83 S.Ct. 1815, 10 L.Ed.2d 818 (1963); Houlihan v. Offerman & Co., Inc., 31 F.3d 692, 695 (8th Cir.1994) ("Thus, a court can consider a claim that a party was fraudulently induced to include an arbitration clause in a contract, but not a claim that an entire contract was the product of fraud.").

20. Cohen, 841 F.2d 282.

21. 67 Cal.App.3d 19, 136 Cal.Rptr. 378 (1977).

22. *Id.* at 33, 136 Cal.Rptr. at 386. *See also* Ford v. Shearson Lehman/American Express, Inc., 180 Cal.App.3d 1011, 225 Cal. Rptr. 895 (1986) (Client alleged he was unduly influenced by a psychotherapist-business advisor who colluded with the stockbroker to take advantage of him. The court found the allegations sufficient to include the arbitration clause.).

(c) Duress, Undue Influence

Lack of voluntary assent to the arbitration agreement is a defense to enforcement. While there is scant authority in the federal courts addressing this particular standard, there are state law cases that provide some guidance.[23]

(d) Unconscionability

The Federal Arbitration Act defers to state contract law in determining enforceability of arbitration agreements. Federal courts will, however, refuse enforcement of arbitration clauses "where the party opposing arbitration presents 'well-supported claims that the agreement to arbitrate resulted from ... overwhelming economic power that would provide grounds for the revocation of any contract.' "[24] In evaluating a claim for unconscionability, a federal court must evaluate the arbitration clause by the same standard applied to other basic terms in the contract (e.g., price). To apply a higher standard to arbitration agreements would violate the fundamental policy of the FAA: "that kind of policy would place arbitration clauses on an unequal 'footing' directly contrary to the Act's language and Congress' intent."[25]

Claims that the arbitration procedures are unfair will generally fail when the underlying procedures are those of a national organization such as the American Arbitration Association or the New York Stock Exchange.[26] On the other hand, arbitration clauses that purport to waive or limit rights or benefits required by federal law will *not* be given effect.[27] For example, in *Graham Oil Company v. ARCO Products Company*,[28] a franchise agreement contained an arbitration clause that limited rights expressly provided by federal law, including claims for punitive damages, attorneys' fees, and a one-year period within which to sue. The Ninth Circuit found such a limitation was invalid.

(e) Waiver

The right to compel arbitration, consistent with other contractual

---

23. Ford, 180 Cal.App.3d at 1019, 225 Cal.Rptr. at 898; Bayscene Resident Negotiators v. Bayscene Mobilehome Park, 15 Cal. App.4th 119, 129, 18 Cal.Rptr.2d 626, 632 (1993).

24. Rodriguez de Quijas v. Shearson/American Express, Inc., 490 U.S. 477, 483–84, 109 S.Ct. 1917, 1921–22, 104 L.Ed.2d 526 (1989).

25. Allied–Bruce Terminix Cos., Inc. v. Dobson, 513 U.S. 265, 115 S.Ct. 834, 130 L.Ed.2d 753 (1995).

26. The Securities Exchange Commission has specifically approved the arbitration proceedings of the New York Stock Exchange, National Association of Securities Dealers, and other exchanges. Shearson/American Express, Inc. v. McMahon, 482 U.S. 220, 234, 107 S.Ct. 2332, 2341, 96 L.Ed.2d 185 (1987). *See also* Cohen v. Wedbush, Noble, Cooke, Inc., 841 F.2d 282, 286 (9th Cir.1988) ("The strong federal policy favoring arbitration coupled with the extensive regulatory oversight performed by the SEC in this area, compel the conclusion that agreements to arbitrate disputes in accordance with SEC-approved procedures are not unconscionable as a matter of law.").

27. Graham Oil Co. v. Arco Products Co., 43 F.3d 1244, 1248 (9th Cir.1994), *cert. denied,* 516 U.S. 907, 116 S.Ct. 275, 133 L.Ed.2d 195 (1995).

28. *Id.*

rights, is subject to waiver.[29] A party seeking to prove waiver of a right to arbitration must demonstrate "(1) knowledge of an existing right to compel arbitration, (2) acts inconsistent with that existing right, and (3) prejudice to the party opposing arbitration."[30] Importantly, it is for the arbitrator to determine whether the delay in demanding arbitration was "unreasonable" and "prejudicial to the other party."[31] For this reason, waiver as a defense to the enforceability of an arbitration agreement is frequently made to the arbitrator rather than to the court in the context of opposing a petition to compel arbitration.

The defense of waiver frequently arises in the context where one party has initiated litigation. The issue, therefore, is whether the acts of litigating constituted a waiver. The Tenth Circuit has held that filing of a lawsuit regarding an arbitrable claim does not per se waive a plaintiff's right to demand arbitration later.[32] However, obtaining judgment on a related claim may bar later arbitration on claims that would be res judicata of the previous litigation.[33]

Library References:

West's Key No. Digests, Arbitration ⟐6.2, 23.3.
Wright, Miller, Cooper & Graham, Federal Practice and Procedure: Civil 2d §§ 1297, 3914.17, 3923, 5460.

§ 9.6 Arbitration Awards in the Courts: Procedures for Confirmation, Vacation, Modification

A commercial litigator will be confronted with the question of whether to confirm or seek to vacate an award at the conclusion of any arbitration. An arbitrator's award without confirmation has the force and effect of a contract. In order to attach assets or ensure compliance, *i.e.* to have the force of a judgment, the award must be confirmed. A confirmed award also has the added advantage of res judicata effect and, in certain instances, collateral estoppel.[1]

The procedures for vacating an award are discussed in detail in the following sections. At the outset, however, it is important to note that the FAA may be seen as establishing a floor for the judicial review of arbitration awards but not a ceiling. The parties may agree to expand the scope of review beyond the parameters provided by the statute. Thus, the boundaries established by the arbitration agreement ultimately define the scope of judicial review. As the Supreme Court repeatedly has held, commercial arbitration agreements are creatures of contract.

29. Fisher v. A.G. Becker Paribas, Inc., 791 F.2d 691, 694 (9th Cir.1986).

30. Britton v. Co-Op Banking Group, 916 F.2d 1405, 1412 (9th Cir.1990).

31. ATSA of California, Inc. v. Continental Insurance Company, 702 F.2d 172, 175 (9th Cir.1983).

32. Hart v. Orion Insurance Co., 453 F.2d 1358, 1361 (10th Cir.1971).

33. Hoffman Construction Co. v. Active Erectors & Installers, Inc., 969 F.2d 796, 799 (9th Cir.1992).

§ 9.6

1. Establishing collateral estoppel from an arbitration is difficult because a party must show the issue was "actually" litigated and "determined." Frequently, arbitrations will not involve a written record or a written opinion.

Federal courts with jurisdiction must enforce those contracts as written by the parties, just as they enforce other kinds of commercial contracts.[2]

(a) Subject Matter Jurisdiction

The domestic FAA does not create federal subject matter jurisdiction.[3] Thus, access to federal court for the purpose of confirming, vacating, or modifying an arbitration award requires the existence of some basis for federal jurisdiction, such as diversity of citizenship,[4] admiralty jurisdiction, or a federal question.[5]

As a practical matter, a federal court may exercise jurisdiction over matters relating to the *arbitration award* by re-invoking the basis of jurisdiction created at an earlier stage, such as a motion to compel arbitration. In this case, the federal court may retain jurisdiction to hear motions relating to the arbitration award.[6]

Under the prevailing view, confirmation of an arbitration award is available even if the agreement contains no provision for consent to entry of judgment by a court.[7] A majority of courts interpret FAA § 9 as

2. In *Gateway Technologies, Inc. v. MCI Telecommunications Corp.*, 64 F.3d 993 (5th Cir.1995), the Fifth Circuit held that contractual provisions calling for expanded review of arbitration awards by federal district courts must be enforced. *Id.* at 997. The *Gateway* parties' agreement provided that "the arbitration decision shall be final and binding on both parties, *except that errors of law shall be subject to appeal.*" *Id.* at 996 (emphasis in original). *See, e.g.,* First Options of Chicago, Inc. v. Kaplan, 514 U.S. 938, 115 S.Ct. 1920, 131 L.Ed.2d 985 (1995); Mastrobuono v. Shearson Lehman Hutton, Inc., 514 U.S. 52, 115 S.Ct. 1212, 131 L.Ed.2d 76 (1995); Volt Information Sciences, Inc. v. Board of Trustees of Leland Stanford Jr. University, 489 U.S. 468, 475–76, 109 S.Ct. 1248, 1253–54, 103 L.Ed.2d 488 (1989); Dean Witter Reynolds Inc. v. Byrd, 470 U.S. 213, 219–21, 105 S.Ct. 1238, 1241–43, 84 L.Ed.2d 158 (1985).

Relying on *Volt* and *Mastrobuono*, the Fifth Circuit held that the district court must enforce the parties' agreement that the court would review the award for errors of law:

When, as here, the parties agree contractually to subject an arbitration award to expanded judicial review, federal arbitration policy demands that the court conduct its review according to the terms of the arbitration contract. Gateway, 64 F.3d at 997.

Accord Fils et Cables d'Acier de Lens v. Midland Metals Corp., 584 F.Supp. 240,

243–44 (S.D.N.Y.1984). *See also* Kyocera Corp. v. Prudential–Bache Trade Services Inc., 130 F.3d 884 (9th Cir.1997).

3. Southland Corp. v. Keating, 465 U.S. 1, 16, 104 S.Ct. 852, 861, 79 L.Ed.2d 1 (1984) (requiring a basis of federal jurisdiction to be established before proceeding to compel arbitration may be filed in federal court).

4. *See* Westinghouse Electric Corp. v. New York City Transit Authority, 14 F.3d 818 (2d Cir.1994) (federal subject matter jurisdiction based on diversity of citizenship).

5. *See* Garrett v. Merrill Lynch, Pierce, Fenner & Smith, Inc., 7 F.3d 882, 884 (9th Cir.1993) (dismissing for lack of federal subject matter jurisdiction a petition to vacate award under FAA § 10 where there was neither diversity of citizenship nor a federal question).

6. *See* Wing v. J.C. Bradford & Co., 678 F.Supp. 622 (N.D.Miss.1987) (court that exercised original subject matter jurisdiction to issue order under FAA § 4 compelling arbitration retained jurisdiction to confirm arbitration award).

7. A minority of courts have interpreted FAA § 9 as imposing a subject matter jurisdiction requirement. According to this reading, FAA § 9 conditions federal subject matter jurisdiction on the inclusion of an entry of judgment clause in an arbitration

enabling parties to choose which court they want to enter a judgment on the award, or in the absence of a choice by the parties, jurisdiction is proper in the court in the district where the award was made.[8] Frequently, parties to an arbitration agreement will designate a court (*e.g.*, the Eastern District of New York). Absent any express provision, the court in the district where either party resides; where the contract is to be performed; where the arbitration was held; or where assets are located may have jurisdiction.

(b) Personal Jurisdiction

A United States district court must have personal jurisdiction over a party to the arbitration agreement before it may compel the party to arbitrate. General principles of personal jurisdiction apply to proceedings respecting confirmation, vacation, and modification of arbitration awards.[9] Exercise of personal jurisdiction over a party requires satisfaction of either the minimum contacts test established in *International Shoe Co. v. Washington*,[10] or the physical presence test of *Burnham v. Superior Court of California*.[11]

Parties may consent in an arbitration agreement to personal jurisdiction in a proceeding for enforcement of an arbitration award.[12] One issue that is raised by these cases is the level of specificity that is required. For example, arbitration agreements frequently include language to the effect that the award may be confirmed in "any court with jurisdiction." In a significant number of agreements, however, the parties have specified a particular court, a city, or a state. In cases where the location of assets is of primary importance, it is advisable to include a clause selecting a court. In the majority of cases, however, it is sufficient to state "any court with jurisdiction."

(c) Venue

(1) Confirmation

Under FAA § 9, venue is in the court specified by the parties in their agreement, or, in the absence of a designated venue, in the "United States court in and for the district within which such award was made." There is no apparent limit on which court parties may select as a forum

agreement. Failure to insert it bars confirmation under FAA § 9. Oklahoma City Associates v. Wal–Mart Stores, Inc., 923 F.2d at 794; *see also* Varley v. Tarrytown Assocs., 477 F.2d 208 (2d Cir.1973).

8. Booth v. Hume Publishing, Inc., 902 F.2d 925, 929–30 (11th Cir.1990); Smiga v. Dean Witter Reynolds, Inc., 766 F.2d 698 (2d Cir.1985), *cert. denied*, 475 U.S. 1067, 106 S.Ct. 1381, 89 L.Ed.2d 607 (1986).

9. *See* Transatlantic Bulk Shipping Ltd. v. Saudi Chartering S.A., 622 F.Supp. 25

(S.D.N.Y.1985) (dismissing motion to confirm arbitral award rendered in London for lack of personal jurisdiction).

10. 326 U.S. 310, 66 S.Ct. 154, 90 L.Ed. 95 (1945). *See also* Chapter 2 "Personal Jurisdiction and Service," *supra*.

11. 495 U.S. 604, 110 S.Ct. 2105, 109 L.Ed.2d 631 (1990).

12. *See* Bergesen v. Joseph Muller Corp., 548 F.Supp. 650 (S.D.N.Y.1982), *aff'd*, 710 F.2d 928 (2d Cir.1983) (U.N. Convention).

for the enforcement of the award.[13] Many of the procedural rules applied by providers of arbitration services include a provision identifying where the award is "made."[14] If the parties do not specify the location in their agreement, for the purpose of determining venue under FAA § 9, the award is "made" in the district where arbitration hearings are held.[15]

Venue under FAA § 9 is permissive. A district court may determine venue according to the provisions of the general venue statute,[16] irrespective of whether the parties have agreed to a particular venue under FAA § 9.[17]

Courts are reluctant to deviate from the standard established in FAA § 9 providing for venue either in the district designated by the parties or where the award was made. Consequently, motions to transfer venue are seldom granted.[18] Motions to transfer venue are governed by 28 U.S.C.A. § 1404. The transferee court must be in a "district or division where [the proceeding] might have been brought" and venue may be transferred only for the "convenience of parties and witnesses, in the interest of justice."[19]

(2) Vacation and Modification

Under FAA §§ 10 and 11, if the conditions for vacation, modification, or correction are satisfied, the "United States court in and for the district wherein the award was made" may enter an order vacating or modifying the award. There is a split in authority as to whether venue provisions are mandatory or permissive under FAA §§ 10 and 11.

The majority view, adopted by both the Fifth and Ninth Circuits, treats the venue provisions in FAA §§ 10 and 11 as mandatory.[20] Where

13. *See* Reed & Martin, Inc. v. Westinghouse Elec. Corp., 439 F.2d 1268, 1275–76 (2d Cir.1971) (the court in the district where arbitration was conducted was proper venue to confirm award).

14. *See, e.g.,* American Arbitration Association Guidelines for Commercial Arbitration.

15. *See* T & R Enterprises., Inc. v. Continental Grain Co., 613 F.2d 1272, 1279 (5th Cir.1980) (refusing to construe "made" under FAA § 9 to apply to place where document was signed, "rather than the place where the [arbitration] proceedings were held and concluded").

16. 28 U.S.C.A. § 1391 (West 1993 & Supp. 1997).

17. *See* Stroh Container Co. v. Delphi Industries, Inc., 783 F.2d 743 (8th Cir.), *cert. denied,* 476 U.S. 1141, 106 S.Ct. 2249, 90 L.Ed.2d 695 (1986) (under FAA § 9, court has discretion to transfer case to court in district in which award was made, although parties had agreed to a different

venue for confirmation proceeding); Smiga v. Dean Witter Reynolds, Inc., 766 F.2d 698, 706–707 (2d Cir.1985), *cert. denied,* 475 U.S. 1067, 106 S.Ct. 1381, 89 L.Ed.2d 607 (1986) (where parties had not agreed on venue for confirmation, federal court having subject matter jurisdiction over the action as a result of an earlier motion to compel could confirm arbitration award, although it was not in the district where the award was made).

18. *See* City of Naples v. Prepakt Concrete Co., 490 F.2d 182 (5th Cir.), *reh'g denied,* 494 F.2d 511 (5th Cir.) *cert. denied,* 419 U.S. 843, 95 S.Ct. 76, 42 L.Ed.2d 71 (1974).

19. 28 U.S.C.A. § 1404(a) (West 1993).

20. City of Naples, 490 F.2d 182 (venue provision in FAA § 10 is mandatory). *See* Sunshine Beauty Supplies, Inc. v. United States Dist. Court, 872 F.2d 310, 311–12 (9th Cir.1989) (FAA § 10 "limits jurisdiction to vacate an award to the district where the award was made").

venue provisions in FAA §§ 10 and 11 are viewed as mandatory, an application under §§ 10 and 11 must be brought in a court in the district in which the award was made and may not be transferred elsewhere.

A minority of courts treat FAA §§ 10 and 11 as establishing only permissive venue requirements.[21]

(d) Standing

A "party to the arbitration" has standing to confirm, vacate, or modify an award.[22] Essentially, a person is a "party to the arbitration" if the arbitration award binds or has preclusive effect on that person. A "party to the arbitration" thus includes: (1) a person who assented to the written agreement to arbitrate or submit the dispute to arbitration; and (2) a nonparty to the arbitration agreement who has rights or duties under the agreement, such as a subsidiary who may be subject to potential indemnity liability.[23]

Library References:

West's Key No. Digests, Arbitration ⊙72, 73.9, 77.
Wright, Miller & Cooper, Federal Practice and Procedure: Civil 2d §§ 1063, 3923.

§ 9.7   Confirming the Award: FAA § 9

(a) Timing

Section 9 of the FAA imposes a one-year time limitation on applications for orders confirming arbitral awards.[1] Under FAA § 9, "at any time within one year after the award is made any party to the arbitration may apply to the court so specified for an order confirming the award." If the application to the court for confirmation under FAA § 9 is late, the opposing party may oppose confirmation and move for a

21. *See* Concourse Beauty School, Inc. v. Polakov, 685 F.Supp. 1311 (S.D.N.Y.1988) (concluding that, given the essential identicality of motions to confirm and motions to vacate, the venue provisions of both FAA § 9 and FAA § 10 should be characterized as permissive). Todd Shipyards Corp. v. Cunard Line Ltd., 708 F.Supp. 1440, 1446–47 (D.N.J.1989) (concluding that venue is permissive with respect to FAA §§ 9, 10, and 11, but reserving judgment where FAA § 8 is concerned).

22. FAA §§ 9–11.

23. *See* Fried, Krupp, GmbH, Krupp Reederei Und Brennstoff–Handel–Seeschiffarht v. Solidarity Carriers, Inc., 674 F.Supp. 1022 (S.D.N.Y.), *aff'd*, 838 F.2d 1202 (2d Cir.1987) (petitioner asserting claim of subsidiary who was not a party to the arbitration agreement permitted to

challenge award, as it faced potential indemnity liability to subsidiary); Dundas Shipping & Trading Co. v. Stravelakis Bros. Ltd., 508 F.Supp. 1000, 1003 (S.D.N.Y. 1981) (petitioner who was neither a party to the contract containing the arbitration agreement, a signatory agreeing to submit the dispute to arbitration, nor bound under the award lacked standing to attack the award).

§ 9.7

1. *But see* Sverdrup Corp. v. WHC Constructors, Inc., 989 F.2d 148 (4th Cir.1993) (interpreting the one-year time limit under FAA § 9 to be permissive, thereby leaving application and interpretation of the limitations period within the discretion of the court).

dismissal, thereby barring confirmation in any federal court under the FAA. This motion is made as a response to a motion to confirm rather than as a motion preceding a motion to confirm. Although there is no explicit statement in FAA § 9 as to when the award is "made" for the purpose of assessing the timeliness of the confirmation application, the clock begins ticking when a "final" award is filed or delivered. An award is considered "final" when it ends the arbitration and nothing remains to arbitrate.[2]

The one-year time limit under FAA § 9 is waived if not raised by the adverse party. In the absence of an objection by the opposing party, a court will not refuse to confirm an award upon a late application.[3]

(b) Procedure

(1) Initiation of Confirmation Proceeding

Section 9 of the FAA prescribes the procedure for serving notice of the application for confirmation upon the opposing party: "Notification of the application shall be served upon the adverse party, and thereupon the court shall have jurisdiction of such party as though he had appeared generally in the proceeding." Section 9 of the FAA distinguishes between residents and nonresidents of the "district within which the award was made" for the purpose of service of notice requirements. If the adverse party is a *resident*, "service shall be made upon the adverse party or his attorney as prescribed by law for service of notice of motion in an action in the same court."[4] If the adverse party is a *nonresident*, "notice of the application shall be served by the marshal of any district within which the adverse party may be found in like manner as other process of the court."[5]

(2) Application for Confirmation

Application for confirmation of an arbitral award should be made by motion where an action has been filed or by petition where there is no underlying action.[6] The application must be in writing and must state the grounds for relief and what relief is sought with particularity, as prescribed under FRCP 7(b)(1). The FAA does not set forth the contents of a motion to confirm. Nevertheless, the application should contain at minimum the following information:

(a) names and addresses of the parties and their counsel of record;

(b) where the award was "made";[7]

(c) acts supporting the court's exercise of jurisdiction;

---

2. *See* Kerr–McGee Refining Corp. v. M/T Triumph, 924 F.2d 467, 471 (2d Cir.), *cert. denied*, 502 U.S. 821, 112 S.Ct. 81, 116 L.Ed.2d 54 (1991) (finding award not final and questioning whether one-year time limit under § 9 should apply to any award which does not end the arbitration).

3. Markowski v. Atzmon, 1994 WL 162407 (D.D.C.1994).

4. FAA § 9.

5. *Id.*

6. FAA § 6.

7. *See supra* § 9.6(c)(1).

(d) facts establishing that the parties entered into a contract that contained an arbitration clause that encompasses the dispute, accompanied by a copy of the agreement to arbitrate;

(e) facts establishing that a hearing was conducted before a duly appointed arbitrator;

(f) assertion that the arbitrators granted an award in favor of the petitioner on a particular date including an outline of the essential terms of the arbitral award;

(g) request that order be entered under FAA § 9 confirming the award and that judgment be entered on the award in favor of the petitioner including where appropriate, interest and costs; and

(h) a copy of the award.

(3) Opposing Confirmation

Under FAA § 9, a motion to confirm "must" be granted "unless the award is vacated, modified, or corrected as prescribed in Sections 10 and 11." Parties opposing the award must petition to vacate or modify the award in a timely fashion, as prescribed under FAA § 12, or risk the automatic confirmation of the award under FAA § 9. It is not enough to merely oppose confirmation, a party must seek to modify, correct, or vacate the award. Under FAA § 12, "[n]otice to vacate, modify, or correct an award must be served upon the adverse party or his attorney within three months after the award is filed or delivered." The court will then stay enforcement proceedings "for the purpose of the motion [to vacate or modify]."[8] If there is a timely application to confirm an award, and the three-month window of time to petition to vacate or modify has been closed, the court must confirm the award under the automatic confirmation provisions of FAA § 9. For this reason, it is frequently advisable to wait until the three-month window has closed to bring a motion to confirm.

(4) Hearing

Hearings are not required and an award may be confirmed automatically if: (1) no motion to vacate or modify the award is made within the prescribed three-month time period after the award is filed or delivered under FAA § 12; and (2) none of the allegations in the application or the application itself are challenged.[9] A hearing is required if the application is challenged. Absent a motion to vacate or modify, the hearing will be limited to the requisite representations in the application.

(5) Entry of Judgment on Confirmation Order

Under FAA § 13, a court order confirming an award must be filed with the court clerk for "entry of judgment thereon." When the order is

---

8. FAA § 12.

9. See Ottley v. Schwartzberg, 819 F.2d 373, 376 (2d Cir.1987) (in responding to petition seeking confirmation order, court erred by vacating and remanding in the absence of petition by losing party).

filed, FAA § 13 requires the moving party to file with the clerk the following papers:

(a) The agreement; the selection or appointment, if any, of the additional arbitrator or umpire; and each written extension of the time (granted by the parties), if any, within which to make the award.

(b) The award.

(c) Each notice, affidavit, or other paper used upon an application to confirm, modify, or correct the award, and a copy of each order of the court upon such an application.

Upon the filing of these papers, the "judgment shall be docketed as if it was rendered in an action."[10]

Library References:

West's Key No. Digests, Arbitration ☞72.3.
Wright, Miller & Cooper, Federal Practice and Procedure: Civil 2d § 3569.

§ 9.8   Vacating the Award: FAA § 10

Section 10(a)(1)–(4) of the FAA lists the statutory grounds for vacating arbitration awards. Under FAA § 10, an award may be vacated "upon the application of any party to the arbitration—

● Where the award was procured by corruption, fraud, or undue means.

● Where there was evident partiality or corruption in the arbitrators, or either of them.

● Where the arbitrators were guilty of misconduct in refusing to postpone the hearing, upon sufficient cause shown, or in refusing to hear evidence pertinent and material to the controversy; or of any other misbehavior by which the rights of any party have been prejudiced.

● Where the arbitrators exceeded their powers, or so imperfectly executed them that a mutual, final and definite award upon the subject matter submitted was not made."

Establishing any of the four grounds under FAA § 10 is difficult where the parties have adopted a broad clause that does not limit the authority or jurisdiction of the arbitrator. For example, the American Arbitration Association's standard clause imposes no limits on the discretion of the arbitrator. In these cases, it is difficult to establish that the arbitrators acted "in excess of their powers." Accordingly, if the parties are concerned with having judicial scrutiny of the award, they should carefully consider circumscribing the authority of the arbitrator. At the same time, limiting the authority of the arbitrator creates another layer of litigation regarding whether the award is within the scope of the arbitrator's designated authority.[1]

10. FAA § 13.

§ 9.8

1. A set of standard clauses with commentary is included in § 9.14, *infra*.

(a) Award Procured by Corruption, Fraud, or Undue Means: FAA § 10(a)(1)

Under FAA § 10(a)(1), the court "may make an order vacating the award ... (1) Where the award was procured by corruption, fraud, or undue means." While the broad language of this subsection encompasses misconduct on the part of arbitrators, parties, and their representatives, challenges brought under this provision usually involve allegations of misbehavior by only *parties or their representatives* in the procurement of an award. Section 10(a)(2), which provides for vacatur for "evident partiality or corruption in the arbitrators," is the vehicle for challenging alleged misconduct on the part of the *arbitrators*.

To have an award vacated under FAA § 10(a)(1), it is insufficient to show corruption, fraud, or undue means by one of the parties or their representatives. A party must satisfy the "nexus requirement" by demonstrating that in fact, the *"award was procured"* by such misconduct. In *Forsythe International, S.A. v. Gibbs Oil Co. of Texas,*[2] the court required the party seeking vacatur to show the existence of a "nexus between the alleged fraud and the basis for the panel's decision." The court concluded that the award was not procured by the party's obvious misconduct and fraud. As the court found the arbitrator's decision to be supported by a sufficient evidentiary basis, vacatur was unwarranted.[3]

Seeking to protect the finality of awards, courts are hesitant to vacate them, as evidenced by their imposition of strict requirements for establishing the existence and impact of the alleged misconduct. Under *Bonar v. Dean Witter Reynolds, Inc.,*[4] fraud must be established by clear and convincing evidence, materially related to an issue in the arbitration. Moreover, the fraud must not have been brought to the attention of the arbitrators with respect to the issue they were handling, nor have been discoverable upon the exercise of due diligence before arbitration.

(b) Arbitrator Misconduct: FAA § 10(a)(3)

Under FAA § 10(a)(3), a court "may make an order vacating the award ... [w]here the arbitrators were guilty of misconduct in refusing to postpone the hearing, upon sufficient cause shown, or in refusing to hear evidence pertinent and material to the controversy ..."

To obtain vacatur under FAA § 10(a)(3), a party must demonstrate that the misbehavior of the arbitrators *actually prejudiced the party's rights*. The misconduct of the arbitrator must have been such that it deprived a party of a "fundamentally fair hearing."[5] Deprivation of a "fundamentally fair hearing" essentially means that a party was denied an opportunity to be heard, such as prohibiting a key witness to testify

2. 915 F.2d 1017, 1022 (5th Cir.1990).
3. *Id.* at 1022–23.
4. 835 F.2d 1378, 1383 n. 7, 1383, 1385 (11th Cir.1988).

5. Apex Fountain Sales, Inc. v. Kleinfeld, 818 F.2d 1089, 1094 (3d Cir.1987).

or, prohibiting cross-examination of an opponent's witness.[6]

Section 10(a)(3) of the FAA also contains a "catch-all" provision, under which an award may be vacated in the event of *"any other misbehavior"* by which the rights of any party have been prejudiced."[7] This provision is rarely utilized, as there is little actionable arbitrator misconduct that falls outside of the misbehavior *specifically* prohibited under the statute.[8]

(c) Arbitrators Exceeded Their Powers: FAA § 10(a)(4)

The most frequently cited grounds for vacating an award is where the arbitrators exceeded their powers. Under FAA § 10(a)(4), a court may vacate an award "[w]here the arbitrators exceeded their powers, or so imperfectly executed them that a mutual, final, and definite award upon the subject matter submitted was not made."

The arbitration agreement defines the powers of the arbitrators. The arbitrator's scope of authority is created and defined by the consent of the parties as expressed in the arbitration agreement.[9] Arbitrators must stay within the boundaries of authority erected by the parties in their agreement.[10]

An arbitrator's failure to adhere to the parties' directives exposes the award to potential vacatur under FAA § 10(a)(4) on the ground that the "arbitrators exceeded their powers." Courts have used different phraseology to signify that an arbitrator has exceeded the scope of his authority. The Ninth Circuit interprets the "excess of power" standard to be the equivalent of the "manifest disregard for the law" standard.[11]

When deciding if the arbitrator exceeded his authority, the court is required to determine whether the award conformed to particular contractual terms.[12] In *Barbier v. Shearson Lehman Hutton, Inc.*,[13] the

6. Cobec Brazilian Trading v. Isbrandtsen, 524 F.Supp. 7 (S.D.N.Y.1980); Cofinco, Inc. v. Bakrie & Bros., 395 F.Supp. 613, 615 (S.D.N.Y.1975).

7. FAA § 10(a)(3) (emphasis added).

8. *See* Ballantine Books, Inc. v. Capital Distributing Co., 302 F.2d 17, 21 (2d Cir. 1962) (rejecting challenge to confirmation of award and holding that the arbitrator's off-the-record comment predicting a favorable outcome for a party who then received an award three months later "neither constituted prejudicial behavior, nor demonstrated evident partiality").

9. Wright Lumber Co. v. Herron, 199 F.2d 446 (10th Cir.1952).

10. *See* Wilko v. Swan, 346 U.S. 427, 436, 74 S.Ct. 182, 187, 98 L.Ed. 168 (1953) (noting that agreement required arbitrators to make "subjective findings on the purpose and knowledge of an alleged violation

of the [Securities Exchange Act of 1934]," where the contract provided that the Act governed all transactions); United States v. ASCAP, 32 F.3d 727, 732–33 (2d Cir.1994) (concluding that arbitrator lacked power to establish new royalty rate under controlling ASCAP rules); Mutual Serv. Corp. v. Spaulding, 871 F.Supp. 324 (N.D.Ill.1994) (NASD Code § 15 barred award that permitted claims older than six years).

11. *See* Todd Shipyards Corp. v. Cunard Line, Ltd., 943 F.2d 1056 (9th Cir.1991).

12. *See* Executive Life Insurance Co. v. Alexander Insurance Ltd., 999 F.2d 318, 319 (8th Cir.1993) (upholding award refunding unearned prepaid premiums to Executive, although contract did not address that subject, where contract empowered arbitrators to make decision based on "equity and customary practices of the insurance and reinsurance industry").

13. 948 F.2d 117 (2d Cir.1991).

contract contained a choice of law provisions selecting New York law to govern the agreement. The arbitrators awarded punitive damages, even though they were unavailable under New York law. The appellate court vacated the punitive damages portion of the award, concluding that the arbitrators exceeded their authority in awarding punitive damages.

Seeking to uphold the finality of arbitration awards, courts are reluctant to vacate them on the ground that arbitrators exceeded their authority.[14] Consequently, courts have construed the "excess of power" standard narrowly.[15]

Misconstruction of a contract is an insufficient basis for setting aside an award under FAA § 10(a)(4).[16] Mistaken decisions of facts[17] or law[18] are also insufficient grounds for vacatur under FAA § 10(a)(4).[19]

On the other hand, arbitrators exceed their powers by granting an award that fails to correspond to the dictates of the arbitration agreement. In *Western Employers Ins. Co. v. Jefferies & Co.*,[20] the parties' agreement required the arbitrators to furnish findings of fact and conclusions of law with the award. No such findings or conclusions were set forth in the arbitrators' decision. The court held that the award exceeded the arbitrators' powers because in failing to provide the re-

---

14. *See* Wall Street Assocs. v. Becker Paribas, Inc., 27 F.3d 845 (2d Cir.1994) (confirming lump-sum award where there was no showing that specific fraud claim, found to be outside the scope of the arbitration clause, was the only basis for arbitrator's decision, and there were alternative fraud theories upon which result could be based).

15. *See* Blue Tee Corp. v. Koehring Co., 999 F.2d 633, 637–38 (2d Cir.1993) (concluding that arbitrator did not exceed powers under governing arbitration clause by quantifying liability decision); Folkways Music Publishers, Inc. v. Weiss, 989 F.2d 108, 111–12 (2d Cir.1993); Lee v. Chica, 983 F.2d 883, 887–88 (8th Cir.), *cert. denied*, 510 U.S. 906, 114 S.Ct. 287, 126 L.Ed.2d 237 (1993) (no excess of powers where punitive damages were awarded under American Arbitration Association rules incorporated into agreement); R. M. Perez & Associates, Inc. v. Welch, 960 F.2d 534, 538 (5th Cir.1992) (finding that arbitrators had authority to decide fraud claims, as they were within scope of arbitration agreement).

16. Bernhardt v. Polygraphic Co. of America, 350 U.S. 198, 203 n. 4, 76 S.Ct. 273, 276 n. 4, 100 L.Ed. 199 (1956) ("Whether the arbitrators misconstrued a contract is not open to judicial review."). *See also* Miller v. Prudential Bache Securi-

ties, Inc., 884 F.2d 128, 130 (4th Cir.1989), *cert. denied*, 497 U.S. 1004, 110 S.Ct. 3240, 111 L.Ed.2d 751 (1990) (stating that "[t]he federal courts ... have consistently held that contract misconstruction is an insufficient basis for vacating an arbitration award").

17. Shearson Hayden Stone, Inc. v. Liang, 653 F.2d 310, 312 (7th Cir.1981) (stating that award would not be vacated because the arbitrator might have reached "the wrong result from conflicting evidence").

18. Miller, 884 F.2d at 130 ("mere" error of law insufficient to support vacatur under "excess of power" standard); Moseley, Hallgarten, Estabrook & Weeden, Inc. v. Ellis, 849 F.2d 264, 272 (7th Cir.1988) ("mistake" of law insufficient to establish that arbitrator exceeded scope of authority).

19. *See* Advest, Inc. v. McCarthy, 914 F.2d 6, 8 (1st Cir.1990) (stating that courts are not permitted to hear claims of either factual or legal error "even where such error is painfully clear"); Siegel v. Titan Industries Corp., 779 F.2d 891, 892–93 (2d Cir.1985) (asserting that "erroneous application of rules of law is not a ground for vacating an arbitrator's award.... nor is the fact that an arbitrator erroneously decided the facts").

20. 958 F.2d 258 (9th Cir.1992).

quired factual findings and legal conclusions, it did not comply with the requirements of the arbitration agreement.[21]

In the context of remedies, courts apply the "essence" test to determine whether the remedies granted were contemplated or anticipated by the parties in their agreement. An award must *"draw its essence"* from the underlying agreement.[22]

In *Valentine Sugars, Inc. v. Donau Corp.*,[23] Valentine argued that the arbitrators exceeded their authority by deciding an issue regarding a joint venture allegedly beyond the scope of the arbitration agreement. The court confirmed the award, focusing on language in the agreement which it found conferred power on the arbitrators to do "whatever was necessary to resolve any disputed matter arising out of the joint venture."[24] The court justified confirmation on the absence of an explicit restriction on the arbitrators' power to resolve the dispute and on the lack of evidence that Valentine intended to exclude the issue from resolution.[25]

(d) Award Contrary to Terms of Contract

Courts rarely vacate awards on the ground that they are "contrary to the terms of the contract."[26] The relatively small number of cases that have applied this standard as a grounds for vacating an arbitration award reflects, in part, a preference for the "excess of powers" standard set forth in Section 10(a)(4). While there is considerable overlap in these two approaches, the "contrary to terms of contract" standard focuses principally on the scope of an arbitration agreement rather than the authority of the arbitrator.

21. *Id.* at 262. *See also* Ottley v. Schwartzberg, 819 F.2d 373, 376 (2d Cir. 1987) (agreement identifies and limits powers of arbitrators); Island Creek Coal Sales v. City of Gainesville, 729 F.2d 1046, 1048 (6th Cir.1984); Wright Lumber Co. v. Herron, 199 F.2d 446 (10th Cir.1952).

22. United Steelworkers of America v. Enterprise Wheel & Car Corp., 363 U.S. 593, 597, 80 S.Ct. 1358, 1361, 4 L.Ed.2d 1424 (1960) (emphasis added).

23. 981 F.2d 210, 213 (5th Cir.), *cert. denied*, 509 U.S. 923, 113 S.Ct. 3039, 125 L.Ed.2d 725 (1993), *relief under FRCP 60(b) denied, sub nom.* Valentine Sugars, Inc. v. Sudan, 34 F.3d 320 (5th Cir.1994).

24. *Id.*

25. *Id.* at 213–14.

26. Employers Insurance of Wausau v. National Union Fire Insurance Co., 933 F.2d 1481, 1486–87 (9th Cir.1991) (refusing to vacate award where arbitrator's interpretation, although making significant claim "read rather awkwardly and with some repetition," was nevertheless "plausible");

Chameleon Dental Products, Inc. v. Jackson, 925 F.2d 223, 226 (7th Cir.1991) (concluding that arbitrators' termination of *three* agreements, when *only two* contained specific provisions for termination, was an appropriate remedy for violating the agreements and refusing to vacate award) (emphasis added); Raiford v. Merrill Lynch, Pierce, Fenner & Smith, Inc., 903 F.2d 1410, 1412–13 (11th Cir.1990) (upholding award in churning case which was substantially lower than typical awards in such cases); Anderman/Smith Operating Co. v. Tennessee Gas Pipeline Co., 918 F.2d 1215, 1218 (5th Cir.1990), *cert. denied,* 501 U.S. 1206, 111 S.Ct. 2799, 115 L.Ed.2d 972 (1991) (upholding award where arbitrators held that buyer could set the price *only when it demonstrated* that the existing price was too high to enable it remain competitive, although the contract authorized the buyer to set the price when, in its *own judgment*, the price was too high for it to remain competitive) (emphasis added).

(e) Manifest Disregard of the Law

The "manifest disregard" doctrine as a nonstatutory basis for vacating an arbitration award originated in dictum in *Wilko v. Swan*,[27] where the Supreme Court stated that "interpretations of the law by the arbitrators *in contrast to manifest disregard* are not subject, in federal courts, to judicial review for error in interpretation." (emphasis added).

Recently, the United States Supreme Court touched on the "manifest disregard of the law" doctrine in *First Options of Chicago v. Kaplan*.[28] The Court asserted:

> [T]he court will set [the award] aside only in very unusual circumstances. *See, e.g.*, 9 U.S.C.A. section 10 (award procured by corruption, fraud, or undue means; arbitrator exceeded his powers); *Wilko v. Swan*, . . . (parties bound by arbitrator's decision not in "manifest disregard" of the law) . . .[29]

The import of the Supreme Court's treatment of the "manifest disregard" doctrine in *First Options* is open to debate. Some authorities characterize the Court's pronouncement as approving, re-enforcing, and re-invigorating the doctrine as a separate, nonstatutory ground for setting aside an award.[30]

The aforementioned interpretation is founded on mere dictum. In *First Options*, the Court was not deciding the issue of whether the "manifest disregard" standard existed as an independent, nonstatutory ground for vacatur. The following discussion proceeds from the premise that the Supreme Court's cursory treatment of the "manifest disregard" doctrine in *First Options* does not resolve definitively the split in the circuits.

The District of Columbia,[31] First,[32] Second,[33] Sixth,[34] Ninth,[35] and

---

27. 346 U.S. 427, 436–37, 74 S.Ct. 182, 187–88, 98 L.Ed. 168 (1953).

28. 514 U.S. 938, 115 S.Ct. 1920, 131 L.Ed.2d 985 (1995).

29. *Id.* at 938.

30. *See* 4 Ian R. MacNeil, Richard E. Speidel, & Thomas J. Stipanowich, Federal Arbitration Law §§ 38–44, at § 40.7.1, at 40:26 (Supp. 1996) (interpreting *First Options* as the Supreme Court's "seal of approval" on the manifest disregard doctrine and extrapolating that "all decisions in lower courts refusing to adopt the doctrine appear to be no longer good law").

31. Kanuth v. Prescott, Ball & Turben, Inc., 949 F.2d 1175 (D.C.Cir.1991); Sargent v. Paine Webber Jackson & Curtis, Inc., 882 F.2d 529, 532 (D.C.Cir.1989), *cert. denied*, 494 U.S. 1028, 110 S.Ct. 1474, 108 L.Ed.2d 612 (1990).

32. Advest, Inc. v. McCarthy, 914 F.2d 6, 7–9 (1st Cir.1990).

33. *See, e.g.*, W. K. Webster & Co. v. American President Lines, Ltd., 32 F.3d 665, 669 (2d Cir.1994); Carte Blanche (Singapore Pte., Ltd.) v. Carte Blanche Int'l, 888 F.2d 260, 265 (2d Cir.1989); Government of India v. Cargill, Inc., 867 F.2d 130, 133 (2d Cir.1989); Merrill Lynch, Pierce, Fenner & Smith, Inc. v. Bobker, 808 F.2d 930, 933–34 (2d Cir.1986).

34. Federated Dept. Stores, Inc. v. J.V.B. Indus., Inc., 894 F.2d 862 (6th Cir. 1990).

35. *See* Todd Shipyards Corp. v. Cunard Line, Ltd., 943 F.2d 1056 (9th Cir.1991); French v. Merrill Lynch, Pierce, Fenner & Smith, Inc., 784 F.2d 902 (9th Cir.1986).

Tenth[36] Circuits all have adopted the "manifest disregard" doctrine. For example, the Ninth Circuit in *Todd Shipyards Corp. v. Cunard Line, Ltd.*, analyzed the question of whether an award of punitive damages was "legally appropriate" in light of New York's substantive law regarding punitive damages. The Ninth Circuit compared New York law which provides for punitive damages for fraud "upon a showing of willful and wanton conduct" with the arbitrator's findings of "deceptive practices and knowingly making incorrect misrepresentations."[37]

The Fourth Circuit mentioned the "manifest disregard" standard in *Remmey v. PaineWebber, Inc.*[38] In discussing the doctrine, the court relied upon *National Wrecking Co. v. International Brotherhood of Teamsters, Local 731.*[39] The court asserted that the doctrine requires a showing that the "arbitrators were aware of the law, understood it correctly, found it applicable to the case before them, and yet chose to ignore it in propounding their decision."[40]

The Seventh Circuit, through Chief Judge Posner in *Baravati v. Josephthal, Lyon & Ross, Inc.*,[41] emphatically rejected the "manifest disregard" doctrine as an independent, nonstatutory ground for vacating arbitration awards. The court announced:

> We can understand neither the need for the formula nor the role that it plays in judicial review of arbitration (we suspect none—that it is just words).... The grounds for setting aside arbitration awards are exhaustively stated in the statute [FAA]. Now that *Wilko* is history, there is no reason to continue to echo its gratuitous attempt at nonstatutory supplementation.[42]

The authority of this pronouncement may be in question in light of *First Options.*[43]

The Eighth Circuit has been inconsistent in its treatment of the "manifest disregard" standard. In *Marshall v. Green Giant Co.*,[44] the court asserted that it has never adopted the "manifest disregard" standard as an independent, nonstatutory basis for setting aside an award, but declined to consider the issue of adoption because it found no manifest disregard in the case at hand. However, in *FSC Sec. Corp. v. Freel*,[45] the court concluded in a case *not* based on the adoption of the manifest disregard doctrine that the arbitration panel "did not exceed its powers or act in manifest disregard of the law."

36. Jenkins v. Prudential–Bache Securities, Inc., 847 F.2d 631 (10th Cir.1988).

37. Todd Shipyards, 943 F.2d at 1063.

38. 32 F.3d 143, 149 (4th Cir.1994), *cert. denied*, 513 U.S. 1112, 115 S.Ct. 903, 130 L.Ed.2d 786, (1995).

39. 990 F.2d 957, 961 (7th Cir.1993) (LMRA § 301).

40. Remmey, 32 F.3d at 149.

41. 28 F.3d 704 (7th Cir.1994).

42. *Id.* at 706.

43. *See* 4 MacNeil, *supra* note 30, §§ 38–44, at § 40.7.1, at 40:28 (observing that "[h]owever sympathetic one may be to Chief Judge Posner's views on this subject, ... the 'manifest disregard' aspect of Wilko seems to be alive and well, having been resurrected, if ever dead, by [*First Options*]").

44. 942 F.2d 539, 550 (8th Cir.1991).

45. 14 F.3d 1310, 1313 (8th Cir.1994).

The Eleventh Circuit also has declared that it never adopted the manifest disregard doctrine.[46] Later, in *Brown v. Rauscher Pierce Refsnes, Inc.*[47] and *Robbins v. Day*,[48] the Eleventh Circuit definitively rejected the manifest disregard doctrine.[49]

In practice, it is extremely difficult to establish the "manifest disregard of the law" standard. The party seeking to vacate the award must establish that the arbitrator clearly must have "understood and correctly stated the law but proceeded to ignore it."[50] Mere error in understanding, interpreting, or applying the law is insufficient to constitute manifest disregard.[51] "Manifest disregard" contemplates that the arbitrator "appreciates the existence of a clearly governing legal principle but decides to ignore or pay no attention to it," and that the error is "obvious and capable of being readily and instantly perceived by a qualified arbitrator."[52]

Application of the manifest disregard test is illustrated in *Advest, Inc. v. McCarthy*.[53] The arbitrator awarded McCarthy $22,500 in addition to the restoration of 6,800 shares of stock that Advest improperly sold, adjusting for all splits and dividends through the date of the award. The district court rejected *Advest's* application for vacatur. On appeal, the First Circuit focused on the fact that the arbitrators' choice of remedies was not limited by contract to damages.[54] The court concluded that *Advest* failed to establish that the arbitrators knew that damages were the only available legal remedy and intentionally failed to apply it.[55] Thus, the court upheld the award.[56]

(f) Violates Public Policy

An additional nonstatutory basis for vacating an award is when its enforcement would violate public policy. The public policy defense is rarely raised and usually rejected in the context of arbitration awards

46. Raiford v. Merrill Lynch, Pierce, Fenner & Smith, Inc., 903 F.2d 1410 (11th Cir.1990), citing O.R. Securities, Inc. v. Professional Planning Assocs., Inc., 857 F.2d 742, 746–47 (11th Cir.1988) (asserting that "[the Eleventh Circuit] has never adopted the manifest-disregard-of-the-law standard; indeed we have expressed some doubt as to whether it should be adopted since the standard would likely never be met when the arbitrator provides no reasons for its award (which is typically the case)").

47. 994 F.2d 775 (11th Cir.1993).

48. 954 F.2d 679 (11th Cir.), *cert. denied*, 506 U.S. 870, 113 S.Ct. 201, 121 L.Ed.2d 143 (1992).

49. *But see* 4 MacNeil, *supra* note 30, §§ 38–44, at § 40.7.1, at 40:29 (stating that *Brown* and *Robbins* "are no longer good law" on the manifest disregard doctrine in light of *First Options*).

50. Siegel v. Titan Indus. Corp., 779 F.2d 891, 892–93 (2d Cir.1985).

51. Todd Shipyards Corp. v. Cunard Line, Ltd., 943 F.2d 1056 (9th Cir.1991), quoting French v. Merrill Lynch, Pierce, Fenner & Smith, 784 F.2d 902 (9th Cir. 1986) (noting that "confirmation is required even in the face of 'erroneous ... misinterpretations of law.' ... An arbitrator's decision must be upheld unless it is 'completely irrational,' or it constitutes a 'manifest disregard of law.' ").

52. Merrill Lynch, Pierce, Fenner & Smith, Inc. v. Bobker, 808 F.2d 930, 933–34 (2d Cir.1986).

53. 914 F.2d 6 (1st Cir.1990).

54. *Id.* at 10.

55. *Id.* at 11.

56. *Id.*

under the FAA.[57]

On occasion, courts have vacated awards that would violate public policy. In *Northrop Corp. v. Triad Financial Establishment,*[58] the court upheld the public policy defense. In *Northrop*, the parties included in their agreement a choice of law provision selecting California law to govern a contract in which Triad was designated to be Northrop's sole sales representative in Saudi Arabia. In a dispute concerning commissions, the arbitrators ordered payment of commissions, which the court found would violate Saudi Arabian law, United States Department of Defense regulations, and the Foreign Corrupt Practices Act. Applying California law providing for the nonenforceability of illegal agreements, the court vacated the parts of the award that violated the aforementioned laws or regulations on the ground that their enforcement would violate public policy.

(g) Procedure

A party must file a petition in district court to vacate an award (or a motion in an action already pending).[59] The motion must be in writing, state the grounds supporting it with particularity, and set out the relief or order sought.[60]

The motion to vacate the award should contain the following information, unless such information is already before the court pursuant to an application to confirm:

     (a) names and addresses of the parties and their counsel of record;

     (b) where the award was "made";[61]

     (c) facts supporting the court's exercise of jurisdiction;

     (d) assertion that parties entered into the contract that contained an arbitration clause on a particular date, accompanied by a copy of the agreement to arbitrate;

57. *See* Brown v. Rauscher Pierce Refsnes, Inc., 994 F.2d 775, 782 (11th Cir.1993) (where arbitrator erroneously interpreted applicable state regulatory legislation to warrant damages instead of a statutory remedy, arbitrator's failure to interpret the law correctly is not a ground for vacatur); Remmey v. Paine-Webber, Inc., 32 F.3d 143 (4th Cir.1994), *cert. denied*, 513 U.S. 1112, 115 S.Ct. 903, 130 L.Ed.2d 786 (1995) (where there was no evidence that the arbitrators had found a violation of the law, granting award did not violate public policy); Board of County Commissioners v. L. Robert Kimball & Associates, 860 F.2d 683, 685–88 (6th Cir.1988), *cert. denied*, 494 U.S. 1030, 110 S.Ct. 1480, 108 L.Ed.2d 617 (1990) (rejecting claim that award enforcing contract with an indefinite term between a county and an engi-

neering firm was against Ohio public policy relating to contracts of public bodies); Osceola County Rural Water System, Inc. v. Subsurfco, Inc., 914 F.2d 1072 (8th Cir. 1990) (where there was no basis for believing that arbitrators accepted testimony alleging that contractor falsified test results, district court erred in vacating award on public policy ground that award impermissibly rewarded party for alleged falsification).

58. 593 F.Supp. 928 (C.D.Cal.1984).

59. FAA § 6. *See* O.R. Securities, Inc. v. Professional Planning Associates, Inc. 857 F.2d 742 (11th Cir.1988) (proper procedure for seeking to vacate an arbitration award is a motion to vacate under FRCP 7(b)).

60. FRCP 7(b)(1).

61. *See* § 9.6(c)(1), *supra*.

(e) facts establishing that a hearing was conducted before a duly appointed arbitrator;

(f) assertion that the arbitrators granted award in favor of the petitioner on a particular date including an outline of the essential terms of the arbitral award;

(g) statement of the grounds for challenging the award, corresponding to the applicable section(s) of FAA § 10;

(h) a copy of the award; and

(i) request that the court vacate the award under FAA § 10.

Section 12 of the FAA prescribes the procedure for serving notice of the application to vacate upon the opposing party. A time limit is imposed under FAA § 12, as notice must be served "within *three months* after the award is filed or delivered."[62] Section 12 distinguishes between residents and nonresidents of the "district within which the award was made" for the purpose of service of notice requirements. If the adverse party is a *resident*, "service shall be made upon the adverse party or his attorney as prescribed by law for service of notice of motion in an action in the same court."[63] If the adverse party is a *nonresident*, "notice of the application shall be served by the marshal of any district within which the adverse party may be found in like manner as other process of the court."[64]

Library References:

West's Key No. Digests, Arbitration ⚏56, 57.1, 63.1, 64.1, 64.2, 77.
Wright & Miller, Federal Practice and Procedure: Civil 2d § 1241.

§ 9.9 Modifying or Correcting the Award: FAA § 11

(a) Scope

Under FAA § 11, a court may make an order modifying or correcting the award upon the application of any party to the arbitration—

(a) Where there was an evident material miscalculation of figures or an evident material mistake in the description of any person, thing, or property referred to in the award.

(b) Where the arbitrators have awarded upon a matter not submitted to them, unless it is a matter not affecting the merits of the decision upon the matter submitted.

(c) Where the award is imperfect in matter of form not affecting the merits of the controversy.

Finally, Section 11 provides that a court has discretionary power to modify or correct an award to effectuate the intentions of the arbitrators and to promote justice between the parties.[1] Under the prevailing view,

---

62. FAA § 12 (emphasis added).

63. *Id.*

64. *Id.*

§ 9.9

1. *See* Sociedad Armadora Aristomenis Panama, S.A. v. Tri–Coast S.S. Co., 184 F.Supp. 738 (S.D.N.Y.1960) (court has dis-

this discretionary power does not create an independent ground for modification or correction by a court; rather, it is limited by the three subsections, which empower a court to modify or correct an award only under the specifically enumerated circumstances.[2]

(b) Evident Material Miscalculation or Mistake: FAA § 11(a)

Under FAA § 11(a), an award may be modified or corrected "[w]here there was an evident material miscalculation of figures or an evident material mistake in the description of any person, thing, or property referred to in the award." A miscalculation or mistake is clearly "evident" if the basis for the calculation or description appears either in the award itself, or in the arbitrator's opinion.[3]

If the basis for the alleged mistake is not readily discernible, the court may remand the case to the arbitrator to clarify the ambiguity or to provide information necessary to correct the apparent error. A miscalculation or mistake is "material" if the alleged error would cause "significant disadvantage" were it not corrected.[4]

Section 11(a) of the FAA contemplates actual errors in mathematical calculations or mistakes in descriptions referred to in the award. Courts are generally unwilling to expand the scope of this provision beyond such mathematical miscalculations or descriptive mistakes.[5] In *Siegel v. Titan Indus. Corp.*,[6] the basis for calculating the value of stock was contested. The arbitrator provided no written opinion illuminating the reasoning underlying the decision, and the award did not reveal the basis for calculating the value. The court asserted that it possessed the authority to remand the case to the arbitrator for clarification.[7] Nevertheless, the court neither remanded the case, nor corrected the award, since it found that the absence of a contractual provision for calculating the award placed the issue firmly within the arbitrator's discretion.[8]

---

cretionary power to modify or correct an award under FAA § 11).

2. *But see* Transnitro, Inc. v. M/V Wave, 943 F.2d 471 (4th Cir.1991) (declining to resolve whether the last sentence of FAA § 11 creates "an independent basis for modification" or whether the court is limited in its authority to modify or correct an award by the preceding subsections).

3. *See* Ehrich v. A.G. Edwards & Sons, Inc., 675 F.Supp. 559, 565 (D.S.D.1987) (correcting award that contained mathematical error in calculating the number of months to which interest should have been applied).

4. *See* South East Atlantic Shipping Ltd. v. Garnac Grain Co., 356 F.2d 189, 192 (2d Cir.1966) ("rounding off" of damage amount produced by particular calculations

was not "material," since party incurred no "significant disadvantage").

5. *See* Merrill Lynch, Pierce, Fenner & Smith, Inc. v. Burke, 741 F.Supp. 191 (N.D.Cal.1990) (finding no evident material miscalculation in award of compensatory damages, despite evidence that settlement did not produce reduction in compensatory damages and investor's net loss was less than the amount awarded).

6. 779 F.2d 891 (2d Cir.1985).

7. *Id.* at 894.

8. *See also* McIlroy v. PaineWebber, Inc., 989 F.2d 817, 821 (5th Cir.1993) (declining to modify award to reflect damages actually requested where there was sufficient evidence to support the amount actually awarded).

(c) Award on Matter Not Submitted: FAA § 11(b)

Under FAA § 11(b), a court may modify or correct an award "[w]here the arbitrators have awarded upon a matter not submitted to them, unless it is a matter not affecting the merits of the decision upon the matter submitted." There is very limited authority applying FAA § 11(b). In *Executone Information Systems, Inc. v. Davis,*[9] one of the rare cases actually applying FAA § 11(b), the court examined whether a certain issue had been submitted to the arbitrators. As the court found that the matter had been submitted, it did not have occasion to apply the remaining language of FAA § 11(b).

(d) Award Imperfect in Form: FAA § 11(c)

FAA § 11(c) provides that an award may be modified or corrected "[w]here the award is imperfect in matter of form not affecting the merits of the controversy." There are very few cases applying this provision of the FAA. In *Fischer v. CGA Computer Assocs., Inc.*[10] one of the rare cases applying FAA § 11(c), the court modified language in an award to clarify that a particular sentence was in fact a statement of declaratory relief.

In the small number of cases where a party has attempted to utilize FAA § 11(c) to obtain modification or correction of an award, such efforts consistently have been rejected on the ground that the matters involved *"affect[ed] the merits of the controversy"* and thus were not modifiable under FAA § 11(c). In *Olympia & York Florida Equity Corp. v. Gould,*[11] the court found an award ambiguous because it did not expressly address the contingency that had developed between the parties. Specifically, the award provided one party to the arbitration with an option to purchase property within a certain time frame. The award was silent, however, as to what would happen if the party failed to exercise that option. Finding the arbitration award was incomplete, the Second Circuit remanded the case to the district court with instructions to remand the case to the arbitrators "for a declaration of what their intent was" in the event the party did not elect to exercise their option. In *Diapulse Corp. of America v. Carba, Ltd.,*[12] the Second Circuit held that the district court improperly modified an award under FAA § 11(c). The district court had *limited* in time and geographical area the *unlimited* permanent injunction issued by the arbitrator. The appellate court found this modification to be impermissible under FAA § 11(c) because it affected "matters of substance that were at the heart of the controversy between Carba and Diapulse."[13]

---

9. 26 F.3d 1314 (5th Cir.1994).
10. 612 F.Supp. 1038 (S.D.N.Y.1985).
11. 776 F.2d 42, 45–46 (2d Cir.1985).

12. 626 F.2d 1108 (2d Cir.1980).
13. *Id.* at 1110.

(e) Procedure

A party must file a petition in district court to modify or correct an award (or a motion if an action is pending).[14] The motion to modify or correct the award must be in writing, state the grounds supporting it with particularity, and set out the relief or order sought.[15]

The motion to modify or correct the award should contain the following information, unless such information is already before the court pursuant to an application to confirm:

(a) names and addresses of the parties and their counsel of record;

(b) where the award was "made";[16]

(c) facts supporting the court's exercise of jurisdiction;

(d) assertion that parties entered into a contract which contained an arbitration clause on a particular date, accompanied by a copy of the agreement to arbitrate;

(e) facts establishing that a hearing was conducted before a duly appointed arbitrator;

(f) assertion that the arbitrator granted award in favor of the petitioner on a particular date including an outline of the essential terms of the arbitral award;

(g) statement of the grounds for challenging the award, corresponding to the applicable section(s) of FAA § 11;

(h) a copy of the award; and

(i) request that the court modify or confirm the award under FAA § 11.

Section 12 of the FAA prescribes the procedure for serving notice of the application to modify or correct the award upon the opposing party. A time limit is imposed under FAA § 12, as notice must be served "within *three months* after the award is filed or delivered."[17] Section 12 distinguishes between residents and nonresidents of the "district within which the award was made" for the purpose of service of notice requirements. If the adverse party is a *resident*, "service shall be made upon the adverse party or his attorney as prescribed by law for service of notice of motion in an action in the same court."[18] If the adverse party is a *nonresident*, "notice of the application shall be served by the marshal of any district within which the adverse party may be found in like manner as other process of the court."[19]

Library References:

West's Key No. Digests, Arbitration ⚖73.9.
Wright & Miller, Federal Practice and Procedure: Civil 2d §§ 1241, 1247.

---

14. FAA § 6.
15. FRCP 7(b)(1).
16. *See supra* § 9.6(c)(1).
17. FAA § 12 (emphasis added).
18. *Id.*
19. *Id.*

§ 9.10   The International FAA: Scope and Application

The FAA includes specific provisions dealing with "international" arbitration beginning at 9 U.S.C.A. § 201. This section describes practices and procedures for the enforcement of agreements to arbitrate and arbitration awards under the "international FAA," which enforces the New York Convention and the Inter-American Convention. Specifically, this section focuses on the unique aspects of litigation under these international regimes.[1] Examples of the application of these provisions include arbitrations involving an American party overseas which is being enforced in the United States and an arbitration conducted in the United States involving one or more foreign parties.

The United States is party to two treaties requiring the enforcement of international arbitration awards and agreements to arbitrate—

● the United Nations Convention on the Recognition and Enforcement of Foreign Arbitral Awards ("New York Convention")[2] and

● the Inter-American Convention on International Commercial Arbitration ("Inter-American Convention" or "IAC").[3]

The provisions of the Conventions are incorporated into U.S. law through 9 U.S.C.A. §§ 201 and 301.[4] These sections comprise the international FAA. These provisions require U.S. federal courts to support international arbitrations over and above the provisions of the domestic FAA.

(a) History and Purpose of the New York Convention

The New York Convention was adopted by the United Nations Social and Economic Council in 1958. Previously, the enforcement of agreements to arbitrate and international arbitration awards had largely depended on norms of comity, a handful of bilateral treaties, and the Geneva treaties of 1923 and 1927 to which only a few States had acceded.[5]

The New York Convention and its American implementation were designed to satisfy "the need of the international commercial system for

§ 9.10

1. The word "State" capitalized shall be used to refer to international states, *i.e.*, countries; the word "state" without capitalization shall be used to refer to domestic U.S. states.

2. June 10, 1958, 21 U.S.T. 2517, 330 U.N.T.S. 38 *reprinted in* Note, 9 U.S.C.A. § 201 (entered into force for the United States on Dec. 29, 1970) (hereinafter New York Convention).

3. Jan. 30, 1975, OAS/SER.A/20 (SEPF) *reprinted in* 14 I.L.M. 336 (1975); Note, 9 U.S.C.A. § 301 (entered into force for the

United States on Oct. 27, 1990) (hereinafter IAC).

4. The enabling legislation, 9 U.S.C.A. §§ 201–208 (New York Convention) and 9 U.S.C.A. §§ 301–307 (IAC), differs from the Conventions in a few minor ways, and in so much as the provisions conflict with the actual words of the Conventions, the enabling legislation governs.

5. *See* Leonard V. Quigley, *Accession by the United States to the United Nations Convention on the Recognition and Enforcement of Foreign Arbitral Awards*, 70 Yale L. J. 1049, 1049–55 (1961).

predictability in the resolution of disputes" by "encourage[ing] the recognition and enforcement of [international arbitration] and unify[ing] ... standards" for recognition and enforcement.[6] One of the primary goals of the delegates who drafted the New York Convention was to limit the grounds upon which domestic courts could refuse to enforce international arbitration. They were concerned "that courts ... not be permitted to decline enforcement of such agreements on the basis of parochial views of their desirability."[7]

Although the United States initially expressed ambivalence towards the Convention, the United States acceded to the Convention in 1970.

(b) History and Purpose of the IAC

The general purpose, content, and structure of the IAC are the same as that of the New York Convention. For example, Article V of the IAC mirrors almost word-for-word Article V of the New York Convention, the limited set of defenses to enforcement which was one of the central achievements of the U.N. Convention. The Inter–American treaty might, thus, appear to be a redundant imitation of the New York Convention. However, the 1975 IAC is not the progeny of the New York Convention but has an independent history.[8] The IAC is only the latest step in a century-old effort by the countries of the Western Hemisphere to regulate the enforcement of international arbitration.[9]

Despite the apparent redundancy, the IAC is of great importance in enforcing international arbitration because until recently very few members of the Organization of American States ("OAS") had adhered to the New York Convention.[10] Unlike the New York Convention, the IAC provides a comprehensive procedural system for arbitrations.[11] Finally, and most importantly, the international FAA gives the IAC precedence over the New York Convention in cases where both apply. The IAC entered into force for the United States in October of 1990.

(c) Strong Pro–Arbitration Federal Policy Under the International FAA: *Mitsubishi Motors v. Soler Chrysler–Plymouth*

The Conventions and the international FAA should be construed with due regard for the doctrine that the "emphatic federal policy in

6. Mitsubishi Motors Corp. v. Soler Chrysler–Plymouth, Inc., 473 U.S. 614, 629, 105 S.Ct. 3346, 3355, 87 L.Ed.2d 444 (1985).

7. Scherk v. Alberto–Culver Co., 417 U.S. 506, 520 n. 15, 94 S.Ct. 2449, 2457 n. 15, 41 L.Ed.2d 270 (1974). For a brief "legislative history" of each provision of the New York Convention, *see* Quigley, *supra* note 5; G. W. Haight, *Convention on the Recognition and Enforcement of Foreign Arbitral Awards: Summary Analysis of Record of U.N. Conference*, May/June 1958 (1958).

8. *See* Charles R. Norberg, *Recent Developments in Inter–American Commercial Arbitration*, 13 Case W. Res. J. Intl. L. 107, 108–11 (1981).

9. *Id.*

10. Marian N. Leich, Current Development: *The Inter–American Convention on International Commercial Arbitration*, 75 A.J.I.L. 982, 982 (1981).

11. IAC, Article III discussed *infra* § 9.11.

favor of arbitral dispute resolution ... applies with special force in the field of international commerce."[12]

The doctrine has its origins in *Scherk v. Alberto–Culver Co.*[13] In *Scherk*, the Supreme Court required enforcement of an international agreement to arbitrate a dispute under the Securities and Exchange Act of 1934, even assuming, *arguendo*, that an identical domestic arbitration agreement would be unenforceable. The Court did not even rely on the then recently adopted New York Convention,[14] but instead relied on the proposition that an "almost indispensable precondition ... to any international business transaction" is respect for choice of law and forum selection clauses.[15] The Court feared that the failure to enforce international arbitration agreements "would invite unseemly and mutually destructive jockeying by the parties to secure tactical litigation advantages."

The *Scherk* policy was reiterated in *Mitsubishi Motors Corp. v. Soler Chrysler–Plymouth.*[16] In *Mitsubishi*, parties to an international commercial transaction agreed to arbitrate their disputes in Japan.[17] The district court ordered the parties to abide by the arbitration agreement, even with regard to federal antitrust issues that were raised.[18] However, the court of appeals for the First Circuit reversed the judgment of the district court insofar as it had ordered the parties to arbitrate antitrust issues, reasoning that the general doctrine precluding arbitration of antitrust claims should not be abandoned in the face of international transactions.[19] The Supreme Court disagreed, reversed the court of appeals, and reiterated that the presumption in favor of freely negotiated choice of forum provisions is reinforced by the "emphatic federal policy in favor of arbitral dispute resolution."[20] The Court held that although Soler's antitrust claims may have been unarbitrable if the arbitration agreement arose from a domestic transaction, it was enforceable in the international context because "concerns of international comity ... and sensitivity to the need of the international commercial system for predictability in the resolution of disputes require that we enforce the parties' agreement, *even assuming that a contrary result would be forthcoming in a domestic context.*"[21]

Thus, in the international context, courts will construe the provisions of arbitration agreements, the FAA, and the Conventions with an even stronger pro-arbitration bias than in the domestic context.[22] The Conventions and the FAA have been "broadly interpreted to effectuate

---

12. Mitsubishi Motors Corp. v. Soler Chrysler–Plymouth, 473 U.S. 614, 631, 105 S.Ct. 3346, 3356, 87 L.Ed.2d 444 (1985).

13. 417 U.S. 506, 94 S.Ct. 2449, 41 L.Ed.2d 270 (1974).

14. *Id.* at 520 n.15, 94 S.Ct. at 2457, n.15.

15. *Id.* at 516–17, 94 S.Ct. at 2455, 56.

16. 473 U.S. 614, 629, 631, 105 S.Ct. 3346, 3355, 3356, 87 L.Ed.2d 444 (1985).

17. *Id.* at 617, 105 S.Ct. at 3349.

18. *Id.* at 620, 105 S.Ct. at 3350.

19. *Id.* at 623, 105 S.Ct. at 3352.

20. *Id.* at 631, 105 S.Ct. at 3356.

21. *Id.* at 629, 105 S.Ct. at 3355 (emphasis added).

22. *See* David L. Threlkeld & Co. v. Mettallgesellschaft Ltd., 923 F.2d 245, 248 (2d Cir.1991).

the goals of the legislation" and the federal pro-arbitration policy.[23] In addition to ignoring some defenses which might apply to domestic arbitration,[24] lower courts have relied on the *Scherk-Mitsubishi* policy to increase burdens of proof on parties opposing the enforcement of international arbitration.[25]

(d) Relationship Between the Domestic FAA, the New York Convention, and the IAC

Sections 208 and 307 of the international FAA explicitly incorporate the provisions of the domestic FAA into actions brought under the international FAA "to the extent that that chapter [the domestic FAA] is not in conflict with" the international FAA or the Conventions.[26] Thus, most courts in international FAA cases borrow freely from the provisions and case law of the domestic FAA.

(e) Choice of Law

There are a number of statutory regimes under which a party might seek to enforce an international arbitration agreement or arbitration award. In addition to the domestic FAA and the two Conventions, most states have provisions for the enforcement of arbitration awards.[27] Though the Conventions provide the strongest presumption regarding the enforceability of arbitration agreements and among the most expedited enforcement provisions among these regimes, they are the most limited in scope. Parties may often need to resort to either the domestic FAA or state arbitration laws. Where both Conventions are applicable, Congress has mandated that the IAC take precedence over the New York Convention.

(1) Using the Domestic FAA to Enforce International Awards

The international FAA is generally more favorable than the domestic FAA to parties seeking enforcement, and where the provisions in the international FAA are silent, the provisions of the domestic FAA are incorporated by Sections 208 and 307 of the international FAA.

Parties only bring actions under the domestic FAA when they are unable to meet the threshold requirements for application of the international FAA.[28] For example, in *National Iranian Oil v. Ashland Oil,*[29] the

---

23. Cargill Intl. S.A. v. M/T Pavel Dybenko, 991 F.2d 1012, 1018 (2d Cir.1993).

24. *See, e.g.,* Mitsubishi and Scherk, discussed in text, *supra.*

25. *See, e.g.,* Republic of Nicaragua v. Standard Fruit Co., 937 F.2d 469 (9th Cir. 1991) ("the most minimal indication of the parties' intent to arbitrate must be given full effect, especially in international disputes").

26. Conflicts between the domestic and international FAA are rare. The most obvi-

ous conflict is the difference in the statute of limitations. *See* Bergesen v. Joseph Muller Corp., 710 F.2d 928 (2d Cir.1983) (international FAA's three-year statute of limitations takes precedence over domestic FAA's one-year limit).

27. *See, e.g.,* Cal. Civ. Pro. Code § 1280 (West 1982 & Supp. 1997); N.Y. C.P.L.R. 7501 (McKinney 1980).

28. *See infra* § 9.12.

29. 817 F.2d 326, 334 (5th Cir.1987).

parties' arbitration agreement provided for arbitration in Iran, a nonsignatory to the New York Convention. The agreement failed the reciprocity requirement of the international FAA,[30] and the court was thus unable to order arbitration in Iran. The court refused to order arbitration under the domestic FAA in its own district, because to do so would re-write the parties' agreement. Courts under the domestic FAA are, in any case, generally limited to ordering arbitration within their own district,[31] so an agreement to arbitrate outside the United States is virtually impossible to enforce under the domestic FAA. Enforcement under the domestic FAA of an unenforceable agreement might also conflict with the polices underlying the international FAA.

Finally, the domestic FAA does not itself grant federal courts subject matter jurisdiction;[32] parties must establish an independent basis for federal jurisdiction, such as diversity jurisdiction. Because of these limitations, parties may be forced to proceed under state arbitration laws.

(2) State Arbitration Laws

Courts will not accept state law defenses to actions under the international FAA and the Conventions.[33] However, where state law does not conflict with the Conventions and the international FAA, it is still viable. For example, foreign judgments confirming awards are not enforceable under the Conventions or the FAA, but may be enforced under state laws of comity. Awards and agreements which are not enforceable under the international or domestic FAA may be enforceable under appropriate state arbitration laws.

(f) Scope of the International FAA: Which Agreements and Awards Can Be Enforced?

The substantive provisions of the international FAA deal with recognition and enforcement of both arbitration agreements and arbitral awards.

FAA § 202 establishes five threshold requirements necessary for jurisdiction to be conferred upon the district court under the international FAA.

(1) Legal Relationship

Section 202 of the FAA requires, "[a]n arbitration agreement or arbitral award arising out of a legal relationship, whether contractual or

---

30. *Id.*

31. 9 U.S.C.A. § 4 (West 1970).

32. *Id.*

33. *See, e.g.,* David L. Threlkeld & Co. v. Metallgesellschaft, 923 F.2d 245, 250 (2d Cir.1991) (refusing to apply Vermont requirement of signed writing for agreement to arbitrate since it "directly clash[es] with the Convention" requirement of simply a "writing"); Ledee v. Ceramiche Ragno, 684 F.2d 184 (1st Cir.1982) (ordering arbitration despite unenforceability of agreement under Puerto Rico law).

not, ... falls under the Convention." There is, however, no case law directly addressing what constitutes a "legal" relationship.

(2) Commercial Relationship

Federal courts can recognize and enforce only those foreign arbitral agreements or awards which arise out of relationships "considered commercial."[34] The definition of "commercial" relationships in international arbitrations is the same as in domestic arbitrations and has been interpreted broadly recognizing agreements in contracts evidencing a transaction involving commerce, interstate or foreign.[35] This definition parallels the federal power over interstate commerce and is not concerned with the actual commercial nature of international relationships. Note that the definition of "commercial" under the FAA is broader than the international definition. The international definition, for example, excludes employment contracts.[36]

(3) International in Nature

Not surprisingly, the international FAA is limited to enforcement of awards which are "foreign" in nature. Pursuant to Article I(1) of the New York Convention coverage is limited to agreements and awards which are either "nonterritorial" or "nondomestic" under national law. FAA § 202 places further restrictions on the enforcement of agreements and awards between U.S. citizens. Although the IAC contains no "foreign" requirement like the New York Convention, FAA § 302 incorporates FAA § 202, and thus includes the same limitations on the enforcement of awards and agreements between U.S. citizens.

Nonterritorial. An award is nonterritorial if it is made in the territory of a State other than the United States.[37] An agreement to arbitrate is nonterritorial if it requires arbitration in the territory of a State other than the United States. For awards and agreements between U.S. citizens, the requirements of FAA § 202 must still be met.

Nondomestic. The New York Convention leaves the definition of "nondomestic" to national law.[38] The FAA fails to define "nondomestic" except to place certain limits in § 202 on the coverage of awards and agreements between U.S. citizens.[39] In the leading case of *Bergesen v. Joseph Muller Corp.*,[40] the Second Circuit posited a two prong test for nondomestic awards. In *Bergesen*, a Norwegian and a Swiss company

---

34. The New York Convention allows States to adopt this limitation. New York Convention Article I(3). Article I of the IAC explicitly limits the scope of the Convention to commercial relationships.

35. *See supra* § 9.3(a), as to the definition of commercial under domestic FAA.

36. *See* Ian R. MacNeil, Richard E. Speidel & Thomas J. Stipanowich, Federal Arbitration Law at § 44.9.3.2 (Supp. 1996).

37. The New York Convention covers "awards made in the territory of a State other than the State where the recognition and enforcement of such awards are sought." *See* Bergesen v. Joseph Muller Corp., 710 F.2d 928 (2d Cir.1983).

38. New York Convention Art. I(1). Section 202 of the FAA includes this provision. Section 302 incorporates the provision by reference.

39. *Id.*

40. 710 F.2d 928 (2d Cir.1983).

entered into an contract providing for the transportation of chemicals from the United States to Europe that included an arbitration agreement providing for arbitration in New York. The court interpreted the Convention broadly, reasoning that since the Convention did not define "domestic," it covers "as wide a variety of eligible awards as possible, while permitting the enforcing authority to supply its own definition of 'nondomestic' in conformity with its own national law."[41] An award is nondomestic if:

- it is made within the legal framework of another country, or it involves parties domiciled or

- having their principal place of business outside the enforcing jurisdiction.[42]

The court in *Dworkin-Cosell Interair Courier Serv. v. Avraham*,[43] held that a shareholders' agreement concerning a sale of a New York corporation's stock to an Israeli corporation was "nondomestic" as the principal place of business was outside the enforcing jurisdiction.[44] The court, however, rejected the argument that the "mere presence of a foreign shareholder in ... an employment dispute and a shareholders dispute concerning a New York corporation [with an Israeli shareholder] ... [is] sufficient in and of itself to bring such a dispute within the ambit of the convention."[45]

Agreements and Awards Between United States Citizens. FAA § 202 excludes from the scope of the international FAA awards or agreements arising out of a legal relationship entirely between citizens of the United States,[46] *unless* the agreement or award.

- involves property located abroad,

- envisages performance or enforcement abroad, or

- has some other reasonable relation with one or more foreign States.

The enforcement of an award or agreement between U.S. citizens under the international FAA must meet one of these criteria, even if it is a nonterritorial award or agreement. If the award or agreement is territorial, *i.e.* made or enforceable within U.S. territory, then it is unclear if these provisions themselves satisfy the "nondomestic" require-

---

41. *Id.* at 932.

42. This test applies to cases arising under the IAC as well. In *Productos Mercantiles E Industriales, S.A. v. Faberge USA*, 23 F.3d 41 (2d Cir.1994), the court held that an award which would be considered nondomestic under the New York Convention would also be considered nondomestic under the IAC.

43. 728 F.Supp. 156 (S.D.N.Y.1989).

44. *Id.* at 159.

45. *Id.*

46. For purposes of this exception to the applicability of the Conventions, a foreign corporation with a principal place of business in the United States will be deemed a "citizen of the United States." *See* Coastal States Trading, Inc. v. Zenith Navigation S.A. 446 F.Supp. 330 (S.D.N.Y.1977). *See* FAA § 202, which also provides that "a corporation is a citizen of the United States if it is incorporated or has its principal place of business in the United States."

ment of Section 202 or if the *Bergesen* nondomestic test must also be met.

Property Located Abroad. The international FAA provisions may apply where the "property" is located abroad. In the real property context, this criteria will be easy to determine. However, the potential for disagreements among other forms of property and whether it is "located abroad" are more difficult to discern. Unfortunately, there are no cases that shed any light on this point.

Envisages Performance or Enforcement Abroad. In *Fuller Co. v. Bauxite*,[47] the court held that a contract between two United States corporations to design, manufacture, and sell a drying and calcinating plant and certain related equipment to be used in the Republic of Guinea met the jurisdictional requirements of Section 202 by both bearing a "sufficient connection with the Republic of Guinea" and "envisaging performance abroad." Evidence indicated that the contract envisaged that Fuller personnel would provide extensive technical services in Guinea.[48] Additionally, "the question is not where most of the contract was performed but whether a 'significant enough portion of the making or performance' " occurred abroad.[49]

Incidental connections to a foreign state will not satisfy the "envisaging of performance" requirement. In *Wilson v. Lignotock U.S.A., Inc.*,[50] the court held that an employment contract did not contemplate enforcement or performance abroad just because the employee made many business trips abroad. The plaintiff's business trips to a foreign State were "incidental to the performance of the plaintiff's contractual duty," and the agreement to arbitrate abroad was unenforceable under the New York Convention.[51]

Some Other Reasonable Relation Between One or More Foreign States. A contract designating foreign law and a foreign forum for arbitration, alone, generally will not be sufficient to bring the dispute under the jurisdiction of the Conventions. In *Jones v. Sea Tow Services Freeport New York, Inc.*,[52] the court concluded that a standard salvage agreement containing a provision calling for arbitration in England was insufficient on its own to confer jurisdiction under the New York Convention. More specifically, the court found that "[n]either the salvor-casualty relationship, nor the LOF [Lloyd's Open Form] agreement relationship has any *reasonable* relation with England in this case." Moreover, the salvage operation took place just off the coast of the United States, and the parties signed the agreement in the United States.

(4) Reciprocity

On ratifying both the New York and Inter–American Conventions, the United States required reciprocity among signatory states, rendering

---

47. 421 F.Supp. 938 (1976).

48. *Id.* at 942, 943.

49. *Id.* at 944 n. 12.

50. 709 F.Supp. 797 (E.D.Mich.1989).

51. *Id.* at 799.

52. 30 F.3d 360 (2d Cir.1994).

unenforceable awards and agreements in noncontracting States.[53] Article I(3) of the New York Convention provides that a contracting State "may on the basis of reciprocity declare that it will apply the Convention to the recognition and enforcement of awards made only in the territory of another contracting State." Section 304 of the FAA provides that "[a]rbitral decisions or awards made in the territory of a foreign State shall, on the basis of reciprocity, be recognized and enforced under this chapter only if that State has ratified or acceded to the IAC." The principle of reciprocity is concerned only with the arbitration forum, the nationalities of the parties are immaterial. Thus, the court in *E.A.S.T., Inc. v. M/V Alaia*[54] upheld jurisdiction under the Convention of an agreement to arbitrate in England, a signatory country, even though the party seeking to arbitrate, a Liberian corporation, was a citizen of a nonsignatory state.[55]

When reciprocity is not satisfied, the domestic FAA or state provisions are possible alternatives. An annually updated list of signatories to the two Conventions is available in Note, 9 U.S.C.A. §§ 201, 301.

(5) Writing

Both Conventions cover only agreements that have been reduced to writing.[56] Article II(2) of the New York Convention explains that the "term 'agreement in writing' shall include an arbitral clause in a contract or an arbitration agreement, signed by the parties or contained in an exchange of letters or telegrams." Similarly, Article I of the IAC provides that "[t]he agreement shall be set forth in an instrument signed by the parties, or in the form of an exchange of letters, telegrams, or telex communications." The determination of the "writing" is governed by federal law.[57] In determining whether an agreement under the Convention has been reduced to writing, district courts will look to general concepts of contract law, including those of the Uniform Commercial Code.[58]

---

53. *See* National Iranian Oil Co. v. Ashland Oil, Inc., 817 F.2d 326, 331 (5th Cir. 1987) (while the United States district courts, under the Convention, have the power to compel arbitration, their power is limited to compelling arbitration in signatory countries).

54. 876 F.2d 1168 (5th Cir.1989).

55. *See also* Imperial Ethiopian Government v. Baruch–Foster Corp., 535 F.2d 334, 335 (5th Cir.1976) (confirming arbitration award involving the Ethiopian government, even though Ethiopia is not signatory to the Convention).

56. *See* Ledee v. Ceramiche Ragno, 684 F.2d 184, 186 (1st Cir.1982) (a court presented with a request to refer a dispute to arbitration pursuant to the FAA must resolve the preliminary question of whether the agreement to arbitrate was in writing).

57. David L.Threlkeld & Co. v. Metallgesellschaft, Ltd., 923 F.2d 245, 250 (2d Cir.1991).

58. *See* Genesco Inc. v. T. Kakiuchi & Co., 815 F.2d 840, 845–46 (2d Cir.1987) (applying general contract law and the U.C.C. in finding that the exchange of telexes, some of which were signed, was a valid writing under arbitration clause); Beromun Aktiengesellschaft v. Societa Industriale Agricola "Tresse," 471 F.Supp. 1163, 1165–70 (S.D.N.Y.1979) (using generally accepted principles of contract law and the U.C.C. to find arbitration clause valid in exchange of letters). *Cf.* Sen Mar, Inc. v. Tiger Petroleum Corp., 774 F.Supp. 879, 882–83 (S.D.N.Y.1991) (agreement to arbitrate embodied in one telex that the party charged did not sign nor consent to does not constitute a "writing" under the Convention).

In the exceptional case of *Ministry of Defense v. Gould Inc.*,[59] the court held that the writing requirement was satisfied by the President's entrance into a settlement agreement with the government of Iran.[60] Even though there was not a written arbitration agreement between the parties, the Convention requirement was satisfied by the execution of the Algiers Accords between the United States on behalf of private claimants and the government of Iran.

Library References:

West's Key No. Digests, Arbitration ⊜2.
Wright, Miller & Cooper, Federal Practice and Procedure: Civil 2d § 4103.

§ 9.11   The   International   FAA   Enforcement   of Agreements to Arbitrate

(a) Actions to Compel Arbitration

Parties to an arbitration agreement may bring a motion requesting the court to compel arbitration under international FAA §§ 206 or 303(a). Both sections provide that courts "may direct that arbitration be held in accordance with the agreement." Although the provisions of the international FAA are similar to those found in Section 4 of the FAA, the international FAA gives the court the power to compel arbitration at any place provided in the agreement "whether that place is within or without the United States."

In considering its order to arbitrate, the court in *Filanto v. Chilewich Intl. Corp.*[1] focused on the word "may" in Section 206 and noted that "[t]he language of Section 206 is concededly permissive."[2] Courts may thus have some discretion in deciding whether to order arbitration or not. However, the weight of opinion holds that "enforcing international arbitration agreements is mandatory and not discretionary" in the absence of one of the exceptions described *infra*.[3]

(b) Defendant's Motion to Compel Arbitration

If a party to an arbitration agreement brings suit in a U.S. court, the defendant may rely on the international FAA as a defense. If the action is brought in a state court, the defendant may remove to a federal court. Once in federal court, a defendant may ask the court to stay or dismiss the action in light of the valid arbitration agreement.[4] In cases like *Filanto v. Chilewich Intl.*, the defendant may not wish arbitration to

59. 887 F.2d 1357 (9th Cir.1989).

60. *Id.* at 1363.

§ 9.11

1. 789 F.Supp. 1229 (S.D.N.Y.1992).

2. *Id.* at 1242.

3. *See* Scherk v. Alberto–Culver Co., 417 U.S. 506, 94 S.Ct. 2449, 41 L.Ed.2d 270 (1974); Mitsubishi Motors Corp. v. Soler

Chrysler–Plymouth, 473 U.S. 614, 629, 631, 105 S.Ct. 3346, 3355, 3356, 87 L.Ed.2d 444 (1985); Riley v. Kingsley Underwriting Agencies, Ltd., 969 F.2d 953, 960 (10th Cir.1992); Filanto v. Chilewich Intl., 789 F.Supp. 1229 (S.D.N.Y.1992).

4. *See e.g.*, Filanto, 789 F.Supp. 1229.

proceed, but may wish only to avoid the pending lawsuit. In *Filanto*, the court ordered arbitration on its own motion "in the interests of justice."[5]

One procedural question which has not been resolved is whether a court ordering arbitration under the international FAA should dismiss the action or stay the litigation retaining jurisdiction during the arbitration. The courts have split on this procedural question.[6] This issue may have been resolved by *Vimar Seguros y Reaseguros v. M/V Sky Reefer*.[7] After ordering arbitration under the New York Convention, the Court noted that "the district court has retained jurisdiction over the case."[8]

(c) Exceptions to Enforcing an Agreement

Notwithstanding the New York Convention's general rule of enforceability of arbitration agreements, Articles II(1) and II(3) create a few narrow exceptions. Article II(1) requires courts to refer to arbitration only disputes that "concern a subject matter capable of settlement by arbitration." In addition, Article II(3) of the Convention expressly excepts referrals where the arbitration agreement is "null and void, inoperative or incapable of being performed."

(1) The "Subject Matter Exception" and United States Public Policy: Article II(1)

Although this exception has the potential to be extremely broad, courts have interpreted the public policy defense narrowly. Rarely will this defense, on its own, be used to upset an award. In *Mitsubishi Motors Corp. v. Soler Chrysler–Plymouth, Inc.*,[9] the Supreme Court restricted the potential scope of the public policy defense by interpreting it in the context of the pro-arbitration policy of the New York Convention. The Court found that despite the strong public policy in favor of the enforcement of antitrust laws and for nonarbitrability of antitrust disputes in the domestic context, concerns of international comity and for predictability in international agreements led to a different conclusion when applied to international agreements. The Court reasoned that:

> [w]here the parties have agreed that the arbitral body is to decide a defined set of claims which includes, as in these cases, those arising from the application of American antitrust law, the tribunal therefore should be bound to decide that dispute in accord with the national law giving rise to the claim.

Having agreed to arbitration, the court reasoned, the parties must shed their "understandable unwillingness to cede jurisdiction of a claim arising under domestic law to a foreign or transnational tribunal ...

---

5. *Id.* at 1241.

6. *See id.* at 1241–42 (granting a stay and retaining jurisdiction); *cf.* Astor Chocolate Corp. v. Mikroverk, 704 F.Supp. 30, 35 (E.D.N.Y.1989) (dismissing action after ordering arbitration).

7. 515 U.S. 528, 115 S.Ct. 2322, 132 L.Ed.2d 462 (1995).

8. *Id.*

9. 473 U.S. 614, 105 S.Ct. 3346, 87 L.Ed.2d 444 (1985).

[and] subordinate domestic notions of arbitrability to the international policy favoring commercial arbitration."[10]

Arbitration agreements will be enforced even when the subject matter of the arbitration concerns matters of sensitive public policy, unless Congress has expressly singled out categories of claims as being nonarbitrable.[11] *Mitsubishi* set the tone for later decisions respecting public policy concerns, and cases decided since *Mitsubishi* have recognized the strong presumption in favor of enforcing freely negotiated arbitration agreements by narrowly construing the "subject matter" exception.

There is an almost identical subject matter/public policy defense to the enforcement of an award.[12] Courts have applied this defense similarly to agreements to arbitrate,[13] giving the public policy defense a narrow construction in both instances.[14]

(2) Consensual Defenses to Enforcement: Article II(3)

Under Article II(3) of the Convention, an arbitration agreement is "null and void" only when it is subject to an internationally recognized defense which undermines the consensual nature of the agreement, such as fraud,[15] mistake, duress, and waiver, or when the arbitration agreement conflicts with the fundamental policies of the forum nation. The results of cases decided under Article II(3) are in accord with *Mitsubishi*; and the "null and void" language has been read narrowly to further the general policy of enforceability.[16] Courts have held that neither the "parochial interests of the forum state, nor those of states having more significant relationships with the dispute, should be permitted to supersede the presumption of enforceability."[17]

10. *Id.* at 637–39.

11. *See* Scherk v. Alberto–Culver Co., 417 U.S. 506, 94 S.Ct. 2449, 41 L.Ed.2d 270 (1974) (securities fraud claims are arbitrable in international disputes).

12. *See infra* § 9.12(c)(7).

13. *See* Antco Shipping Co., Ltd. v. Sidermar S.p.A., 417 F.Supp. 207, 216 (S.D.N.Y.1976) (comparable questions of public policy arise in cases involving both enforcement of awards and agreements).

14. Parsons & Whittemore Overseas Co., Inc. v. Societe Generale De L'Industriale Du Papier, 508 F.2d 969, 975 (2d Cir. 1974) ("The mere fact that an issue of national interest may incidentally figure into the resolution of a breach of contract claim does not make the dispute not arbitrable."); Fotochrome, Inc. v. Copal Co., Ltd., 517 F.2d 512, 516 (2d Cir.1975) (public policy exception to be narrowly construed); Geotech Lizenz AG v. Evergreen

Systems, 697 F.Supp. 1248 (E.D.N.Y.1988) (same).

15. Lower courts have generally been reluctant to conclude that an agreement to arbitrate was procured by fraud. *See* Waterside Ocean Navigation Co. v. Int'l Nav., Ltd., 737 F.2d 150, 153 (2d Cir.1984) (upholding dismissal of fraud counterclaim).

16. *See, e.g.*, Riley v. Kingsley Underwriting Agencies, Ltd., 969 F.2d 953, 960 (10th Cir.1992) (construing "null and void" exception narrowly, holding that an agreement to arbitrate a Securities Act claim in England under English law was valid and enforceable).

17. *See* Rhone Meditarranee Compagnia Francese Di Assicurazioni E Riassicurazoni v. Lauro, 712 F.2d 50, 53–54 (3d Cir.1983) (rule requiring odd number of arbitrators does not implicate fundamental concerns of either the international system or the forum).

Similarly, when considering whether an arbitration agreement violates a statute, the "null and void" provision will be construed narrowly, requiring the party challenging enforcement to show that the "essence of the obligation or remedy is prohibited by a *pertinent* statute or other declaration of public policy" of the forum.[18]

(3) Inconvenience of Arbitration Forum

Courts are very reluctant to consider opposition to contractually selected arbitration forums on grounds of legal or practical inconvenience. Forum selection clauses are almost always enforced. Though not formally related to forum non conveniens, such arguments are drawing on a similar principle.

In *Vimar Seguros y Reaseguros v. M/V Sky Reefer*,[19] the Court ordered arbitration in Japan pursuant to the arbitration agreement, even though the dispute arose under U.S. law and it was not clear whether the Japanese arbitrators would apply U.S. law. The Court accepted the possibility that if the Japanese arbitrators failed to apply U.S. law, the award might not be enforceable in the United States as "repugnant to the public policy of the United States."

By contrast, in *National Iranian Oil v. Ashland Oil, Inc.*,[20] the parties' arbitration agreement provided for arbitration in Iran, a nonsignatory to the New York Convention. The court refused to order arbitration in Iran. In addition, the court refused to order arbitration in its own district, because to do so would re-write the parties' agreement. The court noted that the parties could have easily agreed to arbitration in a signatory country.

Finally, in *Filanto v. Chilewich Intl. Corp.*,[21] the court ordered arbitration in Moscow, in accordance with the arbitration agreement, even though one of the parties opposed arbitration in Moscow due to the "unsettled conditions in Moscow" at the time. The court responded that though conditions were "unsettled, they continue to improve and there is no reason to believe that the Chamber of Commerce in Moscow cannot provide fair and impartial justice."

Library References:

West's Key No. Digests, Arbitration ⊘22–25.
Wright, Miller & Cooper, Federal Practice and Procedure: Civil 2d § 4103.

§ 9.12 Enforcement of International Awards

The international FAA also has separate provisions that govern the enforcement of awards. The New York Convention obligates signatory

18. Antco Shipping Co., 417 F.Supp. at 215 (the exclusion of the use of Israeli ports, which may have violated public policy under the Export Regulation Act, did not render the arbitration agreement null and void) (emphasis added); *see also* Ledee v. Ceramiche Ragno, 684 F.2d 184, 187 (1st Cir.1982) (rejecting the contention that the "null and void" clause was intended to in-

corporate the Dealers Act as an expression of Puerto Rico public policy).

19. 515 U.S. 528, 115 S.Ct. 2322, 132 L.Ed.2d 462, 475–76 (1995).

20. 817 F.2d 326, 334 (5th Cir.1987).

21. 789 F.Supp. 1229, 1242 (S.D.N.Y. 1992).

states to "recognize arbitral awards as binding and enforce them," subject to the exclusive defenses found in Article V. Section 207 of the international FAA implements this requirement along with Section 302 of the international FAA for actions under the IAC.

(a) Foreign Judgments Confirming Awards

The New York Convention is silent respecting the recognition and enforcement of foreign judgments confirming arbitration awards that fall under the Convention. Section 202 of the international FAA provides that only an "arbitration agreement or arbitral award" will fall under the Convention.[1] Several court decisions indicate that the Conventions will *not* apply to such judgments,[2] so state laws of comity govern the enforcement of foreign judgments in state and federal courts.

(b) Confirming Arbitral Awards

(1) The Conventions and International FAA

Under Section 207 of the international FAA, a party seeking to enforce an award under the New York Convention may get an order to confirm the award, and the court shall confirm the award unless one of the seven grounds for nonrecognition is found to exist.[3] Although Section 302 of the international FAA (relating to the IAC) incorporates Section 207 by reference, awards made under the IAC also have the force of a final judgment even without confirmation. The IAC provides that an arbitral award "shall have the force of a final judicial judgment.... [and] [i]ts execution or recognition may be ordered in the same manner as that of decisions handed down by national or foreign ordinary courts, in accordance with the procedural laws of the country where it is to be executed and the provisions of the international treaties."

(2) Procedure

Although the international FAA provisions do not provide detailed procedures relating to the New York Convention to be used in obtaining

---

§ 9.12

1. *See* International Shipping Co. v. Hydra Offshore, Inc., 875 F.2d 388, 391 n. 5 (2d Cir.), *cert. denied*, 493 U.S. 1003, 110 S.Ct. 563, 107 L.Ed.2d 558 (1989) (affirming holding that jurisdiction could not be premised on the Convention because "the party invoking its provisions did not seek either to compel arbitration or to enforce an arbitral award").

2. Victrix S.S. Co. v. Salen Dry Cargo A.B., 825 F.2d 709, 713 (2d Cir.1987) (Convention does not apply to the enforcement of judgments that confirm arbitration awards); Waterside Ocean Navigation Co., Inc. v. International Navigation, Ltd., 737 F.2d 150, 154 (2d Cir.1984) (reasoning that

the goals of the Convention would not be served by allowing a party to confirm an award in England and then seek to enforce that judgment in the U.S.); Island Territory of Curacao v. Solitron Devices, Inc., 489 F.2d 1313, 1319 (2d Cir.1973), *cert. denied*, 416 U.S. 986, 94 S.Ct. 2389, 40 L.Ed.2d 763 (1974) (Convention does not apply to enforcement of judgments that confirm foreign arbitration awards). The decisions of permanent arbitral bodies are not considered judgments of foreign courts. The New York Convention, in fact, explicitly covers awards by such bodies. New York Convention, Art. I, § 2.

3. FAA § 207.

recognition or enforcement of a foreign arbitral award, it does set out basic requirements. A party seeking enforcement or recognition must file (1) an authenticated original award or a certified copy thereof, (2) the original arbitration agreement or a certified copy thereof, and (3) a certified translation of these documents if not in the official language of the enforcing court.[4]

The international FAA's procedures relating to the IAC provide that absent an express agreement otherwise, the arbitration shall be conducted in accordance with the Rules of Procedure of the Inter–American Commercial Arbitration Commission (the "Rules"). The Rules also cover the form of awards. For example, Article 32 of the Rules requires that the award shall (1) be made in writing, (2) state the reasons upon which the award is based, (3) be signed by the arbitrators, and (4) contain the date and place where the award was made.

An expedited procedure for enforcing a foreign arbitral award is set out in the international FAA §§ 207, 208, and 302, following federal motion practice rules.

(3) Time for Bringing an Action

Section 207 of the international FAA provides that an application for an order confirming an arbitral award falling within the scope of the New York Convention must be made within three years after such an award is made. Section 302 of the international FAA relating to the IAC incorporates this provision by reference. The word "made" in Section 207 has been interpreted to mean when the award is originally decided by the arbitrators, *not* when the award becomes final.[5]

(c) Defenses to Enforcement Action

Both the New York and Inter–American Conventions set out seven exclusive grounds for refusal or deferral of enforcement. Section 207 of the international FAA requires the court to confirm an arbitral award, *unless* it finds one of the exclusive grounds for refusal or deferral of recognition. Section 302 of the IAC incorporates Section 207 by reference, thus providing the same seven exclusive grounds for nonenforcement. In general, the exclusive grounds have received a narrow interpretation in the courts.[6]

---

4. Additionally, Article III of the New York Convention requires that signatory States not impose more onerous conditions or higher fees or charges on the enforcement of an arbitral award than are placed on domestic awards.

5. *See* Seetransport Wiking Trader Schiffarhtsgesellschaft MBH & Co. v. Navimpex Centrala Navala, 989 F.2d 572, 581 (2d Cir.1993) *aff'd*, 29 F.3d 79 (2d Cir. 1994).

6. IAC Article V provides that "[t]he recognition and execution of the decision may be refused, at the request of the party against which it is made, *only* if such party is able to prove to the competent authority of the State in which recognition and execution are requested." (emphasis added.) The use of the word "only," along with § 207 ("the courts *shall* confirm the award unless it finds one of the grounds for refusal ...") has led to a narrow construction of the Article's provisions. *See* Parsons & Whittemore Overseas Co., Inc. v. Societe Generale de l'Industrie du Papier, 508 F.2d 969, 976 (2d Cir.1974) (defenses construed narrowly

Both Conventions provide for the refusal to enforce an award or an agreement to arbitrate "at the request of the party against" whom the enforcement is sought but only if that party furnishes to the court where the recognition and enforcement are sought, proof of one or more of the defenses listed in the article. Courts have interpreted this to mean that the party seeking to avoid enforcement has the burden of proof.[7]

(1) Incapacity

Both Conventions provide for nonenforcement of an award if parties to the agreement are under some incapacity. Whether the party was subject to some incapacity is defined under the law applicable to the agreement.[8]

(2) Invalid Agreement

Both Conventions provide for the refusal to enforce an award if the agreement is invalid under the law selected by the parties or, in the absence of such indication, under the law of the country where the award was made.[9] In *Geotech Lizenz AG v. Evergreen Systems, Inc.*,[10] the respondent in a confirmation proceeding challenged the enforcement by arguing that a settlement agreement between the parties superseded the arbitration proceeding and rendered the arbitration agreement invalid.[11] However, the court examined the settlement and found no meeting of the minds as to the settlement agreement.[12] Accordingly, because the dispute was never settled, it became the proper subject of the arbitration mechanism envisioned by the first agreement.[13]

---

to comport with the "enforcement-facilitating thrust of the Convention"); Foto-chrome, Inc. v. Copal Co. Ltd., 517 F.2d 512, 518 (2d Cir.1975); Dworkin–Cosell v. Avraham, 728 F.Supp. 156, 161 (S.D.N.Y. 1989) (public policy defense applied narrowly); American Constr. Mach. & Equip. Corp. v. Mechanised Constr. of Pakistan Ltd., 659 F.Supp. 426, 429 (S.D.N.Y.1987), *cert. denied*, 484 U.S. 1064, 108 S.Ct. 1024, 98 L.Ed.2d 988 (1988) (Article V defense construed narrowly).

7. *See* Parsons & Whittemore Overseas, 508 F.2d at 973 (stating that the New York Convention clearly shifted the burden of proof to the party defending against enforcement and limited its defenses); Imperial Ethiopian Gov't v. Baruch–Foster Corp., 535 F.2d 334, 336 (5th Cir.1976) (burden on party defending against enforcement); Al Haddad Bros. Enterprises, Inc. v. M/S Agapi, 635 F.Supp. 205, 209 (D.Del.1986), *aff'd without opinion*, 813 F.2d 396 (3d Cir. 1987).

8. This is supported by the language of the Conventions. Article V(1)(a) of the New York Convention provides that the law governing questions of incapacity of parties is "the law applicable to them." Likewise, Article V(1)(a) of the Inter–American Convention provides for nonenforcement if the "parties to an agreement were subject to incapacity under the applicable law."

9. Note that the validity of the contract is a matter for the arbitrator to decide at first instance. *See* Prima Paint Corp. v. Flood & Conklin Mfg. Co., 388 U.S. 395, 403–04, 87 S.Ct. 1801, 1805–06, 18 L.Ed.2d 1270 (1967) (claim of fraud in the inducement of the entire contract is to be referred to the arbitrators).

10. 697 F.Supp. 1248 (E.D.N.Y.1988).

11. *Id.* at 1253.

12. *Id.*

13. *Id.*

(3) Lack of Notice of Appointment of Arbitrators or of Arbitration Proceedings and the Inability to Present Case

Both Conventions provide for the refusal of an award if a party against whom the award is invoked can show the failure to provide adequate notice of the appointment of the arbitrator or the foreign proceedings or an inability to present its *case*.[14] These two grounds for refusal essentially sanction the application of the forum State's due process. Most disputes under this section arise when a party is prevented from participating in the arbitration proceedings due to faulty notice or an inability to be heard.

Inadequate Notice. Federal courts usually refuse to enforce or confirm an award only if U.S. due process is denied.[15] In *Sesostris, S.A.E. v. Transportes Navales, S.A.*,[16] the court denied the petitioner's motions to confirm an arbitral award where the defendants received notice after the proceedings had begun, and where a reply to the request for notice contained no reference to the current scheduling of the proceedings which were less than one week away.[17] Conversely, in *Geotech Lizenz AG v. Evergreen Systems, Inc.*[18] the court found proper notice where the respondent was apprised of every step of the arbitration process, but simply chose not to appear at the arbitration.[19]

Inability to Present Case. Courts have placed a heavy burden on parties who submit to international arbitration and then argue that the selected forum is impractical. The "mere fact that participation in a foreign arbitration would be inconvenient ... does not amount to a denial of due process rights."[20] In *Parsons & Whittemore Overseas Co., Inc. v. Societe Generale De L'Industrie Du Papier*,[21] the court rejected the argument that an arbitrator's refusal to delay proceedings in order to accommodate the speaking schedule of a witness prevented Parsons from presenting its case.[22] The court held that the "inability to produce one's witnesses before an arbitral tribunal is a risk inherent in an agreement to submit to arbitration."[23]

14. Note that the IAC allows a party to seek refusal of an award if it was unable to present its *defense*, but no case law has developed under this difference of language between the two Conventions.

15. *See* Parsons & Whittemore Overseas Co., Inc. v. Societe Generale De L'Industrie Du Papier, 508 F.2d 969, 976 (2d Cir.1974).

16. 727 F.Supp. 737 (D.Mass.1989).

17. *Id.* at 742–43.

18. 697 F.Supp. 1248, 1253 (E.D.N.Y. 1988).

19. *Id.* at 1253.

20. *See id.*

21. 508 F.2d 969 (2d Cir.1974).

22. *Id.* at 975.

23. *Id. See also* National Oil Corp. v. Libyan Sun Oil Co., 733 F.Supp. 800 (D.Del. 1990) (rejecting defense that misleading testimony prevented respondent's ability to present case); Biotronik Mess-Und Therapiegeraete GmbH & Co. v. Medford Medical Instrument Co., 415 F.Supp. 133, 139–40 (D.N.J.1976) (respondent's due process rights not infringed because respondent received notice and offered no explanation of its failure to participate). *Cf.* Iran Aircraft Industries v. Avco Corp., 980 F.2d 141, 146 (2d Cir.1992) (denial of opportunity to present case because tribunal never made respondent aware of change in the method of proof required, thus unwittingly preventing respondent from substantiating its claim).

(4) Exceeding the Scope of Submission

Both Conventions provide for the refusal of an award if the award, or an inseverable part of it, stems from a dispute not within the scope of the submission to arbitration.[24] When deciding whether a matter was within the scope of what the parties agreed to submit to arbitration, there is a strong presumption in favor of deferring to the arbitral body's interpretation of the agreement. In *Parsons & Whittemore*,[25] an American company ("Overseas") challenged a component of the award that compensated an Egyptian company for loss of production costs. Overseas argued that because the arbitration agreement contained a clause providing that neither party would be liable for costs associated with loss of production, the award was beyond the scope of what it submitted to arbitration. The court rejected this argument, construing the defense narrowly and stressing the existence of a strong presumption that the arbitral body acted within its powers. The court found that the arbitral body had not simply ignored this clause but had rather "interpreted the provision not to preclude jurisdiction on this matter."[26] The court also expressed reluctance to use this defense to "sanction second-guessing the arbitrator's construction of the parties' agreement."[27]

(5) Improper Composition of Arbitral Tribunal/Improper Procedure

Under both Conventions, an arbitral award may be refused if either the composition of the arbitration board or the hearing procedure was not in accordance with the arbitration agreement, or absent such agreement, with the law of the State where the arbitration took place and the award was made.[28]

However, the international FAA § 207 permits courts to enforce awards despite defects, and may be inclined to do so if the defect is incidental or procedural. In *Rhone Meditarranee Compagnia Francese Di Assicurazioni E Riassicurazoni v. Lauro*,[29] the court emphasized the phrase in Article V "may be refused," and enforced an award despite a procedural defect in the arbitration proceedings.[30] In *Rhone*, the arbitral award was made by an odd number of arbitrators, even though Italian law, which applied, required an even number of arbitrators. The court stated that an American court could enforce the award even though it

24. *See* Articles V(1)(c) of both Conventions.

25. 508 F.2d at 969.

26. *Id.* at 977.

27. *Id. See also* American Const. Mach. & Equip. Corp., Ltd. v. Mechanised Cont. of Pakistan Ltd., 659 F.Supp. 426 (S.D.N.Y. 1987), *cert. denied,* 484 U.S. 1064, 108 S.Ct. 1024, 98 L.Ed.2d 988 (1988) (rejecting defense claim that matter was beyond scope of agreement and noting narrow construction of defense to advance policy of Convention); Management & Technical Consultants S.A.

v. Parsons–Jurden Int'l Corp., 820 F.2d 1531 (9th Cir.1987) (reading broadly the phrase "any dispute" without any limiting words in an agreement to arbitrate; conferring arbitral authority to determine an issue not within the letter agreement).

28. *See* Articles V(1)(d) of both Conventions. *See also* Rhone Meditarranee Compagnia Francese Di Assicurazioni E Riassicurazoni v. Lauro, 712 F.2d 50, 53 (3d Cir. 1983).

29. 712 F.2d 50 (3d Cir.1983).

30. *Id.* at 54.

conflicted with Italian law because the international FAA "permits another forum to disregard the defect and enforce."[31] Furthermore, a party cannot challenge the confirmation of an award based on this defense if the party agreed to use different procedures than required by the applicable law.[32] This defense may also be available to attack the lack of neutrality of an arbitrator.[33]

(6) Award Not Yet Binding

Under both Conventions, an arbitral award may be refused if it is not yet binding on the parties or has been set aside[34] or suspended by a competent authority of the rendering country.[35] An award is binding when made or when it has res judicata effect, *i.e.*, it may be relied upon in litigation of the same subject matter between the parties. An award will be binding if no further recourse may be had to another *arbitral tribunal*; the fact that recourse may be had to a court of law does not prevent an award from being binding.[36] When it is unclear whether an award is binding or not, courts will either remand the case to arbitrators for clarification or stay the decision pending comprehension and application of appropriate law.[37]

(7) Subject Matter Not Arbitrable and/or Award Contrary to Public Policy

Both Conventions reserve to each signatory country the right to refuse enforcement of an award where (1) the subject matter of the difference is not capable of settlement by arbitration under the law of the enforcing country, or (2) the recognition or enforcement of an award would be "contrary to the public policy" of the enforcing forum.[38] Reference should be made to Section 9.11(c)(1) of this chapter, because of the close relation between this defense and the "subject matter exception" to enforcing agreements to arbitrate.

U.S. courts have given the "public policy" exception a narrow construction. Similarly, enforcement of an award will be refused under

---

31. *Id.*

32. *See* American Constr. Mach. & Equip. Corp. v. Mechanised Constr. of Pakistan Ltd., 659 F.Supp. 426, 429 (S.D.N.Y. 1987).

33. *See* Imperial Ethiopian Gov't v. Baruch–Foster Corp., 535 F.2d 334 (5th Cir. 1976).

34. The IAC uses slightly different wording, providing for refusal to enforce if "the decision is not yet binding on the parties or has been *annulled* or suspended by a competent authority ..." (emphasis added).

35. *See* Eurolines Shipping Co., S.A. v. Metal Trans. Corp., 491 F.Supp. 590, 591

(S.D.N.Y.1980) (holding under the domestic FAA that separate, independent claims may be confirmed).

36. *See* Fertilizer Corp. of India v. IDI Management, Inc., 517 F.Supp. 948, 957–58 (S.D.Ohio 1981) (an award was final and binding even though still before Indian courts for review pursuant to law of India requiring such review).

37. *See* Dworkin–Cosell Interair Courier Services, Inc. v. Avraham, 728 F.Supp. 156 (S.D.N.Y.1989); Spier v. Calzaturificio, 663 F.Supp. 871 (S.D.N.Y.1987).

38. *See* Article V(2)(a) & (b) of the New York and Inter–American Conventions.

this defense only if enforcement would violate the forum nation's most basic notions of morality and justice.[39]

Library References:

West's Key No. Digests, Arbitration ☞83.1–85.70.
Wright, Miller & Cooper, Federal Practice and Procedure: Civil 2d §§ 2446, 4473.

§ 9.13   Practice Checklist

(a) To Compel Arbitration (*See* § 9.4)

(1) To move to compel arbitration, prepare a notice of motion if a pleading has been filed in the district court. If there is no previous filing, prepare a petition to compel arbitration. You must give notice to the opposing party.

(2) Your petition to compel arbitration under 9 U.S.C.A. § 4 must include at least the following:

- *Jurisdictional allegations.* 9 U.S.C.A. § 4 provides that the proceeding "may [be brought in] any United States district court which, save for such agreement would have jurisdiction under Title 28, in a civil action or in admiralty of the subject matter of a suit arising out of the controversy between the parties.... " Therefore, the forms of jurisdictional allegations in civil actions generally, set out in FRCP 8(a)(1) are appropriate.

- *Venue.* A petition should also include relevant allegations establishing that venue is proper. For a complete discussion of allegations necessary to establish venue see Chapter 3.

- *Existence of Agreement to Arbitrate.* 9 U.S.C.A. applies only to written agreements to arbitrate involving maritime transactions or interstate commerce. It is necessary, therefore, to include allegations of the written agreement to arbitrate, including the execution date of the underlying agreement, the parties, and the terms of the arbitration clause. In fact, it is advisable to quote the entire arbitration clause in the petition whenever possible.

---

39. *See* Parsons & Whittemore Overseas Co., Inc. v. Societe Generale de l'Industrie di Papier, 508 F.2d 969, 974 (2d Cir.1974) (refusing to deny enforcement of award because of decline in foreign relations between Egypt and the United States, noting that to read the public policy defense as a parochial device protective of national political interests would seriously undermine the Convention's utility). Other relevant cases include Waterside Ocean Navigation Co. v. International Navigation Ltd., 737 F.2d 150, 152 (2d Cir.1984) (the policy against inconsistent testimony is not one of our nation's "most basic notions of morality and justice"); Antco Shipping Co. v. Sidermar S.p.A., 417 F.Supp. 207 (S.D.N.Y.1976) (the fact that a provision in an affreightment contract excluding Israeli ports as designated loading spot violated a provision of New York law forbidding boycotts based on national origin was not sufficient to invoke the public policy defense); *But see* Libyan American Oil Co. v. Socialist People's Libyan Arab Jamahirya, 482 F.Supp. 1175, 1178 (D.D.C.1980) (federal court could not rule on the validity of Libyan nationalization law).

- *Existence of a Controversy Relating to Arbitration.* The petition must also contain some allegations that respondent has failed and refused to consent to the arbitration.

- *Underlying Dispute Is Within Scope of Agreement to Arbitrate.* The petition should also include allegations that the underlying dispute and each claim for relief is within the scope of the arbitration agreement. In most cases, it is sufficient to identify the separate causes of action and a brief description of why each cause of action is within the scope of the arbitration agreement.

(3) The petition to compel arbitration is frequently quite short. Depending on the scope of the proceeding, the above allegations can be adequately set forth in most cases in 12 to 18 separate allegations. The tendency in some cases is to include the level of detail of a complaint. This temptation should be resisted. In most cases, the arbitration agreement provides that "any and all disputes arising under this agreement shall be resolved by arbitration." It is sufficient in this case, therefore, to identify the dispute and allege that it arises under the agreement.

(4) In addition to the petition, the moving party should provide the court with an affidavit (or multiple affidavits if necessary) supplying a copy of the arbitration agreement, verifying the execution date of the underlying agreement, and providing competent evidence that respondent has failed to consent to arbitration. Together with the notice of hearing and petition, these constitute your petition.

(b) To Confirm an Arbitration Award (*See* § 9.7(b))

(1) Application for confirmation of an arbitral award should be made by motion where an action has been filed or by petition where there is no underlying action. (*See* FAA § 6) The application must be in writing and must state the grounds for relief and what relief is sought with particularity, as prescribed under FRCP 7(b). The FAA does not set forth the contents of a petition to confirm. Nevertheless, the application should contain at minimum the following information:

- names and addresses of the parties and their counsel of record;

- where the award was "made"; (*See* § 9.6(c)(1))

- facts supporting the court's exercise of jurisdiction;

- facts establishing that the parties entered into a contract that contained an arbitration clause that encompasses the dispute, accompanied by a copy of the agreement to arbitrate;

- facts establishing that a hearing was conducted before a duly appointed arbitrator;

- assertion that the arbitrators granted an award in favor of the petitioner on a particular date including an outline of the essential terms of the arbitral award;

- request that an order be entered under FAA § 9 confirming the award and that judgment be entered on the award in favor of the petitioner including where appropriate, interest and costs; and

- a copy of the award.

(2) In addition, the petition should include a notice of hearing and an affidavit providing the court with competent evidence relating to the agreement to arbitrate, the completion of the underlying arbitration and the authenticity of the award to be confirmed.

(c) To Vacate an Award (*See* § 9.8(g))

(1) A party must file a petition in district court to vacate an award (or a motion in an action already pending). (*See* FAA § 6) The motion must be in writing, state the grounds supporting it with particularity, and set out the relief or order sought. (*See* FRCP 7(b))

The motion to vacate the award should contain the following information, unless such information is already before the court pursuant to an application to confirm:

- names and addresses of the parties and their counsel of record;

- where the award was "made"; (*See* § 9.6(c)(1));

- facts supporting the court's exercise of jurisdiction;

- assertion that parties entered into the contract that contained an arbitration clause on a particular date, accompanied by a copy of the agreement to arbitrate;

- facts establishing that a hearing was conducted before a duly appointed arbitrator;

- assertion that the arbitrators granted award in favor of the petitioner on a particular date including an outline of the essential terms of the arbitral award;

- statement of the grounds for challenging the award, corresponding to the applicable section(s) of FAA § 10;

- a copy of the award; and

- request that the court vacate the award under FAA § 10.

(2) Section 12 of the FAA prescribes the procedure for serving notice of the application to vacate upon the opposing party. A time limit is imposed under FAA § 12, as notice must be served "within *three months* after the award is filed or delivered."(*See* FAA § 12) Section 12 distinguishes between residents and nonresidents of the "district within which the award was made" for the purpose of service of notice requirements. If the adverse party is a *resident*, "service shall be made upon the adverse party or his attorney as prescribed by law for service of notice of motion in an action in the same court." (*See* FAA § 12) If the adverse party is a *nonresident*,

"notice of the application shall be served by the marshal of any district within which the adverse party may be found in like manner as other process of the court." (*See* FAA § 12)

(d) To Modify or Correct an Award (*See* § 9.9(e))

(1) A party must file a petition in district court to modify or correct an award (or a motion if an action is pending). (*See* FAA § 6) The motion to modify or correct the award must be in writing, state the grounds supporting it with particularity, and set out the relief or order sought. (*See* FRCP 7(b))

(2) The motion to modify or correct the award should contain the following information, unless such information is already before the court pursuant to an application to confirm:

- names and addresses of the parties and their counsel of record;

- where the award was "made"; (*See* § 9.6(c)(1))

- facts supporting the court's exercise of jurisdiction;

- assertion that parties entered into a contract which contained an arbitration clause on a particular date, accompanied by a copy of the agreement to arbitrate;

- facts establishing that a hearing was conducted before a duly appointed arbitrator;

- assertion that the arbitrator granted award in favor of the petitioner on a particular date including an outline of the essential terms of the arbitral award;

- statement of the grounds for challenging the award, corresponding to the applicable section(s) of FAA § 11;

- a copy of the award; and

- request that the court modify or confirm the award under FAA § 11.

(3) Section 12 of the FAA prescribes the procedure for serving notice of the application to modify or correct the award upon the opposing party. A time limit is imposed under FAA § 12, as notice must be served "within *three months* after the award is filed or delivered." (*See* FAA § 12) Section 12 distinguishes between residents and nonresidents of the "district within which the award was made" for the purpose of service of notice requirements. If the adverse party is a *resident*, "service shall be made upon the adverse party or his attorney as prescribed by law for service of notice of motion in an action in the same court." (*See* FAA § 12) If the adverse party is a *nonresident*, "notice of the application shall be served by the marshal of any district within which the adverse party may be found in like manner as other process of the court." (*See* FAA § 12)

§ 9.14   Form Clauses

The following model clauses are presented with commentary. In many cases, the model language has been drafted by one of the principal ADR providers in the domestic and/or international arena. Accompanying each model clause is commentary offering analysis of relevant case law (if any) and a comparison of how the model language would work under a variety of regimes. The commentary analyzes the model language under the following regimes: American Arbitration Association ("AAA"), the International Chamber of Commerce ("ICC"), and the CPR Institute for Dispute Resolution ("CPR").

(a) Standard Arbitration Clause   ⊟

(1) American Arbitration Association   ⊟

(Predispute)

Any controversy or claim arising out of or relating to this contract, or the breach thereof, shall be settled by arbitration administered by the American Arbitration Association in accordance with its [applicable] rules and judgment upon the award rendered by the arbitrator may be entered in any court having jurisdiction thereof.

(Existing disputes)

We, the undersigned parties, hereby agree to submit to arbitration administered by the American Arbitration Association under its [applicable] rules the following controversy [cite briefly]. We further agree that we will faithfully observe this agreement and the rules, and that we will abide by and perform any award rendered by the arbitrators(s) and that a judgment of the court having jurisdiction may be entered upon the award.

The above clause is perhaps the most widely used arbitration clause in the United States. Over 95% of the nearly 70,000 commercial arbitrations currently administered each year by the AAA result from the above standard form agreement.

The final provision in the AAA standard clause ("and judgment upon the award rendered by the arbitrator may be entered in any court having jurisdiction thereof") may be unnecessary in light of Commercial Arbitration Rule 47(c) which provides that "Parties to these rules shall be deemed to have consented that judgment upon the arbitration award may be entered in any federal or state court having jurisdiction thereof." *See Dan River, Inc. v. Cal–Togs, Inc.*, 451 F.Supp. 497 (S.D.N.Y.1978) (where the parties agreed to arbitrate disputes under the AAA rules but did not explicitly consent in the agreement to have a specific court confirm the award, consent was unnecessary in light of Rule 47(c)).

(2) CPR Institute for Dispute Resolution   ⊟

Any dispute arising out of or relating to this contract or the breach, termination or validity thereof, [which has not

been resolved by a nonbinding procedure as provided herein within 90 days of the initiation of such procedure,] shall be settled by arbitration in accordance with the [then current] CPR Institute for Dispute Resolution Rules for Non–Administered Arbitration of Business Disputes [in effect on the date of this agreement,] by [a sole arbitrator] [three independent and impartial arbitrators, of whom each party shall appoint one], [three independent and impartial arbitrators, none of whom shall be appointed by either party]; [provided, however, that if one party has requested the other to participate in a nonbinding procedure and the other has failed to participate, the requesting party may initiate arbitration before expiration of the above period.] The arbitration shall be governed by the United States Arbitration Act, 9 U.S.C.A. 5:1–16, and judgment upon the award rendered by the arbitrator(s) may be entered by any court having jurisdiction thereof. The place of arbitration shall be _____. The arbitrators [are] [are not] empowered to award damages in excess of compensatory damages [and each party hereby irrevocably waives any right to recover such damages with respect to any resolved arbitration.]

(3) JAMS/Endispute

Any controversy, dispute, or claim of whatever nature arising out of, in connection with, or in relation to the interpretation, performance or breach of this agreement, including any claim based on contract, tort or statute, shall be settled, at the request of any party to this agreement, by final and binding arbitration conducted at a location to be determined by the arbitrator in [City and State] administered by and in accordance with the then existing Rules of Practice and Procedure of JAMS/Endispute, and judgment upon any award rendered by the arbitrators may be entered by any state or federal court having jurisdiction thereof.

(b) Standard Clauses of International Providers

(1) International Chamber of Commerce

All disputes arising in connection with the present contract shall be finally settled under the Rules of Conciliation and Arbitration of the International Chamber of Commerce by one or more arbitrators appointed in accordance with said Rules.

(2) United Nations Commission on International Trade Law

Any dispute, controversy or claim arising out of or relating to this contract, or the breach, termination or invalidity thereof, shall be settled by arbitration in accordance with the UNCITRAL Arbitration Rules as at present in force.

(3) Stockholm Chamber of Commerce

Any dispute, controversy or claim arising out of or in connection with this contract, or the breach, termination or invalidity thereof, shall be settled by arbitration in accordance with the Rules of the Arbitration Institute of the Stockholm Chamber of Commerce.

(4) London Court of International Arbitration

Any dispute arising out of or in connection with this contract, including any question regarding its existence, validity or termination, shall be referred to and finally resolved by arbitration under the Rules of the London Court of International Arbitration, which Rules are deemed to be incorporated by reference into this clause. The governing law of this contract shall be the substantive law of _____. The tribunal shall consist of [one or three arbitrators]. The place of the arbitration shall be _____. The language of the arbitration shall be _____.

(c) Special Considerations

(1) Appointment of Arbitrator

All of the major providers allow the parties to designate the number of arbitrators and to create their own selection mechanics. If the parties do not otherwise specify, the rules of the provider provide for the selection of a sole, neutral nonbiased arbitrator, unless it is decided that more arbitrators (generally three) are appropriate. In this regard, note that in practice the AAA will generally appoint three arbitrators in any complex dispute involving more than $200,000. The AAA provides each side with a list of candidates to rank; the AAA then selects based on mutual preference. If this method fails, the AAA selects from a panel. In international disputes, either side may request a neutral national. Under the ICC, unless otherwise agreed, the court selects an arbitrator from a neutral country using its national committee procedures. Both AAA and ICC rules allow the parties to challenge the appointment. Under the CPR Rules, the parties select from a select group of senior attorneys and business persons.

In international arbitration, the major providers' rules allow the parties to request a nationally neutral arbitrator when the arbitral regime selects the arbitrator. It may expedite the selection process if the parties decide at the time they enter into the contract whether or not they waive the right to make such a request. If national neutrality is waived as a selection criterion, the potential pool of neutral arbitrators is much greater.

The parties may prefer to have three arbitrators (which obviously increases costs, but which is generally acknowledged to have distinct advantages in large disputes where the parties may not wish to vest the outcome of their dispute in one arbitrator's hands). In such cases, all regimes effectively allow both sides to select party arbitrators who then select a third neutral arbitrator. However, the ICC "default" provides for the court to select the third arbitrator, and there are other variations in the rules. Generally all of the major providers will select the party arbitrator or neutral arbitrator if the specified selection method fails; providing a defined pool for a back-up could therefore be useful. Some practitioners prefer three neutrals because party arbitrators may have less credibility. The clause set forth below could be limited in use to situations where a monetary claim has been made by one of the parties for an amount in excess of an agreed-upon amount.

a. The arbitration shall be conducted by a panel of three arbitrators, to be selected in the following manner: each party shall select one arbitrator within thirty (30) days [or other time frame] from the date of receipt of the demand to commence arbitration. If one or both of the parties fail to nominate an arbitrator, the [arbitration association] shall have the power to select an arbitrator on the party's behalf. Within thirty (30) days after the appointment of the last of the two arbitrators, the selected party arbitrators shall choose a third arbitrator to serve as the neutral chairperson of the panel.

The ICC rules provide that all appointed arbitrators shall remain independent throughout the case. The AAA's standard domestic rules, however, subject only the "neutral" arbitrator to disqualification for not being impartial (whereas the AAA's international rules appear to subject all arbitrators to the impartiality standard).

The parties may require the arbitrator to be of a certain nationality, to be a resident of the locale of the arbitration, to agree to charge the going rate for commercial matters, or to have skills in particular substantive areas (*e.g.*, law, intellectual property, construction, computer technology, etc.) and/or languages.

b. Each arbitrator appointed under this Section shall be qualified by education and experience in the subject matter of the submitted dispute [or Agreement]. OR [Each arbitrator shall be fluent in (language X) OR [selected from a prearranged list] OR [be from a neutral country]. OR [a lawyer licensed to practice in (x)].

Finally, consider providing that any replacement arbitrator be allowed to continue on the basis of the existing record:

c. In the event of the death or disability of an arbitrator, the parties shall select a new arbitrator as provided in the agreement. The new arbitrator shall have the power to determine the extent to which he shall act on the record already made in the arbitration.

(2) Confidentiality ⊟

Arbitration is a confidential process, and all of the major providers require that the arbitrator permit only directly interested persons to attend hearings. However, the parties may wish explicitly to bind one another, the arbitrator, and any experts to confidentiality requirements.

All papers, documents, or evidence, whether written or oral, filed with or presented to the arbitrator shall be deemed by the parties and the arbitrator to be confidential information. No party, expert, or arbitrator shall disclose in whole or in part to any other person any confidential information submitted by any other person in connection with arbitration proceedings, except to the extent (i) required by law or regulation, (ii) reasonably necessary to assist counsel in the arbitration or preparation for arbitration of the dispute, or (iii) that such "confidential" information was previously disclosed or subsequently becomes known to the disclosing party without restrictions on disclosure, was independently developed by such disclosing party, or becomes publicly known through no fault of the disclosing party. Confidential information may be disclosed to ( ) attorneys, parties, and [( ) "qualified outside experts" requested by any party's counsel to furnish technical or expert services or to give testimony at the arbitration proceedings. Outside experts shall be qualified by agreement of the parties or by order of the arbitrator in the following manner: before disclosure of confidential information is made to a proposed outside expert, the proposed expert's identity shall be notified to the party by whom or at whose instance the confidential information may be disclosed, together with the address of the proposed outside expert and a brief description of the proposed expert's professional and employment background and qualifications. The party originally furnishing the confidential information or on whose behalf it was originally furnished, shall, prior to the disclosure, be entitled to object to such disclosure on the ground that it could reasonably be expected that the disclosure will not remain confidential in accordance with this provision. Such objection shall be served within ten (10) business days after receipt of notice, shall be stated in reasonable detail, and shall be in writing. If the parties are unable to agree as to the merits of the objection within ten (10) business days after its receipt, the matter shall be submitted to the arbitrator. Before an outside expert shall be qualified, the proposed expert shall deliver to counsel for the party originally furnishing the confidential information or on whose behalf it was originally furnished, a legally binding written statement that the expert ( ) is fully familiar with the terms of this Section, ( ) agrees to comply with the confidentiality terms of this Section, and ( ) will not use any disclosed confidential information for personal or business advantage.]

(3) Discovery and Evidentiary Rules ⌨

Typically, parties in arbitration do not have the power to conduct traditional discovery. Moreover, none of the major providers obligates the arbitrator to comply with any evidentiary rules in determining the admissibility of evidence at the arbitral hearings. However, with respect to the arbitrator's subpoena powers, the major providers, in various degrees, all grant the arbitrator some power to obtain evidence which a party may not otherwise wish to present. The AAA rules permit the arbitrator to subpoena witnesses *and* documents based upon a party's or the arbitrator's own request and to conduct inspections. The ICC rules allow the arbitrator to hear any person who a party or the arbitrator requests, provided the person is duly summoned (no rule relates to the arbitrator's power to request additional documents or to conduct inspections).

The parties may wish to modify the discovery and evidentiary rules governing their arbitration and broaden or more strictly circumscribe the arbitrator's subpoena powers relating thereto. For instance, the parties may incorporate state or federal civil procedural rules governing discovery and/or the admissibility of evidence into their agreement. They may also incorporate the evidentiary rules developed for international arbitration by the International Bar Association. With respect to the arbitrator's powers to compel discovery or compel the introduction of evidence, the parties may desire to deprive the arbitrator of any subpoena powers or to waive oral hearings. These choices require serious review and consultation. Requiring some form of discovery may be useful to the parties (particularly parties who will be likely plaintiffs with strong cases), but will also result in prolonged arbitration and increased costs. Moreover, it is important to consider the cultural background of the parties; many civil law countries do not have discovery, and business people operate accordingly. Thus, in some instances, an express exclusion of discovery and involuntary witness testimony may be appropriate in the arbitration agreement.

Alternatives for discovery and evidentiary rules and power of the arbitrator to subpoena evidence follow:

a. There shall be no prehearing discovery of any kind, nor shall either party be required to produce documents or witnesses either at or prior to the arbitration hearing.

OR

b. The parties shall be entitled to discover all documents and other information reasonably necessary for a full understanding of any legitimate issue raised in the arbitration. They may use all methods of discovery customary under [federal] [state] law, including but not limited to depositions, requests for admission, and requests for production of documents. The time periods for compliance shall be set by the arbitrator, who may also set limits on the scope of such discovery.

After the appointment of the arbitrator, the parties to the arbitration shall have the right to take depositions and to obtain discovery regarding the subject matter of the arbitration, and, to that end, to use and exercise all the same rights, remedies, and procedures, and be subject to all of the same duties, liabilities, and obligations in the arbitration with respect to the subject matter thereof, as provided in [the California Code of Civil Procedure,] as if the subject matter of the arbitration were pending in a civil action before a [superior] court in [California,] subject to the reservation that depositions for discovery shall not be taken unless leave to do so is first granted by the arbitrator.

OR

c. The arbitrator shall have sole discretion to permit or prohibit discovery.

AND/OR

d. The arbitrator is empowered to issue, on ex parte application of any party or on his own volition, any subpoena (including any subpoena duces tecum) in accordance with any provision of applicable law, and to make such orders as may be necessary for the arbitrator or persons designated by the arbitrator to inspect the premises of either party. Absent contemporaneous and express agreement by the parties, the arbitrator may not designate representatives or employees of one party to conduct or participate in an inspection of the premises of the other.

AND/OR

e. The Federal [or State] Rules of Evidence [or International Bar Association's Supplementary Rules Governing the Presentation and Reception of Evidence in International Commercial Arbitration] shall apply to the proceedings.

(4) Power of Arbitrators: Provisional Relief   💾

Any provisional remedy which would be available to a court of law shall be available from the arbitrator(s) pending arbitration of the dispute. Either party may make an application to the arbitrator seeking injunctive or other interim relief, and the arbitrator may take whatever interim measures they deem necessary in respect of the subject matter of the dispute, including measures to maintain the status quo until such time as the arbitration award is rendered or the controversy is otherwise resolved.

(5) Power of Arbitrators: Remedies   💾

a. The arbitrator shall have the authority to award any remedy or relief that a court of this state could order or grant, including, without limitation, specific performance or any obligation created under the agreement, the awarding of punitive damages, the issuance of an injunction, or the imposition of sanctions for abuse or frustration of the arbitration process.

b. The arbitrator shall have no authority to award punitive damages or any other remedy not measured by the prevailing party's actual damages, and may not, in any event, make any ruling, finding or award that does not conform to the terms of and conditions of the Agreement.

c. The arbitrator shall be empowered to impose sanctions and to take such other actions with regard to the parties as the arbitrators deem necessary to the same extent a judge could, pursuant to the Federal Rules of Civil Procedure, the [California Code of Civil Procedure] and applicable law.

An arbitrator's powers arise directly from the parties' agreement and include the powers specified in the rules of the chosen arbitral regime and in any applicable law. Only the AAA specifically authorizes arbitrators to render "interim," provisional awards prior to, and without prejudice to, final awards. As a matter of practice, ICC tribunals may render "partial" awards prior to final awards. (With partial awards, it is important to indicate clearly that the award does not finally dispose of the matters at issue.) Such awards may be crucial to the protection of deteriorating assets and the ultimate usefulness of the final arbitral award.

In addition, the AAA rules authorize the arbitrator to grant specific performance as a final remedy. While arbitral remedies may theoretically include specific performance or restitution, monetary relief is the form of award granted in the vast majority of cases. Moreover, many civil law countries (notably Japan) do not provide for effective injunctive relief. Thus, empowering an arbitrator to award injunctive relief in another country, and obtaining such relief, may be useless, as the award may not be enforceable as a practical matter. In any event, consider vesting the right to order interim relief in the courts, as opposed to the arbitrator, in instances where rapid relief for deteriorating assets may be required.

Finally, it is now clear that if parties wish to divest an arbitrator of the power to award punitive damages they must explicitly provide for it in the arbitration agreement. *Mastrobuono v. Shearson Lehman Hutton, Inc.*, 514 U.S. 52, 115 S.Ct. 1212, 131 L.Ed.2d 76 (1995).

(6) Access to the Courts for Interim Relief

Even where the arbitrator is empowered to grant interim relief, the process of selecting an arbitrator and other procedural requirements may be slow, thereby threatening an asset's value or otherwise causing irreversible effects. Furthermore, requests for injunctive relief often involve third parties over whom arbitrators do not have any power. The language below allows the parties to request temporary relief from courts.

A party to an arbitration agreement may file an application in any proper court for a provisional remedy in connection with an arbitrable controversy, but only upon the ground that the award to which the applicant may be entitled may be rendered ineffectual without provisional relief.

(7) Stenographic Records

Producing a transcript of the arbitral proceedings may be useful despite the added expense. If an arbitrator must be replaced, the new arbitrator can review the record; civil law legal professionals are more accustomed to documentary evidence; it adds an air of formality and accountability to the proceedings; and it may prove helpful to the lawyers both in summarizing the case and perhaps later in challenging the proceedings (within or without the arbitral regime). AAA and JCAA rules provide for stenographic records upon a party's request. However, the ICC rules do not. Therefore, if using ICC arbitration, include one of the following:

a. Any party wishing to make a stenographic record of the proceedings may do so at its own expense.

OR

b. The initiating party shall make arrangements for the taking of a stenographic record, the expense of which shall be borne equally by both sides.

(8) Time Limits for Decisions and Relief

Many U.S. jurisdictions, as well as arbitral institutions, impose time limits within which the arbitrator must render an award (these periods are generally extendable by mutual agreement of the parties). The parties may also agree to a tighter time frame in the arbitration clause to help ensure a speedy decision. However, imposing a time limit is dangerous and not recommended; it may force too hasty a decision (if the time limit expires, the arbitrator may lose jurisdiction over the matter). In any case, the time limit should not commence until after the hearings close, otherwise a party could cause the time limit to expire by purposefully delaying the procedures.

In the event the arbitrator appointed hereunder has not rendered a decision within ___ days after the conclusion of the hearings, either party may have the matter determined by equitable proceedings or an action for declaratory relief in any court of competent jurisdiction.

(9) Written Opinion

It is our recommendation that the arbitral tribunal be required to document the reasoning upon which the arbitral award is based. Particularly, unless expressly waived, enforcement of the award in Japan and in certain other countries may not be possible without such a written opinion. This requirement reinforces the need for objectivity on the part of the arbitrator (and increases the costs). The parties may also require the arbitrator to issue findings of fact and of law. While courts are unlikely to overturn findings of fact or law, a court can, at times, overturn the award of an arbitrator, and egregiously incorrect findings of fact or law might compel such a result. In addition, having to explain the reasons for the results reached imposes at least some discipline on the arbitrator. We recommend the following:

The arbitrators shall issue a written explanation of the reasons for the award [and a full statement of the facts as found and the rules of law applied in reaching their decision] to both parties.

(10) Interest 🖫

Whether or not the award will include interest depends upon the parties' agreement and the laws governing the arbitration.

Monetary awards shall include interest from the date of breach or other violation of this Agreement to the date when the award is paid in full. The interest rate or rates applied during such period shall be the prime commercial lending rate announced from time to time by _____ at its principal office in [New York City] [plus x%].

(11) Notice 🖫

As noted above, improper notice of the appointment of the arbitrator or the arbitration proceedings is one of the specific grounds listed in the New York Convention upon which a court may base its refusal to enforce an award. Notice in accordance with the Hague Convention should suffice for the commencement of the arbitration, and the notice section should therefore specifically allow for personal delivery. Note that the Japanese courts have thus far approved notice only if it has been given under the Hague Convention. The Japanese courts have not addressed the sufficiency of notice given through the mail or otherwise or where the parties have specifically agreed on other means of notice. While a notice provision is not essential to an arbitration clause, including it by reference may avoid later disputes regarding what constitutes proper notice.

To the extent this Section is deemed a separate agreement, independent from this [Title] Agreement, Sections [concerning governing law, notices, limitations on liability, and attorneys' fees] are incorporated herein by reference.

(12) Fees and Expenses 🖫

In addition to the usual legal fees and expenses of litigation, the parties must also pay the arbitrator's fees and expenses, various physical facility and communication fees, and the arbitral institution's administrative fees. The arbitrator's fee may be fixed at a given level or may be based on the value of the dispute or time committed to its arbitration.

If the parties desire to give the arbitrator the power to award expenses to the prevailing party, it is important expressly to grant this power to the arbitrator, since some arbitral regimes and legal jurisdictions do not allow the arbitrator to award legal expenses absent an agreement of the parties (this may be done by incorporating the legal fees and expenses provision set forth below into the arbitration clause).

Variations:

a. Each party shall pay fifty percent (50%) of the fees and expenses of the arbitrators and the costs of arbitration. Each party shall otherwise pay its own costs and attorneys' fees.

OR

b. The nonprevailing party in the arbitration shall pay the fees and expenses of the arbitrator[s] and the costs of arbitration and the enforcement of any award rendered therein, including the attorneys' fees and expenses of the prevailing party.

OR

c. The arbitrator shall apportion to each party all costs (other than attorneys' fees) incurred in conducting the arbitration in accordance with what he deems just and equitable under the circumstances.

OR

d. If the arbitrator determines that either party has proceeded in bad faith with respect to the subject matter of the arbitration proceedings, then the arbitrator shall require such party to reimburse the other party for the attorneys' fees and out-of-pocket expenses incurred by the other party in connection with the arbitration.

OR

e. To the extent this Section is deemed a separate agreement, independent from this [Title] Agreement, Sections [concerning governing law, notices, limitations on liability, and attorneys' fees] are incorporated herein by reference.

Also, consider adding language paralleling FRCP 11 with respect to the bringing of meritless claims. Finally, whether through the arbitration clause itself or the cost provision that has been incorporated, make sure that "costs and expenses" include all costs and expenses *through* enforcement of judgment.

(13) *Right to Appeal by Appellate Arbitration Panel* 🖫

If either party is dissatisfied with (a) the decision or award rendered by the arbitrator(s) or (b) a less than unanimous decision or award rendered by a panel of three arbitrators, such dissatisfied party may appeal the arbitrator's award to a panel of three appellate arbitrators by filing a notice of appeal with [insert provider] and the other party within 20 days of the filing of the award. [At least one of the arbitra-

tors selected shall be a retired judge.] **The appealing party shall have the right to submit written briefs not to exceed ___ pages stating the reasons why the panel's decision should be reversed or modified. The responding party may file a response within 20 days after receiving the appeal brief, not to exceed 20 pages.**

(14) Right to Judicial Review 🖫

a. The arbitrator(s) shall set forth their findings of fact and conclusions of law and shall render their award based thereon. Upon application by either party to a court for an order confirming, modifying, or vacating the award, the court shall have the power to review

(a) whether the findings of fact rendered by the arbitrator(s) are supported by substantial evidence and

(b) whether, as a matter of law based on such findings of fact, the award should be confirmed, modified or vacated.

Upon such determination, judgment shall be entered in favor of either party consistent herewith.

The above clause is modeled on a scope of review clause enforced in *Fils et Cables d'Acier de Lens v. Midland Metals Corp.*, 584 F.Supp. 240, 243–44 (S.D.N.Y.1984). In that case, the court held that, since it had subject matter jurisdiction to act as a trial court and determine all issues if the parties had not agreed to arbitration, there was no public policy reason not to make the more limited judicial determination which the parties provided for in their arbitration clause. The court further observed that the parties might not have agreed to submit their matter to arbitration without such a broad provision for judicial review. *See also* Gateway Techs., Inc. v. MCI Telecomm. Corp., 64 F.3d 993, 996–97 (5th Cir.1995). *See also* Kyocera Corp. v. Prudential Bache Trade Services Inc., 130 F.3d 884 (9th Cir.1997).

The risk of nonenforcement can be decreased where the court has subject matter jurisdiction in the first instance. It may also be advisable to include the following language:

b. The parties expressly agree that this Agreement shall confer no power or authority upon the arbitrator(s) to render any judgment or award that is erroneous in its application of substantive law and expressly agree that no such judgment or award shall be eligible for confirmation.

The preceding language may act to bootstrap an expanded judicial review provision. However, it is not clear that a court that disagrees with the logic of *Midland Metals* would be any more impressed with a clause that seeks to provide for expanded judicial review under the excess of powers analysis.

(d) Special Considerations Regarding International Arbitration Agreements

At a minimum, arbitration clauses involving parties from more than one nation must clarify (i) language and any translation requirements, (ii) the choice of law, and (iii) location. In practice, location influences the choice of an arbitrator, and may significantly color the proceedings as well as the enforceability of the clause and arbitral award.

(1) Language ▤

Arbitrators under the ICC, UNCITRAL, Stockholm Chamber of Commerce, and LCIA regimes have great discretion with respect to the language of the arbitration. It is therefore wise to specify the language desired in the arbitration clause. Furthermore, the parties should consider providing for translation and the costs of translation, taking into consideration the added time and cost involved. Two translation methods are possible: iterative (consecutive—where the speaker pauses to allow the translator to speak) and simultaneous. Simultaneous translation is significantly faster but usually of far poorer quality. If it is critical for the audience to understand the content of the proceedings, iterative translation may be preferred.

a. The [x] language shall be used in the arbitral proceedings, and all documents, exhibits, and other evidence shall be translated into the [x] language. If party [y] so elects, iterative translation into the [y] language may be provided at [y]'s, cost.

OR

b. If arbitration is to be conducted in [country x], it shall be conducted in [language x], with iterative translation of the proceedings into [language y]. If it is to be held in [country y], it shall be conducted in [language y], with iterative translation into [language x].

(2) Governing Law ▤

To ensure that the arbitrators construe the arbitration clause under the same governing law as that selected for the basic agreement, many standard clauses contain an "incorporation by reference" provision. There have been instances where arbitrators deemed the arbitration clause a separate agreement, and refused to honor the governing law clause of the basic agreement. The governing law clause should refer to the substantive law of the jurisdiction specified, including applicable federal law, and exclude the operation of the choice of law rules of such jurisdiction.

a. To the extent this Section is deemed a separate agreement, independent from this [Title] Agreement, Sections [concerning governing law, notices, limitations on liability, and attorneys' fees] are incorporated herein by reference.

555

If a U.S. state law is to govern the agreement, to deter the federal/state law preemption issue disputes discussed earlier concerning *Volt Information Sciences, Inc. v. Board of Trustees of the Leland Stanford Junior University*, 489 U.S. 468, 109 S.Ct. 1248, 103 L.Ed.2d 488 (1989), it may be helpful to include:

> **b. It is the express agreement of the parties that the provisions of this Section, including the rules of the [arbitral regime] and the laws of [governing state] referenced herein, as modified by the terms of this Section, shall govern the arbitration of any disputes arising pursuant to this Agreement. In the event of any conflict between the law of [governing-law state], the law of the arbitral location, and the U.S. Arbitration Act (Title 9, U.S.C.), with respect to any arbitration conducted pursuant to this Agreement, to the extent permissible, it is the express intent of the parties that the selected governing law, [or, if that law has a weak arbitration code, the parties may prefer federal law], as modified by this Section, shall prevail.**

In negotiating governing law clauses generally in international agreements, parties often agree to the laws of a neutral forum. However, parties should recognize that the application of the laws of a neutral forum may be more harmful to their positions. Furthermore, a court may refuse to hear a suit or to apply its jurisdiction's laws to a dispute because of insufficient contacts.

The parties may prefer to free the arbitrator of the constraints imposed by various legal principles, and instead vest him or her with equitable, Solomon-like powers in determining a resolution of the dispute (recognizing that an arbitrator may do this anyway). This equitable power is termed "amiable composition," and such arbitrators are known as *amiables compositeurs*. Because of the unrestrained power this gives the decision-maker, we strongly advise against its adoption. (Note also that certain jurisdictions do not allow parties to discard substantive legal principles and therefore would not enforce such an award.)

> **c. The arbitrator shall be bound by no substantive law and shall decide in accordance with: ( ) the language of this Agreement, ( ) the usages and customs of the trade in the country of the party claimed to be responsible for taking or failing to take action, and ( ) what is just and equitable under the circumstances.**

(3) Location 💾

Location is as important to arbitration as it is to real estate. Parties must consider practicality and convenience factors (travel time, expense, security, communication facilities, availability of competent lawyers and an arbitral institution's administrative facilities, etc.), home versus neutral sites, as well as legal issues in selecting a location or locations. Further, even though parties choose a governing law in their agreement, the law of the arbitral location generally fills in the gaps and may override the parties' agreement in whole or in part. Local law and custom influences what can be arbitrated, who may conduct the arbitration, how the arbitration is conducted, and the law that may be applied to the contract. Perhaps most importantly, local law significantly affects whether the arbitration award will be enforceable. The New York Convention of 1958 (the "New York Convention") is the strongest enforcement mechanism; the contracting states provide for recognition and enforcement of commercial arbitration agreements and foreign arbitral awards rendered in other contracting States. However, there are several important exceptions in the New York Convention related to the law of the arbitral location, including whether or not that law recognizes the award. See more information below under "Enforceability."

a. The place of arbitration shall be [place], and the award shall be deemed a [country] award for purposes of the Convention on the Recognition and Enforcement of Foreign Arbitral Awards of 1958 (the "New York Convention").

The AAA and the ICC offer administrative services in countries outside the location of their headquarters (the JCAA does not). In addition, the AAA has agreements with approximately 20 foreign arbitral institutions allowing parties to provide for arbitration either in the foreign country under the rules of the foreign arbitral institution, or arbitration in the U.S. under the AAA rules (*e.g.*, the Japan–American Trade Arbitration Agreement of 1952); if the parties cannot agree on a location, a neutral selection body will do so. Note that this mechanism dictates not only the location, but also the applicable arbitral regime. For these inter-association arbitration agreements to apply to a given agreement, the arbitration clause must include the standard language provided in these inter-association agreements (see *The International Arbitration Kit: A Compilation of Basic and Frequently Requested Documents*, published by the AAA (3d ed. 1986).

For example, in U.S.-Japan agreements where the location and arbitral institution are left open:

b. Such dispute or disagreement may, at the demand of either party, be referred to and decided by arbitration in accordance with the Japan–American Trade Arbitration Agreement of September 16, 1952.

The parties may prefer to structure a shoot-out provision which forces the plaintiff to go to the defendant's home location and perhaps also arbitrate under the defendant's home arbitral organization's rules. Using such a procedure may encourage the parties to resolve their differences using other conciliatory methods; however, if the parties are not financial equals, it may be heavily one-sided. If both parties have sufficient economic strength, and the two regimes' rules do not significantly differ, the provision may have no deterrent effect and may only invite the posturing discussed earlier.

c. The arbitration proceedings shall be held in [Home of Party X], under the commercial rules of the [arbitral association headquartered in X's country] in the event that [Party

Y] requests the commencement of such proceedings and in [Home of Party Y] under the commercial rules of the [arbitral association headquartered in Y's country] in the event that [Party X] requests the commencement of such proceedings.

(4) Sovereign Immunity Waiver, etc. ▣

Some systems of law prohibit a state or state agency from entering into an arbitration agreement (*e.g.*, Saudi Arabia, Belgium, and Luxembourg); no language in the agreement can solve this problem. In addition, sovereign immunity may prevent the enforcement of an award. To mitigate the risk that sovereign immunity will block enforcement, a waiver provision should be included. The provision below contains such a waiver along with language relating to the New York Convention discussed earlier.

a. The Government hereby represents and warrants that it is a signatory to the Convention on the Recognition and Enforcement of Foreign Arbitral Awards, done at New York June 10, 1958 (the "Convention"), and that an award in arbitration can be enforced in the courts of the [country], the United States, or any other signatory nation. The Government hereby agrees that for purposes of the Convention and otherwise, the relationship between the parties pursuant to this Agreement is commercial in nature, and that any disputes between the parties related to this Agreement shall be deemed commercial. The Government hereby unconditionally waives, and agrees not to plead or claim, immunity from jurisdiction on the ground of sovereignty or otherwise from any judicial or arbitration proceedings, or from execution of any judgment to enforce any arbitration decision hereunder.

If the country has a Consul General:

b. The Government irrevocably appoints the person now or in the future acting as or discharging the function of the Consul General of [country] in New York, New York, as its agent to receive, on behalf of it and its property, service of the summons and complaint and any other process that may be served in any action. Nothing in this Section shall affect the right of either party to serve legal process in any other manner permitted by law or affect the right of any party to bring any action or proceeding against the other or its property in the courts of any other jurisdiction.

(5) Enforceability of Award ▣

Providing for judicial recognition and enforcement of the arbitral award is obviously necessary to the ultimate usefulness of an arbitration agreement but is frequently overlooked in the drafting of the clause. The need for a full investigation of the requirements of enforcement prior to drafting the arbitration clause cannot be overemphasized. Arbitration agreements, and foreign arbitral awards that comply with the New York Convention, generally qualify for international recognition and enforcement. However, there are several important qualifications to the New York Convention, including the following: (i) two-thirds of the signatory countries restrict the New York Convention's application to awards rendered by other signatory states (the "reciprocity requirement"); (ii) signatory states may restrict enforcement to contracts which the laws of such states consider "commercial" in nature (approximately a third do so); (iii) the dispute must be arbitrable under the agreement itself, the governing law of the agreement, the arbitral location, and the enforcement location; (iv) the parties must have had legal capacity to enter into the arbitration agreement; (v) the proceedings must have met certain due process related requirements (*e.g.*, the party against whom enforcement is being sought must have received proper notice of the arbitrator's appointment and of the arbitration proceedings—see Article V of the New York Convention); (vi) the composition of the panel must have complied with the parties' agreement or the law of the arbitral location; and (vii) recognition or enforcement of the award cannot be contrary to the public policy of the country in which enforcement is being sought.

Note that notwithstanding the New York Convention, certain jurisdictions have differing requirements for enforceability (written opinion, etc.), and agreeing upon certain actions in advance, such as seeking judicial confirmation of an award in the United States, may assist in enforcement. In addition to the New York Convention, other bilateral and multilateral treaties exist which may be used to secure recognition and enforcement of arbitration clauses and arbitral awards. The first provision or the second provision below should be used to assist in enforcement; the standard AAA-suggested clause includes similar judicial enforcement language; the ICC and JCAA standard clauses do not have any enforcement language. While courts may likely have this power anyway, the language is suggested for arbitrations that will occur in the U.S., to mitigate the argument that its omission indicates that the parties intended to eliminate all court procedures. *See* Domke, Commercial Arbitration (revised ed., 1985) at p. 76, *quoted in* Redfern and Hunter, International Commercial Arbitration (1986) at 122.

a. An award rendered in connection with an arbitration pursuant to this Section shall be final and binding upon the parties, and any judgment upon such an award may be entered and enforced in any court of competent jurisdiction.

b. The parties agree that the award of the arbitral tribunal will be the sole and exclusive remedy between them regarding any and all claims and counterclaims between them with respect to the subject matter of the arbitrated dispute. The parties hereby waive all jurisdictional defenses in connection with any arbitration hereunder or the enforcement of an order or award rendered pursuant thereto (assuming that the terms and conditions of this arbitration clause have been complied with).

c. The parties hereby agree that for purposes of the New York Convention, the relationship between the parties is commercial in nature, and that any disputes between the parties related to this Agreement shall be deemed commercial.

Also, consider having the parties waive defenses arising from Article V(1)(a) of the New York Convention (enforceability of the underlying agreement and agreement to arbitrate). Finally, for enforcement in Japan, waive defenses arising under Article 801(4)-(5) of the Japanese Code of Civil Procedure requiring examination of the party against whom the award was made and a written statement of the reasons for the award.

The parties may wish to specify the jurisdiction where the award may be enforced; although this is not technically necessary in disputes where States are signatories to the New York Convention, at least when attempting to enforce an award in Japan it would be wise to have the award confirmed in a State that the Japanese courts have held grants reciprocal treatment to Japanese judgments. The same is true for Korea. California, New York, and Washington, D.C., among others, fall into this same category.

d. With respect to any order issued by the arbitrator(s) pursuant to this Agreement, the parties expressly agree and consent (i) to the bringing of an action by one party against the other in the federal courts of either to enforce and confirm such order; (ii) that such order shall be conclusive proof of the validity of the determination(s) of the arbitrator(s) underlying such order; and (iii) that either the [ ] or any federal court sitting in either [ ] or [ ] may enter judgment upon and enforce such order, whether pursuant to the New York Convention, the U.S. Arbitration Act, or otherwise.

Clients should be informed, with respect to Japan, that enforcement of a foreign (*e.g.*, U.S.) award *may* take as long as 10–13 years if the other party contests the award to the highest levels of the Japanese court system. (*See Burroughs Corporation v. T. Chung* (1086 Hanrei Jiho 97), which took 8 years to obtain a final judgment in Japan for a United States district court judgment.) With *no* appeals, the process may still take anywhere from 8–50 months, depending on the circumstances, to obtain a final determination in Japan of enforceability.

CHAPTER 10

JOINDER, CONSOLIDATION, AND SEVERANCE

by
Wayne E. Babler, Jr.
and
Peter C. Karegeannes*

Table of Sections

* The authors had assistance from Brian W. Blanchard and Sarah E. Coyne, of Quarles & Brady, Madison, Wisconsin, and from James M. Brennan and Cory L. Nettles, of Quarles & Brady, Milwaukee, Wisconsin.

WESTLAW Electronic Research

See WESTLAW Electronic Research Guide preceding the Summary of Contents.

---

§ 10.1 Scope Note

Multiple claims, counterclaims, and parties are common in business litigation. What claims must or can be asserted, and what parties must or should be joined are issues of law. Joinder, consolidation/separation and severance are procedural rules in the Federal Rules of Civil Procedure, offering considerable latitude for both sides but also mandating certain decisions. Rule 18 of the Federal Rules is directed to joinder of claims and remedies, Rules 19 and 20 are directed to joinder of persons, Rule 21 concerns misjoinder of parties and severance of claims, and Rule 42 concerns consolidation of actions and separate trials of claims.

These Rules, in addition to their legal requirements, present opportunities for implementing strategies to obtain advantages over the other parties and to satisfy the business interests of the litigant. One obvious example of strategy under these Rules: avoid having to bring into a suit persons who the client, for business reasons, wishes to avoid, by asserting claims which do not require that person's participation. There are other obvious examples and more which are subtle but potentially very important to the business interest being represented. Where parties abuse the procedures authorized by the liberal policies of these Rules, happily these same Rules include procedures intended to assure that the litigation can be efficiently resolved without sacrificing justice.

In this chapter an approach is offered for identifying the practical and legal questions presented in business litigation by joinder, consolidation and severance; practical considerations are discussed, and the basic principles of the controlling Federal Rules are reviewed. (The substantive law, while obviously of central importance to the decisions being made, is left to other chapters.) It is not realistic nor even possible to present an exhaustive or authoritative checklist of practical problems other than as raised by the Rules themselves, because such practical problems will vary from client to client and case to case. The discussion below includes typical considerations to the choices available and the legal limitations to joinder, consolidation and severance.

Library References:

West's Key No. Digests, Federal Civil Procedure ⚬⚬8, 81–86, 201–267, 1953–1965.
Wright, Miller, Kane & Cooper, Federal Practice and Procedure: Civil 2d §§ 1362, 1460, 1582, 1585, 1589, 1603, 1605, 1606, 1652, 3914.20.

§ 10.2 Identifying the Legal and Strategic Issues

A business client reports that an unethical competitor is stealing the client's business by hiring away key personnel who know everything about the company's business, including its finances, pricing, customers, suppliers, new product development plans, and manufacturing methods; if not stopped immediately, the client insists, the business will soon be destroyed. Or, the client has just received a summons and complaint containing what the client describes as outrageous and scandalous allegations about patents being infringed that are only intended to interfere with the client's efforts to get an important contract just as the contract is about to be awarded. Business disputes, simple or complex, present legal and practical issues requiring decisions at the outset of the litigation.

Identifying the legal and practical issues raised by a business dispute is essential to arriving at appropriate strategies early in the game, whether on starting legal proceedings or responding to them. Business disputes come in infinite different forms, but early identification of issues and the practical considerations relevant to them can be systematic. Below is such an approach appropriate for plaintiffs and defendants.

Of course, it must be recognized that because the parties have different goals, their strategies will often be in conflict, but the Rules are like chessmen on a board, each with prescribed moves. Nonetheless, the considerations presented here can be useful not only for initial litigation decisions, but for subsequent decisions on the same subject of joinder, consolidation and severance.

(a) The Case Analysis Memorandum

A well thought out and comprehensive case analysis memorandum is a perfect tool for early identification of legal options and strategic considerations of joinder, consolidation and severance. This living document, continuously updated throughout the litigation as circumstances may dictate, should include sections containing,

(i) a list of possible causes of action available arising out of the facts, along with a description of the legal elements to each cause of action and the legal authority;

(ii) a list of all possible parties on either side of the controversy, including additional parties for counterclaims and cross-claims, and identification of possible indispensable parties;

(iii) a list of the client's business needs, ranked according to the client's priorities; and

(iv) a list of practical considerations of the client.

The importance of this process is no less because the party being represented is a defendant. A defendant needs to examine the plaintiff's pleading to determine what joinder issues are potentially present, and it has issues of joinder related to possible defenses, counterclaims, cross-claims, and third-party claims. If the client has been forewarned of imminent suit, counsel will give attention to the legal options open to the client and may conclude to strike first, even if only in the form of a declaratory judgment action. Joinder of claims and parties is a matter of choices and requirements under the Federal Rules, and there are advantages to exploit and disadvantages to avoid. Armed with such a case analysis memorandum, trial counsel, no matter what party is represented, can begin to address issues of joinder, consolidation and severance, from both legal and practical perspectives.

(b) Making Choices of Claims and Parties—Practical Considerations

Federal Rule 18(a) permits a party to join "as independent or as alternate claims, as many claims . . . as the party has. . . ." This authorization is intentionally broad, and historically the courts have strongly encouraged joinder of all potential claims.[1]

It is noteworthy that Rule 18(a) does not make any distinction among the various claims assertable based upon the party's position as plaintiff, counterclaim plaintiff, or cross-claim or third-party plaintiff, no doubt because of the expressed judicial interest in having the whole case tried at one time.[2] Thus, subject to some limitations, it is established federal judicial policy that resolution of all claims, including counterclaims and cross-claims, in one proceeding be encouraged.[3]

Similarly, Rule 20, which authorizes joinder of "all persons" as plaintiffs "if they assert any right to relief jointly, severally, or in the alternative," and "all persons" as defendants "if there is asserted

§ 10.2

1. United Mine Workers of America v. Gibbs, 383 U.S. 715, 724–25, 86 S.Ct. 1130, 1138–39, 16 L.Ed.2d 218 (1966).

2. Hargrave v. Oki Nursery, Inc., 646 F.2d 716, 719 (2d Cir.1980).

3. See Federal Deposit Ins. Corp. v. Loube, 134 F.R.D. 270, 272 (N.D.Cal.1991). Of course, in view of the doctrine of claim preclusion barring claims in a second action which should have been asserted in an earlier action, it is essential for counsel to consider all related claims. See Chapter 12 "Issue and Claim Preclusion," infra.

against them jointly, severally, or in the alternative, any right to relief in respect of or arising out of the same transaction, occurrence," etc., offers wide latitude in party selection, subject to those circumstances where parties are required to be joined under Rule 19.

Liberal though these Rules may be, it is not necessarily desirable to assert all claims or to include all potential parties, either because doing so creates other legal problems such as subject matter or personal jurisdiction problems as evident from a discussion of these Rules below, or because they have practical consequences such as unwanted delay, expense, intrusive discovery, inefficiencies of the legal process, or unwanted disruption to business relationships or transactions. All parties have particular interests which may be, and in all likelihood are, competing interests. Through the Rules on severance, separate trials and consolidation, these interests can be sorted out. The judicial process is only efficient if the parties want it to be efficient. The Federal Rules offer tools to advance efficiency while also assuring fairness and justice.

Subject to the requirements and limitations of Rules 18, 19 and 20, a strategy behind choosing claims and parties or seeking consolidation or severance is driven by business considerations of the client. Once the legal choices are identified, business considerations bear on the decisions to be made, and there are many. These considerations include:

- Relief needed by the client—the client's needs, whether it be a money judgment, injunctive relief, or both; objectives in the litigation, collectibility of judgments and adequacy of preliminary and/or permanent injunctive relief

- Time—speed of the process to final resolution; avoiding depletion of resources in a battle over personal jurisdiction with unessential parties

- Financial burden—avoidable disruption of business relationships, attorneys' fees, witnesses' fees, travel expenses, expert witnesses' fees

- Management burden—attention required of the client's employees, particularly senior management

- Scope of discovery—intrusion into financial, production, manufacturing, engineering and other confidential areas of the client's business; difficulties expected in getting discovery from other parties.

- Settlement—enhancing early settlement favorable to the client

- Persuasion—telling a powerful story to the court or opposing counsel; opting for multiple defendants who will have to fight among themselves on a key issue

- Notoriety—sensitivity to the cost of publicity

These considerations are factors in every business litigation, and they often are in conflict. A discussion of each of them will illustrate how they can influence decisions not just about joinder of claims and parties, but even about how to draft a pleading.

Relief needed by the client is a logical initial practical consideration. The client has a business problem and it necessarily compels the questions, what claim will entitle the client to this vital relief, and who should be parties in order to get it?

There are often disadvantages to including superfluous claims, such as, perhaps, joining a party beyond the jurisdictional long-arm of the preferred federal district court. But there are also more subtle potential disadvantages.

For example, seldom does a client want to sue the hand that feeds it, such as an important vendor, and customer, or a lender. In such a case the party can opt to limit the claims it pursues to those which do not require dragging into the fracas such a party. A plaintiff, content with enforcement of a noncompete or confidentiality agreement with a former employee, might consider resisting the temptation of joining the new employer with various claims like inducing breach of contract and theft of trade secrets if the only practical effect is to add a defendant prepared to use its deep-pocket resources to fight on every front. Or, perhaps the plaintiff would be better off suing the new employer, a large unpopular corporation, for piracy and the like, seeking injunctive relief to stop use of the former employee in certain positions, while omitting the former employee if he, sitting at defense counsel table and with his wife and children sitting in chairs right behind him and who has a pretty good story to tell about unfair employment harassment practices, is likely to enjoy considerable sympathy. If the claim or party is not needed for adequate relief, ask the question: why include it?

Time is an important consideration, especially where a monetary judgment cannot make the party whole or where the litigation has unquantifiable costs such as damage to business relationships. Delay means added expense and prolonged uncertainty. As claims are "piled on" and parties are added, the case grows in legal, procedural and managerial complexity. Discovery takes on a life of its own. Few courts can be expected to bring such cases under control and, more typically, these cases just sit for years until the parties tire. Few plaintiffs want delay, but some defendants may see their interests served by adding claims. If adding claims means unwanted delays, why add them, and if the other side adds them, should severance or separate trials be sought as a means of restoring efficiency?

Financial burdens are increased as a result of many events in litigation, some controllable and some not controllable. At the outset the plaintiff has an opportunity to maintain control at least to the extent of decisions over claims to be brought and parties to be joined. For defendants who are the subject of abuse by a plaintiff business which is using the litigation process to maximize the financial burden of litigation on a small defendant, or for the small plaintiff who finds that the simple contract case is being turned into a major legal war with counterclaims and cross-claims by deep-pocketed resourceful business parties, the Rules have the provisions for keeping the financial burden under some measure of control, at least theoretically. For any party, the prospect of multiple parties in the litigation, each with a team of attorneys ready to demand probing, costly discovery and to file motions, is discouraging, and especially so for the small business. An action for wrongful termination of a dealership under a state fair dealership statute might be brought in a federal court based upon diversity jurisdiction, often with statutory provisions for a preliminary injunction and recovery of attorneys' fees; but increase the ante with charges of antitrust violations, and the financial burdens will skyrocket for expert witnesses, expanded discovery and endless motions. Maybe less is more.

Management burden cannot be underestimated in business litigation. Count on it. Senior management will frequently have to be involved, not just in the policy decisions respecting the case, but in providing evidence and submitting to discovery demands. Actions related to noncompete and confidentiality agreements may not seem likely to command much management attention, but throw in claims like antitrust violations, racketeering, and other complicated claims, and senior management on both sides will likely be drawn into the case on issues such as relevant market, competition, damages, conspiracy, and the like.

Controlling discovery is a most challenging task for trial counsel in virtually all business litigation, and this needs to be factored into strategies from the very start of the case. Neither side relishes the notion that the parties' secrets about finances, customers, prices, profits and profit margins, costs of goods sold, manufacturing, engineering, product development, and so on will be open to discovery. And, few business clients are easily convinced that Rule 26(c) protective orders provide adequate protection against misuse of discovered confidential information.

Settlement early in litigation is always the hope of both parties, and both sides will likely spend a great deal of energy trying to posture for a good settlement position. The selection of claims and parties can have an impact, and consolidation and severance can have an impact. Strategy for obtaining an advantageous early settlement may favor asserting all serious meritorious claims rather than selected claims and adding parties rather than opting to include only one or two, never mind the complexity or added burden, if the potential risk to the other side is too great to bear or if this is the only way to impress upon the other side the commitment and resolve of your client.

Persuasion is what drives the trial counsel's decision-making processes. The powerful story in a pleading can be the beginning point, whether the audience is intended to be opposing counsel, the management of the opposing party, or the court. Claims might be joined as a technique of persuasion in order to get a good settlement or even just to allow the court to quickly obtain a sense of what the clash is all about. Rule 8 instructs that the pleading be a "short and plain statement of the claim showing that the pleader is entitled to relief," but nothing says that the statement must be dry, boring, or devoid of passion. A well written complaint or counterclaim with strong claims joined in a recitation of a compelling story of conspiracy, interference with business relationships and monopolizing markets, might get the attention of a CEO who otherwise has little interest in the litigation of a company subsidiary or division. If Rule 18 permits the joinder, and if getting the attention of a CEO is important strategically, join the claims in the telling of the full story.

A plaintiff corporate subsidiary has filed a frivolous suit for patent infringement in order, the defendant insists, to interfere with the defendant's efforts to obtain a government contract on which bids are being taken. The defendant is a small, independent competitor with nowhere near the resources of the plaintiff. But the defendant, which is on a sure track to being awarded the coveted the contract worth huge sums of money, is faced with the distinct possibility of losing the contract just because the allegations put into jeopardy whether the defendant will ever be able to deliver on the contract. The defendant could seek immediate peace through some settlement arrangement, but this is blackmail. It is a terrible position for the defendant, but the defendant feels that it has the staying power and is insistent that plaintiff pay if the contract is not awarded to defendant. A bland counterclaim for malicious prosecution[4] or violation of the antitrust laws, has no chance of being seriously considered by the other side. But a counterclaim and third-party complaint bringing the parent into the case directly as a third-party defendant with a pleading which tells a compelling story of what is happening might well get the plaintiff's CEO's attention. It will certainly get the attention of opposing counsel and it might prove even more valuable as a means of educating the trial judge about the case. Or, perhaps the pleading would be even more effective in getting attention if filed in a different federal district as a separate suit, naming the parent corporation alone, to reduce the risk of consolidation upon motion of the plaintiff in the first action. Persuasion is an important part of pleading, to be put to early advantage.

Notoriety is an unquantifiable but often dreaded price that the claimant or the opposing side might ultimately pay. A plaintiff for business reasons may not wish to draw attention to itself yet feel compelled to file suit to protect its interests. The choice of claims or parties can affect the likelihood of notoriety and the nature of that notoriety. Of course, there is always the client that insists on the assertion of claims for the notoriety that the client perceives will hurt the opposing party; this consideration needs to be tempered by a careful look at applicable rules of professional conduct. But the practical consid-

---

4. While often a claim for malicious prosecution is asserted by way of counterclaim, this is improper under state common law because of the absence of a final judgment in the maliciously prosecuted action. *See, e.g.,* Shwab v. Doelz, 229 F.2d 749, 753 (7th Cir.1956); Aetna Cas. & Sur. Co. v. Kellogg, 856 F.Supp. 25, 28–29 (D.N.H. 1994); North Triphammer Development Corp. v. Ithaca Associates, 704 F.Supp. 422, 428 (S.D.N.Y.1989); Merrill Lynch Futures, Inc. v. Miller, 686 F.Supp. 1033, 1044 (S.D.N.Y.1988); Zappala v. Hub Foods, Inc., 683 F.Supp. 127, 131 (W.D.Pa.1988); Federal Sav. and Loan Insur. Corp. v. C & J Oil Co., Inc., 632 F.Supp. 1296, 1298 (W.D.Va. 1986); Donovan v. Gingerbread House, Inc., 536 F.Supp. 627, 631–32 (D.Colo.1982); Redman Industries, Inc. v. Tower Properties, Inc., 517 F.Supp. 144, 154 (N.D.Ga. 1981).

eration is present in any case since the courts are open to the public, news media routinely look at court records, and business customers, vendors, suppliers, and competitors seem well informed and are quick to use any information to advantage. A strategy which minimizes the chance of unwanted notoriety may well have substantial importance when considering the legal choices available.

These practical considerations do not dictate the same decisions. Faced with a plurality of claims, some allowing for injunctive relief and some for lost profits damages, some allowing for treble recovery or punitive damages, and some allowing for recovery of attorneys' fees, the decision of joining claims and parties in the first instance and of consolidation or severance later should be premised on a strategy that meets with the client's interests and is most likely to achieve the client's goals efficiently. Exotic antitrust claims may get attention but at too high a cost in terms of intrusive discovery, financial burden and management burden. A limited wrongful dealer termination action may have a small cost but not get attention of senior management. Suing a former employee in order to make an impression on other employees may have short term value but this is all lost if the former employee has such sympathy as to win a preliminary injunction motion. Suing on a claim that gets the desired attention but which makes a favored customer or vendor a necessary party has the same result as shooting one's self in the foot—causing nothing but pain.

While the Rules will control what claims must be pursued at the cost of later claim preclusion and what parties must be joined, the client's objectives in business litigation will determine which claims should be pursued, and which claims might be avoided if business interests or litigation strategies are favored by doing so.

Library References:

West's Key No. Digests, Federal Civil Procedure ⊙8, 81–86, 201–267, 1953–1965.

Wright, Miller & Kane, Federal Practice and Procedure: Civil 2d §§ 1362, 1425, 1434–1436, 1585, 1589.

§ 10.3   Federal Rule 18—Joinder of Claims

Rule 18 broadly states:

A party asserting a claim to relief as an original claim, counterclaim, cross-claim, or third-party claim, may join, either as independent or as alternate claims, as many claims, legal, equitable, or maritime, as the party has against an opposing party.

In the seminal case of *United Mine Workers of America v. Gibbs*,[1] the Supreme Court explained that "the impulse is toward entertaining the broadest possible scope of action consistent with fairness to the parties;

§ 10.3

1. 383 U.S. 715, 86 S.Ct. 1130, 16 L.Ed.2d 218 (1966). The common law pendent jurisdiction doctrine, the subject of this case, was superseded by 28 U.S.C.A. § 1367, enacted in 1990. Whalen v. Carter, 954 F.2d 1087, 1097 n. 10 (5th Cir.1992).

joinder of claims, parties and remedies is strongly encouraged."[2] Although Rule 18 is, therefore, liberal, it must be kept in mind that claims may be severed and proceeded with separately,[3] or they may be separated for trial by the same or a different jury.[4]

There are limitations to Rule 18 as a result of common law, federal jurisdictional and venue requirements[5] and Federal Rules applicable to specific pleadings.[6]

(a) Claims Which Must Be Joined—A Common Law Limitation

FRCP 18 encourages but does not require that claims be joined.[7] However, the doctrine of res judicata, or claim preclusion, may apply to claims not asserted in a prior litigation, if they are based upon facts which arise out of the same transaction or occurrence that is the subject of the prior litigation, irrespective that the legal theory may differ.[8] The tests for claim preclusion may vary, but most often courts apply a "transactional" standard: whether the second lawsuit is based on the same transaction or the same underlying facts as the prior lawsuit.[9] Claim preclusion is discussed in Chapter 12 "Issue and Claim Preclusion," *infra*.

(b) Joinder of Claims in the Complaint and the Diversity Jurisdiction Requirement

The subject matter jurisdiction of the district court is fixed by statute and is not expanded by Rule 18. When jurisdiction is based upon 28 U.S.C.A. § 1332(a), diversity of citizenship, joinder of claims will not present a problem where there is one plaintiff and one defendant and claims in the aggregate equal the requisite amount in controversy, or where there are multiple plaintiffs with claims which are common and undivided, and the claims in the aggregate equal the requisite amount.[10] If there are multiple plaintiffs with separate and distinct claims, or there are claims which are not asserted by all plaintiffs against all defendants, then the amount in controversy requirement must be satisfied separately for those claims.[10.1] If, however, there are claims which are not asserted

2.   383 U.S. at 724, 86 S.Ct. at 1138.

3.   FRCP 21, *see infra* § 10.6.

4.   FRCP 42(b), *see infra* § 10.8.

5.   Rule 82: "These rules shall not be construed to extend or limit the jurisdiction of the United States district courts or the venue of actions therein...."

6.   *See, e.g.*, FRCP 8, 9.

7.   Commercial Box & Lumber Co., Inc. v. Uniroyal, Inc., 623 F.2d 371 (5th Cir. 1980).

8.   *See* Expert Elec., Inc. v. Levine, 554 F.2d 1227, 1234 (2d Cir.1977), *cert. denied*,

434 U.S. 903, 98 S.Ct. 300, 54 L.Ed.2d 190 (1977).

9.   Aunyx Corp. v. Canon U.S.A., Inc., 978 F.2d 3, 6–7 (1st Cir.1992). *See generally*, Chapter 12 "Issue and Claim Preclusion," *infra*.

10.   Shanaghan v. Cahill, 58 F.3d 106, 109 (4th Cir.1995); Troy Bank, Indiana v. G.A. Whitehead & Co., 222 U.S. 39, 40–41, 32 S.Ct. 9, 9–10, 56 L.Ed. 81 (1911).

10.1   Zahn v. International Paper Co., 414 U.S. 291, 294–95, 94 S.Ct. 505, 38 L.Ed.2d 511 (1973) (the holding in *Zahn* is

by all plaintiffs against all defendants, then the amount in controversy requirement must be satisfied separately for those claims. Plaintiffs bringing cases in state courts may use a strategy intended to avoid federal jurisdiction,[11] but this is a subject beyond the scope of this chapter.[12]

(c) Joinder of Claims in the Complaint and the Federal Question Jurisdiction Requirement

Where jurisdiction depends on 28 U.S.C.A. § 1331, federal question jurisdiction, joinder of state claims to the federal question claim is subject to the district court's supplemental jurisdiction controlled by 28 U.S.C.A. § 1367, unless otherwise allowed by specific statute[13] (previous to the statute, such joinder was subject to the court's pendent jurisdiction). Section 1367 grants the court supplemental jurisdiction "over all other claims that are so related to claims in the action within such original jurisdiction that they form part of the same case or controversy under Article III of the United States Constitution."

In the case analysis memorandum discussed in Section 10.2(a), *supra*, causes of action have been listed which may include both federal claims and state claims. A federal claim might offer the potential for a large treble damage recovery but its technical elements might not be so easily established. For example, in restraint of trade cases, injury to competition is often very difficult to prove. More certain state claims can be an essential part of the strategy to intensify pressure on the other side, maximize the likelihood of success and minimize cost through a single lawsuit. If the state claims fall within the court's supplemental jurisdiction, serious consideration to including the claim is warranted.

In *MCI Telecommunications Corp. v. Teleconcepts, Inc.*,[14] the Third Circuit stated that Section 1367 had three requirements: (1) the federal claim must have substance sufficient to confer subject matter jurisdiction on the court; (2) the state and federal claims must derive from a common nucleus of operative facts; and (3) the claims must be such that they would ordinarily be expected to be tried in one judicial proceeding.[15]

in question in view of the enactment of 28 U.S.C.A. § 1367 in 1990). *See* Free v. Abbott Lab. (*in re* Abbott Lab.), 51 F.3d 524, 529 (5th Cir. 1995); Bernard v. Gerber Food Prods. Co., 938 F.Supp. 218, 223–24 (S.D.N.Y. 1996).

11. For example, a plaintiff might pursue claims over which the only basis for federal jurisdiction is diversity of citizenship, and elect to sue in a state court of a state where a defendant resides to avoid removal, *see* 28 U.S.C.A. § 1441(b) (West 1994), or it may join nondiverse parties and sue in state court. *But see* Grassi v. Ciba–Geigy, Ltd., 894 F.2d 181 (5th Cir.1990) (an assignment of a nominal interest in the cause of action to destroy diversity deemed ineffective).

12. *See* Chapter 1 "Subject Matter Jurisdiction," *supra*.

13. *See, e.g.*, 28 U.S.C.A. § 1338(b) (West 1993): "The district courts shall have original jurisdiction of any civil action asserting a claim of unfair competition when joined with a substantial and related claim under the copyright, patent, plant variety protection or trade-mark laws."

14. 71 F.3d 1086 (3d Cir.1995)

15. *Id.* at 1102. Prior to enactment of § 1367, joinder of state claims to a federal question action was allowed under the judi-

The federal question claim must be substantial, but this does not mean that it must be successful;[16] if the federal question claim, even though eventually dismissed, states a cause of action upon which relief can be granted and is not frivolous, the court's jurisdiction over the state claims remains.[17]

Joinder of state and federal questions claims in any action where jurisdiction depends only on federal questions is not a matter of right. The plaintiff may find its interests better served by joining the state claims, but if the defendant, as a matter of its own strategy, wishes to force plaintiff to pursue two lawsuits at the same time, one in federal court and one in state court, or to forego a meritorious state court claim, it can challenge the joinder by appropriate motion under Rule 12. Section 1367(c) authorizes the district court to decline exercising supplemental jurisdiction over state claims where novel or complex issues of state law are raised by the claim, the state claim "substantially predominates" over the federal question claim, the federal question claim is dismissed, or there are other exceptional circumstances. Thus, within the limits of these considerations and considerations of efficiency, fairness to the parties and exigent circumstances, supplemental jurisdiction rests within the district court's sound discretion. *See* Chapter 1 "Subject Matter Jurisdiction," *supra*.

(d) Joinder of Claims and The Venue Requirement

Claims cannot by joined under Rule 18 without regard to the venue limitations of the district court controlled by 28 U.S.C.A. § 1391. An action based upon the court's diversity jurisdiction may be brought (1) in a judicial district where any defendant resides, if all defendants reside in the same state, (2) in "a judicial district in which a substantial part of the events or omissions giving rise to the claim occurred, or a substantial part of property that is the subject of the action is situated," or (3) in a district in which any defendant is subject to personal jurisdiction. If venue is based upon the second circumstance, then only those claims in

---

cial doctrine of pendent jurisdiction which also applied these factors. *See* United Mine Workers of America v. Gibbs, 383 U.S. 715, 86 S.Ct. 1130, 16 L.Ed.2d 218 (1966). However, prior to enactment of § 1367, the district court had discretion to recognize other factors in deciding not to apply pendent jurisdiction. By the enactment of § 1367, Congress defined the exclusive means for a court to decline jurisdiction over claims. *See* Executive Software North America, Inc. v. U.S. Dist. Court for Cent. Dist. of California, 24 F.3d 1545, 1555 (9th Cir.1994).

16. Wal–Juice Bar, Inc. v. Elliott, 899 F.2d 1502 (6th Cir.1990); Brady v. Brown, 51 F.3d 810 (9th Cir.1995).

17. *See, e.g.,* Shanaghan v. Cahill, 58 F.3d 106, 109–11 (4th Cir.1995), and Mizu-

na, Ltd. v. Crossland Federal Sav. Bank, 90 F.3d 650, 654–55 (2d Cir.1996) (in determining whether to retain supplemental jurisdiction, the district court may consider convenience and fairness to parties, underlying federal policy issues, comity and judicial economy); Channell v. Citicorp Nat. Services, Inc., 89 F.3d 379, 386 (7th Cir. 1996)(it is within the district court's discretion to determine whether "compelling" and "exceptional" circumstances warrant that it decline supplemental jurisdiction); Sta–Rite Industries, Inc. v. Allstate Ins. Co., 96 F.3d 281, 285–86 (7th Cir.1996) (the federal court will not allow "contortion of pleadings" by plaintiff to maintain jurisdiction).

which a substantial part of the events or omissions giving rise to them occurred may be joined.

The plaintiff may wish to adopt a litigation strategy which has claims and parties in the correct court, but it may choose to ignore the defect, awaiting the response of the defendant. Joining claims for which the selected venue is improper, is not fatal to the court's authority to act, because objection to venue can be waived if not asserted.[18] A defendant may be content to waive the defect as to one claim as a matter of economy for itself, or it may anticipate that a second lawsuit will be inevitable if it raises the venue objection, probably with a motion to transfer right back to the original court anyway. A plaintiff could consider whether another district could avoid the problem for all defendants, or it could omit the claim or party where venue is defective, but there is little reason not to test the defendant's resolve by going forward with the claim and letting the defendant make the next move. Venue will not be a problem in the case of supplemental jurisdiction under 28 U.S.C.A. § 1367(a), assuming that venue with respect to the federal question claim is proper. *See* Chapter 3 "Venue, Forum Selection and Transfer," *supra*.

(e) Counterclaims, Cross–Claims, and Third–Party Claims

Rule 18 makes no distinction between plaintiffs and defendants. Thus, Rule 18 authorizes joinder of claims whether they be in the complaint, the counterclaim, cross-claim, or third-party complaint, and the above discussion applies equally to such pleadings. However, the right and conditions to asserting counterclaims, cross-claims, and third-party claims are not the subject of Rule 18, but Rules 13 and 14.[19]

(1) Counterclaims

A defendant is required under Rule 13(a) to assert "any claim which at the time of serving the pleading the pleader has against any opposing party, if it arises out of the transaction or occurrence that is the subject matter of the opposing party's claim and does not require for its adjudication the presence of third parties of whom the court cannot acquire jurisdiction." Such compulsory counterclaims do not need to have an independent jurisdictional basis. But failure to assert the claim carries no penalty except the loss of the right to assert the claim in any other action.

Rule 13(b) authorizes counterclaims against an opposing party "not arising out of the transaction or occurrence that is the subject matter of the opposing party's claim." Previous to enactment of Section 1367, permissive counterclaims were required to have independent federal jurisdictional basis.[20] The Seventh Circuit Court of Appeals has held,

---

18. FRCP 12(h)(1).

19. *See supra* §§ 6.12 and 6.13 and Chapter 7 "Third–Party Practice."

20. Valencia v. Anderson Bros. Ford, 617 F.2d 1278, 1290 (7th Cir.1980), *rev'd on other grounds*, 452 U.S. 205, 101 S.Ct. 2266, 68 L.Ed.2d 783 (1981). (The court observed

however, that a district court should look to the rule for supplemental jurisdiction under 28 U.S.C.A. § 1367 and not decide that it lacks jurisdiction simply because the counterclaim, lacking a basis for federal court jurisdiction alone, was permissive.[21] While this authority suggests that the "permissive"/"compulsory" counterclaim distinction is no longer the dispositive inquiry, reported cases since the Seventh Circuit decision have not supported the interpretation.[22] For the business litigant assessing the appropriateness of asserting a Rule 13(b) counterclaim, if there is no independent jurisdictional basis, perhaps the better strategy is to take the plaintiff to state court, rather than spend money on a legal theory that has a serious likelihood of eventually failing.

(2) Cross-Claims

Rule 13(g) authorizes a cross-claim against a co-party for any claim "arising out of the transaction or occurrence that is the subject matter either of the original action or of a counterclaim therein or relating to any property that is the subject matter of the original action." Rule 18 does not alter this rule, but, under Rule 18(a), a party asserting a proper Rule 13(g) cross-claim may join any unrelated, independent claim it has against an opposing party.[23] Whether the cross-claim can be asserted without independent subject matter jurisdiction, is controlled by 28 U.S.C.A. § 1367.[24] Plaintiffs may welcome open litigation warfare between defendants, but if this causes prejudice to plaintiff such as undue delay or confusion, plaintiff can seek severance under Rule 21 or bifurcation under Rule 42(b).[25]

that § 1367 represents a congressional intent that supplemental jurisdiction be broader than the previous doctrines of ancillary jurisdiction as to counterclaims and pendent jurisdiction as to joined claims that it replaced.).

21. Channell v. Citicorp Nat. Services, Inc., 89 F.3d 379, 385 (7th Cir.1996).

22. In *Keegan v. Bloomingdale's Inc.*, 945 F.Supp. 165 (N.D.Ill.1996), the district court ruled that a breach of contract and conversion counterclaim to a COBRA violation claim lacked even a "loose factual connection," much less "a common nucleus of operative fact." In another circuit, a district court rejected the view of the Seventh Circuit in *Channell*, 89 F.3d at 385 and remained true to the original rule. Blue Dane Simmental Corp. v. American Simmental Ass'n, 952 F.Supp. 1399, 1406–08 (D.Neb. 1997). If the requirement of § 1367(a) respecting claims "that are so related to the claims in the action within such original jurisdiction that they form part of the same

case or controversy ... ," is intended to be the same standard as in Rule 13(a) for compulsory counterclaims that a claim which "arises out of the transaction or occurrence that is the subject matter of the opposing party's claim" be joined, then § 1367(a) would not alter the previously accepted rule regarding permissive counterclaims which do not arise out of the same transaction or occurrence.

23. First Nat. Bank of Cincinnati v. Pepper, 454 F.2d 626, 635 (2d Cir.1972) (dismissed unrelated cross-claim reinstated after Rule 13(g) cross-claim erroneously dismissed on summary judgment was reinstated).

24. Allen v. City of Los Angeles, 92 F.3d 842, 846 (9th Cir.1996) (district court did not abuse discretion in exercising jurisdiction over state law indemnity cross-claim remaining following verdict on federal claims brought pursuant to 42 U.S.C.A. § 1983).

25. *See infra* at §§ 10.6(d), 10.8.

(3) Third-Party Claims

A third-party complaint may be served under Rule 14(a) by a defendant third-party plaintiff against another "who is or may be liable to the third-party plaintiff for all or part of the plaintiff's claim against the third-party plaintiff." If the court has jurisdiction of the main action between the original parties, it has supplemental jurisdiction over the Rule 14(a) third-party claim "without regard to whether there is an independent basis of jurisdiction."[26] Pursuant to Rule 18(a), other claims can be added, but such other claims must have independent jurisdictional bases or fall within the court's supplemental jurisdiction under 28 U.S.C.A. § 1367.[27] The third-party complaint does not open the door for the original plaintiff to assert state claims even though arising out of the same transaction or occurrence directly against the third-party defendant, absent an independent basis for jurisdiction, despite the rules for ancillary jurisdiction, because 28 U.S.C.A. § 1332 requires complete diversity and ancillary jurisdiction cannot be used to circumvent this requirement.[28] At the outset, plaintiff will want to assess all these options available not only to itself but to those who are to be potential defendants. Third-party practice can be not only exceedingly complex but certainly very costly. When warfare among defendants slows progress or adds cost, Rule 42(b) offers the plaintiff some avenue to bring order out of chaos.

Library References:

West's Key No. Digests, Federal Civil Procedure ☞81–86.
Wright, Miller & Cooper, Federal Practice and Procedure: Civil 2d § 3964.

§ 10.4 Joinder of Parties—The Indispensable Party

The criteria under FRCP 19 for determining who must be joined as a party are pragmatic with an emphasis on the effect on the parties to the litigation.[1] Perhaps the most succinct statement of the interrelation-

26. King Fisher Marine Service, Inc. v. 21st Phoenix Corp., 893 F.2d 1155, 1158 (10th Cir.1990) (district court's ancillary jurisdiction encompassed not only pass-through third-party claim, but also additional claim for delay damages despite absence of independent basis of jurisdiction). *But see* Aetna Cas. & Sur. Co. v. Spartan Mechanical Corp., 738 F.Supp. 664 (E.D.N.Y.1990) (district court lacked subject matter jurisdiction over third-party claims for indemnification and contribution against nondiverse party).

27. Schwab v. Erie Lackawanna R. Co., 438 F.2d 62, 71 (3d Cir.1971) (railroad sued under FELA for injuries sustained in train-truck accident could make third-party claim for contribution and indemnification against driver and owner of truck involved in accident).

28. Owen Equipment & Erection Co. v. Kroger, 437 U.S. 365, 371, 98 S.Ct. 2396, 2401, 57 L.Ed.2d 274 (1978) (plaintiff may not defeat statutory requirement of complete diversity simply by suing diverse parties and waiting for them to implead nondiverse defendants). *See* Chapter 7 "Third–Party Practice," at § 7.5(b), *supra*.

§ 10.4

1. Challenge Homes, Inc. v. Greater Naples Care Center, Inc., 669 F.2d 667 (11th Cir.1982) (holding that corporate plaintiff's former president and board chairman was not an indispensable party where existing parties with real interests in the matter could be granted complete relief in his absence).

ship between Rule 19(a) and 19(b) was enunciated by the Fourth Circuit. Rule 19(a) sets out whether a person is a "necessary" party; and Rule 19(b) set out whether that person is an "indispensable" party. Only necessary persons can be indispensable, but not all necessary persons are indispensable.[2]

Determining whether an absent person satisfies Rule 19(a) is discussed in Section 10.4(b), *infra*. If Rule 19(a) is satisfied, the absent party must be joined if joinder is feasible. If joinder is not possible because the court would lack personal or subject matter jurisdiction over him, only then does Rule 19(b) discussed in Section 10.4(c), *infra*, become relevant.[3]

"Indispensable" is conclusory. In the words of the Advisory Committee Notes, " ... [A] person is 'regarded as indispensable' when he cannot be made a party and, upon consideration of the factors [noted in Rule 19(b)], it is determined that in his absence it would be preferable to dismiss the action, rather than to maintain it."[4]

A defense of failure to join a party indispensable under Rule 19 may be made in a motion to dismiss (*see* FRCP 12(b)(7)), in any pleading, by motion for judgment on the pleadings, or at trial (*see* FRCP 12(h)(2)). Under FRCP 21, a person may be added as a party at any stage of the action. In complex business litigation, a party contemplating raising the issue of indispensability may wish to defer a decision until the lawsuit has been more fully developed through discovery. This often allows for a more focused and persuasive presentation of the issues Rule 19 presents.

(a) The Roles of State and Federal Law

In a diversity case, in assessing whether a nonparty must be joined, state law determines what interest the nonparty has; but given such state law defined interests, whether a federal court may proceed without the nonparty is a federal matter.[5]

For example, in deciding whether a partnership, whose joinder would destroy diversity in an action among the members of the partnership, was indispensable, the court applied state law in concluding that the partnership had property interests that were implicated by the litigation.[6] However, the court applied federal law in balancing the interests and concluding that the partnership was not indispensable,

---

2. Schlumberger Industries, Inc. v. National Sur. Corp., 36 F.3d 1274, 1285–86 (4th Cir.1994) (held that joinder of *all* insurers who issued policies to insured was mandated in an action regarding an insured's response costs under CERCLA).

3. Burger King Corp. v. American Nat. Bank and Trust Co. of Chicago, 119 F.R.D. 672, 675 (N.D.Ill.1988) (subtenant was an indispensable party in tenant's action against landlord seeking declaration of rights and obligations under leases, but subtenant's joinder was not feasible because it would defeat diversity jurisdiction).

4. FRCP 19, Advisory Committee Note.

5. Provident Tradesmens Bank & Trust Co. v. Patterson, 390 U.S. 102, 123 n. 22, 88 S.Ct. 733, 745 n. 22, 19 L.Ed.2d 936 (1968).

6. HB General Corp. v. Manchester Partners, L.P., 95 F.3d 1185, 1192–93 (3d Cir.1996) (applying Delaware law).

even if the result would be different under state joinder law.[7]

Similarly, the payee of a note whose presence would have defeated diversity jurisdiction was held not to be indispensable under federal law. Among the factors relied on by the court was its determination, based on the application of state law, that the payee's liability was not joint but, rather, was separate and distinct from that of those who were already parties.[8]

(b) Determining Whether Party Should Be Joined

FRCP 19(a) sets forth two alternative grounds for determining whether a person "shall be joined as a party in the action" assuming that the person is subject to service of process and that joinder will not defeat subject matter jurisdiction (*see* Section 10.(4)(d), *infra*). The disjunctive nature of clauses (1) and (2) of Rule 19(a) should be respected; thus, any party whose absence results in the problems identified in *either* subsection "is a party whose joinder is compulsory if feasible," requiring the discretionary determination called for by Rule 19(b).[9]

(1) Rule 19(a)(1)

A person shall be joined if "in the person's absence complete relief cannot be accorded among those already parties." If there are no procedural or jurisdictional bars to joining a party who should be joined under Rule 19(a), the Rule requires joinder.[10] The court looks to the pleadings as they appear at the time of the proposed joinder.[11]

Rule 19(a)(1) requires an inquiry which is "limited to whether the district court can grant complete relief to the persons already parties to the action. The effect a decision may have on the absent party is not material."[12] This commonly turns, in effect, on whether the plaintiff(s) can recover everything that is being sought from those already named.

In a declaratory judgment action filed by certain insurers to determine coverage issues involving their insureds' environmental law obligations, Section 19(a)(1) required the joinder of additional insurers to enable the court to adjudicate the coverage issue as to the entirety of the insureds' obligations.[13] On the other hand, a plaintiff, who was one of the beneficiaries of a voting trust and sought only damages for herself for the alleged breaches of fiduciary duty under a voting trust agree-

---

7. *Id.* at 1195.

8. Inland–Western Inv. Co. v. Winkler Realty Corp., 65 F.R.D. 515 (S.D.N.Y.1975) (applying New York law).

9. Janney Montgomery Scott, Inc. v. Shepard Niles, Inc., 11 F.3d 399, 405 (3d Cir.1993).

10. Schutten v. Shell Oil Co., 421 F.2d 869, 873 (5th Cir.1970) (lessor in action against lessee oil company for eviction and accounting deemed indispensable party who could not be joined requiring dismissal).

11. Faloon v. Sunburst Bank, 158 F.R.D. 378, 380 (N.D.Miss.1994).

12. Janney Montgomery Scott, Inc., 11 F.3d at 405 (second of two co-obligors under investment banking agreement not a party whose joinder is required because complete relief may be granted in suit against only one of them).

13. Schlumberger Industries, Inc. v. National Sur. Corp., 36 F.3d 1274, 1286–87 (4th Cir.1994).

ment, was not required by Rule 19(a)(1) to join two other beneficiaries of the voting trust who were also allegedly damaged.[14]

If it is "not clear" whether complete relief can be accorded among those already parties, at least one court has concluded that Rule 19(a)(1) is satisfied.[15]

(2) Rule 19(a)(2)

Rule 19(a)(2) specifies the criteria governing the second alternative ground for determining whether, assuming jurisdiction, a person "shall be joined." Subdivision 19(a)(1) aside, joinder is required if:

(2) the person claims an interest relating to the subject of the action and is so situated that the disposition of the action in the person's absence may (i) as a practical matter impair or impede the person's ability to protect that interest or (ii) leave any of the persons already parties subject to a substantial risk of incurring double, multiple, or otherwise inconsistent obligations by reason of the claimed interest.

Note that 19(a)(2) has two criteria, both of which must be satisfied. The first is that the absent person must claim "an interest relating to the subject of the action." As discussed in Section 10.4(a), *supra*, state law is applied to determine whether the absent party has such an interest. If that criterion is satisfied, the analysis moves to a consideration of 19(a)(2)(i) or (ii).[16]

Cases which have addressed this "interest" element make clear that it is rarely troublesome. One district court accurately observed that "[c]ourts generally have avoided coming to grips with the [interest] problem by either assuming arguendo that the absent person is necessary and moving directly to the 'indispensability' test, or by disposing of the Rule 19(a) inquiry under another aspect of the subsection."[17]

Interests "relating to the subject of the action" have been held to include outright owners and beneficial owners of voting trust stock,[18] an income beneficiary of a testamentary trust allegedly mishandled by the trustee,[19] and a partnership in whose favor ran an obligation of the defendant partner to provide capital, which was the basis of the plaintiff partners' suit,[20] and persons in addition to parties to a contract whose rescission is being sought who have a substantial interest in the contract.[21] The interest of a parent corporation in a defendant subsidiary

---

14. Pulitzer–Polster v. Pulitzer, 784 F.2d 1305, 1309 (5th Cir.1986). (Note that the Rule 19(a)(2) test may require joinder, however, as discussed in § 10.4(b)(2), *infra*.).

15. H & H Intern. Corp. v. J. Pellechia Trucking, Inc., 119 F.R.D. 352, 353 (S.D.N.Y.1988).

16. Janney Montgomery Scott, Inc., 11 F.3d at 406.

17. Burger King Corp. v. American Nat. Bank and Trust Co. of Chicago, 119 F.R.D. 672, 676 (N.D.Ill.1988).

18. Pulitzer–Polster, 784 F.2d at 1310.

19. Faloon v. Sunburst Bank, 158 F.R.D. 378, 381 (N.D.Miss.1994).

20. HB General Corp. v. Manchester Partners, L.P., 95 F.3d 1185, 1190 (3d Cir. 1996).

21. Naartex Consulting Corp. v. Watt, 722 F.2d 779, 788 (D.C.Cir.1983).

has been held not to be such an interest.[22] Nonetheless, subtleties in interpretation have occasionally arisen.

One case focused on what it called the " 'subject matter' prong of the 'interest relating to the subject matter of the action' requirement."[23]

The court observed that Rule 19(a)(2) requires only that the absent party have an interest "relating to the subject matter of the action," not an interest in the action.[24] In the court's view, this "subject matter" prong confers Rule 19(a)(2) status on "absent persons with legally protected interests which could be affected by the lawsuit, but who have no legal rights vis-a-vis their adversaries in the action."[25] The court's effort reflects an inclination to take a pro-joinder approach to the Rule 19(a)(2) issue.

If the absent person satisfies the "interest" test, the analysis moves to a consideration of the impact resulting from a disposition in that person's absence. Joinder is required if the absent person "is so situated that the disposition of the action in the person's absence may (i) as a practical matter impact or impede the person's ability to protect that interest or (ii) leave any of the persons already parties subject to a substantial risk of incurring double, multiple, or otherwise inconsistent obligations by reason of the claimed interest."[26]

Rule 19(a)(2)(i) focuses on the impact on the absent person, Rule 19(a)(2)(ii) on those already parties.[27] These are alternatives. Consequently, if either is satisfied concerning an absent person who has the required interest discussed above, joinder is required; and the analysis moves to a consideration of the factors listed in Rule 19(b) discussed in Section 10.4(c), *infra*.

The possible settings in which either subdivision (2)(i) or 2(ii) might be met are legion and the analysis is very fact-sensitive. Great latitude for reasoned creativity exists. Case law is generally of use here only if one finds a case involving facts close to one's own. Otherwise it is best to focus one's efforts on developing the facts and law regarding the following factors, which the courts have found the most important in applying (a)(2)(i) and (ii).

Under (a)(2)(i), the principles of res judicata or collateral estoppel are key. If a judgment in the suit would have a legally preclusive effect on the absent person, joinder is required if feasible.[28] However, issue

---

22. La Chemise Lacoste v. General Mills, Inc., 53 F.R.D. 596 (D.Del.1971), *aff'd*, 487 F.2d 312 (3d Cir.1973).

23. Burger King Corp. v. American Nat. Bank and Trust Co. of Chicago, 119 F.R.D. 672, 675 (N.D.Ill.1988).

24. *Id.* at 676.

25. *Id.* (sublessee has interest in the premises which was the subject matter of the dispute and was within Rule 19(a)(2), even though not a party to the lease and may have had no rights under it).

26. FRCP 19(a)(2)(i) and (ii).

27. Challenge Homes, Inc. v. Greater Naples Care Center, Inc., 669 F.2d 667, 670 (11th Cir.1982).

28. Janney Montgomery Scott, Inc. v. Shepard Niles, Inc., 11 F.3d 399, 409 (3d Cir.1993) (recognizing that if issue preclusion or collateral estoppel could be invoked against the absent party in other litigation, Rule 19(a)(2)(i) would require joinder if feasible); Aguilar v. Los Angeles County, 751 F.2d 1089, 1092 (9th Cir.1985) (affirm-

preclusion must be more than just possible. One must show that "some outcome of the federal cases that is reasonably likely can preclude the absent party ... under standard principles governing the effect of prior judgments."[29] However, the absence of a preclusive effect does not end the matter.[30] Something less than being bound by the judgment will suffice. For example, interference with the collection of royalties,[31] a cloud on title to real estate,[32] and prejudice to the ownership and control of stock[33] have been held to be enough.

The possibility that a decision may be "persuasive precedent" or may permit the use of the doctrine of stare decisis against the interests of the absent party has been held sufficient in some cases,[34] but not in all.[35]

The Fifth Circuit, at least where an arguably similar state court action is also pending in which the person absent in the federal action is a party, appears to have acknowledged "that the establishment of a negative precedent can provide the requisite prejudice to the absentee."[36] Yet, comparing the state and federal suits may enable one to avoid the application of (a)(2)(i) by demonstrating that the suits are so different "that any federal precedent established would be inapplicable to the state suit."[37] Where no other suit was pending, one district court disposed of the issue by assessing the likelihood of another suit and concluding that joinder was not required.[38]

Even if the absent party's interest may be impaired or impeded, one may still be able to avoid (a)(2)(i) by demonstrating that an existing party will adequately represent the absent party's interests (where, for example, their interests are aligned), or by persuading the court that the absent party's decision not to intervene indicates that it does not consider its interests "substantially threatened by the litigation."[39]

The role the absent party played in the activities giving rise to the suit should also be explored. If that party was an "active participant" in those activities, (a)(2)(i) may be satisfied[40] and joinder required. Such a

ing dismissal of parent's action to recover premajority damages for child's injuries for failure to join child where child's action for postmajority damages might be collaterally estopped if parents were unsuccessful).

29. Janney Montgomery Scott, Inc., 11 F.3d at 409.

30. Provident Tradesmens Bank & Trust Co. v. Patterson, 390 U.S. 102, 110, 88 S.Ct. 733, 738, 19 L.Ed.2d 936 (1968).

31. Schutten v. Shell Oil Co., 421 F.2d 869 (5th Cir.1970).

32. Id.

33. Haas v. Jefferson Nat. Bank of Miami Beach, 442 F.2d 394 (5th Cir.1971).

34. Janney Montgomery Scott, Inc., 11 F.3d at 407; Pujol v. Shearson/American Exp., Inc., 877 F.2d 132, 136 (1st Cir.1989).

35. Acton Co., Inc. of Massachusetts v. Bachman Foods, Inc., 668 F.2d 76, 78 (1st Cir.1982).

36. Pulitzer–Polster v. Pulitzer, 784 F.2d 1305, 1310 (5th Cir.1986).

37. Id.

38. Faloon v. Sunburst Bank, 158 F.R.D. 378, 381 (N.D.Miss.1994).

39. See Burger King Corp. v. American Nat. Bank and Trust Co. of Chicago, 119 F.R.D. 672, 678–79 (N.D.Ill.1988)(discussion of factors).

40. Haas v. Jefferson Nat. Bank of Miami Beach, 442 F.2d 394, 398 (5th Cir.1971) (absent party involved in conversion of plaintiff's stock); Whyham v. Piper Aircraft Corp., 96 F.R.D. 557, 561 (M.D.Pa.1982)

party's ability to protect his resulting interest in the suit may otherwise be impaired or impeded.

If joinder is not required under Rule 19(a)(1) and 19(a)(2)(i), then 19(a)(2)(ii) must be considered. It provides for joinder if the absent person "is so situated that the disposition of the action in the person's absence may . . . (ii) leave any of the persons already parties subject to a substantial risk of incurring double, multiple, or otherwise inconsistent obligation by reason of the claimed interest."

Rule 19(a)(2)(ii) focuses on those already parties.[41] The phrase "substantial risk" in (a)(2)(ii) has lead to the conclusion that joinder was not required because it was unlikely that the absent party would seek legal redress against a present party at a later time. The chance or possibility that this might occur is not enough;[42] the possibility must be "real," not "unsubstantiated or speculative."[43] The key factors here are an assessment of the substantiality of the absent party's claim and a determination as to whether the absent party would be concerned that his interest would likely be adversely affected by the relief sought.

In cases involving joint tortfeasors or co-obligors on a contract who may be jointly and severally liable, it is also not enough for joinder under (a)(2)(ii) that a person already a party defendant if found liable, may have a claim for indemnification or contribution against the absent party.[44] A party defendant who has such a claim against the absent person may implead that person under FRCP 14; and, if the party chooses not to use impleader, it may bring a separate action for contribution or indemnity.[45] In addition, the possibility that the party defendant may bear the whole loss, assuming it is unsuccessful in a separate indemnification or contribution action, is not "double liability" within the meaning of (a)(2)(ii).[46]

An impleaded claim by a defendant under Rule 14 is ancillary and can proceed despite the lack of complete diversity. A plaintiff's claims against a third-party defendant, however, must have an independent jurisdictional basis.[47] Thus, proper joinder of an impleaded party does not deprive the court of subject matter jurisdiction under Rule 19(a).

Determining whether an existing party is subject to the prejudice (a)(2)(ii) addresses often requires careful and detailed analysis. This is especially so in complicated cases. For example, joinder of absent parties

---

(absent parties were owner and maintainer of plane involved in crash).

41. Challenge Homes, Inc. v. Greater Naples Care Center, Inc., 669 F.2d 667, 670 (11th Cir.1982).

42. Klockner Stadler Hurter Ltd. v. Insurance Co. of State of Pennsylvania, 785 F.Supp. 1130, 1133 (S.D.N.Y.1990).

43. Faloon v. Sunburst Bank, 158 F.R.D. 378, 381 (N.D.Miss.1994).

44. Field v. Volkswagenwerk AG, 626 F.2d 293, 298 (3d Cir.1980) (joint tortfeasors); Janney Montgomery Scott, Inc. v.

Shepard Niles, Inc., 11 F.3d 399, 412 (3d Cir.1993) (co-obligors).

45. Janney Montgomery Scott, Inc., 11 F.3d at 412; Challenge Homes, Inc. v. Greater Naples Care Center, Inc., 669 F.2d 667, 671 (11th Cir.1982) (absent party allegedly breached fiduciary duty to plaintiff).

46. Janney Montgomery Scott, Inc., 11 F.3d at 411, 412.

47. Challenge Homes, 669 F.2d at 671 n. 5.

was required where one suit involved a shareholder's individual claims and the other involved shareholder derivative claims,[48] and where not all claimants to the defendant's stock were plaintiffs.[49]

An analysis not only of the claims and theories involved or potentially involved in the present and any later or currently pending action but also of their consequences on those already parties is far more important than the likely futile search for controlling case authority. This analysis should include a consideration of whether respective juries "might proportion liability differently or make contradictory findings of fact resulting in inconsistent obligations."[50] This requires a careful parsing of the factual issues in the case to identify those as to which contrary jury findings would lead to different results or as to which different juries would give different reasons, such as those involving comparisons of fault.

If a state court action already exists, a later federal action may, in certain cases, subject the federal defendants to "needless multiple litigation" which may satisfy (a)(2)(ii), even if they face no substantial risk of multiple or inconsistent obligations.[51]

(c) Determining Whether Joinder Is Feasible

FRCP 19(b) provides:

(b) Determination by Court Whenever Joinder not Feasible. If a person as described in subdivision (a)(1)-(2) hereof cannot be made a party, the court shall determine whether in equity and good conscience the action should proceed among the parties before it, or should be dismissed, the absent person being thus regarded as indispensable. The factors to be considered by the court include: first, to what extent a judgment rendered in the person's absence might be prejudicial to the person or those already parties; second, the extent to which, by protective provisions in the judgment, by the shaping of relief, or other measures, the prejudice can be lessened or avoided; third, whether a judgment rendered in the person's absence will be adequate; fourth, whether the plaintiff will have an adequate remedy if the action is dismissed for nonjoinder.

If an absent party is a person who should be joined under Rule 19(a) but cannot be because he is not subject to service of process or his joinder will defeat diversity jurisdiction, Rule 19(b) addresses whether the court should dismiss the action or proceed without him. In the

---

48. Pulitzer–Polster v. Pulitzer, 784 F.2d 1305 (5th Cir.1986) (held: two remaining shareholders indispensable because defendant might face double liability as result of a federal suit if they were not joined as plaintiffs).

49. Haas v. Jefferson Nat. Bank of Miami Beach, 442 F.2d 394 (5th Cir.1971) (defendant faced threat of inconsistent obligations if other claimant was not joined).

50. Whyham v. Piper Aircraft Corp., 96 F.R.D. 557, 561 (M.D.Pa.1982).

51. Angst v. Royal Maccabees Life Ins. Co., 77 F.3d 701, 706 (3d Cir.1996); Whyham, 96 F.R.D. at 561 (although court may not have deemed an "unnecessary second suit" sufficient to require joinder absent other concerns generated by other aspects of Rule 19(a)).

language of the Supreme Court, "a court does not know whether a particular person is 'indispensable' until it [has] examined the situation [by applying the Rule 19(b) factors] to determine whether it can proceed without him."[52]

The four criteria listed in Rule 19(b) for determining whether, in equity and good conscience, the court should proceed without a person who cannot be made a party will be discussed in turn. The rule "does not accord a particular weight to any of them."[53] Some factors will be "substantive, some procedural, some compelling by themselves, and some subject to balancing against opposing interests."[54] The factors overlap and are not intended to exclude considerations applicable in particular situations.[55]

(1) Prejudice to the Person or Those Already Parties

The assessment of to what extent a judgment rendered in the person's absence might be prejudicial to the person or those already parties has consistently, since the Supreme Court's decision in *Provident Tradesmens Bank & Trust Co. v. Patterson*, tracked the considerations established by Rule 19(a)(2)(i) and (ii)[56] discussed in Section 10.4(b), *supra*. Some courts, while not expressly making a reference back to (a)(2)(i) or (ii), assess the same concerns. These include, as to those already parties, subjecting them to sole responsibility for possibly shared liability, recognizing their interest in having liability decided consistently as to all alleged wrongdoers, or avoiding a second action or the possibility of inconsistent verdicts.[57] As to absent parties, their being bound by findings in the action, while often dispositive as to this factor if present,[58] is not required.[59] Other concerns as to absent parties include the impact of negative precedent on them, at least in jurisdictions where this is recognized as a type of prejudice under Rule 19,[60] the impact of

52. Provident Tradesmens Bank & Trust Co. v. Patterson, 390 U.S. 102, 119, 88 S.Ct. 733, 743, 19 L.Ed.2d 936 (1968).

53. Angst, 77 F.3d at 706.

54. Provident Tradesmens, 390 U.S. at 118, 88 S.Ct. at 742.

55. FRCP 19, Advisory Committee Notes.

56. *E.g.*, Haas v. Jefferson Nat. Bank of Miami Beach, 442 F.2d 394, 399 (5th Cir. 1971) (dismissing action for failure to join person who may claim title to stock certificates that were at issue, given the prejudice that might result), citing Provident Tradesmens; Faloon v. Sunburst Bank, 158 F.R.D. 378, 382 (N.D.Miss.1994) (no prejudice found because absent party who was trust beneficiary unlikely to commence litigation later against defendant trustee).

57. Schlumberger Industries, Inc. v. National Sur. Corp., 36 F.3d 1274, 1287 (4th Cir.1994)(complete relief to insured was not possible in declaratory action for some in-

surers relating to insured's liability under CERCLA in absence of all insurers that issued policies to insured); Whyham v. Piper Aircraft Corp., 96 F.R.D. 557, 562 (M.D.Pa.1982) (defendant would be prejudiced by being judged solely responsible for a liability it possibly shared); Pasco Intern. (London) Ltd. v. Stenograph Corp., 637 F.2d 496, 503, 505 (7th Cir.1980)(absent party not indispensable based on prejudice to defendant corporation where inconsistent verdicts in later litigation could be avoided by impleader and collateral estoppel).

58. Aguilar v. Los Angeles County, 751 F.2d 1089, 1094 (9th Cir.1985).

59. Provident Tradesmens Bank & Trust Co. v. Patterson, 390 U.S. 102, 110, 88 S.Ct. 733, 738, 19 L.Ed.2d 936 (1968).

60. Pulitzer–Polster v. Pulitzer, 784 F.2d 1305, 1313 (5th Cir.1986).

injunctive relief or damage to business reputation (for example, where fraud or RICO activity is alleged), particularly where the absent person is not an agent of the party,[61] the impact of a judgment having the effect of adjudicating a claim of ownership,[62] whether the absent person's interests are adequately represented by the parties (*i.e.*, are his or her interests substantially aligned with the interests of present parties),[63] and whether the absent person could intervene under FRCP 24(a).[64]

(2) *The Extent to Which Prejudice Can Be Lessened or Avoided*

By its terms, this factor encourages flexible remedy shaping as to either present parties or the absent person, or both, to lessen or avoid any prejudice identified in the consideration of the first factor just discussed. The greater the potential prejudice in a given case, the more important it is to focus on the ameliorative possibilities of remedy shaping.

Remedy shaping may include enjoining the partners who are parties from suing later on behalf of the absent partnership or requiring the general partner to cause the partnership to release certain claims as a condition of judgment.[65] In some cases, it may be too difficult to shape relief because the parties disagree about the nature or importance of the interests of the absentee.[66] This prospect is far more likely in complex business litigation, because the typical range of subtleties makes agreement on that front unlikely.

The wording of a judgment for money might make clear that plaintiffs are entitled only to those damages that relate to them and not to the damages of an absent person.[67]

One court has noted that "the phrase 'other measures' includes measures open to the defendant to avoid any prejudice [to it],"[68] such as by adding absent parties under FRCP 14 and 13(h).

---

61. Pasco Intern. (London) Ltd. v. Stenograph Corp., 637 F.2d 496, 501–02 (7th Cir.1980) (no cognizable prejudice to absent engineer based on potential injunctive relief against defendant corporation in plaintiff's action against corporations with which plaintiff's former engineer entered in exclusive agency agreement).

62. Schutten v. Shell Oil Co., 421 F.2d 869, 874 (5th Cir.1970) (unjoined party would be prejudiced despite technically retaining ownership interest where royalty interest would cease).

63. HB General Corp. v. Manchester Partners, L.P., 95 F.3d 1185, 1193 (3d Cir. 1996) (absent partnership's interests were adequately represented by the partners); H & H Intern. Corp. v. J. Pellechia Trucking, Inc., 119 F.R.D. 352, 354 (S.D.N.Y.1988).

64. Thunder Basin Coal Co. v. Southwestern Public Service Co., 104 F.3d 1205, 1211 (10th Cir.1997) ("we specifically hold that an entity or individual subject to impleader ... and entitled to intervene ... is never an indispensable party").

65. HB General Corp., 95 F.3d at 1191–92.

66. H & H Intern Corp., 119 F.R.D. at 354.

67. Faloon v. Sunburst Bank, 158 F.R.D. 378, 382 (N.D.Miss.1994).

68. Pasco Intern. (London) Ltd. v. Stenograph Corp., 637 F.2d 496, 504 (7th Cir. 1980).

Where the litigation involves conflicting claims of ownership, however, remedy shaping to protect the ownership claims or interests of an absent party probably cannot be achieved.[69] In these circumstances, the fundamental nature of the ownership issue does not permit much flexibility.

(3) Whether a Judgment Rendered in the Person's Absence Will Be Adequate

The Supreme Court has read this factor as referring to "the interest of the courts and the public in complete, consistent and efficient settlement of controversies[,]" *i.e.*, a "public stake in settling disputes by wholes, whenever possible[.]"[70] This puts the focus on the prospects for other or duplicative litigation.[71]

Courts after *Provident Tradesmens Bank & Trust Co. v. Patterson* have also, however, observed the close relationship between this third factor and the Rule 19(a)(i) analysis discussed in Section 10.4(b)(1), *supra*, which addresses whether "in the person's absence complete relief [can] be accorded among those already parties."[72] Without repeating the earlier discussion, it is important to note that most courts have done little more in analyzing this 19(b) factor than refer to their own earlier analyses of 19(a)(i),[73] or to make a relatively conclusory statement that this factor is satisfied based on an earlier discussion of Rule 19(a) in which later litigation was deemed probable.[74]

Consequently, like the first Rule 19(b) factor, a court's conclusion as to this third factor will often be driven, if not determined, by conclusions reached in its Rule 19(a) analysis.

(4) Adequacy of Plaintiff's Remedy if the Action Is Dismissed

According to the Supreme Court, "the strength of this interest obviously depends upon whether a satisfactory alternative forum exists [for the plaintiff]."[75]

The court's inquiry here is whether plaintiff could pursue its claims against present parties and the absent party in state court,[76] or in the courts of plaintiff's home country where the absent persons were not U.S. citizens.[77] If so, this fourth factor is satisfied.

---

69. Schutten v. Shell Oil Co., 421 F.2d 869, 875 (5th Cir.1970).

70. Provident Tradesmens Bank & Trust Co. v. Patterson, 390 U.S. 102, 111, 88 S.Ct. 733, 739, 19 L.Ed.2d 936 (1968).

71. *E.g.*, Schlumberger Industries, Inc. v. National Sur. Corp., 36 F.3d 1274, 1288 (4th Cir.1994); Schutten, 421 F.2d at 875.

72. Schlumberger Industries, Inc., 36 F.3d at 1288; Burger King Corp. v. American Nat. Bank and Trust Co. of Chicago, 119 F.R.D. 672, 679 (N.D.Ill.1988).

73. Haas v. Jefferson Nat. Bank of Miami Beach, 442 F.2d 394, 399 (5th Cir.1971);

Faloon v. Sunburst Bank, 158 F.R.D. 378, 382 (N.D.Miss.1994).

74. Whyham v. Piper Aircraft Corp., 96 F.R.D. 557, 560–61 (M.D.Pa.1982).

75. Provident Tradesmens Bank & Trust Co., 390 U.S. at 109, 88 S.Ct. at 738.

76. *E.g.*, Pasco Intern. (London) Ltd. v. Stenograph Corp., 637 F.2d 496, 500 (7th Cir.1980); Angst v. Royal Maccabees Life Ins. Co., 77 F.3d 701, 706 (3d Cir.1996).

77. Whyham, 96 F.R.D. at 563.

Discussion of this factor in the cases is usually relatively summary,[78] or extends no further than an assertion that all desirable parties or absent persons can be sued in a particular state court,[79] or that a state court is just as convenient or has no less expertise.[80]

How long the federal or any state court action has been pending is relevant to assessing the strength of the plaintiff's interest in a federal forum or the adequacy of plaintiff's remedy in state court. The relatively brief pendency of a federal action against the background of a five-year old state court action militated in favor of dismissal of the federal action.[81] Where, on the other hand, only a few weeks remained before trial, the "remedy in state court would be inadequate."[82]

It has been said that the availability of an alternative state forum is not, "standing alone, ... a sufficient reason [for dismissal].... To outweigh the plaintiff's choice some additional interest of the absent person, the other parties or the judicial system must be found."[83] Where, however, the plaintiff has an "adequate remedy" because of an existing state court action involving all the parties plaintiff desires in the federal action, this fourth factor "is dispositive."[84]

(d) Service of Process, Jurisdiction and Party Alignment

The second and third sentences of Rule 19(a) provide:

"If the person has not been so joined, the court shall order that the person be made a party. If the person should join as a plaintiff but refuses to do so, the person may be made a defendant, or, in a proper case, an involuntary plaintiff."

Under the second sentence, if an absent person described in subdivision (a)(1) and (2) should be aligned as a defendant, is subject to service of process and can be joined without defeating subject matter jurisdiction, the court must order him to be brought into the action. This is accomplished by motion under FRCP 21 discussed in Section 10.6, *infra.*

If the absent person meets the Rule 19(a)(1) and (a)(2) criteria and should be aligned as a defendant, but is not subject to service of process or cannot be joined without defeating subject matter jurisdiction, he cannot be joined under 19(a).[85] Rather, the court must determine wheth-

78. *E.g.,* Schlumberger Industries, Inc. v. National Sur. Corp., 36 F.3d 1274, 1288 (4th Cir.1994).

79. H & H Intern. Corp. v. J. Pellechia Trucking, Inc., 119 F.R.D. 352, 354 (S.D.N.Y.1988); Pasco Intern. (London) Ltd. v. Stenograph Corp., 637 F.2d 496, 500–01 (7th Cir.1980).

80. Pulitzer–Polster v. Pulitzer, 784 F.2d 1305, 1312 (5th Cir.1986).

81. *Id.*

82. Faloon v. Sunburst Bank, 158 F.R.D. 378, 382 (N.D.Miss.1994).

83. Pasco Intern., 637 F.2d at 501, cited with approval in Thunder Basin Coal Co. v. Southwestern Public Service Co., 104 F.3d 1205, 1211 (10th Cir.1997).

84. Angst v. Royal Maccabees Life Ins. Co., 77 F.3d 701, 706 (3d Cir.1996).

85. *E.g.,* Pasco Intern., 637 F.2d at 500 (subject matter jurisdiction); Steinberg & Lyman v. Takacs, 690 F.Supp. 263, 266 (S.D.N.Y.1988) (personal jurisdiction).

er or not to dismiss the action by applying Rule 19(b).[86]

The third sentence authorizes two means of dealing with an absent party who resists voluntarily joining as a plaintiff.

The first route is to make such an absent party an involuntary plaintiff in a "proper case." While the "precise scope of the 'proper case' qualification has never been authoritatively resolved," it is a limited device; and "[t]he Rule clearly does not mean that whenever an absent party is properly alignable as a plaintiff in a lawsuit, he should be brought in under 19(a) as an 'involuntary plaintiff.' "[87] The cases are inconsistent.[88] In the Fifth Circuit's view, the "proper case" covers "only those instances where the absent party has either a duty to allow the plaintiff to use his name in the action or some sort of an obligation to join plaintiff in the action."[89] For example, a plaintiff licensee under a patent can make the patent owner an involuntary plaintiff.

Involuntary plaintiff status allows the plaintiff to bring an absent party into the action even though the party is beyond the personal jurisdiction of the court, assuming the party has been given notice of the suit and refuses to join voluntarily as a plaintiff.[90] Such a party is aligned as a plaintiff for diversity jurisdiction purposes.

The second route is available absent a "proper case." If the absent party is within the jurisdiction of the court, and he refuses to join voluntarily as a plaintiff following notice, he may be joined as a defendant if he is amenable to service of process, regardless of the appropriate interest alignment.[91] However, if his interests are aligned with the plaintiff, he will be treated as a plaintiff for diversity purposes.[92] Consequently, assuming the absent party were a citizen of the plaintiff's state, diversity jurisdiction would be preserved, even though he was joined as a defendant.

The pleading or moving papers requesting joinder should allege or show that the absent party has been notified of the action and has refused to join voluntarily as a plaintiff.[93] They should also demonstrate that the absent person's interests satisfy the "involuntary plaintiff" criteria or are aligned with plaintiff based on the pleadings or other contentions of the parties.

Without these additional means under the third sentence of Rule 19(a) for obtaining personal or preserving diversity jurisdiction over a person who must be joined under Rule 19(a), the action would be subject

---

86. *E.g.*, Haas v. Jefferson Nat. Bank of Miami Beach, 442 F.2d 394, 398 (5th Cir. 1971).

87. Eikel v. States Marine Lines, Inc., 473 F.2d 959, 961 (5th Cir.1973).

88. *Id.*(also noting that the cases rarely discuss this aspect of Rule 19(a) explicitly).

89. *Id.*, citing Independent Wireless Telegraph Co. v. Radio Corporation of America, 269 U.S. 459, 46 S.Ct. 166, 70 L.Ed. 357 (1926) (exclusive licensee of a patent entitled to make patent's owner a co-plaintiff without his consent).

90. Independent Wireless, 269 U.S. 459, 46 S.Ct. 166, 70 L.Ed. 357.

91. Eikel, 473 F.2d at 962.

92. *Id.* at 963.

93. Hicks v. Intercontinental Acceptance Corp., 154 F.R.D. 134, 136 (E.D.N.C. 1994).

to dismissal under Rule 19(b). Recall that if the court cannot obtain personal or subject matter jurisdiction over a party who must be joined under Rule 19(a)(1) and (2), the party's "indispensability" must be examined under Rule 19(b).

(e) Venue

The last sentence of Rule 19(b) states:

"If the joined party objects to venue and joinder of that party would render the venue of the action improper, that party shall be dismissed from the action."

Unlike lack of personal or subject matter jurisdiction, improper venue is not grounds for the court to decline to join an absent party who must be joined if feasible under Rule 19(a).[94] Even if concerns about venue exist or are expressed by the parties, the absent party should be joined.[95] Only if the absent party makes a valid venue objection after joinder should he be dismissed. "Then the court may properly consider whether under Rule 19(b) the action should proceed in his absence."[96] Thus, parties seeking or opposing a joinder need not address venue concerns in their submissions. The burden is on the absent party following joinder to object.

(f) Pleading Reasons for Nonjoinder

Rule 19(c) provides as follows:

(c) Pleading Reasons for Nonjoinder. A pleading asserting a claim for relief shall state the names, if known to the pleader, of any persons as prescribed in subdivision (a)(1)-(2) hereof who are not joined, and the reasons why they are not joined.

Subsection (c) obliges one asserting a claim for relief in a pleading to alert the court and other parties to the identities, if known, of persons as to whom the issues of feasible joinder or indispensability might be raised. The requirement of stating the reasons for nonjoinder is designed to encourage conscientiousness in deciding at the pleading stage who ought properly to be joined.

The obligation imposed by Rule 19(c) should not be taken lightly, especially if sound reasons for nonjoinder exist. One court has decided that a plaintiff's failure to comply with 19(c) permitted the assumption that joinder of a person not named in the complaint who met Rule 19(a)(1)-(2) criteria would destroy the court's jurisdiction rendering joinder not feasible. A dismissal of the case under Rule 19(b) followed.[97] Where only future discovery would reveal the information required by Rule 19(c), a general description has been held to save the action from

94. Turner v. CF&II Steel Corp., 510 F.Supp. 537, 546 (E.D.Pa.1981).

95. Patterson v. MacDougall, 506 F.2d 1, 5 (5th Cir.1975).

96. *Id.*

97. Hinsdale v. Farmers Nat. Bank and Trust Co., 93 F.R.D. 662, 665 (N.D.Ohio 1982).

dismissal for noncompliance, although the court still considered the issue of indispensability under Rule 19(b).[98]

(g) Class Actions

Rule 19 is subject to the provisions of Rule 23 governing class actions.[99] Consequently, the provisions of Rule 23 control joinder issues in the class action setting.

Library References:

West's Key No. Digests, Federal Civil Procedure ⊕201–233.
Wright, Miller & Kane, Federal Practice and Procedure: Civil 2d §§ 1601–1603.

§ 10.5   Permissive Joinder of Parties

FRCP 20(a) provides:

(a) Permissive Joinder. All persons may join in one action as plaintiffs if they assert any right to relief jointly, severally, or in the alternative in respect of or arising out of the same transaction, occurrence, or series of transactions or occurrences and if any question of law or fact common to all these persons will arise in the action. All persons (and any vessel, cargo or other property subject to admiralty process in rem) may be joined in one action as defendants if there is asserted against them jointly, severally, or in the alternative, any right to relief in respect of or arising out of the same transaction, occurrence, or series of transactions or occurrences and if any question of law or fact common to all defendants will arise in the action. A plaintiff or defendant need not be interested in obtaining or defending against all the relief demanded. Judgment may be given for one or more of the plaintiffs according to their respective rights to relief, and against one or more defendants according to their respective liabilities.

Three preliminary points should be made. First, the common question of law or fact requirement applies to parties, not to claims. FRCP 18(a), covering joinder of claims, operates independently. In other words, where multiple parties are properly joined under Rule 20(a), any additional claim by a party against an opposing party may be joined even though the additional claim does not meet the requirements of Rule 20(a). For example, RICO claims may be brought against several defendants if they arise out of the same transaction and there is a question of law or fact common to all of the defendants. The plaintiff may also bring a securities law claim against one of the defendants, even though it arises out of a different transaction and does not involve a legal or factual question common to either of the other two defendants.

98. Jones v. Local 520, Intern. Union of Operating Engineers, 524 F.Supp. 487, 493–94 (S.D.Ill.1981) ("similarly situated contractors").

99. FRCP 19(d). *See* Chapter 15 "Class Actions," *infra.*

Second, joinder of parties under Rule 20(a) is limited by jurisdictional and venue considerations. *See* Section 10.5(b), *infra*.

Third, Rule 20(a) should be read in conjunction with Rule 21 "Misjoinder and Nonjoinder of Parties."[1] *See* Section 10.6, *infra*.

(a) The Requirements for Permissive Joinder

Rule 20 is to be construed liberally to promote trial convenience.[2] Both the same transaction or occurrence and the common question requirements must be met.[3] The analysis in a particular case is fact specific. Courts have decided joinder issues on a case-by-case basis rather than by developing general rules.[4]

Any question of law or fact in common suffices. That some questions relate only to certain plaintiffs or defendants does not prevent joinder, if one question is common to all plaintiffs or to all defendants.

The most commonly used test to determine whether the "same transaction, occurrence, or series of transactions or occurrences" requirement is satisfied is the "logically related events" standard established in *Mosley v. General Motors*.[5] "Absolute identity of all events is unnecessary."[6] *Mosley* was a race discrimination and unlawful employment practice case brought by 10 separate plaintiffs. The complaint contained 12 counts, two of which were class action counts. The district court withheld a determination of the propriety of the class action claims pending discovery. This part of the district court's opinion was affirmed. The district court had also disallowed joinder of the 10 individual counts and had ordered them severed into 10 separate actions. This severance order was reversed.

As to the same transaction or occurrence requirement of Rule 20, the Eighth Circuit reasoned that the plaintiff's allegation that each had been injured by the "same general policy of discrimination" rendered their claims "logically related," thus "comprising a transaction or occurrence" even though there was not "absolute identity of all events."[7]

Regarding the common law or fact requirement, the court found that the alleged existence of discriminatory conduct and policies affecting all of the plaintiffs was "basic" to each claim and thus common to all.

§ 10.5

1. *See* Stark v. Independent School Dist. No. 640, 163 F.R.D. 557, 564 (D.Minn.1995) (the relevance of Rule 21 is based in part on the fact that Rule 20, if satisfied, states that a party "may," not "shall," be added).

2. *See, e.g.,* Mosley v. General Motors Corp., 497 F.2d 1330, 1332–33 (8th Cir.1974)(joinder of claims is strongly encouraged); citing United Mine Workers of America v. Gibbs, 383 U.S. 715, 724, 86 S.Ct. 1130, 1138, 16 L.Ed.2d 218 (1966).

3. Blesedell v. Mobil Oil Co., 708 F.Supp. 1408, 1421 (S.D.N.Y.1989). ("Both requirements must be satisfied for joinder to be proper under Rule 20.") (citation omitted).

4. Mosley, 497 F.2d at 1333. ("In ascertaining whether a particular factual situation constitutes a single transaction for purposes of Rule 20, a case by case approach is generally pursued.") (citation omitted).

5. *Id.* at 1330.

6. *Id.* at 1333.

7. *Id.*

That each plaintiff "suffered different effects" was deemed "immaterial."[8]

Two other less widely utilized standards have also been articulated. The first is that "[there] are enough factual concurrences that it would be fair to the parties to require them to defend jointly against them[.]"[9] The second asks would there "be an overlapping of proof and the duplication of testimony" if joinder were denied, resulting in the delay, inconvenience and added expense associated with another action.[10]

To sustain joinder in cases involving fraud or antitrust claims, it is advisable to allege, if possible, that the fraudulent acts were part of a scheme, or that the antitrust activities involved a conspiracy, which affected all plaintiffs.[11]

In product defect cases in which multiple plaintiffs sought joinder, a warranty common to the plaintiffs did not permit their joinder where there was not a common defect.[12] Thus, the practitioner should emphasize to the fullest extent possible the absence or presence of a common defect or common elements in different defects, depending on whether joinder is being urged or resisted.

In the securities law context, the logically related and common issue factors together have been held to require the plaintiffs to "allege that their claims arise from one or more uniform misrepresentations."[13]

In complex business cases, the extent of the similarity among the transactions involved in the claims may be a close question. If so, discovery may provide the specifics necessary to mount a successful challenge to joinder.[14] A motion under Rule 21 challenging joinder may be made "at any stage." (*See* Section 10.6, *infra.*) Thus, it may often be wiser not to make the motion so early that it can only be based on the

---

8. *Id.* at 1334.

9. Eastern Fireproofing Co. v. U. S. Gypsum Co., 160 F.Supp. 580, 581 (D.Mass. 1958) (variations in loan policies and practices too substantial to permit joinder of 11 banks as defendants in usury action).

10. U.S. for Use and Benefit of Saunders Concrete Co., Inc. v. Tri–State Design Const. Co., 899 F.Supp. 916, 918 (N.D.N.Y. 1995).

11. *See* Mesa Computer Utilities, Inc. v. Western Union Computer Utilities, Inc., 67 F.R.D. 634, 637 (D.Del.1975) (incomplete pleadings and early stage of litigation caused the court to decline ruling that joinder was improper where claims were based on fraud and antitrust conspiracies which affected all plaintiffs).

12. *Compare* Saval v. BL Ltd., 710 F.2d 1027, 1031–32 (4th Cir.1983) (joinder of plaintiffs denied because no common defects) *with In re* General Motors Corp. En-

gine Interchange Litig., 594 F.2d 1106 (7th Cir.), *cert. denied*, 444 U.S. 870, 100 S.Ct. 146, 62 L.Ed.2d 95 (1979) (institutionalized engine swap was a common defect not dependent on individual or different uses, history and service) *and with* Dayton Independent School District v. U.S. Mineral Products Co., 1989 WL 237732 (E.D.Tex. 1989) (defect in asbestos containing material the same, even though purchased and installed at different times, by different contractors, with different designs by different architects).

13. McLernon v. Source Intern., Inc., 701 F.Supp. 1422, 1425 (E.D.Wis.1988).

14. *See* Dougherty v. Mieczkowski, 661 F.Supp. 267, 280 (D.Del.1987) (securities laws; court held that discovery was pending, and the record was not yet developed enough to rule on joinder challenge).

pleadings; although to avoid issues of timeliness, it may be advisable to alert the court to future intentions in some appropriate manner.

The second to last sentence of Rule 20(a) provides that, if the requirements of the Rule are met, "[a] plaintiff or defendant need not be interested in obtaining or defending against all the relief demanded."

A counterclaiming or cross-claiming defendant may join other parties if Rule 20 is satisfied. In that event, such a defendant is treated as a plaintiff and any added parties as plaintiffs or defendants as determined by their interests.

Even if permissive joinder is proper, subdivision (b) authorizes separate trials on grounds that are substantially identical to those set forth in FRCP 42(b) discussed in Section 10.8, *infra*.

(b) Jurisdiction and Venue

Even though the joinder of a party meets the requirements of Rule 20, joinder might still be impermissible for lack of subject matter jurisdiction or on grounds of improper venue. For a detailed discussion, *see* Chapter 1 "Subject Matter Jurisdiction," and Chapter 3 "Venue, Forum Selection and Transfer," *supra*.

(1) *Jurisdiction*

Jurisdictional problems arise under Rule 20 when the main claims are based upon either diversity or federal question grounds, but other claims by or against one of the joined parties are not. Jurisdiction, if any, over such joined parties must then be based upon supplemental jurisdiction or joinder is improper even if there is compliance with Rule 20.

(2) *Venue*

Because venue objections are waivable and must be raised quickly, they are not litigated in multi-party settings as often as jurisdictional limitations which the parties cannot waive by consent or inaction.

(c) Jurisdiction Following Removal

Removal premised on the presence of a separate and independent claim involving a federal question which is joined with nonremovable claims is governed by 28 U.S.C.A. § 1441(c).

The attempted addition of a defendant whose presence would destroy the complete diversity necessary to subject matter jurisdiction is addressed by 28 U.S.C.A. § 1447(e). Section 1447(e) provides that "the court may deny joinder, or permit joinder and remand the action to the State court." For a recent discussion of factors governing how a court applies Section 1447(e), *see Winner's Circle of Las Vegas, Inc. v. AMI Franchising, Inc.*[15] For a detailed discussion of removal, *see* Chapter 8, "Removal to Federal Court," *supra*.

---

15. 916 F.Supp. 1024, 1027 (D.Nev. 1996).

Library References:

West's Key No. Digests, Federal Civil Procedure ☞241–267.
Wright, Miller & Kane, Federal Practice and Procedure: Civil 2d §§ 1604–1606,
1609–1611.

§ 10.6 Misjoinder and Nonjoinder of Parties

FRCP 21 provides:

Misjoinder and Nonjoinder of Parties. Misjoinder of parties is not ground for dismissal of an action. Parties may be dropped or added by order of the court on motion of any party or of its own initiative at any stage of the action and on such terms as are just. Any claim against a party may be severed and proceeded with separately.

(a) Practice

In general, Rule 21 applies when Rules 18, 19 or 20 have not been followed. It also interrelates with other Rules dealing with parties, such as Rules 13(h), 15(a) and (c), 17(a) and 23. The relationship between Rule 21 and Rule 42 (consolidation and separate trials) is discussed in Section 10.6(d), *infra*.

A court has broad discretion in the adding or dropping of parties under Rule 21. The motion may be made by "any party"; and the court may grant the motion "on such terms as are just." If a party is added after motion or on the court's initiative, there must be service of process, except where appearance is voluntary or "involuntary plaintiff" status is appropriate (*see* Section 10.4(d), *supra*). Motions under Rule 21 should be made promptly after the grounds become clear. This is especially important where a party is to be added, since the opportunity for the added party to prepare for trial will be of paramount importance to the court.

(b) Misjoinder

The Rule itself says that "[m]isjoinder of parties is not ground for dismissal of an action." Instead, the misjoined party is to be dropped and "may be dropped ... at any stage of the action." Any claim misjoined because of its improper joinder may be severed, as discussed in Section 10.6(d), *infra*. Because dismissal is not appropriate, the practitioner should move to drop or sever, not to dismiss under Rule 12, and should do so promptly to avoid waiver.

Rule 19 does not expressly authorize the dropping of a dispensable party. The trial court's authority to do so "is derived from either Rule 21 or Rule 15."[1] Thus, a motion to drop a dispensable party should properly invoke either or both of these latter rules.

---

§ 10.6

1. Caperton v. Beatrice Pocahontas Coal

Co., 585 F.2d 683, 692 n. 23 (4th Cir.1978).

Parties are also misjoined when they fail to satisfy the permissive joinder requirements of Rule 20(a).[2] These requirements are discussed in Section 10.5, *supra*.

Where a misjoined party defeats the court's subject matter jurisdiction, defendants who are not indispensable parties[3] and plaintiffs[4] may be dropped, thereby establishing jurisdiction retroactively.[5] This may be done even after judgment has been rendered.[6] If the misjoined party is indispensable, the case must be dismissed for lack of subject matter jurisdiction.[7]

(c) Nonjoinder

"Parties may be ... added ... at any stage of the action" according to Rule 21. This would apply, for example, to the addition of a party whose joinder is required under Rule 19(a) or one who is a proper party under Rule 20. A failure to join a person required to be joined is, strictly speaking, not an issue to be raised by motion under Rule 21. Rather, such a failure should be raised early in response to the complaint by motion to dismiss under Rule 12(b)(7). It can be raised as late as at the trial under Rule 12(h)(2); but one should not wait that long unless the failure was not clear earlier.

By order under Rule 21, dismissal should be withheld to allow joinder, if feasible, as defined in Rule 19(a).[8] If joinder is not feasible, because the absent party is not subject to process or its joinder will defeat diversity, the court must determine under Rule 19(b) whether the absent party is indispensable; if so, the action must be dismissed.

If a proper party under Rule 20 has not been joined, a Rule 21 motion to add him will not be granted if doing so would defeat jurisdiction.[9]

In supporting or opposing a motion to add parties, assuming indispensability is not an issue, the focus should be on the potential for undue

2. *E.g.*, Glendora v. Malone, 917 F.Supp. 224 (S.D.N.Y.1996).

3. Tuck v. United Services Auto. Ass'n, 859 F.2d 842, 845 (10th Cir.1988) (dismissal of nonessential defendants did not require dismissal of action); Ralli–Coney, Inc. v. Gates, 528 F.2d 572, 575 (5th Cir.1976) (district court properly dismissed nondispensable party when plaintiff could still receive adequate remedy).

4. *See* Publicker Industries, Inc. v. Roman Ceramics Corp., 603 F.2d 1065, 1068 (3d Cir.1979) (subsidiary which destroyed diversity jurisdiction properly dismissed from suit in which parent joined).

5. Continental Airlines, Inc. v. Goodyear Tire & Rubber Co., 819 F.2d 1519, 1522 (9th Cir.1987); Parker v. Mazda American

Credit, 35 Fed. R. Serv. 3d 340 (W.D.Va. 1996).

6. *E.g.*, Enza, Inc. v. We The People, Inc., 838 F.Supp. 975, 977 (E.D.Pa.1993). For a discussion of Rule 21 in the context of the post-removal addition of a nondiverse party, see Munford v. MacLellan, 682 F.Supp. 521 (N.D.Ga.1988).

7. Enza, 838 F.Supp. at 977.

8. Neighborhood Development Corp. v. Advisory Council on Historic Preservation, Dept. of Housing and Urban Development, City of Louisville, 632 F.2d 21, 24 (6th Cir.1980); *see also* School Dist. of Kansas City, Mo. v. State of Mo., 460 F.Supp. 421, 442 (W.D.Mo.1978).

9. Reynolds v. Wabash R. Co., 236 F.2d 387, 390 (8th Cir.1956).

delay of the hearing or trial, the degree of prejudice to the nonmoving party and the prospect of avoiding multiple litigation. Making such a motion early and well before trial negates the prospect of delaying the trial and reduces the nonmoving party's ability to sustain a claim of prejudice. Even if trial is not imminent, the fact that substantial discovery has already taken place may be enough to keep a party out of the case. Both sides should carefully assess whether the threat of multiple litigation is real or imagined. If it is real, stress why adding the party is the better course. If it is imagined, detail why that is so. In addition, explain or attack, depending on your position on the motion, the reasons why the motion is being brought at this time.

(d) Severance

Under the last sentence of Rule 21, "[a]ny claim against a party may be severed and proceeded with separately." Unlike this provision, FRCP 42(b),[10] which is related, operates independently of the requirements of Rules 18 and 20. The standards established by Rule 42 to separate joined claims for trial do not include curing defects under those Rules. In other words, the availability of severance under Rule 42 is determined solely with reference to the criteria set forth in that Rule, quite apart from whether severance would also be available under Rule 21 on grounds of misjoinder.

The disposition of a joined claim tried separately under Rule 42 cannot be appealed unless it is made final under FRCP 54(b).[11] This is because the joined claim, while tried separately, is still a part of the main action which is still pending. Severance under Rule 21, on the other hand, makes the severed claim a separate action, and any judgment is final and appealable.[12]

Because severance cures misjoinder by making the severed claim a separate action, the severed claim must independently meet subject matter jurisdiction requirements. After severance, it may then be consolidated with the original action, if desired, in accordance with Rule 42(a). The parties may, in effect, end up in the same place. However, severance followed by consolidation assures, in appropriate circumstances, that a claim may properly be severed on misjoinder grounds while still permitting it to be consolidated for trial with other claims where judicial economy warrants.

If the claims are maintainable as separate actions, severance is an alternative to dropping a party because of improper joinder.[13] A party

---

10. See infra § 10.8.

11. Vann v. Citicorp Sav. of Illinois, 891 F.2d 1507, 1509 (11th Cir.1990) (purpose of Rule 42 is prevention of piecemeal litigation).

12. United States v. O'Neil, 709 F.2d 361, 368 (5th Cir.1983)(appeal proper because severance effected under Rule 21).

13. For a discussion of the limited circumstances where Rule 21 severance has been extended beyond instances of misjoinder, see 3A Moore's Federal Practice, ¶ 21.05(2) at 36–44 (2d ed. 1963), and 7 Charles Alan Wright, Arthur R. Miller and Mary Kay Kane, Federal Practice and Procedure § 1689, at 477–481 (2d ed. 1986).

may favor severance in order to enable it to continue to pursue its claim against the misjoined party after a considerable investment in discovery regarding that claim has been made. Severance should be opposed by a misjoined defendant, because such a party obviously would prefer dismissal to being forced to continue to litigate the claim after severance.

A court has broad discretion in ruling on a request for severance under Rule 21, and considerations of delay and prejudice are relevant.[14] Where a party seeks severance of a claim asserted by or against it, the court will assess whether the claim arises "out of the same transaction or occurrence or [presents] some common question of law or fact," as required by Rule 20,[15] discussed in Section 10.5, *supra.* For a party opposing severance, the more clear it is that Rule 20 may require severance, the more important it is to emphasize any delay or prejudice which severance would create.

Where appropriate, a court, in ruling on a Rule 21 motion for severance, may need to address whether a party who could not be a party in a severed action is indispensable to that action under Rule 19.[16]

Library References:

West's Key No. Digests, Federal Civil Procedure ⚬384–388.
Wright, Miller & Kane, Federal Practice and Procedure: Civil 2d §§ 1681–1689.

§ 10.7   Consolidation of Separate Actions; Separation of Claims

(a) Policies and Limits of Consolidation

Rules 18, 19 and 20 are premised upon a public policy of encouraging the resolution of all disputes in a single proceeding as a matter of judicial economy. But economies are not always achieved or might come at the price of prejudice, undue delay or burden. One plaintiff's interests might be served by bringing together all claims or parties, while another plaintiff's interests are served by filing separate actions. One defendant might file a separate action rather than file counterclaims, cross-claims or third-party claims, while another might load on many claims, assert cross-claims, or serve third-party complaints, and so on. Obviously the strategy of one party can frustrate the strategies of another, with significant prejudicial effects, substantial delay, and inefficiency. Rule 42 offers litigants help in the form of consolidation or separation for trials.

Consolidation—bringing separate actions into a single proceeding— is the subject of Rule 42(a). It provides that separate actions pending in

14. E.I. Du Pont De Nemours & Co. v. Fine Arts Reproduction Co., Inc., 1995 WL 312505 (S.D.N.Y.1995) (granting severance).

15. Hohlbein v. Heritage Mut. Ins. Co., 106 F.R.D. 73, 78 (E.D.Wis.1985); Jonas v. Conrath, 149 F.R.D. 520, 523 (S.D.W.Va. 1993).

16. E.I. Du Pont, 1995 WL 312505 (defendant was in bankruptcy and current action was automatically stayed; bankrupt was not an indispensable party and severance was granted on finding that it would not interfere with bankruptcy proceedings).

the same court having common questions of law or fact may be consolidated at the discretion of the trial court:

(a) Consolidation. When actions involving a common question of law or fact are pending before the court, it may order a joint hearing or trial of any or all the matters in issue in the actions; it may order all the actions consolidated; and it may make such orders concerning proceedings therein as may tend to avoid unnecessary costs or delay.

Consolidation is available for parties to use defensively, bringing about consolidation of claims of an adverse party, or offensively, bringing about consolidation of a party's own claims.

For example, a plaintiff files suit alleging a claim for trade dress and trademark infringement, a claim under a state antidilution statute, and unfair competition. The defendant denies the allegations. It wishes to assert claims against the plaintiff based upon strong evidence that plaintiff's sales people have been telling defendant's customers that defendant's products are of poor quality and unsafe to use, and that defendant uses unethical business practices by copying the trade dress of its competitors' products. Assuming there is diversity, the defendant may elect to deny the infringements in one action and assert claims for unfair competition, defamation, and wrongful interference with business opportunities in a counterclaim. Or, the defendant may conclude that a separate lawsuit for its claims would be preferable, because it wants the advantage of leading off with the proof as a plaintiff on its claims and because these claims are less likely to get lost in the evidence of defendant's conduct. The defendant opts for filing a separate lawsuit, and it files the suit in a different district to reduce the chance of consolidation.

The plaintiff can do something about it—move to transfer under 28 U.S.C.A. § 1404(a) and, upon transfer, move for consolidation in a defensive use of Rule 42(a). Both motions will lead to a judicial airing of the relative prejudices that the parties face by their conflicting strategies.

A plaintiff might be confronted with a situation where it has multiple claims but cannot assert them all in the same federal district court. The plaintiff is compelled to forego some claims or file two lawsuits. The plaintiff might try for a transfer under 28 U.S.C.A. § 1404(a) and then use Rule 42(a) offensively to get its claims consolidated into a single proceeding.

Consolidation is considered to be a matter of broad judicial discretion,[1] and courts are encouraged to consolidate actions to speed up the

§ 10.7

1. Hendrix v. Raybestos–Manhattan, Inc., 776 F.2d 1492, 1495–96 (11th Cir. 1985) (consolidation of asbestos actions "was entirely reasonable," the cases having "striking similarity"); Johnson v. Celotex

Corp., 899 F.2d 1281, 1284 (2d Cir.1990) (consolidation of asbestos cases approved, after weighing specific risks of prejudice and confusion in light of cautionary jury instructions, and risks of inconsistent re-

trial process and eliminate needless repetition and confusion.[2] It can be ordered by the court upon motion by a party or sua sponte over objection of all of the parties.[3] Consolidation can be ordered for purposes of trial or pretrial proceedings or both.[4] The only circumstance where the court lacks such discretion is in the case of consolidating multiple arbitration proceedings.[5]

The purpose for consolidation is promotion of convenience and economy for the benefit of the court, counsel and the parties,[6] and, as one might expect, motions for consolidation are typically based upon these considerations. Parties have their reasons, too. The situation above where the defendant filed a separate action for unfair competition and interference is an example. Recall that the defendant wanted the advantage of being able to lead off with the proof in these claims and avoid having them lost in the evidence of plaintiff's case. Plaintiff should want consolidation so that it leads off at trial with evidence of defendant's intentional copying of the design of plaintiff's products and defendant's scheme to take plaintiff's business through the use of trade dress and

sults on common issues, burden on parties and witnesses, and judicial resources).

2. Hendrix, 776 F.2d at 1495 ("We have encouraged trial judges 'to make good use of Rule 42(a) . . . in order to expedite the trial and eliminate unnecessary repetition and confusion,' " quoting, Dupont v. Southern Pac. Co., 366 F.2d 193, 195–96 (5th Cir.1966), *cert. denied*, 386 U.S. 958, 87 S.Ct. 1027, 18 L.Ed.2d 106 (1967).

3. Gentry v. Smith, 487 F.2d 571, 581 (5th Cir.1973) (plaintiffs and defendant opposed joining additional party in order to get all related issues before court and plaintiffs opposed consolidation of later suit by defendant against such additional party); Miller v. U.S. Postal Service, 729 F.2d 1033, 1036 (5th Cir.1984); *In re* Air Crash Disaster at Florida Everglades on December 29, 1972, 549 F.2d 1006, 1013 (5th Cir.1977); Ellerman Lines, Limited v. Atlantic & Gulf Stevedores, Inc., 339 F.2d 673, 675 (3d Cir. 1964) (Court of Appeals instructed district court on remand to consider consolidation on its own motion and order consolidation if no disadvantages outweigh the "obvious advantages.").

4. MacAlister v. Guterma, 263 F.2d 65, 68 (2d Cir.1958); 28 U.S.C.A. § 1407 (West 1993).

5. The Second Circuit Court of Appeals ruled in 1975 that the district court *could* order consolidation of arbitrations covered by separate agreements without consent of the parties. Compania Espanola de Petrol-

eos, S.A. v. Nereus Shipping, S.A., 527 F.2d 966, 974 (2d Cir.1975), *cert. denied*, 426 U.S. 936, 96 S.Ct. 2650, 49 L.Ed.2d 387 (1976). This position was not followed in other circuits. *See* Weyerhaeuser Company v. Western Seas Shipping Co., 743 F.2d 635, 636 (9th Cir.1984); American Centennial Ins. Co. v. National Cas. Co., 951 F.2d 107, 108 (6th Cir.1991); Protective Life Ins. Corp. v. Lincoln Nat. Life Ins. Corp., 873 F.2d 281, 282 (11th Cir.1989). In 1993 the Second Circuit Court of Appeals retreated, stating that its earlier decision to the contrary was no longer good law. Government of the United Kingdom of Great Britain and Northern Ireland, Through United Kingdom Defense Procurement Office, Ministry of Defense v. Boeing Co., 998 F.2d 68, 70–71 (2d Cir.1993).

6. Katz v. Realty Equities Corp. of New York, 521 F.2d 1354, 1358–59 (2d Cir. 1975)(court also mentions avoiding unnecessary paperwork); Harris v. Illinois–California Exp., Inc., 687 F.2d 1361, 1368 (10th Cir.1982); Hanes Companies, Inc. v. Ronson, 712 F.Supp. 1223, 1230 (M.D.N.C. 1988). In *Arroyo v. Chardon*, 90 F.R.D. 603, 605 (D.P.R.1981) the district court explained the purpose of consolidation for trial to be "to avoid: 1) overlapping trials containing duplicative proof; 2) excess cost incurred by all parties and the government; 3) the waste of valuable court time in the trial of repetitive claims; and 4) the burden placed on a new judge in gaining familiarity with the cases." Avoiding unnecessary paperwork could be added to the list as well.

trademark infringement, followed by evidence of both lost sales and irreparable harm through sales of potentially shoddy manufacture. This is a preemption strategy, and a defendant, wise to it, will insist on prejudice as reason for disallowing the consolidation. The court will look for the best of both worlds—allow consolidation but provide for special jury instructions and verdict forms to avoid the prejudice. This is what Rule 42(a) is all about.

The party asking for consolidation has the burden of establishing commonality of factual or legal issues[7] and that convenience and economy are promoted by consolidation or that a prejudice such as potential inconsistent findings can result without consolidation.[8]

The court can order consolidation where parties are the same[9] and where they are different.[10] It can do so where the defendants are not only different, but where plaintiff could not have joined them initially in a single action under Rule 20,[11] because it could not sue both defendants in the same district; in this situation, although a court has authority only over cases pending before it, actions pending before another district court can be transferred under 28 U.S.C.A. § 1404(a) in order that they might be consolidated.[12]

Whatever efficiencies are obtainable with consolidation, the court's discretion to order it has limits: "considerations of convenience and economy must yield to a paramount concern for a fair and impartial trial."[13] Therefore, parties opposed to consolidation should argue that consolidation will cause it unfair prejudice. A defendant, for example, alleged to infringe plaintiff's patent, files a separate suit against the plaintiff for infringement of its own patent, electing not to file a counterclaim because it found it important to avoid having its own patent infringement conduct (copying plaintiff's product) prejudice the jury against it, were the opposing but independent patent claims tried together. If the plaintiff moves for consolidation, the defendant should be

---

7. In re Repetitive Stress Injury Litig., 11 F.3d 368, 373, 374 (2d Cir.1993).

8. Shump v. Balka, 574 F.2d 1341, 1344 (10th Cir.1978).

9. Hanes Companies, Inc., 712 F.Supp. at 1230.

10. Bottazzi v. Petroleum Helicopters, Inc., 664 F.2d 49, 50 (5th Cir.1981).

11. Stanford v. Tennessee Val. Authority, 18 F.R.D. 152, 154 (M.D.Tenn.1955); Kenvin v. Newburger, Loeb & Co., 37 F.R.D. 473, 475 (S.D.N.Y.1965).

12. Continental Grain Co. v. The FBL–585, 364 U.S. 19, 26, 80 S.Ct. 1470, 1475, 4 L.Ed.2d 1540 (1960) (related admiralty in rem action properly transferred to district where damage action pending, for consolidation in view of identical issues raised). For transfer of cases under the multi-district litigation procedure, see 28 U.S.C.A.

§ 1407(a) (West 1993) and Chapter 11 "Multi–District Litigation," infra.

13. Johnson v. Celotex Corp., 899 F.2d 1281, 1285 (2d Cir.1990) (no unfairness in consolidation of asbestos-related personal injury actions where there were common facts, same counsel represented all plaintiffs, cases were in similar stage of readiness for trial, and, importantly, there were jury instructions to consider claims separately and the court used separate verdict forms); Flintkote Co. v. Allis–Chalmers Corp., 73 F.R.D. 463, 465 (S.D.N.Y.1977) (denying motion to consolidate two breach of contract actions despite similar theories of recovery where contracts were different, different state laws would probably be involved, and different equipment was alleged to be defective).

as explicit as possible regarding the prejudice certain to befall it. Such prejudice is not just to be found in patent infringement claims, of course, but they are easy examples. What should be clear is that the two patent cases, although possibly having some common questions of technology or prior art, are not mutually dependent and in those cases the prejudice resulting from evidence of one claim, irrelevant to the other but nonetheless likely to influence the jurors' attitudes toward the party on other claims, should warrant denial of consolidation.[14]

Courts are required to use caution when consolidating actions to insure that the rights of parties are not prejudiced.[15] Courts have explained:

> The critical question for the district court in the final analysis [is] whether the specific risks of prejudice and possible confusion [are] overborne by the risk of inconsistent adjudications of common factual and legal issues, the burden on parties, witnesses and available judicial resources posed by multiple lawsuits, the length of time required to conclude multiple suits as against a single one, and the relative expense to all concerned of their single-trial, multiple-trial alternatives.[16]

The answer to the critical question does not mean that consolidation may not be ordered where prejudice or confusion will outweigh the considerations. Sometimes the benefits of consolidation can be obtained without risk of prejudice to parties by limiting consolidation to specific matters[17] or by using separate verdicts or special jury instructions.[18] The Seventh Amendment right of jury trial must, of course, be preserved, and, therefore, it has been held that where the jury trial right has been preserved in one of the consolidated actions, the right will attach with respect to the other actions consolidated even though previously waived in the other cases.[19]

---

14. This prejudice is recognized as a "spill-over effect," and it is often argued as a reason for granting separate trials under Rule 42(b). *See infra* § 10.8.

15. Dupont v. Southern Pac. Co., 366 F.2d 193, 196 (5th Cir.1966). The district court ordered consolidation of actions having plaintiffs with conflicting interests among themselves and ordered that all plaintiffs be represented by a single lead counsel. The appellate court saw this as an "impossible situation." *Id.* at 197. There was no intimation, however, that consolidation was itself an abuse of discretion.

16. Arnold v. Eastern Air Lines, Inc., 681 F.2d 186, 193 (4th Cir.1982), *cert. denied*, 460 U.S. 1102, 103 S.Ct. 1801, 76 L.Ed.2d 366 (1983), *quoted in* Johnson, 899 F.2d at 1285; Malcolm v. National Gypsum Co., 995 F.2d 346, 350 (2d Cir.1993); Hendrix v. Raybestos–Manhattan, Inc., 776 F.2d 1492, 1495 (11th Cir.1985).

17. Katz v. Realty Equities Corp. of New York, 521 F.2d 1354, 1361 (2d Cir. 1975) (limited to pretrial stages).

18. Johnson, 899 F.2d at 1285 (instructions were given during trial and in the jury charge, and separate verdict forms were used). *See also*, Hendrix, 776 F.2d at 1495 (jurors given notebooks with separate sections for each plaintiff and each defendant, and they were encouraged to prepare notes; the court also repeatedly gave cautionary instructions reminding jurors they would be deciding each plaintiff's claim separately); Stanford v. TVA, 18 F.R.D. 152, 155 (M.D.Tenn.1955) (separate verdicts to preserve the advantages of a separate trial including the right of peremptory challenges).

19. Cedars–Sinai Medical Center v. Revlon, Inc., 111 F.R.D. 24, 32 (D.Del.1986). But the court may review the facts to deter-

(b) Effect of Consolidation

It is important to know that consolidation under Rule 42(a) may affect appellate rights. If consolidation merges the actions into a single action, appeal from a final disposition of one of the consolidated cases (*e.g.*, the grant of a motion for a summary judgment) must await a final judgment in all actions, absent the certification prescribed in Rule 54(b). On the other hand, if the consolidated actions nonetheless remain separate and a final disposition of one action is entered (*e.g.*, summary judgment), the clock on the time for appeal is running at the moment of the disposition of one of the actions even though the remainder of the consolidated actions have not been tried.

In 1933 the Supreme Court held that consolidation, then controlled by 28 U.S.C.A. § 734, did not have the effect of merging actions into a single action.[20] Therefore, the Supreme Court concluded, appeal from a final judgment or order in one consolidated action did not have to wait disposition of all other consolidated actions. This decision adhered to the analysis of a Supreme Court decision 41 years earlier in which it was held that notwithstanding consolidation, separate verdicts and judgments were required and that consolidation may not alter any rights of the parties available to them if the actions were not consolidated, such as, specifically, the right of peremptory challenge of jurors.[21] These holdings were consistently applied in regard to consolidation under Rule 42(a) for many years.[22]

More recently, however, some courts have held that consolidation can have the effect of a merger of actions, thus precluding appeal before final disposition of all actions consolidated, absent a Rule 54(b) certification.[23] These cases do not have a common basis for distinction, and the basis for departing from the old Supreme Court cases is only the adoption of Rule 42 itself. Because the time for appeal is at issue, and untimely appeals are dismissed for lack of jurisdiction if too early or too late, it is imperative that cases in the circuits involved be reviewed.[24]

mine whether the consolidation motion is a means of avoiding a missed deadline for a jury demand in one of the cases, and, if so, it can order consolidation without restoring the right to a jury trial. *Id. See also* Walton v. Eaton Corp., 563 F.2d 66, 71 (3d Cir. 1977).

20. Johnson v. Manhattan Ry. Co., 289 U.S. 479, 496–97, 53 S.Ct. 721, 727–28, 77 L.Ed. 1331 (1933).

21. Mutual Life Ins. Co. of New York v. Hillmon, 145 U.S. 285, 293–94, 12 S.Ct. 909, 912, 36 L.Ed. 706 (1892).

22. *See, e.g.*, Greenberg v. Giannini, 140 F.2d 550, 552 (2d Cir.1944); Katz, 521 F.2d at 1358; *In re* Massachusetts Helicopter Airlines, Inc., 469 F.2d 439, 441 (1st Cir.

1972); Kraft, Inc. v. Local Union 327, Teamsters, Chauffeurs, Helpers and Taxicab Drivers, 683 F.2d 131, 133 (6th Cir. 1982).

23. *See, e.g.*, Bergman v. City of Atlantic City, 860 F.2d 560, 563 (3d Cir.1988); Ringwald v. Harris, 675 F.2d 768, 770 (5th Cir. 1982); Huene v. United States, 743 F.2d 703 (9th Cir.1984).

24. For a survey of cases by circuits, see G. Virden, *Consolidation Under Rule 42 of the Federal Rules of Civil Procedure: The U.S. Courts of Appeals Disagree on Whether Consolidation Merges the Separate Cases and Whether the Cases Remain Separately Final for Purposes of Appeal*, 141 F.R.D. 169 (1992).

(c) Common Question of Law or Fact

Cases are legion analyzing claims to determine whether given actions have common questions of law or fact. In some instances the courts make the determination of commonality based upon a review of the pleadings[25] while in others courts refer to the pleadings and "subsequent proceedings."[26] There is no authority which holds that a court may not consider facts and evidence outside the pleadings, and courts do consider matters extrinsic to the pleadings.[27] What is certain is that a common question of law or fact must exist for consolidation to be granted,[28] and the moving party has the burden of demonstrating that commonality.[29]

Mere similarity of theories of recovery among cases is not sufficient commonality of questions of law or fact.[30] Thus, two actions for breach of contracts involving different but related equipment with common underlying technology and process do not meet the commonality requirement where the common underlying technology and process were not factual issues "framed by the complaint and subsequent proceedings."[31] Where two actions asserted violation of a state franchise statute by the same defendant, there was no commonality beyond the theory of recovery because the franchise statute itself specifically required consideration of facts unique to the individual plaintiffs to understand the rights being protected by the statute.[32]

On the other hand, commonality of questions of law and fact can exist even though only the subject matters of the cases may be related, while the claims are entirely independent. When drafting motion papers, the moving party will want to present a listing of common questions to demonstrate commonality is more than metaphysical, and, undoubtedly, trial counsel can be very creative in developing such a list since fact issues need not be ultimate facts as a special verdict form might read.

---

25. *In re* Repetitive Stress Injury Litig., 11 F.3d 368, 373 (2d Cir.1993) ("The allegations of the complaints afford no support to the district courts' conclusion that these cases are sufficiently related to warrant consolidation."); Bottazzi v. Petroleum Helicopters, Inc., 664 F.2d 49, 50 (5th Cir.1981) ("As a basis for our ruling [ordering consolidation], we need seek no further than the suits' allegations regarding [plaintiff's] psychological condition.").

26. Flintkote Co. v. Allis–Chalmers Corp., 73 F.R.D. 463, 465 (S.D.N.Y. 1977)("We are concerned ... with factual issues as framed by the complaint and subsequent proceedings.").

27. State Mut. Life Assur. Co. of America v. Peat, Marwick, Mitchell & Co., 49 F.R.D. 202, 208 (S.D.N.Y.1969) (referring to evidence submitted by affidavits, as well as the pleadings, from which it found the existence of sufficient commonality of questions or law and fact).

28. Flintkote Co., 73 F.R.D. at 463; Werner v. Satterlee, Stephens, Burke & Burke, 797 F.Supp. 1196, 1211 (S.D.N.Y. 1992); *In re* Prudential Securities Inc. Ltd. Partnerships Litig., 158 F.R.D. 562, 570 (S.D.N.Y.1994).

29. *In re* Repetitive Stress Injury Litig., 11 F.3d at 373.

30. Flintkote Co., 73 F.R.D. at 465; Liberty Lincoln Mercury, Inc. v. Ford Marketing Corp., 149 F.R.D. 65, 81 (D.N.J.1993).

31. Flintkote Co., 73 F.R.D. at 465.

32. Liberty Lincoln Mercury, 149 F.R.D. 65, 81–82 (plaintiffs separately alleged Ford's warranty policies violated the state franchising law which required manufacturers to reimburse dealers for warranty repairs at the retailer's "prevailing retail price" not to exceed what is reasonable for the area in which the dealer was located).

Thus, two patent infringement actions over separate patents were consolidated where the patents were "closely related," one patent employed the technology of the other patent, much of the prior art was the same, contested elements were common to both patents, the parties were the same, and collateral estoppel would likely apply.[33]

When two actions share a central question of law or fact, consolidation is appropriate absent prejudice not avoidable by a jury instruction or jury verdict form.[34] The common questions of law or fact must be substantial,[35] and where individual questions of law or fact predominate, consolidation has been denied because it would not significantly promote efficiency.[36] The court is expected to examine the specific underlying facts to determine similarities, and where differences outweigh the similarities, consolidation should be denied.[37] Thus the opponent to a motion for consolidation will want to develop a list of dissimilarities, with a view of emphasizing the extent and importance of facts for each case and demonstrating how they differ.

Similarity or dissimilarity of plaintiffs will not be dispositive of a motion to consolidate. Two actions involving the same parties will not be consolidated on that fact alone when the actions involve two separate transactions.[38] The fact that plaintiffs are unrelated does not preclude the existence of common questions of law and fact, even though each plaintiff might take a different approach to the action; in such circumstances, where the claims asserted have common questions of law or fact, special verdicts can reflect the different approaches.

Library References:
West's Key No. Digests, Federal Civil Procedure ⏘8.
Wright & Miller, Federal Practice and Procedure: Civil 2d §§ 2381–2392.

§ 10.8 Separate Trials—Policies, Limits, and Effect

The policies and protections for preservation of a fair and just adjudication of a dispute with judicial economy and avoidance of preju-

33. Cedars–Sinai Medical Center v. Revlon, Inc., 111 F.R.D. 24, 31–33 (D.Del.1986).

34. Kershaw v. Sterling Drug, Inc., 415 F.2d 1009, 1012 (5th Cir.1969) (personal injury actions against drug company consolidated day before trial).

35. Arnold v. Eastern Air Lines, Inc., 681 F.2d 186, 194 (4th Cir.1982).

36. Servants of Paraclete, Inc. v. Great American Ins. Co., 866 F.Supp. 1560, 1573 (D.N.M.1994) (consolidation denied for sexual abuse cases involving different priests); cf. Shumate & Co., Inc. v. National Ass'n of Securities Dealers, Inc., 509 F.2d 147, 155 (5th Cir.1975) (common questions of fact did not predominate to warrant granting plaintiffs class action status under Rule 23).

37. In re Repetitive Stress Injury Litig., 11 F.3d 368, 373–74 (2d Cir.1993)(fact that the consolidated cases—unrelated repetitive stress injury cases—involved a "mass tort" does not meet requirements for ordering consolidation, and the court abused its discretion when consolidating 44 suits against manufacturers of office equipment by workers in various occupations alleging repetitive stress injuries, despite commonality of counsel and readiness for trial where plaintiffs had different work sites, different occupations and different injuries, each of which might have cause other than a defendant's tortious conduct).

38. Thorne, Neale & Co. v. Atlantic Gulf Export Corp., 10 F.R.D. 59, 60 (S.D.N.Y.1949) (two different actions between the same parties regarding two unrelated shipments of coal held not sufficiently related).

dice underlying the Rules on joinder and consolidation would not be complete without provision for separation of claims and parties for trial. The plaintiff, suing several defendants, may have joined several claims into a single action, but with no claim against all defendants; or, it might be that there are multiple plaintiffs with different claims against multiple defendants, again, with no claim involving all plaintiffs and all defendants. Any defendant may have a genuine concern that evidence against another defendant will prejudice the jury's determination of issues respecting claims against it. Separate trials will avoid this prejudice, and judicial economy can be promoted if individual trials can be managed efficiently without the likely confusion caused by the different claims with different proofs against different defendants. This is the subject of Rule 42(b):

> **(b) Separate Trials.** The court, in furtherance of convenience or to avoid prejudice, or when separate trials will be conducive to expedition and economy, may order a separate trial of any claim, cross-claim, counterclaim, or third-party claim, or of any separate issue or of any number of claims, cross-claims, counterclaims, third-party claims, or issues, always preserving inviolate the right of trial by jury as declared by the Seventh Amendment to the Constitution or as given by a statute of the United States.

(a) Policies and Limits of Orders for Separate Trials

Multiple claims, the addition of counterclaims, cross-claims and third-party claims, and addition of parties can make a simple case become a very complex and unmanageable collection of claims and issues of law and fact. There can be protracted and expensive discovery and other pretrial proceedings, conflicting interests among parties or issues or evidence, long trials, jury confusion, evidence relevant to only one claim affecting a jury decision on another claim, and mounting costs on parties and the court.

Just as Rule 42(a) is designed to promote efficiencies and fairness where claims were not joined but could have been joined, Rule 42(b) is designed to assure fairness where joinder of claims leads to delay and prejudice. Balancing between the policy of Rule 18 encouraging a single proceeding for the resolution of all disputes, and fairness, is the function of Rule 42(b).

Rule 42(b) gives to the court the discretion to divide the case into separate trials on claims or issues in order to promote convenience, avoid prejudice and contribute to speed and economy.[1] However, courts have made clear that "separate trials should be the exception, not the rule,"[2] and that "the normal lawsuit seldom requires a separate trial of the

---

§ 10.8

1. For the distinction between separate trials under Rule 42(b) and severance as provided in Rules 14 and 21, see *infra* § 10.8(b).

2. Laitram Corp. v. Hewlett–Packard Co., 791 F.Supp. 113, 114 (E.D.La.1992).

issues."[3] Thus there is the unstated presumption that a single trial is economical and nonprejudicial. Nonetheless, in business litigation there is frequently the danger that evidence of limited relevance may offend a juror's sense of business morality or ethics and very likely prejudice a party in relation to the determination of unrelated issues where a separate trial is essential to avoid the prejudice.

The Rule explicitly sets forth the criteria: convenience, avoidance of prejudice, and expedition and economy, and as in the case of consolidation, the cases are legion applying these criteria on a case-by-case factual context.[4] As with consolidation, the decision to order separate trials is left to the trial court's sound discretion.[5]

Rule 42(b) is intended to "serve the ends of justice," and separate trials are only appropriate when the court believes that this purpose will be served.[6] Like consolidation, separation can be ordered upon motion or sua sponte by the court over objection of all parties.[7] No deadline exists for either a motion to bifurcate or for the court to order it sua sponte, and courts have even ordered bifurcation upon motion or sua sponte after trial is underway and plaintiff has rested,[8] where circumstances warranted bifurcation to prevent prejudice and the issues were not related.

Separate trials for liability and damages are ordered as a matter of economy (avoid wasting time on an issue which is moot if there is no liability) and because evidence on damages might prejudice a party in regard to a jury's view of the liability issue. One district court has a local rule providing for separate trials on liability and damages.[9]

While separation of issues or claims is frequently desirable for efficiency, convenience, expedition, and fairness (all legal considerations) business interests are something for individual parties to consider even if they are not factors for the court to apply. An example is the business concern about misuse of financial information required to be disclosed in discovery on the issue of damages—it is not unusual for one party to want damages tried separately from liability, with a stay of discovery as

---

3. Swofford v. B & W, Inc., 336 F.2d 406, 415 (5th Cir.1964).

4. Lis v. Robert Packer Hospital, 579 F.2d 819, 824 (3d Cir.1978) ("[I]n this circuit ... the decision to bifurcate *vel non* is a matter to be decided on a case-by-case basis and must be subject to an informed discretion by the trial judge in each instance.").

5. De Anda v. City of Long Beach, 7 F.3d 1418, 1421 (9th Cir.1993); Idzojtic v. Pennsylvania R. Co., 456 F.2d 1228, 1230 (3d Cir.1972).

6. R.E. Linder Steel Erection Co., Inc. v. Wedemeyer, Cernik, Corrubia, Inc., 585 F.Supp. 1530, 1534 (D.Md.1984) (bifurcation denied).

7. Hosie v. Chicago & N. W. Ry. Co., 282 F.2d 639, 643 (7th Cir.1960).

8. Saxion v. Titan–C–Manufacturing, Inc., 86 F.3d 553, 556 (6th Cir.1996) (bifurcation ordered after plaintiff rested because parties were confused about what issues were being tried); Helminski v. Ayerst Laboratories, a Div. of American Home Products Corp., 766 F.2d 208, 212 (6th Cir.1985) (bifurcation ordered during trial in order to protect against undue prejudice from evidence only relevant to damage phase).

9. *See, e.g.,* E.D. Ill. Local Rule 21; Hosie v. Chicago & N. W. Ry. Co., 282 F.2d 639, 643 n. 1 (7th Cir.1960).

well in order to keep financial disclosures to a minimum until liability has been established.[10] Other considerations are confusion, waste of time because some issues might be dispositive, and delay. Actions seeking perceived anti-competitive relief, as in the case of an action to protect proprietary rights, met with counterclaims for violations of the antitrust and RICO laws, and for unfair competition, are likely to crawl, taking on lives of their own; they can be wasteful without separation.[11] An important business consideration is cost, where one issue or claim might be dispositive of some or all other claims and can be tried without confusion.[12] Piecemeal litigation is not favored, but when judicial economy is served by separation of issues such as liability and damages or claims such as principal claims from defensive broadly stated and vague claims about monopoly, separation is appropriate.[13]

Separation of issues or claims must not have the effect of denying a party its Seventh Amendment right to a jury trial.[14] This effect might, however, be avoided by simply trying the jury issues first.[15] Trials can be separated into phases before the same jury,[16] avoiding any Seventh Amendment problem, or into entirely separate proceedings before a second jury[17] as long as the second jury is not deciding the same factual issue decided by the first jury.[18] A party might prefer a second jury rather than separate trials before the same jury if the evidence in one trial might prejudice that party in regard to trial of other issues or claims. If there are claims among various parties but no claims among all parties, counsel certainly should consider how a single trial might prejudice his client where evidence pertaining to other parties is particularly damaging.

10. See, e.g., Laitram Corp. v. Hewlett–Packard Co., 791 F.Supp. 113, 114 (E.D.La. 1992).

11. Brandt, Inc. v. Crane, 97 F.R.D. 707, 708 (N.D.Ill.1983).

12. Ellingson Timber Co. v. Great Northern Ry. Co., 424 F.2d 497, 499 (9th Cir.1970) (separate trial ordered with discovery proceeding on just the dispositive issue); Kahn v. General Motors Corp., 865 F.Supp. 210, 215 (S.D.N.Y.1994) (patent ownership potentially dispositive, separate trial ordered).

13. Smith v. Alyeska Pipeline Service Co., 538 F.Supp. 977, 983 (D.Del.1982).

14. De Anda v. City of Long Beach, 7 F.3d 1418, 1421 (9th Cir.1993) (separation resulted in plaintiff never having had his claim against the individual tried because the individual for no reason was separated from others alleged to be parties to a conspiracy and the case against him became moot after the jury rendered a verdict for the defendants).

15. Beacon Theatres, Inc. v. Westover, 359 U.S. 500, 510–11, 79 S.Ct. 948, 956–57, 3 L.Ed.2d 988 (1959).

16. Laitram Corp. v. Hewlett–Packard Co., 791 F.Supp. 113, 115 (E.D.La.1992); TBG, Inc. v. Bendis, 160 F.R.D. 621, 623 (D.Kan.1995) ("Separate trials to the same jury will alleviate the defendants' concerns about duplication of evidence and inconsistent verdicts.").

17. Arthur Young & Co. v. U.S. Dist. Court, 549 F.2d 686, 693 (9th Cir.1977)(Seventh Amendment does not require that all evidence be presented to trier of fact at one hearing; distinct factual issues may be considered by separate juries); Arnold v. United Artists Theatre Circuit, Inc., 158 F.R.D. 439, 459–60 (N.D.Cal.1994). Cf. Whelan v. Abell, 939 F.Supp. 44, 46–47 (D.D.C.1996) (Seventh Amendment not violated when a new trial on damages resulted in a jury finding of no damages despite first jury finding of liability).

18. Matter of Rhone–Poulenc Rorer Inc., 51 F.3d 1293, 1303 (7th Cir.1995).

(b) Effect of Order for Separate Trials

The effect of separation under Rule 42(b) is important to a party's right of immediate appeal, just as in the case of consolidation under Rule 42(a). Rule 42(b) empowers a court to order a "separate trial," not a "severance of the action." The terms "separate trial" and "severance," often erroneously used interchangeably, have distinctly different meanings and results under the Federal Rules.[19]

An order for separate trials under Rule 42(b) does not result in the creation of separate legal actions. Therefore, there is still a single judgment at the end of all separate trials, with no right of appellate review until all trials are concluded, unless a Rule 54(b) certification is entered.[20]

When claims are "severed" under Rules 14 and 21, the original action is actually divided into two or more separate, independent actions, and a trial in one concludes with a final appealable judgment irrespective of the status of the other severed claims.[21]

When moving for bifurcation based upon Rule 42(b), care should be taken to make specific reference to the Rule and to adhere to its words.

(c) Criteria for Separate Trials

Rule 42(b) states the relevant criteria: need to achieve greater convenience or to avoid prejudice, or when separate trials will lead to expedition and economy. A moving party will probably recite all of these criteria, but only one need be established,[22] and the party seeking separate trials has the burden of showing it.[23] Inherent is the limitation that the issue to be tried separately be so distinct and separate that a separate trial will not cause an injustice.[24] These criteria have been explained by different courts, such as this:

> A scholarly authority on pretrial procedure counsels that the following factors should be considered in assessing whether bifurcation is appropriate: (1) the complexity of the issues; (2) whether there would be a risk of jury misunderstanding in a nonbifurcated trial; (3) whether bifurcation would facilitate disposition of the issues; and (4) whether bifurcation would prejudice either of the parties.[25]

Another court identified the controlling factors as "1) whether holding separate trials is unfair ...; 2) whether separate trials would truly

---

19. McDaniel v. Anheuser–Busch, Inc., 987 F.2d 298, 304 (5th Cir.1993).

20. Chrysler Credit Corp. v. Country Chrysler, Inc., 928 F.2d 1509, 1519 (10th Cir.1991); Atari, Inc. v. JS & A Group, Inc., 747 F.2d 1422 (Fed.Cir.1984).

21. United States v. O'Neil, 709 F.2d 361, 365–72 (5th Cir.1983).

22. Saxion v. Titan–C–Manufacturing, Inc., 86 F.3d 553, 556 (6th Cir.1996).

23. Lowe v. Philadelphia Newspapers, Inc., 594 F.Supp. 123, 125 (E.D.Pa.1984).

24. Swofford v. B & W, Inc., 336 F.2d 406, 415 (5th Cir.1964); McDaniel, 987 F.2d at 305.

25. Arnold v. United Artists Theatre Circuit, Inc., 158 F.R.D. 439, 459 (N.D.Cal. 1994) (citation omitted).

expedite the litigation …; [and] 3) whether claims at issue arise out of the same set of facts as main claims. . . . "[26]

The criteria of Rule 42(b) have been applied narrowly. Courts frequently include boilerplate comments such as that separate trials are the exception, not a matter of routine;[27] that bifurcation is not the usual course;[28] that separate trials are ordered only when clearly necessary;[29] that single trials are generally more efficient and expedient;[30] that the moving party has the burden of demonstrating a proper basis for bifurcation;[31] that the decision is left to the court's informed discretion;[32] that determination of the issue is on a case-by-case basis.[33]

Of the three considerations identified in Rule 42(b), prejudice is paramount, and if there is likely to be substantial prejudice with a single trial, convenience and economy will not warrant denying a motion for separate trials.[34] However, prejudice cannot be a mere possibility,[35] and where instructions and jury verdicts can be designed to avoid the prejudice, separation of issues or claims will be denied.[36]

A prejudice often argued is the "spill-over" effect from evidence relevant to one issue or claim, on the jury's decision of an issue or claim with respect to which the evidence is irrelevant.[37] In "antitrust conspiracy to monopolize" litigation, a party should consider the spill-over effect of evidence related to one party but not another among alleged conspirators.[38] In patent litigation, a defendant may have reason to fear that evidence of willful infringement, which is relevant to the court's discretion (not the jury's determination) to award enhanced damages, will impact on the jury's decision on infringement itself.[39] Emotionally

26. TBG, Inc. v. Bendis, 160 F.R.D. 621, 622 (D.Kan.1995) (citations omitted).

27. Keyes Fibre Co. v. Packaging Corp. of America, 763 F.Supp. 374, 375 (N.D.Ill. 1991); Marshall v. Overhead Door Corp., 131 F.R.D. 94, 97 (E.D.Pa.1990); Corrigan v. Methodist Hospital, 160 F.R.D. 55, 56–57 (E.D.Pa.1995).

28. Keyes Fibre Co., 763 F.Supp. at 375.

29. Corrigan, 160 F.R.D. at 56–57.

30. Id.; Lowe v. Philadelphia Newspapers, Inc., 594 F.Supp. 123, 125 (E.D.Pa. 1984); Miller v. New Jersey Transit Authority Rail Operations, 160 F.R.D. 37, 40 (D.N.J.1995).

31. Marshall, 131 F.R.D. at 97.

32. Id.; Keyes Fibre Co., 763 F.Supp. at 375; Miller, 160 F.R.D. at 40.

33. Lowe, 594 F.Supp. at 125; Miller, 160 F.R.D. at 40.

34. Tri–R Systems, Ltd. v. Friedman & Son, Inc., 94 F.R.D. 726, 728 (D.Colo.1982) ("Where there is substantial prejudice, considerations of time, economy and convenience must yield thereto.") (citation omitted).

35. Id.

36. Id.; Keister v. Dow Chemical Co., 723 F.Supp. 117, 121 (E.D.Ark.1989) (in action against chemical manufacturer and chemical plant owners, court did not find spill-over effect so likely as to warrant separate trials, and prejudice was avoidable).

37. Corrigan v. Methodist Hospital, 160 F.R.D. 55, 56–57 (E.D.Pa.1995).

38. See, e.g., Tri–R Systems, Ltd., 94 F.R.D. 726 (separate trial denied).

39. See, e.g., Sage Products, Inc. v. Devon Industries, Inc., 1994 WL 791601 (C.D.Cal.1994) (bifurcation granted on willfulness); Swofford v. B & W, Inc., 336 F.2d 406, 415 (5th Cir.1964) (bifurcation between liability and damages affirmed). Patent cases are far from consistent, however. See, e.g., Cameco Industries, Inc. v. Louisiana Cane Mfg., Inc., 1995 WL 468234 (E.D.La.1995) (bifurcation between liability and damages denied); Home Elevators, Inc. v. Millar Elevator Service Co., 933 F.Supp.

charged evidence related to damages in any case, can have a spill-over effect on liability where it may be irrelevant.[40] Nonetheless, the mere assertion that the jury will be influenced by emotions associated with the damages evidence, without identifying actual prejudice specific to the case, will not be adequate.[41]

Prejudice also arises where a party is faced with the dilemma of having to choose a defense to one issue that may undermine the defense of another issue. This is a problem often found in patent infringement and other cases where reliance on opinion of counsel may have relevance to damages but not liability. A patent infringer is liable for damages and the court has discretion to award up to three-fold the damages found, if the infringement is willful.[42] An infringer can avoid a finding of willful infringement by offering evidence that on good faith it relied upon opinion of counsel. Of course, this defense requires waiver of the attorney-client privilege.[43] The patent owner almost always alleges the infringement was willful and seeks discovery on such subjects as attorney opinions intended to be relied upon in defense. The opinion often contains what another party would deem admissions regarding certain issues, assessment of the probabilities as to issues, disclosure of facts not previously known, or discussion of strategies and legal theories. Without separation of issues, a party is forced to decide on waiver of the privilege before liability has been established.

The Federal Circuit has signaled its belief that bifurcation would be an appropriate solution.[44] Nonetheless motions for separate trials of infringement and willfulness/damages, based upon this prejudice, are still frequently denied.[45] In 1991 the Federal Circuit stated that courts

1090, 1091–92 (N.D.Ga.1996) (bifurcation denied); Keyes Fibre Co. v. Packaging Corp. of America, 763 F.Supp. 374, 377 (N.D.Ill. 1991) (bifurcation denied); Remcor Products Co. v. Servend Intern., Inc., 1994 WL 594723 (N.D.Ill.1994) (bifurcation denied).

40. See, e.g., Helminski v. Ayerst Laboratories, a Div. of American Home Products Corp., 766 F.2d 208, 212 (6th Cir.1985) (bifurcation ordered where deformed child would be shown to jury on issue of damages but not liability).

41. Marshall v. Overhead Door Corp., 131 F.R.D. 94, 97–98 (E.D.Pa.1990) (bifurcation denied for lack of showing of specific prejudice from trying liability and damages together).

42. 35 U.S.C.A. § 284 (West 1984). See Chapter 63 "Patents" at § 63.6(c), infra.

43. Thorn Emi North America, Inc. v. Micron Technology, Inc., 837 F.Supp. 616, 620–21 (D.Del.1993) (reliance on opinion of counsel relevant and privilege waived); Abbott Laboratories v. Baxter Travenol Laboratories, Inc., 676 F.Supp. 831, 832 (N.D.Ill. 1987) (infringer cannot selectively waive

privilege; all opinions on same subject matter must be produced).

44. See Fromson v. Western Litho Plate & Supply Co., 853 F.2d 1568, 1572 (Fed.Cir. 1988).

45. See, e.g., Keyes Fibre Co. v. Packaging Corporation of America, 763 F.Supp. 374, 375 (N.D.Ill.1991)(privilege notwithstanding, bifurcation denied because state of mind evidence not "neatly" separable from liability); Foseco, Inc. v. Consolidated Aluminum Corp., 851 F.Supp. 369, 371 (E.D.Mo.1991)(patent infringement and damages bifurcated but willfulness issue tried in liability phase: "In a majority of cases, the issue of willfulness has generally been developed during the liability phase of a bifurcated trial."); United Air Lines, Inc. v. Wiener, 286 F.2d 302 (9th Cir.1961)(damages "interwoven" with liability); Swofford v. B & W, Inc., 336 F.2d 406, 415 (5th Cir.1964) (bifurcation affirmed: "[W]e cannot think of an instance in a patent action where the damage issue is so interwoven with the other issues that it cannot be

should "seriously consider" bifurcation to preserve the privilege, suggesting that the trial court judge review opinions in camera to ascertain the existence of prejudice.[46] Despite this strong endorsement for separate trials, courts still deny bifurcation requested in patent cases.[47]

The factors of confusion and inefficiency are the same as in the case of motions for consolidation under Rule 42(a). Likely jury confusion warranting separate trials may be established based upon anticipated length of trial[48] and complexity of issues and numbers of parties.[49] Where resolution of one issue can obviate the need for deciding other more complicated issues, separate trials are normally warranted to avoid confusion and foster economy.[50] Although separation may be the exception, it can still improve judicial economy and avoid prejudice in some litigation.

Library References:

West's Key No. Digests, Federal Civil Procedure ⊗1953–1965.
Wright, Miller, Kane & Cooper, Federal Practice and Procedure: Civil 2d §§ 1437, 1660, 2387, 3724.

§ 10.9   Practice Checklist

(a) Analysis of the Case and Determination of Strategies

(1) Initial and long term strategies involve multiple considerations. The object is to intelligently adopt a strategy consistent with the client's needs, legal requirements, and legal choices based upon business and legal interests. These strategies, included selecting claims, joining claims, filing separate actions, and choosing forums and venue. (*See* § 10.2)

(2) Prepare list of causes of action, persons having an interest, and potential parties. (*See* § 10.2)

submitted to the jury independently of the others without confusion and uncertainty, which would amount to a denial of a fair trial.").

46. Quantum Corp. v. Tandon Corp., 940 F.2d 642, 643–44 (Fed.Cir.1991).

47. Home Elevators, Inc. v. Millar Elevator Service Co., 933 F.Supp. 1090, 1092 (N.D.Ga.1996) (The *Quantum* decision notwithstanding, "such an in camera inspection is not required" and willfulness " 'is a finding of fact inextricably bound to the facts underlying infringement.' ") (citations omitted); Remcor Products Co. v. Servend International, Inc., 1994 WL 594723 (N.D.Ill.1994) (willfulness is " 'inextricably bound to the facts underlying the alleged infringement' "); Cameco Industries, Inc. v. Louisiana Cane Manufacturing, Inc., 1995 WL 468234 (E.D.La.1995) (no attorney opinion submitted for review). *But see* Sage

Products, Inc. v. Devon Industries, Inc., 1994 WL 791601 (C.D.Cal.1994)(attorney letters detailed tactical differences and legal theories, and defendant faced with a "catch-22," unless case bifurcated).

48. *In re* Beverly Hills Fire Litigation, 695 F.2d 207, 217 (6th Cir.1982)(separate trial ordered on issue of causation, alone requiring 32 days to try); Keister v. Dow Chemical Co., 723 F.Supp. 117, 121 (E.D.Ark.1989).

49. TBG, Inc. v. Bendis, 160 F.R.D. 621, 622–23 (D.Kan.1995) (securities fraud case with numerous parties and complex legal and factual issues, bifurcation ordered, with separate trials to same jury).

50. Sogmose Realties v. Twentieth Century–Fox Film Corp., 15 F.R.D. 496, 497 (S.D.N.Y.1954); Beeck v. Aquaslide 'N' Dive Corp., 562 F.2d 537, 541 (8th Cir.1977).

(3) Ascertain client litigation objectives, and essential relief; review with the client issues such as urgency, financial burden, management burden, scope of discovery, settlement, persuasion, and notoriety. Consider the likelihood that there will be counterclaims, cross claims, and third-party claims, and consider how they would impact on the interests of the client. Pursue claims which will not invite unwanted counterclaims. (*See* §§ 10.2, 10.3)

(4) Identify persons who are necessary parties with respect to particular causes of action and in the case of a defendant, identify any compulsory counterclaims. (*See* FRCP 13, 19; §§ 10.3(e), 10.4).

(5) Consider issues of federal court jurisdiction, venue, and personal jurisdiction of defendants and third-party defendants. Remember that Rule 18(a) encourages joinder of all claims in a single proceeding but it does not alter the requirements of federal jurisdiction and venue. If one claim is a federal claim and the other claims are state claims with respect to which there is no diversity, consider whether the state claims fall within the court's supplemental jurisdiction under 28 U.S.C.A. § 1367. (*See* § 10.5)

(6) Remember, venue can be waived. Therefore, consider ignoring the venue issue and wait for the defendant to raise the issue, unless the defendant can use the issue as a way to defeat your action and proceed with a declaratory judgment action that puts the defendant in the position of a plaintiff for trial strategy purposes. (*See* §§ 10.3(d), 10.4(e), 10.5(b))

(7) If reason exists to pursue multiple claims in separate proceedings, consider filing actions in separate districts with different parties to reduce the chances of transfer and consolidation. If one action is to be filed in state court, remember to use techniques for preempting removal to the federal court, such as filing the action in the state courts of defendant's state of residence or including among the defendants a party whose citizenship is not diverse to all plaintiffs. (*See* §§ 10.3, 10.4, 10.7)

(8) Choose an early litigation strategy respecting joinder of claims and parties suited to the clients objectives and draft pleadings which tell a powerful story for its effect on opposing counsel, the court and senior management of the opposing party. (*See* § 10.2)

(b) Maintenance of Control in Execution of Strategy

(1) If your strategies as plaintiff are frustrated by opposing strategies which burden the case with costly counterclaims, cross-claims, and third-party claims, or which burden plaintiff with multiple lawsuits, remember that Rules 21 and 42 provide help with consolidation, severance and separate trials. Prejudice is the paramount consideration. (*See* § 10.7, 10.8)

(2) All parties should consider whether there is likely to be a spill-over effect respecting evidence only relevant to one claim or party.

In addition, as a defendant faced with a complaint joining many claims, consider whether a defense to one claim will prejudice a defense to another claim. So long as you can be specific in identifying the evidence, such circumstances are clearly prejudicial and ample case authority holds that separate trials may be ordered to avoid the prejudice. (*See* § 10.8)

(3) Before seeking severance or separate trials, consider the effects of such an order on the rules for appeal. A severance under Rules 14 and 21 results in distinct, independent proceedings, and an appeal in one does not await a final disposition in the other severed proceedings. An order for separate trials under FRCP 42(b) does not create distinct and independent proceedings, and, therefore, a disposition of one claim will not be immediately appealable. Cite the Rule under which severance or a separate trial is sought and know the effect of which Rule is used. (*See* §§ 10.7(b), 10.8(b))

(4) If a plaintiff files separate actions and fact or legal issues are common, or if a defendant files a separate action in reply, asserting a claim which could have been asserted in a counterclaim, Rule 42(a) is available for getting these actions consolidated, and if they are pending in separate districts, move to transfer under 28 U.S.C.A. § 1404(a). If consolidation is opposed, remember that prejudice from consolidation might be avoided by appropriate jury instructions, special verdict questions, and bifurcated proceedings. (*See* § 10.7)

(5) Consolidation under Rule 42(a) can affect appellate rights. Some circuits do not treat consolidation as a merger of actions, and therefore appeal in one consolidated action does not await final disposition of the other consolidated action. Other circuits regard consolidation as a merger of the actions into the single action, and no appeal can be taken until final disposition of the entire merged action except where a Rule 54(b) certification is made. (*See* § 10.7(b))

§ 10.10   Forms

(a) Plaintiff's Motion for Consolidation of Separate Action Filed by Defendant 🖫

ABC, plaintiff	)))	
v.	))	Civil Action No. 97–C–123
XYZ, defendant	)))	

MOTION FOR ORDER OF CONSOLIDATION

Plaintiff, ABC, by its undersigned counsel, moves for an order pursuant to FRCP 42(a) consolidating this action with an action filed in this district by defendant against plaintiff entitled XYZ v. ABC, Civil Action No. _____, for the reasons that there exist common questions of law and fact to the said actions, this action was filed first, defendant's claims in the separate action could be assert-ed herein as counterclaims, and judicial economy is enhanced by such consolidation. Plaintiff submits herewith its affidavit of [insert name of counsel or other appropriate person] and brief in support of this motion, setting forth the common questions of law and fact and legal authorities demonstrating that consolidation is warranted and within the discretionary authority of this court to order.

(b) Defendant's Motion to Consolidate Separate Actions Filed by Plaintiff 🖫

ABC, plaintiff	)	
	)	
v.	)	Civil Action No. 97–C–124
	)	
XYZ, defendant	)	

MOTION FOR ORDER OF CONSOLIDATION

Defendant, XYZ, by its undersigned counsel moves for an order pursuant to FRCP 42(a) consolidating this action with an action filed by plaintiff against defendant entitled ABC v. XYZ, Civil Action No. _____, for the reasons that there exist common questions of law and fact to said actions, plaintiff under Rule 18(a) could have joined the claims asserted in the second action with its claims asserted herein, judicial economy is enhanced by such consolidation, and without consolidation inconsistent results can occur. Defendant submits herewith its affidavit of [insert name of counsel or other appropriate person] and brief in support of this motion, setting forth the common questions of law and fact, demonstrating that inconsis-tent results can occur if consolidation is not ordered, and the legal authorities demonstrating that consolidation is warranted and with-in the discretionary authority of this court to order.

(c) Motion for Severance Under Rules 14(a) and 21, and, for Alternatively, Separate Trial Under Rule 42(b) 🖫

ABC, plaintiff	)	
	)	
v.	)	Civil Action No. 97–C–125
	)	
XYZ, defendant, third-party plaintiff	)	
	)	
v.	)	
	)	
DEF, third-party defendant	)	

*MOTION FOR SEVERANCE OF THIRD–PARTY COMPLAINT,
AND ALTERNATIVE MOTION FOR SEPARATE TRIAL*

Plaintiff, ABC, by its undersigned attorneys moves under FRCP 14(a) and 21 for severance of the third-party complaint made by defendant third-party plaintiff XYZ against third-party defendant DEF, for the reason that plaintiff has no interest in said claims asserted in the third-party complaint, proceedings with respect to the third-party complaint will cause undue delay in the disposition of plaintiff's complaint, and plaintiff is prejudiced by the added expense, delay, and likely jury confusion resulting from proceeding with the third-party complaint.

In the alternative plaintiff moves for an order under FRCP 42(b) that a separate trial be had with respect to the claims asserted in the third-party complaint and the counterclaims of the third-party defendant for the reasons stated above.

Submitted herewith is the affidavit of [insert name of counsel or other appropriate person] and brief of plaintiff in support of this motion setting forth the basis for this motion and the legal authorities establishing that severance or alternatively, a separate trial, is warranted and within the discretionary authority of this court to order.

(d) Motion for Separate Trial Under Rule 42(b) ▣

	)	
ABC, plaintiff	)	
	)	
v.	)	Civil Action No. 97–C–126
	)	
XYZ, defendant	)	
	)	

*MOTION FOR SEPARATE TRIAL UNDER RULE 42(b) ON
CLAIM THAT INFRINGEMENT WAS WILLFUL*

Defendant, XYZ, by its undersigned counsel moves for an order under FRCP 42(b) that plaintiff's Count II of its complaint, alleging that the infringement by defendant alleged in Count I was willful, be tried in a separate trial from the trial on Count I because (i) the claim of willful infringement in Count II only has relevance to this court's discretionary authority under 35 U.S.C.A. § 284 to enhance damages, if the jury finds infringement as alleged in Count I, the determination to award enhanced damages is not made by the jury; and, (ii) a single trial on both Counts I and II is unfairly prejudicial to defendant for the reason that the jury will implicitly consider such actions when deciding the issue of liability, and a jury instruction against making such implicit consideration will be ineffective, and for the reason that a single trial will compel defendant to make an election to defend the willful claim without evidence of reliance upon opinion of counsel or waive the attorney-client privilege giving plaintiff the advantage of defense trial counsel strategies and assessments of the merits of the liability claim before it is decided.

Defendant submits herewith the affidavit of [insert name of counsel or other appropriate person] and brief in support of this motion demonstrating that a separate trial is warranted and that this court has the discretionary authority to enter the order requested. In accordance with the decision of the Federal Circuit Court of Appeals, which has exclusive appellate jurisdiction under 28 U.S.C.A. § 1295, stated in *Quantum Corp. v. Tandon Corp.*, 940 F.2d 642, 643–44 (Fed.Cir.1991), defendant consents to submit all opinions of counsel relevant to the defense for its in camera review.

CHAPTER 11

MULTIDISTRICT LITIGATION

by
John L. Strauch
and
Robert C. Weber*

Table of Sections

* The authors gratefully acknowledge the substantial contributions of their partners, Charles H. Moellenberg, Jr., Laura E. Ellsworth and John D. Goetz of Jones, Day, Reavis & Pogue's Pittsburgh Office in the drafting of this chapter. In addition, the authors would like to thank the Clerk to the Judicial Panel on Multidistrict Litigation, Patricia D. Howard, and her staff for their generous and courteous help in providing statistical and other information for use in this chapter.

WESTLAW Electronic Research

See WESTLAW Electronic Research Guide preceding the Summary of Contents.

---

§ 11.1 Scope Note

This chapter will discuss multidistrict litigation primarily under 28 U.S.C.A. § 1407 ("MDL"). The chapter will focus initially on preliminary strategy considerations, including whether to request or oppose MDL, advising the client about its strategic options, and preparing for and organizing MDL. Next, the chapter will address the overall structure of MDL, including general MDL procedures, the factors considered in transfer decisions, the effect of a transfer, the role of transferor and transferee courts, and appeal issues. Finally, issues of case management, discovery and settlement strategy unique to MDL will be discussed.

Library References:

West's Key No. Digests, Federal Civil Procedure ☞9; Federal Courts ☞151–157.
Wright, Miller & Cooper, Federal Practice and Procedure: Civil 2d § 3861.

§ 11.2 Overview of the MDL Process

MDL is a creature of statute: 28 U.S.C.A. § 1407. This statute established a panel of seven federal judges known as the Judicial Panel On Multidistrict Litigation ("Panel"). The sole function of the Panel is to decide whether cases pending in different districts should be aggregated and transferred to a single district for pretrial purposes and whether those cases should be remanded to the originating district at a later date.[1] The Panel makes no decisions about the substantive merits of a case, nor does it exercise any appellate oversight.[2] The Panel simply decides which district court will handle the cases.

§ 11.2

1. 28 U.S.C.A. § 1407(a)(1) (West 1993 & Supp. 1997).

2. *See* State of Utah v. American Pipe and Const. Co., 316 F.Supp. 837, 838–40 (C.D.Cal.1970); *In re* Glenn W. Turner En-ters. Litig., 368 F.Supp. 805, 806 (J.P.M.L. 1973).

The legislative intent behind creation of the Panel was to provide a mechanism by which cases involving common issues of fact could be transferred to a single district court for coordinated pretrial (principally discovery) proceedings. A mechanism for consolidation was perceived to be necessary to avoid duplicative discovery and potentially conflicting rulings between the district courts, and thus to achieve efficiencies for the judicial system as a whole.

Because common questions of fact and the attendant potential efficiencies in discovery are the linchpins of the MDL process,[3] the most common candidates for MDL treatment are cases in which a single event has allegedly caused harm to multiple plaintiffs living in diverse jurisdictions. Examples of such cases include air crash disaster cases, securities actions, and product liability suits alleging a common defect across a product line.[4]

The essential mechanics of the MDL process can be illustrated by a hypothetical case. Assume that an airplane crash in Pittsburgh, Pennsylvania has spawned five lawsuits by families of passengers in federal courts in their home states of Ohio, California, Texas, Pennsylvania and Florida. Any party in any of those actions can file a motion before the Panel asking for the transfer of all actions to a single district for pretrial proceedings pursuant to 28 U.S.C.A. § 1407. Alternatively, the Panel can issue orders sua sponte requiring the parties to these actions to present arguments to the Panel as to whether the actions should be transferred.

If the Panel concludes that transfer should occur, all five cases will be transferred to a single district court, which may or may not be one of the five original jurisdictions.[5] The five district courts in which the actions were originally filed are called *transferor courts* within the MDL framework. The single district court to which the cases are transferred is called the *transferee court.*

When the cases are ready for remand, the reverse occurs. The transferee court or one or more parties notifies the Panel that they believe remand would be appropriate.[6] The Panel then decides if the cases should be remanded[7] and, if so, enters an order returning the cases to their transferor districts.

Another term frequently used within the MDL process is "tag-along action," which is "a civil action pending in a district court and involving common questions of fact with actions previously transferred under Section 1407."[8] In other words, if the Panel has already transferred all cases arising out of the airplane crash to a single district, creating a new MDL proceeding, the next case filed by a passenger would likely be

---

3. *See infra* § 11.9 for the various factors considered in deciding whether to transfer.

4. *See infra* § 11.24 for a comprehensive listing of MDL cases by case type.

5. *See infra* § 11.10 for the considerations applied to determine the court to which the cases are transferred.

6. *See infra* § 11.20 for remand procedure.

7. *See infra* § 11.20 for factors considered in remand.

8. JPML Rule 1.

considered a "tag-along." Tag-along actions typically become part of an MDL through the Panel's issuance of Conditional Transfer Orders.[9] The transfer of cases filed after the initial MDL transfer order is not automatic and requires an additional order.

Before the Panel's transfer order, the transferor courts have complete control over their actions as if no MDL existed.[10] Once the transfer order becomes effective, however, the transferor courts lose all power and the transferee court assumes full responsibility.[11] If the cases are remanded, the transferor court once again resumes full authority. In both the transferor and transferee courts, the litigation proceeds as normal litigation under the Federal Rules of Civil Procedure and the Local Rules of the particular district. The only procedural difference in an MDL setting is that more aggressive case management techniques will probably be applied in an MDL transferee court.[12]

Although the literal wording of the MDL statute appears to mandate the remand of cases at the conclusion of pretrial proceedings, it is important to recognize that, in practice, cases almost never return to their home forum for trial. Since the statute was passed in 1968, 109,410 cases have been transferred but only 3,757 have been remanded by the Panel.[13] This is due in large part to the exercise by transferee courts of the power to make dispositive rulings or approve settlements.[14] In part, however, the statistics also result from the frequent practice of transferee courts to transfer the cases to themselves for trial pursuant to 28 U.S.C.A. § 1404 (convenience transfers).[15] In light of this practice, it is highly likely that, absent a definitive future ruling requiring remand of all such cases for trial,[16] an MDL transfer order will result in final disposition in the transferee court including the possibility of a full trial in that forum.

Consequently, plaintiff counsel considering whether to use MDL are well-advised to assume that there is a significant chance that the MDL process could result in a trial in a jurisdiction different from the one in

---

9. *See infra* § 11.7.

10. However, as a practical matter, the pendency of Panel proceedings may accelerate or postpone certain activity in the transferor court. *See infra* § 11.13.

11. *See infra* § 11.13 for the relative responsibilities of transferor and transferee courts.

12. *See infra* §§ 11.15–11.17, 11.19 for discussion of case management techniques in MDL. Although the basic procedural rules applicable in the transferee court will be generally familiar to practitioners, there are unique strategic considerations.

13. Administrative Office of the United States Courts: 1996 Report of the Director, Table S–22.

14. *See infra* § 11.13 (powers of transferee court to make dispositive rulings);

§ 11.21 (reasons why MDL can increase settlement pressures).

15. *See infra* § 11.18.

16. At the time this chapter went to print, it was common practice for transferee courts to approve § 1404 transfers to themselves for trial. However, in Lexecon Inc. v. Milberg Weiss Bershad Hynes & Lerach, ___ U.S. ___, 118 S.Ct. 956, 140 L.Ed.2d 62 (1998), the United States Supreme Court held that the transferee court may not assign an MDL transferred case to itself for trial. The decision leaves open the questions whether a transferor court may use § 1404(a) to assign the case back to the transferee court or whether the parties may stipulate to trial before the transferee court.

which they have filed. Similarly, all counsel participating in pretrial proceedings in a transferee court must be cognizant of the fact that the judge handling the discovery phase of the case may turn out to be the trial judge. Such a possibility should strongly influence counsel's decisions about the manner in which discovery and motions are handled, as well as the nature of settlement discussions held with the transferee court.

Library References:

West's Key No. Digests, Federal Civil Procedure ☞9.
Wright, Miller & Cooper, Federal Practice and Procedure: Civil 2d § 3862.

§ 11.3 Preliminary Considerations and Strategy

(a) Procedural Alternatives to MDL

Multidistrict litigation comes in diverse shapes and sizes. Since many commercial products and services, from consumer products to securities to insurance policies, are sold nationwide, the potential for nationwide litigation arising out of a common or related set of events, but filed in a number of different forums, is substantial and covers a wide range of business activity.

Although this chapter will focus on multidistrict litigation in the federal courts under the federal statutory scheme, it is important to bear in mind that numerous procedural devices other than MDL are available to assist in the coordination of widespread litigation. Thus, although one important issue confronting the attorney and client facing the prospect of mass litigation with federal court involvement will be whether to choose the federal multidistrict litigation procedure available under 28 U.S.C.A. § 1407, that procedure should be considered along with other available procedures. The alternative procedures include:

- Rule 16 pretrial orders;[1]
- Joinder rules (FRCP 19 and 20);[2]

§ 11.3

1. FRCP 16(c) expressly authorizes a federal judge to "take appropriate action, with respect to: * * * (12) the need for adopting special procedures for managing potentially difficult or protracted actions that may involve complex issues, multiple parties, difficult legal questions, or unusual proof problems." The court has broad discretion under Rule 16 to consider any matter and to enter orders "as may facilitate the just, speedy, and inexpensive disposition of the action." This rule gives the federal courts considerable flexibility in the absence of a formal MDL proceeding, or in the event of a perceived need for state and federal court coordination, to fashion proce-dures to streamline litigation which cuts across forum and jurisdictional lines. Of course, a court's orders are limited to the cases over which it has jurisdiction. Therefore, without the agreement and coopera-tion of other courts, the reach of a court's Rule 16 orders is limited to the cases on its docket.

2. Compulsory joinder under Rule 19 is rarely required, because the consequences of such a finding could be dismissal of the entire action or certain claims. FRCP 19(b). Typically courts do not find that compulso-ry joinder is required of joint tortfeasors or injured parties. *See* Temple v. Synthes Corp., 498 U.S. 5, 7, 111 S.Ct. 315, 316, 112 L.Ed.2d 263 (1990) (holding that joint tort-

- Interpleader (FRCP 22);[3]
- Class actions (FRCP 23);
- Intervention (FRCP 24);[4]
- Consolidation (FRCP 42(a));[5]
- Appointment of a single judge to hear related cases (28 U.S.C.A. § 292);[6]

feasors are not necessary parties under Rule 19); Complex Litigation: Statutory Recommendations and Analysis with Reporter's Study: A Model System for State-To-State Transfer and Consolidation, The American Law Inst. (1994). Thus, where potential plaintiffs or defendants are not within the jurisdiction and do not want to combine their actions voluntarily, Rule 19 usually will not require consolidation. Indeed, arguments for misjoinder can be made if the different claims arise in different jurisdictions and involve potentially different facts, applicable laws and other issues, such as appropriate venue. See Tick v. Cohen, 787 F.2d 1490, 1493–94 (11th Cir. 1986) (venue and jurisdictional limitations may bar joinder); 7 Charles Alan Wright, Arthur R. Miller & Mary Kay Kane, Federal Practice and Procedure §§ 1604–06 (2d ed. 1986); 4 James Wm. Moore, et al., Moore's Federal Practice ¶ 19.04 (3d ed. 1997).

Joinder under Rule 20 has limited utility because the joinder is discretionary to the parties and each new party must individually satisfy the requirements for jurisdiction and venue. See Wright & Miller, supra, § 1659; Moore, supra, ¶ 20.02[5]. See also 28 U.S.C.A. § 1367 (West 1993 & Supp. 1997) (supplemental jurisdiction rules). Each party must personally appear, unlike with representative class actions. Though the standards for Rule 20 joinder are sufficiently lax to permit some joinder in most mass litigation, it is typically used only to join small groups of parties having similar claims within a single jurisdiction. See Chapter 10 "Joinder, Consolidation and Severance," at §§ 10.4 and 10.5, supra.

3. Situations calling for the use of interpleader are rare. Interpleader is typically used where a stakeholder of certain property seeks to determine in one action the contesting rights of those claiming entitlement to that property. See Chapter 14 "Parties," infra.

4. Intervention has some utility in aggregating parties having similar claims. The breadth of the rule for permissive intervention under FRCP 24(b), which requires only "a question of law or fact in common," would permit intervention in most cases of mass litigation. However, intervention is limited by the parties' voluntary initiative, the courts' discretion, and rules for subject matter jurisdiction and venue. FRCP 82. See 7C Charles Alan Wright and Arthur R. Miller, Federal Practice and Procedure, § 1913 (2d ed. 1986); Moore, supra note 2, at ¶ 24.10[1]. Intervention as a matter of right will rarely apply in the context of mass litigation, since the intervenors' rights can be protected by existing parties or in other lawsuits. See 7C Wright & Miller, supra § 1909; Moore, supra note 2, at ¶ 24.03[4][a].

5. Consolidation under FRCP 42(a) is limited to pending cases before a single court. Individual parties and counsel continue to appear and can have an opportunity to control their own destinies. Courts may creatively use consolidation for certain pretrial proceedings, case organization, discovery, settlement or certain issues for trial. Its broad standard, requiring only "a common question of law or fact," is easily met in complex litigation, giving federal judges the mechanism for innovative and coordinated judicial management of similar litigation within their courts. In combination with Rule 42(b), judges can consolidate certain claims or issues to advance judicial economy and efficiency, yet still separate parties, claims or defenses for trial to avoid unnecessary complexity, to allow full presentation of individual issues, and to prevent an unduly long or complicated trial for a single jury. See Chapter 10 "Joinder, Consolidation and Severance," supra.

6. This statute allows the appointment of one district judge to handle and hear all similar cases within a circuit. 28 U.S.C.A. § 292(b) (West 1993 & Supp. 1997). The Chief Justice of the United States similarly may appoint a single district judge to hear all similar cases nationwide (§ 292(d)), but the MDL procedure is more likely to be

- Change of venue (28 U.S.C.A. § 1404);[7]
- Coordination between courts through joint conferences and other proceedings.[8]

These procedures can be used in various combinations, limited though by the rules themselves, principles of due process, and the needs and creativity of the courts and counsel.

(b) Strategic Options

The attorney will need to provide early advice on the alternative approaches available to handle mass litigation and the advantages and disadvantages of each approach. Among the various options listed above, as a practical matter the main alternative approaches to be considered will be: (1) no consolidation of the cases; (2) consolidation of cases within each judicial district; (3) class action; and (4) multidistrict transfer of cases pursuant to 28 U.S.C.A. § 1407.

(1) No Consolidation of Cases

No consolidation of cases is a practical alternative when the number of cases is small. This often occurs when plaintiffs bring individual test cases, because the cases present novel issues of law or difficult issues of proof. In this situation, plaintiffs might opt to bring only a few test cases in jurisdictions viewed to be most favorable to plaintiffs, before making a large investment in starting mass litigation.

used in that situation. This statute could provide authority to overcome the MDL statute's literal limitation of MDL transfers to pretrial proceedings should that become necessary.

7. Under the authority of the change of venue rule, a federal court may transfer a case to any district "where [the case] might have been brought" upon a finding that a transfer is "[f]or the convenience of parties and witnesses" and "in the interest of justice." The utility of this rule is limited by the need for coordination of many federal courts in typical mass litigation and also by jurisdiction and venue rules. *See also infra* § 11.18. *See* Chapter 3 "Venue, Forum Selection and Transfer," *supra*.

8. Federal and state courts have certain latitude to hold joint conferences; to issue parallel case management, pretrial and discovery orders; to make joint appointments of lead or liaison counsel and discovery or settlement masters; and to enter orders limiting duplicative discovery. Manual for Complex Litigation, (Third) §§ 31.14, 31.3 (1997). Coordination, though, is discretion-ary and becomes increasingly difficult as the litigation becomes more widely dispersed throughout the federal and state courts. Moreover, the prospect of federal and state court coordination must not imperil the rights of the individual litigants under the rules of civil procedure and constitutional due process. *See* FRCP 1; 4 Charles Alan Wright & Arthur R. Miller, Federal Practice and Procedure § 1029 (2d ed. 1987); Moore's, *supra* note 2, ¶ 1.21[1][a]; Moss v. Associated Transp., Inc., 344 F.2d 23, 26 (6th Cir.1965) (considerations of economy of time and money must yield to the paramount consideration of the administration of justice in a fair and impartial trial). Judicial efficiency may not sacrifice the fundamental procedural rights and opportunity to be heard of the individual litigants. Informal coordination and communications among different courts, outside the defined procedural rules and MDL proceedings, presents this risk. *Cf.* Mathews v. Eldridge, 424 U.S. 319, 96 S.Ct. 893, 47 L.Ed.2d 18 (1976) (due process requires that individuals receive adequate procedures to protect their rights).

When pursuing a "test case" strategy in one or only a few jurisdictions, plaintiffs might also agree among themselves which of those test cases should be brought to trial first.[9] Unless legal theories and factual development prove successful in the test cases or the statute of limitations compels the filing of many actions, the litigation may not spread quickly and may be centered in a few jurisdictions. In this situation, there is no request for MDL by plaintiffs and no need for MDL for purposes of judicial economy.

A defendant still might consider an MDL strategy in order to try to put all test cases in a jurisdiction which the defendant views as favorable, or because the defendant anticipates or wants to be protected in the event that the litigation expands. But if the defendant does not request an MDL transfer order, then the litigation strategy of all parties will focus on choosing the best jurisdiction in which to prosecute the test cases, considering, among other factors, applicable law, discovery rules, development of individual case facts, procedural rules and practices regarding dispositive motions and jury trials, and the likely timing of case resolution in each jurisdiction.

(2) Factors to Consider Regarding Consolidation

If a number of cases have been filed in the same jurisdiction, then the plaintiffs or the defendants should consider whether to ask for consolidation of the cases for purposes of discovery, motions, settlement or trial. Factors for plaintiffs and defendants to consider include:

- whether, based on the facts of the case or the applicable law, a case warrants being a leader or a follower;

- whether, from the plaintiffs' point of view, there are benefits from pooling resources and cooperating with other plaintiffs and their counsel;

- whether, from the defendant's point of view, there are benefits from making it more difficult for plaintiffs to pool resources;

- the extent to which potential conflicts exist among the plaintiffs or their counsel (such as fee or cost sharing, who will take the lead, which cases will be tried first, how to present individual issues, or how to negotiate settlements and divide the proceeds);

- whether the cases present important, unique issues, or instead present a number of common issues of law and fact, including the need for joinder of or evidence regarding the conduct of third parties;

- whether consolidation will expedite or delay case resolution for each party;

- whether consolidation might lead to limitations on pleadings, discovery, briefing or opportunities to present evidence at trial;

9. *See, e.g.,* American Law Institute, Complex Litigation: Statutory Recommen- dations and Analysis, 9–10 (1994) (plaintiffs' coordination of MER/29 litigation).

- whether all claims can be tried together efficiently and effectively before the same jury in one trial;

- whether the judge who is likely to receive the consolidated cases is likely to be more favorable on the substantive law or procedure than other judges who have some of the cases;

- whether the cases have the same or many overlapping counsel;

- presence of prior favorable rulings or jury verdicts in any transfer- or jurisdiction;

- the stage of development of the individual cases;

- the effect of consolidation on litigation costs and attorney's fees;

- the advantages or disadvantages of uniformity in rulings;

- the potential impact of consolidation on settlement and each party's settlement strategy;

- the possible effect of consolidation on collateral estoppel, law-of-the-case or res judicata arguments.

Local related-case rules might lead to an assignment of the cases to the same judge within a jurisdiction, even without formal consolidation. Even absent such a local rule, once a significant number of similar cases are filed, the court may act on its own to assign all of the cases to the same judge, producing some of the effects of consolidation.

If litigation is concentrated in one or a few federal judicial districts, the use of the MDL procedure is probably unnecessary. Consolidation of the cases within a particular judicial district can be accomplished under FRCP 42(a) or through each district's related-case procedure. Transfers under the change of venue statute, 28 U.S.C.A. § 1404, might also be practical. If only a few judicial districts are involved, the litigation is likely to be manageable without resort to MDL, and the MDL Judicial Panel is not likely to use its statutory powers.[10] Moreover, the defendants, and perhaps the plaintiffs, will have the advantage of spreading the litigation risk among several jurisdictions. It may also be advantageous to the parties to focus more particularly on the differences in the law among the jurisdictions and to develop the facts for the individual claims in order to emphasize the best arguments of law and evidence to win in each case.[11] The more important issues in this situation will be whether and how discovery will be organized and coordinated among the pending cases; how to achieve consistency in discovery responses, litigation positions and strategy; how the consolidated cases will be tried within each jurisdiction; whether plaintiffs or defendants are interested in attempting a global settlement of the cases; and whether the defen-

---

10. It should be noted, however, that MDL proceedings have sometimes been used to consolidate as few as two or three cases in different jurisdictions. Manual for Complex Litigation, (Third) § 31.13 at 251–52 (1997). *See, e.g., In re* Clark Oil and Ref. Corp. Antitrust Litig., 364 F.Supp. 458 (JPML 1973).

11. Of course, this potential rationale assumes that the individual cases transferred to an MDL proceeding are not returned to their original courts for final disposition after pretrial proceedings.

dants will be subject to issue or claim preclusion in other jurisdictions if they receive an adverse verdict.

(3) Class Actions

Plaintiffs may consider a class action as an alternative to the filing of numerous individual cases, either in a single jurisdiction or across a number of jurisdictions. Of course, class actions might also be included among the cases transferred to an MDL proceeding. The class action device differs fundamentally from the transfer of cases for pretrial and discovery purposes under 28 U.S.C.A. § 1407. Because class actions are representational and a judgment is binding on all members of the class, due process[12] and FRCP 23 provide a number of procedural safeguards to protect the absent class members.

In considering whether to use the class action as an alternative to requesting the transfer of numerous individual actions into an MDL proceeding, plaintiffs must initially assess their prospects of satisfying the criteria set forth in the Federal Rules for class certification, particularly in light of the skepticism recently exhibited by federal appellate courts to approve class certification in mass tort litigation.[13] Consolidation does not require satisfaction of the same criteria and is more subject to the discretion of the trial court. Likewise, the criteria for MDL treatment are much less stringent than those for class certification.[14]

Additional practical considerations for deciding whether to launch a class action rather than seeking MDL proceedings for a collection of individual cases are:

- the ability in a class action to choose the jurisdiction in which the case will proceed for all purposes;

- the certainty of having the same judge for all proceedings;

- the ability of one or few class counsel to control the entire case (and collect the attorneys' fees, but also bear the expense);

- the size of the individual claims in terms of warranting individual suits or meeting jurisdictional requirements;

- whether the class is seeking injunctive relief or relief against a limited fund;

- the extent to which putative class members might choose to opt-out;

---

12. *See, e.g.*, Phillips Petroleum Co. v. Shutts, 472 U.S. 797, 105 S.Ct. 2965, 86 L.Ed.2d 628 (1985) (application of law of jurisdiction of state court violated due process rights when applied to out of state transactions; due process requires procedural safeguards for absent class members).

13. *E.g.*, Amchem Prods., Inc. v. Windsor, ___ U.S. ___, 117 S.Ct. 2231, 138 L.Ed.2d 689 (1997); Castano v. American Tobacco Co., 84 F.3d 734 (5th Cir.1996); *In* re Rhone–Poulenc Rorer Inc., 51 F.3d 1293 (7th Cir.), *cert. denied*, 516 U.S. 867, 116 S.Ct. 184, 133 L.Ed.2d 122 (1995).

14. The three statutory criteria for MDL transfer are: "one or more common questions of fact," "the convenience of the parties and witnesses," and "the just and efficient conduct of such actions." 28 U.S.C.A. § 1407(a) (West 1993 & Supp. 1997).

- the proposed size of the class in the various jurisdictions;

- anticipated differences in applicable law among class members' claims;

- the significance of unique individual issues and need for individualized proofs for liability or damages;

- the costs of class litigation, such as notice, compared to the costs of litigating an individual, though consolidated, claim;

- the benefit and risk of a single binding judgment on all class members, affected substantially by the claims and presentation of the named plaintiffs, as compared against the individualized judgments for each plaintiff in an MDL proceeding;

- the limitation of MDL to currently pending cases and plaintiffs, unlike class actions which merely define categories of people within the class but those categories or the persons within them may vary throughout the litigation;

- the increased leverage for settlement, from a plaintiff's point of view, that a class action presents, with the risk of a huge, single class action verdict that might cripple or bankrupt a defendant, giving that defendant an incentive to limit the risk through settlement;

- required court approval of settlements and attorneys' fees in a class action (FRCP 23(e)), unlike consolidated individual cases.[15] See Chapter 15 "Class Actions," infra

Notwithstanding federal judicial reluctance to certify classes in mass tort litigation, plaintiffs seem to favor class actions over the use of MDL procedures, because of the increased settlement leverage, the opportunity for greater control of the case and choice of forum, and the prospect for large, undivided attorneys' fees. This has resulted in many such class actions, even those seeking certification of national classes, being filed in state courts, in jurisdictions which are becoming identified as friendly to class actions, in some instances with defendants who are interested in a class action settlement cooperating.

(4) Advantages to Plaintiffs of MDL

The final strategic option for consideration is an MDL proceeding. Either plaintiffs or defendants may request the Judicial Panel on Multidistrict Litigation to transfer all pending cases to one court, or the Panel may act sua sponte to consolidate the cases. Plaintiffs are likely to favor an MDL proceeding if:

- the cases are not appropriate for class certification;

---

15. Federal courts have the power under FRCP 23(c)(4) to create partial classes for particular issues and to establish subclasses. Further, the federal courts have broad discretion under FRCP 23(d), which refers to FRCP 16, to customize and manage class actions. Therefore, there is little difference in the courts' flexibility to manage a class action compared to an MDL or consolidated proceeding, once the strict criteria of FRCP 23 are met and a class is certified.

- the litigation is widely dispersed in many federal jurisdictions;

- plaintiffs are not organized to share litigation information and require a formal structure such as MDL to achieve that organization;

- plaintiffs and their counsel have a strong opportunity to be the lead plaintiffs and counsel;

- plaintiffs anticipate assignment of the MDL to a (more) favorable jurisdiction and judge;[16]

- plaintiffs view the MDL as a mechanism for a desired global settlement;

- plaintiffs believe that the MDL will cut through delay in the courts in which their cases are pending;

- the lead plaintiffs and their counsel want to obtain the sharing of litigation expense with other plaintiffs and their counsel, and that cost-sharing is tolerated by the other plaintiffs' counsel who must pay for the liaison costs.

(5) Disadvantages to Plaintiffs of MDL

Plaintiffs might not benefit, however, from an MDL proceeding because it moves the litigation away from the home jurisdictions of many plaintiffs, could produce conflicts among the lead plaintiffs and their counsel and the remaining plaintiffs and counsel, might increase costs for nonlead plaintiffs, might delay the trial of cases that are in later stages of discovery, might transfer settlement value from high-value to low-value plaintiffs, and is limited to consolidation of the cases for pretrial purposes and may not avoid a series of trials that only bind the individual parties. Invocation of the MDL process may also deprive a plaintiff of his or her choice of trial forum.[17] An MDL proceeding can raise numerous practical and ethical issues for lead plaintiffs' counsel, who represent only individual clients but are in effect acting on behalf of all plaintiffs and performing work benefitting all plaintiffs.[18]

(6) Advantages to Defendants of MDL

Defendants may favor the use of an MDL proceeding for at least three reasons:

16. The Panel may, however, assign the cases to any judge in any district, even districts in which no cases are currently pending. This type of assignment occurred with the appointment of Judge Sam C. Pointer in the Northern District of Alabama to handle the breast implant litigation. *In re* Silicone Gel Breast Implants Prods. Liab. Litig., 793 F.Supp. 1098 (J.P.M.L. 1992). The Panel may also transfer the cases to one district, but assign a district judge from another district to pre-side. *E.g., In re* Olympia Brewing Co. Antitrust Litig., 415 F.Supp. 398 (J.P.M.L. 1976). Thus, making decisions based on assumptions of the likely district court and judge to handle the transferred cases is not without risk.

17. *See infra* § 11.18.

18. *See* Judith Resnick, et al., *Individuals Within the Aggregate: Relationships, Representation and Fees*, 71 N.Y.U. L. Rev. 296 (Apr.-May 1996).

- Consolidation in an MDL proceeding may reduce the costs of litigation significantly, by eliminating multiple, duplicative motions, discovery and hearings on the same issues in numerous jurisdictions;

- An MDL eliminates the problems caused by inconsistent rulings among jurisdictions, such as some jurisdictions permitting much broader discovery than others;

- The MDL proceeding may transfer the litigation to an outstanding trial judge who is experienced and skilled at managing complex litigation.

(7) Disadvantages to Defendants of MDL

Defendants typically perceive some disadvantages to the MDL device:

- MDL proceedings tend to breed the filing of more litigation and to lend credibility to the claims;

- MDL proceedings can focus more attention on case administration and management than the merits of the claims and defenses;

- judicial administration of MDL proceedings often leads to a concentration on case resolution through settlement;[19]

- judicial management can restrict defendants' control and development of their defenses, such as restricting discovery or requiring fragmented and early dispositive motions; or, a transfer of cases to an MDL proceeding might remove the opportunity for early dispositive motions in jurisdictions having favorable law or in cases having favorable facts;

- MDL proceedings focus more on the defendants' alleged misconduct and general injury causation issues, as opposed to individual plaintiff facts and causation issues;

- MDL proceedings most often do not return the cases to the original transferor courts for trial, but when they do, the transferor courts have not been educated on the discovery or issues in the case. Moreover, when the individual plaintiffs' attorneys were not part of the MDL proceedings, the transferor courts are less inclined to hold the plaintiffs, unlike the defendants, to adverse rulings made by the MDL court.[20]

19. The Second Circuit has recognized that the MDL proceeding engenders a "great pressure to settle. Indeed, a settlement in a case such as [this] ... seems almost as inevitable as the sunrise." *In re* "Agent Orange" Prod. Liab. Litig., 818 F.2d 145, 166 (2d Cir.1987) *cert. denied*, 484 U.S. 1004, 108 S.Ct. 695, 98 L.Ed.2d 648 (1988).

20. As a general rule, the transferor court should and does adhere to the rulings of the MDL transferee court under the law of the case doctrine. *See In re* Multi–Piece Rim Prods. Liab. Litig., 653 F.2d 671, 678 (D.C.Cir.1981); Allegheny Airlines, Inc. v. LeMay, 448 F.2d 1341, 1345 (7th Cir.), *cert. denied*, 404 U.S. 1001, 92 S.Ct. 565, 30 L.Ed.2d 553 (1971); Sentner v. Amtrak, 540 F.Supp. 557, 558 n. 3 (D.N.J.1982). For an extensive discussion of the law of the case rules as applied to MDL proceedings, *see* Joan Steinman, *Law of the Case: A Judicial Puzzle in Consolidated and Transferred*

(8) Disadvantages to Plaintiffs and Defendants of MDL

Plaintiffs and defendants both may consider an MDL proceeding to be disadvantageous for several reasons:

- an MDL proceeding multiplies the risk from an adverse decision and makes the cases depend on the predilections of one, yet unidentified judge;

- an MDL proceeding might hinder the discovery and presentation of individual issues, claims, or defenses;

- favorable decisions made by the transferor court can be reconsidered and reversed by the MDL transferee court;[21]

- favorable law applicable in transferor courts might not be applied when the MDL transferee court fashions its choice of law rulings;[22]

(9) Advantages to All Parties of MDL

Most justifications for MDL proceedings discuss the benefits for the judicial system from the consolidation of the cases for pretrial purposes and often for settlement, rather than the benefit to individual parties. Nevertheless, the litigants may perceive potential advantages of an MDL proceeding that might outweigh the disadvantages in certain cases, principally: (a) the reduction in costs of litigation and the greater

Cases and in Multidistrict Litigation, 135 U. Pa. L. Rev. 595 (Mar. 1987). *See also* *infra* § 11.13.

21. *E.g.*, Astarte Shipping Co. v. Allied Steel & Export Service, 767 F.2d 86 (5th Cir.1985); *In re* Upjohn Co. Antibiotic Cleocin Prods. Liab. Litig., 81 F.R.D. 482, 486–87 (E.D.Mich.1979), *aff'd*, 664 F.2d 114 (6th Cir.1981). *See also* Steinman, *supra*, note 20, at 595, 667–68 ("'[T]he very facts of transfer and consolidation with other cases under section 1407, after the initial decision of an issue, often will constitute a change in circumstances that warrants reconsideration. Thus, when transferor court rulings are questioned in the section 1407 transferee court or in a discovery court, reconsideration often will be appropriate even for rulings that otherwise should stand.'") Of course, a transferor court's rulings can only apply, consistent with due process and law-of-the-case principles, to the parties which were before the transferor court. Consequently, the MDL transferee court will often need to decide issues that were previously decided by some, but not all, transferor courts.

22. Under the United States Supreme Court authority, the MDL transferee court is required to apply the substantive law which would apply to each case when pending in the transferor court. Van Dusen v. Barrack, 376 U.S. 612, 84 S.Ct. 805, 11 L.Ed.2d 945 (1964); Klaxon Co. v. Stentor Elec. Manufacturing. Co., 313 U.S. 487, 61 S.Ct. 1020, 85 L.Ed. 1477 (1941). This result is also mandated by federal statute, because the parties' substantive rights should not change based on the procedural transfer of the cases under the MDL rule. *See* 28 U.S.C.A. § 1652 (West 1993 & Supp. 1997) (Rules of Decision Act); § 2072(b) (federal courts' procedural rules "shall not abridge, enlarge or modify any substantive right").

However, in practice, MDL transferee courts have sometimes avoided the complexity of a multiplicity of divergent state laws by means of a choice of law analysis finding one state's law to apply uniformly or by creating national law. *See In re* Bendectin Litig., 857 F.2d 290, 304–05 (6th Cir.1988) *cert. denied*, 488 U.S. 1006, 109 S.Ct. 788, 102 L.Ed.2d 779 (1989); *In re* "Agent Orange" Prod. Liab. Litig., 580 F.Supp. 690, 693–96 (E.D.N.Y.1984). Thus, in practice, MDL transfers have resulted in a change of a party's substantive rights. *See infra* § 11.14.

efficiency and administrative control possible through consolidation;[23] (b) the increased ease of a global resolution, through dispositive motions or settlement, when all parties are in front of the same court and have some degree of organization through lead counsel; (c) the ability to move the cases away from jurisdictions seen as hostile or less favorable; and (d) the decreased risk of aberrant rulings and verdicts in favor of consistency and uniformity. Efficiency, economy and convenience of litigation and settlement for the plaintiffs and a desire on the part of defendants to reduce litigation expense while striving for a quick, global settlement are likely to be the driving factors to a decision to request or agree to an MDL proceeding.

(c) Case Organization and Client Counseling of Defendants in MDL

(1) Client Organization and Resources

While the amount of resources devoted to the task will depend upon the number of cases involved in the MDL and the nature and size of the risk they present, the client, in order to adequately manage MDL litigation internally and support outside counsel, will usually need to assemble a team of in-house attorneys, legal assistants, and business personnel from a number of different areas. The client must make a commitment to support MDL litigation, and management must be well informed of the litigation status and significant developments. Management must communicate to the organization the importance of the litigation and the need to assist and cooperate with counsel upon request, and a business person should be assigned to work with counsel

---

23. The parties and counsel should carefully consider whether asserted benefits of consolidation are overstated in their litigation. Professor Kramer, among others, has questioned the assumed benefits of MDL consolidation:

> The topic of consolidation does, however, require further exploration. Most commentators, for example, appear to calculate the costs of dispersed litigation as if each separate action were the first and only one. Yet there are mechanisms for achieving economies of scale even without formal consolidation. First, because the defendants are mostly the same from action to action, they need not duplicate much of their work and can be expected to share costs. Second, plaintiff and defendant bar organizations can coordinate efforts and arrange for the sharing of information and costs. Third, with some modification to prevent unfairness to defendants, offensive collateral estoppel can help limit duplicative litigation. Fourth,

once a pattern of results begins to emerge, settlements take place with increasing ease and dispatch. By no means are these points sufficient to refute the argument for consolidation. But they suggest that, while dispersed litigation may be less cost effective than consolidation, it may also be nowhere near as bad as generally assumed. This is important because allowing individualized adjudication has advantages—not the least of which is that it enables plaintiffs to control their own fate.

Larry Kramer, *Choice of Law in Complex Litigation*, 71 N.Y.U. L. Rev. 547, 589 n.129 (Apr.–May 1996). *See also In re* Rhone–Poulenc Rorer Inc., 51 F.3d 1293, 1300 (7th Cir.) *cert. denied* 516 U.S. 867, 116 S.Ct. 184, 133 L.Ed.2d 122 (1995) (might be preferable to submit the cases "to multiple juries constituting in the aggregate a much larger and more diverse sample of decision-makers").

in the litigation.[24]

A coherent MDL litigation plan must be developed by counsel and then approved by management, including an appreciation of the litigation risks and costs. Management's goals in the litigation should be identified as early as feasible to permit the development of a corresponding litigation strategy and budget. For example, management should not be driven prematurely to a settlement because of the MDL judge's pressure to resolve the litigation; a decision by management to adopt an MDL strategy should be made as part of a thoughtfully considered settlement strategy. The process of MDL litigation should not drive management decisions; management should set the litigation goals at the outset, modifying them if necessary as the litigation defines itself.

The client should identify a lead in-house attorney to handle the MDL litigation. The in-house attorney may require support from other in-house attorneys in view of the scope of the litigation and the extent of responsibilities that in-house counsel will handle. Because in-house counsel typically have primary responsibility for locating relevant documents and current or former employees having relevant information,[25] and for making the necessary client decisions, sufficient in-house counsel resources must be committed at the outset of the litigation. An attorney or business person experienced in the organization's document filing systems and in document database technology management can be especially useful. In-house counsel should participate in determining the organization of the litigation team, deciding how information and documents will be gathered and organized, setting the litigation plan and strategy, selecting national and local counsel and defining their roles, informing and advising management, establishing budgets, and establishing company directives for document retention during the litigation. These responsibilities require adequate time, experience and expertise.

Depending on the MDL litigation issues and the client's internal organization, in-house counsel in various substantive areas as well as different parts of the organization might be needed. The litigation, for example, might raise corporate restructuring, securities disclosure, bankruptcy planning, environmental, and regulatory issues, each of which could benefit from in-house counsel with expertise in that area. Communications with financial analysts, shareholders and auditors may be necessary and will raise for publicly traded corporations sensitive disclo-

24. *See generally*, Ann T. Burks, *Managing Complex Industrywide Litigation Effectively: The View from the Inside* (Defense Research Institute March 1997); William A. Sowinski, Jr. & C. Paul Cavender, *In-House Management of Mass Tort Litigation and What Field Counsel Should Know*, in *Current Issues in Industrywide Litigation*, Vol. 1995, No.4 (Defense Research Institute, 1995).

25. A methodology and means for communicating with current and former employees and protecting against improper or unknown contacts by opposing counsel should be considered and implemented at an early stage of the litigation. *See* John E. Iole and John D. Goetz, *Ethics or Procedure? A Discovery–Based Approach to Ex Parte Contacts with Former Employees of a Corporate Adversary*, 68 Notre Dame L. Rev. 81 (1992).

sure issues regarding the status and potential financial risks of the litigation.

The client should also include on the litigation team in-house counsel and business persons skilled in the areas of insurance coverage, media strategy[26] and investor relations. Each of these areas is likely to assume major importance during the life of the litigation. Early planning can avoid mistakes, such as late notice of claims to insurers or misguided media statements, and develop a more thoughtful pro-active rather than reactive strategy.

(2) Organization of National and Local Counsel

Because multidistrict litigation involves big stakes, it warrants the use of an experienced and expert team of national counsel, which will represent the client in all proceedings throughout the United States on that matter. The sheer size of MDL litigation may require an outside law firm with substantial resources available. Local counsel will be needed for the individual cases, and a significant role can be anticipated for local counsel in the jurisdiction to which the consolidated MDL proceeding is transferred.

National counsel usually assume responsibility for all aspects of the MDL, including discovery responses, offensive discovery, fact investigation, selection and preparation of experts, jury research, legal research and preparation of dispositive motions, motions in limine, development of demonstrative aids and trial. National counsel will likely become involved in other areas affected by the litigation, such as corporate structure, insurance and securities disclosure issues.

One of the early priorities for national counsel, in conjunction with in-house counsel, will be to identify the documents that must be preserved, to collect all potentially relevant documents, and to determine and implement a system for document management and retrieval. Describing and implementing a methodology for protecting privileged documents is particularly important to avoid inadvertent disclosures.

---

26. Media relations and statements assume added importance in a highly visible and monitored MDL proceeding. Media statements often become a significant part of the overall business strategy, and typically play a role in litigation strategy. The media is often used to try to affect the settlement value of the cases. *See* Stephanie A. Scharf & Steven M. Wernikoff, *The Media and Products Litigation*, Defense 15 (Oct. 1996). A coherent, thoughtful media approach is essential. *See, e.g.*, William T. Hangley, *Winning in The Press, Litigation*, Vol. 23, No. 3, 14 (Spring 1997); Janell M. Gabor, *When the Media Call: The Court of Law vs. the Court of Public Opinion*, (Mar. 1997); Jeffrey R. Johnson, Manufacturer and the Media: Coexistence or Combat, (1995).

Because of its public visibility, MDL litigation can spawn significant tangential litigation over the media's right of access to pretrial materials or the propriety of pretrial protective orders. The First Amendment might collide with an MDL court's interest in judicial efficiency in discovery, pretrial management and settlement and a party's interest in privacy and confidentiality. *See, e.g.*, Seattle Times Co. v. Rhinehart, 467 U.S. 20, 104 S.Ct. 2199, 81 L.Ed.2d 17 (1984); Richmond Newspapers, Inc. v. Virginia, 448 U.S. 555, 100 S.Ct. 2814, 65 L.Ed.2d 973 (1980); Anderson v. Cryovac, Inc., 805 F.2d 1 (1st Cir.1986). *See generally*, Arthur R. Miller, *Confidentiality, Protective Orders, and Public Access to the Courts*, 105 Harv. L. Rev. 427 (1991).

Plaintiffs have learned that the retention, collection and production of documents is often the Achilles' heel of large corporations. The vigorous pursuit by plaintiffs of documents in discovery can, if the defendant company does not have in place an efficient and reliable system for responding to such discovery, produce errors or unreasonable delay by the defendant which can, in turn, be used by plaintiffs to begin to influence a court's attitude toward the defendant and the merits of its defenses. Aggressive discovery in the hope of having discovery sanctions imposed on error-prone defendants is now part of sophisticated plaintiffs' litigation strategy, and defendants must be well prepared early in the litigation to defend against such tactics.[27]

Once the documents are gathered, MDL counsel must begin synthesizing the important facts and compiling information memoranda, including key documents and interview reports, that can educate counsel and ultimately provide the basis for depositions and the presentation of evidence. This process will require a substantial team of attorneys to accomplish the document collection, and review and compilation of information in a short period of time. Early interviews of persons having relevant information are important. There may be a need to take depositions quickly to preserve relevant evidence from elderly or ill witnesses.

Similarly, defendants must quickly prepare for their discovery of plaintiffs. Defendants might want to begin discovery in individual cases before an MDL proceeding is put in place, particularly to focus on facts specific to individual plaintiffs. In an MDL proceeding, the court is likely to manage discovery aggressively, and taking discovery in phases is common. Defendants must plan their priorities in discovery of plaintiffs, as well as plan for issues of evidence preservation in the event that certain areas of discovery are stayed.

Another early priority will be to define and research the significant issues of law. Research is imperative in order to develop the MDL legal strategy of which issues to present and in what order. Without knowing the facts and the applicable law, the attorneys cannot adequately advise the clients of the litigation risks or costs, nor can the defendants be prepared to advise whether to request or concur in an MDL proceeding. If an MDL proceeding takes place, early knowledge of the facts and law sufficient to consider and present a plan for handling the MDL litigation is essential. Because the MDL court is likely to manage the timing of the filing and resolution of dispositive motions, a coherent, well developed plan is critical. Choice of law issues will be prominent in many MDL proceedings, and even on issues of federal law there might be conflicts within the circuits that the MDL court must recognize and resolve.

Attorneys should be assigned the task of identifying issues on which expert consultants and expert testimony will be needed, and then finding

---

27. See *In re* E.I. DuPont de Nemours & Company–Benlate Litig., 99 F.3d 363 (11th Cir.1996) *petition for cert. filed*, 65 U.S.L.W. 3767 (U.S. May 8, 1997). *See* Chapter 20 "Document Discovery," at § 20.2, *infra* regarding counsel's role in document management.

and retaining those experts. A team combining nationally recognized experts and outstanding local experts is typically preferred. Careful review of each expert's qualifications, writings and prior testimony is essential, as well as early consideration of any issues governing the admissibility of expert testimony. Legal research may be necessary to support the admissibility of the anticipated expert testimony.

Finally, in cases with multiple defendants, the defendants should consider the prospects and advantages of joint coordination of their defense. Even when conflicts may potentially exist among defendants, there are usually areas of common interest which could be the subject of a joint defense arrangement. MDL defendants should weigh such considerations in determining whether a joint defense agreement is necessary or desirable for purposes of protecting joint attorney work-product and communications from discovery, and in order to establish a clear understanding of cost-sharing arrangements.[28]

(d) Organization of Plaintiffs' Counsel

The development and presentation of plaintiffs' cases mirrors the defendants' preparation in many ways. Plaintiffs' counsel will need to organize to litigate against the defendants, will need resources to sustain the litigation, and will need a coordinated effort in presenting their litigation plans to the MDL court. Plaintiffs will face three additional, potentially contentious, issues: representing their individual clients and attempting to deal with conflicts within the group of plaintiffs over issues important to their individual clients; the selection of lead counsel and issues related to the division of labor, such as information-sharing, work-sharing, fee-sharing and cost-sharing; and handling the burdensome logistics of communicating with and periodically informing all plaintiffs' counsel of case developments. Resolution of these difficult issues is not guided by explicit procedural or ethical rules, and will require frank discussions, and often express agreements, even before a request for an MDL proceeding is lodged. Conflicts among the plaintiffs might raise difficult ethical issues for the lead attorneys and create case management issues for the MDL court.[29] These issues, for example, include:

- must or can the lead attorneys sacrifice the interests of their individual clients when those interests conflict with other plaintiffs in the MDL?

---

28. *See* Gerald F. Uelmen, *The Joint Defense Privileges: Know the Risks*, Litigation, Vol. 22 at 35 (Summer 1988).

29. For an extensive discussion of these issues and the many difficult questions for resolution, *see* Judith Resnick, et al., *Individuals Within the Aggregate: Relationships, Representation, and Fees*, 71 N.Y.U. L. Rev. 296 (Apr.–May 1996). *See also* Jack Weinstein, Individual Justice in Mass Tort Litigation 40–41 (1995) (arguing that ethi-

cal issues in mass torts have not "been given the special attention they deserve"); Carrie Menkel–Meadow, *Ethics and the Settlements of Mass Torts: When the Rules Meet the Road*, 80 Cornell L. Rev. 1159, 1172 (1995); Joan Steinman, *The Effects of Case Consolidation on the Procedural Rights of Litigants: What They Are, What They Might Be: Non–Jurisdictional Matters (pt. 2)*, 42 UCLA L. Rev. 967, 1051 (1995).

- must or can the lead attorneys present unique issues relating to individual plaintiffs who are not their clients?

- can the lead attorneys effectively and zealously represent plaintiffs who are not their clients?

- how much will the lead attorneys take in legal fees, and should those fees be deducted from the nonlead attorneys' fees?

- are fee agreements signed before the MDL proceeding was contemplated still valid, and should they be enforced?

- will individual plaintiffs pay more in fees and costs because of the MDL and, if so, should their counsel object to an MDL proceeding?

- how should attorneys who assist the lead attorneys be compensated?

- how should the lead attorneys act if some plaintiffs approve of a course of action and others do not?

- to what extent should lead attorneys keep the other attorneys informed?

Because an MDL proceeding in theory is simply to consolidate pending lawsuits in which individual plaintiffs have already retained attorneys, MDL rules have not dealt with this complex set of issues.

The extent of aggregation or disaggregation of plaintiff counsel's work will also vary according to the type of case involved. For example, securities cases tend to focus less on individual plaintiff issues, while personal injury cases will frequently focus heavily on the individual plaintiffs' conduct, injuries and damages.

Library References:

West's Key No. Digests, Federal Civil Procedure ⚖9.
Wright, Miller & Cooper, Federal Practice and Procedure: Civil 2d §§ 3862–3864.

§ 11.4 Sources of Authority

There are six essential sources of authority that must be consulted with respect to the MDL process: (1) 28 U.S.C.A. § 1407; (2) the Rules of the Judicial Panel on Multidistrict Litigation; (3) the decisions of the Panel and of the courts relating to Panel conduct; (4) The Manual for Complex Litigation, Third; (5) the Federal Rules of Civil Procedure; and (6) Local Rules.

(1) **28 U.S.C.A. § 1407**. The Multidistrict Litigation mechanism was created in 28 U.S.C.A. § 1407, passed in 1968. The statute, itself, sets forth the prerequisites for the transfer and remand of cases,[1] the composition and operation of the Panel,[2] and the process by which to appeal Panel determinations.[3]

§ 11.4

1. *See infra* §§ 11.9, 11.20.

2. *See infra* §§ 11.5–11.11.

3. *See infra* § 11.12.

(2) **Rules of Procedure of the Judicial Panel On Multidistrict Litigation.** Pursuant to the authority granted to the Panel in 28 U.S.C.A. § 1407(f), the Panel has promulgated Rules of Procedure,[4] which set forth the specific rules to be followed in all proceedings before the Panel.

(3) **Opinions of Panel and Courts**. The opinions of the Panel are reported in the Federal Supplement and Federal Rules Decisions.

(4) **Federal Rules of Civil Procedure**. The Federal Rules of Civil Procedure govern practice within the transferor and transferee courts. Because practice before the Panel represents only two discrete phases of MDL (the transfer and remand of actions), the Federal Rules constitute the authority that will govern the vast majority of practice within MDL.[5]

(5) **Local Rules**. The local rules of the transferor and transferee courts will apply at various times in the MDL process when the action is pending in that district.

(6) **Manual for Complex Litigation, Third**. Although not formally authoritative, the manual, published by the Federal Judicial Center, is frequently cited in MDL proceedings and is generally treated as highly persuasive. The manual addresses virtually every aspect of complex litigation practice, focusing primarily on practical techniques to manage litigation.

The manual can be used not only to manage the MDL process itself, but to provide arguments for and against transfer in the first instance. Proponents of transfer often argue that the case management techniques in the manual mitigate any confusion, complexity, or prejudice claimed by opponents to be created by the MDL.[6]

Library References:

West's Key No. Digests, Federal Civil Procedure ⟜9.
Wright, Miller & Cooper, Federal Practice and Procedure: Civil 2d § 3868.

§ 11.5   Composition of the Panel

The Panel consists of seven circuit and district judges appointed "from time to time" by the Chief Justice of the United States.[1] No two members of the Panel may be from the same circuit and the concurrence of four members is required for any Panel action.[2]

The present and former Panel members are as follows:

4. The rules can be found immediately following the annotations of 28 U.S.C.A. § 1407 (West 1993) and are cited herein as "JPML Rule ___ ."

5. The substantive provisions of the Federal Rules, such as regarding discovery, motions, and the like, are addressed in other chapters of this treatise and are not addressed in detail here.

6. *See infra* § 11.15.

§ 11.5

1. 28 U.S.C.A. § 1407(d) (West 1993 & Supp. 1997).

2. *Id.*

Judge	District	Appointment	Termination
John F. Nangle	S. Dist. GA	06/01/90	
Robert R. Merhige Jr.	E. Dist. VA	11/19/90	
William B. Enright	S. Dist. CA	11/19/90	
Clarence A. Brimmer	Dist. WY	10/26/92	
John F. Grady	N. Dist. IL	10/26/92	
Barefoot Sanders	N. Dist. TX	10/26/92	
Louis C. Bechtle	E. Dist. PA	12/06/94	
Halbert O. Woodward	N. Dist. TX	03/02/89	06/23/92
S. Hugh Dillin	S. Dist. IN	10/01/83	10/26/92
Milton Pollock	S. Dist. NY	10/01/83	12/06/94
Louis H. Pollak	E. Dist. PA	10/01/83	10/26/92
Frederick A. Daugherty	E. Dist. OK	03/01/80	11/19/90
Sam C. Pointer Jr.	N. Dist. AL	03/01/80	11/20/87
Murray I. Gurfein	2nd Circuit	11/15/78	12/16/79
Charles R. Weiner	E. Dist. PA	10/25/78	09/30/83
Robert H. Schnacke	N. Dist. CA	07/01/79	11/19/90
Edward S. Northrop	Dist. MD	06/06/79	09/30/83
Roy W. Harper	E. Dist. MO	02/01/77	09/30/83
Andrew A. Caffrey	Dist. MA	11/06/75	06/01/90
Alfred P. Murrah	10th Circuit	05/29/68	10/30/75
John M. Wisdom	5th Circuit	05/29/68	10/26/78
Edwin A. Robson	N. Dist. IL	05/29/68	07/01/79
William H. Becker	W. Dist. MO	05/29/68	01/17/77
Edward Weinfeld	S. Dist. NY	05/29/68	11/15/78
Joseph S. Lord III	E. Dist. PA	05/29/68	07/17/78
Stanley A. Weigel	N. Dist. CA	05/29/68	07/01/79

Library References:

West's Key No. Digests, Federal Civil Procedure ⊚9.

Wright, Miller & Cooper, Federal Practice and Procedure: Civil 2d § 3865.

§ 11.6 Qualifications to Practice Before the Panel and in the MDL Process

No special qualifications and no separate admissions are required to practice before the Panel or in the transferee court. Every member in good standing of the bar of any federal district court is entitled without condition to practice before the Panel.[1] If an action is transferred to a different district, any attorney of record in the transferred action may continue to represent his or her client in the transferee district court.[2]

No party is required to obtain local counsel in the transferee district.[3] However, as in any litigation located in an unfamiliar forum, it is prudent to retain local counsel to provide advice on the nuances of local practice or the preferences and proclivities of the judge. As a practical matter, the practice of appointing liaison counsel in MDL proceedings[4] will frequently minimize local counsel's direct interaction with the court.

§ 11.6

1. JPML Rule 6.

2. *Id.*

3. *Id.*

4. *See infra* § 11.15(b)(1).

§ 11.7　Initiation of MDL Proceedings

The MDL process can be initiated in four different ways: (a) by a motion to transfer filed by a party in any case that is a candidate for the MDL; (b) by the Panel, sua sponte, through a conditional transfer order; (c) by the Panel, sua sponte, through a show cause order; or, (d) by administrative intradistrict transfer under that district's local rules, if the MDL is already located in the district in which the new action is filed.[1]

(a) Initiation of MDL By Motion

(1) Who May Make a Motion

Any party in any action in which transfer under 28 U.S.C.A. § 1407 may be appropriate may file a motion to transfer.[2] As a result, counsel in an entirely separate action may file the motion that brings your case before the Panel. To return to the earlier airplane crash hypothetical,[3] counsel in the Ohio action may decide to move the Panel to create an MDL proceeding for the crash. As a result of such a motion, all parties in all five pending federal cases will be called before the Panel to determine if the cases should be consolidated in one court. Thus, while neither plaintiff nor defendant in the Texas action may have wanted an MDL, they would still be required to appear before the Panel and might, in fact, find their case incorporated into an MDL over their united objection.[4]

(2) Form of Motion

All motions must be in numbered paragraphs and responses are to be in correspondingly numbered paragraphs.[5] Each paragraph should be limited to a single averment of fact.[6] Responses must admit or deny, in whole or in part, each allegation; unless an allegation is wholly admitted, the response must provide the respondent's version of the issue.[7]

(3) Accompanying Papers

Together with the motion itself, the movant must file (a) a supporting brief and (b) a schedule giving (1) the complete case name of every action known to be involved; (2) the district court in which each action is

---

§ 11.7

1. 28 U.S.C.A. § 1407(c) (West 1993 & Supp. 1997); JPML Rules 10 (motions), 11 (show cause orders), and 12 (conditional orders).

2. 28 U.S.C.A. § 1407 (c)(ii) (West 1993 & Supp. 1997).

3. See supra § 11.2

4. In re Air Crash Disaster at Stapleton Int'l Airport, 720 F.Supp. 1505, 1513 (D.Colo.1989) rev'd sub nom. Johnson v.

Continental Airlines Corp., 964 F.2d 1059 (10th Cir.1992) (transfer may be ordered over objection of the parties); In re Natural Gas Liquids Regulation Litig., 434 F.Supp. 665 (J.P.M.L. 1977) (Panel has power to order transfer even if no party favors transfer.).

5. JPML Rule 9(a), (b).

6. JPML Rule 9(a).

7. JPML Rule 9(b).

pending and the civil action number of each action; and (3) the name of the judge assigned to each action, if known.[8]

A proposed order should not be submitted; in fact, the Rules specifically provide that "[p]roposed Panel orders shall not be submitted with papers for filing."[9]

Briefs are limited to 20 pages, exclusive of exhibits.[10] If the exhibits, themselves, exceed 25 pages, they must be bound separately.[11] If the movant wishes to reply, a single brief in reply to any opposition is permitted.[12]

(4) Service

The motion to transfer and accompanying papers must be served on all other parties in all actions involved in the litigation.[13] Proof of service must be included with the motion at the time of filing.[14]

The proof of service must comply with FRCP 5 and 6 and must indicate the name and address of each person served, as well as the party represented by that person.[15] Once initial appearances are received, the Clerk of the Panel will issue to all parties a "Panel Service List," which is thereafter to be used as the service list (supplemented as necessary by any more current information).[16]

If liaison counsel have been appointed and receipt of service is within their designated responsibility,[17] service on liaison counsel is sufficient to comply with service requirements.[18]

(5) Time for Appearance, Response, and Reply

Upon receipt of a motion to transfer, the Clerk of the Multidistrict Panel will notify all recipients of the motion of the filing date,[19] caption, MDL docket number, briefing schedule and pertinent Panel policies.[20]

Within 11 days of the filing of a motion to transfer, each party must notify the Clerk of the Panel, in writing, of the name and address of the attorney designated to receive service of all papers related to practice before the Panel.[21] Only one attorney may be designated for each party.[22] Extensions of this deadline are not granted, except in extraordinary circumstances.[23]

---

8. JPML Rule 10(a)(i), (ii).

9. JPML Rule 9(g).

10. JPML Rule 9(f).

11. *Id.*

12. JPML Rule 10(d).

13. JPML Rule 8(a).

14. *Id.*

15. *Id.*

16. JPML Rule 8(a), (d).

17. *See infra* § 11.15(b)(1) for discussion of liaison counsel issues.

18. JPML Rule 8(e).

19. Within the MDL process, deadlines generally run from date of *filing* as opposed to the date of *service.*

20. JPML Rule 10(b).

21. JPML Rule 8(c).

22. *Id.*

23. *Id.*

Responses to the motion to transfer are due within 20 days of the filing of the motion.[24] Failure to respond is treated as acquiescence to the motion.[25]

Any reply is due within 25 days of the date of filing of the *original* motion to transfer.[26] Only one reply may be filed, regardless of the number of responses.[27]

Applications for extension of the time[28] to respond and reply must be in writing, must request a specific number of additional days, must set forth the reason for the request, and may be acted upon by the Clerk of the Panel.[29] The application is evaluated in relation to the impact on the Panel's calendar and on the basis of the reasons set forth in the application.[30] Any party aggrieved by the Clerk of the Panel's action on the application may submit its objections to the Panel for consideration.[31]

(6) Disclosure of Potential Tag–Along Actions

Any party or counsel in an action previously transferred or under consideration by the Panel must "promptly" notify the Clerk of the Panel of any potential "tag-along actions" in which that party is also named or in which that counsel appears.[32] The use of the phrase "previously transferred" imposes a continuing duty to disclose—a duty made explicit in other provisions of the Rules.[33]

(b) Initiation of MDL by the Panel Generally

The Panel possesses the statutory power to trigger the MDL process on its own initiative.[34] If the Panel elects to do so, it may issue either a show cause order or a conditional transfer order.[35]

Show cause orders are generally used where there is no MDL proceeding pending or where the Panel has some question as to the propriety of adding the specific action for which it issues the order.[36] Conditional transfer orders are typically used for noncontroversial "tag-along" actions.

---

24. JPML Rule 10(c).

25. *Id.*

26. JPML Rule 10(d). The Rule is actually phrased "within five days after the lapse of the time period for filing responsive briefs," which, under JPML 10(c), is 20 days from filing of the motion.

27. JPML Rule 10(d).

28. For special rules relating to notice of opposition to conditional transfer and conditional remand orders, *see infra* §§ 11.7(d) and 11.20(c). Time periods relating to these notices are not extended absent extraordinary circumstances. JPML Rule 15.

29. JPML Rule 15.

30. *Id.*

31. *Id.*

32. *See* JPML Rule 13(e).

33. *See* JPML Rule 11(a).

34. 28 U.S.C.A. § 1407(c)(i) (West 1993 & Supp. 1997).

35. *See* JPML Rules 10 (show cause), 11 (conditional transfer).

36. JPML Rule 13(b), for example, provides that an order to show cause may be used if the Panel has reasonable anticipation of opposition to transfer of a potential tag-along action.

(c) Show Cause Order (Transfer)

A show cause order, as its name implies, directs the parties to an action or actions to show cause why the action or actions should not be transferred under Section 1407.[37] Upon receipt of such an order, any party or counsel is required to notify the Clerk of the Panel of any other federal district court actions related to the litigation.[38] This is a continuing duty, and counsel to the parties must similarly report all future-filed related federal actions as well.[39]

(1) Time for Appearance, Response and Reply

Within 11 days of the filing of the show cause order, each party must notify the Clerk of the Panel, in writing, of the name and address of the attorney designated to receive service of all papers related to practice before the Panel.[40] Only one attorney may be designated for each party.[41] Extensions of this deadline are not granted, except in extraordinary circumstances.[42]

Any party may file a response to the show cause order.[43] Responses must be filed within 20 days of the filing of the order, unless otherwise specified therein.[44] Failure to respond is treated as a party's acquiescence to the Panel action contemplated in the order.[45]

Any reply must be filed within 25 days of the date of the filing of the show cause order.[46] Unlike the reply concerning a motion to transfer, a reply concerning a show cause order is specifically "limited to new matters."[47]

Extensions of these time periods are subject to the same rules as general motions.[48]

(d) Conditional Transfer Order

If the Panel learns of a potential tag-along action, the Clerk of the Panel may enter an order transferring that action to the previously designated transferee court on the basis of the prior hearing or hearings and for the reasons expressed in the prior opinions and rulings of the Panel.[49] Potential tag-along actions include actions which were filed or came to the attention of the Panel either after the initial hearing or too late to be included in the initial hearing.[50]

Within 11 days of the filing of the conditional order each party must notify the Clerk of the Panel, in writing, of the name and address of the

---

37. JPML Rule 11(a).

38. Id.

39. Id.

40. JPML Rule 8(c).

41. Id.

42. Id.

43. JPML Rule 11(b).

44. Id.

45. Id.

46. JPML Rule 11(c). The Rule is actually phrased "within five days after the lapse of the time period for filing a response."

47. Id.

48. See supra § 11.7(a)(5) and infra § 11.11.

49. JPML Rule 12(a).

50. JPML Rule 13(d).

attorney designated to receive service of all papers related to practice before the Panel.[51] Only one attorney may be designated for each party.[52] Extensions of this deadline are not granted, except in extraordinary circumstances.[53]

The conditional transfer order is served on all parties to the litigation.[54] However, it is not served on the Clerk of the transferee court (*i.e.*, it is not made effective[55]) for 15 days from the entry of the conditional order.

Within that 15–day period, any party opposing the transfer must file a notice of opposition with the Clerk of the Panel.[56] Extensions of this time period are permitted only in exceptional circumstances.[57] If the action subject to the order is no longer pending, the parties must so notify the Clerk of the Panel within this 15–day period.[58] Upon the receipt of a notice of opposition, the Clerk of the Panel will hold the conditional order until further order of the Panel.[59] The notice of opposition thus precludes any transfer until further Panel action, since the Conditional Order does not become effective until it is filed with the transferee court.[60]

Within 15 days of the filing of the notice of opposition, the party opposing transfer must file a motion to vacate the conditional transfer order and brief in support.[61] Failure to file a motion and brief are treated as withdrawal of the opposition and the Clerk of the Panel "shall forthwith" transmit the order to the transferee court, thus, making the transfer effective.[62]

(e) Intradistrict Transfers

If a new case is filed in the transferee district after the MDL is transferred there, no Panel proceedings are involved and any transfer is handled under that district's administrative rules for related-cases.

Library References:

West's Key No. Digests, Federal Civil Procedure ⊙9.
Wright, Miller & Cooper, Federal Practice and Procedure: Civil 2d § 3861.

§ 11.8   Hearing and Oral Argument

In a notice of hearing, the Clerk of the Panel will provide a date by which counsel must notify the Clerk, in writing, that counsel either: (1) waives oral argument; (2) will present argument; or (3) will waive oral

---

51. JPML Rule 8(c).

52. *Id.*

53. *Id.*

54. JPML Rule 12(a).

55. Transfer orders become effective upon filing in the transferee court. JPML Rule 12(e); 28 U.S.C.A. § 1407(c) (West 1993 & Supp. 1997).

56. JPML Rule 12(c).

57. JPML Rule 15.

58. JPML Rule 12(b).

59. JPML Rule 12(c).

60. JPML Rule 12(e); 28 U.S.C.A. § 1407(c) (West 1993 & Supp. 1997).

61. JPML Rule 12(d).

62. *Id.*

argument if all other counsel do so.[1] If all parties agree to waive oral argument, the issue will be decided on the papers.[2]

Unless all parties consent or agree to a decision on the papers, no transfer or remand determination can be made unless a hearing is held.[3] Unless otherwise ordered, all other matters are considered on the papers.[4]

Except for leave of the Panel on good cause shown, only parties who have filed a motion or written response to a motion or order are permitted to appear before the Panel and present argument.[5] If a party is not present when the case is called, the party is deemed to have submitted to decision on the papers.[6]

On the issues of transfer or remand, counsel favoring the relief requested and counsel opposing the relief are to confer separately prior to the hearing to organize their arguments and to select representatives to "present all views without duplication."[7] Counsel are well-advised to adhere to this, because time for argument is very limited: a maximum of 30 minutes for any new group of actions and a maximum of 20 minutes for any other matters, the time being divided equally among those with varying view points.[8]

Oral testimony is disfavored and is generally not received.[9] If a party wishes to submit oral testimony, that party must provide notice and a motion to the Panel and the Panel must issue an order allowing testimony.[10]

Proof at the hearing is submitted pursuant to the Federal Rules of Civil Procedure.[11] Given the Panel's disinclination to entertain oral testimony, evidence should generally be submitted by affidavit.

Because of the brevity of argument and the requirement that "like" positions must share time, it is critical that all counsel on a given side of an issue confer in advance of the hearing to distill their arguments as thoroughly as possible. The number of counsel presenting argument should also be reduced to the extent possible. It is preferable to have all parties' arguments synthesized into one cohesive argument, rather than to have multiple counsel presenting discreet facts applicable solely to their cases. A unified presentation tends to marshal favorable facts from different cases and thus strengthen the overall argument, whereas a multiplicity of counsel is likely to splinter the issues.

Selection of counsel to present the argument depends upon a number of factors, including prior practice before Panel members, prior practice before the Panel itself, the number of cases subject to transfer in which counsel appears, familiarity with the underlying facts of the

---

§ 11.8

1. JPML Rule 17(a).
2. JPML Rule 17(b).
3. JPML Rule 16(b).
4. *Id.*
5. JPML Rule 16(c).
6. JPML Rule 17(b).

7. JPML Rule 16(d).
8. JPML Rule 16(e).
9. JPML Rule 16(f).
10. *Id.*
11. *Id.*

cases, and ability (and willingness) to effectively incorporate the arguments of other parties on his or her side of the issue.

At the argument itself, counsel should assume the Panel's familiarity with the papers and with pertinent precedent. Argument should focus principally on the factors that the Panel must weigh[12] in making its decision.

Parties opposing transfer should also be prepared to address why available MDL case management techniques are insufficient to mitigate any claimed prejudice or hardship. For example, counsel frequently argue that pretrial proceedings in a foreign transferee district would impose severe cost burdens, including travel costs and the retention of local counsel. The Panel, however, often finds that such hardship can be minimized by telephonic hearings and the appointment of liaison counsel. Consequently, at argument before the Panel, counsel opposing transfer should be prepared to explain, with some specificity, why case management techniques would be insufficient to mitigate burdens, while proponents should argue that effective case administration can alleviate such burdens.

Library References:

West's Key No. Digests, Federal Civil Procedure ⬤9.
Wright, Miller & Cooper, Federal Practice and Procedure: Civil 2d § 3980.1.

§ 11.9   Factors in Deciding on Transfer

There are three statutory prerequisites to transfer under 28 U.S.C.A. § 1407, as to which the moving party bears the burden of proof:

    (1) there are multiple cases sharing one or more common issues of fact;

    (2) transfer will be for the convenience of the parties and witnesses; and

    (3) transfer will promote the just and efficient conduct of the actions.[1]

These factors are fluid and the ultimate decision is often fact-specific. However, several generalizations can be drawn. The Panel is typically most focused on the "just and efficient conduct of the actions" and will tend to find that the individual hardship on particular parties is outweighed by overall efficiencies from the MDL, particularly where the hardships can be minimized by case management techniques such as liaison counsel, telephonic hearings and the like.

Certain factors weigh in favor of transfer:

● discovery in candidate actions is in early phase;

---

12. *See infra* § 11.9.

§ 11.9

1. 28 U.S.C.A. § 1407(a) (West 1993 & Supp. 1997).

- there are numerous cases;
- there are numerous common fact issues;[2]
- there are complex fact issues;[3]
- the parties consent to transfer.

Other factors weigh against transfer:

- discovery in candidate actions is in advanced stage;[4]
- a decision by transferor court of a potentially dispositive issue is imminent;[5]
- there are few cases;[6]
- there is a lack of sufficient common issues;[7]
- complex issues are lacking;
- the parties oppose transfer.[8]

Library References:

West's Key No. Digests, Federal Civil Procedure ⚮9; Federal Courts ⚮151157.
Wright, Miller & Cooper, Federal Practice and Procedure: Civil 2d §§ 3682, 3863.

§ 11.10   Selection of Transferee Court and Judge

The Panel selects both the transferee district and the specific judge who will handle the matter.[1] In many cases there is little dispute that an MDL proceeding will be invoked; the real issue is which district court and judge will be designated to handle the MDL. This is a critical decision and one on which counsel should be prepared to address significant argument, even if opposing MDL treatment.

2. *See In re* Temporomandibular Joint (TMJ) Implants Prods. Liab. Litig., 844 F.Supp. 1553 (J.P.M.L. 1994).

3. *See In re* Garrison Diversion Unit Litig., 458 F.Supp. 223, 225 (J.P.M.L. 1978) (even minimal number of cases may be transferred if issues are sufficiently complex).

4. *See In re* Motion Picture Licensing Antitrust Litig., 479 F.Supp. 581, 590 (J.P.M.L. 1979); *In re* Luminex Int'l, Inc. Prods. Liab. Litig., 434 F.Supp. 668, 670 (J.P.M.L. 1977); *In re* A. H. Robins Co., Inc. "Dalkon Shield" IUD Prods. Liab. Litg., 570 F.Supp. 1480, 1481–82 (J.P.M.L. 1983).

5. *See In re* Bourns Patent Litig., 385 F.Supp. 1260, 1261 (J.P.M.L. 1974).

6. *See In re* Magic Marker Sec. Litig., 470 F.Supp. 862, 865 (J.P.M.L. 1979) (where only a minimal number of actions are involved, the movant has a strong burden to establish sufficient complexity to warrant transfer).

7. *See In re* Repetitive Stress Injury Litig., 11 F.3d 368, 373 (2d Cir.1993) (transfer denied where only common issue was generalized injury claim for which there were numerous possible causes other than the alleged tort and, as a result, individual issues predominated); *In re* McDonnell Douglas "Wild Weasel AN/APR–38" Contract Litig., 415 F.Supp. 387, 389 (J.P.M.L. 1976); *In re* United Gas Pipe Line Co. Litig., 391 F.Supp. 774, 776 (J.P.M.L. 1975).

8. *In re* Asbestos & Asbestos Insulation Material Prods. Liab. Litig., 431 F.Supp. 906, 910 (J.P.M.L. 1977) (virtually unanimous opposition of parties is a "very persuasive factor"). *But see In re* Air Crash Disaster at Stapleton Int'l Airport, 720 F.Supp. 1505, 1513 (D.Colo.1989) (transfer may be ordered over objection of the parties.

§ 11.10

1. 28 U.S.C.A. § 1407(a) (court), (b) (judge) (West 1993 & Supp. 1997).

(a) Selection of Transferee Court

The Panel may select any district court; the transferee district need not be one of the transferor districts, nor is the Panel limited by venue or personal jurisdiction considerations.[2] The paramount consideration for selection of the transferee district is the "just and efficient conduct of such actions."[3]

Specific factors that the Panel will consider in selecting the transferee court include:

- whether it is a district "in which the action could have been brought";[4]

- the parties' residences and principal places of business;[5]

- the location of relevant evidence, documents and witnesses;[6]

- the geographic proximity to the various transferor districts;[7]

- the district selected for prior transfers under 28 U.S.C.A. § 1404 (convenience transfers);[8]

- which district has the largest number of significant candidate cases already pending;[9]

- the congestion of the transferee court's docket;[10]

- the location of related proceedings;[11]

- the location of related state court cases;[12]

---

2. 28 U.S.C.A. § 1407(a) (West 1993 & Supp. 1997); *see In re* Ivy, 901 F.2d 7, 9 (2d Cir.1990); *In re* Vernitron Sec. Litig., 462 F.Supp. 391, 394 (J.P.M.L. 1978); *In re* Falstaff Brewing Corp. Antitrust Litig., 434 F.Supp. 1225, 1229 (J.P.M.L. 1977).

3. 28 U.S.C.A. § 1407(a).

4. This may allow the transferee court to retain the matter for trial. *See infra* § 11.18; *see* Blake M. Rhodes, *The Judicial Panel On Multidistrict Litigation: Time For Rethinking,* 140 U. Pa. L. Rev. 711, 747–48 (1991).

5. *See In re* "Factor VIII or IX Concentrate Blood Prod." Prods. Liab. Litig., 853 F.Supp. 454, 455 (J.P.M.L. 1993).

6. *See In re* Air Crash Disaster Near Coolidge, Arizona on May 6, 1971, 362 F.Supp. 572, 573 (J.P.M.L. 1973).

7. *See In re* Rio Hair Neutralizer Prods. Liab. Litig., 904 F.Supp. 1407, 1408 (J.P.M.L. 1995) (central location); *see In re* Wheat Farmers Antitrust Class Action Litig., 366 F.Supp. 1087, 1088 (J.P.M.L. 1973) (centralized location selected).

8. *See In re* Warehouse Constr. Contract Litig., 387 F.Supp. 734, 735–36 (J.P.M.L. 1975).

9. *See In re* Regents of the University of California, 964 F.2d 1128, 1136 (Fed.Cir. 1992) (look to location of number of cases of significance); *In re* Republic National–Realty Equities Sec. Litig., 382 F.Supp. 1403, 1407 (J.P.M.L. 1974) (numerically most cases); *In re* Plywood Antitrust Litig., 376 F.Supp. 1405, 1407 (J.P.M.L. 1974) (judge already familiar with issues because of cases already located there).

10. *See In re* Peruvian Rd. Litig., 380 F.Supp. 796, 798 (J.P.M.L. 1974).

11. *See In re* American Continental Corp./Lincoln Sav. and Loan Sec. Litig., 130 F.R.D. 475, 476 (J.P.M.L. 1990) (district where defendant's bankruptcy proceedings were located); *In re* Cement and Concrete Antitrust Litig., 437 F.Supp. 750, 753 (J.P.M.L. 1977) (district where grand jury investigating antitrust allegations was sitting).

12. Although state cases cannot be transferred in the MDL process, location of

- the position(s) of the parties on the appropriate district;[13]
- the location of judges experienced in the litigation or in complex litigation generally.[14]

(b) Selection of Transferee Judge

As a general rule, the Panel selects a judge already sitting within the transferee district and, indeed, one factor in selecting that district may be the fact that a particular judge is located there. However, the Panel also possesses the statutory power to request that a circuit or district judge be designated and assigned temporarily for service in the transferee district.[15] This power, however, is rarely used.

The paramount factor in selection of a judge is his or her ability to handle complex litigation. In that vein, selection factors include:

- prior experience in successfully handling complex litigation;
- ability to devote sufficient time to the matter; and
- expressed willingness to undertake the responsibility.

Not surprisingly, it is not uncommon for significant cases to be assigned to a former Panel member with experience in complex litigation.[16]

Since selection of an experienced judge is a significant factor in the Panel's decision on the appropriate transferee district, it is advisable, when arguing for a specific transferee court, to identify appropriate judges within the requested district and to speak to their expertise. Prior service on the Panel or on other judicial bodies which address case management issues and techniques (such as the Federal Judicial Center, Board of Editors of the Manual for Complex Litigation, or Judicial Conference Advisory Committee on Civil Rules) should be emphasized.

Library References:

West's Key No. Digests, Federal Civil Procedure ⚷9; Federal Courts ⚷151–157.
Wright, Miller & Cooper, Federal Practice and Procedure: Civil 2d § 3864.

the MDL in a district where state court cases are pending can facilitate voluntary informal communication and coordination between federal and state proceedings. *See In re* Air Crash Disaster at Sioux City, Iowa on July 19, 1989, 128 F.R.D. 131, 132–33 (J.P.M.L. 1989); *In re* Oil Spill by the "Amoco Cadiz" off Coast of France on March 16, 1978, 471 F.Supp. 473, 478–79 (J.P.M.L. 1979).

13. *In re* Cutter Lab., Inc. "Braunwald–Cutter" Aortic Heart Valve Prods. Liab. Litig., 465 F.Supp. 1295, 1297–98 (J.P.M.L. 1979) (if other factors are equal, Panel will follow suggestion of majority of litigants); *but see In re* Silicone Gel Breast Implants Prods. Liab. Litig., 793 F.Supp. 1098, 1101 (J.P.M.L. 1992) (litigants unable to agree on appropriate transferee district and Panel selected entirely different one).

14. *See In re* Silicone Gel Breast Implants Prods. Liab. Litig., 793 F.Supp. at 1101. *In re* Data Gen. Corp. Antitrust Litig. 470 F.Supp. 855, 859 (J.P.M.L. 1979).

15. 28 U.S.C.A. § 1407(b) (West 1993 & Supp. 1997); appointment is made by the Chief Justice of the United States or the chief judge of the circuit. *See In re* Olympia Brewing Co. Antitrust Litig., 415 F.Supp. 398 (J.P.M.L. 1976).

16. *See infra* § 11.24.

§ 11.11   Extensions of Time

Applications for extension of any time specified in the Rules must be made in writing and must specify the reason for the request and propose a specific number of additional days needed.[1] The Clerk of the Panel may act upon the application, taking into account the reasons set forth and the impact of the extension on the Panel's calendar.[2] A party dissatisfied with the decision of the Clerk of the Panel may submit objections to the Panel.[3]

Extensions of the deadlines for entry of appearance and for notice of opposition to conditional transfer or remand orders are not granted, except in extraordinary circumstances.[4] Similarly, once a hearing has been scheduled, it may only be continued by order of the Panel on good cause shown.[5]

§ 11.12   Appeal from Panel Decisions

There is no appeal or review of an order denying transfer.[1] With respect to all other Panel orders, the exclusive route for appeal is an extraordinary writ pursuant to 28 U.S.C.A. § 1651.[2]

The particular appellate court in which the petition for a writ must be filed, however, depends on the type of order at issue. For all Panel orders issued prior to an order granting or denying transfer, appeals should be filed in the appellate court with "jurisdiction over the district in which [the Panel's transfer] hearing is to be or has been held."[3] For appeal of a transfer order and any subsequent orders (such as remand orders), the proper appellate court is that with jurisdiction over the transferee court.[4]

§ 11.13   Powers of Transferor and Transferee Courts

(a) Effect of Pendency of Action Before Panel

The Panel's order directing a transfer does not become effective until it is filed in the transferee court by the Clerk of the Panel.[1] Until that time, the transferor court retains full control of the action and the MDL proceedings do not affect or suspend orders or proceedings or in any way limit the jurisdiction of the transferor court. After entry of the

§ 11.11

1. JPML Rule 15.

2. Id.

3. Id.

4. JPML Rules 8(c); 15.

5. JPML Rule 16(g).

§ 11.12

1. 28 U.S.C.A. § 1407(e) (West 1993 & Supp. 1997).

2. Id.

3. Id.

4. For appeals of deposition orders, see infra § 11.13(b).

§ 11.13

1. JPML Rule 12(e), 18; 28 U.S.C.A. § 1407(c) (West 1993 & Supp. 1997).

transfer order, the transferor court jurisdiction is terminated.[2] Reciprocally, a remand order becomes effective when it is filed with the clerk of the transferee court and, until such time, the transferee court retains all jurisdiction over the matter.[3]

While these basic rules are simple to state, actual practice is often more complicated. If motions are pending at the time MDL procedures are initiated, some transferor judges will accelerate their decisional process in order to enter their ruling prior to any transfer order that would deprive them of power over the case; other transferor judges will delay ruling, preferring to allow the transferee court to rule on the matters at issue. Conversely, the Panel may delay its own transfer decisions pending rulings on dispositive motions in either the transferor or transferee courts.[4] These subtle timing issues depend on the proclivities of the judges involved and the specific matters at issue. For example, a transferor judge may be more inclined to defer to the transferee judge on discovery issues than dispositive issues. The Panel may be more inclined to delay ruling as a result of the pendency of case-dispositive motions, rather than merely issue-dispositive motions.

(b) Powers of the Transferee Judge

After transfer, the authority of the transferee court is very broad and includes the power:

- to modify, expand or vacate orders previously issued by the transferor courts;[5]

- to exclude trial issues by pretrial order;[6]

- to permit amendment of pleadings;[7]

- to decide dispositive motions, including motions to dismiss, motions for judgment on the pleadings, motions for summary judgment, or motions for involuntary dismissal;[8]

---

2. *In re* Upjohn Co. Antibiotic Cleocin Prods. Liab. Litig., 664 F.2d 114, 118 (6th Cir.1981); General Electric Co. v. Byrne, 611 F.2d 670, 673 (7th Cir.1979).

3. JPML Rule 18.

4. *See, e.g., In re* Resource Exploration, Inc. Sec. Litig., 483 F.Supp. 817, 821–22 (J.P.M.L. 1980) (principles of comity cause Panel to delay action pending resolution of potentially dispositive issue).

5. *See In re* Plumbing Fixture Cases, 298 F.Supp. 484, 489 (J.P.M.L. 1968); *In re* Multi–Piece Rim Products Liability Litigation, 653 F.2d 671, 676–77 (D.C.Cir.1981) (pretrial order); *In re* Upjohn Co. Antibiotic Cleocin Prods. Liab. Litig., 664 F.2d at 118 (protective order).

6. *See In re* Multi–Piece Rim Prods. Liab. Litig., 464 F.Supp. 969, 975 (J.P.M.L. 1979).

7. *See In re* Equity Funding Corp. of America Sec. Litig., 416 F.Supp. 161, 177 (C.D.Cal.1976).

8. *See* 28 U.S.C.A. § 1407(b) (West 1993 & Supp. 1997); *In re* Temporomandibular Joint (TMJ) Implants Prods. Liab. Litig., 872 F.Supp. 1019, 1024 (D.Minn.1995) *aff'd*, 97 F.3d 1050 (8th Cir.1996), *reh'g denied* (1996); *In re* Donald J. Trump Casino Sec. Litig.-Taj Mahal Litig., 7 F.3d 357, 367–68 (3d Cir.1993), *cert. denied sub nom.* Gollomp v. Trump, 510 U.S. 1178, 114 S.Ct. 1219, 127 L.Ed.2d 565 (1994); Humphreys v. Tann, 487 F.2d 666, 667–68 (6th Cir. 1973), *cert. denied*, 416 U.S. 956, 94 S.Ct. 1970, 40 L.Ed.2d 307 (1974) (summary judgment and involuntary dismissal under FRCP 41(a)); *In re* King Resources Co. Sec. Litig., 385 F.Supp. 588, 590 (J.P.M.L. 1974) (motion to dismiss); Kaiser Indus. Corp. v.

- to determine class certification issues;[9]
- to approve consent decrees;[10]
- to approve settlements;[11] and
- to quash service of process.[12]

If a motion was pending at the time of transfer, it is wise to renew it in the transferee court to avoid any question as to its continued vitality.[13] This is done most efficiently at the initial conference with the judge handling the MDL. Because the transferee judge will often have a large volume of materials to master, it is helpful to submit a list of those motions which remain pending.

Both transferee judges and the Panel judges are statutorily empowered to exercise the powers of district judge in *any* district for the purpose of conducting pretrial depositions in MDL proceedings.[14] Thus, if an MDL is pending in a district in Pennsylvania, disputes at a third-party deposition being taken in a district in Texas should be referred to the transferee judge in the Pennsylvania district. One procedural anomaly is that an appeal of an order relating to such a deposition is made to the circuit in which the deposition is taken, in which the transferee judge is deemed to be sitting for purposes of that particular ruling, and not to the circuit in which the transferee district is located.[15]

(c) Amendment of Prior Rulings

Comity and law-of-the-case issues may arise in instances where the transferee judge revisits prior rulings of the transferor judge after the transfer, as well as when the reverse occurs after remand. It is not uncommon for the transferee judge to amend prior rulings of the transferor judge, particularly on discovery related issues or case management issues. Counsel should not assume that prior favorable rulings are set in stone, or that opportunities to contest unfavorable rulings are lost.

The issue of modification of prior orders is particularly troublesome in the event of a remand, where many of the transferee judge's rulings

Wheeling–Pittsburgh Steel Corp., 328 F.Supp. 365, 371 (D.Del.1971) (judgment on pleadings); *In re* Four Seasons Sec. Laws Litig., 63 F.R.D. 115, 120 (W.D.Okla.1974) (involuntary dismissal under FRCP 41(b)).

9. *See In re* Copley Pharmaceutical, Inc. "Albuterol" Prods. Liab. Litig., 161 F.R.D. 456 (D.Wyo.1995); *In re* Phar–Mor, Inc. Sec. Litig., 875 F.Supp. 277, 278–80 (W.D.Pa. 1994).

10. *See* Temporomandibular Joint (TMJ) Implants Prod. Liab. Litig., 872 F.Supp. at 1024.

11. *See In re* Corrugated Container Antitrust Litig., 659 F.2d 1332, 1335 (5th Cir. 1981), *cert. denied sub nom.* Three J. Farms

v. Plaintiffs' Steering Committee, 456 U.S. 936, 102 S.Ct. 1993, 72 L.Ed.2d 456 (1982).

12. *See In re* King Resources Co. Sec. Litig., 385 F.Supp. at 590.

13. *See In re* Norplant Contraceptive Prods. Liab. Litig., 898 F.Supp. 433, 436 n. 2 (E.D.Tex.1995) (motion pending in transferor court at time of transfer deemed withdrawn when not renewed in transferee court).

14. 28 U.S.C.A. § 1407(b) (West 1993 & Supp. 1997).

15. *See In re* Corrugated Container Antitrust Litig., 662 F.2d at 879.

may have related to trial matters.[16] The commentators generally agree that, after remand back to the original transferor judge, that judge should not be permitted to modify orders issued by the transferee judge.[17] As one long-time Panel member has observed:

> If transferor judges were permitted to upset rulings of transferee judges, the result would be an undermining of the purposes and usefulness of transfer under Section 1407 for coordinated or consolidated pretrial proceedings because those proceedings would then lack the finality (at the trial court level) requisite to the convenience of witnesses and parties and to efficient conduct of actions.[18]

While this position is consistent with principles of comity and law-of-the-case rules, it is not necessarily implemented in practice.[19] The transferor judge, now having received back the case originally assigned to him or her, has an interest in exercising control over the case again. It is also difficult for many judges to adopt prior rulings with which they disagree and particularly difficult to implement such rulings consistently throughout trial. Furthermore, many transferor judges are receptive to the argument by trial counsel that the MDL process, with its massing of issues and use of liaison counsel, prevented them from effectively arguing their own motions or their unique facts.

Consequently, the best practice is to be prepared for the possibility that the transferor judge may reopen issues. Parties wanting to maintain existing rulings should argue not only the merits of the issue itself, but also principles of comity, law-of-the-case, and the effect that relitigation of issues will have in undermining the purposes of the MDL process.

§ 11.14   Choice of Law Within an MDL

(a) State Law

Choice of law is a turbulent and problematic area of MDL practice.[1] The United States Supreme Court has established two basic choice of law principles: (1) absent applicable federal statutory or common law, a

---

16. See infra § 11.13(b).

17. See, e.g., 15 Charles Alan Wright, Arthur R. Miller & Edward H. Cooper, Federal Practice and Procedure § 3866 (2d ed. 1986); 4 James Wm. Moore, et al. Moore's Federal Practice, § 112.06[3] at 112–62 (3d ed. 1997); Stanley A. Weigel, The Judicial Panel on Multidistrict Litigation, Transferor Courts and Transferee Courts, 78 F.R.D. 575, 577 (1978).

18. Weigel, 78 F.R.D. at 577.

19. As a general rule, the transferor court should and does adhere to the rulings of the MDL transferee court under the law-of-the-case doctrine. See In re Multi–Piece Rim Prods. Liab. Litig., 653 F.2d 671, 678 (D.C.Cir.1981); Allegheny Airlines, Inc. v.

LeMay, 448 F.2d 1341, 1345 (7th Cir.), cert. denied, 404 U.S. 1001, 92 S.Ct. 565, 30 L.Ed.2d 553 (1971); Sentner v. Amtrak, 540 F.Supp. 557, 558 n. 3 (D.N.J.1982). For an extensive discussion of the law-of-the-case rules as applied to MDL proceedings, see Joan Steinman, Law of the Case: A Judicial Puzzle in Consolidated and Transferred Cases and in Multidistrict Litigation, 135 U. Pa. L. Rev. 595 (Mar. 1987).

§ 11.14

1. See Larry Kramer, Choice of Law in Complex Litigation, 71 N.Y.U. L. Rev. 547 (1996); Robert A. Ragazzo, Transfer and Choice of Federal Law: The Appellate Model, 93 Mich. L. Rev. 703 (1995).

federal court must apply the substantive law, including choice of law rules, of the state in which it sits;[2] and (2) where a case has been transferred to another district, the law of the state of the transferor district should apply, including its choice of law rules.[3]

As a general matter, these principles should not disturb the analysis that would be applied by a plaintiff who has given attention to both choice of law rules and substantive law in selecting the initial forum in which to file the action. The law of the transferor district (which has led to the selection of that district as the initial forum) would theoretically be carried over into the MDL.

In an MDL proceeding, however, the result may not be that simple. Using our 5–case MDL hypothetical described in Section 11.2, *supra,* the transferee court would need to look at the choice of law rules for each of the transferor districts. Assuming each district's choice of law rule (which would be the rule of the state in which it sits) fortuitously required application of governing state law which would be the same for all cases, there would be no problem. In practice, however, such simplicity rarely exists. Instead, it is common to encounter different choice of law rules which point to different state laws for resolution of the substantive issues. In our hypothetical, for example, it could well be that a different state's law applies to each of the five cases, and that there are material differences between the laws of those states with respect to material issues.

Because diverse substantive laws within a single MDL present complex management problems for the MDL judge, there is an understandable tendency to find that a single law applies. As one commentator has observed, "it is remarkable how often courts adjudicating mass actions nevertheless find that one law applies to all the claims or to each issue."[4] The intrinsically subjective character of choice of law analysis, combined with the natural tendency of an MDL judge to standardize proceedings as much as possible, creates an impetus to find that a single state law governs all cases. However, a problem results from this dynamic:

2. Klaxon Co. v. Stentor Elec. Manufacturing. Co., 313 U.S. 487, 496, 61 S.Ct. 1020, 1021, 85 L.Ed. 1477 (1941); Erie R. Co. v. Tompkins, 304 U.S. 64, 72–73, 58 S.Ct. 817, 819–20, 82 L.Ed. 1188 (1938).

3. Van Dusen v. Barrack, 376 U.S. 612, 638–39, 84 S.Ct. 805, 820–21, 11 L.Ed.2d 945 (1964) (discussing convenience transfers under 28 U.S.C.A. § 1404(a), the Court observed that "we should ensure that the 'accident' of federal diversity jurisdiction does not enable a party to utilize a transfer to achieve a result in federal court which could not have been achieved in the courts of the State where the action was filed .... We conclude, therefore, that in cases ... where the defendants seek transfer, the transferee district must be obligated to ap-

ply the state law that would have been applied if there had been no change of venue. A change of venue under § 1404(a) generally should be, with respect to state law, but a change of courtrooms."); Ferens v. John Deere Co., 494 U.S. 516, 523, 110 S.Ct. 1274, 1280, 108 L.Ed.2d 443 (1990) (*Van Dusen* rule applies regardless of which party initiates the § 1404(a) transfer; "[a] transfer under § 1404(a) ... does not change the law applicable to a diversity case").

4. Kramer, *supra* note 1, at 552; *see In re* Bendectin Litig., 857 F.2d 290, 302–05 (6th Cir.1988); *In re* "Agent Orange" Litig., 580 F.Supp. 690 (E.D.N.Y.1984).

If choice of law is substantive (in the sense that it defines the parties' rights), then courts should not alter choice-of-law rules for complex cases. The reasoning is straightforward. We start with claims that everyone concedes would otherwise be adjudicated under different laws. We combine these claims [through MDL] ... on the ground we can adjudicate the parties' rights more effectively and efficiently in one big proceeding.... Then, having constructed this proceeding, we are told we must change the parties' rights to facilitate the consolidated adjudication. And that makes no sense. If the reason for consolidating is to make adjudication of the parties' rights more efficient and effective, then the fact of consolidation itself cannot justify changing those rights. To let it do so is truly to let the tail wag the dog.[5]

In practice, different analyses may emerge, depending on the transferee judge. In some instances, the "drive for uniformity" will color the analysis and the court will find a single law applies.[6] In other cases, the court will adopt different law for different parties or issues.[7]

The best practical advice is that it is unwise to presume that any particular choice of law will be made; significant risk must be factored in by all parties on choice of law issues.

(b) Federal Law

The majority view is that *Van Dusen* and *Ferens,* discussed above, are limited to requiring application of the state law that would have been applied by the transferor court. In the case of how applicable federal law is to be determined, a number of courts have held that while the law of the transferor court is entitled to close consideration, a transferee court should be free to decide federal law issues on its own.[8] This rule is

---

5. Kramer, *supra* note 1, at 572.

6. *See In re* Silicone Gel Breast Implant Prods. Liab. Litig., 887 F.Supp. 1463, 1465–68 (N.D.Ala.1995); *In re* Air Crash Disaster Near Chicago, Illinois on May 25, 1979, 644 F.2d 594 (7th Cir.1981); *In re* Bendectin Litig., 857 F.2d 290 (6th Cir.1988). *See also* James A.R. Nafzinger, *Choice of Law in Air Disaster Cases: Complex Litigation Rules and the Common Law*, 54 La. L. Rev. 1001, 1015–84 (1994) (containing survey of cases from 1975–1993).

7. *See In re* Air Crash Disaster at Sioux City, Iowa on July 19, 1989, 734 F.Supp. 1425, 1425–26 (N.D.Ill.1990) (applying California, Ohio, and Illinois law to different defendants); *In re* Lou Levy & Sons Fashions, Inc., 988 F.2d 311, 313 (2d Cir.1993) ("In multidistrict litigation transfers, the law of the transferor district must be applied."); *In re* Integrated Resources Real Estate Limited Partnerships Sec. Litig., 815

F.Supp. 620, 649 (S.D.N.Y.1993) (applying Alabama, Connecticut, D.C., Florida, Illinois, Iowa, Maryland, Missouri, Mississippi, North Carolina, New Jersey, Pennsylvania and Tennessee law); *In re* School Asbestos Litig., 977 F.2d 764, 796–98, n. 34 (3d Cir. 1992) (division of state laws into four categories that encompass the variations in the product liability laws of the states may prove successful; plaintiff's proposal to pursue the strictest state standards of liability would raise constitutional issues about whether class members from a state with a less strict law could be precluded from challenging an adverse decision based on another state's stricter standard); Manual for Complex Litigation, (Third) § 31.132 at 254 (1995).

8. *See In re* Korean Air Lines Disaster of September 1, 1983, 829 F.2d 1171, 1173–76 (D.C.Cir.1987), *aff'd*, 490 U.S. 122, 109 S.Ct. 1676, 104 L.Ed.2d 113 (1989); Menow-

premised on the principle that "federal law" is uniform throughout the land, although even the federal courts candidly admit that this is not always true in fact.[9] Given this acknowledged reality, allowing the transferee court to decide the federal law issues on its own would appear to present the problem of a Section 1407 transfer changing substantive rights: a different rule of law will apply simply because the case is now in a different federal district by virtue of Section 1407.[10] The Seventh Circuit recognized this problem in *Eckstein v. Balcor Film Investors*,[11] holding that where federal law is in conflict, the rationale of *Van Dusen* applies and the law of the transferor court should govern. This is, at present, a minority view, but it appears more in keeping with the fundamental principle underlying the Supreme Court's decisions in *Van Dusen* and *Ferens* that transfers ordered in the name of administrative efficiency and convenience should not affect substantive rights.

§ 11.15 Case Administration Following Transfer

Initial case management following transfer involves establishing administrative procedures, appointing responsible counsel to certain positions and committees, planning for an effective initial pretrial conference with the transferee court, and negotiating the entry of a comprehensive initial case management order. Though these tasks are administrative and preliminary in nature, they offer MDL counsel an early opportunity to focus their litigation strategies and sensitize the transferee court to important issues.

(a) Notices and Docketing

Plaintiff and defense counsel should request a concise statement of the housekeeping measures that will govern the MDL proceeding. The clerk of court, or transferee judge, will address certain matters in either an administrative order or the initial case management order:[1]

- creation of a master or "all actions" file by the clerk of the transferee court for pleadings, motions, memoranda and other papers;
- establishment of a uniform case caption and docket numbers for the master file and each individual case;

itz v. Brown, 991 F.2d 36, 40–42 (2d Cir. 1993); *In re* Temporomandibular Joint (TMJ) Implants Prods. Liab. Litig., 872 F.Supp. 1019, 1024 (D.Minn.1995), *aff'd*, 97 F.3d 1050 (8th Cir.), *reh'g denied* (1996); Newton v. Thomason, 22 F.3d 1455, 1460 (9th Cir.1994). *Cf. In re* United Mine Workers of America Employee Benefit Plans Litig., 854 F.Supp. 914, 919–22 (D.D.C.1994) (applying *Van Dusen* rule to federal law issue).

9. *See* Menowitz v. Brown, 991 F.2d 36, 40 (2d Cir.1993) (quoting *In re* Pittsburgh & Lake Erie R.R. Co. Sec. & Antitrust Li-

tig., 543 F.2d 1058, 1065 n. 19 (3d Cir.1976) ("federal law . . . is assumed to be nationally uniform, whether or not it is in fact").

10. *See* Robert A. Ragazzo, *Transfer and Choice of Law: The Appellate Model*, 93 Mich. L. Rev. 703 (1995) (arguing that transferor law should apply).

11. 8 F.3d 1121, 1126–27 (7th Cir.1993).

§ 11.15

1. For a discussion of Case Management Orders, *see infra* § 11.16.

- creation of a master service list for counsel who have entered appearances;

- instructions for filing materials with the clerk and for delivering courtesy copies to the transferee judge;

- procedures for serving papers on steering committee counsel, plaintiff and defense liaison counsel, and counsel in individual actions; service is typically required to be made by facsimile or overnight mail;

- requirements that all counsel familiarize themselves with the local rules of the transferee court, along with the Manual for Complex Litigation, Third Edition;

- procedures for notifying the transferee court, and all counsel, of "tag-along" actions;

- whether retention of local counsel is advisable or necessary, and any requirements that counsel be admitted pro hac vice for the MDL proceedings.

(b) Counsel Arrangements

Because MDL proceedings generally involve multiple individual actions and complex liability issues, counsel on each side should jointly coordinate their discovery activities. Often, this is done by appointing liaison counsel, setting up plaintiff and defense steering committees and selecting lead trial counsel. Obtaining appointment to one of these positions is seen, by some, as a way to gain a prominent role in the MDL proceeding or to realize additional fees. Both sides, however, will be better served if individuals are recommended to these positions because of their credentials and expertise, their firm resources, and their ability to work smoothly with colleagues.

Plaintiff and defense counsel should meet as a group to discuss appointments to the following positions:[2]

(1) Plaintiff and Defense Liaison Counsel

To be effective, liaison counsel should have offices in the locality of the transferee court. Liaison counsel are typically responsible for administrative matters, such as maintaining a current master service list and communicating with, and distributing notices, orders, motions, etc. to counsel on each side. Plaintiffs' liaison counsel is also responsible for maintaining records of disbursements for discovery and investigation costs. Because administrative matters must be faithfully attended to if MDL proceedings are to remain on track, liaison counsel should be selected on the basis of their diligence, thoroughness, and law firm resources.

---

2. For a discussion of various organizational structures and counsel positions in complex litigations, *see* Manual for Complex Litigation, (Third) §§ 20.21, 20.221–222 (1997).

(2) Steering Committees

Steering committees for each side of the MDL litigation are formed to perform a wide range of management functions, as assigned by the transferee court or the parties. Plaintiffs and defendants should each select counsel for steering committees who can carry out certain substantive responsibilities:

- consolidate and coordinate discovery and prevent duplication of effort or duplicative papers;
- advance the common interests of all plaintiffs or defendants in the prosecution of liability issues;
- brief and argue motions;
- draft and answer written discovery;
- determine which attorneys should examine witnesses in depositions, subject to the right of nonsteering committee members to attend and submit questions to the examining attorney;
- act as a spokesperson at pretrial conferences;
- call joint meetings of counsel as necessary and appropriate;
- generally coordinate discovery and other pretrial activities of counsel and delegate work responsibilities to selected counsel, including nonsteering committee members;
- coordinate the matter with any other related litigation;
- provide periodic reports to noncommittee members on the status of the litigation;
- submit to the court and distribute to counsel for a given side, including counsel for tag-along actions, all documents, notices of depositions, written interrogatories, requests for production and inspection of documents, requests for admissions, and motions;
- establish and maintain a depository for all documents produced by the adverse parties and make such files available to noncommittee counsel upon request; and
- perform such other functions as may be authorized by further order of court.[3]

(3) Chair of Steering Committee

The Chair acts for the group—either personally or by coordinating the efforts of others—in presenting written and oral arguments and suggestions to the court, working with opposing counsel in developing and implementing a litigation plan, initiating and organizing discovery requests and responses, conducting the principal examination of deponents, employing experts, arranging for support services, and seeing that schedules are met.[4] Because these responsibilities are significant, a

---

3. These types of responsibilities were assigned to members of the plaintiffs' steering committee in *In re* Air Crash Near Pittsburgh on September 8, 1994, Misc. No. 94–1014, MDL Docket No. 1040, Case Management Order No. 1 (W.D. Pa. 12/16/94).

4. *See* Manual for Complex Litigation, (Third) § 20.221, at 27–28 (1997).

senior, experienced member of the bar should be selected for this position.

(4) Lead Trial Counsel

If trial proceeds on a consolidated basis,[5] lead trial counsel serves as the principal attorney for the group at trial in presenting arguments, making objections, examining witnesses, and generally organizing and coordinating the work of the other attorneys on the trial team.[6] Each side typically designates lead trial counsel as discovery nears completion. Some transferee courts, however, require that lead trial counsel be named shortly after initial transfer to ensure that each side analyzes and raises the trial implications of any discovery issues addressed by the transferee court.

A careful and prudent selection process should obviously be followed before naming lead trial counsel. Lead trial counsel will be the individual with whom the jury becomes most familiar during the trial and the person most identified with the party and its cause. Several practical factors, such as whether a prospective trial counsel's own action(s) are likely to settle before trial, and whether remand is likely after the completion of discovery, may also influence the appointment process.

(5) Selection Process

Counsel should understand that competition for appointment to these select positions is often intense. Alliances and negotiations among attorneys vying for selection may influence the nominating process, and informal agreements may affect the various arguments advanced by counsel at appointment hearings.[7] For these reasons, counsel should insist that each attorney interested in appointment file a submission outlining his or her professional qualifications, experience, specialty of practice and relevant personal background.[8]

Counsel should request that the court conduct a hearing before appointments are approved to ensure an independent assessment of the qualifications, collegiality and proposed compensation of designated counsel. Counsel should also request that the responsibilities of liaison, lead and trial counsel, along with those of each steering committee, be outlined in a court order or stipulation signed by all counsel and approved by the court.[9] Typically, if substantially all parties agree on the appointments, the court will endorse the appointments. But if there is

---

5. See infra § 11.18.

6. Manual for Complex Litigation, (Third) § 20.221 at 28 (1997).

7. To this end, some transferee courts may direct attorneys interested in serving as lead, liaison or coordinating counsel to submit information showing how and at what rates they propose to be compensated and to disclose any agreements they have made on the role and responsibility of other attorneys in conducting pretrial proceedings, discovery, and trial.

8. For example, experienced plaintiffs' counsel who are also licensed pilots with substantial flying experience may be appropriate candidates for appointment to the Plaintiffs' Steering Committee in an MDL proceeding involving an air disaster.

9. See Manual for Complex Litigation, (Third) § 20.222 (1997).

disagreement, the court will make its independent decision following a hearing.

(c) Compensation and Trust Accounts

Once liaison and trial counsel, along with the two steering committees, are appointed, procedures must be established to reimburse selected counsel for expenses and fees incurred in performing their duties. All parties benefitting from their services are usually required to share the resulting expenses and fees.[10] Appointed counsel should initially circulate a proposed compensation procedure among all counsel on a given side and work toward a consensus. Individual counsel should review the procedures for reasonableness and request that the procedures be approved by the court and be subject to continuing judicial oversight.[11]

Plaintiffs' steering committee ("PSC") expenses should be paid from an expense fund approved by the court and administered by liaison counsel.[12] A newly-formed PSC may seek an agreement whereby counsel for each individual plaintiff deposits an initial amount with the Chair of the PSC to be used on an ongoing basis to help defray PSC costs and expenses.[13] Liaison counsel are then responsible for monitoring disbursements from the account.

Because this initial assessment probably will prove inadequate to cover all expenses, additional resources will be necessary to fully compensate and reimburse designated counsel. Steering committee counsel may seek to have the court impose an additional assessment on each settlement reached in individual cases. The PSC may propose, for example, that the court order, before an individual action is terminated by the entry of judgment or settlement and before any proceeds from a

---

10. See id. § 20.223, at 30–31; Smiley v. Sincoff, 958 F.2d 498 (2d Cir.1992); In re Air Crash Disaster at Florida Everglades on December 29, 1972, 549 F.2d 1006 (5th Cir.1977); In re Silicone Gel Breast Implant Prods. Liab. Litig., MDL No. 926, Order No. 13 (N.D. Ala. July 23, 1992). Any procedure that is adopted to determine or change the allocation of fees should, of course, afford interested parties with an opportunity to be heard. See In re Nineteen Appeals Arising out of San Juan Dupont Plaza Hotel Fire Litig., 982 F.2d 603, 610–15 (1st Cir.1992). Objections to fees and assessments, and proposals to amend the fee structure, may be assigned to a special master. See In re Shell Oil Refinery, Civil Action No. 88–1935, Order and Reasons (E.D. La. January 13, 1989).

11. A transferee court has the discretion to order reimbursement and compensation for designated counsel, along with the obligation to ensure that the amounts are reasonable. See, e.g., Walitalo v. Iacocca, 968 F.2d 741, 747 (8th Cir.1992); Smiley, 958 F.2d at 501–02; In re FTC Line of Business Report Litig., 626 F.2d 1022, 1027 (D.C.Cir. 1980); In re Air Crash Disaster at Florida Everglades on December 29, 1972, 549 F.2d at 1016.

12. While expenses incurred by defense steering committees are also commonly shared among defendants, a different procedure is typically used. The defendants in a MDL proceeding are generally fewer in number, involve a less diverse group, and consist of substantial, credit-worthy corporations. For these reasons, defendants often share expenses in an MDL proceeding on an informal basis and without the continuing supervision of the transferee court.

13. Counsel should determine whether all individual cases should be treated equally for purposes of this initial assessment, or whether payments should be based on the size or potential damages of an individual case.

settlement are disbursed, that counsel for the individual plaintiffs remit a certain percentage of the proceeds to the PSC to cover disbursements and fees.[14]

Counsel for individual parties should request that periodic billings be submitted to the court for approval and that status reports detailing disbursements from the expense fund be circulated. Final determination of the appropriate fee to be awarded to PSC members and liaison counsel should typically be made at the conclusion of pretrial proceedings.[15] Appointed counsel should submit a compensation plan that outlines services performed, time spent in discovery proceedings and coordination activities, and proposed fees. The court may direct that assessments for PSC counsel fees shall not increase the amount of fees to which individual clients agreed in advance. The court may require that some or all of the fees be taken out of individual counsel's shares for each action, so that the parties themselves do not entirely bear the cost burden for the MDL litigation structure.

Counsel appointed to an MDL position should take care to avoid unnecessary discovery activities, limit attendance at meetings, conferences and depositions, and coordinate work on briefs and other tasks. Individual counsel should monitor designated counsel's activities to ensure that they are reasonable, will benefit all cases, and do not constitute duplicative work. Counsel on each side should also agree on what type of records will be kept to support fee and expense applications.[16]

(d) Initial Pretrial Conference

The initial pretrial conference in an MDL proceeding will be held as soon as practical, typically 30 to 60 days after an initial transfer order, even if some parties have not yet appeared or been served.[17] The

---

14. The expense assessment is typically calculated based on the gross proceeds recovered or, in the case of structured settlements, the gross amount or present cash value of a particular structure. *See In re* Air Crash Near Pittsburgh on September 8, 1994, Misc. No. 94–1014, MDL Docket No. 1040, Case Management Order No. 3 (7/19/95).

The assessment typically applies to all cases that are resolved after an initial period, such as six months after the initial conference conducted by the transferee court. This gives individual counsel an opportunity to resolve their cases without being "taxed" for the services of an MDL counsel structure. Assessments are then made on each case that is settled after the initial period. This procedure was followed in the *Pittsburgh Air Crash* litigation to balance the need for reimbursement of des-

ignated counsel with the desire of individual counsel to resolve their cases quickly, without resort to case coordination or assistance.

15. *Id.*

16. Though these records may be filed under seal, courts will monitor them to determine whether the expenditures of time or other costs are appropriate.

17. FRCP 16(a) empowers a district court to direct all counsel to appear for a conference before trial "for such purposes as (1) expediting the disposition of the action; (2) establishing early and continuing control so that the case will not be protracted because of lack of management; (3) discouraging wasteful pretrial activities; (4) improving the quality of the trial through more thorough preparation; and; (5) facilitating the settlement of the case." FRCP 16(a).

conference usually occurs before preanswer motions are filed and discovery begins.[18] Appointments to the steering committee, of liaison counsel and of other positions in the MDL governance structure should be well under way or completed to ensure that each side will know who is responsible for presenting and arguing positions at the conference.

To ensure that the initial conference addresses the global aspects of an MDL proceeding, and not the peculiarities of any individual action, a transferee court may order plaintiff and defense counsel to meet and confer before the conference:

● to identify claims and defenses common to the MDL action and to discuss a plan for initial disclosures;

● to identify substantive issues common to all actions that should be raised at the conference;

● to draft a joint statement detailing disputed issues of fact or law as specifically as possible;

● to discuss a proposed schedule for conducting the MDL proceeding, including a detailed discovery plan that takes into account the number of actions filed to date, the likelihood of future filings and the possibility and rate of settlements in individual actions;

● to draft brief factual statements to assist the court in understanding the background, setting, and likely dimensions of the MDL proceeding; and

● to share information about all related litigation pending in other courts.[19]

The Advisory Committee notes that pretrial conferences should "shift[] the emphasis away from a conference focused solely on the trial and toward a process of judicial management that embraces the entire pretrial phase, especially motions and discovery." Advisory Committee Notes, Subdivision (a).

18. The transferee court's order setting the conference often stays discovery until after the conference.

19. See Manual for Complex Litigation, (Third) § 21.11 (1997). The court may also order several interim measures pending the initial conference, such as temporarily suspending some local rules requiring the entries of appearance or retention of local counsel, extending the time for filing responses to complaints until after the initial conference, and suspending the FRCP 26(a)(1) requirement of initial discovery disclosures. See id. at § 21.12.

Some districts have opted-out of Rule 26(a)(1) or have adopted different disclosure requirements. See Chapter 18 "Discovery Strategy and Privileges" and Chapter

20 "Document Discovery," infra. See Smith v. Union Pacific R.R. Co., 168 F.R.D. 626, 627 (N.D.Ill.1996) ("[The 1996 amendments to Rule 26] were revolutionary—so much so that the highly controversial new requirement for advance disclosure without a discovery request, embodied in Rule 26(a)(1), created a sharp split among the district courts, with a majority of them (including this one) opting out of that requirement by local rule (as the Rule itself permitted)."). See also 8 Charles Alan Wright, Arthur R. Miller & Richard L. Marcus, Federal Practice and Procedure (2d ed. Supp. 1997); Donna Stienstra, Implementation of Disclosure in United States District Courts, with Specific Attention to Courts' Responses to Selected Amendments to Federal Rule of Procedure 26, in 6 Moore's Federal Practice, Chapter 26 (3d ed. 1997) (noting that, as of March 22, 1996, Rule 26 was in effect in forty-nine districts, was rejected in forty-five districts, with seven districts adopting the Rule with significant revisions). In MDL litigation, application of this Rule typically places unreasonable burdens on de-

Counsel should understand that the initial conference provides the transferee court with its first opportunity to hear the factual background and relevant legal issues that will be unique to the MDL proceeding. The conference will set the tone for future conferences and proceedings. Because counsel will initially be more familiar than the transferee court with the challenges presented by the MDL proceeding and the management issues that should be addressed, counsel should plan to present case management proposals that are tailored to the specifics of the action and are designed to simplify and streamline pretrial proceedings. Counsel should also be prepared to discuss:

- the nature and potential dimensions of the MDL litigation;
- procedures for the early resolution of dispositive legal issues;[20]
- the unique procedural and substantive problems likely to be encountered;
- procedures for coordinating discovery applicable to all individual actions so that duplication can be avoided; and
- a proposed schedule for MDL discovery, disclosure of experts and trial.[21]

· Plaintiff's counsel in an MDL action should seek to enlist the early and active involvement of the transferee court to expedite discovery. For plaintiffs, delay is undesirable. Conveying a focused view of the claims likely to be asserted in the MDL proceeding to the court and proposing a tailored discovery plan will reduce the ability of defendants to delay the cases or overly tax plaintiffs' resources.

Defendants, on the other hand, should seek to educate the transferee court about the defense themes that will be advanced in the MDL proceeding. Defense counsel should advocate a discovery plan that will quickly weed out nonmeritorious claims. Counsel should seek to narrow the issues and accelerate the disposition of individual cases through dispositive motions or settlement. Defendants should raise threshold dispositive issues, such as statute of limitations, product identification,

---

fendants, making its modification or suspension appropriate.

20. For example, in the *Agent Orange* litigation, the transferee court ordered both sides to brief and argue the effect of the "government contract" defense on the case and discovery. *In re* "Agent Orange" Prod. Liab. Litig., 506 F.Supp. 762, 796 (E.D.N.Y. 1980) ("[T]he court believes that early resolution of this potentially dispositive issue will serve the interests of justice and judicial efficiencies."). The court ordered initial, limited discovery to determine whether the defense was applicable, before general discovery could commence on the general issues of liability, causation and damages. *Id.* at 797.

21. FRCP 16(c) sets forth an exhaustive list of subjects properly considered at the initial pretrial conference. The Rule provides that a court may take appropriate action with respect to, among other things, the formulation and simplification of the issues, the necessity or desirability of amendments to the pleadings, stipulations of fact, the avoidance of unnecessary proofs, the timing of dispositive motions, control and scheduling of discovery, identification of witnesses and documents, and settlement. *Id.* Rule 16(c) also empowers a court to adopt "special procedures for managing potentially difficult or protracted actions that may involve complex issues, multiple parties, difficult legal questions or unusual proof problems." Rule 16 (c)(12). *See* Chapter 27 "Scheduling and Pretrial Conferences and Orders," *infra.*

absence of injury or causation, and advocate that the transferee court set up a schedule or process to quickly resolve them. To build credibility, defendants should also propose a reasonable discovery plan for individual actions likely to survive a motion to dismiss.

Plaintiff and defense counsel each should consider requesting the transferee court to order briefing on significant legal issues, such as choice of law or the effect of ongoing regulatory proceedings.[22] In mass disaster litigation, the court may find, upon analysis of applicable choice of law rules, that one state's law governs all cases, or that subclasses or other consolidated groups should be created.[23]

§ 11.16   Case Management Orders

Case management orders in an MDL proceeding are entered after the initial pretrial conference and serve as a roadmap for pretrial discovery.[1] Counsel should ensure that the initial case management order addresses any nuances unique to the particular MDL proceeding along with the following:

- administrative matters, such as creation of an MDL Master File and service requirements;[2]

- procedures for appointment of MDL liaison counsel, steering committees, lead and trial counsel;[3]

- deadlines and limits on joinder of parties in the transferee court and amended or additional pleadings;

- coordination with related litigation in state court that cannot be removed and consolidated with the MDL proceeding and procedures for later-transferred actions;

---

22. For example, a Federal Aviation Administration or National Transportation Safety Board investigation of an air disaster may limit the availability of witnesses for deposition and may restrict the parties' access to evidence such as cockpit voice recorder tapes or pieces of the aircraft. Similarly, an ongoing Food and Drug Administration investigation may impair the parties' ability to pursue discovery in an MDL proceeding arising out of a pharmaceutical that is recalled or voluntarily removed from the market.

23. *See supra* § 11.14.

§ 11.16

1. Case management orders are enjoying a renewed emphasis nationwide as a device for accelerating the disposition of otherwise protracted and complicated litigation. The Judicial Improvements Act of 1990, P.L. No. 101–650, among other things, mandated district courts to formulate a plan designed to "facilitate deliberate adjudication of civil cases on the merits, monitor discovery, improve litigation management, and ensure just, speedy, and inexpensive resolutions of civil disputes." Congress outlined several "principles" and "techniques" for litigation management and cost and delay reduction. These include: "early and ongoing control of the pretrial process through involvement of a judicial officer in ... controlling the extent of discovery and time for completion of discovery ... setting, at the earliest practical time, deadlines for filing motions and a time framework for their disposition ..., identif[ying] or formulat[ing] the principal issues in contention and, in appropriate cases, provid[ing] for the staged resolution or bifurcation of issues for trial ..., [and] present[ing] a discovery case management plan for the case at the initial pretrial conference...."

2. *See supra* § 11.15.

3. For a discussion of the initial pretrial conference, *see supra* § 11.15(d).

- briefing schedules for early resolution of jurisdictional or other dispositive issues applicable to all parties and/or unique to the MDL action;

- motion practice and briefing requirements (*i.e.*, length of briefs, schedules, necessity of complying with local rules regarding format and other requirements);

- management of MDL document disclosure and discovery;

- schedules and deadlines for completion of various pretrial phases of the case and the setting of a trial date;

- appointment of magistrate judges or special masters to resolve global discovery or other pretrial issues;

- prospects for settlement of individual actions or possible referral to mediation or other ADR procedure.

- schedules for future case management conferences, typically held every four to six months. The order may require that the PSC and defense counsel confer and circulate a proposed agenda for each conference;

- procedures for filing motions with the transferee court under Rule 11 or Rule 56; typically, leave of court is required; and

- any other special procedures that may facilitate management of the MDL litigation.[4]

The process of negotiating a case management order in an MDL proceeding requires a considerable amount of advance thought and coordination, especially if individual case counsel raise competing or inconsistent discovery plans.[5] Both sides should refine and propose procedures and deadlines that will favorably advance their goals concerning the pace and direction of the MDL pretrial phase.

(a) Discovery Plan

4. Case Management Orders in several recent MDL proceedings contained comprehensive provisions addressing all of these subjects. *See In re* Air Crash Near Pittsburgh, MDL Docket No. 1040 (W.D. Pa. 12/16/94); *In re* Abbott Laboratories Omniflox Products Liability Litig. (MDL 1004) (N.D. Ill. 9/7/94); *In re* Silicone Gel Breast Implant Prods. Liab. Litig., MDL No. 926, Case Management Order No. 1, 5 (N.D. Ala. 6/26/92, 9/15/92).

5. The Manual for Complex Litigation (Third) (1997) contains comprehensive checklists and detailed sample orders that counsel should consult for guidance. *See* §§ 21.211 (case-management plans), 40.1 (agenda items for initial pretrial conference), 40.2 (disclosure and discovery), 41.2 (sample order setting initial conference),

41.3 (sample case management order), 41.33 (sample scheduling order).

Several recent articles also contain practical advice about strategies to employ in negotiating a case management order. *See, e.g.*, Arvin Maskin, *Case Management Orders: An Important Tool for Civil Litigation Management Comes of Age, in Managing Complex Litigation: Procedures and Strategies for Lawyers and Courts* 145 (Am. Bar Assoc. 1992); Elizabeth Joan Cabraser, *Preparing, Proposing and Implementing Case Management Orders, in Managing Complex Litigation: Procedures and Strategies for Lawyers and Courts* 173 (Am. Bar Assoc. 1992); Elizabeth Joan Cabraser, *Tailor a Case Management Order to Your Controversy, available on* WESTLAW, 21–SUM Brief 13 (Summer 1992).

A realistic discovery plan should be negotiated as part of the case management order that will govern the MDL proceeding. Counsel for both sides should confer before the initial pretrial conference to develop a workable plan and discuss whether phased or sequenced discovery makes the most sense given any facts and issues unique to the MDL action. Several other issues should be discussed:

- whether written discovery will be the initial form of discovery to be used, and the time period for such discovery;

- whether coordination of discovery will be required, *e.g.*, plaintiffs' steering committee to consolidate and serve joint discovery on MDL liability issues; defendants to serve joint written discovery on liability or damage issues;

- limits on the numbers of interrogatories, requests for production, and requests for admission;

- whether individual case counsel are permitted to serve written discovery focused on issues specific to that plaintiff's case, and the limits of such discovery;

- voluntary disclosure of categories of documents, either from related cases or relevant to the MDL proceeding;

- the extent to which the MDL proceeding will be governed by the revised FRCP 26(a)(1);

- setting up document depositories and computerized storage;

- establishing a uniform Bates numbering system to identify the source of documents produced in the MDL action;

- establishing a date for the commencement of depositions, including nonparty depositions to obtain documents and tangible things;

- whether depositions may be recorded by video as well as by stenographic means and the procedures for videotaping (numbers of cameras, where focused, etc.);

- whether depositions of government officials involved in any investigation relevant to the MDL action may proceed, or will be delayed until the investigation is over or sufficiently complete to avoid interference;[6]

- procedures for filing motions to compel; typically the transferee court will not consider such motions until steering committee counsel or their designees meet and confer in good faith in an attempt to resolve the motion;

- deposition procedures;[7]

---

6. This is especially crucial in MDL litigation arising out of an air disaster, when FAA and NTSB personnel are typically enmeshed in post-accident hearings and investigation that may stretch over many months or years after the disaster has occurred.

7. Provisions regarding MDL deposition procedures typically address matters such as the location of depositions of parties and nonparties, who can attend (*i.e.*, whether individual case counsel are permitted to attend, whether personnel other than coun-

- whether independent medical examinations of plaintiffs will be permitted, and the terms and conditions of same;[8]

- timetables for completion of third-party fact discovery (liability and damages);

- procedures for completing records depositions and producing copies of records obtained at or before the depositions;

- timetables and procedures for expert disclosure, production of expert reports, and expert depositions (including the order of such depositions); and

- discovery cut-off, and dates for the filing of dispositive motions and pretrial statements.

Counsel should also consider whether to propose the submission of MDL discovery issues to a magistrate judge or special master for speedy disposition.

(b) Protective Orders and Procedures for Handling Claims of Confidentiality

Early in discovery, the defendants' steering committee should negotiate a protective order to protect sensitive information or documents that will be disclosed in the MDL proceeding. "Umbrella" protective orders, favored by defendants and most transferee courts, provide that all material designated as "confidential" by the producing party is presumptively protected and can only be disclosed to certain categories of individuals unless challenged.[9] The transferee court signs the agreed upon order without a particularized showing to support the claim for

sel, representatives of parties, and experts can attend), procedures and order of questioning (typically plaintiffs' liaison counsel is required to coordinate with other plaintiffs' counsel to designate one examiner for each deponent), and whether witnesses can only be examined by certain counsel (such as by PSC members or trial counsel). *See generally* Manual for Complex Litigation, (Third) § 21.45 (1997). The court may also require deposing counsel to produce copies of all documents upon which he or she intends to examine the witness no less than five business days before the deposition, unless surprise is important for impeachment or other purposes. The court may also limit the depositions to a reasonable length, such as seven hours, not including breaks. *See, e.g., In re* Abbott Laboratories Omniflox Products Liability Litig. (MDL 1004), Case No. 94–C–2469 (N.D. Ill.) (9/7/94 Case Management Order). Even though numerous individual actions are filed in an MDL proceeding, resulting in the entries of appearance of armies of counsel, an individual should be deposed only once, unless a party

obtains leave of court upon showing of good cause.

8. Such terms and conditions may include where the examination may be scheduled (usually in the transferor district), who may conduct the examination (typically limited to no more than three physicians, not as a panel, each in different areas of specialty), and who will bear the costs of the medical examination, including plaintiff's reasonable transportation expenses (typically the defendant). The court will also generally require the defendant to coordinate the examinations to the extent practicable to minimize inconveniences to the individual plaintiffs, and to provide a detailed report of the examining physician within 45 days of the examination setting forth all findings and diagnoses and the results of all tests.

9. For a discussion of appropriate protective orders in complex litigation, *see* Manual for Complex Litigation, (Third) § 21.432 (1997).

protection. Such a showing is required, however, if the receiving party challenges the claim within a reasonable, or the required, time following production.[10]

Applications for umbrella protective orders in MDL proceedings are usually presented to the transferee court for approval following stipulation by the Chair of each steering committee. The plaintiffs' steering committee should scrutinize the order proposed by defendants to make sure that it is narrowly tailored to protect truly confidential information rather than information that may merely prove embarrassing if it becomes publicly known.

Umbrella protective orders in MDL proceedings usually address several topics:

- the categories of MDL information and documents subject to the order;

- the option and procedure for a party to designate materials, documents or information as "Confidential";[11]

- procedures for producing documents to a central MDL document depository, its location and operation and the procedures for accessing the depository;

- Bates numbering of documents to identify the parties producing them;

- the procedures and extent to which "Confidential" documents may be used in MDL depositions, attached to motions, used as trial exhibits, or summarized in court papers;

- procedures for individual case counsel or steering committees to challenge or object to the designation of documents as "Confidential"[12];

---

10. The alternative to an "umbrella" protective order is a particularized protective order, where a party, typically a defendant in an MDL proceeding, moves under Rule 26(c) to limit disclosure or provide safeguards to protect the confidentiality of specific information to be produced. The movant must make a particularized showing of "good cause," by affidavit or testimony of a witness, of the harm that would result from disclosure or loss of confidentiality. *See id.* § 21.432, at 73; FRCP 26(c) (protective orders). *See also* Chapter 18 "Discovery Strategy and Privileges." at § 18.5(d), *infra.*

Particularized protective orders require a document-by-document assessment by the court and, therefore, are not favored in MDL proceedings, which are usually document intensive.

11. Items produced in a MDL action under a claim of confidentiality are identi-

fied with a special marking or legend to ensure that all personnel know what is confidential. Portions of depositions may also be so designated. Documents produced in MDL proceedings often bear a stamp:

CONFIDENTIAL

Subject to Protective Order in Cases

Consolidated under Docket ___ in the

United   States   District   Court

_____ .

Do not copy or disclose, except under terms of the Protective Order or upon leave of Court.

12. The opposing party generally has a specified period, such as 30 days following production, within which to contest the designation. *See* Manual for Complex Litigation, (Third) § 21.432 at 72 and n.149 (1997); Poliquin v. Garden Way, Inc., 989

- the extent to which Confidential and Nonconfidential documents may be used in related state court litigation not consolidated with the MDL action; and

- procedures for returning documents and all copies at the conclusion of the MDL proceedings.[13]

An MDL protective order should especially address the persons who may have access to protected materials. All individual case counsel, liaison counsel and steering committee counsel should be permitted to disclose such information to their office personnel, expert witnesses, the transferee court, and qualified persons taking testimony through stenographic and videotape means. Parties should also normally be entitled to have access to Confidential materials, unless the material has commercial or trade secret value. If so, the order should (1) limit disclosure to named individuals not involved in relevant corporate activity, (2) create a special class of highly confidential documents "for counsel's eyes only," and (3) require a log to be kept to record the personnel viewing the documents.[14]

Defense counsel in an MDL proceeding should also consider terms requiring plaintiffs to show the order to each individual who will view the document and obtain his or her signature indicating agreement not to misuse the information. Defendants also may request opposing counsel to provide in advance the names and addresses of persons to whom the disclosure will be made and to identify with particularity the documents to be disclosed. The producing party will then have the option of filing a motion objecting to the proposed disclosure.

Once the terms of an MDL protective order are in place, plaintiffs' counsel should review documents and portions of testimony designated as Confidential to determine if grounds exist to challenge the designation. Challenges should be raised quickly, if it appears that the Confidential designation has been used overbroadly. Plaintiffs should be vigilant to ensure that MDL protective orders are not used to block a party's or an expert's access to information relevant to liability issues.

(c) Preservation of Physical Evidence

The parties to an MDL proceeding should immediately consider and, where appropriate, propose procedures for the preservation of relevant physical evidence. Procedures for collecting, relocating, preserving, inspecting and testing physical evidence such as aircraft wreckage, allegedly defective products, or evidence from a mass disaster such as a hotel fire, should be outlined in a protective order entered by the transferee court.

Typical preservation orders in MDL proceedings require a defendant to preserve and keep safe all physical evidence or wreckage and relocate

---

F.2d 527, 529 (1st Cir.1993). The burden then shifts to the party seeking protection to justify the claim, usually through affidavits. *Id.* at 531.

13. *See* Manual for Complex Litigation, (Third) § 21.432, at 72–73 (1997).

14. *See id.* at 72 n.146.

it to an approved location. Plaintiffs' counsel should consider requesting additional provisions that address how the evidence will be stored and displayed (*e.g.*, boxing, master inventory list, inventories of each box). All related evidence or parts should be segregated and boxed together. Defendants may also be required, in air disaster cases, to create a master template to re-configure physical evidence or wreckage. Counsel should also discuss who will bear the costs and fees associated with preserving and keeping the wreckage. This is generally a defendant's responsibility.[15]

Protective orders in an MDL action should also address the conditions for photographing, videotaping and inspecting the evidence. An order from the transferee court is typically required, after a showing of exceptional need, before any destructive testing by an expert can take place or before the condition of parts is altered in any manner. Plaintiffs may also request that a defendant provide for deposition one or more witnesses who are knowledgeable as to how the MDL evidence or wreckage was collected, categorized and displayed in its approved location.

Defendants should request that any preservation order entered by the transferee court contain terms addressing how long cumbersome evidence such as aircraft wreckage must be preserved. Storage and maintenance of large pieces of physical evidence is costly, especially considering the potential length of an MDL proceeding. The transferee court, therefore, should only require that nonessential evidence or wreckage be preserved for a reasonable time (*e.g.*, one year after the commencement of proceedings in the transferee court). Individual case counsel and steering committees are well-advised to examine and thoroughly document MDL evidence at an early stage to allow sufficient time for further or follow-up inspections at a later time.

§ 11.17   Federal and State Court Coordination

Air crash disaster and mass tort litigation frequently involve filings in both federal and state courts. While multidistrict treatment of the federal cases under Section 1407 may be possible,[1] some state court cases

---

15. Plaintiffs may also be required to assemble and preserve relevant physical evidence in one central location. For example, in a MDL proceeding arising out of the federal recall of a pharmaceutical, plaintiffs should be required to preserve any unused prescription drugs. If appropriate, therefore, a preservation order should impose equal obligations on both sides.

§ 11.17

1. The Judicial Panel has consolidated a number of mass tort and air crash cases for centralized pretrial management. *E.g.*, *In re* Abbott Laboratories Omniflox Products Li-

ability Litigation, MDL Docket No. 1004, No. 94 C 2469, 1995 WL 55218 (N.D.Ill. 1995); *In re* Asbestos Prods. Liab. Litig., 771 F.Supp. 415 (J.P.M.L. 1991); *In re* Silicone Gel Breast Implants Prods. Liab. Litig. (MDL Docket No. 926), 793 F.Supp. 1098 (J.P.M.L. 1992); *In re* Air Crash Near Pittsburgh on September 8, 1994, Misc. No. 94–1014, MDL Docket No. 1040 (W.D. Pa.). *See also In re* Swine Flu Immunization Prod. Liab. Litig., 464 F.Supp. 949 (1979); *In re* A.H. Robins Co. "Dalkon Shield" IUD Prods. Liab. Litig., 406 F.Supp. 540 (J.P.M.L. 1975).

may not be removable—and therefore may not be subject to Section 1407 transfer.[2]

When consolidated treatment in a single court is not possible, counsel in the state and federal court actions should consider closely coordinating the proceedings to reduce duplication of effort and minimize conflicting rulings. Counsel may request that the courts coordinate scheduling and discovery plans, appoint joint special masters and lead counsel, create federal-state depositories, preside jointly at hearings, and conduct joint settlement and alternative dispute resolution procedures.[3]

The *Manual for Complex Litigation* suggests the above as well as several other techniques to coordinate state and federal court proceedings:

- appoint one or more attorneys to serve as a liaison with each state court in which a significant number of similar cases have been filed;

- appoint a special master with primary responsibility for monitoring, coordinating, and disseminating information about state and federal activities;

- negotiate consistent case management orders, master pleadings, and discovery protocols to adopt similar approaches to discovery and pretrial management;

- coordinate discovery schedules and trial dates;

- create joint federal-state, plaintiff-defendant document depositories that will be accessible to attorneys in all states;

- schedule joint status conferences;

- request that discovery materials from prior state and federal cases be included in the document depository;

- request that the state courts enjoin attorneys who conduct federal discovery from objecting to its use in state proceedings on the grounds that it originated in a federal court;

- request joint orders for the preservation of evidence and coordinate the examination of evidence by experts in both state and federal proceedings; and

2. For example, the numerous federal court actions that were filed after the crash of USAir Flight 427 near Pittsburgh, Pennsylvania in 1994 were consolidated for centralized pretrial proceedings in the Western District of Pennsylvania. *In re* Air Crash Near Pittsburgh on September 8, 1994, Misc. No. 94–1014, MDL Docket No. 1040 (W.D. Pa.). Numerous state court actions, however, were also filed in various jurisdictions, including in Cook County, Illinois which named certain nondiverse individuals as defendants. *See, e.g.,* Sarah McCoy, et al. v. USAir, Inc., The Boeing Company, Gerald E. Fox, No. 94L11726 (Consolidated), Circuit Court of Cook Cty. (Law Div.), Illinois. These state court suits were not removable and, therefore, could not be consolidated with the federal MDL proceedings.

3. *See* William W. Schwarzer et al., *Judicial Federalism in Action: Coordination of Litigation in State and Federal Courts,* 78 Va. L. Rev. 1689, 1700–06 (1992), which discusses eleven case studies of such cooperation. Most of the cases involved mass torts, including three major air crashes, two groups of asbestos cases, two hotel fires, two building collapses, an investment fraud case, and an oil spill.

- request that federal and state judges preside jointly at status conferences, motion hearings, and perhaps even at trial to ensure, where possible, consistency in rulings and deadlines.[4]

These suggestions are widely followed in practice.[5]

§ 11.18   Transferee Court Retention of Case for Trial

On its face, Section 1407(a) only permits transfer for pretrial proceedings; it does not expressly authorize transfer for a consolidated trial.[1] Rather, Section 1407(a) mandates that "actions may be transferred ... *for ... pretrial proceedings*.... Each action so transferred *shall be remanded* by the panel at or before the conclusion of pretrial proceedings to the district from which it was transferred unless it shall have been previously terminated[.]"[2]

In practice, however, very few transferred cases are actually remanded to the original district court.[3] One explanation for the low incidence of remand is settlement; many MDL cases settle and, therefore, are not remanded because they are terminated in the transferee district.[4] Many other actions are terminated by dispositive rulings on motions, such as motions to dismiss and for summary judgment.[5] Another explanation for infrequent remand is that the Panel normally will not remand without approval from the transferee judge.[6] In addition, a

---

4. Manual for Complex Litigation, (Third) § 33.24, at 354 (1997); *see also* George A. Lehner, *Protecting Your Clients' Rights in Multidistrict Litigation* (Defense Research Institute 3/13/97).

5. For example, in the USAir 427 air crash litigation, the federal and state judges have frequently held joint hearings to coordinate discovery rulings concerning the production of documents and items of physical evidence, such as copies of the cockpit voice recorder tape.

§ 11.18

1. 28 U.S.C.A. § 1407(a) (West 1993 & Supp. 1997). *See also* Blake M. Rhodes, *The Judicial Panel on Multidistrict Litigation: Time for Rethinking,* 140 U. Pa. L. Rev. 711, 722 (1991); H.R. Rep. No. 90–1130 (1968), *reprinted in* 1968 U.S.C.C.A.N. 1898, 1900 (stating "the proposed statute affects only the pretrial stages in multidistrict litigation").

2. 28 U.S.C.A. § 1407(a) (West 1993 & Supp. 1997)(emphasis added).

3. Since 1968, the Panel has transferred 109,410 cases pursuant to 28 U.S.C.A. § 1407. Only 3,757 of those cases have been remanded by the Panel. Administrative Office of the United States Courts, Judicial

Business of the United States Courts: 1996 Report of the Director, Table S–22.

4. *Id.*

5. *See* 28 U.S.C.A. § 1407(a); JPML Rule 14(a) (stating that "[a]ctions terminated in the transferee district court by valid judgment, including but not limited to summary judgment, judgment of dismissal and judgment upon stipulation, shall not be remanded by the Panel and shall be dismissed by the transferee district court").

In multidistrict litigation, the transferee court has authority to dispose of cases transferred to it by means of summary judgment or dismissal. *See* 28 U.S.C.A. § 1407(a). *See also In re* American Continental Corp./Lincoln Sav. & Loan Sec. Litig., 102 F.3d 1524 (9th Cir.1996), *cert. granted sub nom.* Lexecon, Inc. v. Milberg Weiss Bershad Hynes & Lerach, 117 S.Ct. 1818, 137 L.Ed.2d 1026 (1997).

6. *See* Rhodes, *The Judicial Panel on Multidistrict Litigation: Time for Rethinking,* 140 U.Pa.L.Rev. 711, 723, n. 75 (1991) (citing *In re* Richardson–Merrell, Inc. "Bendictin" Prods. Liab. Litig., 606 F.Supp. 715, 716 (J.P.M.L. 1985)); *In re* Evergreen Valley Project Litig., 435 F.Supp. 923, 924

transferee court can retain a case for trial if it secures the consent of all parties.

Prior to 1998, the primary method that transferee courts used to retain cases for trial was by transferring the case to themselves pursuant to 28 U.S.C.A. § 1404(a) or § 1406, the general transfer provisions in the United States Code.[7] As discussed in the next section, however, this widespread practice has now been prohibited by the United States Supreme Court.[8]

(a) Sections 1404(a) and 1406 Transfer of Venue

Prior to 1998, transferee courts often retained MDL cases for trial by transferring the case to their own districts, invoking either 28 U.S.C.A. § 1404(a), the general transfer provision, or 28 U.S.C.A. § 1406, the provision governing waiver and defects. Thus, a transferee court could retain a case for trial by using Section 1404(a) or Section 1406 to transfer the case to itself.

In *Lexecon, Inc. v. Milberg Weiss Bershad Hynes & Lerach*, however, the United States Supreme Court held that this widespread and long-standing practice violated the clear statutory language of Section 1407. In a spirited dissent in the circuit court opinion under review, Judge Kozinski, while recognizing that "[e]very court that has examined the issue ... has held or assumed that such authority exists," had opined that the practice:

> tell[s] the story of a remarkable power grab by federal judges who have parlayed a narrow grant of authority to conduct consolidated discovery into a mechanism for systematically denying plaintiffs the right to trial in the forum of their choice.

> You don't have to stare very long at the statutory language and drafting history to realize this is not at all what Congress had in mind when it passed 28 U.S.C. § 1407....

> Soon after the MDL process got underway, a peculiar thing started happening: Judges began to develop proprietary feelings toward the cases entrusted to them; they began using 28 U.S.C. § 1404(a) ... to hold onto these cases for trial....

(J.P.M.L. 1977); JPML Rule 14(d) ("the Panel is reluctant to order remand absent a suggestion of remand from the transferee district court").

7. Section 1404(a) provides: "For the convenience of parties and witnesses, in the interest of justice, a district court may transfer any civil action to any other district or division where it might have been brought." 28 U.S.C.A. § 1404(a) (West 1993 & Supp. 1997).

Section 1406 provides:

(a) The district court of a district in which is filed a case laying venue in the wrong division or district shall dismiss, or if it be in the interest of justice, transfer such case to any district or division in which it could have been brought.

(b) Nothing in this chapter shall impair the jurisdiction of a district court of any matter involving a party who does not interpose timely and sufficient objection to the venue.

8. *See* Lexecon, Inc. v. Milberg Weiss Bershad Hynes & Lerach, ___ U.S. ___, 118 S.Ct. 956, 140 L.Ed.2d 62 (1998).

Section 1404(a), thus, has not only been conscripted by the federal courts to serve ends Congress never had in mind for it, it also has been stripped of the prudential constraints designed to protect plaintiff's choice of forum.... [S]elf-transfers are not occasional, isolated events based on an unusually strong showing of judicial economy; they are the norm. The simple reality is that once a case is sucked into the MDL vortex, it seldom comes back.[9]

The United States Supreme Court agreed, holding:

If we do our job of reading the statute whole, we have to give effect to this plain command [to remand after pretrial proceedings], even if doing that will reverse the longstanding practice under the rule. "Age is no antidote to clear inconsistency with a statute."[10]

The Court left open the issue of whether the transferor court can, after remand, transfer the case back to the transferee court for trial using Section 1404, but gave an indication that such "retransfer" would be acceptable.[11] The Court noted, however, that such Section 1404 transfers back to the transferee court will be limited by venue considerations, whereas the original transfer was not.[12] This factor may well be considered by the Panel in making its initial transfer decision, because if venue requirements are met by the transferee court initially, then that court could receive the case back for trial under Section 1404.

(1) Factors That Courts Consider

Because of the possibility that, after remand, the transferor court might use Section 1404 to send the case back to the transferee court for trial, the case law involving the Section 1404 transfers invalidated in *Lexecon* remains instructive, since it addresses how the Section 1404 factors can apply in an MDL setting. The statutory test under Section 1404(a) involves three requirements: first, transfer must serve the convenience of the parties and witnesses; second, transfer must be in the interests of justice; and third, the proposed district must be a district "where [the case] might have been brought."[13] If these three requirements are satisfied then the action may be transferred.

A good illustration of the application of this test is found in *Pfizer, Inc. v. Lord*,[14] in which the Second Circuit found that the district court judge did not abuse his discretion in transferring a case. The factors that the judge considered in making his decision included:

(1) The waiver by the plaintiffs of the original choice of forum.

(2) The lack of showing that any important witness would be unavailable or even inconvenienced by the transfer.

---

9. *In re* American Continental Corp/Lincoln Sav. & Loan Sec. Litig., 102 F.3d 1524, 1540–41, 1547 (9th Cir.1996), *cert. granted sub nom.* Lexecon, Inc. v. Milberg Weiss Bershad Hynes & Lerach, ___ U.S. ___, 117 S.Ct. 1818, 137 L.Ed.2d 1026 (1997).

10. 1998 WL 85319, at *6 (citations omitted).

11. *See* 1998 WL 85319, at *8 n. 2.

12. *Id.*

13. *See supra* Chapter 3 "Venue, Forum Selection and Transfer" for detailed discussion of transfer factors.

14. 447 F.2d 122 (2d Cir.1971).

(3) The fact that there was already one substantial case pending in the transferee district.

(4) The fact that each of the defendants had already retained experienced counsel in Minnesota who had been active in the pretrial preparation of these cases.

(5) The fact that the civil docket in Minnesota was the least burdened of any of the eleven districts where the actions had originally been filed.[15]

Significantly, the *Pfizer* court noted that "because of the complexity of these cases the interests of judicial efficiency make it highly desirable that the judge who conducted the pretrial proceedings continue as the trial judge ..."[16] As a practical matter, this will be true in almost every MDL setting. Given this rationale, then, the very creation of the MDL provides a virtually self-effectuating justification for Section 1404 transfer to the transferee court.

Similarly, the first two elements of Section 1404(a) also apply to Section 1407(a) transfers: both statutes consider convenience of parties and witnesses and the interests of justice.[17] Thus, if circumstances warrant transfer under Section 1407, they will probably warrant transfer under Section 1404 as well.

However, the third element of the Section 1404 analysis may create an obstacle to transfer in light of *Hoffman v. Blaski,* the seminal case on transfer of venue. In *Hoffman,* the United States Supreme Court interpreted the phrase "where it might have been brought." The issue before the Court was whether a district court could transfer a case to a district where venue or personal jurisdiction would be unattainable without a waiver from the defendant. The Court held that a district court has no power to transfer an action pursuant to 28 U.S.C.A. § 1404(a) despite the consent or waiver of the defendant,[18] to a district where plaintiff did not have a right to bring it. In sum, a district court can only transfer a case to a district where the plaintiff would have been entitled to bring the case in the first place. Thus, the requirements for transfer pursuant to Section 1404(a) are harder to meet in an MDL case because many different plaintiffs are involved.

(b) Securing the Consent of All Parties Involved

As an alternative to Section 1404(a), a transferee court can retain an MDL case for trial if all parties consent to trial in the transferee district, "even if the Section 1407 forum would not have been a proper court for venue purposes."[19] Thus, trial by consent, if it can be obtained, can

---

15. *Id.* at 125.

16. *Id.*

17. *See* 28 U.S.C.A. § 1407(a): the Panel may only transfer related actions upon a determination that transfers will be "for the convenience of parties and witnesses

and will promote the just and efficient conduct of such actions."

18. Hoffman v. Blaski, 363 U.S. 335, 343–44, 80 S.Ct. 1084, 1089–90, 4 L.Ed.2d 1254 (1960).

19. *See* Rhodes, *supra* note 1, at 742 n.168, citing, *In re* Alien Children Educ.

obviate the difficult and intricate analysis required for transfer under Section 1404(a). While this practice might technically be problematic under *Hoffman v. Blaski*,[20] the practical reality is that the transferee court can conduct the trial if all parties consent.

Library References:

West's Key No. Digests, Federal Courts ⊙151–157.
Wright, Miller & Cooper, Federal Practice and Procedure: Civil 2d § 3866.

§ 11.19 Management of MDL Cases Retained for Trial

(a) Bifurcation

If a transferee court tries an MDL proceeding, counsel should consider whether to request bifurcated trials on certain issues. A transferee court (like all district courts) has discretion to order separate trials on certain issues pursuant to Rule 42(b).[1] In some multidistrict proceedings, counsel for all parties may stipulate that the transferee court conduct a consolidated trial on certain issues, such as causation in MDL proceedings involving a pharmaceutical.[2] Similarly, in air disaster cases,

---

Litig., 501 F.Supp. 544, 551 n. 7 (S.D.Tex. 1980) (the court noted that while a Section 1404(a) transfer was not possible, the parties waived venue and consented to the resolution of a particular issue in the transferee court.); 15 Charles Alan Wright, Arthur R. Miller & Edward H. Cooper, Federal Practice & Procedure § 3866 (2d ed. 1986).

20. *See* Rhodes, *supra* note 1, at 742.

§ 11.19

1. Rule 42(b) authorizes a court to order a separate trial "of any claim, ... or ... issue or of any number of claims ... or issues ..." Rule 42(b) states that courts can order separate trials: (1) in furtherance of convenience; (2) to avoid prejudice; or (3) when separate trials will promote efficiency and economy. *Id.* In addition, a court can order separate trials only if the Seventh Amendment right to trial by jury will be preserved. *Id.*

Courts have held that a party's Seventh Amendment right to trial by jury will be preserved where: (1) the same jury decides all issues; or (2) where different juries decide separate and distinct issues. *See generally* Gasoline Products Co. v. Champlin Refining Co., 283 U.S. 494, 500, 51 S.Ct. 513, 515, 75 L.Ed. 1188 (1931); Castano v. American Tobacco Co., 84 F.3d 734, 750–51 (5th Cir.1996); *In re* Beverly Hills Fire Li-

tig., 695 F.2d 207, 216 (6th Cir.1982) (in deciding whether to order separate trials the court must consider the "potential prejudice to the parties, potential confusion to the jury, and the relative convenience and economy"), *cert. denied*, 461 U.S. 929, 103 S.Ct. 2090, 77 L.Ed.2d 300 (1983); *In re* Bendectin Litig., 857 F.2d 290, 307–09 (6th Cir.1988), *cert. denied*, 488 U.S. 1006, 109 S.Ct. 788, 102 L.Ed.2d 779 (1989).

Several courts have ordered bifurcated trials in MDL proceedings on liability and damages. *See, e.g., In re* Lower Lake Erie Iron Ore Antitrust Litig., No. MDL 587, Civ. A. No. 94–2010, 1994 WL 114904, *1 (E.D.Pa.1994) (bifurcating liability and damages in MDL trial before transferee court. Following appellate reversal on certain damage verdicts, the transferee court suggested that the Judicial Panel remand the damage issues to the transferor court for retrial); *In re* Air Crash Disaster at Detroit Metropolitan Airport on August 16, 1987, 737 F.Supp. 391, 395 (E.D.Mich.1987) (bifurcating liability and damages following no objections by counsel). *See also In re* Ampicillin Antitrust Litig., 88 F.R.D. 174, 178–79 (D.D.C.1980) (bifurcating liability and damages in multidistrict antitrust litigation).

2. *See In re* Richardson–Merrell, Inc. "Bendectin" Prods. Liab. Litig. (No. II), 606 F.Supp. 715, 716 (J.P.M.L. 1985)

a transferee court may conduct a consolidated trial on liability issues, since there is only one operative set of facts and remand might produce inconsistent results.[3]

Whether a transferee court can conduct a consolidated trial on liability and then transfer individual cases to the transferor districts for trials on damages is less clear. While the *Manual for Complex Litigation* suggests that a transferee court does not have authority to bifurcate an action in such a manner,[4] transferee courts have followed the practice, especially when counsel for all parties in an MDL proceeding consent to such a procedure.[5]

For example, the transferee judge in *In re* Air Crash Disaster at Sioux City, Iowa allowed this type of bifurcation.[6] The transferee court determined that it would conduct a trial on the issues of liability and punitive damages. The court resolved that, after the initial trial, the "individual cases will be returned to the transferor courts, where the issue of compensatory damages will be separately tried if plaintiffs receive a favorable verdict on the issue of liability."[7]

Similarly, in *In re* Air Crash Disaster at Detroit Metropolitan

(plaintiffs refusing to opt into consolidated causation trial).

3. *See In re* Aircrash Near Duarte, California on June 6, 1971, 357 F.Supp. 1013 (C.D.Cal.1973). In justifying the joint trial, the transferee court noted that each of the individual actions could have been originally filed in that district. *Id.* at 1016. In *In re* Air Crash Near Cerritos, California August 31, 1989, No. MDL 717 KN, 1989 WL 330820, *1 (C.D.Cal.1989), *aff'd sub nom.* Steering Committee v. United States, 6 F.3d 572 (9th Cir.1993), numerous actions arose from a mid-air collision between an Aeromexico DC–9 passenger jet and a single-engine Piper aircraft. All cases were consolidated in the Central District of California pursuant to § 1407. Upon the joint request of all parties, the issues of liability and damages were bifurcated and the Central District of California proceeded to try liability issues against certain defendants.

In re Air Crash Disaster at Mannheim Germany on 9/11/82, 769 F.2d 115, 117 (3d Cir.1985), *cert. denied*, 474 U.S. 1082, 106 S.Ct. 851, 88 L.Ed.2d 891 (1986), survivors and personal representatives of deceased servicemen who died in a helicopter crash brought suit against the manufacturer of the helicopter. The Judicial Panel transferred all cases to the Eastern District of Pennsylvania under § 1407, and the Eastern District consolidated all cases for purposes of trial on the issue of liability. *Id.* at 119 n.2. Trial was bifurcated with the is-

sues of liability and damages to be tried separately. *Id.* at 119.

In *In re* Korean Air Lines Disaster of September 1, 1983, 814 F.Supp. 592, 594–95 (E.D.Mich.1993), numerous wrongful death actions arising from an air disaster were transferred to the District Court for the District of Columbia pursuant to § 1407. There, the court conducted a consolidated trial on the issue of liability. Following a verdict on liability for plaintiffs, the individual cases were returned by the Judicial Panel to their original courts for trial on the question of damages.

4. Manual for Complex Litigation, (Third) § 31.132, at 283 (1997) ("Whether under § 1404(a) a case may be transferred only for the determination of certain issues and whether a retransfer or second transfer may be ordered is not clear.").

5. *See, e.g., In re* Lower Lake Erie Iron Ore Antitrust Litig., No. MDL 587, 1994 WL 114904; *cf. In re* Korean Air Lines Disaster, 814 F.Supp. at 594–95; *In re* Air Crash Disaster at Sioux City, Iowa, on July 19, 1989, 734 F.Supp. 1425, 1426 (N.D.Ill. 1990); *In re* Air Crash Disaster at Detroit Metropolitan Airport, 737 F.Supp. at 395; Dispenza v. Eastern Air Lines, Inc., 508 F.Supp. 239, 241–43 (E.D.N.Y.1981).

6. *In re* Air Crash Disaster at Sioux City, Iowa, on July 19, 1989, 1991 WL 279286 (N.D.Ill. 1991).

7. *Id.* at *1.

Airport,[8] multidistrict litigation arose out of an aircraft disaster in Michigan. The Judicial Panel transferred all cases arising from the crash to the Eastern District of Michigan for pretrial proceedings and, ultimately, the Eastern District transferred the case to itself for trial.[9]

The transferee court bifurcated liability and damages issues, holding that bifurcation would simplify the jury's task in deciding liability issues, would not prejudice the parties and could obviate the need for a damages trial.[10] Moreover, the court found that the evidence regarding liability and damages was not intertwined. Finally, and importantly, no party objected to the proposed bifurcation. Accordingly, issues regarding compensatory and punitive damages were severed and were reserved for a subsequent trial. The court held that if plaintiffs prevailed in the joint liability trial, "those claimants who originally filed their cases in a transferor court may move to remand the issue of damages to the transferor district for a final determination."[11] Thus, like the court in *Sioux City*, the transferee court decided the issue of liability and then returned the case to the transferor courts for trials on damages.[12]

(b) Final Pretrial Conference

If an MDL proceeding proceeds to trial in the transferee court, steering committee and individual case counsel should seek to conduct the final pretrial conference to "improv[e] the quality of the trial

---

8. 737 F.Supp. 391 (E.D.Mich.1989).

9. *Id.* at 392; 28 U.S.C.A. §§ 1407, 1404(a) (West 1993 & Supp. 1997).

10. *In re* Air Crash Disaster at Detroit Metropolitan Airport, 737 F.Supp. at 395.

11. *Id.*

12. *Id. See also In re* Lower Lake Erie Iron Ore Antitrust Litig., No. MDL 587, Civ. A. No. 94–2010, 1994 WL 114904 (E.D.Pa.1994) (suggesting that plaintiffs' claims be remanded to the Northern District of Ohio, the transferor district, for retrial on the issue of damages); Dispenza v. Eastern Air Lines, Inc., 508 F.Supp. 239, 242–43 (E.D.N.Y.1981) (concluding that after liability was tried "the convenience of parties and witnesses and the interests of justice command that the cases at bar be transferred to the districts ... in which they were commenced" for determination of the issue of damages).

In some cases, different juries deciding the issues of liability and damages can raise constitutional concerns under the Seventh Amendment. Separate trials before different juries will satisfy Seventh Amendment requirements if liability and damage issues are separate and distinct. Mag Instrument,

Inc. v. J. Baxter Brinkmann Int'l Corp., 123 F.R.D. 543, 545 (N.D.Tex.1988) ("[t]he prohibition is not against having two juries review the same evidence but rather against having two juries decide the same essential issues"); *see also In re* Innotron Diagnostics, 800 F.2d 1077, 1086 (Fed.Cir. 1986); Martin v. Bell Helicopter Co., 85 F.R.D. 654, 658–59 (D.Colo.1980).

Two different juries cannot decide the same essential issues because the resulting confusion would preclude a fair jury trial. *See In re* Lower Lake Erie Iron Ore Antitrust Litig., 998 F.2d 1144, 1181–85 (3d Cir.1993) (reversing bifurcated damages verdict in MDL antitrust trial on the grounds that the jury which tried the damages issues had been improperly permitted to second-guess an implicit determination by an earlier jury that tried liability issues), *cert. dismissed*, 510 U.S. 1021, 114 S.Ct. 625, 126 L.Ed.2d 589 (1993); Martin, 85 F.R.D. at 659; Mag Instrument, 123 F.R.D. at 545. Issues are separate and distinct if they are not "so interwoven," that their independent trial would cause "confusion and uncertainty." Gasoline Prods. Co. v. Champlin Refining Co., 283 U.S. 494, 500, 51 S.Ct. 513, 515, 75 L.Ed. 1188 (1931).

through more thorough preparation" and to "facilitat[e] the settlement of the case."[13] The conference takes on added importance in an MDL proceeding, given the typically complex nature of the litigation, the number of individual cases involved, and the document-intensive nature of most MDL trials.

The final pretrial conference in an MDL action is usually held shortly before the time of trial, after the parties have submitted a joint plan for the MDL trial, including a program to facilitate the admission of evidence.[14] Lead trial counsel for all parties are required to attend and participate in the conference. Steering committee counsel are also typically required to attend, and generally provide additional support for lead trial counsel.

If not already required to do so, counsel in an MDL proceeding should file all motions for summary judgment and motions in limine with sufficient lead time to ensure rulings before or at the final pretrial conference. Unnecessary preparation, expense and uncertainty will result if such motions are deferred until immediately before or after the conference.

Transferee courts generally require lead and other counsel for both sides to meet in good faith before the conference to exchange the following information:

- lists of witnesses to be called and the subject matter of their testimony (including designation of deposition testimony);
- copies and lists of all exhibits and demonstrative aids;
- proposed questions and procedures for voir dire;
- stipulations of fact believed to be undisputed; and
- proposed findings of fact and conclusions of law (in nonjury cases).[15]

Lead trial counsel should also, before the final pretrial conference, discuss jury instructions on substantive issues and special jury verdict forms. Counsel should submit a single set of instructions on issues for which there is no disagreement. Providing undisputed instructions to the transferee court will expedite the presentation of evidence in the MDL trial. Each side should then submit additional proposed instructions on disks in compatible word processing format to the transferee judge. Briefs also should be prepared on any legal issues that remain open after rulings on dispositive motions.

The transferee court will typically enter an order following the final pretrial conference that encompasses all rulings made at the conference with respect to the conduct of the MDL trial. The order will govern the trial and will not be modified except "to prevent manifest injustice."[16] Counsel should ensure that the order addresses:

---

13. FRCP 16(a)(4) and (5).

14. FRCP 16(d).

15. *See* Manual for Complex Litigation, (Third) § 21.6 (1997).

16. FRCP 16(e).

- the precise issues to be tried in the MDL proceeding;
- if separate trials are to be held, the issues to be tried at the initial MDL trial;
- the witnesses to be called and the exhibits to be offered by each side (other than for impeachment);
- whether additional undisclosed or other specified evidence is precluded;
- which objections are to be deemed waived;
- procedures for consolidation, severance or remand of cases back to transferor courts;
- procedures for the presentation of testimony and exhibits;
- scheduling conferences with lead trial counsel at the end of each trial day, after the jury has been excused, to plan the next day's proceedings and to fix the order of witnesses and exhibits. The transferee court can also address anticipated objections and hear offers of proof to eliminate side-bars and adjournments;
- the starting date of the MDL trial and the schedule to be followed; and
- other housekeeping matters to expedite the MDL trial.[17]

(c) Expediting the Presentation of Evidence

Trial in an MDL proceeding often promises to be time-consuming and complex. To facilitate the presentation of evidence, the transferee court at the final pretrial conference will review the parties' anticipated proofs. To ensure adequate focus, the transferee court may require each side, through lead trial counsel, to file a statement before the conference listing in detail the facts it intends to establish at trial and the evidence that supports each fact. Counsel should also consider submitting glossaries of technical or important terms, names, dates and events, indices of exhibits and timelines of key events to aid the transferee court's understanding of relevant subject matter and to improve the flow of the trial.

Lead trial counsel should raise objections at the final pretrial conference regarding evidence and exhibits, particularly computer-generated animations, simulations, or other demonstrative evidence.[18] Counsel should also review proposed narratives or data summaries to determine if they constitute objectionable hearsay. Counsel should consider proposing limiting instructions to clarify the purpose for which evidence is being offered, and counsel should determine whether the data underlying any exhibit has the necessary foundation of authenticity and reliability.

To streamline an MDL trial, a transferee court may impose limits on the presentation of evidence, including limits on the number of witnesses

---

17. *See* Manual for Complex Litigation, (Third) § 21.67, at 136, § 40.3 (checklist) (1997).

18. *Id.* at § 21.642.

or exhibits that a party can call or offer in the aggregate, the length of examinations and cross-examinations of witnesses, and the total time to be allowed each party for presentations of their case.[19] The transferee court will also encourage counsel to further narrow the evidence by stipulating to certain facts before trial.[20]

Finally, counsel should agree on a daily trial schedule. Because MDL trials involve numerous witnesses, some of whom are required to travel great distances, the schedule should specify the days of the week and the hours each day that trial will be held. All equipment necessary to display demonstrative aids, computer simulations or other graphic or visual media should be set up and tested before the start of each trial day.

(d) Bellwether Trials

Bellwether trials[21] have been used with varying degrees of success in multidistrict proceedings. In *In re* Air Crash Disaster at Stapleton

19. *See id.* § 21.643, at 134; United States *ex rel.* Nelson v. Follette, 430 F.2d 1055, 1059 (2d Cir.1970) (noting that the trial judge maintains broad discretion in controlling the conduct of the trial and the presentation of evidence), *cert. denied*, 401 U.S. 917, 91 S.Ct. 899, 27 L.Ed.2d 818 (1971); United States v. Gray, 507 F.2d 1013, 1016 (5th Cir.) (court has discretion to limit the number of witnesses), *cert. denied*, 423 U.S. 824, 96 S.Ct. 38, 46 L.Ed.2d 40 (1975). A court has authority under Fed. R.Evid. 611(a) to "exercise reasonable control over the mode and order of interrogating witnesses and presenting evidence." *Id.* Any limits imposed by the transferee court should be uniform and be subject to modification for cause shown. In fashioning such limits, the court should balance the need for expediting a multidistrict trial against the parties' right to a fair trial. The parties' respective evidentiary burdens should also be considered.

20. Such stipulations were effectively used in *In re* Washington Public Power Supply System Sec. Litig., MDL No. 551, a case involving multiple consolidated securities class actions against hundreds of defendants. That litigation involved more than three million document pages and over 300,000 pages of deposition testimony. Notwithstanding the complexity of the factual issues and the mountain of evidence, the parties were able, through extended negotiation, to assemble a multi-volume stipulation with respect to factual claims and legal issues.

21. "The term 'bellwether' is derived from the ancient practice of belling a weth-

er (a male sheep) selected to lead his flock." *In re* Chevron U.S.A., Inc., 109 F.3d 1016, 1019 (5th Cir.1997). Ultimately, the success of the wether selected to wear the bell hinged upon whether the flock had confidence that the selected wether would not lead them astray. *Id.*

Bellwether trials of selected plaintiffs' claims is an increasingly common practice in mass tort litigation. *See* Manual for Complex Litigation (Third) § 33.28, at 369 (1995). One court has observed that the bellwether concept "is particularly useful and appropriate" where there is a relatively large number of actions and plaintiffs are proceeding on the same theory or claim; such trials can aid in judicial economy and manageability. *In re* Ampicillin Antitrust Litigation, 88 F.R.D. 174, 178 (D.D.C.1980); *see* Chevron, 109 F.3d at 1019 ("The notion that the trial of some members of a large group of claimants may provide a basis for enhancing prospects of settlement or for resolving common issues or claims is a sound one that has achieved general acceptance by both bench and bar.").

Bellwether trials, however, are not without substantial critics. *See id.* at 1021 (Jones, J., concurring) ("I also have serious doubts about the major premise of Judge Parker's opinion, *i.e.*, his confidence that a bellwether trial of representative cases is permissible to extrapolate findings relevant to and somehow preclusive upon a larger group of cases."). Judge Jones cogently noted that a district court's selection of a certain number of "bellwether" cases, whose

International Airport,[22] an exemplar or bellwether trial of one passenger injured in an aircrash and her husband was held to resolve issues of common law tort liability, punitive damages liability, and common issues under a state's deceptive practices act for all cases consolidated under the Panel's transfer order.[23] The transferee court held that all consolidated cases pending on a certain date were bound by the verdicts of the exemplar trial, including the jury's finding that defendants were not liable for punitive damages.[24] The court entered judgment accordingly, finding that "plaintiffs were afforded a full and fair opportunity to litigate their claims...."[25]

Bellwether trials also have been used in MDL antitrust proceedings. In *In re Ampicillin Antitrust Litigation*,[26] the court endorsed bellwether trials for a certain class of plaintiffs raising claims under Section 1 of the Sherman Act.[27] The court also addressed the selection process regarding the number and identity of the bellwether actions to be tried in the initial liability stage of the proceeding.[28] Five bellwethers were eventually chosen. The court overruled defendant's objections that the trial would be unmanageable and would violate the Seventh Amendment.[29]

Other courts have embraced the bellwether concept as a way to expedite the trial of a multidistrict proceeding. In *In re Norplant*

---

results would bind all parties on issues such as general liability or causation, "is probably not effectively reviewable after trial. The pressure on the parties to settle in fear of the result of a perhaps all-or-nothing 'bellwether' trial is enormous." *Id.* The troubling due process, fairness and statistical issues inherent in the bellwether format deserve serious consideration before such a trial is proposed or adopted in a MDL proceeding. *See id.* at 1023 (Jones, J., concurring).

While the debate on bellwether trials continues, MDL plaintiffs should nevertheless consider whether common issues, or perhaps even general liability, can be fairly resolved in this format. However, "[a] bellwether trial designed to achieve its value ascertainment function for settlement purposes or to answer troubling causation or liability issues common to the universe of claimants has as a core element representativeness...." *Id.* at 1019. The *Chevron* court held that "before a trial court may utilize results from a bellwether trial for a purpose that extends beyond the individual cases tried, it must, prior to any extrapolation, find that the cases tried are representative of the larger group of cases or claims from which they are selected." *Id.* at 1020. Typically, such a finding must be based on competent scientific or statistical evidence that the sample is of sufficient size to permit a level of confidence that the results

obtained reflect results that would be obtained from trials of the whole. *See id.*; Castaneda v. Partida, 430 U.S. 482, 97 S.Ct. 1272, 51 L.Ed.2d 498 (1977) (using statistical data to prove discrimination in jury selection); Capaci v. Katz & Besthoff, Inc., 711 F.2d 647, 653–57 (5th Cir.1983) (using census data in gender discrimination case); Michael J. Saks and Peter David Blanck, *Justice Improved: The Unrecognized Benefits of Aggregation and Sampling in Mass Torts*, 44 Stan. L. Rev. 815 (1992).

22. 720 F.Supp. 1505 (D.Colo.1989).

23. *Id.* at 1510.

24. *Id.* at 1513–15.

25. *Id.* at 1513.

26. 88 F.R.D. 174, 177–78 (D.D.C.1980)

27. 15 U.S.C.A. § 1 (West 1997).

28. *In re* Ampicillin Antitrust Litig., 88 F.R.D. at 179. Along with conducting bellwether trials, the transferee court also bifurcated the trials on liability and damages issues. *Id.* at 178.

29. *In re* Ampicillin Antitrust Litig., MDL Docket No. 50, 1981 WL 2008 (D.D.C. 1981). The court held that the collateral estoppel effect of the bellwether trials on the other claims in the MDL proceeding would be determined after the trials were completed. *Id.* at *5.

Contraceptive Products Liability Litigation,[30] a multidistrict proceeding involving product liability claims, the court denied plaintiffs' motion for class certification but scheduled three bellwether trials of five plaintiffs. The court required all counsel to propose appropriate plaintiffs for the trials, after outlining selection criteria.[31] Three bellwether trials were also conducted in *Friends for All Children, Inc. v. Lockheed Aircraft Corp., et al.,*[32] a multidistrict proceeding arising out of the tragic aircrash of a military transport plane airlifting children out of South Vietnam in the last days of the U.S. presence. While the cases resulted in plaintiffs' verdicts, the verdicts were set aside on appeal because of certain evidentiary rulings.[33]

§ 11.20 Remand

If an MDL proceeding is not resolved or retained for trial by the transferee court, it is remanded back to the various transferor districts for trial. The Panel is the only entity authorized to remand an action to the transferor court for trial.[1] The transferee court lacks the power to effect remand.[2] Significantly, the Panel has the authority to separately remand any claim, counterclaim or third-party claim before the remainder of the action is remanded.[3]

Remand of an action or claim can arise in one of three ways: (1) motion of a party; (2) suggestion of the transferee court; (3) sua sponte action of the Panel, either through a show cause order or conditional remand order.[4] As a practical matter, remand is rarely ordered absent suggestion of the transferee court that all pretrial proceedings are concluded and the case is ready to be sent back to the transferor jurisdiction for trial.[5]

30. 955 F.Supp. 700, 702 (E.D.Tex. 1997). Summary Judgment was granted to defendants before the trials could occur. *See also In re* Copley Pharmaceutical Inc. "Albuterol" Products Liability Litig., 161 F.R.D. 456, 468 (D.Wyo.1995) (denying use of bellwether plaintiffs at trial of national class action product liability lawsuit, but only because the proposal was not advanced until shortly before trial).

31. *See In re* Norplant Contraceptive Products Liability Litig., 1996 WL 608470 (E.D.Tex.1996) (directing parties to select 15 bellwether trial plaintiffs and eliminating certain "exotic cases" from the pool); *In re* Norplant, 1996 WL 571535 (E.D.Tex. 1996) (addressing criteria to select the pool of bellwether plaintiffs, including residence of plaintiffs, randomness of plaintiffs).

32. 497 F.Supp. 313, 315–16 (D.D.C. 1980), *rev'd on different grounds*, Schneider v. Lockheed Aircraft Corp., 658 F.2d 835 (D.C.Cir.1981), *cert. denied*, 455 U.S. 994, 102 S.Ct. 1622, 71 L.Ed.2d 855 (1982).

33. Schneider, 658 F.2d 835. In its opinion, the circuit court also provided direction on the collateral estoppel effect of any further bellwether verdicts. *Id.* at 852. The court held that defendants could not be denied the opportunity to adjudicate in future cases whether the crash caused the *particular* injuries claimed by the remaining plaintiffs. *Id.*

§ 11.20

1. JPML Rule 14(b); 28 U.S.C.A. § 1407(a) (West 1993 & Supp. 1997).

2. *Id.*

3. 28 U.S.C.A. § 1407(a).

4. JPML Rule 14(c).

5. JPML Rule 14(d); *In re* Multi–Piece Rim Prods. Liab. Litig., 464 F.Supp. 969, 975 (J.P.M.L. 1979) (transferee judge is in best position to know if remand is appropriate); *In re* Asbestos Prods. Liab. Litig. (No. VI), 771 F.Supp. 415, 422 n. 8 (J.P.M.L. 1991) (noting Panel's "reluctance" to re-

(a) Motion to Remand

Any remand motion must be accompanied by a supporting brief, the transferee court's final pretrial order, if one has been issued, and an affidavit stating:

* whether the movant has requested a suggestion of remand from the transferee court;

* how the court responded to any such request;

* if no such request was made, why;

* whether all common discovery and other pretrial proceedings have been concluded and, if not, what remains to be done;

* whether all orders of the transferee court have been satisfactorily complied with and, if not, what remains to be done.[6]

(b) Show Cause Order (Remand)

When the Panel issues an order to show cause why the action should not be remanded, any party may file a response within 20 days of the filing of the order.[7] Failure of a party to respond is considered acquiescence in the remand.[8] Within five days of the filing of the response, a party may file a reply brief, which must be limited to new matters.[9]

(c) Conditional Remand Orders

When the Panel has been advised by the transferee court, or otherwise has reason to believe that the pretrial proceedings are concluded or that remand of the action is otherwise appropriate, the Clerk of the Panel may issue a conditional remand order.[10] This order is held by the Clerk, however, and not transmitted to the transferee court (*i.e.*, not made effective) for 15 days to give the parties an opportunity to oppose remand.[11]

Any party opposing remand must file a notice of opposition with the Clerk of the Panel within the 15–day period.[12] Extensions of this period are permitted only in exceptional circumstances.[13] If such notice is received, the order will not be made effective until further order of the

mand without suggestion of transferee judge); *In re* Data Gen. Corp. Antitrust Litig., 510 F.Supp. 1220, 1226 (J.P.M.L. 1979) (party moving for remand without concurrence of transferee judge bears heavy burden of proof).

cause order relating to transfer, which is 25 days from the date of the order. Here, the reply is due 5 days from the actual filing of the response and therefore a reply may be due sooner if the response is filed before the expiration of the 20–day response period.

6.   JPML Rules 10(a), 14(d).

7.   JPML Rule 14(e).

8.   *Id.*

9.   *Id.* Note that this period differs from the deadline provided for a reply to a show

10.   JPML Rule 14(f)(i).

11.   *Id.*

12.   JPML Rule 14(f)(ii).

13.   JPML Rule 15.

Panel.[14]

The party opposing remand must then file a motion to vacate and supporting brief within 15 days of filing its notice of opposition.[15] Failure to file such motion and brief is considered a withdrawal of the opposition and the Clerk will transmit the conditional order to the transferee court, making remand effective.[16]

Upon receipt of a remand order, the parties must "forthwith" file with the transferee court a stipulation or designation of the contents of the record to be remanded.[17]

§ 11.21 Settlement Strategy in MDL

An important consequence of an MDL proceeding is the opportunity that it offers for settlement by bringing all parties and counsel in pending federal court claims together in one forum. *The Manual for Complex Litigation*, emphasizes this "unique opportunity" and encourages the transferee court to "take appropriate steps to make the most of this opportunity and facilitate the settlement of the federal and any related state cases."[1]

The great majority of cases transferred to an MDL proceeding are not transferred back to their original courts. The MDL proceeding disposes of most cases either through dispositive motions or settlement.[2] Therefore, the pretrial decisions and proceedings in the MDL are influential factors in gauging the settlement value of the cases.

The transferee MDL court may exercise, and is encouraged by the *Manual for Complex Litigation*, to exercise the full panoply of powers and options to promote settlement, from the way in which discovery is structured, to the ordering and deciding of dispositive motions, to the appointment of special masters or mediators to conduct settlement negotiations.[3] The coordination of the widespread cases in one forum invites settlement, and the aggregation of the cases lends legitimacy to them. Thus, from all parties' perspective, whether one wants the "unique opportunity" for a global settlement of the mass litigation is a critical factor in deciding whether to seek or oppose an MDL proceeding.

In view of the enormous incentive placed on the transferee court to resolve the litigation while it is within the MDL proceeding, every party entering an MDL must immediately consider and develop a settlement position and strategy. It should be anticipated that the MDL court will

---

14. JPML Rule 14(f)(ii).

15. JPML Rule 14(f)(iii).

16. JMPL Rule 14(f)(iv); 28 U.S.C.A. § 1407(c) (West 1993 & Supp. 1997).

17. JPML Rule 14(g).

§ 11.21

1. Manual for Complex Litigation, (Third) § 31.132, at 284 (1997).

2. *Id.*; Patricia D. Howard, *A Guide to Multidistrict Litigation*, 124 F.R.D. 479 (1989).

3. *See* Manual for Complex Litigation, (Third) § 23.11 (1997). For a full discussion of a court's settlement powers and options, *see infra* Chapter 28 "Settlement."

take into account how its organization and structure of the proceeding will affect the possibility of settlement.

Consequently, one of the early determinations by all parties will be whether to posture the case for settlement or instead for trial (though the best settlement approach typically involves being well prepared for trial, that dynamic being among the most effective leverage tools in settlement negotiations). The parties and their counsel need to consider promptly the information that will be needed both from internal investigation and from discovery in order to make that determination and then, if the determination is to head toward settlement, the information needed to determine settlement values[4] and to put the case in the best light during settlement negotiations. The parties should consider adverse information that should not be disclosed, if possible, before settlement, and therefore suggest priorities for discovery management orders, protective orders or dispositive motions that will avoid or postpone disclosure. The centralized control of the MDL is a strategic tool that every party will try to use to its advantage to gain settlement leverage; the procedural and organizational issues will assume heightened importance.

In any settlement negotiation, the parties must determine whether they are comfortable with the transferee judge's participation in pretrial settlement discussions. If they are not, then another judge or special settlement master can be suggested to handle settlement negotiations. Though the MDL transferee court's statutory authority is limited to pretrial proceedings, concern about participation in settlement discussions by the transferee judge is very much in order, because many MDL cases are not transferred back to their original courts for trial.

Each party must consider whether a global settlement in the MDL proceeding is more advantageous to it than individual case settlements before or after the MDL proceeding. Initially, the MDL judge is likely to be more knowledgeable about the case facts and legal issues than a transferor court, which often has had little involvement with the case before it is sent back for trial. MDL proceedings are also assigned to judges who are believed to have the necessary experience and expertise to handle the complex proceedings and who, therefore, might be expected to have well honed skills in supervising and steering settlement negotiations. Moreover, because an MDL proceeding provides a better opportunity for coordination of the federal court with state courts in which related cases have been filed, it offers a greater likelihood of achieving a global settlement of all federal and state cases. However, the transferor court may be located in a jurisdiction the nature of which enhances or diminishes the settlement value of a case, and that court may thus be a more favorable jurisdiction from one side's perspective. Individual cases may also have particularly high or low settlement values that may persuade a party to eschew settlement within the MDL proceeding in favor of a settlement forum which deals more intensely with the details of a specific case.

---

4. Expert consultants, especially economists and statisticians, will likely be required to assist in determining settlement values and strategies.

Though the MDL proceeding is likely to use lead or liaison counsel to carry out settlement negotiations, the individual differences among the parties and the perceived strengths and values of their claims should be considered. Unlike a class action having representative parties and counsel and procedural protections such as notice,[5] opting-out[6] and court approval of the settlement for fairness,[7] the MDL proceeding is only a mechanism to obtain the aggregation of individual parties, counsel and claims in one forum, which can facilitate settlement, but may not impose settlement on any party. It will be particularly important for plaintiffs' lead counsel and the judge or master who is conducting the settlement negotiations to have clear and open lines of communication with counsel for all plaintiffs. Differences among plaintiffs' claims and limits of lead counsel's authority are important for the plaintiffs' lead counsel to identify and for the defense counsel and court to consider.

Choice of law issues for cases in which state law provides the governing substantive law may arise again at the settlement stage.[8] Differences in state laws regarding set-off or apportionment of settlements and rights of contribution should be considered. State laws might also differ on rights to obtain disclosure of settlement agreements, to inform the jury of settlements and to enforce or strike down certain side agreements, such as "Mary Carter" agreements, limitations on counsel pursuing future cases, confidentiality agreements, or limitations on assisting other counsel in the litigation after settlement.[9]

Finally, a settlement within an MDL proceeding can only govern the pending cases within the MDL proceeding and any coordinated state cases in which the parties have voluntarily participated in the settlement negotiations. The settlement does not extend to future cases, and, contrary to the situation obtaining in class actions, there is no procedure by which a representative can be appointed to protect the interests of future claimants. Therefore, the MDL settlement cannot protect defendants from future claims, unless the MDL also includes an appropriate class action suitable for certification.[10]

---

5. FRCP 23(c)(2), (e).

6. FRCP 23(b)(3), (c)(2).

7. FRCP 23(e). *See* Chapter 15 "Class Actions," *infra*.

8. *See* Robert G. Bone, *Case Five: Complex Litigation and Prior Rulings Issues*, 29 New Eng. L. Rev. 711, 715–16 (1995).

9. *See* Manual for Complex Litigation, (Third) §§ 23.22, 23.23 (1997); Lisa Berstein & Daniel Klerman, *An Economic Analysis of Mary Carter Settlement Agreements*, 83 Geo. L.J. 2215, 2215–18 (1995).

Se also Chapter 28 "Settlement" at § 28.10(b)(1), *infra*.

10. The procedural and due process limitations on the use of settlement classes, and the conflict posed by attempting to settle current and future claims through representation by the same plaintiffs' counsel and same representative plaintiffs, are discussed in *Amchem Prods., Inc. v. Windsor*, ___ U.S. ___, 117 S.Ct. 2231, 138 L.Ed.2d 689 (1997).

§ 11.22   Practice Checklist

(a) Motions

(1) All motions must be accompanied by:

a. a supporting brief; and

b. schedule giving:

- the complete (not short form) name of each action involved;
- the district court in which each action is pending;
- the civil action number of each action; and
- the name of the judge assigned to each action, if known. (*See* § 11.7(a)(2); JPML Rule 10(a))

(2) Motions for remand must be accompanied by:

a. a supporting brief;

b. any final pretrial order that the transferee court has entered; and

c. an affidavit reciting:

- whether the movant has requested a suggestion of remand from the transferee court;
- how the court responded to any such request;
- if no such request was made, why;
- whether all common discovery and other pretrial proceedings have been concluded and, if not, what remains to be done;
- whether all orders of the transferee court have been satisfactorily complied with and, if not, what remains to be done. (*See* § 11.20(a); JPML Rules 10(a), 14(d))

(3) Motions are to be in numbered paragraphs; responses are to be in correspondingly numbered responsive paragraphs (*See* JPML Rule 9(a), (b))

(4) Each paragraph should be limited to a single averment of fact (*See* JPML Rule 9(a))

(5) Responses must admit or deny, in whole or in part, each allegation. If an allegation is not wholly admitted, the response must contain the respondent's version of the matter (*See* JPML Rule 9(b))

(6) Proposed orders should not be filed (*See* § 11.7(a)(2); JPML Rule 9(g))

(b) Briefs

(1) Briefs are limited to 20 pages exclusive of exhibits (*See* JPML Rule 9(f))

(2) If the exhibits exceed 25 pages, they must be bound separately (*See* JPML Rule 9(f))

(3) For reply briefs, a movant must file a single brief in reply to any opposition (*See* § 11.7(a)(2), (3); JPML Rule 10(d))

(c) Time Requirements

(1) Appearance, entry of: must be filed within 11 days of the filing of a motion to transfer, an order to show cause or a conditional transfer order (*see* JPML Rules 10(b), 8(c))

(2) Motions:

    a. responses are due within 20 days after the filing of motion (*See* JPML Rule 10(c));

    b. any reply is due within 5 days after the lapse of time for filing responsive briefs, *i.e.* 25 days from the date of the filing of the motion (*See* § 11.7(a)(5), (c)(1); JPML Rule 10(d))

(3) Conditional Transfer or Remand Orders:

    a. if action is no longer pending, notification must be made to the Clerk of the Panel within 15 days from entry of the conditional order (*See* JPML Rule 12(b));

    b. notice of opposition must be filed within 15 days from entry of conditional order (*see* JPML Rule 12(c));

    c. a motion to vacate must be filed within 15 days of the filing of the notice of opposition (*See* §§ 11.7(d), 11.20); JPML Rule 12(d))

(4) Show Cause Orders for Transfer:

    a. responses must be filed within 20 days of the filing of the order (unless otherwise specified in order) (*See* JPML Rule 11(b));

    b. replies must be filed within 5 days after the lapse of time for response (*i.e.* 25 days from date of filing of order) (*See* JPML Rule 11(c). [Note that show cause orders for remand have a shorter deadline (*see* subsection (5) below)]. (*See* § 11.7(c))

(5) Show Cause Orders for Remand:

    a. responses must be filed within 20 days of the filing of the order (unless otherwise specified therein) (*See* JPML Rule 14(e));

    b. replies must be filed within 5 days of the filing of the response (*See* JPML Rule 14(e)). [Note that this time is shorter than that applicable to Show Cause Orders concerning transfer.] (*See* § 11.20(b))

(6) Notice of Potential Tag–Along: "promptly" (*See* § 11.7(a)(6); JPML Rule 13(e))

(7) Extensions:

    a. Applications for extension of time must be in writing, must set forth specific reasons, and must request a specific number of additional days (*See* JPML Rule 15)

    b. Applications for extension of time relating to the following actions will be granted only in exceptional circumstances:

- notice of opposition to conditional transfer order (*See* JPML Rule 8(c));

- notice of opposition to conditional remand order (*see* JPML Rule 15);

- entry of appearance (*See* §§ 11.7(a)(5), (d), 11.20(c); (JPML Rule 8(c))

(d) Service

(1) All papers must contain a Proof of Service which complies with FRCP 5 and 6. The Proof of Service must indicate the name and address of each person served, as well as the party represented by that person (*See* JPML Rule 8(a)).

(2) If the Panel has issued a Panel Service List, this should be used for the Proof of Service, with any necessary supplementation (*See* JPML Rule 8(a)).

(3) For a motion to transfer or a motion to remand, the Proof of Service must also certify that the motion has been mailed or delivered to the courts required by JPML Rule 8(b).

(4) The Proof of Service must be served on all parties (*See* JPML Rule 8(a)).

(5) If liaison counsel have been appointed, Proof of Service may be satisfied by service on each such counsel, provided their designated responsibilities include receipt and distribution of pleadings (*See* § 11.7(a)(4); JPML Rule 8(e))

(e) Filing Requirements

(1) The address for filings with the Judicial Panel is:

Clerk of the Panel

Judicial Panel on Multidistrict Litigation

Thurgood Marshall Federal Judiciary Building

One Columbus Circle, N.E.

Room G–255, North Lobby

Washington, D.C. 20002

FAX: 202–273–2810

(2) Only the original of the following documents must be filed; filing may be made by fax with prior approval from the Clerk of the Panel (*See* JPML Rule 7(a), (d)):

    a. proof of service (*See* JPML Rule 8(a));

    b. notice of appearance (*See* JPML Rule 8(c));

    c. status notice (*See* JPML Rules 10(e), 11(e) and 12(b));

    d.   notice of related action (*See* JPML Rule 13(e));

    e.   notice of opposition (*See* JPML Rules 12(c), 14(f)(ii));

    f.   application for extension of time (*See* JPML Rule 15); and

    g.   notice of presentation or waiver of oral argument. (*See* JPML 17(a)).

(3) The original plus 11 copies of all other documents must be filed; filing may not be made by fax (*See* JPML Rule 7(a), (d)). Such documents include but are not limited to:

    a.   motions for or in opposition to transfer; and

    b.   motions for or in opposition to remand.

(4) Additional Filings Required.

    a.   *Motions to Transfer*: copies must be filed with the Judicial Panel (as specified above) and a copy must be filed in: (1) the district court in which the action is pending; and (2) in each district court in which an action is pending that would be affected by the motion (*See* 28 U.S.C.A. § 1407(c)(ii))

    b.   *Motions to Remand*: Copies must be filed with the Judicial Panel (as specified above) and a copy must be filed in the transferee court (*See* JPML Rule 7(c)).

(f) Format of Papers Filed with Judicial Panel

(1) All papers must be:

    a.   typewritten on plain 8½" x 11" paper

    b.   double-spaced

    c.   fastened in top left hand corner

    d.   no front or back covers. (*See* JPML Rule 9(c))

(2) The heading on the first page must bear:

    a.   the heading "Before the Judicial Panel On Multidistrict Litigation"

    b.   the identification "MDL Docket No. _____ "

    c.   the descriptive title designated by the Panel; if no descriptive title has been designated yet, the filing party should determine an appropriate descriptive title to use. (*See* JPML Rule 9(d))

(3) The last page of each pleading must contain the name, address and telephone number of the attorney or party in active charge of the case. (*See* JPML Rule 9(e)) Only 1 attorney may be designated. (*See* JPML Rule 8(c))

§ 11.23   Forms

    The Panel maintains certain forms which are sent out to the parties from time to time throughout the litigation. Those forms are substantially the same as those set forth below, but may contain specific due dates and filing instructions (which are consistent with the general rules explained in this chapter).[1]

(a) Notice of Appearance. ▦

MDL Docket No. _____ In Re [case name]

To: Clerk of the Panel

     Judicial Panel on Multidistrict Litigation

     One Columbus Circle, NE

     Thurgood Marshall Federal Judiciary Building

     Room G–255, North Lobby

     Washington, DC 20002

NOTICE OF APPEARANCE

In compliance with Rule 8(c) R.P.J.P.M.L., the following designated attorney is authorized to receive service of all pleadings, notices, orders, and other papers relating to practice before the Judicial Panel on Multidistrict Litigation on behalf of the following [plaintiff(s)/defendant(s)]. I am aware that only one attorney can be designated for each party.

_____   _____

Date   Name

* * * * * * * * * * * *

Name and Address of Designated Attorney:

Telephone No. _____   Fax No. _____

* * * * * * * * * * * *

List of Represented Parties With Case's Short Caption, District, Civil Action No.

         [Separate list may be attached if necessary]

(b) Proof of Service ▦

PROOF OF SERVICE

I hereby certify that on this date a true and correct copy of the foregoing [name of document] was served on each of the following by [method of service].

§ 11.23

1. For additional Forms, *see* Federal Procedural Forms, Lawyers Edition, Chap-

ter 49; Multidistrict Litigation, (1988).

[List parties and counsel served or attach Service List]

Date: _____   _____
                              [signature]

(c) Motion to Transfer 💾

BEFORE THE JUDICIAL PANEL
ON MULTIDISTRICT LITIGATION

In re _____)   MDL Docket No. _____
_____)

MOTION BY [MOVANT] FOR TRANSFER OF ACTIONS
FOR CONSOLIDATED PRETRIAL PROCEEDINGS
PURSUANT TO 28 U.S.C.A. § 1407

[Movant], by [his/her/its] undersigned counsel, moves the Panel for an order, pursuant to 28 U.S.C.A.§ 1407, transferring the actions described in the attached Schedule of Actions Involved to the United States District Court for the _____ District of _____ for coordinated or consolidated pretrial proceedings. In support of this motion, [Movant] alleges as follows:

1. [Movant] is a defendant in 37 actions ("Actions") currently pending in 11 different federal district courts, all arising from an allegedly defective [component] of the [product] manufactured by [Movant]. These actions are listed in the Schedule of Actions Involved, attached as Exhibit 1.

2. All of these Actions involve common questions of law and fact in that all allege that the [component] of the [product] manufactured by [Movant] was defectively designed, tested, and manufactured and that [Movant] failed to warn the general public (including the plaintiffs in the Actions) of the risk associated with the product. Development of facts relating to these common issues will be essential to the disposition of all Actions for which transfer is sought.

3. Transfer of these Actions to a single district for coordinated or consolidated pretrial proceedings will promote the just and efficient conduct of the Actions and would be in the interest of the majority of the parties and witnesses.

4. _____ [number] of the Actions are currently pending in the United States District Court for the _____ District of _____ and have been assigned to the docket of Judge _____, who has been handling those cases for several months.

5. In addition, [Movant]'s manufacturing and testing facility is located in that district and a majority of the pertinent witnesses and documents are already located there.

WHEREFORE, [Movant] respectfully requests that, pursuant to 28 U.S.C.A. § 1407, the Panel order the transfer of the Actions listed on Exhibit 1 to the United States District Court for the _____ District of

_____ for consolidated pretrial proceedings and, with the consent of that court, to the docket of Judge _____.

Dated: _____   Respectfully submitted,
                                 [Name, address, telephone, party represented]

(d) Order To Show Cause

BEFORE THE JUDICIAL PANEL
ON MULTIDISTRICT LITIGATION

In re _____)   MDL Docket No. _____
_____)

ORDER TO SHOW CAUSE

You and each of you are hereby ordered to show cause why the actions listed on the attached Schedule should not be transferred pursuant to 28 U.S.C.A. § 1407 to a single district for coordinated or consolidated pretrial proceedings.

Responses to this Order shall conform to RPJPML 11.

You are further notified that the issuing of this Order by the Panel does not affect or suspend orders and discovery proceedings in the district courts in which said multidistrict litigation is pending (RPJPML 18).

                     FOR THE PANEL: [name]

(e) Response to Order to Show Cause

BEFORE THE JUDICIAL PANEL
ON MULTIDISTRICT LITIGATION

In re _____)   MDL Docket No. _____
_____)

[RESPONDENTS]' RESPONSE TO ORDER TO SHOW CAUSE

I. BACKGROUND.

1. On _____, the Panel issued an Order to Show Cause ("Order") directing the parties involved in the actions listed on the Schedule attached to the Order ("Actions") to show cause why the Actions should not be transferred to a single district pursuant to 28 U.S.C.A. § 1407.

2. [Respondents] are the plaintiffs in eight of the actions as follows:

[list actions]

II. SUMMARY OF POSITION

3. It is [Respondents]' position that transfer by the Panel is not appropriate at this time. If, however, transfer is ordered, it should be to the United States District Court for the _____ District of _____.

III. DISCUSSION

4. The Actions lack sufficient common questions of law and fact to justify transfer. First, the law applicable to each case will be determined by state, not federal, law and that law differs from state to state. Since each of the actions arose in a different state, the legal framework applicable to each case will be significantly different. For example [explain].

5. Second, common questions of fact do not predominate. While the cases all involve similar issues of product design and testing, five of them involve testing done at a substantially different time under a different protocol than that at issue in the other cases. Moreover, the more significant pretrial activities in these cases will concern the specific use of the product by the individual plaintiffs and the unique damages each plaintiff sustained. These issues are not common to all of these Actions.

6. The convenience of parties and witnesses also weighs against transfer. The witnesses to the actual incidents that gave rise to these claims are located in the jurisdictions where the Actions are currently pending, as are the voluminous documents relating to the individual injuries sustained by the plaintiffs.

7. Transfer would not promote the just and efficient conduct of these actions. [Respondents'] cases are already at a very advanced stage and discovery is almost closed. In addition, a summary judgment motion has already been briefed and argued; if granted, the motion would conclude the cases in which [Respondents] are involved.

8. In the event transfer is ordered, the Actions should be transferred to the _____ District of _____, because the four most-advanced cases are located there, it is centrally-located geographically, and the majority of counsel involved in these actions maintain their offices there.

IV. CONCLUSION

9. For the reasons set forth above, transfer under 28 U.S.C.A. § 1407 would be inappropriate at this time. In the event the Panel decides otherwise, the most just and convenient district is the _____ District of _____.

> Respectfully submitted,
> [Name, address, telephone, party represented]

(f) Notice of Tag–Along Action 🖫

BEFORE THE JUDICIAL PANEL
ON MULTIDISTRICT LITIGATION

In re _____)   MDL Docket No. _____
_____)

To the Clerk of the Multidistrict Panel:

Please take notice that on [date], [party giving notice] was served with a Summons and Complaint filed in the United States District Court for the _____ District of _____ at docket number _____ captioned _____, a copy of which is attached as Exhibit 1.

The Complaint is identical in all material respects to the other complaints that are the subject of the matter presently pending before the Panel pursuant to 28 U.S.C.A. § 1407.

Date: _____

Respectfully submitted,
[Name, address, telephone, party represented]

(g) Notice of Opposition to Conditional Order 💾

BEFORE THE JUDICIAL PANEL
ON MULTIDISTRICT LITIGATION

In re _____)   MDL Docket No. _____
_____)

[List of cases that are specific subject of notice]

NOTICE OF OPPOSITION TO CONDITIONAL
[TRANSFER/REMAND] ORDER

[Party] opposes the [transfer/remand] of the case[s] captioned above under 28 U.S.C.A. § 1407, as conditionally ordered by the Judicial Panel on [date].

Pursuant to RPJPML Rule [12(d)/14(f)(iii)], [party] will file within fifteen days of the filing of this notice a motion to vacate the conditional order and brief in support thereof.

Respectfully submitted,
[Name, address, telephone, party represented]

(h) Motion to Vacate Conditional Order 💾

BEFORE THE JUDICIAL PANEL
ON MULTIDISTRICT LITIGATION

In re _____)   MDL Docket No. _____
_____)

MOTION TO VACATE CONDITIONAL
[TRANSFER/REMAND] ORDER

[Movant], pursuant to RPJPML [12(d)/14(f)(iii)], moves the Panel to vacate its order of [date] conditionally [transferring/remanding] the above-captioned case[s] to the United States District Court for the _____ District of _____.

In support of this motion, [Movant] submits the attached Brief in Support of Motion to Vacate Conditional [Transfer/Remand] Order, [affidavits, if any], and such other materials and evidence as may be presented to the panel at time of hearing.

Respectfully submitted,

[Name, address, telephone, party represented]

(i) Notice of Presentation or Waiver of Oral Argument 🖫

MDL DOCKET NO. _____ In re _____.

TO: Clerk of the Panel
    Judicial Panel on
    Multidistrict Litigation
    One Columbus Circle, NE
    Thurgood Marshall Federal
    Judiciary Building
    Room G–255, North Lobby
    Washington, DC 20002–8004

NOTICE OF [PRESENTATION/WAIVER] OF ORAL ARGUMENT

[Select one of the following]

[Please take notice that the following designated attorney shall PRESENT ORAL ARGUMENT at the Panel hearing on behalf of the designated [party/parties] pursuant to RPJPML 17.]

[Please take notice that the [party/parties] noted herein will WAIVE ORAL ARGUMENT pursuant to RPJPML 17(b).]

[Please take notice that the [party/parties] noted herein will WAIVE ORAL ARGUMENT IF ALL OTHER PARTIES IN THIS MATTER WAIVE ORAL ARGUMENT.

Otherwise, the following designated attorney shall present oral argument at the Panel hearing on behalf of the designated [party/parties] pursuant to RPJPML 17.

Date: _____   _____
                                   Authorized Signature

* * *

Name and Address of Attorney Designated to Present Oral Argument:

Telephone No.: _____

[Party/Parties] Represented:

§ 11.24 Appendix

This Appendix is organized by general type of litigation, and identifies the case type, name, disposition, all opinions, transferee judge and transferee court of the MDL proceedings reported to date. The Appendix does not include unpublished opinions, nor does it include subsequent case histories. For simplicity, only the shortform case name is cited and the transferee judge and court are noted in parentheses.

Case Type
(a) Air Disaster
(b) Common Disaster
(c) Product Liability
(d) Contract
(e) Antitrust
(f) Securities
(g) Employment Practices
(h) Patent
(i) Trademark
(j) Copyright
(k) Miscellaneous

(a) Air Disaster[1]

Cases Transferred: Cincinnati Airport—11/8/65 (Swinford, M.; E.D. Ky.), 298 F.Supp. 353 (J.P.M.L. 1968), 298 F.Supp. 358 (J.P.M.L. 1969), 298 F.Supp. 355 (J.P.M.L. 1969), 354 F.Supp. 275 (J.P.M.L. 1973); Cincinnati Airport—11/21/67 (Swinford, M.; E.D. Ky.), 354 F.Supp. 275 (J.P.M.L. 1973); Ardmore, Oklahoma—4/22/66 (Langley, E.; E.D. Okla.) 295 F.Supp. 45 (J.P.M.L. 1968); Hendersonville, N.C.—7/19/67 (Jones, W.W.; W.D. N.C.), 297 F.Supp. 1039 (J.P.M.L. 1969); Hong Kong—6/30/67 (Hall, P.M.; N.D. Cal.), 298 F.Supp. 390 (J.P.M.L. 1969); Fairland, Indiana—9/9/69 (Holder, C.J.; S.D. Ind.), 309 F.Supp. 621 (J.P.M.L. 1970); Dayton, Ohio—3/9/67 (Weinman, C.A.; S.D. Ohio), 310 F.Supp. 798 (J.P.M.L. 1970), 386 F.Supp. 908 (J.P.M.L. 1975); Hanover, N.H.—10/25/68 (Bownes, H.H.; D.N.H.), 314 F.Supp. 62 (J.P.M.L. 1970); San Juan, P.R.—3/5/69 (Weinfeld, E.; D.P.R.), 316 F.Supp. 981 (J.P.M.L. 1970); New Orleans, LA—3/20/69 (McRae, R.M.; W.D. Tenn.), 331 F.Supp. 554 (J.P.M.L. 1971); San Antonio, Venezuela—4/69 (Kelleher, R.J.; C.D. Cal.), 331 F.Supp. 547 (J.P.M.L. 1971); Las Vegas, Nevada—10/8/68 (Hill, R.M.; N.D. Tex.), 336 F.Supp. 414 (J.P.M.L. 1972); Denver, Colorado—10/3/69 (Winner, F.M.; D. Colo.), 339 F.Supp. 415 (J.P.M.L. 1972); Huntington, WV—11/14/70 (Hall, K.K.; S.D. W.Va.), 342 F.Supp. 1400 (J.P.M.L. 1972); Tweed/New Haven—6/7/71 (Blumenfeld, M.J.; D. Conn.), 343 F.Supp. 951 (J.P.M.L. 1972), 368 F.Supp. 815 (J.P.M.L. 1973); Toronto Airport—7/5/70 (Hall, P.M.; C.D. Cal.), 346 F.Supp. 533 (J.P.M.L. 1972); Duarte, California—6/6/71 (Hall, P.M.; C.D. Cal.), 346 F.Supp. 529 (J.P.M.L. 1972), 354 F.Supp. 278 (J.P.M.L. 1973); Juneau, Alaska—9/4/71 (Hall, P.M.; N.D. Cal.), 350 F.Supp. 1163 (J.P.M.L. 1972), 360 F.Supp. 1406 (J.P.M.L. 1973); Silver Plume, Colorado—10/2/70 (Theis, F.G.; D. Kan.), 352 F.Supp. 968 (J.P.M.L. 1972), 368 F.Supp. 810 (J.P.M.L. 1973); Atlantic City, N.J.—7/26/69 (Sharpe, M.E.; W.D. Wash.), 352 F.Supp. 969 (J.P.M.L. 1973); Pellston, Michigan—5/9/70 (Higginbotham, A.L.; E.D. Pa.), 357 F.Supp. 1286 (J.P.M.L. 1973); Florida Everglades—12/29/72 (Fay, P.T.; S.D. Fla.), 360 F.Supp. 1394 (J.P.M.L. 1973), 368 F.Supp. 812 (J.P.M.L. 1973); Coolidge, Arizona—5/6/71 (Muecke, C.A.; D. Ariz.), 362 F.Supp. 572 (J.P.M.L. 1973); Boston,

§ 11.24

1. Transferee Judge in parentheses.

Massachusetts—7/31/73 (Nelson, D.S.; D. Mass.), 373 F.Supp. 1406
(J.P.M.L. 1974), 395 F.Supp. 1405 (J.P.M.L. 1975); Paris, France—3/3/74
(Hall, P.M.; C.D. Cal.), 376 F.Supp. 887 (J.P.M.L. 1974), 386 F.Supp.
1404 (J.P.M.L. 1975); Pago Pago, American Samoa—1/30/74 (Byrne, Jr.,
W.M.; C.D. Cal.), 383 F.Supp. 501 (J.P.M.L. 1974), 394 F.Supp. 799
(J.P.M.L. 1975), 424 F.Supp. 1075 (J.P.M.L. 1977); Natchitoches Parish,
LA—9/20/73 (Dawkins, Jr., B.C.; W.D. La.) 391 F.Supp. 765 (J.P.M.L.
1975), 407 F.Supp. 1401 (J.P.M.L. 1976); Upperville, VA—11/27/73
(Bryan, A.V.; E.D. Va.), 393 F.Supp. 1089 (J.P.M.L. 1975), 430 F.Supp.
1295 (J.P.M.L. 1977); Chattanooga, Tennessee—11/27/73 (Wilson, F.W.;
E.D. Tenn.), 393 F.Supp. 1406 (J.P.M.L. 1975); Charlotte, N.C.—9/11/74
(McMillan, J.B.; W.D. N.C.), 393 F.Supp. 1404 (J.P.M.L. 1975); Papeete,
Tahiti—7/22/73 (Hall, P.M.; C.D. Cal.), 397 F.Supp. 886 (J.P.M.L. 1975);
Bali, Indonesia—4/22/74 (Williams, D.W.; C.D. Cal.), 400 F.Supp. 1402
(J.P.M.L. 1975); Saigon, South Vietnam—4/4/75 (Oberdorfer, L.F.;
D.D.C.), 404 F.Supp. 478 (J.P.M.L. 1975); John F. Kennedy Airport—
6/24/75 (Bramwell, H.; E.D.N.Y.), 407 F.Supp. 244 (J.P.M.L. 1976);
Ionian Sea—9/8/74 (Duffy, K.T.; S.D.N.Y.), 407 F.Supp. 238 (J.P.M.L.
1974), 438 F.Supp. 932 (J.P.M.L. 1977); Taipei International Airport—
7/31/95 (Bryant, W.B.; D.D.C.), 433 F.Supp. 1120 (J.P.M.L. 1977); Helicopter Crash—Germany—9/26/75 (Burns, E.B.; D. Conn.), 443 F.Supp.
447 (J.P.M.L. 1978); Tenerife, Canary Islands—3/27/77 (Ward, R.J.;
S.D.N.Y.), 435 F.Supp. 927 (J.P.M.L. 1977), 461 F.Supp. 671 (J.P.M.L.
1978); Denver, Colorado—8/7/75 (Finesilver, S.G.;D. Colo.), 447 F.Supp.
1071 (J.P.M.L. 1978); Marsh Island, LA—12/8/77 (Davis, W.E.; W.D.
La.), 461 F.Supp. 675 (J.P.M.L. 1978); Bombay, India—1/1/78 (Fitzgerald; W.D. Wash.), 463 F.Supp. 158 (J.P.M.L. 1979); Barrow, Alaska—
10/13/78 (Robinson, Jr., A.E.; D.D.C.), 474 F.Supp. 996 (J.P.M.L. 1979);
Pittsburgh, PA—8/21/77 (McCune, B.P.; W.D. Pa.), 510 F.Supp. 1228
(J.P.M.L. 1979); Chicago, Illinois—5/25/79 (Robson, E.A./Will, H.L.; N.D.
Ill.), 476 F.Supp. 445 (J.P.M.L. 1979); Van Cleve, Mississippi—8/13/77
(Cook, H.D.; N.D. Okla.), 486 F.Supp. 926 (J.P.M.L. 1980); Denver,
Colorado—11/16/76 (Kelleher, R.J.; C.D. Cal.), 486 F.Supp. 241 (J.P.M.L.
1980); Washington, D.C.—1/13/82 (Green, J.H.; D.D.C.), 533 F.Supp.
1350 (J.P.M.L. 1982); New Orleans, LA—7/9/82 (Duplantier, A.G.; E.D.
La.), 548 F.Supp. 1268 (J.P.M.L. 1982); Korean Air Lines—9/1/83 (Rob-
inson, A.E.; D.D.C.), 575 F.Supp. 342 (J.P.M.L. 1983); Covington, KY—
6/2/83 (Waters, L.E.; C.D. Cal.), 579 F.Supp. 1057 (J.P.M.L. 1984);
Dallas/Fort Worth Airport—8/2/85 (Belew, Jr., D.O.; N.D. Tex.), 623
F.Supp. 634 (J.P.M.L. 1985); Gander, Newfoundland—12/12/85 (John-
stone, E.H.; W.D. Ky.), 633 F.Supp. 50 (J.P.M.L. 1986); Detroit, MI—
8/16/87 (Cook, J.A.; E.D. Mich.), 674 F.Supp. 27 (J.P.M.L. 1987); Denver,
CO—11/15/87 (Finesilver, S.G.; D. Colo.) 683 F.Supp. 266 (J.P.M.L.
1988); Lockerbie, Scotland—12/21/88 (Platt, Jr., T.C.; E.D.N.Y.), 709
F.Supp. 231 (J.P.M.L. 1989); Sioux City, IA—7/19/89 (Conlon, S.B.; N.D.
Ill.), 128 F.R.D. 131 (J.P.M.L. 1989).

Transfer Denied: Falls City, Nebraska—9/6/66, 298 F.Supp. 1323
(J.P.M.L. 1969); Anchorage, Alaska—11/27/70, 342 F.Supp. 755 (J.P.M.L.
1972); Cameron, Louisiana—4/23/76, 443 F.Supp. 1022 (J.P.M.L. 1978).

(b) Common Disaster

Cases Transferred: Silver Bridge Disaster (Kaufman, F.A.; S.D. W.Va.), 311 F.Supp. 1345 (J.P.M.L. 1970); Roseville, California—4/28/73 (MacBride, T.J.; E.D. Cal.), 399 F.Supp. 1400 (J.P.M.L. 1975); Radiation Incident—4/5/74 (Hart, G.L.; D.D.C.), 400 F.Supp. 1404 (J.P.M.L. 1975); USS NEWPORT NEWS—10/1/72 (Collinson, W.R.; W.D. Mo.), 411 F.Supp. 790 (J.P.M.L. 1976); Frankewing, Tennessee—10/1/75 (Morton, L.C.; M.D. Tenn.), 431 F.Supp. 916 (J.P.M.L. 1977); Sinking of Motor Vessel UKOLA (Eaton, J.; S.D. Fla.), 462 F.Supp. 385 (J.P.M.L. 1978); "Amoco Cadiz" Oil Spill (Norgle, C.R.; N.D. Ill.), 471 F.Supp. 473 (J.P.M.L. 1979); Continental Grain Disaster (Mitchell, L.L.; E.D. La.), 482 F.Supp. 330 (J.P.M.L. 1979); Union Carbide, Bhopal, India (Keenan, J.F.; S.D.N.Y.), 601 F.Supp. 1035 (J.P.M.L. 1985); Dupont Plaza Hotel Fire, PR—12/31/86 (Acosta, R.L.; D.P.R.), 660 F.Supp. 982 (J.P.M.L. 1987); Rail Collision Near Chase, MD—1/4/87 (Harvey, A.; D. Md.), 661 F.Supp. 69 (J.P.M.L. 1987).

Transfer Denied: Galveston, Texas Oil Explosion, 322 F.Supp. 1405 (J.P.M.L. 1971); USS Trenton, 383 F.Supp. 1406 (J.P.M.L. 1974); Alamagordo, NM—6/18/69, 387 F.Supp. 732 (J.P.M.L. 1975); Rockville, Connecticut—12/30/72, 388 F.Supp. 574 (J.P.M.L. 1975); Washington, D.C.—5/3/74, 405 F.Supp. 1304 (J.P.M.L. 1976).

(c) Product Liability

Cases Transferred: Aviation (Sharp, M.E.; S.D. Ind.), 347 F.Supp. 1401 (J.P.M.L. 1972); Celotex Corp. "Technifoam" (Weiner, C.R.; D. Minn.), 68 F.R.D. 502 (J.P.M.L. 1975), 424 F.Supp. 1077 (J.P.M.L. 1977); A.H. Robins Co., Inc., Dalkon Shield IUD (Theis, F.G.; D. Kan.), 406 F.Supp. 540 (J.P.M.L. 1975), 419 F.Supp. 710 (J.P.M.L. 1976), 438 F.Supp. 942 (J.P.M.L. 1977), 453 F.Supp. 108 (J.P.M.L. 1978), 505 F.Supp. 221 (J.P.M.L. 1981), 570 F.Supp. 1480 (J.P.M.L. 1983), 610 F.Supp. 1099 (J.P.M.L. 1985); Swine Flu Immunization (Gesell, G.A.; D.D.C.), 446 F.Supp. 244 (J.P.M.L. 1978), 453 F.Supp. 648 (J.P.M.L. 1978), 464 F.Supp. 949 (J.P.M.L. 1979); Upjohn Co. "Cleocin" (Kennedy, C.G.; E.D. Mich.), 450 F.Supp. 1168 (J.P.M.L. 1978); Multi–Piece Rim (Collinson, W.R.; W.D. Mo.), 464 F.Supp. 969 (J.P.M.L. 1979); Aortic Heart Valve (Weinstein, J.B.; E.D.N.Y.), 465 F.Supp. 1295 (J.P.M.L. 1979); Richardson–Merrell, Inc., "Bendectin" (Rubin, C.B.; S.D. Ohio), 533 F.Supp. 489 (J.P.M.L. 1982), 582 F.Supp. 890 (J.P.M.L. 1984), 588 F.Supp. 1448 (J.P.M.L. 1984), 606 F.Supp. 715 (J.P.M.L. 1985); Asbestos (No. VI) (Weiner, C.R.; E.D. Pa.), 771 F.Supp. 415 (J.P.M.L. 1991); Silicone Gel Breast Implants (Pointer, S.C.; N.D. Ala.), 793 F.Supp. 1098 (J.P.M.L. 1992); Factor VIII or IX Concentrate Blood (Grady, J.F.; N.D. Ill.), 853 F.Supp. 454 (J.P.M.L. 1993); Temporomandibular Joint (TMJ) Implants (Magnuson, P.A.; D. Minn.) 844 F.Supp. 1553 (J.P.M.L. 1994), 872 F.Supp. 1018 (J.P.M.L. 1994); Rio Hair Naturalizer (Rosen, G.; E.D. Mich.), 904 F.Supp. 1407 (J.P.M.L. 1995), 904 F.Supp. 1407 (J.P.M.L. 1995).

Transfer Denied: Oral Contraceptives, 322 F.Supp. 1011 (J.P.M.L. 1971); Boncoat, 353 F.Supp. 1302 (J.P.M.L. 1973); Asbestos Insulation Material, 431 F.Supp. 906 (J.P.M.L. 1977); "Polystyrene Foam", 429 F.Supp. 1035 (J.P.M.L. 1977); Luminex International Inc., 434 F.Supp. 668 (J.P.M.L. 1977); Ortho Pharmaceutical, 447 F.Supp. 1073 (J.P.M.L. 1978); G.D. Searle & Co. "Copper 7" IUD, 483 F.Supp. 1343 (J.P.M.L. 1980); Rely Tampon, 533 F.Supp. 1346 (J.P.M.L. 1982); Eli Lilly & Co. "Oraflex", 578 F.Supp. 422 (J.P.M.L. 1984); Asbestos School, 606 F.Supp. 713 (J.P.M.L. 1985); A.H. Robins Co., Inc. (No. II), 610 F.Supp. 1099 (J.P.M.L. 1985).

(d) Contract

Cases Transferred: Grain Shipments (Templar, G.; D. Kan.), 300 F.Supp. 1402 (J.P.M.L. 1969), 304 F.Supp. 457 (J.P.M.L. 1969), 305 F.Supp. 3 (J.P.M.L. 1969), 319 F.Supp. 533 (J.P.M.L. 1970), 325 F.Supp. 318 (J.P.M.L. 1971), 332 F.Supp. 588 (J.P.M.L. 1971), 327 F.Supp. 1313 (J.P.M.L. 1971); Grain Shipments (No. II) (Becker, W.H.; W.D. Mo.), 364 F.Supp. 462 (J.P.M.L. 1973); AMF Computer Cash Register (McLaren, R.W.; N.D. Ill.), 360 F.Supp. 1404 (J.P.M.L. 1973); Warehouse Construction (Morton, L.C.; M.D. Tenn.), 387 F.Supp. 734 (J.P.M.L. 1975); Westinghouse Electric Corp. Uranium (Merhige, Jr., R.R.; E.D. Va.), 405 F.Supp. 316 (J.P.M.L. 1975), 436 F.Supp. 990 (J.P.M.L. 1977).

Transfer Denied: Homemakers Franchise, 337 F.Supp. 1342 (J.P.M.L. 1972); Times Square Shopping Center, 405 F.Supp. 310 (J.P.M.L. 1975); U.S. Navy Re-enlistment Bonus, 407 F.Supp. 1405 (J.P.M.L. 1976); Wild Weasel, 415 F.Supp. 387 (1976); Commercial Lighting Products, 415 F.Supp. 392 (J.P.M.L. 1976); Royal Typewriter Co., 435 F.Supp. 925 (J.P.M.L. 1977).

(e) Antitrust

Cases Transferred: Children's Books (Decker, B.M.; N.D. Ill.), 297 F.Supp. 385 (J.P.M.L. 1968), 297 F.Supp. 1352 (J.P.M.L. 1968), 299 F.Supp. 1139 (J.P.M.L. 1969); Plumbing Fixtures (Harvey, A.; E.D. Pa.), 295 F.Supp. 33 (J.P.M.L. 1968), 298 F.Supp. 483 (J.P.M.L. 1968), 298 F.Supp. 484 (J.P.M.L. 1968), 302 F.Supp. 795 (J.P.M.L. 1969), 308 F.Supp. 242 (J.P.M.L. 1970), 311 F.Supp. 349 (J.P.M.L. 1970), 332 F.Supp. 1047 (J.P.M.L. 1971), 343 F.Supp. 756 (J.P.M.L. 1972); Protection Devices (Metzner, C.M.; S.D.N.Y.), 295 F.Supp. 39 (J.P.M.L. 1968), 297 F.Supp. 622 (J.P.M.L. 1968); Antibiotic Drugs (Group I) (Lord, M.W.; D. Minn.), 295 F.Supp. 1402 (J.P.M.L. 1968), 297 F.Supp. 1126 (J.P.M.L. 1968), 299 F.Supp. 1403 (J.P.M.L. 1969), 301 F.Supp. 1158 (J.P.M.L. 1969), 303 F.Supp. 1056 (J.P.M.L. 1969), 309 F.Supp. 155 (J.P.M.L. 1970), 320 F.Supp. 586 (J.P.M.L. 1970); Antibiotic Drugs (Lord, M.W.; S.D.N.Y.), 320 F.Supp. 586 (J.P.M.L. 1970); Antibiotic Drugs (Group II), (Lord, M.W.; D. Minn.), 327 F.Supp. 617 (J.P.M.L. 1971), 355 F.Supp. 1400 (J.P.M.L. 1973), 384 F.Supp. 607 (J.P.M.L. 1974), 405 F.Supp. 1302 (J.P.M.L. 1976); Concrete Pipe (Davis, J.M.;

E.D. Pa.), 297 F.Supp. 1125 (J.P.M.L. 1968), 303 F.Supp. 507 (J.P.M.L. 1969), 302 F.Supp. 244 (J.P.M.L. 1969), 302 F.Supp. 244 (J.P.M.L. 1969); Gypsum Wallboard (Zirpoli, A.J.; N.D. Cal.), 297 F.Supp. 1350 (J.P.M.L. 1969), 303 F.Supp. 510 (J.P.M.L. 1969), 302 F.Supp. 794 (J.P.M.L. 1969), 340 F.Supp. 990 (J.P.M.L. 1972); IBM (Neville, P.; D. Minn.) 302 F.Supp. 796 (J.P.M.L. 1969), 314 F.Supp. 1253 (J.P.M.L. 1970), 316 F.Supp. 976 (J.P.M.L. 1970), 319 F.Supp. 926 (J.P.M.L. 1970), 328 F.Supp. 509 (J.P.M.L. 1971), 342 F.Supp. 200 (J.P.M.L. 1972); Koratron (Renfrew, C.B.; N.D. Cal.), 302 F.Supp. 239 (J.P.M.L. 1969), 314 F.Supp. 60 (J.P.M.L. 1970), 327 F.Supp. 559 (J.P.M.L. 1971); Admission Ticket (Robson, E.A.; N.D. Ill.), 302 F.Supp. 1339 (J.P.M.L. 1969); Water Meters (Boldt, G.H.; N.D. Cal.), 304 F.Supp. 873 (J.P.M.L. 1969); Western Liquid Asphalt (Smith, R.E.; N.D. Cal.), 303 F.Supp. 1053 (J.P.M.L. 1969), 309 F.Supp. 157 (J.P.M.L. 1970); Concrete Pipes (W. Rockies) (Pence, M.; C.D. Cal.), 303 F.Supp. 507 (J.P.M.L. 1969); Air Pollution Control Equipment (Real, M.L.; C.D. Cal.), 311 F.Supp. 1349 (J.P.M.L. 1970); Master Key (Blumenfeld, M.J.; D. Conn.), 320 F.Supp. 1404 (J.P.M.L. 1971); Ampicillin (Richey, C.R.; D.D.C.), 315 F.Supp. 317 (J.P.M.L. 1970); CBS Licensing (Troutman, E.M.; E.D. Pa.), 328 F.Supp. 511 (J.P.M.L. 1971), 342 F.Supp. 1177 (J.P.M.L. 1972); Government Auto Fleet Sales (McGarr, F.J.; N.D. Ill.), 328 F.Supp. 218 (J.P.M.L. 1971), 352 F.Supp. 966 (J.P.M.L. 1972); Refrigerant Gas (Battisti, F.J.; N.D. Ohio), 334 F.Supp. 996 (J.P.M.L. 1971); International House of Pancakes (Collinson, W.R.; W.d. Mo.), 331 F.Supp. 556 (J.P.M.L. 1971), 343 F.Supp. 948 (J.P.M.L. 1972), 374 F.Supp. 1406 (J.P.M.L. 1974); Kauffman Mutual Fund (Pettine, R.J.; D. Mass.) 337 F.Supp. 1337 (J.P.M.L. 1972); Midwest Milk Monopolization (Oliver, J.W.; W.d. Mo.) 379 F.Supp. 989 (J.P.M.L. 1974), 379 F.Supp. 992 (J.P.M.L. 1974), 386 F.Supp. 1401 (J.P.M.L. 1975), 398 F.Supp. 676 (J.P.M.L. 1975), 435 F.Supp. 930 (J.P.M.L. 1977), 441 F.Supp. 930 (J.P.M.L. 1977), 483 F.Supp. 823 (J.P.M.L. 1980); Hotel Telephone Charge (Lucas, M.M.; C.D. Cal.), 341 F.Supp. 771 (J.P.M.L. 1972), 374 F.Supp. 1402 (J.P.M.L. 1974); 7–Eleven Franchise (Schnacke, R.H.; N.D. Cal.), 358 F.Supp. 286 (J.P.M.L. 1973); Career Academy, Inc. (Gordon, M.L.; E.D. Wis.) 342 F.Supp. 753 (J.P.M.L. 1972); Commodities Exchange Rate (Bauer, W.J.; N.D. Ill.), 342 F.Supp. 1405 (J.P.M.L. 1972); Convenient Food Mart (Marshall, P.H.; N.D. Ill.), 350 F.Supp. 1166 (J.P.M.L. 1972); Transit Co. Tires (Hunter, E.B.; W.D. Mo.), 350 F.Supp. 1165 (J.P.M.L. 1972); REA Express, Inc. (Becker, E.; E.D. Pa.), 352 F.Supp. 803 (J.P.M.L. 1972), 386 F.Supp. 1406 (J.P.M.L. 1975); Professional Hockey (Higginbottom, A.; E.D. Pa.), 352 F.Supp. 1405 (J.P.M.L. 1973), 369 F.Supp. 1117 (J.P.M.L. 1974), 369 F.Supp. 1119 (J.P.M.L. 1974); Nissan Motor Corp. (Atkins, C.C.; S.D. Fla.), 352 F.Supp. 960 (J.P.M.L. 1973), 385 F.Supp. 1253 (J.P.M.L. 1974), Cessna Aircraft (Roberts, R.T.; W.D. Mo.), 359 F.Supp. 543 (J.P.M.L. 1973), 460 F.Supp. 159 (J.P.M.L. 1978); General Adjustment Bureau (Werker, H.F.; S.D.N.Y.), 375 F.Supp. 1405 (J.P.M.L. 1973); Wheat Farmers (No. I) (Daugherty, F.A.; W.D. Okla.), 366 F.Supp. 1087 (J.P.M.L. Okla. 1973); Mutual Funds Sales (Corcoran, H.F.; D.D.C.), 361 F.Supp. 638 (J.P.M.L. 1973); Clark Oil & Refining Corp. (Reynolds, J.W.; E.D. Wis.) 364 F.Supp. 458 (J.P.M.L. 1973); West

Coast Bakery Flour (Boldt, G.H.; W.D. Wash.), 368 F.Supp. 808
(J.P.M.L. 1974), 383 F.Supp. 842 (J.P.M.L. 1974); Petroleum Products
(Tashima, A.W.; C.D. Cal.), 393 F.Supp. 1091 (J.P.M.L. 1975), 407
F.Supp. 249 (J.P.M.L. 1976), 419 F.Supp. 712 (J.P.M.L. 1976), 476
F.Supp. 455 (J.P.M.L. 1979); Plywood (Pointer, S.C.; E.D. La.), 376
F.Supp. 1405 (J.P.M.L. 1974); IBM Peripheral EDP Devices (McNichols,
R.; N.D. Cal.), 375 F.Supp. 1376 (J.P.M.L. 1974), 394 F.Supp. 796
(J.P.M.L. 1975), 407 F.Supp. 254 (J.P.M.L. 1976), 411 F.Supp. 791
(J.P.M.L. 1976); Gas Vent Pipe (Byrne, W.M.; N.D. Cal.), 380 F.Supp.
799 (J.P.M.L. 1974); Mack Truck, Inc. (Voorhees, D.S.; W.d. Wash.), 383
F.Supp. 503 (J.P.M.L. 1974), 405 F.Supp. 1400 (J.P.M.L. 1975); Toilet
Seat (Keith, D.J.; E.D. Mich.), 387 F.Supp. 1342 (J.P.M.L. 1975); L.E.
Lay & Co., Inc. (Justice, W.W.; E.D. Tex.), 391 F.Supp. 1054 (J.P.M.L.
1975); Japanese Electronic Products (Becker, E.R.; E.D. Pa.), 388
F.Supp. 565 (J.P.M.L. 1975); Amerada Hess Corporation (Cannella, J.M.;
S.D.N.Y.), 395 F.Supp. 1404 (J.P.M.L. 1975); Sugar Industry
(Boldt/Cahn; N.D. Cal.), 395 F.Supp. 1271 (J.P.M.L. 1975), 399 F.Supp.
1397 (J.P.M.L. 1975), 405 F.Supp. 1404 (J.P.M.L. 1975), 427 F.Supp.
1018 (J.P.M.L. 1977), 433 F.Supp. 1122 (J.P.M.L. 1977); Sugar Industry
(East Coast) (Cahn/Boldt; E.D. Pa.), 405 F.Supp. 1404 (J.P.M.L. 1975),
427 F.Supp. 1018 (J.P.M.L. 1977), 433 F.Supp. 1122 (J.P.M.L. 1977), 437
F.Supp. 1204 (J.P.M.L. 1977), 471 F.Supp. 1089 (J.P.M.L. 1979); Griseo-
fulvin (Robinson, Jr., A.E.; D.D.C.), 395 F.Supp. 1402 (J.P.M.L. 1975);
Piper Aircraft Distribution (Sachs, H.F.; W.D. Mo.), 405 F.Supp. 1402
(J.P.M.L. 1975); Chicken "Broiler" (O'Kelley, W.C.; N.D. Ga.) 411
F.Supp. 788 (J.P.M.L. 1976); Olympia Brewing Co. (Weiner, C.R.; D.
Minn.), 415 F.Supp. 398 (J.P.M.L. 1976); Beef Industry (Kazen, G.P.;
N.D. Tex.), 419 F.Supp. 720 (J.P.M.L. 1976), 432 F.Supp. 211 (J.P.M.L.
1977); Alaska Salmon Fishery (Fitzgerald; W.D. Wash.), 424 F.Supp. 504
(J.P.M.L. 1976); Folding Carton (Will, H.L./Robson, E.A.; N.D. Ill.), 415
F.Supp. 384 (J.P.M.L. 1976); Falstaff Brewing Corp. (Wangelin, H.K.;
E.D. Mo.), 434 F.Supp. 1225 (J.P.M.L. 1977); Independent Gasoline
(Young, J.H.; D. Md.), 439 F.Supp. 267 (J.P.M.L. 1977); South Central
States Bakery (Schwartz; M.D. La.), 433 F.Supp. 1127 (J.P.M.L. 1977),
462 F.Supp. 388 (J.P.M.L. 1978); Anthracite Coal (Muir, M.; M.D. Pa.),
436 F.Supp. 402 (J.P.M.L. 1977); Cement and Concrete (Real, M.L.; D.
Ariz.), 437 F.Supp. 750 (J.P.M.L. 1977), 465 F.Supp. 1299 (J.P.M.L.
1979); Preferential Drug Products (Hill, I.; C.D. Cal.), 429 F.Supp. 1027
(J.P.M.L. 1977); Hawaiian Hotel Room Rate (King, S.P.; D. Hawaii), 438
F.Supp. 935 (J.P.M.L. 1977); Corrugated Container (Singleton, Jr., J.V.;
S.D. Tex.), 441 F.Supp. 921 (J.P.M.L. 1977), 447 F.Supp. 468 (J.P.M.L.
1978); Armored Car (Freeman, R.C.; N.D. Ga.), 441 F.Supp. 921
(J.P.M.L. 1977), 462 F.Supp. 394 (J.P.M.L. 1978); "Fine Paper"
(McGlynn, Jr., J.L.; E.D. Pa.), 446 F.Supp. 759 (J.P.M.L. 1978), 453
F.Supp. 118 (J.P.M.L. 1978); Wiring Device (Weinstein, J.B.; E.D.N.Y.),
444 F.Supp. 1348 (J.P.M.L. 1978); Airport Car Rental (Schwarzer, W.W.;
N.D. Cal.), 448 F.Supp. 273 (J.P.M.L. 1978), 459 F.Supp. 1006 (J.P.M.L.
1978); Uranium Industry (Marshall, P.H.; N.D. Ill.), 458 F.Supp. 1223
(J.P.M.L. 1978), 466 F.Supp. 958 (J.P.M.L. 1979); General Aircraft Corp.
(Green, J.L.; D.D.C.), 449 F.Supp. 604 (J.P.M.L. 1978); Gas Meter

(Weiner, C.R.; E.D. Pa.), 464 F.Supp. 391 (J.P.M.L. 1979); Motion Picture Licensing (Singleton, Jr., J.V.; S.D. Tex.), 468 F.Supp. 837 (J.P.M.L. 1979), 479 F.Supp. 581 (J.P.M.L. 1979); Data General Corp. (Patel, M.H.; N.D. Cal.), 470 F.Supp. 855 (J.P.M.L. 1979), 510 F.Supp. 1220 (J.P.M.L. 1979); California Armored Car (Hill, I.; C.D. Cal.), 476 F.Supp. 452 (1979); New Mexico Natural Gas (Winder, D.K.; D.N.M.), 482 F.Supp. 333 (J.P.M.L. 1979); Corn Derivatives (Debevoise, D.R.; D.N.J.), 486 F.Supp. 929 (J.P.M.L. 1980); Marine Construction (Sear, M.L.; E.D. La.), 487 F.Supp. 1355 (J.P.M.L. 1980); Cuisinart Food Processor (Cabranes, J.A.; D. Conn.), 506 F.Supp. 651 (J.P.M.L. 1981); Amino Acid Lysine (Shadur, M.I.; N.D. Ill.), 910 F.Supp. 696 (J.P.M.L. 1995); Corn Sweeteners (Mihm, M.M.; C.D. Ill.), 910 F.Supp. 696 (J.P.M.L. 1995); Citric Acid (Smith, F.M.; N.D. Cal.), 910 F.Supp. 696 (J.P.M.L. 1995).

Transfer Denied: Scotch Whiskey, 299 F.Supp. 543 (J.P.M.L. 1969); Concrete Pipes (Texas), 302 F.Supp. 1342 (J.P.M.L. 1969); Motion Picture Standard Accessories, 339 F.Supp. 1278 (J.P.M.L. 1972); Professional Basketball, 344 F.Supp. 1405 (J.P.M.L. 1972); Brandywine Associates, 407 F.Supp. 236 (J.P.M.L. 1976); Women's Clothing, 455 F.Supp. 1388 (J.P.M.L. 1978); McDonald's Franchise, 472 F.Supp. 111 (J.P.M.L. 1979); Gasoline Lessee Dealers, 479 F.Supp. 578 (J.P.M.L. 1979); Chiropractic, 483 F.Supp. 811 (J.P.M.L. 1980); Insulin Manufacturing, 487 F.Supp. 1359 (J.P.M.L. 1980); Citric Acid, Corn Sweeteners & Lysine, 910 F.Supp. 696 (J.P.M.L. 1995).

(f) Securities

Cases Transferred: WESTEC Corp. (Hannay, A.B.; S.D. Tex.), 307 F.Supp. 559 (J.P.M.L. 1969); Revenue Properties Company, Ltd. (Caffrey, A.A.; D. Mass.), 309 F.Supp. 1002 (J.P.M.L. 1970), 314 F.Supp. 1255 (J.P.M.L. 1970), 333 F.Supp. 558 (J.P.M.L. 1971); Seeberg–Commonwealth United Merger (McFadden, F.H.; S.D.N.Y.), 312 F.Supp. 909 (J.P.M.L. 1970), 331 F.Supp. 552 (J.P.M.L. 1971), 333 F.Supp. 911 (J.P.M.L. 1971), 362 F.Supp. 568 (J.P.M.L. 1973), 415 F.Supp. 393 (J.P.M.L. 1976); Four Seasons (Thomsen, R.C.; W.D. Okla.), 328 F.Supp. 221 (J.P.M.L. 1971), 331 F.Supp. 559 (J.P.M.L. 1971), 342 F.Supp. 758 (J.P.M.L. 1972), 344 F.Supp. 1404 (J.P.M.L. 1972), 352 F.Supp. 962 (J.P.M.L. 1972), 352 F.Supp. 964 (J.P.M.L. 1973), 355 F.Supp. 1405 (J.P.M.L. 1973), 361 F.Supp. 636 (J.P.M.L. 1973), 362 F.Supp. 574 (J.P.M.L. 1973), 373 F.Supp. 975 (J.P.M.L. 1974), 429 F.Supp. 527 (J.P.M.L. 1976); Penn Central (Lord, III, J.S.; E.D. Pa.), 322 F.Supp. 1021 (J.P.M.L. 1971), 325 F.Supp. 309 (J.P.M.L. 1971), 333 F.Supp. 382 (J.P.M.L. 1971), 349 F.Supp. 1029 (J.P.M.L. 1972), 358 F.Supp. 284 (J.P.M.L. 1973), 374 F.Supp. 1400 (J.P.M.L. 1974); Penn Central Commercial Paper (Edelstein, D.N.; S.D.N.Y.), 325 F.Supp. 309 (J.P.M.L. 1971), 337 F.Supp. 1335 (J.P.M.L. 1972), 358 F.Supp. 284 (J.P.M.L. 1973); Brown Co. (Rubin, A.B.; S.D.N.Y.), 325 F.Supp. 307 (J.P.M.L. 1971); Value Line Spec. Situations (Tenney, C.H.; S.D.N.Y.), 334 F.Supp. 999 (J.P.M.L. 1971); King Resources, Co. (Finesilver, S.G.; D. Colo.), 342

F.Supp. 1179 (J.P.M.L. 1972), 352 F.Supp. 974 (J.P.M.L. 1972), 352
F.Supp. 975 (J.P.M.L. 1972), 385 F.Supp. 588 (J.P.M.L. 1974), 458
F.Supp. 220 (J.P.M.L. 1978); Texas Gulf Sulphur (Bonsal, D.B.;
S.D.N.Y.), 344 F.Supp. 1398 (J.P.M.L. 1972); National Student Market-
ing (Parker, B.D.; D.D.C.), 368 F.Supp. 1311 (J.P.M.L. 1972), 358
F.Supp. 1303 (J.P.M.L. 1973); Glenn W. Turner Enterprises (Weber,
G.J.; W.D. Pa.), 355 F.Supp. 1402 (J.P.M.L. 1973), 368 F.Supp. 805
(J.P.M.L. 1973), 383 F.Supp. 844 (J.P.M.L. 1974), 476 F.Supp. 459
(J.P.M.L. 1979); Caeser's Palace (Weiner, C.R.; S.D.N.Y.), 385 F.Supp.
1256 (J.P.M.L. 1974); Atlantic Department Stores (Weiner, C.R.;
S.D.N.Y.), 352 F.Supp. 971 (J.P.M.L. 1972); Evergreen Valley Project
(Bownes, H.H.; D. Mass.), 366 F.Supp. 510 (J.P.M.L. 1973), 435 F.Supp.
923 (J.P.M.L. 1977); Holiday Magic SEC & AT (Burke, L.H.; N.D. Cal.),
368 F.Supp. 806 (J.P.M.L. 1973), 372 F.Supp. 1167 (J.P.M.L. 1974), 375
F.Supp. 1400 (J.P.M.L. 1974), 384 F.Supp. 1403 (J.P.M.L. 1974), 433
F.Supp. 1125 (J.P.M.L. 1977); Stirling Homex Corp. (Bonsal, D.B.;
S.D.N.Y.), 388 F.Supp. 567 (J.P.M.L. 1975), 388 F.Supp. 570 (J.P.M.L.
1975), 405 F.Supp. 314 (J.P.M.L. 1975), 442 F.Supp. 547 (J.P.M.L. 1977);
Boise Cascade (Sharp, M.E.; W.D. Wash.), 364 F.Supp. 459 (J.P.M.L.
1973); Stirling Homex Banking (Bonsal, D.B.; S.D.N.Y.), 388 F.Supp. 572
(J.P.M.L. 1975); Pittsburgh & Lake Erie Railroad Co. SEC (Troutman,
E.M.; E.D. Pa.), 374 F.Supp. 1404 (1974); Clinton Oil Company (Brown,
W.E./Rogers; D. Kan.), 368 F.Supp. 813 (J.P.M.L. 1973); Viatron Com-
puter Systems (Tauro, J.L.; D. Mass.), 462 F.Supp. 382 (J.P.M.L. 1978);
Equity Funding Corp. (Lucas, M.M.; C.D. Cal.), 375 F.Supp. 1378
(J.P.M.L. 1973), 385 F.Supp. 1262 (J.P.M.L. 1974), 391 F.Supp. 767
(J.P.M.L. 1975), 396 F.Supp. 1277 (J.P.M.L. 1975), 397 F.Supp. 884
(J.P.M.L. 1975); Great Western Ranches (Zirpoli, A.J.; N.D. Cal.), 369
F.Supp. 1406 (J.P.M.L. 1974); Natural Resources, Inc. (Rogers, R.D.; D.
Kan.), 372 F.Supp. 1403 (J.P.M.L. 1974); Sta–Power Industries, Inc. SEC
& AT (Burke, L.H.; N.D. Cal.), 372 F.Supp. 1398 (J.P.M.L. 1974), 404
F.Supp. 476 (J.P.M.L. 1975); Scientific Control Corp. (Brieant, Jr., C.L.;
S.D.N.Y.), 380 F.Supp. 791 (J.P.M.L. 1974); U.S. Financial (Turrentine,
H.B.; S.D. Cal.), 375 F.Supp. 1403 (J.P.M.L. 1974), 385 F.Supp. 586
(J.P.M.L. 1974); Bestline Products SEC & AT (Marcus, S.; S.D. Fla.), 375
F.Supp. 926 (J.P.M.L. 1974), 405 F.Supp. 313 (J.P.M.L. 1975); Alodex
Corporation (Hanson, W.C.; S.D. Iowa), 380 F.Supp. 790 (J.P.M.L. 1974);
Rep. National Realty Equities (Pollack, M.; S.D.N.Y.), 382 F.Supp. 1403
(J.P.M.L. 1974); Air West, Inc. (Zirpoli, A.J.; N.D. Cal.), 384 F.Supp. 609
(J.P.M.L. 1974); Pennsylvania Life Co. (Real, M.L.; C.D. Cal.), 389
F.Supp. 981 (J.P.M.L. 1975), 436 F.Supp. 406 (J.P.M.L. 1977); Industrial
Wine Contracts (MacKenzie, J.A.; E.D. Va.), 386 F.Supp. 909 (J.P.M.L.
1975); Franklin National Bank (Weinstein, J.B.; E.D.N.Y.), 393 F.Supp.
1093 (J.P.M.L. 1975), 407 F.Supp. 248 (J.P.M.L. 1976); TransOcean
Tender Offer (Will, H.L.; N.D. Ill.), 415 F.Supp. 382 (J.P.M.L. 1976);
Haven Industries, Inc. (Gagliardi, L.P.; S.D.N.Y.), 415 F.Supp. 396
(J.P.M.L. 1976); Tenneco, Inc. (Singleton, Jr., J.V.; S.D. Tex.), 426
F.Supp. 1187 (J.P.M.L. 1977); Colocotronis Tanker (Tenney, C.H.;
S.D.N.Y.), 420 F.Supp. 998 (J.P.M.L. 1976); General Tire & Rubber Co.
(Battisti, F.J.; N.D. Ohio), 429 F.Supp. 1032 (J.P.M.L. 1977); Ascott Oils,

Inc. (Schwartz, Jr., C.; E.D. La.), 433 F.Supp. 1118 (J.P.M.L. 1977); Investors Funding Corp. (Conner, W.C.; S.D.N.Y.), 437 F.Supp. 1199 (J.P.M.L. 1977), 461 F.Supp. 673 (J.P.M.L. 1978); Cenco, Inc. (Aspen, M.E.; N.D. Ill.), 434 F.Supp. 1237 (J.P.M.L. 1977); New York City Municipal (Owen, R.; S.D.N.Y.), 439 F.Supp. 267 (J.P.M.L. 1977); Teledyne, Inc. (Real, M.L.; C.D. Cal.), 440 F.Supp. 58 (J.P.M.L. 1977); Sunshine Mining Co. (Knapp, W.; S.D.N.Y.), 444 F.Supp. 223 (J.P.M.L. 1978); Amtel, Inc. (Goettel, G.L.; S.D.N.Y.), 447 F.Supp. 466 (J.P.M.L. 1978); First National Bank, Heavener, OK (Thompson, R.G.; W.D. Okla.), 451 F.Supp. 995 (J.P.M.L. 1978); Commonwealth/Oil Tesoro (Higginbotham; W.D. Tex.), 458 F.Supp. 225 (J.P.M.L. 1978); Vernitron (Byrne, Jr., W.M.; C.D. Cal.), 462 F.Supp. 391 (J.P.M.L. 1978), 469 F.Supp. 297 (J.P.M.L. 1979); Capital Underwriters, Inc. (Orrick, Jr., W.H.; N.D. Cal.), 464 F.Supp. 955 (J.P.M.L. 1979); Food Fair (Huyett, III, D.H.; E.D. Pa.), 465 F.Supp. 1301 (J.P.M.L. 1979); LTV (Higginbotham, P.E.; N.D. Tex.), 470 F.Supp. 859 (J.P.M.L. 1979); Resource Exploration, Inc. (Brieant, C.L.; S.D.N.Y.), 483 F.Supp. 817 (J.P.M.L. 1980); Longhorn (Eubanks, L.B.; W.D. Okla.), 552 F.Supp. 1003 (J.P.M.L. 1982); Washington Public Power Supply (Browning, W.D.; W.D. Wash.), 568 F.Supp. 1250 (J.P.M.L. 1983); General Motors Class E (Robinson, S.L.; D. Del.), 696 F.Supp. 1546 (J.P.M.L. 1988); American Continental/Lincoln Savings (Bilby, R.M.; D. Ariz.), 130 F.R.D. 475 (J.P.M.L. 1990).

Transfer Denied: Royal American Ind., Inc., 407 F.Supp. 242 (J.P.M.L. 1976); Harmony Loan Co., 372 F.Supp. 1406 (J.P.M.L. 1974); Hamilton Bank (of Atlanta), 438 F.Supp. 940 (J.P.M.L. 1977); Raymond Lee Organization, 446 F.Supp. 1266 (J.P.M.L. 1978); Magic Marker Corp., 470 F.Supp. 862 (J.P.M.L. 1979).

(g) Employment Practices

Cases Transferred: Roadway Express (Real, M.L.; W.D. Tex.), 384 F.Supp. 612 (J.P.M.L. 1974); Eastern Air Lines, Inc. (Merhige, Jr., R.R.; E.D. Va.), 391 F.Supp. 763 (J.P.M.L. 1975); Southwestern Bell/Maternity (Harper, R.W.; E.D. Mo.), 400 F.Supp. 1400 (J.P.M.L. 1975); National Airlines, Inc. (Roettger, Jr., N.C.; S.D. Fla.), 399 F.Supp. 1405 (J.P.M.L. 1975); Ryder Truck Lines, Inc. (Moye, Jr., C.A.; N.D. Ga.), 405 F.Supp. 308 (J.P.M.L. 1975); Ironworkers Union (Hannum, J.B.; E.D. Pa.), 424 F.Supp. 1072 (J.P.M.L. 1976); Southern Pacific Trans. Co. (Sterling, R.N.; S.D. Tex.), 429 F.Supp. 529 (J.P.M.L. 1977); Petrol Stops Northwest (Belloni, R.C.; D. Or.), 446 F.Supp. 241 (J.P.M.L. 1978).

Transfer Denied: Trucking Industry, 384 F.Supp. 614 (J.P.M.L. 1974); Braniff Airways, 411 F.Supp. 798 (J.P.M.L. 1976); Delta Air Lines, Inc., 411 F.Supp. 795 (J.P.M.L. 1976); Pan American World Airways, 414 F.Supp. 1232 (J.P.M.L. 1976); Westinghouse Electric Corp., 438 F.Supp. 937 (J.P.M.L. 1977); Southern Railway, 441 F.Supp. 926 (J.P.M.L. 1977); Texas Instruments Inc., 441 F.Supp. 928 (J.P.M.L. 1977); Airline "Age of Employees," 483 F.Supp. 814 (J.P.M.L. 1980); Sears, Roebuck & Co., 487 F.Supp. 1362 (J.P.M.L. 1980).

(h) Patent

Cases Transferred: Butterfield (Will, H.L.; N.D. Ill.), 328 F.Supp. 513 (J.P.M.L. 1970), 328 F.Supp. 513 (J.P.M.L. 1970); Kaehni Patent (Northrop, E.S.; D. Md.), 311 F.Supp. 1342 (J.P.M.L. 1970); Frost (Wright, C.M.; D. Del.), 316 F.Supp. 977 (J.P.M.L. 1970); Embro (Whelan, F.C.; C.D. Cal.), 328 F.Supp. 507 (J.P.M.L. 1971); CBS Color Tube (Caffrey, A.A.; D. Mass.), 329 F.Supp. 540 (J.P.M.L. 1971), 342 F.Supp. 1403 (J.P.M.L. 1972); Suess (Rosenberg, L.; W.D. Pa.), 331 F.Supp. 549 (J.P.M.L. 1971), 384 F.Supp. 1405 (J.P.M.L. 1974); Yarn Processing (Atkins, C.C.; S.D. Fla.), 341 F.Supp. 376 (J.P.M.L. 1972); Camco (Brewster, L.; N.D. Tex.), 343 F.Supp. 1406 (J.P.M.L. 1972); Molinaro/Catanzaro (Metzner, C.M.; S.D.N.Y.), 380 F.Supp. 794 (J.P.M.L. 1974), 402 F.Supp. 1404 (J.P.M.L. 1975); Triax Company (Manos, J.M.; N.D. Ohio), 385 F.Supp. 590 (J.P.M.L. 1974); Panty Hose Seaming (Jones, W.W.; W.D. N.C.), 402 F.Supp. 1401 (J.P.M.L. 1975); Joseph F. Smith (Ward, H.H.; M.D. N.C.), 407 F.Supp. 1403 (J.P.M.L. 1976); Western Electric Co., Inc. (Warriner, D.D.; E.D. Va.), 415 F.Supp. 378 (J.P.M.L. 1976), 436 F.Supp. 404 (J.P.M.L. 1977); FMC Corporation (O'Connor, E.E.; D. Kan.), 422 F.Supp. 1163 (J.P.M.L. 1976); Sundstrand Data Control, Inc. (Fitzgerald; W.D. Wash.), 443 F.Supp. 1019 (J.P.M.L. 1978); Amoxicillin PAT & AT (Richey, C.R.; D.D.C.), 449 F.Supp. 601 (J.P.M.L. 1978).

Transfer Denied: Eisler, 297 F.Supp. 1034 (J.P.M.L. 1968); SCM Photocopy Paper, 305 F.Supp. 60 (J.P.M.L. 1969); Deering–Milliken, 328 F.Supp. 504 (J.P.M.L. 1970); Disposable Diaper, 362 F.Supp. 567 (J.P.M.L. 1973); Lehman Equipment Company, 360 F.Supp. 1402 (J.P.M.L. 1973); Shipley Co., Inc., 383 F.Supp. 847 (J.P.M.L. 1974); Molinaro/Catanzaro (II), 464 F.Supp. 966 (J.P.M.L. 1979); Bourns, Inc., 385 F.Supp. 1260 (J.P.M.L. 1974); Allen Archery, Inc., 446 F.Supp. 248 (J.P.M.L. 1978); Wyeth (Pet), 445 F.Supp. 992 (J.P.M.L. 1978); Eli Lilly & Company, 446 F.Supp. 242 (J.P.M.L. 1978); Deering Milliken, 476 F.Supp. 461 (J.P.M.L. 1979); Cable Tie, 487 F.Supp. 1351 (J.P.M.L. 1980); Sicilla Di. R. Biebow & Co. PAT & AT, 490 F.Supp. 513 (J.P.M.L. 1980).

(i) Trademark

Cases Transferred: Carrom (Tyler, Jr., H.R.; S.D.N.Y.), 322 F.Supp. 1016 (J.P.M.L. 1971).

Transfer Denied: Grand Funk Railroad, 371 F.Supp. 1084 (J.P.M.L. 1974); "Lite Beer," 437 F.Supp. 754 (J.P.M.L. 1977).

(j) Copyright

Cases Transferred: "The Exorcist" (Williams, D.W.; C.D. Cal.), 411 F.Supp. 793 (J.P.M.L. 1976).

Transfer Denied: "Truckin" Cartoon Characters, 372 F.Supp. 1400 (J.P.M.L. 1974).

(k) Miscellaneous

Cases Transferred: Fourth Class Postage (Augelli, A.T.; D.N.J.), 298 F.Supp. 1326 (J.P.M.L. 1969); Alsco–Harvard Fraud (Oberdorfer, L.F.; D.D.C.), 325 F.Supp. 315 (J.P.M.L. 1971), 328 F.Supp. 1405 (J.P.M.L. 1971); Air Fare (Will, H.L.; N.D. Ill.), 322 F.Supp. 1013 (J.P.M.L. 1971); Cross–Florida Barge Canal (Bechtle, L.C.; M.D. Fla.), 329 F.Supp. 543 (J.P.M.L. 1971); Public Air Travel Tariff (McNichols, R.; C.D. Cal.), 360 F.Supp. 1397 (J.P.M.L. 1973); Regional Rail Reorganization Act (Wisdom, J.M.; D.D.C.), 373 F.Supp. 1401 (J.P.M.L. 1974), 373 F.Supp. 1404 (J.P.M.L. 1974), 404 F.Supp. 477 (J.P.M.L. 1975); Peruvian Road (McNichols, R.; D. Idaho), 380 F.Supp. 796 (J.P.M.L. 1974); Fireman's Fund Insurance Co. (Debevoise, D.R.; D.N.J.), 422 F.Supp. 287 (J.P.M.L. 1976); Liquid Carbonic Chemical Poisoning (Sear, M.L.; E.D. La.), 423 F.Supp. 937 (J.P.M.L. 1976); Longoria Bank Deposits (Hughes, S.T.; N.D. Tex.), 431 F.Supp. 913 (J.P.M.L. 1977); Practice of Naturopathy (Young, J.H.; D. Md.), 434 F.Supp. 1240 (J.P.M.L. 1977); Westinghouse Electric Corp. (Weinstein, J.B.; E.D.N.Y.), 436 F.Supp. 990 (J.P.M.L. 1977); General Motors Corp. Engine Interchange (McGarr, F.J.; N.D. Ill.), 441 F.Supp. 933 (J.P.M.L. 1977); Federal Election Campaign (Richey, C.R.; D.D.C.), 511 F.Supp. 821 (J.P.M.L. 1979); Stripper Well Exemption (Theis, F.G.; D. Kan.), 472 F.Supp. 1282 (J.P.M.L. 1979); Alien Children of Tex. Ed. (Seals, W.B.; S.D. Tex.), 482 F.Supp. 326 (J.P.M.L. 1979); Iowa Beef Processors (McManus, E.J.; N.D. Iowa), 491 F.Supp. 1359 (J.P.M.L. 1980); 1980 Decennial Census (Northrop, E.S.; D. Md.), 506 F.Supp. 648 (J.P.M.L. 1981); Baldwin United Corp. (Brieant, C.L.; S.D.N.Y.), 581 F.Supp. 739 (J.P.M.L. 1984); Gross Common Carrier, Inc. (Shabaz, J.C.; W.d. Wis.), 843 F.Supp. 1506 (J.P.M.L. 1994).

Transfer Denied: Iowa Beef Packers,Inc. & Amalgamated, 309 F.Supp. 1259 (J.P.M.L. 1970); Molecular Weight Polyethylene, 339 F.Supp. 1278 (J.P.M.L. 1972); Pension Fund, 360 F.Supp. 1400 (J.P.M.L. 1973); United Gas Pipe Line Company, 391 F.Supp. 774 (J.P.M.L. 1975); Fotomat Franchise, 394 F.Supp. 798 (J.P.M.L. 1975); Klein Medical Malpractice, 398 F.Supp. 679 (J.P.M.L. 1975); Good Samaritan Nursing Center, 415 F.Supp. 389 (J.P.M.L. 1976); Buffalo Valley Gas Authority, 429 F.Supp. 1029 (J.P.M.L. 1977); Natural Gas Liquids, 434 F.Supp. 665 (J.P.M.L. 1977); American Financial Corp., 434 F.Supp. 1232 (J.P.M.L. 1977); EPA Pesticide Listing, 434 F.Supp. 1235 (J.P.M.L. 1977); 21st Century Productions, Inc., 448 F.Supp. 271 (J.P.M.L. 1978); American Home Products Corp., 448 F.Supp. 276 (J.P.M.L. 1978); Garrison Diversion Unit, 458 F.Supp. 223 (J.P.M.L. 1978); Penitentiary Postal Procedure, 465 F.Supp. 1293 (J.P.M.L. 1979); Oklahoma Ins. Holding Co., 464 F.Supp. 961 (J.P.M.L. 1979); Ecuadorian Oil Concession, 487 F.Supp. 1364 (J.P.M.L. 1980).

CHAPTER 12

ISSUE AND CLAIM PRECLUSION

by

H. Robert Fiebach
Douglas R. Widin
and
James E. Brown

Table of Sections

WESTLAW Electronic Research

See WESTLAW Electronic Research Guide preceding the Summary of Contents.

---

§ 12.1 Scope Note

With the rise in litigation comes a concomitant rise in the potential that causes of action or issues of fact or law have previously been the subject of litigation. This requires the astute litigator to be sensitive to the possible application of preclusionary doctrines that prevent relitigation of claims or issues. These doctrines are important to both plaintiffs and defendants, because they may be used both offensively and defensively.

When litigating in the federal courts, the practitioner must be sensitive to a number of considerations inherent in our federal system. Care must be taken that the proper body of law, state or federal, is identified for purposes of the particular preclusionary doctrine at issue. Further due, to the highly fact-sensitive nature of many of the preclusionary doctrines, early and thorough investigation should be undertaken. Early identification of prior or concurrently pending related litigation is essential. Additionally, when a party is subject to multiple pieces of litigation involving similar claims or issues, tactics can become extremely important, in terms of which cases are tried or settled and the speed at which they are processed, in seeking to avoid or take advantage of potential preclusive effects.

In this chapter, we review the major preclusionary doctrines of res judicata and collateral estoppel. Their elements and application in different circumstances are examined. The rules governing the effect of state court judgments on federal litigation are also explored. Certain special circumstances holding potential for preclusion, including the relationship between criminal and civil proceedings and class actions, receive separate treatment. The preclusive effect given to administrative proceedings is also discussed.

Library References:

West's Key No. Digests, Judgment ☞540–633, 634–751.

Wright, Miller & Cooper, Federal Practice and Procedure: Civil 2d §§ 4406, 4416.

§ 12.2　Distinction Between Issue and Claim Preclusion

The rules of the finality of judgments consist of two doctrines: (1) "res judicata," or what is known in more modern parlance as "claim preclusion," and (2) "collateral estoppel," or "issue preclusion." Although the two doctrines are related, each has distinct elements and application.[1]

Under res judicata, or claim preclusion, "a final judgment on the merits of an action precludes the parties or their privies from relitigating issues that were or could have been brought in that action."[2] It precludes not only relitigating a claim previously adjudicated, but also any related claim or defense that could have been raised, but was not, in connection with the previously adjudicated claim.[3]

Under collateral estoppel, or issue preclusion, "once a court decides an issue of fact or law necessary to its judgment, that decision precludes relitigation of the same issue on a different cause of action between the same parties."[4] Collateral estoppel applies not only against actual parties to prior litigation, but also against a party that is in privity with a party to the previous litigation.[5] Courts have been cautious, however, when

---

§ 12.2

1. The terminology of res judicata and collateral estoppel is often inconsistently used by litigants, courts, and commentators. The term "res judicata" is sometimes used to encompass both claim and issue preclusion. *See* Americana Fabrics, Inc. v. L & L Textiles, Inc., 754 F.2d 1524, 1529 & n. 1 (9th Cir.1985); Ross v. Communications Satellite Corp., 759 F.2d 355, 362 n. 8 (4th Cir.1985); Jones v. City of Alton, 757 F.2d 878, 879–80 n. 1 (7th Cir.1985). The confusion engendered by over a century of misuse has led most modern courts and commentators to prefer the terms "claim preclusion" and "issue preclusion." *See, e.g.,* Horwitz v. Alloy Automotive Co., 992 F.2d 100, 103 (7th Cir.1993); Clark v. Bear Stearns & Co., 966 F.2d 1318, 1320 (9th Cir.1992); Carter v. City of Emporia, 815 F.2d 617, 619 n. 2 (10th Cir.1987); Wade v. City of Pittsburgh, 765 F.2d 405, 408 (3d Cir.1985).

The Restatement (Second) of Judgments speaks of res judicata as "claim preclusion" and of collateral estoppel as "issue preclusion." United States v. Mendoza, 464 U.S. 154, 104 S.Ct. 568, 78 L.Ed.2d 379 (1984). *See also* Allen v. McCurry, 449 U.S. 90, 94, 101 S.Ct. 411, 414, 66 L.Ed.2d 308 (1980) (distinguishing between res judicata and collateral estoppel).

Consistent with the Restatement (Second) of Judgments and United States Supreme Court jurisprudence, for purposes of this chapter, we will speak of "res judicata" as a separate doctrine from "collateral estoppel," and will use the term "res judicata" interchangeably with "claim preclusion," and "collateral estoppel" interchangeably with "issue preclusion."

2. Kremer v. Chemical Construction Corp., 456 U.S. 461, 102 S.Ct. 1883, 72 L.Ed.2d 262 (1982).

3. Federated Department Stores, Inc. v. Moitie, 452 U.S. 394, 398, 101 S.Ct. 2424, 2427, 69 L.Ed.2d 103 (1981); Nevada v. United States, 463 U.S. 110, 129–30, 103 S.Ct. 2906, 2918–19, 77 L.Ed.2d 509 (1983); Interoceanica Corp. v. Sound Pilots, Inc., 107 F.3d 86, 90 (2d Cir.1997); Roy v. Jasper Corp., 666 F.2d 714, 717 (1st Cir.1981).

4. Kremer, 456 U.S. at 466 n.6, 102 S.Ct. at 1889 n.6. *See also* Montana v. United States, 440 U.S. 147, 153, 99 S.Ct. 970, 973, 59 L.Ed.2d 210 (1979); Allen, 449 U.S. at 414–16, 101 S.Ct. at 693–94.

The elements and application of claim and issue preclusion are discussed in more detail in §§ 12.6, 12.7, *infra.*

5. *E.g.,* Shaw v. Hahn, 56 F.3d 1128, 1131 (9th Cir.), *cert. denied,* 516 U.S. 964, 116 S.Ct. 418, 133 L.Ed.2d 336 (1995).

applying collateral estoppel against parties that were not in a position of adversity in the earlier litigation regarding the issue as to which collateral estoppel is currently invoked and generally determine whether the former co-parties had a full and fair opportunity to litigate the issues under consideration.[6]

The purpose of both claim and issue preclusion is to relieve parties of the cost and vexation of multiple lawsuits, conserve judicial resources, and, by preventing inconsistent decisions, encourage reliance on adjudication.[7]

Library References:

West's Key No. Digests, Judgment ⚌540, 634.
Wright, Miller & Cooper, Federal Practice and Procedure: Civil 2d §§ 4408, 4417.

§ 12.3 What Law Applies

Generally, the rendering court does not determine the later preclusive effect of its own judgments; rather, the second court confronted with a previously litigated claim or issue must decide for itself what matters were settled in the first case.[1] The applicability of res judicata or collateral estoppel is primarily a question of law for the court, although it may necessitate resolution of factual questions.[2] Whether state or

6. See, e.g., Steen v. John Hancock Mutual Life Insurance Co., 106 F.3d 904, 911 (9th Cir.1997); Alumax Mill Prods. v. Congress Financial Corp., 912 F.2d 996, 1012 (8th Cir.1990); Clark–Cowlitz Joint Operating Agency v. Federal Energy Regulation Commission, 826 F.2d 1074, 1080 (D.C.Cir. 1987), cert. denied, 485 U.S. 913, 108 S.Ct. 1088, 99 L.Ed.2d 247 (1988); Franklin Stainless Corp. v. Marlo Transport Corp., 748 F.2d 865, 867 (4th Cir.1984); see also Restatement (Second) of Judgments § 38 (1982) ("Parties who are not adversaries to each other under the pleadings in an action involving them and a third party are bound by and entitled to the benefits of issue preclusion with respect to issues they actually litigate fully and fairly as adversaries to each other and which are essential to the judgment rendered.").

7. Kremer, 456 U.S. at 466 n.6, 102 S.Ct. at 1889 n.6; Allen, 449 U.S. at 94, 101 S.Ct. at 414.

§ 12.3

1. Guillermo v. Brennan, 657 F.Supp. 216, 220 (N.D.Ill.1987) (opinion of judge in first court was not controlling as to preclusive effect of her ruling); Teamsters Local 282 Pension Trust Fund v. Angelos, 762 F.2d 522, 525 (7th Cir.1985); EDO Corp. v. Beech Aircraft Corp., 755 F.Supp. 985, 987 (D.Kan.1991); National Union Fire Insur-

ance Co. of Pittsburgh, Pennsylvania v. Continental Illinois Corp., 673 F.Supp. 267, 270 n. 7 (N.D.Ill.1987).

There may be certain circumstances in which the rendering court has power to narrow the ordinary rules of claim preclusion. See 18 Charles Alan Wright, Arthur R. Miller & Edward H. Cooper, Federal Practice and Procedure § 4413 (2d ed. 1981); see also infra § 12.4(c), discussing the rendering court's power to issue preliminary or permanent injunctions against future litigation.

2. E.B. Harper & Co., Inc. v. Nortek, Inc., 104 F.3d 913, 922 (7th Cir.1997); Baker Electric Coop., Inc. v. Chaske, 28 F.3d 1466, 1475 (8th Cir.1994); Harbeson v. Parke Davis, Inc., 746 F.2d 517, 520 (9th Cir.1984); Coates v. Kelley, 957 F.Supp. 1080, 1082 (E.D.Ark.1997); United States ex rel. The Yankton Sioux Tribe v. Gambler's Supply, Inc., 925 F.Supp. 658, 662–63 (D.S.D.1996).

Some courts treat "privity" for purposes of applying res judicata or collateral estoppel as a question of fact, see, e.g., Vulcan, Inc. v. Fordees Corp., 658 F.2d 1106, 1109 (6th Cir.1981), cert. denied, 456 U.S. 906, 102 S.Ct. 1752, 72 L.Ed.2d 162 (1982), while others have held that it is a conclusion of law, see First Options of Chicago,

federal law applies to determine the preclusive effect of a prior judgment depends initially upon the origin of the prior judgment.

(a) Prior Judgments from State Courts

The Full Faith and Credit Clause of the United States Constitution[3] and its enabling statute, 28 U.S.C.A § 1738,[4] require that "every court within the United States" give full faith and credit to "[s]uch state Acts, records, and judicial proceedings or copies thereof, so authenticated." It is well-established law that this statute requires a federal court to give a state court judgment the same preclusive effect as would be given that judgment under the law of the state in which the judgment was rendered.[5] Section 1738 embodies concerns of comity and federalism that allow the states to determine, subject to the requirements of the statute and the Due Process Clause, the preclusive effect of judgments rendered in their own courts.[6] In instances where state law is unsettled regarding the preclusionary effect of a prior judgment potentially applicable to a case, the practitioner should give careful consideration to forum selection between state and federal court, when available.

Inc. v. Kaplan, 913 F.Supp. 377, 384 (E.D.Pa.1996).

3. This provision reads: "Full Faith and Credit shall be given in each State to the public Acts, Records, and judicial Proceedings of every other State. And the Congress may by general Laws prescribe the Manner in which such Acts, Records and Proceedings shall be proved, and the Effect thereof." U.S. Const., art. IV, § 1.

4. This statute provides:

The Acts of the legislature of any State, Territory, or Possession of the United States, or copies thereof, shall be authenticated by affixing the seal of such State, Territory or Possession thereto.

The records and judicial proceedings of any court of any such State, Territory or Possession, or copies thereof, shall be proved or admitted in other courts within the United States and its Territories and Possessions by the attestation of the clerk and seal of the court annexed, if a seal exists, together with a certificate of a judge of the court that the said attestation is in proper form.

Such Acts, records and judicial proceedings or copies thereof, so authenticated, shall have the same full faith and credit in every court within the United States and its Territories and Possessions as

they have by law or usage in the courts of such State, Territory or Possession from which they are taken.

28 U.S.C.A. § 1738 (West 1994), by its terms, only applies to state court judgments.

5. "It has long been established that § 1738 does not allow federal courts to employ their own rules of res judicata in determining the effect of state judgments. Rather, it goes beyond the common law and commands a federal court to accept the rules chosen by the State from which the judgment is taken." Kremer v. Chemical Construction Corp., 456 U.S. 461, 481–82, 102 S.Ct. 1883, 1897–98, 72 L.Ed.2d 262 (1982); see also Allen v. McCurry, 449 U.S. 90, 96, 101 S.Ct. 411, 415, 66 L.Ed.2d 308 (1980).

See also Patin v. Allied Signal, Inc., 77 F.3d 782, 789 (5th Cir.1996); International Evangelical Church v. Church of the Soldiers, 54 F.3d 587, 590 (9th Cir.1995); Davis v. United States Steel Supply, 688 F.2d 166, 170 (3d Cir.1982), cert. denied, 460 U.S. 1014, 103 S.Ct. 1256, 75 L.Ed.2d 484 (1983); Hwang v. Dunkin' Donuts, Inc., 840 F.Supp. 193, 197–98 (N.D.N.Y.), aff'd, 28 F.3d 103 (2d Cir.1994).

6. Kremer, 456 U.S. at 478, 481–83, 102 S.Ct. at 1896, 1897–99. See infra § 12.9.

(b) Prior Judgments from Federal Courts

In general, "[f]ederal law determines the effects under the rules of res judicata of a judgment of a federal court."[7] There may be exceptions to this rule, depending upon the substance of the prior federal judgment and the jurisdictional basis of the two federal actions. There are four situations in which these rules emerge:

- In a current federal question case, where the court is asked to determine the preclusive effect of a prior federal judgment that determined a federal question;

- In a current federal question case, where the court is asked to determine the preclusive effect of a prior federal judgment that determined an issue of state law;

- In a current diversity case, where the court is asked to determine the preclusive effect of a prior federal judgment that determined a federal question; and

- In a current diversity case, where the court is asked to determine the preclusive effect of a prior federal judgment that determined an issue of state law.

The cases are consistent in determining the applicable law in federal question cases; however, courts vary significantly in their approaches when diversity of citizenship is the basis for jurisdiction.

(1) Current Federal Question Case

In a federal question case, federal law governs the preclusive effects of a prior federal court judgment that determined a federal question,[8]

---

7. Restatement (Second) of Judgments § 87. The rules governing claim and issue preclusion in federal court find their source in federal common law. Allen, 449 U.S. at 96, 101 S.Ct. at 415; United States v. Manning Coal Corp., 977 F.2d 117, 121 (4th Cir.1992); Premier Electrical Construction Co. v. National Electrical Contractors Assoc., 814 F.2d 358 (7th Cir.1987) (because the rules are developed as a matter of common law, they should yield to the contrary command of formal rules of procedure or statute). Although federal common law generally is consistent on the doctrines of claim and issue preclusion, the court in *Continental Airlines, Inc. v. American Airlines, Inc.,* 824 F.Supp. 689 (S.D.Tex.1993), found that there was a conflict between two federal circuits on the precise issue before it, and the court, sitting in Texas, followed the federal common law of the Fifth Circuit:

This Court is absolutely bound to follow the pronouncements of the Fifth Circuit and the Supreme Court as to what is, and what is not, federal law. Where neither has spoken, the Court may determine federal law for itself, and in so doing, it may be guided by the nonbinding decisions of other courts. Where the Fifth Circuit has spoken, however, this court is not free to deviate from that court's mandate, even if this entails giving an effect to an order of another federal court that is different from the effect that would be given to that order by the courts of another circuit.

Id. at 710–11.

8. Blonder–Tongue Laboratories, Inc. v. University of Illinois Foundation, 402 U.S. 313, 324 n. 12, 91 S.Ct. 1434, 1440 n. 12, 28 L.Ed.2d 788 (1971); Gonzalez v. Banco Cent. Corp., 27 F.3d 751, 755 (1st Cir.1994); Hudson v. Hedge, 27 F.3d 274, 276 (7th Cir.1994); Zip Dee, Inc. v. Dometic Corp., 886 F.Supp. 1427, 1431 (N.D.Ill.1995); Branning v. Morgan Guaranty Trust Co. of New York, 739 F.Supp. 1056, 1062 n. 4 (D.S.C.1990).

while state law governs the preclusive effect of a prior federal court judgment that decided an issue of state law.[9]

Recently, the United States Supreme Court put to rest any suspicion that the preclusive effect of a prior federal court judgment could serve as the jurisdictional foundation to support removal, premised on presence of a federal question, of a state court action involving the same issues.[10]

(2) Current Diversity Case

In a diversity case, some courts apply federal law to determine the preclusive effect of a prior federal judgment that determined a federal question,[11] while others apply the law of the forum state.[12]

The circuits are split as to what law a federal court sitting in diversity is to apply to a prior federal judgment that was rendered in an action also founded upon diversity jurisdiction. The Second, Fourth, Fifth, Sixth, Seventh, and Eleventh Circuits hold that federal common law applies in this circumstance.[13] The Third, Eighth, Ninth, and D.C. Circuits hold that the law of the forum state governs.[14] The Tenth Circuit has rendered somewhat inconsistent results, finding in some

---

9. Oklahoma Packing Co. v. Oklahoma Gas & Electric Co., 309 U.S. 4, 60 S.Ct. 215, 84 L.Ed. 537 (1940); Pennsylvania v. Brown, 260 F.Supp. 323 (E.D.Pa.1966); Maryland Use of Gliedman v. Capital Airlines, Inc., 267 F.Supp. 298 (D.Md.1967).

10. See Rivet v. Regions Bank of Louisiana, ___ U.S. ___, 118 S.Ct. 921, 139 L.Ed.2d 912 (1998). The court distinguished the case before it from one where a plaintiff attempts to evade federal removal jurisdiction by disguising the federal quintessence of a claim in state law lexicon.

11. Jaramillo v. Burkhart, 999 F.2d 1241, 1245 (8th Cir.1993); Johnson v. SCA Disposal Services, Inc., 931 F.2d 970, 974 (1st Cir.1991); Precision Air Parts, Inc. v. Avco Corp., 736 F.2d 1499, 1503 (11th Cir. 1984), cert. denied, 469 U.S. 1191, 105 S.Ct. 966, 83 L.Ed.2d 970 (1985); Sanders v. Venture Stores, Inc., 899 F.Supp. 387, 388 (N.D.Ill.1995), aff'd, 82 F.3d 420 (7th Cir. 1996).

12. Costantini v. Trans World Airlines, 681 F.2d 1199, 1201 (9th Cir.), cert. denied, 459 U.S. 1087, 103 S.Ct. 570, 74 L.Ed.2d 932 (1982); Bryant v. American National Bank & Trust Co. of Chicago, 407 F.Supp. 360 (N.D.Ill.1976) (federal court sitting in diversity looks to state law to determine preclusive effect of order of federal bankruptcy court).

13. RecoverEdge L.P. v. Pentecost, 44 F.3d 1284, 1290 (5th Cir.1995); Havoco of America, Ltd. v. Freeman, Atkins & Coleman, Ltd., 58 F.3d 303, 307 & n. 7 (7th Cir.1995); Gelb v. Royal Globe Insurance Co., 798 F.2d 38, 42 n. 3 (2d Cir.1986), cert. denied, 480 U.S. 948, 107 S.Ct. 1608, 94 L.Ed.2d 794 (1987); Harnett v. Billman, 800 F.2d 1308, 1312–13 (4th Cir.1986), cert. denied, 480 U.S. 932, 107 S.Ct. 1571, 94 L.Ed.2d 763 (1987); Precision Air Parts, Inc. v. Avco Corp., 736 F.2d 1499, 1502 (11th Cir.1984), cert. denied, 469 U.S. 1191, 105 S.Ct. 966, 83 L.Ed.2d 970 (1985); Silcox v. United Trucking Service, Inc., 687 F.2d 848, 852 (6th Cir.1982); B.N.E., Swedbank, S.A. v. Banker, 791 F.Supp. 1002, 1005–06 (S.D.N.Y.1992); Prudential Securities Inc. v. Arain, 930 F.Supp. 151, 156 (S.D.N.Y.1996); In re Air Crash at Detroit Metropolitan Airport, 776 F.Supp. 316, 319–23 (E.D.Mich.1991); Palmer Exploration, Inc. v. Dennis, 759 F.Supp. 332, 334 n. 1 (S.D.Miss.1991).

Cf. Kachler v. Taylor, 849 F.Supp. 1503 (M.D.Ala.1994) (finding conflict within the circuit, but holding that federal law governs preclusive effect of prior judgment in diversity action in subsequent diversity action).

14. Bates v. Union Oil Co. of California, 944 F.2d 647, 649 (9th Cir.1991); Austin v. Super Valu Stores, Inc., 31 F.3d 615, 617 (8th Cir.1994); Donegal Steel Foundry Co. v. Accurate Products Co., 516 F.2d 583, 587 & n. 5 (3d Cir.1975); Answering Service, Inc. v. Egan, 728 F.2d 1500, 1505–06 (D.C.Cir.1984).

instances that state law will apply in diversity cases,[15] and in other instances, applying federal preclusion law except for those aspects which are clearly substantive.[16]

The distinction may not always be as acute as it initially seems because many states apply federal law to determine the preclusive effect of a prior federal judgment.[17] Nevertheless, this dichotomy of approach may make forum selection crucial to the final outcome of issues of preclusion and, therefore, forum selection must be carefully analyzed.

Library References:

West's Key No. Digests, Federal Courts ⬤⚊420.
Wright, Miller & Cooper, Federal Practice and Procedure: Civil 2d §§ 4411–4413, 4419, 4420.

§ 12.4 Manner and Timing of Raising Issue

(a) Affirmative Defenses and Waiver

Under FRCP 8(c), res judicata and collateral estoppel must be pled as affirmative defenses, and failure to so plead may result in a waiver.[1] Generally, this rule is strictly applied, but courts have recognized several exceptions. Amendments are often allowed under FRCP 15.[2] Courts also

15. Federal Insurance Co. v. Gates Learjet Corp., 823 F.2d 383 (10th Cir.1987).

16. Lowell Staats Mining Co. v. Philadelphia Electric Co., 878 F.2d 1271 (10th Cir.1989) ("as a general rule, we apply federal law to the res judicata issue in successive diversity actions, but federal law will incorporate state law when the issue is more distinctly substantive, as with the concept of 'privity' ").

17. See, e.g., Intermedics, Inc. v. Ventritex, Inc., 804 F.Supp. 35, 39 (N.D.Cal.1992) (applying California law to find that federal law applied to the preclusive effect of a prior federal judgment); Alcantara v. Boeing Co., 41 Wash. App. 675, 678, 705 P.2d 1222, 1225 (1985); Levy v. Cohen, 19 Cal.3d 165, 172–73, 137 Cal.Rptr. 162, 167, 561 P.2d 252, 257, cert. denied, 434 U.S. 833, 98 S.Ct. 119, 54 L.Ed.2d 94 (1977).

§ 12.4

1. Garry v. Geils, 82 F.3d 1362, 1367 n. 8 (7th Cir.1996); Old Republic Insurance Co. v. Chuhak & Tecson, 84 F.3d 998, 1000–01 (7th Cir.1996); Russell v. SunAmerica Securities, Inc., 962 F.2d 1169, 1172 (5th Cir.1992); Clements v. Airport Authority of Washoe County, 69 F.3d 321, 328–29 (9th Cir.1995); Totalplan Corp. of America v. Colborne, 14 F.3d 824, 832 (2d Cir.1994).

The failure of a defendant to object to the prosecution of dual proceedings while both proceedings are pending also constitutes waiver. Clements, 69 F.3d at 328–29; Bradley v. Pittsburgh Board of Education, 913 F.2d 1064, 1072–73 (3d Cir.1990); Calderon Rosado v. General Electric, 805 F.2d 1085 (1st Cir.1986); Restatement (Second) of Judgments § (1)(a) (1982).

A party may validly waive the defenses of res judicata and collateral estoppel by stipulation. Sinicropi v. Milone, 915 F.2d 66 (2d Cir.1990).

2. See, e.g., Stoebner v. Parry, Murray, Ward & Moxley, 91 F.3d 1091, 1093 (8th Cir.1996) (construing summary judgment motion as motion to amend answer to add estoppel defense and granting motion); North Georgia Electric Membership Corp. v. City of Calhoun, 989 F.2d 429, 431–32 (11th Cir.1993); Atiya v. Salt Lake County, 988 F.2d 1013, 1017–18 (10th Cir.1993); Phyfer v. San Gabriel Development Corp., 884 F.2d 235, 241 (5th Cir.1989).

Cf. Banc One Capital Partners Corp. v. Kneipper, 67 F.3d 1187, 1199–1200 (5th Cir.1995) (seller of securities and law firm which represented seller were not entitled to amend their answer to assert defense of res judicata and, thus, seller and law firm waived res judicata defense in securities

may raise the issue on their own motion, where all relevant information is before the court and considerations of judicial economy, comity, and continuity in the law warrant judicial invocation of the doctrine.[3] Moreover, a party opposing the defense of res judicata or collateral estoppel may be held to have "waived the waiver" by not bringing the issue of waiver before a lower court.[4]

In *Blonder-Tongue Laboratories v. University of Illinois Foundation*,[5] the Supreme Court observed: "The purpose of [requiring res judicata and collateral estoppel to be pled] is to give the opposing party notice of the plea of estoppel and the chance to argue, if he can, why the imposition of an estoppel would be inappropriate." Accordingly, courts may allow late assertions of claim and issue preclusion, either through amendments of answers, motions to dismiss[6] or for summary judgment,[7]

fraud and malpractice action, where seller and law firm did not attempt to amend their answer until ten months after deadline, and seller and law firm could have discovered and asserted res judicata defense earlier).

3. Columbia Steel Fabricators, Inc. v. Ahlstrom Recovery, 44 F.3d 800, 802–03 (9th Cir.1995) (res judicata doctrine preserves scarce resources, as well as protecting litigants from multiple lawsuits, so courts have independent interest in raising it, even if party does not); Bechtold v. City of Rosemount, 104 F.3d 1062, 1068 (8th Cir.1997); Carbonell v. Louisiana Department of Health & Human Resources, 772 F.2d 185, 189 (5th Cir.1985); Kratville v. Runyon, 90 F.3d 195, 198 (7th Cir.1996); Salahuddin v. Jones, 992 F.2d 447, 448–49 (2d Cir.), *cert. denied*, 510 U.S. 902, 114 S.Ct. 278, 126 L.Ed.2d 229 (1993); United States v. Real Property Located in El Dorado County at 6380 Little Canyon Road, 59 F.3d 974, 979 n. 4 (9th Cir.1995).

Cf. Warnock v. Pecos County, Texas, 116 F.3d 776 (5th Cir.1997)(district court should not have raised issue of res judicata sua sponte where it did not have the relevant records before it and was not confronted with "the demands of comity, continuity in the law, and essential justice"); State of Nevada Employees Assoc., Inc. v. Keating, 903 F.2d 1223, 1225–26 (9th Cir.) (res judicata must generally be affirmatively pleaded or waived, and district court should not have raised res judicata sua sponte without allowing parties to submit post-trial briefs on res judicata), *cert. denied*, 498 U.S. 999, 111 S.Ct. 558, 112 L.Ed.2d 565 (1990).

4. Kratville, 90 F.3d at 198; United States v. Baker, 40 F.3d 154, 160 (7th Cir.

1994), *cert. denied*, 514 U.S. 1028, 115 S.Ct. 1383, 131 L.Ed.2d 237 (1995).

Courts may alternatively hold that issue of res judicata or collateral estoppel was tried with the "implied consent" of the parties under FRCP 15(b). *See* United States v. Shanbaum, 10 F.3d 305, 312–13 (5th Cir.1994).

5. 402 U.S. 313, 350, 91 S.Ct. 1434, 1453, 28 L.Ed.2d 788 (1971).

6. Meagher v. Board of Trustees of Pension Plan, Cement and Concrete Workers, 921 F.Supp. 161, 165 (S.D.N.Y.1995) ("when all relevant facts are shown by the court's own records, of which the court takes notice, the defense may be upheld on a Rule 12(b)(6) motion without requiring an answer"), *aff'd*, 79 F.3d 256 (2d Cir.1996); Weldon v. United States, 845 F.Supp. 72, 81 (N.D.N.Y.1994), *aff'd*, 70 F.3d 1 (2d Cir. 1995); American Furniture Co., Inc. v. International Accommodations Supply, 721 F.2d 478, 482 (5th Cir.1981); Thomas v. Consolidation Coal Co., 380 F.2d 69 (4th Cir.1967); Williams v. Murdoch, 330 F.2d 745 (3d Cir.1964); Suckow Borax Mines Consolidated v. Borax Consolidation, Ltd., 185 F.2d 196 (9th Cir.1950); Lambert v. Conrad, 536 F.2d 1183, 1186–87 (7th Cir. 1976).

7. Oldham v. Pritchett, 599 F.2d 274, 276 (8th Cir.1979); In re Multidistrict Litig. Concerning Air Crash Disaster Near Brunswick, Georgia, 879 F.Supp. 1196, 1200 (N.D.Ga.1994) (considering res judicata raised for the first time in summary judgment motion because the filing was timely and gave plaintiffs sufficient time to respond, nor did plaintiffs raise issue of waiver in responsive brief); Johnston v. So, 859

where the opposing party was on notice of the assertion and has suffered little or no prejudice.[8]

An early tactical decision for the defendant is whether to raise the issue in a motion under FRCP 12(b)(6). Generally, collateral estoppel will not lend itself to this type of motion, because the court will probably need to review salient portions of the record from the earlier case before being able to determine whether the elements of collateral estoppel have been met. Frequently, however, a motion to dismiss will be an appropriate vehicle for raising the defense of res judicata, since courts will often take judicial notice of the judgment and essential pleadings in the earlier case, especially when the earlier judgment was rendered in the same district.[9]

(b) Burden of Proof

Whatever the method by which the question is raised, the burden of establishing preclusion is placed on the party claiming it.[10] In some circumstances, it may be possible to rely on judicial notice of earlier proceedings,[11] but, ordinarily, sufficient proof must be introduced to

F.Supp. 1197, 1201 (N.D.Ind.1994); Kachler v. Taylor, 849 F.Supp. 1503, 1515 (M.D.Ala. 1994); Conte v. Justice, 802 F.Supp. 997, 1002 (S.D.N.Y.1992) (if unavailable at time of answer, claim or issue preclusion may be raised at summary judgment stage), *aff'd in part, rev'd in part*, 996 F.2d 1398 (2d Cir. 1993); Carino v. Town of Deerfield, 750 F.Supp. 1156, 1162 n. 9 (N.D.N.Y.1990), *aff'd*, 940 F.2d 649 (2d Cir.1991).

8. Stoebner v. Parry, Murray, Ward & Moxley, 91 F.3d 1091, 1093–94 (8th Cir. 1996); United States v. Shanbaum, 10 F.3d 305, 312 (5th Cir.1994) (if party fails to raise issue or claim preclusion in pleading but nevertheless raises it at "pragmatically sufficient time" and opposing party was not prejudiced, court may hold that defense was not waived).

9. *See infra* note 10.

10. Dowling v. United States, 493 U.S. 342, 350, 110 S.Ct. 668, 673, 107 L.Ed.2d 708 (1990) (defendant seeking to foreclose relitigation of issue in second case has burden of demonstrating that issue sought to be foreclosed was actually decided in first proceeding); Offshore Sportswear, Inc. v. Vuarnet International, B.V., 114 F.3d 848, 850 (9th Cir.1997) (party asserting issue preclusion has burden of showing with clarity and certainty what was determined by prior judgment); In re Sokol, 113 F.3d 303, 306 (2d Cir.1997) (under New York law, party seeking benefit of collateral estoppel

has burden of demonstrating identity of issues and necessity of their having been decided, and party opposing its use has responsive burden of establishing absence of full and fair opportunity to litigate issue in prior action); E.B. Harper & Co., Inc. v. Nortek, Inc., 104 F.3d 913, 922 (7th Cir. 1997); Berger Transfer & Storage v. Central States, Southeast and Southwest Areas Pension Fund, 85 F.3d 1374, 1377 (8th Cir. 1996); Connors v. Tanoma Mining Co., Inc., 953 F.2d 682, 684 (D.C.Cir.1992).

Cf. Richardson v. Miller, 101 F.3d 665 (11th Cir.1996) (showing of lack of counsel at first action makes out prima facie case of lack of full and fair opportunity to litigate issues decided in first action); Ressler v. White, 968 F.2d 1478, 1480 (2d Cir.1992) (district court acted within its discretion in holding that prior judgment did not collaterally estop underwriters from denying their liability to loss payee because loss payee did not establish that parties were identical, loss payee clauses in respective policies differed significantly, and decision rendered on prior judgment seemed contrary to trend of New York law).

11. Mack v. South Bay Beer Distributors, Inc., 798 F.2d 1279, 1282 (9th Cir. 1986); Mandarino v. Pollard, 718 F.2d 845, 849 (7th Cir.1983); Forest Hills Early Learning Center, Inc. v. Lukhard, 487 F.Supp. 1378 (E.D.Va.1980).

show litigation of the claim or issue involved.[12] Reasonable doubt is resolved against an asserted preclusion.[13]

(c) Injunctions

Instead of undertaking the burden of persuading a second court to honor the preclusive effects of a prior judgment, a party may seek protection through an injunction from the initial court against later litigation.[14] Any such injunction must satisfy the general requirements of injunctions, and injunctions against state court proceedings must further satisfy special concerns of comity and federalism.[15] Injunctions may, however, be subject to stringent requirements reserved only for instances of vexatious, multiplicitous, and harassing litigation of the same claim that has not been deterred effectively by ordinary methods of defensive pleading.[16]

12. Jones v. Gann, 703 F.2d 513, 515 (11th Cir.1983); Allen v. Zurich Insurance Co., 667 F.2d 1162, 1166 (4th Cir.1982); Hernandez v. City of Los Angeles, 624 F.2d 935, 937 (9th Cir.1980); United States v. Nicolet, Inc., 712 F.Supp. 1193, 1200 (E.D.Pa.1989); Wetherill v. University of Chicago, 548 F.Supp. 66, 68–69 (N.D.Ill. 1982).

Cf. Guillen v. The National Grange, 955 F.Supp. 144 (D.D.C.1997) (record was completely devoid of any information from which district court could determine that res judicata barred action, and, thus, motion to dismiss based on res judicata was denied; although employer alleged employee filed identical action in Superior Court for the District of Columbia, provided case number and indicated that case was ultimately dismissed with prejudice, employer gave no details of nature of prior lawsuit and did not submit copies of order dismissing complaint).

13. Dici v. Commonwealth of Pennsylvania, 91 F.3d 542, 551 (3d Cir.1996); Welch v. Johnson, 907 F.2d 714, 719–20 (7th Cir.1990); Villas of Lake Jackson, Ltd. v. Leon County, 906 F.Supp. 1509, 1523 (N.D.Fla.1995), *aff'd*, 121 F.3d 610 (11th Cir.1997).

14. Sassower v. American Bar Assoc., 33 F.3d 733, 734–36 (7th Cir.1994); *In re March*, 988 F.2d 498, 499–500 (4th Cir. 1993); Daewoo Electonics Corp. of America, Inc. v. Western Auto Supply Co., 975 F.2d 474, 478–79 (8th Cir.1992); Moy v. United States, 906 F.2d 467 (9th Cir.1990); *In re Corrugated Container Antitrust Litig.*; Three J Farms, Inc. v. Plaintiffs' Steering Committee, 659 F.2d 1332 (5th Cir.1981); Harper Plastics, Inc. v. Amoco Chemicals Corp., 657 F.2d 939, 947 (7th Cir.1981); Morgan Consultants v. American Tel. & Tel. Co., 546 F.Supp. 844, 848–49 (S.D.N.Y. 1982).

15. Merle Norman Cosmetics, Inc. v. Victa, 936 F.2d 466, 468 (9th Cir.1991); First Alabama Bank v. Parsons Steel, Inc., 825 F.2d 1475, 1482–86 (11th Cir.1987) (it was within discretion of district court to enjoin further conduct of state proceedings after state court had rejected defense of claim preclusion based on prior federal judgment, had decided the case on the merits, but had not yet disposed of motions for judgment n.o.v. or for a new trial), *cert. denied*, 484 U.S. 1060, 108 S.Ct. 1015, 98 L.Ed.2d 980 (1988).

Cf. Regional Properties, Inc. v. Financial & Real Estate Consulting Co., 678 F.2d 552, 565–66 (5th Cir.1982) (principles of comity, equity, and federalism require that there be a strong and unequivocal showing to overcome the disinclination to meddle in state court proceedings; in this case, the state proceeding would not directly interfere with the federal judgment, since at most it would be barred by failure to advance claim as counterclaim in federal action).

16. *See* Daewoo Electronics Corp., 975 F.2d at 478–79; De Long v. Hennessey, 912 F.2d 1144 (9th Cir.) (before filing a "vexatious litigant order" enjoining plaintiff from filing any future actions without leave of court, plaintiff must be afforded a hearing, a record must be made that shows number or abusive character of past actions, must

(d) Rule 11 Sanctions

In addition to dismissal or limitation of the issues open in a second suit, sanctions may be imposed under FRCP 11 or FRAP 38 for pursuing repetitive litigation of matters clearly barred by res judicata.[17]

Library References:

West's Key No. Digests, Judgment ☞948(1), 956(1).
Wright, Miller & Cooper, Federal Practice and Procedure: Civil 2d §§ 1285, 4423.

§ 12.5 Mode of Proof

(a) Certified Copies of Judgments

Section 1738 of Title 28 of the United States Code dictates the preclusive effect to be given to state court judgments in federal courts.[1] That section also dictates the manner of proving state court judgments in order to obtain the benefit of that preclusive effect.

> The records and judicial proceedings of any court of any such State, Territory or Possession, or copies thereof, shall be proved or admitted in other courts within the United States and its Territories and Possessions by the attestation of the clerk and seal of the court annexed, if a seal exists, together with a certificate of a judge of the court that the said attestation is in proper form.[2]

No hard and fast rule regarding the requisites of authentication under Section 1738 can be given, because the practices of different courts in different states vary. Thus, the practitioner should be certain to consult local counsel and court personnel in the jurisdiction rendering the judgment in order to comply with the requirements of Section 1738. Failure to comply with those requirements could result in a federal court refusing to consider the preclusive effect of a judgment that otherwise fits all of the criteria for application of a preclusive doctrine.[3]

be substantive findings as to the frivolous or harassing nature of the actions, and "these orders must be narrowly tailored to closely fit the specific vice encountered"), *cert. denied*, 498 U.S. 1001, 111 S.Ct. 562, 112 L.Ed.2d 569 (1990); Safir v. United States Lines, Inc., 792 F.2d 19, 23–25 (2d Cir.1986); Castro v. United States, 775 F.2d 399, 408–10 (1st Cir.1985).

17. Westcott Construction Corp. v. Firemen's Fund, 996 F.2d 14, 17 (1st Cir.1993) (double costs were awarded against appellant for taking an appeal on a claim so clearly foreclosed by preclusion effects of state judgment); Paganucci v. City of New York, 993 F.2d 310, 312–13 (2d Cir.) (the "audacious attempt to revisit" issues resolved in earlier proceedings "is patently

frivolous. Even a cursory review of the doctrine of res judicata would have so indicated."), *cert. denied*, 510 U.S. 826, 114 S.Ct. 90, 126 L.Ed.2d 58 (1993); In re Lane, 991 F.2d 105, 108 (4th Cir.1993); King v. Hoover Group, Inc., 958 F.2d 219, 223 (8th Cir.1992); Foret v. Southern Farm Bureau Life Insurance Co., 918 F.2d 534, 539–40 (5th Cir.1990); West Coast Theater Corp. v. City of Portland, 897 F.2d 1519, 1527 (9th Cir.1990).

§ 12.5

1. *See infra* § 12.9.

2. 28 U.S.C.A. § 1738 (West 1994).

3. *See, e.g.,* Horwitz v. State Board of Medical Examiners, 822 F.2d 1508, 1512

(b) Self–Authenticating Documents

Especially when collateral estoppel is asserted, documents other than judgments from earlier litigation may be needed for presentation to the court. For example, in order to demonstrate that resolution of a particular issue was, in fact, necessary to an earlier judgment, opinions rendered by the first court may be pertinent. Depositions or other forms of discovery may also be used to demonstrate the scope of earlier litigation, as well as transcripts of hearings or trials.

All of these documents should be considered in terms of the requisites necessary to their admission in the pending litigation when they are obtained in the course of investigation or discovery. In particular, the terms of Federal Rule of Evidence 902 should be considered. That Rule provides that "[e]xtrinsic evidence of authenticity as a condition of admissibility is not required" with regard to certain classes of documents. By planning ahead and satisfying the requirements of this Rule, the proper foundation for admission of many of the types of proof necessary to demonstrate the application of a preclusive doctrine can be easily obtained.

Depositions that are certified by a notary may qualify as self-authenticated.[4] Interrogatory answers or answers to requests for admission may, depending upon local practice in the court where the earlier proceeding was adjudicated, qualify as "acknowledged documents."[5] Otherwise, if discovery is or can be filed with the court, discovery may be authenticated by obtaining certified copies.[6] In all circumstances, counsel should take care that proof of the judgment is properly demonstrated as a predicate to affording the judgment preclusive effect.

(c) Judicial Notice

While the better practice is always to obtain certified copies or other forms of judgments and other documents necessary to proving the preclusive effect of a prior proceeding, counsel may be able to fall back on judicial notice as a means of gaining admission of necessary facts. For example, in the event the judgment in an earlier litigation is contended to have preclusive effect and that judgment was rendered in the same district court in which the current action is now pending, the presiding judge may take judicial notice of that judgment without the need for

(10th Cir.)(refusing to consider preclusive effect of state court judgment for, *inter alia*, lack of certified record of judgment in record), *cert. denied*, 484 U.S. 964, 108 S.Ct. 453, 98 L.Ed.2d 394 (1987).

4. *See* Fed.R.Evid. 902(8). This Rule eliminates the necessity to authenticate extrinsically: "Documents accompanied by a certificate of acknowledgment executed in the manner provided by law by a notary public or other officer authorized by law to take acknowledgments." Local discovery practice regarding the variety of certification necessary for a deposition transcript should be consulted to insure compliance with the Rule.

5. *See id.*

6. *See* Fed.R.Evid. 902(4).

certified copies being presented.[7]

§ 12.6 Res Judicata: Elements and Application

The elements of the doctrine of res judicata in the federal courts have been recited often and are well-established.[1] Succinctly stated, the doctrine provides that, "A final judgment on the merits of an action precludes the parties or their privies from relitigating issues that were or could have been raised in that action."[2] Res judicata is an extremely powerful doctrine,[3] and it goes to the very heart of the purpose of the federal judicial system.[4]

---

7. Fed.R.Evid. 201 controls judicial notice. "A judicially noticed fact must be one not subject to reasonable dispute in that it is either (1) generally known within the territorial jurisdiction of the trial court or (2) capable of accurate and ready determination by resort to sources whose accuracy cannot reasonably be questioned."

§ 12.6

1. In fact, in 1981, then Justice Rehnquist was prompted to state: "There is little to be added to the doctrine of res judicata as developed in the case law of this Court." Federated Department Stores, Inc. v. Moitie, 452 U.S. 394, 398, 101 S.Ct. 2424, 2427, 69 L.Ed.2d 103 (1981)

2. *Id.* at 398, 101 S.Ct. at 2427.

Simply put, the doctrine of res judicata provides that when a final judgment has been entered on the merits of a case, "[i]t is a finality as to the claim or demand in controversy, concluding the parties and those in privity with them, not only as to every matter which was offered and received to sustain or defeat the claim or demand, but as to any other admissible matter which might have been offered for that purpose." Cromwell v. Sac County, 94 U.S. (4 Otto) 351, 352, 24 L.Ed. 195 (1877). The final "judgment puts an end to the cause of action, which cannot again be brought into litigation between the parties upon any ground whatever." Commissioner v. Sunnen, 333 U.S. 591, 597, 68 S.Ct. 715, 719, 92 L.Ed. 898 (1948). See Chicot County Drainage District v. Baxter State Bank, 308 U.S. 371, 378, 60 S.Ct. 317, 320, 84 L.Ed. 329 (1940).

Nevada v. United States, 463 U.S. 110, 129–30, 103 S.Ct. 2906, 2918–19, 77 L.Ed.2d 509 (1983); Allen v. McCurry, 449 U.S. 90, 94, 101 S.Ct. 411, 414, 66 L.Ed.2d 308 (1980);

Parklane Hosiery Company, Inc. v. Shore, 439 U.S. 322, 327 n. 5, 99 S.Ct. 645, 649 n. 5, 58 L.Ed.2d 552 (1979).

3. "[R]es judicata renders white that which is black; and straight that which is crooked. *Facti excurvo rectum, ex albo nigrum.*" Jeter v. Hewitt, 63 U.S. (22 How.) 352, 364, 16 L.Ed. 345 (1860). The Court has also counselled caution in the application of the doctrine due to its far-reaching effect.

Because res judicata may govern grounds and defenses not previously litigated, however, it blockades unexplored paths that may lead to truth. For the sake of repose, res judicata shields the fraud and the cheat as well as the honest person. It is therefore to be invoked only after careful consideration.

Brown v. Felsen, 442 U.S. 127, 132, 99 S.Ct. 2205, 2210, 60 L.Ed.2d 767 (1979).

4. But what we said with respect to this doctrine more than 80 years ago is still true today; it ensures "the very object for which civil courts have been established, which is to secure the peace and repose of society by the settlement of matters capable of judicial determination. Its enforcement is essential to the maintenance of social order; for, the aid of judicial tribunals would not be invoked for the vindication of rights of person and property, if ... conclusiveness did not attend the judgments of such tribunals." Nevada, 463 U.S. at 129, 103 S.Ct. at 2918 (quoting Southern Pacific R. Co. v. United States, 168 U.S. 1, 49, 18 S.Ct. 18, 27, 42 L.Ed. 355 (1897). *See* Jeter, 63 U.S. (22 How.) at 364 ("[T]he maintenance of public order, the repose of society, and the quiet of families, require that what has been definitively determined by competent tribunals shall be accepted as irrefragable legal truth."); Medina v. Immigration and Natu-

Virtually all formulations of the federal version of res judicata incorporate three core analytical elements.[5]

To prevail on a defense of *res judicata* requires a defendant to establish: (1) a final judgment on the merits in the prior action, (2) the claims raised in the subsequent action were identical to those decided in the prior action, and (3) the prior action involved the same parties or their privies.[6]

These elements will be examined individually.[7]

(a) Final Judgment on the Merits

Only final judgments on the merits support application of res judicata to a subsequent claim.[8] Under the Federal Rules of Civil Procedure, "[a] judgment is effective only . . . when entered as provided

ralization Service, 1 F.3d 312, 313 (5th Cir. 1993)("Few legal doctrines are more intrinsic or necessary to our system than res judicata.").

5. The formulations stated by the federal courts for the elements of res judicata vary in both the number of elements and the precise elements, themselves. Three elements appears to be the most common number. For example, in *Gonzalez v. Banco Central Corp.*, 27 F.3d 751, 755 (1st Cir. 1994), the court identified the elements as follows: "Accordingly, the elements of res judicata are (1) a final judgment on the merits in an earlier suit, (2) sufficient identicality between the causes of action asserted in the earlier and later suits, and (3) sufficient identicality between the parties in the two suits." Nevertheless, the three elements are not static. "Res judicata bars a party from asserting a claim in court if three requirements are met: (1) the prior judgment was rendered by a court of competent jurisdiction; (2) the decision was a final judgment on the merits; and (3) the same cause of action and the same parties or their privies were involved in both cases." United States v. Brekke, 97 F.3d 1043, 1047 (8th Cir.1996). Furthermore, four element formulations are not uncommon. "Application of res judicata is proper only if the following four requirements are met: (1) the parties must be identical in the two suits; (2) the prior judgment must have been rendered by a court of competent jurisdiction; (3) there must be a final judgment on the merits; and (4) the same cause of action must be involved in both cases." Russell v. SunAmerica Securities, Inc., 962 F.2d 1169, 1172 (5th Cir.1992). *Accord, e.g.,*

Travelers Insurance Company v. St. Jude Hospital of Kenner, Louisiana, Inc., 37 F.3d 193, 195 (5th Cir.1994). *See In re* Varat Enterprises, Inc., 81 F.3d 1310, 1315 (4th Cir.1996)(noting other cases stating same three criteria for application of res judicata as four elements).

6. Hoxworth v. Blinder, 74 F.3d 205, 208 (10th Cir.1996). *Accord, e.g.,* People Who Care v. Rockford Board of Education, 68 F.3d 172, 177 (7th Cir.1995); Brzostowski v. Laidlaw Waste Systems, Inc., 49 F.3d 337, 338 (7th Cir.1995); Gonzalez v. Banco Central Corp., 27 F.3d 751, 755 (1st Cir. 1994); Satsky v. Paramount Communications, Inc., 7 F.3d 1464, 1467 (10th Cir. 1993).

7. Even when counsel determines that a judgment in a case on appeal should qualify as "final" for preclusion purposes, tactical considerations should be taken into account before pressing the preclusive effect before the appellate process has been completed. A court could simply defer ruling on the issue involved until the appeal in the first case is completed. Then, counsel loses control over an aspect of the litigation and extraneous factors that affect the earlier case and its appeal become injected into the present case. Additionally, by urging application of preclusionary effect before the appellate process is complete, counsel may highlight application of a preclusionary doctrine for use against his own client in the event of an adverse appellate result.

8. *See, e.g.,* Federated Department Stores, Inc. v. Moitie, 452 U.S. 394, 398, 101 S.Ct. 2424, 2427, 69 L.Ed.2d 103 (1981).

in Rule 79(a),"[9] which requires notation on the "civil docket" of the substance and date of entry of the judgment.[10] The formality of formal entry is not necessarily required for res judicata to apply to an adjudication[11] as a "final judgment."[12] In order to qualify as final, appellate remedies need not have yet been exhausted.[13] As with most aspects of preclusion doctrine, cases must be examined individually.

Some general principles can, however, be stated. Not surprisingly, a court ordered dismissal with prejudice of an action constitutes a final judgment on the merits sufficient to implicate res judicata in the event a second suit is brought.[14] A voluntary dismissal with prejudice also constitutes a final adjudication on the merits.[15] On the other hand, a stipulation of dismissal without prejudice is not a final adjudication on the merits.[16]

A stipulated judgment is a final judgment on the merits.[17] Neither a dismissal for lack of subject matter jurisdiction[18] nor for lack of personal jurisdiction[19] will operate to preclude a later suit on the same claim between the same parties. Dismissal of an in forma pauperis action under 28 U.S.C.A. § 1915A(b)(1) is not a final adjudication on the merits

9. FRCP 58.

10. FRCP 79(a).

11. An adjudication implies judicial activity. In that vein, it should be noted that arbitration awards that are not subject to court review are not generally given res judicata effect under federal law. E.g., McDonald v. City of West Branch, 466 U.S. 284, 104 S.Ct. 1799, 80 L.Ed.2d 302 (1984) (unreviewed award from arbitration of police officer's claim under collective bargaining agreement has no claim preclusive affect on later action under 42 U.S.C.A. § 1983); Barrentine v. Arkansas–Best Freight System, Inc., 450 U.S. 728, 101 S.Ct. 1437, 67 L.Ed.2d 641 (1981)(wage claim under Fair Labor Standards Act not precluded by unreviewed arbitration award); Alexander v. Gardner–Denver Co., 415 U.S. 36, 94 S.Ct. 1011, 39 L.Ed.2d 147 (1974)(subsequent Title VII action not precluded by unreviewed arbitration award). As to the preclusive effect given to determinations of administrative bodies, see infra § 12.13.

12. E.g., Golden v. Barenborg, 53 F.3d 866, 868–69 (7th Cir.1995)(holding that unfiled stipulation of dismissal contained in release was effective as a final judgment for res judicata purposes). See Amcast Industrial Corp. v. Detrex Corp., 45 F.3d 155, 158 (7th Cir.1995)(discussing whether finality in terms appealability under 28 U.S.C.A. § 1291 is required for res judicata finality).

13. E.g., Amcast Industrial Corp., 45 F.3d at 158 ("But we shall see that a final judgment is res judicata even if it is still appealable."). Even the end of the appellate process regarding a judicial ruling does not necessarily signify "finality" for res judicata purposes. Id. ("the denial of certiorari is a red herring. It marks the end of the appellate process and so, if the judgment from which certiorari was sought were itself a final judgment . . . , it establishes finality in a strong sense").

14. E.g., In re Tomlin, 105 F.3d 933, 936–37 (4th Cir.1997).

15. NBN Broadcasting v. Sheridan Broadcasting Networks, Inc., 105 F.3d 72, 78 (2d Cir.1997); Chase Manhattan Bank v. Celotex Corp., 56 F.3d 343, 345 (2d Cir. 1995).

16. Cooter & Gell v. Hartmarx Corp., 496 U.S. 384, 396, 110 S.Ct. 2447, 2456, 110 L.Ed.2d 359 (1990).

17. E.g., In re Baker, 74 F.3d 906, 910 (9th Cir.1996), cert. denied sub nom. Baker v. Internal Revenue Service, ___ U.S. ___, 116 S.Ct. 1683, 134 L.Ed.2d 784 (1996).

18. E.g., Northeast Erectors Ass'n of the BTEA v. Secretary of Labor, 62 F.3d 37, 39 (1st Cir.1995); Robinson v. Overseas Military Sales Corp., 21 F.3d 502, 507 n. 4 (2d Cir.1994).

19. E.g., Robinson, 21 F.3d at 507 n.4.

that will receive res judicata recognition.[20]

Dismissal of an action on the grounds of the statute of limitations may qualify for res judicata treatment as a final judgment on the merits,[21] but generally does not.[22]

(b) Identical Claims

Because res judicata precludes assertion of entire claims, it is necessary to compare the two actions involved to determine whether there is identity of claims or causes of action.[23] Generally, federal law involves an analysis of the transactions underlying the cause of action or claim.[24] Some courts expressly adopt the "transactional approach" to analyze identity between claims,[25] which "recognizes that a valid and final judgment in an action will extinguish subsequent claims 'with respect to all or any part of the transaction, or series of connected transactions, out of which the action arose.' "[26]

---

20. Denton v. Hernandez, 504 U.S. 25, 34, 112 S.Ct. 1728, 1734, 118 L.Ed.2d 340 (1992).

21. See Reinke v. Boden, 45 F.3d 166, 169–70 (7th Cir.), cert. denied, 516 U.S. 817, 116 S.Ct. 74, 133 L.Ed.2d 34 (1995)(discussing differences in treatment, under state law, given statutes of limitations depending upon whether the statute destroys the cause of action or simply precludes institution of an action in the particular forum).

22. Martel v. Stafford, 992 F.2d 1244, 1245–46 (1st Cir.1993).

23. "To determine the applicability of res judicata to the facts before us, we must decide first if the 'cause of action' which the Government now seeks to assert is the 'same cause of action' that was asserted in [the first action]." Nevada v. United States, 463 U.S. 110, 130, 103 S.Ct. 2906, 2918, 77 L.Ed.2d 509 (1983). The cases alternatively and interchangeably use claims and causes of action when stating the unit of litigation that is being compared for purposes of application of res judicata without appearing to intend any distinction in meaning. Compare Hoxworth v. Blinder, 74 F.3d 205, 208 (10th Cir.1996)("claims raised in the subsequent action were identical to those decided in the prior action") with Brzostowski v. Laidlaw Waste Systems, Inc., 49 F.3d 337, 338 (7th Cir.1995)("identity of the cause of action between both suits"). But see Goldberg v. R.J. Longo Construction Co., Inc., 54 F.3d 243, 246 (5th Cir.1995)("Under federal law, res judicata bars all claims that were or could have been advanced in

support of the cause of action.... ")(italics added).

24. E.g., Interoceanica Corp. v. Sound Pilots, Inc., 107 F.3d 86, 90 (2d Cir.1997)("Whether or not the first judgment will have preclusive effect depends in part on whether the same transaction or connected series of transactions is at issue,.... "); Gonzalez v. Banco Central Corp., 27 F.3d 751, 755 (1st Cir.1994)("To determine whether sufficient subject matter identity exists between an earlier and a later suit, federal courts employ a transactional approach."); Agrilectric Power Partners, Ltd. v. General Electric Co., 20 F.3d 663, 665 (5th Cir.1994)("We have adopted a transactional test for determining whether two complaints involve the same cause of action."); Eubanks v. Federal Deposit Ins. Corp., 977 F.2d 166, 171 (5th Cir.1992)("To determine whether the same claim is involved in two actions, we apply the transactional test of the Restatement (Second) of Torts § 24."). See, e.g., In re International Nutronics, Inc., 28 F.3d 965, 970 (9th Cir. 1994)(One part of four-part test is "whether the two suits arise out of the same transactional nucleus of facts."); Clark v. Bear Stearns & Co., Inc., 966 F.2d 1318, 1320 (9th Cir.1992).

25. See, e.g., Interoceanica Corp., 107 F.3d at 90; Gonzalez, 27 F.3d at 755; Agrilectric Power Partners, 20 F.3d at 665; Eubanks, 977 F.2d at 171.

26. Gonzalez, 27 F.3d at 755 (quoting Manego v. Orleans Bd. of Trade, 773 F.2d 1, 5 (1st Cir.1985), cert. denied, 475 U.S. 1084,

Under this [transactional] approach, a cause of action is defined as a set of facts which can be characterized as a single transaction or a series of related transactions. The cause of action, therefore, is a transaction that is identified by a common nucleus of operative facts. Although a set of facts may give rise to multiple counts based on different legal theories, if the facts form a common nucleus that is identifiable as a transaction or series of transactions, then those facts represent one cause of action.[27]

The forms of relief sought or legal theories advanced are not of great relevance in this inquiry.[28] Some court eschew reliance on detailed factual circumstances, such as comparison of the evidence necessary to proving each claim,[29] while other courts do factor these matters into the determination of identity between claims.[30] Even those courts adhering formally to the transactional test, however, refine the analysis by supplying aids for determining whether the same transaction is involved.

This Court has enumerated several factors which are useful in determining whether a party has advanced claims in multiple litigations which derive from the same nucleus of operative facts. [Citation omitted.] These factors include: 1) whether the facts are related in time, space, origin or motivation; 2) whether the facts form a convenient trial unit; and 3) whether treating the facts as a unit conforms to the parties' expectations. [Citation omitted.] Additionally, when defining the contours of the common nucleus of operative

---

106 S.Ct. 1466, 89 L.Ed.2d 722 (1986) and Restatement (Second) of Judgments § 24).

27. Apparel Art International v. Amertex Enterprises, 48 F.3d 576, 583–84 (1st Cir.1995). Accord, e.g., Gonzalez, 27 F.3d at 755–56; Agrilectric Power Partners, Ltd., 20 F.3d at 664. See, e.g., Brzostowski, 49 F.3d at 338–39 ("A claim has 'identity' with a previously litigated matter if it emerges from the same 'core of operative facts' as that earlier action."); Facchiano Construction Co., Inc. v. U.S. Department of Labor, 987 F.2d 206, 212 (3d Cir.1993)(One part of four-part test is "whether the material facts alleged are the same.").

28. "Under this approach, the critical issue is not the relief requested or the theory asserted but whether the plaintiff bases the two actions on the same nucleus of operative facts." If the factual scenario of the two actions parallel, the same cause of action is involved in both. The substantive theories advanced, forms of relief requested, types of rights asserted, and variations in evidence needed do not inform this inquiry. Agrilectric Power Partners, Ltd., 20 F.3d at 665 (note omitted). See Shaver v. F.W. Woolworth Co., 840 F.2d 1361, 1365 (7th

Cir.), cert. denied, 488 U.S. 856, 109 S.Ct. 145, 102 L.Ed.2d 117 (1988)("Although this single group of facts may conceivably give rise to different theories of recovery, under the federal definition a single cause of action remains."). But see Facchiano Construction Co., Inc., 987 F.2d at 212 ("The test for whether there is a single cause of action is: (1) whether the acts and the demand for relief are the same[,] (2) whether the theory of recovery is the same, (3) whether the witnesses and documents necessary at trial are the same, and (4) whether the material facts alleged are the same.").

29. E.g., Agrilectric Power Partners, Ltd., 20 F.3d at 665 ("variations in evidence needed do not inform this inquiry").

30. "Whether or not the first judgment will have preclusive effect depends in part on whether the same transaction or connected series of transactions is at issue, [and] whether the same evidence is needed to support both claims." Interoceanica Corp., 107 F.3d at 90. See Facchiano Construction Co., Inc., 987 F.2d at 212 (expressly mandating consideration of whether witnesses and documents necessary at trial are identical).

facts, it is often helpful to consider the nature of the injury for which the litigant seeks to recover.[31]

Merely stating these additional factors does not particularly illuminate the mechanics of the inquiry, but the Second Circuit has provided a useful discussion of the process of determining identity of claims for res judicata purposes.

> With respect to the determination of whether a second suit is barred by res judicata, the fact that both suits involved essentially the same course of wrongful conduct is not decisive; nor is it dispositive that the two proceedings involved the same parties, similar or overlapping facts, and similar legal issues. A first judgment will generally have preclusive effect only where the transaction or connected series of transactions at issue in both suits is the same, that is where the same evidence is needed to support both claims, and where the facts essential to the second were present in the first.

> If the second litigation involved different transactions, and especially subsequent transactions, there generally is no claim preclusion. For example, when a contract was to be performed over a period of time and one party has sued for a breach but has not repudiated the contract, res judicata will preclude the party's subsequent suit for any claim of breach that had occurred prior to the first breach-of-contract suit, but will not preclude a subsequent suit for a breach that had not occurred when the first suit was brought.[32]

As the Second Circuit's exposition implies, the determination of identity must, essentially, be accomplished on a case-by-case basis without resort to hard-and-fast rules of decision.

Certain exceptions to the rule of identity of claims should be kept in mind. Res judicata will not be applied to preclude assertion of a claim arising subsequent to the assertion of an initial claim, even though the same circumstances give rise to both claims.[33] Res judicata is not applicable to nondischargeability proceedings in bankruptcy.[34] A second suit directed at wrongful conduct that might have been prevented by an

31. Apparel Art International, 48 F.3d at 584. *Accord, e.g.,* Interoceanica Corp., 107 F.3d at 90; Gonzalez, 27 F.3d at 756. This amplification of the transactional approach is derived from § 24 of the Restatement (Second) of Judgments.

32. Securities and Exchange Commission v. First Jersey Securities, Inc., 101 F.3d 1450, 1463–64 (2d Cir.1996)(citations omitted and internal quotations omitted).

33. Lawlor v. National Screen Service Corp., 349 U.S. 322, 328, 75 S.Ct. 865, 869, 99 L.Ed. 1122 (1955)(prior judgment "cannot be given the effect of extinguishing claims which do not even then exist and which could not possibly have been sued upon in the previous case"). *See* Lovilia

Coal Co. v. Harvey, 109 F.3d 445, 450 (8th Cir.1997)(Black Lung claimant not precluded from bringing subsequent suit based on alleged change in physical condition, because "health of a human being is not susceptible to once-in-a-lifetime adjudication."); NBN Broadcasting, Inc. v. Sheridan Broadcasting Networks, Inc., 105 F.3d 72, 78 (2d Cir.1997)(party has no duty to supplement an action to state claims arising after initial filing, so "later suit based on the subsequent conduct is not barred by *res judicata*").

34. Brown v. Felsen, 442 U.S. 127, 99 S.Ct. 2205, 60 L.Ed.2d 767 (1979); *In re* Pancake, 106 F.3d 1242, 1244 (5th Cir. 1997).

injunction available, but not obtained, in a first action will not precluded by res judicata.[35] Further, the preclusive effect of declaratory judgments is limited to those matters actually declared, and additional actions to obtain coercive or damages relief are not necessarily barred.[36]

(c) Identical Parties or Their Privies

In order to be bound by the claim preclusive effect of a prior adjudication, a party must have either been a participant in the prior adjudication or have been so intimately involved in that adjudication that it is fair and equitable to require that party to accept the burden of the earlier judgment.[37]

Determining whether the parties to two actions are identical often presents little more than a mechanical task. In certain instances, the issue may be confused at first inspection. For example, there may be instances where a party is present in the first action in a capacity different from that in which he participates in the second action where res judicata is sought to be applied. In that circumstance, there must be an examination of the role played by the party, rather than a simple mechanical observation of the names of the parties. The more difficult situations, which call for the exercise of judgment, require identification of those parties whose interests are sufficiently closely aligned with one of the parties to the prior litigation so that application of res judicata is appropriate. In the lexicon of res judicata, that quality of sufficiently close alignment of interests is referred to as "privity."

The cases frequently state that res judicata will bind those in privity with parties to an earlier action or will bind the parties and their privies.[38] Privity is, however, only a descriptive concept[39] and not a test

---

35. Lawlor, 349 U.S. at 328–29, 75 S.Ct. at 869; Russo v. Baxter Healthcare Corp., 919 F.Supp. 565, 569 (D.R.I.1996).

36. A plaintiff who wins a declaratory judgment may go on to seek further relief, even in an action on the same claim which prompted the action for a declaratory judgment. This further relief may include damages which had accrued at the time the declaratory relief was sought; it is irrelevant that the further relief could have been requested initially.

Restatement (Second) of Judgments § 33 (1995). *See, e.g.,* Harborside Refrigerated Serv. v. Vogel, 959 F.2d 368, 372 (2d Cir. 1992); Umhey v. County of Orange, 957 F.Supp. 525, 528 (S.D.N.Y.1997)("[T]here is an exception to res judicata for declaratory judgment actions recognized both by New York and federal courts.").

37. "The concept of privity is protean, and federal courts are no longer bound by inflexible definitions. [Citation omitted.]

The fundamental requirement, courts have consistently held, is fairness." Coates v. Kelley, 957 F.Supp. 1080, 1086 (E.D.Ark. 1997). At some point, due process of law, rather than prudential concerns of judicial decision making, circumscribes the reach of res judicata in order that litigants are afforded a fair opportunity to be heard. *See, e.g.,* Richard v. Jefferson County, 517 U.S. 793, 116 S.Ct. 1761, 135 L.Ed.2d 76 (1996)(application of Fourteenth Amendment due process to state court invocation of res judicata).

38. *E.g.,* Satsky v. Paramount Communications, Inc., 7 F.3d 1464, 1468 (10th Cir.1993)("Res judicata is applicable only to parties to the first suit or their privies."). *See, e.g.,* cases cited in note 36 *supra.*

39. The Fifth Circuit recently described it well: "As the case law and scholars recognize, 'privity' is not a requirement we can satisfy through inquiry; rather the existence of 'privity' is the inquiry satisfied."

for application of res judicata.[40]

Courts have enunciated general rules of application regarding privity.

> First, a nonparty who has succeeded to a party's interest in property is bound by any prior judgments against the party ..... Second, a nonparty who controlled the original suit will be bound by the resulting judgment ..... Third, federal courts will bind a nonparty whose interests were represented adequately by a party in the original suit.[41]

Reviewing the above-quoted passage even cursorily, however, reveals that it provides little more than broad-based generalities amounting to a finding of "privity." In reality, privity eludes categorical description,[42] and no definition of it is possible that will easily resolve the myriad fact patterns that can be presented.[43] Privity can only be determined by the district court through a fact-intensive examination of the circumstances of each individual case.[44] From the appellate perspective, courts do not necessarily agree regarding whether privity is a factual or legal issue,[45]

Russell v. SunAmerica Securities, Inc., 962 F.2d 1169, 1174 (5th Cir.1992).

40. "Privity states no reason for including or excluding one from the estoppel of a judgment. It is merely a word used to say that the relationship between the one who is a party on the record and another is close enough to include that other within the res judicata." Bruszewski v. United States, 181 F.2d 419, 423 (3d Cir.)(Goodrich, J., concurring), *cert. denied*, 340 U.S. 865, 71 S.Ct. 87, 95 L.Ed. 632 (1950).

41. Becherer v. Merrill Lynch Pierce Fenner & Smith, Inc., 43 F.3d 1054, 1069–070 (6th Cir.1995)(quoting Southwest Airlines Co. v. Texas Int'l Airlines, Inc., 546 F.2d 84, 95 (5th Cir.), *cert. denied*, 434 U.S. 832, 98 S.Ct. 117, 54 L.Ed.2d 93 (1977).

42. "Privity is an elusive concept." *In re* L & S Industries, Incorporated, 989 F.2d 929, 932 (7th Cir.1993). *See* People Who Care v. Rockford Board of Education, 68 F.3d 172, 177 (7th Cir.1995).

43. " 'There is no definition of "privity" which can be automatically applied to all cases involving the doctrines of res judicata and collateral estoppel,' Lowell Staats, 878 F.2d at 1274–75, since 'privity depends upon the circumstances,' 1B Moore's Federal Practice ¶ 0.411[1] at III–215 (1993)." Satsky, 7 F.3d at 1469–69.

44. The inquiry into the existence of privity is of "fact-intensive nature." *In re* L

& S Industries, Incorporated, 989 F.2d at 932.

> Privity may exist for the purpose of determining one legal question but not another depending on the circumstances and legal doctrines at issue. Whether there is privity between a party against whom claim preclusion is asserted and a party to prior litigation is a functional inquiry in which the formalities of legal relationships provide clues but not solutions. Some courts have thus held that the inquiry is a factual one.

Chase Manhattan Bank, N.A. v. Celotex Corporation, 56 F.3d 343, 346 (2d Cir.1995). As one legal treatise has described the evolution of the privity inquiry:

> As the preclusive effect of judgments has been expanded to include nonparties in more and more situations, however, it has come to be recognized that the privity label simply expresses a conclusion that preclusion is proper. Modern decisions search directly for circumstances that justify preclusion.

18 Charles Alan Wright, Arthur R. Miller & Edward H. Cooper, Federal Practice and Procedure: Jurisdiction § 4449, at 418–19 (2d ed. 1981).

45. *Compare* Vulcan, Inc. v. Fordees Corp., 658 F.2d 1106, 1109 (6th Cir.1981), *cert. denied*, 456 U.S. 906, 102 S.Ct. 1752,

and the answer may well be that it can be either depending upon the circumstances.[46]

The federal courts have considered any number of different circumstances in determining whether privity exists.[47] For example, the relationship of landlord and tenant does not necessarily represent a relationship sufficiently close in interest to justify imposing the burdens of an earlier judgment.[48]

Although privity represents the central analytical tool for determining that interests of parties are sufficiently closely aligned to justify application of res judicata,[49] there is another construct for judging the relationship of parties that has been introduced into federal jurisprudence—virtual representation.

Res judicata may bar nonparties to earlier litigation not only when there was a formal arrangement for representation in, or actual control of, the earlier action but also when the interests involved in the prior litigation are virtually identical to those in later litigation. See Allan D. Vestal, Res Judicata/Preclusion V–125–26 (1969). As Professor Vestal has written, "the key seems to be that [the] interests [of the nonparty] have been adequately represented by others who have litigated the matter and have lost ..." Id. at 128. Federal courts have sometimes called this "virtual representation."[50]

72 L.Ed.2d 162 (1982)(concluding privity is a fact issue) *with* Southwest Airlines Co. v. Texas Int'l Airlines, Inc., 546 F.2d 84, 95 (5th Cir.), *cert. denied*, 434 U.S. 832, 98 S.Ct. 117, 54 L.Ed.2d 93 (1977)(privity represents a legal conclusion).

46. *In re* L & S Industries, Incorporated, 989 F.2d at 932–33, presents an insightful commentary on the issue of privity and its characterization as a factual or legal question.

In other words, the legal authority of a party to act on behalf of a nonparty in previous litigation may not be easily characterized as factual or legal. For example, a question of whether a nonparty effectively agreed to be represented in previous litigation—such as by implied consent or by conduct—would involve the sort of factual inquiry by a district court that we would review for an abuse of discretion. [Citation omitted.] On the other hand, a question of whether representation of a nonparty falls within some preexisting relationship—as defined by statute, for example—would call for the kind of legal conclusion that we would review *de novo*. [Citation omitted.] The question of privity is therefore particularly amenable to a sliding-scale standard of review.

47. Because the inquiry is fact-intensive, an exhaustive catalog of rulings regarding privity is well beyond the scope and intent of this work. The intention is merely to give the reader an overview of the decisions regarding privity.

48. Casa Marie, Inc. v. Superior Court of Puerto Rico, 988 F.2d 252, 265 n. 13 (1st Cir.1993) ("As a general rule, holders of concurrent interests in property, unlike successors in interest, are not considered in privity for *res judicata* purposes.").

49. "The most familiar mechanism for extending res judicata to nonparties without savaging important constitutional rights is the concept of privity—a concept that furnishes a serviceable framework for an exception to the rule that res judicata only bars relitigation of claims by persons who were parties to the original litigation." Gonzalez v. Banco Central Corp., 27 F.3d 751, 757 (1st Cir.1994).

50. Chase Manhattan Bank, N.A. v. Celotex Corporation, 56 F.3d 343, 345 (2d Cir. 1995). The terminology of adequate representation has also been used to describe this concept. Becherer v. Merrill Lynch Pierce Fenner & Smith, Inc., 43 F.3d 1054, 1070 (6th Cir.1995).

Virtual representation enjoyed favor relatively recently among several federal courts as a mechanism for expanding the scope of the preclusive net cast by res judicata. The theory was originally nearly exclusively premised upon the consonance of interest between the party against whom the preclusion was sought and a party to the prior litigation.[51] Today, courts have recognized that greater limitations are necessary on application of virtual representation theory,[52] but it is quite difficult to state any cogent formula for its application.[53]

Library References:

West's Key No. Digests, Judgment ⟜562, 564, 585, 667, 678.
Wright, Miller & Cooper, Federal Practice and Procedure: Civil 2d §§ 1225, 2735, 4401–4405.

§ 12.7 Collateral Estoppel

(a) General Requirements

Res judicata and collateral estoppel, while related and often confused, are distinct doctrines that perform different, yet related, functions.[1] "Under collateral estoppel, once an issue is actually and necessarily determined by a court of competent jurisdiction, that determination is conclusive in subsequent suits based on a different cause of action involving a party to the prior litigation."[2] The requirements for preclud-

---

51. E.g., Aerojet–General Corp. v. Askew, 511 F.2d 710, 719 (5th Cir.), cert. denied, 423 U.S. 908, 96 S.Ct. 210, 46 L.Ed.2d 137 (1975); In re Medomak Canning Co., 922 F.2d 895, 901 (1st Cir.1990). Gonzalez, 27 F.3d at 760.

52. "The upshot is that, today, while identity of interests remains a necessary condition for triggering virtual representation, it is not alone a sufficient condition. More is required to bring the theory to bear." Gonzalez, 27 F.3d at 760 (note omitted). See Griffin v. Burns, 570 F.2d 1065, 1071 (1st Cir.1978).

53.

To say that a litigant advocating virtual representation, and seeking thereby to preclude a nonparty's suit, must show more than an identity of interests is to state the nature of the problem, not to solve it. Many of the ensuing questions— questions like "how much more?" and "what comprises 'more'?"—seem to have no categorical answers. Not surprisingly, then, the cases in which courts have dealt with the doctrine, taken as an array, are resistant to doctrinal rationalization in the form of a single limiting principle of the "one size fits all" variety. There is no

black-letter rule. [Citations omitted.] In the end, virtual representation is best understood as an equitable theory rather than as a crisp rule with sharp corners and clear factual predicates, see 18 Wright & Miller, supra, § 4457 at 502, such that a party's status as a virtual representative must be determined on a case-by-case basis, see Bonilla Romero, 836 F.2d at 43.

See Gonzalez, 27 F.3d at 761.

§ 12.7

1. Under the doctrine of res judicata, a judgment on the merits in a prior suit bars a second suit involving the same parties or their privies based on the same cause of action. Under the doctrine of collateral estoppel, on the other hand, the second action is upon a different cause of action and the judgment in the prior suit precludes relitigation of issues actually litigated and necessary to the outcome of the first action.

Parklane Hosiery Co., Inc. v. Shore, 439 U.S. 322, 326 n. 5, 99 S.Ct. 645, 649 n. 5, 58 L.Ed.2d 552 (1979).

2. Montana v. United States, 440 U.S. 147, 153, 99 S.Ct. 970, 973, 59 L.Ed.2d 210

---

ing relitigation of an issue through application of the doctrine of collateral estoppel in the federal courts are generally identified[3] as follows:

1.   The current issue against which the preclusive effect of collateral estoppel is to be invoked must be identical to the issue presented in the previous litigation;[4]

2.   The issue must have actually been litigated in the prior action;[5]

3.   Adjudication of the issue must have been necessary to resolution of the prior action;[6] and

4.   There must have been a full and fair opportunity to litigate the issue in the previous litigation.[7]

The party seeking to assert collateral estoppel bears the burden of demonstrating that the identical issues as to which preclusion is sought were the subject of earlier litigation.[8]

In determining whether there is identity of issues, four factors for consideration have been endorsed:

(1) is there a substantial overlap between the evidence or argument to be advanced in the second proceeding and that advanced in the first?

(2) does the new evidence or argument involve the application of the same rule of law as that involved in the prior proceeding?

(1979). *See* Southern Railroad v. United States, 168 U.S. 1, 48–49, 18 S.Ct. 18, 27–28, 42 L.Ed. 355 (1897)(containing oft-quoted and eloquent statement of function and purpose of collateral estoppel by Justice Harlan).

3. Some cases identify three elements necessary to the invocation of collateral estoppel, *e.g.*, Town of North Bonneville v. Callaway, 10 F.3d 1505, 1508 (9th Cir. 1993), some identify four elements, *e.g.*, People Who Care v. Rockford Board of Education, 68 F.3d 172, 178 (7th Cir.1995), and some identify five elements, *e.g.*, Ramsay v. U.S. Immigration & Naturalization Service, 14 F.3d 206, 210 (4th Cir.1994). These variations do not, based on reviewing the holdings and rationales, appear to imply any substantial doctrinal differences.

4. *E.g.*, Hirschfeld v. Spanakos, 104 F.3d 16, 19 (2d Cir.1997)(issue must be "identical"); Trevino v. Gates, 99 F.3d 911, 923 (9th Cir.1996)(issue must be "identical"), *cert. denied*, ___ U.S. ___, 117 S.Ct. 1249, 137 L.Ed.2d 330 (1997); Burlington Northern Railroad Co. v. Hyundai Merchant Marine Co., Ltd., 63 F.3d 1227, 1232–233 (3d Cir.1995)(issue must be "same").

5. *E.g.*, Hirschfeld, 104 F.3d at 19 (issue must have been "actually litigated and decided"); Trevino, 99 F.3d at 923 (issue must have been "actually litigated"); Freeman

United Coal Mining Co. v. Office of Workers' Compensation Program, 20 F.3d 289, 293 (7th Cir.1994)(issue must have been "actually litigated").

6. *E.g.*, Hirschfeld, 104 F.3d at 19 ("issues were necessary to support a valid and final judgment on the merits"); Freeman United Coal Mining, 20 F.3d at 293 ("issue must have been essential to the final judgment"); Town of North Bonneville v. Callaway, 10 F.3d 1505, 1508 (9th Cir.1993)("issue in the prior litigation must have been a critical and necessary part of the judgment").

7. *E.g.*, Hirschfeld, 104 F.3d at 19 ("there must have been 'full and fair opportunity' for the litigation of the issues in the prior proceeding"); People Who Care, 68 F.3d at 178 ("the party against whom estoppel is invoked must be fully represented in the prior action"); Ramsay, 14 F.3d at 210; Town of North Bonneville, 10 F.3d at 1508.

8. *E.g.*, Steen v. John Hancock Mutual Life Ins. Co., 106 F.3d 904, 912 (9th Cir. 1997). *See* Levy v. Kosher Overseers Association of America, Inc., 104 F.3d 38, 41 (2d Cir.1997)(comparison of trademark cancellation and trademark infringement issues).

(3) could pretrial preparation and discovery related to the matter presented in the first action reasonably be expected to have embraced the matter sought to be presented in the second?

(4) how closely related are the claims in the two proceedings?[9]

If a different legal standard is applicable in the two actions, then the issue is necessarily not identical.[10] The inquiry the court will make regarding identity of the issues is not a perfunctory one and will consider the intricacies of the issues presented.[11]

Because collateral estoppel is narrower than res judicata, with the latter applying to preclude all issues whether raised or not, examination of the issues actually litigated is necessary to application of collateral estoppel. In practice, the question of identity of issues and actual litigation of issues sometimes overlap.[12] If there is any doubt that the issue as to which preclusion is sought was actually litigated, collateral estoppel should not be applied.[13] A court may, however, draw reasonable inferences from the issues raised in the prior litigation, where no express findings were made by the court in the earlier litigation.[14] Decisions on motion for judgment on the pleadings or summary judgment are sufficient to satisfy the actually litigated requirement.[15] A judgment based solely on consent will probably not be considered as actual litigation of the issues it encompasses,[16] unless it incorporates specific factual findings made by the court.[17] A default judgment may constitute actual litigation sufficient for collateral estoppel purposes, as may a judgment rendered upon an unopposed motion.[18]

---

9. Steen, 106 F.3d at 912 (quoting Restatement (Second) of Judgments § 27 cmt. C).

10. *E.g.,* Freeman United Coal Mining Co. v. Office of Workers' Compensation Program, 20 F.3d 289, 294 (7th Cir.1994).

11. *See, e.g.,* Levy, 104 F.3d at 41 (comparison of trademark cancellation and trademark infringement issues); Freeman United Coal, 20 F.3d at 294 (comparing issues presented in workers' compensation and Black Lung benefits claims); Stop & Shop Companies, 946 F.Supp. at 106 (different state law applicable in second action to interpretation of contract, so issues not identical). The Supreme Court has pointed out the importance of identity of the issues in that even a change in the underlying factual undergirding of a judgment may support denial of collateral estoppel effect: "It is, of course, true that changes in facts essential to a judgment will render collateral estoppel inapplicable in a subsequent action raising the same issues." Montana v. United States, 440 U.S. 147, 159, 99 S.Ct. 970, 976, 59 L.Ed.2d 210 (1979).

12. *See* People Who Care, 68 F.3d at 178.

13. Steen, 106 F.3d at 912. The *Steen* court also noted that collateral estoppel should not apply in the situation where there are potential alternative grounds for the ruling in the earlier litigation, with at least one of those alternatives differing from the issue under examination. *Id.*

14. *See* Westinghouse Electric Corporation v. General Circuit Breaker & Electric Supply, Inc., 106 F.3d 894, 901 (9th Cir. 1997).

15. Steen, 106 F.3d at 912.

16. People Who Care, 68 F.3d at 178.

However, "[c]onsent judgments, while settling the issue definitively between the parties, normally do not support an invocation of collateral estoppel." [Citation omitted.] The reason behind this general rule is that "issues underlying a consent judgment generally are neither actually litigated nor essential to the judgment."

17. *Id.* at 178 n.5.

18. *In re* Daily, 47 F.3d 365, 368 (9th Cir.1995).

A party who deliberately precludes resolution of factual issues through normal

As is the case with res judicata, collateral estoppel applies against a party to prior litigation or one in privity with that party.[19] "When two parties are so closely aligned in interest that one is the virtual representative of the other, a claim by or against one will serve to bar the same claim by or against the other."[20] Even without an existing legal relationship, a party can be found in privity and bound by a prior adjudication, if that party exercised sufficient control over the prior action.[21] Nevertheless, due process operates as a limitation upon the application of collateral estoppel against one that was not a party or in privity with a party to the prior litigation.[22]

There must also be a final determination of the issues in prior litigation in order for the preclusive effect of collateral estoppel to attach.[23] Nevertheless, the finality required for application of collateral estoppel is not necessarily finality for purposes of appeal,[24] and the finality required for application of collateral estoppel is flexible.[25]

Counsel should be aware of potential pratfalls for the unwary practitioner. Issues may be precluded in a second trial after a new trial is granted on limited issues.[26] If a trial court decision rests on alternative grounds in deciding an issue and an appellate court affirms on only one alternative, the preclusive effect is limited to the single ground on which the judgment was affirmed.[27] Conversely, a judgment rendered moot by subsequent developments pending appeal may still have preclusive effect unless vacated on motion.[28]

adjudicative procedures may be bound, in subsequent, related proceedings involving the same parties and issues, by a prior judicial determination reached without completion of the usual process of adjudication. In such a case the "actual litigation" requirement may be satisfied by substantial participation in an adversary contest in which the party is afforded a reasonable opportunity to defend himself on the merits but chooses not to do so. *Id.* (note omitted).

19. *E.g.*, Steen, 106 F.3d at 904.

20. Shaw v. Hahn, 56 F.3d 1128, 1131 (9th Cir.1995). Mere similarity of interest among parties, without more in the form of privity, is insufficient to permit application of collateral estoppel. *See* Beacon Oil Co. v. O'Leary, 71 F.3d 391, 395 (Fed.Cir.1995).

21. Montana v. United States, 440 U.S. 147, 99 S.Ct. 970, 59 L.Ed.2d 210 (1979).

22. *E.g.*, Shaw, 56 F.3d at 1131.

23. *E.g.*, Amcast Industrial Corp. v. Detrex Corp., 45 F.3d 155, 158 (7th Cir.1995)("collateral estoppel like res judicata applies only when there has been a final judgment").

24. Burlington Northern Railroad Co. v. Hyundai Merchant Marine Co., Ltd., 63 F.3d 1227, 1233 n. 8 (3d Cir.1995). *But see* Spink v. Lockheed Corp., 60 F.3d 616, 625 (9th Cir.1995) (interlocutory order not sufficient for application of collateral estoppel, because not appealable), *rev'd on other grounds*, 517 U.S. 882, 116 S.Ct. 1783, 135 L.Ed.2d 153 (1996). *See also* Biggins v. Hazen Paper Company, 111 F.3d 205, 210 (1st Cir.1997)("[C]ollateral estoppel is no longer limited to ultimate issues; necessary *intermediate* findings can now be used to preclude relitigation.")(emphasis in original).

25. Burlington Northern Railroad Co., 63 F.3d at 1233 n.8; Amcast Industrial Corp., 45 F.3d at 158 ("Yet a good deal more latitude is allowed when collateral estoppel is invoked rather than res judicata.").

26. Westinghouse Electric Corporation v. General Circuit Breaker & Electric Supply, Inc., 106 F.3d 894, 901 n. 3 (9th Cir. 1997). *See* Biggins, 111 F.3d at 209.

27. Synanon Church v. United States, 820 F.2d 421, 424–25 (D.C.Cir.1987).

28. *See In re* Otasco, Inc., 18 F.3d 841, 843–44 (10th Cir.1994).

In determining whether there has been a full and fair opportunity to litigate an issue, the court should rely on its "sense of justice and equity."[29] This aspect of the test for application of collateral estoppel involves a more demanding inquiry into the circumstances of the earlier judgment than due process and is substantial.

> Although neither judges, the parties, nor the adversary system performs perfectly in all cases, the requirement of determining whether the party against whom an estoppel is asserted had a full and fair opportunity to litigate is a most significant safeguard.[30]

While the appeal to the court's perception of fairness of the proceedings below necessarily dictates a case-by-case examination, certain indicia, such as the absence of representation by counsel in the first litigation,[31] will inform the court's decision.[32]

Classic discussions of collateral estoppel law state that collateral estoppel can apply to preclude relitigation of issues of both fact and law.[33] The Supreme Court has, however, carved out an exception to that rule so that collateral estoppel is not applied to "unmixed questions of law."[34] Although the exception is ill-defined in both application[35] and purpose,[36] it still has vitality.[37] This exception was stated in *United States v. Moser*[38] as follows:

29. Robinson v. Volkswagenwerk AG, 56 F.3d 1268, 1274 (10th Cir.1995).

30. Blonder–Tongue Laboratories, Inc. v. University of Illinois Foundation, 402 U.S. 313, 329, 91 S.Ct. 1434, 1443, 28 L.Ed.2d 788 (1971).

31. *See* Richardson v. Miller, 101 F.3d 665, 669 (11th Cir.1996).

32. *See* Robinson, 56 F.3d at 1274 ("this inquiry normally focuses on whether there were procedural limitations or a lack of incentive to fully litigate an issue in the prior proceeding"); Restatement (Second) of Judgments § 29. *See also* note 69 *infra*.

33. *See* United States v. Stauffer Chemical Company, 464 U.S. 165 170–71, 104 S.Ct. 575, 578–79, 78 L.Ed.2d 388 (1984)("As commonly explained, the doctrine of collateral estoppel can apply to preclude relitigation of both issues of law and issues of fact if those issues were conclusively determined in a prior action.").

34. *See id.* at 170–72, 104 S.Ct. at 578–79; Montana v. United States, 440 U.S. 147, 162–63, 99 S.Ct. 970, 978–79, 59 L.Ed.2d 210 (1979); United States v. Moser, 266 U.S. 236, 242, 45 S.Ct. 66, 67, 69 L.Ed. 262 (1924).

35. "While our discussion in *Montana* indicates that the exception is generally recognized, we are frank to admit uncertainty as to its application." Stauffer, 464 U.S. at 170, 104 S.Ct. at 578. "To be sure, the scope of the *Moser* exception may be difficult to delineate." Montana, 440 U.S. at 163, 99 S.Ct. at 978.

36. In *Stauffer Chemical*, the Supreme Court displayed significant doubt regarding the purpose of the exception. "Admittedly the purpose underlying the exception for 'unmixed questions of law' in successive actions on unrelated claims is far from clear." 464 U.S. at 172, 104 S.Ct. at 579. In *Montana*, 440 U.S. 147, 162–63, 99 S.Ct. 970, 978–79, 59 L.Ed.2d 210 (1979), the Court seemed far less confounded as to the raison d'etre of the exception for unmixed questions of law.

> This exception is of particular importance in constitutional adjudication. Unreflective invocation of collateral estoppel against parties with an ongoing interest in constitutional issues could freeze doctrine in areas of the law where responsiveness to changing patterns of conduct or social mores is critical.

37. Burlington Northern Railroad Co. v. Hyundai Merchant Marine Co., Ltd., 63 F.3d 1227, 1229 (3d Cir.1995)("we conclude that such an exception for questions of law continues to apply").

38. 266 U.S. 236, 45 S.Ct. 66, 69 L.Ed. 262 (1924).

Where, for example, a court in deciding a case has enunciated a rule of law, the parties in a subsequent action upon a different demand are not estopped from insisting that the law is otherwise, merely because the parties are the same in both cases. But a fact, question or right distinctly adjudged in the original action cannot be disputed in a subsequent action, even though the determination was reached upon an erroneous view or by an erroneous application of the law.[39]

The exception has been questioned,[40] but continues to receive recognition and interpretation.[41]

(b) Nonmutual Defensive Use of Collateral Estoppel

At common law, mutuality was required in order for preclusive effect to be given to a judgment.[42] The concept of mutuality required that, in order for a party to take advantage of the preclusive effect of a judgment, that party must also have been bound by that judgment.[43] The concept became entrenched in American law through decisions such as *Triplett v. Lowell*.[44] In *Triplett*, the Supreme Court held that a patentee

---

39. *Id.* at 242, 45 S.Ct. at 67 (*quoted in* Montana, 440 U.S. at 162, 99 S.Ct. at 978). In *Stauffer Chemical*, the Court stated that, "The exception seems to require a determination as to whether an 'issue of fact' or an 'issue of law' is sought to be relitigated and then a determination as to whether the 'issue of law' arises in a successive case that is so unrelated to the prior case that relitigation of the issue is warranted." 464 U.S. at 170, 104 S.Ct. at 578.

40. *See* Burlington Northern Railroad Co., 63 F.3d at 1229.

41. Recently, the Third Circuit attempted to harmonize the law regarding this nebulous exception to the rule of collateral estoppel.

While continued viability of this exception has been called into question by the Supreme Court's decision in United States v. Stauffer Chemical Co., 464 U.S. 165, 104 S.Ct. 575, 78 L.Ed.2d 388 (1984), we conclude that such an exception for questions of law continues to apply, and that it is satisfied only so long as the issue involved is one of law and either (1) the two actions involve claims that are substantially unrelated or (2) a new determination of the legal issue is warranted in order to take account of an intervening change in the applicable legal context or otherwise to avoid inequitable administration of the laws.

Burlington Northern Railroad Co., 63 F.3d at 1229.

42. *See, e.g.,* Triplett v. Lowell, 297 U.S. 638, 56 S.Ct. 645, 80 L.Ed. 949 (1936), *overruled in* Blonder–Tongue Laboratories, Inc. v. University of Illinois Foundation, 402 U.S. 313, 350, 91 S.Ct. 1434, 1453, 28 L.Ed.2d 788 (1971). In an earlier decision, the United States Supreme Court described mutuality of estoppel as "a principle of general elementary law." Bigelow v. Old Dominion Copper Co., 225 U.S. 111, 127, 32 S.Ct. 641, 642, 56 L.Ed. 1009 (1912).

43. The "judge-made" rule of mutuality required "that unless both parties (or their privies) in a second action are bound by a judgment in a previous case, neither party (nor his privy) in the second action may use the prior judgment as determinative of an issue in the second action." Blonder–Tongue, 402 U.S. at 321–22, 91 S.Ct. at 1439. As the mutuality requirement was described by Jeremy Bentham, "Nobody can take benefit by a verdict, who had not been prejudiced by it, had it gone contrary." Zdanok v. Glidden Company, 327 F.2d 944 954 (2d Cir.1964)(quoting Jeremy Bentham, Rationale of Judicial Evidence, in 7 Works of Jeremy Bentham 171 (Bowring ed. 1843).

44. 297 U.S. 638, 56 S.Ct. 645, 80 L.Ed. 949 (1936). The rule of mutuality was reflected in the original Restatement of Judgments § 93.

or its licensee was not precluded, by an adverse judgment in a prior suit to enforce the patent rendered on the basis of invalidity of the patent, from later suing another party for infringement of the same patent.[45]

In 1971, *Blonder-Tongue Laboratories, Inc. v. University of Illinois Foundation*[46] changed forever the manner in which the federal courts give preclusive effect to a prior adjudication. In *Blonder-Tongue*, the Supreme Court expressly overruled *Triplett* and abandoned the doctrine of mutuality for purposes of defensive[47] use of collateral estoppel.[48]

The *Blonder-Tongue* opinion, rather than truly breaking ground, traced the origins of the attack upon the doctrine of mutuality of estoppel. It noted Bentham's description of mutuality "as destitute of any semblance of reason, and as 'a maxim which one would suppose to have found its way from the gaming-table to the bench.' "[49] Justice Traynor's watershed denouncement of mutuality[50] in *Bernhard v. Bank of America National Trust & Savings Ass'n*[51] was also reviewed.[52]

The *Blonder-Tongue* Court, after establishing this backdrop of justi-

---

45. *Id.* The *Triplett* Court stated:

Neither reason nor authority supports the contention that an adjudication adverse to any or all the claims of a patent precludes another suit upon claims against a different defendant. While the earlier decision may by comity be given great weight in a later litigation and thus persuade the court to render a like decree, it is not res adjudicata and may not be pleaded as a defense.

Id. at 642, 56 S.Ct. at 647.

46. 402 U.S. 313, 350, 91 S.Ct. 1434, 1453, 28 L.Ed.2d 788 (1971).

47. "Defensive use [of collateral estoppel] occurs when a defendant seeks to prevent a plaintiff from asserting a claim the plaintiff has previously litigated and lost against another defendant." Parklane Hosiery Co., Inc. v. Shore, 439 U.S. 322, 326 n. 4, 99 S.Ct. 645, 649 n. 4, 58 L.Ed.2d 552 (1979). *Accord, e.g.,* Burlington Northern Railroad Co. v. Hyundai Merchant Marine Co., Ltd., 63 F.3d 1227, 1232 (3d Cir.1995).

48. According to its opinion, the *Blonder-Tongue* Court did not consider and rule upon the vitality of mutuality in federal collateral estoppel doctrine generally. *See* 402 U.S. at 327, 91 S.Ct. at 1442. Instead, the Court purported merely to "re-examine whether mutuality of estoppel is a viable rule where a patentee seeks to relitigate the validity of a patent once a federal court has declared it to be invalid." *Id.* Eight years later, the Supreme Court, while recognizing the limitations that had been expressly

placed on the *Blonder-Tongue* opinion, stated, "The 'broader question' before the Court, however, was 'whether it is any longer tenable to afford a litigant more than one full and fair resolution of the same issue.' " Parklane Hosiery Co., 439 U.S. at 327–28, 99 S.Ct. at 649–50.

49. Zdanok v. Glidden Company, 327 F.2d 944, 954 (2d Cir.1964)(quoting Bentham, *supra,* note 43. *See* Bruszewski v. United States, 181 U.S. 419, 421 (3d Cir.) *cert. denied,* 340 U.S. 865, 71 S.Ct. 87, 95 L.Ed. 632 (1950).

50. The California Supreme Court left little room for doubt when it stated: "There is no compelling reason, however, for requiring that the party asserting the plea of res judicata must have been a party, or in privity with a party to the earlier litigation." Bernhard v. Bank of America National Trust & Savings Ass'n, 19 Cal.2d 807, 122 P.2d 892, 894 (1942).

51. *Id.*

52. Blonder–Tongue, 402 U.S. at 323–24, 91 S.Ct. at 1439–40. The outline of crucial inquiries espoused by Justice Traynor was recounted with favor. "In determining the validity of a plea of res judicata three questions are pertinent: Was the issue decided in the prior adjudication identical with the one presented in the action in question? Was there a final judgment on the merits? Was the party against whom the plea is asserted a party or in privity with a party to the prior adjudication?"

fication, turned to its own examination of defensive use[53] of collateral estoppel and the role of mutuality. After noting the costs imposed by adherence to mutuality in the context of defensive collateral estoppel,[54] the Court clearly lamented the effects of the doctrine.

> Permitting repeated litigation of the same issue as long as the supply of unrelated defendants holds out reflects either the aura of the gaming table or "a lack of discipline and of disinterestedness on the part of the lower courts, hardly a worthy or wise basis for fashioning rules of procedure."[55]

Nevertheless, the Court did identify certain considerations necessary to ensure that unfettered use of nonmutual collateral estoppel would not become a tool of inequity and unfairness.[56]

In delineating the elements of defensive, nonmutual collateral estoppel, the Court first allocated to the defendant the burden of identifying "the issue in suit as the identical question finally decided against the [plaintiff] or one of his privies in the previous litigation."[57] Next, the Court offered to those against whom the plea of estoppel is invoked an opportunity to demonstrate why it should not be imposed. "[P]laintiff must be permitted to demonstrate, if he can, that he did not have a fair

---

53. The Supreme Court expressly noted it was not confronting issues of offensive use of collateral estoppel in *Blonder-Tongue. Id.* at 330, 91 S.Ct. at 1443.

54.

In any lawsuit where a defendant, because of the mutuality principle, is forced to present a complete defense on the merits to a claim which the plaintiff has fully litigated and lost in a prior action, there is an arguable misallocation of resources. To the extent the defendant in the second suit may not win by asserting, without contradiction, that the plaintiff had fully and fairly, but unsuccessfully, litigated the same claim in the prior suit, the defendant's time and money are diverted from alternative uses—productive or otherwise—to relitigation of a decided issue. And still assuming that the issue was resolved correctly in the first suit, there is reason to be concerned about the plaintiff's allocation of resources.

Id. at 329, 91 S.Ct. at 1443.

55. *Id.* at 329, 91 S.Ct. at 1443.

56. One highly important exception to the general rule permitting the use of nonmutual collateral estoppel has been created. That exception, created in *United States v. Mendoza*, 464 U.S. 154, 104 S.Ct. 568, 78 L.Ed.2d 379 (1984), eliminates application of nonmutual collateral estoppel, whether defensive or offensive, to preclude relit-

igation by the United States. This exception was imposed, because a contrary rule "would substantially thwart the development of important questions of law by freezing the first final decision rendered on a particular legal issue." *Id.* at 160, 104 S.Ct. at 572.

57. Blonder–Tongue, 402 U.S. at 332–33, 91 S.Ct. at 1444–45 (note omitted). Before enunciating the considerations pertinent to erecting a defensive collateral estoppel absent mutuality, the Court noted the role of the constitutional limitation of due process of law.

> Some litigants—those who never appeared in a prior action—may not be collaterally estopped without litigating the issue. They have never had a chance to present their evidence and arguments on the claim. Due process prohibits estopping them despite one or more existing adjudications of the identical issue which stand squarely against their position.

Id. at 329, 91 S.Ct. at 1443. These observations were made despite the fact that "the case before us involves neither due process nor 'offensive use' questions." *Id.* at 330, 91 S.Ct. at 1443. This demonstrates the sensitivity of the courts to due process concerns and alerts the practitioner to address those concerns whenever nonmutual collateral estoppel issues arise.

opportunity procedurally, substantively and evidentially to pursue his claim the first time."[58] In the final analysis, however, the trial court is invested with significant discretion in determining whether collateral estoppel will be permitted in a given set of circumstances.

But as so often is the case, no one set of facts, no one collection of words or phrases, will provide an automatic formula for proper rulings on estoppel pleas. In the end, decision will necessarily rest on the trial courts' sense of justice and equity.[59]

(c) Nonmutual Offensive Use of Collateral Estoppel

Parklane Hosiery Co., Inc. v. Shore[60] is at once both the final nail in the coffin of mutuality in federal collateral estoppel doctrine and the seminal case on offensive[61] use of collateral estoppel. In *Parklane Hosiery*, a stockholder class action was brought against Parklane Hosiery Co., Inc. and 13 of its officers, directors, and stockholders based on a false and misleading proxy statement issued in connection with a merger. While that first suit was pending, the Securities and Exchange Commission brought suit on the basis of the same proxy statement, seeking injunctive and declaratory relief. The SEC suit went to trial first and resulted in a declaratory judgment by the district court that the proxy statement was materially false and misleading, which was affirmed on appeal. The plaintiff in the class action then moved for partial summary judgment based on the ruling in the SEC action.[62]

The district court denied the partial summary judgment motion on the ground that the estoppel sought to be worked on the basis of the SEC case would deprive the defendants of their Seventh Amendment right to jury trial. The Second Circuit reversed. The Supreme Court granted certiorari[63] and specifically addressed the mutuality question presented by the case.

---

58. *Id.* at 333, 91 S.Ct. at 1445. The Court specifically noted that the determination of whether the plaintiff has previously had a full and fair opportunity to litigate its case "is of necessity not a simple matter." *Id.* Considerations of choice of forum, incentive to litigate, the failure (in rare instances) of the court to grasp technical subject matter, inability to present critical evidence, and unavailability of witnesses were identified as pertinent to the question of full and fair opportunity to litigate. *Id.* These issues are critical to any effort to block a plea of estoppel as they will provide the basis for arguing it is not "just and equitable" to sustain the plea. Additionally, issues such as higher standards or differences in allocations of burdens of proof faced by a litigant in the first action are highly pertinent to overcoming collateral estoppel in a second action. *See, e.g.,* Free-

man United Coal Mining Company v. Office of Workers' Compensation Program, 20 F.3d 289, 295 (7th Cir.1994).

59. Blonder–Tongue, 402 U.S. at 333–34, 91 S.Ct. at 1445–46.

60. 439 U.S. 322, 99 S.Ct. 645, 58 L.Ed.2d 552 (1979).

61. "In this context, offensive use of collateral estoppel occurs when the plaintiff seeks to foreclose the defendant from litigating an issue the defendant has previously litigated unsuccessfully in an action with another party." *Id.* at 326 n.4, 99 S.Ct. at 649 n.4.

62. *See id.* at 324–25, 99 S.Ct. at 648–49.

63. The constitutional question involved in the case was the Seventh Amendment right to jury trial. The Supreme Court,

Specifically, we must determine whether a litigant who was not a party to a prior judgment may nevertheless use that judgment "offensively" to prevent a defendant from relitigating issues resolved in the earlier proceeding.[64]

The *Parklane Hosiery* Court first ascribed to *Blonder-Tongue* the effect, much more far-reaching than had been its stated intention, of abandoning mutuality in defensive collateral estoppel law.[65] Then, the Court recited the traditional justifications offered for treating offensive use of collateral estoppel differently, in terms of requiring mutuality, from defensive use:

> If plaintiffs are permitted to rely upon judgments to which they are not bound, there will be incentive for potential plaintiffs to wait in the shadows until conclusion of the first litigation by another plaintiff against the potential defendant. If the first plaintiff wins, then the waiting plaintiff uses the judgment offensively through collateral estoppel. If the first plaintiff loses, the awaiting plaintiff is not bound. This potential for a "free shot" for estoppel purposes leads to more litigation, because plaintiffs are less likely to join or intervene in impending litigation.[66]

It is unfair to a defendant to allow offensive use of collateral estoppel, because:

> a. In a prior suit where the damages were fairly small, especially in the event future litigation was not foreseen, the defendant may not have defended against the judgment particularly vigorously;[67]

> b. The judgment relied upon as the basis of the estoppel may, itself, be inconsistent with earlier judgments in favor of that defendant that could not, based on due process limitations, be asserted against that defendant's later opponents;[68]

> c. There may be procedural advantages available to the defendant in the second action that were unavailable in the first that could cause a change in the resulting judgment.[69]

however, following the time-honored tradition of avoiding constitutional questions whenever possible, addressed first the issue of offensive use of collateral estoppel. *See id.* at 326, 99 S.Ct. at 649.

64. *Id.* at 326, 99 S.Ct. at 649 (note omitted).

65. *See id.* at 327–28, 99 S.Ct. at 649–50. The *Parklane Hosiery* Court also noted, with approval and without any reference to either defensive or offensive use of collateral estoppel, the indictment of mutuality delivered by Justice Traynor in *Bernhard v. Bank of America National Trust & Savings*, 19 Cal.2d 807, 122 P.2d 892, 895 (1942).

No satisfactory rationalization has been advanced for the requirement of mutuality. Just why a party who was not bound by a previous action should be precluded from asserting it as res judicata against a party who was bound by it is difficult to comprehend.

66. Parklane Hosiery, 439 U.S. at 330, 99 S.Ct. at 651.

67. *Id.*

68. *Id.*

69. *Id.* at 330–31, 99 S.Ct. at 651–52.

If for example, the defendant in the first action was forced to defend in an inconvenient forum and therefore was unable to engage in full scale discovery or call witnesses, application of offensive col-

None of these considerations, however, in the Court's opinion, presented an insurmountable obstacle to allowing the offensive use of nonmutual collateral estoppel. Instead, the Court determined that, in addition to requiring fulfillment of the usual elements of collateral estoppel, the lower courts would be charged with the responsibility of policing fairness in individual situations.

> We have concluded that the preferable approach for dealing with these problems in the federal courts is not to preclude the use of offensive collateral estoppel, but to grant trial courts broad discretion to determine when it should be applied. The general rule should be that in cases where a plaintiff could easily have joined in the earlier action or where, either for the reasons discussed above or for other reasons, the application of offensive estoppel would be unfair to a defendant, a trial judge should not allow the use of offensive collateral estoppel.[70]

In the end, the Court allowed the judgment from the SEC action to estop the defendants from contesting the materially false and misleading nature of the proxy statement in the class action.[71]

The potential adverse effects of nonmutual offensive use of collateral estoppel may require difficult decisions at early stages of the litigation. For example, when a client is confronted with several similarly situated claimants whose cases involve common issues of fact, an adverse ruling in any one of those cases may be disastrous for defense of the others due to its collateral estoppel effects. Careful analysis of the various cases in order to determine which are the cases to try first or even which cases

---

lateral estoppel may be unwarranted. Indeed, differences in available procedures may sometimes justify not allowing a prior judgment to have estoppel effect in a subsequent action even between the same parties, or where defensive estoppel is asserted against a plaintiff who has litigated and lost. The problem of unfairness is particularly acute in cases of offensive estoppel, however, because the defendant against whom estoppel is asserted typically will not have chosen the forum in the first action.

Id. at 331 n.15, 99 S.Ct. at 651 n.15.

70. *Id.* at 331, 99 S.Ct. at 652. Later in its opinion, the *Parklane Hosiery* Court implied that the considerations of fairness it had enunciated specifically and that resulted in the explicit investment of discretion in the district courts regarding application of offensive collateral estoppel were all encompassed within the general concept of a full and fair opportunity to litigate claims in the prior action. *See id.* at 332–33, 99 S.Ct. at 652–53. Obviously, those opposing application of the estoppel will seek to accentuate the distinctiveness of these considerations,

whereas those advancing the estoppel will cast them as simply another aspect of the usual requirement of a full and fair opportunity to litigate.

71. The Seventh Amendment attack on the offensive use of the prior judgment was also rejected.

> The law of collateral estoppel, like the law in other procedural areas defining the scope of the jury's function, has evolved since 1791. under the rationale of the Galloway case, these developments are not repugnant to the Seventh Amendment simply for the reason that they did not exist in 1791. Thus if, as we have held, the law of collateral estoppel forecloses the petitioners from relitigating the factual issues determined against them in the SEC action, nothing in the Seventh Amendment dictates a different result, even though because of lack of mutuality there would have been no collateral estoppel in 1791.

Id. at 337, 99 S.Ct. at 655 (note omitted).

must be settled may be critical to avoiding adverse collateral estoppel effects. This analysis may not always be limited to the legal issues. For example, in the context of similar securities claims, the claim brought by a widow living on a fixed income may well be one that requires settlement, whereas the same claim by a sophisticated, professional investor may be a case to try. Conversely, when acting as plaintiff's counsel, recognition of the possible collateral estoppel effect your case presents for the defendant may be important to achieving full settlement potential of the case.

Library References:

West's Key No. Digests, Judgment ☞632, 634.
Wright, Miller & Cooper, Federal Practice and Procedure: Civil 2d §§ 1225, 2735.

§ 12.8   Judicial Estoppel

The doctrine of judicial estoppel is designed principally to protect the integrity of the judicial process.[1] Judicial estoppel is a creature of equity and, as such its application lies in the discretion of the court.[2] It has also been called the "doctrine of preclusion of inconsistent positions."[3] Judicial estoppel, although intended to protect the integrity of the judicial process, is a defense capable of being lost through failure to assert it in a timely manner.[4]

The doctrine can arise in many different situations. One common, fertile ground for its application lies in the tension between an individual's business interests and interests that arise in the course of a divorce proceeding. In a divorce proceeding, the wealthier spouse may well desire to minimize the value of certain business holdings. This position may be diametrically opposed to an interest in other litigation, such as valuation of a partnership interest upon dissolution. Counsel should always be aware of the potential for inconsistent positions created by the effects of different valuations of property. Another issue that often engenders inconsistent positions is that of agency. For example, a litigant may seek to deny agency to avoid imputation of knowledge in one instance, but

§ 12.8

1. United States v. Garcia, 37 F.3d 1359, 1366 (9th Cir.1994); Bates v. Long Island R. Co., 997 F.2d 1028, 1037–38 (2d Cir.1993); Morris v. State of California, 966 F.2d 448, 453 (9th Cir.1991).

The policies underlying the doctrine include preventing internal inconsistency, precluding litigants from playing "fast and loose" with the courts, and prohibiting parties from deliberately changing positions according to the exigencies of the moment.

United States v. McCaskey, 9 F.3d 368, 378 (5th Cir.1993). Other courts recognize protection of a party when "his opponent seeks to repudiate an earlier position successfully

asserted." Chaveriat v. Williams Pipe Line Co., 11 F.3d 1420, 1427 (7th Cir.1993).

2. *E.g.,* Morris, 966 F.2d at 453. "The decision whether to invoke judicial estoppel lies within the court's discretion, and a refusal to apply the doctrine is reviewed under the 'abuse of discretion' standard." Data General Corp. v. Johnson, 78 F.3d 1556, 1565 (Fed.Cir.1996).

3. United States v. Nix, 21 F.3d 347, 352 (9th Cir.1994).

4. *E.g.,* Altman v. Altman, 653 F.2d 755, 758 (3d Cir.1981)(absent exceptional circumstances party will not be permitted to raise judicial estoppel on appeal for first time).

seek to support agency in another context to establish, for example, formation of a contract with another party. The conflict in the positions may be fatal to whichever position is asserted later, assuming all other elements of judicial estoppel are met.

The elements of judicial estoppel are not uniformly recognized. All courts applying the doctrine agree that the doctrine is triggered by a party seeking to take a position in a later proceeding that is inconsistent with a position advanced earlier,[5] but there is disagreement regarding whether a second element exists.

> The majority of courts recognizing the doctrine hold that it is inapplicable unless the inconsistent statement was actually adopted by the court in the earlier litigation; only in that situation, according to those circuits, is there a risk of inconsistent results and a threat to the integrity of the judicial process. [Citations omitted.] the minority view, in contrast, holds that the doctrine applies even if the litigant was unsuccessful in asserting the inconsistent position, if by his change of position he is playing "fast and loose" with the court. [Citations omitted.] In either case, the purpose of the doctrine is to protect the integrity of the judicial process.[6]

Obviously, the effect of the doctrine will vary significantly depending upon whether the court involved imposes a requirement on application of the doctrine that a court actually adopted the previous position advanced by the party against whom the estoppel is sought.[7]

It should be noted that the doctrine does not freeze a party's position forever irrespective of subsequent developments. A change in the operative facts will not preclude a change in legal position.[8]

The propriety of application may be more difficult to ascertain for judicial estoppel than for other preclusionary doctrines, because it requires an in-depth knowledge of positions taken by a litigant in earlier litigation that may not necessarily be obvious from earlier court decisions or judgments. Thus, it may require greater investigation of the details of earlier litigation to be aware of the potential application of the

---

5. *E.g.*, Nix, 21 F.3d at 352; Bates, 997 F.2d at 1038.

6. Morris, 966 F.2d at 452–53. *Accord, e.g.*, Garcia, 37 F.3d at 1367.

7. In this vein, there may be a significant difference regarding the effect of a settlement, especially one that is memorialized in an order or judgment. *See* Bates, 997 F.2d at 1038 ("A 'settlement neither requires nor implies any judicial endorsement of either party's claims of theories, and thus a settlement does not provide the prior success necessary for judicial estoppel.' ").

8.

[T]he doctrine of judicial estoppel is not an absolute bar to obtaining legal relief on the basis of new information, even if inconsistent old information had gotten the party an advantage in some other proceeding. It would be odd to apply this rather esoteric though we think salutary doctrine more strictly than collateral estoppel or law of the case, related bars to changing one's position after it has been adopted by a court.

Chaveriat v. Williams Pipe Line Co., 11 F.3d 1420, 1428 (7th Cir.1993). In this regard, counsel should liken a change in facts requiring an adjustment of legal position to the situation where res judicata is found inapplicable due to lack of identity between claims. *See supra* § 12.6(b).

doctrine. Also, because changing facts may affect its application even after a detailed investigation has been conducted, the expense of fully pursuing investigation of judicial estoppel may outweigh its eventual utility and should be considered at the outset.

Library References:

West's Key No. Digests, Estoppel ☞68(2).
Wright, Miller, Kane & Cooper, Federal Practice and Procedure: Civil 2d § 1500, 4418, 4453.

§ 12.9   Section 1738 and State Court Judgments

(a) Full Faith and Credit and Its Enabling Act

Any analysis of the preclusive effect of prior state court adjudications is both constitutionally and statutorily based. The Full Faith and Credit Clause of the Constitution[1] specifically provides that "Full Faith and Credit shall be given in each State to the public Acts, Records and judicial Proceedings of every other State."[2] Nothing is mandated in the Constitution, however, regarding the effect to be given to state court judgments in federal courts. Nevertheless, the Constitution supplies congressional authority to make that determination.[3] Soon after the birth of the republic, Congress put into effect that authority by enacting what is now codified as Section 1738 of Title 28 of the United States Code.[4]

The Acts of legislature of an State, Territory, or Possession of the United States, or copies thereof, shall be authenticated by affixing the seal of such State, Territory or Possession thereto.

The records and judicial proceedings of any court of any such State, Territory or Possession, or copies thereof, shall be proved or admitted in other courts within the United States and its Territories and Possessions by the attestation of the clerk and seal of the court annexed, if a seal exists, together with a certificate of the court that the said attestation is in proper form.

Such Acts, records and judicial proceedings or copies thereof, so authenticated, shall have the same full faith and credit in every court within the United States and its Territories and Possessions as

§ 12.9

1. U.S. Const., art. IV, § 1.

2. *Id.*

3. "And the Congress may by general Laws prescribe the Manner in which such [state] Acts, Records and [judicial] Proceedings shall be proved, and the Effect thereof." U.S. Const., art. IV, § 1, cl. 2.

4. "As one of its first acts, Congress directed that all United States courts afford the same full faith and credit to state court

judgments that would apply in the State's own courts." Kremer v. Chemical Construction Corp., 456 U.S. 461, 463, 102 S.Ct. 1883, 1888, 72 L.Ed.2d 262 (1982). The original predecessor to 28 U.S.C.A. § 1738 (West 1994) was enacted May 27, 1790. The statute has existed in essentially the same form as it stands today since its initial passage. *See* Allen v. McCurry, 449 U.S. 90, 96 n. 8, 101 S.Ct. 411, 415 n. 8, 66 L.Ed.2d 308 (1980).

they have by law or usage in the courts of such State, Territory or Possession from which they are taken.[5]

While this statute does not state any uniform or express preclusive effect that state court judgments will receive in the federal courts, it does command adherence by the federal courts to state standards and precludes application of federal common law of preclusion to state court judgments.[6]

(b) Application and Interpretation of Section 1738

At first examination, the application of Section 1738 would appear rather straightforward, but much litigation has been engendered by its effect in differing circumstances.

In *Allen v. McCurry*,[7] the United States Supreme Court considered the scope of Section 1738 in precluding federally created claims based upon state court adjudications. The particular issue under consideration in *Allen* was whether a state court's determination in a pretrial suppression hearing of the constitutionality of a warrantless search would control a later civil rights action under 42 U.S.C.A. § 1983. In *Allen*, undercover agents had effected an arrest of McCurry and searched his house after attempting to effect a purchase of heroin from him.[8] After his state conviction, which was based on certain evidence seized in a warrantless search after his arrest, McCurry brought a federal action for damages under 42 U.S.C.A. § 1983 against the officers based on alleged unconstitutionality of the search of his house.

The district court applied collateral estoppel to McCurry's claims, based on the state court's decisions at the suppression hearing, and granted summary judgment in favor of the officers. The Eighth Circuit reversed, reasoning that the unavailability of federal habeas corpus relief

---

5. 28 U.S.C.A. § 1738. The current version of § 1738 that appears in the text is that enacted June 25, 1948.

6.

Indeed, though the federal courts may look to the common law or to the policies supporting res judicata and collateral estoppel in assessing the preclusive effect of decisions of other federal courts, Congress has specifically required all federal courts to give preclusive effect to the state-court judgments whenever the courts of the State from which the judgments emerged would do so. . . .

Allen, 449 U.S. at 96, 101 S.Ct. at 415. *Accord, e.g.*, Migra v. Warren City School District Board of Education, 465 U.S. 75, 81, 104 S.Ct. 892, 896, 79 L.Ed.2d 56 (1984).

7. 449 U.S. 90, 101 S.Ct. 411, 66 L.Ed.2d 308 (1980).

8. According to the Supreme Court's opinion, officers attempted to buy heroin from McCurry based on a tip. Two officers went to McCurry's door and several others hid nearby. When McCurry answered the door, the two agents asked to buy heroin. McCurry retreated into the house, only to return brandishing and firing a pistol. Two officers were wounded. A subsequent warrantless search of the house resulted in seizure of heroin in plain view and more contraband that was located in dresser drawers and in old tires on the porch. In a suppression hearing, the state court held that the evidence in plain view had been properly seized, but the contraband found in the dresser drawers and old tires was excluded from trial as having been found pursuant to a constitutionally impermissible warrantless search. McCurry was convicted on charges of possession of heroin and assault. *Id.* at 92, 101 S.Ct. at 413.

in this context,[9] made application of collateral estoppel inconsistent with "the special role of the federal courts in protecting civil rights."[10]

The Supreme Court began its analysis by noting the historic adherence to principles of res judicata and collateral estoppel, even in situations involving prior state court adjudications. This practice, the Court stated, served to "not only reduce unnecessary litigation and foster reliance on adjudication, but also promote the comity between state and federal courts that has been recognized as a bulwark of the federal system."[11] Only then, did the Court acknowledge the existence and mandatory nature of 28 U.S.C.A. § 1738. The issue addressed by the Court was whether Section 1983 presented a situation of sufficiently compelling federal interest that claim and issue preclusion dictated by Section 1738,[12] should not control.

The Court found that nothing short of a limited repeal of Section 1738 by Section 1983 would justify ignoring the former's dictates. Since Section 1983 is silent regarding preclusive effect, any repeal of Section 1738 would be implied. The Supreme Court clearly recognized that

9. *See* Stone v. Powell, 428 U.S. 465, 96 S.Ct. 3037, 49 L.Ed.2d 1067 (1976).

10. McCurry v. Allen, 606 F.2d 795 (8th Cir.1979), *rev'd*, 449 U.S. 90, 101 S.Ct. 411, 66 L.Ed.2d 308 (1980). The court of appeals, concerned that the action under Section 1983 was the only avenue of federal review available to McCurry regarding his constitutional claim, directed the district court to allow the suit to proceed forward unencumbered by collateral estoppel sourced from the state criminal proceedings. Nevertheless, concerned also about the integrity of state/federal relations, the court of appeals further directed abstention by the district court until pursuit of state appellate remedies in the criminal context were completed. *See id.* at 93 & 93 n.4, 101 S.Ct. at 414 & 414 n.4.

11. *Id.* at 96–97, 101 S.Ct. at 415–17.

12. The effect of 28 U.S.C.A. § 1738 (West 1994) which treats the preclusive effect to be given to a state court judgment, must be distinguished from the jurisdictional *Rooker-Feldman* doctrine. The latter legal precept, derived from *Rooker v. Fidelity Trust Co.*, 263 U.S. 413, 44 S.Ct. 149, 68 L.Ed. 362 (1923), and *District of Columbia Court of Appeals v. Feldman*, 460 U.S. 462, 103 S.Ct. 1303, 75 L.Ed.2d 206 (1983), is a recognition that lower federal courts have no power to conduct appellate review of state court judgments.

We have consistently emphasized the distinction between *res judicata* and *Rooker-Feldman* and insisted that the applicability of *Rooker-Feldman* be decided before considering *res judicata* ..... We noted that res judicata and the *Rooker-Feldman* doctrine "are not coextensive." [Citation omitted.] While res judicata and preclusion are founded upon the Full Faith and Credit Statute, 28 U.S.C.A. § 1738, which requires federal courts to give state court judgments the same effect that the rendering state would, *Rooker-Feldman* is based on the separate principle that only the Supreme Court has appellate jurisdiction over the civil judgments of state courts.

In order to determine the applicability of the *Rooker-Feldman* doctrine, the fundamental and appropriate question to ask is whether the injury alleged by the federal plaintiff resulted from the state court judgment itself or is distinct from that judgment. If the injury alleged resulted from the state court judgment itself, *Rooker-Feldman* directs that the lower federal courts lack jurisdiction. If the injury alleged is distinct from that judgment, *i.e.*, the party maintains an injury apart from the loss in state court and not "inextricably intertwined" with the state judgment, res judicata may apply, but *Rooker-Feldman* does not.

Garry v. Geils, 82 F.3d 1362, 1365–66 (7th Cir.1996). *But cf.* Thaler v. Casella, 960 F.Supp. 691, 698 (S.D.N.Y.1997)(*Rooker-Feldman* doctrine is at least coextensive with preclusion principles).

Congress intended to change the relationship of the state and federal courts through passage of Section 1983 in the post-reconstruction era,[13] but found the legislative history "lends only the most equivocal support to any argument that ... congress intended to override § 1738 or the common-law rules of collateral estoppel and res judicata."[14] In the end, the Supreme Court found nothing in the text or legislative history to justify overriding Section 1738, despite the fact that federal habeas corpus relief was unavailable as a mechanism for bringing the Fourth Amendment issues before a federal court for adjudication. In a statement that serves as a distillation of many of the decisions regarding the scope of Section 1738, the Court wrote:

> There is, in short, no reason to believe that Congress intended to provide a person claiming a federal right an unrestricted opportunity to relitigate an issue already decided in state court simply because the issue arose in a state proceeding in which he would rather not have been engaged at all.[15]

As was the case in *Allen*, where a state court has rendered a judgment on a claim over which state and federal courts have concurrent jurisdiction, Section 1738 mandates application of state law in determining the preclusive effect of the state court judgment.[16] That same result

---

13. Allen, 449 U.S. at 99–100, 101 S.Ct. at 417–18.

14. *Id.* at 99, 101 S.Ct. at 417. The Court specifically found, however, that the congressional lack of concern was for "cases where the state courts have recognized and provided fair procedures for determining them." *Id.* The Court went on to acknowledge that § 1983 was intended to supply an independent federal remedy when the state court did not "allow full litigation of a constitutional claim." *Id.* at 100–01, 101 S.Ct. at 418–19.

This understanding of § 1983 might well support an exception to res judicata and collateral estoppel where state law did not provide fair procedures for the litigation of constitutional claims, or where a state court failed to even acknowledge the existence of the constitutional principle on which a litigant based his claim. Such an exception, however, would be essentially the same as the important general limit on rules of preclusion that already exists: collateral estoppel does not apply where the party against whom an earlier court decision is asserted did not have a full and fair opportunity to litigate the claim or issue decided by the first court.

Id. at 101–02, 101 S.Ct. at 418–19.

15. *Id.* at 104, 101 S.Ct. at 420.

The Supreme Court has also held that no partial repeal of § 1738 was intended by Title VII of the Civil Rights Act of 1964. Kremer v. Chemical Construction Corp., 456 U.S. 461, 102 S.Ct. 1883, 72 L.Ed.2d 262 (1982). In *Kremer*, the Court also addressed the preclusive effect to be given to state administrative rulings. *See infra* § 12.13. It has also been held that § 1738 is not disturbed by the Dealer Day In Court Act, 15 U.S.C.A. §§ 1221–1225 (West 1998). Bethesda Ford, Inc. v. Ford Motor Company, 572 F.Supp. 623, 628–29 (D.Md.1983).

16. Migra v. Warren City School District Board of Education, 465 U.S. 75, 104 S.Ct. 892, 79 L.Ed.2d 56 (1984); Kaufman v. BDO Seidman, 984 F.2d 182, 183 (6th Cir. 1993).

The Tenth Circuit in *Fox v. Maulding*, 112 F.3d 453 (10th Cir.1997), held that where it was unclear whether state and federal courts had concurrent jurisdiction over RICO claims at the time that the plaintiffs filed a lawsuit in state court, the plaintiffs were obligated at least to attempt to litigate their RICO claims in state court along with their related state law claims, and where they failed to do so, their subsequent RICO claims brought in federal court were barred. *Id.* at 459. *See also* Diversified Foods, Inc. v. First National Bank of Boston, 985 F.2d 27, 31 (1st Cir.) (plaintiffs' mistaken belief in exclusive federal jurisdic-

obtains in the case of a state court judgment on a claim that lies within the exclusive jurisdiction of the federal courts. In *Marrese v. American Academy of Orthopaedic Surgeons*,[17] the Court held that a federal court is bound by Section 1738 to apply state law to determine the preclusive effect of a state judgment on a federal antitrust claim that could not have been brought in the state proceeding:

> The fact that petitioners' antitrust claim is within the exclusive jurisdiction of the federal courts does not necessarily make § 1738 inapplicable to this case. Our decisions indicate that a state court judgment may in some circumstances have preclusive effect in a subsequent action within the exclusive jurisdiction of the federal courts. Without discussing § 1738, this Court has held that the issue preclusive effect of a state court judgment barred a subsequent patent suit that could not have been brought in state court. Moreover, *Kremer* held that § 1738 applies to a claim of employment discrimination under Title VII of the Civil Rights Act of 1964, 78 Stat. 253, as amended, 42 U.S.C.A. § 2000e *et seq.*, although the Court expressly declined to decide whether Title VII claims can be brought only in federal courts. *Kremer* implies that absent an exception to § 1738, state law determines at least the issue preclusive effect of a prior state judgment in a subsequent action involving a claim within the exclusive jurisdiction of the federal courts.[18]

Under *Marrese*, a federal court determining the preclusive effect of a state judgment on a claim that is within the exclusive jurisdiction of the federal courts must look to that state's law to decide whether the state would preclude later litigation in a federal court.[19]

> With respect to matters that were not decided in the state proceedings, we note that claim preclusion generally does not apply where "[t]he plaintiff was unable to rely on a certain theory of the case or to seek a certain remedy because of the limitations on the subject matter jurisdiction of the courts ... "Restatement (Second) of

---

tion did not alter the res judicata effect of state court judgment), *cert. denied*, 509 U.S. 907, 113 S.Ct. 3001, 125 L.Ed.2d 694 (1993).

17. 470 U.S. 373, 105 S.Ct. 1327, 84 L.Ed.2d 274 (1985).

18. *Id.* at 380–81, 105 S.Ct. at 1331–32.

19. *Id.* at 381–82, 105 S.Ct. at 1332–33. The Court recognized that "[t]o be sure, a state court will not have occasion to address the specific question whether a state judgment has issue or claim preclusive effect in a later action that can be brought only in federal court." *Id.* Nevertheless, "a federal court may rely in the first instance on state preclusion principles to determine the extent to which an earlier state judgment bars subsequent litigation." *Id.*

If it is determined that state law bars the subsequent federal claim, the federal court must undertake the second step of determining whether some exception to § 1738 applies. *Id.* at 383, 105 S.Ct. at 1333. An exception to § 1738 would exist where a later statute contained "an express or implied repeal." *Id.* (citing Kremer, 456 U.S. at 468, 102 S.Ct. at 1890). *See also* Murphy v. Gallagher, 761 F.2d 878 (2d Cir.1985) (applying New York law to find that a prior state proceeding barred subsequent federal action under Securities and Exchange Act of 1934, which was under exclusive jurisdiction of federal courts, and that the 1934 Act neither expressly nor impliedly repealed § 1738); Gargallo v. Merrill Lynch, Pierce, Fenner & Smith, Inc., 918 F.2d 658, 662–64 (6th Cir.1990).

Judgments § 26(1)(c) (1982). If state preclusion law includes this requirement of prior jurisdictional competency, which is generally true, a state judgment will not have claim preclusive effect on a cause of action within the exclusive jurisdiction of the federal courts.[20]

Thus, "to the extent that state preclusion law indicates that a judgment normally does not have claim preclusive effect as to matters that the court lacked jurisdiction to entertain, lower courts and commentators have correctly concluded that a state court judgment does not bar a subsequent federal antitrust claim."[21] If the court determines, however, that law would give preclusive effect to the state court judgment even where that state court was without jurisdiction, the federal court in the subsequent action must then "determine if the federal court, as an exception to § 1738, should refuse to give preclusive effect to a state court judgment."[22]

A similar approach is taken with respect to state court settlements that resolve claims that are within exclusive federal jurisdiction.[23]

Library References:

West's Key No. Digests, Judgment ⚯828.4.
Wright, Miller & Cooper, Federal Practice and Procedure: Civil 2d § 4508.

§ 12.10 Interrelationship of Civil and Criminal Cases

(a) Criminal Convictions and Guilty Pleas in Subsequent Federal Civil Actions

Issues actually litigated for purposes of a criminal conviction conclu-

---

20. Marrese, 470 U.S. at 382, 105 S.Ct. at 1333.

21. *Id.* at 383, 105 S.Ct. at 1333. *See, e.g.*, Pension Trust Fund for Operating Engineers v. Triple A Machine Shop, Inc., 942 F.2d 1457 (9th Cir.1991)(denying res judicata effect under § 1738 and California law to state judgment on ERISA claim and examining potential effect under principles of collateral estoppel). It should be noted that federal courts have held that no full faith and credit need be given to a state court judgment where the state court did not have jurisdiction over the subject matter or the parties in the case it adjudicated. *See, e.g.*, *In re* Brady, Texas, Municipal Gas Corp., 936 F.2d 212, 218 (5th Cir.1991).

22. Marrese, 470 U.S. at 383, 105 S.Ct. at 1333. The Court stated that, "We conclude that the basic approach adopted in Kremer [v. Chemical Construction Corp., 456 U.S. 461 (1982),] applies in a lawsuit involving a claim within the exclusive juris-

diction of the federal courts." *Id.* at 381, 105 S.Ct. at 1332.

23. Matsushita Electric Industrial Co., Ltd. v. Epstein, 516 U.S. 367, 116 S.Ct. 873, 134 L.Ed.2d 6 (1996)("In accord with these precedents, we conclude that § 1738 is generally applicable in cases in which the state court judgment at issue incorporates a class action settlement releasing claims solely within the jurisdiction of the federal courts."). Unreviewed arbitration decisions do not receive the same treatment or preclusive effect, because they do not represent judicial proceedings as referenced in § 1738. *See* McDonald v. City of West Branch, 466 U.S. 284, 287–88, 104 S.Ct. 1799, 1801–02, 80 L.Ed.2d 302 (1984). For a discussion of the treatment to be given to arbitration awards that are later reviewed by state court, *see* Lum v. City and County of Honolulu, 728 F.Supp. 1452 (D.Haw. 1989).

sively establish those issues for later federal civil litigation. The application of collateral estoppel to criminal convictions and guilty pleas is incorporated into, but narrower than, the Fifth Amendment's prohibition of double jeopardy:

> The traditional bar of double jeopardy prohibits the prosecution of the crime itself, whereas collateral estoppel, in a more modest fashion, simply forbids the government from relitigating certain facts in order to establish the fact of the crime.[1]

Convictions and guilty pleas in criminal proceedings generally are subject to the same analysis as civil judgments with respect to their preclusive effect on subsequent civil proceedings.[2] Courts must follow state law, pursuant to 28 U.S.C.A. § 1738, in determining the preclusive effect of a state court criminal conviction or guilty plea.[3]

There is often no distinction made between a conviction rendered after a full jury trial and a guilty plea.[4] When faced with either a prior conviction or guilty plea, courts usually apply general principles of collateral estoppel to determine whether the issue sought to be barred was fully litigated in the criminal proceedings, necessarily determined by the conviction or plea, and involved the same parties or privies as those

§ 12.10

1. United States v. Mock, 604 F.2d 341, 343–44 (5th Cir.1979). *See* Ashe v. Swenson, 397 U.S. 436, 445, 90 S.Ct. 1189, 1195, 25 L.Ed.2d 469 (1970).

2. Pleas of nolo contendere, on the other hand, have no preclusive effect. The Federal Rules of Evidence provide that a conviction by plea of nolo contendere is not admissible in any civil or criminal proceeding against the defendant making or participating in the plea. Fed.R.Evid. 410. A plea of nolo contendere is not an admission of guilt and thus cannot be used as such in a subsequent civil or criminal action. *See generally* Annotation, *Plea of Nolo Contendere or Non Vult Contendere*, 89 A.L.R.2d 540, 600–03 (1963); *see also* Doherty v. American Motors Corp., 728 F.2d 334 (6th Cir. 1984). Additionally, a plea of nolo contendere does not estop a defendant from denying facts on which the criminal charge was based. *See* 1 Charles Alan Wright, Arthur R. Miller, & Mary Kay Kane, Federal Practice and Procedure, § 177 at 666 (2d ed. 1982). A plea of nolo contendere may be utilized, however, in certain administrative proceedings. *See* Pearce v. United States Dept. of Justice, 836 F.2d 1028 (6th Cir. 1988) (plea of nolo contendere may be used by Attorney General under Controlled Substances Act to suspend or revoke a physician's license).

3. Haring v. Prosise, 462 U.S. 306, 314, 103 S.Ct. 2368, 2373, 76 L.Ed.2d 595 (1983).

4. *See* Appley v. West, 832 F.2d 1021, 1025–26 (7th Cir.1987) (applying same collateral estoppel principles to criminal convictions and guilty pleas); Gray v. Commissioner of Internal Revenue, 708 F.2d 243 (6th Cir.1983) (guilty plea is as much a conviction as a conviction following jury trial for collateral estoppel purposes), *cert. denied*, 466 U.S. 927, 104 S.Ct. 1709, 80 L.Ed.2d 182 (1984); United States v. Certain Real Property and Premises Known as 4003–4005 Fifth Avenue, Brooklyn, New York, 855 F.Supp. 50 (E.D.N.Y.1994) (criminal conviction, whether by jury verdict or guilty plea, constitutes estoppel in subsequent civil proceedings as to those matters determined by judgment in criminal case), *aff'd*, 55 F.3d 78 (2d Cir.1995).

Some states hold that guilty pleas, as opposed to convictions, are admissible only as admissions against interest in subsequent civil proceedings. *See* United States v. One Parcel of Real Property, 900 F.2d 470, 473 (1st Cir.1990) (applying Massachusetts law); Country Mutual Insurance Co. v. Duncan, 794 F.2d 1211, 1215 (7th Cir.1986) (applying Illinois law) ("A guilty plea, like any other admission, is not necessarily conclusive as to the facts underlying the plea but is subject to explanation by the declarant.").

in the current federal action.[5] Some courts also inquire regarding whether a full and fair trial preceded the conviction "in order to prevent convictions of doubtful validity from being used" to support application of collateral estoppel.[6]

Litigants have successfully used prior convictions or guilty pleas offensively to conclusively establish one or more elements of civil actions such as fraud,[7] civil violations of the Racketeer Influenced and Corrupt

5. *See, e.g.,* Davis v. Gracey, 111 F.3d 1472 (10th Cir.1997) (obscenity conviction and forfeiture of computer equipment did not collaterally estop plaintiffs' § 1983 action against police officer who seized computer equipment, because at least one plaintiff in § 1983 action was not in privity with plaintiff who was subject of criminal proceedings); United States v. Peters, 927 F.Supp. 363 (D.Neb.1996) (defendant's conviction for filing false claims to EPA collaterally estopped him from contesting issue of liability in civil action seeking to impose liability under False Claims Act because identical factual conduct and violation of law raised in civil action were distinctly put in issue and directly determined against defendant in criminal trial), *aff'd,* 110 F.3d 616 (8th Cir.1997); Martinez v. Universal Underwriters Insurance Co., 819 F.Supp. 921 (W.D.Wash.1992) (insured's criminal conviction in state court for first-degree arson precluded relitigation in insured's action against insurer to recover under homeowner's policy for fire loss, of critical issue whether fire was set by insured), *aff'd,* 15 F.3d 1087 (9th Cir.1993).

But see Snyder v. Alexandria, 870 F.Supp. 672, 690 (E.D.Va.1994) (recognizing that under Virginia law, a criminal judgment of conviction has no preclusive effect on subsequent civil actions because the parties, purposes, and standards of proof in criminal and civil proceedings are too different).

Convictions or guilty pleas do not necessarily foreclose an action brought under 42 U.S.C.A. § 1983 for violations of civil rights that occurred in connection with the defendant's arrest or confinement if the issue arising under the civil rights action was not actually litigated or necessary to the convic-

tion or plea. *See* Haring v. Prosise, 462 U.S. 306, 103 S.Ct. 2368, 76 L.Ed.2d 595 (1983); B.C.R. Transport Co., Inc. v. Fontaine, 727 F.2d 7, 11–12 (1st Cir.1984); Presley v. Morrison, 950 F.Supp. 1298, 1305 (E.D.Pa. 1996).

6. United States v. Real Property Located at Grays Harbor County, WA, 976 F.2d 515, 518 (9th Cir.1992).

7. Instituto Nacional De Comercializacion Agricola (Indeca) v. Continental Illinois National Bank and Trust Co., 858 F.2d 1264 (7th Cir.1988) (defendant's conviction of wire fraud and of submitting false statements to a federally insured bank established all elements of defendant's fraud in a subsequent civil proceeding); Rowe v. Marietta Corp., 955 F.Supp. 829, 833–34 (W.D.Tenn.1996) (fact that president of corporation was convicted on securities fraud charges established elements of material false representation and intent to defraud in subsequent fraud action); Chase Manhattan Bank, N.A. v. Harris, 899 F.Supp. 64 (D.Conn.1995) (conviction for bank fraud had collateral estoppel effect with regard to elements of Connecticut common law fraud claim that there must be false representations, that representations be knowingly made, and that representations be made with purpose of obtaining something of value from bank, since those issues were required for conviction and were fully and fairly litigated); Roso v. Saxon Energy Corp., 758 F.Supp. 164 (S.D.N.Y.1991) (defendant's prior convictions for grand larceny and a scheme to defraud conclusively established the claim for common law fraud in a subsequent civil proceeding where every element necessary to prove fraud was fully litigated in the criminal proceeding and necessary to the jury's verdict).

Organizations Act, ("RICO"),[8] and civil securities violations.[9]

(b) Acquittals

An acquittal in a prior criminal proceeding generally does not allow the defendant to use the fact of acquittal defensively as collateral estoppel, because of the different standards of proof in criminal and civil actions.[10] The government's failure to sustain its burden of proof beyond a reasonable doubt on an issue in a criminal trial, does not prevent that issue from being relitigated in a civil action under a lower standard of proof. Moreover, a defendant may not use the fact of acquittal offensively as collateral estoppel on an issue upon which a defendant based its defense in the criminal proceedings.[11]

8. 18 U.S.C.A. § 1961 (West 1983 & Supp. 1997) United States v. Private Sanitation Industry Assoc. of Nassau/Suffolk, Inc., 899 F.Supp. 974 (E.D.N.Y.1994) (defendant's guilty plea in state court to coercion conclusively established that he had committed one predicate racketeering act for purposes of a civil RICO action), aff'd, 47 F.3d 1158 (2d Cir.), cert. denied sub nom. Ferrante v. United States, 516 U.S. 806, 116 S.Ct. 50, 133 L.Ed.2d 15 (1995); County of Oakland v. City of Detroit, 776 F.Supp. 1211 (E.D.Mich.1991).

But see In re Lewisville Properties, Inc., 849 F.2d 946, 949–50 (5th Cir.1988) (defendant's conviction for importing and selling illegal drugs could not be used as collateral estoppel in civil RICO action because plaintiff alleged different enterprise and different racketeering acts from those proven in the criminal proceeding); Appley, 832 F.2d at 1027 ("because the amount of restitution was not a material fact of the indictment on which the guilty plea was based, because the issue of the amount of Ms. Appley's injury was not litigated, because Ms. Appley failed in her burden of establishing that the amount of injury was established by the guilty plea, and, finally, because under the facts of this case, the application of preclusion would be unfair," the court refused to apply guilty plea as collateral estoppel in civil RICO action); Roso, 758 F.Supp. at 169–70 (convictions for grand larceny and scheme to defraud, while conclusively establishing elements of fraud, did not establish claim for RICO violations because the issue

of whether the fraud was accomplished by the use of the mails or means of interstate commerce—an essential element of RICO—was never submitted to the jury in the criminal proceeding).

9. Securities and Exchange Comm. v. Grossman, 887 F.Supp. 649 (S.D.N.Y.1995) (attorney's criminal conviction for securities fraud collaterally estopped him from litigating his liability in civil securities fraud action, even though attorney did not testify in his defense in criminal trial; facts required to convict attorney of securities fraud were identical to allegations underlying civil complaint, and fact that attorney chose not to testify in his own defense did not require relitigation of same issues), aff'd sub nom. S.E.C. v. Estate of Hirshberg, 101 F.3d 109 (2d Cir.1996).

10. See Helvering v. Mitchell, 303 U.S. 391, 58 S.Ct. 630, 82 L.Ed. 917 (1938); United States v. One Assortment of 89 Firearms, 465 U.S. 354, 79 L.Ed.2d 361 (1984); Securities and Exchange Comm. v. Ridenour, 913 F.2d 515, 518 (8th Cir.1990); Traficant v. Commissioner of Internal Revenue Service, 884 F.2d 258, 262–63 (6th Cir. 1989); State Farm Fire & Casualty Co. v. King, 851 F.2d 1369 (11th Cir.1988).

11. Zwak v. United States, 848 F.2d 1179, 1184–85 (11th Cir.1988) (defendant's acquittal for illegal manufacture and transfer of handgun silencers in which his only defense was entrapment did not establish that defendant was entrapped as matter of law).

(c) Prior Civil Judgments in Subsequent Criminal Proceedings

The doctrine of collateral estoppel also may be applicable where the first cause of action is civil and the second is criminal.[12] Courts look to what facts were necessarily determined in the first action and whether the government in a subsequent trial has tried to relitigate facts necessarily established against it in the first trial.[13]

(d) Restitution Orders

The Victim and Witness Protection Act of 1982 ("VWPT")[14] contains restitution provisions[15] that require convicted criminals to compensate their victims to the greatest extent possible for injury or loss resulting from the offense. Because convicted criminals are often sued in subsequent civil proceedings for damages arising out of the offense committed, Congress enacted 18 U.S.C.A. § 3580(e) which permits the victim to forgo establishing the criminal's liability a second time.[16]

Many of the federal courts use the term "res judicata" when discussing the effect the statute had in preventing a convicted criminal from denying the essential allegations of the criminal offense in a subsequent civil suit.[17] However, the federal statute is intended to give issue preclusive, not claim preclusive, effect to criminal convictions.[18] It

---

12. United States v. Mumford, 630 F.2d 1023, 1027 (4th Cir.1980), *cert. denied*, 450 U.S. 1041, 101 S.Ct. 1759, 68 L.Ed.2d 238 (1981).

13. United States v. Mock, 604 F.2d 341, 343 (5th Cir.1979); United States v. Whitaker, 702 F.2d 901 (11th Cir.1983).

See United States v. Rogers, 960 F.2d 1501, 1503–09 (10th Cir.) (prior civil action brought by the SEC in which court found for the defendant operated as collateral estoppel in subsequent criminal action against defendant for fraud, RICO, securities, and tax violations where the SEC case and criminal indictment alleged identical issues with respect to defendant's participation in tax shelter, the SEC action adjudicated the issues on the merits, the parties were identical, and the parties had a full and fair opportunity to litigate the issues), *cert. denied*, 506 U.S. 1035, 113 S.Ct. 817, 121 L.Ed.2d 689 (1992).

14. Pub. L. No. 97–291, 96 Stat. 1248 (1982) (codified as amended in scattered sections of 18 U.S.C.A. & Fed.R.Crim.P. 32(c)(2).

15. 18 U.S.C.A. §§ 3579–3580 (West 1982) (renumbered 18 U.S.C.A. §§ 3663–3664 (West 1987) (effective Nov. 1, 1987)). In addition to restitution, the VWPA has two major provisions. First, the Act strengthens the criminal and civil protections accorded to crime victims and witnesses against harassment and intimidation. 18 U.S.C.A. §§ 1512–15 (West 1982). Second, in order to assess the effect of the crime on the victim, the Act requires the preparation of a "Victim Impact Statement" in every criminal case. Fed. R.Crim.P. 32(c)(2). *See* Thomas D. Sawaya, *Use of Criminal Convictions in Subsequent Civil Proceedings: Statutory Collateral Estoppel Under Florida and Federal Law and the Intentional Act Exclusion Clause*, 40 U. Fla. L. Rev. 479 (1988).

16. 18 U.S.C.A. § 3580(e) provides that: A conviction of a defendant for an offense involving the [Victim and Witness Protection] Act giving rise to restitution under this section shall estop the defendant from denying the essential allegations of that offense in any subsequent Federal civil proceeding or State civil proceeding, to the extent consistent with State law, brought by the victim.

17. *See, e.g.*, United States v. Brown, 744 F.2d 905 (2d Cir.1984); United States v. Ciambrone, 602 F.Supp. 563 (S.D.N.Y. 1984); United States v. Welden, 568 F.Supp. 516 (N.D.Ala.1983), *rev'd sub nom.* United States v. Satterfield, 743 F.2d 827 (11th Cir.1984).

18. For a more detailed discussion, *see* Sawaya, *supra* note 15, at 486–87.

is important to note that the VWPT gives only issue preclusive effect to the use of criminal convictions in subsequent civil suits for damages.[19] Thus, to the extent the civil cause of action requires proof of elements not necessary to the criminal conviction, the civil litigant is still required to prove his claim independently.

Under the federal statute, the plaintiff[20] must initially establish three elements: (1) the plaintiff is a victim of the crime; (2) the defendant in the criminal proceeding was convicted; and (3) the conviction is for an offense that involves the act giving rise to the restitution. Once the plaintiff meets these threshold requirements, the plaintiff may invoke the statute in any subsequent civil proceeding to estop the convicted defendant from denying the essential allegations of the criminal offense for which he was convicted.

Library References:
West's Key No. Digests, Judgment ⊂═559, 648.
Wright, Miller, Cooper, Graham & Gold, Federal Practice and Procedure: Civil 2d § 3533.4, 3575, 3918, 3919, 3936, 3950.8, 4474, 5003, 5383.1, 5413, 5413A, 6186.

§ 12.11   Class Actions

(a) The Effect of Judgments on Class Members' Claims

The above described principles of res judicata (claim preclusion) and collateral estoppel (issue preclusion) apply with equal force in the context of class action litigation.[1] A judgment in a properly entertained class action is binding on the class members in any subsequent litigation.[2]

A judgment in favor of the plaintiff class extinguishes their claim, which merges into the judgment granting relief. A judgment in favor of the defendant extinguishes the claim, barring a subsequent action on that claim. A judgment in favor of either side is conclusive in a subsequent action between them on any issue actually litigated and determined, if its determination was essential to that judgment.[3]

The res judicata effect applies only where the class has been certified and, thus, the dismissal of a class action proceeding before certification is not res judicata against the absent class members.[4] In addition, the res judicata effect only applies to issues that affect all of the class members

19. At least two courts have recognized that the VWPA is premised on the doctrine of collateral estoppel or issue preclusion. See United States v. Palma, 760 F.2d 475 (3d Cir.1985); Satterfield, 743 F.2d 827.

20. The federal statute specifically states that the collateral estoppel provisions will apply to civil proceedings "brought by the victim." 18 U.S.C.A. § 3580(e) (West 1982) (renumbered 18 U.S.C.A. § 3664(e) (West 1987) (effective Nov. 1. 1987).

§ 12.11

1. This section discusses claim preclusion and issue preclusion in the context of class action litigation. See Chapter 15 "Class Actions," infra, for a general discussion of class action practice and § 15.15(b)(1), (2) for discussion of issue and claim preclusion.

2. See, e.g., Supreme Tribe of Ben Hur v. Cauble, 255 U.S. 356, 366, 41 S.Ct. 338, 342, 65 L.Ed. 673 (1921); Restatement (Second) of Judgments § 41(1)(e) (1982); FRCP 23(c)(3).

3. Cooper v. Federal Reserve Bank of Richmond, 467 U.S. 867, 874, 104 S.Ct. 2794, 2798, 81 L.Ed.2d 718 (1984).

4. Larkin General Hospital, Ltd. v. American Telephone and Telegraph Co., 93 F.R.D. 497, 501 (E.D.Pa.1982).

and not to issues that are unique to the named plaintiffs.[5]

The purpose of class actions is to provide a final determination of numerous claims in one proceeding. Class actions conserve judicial resources by resolving common issues of fact and law in one lawsuit.[6] The purpose of class actions would be undermined if they were subject to collateral attack in subsequent litigation.[7] Thus, the application of res judicata and collateral estoppel to class actions allows those procedural devices to serve the judicial interest in consistency, finality and judicial economy.[8]

The principal difficulty in adopting class actions in the United States was the binding effect of a class action decree on absent class members.[9] The application of res judicata to absent parties raises constitutional issues of due process.[10] In order to address the due process issues, individual class members are provided with notice and the right to opt-out of the class action.[11]

The notice requirements for class actions were established by the Supreme Court in *Phillips Petroleum Co. v. Shutts*.[12] According to *Shutts*, due process requires that absent class members be provided with an opportunity to opt-out of the litigation.[13] However, the Court limited its holding, to Rule 23(b)(3) class actions, which "wholly or predominantly" seek monetary relief.[14] Classes seeking monetary relief are normally certified under Rule 23(b)(3). The Supreme Court has been silent with respect to due process notice requirements for the other categories of class actions, including classes seeking equitable relief, which are normally certified under Rule 23(b)(1) or (b)(2).[15]

---

5. *See, e.g.*, Cooper, 467 U.S. at 878–80, 104 S.Ct. at 2800–02 (court's ruling on unique issues raised by claims of class representatives is not res judicata as to individual claims of absent class members).

6. *See* General Telephone Co. of the Southwest v. Falcon, 457 U.S. 147, 155, 102 S.Ct. 2364, 2369, 72 L.Ed.2d 740 (1982).

7. Garcia v. Board of Ed., School District No. 1, 573 F.2d 676, 679 (10th Cir. 1978) ("The policy behind the class action device is, of course, to facilitate the final determination of numerous claims in one suit. This policy is not furthered by allowing subsequent collateral attacks by class members.").

8. *See* King v. South Central Bell Telephone and Telegraph Co., 790 F.2d 524, 528 (6th Cir.1986).

9. *See* Z. Chafee, Some Problems of Equity, 224–25 (1950).

10. *See* Supreme Tribe of Ben Hur v. Cauble, 255 U.S. 356, 366, 41 S.Ct. 338, 342, 65 L.Ed. 673 (1921) (all members of beneficial society bound by state decreeing class action including individuals that were

not parties to the state suit); Hansberry v. Lee, 311 U.S. 32, 61 S.Ct. 115, 85 L.Ed. 22 (1940) (reversing Illinois Supreme Court order that decree in class action enjoining violation of racially restricted covenants bound absent class members).

11. *See* FRCP 23(c)(2) (providing right to opt-out in Rule 23(b)(3) class actions). *See* Howard M. Downs, *Federal Class Actions: Diminished Protection for the Class and the Case for Reform*, 73 Neb. L. Rev. 646 (1994).

12. 472 U.S. 797, 105 S.Ct. 2965, 86 L.Ed.2d 628 (1985). *See also* General Telephone Co. of the Southwest v. Falcon, 457 U.S. 147, 102 S.Ct. 2364, 72 L.Ed.2d 740 (1982).

13. Phillips Petroleum Co., 472 U.S. at 812, 105 S.Ct. at 2974, 86 L.Ed.2d 628.

14. *Id.* at 811–12 n. 3, 105 S.Ct. at 2974–75 n. 3.

15. *See* Lawrence J. Restieri, Jr. *The Class Action Dilemma: The Certification of Classes Seeking Equitable Relief and Monetary Damages After Ticor Title Insurance

In view of the serious consequences of res judicata in class actions, courts scrutinize the protection afforded to the rights of absent class members.[16] Where courts have refused to preclude claims under traditional res judicata rules in the context of class action litigation, they typically have done so out of concern that it is unfair to preclude a nonnamed class member. These courts have recognized that, due to the impact on the rights of nonnamed class members, res judicata must be applied carefully in this context.[17]

(b) The Effect of Prior Class Action Determinations from Other Jurisdictions on Subsequent Federal Class Actions

It is common for there to be multiple class action lawsuits in different jurisdictions all presenting the same claims.[18] Where multiple class actions are pending simultaneously in different federal district courts, they are subject to consolidation.[19] In addition, after entry of judgment in federal court in one class action, subsequent class actions in federal court will be barred under the doctrine of res judicata. Where there is a judgment in previous class action litigation in state court, the federal court is bound by the full faith and credit statute to accept the state court judgment giving it the same preclusive effect it would be given by a court of that state.[20] Where a final judgment is entered in

Co. v. Brown, 63 Fordham L. Rev. 1745, 1751 (1995).

16. See, e.g., Gonzales v. Cassidy, 474 F.2d 67 (5th Cir.1973) (refusing to give res judicata effect to class action judgment because of inadequate representation of the class); Gibson v. Local 40, Supercargoes and Checkers of the Int'l Longshoremen's and Warehousemen's Union, 543 F.2d 1259, 1265 n. 8 (9th Cir.1976) (court has duty to carefully consider fairness of proceedings to absent class members).

17. See Richards v. Jefferson County, Alabama, 517 U.S. 793, 116 S.Ct. 1761, 135 L.Ed.2d 76 (1996) ("Because petitioners received neither notice of, nor sufficient representation in, [the state court class action litigation] that adjudication, as a matter of federal due process, may not bind them and thus cannot bar them from challenging an allegedly unconstitutional deprivation of their property."); see also Hiser v. Franklin, 94 F.3d 1287, 1293 (9th Cir.1996) (application of res judicata to overly broad class action would lead to unfair deprivation of claims of nonnamed class members), cert. denied, ___ U.S. ___, 117 S.Ct. 1106, 137 L.Ed.2d 308 (1997). But see Federal Class Actions, 73 Neb. L. Rev. 646 (1994) (inadequate consideration being given by the

courts to the due process of absent class members).

18. See Geoffrey P. Miller, Overlapping Class Actions, 71 N.Y.U. L. Rev. 514, 519 (1996).

19. Id. at 520 n. 11 (under 28 U.S.C.A. § 1407(a) "[w]hen civil actions involving one or more common questions of fact are pending in different districts, such actions may be transferred to any district for coordinated or consolidated pretrial proceedings").

20. See Matsushita Electric Industrial Co. v. Epstein, 516 U.S. 367, 372–75, 116 S.Ct. 873, 877–78, 134 L.Ed.2d 6 (1996) (state courts have power to approve settlement agreements that effectively release defendants from claims under exclusive jurisdiction of federal court); Grimes v. Vitalink Communications Corp., 17 F.3d 1553, 1563–64 (3d Cir.) (state court has power to approve settlement releasing federal claims), cert. denied, 513 U.S. 986, 115 S.Ct. 480, 130 L.Ed.2d 393 (1994). See, e.g., Class Plaintiffs v. City of Seattle, 955 F.2d 1268, 1287 (9th Cir.) court approved settlement of class action claim in federal court extinguishes all claims arising out of common facts including state law claims outside of

federal court on a class action claim, that judgment should preclude future class actions in state court under the doctrines of res judicata and under the full faith and credit statute.

The preclusive effect of a judgment in a class action lawsuit dictates that counsel consider the impact of class actions pending in other jurisdictions. For example, plaintiffs' counsel in a jurisdiction with favorable law should press for the resolution of the claim in order to avoid the impact of an adverse ruling in another, less favorable jurisdiction. Conversely, where the law is favorable to defendants, defense counsel should press for the early resolution of defenses by, for example, summary judgment. This ruling can then be used in class actions pending in other jurisdictions.

Library References:

West's Key No. Digests, Judgment ⟐678(7), 828.14(8).
Wright, Miller & Kane, Federal Practice and Procedure: Civil 2d §§ 1231, 1626, 1751–1806.

§ 12.12 Special Cases

(a) Actions Twice Voluntarily Dismissed—Rule 41(a)(1)

Ordinarily, the voluntary dismissal of an action pursuant to Rule 41(a)(1)[1] is "without prejudice," meaning it does not operate as an adjudication upon the merits and, thus, does not have res judicata effect.[2] However, where the plaintiff has already dismissed an action based on the same claim, a second voluntary dismissal operates as an adjudication upon the merits and bars future lawsuits based on the claim. This rule, which is referred to as the "two dismissal rule," prevents delay and harassment by plaintiffs by securing numerous voluntary dismissals without prejudice.[3]

The two dismissal rule applies where the second dismissal was in federal court, regardless of whether the first dismissal was in state or

the federal courts' subject matter jurisdiction, *cert. denied*, 506 U.S. 953, 113 S.Ct. 408, 121 L.Ed.2d 333 (1992).

§ 12.12

1. Rule 41(a)(1) provides as follows:

Dismissal of Actions.

(a) Voluntary Dismissal: Effect Thereof

(1) ... an action may be dismissed by the plaintiff without order of court (i) by filing a notice of dismissal at any time before service by the adverse party of an answer or of a motion for summary judgment, whichever first occurs, or (ii) by filing a stipulation of dismissal signed by all parties who have appeared in the action. Unless otherwise stated in the no-

tice of dismissal or stipulation, the dismissal is without prejudice, except that a notice of dismissal operates as an adjudication upon the merits when filed by a plaintiff who has once dismissed in any court of the United States or of any state an action based on or including the same claim.

2. Cooter & Gell v. Hartmarx Corp., 496 U.S. 384, 396–97, 110 S.Ct. 2447, 2456–57, 110 L.Ed.2d 359 (1990).

3. *See, e.g.,* Lake at Las Vegas Investors Group, Inc. v. Pacific Malibu Dev. Corp., 933 F.2d 724, 728 (9th Cir.1991) (holding that two dismissals of claim under Rule 41(a)(1) barred third claim under principles of res judicata), *cert. denied*, 503 U.S. 920, 112 S.Ct. 1295, 117 L.Ed.2d 518 (1992).

federal court.[4] Courts have held that the rule does not apply, however, where the second dismissal occurs in state court.[5]

The two dismissal rule applies to voluntary dismissals under Rule 41(a)(1) and, thus, by its terms does not apply to dismissals by stipulation of the parties or by order of the court. "Voluntary" under Rule 41 "means that the party is filing the dismissal without being compelled by another party or the court.... [I]t does not mean that other circumstances might not have compelled the dismissal or that the party desired it."[6] Rule 41 distinguishes between voluntary (Section (a)) dismissals and involuntary (Section (b)) dismissals on the basis of the party that initiates the dismissal. The two dismissal rule does not require the court to inquire into plaintiff's reasons for seeking dismissal. Thus, it is not necessary to prove that the purpose of the dismissals was to harass or abuse the defendant. However, certain courts have indicated that the intent of the parties is relevant to the issue of whether a second dismissal bars future claims. For example, in *Poloron Products, Inc. v. Lybrand Ross Bros. & Montgomery*,[7] the Second Circuit held that the two dismissal rule does not apply where one of the prior voluntary dismissals was knowingly consented to by all parties. Under the circumstances, the court held that the dismissal posed little danger of harassment and therefore should not bar a future lawsuit based on the same claims.[8]

The two dismissal rule is typically applied where the previous dismissals involved the same defendant. The rule also applies, however, in instances where the defendants are substantially the same, or are in privity. For example, in *Manning v. South Carolina Department of Highway and Public Transportation*,[9] the plaintiff sued the South Carolina Department of Highway and Public Safety and certain "John Doe" defendants. Plaintiff voluntarily dismissed the suit and then filed a second action naming, among others, the highway department and an individual state official. Plaintiff then voluntary dismissed the second action. Plaintiff filed a third lawsuit naming the state official. The court dismissed the state official from the third lawsuit on the basis of the two dismissal rule. The court of appeals affirmed noting that the rule extends not only to the named parties to an action but also to their privies. The court explained that in the context of a judgment or decree, "privy" means one so identified in interest with another that he represents the same legal right and, thus, whose legal interests were litigated in the former proceeding. In *Manning*, plaintiff's lawyers admitted that the

---

4. *Id.* at 728 (two dismissal rule applies where first suit filed in state court).

5. *See* Rader v. Baltimore & O. R. Co., 108 F.2d 980, 986 (7th Cir.), *cert. denied*, 309 U.S. 682, 60 S.Ct. 722, 84 L.Ed. 1026 (1940) (two dismissal rule does not apply where the second dismissal was in state court); Stewart v. Stearman, 743 F.Supp. 793, 794 (D.Utah 1990) (two dismissal rule does not bar third suit in federal court where two previous dismissals were in state court).

6. Randall v. Merrill Lynch, 820 F.2d 1317, 1321 (D.C.Cir.1987), *cert. denied*, 484 U.S. 1027, 108 S.Ct. 753, 98 L.Ed.2d 765 (1988).

7. 534 F.2d 1012, 1017–18 (2d Cir.1976).

8. *Id.*

9. 914 F.2d 44, 48 (4th Cir.1990).

state official was intended to be the defendant named as "John Doe" in the first lawsuit.[10]

(b) Compulsory Counterclaims

Rule 13 of the Federal Rules of Civil Procedure sets forth the circumstances under which a defendant must assert a counterclaim in order to preserve the claim. Rule 13(a) provides as follows in pertinent part:

> A pleading shall state as a counterclaim any claim which at the time of serving the pleading the pleader has against any opposing party, if it arises out of the transaction or occurrence that is the subject matter of the opposing party's claim and does not require for its adjudication the presence of third parties of whom the court cannot acquire jurisdiction.[11]

A party's failure to present claims that are "compulsory counterclaims" under Rule 13(a) bars a subsequent assertion of those claims in federal court. The effect of the failure to assert a compulsory counterclaim is not set forth explicitly in Rule 13; however, it is well established that the claim is barred.[12] This result is justified either under a theory of res judicata or a theory of waiver or estoppel.[13]

Courts construing the compulsory counterclaim rule have given Rule 13 "flexible and realistic constructions in order to effect 'judicial economy' i.e., trial in one action of all related controversies between the parties and, of course, the avoidance of multiplicity of suits."[14] Courts

---

10. See also Lake at Las Vegas Investors Group, Inc. v. Pacific Malibu Dev. Corp., 933 F.2d 724, 728 (9th Cir.1991) (two dismissal rule applies where one lawsuit filed against wholly-owned subsidiary and another filed against partnership in which the subsidiary was a general partner). But see Murray v. Sevier, 145 F.R.D. 563, 567 (D.Kan.1993) (application of two dismissal rule is inappropriate where there are multiple defendants and the interests of the defendants are not so interrelated that each represents the same legal right).

11. FRCP 13(a).

12. Noncompulsory counterclaims and cross-claims are not governed by Rule 13(a); however, these claims may still be barred under the doctrine of collateral estoppel. Specifically where a party failed to plead a noncompulsory counterclaim or cross-claim in the prior action, they may be barred from pursuing that claim in a subsequent case if that claim was necessarily determined in the first action.

In addition, noncompulsory counterclaims and cross-claims may be barred where the successful prosecution of the second action would nullify a judgment obtained in the first action or would, thus, impair rights established in the first action. See Martino v. McDonald's System, Inc., 598 F.2d 1079, 1085 (7th Cir.), cert. denied, 444 U.S. 966, 100 S.Ct. 455, 62 L.Ed.2d 379 (1979); Billingsley v. Seibels, 556 F.2d 276 (5th Cir.1977), cert. denied, 435 U.S. 929, 98 S.Ct. 1499, 55 L.Ed.2d 524 (1978). See Restatement (Second) of Judgments § 22(2)(b) and cmt. f (1980).

13. See 6 Charles Alan Wright, Arthur R. Miller & Mary Kay Kane, Federal Practice & Procedure § 1417, at 131–34 (2d ed. 1990).

14. Pipeliners Local Union No. 798 v. Ellerd, 503 F.2d 1193, 1198 (10th Cir.1974). A nonparty may also obtain the benefits of the compulsory counterclaim rule where that party was an indispensable party to the prior litigation, but was not joined by the defendant. See Akin v. PAFEC Ltd., 991 F.2d 1550, 1559 (11th Cir.1993).

have determined the nature of specific counterclaims based on the following guidelines:

> (1) Are the issues of fact and law raised by the claim and counterclaim largely the same? (2) Would res judicata bar a subsequent suit on defendants' claim absent the compulsory counterclaim rule? (3) Will substantially the same evidence support or refute plaintiffs' claims as well as defendants' counterclaim? (4) Is there any logical relation between the claim and the counterclaim?[15]

A claim that should have been pleaded as a compulsory counterclaim will be barred in a subsequent lawsuit only if a responsive pleading was served or was required to be served in the first action.[16] For example, where a party successfully moves to dismiss an action for failure to state a claim under Rule 12(b)(6), that party is not barred from filing a lawsuit against the plaintiff based on a claim arising out of the same transaction or occurrence.[17] In addition, a compulsory counterclaim is not barred unless a final judgment was entered in the first suit.[18]

Courts have applied Rule 13(a) where a default judgment was entered in holding that a compulsory counterclaim that should have been asserted in the action is barred in any future lawsuits.[19] Where judgment is entered by consent, however, the defendant can reserve counterclaims for prosecution in a separate lawsuit.[20] Thus, whenever a consent judgment is to be entered, defense counsel should take care to reserve any potential counterclaims to avoid preclusion.

Rule 13(a) ordinarily arises where judgment has been entered and a party seeks to assert what should have been pled as a compulsory counterclaim in a subsequent lawsuit. This issue also arises, however, where the first lawsuit is still pending when a second lawsuit is filed asserting what would be a compulsory counterclaim in the first suit.

---

15. Pipeliners, 503 F.2d at 1198. *See also* Fox v. Maulding, 112 F.3d 453, 457 (10th Cir.1997) (where issues of fact and law in claim and counterclaim arise out of the same relationship between plaintiff and defendant and successful prosecution of defendant's counterclaim in separate litigation would impair rights established in the first action, counterclaim is compulsory and barred by doctrine of res judicata).

16. United States v. Snider, 779 F.2d 1151, 1157 (6th Cir.1985)(compulsory counterclaim not barred where defendant not required to serve responsive pleading in first action).

17. *See* Lawhorn v. Atlantic Refining Co., 299 F.2d 353 (5th Cir.1962).

18. *See* Dillard v. Security Pacific Brokers, Inc., 835 F.2d 607, 608 (5th Cir.1988)(where action dismissed with prejudice at any stage of proceeding, dismissal constitutes final judgment on merits barring later suit on same claim).

19. *See* Greyhound Exhibitgroup, Inc. v. E.L.U.L. Realty Corp., 973 F.2d 155, 160 (2d Cir.1992)(Rule 13(a) bars assertion of offset that was a compulsory counterclaim in action resolved by default judgment), *cert. denied*, 506 U.S. 1080, 113 S.Ct. 1049, 122 L.Ed.2d 357 (1993); Dillard, 835 F.2d at 608, (default judgment is judgment on the merits barring subsequent suit on same claim); Carteret Sav. & Loan Ass'n v. Jackson, 812 F.2d 36, 38–39 (1st Cir.1987)(default judgment entered against defendant in contract action barred subsequent assertion of tort claims that were compulsory counterclaims in first lawsuit).

20. Benjamin v. United States, 348 F.2d 502, 513 (Ct.Cl.1965)(Rule 13(a) does not bar second lawsuit where it was understood by all parties and court that right to bring second lawsuit was preserved).

Courts have held that Rule 13(a) does not apply until a judgment has been entered in the first lawsuit.[21] The court can, however, enjoin the defendant from bringing the compulsory counterclaim in a separate lawsuit.[22]

(c) The New Jersey Entire Controversy Doctrine

As discussed above, federal courts assessing the effect of a prior state judgment must apply the governing law of the state issuing the judgment.[23] It is therefore essential that practitioners consider unique state law principles with respect to claim preclusion and issue preclusion.[24] For example, the State of New Jersey has one of the most comprehensive set of rules in the United States relating to joinder of claims and parties.[25] New Jersey has adopted the "entire controversy doctrine,"[26] which requires that all parties involved in a dispute be joined in one litigation and that all of their claims and defenses be presented in this litigation or be waived.[27] The entire controversy doctrine expands the res judicata effect of a prior judgment to claims arising from the same controversy that were omitted from the lawsuit.

The entire controversy doctrine has been codified in the New Jersey Court Rules at R. 4:30A, which provides:

Nonjoinder of claims or parties required to be joined by the entire controversy doctrine shall result in the preclusion of the omitted

21. J. Lyons & Co. Ltd. v. Republic of Tea, Inc., 892 F.Supp. 486, 490 (S.D.N.Y.1995)(filing of compulsory counterclaim in second lawsuit while first lawsuit still pending does not violate Rule 13(a), but undermines purpose of Rule).

22. See Asset Allocation and Management Co. v. Western Employers Ins. Co., 892 F.2d 566, 572–73 (7th Cir.1989) (court has equitable power to enjoin defendants from bringing compulsory counterclaim in separate litigation).

23. See Migra v. Warren City School District Board of Education, 465 U.S. 75, 81, 104 S.Ct. 892, 896, 79 L.Ed.2d 56 (1984).

24. See, e.g., Rycoline Products, Inc. v. C & W Unlimited, 109 F.3d 883 (3d Cir. 1997) (a federal court construing New Jersey judgment is bound by the entire controversy doctrine by virtue of Full Faith and Credit Clause).

25. See Electro-Miniatures Corp. v. Wendon Co., Inc., 889 F.2d 41, 44 n. 5 (3d Cir.1989)(entire controversy doctrine is inextricably related to general principle of res judicata); Prevratil v. Mohr, 145 N.J. 180, 187, 678 A.2d 243, 246 (1996) (entire controversy doctrine "stems directly from the

principles underlying the doctrine of res judicata or claim preclusion").

26. N.J. Ct. R. 4:30A.

27. The entire controversy doctrine requires "the joinder of virtually all causes, claims, and defenses relating to a controversy between the parties engaged in litigation." Cogdell v. Hospital Center at Orange, 116 N.J. 7, 16, 560 A.2d 1169, 1173 (1989). The principle objectives of the doctrine are as follows:

(1) to encourage the comprehensive and conclusive determination of a legal controversy;

(2) to achieve party fairness, including both parties before the court as well as prospective parties; and

(3) to promote traditional economy and efficiency by avoiding fragmented, multiple and duplicative litigation.

Mystic Isle Development Corp. v. Perskie & Nehmad, 142 N.J. 310, 323–24, 662 A.2d 523, 529–30 (1995). See also Rycoline, 109 F.3d at 885–86 (providing summary of the entire controversy doctrine). See also Chapter 6 "Responses to Complaints," at § 6.12(a)(2), supra discussing doctrine.

claims to the extent required by the entire controversy doctrine, except as otherwise provided by R. 4:64–5 (foreclosure actions) and by R. 4:67–4(a)(leave required for counterclaims or crossclaims in summary actions).[28]

The rule includes "all affirmative claims that a party might have against another party, including counterclaims and crossclaims, as well as joinder of all parties with a material interest in the controversy, *i.e.*, those who can affect or be affected by the judicial outcome of the controversy."[29]

A party's failure to join a claim pursuant to the entire controversy doctrine bars future actions against the parties to the initial litigation and against nonparties that should have been joined in the initial litigation. The New Jersey approach to claim preclusion is unique and not well known to practitioners outside of New Jersey.[30] Practitioners in other jurisdictions must be conscious of the entire controversy doctrine because the Supreme Court of New Jersey has held that it applies to bar litigation in New Jersey where related claims were previously litigated in other jurisdictions.

Specifically, in *Mortgagelinq Corp. v. Commonwealth Land Title Ins. Co.*,[31] the New Jersey Supreme Court addressed the issue of whether New Jersey courts will hear claims that the plaintiff could have joined with similar claims it had previously filed in another state. In *Mortgagelinq*, a defrauded mortgage lender, brought suit against the principal perpetrators of the alleged fraud in federal court in Pennsylvania. The plaintiffs reserved claims against several New Jersey title insurance companies, which they alleged were accessories to the fraud. Plaintiffs brought a separate lawsuit in New Jersey state court against the title insurance companies. The New Jersey Supreme Court held that plaintiffs' deliberate fragmentation of the suit justified dismissal of the claims asserted against the New Jersey title insurance companies based on the entire controversy doctrine.

The court acknowledged that its decision imposed the law of New Jersey on a judgment from other jurisdictions. "If Pennsylvania courts do not have a comparable party-joinder rule, principles of comity suggest that New Jersey should not seek to export its entire controversy doctrine to regulate the conduct of attorneys in that jurisdiction."[32] However, the court stated that there is a "corollary" to that proposition, that "New

---

28. N.J. Ct. R. 4:30A.

29. Circle Chevrolet v. Giordano, Halleran & Ciesla, 142 N.J. 280, 662 A.2d 509, 513 (1995)(citations omitted). According to the Supreme Court of New Jersey, the entire controversy doctrine is discretionary and "should not be applied when 'joinder would result in significant unfairness [to the litigants] or jeopardy to a clear presentation of the issues and just result.'" *Id.*

30. Mortgagelinq Corp. v. Commonwealth Land Title Insurance Co., 142 N.J.

336, 350–51, 662 A.2d 536, 543 (1995), (Pollack, J., dissenting). New Jersey's entire controversy doctrine is in contrast to federal practice where only certain claims must be joined or be barred in future proceedings. *See* FRCP 13(a), (b), (g), 19(a), 20(a) (compulsory counterclaims, permissive counterclaims, permissive cross-claims and joinder).

31. 142 N.J. 336, 662 A.2d 536.

32. *Id.* at 345, 662 A.2d at 541.

Jersey courts need not necessarily grant relief when parties deliberately refrain from seeking relief in other jurisdictions when doing so would have been much fairer to all parties involved."[33] The court applied this corollary, holding that plaintiffs were barred from bringing suit in New Jersey under the entire controversy doctrine.[34]

As a result of the *Mortgagelinq* decision, practitioners must consider the New Jersey entire-controversy doctrine not only when litigating claims in New Jersey but also in any other jurisdiction if there is a possibility that the claims may give rise to litigation in New Jersey.[35]

The New Jersey Supreme Court has retreated somewhat from the expansive application of the entire controversy doctrine that it had previously espoused. In *Circle Chevrolet v. Giordano, Halleran & Ciesla*,[36] the Supreme Court held in 1995 that a former client was barred from pursuing a legal malpractice claim against its former lawyer because the client had failed to raise this claim in the context of the prior litigation in which the lawyer's mistake came to light. Two years later, the court realized the difficulties this posed to practitioners and rejected the *Circle Chevrolet* rule, holding in *Olds v. Donnelly*[37] that the entire controversy doctrine did *not* preclude a former client from bringing a legal malpractice claim against its former attorney, even where the former attorney's mistakes had been discovered during the prior litigation, because the legal malpractice claim had not accrued until the client had actually suffered damage—which was at the time that the court entered judgment dismissing the prior litigation for the client's failure to prosecute.[38]

The court acknowledged the substantial criticism that had arisen among the bar following *Circle Chevrolet* and suggested that the entire controversy doctrine embodied in Rule 4:30A would be reviewed and possibly revised at the next biannual review of New Jersey's Rules of Practice. For the moment, the entire controversy doctrine was left intact, with the exception of legal malpractice claims. The court specifi-

---

33. *Id.*

34. The court noted that under New Jersey rules, dismissal under the entire controversy was not a ruling on the merits and, thus, the dismissal of plaintiffs' suit would not preclude plaintiffs from bringing suit in another jurisdiction. *Id.* at 347, 662 A.2d at 542.

35. *Id.* at 354, 662 A.2d at 545 (Pollock, J., dissenting). According to the United States Court of Appeals for the Third Circuit, the application of the entire controversy doctrine to claims previously brought in other jurisdictions may compel counsel:

to raise all related claims and issues and seek all available remedies in a single proceeding, because of the possibility that a subsequent claim might arise in New Jersey. In this way, New Jersey would be

imposing on litigants and courts in other states its policy choice to encourage parties to litigate all claims, defenses, issues, and remedies related to a particular transaction.

Electro–Miniatures Corp. v. Wendon, 889 F.2d 41, 45 n. 6 (3d Cir.1989).

36. 142 N.J. 280, 662 A.2d 509 (1995).

37. 150 N.J. 424, 696 A.2d 633 (1997).

38. The New Jersey Supreme Court decided three cases on the same day, all holding that a former client was not barred by the entire controversy doctrine from bringing a legal malpractice claim against its former attorney. In addition to *Olds v. Donnelly*, the court also decided *Donohue v. Kuhn*, 150 N.J. 484, 696 A.2d 664 (1997), and *Karpovich v. Barbarula*, 150 N.J. 473, 696 A.2d 659 (1997).

cally noted, however, that its holding did not reach other claims, such as second-litigation malpractice claims against accountants, architects, engineers, physicians or psychologists, and that the underlying purpose of the entire controversy doctrine—to require submission to a court of issues concerning joinder so that the court could determine how best to manage them—remained an important state policy.

Library References:

West's Key No. Digests, Judgment ⬤570(3), 585(4), 592, 654.
Wright, Miller, Kane & Cooper, Federal Practice and Procedure: Civil 2d §§ 1409, 1411, 1412, 1417, 1418, 2362, 3914.8.

§ 12.13   Effect of Administrative Agency Proceedings

The doctrines of res judicata and collateral estoppel apply to determinations of governmental administrative agencies so long as the "administrative agency is acting in a judicial capacity and resolves disputed issues of fact properly before it which the parties have had an adequate opportunity to litigate. . . . "[1] According to the Supreme Court, the principle of judicial economy and fairness to successful litigants is equally applicable in the context of administrative proceedings.[2] Thus, the policy justifications for res judicata and collateral estoppel apply "equally when the issue has been decided by an administrative agency, be it state or federal, which acts in a judicial capacity."[3]

Federal administrative agency decisions will be given preclusive effect under the doctrines of res judicata and collateral estoppel if (1) the original action was properly before the agency, (2) the same disputed issues of fact are before the court as were before the agency, (3) the agency acted in a judicial capacity, and (4) the parties had an adequate opportunity to litigate the issue before the agency.[4]

When state administrative agency decisions are involved, however, the Supreme Court has drawn a distinction, however, between state administrative agency decisions that are reviewed and approved by state courts and those that are unreviewed. Unreviewed state agency determi-

---

§ 12.13

1. Astoria Federal Savings and Loan Association v. Solimino, 501 U.S. 104, 107, 111 S.Ct. 2166, 2169, 115 L.Ed.2d 96 (1991) (citing United States v. Utah Construction and Mining Co., 384 U.S. 394, 422, 86 S.Ct. 1545, 1560, 16 L.Ed.2d 642 (1966)).

2. *Id.* at 107, 111 S.Ct. at 2169.

3. *Id.* at 108, 111 S.Ct. at 2169 (citing University of Tennessee v. Elliott, 478 U.S. 788, 798, 106 S.Ct. 3220, 3226, 92 L.Ed.2d 635 (1986).

4. Frye v. United Steelworkers of America, 767 F.2d 1216, 1220 (7th Cir.), *cert. denied*, 474 U.S. 1007, 106 S.Ct. 530, 88

L.Ed.2d 461 (1985). *See also* Utah Construction & Mining Co., 384 U.S. at 421–22, 86 S.Ct. at 1560, 16 L.Ed.2d 642 (res judicata principles apply in the context of administrative proceedings where the agency is acting in a judicial capacity and resolves disputed issues of fact properly before it which the parties have had an adequate opportunity to litigate); Alexander v. Pathfinder, 91 F.3d 59, 62–63 (8th Cir.1996) (collateral estoppel is also applied to administrative agency rulings to prevent re-litigation of factual disputes previously presented to the administrative agency).

nations do not bar subsequent federal court litigation under the doctrine of res judicata.[5]

While res judicata and collateral estoppel are presumed to apply to federal administrative agency decisions, this presumption may be overcome where the statutory scheme enacted by the legislature indicates an intention that a particular agency determination is not subject to these rules.[6] The issue is "whether a common law rule of preclusion would be consistent with Congress' intent in enacting [the statute]."[7]

Thus, an administrative agency decision will not be given preclusive effect when the legislature either expressly or impliedly indicates that none is intended.[8] For example, discrimination claims under Title VII or other federal anti-discrimination statutes typically must first be brought to a state administrative agency responsible for enforcement of anti-discrimination laws. Claims under federal anti-discrimination laws may only be filed after the state agency has concluded its investigation and made a determination.[9] Under these circumstances, application of res judicata and collateral estoppel to the state agency determination would effectively preclude the relief envisioned in the federal anti-discrimination statutes.[10]

In *Kremer v. Chemical Construction Corp.*,[11] the Supreme Court held that final state court judgments disposing of discrimination claims are entitled to full faith and credit when the same claims are brought in federal court under Title VII. In *Kremer* an employee filed a Title VII discrimination claim with the Equal Employment Opportunity Commission ("EEOC"), which, in turn, referred the case to a state agency charged with administering the state's employment discrimination laws pursuant to 42 U.S.C.A. § 2000e–5. The state agency rejected the discrimination claim and this judgment was affirmed by a state court. The employee then brought a Title VII action in which the employer raised

---

5. *See* Garner v. Giarrusso, 571 F.2d 1330 (5th Cir.1978); Cooper v. Phillip Morris, Inc., 464 F.2d 9 (6th Cir.1972); Voutsis v. Union Carbide Corp., 452 F.2d 889 (2d Cir.1971), *cert. denied*, 406 U.S. 918, 92 S.Ct. 1768, 32 L.Ed.2d 117 (1972).

6. Astoria, 501 U.S. at 108–09, 111 S.Ct. at 2169–70.

7. *Id.* at 110, 111 S.Ct. at 2170 (citing University of Tennessee v. Elliott, 478 U.S. 788, 796, 106 S.Ct. 3220, 3225, 92 L.Ed.2d 635 (1986).

8. *Id.* at 110, 111 S.Ct. at 2170. *See also* Texas Instruments, Inc. v. Cypress Semiconductor Corp., 90 F.3d 1558, 1569 (Fed. Cir.1996), *cert. denied*, ___ U.S. ___, 117 S.Ct. 1818, 137 L.Ed.2d 1027 (1997) (decisions of the International Trade Commission on patent issues do not have collateral estoppel effect in subsequent infringement action).

9. Astoria, 501 U.S. at 110, 111 S.Ct. at 2170 (citing Section 14(b) of the Age Discrimination in Employment Act, 29 U.S.C.A. § 633(b) which precludes filing of claims with the EEOC or filing suit until the state administrative agency has had an opportunity to address the claim).

10. *Id.* at 111, 111 S.Ct. at 2171. *See also* University of Tennessee, 478 U.S. at 795, 106 S.Ct. at 3224, 92 L.Ed.2d 635 (Title VII requires that federal agency accord "substantial weight to final findings and orders made by State or local authorities in proceedings commenced under State or local law," indicating that Congress did not intend for State agency findings to have preclusive effect.).

11. 456 U.S. 461, 102 S.Ct. 1883, 72 L.Ed.2d 262 (1982).

res judicata as a defense. The Supreme Court held that under 28 U.S.C.A. § 1738 the state court's judgment affirming the state administrative agency's finding was entitled to preclusive effect in the employee's Title VII action.

Similarly in actions under Section 1983, the Supreme Court has held that "federal courts must give [an] agency's fact finding the same preclusive effects to which it would be entitled in the State's courts."[12]

§ 12.14   Practice Checklist

(a) Res Judicata

(1) Res judicata is an affirmative defense that must be raised in the pleadings to be preserved. (*See* FRCP 8(c); § 12.4(a))

(2) To support application of res judicata, a certified copy of the prior judgment should be obtained. (*See* § 12.5)

(3) Counsel should determine at the outset whether federal law or the law of a particular state controls the preclusive effect of the prior judgment (*See* §§ 12.4, 12.9)

(4) The relationship between the parties to the current action and the prior action must be assessed to determine whether "privity" exists for purposes of binding the current parties to the earlier judgment. (*See* § 12.6(b)).

(5) Counsel must determine that the claims in the earlier litigation and the prior litigation are, in fact, the same claims in order for preclusionary effect to be given to the earlier judgment (*See* § 12.6(c))

(b) Collateral Estoppel

(1) Like res judicata, collateral estoppel is an affirmative defense that must be pleaded to avoid waiver. (*See*, FRCP 8(c); § 12.4(a))

(2) Counsel will be required to obtain proof in the proper form from the earlier litigation to allow the court to find a proper evidentiary basis for application of collateral estoppel. (*See* § 12.5)

(3) Collateral estoppel does not require mutuality of estoppel and it may be used both offensively and defensively. (*See* § 12.7(b), (c))

(4) For application of collateral estoppel, there must be identical issues presented in the earlier and current litigation, actual litigation of the issue in the earlier case, necessary resolution of the issue in the earlier case and a full and fair opportunity to litigate the issue in the earlier case. (*See* § 12.7)

---

12. *See* Elliott, 478 U.S. at 799, 106 S.Ct. at 3226 (note omitted). *See also* Clark v. Alexander, 85 F.3d 146 (4th Cir.1996) (where recipient of federal housing benefits brought Section 1983 action against local housing authority, authority's adjudicative decision interpreting federal regulations was granted deference by federal court).

(5) Depending upon the forum in which the earlier litigation was pending, the preclusive effect of issues decided in it may be determined by either federal or state law. (*See* § 12.9)

(c) Other Preclusionary Doctrines

(1) Judicial estoppel prevents a party, having once successfully obtained judicial relief based on advocating a particular position on an issue, from changing its position later to gain relief again. (*See* § 12.8)

(2) Any time a related criminal action exists, counsel should be mindful of the potential preclusive effect of either a guilty plea or a conviction in pending or subsequent civil litigation. (*See* § 12.10)

(3) Class actions present unique considerations in terms of potential preclusive effect and must be scrutinized closely at all stages. (*See* § 12.11)

(4) Administrative proceedings, depending upon the circumstances, may or may not have preclusive effect in later litigation depending upon the character and venue of the earlier administrative proceeding. (*See* § 12.13)

§ 12.15   Forms

(a) Motion for Summary Judgment Based on Res Judicata 🖫

IN THE UNITED STATES DISTRICT COURT
FOR THE _____ DISTRICT OF _____

_____,	)	Civil Action
Plaintiff	)	
	)	
vs.	)	
	)	
	)	No.
_____,	)	
Defendant	)	
	)	

MOTION FOR SUMMARY JUDGMENT

Defendant, by and through its attorneys, now moves this Honorable Court, pursuant to FRCP 56, for an Order entering judgment against plaintiff and in favor of defendant on the ground that plaintiff's claim is barred by the doctrine of res judicata, and in support thereof states as follows:

1. Plaintiff commenced this action against defendant on [state date action commenced].

2. In this action, plaintiff seeks judgment against defendant on a claim that [state essential nature of plaintiff's cause of action].

3. The same claims encompassed in this action have previously been the subject of litigation between plaintiff and defendant in [identify the court where previous action was instituted] in an action entitled [state name of earlier case] and identified on that court's docket as [state identifying index or action numbers from other court]. A copy of the Complaint in that earlier action is attached hereto as Exhibit A.

[Note: To the extent the motion is based on earlier litigation by parties in privity with plaintiff and/or defendant, the motion should state the identity of those parties, the nature of those parties' relationship to the current litigants, and that the nature of that relationship is sufficient to constitute privity between those parties and the current litigants.]

4. In that earlier action, judgment was rendered on [state date] on claims identical to those now brought by plaintiff. A certified copy of the judgment order from that earlier action is attached hereto as Exhibit B.

5. Plaintiff [or those in privity with plaintiff] had a full and fair opportunity to litigate its claims in the earlier action and, in fact, did so.

6. Consequently, all of the elements of the doctrine of res judicata are established by the proceedings and judgment in the earlier action, and plaintiff is barred from bringing this action on those same claims against defendant.

WHEREFORE, defendant requests this Honorable Court to enter an Order entering judgment in its favor and against plaintiff on the claims set forth in the Complaint in this action, together with any and all further relief this Court may deem just and proper.

Respectfully submitted,

BY: _____

Attorney for Defendant

(b) Interrogatories Directed to Res Judicata Issues 💾

IN THE UNITED STATES DISTRICT COURT
FOR THE _____DISTRICT OF _____

_____,	)	
Plaintiff	)	Civil Action
	)	
vs.	)	
	)	
	)	No.
_____,	)	
Defendant	)	
	)	

INTERROGATORIES DIRECTED TO RES JUDICATA ISSUES

1. Have any of the claims set forth in the Complaint in this action ever been the subject of any prior or ongoing litigation or administrative proceeding?

2. If your answer to the preceding interrogatory is in the affirmative, then state the following for each prior or ongoing litigation or administrative proceeding;

(a) The caption of the other litigation or administrative proceeding involving the claims set forth in the Complaint;

(b) The identity of the parties between whom those claims that are set forth in the Complaint were litigated;

(c) The Court or agency in which the prior or ongoing litigation or administrative proceeding was instituted;

(d) Any identifying docket or index numbers assigned to the prior or ongoing litigation;

(e) Your relationship to the parties to the prior or ongoing litigation or administrative proceeding between whom the claims that are set forth in the Complaint were litigated;

(f) The terms of any judgment, order, or decree entered on the claims that are set forth in the Complaint.

3. Do you contend that the claims in the prior or ongoing litigation or administrative proceeding identified in response to Interrogatory No. 2 were not fully litigated?

4. If your answer to Interrogatory No. 3 is in the affirmative, then set forth the manner in which you contend those claims were not fully litigated?

5. Do you contend that the claims in the prior or ongoing litigation or administrative proceeding identified in response to Interrogatory No. 2 were not fairly litigated?

6. If your answer to Interrogatory No. 5 is in the affirmative, then set forth the manner in which you contend those claims were not fairly litigated.

7. Do you contend, other than by way of the identity of the parties, that the factual circumstances of the claims in any prior or ongoing litigation or administrative proceeding identified in response to Interrogatory No. 2 differ from the factual circumstances forming the basis for the claims set forth in the Complaint in this action?

8. If your answer to Interrogatory No. 7 was in the affirmative, then for each prior or ongoing litigation or administrative proceeding identified in response to Interrogatory No. 2, set forth the manner in which you contend the factual circumstances of the claims in that litigation differ from the factual circumstances in this litigation.

Respectfully submitted,

BY:_____

Attorney for Defendant

(c) Interrogatories Directed to Collateral Estoppel Issues 🖫

1. Have you ever been involved in any litigation or administrative proceeding in which the claims at issue required proof of any of the same facts as form the basis for the claims in this action.

2. If your answer to the preceding interrogatory is in the affirmative, then state the following for each such prior or ongoing litigation or proceeding:

    (a) The caption of the other litigation or administrative proceeding that required proof of the same facts.

    (b) The identity of the parties to that prior or ongoing litigation or administrative proceeding between whom were asserted the claims requiring proof of any of the same facts as form the basis for the claims in this action;

    (c) The Court or agency in which the prior or ongoing litigation or administrative proceeding was instituted;

    (d) Any identifying docket or index numbers assigned to the prior or ongoing litigation or administrative proceeding;

    (e) Your relationship to the parties to the prior or ongoing litigation or administrative proceeding between whom were asserted the claims that required proof of any of the same facts as form the basis for the claims in this action;

    (f) The date of any judgment, order, decree, opinion, or memorandum issued by the Court or administrative body that stated or contained any finding with regard to any of the same facts as form the basis for the claims in this action.

3. Do you contend that the factual findings made in any of the actions or administrative proceedings identified in response to Interrogatory No. 2 with regard to any of the same facts as form the basis for the claims in this action were unnecessary to resolution of that prior or ongoing litigation or administrative proceeding.

4. If your answer to Interrogatory No. 3 is in the affirmative, then, for each fact in each prior or ongoing litigation or administrative proceeding as to which you make that contention, state the basis for your contention.

5. Do you contend that the issues of fact determined in any of the prior or ongoing litigation or administrative proceedings identified in response to Interrogatory No. 2 were not fully litigated.

6. If your answer to Interrogatory No. 5 is in the affirmative, then, for each fact in each prior or ongoing litigation or administrative proceeding as to which you make that contention, state the basis for that contention.

7. Do you contend that the issues of fact determined in any of the prior or ongoing litigation or administrative proceedings identified in response to Interrogatory No. 2 were not fairly litigated.

8. If your answer to Interrogatory No. 7 is in the affirmative, then, for each fact in each prior or ongoing litigation or administrative proceeding as to which you make that contention, state the basis for that contention.

(d) Motion in Limine to Preclude Evidence Contradictory to Earlier Adjudication Based on Offensive Collateral Estoppel in Connection with Injunction Hearing 💾

IN THE UNITED STATES DISTRICT COURT
FOR THE _____ DISTRICT OF _____

_____,	)	
Plaintiff	)	Civil Action
	)	
vs.	)	
	)	
	)	No.
_____,	)	
Defendant	)	
	)	

MOTION IN LIMINE

[Name of Movant] by and through its attorneys, now moves this Honorable Court for an order precluding [name of respondent] from offering any evidence at trial contradictory to the determination of the court in [name of other case], and in support thereof states as follows:

1. This action is brought by plaintiff against defendant seeking damages on claims of [state essential nature of claims].

2. On [state date], another action was brought against the current defendant in [identify court where prior adjudication was rendered], docketed in that court as [state identifying action, docket, or index numbers] (hereinafter the "First Action").

3. In the First Action, the plaintiff brought suit against the defendant based on claims of [state essence of earlier claims]. A certified copy of the Complaint in the First Action is attached hereto as Exhibit A.

4. As part of the First Action, the plaintiff therein moved for partial summary judgment against the defendant, and that motion was granted by the court in the First Action. A certified copy of the unpublished memorandum opinion of the court in the First Action granting partial summary judgment against defendant is attached hereto as Exhibit B.

5. In the course of its memorandum opinion granting partial summary judgment against defendant, the court in the First Action determined that [state fact at issue in current action that was determined adversely to current respondent].

770

6. The identified issue of fact determined in the First Action as part of the partial summary judgment against defendant is identical to an issue of fact involved in the current action.

7. Defendant had a full and fair opportunity to litigate the identified issue of fact in the First Action.

8. The determination of fact made by the court in the First Action was a necessary element of its ruling on the motion for partial summary judgment.

9. The adjudication of fact rendered as part of the ruling in the First Action on the motion for partial summary judgment meets all of the criteria for application of the doctrine of collateral estoppel, and therefore, defendant is bound by and may not contest the existence of the fact determined in the First Action.

10. Currently, the Court has scheduled before it a hearing on plaintiff's motion for preliminary injunction on [state date and time of hearing].

11. Plaintiff believes that, at the preliminary injunction hearing, defendant will seek to contest the existence of the fact determined in the First Action by offering evidence and argument.

12. Due to the adjudication of fact in the First Action, the existence of [state the essential fact and issue] must be considered conclusively established by reason of the doctrine of collateral estoppel, and the defendant must be precluded from challenging the existence of that fact.

13. To allow defendant, after having had the full and fair opportunity to litigate the existence of this fact in the First Action, to challenge the existence of that fact in this Court would unjustifiably call into question the judgment rendered by the Court in the First Action, reduce public respect for and ability to rely upon existing judgments rendered by courts of competent jurisdiction, and result in unnecessarily prolonging the preliminary injunction hearing and wasting scarce judicial resources.

WHEREFORE, plaintiff requests this Honorable Court enter an Order, in the form submitted herewith, precluding defendant from offering any evidence or argument seeking to disprove or challenge the existence of [state essential fact at issue].

Respectfully submitted,

COZEN AND O'CONNOR

BY:_____
Attorneys for Plaintiffs

CHAPTER 13

PROVISIONAL REMEDIES

by

Paul H. Dawes

and

William J. Meeske*

Table of Sections

* The authors wish to thank Eyal Gamliel (JD USC 1996) and Randy Merritt (JD Iowa 1996), who are associates at Latham & Watkins, for their extraordinary effort in researching and writing this chapter. The authors also thank Estela de Llanos (Pennsylvania 1998), Tisha Greene (Howard 1998) and Christopher Lenhart (Cornell 1998), summer associates at Latham & Watkins, for similar extraordinary effort on this project.

WESTLAW Electronic Research

See WESTLAW Electronic Research Guide preceding the Summary of Contents.

---

§ 13.1 Scope Note

This chapter discusses the practice and procedures that govern the provisional remedies under the FRCP: preliminary injunction, temporary restraining order, receivership, prejudgment seizures of person or property and lis pendens. These remedies provide provisional relief because they offer a moving party interim security or protection during the pendency of an action. Other than the doctrine of lis pendens, under which a notice of lis pendens may be filed without prior court approval, each of these remedies requires court intervention before a final decision on the merits of an action and prevents the affected party from taking some action that he otherwise is legally authorized to take. As a result, courts view these remedies as "extraordinary" relief, which is granted only in exceptional circumstances.

The section on preliminary injunction discusses the provisions of FRCP 65, which governs preliminary injunctions, the issues raised by the notice requirement, evidence submitted in support of a motion, the hearing, the tests for and factors considered by the courts in granting preliminary injunctions, and issues related to appeal from the grant or denial of preliminary injunctions.

The section on temporary restraining order ("TRO") discusses applications and standards for granting a TRO, including the notice and hearing requirements, as well as the requirement of security, duration, form and scope and appealability of the order granting a TRO.

The section on receivership addresses the provisions of FRCP 66, the definition and role of receivers, the appointment of receivers, the federal and state laws that apply to receivers, different kinds of receiverships, jurisdiction over property after the appointment of a receiver, actions brought by and against receivers, and interlocutory appeals of orders involving receivers.

The section on prejudgment seizure discusses state law remedies collectively referred to as prejudgment seizures such as attachment, garnishment, replevin, sequestration and similar remedies, and federal statutory and constitutional limitations affecting prejudgment seizures.

The section on lis pendens addresses the doctrine of lis pendens and the general treatment of pendente lite transfers. The section discusses FRCP 64, common law implications, jurisdictional and notice requirements, due diligence and the duration of lis pendens remedies. Since lis pendens is a matter of state substantive real property law, this discussion primarily involves state statutory and common law doctrines that are applied in federal court actions.

Library References:

West's Key No. Digests, Injunction ⊗132–188.
Wright, Miller & Kane, Federal Practice and Procedure: Civil 2d § 2932.

§ 13.2   Preliminary Injunction

(a) Practical and Strategic Aspects of Preliminary Injunctions

(1) Effect of Seeking a Preliminary Injunction on Continued Litigation and Settlement

The decision to seek a preliminary injunction involves a number of strategic and tactical considerations. In addition to the obvious goal of avoiding perceived irreparable harm, by seeking such preliminary relief, a party discloses its case early in the proceedings, before substantial discovery, and forces the opposing parties to do so as well. Such disclosure also causes early evaluation of the case by the parties and the court. That evaluation may lead to more expeditious and less expensive resolution of the dispute than would otherwise occur. As does the court, the defendant is forced to make a quick evaluation of the likelihood of success on the merits and the impact that injunctive relief will have on the defendant, its business or other conduct. The defendant may conclude that an early settlement will provide a better option than the risk of an injunction.

Settlement may also be more attractive to the defendant after an injunction is entered. An early, major victory by the plaintiff may dampen the defendant's enthusiasm for litigation. In particular, the defendant may wish to avoid the cost of discovery and trial, especially if the court's ruling on the preliminary injunction signals clearly that, absent a substantial difference in the evidence presented at the trial on the merits, the entry of a permanent injunction as well as the award of damages appears inevitable.

The same considerations affect the plaintiff. A motion for preliminary injunction educates the court and the opposition to the nature and strength of the plaintiff's claim. By seeking a preliminary injunction, the plaintiff may disclose potential weaknesses in its case and risk the chance that the court will make damaging preliminary findings. The plaintiff also takes the risk that the court may gain a view of the facts and the parties that will be difficult to alter during the rest of the proceeding.

Finally, the parties may feel they have had their "day in court" and have received consideration of their arguments from a neutral decision-maker. As a result, both may be more inclined to view the case realistically.

(2) The Decision to Seek a Preliminary Injunction

The plaintiff first should consider whether seeking a preliminary injunction is the appropriate course of action. For example, the plaintiff should consider whether it can avoid the anticipated harm from the defendant's conduct by agreement with the defendant, especially if confirmed by a stipulation and order. The plaintiff may also consider the possibility of moving for an early trial, explaining to the court that the granting of such a motion might avoid the need to seek a preliminary injunction. As with a TRO, counsel must consider whether the need for a preliminary injunction is caused by the client's delay, rather than the unexpected threat of harmful conduct by the defendant. Counsel must carefully consider whether the threatened harm is truly irreparable or whether money damages will suffice. Without this preliminary analysis, an ill-considered decision to file a motion for preliminary injunction will instigate expensive and time-consuming activity, perhaps including extensive expedited discovery. If the chances of success are small, unless there is no alternative, it may be unwise to "let loose the dogs of war."

If the client and counsel decide to proceed, a party may seek a preliminary injunction by filing a noticed motion. If the party believes that it will suffer irreparable harm before the court can decide that motion, counsel must consider seeking a TRO to protect the status quo pending the hearing on the preliminary injunction. On the considerations affecting the decision to seek a TRO, see Section 13.3(a), *infra*. If the party seeks a TRO, then it normally seeks a preliminary injunction by the same application, by including an order to show cause ("OSC") why the injunction should not be issued. The OSC is served with and included in the proposed TRO and is normally granted by the court even if the TRO is denied.

Counsel should consider whether the client can make the necessary showing to obtain a preliminary injunction without the expense and delay of expedited discovery. If the party already has sufficient facts to justify a preliminary injunction order, simply filing the complaint and the motion places pressure on the defendant to evaluate the strength of its case. If the defendant then seeks expedited discovery, the plaintiff may be in a position to argue that the facts are simple and straightforward and that no expedited discovery is necessary.

The defendant faces similar considerations. If the plaintiff simply files a motion for preliminary injunction, without seeking a TRO or expedited discovery, it may be to the defendant's advantage to avoid escalating the dispute by seeking expedited discovery. The defendant may be able to introduce evidence that the plaintiff cannot controvert without taking any discovery, or to argue that the plaintiff's showing is insufficient to justify extraordinary relief.

The plaintiff may also decide that expedited discovery is necessary to support its motion. If the plaintiff does not yet have enough facts to support a motion and no claim of immediate harm to justify a TRO application, counsel should file only an ex-parte application for leave to take expedited discovery. To make it more likely that the application will be granted, the discovery should be narrowly tailored to obtain the facts necessary to support the preliminary injunction. The court is much more likely to grant an application for expedited discovery than a TRO. The quick, early victory and the initiation of expedited discovery sends a message that the plaintiff is serious and that this action will be time-consuming and expensive. That alone may bring the defendant to the settlement table.

If the defendant successfully seeks expedited discovery, the court will almost certainly permit the plaintiff to take advantage of the opportunity for early discovery as well. By engaging in extensive expedited discovery, the parties increase the chances that the trial on the merits will be advanced, or consolidated with the preliminary injunction hearing. Even without advancement or consolidation, if the court considers the preliminary injunction motion on an extensive record, there may be little new left to try and the court may gain a view of the case that is difficult to change. On the other hand, if the effect of the entry of a preliminary injunction on the defendant's business would be extremely harmful, the defendant may have no choice but to seek expedited discovery and a full record for consideration by the court. Such an application also tells the plaintiff that the defendant intends to fight and may thus lead to a more favorable early resolution in the defendant's favor.

(3) Drafting the Proposed Order

Draft the proposed order first. Defining the specific conduct that the plaintiff seeks to enjoin will immediately disclose problems with the motion. For example, is the client seeking a mandatory injunction? Can the order be reframed to become a prohibitory injunction? Can the conduct be specifically described? Will the injunction sought protect the plaintiff's interests that are being harmed? The thought and analysis that goes into drafting that specific order will help counsel draft affidavits and other supporting documents that are aimed specifically at the offending conduct. A failure to draft the order first leads to an unfocused and sometimes wasteful effort.

In seeking preliminary relief, while counsel should attempt to obtain a sufficiently broad order that will protect the client's legitimate interests, it is important to be reasonable. Overreaching damages credibility, while a reasonably drafted preliminary injunction order builds credibility. A preliminary injunction that seeks reasonable relief that is justified by the facts also minimizes haggling and reduces the court's role in redrafting the order, which may otherwise cause a delay in obtaining that order. Clear, unambiguous language may strengthen a later position in a contempt proceeding or on appeal. Carefully consider the parties against whom the injunction should run and the activities to which the enjoined party may alternatively resort that might circumvent the order as worded but which would continue to injure the applicant. Determine who is most likely to violate the order and be prepared to serve them individually.

(4) Supporting Affidavits

In drafting supporting affidavits, consider summarizing the contents of and the purpose for submitting the affidavit in the initial paragraph of the affidavit and placing the sections on qualifications and background at the end. Avoid hearsay, conclusions and vituperation. The facts stated in the affidavit must be within the witness' personal knowledge; be sure to establish a sufficient foundation. Lay the proper foundation for any attached exhibits. Avoid having counsel sign affidavits. For the reasons stated above, it is preferable to use the client or one who has personal knowledge. Use affidavits, rather than a verified complaint, to support the motion. The allegations of a verified complaint are normally too conclusory and may not be supported by adequate foundation. To minimize the amount of bond required, consider including an evidentiary showing that the opposing party will suffer little or no damage if the injunction is granted.

(5) Defensive Considerations

In defending against a preliminary injunction, it is important to obtain a bond amount which will adequately compensate the defendant for all possible damage. The bond is the sole source of any recovery if the preliminary injunction has been improvidently granted. On occasions, a party that wins a preliminary injunction ends up losing because the party is unable to post a substantial bond. To support the imposition of a large bond, include in the opposing papers evidence of the substantial monetary harm that the defendant will suffer if the preliminary injunction is granted.

Be sure to preserve evidentiary objections in the memorandum of law for possible appeal. Make separate written objections to the plaintiff's affidavits and exhibits.

In opposing a preliminary injunction, consider attacking the underlying complaint with a FRCP 12(b)(6) motion or a motion to strike. Such motions tend to emphasize the strength of the argument that plaintiff will not succeed on the merits of its claims and puts the moving party on the defensive.

Pursue any affirmative defenses and equitable defenses. Credible arguments of laches or unclean hands may tip the scales in your direction, especially in a close case. If the plaintiff has delayed in seeking the preliminary injunction, set forth the facts in detail, including the prejudice to the defendant caused by such delay. Courts will often deny a preliminary injunction sought by a plaintiff which demands that the court act quickly because the plaintiff has not done so. Likewise, specific evidence of misconduct that can be characterized as unclean hands will cause the court to pause before granting the plaintiff extraordinary relief.

Even if counsel cannot defeat the preliminary injunction, try to narrow it in order to minimize its effect. Also, offer to work with the plaintiff, possibly to fashion a stipulated order which will minimize the court's role and may allow for more flexibility in the defendant's conduct than the proposed injunction would permit.

(6) The Hearing

Find out whether the court expects or will permit live testimony. A party that believes that an evidentiary hearing will emphasize the strength of its evidence and the weakness of its opponent's evidence should consider requesting such a hearing, especially where the opposing witnesses may not be available.

At oral argument, both parties should normally emphasize the irreparable injury factor. Prepare arguments for offensive, defensive, and fallback positions. Anticipate arguments on the merits, bond amount, and the language of the order. Defense counsel should try to force the plaintiff to choose between obtaining partial relief and risking losing the entire motion. To avoid the entry of an order, offer relief through a private agreement, rather than a court order. If the entry of an injunction would be devastating to the client, and if the plaintiff's claim of irreparable harm is based upon an argument that money damages are too speculative to recover, consider offering a stipulation that the defendant will not challenge the plaintiff's damage claims at trial as too speculative. This is a major concession that should not be considered lightly.

To avoid a preliminary injunction, offer to agree that at the trial the defendant will not rely on any claim that the defendant would be harmed by entry of a permanent injunction because the defendant changed his position or engaged in conduct in the absence of a preliminary injunction. Focus on the lack of any real threat of immediate injury as well as the ensuing harm to defendant if it were to be enjoined for even a brief period. Counsel may be able to limit the order or obtain an increased bond amount. Be prepared to offer alternatives to the relief sought by the plaintiff.

Some courts will press hard for a stipulation between the parties short of an actual preliminary injunction to preserve the status quo. Among other advantages, no bond is required. If agreement is reached, the plaintiff should request that the stipulation be entered on the record so that there will be no later misunderstanding as to the content of the stipulation. Counsel must understand the limits and variants of the client's bargaining positions, have the authority to enter into such a stipulation, and make the client cognizant of the impact of any stipulation agreed upon.

(b) Overview of Preliminary Injunctions

A preliminary injunction is a provisional remedy granted by a court in equity to protect the plaintiff from irreparable injury and to preserve the court's power to render a meaningful decision.[1] These goals are

---

§ 13.2

1. WarnerVision Entertainment v. Empire of Carolina, Inc., 101 F.3d 259, 261 (2d Cir.1996) (A court must "preserve a state of affairs such that it will be able upon conclusion of the full trial to render a meaningful decision for either party."); Caplan v. Fellheimer Eichen Braverman & Kaskey, 68 F.3d 828 (3d Cir.1995) ("[T]he purpose of [a preliminary] injunction is to protect the moving party from irreparable injury until the court can render a meaningful decision on the merits."); United States v. Alabama, 791 F.2d 1450, 1459 (11th Cir.1986) ("Preliminary injunctive relief may be necessary to insure that a remedy will be available."); Hunt v. City of Longview, 932 F.Supp. 828, 842 (E.D.Tex.1995) (" 'The purpose of a preliminary injunction is always to prevent irreparable injury so as to preserve the

generally accomplished by an order preserving the status quo until the court makes a final decision on the merits.[2] The grant or denial of a preliminary injunction is not a disposition of the merits of the case.[3] The court, therefore, may issue a preliminary injunction even though the plaintiff's right to permanent relief is uncertain.[4] Because the remedy imposes a restraint on the defendant before the parties' rights have been adjudicated, courts usually view a preliminary injunction as an extraordinary[5] and drastic[6] measure to be granted reluctantly.

Despite the temporary nature of this remedy, a preliminary injunction has the full force of a permanent injunction during its effective period.[7] A preliminary injunction is generally effective until the trial on the merits concludes[8] or the matter is dismissed.[9] The injunction may also expire according to its terms, the consent of the parties,[10] modification by the court,[11] or a reversal of the injunction on appeal.[12]

court's ability to render a meaningful decision on the merits.' ") (citation omitted);

2. University of Tex. v. Camenisch, 451 U.S. 390, 395, 101 S.Ct. 1830, 1834, 68 L.Ed.2d 175 (1981); Board of Educ. of Oak Park & River Forest High Sch. Dist. 200 v. Ill. State Bd. of Educ., 79 F.3d 654, 657 (7th Cir.1996); Acierno v. New Castle County, 40 F.3d 645, 647 (3d Cir.1994); Zepeda v. U.S. Immigration & Naturalization Serv., 753 F.2d 719, 728 (9th Cir.1983).

3. Camenisch, 451 U.S. at 395, 101 S.Ct. at 1834 (explaining that a decision on the merits is inappropriate at the preliminary injunction stage because preliminary injunction proceedings are based on informal and incomplete evidence and are granted in haste for the limited purpose of maintaining the relative positions of the parties until the trial on the merits); N.J. Hosp. Ass'n v. Waldman, 73 F.3d 509, 519 (3d Cir.1995) (noting that the findings of fact and conclusions of law made in conjunction with preliminary injunction proceedings are "indeed preliminary" and subject to contrary findings basing the final decision on the merits); Hunt, 932 F.Supp. at 841 n.8 ("This ruling should not be construed as a final determination on the merits. In the preliminary injunction context, Plaintiffs need not prove their case.... A final determination is possible only after a full evidentiary trial on the merits.").

4. Republic of the Philippines v. Marcos, 862 F.2d 1355, 1362 (9th Cir.1988); SK & F, Co. v. Premo Pharm. Lab., Inc., 625 F.2d 1055, 1066 (3d Cir.1980); Benson Hotel Corp. v. Woods, 168 F.2d 694 (8th Cir. 1948).

5. Intel Corp. v. ULSI Sys. Tech., Inc., 995 F.2d 1566, 1568 (Fed.Cir.1993); Lakedreams v. Taylor, 932 F.2d 1103, 1107 (5th Cir.1991); GTE Corp. v. Williams, 731 F.2d 676, 678 (10th Cir.1984).

6. Crochet v. Housing Authority of Tampa, 37 F.3d 607 (11th Cir.1994); Borey v. National Union Fire Ins. Co. of Pittsburgh, PA., 934 F.2d 30, 33 (2d Cir.1991); United States v. Overton, 834 F.2d 1171, 1177 (5th Cir.1987).

7. Paschall v. Kansas City Star Co., 441 F.Supp. 349, 355 (W.D.Mo.1977).

8. Burbank–Glendale–Pasadena Airport Auth. v. City of Los Angeles, 979 F.2d 1338, 1340 n. 1 (9th Cir.1992) (appeal of the preliminary injunction was improper because the preliminary injunction did not survive the adjudication of the merits by summary judgment).

9. Venezia v. Robinson, 16 F.3d 209 (7th Cir.1994) (vacating a preliminary injunction granted in state court before removal because, among other reasons, the district court dismissed plaintiff's claim).

10. JAK Prod., Inc. v. Wiza, 986 F.2d 1080, 1090 (7th Cir.1993) (district court had discretion to enjoin defendant from soliciting plaintiff's customers for one year pursuant to the terms of their noncompetition agreement).

11. *In re* Detroit Auto Dealers Ass'n, Inc., 84 F.3d 787, 789–90 (6th Cir.1996) (noting that the court has continuing jurisdiction to terminate or modify an injunction when either a change in the law or the facts warrant modification).

12. Arkansas Peace Ctr. v. Arkansas Department of Pollution Control, 999 F.2d 1212 (8th Cir.1993).

(c) Statutory Framework and Procedural Requirements

(1) The Provisions of FRCP 65

FRCP 65 governs preliminary injunctions and temporary restraining orders in the federal courts. Sections 65(a), (c), (d) and (e) relate to preliminary injunctions.[13]

FRCP 65 does not provide the procedures for obtaining a preliminary injunction. Rule 65(a) discusses only 1) the requirement of notice, 2) the possibility of an advanced or consolidated trial with the preliminary injunction hearing and 3) the preservation of evidence obtained in injunction proceedings for a later trial when the hearing has not been consolidated. Rule 65(c) discusses the requirement of security; 65(d) governs the form and scope of the injunction or restraining order; and 65(e) limits the application of Rule 65 in certain circumstances. Otherwise, the party must look to other Federal Rules and the local rules of court to learn the proper procedures for seeking a preliminary injunction or temporary restraining order. FRCP 65 likewise does not specify the equitable principles that govern application for an injunction; traditional federal equity principles apply.

13. Rule 65. Injunctions

(a) Preliminary Injunction.

(1) Notice. No preliminary injunction shall be issued without notice to the adverse party.

(2) Consolidation of Hearing with Trial on the Merits. Before or after the commencement of the hearing of an application for preliminary injunction, the court may order the trial of the action on the merits to be advanced and consolidated with the hearing of the application. Even when this consolidation is not ordered, any evidence received upon an application for a preliminary injunction which would be admissible upon the trial on the merits becomes a part of the record on the trial and need not be repeated upon the trial. This subdivision (a)(2) shall be so construed and applied as to save to the parties any rights they may have to trial by jury.

* * *

(c) Security. No restraining order or preliminary injunction shall issue except upon the giving of security by the applicant, in such sum as the court deems proper, for the payment of such costs and damages as may be incurred or suffered by any party who is found to have been wrongfully enjoined or restrained. No such security shall be required of the United States or of an officer or agency thereof. The provisions of Rule 65.1 apply to a surety upon a bond or undertaking under this rule.

(d) Form and Scope of Injunction or Restraining Order. Every order granting an injunction and every restraining order shall set forth the reasons for its issuance; shall be specific in terms; shall describe in reasonable detail, and not by reference to the complaint or other document, the act or acts sought to be restrained; and is binding only upon the parties to the action, their officers, agents, servants, employees, and attorneys, and upon those persons in active concert or participation with them who receive actual notice of the order by personal service or otherwise.

(e) Employer and Employee; Interpleader; Constitutional Cases. These rules do not modify any statute of the United States relating to temporary restraining orders and preliminary injunctions in actions affecting employer and employee; or the provisions of Title 28, U.S.C., § 2361, relating to preliminary injunctions in actions of interpleader or in the nature of interpleader; or Title 28, U.S.C., § 2284, relating to actions required by Act of Congress to be heard and determined by a district court of three judges.

(2) FRCP 65 Does Not Create Federal Jurisdiction

FRCP 65 does not confer an independent basis for federal jurisdiction.[14] A district court may not issue a preliminary injunction unless the applicant has shown grounds for federal subject matter jurisdiction,[15] such as diversity of citizenship with the requisite amount in controversy,[16] a federal question[17] or some other ground that confers federal jurisdiction.[18]

The district court must also have personal jurisdiction over the party against whom the injunction is sought.[19] When the party is the defendant, personal jurisdiction attaches by the defendant's voluntary appearance or effective service of process.[20] If the defendant counterclaims for injunctive relief, personal jurisdiction over the plaintiff arises through the plaintiff's submission to the jurisdiction of the court by filing suit in that court.[21] A preliminary injunction issued against a party

---

14. White v. National Football League, 41 F.3d 402, 409 (8th Cir.1994) (noting that the All–Writs Act, 28 U.S.C.A. § 1651 (West 1994), gives the district court power to issue injunctions in aid of its jurisdiction, but does not independently grant jurisdiction); Citizens Concerned for Separation of Church and State v. City and County of Denver, 628 F.2d 1289, 1299 (10th Cir. 1980); Miller v. Heckler, 601 F.Supp. 1471, 1488 (E.D.Tex.1985) ("[T]he power of federal courts to issue declaratory and injunctive relief, cannot provide the independent basis for jurisdiction....").

15. Arkansas Peace Ctr. v. Arkansas Department of Pollution Control, 999 F.2d 1212 (8th Cir.1993) (vacating preliminary injunction for lack of subject matter jurisdiction under federal environmental statutes); Zepeda v. U.S. I.N.S., 753 F.2d 719, 727 (9th Cir.1983).

16. See 28 U.S.C.A. § 1332 (West 1993 & Supp. 1997); Occidental Chem. Corp. v. Bullard, 995 F.2d 1046, 1047 (11th Cir. 1993) (noting that the amount in controversy for federal diversity jurisdiction, in actions seeking declaratory or injunctive relief, is measured by the value of the object of litigation).

17. American–Arab Anti–Discrimination Comm. v. Reno, 70 F.3d 1045, 1070 (9th Cir.1995) (found federal question jurisdiction in action to enjoin enforcement of the Immigration and Nationality Act, 8 U.S.C.A. § 1329 (West 1970 & Supp. 1997)); See 28 U.S.C.A. § 1331 (West 1993); In re Estate of Ferdinand Marcos, 25 F.3d 1467, 1473–75 (9th Cir.1994) (rejecting argument that the Alien Tort Action, 28 U.S.C.A. § 1350 (West 1993), was exclusively jurisdictional and therefore could not satisfy the "arising under" requirement of federal question jurisdiction).

18. Examples: *statutory interpleader*, 28 U.S.C.A. § 1335 (West 1993), Truck–A–Tune, Inc. v. Re, 23 F.3d 60 (2d Cir.1994); *action under Freedom of Information Act*, 5 U.S.C.A. § 552 (West 1996 & Supp. 1997), Senate of the State of Cal. v. Mosbacher, 968 F.2d 974 (9th Cir.1992); *action to enjoin arbitration*, 9 U.S.C.A. § 4 (West 1970), PaineWebber, Inc. v. Hartmann, 921 F.2d 507 (3d Cir.1990); *action under postal laws*, 28 U.S.C.A. § 1339 (West 1993), American Bible Soc'y v. Blount, 446 F.2d 588 (3d Cir.1971).

19. Weitzman v. Stein, 897 F.2d 653, 658–659 (2d Cir.1990) (vacating preliminary injunction order because " '[a] prima facie showing of jurisdiction will not suffice.... A court must have in personam jurisdiction over a party before it can validly enter even an interlocutory injunction against him.' ") (citation omitted); Zepeda, 753 F.2d at 727.

20. Audio Enter., Inc. v. B & W Loudspeakers of Am., 957 F.2d 406 (7th Cir. 1992) (where service of process was never completed, the district court lacked jurisdiction to issue the preliminary injunction); *cf.* Cargill v. Sabine Trading & Shipping Co., Inc., 756 F.2d 224 (2d Cir.1985) (holding that defendants did not submit to personal jurisdiction by filing an answer and counterclaim for damages caused by attachment).

21. Leman v. Krentler–Arnold Hinge Last Co., 284 U.S. 448, 451, 52 S.Ct. 238, 239, 76 L.Ed. 389 (1932); Depew v. Secre-

over whom the court had no jurisdiction is erroneous as a matter of law.[22]

(3) Notice

FRCP 65(a)(1) provides that notice to the adverse party is mandatory before seeking a preliminary injunction.[23] "Adverse party" includes any opposing party and certain nonparties whom the injunction will directly affect.[24] While notice is mandatory, FRCP 65 does not specify what constitutes sufficient notice. The court exercises its discretion in determining whether the moving party has given adequate notice.[25]

A party seeking injunctive relief generally provides notice by serving a motion for preliminary injunction on the adverse party.[26] The motion should conform to the requirements of FRCP 7(b)[27] by describing the injunction sought and stating with particularity the grounds for granting it.[28] It should also conform to the timing requirements of FRCP 6(d), which provides that motions "shall be served not later than 5 days before the time specified for the hearing,"[29] unless court rules[30] or a court order designates otherwise.[31] A shorter notice period may compro-

---

tary of the Treasury, 1995 WL 776925, at *3 (D.Colo.).

22. United Elec. Radio & Machine Workers of Am. v. 163 Pleasant St. Corp., 987 F.2d 39 (1st Cir.1993) (vacating preliminary injunction for lack of personal jurisdiction where appellate review of personal jurisdiction is nondeferential and plenary); Visual Sciences, Inc. v. Integrated Communications, Inc., 660 F.2d 56 (2d Cir.1981).

23. See FRCP 65(a)(1); Granny Goose Foods, Inc. v. Brotherhood of Teamsters Auto Truck Drivers Local No. 70 of Alameda County, 415 U.S. 423, 94 S.Ct. 1113, 39 L.Ed.2d 435 (1974); Rosen v. Siegel, 106 F.3d 28, 31–32 (2d Cir.1997); Weitzman, 897 F.2d 653 ("The court may not properly enter a preliminary injunction sua sponte without notice."); Commerce Park at DFW Freeport v. Mardian Constr. Co., 729 F.2d 334, 341 (5th Cir.1984).

24. Parker v. Ryan, 960 F.2d 543, 545 (5th Cir.1992) (nonparty whose assets were to be frozen was considered "adverse party"); Phillips v. Chas. Schreiner Bank, 894 F.2d 127, 130–131 (5th Cir.1990) (failure to give notice to adverse party resulted in dissolution of preliminary injunction).

25. People of Ill. *ex rel*. Hartigan v. Peters, 871 F.2d 1336, 1340 (7th Cir.1989); United States v. Alabama, 791 F.2d 1450, 1458 (11th Cir.1986); White v. Roughton, 530 F.2d 750, 755 n. 1 (7th Cir.1976) ("The district court should determine what sort of

procedures due process requires be afforded to applicants.").

26. Dillard v. Merrill Lynch, Pierce, Fenner & Smith, Inc., et al., 961 F.2d 1148, 1155 (5th Cir.1992); James Luterbach Constr. Co. v. Adamkus, 781 F.2d 599, 603 n. 1 (7th Cir.1986) ("As a matter of professional practice, counsel who seek temporary relief usually make a motion for a preliminary injunction separate from the prayer for relief contained in the complaint. In addition ... Rule 65(c)(2) ... seems to require a separate motion for temporary relief when it refers to 'an *application* for a preliminary injunction.'") (emphasis added); Lermer Germany v. Lermer Corp., 94 F.3d 1575, 1577 (Fed.Cir.1996) (refusing to construe the plaintiffs' request for a permanent injunction as incorporating a request for a preliminary injunction).

27. See FRCP 7(b).

28. See infra § 13.3(c).

29. See FRCP 6(b); Parker, 960 F.2d at 544.

30. Local rules of the district courts generally provide for greater notice than FRCP 7.

31. Parker, 960 F.2d 543 (validating four day notice); American Benefit Life Ins. Co. v. United Founders Life Ins. Co., 515 F.Supp. 800, 802 (W.D.Okla.1980) (rejecting defendant's objection of insufficient notice of plaintiff's motion because the court, by

---

mise the defendant's ability to gather evidence to defend against the requested injunction and thereby violate due process.[32] A written motion and designation of the time and place of the preliminary injunction hearing generally provides sufficient notice.[33]

When the court issues or denies a temporary restraining order, the court gives notice of the preliminary injunction through an order to show cause regarding the preliminary injunction.[34] An order to show cause will provide sufficient notice to the parties when it indicates the time and place of the hearing.[35] If the court issues the temporary restraining order without notice, the preliminary injunction hearing will "be set down for hearing at the earliest possible time."[36]

(4) Evidence in Support of or in Opposition to a Preliminary Injunction

The preliminary injunction motion must include evidence that goes beyond the unverified allegations in the pleadings.[37] Parties typically support preliminary injunction motions and oppositions with sworn affidavits[38] or declarations[39] and deposition testimony.[40] Verified pleadings[41] are sometimes also acceptable so long as the facts alleged do not consist largely of general assertions that are substantially controverted.[42] Normally, it is preferable to introduce evidence through affidavits, rather than relying on the allegations of the compliant, which are often

order, shortened the notice period under FRCP 6(d)).

32. Granny Goose Foods, Inc. v. Brotherhood Teamsters & Auto Truck Drivers Local No. 70 of Alameda County, 415 U.S. 423, 94 S.Ct. 1113, 39 L.Ed.2d 435 (1974).

33. People of Ill. *ex rel.* Hartigan v. Peters, 871 F.2d 1336, 1341 (7th Cir.1989).

34. Plaquemines Parish Sch. Bd. v. United States, 415 F.2d 817, 824 (5th Cir. 1969); Walling v. Moore Milling Co., Inc., 62 F.Supp. 378, 381–82 (W.D.Va.1945) (denying defendant's motion to quash order to show cause; holding that notice of plaintiff's preliminary injunction was procedurally improper, however, service of the order to show cause indicating the time and place of hearing with a copy of complaint and supporting affidavit took the place of notice by motion and in no way prejudiced defendant).

35. Plaquemines Parish Sch. Bd., 415 F.2d 817.

36. *See* FRCP 65(b).

37. Societe Comptoir De L'Industrie Cotonniere, Etablissements Boussac v. Alexander's Dep't Stores, Inc., 190 F.Supp. 594 (S.D.N.Y.1961) ("As support for a preliminary injunction the court can consider only

facts presented by affidavit or testimony and cannot consider facts provable under the modern liberal interpretation of the complaint[] which have not been proved."), *aff'd,* 299 F.2d 33 (2d Cir.1962).

38. Republic of the Philippines v. Marcos, 862 F.2d 1355, 1363 (9th Cir.1988); K–2 Ski Co. v. Head Ski Co., 467 F.2d 1087, 1088–89 (9th Cir.1972) ("A verified complaint or supporting affidavits may afford the basis for a preliminary injunction. . . .").

39. To avoid unnecessary verbiage, the term "affidavit" will be used to refer to both affidavits and declarations.

40. Levi Strauss & Co. v. Sunrise Int'l Trading Inc., 51 F.3d 982, 985 (11th Cir. 1995) ("At the preliminary injunction stage, a district court may rely on affidavits and hearsay materials which would not be admissible evidence for a permanent injunction, if the evidence is 'appropriate given the character and objectives of the injunctive proceeding.' ") (citation omitted); Asseo v. Pan Am. Grain Co., Inc., 805 F.2d 23, 26 (1st Cir.1986).

41. United States v. Quadro Corp., 916 F.Supp. 613, 617 (E.D.Tex.1996).

42. K–2 Ski Co., 467 F.2d at 1088–89.

conclusory and lack the necessary foundation to constitute admissible evidence. Under FRCP 6(d) affidavits must be served no later than one day before the hearing, although local rules normally provide for different filing requirements.[43]

FRCP 65 does not address the substantive requirements of supporting affidavits, which are generally governed by the Federal Rules of Evidence. The rigid requirements for affidavits filed in support of summary judgment motions under FRCP 56 do not apply to affidavits filed in connection with preliminary injunction motions.[44] Because the grant of a preliminary injunction is discretionary, the district court may use that discretion to weigh the evidence. The court, therefore, has the power to prevent irreparable harm before trial by giving some weight to evidence that may be inadmissible at trial.[45] In fact, hearsay testimony is sometimes used in adjudicating a motion for preliminary injunction.[46] Nevertheless, the court typically assigns less credibility to hearsay statements, as opposed to direct statements of fact.[47] When a preliminary injunction is sought solely on allegations based on information and belief, rather than personal knowledge, the court generally will find the evidence insufficient to grant the motion.[48]

As a matter of strategy, counsel should not rely on the court ruling leniently with respect to hearsay or other inadmissible evidence. Since the court has great discretion to grant or deny the motion, the failure to produce admissible evidence provides the court with sufficient reason to reject a party's position. The court is far more likely to be impressed favorably by the party which presents evidence in admissible form, compared to opposing evidence that lacks foundation, constitutes hearsay, or is otherwise inadmissible, particularly if the deficiency could have been cured. Despite the court's willingness to consider such evidence under certain circumstances, counsel should still file objections to all inadmissible evidence to emphasize the weakness of the opposing party's showing and to preserve objections for appeal.

Courts will more easily decide applications for preliminary injunctions when the documentary evidence is undisputed.[49] Written evidence

43. *See* FRCP 6(d).

44. Bracco v. Lackner, 462 F.Supp. 436, 442 n. 3 (N.D.Cal.1978).

45. Sierra Club, Lone Star Chapter v. FDIC, 992 F.2d 545, 551 (5th Cir.1993).

46. *Id.*, at 551 (court accepted evidence in the form of deposition transcripts and affidavits); Asseo v. Pan Am. Grain Co., Inc., 805 F.2d 23, 26 (1st Cir.1986); Fed. Sav. & Loan Ins. Corp. v. Dixon, 835 F.2d 554, 558 (5th Cir.1987) (recognizing the propriety of hearsay evidence in preliminary injunction proceedings when all the attendant factors, including the need for expedition warranted the use of such evidence).

47. United States v. Quadro Corp., 916 F.Supp. 613, 617 (E.D.Tex.1996) (less credence given to deposition transcripts and affidavits than direct allegations); Asseo, 805 F.2d at 25–26 (court considered transcript of testimony at administrative proceeding).

48. E.E. Maxwell Co., Inc. v. Arti Decor, Ltd., 638 F.Supp. 749, 754 (N.D.Tex.1986).

49. Commerce Park at DFW Freeport v. Mardian Constr. Co., 729 F.2d 334, 341 (5th Cir.1984) (no evidentiary hearing was necessary where submitted evidence was not in dispute).

may be presumed to be true when it is uncontradicted.[50] Courts will often deny a preliminary injunction supported only by disputed written evidence.[51]

(5) Hearing

The notice requirement of FRCP 65(a)(1) implies a hearing that affords the adverse party a fair opportunity to oppose the motion for preliminary injunction.[52] The party seeking the injunction bears the burden of persuasion.[53]

Courts have discretion not to hold a hearing when no factual issues are in dispute.[54] The court may abuse its discretion if it grants a preliminary injunction without a hearing when a factual dispute exists[55] or if the injunction is based on insufficient facts in the affidavits.[56] Many courts decide motions for preliminary injunctions on the papers, and do not hold evidentiary hearings.

When written evidence is disputed, the court may prefer oral testimony so that it may observe the witness' demeanor to assess the credibility of the testimony.[57] Some courts have even compelled oral testimony from affiants who provide evidence that is challenged in an opposing affidavit.[58] A party who believes that an evidentiary hearing will emphasize the strength of its evidence and the weakness of its opponent's evidence, should consider requesting such a hearing, especially where the opposing witnesses may not be available for a hearing.

Sometimes, to shorten an evidentiary hearing, the court will not require direct examination of affiants but will accept their affidavits and then permit the adversary to cross-examine them on the affidavits. Sometimes the court will direct the party opposing the preliminary injunction to present its evidence or submit to cross-examination first,

50. Huk–A–Poo Sportswear, Inc. v. Little Lisa, Ltd., 74 F.R.D. 621, 623–24 (S.D.N.Y.1977); Williams v. San Francisco Unified Sch. Dist., 340 F.Supp. 438, 442 (N.D.Cal.1972).

51. Digital Equip. Corp. v. Emulex Corp., 805 F.2d 380 (Fed.Cir.1986); SEC v. Frank, 388 F.2d 486 (2d Cir.1968) (holding order for preliminary injunction was procedurally defective for failure to conduct evidentiary hearing where affidavits revealed dispute).

52. Granny Goose Foods, Inc. v. Brotherhood Teamsters & Auto Truck Drivers Local No. 70 of Alameda County, 415 U.S. 423, 94 S.Ct. 1113, 39 L.Ed.2d 435 (1974); Rosen v. Siegel, 106 F.3d 28, 31 (2d Cir. 1997); Williams v. McKeithen, 939 F.2d 1100, 1105 (5th Cir.1991).

53. Church v. City of Huntsville, 30 F.3d 1332, 1342 (11th Cir.1994); Lakedreams v. Taylor, 932 F.2d 1103, 1107 (5th Cir.1991); Cox v. City of Chicago, 868 F.2d 217, 219 (7th Cir.1989); West Point–Pepperell, Inc. v. Donovan, 689 F.2d 950, 956 (11th Cir.1982).

54. Cohen v. Cook County, Ill., 677 F.Supp. 547 (N.D.Ill.1988).

55. Forts v. Ward, 566 F.2d 849 (2d Cir.1977).

56. United States v. Board of Educ. of Chicago, 11 F.3d 668, 672 (7th Cir.1993).

57. General Elec. Co. v. American Wholesale Co., 235 F.2d 606, 609 (7th Cir. 1956) ("Where averments of affidavits are conflicting, the conflicts should be resolved by oral testimony.").

58. Wounded Knee Legal Defense/Offense Comm. v. F.B.I., 507 F.2d 1281, 1287 (8th Cir.1974) ("[W]here the affidavits relate to controverted factual issues . . . [t]he court should insist . . . on the presentation of oral testimony . . . ." citation omitted).

particularly if the judge is inclined to rule in favor of that party but wants to see how its position holds up under cross-examination.

At the hearing, counsel should consider expressing a willingness to have its primary witnesses testify if the court determines that oral testimony would be helpful. Counsel may indicate that, based upon the papers, the outcome is clear, but if the court has any doubt, or wishes to hear any witnesses, they will be available. The opposing party may be caught off guard or unprepared to call its witnesses or subject them to cross-examination. If there is an opportunity at the TRO hearing, or by a call to the clerk, it is helpful to inquire as to the court's practice with respect to live testimony, so that counsel will not be unprepared or fail to appear with witnesses when expected to do so.

Where a factual dispute exists, some courts favor hearing oral testimony[59] on the rationale that the court would be unable to make the findings of fact required by FRCP 52(a) without oral evidence.[60]

Since all preliminary injunctions are based on the court's discretion, it is important for courts to allow legal argument on how the court should apply its discretion to the facts of the case. Such hearings on legal issues should be distinguished from oral testimony about disputed facts.[61] Different districts and individual judges within those districts have different attitudes toward evidentiary hearings. It is essential to consult the local rules of court and inquire into the individual judge's practice in preparing for a hearing in a preliminary injunction motion.

(6) Advancement or Consolidation with the Trial on the Merits

FRCP 65(a)(2) provides for the advancement or consolidation of the preliminary injunction hearing with the trial on the merits by motion of the court or a party.[62] The grant of such an order is discretionary.[63] The

59. See FRCP 43(e); Atari Games Corp. v. Nintendo of Am., Inc., 897 F.2d 1572, 1575 (Fed.Cir.1990) ("As a general rule, a preliminary injunction should not issue on the basis of affidavits alone.") (citations omitted); Charlton v. Estate of Charlton, 841 F.2d 988, 989 (9th Cir.1988).

60. See Two Wheel Corp. v. American Honda Corp., 506 F.Supp. 806 (E.D.N.Y. 1980) (setting forth findings of fact and conclusions of law).

61. Duer Spring & Mfg. Co., Inc. v. Commonwealth of Pa. Dep't of Labor & Indus., 906 F.2d 968, 969 (3d Cir.1990) (holding the lower court's denial of plaintiff's motion for preliminary injunction turned on a legal issue, therefore, the court did not abuse its discretion in declining an evidentiary hearing and hearing legal argument only); Johnston v. J.P. Stevens & Co., 341 F.2d 891 (4th Cir.1965) (the court allowed several days of argument on a motion

for preliminary injunction submitted on affidavits and denied oral testimony to explain submitted affidavits).

62. Holly Sugar Corp. v. Goshen County Coop. Beet Growers Ass'n, 725 F.2d 564, 568 (10th Cir.1984) (district court consolidated the preliminary injunction proceedings with trial on merits sua sponte); Oregon Natural Resources Council v. Marsh, 628 F.Supp. 1557, 1569 (D.Or.1986) (granting plaintiff's motion to consolidate preliminary injunction proceedings with trial on merits).

63. Commonwealth Life Ins. Co. v. Neal, 669 F.2d 300, 303 (5th Cir.1982) (consolidation was not required because counsel objected); United States v. School Dist. 151 of Cook County, Ill., 404 F.2d 1125, 1129 n. 4 (7th Cir.1968) (The validity of the injunction in a school desegregation case was not defective for failure to consolidate the hear-

acceleration of the trial is generally appropriate when a preliminary injunction is requested because it would shorten the periods during which the plaintiff may face a threat of irreparable harm, or would minimize the harm to the defendant from what may prove to be an unjustified restraint.[64] Acceleration of the trial on the merits is often practical where the parties have engaged in extensive accelerated discovery and are essentially prepared for the trial on the merits and little new evidence would be introduced at a later trial. Consolidation of the trial with preliminary injunction proceedings is encouraged for similar reasons.[65] The Advisory Committee has recognized the efficiency of consolidated proceedings.[66]

A party's failure to object to consolidation at the time of notice will preclude an objection on appeal.[67] If the court orders consolidation, the record must include explicit notice.[68] The court must give the parties "clear and unambiguous" notice of its intent to consolidate at a time that affords the parties the time to present their respective cases.[69] Sufficient notice is assessed by equitable principles, and therefore, will vary according to circumstances.[70] Notice at, or even after, the time of

ing for preliminary injunction with permanent injunction proceedings. "The court was not required to use its power under Rule 65(a)(2) . . . . ").

64. Helfant v. Kugler, 484 F.2d 1277, 1283 (3d Cir.1973) ("Mindful that present or even potential interference with a pending state prosecution is a matter of utmost gravity, this case should on remand receive accelerated consideration, and the court should enter an order consolidating the hearing . . . ."); Brass v. Hoberman, 295 F.Supp. 358, 364–65 (S.D.N.Y.1968) (holding the trial on the merits should be advanced because the case raises constitutional questions with wide impact on public administration and all issues that must be litigated to issue or deny a preliminary injunction are involved with the claim for permanent relief).

65. See F.D.I.C. v. Cafritz, 762 F.Supp. 1503, 1504 (D.D.C.1991) ("The Court prefers to consolidate a hearing on the preliminary injunction with a hearing on the merits.").

66. See FRCP 65(a)(2) Advisory Committee Note, 1966 amendment.

67. New England Anti–Vivisection Soc'y, Inc. v. United States Surgical Corp., Inc., 889 F.2d 1198, 1201 (1st Cir.1989); but see Paris v. U.S. Dep't of Housing & Urban Dev., 713 F.2d 1341, 1346–47 (7th Cir.1983) (issue of improper consolidation was preserved for appeal where consolidation was

ordered at last moments of hearing on preliminary injunction and court was adjourned immediately thereafter); Nordic-Track, Inc. v. Consumer Direct, Inc., 158 F.R.D. 415, 427–28 (D.Minn.1994).

68. United States v. Owens, 54 F.3d 271, 277 (6th Cir.1995) (district court improperly consolidated preliminary injunction proceedings with permanent injunction without providing "clear and unambiguous notice" despite "several inconclusive statements about making a final decision in the case").

69. University of Tex. v. Camenisch, 451 U.S. 390, 395, 101 S.Ct. 1830, 1834, 68 L.Ed.2d 175 (1981); Owens, 54 F.3d at 277; Air Line Pilots Ass'n, Int'l v. Alaska Airlines, Inc., 898 F.2d 1393, 1397 (9th Cir. 1990).

70. Woe v. Cuomo, 801 F.2d 627, 629 (2d Cir.1986) ("Neither the district court's oblique references during the hearing to the dispositive nature of the proceedings . . . , nor the request for permanent relief in appellees' post-hearing memorandum constitute timely, 'clear and unambiguous notice.' "); Holly Sugar Corp. v. Goshen County Coop. Beet Growers Ass'n, 725 F.2d 564, 568 (10th Cir.1984) (the district court's notice of its intent to consolidate on the second day of testimony was not error where the adverse party failed to ask for a continuance to present additional evidence and admitted in oral argument that it would not have significantly changed the presen-

the hearing will sometimes be acceptable, as long as it gives each party a full opportunity to present its case.[71] Insufficient notice may be excused when no prejudice to the parties would result.[72]

A party seeking a preliminary injunction may choose not to produce its entire case at the preliminary injunction hearing because the standard for granting a preliminary injunction does not require the movant to show a certainty of success on the merits.[73]

Most counsel would not normally risk holding back evidence that supports the party's case for a future trial that may never occur. As a matter of strategy, however, counsel will usually emphasize the client's strongest evidence or avoid complex issues that could be developed further with more time for discovery and trial preparation. Counsel may choose not to introduce other evidence to avoid trying the patience of a busy court. It is, therefore, crucial for parties to know that the court will adjudicate all of the issues in their case at only one proceeding.

Since a preliminary injunction is an equitable remedy, there is no right to a jury.[74] If the hearing on a preliminary injunction is joined with a legal claim for which a party has the right to a jury,[75] the judge in the combined proceeding may not make any binding findings that are reserved for the jury.[76] This limitation, however, does not affect the

---

tation of its evidence even if it had received more timely notice); Reese Pub. Co., Inc. v. Hampton Int'l Communications, Inc., 620 F.2d 7, 12 (2d Cir.1980) (notice of consolidation given at the close of preliminary injunction proceedings was valid where court made clear its intention to consolidate during hearing if no material facts remained in dispute and where appellant's assertion that questions of secondary meaning remained were immaterial to resolution of the trademark protection action).

71. Camenisch, 451 U.S. at 395, 101 S.Ct. at 1834; Holly Sugar Corp., 725 F.2d 564; Reese Publ'g Co., Inc., 620 F.2d at 12 (holding the district court did not err in providing notice of consolidation at the close of preliminary injunction proceedings because the parties were not prejudiced).

72. Holly Sugar Corp., 725 F.2d at 568; Wohlfahrt v. Memorial Med. Ctr., 658 F.2d 416, 418 (5th Cir.1981) (remanded dismissal of civil rights action to determine whether plaintiff was prejudiced by the insufficient notice of the court's consideration of the merits of his claim following an evidentiary hearing for temporary injunctive relief); Reese Publ'g Co., Inc., 620 F.2d at 12.

73. Camenisch, 451 U.S. at 395, 101 S.Ct. at 1834 (noting the lower standard of preliminary injunction proceedings due to the limited purpose and haste in which

preliminary injunctions are decided and the notice requirement which protects the parties' opportunity to present their case in the event of consolidation).

74. Reich v. Tiller Helicopter Services, Inc., 8 F.3d 1018, 1031 (5th Cir.1993) (suit seeking injunction under statute is in equity with no right to jury trial); Wilson v. Bailey, 934 F.2d 301, 305 (11th Cir.1991) (same); K–Mart Corp. v. Oriental Plaza, Inc., 875 F.2d 907, 914 (1st Cir.1989) (no right to jury trial for injunction based on breach of contract claim).

75. U.S. Const. amend VII; Curtis v. Loether, 415 U.S. 189, 194, 94 S.Ct. 1005, 1008, 39 L.Ed.2d 260 (1974).

76. Beacon Theatres, Inc. v. Westover, 359 U.S. 500, 510, 79 S.Ct. 948, 956, 3 L.Ed.2d 988 (1959) (cases involving both equitable and legal claims require the court's discretion to decide which should be tried first, yet this discretion is "very narrowly limited and must, whenever possible, be exercised to preserve jury trial"); Hensley v. E.R. Carpenter Co., Inc., 633 F.2d 1106, 1110 (5th Cir.1980); Bowles v. Bennett, 629 F.2d 1092, 1094 (5th Cir.1980) (holding that consolidation of preliminary injunction proceedings with the trial on the merits "must be done in such a way that the parties' rights to trial by jury are protected").

court's ability to decide the preliminary injunction based on its own determination of issues that the jury will ultimately decide.[77]

As a matter of strategy, a party that believes that it has a strong case on the merits should consider seeking acceleration or consolidation. This is particularly true for a defendant that believes that the plaintiff has strong equitable arguments but a weak case on the merits. By seeking acceleration or consolidation, the defendant can avoid the harm, inconvenience and expense of preliminary injunction while waiting for a trial on the merits. The plaintiff in such a case will undoubtedly oppose either procedure, as the grant of a preliminary injunction may provide leverage for settlement, without risking an adverse judgment at the trial on the merits. A party, most likely the defendant, that believes that the case is complicated and will require extensive discovery before trial should oppose consolidation or acceleration, lest the court rule on an inadequate record. That is particularly true when the defendant believes that the plaintiff does not have the financial resources for extended discovery and a lengthy trial and is thus more likely to settle on favorable terms if faced with that prospect. The plaintiff in such a situation will undoubtedly prefer the less expensive and quicker route of consolidation or acceleration.

(7) Use of Evidence from Preliminary Injunction Hearing at Trial

FRCP 65(a)(2) provides that when preliminary injunction proceedings are not consolidated with the trial on the merits, the evidence received at the preliminary injunction hearing that would be admissible at the trial on the merits becomes part of the trial record and need not be repeated at trial.[78] The Advisory Committee clarified that the Rule does not preclude the repetition of evidence at trial.[79] For example, the court may desire to repeat evidence at trial for the sake of continuity or because a different trial judge is hearing the matter.[80] The parties normally will wish to repeat their evidence, or at least the most impor-

---

77. Bowles, 629 F.2d 1092 (consolidation of preliminary injunction motion with trial on the merits must be done in such a way that the parties' right to a jury trial is protected).

78. Project Strategies Corp. v. National Communications Corp., 948 F.Supp. 218, 221 (E.D.N.Y.1996) ("The evidence received during the course of the [injunction] proceedings culminating in the bench trial required no repetition upon trial and are deemed part of the trial record."); United States v. City of Chicago, 411 F.Supp. 218, 229 (N.D.Ill.1976); SEC v. Commonwealth Chem. Sec., Inc., 410 F.Supp. 1002, 1008 n. 4 (S.D.N.Y.1976).

79. See FRCP 65(a)(2) Advisory Committee Note, 1966 amendment ("[R]epetition is not altogether prohibited.").

80. SEC v. North Am. Research & Dev. Corp., 511 F.2d 1217, 1218 (2d Cir. 1975) (judge did not abuse his discretion by issuing the permanent injunction based on evidence obtained at the preliminary injunction hearing without repetition of such evidence); Knox v. Milwaukee County Bd. of Election Comm'rs, 607 F.Supp. 1112, 1126 (E.D.Wis.1985) ("[S]ome repetition of testimony may be called for where the trial is conducted by a judge who did not hear the application for the preliminary injunction."); Sheet Metal Workers Int'l Ass'n, Local Union No. 292, AFL–CIO v. Wer–Coy Fabrication Co., Inc., 578 F.Supp. 296, 298 (E.D.Mich.1984) ("It is clear that repetition of evidence is permitted. . . .").

tant evidence, at trial, especially when there is any substantial time lapse between the hearing and the trial. A busy judge is likely to forget the details of the case over that period. In a jury trial, when the trial is not consolidated with the preliminary injunction hearing, the evidence from preliminary injunction proceedings must be repeated to the jury at the trial on the merits.[81]

Parties may also use evidence submitted at preliminary injunction proceedings to support or oppose a motion for summary judgment, although the Rule does not explicitly address such use.[82] Nor does the Rule deal with findings of fact made by the court in preliminary injunction proceedings. Such findings are not binding at the trial on the merits because the urgency and lower burden used in preliminary injunction proceedings may have precluded parties from presenting additional evidence at that time.[83] Consequently, the court may not use such findings of fact to resolve factual issues in summary judgment proceedings.[84]

(8) Security

FRCP 65(c) requires the applicant for a temporary restraining order[85] or a preliminary injunction to post a security bond to protect the adverse party from damages caused by a wrongfully granted injunction[86] and to deter frivolous claims.[87] This security is not required until the

---

81. See FRCP 65(a)(2) Advisory Committee Note, 1966 amendment (stating that when there is a right to a trial by jury, "the jury will have to hear all the evidence bearing on its verdict, even if some part of the evidence has already been heard by the judge alone on the application for the preliminary injunction."); see also Crane Co. v. American Standard, Inc., 326 F.Supp. 766, 772 (S.D.N.Y.1971).

82. Cohen v. San Bernardino Valley College, 883 F.Supp. 1407, 1410 n. 1 (C.D.Cal.1995), aff'd in part, reversed in part, 92 F.3d 968 (9th Cir.1996).

83. University of Tex. v. Camenisch, 451 U.S. 390, 395, 101 S.Ct. 1830, 1834, 68 L.Ed.2d 175 (1981) (recognizing that findings of fact and conclusions of law made by a court granting a preliminary injunction are not binding in trial on the merits); Henderson v. Bodine Aluminum, Inc., 70 F.3d 958, 962 (8th Cir.1995).

84. Country Floors, Inc. v. Partnership Composed of Gepner & Ford, 930 F.2d 1056, 1062–63 (3d Cir.1991) (in light of the different standard and policy considerations of preliminary injunctions, the district court erred in using the factual findings developed at the preliminary injunction hearing for the manufacturer to assess the competitor's summary judgment motion in a trade-

mark infringement case); Brooks v. Nacrelli, 415 F.2d 272, 275 (3d Cir.1969) (holding that the district court erred in dismissing plaintiff's complaint because "resisting motion for preliminary injunction where factual issues are presented does not entitle the defendant to summary judgment without an opportunity to present additional evidence, if need be, on final hearing") (citations omitted).

85. See discussion infra § 13.3(b)(9).

86. See FRCP 65(c) (security required "for payment of such costs and damages as may be incurred or suffered by any party who is found to have been wrongfully enjoined or restrained"); Continuum Co., Inc. v. Incepts, Inc., 873 F.2d 801, 803 (5th Cir.1989) (noting the bond requirement serves two functions: "(1) it assures the enjoined party that it may readily collect damages from the funds posted or the surety ...in the event that it was wrongfully enjoined, without further litigation and without regard to the possible insolvency of the assured and (2) it provides the plaintiff with notice of the maximum extent of its potential liability...." footnote omitted).

87. Elliott v. Kiesewetter, 98 F.3d 47, 60 (3d Cir.1996) (court must make specific findings regarding relative hardships before waiving bond requirement).

court is ready to grant injunctive relief.[88] FRCP 65(c) exempts the United States government from the obligation to provide security.[89]

The Rule leaves the amount of security to the discretion of the court.[90] In noncommercial cases, the court will weigh the extent of any possible loss to the enjoined party against the potential hardship on the applicant of supplying the bond.[91] In commercial cases, however, the hardship factor assumes less importance because the court assumes that the party is able to bear the burden of the bond.[92] In rare circumstances, however, a court may dispense with the bond requirement altogether. These situations include where the bond requirement would frustrate a suit to enforce federal rights[93] or to protect the public interest,[94] where the preliminary injunction would present no monetary risk to the defendant,[95] where the preliminary injunction would protect the court's jurisdiction over the subject matter,[96] or where indigent parties are involved.[97] However, other courts have refused to recognize any exception to the security requirement.[98]

88. Shakman v. Democratic Org. of Cook County, 310 F.Supp. 1398, 1400 (N.D.Ill.1969) (civil rights action was not subject to dismissal where motion for preliminary injunction was not accompanied by a bond because "security is not required unless and until the equitable relief is to be granted"); Thermex Co. v. Lawson, 25 F.Supp. 414, 415 (E.D.Ill.1938) ("Rule 65(c) prescribes security for payment of costs and damages to be given by applicant only as a prerequisite of the issuance of a . . . preliminary injunction. Until such relief is ready to be granted indemnifying security is not required.").

89. See FRCP 65(c) ("No such security shall be required of the United States or of an officer or agency thereof."); FTC v. Career Info. Serv., Inc., 1996 WL 435225, at * 6 (N.D.Ga.) ("No security is required of any agency of the Federal government, including the Commission, for the issuance of a preliminary injunction.").

90. Wilderness Soc'y v. Tyrrel, 701 F.Supp. 1473, 1492 (E.D.Cal.1988) (using its discretion, the court set the nonprofit organization plaintiffs' bond at a nominal amount of $100, " 'unwilling to close the courthouse door to public interest litigation' "), supplemented by, 1989 WL 315186 (E.D.Cal.1989), reversed on other grounds 918 F.2d 813 (9th Cir.1990) (citation omitted).

91. See Pharmaceutical Soc'y v. New York State Dep't of Soc. Servs., 50 F.3d 1168, 1174–75 (2d Cir.1995); Temple Univ. v. White, 941 F.2d 201, 219–20 (3d Cir. 1991).

92. See 13 James Wm. Moore, et al., Moore's Federal Practice § 65.52 (3d ed. 1997).

93. Waterfront Comm'n of New York Harbor v. Construction and Marine Equip. Co., Inc., 928 F.Supp. 1388 (D.N.J.1996).

94. Moltan Co. v. Eagle–Picher Indus., Inc., 55 F.3d 1171 (6th Cir.1995) (bond waived where public interest was workers' health); City of Atlanta v. Metropolitan Atlanta Rapid Transit Auth., 636 F.2d 1084, 1094 (5th Cir.1981) (no bond required where parties were seeking to protect citizens in the Atlanta area from perceived adverse economic and social consequences).

95. International Controls Corp. v. Vesco, 490 F.2d 1334, 1356 (2d Cir.1974) (interpreting the language "as the court deems proper" in FRCP 65(c) as allowing the court discretion to dispense with security where there has been no proof of likelihood of harm to the party enjoined) (citation omitted); McCormack v. Township of Clinton, 872 F.Supp. 1320, 1328 (D.N.J. 1994) ("[I]f the imposition of an injunction imposes no risk of monetary harm to defendant, the court need not address whether it may dispense with the security requirement.").

96. Doctor's Assocs., Inc. v. Stuart, 85 F.3d 975, 985 (2d Cir.1996).

97. See, e.g., Doe v. Perales, 782 F.Supp. 201 (W.D.N.Y.1991).

98. See Maryland Dep't of Human Resources v. United States Dep't of Agric., 976 F.2d 1462, 1483 n. 20 (4th Cir.1992) ("The

Some courts suggest that a defendant waives its right to damages if it fails to request a bond.[99] Many circuits hold that the district court's failure to require the security mandated by FRCP 65(c) is reversible error,[100] unless the error was harmless.[101] Others hold that the district court's failure to consider whether to require a bond at all is legal error.[102]

Courts usually require the moving party to post a bond equal to the amount the court estimates is necessary to protect the adverse party from damages directly attributable to the injunction.[103] The amount is left to the discretion of the court[104] and therefore may be difficult to predict. A party may move the court to increase or decrease the bond during the effective period of the injunction.[105]

The amount of the bond can become a crucial issue in a preliminary injunction matter. The normal roles of plaintiff and defendant are reversed. If the defendant can establish that it will suffer substantial damages if the injunction is improvidently granted, the court may order the plaintiff to post a bond in an amount that it cannot afford, or that the plaintiff concludes is not worth the benefit of the injunction obtained. For example, if the plaintiff persuades the court to enjoin a substantial corporate transaction but is required to post a multi-million dollar bond to protect the defendant from the loss of a substantial business opportunity, the plaintiff might decide that it is both less expensive and less risky for the plaintiff to permit the transaction to close and to seek money damages. To support a large bond, the defen-

rule's only exception to the security requirement exempts 'the United States or . . . an officer or agency thereof.' . . . There are no other exceptions.'').

99. Clarkson Co., Ltd. v. Shaheen, 544 F.2d 624, 632 (2d Cir.1976).

100. District 17, United Mine Workers of Am. v. A & M Trucking, Inc., 991 F.2d 108, 110 (4th Cir.1993) (" '[F]ailure to require a bond before granting preliminary injunctive relief is reversible error.' ") (citation omitted); Phillips v. Chas. Schreiner Bank, 894 F.2d 127, 131 (5th Cir.1990); *See also* Coquina Oil Corp. v. Transwestern Pipeline Co., 825 F.2d 1461, 1462 (10th Cir.1987) ("[W]hen a trial court fails to contemplate the imposition of the bond, its order granting a preliminary injunction is unsupportable.").

101. Ferguson v. Tabah, 288 F.2d 665, 675 (2d Cir.1961) (allowing injunction without security bond because absence of bond would not cause financial harm to defendant); Urbain v. Knapp Bros. Manuf. Co., 217 F.2d 810, 815 (6th Cir.1954) (same).

102. Rathmann Group v. Tanenbaum, 889 F.2d 787, 789 (8th Cir.1989); Reinders

Bros., Inc. v. Rain Bird Eastern Sales Corp., 627 F.2d 44, 54 (7th Cir.1980) (recognizing that while the mandatory requirement to issue a bond has been relaxed, a district court's decision "to ignore defendant's request completely" is not sanctioned so "the court shall entertain and expressly rule on the request [for bond]."); Hinckley v. Kelsey–Hayes Co., 866 F.Supp. 1034, 1046 (E.D.Mich.1994).

103. Instant Air Freight Co. v. C.F. Air Freight, Inc., 882 F.2d 797, 805–06 n. 9 (3d Cir.1989); Johnson Chemical Co. v. Home Care Products, Inc., 823 F.2d 28, 29 (2d Cir.1987); USACO Coal Co. v. Carbomin Energy, Inc., 689 F.2d 94, 99 (6th Cir.1982); Alexander v. Primerica Holdings, Inc., 811 F.Supp. 1025, 1038 (D.N.J.1993); Storck USA, L.P. v. Farley Candy Co., 797 F.Supp. 1399, 1413 (N.D.Ill.1992).

104. Rathmann Group, 889 F.2d 787.

105. Continuum Co., Inc. v. Incepts, Inc., 883 F.2d 333, 334 (5th Cir.1989); LeSportsac, Inc. v. K Mart Corp., 754 F.2d 71 (2d Cir.1985); International Ladies' Garment Workers' Union v. Donnelly Garment Co., 147 F.2d 246, 252 (8th Cir.1945).

dant may wish to provide substantial evidence, including expert witness testimony, of the damages the defendant will suffer if the injunction is entered. The calculation should be supported by evidence as strong as the evidence supporting a damage calculation submitted at trial.

The plaintiff, on the other hand, will want to prove that the defendant's claimed damages from an improvidently granted injunction are without foundation and highly speculative. In an appropriate case, the plaintiff may argue that where there has been a strong showing of irreparable harm and where the public interest is affected by the proposed injunction, a high bond will effectively deprive the plaintiff and the public of the benefits of injunctive relief that is clearly warranted.

The plaintiff must make a judgment whether to address the bond issue in its moving papers. Since FRCP 65(c) makes a bond mandatory, counsel normally would include such a discussion. In light of authority that a defendant may waive the right to a bond if it fails to request a bond, set forth above, and without knowledge of the defendant's position on the issue, it may be a better approach to wait for the reply brief to respond to the defendant's specific arguments about the bond issue. Otherwise, the plaintiff may not anticipate the defendant's arguments correctly, alert the defendant to the issue or concede too much.

The amount of the bond can be significant to the plaintiff. If the plaintiff uses a bonding company, it will have to establish that it has sufficient assets to pay the amount of the bond or provide sufficient collateral. The plaintiff would then pay the bonding company a premium, usually a percentage of the amount of the bond, for issuance of the bond by the bonding company. The plaintiff may also secure payment of the bond by obtaining a letter of credit.

The defendant may only recover costs and damages directly attributable to the injunction under the bond.[106] Federal law dictates what "costs and damages" are recoverable.[107] Generally, attorney's fees cannot be recovered under federal law.[108] Attorney's fees can be recovered when the preliminary injunction is sought for a claim under a federal statute that provides for such recovery.[109]

106. Board of Educ. v. Illinois State Board of Educ., 79 F.3d 654, 659 (7th Cir. 1996); Blumenthal v. Merrill, Lynch, Pierce, Fenner & Smith, Inc., 910 F.2d 1049, 1051 (2d Cir.1990); Division No. 1, Detroit, Brotherhood of Locomotive Engineers v. Consolidated Rail Corp., 844 F.2d 1218, 1225 (6th Cir.1988).

107. Fireman's Fund Ins. Co. v. S.E.K. Construction Co., 436 F.2d 1345, 1351 (10th Cir.1971); But see Bulova Watch Co. v. Rogers–Kent, Inc., 181 F.Supp. 340, 344–45 (E.D.S.C.1960) (applying state law in diversity case in action on injunction bond, court awarded attorney's fees after determining that preliminary injunction was wrongly issued).

108. International Ass'n of Machinists & Aerospace Workers v. Eastern Airlines, Inc., 925 F.2d 6 (1st Cir.1991); Matek v. Murat, 862 F.2d 720, 734 (9th Cir.1988); Fireman's Fund Ins. Co., 436 F.2d at 1351.

109. Locust Lane v. Swatara Township Authority, 636 F.Supp. 534, 539 (M.D.Pa. 1986) (under Clean Water Act, court may consider in determining amount of bond the possible award of attorney's fees to prevailing party permitted by statute); Pymatuning Water Shed Citizens for a Hygienic Environment v. Eaton, 506 F.Supp. 902, 906 (W.D.Pa.1980), aff'd, 644 F.Supp. 995 (3d Cir.1981) (same).

Separate bonds must issue for a temporary restraining order and a preliminary injunction, as the bond for one remedy cannot cover the liability incurred by the other.[110] When the trial court issues a permanent injunction, it may discharge the security bond covering the preliminary injunction. If the permanent injunction is later reversed, some courts will permit the defendant to obtain damages up to the sum of the preliminary and permanent bonds.[111] Other courts find that the defendant's failure to address the wrongfully discharged bond on appeal ends the court's jurisdiction over the bond.[112] According to these courts, the reversal of the permanent injunction does not implicitly reverse the discharge of the preliminary bond.[113]

If the plaintiff is not required to post a bond, the defendant cannot recover damages for an improperly granted preliminary injunction,[114] unless the claim was maliciously prosecuted without probable cause.[115] Even if the injunction was issued in error, the party obtaining it is not liable for damages beyond the posted bond, unless it was sought maliciously and without probable cause.[116] Also, the court may require the party that had wrongfully obtained the injunction to make restitution of gains made at the other's expense while the injunction was in effect.[117]

The court retains discretion to deny recovery under the bond.[118] Some courts interpret this discretion broadly where the preliminary injunction was sought and obtained in good faith.[119] The majority of

---

110. District 17, United Mine Workers of America v. A & M Trucking, Inc., 991 F.2d 108, 110 (4th Cir.1993); Rathmann Group v. Tanenbaum, 889 F.2d 787, 789 (8th Cir.1989).

111. Atomic Oil Co. v. Bardahl Oil Co., 419 F.2d 1097 (10th Cir.1969).

112. Buddy Systems, Inc. v. Exer–Genie, Inc., 545 F.2d 1164, 1169 (9th Cir. 1976), cert. denied, 431 U.S. 903, 97 S.Ct. 1694, 52 L.Ed.2d 387 (1977).

113. Id. at 1169 n.10.

114. W.R. Grace Co. v. Local Union 759, Int'l Union of the United Rubber, Cork, Linoleum & Plastic Workers of Am., 461 U.S. 757, 769 n. 14, 103 S.Ct. 2177, 2185 n. 14, 76 L.Ed.2d 298 (1983) ("A party injured by the issuance of an injunction later determined to be erroneous has no action for damages in the absence of a bond."); International Ass'n of Machinists & Aerospace Workers v. Eastern Airlines, Inc., 925 F.2d 6 (1st Cir.1991); Commerce Tankers Corp. v. National Maritime Union, 553 F.2d 793, 800 (2d Cir.1977).

115. Adolph Coors Co. v. A & S Wholesalers, Inc., 561 F.2d 807, 813 (10th Cir. 1977); Casas Office Machines, Inc. v. Mita Copystar America, Inc., 961 F.Supp. 353, 359 (D.P.R.1997).

116. See Buddy Sys., Inc., 545 F.2d at 1167–68; Northern Oil Co. v. Socony Mobil Oil Co., 347 F.2d 81 (2d Cir.1965) (applying Vermont law to allow for recovery for malicious prosecution).

117. See Arkadelphia Milling Co. v. St. Louis Southwestern Ry. Co., 249 U.S. 134, 145, 39 S.Ct. 237, 242, 63 L.Ed. 517 (1918).

118. Blumenthal v. Merrill, Lynch, Pierce, Fenner, Smith, Inc., 910 F.2d 1049, 1054–55 (2d Cir.1990); Coyne–Delany Co., Inc. v. Capital Development Board, 717 F.2d 385 (7th Cir.1983); Cappaert Enterprises v. Citizens & So. Int'l Bank of New Orleans, 564 F.Supp. 214 (E.D.La.1983).

119. H & R Block, Inc. v. McCaslin, 541 F.2d 1098, 1099 (5th Cir.1976) (where company obtained preliminary injunction pursuant to a covenant not to compete in its contract with its former employee, no damages were awarded to former employee even though the covenant not to compete was later found unenforceable and even though preliminary injunction caused former employee to shut his business down for over a year, because company pursued in good faith its claim based on the covenant); Page Communications Eng'rs, Inc. v. Froehlke, 475 F.2d 994, 997 (D.C.Cir.1973) (refusal to assess damages against unsuccessful offeror

courts, however, limit this discretion, holding that damages should be granted to a prevailing defendant unless the plaintiff shows sufficient justification to deny such damages under the particular circumstances of the case.[120]

The leading majority case addressing factors to be considered when assessing damages is *Coyne-Delany Co. v. Capital Development Board.*[121] According to *Coyne*, courts may consider the respective resources of the parties,[122] the defendant's efforts in mitigating damages[123] and the disposition of the underlying suit.[124] A change in the law[125] and the plaintiff's good faith[126] are additional factors helpful to the plaintiff that the court may use to determine damages for a wrongful injunction.

If recovery is permitted, FRCP 65.1 allows for summary proceedings by motion against the surety. Under FRCP 65.1, the surety is required to submit to the jurisdiction of the court and "irrevocably" appoint the court clerk as an agent who may be served with papers affecting the surety's liability on the bond.[127] This Rule obviates the need for an independent action.[128]

Recovery is usually limited to the bond amount.[129] However, courts have held that a defendant may recover in excess of the bond amount when the plaintiff has acted in bad faith.[130] When the case is settled or the injunction is withdrawn by stipulation without addressing the bond, recovery on the bond is not allowed.[131] The plaintiff may be liable under the bond, however, if the plaintiff voluntarily dismisses the case.[132] In fact, some courts have ruled that voluntary dismissal of an injunction

---

on Government contract for damage the Government sustained by reason of wrongful issuance of preliminary injunction restraining performance pursuant to award of contract to competing offeror was not an abuse of discretion where suit was not a frivolous one, suit was brought in good faith).

120. Coyne–Delany Co., 717 F.2d at 392; Zenith Radio Corp. v. United States, 823 F.2d 518, 521 (Fed.Cir.1987).

121. 717 F.2d 385 (7th Cir.1983).

122. *Id.* at 392; Zenith Radio Corp., 823 F.2d at 520.

123. Coyne–Delany Co., 717 F.2d at 392; Zenith Radio Corp., 823 F.2d at 520.

124. Coyne–Delany Co., 717 F.2d at 392.

125. *Id.*; Zenith, 823 F.2d at 520.

126. Coyne–Delany Co., 717 F.2d at 392; H & R Block, Inc. v. McCaslin, 541 F.2d 1098, 1100 (5th Cir.1976).

127. FRCP 65.1.

128. *Id.*

129. Continuum Co., Inc. v. Incepts, Inc., 873 F.2d 801, 803 (5th Cir.1989); Phillips Bus. Sys., Inc. v. Executive Comm. Sys., Inc., 744 F.2d 287, 290 (2d Cir.1984); Lucsik v. Board of Ed., 621 F.2d 841, 842 (6th Cir.1980); Buddy Sys., Inc. v. Exer–Genie, Inc., 545 F.2d 1164 (9th Cir.1976), *cert. denied*, 431 U.S. 903, 97 S.Ct. 1694, 52 L.Ed.2d 387 (1977).

130. Merck & Co. Inc. v. Lyon, 941 F.Supp. 1443, 1464 (M.D.N.C.1996) (defendant's attorney's fees not limited to bond amount due to plaintiff's bad faith) (citing Continuum Co., 873 F.2d 801); qad. inc. v. ALN Assocs., Inc., 781 F.Supp. 561 (N.D.Ill. 1992) (plaintiff's bad faith lifts ceiling amount for defendant's recovery).

131. Janssen v. Shown, 53 F.2d 608 (9th Cir.1931) (Where an action involving an injunction is dismissed by agreement of the parties, defendant may not maintain action against the sureties on the bond.).

132. J.A. Jones Construction Co. v. Plumbers & Pipefitters Local 598, 568 F.2d 1292, 1294 (9th Cir.1978); Golden Gate Mechanical Contractors Ass'n v. Seaboard Sur. Co., 389 F.2d 892 (9th Cir.1968).

action by the plaintiff without the consent of the defendant renders the plaintiff liable on the surety bond.[133] Finally, even though a preliminary injunction may have run its course or otherwise has become moot, the presence of an injunction bond may preclude dismissal of the case for mootness, as liability on the bond may remain to be adjudicated.[134]

(9) Order

FRCP 65(d) requires that every order granting an injunction or restraining order 1) set forth the reasons for its issuance, 2) be specific in terms and 3) describe in reasonable detail, without reference to other documents, the act or acts sought to be restrained.

While these are mandatory provisions that the court must scrupulously follow,[135] failure to conform strictly to this rule does not render an order for preliminary injunction void.[136] However, material nonconformities may cause an appellate court to vacate or reverse the injunction.[137]

The order should set forth the specific reasons for the injunctive relief.[138] This requirement furthers effective appellate review by allowing the reviewing court to understand the basis for the trial court's decision.[139] In addition, requiring the trial court to explain its reasoning encourages the trial judge to ascertain the facts and make the decision after fair consideration of all the facts and applicable law.[140]

133. Middlewest Motor Freight Bureau. v. United States, 433 F.2d 212, 243 (8th Cir.1970). *See also* Wainwright Sec., Inc. v. Wall Street Transcript Corp., 80 F.R.D. 103 (S.D.N.Y.1978).

134. University of Tex. v. Camenisch, 451 U.S. 390, 396, 101 S.Ct. 1830, 1834, 68 L.Ed.2d 175 (1981) (recognizing that an injunction bond prevents a case from becoming moot, while distinguishing an appellate court's ability to resolve issues preserved by a permanent injunction bond from the appellate court's inability to resolve issues which were never adjudicated at a trial on the merits yet preserved by a preliminary injunction bond); Liner v. Jafco, Inc., 375 U.S. 301, 84 S.Ct. 391, 11 L.Ed.2d 347 (1964); Henco, Inc. v. Brown, 904 F.2d 11, 13 (7th Cir.1990); *see also* Medtronic, Inc. v. Janss, 729 F.2d 1395, 1398 (11th Cir.1984) (temporary restraining order bond prevented mootness).

135. Schmidt v. Lessard, 414 U.S. 473, 94 S.Ct. 713, 38 L.Ed.2d 661 (1974) ("specificity provisions are no mere technical requirements"); Citizen Band Potowatomi Indian Tribe of Okla. v. Oklahoma Tax Comm'n, 969 F.2d 943, 946 n. 3 (10th Cir. 1992); *See also* Pasadena City Bd. of Educ. v. Spangler, 427 U.S. 424, 439, 96 S.Ct. 2697, 2706, 49 L.Ed.2d 599 (1976).

136. Citizen Band Potowatomi Indian Tribe of Okla., 969 F.2d at 946 n.3; Combs v. Ryan's Coal Co., Inc., 785 F.2d 970, 978 (11th Cir.), *cert. denied sub nom.* Simmons v. Combs, 479 U.S. 853, 107 S.Ct. 187, 93 L.Ed.2d 120 (1986).

137. Chicago & North Western Transp. Co. v. Railway Labor Exec. Ass'n, 908 F.2d 144, 149 (7th Cir.1990); Seattle–First National Bank v. Manges, 900 F.2d 795 (5th Cir.1990).

138. FRCP 65(d); *See* Rosen v. Siegel, 106 F.3d 28, 32–33 (2d Cir.1997) (orders must set forth specific reasons for relief granted); *but see* Board of Educ. v. Illinois State Bd. of Educ., 103 F.3d 545, 550 (7th Cir.1996) (affirming injunctions with only reason stated as to protect the status quo).

139. Gunn v. University Committee to End the War, 399 U.S. 383, 388, 90 S.Ct. 2013, 2016, 26 L.Ed.2d 684 (1970); Rosen v. Siegel, 106 F.3d 28 (2d Cir.1997); TEC Engineering Corp. v. Budget Molders Supply, Inc., 82 F.3d 542, 544 (1st Cir.1996).

140. Rosen, 106 F.3d at 32 (specific reasons encourages judge to ascertain facts with care and render a decision according to the fair evaluation of facts and law).

Additionally, FRCP 65(d) requires the order to describe with specificity[141] the prohibited acts in reasonable, though not elaborate, detail on the face of the order such that an ordinary person should be able to ascertain exactly the proscribed conduct.[142] The primary purpose of this requirement is to provide notice to enjoined parties of the restrictions that could expose them to contempt,[143] to enable effective appellate review,[144] and to avoid unnecessary restraint on parties or others affected by an order[145] that is too broad.[146] While FRCP 65(d) prohibits achieving such detailed description via reference to another document, some courts have allowed reference to extraneous documents, observing that a less strict interpretation does not conflict with the purpose of the Rule.[147] Nevertheless, one court has suggested that "complete agreement of counsel" may waive the specificity required by FRCP 65(d).[148]

An injunctive order binds parties to the action, their officers, agents, servants, employees and attorneys and persons in active concert or participation with them who receive actual notice of the order by personal service or otherwise.[149] Notice is not required to persons in privity with a party who has actual notice, unless due process is

141. McComb v. Jacksonville Paper Co., 336 U.S. 187, 192, 69 S.Ct. 497, 500, 93 L.Ed. 599 (1949) (injunction need not be laboriously detailed, but must at least say something about conduct enjoined); Reich v. ABC/York–Estes Corp., 64 F.3d 316, 319 (7th Cir.1995).

142. FRCP 65(d). *See also* Federal Election Comm'n v. Furgatch, 869 F.2d 1256, 1263–64 (9th Cir.1989) (requiring remand of TRO "because the injunction is susceptible to more than one interpretation.... [and] therefore fails to satisfy the exacting requirements of Rule 65(d)").

143. Schmidt v. Lessard, 414 U.S. 473, 476, 94 S.Ct. 713, 715, 38 L.Ed.2d 661 (1974); EFS Marketing, Inc. v. Russ Berrie & Co., Inc., 76 F.3d 487, 493 (2d Cir.1996).

144. Schmidt, 414 U.S. at 477, 94 S.Ct. at 715 (Persons affected by the injunction who are unsuccessful in modifying the order by motion are entitled to a "definitive disposition of their objections" on appeal.); Pasadena City Bd. of Educ. v. Spangler, 427 U.S. 424, 439, 96 S.Ct. 2697, 2706, 49 L.Ed.2d 599 (1976).

145. Gemveto Jewelry Co., Inc. v. Jeff Cooper, Inc., 800 F.2d 256, 258 (Fed.Cir. 1986) (vacating injunction that imposed unnecessary restraints on defendant's lawful activity); Zepeda v. U.S. I.N.S., 753 F.2d 719, 727–31 (9th Cir.1983) (vacating an over-broad preliminary injunction which restricted defendant's contact with persons outside of the class certification and re-

quired acts beyond what was necessary to comport with constitutional requirements); Globe Slicing Machine Co. v. Hasner, 333 F.2d 413, 416 (2d Cir.1964) (requiring modification of injunction that impinged on defendant's legal rights).

146. Regal Knitwear Co. v. N.L.R.B., 324 U.S. 9, 12, 65 S.Ct. 478, 480, 89 L.Ed. 661 (1945) (courts "may not grant ... injunction so broad as to make punishable the conduct of persons who act independently and whose rights have not been adjudged according to law"); Martin's Herend Imports, Inc. v. Diamond & Gem Trading Co., 112 F.3d 1296, 1303 (5th Cir.1997) (modifying injunction as over-broad in restricting defendant's noninfringing activity); Zepeda, 753 F.2d at 727–31 (vacating preliminary injunction with over-broad scope).

147. *See* United States v. Goehring, 742 F.2d 1323, 1324 (11th Cir.1984) (per curiam) (Rule 65(d) not specifically invoked, but contempt order upheld that incorporated earlier order because later order "contain[ed], sufficient findings of fact and conclusions of law for this court to perform its proper function and for the appellant to clearly understand the basis for the contempt order"); Seagram–Distillers Corp. v. New Cut Rate Liquors, 221 F.2d 815, 821 (7th Cir.1955).

148. Brumby Metals, Inc. v. Bargen, 275 F.2d 46 (7th Cir.1960).

149. FRCP 65(d).

threatened.[150] In a class action, only those class members over whom the court has jurisdiction are enjoined by the order, and until the class is certified, only the named plaintiffs are bound.[151]

An order of injunction binds nonparties when the nonparty is identified with a defendant against whom the injunction is issued[152] or the nonparty participated in the enjoined activity.[153] For example, an assignee or successor in the defendant's interest will be bound by the order if the court finds the relationship was designed to circumvent the preliminary injunction.[154] Otherwise, such orders do not bind nonparties because they were not afforded an opportunity to oppose the preliminary injunction before it was issued.[155]

As discussed in Section 13.2(a)(3), *supra*, it is important to be reasonable in drafting the proposed order. Do not overreach, or counsel and the client may both lose credibility and valuable time negotiating or redrafting the order. Be precise in the language describing the prohibited conduct and identifying the parties against which the order will be enforced. Serve the order individually on anyone whom counsel believes is likely to violate it.

When the injunction is a restraint in personam, the court must have personal jurisdiction over the individual to issue the injunction at all.[156] Injunctions in actions in rem bind anyone dealing with property falling within the subject matter of the order.[157]

---

150. Golden State Bottling Co. Inc. v. N.L.R.B., 414 U.S. 168, 178, 94 S.Ct. 414, 422, 38 L.Ed.2d 388 (1973) (decree of injunction binds parties in privity with defendants); Regal Knitwear Co. v. N.L.R.B., 324 U.S. 9, 14–15, 65 S.Ct. 478, 481–82, 89 L.Ed. 661 (1945) (same); Travelhost, Inc. v. Blandford, 68 F.3d 958, 961 (5th Cir.1995) (same); Stolberg v. Members of Bd. of Trustees for State Colleges of Conn., 541 F.2d 890 (2d Cir.1976) (same); *see also* United States v. Baker, 641 F.2d 1311, 1318 (9th Cir.1981) (requiring actual notice to nonparty for privity with party to avoid due process concerns in criminal contempt).

151. *See* Zepeda v. United States INS, 753 F.2d 719, 727 (9th Cir.1983).

152. Regal Knitwear Co., 324 U.S. at 14, 65 S.Ct. at 481 ("Successors and assigns may ... be instrumentalities through which defendant seeks to evade an order...."); NBA Properties, Inc. v. Gold, 895 F.2d 30, 33 (1st Cir.1990) (franchisors could not be held in contempt on the theory that granting the franchises enabled the violation by the franchisees or on ground that decree prohibited any persons acting in concert or participation with franchisors from using the marks without permission).

153. Regal Knitwear Co., 324 U.S. at 14–15, 65 S.Ct. at 481–82; Rockwell Graph-

ic Sys., Inc. v. DEV Indus., Inc., 91 F.3d 914, 419 (7th Cir.1996); G & C Merriam Co. v. Webster Dictionary Co., Inc., 639 F.2d 29, 35 (1st Cir.1980) (corporation and its president could not be held in contempt on basis of aiding or abetting former corporation and named individuals in violating injunction previously issued against former corporation where acts of corporation and its president occurred after president had withdrawn from all participation in former corporation, and where there was no evidence that former corporation was involved in acts by corporation and its president).

154. People v. Operation Rescue Nat'l, 80 F.3d 64 (2d Cir.1996).

155. Alemite Mfg. Corp. v. Staff, 42 F.2d 832 (2d Cir.1930); Martin v. Carroll Graphics Corp., 804 F.Supp. 311, 313 (M.D.Fla.1992).

156. Zenith Radio Corp. v. Hazeltine Research, Inc., 395 U.S. 100, 89 S.Ct. 1562, 23 L.Ed.2d 129 (1969); United Elec., Radio & Machine Workers of Am. v. 163 Pleasant Street Corp., 960 F.2d 1080, 1099 (1st Cir. 1992); Zepeda, 753 F.2d 719.

157. United States v. Hall, 472 F.2d 261, 265–66 (5th Cir.1972).

The geographic scope of injunction orders generally extends nation-wide,[158] and may even extend worldwide.[159] International injunctions, however, cannot enjoin a foreign national to act or refrain from acting in a manner violating that country's laws while in that country.[160]

(10) When FRCP 65 Does Not Apply

FRCP 65(e) states "these rules do not modify any statute of the United States relating to temporary restraining orders and preliminary injunctions in actions affecting employer and employee...." Under specific circumstances, federal labor laws prevent courts from granting injunctions.[161] FRCP 65(e) simply acknowledges that the provisions of Rule 65 do not preempt such federal law. Nevertheless, the Rule does not bar courts from exercising equitable jurisdiction in actions which merely involve labor issues.[162]

FRCP 65(e) further states that the FRCP also does not modify "the provisions of Title 28, U.S.C., § 2361, relating to preliminary injunctions in actions of interpleader or in the nature of interpleader"[163] and "Title 28, U.S.C., § 2284, relating to actions required by Act of Congress to be heard and determined by a district court of three judges." The Supreme Court has held that "the three-judge court procedure is brought into play in any 'suit which seeks to interpose the Constitution against enforcement of a state policy, whether such policy is defined in a state constitution or in an ordinary statute or through the delegated legislation of an administrative board or commission.' "[164] In such cases, a majority of the three-judge court is required for issuance of a preliminary injunction.[165]

FRCP 65(b) does not apply to TROs granted by a court of appeals.[166] Also, before passage of Bankruptcy Rule 7065, courts were unsure about

---

158. Waffenschmidt v. MacKay, 763 F.2d 711, 716 (5th Cir.1985).

159. Lamb–Weston, Inc. v. McCain Foods, Ltd., 941 F.2d 970 (9th Cir.1991) (defendant enjoined from utilizing trade secrets worldwide).

160. Reebok Int'l, Ltd. v. McLaughlin, 49 F.3d 1387 (9th Cir.1995) (no contempt for complying with foreign court order that conflicted with district court's temporary restraining order).

161. 29 U.S.C.A. § 104(a) ("Norris–La-Guardia Act") (West 1973).

162. Boys Markets, Inc. v. Retail Clerks Union, 398 U.S. 235, 90 S.Ct. 1583, 26 L.Ed.2d 199 (1970); Reuter v. Skipper, 4 F.3d 716 (9th Cir.1993); American Broadcasting Co., Inc. v. American Fed'n of TV & Radio Artists, 412 F.Supp. 1077, 1081–82 (S.D.N.Y.1976); but see Camping Constr. Co. v. District Council of Iron Workers, 915 F.2d 1333, 1343–49 (9th Cir.1990) (discussing situations where Norris–LaGuardia Act

does not bar injunctive relief). See Chapter 66 "Labor Law" at § 66.3(a), infra.

163. General Ry. Signal Co. v. Corcoran, 921 F.2d 700, 702 (7th Cir.1991); Sotheby's, Inc. v. Garcia, 802 F.Supp. 1058, 1066–67 (S.D.N.Y.1992); see also 28 U.S.C.A. §§ 1335, 2361 (West 1996).

164. Morales v. Turman, 430 U.S. 322, 323, 97 S.Ct. 1189, 1190, 51 L.Ed.2d 368 (1977) (citation omitted); see also Puerto Rican Legal Defense & Educ. Fund v. City of New York, 769 F.Supp. 74, 79 (E.D.N.Y. 1991) (plan under § 5 of Federal Voting Rights Act of 1965, 42 U.S.C.A. § 1973(b) (West 1994), required approval by three-judge district court).

165. See Breswick & Co. v. United States, 75 S.Ct. 912 (1955) (signature of one judge conforming to majority opinion satisfied 28 U.S.C.A. § 2284).

166. See Board of Governors of Fed. Reserve Sys. v. Transamerica Corp., 184 F.2d 311 (9th Cir.1950) (order of court of

the application of FRCP 65(b) to bankruptcy proceedings. After the passage of Bankruptcy Rule 7065, however, all courts apply FRCP 65(b) to adversary proceedings in bankruptcy.[167]

(11) Enforcement

The effectiveness of an injunction depends predominantly on the court's power to punish noncompliance by civil and criminal contempt.[168] "Both forms of contempt typically carry a monetary fine in this context, and the classification as civil or criminal simply depends on the purpose of such fine."[169] Civil contempt is a remedial measure, designed to coerce compliance with the court's order and/or compensate the complainant for losses.[170] Coercive fines should take into account the fined party's "financial resources and consequent seriousness of the burden."[171] Civil contempt must be proven by clear and convincing evidence.[172]

Criminal contempt is designed to vindicate the authority of the court.[173] As such, an appellate court's reversal of a wrongly granted TRO may affect a finding of civil contempt, yet have no impact on a finding of criminal contempt.[174] Imposition of criminal contempt penalties requires adherence to the full protection of criminal process, including the rights to counsel and jury trial and the need for proof beyond a reasonable doubt.[175] Fewer procedural protections are necessary for civil contempt

appeals temporarily restraining threatened transfer to another bank of assets of banks was not invalid on ground that order did not recite matters specified in rule prescribing contents of restraining order, in view of rule limiting its application to proceedings in district courts).

167. Bankruptcy Rule 7065 reads: "Rule 65 F.R.Civ.P. applies in adversary proceedings, except that a temporary restraining order or preliminary injunction may be issued on application of a debtor, trustee, or debtor in possession without compliance with Rule 65(c)."

168. Spallone v. United States, 493 U.S. 265, 276, 110 S.Ct. 625, 632, 107 L.Ed.2d 644 (1990); Pierce v. Vision Invs., Inc., 779 F.2d 302, 309 (5th Cir.1986).

169. Bingman v. Ward, 100 F.3d 653 (9th Cir.1996), cert. denied, ___ U.S. ___, 117 S.Ct. 1473, 137 L.Ed.2d 686 (1997) (fines imposed against the noncomplying party, one of $500 to the aggrieved party and $1450 to the court, were criminal in nature because they were intended to punish not compensate).

170. Weitzman v. Stein, 98 F.3d 717 (2d Cir.1996).

171. Dole Fresh Fruit Co. v. United Banana Co., 821 F.2d 106, 110 (2d Cir.1987); New York State Nat'l Org. for Women v.

Terry, 886 F.2d 1339, 1352 (2d Cir.1989) (quoting Dole).

172. Glaxo, Inc. v. Novopharm, Ltd., 110 F.3d 1562 (Fed.Cir.1997) (violation of protective order); United States v. Ayer, 866 F.2d 571 (2d Cir.1989) (violation of injunction).

173. Gompers v. Buck's Stove & Range Co., 221 U.S. 418, 441, 31 S.Ct. 492, 498, 55 L.Ed. 797 (1911); Finn v. Schiller, 72 F.3d 1182, 1188 (4th Cir.1996); Roe v. Operation Rescue, 920 F.2d 213, 216 (3d Cir.1990); In re Sequoia Auto Brokers, Inc., 827 F.2d 1281, 1283 n. 1 (9th Cir.1987); Falstaff Brewing Corp. v. Miller Brewing Co., 702 F.2d 770, 778 (9th Cir.1983).

174. See Walker v. City of Birmingham, 388 U.S. 307, 315, 87 S.Ct. 1824, 1829, 18 L.Ed.2d 1210 (1967). See generally Blalock v. United States, 844 F.2d 1546, 1558–60 (11th Cir.1988) (contrasting civil and criminal contempt).

175. International Union, United Mine Workers of America v. Bagwell, 512 U.S. 821, 834, 114 S.Ct. 2552, 2561, 129 L.Ed.2d 642 (1994); United States v. McMahon, 104 F.3d 638 (4th Cir.1997) (violation of sequestration order); United States v. Oberhellmann, 946 F.2d 50 (7th Cir.1991) (attorney misconduct).

penalties.[176]

The distinction between acts that trigger one type of contempt versus the other is ambiguous, especially since some acts result in both civil and criminal contempt.[177] Although the line between civil and criminal contempt is fuzzy, the Supreme Court has indicated factors which should be considered in making the determination.[178] These factors include the nature of the injunction itself as either a simple injunction restricting limited types of conduct or a complex injunction involving an "entire code of conduct" which governs extensive activities.[179] The violation of the former results in civil contempt, while violating the latter may constitute criminal contempt. Another factor is whether the offending conduct takes place in the court's presence and affects the ability of the court to adjudicate the case.[180] The amount of the contempt fine may also be a factor—the more serious the fine, the more likely the contempt is criminal.[181]

A civil contempt proceeding does not continue past the effective period of the injunction if the purpose of the sanction was to coerce compliance with the court order.[182] However, if the civil contempt sanction was intended to compensate the aggrieved party, the contempt proceeding will not be mooted.[183] Also, neither the mootness of an underlying action nor the reversal of the order affects a criminal contempt order.[184]

Civil contempt proceedings are instituted on the motion of the aggrieved plaintiff and are part of the underlying action.[185] This pleading must conform to the requirements of FRCP 8 by showing facts sufficient to constitute contempt.[186] The propriety of the injunction is not at issue at a contempt hearing,[187] and the only defenses available to the party subject to contempt are that it did not receive notice of the order,[188] that it was unable to comply or did in fact substantially comply with the order,[189] or that it acted in good faith. Lack of personal jurisdiction is

176. International Union, 512 U.S. at 831, 114 S.Ct. at 2559.

177. See United States v. Rylander, 714 F.2d 996, 1000 (9th Cir.1983) ("The same conduct may result in citations for both civil and criminal contempt."), cert. denied, 467 U.S. 1209, 104 S.Ct. 2398, 81 L.Ed.2d 355 (1984).

178. International Union, 512 U.S. at 837–38, 114 S.Ct. at 2562–63, 129 L.Ed.2d 642.

179. Id.

180. Id.

181. Id.

182. Petroleos Mexicanos v. Crawford Enterprises, Inc., 826 F.2d 392, 399 (5th Cir.1987).

183. Id.

184. United States v. United Mine Workers of Am., 330 U.S. 258, 293, 67 S.Ct.

677, 696, 91 L.Ed. 884 (1947); Johnson v. Kay, 860 F.2d 529, 539 n. 3 (2d Cir.1988).

185. Latrobe Steel Co. v. United Steelworkers, Etc., 545 F.2d 1336, 1343–44 (3d Cir.1976).

186. See FRCP 8.

187. See Backo v. Local 281, United Bhd. of Carpenters and Joiners of Am., 308 F.Supp. 172, 176 (N.D.N.Y.1969) (TRO was not open to collateral attack in a contempt proceeding based on disobedience of that order), aff'd, 438 F.2d 176 (2d Cir.1970), cert. denied, 404 U.S. 858, 92 S.Ct. 110, 30 L.Ed.2d 99 (1971).

188. Dorsey v. Warden, Southern Mich. State Prison, 421 F.Supp. 1133 (E.D.Mich. 1976).

189. Rolex Watch U.S.A., Inc. v. Crowley, 74 F.3d 716 (6th Cir.1996) (holding that defendant must show categorically and in

also a defense in a subsequent contempt proceeding, but this will be unavailing if the entity knowingly aided or abetted the violation of the order or was in privity with the party violating the order.[190]

Under the collateral bar doctrine, a restrained party may not challenge a district court's order by violating it. Instead, the restrained party must move to vacate or modify the order. If the party fails to do so, that party may not challenge the order on appeal unless it was transparently invalid or exceeded the district court's jurisdiction.[191]

Criminal contempt proceedings may be instituted by the judge or a United States Attorney.[192] Notice and a hearing must be afforded the defendant, unless the judge certifies that he or she saw or heard the conduct constituting the contempt, in which case criminal contempt may be punished summarily.[193]

Contempt proceedings are usually summarily adjudicated, especially when no factual dispute exists.[194] In the interest of efficiency, the court may adjudicate both civil and criminal contempt in one proceeding so long as it affords to defendant the same rights and privileges given a criminal defendant.[195]

(12) Appealability

Although the general rule is that an appellate court can review only final judgments, 28 U.S.C.A. § 1292(a)(1) creates an exception for certain interlocutory orders, including injunctions.[196] Appeals from a preliminary injunction are appeals as a matter of right pursuant to that section.[197]

Because a preliminary injunction is a discretionary remedy, the standard for appellate review is whether the court abused its discretion

---

detail why he or she is unable to comply with court order).

190. See Geneva Assurance Syndicate, Inc. v. Medical Emergency Servs. Ass'n, 964 F.2d 599, 600 (7th Cir.1992) (order granting TRO held not appealable); Petraco–Valley Oil & Ref. Co. v. United States Dep't of Energy, 633 F.2d 184, 199 (Temp. Emer. Ct. App. 1980) (denial of TRO is generally not appealable).

191. See Walker v. City of Birmingham, 388 U.S. 307, 317–21, 87 S.Ct. 1824, 1830–32, 18 L.Ed.2d 1210 (1967); United States v. Cutler, 58 F.3d 825 (2d Cir.1995); United States v. Terry, 17 F.3d 575, 579 (2d Cir. 1994); In re Providence Journal Co., 820 F.2d 1342, 1346–47 (1st Cir.1986), modified, 820 F.2d 1354 (1st Cir.1987), cert. dismissed, United States v. Providence Journal Co., 485 U.S. 693, 108 S.Ct. 1502, 99 L.Ed.2d 785 (1988).

192. See Fed.R.Crim.P. 42.

193. See id.

194. Harris v. City of Philadelphia, 47 F.3d 1333 (3d Cir.1995) (no evidentiary hearing required before imposing contempt sanction where facts were undisputed).

195. See United States v. United Mine Workers of Am., 330 U.S. 258, 67 S.Ct. 677, 91 L.Ed. 884 (1947) (One proceeding for both civil and criminal contempt is permissible so long as contemnor does not suffer substantial prejudice.).

196. 28 U.S.C.A. § 1292(a) (West 1993) provides that "the courts of appeals shall have jurisdiction of appeals from: 1) Interlocutory orders of the district courts ... granting, continuing, modifying, refusing or dissolving injunctions, or refusing to dissolve or modify injunctions...."

197. Sierra Club v. Robertson, 28 F.3d 753, 756 n. 3 (8th Cir.1994); United States v. Bayshore Assocs., Inc., 934 F.2d 1391, 1395 (6th Cir.1991).

by granting or denying the relief.[198] A factual finding must be "clearly erroneous" to justify reversal.[199] The standard for appeal of a preliminary injunction places a heavy burden on the appellant.[200]

A court may issue orders controlling a defendant's actions which are not appealable injunctions.[201] An order appealable as an injunction must either restrain or require conduct that lies at the core of the underlying case, or protect the court's jurisdiction over the subject matter.[202]

(d) Grounds for the Grant or Denial of Preliminary Injunctions

(1) Generally

Rule 65 does not provide the specific standards for granting a preliminary injunction. The grant or denial of a preliminary injunction is left within the discretion of the court pursuant to traditional equitable principles and the substantive law applicable to the claim upon which the application for the injunction is based.[203]

(2) Standards for Granting a Preliminary Injunction

In deciding whether to grant a preliminary injunction, a court must balance the competing claims of injury to the defendant if the injunction is granted and to the plaintiff if the injunction is denied.[204] Since a preliminary injunction is considered a drastic remedy,[205] the applicant must show clearly that equitable considerations warrant the preliminary

---

198. Thornburgh v. American College of Obstetricians & Gynecologists, 476 U.S. 747, 818, 106 S.Ct. 2169, 2208, 90 L.Ed.2d 779 (1986); San Antonio Comm. Hosp. v. Southern Cal. Dist. Council of Carpenters, 115 F.3d 685, 688 (9th Cir.1997); Landscape Forms, Inc. v. Columbia Cascade Co., 113 F.3d 373, 376 (2d Cir.1997); Sierra Club v. San Antonia, 112 F.3d 789, 793 (5th Cir.1997).

199. San Antonio Comm. Hosp., 115 F.3d 685; Fun–Damental Too, Ltd. v. Gemmy Indus. Corp., 111 F.3d 993 (2d Cir.1997).

200. International Comm. Materials, Inc. v. Ricoh Co., 108 F.3d 316, 317 (Fed. Cir.1997); Eli Lilly & Co. v. Premo Pharm. Lab., 630 F.2d 120, 136 (3d Cir.1980).

201. McLaughlin Gormley King Co. v. Terminix Int'l Co., 105 F.3d 1192, 1194 (8th Cir.1997) ("injunction" against arbitration affirmed as nonappealable order); Allendale Mut. Ins. Co. v. Bull Data Sys., Inc., 32 F.3d 1175, 1177 (7th Cir.1994) (discovery order not appealable injunction); Bogosian v. Woloohojian Realty Corp., 923

F.2d 898, 901 (1st Cir.1991); Cox v. Piper, Jaffray & Hopwood, Inc., 848 F.2d 842, 843 (8th Cir.1988) (order denying motion for stay of arbitration not appealable injunction); Teradyne, Inc. v. Mostek Corp., 797 F.2d 43, 47 (1st Cir.1986) (order of attachment is appealable injunction); Rosenfeldt v. Comprehensive Accounting Service Corp., 514 F.2d 607, 608 (7th Cir.1975) (order of attachment is nonappealable).

202. Bogosian, 923 F.2d at 901; United States v. Crozier, 777 F.2d 1376 (9th Cir. 1985) (order freezing assets).

203. San Antonio Comm. Hosp., 115 F.3d 685; Carillon Importers, Ltd. v. Frank Pesce Intern. Group, Inc., 112 F.3d 1125 (11th Cir.1997).

204. Ross–Simons of Warwick, Inc. v. Baccarat, Inc., 102 F.3d 12 (1st Cir.1996); Storck USA, L.P. v. Farley Candy Co., 14 F.3d 311 (7th Cir.1994).

205. Crochet v. Housing Auth. of Tampa, 37 F.3d 607 (11th Cir.1994); Borey v. National Union Fire Ins. Co. of Pittsburgh, 934 F.2d 30 (2d Cir.1991).

injunction.[206]

The traditional factors courts consider in deciding an application for a preliminary injunction include the following: 1) whether the applicant would suffer irreparable injury if the preliminary injunction is denied, 2) whether the applicant is likely to succeed on the merits, 3) whether injury to the applicant, if the preliminary injunction is denied, outweighs injury to the adverse party if the preliminary injunction is granted and 4) whether the preliminary injunction is in the public interest.[207]

The federal courts have developed different and changing formulations of these basic standards, and the standard for issuing a preliminary injunction varies among the circuits. The traditional considerations, however, play essential roles in every circuit.

The traditional four factor test[208] is used in most of the federal circuits, although each circuit varies slightly in its application of these factors. The Third,[209] Sixth,[210] Eighth,[211] District of Columbia[212] and Federal[213] Circuits apply the traditional test, using their discretion to balance all four factors where no single factor is determinative. In the D.C. Circuit, however, a party that moves for a preliminary injunction that would intrude on the core concerns of the government must make an extraordinarily strong showing for each factor, beyond the typical burden applicable to other claims.[214] The Federal Circuit uses the traditional test when it has exclusive jurisdiction over the substantive issues,[215] otherwise it applies the test of the circuit from which the appeal is taken.[216]

The First[217] and Fourth[218] Circuits also use the traditional test;

206. Giddens v. City of Shreveport, 901 F.Supp. 1170 (W.D.La.1995); Romm Art Creations Ltd. v. Simcha Int'l Inc., 786 F.Supp. 1126 (E.D.N.Y.1992).

207. Nnadi v. Richter, 976 F.2d 682 (11th Cir.1992); Chevron, U.S.A. Production Co. v. O'Leary, 958 F.Supp. 1485 (E.D.Cal.1997).

208. See discussion *infra* § 13.2(d)(3).

209. University of Maryland v. Peat, Marwick, Main & Co., 996 F.2d 1534 (3d Cir.1993); Hoxworth v. Blinder, Robinson & Co., Inc., 903 F.2d 186 (3d Cir.1990); Kershner v. Mazurkiewicz, 670 F.2d 440 (3d Cir.1982).

210. *In re* DeLorean Motor Co., 755 F.2d 1223 (6th Cir.1985); Friendship Materials, Inc. v. Michigan Brick, Inc., 679 F.2d 100 (6th Cir.1982).

211. Sanborn Mfg. v. Campbell Hausfeld/Scott Fetzer Co., 997 F.2d 484 (8th Cir.1993); Glenwood Bridge, Inc. v. City of Minneapolis, 940 F.2d 367 (8th Cir.1991).

212. Sea Containers Ltd. v. Stena AB, 890 F.2d 1205 (D.C.Cir.1989).

213. Payless Shoesource, Inc. v. Reebok Intern. Ltd., 998 F.2d 985 (Fed.Cir.1993); FMC Corp. v. United States, 3 F.3d 424 (Fed.Cir.1993).

214. Reporters Committee for Freedom of the Press v. AT & T, 593 F.2d 1030, 1065 (D.C.Cir.1978) ("A party invoking equitable intervention in the criminal investigative process has a particularly heavy burden.... The powers of criminal investigation are committed to the Executive branch."), *cert. denied*, 440 U.S. 949, 99 S.Ct. 1431, 59 L.Ed.2d 639 (1979); Adams v. Vance, 570 F.2d 950 (D.C.Cir.1978) (departing from traditional standards where a request for an order directing action by the Secretary of State in foreign affairs was made).

215. Chrysler Motors Corp. v. Auto Body Panels of Ohio, 908 F.2d 951, 952 (Fed.Cir.1990).

216. *Id.*

217. Coastal Fuels v. Caribbean Petroleum, 990 F.2d 25 (1st Cir.1993).

218. Virginia Carolina Tools v. International Tool, 984 F.2d 113 (4th Cir.), *cert.*

however, the First Circuit views the plaintiff's likelihood of success[219] as the most important factor while the Fourth Circuit considers the balance of hardships[220] the most important factor. In fact, the balance of hardships must be determined in the Fourth Circuit before any of the other factors are even considered.[221]

The Fifth,[222] Seventh,[223] Tenth[224] and Eleventh[225] Circuits use the traditional test, yet unlike circuits which balance all of the factors, these circuits require the movant to produce sufficient evidence to carry the burden of proof on each factor. Some courts in the Seventh Circuit recognize a fifth factor, whether the movant has an adequate remedy at law,[226] but most courts integrate this consideration into the assessment of whether the movant would suffer irreparable injury without the preliminary injunction.[227]

Some jurisdictions use an alternative test which requires the applicant to prove either: 1) probable success on the merits and possibility of irreparable harm or 2) serious questions on the merits and the balance of hardships tipping sharply in the applicant's favor.[228] These are not two separate tests, but a single test stating the extremes of a single continuum.[229] "[T]he greater the relative hardship to the moving party, the less [the] probability of success must be shown."[230] District courts have employed the alternative test in the Second[231] and Ninth[232] Cir-

denied, 508 U.S. 960, 113 S.Ct. 2930, 124 L.Ed.2d 681 (1993); Blackwelder Furniture Co. of Statesville, Inc. v. Seilig Mfg. Co., 550 F.2d 189 (4th Cir.1977); Merrill Lynch, Pierce, Fenner & Smith v. Bradley, 756 F.2d 1048 (4th Cir.1985).

219. Lancor v. Lebanon Housing Authority, 760 F.2d 361 (1st Cir.1985).

220. Hughes Network Systems v. Inter-Digital Communications Corp., 17 F.3d 691 (4th Cir.1994); Rum Creek Coal Sales, Inc. v. Caperton, 926 F.2d 353 (4th Cir.1991).

221. Virginia Carolina Tools, 984 F.2d 113.

222. Doe v. Ducanville Ind. Sch. Dist., 994 F.2d 160 (5th Cir.1993); Roho, Inc. v. Marquis, 902 F.2d 356 (5th Cir.1990)

223. Diginet, Inc. v. Western Union ATS, Inc. 958 F.2d 1388 (7th Cir.1992); Roland Machinery Co. v. Dresser Industries, Inc., 749 F.2d 380 (7th Cir.1984); Cox v. City of Chicago, 868 F.2d 217 (7th Cir. 1989); Shaffer v. Globe Protection, Inc., 721 F.2d 1121 (7th Cir.1983).

224. Resolution Trust Corp. v. Cruce, 972 F.2d 1195 (10th Cir.1992); SCFC ILC, Inc. v. Visa USA, Inc., 936 F.2d 1096 (10th Cir.1991); Equifax Servs., Inc. v. Hitz, 905 F.2d 1355 (10th Cir.1990).

225. United States v. Jefferson County, 720 F.2d 1511 (11th Cir.1983); United

States v. Lambert, 695 F.2d 536 (11th Cir. 1983).

226. JAK Productions, Inc. v. Wiza, 986 F.2d 1080 (7th Cir.1993); Roland Machinery Co., 749 F.2d 380.

227. JAK Productions, Inc., 986 F.2d 1080.

228. Marbled Murrelet v. Babbitt, 83 F.3d 1068, 1073 (9th Cir.1996); Sweeney v. Bane, 996 F.2d 1384 (2d Cir.1993); United States v. Nutri-cology, Inc., 982 F.2d 394 (9th Cir.1992); Senate of Cal. v. Mosbacher, 968 F.2d 974, 977 (9th Cir.1992); Rent–A–Center, Inc. v. Canyon Television & Appliance, 944 F.2d 597 (9th Cir.1991); Cliffs Notes, Inc. v. Bantam Doubleday Dell Publ'g Group, Inc., 886 F.2d 490, 497 (2d Cir.1989); Dataphase Sys., Inc. v. C L Sys., Inc., 640 F.2d 109, 112 (8th Cir.1981).

229. Westlands Water Dist. v. Natural Resources Defense Council, 43 F.3d 457, 459 (9th Cir.1994); Topanga Press, Inc. v. City of Los Angeles, 989 F.2d 1524 (9th Cir.1993).

230. White Mountain Apache Tribe v. Smith Plumbing Co., Inc., 856 F.2d 1301, 1304 (9th Cir.1988) (citation omitted).

231. Jayaraj v. Scappini, 66 F.3d 36 (2d Cir.1995) (applying the alternative test).

232. Johnson v. California State Bd. of Accountancy, 72 F.3d 1427 (9th Cir.1995) (applying the alternative test).

cuits. The plaintiff's likelihood of success in prevailing on the merits is articulated by the courts in various ways.[233]

Despite these semantic differences, all circuits require the plaintiff to present a prima facie case and no circuit requires the plaintiff to show a certainty of success on the claim.[234] The likelihood of success is not always determinative. Courts must balance the plaintiff's likelihood of success with the respective injuries of the parties.[235] This balancing is often referred to as a "sliding scale."[236] When the plaintiff does not seem likely to win on the merits, a preliminary injunction may still issue if the balance of hardships tips strongly in the plaintiff's favor.[237] Conversely, when the balance of hardships tips away from the plaintiff, a preliminary injunction may still issue if the plaintiff makes a strong showing of ultimate success on the merits.[238] Similarly, if evidence of irreparable injury to the plaintiff is minimal, the plaintiff carries a higher burden of proving likelihood of success on the claim.[239]

Sometimes, cases with significant conflict over facts or profound legal questions will raise sufficient doubt about the merits of the case to justify denying a preliminary injunction.[240]

(3) Irreparable Harm

Irreparable harm is an injury for which there is no adequate remedy at law.[241] Relief under federal or state statutory law may provide an

233. Statewide Detective Agency v. Miller, 115 F.3d 904 (11th Cir.1997) ("substantial likelihood"); Blue Cross & Blue Shield Mut. of Ohio v. Blue Cross and Blue Shield Ass'n, 110 F.3d 318, 322 (6th Cir.1997) ("strong likelihood"); Gilliam v. Foster, 61 F.3d 1070, 1078 n. 5 (4th Cir.1995) ("probable"); S.E.C. v. Unifund SAL, 910 F.2d 1028, 1037 (2d Cir.1990) ("reasonable certainty").

234. Curtis 1000, Inc. v. Suess, 843 F.Supp. 441 (C.D.Ill.), aff'd, 24 F.3d 941 (7th Cir.1994); Gilder v. PGA Tour, Inc., 936 F.2d 417 (9th Cir.1991).

235. Blue Cross & Blue Shield Mut. of Ohio, 110 F.3d at 322; Haan Crafts Corp. v. Craft Masters, Inc., 683 F.Supp. 1234 (N.D.Ind.1988).

236. Vencor, Inc. v. Webb, 33 F.3d 840, 845 (7th Cir.1994) ("sliding scale"); United States v. Nutri–cology, Inc., 982 F.2d 394, 397 (9th Cir.1992) ("sliding scale").

237. Grossbaum v. Indianapolis–Marion County Bldg. Auth., 909 F.Supp. 1187 (S.D.Ind.1995), aff'd, 100 F.3d 1287 (7th Cir.1996), cert. denied, ___ U.S. ___, 117 S.Ct. 1822, 137 L.Ed.2d 1030 (1997); Dy-

namics Corp. of Am. v. CTS Corp., 805 F.2d 705 (7th Cir.1986).

238. See Direx Israel, Ltd. v. Breakthrough Med. Corp., 952 F.2d 802, 818 (4th Cir.1991) (Where the hardship balance does not tilt decidedly in plaintiff's favor, a strong showing of likelihood of success is required.).

239. American Hosp. Ass'n v. Harris, 625 F.2d 1328, 1331 (7th Cir.1980) (" '[W]here it appears that a lack of showing of irreparable damage exists ... the party seeking a preliminary injunction has a burden of convincing with reasonable certainty that it must succeed at [the] final hearing.' ") (citation omitted).

240. Stop & Shop Supermarket Co. v. Big Y Foods, Inc., 943 F.Supp. 120 (D.Mass. 1996) (complex legal issues); Sovereign Order of Saint John of Jerusalem–Knights of Malta by Coleman v. Messineo, 572 F.Supp. 983, 990 (E.D.Pa.1983) (conflicting facts).

241. Sampson v. Murray, 415 U.S. 61, 94 S.Ct. 937, 39 L.Ed.2d 166 (1974); Caplan v. Fellheimer Eichen Braverman & Kaskey, 68 F.3d 828, 839 (3d Cir.1995) (stating that the movant must demonstrate a potential harm which cannot be redressed by a legal or equitable remedy after trial, whereby a

applicant with an adequate remedy at law.[242] Also, the court will not grant a preliminary injunction when a trial on the merits could be conducted before the threatened injury occurs.[243] Courts assess irreparable injury at the time of the application for preliminary injunction, not at the time the action begins.[244] A self-inflicted injury will not satisfy the irreparable harm standard.[245]

Further, the court must find that the threatened injury is likely to occur.[246] The injury must be imminent not remote.[247] Mere speculation or an unsubstantiated fear of harm does not show irreparable injury.[248]

Claimed injuries of economic loss[249] or injuries for which damages

preliminary injunction is the only way to protect the movant from harm); JAK Prod., Inc. v. Wiza, 986 F.2d 1080, 1084 (7th Cir. 1993) (finding inadequate legal remedy for the threat of a former employee's continued contact with clients of plaintiff's fund raising business which depends upon personal relationships with its customers); Loveridge v. Pendleton Woolen Mills, Inc., 788 F.2d 914, 918 (2d Cir.1986) (stating "where money damages are adequate compensation, a preliminary injunction will not issue since equity should not intervene where there is an adequate remedy at law").

242. *See* Youngstown Sheet & Tube Co. v. Sawyer, 103 F.Supp. 978 (D.D.C.1952) (stating the plaintiff had adequate remedy under the Federal Tort Claims Act that precluded grant of a TRO).

243. Bascom Food Products Corp. v. Reese Finer Foods, Inc., 715 F.Supp. 616, 624 (D.N.J.1989) (In considering irreparable harm, "consideration can be given to whether the plaintiff will get an early trial on the merits.").

244. SI Handling Sys. Inc. v. Heisley, 753 F.2d 1244, 1263 (3d Cir.1985) ("the relevant inquiry is whether the movant is in danger of suffering irreparable harm at the time the preliminary injunction is to be issued"); Stewart B. McKinney Foundation v. Town Plan & Zoning Commission, 790 F.Supp. 1197, 1209 (D.Conn.1992).

245. Caplan v. Fellheimer Eichen Braverman & Kaskey, 68 F.3d 828, 839 (3d Cir.1995) (in former employer's attempt to obtain preliminary injunction precluding former employer's insurer from settling claim, damage to former employer's ability to bring future malicious prosecution action against its former employee was not irreparable because employer contracted with insurer to authorize insurer to settle this

litigation); Fiba Leasing Co., Inc. v. Airdyne Indus., Inc., 826 F.Supp. 38 (D.Mass.1993) (lessor's irreparable harm argument resting on the claim that it could now be held liable if lessee causes a third party damage through use of unregistered equipment failed because lessor was responsible for the equipment not being registered).

246. Hunt v. City of Longview, 932 F.Supp. 828, 842 (E.D.Tex.1995) (granting a preliminary injunction where plaintiffs proved a "substantial threat," not "absolute certainty" that irreparable injury would result from the denial of the injunction).

247. Tom Doherty Assocs., Inc. v. Saban Entertainment, Inc., 60 F.3d 27, 34 (2d Cir.1995); Direx Israel Ltd. v. Breakthrough Med. Corp., 952 F.2d 802, 812 (4th Cir. 1991); Reuters Ltd. v. United Press Int'l, 903 F.2d 904, 907 (2d Cir.1990).

248. Goff v. Harper, 60 F.3d 518 (8th Cir.1995) (possibility that defendant would participate in a disciplinary hearing and discriminate against plaintiff during pendency of litigation deemed too speculative); Kaplan v. Board of Educ. of City Sch. Dist. of New York, 759 F.2d 256 (2d Cir.1985) (prediction of havoc and unrest due to filing financial disclosure forms deemed too speculative).

249. Acierno v. New Castle County, 40 F.3d 645, 653 (3d Cir.1994) (holding that plaintiff's claim of economic loss resulting from defendant's denial of a permit to build a shopping center was compensable in money and therefore did not justify a preliminary injunction); Loveridge v. Pendleton Woolen Mills, Inc., 788 F.2d 914, 918 (2d Cir.1986) ("It is well established that irreparable injury means injury for which a monetary award cannot be adequate compensation.").

can be calculated[250] generally are not considered irreparable because the plaintiff can be compensated later by money damages. Extraordinary circumstances, such as the threat of defendant's insolvency at the time of award, may warrant a finding of irreparable harm for an otherwise compensable injury.[251] Some courts grant preliminary injunctions freezing the defendant's assets, thereby preserving the defendant's ability to pay at the time an award is made.[252] Other courts are reluctant to take such action when the assets have no relation to the plaintiff's claim.[253]

Courts have declined to find irreparable injuries for harms such as discharge from employment,[254] threat of litigation,[255] the cost of litigation[256] or the cost of compliance with a government regulation.[257] Injuries which the courts have commonly found to be irreparable include cases involving possible bankruptcy,[258] injury to goodwill of a business or reputation,[259] the loss of a unique product or contractual right,[260] and the

250. Roland Mach. Co. v. Dresser Indus., Inc., 749 F.2d 380, 386 (7th Cir.1984) (irreparable harm is shown when monetary damages are difficult to calculate); Progressive Games, Inc. v. Bally's Olympia, L.P., 967 F.Supp. 193 (S.D.Miss.1997); Burger King Corp. v. Agad, 911 F.Supp. 1499, 1506 (S.D.Fla.1995); FMC Corp. v. Cyprus Foote Mineral Co., 899 F.Supp. 1477, 1483 (W.D.N.C.1995).

251. Performance Unlimited, Inc. v. Questar Publishers, Inc., 52 F.3d 1373 (6th Cir.1995); Interpoint Corp. v. Truck World, Inc., 656 F.Supp. 114 (N.D.Ind.1986).

252. *In re* Estate of Marcos 25 F.3d 1467, 1480 (9th Cir.1994); Teradyne, Inc. v. Mostek Corp., 797 F.2d 43, 53 (1st Cir. 1986).

253. Rosen v. Cascade Int'l, Inc., 21 F.3d 1520, 1527 (11th Cir.1994); *In re* Fredeman Litigation, 843 F.2d 821, 826 (5th Cir.1988).

254. Sampson v. Murray, 415 U.S. 61, 92 n. 68, 94 S.Ct. 937, 954 n. 68, 39 L.Ed.2d 166 (1974) (absent a "generally extraordinary situation," financial distress or difficulty caused by termination of employment is not irreparable harm); Adam–Mellang v. Apartment Search, Inc., 96 F.3d 297, 299 (8th Cir.1996); *But see* Arcamuzi v. Continental Air Lines, Inc., 819 F.2d 935, 939 (9th Cir.1987) (discharge for union involvement may constitute irreparable harm); Morgan v. Fletcher, 518 F.2d 236, 239 (5th Cir.1975).

255. O'Shea v. Littleton, 414 U.S. 488, 502, 94 S.Ct. 669, 679, 38 L.Ed.2d 674 (1974); Rushia v. Town of Ashburnham, Massachusetts, 701 F.2d 7, 9 (1st Cir.1983).

256. Renegotiation Bd. v. Bannercraft Clothing Co., 415 U.S. 1, 24, 94 S.Ct. 1028, 1040, 39 L.Ed.2d 123 (1974) ("Mere litigation expense, even substantial and unrecoupable cost, does not constitute irreparable injury."); PaineWebber, Inc. v. Farnam, 843 F.2d 1050, 1051 (7th Cir.1988); Emery Air Freight Corp. v. Local Union 295, 786 F.2d 93, 100 (2d Cir.1986) (cost of arbitration is not irreparable injury); United States v. City of Los Angeles, 595 F.2d 1386, 1391 (9th Cir.1979).

257. American Hosp. Ass'n v. Harris, 625 F.2d 1328, 1331 (7th Cir.1980); A.O. Smith Corp. v. FTC, 530 F.2d 515 (3d Cir. 1976).

258. Doran v. Salem Inn, Inc., 422 U.S. 922, 932, 95 S.Ct. 2561, 2568, 45 L.Ed.2d 648 (1975) (threat of bankruptcy constitutes irreparable harm); Performance Unlimited, Inc. v. Questar Publishers, Inc., 52 F.3d 1373, 1382–83 (6th Cir.1995); Atwood Turnkey Drilling, Inc. v. Petroleo Brasileiro, S.A., 875 F.2d 1174, 1179 (5th Cir.1989).

259. Ross–Simons of Warwick, Inc. v. Baccarat, Inc., 102 F.3d 12 (1st Cir.1996) (dealer would suffer irreparable harm to its goodwill if distributor were allowed to cut off supply of goods); Tom Doherty Assocs., Inc. v. Saban Entertainment, Inc., 60 F.3d 27 (2d Cir.1995) (book publisher's goodwill would be irreparably harmed if not allowed to publish book and establish itself in children's book market); Rent–A–Center, Inc. v. Canyon Television and Appliance Rental, Inc., 944 F.2d 597 (9th Cir.1991) (competitor's continued operation of store in violation of agreement would cause irreparable harm to purchaser's advertising efforts and goodwill).

260. Sportsmen's Wildlife Defense Fund v. United States Dept. of the Interior, 949

deprivation of a statutory right.[261]

In limited situations, irreparable injuries are presumed. When a preliminary injunction is sought pursuant to express provisions of a statute, a demonstration of irreparable harm is unnecessary when the plaintiff has satisfied all of the statutory provisions.[262] Additionally, an alleged deprivation of a constitutional right requires no further showing of irreparable harm.[263] When a claimant makes a prima facie case for a copyright action, a rebuttable presumption of irreparable injury exists.[264] The claimant in a trademark infringement case need only prove a likelihood of confusion between trademarks to show irreparable injury.[265] In the same vein, courts will presume irreparable injury when trade secrets and confidential information are used or disclosed.[266] An irreparable injury may be presumed by the violation of a noncompetition covenant, depending on state law governing such restrictive covenants.[267]

F.Supp. 1510 (D.Colo.1996) (loss of real property is per se irreparable injury); Arias v. Solis, 754 F.Supp. 290 (E.D.N.Y.1991) (boxer's services were unique and permitting fight to go forward would cause irreparable harm to manager).

261. Sullivan v. Pittsburgh, 811 F.2d 171, 180 (3d Cir.1987); OKI Electric Industry Co., Ltd. v. United States, 669 F.Supp. 480, 486 (Court of Int'l Trade, 1987).

262. CSX Transp. v. Tennessee State Board of Equalization, 964 F.2d 548, 551 (6th Cir.1992) 49 U.S.C.A. § 11503 (West 1978), omitted by Pub. L. 104–88, § 102(a) (1995), prohibiting discriminatory state taxation of railroads, expressly provided for injunctive relief); Burlington Northern R.R. Co. v. Bair, 957 F.2d 599, 601 (8th Cir. 1992) (same); Capital Tool & Mfg. Co. v. Maschinenfabrik Herkules, 837 F.2d 171, 172 (4th Cir.1988) (affirming denial of preliminary injunction where state statute on trade secrets merely permitted such relief in discretion of court); United States v. Odessa Union Warehouse Co-op, 833 F.2d 172, 175–76 (9th Cir.1987) (applying this principle to violations of the Food, Drug, and Cosmetic Act, 21 U.S.C.A. § 331(a)); EEOC v. Cosmair, Inc., 821 F.2d 1085, 1090 (5th Cir.1987) (irreparable harm presumed where civil rights statute was violated); SEC v. Management Dynamics, Inc., 515 F.2d 801, 808 (2d Cir.1975) (applying this principle to securities laws context).

263. Deerfield Med. Ctr. v. City of Deerfield Beach, 661 F.2d 328 (5th Cir.1981) (violation of right to privacy mandates finding of irreparable harm); SAC and Fox Nation of Mo. v. La Faver, 946 F.Supp. 834, 887 (D.Kan.1996) ("Where ... plaintiffs allege deprivation of a constitutional right, no further showing of irreparable injury is generally necessary."). But see Hamlyn v. Rock Island County Metro. Mass Transit Dist., 960 F.Supp. 160, 163 (C.D.Ill.1997) ("[I]n a procedural due process action, there is no harm where the injury is ultimately redressable through monetary compensation.").

264. Richard Feiner & Co., Inc. v. Turner Entertainment Co., 98 F.3d 33, 34 (2d Cir.1996); Triad Sys. Corp. v. Southeastern Express Co., 64 F.3d 1330, 1334 (9th Cir. 1995); Concrete Machinery Co., Inc. v. Classic Lawn Ornaments, Inc., 843 F.2d 600, 611 (1st Cir.1988). See Chapter 65 "Copyright" at § 65.13(a), infra.

265. Metro Pub'g, Ltd. v. San Jose Mercury News, 987 F.2d 637 (9th Cir.1993); Vision Sports, Inc. v. Melville Corp., 888 F.2d 609, 612 n. 3 (9th Cir.1989). See Chapter 64 "Trademark," at § 64.5(b)(2) infra.

266. FMC Corp. v. Varco Int'l, Inc., 677 F.2d 500, 503 (5th Cir.1982) (fact that a single trade secret may be disclosed satisfied irreparable harm); Picker Int'l, Inc. v. Blanton, 756 F.Supp. 971, 981 (N.D.Tex. 1990) (citing FMC Corp. in the context of confidential information).

267. AMP, Inc. v. Fleischhacker, 823 F.2d 1199, 1206 (7th Cir.1987); Overholt Crop Ins. Serv. Co. v. Travis, 941 F.2d 1361, 1371 (8th Cir.1991); but see Hester Indus., Inc. v. Tyson Foods, Inc., 882 F.Supp. 276, 277 (rejecting presumption theory under New York law) (N.D.N.Y. 1995).

Courts may also grant injunctions absent irreparable harm, if necessary to protect its jurisdiction, typically in an attempt to restrain prolific and vexatious litigators.[268]

(4) Balancing the Hardships

Balancing the hardships requires the court to weigh the injury that the plaintiff would suffer if the preliminary injunction were denied against the injury the defendant would incur if the injunction were granted. A preliminary injunction is often granted when the balance of hardships favors the plaintiff[269] and usually denied when the balance tips in favor of the defendant.[270] Furthermore, if an injunction bond can compensate the defendant for any harm likely to occur from the injunction, the court may balance in favor of the plaintiff.[271]

When evaluating the balance of hardships the courts sometimes consider whether the preliminary injunction would give the plaintiff all or most of the relief that would be awarded in a successful trial[272] and whether the application is for a mandatory as opposed to a prohibitory injunction.[273] While courts are reluctant to provide a plaintiff full relief in granting a preliminary injunction, they are not precluded from issuing a preliminary injunction simply because the plaintiff would temporarily obtain all of the relief sought.[274] If the application is for a mandatory

---

268. In re Martin–Trigona, 737 F.2d 1254, 1261 (2d Cir.1984) (Under its own inherent power to protect its jurisdiction, federal district court was authorized to enjoin party's further litigation activities upon determination that party had used legal processes solely for harassment, had deprived other parties of their right to unimpaired access to federal courts and efficient adjudication, and had diverted considerable judicial resources to his voluminous and largely frivolous litigation); Green v. Warden, U.S. Penitentiary, 699 F.2d 364, 368 (7th Cir.1983) (court of appeals had authority under All Writs Act to issue original injunction against prison inmate requiring that all of his future claims be original, particularly since claim presented by prisoner had no basis in law or fact, was taken in bad faith and was presented by litigant whose avowed intent was to frustrate and harass federal judicial system); Gordon v. United States Dept. of Justice, 558 F.2d 618 (1st Cir.1977) (it was "proper and necessary" to issue injunction barring a party from filing and processing frivolous and vexatious lawsuits against federal judges for ruling against him).

269. JAK Prod., Inc. v. Wiza, 986 F.2d 1080, 1085 (7th Cir.1993) (balancing the hardships in favor of the employer plaintiff who sought preliminary injunction to protect customers from solicitation by former

employee defendant who admitted such customers are a small percentage of their potential customers).

270. Quon v. Stans, 309 F.Supp. 604, 607 (N.D.Cal.1970) ("Unless such balance tips in favor of the plaintiffs, relief is normally denied.").

271. Gateway Eastern Ry. Co. v. Terminal R.R. Ass'n of St. Louis, 35 F.3d 1134, 1140 (7th Cir.1994) ("So long as an adequate bond is posted during the injunction, [defendant] will not suffer irreparable harm.").

272. Diversified Mortgage Investors v. United States Life Ins. Co. of New York, 544 F.2d 571, 576 (2d Cir.1976) ("[A preliminary injunction] should not grant relief properly awarded only in a final judgment.").

273. Acierno v. New Castle County, 40 F.3d 645, 653 (3d Cir.1994); Silverman v. Major League Baseball Player Relations Committee, 880 F.Supp. 246, 254 n. 6 (S.D.N.Y.1995). See also discussion supra § 13.2(d)(2).

274. Boston Celtics Ltd. Partnership v. Shaw, 908 F.2d 1041 (1st Cir.1990) (basketball player forced to cancel playing for Italian team and play instead for domestic team).

preliminary injunction, the courts are less likely to grant the application since they often view mandatory injunctions as a greater burden on the defendant than prohibitory orders.[275] There is, however, no litmus test for whether an injury to one party is a disproportionate burden; therefore, the court uses its discretion to balance the hardships between the parties.

(5) The Public Interest

The Supreme Court has held that the public interest must be considered in any injunctive action where it is affected.[276] The public interest factor requires the court to evaluate the policy implications of the requested preliminary injunction. Public interest is a significant consideration in claims where the public interest may be furthered[277] or injured[278] by the requested remedy. Areas of public concern that courts have considered include law enforcement,[279] employment discrimination,[280] public health,[281] and political representation and activity.[282]

Sometimes a court will enjoin the enforcement of a statute because it finds that enforcement will injure the public.[283] On the other hand, a statute may declare public policy. For instance, a federal statute that prohibits the threatened acts sought to be enjoined[284] will be weighed

275. *See also, infra* § 13.2(d)(6); Aciero, 40 F.3d at 653.

276. Weinberger v. Romero–Barcelo, 456 U.S. 305, 312, 102 S.Ct. 1798, 1803, 72 L.Ed.2d 91 (1982).

277. Rivera–Vega v. ConAgra, Inc., 70 F.3d 153 (1st Cir.1995) (public interest furthered by ending lockout and returning people to work); Ronald Mayotte Assocs. v. MGC Bldg. Co., 885 F.Supp. 148 (E.D.Mich. 1994) (public interest of encouraging creativity facilitated by enjoining copyright infringers).

278. Grigsby Brandford & Co., Inc. v. United States, 869 F.Supp. 984 (D.D.C. 1994) (injunction would harm public interest by halting a financing program that facilitates funding for historically black schools).

279. Spiegel v. City of Houston, 636 F.2d 997, 1000 (5th Cir.1981); Oburn v. Shapp, 521 F.2d 142, 151 (3d Cir.1975) (potential police force understaffing).

280. EEOC v. Astra USA, Inc., 94 F.3d 738, 744 (1st Cir.1996); Stanley v. University of S. Cal., 13 F.3d 1313, 1325 (9th Cir. 1994); EEOC v. Recruit U.S.A., Inc., 939 F.2d 746, 754 (9th Cir.1991); Hybritech Inc. v. Abbott Lab., 4 U.S.P.Q. 2d 1001, 1015, 1987 WL 123997 (C.D.Cal.1987) (not enjoining distribution of hepatitis test kits by

defendant even though as patent holder, plaintiff was likely to succeed on merits), *aff'd*, 849 F.2d 1446, 1458 (Fed.Cir.1988); United States v. Odessa Union Warehouse Co-op, 833 F.2d 172, 176 (9th Cir.1987) (public interest in availability of noncontaminated content).

281. Hybritech Inc., 4 U.S.P.Q.2d 1001; Odessa Union Warehouse Co-op, 833 F.2d at 176.

282. Chisom v. Roemer, 853 F.2d 1186, 1192 (5th Cir.1988) (reversing injunction of election); Carey v. Klutznick, 637 F.2d 834, 839 (2d Cir.1980) (apportionment); Republican Party of North Carolina v. Hunt, 841 F.Supp. 722, 731 (E.D.N.C.1994) (constitutional protections attaching to the franchise and opportunity to choose from any of the most qualified candidates available).

283. Gately v. Massachusetts, 811 F.Supp. 26 (D.Mass.1992) (enjoining enforcement of a statute that discriminated according to age); Telco Communications, Inc. v. Barry, 731 F.Supp. 670 (D.N.J.1990) (preventing enforcement of a statute that violated the First Amendment).

284. United States v. Ingersoll–Rand Co., 320 F.2d 509 (3d Cir.1963) (court need not demonstrate precise injury to public interest so long as the threatened act was within declared prohibition of Congress).

heavily in favor of a preliminary injunction. Such threatened acts must, however, be likely to occur.[285]

When the threatened acts are clearly against public interest or have been declared unlawful by statute, an applicant for a preliminary injunction is not required to show irreparable injury,[286] a favorable balance of hardships,[287] or a likelihood of success on the merits.[288] This is true especially when the cited statute provides for a preliminary injunction.[289] Alternatively, some statutes prohibit the grant of a preliminary injunction under certain circumstances.[290]

(6) Prohibitory Versus Mandatory Injunction

Generally, preliminary injunctions preserve the status quo until the court makes a final decision on the merits.[291] A prohibitory injunction[292] enjoins certain conduct by the defendant to maintain the status quo, whereas a mandatory injunction[293] alters the status quo by requiring an affirmative act. A mandatory preliminary injunction is usually disfavored over a prohibitory injunction because of its effect on the status quo.[294] Therefore, a mandatory preliminary injunction requires a greater showing of need than a prohibitory injunction and a greater likelihood of success on the merits.[295] A mandatory injunction, however, may be

---

285. See Reuters Ltd. v. United Press Int'l, Inc., 903 F.2d 904, 906 (2d Cir.1990) ("[T]he moving party must first demonstrate that such injury is likely....").

286. United States v. Nutri-cology, Inc., 982 F.2d 394, 398 (9th Cir.1992) (irreparable harm presumed "because the passage of the statute is itself an implied finding by Congress that violations will harm the public").

287. Central Presbyterian Church v. Black Liberation Front, 303 F.Supp. 894, 901 (E.D.Mo.1969) ("If defendants are committing illegal acts, then it is unnecessary to weigh the injuries.").

288. X Corp. v. Doe, 805 F.Supp. 1298, 1304 (E.D.Va.1992) (no need to show likelihood of success on the merits where case involved difficult and troubling ethical issues).

289. Ringling Bros.-Barnum & Bailey Combined Shows, Inc. v. Celozzi-Ettelson Chevrolet, Inc., 855 F.2d 480, 484 n. 4 (7th Cir.1988) (consideration of other factors not necessary where statute provides for preliminary injunction).

290. Camping Constr. Co. v. District Council of Iron Workers, 915 F.2d 1333 (9th Cir.1990) (discussing prohibition on preliminary injunction under Norris-LaGuardia Act), cert. denied sub nom. District Council of Iron Workers of Cal. and Vicinity, AFL-CIO v. Camping Constr. Co., 500 U.S. 905, 111 S.Ct. 1684, 114 L.Ed.2d 79

(1991), and cert. denied, Camping Constr. Co. v. District Council of Iron Workers of Cal. and Vicinity, AFL-CIO, 500 U.S. 953, 111 S.Ct. 2260, 114 L.Ed.2d 713 (1991).

291. See cases cited supra note 2.

292. Legal Aid Soc'y of Haw. v. Legal Servs. Corp., 961 F.Supp. 1402 (D.Haw. 1997) (action by legal aid organizations receiving federal funds from the Legal Services Corporation to enjoin Legal Services Corporation from enforcing restrictions placed on their activities was prohibitive, not mandatory).

293. Tom Doherty Assocs., Inc. v. Saban Entertainment, Inc., 60 F.3d 27 (2d Cir. 1995); Acierno v. New Castle County, 40 F.3d 645, 647 (3d Cir.1994) ("A mandatory preliminary injunction compelling issuance of a building permit fundamentally alters the status quo.").

294. Stanley v. University of S. Cal., 13 F.3d 1313, 1314 (9th Cir.1994) (mandatory injunction compelling school to install plaintiff as head coach disturbed status quo); Martin v. International Olympic Committee, 740 F.2d 670, 674-75 (9th Cir.1984) (denying mandatory injunction for inclusion of two women's races in the 1984 Summer Olympic Games).

295. Tom Doherty Assoc., Inc., 60 F.3d at 34; Taylor v. Freeman, 34 F.3d 266, 269, n. 2 (4th Cir.1994); Stanley, 13 F.3d at

necessary to compel a defendant to correct an injury already inflicted on the plaintiff. When such a remedy is necessary, the courts justify the mandatory injunction by defining the status quo as the "last peaceable uncontested status" between the parties.[296] Then the court may issue a mandatory injunction to restore the situation existing before the dispute arose.[297]

A problem arises when the movant seeks a mandatory preliminary injunction to prevent some future injury. Compliance with such an injunction would effect a change in the current situation of the parties. Nonetheless, the court may still grant a mandatory preliminary injunction when necessary to protect the movant from irreparable harm and to preserve the court's ability to render a meaningful decision.[298]

A mandatory injunction often can be creatively rephrased in prohibitory form.[299] In fact, this concept of preserving the status quo and distinguishing between mandatory and prohibitory injunctions has been criticized by academics[300] and often ignored by the courts.[301]

1314; Martin, 740 F.2d at 674–75; Ferry–Morse Seed Co. v. Food Corn, Inc., 729 F.2d 589, 593 (8th Cir.1984); Citizens Concerned for Separation of Church and State v. City and County of Denver, 628 F.2d 1289, 1299 (10th Cir.1980).

296. Canal Auth. of Fla. v. Callaway, 489 F.2d 567 (5th Cir.1974); United Steelworkers of Am. v. Textron, 836 F.2d 6, 10 (1st Cir.1987); Montgomery v. Carr, 848 F.Supp. 770 (S.D.Ohio 1993).

297. Sara Lee Corp. v. Kayser–Roth Corp., No. 6:92CV00460, 1992 WL 436279 (M.D.N.C.1992).

298. Ferry–Morse Seed Co., 729 F.2d at 593 (maintenance of status quo required developer of hybrid seed corn to turn over seed corn to seed company which was marketing corn under license agreement); Crowley v. Local No. 82, Furniture and Piano Moving, Furniture Store Drivers, Helpers, Warehousemen & Packers, 679 F.2d 978, 1000 (1st Cir.1982) (district court did not abuse its discretion in ordering new, supervised nomination meeting and election of union local officers, in view of plaintiffs' showing of violations of provisions of Labor–Management Reporting and Disclosure Act and in view of defendants' stipulations); Guinness Harp Corp. v. Joseph Schlitz Brewing Co., 613 F.2d 468 (2d Cir.1980) (court granted mandatory preliminary injunction against termination of distributorship pending arbitration between the parties); Martinez v. Mathews, 544 F.2d 1233, 1243 (5th Cir.1976) (migrant and seasonal farm workers were entitled to preliminary injunctive relief requiring provider of

health services under Migrant Health Act to comply with Act's requirement that individuals being served by provider comprise majority of migrant health center's governing board and requiring that new board be selected as soon as plan for its selection is approved by district court).

299. Jolly v. Coughlin, 76 F.3d 468, 473 (2d Cir.1996) ("The injunction could be viewed as mandating that the defendants release [prisoner] from medical keeplock during the pendency of this suit, or as prohibiting the defendants from continuing to confine [prisoner] to medical keeplock."); Abdul Wali v. Coughlin, 754 F.2d 1015, 1026 (2d Cir. 1985) (although a group of prisoners sought to require prison officials to deliver to them a published report discussing prison conditions, injunction issued was prohibitory in nature because it prevented prison officials from interfering with the delivery of documents sent to the prisoners by a third party).

300. Frederick P. Santarelli, Note, *Preliminary Injunctions in Delaware: The Need for a Clearer Standard*, 13 Del. J. Corp. L. 107, 135 (1988); *Developments in the Law—Injunctions*, 78 Harv. L. Rev. 994, 1062 ("The 'mandatory' injunction has not yet been devised that could not be stated in 'prohibitory' terms.").

301. Innovative Health Sys., Inc. v. City of White Plains, 117 F.3d 37, 43 (2d Cir. 1997) ("[T]he distinction between mandatory and prohibitory injunctions is often 'more semantical than substantive.' ") (citation omitted).

(7) Equitable Defenses

Equitable defenses may defeat an otherwise meritorious motion for preliminary injunction. Underlying these defenses is the equitable concept that courts should not grant the extraordinary relief of a preliminary injunction to claimants who have acted in bad faith.[302]

The court may consider the unclean hands of the plaintiff in deciding whether to grant a preliminary injunction.[303] The plaintiff requesting the court to intervene on its behalf must act in good faith. The plaintiff's bad faith is not, however, an absolute bar to relief,[304] because the defendant's misconduct may be more unconscionable than that of the plaintiff's.[305]

The court in equity will also apply the maxim "equity aids the vigilant, not those who slumber on their rights." Plaintiffs who have "slept" on their rights are guilty of laches and may be denied injunctive relief.[306] Unnecessary delay in an application for preliminary injunction may also contradict a plaintiff's claim of imminent irreparable injury.[307] Delay alone, however, will not bar relief based on laches.[308] When a defendant's continued conduct would cause further harm to a plaintiff

---

302. See qad. inc. v. ALN Assocs., Inc., 781 F.Supp. 561 (N.D.Ill.1992) (preliminary injunction vacated and defendant recovered damages above bond amount against plaintiff who acted in bad faith by deceiving court and causing issuance of preliminary injunction).

303. Estate of Lennon by Lennon v. Screen Creations, Ltd., 939 F.Supp. 287, 293 (S.D.N.Y.1996) (applying equitable defense of unclean hands and denying preliminary injunction to plaintiff who engaged in misrepresentations during negotiations with defendant).

304. E.E.O.C. v. Recruit U.S.A., Inc., 939 F.2d 746, 752 (9th Cir.1991) ("[T]he substantial public interest permeating this case warrants a departure from the 'clean hands' doctrine.").

305. Duggal v. Krishna, 554 F.Supp. 1043, 1047 (D.D.C.1983) ("[T]he doctrine of unclean hands . . . 'may be relaxed if defendant has been guilty of misconduct that is more unconscionable than that committed by plaintiff.'") (citation omitted); See also Shondel v. McDermott, 775 F.2d 859, 868 (7th Cir.1985) ("Today, unclean hands really just means that in equity as in law the plaintiff's fault, like the defendant's, may be relevant to the question of what if any remedy the plaintiff is entitled to."); Houston Oilers, Inc. v. Neely, 361 F.2d 36, 42 (10th Cir.1966) ("But the doctrine does not exclude all wrongdoers from a court of equity nor should it be applied in every case

where the conduct of a party may be considered unconscionable or inequitable.").

306. Clark Equip. Co. v. Harlan Corp., 539 F.Supp. 561, 570 (D.Kan.1982) (three years from time plaintiffs first saw evidence of defendant's copyright infringement held unreasonable delay in bringing action); American Fabrics Co. v. Lace Art, Inc., 291 F.Supp. 589, 592 (S.D.N.Y.1968) (seven month delay in bringing suit and delaying of preliminary injunction hearing was unreasonable delay in copyright infringement case). Courts have used laches to also deny TROs when the plaintiff failed to seek a preliminary injunction instead of an eleventh-hour TRO. See Lydo Enterprises v. City of Las Vegas, 745 F.2d 1211, 1213 (9th Cir.1984); 11A Charles Alan Wright, Arthur R. Miller, & Mary Kay Kane, Federal Practice and Procedure § 2942 (2d ed. 1995). See also Local R. 231 (E.D. Cal.) (the court will consider whether the applicant could have earlier sought a motion for preliminary injunction instead of the eleventh-hour TRO).

307. Citibank, N.A. v. Citytrust, 756 F.2d 273, 276 (2d Cir.1985) (noting that although delays may not rise to level of laches, it may indicate absence of irreparable harm).

308. See Ocean Garden, Inc. v. Marktrade Co., Inc., 953 F.2d 500, 508 (9th Cir. 1991) (laches did not bar relief where no harm resulted from delay).

guilty of laches, the court may grant prospective relief while denying damages for past conduct.[309]

Finally, courts may not grant injunctive relief when enforcement of the remedy would require "constant supervision" by the court.[310]

(e) Preliminary Injunction in Particular Areas of Law

Federal courts frequently hear motions for preliminary injunction in certain types of federal cases, discussed below.

(1) Securities

The standard for issuance of a preliminary injunction in the federal securities context depends on whether the Securities and Exchange Commission or a private litigant is seeking the relief.

"Unlike a private litigant, the SEC is not required to show irreparable injury or a balance of equities in its favor. Instead, it must make out a 'strong *prima facie* case of previous violations' and show that there is 'a reasonable likelihood that the wrong will be repeated.' "[311] A court may look to such factors as the egregiousness of the defendant's actions, the isolated or recurrent nature of the infraction, the degree of scienter, the sincerity of the defendant's assurances against future violations, the defendant's recognition of the wrongful nature of his conduct, and the likelihood that the defendant's occupation will present opportunities for future violations.[312] Furthermore, in deciding on a preliminary injunction, the district court must view the evidence in the light most favorable to the SEC, and the SEC is entitled to the benefit of all reasonable inferences.[313]

A private litigant must satisfy all the traditional requirements.[314] *See* Chapter 54 "Securities," at Section 54.15 for further discussion of injunctive relief in securities cases.

---

309. James Burrough Ltd. v. Sign of Beefeater, Inc., 572 F.2d 574, 578 (7th Cir. 1978) ("By reason of laches, a plaintiff in a trademark infringement action may lose the right to recover damages or wrongfully derived profits during the period prior to the filing of suit. Upon a showing of infringement, however, the plaintiff may still be entitled to injunctive relief ... and to damages and profits for the period subsequent to the filing of suit.").

310. Zurn Constructors, Inc. v. B.F. Goodrich Co., 685 F.Supp. 1172, 1182 (D.Kan.1988) ("The need for court supervision is one of the ingredients in the court's discretionary formula for determining whether to issue a preliminary injunction.").

311. SEC v. Life Partners, Inc., 898 F.Supp. 14, 18 (D.D.C.1995) (citing SEC v. International Loan Network, 770 F.Supp. 678, 688 (D.D.C.1991), aff'd, 968 F.2d 1304 (D.C.Cir. 1992)).

312. SEC v. Warner, 674 F.Supp. 841, 844 (S.D.Fla.1987) (citing SEC v. Blatt, 583 F.2d 1325, 1334 n. 29 (5th Cir.1978)).

313. Warner, 674 F.Supp. at 844.

314. Crouch v. Prior, 905 F.Supp. 248, 259 (D.Vi.1995) (private litigant "must satisfy the traditional prerequisites of extraordinary equitable relief by establishing irreparable harm") (citing Gulf Corp. v. Mesa Petroleum, Co., 582 F.Supp. 1110, 1116 (D.Del.1984)).

(2) Antitrust

The standard for issuance of a preliminary injunction in the antitrust context varies depending on who is seeking the relief.

Often in Clayton Act cases, the suit is brought by the Federal Trade Commission ("FTC") pursuant to 15 U.S.C.A. § 53(b), which provides the FTC with authority to seek such relief whenever it has reason to believe "that any person, partnership, or corporation is violating, or is about to violate, any provision of law enforced by the [FTC]."[315] In such cases, the standard for a preliminary injunction is the statutory "public interest" test: whether "[u]pon a proper showing that, weighing the equities and considering the Commission's likelihood of ultimate success, such action would be in the public interest."[316]

Private parties may also seek injunctive relief for antitrust violations. "Any person . . . shall be entitled to sue for and have injunctive relief . . . when and under the same conditions and principles as courts of equity . . . upon . . . a showing that the danger of irreparable loss or damage is immediate. . . ."[317] Courts have held that the standard for a preliminary injunction in such cases is no different than in other cases.[318] A preliminary injunction involving antitrust claims in the mergers and acquisitions context is considered to be an especially drastic remedy. "[T]he issuance of a preliminary injunction blocking an acquisition or merger may prevent the transaction from ever being consummated."[319]

In light of the severity of a preliminary injunction in this context, courts have required the FTC to meet a "substantial burden."[320] The FTC must first prove a "likelihood of ultimate success."[321] This requires a showing that the merger in question will "probably have [an anticompetitive] effect."[322] Next, the FTC must prove that " 'the equities' favor enjoining the transaction."[323] This requires a showing that the "harm to the parties and to the public that would flow from a preliminary injunction is outweighed by the harm to competition, if any, that would occur in the period between denial of a preliminary injunction and the final adjudication of the merits."[324]

---

315. 15 U.S.C.A. § 53(b)(1) (West 1996).

316. 15 U.S.C.A. § 53(b) (West 1996). *See* Federal Trade Comm'n v. Freeman Hosp., 69 F.3d 260 (8th Cir.1995) (applying the "public benefit" test in a hospital merger case).

317. 15 U.S.C.A. § 26 (West 1996).

318. *See* Blanksteen v. New York Mercantile Exch., 879 F.Supp. 363 (S.D.N.Y. 1995) (irreparable harm must be showed for preliminary injunction under 15 U.S.C.A. § 26).

319. Federal Trade Comm'n v. Exxon Corp., 636 F.2d 1336, 1343 (D.C.Cir.1980) (*cited in* United States v. BNS Inc., 848

F.2d 945 (9th Cir.1988); Federal Trade Comm'n, 911 F.Supp. 1213).

320. Federal Trade Comm'n v. Great Lakes Chem. Corp., 528 F.Supp. 84, 86 (N.D.Ill.1981).

321. *Id.*

322. *Id.* (citation omitted).

323. *Id.*

324. *Id.* (denying FTC request for preliminary injunction barring integrated elemental bromine and bromine derivative producer from acquiring the bromine-related assets of another corporation on the grounds that evidence did not establish a likelihood that the acquisition would lead to

(3) Taxation

A district court may not issue a preliminary injunction interfering with the levy or collection of any state tax where a speedy remedy may be acquired in state court.[325] Nor can the court issue a preliminary injunction to enjoin the levy or collection of a federal tax.[326]

(4) Against State Court Proceedings

28 U.S.C.A. § 2283, the "Anti–Injunction Act," was enacted to prevent needless conflict between state and federal courts.[327] It provides that "[a] court of the United States may not grant an injunction to stay proceedings in a State court except as expressly authorized by Act of Congress, or where necessary in aid of its jurisdiction, or to protect or effectuate its judgments."

The exceptions to the Anti–Injunction Act are narrowly construed and doubts as to the propriety of a federal injunction against a state court are resolved in favor of permitting the state action to proceed.[328]

The "Act of Congress" exception requires a specific and uniquely federal right or remedy, enforceable in a federal court of equity, that could be frustrated if the federal court were not empowered to enjoin a state court proceeding.[329] "The test ... is whether an Act of Congress, clearly creating a federal right or remedy enforceable in a federal court of equity, could be given its intended scope only by the stay of a state court proceeding."[330] In order to qualify under this exception, the federal law need not contain express reference to the anti-injunction statute.[331] However, this exception does not apply merely because it involves a statute that permits injunctive relief in general terms.[332]

The general rule under the "necessary in aid of its jurisdiction" exception is that where state and federal courts have concurrent jurisdiction over a case, neither court may prevent the parties from simultaneously pursuing claims in both courts.[333] The requisite interference to justify enjoining state proceedings often exists when a case is one in rem. This exception allows a federal court that has jurisdiction over a res to

---

a lessening of competition in the flame retardant market). *See* Chapter 53 "Antitrust," at §§ 53.5(b) and 53.9(b), *infra*.

325. 28 U.S.C.A. § 1341 (West 1996); Bidart Bros. v. California Apple Comm'n, 73 F.3d 925, 928–29 (9th Cir.1996).

326. 26 U.S.C.A. § 7421(a) (West 1996); O'Hagan v. United States, 86 F.3d 776, 778 (8th Cir.1996) (noting statutory and judicial exception to the Act).

327. NLRB v. Nash–Finch Co., 404 U.S. 138, 92 S.Ct. 373, 30 L.Ed.2d 328 (1971).

328. Kansas Pub. Employees Retirement Sys. v. Reimer & Koger Assocs., Inc., 77 F.3d 1063 (8th Cir.1996) (citing Atlantic Coast Line R.R. v. Brotherhood of Locomotive Eng'rs, 398 U.S. 281, 90 S.Ct. 1739, 26

L.Ed.2d 234 (1970)); Lou v. Belzberg, 834 F.2d 730, 739 (9th Cir.1987) (citing Vendo Co. v. Lektro–Vend Corp., 433 U.S. 623, 97 S.Ct. 2881, 53 L.Ed.2d 1009 (1977); Alton Box Bd. Co. v. Esprit de Corp., 682 F.2d 1267 (9th Cir.1982)).

329. Mitchum v. Foster, 407 U.S. 225, 236, 92 S.Ct. 2151, 2159, 32 L.Ed.2d 705 (1972) (applying this exception in the civil rights context).

330. *Id.*

331. *Id.*

332. Tampa Phosphate R. Co. v. Seaboard C.L.R. Co., 418 F.2d 387 (5th Cir. 1969).

333. Lou, 834 F.2d at 740.

proceed as to that res without interference from other courts involving the same res.[334] Furthermore, a court may invoke this exception to avoid interference with its attempts to settle a complex matter.[335]

The third exception, known as the "relitigation exception," is founded in well-recognized concepts of res judicata and collateral estoppel. It allows a federal court to prevent state litigation of issues previously presented to and decided by the federal court.[336] The prerequisite for applying this exception is that the claims or issues actually have been decided by the federal court.[337] Moreover, a reviewing court will construe this prerequisite narrowly by looking closely at the record to determine what the federal trial court actually held, so as to prevent that court from rendering post hoc judgment regarding what its previous decision was intended to say.[338]

(5) Intellectual Property

Federal courts have statutory authorization to grant preliminary injunctive relief in trademark, copyright, and patent actions.[339] Federal courts exercising supplemental jurisdiction over trade secret actions have authority to issue an injunction under the governing state law.[340]

Courts evaluate intellectual property motions for preliminary injunctions according to the preliminary injunction test governing their respective circuits.[341] In trademark and copyright actions, however, most circuits recognize a rebuttable presumption of irreparable harm once the plaintiff has demonstrated a likelihood of success on the merits.[342]

---

334. Morongo Band of Mission Indians v. Stach, 951 F.Supp. 1455 (C.D.Cal.1997) (citing Kline v. Burke Const. Co., 260 U.S. 226, 43 S.Ct. 79, 67 L.Ed. 226 (1922)).

335. *In re* Baldwin–United Corp., 770 F.2d 328, 337 (2d Cir.1985) (comparing an advanced class action to a res, over which the judge required complete control).

336. Chick Kam Choo v. Exxon Corp., 486 U.S. 140, 147, 108 S.Ct. 1684, 1690, 100 L.Ed.2d 127 (1988).

337. *Id.*

338. *Id.*

339. *See* 15 U.S.C.A. § 1116(a) (West 1998) (trademark); 17 U.S.C.A. § 502 (West 1996) (copyright); and 35 U.S.C.A. § 283 (West 1996) (patent). *See* § 65.13(a) "TROs and Preliminary Injunctions," in Chapter 65 "Copyright," *infra.*

340. *See, e.g.,* Uniform Trade Secret Act Sec. 2 (as adopted by 42 states); PepsiCo v. Redmond, 54 F.3d 1262, 1268 (7th Cir. 1995) (affirming injunction based on the Uniform Trade Secret Act as adopted into Illinois law).

341. Advent Elecs., Inc. v. Buckman, 112 F.3d 267, 274 (7th Cir.1997) (applying

traditional four-factor test used by Seventh Circuit); Warner–Lambert Co. v. Northside Development Corp., 86 F.3d 3, 5 (2d Cir. 1996) (applying alternative test used by Second Circuit); Country Kids 'N City Slicks, Inc. v. Sheen, 77 F.3d 1280, 1283 (10th Cir.1996) (applying traditional four-factor test adopted by Tenth Circuit).

342. *See, e.g.,* Country Kids 'N City Slicks, Inc., 77 F.3d at 1283 (applying presumption of irreparable harm); Triad Systems Corp. v. Southeastern Express Co., 64 F.3d 1330, 1335 (9th Cir.1995) (same); Johnson Controls, Inc. v. Phoenix Control Sys., Inc., 886 F.2d 1173, 1174 (9th Cir. 1989) (same); National Football League v. McBee & Bruno's, Inc., 792 F.2d 726, 729 (8th Cir.1986) (same); Hasbro Bradley, Inc. v. Sparkle Toys, Inc., 780 F.2d 189, 192 (2d Cir.1985) (same). *But see* Plains Cotton Coop. Ass'n v. Goodpasture Computer Service, Inc., 807 F.2d 1256, 1261 (5th Cir. 1987) (rejecting presumption of irreparable injury rule). *See* § 64.5 "Preliminary Injunctions," in Chapter 64 "Trademark," *infra.*

Before the creation of the Federal Circuit in 1982, courts rarely granted preliminary injunctions in patent actions.[343] Since that time, however, courts have issued injunctive relief in numerous patent cases.[344] Because all appeals of patent cases fall within the exclusive jurisdiction of the Federal Circuit, all preliminary injunction motions are evaluated according to the traditional four-factor test used by the Federal Circuit.[345] Similar to trademark and copyright actions, a clear showing of the likelihood of success on the patent infringement claim gives rise to rebuttable presumption of irreparable harm.[346]

To demonstrate the probability of irreparable harm in a trade secret action, some courts will require the plaintiff to demonstrate the existence of an imminent threat of disclosure of the trade secret.[347] Other courts will find irreparable harm and grant the injunction if the defendant had access to trade secrets that would be impossible to disregard in performing duties as a competitor with the owner of the trade secrets.[348]

Library References:

West's Key No. Digests, Injunction ⬦132–188.
Wright, Miller & Kane, Federal Practice and Procedure: Civil 2d §§ 2947–2950, 2954.

§ 13.3 Temporary Restraining Order

(a) Strategy

(1) Avoid TRO Applications if Another Approach Is Available

In general, courts prefer to avoid TRO applications, which require fast decisions based on an incomplete record and which may have substantial impact on the rest of the case. A TRO is available only to avoid irreparable harm between the date of the TRO application and the hearing on a preliminary injunction. A party should be certain that a TRO is required rather than an order shortening time for a hearing on a

---

343. Smith Int'l, Inc. v. Hughes Tool Co., 718 F.2d 1573, 1578 (Fed.Cir.1983) (discussing the "unusually stringent" requirements for preliminary injunctions in patent actions before 1982).

344. See, e.g., H.H. Robertson Co. v. United Steel Deck, Inc., 820 F.2d 384, 387 (Fed.Cir.1987) ("The standards applied to the grant of a preliminary injunction are no more nor less stringent in patent cases than in other areas of the law.").

345. See, e.g., High Tech Med. Instrumentation, Inc. v. New Image Indus., Inc., 49 F.3d 1551, 1553 (Fed.Cir.1995) (using traditional four-factor test); Reebok, Int'l Ltd. v. J. Baker, Inc., 32 F.3d 1552, 1555 (Fed.Cir.1994) (same).

346. Polymer Techs., Inc. v. Bridwell, 103 F.3d 970 (Fed.Cir.1996); Eli Lilly & Co. v. American Cyanamid Co., 82 F.3d 1568, 1578 (Fed.Cir.1996) (failure to make a "strong showing" of infringement precludes presumption of irreparable harm); Smith Int'l, Inc. v. Hughes Tool Co., 718 F.2d 1573 (Fed.Cir.1983) (same). See Chapter 63 "Patents," at § 63.6(a), infra.

347. Continental Group, Inc. v. Amoco Chems. Corp., 614 F.2d 351, 358–59 (3d Cir.1980) (mere possibility of inadvertent disclosure is insufficient).

348. PepsiCo, Inc. v. Redmond, 54 F.3d 1262, 1270–71 (7th Cir.1995) (adopting "inevitability of disclosure" standard); Merck & Co., Inc. v. Lyon, 941 F.Supp. 1443, 1457–58 (M.D.N.C.1996).

preliminary injunction or an application for an order shortening time to initiate discovery for the preliminary injunction hearing. A TRO is rarely appropriate to enjoin the holding of a corporate meeting or the closing of a corporate transaction, for example, where advance substantial notice to stockholders of the meeting or the effectuation of the transaction is required. Of course, a party is unlikely to obtain a TRO if the reason for the emergency is the client's delay in seeking the TRO, rather than a lack of notice of the action the party seeks to restrain.

(2) Notice

Although FRCP 65(b) contemplates the grant of a TRO without notice, in practice the courts demand that notice be given in all but the most exceptional circumstances. The party seeking the TRO must at least attempt to give actual notice of when and where it will make its application. Such notice may be made informally, however, often by telephone. With recent advances in technology, leaving a voice-mail message to provide notice is common, but counsel who does not speak directly with opposing counsel takes the risk that such opposing counsel will claim that he or she did not receive the message in time to respond adequately. Similarly, if opposing counsel is not available, counsel sometimes gives notice to a secretary or paralegal. In that circumstance, it is important to obtain the name and position of the law firm employee to include in the affidavit regarding notice. In providing notice, counsel should inform the opposing party (1) of the intent to seek a TRO, (2) the date, time and in which courtroom that counsel will seek the TRO, and (3) the nature of the relief requested. The declaration or affidavit describing the notice given should include a statement as to whether the opposing counsel indicated an intent to be present at the hearing or to oppose the TRO application.

It is important to be clear and specific regarding the steps taken to notify the other side. Include the names and telephone numbers of all persons spoken with in attempting to notify the opposition as well as the dates and times of the calls and what was said. The fact that Rule 11 sanctions are available and that the same judge who will hear the motion for the TRO will probably also hear the motion for preliminary injunction and the trial should dissuade the applicant from fudging on the notice requirement.

If no notice is given, the attorney must certify in writing the efforts, if any, made to notify the other side and why notice is not required. Even if the application is otherwise meritorious, the court may still deny the TRO if notice is inadequate or if the reason offered for not giving notice is deficient. Local rules often require notice unless a true emergency exists, and the courts are extremely reluctant to grant a TRO if it was at all possible to give notice and yet none was given. A clear factual showing of immediate, irreparable injury occurring before the applicant could otherwise be heard must be made if a TRO is to be granted without notice. For example, a court may be willing to grant a TRO without notice if the plaintiff makes a strong factual showing that giving notice would likely cause the defendant to take the action which the plaintiff seeks to restrain, or hide or transfer an asset that is the subject of the TRO, thus making the TRO ineffective. Absent such an emergency, the court may view negatively a party or counsel who appears to be seeking unfair advantage and deny or limit the relief sought.

Counsel should consider the timing of notice in another context. Normally, counsel for the plaintiff gives the opposing party or its counsel the minimum notice required and files the TRO application at the last moment, giving the court little time to decide the matter. In most cases, such short notice to the court is sufficient and may be unavoidable. In a difficult case, however, consider filing the TRO application, and thus notice to the opposing party, as much in advance as possible of the date on which a ruling is required. It is better to file papers as early as possible, even though the opponent may gain more time to respond, than to force the court to decide the matter too quickly; the court is more likely to deny the TRO in such a situation. Also, never give the court a false deadline. Both lawyer and client lose credibility when that fact is exposed by opposing counsel.

(3) The Pleadings

The court likely will have no prior knowledge of the facts and little time to review the documents. However, the court will probably already know the law and will rule on a TRO application quickly. Relief is usually not granted or denied based upon technical arguments, so it is more helpful to emphasize the facts. Tell the entire story in the first 50 words of every pleading. Documentation should be short and specific, but facts pertaining to the need for immediate relief before a full hearing should be set forth in detail.

Draft the proposed TRO first. Focusing on the exact relief to be sought forces counsel to structure the other papers to support that relief, and any problems with the relief sought will quickly become apparent.

Make sure the proposed order complies with Rule 65 by stating the reasons for issuance and by meeting the requirements for specificity. Do not refer to other documents in the order.

Usually, the TRO is combined with an order to show cause regarding preliminary injunction. Include in the proposed order blanks to be filled in with the date of the preliminary injunction hearing, the briefing schedule, and the manner and time of service of papers, so that the opponent has notice of all of these matters when served with the TRO.

In drafting the proposed order, include any forms of relief that the court is unlikely to grant in separate paragraphs so that they can be jettisoned easily if the court balks at those provisions. Do not overreach by seeking relief that the court is highly unlikely to grant. That approach is likely to undermine the credibility of the party and its counsel and the court may deny relief to which the party may be entitled. Likewise, consider putting the forms of relief the court is most likely to grant in separate paragraphs at the beginning of the order so that they are more likely to be salvaged if the court grants only some of the relief sought. Courts are more willing to grant a TRO prohibiting conduct than one mandating conduct (some require a greater showing for a mandatory TRO), so draft carefully to frame the order as prohibitory. Try to obtain the full 10–day duration for the TRO provided in FRCP 65(b).

In seeking preliminary relief, while counsel should attempt to obtain a sufficiently broad order which will protect the client's legitimate interests, it is important to be reasonable. As noted above in the discussion of preliminary injunction strategy, overreaching damages credibility, while a reasonably drafted TRO builds credibility. A TRO which seeks reasonable relief justified by the facts also minimizes haggling and reduces the court's role in redrafting the order, which may otherwise cause a delay in obtaining that order. Clear, unambiguous language may strengthen a later position in a contempt proceeding or on appeal. Carefully consider the parties against whom the restraining order should run and the activities to which the enjoined party may alternatively resort that might circumvent the order as worded but continue to injure the applicant. Determine who is most likely to violate the order and be prepared to serve them individually.

At a TRO hearing, the judge likely will read the TRO first and then the affidavit(s) to assess the supporting evidence. Consider summarizing the contents of and the purpose for submitting the affidavit in the initial paragraph of the affidavit and placing the sections on qualifications and background at the end. Avoid hearsay, conclusions and vituperation. The facts stated in the affidavit must be within the witness' personal knowledge; be sure to establish a sufficient foundation. Lay the proper foundation for any attached exhibits. Since there may not be an opportunity to reply on a TRO application, consider including facts that will defeat anticipated defenses. To minimize the amount of bond required, consider including an evidentiary showing that the opposing party will suffer little or no damage if the TRO is granted, in particular due to the brief period between the grant of the TRO and the hearing on the preliminary injunction.

At a TRO hearing, the court may read the complaint third. A verified complaint may sometimes be used as a supporting affidavit and thus avoid duplicative material for the court. Normally, however, it is preferable not to rely on the complaint for evidentiary support because it tends to be too conclusory and argumentative to meet the evidentiary standards required to support the grant of a TRO. Begin the complaint with a persuasive introduction and avoid overly aggressive theories and claims. This is not the time for novel propositions of law. Counsel may decide to plead more exotic theories, but leave these to the end of the complaint and do not base the TRO application on them. Since the court probably already knows the applicable law, the court may read the memorandum of law last, if at all. If the legal questions are more complicated, the court may pay more attention to the legal argument, but in any event this document should be succinct. Clearly set out persuasive headings and a table of contents to act as the argument's outline; this may be all the court has time to read.

(4) Defensive Considerations

In defending against a TRO, it is important to obtain a bond amount that will adequately compensate the defendant for all possible damage. The bond is the sole source of any recovery if the TRO has been granted in error. On occasions, a party that wins a TRO ends up losing because the party is unable to post a substantial bond. To support the imposition of a large bond, include in the opposing papers evidence of the substantial harm, especially monetary harm, that the defendant will suffer if the TRO is granted.

Be sure to preserve evidentiary objections in the memorandum of law for possible appeal. Make separate written objections to the plaintiff's affidavits and exhibits.

Pursue any affirmative defenses and equitable defenses. Credible arguments of laches or unclean hands may tip the scales in your direction, especially in a close case. If the plaintiff has delayed in seeking the TRO, set forth the facts in detail, including the prejudice to the defendant caused by such delay. Courts will often deny a TRO sought by a plaintiff that demands that the court act quickly because the plaintiff has not done so. Likewise, specific evidence of misconduct that can be characterized as unclean hands will cause the court to pause before granting the plaintiff extraordinary relief.

Even if counsel cannot defeat the TRO, try to narrow it in order to minimize its effect. Also, offer to work with the plaintiff, possibly to fashion a stipulated order that will minimize the court's role and may allow for more flexibility in the defendant's conduct than the proposed TRO would permit.

(5) Filing

If no complaint has yet been filed, the first step in obtaining a TRO is to file the complaint. In extreme emergencies, however, it may not be necessary to file the complaint. If the complaint is verified it can also serve as the required affidavit, but normally this should be avoided as complaints are generally too conclusive and argumentative in nature to prove useful in convincing the court. The TRO application and supporting papers are generally filed at the same time. Check the local court rules for any additional requirements. If discovery is needed in order to prepare for the preliminary injunction hearing, make an application for expedited discovery at this time as well. Avoid having counsel sign affidavits; it is preferable to use the client or one who has personal knowledge.

The date of the hearing on the preliminary injunction is usually set by an order to show cause, which will issue even if the court denies the TRO. If the TRO is granted without notice, the date for the preliminary injunction hearing must be set for the earliest possible time and takes precedence over all other matters.

If the TRO is sought contemporaneously with the filing of the complaint, file the complaint and accompanying papers with the docket clerk. Take the file-stamped copies to the courtroom clerk or judge's secretary, and to opposing counsel if he or she appears. If the complaint has already been filed, contact the clerk before filing the TRO application to determine the time to apply for the TRO. If the judge is unavailable, check with the docket clerk. Generally, counsel will be directed to the chief judge or a "general duty" judge. Since the TRO is not effective until the bond is obtained, be prepared to obtain the bond immediately. If necessary, have the representative of the security company in the courtroom.

(6) The Hearing

Procedures vary as to oral argument. Some courts will allow oral argument before a clerk or magistrate, some do so in open court and on the record, others in chambers, and some will decide based solely on the papers. If the court holds a hearing on a TRO, the judge will usually review the papers and then summon counsel into chambers. Even if the court hears oral argument on TRO applications, often there will be no set time in which the court will hear the application and the court will attempt to squeeze the hearing in between other matters, so be prepared to spend the entire day in court. Some law firms will send a junior lawyer to the courthouse with the TRO application; the junior lawyer is directed to call the lawyer at the firm with responsibility for the matter as soon as the judge is able to hear the application. Some firms assume that counsel will not be able to speak to the judge and that only a junior lawyer therefore need appear. Although this approach may work under some circumstances, the presence of a senior lawyer in court to submit the application can send a message about the urgency and the importance counsel attaches to the application; the presence of only a junior lawyer may send the opposite message. The client probably has a substantial investment in both time and money in the application by the time counsel enters the courthouse. It would be unfortunate to jeopardize that investment by treating the matter at the last moment as if it is unimportant.

At oral argument both parties should emphasize the irreparable injury factor, prepare arguments for offensive, defensive, and fallback positions, and anticipate arguments on the merits, bond amount, and the language of the order. Counsel for the defendant should focus on the lack of any real threat of immediate injury as well as the ensuing harm to the defendant if it were to be enjoined for even a brief period. Counsel may be able to limit the order or obtain an increased bond amount. Be prepared to offer alternatives to the relief sought by the plaintiff. Force the applicant to choose between obtaining partial relief and risking losing the entire application. To avoid the entry of an order, offer relief through a private agreement, rather than a court order. To avoid a TRO, offer to agree that in opposing the preliminary injunction, the defendant will not rely on any argument that the defendant would be harmed by entry of a preliminary injunction because the defendant changed his position or engaged in conduct in the absence of a TRO.

Some courts will press hard for a stipulation between the parties short of an actual TRO to preserve the status quo. Among other advantages, no bond is required. If agreement is reached, the plaintiff should request that the stipulation be entered on the record so that there will be no later misunderstanding as to the content of the stipulation. Counsel must understand the limits and variants of the client's bargaining positions, have the authority to enter into such a stipulation, and make the client cognizant of the impact of any stipulation agreed upon.

(b) Procedures for Obtaining a TRO

(1) FRCP 65

TROs allow swift injunctive relief pending a hearing on a preliminary injunction. FRCP 65(b) outlines certain basic procedures for obtaining a TRO in federal court. FRCP 65(b) provides as follows:[1]

> (b) Temporary Restraining Order; Notice; Hearing; Duration. A temporary restraining order may be granted without written or oral notice to the adverse party or that party's attorney only if (1) it clearly appears from specific facts shown by affidavit or by the verified complaint that immediate and irreparable injury, loss, or damage will result to the applicant before the adverse party or that party's attorney can be heard in opposition, and (2) the applicant's attorney certifies to the court in writing the efforts, if any, which have been made to give the notice and the reasons supporting the claim that notice should not be required. Every temporary restraining order granted without notice shall

---

§ 13.3

1. FRCP 65(c)–(e) relates to both preliminary injunctions and TROs and provides as follows:

(c) Security. No restraining order or preliminary injunction shall issue except upon the giving of security by the applicant, in such sum as the court deems proper, for the payment of such costs and damages as may be incurred or suffered by any party who is found to have been wrongfully enjoined or restrained. No such security shall be required of the United States or of an officer or agency thereof. The provisions of Rule 65.1 apply to a surety upon a bond or undertaking under this rule.

(d) Form and Scope of Injunction or Restraining Order. Every order granting an injunction and every restraining order shall set forth the reasons for its issuance; shall be specific in terms; shall describe in reasonable detail, and not by reference to the complaint or other document, the act or acts sought to be restrained; and is binding only upon the parties to the action, their officers, agents, servants, employees, and attorneys, and upon those persons in active concert or participation with them who receive actual notice of the order by personal service or otherwise.

(e) Employer and Employee; Interpleader; Constitutional Cases. These rules do not modify any statute of the United States relating to temporary restraining orders and preliminary injunctions in actions affecting employer and employee; or the provisions of Title 28, U.S.C., § 2361, relating to preliminary injunctions in actions of interpleader or in the nature of interpleader; or Title 28, U.S.C., § 2284, relating to actions required by Act of Congress to be heard and determined by a district court of three judges.

be indorsed with the date and hour of issuance; shall be filed forthwith in the clerk's office and entered of record; shall define the injury and state why it is irreparable and why the order was granted without notice; and shall expire by its terms within such time after entry, not to exceed 10 days, as the court fixes, unless within the time so fixed the order, for good cause shown, is extended for a like period or unless the party against whom the order is directed consents that it may be extended for a longer period. The reasons for the extension shall be entered of record. In case a temporary restraining order is granted without notice, the motion for a preliminary injunction shall be set down for hearing at the earliest possible time and takes precedence of all matters except older matters of the same character; and when the motion comes on for hearing the party who obtained the temporary restraining order shall proceed with the application for a preliminary injunction and, if the party does not do so, the court shall dissolve the temporary restraining order. On 2 days' notice to the party who obtained the temporary restraining order without notice or on such shorter notice to that party as the court may prescribe, the adverse party may appear and move its dissolution or modification and in that event the court shall proceed to hear and determine such motion as expeditiously as the ends of justice require.

FRCP 65 does not purport to describe all procedures involved nor the applicable local rules and procedures followed by district courts or the individual judge. Traditional equity principles govern the substantive requirements for obtaining injunctive relief, including TROs. Substantive law, not FRCP 65, determines a plaintiff's right to a TRO. However, courts will scrupulously observe the requirements of FRCP 65 "in the delicate business of granting temporary restraining orders."[2]

Like the preliminary injunction, the TRO is a form of injunctive relief used by the court to protect a party where the threat of future harm exists. The TRO, however, serves as a temporary device to protect the status quo for the brief period while the parties prepare for the hearing on a preliminary injunction. Thus, the TRO differs from the preliminary injunction as it may be issued without notice or with only informal notice to the restrained party, different weight is given to considered factors, the duration of the TRO is much shorter than a preliminary injunction, and the TRO appeal process differs from the appeal of a grant or denial of a preliminary injunction.

The requirements, form, and function of TROs issued under FRCP 65 are shaped by local rules as well. Local rules may require specific documents to accompany the TRO application,[3] such as a proposed draft

---

2. Austin v. Altman, 332 F.2d 273, 275 (2d Cir.1964).

3. *See, e.g.,* E.D. Cal. Civ. Local Rule 231; N.D. Cal. Civ. Local Rule 65–1; C.D.

Cal. Local Rule 7.18; S.D. Cal. Local Rule 65.1.

of the TRO[4] or a separate affidavit supporting the existence of irreparable injury.[5] Additionally, local rules may expand upon the notice requirement of FRCP 65,[6] specifying types of informal notice which may be appropriate[7] or clarifying the legal standard by which the plaintiff's efforts to give notice will be judged.[8] Local rules may also provide the adverse party with defenses to the motion for TRO.[9]

(2) Not a Basis for Jurisdiction

FRCP 65 does not provide an independent basis of federal subject matter jurisdiction. The basis of federal jurisdiction, including personal and subject matter jurisdiction, must appear in the complaint.[10] Even if jurisdiction is disputed, however, the court may still issue a TRO pending resolution of the jurisdictional question.[11] If the court has personal jurisdiction, a TRO may enjoin an entity's conduct outside of the jurisdiction.[12]

(3) Types of TROs

The most common restraining order prohibits certain conduct ("prohibitory" TROs).[13] Other restraining orders require specific performance

4. *See, e.g.*, S.D. Cal. Local Rule 65.1(c).

5. *See, e.g.*, E.D. Cal. Civ. Local Rule 231(c).

6. *See, e.g.*, E.D. Cal. Civ. Local Rule 231; N.D. Cal. Civ. Local Rule 65–1; C.D. Cal. Local Rule 7.18.

7. *See, e.g.*, E.D. Cal. Civ. Local Rule 231(a) (stating that telephonic notice may suffice).

8. *See, e.g.*, C.D. Cal. Local Rule 7.18.1 (stating that applicants must make a "good faith effort" to advise opposing counsel of the motion).

9. *See, e.g.*, E.D. Cal. Civ. Local Rule 231(b) (stating that if court finds that plaintiff delayed in seeking the TRO, the court may deny the application solely on that ground).

10. Suster v. Marshall, 951 F.Supp. 693, 701 n. 12 (N.D.Ohio 1996) (stating "the court 'may not attempt to determine the rights of persons not before the court . . . [and] must, therefore, tailor the injunction to affect only those persons over which it has power'") (citation omitted); *See* Lathrop v. Unidentified, Wrecked, & Abandoned Vessel, 817 F.Supp. 953, 961 (M.D.Fla.1993) (citing Zepeda v. United States, 753 F.2d 719 (9th Cir.1983)) ("A federal court may issue an injunction if it has personal jurisdiction over the parties and subject matter jurisdiction over the claim.").

11. *See* United States v. United Mine Workers of America, 330 U.S. 258, 293, 67 S.Ct. 677, 696, 91 L.Ed. 884 (1947) (stating that the district court had the power to preserve existing conditions while it was determining its own authority to grant injunctive relief); Alaska v. Native Village of Venetie, 856 F.2d 1384 (9th Cir.1988); Fernandez–Roque v. Smith, 671 F.2d 426, 431 (11th Cir.1982); Stewart v. Dunn, 363 F.2d 591, 598 (5th Cir.1966).

12. *See* Ocean Garden, Inc. v. Marktrade Co., 953 F.2d 500 (9th Cir.1991) (enjoining trademark infringement in Asia). *See generally*, 11A Charles Alan Wright, Arthur R. Miller, & Mary Kay Kane, Federal Practice and Procedure § 2945 (2d ed. 1995) (discussing extraterritorial effect of injunctive relief).

13. Clark Pacific v. Krump Constr., Inc., 942 F.Supp. 1324 (D.Nev.1996) (granting TRO prohibiting state and general contractor from using substitute subcontractor); *see* Towers Fin. Corp. v. Dun & Bradstreet, Inc., 803 F.Supp. 820 (S.D.N.Y.1992) (TRO sought to prohibit publication of business-information report); VanLeeuwen v. Farm Credit Administration, 577 F.Supp. 264 (D.Or.1983) (TRO prohibiting FCA from appointing receiver and liquidating credit association).

of acts to remedy past wrongs ("mandatory" TROs).[14] In addition, a TRO may be issued to stay a federal action from being brought in another district if such action is brought to harass or if the court determines that it is the more convenient forum ("jurisdictional" TROs).[15] Because restraining a party from filing in state court, however, implicates principles of federalism, a TRO will issue in those instances only when it is expressly authorized by Congress, is necessary to aid the court's jurisdiction, or protects or effectuates the court's jurisdiction.[16]

(4) Not an Adjudication on the Merits

The issuance of a TRO does not affect the merits of either party's case. While courts often consider the likelihood of the plaintiff's success on the merits to issue the restraining order, parties may not invoke this initial determination in later proceedings to prove the merits of their case. Courts have granted TROs and subsequently denied preliminary injunctions enjoining the same acts.[17]

(5) Pleading

Plaintiffs may request TROs in the complaint or, as is more common, by separate motion or application. Some local rules require TRO requests, when the TRO is sought without notice to the opposing party, to be filed in separate documents.[18] As one court has noted, "the submission of affidavits in support of or opposition to a preliminary injunction is both customary and appropriate."[19]

(6) Notice

It is generally held that orders sought without notice "run[] counter to the notion of court action taken before reasonable notice and an opportunity to be heard has been granted both sides of a dispute...."[20]

To secure a TRO without notice to the opposing party,[21] FRCP 65 requires the application to assert two conditions. First, the complaint or

---

14. Dolan v. Transport Workers Union, 746 F.2d 733 (11th Cir.1984) (TRO sought to require union to place applicant's name on ballot); *See* The Nation Magazine v. Department of State, 805 F.Supp. 68 (D.D.C. 1992) (TRO sought to expedite processing of magazine's FOIA requests); Benjamin v. Malcolm, 629 F.Supp. 713 (S.D.N.Y.), *aff'd,* 803 F.2d 46 (2d Cir.1986) (TRO requiring state commissioner to accept custody of prisoners).

15. *See* Northwest Airlines v. American Airlines, 989 F.2d 1002 (8th Cir.1993) (applying "first-filed" rule to enjoin parallel proceeding in another federal jurisdiction); Terra Int'l, Inc. v. Mississippi Chemical Corp., 896 F.Supp. 1468 (N.D.Iowa 1995) (applying "first-filed" rule).

16. *See* 28 U.S.C.A. § 2283 (West 1994) (Anti–Injunction Statute); Vendo Co. v.

Lektro–Vend Corp., 433 U.S. 623, 97 S.Ct. 2881, 53 L.Ed.2d 1009 (1977).

17. *See* Interox Am. v. PPG Indus., Inc., 736 F.2d 194, 198 (5th Cir.1984) (TRO granted, preliminary injunction denied); Pabst Brewing Co. v. Corrao, 940 F.Supp. 217 (E.D.Wis.1996) (TRO granted, preliminary injunction denied).

18. E.D & W.D. Ark. Local Rule C–7(e), D. Haw. Local Rule 120–2(f).

19. Bracco v. Lackner, 462 F.Supp. 436, 442 n. 3 (N.D.Cal.1978).

20. Granny Goose Foods, Inc. v. Brotherhood of Teamsters, Local No. 70, 415 U.S. 423, 94 S.Ct. 1113, 39 L.Ed.2d 435 (1974).

21. FRCP 65 refers to a TRO sought without notice to the opposing party as an ex parte TRO. However, because ex parte is

affidavits accompanying the application must clearly set forth specific facts demonstrating that "irreparable injury, loss, or damage" will occur before the adverse party has the opportunity to present its case in court.[22] While courts require the affidavit to be based upon personal knowledge and to avoid vague or conclusory[23] statements, the more stringent requirements for the form of affidavits imposed by FRCP 56(e) governing summary judgment need not be met.[24] The affidavit must convince the court of the danger of immediate and irreparable injury. Second, the plaintiff's attorney must certify in writing any effort to give the restrained party notice and the reasons that formal notice should not be required.[25] The FRCP does not set forth what efforts or reasons are sufficient. Formal procedures under FRCP 4 for service of a summons are probably not required, and compliance with FRCP 5(b) regarding service of a pleading upon a party's attorney should suffice.[26] Nonetheless, FRCP 65 is clear that TROs may issue without notice where circumstances require.

While FRCP 65(b) recognizes the possibilities of TROs issuing without notice, courts prefer some form of notice, whether formal or informal,[27] such as by telephone.[28] Some courts have required notice "absent exigent or extraordinary circumstances,"[29] while other courts have granted TROs without notice where "no reasonable alternative" to proceeding without notice exists.[30] Courts have refused to grant a TRO without notice when time to give notice existed and the applicant knew the identity and location of the opposing party, but gave no notice.[31] However, when the adverse party was unknown or unable to be found, courts have not required notice.[32] Courts have also foregone notice where

used in some jurisdictions to mean quick legal action with or without notice, this text will use "without notice" in lieu of "ex parte."

22. FRCP 65(b).

23. See 11A Charles Alan Wright, Arthur R. Miller, & Mary Kay Kane, Federal Practice and Procedure § 2952 (2d ed. 1995).

24. See Bracco, 462 F.Supp. at 442 n.3.

25. FRCP 65(b).

26. See 11A Charles Alan Wright, Arthur R. Miller, & Mary Kay Kane, Federal Practice and Procedure § 2952 (2d ed. 1995).

27. See, e.g., United States v. Atlantic Richfield Co., 297 F.Supp. 1060 (S.D.N.Y. 1969) (ordering a party who arrived in court at 4:45 P.M. requesting a TRO to return the next day "so that everybody will be in a position to come here and present whatever facts there are").

28. Elsinore Shore Associates v. Local 54, Hotel Employees and Restaurant Employees Intern. Union, 820 F.2d 62, 64 (3d Cir.1987).

29. EEOC v. Steamship Clerks Union, Local 1066, 48 F.3d 594, 608 (1st Cir.1995); United States v. Monsanto, 924 F.2d 1186 (2d Cir.), cert. denied, 502 U.S. 943, 112 S.Ct. 382, 116 L.Ed.2d 333 (1991) (because of the exigent circumstances presented, notice and hearing are not required by due process before ex parte restraining order is entered pursuant to statute with respect to assets of defendant which would be subject to forfeiture in event of conviction).

30. American Can Co. v. Mansukhani, 742 F.2d 314, 322 (7th Cir.1984); United States v. 408 Peyton Road, S.W., Atlanta, Fulton County, Ga., 112 F.3d 1106, 1112, (11th Cir.1997) ("If an owner seems likely to destroy his property when advised of the forfeiture action, the Government may obtain an ex parte restraining order ... upon a proper showing in district court.").

31. See American Can Co., 742 F.2d at 321–22.

32. See First Tech. Safety Sys., Inc. v. Depinet, 11 F.3d 641, 650 (6th Cir.1993) ("The normal circumstances for which the district court would be justified in proceed-

it may render moot further prosecution of the action.[33]

(7) Hearing

The court may require a hearing where the plaintiff's application has not clearly established that the risk of harm outweighs the adverse party's right to adequate notice of the action. Additionally, the court may order a hearing when the adverse party, after giving notice to the plaintiff, seeks dissolution or modification of a TRO after its initial issuance.[34] In either case, such hearing will often convert the TRO request into a preliminary injunction hearing. A TRO issued after a full hearing may be treated as a preliminary injunction and is not limited to 10 days.[35]

Issuance of a TRO requires the court to calendar a hearing on the preliminary injunction on the earliest possible date the court can accommodate.[36] It also requires the hearing to take precedence over any other matters, except for older hearings of the same character.[37]

(8) Duration

FRCP 65(b) requires the court to fix the duration of a TRO, up to a maximum 10–day period.[38] A properly drawn TRO sought without notice should state the time of expiration, which should not exceed 10 days. Otherwise, the duration is automatically 10 days, absent an extension. FRCP 65 does not specify the maximum time period allowable if notice has been given, but the courts generally treat the duration of such a TRO the same as one without notice.[39]

The court may extend such period for good cause for up to another 10 days, or beyond when the party against whom the order is directed consents.[40] The plaintiff probably demonstrates good cause if the condi-

---

ing ex parte is where notice to the adverse party is impossible, as in the case where the adverse party is unknown or is unable to be found.").

33. *See In re* Vuitton et Fils, S.A., 606 F.2d 1, 5 (2d Cir.1979) (directing the district court to issue an ex parte temporary restraining order in a trademark infringement case where notice repeatedly in the past had enabled the defendant to dispose of infringing materials and "serve[d] only to render fruitless further prosecution of the action").

34. See FRCP 65(b).

35. *See* Kansas Hosp. Ass'n v. Whiteman, 835 F.Supp. 1548, 1551 (D.Kan.1993) ("When the opposing party has been notified and a hearing held prior to the issuance of a temporary restraining order, the specific requirements of Fed.R.Civ.P. 65(b), including the ten-day limitation on the duration of such an order, do not apply."); New Jersey Dept. of Envtl. Protection v. Briar

Lake Dev. Corp., 736 F.Supp. 62, 65 n. 3 (D.N.J.1990); Delaware Valley Transplant Program v. Coye, 678 F.Supp. 479 (D.N.J. 1988).

36. FRCP 65(b).

37. *Id.*

38. *Id.*

39. *Cf.* Granny Goose Foods v. Brotherhood of Teamsters, Local No. 70, 415 U.S. 423, 432 n. 7, 94 S.Ct. 1113, 1122 n. 7, 39 L.Ed.2d 435 (1974) ("We think it clear ... informal notice and hearing does not convert the temporary restraining order into a preliminary injunction of unlimited duration under state law."); Horn Abbot Ltd. v. Sarsaparilla Ltd., 601 F.Supp. 360, 370 n. 12 (N.D.Ill.1984) (if notice is obtained in advance and a hearing is held, the TRO can remain in effect for 20 days).

40. *Id. See also, e.g.,* Project Strategies Corp. v. National Communications Corp., 948 F.Supp. 218 (E.D.N.Y.1996).

tions originally justifying the TRO continue. Good cause also will probably exist if an earlier hearing on a preliminary injunction is unavailable or if more lengthy discovery is needed for such hearing.[41] The length of an extension for good cause is "a like period."[42] While the FRCP does not explicitly limit the number or duration of extensions, most courts interpret this to mean the TRO may remain in effect no more than a combined 20 days.[43] The plaintiff must request an extension before the expiration of the initial 10–day period.[44] When the parties consent to such an extension, the TRO may remain in effect longer than 20 days.[45]

When an action is removed to federal court, any TRO granted by the state court will subsequently be governed by federal law.[46] Under 28 U.S.C.A. § 1450, the injunction remains in full force and effect until the district court dissolves or modifies it.[47]

(9) Security

The same basic principles regarding posting of security in the preliminary injunction context apply in the TRO context.[48]

While the amount of the bond is at the court's discretion, such amount should be sufficient to cover consequential costs and injuries that a wrongfully granted TRO will cause the restrained party between TRO application and the preliminary injunction hearing.[49]

In the discussion of the bond requirement in connection with a motion for preliminary injunction, at Section 13.2(c)(8) *supra*, it was suggested that a plaintiff might decide not to address the bond issue in the moving papers, to avoid anticipating (incorrectly) defendant's arguments or alerting the defendant to the issue. The plaintiff takes a substantial risk if it does not discuss the bond issue in its moving papers in a TRO application. In light of the time constraints of a TRO application, the plaintiff may not have the opportunity to file a reply brief. The defendant's arguments concerning the bond then may go unaddressed, particularly where the court decides the TRO application on the papers

---

41. *See* Maine v. Fri, 483 F.2d 439 (1st Cir.1973) (more than 20 days if plaintiff has been unable in good faith to obtain a date for a preliminary injunction hearing).

42. FRCP 65(b).

43. *See* Casey v. Planned Parenthood of Southeastern Pa., 14 F.3d 848, 855 (3d Cir. 1994).

44. *See* SEC v. Unifund SAL, 910 F.2d 1028, 1034–35 (2d Cir.1990).

45. *See* SEC v. Comcoa, Ltd., 887 F.Supp. 1521, 1526–27 (S.D.Fla.1995), *aff'd*, 70 F.3d 1191 (11th Cir.1995) (finding party gave implied consent to extension).

46. *See* Billy Jack for Her, Inc. v. New York Coat, Suit, Dress, Rainwear and Allied Workers' Union, 511 F.Supp. 1180 (S.D.N.Y.1981) ("An ex parte temporary re-

straining order issued by a state court prior to removal remains in force after removal no longer than it would have remained in effect under state law, but in no event does the order remain in force longer than the time limitations imposed by Rule 65(b), measured from the date of removal.").

47. *See* Granny Goose Foods v. Brotherhood of Teamsters, Local No. 70, 415 U.S. 423, 436–37, 94 S.Ct. 1113, 1122–23, 39 L.Ed.2d 435 (1974).

48. *See* discussion *supra* § 13.2(c)(8).

49. *See* LTD Commodities, Inc. v. Perederij, 699 F.2d 404, 408 (7th Cir.1983) ("[I]f [the plaintiff] failed to obtain equitable relief by way of preliminary injunction, it should be in no better position than it was before the status quo was changed by the [TRO].").

without a hearing. Moreover, the TRO bond is required to protect the defendant from damages only for the short period between the issuance of the TRO and the hearing on the preliminary injunction motion. Under that circumstance, the plaintiff can often argue persuasively for a low bond. If the defendant makes a strong argument of damage from the issuance of the TRO, the plaintiff can suggest that the hearing on the preliminary injunction be scheduled on a very short time frame, to avoid the alleged damages.

(10) Form and Scope

The court issuing the TRO must set forth in its order the reasons for granting the TRO and set forth with specificity the terms of the TRO.[50] Without such specificity, uncertainty could chill the restrained party from engaging in otherwise unrestrained activity. Specific terms, therefore, should prevent the restrained party from violating the order due to its vagueness. Moreover, it should allow for informed, intelligent appellate review. A common benchmark for an acceptable TRO is the "four corners" test—the order on its face should enable the party to ascertain what is enjoined and why.[51] If the order is not sufficiently specific, the appellate court may vacate the order.[52]

When the court does not comply with the form and scope requirements of FRCP 65(d), a TRO is not necessarily void. TROs granted pursuant to an order that contains material defects may still be valid, requiring the enjoined party to conform to the order.[53] In these cases, however, courts have cautioned that strict adherence to the requirements of FRCP 65(d) will protect such TROs from modification or dissolution at a later hearing. The specificity requirements are largely the same as those for preliminary injunctions.[54]

If the TRO is issued without notice, the order must also be endorsed with the date and hour of issuance, define the injury, state why such injury is irreparable and state why the TRO was granted without notice.[55]

Some TROs have been struck down for being overbroad,[56] while other appellate courts struck down TROs which encroached upon lawful activity, or which infringed upon the constitutional rights of the

---

50. FRCP 65(d).

51. See Seattle–First Nat. Bank v. Manges, 900 F.2d 795, 800 (5th Cir.1990) (applying four-corners test); Sanders v. Air Line Pilots Ass'n, 473 F.2d 244 (2d Cir. 1972) (same).

52. See SEC v. Lorin, 76 F.3d 458, 461 (2d Cir.1996); Young v. Pierce, 822 F.2d 1368, 1374 (5th Cir.1987).

53. See Combs v. Ryan's Coal Co., 785 F.2d 970, 978–79 (11th Cir.1986) (finding that despite problem with specificity of the TRO, restrained party had adequate notice regarding prohibited acts); Clarkson Co. v.

Shaheen, 544 F.2d 624, 632 (2d Cir.1976) (stating that lack of formal injunction order did not render the injunctive relief invalid).

54. See discussion supra § 13.2 (c)(9).

55. FRCP 65(d).

56. See Louis W. Epstein Family Partnership v. Kmart Corp., 13 F.3d 762, 771 (3d Cir.1994) ("[I]njunctions, which carry possible contempt penalties for their violation, must be tailored to remedy the specific harms shown rather than to enjoin all possible breaches of the law.") (citations omitted); E.W. Bliss Co. v. Struthers–Dunn, Inc., 408 F.2d 1108 (8th Cir.1969).

adverse party.[57] However, the temporary nature of the decree and the short time in which the court has to adjudicate and issue the TRO often make timeliness more important than concerns with broadness.

The three classes of persons bound by a TRO are the same as those bound by a preliminary injunction.[58] For a TRO to cover a third party, however, the third party must receive actual notice of the order.[59] Because this notice can be "by personal service or otherwise," original process need not be followed. Knowledge of the existence of the TRO and its basic terms fulfills this notice requirement.[60]

(11) When FRCP 65 Does Not Apply

The same principles apply to TROs as to preliminary injunctions regarding the inapplicability of FRCP 65.[61]

(12) Dissolution/Modification

FRCP 65(b) expressly provides for modification or dissolution of a TRO issued without notice. If the TRO is granted without notice, the court will set a hearing for a preliminary injunction for the earliest possible date and this hearing takes precedence over all other matters except older matters of the same kind.[62] At the hearing, the party initially obtaining the TRO must proceed with the motion for a preliminary injunction. Failure to do so requires the court to dissolve the TRO automatically.[63]

A party enjoined without notice may move the court to dissolve or modify the TRO upon two days' notice, or less as the court decides.[64] In doing so, the defendant may challenge the propriety, breadth, vagueness or bond amount of the TRO. Additionally, the restrained party may prove that the circumstances requiring the order have changed,[65] or that the underlying law supporting the order has been amended or repealed.[66]

57. See Consolidation Coal Co. v. Disabled Miners of Southern W. Va., 442 F.2d 1261, 1267 (4th Cir.1971) (First Amendment).

58. See discussion supra § 13.2(c)(9).

59. FRCP 65(d).

60. See Multi–Channel TV Cable Co. v. Charlottesville Quality Cable Operating Co., 22 F.3d 546, 550–51 (4th Cir.1994) (when unnamed party attended the hearing and had notice of the injunction, injunction may properly apply to party); United States v. Hochschild, 977 F.2d 208, 211–12 (6th Cir. 1992).

61. See discussion supra § 13.2(c)(10).

62. FRCP 65(b).

63. Id. See also Hudson v. Barr, 3 F.3d 970, 975–76 (6th Cir.1993).

64. FRCP 65(b).

65. See, e.g., United States v. George, 239 F.Supp. 752 (D.Conn.1965) (quashing TRO requiring VA hospital to give patient blood transfusion when patient's condition improved sufficiently to allow for careful consideration of further transfusions).

66. This is done pursuant to FRCP 60(b), which provides as follows:

[o]n motion and upon such terms as are just, the court may relieve a party ... from a final judgment, order, or proceeding for the following reasons: (1) mistake, inadvertence, surprise, or excusable neglect; (2) newly discovered evidence which by due diligence could not have been discovered in time to move for a new trial under Rule 59(b); (3) fraud (whether heretofore denominated intrinsic or extrinsic), misrepresentation, or other misconduct of an adverse party; (4) the judgment is void; (5) the judgment has been satisfied, released, or discharged, or a prior judgment upon which

If both parties are prepared to present evidence and legal arguments for or against a preliminary injunction, the court may treat this hearing for modification or dissolution of the TRO as one for a preliminary injunction.[67]

(13) Enforcement

The same general principles applicable to enforcement of a preliminary injunction apply to enforcement of a TRO.[68] When the party subject to the TRO believes that the TRO was transparently invalid or exceeded the district court's jurisdiction, some courts have allowed the restrained party to deviate from the normal appeals process.[69] In order to make such a challenge, the restrained party must first seek emergency appellate relief or show compelling circumstances excusing the decision not to seek some kind of emergency relief.[70] However, if timely access to the appellate court is not available or if a timely decision is not forthcoming, a party may proceed to violate the TRO and challenge its constitutionality in the contempt proceedings.[71]

(14) Appealability

Unlike preliminary injunctions, a court's decision to grant or deny a TRO generally is not appealable.[72] Courts have ruled TROs do not fall under the same statutory exception to the final judgment rule, codified at Section 1292(a)(1) of the Judicial Code, which permits appeal of a preliminary injunction. An exception to this rule arises when denial of the TRO would be "tantamount to the denial of a preliminary injunc-

it is based has been reversed or otherwise vacated, or it is no longer equitable that the judgment should have prospective application; or (6) any other reason justifying relief from the operation of the judgment. The motion shall be made within a reasonable time, and for reasons (1), (2), and (3) not more than one year after the judgment, order, or proceeding was entered or taken.

See, e.g., Protectoseal Co. v. Barancik, 23 F.3d 1184 (7th Cir.1994) (lifting an injunction pursuant to FRCP 60(b)(5)).

67. *See* Granny Goose Foods v. Brotherhood of Teamsters, Local No. 70, 415 U.S. 423, 441, 94 S.Ct. 1113, 1125, 39 L.Ed.2d 435 (1974).

68. *See* discussion *supra* § 13.2(c)(11).

69. *See In re* Providence Journal Co., 820 F.2d 1354, *cert. dismissed*, United States v. Providence Journal Co., 485 U.S. 693, 108 S.Ct. 1502, 99 L.Ed.2d 785 (1988) (on rehearing en banc, the court of appeals held that publisher, even when it thinks it is subject of transparently unconstitutional

order of prior restraint, must make good faith effort to seek emergency relief from appellate court and, if timely access to appellate court is not available or if timely decision is not forthcoming, publisher may then proceed to publish and challenge constitutionality of order in contempt proceedings).

70. *See id.*

71. *See id.*

72. *See* Office of Personnel Management v. American Fed'n of Gov't Employees, 473 U.S. 1301, 1303, 105 S.Ct. 3467, 3468, 87 L.Ed.2d 603 (1985) ("[T]he established rule is that denials of temporary restraining orders are ordinarily not appealable."); Board of Governors of Federal Reserve Sys. v. DLG Financial Corp., 29 F.3d 993, 1000 (5th Cir.1994) ("[A] TRO is not appealable [because] TROs are usually effective for only very brief periods of time, far less than the time required for an appeal ... and are then generally supplanted by appealable temporary or permanent injunctions.").

tion."[73] In such a case, the appealing party may take appeal by invoking the collateral order doctrine.[74]

Deciding the question of appealability requires appellate courts to categorize the order as a preliminary injunction or a TRO. The label that the district court gives the order does not necessarily control. TROs granted after notice and a hearing,[75] or TROs which run beyond the time limits given in FRCP 65(b),[76] can be recharacterized as preliminary injunctions, which are appealable. However, courts have reached conflicting decisions when deciding whether a TRO granted with notice or an extended-period TRO are preliminary injunctions for the purposes of appeal.[77] Additionally, it is possible to seek a writ of mandamus or prohibition, but such procedures are expensive and time-consuming and because they are such drastic remedies[78] are seldom granted.[79]

(c) Legal Principles Applicable to the Grant or Denial of a TRO

(1) Substantive Law

Whether a party has a right to a TRO is a question of substantive law, governed by the court's equity powers.[80] If a federal statute provides

73. See Religious Tech. Ctr., Church of Scientology Int'l v. Scott, 869 F.2d 1306 (9th Cir.1989) ("[T]he denial of the TRO [is] tantamount to the denial of a preliminary injunction because of the presence of two factors: the denial of the TRO followed a 'full adversary hearing' and 'in the absence of review, the appellants would be effectively foreclosed from pursuing further interlocutory relief.' ") (citing Environmental Defense Fund, Inc. v. Andrus, 625 F.2d 861, 862 (9th Cir.1980)).

74. The collateral order doctrine is a narrow exception to the final judgment rule allowing appeal of a trial court's prejudgment order when such order affects rights that will be lost without immediate appeal. For a party to invoke the exception, the order must satisfy three conditions: "it must conclusively determine the disputed question, resolve an important issue completely separate from the merits of the action, and be effectively unreviewable on appeal from a final judgment." Richardson–Merrell, Inc. v. Koller, 472 U.S. 424, 431, 105 S.Ct. 2757, 2761, 86 L.Ed.2d 340 (1985). See Chapter 49 "Appeals to the Court of Appeals," at § 49.5(a)(4), infra.

75. See Sampson v. Murray, 415 U.S. 61, 86–88, 94 S.Ct. 937, 951–52, 39 L.Ed.2d 166 (1974).

76. See id.; Diginet, Inc. v. Western Union ATS, Inc., 958 F.2d 1388, 1392 (7th Cir.1992); Professional Plan Examiners of N.J., Inc. v. Lefante, 750 F.2d 282, 287 (3d Cir.1984).

77. For cases that did not convert such TROs into preliminary injunctions, see Connell v. Dulien Steel Prods., Inc., 240 F.2d 414 (5th Cir.1957); Pennsylvania Motor Truck Ass'n v. Port of Philadelphia Marine Terminal, 276 F.2d 931 (3d Cir.1960).

78. Kerr v. U. S. Dist. Court for Northern Dist. of California, 426 U.S. 394, 402, 96 S.Ct. 2119, 2123, 48 L.Ed.2d 725 (1976) ("The remedy of mandamus is a drastic one, to be invoked only in extraordinary situations.").

79. In United States v. Noriega, 917 F.2d 1543 (11th Cir.1990), the court denied CNN's writ of mandamus to correct the district court's alleged abuse in granting a TRO against CNN from broadcasting taped conversations between Noriega and his attorneys.

80. See Hecht Co. v. Bowles, 321 U.S. 321, 329, 64 S.Ct. 587, 591, 88 L.Ed. 754 (1944) ("An appeal to the equity jurisdiction conferred on federal district courts is an appeal to the sound discretion which guides the determinations of courts of equity."). See also Wagner v. Taylor, 836 F.2d 566, 571 (D.C.Cir.1987) ("If the court may eventually have jurisdiction of the substantive claim, the court's incidental equitable

the substantive law, federal courts are free to exercise their equitable powers to issue injunctions "[a]bsent the clearest command to the contrary from Congress."[81] When a federal statute specifically provides for certain remedies but omits any reference to a TRO, however, some courts refuse to issue a TRO.[82]

If state law provides the underlying substantive law and the state law does not specifically provide for equitable relief, a TRO should still be available.[83] If the state law specifies that injunctive relief is not available, however, the *Erie* doctrine may preclude granting a TRO.[84] However, since TROs provide only temporary relief, they do not substantially impair state interests and hence they may not implicate the same concerns that the *Erie* doctrine addresses.[85] Even when damages provide the sole remedy, a TRO may still be available to protect the applicant's right to an effective damages remedy.[86]

(2) Balancing of Equitable Considerations

The tests that the circuits have adopted for preliminary injunctions, discussed above, similarly apply to TROs and the equitable considerations are similar.[87]

jurisdiction, despite the agency's primary jurisdiction, gives the court authority to impose a temporary restraint in order to preserve the status quo pending ripening of the claim for judicial review.").

81. Califano v. Yamasaki, 442 U.S. 682, 705, 99 S.Ct. 2545, 2559, 61 L.Ed.2d 176 (1979). *See* Frio Ice, S.A. v. Sunfruit, Inc., 918 F.2d 154 (11th Cir.1990).

82. *See* Religious Tech. Center v. Wollersheim, 796 F.2d 1076, 1088 (9th Cir. 1986) (RICO statutes do not expressly allow for an injunctive remedy in a private action).

83. *See* Ferrero v. Associated Materials Inc., 923 F.2d 1441, 1448 (11th Cir.1991) (finding federal procedure, rather than state law, applied in determining appropriateness of issuing injunction restraining employee from violating covenant not to compete).

84. *See* Sims Snowboards, Inc. v. Kelly, 863 F.2d 643, 647 (9th Cir.1988) (denying TRO when California anti-injunction statute expressly prohibited the issuance of injunctions in contract dispute); *cf.* Kaiser Trading Co. v. Associated Metals & Minerals Corp., 321 F.Supp. 923, 931 n. 14 (N.D.Cal.1970) (stating that "the best approach would be to look to state law to determine if a preliminary injunction is permissible ... [and then to] look to federal law to determine whether the court should exercise its discretion"). *But see* Perfect Fit

Indus., Inc. v. Acme Quilting Co., 646 F.2d 800, 806 (2d Cir.1981) (stating it does not matter if state law bars a certain remedy because state law does not govern the scope of a federal court's equitable power); Irving Trust Co. v. Braswell, 596 F.Supp. 1441, 1444 (S.D.N.Y.1984) (citing Perfect Fit).

85. *See* 11A Charles Alan Wright, Arthur R. Miller, & Mary Kay Kane, Federal Practice and Procedure § 2943 (2d ed. 1995).

86. *See* Airlines Reporting Corp. v. Barry, 825 F.2d 1220, 1227 (8th Cir.1987) ("clear probability that defendants will not be able to satisfy an award of adequate damages"); Productos Carnic, S.A. v. Central Am. Beef and Seafood Trading Co., 621 F.2d 683, 686 (5th Cir.1980) (foreign entity plans to transfer property and its proceeds out of country which will "frustrate any judgment on the merits"); In re Clawson Med. Rehabilitation, 9 B.R. 644, 650–51 (Bankr.E.D.Mich.), (reorganization is unlikely for entity facing impending bankruptcy and losses will be "difficult if not impossible" to recover in damages), *rev'd on other grounds,* 12 B.R. 647 (E.D.Mich.1981).

87. *See* Local 1814, Int'l Longshoremen's Ass'n v. New York Shipping Ass'n, 965 F.2d 1224, 1228 (2d Cir.1992); Charleston West 76 Auto/Truckstop, Inc. v. National Auto/Truckstops, Inc., 1997 WL 528491 (N.D.W.Va.1997); Bieros v. Nicola, 857

Library References:

West's Key No. Digests, Injunction ⬡150.
Wright, Miller & Kane, Federal Practice and Procedure: Civil 2d §§ 2951–2954.

§ 13.4   Receivership

(a) Strategy

A party to litigation, usually the plaintiff, may seek an order appointing a receiver to protect that party's interest in property that is the subject of that litigation. The receiver takes possession of, preserves and protects assets that are the subject of the litigation. When that litigation is decided, the receiver then distributes those assets in accordance with the judgment.

The plaintiff must consider what type of receiver to seek. A general equity receiver has broad power to protect assets for all creditors, but is the most expensive approach. A "rents, issues and profits" receiver takes possession of property securing a loan for a limited period while a foreclosure is in process. Such a receiver has more limited powers and is less expensive than a general equity receiver. A receiver appointed for a specific purpose has a limited role, for example, to receive and disburse rents or to monitor payment of expenses. The special receiver is also less expensive than a general equity receiver.

There are a number of advantages to the plaintiff in the appointment of a receiver. The receiver may be able to increase the value of the assets involved, for example by continuing business operations or selling the assets. The receiver may also be able to preserve the value of those assets by preventing the defendant from taking or misusing them. The plaintiff is further protected because the receiver reports to the court and his performance is monitored.

In addition, as with other provisional remedies, the plaintiff can use the appointment of a receiver to obtain settlement leverage. A defendant that loses control over the assets held by the receiver may settle on more favorable terms to regain possession of the assets.

There are also numerous risks and disadvantages to appointing a receiver. The cost of appointment, monitoring and compensation of the receiver and his support staff and consultants can be high. The receiver must post a bond and follow rigorous reporting requirements. The receiver must seek court authorization to take certain actions or hire accountants or lawyers. If the cash flow from the assets is not sufficient to compensate the receiver, the plaintiff will likely have to do so. Although the receiver may seek court authorization to borrow money to cover the expenses of receivership, the debt may become a lien on the assets.

F.Supp. 445, 446 (E.D.Pa.1994); Hunt v. Bankers Trust Co., 646 F.Supp. 59 (N.D.Tex.1986); United States v. Phillips, 527 F.Supp. 1340, 1343 (N.D.Ill.1981); *See* *also supra* § 13.2(d)(4) (discussing the different tests used by the circuits for preliminary injunctions).

There may also be harmful delay in the operation of a business while the receiver seeks court approval for his proposed actions. Since the receiver is a neutral party who reports to the court, the plaintiff that sought the receiver may disagree with the receiver's management of the assets but have little ability to affect his decisions.

The cost of the proceedings may also be increased if the defendant opposes the appointment of the receiver, moves to vacate the appointment after it is made, appeals the appointment or files a writ of prohibition challenging the appointment. If the court finds the plaintiff wrongfully obtained a receiver, the court may require the plaintiff to pay all of the costs of the receivership. The appointment of a receiver also may cause other creditors or the defendant to file a bankruptcy petition, which may cause further complications and delay.

The plaintiff that moves for a receiver may face liability as well. The plaintiff and the receiver may become exposed to liability under environmental laws, and the receiver may seek indemnity from the plaintiff for such liability.

In light of the expense of a receivership, a party contemplating a motion to appoint a receiver should consider the alternatives, such as a workout of a loan agreement, imposition of limits and controls on the assets involved, the appointment of an agreed upon manager for the assets without court approval, an injunction against the transfer or waste of the assets or an attachment of the assets.

(b) FRCP 66

FRCP 66 governs the appointment of receivers in the district courts. FRCP 66 provides as follows:

> An action wherein a receiver has been appointed shall not be dismissed except by order of the court. The practice in the administration of estates by receivers or by other similar officers appointed by the court shall be in accordance with the practice heretofore followed in the courts of the United States or as provided in rules promulgated by the district courts. In all other respects the action in which the appointment of a receiver is sought or which is brought by or against a receiver is governed by these rules.

By its language, FRCP 66 does not authorize the courts to appoint receivers, but assumes the power of the court to appoint a receiver to manage or control property involved in any action or civil proceeding. Nor does FRCP 66 set forth any procedures related to the appointment of receivers. FRCP 66 states generally that actions in which receivers have been appointed shall not be dismissed without a court order. The Rule further provides that the appointment and practice of receivers in the administration of estates shall be in accordance with the practice that has been followed in federal courts or rules promulgated by district courts. Other than these two items, FRCP 66 provides merely that in all other respects actions involving receivers are governed by the Federal Rules of Civil Procedure. Although not mentioned in the Rule, FRCP 66 does not apply to bankruptcy cases, which are governed by the Bankruptcy Code and the General Orders. Furthermore, a bankruptcy judge may not appoint a receiver instead of a trustee.[1]

(c) Jurisdiction

An application for a receiver does not create federal jurisdiction. To appoint a receiver, a federal court must have subject matter jurisdiction over the action under an independent basis[2] and, as in any action, the district court may exercise supplemental jurisdiction over state law claims. A receiver appointed under the proper subject matter jurisdiction, therefore, may bring any subsequent suit under the court's supplemental jurisdiction.[3]

(d) Applicable Federal and State Law

(1) FRCP Applies to Receivers in Federal Court

The *Erie* doctrine does not apply to federal equity receivers[4] and federal law and practice thus govern their appointment. In diversity cases, for purposes of the *Erie*[5] doctrine, the appointment of a receiver does not directly affect the outcome of the suit and therefore is considered a procedural issue governed by federal law. In practice, state and federal standards for receivership appointments are often similar, so that there is little benefit from forum shopping between federal and state court. Where there is no substantial federal precedent regarding particular issues, federal courts will likely look to state law for direction.

---

§ 13.4

1. 11 U.S.C.A. § 105(b) (West 1993).

2. *See* 28 U.S.C.A. §§ 1331 (West 1993) (federal question); 1332 (West 1993 & Supp. 1997) (diversity); 1333 (West 1993) (admiralty, maritime and prize cases); 1334 (West 1993 & Supp. 1997) (bankruptcy cases); 1336 (West 1993 & Supp. 1997) (commerce and antitrust cases); 1338 (West 1993) (patent, copyright and trademark cases); 1339 (West 1993) (cases involving Acts of Congress related to the post office); 1340 (West 1993) (internal revenue cases); 1343 (West 1993) (civil rights cases); 1345 (West 1993) (cases with the United States as plaintiff); 1346 (West 1993 & Supp. 1997) (specific types of cases with the United States as defendant).

3. Haile v. Henderson Nat'l Bank, 657 F.2d 816, 822 (6th Cir.1981), *cert. denied sub nom.* First Nat'l Bank v. Haile, 455 U.S. 949, 102 S.Ct. 1450, 71 L.Ed.2d 663 (1982). *See* United States v. Franklin Nat'l Bank, 512 F.2d 245, 249–50 (2d Cir.1975); City of Detroit v. Michigan, 538 F.Supp. 1169 (E.D.Mich.1982). *See* 28 U.S.C.A. § 1367 (West 1993); O'Neal v. General Motors Corp., 841 F.Supp. 391, 395 (M.D.Fla. 1993).

4. New York Life Ins. Co. v. Watt West Inv. Corp., 755 F.Supp. 287, 290 (E.D.Cal. 1991) (discussing the Advisory Committee Note to FRCP 66 that "the final sentence of the Rule was added in 1948 to assure 'the application of the federal rules to all matters except actual administration of the receivership estate itself.'"); *see also* Hanna v. Plumer, 380 U.S. 460, 85 S.Ct. 1136, 14 L.Ed.2d 8 (1965) (discussing the validity of using FRCP in diversity case).

5. Erie Railroad Company v. Tompkins, 304 U.S. 64, 58 S.Ct. 817, 82 L.Ed. 1188 (1938).

(2) State Law Governs the Rights, Duties and Liabilities of a Receiver

Under Title 28 U.S.C.A. § 959(b), the substantive rights, duties and liabilities of the receiver are determined by state law and a receiver must administer the receivership property according to the applicable laws of the state in which the property is located, in the same way the owner would be bound.[6] This statute refers only to the receiver's operation of the property. For example, the receiver in charge of a railroad must follow state laws requiring weekly payment of wages[7] and the receiver charged with operating an oil refining and distribution business must follow state licensing and bond requirements.[8] State law also controls actions in which a receiver is sued for tort liability.[9]

Under 28 U.S.C.A. § 960, tax liability attaches to the receiver just as if the defendant still managed the property and a receiver is responsible for all applicable local, state, and federal taxes.[10] Any tax expenses are deemed administrative expenses that have priority over claims of general creditors.[11] Section 960 also applies to receivers appointed in mortgage foreclosure suits brought by the United States.[12]

(e) Role of Receiver and Eligibility for Appointment

(1) Definition and Role of Receiver

Generally, a receiver assumes control over, takes custody of, or manages property that is involved or likely to become involved in litigation. The receiver conserves the property by taking appropriate actions pending the final outcome of the suit.[13] The receiver's primary

---

6. 28 U.S.C.A. § 959(b) (West 1993). "Except as provided in § 1166 of title 11, a trustee, receiver or manager appointed in any cause pending in any court of the United States, including a debtor in possession, shall manage and operate the property in his possession as such trustee, receiver or manager according to the requirements of the valid laws of the State in which such property is situated, in the same manner that the owner or possessor thereof would be bound to do if in possession thereof."

28 U.S.C.A. § 959(b) (West 1993).

7. Burke v. Morphy, 109 F.2d 572 (2d Cir.), cert. denied, 310 U.S. 635, 60 S.Ct. 1078, 84 L.Ed. 1404 (1940).

8. Gillis v. California, 293 U.S. 62, 55 S.Ct. 4, 79 L.Ed. 199 (1934).

9. Erb v. Morasch, 177 U.S. 584, 20 S.Ct. 819, 44 L.Ed. 897 (1900); Peirce v. Van Dusen, 78 Fed. 693 (6th Cir.1897), appeal dismissed, 19 S.Ct. 879, 43 L.Ed. 1184 (1899) (statute modifying fellow-servant rule); Hornsby v. Eddy, 56 Fed. 461

(8th Cir.1893) (statute abrogating fellow-servant rule).

10. Gillis, 293 U.S. 62, 55 S.Ct. 4, 79 L.Ed. 199; Coy v. Title Guarantee & Trust Co., 220 Fed. 90 (9th Cir.1915); Ex parte Tyler, 149 U.S. 164, 13 S.Ct. 785, 37 L.Ed. 689 (1893).

11. Michigan v. Michigan Trust Co., 286 U.S. 334, 52 S.Ct. 512, 76 L.Ed. 1136 (1932).

12. The Southern Cross, 120 F.2d 466 (2d Cir.1941).

13. Booth v. Clark, 58 U.S.(17 How.) 322, 331, 15 L.Ed. 164 (1854) (receiver brings and defends actions, leases the estate and repairs the property as necessary); Santibanez v. Wier McMahon & Co., 105 F.3d 234 (5th Cir.1997) (receiver appointed to take possession and sell assets subject to the court's "turnover" order); Citibank, N.A. v. Nyland Ltd., 839 F.2d 93 (2d Cir. 1988) (receiver appointed at request of mortgagee was entitled to injunctive relief precluding mortgagor's agent from interfer-

role is to manage the property in an orderly and efficient manner preserving the property for all interested parties.[14] Receivers are often appointed in actions by creditors. Most commonly, receivers are appointed to preserve or rehabilitate an enterprise as opposed to liquidating it in a bankruptcy-like proceeding.[15]

A receiver takes direction from the court, not the parties. A receiver is "an officer of the court to receive, collect, care for, administer and dispose of the property or the fruits of the property of another or others brought under the orders of the court by the institution of a proper action or actions."[16] As officers of the court, receivers are not agents of the parties,[17] and their appointment is incident to the primary proceedings of the litigation.[18] Generally, the district court has broad discretion

---

ing with receiver's duties); *In re* Armstrong Glass Co., Inc., 502 F.2d 159 (6th Cir.1974) (receiver appointed before bankruptcy proceeding for legal and accounting services); View Crest Garden Apartments Inc. v. United States, 281 F.2d 844 (9th Cir.) *cert. denied,* 364 U.S. 902, 81 S.Ct. 235, 5 L.Ed.2d 195 (1960) (receiver appointed to collect rents and manage property pending foreclosure proceeding); Ledbetter v. Farmers Bank & Trust Co., 142 F.2d 147 (4th Cir.), *cert. denied,* 323 U.S. 719, 65 S.Ct. 48, 89 L.Ed. 578 (1944) (mortgage receiver found not liable for failure to insure property lost in fire); Commissioner of Internal Revenue v. Owens, 78 F.2d 768 (10th Cir. 1935) (receiver appointed to lease lands for oil and gas purposes held "fiduciary" for tax purposes); Adelman v. CGS Scientific Corp., 332 F.Supp. 137 (E.D.Pa.1971) (receiver appointed in Securities Act action to rescind a fraudulently induced sale); Haase v. Chapman, 308 F.Supp. 399 (W.D.Mo. 1969) (receiver appointed in supplemental action for collection of judgment); Gross v. Missouri & A. Ry. Co., 74 F.Supp. 242 (D.Ark.1947) (receiver appointed to take charge of railroad where railroad was solvent but unable to pay all debts and Interstate Commerce Commission had filed pending action).

14. *See* Rosen v. Siegel, 106 F.3d 28 (2d Cir.1997) (appointment of receiver to manage defendant's assets during litigation is considered to be extraordinary remedy, and should be employed cautiously and granted only when clearly necessary to protect plaintiff's interests in property); SEC v. Hardy, 803 F.2d 1034, 1038–39 (9th Cir. 1986); SEC v. Safety Fin. Serv., Inc., 674 F.2d 368, 372–73 (5th Cir.1982); Levin v. Garfinkle, 514 F.Supp. 1160 (E.D.Pa.1981).

15. The most common use of the equity receivership nowadays is in the rehabilitation of business enterprises after they have encountered financial difficulties. The aim usually is not, as with bankruptcy, a prompt liquidation with sale of assets and payment of the proceeds to creditors. The aim is rather to administer the assets, often over years, to scale down or extend fixed money obligations, and generally restore an ailing enterprise to health. Dawson & Harvey, Cases on Contracts and Contract Remedies 132 (2d ed. 1969).

16. 1 Clark on Receivers § 11(a) (3d ed. 1959): *See* Booth v. Clark, 58 U.S. (17 How.) 322, 331, 15 L.Ed. 164 (1854) ("A receiver is an indifferent person between parties, appointed by the court to receive the rents, issues, or profits of land, or other thing in question in this court, pending the suit, where it does not seem reasonable to the court that either party should do it.") (*cited in* Holland v. Sterling Enterprises, Inc., 777 F.2d 1288, 1292 (7th Cir.1985)).

17. Booth, 58 U.S. at 331, 15 L.Ed. 164; United States v. Smallwood, 443 F.2d 535 (8th Cir.) *cert. denied,* 404 U.S. 853, 92 S.Ct. 95, 30 L.Ed.2d 93 (1971); Ledbetter, 142 F.2d at 150; American Brake Shoe and Foundry Co. v. Interborough Rapid Transit Co., 6 F.Supp. 215 (S.D.N.Y.1933).

18. Zittman v. McGrath, 341 U.S. 446, 71 S.Ct. 832, 95 L.Ed. 1096 (1951) (receiver appointed under New York statute to liquidate assets of foreign debtor corporation); Credit Managers Ass'n of Southern Cal. v. Kennesaw Life and Accident Ins. Co., 809 F.2d 617 (9th Cir.1987) (receivership ancillary to liquidation under Insurance Code); Resolution Trust Corp. v. Fountain Circle Assocs. Ltd. Partnership, 799 F.Supp. 48 (N.D.Ohio 1992) (receiver appointed to col-

to establish any methods necessary to insure proper management and conservation of the property. The court may exercise whatever methods it deems appropriate to supervise the receiver.[19]

(2) Persons Prohibited from Acting as Receivers

Federal and state statutes prohibit certain persons from serving as receivers. Under 28 U.S.C.A. § 957(a), no clerk or deputy clerk of the district court may be appointed a receiver absent special reasons set forth in the order of appointment.[20] The district court may not appoint as a receiver anyone holding any civil or military office or employment under the United States, or anyone employed by a judge or justice of the United States.[21] 28 U.S.C.A. § 458 prohibits any person "appointed to or employed in any office or duty in any court who is related by affinity or consanguinity within the degree of first cousin to any justice or judge of such court" from serving as a receiver.[22] Similarly, under 18 U.S.C.A. § 1910, a judge may not appoint as a receiver anyone related to him or her "by consanguinity, or affinity, within the fourth degree."[23]

Typically, interested parties are not appointed as receivers.[24] In some cases, state statutes prohibit interested parties from serving as receivers.[25] Elsewhere, however, an interested party may serve as a receiver if the parties consent or if special circumstances exist to make such an appointment in the best interests of all concerned.[26] When not contrary to state or local law, a national bank may obtain a permit from the Comptroller of the Currency to act as a receiver.[27]

Subject to the foregoing rules and restrictions, a court has broad discretion in selecting a qualified receiver.[28]

(f) Appointment of a Receiver

Courts consider several issues in deciding on the appointment of a

lect rents during pendency of foreclosure action).

19. *See* 28 U.S.C.A. § 959(b) (West 1993). In *SEC v. Hardy*, 803 F.2d 1034, 1038–39 (9th Cir.1986), the Ninth Circuit held that the district court had discretion to establish deadlines for filing claims to bar untimely claims.

20. This statute does not bar appointment of a clerk to avoid the expense of an outside receiver of a check to be deposited with the court, if that receiver's duties are restricted to endorsing and depositing the check. United States v. Jacobs, 187 F.Supp. 630 (D.Md.1959), *aff'd,* 298 F.2d 469 (4th Cir.1961).

21. 28 U.S.C.A. § 958 (West 1993).

22. 28 U.S.C.A. § 458 (West 1993).

23. 18 U.S.C.A. § 1910 (West 1984 & Supp. 1997).

24. Lewis v. City of Grand Rapids, 222 F.Supp. 349 (W.D.Mich.1963), *rev'd in part,* 356 F.2d 276 (6th Cir.), *cert. denied,* 385 U.S. 838, 87 S.Ct. 84, 17 L.Ed.2d 71 (1966).

25. Adams v. Spillyards, 187 Ark. 641, 61 S.W.2d 686 (1933).

26. Northern Brewery Co. v. Princess Hotel, 78 Or. 453, 153 P. 37 (1915) (finding no acquiescence to designated receiver) (citing Bartelt v. Smith, 145 Wis. 31, 129 N.W. 782 (1911); Penn Mut. Life Ins. Co. v. Cudd, 172 S.C. 88, 172 S.E. 787 (1934).

27. 12 U.S.C.A. § 92(a) (West 1989).

28. General Motors Truck Co. of Louisiana v. Caddo Transfer & Warehouse Co., 176 La. 181, 186, 145 So. 372, 373 (1932); People *ex rel.* Gore v. Illinois Building & Loan Ass'n, 56 Ill.App. 642 (1895).

receiver, including the court's jurisdiction, applicable federal and state law, grounds for appointing the receiver, due process issues and the duration of the appointment.

(1) Motion to Appoint a Receiver

A moving party seeks the appointment of a receiver in the principal action.[29] Generally, any party having an interest in property eligible for receivership, or a relation to a party in control of such property, may petition for a receiver[30] by filing a complaint or motion[31] justifying court intervention. The petitioner must demonstrate a provable interest or right in the property when requesting a receiver.[32] Some courts will entertain requests based on a mere probable interest or right in the property,[33] but a plaintiff who merely asserts a claim against the defendant may not seek a receivership.[34]

The complaint for and the motion requesting the appointment must sufficiently allege that the defendant is unable to manage the property appropriately or that the defendant's continued involvement will result in the loss or dissipation of the property.[35] The pleading requirements

29. Zittman v. McGrath, 341 U.S. 446, 71 S.Ct. 832, 95 L.Ed. 1096 (1951). In *Kelleam v. Maryland Casualty Co.*, 312 U.S. 377, 61 S.Ct. 595, 85 L.Ed. 899 (1941), the Court held that a receiver could not be appointed to conserve the property or impress a lien upon it where ownership remained to be determined by a pending state court suit and the plaintiff had no interest in the property, but merely wanted to conserve it to protect his contingent liability as surety on the bond of the administrator of the estate which included the property.

30. Crowley v. Valley West Water Co., 267 Mont. 144, 882 P.2d 1022 (1994); Abella v. Knight Oil Tools, 945 S.W.2d 847 (Tex.App.1997); Williams v. Liggett, 113 N.C.App. 812, 440 S.E.2d 331 (1994).

31. The form of the request to appoint a receiver takes on several forms, depending on the stage of the litigation at which the request is made. *See* 65 Am. Jur. 2d Receivers 110 (1972).

32. Piambino v. Bailey, 757 F.2d 1112 (11th Cir.1985) (receivership not available to plaintiffs in tort action seeking unliquidated money damages); State *ex rel.* James v. Marion Superior Ct., 222 Ind. 26, 51 N.E.2d 844 (1943) (bank commissioner had sufficient right or interest to request receiver); State *ex rel.* Nenzel v. Second Judicial Dist. Ct., 49 Nev. 145, 241 P. 317 (1925).

33. Sheridan Brick Works v. Marion Trust Co., 157 Ind. 292, 61 N.E. 666 (1901).

34. DeTar Distrib. Co. v. Tri–State Motor Transit Co., 379 F.2d 244 (10th Cir. 1967); Mintzer v. Arthur L. Wright & Co., 263 F.2d 823, 825 (3d Cir.1959).

35. Consolidated Rail Corp. v. Fore River Ry. Co., 861 F.2d 322 (1st Cir.1988) (appointment of receiver for assets of railway company was proper in action brought to recover unpaid freight charges allegedly collected by railway company on another company's behalf, where there was sufficient evidence that property would be imminently squandered, that railway company failed to account for collected freight charges, and that such funds had been intermingled with other funds of either railway company or of its officers); Tanzer v. Huffines, 408 F.2d 42 (3d Cir.1969) (trial court did not abuse its discretion by appointing receiver for diversified management investment company that failed to file annual report with Securities and Exchange Commission, sent stockholder misleading annual report and whose directors indicated almost flagrant disregard for affairs of company); American Maganese Steel Co. v. Alaska Mines Corp., 250 Fed. 614 (9th Cir. 1918) (where defendant was not insolvent, and no irreparable injury could result from refusal, the denial of complainant's motion for appointment of a receiver, to take into custody property which complainant asserted it was entitled to subject to its claim, was not error); Haase v. Chapman, 308 F.Supp. 399 (W.D.Mo.1969) (where identity

differ depending on whether notice was given[36] or not.[37]

In typical cases corporate stockholders and mortgagees may petition for a receiver.[38] Courts have appointed receivers in cases involving enforcement of the Securities Acts,[39] preservation of property pending its

of party possessing bearer note was not proved, note was readily transferrable and place of payment on note was known, appointment of receiver for payments on note was proper even though alleged transferee was not party to supplemental action in equity to collect judgment); Wickes v. Belgian American Educational Found., Inc., 266 F.Supp. 38 (S.D.N.Y.1967) (the mere possibility that gift by charitable corporation to corporate foundation might have been invalid was insufficient basis upon which to grant injunction pendente lite and appointment pendente lite of receiver of assets of charitable corporation in derivative action by its members and directors for relief in connection with the gift); Tcherepnin v. Franz, 277 F.Supp. 472 (N.D.Ill.1966) (general allegations to the effect that present liquidators of a savings and loan association were either corrupt, inefficient, or both, did not warrant granting extraordinary relief of appointment of a receiver, in view of fact such allegations were not specific, and in view of fact appointment of a receiver might impede expeditious resolution of investors' claims).

36. Citicorp Sav. of Illinois, F.A. v. Occhipinti, 136 Ill.App.3d 835, 91 Ill.Dec. 360, 483 N.E.2d 706 (1985) (appointment of receiver was not fatal where sole defect alleged in procedure by which receiver was appointed was failure to allege in petition sufficient facts regarding waste, since the concept of waste, particularly as it applies to residential property, was well understood, and where the concept of waste was amplified upon by plaintiff's counsel at the hearing and was responded to by the attorney for defendant on a point-by-point basis); Wolf v. Greek Am. Realty Co., 40 Ill. App.2d 292, 189 N.E.2d 406 (1963) (where receiver was appointed based solely upon allegations of amended complaint without regard to verified denials set forth in the answer and the affirmative defenses interposed, it was improvident to appoint receiver pendente lite without a hearing of the many controverted issues made up by the pleadings).

37. Environmental Control Systems, Inc. v. Allison, 161 Ind.App. 148, 314 N.E.2d 820 (1974) (allegations of complaint

seeking appointment of a receiver without notice, and purported verification thereof, were not sufficient upon which to base an order appointing a receiver without notice, where allegations of complaint were couched in terms that were mere conclusory statements, some of them hearsay, supported only by plaintiffs' statements that "they believed" or that they "verily believed," where no facts were pleaded upon which the drastic, extraordinary remedy of appointment of receiver without notice could possibly be founded, and where, additionally, the complaint was not supported by separate affidavit and was not verified in positive terms); Head v. Roberts, 291 S.W.2d 483 (Tex.Civ.App.1956) (to be sufficient to authorize ex parte appointment of receiver, petition must allege facts showing that it is extreme and exceptional case and that there is a great emergency and such an imperious and most stringent necessity for haste that applicant would likely suffer material injury by delay necessary to give notice).

38. Kessler v. United Agencies, 243 S.W.2d 779 (Mo.App.1951) (in action by minority stockholders seeking appointment of a receiver to liquidate and dissolve corporation on ground that corporate assets were being misapplied and wasted, plaintiffs had the burden of proving the essential allegations in their petition); see also Burnrite Coal Briquette Co. v. Riggs, 274 U.S. 208, 47 S.Ct. 578, 71 L.Ed. 1002 (1927); Union Trust Co. v. Illinois Midland R. Co., 117 U.S. 434, 6 S.Ct. 809, 29 L.Ed. 963 (1886); Chase Manhattan Bank v. Turabo Shopping Center, Inc., 683 F.2d 25 (1st Cir.1982); View Crest Garden Apartments, Inc. v. United States, 281 F.2d 844 (9th Cir.) cert. denied, 364 U.S. 902, 81 S.Ct. 235, 5 L.Ed.2d 195 (1960).

39. See, e.g., SEC v. American Bd. of Trade, 830 F.2d 431 (2d Cir.1987); SEC v. Hardy, 803 F.2d 1034 (9th Cir.1986); United States v. Smallwood, 443 F.2d 535 (8th Cir.) cert. denied, 404 U.S. 853, 92 S.Ct. 95, 30 L.Ed.2d 93 (1971).

distribution in proceedings in aid of execution,[40] and in enforcement of carriers' obligations to render services.[41] An unsecured creditor is not entitled to an appointment of a receiver[42] absent extraordinary circumstances[43] or a statute[44] providing for such a right. An unsecured creditor may also request an appointment of a receiver regarding the general administration of debtor assets, the seizure of assets not subject to execution, levy, or fraudulent conveyances.

(2) Standards upon Which Appointment of Receiver Is Granted or Denied

As with injunctions, a court has the discretion to grant or deny the appointment of a receiver.[45] A court exercises its discretion only after it has determined that circumstances require the extraordinary remedy of a receivership.[46] Courts consider a variety of factors to varying

40. Santibanez v. Wier McMahon & Co., 105 F.3d 234 (5th Cir.1997); Haase, 308 F.Supp. 399.

41. Montgomery Ward & Co. v. Northern Pac. Terminal Co. of Or., 128 F.Supp. 475 (D.Or.1953).

42. Zechiel v. Firemen's Fund Ins. Co., 61 F.2d 27 (7th Cir.1932) (in Indiana, order appointing receiver of individual at suit of unsecured simple contract creditor was void for lack of jurisdiction in court to make appointment), *cert. denied*, 288 U.S. 602, 53 S.Ct. 387, 77 L.Ed. 978 (1933); State *ex rel.* Makar v. St. Joseph County Circuit Court, 242 Ind. 339, 179 N.E.2d 285 (1962) (in action for foreclosure of mortgage upon specific property, not including business as going concern, court may not appoint general receiver to take charge of all assets of individual proprietor and operate his businesses for benefit of general unsecured creditors, in absence of extraordinary circumstances, which did not exist); Frigidraft, Inc. v. Michel, 198 Md. 509, 511, 84 A.2d 695, 696 (1951) ("To allow [the appointment of a receiver] to be done at the behest of an unsecured creditor, who may never be able to get a judgment in a court of law is an improper assumption of power by the equity court.").

43. *See* Whisenhunt v. Park Lane Corp., 418 F.Supp. 1096, 1098 (N.D.Tex.1976) (discussing the "trust fund doctrine" exception, which allows unsecured creditors to obtain appointment of receiver to prevent misappropriation and a fraud on creditors); Mathias v. Segaloff, 187 Md. 690, 51 A.2d 654 (1947) (unsecured creditor cannot file a bill for the appointment of a receiver, but where defendant assents, thereby giving court the power to appoint a receiver, de-

fendant cannot thereafter restrict the court in power given to that receiver).

44. Griner v. Starling, 223 Ga. 282, 154 S.E.2d 604 (1967) (petition by unsecured creditor, whose claim represented more than one-third of debtors' unsecured debts, alleging that debtors were insolvent and were permitting assets of business to be squandered and physical assets to deteriorate from lack of proper upkeep, stated cause of action entitling creditor to appointment of receiver under statutes governing insolvent traders).

45. Santibanez, 105 F.3d 234; Security Pacific Mortgage and Real Estate Servs., Inc. v. Republic of the Philippines, 962 F.2d 204 (2d Cir.1992); Consolidated Rail Corp. v. Fore River Ry. Co., 861 F.2d 322 (1st Cir.1988); Guy v. Citizens Fidelity Bank & Trust Co., 429 F.2d 828 (6th Cir.1970); Tanzer v. Huffines, 408 F.2d 42 (3d Cir. 1969); Mintzer v. Arthur L. Wright & Co., 263 F.2d 823 (3d Cir.1959); Lias v. United States, 196 F.2d 90 (4th Cir.1952); Connolly v. Gishwiller, 162 F.2d 428 (7th Cir.) *cert. denied*, 332 U.S. 825, 68 S.Ct. 166, 92 L.Ed. 400 (1947); Ledbetter v. Farmers Bank & Trust Co., 142 F.2d 147 (4th Cir.) *cert. denied*, 323 U.S. 719, 65 S.Ct. 48, 89 L.Ed. 578 (1944); Skirvin v. Mesta, 141 F.2d 668 (10th Cir.1944).

46. Courts have discretion to evaluate the form and the amount of evidence required for a motion requesting the appointment of a receiver. For example, courts have held that further argument for the appointment of a receiver is a privilege which judges need not grant, and that if no important allegations are controverted in

degrees[47] in ordering the appointment of a receiver.[48] The grounds for granting a receiver may be likened to a demonstration of irreparable harm and a likelihood of success on the merits required for grant of a preliminary injunction.[49] Some courts, in fact, specifically require such a showing by the moving party before considering the appointment.[50]

The application of those standards in the receivership context requires a party to show irreparable harm by demonstrating clearly a need to protect his or her interests in a property.[51] Thus, courts generally examine the validity of the plaintiff's claim; immediate danger to the property; the adequacy of legal remedies;[52] the availability of less drastic, yet sufficient, remedies; the probability that the receiver will be more beneficial than harmful to the property; whether the appointment will

the request for a receiver, the motion does not need to be verified with affidavits. *See* United States v. O'Connor, 291 F.2d 520 (2d Cir.1961) and Haase v. Chapman, 308 F.Supp. 399 (W.D.Mo.1969).

47. Meyer Jewelry Co. v. Meyer Holdings, Inc., 906 F.Supp. 428, 432–34 (E.D.Mich.1995); New York Life Ins. Co. v. Watt West Inv. Corp., 755 F.Supp. 287, 292–93 (E.D.Cal.1991).

48. *See* Aviation Supply Corp. v. R.S.B.I. Aerospace, Inc., 999 F.2d 314, 316–17 (8th Cir.1993) (Court will consider, among other things, potential fraud, imminent danger of property loss, lack of alternative remedies, potential benefits of receiver's appointment.); Consolidated Rail Corp. v. Fore River Ry., 861 F.2d 322, 326–27 (1st Cir.1988) (property in danger of being imminently squandered); Select Creations, Inc. v. Paliafito Am., Inc., 828 F.Supp. 1301, 1367 (E.D.Wis.1992) (discussing factors in appointing receivers for assets attached prior to judgment).

49. New York Life Ins. Co. v. Watt West Inv. Corp., 755 F.Supp. 287, 292–93 (E.D.Cal.1991); Commodity Futures Trading Comm'n v. Comvest Trading Corp., 481 F.Supp. 438, 441 (D.Mass.1979).

50. *See* New York Life Ins. Co., 755 F.Supp. at 292–93 (plaintiff demonstrated likelihood of success and imminent threat of harm); Commodity Futures Trading Comm'n, 481 F.Supp. at 441 (plaintiff was required to clearly demonstrate extraordinary necessity for receiver).

51. Kelleam v. Maryland Cas. Co. of Baltimore, Maryland, 312 U.S. 377, 61 S.Ct. 595, 85 L.Ed. 899 (1941); Gordon v. Washington, 295 U.S. 30, 39, 55 S.Ct. 584, 589, 79 L.Ed. 1282 (1935); Aviation Supply

Corp., 999 F.2d 314; Republic of the Philippines v. New York Land Co., 852 F.2d 33 (2d Cir.1988); Citibank v. Nyland (CF8) Ltd., 839 F.2d 93, 97 (2d Cir.1988); Mintzer, 263 F.2d 823; Macon Lumber Co. v. Bishop, 229 F.2d 305 (6th Cir.1956); Tucker v. Baker, 214 F.2d 627, 631 (5th Cir.1954); Connolly, 162 F.2d 428; Skirvin, 141 F.2d at 673; Rubert Hermanos, Inc. v. People of Puerto Rico, 118 F.2d 752 (1st Cir.1941) (circuit court's reversal of the appointment of a receiver reversed), 315 U.S. 637, 62 S.Ct. 771, 86 L.Ed. 1081 (1942); Meyer Jewelry Co., 906 F.Supp. 428; Zinke–Smith, Inc. v. Marlowe, 323 F.Supp. 1151 (D.Vi. 1971); Hasse, 308 F.Supp. 399 (W.D.Mo. 1969); Tanzer, 287 F.Supp. 273; Wickes v. Belgian Am. Educ. Foundation, Inc., 266 F.Supp. 38 (S.D.N.Y.1967); Tcherepnin v. Franz, 277 F.Supp. 472 (N.D.Ill.1966); Youngstown Sheet & Tube Co. v. Patterson–Emerson–Comstock of Indiana, 227 F.Supp. 208 (N.D.Ind.1963); Margolis v. Franks, 138 F.Supp. 9 (S.D.N.Y.1956).

52. Leighton v. One William St. Fund, Inc., 343 F.2d 565 (2d Cir.1965) (money damages sufficient compensation); Macon Lumber Co. v. Bishop, 229 F.2d 305 (6th Cir.1956) (imminent danger of loss to stockholders and no adequate remedy at law); Meyer Jewelry Co., 906 F.Supp. 428 (no receivership where money damages were easily calculated); *See also* View Crest Garden Apartments, Inc. v. United States, 281 F.2d 844 (9th Cir.), *cert. denied,* 364 U.S. 902, 81 S.Ct. 235, 5 L.Ed.2d 195 (1960) (receiver appointed to collect rents, issues and profits where security is inadequate or mortgagee is insolvent); *Compare* Brown, Bonnell & Co. v. Lake Superior Iron Co., 134 U.S. 530, 10 S.Ct. 604, 33 L.Ed. 1021 (1890).

actually benefit the person seeking it[53] and whether the plaintiff would suffer more harm from the denial of the appointment than the defendant would suffer if it were granted.[54] Courts also consider individual circumstances. For example, courts have appointed receivers in response to a defendant's lack of cooperation during discovery,[55] a defendant's refusal to answer questions relating to relevant business operations,[56] an immediate threat that the property may be lost, hidden, harmed, squandered, or diminished in value[57] and the defendant's fraudulent acts.[58]

(3) Notice and Hearing

Although neither FRCP 66 nor any other statute requires notice to all affected parties of the application for an appointment, courts generally require such notice.[59] Courts, however, may make emergency appointments without notice.[60] In *Fahey v. Mallonee,*[61] the practice of emergency ex parte appointments survived constitutional challenge. The Supreme Court found that ex parte procedures for appointing a conservator or

53. *See* Aviation Supply Corp. v. R.S.B.I. Aerospace, Inc., 999 F.2d 314 (8th Cir.1993); Consolidated Rail Corp., 861 F.2d 322; Select Creations, Inc., 828 F.Supp. 1301.

54. Mintzer, 263 F.2d at 825 ("showing that harm accruing to plaintiff by denial clearly outbalance[s] harm to defendant upon granting the appointment" warrants receivership); Meyer Jewelry Co., 906 F.Supp. 428 (receivership would do more harm than good to solvent company); Haase, 308 F.Supp. 399; *See also* Adelman v. CGS Scientific Corp., 332 F.Supp. 137 (E.D.Pa.1971).

55. *See* Aviation Supply Corp., 999 F.2d at 317 (court appointed receiver after defendant's willful and deceitful nondisclosure).

56. *See* United States v. Ianniello, 824 F.2d 203, 208 (2d Cir.1987) (in appointing receiver to prevent embezzlement, court could consider defendants' refusal to answer questions regarding business operations).

57. Gordon v. Washington, 295 U.S. 30, 39, 55 S.Ct. 584, 589, 79 L.Ed. 1282 (1935) (receivership "should be resorted to only on a plain showing of some threatened loss or injury to the property, which the receivership would avoid"); Santibanez v. Wier McMahon & Co., 105 F.3d 234 (5th Cir. 1997) (imminent threat that defendant would transfer assets); Consolidated Rail Corp., 861 F.2d 322 (threat that property would be immediately squandered); Tanzer v. Huffines, 408 F.2d 42 (3d Cir.1969);

(finding that violations of federal securities laws threatened the company).

58. *See, e.g.,* Burnrite Coal Briquette Co. v. Riggs, 274 U.S. 208, 47 S.Ct. 578, 71 L.Ed. 1002 (1927) ("gross fraud and mismanagement" of corporation officers); Santibaniz, 105 F.3d 234 (fraudulent ERISA violations, concealment of assets and fraudulent conveyances); Aviation Supply Corp., 999 F.2d 314 (transfers of interests to family members pending writ of execution and defendant's refusal to answer questions); Consolidated Rail Corp., 861 F.2d 322 (intermingling of company and officer funds); *But compare*: Tcherepnin v. Franz, 277 F.Supp. 472 (N.D.Ill.1966) (general allegations that defendants were corrupt or inefficient did not warrant receivership); Ivey v. Housing Foundation of America, 73 F.Supp. 201 (M.D.Pa.1947) (fraudulent false representations insufficient to warrant receivership).

59. Britton v. Green, 325 F.2d 377 (10th Cir.1963); Argonaut Ins. Co. v. Halvanon Ins. Co., 545 F.Supp. 21 (S.D.N.Y.1981); Haase, 308 F.Supp. 399; Ford v. Taylor, 137 Fed. 149 (D.Nev.1905).

60. Arkansas Louisiana Gas Co. v. Kroeger, 303 F.2d 129 (5th Cir.), *cert. denied,* 371 U.S. 887, 83 S.Ct. 183, 9 L.Ed.2d 121 (1962); 1 Clark, Receivers, § 82 (3d ed. 1959). *See also* Local Court Rule 125 (b) and (c) for the Northern District of California.

61. 332 U.S. 245, 67 S.Ct. 1552, 91 L.Ed. 2030 (1947).

receiver under the Federal Home Loan Bank Board regulations did not violate constitutional procedural due process.

In general, a temporary restraining order[62] will often obviate the need for emergency appointment of a receiver, by maintaining existing conditions pending a hearing.[63]

In deciding whether to appoint a receiver, a court may, at its discretion, consider testimony at a hearing in addition to the moving papers, answers, affidavits or declarations.[64] The hearing on a motion for appointment of receiver may be held in chambers.[65]

(4) Retaining Jurisdiction for All Creditors

FRCP 66 provides that "[a]n action wherein a receiver has been appointed shall not be dismissed except by order of the court." Once a court has taken jurisdiction over a debtor's property by appointing a receiver at the request of one creditor, for example, it may retain jurisdiction for the benefit of other creditors, even though the primary claim has been satisfied.[66] In consolidated actions in which a receiver has been appointed for only one of the actions,[67] a court will retain jurisdiction.

(5) Bond

State statutes generally require the posting of a bond sufficient to indemnify the litigants from possible breaches of the receiver's official duties. Some statutes require the receiver to post the bond.[68] Other

---

62. *See supra* § 13.3.

63. Marion Mtg. Co. v. Edmunds, 64 F.2d 248 (5th Cir.1933). *See also* Maxwell v. Enterprise Wall Paper Mfg. Co., 131 F.2d 400 (3d Cir.1942); Cabaniss v. Reco Min. Co., 116 Fed. 318 (5th Cir.1902); North American Land & Timber Co. v. Watkins, 109 Fed. 101 (5th Cir.1901).

64. Bookout v. First Nat'l Mortgage & Discount Co., Inc., 514 F.2d 757, 758 (5th Cir.1975) ("The appointment of a receiver, otherwise proper, is not to be defeated for lack of sworn pleading or the absence of a full evidentiary hearing."); United States v. O'Connor, 291 F.2d 520 (2d Cir.1961) (a judge may or may not grant further argument on a request for a receiver); Haase, 308 F.Supp. 399 (if no important facts are controverted, the appointment of a receiver may be granted as a summary judgment).

65. FRCP 77(a), (b); Horn v. Pere Marquette R. Co., 151 Fed. 626 (E.D.Mich. 1907).

66. Brown v. Lake Superior Iron Co., 134 U.S. 530, 10 S.Ct. 604, 33 L.Ed. 1021 (1890); Consolidated Rail Corp. v. Fore River Ry., 861 F.2d 322 (1st Cir.1988); Guy v.

Citizens Fidelity Bank & Trust Co., 429 F.2d 828 (6th Cir.1970).

67. This issue was addressed in *United States v. Altman,* 750 F.2d 684 (8th Cir. 1984), when several foreclosure actions were consolidated with other litigation and collateral receiverships. The parties to the foreclosure reached an agreement, but the district court denied approval of the settlement because the receiver had not joined in the agreement. The court of appeals reversed that decision, holding that the consolidation of several actions, including one involving a receiver, does not make that receiver a receiver for the entire consolidated action. The court of appeals found that in order for the settlement to be valid, it was not necessary for the receiver to agree to it, nor for the court to approve it since the receiver had not been appointed in the foreclosure action.

68. Iowa Code Ann. § 657A.6 (West 1987); Minn. Stat. Ann. § 576.01 (West 1988 & Supp. 1997); R.I. Gen. Laws § 34–44–6 (1995); Wash. Rev. Code Ann. § 35A.15.060 (West 1990). Other statutes leave the receiver's bond in the court's dis-,

statutes place this burden on the applicant requesting the receiver.[69] However, courts will not require posting the bond if it would further deplete the property, unless the bond is necessary to protect the interest in the property.[70] In the absence of such statutory requirement, a district court may, in its discretion, order a receiver to post a bond and may determine the terms and conditions of that bond.[71]

State statutes may also require the posting of a plaintiff's bond. In the absence of statutory requirements, a court may, in its discretion, require the party requesting the appointment to post a plaintiff's bond.[72]

(6) Duration, Modification and Termination

The appointment of a receiver remains in effect until the termination of the principal action or until the court discharges the receiver of his or her duties. The court may vacate the receivership order,[73] dismiss the receivership and restore the property to the debtor if the debtor offers to discharge his or her debts,[74] or create a temporary receivership which will terminate if the plaintiff fails to pursue the primary action in a timely fashion.[75]

A court may terminate or modify a receivership at any point in the proceedings.[76] If the reason or necessity for the receivership no longer exists, the appointment automatically terminates by the terms of the order appointing the receiver, as when the receiver disposes of the property according to his or her duties.[77] Once the receivership is terminated, a court loses its jurisdiction over the property[78] and other

---

cretion. Ind. Code Ann. § 23–1–47–3 (Michie 1995); N.M. Stat. Ann. § 44–8–6 (Michie 1997).

69. See La. Rev. Stat. Ann. § 12:151 (West 1994).

70. SEC v. Universal Fin., 760 F.2d 1034, 1039 (9th Cir.1985) (no abuse of discretion for failure to require bond that would further diminish value of receivership estate).

71. See FTC v. World Wide Factors, Ltd., 882 F.2d 344, 348 (9th Cir.1989) (special master rendered receiver, and district court instructed to direct receiver to post bond); Ferguson v. Tabah, 288 F.2d 665 (2d Cir.1961).

72. Universal Fin., 760 F.2d 1034; Ferguson, 288 F.2d 665; Bowler v. Leonard, 70 Nev. 370, 269 P.2d 833 (1954); Benton v. Turk, 188 Ga. 710, 4 S.E.2d 580 (1939).

73. United States v. Amodeo, 44 F.3d 141, 146 (2d Cir.1995) ("The discharge of a receiver is ordinarily a matter within the discretion of the district court."); Skirvin v. Mesta, 141 F.2d 668 (10th Cir.1944).

74. Consolidated Rail Corp. v. Fore River Ry. Co., 861 F.2d 322 (1st Cir.1988); In re Missouri Pac. R. Co., 93 F.Supp. 832

(E.D.Mo.1950), aff'd sub nom. State of Texas v. Group of Institutional Investors, 191 F.2d 265 (8th Cir.1951), cert. denied, 342 U.S. 904, 72 S.Ct. 293, 96 L.Ed. 676 (1952), and Chemical Bank & Trust Co. v. Group of Institutional Investors, 343 U.S. 929, 72 S.Ct. 757, 96 L.Ed. 1339 (1952).

75. Levin v. Ruby Trading Corp., 352 F.2d 508 (2d Cir.1965) (plaintiff given four months to bring his action to trial).

76. See Amodeo, 44 F.3d 141 (discharge of receiver is within discretion of district court; State ex rel. Sullivan v. Reynolds, 209 Mo. 161, 107 S.W. 487 (1907).

77. Federal Sav. & Loan Ins. Corp. v. PSL Realty Co., 630 F.2d 515, 521 (7th Cir.1980), cert. denied sub nom. Granite Inv. Co. v. Federal Sav. & Loan Ins. Corp., 452 U.S. 961, 101 S.Ct. 3109, 69 L.Ed.2d 971 (1981); Strategis Asset Valuation & Management, Inc. v. Pacific Mut. Life Ins. Co., 805 F.Supp. 1544, 1553 (D.Colo.1992); See also Amodeo, 44 F.3d at 146; In re Still, 963 F.2d 75, 77 (5th Cir.1992).

78. Tanzer v. Huffines, 315 F.Supp. 1140 (D.Del.1970) (court will not hear motions regarding a receivership that has been terminated).

courts are free to decide controversies involving the property. In the alternative, to satisfy outstanding court orders[79] or creditor claims,[80] the court may at its discretion discharge the receiver before the disposition of the property and retain jurisdiction and supervision over the property. Even after the termination of a receivership, however, the court retains personal jurisdiction over the receiver to hear claims of the receiver's improper conduct beyond the scope of his or her duties.[81]

(g) Types of Receiverships

(1) Primary and Ancillary Receiverships

A party may seek a receiver on a primary or ancillary basis. The term primary receivership describes the appointment of the original receiver in an action. The term ancillary receivership refers to a receiver appointed after the primary receiver. An ancillary receiver assists the primary receiver in maintaining or controlling the disputed property. Ancillary receivers most significantly play a role when the assets in dispute are located within the jurisdiction of another district court.[82] Although ancillary receivers are appointed independently of primary receivers,[83] the receiverships generally exist in harmony with each other to promote efficient management of the property.

If the primary receiver files for an ancillary receiver to acquire control over property located in another district, that proceeding may be termed "ancillary" to the action in which the primary receiver was appointed.[84] The primary receiver obtains such jurisdiction by filing copies of the complaint and order of appointment with other districts within 10 days of the appointment.[85]

Under 28 U.S.C.A. § 754 receivers appointed in federal court now have the capacity to sue in any district court without ancillary appointment. Thus, ancillary receivers are no longer required in federal court in order to obtain jurisdiction over property in other districts and to bring suit in a forum outside the jurisdiction of the appointing district court.

(2) Consent Receiverships and Reorganization

Before 1933, debtors and mortgagees or other creditors used consent receiverships as a cooperative means to effectuate reorganizations. In

---

79. Wabash R.R. Co. v. Adelbert College of the W. Reserve Univ., 208 U.S. 38, 28 S.Ct. 182, 52 L.Ed. 379 (1908); Tanzer, 315 F.Supp. 1140.

80. Brown, Bonnell & Co. v. Lake Superior Iron Co., 134 U.S. 530, 10 S.Ct. 604, 33 L.Ed. 1021 (1890).

81. Federal Sav. & Loan Ins. Corp., 630 F.2d at 521 (in personam action against receiver could be brought after termination of receivership).

82. Great Western Min. & Mfg. Co. v. Harris, 198 U.S. 561, 25 S.Ct. 770, 49 L.Ed. 1163 (1905).

83. Paxton v. McCartney, 103 Ind.App. 697, 6 N.E.2d 719 (1937).

84. American Freedom Train Found. v. Spurney, 747 F.2d 1069, 1073 (1st Cir. 1984); Haile v. Henderson Nat'l Bank, 657 F.2d 816, 822 (6th Cir.1981) (action in which receiver is appointed is primary suit and any suit brought by receiver is ancillary), cert. denied sub nom. First Nat'l Bank v. Haile, 455 U.S. 949, 102 S.Ct. 1450, 71 L.Ed.2d 663 (1982).

85. 28 U.S.C.A. § 754 (West 1993).

1933, Congress amended the Bankruptcy Act by adding Section 77, allowing for the reorganization of railways.[86] In 1934, Congress added Section 77(b), ultimately replaced in 1938 by Chapter X of the Bankruptcy Act and in 1978 by Chapter XI of the Bankruptcy Act, authorizing the reorganization of other corporations. The use of equity receiverships in corporate reorganizations has been virtually replaced by these statutes.

(3) Equitable Receiverships and Bankruptcy

Under 11 U.S.C.A. § 105, receivers may not be appointed in lieu of trustees in bankruptcy cases.[87] In limited circumstances, however, receivers may become involved in bankruptcy proceedings. For example, once a debtor files for bankruptcy, the trustee or creditor may commence a foreclosure proceeding in federal court or continue one removed from state court. While the foreclosure action is pending, the court may appoint a receiver for the property.[88] Because the involvement of this receiver is limited to the foreclosure, the appointment does not violate the prohibition on the use of receivers in bankruptcy proceedings. The appointment of such a receiver lasts only for the duration of the foreclosure proceeding.

A receiver may also become involved in a bankruptcy proceeding when a corporation files for reorganization under chapter 11 of the Bankruptcy Code, pending a governmental civil enforcement proceeding.[89] Under the Bankruptcy Code's automatic stay provision, 11 U.S.C.A. § 362 (b)(5), a bankruptcy petition does not stay the enforcement of a nonmonetary judgment obtained by a governmental unit exercising its police or regulatory powers. Thus, courts have held that receivers appointed in civil enforcement proceedings by governmental agencies are exempt from Section 362.[90]

Courts have also held that debtors subject to federal receiverships have no absolute right to file bankruptcy petitions without permission from the district court.[91] When a court so precludes a bankruptcy liquidation, it must expressly state its reasons.[92] In *United States v. Royal Business Funds Corp.*,[93] the Second Circuit stayed bankruptcy

---

86. 11 U.S.C.A. § 105 (West 1993 & Supp. 1997).

87. The Bankruptcy Code has ample provision for the appointment of a trustee when needed and appointment of a receiver would simply circumvent the established procedures.

88. *In re* Memorial Estates, 797 F.2d 516 (7th Cir.1986); *In re* Cassidy Land & Cattle Co., 69 B.R. 649 (D.Neb.1987), *aff'd*, 836 F.2d 1130 (8th Cir.1988).

89. SEC v. First Fin. Group of Tex., 645 F.2d 429 (5th Cir.1981) (appointment of receiver in continuing injunctive enforcement proceeding brought by the Securities and Exchange Commission against securities dealer against which involuntary bankruptcy proceeding had been instituted was proper and was not precluded).

90. First Fin. Group of Tex., 645 F.2d 429; Commodity Futures Trading Comm'n v. F.I.T.C., Inc., 52 B.R. 935 (N.D.Cal.1985) (filing of bankruptcy proceedings under chapter 11 by corporation's president did not deprive district court of jurisdiction in receivership proceedings brought by the Commodity Futures Trading Commission).

91. United States v. Royal Business Funds Corp., 724 F.2d 12, 15–16 (2d Cir. 1983).

92. SEC v. Lincoln Thrift Ass'n, 577 F.2d 600, 609 (9th Cir.1978).

93. 724 F.2d 12 (2d Cir.1983).

proceedings initiated without the district court's consent after the debtor had agreed in writing to a receivership and received loans from the Small Business Administration based on the appointment.[94]

When a liquidation under a federal equity receiver is well under way or nearly complete and creditors would not benefit from bankruptcy proceedings, courts have disallowed initiation of chapter 11 proceedings.[95] Generally, however, appellate courts have preferred bankruptcy court to receiverships for liquidation proceedings.[96]

(h) Jurisdiction over Property After Appointment of Receiver

A receiver's jurisdiction over property is governed by 28 U.S.C.A. § 754. Section 754 grants the receiver exclusive jurisdiction and control over property located within the appointing court's district. The receiver may also exercise control over properties located in other districts if he or she complies with the following procedures.

(1) Property Located in Different Districts

To exercise control over property located in another district, a federal receiver must file copies of the complaint and the order of appointment in that district within 10 days of entry of the appointment order.[97] Failure to file complaints in a timely fashion normally results in divestment of jurisdiction in those districts,[98] although some courts have been flexible.[99]

Once a receiver controls certain property within a district, state and federal courts sitting in that district may not exercise jurisdiction over those properties or the receiver,[100] nor may they grant leave to sue the receiver. Furthermore, the rights of creditors to the property subject to the receivership are fixed as of the moment of the entry of appointment, thus continuing all valid, preexisting liens.[101] Until the receivership is terminated, the appointing court must determine all rights to the

---

94. *Id.*

95. Lincoln Thrift Ass'n, 577 F.2d 600; SEC v. Bartlett, 422 F.2d 475 (8th Cir. 1970); Esbitt v. Dutch–American Mercantile Corp., 335 F.2d 141 (2d Cir.1964).

96. *See* SEC v. American Bd. of Trade, 830 F.2d 431 (2d Cir.1987); Bartlett, 422 F.2d 475; SEC v. S & P Nat'l Corp., 360 F.2d 741 (2d Cir.1966); *See also* Los Angeles Trust Deed & Mortgage Exch. v. SEC, 285 F.2d 162 (9th Cir.1960), *cert. denied,* 366 U.S. 919, 81 S.Ct. 1095, 6 L.Ed.2d 241 (1961).

97. 28 U.S.C.A. § 754 (West 1993).

98. *Id.*

99. SEC v. Equity Service Corp., 632 F.2d 1092 (3d Cir.1980) (receiver who has

failed to file copies of complaint and order of appointment within 10 days after entry of order of appointment and has been divested of jurisdiction and control of property may reassume jurisdiction by later filing, as long as rights of others have not been prejudiced during intervening period).

100. Guaranty Trust Co. of New York v. Chicago, M. & St. P. Ry. Co., 13 F.2d 129 (D.Wash.1926); 1 Clark, Receivers § 280(a) (3d ed. 1959); Payne, *The General Administration of Equity Receiverships of Corporations* 31 Yale L.J. 685, 686 (1922).

101. Modart, Inc. v. Penrose Indus. Corp., 293 F.Supp. 1116, 1120 (E.D.Pa. 1967), *aff'd per curiam,* 404 F.2d 72 (3d Cir.1968); 1 Clark, Law of Receivers § 280(a) (3d ed. 1959).

property. A creditor may prosecute an action to judgment but must present that judgment to the receivership court for payment. The judgment results in no preference or right to execution against the receivership assets.[102] 28 U.S.C.A. § 1692 further reinforces the appointing court's exclusive jurisdiction by providing that "process may issue and be executed in any such district as if the property lay wholly within one district, but orders affecting the property shall be entered of record in each of such districts."[103]

(2) Conflicts Among Courts

Conflicts of jurisdiction may arise between state and federal courts when competing suits involving receiverships concern the same property or defendant. In *Harkin v. Brundage*,[104] the Supreme Court articulated the test now generally used to resolve such conflicts. According to this test, if two or more actions involving receiverships substantially concern the same controversy, the court in which the bill was first filed has jurisdiction over the property since filing the bill conferred constructive possession upon the court.[105] This is true even if another court first takes possession of the property through a receiver.[106] If the actions involve substantially different controversies, the first court to acquire possession will have jurisdiction.[107]

The first court to acquire possession will not have jurisdiction if, for example, the defendant in the first action delays that court from taking possession of the property to allow the subsequent court to acquire the property; the court in the first action still has jurisdiction.[108] Also, if the defendant has used the receivership to continue fraudulent practices, the court without possession assumes jurisdiction.[109] In addition, for the liquidation of certain kinds of debtors, such as insurance companies and

---

102. Grocery Supply v. McKinley Park Servs., 128 F.Supp. 694, 15 Alaska 469 (D.Alaska 1955).

103. 28 U.S.C.A. § 1692 (West 1994).

104. 276 U.S. 36, 43, 48 S.Ct. 268, 271, 72 L.Ed. 457 (1928):

As between two courts of concurrent and coordinate jurisdiction, the court which first obtains jurisdiction and constructive possession of property by filing the bill is entitled to retain it without interference and cannot be deprived of its right to do so, because it may not have obtained prior physical possession by its receiver of the property in dispute; but where the jurisdiction is not the same or concurrent, and the subject-matter in litigation in the one is not within the cognizance of the other, or there is no constructive possession of the property in dispute by the filing of a bill, it is the date of the actual possession of the receiver that determines the priority of jurisdiction.

105. *Id.*

106. United States v. Goldberg, 349 F.2d 633 (3d Cir.1965); Farmers' Loan & Trust Co. v. Lake Street Elevated Railroad Co., 177 U.S. 51, 61, 20 S.Ct. 564, 568, 44 L.Ed. 667 (1900); Lee v. Edmunds, 66 F.2d 122 (5th Cir.1933); McKinney v. Landon, 209 F.300 (8th Cir.1913); Lewis v. American Naval Stores Co., 119 Fed. 391 (E.D.La. 1902); *Cf.* Wiswall v. Sampson, 55 U.S. (14 How.) 52, 14 L.Ed. 322 (1852).

107. Harkin v. Brundage, 276 U.S. 36, 48 S.Ct. 268, 72 L.Ed. 457 (1928); Empire Trust Co. v. Brooks, 232 Fed. 641 (5th Cir.1916).

108. Harkin, 276 U.S. 36, 48 S.Ct. 268, 72 L.Ed. 457.

109. *Id.*; SEC v. Wencke, 577 F.2d 619 (9th Cir.1978); First Nat'l Bank v. Horuff, 65 F.2d 318 (5th Cir.1933).

building and loan associations, courts adhere to special statutory schemes.[110] Depending upon the application of these principles to its circumstances, a federal court must either relinquish jurisdiction or, if necessary, enjoin interfering proceedings in state or other federal courts.[111] Once a court relinquishes jurisdiction, other courts may decide any outstanding issues involving the property.[112]

A conflict of jurisdiction also arises between federal courts if several motions to appoint a receiver for the same debtor are filed in more than one court. In such situations, the court in which the first motion for receivership is filed may carry on as the primary court, if the plaintiff establishes the need for appointment of a receiver.

(3) Broad Supervisory Powers

Procedures for the administration of the receivership property are left to the discretion of the district court.[113] The standard for review of a district court's administration of a receivership is abuse of that discretion.[114]

The district court has discretion to use summary procedures, as opposed to plenary proceedings under the FRCP,[115] for the protection of receivership assets.[116] The Ninth Circuit, for example, has held it proper for the district court to hold summary proceedings in which the court determined only who was entitled to interim possession of certain funds where the creditor had ample notice and opportunity to contest the receiver's challenge.[117] In that same decision, the court held that no right

---

110. *See, e.g.,* Pennsylvania v. Williams, 294 U.S. 176, 55 S.Ct. 380, 79 L.Ed. 841 (1935).

111. *See* 28 U.S.C.A. § 2283 (West 1994); Princess Lida v. Thompson, 305 U.S. 456, 59 S.Ct. 275, 83 L.Ed. 285 (1939); Kline v. Burke Constr. Co., 260 U.S. 226, 43 S.Ct. 79, 67 L.Ed. 226 (1922); Moran v. Sturges, 154 U.S. 256, 14 S.Ct. 1019, 38 L.Ed. 981 (1894) (admiralty); *In re* Mt. Forest Fur Farms of Am., 103 F.2d 69 (6th Cir.), *cert. denied,* 308 U.S. 583, 60 S.Ct. 105, 84 L.Ed. 488 (1939) (bankruptcy). *See also* Green v. Porter, 123 Fed. 351 (D.Mass. 1903) (patents).

112. *See* Palmer v. Texas, 212 U.S. 118, 29 S.Ct. 230, 53 L.Ed. 435 (1909); Shields v. Coleman, 157 U.S. 168, 15 S.Ct. 570, 39 L.Ed. 660 (1895).

113. *See* SEC v. Hardy, 803 F.2d 1034 (9th Cir.1986); SEC v. Safety Finance Serv., Inc., 674 F.2d 368 (5th Cir.1982); SEC v. An–Car Oil Co., 604 F.2d 114 (1st Cir. 1979).

114. Matter of McGaughey, 24 F.3d 904 (7th Cir.1994); Hardy, 803 F.2d 1034; Lyman v. Spain, 774 F.2d 495 (D.C.Cir.1985).

115. *See* Central Republic Bank & Trust Co. v. Caldwell, 58 F.2d 721, 731 (8th Cir.1932):

The main characteristic differences between a summary proceeding and a plenary suit are: The former is based upon a petition, and proceeds without formal pleadings; the latter proceeds upon formal pleadings. In the former, the necessary parties are cited in by order to show cause; in the latter, formal summons brings in the parties other than the plaintiff. In the former, short time notice of hearing is fixed by the court; in the latter, time for pleading and hearing is fixed by statute or rule of court. In the former, the hearing is quite generally upon affidavits; in the latter, examination of witnesses is the usual method. In the former, the hearing is sometimes ex parte; in the latter, a full hearing is had.

116. Hardy, 803 F.2d 1034; F.D.I.C. v. Bernstein, 786 F.Supp. 170 (E.D.N.Y.1992).

117. United States v. Arizona Fuels Corp., 739 F.2d 455 (9th Cir.1984).

to a jury trial exists in equitable proceedings over the administration of receiverships, even if that right would have attached had the receiver instituted a plenary proceeding against the creditor.[118] The use of summary procedures in situations involving investors' claims and filing deadlines was upheld in *SEC v. Hardy*.[119] Summary proceedings may not be used, however, to determine the ultimate merits of a party's claims.[120]

(i) Suits by Receiver

Receivers may sue in their appointing courts for claims that the defendant failed to bring before the receivership appointment[121] or on any claim arising during the receivership[122] without independent jurisdictional grounds.[123] Jurisdiction of the appointing court over actions brought by the receiver is based upon the court's jurisdiction over the underlying action in which the receiver was appointed.[124] This ancillary jurisdiction is probably limited to suits brought by the receiver in the appointing court.[125] For a receiver to bring a suit in another federal court, the receiver probably needs to establish independent jurisdictional grounds.

A receiver's capacity to sue depends on the law of the state in which the federal court is located.[126] A receiver has no more capacity to sue than the person or entity whose assets are subject to the receivership. Thus, when a court appoints a receiver to represent a corporation, the receiver may only assert the claims the corporation could have asserted.[127]

118. *Id.*

119. Hardy, 803 F.2d 1034.

120. *See* Arizona Fuels Corp., 739 F.2d 455; American Brake Shoe & Foundry Co. v. New York Ry. Co., 10 F.2d 920 (2d Cir. 1926); Dold Packing Co. v. Doermann, 293 Fed. 315 (8th Cir.1923).

121. White v. Ewing, 159 U.S. 36, 15 S.Ct. 1018, 40 L.Ed. 67 (1895).

122. Klages v. Cohen, 146 F.2d 641 (2d Cir.1945); Wilson v. Kansas City Power & Light Co., 300 Fed. 185 (W.D.Mo.1925).

123. American Freedom Train Found. v. Spurney, 747 F.2d 1069 (1st Cir.1984); Haile v. Henderson Nat'l Bank, 657 F.2d 816 (6th Cir.1981), *cert. denied,* 455 U.S. 949, 102 S.Ct. 1450, 71 L.Ed.2d 663 (1982); United States v. Franklin Nat'l Bank, 512 F.2d 245 (2d Cir.1975); Tcherepnin v. Franz, 439 F.Supp. 1340 (N.D.Ill.1977).

124. Pope v. Louisville, New Albany & Chicago Ry. Co., 173 U.S. 573, 577, 19 S.Ct. 500, 501, 43 L.Ed. 814 (1899), *cited in* American Freedom Train Foundation, 747 F.2d at 1073; O'Leary v. Moyer's Landfill, Inc., 677 F.Supp. 807, 816 (E.D.Pa.1988).

125. Franklin National Bank, 512 F.2d 245 (quoting 12 Charles Alan Wright & Arthur R. Miller, Federal Practice and Procedure § 2984, at 31, § 2985, at 45 (1973) for the proposition that "[i]t is uncertain whether ancillary jurisdiction only exists in the appointing court, although this probably is the case"); Gableman v. Peoria, D. & E. Ry. Co., 179 U.S. 335, 21 S.Ct. 171, 45 L.Ed. 220 (1900); Texas & Pacific Ry. Co. v. Cox, 145 U.S. 593, 12 S.Ct. 905, 36 L.Ed. 829 (1892); *see also* Mitchell v. Maurer, 293 U.S. 237, 55 S.Ct. 162, 79 L.Ed. 338 (1934); Capital Nat'l Bank v. First Nat'l Bank, 172 U.S. 425, 19 S.Ct. 202, 43 L.Ed. 502 (1899).

126. *See* FRCP 17(b), 66; Meyers v. Moody, 693 F.2d 1196, 1206 (5th Cir.1982), *cert. denied,* 464 U.S. 920, 104 S.Ct. 287, 78 L.Ed.2d 264 (1983); O'Neal v. General Motors Corp., 841 F.Supp. 391, 398 (M.D.Fla. 1993).

127. Hunt v. American Bank & Trust Co. of Baton Rouge, 606 F.Supp. 1348 (N.D.Ala.1985), *aff'd,* 783 F.2d 1011 (11th Cir.1986).

This issue is especially prevalent in cases of securities law violations. For example, a receiver lacks standing to bring a cause of action against issuers of securities for alleged violations of securities regulations if the corporation subject to the receivership suffers no harm.[128] If the receiver represents the corporation, any causes of action pertaining to investors must be brought by the investors.[129] On the other hand, the receiver may pursue any fraud committed on the corporation that damages the corporation as a receivership entity.[130] In addition, the receiver could assert claims on behalf of and for the protection of creditors who have claims against the property.[131] A receiver may also sue to remedy injuries to the property.[132]

Under 28 U.S.C.A. § 754, receivers appointed by a federal court and charged with property in different districts "shall have capacity to sue in any district without ancillary appointment, and may be sued with respect thereto as provided in section 959 of this title."[133]

(j) Suits Against Receivers

Receivers are liable for their actions while managing a property just as the owners of the property would be. 28 U.S.C.A. § 959(a) governs proceedings against receivers.[134]

---

128. *See, e.g.,* Baker v. Heller, 571 F.Supp. 419, 421 (S.D.Fla.1983).

129. Scholes v. Schroeder, 744 F.Supp. 1419, 1422–23 (N.D.Ill.1990). *See* Fleming v. Lind–Waldock & Co., 922 F.2d 20, 25 (1st Cir.1990); Commodity Futures Trading Comm'n v. Chilcott Portfolio Management, 713 F.2d 1477, 1482 (10th Cir.1983); Johnson v. Chilcott, 590 F.Supp. 204, 207–208 (D.Colo.1984).

130. Commodity Futures Trading Comm'n, 713 F.2d at 1482 (10th Cir. 1983) (equity receiver appointed in action by Commodities Futures Trading Commission action against registered commodity pool operator had capacity to initiate separate, ancillary action against the broker individually and several persons who allegedly dealt with broker in soliciting investors and investing assets of the pool, which allegedly was run as a "Ponzi" scheme, and was proper real party in interest to maintain that suit).

131. Southmark Corp. v. Cagan, 999 F.2d 216, 221 (7th Cir.1993) (partners were "creditors" under Arkansas law and receiver was allowed to assert their cause of action against mortgagee of property); Downriver Community Federal Credit Union v. Penn Square Bank Through F.D.I.C., 879 F.2d 754, 764 (10th Cir.1989) ("Any remedy

for fraudulent representations that affects, or potentially affects, all creditors belongs to the receiver, who asserts such claims for the benefit of all creditors."), *cert. denied,* 493 U.S. 1070, 110 S.Ct. 1112, 107 L.Ed.2d 1019 (1990).

132. *See* Scholes v. Lehmann, 56 F.3d 750, 753 (7th Cir.) (receiver for corporations owned by Ponzi scheme principal had standing to assert fraudulent conveyance claims), *cert. denied sub nom.* African Enter. Inc. v. Scholes, ___ U.S. ___, 116 S.Ct. 673, 133 L.Ed.2d 522 (1995).

133. 28 U.S.C.A. § 754 (West 1993) provides as follows:

A receiver appointed in any civil action or proceeding involving property, real, personal or mixed, situated in different districts shall, upon giving bond as required by the court, be vested with complete jurisdiction and control of all such property with the right to take possession thereof.... He shall have capacity to sue in any district without ancillary appointment, and may be sued with respect thereto as provided in section 959 of this title....

134. 28 U.S.C.A. § 959(a) (West 1993) provides as follows:

Trustees, receivers or managers of any property, including debtors in possession,

After a receiver has been appointed,[135] claims that a receiver has wrongfully or negligently administered the property must be brought against the receiver and not the property owners.[136] Consent of the appointing court is not necessary for claims against the receiver involving acts or transactions connected with the receivership property arising after the appointment of the receiver. However, the appointing court must consent to a suit against a receiver on claims arising from the owner's conduct or the property itself, rather than the receiver's actions.[137] In addition, the appointing court typically must grant express permission for a receiver to be sued in his or her individual capacity.[138]

To insure that the receiver exercises the maximum discretion in managing the property, suits against receivers are normally brought against the receivership entity or the property in receivership, not the receiver personally and the receiver usually faces no personal liability.[139] If a receiver acts outside the scope of his or her authority, however, the receiver is individually and personally liable for damages and other relief.[140] As a practical matter, however, such a suit is rare.[141]

may be sued, without leave of the court appointing them, with respect to any of their acts or transactions in carrying on business connected with such property. Such actions shall be subject to the general equity power of such court so far as the same may be necessary to the ends of justice, but this shall not deprive a litigant of his right to trial by jury.

See also, Eddy v. Lafayette, 163 U.S. 456, 16 S.Ct. 1082, 41 L.Ed. 225 (1896); SEC v. United Fin'l Group, Inc., 576 F.2d 217 (9th Cir.1978) (leave of court not required for suit against receiver involving receiver's carrying on business connected with receivership property); Barber v. Powell, 135 F.2d 728 (4th Cir.), *cert. denied,* 320 U.S. 752, 64 S.Ct. 56, 88 L.Ed. 447 (1943).

135. Erb v. Morasch, 177 U.S. 584, 20 S.Ct. 819, 44 L.Ed. 897 (1900); Eddy, 163 U.S. 456, 16 S.Ct. 1082, 41 L.Ed. 225; Texas & P. Ry. Co. v. Cox, 145 U.S. 593, 12 S.Ct. 905, 36 L.Ed. 829 (1892).

136. Ledbetter v. Farmers Bank & Trust Co., 142 F.2d 147 (4th Cir.), *cert. denied,* 323 U.S. 719, 65 S.Ct. 48, 89 L.Ed. 578 (1944).

137. *See* SEC v. Lincoln Thrift Ass'n, 557 F.2d 1274 (9th Cir.1977) (suit for possession of property held by receiver was outside 28 U.S.C.A. § 959(a) and therefore required leave of court); American Brake Shoe & Foundry Co. v. Interborough Rapid Transit Co., 10 F.Supp. 512, (S.D.N.Y.) (leave denied to sue receiver in state court),

aff'd per curiam, 76 F.2d 1002 (2d Cir.), *cert. denied,* 295 U.S. 760, 55 S.Ct. 923, 79 L.Ed. 1702 (1935).

138. *See, e.g.,* FDIC v. J.D.L. Assocs., 866 F.Supp. 76, 78 (D.Conn.1994); Strategis Asset Valuation & Management, Inc. v. Pacific Mut. Life Ins. Co., 805 F.Supp. 1544, 1553–54 (D.Colo.1992).

139. *See* FRCP 66; Capitol Indem. Corp. v. Curiale, 871 F.Supp. 205, 209 (S.D.N.Y. 1994).

140. *See* New Alaska Dev. Corp. v. Guetschow, 869 F.2d 1298, 1303 (9th Cir. 1989) (receiver was not immune from allegations that he stole estate assets or slandered parties, in that such alleged acts were not judicial acts); Federal Home Loan Mortgage Corp. v. Tsinos, 854 F.Supp. 113, 116 (E.D.N.Y.1994) ("Only in the rare instance where a receiver has acted outside the scope of his or her authority may the receiver be sued in his or her individual capacity."); Anes v. Crown Partnership, Inc., 113 Nev. 195, 932 P.2d 1067 (1997) (lessee could sue receiver for leased property, who acted as lessor, for breach of contract, breach of covenant of quiet enjoyment, and breach of duty of good faith and fair dealing, without leave of court, given that order appointing receiver granted receiver right to defend all legal proceedings and claims involving the property, and lessee's claims concerned receiver's liability for actions performed outside scope of its authority); Krist v. Aetna Cas. & Sur., 667 P.2d 665 (Wyo.1983) (successor receiver was not entitled to recover

141. See note 141 on page 860.

Generally, the court which appoints a receiver has supplemental jurisdiction over all suits by or against that receiver. Suits brought against receivers may be brought in the appointing court with no showing of independent jurisdictional grounds.[142]

Actions brought in state court against a receiver may be removed to federal court if a federal question exists under 28 U.S.C.A. § 1441 or the claims are against the receiver in his or her capacity as an "officer of the court" under 28 U.S.C.A. § 1442.[143] Courts have limited this doctrine to suits involving acts for which the receiver may be personally liable.[144] A federal question is not raised by the mere fact that a federal court appointed the receiver. State court actions by or against a federal receiver may also be removed on diversity grounds.[145] In determining diversity, the citizenship of the receiver, not that of the debtor or the creditor or the state of the appointing court, controls.[146]

Other statutes further limit removal. For example, 15 U.S.C.A. § 77v prohibits removal of cases brought under the Securities Act of 1933 and 28 U.S.C.A. § 1445(b) limits removal of FELA cases brought against the receivers of common carriers.[147]

(k) Interlocutory Appeal of Orders Involving Receivers

Although the appointment of a receiver is considered an interlocutory order, 28 U.S.C.A. § 1292(a)(2) explicitly makes an order appointing a receiver appealable as a matter of right.[148] While the appointment of

attorney's fees and litigation expenses incurred in action against first receiver and his surety, where successor receiver neither sought nor obtained authorization of the court to proceed with such action); *see also* FDIC v. J.D.L. Assoc., 866 F.Supp. 76, 78 (D.Conn.1994); Capitol Indem. Corp. v. Curiale, 871 F.Supp. 205, 209 (S.D.N.Y. 1994).

141. *See In re* Still, 963 F.2d 75, 77 (5th Cir.1992) (no personal liability where receiver did not assume liabilities).

142. Fulton National Bank v. Hozier, 267 U.S. 276, 45 S.Ct. 261, 69 L.Ed. 609 (1925); Rouse v. Hornsby, 161 U.S. 588, 16 S.Ct. 610, 40 L.Ed. 817 (1896); Eddy v. Lafayette, 163 U.S. 456, 16 S.Ct. 1082, 41 L.Ed. 225 (1896); Rouse v. Letcher, 156 U.S. 47, 15 S.Ct. 266, 39 L.Ed. 341 (1895).

143. 13 James Wm. Moore et al., Moore's Federal Practice § 66.08 (3d ed. 1997).

144. Gay v. Ruff, 292 U.S. 25, 54 S.Ct. 608, 78 L.Ed. 1099 (1934); Caddell v. Powell, 70 F.2d 123 (4th Cir.1934); American Locomotive Co. v. Histed, 18 F.2d 656 (D.C.Mo.1926).

145. Gay, 292 U.S. 25, 54 S.Ct. 608, 78 L.Ed. 1099; Barnette v. Wells Fargo Nevada Nat. Bank of San Francisco, 270 U.S. 438, 46 S.Ct. 326, 70 L.Ed. 669 (1926); Gableman v. Peoria, D & E Ry. Co., 179 U.S. 335, 340, 21 S.Ct. 171, 193, 45 L.Ed. 220 (1900); Barber v. Powell, 135 F.2d 728 (4th Cir.), *cert. denied,* 320 U.S. 752, 64 S.Ct. 56, 88 L.Ed. 447 (1943); Thompson v. St. Louis–San Francisco Ry. Co., 5 F.Supp. 785 (D.Okla.1934); Elliott v. Wheelock, 34 F.2d 213 (W.D.Mo.1929); Newell v. Byram, 18 F.2d 657 (D.Minn.1927), *aff'd,* 26 F.2d 200 (8th Cir.1928); Matarazzo v. Hustis, 256 Fed. 882 (N.D.N.Y.1919).

146. Clarkson Co., Ltd. v. Shaheen, 544 F.2d 624 (2d Cir.1976); Barber, 135 F.2d 728; Pepper v. Rogers, 128 Fed. 987 (D.Mass.1904); Brisenden v. Chamberlain, 53 Fed. 307 (D.S.C.1892); Davies v. Lathrop, 12 Fed. 353 (S.D.N.Y.1882).

147. 15 U.S.C.A. § 77v (West 1997); 28 U.S.C.A. § 1445 (West 1994 & Supp. 1997).

148. *See* Lyman v. Spain, 774 F.2d 495, 497–98 (D.C.Cir.1985) (despite claim that receivership appointment was not appealable because order was timely, court held it appealable as a matter of law).

the receiver is appealable under the statute, a refusal to vacate the appointment is not.[149] Section 1292 also expressly makes appealable "[i]nterlocutory orders ... refusing orders to wind up receiverships or to take steps to accomplish the purposes thereof, such as directing sales or other disposals of property." Section 1292 governs "orders in the nature of 'executions before judgment,' [that] in effect either oust parties from the possession of property or injuriously control[ ] the management and disposition of property."[150] If one order is reviewable and another substantially inter-related order is not reviewable, the court may review both, provided that limiting the review of only the reviewable action would be useless.[151]

Library References:

West's Key No. Digests, Receivers ⊕1–28.
Wright, Miller, Kane, Marcus & Cooper, Federal Practice and Procedure: Civil 2d
§§ 1567, 2981–2986, 3925.

§ 13.5   Prejudgment Seizure

(a) Strategy

This section discusses a number of state law remedies which may be pursued in federal district court. The most common type of prejudgment seizure that a business litigator might seek in federal court is the writ of attachment. A brief discussion of the strategy regarding writ of attachment, is included here. In general, counsel should consult the state law for the appropriate forms and procedures to be followed in pursuing any of these remedies in the district courts.

A writ of attachment allows the plaintiff to levy on the defendant's property to ensure that a judgment against the defendant can be satisfied. Generally speaking, under state law, the plaintiff must have an unsecured claim for a specific or easily ascertainable amount of money based on contract and must establish a sufficiently high likelihood of prevailing on the claim. (For example, in California, the plaintiff must establish the "probable validity" of its claim.)

The advantage of attachment to a plaintiff is that the attachment allows an unsecured creditor to become a secured creditor with a preference in bankruptcy, as a judgment on the plaintiff's claim will become a lien on the property attached. However, if the debtor declares bankruptcy (or a competing creditor files an involuntary bankruptcy)

---

149. 28 U.S.C.A. § 1292(a)(2) (West 1993); Illinois *ex rel.* Hartigan v. Peters, 861 F.2d 164 (7th Cir.1988); Warren v. Bergeron, 831 F.2d 101 (5th Cir.1987); Guy v. Citizens Fidelity Bank & Trust Co., 429 F.2d 828 (6th Cir.1970); Waylyn Corp. v. Casalduc, 219 F.2d 888 (1st Cir.1955); Skirvin v. Mesta, 141 F.2d 668 (10th Cir.1944); Orth v. Transit Inv. Corp., 132 F.2d 938 (3d Cir.1942); Adler v. Seaman, 266 Fed. 828 (8th Cir.), *cert. denied*, 254 U.S. 655, 41 S.Ct. 218, 65 L.Ed. 460 and *appeal dismissed*, 254 U.S. 621, 41 S.Ct. 320, 65 L.Ed. 443 (1920).

150. Gulf Ref. Co. of Louisiana v. Vincent Oil Co., 185 Fed. 87, 89 (5th Cir.1911).

151. Illinois *ex rel.* Hartigan, 861 F.2d at 166 (preliminary injunction freezing assets, and order appointing receiver were "the head and tail of the same coin").

within 90 days, or the defendant makes a general assignment for the benefit of creditors, the plaintiff's attachment lien is terminated and the expense of the attachment procedure is wasted. In addition, by attaching assets, the plaintiff can obtain quasi in rem jurisdiction over the assets of an out of state defendant.

As with the other provisional remedies, obtaining a writ of attachment increases the plaintiff's settlement leverage. Not only does the attachment provide a source of payment for the later judgment, but it also focuses the attention of the defendant on the plaintiff's claim. The court's finding of "probable validity" of the plaintiff's claim in granting the writ of attachment may persuade the defendant not to incur additional costs of defense and force an early settlement.

The disadvantage of a writ of attachment for the plaintiff is that the court may view an attachment as an election of the contract remedy where the plaintiff has alleged both tort and contract claims. The attachment procedure may also add to the cost of the collection effort, especially if the defendant has few assets.

In addition, if the defendant wins the underlying action, the defendant may pursue a claim of wrongful attachment, in which the plaintiff will be liable for damages, costs and expenses. Normally, however, the plaintiff's liability is limited by the amount of the undertaking required upon grant of the writ of attachment. The plaintiff also risks a claim by third parties if the plaintiff wrongfully attaches property owned by such third parties.

(b) FRCP 64

FRCP 64 governs certain state law remedies providing for seizure of person or property used to secure the satisfaction of a judgment which the plaintiff may ultimately obtain. FRCP 64 provides as follows:

> At the commencement of and during the course of an action, all remedies providing for seizure of person or property for the purpose of securing satisfaction of the judgment ultimately to be entered in the action are available under the circumstances and in the manner provided by the law of the state in which the district court is held, existing at the time the remedy is sought, subject to the following qualifications: (1) any existing statute of the United States governs to the extent to which it is applicable; (2) the action in which any of the foregoing remedies is used shall be commenced and prosecuted or, if removed from a state court, shall be prosecuted after removal, pursuant to these rules. The remedies thus available include arrest, attachment, garnishment, replevin, sequestration, and other corresponding or equivalent remedies, however designated and regardless of whether by state procedure the remedy is ancillary to an action or must be obtained by an independent action.

While other Rules create remedies to enforce judgments,[1] FRCP 64 covers certain remedies available before judgment. Prejudgment seizure

---

§ 13.5

1. FRCP 69 (execution); FRCP 70 (judgment for specific acts; vesting title; United States v. Overlie, 730 F.2d 1159, 1161 (8th Cir.1984).

protects litigants who may otherwise forego specific property or the ability to collect damages pending the outcome of the trial. Because these remedies are often summarily granted under severe time constraints, they pose a threat to procedural due process.

(c) State Law Primarily Governs Prejudgment Remedies While the Federal Rules Govern Procedures Applicable to Prejudgment Seizures

FRCP 64 provides that except to the extent the Constitution or an applicable United States statute governs, state law determines what remedies are available in a particular jurisdiction. State laws often limit the use of provisional remedies to those actions historically considered actions at law, as opposed to actions in equity,[2] and may also restrict the circumstances and manner in which remedies may be used in other respects.

Although state law generally governs the availability, timing and method of obtaining a remedy, FRCP 64 makes it clear that the underlying federal action proceeds under the Federal Rules of Civil Procedure. State procedures employed in exercising provisional remedies have no effect on the federal action.[3] Furthermore, federal courts have inherent powers to limit the scope of prejudgment remedies available under state law.[4]

Under FRCP 64, state provisional remedies are available only upon the commencement and during the prosecution of an action. Under FRCP 3, the commencement of an action occurs upon filing the com-

---

2. De Beers Consol. Mines v. United States, 325 U.S. 212, 218, 65 S.Ct. 1130, 1133, 89 L.Ed. 1566 (1945); Mitsubishi Int'l Corp. v. Cardinal Textile Sales, Inc., 14 F.3d 1507 (11th Cir.1994), cert. denied, 513 U.S. 1146, 115 S.Ct. 1092, 130 L.Ed.2d 1061 (1995); EBSCO Indus., Inc. v. Lilly, 840 F.2d 333 (6th Cir.), cert. denied, 488 U.S. 825, 109 S.Ct. 73, 102 L.Ed.2d 50 (1988); Hamilton v. MacDonald, 503 F.2d 1138, 1149 (9th Cir.1974).

3. United States for Use of Tanos v. St. Paul Mercury Ins. Co., 361 F.2d 838 (5th Cir.) (Pursuant to FRCP 4, United States Marshal should have served writ of garnishment as opposed to Florida sheriff as provided by Florida Rule addressing service generally), cert. denied, 385 U.S. 971, 87 S.Ct. 510, 17 L.Ed.2d 435 (1966); Consumers Time Credit, Inc. v. Remark Corp., 227 F.Supp. 263 (E.D.Pa.1964) (Although federal court action upon an accounts receivable financing agreement was commenced under a state law writ of attachment, state rules of civil procedure did not apply.); Prozel & Steigman, Inc. v. International Fruit Distribs., 171 F.Supp. 196 (D.N.J.1959) (In a proceeding involving a prejudgment seizure of property which has been removed to a federal court from a state court, the manner of seizing the property is governed by state law subject to the federal court rules.); Grant v. Kellogg Co., 3 F.R.D. 229 (S.D.N.Y. 1943) (a defendant's special appearance is not authorized by the rules if only to protect attached property).

4. Bridgestone/Firestone, Inc. v. Recovery Credit Servs., Inc., 147 F.R.D. 66 (S.D.N.Y.1993) (A federal court has the power to limit the scope of prejudgment remedies under the inherent power to grant a lesser thing if a greater one could have been granted, unless used to encroach upon constitutional or otherwise protected rights in a way that contravenes the purpose behind those rights.).

plaint.[5] Therefore, any state schemes allowing for prejudgment seizure remedies before the plaintiff files the complaint in federal court are not allowed.

FRCP 64 applies to actions that are removed from state to federal court. Under FRCP 64, any injunctions, orders, attachments, garnishments and other remedies obtained during state court proceedings remain in effect after an action has been removed to federal court.[6] Once a case has been removed, more property may be attached or garnished if state laws so provide.

(d) Limitations Imposed on Prejudgment Seizure by Federal Statutes and the United States Constitution

(1) Limitation Imposed by Federal Statutes

FRCP 64 provides that the application of state law to prejudgment seizures is subject to United States statutes that may affect such remedies. Various federal statutes grant immunity or otherwise limit the applicability of state law remedies. Examples of such federal statutes include those involving foreign sovereigns[7] (28 U.S.C.A. §§ 1609–1611), imprisonment for debt (28 U.S.C.A. § 2007), garnishment by the United States (28 U.S.C.A. § 2405) property taken according to revenue laws (28 U.S.C.A. § 2463),[8] or immunity of military service persons under the Soldiers' and Sailors' Relief Act (50 App. U.S.C.A. § 464).

---

5. FRCP 3.

6. 28 U.S.C.A. § 1450 (West 1994).

7. Foreign sovereigns are usually immune from attachment unless immunity is waived. Atwood Turnkey Drilling, Inc. v. Petroleo Brasileiro, S.A., 875 F.2d 1174 (5th Cir.1989) (waiver provision in letter of credit enough to waive national oil company of Brazil immunity to prejudgment attachment), *cert. denied*, 493 U.S. 1075, 110 S.Ct. 1124, 107 L.Ed.2d 1030 (1990); O'Connell Machinery Co. v. M.V. Americana, 734 F.2d 115 (2d Cir.) (Italian government immune from prejudgment attachment because the "or any other liability" clause in Treaty of Friendship, Commerce and Navigation between U.S. and Italy is not sufficiently broad to include such remedies.) *cert. denied*, 469 U.S. 1086, 105 S.Ct. 591, 83 L.Ed.2d 701 (1984); Moore v. National Distillers & Chem. Corp., 143 F.R.D. 526 (S.D.N.Y.1992); Liberian Eastern Timber Corp. v. Government of Liberia, 659 F.Supp. 606 (D.D.C.1987) (Immunity from attachment to satisfy a civil judgment was found under Foreign Sovereign Immunities Act in situation where only a portion of a bank account was used to run embassy,

that portion was deemed auxiliary, and did not denote the necessary character of the use of the funds in question.); Security Pacific Nat. Bank v. Government of Iran, 513 F.Supp. 864 (S.D.Cal.1981) (Treaty of Amity did not affect Iran's immunity from prejudgment attachments.); New England Merchants Nat. Bank v. Iran Power Generation & Transmission Co., 502 F.Supp. 120 (S.D.N.Y.1980) (waiver of immunity from prejudgment attachments must be unequivocal and absolutely explicit in order to subject a foreign state to such a remedy); Note, *Prejudgment Attachment Under the United States Foreign Sovereign Immunities Act: a Loophole in Need of Repair*, 1987, 66 Or. L. Rev. 627; Birch Shipping Corp. v. Embassy of United Republic of Tanzania, 507 F.Supp. 311 (D.D.C.1980) (Where Republic of Tanzania had agreed to arbitration and judicial enforcement of resulting awards, and checking account was used for commercial activity, that checking account was not immune from garnishment.).

8. The remedy of replevin is not available for property that has been taken according to revenue laws. Raffaele v. Granger, 196 F.2d 620 (3d Cir.1952); Starr v. Salemi, 329 F.Supp. 1150 (D.Ill.1971).

(2) Constitutional Limitations

The United States Constitution also limits the extent to which district courts may order prejudgment seizure remedies. The Fifth and Fourteenth Amendments of the Constitution guarantee that certain due process protections accompany any governmental deprivation of liberty or property. Because prejudgment seizure remedies are sought before the full adjudication of the merits of a case, a defendant who ultimately prevails in the underlying action could be deprived of liberty or due process by such remedies. Although cases on this issue have placed considerable constitutional limitations on state law remedies, significant debate continues over the specific requirements of procedural due process.

In *Sniadach v. Family Finance Corp. of Bayview*,[9] the Supreme Court held that a defendant's wages could not be garnished before judgment without notice or opportunity to be heard. In that case, a lender sued the defendant over her failure to pay $420 on a promissory note. The lender obtained a writ of garnishment ordering the defendant's employer to retain half of the defendant's salary pending the outcome of the trial. The Supreme Court found that the prejudgment seizure of a person's income posed great hardship and could not be exercised without notice and an opportunity to be heard on the matter.

After *Sniadach*, the law was unclear whether the holding of *Sniadach* applied to prejudgment remedies other than garnishment of wages. In *Fuentes v. Shevin*,[10] the Supreme Court held that prejudgment replevin under Florida and Pennsylvania laws was unconstitutional because defendants have a due process right to be heard before a court permits the seizure of their chattels.[11] The state statutes involved in *Fuentes* provided for the issuance of ex parte writs on behalf of anyone who claimed a right to another person's possessions and who posted a security bond. Neither statute required notice to the possessor or an opportunity to challenge the seizure at a hearing.

Unlike *Sniadach*, the household chattels seized in *Fuentes* were not found to be essential to the defendant. The Court nevertheless found that the lack of notice and hearing was an unconstitutional violation of due process[12] and held that notice and a hearing must precede the seizure. Although a post-seizure hearing might call for the return of property and damages might even be awarded for wrongful deprivation of that property, the Court stated that "no later hearing and no damage

---

9. 395 U.S. 337, 89 S.Ct. 1820, 23 L.Ed.2d 349 (1969). Kennedy, *Due Process Limitations on Creditors' Remedies: Some Reflection on Sniadach v. Family Finance Corp.*, 19 Amer. U. L. Rev. 158 (1970). West & Berman, *The Issue of Sniadach*, 79 Com. L. J. 49 (1974). *See also*, Lynch v. Household Fin. Corp., 405 U.S. 538, 92 S.Ct. 1113, 31 L.Ed.2d 424 (1972); Fuentes v. Shevin, 407 U.S. 67, 88–89, 92 S.Ct. 1983, 1998–99, 32 L.Ed.2d 556 (1972).

10. 407 U.S. 67, 92 S.Ct. 1983, 32 L.Ed.2d 556.

11. *Id.*

12. *Id.*

award [could] undo the fact that the arbitrary taking that was subject to the right of procedural due process [had] already occurred."[13]

Finally, the Court found that procedural due process protections were triggered even though the defendant held only a conditional sales interest in the seized chattels. The fact that the defendant did not fully own the household goods did not avoid the need for due process protections. The Court narrowed its holding, however, by stating that state legislatures possess much latitude in determining what criteria satisfy the requirements for a constitutional hearing.

Some debate still surrounds the legal effect of *Fuentes*. *Fuentes*, for example, implies that special circumstances may exist in which a sufficiently narrow statute may allow for prejudgment seizure in summary proceedings.[14] At the same time, the decision suggests that any state statute allowing prejudgment seizure without a hearing may not be utilized.[15] Later cases have addressed the issues left open by *Fuentes*.[16]

In *Mitchell v. W.T. Grant*,[17] the Court appeared to limit or perhaps overrule *Fuentes*, holding that an immediate post-seizure hearing, combined with the presence of certain safeguards, adequately protected a defendant's due process rights. In *Mitchell*, a Louisiana retailer alleged overdue payments on several household items. Under state law, a plaintiff could seek prejudgment seizure by claiming a right to property and a belief that the defendant might somehow dispose of or conceal it. Based on an affidavit asserting those required elements, the plaintiff obtained an order of sequestration from a judge in accordance with the statute, enabling the court to take possession of the encumbered property. Although the defendant received no notice of the seizure, the Supreme Court upheld the Louisiana statute.

Insofar as it did not require a preseizure hearing, *Mitchell* appears to overrule *Fuentes*. The majority in *Mitchell* upheld the statute because it provided for judicial authorization of the seizure, whereas in *Fuentes*, a court functionary ordered the ex parte seizure. The four dissenters in *Mitchell* argued that *Mitchell* is not constitutionally distinguishable from *Fuentes*. Some commentators have agreed with this conclusion, while others have questioned *Mitchell's* failure to explicitly overrule *Fuentes*.[18]

---

13. *Id.*

14. *Id.* at 93 ("There may be cases in which a creditor could make a showing of immediate danger that a debtor will destroy or conceal disputed goods. But the statutes before us are not 'narrowly drawn to meet any such unusual condition.' ") (citing Sniadach).

15. *Id.* at 96–97; Bergesen d.y. A/S v. Lindholm, 760 F.Supp. 976 (D.Conn.1991); Terranova v. AVCO Financial Servs. of Barre, Inc., 396 F.Supp. 1402 (D.Vt.1975).

16. In *Flagg Bros., Inc. v. Brooks*, 436 U.S. 149, 166, 98 S.Ct. 1729, 1738, 56 L.Ed.2d 185 (1978), for example, the Court found that violations of Fourteenth Amendment due process require state action.

17. 416 U.S. 600, 94 S.Ct. 1895, 40 L.Ed.2d 406 (1974), *noted in* 36 Mont. L. Rev. 103 (1974), 6 Seton Hall L. Rev. 150 (1974), 27 U. Fla. L. Rev. 273 (1974).

18. 416 U.S. at 623, 94 S.Ct. at 1908. *See*, 35 La. L. Rev. 221 (1974), 5 Mem. St. U. L. Rev. 74, 1974 Wash. U. L.Q. 653; 52 Denver L.J. 619 (1975), 54 Neb. L. Rev. 206 (1975); 49 Tul. L. Rev. 467 (1975). *Compare* Anderson & Guidry, *Mitchell v. W.T.Grant Co.: Recognition of Creditors' Rights*, 80 Com. L. J. 63 (1975).

Later circuit court decisions followed *Mitchell*, finding that a post-seizure hearing protects a debtor's due process rights if additional safeguards, such as the posting of a bond or the participation of a judge in approving the writ, are provided; these courts have differed, however, on the issue of what particular safeguards should be imposed.[19]

The Supreme Court revived *Fuentes* to some extent in *North Georgia Finishing, Inc. v. Di–Chem, Inc.*,[20] in which it held unconstitutional Georgia statutes authorizing the garnishment of a defendant's business bank account without safeguard procedures. Like the Louisiana statute in *Mitchell*, the Georgia statutes in *Di-Chem* permitted plaintiffs to obtain a writ of garnishment if they submitted an affidavit alleging an amount due and a reason to believe that the amount might be lost pending trial. Di–Chem obtained a writ of garnishment from the court clerk based on such an affidavit. The defendant's bank account was frozen without notice.

Applying *Fuentes*, the Court struck down the Georgia statute, stating that it lacked the requisite safeguards required by *Mitchell*. Under the Georgia statute, a creditor or an attorney, without personal knowledge of the facts, could sign an affidavit for the purpose of obtaining a writ. Based on an affidavit containing only conclusory allegations, a court clerk, rather than a judge, could issue the writ and the statute did not provide for an immediate post-seizure hearing. The absence of such safeguards was sufficient to render the statutory scheme unconstitutional.

Subsequent decisions continue the return to *Fuentes'* due process requirements.[21] In *Connecticut v. Doehr*,[22] the Court applied a procedural due process balancing test, described in *Mathews v. Eldridge*,[23] to find a prejudgment seizure of real estate unconstitutional. In *Doehr*, a Connecticut statute authorized prejudgment attachment of real estate without prior notice or hearing, a showing of extraordinary circumstances or the moving party posting a security bond. The statute merely required a

---

19. Watertown Equip. Co. v. Norwest Bank Watertown, N.A., 830 F.2d 1487, 1492 (8th Cir.1987), *cert. denied,* 486 U.S. 1001, 108 S.Ct. 1723, 100 L.Ed.2d 188 (1988) (requiring the posting of a security bond as well as the active participation of a judge in approving a writ of attachment); Jonnet v. Dollar Savs. Bank of New York, 530 F.2d 1123, 1130 (3d Cir.1976) (requiring the posting of a security bond and official approval of seizure writs).

20. 419 U.S. 601, 608, 95 S.Ct. 719, 723, 42 L.Ed.2d 751 (1975).

21. *See* Degen v. United States, 517 U.S. 820, ___, 116 S.Ct. 1777, 1780, 135 L.Ed.2d 102 (1996); United States v. James Daniel Good Real Property, 510 U.S. 43, 48, 114 S.Ct. 492, 498, 126 L.Ed.2d 490 (1993); Richmond Tenants Org. Inc. v. Kemp, 956

F.2d 1300, 1307 (4th Cir.1992); United States v. Monsanto, 924 F.2d 1186, 1191 (2d Cir.1991); United States v. Veritol, H21C Reg. No. N8540, 545 F.2d 648 (9th Cir.1976); Jonnet, 530 F.2d at 1130; Terranova, 396 F.Supp. 1402.

22. 501 U.S. 1, 11, 111 S.Ct. 2105, 2112, 115 L.Ed.2d 1 (1991).

23. Mathews v. Eldridge, 424 U.S. 319, 347, 96 S.Ct. 893, 908, 47 L.Ed.2d 18 (1976). In *Mathews*, the Court enunciated a three-part balancing test to be applied in situations involving government actions to effect deprivations. The three factors to be considered were (1) the private interest involved; (2) the risk of erroneous deprivation and the probable value; and (3) the government's interest in avoiding more costly procedures. *Id.* at 335, 96 S.Ct. at 903.

verified statement of probable cause and that the attachment be limited to real property.

Under the *Mathews* test, the Court reasoned that the Connecticut statutory scheme posed too great a risk of erroneous deprivation of property. The plaintiff's belief in the defendant's liability, the Court found, should not be considered enough for a prejudgment seizure. Furthermore, in the absence of extraordinary circumstances, the governmental interest in protecting the plaintiff's rights did not warrant such a drastic form of relief.

At present, although the standards remain unclear, the Constitution limits the ability of the federal government and state governments to permit or order prejudgment seizures without prior notice or hearing. Courts examine statutory schemes on a case-by-case basis, balancing the interests of both plaintiffs and defendants and requiring sufficient due process safeguards.

(e) State Remedies Available Under FRCP 64

FRCP 64 provides for several available remedies, including attachment, arrest, garnishment, replevin, sequestration, and "other corresponding or equivalent remedies." This section briefly describes those remedies. Counsel should look to the law of the appropriate jurisdiction for applicable statutes, cases and forms to pursue for such remedies.

Attachment refers to the seizure of a defendant's property for the purpose of securing eventual relief before the court renders judgment.[24] Attachment applies to debt-collection cases.[25]

If state law provides for civil arrest, a defendant may be apprehended for the purpose of answering to the demands of a civil action. However, this remedy is largely obsolete.[26]

---

24. Mitsubishi Int'l Corp. v. Cardinal Textile Sales, Inc., 14 F.3d 1507 (11th Cir. 1994), *cert. denied,* 513 U.S. 1146, 115 S.Ct. 1092, 130 L.Ed.2d 1061 (1995); Inter–Regional Financial Group, Inc. v. Hashemi, 562 F.2d 152 (2d Cir.1977), *cert. denied,* 434 U.S. 1046, 98 S.Ct. 892, 54 L.Ed.2d 798 (1978); Crist v. United Underwriters, Ltd., 343 F.2d 902 (10th Cir.1965); Ross v. Peck Iron & Metal Co., 264 F.2d 262, 268 (4th Cir.1959); Foreign Exchange Trade Assoc., Inc. v. Oncetur, S.A., 591 F.Supp. 1496 (S.D.N.Y.1984); Harman Elec. Co. v. First Real Estate Inv. Co., 55 F.R.D. 195 (W.D.Pa.1972); Kend v. Chroma–Glo, Inc., 51 F.R.D. 547 (D.Minn.1970); Davenport v. Ralph N. Peters & Co., 274 F.Supp. 99 (D.N.C.1966), *rev'd on other grounds* 386 F.2d 199 (4th Cir.1967); Warner Co. v. Brann & Stuart Co., 198 F.Supp. 634 (E.D.Pa.1961); United States v. J. Tirocchi & Sons, Inc., 180 F.Supp. 645 (D.R.I.1960);

Reiber v. Trailmobile Co., 11 F.R.D. 431 (W.D.Mo.1951); Stanley Trading Co. v. Bensdorp, Inc., 95 F.Supp. 502 (D.Miss. 1950); Eagle Pencil Co. v. U. & L. Corp., 83 F.Supp. 1011 (D.Mass.1949).

25. Wilder v. Inter–Island Steam Nav. Co., 211 U.S. 239, 29 S.Ct. 58, 53 L.Ed. 164 (1908) (*cited in* MBank New Braunfels, N.A. v. FDIC, 721 F.Supp. 120, 126 (N.D.Tex.1989).

26. United Refrigerator Co. v. Gershel, 276 F.2d 573, 574 (2d Cir.1960); *In re* Harris, 69 Cal.2d 486, 72 Cal.Rptr. 340, 446 P.2d 148 (1968); *Civil Arrest of Fraudulent Debtors: Toward Limiting the Capias Process,* 26 Rutgers L.Rev. 853 (1973), suggesting attachment as a constitutionally preferable alternative to civil arrest; *Body Attachment and Body Execution: Forgotten but Not Gone,* 17 Wm. & Mary L. Rev. 543 (1976).

Garnishment refers to the process by which a debt owed by a third person to the defendant, such as the wages owed by an employer to the defendant employee, or the defendant's property in the hands of a third person, such as the defendant's bank account, may be made subject to a plaintiff's claim.[27]

Under the remedy of replevin, a court can compel a person with wrongful possession of a property to return that property to the rightful owner.[28]

Sequestration refers to the process of seizing property pending the outcome of litigation or the compliance of a defendant with a court order. Unlike attachment, sequestration includes seizures of property that are not for the sole purpose of securing the collectibility of the judgment but also to preserve specific property which may be the subject of conflicting claims of ownership.[29] As such, a court normally sequesters specific property over which a plaintiff claims ownership, a right, lien, or other privilege.[30]

FRCP 64 remedies also include "other corresponding or equivalent" measures. Such methods include writs of *ne exeat*, which restrain people from leaving or removing property from the jurisdiction; trustee writs, by which intangibles may be garnished; impoundment, by which property is seized and taken into the custody of the law or a court; and writs of *distringas*, mostly obsolete, by which defendants are compelled to appear by seizure of their property. Other such remedies are applicable regardless of how they are designated and whether the state procedure by which the remedy is obtained is ancillary to an action or independent of it.[31]

27. United States v. Harkins Builders, Inc., 45 F.3d 830 (4th Cir.1995); Millard v. United States, 916 F.2d 1 (Fed.Cir.1990); Frost v. Davis, 288 F.2d 497 (5th Cir.1961); Cold Metal Process Co. v. McLouth Steel Corp., 126 F.2d 185 (6th Cir.1942); Lloyd v. Lawrence, 60 F.R.D. 116 (S.D.Tex.1973); Tate v. SS Suzanne, 58 F.R.D. 522 (E.D.La. 1970); General Elec. Credit Corp. v. Waukesha Bldg. Corp., 259 F.Supp. 958 (D.Ark. 1966); C.S. Foreman Co. v. H.B. Zachry Co., 122 F.Supp. 859 (W.D.Mo.1954); Robert W. Irwin Co. v. Sterling, Inc., 14 F.R.D. 250 (W.D.Mich.1953); United States v. Schuermann, 106 F.Supp. 86, 88 (E.D.Mo.1952).

28. Dennis Garberg & Assocs., Inc. v. Pack–Tech Int'l Corp., 115 F.3d 767 (10th Cir.1997); Howell v. United States Marshal, 241 F.2d 119 (3d Cir.1957); Diamond v. T. Rowe Price Assocs., Inc., 852 F.Supp. 372 (D.Md.1994); Kovatch Mobile Equip. Corp. v. Warren Township, 831 F.Supp. 665 (S.D.Ind.1993); Bridgestone/Firestone, Inc. v. Recovery Credit Servs., Inc., 147 F.R.D. 66 (S.D.N.Y.1993); Savada Bros. v. Conville,

8 F.R.D. 127 (M.D.Pa.1948); Commonwealth Trust Co. of Pittsburgh v. Reconstruction Fin. Corp., 28 F.Supp. 586, 587–88 (W.D.Pa.1939).

29. Baxter v. United Forest Prods. Co., 406 F.2d 1120 (8th Cir.) *cert. denied,* 394 U.S. 1018, 89 S.Ct. 1635, 23 L.Ed.2d 42 (1969); J.C. Trahan Drilling Contractor, Inc. v. Sterling, 335 F.2d 65 (5th Cir.1964); Altherr v. Swiss Am. of Miss., Inc., 446 F.Supp. 17, 18 (N.D.Miss.1977); United States v. Stone, 59 F.R.D. 260 (D.Del.1973).

30. Manning v. Mercantile Sec. Co., 242 Ill. 584, 90 N.E. 238 (1909), *aff'd,* 217 U.S. 597, 30 S.Ct. 696, 54 L.Ed. 896 (1910) (writ of sequestration was appropriate for receiver to obtain corporation records).

31. Mitsubishi Int'l Corp., 14 F.3d 1507; Bricklayers Fringe Benefit Funds v. North Perry Baptist Church of Pontiac, 590 F.2d 207 (6th Cir.) *cert. denied,* 444 U.S. 834, 100 S.Ct. 66, 62 L.Ed.2d 43 (1979); DeMoss v. Kelly Servs., Inc., 493 F.2d 1012 (1st Cir.1974); Kinderhill Select Bloodstock, Inc.

(f) Appellate Review

An order granting or denying prejudgment seizure is not appealable as a final judgment. Plaintiffs seek these provisional remedies for the purpose of securing the satisfaction of the expected judgment or to prevent further harm pending the final judgment. Until such judgment is rendered, no finality exists. If a district court, however, refuses to grant such a remedy and dismisses the action as well, the dismissal is final and the ruling denying the provisional remedy is thereby reviewable.[32]

Provisional remedy orders do not attach to independent claims in multiple claim actions and are therefore not given finality for purposes of appeal under FRCP 54(b).[33] Such orders are not appropriate orders for interlocutory appeals under 28 U.S.C.A. § 1292(b).[34]

A small class of "collateral orders" are appealable as final orders regardless of the posture of the principal litigation. To qualify as a "collateral order," the Supreme Court has held that the order must be "a final disposition of a claimed right which is not an ingredient of the cause of action and does not require consideration with it."[35] According to the Court, orders vacating attachments fall within this class and are appealable but orders sustaining attachments are probably not.[36]

Courts have applied the collateral order doctrine to hold that denials or vacations of attachment orders generally are appealable, while grants and continuances of attachment orders are not.[37] Practical considerations are taken into account, however. Vacations of attachment orders have been found not appealable where no security risk existed.[38] Further, an order sequestering defendant's monies when that order did not comply with state law protective provisions was appealable.[39]

Library References:

West's Key No. Digests, Federal Civil Procedure ☞581–590.
Wright, Miller & Kane, Federal Practice and Procedure: Civil 2d §§ 2931–2936.

v. United States, 835 F.Supp. 699 (N.D.N.Y. 1993); United States v. City of New Orleans, 215 F.Supp. 895 (E.D.La.1963); Daley v. Ort, 98 F.Supp. 151 (D.Mass.1951); Intra–Mar Shipping (Cuba) S.A. v. John S. Emery & Co., 11 F.R.D. 284 (S.D.N.Y.1951); Chappell & Co. v. Haddad, 1 F.R.D. 221 (D.Miss.1940).

32. Davis v. Operation Amigo, Inc., 378 F.2d 101 (10th Cir.1967).

33. Baxter, 406 F.2d at 1123.

34. *Id.*

35. Cohen v. Beneficial Indus. Loan Corp., 337 U.S. 541, 546–547, 69 S.Ct. 1221, 1226, 93 L.Ed. 1528 (1949); Mitsubishi Int'l Corp., 14 F.3d 1507. *See* Chapter 49 "Appeals to the Court of Appeals," at § 49.5(a)(4) .

36. Swift & Co. Packers v. Compania Colombiana Del Caribe, 339 U.S. 684, 689, 70 S.Ct. 861, 865, 94 L.Ed. 1206 (1950).

37. F.D.I.C. v. Elio, 39 F.3d 1239 (1st Cir.1994); *In re* Jenson, 980 F.2d 1254 (9th Cir.1992); Victrix S.S. Co., S.A. v. Salen Dry Cargo A.B., 825 F.2d 709 (2d Cir.1987); American Oil Co. v. McMullin, 433 F.2d 1091 (10th Cir.1970); American Mortgage Corp. v. First Nat. Mortgage Co., 345 F.2d 527 (7th Cir.1965).

38. 21 Turtle Creek Square, Ltd. v. New York State Teachers' Retirement Sys., 404 F.2d 31 (5th Cir.1968), *modified on other grounds,* 432 F.2d 64 (5th Cir.1970).

39. Baxter v. United Forest Prods. Co., 406 F.2d 1120, 1123–24 (8th Cir.), *cert. denied* 394 U.S. 1018, 89 S.Ct. 1635, 23 L.Ed.2d 42 (1969).

§ 13.6   Lis Pendens

(a) Strategy

A party to a federal civil action which claims that it has an interest in real property (the "claimant") may gain certain tactical advantages by recording a lis pendens in the appropriate state or county department and then filing a notice of that recording in district court. The recording and filing are made pursuant to the law of the state in which the district court is located.

A primary advantage of recording a lis pendens is settlement leverage. The notice prevents any party that obtains some interest in that property (a "purchaser," which includes a lender or other encumbrancer) from being a bona fide purchaser and thus subject to the claims of the claimant that records the lis pendens. If the claimant does not file the lis pendens, a purchaser that does not have actual knowledge of the claim may acquire an interest in the property without being bound by the judgment in the claimant's pending action.

As a result of the lis pendens, the owner often cannot sell or encumber the property because purchasers will not be willing to proceed with the transaction subject to the claimant's adverse claim. To make the property marketable, the owner may settle with the claimant on better terms than the merits of the claimant's case might otherwise justify. This is particularly true when the owner is facing time constraints (for example, a hearing seeking a date for a governmental permit to develop the land or the closing of a pending sale) or financial constraints (the cost of a motion to expunge or filing a bond), or the concern that the owner might lose a motion to expunge.

On the other hand, the claimant faces a number of risks by recording a lis pendens. The owner may file a motion to expunge the lis pendens. If the owner prevails and the lis pendens is expunged, usually only a party to the claimant's action is deemed to have actual notice of the claims. No other person is deemed to have constructive knowledge and a third party, even with actual knowledge, could become a bona fide purchaser of the property. Thus, a claimant with a weak claim, or a claim for which the owner could pay money damages or file the necessary bond, could lose the motion to expunge and risk the sale of the property to a third party. Depending upon the state law, the claimant that loses a motion to expunge may also be liable for attorney's fees and costs. Later, the owner could also sue the claimant for slander of title.

The claimant that records a lis pendens also risks the possibility that, upon motion by the owner to expunge the lis pendens, the court may decide not to expunge on condition that the claimant file an undertaking. The claimant may prevail but be unable to afford the undertaking or decide that the cost of the undertaking is not justified by the weakness of his claim.

A claimant that is unwilling to risk the outcome of a motion to expunge may decide that it is more advantageous to give actual notice of its claim to potential purchasers of the property of which he becomes aware. The owner cannot avoid the effects of the actual notice as he can avoid the lis pendens by a motion to expunge. Of course, the claimant takes the risk that it does not become aware of a potential purchaser, and fails to give actual notice. The potential purchaser then may become a bona fide purchaser.

Although the standards vary in different states, in general, on a motion to expunge the claimant must establish that his claim has merit. For example, the standard in California is "probable validity." If the claimant fails to meet that standard, sometimes based on an incomplete record early in the proceedings, it may lose the motion to expunge, despite the fact that it has a meritorious claim. The owner that files a motion to expunge takes a similar risk of the disclosure of the weakness of its case. Of course, both claimant and owner may be able to avoid this risk by seeking discovery, although that approach increases all party's attorney's fees, as well as the cost of reimbursing the opposing party for attorney's fees if they are recoverable under state law.

An owner, especially one with a strong argument on a motion to expunge, should consider agreeing to expedite discovery to avoid a continuance for discovery sought by the claimant and thus avoid having such a continuance affect a time-sensitive sale or other transaction. If the claimant seeks a continuance for discovery, the owner might also seek an undertaking to compensate it for any damage caused by delay.

The claimant must also consider whether it needs to seek injunctive relief against a transfer if the owner finds a purchaser willing to proceed with the purchase despite the filing of the lis pendens. For example, such a purchaser might agree to proceed with the transaction if it obtains from the owner indemnity against claims by the claimant. The purchaser could also agree with the owner to put aside some of the purchase price in an escrow account to provide money damages if the claimant wins its case.

The claimant also faces the risk that an owner that prevails in the action will seek damages for the loss in value or marketability of the property, or other consequential damages, or even for malicious prosecution.

A major tactical decision for the owner is whether to file a motion to expunge the lis pendens. Such a motion puts the claimant to its burden of proof to establish its claim under the standards provided by the applicable state law. This may involve an evidentiary hearing or a more typical motion procedure. The owner may join a motion to expunge with a summary judgment motion. If it is possible in the district court in which the action is pending, the owner might also consider requesting an early trial date in lieu of a motion to expunge, or after such a motion is denied.

The usual grounds for motions to expunge are that the claimant is not pursuing a claim involving the property that justifies the filing of a lis pendens or that the claimant cannot satisfy its burden of proving the strength of its claim. In deciding a motion to expunge, the court could order expungement of the lis pendens, require the owner to file an undertaking if monetary relief can protect the claimant, or continue the lis pendens subject to an undertaking by the claimant. The owner acquires leverage by such a motion; even if the claimant prevails, it may be unwilling or unable to comply with an undertaking ordered by the court and the lis pendens will be expunged as a result. If the owner can bear the cost of an undertaking imposed by the court, it will be able to sell or encumber property. The owner should produce strong factual support for its claim of damages if expungement is denied (e.g. the profits from a lost sale) and the low amount of damages to the claimant if the motion is granted. The prevailing party will likely be entitled to recover the cost of the undertaking as a recoverable cost.

(b) Generally

The doctrine of lis pendens protects a party's interest in real or personal property while litigation involving that property is pending. "Lis pendens" literally means pending litigation. This doctrine supports the traditional view that a party who purchases or acquires an interest in property involved in litigation takes that property subject to any valid judgment rendered in that litigation. While no formal notice was required at common law, and while some states have adopted the common law view,[1] many states statutes now require a party to file a formal notice of pending litigation in order to protect its interest.

Once notice is established, the doctrine of lis pendens provides that the property remains subject to the jurisdiction and control of the court until the controversy is resolved.[2] As a result, those who attempt to buy, sell, or otherwise deal with the property while the litigation is pending do so at their peril;[3] that is, they assume the risk that the court will determine ownership or interests in that property inconsistent with their position. The doctrine thus prevents third parties from acquiring interests in property that is the subject matter of a pending lawsuit.[4] A person who acquires such property accepts the property subject to any provisional remedies and subsequent valid judgments that affect it,[5] and

§ 13.6

1. See 51 Am Jur. 2d, Lis Pendens 5 (1970).

2. Massachusetts Bonding & Ins. Co. v. Knox, 220 N.C. 725, 18 S.E.2d 436 (1942); Marchand v. De Soto Mortg. Co., 149 So.2d 357 (Fla.App.1963); Hulen v. Chilcoat, 79 Neb. 595, 113 N.W. 122 (1907); Stuart v. Coleman, 78 Okla. 81, 188 P. 1063 (1920).

3. Presidio County v. Noel–Young Bond & Stock Co., 212 U.S. 58, 29 S.Ct. 237, 53 L.Ed. 402 (1909); Union Trust Co. v. Southern Inland Nav. & Improv. Co., 130 U.S. 565, 9 S.Ct. 606, 32 L.Ed. 1043 (1889); Warren County v. Marcy, 97 U.S. (7 Otto) 96, 24 L.Ed. 977 (1877); Tuft v. Federal

Leasing, 657 P.2d 1300 (Utah 1982); Blakely & Son, Ltd. v. Humphreys, 148 Ga.App. 281, 250 S.E.2d 826 (1978).

4. Merrill v. Wright, 65 Neb. 794, 91 N.W. 697 (1902); Roberts v. Cardwell, 154 Ky. 483, 157 S.W. 711 (1913).

5. Mackenzie v. A. Engelhard & Sons Co., 266 U.S. 131, 45 S.Ct. 68, 69 L.Ed. 205 (1924); Lewers & Cooke v. Atcherly, 222 U.S. 285, 32 S.Ct. 94, 56 L.Ed. 202, (1911); Thompson v. Baker, 141 U.S. 648, 12 S.Ct. 89, 35 L.Ed. 889 (1891); American Automobile Insurance Co. of St. Louis v. Sansone, 206 A.D.2d 445, 614 N.Y.S.2d 550 (1994) (purchaser bound to same extent as vendor).

may be bound to transfer his or her interest in the property to the successful litigant.[6] Pendente lite transferees who refuse to transfer their interest in the property after judgment has been rendered may be forced to surrender the property according to the terms of a writ of assistance.[7] Such transferees may also be subject to equitable proceedings and may also be held in contempt of court.[8]

(c) State Substantive Law Governs Lis Pendens

Although the text of FRCP 64 does not mention lis pendens, the original Advisory Committee Notes refer to the doctrine, indicating that notice of lis pendens is a matter of substantive state property law.[9] Under 28 U.S.C.A. § 1964, parties in federal court actions must comply with state laws requiring notice of pending actions concerning real property.[10] The Advisory Committee Notes to FRCP 64 also state that in the absence of state statutes requiring formal notice, the mere commencement of a federal action may serve as notice to anyone affected.[11]

(d) Property Affected

The doctrine of lis pendens may apply to various forms of real property,[12] including water rights,[13] timber,[14] and other attachments to

6. Powell v. Campbell, 20 Nev. 232, 20 P. 156 (1889); Moffatt v. Shepard, 1847 WL 1490 (1847).

7. Lacassagne v. Chapuis, 144 U.S. 119, 12 S.Ct. 659, 36 L.Ed. 368 (1892); Terrell v. Allison, 88 U.S. (21 Wall.) 289, 22 L.Ed. 634 (1874).

8. Lamb v. Cramer, 285 U.S. 217, 52 S.Ct. 315, 76 L.Ed. 715 (1932).

9. Original Committee Note of 1937 to FRCP 64. *See also* Beefy King Int'l, Inc. v. Veigle, 464 F.2d 1102 (5th Cir.1972); Daniels v. Universal Inv. Corp., 355 F.Supp. 693 (D.P.R.1972); McGregor v. McGregor, 101 F.Supp. 848 (D.C.Colo.1951). Frederick v. Baxter Arms Corp., 39 F.Supp. 609 (E.D.N.Y.1941) (Under FRCP 64 and *Erie-Tompkins* authority, lis pendens cancelled according to New York State law); United States v. Calcasieu Timber Co., 236 Fed. 196 (5th Cir.1916) (State lis pendens statutes are binding.).

10. 28 U.S.C.A. § 1964 (West 1994) provides,

"Where the law of a State requires a notice of an action concerning real property pending in a court of the State to be registered, recorded, docketed, or indexed in a particular manner, or in a certain

office or county or parish in order to give constructive notice of the action as it relates to the real property, and such law authorizes a notice of an action concerning real property pending in a United States district court to be registered, recorded, docketed, or indexed in the same manner, or in the same place, those requirements of the State law must be complied with in order to give constructive notice of such an action pending in a United States district court as it relates to real property in such State."

11. FRCP 64, Advisory Committee Note (citing King v. Davis, 137 Fed. 198 (W.D.Va. 1903)).

12. Union Trust Co. v. Southern Inland Nav. & Improv. Co., 130 U.S. 565, 9 S.Ct. 606, 32 L.Ed. 1043 (1889); Lacassagne v. Chapuis, 144 U.S. 119, 12 S.Ct. 659, 36 L.Ed. 368 (1892).

13. Rickey Land & Cattle Co. v. Miller & Lux, 218 U.S. 258, 31 S.Ct. 11, 54 L.Ed. 1032 (1910).

14. Goff v. McLain, 48 W.Va. 445, 37 S.E. 566 (1900); McCord v. Akeley, 132 Wis. 195, 111 N.W. 1100 (1907); Alliance Trust Co. v. Nettleton Hardwood Co., 74 Miss. 584, 21 So. 396 (1897).

the soil as well as trees removed from land[15] and leasehold interests in real property.[16] In determining whether the doctrine of lis pendens covers a particular property, courts give special attention to how the litigation involves or affects the property. The doctrine is not triggered unless some identifiable "property"[17] is the subject of the litigation.[18] For example, lis pendens does not apply where property is sold but the litigation merely involves the ownership of the mortgage on the land.[19]

Although the doctrine of lis pendens has been said not to apply to "articles of ordinary commerce sold in the usual way,"[20] courts have recognized the need to apply the doctrine to items that are readily transferred without notice of pending litigation.[21] The doctrine has been applied to cases involving various forms of personal property, including mules,[22] logs,[23] machinery,[24] locomotives,[25] boats,[26] wheat,[27] stocks,[28] and

15. Goff, 48 W.Va. 445, 37 S.E. 566 (lis pendens did not apply to buildings considered "personalty" because they were intended to be portable). *But see* Hubbard v. Hardeman County Bank, 868 S.W.2d 656 (Tenn.App.1993).

16. Westbrook v. Superior Court (Fairchild), 176 Cal.App.3d 703, 222 Cal.Rptr. 317 (1986).

17. Miller v. Sherry, 69 U.S. (2 Wall.) 237, 17 L.Ed. 827 (1864).

18. Richard J. Zitz, Inc. v. Pereira, 965 F.Supp. 350 (E.D.N.Y.1997) (under New York law, action seeking damages for breach of contract to design house to be built on real property owned by respondent was not one that directly affects title, possession, use or enjoyment of real property in question, and therefore notice of pendency could not be filed); Tsiporin v. Ziegel, 203 A.D.2d 451, 610 N.Y.S.2d 603 (1994) (action to recover down payment under contract for sale of real property did not directly affect title to or possession of subject property and, thus, notice of pendency was not appropriate); Levin v. George Fraam & Sons, Inc., 65 Ohio App.3d 841, 585 N.E.2d 527 (1990) (property in suit which originated as breach of contract action in which property described would be one of sources from which plaintiff would be compensated was not subject to doctrine of lis pendens); Grabowski v. S & E Const. Co., 72 N.J.Super. 1, 177 A.2d 576 (Ch.Div.1962) (subcontractor, who was hired by contractor to complete subdivision improvements on land of subdivision owner, whose sole business was erecting and selling of dwellings, was not entitled to a lis pendens when subcontractor had not obtained a judgment against contractor and when sole relief sought was a money judgment); Domino v. Domino, 99

N.E.2d 825 (Ohio Com.Pl.1951) (lis pendens did not apply to an action for divorce and for alimony to be paid out of the husband's estate); *see also* Flanagan v. Clark, 156 Okla. 230, 11 P.2d 176 (1932); Leuders v. Thomas, 35 Fla. 518, 17 So. 633 (1895); Hailey v. Ano, 136 N.Y. 569, 32 N.E. 1068 (1893); Wilkinson v. Elliott, 43 Kan. 590, 23 P. 614 (1890); Powell v. Campbell, 20 Nev. 232, 20 P. 156 (1889).

19. Green v. Rick, 121 Pa. 130, 15 A. 497 (1888).

20. Presidio County v. Noel–Young Bond & Stock Co., 212 U.S. 58, 77, 29 S.Ct. 237, 243, 53 L.Ed. 402 (1909). *See* Warren County v. Marcy, 97 U.S. (7 Otto) 96, 24 L.Ed. 977 (1877).

21. Carr v. Lewis Coal Co., 96 Mo. 149, 8 S.W. 907 (1888). *See* Di Iorio v. Di Iorio, 254 N.J.Super. 172, 603 A.2d 127 (1991) (Kansas lis pendens statute applies to real property and personal property except for negotiable instruments and articles of ordinary commerce sold in the usual way); *In re* Washington, 623 F.2d 1169, 6 Bankr. Ct. Dec. 943 (6th Cir.1980) (Ohio's lis pendens statute applies to personal property.).

22. Schwantz v. Pillow, 50 Ark. 300, 7 S.W. 167 (1888).

23. Bergman v. Inman, Poulsen & Co., 43 Or. 456, 72 P. 1086 (1903).

24. Sowden v. Craig, 26 Iowa 156 (1868).

25. North Carolina Land & Lumber Co. v. Boyer, 191 Fed. 552 (6th Cir.1911).

26. Carr v. Lewis Coal Co., 96 Mo. 149, 8 S.W. 907 (1888).

27. Hubbard v. Johnson, 89 Wash. 310, 154 P. 457 (1916).

28. Sailfish Point, Inc. v. Sailfish Point Owners Representatives by Jaffe, 679 So.2d 1283 (Fla.App.1996).

nonnegotiable bonds and notes.[29]

(e) Statutory Notices

Notices of lis pendens required by statute typically must include the "style, number, and objective of the action,"[30] the title of the court of litigation, the names of the parties involved, and a description of the property in question.[31] Unless otherwise mandated by statute, a required formal notice of lis pendens, not the pleadings, must adequately describe the property in question.[32] Most state statutes require that the formal notice be filed in the office of the recorder in the county in which the subject property is located.[33]

(f) Effect of Common Law

State courts have generally viewed statutes governing the notice of lis pendens as further defining the common law rather than replacing or abrogating the doctrine.[34] While most states have enacted statutes requiring formal notice, in the absence of applicable statutes courts typically apply the common law.[35]

According to the common law, the mere pendency of litigation triggers the doctrine of lis pendens; formal notice is not required.[36] For example, even if the applicable lis pendens statute refers only to real property, some courts have held that a person who buys personal property involved in litigation acquires that property subject to the outcome of litigation even without formal notice of lis pendens, provided

---

29. Steger v. Traveling Men's Bldg. & Loan Ass'n, 208 Ill. 236, 70 N.E. 236 (1904); Jones v. Williams, 155 N.C. 179, 71 S.E. 222 (1911). Broom v. Armstrong, 137 U.S. 266, 11 S.Ct. 73, 34 L.Ed. 648 (1890); Enfield v. Jordan, 119 U.S. 680, 7 S.Ct. 358, 30 L.Ed. 523 (1887).

30. 51 Am. Jur. 2d, Lis Pendens § 22 (1970).

31. Smith v. Gale, 144 U.S. 509, 12 S.Ct. 674, 36 L.Ed. 521 (1892); State ex rel. Parkland Development, Inc. v. Henning, 189 W.Va. 186, 429 S.E.2d 73 (1993); Tennis Coal Co. v. Sackett, 172 Ky. 729, 190 S.W. 130 (1916); McIlwrath v. Hollander, 73 Mo. 105 (1880).

32. Clopine v. Kemper, 140 Colo. 360, 344 P.2d 451 (1959), disapproving Central Sav. Bank v. Smith, 43 Colo. 90, 95 P. 307 (1908).

33. See Cal. Civ. Code § 3146 (West 1993); Colo. Rev. Stat. Ann. § 38–35–110 (West 1990 & Supp. 1997); Idaho Code § 5–

505 (1990); 735 Ill. Comp. Stat. Ann. § 5/2–1901 (West 1992); Mont. Code Ann. § 70–29–109 (1997).

34. First Ave. Coal & Lumber Co. v. Rimer, 222 Ala. 545, 133 So. 589 (1931) (State statutes limit but do not repeal common law doctrine of lis pendens.); Shuck v. Quackenbush, 75 Colo. 592, 227 P. 1041 (1924) (Statutory provision modified or restricted common law rather than creating lis pendens.); P. A. Stark Piano Co. v. Fannin, 212 Ky. 640, 279 S.W. 1080 (1926); Rardin v. Rardin, 85 W.Va. 145, 102 S.E. 295 (1919).

35. First Ave. Coal & Lumber Co., 222 Ala. 545, 133 So. 589; P.A. Stark Piano Co., 212 Ky. 640, 279 S.W. 1080; Rardin, 85 W.Va. 145, 102 S.E. 295; Brown v. Cohn, 95 Wis. 90, 69 N.W. 71 (1896).

36. American Roofing Supply of Colorado Springs, Inc. v. Capps, 890 P.2d 133 (1994); P.A. Stark Piano Co. v. Fannin, 212 Ky. 640, 279 S.W. 1080; Rardin, 85 W.Va. 145, 102 S.E. 295.

that the common law doctrine of lis pendens in that jurisdiction applies to the particular kind of personal property in question and absent state law to the contrary.[37] The common law doctrine of lis pendens will not always apply to actions involving only personal property.

(g) Misfiling or Failure to File

Although some statutes might invalidate judgments as to third parties to whom no notice of lis pendens was given,[38] the typical statutory lis pendens scheme does not make the filing of formal notice a prerequisite to maintaining the primary litigation. Notice, however, may be required to enforce a judgment.[39] Moreover, the doctrine of lis pendens usually does not apply to acquisitions occurring after judgment has been rendered.[40]

(h) Notice Imputed to Purchaser

Under the early common law doctrine of lis pendens, the mere filing of a lawsuit affecting property imparted constructive notice of the pendency of the suit, such that anyone who acquired an interest in the property during the pendency took the property subject to the outcome of the suit.[41] This was intended to protect the litigants by preserving the property so that the court could render an effective final judgment.[42] The drastic common law doctrine no longer operates against a person who purchases in good faith property subject to litigation before judgment is rendered, without actual or constructive notice of the litigation.[43]

Under current law, the filing of a notice of lis pendens protects the litigants by providing the requisite constructive notice.[44] A party with

37. P.A. Stark Piano Co., 212 Ky. 640, 279 S.W. 1080, cited with approval in New Holland Machinery Co., Division of Sperry Rand Corp. v. Bell, 357 S.W.2d 868, 869 (Ky.1962); Kellogg v. Fancher, 23 Wis. 21, 99 Am. Dec. 96 (1868).

38. See Hughes v. North Carolina State Highway Comm'n, 275 N.C. 121, 165 S.E.2d 321 (1969) (requiring strict adherence to lis pendens statute); R.M. Hacker v. Hollymount Bowl, 146 Cal.App.2d Supp. 875, 303 P.2d 387 (Cal. App. Dep't Super. Ct. 1956) (under statute, failure to file notice of lis pendens to foreclose mechanic's lien within 90 days of claim barred right to enforce lien).

39. See statutes discussed in P.A. Stark Piano Co., 212 Ky. 640, 279 S.W. 1080; McVay v. Tousley, 20 S.D. 258, 105 N.W. 932 (1905).

40. Federal Intermediate Credit Bank of Spokane v. O/S Sablefish, 111 Wash. 2d 219, 758 P.2d 494 (1988); London & San Francisco Bank v. Dexter Horton & Co.,

126 Fed. 593 (9th Cir.) (lis pendens statute is inapplicable after judgment has been rendered) cert. denied, 194 U.S. 631, 24 S.Ct. 856, 48 L.Ed. 1158 (1903).

41. See Chrysler Corp. v. Fedders Corp., 670 F.2d 1316, 1319 (3d Cir.1982) (discussing the historical developments of lis pendens).

42. See id.

43. Todd v. Romeu, 217 U.S. 150, 30 S.Ct. 474, 54 L.Ed. 705 (1910); Smith v. Gale, 144 U.S. 509, 12 S.Ct. 674, 36 L.Ed. 521 (1892); Bensley v. Mountain Lake Water Co., 13 Cal. 306 (1859).

44. See also Orange County v. Hongkong and Shanghai Banking Corp. Ltd., 52 F.3d 821 (9th Cir.1995) (applying California law); United States v. Premises Known as 2930 Greenleaf Street, Allentown, Pa., 920 F.Supp. 639 (E.D.Pa.1996) (applying Pennsylvania law).

actual notice of the litigation takes the property subject to the outcome of litigation whether or not a statute requires constructive notice for the doctrine to operate.[45] Furthermore, unless the relevant statute provides otherwise, anyone other than a "bona fide purchaser" who acquires property during litigation does so subject to the outcome of litigation whether or not statutory notice of lis pendens was filed.[46]

Although a party directly interested in litigation regarding the title to real property generally cannot convey good title pending the judicial proceeding,[47] transferees may obtain good title providing that they purchase the property for value and have neither actual nor constructive notice of the litigation.[48] Such a purchase serves as an affirmative defense against a person claiming the property pursuant to the outcome of litigation. A party's attorney who purchases real property involved in litigation from the client while serving as counsel in the matter cannot claim to be a bona fide purchaser.[49] Also, a purchaser of real property in a mortgage foreclosure action with knowledge of the pending litigation, who fails to record the transfer in violation of a statute requiring such a recording for the transfer to be valid against subsequent, good faith purchasers, buys the property subject to the foreclosure proceeding even if no formal notice of lis pendens was filed as the statute provides.[50]

(i) Persons Acquiring Interest Before Filing of Lis Pendens

In general, the doctrine of lis pendens will not apply to an interest acquired in a property before the commencement of litigation[51] or before the filing of any applicable statutory notice.[52] This is true for both legal and equitable interests.[53] However, the outcome of litigation may bind

45. Goodson v. Lehmon, 225 N.C. 514, 35 S.E.2d 623 (1945); Packard Bell Elec. Corp. v. Theseus, Inc., 244 Cal.App.2d 355, 53 Cal.Rptr. 300 (1966).

46. See generally Wood v. Price, 79 N.J.Eq. 620, 81 A. 983 (Err. & App. 1911); Brown v. Cohn, 95 Wis. 90, 69 N.W. 71 (1896) (issuing subpoena and subsequent judicial proceedings did not constitute constructive notice).

47. 51 Am. Jur. 2d, Lis Pendens § 24 (1970).

48. Whitehurst v. Abbott, 225 N.C. 1, 33 S.E.2d 129 (1945).

49. Gay v. Parpart, 106 U.S. 679, 1 S.Ct. 456, 27 L.Ed. 256 (1883).

50. Ray v. Hocker, 65 Fla. 265, 61 So. 500 (1913).

51. Abraham & Son v. Casey, 179 U.S. 210, 21 S.Ct. 88, 45 L.Ed. 156 (1900) (Lis pendens did not prevent right to foreclose mortgage nor did it interfere with title acquired in foreclosure proceedings.); Pittsburgh, C., C. & St. L.R. Co. v. Long Island

Loan & T. Co., 172 U.S. 493, 19 S.Ct. 238, 43 L.Ed. 528 (1899) (Lis pendens due to second mortgage did not prevent lien on property under first mortgage.); Machover v. Abdallah, 329 F.2d 800 (3d Cir.1964) (Lis pendens not applicable to tenant who acquired his interest before action was brought.).

52. Applegate Apartments Ltd. Partnership v. Commercial Coin Laundry Systems, 276 Ill.App.3d 433, 212 Ill.Dec. 827, 657 N.E.2d 1172 (1995); General Electric Credit Corp. v. American Nat. Bank & Trust Co. of Chicago, 562 F.Supp. 456 (N.D.Ill.1983); Urez Corp. v. Superior Court (Keefer), 190 Cal.App.3d 1141, 235 Cal.Rptr. 837 (1987); In re Lane, 980 F.2d 601, 27 Collier Bankr. Cas. 2d 1724, 23 Bankr. Ct. Dec. 1197 (9th Cir.1992); Bowen v. Jameson, 223 Ky. 493, 4 S.W.2d 401 (1927); Moulton v. Kolodzik, 97 Minn. 423, 107 N.W. 154 (1906); Munger v. T.J. Beard & Bros., 79 Neb. 764, 113 N.W. 214 (1907).

53. Warnock v. Harlow, 96 Cal. 298, 31 P. 166 (1892); Moulton, 97 Minn. 423, 107 N.W. 154; Bowen, 223 Ky. 493, 4 S.W.2d

both the new owner and the property if the new owner is properly made a party to the litigation before the court renders judgment.[54]

Courts disagree over the implications of the lis pendens doctrine concerning property acquired through transfers made before statutory notice of lis pendens, or, in common law jurisdictions, property acquired before commencement of the action, but not recorded until later.[55]

Under a statute requiring the filing of a notice of lis pendens,[56] some courts have held that in the absence of required filing, a party who has obtained, but not recorded, the deed to the property in question cannot rely upon the doctrine.[57] Statutes in other states provide that if a transfer has not been recorded as of the time that statutory notice has been filed, the property is subject to the outcome of litigation.[58] Properties have also been bound by the outcome of litigation when applicable statutes invalidate unrecorded instruments unless parties have actual knowledge of the instruments.[59]

(j) Jurisdictional Requirements

Before applying the doctrine of lis pendens, a court must have subject matter jurisdiction.[60] If, for example, a court does not have subject matter jurisdiction over an action involving property outside the district, "pendente lite transferees" of such property will not be bound by the outcome of litigation.[61] In some situations, such as where service

401; Palisade Gardens v. Grosch, 120 N.J.Eq. 294, 185 A. 27 (Ch. 1936), aff'd, 121 N.J.Eq. 240, 189 A. 622 (Err. & App. 1937); Trimble's Lessee v. Boothby, 14 Ohio 109 (1846).

54. Pittsburgh, C., C. & St. L.R. Co. v. Long Island Loan & T. Co., 172 U.S. 493, 19 S.Ct. 238, 43 L.Ed. 528 (1899).

55. Dime Sav. Bank of New York, FSB v. Sandy Springs Associates, 261 Ga. 485, 405 S.E.2d 491 (1991)(Lis pendens has no affect on prior unrecorded conveyance to bona fide purchaser for value.); J. & S. Corp. v. Mortgage Associates, Inc., 41 Wis.2d 418, 164 N.W.2d 221 (1969) (Under lis pendens statute, prior unrecorded interest is subject to legal proceedings.); Wolfenberger v. Hubbard, 184 Ind. 25, 110 N.E. 198 (1915); See Jones v. Jones, 249 Miss. 322, 161 So.2d 640 (1964) (lis pendens not in effect until interest was recorded).

56. See, e.g., Moulton v. Kolodzik, 97 Minn. 423, 107 N.W. 154 (1906).

57. Dime Sav. Bank of New York, FSB, 261 Ga. 485, 405 S.E.2d 491 (1991); Shuck v. Quackenbush, 75 Colo. 592, 227 P. 1041 (1924); Moulton, 97 Minn. 423, 107 N.W. 154; Baker v. Bartlett, 18 Mont. 446, 45 P.

1084 (1898); Warnock, 96 Cal. 298, 31 P. 166.

58. See, e.g., J. & S. Corp. v. Mortgage Associates, Inc., 41 Wis.2d 418, 164 N.W.2d 221 (1969); Jones v. Jones, 249 Miss. 322, 161 So.2d 640 (1964); Wilson v. Robinson, 21 N.M. 422, 155 P. 732 (1916); Wolfenberger v. Hubbard, 184 Ind. 25, 110 N.E. 198 (1915); Munger v. T.J. Beard & Bros., 79 Neb. 764, 113 N.W. 214 (1907).

59. Poncelet v. English, 243 Mont. 481, 795 P.2d 436 (1990); Lind v. Goble, 117 Okla. 195, 246 P. 472 (1926); Shuck, 75 Colo. 592, 227 P. 1041; Nuckles v. Tallman, 106 Kan. 264, 187 P. 654 (1920); Heckmann v. Detlaff, 283 Ill. 505, 119 N.E. 639 (1918); Wilson v. Robinson, 21 N.M. 422, 155 P. 732 (1916); Noyes v. Crawford, 118 Iowa 15, 91 N.W. 799 (1902).

60. Rickey Land & Cattle Co. v. Miller & Lux, 218 U.S. 258, 31 S.Ct. 11, 54 L.Ed. 1032 (1910); Levin v. George Fraam & Sons, Inc., 65 Ohio App.3d 841, 585 N.E.2d 527 (1990); People ex rel. Fahner v. Steel Container Corp., 102 Ill.App.3d 369, 58 Ill. Dec. 126, 430 N.E.2d 68 (1981).

61. Benton v. Shafer, 47 Ohio St. 117, 24 N.E. 197 (1890).

of process is required before lis pendens comes into effect, personal jurisdiction over the defendant may be necessary for the final judgment to be binding.[62]

(k) Due Diligence in Pursuing Litigation

To protect innocent third parties, the doctrine of lis pendens often requires the litigant seeking to apply the doctrine to pursue the litigation with adequate diligence. The standard sometimes required has been "close and continuous prosecution."[63]

Although the concept of laches usually applies to actions in equity, the idea that litigation that is not timely commenced or diligently pursued effectively precludes relief may apply to lis pendens actions. A bona fide purchaser may successfully assert the defense that the party seeking to apply the doctrine of lis pendens has not prosecuted its claims with diligence, thereby making the property not subject to the judgment.[64] The party seeking lis pendens protection may rebut the defense if it satisfactorily explains its lack of diligence.[65]

Some courts have required more than a mere failure to exercise ordinary diligence before rejecting the doctrine of lis pendens, calling for "unusual and unreasonable negligence" or negligence sufficient to cause a belief that the matter has been abandoned.[66] Many authorities, however, require a less extreme standard, such as "reasonable" or "due" diligence.[67] Generally, the question of how much time must elapse before the doctrine of lis pendens will not apply is one of fact.[68] Thus, courts have found claims inexplicably delayed for periods from two[69] to 40[70] years not subject to the doctrine of lis pendens.[71]

62. Federal Land Bank of New Orleans v. Ozark City Bank, 225 Ala. 52, 142 So. 405 (1931); Norris v. Ile, 152 Ill. 190, 38 N.E. 762 (1894); Wilkinson v. Elliott, 43 Kan. 590, 23 P. 614 (1890); Powell v. Campbell, 20 Nev. 232, 20 P. 156 (1889); Hailey v. Ano, 136 N.Y. 569, 32 N.E. 1068 (1893); Flanagan v. Clark, 156 Okla. 230, 11 P.2d 176 (1932); Houston v. Timmerman, 17 Or. 499, 21 P. 1037 (1889).

63. Robinson v. Bierce, 102 Tenn. 428, 52 S.W. 992 (1899).

64. Bridger v. Exchange Bank, 126 Ga. 821, 56 S.E. 97 (1906); Johnston v. Standard Min. Co., 148 U.S. 360, 13 S.Ct. 585, 37 L.Ed. 480 (1893); Redfield v. Ystalyfera Iron Co., 110 U.S. 174, 3 S.Ct. 570, 28 L.Ed. 109 (1884).

65. Redfield, 110 U.S. 174, 3 S.Ct. 570, 28 L.Ed. 109.

66. Norris, 152 Ill. 190, 38 N.E. 762 (No estoppel against lis pendens unless negligence induces belief that prosecution has been abandoned.); Gossom v. Donaldson, 57 Ky. 230 (1857).

67. See Louisville Asphalt Co. v. Cobb, 310 Ky. 126, 220 S.W.2d 110 (1949).

68. Hammock v. Qualls, 139 Tenn. 388, 201 S.W. 517 (1918); Olson v. Leibpke, 110 Iowa 594, 81 N.W. 801 (1900); Robinson, 102 Tenn. 428, 52 S.W. 992; Watson v. Wilson, 32 Ky. 406 (1834).

69. Watson, 32 Ky. 406.

70. Hayes v. Nourse, 114 N.Y. 595, 22 N.E. 40 (1889).

71. Redfield v. Ystalyfera Iron Co., 110 U.S. 174, 3 S.Ct. 570, 28 L.Ed. 109 (1884); Dice v. Bender, 383 Pa. 94, 117 A.2d 725 (1955); Louisville Asphalt Co., 310 Ky. 126, 220 S.W.2d 110; Robinson, 102 Tenn. 428, 52 S.W. 992; Taylor v. Carroll, 89 Md. 32, 42 A. 920 (1899); Pipe v. Jordan, 22 Colo. 392, 45 P. 371 (1896); Fox v. Reeder, 28 Ohio St. 181 (1875).

(l) Duration

In general, once the doctrine of lis pendens is triggered, it remains in effect until the litigation ends, upon entry of a final judgment.[72] Statutes may limit the operation of a notice of lis pendens or place conditions that will extend the term beyond when it would ordinarily expire.[73]

(m) Termination

Generally, dismissal of an action without provision for further litigation terminates the doctrine of lis pendens.[74] In cases involving a dismissal in which the litigation is subsequently renewed, the outcome depends upon whether the owner acquired the property in question before the dismissal or between the dismissal and the renewal of litigation. If the owner acquired the property before the dismissal and received notice of the original lis pendens and the litigation has been renewed within a reasonable amount of time, the property will remain subject to the doctrine of lis pendens.[75] By contrast, some courts have held that the doctrine of lis pendens does not apply to property acquired after the dismissal and before the reinstatement of litigation.[76]

(n) Cancellation

Statutes may also condition a notice of lis pendens on specific criteria, such as proper service,[77] or the posting of a bond.[78] Failure to meet those criteria may result in cancellation of the notice.[79] Courts have

72. Duncan v. Farm Credit Bank of St. Louis, 940 F.2d 1099 (7th Cir.1991); Roberts v. Cardwell, 154 Ky. 483, 157 S.W. 711 (1913); Olson, 110 Iowa 594, 81 N.W. 801; Wingfield v. Neal, 60 W.Va. 106, 54 S.E. 47 (1906); McVay v. Tousley, 20 S.D. 258, 105 N.W. 932 (1905); Dupee v. Salt Lake Valley Loan & T. Co., 20 Utah 103, 57 P. 845 (1899); Fox, 28 Ohio St. 181.

73. See Fla. Stat. Ann. § 48.23 (West 1994), providing as follows:

No notice of lis pendens is effectual for any purpose beyond 1 year from the commencement of the action unless the relief sought is disclosed by the initial pleading to be founded on a duly recorded instrument or on a lien claimed under part I of chapter 713 against the property involved, except when the court extends the time on reasonable notice and for good cause. The court may impose such terms for the extension of time as justice requires.

74. State ex rel. Shannon v. Crouch, 645 S.W.2d 204 (Mo.App.1983); Blackwell v.

Hunt Oil Co., 217 Miss. 686, 64 So.2d 901 (1953).

75. See Goodson v. Lehmon, 225 N.C. 514, 35 S.E.2d 623 (1945).

76. Jones v. Robb, 35 Tex.Civ.App. 263, 80 S.W. 395 (1904); See McIlwrath v. Hollander, 73 Mo. 105 (1880).

77. See Conn. Gen. Stat. Ann. § 52–325 (1991 & Supp. 1997).

78. See Fla. Stat. Ann. § 48.23 (West 1994).

79. See, e.g., Allied Eastern Financial v. Goheen Enterprises, 265 Cal.App.2d 131, 71 Cal.Rptr. 126 (1968); Cutter v. Cutter Realty Co., 265 N.C. 664, 144 S.E.2d 882 (1965); Brownlee v. Vang, 206 Cal.App.2d 814, 24 Cal.Rptr. 158 (1962); Israelson v. Bradley, 308 N.Y. 511, 127 N.E.2d 313 (1955); McGurk v. Moore, 234 N.C. 248, 67 S.E.2d 53 (1951); Continental Securities Corp. v. Wetherbee, 187 La. 773, 175 So. 571 (1936) (under statute, filed notice of lis pendens canceled if court rendered judgment for plaintiff).

held the cancellation of a notice of lis pendens to be appealable.[80]

Library References:

West's Key No. Digests, Lis Pendens ☞1–26.
Wright, Miller & Kane, Federal Practice and Procedure: Civil 2d § 2935.

§ 13.7   Practice Checklists

(a) Preliminary Injunction

(1) Consider alternatives to preliminary injunction such as motion for early trial setting, receivership or prejudgment seizure. (*See* § 13.2(a)(2))

(2) Prepare a notice of motion or an order to show cause to be filed and served. Include memorandum of points and authorities, declarations or affidavits and other evidence, and a proposed order. Give notice to opponent. (*See* FRCP 65(a); § 13.2(c))

(3) Check the law of the particular circuit to determine the proper standard to be met. Set forth facts, not speculation, demonstrating likelihood of success on the merits, irreparable harm and favorable balance of equities. (*See* § 13.2(d)(2))

(4) Be prepared to provide the undertaking. (*See* FRCP 65(c); § 13.2(c)(8))

(b) Temporary Restraining Order

(1) Consider alternatives to temporary restraining order such as expedited discovery, receivership or prejudgment seizure. (*See* § 13.3(a))

(2) Prepare complaint, application for TRO, supporting declarations or affidavits, memorandum of points and authorities, and other evidence. Check the law of the particular circuit to determine the proper standard to be met. Set forth facts, not speculation, demonstrating likelihood of success on the merits, immediate and irreparable harm and favorable balance of equities. (*See* § 13.3(b))

(3) Attach a proposed TRO with provisions for a bond. Include an order to show cause to fix the time and date for hearing on preliminary injunction. (*See* § 13.3(a))

(4) Give notice to the affected party of time and place for hearing of TRO. If unable to give notice, certify in writing the efforts made and reasons for not giving notice. (*See* FRCP 65(b); § 13.3(a)(2))

(5) Be prepared to provide the undertaking. (*See* FRCP 65(c); § 13.3(b)(9))

---

80. Rehnberg v. Minnesota Homes, 236
Minn. 230, 52 N.W.2d 454 (1952).

(c) Receivership

(1) Determine whether requisite facts exist to establish grounds for appointment of a receiver. (*See* FRCP 66; § 13.4(b), (f)(2))

(2) Consider less drastic alternatives to receivership such as temporary restraining order, prejudgment seizure or lis pendens. (*See* § 13.4(a))

(3) Determine whether immediate, ex parte appointment is required. If so, be prepared to furnish bond immediately. (*See* § 13.4(f)(5))

(4) Prepare notice of motion and motion, supporting declarations or affidavits and other evidence, memorandum of points and authorities and proposed order of appointment. (*See* § 13.4(f))

(5) Follow local rules in each district for procedural matters such as notice, bonding and nominating a receiver. (*See* § 13.4(d), (f))

(d) Prejudgment Seizure

(1) Consider alternatives to prejudgment seizure such as temporary restraining order, receivership or lis pendens. (*See* § 13.5(a))

(2) Determine whether a federal statute applies. If not, state law will govern. (*See* FRCP 64; § 13.5(c), (d))

(3) Determine which specific state law remedy is most appropriate (*i.e.* arrest, attachment, garnishment, replevin or sequestration). (*See* FRCP 64; § 13.5(e))

(4) Follow applicable state substantive law. (*See* § 13.5(c), (e))

(e) Lis Pendens

(1) Locate the relevant state law. (*See* § 13.6(c))

(2) Determine whether the subject property is appropriate for recording a lis pendens. (*See* § 13.6(d))

(3) Determine whether the relevant cause of action is appropriate for recording a lis pendens. (*See* § 13.6(a))

(4) Consider more aggressive alternatives to lis pendens such as temporary restraining order, receivership or prejudgment seizure. (*See* § 13.6(a))

(5) Comply with the relevant state filing, recording and notice requirements. (*See* § 13.6(c), (e))

§ 13.8   Forms

(a) Ex Parte Application for Order to Show Cause re Preliminary Injunction and Temporary Restraining Order 💾

UNITED STATES DISTRICT COURT

_____ DISTRICT OF _____

Plaintiff,	) CASE NO.
	) EX PARTE APPLICATION FOR
	) ORDER TO SHOW CAUSE RE
vs.	) PRELIMINARY INJUNCTION AND
	) TEMPORARY RESTRAINING ORDER
	) DATE:
Defendant.	) TIME:
	) DEPT.:
	) TRIAL DATE: NOT SET
	) MOTION CUT–OFF DATE: NOT SET
_____)	DISCOVERY CUT–OFF DATE: NOT SET

Petitioner, _____ ("Petitioner"), moves this Court pursuant to Federal Rule of Civil Procedure 65 and Local Rule _____ for an Order to Show Cause re Preliminary Injunction and Temporary Restraining Order in the form attached to this application.

This Application is made upon the ground that defendant will, unless restrained, continue to [specify harmful activity by defendant]. If defendant is not enjoined, Petitioner will suffer irreparable harm in that [specify irreparable harm to Petitioner].

This Application is based on this Application, Petitioner's Memorandum of Points and Authorities, the Declarations of _____ and _____, and the exhibits thereto, filed concurrently herewith, the Complaint on file herein, any other pleadings, files and records in this action and any further argument or evidence introduced at the hearing of this Application.

DATED: _____

[NAME OF LAW FIRM OR
ATTORNEY]

By _____
Attorneys for Plaintiff

(b) Declaration re Certification of Giving Notice 💾

UNITED STATES DISTRICT COURT

_____ DISTRICT OF _____

Plaintiff,	) CASE NO.
	) DECLARATION RE
	) CERTIFICATION OF GIVING NOTICE
vs.	) DATE:

Defendant.	) TIME:) DEPT.:) TRIAL DATE: NOT SET) MOTION CUT–OFF DATE: NOT SET) DISCOVERY CUT–OFF DATE: NOT SET))

_____ declares:

1. I am counsel of record for plaintiff in the above-entitled action. I have personal and first-hand knowledge of the facts set forth in this declaration and could testify competently to such facts if called upon to do so. Pursuant to Fed.R.Civ.P. 65 and Local Rule _____, I make this declaration regarding the notice given to [Defendant/Defendants' counsel if known].

2. At ___*[time and date]*___, I called Defendant [at his residence/business] and asked to speak to Defendant. He was not present. I informed the person who answered the telephone that my client intended to file the within action as soon as the papers could be prepared, and that my client would seek a temporary restraining order. I asked that she have Defendant or his attorney contact me as soon as possible.

(a) At about _____ Defendant called me. I described to him each of the causes of action plaintiff intended to bring, and told him plaintiff would seek a temporary restraining order [describe relief to be sought.]

(b) At _____, Mr. _____ called me and identified himself as counsel for Defendant. I described each cause of action plaintiff intended to bring, and told him plaintiff would seek a temporary restraining order [describe relief to be sought]. He requested that he be given sufficient notice to appear and oppose the application.

(c) At _____ on _____, immediately on learning of the date, place and time for the hearing on plaintiff's application, I called Defendant counsel's office and advised him accordingly. At the same time I dispatched a messenger with a copy of all papers filed by plaintiff relating to the application.

Executed at _____, _____ this ___ day of _____, _____.

I declare under penalty of perjury under the laws of the United States of America that the foregoing is true and correct.

By _____
Attorneys for Plaintiff

(c) Order to Show Cause re Preliminary Injunction and Temporary Restraining Order 🖫

UNITED STATES DISTRICT COURT
_____ DISTRICT OF _____

	) Case No. _____
	)
Plaintiffs,	)
	) ORDER TO SHOW CASE RE
vs.	) PRELIMINARY INJUNCTION
	) AND TEMPORARY
	) RESTRAINING ORDER
	)
Defendant.	)
	)
_____	)

The Court has read the Complaint, the Application for an Order to Show Cause re Preliminary Injunction and Temporary Restraining Order, the Memorandum of Points and Authorities, the Affidavits of _____ and _____ and the attached exhibits, all filed concurrently herewith, and the pleadings, files and records in this action. The Court has considered the further argument or evidence introduced at the time this application was made. Based on such consideration, it appears that the defendant has [specify harm to plaintiff] and that unless restrained, will continue to [specify harm to plaintiff]. Such conduct will cause irreparable harm to the plaintiff by causing the following: [set forth specific injuries to plaintiff]. It further appears that (i) the plaintiff is likely to succeed on the merits of this action; (ii) immediate and irreparable injury, loss or damage will result to the plaintiff if the requested relief is not granted; (iii) serious questions are raised by plaintiff's Application; and (iv) the balance of hardships tips sharply in favor of the plaintiff,

IT IS HEREBY ORDERED, that defendant show cause before the Honorable _____ of this Court located at _____, at ____ o'clock ____.m., or as soon thereafter as counsel can be heard, on _____, 19__, why a preliminary injunction should not issue herein ordering said defendant, and its owners, representatives, stockholders, directors, agents, employees and all persons acting in concert or participation with them, during the pendency of this action, do all of the following: [specify conduct to be restrained].

IT IS FURTHER HEREBY ORDERED, that pending the hearing and determination of the Order to Show Cause re Preliminary Injunction, said defendant, and its owners, representatives, stockholders, directors, officers, agents, employees and all persons acting in concert or participation with them, be and they hereby are [specify conduct to be restrained].

IT IS FURTHER ORDERED that this order shall expire on _____, 19__ unless within such time the Order for Good Cause Shown is extended or unless the defendant consents that it may be extended for a longer period.

IT IS FURTHER ORDERED, that service of this Order to Show Cause re Preliminary Injunction and Temporary Restraining Order together with a copy of the papers filed with the Application therefor by hand delivery to [defendant's address] on or before _____, 19__, at ___ o'clock __.m. be deemed sufficient service. Defendant's opposition, if any, shall be filed and served by personal delivery on or before ___ a.m. on _____, 19__, and the plaintiff's reply, if any, shall be filed and served by personal delivery on or before ___.m. on _____, 19__.

Let the above orders issue on plaintiff's filing of a bond in the sum of $_____.

_____
United States District Judge

(d) Ex Parte Application for Appointment of Receiver or Alternatively, for Order to Show Cause re Appointment of Receiver; and Issuance of a Temporary Restraining Order and Order to Show Cause re Preliminary Injunction 🖫

UNITED STATES DISTRICT COURT
_____ DISTRICT OF _____

Plaintiffs, vs. Defendants.	) CASE NO.) EX PARTE APPLICATION FOR) APPOINTMENT OF RECEIVER OR) ALTERNATIVELY, FOR ORDER) TO SHOW CAUSE RE) APPOINTMENT OF RECEIVER;) AND ISSUANCE OF) TEMPORARY RESTRAINING) ORDER AND ORDER TO SHOW) CAUSE RE PRELIMINARY INJUNCTION) DATE:) TIME:) DEPT.:) TRIAL, MOTION AND) DISCOVERY CUTOFF DATES: NOT SET

Plaintiffs, the "Minority Shareholders," have filed this application in an effort to preserve the assets, books and records of defendant Corporation pending an involuntary dissolution of Corporation. Immediate relief is required because Corporation's majority shareholder, [   ], has excluded the Minority Shareholders from Corporation's affairs, defaulted on obligations to the Minority Shareholders exceeding $17 million, paid himself huge sums from Corporation's coffers, and otherwise brought Corporation to the brink of insolvency.

Specifically, the Minority Shareholders hereby apply ex parte for an order appointing a receiver to take possession of, conserve, manage, and collect any and all rents and profits from Corporation. Alternatively, Minority Shareholders seek an order to show cause why a receiver should not be appointed. The Minority Shareholders also request this Court to issue a temporary restraining order and an Order to Show Cause regarding the preliminary injunction in the form filed concurrently with this Application preventing defendants from interfering with the receiver's duties.

This Application is made on the grounds that absent immediate appointment of receiver and issuance of an order restraining interference with the receiver, the interests of Corporation and the Minority Shareholders will suffer pending the hearing and determination of the complaint for dissolution.

This Application is based upon the concurrently-filed Memorandum of Points and Authorities; Declarations of _____ ; the Verified Complaint for Dissolution; the pleadings, records and files herein; and on such other and further evidence and argument as may be presented at or before the hearing.

DATED: _____

By _____
Attorneys for Plaintiffs

(e) Application for Attachment, Temporary Protective Order, etc.[1] 🖬

ATTORNEY OR PARTY WITHOUT ATTORNEY (*Name and Address*):	TELE-PHONE NO.:	*FOR COURT USE ONLY*
ATTORNEY FOR (*Name*):		
NAME OF COURT: STREET ADDRESS: MAILING ADDRESS: CITY AND ZIP CODE: BRANCH NAME:		
PLAINTIFF: DEFENDANT:		

APPLICATION FOR	CASE NUMBER:
☐ **RIGHT TO ATTACH ORDER** ☐ **TEMPORARY PROTECTIVE ORDER** ☐ **ORDER FOR ISSUANCE OF WRIT OF ATTACHMENT** ☐ **ADDITIONAL WRIT OF ATTACHMENT** ☐ **After Hearing** ☐ **Ex Parte** ☐ **Against Property of Nonresident**	

1. Plaintiff (*name*):
   makes application
   ☐ after hearing
   ☐ ex parte for
   a. ☐ right to attach order and writ of attachment.
   b. ☐ writ of attachment.
   c. ☐ additional writ of attachment.
   d. ☐ temporary protective order.
   e. ☐ an order directing the defendant to transfer to the levying officer possession of
      (1) ☐ property in defendant's possession.
      (2) ☐ documentary evidence in defendant's possession of title to property.
      (3) ☐ documentary evidence in defendant's possession of debt owed to defendant.

2. Defendant (*name*):
   a. ☐ is a corporation
      (1) ☐ qualified to do business in California.
      (2) ☐ not qualified to do business in California.
   b. ☐ is a California partnership or other unincorporated association.

§ 13.8

1. This is a California Judicial Form.
Check your state for official forms.

SHORT TITLE:	CASE NUMBER:

   c. ☐ is a foreign partnership which

      (1) ☐ has filed a designation under Corp C 15700.

      (2) ☐ has not filed a designation under Corp C 15700.

   d. ☐ is a natural person who

      (1) ☐ resides in California.

      (2) ☐ does not reside in California.

3. ☐ Attachment is not sought for a purpose other than recovery on a claim for money which is not secured within the meaning of CCP 483.010.

   and is based upon a contract; the facts showing plaintiff is entitled to a judgment are set forth in the

   a. ☐ verified complaint.

   b. ☐ attached affidavit.

   c. ☐ following facts:

4. ☐ The claim arises out of conduct by the defendant who is a natural person of a trade, business or profession. The claim is not based on the sale or lease of property, a license to use property, the furnishing of services, or the loan of money where any of the foregoing was used by the defendant primarily for personal, family, or household purposes.

5. The amount to be secured by the attachment is $

   a. ☐ which includes estimated costs of $

   b. ☐ which includes estimated allowable attorney fees of $

6. Plaintiff has no information or belief that the claim is discharged or the prosecution of the action is stayed in a proceeding under Title 11 of the United States Code (Bankruptcy).

7. Plaintiff is informed and believes that the following property sought to be attached for which a method of levy is provided is subject to attachment:

   a. ☐ Any property of a defendant who is **not** a natural person.

   b. ☐ Any property of a nonresident defendant.

   c. ☐ Property of a defendant who is a natural person (*describe property and identify statute providing for method of levy*):

   Where required provide the following additional information:

   (1) ☐ The Property is in the possession, custody, or control of a nondefendant or a nondefendant has an interest in the property (*state the name and address of the nondefendant*):

   (2) ☐ The property is a crop, timber, or mineral or the like (*describe the real property on which it is located*):

                          (Page two of four)

SHORT TITLE:	CASE NUMBER:

(3) ☐ The property is covered by a bulk sales notice or escrow.

(4) ☐ The property is plaintiff's share of proceeds from an escrow in which defendant's liquor license is sold (*specify license number*):

(5) ☐ The property is money of a defendant who is a natural person, and the property is

    (a) ☐ located on the premises where a trade, business, or profession is conducted by defendant;

    (b) ☐ in excess of $1,000 located elsewhere than on the premises where a trade, business, or profession is conducted by defendant and not in deposit accounts;

    (c) ☐ located in a deposit account in excess of $1,000;

    (d) ☐ in excess of an aggregate amount of $1,000 located
        ☐ in deposit accounts.

        ☐ in a deposit account and money located elsewhere than on the premises where a trade, business, or profession is conducted by defendant.

8. Plaintiff is informed and believes that the property sought to be attached is not exempt from attachment.

9. ☐ The court issued a Right to Attach Order on (*date*):

    ☐ pursuant to CCP 484.090 (on hearing)

    ☐ and Order for Writ of Attachment pursuant to CCP 492.030 (nonresident).

    ☐ and Order for Writ of Attachment pursuant to CCP 485.220 (ex parte).

10. The court found plaintiff is entitled to a Right to Attach Order pursuant to CCP 485.240 on (*date*):

11. ☐ Nonresident defendant has not filed a general appearance.

12. ☐ Plaintiff

    ☐ alleges on ex parte application for order for writ of attachment

    ☐ is informed and believes on application for temporary protective order that plaintiff would suffer great or irreparable injury if the order is not issued before the matter can be heard on notice because

    a. ☐ it may be inferred that there is a danger that the property sought to be attached would be

        ☐ concealed

        ☐ substantially impaired in value

        ☐ made unavailable to levy by other than concealment or impairment in value and the inference is supported by facts set forth in the
        ☐ verified complaint

        ☐ attached affidavit

        ☐ following facts (*specify*):

    b. ☐ a bulk sales notice was recorded and published pursuant to Division 6 of the Commercial Code with respect to a bulk transfer by the defendant.

    c. ☐ an escrow has been opened pursuant to the provisions of Bus & PC 24074 with respect to the sale by the defendant of a liquor license (*specify license number*):

    d. ☐ other circumstances (*specify*):

13. ☐ Plaintiff requests the following relief in the temporary protective order (*specify*):

(Page three of four)

SHORT TITLE:	CASE NUMBER:

14.   ☐ Plaintiff

a.   ☐ has filed an undertaking in the amount of
$

b.   ☐ has not filed an undertaking.

Date:

....▶

(TYPE OR PRINT NAME OF PLAINTIFF)
(SIGNATURE OF PLAINTIFF)

By: ....
(NAME AND TITLE)

DECLARATION

I declare under penalty of perjury under the laws of the State of California that the foregoing is true and correct.

Date:

....▶

(TYPE OR PRINT NAME)(SIGNATURE OF DECLARANT)

15.   Total number of pages attached:

(f) Notice of Pendency of Action (Lis Pendens)   🖫

UNITED STATES DISTRICT COURT
_____ DISTRICT OF _____

Plaintiffs,	) CASE NO.
	) NOTICE OF PENDENCY OF ACTION
	) (LIS PENDENS)
	)
vs.	) DATE:
	) TIME:
	) DEPT.:
Defendants.	) TRIAL DATE: NOT SET
	) MOTION CUT–OFF DATE: NOT SET
_____)	DISCOVERY CUT–OFF DATE: NOT SET

PLEASE TAKE NOTICE THAT the above-captioned action, by plaintiff _____ against _____, affects title to and/or possession of real property in that plaintiff seeks specific performance of a contract to purchase the real property located in _____ County at (street address) and described as:

[LEGAL DESCRIPTION OF PROPERTY]

DATED: _____, 19__

By _____

Attorneys for _____

CHAPTER 14

PARTIES

by
Samuel Adams
and
James J. Arguin

Table of Sections

WESTLAW Electronic Research

See WESTLAW Electronic Research Guide preceding the Summary of Contents.

---

§ 14.1 Scope Note

This chapter discusses the rules, statutes and procedures governing which individuals or entities may bring suit in their own name; the capacity of an individual or entity to sue or be sued; the right of a disinterested stakeholder to resolve in one proceeding multiple, competing claims to a single liability; the ability of a nonparty to intervene and participate in pending litigation; and the substitution of parties in the event of death, incompetency or the transfer of interest occurring during the course of pending litigation. Of primary concern are FRCP 17, establishing the real party in interest and capacity requirements; FRCP 22, establishing the requirements for interpleader; FRCP 24, establishing the requirements for intervention; and FRCP 25, establishing the requirements for substitution of parties. Like the rules of joinder, which are addressed in Chapter 10 "Joinder, Consolidation and Severance," *supra*, the purpose of the rules, statutes and procedures discussed in this chapter is to avoid multiplicity of suits by facilitating the resolution of all pending controversies among interested parties in one proceeding. As such, the rules, statutes and procedures discussed in this chapter are of critical importance not only to the individual parties interested in the resolution of a particular lawsuit, but also to the efficient administration of the entire litigation process.

Library References:

West's Key No. Digests, Federal Civil Procedure ⊕101–392.
Wright, Miller & Kane, Federal Practice and Procedure: Civil 2d § 1541.

§ 14.2 Practical Considerations

(a) Real Party in Interest

FRCP 17(a) requires that every action be brought in the name of the party possessing the substantive right to relief. [1] The ultimate beneficiary of the action is entirely irrelevant, as illustrated by the fact that the Rule expressly authorizes executors, administrators and other named representatives to sue in their own name without joinder of the party for whose benefit the action is brought. The Rule serves as an important, albeit perhaps unnecessary, reminder that no party can bring suit unless the suit is brought in the name of the person possessing the right to relief under the substantive law. Strategically, this means that a defendant may insist upon having an action maintained by a plaintiff against whom it can assert the res judicata principles of finality of judgment when the litigation is carried through to a judgment on the merits.

§ 14.2

1. *See infra* § 14.3.

In practice, the Rule is most commonly applied with regard to assignments and subrogation. It is now settled that the assignee of a chose in action is a real party in interest, and that an assignor who has assigned his entire claim is not. Where, on the other hand, there is a partial assignment, both the assignor and assignee are real parties in interest. In such a situation, a defendant is faced with the threat of a split judgment and should move to compel the joinder of both the assignor and assignee as plaintiffs.

A similar situation is presented when an insurer pays its insured's loss and thus is subrogated to the insured's right against some third party. Where the insurer has paid the entire loss, it is the real party in interest and must sue in its own name. The insured, which no longer has any interest in any potential recovery, cannot bring suit in its own name. If the insurer has paid only part of the loss, both the insured and insurer remain real parties in interest and a defendant faced with such a situation should move to join both parties as plaintiffs in order to avoid multiplicity of suits.

Procedurally, a defendant seeking to challenge the plaintiff's standing as a real party in interest should file a motion to dismiss pursuant to FRCP 12(b)(1) (lack of subject matter jurisdiction), (6) (failure to state a claim), or (7) (failure to name an indispensable party). While such a motion may be filed during trial or, in the case of a motion asserting lack of subject matter jurisdiction, on appeal, it is advisable to file the motion as early in the litigation as possible to avoid any potential waiver of the defense. A plaintiff faced with such a motion must show that it possesses the legal right under the applicable law or that the defendant has unreasonably delayed the filing of its motion. Since one of the purposes of the Rule is to avoid the forfeiture of meritorious claims, courts are particularly wary of allowing dismissal where the defendant's delay in raising the real party in interest challenge would prejudice the real party in interest, e.g., where, as a result of a mistake as to real party status, the applicable limitations period has expired.

Moreover, the plaintiff is entitled to a "reasonable time" within which to cure any defect by joining, substituting or obtaining ratification from the real party in interest before the action may be dismissed. To avoid any potential ambiguity as to the plaintiff's compliance with this provision, it is advisable to include in a motion to dismiss on real party in interest grounds a request that the court specify the time within which the plaintiff must effectuate its cure or face dismissal.

(b) Capacity to Sue and Be Sued

An important procedural distinction exists between the concept of a "real party in interest" under Rule 17(a) and "capacity to sue and be sued," which is governed by Rule 17(b). While a party may be the real party in interest, it may nevertheless lack capacity to sue, as for example when a party becomes mentally incompetent. The converse is also true. A party may possess the capacity to sue, but it may not be the real party in interest, as for example when a corporation has assigned all of its interest in a claim to another party. The distinction is significant because FRCP 9(a) generally requires a specific negative averment if a defendant seeks to challenge a plaintiff's capacity to sue. A plaintiff, in contrast, generally has the burden of establishing its substantive right to recovery when its real party in interest status is challenged.

FRCP 17(b) sets forth the rules by which the legal capacity of business entities, such as partnerships and corporations is to be determined.[2] FRCP 17(c) permits a "next friend" to sue on behalf of an infant or incompetent person without being appointed by the court. In practice, such next friends are typically parents or relatives, who will not usually have interests adverse to those of the infant or incompetent person and who can pursue the action without the necessity of the appointment of a guardian ad litem. Nevertheless, when a case pursued by a next friend is settled, it is advisable for the defendant to request that the court approve the settlement. While court approval is not required by any Rule, it will help deter any later challenge to the settlement claiming that it was not in the best interests of the infant or incompetent person. In those situations where parents or relatives have interests that may conflict with those of the infant or incompetent person, it is advisable to seek appointment of a guardian ad litem by the court, which appointment may be sought concurrently with the commencement of the action.

When defending an infant or incompetent person who does not have a representative, the appointment of a guardian ad litem should be sought as soon as possible after service of the complaint and summons. In contrast to actions brought by a "next friend," prior court approval generally is required before a "next friend" may defend an action on behalf of an infant or incompetent person. In all instances, court approval of a proposed settlement with a minor or incompetent person is advisable to avoid later challenge.

(c) Interpleader

Interpleader allows a party facing conflicting claims to the same liability to avoid satisfying the wrong claim and incurring multiple adverse judgments in different courts by providing a mechanism requiring that all of the claims be litigated in one proceeding.[3] In practice, the procedure most commonly arises when two or more persons claim adverse interest in the proceeds of a life insurance policy. Rather than paying any one claimant, the insurance company may require all the claimants to litigate the merits of their claims in a single proceeding. Interpleader also arises where, for instance, a defendant is exposed to double liability on claims asserted by a plaintiff and co-defendant. In such a situation, interpleader allows the defendant to interplead the plaintiff by counterclaim and the co-defendant by cross-claim, thereby avoiding the threat of double liability and affording the defendant

---

2. *See infra* § 14.4.   **3.** *See infra* § 14.5.

important strategic options. For instance, a secondary beneficiary may bring suit against an insurer and the principal beneficiary, alleging that the insurer's payment to the principal beneficiary was improper, *e.g.*, because the principal beneficiary was suspected of murdering the insured. The insurer may defend by bringing claims for interpleader against the multiple claimants to the fund.

Where the party seeking interpleader is truly an innocent stakeholder with respect to the disputed fund (that is where the interpleader acknowledges that the fund is due and owing to at least one of the claimants), it is entitled to be discharged of full responsibility regarding the disputed fund once those funds are paid into the court's registry. In addition, the court, in its discretion, may award an innocent stakeholder its reasonable attorneys' fees and costs incurred in connection with the interpleader action. Increasingly, however, courts have declined to award attorneys' fees and costs to insurance companies that are in the business of distributing proceeds from insurance policies. In the absence of such an award, there may be less of an impetus for insurance companies to initiate an interpleader action in smaller cases (smaller, that is, in terms of the number of potential claimants and relative value of the claims) since, as a practical matter, it may be more cost efficient for the insurer to simply wait to defend an action brought by one of the claimants. Where, however, there is a large class of potential claimants seeking recovery from a single fund (*e.g.*, the proceeds of an insurance policy), as for instance in the product liability or environmental tort arena, interpleader continues to provide an orderly and efficient mechanism for resolving competing claims in one proceeding.

(d) Intervention

Intervention is the mechanism by which persons claiming an interest in a pending action, who were not originally included in the action, may seek to participate.[4] To intervene as of right, the person must qualify as a real party in interest within the meaning of FRCP 17 or as a person required for just adjudication within the meaning of FRCP 19. FRCP 24(b) also provides for permissive intervention where a person eligible for permissive joinder under FRCP 20(a) may seek to join in an action after it has commenced.

Prior to moving for intervention, careful consideration must be given to determining whether the movant's interest in the pending litigation is compelling enough to risk being bound by an adverse judgment. Once a motion to intervene is allowed, the intervenor generally has the right to fully participate in the litigation in the same manner and to the same extent as the original parties. The intervenor, therefore, risks being bound by the res judicata effect of a potentially adverse judgment that it otherwise could have avoided by remaining on the side lines. As a practical matter, therefore, careful consideration must be given to the posture of the pending litigation and the intervenor's

---

4. *See infra* § 14.6.

likelihood of success on the merits of its claim. The intervenor also generally should be prepared to assume an active role in the conduct of the litigation by staking out its position on the issues that are of interest to it.

An application to intervene should be timely made and accompanied by a copy of the proposed pleading in intervention (*e.g.*, complaint or answer). When a motion to intervene is filed long after the action was commenced, it may be opposed as being untimely and the party seeking intervention should be prepared to demonstrate that no unreasonable prejudice or delay will result from allowance of intervention.

(e) Substitution of Parties

If a party (either plaintiff or defendant) dies after commencement of the action, and the action survives in favor of the decedent's estate or against it, FRCP 25(a)(1) controls, with the decedent's representative bearing the burden of compliance.[5] Although the Rule does not set any time limit as to when a suggestion of death must be made, it contains a spring trap for the unwary representative of the deceased party in that it allows any party, not just the decedent's representative, to enter a suggestion of death on the record. Once the suggestion of death is properly entered, a motion to substitute the decedent's representative must be made within 90 days or the cause of action will be dismissed as to the deceased party. The 90–day time limit may present difficulties to the decedent's representative since appointment procedures for qualified representatives often take substantially longer to complete. However, the decedent's representative may obtain additional time for substitution by filing a motion pursuant to FRCP 6(b).

Even assuming that additional time remains, substitution may be denied where it would be otherwise unfair or inequitable to allow substitution. Substitution has been denied, for instance, where the settlement and distribution of the decedent's estate was near completion at the time the motion for substitution was made. The safest course for a decedent's representative is not to wait for a suggestion of death to be filed, but to move for substitution as soon as the fact of death becomes known.

Library References:

West's Key No. Digests, Federal Civil Procedure ⊶101–392.
Wright, Miller & Kane, Federal Practice and Procedure: Civil 2d § 1542.

§ 14.3 Real Party in Interest

FRCP 17(a) provides that "[e]very action shall be prosecuted in the name of the real party in interest."[1] The Rule does not purport to identify the "real party in interest" in any particular case; instead, that issue is resolved by reference to substantive statutory and common law.

---

5. *See infra* § 14.7.

§ 14.3

1. FRCP 17(a).

The provisions of FRCP 17(a) are, therefore, purely procedural. Unlike capacity to sue or be sued, which is discussed *infra* at Section 14.4, the requirement of bringing suit in the name of the real party in interest applies only to plaintiffs, not to defendants.[2]

(a) Protection from Multiple Suits

The purpose of the Rule is to ensure that the person who brings a claim is entitled to enforce the claim.[3] Thus, the Rule protects a defendant who is subject to liability in a pending action from being called upon to defend a subsequent suit initiated by the true claimant. In this way, the Rule ensures that a defendant will be called upon to defend only once and that any action taken to judgment will have its proper effect as res judicata.[4]

(b) Party Must Possess Legal Right or Interest

Courts uniformly identify the real party in interest as the person holding the substantive right that is sought to be enforced in the subject litigation.[5] Thus, to determine the plaintiff's status as the real party in interest, courts look to the substantive statutory or common law creating the right being sued upon to ascertain whether the plaintiff possesses a substantive right to relief.[6] A party not possessing a right under the substantive law is not the real party in interest with respect to that right and may not enforce it.[7]

The real party in interest need not be the party who ultimately will benefit from the recovery.[8] For instance, a shareholder may be the real party in interest in a shareholder derivative action, although any recovery will inure to the corporation's benefit.[9] Similarly, an executor or

---

2. University of Texas v. Vratil, 96 F.3d 1337, 1340 n. 2 (10th Cir.1996).

3. Audiotext Communications Network, Inc. v. US Telecom, Inc., 912 F.Supp. 469, 477 (D.Kan.1995) ("The purpose of Rule 17(a) is to ensure that the person who brings an action is entitled to enforce the right.").

4. Allwaste Envtl. Servs./North Atl., Inc. v. Pastore, 911 F.Supp. 29, 31 (D.Me. 1996) (the purpose of FRCP 17(a) is to protect a defendant from facing a subsequent similar action by one not a party to the present proceeding and to ensure that judgments will have proper finality); Naghiu v. Inter–Continental Hotels Group, Inc., 165 F.R.D. 413, 419 (D.Del.1996) (the underlying aim of FRCP 17(a) is to ensure fairness to the defendant by protecting it against a subsequent action by the party actually entitled to relief).

5. Farrell Constr. Co. v. Jefferson Parish, 896 F.2d 136, 140 (5th Cir.1990).

6. Naghiu v. Inter–Continental Hotels Group, Inc., 165 F.R.D. 413, 419 (D.Del. 1996) (bailee's status as real party in interest determined by reference to substantive law of the state in which the district court sits); United States v. Gambler's Supply, Inc., 925 F.Supp. 658, 668–69 (D.S.D.1996) (government's status as real party in interest in statutory qui tam action determined by reference to federal statute).

7. Farrell Constr. Co., 896 F.2d at 140.

8. *Id.* at 140–41 (while subcontractor lacked right under substantive state law to sue owner for breach of contract, suit could be maintained on subcontractor's behalf by prime contractor who was in privity with owner and any recovery would "pass through" to subcontractor).

9. Ross v. Bernhard, 396 U.S. 531, 538, 90 S.Ct. 733, 738, 24 L.Ed.2d 729 (1970) (corporation is the real party in interest in a shareholder derivative action). *See gener-*

administrator may be the real party in interest to maintain a wrongful death action under the applicable state law, even though any recovery would pass through the decedent's estate and go directly to the statutory beneficiaries.[10] In fact, the second sentence of FRCP 17(a) expressly envisions just this situation by providing that an "executor, administrator, guardian, bailee, trustee of an express trust, a party with whom or in whose name a contract has been made for the benefit of another, or a party authorized by statute may sue in that person's own name without joining the party for whose benefit the action is brought.... "[11]

Moreover, there may be multiple real parties in interest for a given claim, and if the plaintiff is a real party in interest under the substantive law, FRCP 17(a) does not require the addition of other parties also fitting that description.[12] However, such additional parties may need to be joined to the lawsuit pursuant to the requirements of FRCP 19(a).[13]

(1) Executors, Administrators, Guardians

As noted in Section 14.3(b), *supra,* FRCP 17(a) allows an executor, administrator, guardian, bailee, or trustee of an express trust to sue in his own name without joining as a plaintiff the party for whose benefit the action is brought.[14] This is not an exception to the real party in interest requirement; rather, these parties are deemed by the Rule to possess the substantive right to sue in their own names, without the need for joinder of the person for whose benefit the action has been brought. The Rule extends this same permission to sue in his own name without joinder of the party for whose benefit the action has been brought to a person who contracts in his own name for the benefit of another and to a person authorized by statute.[15] Once again, it is immaterial for real party in interest purposes that the ultimate beneficiary of any recovery is not a party to the action, so long as the party bringing suit is authorized by the applicable substantive law to do so.[16] For instance, where state law delegates to the general partner the power to sue directly on behalf of a partnership, the general partner is the real party in interest for the partnership's claims, even though any recovery will inure to the partnership's benefit.[17]

---

ally Chapter 16 "Derivative Actions by Stockholders" *infra* (discussing FRCP 23.1 and derivative actions).

10. *See* Cruz v. Korean Air Lines Co., 838 F.Supp. 843, 847 (S.D.N.Y.1993) (administrator of decedent's estate was real party in interest in wrongful death action brought for benefit of statutory beneficiaries).

11. FRCP 17(a).

12. HB Gen. Corp. v. Manchester Partners, L.P., 95 F.3d 1185, 1194–97 (3d Cir. 1996) (allowing general and limited partners to maintain suit "derivatively or otherwise" for the benefit of partnership where

under the substantive state law the plaintiffs were among the parties authorized to bring such claims).

13. Farrell Constr. Co., 896 F.2d at 140 (noting that joinder of indispensable parties may be required under FRCP 19(a), but not FRCP 17(a)). *See generally* Chapter 10 "Joinder, Consolidation and Severance," *supra* (discussing the rules and procedures of joinder).

14. FRCP 17(a).

15. *Id.*

16. *See supra* § 14.2.

17. HB Gen. Corp., 95 F.3d at 1194.

The list of persons set out in FRCP 17(a) who are regarded as real parties in interest is meant to be illustrative, and not exhaustive.[18] Thus, any party possessing a substantive right under the applicable law may bring suit, without regard to particular factual context in which the case may arise.[19] Moreover, the Rule does not prevent suit by the ultimate beneficiary in his own name. Thus, although Rule 17(a) permits a promisee in a contract for the benefit of a third party to sue as a real party in interest, it is clear that the third party beneficiary may also maintain an action when the applicable substantive law recognizes that right.[20] Where, for instance, the applicable state law provides that a partnership may enforce a contract entered into by one of its partners, Rule 17(a) provides that either or both the partner, in whose name the contract was entered into, and the partnership, for whose benefit the contract was made, are real parties in interest entitled to recover,[21] so too in the case of a beneficiary under an express trust or a bailor in a bailment situation.[22]

(2) Attorneys-In–Fact/Agents

An attorney-in-fact is not a real party in interest and cannot maintain suit in his own name. An attorney-in-fact with authority to initiate a suit on behalf of the principal is entitled to bring suit, but the principal remains the real party in interest; the attorney-in-fact brings suit only in the name of the principal, not on his own behalf.[23] This is consistent with the general rule that an agent does not acquire the real party status of its principal, absent a valid assignment or subrogation of the claim.[24]

(3) Fictitious Names

While a court has discretion to permit a real party in interest to proceed in litigation under a fictitious name, this practice is unusual and has been allowed only in "exceptional circumstances where the party has

18. Advisory Committee Notes to 1966 amendment to FRCP 17 (noting that "the rule is designed to make it clear that the specific instances enumerated are not exceptions to, but illustrations of, the rule").

19. *Id.* ("These illustrations, of course, carry no negative implication to the effect that there are not other instances of recognition as the real party in interest of one whose standing as such may be in doubt.").

20. *Id.*

21. Autin's Cajun Cookery Joint Venture v. Kroger Co., No. 89–3902, 1989 WL 133103, at *2 (E.D.La.1989).

22. *See In re* Narciso, 149 B.R. 917, 918 (E.D.Ark.1993) (recognizing both administrator and heir as real party in interest); Gulf Oil Corp. v. Gilbert, 330 U.S. 501, 67 S.Ct. 839, 91 L.Ed. 1055 (1947) (owner of warehouse in which furniture was stored held to be equally entitled to sue on behalf of the numerous owners of the stored furniture).

23. *See* Advanced Magnetics, Inc. v. Bayfront Partners, Inc., 106 F.3d 11, 17–18 (2d Cir.1997) (power of attorney is not the equivalent of an assignment of ownership; and, standing alone, it does not enable the grantee to bring suit in his own name); Choi v. Kim, 50 F.3d 244, 246–47 (3d Cir. 1995) (reversing dismissal of suit where district court improperly concluded that attorney-in-fact was suing on his own behalf and not merely as agent for principal).

24. Hanna Mining Co. v. Minnesota Power & Light Co., 573 F.Supp. 1395, 1398 (D.Minn.1983) (an agent does not possess real party status), *aff'd*, 739 F.2d 1368 (8th Cir.1984).

a privacy right so substantial as to outweigh the customary and constitutionally-embedded presumption of openness in judicial proceedings."[25] This concern for openness in judicial proceedings reflects another important policy underlying the real party in interest rule.

By requiring that all civil actions be prosecuted in the name of the real party in interest, FRCP 17(a) protects the public's legitimate interest in knowing what disputes involving what parties are pending in the judicial system.[26] Because the use of fictitious names undermines this legitimate policy interest, courts have been willing to allow real parties to maintain suit under a fictitious name only if there are substantial privacy interests at stake, such as, where the interests of children are involved or where the claims involve highly sensitive personal issues, such as, abortion, mental illness, personal safety or intimacy.[27]

(c) Effect of Assignment or Subrogation of Claim

(1) Valid Assignment Shifts Real Party Status

FRCP 17(a) makes the assignee of a valid assignment, written or oral, a real party in interest.[28] The Rule applies only to transfers of interest that occur prior to the commencement of an action; transfers that take place during the action are governed by FRCP 25(c).[29] Where the assignment is total, the assignee is the only real party in interest and suit must be brought in its name.[30] Where, on the other hand, the assignment is partial and the assignor still retains part of the substantive right being sued upon, both the assignee and assignor remain as real parties in interest and each must sue in its own name, with judgment to be entered proportionally.[31] If the assignor and assignee sue separately, the defendant may move for joinder under FRCP 19 and 21, so as to litigate the validity of the underlying claim in one proceeding.[32] The fact

25. Doe v. Indiana Black Expo, Inc., 923 F.Supp. 137, 139–40 (S.D.Ind.1996) (discussing the use of fictitious names in federal court proceedings and the limited circumstances under which it has been allowed).

26. *Id.* at 139; *see also* Doe v. Frank, 951 F.2d 320, 324 (11th Cir.1992) ("Lawsuits are public events.").

27. Indiana Black Expo, Inc., 923 F.Supp. at 139–40 (collecting cases where the use of fictitious names has been allowed).

28. *See* HB Gen. Corp. v. Manchester Partners, L.P., 95 F.3d 1185, 1197 (3d Cir. 1996) ("the original purpose of the real party in interest rule was … to allow an assignee to sue in his or her own name").

29. Barker v. Jackson Nat'l Life Ins. Co., 163 F.R.D. 364, 365 (N.D.Fla.1995); *see infra* § 14.7(d).

30. Overseas Dev. Disc Corp. v. Sangamo Constr. Co., 686 F.2d 498, 505 n. 17

(7th Cir.1982) (noting that courts are in "full accord" in holding that an assignee under a valid assignment is the real party in interest and that suit must be brought in his name).

31. *See* Scheufler v. General Host Corp., 895 F.Supp. 1416, 1417–18 (D.Kan.1995) (purported assignment of claims between landowner and tenants was insufficient to confer real party in interest status on landowner as to the portion of damages attributable to injury to tenants where, under applicable state law, landowner and tenants could each recover only the damage to his or her own interests), *aff'd,* 126 F.3d 1261 (10th Cir.1997).

32. *See supra* Chapter 10 "Joinder, Consolidation and Severance."

that the assignor may be the ultimate beneficiary of any recovery does not usually prevent the assignee from becoming the real party in interest.[33]

While FRCP 17(a) in no way attempts to determine the underlying validity of the assignment since that is a matter governed by the applicable substantive law,[34] the general rule that an assignee may sue in his or her own name is subject to two important limitations: an assignment may not be used merely as a vehicle to circumvent the applicable limitations period, nor to confer federal jurisdiction where none otherwise would exist.[35]

(2) Valid Subrogation Shifts Real Party Status

Like assignments, a valid subrogation shifts real party status to the subrogee.[36] Subrogation typically arises when an insurance company pays its insured pursuant to a policy, and the company is then subrogated to the cause of action of its insured.[37] The general rule is that if an insurer has paid the entire loss suffered by the insured, it is the only real party in interest and must sue in its own name.[38] However, if the insurer has paid only part of the loss, both the insured and the insurer have substantive rights against the tortfeasor which qualify them as real parties in interest.[39]

A question arises in a loan receipt situation as to whether the insurer or the insured is the real party in interest. A loan receipt is an arrangement under which the insurer advances an amount of money to its insured as a loan. The loan is repayable only in the event and to the extent of any net amount recovered by that insured from a third party.[40] Technically, the insurer is not the real party in interest, since it has not paid the insured's claims and, therefore, is not subrogated to his rights.[41]

---

33. Klamath-Lake Pharm. Ass'n v. Klamath Med. Serv. Bureau, 701 F.2d 1276, 1282 (9th Cir.) ("An assignment of claims does not prevent the assignors from receiving the benefits of the litigation."), *cert. denied*, 464 U.S. 822, 104 S.Ct. 88, 78 L.Ed.2d 96 (1983). *But see In re* Stevens, 184 B.R. 584, 586 (Bankr.W.D.Wash.1995) (holding that assignee was not real party in interest where the assignment was for collection purposes only and assignor would receive 100% of any recovery).

34. Weaver v. Employers Fire Ins. Co., No. 88–1189–C, 1989 WL 46263, at *2 (D.Kan.1989) ("The question of who owns the cause of action is a matter of state substantive law in diversity cases."). *See also* Scheufler, 895 F.Supp. at 1417–18 (looking to state substantive law to determine validity of assignment).

35. *See infra* § 14.3(d).

36. 18 George J. Couch, Couch on Insurance § 74.381 (2d rev. ed. 1983).

37. *See id.* at §§ 74.378 to 74.381.

38. Underwriters At Interest On Cover Note JHB92M10582079 v. Nautronix, Ltd., 79 F.3d 480, 484 (5th Cir.1996) (reversing trial court's order replacing insurer for insured in partial subrogation case since both insurer and insured were real parties in interest); Krueger v. Cartwright, 996 F.2d 928, 931–32 (7th Cir.1993) (where insurer has paid entire claim it is the real party in interest and must sue in its own name; where insurer has paid only part of the loss, both the insurer and insured own portions of the substantive rights and should sue in their own names).

39. *Id.*

40. T.S.I. Holdings, Inc. v. Buckingham, 885 F.Supp. 1457, 1462 (D.Kan.1995).

41. *See id.* (noting that there is a split of authority among courts as to the validity of loan receipt agreements).

However, where the loan receipt arrangement is valid under state law, federal courts generally have held that the insured remains the real party in interest under FRCP 17(a).[42] Where permissible, this allows the insurance company to pay the full value of the insured's loss, and preserve the right to bring suit in the insured's name, as opposed to its own.[43]

(d) Dismissal and Relation Back

(1) Defenses and Objection

Although the Federal Rules of Civil Procedure do not specifically address the defense that the plaintiff is not a real party in interest, courts have permitted the defense to be raised either by answer or motion.[44] Even absent an objection by the defendant, the court may raise a FRCP 17(a) objection on its own initiative.[45]

A defendant's motion to dismiss on real party in interest grounds may assert that an indispensable party (the real party in interest) has been omitted from the action or that the plaintiff's complaint fails to state a claim upon which relief may be granted.[46] In either event, the defense may be raised by motion filed after pleading, even during trial.[47] Moreover, if joinder or substitution of the real party in interest destroys subject matter jurisdiction,[48] then the motion to dismiss may be brought at any time, even on appeal.[49] Despite the seeming liberality of the Rule, in practice courts have broad discretion to deny "untimely" motions to dismiss on real party in interest grounds.[50] For instance, an objection to real party in interest status generally will be denied when raised for the

42. R.J. Enstrom Corp. v. Interceptor Corp., 520 F.2d 1217, 1219–20 (10th Cir. 1975).

43. See T.S.I. Holdings, Inc., 885 F.Supp. at 1462 (in loan receipt situation holding that insured, not insurer, was real party in interest, possessing substantive right to recovery under state law).

44. Whelan v. Abell, 953 F.2d 663, 672 (D.C.Cir.) (FRCP 17(a) defense may be raised either as an affirmative defense under FRCP 8(c) or in a motion to dismiss under FRCP 12(b)(6)), cert. denied, 506 U.S. 906, 113 S.Ct. 300, 121 L.Ed.2d 223 (1992); Gogolin & Stelter v. Karn's Auto Imports, Inc., 886 F.2d 100, 102–03 n. 3 (5th Cir.1989) (noting that the real party in interest defense, unlike capacity, need not be raised by specific negative averment in pleading, but need only be timely asserted), cert. denied, 494 U.S. 1031, 110 S.Ct. 1480, 108 L.Ed.2d 617 (1990).

45. See, e.g., Weissman v. Weener, 12 F.3d 84, 86 (7th Cir.1993) (real party issue raised sua sponte by court).

46. See FRCP 12(b)(6) and (7).

47. See FRCP 12(h)(2) (a defense for failure to state a claim or failure to join an indispensable party may be raised "at a trial on the merits").

48. When the real party in interest has been brought into the lawsuit by substitution, joinder or ratification, the court must assure itself that subject matter jurisdiction (i.e., diversity of citizenship) still exists. See Certain Interested Underwriters at Lloyd's v. Layne, 26 F.3d 39, 42–43 n. 1 (6th Cir. 1994).

49. See FRCP 12(b)(1) and (h)(3). See also Attorneys Trust v. Videotape Computer Prods., Inc., 93 F.3d 593, 595 (9th Cir. 1996) (noting that court will consider a jurisdictional challenge even when it is raised for the first time on appeal).

50. See infra § 14.3(d)(2) (discussing waiver).

first time on the eve of trial.[51]

(2) Waiver

Because the requirements of FRCP 17(a) are for the benefit of the defendant, courts have held that an objection on real party grounds must be raised with "reasonable promptness."[52] By raising the defense early on in the proceeding, the court and the parties are better able to comply with FRCP 17(a)'s mandate that the plaintiff be given a reasonable opportunity to join, substitute or obtain ratification from the real party in interest.[53] If not raised in a timely and seasonable fashion, the objection may be deemed waived, particularly where the real party would be prejudiced by the defendant's delay.[54]

(3) Opportunity to Cure Defect

FRCP 17(a) contemplates the dismissal of a plaintiff who is not a real party in interest.[55] However, the last sentence of the Rule provides plaintiffs with a safe harbor "when an honest mistake has been made in choosing the party in whose name the action is to be filed.... "[56] Indeed, the Rule provides that "[n]o action shall be dismissed on the ground that it is not prosecuted in the name of the real party in interest until a reasonable time has been allowed after objection for ratification of commencement of the action by, or joinder or substitution of, the real party in interest."[57] In addition, the Rule provides that the ratification, joinder or substitution of the real party in interest "shall have the same effect as if the action had been commenced in the name of the real party in interest." In this way, the Rule is intended to prevent the loss of substantial rights by allowing the correction of the plaintiff's identity, despite the intervening running of the statute of limitations.

Read literally, the language of the Rule is without limitation, permitting relation back in all cases, even where suit is commenced in the name of a fictitious plaintiff. However, the Advisory Committee Notes make clear that this language is intended to protect only against the "forfeiture and injustice" that could result from a good faith or honest mistake in selecting the party in whose name the action is filed.[58] Relief

---

51. See, e.g., United HealthCare Corp. v. American Trade Ins. Co., 88 F.3d 563, 569 (8th Cir.1996) (real party in interest defense waived when raised on the first day of trial where defendant was on notice at least two years prior to trial, but raised no objection until trial); Whelan v. Abell, 953 F.2d 663, 671–72 (D.C.Cir.) (holding that "Where a Rule 17(a) defense is made, judges abuse their discretion in allowing the plea as late as the start of the trial if the real party has been prejudiced by the defendant's laxness." cert.denied 506 U.S. 906, 113 S.Ct. 300, 121 L.Ed.2d 223 (1992)); Hefley v. Jones, 687 F.2d 1383, 1388 (10th Cir.1982) (real party in interest defense raised 16 days prior to trial deemed waived).

52. United HealthCare Corp., 88 F.3d at 569.

53. Gogolin & Stelter v. Karn's Auto Imports Inc., 886 F.2d 100, 102 (5th Cir. 1989).

54. See supra note 51.

55. Classic Communications, Inc. v. Rural Tel. Serv. Co., 956 F.Supp. 910, 916 (D.Kan.1997).

56. FRCP 17(a) Advisory Committee Notes to 1966 amendment.

57. FRCP 17(a).

58. FRCP 17(a) Advisory Committee Notes to 1966 amendment. See, e.g., Crowder v. Gordons Transports, Inc., 387 F.2d

under the last sentence of FRCP 17(a) will not be allowed where the plaintiff improperly seeks to manipulate the Rule for strategic advantage. Thus, courts have denied relief under the last sentence of Rule 17(a) where the plaintiff attempted to use the Rule to circumvent a state law prohibition on the assignment of claims,[59] avoid the running of the applicable limitations period,[60] or create subject matter jurisdiction where none would otherwise exist.[61]

(4) How to Cure Defect

A defect in real party status may be cured by joining the real party in interest to the action,[62] by allowing substitution of the real party in interest for the misnamed plaintiff[63] or by ratification.[64] The substitution contemplated by FRCP 17(a) applies only to a substitution of the real party in interest for the original named plaintiff, and is distinct from the substitution contemplated by FRCP 25, which is discussed *infra* at § 14.7, involving substitution in the event of the subsequent incapacity or death of an original party.[65] A proper ratification under FRCP 17(a) requires the ratifying party to (1) authorize continuation of the action and (2) agree to be bound by the lawsuit's result.[66]

There is substantial authority indicating that it would be error to dismiss an action without allowing the plaintiff the opportunity to correct a real party in interest error by one of the means contemplated

413 (8th Cir.1967) (reversing trial court's allowance of motion to dismiss based on the liberal relation-back provisions of FRCP 15(c) and the last sentence of FRCP 17(a) where plaintiff, mistakenly believing that her action was governed by the state's wrongful death statute, sued as administratrix of her husband's estate and, after the limitation period had expired, moved to substitute herself as plaintiff in the capacity as next friend to her minor children).

59. See *infra* § 14.3(e)(1) (discussing procedural manipulation). See, e.g., Star Mfg. Co. v. Mancuso, 680 F.Supp. 1496, 1499 (D.Kan.1988) (assignment of tort claim, which was unlawful under state law, could not be "cured" by ratification of real party in interest under FRCP 17(a)).

60. See *infra* § 14.3(e)(1) (discussing procedural manipulation). See, e.g., Del Re v. Prudential Lines, Inc., 669 F.2d 93, 95–96 (2d Cir.) (ratification by real party in interest under Rule 17(a) denied where it would circumvent limitations period applicable to workers' compensation claim), *cert. denied*, 459 U.S. 836, 103 S.Ct. 81, 74 L.Ed.2d 77 (1982).

61. See *infra* § 14.3(e)(2) (discussing jurisdictional manipulation).

62. See, e.g., Jaramillo v. Burkhart, 999 F.2d 1241, 1246 (8th Cir.1993) (court allowing joinder of father, as real party in interest of minor child in personal injury action initiated by grandparent).

63. See, e.g., Underwriters At Interest On Cover Note JHB92M10582079 v. Nautronix, 79 F.3d 480, 484 (5th Cir.1996) (holding that if substitution were necessary to correct real party in interest defect, then the "trial court's decision to permit the amendment would not only be correct but it would have been required by Rule 17").

64. See, e.g., Allwaste Envtl. Servs. /North Atl., Inc. v. Pastore, 911 F.Supp. 29, 31–32 (D.Me.1996) (FRCP 17(a) expressly permits ratification as an alternative cure to substitution or joinder).

65. See Glickstein v. Sun Bank/Miami, N.A., 922 F.2d 666, 672 n. 10 (11th Cir. 1991) (noting that FRCP 25 applies only "when the case originally had the correct parties," whereas FRCP 17(a) applies when the wrong party has mistakenly brought suit).

66. Mutuelles Unies v. Kroll & Linstrom, 957 F.2d 707, 712 (9th Cir.1992).

by FRCP 17(a).[67] However, if a plaintiff fails to cure the defect within a reasonable time after an objection, then dismissal should be allowed.[68] The court, in the exercise of its sound discretion, may determine what is a "reasonable time" to cure a real party defect and may impose appropriate time limits within which such action must be taken.[69] Dismissal on this ground should not be on the merits, at least as to the absent real party in interest, whose right to commence his or her own action against the defendant should not in any way be precluded.[70]

(e) Procedural and Jurisdictional Limitations

(1) Limitation on Procedural Manipulation

FRCP 17(a) does not apply to a situation where a party with no cause of action files a lawsuit to toll the statute of limitations and later obtains a cause of action through a valid assignment or otherwise.[71] The party bringing suit must possess the right being asserted at the time suit is commenced.[72] As the Advisory Committee Notes to the 1966 amendment clearly state, the safe harbor provisions of FRCP 17(a) do "not mean for example, that, following an airplane crash in which all aboard were killed, an action may be filed in the name of John Doe (a fictitious person), as personal representative of Richard Roe (another fictitious person), in the hope that at a later time the attorney filing the action may substitute the real name of the real personal representative of a real victim, and have the benefit of suspension of the limitation period."[73] Thus, courts uniformly have held that FRCP 17(a) cannot be manipulated to circumvent limitations periods.[74]

---

67. See, e.g., Crowder v. Gordons Transports, Inc., 387 F.2d 413 (8th Cir.1967) (reversing trial court's allowance of motion to dismiss based on the liberal relation-back provisions of FRCP 15(c) and the last sentence of FRCP 17(a) where plaintiff, mistakenly believing that her action was governed by the state's wrongful death statute, sued as administratrix of her husband's estate and, after the limitation period had expired, moved to substitute herself as plaintiff in the capacity as next friend to her minor children); Sun Refining & Marketing Co. v. Goldstein Oil Co., 801 F.2d 343, 345 (8th Cir.1986) (holding that the trial court erred in refusing to accept ratification by the real party in interest, where ratification would not result in any prejudice to the defendants and failure to accept plaintiff's cure would result in forfeiture of the claim).

68. Naghiu v. Inter–Continental Hotels Group, Inc., 165 F.R.D. 413, 421 (D.Del. 1996) (dismissing action based on plaintiff's failure to sue in the name of real party in interest after providing plaintiff with a reasonable opportunity to locate and formally join, substitute or seek ratification from the real parties in interest).

69. See id.; see also National Safe Corp. v. Texidor Sec. Equip., Inc., 101 F.R.D. 467, 472 (D.P.R.1984) (ordering plaintiff to cure real party defect within 10 days or face dismissal).

70. See Ronsick v. Phariss, 286 F.2d 316, 318 (10th Cir.1960).

71. United States v. CMA, Inc., 890 F.2d 1070, 1074 (9th Cir.1989).

72. Id.

73. FRCP 17(a) Advisory Committee Note to 1966 amendment.

74. CMA, Inc., 890 F.2d at 1074; RTC v. Scaletty, 810 F.Supp. 1505, 1509 (D.Kan. 1992) (relief under FRCP 17(a) "should not be allowed where it would reflect an abuse of process, such as the use of John Doe or fictitious names in the hope that the real party subsequently may be discovered"). See also Barker v. Jackson Nat'l Life Ins. Co., 163 F.R.D. 364, 365 (N.D.Fla.1995) (where a transfer is made solely for the

(2) Limitation on Jurisdictional Manipulation

Similarly, courts have refused to recognize the validity of even facially valid assignments where the assignment violates the statutory prohibition against collusive joinder.[75] Collusive joinder occurs when "any party, by assignment or otherwise, has been improperly or collusively made or joined to invoke the jurisdiction of [the district court]."[76] In such cases, Congress has declared that the district court shall not have jurisdiction to hear the case.[77] The prohibition against collusive joinder is intended to prevent parties from manufacturing diversity jurisdiction and thereby inappropriately federalizing claims that properly belong in the state courts.[78]

A common example of jurisdictional manipulation involves the transfer of interest from a nondiverse corporation to a diverse subsidiary or shell corporation.[79] Whether such a transfer will be deemed improper or collusive will turn on the facts of each individual case.[80] Among the factors to be considered in making this determination are the following: (1) were there good business reasons for the assignment or transfer; (2) did the assignee or transferee have a prior interest in the item or was the transfer timed to coincide with the commencement of the litigation; (3) was any consideration provided by the assignee or transferee; (4) was the assignment/transfer partial or complete; and (5) was there other evidence tending to show that the motivation for the assignment/transfer was to create federal jurisdiction.[81] At bottom, the central focus is whether the assignee/transferee has some independent, legitimate interest in the dispute, as opposed to being merely a straw put forward to invoke diversity jurisdiction.[82]

---

purpose of legal tactics, the court may ignore the transfer and continue to treat the transferor as the real party in interest).

75. Kramer v. Caribbean Mills, Inc., 394 U.S. 823, 829–30, 89 S.Ct. 1487, 1491, 23 L.Ed.2d 9 (1969) (subject matter jurisdiction lacking where assignment, while valid under substantive state law, violated statutory prohibition against collusive joinder); Attorneys Trust v. Videotape Computer Prods., Inc., 93 F.3d 593, 595 (9th Cir.1996) (corporation assigned its claim for collection to plaintiff, which, following trial, unsuccessfully challenged the court's exercise of subject matter jurisdiction over assigned claim).

76. 28 U.S.C.A. § 1359 (West 1993).

77. Id.

78. Yokeno v. Mafnas, 973 F.2d 803, 809 (9th Cir.1992) ("The federal anti-collusion statute is aimed at preventing parties from manufacturing diversity jurisdiction to inappropriately channel ordinary business litigation into the federal courts."). See generally Chapter 1 "Subject Matter Jurisdic-

tion," supra at § 1.7(e) (discussing jurisdictional manipulation).

79. See, e.g., Toste Farm Corp. v. Hadbury, Inc., 70 F.3d 640, 642, 646 (1st Cir. 1995) (merger of corporation into another corporate shell deemed ineffective to create diversity jurisdiction); Nike, Inc. v. Comercial Iberica De Exclusivas Deportivas, S.A., 20 F.3d 987, 993 (9th Cir.1994) (assignment by wholly-owned corporate subsidiary of its rights to parent corporation deemed ineffective to create diversity jurisdiction).

80. See J.F. Pritchard & Co. v. Dow Chem. of Canada, Ltd., 331 F.Supp. 1215, 1220–22 (W.D.Mo.1971) (whether assignment by wholly-owned corporate subsidiary of its rights to parent corporation was collusive presented "question of law and fact"), aff'd, 462 F.2d 998 (8th Cir.1972).

81. Attorneys Trust, 93 F.3d at 595.

82. See Haskin v. Corporacion Insular de Seguros, 666 F.Supp. 349, 353–54 (D.P.R.1987) (holding that the assignee must have "some independent, legitimate interest in the dispute that predated the

Library References:

West's Key No. Digests, Federal Civil Procedure ☞131–149.
Wright, Miller & Kane, Federal Practice and Procedure: Civil 2d §§ 1543–1558.

§ 14.4   Capacity to Sue and Be Sued

(a) Applicable to All Parties

While the real party in interest requirements of FRCP 17(a) are applicable only to plaintiffs, the remaining portions of the Rule are applicable to all parties.[1] FRCP 17(b) provides that every party to a lawsuit must have the legal capacity to sue or be sued, and it sets forth the manner in which that capacity is to be determined. The distinction between these issues—real party in interest and capacity to maintain the action—is significant. Capacity to sue and be sued relates to the right of a party to come into court and maintain suit on his or her own behalf; whereas the real party in interest requirement is intended to make sure that the party bringing suit possesses the substantive right to the relief that is being sought.[2] A party may be the real party in interest, but it nevertheless may be unable to maintain suit because it lacks the capacity to sue under the substantive law, as for example when a party is mentally incompetent. Unlike the defense that the plaintiff is not a real party in interest, which may be raised during trial or on appeal,[3] lack of capacity generally will be waived if not attacked by a specific negative averment at the pleading stage.[4]

The manner in which the capacity of a party to sue and be sued is determined turns on the type of party that is involved—that is, whether the party is an individual, representative of another party, corporation, or some other entity.

(b) Individuals

The capacity of an individual, other than one acting in a representative capacity, is determined by the law of the individual's domicile.[5] For purposes of the Rule, "domicile" has the same meaning as is used in connection with the determination of diversity jurisdiction.[6] This typically requires a combination of physical presence and an intent to remain or, when absent, an intent to return.[7] As with the existence of subject

assignment and was not a complete stranger to the transaction").

§ 14.4

1. *See* FRCP 17(a)-(c).

2. *See* Citizens Concerned for Separation of Church and State v. City of Denver, 628 F.2d 1289, 1300 (10th Cir.1980) (distinguishing capacity from standing), *cert. denied*, 452 U.S. 963, 101 S.Ct. 3114, 69 L.Ed.2d 975 (1981). *See also supra* § 14.3(a).

3. *See supra* § 14.3(c).

4. *See infra* § 14.4(d).

5. FRCP 17(b).

6. *See* Chapter 1 "Subject Matter Jurisdiction," *supra*.

7. Juvelis v. Snider, 68 F.3d 648, 654 (3d Cir.1995) (" 'In general, the domicile of an individual is his true, fixed and permanent home and place of habitation. It is the place to which, whenever he is absent, he has the intention of returning.' " quoting

matter jurisdiction, capacity is determined at the time the suit is filed and is not affected by a subsequent change of citizenship.[8]

(1) Infants and Incompetent Persons

The most common bases for which an individual is deemed to lack the capacity to sue or be sued are infancy or incompetency. If by the law of his domicile an individual may sue or be sued without regard to infancy or incompetency, then FRCP 17(b) provides that the individual may sue and be sued in the federal courts.[9] On the other hand, where the individual is precluded under the law of his domicile from doing so, FRCP 17(c) ensures that the individual's interests are adequately protected by providing that the "court shall appoint a guardian ad litem for an infant or incompetent person not otherwise represented in an action or shall make such other order as it deems proper for the protection of the infant or incompetent person."[10] Thus, while the law of the individual's domicile may confer the capacity to sue or be sued in federal court, state law cannot deny an individual the right to sue or defend in federal court.[11] The only effect that a party's incapacity has on the maintenance of a federal action is the possible need for the appointment of a guardian ad litem or entry of any other order suitable to protect the infant or incompetent's interests (e.g., court review of any settlement agreement), where the infant or incompetent is not otherwise represented.[12]

The phrase "otherwise represented" as used in FRCP 17(c) refers to those infants or incompetent persons who, at the initiation of the action, are represented by a guardian, conservator or other like fiduciary. FRCP 17(c) permits a guardian, conservator or other like fiduciary to sue or defend on behalf of the infant or incompetent person.[13] Where no such representative has been appointed, the individual lacking capacity may sue by his "next friend" or by a guardian ad litem. It is only when the court determines that the interests of the person lacking capacity are not adequately protected either because there is no other representative or because the existing representative is inadequate, that the court need

---

Vlandis v. Kline, 412 U.S. 441, 93 S.Ct. 2230, 37 L.Ed.2d 63 (1973)).

8. See Chapter 1 "Subject Matter Jurisdiction," supra. See also Felson v. Miller, 674 F.Supp. 975, 977 (E.D.N.Y.1987) (capacity determined by domicile at time suit was filed). Bank One, Texas, N.A. v. Montle, 964 F.2d 48, 49 (1st Cir.1992) ("Domicile is determined as of the time suit is filed, and once diversity jurisdiction is established, it is not lost by a later change in domicile.").

9. FRCP 17(b).

10. FRCP 17(c).

11. Donnelly v. Parker, 486 F.2d 402, 406–07 (D.C.Cir.1973) ("state law may confer but not deny capacity to sue or defend federally . . . In no event is federal jurisdic-

tion to entertain the cause diminished."). See also Thomas v. Humfield, 916 F.2d 1032, 1035 (5th Cir.1990) (while the appointment of a guardian ad litem may deprive the individual of his right to control the litigation, it preserves his day in court).

12. Donnelly, 486 F.2d at 406–07 ("the only effect of a party's incompetence upon the maintenance of the action is the possible need for appointment of a guardian ad litem or entry of a protective order"); Thomas, 916 F.2d at 1035 ("in the context of someone seeking to pursue litigation in federal court on his own behalf, we interpret the term 'incompetent person' in Rule 17(c) to refer to a person without capacity to litigate under the law of his state of domicile and, hence, under Rule 17(b)").

13. FRCP 17(c).

appoint a guardian ad litem or make any other order necessary to protect the interests of the person lacking capacity.[14] A federal court's ability to appoint a guardian to represent a person lacking capacity is not subject to any restrictions that may be imposed by state law.[15]

As discussed in Section 14.3, *supra*, in an action prosecuted or defended by a "next friend" or guardian ad litem, the minor or incompetent person—not the representative—is the proper plaintiff or defendant.[16] An action prosecuted or defended by a general guardian or conservator may be brought either in the name of the minor or incompetent or in the name of the guardian or conservator, or in the names of both.[17]

(2) Other Persons

A narrow exception to the general rule that an individual's capacity is determined by the law of his domicile is recognized where operation of the rule would deprive the individual of important substantive rights secured by federal law. For instance, courts have allowed prisoners to maintain actions for alleged violations of the federal Civil Rights Act, even though the prisoners lack capacity under the law of their state of domicile, because a contrary result would thwart express provisions of federal law extending the right to sue under the Act to all citizens.[18]

(c) Representatives of Another Party

The capacity of an individual suing or defending in a representative capacity such as a trustee, executor, administrator, guardian or the like, is determined by the "law of the state in which the district court is held."[19] Thus, only the law of the forum state, not the law of the state in which the representative was appointed nor the law of the state of the individual for whom the representative is appointed, can grant capacity to sue or defend on a state law claim.[20] Where, however, a federal claim is involved, federal law may preempt state law by providing an independent basis upon which capacity to sue or defend may be found.[21] Such

---

14. *Id.*; *see also* Rubin v. Smith, 882 F.Supp. 212, 216–17 (D.N.H.1995) (court has discretion to determine what type of order is necessary to adequately protect the best interests of a person lacking capacity).

15. Slade v. Louisiana Power & Light Co., 418 F.2d 125, 126 (5th Cir.1969), *cert. denied*, 397 U.S. 1007, 90 S.Ct. 1233, 25 L.Ed.2d 419 (1970).

16. FRCP 17(a). *See supra* § 14.3.

17. *Id.*

18. Almond v. Kent, 459 F.2d 200, 202–03 (4th Cir.1972) (holding that the specific language of the federal Civil Rights Act, which provides every citizen with the right to sue under the Act, should prevail over the general rule contained in FRCP 17(b),

at least where application of the law of the domicile would result in complete incapacity).

19. FRCP 17(b).

20. *See, e.g.*, Turton v. Turton, 644 F.2d 344, 348 (5th Cir.1981) (holding that an administrator duly appointed under the law of foreign state nevertheless lacked capacity under the law of the forum state).

21. AM Properties Corp. v. GTE Products Corp., 844 F.Supp. 1007, 1011–12 (D.N.J.1994) (recognizing federal preemption of state law regarding capacity of dissolved corporation to be sued for environmental contamination under CERCLA).

independent bases for capacity have been deemed to exist under various federal statutes, including the Comprehensive Environmental Response Compensation and Liability Act ("CERCLA") and the Federal Employers' Liability Act ("FELA").[22]

The same rules apply in the case of state appointed receivers and officers who seek to sue or defend in their representative capacity.[23]

(d) Corporations

The capacity of a corporation to sue or be sued is determined by the "law under which it was organized."[24] The same rule applies to determine the capacity of a defunct or dissolved corporation. Thus, if under the law of the state of incorporation, a dissolved corporation possesses the capacity to sue or be sued, then it may sue or defend in federal court.[25] Once again, the general rule is subject to a limited exception when a federal statute is deemed to preempt state law regarding capacity to sue or be sued.[26]

(e) Partnerships and Unincorporated Associations

Under common law, partnerships and unincorporated associations have no legal existence apart from their members and, therefore, have no capacity to sue or defend in their common names.[27] FRCP 17(b) modified the common law rule by providing that "capacity to sue or be sued shall be determined by the law of the state in which the district court is held, except (1) that a partnership or other unincorporated association, which has no such capacity by the law of such state, may sue or be sued in its common name for the purpose of enforcing for or against it a substantive right existing under the Constitution or laws of the United States...."[28] Thus, under the Rule, a partnership or unincorporated association can sue or be sued in its common name in a federal court under two circumstances: (1) when the claim arises under federal law; or (2) when the forum state law allows suits by or against the partnership or unincorporated association.[29] This eliminates the need

22. See id.; but see Witco Corp. v. Beekhuis, 38 F.3d 682, 689 (3d Cir.1994) (holding that federal preemption of state law by CERCLA is limited to liability, and does not alter the general rule set forth in FRCP 17(b) that capacity is determined by the law of the state of incorporation). See also 45 U.S.C.A. § 59 (West 1983) (permitting suit under FELA to be maintained by decedents' personal representative or, if none, by decedents' surviving dependents).

23. FRCP 17(b). See Baxley v. Rutland, 409 F.Supp. 1249, 1256 (M.D.Ala.1976) (capacity of state officer to sue determined by law of the forum state); Gross v. Hougland, 712 F.2d 1034, 1040 (6th Cir.1983) (capacity of receiver appointed by state law to sue

determined by law of the forum state), cert. denied, 465 U.S. 1025, 104 S.Ct. 1281, 79 L.Ed.2d 684 (1984).

24. FRCP 17(b).

25. Gross, 712 F.2d at 1040 (capacity of dissolved corporation to defend in federal court determined by law of state of incorporation).

26. See supra note 22.

27. Moffat Tunnel League v. United States, 289 U.S. 113, 118–19, 53 S.Ct. 543, 545, 546, 77 L.Ed. 1069 (1933).

28. FRCP 17(b).

29. See Country Club Assocs. Ltd. Partnership v. FDIC, 918 F.Supp. 429, 438

in an action by or against a partnership or unincorporated association to join or name all of the individual partners or members.[30] The determination of what constitutes a partnership or an "unincorporated association" is a question of federal law.[31] Federal courts have defined an "unincorporated association" generally as "a voluntary group of persons, without a charter, formed by mutual consent for the purpose of promoting a common objective."[32]

The purpose of the Rule, insofar as it allows federal claims against unincorporated associations in their own names, even if state law does not so provide, is to prevent state law from frustrating the enforcement of substantive federal rights.[33] However, FRCP 17(b)(1) is procedural only, and it does not create any substantive rights where none existed previously.[34] When the federal law under which the alleged substantive right arises is silent as to its application to partnerships and unincorporated associations, such as where the law speaks only in terms of individuals but does not expressly exclude partnerships and unincorporated associations from its scope, the court is free to decide the applicability of the FRCP 17(b) substantive right exception on the merits of the particular case before it.[35] This same rule applies with regard to the unincorporated plaintiff's right to sue, as well as the capacity of an unincorporated defendant's right to be sued.[36]

(D.D.C.1996) (in the absence of an applicable federal claim, the capacity of a partnership or unincorporated association to sue or be sued is determined by the law of the state in which the district court sits); Orraca v. City of New York, 897 F.Supp. 148, 151–52 (S.D.N.Y.1995) (capacity of city police department to be sued on tort claims properly determined by state law).

30. *See also* FRCP 23.2 Advisory Committee Notes to the 1966 Addition (although an action by or against representatives of the membership of an unincorporated association has often been viewed as a class action, the purpose of this characterization is to give "entity treatment" to the association when for formal reasons it cannot sue or be sued as a jural person under FRCP 17(b)). Class actions are discussed in Chapter 15 "Class Actions," *infra.*

31. Committee for Idaho's High Desert, Inc. v. Yost, 92 F.3d 814, 819–20 (9th Cir. 1996).

32. *Id.*; *see also* Four Way Plant Farm, Inc. v. National Council on Compensation Ins., 894 F.Supp. 1538, 1546 (M.D.Ala.1995)

(an unincorporated association is a collection of persons "created and formed by the voluntary action of a number of individuals in associating themselves together under a common name for the accomplishment of some lawful purpose").

33. Klinghoffer v. S.N.C. Achille Lauro, 739 F.Supp. 854, 858 (S.D.N.Y.1990), *vacated on other grounds*, 937 F.2d 44 (2d Cir. 1991).

34. *See* University of Texas v. Vratil, 96 F.3d 1337, 1340 (10th Cir.1996) (although FRCP 17(b) is purely procedural, an association's jural existence under the Rule extends beyond the mere service of process to all other procedural incidents under the Federal Rules, including compliance with all of the applicable discovery rules).

35. Elliott v. Sherwood Manor Mobile Home Park, 947 F.Supp. 1574, 1577 (M.D.Fla.1996) (finding that unincorporated defendant had the capacity to be sued by tenant under the provisions of the federal Fair Housing Act, even though defendant had no legal existence under state law).

36. *Id.*

(f) Defenses and Objections

Capacity is a defense that is waived if not timely asserted.[37] Some courts have held that a party desiring to challenge an opponent's capacity to sue must raise the issue by specific negative averment at the pleading stage and must include in its answer "such supporting particulars as are peculiarly within the pleader's knowledge" as required by FRCP 9(a).[38] Other courts have been less rigorous, holding that waiver occurs only if the defense is not raised in a "timely manner, *i.e.* at the outset of a lawsuit"[39] when the risk of prejudice is slight.[40] Despite the somewhat liberal approach adopted by some courts, the better practice is to raise the capacity defense by specific negative averment at the pleading stage to avoid any risk of waiver.[41] This may be done by either a specific negative averment or by motion. In either event the party asserting lack of capacity should include in its pleading all of the facts within its possession bearing on the opposing party's alleged lack of capacity, *e.g.*, in the case of a dissolved corporation lacking capacity under the applicable state law, copies of any corporate minutes or filings with the Secretary of State reflecting that fact.

Library References:

West's Key No. Digests, Federal Civil Procedure ⟨Key⟩111–116.
Wright, Miller & Kane, Federal Practice and Procedure: Civil 2d §§ 1559–1569.

§ 14.5 Interpleader

(a) Purpose to Avoid Double or Multiple Liability

Interpleader is a remedial device that is intended to protect a party from multiple liability and the vexation of defending multiple claims to the same fund.[1] In practice, interpleader typically arises in the insurance context where two or more parties claim adverse interests in the pro-

---

37. *In re* Hashim, 188 B.R. 633, 650 (Bankr.D.Ariz.1995) (holding that capacity is a defense that is waivable).

38. Swaim v. Moltan Co., 73 F.3d 711, 717 (7th Cir.) (failure to raise capacity in a responsive pleading amounts to a waiver of that right), *cert. denied*, 517 U.S. 1244, 116 S.Ct. 2499, 135 L.Ed.2d 191 (1996); NAACP Labor Committee v. Laborers' Int'l Union of N.A., 902 F.Supp. 688, 699 (W.D.Va. 1993) (challenge to plaintiff's capacity to maintain suit as personal representative of decedent waived based on defendant's failure to include a "specific negative averment" as required by FRCP 9(a) in answer), *aff'd*, 67 F.3d 293 (4th Cir.1995).

39. Pressman v. Estate of Steinvorth, 860 F.Supp. 171, 176 (S.D.N.Y.1994) (capacity defense must be raised in a timely manner).

40. *Compare* Asbestos Workers Syracuse Pension Fund v. M.G. Indus. Insula-

tion Co., 875 F.Supp. 132, 137–38 (N.D.N.Y. 1995) (no waiver where capacity defense raised six months after commencement of litigation, but not in answer, where no prejudice would result to other party) *with* Wagner Furniture Interiors, Inc. v. Kemner's Georgetown Manor, Inc., 929 F.2d 343, 345–46 (7th Cir.1991) (waiver found where defendant did not raise capacity defense until final pretrial conference, only two weeks before trial).

41. *In re* Narcisco, 149 B.R. 917, 918 (E.D.Ark.1993) (general denial of plaintiff's capacity to sue constitutes a waiver of the defense).

§ 14.5

1. State Farm Fire & Cas. Co. v. Tashire, 386 U.S. 523, 533, 87 S.Ct. 1199, 1205, 18 L.Ed.2d 270 (1967) (interpleader is a remedial device that is to be applied liberally); Washington Elec. Co-op., Inc. v. Pa-

ceeds of a life insurance policy.[2] Rather than paying any one claimant, the insurance company may require all of the claimants to litigate the merits of their competing claims in a single proceeding by invoking the rules of interpleader.[3]

(b) Two Forms of Interpleader

In federal courts, there are two forms of interpleader: rule interpleader and statutory interpleader.[4] While similar in purpose and function, there are important procedural and substantive distinctions between the two types of interpleader and it is important to analyze separately each potential basis for interpleader.[5] Perhaps most significantly, rule interpleader is merely a procedural device that does not confer any independent jurisdiction on the district court; statutory interpleader, on the other hand, provides an independent jurisdictional basis when the requirements of the statute are satisfied.[6]

(c) Rule Interpleader

(1) Relationship to Other Rules

FRCP 20 allows a plaintiff to sue two or more defendants when he is unsure which one is liable to him; it also permits several persons to sue as plaintiffs when they are uncertain as to which one of them possesses the asserted legal right.[7] FRCP 22 supplements FRCP 20; it allows a person against whom two or more persons are asserting claims entailing possible double or multiple liability to join the claimants as defendants and requires them to interplead their claims.[8] FRCP 22 expressly allows interpleader to be used offensively by way of a complaint against multiple claimants, or defensively by way of counterclaim or cross-claim.[9] In this way, the Rule enables a party faced with conflicting claims to avoid the risk of satisfying the wrong claim and incurring multiple adverse judgments by different courts.

(2) Standard for Application

The standard for rule interpleader appears in the first sentence of FRCP 22(1): the claims must be such "that the plaintiff [or defendant] is

---

terson, Walke & Pratt, P.C., 985 F.2d 677, 679 (2d Cir.1993) ("Rooted in equity, interpleader is a handy tool to protect a stakeholder from multiple liability and the vexation of defending multiple claims to the same fund.").

2. See infra § 14.9(c).

3. See, e.g., Aetna U.S. Healthcare v. Higgs, 962 F.Supp. 1412, 1414 (D.Kan. 1997) (insurer brought interpleader action pursuant to FRCP 22 against beneficiary and contingent beneficiaries of life insurance policy alleging that it faced the possibility of exposure to multiple liability where

primary beneficiary was suspected of murdering insured, thereby potentially disqualifying primary beneficiary from recovery under the policy).

4. Blackmon Auctions, Inc. v. Van Buren Truck Center, Inc., 901 F.Supp. 287, 289 (W.D.Ark.1995).

5. See infra § 14.5(c)-(d).

6. Id.

7. FRCP 22(1).

8. Id.

9. Id.

or may be exposed to double or multiple liability."[10] The Rule is intended to be interpreted liberally.[11] Therefore, to meet this requirement, the party seeking interpleader relief need only demonstrate that there is a possibility of multiple liability or litigation.[12] It is not ground for objection that the possibility of multiple liability or litigation is remote or rests on tenuous grounds, so long as the possibility exists either presently or prospectively.[13] Interpleader relief should be allowed whenever there is a "legitimate fear of multiple litigation, irrespective of the merits of the competing claims."[14] This is because "a party is not required to evaluate the merits of conflicting claims at its peril; rather, it need only have a good faith concern about duplicitous litigation and multiple liability if it responds to the requests of certain claimants and not to others."[15]

In addition to presenting the possibility of multiple liability or litigation, the claims sought to be interpleaded must be adverse.[16] If, for example, the plaintiff (or defendant in a defensive interpleader action) is probably liable to both claimants, then the interpleader action should be dismissed.[17] Similarly, if only one claim has any substance and the interpleader's fears of double or multiple liability are unreasonable, the interpleader action also should be dismissed because there is no threat of double or multiple liability.[18]

---

10. *Id.* ("Persons having claims against the plaintiff may be joined as defendants and required to interplead when their claims are such that the plaintiff is or may be exposed to double or multiple liability.... A defendant exposed to similar liability may obtain such interpleader by way of cross-claim or counterclaim."); *see also* Bankers Trust Co. v. Manufacturers Nat'l Bank, 139 F.R.D. 302, 308 (S.D.N.Y.1991) ("Both statutory and rule interpleader may be brought by way of cross-claim or counterclaim.").

11. State Farm Fire & Cas. Co. v. Tashire, 386 U.S. 523, 533, 87 S.Ct. 1199, 1205, 18 L.Ed.2d 270 (1967) (interpleader is a remedial device that is to be applied liberally).

12. Aetna U.S. Healthcare v. Higgs, 962 F.Supp. 1412, 1414 (D.Kan.1997) (FRCP 22 permits a stakeholder to bring an interpleader action when it may be exposed to multiple liability—a possibility is all that is required). *See also* Catizone v. Memry Corp., 897 F.Supp. 732, 739–40 (S.D.N.Y. 1995) (the party seeking interpleader bears the burden of establishing that an interpleader action is necessary).

13. *See* First Interstate Bank of Oregon, N.A. v. United States, 891 F.Supp. 543, 546 (D.Or.1995) (it is sufficient for the interpleader to show that there is a possibility of multiple liability or litigation, even if that possibility is remote or tenuous). *See also* 6247 Atlas Corp. v. Marine Ins. Co., 155 F.R.D. 454, 463 (S.D.N.Y.1994) (FRCP 22 allows interpleader where adverse claims are prospective only).

14. *See* First Interstate Bank of Oregon, N.A., 891 F.Supp. at 547.

15. *See* Massachusetts Mut. Life Ins. Co. v. Morris, 61 F.2d 104, 105 (9th Cir. 1932).

16. *See* Bradley v. Kochenash, 44 F.3d 166, 167 (2d Cir.1995) (denying interpleader where plaintiff was potentially liable to both claimants based on its breach of duties owed to each claimant, respectively); Catizone, 897 F.Supp. at 739–40 (interpleader will not be available unless there are two or more adverse claimants to the disputed fund).

17. *Id.*

18. *Compare* Francis I. duPont & Co. v. O'Keefe, 365 F.2d 141, 143 (7th Cir.1966) (statutory interpleader suit dismissed where none of the defendant claimants were claiming to be entitled to any part of the sum involved) *with* Sotheby's, Inc. v. Garcia, 802 F.Supp. 1058, 1065 (S.D.N.Y. 1992) (threat of potential future lawsuit based on letter from adverse claimant to

A party seeking interpleader need not be "wholly disinterested" with respect to the subject matter of the dispute.[19] FRCP 22 abolishes the prior distinction between strict interpleader and bills in the nature of interpleader, and allows the plaintiff to avoid the role of a mere stakeholder. It is no longer a ground for objection that the interpleader is not neutral because he is independently liable to one of the claimants.[20] Instead, FRCP 22 expressly permits the interpleader to plead in the alternative that (1) he is not liable to any of the claimants, but (2) if he is liable in whole or in part, the court should determine which of the competing defendants has the rightful claim. Nor is it a ground for objection to interpleader that the claims lack a common origin or are not identical but are adverse to and independent of one another.[21]

(3) Deposit in Court Registry

Rule 22 does not require the deposit of disputed funds into the registry of the court.[22] However, the law normally regards the plaintiff in an interpleader action as having been discharged of full responsibility regarding the interpleaded funds when the funds have been paid into the registry of the court and the parties have had notice and an opportunity to be heard.[23] Additionally, the court may enter an order relieving the interpleader plaintiff of further responsibility, awarding costs and fees, and enjoining the interpleaded defendants from bringing further action against the plaintiff with regard to the disputed funds.[24] Thus, where possible, it generally is in the interpleader's best interest to deposit the disputed funds in the court registry, even though not expressly required by the Rule.[25]

(4) Jurisdiction, Service and Venue

FRCP 22 does not enlarge the jurisdiction of the federal courts.[26] Instead, district courts may hear interpleader actions only if federal subject matter jurisdiction exists on some other basis, such as diversity

property is sufficient to invoke interpleader relief).

19. State Farm Fire & Cas. Co. v. Tashire, 386 U.S. 523, 532 n. 9, 87 S.Ct. 1199, 1205 n. 9, 18 L.Ed.2d 270 (1967) (affirming exercise of interpleader jurisdiction despite interpleader's alternative plea for declaratory judgment regarding its liability for insurance coverage).

20. FRCP 22(1); see also First Interstate Bank of Oregon, N.A. v. United States, 891 F.Supp. 543, 546 n. 5 (D.Or. 1995) ("the existence of a neutral stakeholder is not a prerequisite to interpleader jurisdiction").

21. See Aetna U.S. Healthcare, 962 F.Supp. 1412, 1414 (D.Kan.1997) (it is not ground for objection under FRCP 22 that the claims of the several claimants to the

fund lack a common origin or are not identical).

22. Kurland v. United States, 919 F.Supp. 419, 421 (M.D.Fla.1996).

23. Id.

24. Id. ("It is a generally accepted principle that a disinterested stakeholder filing an action in interpleader may be dismissed from the case, discharged from further liability, and, in the court's discretion, awarded attorneys' fees and costs.")

25. See infra § 14.5(e)(1)-(2).

26. Hat Ranch, Inc. v. Babbitt, 932 F.Supp. 1, 3 (D.D.C.1995) (denying rule interpleader where dispute with the United States was beyond the court's subject matter jurisdiction), aff'd, 102 F.3d 1272 (D.C.Cir.1996).

of citizenship or a federal question.[27] Subject matter jurisdiction over an interpleader claim also may be established by reliance on the court's supplemental jurisdiction under 28 U.S.C.A. § 1367, such as where diversity is established for purposes of a declaratory judgment claim (but defeated when all interpleaded complainants are brought into the action).[28]

Plainly, the court's jurisdiction in an interpleader matter extends to all matters necessary to the determination of rights with respect to who owns the deposited funds, but there is some confusion as to whether it extends any further.[29] Some courts have adopted a narrow interpretation that the court should limit itself to a determination of who owns the interpleaded funds;[30] other courts have taken a broader view, allowing the defendants/claimants, for instance, to file permissive and compulsory counterclaims in the interpleader action, as well as to assert cross-claims, even against nonresident defendants where there is a basis for the exercise of supplemental jurisdiction.[31]

With regard to service of process and venue, there are no special rules applicable to interpleader actions brought under FRCP 22.[32] Thus, the rule interpleader must comply with both FRCP 4, governing the service of process, and 28 U.S.C.A. § 1391, setting forth the rules of venue.[33]

(d) Statutory Interpleader

(1) Comparison to Rule Interpleader

Like rule interpleader, the Federal Interpleader Act, 28 U.S.C.A. § 1335, is a procedural device which enables a person holding property or money to compel two or more persons asserting mutually exclusive rights to the fund to join and litigate their respective claims in one action.[34] As with rule interpleader, statutory interpleader relieves a

27. Blackmon Auctions, Inc. v. Van Buren Truck Center, 901 F.Supp. 287, 289 (W.D.Ark.1995)(no independent basis for jurisdiction exits under FRCP 22).

28. See 6247 Atlas Corp. v. Marine Ins. Co., 155 F.R.D. 454, 464–65, n. 7 (S.D.N.Y. 1994) (holding that the limitations set forth in 28 U.S.C.A. § 1367(b) relating to the exercise of supplemental jurisdiction "may not be ... used to limit the scope of Rule 22").

29. Priority Records, Inc. v. Bridgeport Music, Inc., 907 F.Supp. 725, 728–29 (S.D.N.Y.1995).

30. Humble Oil & Ref. Co. v. Copeland, 398 F.2d 364, 368 (4th Cir.1968) ("[i]nterpleader is based upon *in personam* jurisdiction which extends only to the funds deposited in court").

31. Priority Records, Inc., 907 F.Supp. at 732 (invoking principles of supplementa-ry jurisdiction to allow cross-claims to be asserted against nonresident defendant in interpleader action); Bell v. Nutmeg Airways Corp. 66 F.R.D. 1, 4 (D.Conn.1975) (permissive and compulsory counterclaims may be brought in interpleader action).

32. General Accident Group v. Gagliardi, 593 F.Supp. 1080, 1087 (D.Conn.1984) (service of process for rule interpleader is subject to compliance with FRCP 4), *aff'd*, 767 F.2d 907 (2d Cir.1985); Leader Nat'l Ins. Co. v. Shaw, 901 F.Supp. 316, 320 (W.D.Okla.1995) (venue in rule interpleader action is determined by the general venue provisions of 28 U.S.C.A. § 1391).

33. *Id.*

34. NYLife Distribs., Inc. v. Adherence Group, Inc., 72 F.3d 371, 374 (3d Cir.1995), *cert. denied*, 517 U.S. 1209, 116 S.Ct. 1826, 134 L.Ed.2d 931 (1996).

stakeholder from determining at his peril the merits of the competing claims and shields him from the prospect of multiple liability or litigation.[35] Also, like rule interpleader, the absence of a threat of multiple litigation or liability is fatal to an application for interpleader under the statute.[36] Moreover, like rule interpleader, statutory interpleader permits the stakeholder to maintain an interest in the outcome of the action by not admitting liability when it deposits the contested fund in the court.[37] Statutory interpleader also may be used either offensively or defensively.[38] Despite these similarities, there are important substantive and procedural differences between the two types of interpleader, particularly in terms of jurisdiction, service and venue.[39]

(2) Jurisdiction, Service and Venue

Unlike rule interpleader, statutory interpleader provides an independent basis for federal jurisdiction when there is minimal diversity between the claimants, that is, when at least two of the claimants are citizens of different states.[40] In order for a court to exercise jurisdiction under 28 U.S.C.A. § 1335, the interpleader must establish the following three prerequisites: (1) the interpleader has custody or possession of money or property valued at $500 or more; (2) two or more adverse claimants of diverse citizenship claim rights to the money or property; and (3) the interpleader has deposited such money or posted bond in an amount and with such surety as the court deems proper.[41]

The focus of the first element is simply on the total value of the stake. By setting the amount in controversy at $500, statutory interpleader sets a significantly lower threshold than normally required to invoke federal jurisdiction in diversity cases which requires an amount in controversy in excess of $75,000.[42] Similarly, the statute requires only that two or more of the adverse claimants have diverse citizenship.[43]

35. Id.

36. Alfa Fin. Corp. v. Key, 927 F.Supp. 423, 428–29 (M.D.Ala.1996) (multiple adverse claims to a single liability are at the core of any interpleader action), aff'd, 112 F.3d 1172 (11th Cir.1997).

37. Id.

38. Bankers Trust Co. v. Manufacturers Nat'l Bank, 139 F.R.D. 302, 308 (S.D.N.Y. 1991) ("Both statutory and rule interpleader may be brought by way of cross-claim or counterclaim.").

39. See Blackmon Auctions, Inc. v. Van Buren Truck Center, Inc., 901 F.Supp. 287, 289 (W.D.Ark.1995) (comparing the two forms of interpleader).

40. Id.

41. NYLife Distribs., Inc. v. Adherence Group, Inc., 72 F.3d at 374–75 (statutory interpleader "calls for diversity of citizenship between two or more of the adverse claimants, requires that the amount in controversy, which is measured by the value of the stake, be $500, and compels the stakeholder to deposit the money or property at issue in the court's Registry or, in the alternative, to give a bond payable to the clerk of courts in the appropriate amount"); Network Solutions, Inc. v. Clue Computing, Inc., 946 F.Supp. 858, 860 (D.Colo.1996) (setting forth the three prerequisites to exercise of jurisdiction in statutory interpleader action).

42. See 28 U.S.C.A. § 1332 (West 1993), Chapter 1 "Subject Matter Jurisdiction," supra.

43. 28 U.S.C.A. § 1335 (West 1993); State Farm Fire & Cas. Co. v. Tashire, 386 U.S. 523, 530, 87 S.Ct. 1199, 1203, 18 L.Ed.2d 270 (1967) (noting that only "minimal diversity" is required for statutory intervention).

Complete diversity is not required, and the citizenship of the party seeking interpleader is irrelevant.[44] The final requirement is that the interpleader deposit the res into the court's registry. This is intended to ensure the safety of the disputed property and to facilitate the distribution of funds once the competing claims have been resolved.[45] It is not enough for the interpleader to promise that it will maintain the status quo and abide by the court's determination of rights with regard to the disputed funds; the funds must be deposited or an adequate bond must be posted.[46]

Statutory interpleader provides for nationwide service on all claimants and allows a district court to enjoin any state or federal proceeding affecting the stake.[47] In addition, venue for a statutory interpleader action is proper where one or more of the claimants reside.[48]

(e) Form of Trial

An interpleader action typically encompasses two distinct procedural stages. In the first stage, the court determines whether the plaintiff has established the right under the rule or statute to require the claimants to interplead their claims.[49] This is a court-tried, equitable issue, historically not entitled to a trial by jury.[50] In the second phase, the court adjudicates the competing claims of the defendant claimants and determines which claimant is entitled to recover.[51] Arguably, the plaintiff in an interpleader action may be taken to have waived his right to a jury trial based on the historically equitable nature of interpleader. Following the merger of law and equity, however, a jury trial should be accorded, as of right, to both parties in an interpleader action because, despite the equitable nature of the interpleader procedure, both the underlying claims and the relief sought typically are legal in nature.[52]

44. CNA Ins. Cos. v. Waters, 926 F.2d 247, 249 n. 5 (3d Cir.1991) (citizenship of stakeholder is "irrelevant" for purposes of statutory interpleader).

45. Network Solutions, Inc., 946 F.Supp. at 860.

46. *Id.* (the res must be deposited); National Union Fire Ins. Co. v. Coric, 924 F.Supp. 373, 382 (N.D.N.Y.1996) (posting of a bond in the highest amount claimed by the defendants with respect to the res in the interpleader action is a requirement for statutory interpleader), *aff'd in part, rev'd in part on other grounds*, 108 F.3d 17 (2d Cir.1997).

47. 28 U.S.C.A. § 2361 (West 1994) (providing for nationwide service of process in statutory interpleader action and authorizing the district court to enjoin other proceedings affecting the stake deposited in a statutory interpleader action).

48. 28 U.S.C.A. § 1397 (West 1993) (venue for statutory interpleader claim

proper where one or more of the claimants reside).

49. First Interstate Bank of Oregon, N.A. v. United States, 891 F.Supp. 543, 546 (D.Or.1995) (rule interpleader); NYLife Distribs., Inc. v. Adherence Group, Inc., 72 F.3d 371, 375 (3d Cir.1995) (statutory interpleader).

50. *See* Ross v. Bernhard, 396 U.S. 531, 540–41, 90 S.Ct. 733, 739–40, 24 L.Ed.2d 729 (1970) (discussing the right to a jury trial in actions historically tried to courts in equity).

51. First Interstate Bank of Oregon, N.A., 891 F.Supp. at 546; NYLife Distribs, Inc., 72 F.3d at 375.

52. *See* Ross, 396 U.S. at 538, 541 n. 15, 90 S.Ct. at 738, 739 n. 15 (in determining right to a jury trial, court considers both the nature of the underlying claims and relief sought).

(1) Discharge

The typical plaintiff in an interpleader action—whether pursuant to the rule or statute—is an innocent stakeholder who is subject to competing claims. So long as the interpleader action is commenced in good faith to resolve competing claims,[53] the interpleader is entitled to be discharged from liability upon deposit of the disputed funds in the court's registry or posting of an adequate bond and surety.[54]

(2) Recovery of Costs and Fees

The court has discretion to award attorneys' fees and costs to a disinterested stakeholder in an interpleader action, and such an award is made routinely in the absence of bad faith.[55] Typically, the stakeholder will be compensated out of the interpleader funds deposited with the court, provided that it does not jeopardize satisfaction of a federal tax lien.[56] The theory behind permitting an award of costs and fees to a disinterested stakeholder is that it would be inequitable to require such an innocent party, willing to pay the entire claim, to bear the costs of litigation stemming from a dispute solely between two other parties. Those considerations are not involved when the stakeholder is not truly disinterested or innocent.[57] Thus, an award of costs and fees generally will be denied where, for instance, the stakeholder has contested liability on the underlying claim because in such a situation the stakeholder is not truly disinterested.[58]

(3) Equitable Limitations

Regardless of the manner in which interpleader is invoked, it remains an equitable device and it is within the discretion of the court to withhold relief where the party seeking interpleader is not free from blame in causing the controversy[59] or has engaged in some other type of

---

53. See infra § 14.5(e)(3).

54. See New York Life Ins. Co. v. Connecticut Dev. Auth., 700 F.2d 91, 96 (2d Cir.1983) (disinterested stakeholder may be ordered discharged unless there exists serious charges that interpleader action was commenced in bad faith); Connecticut Gen. Life Ins. Co. v. Thomas, 910 F.Supp. 297, 300 (S.D.Tex.1995) (allowing stakeholder insurance company to be dismissed from lawsuit between named beneficiary and alleged intended beneficiary of life insurance policy upon deposit of full amount of benefits due under insurance policy).

55. See First Interstate Bank of Oregon, N.A., 891 F.Supp. 543, 548 (costs and fees should be routinely allowed in the absence of bad faith).

56. See id. (costs and fees are typically paid out of funds deposited with the court, but no award will be made where it would jeopardize payment of a federal tax lien).

See also Hoover, Inc. v. McCullough Indus., Inc., 351 F.Supp. 1023, 1027, 1031 (S.D.Ala. 1972) (where there is a dispute as to the correctness of the amount deposited, the court may prorate its award of attorneys' fees by disallowing recovery for fees allocated to the dispute over the amount of the funds deposited, but allowing recovery for fees incurred in bringing the interpleader action).

57. See infra § 14.5(e)(3).

58. Perkins State Bank v. Connolly, 632 F.2d 1306, 1311 (5th Cir.1980) (where interpleader contests liability, he is not a disinterested stakeholder entitled to an award of fees and costs).

59. Network Solutions, Inc. v. Clue Computing, Inc., 946 F.Supp. 858, 860–61 (D.Colo.1996) (denying interpleader where plaintiff was not free from blame, but was alleged in a separate state court action to

wrongdoing,[60] such as manipulating the interpleader procedure to avoid liability on a substantive claim[61] or using it as a pretext to shift the ordinary costs of doing business.[62] The latter situation arises most frequently in the context of insurance companies, for whom the settlement of disputed claims has been regarded by some courts as a routine part of their business, the cost of which should not be taken out of the disputed fund.[63]

Library References:

West's Key No. Digests, Interpleader ⊜1–43.
Wright, Miller & Kane, Federal Practice and Procedure: Civil 2d §§ 1701–1721.

§ 14.6 Intervention

FRCP 24 allows an outsider to intervene in a pending action. It complements FRCP 19, which requires that existing parties to an action in some instances join other parties,[1] and FRCP 20, which allows, but does not compel, joinder of parties under certain conditions.[2] The purpose of the Rule is similar to the rules of joinder in that it provides a mechanism by which an outsider, whose interests may be detrimentally affected by a pending litigation, may participate in the litigation.[3] The Rule also seeks to conserve judicial resources and avoid the expense of multiple litigation by allowing an uninvited, but interested outsider to join in a pending action, even against the wishes of existing parties.[4] Before an outsider will be allowed to intervene, he must satisfy certain prerequisites, which are more stringent depending on whether the outsider is seeking intervention as of right or permissive intervention.[5]

have breached contractual obligations to the claimants).

60. *See* Kurland v. United States, 919 F.Supp. 419, 422 (M.D.Fla.1996) (where interpleader has engaged in improper conduct, such as wrongfully disbursing funds after being put on notice of a lien, and is not an innocent stakeholder, the equitable relief available through interpleader will not be allowed); National Union Fire Ins. Co. v. Coric, 924 F.Supp. 373, 381 (N.D.N.Y.1996) (interpleader relief may be withheld where allowing it might reward inequitable or improper conduct), *aff'd in part, rev'd in part on other grounds*, 108 F.3d 17 (2d Cir.1997); Truck–A–Tune, Inc. v. Re, 856 F.Supp. 77, 81 (D.Conn.1993) ("An interpleader action is equitable in nature, and the doctrine of unclean hands can thus bar a stakeholder from successfully invoking it."), *aff'd*, 23 F.3d 60 (2d Cir. 1994).

61. *See* Emcasco Ins. Co. v. Davis, 753 F.Supp. 1458, 1464–65 (W.D.Ark.1990) (costs and fees denied where insurance

company brought interpleader action as a pretext to avoid duty to defend insured).

62. *See* Aetna U.S. Healthcare v. Higgs, 962 F.Supp. 1412, 1414 (D.Kan.1997) (no costs awarded to interpleader insurance company where court deemed it an ordinary cost of business to settle such claims); Metropolitan Property & Cas. Ins. Co. v. Long, 1995 WL 781215, at *2 (D.Kan.1995) (inappropriate in interpleader action to award fees to plaintiff insurance company where it would typically incur those costs in the settlement of any claim).

63. *Id.*

§ 14.6

1. FRCP 19; *see supra* Chapter 10 "Joinder, Consolidation and Severance."

2. FRCP 20; *see supra* Chapter 10 "Joinder, Consolidation and Severance."

3. *See infra* § 14.6(a).

4. *See infra* § 14.6(a)-(b).

5. *See id.*

(a) Intervention as of Right

FRCP 24(a) provides that a timely[6] application for intervention shall be permitted when either: (1) a statute of the United States confers an unconditional right to intervene; or (2) the applicant (a) claims an interest relating to the property or transaction which is the subject of the action, (b) is so situated that the disposition of the action may, as a practical matter, impair or impede his ability to protect that interest, and (c) his interest is not adequately represented by the existing parties to the lawsuit.[7] The inquiry under this Rule is intended to be flexible, focusing on the particular facts and circumstances of each application.[8] Accordingly, an application for intervention as of right should be measured by a practical, rather than technical yardstick.[9] However, each element must be satisfied or the application for intervention as of right will be denied.[10]

(1) Federal Statutory Basis

There are relatively few statutes that confer an unambiguous right to intervene on private litigants under FRCP 24(a)(1).[11] Most of the cases arising under this section relate to the ability of the state or federal government or its officers and agents to intervene in cases challenging the constitutionality of state and federal laws or other matters of public interest.[12] In practice, therefore, applications for intervention generally turn on the alternative requirements of FRCP 24(a)(2), to wit, proving a

---

6. *See infra* § 14.6(c)(2) (discussing the timeliness requirement).

7. FRCP 24(a); *see also* Chiglo v. City of Preston, 104 F.3d 185, 187 (8th Cir.1997) (FRCP 24(a) imposes four requirements for intervention as of right: (1) the application must be timely, (2) the movant must have a cognizable interest relating to the property or transaction which is the subject of the action, (3) the movant must be so situated that the disposition of the action may impair her ability to protect the interest, and (4) the movant's interest must be inadequately represented by the existing parties); Michigan State AFL–CIO v. Miller, 103 F.3d 1240, 1245 (6th Cir.1997) (same).

8. Swann v. City of Dallas, 172 F.R.D. 211, (N.D.Tex.1997) (standard for intervention as of right is intended to be applied with flexibility to meet the facts and circumstances involved in each particular case).

9. *Id.*; *see also In re* Pantopaque Prods. Liab. Litig., 938 F.Supp. 266, 273–74 (D.N.J.1996) ("a district court may at its discretion accept a procedurally deficient motion to intervene or construe a motion of

a different stripe to be a constructive or implied motion to intervene").

10. Chiglo, 104 F.3d at 187 (each of the requirements of FRCP 24(a) must be met before a court will grant a motion to intervene as of right); Reich v. ABC/York–Estes Corp., 64 F.3d 316, 321 (7th Cir.1995) (failure to satisfy one of the necessary prerequisites to intervention as of right mandates denial of application).

11. *See, e.g.*, United States v. Mississippi, 958 F.2d 112, 115 (5th Cir.1992) (allowing intervention as of right pursuant to express provisions of the Clean Water Act); International Union, Local 283 v. Scofield, 382 U.S. 205, 212–13, 86 S.Ct. 373, 378–79, 15 L.Ed.2d 272 (1965) (holding that under the National Labor Relations Act any party that was successful in proceeding before NLRB must be allowed to intervene as of right in any subsequent appeal).

12. *See, e.g., In re* Benny, 812 F.2d 1133, 1139–42 (9th Cir.1987) (trial court allowed intervention by government agencies and representatives in suit challenging the constitutionality of certain provisions of the federal Bankruptcy Act).

sufficient interest in the subject matter of the litigation that will be adversely affected if intervention as of right is not allowed.

(2) Applicant Must Have Sufficient Interest

There is no clear definition of what constitutes a litigable "interest" for purposes of intervention under FRCP 24(a)(2).[13] Most courts adopt a rather expansive notion of the interest sufficient to invoke the intervention as of right.[14] The Supreme Court, for instance, has noted that "[w]hat is obviously meant [by Rule 24(a)(2)] is a significantly protectable interest."[15] Lower courts similarly have required a direct, substantial interest in the litigation which must be sufficiently protectable.[16]

Despite the general willingness of courts to apply a rather expansive concept of the interest sufficient to invoke intervention as of right, intervention will not be allowed where the movant has shown nothing more than a remote, hypothetical or contingent interest.[17] Similarly, a mere economic interest in the outcome of the pending litigation generally is not sufficient in itself, unless the substantive law recognizes that interest as one belonging to or being owned by the movant.[18] This is just another way of saying that a party cannot assert the legal rights of a third party—the intervenor must be the real party in interest with respect to its claim.[19] That is, it generally must have a legally recognized interest in either the property or transaction that is the subject of the action.[20] Nor will mere convenience to the prospective intervenor suffice;

---

13. Redland Ins. Co. v. Chillingsworth Venture, Ltd., 171 F.R.D. 206, 206 (N.D.Ohio 1997) (discussing the interest requirement of FRCP 24(a)(2)).

14. Michigan State AFL–CIO v. Miller, 103 F.3d 1240, 1245 (6th Cir.1997) (courts generally apply an expansive interpretation to the interest requirement).

15. Donaldson v. United States, 400 U.S. 517, 531, 91 S.Ct. 534, 542, 27 L.Ed.2d 580 (1971).

16. See Edwards v. City of Houston, 78 F.3d 983, 1004 (5th Cir.1996) (movant seeking intervention must have a "direct, substantial, [and] legally protectable interest in the proceedings"); Jansen v. City of Cincinnati, 904 F.2d 336, 341 (6th Cir.1990) (intervenor must have a direct, substantial interest in the litigation which must be sufficiently protectable).

17. Redland Ins. Co., 171 F.R.D. at 206 (denying intervention as of right to representatives of passengers killed in a helicopter accident where the subject declaratory judgment action concerned only the insurer's duty to defend and indemnify the owner and pilot of the helicopter, and where

there had not been any liability determination in any tort action); League of United Latin American Citizens v. Clements, 884 F.2d 185, 188 (5th Cir.1989) (intervention as of right cannot rest on an interest that is remote or collateral to the main action).

18. Swann v. City of Dallas, 172 F.R.D. 211, 213 (N.D.Tex.1997) (economic interests unaccompanied by any legally recognized right generally do not satisfy interest requirement for intervention as of right); New Orleans Pub. Serv., Inc. v. United Gas Pipe Line Co., 732 F.2d 452, 456 (5th Cir.) (motion of consumers and city officials to intervene denied where prospective intervenors were not parties to the pending contract dispute between utility company and its supplier), cert. denied, 469 U.S. 1019, 105 S.Ct. 434, 83 L.Ed.2d 360 (1984).

19. New Orleans Pub. Serv., Inc., 732 F.2d at 456–58 (intervention in pending contract dispute denied where prospective intervenors were neither parties nor intended third-party beneficiaries of contract and, thus, were not the real parties in interest with respect to that claim).

20. Id.; see also FRCP 24(a)(2).

the interest must be "significantly protectable such that it will be directly and immediately affected by the litigation."[21]

Some courts have recognized an even broader interpretation of the interest requirement where intervention is sought by a public interest group in actions challenging the validity of general legislation, at least where the group was actively involved in the process leading up to the adoption of the subject legislation or has a history of representing the interests that are at stake in the litigation.[22]

(3) Applicant's Ability to Protect Interest Will Be Impaired or Impeded

The nature of the applicant's interest in the subject of the action relates closely to its inability to otherwise protect that interest. The kind of interest that suffices depends upon the nature of the action in which the applicant seeks to intervene. The wording of Rule 24(a)(2) ("may as a practical matter impair or impede the applicant's ability to protect that interest") obviates any need to show that disposition of the action would preclude the applicant, on the res judicata principle, from pursuing his remedy elsewhere. The standard is simply whether, as a practical matter, the applicant's ability to protect its interest will be impaired, not whether the applicant will be bound by the disposition of the action in its absence.[23] To satisfy this element, a would-be intervenor must show only that impairment of its substantial legal interest is possible if intervention is denied; this burden is minimal and may be satisfied simply by showing that the decision may have an adverse precedential impact on a future litigation.[24]

(4) Applicant's Interest Must Be Inadequately Represented

The intervenor also bears the burden of showing that its interests are not adequately represented by existing parties, but this burden is minimal.[25] Once again, the would-be intervenor need only show that the

21. Werbungs Und Commerz Union Austalt v. Collectors' Guild, Ltd., 782 F.Supp. 870, 874 (S.D.N.Y.1991) United States v. Massachusetts Maritime Academy, 76 F.R.D. 595, 597 (D.Mass.1977) (mere convenience to prospective intervenor is inadequate to meet interest requirement).

22. See Michigan State AFL–CIO v. Miller, 103 F.3d 1240, 1245 (6th Cir.1997) (intervention by Chamber of Commerce allowed where members of the Chamber had played a key role in obtaining passage of the subject legislation); Idaho Farm Bureau Fed'n v. Babbitt, 58 F.3d 1392, 1398–99 (9th Cir.1995) (intervention of public interest group allowed where members of the group had direct contact with the subject of the litigation and government agency had failed to appeal an issue of great significance to the group).

23. United States v. Texas E. Transmission Corp., 923 F.2d 410, 413 (5th Cir.1991) (possibility of impairment of interest is all that is required).

24. Michigan State AFL–CIO, 103 F.3d at 1247 (burden of proving impairment is minimal). See also American Nat'l Bank and Trust Co. v. City of Chicago, 865 F.2d 144, 147–48 (7th Cir.1989) (impairment exists when there is a possibility that the stare decisis effect of decision will foreclose the rights of the proposed intervenor in a subsequent proceeding); Atlantis Dev. Corp. v. United States, 379 F.2d 818, 828–29 (5th Cir.1967) (same).

25. Swann v. City of Dallas, 172 F.R.D. 211, 213 (N.D.Tex.1997) (the applicant's burden under the inadequate representation requirement of FRCP 24(a) is "minimal").

present representation may be inadequate to protect its interest; one is not required to show that the representation is in fact inadequate.[26] In determining whether the representation by existing parties precludes intervention as of right, courts generally consider the following factors: (1) the extent to which the present party's interests coincide with the applicant's; (2) the presence or absence of any adverse interest between the applicant and the present party; (3) the diligence, or lack thereof, of the present party in pursuing the action; and (4) the presence or absence of collusion between the present party and his opponent.[27] Any doubt as to the adequacy of representation should be resolved in favor of the proposed intervenor.[28]

Inadequate representation may, of course, be shown by misfeasance or nonfeasance in the course of the representation or by divergent interests.[29] However, the mere failure to pursue an appeal, without more, ordinarily will not be sufficient to show inadequate representation since a decision to take an appeal is ordinarily within the discretion of the representative.[30] Similarly, mere disagreement as to trial tactics does not constitute inadequate representation, although it may be enough to show that the existing party who purports to seek the same outcome as the proposed intervenor does not share the same perspective on significant legal issues and, as such, will not make all of the arguments that are of concern to the proposed intervenor.[31]

A presumption of adequate representation arises where an existing party to the suit is charged with representing the intervenor's interests.[32] This situation frequently arises where, for instance, one of the parties is an arm or agency of the government, acting in a matter of sovereign interest. In such cases, the governmental entity is presumed to adequately represent the interests of its citizens, so long as those interests are shown to be coextensive with those of the proposed intervenor. Where, however, the proposed intervenor stands to gain or lose something from the litigation in a way different from the public at large, the government agency should not be presumed to adequately represent the intervenor's interests.[33] Private landowners, for instance, have been

---

26. Michigan State AFL–CIO, 103 F.3d at 1247 (possibility of inadequate representation is all that is required); Sierra Club v. Espy, 18 F.3d 1202, 1207 (5th Cir.1994) (applicant for intervention as of right need only show that the current representation "may be" inadequate).

27. United States v. International Bus. Machs. Corp., 62 F.R.D. 530, 536–37 (S.D.N.Y.1974) (setting forth criteria normally considered by court in evaluating adequacy of representation).

28. See id.

29. See Chiglo v. City of Preston, 104 F.3d 185, 188 (8th Cir.1997) (inadequate representation may be shown by misfea-

sance, nonfeasance or divergence of interests).

30. Cf. Michigan State AFL–CIO, 103 F.3d at 1248 ("a decision not to appeal by an original party to the action can constitute inadequate representation of another party's interest").

31. See B.H. v. McDonald, 49 F.3d 294, 297 (7th Cir.1995) (disagreement as to trial tactics does not amount to inadequate representation).

32. See Chiglo, 104 F.3d at 187 (where government agency is representing interests of public at large, a presumption of adequate representation arises).

33. Id. at 187–88.

allowed to intervene in an action brought by the state to protect fish and wildlife based on the court's determination that the landowners' interest in preserving the value of their nearby land values, which might be negatively impacted by the depletion of fish and game, was distinct from the general public's interest in protecting fish and wildlife.[34]

(b) Permissive Intervention

Where a party cannot meet the requirements for intervention as of right, intervention may nevertheless be allowed in the court's discretion pursuant to the provisions of FRCP 24(b).[35] By its terms, the Rule allows intervention upon timely[36] motion when (1) a statute of the United States confers a conditional right to intervene, or (2) there are common questions of law or fact presented by the applicant's claim or defense and the main action, provided that intervention will not unduly delay or prejudice the adjudication of the rights of the original parties.[37] The court has broad discretion in resolving applications for permissive intervention.[38] Unlike intervention as of right, an applicant for permissive intervention need not demonstrate an interest in the subject litigation nor that the existing representation is inadequate.[39] However, as discussed in Section 14.6(b)(3), *infra*, those factors may properly weigh in the court's determination as to whether permissive intervention should be allowed.

(1) Federal Statutory Basis

The standard for permissive intervention on a federal statutory basis is essentially the same as that applied under FRCP 24(a)(1), except that FRCP 24(b)(1) makes clear that permissive intervention will be denied if it would unduly delay or prejudice the adjudication of the original parties' rights.[40] Where, however, a federal statute unambiguously confers a right to intervene on a party, there is no need to rely on the permissive requirements of subsection (b) since the applicant in such circumstances would be entitled to intervene as of right, provided that all of the conditions set forth in the statute are complied with.[41] Absent

---

34. Mille Lacs Band of Chippewa Indians v. Minnesota, 989 F.2d 994, 1001 (8th Cir.1993).

35. Henry v. First Nat'l Bank of Clarksdale, 50 F.R.D. 251, 261–62 (N.D.Miss.1970) (allowing permissive intervention despite intervenor's inability to meet requirements for intervention as of right), *vacated on other grounds*, 444 F.2d 1300 (5th Cir. 1971), *cert. denied*, 405 U.S. 1019, 92 S.Ct. 1284, 31 L.Ed.2d 483 (1972).

36. *See infra* § 14.6(c)(2) (discussing the timeliness requirement).

37. FRCP 24(b).

38. Rosenshein v. Kleban, 918 F.Supp. 98, 106 (S.D.N.Y.1996) (court has "broad

discretion in resolving applications for permissive intervention").

39. *Compare* FRCP 24(a) *with* FRCP 24(b); *see also* SEC v. United States Realty & Improvement Co., 310 U.S. 434, 459, 60 S.Ct. 1044, 1055, 84 L.Ed. 1293 (1940) (FRCP 24(b) "dispenses with any requirement that the intervenor shall have a direct personal or pecuniary interest in the subject of the litigation").

40. FRCP 24(b); *see also* § 14.6(a)(1), *supra*.

41. *See, e.g.*, Phar–Mor, Inc. v. Coopers & Lybrand, 22 F.3d 1228, 1230–31 (3d Cir. 1994) (Section 1109(b) of the Bankruptcy Code gives creditors an unconditional right

such an express statutory right to intervene, the applicant for permissive intervention must demonstrate that there is at least one common question of law or fact to be resolved.[42]

(2) Common Question of Law or Fact

Apart from a statutory conditional right to intervene, the threshold requirement for an application for permissive intervention is the existence of at least one common question of law or fact between the applicant's claim or defense and the main action.[43] Courts tend to read this requirement literally so that the standard is satisfied when there is either a common question of law or fact; the applicant need not show both.[44] As a general rule, therefore, intervention will be allowed whenever the claims or defenses are identical or share a common factual or legal basis.[45] As discussed in the following section, however, the court retains discretion to deny intervention, such as where intervention would result in undue prejudice or delay to the existing parties.

(3) Factors Relevant to Exercise of Discretion

In addition to being timely and presenting a common question of law or fact, an application for permissive intervention must demonstrate that its allowance will not result in the likelihood of undue delay or prejudice to the rights of the existing parties.[46] This requires balancing the advantages of intervention to the applicant against any disadvantages to the existing parties.[47] Among the factors that should be considered are the stage of the proceedings at which intervention is sought,[48] the likelihood of any delay that may result,[49] any unique perspective or expertise that the intervenor may bring to the resolution of the dispute,[50] whether the intervenor's interests are already represented by an existing party,[51] and whether intervention will unnecessarily complicate

---

to intervene in pending bankruptcy proceedings).

42. *See infra* § 14.6(b)(2).

43. Michigan State AFL–CIO v. Miller, 103 F.3d 1240, 1248 (6th Cir.1997) (application for permissive intervention must present one common question of law or fact with the main action).

44. *See* Lee v. State of Oregon, 891 F.Supp. 1421, 1427 (D.Or.1995) (permissive intervention should be allowed where there is at least one common question of law or fact).

45. *See, e.g.,* McNeill v. New York City Hous. Auth., 719 F.Supp. 233, 250–51 (S.D.N.Y.1989) (commonality for purposes of FRCP 24(b) established where claims were identical, even though facts underlying claims differed).

46. FRCP 24(b).

47. *See* Redland Ins. Co. v. Chillingsworth Venture, Ltd., 171 F.R.D. 206, 207

(N.D.Ohio 1997) (in exercising its discretion to allow permissive intervention, the court must consider whether the intervention will unduly delay or prejudice the adjudication of the rights of the original parties).

48. *See infra* § 14.6(c)(2).

49. United States v. Texas E. Transmission Corp., 923 F.2d 410, 416 (5th Cir.1991) (intervention should be denied where it would result in undue delay in the proceedings).

50. Johnson v. Mortham, 915 F.Supp. 1529, 1538–39 (N.D.Fla.1995) (allowing NAACP to intervene in redistricting case where it offered a unique and valuable perspective).

51. Lee v. State of Oregon, 891 F.Supp. 1421, 1427–28 (D.Or.1995) (permissive intervention should be denied where the applicant's interests were adequately represented by other named parties).

or prolong the proceedings.[52] A district court has broad discretion to deny an applicant's motion for permissive intervention. In fact, a denial of permissive intervention has "virtually never been reversed."[53]

(c) Procedure

(1) Motion to Intervene

A person seeking to intervene must serve an appropriate FRCP 5–type motion on the present parties in the action.[54] The motion must (1) state the grounds supporting intervention and (2) be accompanied by a pleading (*i.e.*, complaint or answer) setting forth the claim or defense sought to be asserted.[55] Failure to comply with either requirement will usually result in denial of the motion.[56] The Supreme Court has held that if it is clear from the face of the application or pleading that the motion should be denied, no hearing on the application for intervention need be held.[57] In all other cases, a hearing will usually be held. A party seeking to oppose a motion to intervene, must promptly object to the application or risk waiver.[58] The burden of justifying intervention rests with the prospective intervenor.[59]

(2) Timeliness

A motion for intervention, whether permissive or as of right, must be timely made.[60] This requirement is intended to prevent a tardy intervenor from derailing the lawsuit that is near completion. The test is one of reasonableness—potential intervenors must be reasonably diligent in learning of a suit that might affect their rights, and upon so learning they need to act reasonably promptly.[61] Among the factors that courts normally consider in making this determination are the following: (1) the point to which the suit has progressed; (2) the purpose for which

52. Arney v. Finney, 967 F.2d 418, 421–22 (10th Cir.1992) (intervention denied where it would unnecessarily prolong litigation).

53. Catanzano v. Wing, 103 F.3d 223, 234 (2d Cir.1996) (affirming district court's denial of application for permissive intervention where motion was not timely filed).

54. FRCP 24(c).

55. *Id.*

56. Ryer v. Harrisburg Kohl Bros. Inc., 53 F.R.D. 404, 411 (M.D.Pa.1971) (motion requirement); Associated Students of Univ. of Cal. at Riverside v. Kleindienst, 60 F.R.D. 65, 68 (C.D.Cal.1973) (pleading requirement).

57. Sam Fox Publ'g Co. v. United States, 366 U.S. 683, 693–94, 81 S.Ct. 1309, 1315, 6 L.Ed.2d 604 (1961).

58. Exchange Nat'l Bank v. Abramson, 45 F.R.D. 97, 101–02 (D.Minn.1968).

59. *See* Michigan State AFL–CIO v. Miller, 103 F.3d 1240, 1247 (6th Cir.1997) (intervenor bears burden of proof).

60. FRCP 24(a) and (b) (stating that intervention must be "upon timely application").

61. *See* Save Our Springs Alliance Inc. v. Babbitt, 115 F.3d 346, 347–48 (5th Cir. 1997) (affirming denial of motion to intervene where intervenor delayed three months before filing, filed the day before summary judgment briefs were due, and offered no plausible explanation for its delay); Burdick v. Koerner, 173 F.R.D. 242, 1997 WL 269128, at *1 (E.D.Wis.1997) (denying intervention where motion was filed five months after proposed intervenor learned of the lawsuit, two months before the close of discovery and nearly four months before trial, all without any reasonable explanation for the intervenor's delay).

intervention is sought; (3) the length of time preceding the application during which the proposed intervenors knew or should have known of their interest in the case; (4) the prejudice to the original parties due to the proposed intervenor's failure to promptly intervene after it knew or reasonably should have known of its interest in the case; and (5) the existence of unusual circumstances mitigating against or in favor of intervention.[62] Timeliness, in short, requires consideration of all the relevant facts and circumstances involved in a given case, not just the mere passage of time. In fact, intervention has even been allowed after entry of judgment to permit the intervenor to pursue an appeal that the original party had abandoned.[63] In that case, however, the intervenor must establish a compelling basis to allow intervention at such a late stage in the proceedings and provide a strong justification for its failure to intervene earlier.[64]

The trial judge is entitled to a full range of reasonable discretion in determining whether the timeliness and other requirements for intervention have been met, and only an abuse of discretion will cause reversal.[65]

(3) Jurisdiction and Venue

There is no separate or independent jurisdictional basis for intervention. Therefore, a party seeking intervention generally must demonstrate either the existence of a federal question or diversity jurisdiction.[66] However, if an intervenor's entry in the case can be supported by ancillary or supplemental jurisdiction,[67] a federal question or diversity of citizenship between the intervenor and the other parties to the litigation is unnecessary, provided that the nondiverse intervenor was not an indispensable party under FRCP 19 at the time the action was filed.[68]

62. *See* Grubbs v. Norris, 870 F.2d 343, 345 (6th Cir.1989) (setting forth factors to be considered in making timeliness determination); *see also* Calvert v. Huckins, 109 F.3d 636, 638 (9th Cir.1997) (three factors are weighed in determining timeliness: (1) the stage of the proceeding at which an applicant seeks to intervene; (2) the prejudice to the other parties; and (3) the reason for and length of the delay).

63. *See* United Airlines, Inc. v. McDonald, 432 U.S. 385, 395–96, 97 S.Ct. 2464, 2470–71, 53 L.Ed.2d 423 (1977) (the critical inquiry to permit post-judgment intervention is whether in view of all the circumstances the intervenor acted promptly after judgment and meets all the traditional criteria for intervention); United States v. City of Oakland, 958 F.2d 300, 302 (9th Cir.1992) (intervention allowed post-judgment to pursue significant issues on appeal).

64. *See* McDonald, 432 U.S. at 395, 97 S.Ct. at 2470; Banco Popular de Puerto Rico v. Greenblatt, 964 F.2d 1227, 1231 (1st Cir.1992) ("The more advanced the litigation, the more searching the scrutiny which the motion [to intervene] must withstand.").

65. Maddow v. Procter & Gamble Co., 107 F.3d 846, 854 (11th Cir.1997) (timeliness determination is in the court's discretion).

66. *See* International Paper Co. v. Inhabitants of Town of Jay, 887 F.2d 338, 345–46 (1st Cir.1989) (affirming denial of intervention where there was no independent basis for federal jurisdiction under either federal question or diversity).

67. *See* Chapter 1 "Subject Matter Jurisdiction," *supra.*

68. Angst v. Royal Maccabees Life Ins. Co., 77 F.3d 701, 704–05 (3d Cir.1996) (where diversity of citizenship is lacking, intervenor may seek to rely on court's supplemental jurisdiction).

A party seeking intervention consents to the venue of the main action and waives any objection on that basis.[69]

(4) Appeal from Denial

The denial of a motion for intervention under FRCP 24 is immediately appealable as a collateral order, provided that all aspects of the decision are final.[70]

(d) Rights of Intervenor

(1) Conditional or Limited Intervention

Because an application for permissive intervention is directed to the court's discretion, the court may impose conditions on its allowance.[71] Despite some initial dispute, it is now established that, even though a party is entitled to intervene as of right under FRCP 24(a), the court may, in the exercise of its discretion, impose reasonable conditions on intervention.[72] This conclusion is supported by the Advisory Committee Notes to the 1966 amendments to FRCP 24, which expressly state that an "intervention of right under the amended rule may be subject to appropriate conditions or restrictions responsive among other things to the requirements of efficient conduct of the proceedings." In its discretion, the court also may impose reasonable restrictions on the scope of the intervenor's participation in the subject litigation.[73]

(2) Procedure Following Intervention

Subject to any conditions imposed on the allowance of intervention, the intervenor enjoys the rights of the original parties.[74] The intervenor

69. Commonwealth Edison Co. v. Train, 71 F.R.D. 391, 394 (N.D.Ill.1976) (intervenor may not challenge venue).

70. *See* Ozee v. American Council On Gift Annuities, Inc., 110 F.3d 1082, 1094 (5th Cir.1997) (denial of Rule 24(a) motion to intervene is a final appealable collateral order); Edwards v. City of Houston, 78 F.3d 983, 992 (5th Cir.1996) (same), *petition for cert. filed*, 66 U.S.L.W. 3170 (Aug. 19, 1997). *Cf.* Stringfellow v. Concerned Neighbors in Action, 480 U.S. 370, 377–78, 107 S.Ct. 1177, 1183, 94 L.Ed.2d 389 (1987) (conditional allowance of motion to intervene is not immediately appealable).

71. Beauregard, Inc. v. Sword Servs. LLC, 107 F.3d 351, 352–53 (5th Cir.1997) (noting that there is no dispute that virtually any condition may be attached to the allowance of a motion for permissive intervention).

72. *Id.* (affirming district court order allowing intervention as of right on condition that intervenor share its portion of the costs of maintaining the disputed res); United Nuclear Corp. v. Cranford Ins. Co., 905 F.2d 1424, 1427 (10th Cir.1990) (intervention sought for discovery purposes only), *cert. denied*, 498 U.S. 1073, 111 S.Ct. 799, 112 L.Ed.2d 860 (1991).

73. *See* Massachusetts School of Law at Andover, Inc. v. United States, 118 F.3d 776, 781–82 (D.C.Cir.1997) (law school permitted to intervene in antitrust action against American Bar Association on limited issue regarding disclosure of government consent decree); Swann v. City of Dallas, 172 F.R.D. 211, 213 (N.D.Tex.1997) (allowing intervention of right for the limited purpose of modifying a supersedeas bond).

74. Hallmark Cards, Inc. v. Lehman, 959 F.Supp. 539, 541 n. 1 (D.D.C.1997) (intervenor is to be treated as if it were an original party to the claim once intervention has been allowed).

may, for instance, demand a jury trial,[75] move to dismiss the action,[76] or challenge the court's subject matter jurisdiction.[77] While an intervenor may not change the issues between the original parties,[78] it is entitled to fully litigate its claims or defenses.[79] An intervenor of right may (and, in fact, must) assert a compulsory counterclaim.[80] As to other situations, federal courts generally allow an intervenor as of right to counterclaim (whether compulsory or permissive), cross-claim or interplead a third-party defendant; but it is a matter of judicial discretion whether to allow such claims to be asserted by a permissive intervenor.

Library References:

West's Key No. Digests, Federal Civil Procedure ⚷311–345.

§ 14.7   Substitution of Parties

(a) In General

(1) Post-Commencement Events

In contrast to FRCP 17(a), which governs transfers of interest prior to the commencement of an action, FRCP 25 governs the substitution of a party (plaintiff or defendant) due to a change of circumstances occurring during the course of the action.[1] The Rule contemplates: (1) death of a party; (2) incompetency of a party; (3) transfer of an interest (e.g., resignation of a trustee and appointment of a successor); and (4) death or separation from office of a public officer.[2] The Rule is solely procedural and does not determine the substantive rights of parties in the situations to which it applies.[3] Thus, regardless of whether or not substitution is ordered, the respective substantive rights of the parties will remain the same.

75. United States v. California Mobile Home Park Management Co., 107 F.3d 1374, 1379 (9th Cir.1997) (intervenor may demand jury trial despite lack of jury demand by original parties).

76. Hallmark Cards, Inc., 959 F.Supp. at 539, 541 n.l (allowing intervenor's motion to dismiss underlying action).

77. National Metalcrafters v. McNeil, 103 F.R.D. 536, 538 (N.D.Ill.1984) ("intervenors as of right may challenge the subject matter jurisdiction of the court").

78. Tropical Cruise Lines, S.A. v. Vesta Ins. Co., 805 F.Supp. 409, 414 (S.D.Miss. 1992) ("[I]ntervenor 'cannot change the issue that is framed between the original parties.' ").

79. Crosby Yacht Yard, Inc. v. Yacht Chardonnay, 159 F.R.D. 1, 4 (D.Mass.1994) ("[a]n intervenor has the right to bring a counterclaim or a cross-claim against an existing party").

80. Exchange Nat'l Bank of Chicago v. Abramson, 45 F.R.D. 97, 103–04 (D.Minn. 1968) (commenting that "[m]any authoritative commentators on federal procedure state that an intervenor of right can file any counterclaim then available, either compulsory or permissive....").

§ 14.7

1. Barker v. Jackson Nat'l Life Ins. Co., 163 F.R.D. 364, 365 (N.D.Fla.1995) (substitution under FRCP 25 refers to substitution due to changes occurring after the commencement of the action); Veverica v. Drill Barge Buccaneer No. 7, 488 F.2d 880, 886 (5th Cir.1974) (transfer two days after suit filed governed by Rule 25(a), not Rule 17(a)).

2. FRCP 25(a)-(d).

3. Barker, 163 F.R.D. at 365 (FRCP 25 is solely procedural).

(2) Within Court's Discretion

The disposition of a motion pursuant to FRCP 25 is committed to the sound discretion of the trial court.[4] Substitution of parties under the Rule is never mandatory; it is "purely a matter of convenience."[5] The court may in its discretion order that the original party continue the action alone, that the new party be substituted for the original party, or that the new party be joined as an additional party.[6] Substitution may be denied where, for instance, the request is unreasonably delayed such that its allowance would prejudice the rights of the original parties.[7]

(3) No Effect on Jurisdiction or Venue

The Supreme Court's decision in *Freeport-McMoRan, Inc. v. KN Energy, Inc.*,[8] establishes that the addition of a nondiverse party pursuant to Rule 25(c) generally does not deprive the court of subject matter jurisdiction, and hence does not require remand or dismissal, at least where the new party was not an indispensable party at the beginning of the litigation.[9] Similarly, substitution of parties under FRCP 25 has no effect on venue that has been properly established at the outset of the litigation.[10]

(b) Death

If a party (either plaintiff or defendant) dies after commencement of the action, and the action survives either in favor of the decedent's estate or against it, FRCP 25(a)(1) controls, with the decedent's representative bearing the burden of compliance. It applies if the decedent is the sole plaintiff or defendant, or if he is one of several plaintiffs or

---

4. Virgo v. Riviera Beach Assocs., Ltd., 30 F.3d 1350, 1357 (11th Cir.1994); National Independent Theatre Exhibitors, Inc. v. Buena Vista Distribution Co., 748 F.2d 602, 610 (11th Cir.1984), *cert. denied*, 474 U.S. 1013, 106 S.Ct. 544, 88 L.Ed.2d 473 (1985); *see also* FRCP 25(a) (court "may" allow substitution).

5. Barker, 163 F.R.D. at 365.

6. *Id.* at 366.

7. *Id.* (denying transferee's motion for substitution where it was brought three years into the proceedings and would result in a disruption of the scheduled trial).

8. 498 U.S. 426, 428, 111 S.Ct. 858, 860, 112 L.Ed.2d 951 (1991) (holding that "diversity of citizenship is assessed at the time the action is filed ... [and] if jurisdiction exists at the time an action is commenced, such jurisdiction may not be divested by subsequent events ... [including] the addition of a nondiverse party to the action" pursuant to FRCP 25).

9. *See* Burka v. Aetna Life Ins. Co., 87 F.3d 478, 482 (D.C.Cir.1996) ("In other words, under Freeport–McMoRan, it is clearly understood that, as a general rule, the addition of a nondiverse party pursuant to Rule 25(c) does not deprive the District Court of subject matter jurisdiction. This general rule is equally applicable both in removal cases and cases originally brought in federal court.... The only potential caveat alluded to in Freeport–McMoRan is that a Rule 25(c) addition of a nondiverse party may destroy diversity jurisdiction (and, hence, in a case removed from state court, require remand) if the added party was *indispensable at the time the action began*."). (emphasis in original).

10. Minnesota Mining & Mfg. Co. v. Eco Chem, Inc., 757 F.2d 1256, 1264 (Fed.Cir. 1985) ("Just as joinder of a new party does not disturb the district court's jurisdiction, we see no logical rationale for concluding that joinder in any way disturbs venue properly established as an initial matter.").

defendants. The Rule establishes a two-step process before substitution may be ordered: first, the fact of the death must be formally suggested on the record; second, a motion for substitution must be filed not later than 90 days after the fact of the death is suggested on the record.[11] If a party or the representative of the deceased party wants to limit the time within which another may move for substitution, he may do so by suggesting the death upon the record, thereby starting the 90–day clock within which a motion for substitution ordinarily must be filed.[12]

(1) Suggestion of Death

The case law holds that strict formalities must be observed in serving a formal suggestion of death.[13] To be valid, a suggestion of death must be made by a surviving party or on behalf of the decedent's heirs or successors or as a representative of his estate.[14] The attorney for a deceased party may not make the suggestion of death since he is not himself a party to the action and, since his authority to represent the deceased terminated on the death, he is not a representative of the deceased party of the sort contemplated by the Rule.[15] As one court has held, "[d]eath withdrew from the attorney every iota of authorization he had to act for or in [his client's] behalf."[16]

Additionally, the suggestion of death must be served on all parties to the litigation as provided in FRCP 5, and on the successors or representatives of the deceased party who are not parties to the action, in the manner provided by FRCP 4.[17] Service of a formal suggestion of death is "absolutely necessary" to trigger the running of the 90–day clock for filing of a motion to substitute.[18] Actual knowledge of the party's death is not sufficient, nor is mention of the death in court proceedings or pleadings.[19]

In addition, a valid suggestion of death must identify the representative of the successor who may be substituted as a party, at least where it

---

11. FRCP 25(a)(1).

12. Id.

13. See International Cablevision, Inc. v. Sykes, 172 F.R.D. 63 (W.D.N.Y.1997) (a mere letter sent by counsel for the deceased party notifying the other parties of his client's death fails to meet the formal requirements of FRCP 25(a)). See illustrative suggestion of death set forth in § 14.9(e), infra.

14. FRCP 25(a)(1) (suggestion of death shall be made in the same manner as service of a motion for substitution, by "any party or by the successors or representatives of the deceased party").

15. See Hilsabeck v. Lane Co., 168 F.R.D. 313, 314 (D.Kan.1996) (attorney for deceased party is not proper party to make suggestion of death).

16. Al-Jundi v. Estate of Rockefeller, 757 F.Supp. 206, 210 (W.D.N.Y.1990).

17. FRCP 25(a)(1). See Chobot v. Powers, 169 F.R.D. 263, 266 (W.D.N.Y.1996) (service of suggestion of death by mailing a copy to the deceased plaintiff's last known address deemed effective, even though it was returned by the postal service).

18. See International Cablevision, Inc., 172 F.R.D. 63 (letter sent by counsel for the deceased party notifying the other parties of his client's death is ineffective to trigger the 90–day filing period under FRCP 25(a)).

19. Hawes v. Johnson & Johnson, 940 F.Supp. 697, 699 (D.N.J.1996) (actual knowledge of a party's death or the disclosure of that fact in court pleadings does not excuse party's failure to adhere to formal requirements for filing and service of suggestion of death).

is filed by the successors or representatives of the deceased party.[20] Where, however, the suggestion of death is filed by a surviving party to the action, courts have been less demanding. As one court has explained, the Advisory Committee that drafted FRCP 25 plainly contemplated that "the suggestion of death emanating from the side of the deceased would identify a representative of the estate," but that requiring the surviving party to locate the representative of the deceased party's estate was an imposition of an undue burden.[21] Thus, where the suggestion of death is filed by a surviving party, as opposed to the representative of the deceased party, the surviving party generally is not required to identify the representative of the deceased party's estate in the suggestion of death because such a requirement would be unduly burdensome.[22] However, this approach seems inconsistent with the requirement that the suggestion of death be served on both parties and nonparties since implicit in this requirement is an obligation to identify the deceased party's successor or representative.[23] Accordingly, the better practice is to make a reasonable effort to identify the party to be substituted whenever possible by, for example, reviewing any available probate records.

(2) Motion for Substitution

Where a party dies after commencement of an action which survives, the court may on motion substitute the decedent's representative for the decedent.[24] Either an existing party or the representative may make the motion, which should be served, together with a notice of hearing, on each existing party in the normal FRCP 5 manner, and on the nonparty successors or representatives of the deceased party in the manner provided by FRCP 4, *i.e.,* as though they were being served with fresh process.[25]

The motion for substitution must be made within 90–days after the suggestion of death is entered on the record.[26] Absent timely substitution, the "action shall be dismissed as to the deceased party."[27] In

---

20. Hilsabeck, 168 F.R.D at 314 n.1 (at least with regard to plaintiffs, FRCP 25 implicitly requires the party making the suggestion of death to identify the substitute party).

21. Chobot v. Powers, 169 F.R.D. 263, 267 (W.D.N.Y.1996). *See* Yonofsky v. Wernick, 362 F.Supp. 1005, 1012 (S.D.N.Y. 1973) (holding that service of a suggestion of the plaintiff's death on counsel for the deceased plaintiff which failed to name the plaintiff's representative was sufficient under FRCP 25(a) since the surviving party is not in the same position to know the representative of the deceased plaintiff's estate as counsel for the deceased party).

22. Chobot, 169 F.R.D. at 267 (holding that it would be "unduly burdensome" to

require a surviving party to identify the representative of a deceased party).

23. *See* Hilsabeck, 168 F.R.D. at 314 n. 1 (noting that implicit in the requirement for service on parties and nonparties is the burden of identifying the party to be substituted).

24. Ambruster v. Monument 3: Realty Fund VIII, Ltd., 963 F.Supp. 862, 864 (N.D.Cal.1997) (substitution of parties in the event of death is discretionary).

25. FRCP 25(a)(1).

26. Harris v. Commonwealth Nat'l Life Ins. Co., 929 F.Supp. 393, 395 (M.D.Ala. 1996) (filing motion to substitute within 90 days of suggestion of death on the record complies with the requirements of Rule 25).

27. FRCP 25(a)(1).

practice, however, the court may in its discretion allow additional time where the failure to act within the 90–day time limit was the result of excusable neglect.[28]

Although ordinarily a timely motion for substitution will be granted, FRCP 25(a)(1) gives the court considerable discretion ("the court may order substitution of the proper parties"). Undue delay in suggesting the death on the record or in seeking the appointment of an administrator, for example, might result in denial of the motion, particularly where circumstances have arisen rendering it unfair to allow substitution.[29] Accordingly, a party seeking substitution should not assume that he can wait indefinitely for the suggestion of death before filing his motion to substitute.[30]

Significantly, no time limit is set for when the actual substitution of the deceased party's representative must be consummated; the Rule deals only with the filing of a motion for substitution. [31] However, it is clearly within the court's discretion to set a reasonable time limit within which the substitution must be consummated.[32]

Finally, as with the suggestion of death, a proper motion for substitution must identify the party to be substituted or it will be denied.[33]

(3) Survival Statutes

Since FRCP 25 is purely procedural, the determination of whether a cause of action survives the death of the party must be made by reference to the underlying substantive law.[34] Absent some specific direction by Congress, whether an action created by federal statutory law survives the death of the plaintiff is a matter of federal common law.[35] Federal common law has long recognized that actions which are

28. *See* Dubuc v. Green Oak Township, 958 F.Supp. 1231, 1240 (E.D.Mich.1997) (it is within the court's discretion to allow additional time for the filing of a motion for substitution where the failure to act was the result of excusable neglect within the meaning of FRCP 6(b)(2)).

29. *See* Anderson v. Yungkau, 329 U.S. 482, 485–86, 67 S.Ct. 428, 430–31, 91 L.Ed. 436 (1947) (noting that settlement and distribution of the estate of a deceased defendant might be so far advanced as to warrant denial of a motion to substitute, even though filed within the time prescribed by the Rule).

30. *See* Advisory Committee Note to the 1963 amendment of FRCP 25 (discussing the permissive language of Rule 25(a)(1)).

31. Escareno v. Carl Nolte Sohne GmbH & Co., 77 F.3d 407, 411 (11th Cir. 1996) (reversing trial court's dismissal where motion to substitute was filed within 90–day period, but substitution was not effectuated).

32. *See* Escareno v. Noltina Crucible and Refractory Corp., 172 F.R.D. 522, 526 (N.D.Ga.1997) (on remand, court dismissed complaint where substitution was not consummated despite the passage of at least 280 days since the suggestion of death was entered).

33. *See* Fehrenbacher v. Quackenbush, 759 F.Supp. 1516, 1519 (D.Kan.1991) (motion for substitution, filed after expiration of 90–day time limit, denied where it failed to identify the representative of the decedent's estate).

34. *See* Barker v. Jackson Nat'l Life Ins. Co., 163 F.R.D. 364, 365 (N.D.Fla.1995) (FRCP 25 is purely procedural and does not purport to determine the substantive rights of the parties).

35. *See* Estwick v. U.S. Air Shuttle, 950 F.Supp. 493, 498 (E.D.N.Y.1996) (survival of action brought under federal statute is a matter of federal common law).

penal in nature do not survive the death of a party, whereas actions that are remedial in nature do survive.[36]

Where state law claims are involved, the federal court must look to state law to determine whether a particular cause of action survives the death of a party.[37] This typically requires consideration of the survival statute enacted in the state in which the district court sits.[38]

(4) Effect of Substitution

Where substitution has been allowed, the case continues as though the substituted party were the original party, and the substituted party is subject to all prior rulings in the action.[39] FRCP 25(a)(2) makes clear that if the deceased was one of several plaintiffs or defendants, and the action did not survive his death, the nonsurvival does not affect the decedent's remaining co-parties. They remain, and the action proceeds unabated in their favor or against them.[40]

(c) Incompetency

(1) Incompetency Must Arise During Litigation

FRCP 25(b) provides that "[i]f a party becomes incompetent, the court upon motion served as provided in subdivision (a) of this rule may allow the action to be continued by or against the party's representative."[41] For the Rule to apply, the incompetency must arise during the suit, not before the action is commenced.[42]

(2) Procedure

The Rule expressly makes applicable to the incompetency of a previously-competent party, selected portions of FRCP 25(a) relating to substitution in the event of death.[43] Significantly, the Rule does not incorporate any provision relating to the necessity of filing a suggestion of death, nor to the 90–day time period for filing a motion for substitution.[44] Instead, the reference in FRCP 25(b) is limited to the filing of a motion for substitution.[45] Therefore, substitution on the basis of incompetency requires the service of a motion, together with a notice of

---

36. See Holford USA Ltd. v. Harvey, 169 F.R.D. 41, 43 (S.D.N.Y.1996) (a claim survives the death of a party if it is remedial, rather than punitive).

37. See Knauer v. Johns–Manville Corp., 638 F.Supp. 1369, 1387 (D.Md.1986) (where state law claims are involved, court must look to substantive state law and apply the appropriate survival statute of the state in which the district court is located).

38. Id.

39. See Brook, Weiner, Sered, Kreger & Weinberg v. Coreq, Inc., 53 F.3d 851, 852 (7th Cir.1995) (substituted party assumes

the role of the original party and is subject to all prior rulings).

40. FRCP 25(a)(2).

41. FRCP 25(b).

42. See Schwartz v. Metropolitan Life Ins. Co., 2 F.R.D. 167, 168 (D.Mass.1941) (substitution under FRCP 25(b) denied where the incompetency did not arise during the action, but existed prior to filing suit).

43. FRCP 25(b).

44. Id.

45. Id.

hearing, in the manner required by FRCP 4 and 5 for service on parties and nonparties.[46]

(3) Effect of Substitution

Moreover, since the provisions of FRCP 25 are purely procedural, the Rule has no effect on the substantive determination as to the party's competence.[47] That determination is properly made under the applicable substantive state law.[48]

(d) Transfer of Interest

(1) Transfer Must Occur During Litigation

As noted in Section 14.3(a), *supra*, FRCP 17(a) requires that the assignee of a claim maintain the action in his own name as the real party in interest. When an interest is assigned or transferred during the pendency of an action, FRCP 25(c) controls.[49] Besides the ordinary assignment cases, other common FRCP 25(c) situations include: resignation of a trustee and appointment of a new trustee; appointment of a trustee in bankruptcy for one of the parties; and a corporate merger involving one of the parties.[50]

(2) Procedure

The procedure for the filing of a motion for substitution following a transfer of interest is the same as that for filing a motion for substitution of a party on the basis of incompetency under FRCP 25(b).[51] Following service of the motion, together with notice of hearing, in the manner provided by subsection (a), the court may in its discretion: (1) order that the transferee be substituted for the transferor;[52] or (2) order that the transferee be joined as a party with the transferor;[53] or (3) if the transferee is already a party, order a dismissal as to the transferor;[54] or (4) deny the motion and continue with the original parties.[55]

---

46. *Id.*

47. *See* Barker v. Jackson Nat'l Life Ins. Co., 163 F.R.D. 364, 365 (N.D.Fla.1995) (FRCP 25 is purely procedural and does not purport to determine the substantive rights of the parties).

48. *See id.*

49. *See id.* (FRCP 17(a) applies when transfer takes place prior to suit being filed; FRCP 25(c) applies when transfer occurs during pendency of case); *see also* Veverica v. Drill Barge Buccaneer No. 7, 488 F.2d 880 (5th Cir.1974) (substitution under FRCP 25(c) allowed where plaintiff assigned his contract two days after commencement of action).

50. *See* Luxliner P.L. Export, Co. v. RDI/Luxliner, Inc., 13 F.3d 69 (3d Cir.1993) (transfer following corporate merger); Minnesota Mining & Mfg. Co. v. Eco Chem,

Inc., 757 F.2d 1256, 1262–63 (Fed.Cir.1985) (substitution proper following sale of assets by defendant corporation to another entity).

51. *See* FRCP 25(c); *see also supra* § 14.7(c)(2).

52. DeVilliers v. Atlas Corp., 360 F.2d 292, 297 (10th Cir.1966) (order of substitution).

53. Television Reception Corp. v. Dunbar, 426 F.2d 174, 178 (6th Cir.1970) (transferee joined as party with transferor).

54. Hyatt Chalet Motels, Inc. v. Salem Bldg. & Constr. Trades Council, 298 F.Supp. 699, 704 (D.Or.1968) (transferor dismissed where transferee already a party).

55. Homestake Mining Co. v. Mid–Continent Exploration Co., 282 F.2d 787, 803–04 (10th Cir.1960) (motion for substitution denied).

(3) Effect of Substitution

The provisions of FRCP 25(c) are purely procedural.[56] Therefore, the Rule has no effect on the substantive determination as to the validity of the transfer or any other rights; those determinations are properly made under the applicable substantive law.[57]

(e) Public Officers

When during the pendency of an action a public officer, a party in his official capacity, dies, resigns, or otherwise ceases to hold the office, FRCP 25(d)(1) provides for an automatic substitution of his successor.[58] The court may enter an order of substitution; but the failure to do so does not affect the substitution.[59] If a public officer sues or is sued in his official capacity, FRCP 25(d)(2) allows him to be described as a party by his official title rather than by name (*e.g.* "Secretary of Health and Human Services"); but the court may require his name to be added.

Library References:

West's Key No. Digests, Federal Civil Procedure ⟐351–366.
Wright, Miller & Kane, Federal Practice and Procedure: Civil 2d §§ 1799–1800, 1901–1913.

§ 14.8   Practice Checklist

(a) Real Party in Interest

(1) Every action must be prosecuted in the name of the real party in interest. The real party in interest is the person holding the substantive right sought to be enforced. (*See* FRCP 17(a); § 14.3(a)–(b))

(2) To determine a plaintiff's status as a real party in interest, courts look to the substantive state or federal law to ascertain whether the plaintiff possesses a substantive right to relief. An executor, administrator, guardian, bailee, trustee of an express trust, a party with whom or in whose name a contract has been made for the benefit of another, or a party authorized by statute may sue in that party's own name without joining the party for whose benefit the action is brought. Similarly, a valid assignment or subrogation shifts real party status to the assignee or subrogee. (*See* FRCP 17(a); § 14.3(b)–(c))

(3) An objection that the plaintiff is not the real party in interest may be raised by either answer or motion. If raised by motion, the

---

56. *See* Barker v. Jackson Nat'l Life Ins. Co., 163 F.R.D. 364, 365 (N.D.Fla.1995) (FRCP 25 is purely procedural and does not purport to determine the substantive rights of the parties).

57. *See id.*

58. Dubuc v. Green Oak Township, 958 F.Supp. 1231, 1240 (E.D.Mich.1997) (the death of parties sued in their official capacities does not require substitution by motion, rather substitution is automatic).

59. *Id.*

objection must be presented with reasonable promptness or it may be deemed waived. (*See* FRCP 17(a); § 14.3(d)(1)–(2))

(4) No action shall be dismissed on the ground that it is not prosecuted in the name of the real party in interest until a reasonable time has been allowed after objection for ratification of the commencement of the action by, or joinder or substitution of, the real party in interest. (*See* FRCP 17(a); § 14.3(d)(3))

(5) The ratification, joinder or substitution of the real party in interest must be accomplished within a reasonable time after the objection. The ratification, joinder or substitution of the real party in interest relates back to the commencement of the action, and has the same effect as if the action had been commenced in the name of the real party in interest. (*See* FRCP 17(a); § 14.3(d)(3)–(4))

(b) Capacity to Sue and Be Sued

(1) The capacity of an individual, other than one acting in a representative capacity, is determined by the law of the individual's domicile. (*See* FRCP 17(b); § 14.4(b))

(2) Where an individual lacks capacity under the law of his or her domicile, whether by reason of infancy or incompetency, the court may permit a guardian, conservator or other like fiduciary to sue or defend on behalf of the infant or incompetent person, or the individual lacking capacity may sue by his "next friend" or guardian ad litem. (*See* FRCP 17(b)–(c); § 14.4(b)(1))

(3) Where an individual lacks capacity under the law of his or her domicile, whether by reason of infancy or incompetency and is otherwise unrepresented, the court in its discretion may appoint a guardian ad litem or make such other order as it deems proper to protect the interests of the infant or incompetent person. (*See* FRCP 17(b)-(c); § 14.4(b)(1))

(4) In all other cases, the capacity of an individual, such as one suing or defending in a representative capacity as a trustee, executor, administrator, guardian or the like, is determined by the law of the state in which the district court sits. (*See* FRCP 17(b); § 14.4(c))

(5) The capacity of a corporation to sue or be sued is determined by the law under which it was organized. (*See* FRCP 17(b); § 14.4(d))

(6) The capacity of a partnership or other unincorporated association is determined by the law of the state in which the district court sits, except that a partnership or other unincorporated association, which has no capacity under the law of such state, may sue or defend in its common name whenever the claim arises under federal law. (*See* FRCP 17(b); § 14.4(e))

(7) Capacity is a defense that is waived if not timely asserted. To avoid waiver, the defense generally must be raised by specific negative averment at the pleading stage by including in the pleading

any such supporting particulars as are within the pleader's knowledge. (*See* FRCP 9(a); § 14.4(f))

(c) Interpleader

(1) Interpleader may be brought pursuant to either FRCP 22 or the Federal Interpleader Act. In either event, an interpleader action may be initiated by the filing of a complaint, counterclaim or crossclaim. Thus, interpleader may be used either offensively or defensively. (*See* FRCP 22; 28 U.S.C.A. 1335; § 14.5(b)–(d))

(2) A party seeking interpleader relief under either the Rule or statute must demonstrate that it is exposed to the possibility of double or multiple liability or litigation resulting from one or more competing claims to money or property in its custody or control. The adverse claims may be presently existing or prospective. (*See* FRCP 22; 28 U.S.C.A. 1335; § 14.5(c)(2) and(d)(1))

(3) A party seeking interpleader relief must establish subject matter jurisdiction over the interpleader action. Where a party is relying on rule interpleader, the party must establish jurisdiction under the normal rules for diversity of citizenship or a federal question. Where a party is relying on statutory interpleader, subject matter jurisdiction is established where: (1) the interpleader had custody or possession of money or property valued at $500 or more, (2) two or more adverse claimants of diverse citizenship claim a right to the money or property, and (3) the interpleader has deposited such money or posted a bond in an amount that the court deems sufficient to cover the value of the stake. (*See* FRCP 22; 28 U.S.C.A. § 1335; § 14.5(c)(4) and (d)(2))

(4) A party seeking interpleader relief must establish proper venue. A party relying on rule interpleader must establish venue under the general venue provisions of 28 U.S.C.A. § 1391. Venue in a statutory interpleader action is proper where one or more of the claimants reside. (*See* 28 U.S.C.A. §§ 1391 and 1397; FRCP 22; § 14.5(c)(4) and (d)(2))

(5) The party seeking interpleader relief must establish proper service of process. A party relying on rule interpleader must comply with the manner of service set forth in FRCP 4. Nationwide service of process is provided for in an action for statutory interpleader. (*See* FRCP 22; FRCP 4; 28 U.S.C.A. § 2361; § 14.5(c)(4) and (d)(2))

(6) A party relying on rule interpleader is not required to deposit the disputed fund into the registry of the court or to post a bond, although, as a practical matter, such conditions may be imposed by the court before allowing the interpleader to be discharged from liability or be awarded its costs and fees. A party relying on statutory interpleader must deposit the disputed fund into the registry of the court or post a bond in an amount and with such surety as the court deems proper. (*See* FRCP 22; 28 U.S.C.A. § 1335; § 14.5(c)(3) and (d)(2))

(7) Upon deposit with the court of the disputed fund or the posting of an adequate bond, the court in its discretion may discharge an innocent stakeholder from all liability with regard to the disputed fund. In addition, in its discretion, the court may award an innocent stakeholder its costs and fees incurred in connection with bringing the interpleader action. (*See* § 14.5(e)(1), (2))

(d) Intervention

(1) Intervention as of right shall be permitted when either: (1) a statute of the United States confers an unconditional right to intervene; or (2) the applicant (a) claims an interest relating to the property or transaction which is the subject of the action, (b) is so situated that the disposition of the action may as a practical matter impair or impede his ability to protect that interest, and (c) his interest is not adequately represented by the existing parties to the lawsuit. (*See* FRCP 24(a); § 14.6(a))

(2) Permissive intervention may be allowed when (1) a statute of the United States confers a conditional right to intervene, or (2) there are common questions of law or fact presented by the applicant's claim or defense and the main action, provided that intervention will not unduly delay or prejudice the adjudication of the rights of the original parties. (*See* FRCP 24(b); § 14.6(b))

(3) Regardless of whether intervention is as of right or permissive, a party seeking intervention must file a timely motion setting forth the grounds supporting intervention. The district court has broad discretion in determining whether a motion to intervene is timely and its determination is almost never reversed. *(See* FRCP 24(c); § 14.6(c)(1)–(2))

(4) The motion must be accompanied by a copy of the pleading (*i.e.* complaint or answer) setting forth the claim or defense that is sought to be asserted. Failure to comply with this requirement warrants denial of the motion for intervention. (*See* FRCP 24(c); § 14.6(c)(1))

(5) The prospective intervenor must also demonstrate the existence of subject matter jurisdiction over the claims sought to be asserted. In addition, a party seeking intervention waives any objection to the action's existing venue. (*See* § 14.6(c)(3))

(e) Substitution of Parties

(1) If a party dies after the commencement of the action, and the action survives either in favor of the decedent's estate or against it, substitution of the decedent's representative may be ordered where: (a) the fact of the death is formally suggested on the record; and (b) a motion for substitution is filed within 90 days after the fact of the death is suggested on the record. (*See* FRCP 25(a)(1); § 14.7(b))

(2) A valid suggestion of death must be made by a surviving party or on behalf of the decedent's heirs or successors by a representative of

his estate. It must be served on all parties to the litigation in the manner provided by FRCP 5 and on the nonparty successors or representatives of the deceased party in the manner provided by FRCP 4. In addition, the suggestion of death generally must identify the representative or successor who may be substituted as a party, at least where it is filed on behalf of the deceased party, as opposed to by one of the surviving parties. (*See* FRCP 25(a)(1); § 14.7(b)(1))

(3) Within 90 days after a valid suggestion of death has been entered on the record, either an existing party or the representative of a deceased party may move to substitute the decedent's representative for the deceased party. The motion should be served, together with a notice of hearing, on each existing party in the manner provided by FRCP 5, and on the nonparty successors or representatives in the manner provided by FRCP 4. (*See* FRCP 25(a)(1); § 14.7(a)(2))

(4) Where a party becomes incompetent during the course of a proceeding, a motion for substitution may be filed by any party or by a representative of the incompetent party. The motion must be filed in the same manner as a motion for substitution resulting from the death of a party. (*See* FRCP 25(b); § 14.7(c))

(5) Where there is a transfer of interest in the course of a proceeding, a motion for substitution may be filed by any party or by the transferee. The motion must be filed in the same manner as a motion for substitution resulting from the death of a party. (*See* FRCP 25(c); § 14.7(d))

(6) When during the pendency of an action a public officer, a party in his official capacity, dies, resigns, or otherwise ceases to hold the office, his successor is automatically substituted, without the need for filing a motion. (*See* FRCP 25(d); § 14.7(e))

§ 14.9 Forms

(a) Motion to Dismiss/to Require Ratification, Joinder or Substitution by Real Party in Interest 💾

UNITED STATES DISTRICT COURT
FOR THE DISTRICT OF MASSACHUSETTS

General Corporation, Plaintiff.)	
)	Civil Action
v.)	No.
)	
John Doe, Defendant.)	
)	

Motion to Dismiss/to Require Ratification, Joinder
or Substitution by Real Party in Interest

Pursuant to Rule 17(a) of the Federal Rules of Civil Procedure, the defendant John Doe hereby moves to require Acme Corporation to ratify the commencement of this action, to join with or be substituted for the plaintiff General Corporation, which is not the real party in interest.

In support of this motion, defendant Doe states that, by virtue of a comprehensive sale of assets from General Corporation to Acme Corporation which preceded the initiation of this action (a copy of which is attached hereto), General Corporation does not possess any right, title or interest in the contract that is the subject of this suit. As such, General Corporation is not the real party in interest to prosecute this breach of contract claim.

Doe is entitled to have this action prosecuted in the name of the real party in interest to avoid the threat of multiple liability and so that any judgment will have its proper res judicata effect. Accordingly, Doe requests that this Court dismiss this cause of action unless, within 30 days of the date of the hearing on this motion, General Corporation either joins, substitutes or obtains the written ratification of the commencement of this action from Acme Corporation, the real party in interest.

Respectfully submitted,
[Signature & Address]

(b) Motion for Appointment of Guardian Ad Litem 💾

UNITED STATES DISTRICT COURT
FOR THE DISTRICT OF MASSACHUSETTS

_____, Plaintiff	)	
	)	Civil Action
v.	)	No.
_____, Defendant	)	

Motion for Appointment of Guardian Ad Litem

In accordance with Rule 17(c) of the Federal Rules of Civil Procedure, defendant John Doe hereby moves this Court to appoint [name of proposed guardian ad litem] to act as guardian ad litem to represent and protect his interests in this action.

In support of this motion, the defendant states that he was born on January 1, 1992 and is an infant who cannot represent himself in this action. The defendant seeks the appointment of [name of proposed guardian ad litem] because he is an attorney with over 10 years' experience, is a disinterested person and will faithfully represent the interests of John Doe in these proceedings.

Respectfully submitted,
[Signature & Address]

(c) Complaint for Interpleader[1] ⌘

UNITED STATES DISTRICT COURT
FOR THE DISTRICT OF MASSACHUSETTS

_____, Plaintiff	))))	Civil Action
v.	))	No.
_____, Defendants	))))	

Complaint for Interpleader

1. Allegation of jurisdiction.

2. On or about July 10, 1996, plaintiff issued a life insurance policy to John Doe whereby plaintiff promised to pay Jane Smith as beneficiary the sum of $100,000 dollars upon the death of John Doe.

3. John Doe and Jane Smith died on June 10, 1997.

4. Defendant A is the duly appointed and acting executor of the will of John Doe; defendant B is the duly appointed and acting executor of the will of Jane Smith; defendant C claims to have been duly designated as beneficiary of said policy in place of Jane Smith.

5. Each of defendants A, B and C is claiming to be the only person entitled to receive payment of the amount of the policy and has made demand for payment thereof.

6. By reason of these conflicting claims of the defendants, plaintiff is uncertain as to which defendant is entitled to be paid the amount of the policy.

Wherefore, plaintiff respectfully requests that the court adjudge:

(1) That the defendants be required to interplead and settle among themselves their respective claims to the money due under said policy;

(2) That plaintiff be permitted to pay into the registry of the court all amounts due under the policy and upon such deposit be discharged from all liability arising from the policy; and

(3) That plaintiff be awarded its costs and attorneys' fees.

> Respectfully submitted,
> [Signature & Address]

§ 14.9   Form 18.

1. *See also* FRCP Appendix of Forms at

(d) Motion to Intervene[2] 💾

UNITED STATES DISTRICT COURT
FOR THE DISTRICT OF MASSACHUSETTS

_____, Plaintiff)	
)	Civil Action
v.)	No.
)	
_____, Defendant)	
_____, Applicant for)	
Intervention,)	

Motion to Intervene

In accordance with Rule 24(a) of the Federal Rules of Civil Procedure, Doe Corporation hereby moves for leave to intervene as of right as a defendant in this action, in order to assert the defenses set forth in the proposed answer, a copy of which is attached hereto.

In support of this motion, the intervenor states that it has an interest in the property that is the subject matter of this action in that it is the [describe relationship to subject matter of action]. As such, the intervenor is so situated that disposition of this action in its absence may, as a practical matter, impair or impede its ability to protect that interest in that [describe nature of impairment]. Additionally, the intervenor's interests are not adequately represented by the existing parties because [describe why representation is inadequate].

Wherefore, this motion to intervene as of right should be allowed, and the accompanying answer should be accepted for filing.

Respectfully submitted,
[Signature & Address]

2. *See also id.* at Form 23.

(e) Suggestion of Death Upon the Record[3] 💾

UNITED STATES DISTRICT COURT
FOR THE DISTRICT OF MASSACHUSETTS

_____, Plaintiff	)
	)
	)
	) Civil Action
v.	) No.
	)
_____, Defendant	)
	)
	)

Suggestion of Death Upon the Record

In accordance with Rule 25(a)(1) of the Federal Rules of Civil Procedure, the defendant John Doe hereby suggests upon the record the death of the plaintiff Jane Smith during the pendency of this action.

Respectfully submitted,
[Signature & Address]

---

3.   *See also id.* at Form 30.

CHAPTER 15

CLASS ACTIONS

by

John F.X. Peloso
Peter Buscemi
and
James D. Pagliaro*

Table of Sections

* The authors acknowledge with gratitude and appreciation the assistance of the following colleagues at Morgan, Lewis & Bockius LLP in the preparation of this chapter: Jennifer A. Davidson, Kevin M. Donovan, Joseph B.G. Fay, Joseph A. Hennessey, Margaret Scott Izzo, Stanley M. Lechner, Laura A. Livaccari, David M. Lubitz, Richard S. Meyer, David E. Plunkett, Brian O. Quinn, Kevin T. Rover, Brian W. Shaffer, Robert J. Smith and Jennifer Rand Stein.

WESTLAW Electronic Research

See WESTLAW Electronic Research Guide preceding the Summary of Contents.

---

§ 15.1 Scope Note

This chapter discusses class actions in federal business and commercial litigation. The chapter begins by examining the provisions of FRCP 23 and the prerequisites for class litigation. The chapter then addresses a number of special procedural and constitutional issues that arise in the class action context, including issues relating to class certification procedure, notice to absent class members, subject matter jurisdiction, defendant classes, settlement classes, and the due process concerns that inevitably arise when binding judgments can be entered against absent class members. The chapter also discusses issues relating to awards of attorneys' fees in class actions and several specific ethical issues that can arise in class actions. Finally, the chapter considers the use of the class action device in a variety of substantive contexts, to illustrate the interaction between the class procedure and different bodies of substantive law and to identify particular issues likely to arise in class actions in particular substantive areas. This final portion of the chapter focuses on the actual use of class actions in particular kinds of cases, with special emphasis on the practical considerations counsel are likely to encounter in prosecuting or defending class actions in different substantive settings.

Library References:
West's Key No. Digests, Federal Civil Procedure ⊕161–189.
Wright, Miller & Kane, Federal Practice and Procedure: Civil 2d § 1751.

§ 15.2   Strategic Considerations for the Practitioner

(a) The Advantages of Class Actions

The structure of the modern class action, in federal and most state courts, is the product of the 1966 amendments to Rule 23 of the Federal Rules of Civil Procedure. The frequency and subject matter of class actions, however, has expanded dramatically since the Rule's promulgation. With the widespread docket congestion of the 1980s, courts across the country grew increasingly receptive to procedural devices that promised to lower transaction costs and resolve more cases quickly. The class action emerged as a principal method of achieving these goals. Embraced by some, the move away from individual case treatment has been disparaged by others on the grounds that it subjugates individual justice to the goals of efficiency and conservation of judicial resources.[1] Nonetheless, Rule 23 class actions (as well as other procedural vehicles of mass adjudication, such as Rule 19 joinder and multidistrict litigation) are frequently used to aggregate claims for resolution.

With the encouragement and prompting of the plaintiffs' bar, courts have recognized the advantages of class action suits over other alternatives. The power of numbers is great. The fact that hundreds, thousands, or even millions of potential claims may be aggregated in one case provides a substantial impetus for resolution by settlement, which courts value in their efforts to manage litigation and control dockets. The aggregate force of numbers also has an impact on defendants, which often conclude that early settlement is the only viable alternative to a serious risk of economic ruin. Placing the fate of an entire company, or even an industry, in the hands of a single jury is a real and frightening possibility, and ensures serious consideration of settlement options where no such incentives might exist in a more conventional litigation setting.

The class action vehicle provides procedural advantages to plaintiffs, including greater weight when a court must balance the countervailing hardships between the parties in determining the appropriateness of injunctive relief. A class action may be used to obtain a declaratory or injunctive determination that can operate preclusively as to liability in subsequent damage actions by individual class members or sub-classes. In addition, the broad discovery rights allowed in class actions permit a limited group of class representatives to obtain discovery relevant to claims against a company or industry in an organized, uniform, and cost-effective manner, as opposed to pursuing repetitive discovery regarding the same defendant or industry in the context of litigating numerous individual claims. The economic benefit of class actions is also significant because it allows for sharing expenses and fees. The sharing of expenses among a pool of plaintiffs can assist in amortizing the significant costs of

---

§ 15.2

1. *See* David Rosenberg, *Individual Justice and Collectivizing Risk–Based Claims* *in Mass–Exposure Cases*, 71 N.Y.U. L. Rev. 210, 210–11 (1996).

major litigation. In addition, the opportunities for attorneys' fees awards are exponentially increased in the context of the class action as well.

Class actions have a tendency to raise public awareness. With the increased profile conferred by large numbers and potentially greater media attention, class actions present an opportunity to generate and strengthen public support for resolving issues or redressing a perceived wrong. Plaintiffs may use the class action vehicle to magnify the wrongful conduct of a group of defendants, a trade association, or an entire industry. Public sympathies may be particularly heightened when the defendants' alleged wrongful conduct has caused grievous bodily injury or financial loss to a large number of claimants.

Although there are obvious risks for absent class members in the conduct of a class action, there are also potential advantages. In many instances, the filing of a class action tolls the running of a statute of limitations for the members of the putative class as defined in the complaint. In addition, plaintiffs with weak, small, or uncertain individual claims can, in effect, have the value of their claims clarified and augmented through class treatment. If the named plaintiff loses standing during the pendency of the class action, a substitute may be found, thus avoiding the mootness problem and obviating the need for repetition of preliminary proceedings. Thus, class actions are frequently viewed by plaintiffs' lawyers as a valuable alternative to the traditional case-by-case adjudication of disputes in litigation.

(b) Weighing the Pros and Cons of the Class Action Alternative

From the standpoint of judicial economy, class certification may not be appropriate if some class members with large claims have the practical ability to pursue their claims individually, rather than as part of a class action. The relevant inquiry is not so much whether some class members *can* pursue separate litigation, but rather whether or not the class members will *desire* to litigate individually. The potential tension between strong and weak claims may present an obstacle to certification of a class action. This is one of many issues of likely conflict between groups or subgroups of plaintiffs, whose alleged injuries or amount of damages may differ significantly from those of named class representatives. The analysis of whether this divergence precludes class certification is often undertaken in applying the requirement that the named plaintiffs be "adequate representatives" of the interests of the class.

A further issue for consideration, from the perspective of class members, is the so-called surrender of individual rights by some members of the class. There is some likelihood that a class action may delay individual relief. The process of certifying the class, taking class discovery, providing notice, and complying with other procedural formalities frequently delays the resolution of a class action far beyond what would be expected in other forms of aggregation involving other methods of joinder. These intricacies can often extend the cumulative duration of the various phases of a class action well beyond a single decade.[2] An empirical comparison between nonclass civil actions and class actions reveals that "class actions are not routine in terms of their longevity."[3] Indeed, one study estimates that the average time from filing to disposition is roughly two to three times longer for class actions.[4]

Absent class members not only do not get to select their own counsel, but often are unaware that their legal rights may be bartered and compromised by counsel who are not constrained by a traditional attorney-client relationship with the absent class members. The process of settlement of a class action also does not allow meaningful participation by the typical absent class member. Thus, the mantle of class counsel provides tremendous power to the attorneys who act in that capacity. In addition, even the class representative has little say over the selection of the forum or the claims asserted. Class certification procedures consume considerable resources determining matters unrelated to the merits of the case. Finally, absent plaintiffs can be exposed to defense counterclaims, often without their knowledge or informed consent.

As in other litigation, there is always the risk that the class action ultimately will fail on the merits. The litigation expenses and opportunity costs of an unsuccessful class action can be massive. Even the failure of class certification can undermine subsequent individual efforts to obtain settlements on a case-by-case basis. Further, the res judicata effect of a class action may effectively block re-litigation of an individual claim in another forum. Moreover, class actions tend to shift the focus of settlement negotiations from the facts of individual cases to the facts of the named plaintiffs' cases. Thus, where the named plaintiffs have strong claims, it tends to create great pressure for defendants to settle cases for an amount greater than their true value. By the same token, where the named plaintiffs' claims are weaker, it may result in undercompensation of absent class members. Although when squarely and explicitly faced with the issue, courts are quick to rhetorically exalt individual rights,[5] the reality is that often these considerations are quietly disregarded when the court and the representative parties have coalesced behind a proposed settlement.

(c) Plaintiffs' Strategies

In determining whether to proceed with a class action, a claimant should assess the potential defendants' amenability to class certification and the likely effects of resistance to certification. Some defendants

---

2. *See In re* School Asbestos Litig., Master File No. 83–0268, hearings of Sept. 13, 1995 (E.D. Pa.).

3. Thomas E. Willging et al., *An Empirical Analysis of Rule 23 to Address the Rulemaking Challenges*, 71 N.Y.U. L. Rev. 74, 92 (1996).

4. *See id.*

5. *See, e.g., In re* Fibreboard Corp., 893 F.2d 706, 709–11 (5th Cir.1990) (invoking constitutional norms of due process to reject class-wide proportionate determinations of causation and damages in asbestos class action).

prefer to defend against class claims rather than individual actions, reasoning that unitary litigation will conserve resources and, upon conclusion of the litigation, provide a broad bar against future claims brought by individuals falling within the class definition. In addition, class treatment can, in some limited instances, expedite and simplify the settlement process.

Generally, however, plaintiffs can expect that the decision to assert class claims will substantially increase the stakes in the litigation. Although the class action device provides a greater, and in some cases excessive, "hammer" for compelling ultimate settlement of claims, the response it elicits from many defendants will force the plaintiffs to expend time and money far beyond that which would have been required to bring a series of individual actions. The litigation almost undoubtedly will be lengthened, and plaintiffs' counsel will need to master numerous complex legal issues relating to the certification of the class.

If and when claimants elect to pursue class treatment, the selection of adequate class representatives is a critical threshold step in the class certification process. An analysis must be undertaken to ensure that the named class representatives have no conflict with other class members, that they understand the special responsibilities of being the named representatives, including the burden of discovery and, finally, that their selection as class representatives may impair their ability to settle individually, because the class representatives must act in the best interests of the class. The importance of the adequacy of the named class representatives has been highlighted in the settlement context by the Supreme Court's recent decision in *Amchem Products, Inc. v. Windsor.*[6] In *Amchem*, the Court held, in relevant part, that a common interest in obtaining a fair settlement provided an insufficient basis on which to conclude that class-wide issues predominated over individual issues.[7] Conversely, the inquiry into the adequacy of the class representatives, even in the settlement context, "trains on the legal or factual questions that qualify each class member's case as a genuine controversy, questions that preexist any settlement."[8]

The process of drafting the class action complaint and selecting the appropriate legal forum for filing is complex and requires careful consideration by plaintiff's counsel. The description of the class, including its defining boundaries and objective characteristics, often will be the subject of controversy in the certification process. The claims included might depend on a strategic choice of whether it is preferable to litigate the action in federal or state court. In the mass tort area, for example, recovery of costs associated with medical monitoring or increased risk or fear of cancer may depend on the forum chosen and its applicable common law. Additionally, the selection of defendants may require deliberation. Selecting industry representatives, determining the role of trade associations and ensuring that all appropriate defendants are

---

6. ___ U.S. ___, 117 S.Ct. 2231, 138 L.Ed.2d 689 (1997), *aff'g* Georgine v. Amchem Prods. Inc., 83 F.3d 610 (3d Cir.1996).

7. *See id.* at ___, 117 S.Ct. at 2249–50.

8. *Id.* at ___, 117 S.Ct. at 2249 (footnote omitted).

named in the suit often involves extensive investigation prior to filing the complaint. Finally, plaintiffs' counsel will certainly want to carefully research and consider the historical attitude of the forum court to class certification.

Carefully defining the core or common issues for certification requires a significant expenditure of class resources. Claims involving individual reliance or particularized causation must be avoided and sometimes abandoned. The alleged conduct of defendants, including whether or not punitive damages are appropriate, often presents issues common to the class. In most cases, the defendants' conduct or behavior constitutes the core issue for certification. Plaintiffs' attorneys must draft a complaint drawing attention to the commonality and predominance of these issues over the individual issues. Another strategic choice for plaintiffs' counsel—especially with respect to consumer fraud claims—is whether to pursue a nationwide or statewide class certification. The process of certifying a nationwide class has come under considerable criticism due to the frequent necessity to consider the separate laws of numerous jurisdictions in the context of determining both liability and damages.[9]

(d) Defense Strategies

From the defendants' perspective, class actions are often perceived as "bet your company" cases that require careful consideration of settlement options because of the enormous economic threat posed by the aggregation of what may be marginal claims. Defending class actions is also time-consuming and expensive. A defendant's participation in a class action may be required for upwards of 10 to 15 years, and because of the procedural steps, e.g., certification, broad discovery, notice, and the delays inherent in the litigation of peripheral issues, the costs are often immense. The effect of a class action on statutes of limitations is often viewed as a distinct disadvantage for defendants in that the running of such statutes as to the claims of absent class members may be tolled, thus preserving for years the possibility of numerous individual claims if the case ultimately does not proceed on a class basis.

Defendants may view class actions as beneficial in some situations. The possibility of obtaining broad res judicata protection against future claims, the potential for a broad release from a large group of absent class members in a settlement, and general protection against the cost and unfairness of repeated serial litigation are some of the benefits defendants might garner from a class action.

The process of class discovery and certification as well as the broad scope of discovery on the merits permit defendants some flexibility with regard to scheduling and the sequence of discovery. Punitive damages exposure also may be lessened by a class action because many courts are

9. *See In re* Schools Asbestos Litig., 13, 1995 (E.D. Pa.).
Master File No. 83–0268, hearing of Sept.

sensitive to the limited availability of funds to satisfy large punitive damage judgments. Furthermore, defendants gain the benefit of avoiding repeated exposure to punitive damages that may arise in a series of individual actions. Further, when serial litigation is the alternative, there may actually be reduced costs and less time invested in defending a single unitary class action, as opposed to defending hundreds of individual claims around the state or the country. Finally, the proposed revision to Rule 23 allowing some interlocutory appeals immediately after class certification is certain to make class actions more attractive to defendants—even defendants that desire class treatment—because it will create at least the possibility of a prompt appeal and thus will provide an avenue for challenging and perhaps correcting class definition errors before the entire expense of litigating the action is incurred.[10]

(1) Opposition to Class Certification

One critical consideration for a defendant in determining whether to attack class certification is the number of individual cases likely to arise in the absence of a class action. This issue is often complex and not capable of precise determination. It is clear, however, that class actions are frequently pursued where there are large numbers of either small or weak claims. Further, the opt-out right in classes certified under Rule 23(b)(3) permits those plaintiffs with strong or large claims to opt-out and pursue individual relief. Thus, in many cases defendants get the worst of both worlds in having to face the strong individual claims in the opt-out individual actions, while defending a large number of aggregated weak claims in a class action setting.

In many instances, class action resolution of matters may provide some business certainty for clients that are potential defendants. There is a value in capping liability at a known amount rather than being forced to anticipate which claimants may pursue individual actions. In this regard, defendants find significant benefit in obtaining broad releases from absent class members, which may make settlement of a class action a better business decision than defending myriad individual claims around the country, where the ultimate exposure is necessarily unknown.

(2) Timing the Opposition

The timing of an attack on class certification deserves careful attention. One option is to attack class certification at the outset, prior to merits discovery. Another option is to wait until after the class is certified and to seek decertification if and when discovery on the merits reveals problems with manageability or adequacy of class representatives. Particularly when such problems seem likely, it may be tempting to allow certification to proceed—for unsuccessful opposition early on

---

10. *See* Committee on Rules of Practice of the Judicial Conference of the United States, Proposed Amendments to the Federal Rules of Civil Procedure (May 1996), *reprinted in* 167 F.R.D. 523, 559–60 (1996) setting forth proposed new Rule 23(f). The amendment would authorize a permissive interlocutory appeal, in the sole discretion of the court of appeals, from an order granting or denying class certification.

will make later opposition more difficult—and then move to decertify the class when the record better supports opposition to class certification. The better approach appears to be to undertake class discovery early, and make a strong initial attack on the weak points in the arguments in favor of certification, developing differences or tensions between the named class representatives and absent class members in an effort to undermine the representativeness of the named class representatives, and to demonstrate the lack of predominance of common issues over the individual issues.

In the mass tort setting, an initial challenge to class treatment because of an inadequate causal link between the claimed injuries and the instrumentalities alleged to have caused the harm has additional advantages. In doing so, defendants can make a full record as to the inability of the named plaintiffs with their limited injuries to represent adequately the myriad injuries alleged to be suffered by members of the class. Through discovery relating to individual medical histories, environmental exposures, and personal habits, defendants may be able to demonstrate that the individual causation issues outnumber and therefore predominate over the common issues so that plaintiffs cannot meet their predominance burden under FRCP 23(b)(3). Defendants can also shift the focus from the conduct of defendant to the conduct of the plaintiffs (under a contributory or comparative negligence theory, for example) or to the knowledge of the plaintiffs (for example, to establish a statute of limitations defense). These strategies have the benefit of not only destroying commonality and predominance of issues relevant to the entire class, but also can establish a defense on the merits. Defendants may have a right to a jury trial on these defenses, which will often be an additional argument to undermine class certification.

Library References:

West's Key No. Digests, Federal Civil Procedure ⚖︎161–189.
Wright, Miller & Kane, Federal Practice and Procedure: Civil 2d § 1759.

§ 15.3   Requirements for All Class Actions—FRCP 23(a)

The Supreme Court has explained that because class actions depart from "the usual rule that litigation is conducted by and on behalf of the individual named parties only," before a court may certify a class, it should undertake a "rigorous analysis" to determine whether a party seeking class certification has satisfied the requirements of Rule 23.[1] The party seeking certification bears the burden of showing that each of the four requirements of Rule 23(a) (*i.e.*, numerosity, commonality, typicality, and adequacy of representation) is met. The party also must demonstrate the appropriateness of a class action under one of the Rule 23(b)

---

§ 15.3

1. General Tel. Co. of Southwest v. Falcon, 457 U.S. 147, 155, 102 S.Ct. 2364,

2369, 72 L.Ed.2d 740 (1982), quoting Califano v. Yamasaki, 442 U.S. 682, 700–01, 99 S.Ct. 2545, 2557–58, 61 L.Ed.2d 176 (1979).

subparts.[2] Provided that the trial court abides by the framework established by Rule 23, the decision on whether to certify a class lies within the court's sound discretion.[3] One of the most often-recited principles under Rule 23 is that the merits of the controversy are separate from the determination of whether the requirements of the Rule have been satisfied and that a court should not consider the merits in ruling on class certification.[4]

Generally speaking, the first two factors of Rule 23(a), often referred to as numerosity and commonality, focus on the propriety of the proposed class, and factors three and four, typicality and adequacy of representation, focus on the propriety of the class representative.[5] When evaluating the appropriateness of a class action under Rule 23, however, courts often merge one or more of the factors together, finding, for example, that the question of commonality is closely related to the issue of whether the named plaintiff satisfies the typicality requirement, or explaining that the same facts that make the named plaintiff atypical also make him or her an inadequate class representative.[6] Notwithstanding this tendency by courts, a practitioner evaluating a potential class action lawsuit from the standpoint of plaintiff or defendant should analyze each subpart of Rule 23(a) separately.

(a) "Numerosity"—Joinder Impracticable

Before certifying a proposed class, the court must find that the "class is so numerous that joinder of all members is impracticable."[7] This entails a fact-specific inquiry to determine whether joinder is impracticable in the circumstances of the particular case.[8] If joinder is not impracticable, then a class should not be certified, and the putative class representatives may continue the litigation on their own behalf, perhaps joined by other members of the alleged class that elect to join the case as plaintiffs. The party seeking class certification need not show that joinder is impossible to satisfy its burden under the rule.[9] Although the number of members in the proposed class sometimes is the overriding factor in a court's assessment of whether joinder is impractica-

---

2. *In re* Drexel Burnham Lambert Group, Inc., 960 F.2d 285, 290 (2d Cir. 1992); Haley v. Medtronic, Inc., 169 F.R.D. 643, 647 (C.D.Cal.1996). *See infra* §§ 15.5, 15.6.

3. *In re* American Med. Sys. Inc., 75 F.3d 1069, 1079 (6th Cir.1996).

4. Eisen v. Carlisle & Jacquelin, 417 U.S. 156, 177, 94 S.Ct. 2140, 2159, 40 L.Ed.2d 732 (1974); Sandlin v. Shapiro & Fishman, 168 F.R.D. 662, 665 (M.D.Fla. 1996).

5. *See generally* 1 H. Newberg & A. Conte, Newberg on Class Actions § 3.01 at 3–3 to 3–5 (3d ed. 1992).

6. *See generally* General Tel. Co. of Southwest, 457 U.S. at 157–58 n.13, 102 S.Ct. at 2370–71 n. 13; Weiss v. York Hosp., 745 F.2d 786, 809 n. 36 (3d Cir.1984), *cert. denied*, 470 U.S. 1060, 105 S.Ct. 1777, 84 L.Ed.2d 836 (1985).

7. FRCP 23(a)(1).

8. General Tel. Co. of Northwest v. E.E.O.C., 446 U.S. 318, 330, 100 S.Ct. 1698, 1706, 64 L.Ed.2d 319 (1980).

9. Robidoux v. Celani, 987 F.2d 931, 935 (2d Cir.1993).

ble,[10] often the determination does not rest on that fact alone.[11] In addition to the number of members, courts look at additional factors[12] such as 1) geographic dispersion of the class members;[13] 2) the size of the individual claims;[14] 3) the financial resources of class members;[15] 4) the willingness and ability of the individual claimants to bring an action;[16] 5) judicial economy;[17] 6) fear of retaliation or prejudice against members of the putative class if they were to sue on their own behalf;[18] and 7) requests for prospective injunctive relief that may involve future class members.[19]

"There is no set numerical cutoff under the numerosity requirement."[20] The movant need not show the exact number of members in the class to satisfy its burden under Rule 23(a)(1), but must put forth some evidence of the expected class size.[21] A court may rely on "common sense assumptions" when determining whether the numerosity factor has been met.[22] Conclusory allegations, however, are insufficient.[23]

As a general rule, commentators have observed that courts likely will certify classes comprising 40 or more members.[24] In specific cases, however, courts have certified classes with as few as 17 members and refused to certify classes with as many as 350 members.[25]

For example, in *Alvarado Partners, L.P. v. Mehta*,[26] a suit brought under the federal securities law, the court certified a class of 33 members

10. Walco Investments, Inc. v. Thenen, 168 F.R.D. 315, 324 (S.D.Fla.1996).

11. Alvarado Partners, L.P. v. Mehta, 130 F.R.D. 673, 675 (D.Colo.1990).

12. Newberg, *supra* note 5, § 3.06, at 3–27 to 3–28.

13. Alvarado, 130 F.R.D. at 675.

14. Stoudt v. E.F. Hutton & Co., Inc., 121 F.R.D. 36, 38 (S.D.N.Y.1988) ("When the size of each claim is significant, and each proposed class member therefore possesses the ability to assert an individual claim, the goal of obtaining redress can be accomplished without the use of the class action device.").

15. Block v. First Blood Associates, 125 F.R.D. 39, 42 (S.D.N.Y.1989).

16. Liberty Lincoln Mercury, Inc. v. Ford Marketing Corp., 149 F.R.D. 65, 74 (D.N.J.1993).

17. *In re* Drexel Burnham Lambert Group, 960 F.2d 285, 290 (2d Cir.1992).

18. Slanina v. William Penn Parking Corp., 106 F.R.D. 419, 423–24 (W.D.Pa. 1984).

19. *Id.*

20. Christiana Mortgage Corp. v. Delaware Mortgage Bankers Ass'n., 136 F.R.D. 372, 377 (D.Del.1991).

21. Robidoux v. Celani, 987 F.2d 931, 935 (2d Cir.1993).

22. Sandlin v. Shapiro & Fishman, 168 F.R.D. 662, 666 (M.D.Fla.1996), citing Evans v. U.S. Pipe & Foundry Co., 696 F.2d 925, 930 (11th Cir.1983).

23. *See* Sandlin, 168 F.R.D. at 666 (finding that plaintiff failed to put forth adequate proof of the proposed class size where the plaintiff stated that defendant's use of standard forms and standard practices "gives rise to a reasonable inference that the number of class members exceeds the 10–40 requirement").

24. Newberg, *supra* note 5, § 3.05 at 3–26; 5 James Wm. Moore, et al., Moore's Federal Practice § 23.23, at 23–63 (3d ed. 1997).

25. 7A Charles Alan Wright, Arthur R. Miller & Mary Kay Kane, Federal Practice and Procedure § 1762, at 175–77 (2d ed. 1986).

26. 130 F.R.D. 673, 675 (D.Colo.1990); *compare* Christiana Mortgage Corp. v. Delaware Mortgage Bankers Association, 136 F.R.D. 372, 378 (D.Del.1991) (refusing to certify a class of 28 members even though it found that the proposed class fulfilled three other requirements of Rule 23(a) based on the fact that the class members lived within a 100–mile radius).

where it found that the members were located throughout the country. Similarly, in *Allen v. Isaac*,[27] a proposed class action challenging allegedly discriminatory training and promotion practices, the court certified a class of 17 members who were geographically dispersed.

Conversely, in *Liberty Lincoln Mercury, Inc. v. Ford Mktg. Corp.*,[28] the court rejected plaintiff's contention that joinder of 123 class members was impracticable. The court reviewed several of the factors listed above, including the location of the class members and whether the class members would be able to pursue their claims individually, and found that joinder was not impracticable because all class members were known and identifiable by name and address, each was located within the State of New Jersey, and each was a "substantial business capable of litigating for itself."[29] In *Minersville Coal Co. v. Anthracite Export Ass'n*,[30] the court determined that joinder of a proposed class of as many as 330 members was not impracticable, relying on an earlier decision in which a court found that joinder of 350 plaintiffs "was far simpler than a class action." At least one court has ruled that if every member of the proposed class could be and was in fact named as a plaintiff in the action, joinder of all members could not be considered impracticable.[31]

(b) "Commonality"—Common Questions of Law or Fact

Under Rule 23(a)(2), before a court may certify a class, it must find that "there are questions of law or fact common to the class."[32] Courts have not established a uniform rule regarding how many questions must be common to satisfy this factor. Courts generally agree that the rule does not require that every question of law or fact at issue in the litigation be common to all class members.[33] The language of the Rule itself implies that the class representative must proffer more than one issue of law or fact that is common to all members of the class,[34] and some courts have followed this interpretation of the Rule.[35] Many other courts, however, have found the commonality requirement satisfied when the plaintiff identifies only one question of law or fact common to all members of the proposed class.[36] In practice, the commonality re-

27. 99 F.R.D. 45, 53 (N.D.Ill.1983).

28. 149 F.R.D. 65, 74 (D.N.J.1993).

29. *Id.*

30. 55 F.R.D. 426, 428 (M.D.Pa.1971).

31. Joshlin v. Gannett River States Publ'g Corp., 152 F.R.D. 577, 579 (E.D.Ark. 1993) (refusing to certify a class of 95 members named in amended complaint); *see also* Uniondale Beer Co., Inc. v. Anheuser–Busch, Inc., 117 F.R.D. 340, 345 (E.D.N.Y. 1987) (refusing to certify defendant class where class counsel admitted that it could easily name the 124 defendants in the complaint).

32. FRCP 23(a)(2).

33. 1 Newberg, *supra* note 5, § 3.10 at 23–49; *see* Weiss v. York Hosp., 745 F.2d 786, 808–09 (3d Cir.1984), *cert. denied*, 470 U.S. 1060, 105 S.Ct. 1777, 84 L.Ed.2d 836 (1985).

34. 7A Charles Alan Wright, Arthur R. Miller & Mary Kay Kane, Federal Practice and Procedure § 1763, at 196–97 (2d ed. 1986); 5 Moore's, *supra* note 24, § 23.23 at 23–76.

35. *See, e.g.*, Stewart v. Winter, 669 F.2d 328, 335 n. 16 (5th Cir.1982).

36. *See, e.g.*, Baby Neal v. Casey, 43 F.3d 48, 56 (3d Cir.1994); Haley v. Medtronic, Inc., 169 F.R.D. 643, 648 (C.D.Cal. 1996).

quirement of Rule 23(a) generally is a relatively easy one for the moving party to satisfy,[37] because even though commonality remains a distinct requirement under Rule 23(a)(2), courts often consider it together with, and focus principal attention on, Rule 23(b)(3), which requires not only that common questions exist but that they predominate.[38] If a court finds that the moving party has met its burden under Rule 23(b)(3), then necessarily the commonality requirement of Rule 23(a) has been satisfied as well.

The Supreme Court has observed that the commonality requirement (*i.e.*, that there are questions of law or fact common to the class) and the typicality requirement (*i.e.*, that the claims or defenses of the named representatives are typical of those of the class) serve similar functions. The Court explained that "[b]oth serve as guideposts for determining whether under the particular circumstances maintenance of a class action is economical and whether the named plaintiff's claim and the class claims are so interrelated that the interests of the class members will be fairly and adequately protected in their absence."[39] At least one commentator has noted, however, that the commonality and typicality requirements focus on different aspects of the class: the former addresses the propriety of the class, while the latter concerns the sufficiency of the class representative.[40]

(c) "Typicality"—Claims or Defenses of Named Representatives Typical of Class

Rule 23(a)(3) requires a showing that "the claims or defenses of the representative parties are typical of the claims or defenses of the

---

37. Examples of common questions include allegations of a conspiracy to fix prices, allegations of fraud against a corporation arising out of false and misleading news releases regarding the company, allegations of standardized conduct which violates the Truth in Lending Act, or instances where the existence of a discriminatory policy adversely affects members of the proposed class. 7A Charles Alan Wright, Arthur R. Miller & Mary Kay Kane, Federal Practice and Procedure § 1763, at 204–23 (2d. ed. 1986). *But see* Moore Video Distributors, Inc. v. Quest Entertainment, Inc., 823 F.Supp. 1332 (S.D.Miss.1993) (finding that the commonality element was not met where plaintiffs had not shown that the same terms were present in the contracts at issue or that defendants breached the contracts in the same manner); R.W. Brooks v. Southern Bell Tel. & Tel. Co., 133 F.R.D. 54 (S.D.Fla.1990) (denying motion for class certification based on lack of commonality, where plaintiff would be required to look to

the law of four different states to determine whether defendants were contractually bound to provide certain benefits to plaintiffs and where the terms of the contracts and any defenses to the contracts would need to be proven individually.

38. Moore's, *supra* note 24, § 23.23, at 23–78; 7A Charles Alan Wright, Arthur R. Miller & Mary Kay Kane, Federal Practice and Procedure § 1763, at 227–28 (2d ed. 1986).

39. General Tel. Co. of Southwest v. Falcon, 457 U.S. 147, 157–58 n. 13, 102 S.Ct. 2364, 2370–71 n. 13, 72 L.Ed.2d 740 (1982).

40. Moore's, *supra* note 24, § 23.23, at 23–79. Some cases have stated that the commonality element merges with the adequacy of representation factor. General Tel. Co. of Southwest, 457 U.S. at 157–58 n.13, 102 S.Ct. at 2370–71 n. 13; Washington v. Brown & Williamson Tobacco Corp., 959 F.2d 1566, 1569 (11th Cir.1992).

class."[41] Generally, a class representative is considered "typical" when his or her claims and the claims of the other class members arise out of the same series or kind of events, and rely on similar legal theories to prove the defendant's liability.[42] "The typicality requirement is said to limit the class claims to those fairly encompassed by the named plaintiffs' claim."[43] As a result, the typicality requirement is linked closely with a named plaintiff's ability to be an adequate representative. As long as the representative's claims are typical of the class claims, a representative that pursues his or her own claims vigorously can be expected to pursue the class claims vigorously as well.[44] In addition, fewer conflicts are likely to arise if the class representative's interests are closely aligned with the interests of class members.[45]

To satisfy the typicality requirement, the moving party need not show that its claims are identical to the claims of the proposed class.[46] Insignificant factual differences between the class representative's claim and the claims of the class will not destroy typicality if both are pursuing similar legal theories.[47] Thus, where the claims of the named plaintiffs and the claims of absent class members were based on investments in different limited partnerships but on the same course of wrongful conduct and a standardized sales approach, the court found the typicality element satisfied.[48] If, however, the factual differences are material, or if they are numerous, a court may find that the typicality requirement is not satisfied.[49] For example, in a case filed on behalf of a class of students of a bankrupt college for rescission of student loan contracts, the court denied certification for lack of typicality, finding that the claims were based on oral representations and that the degree of reliance by the students differed.[50] A court must inquire whether "the named plaintiff's individual circumstances are markedly different" from those

---

41. FRCP 23(a)(3).

42. *In re* Drexel Burnham Lambert Group, Inc., 960 F.2d 285, 291 (2d Cir. 1992).

43. General Tel. Co. of Northwest v. E.E.O.C., 446 U.S. 318, 330, 100 S.Ct. 1698, 1706, 64 L.Ed.2d 319 (1980).

44. 1 Newberg, *supra* note 5, § 3.13 at 3–75; *see also* Georgine v. Amchem Products, Inc., 83 F.3d 610, 632 (3d Cir.1996), *aff'd sub nom.* Amchem Products, Inc. v. Windsor, ___ U.S. ___, 117 S.Ct. 2231, 138 L.Ed.2d 689 (1997); *In re* American Med. Sys., Inc., 75 F.3d 1069, 1083 (6th Cir.1996) ("The adequate representation requirement overlaps with the typicality requirement because in the absence of typical claims, the class representative has no incentives to pursue the claims of the other class members."). As explained above, some courts discuss typicality with the commonality requirement. General Tel. Co. of Southwest,

457 U.S. at 157–58 n.13, 102 S.Ct. at 2370–71 n. 13. More recently, the Supreme Court noted the relationship between the typicality requirement and the predominance requirement under Rule 23(b)(3). Amchem Products, Inc., ___ U.S. at ___ n. 18, 117 S.Ct. at 2249 n. 18.

45. Eisenberg v. Gagnon, 766 F.2d 770, 786 (3d Cir.), *cert. denied*, 474 U.S. 946, 106 S.Ct. 342, 88 L.Ed.2d 290 (1985); *see also* Baby Neal v. Casey, 43 F.3d 48, 56 (3d Cir.1994).

46. Trief v. Dun & Bradstreet Corp., 144 F.R.D. 193, 200 (S.D.N.Y.1992).

47. *In re* Prudential Secs. Incorp. Ltd. Partnerships Litig., 163 F.R.D. 200, 208 (S.D.N.Y.1995).

48. *Id.*

49. 1 Newberg, *supra* note 5, § 3.15, at 3–78 to 3–81.

50. *Id.* at 3–81 to 3–82.

of the class members he seeks to represent.[51] An argument by defendant that the claimed damages of the class representative differ from the damages suffered by the class members, however, generally will not defeat a motion for class certification.[52] For example, in a case in which plaintiffs challenged defendants' treatment of an employee investment plan and severance payment plan in connection with a merger, the fact that the named plaintiffs and some of the class members made money as a result of the sale of their company stock would not bar certification, where the claims were based on an alleged breach of fiduciary duty as ERISA trustees.[53]

When analyzing the typicality requirement, courts have found, for example, that a named plaintiff whose business transactions with defendants are of a more limited nature than those of the majority of the class does not satisfy the typicality requirement.[54] In *Jackshaw Pontiac, Inc. v. Cleveland Press Publ'g Co.*, the court found that the facts surrounding the named plaintiffs' positions differed greatly from those of the other proposed class members, and denied class certification. Plaintiffs were advertisers that alleged that two newspapers had conspired to close down one of the newspapers with the purpose of establishing a monopoly in the market for daily newspapers, thereby forcing advertisers to pay higher rates.[55] Defendants put forth evidence to show that the rates paid by each advertiser differed greatly, and depended upon a number of variables, including the frequency, size, and place of the ad, among other things.[56] The named plaintiffs conceded that they had paid rates based on only a few of the possible combinations, but claimed that fact irrelevant because of defendants' alleged conspiracy and the resulting injury to all class members.[57]

In rejecting that argument, the court noted that plaintiffs' alleged injuries were not typical of those of other class members, and that this kind of case was inherently unsuitable for a class action because of the great factual differences among potential plaintiffs. The court also noted that "Rule 23(a)(3) may have independent significance if it is used to screen out class actions when the legal or factual position of the representatives is markedly different from that of other members of the class even though common issues of law and fact are raised."[58] Similarly, in *In re American Med. Sys., Inc.*,[59] a products liability action, the court

---

51. Weiss v. York Hospital, 745 F.2d 786, 809 n. 36 (3d Cir.1984), *cert. denied*, 470 U.S. 1060, 105 S.Ct. 1777, 84 L.Ed.2d 836 (1985); Brooks v. Southern Bell Tel. & Tel. Co., 133 F.R.D. 54, 58 (S.D.Fla.1990) ("courts have repeatedly held representatives' claims to be atypical if they are grounded in factual situations differing from those of other class members").

52. 1 Newberg, *supra* note 5, § 3.16, at 3–97 to 3–98; Walsh v. Northrop Grumman Corp., 162 F.R.D. 440, 445 (E.D.N.Y.1995).

53. Walsh, 162 F.R.D. at 445.

54. Jackshaw Pontiac, Inc. v. Cleveland Press Publ'g Co., 102 F.R.D. 183 (N.D.Ohio 1984).

55. *Id.* at 185–86.

56. *Id.* at 190.

57. *Id.* at 189–90.

58. *Id.* at 190, citing 7 Charles Alan Wright, Arthur R. Miller & Mary Kay Kane, Federal Practice and Procedure at § 1764.

59. 75 F.3d 1069, 1082 (6th Cir.1996); *see also* Liberty Lincoln Mercury, Inc. v. Ford Mktg. Corp., 149 F.R.D. 65, 77 (D.N.J.

vacated an order granting class certification, in part because it found that the typicality requirement could not be satisfied where class members used different models of the medical device at issue and suffered different problems as a result of the device. In this case, defendant manufactured ten different types of penile prostheses.[60] The court explained that each named plaintiff had had different protheses implanted, and suffered a range of problems from leakage to malfunctioning of different inflation mechanisms.[61] As a result, the court found that the allegations "fail[ed] to establish a claim typical to [each of the other named plaintiff's claims], let alone a class."[62]

Additionally, a plaintiff class representative is not "typical if the defendant can raise unique defenses against the representative that could not be raised against other class members."[63] For example, in a securities fraud action, the court found the named plaintiff atypical where unique defenses likely would be raised against him: "[Plaintiff's] reliance on the integrity of the market would be subject to serious dispute as a result of his extensive experience in prior securities litigation, his relationship with his lawyers, his practice of buying a minimal number shares of stock in various companies, and his uneconomical purchase of only ten shares of stock in [Defendant company]."[64] The concern with unique defenses is that the resolution of these issues could consume much of the class litigation, thereby diverting the focus from the claims of the class as a whole.[65] As a result, "the presence of even an arguable defense peculiar to the named plaintiff may prevent certification (or it may lead to the substitution of another named class representative, if one is available, to whom the defense is not applicable)."[66] Whether the issue of "unique defenses is properly analyzed under the typicality requirement, Rule 23(a)(3), or the adequacy of representation requirement, Rule 23(a)(4), has not been established uniformly by the case law."[67] Regardless of the provision under which it is assessed,

1993) (finding that the named plaintiff was not "typical" because "highly individualized circumstances" surrounded its claims).

60. *In re* American Med. Sys., 75 F.3d at 1075.

61. *Id.* at 1082.

62. *Id.*

63. Hanon v. Dataproducts Corp., 976 F.2d 497, 508 (9th Cir.1992).

64. *Id.*

65. Gary Plastic Packaging Corp. v. Merrill Lynch, Pierce, Fenner & Smith, Inc., 903 F.2d 176, 180 (2d Cir.1990), *cert. denied*, 498 U.S. 1025, 111 S.Ct. 675, 112 L.Ed.2d 667 (1991).

66. J.H. Cohn & Co. v. American Appraisal Assoc., Inc., 628 F.2d 994, 998 (7th Cir.1980).

67. *See, e.g.,* 7A Charles Alan Wright, Arthur R. Miller & Mary Kay Kane, Federal Practice and Procedure § 1764, at 259–60 (2d ed. 1986) (typicality); 5 Moore's, *supra* note 24, § 23.24 at 23–97 to 23–98 and § 23.25, at 23–125 to 23–126 (analyzing unique defenses under both typicality and adequacy of representation); 1 Newberg, *supra* note 5, § 3.16, at 3–90 to 3–91 (typicality); *compare* Schaefer v. Overland Express Family of Funds, 169 F.R.D. 124 (S.D.Cal. 1996) *and* Gaspar v. Linvatec Corp., 167 F.R.D. 51 (N.D.Ill.1996) (both noting that the presence of unique defenses against the named plaintiff prevents certification under 23(a)(3)) *to* Weigmann v. Glorious Food, Inc., 169 F.R.D. 280 (S.D.N.Y.1996) *and* Barry B. Roseman, D.M.D., M.D., Profit Sharing Plan v. Sports and Recreation, 165 F.R.D. 108 (M.D.Fla.1996) (finding that the presence of unique defenses against the

however, courts universally have raised the same concerns about the effect of "unique defenses on class action lawsuits." As the Second Circuit stated, "whether the issue [of unique defenses] is framed in terms of the typicality of the representative's claims, or the adequacy of its representation, there is a danger that absent class members will suffer if their representative is preoccupied with defenses unique to it."[68]

For a named plaintiff to be typical, he or she must have a claim against each defendant, and must have suffered an injury as a result of the claim.[69] Relatedly, courts routinely have held that a class representative who lacks standing cannot meet the typicality requirement of Rule 23.[70]

Finally, to satisfy the typicality requirement, the court must find that the plaintiff's claims encompass the claims of the class.[71] The Supreme Court addressed this issue in *General Tel. Co. of Southwest v.*

---

class representative renders him an inadequate representative under 23(a)(4)).

68. Gary Plastic Packaging Corp., 903 F.2d at 180 (citations omitted).

69. 5 Moore's, *supra* note 24, § 23.24, at 23–99; La Mar v. H & B Novelty & Loan Co., 489 F.2d 461, 466 (9th Cir.1973) (holding "that a plaintiff who has no cause of action against the defendant can not fairly and adequately protect the interests of those who do have such causes of action") (citations omitted in original). In *La Mar*, the court addressed two cases from the district court that presented the same issue: whether a plaintiff with a cause of action against one defendant can represent a class against that defendant and "an unrelated group of defendants who have engaged in conduct closely similar to that of the single defendant on behalf of all those injured by all the defendants." *Id.* at 462. In the first case, the named plaintiff sought to certify a class of all customers of all pawnbrokers in the State of Oregon for violations of the Truth-in-Lending Act, 15 U.S.C.A. § 1601 to 1677 (West 1998), although he had done business with only one pawnbroker. *Id.* In the second case, plaintiff, a purchaser of round-trip air tickets from two airlines, alleged that he had been overcharged for his ticket in violation of the Federal Aviation Act. *Id.* at 463. He sought to represent a class of individuals that had paid similar overcharges against the two airlines with whom he had dealings and six other carriers. *Id.* The court refused to certify the classes, explaining that "typicality is lacking when the representative plaintiff's cause of action is against a defendant unrelated to the defendants against whom the cause of action of the members of the class

lies." *Id.* at 465. The named plaintiff need not have independent claims against each defendant if the complaint alleges a conspiracy. *Id.*

70. *See* Weiner v. Bank of King of Prussia, 358 F.Supp. 684, 694 (E.D.Pa.1973) (finding that in a case where the named plaintiff sought to represent a class of borrowers against his lender and 19 other banks for violations of federal and state banking laws, certification would be denied where plaintiff had no dealings with the 19 other banks: "[w]ithout standing, one cannot represent a class). Other courts have reached similar results. For example, in *Reichman v. Bureau of Affirmative Action*, 536 F.Supp. 1149 (M.D.Pa.1982), plaintiff sought to represent a class of certain individuals that had been or would be harmed in the future by defendants' use of affirmative action plans. The court found that plaintiff failed to establish actual or threatened harm as a result of these policies, and thus did not have standing to challenge the practices at issue. *Id.* at 1167. Her lack of standing rendered her an atypical plaintiff, thus, the court denied the motion for class certification. *Id.* at 1169; *see* Ramos v. Patrician Equities Corp., 765 F.Supp. 1196 (S.D.N.Y.1991) (holding that a class representative must have individual claims to assert claims on behalf of the class). A plaintiff without standing cannot bootstrap his way past this fatal deficiency by attempting to serve as a class representative in a class action lawsuit. 1 Newberg, *supra* note 5, § 3.19, at 3–114 to 3–115.

71. 1 Newberg, *supra* note 5, § 3.17, at 3–95 to 3–100.

Falcon.[72] In *General Tel. Co. of Southwest*, an employment discrimination suit, the named plaintiff sued on behalf of an alleged class consisting of defendant's current and future employees of Mexican–American descent who had been subjected to discriminatory practices or who might be subjected to such practices in the future.[73] The named plaintiff was an employee who had applied for a promotion, but whose application had been denied.[74] At issue before the Court was whether the named plaintiff could represent the class in an "across the board attack on the allegedly discriminatory hiring and promotion practices of defendant, even though his specific complaint was that he had been denied a promotion."[75]

The Court held that the district court had erred in determining that the named plaintiff's claims were typical of claims of other class members.[76] In doing so, the Court found that the evidence the named plaintiff would adduce in attempting to show that his denial of a promotion was discriminatory would not necessarily support conclusions that the company's promotion practices overall were motivated by discrimination or that the company's hiring practices were discriminatory.[77] The Court concluded, therefore, that the class claims were not " 'fairly encompassed' within the claim of the named plaintiff."[78]

(d) "Adequacy"—Named Representative Will Adequately Protect Class Interests

Rule 23(a)(4) requires that "the representative parties will fairly and adequately protect the interests of the class."[79] Adequate representation is "constitutionally required to afford due process."[80] Courts, therefore, carefully scrutinize this factor to ensure that the interests of absent class members, who will be bound by the results of the litigation, are protected.[81] The court's obligation to ensure the adequacy of the representation continues throughout the lawsuit.[82]

Adequate representation requires findings by the court regarding both the class representative and class counsel. Whether the class

---

72. 457 U.S. 147, 102 S.Ct. 2364, 72 L.Ed.2d 740 (1982).

73. *Id.* at 151, 102 S.Ct. at 2367.

74. *Id.* at 149, 102 S.Ct. at 2366.

75. *Id.* at 155, 102 S.Ct. at 2369.

76. *Id.* at 158–59, 102 S.Ct. at 2371–72.

77. *Id.*

78. *Id.* at 158, 102 S.Ct. at 2370. The Court noted that the plaintiff's identification of common questions of law or fact only identified the company's allegedly discriminatory promotion practices, and did not relate to defendant's hiring practices. *Id.* The Court also gave an example of the type of evidence that would have satisfied the commonality and typicality requirements of Rule 23(a), stating that a "biased testing procedure to evaluate both

applicants for employment and incumbent employees" would have justified "a class action on behalf of every applicant or employee who might have been prejudiced by the test." *Id.* at 159 n.15, 102 S.Ct. at 2371 n.15.

79. FRCP 23(a)(4).

80. Fisher Bros. v. Mueller Brass Co., 102 F.R.D. 570, 576 (E.D.Pa.1984).

81. 7A Charles Alan Wright, Arthur R. Miller & Mary Kay Kane, Federal Practice and Procedure § 1765, at 266–67 (2d ed. 1986).

82. Key v. Gillette Co., 782 F.2d 5, 7 (1st Cir.1986); *In re* Fine Paper Antitrust Litig., 617 F.2d 22, 27 (3d Cir.1980).

representative and class counsel can adequately protect the class depends on the particular facts and circumstances surrounding the case.[83] To certify the class, the court first must find that the interests of the named plaintiffs are sufficiently aligned with the absentees, and that potential conflicts among various members of the class do not exist.[84] Second, the court must find that class counsel is qualified and will be able to serve the interests of the "entire class."[85]

(1) Adequacy of the Class Representative

"[A] class representative must be part of the class and 'possess the same interest and suffer the same injury' as the class members."[86] Rule 23 does not require that the named representative be the best possible representative for the class, nor must he or she occupy a position identical to other members of the class.[87] It is crucial, however, that the named plaintiff's interests are not antagonistic to the interests of the class. Further, "[i]f the class members themselves have conflicting interests in the subject matter of the litigation so that priorities among them must be determined, then the class action device is improper."[88] Speculative allegations of conflicts among class members, however, are insufficient to defeat a motion for class certification.[89]

The recent Supreme Court decision in *Amchem Products, Inc. v. Windsor* provides an illustration of the kind of conflict among class members that will preclude certification under Rule 23(a)(4).[90] In *Amchem*, the Court affirmed a Third Circuit decision that vacated the district court's order certifying a settlement class of persons with current and future asbestos-related claims.[91] Under the terms of the settlement, persons currently suffering from asbestos-related injuries would receive compensation based on their injuries, and persons who had been exposed to asbestos but had no obvious injuries could qualify for benefits in the future under certain circumstances.[92] The Third Circuit ruled that certification of the settlement class was improper for several reasons, including in particular the widely divergent interests between the claim-

83. Kirkpatrick v. J.C. Bradford & Co., 827 F.2d 718, 728 (11th Cir.1987), *cert. denied*, 485 U.S. 959, 108 S.Ct. 1220, 99 L.Ed.2d 421 (1988).

84. Amchem Products, Inc. v. Windsor, ___ U.S. ___, ___, 117 S.Ct. 2231, 2250, 138 L.Ed.2d 689 (1997); *In re* Drexel Burnham Lambert Group, 960 F.2d 285, 291 (2d Cir. 1992).

85. *See* Amchem, ___ U.S. at ___ n. 20, 117 S.Ct. at 2251 n. 20; Drexel Burnham, 960 F.2d at 291.

86. East Texas Motor Freight Sys., Inc. v. Rodriguez, 431 U.S. 395, 403, 97 S.Ct. 1891, 1896, 52 L.Ed.2d 453 (1977), quoting Schlesinger v. Reservists Comm. to Stop the War, 418 U.S. 208, 216, 94 S.Ct. 2925, 2929, 41 L.Ed.2d 706 (1974).

87. Liberty Lincoln Mercury, Inc. v. Ford Mktg. Corp., 149 F.R.D. 65, 78 (D.N.J. 1993).

88. Al Barnett & Son, Inc. v. Outboard Marine Corp., 64 F.R.D. 43, 50 (D.Del. 1974).

89. Alvarado Partners, L.P. v. Mehta, 130 F.R.D. 673, 675 (D.Colo.1990); Walsh v. Northrop Grumman Corp., 162 F.R.D. 440, 447 (E.D.N.Y.1995).

90. *See* Amchem, ___ U.S. ___, 117 S.Ct. 2231, 138 L.Ed.2d 689.

91. *Id.*

92. *Id.* at ___, 117 S.Ct. at 2240–41.

ants with current injuries and exposure-only claimants.[93] Claimants with current injuries, the court of appeals explained, would seek higher current payouts, while persons who might develop injuries in the future would desire a settlement that made accommodations for changes in inflation and health care costs that might occur over time.[94]

The Supreme Court agreed, finding significant "[t]he disparity between the currently injured and exposure-only categories of plaintiffs."[95] The Court explained that the settlement provided "no structural assurance of fair and adequate representation for the diverse groups and individuals affected, thus making certification improper."[96]

A conflict may exist between a class representative and class members if the class representative is seeking relief different from that sought on behalf of the class or if the representative has some interest in the business of the defendant that might prevent him or her from seeking damages.[97] A conflict also may be present if the proof of the named plaintiff's case necessarily would limit the ability of class members to recover. Such was the case in *Yeager's Fuel, Inc. v. Pennsylvania Power & Light Co.*[98] In *Yeager's*, the moving party, a retail fuel oil dealer and supplier and installer of heating equipment, sought certification of a class of persons who sold retail fuel oil or sold, installed, or serviced oil heating equipment within the defendant's service area.[99] The plaintiff contended that defendant violated the antitrust laws by offering and paying rebates to builders and contractors that installed electric heat pumps and to homeowners who converted from fossil fuel to electric heating equipment.[100]

The defendant argued, among other things, that certification would be improper under Rule 23(a)(4) because the named plaintiff's interests were antagonistic to the interests of other class members, and because conflicts existed among class members.[101] Specifically, the defendant contended that because the class consisted of "competitors in a limited market seeking damages for lost business,[102] any proof the class representative would introduce to prove his loss would limit the ability of other class members to prove damages." In addition, the named plaintiff would need to show that it would have obtained business in the absence of the alleged anticompetitive actions of the defendant, proof of which would affect class members' ability to prove the same.[103] Finally, the defendant explained that within the class, some members may have benefitted from the alleged practices.[104] For example, the class included installers of heat pumps who had benefitted from the challenged incentive programs and installers who had not benefitted from defendant's

93. *Id.*

94. *Id.*

95. *Id.* at ___, 117 S.Ct. at 2251.

96. *Id.*

97. Schaefer v. Overland Express Family of Funds, 169 F.R.D. 124, 130 (S.D.Cal. 1996).

98. 162 F.R.D. 471 (E.D.Pa.1995).

99. *Id.* at 475.

100. *Id.*

101. *Id.* at 477.

102. *Id.* at 478.

103. *Id.*

104. *Id.* at 480.

program. The court accepted these arguments, and found that conflicts existed within the class, and that the named plaintiff could not represent these conflicting interests.[105]

A court also may refuse to certify a class where the class representatives attempt to form a class of both former and current business owners.[106] In *Aamco Automatic Transmissions, Inc. v. Tayloe,* the named plaintiffs were former franchisees of defendant, and sought to represent a class of current and former franchisees.[107] The court found that the representatives did not satisfy Rule 23(a)(4), explaining that the current franchisees had an interest in protecting the "economic viability and goodwill of Aamco, an interest which former franchisees did not share."[108] The court noted that the main interest of the former franchisees was to recover the "maximum monetary damages without regard to the possible adverse impact of [the] lawsuit on the present Aamco franchise system."[109] Because these interests were irreconcilable, the court refused to certify the class.[110] Other courts have held that economic competition between the named plaintiff and other class members will not render the representative inadequate.[111]

A court may be hesitant to certify a class in which the class representative is closely affiliated with class counsel.[112] In such cases, courts are especially concerned with the possibility that the representative may sacrifice the interests of the class for a settlement under which class counsel would collect substantial attorneys' fees.[113]

Evaluating the adequacy of the class representative under Rule 23(a)(4) also involves assessing whether the named representative will pursue the action vigorously so that the rights of the class members will be protected.[114] A court may look at whether the representative has the integrity to fulfill his role of a fiduciary,[115] and whether he has at least a

---

105. *Id.*

106. Aamco Automatic Transmissions, Inc. v. Tayloe, 67 F.R.D. 440 (E.D.Pa.1975).

107. *Id.* at 444.

108. *Id.* at 446.

109. *Id.*

110. *Id.* at 447; *but see* Rental Car of New Hampshire, Inc. v. Westinghouse Elec. Corp., 496 F.Supp. 373, 383 (D. Mass.1980) (certifying a class of present and former franchisees).

111. Walsh v. Northrop Grumman Corp., 162 F.R.D. 440, 447 (E.D.N.Y.1995); Uniondale Beer Co. v. Anheuser–Busch, Inc., 117 F.R.D. 340, 342 (E.D.N.Y.1987).

112. 5 Moore's, *supra* note 24, § 23.25, at 23–128; Kirby v. Cullinet Software, Inc., 116 F.R.D. 303, 309–11 (D.Mass.1987); Susman v. Lincoln American Corp., 561 F.2d 86 (7th Cir.1977), *cert. denied,* 445 U.S. 942, 100 S.Ct. 1336, 63 L.Ed.2d 775 (1980).

113. Susman, 561 F.2d at 90–91.

114. *See* 7A Charles Alan Wright, Arthur R. Miller & Mary Kay Kane, Federal Practice and Procedure § 1766, at 302–03 (2d ed. 1986); *see* Hassine v. Jeffes, 846 F.2d 169, 179 (3d Cir.1988) (finding that in evaluating whether the proposed class satisfies Rule 23(a)(4), a court should determine that the named representative "has the ability and the incentive to represent the claims of the class vigorously").

115. Kirkpatrick v. J.C. Bradford & Co., 827 F.2d 718, 726 (11th Cir.1987) (reversing the denial of class certification, in part because of the district court's erroneous conclusion that the class representative lacked sufficient subjective interest in the prosecution of the class claims), *cert. denied,* 485 U.S. 959, 108 S.Ct. 1220, 99 L.Ed.2d 421 (1988).

basic understanding of the nature of the litigation.[116] A court may find that a named plaintiff who has little knowledge or interest in pursuing the action is an inadequate representative.[117] Courts have noted, however, that:

> where the class is represented by competent and zealous counsel, class certification should not be denied simply because of a perceived lack of subjective interest on the part of the named plaintiffs unless their participation is so minimal that they virtually have abdicated to their attorneys the conduct of the case.[118]

(2) Adequacy of Class Counsel

To determine whether the proposed class satisfies Rule 23(a)(4), a court also must evaluate the adequacy of class counsel. Factors such as counsel's experience with class actions, knowledge of the subject matter at issue in the case, and the resources of counsel are relevant to this determination.[119] The fact that counsel files frequent and numerous class action lawsuits is not a basis for a finding of inadequacy, but an attorney's behavior in past class actions may lead a court to conclude that he or she is inadequate.[120] Class counsel must be qualified to serve the interests of the "entire class,[121] and class counsel owes fiduciary obligations to that class."[122] As a result, conflicts between class counsel and members of the class generally will render class counsel inadequate.[123] For example, courts have disqualified class counsel where he or she has a familial or business relationship with the class representative or if the counsel represents another class in another unrelated suit against the same defendant.[124] In addition, if the attorney represents separate groups within the class, a court must scrutinize carefully whether the separate groups possess conflicting interests or whether such conflicts could develop at a later stage of the proceeding. In such a case, a court may disqualify the attorney from representing one or both groups.[125]

116. 5 Moore's, *supra* note 24, § 23.25, at 23–133.

117. *See* Ballan v. Upjohn Co., 159 F.R.D. 473, 486 (W.D.Mich.1994) (finding inadequate the class representative who failed to participate in a number of important decisions that could seriously affect class members).

118. Kirkpatrick, 827 F.2d at 728.

119. Haley v. Medtronic, Inc., 169 F.R.D. 643, 650 (C.D.Cal.1996); *In re* Prudential Secs. Incorp. Ltd. Partnerships Litig., 163 F.R.D. 200, 208 (S.D.N.Y.1995).

120. Sandlin v. Shapiro & Fishman, 168 F.R.D. 662, 668 (M.D.Fla.1996) (finding class counsel inadequate after a judge in a different class action disqualified counsel, stating " 'I can think of no plague worse than to have a Court impose the like of [the named counsel] on absent and unsuspecting class members.' ") (citation omitted in original).

121. *In re* General Motors Corp. Pick–Up Truck Fuel Tank Prods. Liab. Litig., 55 F.3d 768, 801 (3d Cir.), *cert. denied*, 516 U.S. 824, 116 S.Ct. 88, 133 L.Ed.2d 45 (1995).

122. Maywalt v. Parker & Parsley Petroleum Co., 155 F.R.D. 494, 496 (S.D.N.Y. 1994), *aff'd*, 67 F.3d 1072 (2d Cir.1995).

123. Moore's, *supra* note 24, § 23.25, at 23–148.

124. *Id.*

125. *See In re* Corn Derivatives Antitrust Litig., 748 F.2d 157 (3d Cir.1984), *cert. denied sub nom.* Cochrane & Bresnahan v. Plaintiff Class Representatives, 472 U.S. 1008, 105 S.Ct. 2702, 86 L.Ed.2d 718

Library References:

West's Key No. Digests, Federal Civil Procedure ⚮161–189.
Wright, Miller & Kane, Federal Practice and Procedure: Civil 2d §§ 1759–1771.

§ 15.4 Mandatory "No Opt–Out Classes"—FRCP 23(b)(1) and (2)

In addition to satisfying the requirements of FRCP 23(a),[1] to obtain class certification an action must satisfy the requirements of either FRCP 23(b)(1), FRCP 23(b)(2), or FRCP 23(b)(3). This section discusses FRCP 23(b)(1) and 23(b)(2), the so-called "no opt-out classes."[2] As a general matter, FRCP 23(b)(1) authorizes a class action when separate actions pose a risk of establishing incompatible standards of conduct on the party opposing the class or of substantially impeding the ability of absent class members to protect their interests, and FRCP 23(b)(2) authorizes a class action when the claimants seek injunctive or declaratory relief.

Unlike class actions certified under FRCP 23(b)(3), when a class action is certified under either FRCP 23(b)(1) or FRCP 23(b)(2), absent class members generally have no right to notice or the opportunity to opt-out of the class action.[3] When courts have the choice of certifying a class under one of the two "no opt-out" provisions or under Rule 23(b)(3), they often elect to proceed under the available "no opt-out" provision, so as to eliminate the risk that individual class members will opt-out of the class and pursue separate litigation that could prejudice the other class members or the party opposing the class."[4]

(a) Separate Actions Pose Risks of Adverse Effects on Absent Class Members or Party Opposing Class

(1) Incompatible Standards of Conduct for Party Opposing Class

FRCP 23(b)(1)(A) authorizes a class action when separate actions might result in inconsistent or varying adjudications that would "establish incompatible standards of conduct for the party opposing the class."

(1985). In this case, two separate companies retained a law firm to bring separate antitrust actions against corn derivative producers. *Id.* at 160. Later, when other actions were brought around the country, the actions were consolidated by the Multidistrict Litigation Panel. *Id.* The law firm continued to represent its two original clients, in addition to the plaintiff class member. When a settlement was reached, the law firm filed objections on behalf of its two original clients. One company decided to accept the settlement. *Id.* Once the district court entered the settlement, the second company filed a notice of appeal. The law firm then filed a notice of withdrawal as counsel for the first company. *Id.* The court disqualified the law firm from continuing to represent the second company, finding the representation would violate the law firm's duty of loyalty to the first company. *Id.* at 161–62.

§ 15.4

1. See *supra* § 15.3.

2. For a discussion of FRCP 23(b)(3), see *infra* § 15.5.

3. See FRCP 23(c)(2).

4. See 7A Charles Alan Wright, Arthur R. Miller & Mary Kay Kane, Federal Practice and Procedure § 1775 (2d ed. 1986).

Courts generally require claimants seeking certification under FRCP 23(b)(1)(A) to establish that (1) a realistic possibility exists that separate lawsuits concerning the same subject matter will be brought if class certification is not granted,[5] and (2) such separate lawsuits likely will result in judgments imposing incompatible standards of conduct on the party opposing the class.[6] FRCP 23(b)(1)(A) has often been utilized in cases where the party opposing the class is obligated to treat the purported class members in a uniform manner, such as in cases involving a government tax assessment or a corporation's declaration of a dividend.[7]

The risk of individual lawsuits may not be merely speculative.[8] For example, in *Eisen v. Carlisle & Jacquelin*,[9] an odd-lot investor (*i.e.*, an investor purchasing fewer than 100 shares of stock) brought a class action on behalf of all New York Stock Exchange odd-lot investors against two brokerage firms for conspiring to monopolize odd-lot trading and price-fixing. The court held that FRCP 23(b)(1)(A) certification was not appropriate because the individual class members' claims were so small that there was little chance of multiple adjudications in the absence of a class action.[10]

Also, it is not enough to show that the possibility exists that the party opposing the class may win some of the lawsuits and lose others.[11] Rather, the party seeking certification must show that such separate lawsuits likely will result in inconsistent orders such that the party opposing the class would be unable to pursue a uniform course of conduct with respect to the purported class members. For example, in *Mertz v. Harris*,[12] an action by a widower challenging provisions of the Social Security Act that treated widowers differently from widows, class certification was granted under FRCP 23(b)(1)(A) because of the risk that separate adjudications could subject the federal government to

---

5. *See In re* Dennis Greenman Sec. Litig., 829 F.2d 1539, 1544–45 (11th Cir. 1987); Eisen v. Carlisle & Jacquelin, 391 F.2d 555, 564 (2d Cir.1968).

6. *See* Eliasen v. Green Bay & W.R. Co., 93 F.R.D. 408, 412 (E.D.Wis.1982) (denying class certification under FRCP 23(b)(1)(A) because no real risk of inconsistent or varying adjudications where there was no evidence that other similar suits would be initiated), *aff'd,* 705 F.2d 461 (7th Cir.), *cert. denied,* 464 U.S. 874, 104 S.Ct. 206, 78 L.Ed.2d 183 (1983); Ruland v. General Elec. Co., 94 F.R.D. 164, 165–66 (D.Conn.1982) (in an action by river front property owners against alleged corporate polluter certification was denied under FRCP 23(b)(1)(A) where plaintiffs failed to show realistic risk that actions by other property owners would result in decrees imposing conflicting obligations on defendant).

7. *See* 7A Charles Alan Wright, Arthur R. Miller & Mary Kay Kane, Federal Practice and Procedure § 1773 (2d ed. 1986).

8. *See* Eliasen, 93 F.R.D. at 412.

9. 391 F.2d 555, 564 (2d Cir.1968).

10. *Id.*

11. *See In re* Bendectin Prods. Liab. Litig., 749 F.2d 300, 305 (6th Cir.1984) (denying class certification where purported defendant class sought certification based on possibility that it could win and lose different lawsuits); National Union Fire Ins. Co. of Pittsburgh v. Midland Bancor, Inc., 158 F.R.D. 681, 687 (D.Kan.1994); Alexander Grant & Co. v. McAlister, 116 F.R.D. 583, 589–590 (S.D.Ohio 1987).

12. 497 F.Supp. 1134 (S.D.Tex.1980).

incompatible judicial decisions.[13]

As FRCP 23(b)(1)(A) is designed to protect the party opposing the class from being subject to incompatible judgments, a few courts have indicated that certification under FRCP 23(b)(1)(A) is inappropriate if the party opposing the class objects to certification and thereby accepts the risk of separate actions and possible incompatible adjudications.[14] Additionally, some courts have held that certification under Rule 23(b)(1)(A) is inappropriate when specific issues exist as to individual class members; the apparent reasoning is that adjudications involving unique factual issues are unlikely to result in decrees subjecting the party opposing the class to incompatible standards of conduct.[15] Likewise, some courts have found Rule 23(b)(1)(A) inapplicable to actions seeking only damages, because inconsistent judgments as to liability for damages will not necessarily impose incompatible standards of conduct on the party opposing the class.[16] In other words, the mere fact of being required to pay damages in some cases but not others, or the fact of being required to pay damages computed in different ways in different cases, does not in and of itself require the party opposing the class to conform its conduct to incompatible standards. The fact that a class seeks monetary damages in addition to injunctive relief, however, normally will not preclude certification under FRCP 23(b)(1)(A).[17]

---

13. See McDonnell–Douglas Corp. v. U.S. Dist. Ct. for C.D. Cal., 523 F.2d 1083, 1086 (9th Cir.1975) (the " 'incompatible standards of conduct' of subdivision (b)(1)(A) must be interpreted to be incompatible standards of conduct required of the defendant in fulfilling judgments in separate actions"), cert. denied sub nom. Flanagan v. McDonnell Douglas Corp., 425 U.S. 911, 96 S.Ct. 1506, 47 L.Ed.2d 761 (1976); Employers Ins. of Wausau v. Fed. Deposit Ins. Corp., 112 F.R.D. 52, 54 (E.D.Tenn. 1986) ("the risk of 'incompatible standards of conduct' which Rule 23(b)(1)(A) was designed to protect against involves situations where the nonclass party does not know, because of inconsistent adjudications, whether or not it is legally permissible for it to pursue a certain course of conduct").

14. See Pettco Enterprises, Inc. v. White, 162 F.R.D. 151, 155 (M.D.Ala.1995) (ruling that it is inappropriate to certify a FRCP 23(b)(1)(A) class over objection of the party opposing the class); Pruitt v. Allied Chem. Corp., 85 F.R.D. 100, 106–07 (E.D.Va.1980) (questioning the availability of certification of a class under FRCP 23(b)(1)(A) where the party opposing the class does not seek its protection); Alsup v. Montgomery Ward & Co., 57 F.R.D. 89, 92 (N.D.Cal.1972).

15. See Doe v. Guardian Life Ins. Co. of America, 145 F.R.D. 466, 477 (N.D.Ill.1992) (FRCP 23 (b)(1)(A) not satisfied in action against insurer for refusing to accept claims for treatment of bipolar affective disorder where factual issues such as the accuracy of diagnosis, policy, coverage, and estoppel would be unique to each plaintiff; Horowitz v. Pownall, 105 F.R.D. 615, 618 (D.Md. 1985) ("in a securities fraud action where there are some individual questions of reliance and injury, as there are in this case, certification under 23(b)(1) is not appropriate"), aff'd, 800 F.2d 386 (4th Cir.1986).

16. See In re Dennis Greenman Sec. Litig., 829 F.2d 1539, 1545 (11th Cir.1987) ("only actions seeking declaratory or injunctive relief can be certified under [FRCP 23(b)(1)(A)]"); Zimmerman v. Bell, 800 F.2d 386, 389 (4th Cir.1986) (class certification denied in shareholder suit seeking money damages).

17. See Robertson v. National Basketball Ass'n, 556 F.2d 682, 685 (2d Cir.1977) (upholding class certification under Rule 23(b)(1) where claimants sought both equitable and monetary damages); In re Jackson Lockdown/MCO Cases, 107 F.R.D. 703, 711 (E.D.Mich.1985).

Moreover, at least two courts in cases involving mass torts have rejected the proposition that inconsistent liability judgments in separate suits would be compatible and have permitted certification of a class under FRCP 23(b)(1)(A) even though the primary relief sought was damages.[18] Likewise at least one court has allowed certification under FRCP 23(b)(1)(A) where the claimants sought primarily money damages from a limited fund, because in such a situation individual adjudications could result in incompatible judgments concerning distribution of the fund.[19]

(2) Practical Impact on Ability of Absent Class Members to Protect Their Interests

FRCP 23(b)(1)(B) authorizes a class action when separate actions might result in a determination that, as a practical matter, would be dispositive of the interests of other purported class members or substantially impede their ability to protect their interests. A common example of an action to which FRCP 23(b)(1)(B) applies is where a limited fund is insufficient to satisfy the claims of all of the class members.[20] Notably, unlike FRCP 23(b)(1)(A), many courts recognize that FRCP 23(b)(1)(B) does not require the plaintiff to demonstrate the likelihood of separate actions in the absence of class certification.[21]

Generally, the risk that separate actions might create adverse judicial precedent that then would apply to future claims by absent class members will not, standing alone, justify certification under Rule 23(b)(1)(B).[22] Rather, a party also must demonstrate some additional practical impact that may arise from separate actions.[23] For example, in *Eliasen v. Green Bay & W.R. Co.*,[24] bondholders brought suit seeking,

---

18. *See In re* A.H. Robbins Co. Inc., 880 F.2d 709, 742 (4th Cir.), *cert. denied sub nom.* Anderson v. Aetna Cas. and Sur. Co., 493 U.S. 959, 110 S.Ct. 377, 107 L.Ed.2d 362 (1989); *In re* Federal Skywalk Cases, 93 F.R.D. 415, 423–24 (W.D.Mo.), *vacated on other grounds*, 680 F.2d 1175 (8th Cir.), *cert. denied sub nom.* Stover v. Rau, 459 U.S. 988, 103 S.Ct. 342, 74 L.Ed.2d 383 (1982).

19. *See* Berman v. Narragansett Racing Ass'n, 48 F.R.D. 333, 337 (D.R.I.1969) (certification under FRCP 23(b)(1)(A) granted in action brought by horse owners seeking shares of a specific purse), *cert. denied*, 396 U.S. 1037, 90 S.Ct. 682, 24 L.Ed.2d 681 (1970).

20. FRCP 23(b)(1)(B).

21. *See* Eliasen v. Green Bay & W.R. Co., 93 F.R.D. 408, 412 (E.D.Wis.1982), *aff'd*, 705 F.2d 461 (7th Cir.), *cert. denied*, 464 U.S. 874, 104 S.Ct. 206, 78 L.Ed.2d 183 (1983); *see also* 7A Charles Alan Wright, Arthur R. Miller & Mary Kay Kane, Federal Practice and Procedure § 1774 (2d ed.

1986). *But see* Ruland v. General Elec. Co., 94 F.R.D. 164, 165–66 (D.Conn.1982) (certification under Rule 23(b)(1)(B) requires a showing of a realistic risk of separate actions).

22. *See In re* Dennis Greenman Sec. Litig., 829 F.2d 1539, 1546 (11th Cir.1987); La Mar v. H & B Novelty & Loan Co., 489 F.2d 461, 467 (9th Cir.1973). *But see In re* Itel Sec. Litig., 89 F.R.D. 104, 125–26 (N.D.Cal.1981) (questioning the wisdom of refusing to use stare decisis as a basis for certification).

23. *See* Larionoff v. United States, 533 F.2d 1167, 1182 n. 36 (D.C.Cir.1976) (discussing standards and practical considerations of Rule 23(b)(1)(B) certification), *aff'd*, 431 U.S. 864, 97 S.Ct. 2150, 53 L.Ed.2d 48 (1977).

24. 93 F.R.D. 408, 412–13 (E.D.Wis. 1982), *aff'd*, 705 F.2d 461 (7th Cir.), *cert. denied*, 464 U.S. 874, 104 S.Ct. 206, 78 L.Ed.2d 183 (1983).

inter alia, a declaration that an acquisition of the railroad was a de facto sale which entitled the bondholders to a pro rata distribution. In ruling that FRCP 23(b)(1)(B) was appropriate, the court identified two practical factors in support of class certification. First, the plaintiffs requested a liquidation of the railroad if necessary to satisfy their claims, and such a liquidation would have affected the ability of other purported class members to make future claims. Second, because the railroad had a duty to treat all bondholders equally, any judicial determination of the railroad's obligation under the bonds would affect permanently the railroad-bondholder relationship.[25]

As in the case of FRCP 23(b)(1)(A), certification under FRCP 23(b)(1)(B) is generally not appropriate when the purported class members' claims are dependent on facts unique to individual class members,[26] or when the sole relief sought in the action is monetary damages.[27] Again, as is true under FRCP 23(b)(1)(A), certification is not normally precluded merely because the claimants seek monetary damages in addition to equitable relief.[28]

As noted previously, a common use of FRCP 23(b)(1)(B) is in actions in which the plaintiffs' only source of recovery is from a limited fund. The rationale is that a class action is necessary to prevent members of the class from exhausting the entire fund through individual adjudications, to the detriment of other class members.[29] Limited fund class actions are deemed equitable in nature and therefore not precluded by the general rule that FRCP 23(b)(1)(B) certification is inappropriate in actions seeking solely monetary damages.[30]

25. *Id.*

26. *See* Bazemore v. Friday, 478 U.S. 385, 406–07, 106 S.Ct. 3000, 3011–12, 92 L.Ed.2d 315 (1986) (upholding denial of certification because determination of whether a county acted intentionally and discriminatorily towards a particular claimant would not be dispositive of whether the county discriminated against other purported class members).

27. *See* Mateo v. M/S KISO, 805 F.Supp. 761, 773 (N.D.Cal.1991) (denying FRCP 23(b)(1)(B) certification in an action for money damages); Durrett v. John Deere Co., 150 F.R.D. 555, 560 (N.D.Tex.1993) (denying FRCP 23(b)(1)(B) certification in action by property buyers against financing lenders for money damages).

28. *See* White v. National Football League, 822 F.Supp. 1389, 1407–09 (D.Minn.1993) (granting certification under FRCP 23(b)(1)(B) when both injunctive and monetary relief were sought), *aff'd,* 41 F.3d 402 (8th Cir.1994).

29. *See, e.g., In re* Drexel Burnham Lambert Group, 960 F.2d 285, 292 (2d Cir. 1992) (certification was necessary to prevent individual claimants from unfairly diminishing the eventual recovery of other class members); County of Suffolk v. Long Island Lighting Co., 907 F.2d 1295, 1303 (2d Cir.1990).

30. *See In re* Joint E. & S. Dist. Asbestos Litig., 982 F.2d 721, 735 (2d Cir.1992) (a Rule 23(b)(1)(B) class action is appropriate to avoid unfair preferences for early claimants), *modified on other grounds*, 993 F.2d 7 (2d Cir.1993); U.S. Trust Co. of New York v. Alpert, 163 F.R.D. 409, 419 (S.D.N.Y.1995); *In re* Jackson Lockdown/MCO Cases, 107 F.R.D. 703, 712 (E.D.Mich.1985) ("[w]here a limited fund exists in a particular litigation and the projected number of claims would exceed the amount of that fund, it is both equitable and reasonable that the mere fortuitousness of one party filing before another should not be the deciding factor in determining the availability of recompense").

A mere allegation that the fund may be depleted, without more, however, is an insufficient basis for certification under FRCP 23(b)(1)(B).[31] Some courts require that claimants show a risk that claimants who file earlier will deplete the fund,[32] while other courts require that claimants show a "substantial probability that the limit on funds will affect other potential plaintiffs' claims."[33] In the Ninth Circuit a claimant must show that separate actions necessarily will result in the fund being depleted prior to the satisfaction of all class members' claims.[34] Additionally, although in limited fund cases the issue is normally whether the fund will satisfy all the possible compensatory damage awards to the purported class members, some courts have certified limited fund cases on the basis that punitive damage awards may deplete the limited fund.[35]

Of course, certification under FRCP 23(b)(1)(B) is not restricted only to limited fund cases. Courts have certified classes under FRCP 23(b)(1)(B) in a variety of situations, including suits to compel the declaration of interest payments,[36] actions challenging a statute,[37] and breach of contract cases.[38]

(b) Actions for Declaratory or Injunctive Relief

FRCP 23(b)(2) authorizes class certification if (1) "the party opposing the class has acted or refused to act on grounds generally applicable

31. See In re Northern Dist. of Cal., Dalkon Shield IUD Prods. Liab. Litig., 693 F.2d 847, 852 (9th Cir.1982), cert. denied sub nom. A.H. Robins Co., Inc. v. Abed, 459 U.S. 1171, 103 S.Ct. 817, 74 L.Ed.2d 1015 (1983).

32. See, e.g., In re First Commodity Corp. of Boston Customer Accounts Litig., 119 F.R.D. 301, 312 (D.Mass.1987); In re Jackson Lockdown/MCO Cases, 107 F.R.D. at 713.

33. See, e.g., In re Agent Orange Prod. Liab. Litig., 100 F.R.D. 718, 724–25 (E.D.N.Y.1983), aff'd, 818 F.2d 145 (2d Cir. 1987), cert. denied sub nom. Pinkney v. Dow Chem. Co., 484 U.S. 1004, 108 S.Ct. 695, 98 L.Ed.2d 648 (1988); Ahearn v. Fibreboard Corp., 162 F.R.D. 505, 526 (E.D.Tex.1995) ("substantial probability" described as "more than a mere possibility" but "less than a preponderance"); Trautz v. Weisman, 846 F.Supp. 1160, 1169 (S.D.N.Y. 1994).

34. See In re Northern Dist. of Cal., Dalkon Shield IUD Prods. Liab. Litig., 693 F.2d at 852 .

35. See In re First Commodity Corp. of Boston Customer Accounts Litig., 119 F.R.D. at 312; see also In re Northern Dist.

of Cal., Dalkon Shield IUD Prods. Liab. Litig., 693 F.2d at 852 (district court erred by ordering certification of punitive damages class without evidentiary hearing).

36. See U.S. Trust Co. of N.Y. v. Executive Life Ins. Co., 602 F.Supp. 930, 933 (S.D.N.Y.1984), aff'd, 791 F.2d 10 (2d Cir. 1986) (certifying debt holders class action for interest payments because all debt holders would ultimately be affected by any possible decree).

37. See Stewart v. Waller, 404 F.Supp. 206, 213 (N.D.Miss.1975) (certifying defendant class under FRCP 23(b)(1)(B) in action challenging validity of state law mandating at-large elections for alderman positions because the adjudication of the statute's validity could be dispositive as to all class members).

38. See Mungin v. Florida E. Coast Ry. Co., 318 F.Supp. 720 (M.D.Fla.1970), aff'd, 441 F.2d 728 (5th Cir.) (per curiam) (certifying class under FRCP 23(b)(1)(B) for breach of collective bargaining agreement), cert. denied, 404 U.S. 897, 92 S.Ct. 203, 30 L.Ed.2d 175 (1971); Berman v. Narragansett Racing Ass'n, 48 F.R.D. 333 (D.R.I. 1969) (certifying class action under FRCP 23(b)(1)(B) for breach of contract action).

to the class," and (2) the class representatives are seeking "final injunctive relief or corresponding declaratory relief."[39] As to the "general applicability" requirement of FRCP 23(b)(2), the key issue is whether the conduct complained of affects all of the members of a group of similarly situated persons.[40] FRCP 23(b)(2) was adopted to facilitate civil rights actions and has been used for racial discrimination[41] and gender discrimination[42] class action claims.[43]

FRCP 23(b)(2) is not limited to class actions involving civil rights statutes, however. It also has been invoked in actions based on alleged violations of constitutional rights, including First Amendment and due process rights,[44] and in a variety of other circumstances, including patent infringement cases[45] and bondholder suits seeking to compel the conversion of convertible debentures.[46]

(1) The General Applicability Requirement

To satisfy the "general applicability" requirement of FRCP 23(b)(2), the purported class representatives must show either that the defendant acted in a consistent manner toward members of the class so that the defendant's actions may be viewed as part of a pattern of activity, or that the defendant established or acted pursuant to a regulatory scheme common to all class members.[47] Some courts have held that the defendant's conduct need not have harmed all members of the potential

---

39. FRCP 23(b)(2). In determining whether to certify a class under FRCP 23(b)(2), some courts have considered whether a class action is necessary to provide relief for the individual class members. The Supreme Court has held, however, that a class may be certified under Rule 23(b)(2) even if there is no apparent need for a class action. *See* Califano v. Yamasaki, 442 U.S. 682, 99 S.Ct. 2545, 61 L.Ed.2d 176 (1979).

40. *See* 7A Charles Alan Wright, Arthur R. Miller & Mary Kay Kane, Federal Practice and Procedure § 1775 (2d ed. 1986).

41. *See* Paxton v. Union Nat'l Bank, 688 F.2d 552, 563 (8th Cir.1982) ("This case seeking injunctive relief against class-wide race discrimination in bank's promotion practices was appropriately brought under 23 (b)(2)"), *cert. denied*, 460 U.S. 1083, 103 S.Ct. 1772, 76 L.Ed.2d 345 (1983); Buycks–Roberson v. Citibank Fed. Sav. Bank, 162 F.R.D. 322, 328 (N.D.Ill. 1995) (class certified under FRCP 23(b)(2) for purposes of injunctive relief only, in action alleging that loan applications of African–Americans were denied because of defendant's racially discriminatory underwriting criteria).

42. *See* Jordan v. Swindall, 105 F.R.D. 45, 49 (M.D.Ala.1985) (certified class of women police officers under FRCP 23(b)(2) in action alleging that various of the police

department's employment practices discriminated on the basis of gender).

43. Generally, in such cases the representative plaintiffs must exhaust available administrative remedies before turning to class litigation. *See* Gulley v. Orr, 905 F.2d 1383, 1384–85 (10th Cir.1990) (to warrant certification under FRCP 23(b)(2) a class representative must exhaust the administrative remedies available to the class); Briggs v. Anderson, 796 F.2d 1009, 1018 (8th Cir.1986) (holding that every class member need not file an administrative claim, but their class representative must have filed such a claim to have standing); Ekanem v. Health & Hosp. Corp. of Marion County, Ind., 724 F.2d 563, 572 (7th Cir. 1983), *cert. denied*, 469 U.S. 821, 105 S.Ct. 93, 83 L.Ed.2d 40 (1984).

44. *See generally* 7A Charles Alan Wright, Arthur R. Miller & Mary Kay Kane, Federal Practice and Procedure § 1775 (2d ed. 1986).

45. Dale Elecs., Inc. v. RCL Elecs., Inc., 53 F.R.D. 531 (D.N.H.1971).

46. Van Gemert v. Boeing Co., 259 F.Supp. 125 (S.D.N.Y.1966).

47. *See* Hiatt v. County of Adams, Ohio, 155 F.R.D. 605, 609 (S.D.Ohio 1994) (class certified under FRCP 23(b)(2) because de-

class.[48] Rather, the relevant inquiry is whether the defendant's behavior had a similar effect on all of the prospective class members.[49]

(2) Injunctive or Declaratory Relief

Parties seeking class certification under Rule 23(b)(2) also must be seeking final injunctive or corresponding declaratory relief.[50] A request for a temporary restraining order or a preliminary injunction alone does not qualify under Rule 23(b)(2).[51] Also, certification under FRCP 23(b)(2) is inappropriate if the primary relief sought is monetary damages,[52] or if declaratory relief is sought solely to lay the basis for subsequent damage awards.[53] Seeking money damages that are merely incidental to the request for injunctive or declaratory relief, however, will not necessarily preclude certification under FRCP 23(b)(2).[54]

Library References:

West's Key No. Digests, Federal Civil Procedure ⬤180.
Wright, Miller & Kane, Federal Practice and Procedure: Civil 2d §§ 1772–1775.

fendant county's policy and conduct affected entire class of prison inmates); Heastie v. Community Bank of Greater Peoria, 125 F.R.D. 669, 679–80 (N.D.Ill.1989) (FRCP 23(b)(2) requirement of "grounds generally applicable to class" satisfied by bank's requirement that all class members sign a loan document that included a nonresponsibility clause); Calkins v. Blum, 511 F.Supp. 1073, 1088–89 (N.D.N.Y.1981), aff'd, 675 F.2d 44 (2d Cir.1982).

48. See Afro American Patrolmen's League v. Duck, 503 F.2d 294, 298 (6th Cir.1974); Arnold v. United Artists Theatre Circuit, Inc., 158 F.R.D. 439, 454 (N.D.Cal. 1994) ("where action would generally affect members of the class in the same way, but has only affected a subset of the class, (b)(2) certification is still appropriate"); Owens v. Brown, 455 F.Supp. 291, 293 (D.D.C.1978) (the fact that all class members do not share common opinion on merits of action does not bar class certification).

49. See Moore v. Miller, 612 F.Supp. 952, 955 (N.D.Ill.1985) (improper calculation of benefits by Department of Public Assistance constituted action generally applicable to all members of class); Calkins, 511 F.Supp. at 1088–89 (defendant's erroneous computation of Medicare recipient's income satisfied requirement that defendant's conduct be generally applicable to entire class).

50. See McGlothlin v. Connors, 142 F.R.D. 626, 640 (W.D.Va.1992); Bower v. Bunker Hill Co., 114 F.R.D. 587, 596 (E.D.Wash.1986). The words "corresponding declaratory relief," which appear in the

Rule, were defined by the Advisory Committee as referring to any remedy that "as a practical matter ... affords injunctive relief or serves as the basis for later injunctive relief." See FRCP 23, Advisory Committee Note.

51. See McGlothlin, 142 F.R.D. at 640.

52. See Boughton v. Cotter Corp., 65 F.3d 823, 827 (10th Cir.1995) (certification denied because plaintiffs' demand for medical monitoring of their alleged radiation exposure constituted "predominately money damages"); In re School Asbestos Litig., 789 F.2d 996, 1008–09 (3d Cir.); cert. denied sub nom. Celotex Corp. v. School Dist. of Lancaster, 479 U.S. 852, 107 S.Ct. 182, 93 L.Ed.2d 117 (1986).

53. See Sarafin v. Sears, Roebuck, & Co., 446 F.Supp. 611, 616 (N.D.Ill.1978).

54. See Probe v. State Teachers' Retirement Sys., 780 F.2d 776, 780 (9th Cir.) ("class actions certified under Rule 23(b)(2) are not limited to actions requesting only injunctive or declaratory relief but may include cases that also seek monetary damages"), cert. denied, 476 U.S. 1170, 106 S.Ct. 2891, 90 L.Ed.2d 978 (1986); Paxton v. Union Nat'l Bank, 688 F.2d 552, 563 (8th Cir.1982) (holding that certification under FRCP 23(b)(2) was proper even though claimants sought back pay for individual class members in addition to injunctive relief), cert. denied, 460 U.S. 1083, 103 S.Ct. 1772, 76 L.Ed.2d 345 (1983); Parker v. Local Union No. 1466, United Steelworkers of America, 642 F.2d 104, 107 (5th Cir.1981).

§ 15.5 "Opt–Out" Classes in Actions for Damages— FRCP 23(b)(3)

Class actions for money damages are appropriately brought under Rule 23(b)(3).[1] Declaratory or injunctive relief need not be sought in actions under Rule 23(b)(3). In authorizing the use of the class action device in suits for damages, FRCP 23(b)(3) was designed to achieve economies of time, effort, and expense "without sacrificing procedural fairness or bringing about other undesirable results."[2] Class members in an action maintained under this Rule are entitled to the "best notice practicable," and they must be advised that they are entitled to opt-out from the class.[3]

There is considerable overlap between the requirements of Rule 23(a) and those of Rule 23(b)(3).[4]

A class action under FRCP 23(b)(3) may be brought only if the court finds that the requirements of Rule 23(a) are satisfied *and* (1) that common questions of law or fact predominate in the case, and (2) that a class action is superior to other available methods for adjudicating the controversy. Nonetheless, the different portions of the Rule contemplate separate findings and Rule 23(b)(3) specifies several factors to be considered in determining whether the "predominance" and "superiority" requirements are satisfied.[5]

The predominance requirement focuses on the factual or legal issues common to members of the class and the significance of those common issues in the lawsuit as a whole. The superiority requirement involves an inquiry into the advantages and disadvantages of the class action device as compared to other available methods for adjudicating the controversy.[6] Despite Rule 23(b)(3)'s separate statement of the predominance and superiority requirements, courts considering whether to certify a case as a class action frequently blur the distinction between the two requirements.[7]

---

§ 15.5

1. *See* Smith v. Shawnee Library Sys., 60 F.3d 317, 321 (7th Cir.1995); Day v. NLO, 851 F.Supp. 869, 885–86 (S.D.Ohio 1994) (Rule 23(b)(3) certification is the preferred route when monetary damages are plaintiffs' primary goal).

2. FRCP 23(b)(3), Advisory Committee Note, 1966 amendment; *see also* Sterling v. Velsicol Chem. Corp., 855 F.2d 1188, 1196 (6th Cir.1988); Brown v. Cameron–Brown Co., 92 F.R.D. 32, 41 (E.D.Va.1981).

3. *See* FRCP 23(c)(2).

4. *See, e.g.,* Freedman v. Arista Records, Inc., 137 F.R.D. 225, 228 (E.D.Pa.1991) (typicality overlaps requirements of predominance and superiority); Alexander Grant & Co. v. McAlister, 116 F.R.D. 583, 590–91 (S.D.Ohio 1987) (superiority analysis converges with discussions of numerosity, commonality, and typicality). *See also* Jerold S. Solovy et al., Class Action Controversies, in 3 ALI–ABA Resource Materials: Civil Practice and Litigation in Federal and State Courts VI–A–1 at 87 (Sol Schreiber, et al. eds. 5th ed. 1992).

5. *See* FRCP 23(b)(3)(A–D).

6. 5 James Wm. Moore, et al., Moore's Federal Practice § 23.44 (3d ed. 1997); *see also* Riordan v. Smith Barney, 113 F.R.D. 60, 65 (N.D.Ill.1986).

7. *See, e.g.,* Goldwater v. Alston & Bird, 116 F.R.D. 342, 355–56 (S.D.Ill.1987).

(a) Court Must Make Findings, Based on Evidence in Record

(1) Predominance—Common Questions Predominate

The text of Rule 23(b)(3) does not specify what it means for common issues to "predominate," and the courts have not developed a precise test. Essentially, the predominance determination requires a "pragmatic assessment of the entire action and the issues involved."[8] Perhaps as a consequence, courts considering whether common issues predominate have sometimes transformed that inquiry into a more general balancing of the value of individual actions against the economy of a class-wide resolution.[9]

The primary consideration for assessing predominance is the proof necessary to establish the class members' claims under the applicable substantive law. For this reason, certification of a class under Rule 23(b)(3) may depend on some examination of the factual and legal issues underlying the complaint, in order to predict what shape a trial will take on those issues.[10]

Common questions that have been routinely held to predominate are: 1) a common scheme of fraudulent conduct in the context of securities fraud cases, since the defendants' conduct in failing to disclose material information is the same as to all class members, 2) antitrust actions alleging a price-fixing conspiracy, since the fixed price presumably impacts all purchasers, and 3) single incident mass tort actions, even though each plaintiff's damages turn on individual circumstances.[11] Common questions that are generally not held to predominate are: 1) oral misrepresentations in security fraud cases, since such representations are likely to vary from purchaser to purchaser, 2) private consumer fraud actions brought under state law or RICO,[12] since individualized issues of reliance often predominate, and 3) discrimination claims, where evidence of such discrimination can be proved only by the introduction of evidence pertaining to each individual.[13]

In particular, in assessing predominance, courts may evaluate whether and to what extent the claims of each class member will require the same proof to satisfy the elements of the claims.[14] Other formulations include whether resolution of a common issue would "significantly

---

8. Rodriguez v. Carlson, 166 F.R.D. 465, 477 (E.D.Wash.1996); *In re* Copley Pharmaceutical, Inc., 158 F.R.D. 485, 491 (D.Wyo. 1994) (citation omitted).

9. 7A Charles A. Wright, Arthur R. Miller & Mary Kay Kane, Federal Practice and Procedure § 1777, at 519 (2d ed. 1986); *see also* O'Neil v. Appel, 165 F.R.D. 479, 495 (W.D.Mich.1996) (citing Wright, et al.).

10. Retired Chicago Police Ass'n v. City of Chicago, 7 F.3d 584, 598 (7th Cir.1993), *aff'd,* 76 F.3d 856, *cert. denied,* ___ U.S. ___, 117 S.Ct. 305, 136 L.Ed.2d 222 (1996); Wagner v. Taylor, 836 F.2d 578, 587 (D.C.Cir. 1987).

11. *See* 5 Moore's, *supra* note 6, § 23.47, at 23–213–14, 23–236–39, 23–243–45.

12. *See id.* at 23–215–16 and 23–234.

13. *See* 7A Charles A. Wright, Arthur R. Miller & Mary Kay Kane, Federal Practice and Procedure § 1778, at 539 (2d ed. 1986).

14. *See, e.g.,* Anderson v. Bank of South, N.A., 118 F.R.D. 136, 150 (M.D.Fla. 1987) (finding that the common question of proof of a fraudulent scheme in bond sales predominates over any questions affecting only individual members of proposed class).

advance" the underlying individual cases;[15] whether the common issues constitute a significant part of each class member's individual case;[16] and whether common questions are central to all the members' claims.[17] Common theories of liability asserted[18] or the same basic defense raised by all class members may also support predominance.[19] The common issues need not be the only issues in the action; they must only predominate.[20] Nor must the common issues necessarily be dispositive of the litigation.[21] Indeed, one commentator has asserted that the predominance requirement, by its very nature, "contemplates that individual issues will usually remain after the common issues are adjudicated."[22] Two recent decisions, however, have stressed that variations in state law as applied to class claimants from different jurisdictions, amplified by the associated choice of law problems (*i.e.*, the problems associated with looking to the laws of various different states to determine which law should apply to different claimants), may undermine a finding of predominance.[23] A statute of limitations barring some claims, but not all,

15. Jenkins v. Raymark Industries, 782 F.2d 468, 472–73 (5th Cir.1986) (where hundreds of asbestos-related personal injury claims were pending with the district court, findings on the class question will significantly advance the resolution of the underlying cases).

16. Watson v. Shell Oil Co., 979 F.2d 1014, 1022 (5th Cir.1992) (finding that liability issues to be determined in a mass tort action form "integrated elements of the claims asserted by each of the more than 18,000 plaintiffs"); *In re* Energy Sys. Equip. Leasing Sec. Litig., 642 F.Supp. 718, 751–52 (E.D.N.Y.1986) (finding predominance where common claims of misrepresentations and omissions contained in standardized investment materials provided the "dominant core" of the case).

17. Edgington v. R.G. Dickinson & Co., 139 F.R.D. 183, 190–91, 194 (D.Kan.1991) (finding that a "court must discern whether the claims involve a common nucleus of operative facts and whether material variations in the claims exist," and denying certification where class representatives are "subject to unique defenses that predictably will become a major focus of the litigation").

18. Genden v. Merrill Lynch, Pierce, Fenner & Smith, Inc., 114 F.R.D. 48, 52 (S.D.N.Y.1987) (finding predominance where defendant's alleged duty to disclose and the materiality of the alleged omission were common to the class).

19. *See, e.g.*, Alexander Grant & Co. v. McAlister, 116 F.R.D. 583, 590 (S.D.Ohio 1987) (granting certification where "the

theory of liability and all defenses to this theory are identical for all class members").

20. *See, e.g.*, Kirkpatrick v. J.C. Bradford & Co., 827 F.2d 718, 724–25 (11th Cir.1987) (citation omitted) (finding that common questions predominate where oral representations did not vary materially from information disseminated generally); Gavron v. Blinder Robinson & Co., 115 F.R.D. 318, 324–25 (E.D.Pa.1987) (commenting that "possible issues of individualized proof of reliance or individualized defenses of nonreliance that may be raised are subordinate to the core issues of liability in the fraud-on-the-market theory").

21. Riordan v. Smith Barney, 113 F.R.D. 60, 65 (N.D.Ill.1986); *see also* Eisenberg v. Gagnon, 766 F.2d 770, 786 (3d Cir.) (issue of individual reliance does not by itself deny predominance of common questions in securities case), *cert. denied sub nom.* Weinstein v. Eisenberg, 474 U.S. 946, 106 S.Ct. 342, 88 L.Ed.2d 290 (1985); Freedman v. Louisiana–Pacific Corp., 922 F.Supp. 377, 400 (D.Or.1996) ("the fact that questions peculiar to each individual member of the class may remain after the common questions have been resolved does not dictate the conclusion that a class action is not permissible").

22. 1 H. Newberg & A. Conte, Newberg on Class Actions § 4.25 at 4–83 (3d ed. 1992).

23. Castano v. American Tobacco Co., 84 F.3d 734, 741 (5th Cir.1996); Georgine v. Amchem Products, Inc., 83 F.3d 610, 618 (3d Cir.1996), *aff'd sub nom.* Amchem Prod-

ordinarily will not preclude certification.[24]

Predominance is not determined by a simple counting of the number of common issues or by a finding that common issues outnumber individual issues.[25] Nor is it simply a question of the amount of time that will be taken to litigate common issues as opposed to individual issues.[26] Nor does it depend merely on an abstract subjective assessment of the relative importance of common issues.[27] Important individual issues, such as damages or each plaintiff's degree of reliance, can be resolved separately as long as the court properly can find, based on the materials in the record, that common questions predominate.[28]

Courts generally agree that the need for individual proof of damages does not undermine the ability to certify a class. Certification of a class under Rule 23(b)(3) would be virtually impossible if the necessity of individual proof of damages automatically precluded a finding that common issues predominate.[29] Class-wide mathematical formulas for the calculation of individual damages may help to reduce the problem of proof of individual damages.[30]

In summary, a practitioner advocating Rule 23(b)(3) class certification should demonstrate predominance by showing a central link between class members for which the court can provide a remedy. Plaintiffs' counsel should also be prepared to explain how a single action will promote judicial economy. Moreover, a practitioner seeking certification should give some thought to the calculation of individual damages, to help defuse any arguments that damages calculations will be extremely complex or time intensive.

ucts, Inc. v. Windsor, ___ U.S. ___, 117 S.Ct. 2231, 138 L.Ed.2d 689 (1997); *cf.* Walsh v. Chittenden Corp., 798 F.Supp. 1043, 1055 (D.Vt.1992) (certification appropriate despite different laws applying to pendent state claims given that both federal and state claims were predicated on same facts).

24. Hoxworth v. Blinder, Robinson & Co. Inc., 980 F.2d 912, 924 (3d Cir.1992) (citing Cameron v. E.M. Adams & Co., 547 F.2d 473, 478 (9th Cir.1976)); CV Reit, Inc. v. Levy, 144 F.R.D. 690, 699 (S.D.Fla.1992); *In re* Revco Sec. Litig., 142 F.R.D. 659, 663 (N.D.Ohio 1992).

25. Buford v. H & R Block, Inc., 168 F.R.D. 340, 356 (S.D.Ga.1996) (court must make a qualitative, not quantitative analysis).

26. *See* Coleman v. Cannon Oil Co., 141 F.R.D. 516, 526 (M.D.Ala.1992) ("The total amount of time spent on a common issue compared to time spent on individual issues is immaterial.") (quoting *In re* Workers' Compensation, 130 F.R.D. 99, 108 (D.Minn. 1990)).

27. 1 Newberg, *supra* note 22, § 4.25, at 4–85.

28. Caleb & Co. v. E.I. DuPont de Nemours & Co., 110 F.R.D. 316, 321 (S.D.N.Y. 1986).

29. *See, e.g.,* Epstein v. MCA, Inc., 50 F.3d 644, 669 (9th Cir.1995) (damage calculation is invariably an individual question that does not defeat class certification); Sterling v. Velsicol Chem. Corp., 855 F.2d 1188, 1197 (6th Cir.1988) (tort); Bresson v. Thomson McKinnon Sec., Inc., 118 F.R.D. 339, 343 (S.D.N.Y.1988) (antitrust). *See also* Solovy, et al., *supra* note 4, at 89.

30. *See, e.g.,* Blackie v. Barrack, 524 F.2d 891, 905 (9th Cir.1975); Brown v. Pro Football, Inc., 146 F.R.D. 1, 5 (D.D.C.1992); *cf.* Butt v. Allegheny Pepsi–Cola Bottling Co., 116 F.R.D. 486, 492 (E.D.Va.1987) (class certification denied in price-fixing case where damages could be calculated only with "detailed and individualized examination of hundreds of thousands of transactions").

A practitioner opposing Rule 23(b)(3) class certification may succeed even if common issues clearly predominate. Defense counsel in this situation may seek to emphasize that calculation of damages is complex or burdensome, or that counterclaims or conflicting state laws decrease the importance of the predominant issues.

(2) Superiority—Class Action Superior to Other Available Methods for Adjudicating the Controversy

In addition to the predominance of common issues, Rule 23(b)(3) requires a finding that a class action is "superior" to other available methods for adjudicating the controversy. Thus, a court must consider alternative modes of adjudication and compare those possibilities to a class action.[31] Alternative modes of adjudication include: 1) remitting the class members to individual actions, especially when other claimants may likely be permitted to join or intervene in the individual action, 2) proceeding with a single test case, which may have a preclusive effect on the other class members' claims, 3) dividing the class into subclasses with one subclass treated as a test case, 4) consolidation by the Judicial Panel on Multidistrict Litigation, and 5) instituting an administrative proceeding.[32] Under Rule 23(b)(3)'s superiority requirement, a class action must in fact be better than, not merely as good as, these other adjudication methods.[33] The essential inquiry is an evaluation of the efficiency and fairness of alternative methods of adjudication compared to a class action.[34]

The fact that a class action may be burdensome does not preclude certification unless the burden is worse than or the same as that produced by possible alternatives.[35] The burdens of a class action potentially can produce great benefits by resolving many claims in a single litigation. For example, a successful defense on a common liability issue can dispose of all individual claims in a single proceeding.[36] On the other hand, at least one federal court of appeals (the Seventh Circuit) has expressed reservations about the class action mechanism under such circumstances, because forcing defendants to stake the outcome of all suits on one trial may induce them to settle when they otherwise may not have done so in individual suits.[37]

---

31. *See, e.g.,* Curley v. Cumberland Farms Dairy, Inc., 728 F.Supp. 1123, 1133 (D.N.J.1989); Moskowitz v. Lopp, 128 F.R.D. 624, 636 (E.D.Pa.1989).

32. *See* 7A Charles Alan Wright, Arthur R. Miller & Mary Kay Kane, Federal Practice and Procedure § 1779, at 552–62 (2d ed. 1986).

33. Coleman v. Cannon Oil Co., 141 F.R.D. 516, 529 (M.D.Ala.1992) (quoting Rutledge v. Electric Hose & Rubber Co., 511 F.2d 668 (9th Cir.1975)); Beebe v. Pacific Realty Trust, 99 F.R.D. 60, 73 (D.Or. 1983).

34. *See* Watson v. Shell Oil Co., 979 F.2d 1014, 1023 (5th Cir.1992); Perez v. Government of Virgin Islands, 109 F.R.D. 384, 390 (D.Vi.1986).

35. *See* Anderson v. Bank of South, N.A., 118 F.R.D. 136, 150 (M.D.Fla.1987).

36. *See* Roper v. Consurve, Inc., 578 F.2d 1106, 1116 (5th Cir.1978), *aff'd sub nom.* Deposit Guaranty Nat'l Bank v. Roper, 445 U.S. 326, 100 S.Ct. 1166, 63 L.Ed.2d 427 (1980).

37. *See In re* Rhone–Poulenc Rorer Inc., 51 F.3d 1239, 1299 (4th Cir.1995).

The countervailing argument, of course, is that a class action may be the only economically feasible means of litigating a large number of small claims, and that, in such instances, the practical choice is between a class action and no action at all.[38]

In such circumstances, a court should consider carefully whether a class action is truly an expeditious means for resolving a large number of claims or whether the number of individual issues and proceedings that will remain after the decision of common issues still will pose substantial obstacles to the efficient resolution of the claims of individual class members. Such an inquiry can help to separate legitimate class actions from those brought for some improper purpose.[39] A class action may produce a critical mass of potential recovery where individuals have little incentive to bring suit because the amount of each claim is small.[40] Thus, a class action may provide crucial access to the courts by permitting individuals to combine resources to achieve a more powerful litigation posture.[41]

Although the possibility of large individual recovery militates against a finding of superiority,[42] courts have held that, if a class action is the fairest and most efficient method of adjudication, it is superior even though individual class members may have sufficient incentives to bring individual suits.[43] Likewise, superiority may be found where particularly costly or complex litigation otherwise would deter individuals from bringing suit.[44] Where the prevailing party may recover fees and costs, however, superiority of the class action is more difficult to establish.[45]

38. *In re* Tetracycline Cases, 107 F.R.D. 719, 732 (W.D.Mo.1985); 5 Moore's, *supra* note 6, at § 23.48 [1].

39. *See* 7A Charles Alan Wright, Arthur R. Miller & Mary Kay Kane, Federal Practice and Procedure § 1779, at 552 (2d ed. 1986).

40. *See, e.g.,* Deposit Guaranty Nat'l Bank, 445 U.S. at 338, 100 S.Ct. at 1174; *In re* Amerifirst Sec. Litig., 139 F.R.D. 423, 435 (S.D.Fla.1991); Goldwater v. Alston & Bird, 116 F.R.D. 342, 356 (S.D.Ill.1987) (individual suits too inefficient and costly where class consists of many small investors); *In re* Kirschner Med. Corp. Sec. Litig., 139 F.R.D. 74, 80 (D.Md.1991) (individual claims too small to warrant individual suits); Bresson v. Thomson McKinnon Sec., Inc., 118 F.R.D. 339, 345 (S.D.N.Y.1988) (average investment of $8,600 would not justify individual actions).

41. *See* Roper, 578 F.2d at 1116 (citation omitted).

42. *See* Castano v. American Tobacco Co., 84 F.3d 734, 748 (5th Cir.1996) (poten-

tial large individual recovery suggests class action is inferior method of adjudication); *In re* Rhone–Poulenc Rorer, Inc., 51 F.3d at 1300; Stoudt v. E.F. Hutton & Co., 121 F.R.D. 36, 38 (S.D.N.Y.1988) (class certification denied where each plaintiff's claim was at least $60,000; claimants were "fully capable of proceeding on their own").

43. *See* Scholes v. Moore, 150 F.R.D. 133, 138 (N.D.Ill.1993) (large claims of some individuals does not defeat certification); Ardrey v. Federal Kemper Ins. Co., 142 F.R.D. 105, 115 (E.D.Pa.1992); Lubin v. Sybedon Corp., 688 F.Supp. 1425, 1463 (S.D.Cal.1988).

44. Epifano v. Boardroom Business Prods., Inc., 130 F.R.D. 295, 299 (S.D.N.Y. 1990) (despite large individual claims, class certified due to uncertainty that individuals would bring suit); Wehner v. Syntex Corp., 117 F.R.D. 641, 645 (N.D.Cal.1987).

45. Castano, 84 F.3d at 748 (availability of attorneys' fees is common basis for non-superiority finding); Mayo v. Sears, Roebuck & Co., 148 F.R.D. 576, 583 (S.D.Ohio 1993).

The superiority of a class action compared to consolidation depends largely on the feasibility of consolidation of claims.[46] In addition, courts should consider carefully the effectiveness of the multidistrict litigation procedures[47] compared to a class action.[48] When similar litigation is not already pending, consolidation is not possible, unless similar actions are filed promptly by other members of the potential class. Consolidation also is less likely to be feasible when there are numerous, geographically dispersed claims, or when other litigation has progressed to an advanced stage, thus raising practical problems about combining such cases with others more recently filed.[49]

A class action may be superior because of its advantage in apprising potential plaintiffs of their injury and recovery opportunity.[50] Where potential plaintiffs are alerted by wide publicity of a suit, a class may be denied because potential plaintiffs easily could intervene.[51] Intervention may be unworkable, however, if the class is too large.[52] Similarly, joinder cannot be superior when the class is too large.[53] If the class is small, the court may prefer joinder, consistent with the express terms of Rule 23(a), which authorize a class action only if joinder is "impracticable."[54]

Where there are compulsory counterclaims, especially where the complaint is based on a federal question but compulsory counterclaims are predicated on state law, class certification may be denied. Superiority is diminished when a class action would force a federal court to hear matters that it otherwise might be without jurisdiction to hear.[55]

Finally, courts sometimes will approve a "test case" approach in which one class member tries the case with the defendant's agreement that, if the plaintiff prevails, the defendant will be estopped from re-litigating common issues when the remaining members bring suit. The test case may be preferred by courts in order to avoid the complexity of managing individual claims in a class action.[56] One court has found this

---

46. See Datz v. Whitworth, 144 F.R.D. 426, 427 (N.D.Ga.1992) (consolidation found superior).

47. See 28 U.S.C.A. § 1407 (West 1993). See Chapter 11 "Multidistrict Litigation," supra.

48. See, e.g., West Virginia v. Chas. Pfizer & Co., 440 F.2d 1079 (2d Cir.), cert. denied sub nom. Cotler Drugs, Inc. v. Chas. Pfizer & Co., 404 U.S. 871, 92 S.Ct. 81, 30 L.Ed.2d 115 (1971).

49. See Esler v. Northrop Corp., 86 F.R.D. 20, 39 (W.D.Mo.1979). See Chapter 10 "Joinder, Consolidation and Severance," supra.

50. McClendon v. Continental Group, Inc., 113 F.R.D. 39, 45 (D.N.J.1986) (class action superior where most plaintiffs would learn of possible right to recovery only through litigation).

51. Reichert v. Bio–Medicus, Inc., 70 F.R.D. 71, 77 (D.Minn.1974).

52. Brown v. Cameron–Brown Co., 92 F.R.D. 32, 50 (E.D.Va.1981).

53. E.g., In re Texas Int'l Sec. Litig., 114 F.R.D. 33, 46 (W.D.Okla.1987).

54. Christiana Mortgage Corp. v. Delaware Mortg. Bankers Ass'n, 136 F.R.D. 372, 378 (D.Del.1991) (class action inappropriate where claims of 28 mortgage brokers can be adjudicated through joinder).

55. George v. Beneficial Fin. Co. of Dallas, 81 F.R.D. 4, 7 (N.D.Tex.1977).

56. See Castano v. American Tobacco Co., 84 F.3d 734, 750 (5th Cir.1996) (individual trials may establish general causation and pare down plaintiffs' claims to the strongest causes of action); Butt v. Allegheny Pepsi–Cola Bottling Co., 116 F.R.D. 486, 493 (E.D.Va.1987).

mechanism appropriate where notification to the class posed a signifi-cant threat to the defendant's business, where defendant's customers would likely withhold their payments due under their rent-to-own con-tracts if they received notice of the class action.[57] Of course, this approach depends on having a plaintiff willing to bring suit[58] and an attorney willing to commence litigation.[59] The test-case mechanism can be counter-productive, however, if a defendant can avoid a binding ruling on liability by entering into a settlement with the individual bringing the suit. In these circumstances, the purpose of the test case would not be served, and other potential claimants still would need to file their own actions. By settling with the claimants having the resources to bring suit, a defendant could leave the rest of the potential class without a test case basis for their suits.[60] Accordingly, if the parties are entering into an agreement under which a test case is to be used as a substitute for a class action, they may wish to address whether, under what circum-stances, and with what impact on other similarly situated claimants the defendant may settle the designated test case.

(b) Factors to Be Considered in Making Such Findings

In determining whether Rule 23(b)(3)'s predominance and superiori-ty requirements have been satisfied, a court may consider a variety of factors, including four specific factors set out in the text of the Rule:

(A) the interest of members of the class in individually controlling the prosecution or defense of separate actions; (B) the extent and nature of any litigation concerning the controversy already com-menced by or against members of the class; (c) the desirability or undesirability of concentrating the litigation of the claims in the particular forum; (D) the difficulties likely to be encountered in the management of a class action.[61]

The four factors enumerated in the text of the Rule were not intended to be exhaustive. Rather, the Rule declares that these factors are "perti-nent" to the findings of predominance and superiority, and leaves open the possibility that the court will consider others as well.[62] The Rule does not require specific findings with respect to any of the factors.

---

57. Fogie v. Rent–A–Center, Inc., 867 F.Supp. 1398, 1404 (D.Minn.1993), *aff'd sub nom.* Fogie v. THORN Americas, Inc., 95 F.3d 645 (8th Cir.1996), *cert. denied,* ___ U.S. ___, 117 S.Ct. 1427, 137 L.Ed.2d 536 (1997).

58. Brown v. Cameron–Brown Co., 92 F.R.D. 32, 50 (E.D.Va.1981) (test case inap-propriate because no plaintiff willing to in-dividually institute action).

59. Eisen v. Carlisle & Jacquelin, 417 U.S. 156, 161, 94 S.Ct. 2140, 2145, 40 L.Ed.2d 732 (1974) (attorney probably would not take on complex antitrust case where individual's stake is negligible; eco-nomic reality thus may dictate a class ac-tion).

60. 1 Newberg, *supra* note 22, § 4.27, at 4–111.

61. *See* FRCP 23(b)(3)(A–D).

62. Walco Investments, Inc. v. Thenen, 168 F.R.D. 315, 337 (S.D.Fla.1996) (factors are discretionary).

(1) Interest of Class Members in Individual Control of Action

Individual interests a court may consider include emotional involvement, the size of individual damage claims, and the possible need to tailor trial tactics to distinct claims.[63] The interest addressed in Rule 23(b)(3)(A) does not refer merely to some individuals' desire to bring separate suits; rather, the Rule focuses on the efficient and effective conduct of litigation and directs a court to weigh the advantages of individual control of separate actions versus the advantages of a class action.[64]

Where individuals have claims of varying degrees of strength, they may not have common interests, and individual control over litigation may be preferable.[65] The number of individual suits filed compared to the class size also may reflect the degree of individual interest in controlling the litigation; when no other potential class member has filed an individual action, the interest in individual control is not likely to be great.[66] Similarly, relatively little opposition from other class members to class certification may indicate little interest in individual control.[67] Class certification may, however, attract excessive numbers of weak claims from otherwise content persons who may seek to join the class and share in a settlement.[68]

63. *See In re* Three Mile Island Litig., 87 F.R.D. 433, 442 & n. 16 (M.D.Pa.1980) (individual actions appropriate where personal nature of injuries evince high degree of emotional involvement); Stoudt v. E.F. Hutton & Co., 121 F.R.D. 36, 38 (S.D.N.Y. 1988) ("When the size of each claim is significant and each proposed class member therefore possesses the ability to assert an individual claim, the goal of obtaining redress can be accomplished without the use of the class action device. The Rule was not designed to permit large claimants, who are fully capable of proceeding on their own, to strengthen their bargaining position by threatening their adversaries with the prospect of class-wide relief and large attorney fee awards."; *In re* Northern Dist. of Cal., Dalkon Shield IUD Prods. Liab. Litig., 693 F.2d 847, 852–53, 856 (9th Cir.1982) (separate suits superior due to distinct facts with respect to individual claims) ("Dalkon Shield"), *cert. denied sub nom.* A.H. Robins Co., Inc. v. Abed, 459 U.S. 1171, 103 S.Ct. 817, 74 L.Ed.2d 1015 (1983).

64. Klamberg v. Roth, 473 F.Supp. 544, 559 (S.D.N.Y.1979) (noting advantages of class action, especially in light of class members' opt-out opportunity).

65. *In re* "Agent Orange" Prod. Liab. Litig., 818 F.2d 145, 165–66 (2d Cir.1987) (upholding certification despite noting problems of varying strength of claims) ("Agent Orange"), *cert. denied sub nom.* Pinkney v. Dow Chem. Co., 484 U.S. 1004, 108 S.Ct. 695, 98 L.Ed.2d 648 (1988); Dalkon Shield, 693 F.2d at 853, 856 (class certification denied); *cf.* Epstein v. MCA, Inc., 50 F.3d 644, 668 (9th Cir.1995) (little interest in individual control where claims rely on same facts and law).

66. *See* Riordan v. Smith Barney, 113 F.R.D. 60, 66 (N.D.Ill.1986).

67. Central Wesleyan College v. W.R. Grace & Co., 143 F.R.D. 628, 640 (D.S.C. 1992), *aff'd*, 6 F.3d 177 (4th Cir.1993) (few members indicating intention to opt-out suggests class action is superior); Riordan, 113 F.R.D. at 66.

68. *See* "Agent Orange," 818 F.2d at 166–67 (upholding certification despite noting possible excessive number of weak claimants joining class and possibly diluting settlement).

(2) Nature and Extent of Preexisting Litigation Involving Class Members

The pendency of individual actions, particularly if the number of such actions is large or if one or more such actions is far advanced, may have substantial bearing on the class certification decision. An assessment of preexisting suits may demonstrate the feasibility of alternatives to the class action,[69] or it may tend to show that a class action is the only effective means of resolving a large number of very similar claims on a cost-efficient basis. At least one court has rejected the argument that the existence of pending lawsuits indicates a high likelihood of opt-out plaintiffs, who would undermine the stability of the class.[70] On the other hand, certifying an additional class may be unnecessary if one or more other such actions is already pending.[71]

(3) Desirability or Undesirability of Concentrating Litigation in a Single Forum

This factor's assessment generally proceeds along lines similar to change of venue determinations.[72] Geographical dispersion of class members and witnesses may make concentration in a single forum undesirable.[73] Some courts, however, have found that geographical dispersion provides more reason to use the class action device.[74] Additionally, concentration has been found appropriate where all members' claims turn on the same facts and law.[75]

(4) Difficulties of Managing Class Actions

This is probably the most heavily litigated factor of those enumerated in Rule 23(b)(3).[76] Manageability is a factual issue left to the discretion of the court.[77] Virtually any practical problems regarding the conduct or effect of class actions may be considered under this factor.[78] The

---

69. See Kurczi v. Eli Lilly & Co., 160 F.R.D. 667, 680 (N.D.Ohio 1995) (existence of parallel state lawsuits filed by majority of plaintiffs weighs against class action).

70. See In re Crazy Eddie Sec. Litig., 135 F.R.D. 39, 41 (E.D.N.Y.1991).

71. Mitchell v. Texas Gulf Sulphur Co., 446 F.2d 90, 107 (10th Cir.) (certification properly denied where two similar class actions already proceeding in other districts), cert. denied, 404 U.S. 1004, 92 S.Ct. 564, 30 L.Ed.2d 558 (1971); cf. Pennsylvania v. Budget Fuel Co., Inc., 122 F.R.D. 184, 185 (E.D.Pa.1988) (class action deemed inferior where government bringing suit on same issue).

72. See, e.g., Ikonen v. Hartz Mountain Corp., 122 F.R.D. 258, 266 (S.D.Cal.1988).

73. State Sec. Ins. Co. v. Frank B. Hall & Co. Inc., 95 F.R.D. 496, 499 (N.D.Ill. 1982); Causey v. Pan Am. World Airways,

Inc., 66 F.R.D. 392, 398–99 (E.D.Va.1975) (denying certification where parties were from different states and countries).

74. Law v. Nat'l Collegiate Athletic Ass'n, 167 F.R.D. 178, 182 (D.Kan.1996); Riordan v. Smith Barney, 113 F.R.D. 60, 66 (N.D.Ill.1986) (concentration in single forum appropriate where parties were geographically dispersed because single court was already familiar with issues).

75. See Epstein v. MCA, Inc., 50 F.3d 644, 668 (9th Cir.1995).

76. 5 Moore's, supra note 6, § 23.49[5][a], at 23–266.

77. Windham v. American Brands, Inc., 565 F.2d 59, 65 (4th Cir.1977), cert. denied, 435 U.S. 968, 98 S.Ct. 1605, 56 L.Ed.2d 58 (1978).

78. Andrews v. American Tel. & Tel. Co., 95 F.3d 1014, 1023 (11th Cir.1996).

fact that a case presents novel issues does not mean it would be unmanageable as a class action.[79] The mere fact that a case may be difficult to try on a class basis[80] may not be enough to demonstrate that a class action will be unmanageable.[81] The court should focus on actual problems rather than speculative problems that may appear.[82] Although management difficulties can outweigh the benefits of a class action, some courts have been reluctant to deny class certification on manageability grounds.[83]

Among the considerations that bear on the manageability of a class action are whether the class is finite and easily identifiable;[84] whether the potential class members can be contacted;[85] whether the location of class members is known;[86] the size of individual claims;[87] and whether the potential class members are hostile to certification.[88]

The issue of predominance is also often discussed in terms of manageability.[89] Consistent with the Fourth Circuit's approach in *Windham v. American Brands, Inc.*, the court in *Butt v. Allegheny Pepsi–Cola Bottling Co.*,[90] concluded that an antitrust class action would be unmanageable where proof of both fact of injury and amount of damages was "highly individualized and complex." Differing state law applications for various claimants also may make a class action unmanageable.[91] Some courts have found a case unmanageable when the number of individual

79. Bower v. Bunker Hill Co., 114 F.R.D. 587, 596 (E.D.Wash.1986).

80. *See* Buford v. H & R Block, Inc., 168 F.R.D. 340, 363 (S.D.Ga.1996); Goldwater v. Alston & Bird, 116 F.R.D. 342, 356 (S.D.Ill. 1987).

81. *See, e.g., In re* Domestic Air Transp. Antitrust Litig., 137 F.R.D. 677, 694 (N.D.Ga.1991) (class of 12.5 million claimants will not be precluded "unless the only conclusion the Court is able to reach is that the action is unmanageable").

82. *See* Windham, 565 F.2d at 70.

83. Six (6) Mexican Workers v. Arizona Citrus Growers, 904 F.2d 1301, 1305 (9th Cir.1990) (certifying class despite noting that high costs of managing class may outweigh small potential individual recovery); Coleman v. Cannon Oil Company, 141 F.R.D. 516, 526 (M.D.Ala.1992); *In re* Workers' Compensation, 130 F.R.D. 99, 110 (D.Minn.1990). *But see, e.g.,* Gaffney v. United States, 834 F.Supp. 1, 6 (D.D.C. 1993) (difficulties with notification and opt-out procedures are factors in denying certification).

84. Ouellette v. International Paper Co., 86 F.R.D. 476, 483 (D.Vt.1980), *aff'd,* 776 F.2d 55 (2d Cir.1985), *cert. denied,* 475 U.S. 1081, 106 S.Ct. 1457, 89 L.Ed.2d 715 (1986).

85. Mateo v. M/S KISO, 805 F.Supp. 761, 774 (N.D.Cal.1991) (certification denied because too difficult to communicate with class of seamen at sea).

86. *See* Riordan v. Smith Barney, 113 F.R.D. 60, 66 (N.D.Ill.1986).

87. *See* Anderson v. Bank of South, N.A., 118 F.R.D. 136, 150 (M.D.Fla.1987).

88. *See* Riordan, 113 F.R.D. at 66.

89. *E.g.,* Windham v. American Brands, Inc., 565 F.2d 59, 68–70 (4th Cir.1977), *cert. denied,* 435 U.S. 968, 98 S.Ct. 1605, 56 L.Ed.2d 58 (1978) (separate trials for individual damages issues in antitrust case presented unmanageable difficulties); *see also* Zimmerman v. Bell, 800 F.2d 386, 390 (4th Cir.1986); Mattoon v. City of Pittsfield, 128 F.R.D. 17, 21 (D.Mass.1989); *but see, e.g.,* Brown v. Cameron–Brown Co., 92 F.R.D. 32, 48 (E.D.Va.1981) (*Windham* case distinguished as "presenting a set of uniquely intertwined facts").

90. *See* 116 F.R.D. 486, 493 (E.D.Va. 1987); *see also In re* Tetracycline Cases, 107 F.R.D. 719, 735 (W.D.Mo.1985).

91. *See In re* American Med. Sys., Inc., 75 F.3d 1069, 1085 (6th Cir.1996); McBride v. Galaxy Carpet Mills, Inc., 920 F.Supp. 1278, 1286 (N.D.Ga.1995).

issues would require a significant number of separate trials.[92] Other courts have certified classes despite the need for separate trials on certain issues.[93] The Seventh Circuit has held that where an appellee argued unmanageableness as an alternative ground for upholding a district court's denial of class certification, and appellant in her reply brief did not deny that a class action would be unmanageable, denial of class certification must be affirmed. In so holding, the Seventh Circuit commented that it is conceivable that if the district judge had explored manageability he would have found the problem to be less serious than the appellee claimed.[94]

Where damage calculations on an individual basis would be prohibitively burdensome, due to complexities in calculations or large numbers of unclaimed damages, some courts have been willing to consider a "fluid recovery" or "cy pres" method to manage a class action. Under the "fluid recovery method," a court might award damages to the class as a unit, without requiring individual proof of damages; individual damages are then satisfied out of this pot.[95] Such a recovery method, however, has been rejected by most federal courts, unless it is part of a distribution arising out of a settlement.[96] A more accepted recovery method, which is generally known as the "cy pres" remedy,[97] involves the funding of a project likely to benefit the class members. For example, in *Six (6) Mexican Workers v. Arizona Citrus Growers*[98], the court recognized that there would be numerous unlocated class members, and ordered all unclaimed funds over $50,000 to go to a foundation that operates human assistance projects in areas where many of the plaintiffs are believed to reside.

Practitioners bringing a multifarious class action case should point out that class actions are inherently complex, and that many courts have

92. *See* Andrews v. American Tel. & Tel. Co., 95 F.3d 1014, 1023 (11th Cir. 1996); Castano v. American Tobacco Co., 84 F.3d 734, 745 n. 19 (5th Cir.1996); *In re* American Med. Sys., Inc., 75 F.3d at 1085.

93. *E.g., In re* A.H. Robins Co., Inc., 880 F.2d 709, 740 (4th Cir.), *cert. denied sub nom.* Anderson v. Aetna Cas. & Sur. Co., 493 U.S. 959, 110 S.Ct. 377, 107 L.Ed.2d 362 (1989); De La Fuente v. Stokely–Van Camp, Inc., 713 F.2d 225, 233 (7th Cir. 1983); Central Wesleyan College v. W.R. Grace & Co., 143 F.R.D. 628, 641–42 (D.S.C.1992).

94. Hardy v. City Optical, Inc., 39 F.3d 765, 771 (7th Cir.1994).

95. *See* Moore's, *supra* note 6, § 23.49(c)(5), at 23–271.

96. *See* Beecher v. Able, 575 F.2d 1010, 1016 n. 3 (2d Cir.1978) ("fluid" recovery proper where case involved a settlement agreement and defendant had agreed to some "fluidity" with respect to the individ-

ual class members' recovery); Eisen v. Carlisle & Jacquelin, 479 F.2d 1005, 1010 (2d Cir.1973) (denying fluid recovery and noting that case allowing such recovery involved a settlement), *vacated on other grounds,* 417 U.S. 156, 94 S.Ct. 2140, 40 L.Ed.2d 732 (1974).

97. The terms "cy press" and "fluid recovery" are sometimes used interchangeably. *See, e.g.,* 7A Charles A. Wright, Arthur R. Miller & Mary Kay Kane, Federal Practice and Procedure § 1784, at 83 (2d ed. 1986).

98. 904 F.2d 1301, 1307 (9th Cir.1990). *See also In re* "Agent Orange" Prod. Liability Litig., 818 F.2d 179, 186 (2d Cir.1987) (eliminating a private foundation financed from remaining settlement monies and ruling that the district court should manage the funds for projects that would benefit the defined class as precisely as possible), *cert. denied sub nom.* Krupkin v. Dow Chemical Co., 487 U.S. 1234, 108 S.Ct. 2899, 101 L.Ed.2d 932 (1988).

certified seemingly unmanageable class claims.[99] Plaintiffs' counsel should be prepared to explain various management techniques that can help eliminate such complexity, such as bifurcated trials for liability and damages, use of special masters or magistrates, and use of liaison or lead counsel for the parties.[100] Finally, plaintiffs' counsel can advocate a flexible approach for the court—if the litigation proves unmanageable, the class can always be limited or the proceedings can be modified to eliminate the problem.[101]

Practitioners opposing a class action on manageability grounds should look to any possible problem that may render the class action unmanageable. Such common problems, which are discussed above, include obstacles in identifying and/or notifying the entire class and difficulties in computing damages. Defendants' counsel should also attempt to demonstrate why other procedures for resolving the class claims are more fair and efficient. Finally, defense counsel should ensure that their clients do not take actions that would make the adjudication of the class action more difficult, because such actions may adversely affect presumptions concerning manageability.[102]

Library References:
West's Key No. Digests, Federal Civil Procedure ⌖180.
Wright, Miller & Kane, Federal Practice and Procedure: Civil 2d §§ 1777–1784.

§ 15.6   Basic Due Process Issues in Class Litigation

At least where a claim for legal relief in the form of money damages is at stake, each class member's interest in litigation is presumptively sufficient to constitute a property interest for the purposes of the Due Process Clause. In adjudicating such interests, where the interest holders are not fully "present" in the traditional model of two-party litigation, class actions present some unique constitutional issues. Cases addressing constitutional concerns in this context have delineated a number of separate threads of due process analysis that must be considered, under the rubrics of personal jurisdiction, adequacy of representation, and adequacy of notice.

99. See In re Antibiotic Antitrust Actions, 333 F.Supp. 278, 287–89 (S.D.N.Y. 1971) (certifying class where seven states each represented two classes, one composed of governmental entities within the state, and another composed of all retail purchasers of drugs for human consumption within the state); Illinois v. Harper Row Publishers, Inc., 301 F.Supp. 484, 495 (N.D.Ill. 1969) (class action permitted where more than 40 separate antitrust actions were brought in eight judicial districts against 37 defendants).

100. 1 Newberg, supra note 22, § 4.32 at 4–134.

101. See Brady v. LAC, Inc., 72 F.R.D. 22, 29 (S.D.N.Y.1976) (class conditionally

certified so that court could amend its order if individual issues became more significant).

102. See Appleton Elec. Co. v. Advance–United Expressways, 494 F.2d 126, 135 (7th Cir.1974) (rejecting argument that difficulties in notification made class unmanageable where defendants, who had early notice of their possible liability, destroyed records of transactions with plaintiffs); see also Arizona Citrus Growers, 904 F.2d at 1307 (finding manageability where the potential for numerous unlocated class members was largely attributable to defendant's own failure to record and retain the addresses of its workers as required by law.).

(a) Personal Jurisdiction

Class actions raise questions concerning personal jurisdiction over plaintiffs. This is not an issue in most litigation, where plaintiffs obviously consent to personal jurisdiction in the forum by initiating proceedings in that forum. Absent class members do not choose the forum, however, and issues therefore arise as to the circumstances under which absent persons can be deemed to have consented to the jurisdiction of the forum.

In *Phillips Petroleum Co. v. Shutts*,[1] the Supreme Court concluded that a state court could not bind a nonresident class member to a judgment on a damage claim rendered in personam without affording minimal procedural due process protections. In *Phillips Petroleum*, class members were given the opportunity to exclude themselves from the litigation, but had not been required to assent affirmatively to personal jurisdiction. While concluding that the "minimum contacts" analysis of *International Shoe Co. v. State of Washington*,[2] and its progeny is not fully applicable to absent plaintiffs, the Court went on to note that such class members nevertheless must at a minimum be afforded an opportunity to exclude themselves from the action.

Phillips Petroleum leaves room for argument that absent class members may nevertheless be bound to monetary judgments in some cases even if no opt-out right was provided. In particular, *Phillips Petroleum* does not compel the conclusion that as a constitutional matter a *federal* court is inevitably foreclosed from adjudicating a damage claim of an out of state plaintiff that arises under *federal* law, unless that plaintiff has been given the opportunity to "opt-out" as would be the case in an action certified under Rule 23(b)(3). If Congress has indicated that nonresident *defendants* may be subject to personal jurisdiction in federal court under a given statute, *Phillips Petroleum* should not require that nonresident plaintiff class members be afforded broader rights as a matter of due process.

Judge Weinstein has observed that "[t]he standard jurisdictional formulations are, after all, the product of traditional cases which were not decided with mass litigation in mind."[3] Class actions also may present unusual problems with respect to personal jurisdiction over defendants, particularly where jurisdiction is based upon "specific contacts" analysis. The "specific contacts" that form the basis for personal jurisdiction over the defendant with respect to (for example) the representative plaintiff's claim may be insufficient in normal circumstances to justify personal jurisdiction over the defendant for the purposes of some or all absent class members' claims.

§ 15.6

1. 472 U.S. 797, 105 S.Ct. 2965, 86 L.Ed.2d 628 (1985).

2. 326 U.S. 310, 66 S.Ct. 154, 90 L.Ed. 95 (1945).

3. *In re* DES Cases, 789 F.Supp. 552, 576 (E.D.N.Y.1992).

(b) Adequacy of Representation

Adequacy of representation has long been regarded as the central touchstone of due process in the class action context.[4] At a minimum, adequacy in the constitutional sense requires a determination that the interests of absent class members are sufficiently closely aligned with the interests of their representatives that it is fundamentally fair to bind the former to the results of litigation conducted by the latter. The closely related requirements of typicality and adequacy of representation in Rule 23(a) of the Federal Rules of Civil Procedure are designed to meet this underlying constitutional concern.

One important consequence of this constitutional concern may be to limit the merger effect of class judgments. In traditional res judicata analysis all claims a plaintiff has brought or that could have been brought by plaintiff based on the transaction or transactions from which the cause of action arose are presumed to be merged into the judgment rendered in the plaintiff's suit.[5] Although the Supreme Court has observed that "[b]asic principles of res judicata (merger and bar or claim preclusion) and collateral estoppel (issue preclusion) apply" in class litigation,[6] it may be inappropriate to take this statement literally. The constitutional foundation underlying the requirement of adequacy of representation may preclude the full operation of merger principles where, for example, the named plaintiff is an adequate representative only as to certain specified claims among the many claims that absent class members might be capable of asserting (based on their own particular facts). Moreover, merger principles should not logically apply where class certification is limited to specified claims.

This principle may have particular importance where class plaintiffs' claims have been consciously cast in such a way as to maximize the likelihood of class certification, by excluding liability theories dependent on individualized facts that absent class members might pursue if they filed individual cases. Even if the order certifying the class does not by its terms exclude such theories, constitutional barriers may preclude resolution of such theories on a representative basis. When this happens, the superiority of the class device can be greatly undermined.

(c) Adequacy of Notice

Absent class members and parties opposing classes share an interest in adequate notice. Although Rule 23(c)(2) provides for mandatory notice in actions certified under Rule 23(b)(3), and Rule 23(e) requires notice to class members whenever a certified class action is compromised or settled, *actual* notice traditionally has not been regarded as a constitu-

---

4. *See* Hansberry v. Lee, 311 U.S. 32, 61 S.Ct. 115, 85 L.Ed. 22 (1940); *cf.* Richards v. Jefferson County, 517 U.S. 793, 116 S.Ct. 1761, 135 L.Ed.2d 76 (1996).

5. *See* Restatement (Second) of Judgments, §§ 18, 24 (1982).

6. Cooper v. Federal Reserve Bank of Richmond, 467 U.S. 867, 874, 104 S.Ct. 2794, 2798, 81 L.Ed.2d 718 (1984).

tional prerequisite to binding absent persons to judgment. Rather, where Rule 23 requires notice, "the best notice practicable under the circumstances" has been deemed procedurally sufficient.[7] Notice by publication has frequently been deemed adequate where individual notice by first-class mail was not feasible.

The Supreme Court's decision in *Phillips Petroleum Co. v. Shutts* underscored the importance of notice—with a concomitant opportunity to opt-out—in cases involving monetary claims pursued on behalf of out of state plaintiffs. Indeed, to the extent that that decision is based on the notion that absent class members consent to personal jurisdiction, *Phillips Petroleum* logically may suggest an exception to the general principle that actual notice is not required, in that consent cannot logically be inferred from notice not actually received.

Moreover, to the extent an opportunity to be heard ultimately may be regarded as necessary to provide full protection to absent class members under the Due Process Clause, actual notice will become increasingly important.[8] Absent actual notice, class members may be deprived of a procedurally adequate opportunity to participate in the pursuit or defense of their claims. Only time will tell whether increased judicial scrutiny of issues of proper notice will have a significant impact on the class certification process. Practitioners must in the meantime be alert to the fact that inadequate notice is a common basis for collateral attacks on class judgments.

Library References:

West's Key No. Digests, Constitutional Law ⚷309(1.5); Federal Civil Procedure ⚷161–189.

Wright, Miller & Kane, Federal Practice and Procedure: Civil 2d § 1786.

§ 15.7   Procedure for Determining Whether Action Should Be Maintained as Class Action

(a) Timing

FRCP 23(c)(1) states that "[a]s soon as practicable after the commencement of an action brought as a class action, the court shall determine by order whether it is to be so maintained." Although the Rule leaves the precise timing of the certification decision to the discretion of the court,[1] the requirement that the determination be made as soon as practicable is mandatory.[2] In the rare instance, a court may

---

7. *See generally* Eisen v. Carlisle & Jacquelin, 417 U.S. 156, 172–77, 94 S.Ct. 2140, 2150–52, 40 L.Ed.2d 732 (1974).

8. In *Amchem Products, Inc. v. Windsor,* __ U.S. __, 117 S.Ct. 2231, 138 L.Ed.2d 689 (1997), the Supreme Court noted but did not reach serious questions regarding the adequacy of the notice provided in that litigation, notwithstanding the absence of any suggestion that better notice could have

been provided, under the circumstances presented.

§ 15.7

1. Montelongo v. Meese, 803 F.2d 1341, 1351 (5th Cir.1986).

2. *In re* General Motors Corp. Pick–Up Truck Fuel Tank Prod. Liab. Litig., 55 F.3d 768, 787 (3d Cir.1995) (stating that Rule 23

reach its decision on certification based on the pleadings alone.[3] Thus, a party seeking to certify a class must raise the issue at the outset of litigation in a well-pleaded complaint that alleges all the facts needed to demonstrate that the prerequisites for a class action have been met.[4] After the complaint is filed, judicial consideration of the issue of class certification usually occurs as a result of a motion for an order certifying the class.[5] Failure to follow the procedures specified in a jurisdiction's local rules governing such motions may jeopardize court consideration of certification.[6]

Although the timing of class certification must be as soon as practicable, there is no ultimate limit on the amount of time the court, in its discretion, may allot to properly consider the issue.[7] A certification order may be conditional and may be altered or amended at any time before the final decision in the case.[8] It is also within the trial court's

does not authorize the deferral of class certification pending settlement discussions).

3. Huff v. N. D. Cass Co. of Ala., 485 F.2d 710 (5th Cir.1973); Hyatt v. United Aircraft Corp., 50 F.R.D. 242 (D.Conn.1970) (refusing to certify plaintiff's race discrimination suit as a class action based on pleadings alone).

4. *In re* American Med. Sys., Inc., 75 F.3d 1069, 1083 (6th Cir.1996); *cf.* Eisen v. Carlisle & Jacquelin, 391 F.2d 555, 562 (2d Cir.1968) (holding that a plaintiff need not name all of the members of the class in the complaint).

5. East Texas Motor Freight System Inc. v. Rodriguez, 431 U.S. 395, 404–05, 97 S.Ct. 1891, 1897, 52 L.Ed.2d 453 (failure of named plaintiffs to move for class certification "surely bears strongly on the adequacy of the representation that those class members might expect to receive"); Trotter v. Klincar, 748 F.2d 1177, 1185 (7th Cir.1984) (upholding denial of certification where named party never moved to certify class); *but see* Bieneman v. City of Chicago, 838 F.2d 962, 963 (7th Cir.1988) (rejecting district court's determination that it need not reach certification issue in the absence of a proper motion); Senter v. General Motors Corp., 532 F.2d 511, 520–21 (6th Cir.1976) (stating that district court must decide class certification issue even if plaintiff does not move for certification).

6. Davis v. Buffalo Psychiatric Center, 613 F.Supp. 462, 464 (W.D.N.Y.1985) (denying class certification for failure to move for class certification within 60 days of filing complaint as required by Local Rule 8(c)); Walton v. Eaton Corp., 563 F.2d 66, 74–75 (3d Cir.1977) (en banc) (holding that order

denying class certification was appropriate where plaintiff violated Local Rule 45(c) requiring a motion for class certification within 90 days of filing of complaint); *see also* Commander Properties Corp. v. Beech Aircraft Corp., 164 F.R.D. 529, 534 (D.Kan. 1995) (requiring that the complaint contain a definition of the proposed class under Local Rule 23.1(a)(2)(A)). *Cf.* Slanina v. William Penn Parking Corp., 106 F.R.D. 419, 422 (W.D.Pa.1984) (the local rule must yield if its requirements conflict with Rule 23).

7. Montelongo v. Meese, 803 F.2d 1341, 1351 (5th Cir.1986) (decision to certify made three years after institution of suit), *cert. denied*, 481 U.S. 1048, 107 S.Ct. 2179, 95 L.Ed.2d 835 (1987).

8. As the Advisory Committee Note to the 1966 amendment to Rule 23 states, "Subdivision (d)(3) reflects the possibility of conditioning the maintenance of a class action, *e.g.*, on the strength of the representation . . . and recognizes that the imposition of conditions or intervenors may be required for the proper and efficient conduct of the action." *See, e.g., In re* American Honda Motor Co., Inc., 979 F.Supp. 365 (D.Md.1997) (certifying class on the condition that 1) plaintiffs redefine class membership, 2) each member of class file a direct action within the applicable statute of limitations period, and 3) the issue addressed in the class action phase be limited to liability and not address damages); Cullen v. New York State Civil Serv. Comm'n, 435 F.Supp. 546, 563–64 (E.D.N.Y.), *appeal dismissed*, 566 F.2d 846 (2d Cir.1977) (conditioning class certification on the appointment of new counsel so

discretion to revisit its certification decision at any time. The court may consider sua sponte the possibility of certifying a class where the interests of justice require.[9] A court may decertify a class when it appears that the requisites of Rule 23 are no longer met.[10] A class may even be decertified after trial.[11] The timing of such decisions will be a ground for reversal only if it constitutes an abuse of discretion.[12]

As a general matter, a trial court may dispose of a case prior to deciding the certification issue.[13] At times, however, trial courts have been criticized for dismissing an action before determining whether the rights of a class are truly at issue.[14] Such dismissals are said to run counter to the trial court's obligation to decide the question of class certification "as soon as practicable."[15] A defendant therefore must carefully weigh the timing of a dispositive motion. Although dismissal before certification may reduce costs in the particular litigation, dismissal after certification may prove more cost-effective in the long run, by precluding future claims on the same cause of action.

(b) Discovery

District courts are afforded wide latitude in determining the necessity and scope of discovery for purposes of deciding class certification issues.[16] Still, a failure to allow any discovery at all with respect to class certification may well constitute an abuse of discretion.[17] Ideally, discovery going to class certification should be limited to certification issues, and discovery going to the merits of the action should be postponed, or at least limited to nonclass issues (most typically, the facts and circumstances regarding the claim of the named plaintiff), until after the certification decision has been made.[18] As a practical matter, however, such bifurcation may be difficult, since information relevant to class

---

as to assure adequate representation of the absent members of the class).

9. Bieneman, 838 F.2d at 963.

10. Forehand v. Florida State Hosp. at Chattahoochee, 89 F.3d 1562, 1566 (11th Cir.1996) (upholding decertification of class action in Title VII suit filed by black employees against the state hospital where, notwithstanding the fact that the suit had been filed 10 years earlier and had already gone to trial, the definition of class membership was overbroad).

11. Roby v. St. Louis Southwestern Ry. Co., 775 F.2d 959, 962 (8th Cir.1985).

12. Shapiro v. Midwest Rubber Reclaiming Co., 626 F.2d 63, 71 (8th Cir.1980).

13. Floyd v. Bowen, 833 F.2d 529, 534–35 (5th Cir.1987); Christensen v. Kiewit–Murdock Inv. Corp., 815 F.2d 206, 214 (2d Cir.), cert. denied, 484 U.S. 908, 108 S.Ct. 250, 98 L.Ed.2d 209 (1987).

14. Schwarzschild v. Tse, 69 F.3d 293, 295 (9th Cir.1995), cert. denied, 517 U.S. 1121, 116 S.Ct. 1355, 134 L.Ed.2d 523 (1996); Koch v. Stanard, 962 F.2d 605, 607 (7th Cir.1992).

15. Bieneman, 838 F.2d at 964 (holding that FRCP 23(c)(1) would seem to require addressing class certification before reaching the merits of the suit).

16. Villar v. Crowley Maritime Corp., 990 F.2d 1489, 1495 (5th Cir.1993), cert. denied, 510 U.S. 1044, 114 S.Ct. 690, 126 L.Ed.2d 658 (1994); Stewart v. Winter, 669 F.2d 328, 331 (5th Cir.1982).

17. In re American Med. Sys., Inc., 75 F.3d 1069, 1086 (6th Cir.1996); Yaffe v. Powers, 454 F.2d 1362, 1364 (1st Cir.1972).

18. Washington v. Brown & Williamson Tobacco Corp., 959 F.2d 1566, 1570–71 (11th Cir.1992); Stewart, 669 F.2d at 331.

certification may not easily be separated from information relevant to the underlying cause of action. A precertification discovery request for information from absent class members ordinarily will be denied, unless a particularized need can be demonstrated and such discovery is not unduly burdensome on the absent member.[19] After the class has been certified, absent members may, under certain circumstances, be subject to discovery and the sanctions occasioned by failure to comply with discovery obligations.[20]

(c) Possible Need for an Evidentiary Hearing

The Federal Rules do not require an evidentiary hearing prior to a determination on class certification.[21] Such proceedings are often critical, however, to more fully inform the court's decision on the certification issue. This is especially so when discovery fails to provide dispositive evidence on the existence of a class,[22] or when an evidentiary hearing is needed to provide the parties an opportunity to be fully heard on the issue.[23] The decision on whether to conduct an evidentiary hearing is left to the discretion of the trial court.[24] Such a hearing should be limited to the class certification requirements, i.e., a court should not consider the merits of the underlying action or the likelihood of success in making the class determination.[25] Any right to an evidentiary hearing may be waived if such a hearing is not requested.[26] A court may abuse its discretion if it denies[27] or revokes[28] class certification without such a hearing. A district

19. M. Berenson Co. v. Faneuil Hall Marketplace, Inc., 103 F.R.D. 635, 637 (D.Mass.1984).

20. Brennan v. Midwestern United Life Ins. Co., 450 F.2d 999, 1004 (7th Cir.1971), cert. denied, 405 U.S. 921, 92 S.Ct. 957, 30 L.Ed.2d 792 (1972). Cf. Clark v. Universal Builders, 501 F.2d 324, 340 (7th Cir.1974) (holding that district court erred in dismissing with prejudice absent class members who failed to answer interrogatories, where district court failed to consider whether the interrogatories were necessary or whether they were designed as a tactic to take advantage of the class members or as a "mere stratagem to diminish class membership").

21. Franks v. Kroger Co., 649 F.2d 1216, 1223 (6th Cir.1981); Marcera v. Chinlund, 565 F.2d 253, 255 (2d Cir.1977).

22. Twyman v. Rockville Housing Authority, 99 F.R.D. 314, 316 (D.Md., 1983).

23. Bradford v. Sears, Roebuck & Co., 673 F.2d 792 (5th Cir.1982).

24. Grayson v. K Mart Corp., 79 F.3d 1086, 1099 (11th Cir.1996) (failure to hold evidentiary hearing "does not require reversal of the class certification unless the parties can show that the hearing, if held,

would have affected their rights substantially"). See also Burns v. Long, 44 F.3d 1031 (D.C.Cir.1994); United States v. Dynalectric Co., 859 F.2d 1559, 1580 (11th Cir. 1988) cert. denied, 490 U.S. 1006, 109 S.Ct. 1641, 104 L.Ed.2d 157 (1989).

25. See Eisen v. Carlisle & Jacquelin, 417 U.S. 156, 177, 94 S.Ct. 2140, 2152, 40 L.Ed.2d 732 (1974) (holding that the district court erred by imposing most of the cost of notice on the defendants on the basis of a finding, made after a preliminary hearing on the merits of the case, that plaintiff was "more than likely" to prevail on his claims).

26. Morrison v. Booth, 730 F.2d 642, 644 (11th Cir.1984); Marcera v. Chinlund, 565 F.2d 253, 255 (2d Cir.1977).

27. Morrison, 730 F.2d at 644; Marcera, 565 F.2d at 255.

28. Shepard v. Beaird–Poulan, Inc., 617 F.2d 87, 89 (5th Cir.1980); Guerine v. J & W Inv., Inc., 544 F.2d 863, 865 (5th Cir. 1977) (requiring that a trial judge hold an evidentiary hearing before revoking class certification on grounds that the plaintiff would not adequately represent the class' interests).

court may be reversed for premature certification if it has failed to develop a sufficient evidentiary record from which to conclude that the requirements of numerosity, typicality, commonality, and adequacy of representation have been met.[29]

(d) Appealability

Because a trial court may revisit its certification at any time, an order certifying a class action is not a "final decision" within 28 U.S.C.A. § 1291. A certification order does not fall within the "collateral order" exception to the final judgment rule.[30] The certification decision is not appealable even where denial of class certification would induce a party to discontinue its claim.[31] Some circuits hold that if, upon entry of the denial of class certification, a class representative fails to prosecute his or her individual claims and the case is dismissed for that reason, the class certification issue may then be appealed since it is deemed to have merged into the final judgment of dismissal.[32] Other circuits reject this approach.[33] A party may petition the district court to certify its decision on certification for interlocutory appeal under 28 U.S.C.A. § 1292(b).[34] A party may also apply for a writ of mandamus in extraordinary cases in which a grant or denial of class certification not only inflicts irreparable harm but also "so far exceed[s] the proper bounds" of judicial discretion as to be legitimately considered usurpative in character, or in violation of a clear and indisputable legal right, or, at the very least, patently erroneous.[35] Given this high standard, mandamus relief normally will be difficult to obtain.

Library References:

West's Key No. Digests, Federal Civil Procedure ⊕161–189.
Wright, Miller & Kane, Federal Practice and Procedure: Civil 2d § 1785.

§ 15.8   Notice to Absent Members of Rule 23(b)(3) "Opt–Out" Class

A judgment in a class action is conclusive in any subsequent dispute between a represented class member and an opposing party with regard

---

29. Sirota v. Solitron Devices, Inc., 673 F.2d 566, 571 (2d Cir.), *cert. denied,* 459 U.S. 838, 103 S.Ct. 86, 74 L.Ed.2d 80 (1982); Chateau de Ville Productions, Inc. v. Tams–Witmark Music Library, Inc., 586 F.2d 962, 966 (2d Cir.1978).

30. Coopers & Lybrand v. Livesay, 437 U.S. 463, 468–69, 98 S.Ct. 2454, 2457–58, 57 L.Ed.2d 351 (1978).

31. *Id.* at 477, 98 S.Ct. at 2462.

32. Gary Plastic Packaging Corp. v. Merrill Lynch, Pierce, Fenner & Smith, Inc., 903 F.2d 176, 179 (2d Cir.1990), *cert. denied,* 498 U.S. 1025, 111 S.Ct. 675, 112 L.Ed.2d 667 (1991).

33. Huey v. Teledyne, Inc., 608 F.2d 1234, 1240 (9th Cir.1979); Bowe v. First of Denver Mortg. Investors, 613 F.2d 798 (10th Cir.), *cert. denied,* 447 U.S. 906, 100 S.Ct. 2989, 64 L.Ed.2d 855 (1980).

34. Jenkins v. Raymark Industries, Inc., 782 F.2d 468, 471 (5th Cir.1986).

35. *In re* Rhone–Paulenc Rorer Inc., 51 F.3d 1293, 1295 (7th Cir.1995) (decertifying plaintiff class in HIV-related mass tort action); *see also In re* Fibreboard Corp., 893 F.2d 706 (5th Cir.1990).

to any issue actually litigated and essential to judgment.[1] In the Supreme Court's words, "under elementary principles of prior adjudication a judgment in a properly entertained class action is binding on class members in any subsequent litigation."[2] Such a judgment, binding absent class members and those present for the suit, disposes of every matter which was or could have been offered to sustain or defeat the class action.[3] In part because of the substantial due process concerns raised by the binding effect of class action judgments, FRCP 23(c)(2) prescribes procedures designed to provide notice to absent class members in Rule 23(b)(3) class actions.[4] These notice procedures are intended to enable absent class members to safeguard their rights. The usual rule is that a named plaintiff must bear the cost and burden of providing notice to a class that the plaintiff purports to represent.[5] In situations where the defendant may be able to perform a necessary task with less difficulty or expense than could the representative plaintiff, the district court may exercise its discretion under Rule 23(d) to order defendant to cooperate in providing the notice.

(a) Form of Notice: "Best Notice Practicable"

Rule 23 (c)(2) requires that "[i]n any class action maintained under subdivision (b)(3), the court shall direct to the members of the class the best notice practicable under the circumstances, including individual notice to all members who can be identified through reasonable effort." The Supreme Court has stated that "each class member who can be identified through reasonable effort must be notified that he may request exclusion from the action and thereby preserve his opportunity to press his claim separately or that he may remain in the class and perhaps participate in the management of the action."[6]

§ 15.8

1. Cooper v. Federal Reserve Bank of Richmond, 467 U.S. 867, 874, 104 S.Ct. 2794, 2798, 81 L.Ed.2d 718 (1984).

2. *Id.*

3. Helfand v. Cenco, Inc., 80 F.R.D. 1, 5 (N.D.Ill.1977).

4. The specific Rule 23(c)(2) procedures do not apply in the context of class actions under Rule 23(b)(1) or (b)(2). All class actions, however, are subject to the provisions of Rule 23(d)(2), which authorize the court to provide for notice "in such manner as the court may direct" to "some or all" of the absent class members so as to protect the members of the class or otherwise promote the fair conduct of the action. There has been substantial debate in the cases about the extent to which the Due Process Clause may require notice to absent class members in class actions under Rule 23(b)(1) or (b)(2). *See, e.g.,* Larionoff v.

United States, 533 F.2d 1167, 1184–87 (D.C.Cir.1976), *aff'd,* 431 U.S. 864, 97 S.Ct. 2150, 53 L.Ed.2d 48 (1977) (describing debate, citing cases, and concluding that prejudgment notice to absent class members is not constitutionally required in a Rule 23(b)(1) action). For examples of differing points of view on the due process issue in Rule 23(b)(2) actions, *compare, e.g.,* Alexander v. Aero Lodge No. 735, 565 F.2d 1364, 1373–74 (6th Cir.1977), and cases there cited (prejudgment notice not required), *with* Schrader v. Selective Serv. Sys. Local Board No. 76, 470 F.2d 73, 75 (7th Cir.), *cert. denied,* 409 U.S. 1085, 93 S.Ct. 689, 34 L.Ed.2d 672 (1972) (prejudgment notice required).

5. *E.g.,* Silber v. Mabon, 957 F.2d 697, 701 & n. 6 (9th Cir.1992).

6. Eisen v. Carlisle & Jacquelin, 417 U.S. 156, 173, 94 S.Ct. 2140, 2150, 40 L.Ed.2d 732 (1974) (rejecting argument that adequate representation of the class,

In most cases, "the best notice practicable" involves the mailing of individual notice to known class members, and then publication of notice in order to reach class members whose names and addresses are unknown.[7] In certain circumstances, however, the court may require that additional measures be taken.[8]

The notice requirements of Rule 23(c)(2) for 23(b)(3) class actions are mandatory, and may not be waived at the discretion of the district court. In *Eisen v. Carlisle & Jacquelin*,[9] for example, the United States Supreme Court held that where the names and addresses of 2,250,000 class members were easily ascertainable, individual notice to each class member was required, and could not be waived by the district court even though, as the plaintiff argued, providing such notice would be prohibitively expensive, and no absent class member so notified would have a large enough stake to justify separate litigation of his or her individual claim.[10]

rather than individual notice, is more important for due process purposes).

7. *See, e.g.*, Silber, 18 F.3d at 1453–54 (stating that notice by mail plus publication constitutes "best practicable notice"); *In re Southern Florida Waste Disposal Antitrust Litig.*, 896 F.2d 493, 494 (11th Cir.1990) (stating that in waste disposal antitrust class action, notice sent individually to all persons or entities that purchased defined waste disposal services in two county area during 10-year time period, plus publication, comported with due process); *In re Prudential Securities Inc. Ltd. Partnerships Litig.*, 164 F.R.D. 362, 368–70 (S.D.N.Y.) (establishing that in a class action for fraud brought by purchasers of limited partnership interests, due process and Rule 23 were satisfied by mailing of notice to last known address of identifiable class members, and publishing of summary notice on two occasions in national editions of Wall Street Journal, New York Times, and USA Today), *aff'd*, 107 F.3d 4 (2d Cir.1996), and *cert. denied*, ___ U.S. ___, 117 S.Ct. 2509, 138 L.Ed.2d 1013 (1997); Ikonen v. Hartz Mountain Corp., 122 F.R.D. 258, 261 (S.D.Cal.1988) (determining that in class action filed by pet owners against manufacturer of allegedly poisonous flea and tick spray, "best practicable" notice was notice by mail, publication, and radio and television broadcast); Jordan v. Global Natural Resources, Inc., 102 F.R.D. 45, 51–52 (S.D.Ohio 1984) (holding that in an action for securities fraud in which many potential class members would be unidentifiable, due process and Rule 23 were satisfied by mailing notice to those who could be identified

and by publication notice targeted at the unidentified class members).

8. *See, e.g.*, Montelongo v. Meese, 803 F.2d 1341, 1351 (5th Cir.) (determining that in a class action brought by migrant farm workers, many of whom were likely not to be proficient in English, mailing individual notices in English and Spanish, and ordering bilingual radio and newspaper announcements met the requirements of Rule 23), *reh'g denied*, 808 F.2d 56 (5th Cir. 1986), and *cert. denied*, 481 U.S. 1048, 107 S.Ct. 2179, 95 L.Ed.2d 835 (1987) Hartman v. Wick, 678 F.Supp. 312, 329–30 (D.D.C. 1988) (in an employment discrimination class action that involved numerous unidentified class members, Rule 23 would be satisfied by mailing notice, publishing notice in the largest newspapers within 18 of the largest Standard Metropolitan Statistical Areas and in newspapers and magazines where defendant advertised job openings, and posting notice in all government employment offices).

9. 417 U.S. 156, 94 S.Ct. 2140, 40 L.Ed.2d 732 (1974).

10. *Id.* at 173–76, 94 S.Ct. at 2150–52; *see also* Walsh v. Ford Motor Co., 807 F.2d 1000, 1007 (D.C.Cir.1986) (overturning district court's ruling that plaintiff class representatives need not provide individual notice to all members of proposed class in action brought for violation of Magnuson-Moss Warranty and Federal Trade Commission Improvement Act, 15 U.S.C.A. §§ 2301–2312 (West 1994); plaintiffs' financial inability to send requisite notice immaterial, because Rule 23(c)(2) requirement is

Practicability and reasonableness define the obligations under Rule 23. Class representatives must take those steps which are "practicable ... under the circumstances"[11] to ensure that individual class members receive notice. Class representatives are required to make "reasonable efforts"[12] to discover the names and addresses of individual class members. When the names and addresses of potential class members are not reasonably discoverable, constructive notice by publication may be sufficient to satisfy due process and Rule 23.[13]

In securities actions, where shares are held "in street name" by brokers or banks for beneficial owners, due process generally requires that notice be sent to the entity holding the shares, with instructions to forward it to the owner.[14] Class counsel may, however, be required to pay the holder's forwarding costs, in order to make actual notification of

unconditional, and may not be " 'tailored to fit the pocketbooks of particular plaintiffs' ") (quoting Eisen, 417 U.S. at 176, 94 S.Ct. at 2152), cert. denied, 482 U.S. 915, 107 S.Ct. 3188, 96 L.Ed.2d 677 (1987).

11. See, e.g., In re United Telecomm., Inc. Sec. Litig., 151 F.R.D. 127, 129 (D.Kan. 1993) (mem.) (upholding use of folded self-mailer format for mailing notice, in spite of defendant's contention that this format rendered the notice virtually indistinguishable from junk mail, and thus likely to be thrown away by recipient); Roberts v. Heim, 130 F.R.D. 416, 423 (N.D.Cal.1988) (holding that notice to potential class members by registered mail was not required in class actions filed by investors in limited partnerships against the partnership group, alleging violation of RICO and state and federal securities laws).

12. See, e.g., In re Southern Florida Waste Disposal Antitrust Litig., 896 F.2d 493, 494 (11th Cir.1990) (ruling that class counsel had made a "reasonable effort" to ensure that class members received notice when counsel sent notice to all persons or entities that purchased defined waste disposal services in a two county area during ten-year time period); In re Prudential Securities Inc. Ltd. Partnerships Litig., 164 F.R.D. 362, 368–70 (S.D.N.Y.) (ruling that class counsel had made a "reasonable effort" to notify class members when counsel had relied on the defendant's list of purchasers in the limited partnership which had allegedly been the subject of fraud, even though a great many class members had moved and thus did not receive actual notice), aff'd, 107 F.3d 4 (2d Cir.1996), and cert. denied, ___ U.S. ___, 117 S.Ct. 2509, 138 L.Ed.2d 1013 (1997); Sollenbarger v. Mountain States Tel. and Tel. Co., 121

F.R.D. 417, 436–37 (D.N.M.1988) (ruling that class plaintiffs, who alleged violation of federal antitrust and state contract laws with respect to inside wire maintenance service contracts, were not required to notify all of the defendant's inactive customers in light of the tremendous expense and the fact that such a method would not provide any more notice than including notice in the monthly bills sent to current customers); Wehner v. Syntex Corp., 117 F.R.D. 641 (N.D.Cal.1987) (determining, in an environmental contamination class action, that plaintiffs were required to notify only those potential class members "reasonably identifiable" consequent to the confirmation of certain hazardous waste sites).

13. See, e.g., Jordan v. Global Natural Resources, Inc., 102 F.R.D. 45, 51–52 (S.D.Ohio 1984) (rejecting defendant's claim, the fact of a foreign corporation, and existence of foreign shareholders, made effective, individual notice to each potential class member impracticable).

14. See, e.g., Silber v. Mabon, 18 F.3d 1449, 1454 (9th Cir.1994) (ruling that the beneficial owner who, as a consequence of the broker's delay, failed to receive actual notice before the opt-out deadline, was not entitled to an extension because class counsel's mailing of notice with forwarding instruction provided " 'best practicable' notice under circumstances"); Mashburn v. National Healthcare, Inc., 684 F.Supp. 660, 666 (M.D.Ala.1988) (ruling, in a securities action, that settlement notice sent to brokers with instructions to forward to beneficial owners was "best practicable" notice under circumstances); Stoller v. Baldwin–United Corp., 650 F.Supp. 341, 343–44 (S.D.Ohio 1986).

beneficial owners more probable.[15]

Notice to putative class members is not required when an action is dismissed on the merits prior to the certification of an actual class.[16] When an action is settled prior to class certification, a single notice is all that is required to advise potential class members of the pendency of the action and of the proposed settlement.[17]

For class action settlements that establish a res judicata effect for all class members, Rule 23(e) and due process require that notice of the proposed settlement be sent to absent members of the class.[18] This notice procedure serves three functions: (1) it assures that those whose rights would be affected by the settlement have the opportunity to support or oppose it;[19] (2) it protects the rights of those whose interests may not have been given due regard by the negotiating parties; it prevents private arrangements from advancing at the expense of the best interests of the class; [20] and (3) it assures each class member the right to be heard.[21]

FRCP 23(e) states: "a class action shall not be dismissed or compromised without the approval of the court, and notice of the proposed dismissal or compromise shall be given to all members of the class in such manner as the court directs." This rule leaves the mechanics of settlement notice to the discretion of the district court, subject only to the requirements of due process.[22] The notice procedures chosen by the

---

15. See, e.g., In re Victor Technologies Sec. Litig., 792 F.2d 862 , 866 (9th Cir. 1986).

16. See, e.g., Manes v. Goldin, 400 F.Supp. 23 (E.D.N.Y.1975), aff'd, 423 U.S. 1068, 96 S.Ct. 851, 47 L.Ed.2d 80 (1976); Dolgow v. Anderson, 53 F.R.D. 664 (E.D.N.Y.), aff'd, 464 F.2d 437 (2d Cir. 1972).

17. See, e.g., In re Southern Florida Waste Disposal Antitrust Litig., 896 F.2d at 494.

18. See, e.g., In re Pacific Enters. Litig., 47 F.3d 373, 377 (9th Cir.1995) (Rule 23(e) requires notice of any proposed settlement); Gottlieb v. Wiles, 11 F.3d 1004, 1007 (10th Cir.1993) (Rule 23(e) requires that class members be given notice of proposed settlement); Mayfield v. Barr, 985 F.2d 1090, 1092 (D.C.Cir.1993) (Rule 23(e) requires notice of proposed settlement to class members).

This notice requirement does not apply, however, in class actions that settle before the class is certified. See Glidden v. Chromalloy American Corp., 808 F.2d 621, 627 (7th Cir.1986) (stating that putative class members not always required to be notified of settlement); cf. Simer v. Rios, 661 F.2d 655, 665–66 (7th Cir.1981) (same, reasoning

that settlement does not have res judicata effect on absent putative class members), cert. denied, 456 U.S. 917, 102 S.Ct. 1773, 72 L.Ed.2d 177 (1982).

19. See Pearson v. Ecological Science Corp., 522 F.2d 171, 176–77 (5th Cir.1975), cert. denied, 425 U.S. 912, 96 S.Ct. 1508, 47 L.Ed.2d 762 (1976); see also Torrisi v. Tucson Elec. Power Co., 8 F.3d 1370, 1375 (9th Cir.1993) (purpose of notice "to flush out whatever objections might reasonably be raised to the settlement"), cert. denied, 512 U.S. 1220, 114 S.Ct. 2707, 129 L.Ed.2d 834 (1994).

20. See Armstrong v. Board of School Directors, 616 F.2d 305, 313 (7th Cir.1980).

21. See In re "Agent Orange" Product Liability Litigation, 597 F.Supp. 740, 758 (E.D.N.Y.1984).

22. See, e.g., DeBoer v. Mellon Mortgage Co., 64 F.3d 1171, 1176 (8th Cir.1995) (holding that the adequacy of the notice of settlement was to be left to the discretion of the trial court acting within the parameters of due process), cert. denied, 517 U.S. 1156, 116 S.Ct. 1544, 134 L.Ed.2d 648 (1996). Burns v. Elrod, 757 F.2d 151, 152–55 (7th Cir.1985) (explaining that Rule 23(e) requires settlement notice in such form "as

court need not be designed to reach every single class member.[23] They will comply with due process provided that they are reasonable in light of the circumstances.[24] A number of courts have required that settlement notices comply with the Rule 23(c)(2) standard for notice of class action pendency rather than applying the less stringent and more clearly applicable requirements of Rule 23(e).[25] Others have been careful to distinguish the pendency notice requirement of Rule 23(c)(2) and the settlement notice requirement of Rule 23(e).[26]

the court directs"); Harris v. Graddick, 615 F.Supp. 239, 244 (M.D.Ala.1985) (reiterating that the mechanics of notice process are to be left to discretion of the district court, subject only to broad due process "reasonableness standard"); In re "Agent Orange," 597 F.Supp. at 759 (stating that Rule 23(e) leaves manner of giving notice of proposed settlement to discretion of trial court).

23. See, e.g., Torrisi, 8 F.3d at 1375 (explaining that the adequacy of settlement notice procedures depends not on whether individual shareholders got notice, but rather whether a sufficient number of class members received notice so that it might reasonably be expected that all rational objections to the settlement had been raised); Battle v. Liberty Nat'l Life Ins. Co., 770 F.Supp. 1499, 1514–20 (N.D.Ala.1991) (holding that when a class was "cohesive" and the representation had been effective, individual notice to only discrete portion of known absent class members was sufficient notice under Rule 23), aff'd, 974 F.2d 1279 (11th Cir.1992), and cert. denied, 509 U.S. 906, 113 S.Ct. 2999, 125 L.Ed.2d 692 (1993).

24. See, e.g., DeBoer, 64 F.3d at 1176 (holding that notification by mail and publication directed by district court, although not "extensive," was "sufficient to comply with the strictures of due process"); Gottlieb v. Wiles, 11 F.3d 1004, 1013 (10th Cir.1993) (rejecting argument that settlement notice ordered by district court was constitutionally deficient because it did not assure individual notice even to those class members whose names and addresses were easily ascertainable); Burns, 757 F.2d at 152–53 (establishing as reasonable settlement notice procedures that included advertising in Chicago's two daily newspapers, mailing to last known address of each prospective class member, and follow-up mailing to those whose notice was returned as undeliverable yet whose address was ascertainable); Battle, 770 F.Supp. at 1514–20

(upholding, in a class action brought by burial insurance policy holders, settlement notice procedure that relied on publication and then individual notification for policyholders who were still making payments, yet did not include individual notice for class members whose policies were paid in full, on the ground that the interests of class members were "cohesive" and that representation of the class had been effective); In re "Agent Orange," 597 F.Supp. at 763 (notice of settlement by mail to all class members to whom notice of pendency of class action sent, plus all persons whose names and addresses provided through "800" number, in addition to publication, was sufficient).

25. See, e.g., Silber v. Mabon, 18 F.3d 1449, 1453 (9th Cir.1994) (determining that the mailing of over 6,000 long form settlement notices, as well as publication, constituted the best notice practicable); White v. National Football League, 822 F.Supp. 1389, 1400–01 (D.Minn.1993) (stating that mailed and published settlement notices "were reasonably calculated . . . to apprise interested parties of the proposed settlement," and thus satisfied due process and Rule 23), aff'd, 41 F.3d 402 (8th Cir.1994); In re Warner Communications Sec. Litig., 618 F.Supp. 735, 746 & n. 3 (S.D.N.Y.1985) (stating that plaintiffs' counsel "clearly complied" with obligation under 23(c)(2) to provide the " 'best notice practicable' " in securities litigation class action where counsel sent notice of settlement to more than 104,000 class members, banks, brokers, and nominees, and published notice in the New York Times and Wall Street Journal), aff'd, 798 F.2d 35 (2d Cir.1986); Mashburn v. National Healthcare, Inc., 684 F.Supp. 660, 666–67 (M.D.Ala.1988) (mem.) (determining that notice of settlement sent to over 10,-000 potential class members, plus publication in the Wall Street Journal, in securities litigation involving stock held in "street name" for anonymous beneficial owners, "constituted the best notice practicable un-

Compliance with the notice procedures that are established by the district court is what is required of class counsel in order to comply with due process.[27] Compliance with the court ordered settlement notification procedures are also governed by a rule of reason.[28] The Seventh Circuit has excused the defendants' failure to comply with several aspects of the lower court's instructions, holding that their efforts to comply were "reasonabl[e]."[29] In *Burns v. Elrod,* the district court had directed the defendants to "immediately ascertain any later known address, if any, of each prospective class member who failed to receive" the first settlement notice, and then to send a second set of notices to these addresses. The defendants took no steps to update addresses of 500 prospective class members who did not receive the first notice, and never mailed second notices to 37 of these whose addresses were discovered by the plaintiffs, choosing to notify them instead by telephone. Nevertheless, the court found that the defendants' efforts to comply with the district court's order were "reasonable."

Notice of settlement should be sent far enough in advance of the court's fairness determination hearing to allow class members a reasonable opportunity to investigate and reflect on the fairness of the proposed settlement before taking a position on it.[30] What constitutes a "reasonable" time varies from case to case.[31] In securities class actions

der the circumstances," and thus met requirements of due process and Rule 23).

26. *See, e.g.,* Gottlieb, 11 F.3d at 1013 (explaining that Rule 23(e) does not necessarily require, as does Rule 23(c)(2), individual notice when names of class members can be easily ascertained); DeBoer, 64 F.3d at 1176 (stating that notice of settlement proposal must be reasonable in order to satisfy due process).

27. *See, e.g.,* Zimmer Paper Prods., Inc. v. Berger & Montague, P.C., 758 F.2d 86, 88, 90–93 (3d Cir.) (ruling that plaintiffs' counsel did not breach fiduciary duty to member of class by failing to go beyond procedures required by court in notifying class member of proposed settlement, where procedures actually employed, first-class mail and publication, were customary and court-approved), *cert. denied,* 474 U.S. 902, 106 S.Ct. 228, 88 L.Ed.2d 227 (1985).

28. *See, e.g.,* DeBoer, 64 F.3d at 1176 (ruling that although counsel's efforts to notify absent class members were not "remarkably thorough," they were sufficient to satisfy due process; Burns, 757 F.2d at 154–55 ("rejecting suggestion of absent class members who did not receive notice because sent to old address that defendants

should have been required to search records of drivers' licenses kept by Secretary of State; although this method and other avenues of inquiry might have led to the notification of additional class members, Rule 23 does not require defendants to exhaust every conceivable method of identification"); Mashburn, 684 F.Supp. at 666–67 (holding, in securities litigation, where district court ordered individual notice of settlement by mail to absent class members whose addresses were reasonably ascertainable, plaintiffs' counsel who mailed over 10,000 settlement notice packets made reasonable effort to comply: "any additional expense in locating [additional absent class members] ... would be outweighed by the tremendous expense of doing so").

29. *See* Burns, 757 F.2d at 152–55.

30. *In re* "Agent Orange" Product Liability Litigation, 597 F.Supp. 740, 759 (E.D.N.Y.1984).

31. *Compare* Grunin v. International House of Pancakes, 513 F.2d 114, 122 (8th Cir.1975) (finding sufficient notice of proposed settlement 19 days before fairness hearing) *with* Greenfield v. Villager Indus., Inc., 483 F.2d 824 (3d Cir.1973) (allowing one month between notice and fairness

involving class members whose shares are held "in street name" by beneficial holders or nominees, the parties responsible for notifying such members are generally not held accountable for delays attributable to the fact that this arrangement adds a step to the notification process.[32]

When a settlement proposal is amended after notice is sent, due process requires that supplementary notice be provided to those absent class members whose rights are affected by the change.[33] Supplementary notice may also be appropriate when the parties or their counsel have directed unauthorized, misleading communications regarding the terms of the settlement to class members.[34] At least one court has ordered that supplementary notice be sent to those who opted-out of the settlement class, informing them of the opportunity to opt back in, where the opt-outs were geographically distributed in a "highly uneven manner," and the original notice sent was so complex as to have possibly confused many class members.[35]

hearing); White v. National Football League, 822 F.Supp. 1389, 1400 (D.Minn. 1993) (publication of notice four weeks prior to fairness hearing, and mailing of notice three weeks prior, provided dissenters sufficient opportunity to formulate and present objections; *and In re* "Agent Orange," 597 F.Supp. at 759 (determining that three months notice of settlement fairness hearing was sufficient).

32. *See, e.g.*, Silber v. Mabon, 18 F.3d 1449, 1452 (9th Cir.1994) (finding no basis for extending opt-out deadline for class action settlement for class member who received notice after opt-out deadline, where delay in receipt of settlement notice was due to inaction of the nominee for the class member's stock, and not to any failure by the party responsible for sending notice); Torrisi v. Tucson Elec. Power Co., 8 F.3d 1370, 1374–75 (9th Cir.1993) (approving timing of settlement notice, even though notice not mailed to many class members until after deadline for filing objections; delay was caused by fact that class representatives had to obtain these class members' addresses from the brokerages, banks, and institutions who held shares in their street names for the class members in question, and defendant's pending bankruptcy made prompt settlement imperative).

33. *See* White v. National Football League, 836 F.Supp. 1458, 1469 (D.Minn. 1993), *aff'd*, 41 F.3d 402 (8th Cir.1994). *But cf.* Harris v. Graddick, 615 F.Supp. 239, 244 (M.D.Ala.1985) (holding that supplementa-

ry notice to absent class members of an amendment to the consent decree was not necessary, because the amendment was "extremely narrow").

34. Georgine v. Amchem Prods., Inc., 160 F.R.D. 478, 502–03 (E.D.Pa.1995) (approving second notice of settlement to remedy damage done by misleading communications sent to class members by counsel opposing settlement). *See* Georgine v. Amchem Products, Inc., 878 F.Supp. 716, *vacated by*, 83 F.3d 610 (3d Cir.1996) *aff'd sub nom.* Amchem Products Inc. v. Windsor, ___ U.S. ___, 117 S.Ct. 2231, 138 L.Ed.2d 689 (1997).

35. *In re* Baldwin–United Corp., 607 F.Supp. 1312, 1335 (S.D.N.Y.1985). The *Baldwin* case involved 18 separate class actions, comprising over 99,000 members, that arose from the sale of single premium deferred annuities of two life insurance companies by broker dealers. *Id.* In concluding that supplementary notice was required, the court reasoned that although the "form of notice issued to the class members [was] no more complicated or extensive than the matter at hand required," and that the "total presentation of facts in any such notice is ... an essential element of due process," "[t]he risk commonly experienced, and present here, is that on receiving a sufficiently complete notice to satisfy the requirements of due process, some persons may become confused and, affected by the understandable suspicion widely held by lay persons concerning court papers, may

(b) Content of Notice

The purpose of the notice requirement, mandatory in Rule 23(b)(3) class actions, is to present a fair recital of the subject matter of the suit and to inform all class members of their opportunity to be heard.[36] Because the choices presented in a class action notice affect substantial rights, the notice must contain an adequate description of the proceedings written in objective, neutral terms that may be understood by the average absentee class member.[37] Rule 23 (c)(2) requires the court to advise each absent member of the class that (A) the court will exclude the member from the class if the member so requests by a specified date; (B) the judgment, whether favorable or not, will include all members who do not request exclusion; and (C) any member who does not request exclusion may, if the member desires, enter an appearance through counsel.

In *Phillips Petroleum Co. v. Shutts*,[38] the United States Supreme Court established the minimum content standard for class action notice under Rule 23(c)(2). It stated that such notice must be " 'reasonably calculated, under all the circumstances, to apprise interested parties of the pendency of the action and afford them an opportunity to present their objections.' "[39] It also implied that such notice must inform potential class members of their ability to "opt-out" of the class.[40]

It is the responsibility of the district courts to elaborate on these basic requirements in particular cases.[41] One court has explained that

opt-out thoughtlessly and without professional advice." *Id.*

36. *In re* Gypsum Antitrust Cases, 565 F.2d 1123, 1125 (9th Cir.1977).

37. *In re* Nissan Motor Corp. Antitrust Litig., 552 F.2d 1088, 1104 (5th Cir.1977); *In re* Agent Orange Product Liability Litig., 597 F.Supp. 740, 759 (E.D.N.Y.1984), *aff'd*, 818 F.2d 145 (2d Cir.1987), *cert. denied*, 484 U.S. 1004, 108 S.Ct. 695, 98 L.Ed.2d 648 (1988).

38. 472 U.S. 797, 105 S.Ct. 2965, 86 L.Ed.2d 628 (1985).

39. *Id.* at 812, 105 S.Ct. at 2974 (quoting Mullane v. Central Hanover Bank & Trust Co., 339 U.S. 306, 314–15, 70 S.Ct. 652, 657–58, 94 L.Ed. 865 (1950)).

40. Shutts, 472 U.S. at 810–11, 105 S.Ct. at 2973–74 (holding that due process does not require that notice to potential class members give them opportunity to opt-in to the class; rather, all that is required is that such persons be given chance to opt-out of the litigation); *see also* Maywalt v. Parker & Parsley Petroleum Co., 147 F.R.D. 51, 53 (S.D.N.Y.1993) (notice required to inform absent class members that they had 30 days in which to opt-out); Roberts v. Heim, 130 F.R.D. 416, 423 (N.D.Cal.1988) (notice must inform poten-

tial class members that they have 60–day period within which to opt-out of suit); Wehner v. Syntex Corp., 117 F.R.D. 641, 645 (N.D.Cal.1987) (notice must inform absent class members of option to be excluded from class, and that judgment will include absent class members who do not opt-out); Goldwater v. Alston & Bird, 673 F.Supp. 930, 931 (S.D.Ill.1987) (purpose of notice to inform class members of action's pendency and give them opportunity to opt-out); *cf. In re* United Telecomm., Inc. Sec. Litig., 151 F.R.D. 127, 129 (D.Kan.1993) (mem.) (attaching required opt-out form to notice itself, rather than enclosing separate opt-out form, did not violate due process; although form was physically attached to notice, it was set apart on separate page, had appearance of official document with its own caption and signature lines, and thus was not confusing or ambiguous).

41. *See, e.g.,* Schisler v. Heckler, 787 F.2d 76, 86 (2d Cir.1986) (remanding case to district court, which had not had opportunity to examine notice sent out to class members, many of whom were mentally disabled, with instructions that it ensure that the content of the notice was tailored to apprise these particular class members of the pendency of the action).

notice must provide a "balanced and detailed description of the action," including language pertaining to applicable defenses and cross-claims.[42] Another has held that where the issue of responsibility for litigation costs has not yet been determined, the notice should not contain any categorical statements of potential class members' liability or nonliability for such costs, but should instead include a paragraph informing prospective class members of the possibility that a portion of their recovery might be used to cover the costs of litigating the matter.[43] Another court has required that notice of class certification must inform potential class members of the existence of related tax cases.[44]

In general, courts have not required that plaintiffs inform potential class members of their future discovery obligations.[45] One court has rejected defendants' request that the notice sent to potential class members inform them that their failure to opt-out of the class could be interpreted as their adoption of the allegations made in the complaint, reasoning that the defendants' proposed statement would be "nebulous and prejudicial."[46] The same court also rejected the defendants' request that the notice include a "questionnaire to be answered under oath," by all class members. The court determined that such a requirement would have the effect of harassing potential class members, and altering class membership.[47]

In a class action in which the court had already found the defendant liable, the court required that the notice sent to potential class members describe the qualifications for class membership, and the process by which class members could obtain relief.[48]

The content of settlement notice, like the mechanics of providing it,

---

42. *See* Roberts, 130 F.R.D. at 422; *see also* Hartman v. Wick, 678 F.Supp. 312, 330 (D.D.C.1988) (notice to potential class members must include description of lawsuit, and of the court's disposition of the case). *But cf.* Goldwater, 673 F.Supp. at 931 (rejecting defendant's request that notice include more detailed description of its position, reasoning that notice should not be "a long 'brief' of the parties' positions, precise in every detail and slanted in such fashion as to please every litigant").

43. *See* McCarthy v. Paine Webber Group, Inc., 164 F.R.D. 309, 312 (D.Conn. 1995).

44. *See, e.g.,* Roberts, 130 F.R.D. at 422.

45. *See, e.g., id.* at 423 (reasoning that "discovery of nonnamed plaintiffs is both rare and usually inappropriate"); *cf.* McCarthy, 164 F.R.D. at 313 (noting that discovery of absent class members permitted only where defendant is able to make strong showing that information sought (1) has neither purpose nor effect or harassing

class members or altering class membership; (2) is relevant to common questions and unavailable from representative parties; and (3) is necessary at trial of issue common to class). *But see* Otto v. Variable Annuity Life Ins. Co., 730 F.Supp. 145, 150 (N.D.Ill.1990) (in action arising out of investments in fixed annuities, in which plaintiff alleged that defendant failed to disclose method by which it calculated interest, court ordered plaintiff to amend proposed notice to inform potential class members that they might be required to respond to individual discovery requests).

46. *See* McCarthy, 164 F.R.D. at 312. The defendants in *McCarthy* claimed that if class members were found to have adopted the allegations in the complaint, certain deductions and/or credits they had claimed on prior tax returns could be declared invalid by the I.R.S. *Id.*

47. *See id.* at 313.

48. *See* Hartman v. Wick, 678 F.Supp. 312, 330 (D.D.C.1988).

is a matter left largely to the discretion of the district courts.[49] The courts have, however, devised some generally applicable rules. First, notice of settlement must describe the settlement sufficiently to allow class members the opportunity to present their objections.[50] Notice need not, however, include a copy of the settlement agreement itself. All that is necessary is that the notice "fairly apprise" the class members of settlement terms, not that it provide all details of the settlement.[51] Notice need not specify each class member's expected recovery,[52] although several courts have required that the notice of settlement provide class members with the correct formula to be used in calculating the amounts to be awarded them under the proposed settlement terms.[53] In general, however, class members are not expected or entitled to rely on the notice provided by class counsel as a complete source of settlement information.[54]

49. *See, e.g.*, DeBoer v. Mellon Mortgage Co., 64 F.3d 1171, 1176 (8th Cir.1995) (stating that notice of settlement proposal need only be as directed by the district court, and reasonable enough to satisfy due process), *cert. denied*, 517 U.S. 1156, 116 S.Ct. 1544, 134 L.Ed.2d 648 (1996). Burns v. Elrod, 757 F.2d 151, 152–55 (7th Cir.1985) (stating that Rule 23(e) requires settlement notice in such form "as the court directs."); Georgine v. Amchem Prods., Inc., 160 F.R.D. 478, 490, 502–03 (E.D.Pa.1995) (explaining that it is responsibility of district courts to direct best notice practicable to class members, and to safeguard them from unauthorized, misleading communications from parties or counsel); In re "Agent Orange" Prod. Liab. Litig., 597 F.Supp. 740, 759 (E.D.N.Y.1984) (stating that Rule 23(e) leaves form of settlement notice to discretion of trial court), *aff'd*, 818 F.2d 145 (2d Cir.1987), and *cert. denied*, 484 U.S. 1004, 108 S.Ct. 695, 98 L.Ed.2d 648 (1988).

50. *See, e.g.*, Weinberger v. Kendrick, 698 F.2d 61, 70 (2d Cir.1982), *cert. denied*, 464 U.S. 818, 104 S.Ct. 77, 78 L.Ed.2d 89 (1983); In re "Agent Orange," 597 F.Supp. at 759; *cf.* White v. National Football League, 822 F.Supp. 1389, 1401 (D.Minn. 1993) (mailed and published notices "fairly, reasonably and adequately conveyed to class members the requisite information concerning the proposed settlement"), *aff'd*, 41 F.3d 402 (8th Cir.1994).

51. *See* Gottlieb v. Wiles, 11 F.3d 1004, 1013 (10th Cir.1993); Grunin v. International House of Pancakes, 513 F.2d 114, 122 (8th Cir.), *cert. denied*, 423 U.S. 864, 96 S.Ct. 124, 46 L.Ed.2d 93 (1975); In re "Agent Orange," 597 F.Supp. at 759; *see also* In re Cement and Concrete Antitrust

Litig., 817 F.2d 1435, 1440 (9th Cir.1987) ("[n]otice is satisfactory if it generally describes the terms of the settlement in sufficient detail to alert those with adverse viewpoints to investigate and to come forward and be heard"), *rev'd on other grounds*, 490 U.S. 93, 109 S.Ct. 1661, 104 L.Ed.2d 86 (1989).

52. *See* Torrisi v. Tucson Elec. Power Co., 8 F.3d 1370, 1374 (9th Cir.1993) (holding, in securities class action, that the content of proposed settlement was sufficient even though each class member's expected recovery was not specified), *cert. denied*, 512 U.S. 1220, 114 S.Ct. 2707, 129 L.Ed.2d 834 (1994); *cf.* Marshall v. Holiday Magic, 550 F.2d 1173, 1176 (9th Cir.1977) (determining that where class members' potential recovery was a "matter of conjecture," the settlement notice need not provide expected recovery).

53. *See* Torrisi, 8 F.3d at 1374 (settlement notice in securities class action was adequate because it clearly stated aggregate amount of the settlement and the formula for computing awards); Marshall, 550 F.2d at 1176 (settlement notice required to provide aggregate amount and formula for computing recoveries). *But see* Gottlieb, 11 F.3d at 1013 (settlement notice not required to provide exact formula to be used in calculating amounts to be awarded to individual class members).

54. Grunin, 513 F.2d at 122; *see also* Maher v. Zapata Corp., 714 F.2d 436, 452 (5th Cir.1983) (holding that "notice is not required to provide a complete source of settlement information"); White, 822 F.Supp. at 1401–02 (where settlement of class action suit was subject of extensive

Second, notice of settlement must be "scrupulously neutral," expressing no opinion on the merits or on the amount of the settlement.[55] The notice is not required to inform class members of the objections raised by those who oppose the settlement. At least one court has held that a settlement notice satisfies due process without listing the dissenters' objections, provided that it does not misrepresent them.[56]

Third, the notice of settlement should make apparent the options available to dissenting class members in connection with the court's fairness determination proceedings.[57] For example, courts generally agree that class members should be notified of their opportunity to appear and voice objections to the settlement.[58] Whether the list of options must include the notice of the class member's opportunity to opt-out of the settlement, however, appears to be unsettled. Several courts have held that due process does not require a settlement notice to give absent class members the opportunity to opt-out of the settlement.[59] Others have implied, however, that the notice of an opportunity to opt-out of the settlement is required.[60]

media coverage, class members not entitled to rely exclusively on notification by class counsel).

55. See Grunin, 513 F.2d at 122; In re "Agent Orange," 597 F.Supp. at 759; see also Georgine, 160 F.R.D. at 490 (explaining that settlement notice should be impartial); In re Drexel Burnham Lambert Group, Inc., 130 B.R. 910, 924 (S.D.N.Y. 1991) (approving settlement notice on basis that it "neutrally apprised" class members of proposed settlement terms), aff'd, 960 F.2d 285 (2d Cir.1992).

56. Maywalt v. Parker & Parsley Petroleum Co., 67 F.3d 1072, 1079 (2d Cir.1995) (rejecting claims of dissenting class representatives that settlement notice violated due process because their objections not included) (citing Weinberger, 698 F.2d at 70).

57. See Air Lines Stewards and Stewardesses Ass'n v. American Airlines, Inc., 455 F.2d 101, 108 (7th Cir.1972); In re "Agent Orange," 597 F.Supp. at 759; see also Maywalt, 67 F.3d at 1079 (determining that notice of proposed settlement in securities fraud class action against general partners in oil and gas limited partnership satisfied due process because it informed absent members, among other things, of the options open to them in connection with the proceeding); Georgine, 160 F.R.D. at 490 (explaining that settlement notice must inform class members of their rights in litigation); In re Drexel Burnham Lambert Group, 130 B.R. at 924 (determining

that notice of proposed settlement in securities fraud class action against debtor's chapter 11 estate sufficient for due process because it notified class members of options open to them in connection with proceedings).

58. See, e.g., Maywalt, 67 F.3d at 1079 (holding that due process was satisfied where notice of proposed settlement informed absent class members of their right to object); Grimes v. Vitalink Communications Corp., 17 F.3d 1553 (3d Cir.) (holding that due process required that settlement notice give class members " 'opportunity to be heard and participate' ") (quoting Phillips Petroleum Co. v. Shutts, 472 U.S. 797, 812, 105 S.Ct. 2965, 2974, 86 L.Ed.2d 628 (1985)), cert. denied, 513 U.S. 986, 115 S.Ct. 480, 130 L.Ed.2d 393 (1994); In re "Agent Orange," 597 F. Supp. at 759 (requiring that class members who object to settlement must be informed of opportunity to voice objections).

59. See, e.g., Grimes, 17 F.3d at 1560–61 (due process does not require opportunity to opt-out of settlement); In re "Agent Orange," 597 F.Supp. at 759 (class members who object to settlement permitted to voice objections, but not to opt-out).

60. See, e.g., Silber v. Mabon, 18 F.3d 1449, 1451 (9th Cir.1994) (holding that settlement notice comported with due process because, among other things, it informed class members of opportunity to opt-out of settlement).

A sensitive issue is the language that should be used to inform class members of the attorney's fees incurred by the class. In a recent case, the United States District Court for the Eastern District of New York was asked to approve language to absent class members informing them that the defendant had agreed to pay their attorneys' fees and costs, and that such payments would not reduce the benefits paid to the plaintiffs.[61] The district court held that this language did not violate due process or Rule 23(e), notwithstanding the fact that defendant's financial resources were limited, and defendants' failure to meet this obligation could "diminish the monies allocated to a present commitment."[62]

Finally, the settlement notice should be printed in readable type, and should be worded in such a way that the members of the class will be able to understand it.[63] In general, formalities are less important than content. For example, one court held that the class representative's failure to use bold type in one section of the notice, as directed by the court, was merely a technical rather than a substantive deficiency, and thus "was not sufficiently egregious to warrant a supplemental corrective notice."[64]

Library References:

West's Key No. Digests, Compromise and Settlement ⬌68; Federal Civil Procedure ⬌177.

Wright, Miller & Kane, Federal Practice and Procedure: Civil 2d §§ 1786–1788.

§ 15.9   Subject Matter Jurisdiction over Claims in Class Actions

(a) Class Actions in Federal Court

"[I]t is axiomatic that the Federal Rules of Civil Procedure do not

---

61. International Union of Electronic, Elec., Salaried, Mach., and Furniture Workers, AFL–CIO v. Unisys Corp., 858 F.Supp. 1243, 1263 (E.D.N.Y.1994). The suit in *Unisys Corp.* was brought by a class of retirees, their surviving spouses and dependents, alleging that the employer had breached collective bargaining agreements by unilaterally changing medical benefits. *Id.*

62. *Id.; see also* Torrisi v. Tucson Elec. Power Co., 8 F.3d 1370, 1374 (9th Cir.1993) (statement in settlement notice that class counsel would request fee award of 30% of aggregate settlement amount was adequate notice of counsel's interest in settlement).

63. *See, e.g.,* White v. State of Alabama, 74 F.3d 1058, 1066 n. 27 (11th Cir.1996) (holding, in a class action that challenged the mechanism for electing state judges, district court erred when it inferred that the lack of response to a settlement notice indicated that the class members found it unobjectionable where the notice "was

printed in very small type and couched in 'legalese' at times so dense that even a lawyer would have had difficulty determining the settlement's probable impact on Alabama's judicial system and on the rights of Alabama voters"). At least one court has required supplementary notice of an opportunity to opt back into the settlement class, where the notice provided was unnecessarily confusing and resulted in an unusual number of opt-outs. *In re* Baldwin–United Corp., 607 F.Supp. 1312, 1335 (S.D.N.Y. 1985).

64. *In re* United Telecomm., Inc. Sec. Litig., 151 F.R.D. 127, 129 (D.Kan.1993); *cf.* Blum v. BankAtlantic Fin. Corp., 925 F.2d 1357, 1359–60 (11th Cir.1991) (ordering supplemental notices to correct substantive deficiencies in notice); Walker v. Mountain States Tel. & Tel. Co., 112 F.R.D. 44, 48 (D.Colo.1986) (ordering additional notice ordered to correct substantive deficiencies).

create or withdraw federal jurisdiction."[1] Like other Rules, Rule 23 is not a grant of federal subject matter jurisdiction. Nevertheless, the history of class actions in the federal court system reveals a tendency to relax the strictures of diversity jurisdiction in such actions. This tendency has been codified in 28 U.S.C.A. § 1367(b), part of the Judicial Improvements Act of 1990, which as a practical matter gives Rule 23 a jurisdictional dimension.

Prior to the passage of the Judicial Improvements Act of 1990, it was generally agreed that, although it was not necessary for purposes of diversity jurisdiction that each absent class member be diverse from all adverse parties, each class member (at least each class member in a Rule 23(b)(3) class action pursuing money damages) presented a separate matter in controversy for purposes of the diversity statute and was required to assert a claim in excess of the jurisdictional amount. There was no textual argument for this dichotomy in either the diversity statute or the Rule. Rather, the disparate analysis of the two statutory requirements for diversity jurisdiction flowed primarily from three Supreme Court cases—*Supreme Tribe of Ben Hur v. Cauble*,[2] *Snyder v. Harris*[3] (interpreting *Supreme Tribe of Ben Hur* in dicta), and *Zahn v. International Paper Co.*[4] Arguably, much of the pre–1990 confusion arose from reading *Supreme Tribe of Ben Hur* as though it were based on a construction of the diversity statute rather than an analysis of ancillary jurisdiction.

The question of the analytical integrity of pre–1990 jurisprudence in this area was mooted by the codification of supplemental jurisdiction in 28 U.S.C.A. § 1367(b), which, depending on one's perspective, either affirmed this dichotomy or eliminated it by changing the rule as to the jurisdictional amount. The text of Section 1367(b) appears to allow supplemental jurisdiction to the constitutional limit in diversity-based class actions (*i.e.*, without regard to statutory jurisdictional amounts). At the same time, however, the legislative history of the statute unequivocally indicates an intent to preserve the preexisting principle that individual claims in a diversity-based class action under Rule 23(b)(3) must exceed the jurisdictional minimum, and a number of district courts have construed the statute accordingly.[5] The Fifth Circuit in *In re Abbott Laboratories*,[6] by contrast, concluded that the text of the statute so clearly allows supplemental jurisdiction over class claims for less than the jurisdictional minimum that no recourse to the legislative history is

---

§ 15.9

1. Owen Equip. & Erection Co. v. Kroger, 437 U.S. 365, 370, 98 S.Ct. 2396, 2401, 57 L.Ed.2d 274 (1978).

2. 255 U.S. 356, 41 S.Ct. 338, 65 L.Ed. 673 (1921).

3. 394 U.S. 332, 89 S.Ct. 1053, 22 L.Ed.2d 319 (1969).

4. 414 U.S. 291, 94 S.Ct. 505, 38 L.Ed.2d 511 (1973).

5. *See, e.g.*, Bernard v. Gerber Food Products Co., 938 F.Supp. 218, 224 (S.D.N.Y.1996); Russ v. State Farm Mutual Automobile Ins. Co., 961 F.Supp. 808 (E.D.Pa.1997).

6. 51 F.3d 524 (5th Cir.1995).

necessary or appropriate.[7] It remains to be seen how the Supreme Court will ultimately resolve this issue.

Whatever that resolution may be, it is clear that claims are not within the scope of supplemental jurisdiction unless they form part of the same constitutional case as claims within some other jurisdictional grant. This principle is reflected in the text of 28 U.S.C.A. § 1367(a). It is generally assumed—the Supreme Court itself has assumed[8]—that *United Mine Workers v. Gibbs*[9] sets forth the test for determining whether claims involving what were formerly known as "pendent parties" are within the same constitutional case. Under *Gibbs*, claims must share "a common nucleus of operative facts" such that a plaintiff "would ordinarily be expected to try them all in one judicial proceeding"[10] before supplemental jurisdiction can be exercised. Where diversity-based class actions seek to join numerous claims arising from a single event (such as an airplane crash or building fire), this test frequently will be met. It is much less clear, however, that class actions framed around a large number of different transactions involving different parties and, perhaps, different products (such as asbestos property damage cases) will meet the requirements of Section 1367(a). The "common nucleus" test is not the "predominance" test; parties desiring to invoke supplemental jurisdiction over the claims of absent class members must be sensitive to this fact, and must be prepared to demonstrate the factual core shared by all class members' claims.

In sum, 28 U.S.C.A. § 1367 has substantially changed the jurisdictional landscape for diversity-based class actions in federal court. If each absent class member's claim meets the requirements of federal subject matter jurisdiction when viewed independently, as would be true in a class action grounded upon federal question jurisdiction, then no jurisdictional difficulty exists. If this is not the case, then it is necessary under principles of supplemental jurisdiction to determine whether class members' claims are all within the same constitutional case within the meaning of *Gibbs*. Even where this test is met, it may be necessary—depending upon which view of Section 1367(b) prevails—for each class member seeking separate legal relief to present a claim in excess of the prevailing jurisdictional minimum.

As suggested by the foregoing, class actions grounded on federal questions present fewer jurisdictional issues under current law, which does not require that claims based on federal law meet any jurisdictional minimum. However, where a federal statutory scheme requires as a jurisdictional matter that a plaintiff go through certain procedures before bringing suit (such as pursuing an administrative remedy), issues sometimes arise as to federal subject matter jurisdiction over the claims

---

7. *See also* Stromberg Metal Works, Inc. v. Press Mechanical, Inc., 77 F.3d 928, 930 (7th Cir.1996); *In re* Brand Name Prescription Drugs Antitrust Litigation, 123 F.3d 599 (7th Cir.1997).

8. *See* Finley v. United States, 490 U.S. 545, 549, 109 S.Ct. 2003, 2006, 104 L.Ed.2d 593 (1989).

9. 383 U.S. 715, 86 S.Ct. 1130, 16 L.Ed.2d 218 (1966).

10. *Id.* at 725, 86 S.Ct. at 1138.

of absent class members who have not individually complied with such procedures. This subject is best treated in depth as a matter of substantive law rather than class action procedure.

Finally, it should be noted that Rule 23 is not the only class action mechanism available under federal law, and other mechanisms may present different jurisdictional issues. Where joinder is sought under the "opt-in" procedures of the Fair Labor Standards Act, 29 U.S.C.A. § 216(b), for example, courts have rigorously applied the requirement that each class member to be joined take steps indicating that he or she consents to be bound by the judgment in the action.

(b) Class Actions in State Court

State systems typically create courts of general jurisdiction, and there are therefore far fewer issues as to subject matter jurisdiction in state court class actions. Nevertheless, some states have by statute limited the jurisdiction of their courts in ways that directly affect class litigation. For example, it has been held that South Carolina's "door closing" statute[11] precludes certification of a nationwide class in the courts of that state, with respect to claims against out of state defendants. In other circumstances, it may be difficult to determine whether a judicially-fashioned limit on the power of a state court to adjudicate foreign disputes is one of subject matter jurisdiction or personal jurisdiction, but it will be clear that such a limit exists.[12]

Library References:
West's Key No. Digests, Federal Courts ⊚14, 23, 288.
Wright, Miller & Kane, Federal Practice and Procedure: Civil 2d §§ 1755–1758.

§ 15.10   Standing and Mootness in Federal Class Actions

The statutory aspects of federal subject matter jurisdiction as applied in the class context, discussed above, have been the subject of extensive judicial and scholarly writing[1] in recent years. Perhaps less frequently the subject of comment, but of at least equal importance, are the standing and mootness requirements of Article III of the United States Constitution as applied to absent class members and their claims. Class litigation can also present difficult jurisprudential standing problems, in the context of appellate jurisdiction.

(a) Standing to Assert Claims

As a general matter, "a class representative must be part of the class and 'possess the same interest and suffer the same injury' as class

---

11. S.C. Code Ann. § 15–5–150; (Law. Co-op. 1976) (limiting jurisdiction of state court with respect to certain claims of out of state plaintiffs).

12. *See, e.g.,* Klemow v. Time, Inc., 466 Pa. 189, 197 n. 15, 352 A.2d 12, 16 n. 15,

cert. denied, 429 U.S. 828, 97 S.Ct. 86, 50 L.Ed.2d 91 (1976).

§ 15.10

1. The authors do not suggest that these are mutually exclusive categories.

members."[2] The requirements of Rule 23(a) help accomplish this result, in that they "effectively 'limit the class claims to those fairly encompassed by the named plaintiff's claims.' "[3] The foundation for this construction of Rule 23(a) is Article III of the Constitution.

Although it empowers a class representative to join other parties (typically plaintiffs) and act as a fiduciary in pursuing their claims, Rule 23 cannot operate to circumvent the case or controversy requirement of Article III. The class representative must have a sufficiently concrete personal interest in the dispute to have standing, from a constitutional standpoint;[4] the same requirement applies to each class member whose claim is to be adjudicated by a federal court. Accordingly, classes must be defined in such a way as to be limited to those with sufficiently palpable interests to meet these basic requirements.

(b) Mootness

Article III requires that a concrete dispute must exist throughout the life of the litigation. A dispute will become moot "when the issues presented are no longer 'live' or the parties lack a legally cognizable interest in the outcome."[5] Unlike most cases, however, a certified class action may present a "live" controversy even if the named plaintiff's claim on the merits has been mooted by passage of time.[6] A class action may present a concrete controversy for purposes of appeal even if the class representative's only remaining interest is in appealing the denial of class certification,[7] or if a would-be class member desires to appeal denial of class certification.[8] Practitioners should bear in mind that class actions may be "live" in the constitutional sense, for some purposes at least, even when the named plaintiff's claims have been resolved.

(c) Standing to Appeal

There is substantial divergence among the circuits with respect to the law of appellate standing as applied to class litigation. Some courts, led by the Eleventh Circuit, have adopted the view that absent class

2. East Texas Motor Freight v. Rodriguez, 431 U.S. 395, 403, 97 S.Ct. 1891, 1896, 52 L.Ed.2d 453 (1977), quoting Schlesinger v. Reservists Comm. to Stop the War, 418 U.S. 208, 216, 94 S.Ct. 2925, 2929, 41 L.Ed.2d 706 (1974); see Amchem Products, Inc. v. Windsor, ___ U.S. ___, 117 S.Ct. 2231, 138 L.Ed.2d 689 (1997).

3. General Tel. Co. of Southwest v. Falcon, 457 U.S. 147, 156, 102 S.Ct. 2364, 2370, 72 L.Ed.2d 740 (1982), quoting General Tele. Co. of Northwest v. E.E.O.C., 446 U.S. 318, 330, 100 S.Ct. 1698, at 1706, 64 L.Ed.2d 319 (1980).

4. See Simon v. Eastern Kentucky Welfare Rights Org., 426 U.S. 26, 96 S.Ct. 1917, 48 L.Ed.2d 450 (1976); O'Shea v. Littleton, 414 U.S. 488, 494, 94 S.Ct. 669, 675, 38 L.Ed.2d 674 (1974).

5. Powell v. McCormack, 395 U.S. 486, 496, 89 S.Ct. 1944, 1951, 23 L.Ed.2d 491 (1969).

6. See Sosna v. Iowa, 419 U.S. 393, 95 S.Ct. 553, 42 L.Ed.2d 532 (1975).

7. Deposit Guaranty Nat'l Bank v. Roper, 446 U.S. 947, 100 S.Ct. 2177, 64 L.Ed.2d 804 (1980).

8. United Airlines, Inc. v. McDonald, 432 U.S. 385, 97 S.Ct. 2464, 53 L.Ed.2d 423 (1977).

members—*i.e.*, class members who are not named plaintiffs and who have not intervened as individual litigants under FRCP 24—have no standing to appeal trial court determinations.[9] Other appellate courts, however, have indicated that nonnamed class members have standing to appeal final orders in class actions.[10] At least one court of appeals seems to have adopted an intermediate position, allowing standing only if the class member seeking to appeal has attempted to intervene or has been "haled into court."[11]

Although the better standing rule would seem to be to allow timely appeal by anyone bound by a judgment (subject to normal principles limiting appellate willingness to address issues not raised below), this has not been the prevailing view. It remains to be seen how the split in the appellate courts will be resolved.

Library References:

West's Key No. Digests, Federal Civil Procedure ⊕103.7, 164.5.
Wright, Miller & Cooper, Federal Practice and Procedure: Civil 2d § 1785.1.

§ 15.11   Statute of Limitation Issues

(a) Tolling of Statute of Limitations

The filing of a class action suspends the applicable statute of limitations for all members of the purported class.[1] This does not help individuals whose claims are not timely at the commencement of the class action. They must be excluded from the class.[2] The statute of limitations remains tolled as to the class members' claims until the court rules on class certification.[3] When a class is certified and a class member opts-out of the class action, the statute of limitations is deemed tolled as to that claimant until the date the claimant opted-out of the class action.[4] If a court certifies a class but later vacates the certification

---

9. *See* Guthrie v. Evans, 815 F.2d 626 (11th Cir.1987); *See also* Gottlieb v. Wiles, 11 F.3d 1004 (10th Cir.1993); Croyden Assoc. v. Alleco, Inc., 969 F.2d 675 (8th Cir. 1992); Walker v. City of Mesquite, 858 F.2d 1071 (5th Cir.1988).

10. *See also* In the Matter of VMS Ltd. Partnership Sec. Litig., 976 F.2d 362 (7th Cir.1992); *See e.g.*, Carlough v. Amchem Products, Inc., 5 F.3d 707 (3d Cir.1993); *cf.* Bell Atlantic Corp. v. Bolger, 2 F.3d 1304 (3d Cir.1993).

11. *See* Shults v. Champion Int'l Corp., 35 F.3d 1056, 1060 (6th Cir.1994).

§ 15.11

1. American Pipe & Constr. Co. v. Utah, 414 U.S. 538, 554, 94 S.Ct. 756, 766, 38 L.Ed.2d 713 (1974). For the application of this principle to defendant classes, *see infra* § 15.3(c)(1).

2. *See* Wetzel v. Liberty Mut. Ins. Co., 508 F.2d 239, 246 (3d Cir.), *cert. denied*, 421 U.S. 1011, 95 S.Ct. 2415, 44 L.Ed.2d 679 (1975); Laffey v. Northwest Airlines, Inc. 567 F.2d 429, 472–73 (D.C.Cir.1976), *cert. denied*, 434 U.S. 1086, 98 S.Ct. 1281, 55 L.Ed.2d 792 (1978).

3. American Pipe & Constr. Co., 414 U.S. at 554, 94 S.Ct. at 766; Tosti v. City of Los Angeles, 754 F.2d 1485, 1488 (9th Cir. 1985).

4. *See* Doe v. Blake, 809 F.Supp. 1020, 1024 (D.Conn.1992) (statute of limitations begins to run when a plaintiff opts-out of a class action).

order, the statute of limitations is deemed tolled until the date the order was vacated.[5] When a court denies class certification, members of the purported class may either file individual actions or intervene in pending actions,[6] provided that they do so within the remaining limitations period.[7] Purported class members are not permitted, however, to file a subsequent class action that seeks to take advantage of the filing date of a previous class action.[8]

(b) Importance of Notice

A class complaint should notify the defendant of both the generic identities of the potential plaintiffs and their substantive claims. Thus, when purported members file individual actions against the defendant after a denial of class certification, or because the members opted-out of the class action, the primary consideration in evaluating whether the statute of limitations was tolled with respect to the individual claims is whether the class action claims placed the defendant on notice as to the claims of these individual claimants.[9] If the allegations in the class action complaint were not sufficiently specific, then a defendant may not have been adequately on notice of such individual class members' claims so as to justify tolling the statute of limitations.[10] Similarly, the statute of limitations is not tolled for additional claims that individual class members may have that are different from, or peripheral to, the claims alleged in the class action.[11]

(c) Relation Back Doctrine

If a trial court, after its original certification of the class, determines

---

5. See Goldstein v. Regal Crest, Inc., 62 F.R.D. 571, 580 (E.D.Pa.1974).

6. Crown, Cork & Seal Co. v. Parker, 462 U.S. 345, 353–54, 103 S.Ct. 2392, 2397–98, 76 L.Ed.2d 628 (1983).

7. Moreover, if an appellate court reverses a lower court's denial of class certification, the statute of limitations applicable to the class members' claims is tolled from the date the class action was initiated. See Satterwhite v. City of Greenville, Texas, 578 F.2d 987, 997 (5th Cir.1978), vacated on other grounds, 445 U.S. 940, 100 S.Ct. 1334, 63 L.Ed.2d 773 (1980); Gelman v. Westinghouse Elec. Corp., 556 F.2d 699, 701 (3d Cir.1977).

8. See Korwek v. Hunt, 827 F.2d 874, 876 (2d Cir.1987); Salazar–Calderon v. Presidio Valley Farmers Ass'n, 765 F.2d 1334, 1351 (5th Cir.1985), cert. denied, 475 U.S. 1035, 106 S.Ct. 1245, 89 L.Ed.2d 353 (1986).

9. See In re Crazy Eddie Sec. Litig., 802 F.Supp. 804, 813 (E.D.N.Y.1992); Rose v. Arkansas Valley Envtl. & Util. Auth., 562 F.Supp. 1180, 1193–96 (W.D.Mo.1983).

10. See Davis v. Bethlehem Steel Corp. 769 F.2d 210, 212 (4th Cir.) (complaint dismissed as time barred where previous class action complaint was too broad to place defendant on notice as to pending claims for purposes of tolling statute of limitations), cert. denied, 474 U.S. 1021, 106 S.Ct. 573, 88 L.Ed.2d 557 (1985); Camotex, S.R.L. v. Hunt, 741 F.Supp. 1086, 1091–92 (S.D.N.Y.1990) (statute of limitations on individual plaintiff's claims not tolled by class action complaint "asserting generalized grievances of an open-ended group").

11. See Lindner Dividend Fund, Inc. v. Ernst & Young, 880 F.Supp. 49, 54–55 (D.Mass.1995); Burns v. Ersek, 591 F.Supp. 837, 842 (D.Minn.1984) (citing Johnson v. Railway Express Agency, Inc., 421 U.S. 454, 467 n. 14, 95 S.Ct. 1716, 1724 n. 14, 44 L.Ed.2d 295 (1975)).

that certification was improper because the class representative was not a proper representative, for statute of limitations purposes, an amended pleading adding a new named plaintiff relates back to the initial filing date of the class complaint.[12] Accordingly, once a class has been certified, it is generally possible to substitute a new named plaintiff for the original class representative without presenting a statute of limitations problem. Courts have held, however, that the same is not true if some difficulty with the original class representative (*i.e.*, lack of typicality, inability to show adequacy of representation) prevents the certification of a class in the first place. In that event, at least one court has held that the statute is not tolled for purposes of adding a new named plaintiff to represent the class.[13] Such a new representative can seek to proceed in that action on behalf of the class only to the extent that its claim is timely, without regard to any tolling by virtue of the original class action complaint.

When an individual claimant brings an action that is later amended to include a class action claim, the amended complaint does not relate back to the date of the original pleading for purposes of the statute of limitations.[14] Additionally, an amended complaint that expands the purported class does not relate back to the original class action complaint as to claims by persons who are members only of the expanded class, and not members of the class as originally pled.[15]

Library References:

West's Key No. Digests, Limitation of Actions ⊗126.5.
Wright, Miller & Cooper, Federal Practice and Procedure: Civil 2d § 1800.

§ 15.12   Class Actions Only for Particular Issues, and the Use of Subclasses

FRCP 23(c)(4) gives the court and the parties flexibility in determining whether and how a class should be certified. It provides:

> When appropriate (A) an action may be brought or maintained as a class action with respect to particular issues, or (B) a class may be divided into subclasses and each subclass treated as a class, and the provisions of this rule shall then be construed and applied accordingly.

The Rule thus speaks to two different situations, and they may or may not be present together in a single case.[1]

---

12. *See* Haas v. Pittsburgh Nat'l Bank, 526 F.2d 1083, 1097 (3d Cir.1975).

13. *See* Fleck v. Cablevision VII, Inc., 807 F.Supp. 824 (D.D.C.1992). *See also In re* Elscint, Ltd. Securities Litig., 674 F.Supp. 374, 378–79, 382 (D.Mass.1987) (statute of limitations not tolled to allow new class representatives to intervene prior to ruling on class certification where original named plaintiffs were not members of the purported class).

14. *See* Perry v. Beneficial Fin. Co., 81 F.R.D. 490, 495 (W.D.N.Y.1979).

15. *See* Arneil v. Ramsey, 550 F.2d 774, 782–83 (2d Cir.1977).

§ 15.12

1. For a case in which both provisions were invoked, *see* Valentino v. Carter–Wallace, Inc., 97 F.3d 1227, 1228 (9th Cir.1996) (in a products liability action, district court certified a plaintiff class of persons who

A party can ask the court to use the powers conferred by Rule 23(c)(4) or the court can raise the issue sua sponte.[2] The court does not, however, have an obligation to invoke the Rule.[3] The trial court also has broad discretion in deciding whether to certify a limited class or subclasses, and an appellate court will review its decision only for abuse of discretion.[4] A class that is delimited according to the Rule still must meet all of the requirements for class certification.[5]

(a) Limiting Class Actions to Particular Issues

The power to limit a proposed class to particular issues may allow a court to certify a class where it otherwise could not. But, where the noncommon issues are inextricably entangled with the common issues, or where the noncommon issues are too predominant to handle on a class basis, certification will be denied.[6]

used product manufactured by defendant, but limited to issues of strict liability, negligence, failure to warn, breach of implied and express warranty, causation in fact, and liability for punitive damages, and it also certified a "serious injury" subclass of all users "who have developed or will develop aplastic anemia or liver failure, as a result of using" the product).

2. Burka v. New York City Transit Auth., 110 F.R.D. 595, 603 (S.D.N.Y.1986) (denying plaintiff's motion for class certification, including use of subclasses, in action challenging workplace drug testing program because proposed representatives of subclasses did not thoroughly and adequately represent claims of class members).

3. U.S. Parole Comm'n v. Geraghty, 445 U.S. 388, 408, 100 S.Ct. 1202, 1215, 63 L.Ed.2d 479 (1980) (plaintiff's burden to submit proposals to the court regarding the construction of subclasses); Lundquist v. Sec. Pac. Automotive Fin. Servs. Corp., 993 F.2d 11, 14 (2d Cir.) cert. denied, 510 U.S. 959, 114 S.Ct. 419, 126 L.Ed.2d 365 (1993) (affirming district court's denial of motion to certify class and rejecting notion that court should have implemented FRCP 23(c)(4) sua sponte).

4. Diaz v. Romer, 961 F.2d 1508, 1511 (10th Cir.1992) (in litigation brought by prisoners challenging state's HIV policies, trial court did not abuse its discretion in creating subclasses for HIV positive prisoners and HIV negative prisoners); Alexander v. Gino's, Inc., 621 F.2d 71, 75 (3d Cir.), cert. denied, 449 U.S. 953, 101 S.Ct. 358, 66 L.Ed.2d 217 (1980) (per curiam) (in sex

discrimination suit trial court did not abuse its discretion in splitting proposed class into subclasses based on promotion and discharge claims).

5. Eisen v. Carlisle & Jacquelin, 417 U.S. 156, 180, 94 S.Ct. 2140, 2153, 40 L.Ed.2d 732 (1974) (Douglas, J., dissenting) (outlining ways in which subclasses might be created).

6. 7B Charles Alan Wright, Arthur R. Miller & Mary Kay Kane, Federal Practice and Procedure § 1790, at 276 (2d ed. 1986). See, e.g., Harding v. Tambrands, Inc. 165 F.R.D. 623, 632 (D.Kan.1996) (refusing partial certification in a products liability action because noncommon issues of different state negligence formulations are inextricably entangled with common issues of whether defendants were negligent); Caruso v. Celsius Insulation Resources, Inc., 101 F.R.D. 530, 538 (M.D.Pa.1984) (complex factual situation presented by mass tort formaldehyde litigation precluded separation of common issue); In re Tetracycline Cases, 107 F.R.D. 719, 734–35 (W.D.Mo. 1985) (certification inappropriate in litigation against manufacturers of tetracycline-based drugs because a large number of individual issues would remain even after the trial on the common issues, and because separating individual issues from common issues would be a difficult task); Davenport by Fowlkes v. Gerber Prods. Co., 125 F.R.D. 116, 120 (E.D.Pa.1989) (in litigation involving "baby mouth" syndrome "insurmountable" difficulty of separating out individual from common issues, as well as fact that large number of individual issues would remain to be resolved, precluded separation of

As a practical matter, certification of a class with respect to only some of the issues will result in the division of the litigation into two or more phases.[7] Depending on how the issues are divided, use of FRCP 23(c)(4)(A) has the potential to compromise the litigants' constitutional right to a single jury determination of a particular issue under the Seventh Amendment.[8]

In *In re Rhone–Poulenc Rorer, Inc.*[9] the Seventh Circuit disagreed with the trial court's decision to divide the issues in the case and certify a class for decision on some of them pursuant to FRCP 23(c)(4)(A). HIV-infected hemophiliacs brought a negligence claim against the drug companies that manufacture blood solids. The district court partially certified a class to determine a number of questions bearing on whether the defendants were negligent. The appeals court found three problems with this approach. First was a concern with forcing the defendants, which together comprised an entire industry, to stake the future of their companies on a single jury trial or be forced by the risk of bankruptcy to settle.[10] Second was a concern that the negligence determination would be made according to a standard that did not actually exist, because the judge would be forced to craft a jury instruction that took into account the common law of all 50 states and the District of Columbia.[11] Third, noting that the district court had not certified a class with respect to all of the liability issues, the court of appeals found that a litigant's Seventh Amendment right to a jury trial means that a litigant has "a right to have juriable issues determined by the first jury impaneled to hear them . . . and not reexamined by another finder of fact."[12] The court ruled that, because the class had not been certified for some liability issues— causation and comparative negligence—subsequent juries would be forced to revisit some of the underlying issues related to whether the defendants had breached their duty of care. For those reasons, the court of appeals directed the district court to decertify the class.

The Fifth Circuit has adopted the Seventh Circuit's view on this issue.[13] The Ninth Circuit on the other hand, recently declined to accept the analysis presented by the court in *Rhone-Poulenc*.[14] In doing so, it

common issue); *In re* Woodmoor Corp., 4 B.R. 186, 193 (Bankr.D.Colo.1980) (refusing class certification in suit by purchasers of homes in real estate development against bankrupt developer where common questions of law and fact did not predominate over individual issues); Kuhn v. Skyline Corp., No. CIV. A 83–0942, 1984 WL 62775, at *7 (M.D.Pa.1984) (class certification inappropriate because common issues and noncommon issues inextricably entangled in plaintiffs' suit against manufacturer of mobile homes for injuries suffered by exposure to formaldehyde used in homes' construction).

7. *See, e.g., In re* Shell Oil Refinery, 136 F.R.D. 588, 593 (E.D.La.1991), *aff'd*, 979 F.2d 1014 (5th Cir.1992) (adopting four-phase trial plan).

8. *See also* FRCP 42(b) (allowing separate trials of claims so long as Seventh Amendment or statute is not violated).

9. 51 F.3d 1293, 1302–03 (7th Cir.), *cert. denied*, 516 U.S. 867, 116 S.Ct. 184, 133 L.Ed.2d 122 (1995).

10. *Id.* at 1299.

11. *Id.* at 1300–02.

12. *Id.* at 1303.

13. Castano v. American Tobacco Co., 84 F.3d 734, 750–51 (5th Cir.1996) (comparative negligence and reliance).

14. Valentino v. Carter–Wallace, Inc., 97 F.3d 1227, 1232–33 (9th Cir.1996) (deny-

relied on an earlier decision that upheld the bifurcation of issues similar to those that were presented in the *Rhone-Poulenc* case.[15]

(b) Subclasses

Subclasses are used by courts when class members have different or antagonistic claims to assert against opponents.[16] The utility of requesting subclasses under FRCP 23(c)(4)(B) is most clear when the claims of various class members may be antagonistic.[17] Subclasses also may be useful when class members seek to assert different claims against their opponents based on different factual or legal considerations.[18]

The use of subclasses can, however, create other litigation problems. For example, the formation of subclasses may be hindered by the requirement of FRCP 23(a)(1) that the class be too numerous to make the joinder of all members impracticable.[19] Also, attorneys who represent more than one subclass may have a conflict of interest that requires withdrawal from one or both classes.[20]

(c) Procedure

The opportunity to invoke FRCP 23(c)(4) should be considered when formulating the initial motion for class certification to the court or when formulating an opposition to such a motion. Rule 23(c)(4) continues to be applicable throughout the litigation of a case, and modification of a class

ing district court's class certification order on other grounds).

15. Arthur Young & Co. v. U.S. Dist. Court, 549 F.2d 686, 698 (9th Cir.), *cert. denied*, 434 U.S. 829, 98 S.Ct. 109, 54 L.Ed.2d 88 (1977) (causation and duty owed to the claimant).

16. *See generally* Eisen v. Carlisle & Jacquelin, 417 U.S. 156, 179–86, 94 S.Ct. 2140, 2153–57, 40 L.Ed.2d 732 (1974) (Douglas, J., dissenting) (outlining possible uses of FRCP 23(c)(4)(B) for class action pursuant to antitrust and securities laws in which subclasses would be created by dividing plaintiffs by date of purchase of securities or by connection to particular defendants through participation in monthly investment or payroll deduction programs).

17. *See, e.g.,* Coca–Cola Bottling Co. of Elizabethtown, Inc. v. Coca–Cola Co., 98 F.R.D. 254, 270 (D.Del.1983) (proposing to divide proposed class of bottling companies into three subclasses according to applicable contracts and consent decrees because bottlers had different origins which could be significant in determining nature and extent of rights under contracts and consent decrees).

18. *See, e.g.,* Deutschman v. Beneficial Corp., 132 F.R.D. 359, 382–83 (D.Del.1990) (in a class action alleging violation of securities laws, court created two subclasses to differentiate between plaintiffs who purchased securities before appearance of newspaper article that questioned company's financial health and plaintiffs who purchased securities after the appearance of the article); Molina v. Mallah Org. Inc., 144 F.R.D. 37, 41 (S.D.N.Y.1992) (in a class action alleging that employers intentionally interfered with employees' protected rights under union welfare and pension funds, plaintiff employees were given leave to move again for creation of subclasses according to the different employers for whom employees worked if they could present evidence that defendants had different intents for engaging in the alleged scheme to violate the employees' rights and that employers utilized different operating procedures for violating those rights).

19. Manual for Complex Litigation, (Third) § 30.15, at 242 (1995).

20. *See In re* Bendectin Prods. Liab. Litig., 749 F.2d 300, 304 (6th Cir.1984) (reversing trial court's certification order for this and other reasons).

certification to limit the class to particular issues or to create subclasses should be considered whenever new facts are discovered.[21]

When asking the court to bifurcate issues pursuant to FRCP 23(c)(4)(A), or when evaluating a court's decision to bifurcate issues, counsel should consider whether the way in which the issues are to be divided implicates the Seventh Amendment right to a single jury determination of an issue.

When evaluating the claims of proposed class members, counsel should consider whether there are distinct or conflicting claims so that FRCP 23(c)(4)(B) might be implicated.

Library References:

West's Key No. Digests, Federal Civil Procedure ⚷176.
Wright, Miller & Cooper, Federal Practice and Procedure: Civil 2d § 1790.

§ 15.13   Defendant Class Actions

Although class actions are most commonly used as a method for plaintiffs with similar claims to bring an action as a unified class, the provisions of FRCP 23 also apply to defendant classes.[1] FRCP 23 expressly provides that a class member "may sue *or be sued*" on behalf of a class.[2] Thus, for example, a patent holder may bring a defendant class action against a class of alleged infringers where there is a common question as to the patent's validity.[3] Although the language of FRCP 23 does not distinguish between plaintiff and defendant class actions, both plaintiffs and defendants should be aware that there are ways in which courts treat defendant classes differently.[4] This section focuses on the application of FRCP 23 to defendant class actions, with particular attention to their differences from plaintiff class actions and the considerations that are especially relevant to the certification of defendant classes.

---

21. *See, e.g.,* Lo Re v. Chase Manhattan Corp., 431 F.Supp. 189, 199 (S.D.N.Y.1977) (court would entertain motion from defendants to subdivide plaintiff class under 23(c)(4) if discovery showed that interests of some class members in sex discrimination suit would be better represented by separate treatment); McLaughlin v. Wohlgemuth, 398 F.Supp. 269, 275 (E.D.Pa. 1975) (defendants permitted to move for division of plaintiff class into subclasses should reason for doing so become apparent), *vacated on other grounds,* 535 F.2d 251 (3d Cir.1976); Johnson v. ITT–Thompson Indus., Inc., 323 F.Supp. 1258, 1262 (N.D.Miss.1971) (denying employer's motion to restrict class of employment discrimination plaintiffs, but suggesting that it would entertain motion to restrict class under 23(c)(4) at a later date should conflicts arise between present and prospective employees).

§ 15.13

1. Northwestern Nat'l Bank of Minneapolis v. Fox & Co., 102 F.R.D. 507, 510 (S.D.N.Y.1984) ("Although defendant class certification occurs relatively infrequently, there is no question that procedure is available where all of the requirements of Rule 23 are met.").

2. FRCP 23(a) (emphasis added).

3. *See, e.g.,* Dale Electronics, Inc. v. R.C.L. Electronics, Inc., 53 F.R.D. 531 (D.N.H.1971).

4. *See In re* Gap Stores Sec. Litig., 79 F.R.D. 283, 290 (N.D.Cal.1978) (defendant and plaintiff class actions "not entirely the same") (citations omitted).

As a practical matter, plaintiffs are most likely to benefit from defendant class actions where they are seeking declaratory or injunctive relief against a group of defendants who are engaged in the same or similar practices, such as suits against government officials in challenges to state laws or administrative policies.[5] Defendant classes also may be certified in cases seeking monetary damages, such as securities fraud actions,[6] but plaintiffs considering seeking certification in such cases should be aware that collateral proceedings often will be necessary to determine the liability of individual class members because of the frequent presence of individual defenses.[7]

On the other side of the coin, there also are benefits to defendants in having a defendant class certified. As discussed below, so long as there are adequate class representatives, the advantages to defendants of a defendant class include the economies of scale in defending common issues as a class, the possibility of greater exposure if sued on an individual basis, and the ability to litigate unique issues in individual collateral proceedings.[8] Conversely, defendants should oppose certification of a defendant class where there are concerns about the class representative's ability or inclination to mount a vigorous defense or where defendants' individual factual issues or defenses predominate over those common to the class.

(a) Prerequisites to Certification

The four basic prerequisites for certification of defendant classes are nearly identical to those applicable to plaintiff classes: joinder impracticability, common issues, typicality of defenses, and adequate representation.[9] The one obvious distinction between plaintiff and defendant class actions is that these prerequisites to certification focus on common and typical defenses, rather than common and typical claims.[10]

(1) Numerosity/Joinder Impractibility

The requirement of FRCP 23(a)(1) that a class be numerous enough that joinder of all class members is impracticable is "applied more liberally when certifying a defendant class than when certifying a plaintiff class."[11] This more liberal approach results in a lower threshold

---

5. *E.g.*, Thornton v. Butler, 728 F.Supp. 679 (M.D.Ala.1990).

6. *E.g.*, Alexander Grant & Co. Litig., 110 F.R.D. 528 (S.D.Fla.1986).

7. *See* Guy v. Abdulla, 57 F.R.D. 14, 16 (N.D.Ohio 1972).

8. *See infra* § 15.13 (a)(2) and (3) and (b)(4).

9. FRCP 23(a); *see supra* § 15.3 for a general discussion of these requirements.

10. *See* FRCP 23(a).

11. Alvarado Partners, L.P. v. Mehta, 130 F.R.D. 673, 675 (D.Colo.1990) (defen-

dant class of 33 underwriters certified) (citing 1 H. Newberg & A. Conte, Newberg on Class Actions § 3.04, at 138 (3d ed. 1992)); *see also In re* Cardinal Industries, Inc., 105 B.R. 834, 843–44 (Bankr.S.D.Ohio 1989), *supplemented by* 109 B.R. 743 (Bankr. D.Ohio 1989) (requirement applied "more flexibly" to defendant classes) (quoting Newberg, *supra*, § 4.55, at 395 (2d ed. 1985)); Dale Elecs., Inc. v. R.C.L. Elecs., Inc., 53 F.R.D. 531, 534–36 (D.N.H.1971) (defendant class of 13 alleged patent infringers certified). *See supra* § 15.3(a) for a

number of class members normally required for a defendant class than for a plaintiff class.[12]

(2) Common Issues

The FRCP 23(a)(2) requirement that there be questions of law or fact common to the class creates particular concerns with defendant classes because of due process considerations of fairness to absent class members.[13] Because a defendant class representative is normally an unwilling participant in the litigation, courts are, and should be, careful to ensure that only truly common issues are tried as part of the class action to ensure that the representative will defend those issues.[14]

Because of the heightened focus on litigating only truly common issues in defendant class actions and the frequent existence of unique defenses for individual defendants, courts also recognize that additional proceedings often will be necessary to enforce the class judgment against defendant class members.[15] For example, the issue of a patent's validity may be tried as a defendant class action, but each defendant's infringement of the patent normally is determined in subsequent litigation.[16] Nonetheless, as in plaintiff class actions, the commonality requirement of Rule 23(a) generally does not prevent defendant class actions because it can be satisfied in appropriate circumstances by a single question of law or fact common to the defendant class,[17] such as whether offering materials contained material misrepresentations in a securities fraud action against numerous defendants.[18]

(3) Typicality of Defenses

FRCP 23(a)(3) focuses on the proposed class representative by requiring that the defenses of the representative be typical of the class.[19] In a securities fraud action, for example, such common defenses might include (1) that no misrepresentations were made, (2) that the defendants exercised due diligence, or (3) that there was no reliance on the defendants' actions.[20] The representative's defenses do not need to be

general discussion of the numerosity/joinder impractibility requirement.

12. Luyando v. Bowen, 124 F.R.D. 52, 57 (S.D.N.Y.1989) (citations omitted).

13. See In re Cardinal, 105 B.R. at 843–44 (citing Newberg, supra note 11, § 4.56 at 395).

14. Id.

15. E.g., Marcera v. Chinlund, 595 F.2d 1231, 1239 (2d Cir.), vacated on other grounds sub nom. Lombard v. Marcera, 442 U.S. 915, 99 S.Ct. 2833, 61 L.Ed.2d 281 (1979) (citing In re Gap Stores Securities Litig., 79 F.R.D. 283 (N.D.Cal.1978; United States v. Trucking Employers, Inc., 75 F.R.D. 682, 689 n. 2 (D.D.C.1977)).

16. See, e.g., In re Gap Stores, 79 F.R.D. at 293 (citing Technograph Printed Cir-

cuits, Ltd. v. Methode Elecs., Inc., 285 F.Supp. 714 (N.D.Ill.1968)); Dale Elecs. Inc., Inc., 53 F.R.D. at 531, 534–36.

17. See Alexander Grant & Co. v. McAlister, 116 F.R.D. 583, 587 (S.D.Ohio 1987) (commonality satisfied where one issue is common to all defendant class members) (citations omitted); see also supra § 15.3(b) for a general discussion of the commonality requirement.

18. In re Computer Memories Sec. Litig., 111 F.R.D. 675 (N.D.Cal.1986).

19. FRCP 23(a)(3); see supra § 15.3(c) for a general discussion of the typicality requirement.

20. See In re Activision Sec. Litig., 621 F.Supp. 415 (N.D.Cal.1985).

identical to those that might be raised by other class members, but need only be typical of the main defenses shared by the class.[21] As one court has stated, "it is only when there is a unique defense forwarded by the representative which will consume the merits of the case that a court should refuse to certify a class based on typicality."[22]

Because individual defendant class members often have defenses that are unique or shared by only certain members of the class, it is sometimes necessary to have multiple defendant class representatives to ensure that defenses typical of the class will be litigated as common issues in the case.[23] Both plaintiffs attempting to have a defendant class certified and defendants attempting to defeat certification or attack a judgment against the class should be aware of this heightened concern relating to typicality of defenses in defendant class actions.

(4) Adequacy of Representative

While the test for adequate representation of a plaintiff class is generally applicable to determine the adequacy of a representative of a defendant class,[24] there are several issues that arise particularly in defendant class actions. As with plaintiff representatives, defendant class representatives must be represented by qualified counsel, must share common interests with other class members, and must not be antagonistic toward other class members.[25] In addition to these factors, courts and commentators often discuss certain issues unique to defendant class representatives, including (1) the defendant class representative's usual unwillingness to serve as a representative and (2) the ability of the plaintiff to choose a weak or ineffective representative.[26] Neither of these concerns, however, has proven to be much of an impediment to certification of defendant classes.[27] In fact, a defendant's unwillingness to serve as the representative of a class has been viewed by some courts as an

---

21. Alexander Grant, 116 F.R.D. at 588 (citing Thillens, Inc. v. Community Currency Exchange Ass'n of Illinois, Inc., 97 F.R.D. 668, 678 (N.D.Ill.1983)); In re Cardinal, 105 B.R. 834, 844 (Bankr.S.D.Ohio 1989), supplemented by 109 B.R. 743 (Bankr.S.D.Ohio 1989) (citing Alexander Grant) (further citation omitted).

22. See Alexander Grant, 116 F.R.D. at 588.

23. See United States v. Trucking Employers, Inc., 75 F.R.D. 682, 689 (D.D.C. 1977) (inclusion of named defendants that varied in size and location assured that all common defenses would be raised).

24. 7A Charles Alan Wright, Arthur R. Miller & Mary Kay Kane, Federal Practice and Procedure § 1770, at 395 (2d ed. 1986); see supra § 15.3(d) for a general discussion of the adequate representation requirement.

25. In re Alexander Grant & Co. Litig., 110 F.R.D. 528, 535 (S.D.Fla.1986) (citing In re Activision Sec. Litig., 621 F.Supp. at 434); Trucking Employers, 75 F.R.D. at 687 (citations omitted); 7A Charles Alan Wright, Arthur R. Miller & Mary Kay Kane, Federal Practice and Procedure § 1770 at 395–96 (2d ed. 1986).

26. E.g., Doss v. Long, 93 F.R.D. 112, 117 (N.D.Ga.1981) (noting commentators' concern regarding unwilling representatives and plaintiffs' selection of weak representatives) (citing Z. Chaffee, Some Problems of Equity 237 (1950)); In re Gap Stores Securities Litig., 79 F.R.D. 283, 290 (N.D.Cal. 1978) (same) (citing Note, Defendant Class Actions, 91 Harv. L. Rev. 630, 639–40 (1978)).

27. In re Cardinal Industries, Inc., 105 B.R. 834, 844 (Bankr.S.D.Ohio 1989), supplemented by 109 B.R. 743 (Bankr.S.D.Ohio 1989) (citation omitted).

indication that the defendant will vigorously defend the rights of the class if certified.[28] With respect to the concern over a plaintiff choosing a weak defendant class representative, at least one court has recognized that the plaintiff's selection does not raise issues materially different from those potentially created by a plaintiff class representative's self-appointment, *i.e.*, neither defendant nor plaintiff class members have much say about the identity of the representative.[29] Further, a plaintiff's choice of a weak class representative may make any judgment against the class more susceptible to attack in subsequent enforcement actions.[30]

More troubling to courts are the due process concerns that arise from representative adjudication, particularly in defendant class actions.[31] Because absent defendant class members may incur liabilities, rather than simply lose the right to bring a claim, without a true "day in court," courts are especially careful to ensure that the class representative will properly safeguard their interests.[32]

(b) Rule 23(b) Class Categories for Defendant Classes

(1) Rule 23(b)(1)(A)

FRCP 23(b)(1)(A) provides that an action may be brought against a class if the FRCP 23(a) prerequisites are satisfied and if individual litigation could "establish incompatible standards of conduct for the party opposing the class."[33] Although courts have certified defendant classes under this subsection,[34] the mere fact that a plaintiff might prevail in individual litigation against one member of the class but not another does not warrant certification; there must be a risk of imposing

---

28. *E.g., In re* Gap Stores, 79 F.R.D. at 290 (unwilling representative likely to be a vigorous adversary) (citing Note, *Defendant Class Actions, supra* note 26; *see also* Marcera v. Chinlund, 595 F.2d 1231, 1239 (2d. Cir.) *vacated on other grounds sub nom.* Lombard v. Marcera, 442 U.S. 915, 99 S.Ct. 2833, 61 L.Ed.2d 281 (1979) ("Rule 23(a)(4) does not require a willing representative but merely an adequate one."); Research Corp. v. Pfister Associated Growers, Inc., 301 F.Supp. 497, 499 (N.D.Ill.1969) (representative's willingness should not be given more than token weight). In fact, a defendant's willingness to serve as a class representative can raise questions about its relationship with the plaintiff and its adequacy as a representative. *In re* Yarn Processing Patent Litig., 56 F.R.D. 648, 653 (S.D.Fla. 1972) (noting possibility of collusion between plaintiff and proposed defendant class representative).

29. *In re* Gap Stores, 79 F.R.D. at 290.

30. Wolfson, *Defendant Class Actions*, 38 Ohio State L.J. 459, 478–79 (1977).

31. *In re* Gap Stores 79 F.R.D. at 290–92; Alexander Grant & Co. v. McAlister, 116 F.R.D. 583, 588–89 (S.D.Ohio 1987).

32. *See* Alexander Grant, 116 F.R.D. at 588–89 (recognizing "extreme importance" of adequacy of representation in defendant class context); *In re* LILCO Sec. Litig., 111 F.R.D. 663, 672 (E.D.N.Y.1986) (stating "it is widely agreed that adequacy is the most important factor") (citing Charles Alan Wright, Arthur R. Miller & Mary Kay Kane, Federal Practice and Procedure § 1765 n.9 (1986)); *In re* Cardinal, 105 B.R. at 834 (recognizing added importance of adequate representation in defendant class actions) (citing Alexander Grant).

33. FRCP 23(b)(1)(A); *see supra* § 15.4 for a general discussion of FRCP 23(b)(1)(A).

34. *E.g.,* U.S. Trust Co. of N.Y. v. Alpert, 163 F.R.D. 409, 418 (S.D.N.Y.1995); National Broadcasting Co. v. Cleland, 697 F.Supp. 1204, 1217 (N.D.Ga.1988).

incompatible standards of conduct on the plaintiff.[35] Thus, courts often are reluctant to certify a class of defendants under Rule 23(b)(1)(A) where the plaintiff is seeking only money damages, or where declaratory or injunctive relief is incidental to a claim for money damages.[36] The decision in *In re Arthur Treacher's Franchise Litigation*,[37] provides a good example of this reluctance. *Arthur Treacher's* involved an action brought by a fast-food franchisor against franchisees to recover damages for alleged failure to make royalty payments for the use of the franchisor's trademark.[38] Denying certification of a defendant class of franchisees, the court stated that the possibility that the franchisor would be able to enforce its franchise agreement and collect damages from certain franchisees, but not others, would not result in "incompatible standards of conduct" for the franchisor.[39]

There is a split of authority over whether Rule 23(b)(1)(A) can be used to certify classes of defendants in patent infringement cases.[40] Some courts have granted certification in such cases because of the risk that varying results would subject the plaintiff patentee to inconsistent standards of conduct with respect to the enforcement of its patent.[41] Other courts have reached the opposite conclusion, explaining that "[a]lthough the ways in which a plaintiff may be required to act with respect to different parties may be inconsistent, they would not be incompatible since the plaintiff would not find itself with court orders both permitting and prohibiting the enforcement of the patent against a particular alleged patent infringer."[42] Similarly, most courts deny FRCP 23(b)(1)(A) certification of defendant classes in securities fraud actions because the possibility that a plaintiff may win some decisions and lose others against individual class members will not result in incompatible standards of conduct for the plaintiff.[43] As one court has observed in denying certification of a defendant class of securities sellers, "[a] plaintiff may recover from one defendant and not from another, but that

---

35. *E.g.*, Alexander Grant, 116 F.R.D. at 589–90; *In re* Arthur Treacher's Franchise Litig., 93 F.R.D. 590, 592–93 (E.D.Pa.1982); *see also* Wolfson, *supra* note 30, at 493 n.131 (FRCP 23(b)(1)(A) and (B) not suitable for defendant class actions unless limited to claims for declaratory relief).

36. *Id.*

37. 93 F.R.D. 590 (E.D.Pa.1982).

38. *Id.*

39. *Id.* at 592–93 (citing McDonnell–Douglas Corp. v. U.S. Dist. Court for the Central District of Calif., 523 F.2d 1083, 1086 (9th Cir.1975), *cert. denied*, 425 U.S. 911, 96 S.Ct. 1506, 47 L.Ed.2d 761 (1976)); Richardson v. Hamilton Int'l Corp., 62 F.R.D. 413, 420 (E.D.Pa.1974); *see also* McBirney v. Autrey, 106 F.R.D. 240, 245 (N.D.Tex.1985) (no risk of incompatible

standards of conduct where plaintiff seeking money damages).

40. Winder Licensing, Inc. v. King Instrument Corp., 130 F.R.D. 392, 394 (N.D.Ill.1990) (denying certification and recognizing split of authority).

41. *E.g.*, Standal's Patents Ltd. v. Weyerhaeuser Co., Civ. No. 86–219–FR, 1986 WL 582 (D.Or.1986); Dale Elecs., Inc. v. R.C.L. Elecs., Inc., 53 F.R.D. 531, 537 (D.N.H.1971).

42. Winder Licensing, 130 F.R.D. at 394; *see also* Webcraft Techs., Inc. v. Alden Press, Inc., No. 85—3369, 1985 WL 2270, at *4 (N.D.Ill.1985); *In re* Yarn Processing Patent Litig., 56 F.R.D. 648, 654 (S.D.Fla. 1972).

43. *E.g.*, Alexander Grant & Co. v. McAlister, 116 F.R.D. 583, 589–90 (S.D.Ohio 1987); McBirney, 106 F.R.D. at 245.

possibility does not place him in the position of complying with one judgment while violating another."[44]

(2) Rule 23(b)(1)(B) Certification

For a defendant class to be certified under FRCP 23(b)(1)(B), a court must find that individual defendants' interests would be impaired or impeded by separate litigation.[45] There is some disagreement among courts, however, over the utilization of Rule 23(b)(1)(B) in situations where the rights of individual defendants would not be directly affected by the litigation at issue, but where the presence of common issues may lead courts deciding subsequent individual actions to follow the initial decision because of stare decisis or precedential considerations.[46] One area in which there is no dispute that Rule 23(b)(1)(B) can apply, however, is where the proposed class members share a common liability that will be satisfied by a common fund, e.g., professional liability insurance held by a partnership.[47] In such situations, not only would a judgment of liability against a partner be dispositive of other partners' liability in subsequent individual actions, but the presence of a limited insurance fund would impair the ability of the later-sued partners to protect their interests.[48]

(3) Rule 23(b)(2) Certification

There also is a split of authority over whether courts may certify defendant classes under FRCP 23(b)(2),[49] which provides that a class may be certified where "the party opposing the class has acted or refused to act on grounds generally applicable to the class."[50] Courts granting certification under this subsection generally comment (1) the drafters could have made the language explicitly applicable only to plaintiff classes, but did not and (2) that limiting one method of class certification

---

44. McBirney, 106 F.R.D. at 245.

45. See FRCP 23(b)(1)(B).

46. Compare National Union v. Midland Bancor, Inc., 158 F.R.D. 681, 687–88 (D.Kan.1994) ("generally recognized" that precedential or stare decisis effect on later cases is not sufficient to satisfy (b)(1)(B)) (citations omitted) and In re Arthur Treacher's Franchise Litig., 93 F.R.D. 590, 593–94 (E.D.Pa.1982) (possibility of stare decisis or comity effects on subsequent actions does not justify certification under (b)(1)(B); recognizing split of authority) (citations omitted) with Research Corp. v. Pfister Associated Growers, Inc., 301 F.Supp. 497, 500 (N.D.Ill.1969) (certification granted under (b)(1)(B) because of great weight afforded to prior adjudications of patent validity).

47. E.g., Alexander Grant, 116 F.R.D. at 590.

48. Id.

49. Henson v. East Lincoln Township, 814 F.2d 410, 413–17 (7th Cir.) (refusing to certify defendant class under (b)(2), but recognizing split of authority), cert. granted, 484 U.S. 923, 108 S.Ct. 283, 98 L.Ed.2d 244 (1987), cert. dismissed, 506 U.S. 1042, 113 S.Ct. 1035, 122 L.Ed.2d 111 (1993); Leer v. Washington Educ. Ass'n, 172 F.R.D. 439 (W.D.Wash.1997) (same) (citing Henson, 814 F.2d at 414–17) (further citations omitted); 7A Charles Alan Wright, Arthur R. Miller & Mary Kay Kane, Federal Practice and Procedure § 1775, at 461–62 (2d ed. 1986). See also Comment, Defendant Class Actions and Federal Civil Rights Litigation, 33 UCLA L. Rev. 283 (1985); Note, Certification of Defendant Classes Under Rule 23(b)(2), 84 Colum. L. Rev. 1371 (1984).

50. FRCP 23(b)(2).

to plaintiff classes runs contrary to the overall purpose of FRCP 23.[51] The application of these decisions may be limited, however, because they generally involve actions to enjoin public officials from enforcing a locally administered state law or administrative policy.[52] Plaintiffs often seek certification under subsection (b)(2) in civil rights cases where injunctive relief is sought against a large number of defendants,[53] but, in such situations, the proposed defendant class also will often qualify under 23(b)(1)(A) because of the risk that inconsistent adjudications will result in inconsistent standards of conduct for the plaintiff or plaintiffs.[54]

Further, the greater weight of authority is against certification of defendant classes under Rule 23(b)(2), emphasizing the incompatibility of defendant classes with the subsection's language, which provides that "the party opposing the class has acted or refused to act on grounds generally applicable to the class."[55] As the Seventh Circuit has stated, it is the defendant, not the plaintiff, "who will have 'acted or refused to act on grounds generally applicable to the class.' "[56] Denying certification of a proposed defendant class of state welfare officials for allegedly failing to provide written standards for welfare eligibility, the court emphasized that subsection (b)(2) is inapplicable to defendant classes because it is the defendants' conduct that is at issue. Similarly, in reversing certification of a class of defendant school board members throughout the state in a challenge to teacher maternity leave policies, the Fourth Circuit has recognized that certifying defendant classes under Rule 23(b)(2) "would

---

51. *See* United States v. Trucking Employers, 75 F.R.D. 682, 691–93 (D.D.C.1977) (language and context of (b)(2) makes it applicable to defendant classes); *see also* Marcera v. Chinlund, 595 F.2d 1231, 1238 (2d Cir.), *vacated on other grounds sub nom.* Lombard v. Marcera, 442 U.S. 915, 99 S.Ct. 2833, 61 L.Ed.2d 281 (1979) (defendant class of public officials certified under (b)(2) in action for injunctive relief); Thornton v. Butler, 728 F.Supp. 679, 681 n. 6 (M.D.Ala.1990) (defendant class of public officials certified under (b)(2) in challenge to state statutes).

52. *See* Greenhouse v. Greco, 617 F.2d 408, 413 n. 6 (5th Cir.1980) (citing Marcera, 595 F.2d at 1238); Thompson v. Board of Educ., 709 F.2d 1200, 1204 (6th Cir.1983) (citing Greenhouse); *but see* Trucking Employers, 75 F.R.D. at 691–93 (defendant class certified under (b)(2) in employment discrimination action); Research Corp. v. Pfister Associated Growers, Inc., 301 F.Supp. 497, 500 (N.D.Ill.1969) (defendant class certified under (b)(2) in patent infringement action).

53. *E.g.,* Trucking Employers, 75 F.R.D. 682.

54. Angelo N. Ancheta, *Defendant Class Actions and Federal Civil Rights Litigation,* 33 UCLA L. Rev. 283, 314 (1985).

55. *E.g.,* Henson v. East Lincoln Township, 814 F.2d 410, 413–17 (7th Cir.1987) (refusing to certify defendant class under (b)(2) and stating that decisions holding otherwise are not well reasoned); Thompson, 709 F.2d at 1203–04 (language of (b)(2) contemplates plaintiff classes, not defendant classes); Paxman v. Campbell, 612 F.2d 848, 854 (4th Cir.1980) (en banc) ((b)(2) applicable only to a plaintiff class seeking injunctive relief), *cert. denied sub nom.* Paxman v. Henrico County School Bd., 449 U.S. 1129, 101 S.Ct. 951, 67 L.Ed.2d 117 (1981); Leer v. Washington Educ. Ass'n, 172 F.R.D. 439 (the "better view is to restrict Rule 23(b)(2) to plaintiff classes seeking injunctive relief") (W.D. Wash. 1997) (citing Henson 814 F.2d at 414–17) (further citations omitted); National Union v. Midland Bancor, Inc., 158 F.R.D. 681, 688 & n. 6 (D.Kan.1994) (noting that every circuit court to address the issue has held that (b)(2) does not apply to defendant classes, or does so in limited circumstances) (citations omitted).

56. Henson, 814 F.2d at 414 (quoting FRCP 23(b)(2)).

create the anomalous situation in which the plaintiffs' own actions or inactions could make injunctive relief against the defendants appropriate."[57] Agreeing with this view of Rule 23(b)(2), one commentator has stated that "the language is clear, and the better view is to restrict its applicability to plaintiff classes seeking injunctive relief."[58]

(4) Rule 23(b)(3) Certification

Certification under FRCP 23(b)(3) requires that common questions of law or fact predominate over individual issues and that a class action is superior to other methods of adjudication.[59] The first requirement regarding a predominance of common issues generally will be satisfied for defendant classes "if the same theory of liability is asserted against all class members, and the same basic defenses will be raised by all class members."[60] For example, this requirement has been satisfied where basic questions of partner liability were common to both the theory of liability and the defenses of a class of defendant partners in an accounting firm.[61] The question of whether a class action is the superior method of adjudication is dependent on the particular facts of the case, with efficiency as an important consideration.[62]

As discussed in Section 15.5 above, a critical difference between certification under Rule 23(b)(3) and certification under Rule 23(b)(1) or (b)(2) is that class members have the option of opting-out of the class under Rule 23(b)(3).[63] Because of this ability to opt-out of the class, a common argument made by defendants against certification under Rule 23(b)(3) is that certification is futile because defendant class members will opt-out *en masse* rather than face liability as a member of the class.[64] Most courts have not been sympathetic to this argument, however, because of the frequent existence of numerous incentives to stay in the class, including economies of scale in defending as a class, retention of a voice in settlement, and the possibility of exposure to greater liability if sued on an individual basis.[65] Nonetheless, because there is

---

57. Paxman, 612 F.2d at 854.

58. *See* 7A Charles Alan Wright, Arthur R. Miller & Mary Kay Kane, Federal Practice and Procedure § 1775, at 462 (2d ed.1986); *see also* Winder Licensing, Inc. v. King Instrument Corp., 131 F.R.D. 538, 540 (N.D.Ill.1990) (citing Wright & Miller).

59. FRCP 23(b)(3); *see supra* § 15.5 for a general discussion of Rule 23(b)(3).

60. *See* Alexander Grant & Co. v. McAlister, 116 F.R.D. 583, 590 (S.D.Ohio 1987); *see also* McBirney v. Autrey, 106 F.R.D. 240, 246–47 (N.D.Tex.1985) (denying certification under (b)(3) because scienter of individual defendants predominated over common liability issues).

61. *See* Alexander Grant, 116 F.R.D. at 590.

62. *See, e.g.,* Osborn v. Pennsylvania–Delaware Serv. Station Dealers Ass'n, 94 F.R.D. 23, 26 (D.Del.1981); *see also supra* § 15.5.

63. *See supra* § 15.5.

64. *E.g.,* Endo v. Albertine, 147 F.R.D. 164, 171 (N.D.Ill.1993); *In re* Alexander Grant & Co. Litig., 110 F.R.D. 528, 536 (S.D.Fla.1986).

65. *See* Endo, 147 F.R.D. at 171–72 (economies of scale and continued voice in settlement limit threat of opting-out); Alvarado Partners, L.P. v. Mehta, 130 F.R.D. 673, 675 (D.Colo.1990) (speculative concern regarding possible opt-outs not sufficient to defeat certification, especially considering economic incentives to remaining in class) (citations omitted); Alexander Grant, 110 F.R.D. at 536 (remaining in class would

always the possibility that defendants will opt-out of a class and undermine the certification, courts generally view certification under Rule 23(b)(3) as less desirable and will certify defendant classes under Rule 23(b)(1) or (b)(2) if the requirements of those subsections are met.[66]

(c) Other Special Concerns for Defendant Class Actions

(1) Effect of Statutes of Limitation on Defendant Classes

Although very few courts have specifically addressed the issue, the filing of a defendant class action has generally been held to toll the statute of limitations for all purported members of the defendant class.[67] At least one court has held that even where certification is denied, the limitations period is tolled from the time of filing until the denial occurs.[68] The tolling of the statute of limitations for claims against a particular defendant ends, however, if that defendant receives notice of the suit and chooses to opt-out.[69]

(2) Plaintiff Class Suing Defendant Class

A number of courts have held that in order for a plaintiff class to bring an action against a defendant class, due process requires that each plaintiff must have a cause of action against each defendant.[70] Although there are exceptions to this general rule[71] and some courts have ignored

---

minimize expenses and potential losses); *In re* Gap Stores Securities Litig., 79 F.R.D. 283, 305 (N.D.Cal.1978) (opt-out unlikely considering pendency of other suits naming defendants individually and exposing them to greater liability); *but see In re* Arthur Treacher's Franchise Litig., 93 F.R.D. 590, 594–96 (E.D.Pa.1982) (defendants likely to opt-out because desire to control litigation more significant than risk of individual suits) (citations omitted).

66. Williams v. State Bd. of Elections, 696 F.Supp. 1574, 1576–77 (N.D.Ill.1988) (noting preference for certification under (b)(1), but certifying under (b)(3)); Guy v. Abdulla, 57 F.R.D. 14, 17 (N.D.Ohio 1972) (action under (b)(1) or (2) preferable to one brought under (b)(3)); Research Corp. v. Pfister Associated Growers, Inc., 301 F.Supp. 497, 500 (N.D.Ill.1969) (no need to consider (b)(3) where (b)(1) and (2) satisfied).

67. Appleton Elec. Co. v. Graves Truck Line, Inc., 635 F.2d 603, 609–10 (7th Cir. 1980) (citing American Pipe & Constr. Co. v. Utah, 414 U.S. 538, 94 S.Ct. 756, 38 L.Ed.2d 713 (1974)), *cert. denied,* 451 U.S. 976, 101 S.Ct. 2058, 68 L.Ed.2d 357 (1981); *In re* Activision Sec. Litig., No. C–83–4639(A) MHP, 1986 WL 15339, at *2–5 (N.D.Cal.1986) (citing Appleton, American

Pipe); *see also In re* Bestline Products Sec. and Antitrust Litig., No. MDL 162–Civ–JLK, 1975 WL 386, at *3 (S.D.Fla.1975) (statute of limitations tolled despite denial of certification; limitations period began to run once certification denied); *but see* Chevalier v. Baird Savings Ass'n, 72 F.R.D. 140, 155 & n. 45 (E.D.Pa.1976) (statute of limitations not tolled until defendants are added as individual party defendants or until class is certified and notice sent).

68. *In re* Bestline Products Sec. and Antitrust Litig., 1975 WL 386, at *2–3 (statute of limitations tolled despite denial of certification; limitations period began to run once certification denied).

69. Appleton, 635 F.2d at 610; *cf.* Doe v. Blake, 809 F.Supp. 1020, 1024 (D.Conn. 1992) (statute of limitation begins to run when a plaintiff opts-out of a class).

70. *E.g.,* La Mar v. H & B Novelty & Loan Co., 489 F.2d 461, 466 (9th Cir.1973); Haas v. Pittsburgh Nat'l Bank, 526 F.2d 1083, 1095 (3d Cir.1975) (citing La Mar).

71. The exceptions are: (1) situations where the alleged injuries result from a conspiracy among the defendants and (2) situations where the defendants are juridically related such that a single disposition

this issue,[72] plaintiff classes should be especially aware of this case law when considering bringing an action against a defendant class. Such actions are most common in cases where a group of similarly situated plaintiffs brings an action against local officials challenging the enforcement of a state law or administrative practice.[73]

Library References:

West's Key No. Digests, Federal Civil Procedure ☜161–189.
Wright, Miller & Kane, Federal Practice and Procedure: Civil 2d § 1770.

§ 15.14 Absent Class Members

Once the court has defined the class, any judgment will bind its members.[1] This includes, of course, class members who do not actually participate in the litigation. These absent class members nevertheless have certain rights and obligations with respect to the litigation. For example, a court can require the class representative to notify absent class members about the litigation and inform them that they have the right to seek to intervene.[2] On the other hand, absent class members may have relevant information that the defendant seeks to discover, and, under certain limited circumstances, they may be required to divulge that information.

(a) Intervention or Other Participation

An absent class member may have the right to participate directly in the litigation. Intervention in a class action law suit has been treated as being governed by the general rule on intervention.[3] As provided in FRCP 24, the court may be obligated to grant intervention as a matter of right, or intervention may be granted as a permissive matter.[4] Once the court grants an application to intervene, it can impose conditions on intervenors to maintain the "proper and efficient conduct of the action."[5] If an absent class member successfully intervenes in the litiga-

of the dispute would be expeditious. La Mar, 489 F.2d at 466; *see also* Doss v. Long, 93 F.R.D. 112, 120 (N.D.Ga.1981) (juridical link between defendant judges allowed certification of both plaintiff and defendant classes) (citing La Mar).

72. *E.g.,* Kendall v. True, 391 F.Supp. 413 (W.D.Ky.1975).

73. *E.g.,* Doss, 93 F.R.D. 112.

§ 15.14

1. FRCP 23(c)(3).

2. FRCP 23(d)(2) provides:

In the conduct of actions to which this rule applies, the court may make appropriate orders ... requiring, for the protection of the members of the class or otherwise for the fair conduct of the action, that notice be given in such manner

as the court may direct to some or all of the members of any step in the action, or of the proposed extent of the judgment, or of the opportunity of members to signify whether they consider the representation fair and adequate, to intervene and present claims or defenses, or otherwise to come into the action....

3. FRCP 24. *See* Chapter 14 "Parties," *supra.*

4. *Compare* FRCP 24(a) (intervention as of right) *with* FRCP 24(b) (permissive intervention).

5. FRCP 23(d)(3) (court has power to impose conditions on parties and intervenors in the conduct of class action litigation). *See also* Advisory Committee Note (recognizing that conditions may be im-

tion, the intervenor is subject to liability for an award of costs and otherwise exposes himself or herself to discovery.[6]

There are two theories by which a plaintiff may invoke the right to intervene. First, if a plaintiff can show that a statute confers that right, the court must grant the application.[7] The application to intervene, however, must be filed with the court in a timely manner.[8]

The timeliness of an application for intervention is always an element for determining whether a party has the right or should be granted permission to intervene under FRCP 24. An application is timely if the petitioner moves to intervene as soon as it becomes clear that the interests of the unnamed class members no longer will be protected adequately by the named class representatives.[9] Courts will apply the following well-settled factors in determining whether an application for intervention is timely under FRCP 24: (1) the purpose for which the intervention is sought; (2) the length of time the applicant for intervention knew or reasonably should have known of its interest in the suit before moving for leave to intervene; (3) the prejudice to the original parties due to any delay in moving for intervention; (4) any unusual circumstances militating for or against intervention; (5) the point to which suit has progressed; and (6) the prejudice to the applicant if intervention is not permitted.[10]

Second, in the absence of a statute that confers a right to intervene, a class member nevertheless must be granted that right upon a showing that: (1) the application is timely; (2) the applicant has an interest relating to the property or transaction which is the subject of the lawsuit; (3) the applicant is so situated that resolution of the lawsuit would as a practical matter impair or impede the ability to protect that interest; and (4) the applicant's interest is not adequately represented by the existing parties.[11] A request that the court exercise its discretionary

posed for the "proper and efficient conduct of the action").

6. 3 H. Newberg & A. Conte, Newberg on Class Actions § 16.13, at 16–78 (3d ed. 1992).

7. FRCP 24(a)(1). *See, e.g.,* E.E.O.C. v. National Cleaning Contractors, Inc., 1991 WL 161364 (S.D.N.Y.1991) (42 U.S.C.A. § 2000–e5(f)(1), which states that "persons aggrieved shall have the right to intervene in a civil action" brought by the government, gives the original charging party a right of intervention in a Title VII class action brought by the Equal Employment Opportunity Commission on behalf of the original charging party and others.

8. United States v. Union Elec. Co., 64 F.3d 1152, 1158–59 (8th Cir.1995) (filing motion to intervene four months after suit began was nevertheless timely because little progress toward resolution had been made).

9. United Airlines, Inc. v. McDonald, 432 U.S. 385, 394, 97 S.Ct. 2464, 2469, 53 L.Ed.2d 423 (1977) (application to intervene to litigate denial of class certification after final judgment was timely when filed within 30–day period for appeal.)

10. *See* Underwood v. State of New York Office of Court Admin., 1983 WL 504, at *3 (S.D.N.Y.1983) (listing factors) (denying request to intervene) (citations omitted). *See* Chapter 14 "Parties," at § 14.6, *supra.*

11. FRCP 24(a)(2). *See, e.g., In re* Orthopedic Bone Screw Products Liability Litigation, 1997 WL 164237, at *3–*4 (E.D.Pa. 1997) (allowing defendants to intervene in products liability class action because proposed settlement agreement would extinguish nonclass members right to seek contribution from settling defendant); Deutschman v. Beneficial Corp., 132 F.R.D.

power pursuant to FRCP 24(b) will be denied if the court finds that the absent party's interests are adequately protected by the class representatives, intervention would unduly complicate the proceedings or if the class action was instituted solely to enable the intervening party to avoid the effect of a statute that would bar him from bringing the action individually.[12]

(b) Discovery

A defendant's request for discovery of absent class members "should be permitted only to the extent necessary and should be carefully limited to ensure that it serves a legitimate purpose and is not used to harass either the class representatives or the class members."[13]

The form of the discovery should affect whether a court grants the request.[14] A majority of courts appear to allow discovery of absent class members by interrogatory or document request when the following test is met: (1) where the information requested is relevant to the decision of common questions; (2) when the discovery requests are tendered in good faith and are not unduly burdensome; and (3) when the information is not available from the class representative parties.[15]

Where a defendant seeks to take depositions from absent class members, one court has said that discovery is not appropriate unless: (1) the discovery is not designed as a tactic to take undue advantage of the class or as a stratagem to reduce the number of claimants; (2) the discovery is necessary; (3) the discovery does not require the assistance of technical and legal advice in understanding the questions and formulating responses; and (4) the discovery does not seek information on matters already known to the defendant.[16]

Library References:
West's Key No. Digests, Federal Civil Procedure ⚫161–189.
Wright, Miller & Kane, Federal Practice and Procedure: Civil 2d §§ 1796.1, 1799.

§ 15.15   Judgments

(a) Form

The requisite form of a class action judgment depends upon whether the class action was certified under FRCP 23(b)(1), (2), or (3).

359, 380–82 (D.Del.1990) (denying intervention as of right but granting permissive intervention in securities class action because defenses against class representative may not apply to other class members).

12. 7B Charles A. Wright, Arthur R. Miller & Mary Kay Kane., Federal Practice and Procedure § 1799, at 442–45 (2d. ed. 1986).

13. Manual for Complex Litigation, (Third) § 30.232, at 254 (1997).

14. *Id.* at 255.

15. Transamerican Refining Corp. v. Dravo Corp., 139 F.R.D. 619, 621 (S.D.Tex. 1991) (citing cases) (allowing limited discovery of absent class members through interrogatories).

16. Clark v. Universal Builders, Inc., 501 F.2d 324, 340–41 (7th Cir.), *cert. denied*, 419 U.S. 1070, 95 S.Ct. 657, 42 L.Ed.2d 666 (1974) (denying request for depositions of absent class members).

The judgment in an action maintained under FRCP 23(b)(1) or (2) must include and describe those persons whom the court has determined are members of the class.[1] The judgment need not specify the individual members of the class, however.[2]

By contrast, the judgment in an action maintained under FRCP 23(b)(3) must include and specify or describe those to whom the notice required by FRCP 23(c)(2) was directed, and who have not opted-out of the class, and whom the court has determined are members of the class.[3] In particular, a FRCP 23(b)(3) judgment must specify the individual members of the class who have been identified, and describe the others.[4] Such a judgment omits only those who have requested exclusion from the class or who are ultimately found by the court not to be members of the class.[5]

All of these rules apply whether or not the judgment is favorable to the class.[6] Procedural defects in the judgment generally may be corrected following a remand to the trial court.[7]

(b) Effect

Class action judgments constitute an exception to the general rule that one cannot be bound in personam by a judgment in a litigation to which he is not a party.[8] Absent class members who are not identified as parties to the class action nonetheless will be bound by the judgment where their interests were adequately represented by the class representatives and attorneys.[9]

§ 15.15

1. FRCP 23(c)(3). For example, in a Title VII action against a motor carrier employer, the trial court described the scope of the class as including the nominal plaintiff, William E. Bing, "on behalf of himself and all black employees of Roadway Express, Inc." Bing v. Roadway Express, Inc., 485 F.2d 441, 447 (5th Cir.1973). As one remedy, the trial court had ordered Roadway "to notify all of its black employees at [Roadway's] Atlanta terminal to come forward if they desired a road driver position." Id. at 447–48. The Fifth Circuit interpreted the trial court's description of the class in this context and found that the trial court, while "fail[ing] to follow explicitly the mandate of Rule 23(c)(3)," intended the class to include "all black employees at Roadway's Atlanta terminal." Id. at 447, 448.

2. Advisory Committee Notes to FRCP 23(c)(3), 1966 amendment.

3. FRCP 23(c)(3).

4. Advisory Committee Notes to FRCP 23(c)(3), 1966 amendment.

5. Id.

6. Id.; FRCP 23(c)(3).

7. See Vaughter v. Eastern Air Lines, Inc., 817 F.2d 685, 689 (11th Cir.1987) ("[W]here the parties have operated under the understanding that a suit is being maintained as a class action, the failure of the district court to designate in the judgment the class thereby bound may be deemed an oversight or omission subject to correction pursuant to Rule 60(a)."); Young v. Katz, 447 F.2d 431, 435 (5th Cir.1971) (finding that procedural defect in a judgment approving a class action settlement was inadvertent and remanding for correction where the judgment did not specify those to whom notices were directed and who had not requested exclusion and whom the court had found to be members of a class).

8. Hansberry v. Lee, 311 U.S. 32, 40–41, 61 S.Ct. 115, 117–18, 85 L.Ed. 22 (1940).

9. E.g., Sam Fox Publ'g Co. v. United States, 366 U.S. 683, 692, 81 S.Ct. 1309, 1314, 6 L.Ed.2d 604 (1961); E.E.O.C. v. Children's Hosp. Med. Ctr., 719 F.2d 1426, 1434 (9th Cir.1983) ("Courts have consis-

(1) Res Judicata/Claim Preclusion

The res judicata effect of a class action judgment, like that of other judgments, is tested and determined in a subsequent lawsuit.[10] Nevertheless, the court "in framing the judgment in any suit brought as a class action, must decide what its extent or coverage shall be, and if the matter is carefully considered, questions of res judicata are less likely to be raised at a later time and if raised will be more satisfactorily answered."[11] To ensure that the scope of res judicata effect in a class action is neither too wide nor too narrow, the judgment should be worded as precisely as possible, to include all members of the intended class.[12]

The judgment will have binding and preclusive effect on absent class members only where, in addition to the other requisites of res judicata,[13] the requirements of due process have been satisfied. In *Phillips Petroleum Co. v. Shutts*,[14] the Supreme Court held that for a forum state to bind an absent plaintiff regarding claims "wholly or predominately for money judgments," it must provide minimal procedural due process protection.[15] This protection includes notice to the absent class member plus an opportunity to be heard and participate in the litigation.[16] The

tently held that absent class members whose interests are adequately represented are bound by the judgment.").

10. Advisory Committee Notes to FRCP 23(c)(3), 1966 amendment; Harrison v. Lewis, 559 F.Supp. 943, 947 (D.D.C.1983). *See* Chapter 12 "Issue and Claim Preclusion," at § 12.11 *supra*.

11. Advisory Committee Notes to FRCP 23(c)(3), 1966 Amendment; *see* Coleman v. Wilson, 912 F.Supp. 1282, 1299 n. 12 (E.D.Cal.1995) (terms of judgment in prior class action stated that class consisted of all inmates housed at a certain facility and did not expressly include future inmates; thus, those inmates were not precluded from bringing suit).

12. On the other hand, where the judgment describes the class by implication, that description may be sufficient, and the failure of the judgment to describe the class specifically will not necessarily deprive it of its binding effect. *See* Johnson v. General Motors Corp., 598 F.2d 432, 435 (5th Cir. 1979) ("The identity of the class is implicit in the final order in light of the preceding actions of this and the district court; the technical failure of the district court to expressly describe the class does not alter the res judicata effect of the judgment.").

13. *See* Huguley v. General Motors Corp., 999 F.2d 142, 146 (6th Cir.1993) (observing that principles of res judicata apply with "special effect" in the class ac-

tion context); King v. South Cent. Bell Tel. & Tel. Co., 790 F.2d 524, 528 (6th Cir.1986)(holding that to bar an action on the basis of res judicata, in addition to satisfying due process requirements specific to class actions, the parties must have been identical in both actions, the prior judgment must have been rendered by a court of competent jurisdiction, there must have been a final judgment on the merits, and both cases must involve the same cause of action); *see also* Cooper v. Fed. Reserve Bank, 467 U.S. 867, 880–82, 104 S.Ct. 2794, 2801–02, 81 L.Ed.2d 718 (1984) (holding in the context of a racial discrimination case that a class action judgment barred the class members from bringing claims alleging a pattern of discrimination, but was not dispositive of individual discrimination claims); *accord* Cameron v. Tomes, 990 F.2d 14, 17–18 (1st Cir.1993) (res judicata did not bar claims based on special, individualized circumstances).

14. 472 U.S. 797, 105 S.Ct. 2965, 86 L.Ed.2d 628 (1985).

15. *Id.* at 811–12 & n. 3, 105 S.Ct. at 2974 & n. 3.

16. *Id.* at 812, 105 S.Ct. at 2974 ; *see also* Besinga v. United States, 923 F.2d 133, 137 (9th Cir.1991) (holding that appellant was not barred by res judicata from pursuing his claim where the absent class members in a Rule 23(b)(3) class action were not

notice must be "the best practicable, 'reasonably calculated, under all the circumstances, to apprise interested parties of the pendency of the action and afford them an opportunity to present their objections.' "[17] The notice should also describe the action and the plaintiff's rights in it. Second, the absent plaintiff must have the opportunity to opt-out of the class by returning a form to that effect to the court.[18] Finally, the named plaintiff must at all times adequately represent the interests of the absent class members.[19]

Since *Phillips Petroleum* was decided, some lower courts have concluded that the decision's opt-out requirements do not apply to a FRCP 23(b)(1) or (2) action where claims for injunctive relief predominate, and that the *Phillips Petroleum* requirements are limited to FRCP 23(b)(3) suits.[20] Further, it has been held that it is unnecessary that each class member actually receive notice, provided that the notification method selected is reasonably calculated to apprise class members of the pendency of the action.[21] On the other hand, it has also been held that before an absent class member may be barred from pursuing a subsequent individual claim for damages, adequate notice must have been

provided with the requisite notice); *cf.* Schwarzschild v. Tse, 69 F.3d 293, 295 (9th Cir.1995) (holding that where summary judgment was obtained prior to class certification and notice to the class, defendants waived their right to compel the plaintiff to notify the class of the pending action, with the resulting effect that only the named plaintiffs were bound by the judgment), *cert. denied*, 517 U.S. 1121, 116 S.Ct. 1355, 134 L.Ed.2d 523 (1996).

17. *See* Phillips Petroleum, 472 U.S. at 812, 105 S.Ct. at 2974 (quoting Mullane v. Cent. Hanover Bank & Trust Co., 339 U.S. 306, 314–15, 70 S.Ct. 652, 657–58, 94 L.Ed. 865 (1950)).

18. *Id.*

19. *Id.*

20. *In re* Joint E. & S. Dist. Asbestos Litig., 78 F.3d 764 (2d Cir.1996) (upholding district court's denial of motion to opt-out, the court distinguished *Phillips Petroleum* on the ground that that case's ruling was limited to claims for money judgments, as opposed to claims for equitable relief); White v. Nat'l Football League, 822 F.Supp. 1389, 1410, 1412 (D.Minn.1993) (although class members were not permitted to opt-out in a FRCP 23(b)(1) class action, the court held that due process requirements were satisfied where the named plaintiffs and class counsel adequately represented the objectors, and the objectors were provided with adequate notice of the proposed

settlement, given an opportunity to object to the settlement, and assured that the settlement would not be approved unless the court determined it to be fair, reasonable, and adequate), *aff'd*, 41 F.3d 402 (8th Cir.1994); *see also* Battle v. Liberty Nat'l Life Ins. Co., 770 F.Supp. 1499, 1517 n. 51 (N.D.Ala.1991) (further distinguishing *Phillips Petroleum* on the ground that, among other things, the Supreme Court's due process analysis dealt with out of state class members in a state court action, analogizing them to such out of state defendants who are protected by due process' "minimum contacts" requirement), *aff'd*, 974 F.2d 1279 (11th Cir.1992), *cert. denied*, 509 U.S. 906, 113 S.Ct. 2999, 125 L.Ed.2d 692 (1993).

21. *In re* Cherry's Petition to Intervene, 164 F.R.D. 630, 637 (E.D.Mich.1996) (finding that notice scheme passed constitutional muster where the parties mailed notice to the class members at their last known addresses, which were updated if necessary, notice was published in two publications, and the action received front-page news coverage in a city newspaper); *In re* Prudential Secs. Inc. Ltd. Partnerships Litig., 164 F.R.D. 362, 368 (S.D.N.Y.) ("It is widely recognized that for the due process standard to be met it is not necessary that every class member receive actual notice, so long as class counsel acted reasonably to inform persons affected."), *aff'd*, 107 F.3d 4 (2d Cir.1996), *cert. denied* ___ U.S. ___, 117 S.Ct. 2509, 138 L.Ed.2d 1013 (1997).

given that his damages claim would be precluded except as part of the class action suit.[22]

Regardless of the type of class action, due process requires that, before a judgment will be given binding effect, absent class members must have been adequately represented.[23] Adequate representation of the absent class members entails a two-part inquiry: (1) Did the trial court in the first suit correctly determine, initially, that the representative would adequately represent the class and (2) Does it appear, after the termination of the suit, that the class representative in fact adequately protected the interest of the class?[24]

(2) Collateral Estoppel/Issue Preclusion

Even when a class action judgment does not present a res judicata bar to subsequent litigation, a class member still may be precluded from relitigating issues that actually were litigated and decided in the class action.[25]

First, the issue sought to be precluded must be the same as that involved in the prior action.[26] Second, the issue must have been actually litigated.[27] Third, the issue must have been determined by a valid, final

---

22. Wright v. Collins, 766 F.2d 841, 847–48 (4th Cir.1985) (finding class notice to be inadequate to preclude an individual damages claim for civil rights violations where the notice generally informed the class of the existence of the litigation, and the questions raised by it, but did not specify the forms of relief sought or notify class members of the effect of class membership); *accord* Morgan v. Ward, 699 F.Supp. 1025, 1035 (N.D.N.Y.1988).

23. *E.g.*, White, 822 F.Supp. at 1412.

24. Gonzales v. Cassidy, 474 F.2d 67, 72, 75 (5th Cir.1973) (concluding that the absent class members were not adequately represented and would not be bound by the judgment where the class representative failed to appeal a decision that was adverse to all members of the class except the representative); Johnson v. Shreveport Garment Co., 422 F.Supp. 526, 533 (W.D.La.1976) (stating that absent class members' interests must be represented adequately at every stage in a proceeding, and that otherwise a court is powerless to bind them to a judgment), *aff'd*, 577 F.2d 1132 (5th Cir. 1978).

25. Morgan, 699 F.Supp. at 1035 ("An issue necessarily decided in an action for equitable relief can have collateral estoppel effect in a subsequent action for damages.").

26. *In re* Piper Aircraft Distribution Sys. Antitrust Litig., 551 F.2d 213, 218 (8th

Cir.1977); *cf.* TBK Partners, Ltd. v. Western Union Corp., 675 F.2d 456, 461 (2d Cir.1982) (observing in the context of a class action settlement that, as long as the settlement is fair and class members are given sufficient notice and opportunity to object to the release, relitigation of a claim or issue based on an "identical factual predicate" can be barred; "where there is a realistic identity of issues between the settled class action and the subsequent suit, and where the relationship between the suits is at the time of the class action foreseeably obvious to notified class members," the policy of encouraging settlement takes priority).

27. *In re* Piper Aircraft Distribution Sys. Antitrust Litig., 551 F.2d at 218; *see* Detroit Police Officers Ass'n v. Young, 824 F.2d 512, 517 (6th Cir.1987) (holding that it was proper to collaterally estop plaintiffs from relitigating general issues of discrimination that had been litigated and decided in class action, but that collateral estoppel was improperly applied to preclude consideration of the more specific question of the affirmative action remedy imposed by the city where that issue had not been litigated nor decided in the class action); Morgan, 699 F. Supp. at 1036–37 (holding that plaintiffs' due process claims were not collaterally estopped by prior class action where the court in that action had only considered disciplinary proceedings during a time peri-

judgment.[28] Fourth, the determination must have been necessary to the outcome of the prior judgment.[29] Finally, the party against whom estoppel is sought must have had a full and fair opportunity to litigate.[30] At least one court has ruled, in applying this last requirement, that, for members of a class to be collaterally estopped by a decision entered in a prior class action, the two classes need not be "identical," provided that they share a "strong community of interests."[31]

Although it is clear that a class member who has properly elected to opt-out of a class action will not bound by an adverse judgment, it is less certain whether and to what extent such an individual may take advantage of a favorable outcome in a subsequent suit.[32] As one court has reasoned, "To permit a plaintiff who declines to join a class action brought under Rule 26(b)(3) of the Federal Rules of Civil Procedure to later apply collateral estoppel to a prior favorable judgment rendered in the class action could burden the defendants with multiple suits and may be contrary to the notion of promoting judicial efficiency."[33] Although such a view may well be understandable from a practical standpoint, it is not so simple to identify a theoretical basis for the view that persons opting-out of a class action should be precluded thereafter from making any offensive use of the judgment entered in the class action. When a case is decided against defendants outside the class action context, a person not involved in the lawsuit can seek to use the judgment offensively in subsequent litigation against the same defendant. It is not clear why persons opting-out of a class action should not have a comparable opportunity to assert offensive collateral estoppel based on the outcome of the class action.

od subsequent to the time relevant to plaintiffs' claims and the procedures employed at such proceedings had changed since the time relevant to plaintiffs' claims).

28. *In re* Piper Aircraft Distribution Sys. Antitrust Litig., 551 F.2d at 219–20 (vacating and remanding district court's dismissal of class action allegations in six antitrust actions on collateral estoppel grounds where class action had been voluntarily dismissed without prejudice and was, therefore, not a final judgment).

29. Detroit Police Officers Ass'n, 824 F.2d at 515.

30. *Id.*; *see* Coates v. Kelley, 957 F.Supp. 1080, 1085 (E.D.Ark.1997) (dismissing the claim of two disabled plaintiffs, the court accorded collateral estoppel effect to an earlier consent judgment in a class action suit where the plaintiffs were members of the settlement class; plaintiffs had a full and fair opportunity to litigate because the class action parties had provided adequate notice to the class and the class representatives could "be counted on to fairly

and adequately protect the interests of the class, as evidenced by, inter alia, their vigorous negotiation on behalf of the national class to date").

31. Detroit Police Officers Ass.n, 824 F.2d at 515–16 (two different but overlapping classes challenging the same voluntary affirmative action program; second class precluded from relitigating the correctness of the city's determination that it had engaged in past discrimination).

32. *Compare* Sarasota Oil Co. v. Greyhound Leasing & Fin. Corp., 483 F.2d 450, 452 (10th Cir.1973) (prohibiting excluded class member from maintaining an action based on the class action judgment) *with In re* TransOcean Tender Offer Secs. Litig., 455 F.Supp. 999, 1006 (N.D.Ill.1978) (holding that based on collateral estoppel principles, excluded plaintiffs were not prohibited from claiming the benefit of a judgment won by the class).

33. Polk v. Montgomery County, Md., 782 F.2d 1196, 1202 (4th Cir.1986) (footnotes omitted).

Library References:
West's Key No. Digests, Federal Civil Procedure ⊛2572; Judgment ⊛678(7).
Wright, Miller & Cooper, Federal Practice and Procedure: Civil 2d § 1789.

§ 15.16 Settlement Classes

After the 1966 amendments to Rule 23, courts increasingly began to entertain conditionally certified "settlement classes" as vehicles for achieving class-wide resolution of disputes, subject to court approval under FRCP 23(e) (discussed below). In some cases, class certification and settlement approval were sought by the parties simultaneously; in others, a conditional class certification preceded meaningful settlement negotiations. In either situation, settlement classes were to a greater or lesser degree premised on the notion that the parties might tentatively agree to class certification in the context of a possible proposed settlement, without first requiring the court to make definitive findings with respect to the various criteria of FRCP 23. In the event that efforts to settle on a class-wide basis ultimately failed, the party aligned against the putative class might still be able to mount credible opposition to class certification.

Because settlement classes by their very nature spark relatively few adversarial proceedings, little was written about the precise role of the criteria of Rule 23(a) and (b) in formulating such classes. Courts tended in some cases to focus their concerns on the reasonableness of the proposed settlement under Rule 23(e), without significant separate scrutiny of the underlying appropriateness of class certification. In such cases, the fact of settlement might gloss over defects in class certification that would have been exposed in a contested context.

In response to concerns that settlement classes could invite abuse of the class action device—particularly where class certification was otherwise unlikely, and plaintiffs' settlement leverage was therefore quite limited—a line of precedent developed in the Third Circuit holding that the fact of settlement should be regarded as irrelevant to class certification. Under the Third Circuit's analysis, a class should not be certified for settlement purposes unless it also would meet the criteria for class certification as a fully litigated matter.

In *Amchem Products, Inc. v. Windsor*,[1] the Supreme Court disagreed with the extreme position staked out by the Third Circuit that settlement is irrelevant to class certification. Among other things, the Supreme Court noted that issues relating to management of the putative class action are of lesser significance where a settlement has been achieved.[2] Nevertheless, the Court agreed that the requirements of Rule 23(a) and (b) continue to have significance in the settlement context. First, these requirements minimize the likelihood of certifications based on subjective impressions or arbitrary criteria of a trial court.[3] Second, analyzing settlement classes by reference to these criteria discloses

§ 15.16

1. __ U.S. __, 117 S.Ct. 2231, 138 L.Ed.2d 689 (1997)

2. *Id.*

3. *Id.*

whether there is a realistic possibility that a litigation class could be certified, which in turn bears upon the strength of class counsel's negotiating position. If class counsel can only recover on a class-wide basis through settlement—because no litigation class could be certified—there may be reason to believe that the party opposing the class will have an undue advantage in settlement discussions, because class counsel may be tempted to sacrifice a significant portion of the value of class members' individual claims in exchange for an agreement to enter into a settlement on a class-wide basis.

Amchem should bring improved uniformity to practice regarding settlement classes. Although it is possible under *Amchem* to stipulate to class certification for settlement purposes without conceding that a class could properly be certified for litigation purposes, the simple fact that a proposed settlement is reasonable does not, under *Amchem*, justify class certification to achieve that settlement. The basic requirements of Rule 23—and particularly the constitutionally-driven requirements of Rule 23(a)—remain indispensable.

Amchem may also affect the fate of a proposed amendment to FRCP 23, which would have addressed settlement classes specifically. In the wake of the Supreme Court's decision, it is unclear whether there will still be a perceived need for the proposed amendment.

Library References:

West's Key No. Digests, Compromise and Settlement ⟐67.
Wright, Miller & Cooper, Federal Practice and Procedure: Civil 2d § 3914.19.

§ 15.17   Settlement Procedure

According to FRCP 23(e), the settlement of a class action requires court approval and notice "to all members of the class in such manner as the court directs." The general practice followed by courts in implementing Rule 23(e) is to conduct an initial approval hearing, which is attended by counsel for the parties and is held prior to notifying the class of the proposed settlement. The purpose of the preliminary approval hearing is to determine "whether the proposed settlement is 'within the range of possible approval' or, in other words, whether there is 'probable cause' to notify the class of the proposed settlement."[1] A trial judge will take into consideration the arm's length nature of the negotiations, the amount of discovery, the ability and experience of counsel, and the extent of any anticipated opposition by class members.[2] One major concern is to ensure that the settlement is not illegal or collusive.[3] If the

---

§ 15.17

1. Horton v. Merrill Lynch, Pierce, Fenner & Smith, Inc., 855 F.Supp. 825 (E.D.N.C.1994).

2. *In re* General Motors Corp. Pick–Up Truck Fuel Tank Litig., 55 F.3d 768, 785 (3d Cir.), *cert. denied sub nom.* General Motors Corp. v. French, 516 U.S. 824, 116 S.Ct. 88, 133 L.Ed.2d 45 (1995).

3. United States v. City of Miami, Fla., 614 F.2d 1322, 1330–31 (5th Cir.1980) ("A ... careful scrutiny is necessary to guard against settlements that may benefit the class representatives or their attorneys at the expense of absent class members or shareholders.").

court preliminarily approves the settlement, notice is sent to class members. After class members have been given an opportunity to submit objections to the settlement, the court holds a hearing to determine finally whether the proposed settlement is fair, reasonable and adequate.[4]

Rule 23(e) applies to the settlement of all class actions without regard to whether certification under Rule 23(c)(1) has already been obtained.[5] The requirement of court approval is intended to protect absent class members.[6] When presented with a proposed class action settlement for approval, a court is required to assess the fairness, adequacy, and reasonableness of the settlement.[7] The court's role resembles that of a fiduciary as it ensures that the proposed settlement does not unfairly compromise the rights of class members.[8]

Under Rule 23(e), courts have broad discretion in selecting the kind of notice to use in notifying class members of a settlement hearing.[9] Actual notice to absent class members is not required;[10] the notice need only be reasonable enough to satisfy due process.[11] Typically, the Rule 23(e) notice requirement is satisfied by a combination of mailing notice to class members and by publication in a national or local publication, depending on the scope of the class.[12]

In terms of content, the notice "must provide the class members with sufficient information to consider the terms of the settlement and decide whether there is a basis for challenging the settlement."[13] The notice should include the terms of the proposed settlement, the time and place of the fairness hearing, and the procedure for objecting to the settlement or for seeking to be excluded from the settlement.[14]

In securities class actions, Congress has prescribed expressly what information must be contained in a Rule 23(e) notice,[15] including the following:

4. Reed v. Rhodes, 869 F.Supp. 1274, 1278 (N.D.Ohio 1994).

5. E.g., Baker v. America's Mortg. Servicing, Inc., 58 F.3d 321 (7th Cir.1995); Caston v. Mr. T's Apparel, Inc., 157 F.R.D. 31 (S.D.Miss.1994).

6. Detroit Police Officers Ass'n v. Young, 920 F.Supp. 755 (E.D.Mich.1995) (Rule 23(e) is intended to protect class members whose rights may not have been given due regard by negotiating parties.).

7. Malchman v. Davis, 706 F.2d 426, 433 (2d Cir.1983), cert. denied, 475 U.S. 1143, 106 S.Ct. 1798, 90 L.Ed.2d 343 (1986).

8. In re Joint E. and S. Dist. Asbestos Litig., 129 B.R. 710 (E.D.N.Y.1991), vacat-

ed, 982 F.2d 721 (2d Cir.1992), opinion modified on reh'g, 993 F.2d 7 (2d Cir.1993).

9. Franks v. Kroger Co., 649 F.2d 1216, 1222–23 (6th Cir.), vacated on reh'g on other grounds, 670 F.2d 671 (7th Cir.1981).

10. Silber v. Mabon, 18 F.3d 1449 (9th Cir.1994).

11. DeBoer v. Mellon Mortg. Co., 64 F.3d 1171, 1176 (8th Cir.1995), cert. denied, 517 U.S. 1156, 116 S.Ct. 1544, 134 L.Ed.2d 648 (1996).

12. Id.; Handschu v. Special Services Division, 787 F.2d 828 (2d Cir.1986).

13. In re Shell Oil Refinery, 155 F.R.D. 552, 558 (E.D.La.1993).

14. Id.

15. 15 U.S.C.A. § 77z–1(a)(7); 15 U.S.C.A. § 78u–4(a)(7) (West 1995).

- the total amount of the settlement to be distributed to class members, both in the aggregate and on a per share basis;[16]

- a statement on the potential outcome of the litigation including the average amount of damages per share that could be recovered if plaintiffs were to prevail on their claims (if the parties are in agreement on this amount);[17]

- a statement concerning the amount of attorneys' fees and costs that the parties seek to pay from any settlement fund;[18]

- the name, address, and telephone number of one or more representatives of counsel for the plaintiff class who can be contacted for information;[19] and

- a brief statement of the reasons why the settlement is proposed to the class.[20]

Library References:

West's Key No. Digests, Compromise and Settlement ⊕51–72.
Wright, Miller & Cooper, Federal Practice and Procedure: Civil 2d § 3533.2.

§ 15.18   Substantive Factors Governing Court Approval of Settlement

The decision whether to approve or reject a proposed class action settlement is left to the discretion of the trial court.[1] In considering the settlement of a class action, the court is required to determine whether the settlement proposal is "fair, reasonable and adequate."[2] There are two considerations that are essential to this analysis. First, the court must examine the substantive terms of the settlement and compare those terms "with the likely rewards of the litigation."[3] The court also must consider the process by which the proposed settlement was reached. "The settlement must be the result of arms' length negotiations, and plaintiffs' attorney must possess experience and ability and have engaged in sufficient discovery to effectively represent the interests of the class."[4]

---

16. 15 U.S.C.A. § 77z–1(a)(7)(A) (West 1995); 15 U.S.C.A. § 78u–4(a)(7)(A) (West 1995).

17. 15 U.S.C.A. § 77z–1(a)(7)(B) (West 1995); 15 U.S.C.A. § 78u–4(a)(7)(B) (West 1995).

18. 15 U.S.C.A. § 77z–1(a)(7)(C) (West 1995); 15 U.S.C.A. § 78u–4(a)(7)(C) (West 1995).

19. 15 U.S.C.A. § 77z–1(a)(7)(D) (West 1995); 15 U.S.C.A. § 78u–4(a)(7)(D) (West 1995).

20. 15 U.S.C.A. § 77z–1(a)(7)(E) (West 1995); 15 U.S.C.A. § 78u–4(a)(7)(E) (West 1995).

§ 15.18

1. Cohen v. Resolution Trust Corp., 61 F.3d 725, 728 (9th Cir.1995).

2. Weinberger v. Kendrick, 698 F.2d 61, 73 (2d Cir.1982), *cert. denied*, 464 U.S. 818, 104 S.Ct. 77, 78 L.Ed.2d 89 (1983).

3. Protective Comm. for Indep. Stockholders of TMT Trailer Ferry, Inc. v. Anderson, 390 U.S. 414, 424–25, 88 S.Ct. 1157, 1163–64, 20 L.Ed.2d 1 (1968).

4. Neilan v. Value Vacations, Inc., 116 F.R.D. 431, 436 (S.D.N.Y.1987).

Courts typically take the following factors into consideration in carrying out their examination of the substance of the proposed settlement and the process by which the compromise was reached:[5]

    (1) the complexity, expense and likely duration of the litigation;

    (2) the reaction of the class to the settlement;

    (3) the stage of the proceedings and the amount of discovery completed;

    (4) the risks of establishing liability;

    (5) the risks of establishing damages;

    (6) the risks of maintaining the class through trial;

    (7) the ability of the defendants to withstand a greater settlement;

    (8) the range of reasonableness of the settlement fund in light of the best possible recovery;

    (9) the range of reasonableness of the settlement fund in light of all the attendant risks of litigation.

The mere fact that a proposed settlement is only a small fraction of the potential damages asserted in the litigation is not a per se showing of inadequacy.[6] Courts usually apply a higher degree of scrutiny to settlements that are reached before final certification of a class.[7]

Library References:

West's Key No. Digests, Compromise and Settlement ⊕51–72.
Wright, Miller & Kane, Federal Practice and Procedure: Civil 2d § 2784.

§ 15.19   Additional Issues in Nationwide Class Actions Based on State Substantive Law

Prior sections of this chapter have addressed some of the issues that commonly arise in nationwide class actions based on state substantive law. Particularly where such actions are brought in federal court, it may not be possible to exercise subject matter jurisdiction over all class claims.[1] Personal jurisdiction over absent class members who are not residents of the forum state may depend upon providing such individuals a meaningful opportunity to exclude themselves.[2] Beyond these issues, however, such class actions raise additional challenges from the standpoint of manageability, due in large measure to choice of law considerations.

5. Pozzi v. Smith, CCH Federal Securities Law Reporter (Current Binder) & 99,422 (E.D. Pa. 1997), quoting Girsh v. Jepson, 521 F.2d 153, 157 (3d Cir.1975).

6. City of Detroit v. Grinnell Corporation, 495 F.2d 448, 455 (2d Cir.1974).

7. *In re* Drexel Burnham Lambert Group, Inc., 130 B.R. 910 (S.D.N.Y.1991).

§ 15.19

1. *See supra* § 15.9.

2. *See supra* §§ 15.14, 15.15.

(a) Choice of Law in Class Litigation—General Rule

In *Phillips Petroleum v. Shutts*,[3] the Supreme Court observed that the Constitution (through the Due Process Clause, the Full Faith and Credit Clause, or both) limits the circumstances under which a state may apply its own law to all claims asserted in a nationwide class action. Specifically, the Court held that a state "must have a 'significant contact or significant aggregation of contacts' to the claims asserted by each member of the plaintiff class, contacts 'creating state interests' " in order to apply its law to the claim of each member of a plaintiff class.[4] Absent such contacts, the Court noted, the application of the law of the forum state—or any single state—would be arbitrary.

Phillips Petroleum spawned a new dimension in manageability analysis of nationwide class actions based on state substantive law. Where class certification is sought under FRCP 23(b)(3), and multiple states' substantive law may be at issue, a federal court conducting a jury trial must consider whether it will be possible to instruct the jury properly on the applicable law without creating hopeless confusion. This in turn will largely be a function of whether any differences in state law present "false" or "true" conflicts. The greater the number of variations in state law, the more difficult it will be to manage the trial of the action.

The need to apply multiple states' substantive law in a given case underscores the importance of considering at least a preliminary trial plan in such cases at the earliest possible state of litigation, ideally in advance of the class certification decision. A detailed trial plan often will not be possible before substantial exploration of the underlying facts. It is nevertheless normally beneficial to the court and the litigants to consider the question of class certification against the backdrop of a concrete proposal that would result in a class-wide judgment, so that all involved may make a better informed judgment on issues of manageability.

For example, the use of special verdicts under FRCP 49(a) may be proffered as a solution to manageability difficulties flowing from multiplicity of state law. Whether the use of such verdict forms is a practical solution depends upon the nature of the case and the number of different verdict forms that would be necessary.

(b) Choice of Law in Class Litigation—Exceptions

Some important areas of law are not governed by *Phillips Petroleum* analysis on choice of law, and states are therefore free in such areas to apply their own law even if they have no substantial connection to the facts giving rise to the litigation. In *Sun Oil Co. v. Wortman*,[5] for example, the Supreme Court reaffirmed that, notwithstanding *Phillips Petroleum*, states are free to apply their own statutes of limitations. That another state's law might be the source of the substantive duties at issue did not change this result.

---

3. 472 U.S. 797, 105 S.Ct. 2965, 86 L.Ed.2d 628 (1985).

4. 472 U.S. at 821, 105 S.Ct. at 2979.

5. 486 U.S. 717, 108 S.Ct. 2117, 100 L.Ed.2d 743 (1988).

The fact that statutes of limitations are not regarded as substantive for the purposes of the Full Faith and Credit Clause can have important implications in class litigation. A state with a relatively long statute of limitations may be a very attractive class venue from a plaintiff's viewpoint, while a state with a short statute (or a borrowing provision that tends to shorten the applicable period) may be a poor forum from a plaintiff's perspective. Consideration of the issue is complicated by the fact that dismissal of, for example, a nonresident absent class member's claim on the ground that the claim is barred by the forum state's statute of limitations may or may not bar subsequent litigation on the same claim under a different statute of limitations.[6]

(c) The Importance of Limits on State Sovereignty in Nationwide Class Litigation

Phillips Petroleum suggests that the choice of law principles articulated in that opinion flow from the Due Process Clause or the Full Faith and Credit Clause, or perhaps both. *Phillips Petroleum* should be considered in conjunction with a closely related but distinct line of authority—grounded in part on the Commerce Clause as well as principles of state comity—that has prompted the Supreme Court to observe (in a nonclass context) that "a State may not impose economic sanctions on violators of its laws with the intent of changing the tortfeasor's lawful conduct in other states."[7] As a general matter, a state statute may not under the Commerce Clause be applied to commerce wholly outside the state's borders, even if the commerce has effects within the state and the state legislature intended the statute to have extra-territorial effect.[8]

Adding this principle to the Supreme Court's observations in *Phillips Petroleum*, certain kinds of class litigation can be seen to present serious manageability concerns. Even where a class action defendant may be incorporated in a given state, for example, it may not be possible under the Commerce Clause to apply that state's law to every transaction in which that defendant engaged, on a nationwide basis. In sum, there may be situations where no single state's law can be applied to all the claims sought to be joined in a putative class action. Where this problem is present, it tends to undermine the manageability and superiority of the proposed class action.

Library References:

West's Key No. Digests, Federal Civil Procedure ⚲161–189.
Wright, Miller & Kane, Federal Practice and Procedure: Civil 2d § 1758.

6. An example of a borrowing statute that tends to shorten the applicable period is the following from Pennsylvania law: "... [t]he period of limitation applicable to a claim accruing outside the Commonwealth shall either be that provided or prescribed by the law of the place where the claim accrued or by the law of this Commonwealth, whichever first bars the claim."

42 Pa. Cons. Stat. Ann. § 5521(b) (West 1981) (based on the Uniform Statute of Limitations on Foreign Claims Act).

7. BMW of North America, Inc. v. Gore, 517 U.S. 559, 571, 116 S.Ct. 1589, 1597, 134 L.Ed.2d 809 (1996).

8. Healy v. Beer Institute, 491 U.S. 324, 336, 109 S.Ct. 2491, 2496, 105 L.Ed.2d 275 (1989) (citations omitted).

§ 15.20 Attorneys' Fees

Under the "American Rule," a litigant ordinarily pays its own attorneys' fees, even if it prevails on the merits of the case.[1] There are several exceptions to the general rule, however. Two of these exceptions—statutory provisions authorizing recovery of attorneys' fees and awards of fees based on "bad faith" litigation—are applicable to many kinds of litigation, and may apply to a class action in an appropriate case, e.g., a case under the federal antitrust laws.[2] Because of their general applicability, they will not be discussed further in this chapter. A third exception, the common fund or common benefit doctrine, is particularly well-suited to, and therefore arises most frequently in the context of, class action litigation.[3] The common fund doctrine is discussed below in Chapter 28 "Settlements" and Chapter 46 "Court Awarded Attorney's Fees"[4] and therefore is treated here only in connection with its application in the class action context.

In general, federal courts have used two methods to determine attorneys' fees under the common fund doctrine—percentage of the fund and lodestar analysis. The percentage of the fund method awards counsel a percentage of the fund sufficient to provide the attorneys with a reasonable fee.[5] By comparison, the lodestar method calculates the number of hours reasonably spent by counsel in litigation, multiplied by a reasonable hourly rate.[6] Under certain circumstances, courts have adjusted the lodestar amount by a multiplier.[7] The propriety of multipliers has been called into question, however, by the Supreme Court's decision in *City of Burlington v. Dague*.[8] Although *Dague* was decided in the context of individuals suing under a fee-shifting statute, some courts have interpreted its holding more broadly to apply in a class action common fund case as well.[9]

§ 15.20

1. Alyeska Pipeline Serv. Co. v. Wilderness Soc'y, 421 U.S. 240, 247, 95 S.Ct. 1612, 1616, 44 L.Ed.2d 141 (1975); In re Thirteen Appeals Arising out of the San Juan Du-Pont Plaza Hotel Fire Litig., 56 F.3d 295, 304 (1st Cir.1995); Swedish Hosp. Corp. v. Shalala, 1 F.3d 1261, 1265 (D.C.Cir.1993).

2. See also, e.g., Flora v. Moore, 461 F.Supp. 1104 (N.D.Miss.1978) (assessing a reasonable attorney's fee pursuant to statute against the legal services corporation that represented a class of African-American maids and cooks in a racial discrimination case under Title VII where the plaintiffs had conducted the litigation in a "vexatious, wanton and oppressive manner"), aff'd, 631 F.2d 730 (5th Cir.1980). See Chapter 46 "Court Awarded Attorneys' Fees," infra.

3. See In re Thirteen Appeals, 56 F.3d at 305 n.6 ("While class actions furnish the most fertile ground for the [common fund]

doctrine, its reach is not limited to such cases.").

4. See infra §§ 46.4, 46.7.

5. In re Gen. Motors Corp. Pick–Up Truck Fuel Tank Prods. Liab. Litig., 55 F.3d 768, 819 n. 38 (3d Cir.1995) (observing that the percentage method "resembles a contingent fee in that it awards counsel a variable percentage of the amount recovered for the class").

6. Id. at 819 n.37.

7. See infra § 46.8.

8. 505 U.S. 557, 566, 112 S.Ct. 2638, 2643, 120 L.Ed.2d 449 (1992) (holding that enhancement of lodestar was not permitted under the fee-shifting provisions of the Solid Waste Disposal Act and Clean Water Acts).

9. See In re Gen. Motors Corp., 55 F.3d at 822 (holding that the district court erred in applying a multiplier to the lodestar

A full discussion of the advantages and disadvantages of the lodestar method and the percentage of the fund method is contained in the chapter on attorneys' fees.[10] An important development in the general debate on the subject occurred in 1985, when a Task Force convened by the Third Circuit issued its report and concluded that the percentage of the fund method is on the whole better suited to a common fund case than is the lodestar approach.[11]

Since the Third Circuit Task Force's recommendations, courts in several circuits now use the percentage of fund approach as their sole[12] or preferred[13] method for calculating attorneys' fees from a common fund. On the other hand, courts in an increasing number of other circuits have held that the district court has discretion to determine the appropriate method in a given case.[14] The Fifth Circuit continues to adhere to past precedent and use the lodestar approach.[15]

Those courts that have applied the percentage method have awarded to counsel, on average, 20%–30% of the common fund.[16] Some courts start from a "benchmark" percentage, such as 25%, and make adjust-

amount in light of *Dague*); *accord, In re* Bolar Pharmaceutical Co., 800 F.Supp. 1091, 1096–97 (E.D.N.Y.1992). *But see* Florin v. Nationsbank of Georgia, N.A., 34 F.3d 560, 565 (7th Cir.1994) (risk multipliers remain available in a common fund case even after *Dague*).

10. *See infra* Chapter 46, and in particular § 46.8 on lodestar method.

11. Report of the Third Circuit Task Force, Court Awarded Attorney Fees, 108 F.R.D. 237, 255 (1985) (advocating in common fund cases a negotiated percentage fee agreement between counsel that must be approved by the court).

12. Swedish Hosp. Corp. v. Shalala, 1 F.3d at 1261, 1271 (D.C. Cir. 1993); Camden I Condominium Ass'n v. Dunkle, 946 F.2d 768, 774 (11th Cir.1991) ("Henceforth in this circuit, attorneys' fees awarded from a common fund shall be based upon a reasonable percentage of the fund established for the benefit of the class.").

13. Rosenbaum v. MacAllister, 64 F.3d 1439, 1445 (10th Cir.1995); *cf. In re* Gen. Motors Corp., 55 F.3d at 821 (concluding that district courts "probably" should use the percentage method as the "primary determinant," although the ultimate choice rested within the discretion of the court).

14. *In re* FPI/Agretech Secs. Litig., 105 F.3d 469, 472 (9th Cir.1997) (stating that court would defer to district court's choice of fee calculation method); Bowling v. Pfizer, Inc., 102 F.3d 777, 779–80 (6th Cir.1996)

(upholding district court's award of fees based on the percentage method cross-checked against the lodestar); Johnston v. Comerica Mortg. Corp., 83 F.3d 241, 246 (8th Cir.1996) (holding that use of lodestar was not an abuse of discretion); *In re* Thirteen Appeals Arising out of the San Juan DuPont Plaza Hotel Fire Litig., 56 F.3d 295, 307, 308 (1st Cir.1995) (upholding use of percentage method under the circumstances of the case); Florin v. Nationsbank of Ga., N.A., 60 F.3d 1245, 1246 n. 2 (7th Cir.1995) (affirming use of lodestar method); *In re* Fleet/Norstar Secs. Litig., 935 F.Supp. 99, 108 (D.R.I.1996), *supplemented by* 974 F.Supp. 155 (D.R.I.1997) (determining that the "circumstances of the . . . case warrant[ed] utilization of the percentage-of-the-fund approach") (following *In re* Thirteen Appeals, 56 F.3d at 307).

15. Longden v. Sunderman, 979 F.2d 1095, 1099 & n. 9 (5th Cir.1992) (continuing to apply the twelve factors identified in *Johnson v. Georgia Highway Express, Inc.,* 488 F.2d 714, 717–19 (5th Cir.1974), to determine whether the lodestar award should be adjusted upward or downward).

16. Swedish Hosp. Corp., 1 F.3d at 1272 (upholding award of 20%); Slomovics v. All for a Dollar, Inc., 906 F.Supp. 146, 151 (E.D.N.Y.1995) (25%); Gottlieb v. Barry, 43 F.3d 474, 487–88 (10th Cir.1994) (22.5%); *see also In re* Shell Oil Refinery, 155 F.R.D. 552, 573–74 (E.D.La.1993) (observing that a majority of common fund fee awards fall between 20% and 30% of the fund).

ments if appropriate.[17] Other courts use the *Johnson v. Georgia Highway Express, Inc.*[18] twelve-factor test to determine a reasonable percentage, or have developed their own test examining similar factors.[19]

Library References:

West's Key No. Digests, Federal Civil Procedure ☜2737.13.
Wright, Miller & Kane, Federal Practice and Procedure: Civil 2d § 1803.

§ 15.21　Ethical Considerations

(a) Prelitigation Communications

Prior to initiation of a class action, plaintiff's counsel may wish to solicit additional class members either to ensure selection of the class representative best able to withstand any challenge to the adequacy of his representation,[1] or to secure a sufficient number of class members to satisfy any applicable numerical requirements to bring a class action.[2] Although a blanket prohibition against targeted direct-mail solicitation by lawyers, without a finding that the solicitation is false or misleading, violates the First Amendment,[3] states may permissibly supervise and restrict such mailings.[4] Moreover, states may prohibit all in-person

---

17. *See* Torrisi v. Tucson Elec. Power Co., 8 F.3d 1370, 1376 (9th Cir.1993) (stating that the benchmark percentage of 25% should be adjusted or replaced by a lodestar calculation where "special circumstances indicate that the percentage recovery would be either too small or too large in light of the hours devoted to the case or other relevant factors").

18. 488 F.2d 714 (5th Cir.1974). *See* Camden I Condominium Ass'n, Inc. v. Dunkle, 946 F.2d 768, 775 (11th Cir.1991) (stating that "the Johnson factors continue to be appropriately used in evaluating, setting, and reviewing percentage fee awards in common fund cases," the court added that other relevant factors included the time required to reach a settlement, whether there were any substantial objections by class members or other parties to the settlement terms regarding the requested fees, any nonmonetary benefits conferred on the class by the settlement, and the economics involved in prosecuting a class action); *accord,* Brown v. Phillips Petroleum Co., 838 F.2d 451, 454–55 (10th Cir.1988).

19. Bowling, 102 F.3d at 780 (upholding award where district court had considered the following factors, with special emphasis given to the first two: (1) the value of the benefit rendered to the plaintiff class, (2) the value of the services on an hourly basis, (3) whether the services were undertaken

on a contingent fee basis, (4) society's stake in rewarding attorneys who produce such benefits in order to maintain an incentive to others, (5) the complexity of the litigation, and (6) the professional skill and standing of counsel involved on both sides).

§ 15.21

1. *See generally,* 2 H. Newberg & A. Conte, Newberg on Class Actions § 6.03 (3d ed. 1992) (discussing considerations in selecting the class representative.)

2. *See, e.g.,* 15 U.S.C.A. § 2310(d)(3)(C) (West 1998) (requiring a minimum of 100 named plaintiffs in order to file a class action under the Magnuson–Moss Warranty Act in federal court).

3. Shapero v. Kentucky Bar Ass'n, 486 U.S. 466, 108 S.Ct. 1916, 100 L.Ed.2d 475 (1988). *See also* Zauderer v. Office of Disciplinary Counsel, 471 U.S. 626, 644–47, 105 S.Ct. 2265, 2278–80, 85 L.Ed.2d 652 (1985) (holding that a blanket prohibition against solicitation through advertisements containing information or legal advice concerning a specific legal problem violates the First Amendment).

4. Shapero, 486 U.S. at 476–77, 108 S.Ct. at 1923–24 (suggesting steps state might take to regulate targeted direct-mail solicitation); Florida Bar v. Went For It, Inc., 515 U.S. 618, 634, 115 S.Ct. 2371,

solicitation by lawyers.[5] Thus, while written contact with potential class members is permissible, the practitioner should consult the applicable solicitation rules in the relevant jurisdiction prior to undertaking any solicitation.[6]

As a practical matter, plaintiff's counsel often secures additional class members through newspaper advertisements.[7] Moreover, restrictions upon attorney solicitation do not apply to solicitation of additional class members undertaken by the class representative,[8] and representative communications with interested organizations may uncover additional class members.[9]

Once a defendant learns of a potential class action, it may attempt to resolve its disputes with potential class members. Defendants should ensure, however, that their communications cannot be interpreted as

2381, 132 L.Ed.2d 541 (1995) (holding that a rule prohibiting direct-mail solicitation of victims and their relatives within 30 days of an accident or disaster does not violate the First Amendment).

5. Ohralik v. Ohio State Bar Ass'n, 436 U.S. 447, 464–67, 98 S.Ct. 1912, 56 L.Ed.2d 444 (1978) (holding that a state may categorically ban in-person solicitation by lawyers for pecuniary gain). *See generally,* Reed v. Sisters of Charity of the Incarnate Word of Louisiana, Inc., 447 F.Supp. 309, 310–11 (W.D.La.1978) (criticizing class counsel for delivering an "unprofessional, inflammatory, and solicitous" speech to potential class members a month before the class action was filed and suggesting speech was sufficient justification to dismiss the class complaint).

6. *See, e.g.,* Model Rules of Professional Conduct Rule 7.3 (1983) (prohibiting in-person and telephone solicitation "when a significant motive for doing so is the lawyer's pecuniary gain," yet permitting written solicitation to prospective clients known to be in need of legal services, with certain restrictions); Model Code of Professional Responsibility DR 2–104(A) (1980) (restricting lawyer's ability to accept employment resulting from in-person, unsolicited advice). *See also* N.Y. State Bar Ass'n Comm. on Prof. Ethics, Op. 676 (1995) (stating that an attorney may advertise for or solicit by mail additional participants in a class action); Ohio Bd. of Comm'rs on Grievances and Discipline, Op. 92–2 (1992) (stating that class counsel may communicate with potential class members via mail and may accept employment arising from such advertising).

7. *See generally,* Zauderer, 471 U.S. at 630, 641, 655, 105 S.Ct. at 2271, 2276, 2284 (permissible for attorney seeking to represent intrauterine device claimants to publish a truthful advertisement in a newspaper, including an illustration of a Dalkon Shield intrauterine device); Zarate v. Younglove, 86 F.R.D. 80, 85–86, 96, 105–06 (C.D.Cal.1980) (permissible for class counsel to publish truthful newspaper advertisements offering to provide information to Hispanic victims of employment discrimination and seeking information from those who have knowledge of employment discrimination against Hispanics). *See also* Jack B. Weinstein, *Ethical Dilemmas in Mass Tort Litigation,* 88 Nw. U. L. Rev. 469, 532 (1994) (noting "jockeying among potential representatives becomes fierce and some lawyers engage in advertising and overt client-chasing"). John C. Coffee, Jr. *Class Wars: The Dilemma of the Mass Tort Class Action,* 95 Colum. L. Rev. 1343, 1359 n.53 (1995) (describing nationwide roving medical screenings conducted by plaintiff's counsel to locate class members).

8. 3 Newberg, *supra* note 1, at §§ 15.06 & 15.13. *See generally,* Brian J. Waid, *Ethical Problems of the Class Action Practitioner: Continued Neglect by the Drafters of the Proposed Model Rules of Professional Conduct,* 27 Loy. L. Rev. 1047, 1057 (1981) (suggesting that if solicitation of additional class members would benefit a client's cause, an attorney may be required to "advise his client to solicit the needed additions or to do it himself").

9. *See generally,* 3 Newberg, *supra* note 1, at § 15.06.

threatening potential class members.[10]

(b) Precertification Communications

Once a class action is filed, the court must determine whether the action properly may be maintained as a class action.[11] Pending this decision, both class counsel and representatives of the defendant may wish to contact potential class members.

The once-common district court practice of prohibiting all communications between parties to the class action and the putative class members without prior court approval has fallen into disfavor following the Supreme Court's decision in *Gulf Oil Co. v. Bernard*.[12] In *Gulf* the Court vacated a broad order prohibiting communications between the parties and any potential class members without prior court approval, ruling that the district court had abused its discretion in entering the order.[13] According to the Court, "an order limiting communications between parties and potential class members should be based on a clear record and specific findings that reflect a weighing of the need for a limitation and the potential interference with the rights of the parties."[14] Moreover, any such order should limit speech "as little as possible, consistent with the rights of the parties under the circumstances."[15]

In the absence of a local rule or court order to the contrary, class counsel legitimately may contact potential class members to advise of the status of the litigation or to obtain information about the merits of the case, and may respond to inquiries from potential class members, so long as such communications are not abusive or misleading.[16] For example, the U.S. Court of Appeals for the Fifth Circuit reversed the district court's entry of summary judgment in favor of the defendant, finding that in the absence of the district court's gag order, class counsel may

---

10. *See* Nesenoff v. Muten, 67 F.R.D. 500, 502–03 (E.D.N.Y.1974) (holding that defendant may contact potential class members in an effort to settle individual disputes); 3 Newberg, *supra* note 1, at § 15.11 ("When no class action is filed, a prospective defendant is free to communicate with potential class members in order to remedy alleged grievances and obtain releases from liability.... Threatening potential class members ... would, however, raise serious ethical questions of propriety.").

11. *See* FRCP 23(c)(1) ("As soon as practicable after commencement of an action brought as a class action, the court shall determine by order whether it is to be so maintained."). *See also supra* §§ 15.3, 15.5, 15.6, and 15.7.

12. 452 U.S. 89, 101 S.Ct. 2193, 68 L.Ed.2d 693 (1981).

13. *Id.* at 103–04, 101 S.Ct. at 2201–02.

14. *Id.* at 101–02, 101 S.Ct. at 2200–01.

15. *Id.* at 102, 101 S.Ct. at 2201. Following the *Gulf* decision, the Manual for Complex Litigation's discussion of the benefits of broad no-communications orders was removed, and the Manual revised to recommend that eight rules be followed in fashioning an order restricting communications between parties and potential class members. *Compare* Manual for Complex Litigation § 1.41 (4th ed. 1977) *with* Manual for Complex Litigation § 1.41 (5th ed. 1982).

16. Gulf Oil Co., 452 U.S. at 101, 101 S.Ct. at 2200 (noting the district court's order had "interfered with [plaintiff's] efforts to inform potential class members of the existence of this lawsuit" and "the order made it more difficult for respondents, as the class representatives, to obtain information about the merits of the case").

have produced sufficient evidence to withstand summary judgment.[17] The court reasoned that the gag order entered by the district court prohibiting class counsel from communicating with class members, other than those by whom he was employed, "made it impossible for [class counsel] to attempt to find such facts as he may have believed were necessary to support his contention."[18] Thus the case was remanded, and the district court instructed to permit class counsel sufficient time to communicate with class members and complete discovery.[19] However, because antisolicitation rules continue to apply during the precertification stage, they must be consulted prior to undertaking any solicitation.[20]

Prior to certification, a defendant may wish to contact potential class members to negotiate individual settlements or to encourage them to opt-out of the putative class.[21] Although most courts agree that prior to certification no attorney-client relationship exists between putative class members and class counsel,[22] the trend is to require some form of court supervision of all communications between defendants and potential class members.[23] In light of this trend, practitioners may be well

---

17. Marmol v. Adkins, 655 F.2d 594, 597–98 (5th Cir.1981).

18. *Id.* at 598.

19. *Id.*

20. William H. Fortune et al., Modern Litigation and Professional Responsibility Handbook 545 (1996). *See infra* § 15.23(a).

21. Some courts have refused to extend the *Gulf* Court's reasoning to communications between defendants and putative class members. *See, e.g.,* Montgomery v. Aetna Plywood, Inc., No. 95 C3193 1996 WL 189347, at *3 (N.D.Ill.1996) (noting that the Supreme Court's decision in *Gulf* concerned communications between the class and their potential counsel, not the putative class' opposing counsel); Bower v. Bunker Hill Co., 689 F.Supp. 1032, 1033–34 (E.D.Wash.1985) (same); Resnick v. American Dental Ass'n, 95 F.R.D. 372, 376, 378–79 (N.D.Ill.1982) (same). *But see In re* School Asbestos Litig., 842 F.2d 671, 680–84 (3d Cir.1988) (holding that district court's order requiring certain disclosures to appear on nonlitigation related communications between class members and an association comprised of some of the defendant corporations must comply with the standards set forth in *Gulf*).

22. Manual for Complex Litigation, (Third) § 30.24 (1995) ("no formal attorney-client relationship exists between class counsel and the putative members of the purported class prior to class certification"); Resnick, 95 F.R.D. at 377 n. 6 (hold-

ing that prior to certification, potential class members are not yet represented by class counsel); Simpson v. Mellon Bank, No. CIV. A–93–4722, 1993 WL 524784, at *3 (E.D.Pa.1993) ("The filing of a class action does not necessarily create an attorney/client relationship.").

23. Hampton Hardware, Inc. v. Cotter & Co., Inc., 156 F.R.D. 630, 632–35 (N.D.Tex.1994) (ordering defendant to refrain from contacting potential class members about the litigation after defendant sent three letters urging potential class members not to participate in litigation); American Fin. Sys., Inc. v. Harlow, 65 F.R.D. 572, 575–76 (D.Md.1974) (holding that defendant may negotiate settlements with individual claimants before certification, but court will prescreen all such communications); Matarazzo v. Friendly Ice Cream Corp., 62 F.R.D. 65, 69 & n. 4 (E.D.N.Y.1974) (noting no rule precludes defendant from contacting potential class members after a class action complaint is filed, but stating "we believe it a better practice" that communications be approved by court order prior to contact); Weight Watchers of Philadelphia, Inc. v. Weight Watchers Int'l., Inc., 55 F.R.D. 50, 51 (E.D.N.Y.1971) (allowing defendant to contact potential class members to attempt to resolve individual disputes, but requiring that notice be given to class counsel and ordering that class counsel be permitted to attend negotiation sessions). *But see* Fulco

advised to seek court approval before contacting potential class members concerning the class action.[24]

Nonlitigation related contact between a defendant and putative class members with whom the defendant has an ongoing business relationship is permissible. The defendant should take care, however, that its communications cannot be interpreted as threatening potential class members not to join the class.[25] Moreover, applicable local rules or court order may require approval of the court prior to contacting putative class members concerning nonlitigation related matters.

(c) Post–Certification Communications

(1) Before Expiration of Exclusion Period

After certification of a class action under FRCP 23(b)(3), potential class members will be notified of their right to opt-out of the class upon request within a specified period of time.[26] Prior to expiration of the opt-out period, class counsel must comply with all applicable antisolicitation rules, but may communicate with class members regarding the status of the case or in an effort to gather information.[27]

Most authorities agree that an attorney-client relationship exists between class counsel and putative class members upon certification of the class,[28] in effect prohibiting defendant contact with absent class

v. Continental Cablevision, 789 F.Supp. 45, 47–48 (D.Mass.1992) (holding that prior to certification, defendant is free to communicate with potential class members, so long as defendant refrains from threatening them in an effort to convince them not to join the suit); In re Winchell's Donut Houses, L.P. Secs. Litig., 1988 WL 135503, at *1 (Del.Ch.1988) (stating it is "well settled" that prior to certification defendant may settle individual claims, so long as defendant's communications are not misleading); Cada v. Costa Line, Inc., 93 F.R.D. 95, 98–99 (N.D.Ill.1981) (holding that local rule prohibiting contact between parties and potential class members was unconstitutional, and did not require the court to void settlements between defendant and potential class members).

24. See generally, Donald D. Levenhagen, Class Actions: Judicial Control of Defense Communications with Absent Class Members, 59 Ind. L.J. 133 (1984).

25. See Hampton Hardware, Inc., 156 F.R.D. at 635 (defendant may contact class members for business purposes, but may not communicate with class members regarding the litigation); In re International House of Pancakes Franchise Litig., 1972 WL 519, at *1 (W.D.Mo. 1972) (holding that court has the power to enjoin all attempts

by defendant to use its economic power to discourage participation in class action). See also cases cited infra note 31.

26. See FRCP 23(c)(2). See also supra § 15.8.

27. Impervious Paint Indus. v. Ashland Oil, 508 F.Supp. 720, 723 (W.D.Ky.1981) (After certification but prior to expiration of the opt-out period, the relationship between class counsel and absent class members "cannot be stated with precision," but it appears "that contact initiated by class counsel prior to the close of the opt-out period would be unethical as direct solicitation of clients, if the purpose or predictable effect of the contact is to discourage a decision to opt-out of the class.").

28. See Van Gemert v. Boeing Co., 590 F.2d 433, 440 n. 15 (2d Cir.1978) ("A certification under Rule 23(c) makes the class the attorney's client for all practical purposes."), aff'd, 444 U.S. 472, 100 S.Ct. 745, 62 L.Ed.2d 676 (1980); Shores v. Publix Super Markets, Inc., No. 95–1162–CIV–T–25(E), 1996 WL 859985, at *2 (M.D.Fla. 1996) ("[O]nce certification was granted, class members were officially represented by counsel."); Fulco, 789 F.Supp. at 47 (holding that after entry of certification or-

members regarding the litigation.[29] Because the trend is in any event to require court supervision of litigation-related communications between defendants and potential class members, practitioners should, after class certification, obtain court approval before contacting potential class members concerning the class action.[30] Courts generally will not prevent

der, an attorney-client relationship exists between class members and class counsel); *In re* Winchell's Donut Houses, L.P. Sec. Litig., 1988 WL 135503, at *2 (finding that after certification, class counsel is the legal representative of class members); Bower v. Bunker Hill Co., 689 F.Supp. 1032, 1034 (E.D.Wash.1985) (After certification "defense counsel must treat plaintiff-class members as represented by counsel."); Resnick v. American Dental Ass'n, 95 F.R.D. 372, 376 (N.D.Ill.1982) ("Without question the unnamed class members, once the class has been certified, are 'represented by' the class counsel."); Impervious Paint Indus., 508 F.Supp. at 723 (After certification but prior to expiration of the opt-out period, "defendants' counsel must treat plaintiff class members as represented by counsel, and must conduct themselves in accordance with both sections of DR 7–104."). *See also* Manual for Complex Litigation, (Third), § 30.2 ("Once a class is certified, the rules governing communications apply as though each member of class member is a client of class counsel."); Fortune, *supra* note 20, at 549. *But see* Mich. Comm. on Professional and Judicial Ethics, Op. RI–219 (1994) (opining that prior to the expiration of the opt-out period, putative members of a certified class who have not specifically sought representation by class counsel are not "known to be represented in the matter" under Michigan Rule of Professional Conduct 4.2).

29. Model Code of Professional Responsibility, DR 7–104 (1980) (prohibiting contact with a represented person regarding the subject matter of the representation); Model Rules of Professional Conduct 4.2 (1983) (prohibiting contact with a represented party regarding the subject matter of the representation absent consent of the other attorney). *See also* Kleiner v. First Nat'l Bank of Atlanta, 751 F.2d 1193, 1206–07 (11th Cir.1985) (holding that Model Rule of Professional Conduct 4.2 prohibits defense counsel from discussing the litigation with class members as of the date of class certification); Shores, 1996 WL 859985, at *2 (holding that after certification, applicable ethics rules prohibited defense counsel and defendant from communicating with

class members regarding the litigation); Montgomery v. Aetna Plywood, Inc., No. 95–3193, 1996 WL 189347, at *3 (N.D.Ill. 1996) ("Once a class action has been certified ... ethical prohibitions against counsel for one party directly communicating with the other party are in force."); Fulco, 789 F.Supp. at 47 (After entry of certification order, an attorney-client relationship exists between class members and class counsel, and defendant must treat class members as "represented by class counsel for purposes of DR 7–104."); Haffer v. Temple Univ., 115 F.R.D. 506, 510 (E.D.Pa.1987) (holding that defendant's post-certification contact with potential class members regarding the class action violated Rule 7–104 of the Code of Professional Responsibility); Tedesco v. Mishkin, 629 F.Supp. 1474, 1483 (S.D.N.Y. 1986) (holding that attorney violates DR 7–104 by communicating with class members after certification); Bower, 689 F.Supp. at 1034 (After certification "defense counsel must treat plaintiff-class members as represented by counsel and must conduct themselves in accordance with DR–104(A)(1)."); Resnick, 95 F.R.D. at 376–77 (holding that DR 7–104 prohibits defendant from communicating with class members regarding the subject matter of the litigation without the prior consent of the court or class counsel).

30. *See* cases cited *supra* note 23. *See also In re* School Asbestos Litig., 842 F.2d 671, 685 (3d Cir.1988) (holding that district court had the authority under FRCP 23(d) to order an association comprised of defendant corporations to disclose its involvement in the litigation when communicating directly with class members concerning the subject of the class action); *In re* Potash Antitrust Litig., 896 F.Supp. 916, 921 (D.Minn.1995) (imposing restrictions on defendant's communications with potential class members about the merits of the class litigation); *In re* Winchell's Donut Houses, L.P. Sec. Litig., 1988 WL 135503, at *2–3 (holding that defendant may, with court supervision, contact potential class members in an attempt to reach individual settlements with class members after certification of the class, despite the fact that class

a defendant from communicating with potential class members in the ordinary course of business.[31]

(2) After Expiration of Exclusion Period

After expiration of the exclusion period, class counsel represents all class members otherwise unrepresented.[32] Accordingly, class counsel may freely communicate with class members, but should ensure that such communications are not misleading.

Because class members are represented by class counsel, defense counsel may not contact class members concerning the litigation or settlement of claims, except through class counsel.[33] Out of necessity, nonlitigation related contact between defendants and putative class members with whom they have an ongoing business relationship remains permissible.[34]

(d) Issues Regarding Costs of Litigation

Because maintenance of a class action suit can be extraordinarily expensive, funding the class action lawsuit may pose unique problems. Class counsel, with court supervision, may solicit contributions for

counsel is the legal representative of class members); *In re* International House of Pancakes Franchise Litig., 1972 Trade Cas. (CCH) & 73,864 at 91,627–28, 1972 WL 535 (W.D. Mo.1972) (barring defendant from negotiating settlements with individual members of the existing class). *But see* Erhardt v. Prudential Group, Inc., 629 F.2d 843, 846 (2d Cir.1980) (vacating civil contempt citation against CEO of class action defendant who sent a letter concerning the litigation to absent class members prior to expiration of opt-out period on grounds that communication violated no court order).

31. Kleiner, 751 F.2d at 1206 (district court order barring informal contact between defendant and class members was narrowly drawn and "did not impinge on the Bank's ability to speak with customers about routine business matters unrelated to the lawsuit"); *In re* Potash Antitrust Litig., 896 F.Supp. at 921 (imposing restrictions on defendant's communications with potential class members about the merits of the class litigation); Haffer, 115 F.R.D. at 510 (noting that order limiting defendant's contact with potential class members is narrowly drawn, in recognition of the fact that "as a practical matter, defendants and class members necessarily interact daily"); Resnick, 95 F.R.D. at 377 (court will not interfere with defendants' "nonlitigation-oriented business" communications with po-

tential class members.). *See also* Manual for Complex Litigation, (Third) § 30.2 (1995) (post-certification communications with "class members in the ordinary course of business, unrelated to the litigation, are not barred").

32. Fortune, *supra* note 20, at 549–50; 3 Newberg, *supra* note 1, at § 15.18. *See also* cases cited *supra* note 28.

33. Model Code of Professional Responsibility, DR 7–104 (1980) (prohibiting contact with a represented person regarding the subject matter of the representation); Model Rules of Professional Conduct 4.2 (1983) (prohibiting contact with a represented party regarding the subject matter of the representation absent consent of the other attorney). *See also* Hawkins v. Holiday Inns, Inc., 1978–1 Trade Cas. (CCH) & 61,838 at 73,494, 1978 WL 1293 (W.D.Tenn. 1978) (prohibiting defendant from negotiating individual settlements, except through the legal counsel for the class member); cases cited *supra* note 29.

34. Hawkins, 1978–1 Trade Cas. (CCH) at 73,494 (prohibiting defendant from negotiating individual settlements, except through the legal counsel for the class member, but allowing defendant to communicate in the ordinary course of business with its licensees). *See also* cases cited *supra* notes 25, 31.

expenses from absent class members, but must not mislead class members into thinking contribution is required.[35]

The question of whether class counsel may advance costs in a class action when, as a practical matter, the client will be unable to reimburse class counsel if the litigation is unsuccessful is unsettled.[36] In recognition of the difficulty in maintaining a class action if the class representative must be responsible for all expenses, the trend is to allow counsel to advance costs in this situation.[37] Disciplinary rules prohibiting class counsel from advancing costs when reimbursement is contingent upon the outcome of the case have been held inapplicable to class actions under FRCP 23.[38]

Any financing arrangement that has the potential to pit the interests of class counsel against the class members may be found invalid and unenforceable. One court, citing the potential conflict of interest, rejected a creative financing arrangement devised by a nine-member plaintiffs' management committee as a means of securing sufficient resources to

35. ABA Comm. on Ethics and Professional Responsibility, Informal Op. 1326 (1975) (opining that it is ethically permissible for class counsel to solicit funds to be used for expenses, including mailing notices to class members). *See also* Norris v. Colonial Commercial Corp., 77 F.R.D. 672, 673 (S.D.Ohio 1977) (allowing class counsel to contact class members who have not opted-out of class action to seek contributions, but requiring prior court approval of all communications). *But see* Fauteck v. Montgomery Ward & Co., Inc., 91 F.R.D. 393, 394–95 (N.D.Ill.1980) (prohibiting class counsel from contacting class members, before any formal notice had been sent by the court of the class action, to solicit contributions to fund the litigation).

36. *Compare* Model Code of Professional Responsibility DR 5–103(B) (1980) (attorney may advance costs of the litigation only if the plaintiff remains ultimately responsible for the expenses) *with* Model Rules of Professional Conduct Rule 1.8(e) (1983) (attorney may advance all costs, with repayment by the plaintiff contingent upon the outcome of the litigation). *See also* Fortune, *supra* note 20, at 551–53.

37. Rand v. Monsanto Co., 926 F.2d 596, 601 (7th Cir.1991) ("[A] district court may not establish a per se rule that the representative plaintiff must be willing to bear all (as opposed to a pro rata share) of the costs of the action."); County of Suffolk v. Long Island Lighting Co., 710 F.Supp. 1407, 1415 (E.D.N.Y.1989) ("There is nothing unethical about the attorneys advancing the costs of litigation even though their

clients can never pay unless the action is successful."), *aff'd*, 907 F.2d 1295 (2d Cir. 1990); Harris v. General Dev. Corp., 127 F.R.D. 655, 662 (N.D.Ill.1989) (holding that arrangement in which named plaintiffs will not be liable for expenses if no recovery is obtained does not require denial of class certification, as a contrary rule would effectively prevent many plaintiffs from bringing a class action). *But see In re* Mid–Atlantic Toyota Antitrust Litig., 93. F.R.D. 485, 489 (D. Md. 1982) (holding that arrangement in which plaintiff is not responsible for the costs of an unsuccessful class action lawsuit violates Model Code of Professional Responsibility DR 5–103(B)); N.C. State Bar, Op. RPC 124 (1994) (opining that attorney may not agree to be ultimately responsible for the costs of a class action). *See generally*, 1 Newberg, *supra* note 1, at § 3.37; Committee on Prof. Resp., Ass'n of the Bar of the City of N.Y., *Financial Arrangements in Class Actions, and the Code of Professional Responsibility*, 20 Fordham Urb. L.J. 831 (1993) (discussing the ABA Code of Professional Responsibility and the need to finance and maintain class actions).

38. Rand, 926 F.2d at 601 (holding that DR 5–103(B) is inconsistent with FRCP 23, and is therefore inapplicable to class actions); County of Suffolk, 710 F.Supp. at 1415 (stating that any attempt by New York to enforce DR 5–103(B) against a New York lawyer who had violated the rule in federal court after the federal court had approved the departure from the state rule would be barred by the Supremacy Clause).

continue the class action.[39] In exchange for their agreement to contribute money to cover expenses, the fee arrangement permitted "investor" attorneys to share fees based primarily on their financial contribution rather than upon the time and effort they devoted to the litigation, and resulted in a distortion of the fees calculated under the traditional lodestar approach.[40] The court found the fee agreement invalid, reasoning that fees tied to a return on investment create the potential for a conflict of interest between class counsel and the class, as the "investor" attorneys will receive the same return, regardless of when the case is resolved.[41] The court held that in the future, fee sharing arrangements should be disclosed to the district court at the time they are formulated to allow the district court to determine, prospectively, whether the agreement places class counsel "in a position that might endanger the fair representation of their clients and whether they will be compensated on some basis other than for legal services performed."[42]

(e) Preferential Treatment of Class Representatives

Although class representatives typically are entitled to reimbursement of their out-of-pocket expenses, they traditionally have not received a disproportionate share of any judgment or settlement of the class action.[43] However, some courts have permitted payment of small bonuses

39. *In re* "Agent Orange" Prod. Liab. Litig., 818 F.2d 216 (2d Cir.), *cert. denied sub nom.* Newton B. Schwartz, P.C. v. Dean, 484 U.S. 926, 108 S.Ct. 289, 98 L.Ed.2d 249 (1987). In a successful class action, class counsel is typically reimbursed from the common fund for his reasonable litigation expenses. *See* 3 Newberg, *supra* note 1, at § 14.02; Manual for Complex Litigation, (Third) §§ 24.214, 24.215 (1995). Expense awards are often quite sizable. *See, e.g.,* Judgment Entered Awarding $44.5 Million in Fees, 10 No. 16 Mealey's Litig. Rep.: Asbestos 14 (Sept. 22, 1995) (reporting an award of $1.2 million in expenses).

40. *In re* "Agent Orange" Prod. Liab. Litig., 818 F.2d at 217–20.

41. *Id.* at 223–34. *But see* Committee on Prof. Resp., Ass'n of the Bar of the City of N.Y., *supra* note 37 (discussing the *Agent Orange* decision and opining that the decision should not be read to foreclose all forms of creative financing of class actions).

42. Agent Orange Prod. Liab. Litig., 818 F.2d at 224, 226. *See generally,* Vincent R. Johnson, *Ethical Limitations on Creative Financing of Mass Tort Class Actions,* 54 Brook. L. Rev. 539 (1988).

43. *In re* Continental Ill. Secs. Litig., 962 F.2d 566, 571–72 (7th Cir.1992) (affirming denial of incentive award to named

representative); Holmes v. Continental Can Co., 706 F.2d 1144, 1147–48 (11th Cir.1983) (reversing approval of settlement, and ruling that proponents of settlement did not justify distribution of disproportionate amount of settlement fund to the named plaintiffs); Hooks v. General Fin. Corp., 652 F.2d 651, 652 (6th Cir.1981) (holding that denial of class certification is not an abuse of discretion when named plaintiff insists that he recover full statutory award, rather than a pro rata share of any class recovery); Lake v. First Nationwide Bank, 900 F.Supp. 726, 736–37 (E.D.Pa.1995) (rejecting requested $2,000 fee to named representatives, but awarding $250 each to compensate representatives for their actual time and expenses); *In re* U.S. Bioscience Secs. Litig., 155 F.R.D. 116, 120–21 (E.D.Pa.1994) (rejecting plaintiff's request for incentive awards in the amount of $2500 and $5000, but awarding a small per diem payment to reimburse class representatives for expenses such as parking and mileage); Weseley v. Spear, Leeds & Kellogg, 711 F.Supp. 713, 720 (E.D.N.Y.1989) (rejecting plaintiff's request for a $5,000 incentive award to compensate the named plaintiff for the inconvenience of acting as named plaintiff); *In re* Gould Secs. Litig., 727 F.Supp. 1201, 1208–09 (N.D.Ill.1989)

or incentive awards to class representatives to compensate them for their effort expended on the litigation and their assumption of the financial risk of the costs of litigation.[44] Other courts approve incentive payments for those who have accepted personal risks.[45] Class representatives who perform services beyond those provided by the typical class representative may receive extra compensation in the form of consultant fees.[46]

(f) Strike Suits

Class actions have been criticized as devices used by unscrupulous plaintiffs' attorneys to quickly coerce a nuisance value settlement.[47]

(denying plaintiffs' request for five small incentive awards as prohibited preferential treatment of the named plaintiffs). *See generally*, Sofia C. Hubscher, *Making Worth Plaintiffs' While: Extra Incentive Awards to Named Plaintiffs in Class Action Employment Discrimination Lawsuits*, 23 Colum. Hum. Rts. L. Rev. 463 (1992); Clinton A. Krislov, *Scrutiny of the Bounty: Incentive Awards for Plaintiffs in Class Litigation*, 78 Ill. B.J. 286 (1990); Richard Greenfield, *Rewarding the Class Representative: An Idea Whose Time Has Come*, 9 Class Action Reports 4 (1986); Committee on Prof. Resp., Ass'n of the Bar of the City of N.Y., *supra* note 37.

44. *See* Van Vranken v. Atlantic Richfield Co., 901 F.Supp. 294, 299–300 (N.D.Cal.1995) (finding incentive award justified, given named plaintiff's significant involvement in the litigation); Enterprise Energy Corp. v. Columbia Gas Transmission Corp., 137 F.R.D. 240, 251 (S.D.Ohio 1991) (finding incentive award justified, in part, due to the risks undertaken by named plaintiffs); In re Dun & Bradstreet Credit Servs. Consumer Litig., 130 F.R.D. 366, 374 (S.D.Ohio 1990) (finding incentive award justified by extensive time named plaintiffs devoted to the litigation and the financial risks they undertook); Huguley v. General Motors Corp., 128 F.R.D. 81, 85 (E.D.Mich. 1989) (holding that compensation to named plaintiffs for "onerous burden of litigation" was fair), *aff'd*, 925 F.2d 1464 (6th Cir.), *cert. denied*, 502 U.S. 909, 112 S.Ct. 304, 116 L.Ed.2d 247 (1991); Golden v. Shulman, [1988–1989 Transfer Binder] Fed. Sec. L. Rep. (CCH) ¶ 94,060 at 90,954, 1988 WL 144718 (E.D.N.Y.1988) (approving incentive award and noting that named plaintiff was personally liable for the costs of the litigation, and was required to respond personally to discovery requests); Bogosian v. Gulf Oil Corp., 621 F.Supp. 27, 32 (E.D.Pa.1985)

(noting class representatives spent considerable time on pretrial discovery, and approving incentive award); In re Jackson Lockdown/MCO Cases, 107 F.R.D. 703, 710 (E.D.Mich.1985) (finding incentive award justified by degree of effort expended by named plaintiffs).

45. White v. National Football League, 822 F.Supp. 1389 (D.Minn.1993) (finding more generous settlement to named plaintiffs justified, in part, because they risked their careers by filing the action), *aff'd*, 41 F.3d 402 (8th Cir.1994), *cert. denied*, 515 U.S. 1137, 115 S.Ct. 2569, 132 L.Ed.2d 821 (1995); In re First Jersey Secs. Inc. Sec. Litig., MDL No. 681, 1989 WL 69901, at *7 (E.D.Pa.1989) (finding incentive award appropriate, in part, because plaintiff maintained action in face of threat of a five million dollar countersuit); Women's Comm. for Equal Employment Opportunity v. National Broadcasting Co., 76 F.R.D. 173, 181 (S.D.N.Y.1977) (criticizing incentive awards generally, but allowing an incentive award to the named plaintiff, in part because she had risked her job by filing suit).

46. Genden v. Merrill Lynch, Pierce, Fenner & Smith, Inc., 700 F.Supp. 208, 210 (S.D.N.Y.1988) (holding payment of consultant fee to class representative justified, when he used his legal background to further the litigation); Bogosian, 621 F.Supp. at 32 (permitting award to named plaintiffs as compensation for "valuable consultative assistance to plaintiff's counsel"); Aamco Automatic Transmissions, Inc. v. Tayloe, 82 F.R.D. 405, 409 (E.D.Pa.1979) (finding compensation to named plaintiff in the form of a consulting fee was justified, given his expertise concerning the parts at issue in the litigation).

47. In re General Motors Corp. Pick–Up Truck Fuel Tank Prods. Liab. Litig., 55

Ethical rules, as well as the Federal Rules of Civil Procedure, prohibit the initiation of a nonmeritorious action simply to induce a settlement.[48] Moreover, to prevent such misuse of the class action device, FRCP 23 provides that a class action may not be dismissed or compromised without court approval.[49]

(g) Conflict Issues Regarding Settlement and Fees

The negotiated settlement of a class action creates the potential for three notable conflicts with class counsel's duty to diligently or zealously advocate on behalf of the class.[50] First, despite class counsel's obligation to advocate on behalf of the class, a settlement offer conditioned upon class counsel's agreement not to bring further cases against the defendant constitutes an impermissible restriction on class counsel's right to practice and on future litigants' right to select counsel of their choice; such an arrangement may not be accepted by class counsel or offered by defense counsel.[51] Second, commentators have sharply criticized the class action procedure as creating the potential for, and often resulting, in a "collusive" or nonadversarial settlement to the detriment of the class.[52]

Third, class counsel's interest in maximizing their attorneys' fees may create a conflict of interest.[53] The most obvious potential conflict of

F.3d 768, 784 (3d Cir.) ("Another problem is that class actions create the opportunity for a kind of legalized blackmail: a greedy and unscrupulous plaintiff might use the threat of a large class action, which can be costly to the defendant, to extract a settlement far in excess of the individual claims' actual worth") *cert. denied,* 516 U.S. 824, 116 S.Ct. 88, 133 L.Ed.2d 45 (1995); Roper v. Consurve, Inc., 578 F.2d 1106, 1110 (5th Cir.1978) ("One well-publicized danger in the class action is the possibility that it will be used to collect quick, undeserved damages; this type of effort to establish a quick coup has been called a 'strike suit.' "). *See generally,* Lucian A. Bebchuk, *Suing Solely to Extract a Settlement Offer,* 17 J. Legal Stud. 437 (1988).

48. Model Rules of Professional Conduct Rule 3.1 (1983); Model Code of Professional Responsibility DR 7–102(A)(1) (1980); FRCP 11.

49. FRCP 23(e). *See also* Roper, 578 F.2d at 1110 (noting that to prevent strike suits, class actions cannot be dismissed prior to certification merely because the named plaintiffs settle their claims against the defendant); Jack B. Weinstein & Karin S. Schwartz, *Notes from the Cave: Some Problems of Judges in Dealing with Class Action Settlements,* 163 F.R.D. 369, 373 (1995) ("The emerging consensus requires

judicial approval of precertification dismissals or settlements pursuant to Rule 23(e), but considers class notification discretionary."); 3 Newberg, *supra* note 1, at § 15.29 (discussing rules designed to discourage frivolous class actions).

50. *See* Model Code of Professional Responsibility Canon 7 (1980); Model Rules of Professional Conduct Rule 1.3 (1983).

51. To demand or accept such a restriction violates Rule 5.6 of the Model Rules of Professional Conduct. ABA Comm. on Ethics and Professional Responsibility, Formal Op. 371 (1993). *See also* N.C. State Bar, Op. RPC 179 (1994).

52. *See, e.g.,* Susan P. Koniak, *Feasting While the Widow Weeps: Georgine v. Amchem Products, Inc.,* 80 Cornell L. Rev. 1045 (1995) (discussing collusive settlements); Coffee, *supra* note 7, at 1343 (discussing factors favoring collusive settlements of mass tort litigation). *See supra* § 15.16 for a general discussion of settlement classes and the growing criticism of stipulated settlement classes due to the perceived possibility of collusive settlements.

53. *In re* General Motors Corp. Pick–Up Fuel Tank Litig., 55 F.3d 768, 819 (3d Cir.) ("[A] thorough judicial review of fee applications is required in all class action settlements" due to the potential for a conflict of interest occurs when class counsel negotiates a settlement amount and a fee amount simultaneously, because every dollar the defendant agrees to pay in fees likely reduces the fund available to the class. Although there is no absolute bar prohibiting the simultaneous negotiation of a settlement for the class and attorneys' fees,[54] courts view such simultaneous negotiation with suspicion.[55]

To avoid any appearance of conflict, the parties may negotiate a total settlement amount, and allow the court to determine the amount of fees to be awarded from the fund. Often such a settlement agreement is accompanied by class counsel's promise not to seek a fee above an agreed ceiling ("ceiling clause") or an agreement by the defendant not to contest a fee application up to the amount of a ceiling ("clear-sailing agreement"). Use of such agreements also may create a conflict of interest, however. For example, clear-sailing agreements raise conflict of interest concerns because in order to secure the defendant's agreement not to contest fees up to an agreed amount, class counsel may have had to bargain away something of value to the class.[56] Accordingly, any fee application containing a clear-sailing clause will be closely scrutinized.[57]

interest between counsel's self-interest and their duty to the class.) *cert. denied*, 516 U.S. 824, 116 S.Ct. 88, 133 L.Ed.2d 45 (1995). *See also* Weinberger v. Great N. Nekoosa Corp., 925 F.2d 518, 524 (1st Cir. 1991) (stating that class counsel's conflicting financial incentives create the "danger ... that the lawyers might urge a class settlement at a low figure or on a less-than-optimal basis in exchange for red-carpet treatment for fees").

54. Evans v. Jeff D., 475 U.S. 717, 734–38, 106 S.Ct. 1531, 1541–43, 89 L.Ed.2d 747 (1986) (simultaneous negotiation of a class settlement and attorneys' fees is permissible, and class counsel may waive attorneys' fees during such simultaneous negotiations).

55. *In re* General Motors Corp. Pick–Up Truck Fuel Tank Prods. Liab. Litig., 55 F.3d at 803–04 (stating that the possibility of simultaneous fee and settlement negotiations is one factor indicating class counsel may not have been an adequate representative); Mendoza v. Tucson Sch. Dist. No. 1, 623 F.2d 1338, 1352–53 (9th Cir.1980) (simultaneous negotiation of settlement and fees creates a potential conflict of interest, and therefore the district court, when reviewing such a settlement, should "examine with special scrutiny the benefits negotiated

for the class"), *cert. denied*, 450 U.S. 912, 101 S.Ct. 1351, 67 L.Ed.2d 336 (1981).

56. Weinberger, 925 F.2d at 525. *See also In re* Fleet/Norstar Secs. Litig., 935 F.Supp. 99, 104 (D.R.I.1996), *supplemented by* 974 F.Supp. 155 (D.R.I.1997) ("[H]eightened judicial oversight" of fee agreements is necessary, as "the very existence of a clear sailing agreement increases the likelihood that something of value will have been bargained away by counsel."); Malchman v. Davis, 761 F.2d 893, 906–08 (2d Cir.1985) (Newman, J., concurring) (criticizing clear-sailing agreements upon grounds that plaintiffs' counsel, in obtaining defendant's agreement, bargained away something of value to the class).

57. Weinberger, 925 F.2d at 525 (A clear-sailing clause "by its nature deprives the court of the advantages of the adversary process" because the court must rule on the propriety of the requested fee without the benefit of a challenge from the opposing party.); Johnston v. Comerica Mortg. Corp., 83 F.3d 241, 246 n. 11 (8th Cir.1996) ("The district court appropriately noted that the potential for abuse is heightened by the defendants' agreement not to contest fees up to a certain point."). *See generally*, Carrie Menkel–Meadow, *Ethics and the Settlements of Mass Torts: When the Rules Meet the Road*, 80 Cornell L. Rev. 1159 (1995).

§ 15.22   Antitrust Actions

Federal antitrust damage cases—particularly horizontal price-fixing cases under Section 1 of the Sherman Act[1]—have long been regarded as good candidates for class treatment under Rule 23(b)(3). Beginning as early as the so-called "electrical equipment cases"[2] filed shortly after the 1966 amendments to Rule 23 (which created "opt-in" class actions for money damages) treble damage class actions seeking relief under Section 4 of the Clayton Act[3] have become fairly common.

The "violation" phase of most cases under the Sherman Act, like other inquiries in other kinds of litigation that focus entirely on the conduct of the party opposing the class, presents some questions that do not vary from one potential plaintiff to the next. Whether the claim is framed as an alleged per se violation of Section 1 of the Sherman Act, or a form of monopolization under Section 2 of the Sherman Act, plaintiffs' proof regarding defendants' conduct will frequently be common. Moreover, even the "fact of injury" phase of an antitrust case—addressed to whether each plaintiff suffered some injury to its business or property by reason of something unlawful under the antitrust laws—may be well suited to class treatment if all potential class members operate in the same relevant market in the same capacity (*i.e.*, as buyers or sellers).

Differences among class members that go solely to the *amount* of each class member's recovery do not generally defeat class certification under Rule 23(b)(3). Where the question of amount of damages is the only significant issue that varies from class member to class member, federal courts frequently certify antitrust cases as class actions.

Where antitrust cases involve multiple relevant markets or otherwise differentiated classes of plaintiffs, however, problems may arise in the application of Rule 23. Such difficulties may be found in the violation phase of certain cases raising claims under Section 1 of the Sherman Act (tying claims regarding individual proof of coercion, for example) or in the injury phase of such litigation. Whether the disparate proof required in such cases will render a class action improper or unmanageable, or undermine the notion that common questions predominate in such cases within the meaning of Rule 23(b)(3), depends upon the facts of each case.[4]

(a) "Adequacy" and "Typicality" of Proposed Class Representatives

As in any other action under Rule 23, the class representatives in an antitrust class action must meet the "typicality" requirement of Rule 23(a)(3) and the "adequacy of representation" requirement of Rule

---

§ 15.22

1. 15 U.S.C.A. § 1 (West 1997) *See* Chapter 53 "Antitrust," *infra.*

2. Philadelphia Electric Co. v. Anaconda American Brass Co., 43 F.R.D. 452 (E.D.Pa. 1968).

3. 15 U.S.C.A.§ 15 (West 1997).

4. *See, e.g.,* Bogosian v. Gulf Oil Corp., 561 F.2d 434, 454 (3d Cir.1977), *cert. denied*, 434 U.S. 1086, 98 S.Ct. 1280, 55 L.Ed.2d 791 (1978).

23(a)(4). In cases framed under Section 1 of the Sherman Act, the named plaintiff frequently will only have had dealings with one of the alleged co-conspirators; this alone does not render the proffered class representative atypical or inadequate, as the essence of all plaintiffs' claims remains the establishment of the conspiracy alleged.

In some circumstances, the proffered plaintiff's claim may be uniquely subject to defenses. The class representative's claim may be barred entirely by the Clayton Act's four-year statute of limitations; the named plaintiff may for other reasons simply be atypical of the class as a whole. Where this happens, Rule 23(a) will pose a barrier to class certification.

(b) Proving "Fact of Injury" on a Class–Wide Basis

The fact that there has been an antitrust violation does not mean everyone in a properly defined relevant market has been affected in the same way—or affected at all. In order to recover treble damages, plaintiffs bear the burden of demonstrating that each of them suffered some injury to business or property by reason of the anticompetitive effects of the violation. Where multiple markets are involved, this requires proof that (for example) prices in excess of competitive prices were charged by defendants in each market, which in turn requires evidence going to the competitive conditions in each market. If there are two relevant markets in which class members participate, the challenge to manageability may not be great. If there are two hundred such markets, however, the challenge to manageability may be overwhelming.

(c) Proving Amount of Damages for Individual Class Members

One difficult problem that has arisen with some frequency in antitrust class actions has been the issue of so-called "fluid class recovery." It can sometimes be extremely difficult to determine precisely which persons were damaged by conduct violative of the antitrust laws, or in what amounts.

Congress has specifically allowed for statistically oriented proofs of damages in actions brought by states parens patriae under 15 U.S.C.A. § 15d, but it has made no similar provisions for private antitrust class actions under Rule 23. There remains significant uncertainty as to whether anything short of individualized proof of damages is acceptable in litigated antitrust class actions in federal court.[5]

---

5. *Compare In re* Antibiotic Antitrust Actions, 333 F.Supp. 278 (S.D.N.Y.), *amended,* 333 F.Supp. 291 (S.D.N.Y.1971) (suggesting permissibility of class-wide award) *with In re* Hotel Telephone Charges, 500 F.2d 86 (9th Cir.1974) (precluding "gross damages").

(d) Specifying or Describing Members of the Class to be Included in the Judgment

Rule 23(c)(3) provides that in an action certified under Rule 23(b)(3), the judgment shall "specify or describe those to whom the notice ... was directed, and who have not requested exclusion, and whom the court finds to be members of the class." The requirement that there be a definable class is basic to the entire class action procedure, particularly where property rights are at stake and notice is required.[6]

It may not be possible to define a plaintiff class in antitrust litigation with reference to those who "suffered competitive injury" or "paid an overcharge" by virtue of the conduct challenged in a complaint. Rather, class membership should be defined with reference to objective criteria, *e.g.*, persons who purchased particular products from particular sellers during a particular time period. If it is not possible to fashion an accurate class definition from such objective criteria, there may be serious manageability problems with the proposed class.

Library References:
    West's Key No. Digests, Federal Civil Procedure ⚯181.5.
    Wright, Miller & Kane, Federal Practice and Procedure: Civil 2d § 1764, 1781.

§ 15.23   Securities Actions

(a) Requirements Imposed by the Securities Litigation Reform Act of 1995

Unlike the other types of substantive class actions discussed in this chapter, Congress has recently established significant procedural requirements which a plaintiff must satisfy in order to maintain a securities class action. In December 1995, Congress overrode President Clinton's veto and passed the Private Securities Litigation Reform Act of 1995 (the "Reform Act").[1] The Reform Act imposed significant procedural changes which affect the prosecution of federal securities class actions, including changes affecting who may serve as a representative plaintiff in such cases. One of the principal goals which Congress sought to achieve in the Reform Act was to de-emphasize the "race to the courthouse" phenomenon which had characterized many securities class actions. The impetus behind the Reform Act was "the belief that the plaintiff's bar had seized control of class action suits, bringing frivolous suits on behalf of only nominally interested plaintiffs in the hope of obtaining a quick settlement."[2] In order to remove control over the

---

6. *Cf.* Amchem Products, Inc. v. Windsor, ___ U.S. ___, 117 S.Ct. 2231, 138 L.Ed.2d 689 (1997) (noting the gravity of the problem of notice where those to whom the notice must be directed may be unaware that they are within the class definition).

and 15 U.S.C.A. § 78u–4 (West 1995). *See* Chapter 54 "Securities," at §§ 54.2(d), 54.28 *infra*.

2. Greebel v. FTP Software Inc., 939 F.Supp. 57, 58 (D.Mass.1996).

§ 15.23

1. Pub. L. No. 104–67, 109 Stat. 737, codified at 15 U.S.C.A. § 77z–1(West 1995)

prosecution of such actions from the lawyers and instead to place control of securities class actions in the hands of those investors whose interests are most affected by the alleged wrongdoing,[3] Congress chose three principal means to achieve this goal: the requirement of a plaintiff's sworn certification filed simultaneously with the complaint, the prompt selection by the court of a lead plaintiff and the discouragement of so-called "professional" plaintiffs.

The Reform Act now requires that in order to commence a securities class action, a prospective plaintiff must file with the complaint a sworn statement certifying that the plaintiff (i) has reviewed the complaint and authorized its filing;[4] (ii) did not purchase the security which is the subject of the complaint "at the direction of plaintiff's counsel" or in order to participate in the class action;[5] (iii) is willing to serve as a representative plaintiff and provide pretrial and trial testimony;[6] and (iv) will not, absent court approval, accept any payment for serving as a class representative beyond a pro rata share of any recovery.[7] The plaintiff must also set forth in the certification all prior transactions in the security which is the subject of the class action during the proposed class period[8] and identify all other class actions in which the plaintiff has sought to serve as a class representative in the three years preceding the date of the plaintiff's certification.[9]

The Reform Act also provides that not later than 20 days after the filing of the complaint, the plaintiff "shall cause to be published, in a widely-circulated national business-oriented publication or wire service,"[10] a notice[11] advising potential class members of the pendency of the class action, the class period and the claims asserted.[12] The notice shall also advise class members that any member of the purported class may, within 60 days after publication of the notice, apply to the court for appointment as lead plaintiff. Not later than 90 days after the publication date of the notice required by the Reform Act, the court shall

---

3. S. Rep. No. 104–98, at 4 and 6, *reprinted in* 1995 U.S.C.C.A.N. 679, 683 and 685.

4. 15 U.S.C.A. § 77z–1(a)(7); 15 U.S.C.A. § 78u–4(a)(2)(A)(i)(West 1995).

5. 15 U.S.C.A. § 77z–1(a)(2)(A)(ii); 15 U.S.C.A. § 78u–4(a)(2)(A)(ii)(West 1995).

6. 15 U.S.C.A. § 77z–1(a)(2)(A)(iii); 15 U.S.C.A. § 78u–4(a)(2)(A)(iii)(West 1995).

7. 15 U.S.C.A. § 77z–1(a)(2)(A)(vi); 15 U.S.C.A. § 78u–4(a)(2)(A)(vi)(West 1995).

8. 15 U.S.C.A. § 77z–1(a)(2)(A)(iv); 15 U.S.C.A. § 78u–4(a)(2)(A)(iv)(West 1995).

9. 15 U.S.C.A. § 77z–1(a)(2)(A)(v); 15 U.S.C.A. § 78u–4(a)(2)(A)(v)(West 1995). The filing of the certification "shall not be construed to be a waiver of the attorney-client privilege." 15 U.S.C.A. § 77z–1(a)(2)(B); 15 U.S.C.A. § 78u–4(a)(2)(B)(West 1995).

10. By way of example, publication on the Business Wire has been held to comply with this requirement. Greebel v. FTP Software, Inc., 939 F.Supp. 57, 63 (D.Mass. 1996). *Id.*

11. 15 U.S.C.A. § 77z–1(a)(2); 15 U.S.C.A. § 78u–4(a)(3)(A)(i) (West 1995). This notice shall be in addition to any notice required by the Federal Rules of Civil Procedure. 15 U.S.C.A. § 77z–1(a)(3)(A)(iii); 15 U.S.C.A. § 78u–4(a)(3)(A)(iii)(West 1995).

12. If, as often occurs, more than one class action is filed asserting the same or similar claims, only the plaintiff in the first-filed action is required to publish the notice. 15 U.S.C.A. § 77z–1(a)(2)(A)(ii); 15 U.S.C.A. § 78u–4(a)(3)(A)(ii)(West 1995).

consider any motion filed by a class member who wishes to be appointed as lead plaintiff. The court must appoint as lead plaintiff the member or members of the purported class "that the court determines to be most capable of adequately representing the interest of class members."[13] If more than one action has been filed on behalf of a class asserting substantially the same claim or claims, and any party has sought to consolidate, the court must decide the consolidation motion before a lead plaintiff is appointed.[14]

In the Reform Act, Congress also established a procedure whereby a court is required to adopt, as a rebuttable presumption, that the most adequate plaintiff in a securities class action is the person or persons that (i) has filed a complaint or moved for appointment as lead plaintiff; (ii) in the court's determination, has the largest financial stake in the litigation; and (iii) otherwise meets the requirements of Rule 23.[15] This presumption may be rebutted only upon proof by another class member that the "presumptively most adequate plaintiff" will not fairly and adequately protect the interests of the class or is subject to unique defenses that would render that plaintiff incapable of adequate class representation.[16] While a plaintiff may conduct discovery in aid of rebutting the "most adequate plaintiff" presumption,[17] that plaintiff must first demonstrate "a reasonable basis for a finding that the presumptively most adequate plaintiff is incapable of adequately representing the class."[18] Congress further legislated that the most adequate plaintiff selects counsel to represent the class, subject to court approval.[19] Finally, in a move to limit "professional" plaintiffs, the Reform Act prohibits, except with the court's approval, a person from serving as a lead plaintiff or as an officer, director or fiduciary of a lead plaintiff in more than five securities class actions in any three-year period.[20]

In the first 18 months following the passage of the Reform Act, there have been a small number of reported decisions construing these procedural requirements. One such decision was issued in *Greebel v. FTP Software, Inc.,*[21] where the court addressed the Reform Act's provisions concerning certification, notice and lead plaintiffs. Plaintiff Greebel and two other members of the purported class (collectively, "Greebel") timely moved for appointment as lead counsel. Defendants FTP Soft-

---

13. 15 U.S.C.A. § 77z–1(a)(3)(B)(i); 15 U.S.C.A. § 78u–4(a)(3)(B)(i)(West 1995).

14. 15 U.S.C.A. § 77z–1(a)(3)(B)(ii); 15 U.S.C.A. § 78u–4(a)(3)(B)(ii)(West 1995).

15. 15 U.S.C.A. § 77z–1(a)(3)(B)(iii)(I); 15 U.S.C.A. § 78u–4(a)(3)(B)(iii)(I)(West 1995).

16. 15 U.S.C.A. § 77z–1(a)(B)(iii)(II); 15 U.S.C.A. § 78u–4(a) (3) (B) (iii) (II) (West 1995).

17. One court has permitted "any plaintiff" to take discovery of "any other plaintiff." *In re* Cephalon Securities Litigation, 1996 WL 515203 (E.D.Pa.1996).

18. 15 U.S.C.A. § 77z–1(a)(3)(B)(iv); 15 U.S.C.A. § 78u–4(a)(3)(B)(iv)(West 1995).

19. 15 U.S.C.A. § 77z–1(a)(3)(B)(v); 15 U.S.C.A. § 78u–4(a)(3)(B)(v)(West 1995). If the attorney for the class owns or has a beneficial interest in the securities which are the subject of the litigation, the court must determine whether the ownership interest constitutes a disqualifying conflict of interest. 15 U.S.C.A. § 77z–1(a)(9)(West 1995); 15 U.S.C.A. § 78u–4(a)(9)(West 1995).

20. 15 U.S.C.A. § 77z–1(a)(3)(B)(vi); 15 U.S.C.A. § 78u–4(a)(3)(B)(vi).

21. 939 F.Supp. 57 (D.Mass.1996).

ware, Inc. and several of its officers (collectively, "FTP") opposed the motion. The court first confronted the issue of FTP's standing to object to Greebel's motion. Construing the Reform Act, the court held that the requirements of certification and early notice to the purported class are "prerequisites to bringing a class action" and that failure to adhere to the requirements is "fatal to the maintenance of the putative class action."[22] Consequently, permitting a class action defendant to object to a plaintiff's motion for appointment as lead plaintiff on these grounds serves the same interest which is satisfied by permitting a class action defendant to object to a class certification motion.[23] At the same time, the court held that FTP lacked standing to challenge whether Greebel met the requirements for lead counsel status, stating that only potential plaintiffs may be heard on this issue.[24] The court also considered the issue of whether any class member seeking lead plaintiff appointment other than a named plaintiff who has filed a complaint must file a certification and concluded that there is no requirement that such a class member file a certification with his or her motion.[25]

Based upon its review of securities class actions filed in 1996, the SEC has concluded that "Congress' efforts to encourage more active participation by institutional and other large investors has not yet taken hold."[26] The SEC noted that in the 105 securities class actions filed in the year after the Reform Act's passage, institutional investors moved to become lead plaintiffs in only eight cases and in seven of those cases, the institutional investor was represented "by a group of law firms which includes at least one traditional plaintiff's law firm." In the most notable case in which a court adhered to Congress' intent to remove control of securities class actions from the hands of the plaintiff's class action bar, a Texas court appointed a large institutional investor, the State of Wisconsin Investment Board ("SWIB"), as lead plaintiff in *Gluck v. CellStar Corp.*,[27] rejecting the position taken by the original plaintiffs and their counsel, Milberg Weiss Bershad Hynes & Lerach, that SWIB and the original plaintiffs should be co-lead plaintiffs with the ability to

22. *See id.* at 59.

23. *Id.*

24. *Id.* The court also stated that this ruling must be without prejudice to the possible revisiting of the issue at the time of a class certification motion. *Id.; accord* Fischler v. AmSouth Bancorporation, 971 F.Supp. 533 (M.D.Fla.1997).

25. Greebel, 939 F.Supp. at 61.

26. Report to the President and the Congress on the First Year of Practice Under the Private Securities Litigation Reform Act of 1995, [Current Binder] Fed. Sec. L. Rep. (CCH) at & 85,931 (April 1997). The SEC concluded that the dearth of institutional investors seeking appointment as lead plaintiff is attributable to a "cost and perceived liability exposure." Institutional investors as plaintiffs will likely be subject-

ed to depositions at the appointment stage and at the class certification stage. In addition, some institutional investors may fear the possibility of being sued by other plaintiffs for poor management of the litigation.

27. C.A. No: 3:96—CV 1353–R (N.D. Tex. Oct. 3, 1996) (Buchmeyer, J.) At the other end of the spectrum, another judge in the same district granted the motion supported by all plaintiffs in six consolidated class actions to appoint 11 plaintiffs as co-lead counsel and to retain four traditional plaintiff's class action firms as lead counsel. Zuckerman v. Foxmeyer Health Corporation, et al. [Current Binder] Fed. Sec. L. Rep. (CCH), & 99,443 (N.D. Tex. March 28, 1997) (Maloney, J.).

retain co-lead counsels. In *In re Donkenny Securities Litigation*,[28] the court ruled less aggressively as it merely rejected the application of named plaintiffs in two of nine consolidated class actions to be named co-lead plaintiffs and instead designated a limited partnership as the sole lead plaintiff. Noting that "[o]ne of the principal legislative purposes of the [Reform Act] was to prevent lawyer-driven litigation," the court held that "[t]o allow lawyers to designate unrelated plaintiffs as a 'group' and aggregate their financial stakes would allow and encourage lawyers to direct the litigation."[29] The court did permit the single lead plaintiff to select two leading plaintiff's firms as co-lead counsel "provided that there is no duplication of attorneys' services."[30]

(b) Satisfying the Requirements of Rule 23(a)

Rule 23(a) sets forth four factors which a court must first consider on a motion for class certification:

(1) the class is so numerous that joinder of all members is impractical, (2) there are questions of law common to the class, (3) the claims or defenses of the representative parties are typical of the claims or defenses of the class, and (4) the representative parties will fairly and adequately protect the interests of the class.[31]

The Reform Act's requirement for the early appointment of a lead plaintiff who fits the Reform Act's specific parameters leaves undisturbed the requirement of satisfying the Rule 23(a) elements in the context of the class certification motion.[32]

The first two Rule 23(a) elements—numerosity and commonality—rarely raise any significant hurdles. Given the depth and breadth of the capital markets in the United States, it is hard to conceive of a purported securities class action in which the numerosity requirement could not be met.[33] The commonality test is customarily satisfied by focusing on a course of conduct by one or more defendants giving rise to liability which affects all class members, such as misrepresentations or omissions in a registration statement or prospectus.[34] "The questions of law and fact

---

28. 171 F.R.D. 156 (S.D.N.Y.1997).

29. *Id.* at 157–58.

30. *Id.* at 158.

31. FRCP 23(a). *See* Chapter 54 "Securities" at § 54.28, *infra.*

32. Greebel v. FTP Software, Inc., 939 F.Supp. 57, 60 (D.Mass.1996) ("Though neither the text of the [Reform Act] nor its legislative history explicitly describe the relationship between motions for lead plaintiff and motions for class certification, it seems clear that Congress recognized that these motions involved distinct inquiries.").

33. CV Reit, Inc. v. Levy, 144 F.R.D. 690, 696 (S.D.Fla.1992) ("Generally, the numerosity requirement is assumed to have been met in class action suits involving nationally traded securities."); *In re* Drexel Burnham Lambert Group, Inc., 960 F.2d 285, 290 (2d Cir.1992) *cert. dismissed sub nom.* Hart Holding Co. v. Drexel Burnham Lambert Group, 506 U.S. 1088, 113 S.Ct. 1070, 122 L.Ed.2d 497 (1993). ("The entire class comprises nearly 850 claimants dispersed throughout the United States."); Lubin v. Sybedon Corp., 688 F.Supp. 1425, 1458 (S.D.Cal.1988) (Class of 300 investors satisfied numerosity requirements.).

34. Beale v. EdgeMark Fin. Corp., 164 F.R.D. 649, 654 (N.D.Ill.1995).

relative to the existence and the nature of the misrepresentations and omissions are common to all Class members."[35]

In securities class actions, the Rule 23(a)(3) typicality analysis focuses on the nature of the claims alleged in the complaint and not on the specific facts underlying the proposed class representative's purchase or sale of the security at issue.[36] "The test of typicality 'is whether other members have the same or similar injury, whether the action is based on conduct which is not unique to the named plaintiffs, and whether other class members have been injured by the same course of conduct.' "[37]

(c) Satisfying the Requirements of Rule 23(b)(3)

Most securities class actions seeking damages are prosecuted under Rule 23(b)(3),[38] which imposes two additional requirements beyond the Rule 23(a) conditions. A plaintiff seeking Rule 23(b)(3) certification must establish that the common questions of law or fact "predominate" over questions affecting individual class members and that a class action is a "superior" method of adjudication.[39] The predominance test is usually a minor obstacle as courts focus on the issue of liability, typically ruling in favor of class certification by finding that the central issue in the litigation is whether a class of plaintiffs was harmed by a defendant's course of conduct. Courts customarily find class actions "superior" to other available methods when "the expense of bringing individual actions is prohibitive when weighed against the potential recovery"[40] or where class members standing alone do not have sufficient interest in pursuing their claims individually.[41]

(d) Discovery Stay

The Reform Act included one additional procedural change which further distinguish securities class actions from other Rule 23 class actions. Upon the filing of a motion to dismiss, "all discovery and other proceedings shall be stayed during the pendency of any motion to dismiss."[42] The court may make exceptions when a party makes a showing of the necessity to preserve evidence or to prevent prejudice.[43]

Library References:

West's Key No. Digests, Federal Civil Procedure ⊶187.
Wright, Miller & Kane, Federal Practice and Procedure: Civil 2d §§ 1781, 1806.

35. *In re* Alco Int'l Group, Inc. Secs. Litig., 158 F.R.D. 152, 154 (S.D.Cal.1994).

36. Hanon v. Dataproducts Corp., 976 F.2d 497, 508 (9th Cir.1992).

37. *Id.* at 508, quoting Schwartz v. Harp, 108 F.R.D. 279, 282 (C.D.Cal.1985).

38. *Id.*

39. FRCP 23(b)(3).

40. *In re* Alco Int'l Group, Inc. Secs. Litig., 158 F.R.D. 152.

41. *In re* Amerifirst Secs. Litig., 139 F.R.D. 423 (S.D.Fla.1991).

42. 15 U.S.C.A. § 77z–1(b)(3)(B); 15 U.S.C.A. § 78u–4(b)(3)(B)(West 1995).

43. *Id.*

§ 15.24   Mass Tort Actions

(a) Introduction

During the 1980's, tort law practitioners witnessed a significant increase in the use of the class action device in the area of mass torts.[1] Specifically, an increased number of class certifications were sought in three types of tort actions: mass accident, toxic exposure and products liability.

Of the three types of actions, mass accident suits are the mostly likely candidates for class treatment. Mass accidents involve a common immediate cause, such as an airplane crash, that is alleged to have resulted in similar harm to a large number of individuals. In such instances, the existence of common facts relating to the single common event (particularly as to the element of general causation) may make class actions more appealing to the judge than the prospect of multiple lawsuits. This sort of class action may also appeal to potential plaintiffs, particularly those who were less seriously injured or who are disinclined to be actively involved in the pursuit of their claim.

By contrast, the case for class certification is much weaker in cases involving exposure to toxic substances and cases involving alleged product defects. Due to the numerous individual issues of fact (such as causation and injury), it is questionable whether class treatment leads to any significant efficiencies. An example of this type of case is an action brought by residents living in the vicinity of an alleged source of toxins. In such cases, no two plaintiffs will typically have experienced identical exposures, or, for that matter, have sustained identical reactions or injuries to any given exposure. Moreover, because many conditions believed to result from toxic exposures do not exhibit symptoms until years later, class treatment of these cases can jeopardize the rights of potential claimants whose injuries have not fully manifested themselves.[2]

(b) Historical Perspective

Mass tort class actions were largely rejected by courts prior to the 1980's.[3] This long-standing judicial reluctance regarding mass tort class actions was evidenced by the 1966 Advisory Committee Note to Rule 23 of the Federal Rules of Civil Procedure, which cautioned that mass torts should not receive class treatment due to the predominance of individu-

---

§ 15.24

1. Amchem Prods. Inc. v. Windsor, ___ U.S. ___, ___, 117 S.Ct. 2231, 2247, 138 L.Ed.2d 689 (1997) (noting that "[i]n the decades since the 1966 revision of Rule 23, class action practice has become ever more 'adventuresome' ").

2. *Id.*at ___, 117 S.Ct. at 2251 (noting tension among the goals of various diverse groups of injured plaintiffs due to differ-

ences in the nature and severity of their respective injuries).

3. *Id.*at ___, 117 S.Ct. at 2250 (noting the certification of mass tort cases in increasing numbers beginning in the late–1970's). *See also* John C. Coffee, Jr., *Class Wars: The Dilemma of the Mass Tort Class Action*, 95 Colum. L. Rev. 1343, 1356–57 (1995) (recounting efforts to certify mass tort classes in the early–1980's).

al, as opposed to common, questions in such actions.[4]

For approximately two decades, courts heeded this warning and hesitated to certify mass tort classes.[5] However, the Fifth Circuit's 1986 approval of class-treatment in an asbestos-related mass tort action[6] signaled appellate recognition of a trend among the nation's courts to consider the class action device as a means of adjudicating mass tort cases. Other federal appellate courts soon followed suit.[7] The Seventh Circuit Court of Appeals recently sought to explain this change in approach by noting that courts faced with the docket congestion bought on by the asbestos litigation "faced a well-nigh irresistible pressure to bend the rules."[8] Through the late 1980's and early 1990's, this use of the class device continued to receive the support of many courts and commentators.[9] In the mid–1990's, however, the pendulum began to swing back. With a decade of experience illustrating the special problems of mass tort class actions (discussed below), judges across the nation are increasingly denying class certification in mass torts cases.[10]

4. FRCP 23(b)(3), 1966 Advisory Committee Note ("A 'mass accident' resulting in injuries to numerous persons is ordinarily not appropriate for a class action because of the likelihood that significant questions, not only of damages but of liability and defenses of liability, would be present, affecting the individuals in different ways.").

5. *See, e.g., In re* "Agent Orange" Prod. Liab. Litig., 818 F.2d 145, 164 (2d Cir.1987) (collecting cases declining to certify mass exposure/products liability cases), *cert. denied*, 484 U.S. 1004, 108 S.Ct. 695, 98 L.Ed.2d 648 (1988); Hobbs v. Northeast Airlines, Inc., 50 F.R.D. 76, 80 (E.D.Pa. 1970) (collecting cases declining to certify mass accident cases); Coffee, *supra* note 3, at 1357 (discussing cases in which certification was denied).

6. Jenkins v. Raymark Indus., Inc., 782 F.2d 468 (5th Cir.1986) (stating that "[c]ourts have usually avoided class actions in most mass accident or tort settings," but noting recent district court decisions certifying classes for Agent Orange claims and asbestos property damage claims by schools).

7. *In re* School Asbestos Litig., 789 F.2d 996 (3d Cir.) (affirming conditional certification of national asbestos property damage class and stating that despite reservations "we do not wish to foreclose an approach that might offer some possibility of improvement over the methods employed to date"), *cert. denied*, 479 U.S. 852, 107 S.Ct. 182, 93 L.Ed.2d 117 & 479 U.S. 915, 107 S.Ct. 318, 93 L.Ed.2d 291 (1986); *In re* "Agent Orange" Prod. Liab. Litig., 818 F.2d

at 166–67 (noting reservations, but affirming certification of Agent Orange class based upon centrality of one affirmative defense in litigation of claims); *In re* A.H. Robins Co., Inc., 880 F.2d 709 (4th Cir.) (affirming certification of class of claimants in intrauterine device products liability litigation), *cert. denied*, 493 U.S. 959, 110 S.Ct. 377, 107 L.Ed.2d 362 (1989).

8. Matter of Rhone–Poulenc Rorer, Inc., 51 F.3d 1293, 1304 (7th Cir.), *cert. denied*, 516 U.S. 867, 116 S.Ct. 184, 133 L.Ed.2d 122 (1995). *See also* Amchem Products Inc. v. Windsor, ___ U.S. ___, ___ – ___, 117 S.Ct. 2231, 2237–38, 138 L.Ed.2d 689 (1997) (noting the existence of an "asbestos-litigation crisis").

9. *See supra* notes 6–7.

10. *See, e.g.,* Amchem Products, ___ U.S. at ___, 117 S.Ct. at 2250 (declining to certify national asbestos personal injury class and noting that the 1966 Advisory Committee's warning regarding the certification of mass tort classes "continues to call for caution when individual stakes are high and disparities among class members great"); Rhone–Poulenc, 51 F.3d at 1304 (denying certification of class of hemophiliacs who claimed to have contracted AIDS from tainted blood products); Castano v. American Tobacco Co., 84 F.3d 734, 746 (5th Cir.1996) (denying certification of a national class of cigarette smokers); Boughton v. Cotter Corp., 65 F.3d 823, 826 (10th Cir.1995) (denying certification of a class of individuals living in proximity to a uranium mill); Reilly v. Gould, Inc., 965 F.Supp. 588,

(c) "Adequacy" and "Typicality" of Proposed Class Representatives

Of Rule 23(a)'s requirements, typicality and adequacy of representation pose the greatest obstacles to the certification of a proposed mass tort class. Establishing typicality, or a nexus between the class representative and the common claims, can present particular trouble with regard to mass torts. Because mass torts by definition involve numerous plaintiffs, each generally having a particularized claim and injury, it is often difficult to locate named plaintiffs that represent the full spectrum of claims. Thus, in cases in which the range of factual or legal differences is great, it is possible that "no set of representatives can be 'typical' of the proposed class."[11]

The adequacy of representation element contemplates whether there exist conflicts of interests between the class representatives (or their counsel) and absent class members.[12] Potential conflicts abound in the mass tort setting for several reasons. First, a lack of shared interests can create antagonism,[13] such as when the named plaintiff has a weaker claim than that of other class members.[14] Due to the critical role that the named plaintiff's claim plays in valuation of the case, a class representative with a weak claim threatens to diminish the recovery of class members who have more favorable facts in support of their cases or to whom more favorable law is applicable. Similar tension is created when the injuries of the named plaintiff are not similar in nature or severity to the interests of a substantial number of absent class members, especially in cases in which a settlement is structured to provide different relief to different types of injuries.[15]

606 (M.D.Pa.1997) (declining to certify class of individuals living in proximity to battery crushing facility); Arch v. American Tobacco Co., Inc., 175 F.R.D. 469 (E.D.Pa.1997) (denying certification of class of Pennsylvania residents who smoked cigarettes).

11. Georgine v. Amchem Prods. Inc., 83 F.3d 610, 632 (3d Cir.1996), *aff'd sub nom.* Amchem Prods. Inc. v. Windsor, ___ U.S. at ___, 117 S.Ct. at 2251; Walker v. Liggett Group, Inc., 175 F.R.D. 226 (S.D.W.Va. 1997) (decertifying national class of cigarette smokers and noting that "this gargantuan assembly of plaintiffs would appear to defy definition, much less division").

12. FRCP 23(a)(4); Amchem Products, ___ U.S. at ___, 117 S.Ct. at 2250–51.

13. *See* Amchem Products, ___ U.S. at ___, 117 S.Ct. at 2251 (noting that the goals of prospective plaintiffs with different injuries "tug against" each other); *In re* General Motors Corp. Pick-up Truck Fuel Tank Prods. Liab. Litig., 55 F.3d 768 (3d Cir. 1995) (holding that owners of individual

trucks and owners of fleets of trucks have antagonistic interests in products liability litigation such that a representative from one group could not adequately represent the interests of the other), *cert. denied*, 516 U.S. 824, 116 S.Ct. 88, 133 L.Ed.2d 45 (1995).

14. *See* Amchem Products, ___ U.S. at ___ n. 14, 117 S.Ct. at 2243 n. 14 (noting argument that California mesothelioma victims have substantially greater historical recoveries than that provided by proposed settlement of national asbestos personal injury class); Valentino v. Carter–Wallace, Inc., 97 F.3d 1227, 1234 (9th Cir.1996) (vacating certification of national class of users of epilepsy drug, due in part to concern that named plaintiffs did not exhibit the more severe conditions for which recovery was sought).

15. *See* Amchem Products, ___ at ___, 117 S.Ct. at 2251 (stating that named plaintiffs, despite diverse medical conditions, all

Conflicts may also arise in cases in which currently-injured claimants seek to represent individuals who were exposed to a substance but have not yet manifested any injury or illness (sometimes referred to as "future claimants"). The obvious goal for currently-injured claimants is to receive the largest possible immediate recovery.[16] The future claimants, however, generally see themselves as best served by the establishment of an adequately endowed, inflation-protected fund from which they can receive payment upon manifestation of an injury and the existence of sufficient flexibility to respond and adapt the remedy to unforeseen future developments (such as medical advances that alter the understanding of the causation element in toxic exposure cases).[17]

Finally, a conflict may exist if the named plaintiff has separate litigation pending against the class action defendant.[18] This scenario raises the concern that the plaintiff could compromise the class action suit in return for a more favorable settlement of its other litigation.

(d) Satisfying the Requirements of Rule 23(b)(3)[19]

(1) Trends in Considering the Predominance of Common Questions

Increasingly, courts are holding that proposed mass tort classes fail to meet Rule 23(b)'s requirement that common issues predominate.[20]

sought to represent the entire proposed asbestos personal injury class); Walker, 175 F.R.D. 226 (decertifying national class of cigarette smokers due to lack of adequate representation for the diverse groups of individuals and types of claims at issue in the litigation); Reilly, 965 F.Supp. at 606 (declining to certify class of individuals living in proximity to battery crushing facility based, in part, on the existence of "a hodge-podge of factually and legally different issues dispersed among different plaintiffs").

16. See Amchem Products, ___ U.S. at ___, 117 S.Ct. at 2251.

17. See id.; See also In re Masonite Corp. Hardboard Siding Products Liability Litigation, 170 F.R.D. 417, 420 (E.D.La. 1997) (noting potential for similar conflict in context of property damage litigation).

18. See Susan P. Koniak, Feasting While the Widow Weeps: Georgine v. Amchem Products, Inc., 80 Corn. L. Rev. 1045, 1051–57 (May 1995); Eric Watt Wiechmann, Rosanne C. Baxter & John P. McKinney, Mass Tort Class Actions: Is the Tide Turning? 64 Def. Couns. J. 67, 73 (Jan. 1997).

19. Because the primary focus of most mass tort plaintiffs is monetary damages,

the limitation of Rule 23(b)(2) to equitable relief makes it a less inviting option. Rule 23(b)(1) is troublesome for some plaintiffs because of judicial uncertainty as to the meaning of "inconsistent" adjudications. See James D. Pagliaro and Paul J. Greco, Toxic Torts, in Environmental Law Practice Guide § 33.05(2) (1992).

20. See, e.g., Amchem Products, ___ U.S. at ___, 117 S.Ct. at 2249–50 (holding that national class of asbestos personal injury claimants could not be certified due to numerous uncommon issues of fact and differences in applicable state laws); Castano v. American Tobacco Co., 84 F.3d 734, 743 (5th Cir.1996) (vacating certification of national class of cigarette smokers); In re American Medical Systems, Inc., 75 F.3d 1069, 1084–85 (6th Cir.1996) (vacating certification of national class in penile implant products liability litigation due to predominance of individual issues); Boughton v. Cotter Corp., 65 F.3d 823, 827–28 (10th Cir.1995) (affirming order denying certification of class of residents in proximity to uranium mill due to predominance of individual issues); Smith v. Brown & Williamson Tobacco Corp., 174 F.R.D. 90, 94–96 (W.D.Mo.1997); In re Masonite Hardboard Siding Products Liability Litigation, 170

Causation in particular leads many courts to decline class treatment in mass tort actions as there is generally neither a single, common event that triggers damage, nor a single proximate cause that pertains to all plaintiffs or all injuries.[21] Similarly, most affirmative defenses in mass torts cases, such as comparative negligence and the statute of limitations, raise particularized questions which predominate over general issues.[22] Finally, especially in the context of proposed national class

F.R.D. at 421–25; Ilhardt v. A.O. Smith Corp., 168 F.R.D. 613, 619–20 (S.D.Ohio 1996); Harding v. Tambrands, Inc., 165 F.R.D. 623, 629–31 (D.Kan.1996).

21. *See* Castano, 84 F.3d at 750–51 (declining to certify national class of cigarette smokers and noting that individual issues relating to proximate causation permeate the action); Smith, 174 F.R.D. at 96 (declining to certify class of state residents who were cigarette smokers, holding that issues of individual causation predominate over those of general causation); Reilly v. Gould, Inc., 965 F.Supp. 588, 606 (M.D.Pa.1997) (declining to certify class of individuals living in proximity to battery crushing facility and noting that causation must be assessed "property by property and individual by individual"); Ilhardt, 168 F.R.D. at 619 (decertifying national products liability class due, in part, to absence of predominant common issues and noting that "no single proximate cause applies equally to each class member and to each defendant"); Harding, 165 F.R.D. at 630 (declining to certify national class in tampon products liability case, and noting that class action treatment would not resolve individual causation issues); Kurczi v. Eli Lilly & Co., 160 F.R.D. 667, 677, 680 (N.D.Ohio 1995) (declining to certify state class of woman exposed to DES due in part to predominance of individual causation issues); Thomas v. FAG Bearings Corp., Inc., 846 F.Supp. 1400, 1404 (W.D.Mo.1994) (declining to certify class of individuals and entities allegedly exposed to contaminated groundwater due to predominance of individual causation issues); Barnes v. American Tobacco Company, Inc., 1997 WL 643607, at *11 (E.D.Pa.1997) (decertifying (b)(2) medical monitoring class action in state class of cigarette smokers due in part to predominance of individual causation issues); Arch v. American Tobacco Co., Inc., 175 F.R.D. 469, 1997 WL 312112, at *16–*17 (E.D.Pa. 1997) (declining to certify state class of cigarette smokers due in part to predominance of individual causation issues); *In re*

Orthopedic Bone Screw Products Liability Litigation, 1995 WL 273597, at *10–*11 (1995) (declining to certify national class due in part to predominance of individual causation issues); McGuire v. International Paper Co., 1994 WL 261360, at *7 (S.D.Miss.1994) (declining to certify class of individuals living in proximity to paper mill due in part to the predominance of individual causation issues). *See also In re* "Agent Orange" Prod. Liab. Litig., 818 F.2d 145, 164–65 (2d Cir.1987) (expressing skepticism regarding the benefits of a determination of "general causation" in considering claims of injury by class of individuals allegedly exposed to the defoliant Agent Orange), *cert. denied*, 484 U.S. 1004, 108 S.Ct. 695, 98 L.Ed.2d 648 (1988).

22. *See* Castano, 84 F.3d at 749, 750–51 (declining to certify national class of cigarette smokers and noting that individual issues relating to comparative negligence and reliance permeate the action and noting the potential for relitigation of issues in individual comparative negligence trials following adjudication of class issues); *In re* Ford Motor Company Ignition Switch Products Liability Litig., 174 F.R.D. 332, 346–47 (D.N.J.1997) (declining to certify national products liability class due in part to predominance of individual issues relating to affirmative defenses); Smith, 174 F.R.D. at 96; *In re* Masonite Hardboard Siding Products Liability Litig., 170 F.R.D. at 424 n. 16; Ilhardt, 168 F.R.D. at 619–20; Arch, 175 F.R.D. 469, 1997 WL 312112, at *13–*14,- *19 (declining to certify state class of cigarette smokers due in part to predominance of individual issues relating to affirmative defenses); Barnes, 1997 WL 643607, at *12 (decertifying (b)(2) medical monitoring class action in state class of cigarette smokers due in part to predominance of individual issues relating to affirmative defenses); *In re* Stucco Litig., 175 F.R.D. 210, 1997 WL 467147, at *5 (E.D.N.C.1997) (declining to certify national class in products liability action due in part to concerns regarding applicability of multiple states laws);

actions, "variations in state law may swamp common issues and defeat predominance."[23]

Recently, courts have increasingly ventured beyond the four corners of the pleadings in making the determination of whether common claims predominate.[24] In this context, a finding by the court that a plaintiff's theory of common injury or causation is of questionable merit weighs against class treatment.[25] Although this is not strictly a determination on the merits, it does involve some assessment of the validity of the plaintiff's theory, and the likelihood that the "common" issues identified by the plaintiff are really issues of importance in the case.

In cases in which class certification as to all issues is inappropriate, a court may consider the option of certifying a class for the resolution of certain limited issues.[26] In mass tort cases, courts have certified classes for the determination of general liability, general causation and certain defenses, as a means of avoiding the problems in the predominance inquiry that are created by the existence of numerous individual causation and damages issues.[27] Other courts, however, have denied partial certification in mass torts cases, noting that the great overlap between common and plaintiff-specific issues may lead to duplicative litigation

McGuire, 1994 WL 261360, at *7 (declining to certify class of individuals living in proximity to paper mill due in part to the predominance of individual issues relating to affirmative defenses).

23. Castano, 84 F.3d at 740 (citing Georgine v. Amchem Prods. Inc., 83 F.3d 610, 618 (3d Cir.1996), aff'd sub nom. Amchem Prods. Inc. v. Windsor, ___ U.S. at ___, 117 S.Ct. at 2251). See also American Medical Systems, Inc., 75 F.3d at 1085 (stating that district judge would potentially "face an impossible task of instructing a jury on the relevant law"); In re Ford Motor Company Ignition Switch Prods. Liab. Litig., 174 F.R.D. at 349–51 (declining to certify national products liability class due in part to predominance of individual issues relating to affirmative defenses); Smith, 174 F.R.D. at 96 (declining to certify class of state residents who were cigarette smokers and noting that variations in state law can cause complications even in state classes); In re Stucco Litig., 175 F.R.D. 210 (declining to certify national class in products liability action, due in part to concerns regarding applicability of multiple states laws).

24. See Castano, 84 F.3d at 744 (holding that analysis of facts outside pleadings is allowed in conducting predominance inquiry (and in evaluating other Rule 23 factors)

even if it is improper to conduct a preliminary evaluation of the merits of the case).

25. See Harding, 165 F.R.D. at 630 (declining to certify class due to possibility that plaintiffs' common defect theory would fail); Arch, 175 F.R.D. 469 (declining to certify class and holding that the possibility that plaintiffs' common defect theory would fail and splinter the class weighs against a finding of predominance).

26. FRCP 23(c)(4).

27. See In re "Agent Orange" Prod. Liab. Litig., 818 F.2d at 166 (class certification proper to determine applicability of the military contractor defense); In re School Asbestos Litig., 789 F.2d 996, 1008–09 (3d. Cir.) (conditional class certification proper to determine common issues in asbestos property damage action), cert. denied, 479 U.S. 852 & 479 U.S. 915 (1986); Central Wesleyan College v. W.R. Grace & Co., 6 F.3d 177 (4th Cir.1993) (same); In re A.H. Robins Co., Inc., 880 F.2d 709, 747–48 (4th Cir.), cert. denied, 493 U.S. 959, 110 S.Ct. 377, 107 L.Ed.2d 362 (1989); Sterling v. Velsicol Chem. Corp., 855 F.2d 1188, 1197 (6th Cir.1988) (noting need for hearings on individual causation, injury and damages issues following adjudication of common issues); Black v. Rhone–Poulenc, Inc., 173 F.R.D. 156, 159, 166 (S.D.W.Va.1996) (conditionally certifying class of individuals sus-

and potential constitutional problems.[28]

(2) Trends in Considering Superiority

Although the class action was initially viewed as a possible solution to the perceived danger of repeated relitigation of issues in individual mass tort cases, recent cases have grappled with the substantial manageability difficulties that class actions present.[29] In this regard, it recently has been recognized by a number of courts that in its haste to streamline mass tort dockets in the 1980's and early–1990's, the judiciary often created mass tort classes that were replete with difficult, and often intractable, management problems.[30]

In many instances, the size of a proposed class and the complexity of litigating a broad range of claims (in some cases requiring the application of multiple states' laws), make class treatment untenable.[31] The

taining injury from alleged leak of toxic gases for adjudication of common issues).

28. See Castano, 84 F.3d at 750–51 (declining to certify national class of cigarette smokers and noting Seventh Amendment concerns regarding the rehearing of issues); Matter of Rhone–Poulenc Rorer, Inc., 51 F.3d 1293, 1297, 1303 (7th Cir.) (holding that class certification of particular issues for national class of hemophiliacs who allegedly received tainted blood products was beyond the "permissible bounds of discretion" and noting Seventh Amendment concerns regarding the need for relitigation of issues in individual actions following the class determination), cert. denied, 516 U.S. 867, 116 S.Ct. 184, 133 L.Ed.2d 122 (1995); Harding, 165 F.R.D. at 632 (declining to certify individual issues in proposed national class action involving products liability claims relating to tampons due to the fact that "noncommon issues are inextricably entangled with the common issues").

29. The manageability factor of Rule 23(b)(3)(D) is often determinative in assessing the superiority of the class action device in mass tort cases.

30. See Castano, 84 F.3d at 751 n.33 (noting that nine years into In re Asbestos School Litig. conflict of law issues had still yet to be resolved); Rhone Poulenc, 51 F.3d at 1304 (noting that in light of past experience most federal courts decline to certify mass tort classes and those that have permitted certification have been criticized).

31. See Georgine v. Amchem Prods. Inc., 83 F.3d 610, 634 (3d Cir.1996) (reversing certification of national asbestos personal injury class and holding that "[a] series of statewide or more narrowly defined adju-

dications, either through consolidation under Rule 42(a) or as class actions under Rule 23, would seem preferable"), aff'd sub nom. Amchem Prods. Inc. v. Windsor, ___ U.S. ___, ___, 117 S.Ct. 2231, 2251, 138 L.Ed.2d 689 (1997); In re American Medical Systems, Inc., 75 F.3d 1069, 1084–85 (6th Cir.1996) (vacating certification of national class in penile implant products liability litigation and holding that "the economies of scale achieved by class treatment are more than offset by the individualization of numerous issues relevant only to a particular plaintiff"); In re Ford Motor Company Ignition Switch Products Liab. Litig., 174 F.R.D. 332, 353–54 (D.N.J.1997) (holding that treatment under federal multidistrict litigation rules was superior to certification of national products liability class); In re Masonite Hardboard Siding Products Liability Litig., 170 F.R.D. 417, 420 (E.D.La. 1997) (denying certification of national property damage class for siding products and holding that due to manageability problems class litigation would be "less efficient than litigation involving state-wide (or smaller) classes, or even a series of individual suits that implicate collateral estoppel to effect judicial economy"); Reilly v. Gould, Inc., 965 F.Supp. 588, 605–06 (M.D.Pa. 1997) (declining to certify class of individuals living in proximity to battery crushing facility); Haley v. Medtronic, Inc., 169 F.R.D. 643, 653–55 (C.D.Cal.1996) (denying certification of national class in mass product liability case relating to alleged pacemaker defect); Ilhardt v. A.O. Smith Corp., 168 F.R.D. 613, 620–21 (S.D.Ohio 1996) (citing manageability concerns in declining to certify national products liability class);

certification of a class virtually ensures an exponential increase in the amount and complexity of discovery, motion practice, and appeals (interlocutory and otherwise).[32] All of this results in considerable delay, thereby transforming straightforward individual tort actions into complex litigation that often lasts for decades.[33] Additionally, the courts obviously must still try the cases of those individuals who exercise their rights to opt-out of the class litigation. As opt-outs, by their very nature, suggest a pro-active plaintiff with confidence in the facts of his or her particular case, it is likely that the courts will still have to adjudicate some of the most hotly contested claims in addition to the time and effort that is poured into the class adjudication.[34]

Creative class definitions also produce manageability problems due to the difficulty in identifying class members. Examples of this are classes that are defined to include future claimants (who have not yet manifested an illness or injury) or those that consist only of claims meeting the requisite amount to sustain federal diversity jurisdiction. In both instances, the determination of whether an individual is included in the class may be highly speculative, or even impossible to determine, at the time of certification. Moreover, regardless of whether the case is resolved through settlement or trial, the defendants may be forced to incur costs in opposing efforts by class members seeking to exploit the nature of the class definition to avoid the bar of the judgment.[35]

Manageability concerns also arise in cases in which partial certifications under Rule 23(c)(4) adjudicate issues such as general causation or liability only at a class-wide level. These cases present the danger of different juries reaching inconsistent factual conclusions during successive phases of a particular class member's case.[36] Not only does such an outcome lead to confusion in the courts and a lack of confidence in the

Harding, 165 F.R.D. at 631–32 (denying certification of national class in tampon litigation due in part to manageability problems); Kurczi v. Eli Lilly & Co., 160 F.R.D. 667, 681 (N.D.Ohio 1995) (declining to certify state class of woman exposed to DES and noting probable need for individual hearings on choice of law, causation and damages).

32. See, e.g., In re School Asbestos Litig., 977 F.2d 764, 769–772 (3d. Cir.1992) (addressing eight separate mandamus petitions and noting that the case had previously been before the appellate court "numerous times").

33. See Castano, 84 F.3d at 751 (noting that due to conflict of law questions, discovery, subclassing, a class trial (and ensuing appeals), individual trials (and ensuing appeals), "[t]he net result could be that the class action device would lengthen, not shorten, the time it takes for the plaintiffs to reach final judgment").

34. See In re "Agent Orange" Prod. Liab. Litig., 818 F.2d 145, 165 (2d Cir.1987) (noting that plaintiffs with strong cases "may well be better off going it alone"), cert. denied, 484 U.S. 1004, 108 S.Ct. 695, 98 L.Ed.2d 648 (1988).

35. See Smith v. Brown & Williamson Tobacco Corp., 174 F.R.D. 90, 92 n. 2 (W.D.Mo.1997) (noting potential need for a "mini-lawsuit" to determine whether a person is bound by a class-wide determination).

36. See Rhone–Poulenc, 51 F.3d at 1303 (noting potential for overlapping issues relating to inquiry into defendant's alleged negligence and into alleged comparative negligence of the plaintiff and relating to general causation versus proximate individual causation); Castano, 84 F.3d at 750–51 (declining to certify national class of cigarette smokers and discussing possible Seventh Amendment problems regarding rehearing of issues); Smith, 174 F.R.D. at 90; Ilhardt, 168 F.R.D. at 620.

judicial system, but it also may raise serious Seventh Amendment issues.[37]

(e) Factors to Be Considered by Practitioners in Determining the Utility of a Mass Tort Class Action

(1) Factors Relating to the Number of Victims, Type and Amount of Damages and Nature of Injury

Plaintiffs' counsel should consider the strength of an individual client's claim before deciding whether to proceed with a class action. A lawyer representing individual claimants must be certain not to compromise those claims by carelessly immersing them in a class action. Although a plaintiff with a weak claim might seek greater economic power by means of aligning with other claimants, a plaintiff with a strong claim will generally stand a better chance of maximizing his or her recovery, both at trial and in a settlement, by proceeding alone.[38] Even seemingly large class settlement funds, after the deduction of costs and attorneys' fees and division among all class members, may leave named class members with a disappointing return on their claims.[39]

(2) The Core Issues for Trial

Due to the substantial intermingling of common and individual issues in mass tort class actions, the determination of core issues for trial often poses a difficult, but critically important, decision.[40] The most significant issue in a tort case, causation, is very often a poor candidate for core status. Given that proximate cause demands a plaintiff-specific inquiry, courts have repeatedly determined that certifying only general causation accomplishes little because individual causation will still need to be tried independently.[41] Although reliance on the commonality of general causation was once a mainstay of the plaintiffs' assertion that common issues existed, the substantial recent authority undermining the argument suggests that plaintiffs' counsel should focus on other purportedly common issues.

Most affirmative defenses in mass tort actions are also inappropriate for class treatment because they rise or fall upon the particular facts of each individual claimant's case.[42] A limited exception to this is those cases involving defendant-oriented defenses, such as the military-contractor defense.[43] The *Agent Orange* litigation illustrates that even one

---

37. See Rhone–Poulenc, 51 F.3d at 1303; Smith, 174 F.R.D. at 90 n. 7; Ilhardt, 168 F.R.D. at 620.

38. See In re "Agent Orange" Prod. Liab. Litig., 818 F.2d at 165.

39. Susan P. Koniak and George M. Cohen, *Under Cloak of Settlement*, 82 Va. L. Rev. 1051, 1053–54 (Oct. 1996).

40. See Rhone–Poulenc, 51 F.3d at 1303 (discussing constitutional and prudential implications of issue selection for class action trial).

41. See supra note 21.

42. See supra note 22. See also Georgine v. Amchem Prods. Inc., 83 F.3d 610, 628 (3d Cir.1996), aff'd sub nom. Amchem Prods. Inc. v. Windsor, ___ U.S. ___, ___, 117 S.Ct. 2231, 2251, 138 L.Ed.2d 689 (1997); See Rhone–Poulenc, 51 F.3d at 1303 (discussing comparative negligence).

43. In re "Agent Orange" Prod. Liab. Litig., 818 F.2d at 166–67 (describing centrality and commonality of the military contractor defense to all claims).

such dominant, case-dispositive legal issue may warrant the certification of a class.[44] Unlike the military contractor defense, which focuses solely on the defendant's behavior and is case-dispositive, most affirmative defenses, like comparative negligence or the statute of limitations, are fact-intensive inquiries focusing on the unique conduct of each plaintiff.[45]

An issue that is frequently proffered by plaintiffs' counsel as a core issue is the nature of a defendant's conduct. Along these lines, in some cases the question of liability for punitive damages has been certified as a common issue.[46] Although on its face, it might be thought that the potential "limitation" of damages would appeal to defendants, the true effect of this consolidated inquiry is to create enormous settlement pressure, as the defendant is faced with an all or nothing adjudication of the issue before a single finder of fact and a lower chance of success on the merits.[47] In addition, there are constitutional questions regarding the ability of a court to determine punitive damages prior to the determination of compensatory damages and prior (on multi-state classes) to a determination of which states' laws justify recovery.[48]

(3) The Use and Advisability of Subclasses

Faced with problems in meeting the typicality, adequacy and predominance requirements, plaintiffs' counsel should consider the possibility of proceeding by means of certified subclasses which group claimants according to common interests.[49] It should be noted, however, that subclasses cannot be created unless each subclass independently meets the requirements of Rule 23.[50]

Although the certification of separate subclasses with their own counsel may provide a means of alleviating concerns about conflicts of interest for plaintiffs' counsel,[51] subclasses can also create significant case management problems in that they create separate groups of

---

44. See id.

45. See supra note 22.

46. See Sterling v. Velsicol Chemical Corp., 855 F.2d 1188, 1215–16 (6th Cir. 1988).

47. See Castano v. American Tobacco Co., 84 F.3d 734, 746 (5th Cir.1996) (stating that "[a]ggregation of claims ... makes it more likely that a defendant will be found liable and results in significantly higher damage awards") (citations omitted); Rhone–Poulenc, 51 F.3d at 1298.

48. See BMW of North America, Inc. v. Gore, 517 U.S. 559, 571, 116 S.Ct. 1589, 1597, 1602, 134 L.Ed.2d 809 (1996) (discussing need for award of punitive damages to be in proportion to extent of the wrong and not to punish for conduct that occurred

in other jurisdictions was not illegal where it occurred); In re Copley Pharmaceutical, 161 F.R.D. 456, 467–68 (D.Wyo.1995) (same).

49. See Amchem Prods. Inc. v. Windsor, __ U.S. __, __ – __, 117 S.Ct. 2231, 2240–41, 138 L.Ed.2d 689 (1997) (noting the absence of subclasses in the context of discussing potential conflicts among proposed class members); In re Telectronics Pacing Systems, Inc., 172 F.R.D. 271 (S.D.Ohio 1997) (certifying numerous subclasses in mass products liability action).

50. Betts v. Reliable Collection Agency, Ltd., 659 F.2d 1000, 1005 (9th Cir.1981). See also Charles Alan Wright, Arthur R. Miller & Mary Kay Kane, Federal Practice and Procedure § 1790, at 284 (2d ed. 1986).

51. Coffee, supra note 3, at 1445.

plaintiffs with potentially disparate agendas and goals.[52] This, in turn, leads to an increase in pleadings and motion practice (and the consequent drain on judicial and litigant resources) and introduces added complications into the settlement dynamic. It seems, therefore, that in the mass tort context, the advantage of subclassing lies more in the prospect of allowing conflict-free negotiation, than in any substantial increase in judicial efficiency.

(g) Illustrative Mass Tort Class Actions

(1) Asbestos: The Rise and Fall of the "Futures" Settlement Class

When the first waves of asbestos-related tort actions were filed, great pressure was created on both the defendant companies and the courts to find ways to deal with the unprecedented demands that the cases made, both on the defendants' assets and on the courts' resources.[53] A number of asbestos manufacturers declared bankruptcy in an attempt to avoid what was perceived to be potentially ruinous liability arising from thousands of personal injury claims.[54] Contemporaneously, the judiciary searched for ways to handle the impending litigation efficiently. During the 1980's, several courts experimented with the certification or conditional certification of classes of asbestos-related personal injury claimants.[55] This culminating in Justice Rehnquist's formation of an Ad Hoc Committee on Asbestos Litigation. In 1991, the Committee issued its findings, recommending a national centralization of asbestos-related claims under the rubric of a legislatively-created administrative body.[56] Although the proposed legislative solution was never adopted, the focus on mass resolution further fueled those courts that were seeking to employ the class action device. This movement ultimately resulted in the creation of several massive "settlement" classes which, among other things, established enormous funds with quasi-administrative claims procedures designed to compensate claimants whose injuries were unmanifested at the time of settlement. In exchange for this and the release of certain affirmative defenses, the defendants to the settlements were to receive immunity from suits brought by those "future" claimants.[57]

In *Amchem Products, Inc. v. Windsor*, however, the Supreme Court rejected this approach to mass tort claims resolution. In *Amchem Products*, the parties had filed a complaint, answer, motion for class certification and request for approval of class settlement contemporaneously.[58]

---

52. Arch v. American Tobacco Co., Inc., 175 F.R.D. 469, 488 (E.D.Pa.1997).

53. Amchem Products, ___ U.S. at ___, 117 S.Ct. at 2237–38 (noting the existence of an "asbestos-litigation crisis").

54. *See, e.g.,* In re Johns–Manville Corp., 36 B.R. 743 (Bankr.S.D.N.Y.1984), aff'd, 52 B.R. 940 (S.D.N.Y.1985).

55. Matter of Rhone–Poulenc Rorer, Inc., 51 F.3d 1293, 1304 (7th Cir.), *cert. denied,* 516 U.S. 867, 116 S.Ct. 184, 133 L.Ed.2d 122 (1995).

56. Coffee, *supra* note 3, at 1389.

57. Amchem Prods. Inc., ___ U.S. at ___, 117 S.Ct. at 2240–41.

58. *Id.* at ___, 117 S.Ct. at 2239.

The district court granted class certification for an opt-out settlement class of workers exposed to asbestos on the job who had yet to file suit.[59] The Third Circuit, holding that the class was ultimately unmanageable and that the case could never be tried as a class action, decertified the class.[60] The Supreme Court affirmed, holding that the class satisfied neither Rule 23(b)(3)'s predominance requirement, nor Rule 23(a)'s adequacy of representation requirement.[61] The Court held that due to the vast range of individual issues, the mere allegation of exposure to a common product did not establish a predominance of common issues.[62] In addition, the existence of dissimilar injuries among the class members combined with the inherent conflict between present and future claimants made the named plaintiffs inadequate class representatives.[63] Although the Supreme Court seemed to suggest that some of the problems noted in the proposed class could have been resolved by procedural devices such as the use of subclasses with independent counsel,[64] *Amchem Products* appears to sound the death knell for the approval of national settlement classes in mass tort cases.

(2) Agent Orange: The Rare Predominant Affirmative Defense

Following the Vietnam War, a number of veterans asserted claims for injuries allegedly caused by Agent Orange, a defoliant used by the United States military. Ultimately, the federal district court certified a mandatory class as to punitive damages and an opt-out class premised upon general causation and the applicability of a unique "military-contractor defense" to all claims.[65] After almost 2500 claimants opted-out,[66] settlement was reached between many of the manufacturers and both present and future claimants.[67] The district judge approved the settlement and subsequently determined that the claims of the plaintiffs who had opted-out were barred by the military contractor defense.[68]

On appeal, the Second Circuit affirmed certification of the opt-out class only as to the issues presented by the military-contractor defense.[69] The court refused to certify the issue of general causation, reasoning that related proximate causation inquiry was a plaintiff-specific question.[70] Despite this, the effect of its determination was to preserve the

59. *Id.* at ___, 117 S.Ct.at 2241.

60. *Id.* at ___, 117 S.Ct. at 2242–44.

61. *Id.* at ___, 117 S.Ct. at 2249–51.

62. *Id.* at ___, 117 S.Ct. at 2250.

63. *Id.* at ___, 117 S.Ct. at 2251.

64. *Id.* at ___, 117 S.Ct. at 2240–41.

65. *In re* "Agent Orange" Prod. Liab. Litig., 818 F.2d 145, 154 (2d Cir.1987), *cert. denied,* 484 U.S. 1004, 108 S.Ct. 695, 98 L.Ed.2d 648 (1988).

66. Marjorie H. Mintzer & Yasmin Dale–Duncan, *Mass Tort Litigation: Why*

Class Action Suits Are Not the Answer, 22 The Brief 25, 29 (Fall 1992).

67. *In re* "Agent Orange" Prod. Liab. Litig., 597 F.Supp. 740 (E.D.N.Y.1984), *aff'd,* 818 F.2d 145.

68. *Id.* at 157–59.

69. *Id.* at 151.

70. *Id.* at 165 (holding that general causation was not the "relevant question" and is "inextricably intertwined" with the "highly individualistic" determination of proximate causation as to each individual plaintiff).

settlement agreement.[71]

In addition, the Second Circuit has protected the settlement from collateral attack. Recently, a group of veterans brought suit claiming that they could not be bound because at the time of settlement they had no cognizable injury-in-fact and thus had no case or controversy.[72] The court rejected their argument, holding that they had a sufficient injury at settlement and that the settlement treated both present and future claimants even-handedly.[73]

Although the *Agent Orange* case provides an example of a successful settlement of a national class in a mass tort case, the existence of the unique military contractor defense serves to distinguish it from the vast majority of mass tort cases. This, combined with the uncertainty of whether the Second Circuit's analysis would differ in the wake of the Supreme Court's decision in *Amchem Products*, suggests that *Agent Orange* will not be an effective model for future efforts to certify and settle national classes in mass tort cases.[74]

(3) Mass Exposure Claims: The Predominance of Individual Causation Issues

Courts have been increasingly reluctant to certify classes in mass exposure tort suits involving "point source" contamination. In *Sterling v. Velsicol Chemical Corp.*,[75] the district court certified a Rule 23(b)(3) opt-out class of community residents who claimed that they were injured as a result of exposure to hazardous waste dumped in a neighborhood landfill. On appeal, the court upheld the certification, but criticized the lower court for failing to adequately distinguish between general and individual causation issues in its certification process.

More recently, the trend has been for courts to deny certification of mass exposure classes altogether and to require individual trials.[76] It

---

71. *Id.* at 174.

72. *In re* "Agent Orange" Prod. Liab. Litig., 996 F.2d 1425 (2d Cir.1993), *cert. denied*, 510 U.S. 1140, 114 S.Ct. 1125, 127 L.Ed.2d 433(1994).

73. *Id.*

74. Valentino v. Carter–Wallace, Inc., 97 F.3d 1227, 1231–32 (9th Cir.1996) (distinguishing *Agent Orange* case on the basis of the military contractor defense); Haley v. Medtronic, Inc., 169 F.R.D. 643, 655 (C.D.Cal.1996) (same); McGuire v. International Paper Co., 1994 WL 261360, at *6 (S.D.Miss.1994) (same).

75. 855 F.2d 1188, 1200 (6th Cir.1988).

76. Boughton v. Cotter Corp., 65 F.3d 823 (10th Cir.1995) (affirming order declining to certify class of residents in proximity to uranium mill alleged to have emitted hazardous materials); Reilly v. Gould, Inc., 965 F.Supp. 588, 606 (M.D.Pa.1997) (de-

clining to certify class of individuals living in proximity to battery crushing facility); Thomas v. FAG Bearings Corp., Inc., 846 F.Supp. 1400, 1404 (W.D.Mo.1994) (declining to certify class of individuals and entities allegedly exposed to groundwater contamination from an industrial facility); Daigle v. Shell Oil Co., 133 F.R.D. 600, 603–04 (D.Colo.1990) (declining to certify class of individuals living in proximity to toxic waste disposal pond, due to absence of commonality and typicality); Dippery v. Amoco Production Co., 1995 WL 478948, at *1–*2 (D.N.M.1995) (declining to certify class of individuals exposed to methane gas from industrial sites); McGuire v. International Paper Co., 1994 WL 261360, at *6 (S.D.Miss.1994) (declining to certify class of individuals living in proximity to paper mill alleged to have discharged contaminants into a river). Interestingly, many state courts have begun to impose the

appears that in light of the clear trend away from certification of classes in mass exposure cases, plaintiffs and their counsel would be better served by seeking other forms of claim consolidation or by proceeding with individual actions.

(4) Breast Implants: The Pitfalls of Premature Settlement and the Bankruptcy Solution

After the Food and Drug Administration commenced an investigation into the safety of silicone gel breast implants, thousands of women who had received the implants filed suit.[77] After centralization, the trial court appointed a plaintiffs' steering committee to facilitate settlement.[78] The negotiations resulted in a record-setting $4.225 billion global settlement.[79] Although initially praised as a model for future settlements, problems soon ensued.[80]

Estimated benefits to class member proved to be grossly unrealistic due to an unexpectedly large number of claims.[81] This led to a substantial reduction in the estimated level of benefits, which, in turn, triggered a contractual delayed opt-out right.[82] Dow Corning was faced with the need to either pay in an additional $24 billion into the settlement fund (to keep the estimated benefits above the contractual level for triggering of the opt-out) or to allow the opt-out right to accrue.[83] Dow–Corning chose the latter, which resulted in over 15,000 class members choosing to

same limitations, very often borrowing directly from federal court decisions. The fact that this change is occurring, however, is masked, to some extent, by the failure of these courts to publish their opinions. *See, e.g.,* Ford v. Murphy Oil U.S.A., Inc., 703 So.2d 542 (La.1997) (decertifying class of residents living in proximity to petrochemical plants alleged to have emitted chemicals); Cordova v. Hughes Company, No. C–284158 (Ariz. Super. Ct., Pima Cty. 1996) (declining to certify class of residents in proximity to airport and alleging exposure to hazardous chemicals); Greene v. Kemira Inc., No. 94–0540–G (Ga. Super. Ct., Chatham Cty. June 14, 1996) (declining to certify proposed class of residents in proximity to industrial plant alleged to have emitted hazardous gases); Ackerman v. Albright & Wilson Americas, Inc., No. 94–CP–10–3016 (S.C. Ct. of Common Pleas Mar. 1, 1996) (declining to certify a proposed class of individuals and businesses allegedly injured by an industrial plant explosion); Dyer v. Monsanto Co., Civil Action No. CV–93–250 (Ala. Cir. Ct., St. Clair Cty. Aug. 4, 1995) (declining to certify a proposed class of individuals claiming exposure to PCB's allegedly released from an industrial facility); Mulcahey v. Columbia Organic Chemicals

Co., No. 91–CP–40–3491 (S.C. Ct. of Common Pleas Mar. 31, 1995) (declining to certify proposed class of residents living in proximity to industrial plant that was alleged to have released chemical pollutants); Simms v. Amerada Hess, No. 93–5767–B (Tex. Dist. Ct. Nueces Cty.1995) (declining to certify proposed class of residents living in proximity to refineries and pipelines alleged to have emitted underground and airborne toxins). *But see* Watson v. Shell Oil Co., 979 F.2d 1014 (5th Cir.1992) (certifying class of residents in proximity to oil refinery explosion), *rehearing granted,* 990 F.2d 805 (5th Cir.1993), *appeal dismissed,* 53 F.3d 663 (5th Cir.1994); Black v. Rhone–Poulenc, Inc., 173 F.R.D. 156 (S.D.W.Va.1996) (certifying class of residents living in proximity to industrial plant fire).

77. *In re* Dow Corning Corporation, 211 B.R. 545, 551 (Bankr.E.D.Mich.1997).

78. *Id.* at 551–52.

79. *Id.* at 552.

80. *Id.*

81. *Id.*

82. *Id.*

83. *Id.*

opt-out.[84] Faced with almost 100 impending trial dates and the prospect of thousands of others, Dow–Corning filed for bankruptcy.

Although some commentators initially speculated that Dow–Corning filed for bankruptcy in an effort to force claimants to accept the settlement,[85] Dow–Corning took an even more aggressive position. Specifically, Dow–Corning chose to attack the scientific validity of the personal injury claims being asserted against it.[86] In essence, it is seeking to use the bankruptcy as a means of getting a class-wide adjudication on the scientific validity of plaintiffs' evidence that it could not likely have obtained outside the bankruptcy.

Most recently, the bankruptcy court has refused to adopt competing proposals of methods by which the bankruptcy court could "estimate" the value of the claims against Dow–Corning.[87] The estimation process was one of several means by which Dow–Corning sought to have the bankruptcy court make a ruling on the scientific validity of the personal injury claims. Another, a motion for summary judgment, is currently under consideration by the bankruptcy court.[88] Moreover, even if the motion does not prevail, the bankruptcy court has indicated its belief that the bankruptcy proceeding should be held in abeyance while the district court conducts a common issue trial on the question of the toxicity of the implants.[89] Thus, although the case is in a relatively early stage, it appears that Dow–Corning has taken the first successful step toward a new form of defendant-driven, class-wide adjudication.

Library References:
> West's Key No. Digests, Compromise and Settlement ⟐51–72; Federal Civil Procedure ⟐181–189.
> Wright, Miller & Kane, Federal Practice and Procedure: Civil 2d §§ 1783, 1786.

§ 15.25   Consumer Fraud Class Actions

Class action lawsuits are commonly used to bring federal and state claims against consumer service providers for alleged fraudulent and unfair business practices. A number of federal consumer protection statutes explicitly provide for class actions, including the Federal Truth-in-Lending Act ("TILA"),[1] the Fair Debt Collection Practices Act ("FDCPA")[2] and the Equal Credit Opportunity Act ("ECOA").[3] These

---

84. *Id.*

85. Coffee, *supra* note 3, at 1409.

86. *In re* Dow Corning Corporation, 211 B.R. at 554 (noting that "[t]he present case is perhaps the first mass tort bankruptcy where liability has been disputed by a debtor").

87. *Id.* at 562.

88. *Id.* at 603. *See also In re* Dow Corning Corporation, 215 B.R. 346 (Bankr. E.D.Mich.1997)

89. *In re* Dow Corning Corporation, 211 B.R. at 591–92.

§ 15.25

1. 15 U.S.C.A. § 1640(a)(2)(B) (West 1982). TILA requires the affirmative disclosure of certain credit and leasing terms and protects consumers against inaccurate and unfair credit billing and credit card practices. 15 U.S.C.A. § 1601 (West 1982).

2. 15 U.S.C.A. § 1692k(a)(2)(B) (West 1982). FDCPA protects consumers from abusive, deceptive and unfair debt collection practices. 15 U.S.C.A. § 1692(a) (West 1982).

3. 15 U.S.C.A. § 1691e(b) (West 1982). ECOA prohibits any creditor from discrimi-

statutes limit the amount of recoverable damages in both individual actions ($1000 per person) and class action suits (lesser of $500,000 or 1% of defendant's net worth). A prevailing plaintiff in a consumer fraud class action is entitled to recover the costs and reasonable attorneys' fees incurred in bringing the action.

Class action claims are often brought under other federal statutes addressing consumer fraud, including the Magnuson–Moss Warranty— Federal Trade Commission Improvement Act ("Magnuson–Moss"),[4] the Fair Credit Reporting Act ("FCRA")[5] and the civil Racketeer Influenced and Corrupt Organizations ("RICO") Act.[6] In addition, class action suits may also allege violations of subject-specific consumer fraud statutes such as the Telephone Consumer Protection Act of 1991,[7] or state-enacted consumer fraud protection acts and unfair or deceptive business practice laws.

The typical consumer fraud class action is marked by a large number of individual claimants. Generally, the acts complained of are widespread business or financial practices allegedly perpetrated against many consumers. The amount of damages sought by each class member is usually small, however. One reason is that when large class actions are brought under consumer fraud statutes containing aggregate damage limitations, it has the effect of limiting the amount each individual class member can recover. A second reason is that some plaintiffs institute consumer fraud class actions in an attempt to force a defendant to discontinue the conduct offensive to all of its consumers, and the recovery of actual damages may actually be only a secondary concern.

Proper definition of the class, a point of contention in all class actions, takes on special significance in the context of consumer fraud allegations. Courts have generally rejected overly broad definitions that require the court to inquire into the actual merits of the claims, such as "every consumer injured by defendant's unfair business practices."[8] Also, for some class actions, defense counsel may be able to argue that the class must be defined and certified, if at all, as a nationwide class because some of the federal consumer protection laws provide a statutory

---

nating against any credit applicant on the bases of race, color, religion, national origin, age, sex or marital status, or because an applicant's income derives from any public assistance program. 15 U.S.C.A. § 1691(a) (West 1982).

4. 15 U.S.C.A. § 2310(e) (West 1982). Magnuson–Moss regulates the contents of consumer product warranties, mandates the disclosure of such warranties and provides special remedies for breaches of consumer product warranties. 15 U.S.C.A. §§ 2301– 2312 (West 1982).

5. 15 U.S.C.A. § 1681n (West 1982). FCRA controls the disclosure of certain in-

formation by credit reporting agencies and provides for civil liability for willful non-compliance. 15 U.S.C.A. § 1681a-n (West 1982).

6. 18 U.S.C.A. §§ 1961–1964 (West 1984).

7. 47 U.S.C.A. § 227(b)(1) (West Supp. 1998).

8. *See also* Forman v. Data Transfer, Inc., 164 F.R.D. 400, 403 (E.D.Pa.1995) (court rejecting definition of class as "all residents and business who have received unsolicited facsimile advertisements").

limitation of damages for either a single class action or a series of class actions involving the same alleged conduct.[9]

There are several benefits, from a defense perspective, to a requirement that any class which may be certified must be a national class. First, there are inherent problems in certifying a nationwide class—the jury must be charged on various state laws and various defenses and inquiries based on state law will be infused into the case—and therefore the court may be reluctant to certify the case as a class action. Second, the costs of notice and claim coordination for a nationwide class may make bringing the action prohibitively expensive for the plaintiff. Third, settlement or adjudication of a case involving a national class should provide the defendant with a nationwide release of all possible claims (except those of plaintiffs who expressly opt-out) stemming from the alleged offensive conduct.

In addition to a properly defined class, consumer fraud class actions must satisfy the other prerequisites of Federal Rule 23(a)—numerosity, commonality, typicality and adequacy of representation. Numerosity is rarely a problem in consumer fraud cases. The commonality and typicality requirements may be less stringently applied in the consumer fraud area than in other contexts. Courts have indicated that claims of the class members need not be identical, at least in cases in which there is standardized conduct by the defendants.[10] Adequacy of representation will not be satisfied if the class representative has antagonistic or conflicting claims with other class members.[11] In class actions brought under statutes which provide maximum recoveries in both individual and class actions, unless the named plaintiff waives the individual recovery (which, as a practical matter, often is larger) and accepts only her pro rata share of class recovery, her interests may be deemed antagonistic to other class members.[12]

If they satisfy the prerequisites of Federal Rule 23(a), most consumer fraud plaintiffs seek class certification under the broad mandate of Federal Rule 23(b)(3).[13] Under that subsection, the plaintiff must show both the predominance of common issues over individual issues, and that

---

9. The Seventh Circuit has rejected this argument, however, in the context of the FDCPA. Mace v. Van Ru Credit Corp., 109 F.3d 338 (7th Cir.1997). The court noted that while the statutory limitation in TILA capped recovery for a class action *or* a series of class actions involving the same conduct, the damage limitation in the FDCPA only capped damages for a particular class action. If correct, this reasoning means the possibility of multiple class actions based on the same conduct, each exposing the defendant to at least $500,000 of liability, plus actual damages of named plaintiffs, costs and attorneys' fees. In circuits that have not addressed this issue, defense counsel may be able to argue that such logic is contrary to congressional intent, and that if such damage limitations are to remain meaningful, any class certified must be a nationwide class.

10. *E.g.*, Buford v. H & R Block, Inc., 168 F.R.D. 340, 349 (S.D.Ga.1996).

11. *E.g.*, Rosario v. Livaditis, 963 F.2d 1013, 1018 (7th Cir.1992).

12. *E.g.*, Perry v. Beneficial Finance Co. of New York, 81 F.R.D. 490, 496 (W.D.N.Y. 1979).

13. If only injunctive or declaratory relief against the offensive business conduct is sought and is permitted by the statute, then class certification may be proper under FRCP 23(b)(2).

a class action is the superior method to resolve the claims. Where the reliance of individual class members upon the alleged improper business conduct is an essential element of the claim, courts have refused to certify the class, finding that common issues do not predominate.[14] Also, if nationwide class certification is sought or required under a particular statute, variations in state law may lead a court to conclude that common issues do not predominate.[15]

In deciding whether a class action is the superior method to resolve consumer fraud claims, case manageability, including the feasibility of enforcing a nationwide judgment, is a primary concern of the court, as these cases often involve large classes and address widespread business practices. The court will also consider whether a class action will provide any additional deterrent value with respect to the alleged unlawful conduct. If cases involve statutory damage limitations, the court must consider whether the particular action, if certified, will consume the entire aggregate damage award provided for under the statute, and therefore may not be superior to permitting individual claims to be brought or joined. Finally, the court will consider whether, if class certification is denied, individual claimants will be able to obtain counsel and have the proper incentive to pursue their claims individually.

Library References:

West's Key No. Digests, Federal Civil Procedure ☞182.5.
Wright, Miller & Kane, Federal Practice and Procedure: Civil 2d § 1782.

§ 15.26   Patent Actions

Class actions suits concerning intellectual property violations generally involve defendant classes of alleged infringers. Such cases should therefore be considered in light of characteristics unique to defendant classes.[1]

(a) Utility of Defendant Class Actions After *Blonder-Tongue*

In *Triplett v. Lowell,* the Supreme Court held that a defendant in a patent infringement suit must satisfy the requirement of mutuality (requiring that both the defendant and the plaintiff be bound by the judgment in a previous decision before that decision is res judicata) in order to claim collateral estoppel as a defense due to a patent invalidity adjudication against the plaintiff in an earlier case against another

---

14. *E.g.,* Buford, 168 F.R.D. at 356–61 (individual issues of reliance in case involving tax refund anticipation loan program predominated over common issues relating to defendants' conduct; class certification denied).

15. *E.g., In re* Masonite Corp. Hardboard Siding Products Liability Litigation, 170 F.R.D. 417 (E.D.La.1997) (variations in applicable substantive state laws overwhelm common elements of plaintiffs' claims).

§ 15.26

1. *See* the discussion of defendant class actions in § 15.13 *supra; see also* H. Newberg & A. Conte, Newberg on Class Actions, §§ 4.45–4.70 (3d ed. 1992).

defendant.[2]

This decision discouraged plaintiffs from bringing class action suits against a defendant class of infringers since a ruling of patent invalidity in such a suit would have res judicata effect on claims against all members of the class. Under the *Triplett* rule, however, a ruling of patent invalidity against the plaintiff in a suit against an individual defendant would not preclude the plaintiff from relitigating the issue of patent validity against future parties.

The *Triplett* decision was partially overruled in *Blonder-Tongue Laboratories, Inc. v. University of Illinois Foundation,*[3] which allowed a defendant to claim the defense of collateral estoppel without a showing of mutuality provided that the plaintiff had a "full and fair opportunity" to present its claim in the earlier proceeding.[4] This decision was based on three specific findings: (1) that the *Triplett* rule was not "essential to effectuate the purposes of the patent system, or . . . an indispensable or even an effective safeguard against faulty trials and judgments,"[5] (2) that adverse economic consequences of the *Triplett* rule, such as the costs of relitigating decided issues, warranted its modification,[6] and (3) that given the disproportionate length of the average patent infringement suit, judicial economy would be promoted by precluding claims that have already been litigated.[7]

The incentive under *Triplett* for a plaintiff to avoid filing a class action suit against a defendant class of infringers was reversed by *Blonder-Tongue.* Now, plaintiffs can seek the beneficial effect of a ruling of patent validity applied to the entire class of patent infringers rather than litigating each claim separately. A ruling of patent invalidity in a class action claim is no longer a disincentive after *Blonder-Tongue,* because such a ruling is granted virtually the same effect through collateral estoppel.

(b) Availability of Defendant Class Actions

As with any class action, the plaintiff in a patent infringement class action must prove that all elements of FRCP 23(a) and at least one of the elements of FRCP 23(b) are met.[8] Although courts generally have been cautious in determining whether a patent infringement action may be brought as a class action "given the uniqueness and complications of patent litigation,"[9] such actions have been upheld once the threshold requirements of Rule 23 have been established.[10] We address the applicability of these requirements to patent actions below.

---

2. 297 U.S. 638, 644, 56 S.Ct. 645, 648, 80 L.Ed. 949 (1936).

3. 402 U.S. 313, 348, 91 S.Ct. 1434, 1452, 28 L.Ed.2d 788 (1971).

4. *Id.* at 327, 91 S.Ct. at 1442.

5. *Id.* at 334, 91 S.Ct. at 1445.

6. *Id.* at 346, 91 S.Ct. at 1452.

7. *Id.* at 348, 91 S.Ct. at 1452.

8. Standal's Patents Ltd. v. Weyerhaeuser Co., 1986 WL 582 (D.Or.1986).

9. Tracor, Inc. v. Hewlett–Packard Co., 176 U.S.P.Q. (BNA) 505, 507–08 (N.D.Ill. 1973); *see also* Sperberg v. Firestone Tire & Rubber Co., 61 F.R.D. 70, 72–73 (N.D.Ohio 1973).

10. *See supra* §§ 15.3—15.5.

(1) Impracticability of Joinder

In considering the requirements of Rule 23(a)(1), joinder often has been considered impracticable due to venue restrictions imposed on patent cases under 28 U.S.C.A. § 1400(b).[11] However, recent decisions holding that Section 1400(b) must be interpreted in light of the 1988 amendment to 28 U.S.C.A. § 1391(c) may remove some of these venue restrictions in patent class actions involving corporations.[12] Section 1391(c) provides that a corporation may be sued in any judicial district in which it is subject to personal jurisdiction at the time the action is commenced. This section alters the rule under Section 1400(b) that corporate patent infringers can be sued only in states where they are incorporated or in jurisdictions where they have an established place of business and have committed an act of infringement.[13] This expansion of venue in patent cases involving corporate defendants, coupled with the general caution courts use in determining whether a patent infringement claim is suitable for class action treatment, may result in courts holding that joinder is not impracticable for patent infringement cases involving large corporate defendants.

Satisfaction of the numerosity requirement of Rule 23(a)(1) is generally handled on a case-by-case basis,[14] although some classes are clearly large enough to satisfy this requirement.[15]

(2) Differences Among Potential Class Members

Only one common issue is necessary to satisfy the common question of law or fact requirement of Rule 23(a)(2), even if there are other differences present in the claims or defenses of the class members.[16] Patent class actions have been deemed proper when the issues at hand have included the validity of the patent, alleged procurement of the patent through fraud, and alleged misuse of the patent.[17] A class of alleged infringers was denied when the determination of a defendant's membership in the class was dependent upon the eventual outcome of the case.[18]

---

11. See Standal's Patents Ltd., 2 U.S.P.Q.2d (BNA) at 1189; Technograph Printed Circuits Ltd. v. Methode Elecs., Inc., 285 F.Supp. 714, 717 (N.D.Ill.1968); but see Sperberg, 61 F.R.D. at 72–73.

12. VE Holding Corp. v. Johnson Gas Appliance Co., 917 F.2d 1574 (Fed.Cir. 1990); Biosyntec, Inc. v. Baxter Healthcare Corp., 746 F.Supp. 5 (D.Or.1990).

13. See Fourco Glass Co. v. Transmirra Prods. Corp., 353 U.S. 222, 77 S.Ct. 787, 1 L.Ed.2d 786 (1957).

14. Compare Dale Elecs., Inc. v. R.C.L. Elecs., Inc., 53 F.R.D. 531 (D.N.H.1971) (certifying class with 13 members) with Tracor, Inc., 176 U.S.P.Q. 505 (refusing to certify class with 13 members).

15. Research Corp. v. Pfister Associated Growers, Inc., 301 F.Supp. 497 (N.D.Ill.

1969) (certifying a class of at least 400); Technograph Printed Circuits Ltd., 285 F.Supp. 714 (certifying a class of at least 240).

16. Standal's Patents Ltd., 2 U.S.P.Q.2d (BNA) at 1188. In actions for damages under Rule 23(b)(3), the requirement that common questions predominate over questions relating to individual class members also must be satisfied. See supra § 15.5(a)(1). See, e.g., Technograph Printed Circuits Ltd., 285 F.Supp. 714.

17. Technograph Printed Circuits Ltd., 285 F.Supp. at 720; Research Corp., 301 F.Supp. at 499.

18. Sperberg v. Firestone Tire & Rubber Co., 61 F.R.D. 70, 75 (N.D.Ohio 1973). ("Ruling within the strictures set down by Sperberg's definition of the class, the Court

In general, a defense of invalidity or unenforceability has been considered common to the defendant class to satisfy the typicality requirement of Rule 23(a)(3).[19] Defenses against infringement claims, particularly defenses contending that specific products do not in fact infringe the patent at issue, have been considered to be too individualized, and thus not typical enough to warrant class certification.[20]

Library References:

West's Key No. Digests, Federal Civil Procedure ⊶181.
Wright, Miller & Kane, Federal Practice and Procedure: Civil 2d §§ 2591, 2761.

§ 15.27   Copyright and Trademark Actions

While there are some examples of class action suits involving both copyright[1] and trademark infringement,[2] there are markedly fewer class actions in these intellectual property areas than patent cases. Copyright and trademark infringement actions rarely involve industry-wide infringement and thus are less likely to be appropriate for class action treatment.

Library References:

West's Key No. Digests, Federal Civil Procedure ⊶181.
Wright, Miller & Kane, Federal Practice and Procedure: Civil 2d § 2761.

§ 15.28   Employment Class Actions

Two types of class actions are prominent under federal employment law statutes, and each has special rules and considerations that differ from class actions outside the employment context. The two types of employment class actions discussed in this section are (a) Rule 23 class actions filed under statutes such as Title VII of the Civil Rights Act of 1964 ("Title VII")[1] and the Americans with Disabilities Act of 1990 ("ADA"),[2] and (b) opt-in collective actions filed under the Age Discrimi-

---

would have to await outcome of the jury trial or trials requested by Sperberg to determine how many alleged class members, if any, were held to have infringed patent # 088. It is apparent that under the circumstances of this case a class action is inappropriate."). *But see* Research Corp., 301 F.Supp. at 499 (where the issue was moot since most of the named defendants had "almost admitted infringement" and a ruling on validity would be dispositive of most of the issues in the case).

19. Standal's Patents Ltd., 2 U.S.P.Q.2d (BNA) at 1189; Research Corp., 301 F.Supp. at 499; Technograph Printed Circuits, Ltd., 285 F.Supp. at 720–21.

20. Standal's Patents Ltd., 2 U.S.P.Q.2d (BNA) at 1189; Research Corp., 301 F.Supp. at 499 (finding the defense of noninfringement to be more "tailored to the individual").

§ 15.27

1. David v. Showtime/The Movie Channel, Inc., 697 F.Supp. 752 (S.D.N.Y.1988) (plaintiff class of copyright holders in infringement action).

2. Cross v. Oneida Paper Products Co., 117 F.Supp. 919 (D.N.J.1954) (certification of plaintiff class of union members in trademark infringement case).

§ 15.28

1. 42 U.S.C.A. §§ 2000e to 2000e–17 (West 1994). *See* Chapter 67 "Employment Discrimination," at § 67.10 discussing Title VII.

2. 42 U.S.C.A. §§ 12101–12213 (West 1994). *See* Chapter 67 "Employment Discrimination," at § 67.13 discussing the ADA.

nation in Employment Act Amendments of 1967 ("ADEA"),[5] the Fair
Labor Standards Act of 1938 ("FLSA"),[6] or the Equal Pay Act of 1963
("EPA").[7]

(a) Rule 23 Employment Class Actions

Until the Supreme Court's 1977 decision in *East Texas Motor
Freight System, Inc. v. Rodriguez,*[8] many courts had held that employment discrimination actions were "by nature" class actions because the
wrong complained of was discrimination based on a common class
characteristic, such as race, sex, religion, or national origin.[9] In *Rodriguez,*[10] the Supreme Court rejected this view and stated that careful
attention must be given to the requirements of Rule 23(a) in racial or
ethnic discrimination suits. Five years later, in *General Telephone Co. v.
Falcon,*[11] the Supreme Court emphasized that courts must undertake a
"rigorous analysis" of Rule 23(a)'s requirements of numerosity, commonality, typicality and adequacy of representation before certifying a
class action under Title VII.

The decisions in *Rodriguez* and *Falcon* have severely limited the use
of across-the-board discrimination claims under Title VII where plaintiffs attempt to assert class-wide claims of discrimination in virtually all
aspects of the employment relationship. To bring an across-the-board
class action after *Rodriguez* and *Falcon*, plaintiffs generally must present
significant proof that the employer operated under a general policy of
discrimination, and that the discrimination manifested itself in the same
fashion across the entire employing organization.[12]

(1) Administrative Charges and the Single–Filing Rule

Several employment statutes such as Title VII, the ADA, and the
ADEA require the filing of administrative charges of discrimination
before initiating an action in federal court. In employment class actions,
however, rather than requiring all plaintiffs to file individual charges of
discrimination with the EEOC, many courts have adopted the "single-
filing rule."[13] Also known as the "piggybacking rule," this doctrine
allows potential class members, in certain limited circumstances, to
bypass the EEOC's administrative process and "piggyback" on timely
EEOC charges filed by named plaintiffs serving as class representatives.[14]

5. 29 U.S.C.A. §§ 621–634 (West 1994).

6. 29 U.S.C.A. §§ 201–219 (West 1994).

7. 29 U.S.C.A. § 206(d) (West 1994).

8. 431 U.S. 395, 97 S.Ct. 1891, 52
L.Ed.2d 453 (1977).

9. *See* Bowe v. Colgate–Palmolive Co.,
416 F.2d 711, 719 (7th Cir.1969).

10. *See* Rodriguez, 431 U.S. at 405, 97
S.Ct. at 1897.

11. 457 U.S. 147, 161, 102 S.Ct. 2364,
2372, 72 L.Ed.2d 740 (1982).

12. *See id.* at 159 n.15.

13. *See, e.g.,* Calloway v. Partners National Health Plans, 986 F.2d 446, 450
(11th Cir.1993) (citing Oatis v. Crown Zellerbach Corp., 398 F.2d 496, 498–99 (5th
Cir.1968)); Tolliver v. Xerox Corp., 918 F.2d
1052, 1056 (2d Cir.1990).

14. *See* Tolliver, 918 F.2d at 1058.

The standards for applying the single-filing rule differ in various courts. Most courts look closely at the EEOC charge that was filed by a named plaintiff to determine whether it provides adequate notice to both the employer and the EEOC of alleged class-wide discrimination. Some cases favorable to plaintiffs find that adequate notice of class-wide discrimination is provided if the EEOC charge and the subsequent class claims arise out of the same circumstances and occur within the same general time frame.[15] A more narrow test favored by employers provides that the EEOC charge must "not only allege discrimination against the class but also allege that the claimant purports to represent a class or others similarly situated."[16]

(2) Statutory Defenses and Strategies

In litigating employment class actions under statutes such as Title VII and the ADA that require the filing of administrative charges with the EEOC, employers frequently develop defenses related to the statutory charge-filing requirement. Employers carefully scrutinize the content of the EEOC charges filed by the named plaintiffs to determine, among other things, the scope and timing of the charges and whether the claims of employees who filed charges arise out of the same alleged discriminatory conduct, or occur within the same time frame, as the claims of putative class members who did not file charges.

Courts have held that Title VII actions can be filed only on claims that are " 'like or related to' " the practices alleged in the EEOC charge.[17] Articulating the standard another way, the Eleventh Circuit has stated that "[t]he judicial complaint is limited to the scope of the administrative investigation which could reasonably be expected to grow out of the [EEOC] charge of discrimination."[18] This limits the judicial claims that can be filed by the individually named plaintiffs who have filed charges with the EEOC, and likewise limits the judicial claims of putative class members who have not filed charges and attempt to invoke the single-filing rule. For example, an EEOC charge limited to alleged racial discrimination in promotions generally will not support individual or class-based claims of racial discrimination in hiring or terminations.[19]

Similarly, based on the statutory requirement of filing timely charges of discrimination with the EEOC, courts have held that the single-filing rule can be invoked only on behalf of putative class members who could have filed a timely EEOC charge when the named plaintiff

---

15. *See* Snell v. Suffolk County, 782 F.2d 1094, 1101 (2d Cir.1986).

16. *See* Tolliver, 918 F.2d at 1058 (citing Naton v. Bank of California, 649 F.2d 691, 697 (9th Cir.1981)). The court in *Tolliver* declined to adopt the standard from *Naton*.

17. *See, e.g.*, Sanchez v. Standard Brands, Inc., 431 F.2d 455, 466 (5th Cir. 1970) (quoting King v. Georgia Power Co., 295 F.Supp. 943, 947 (N.D.Ga.1968)).

18. Griffin v. Carlin, 755 F.2d 1516, 1522 (11th Cir.1985) (citing Evans v. U.S. Pipe & Foundry Co., 696 F.2d 925, 929 (11th Cir.1983)).

19. *See, e.g.*, Griffin v. Dugger, 823 F.2d 1476, 1492–94 (11th Cir.1987).

did.[20] Thus, in litigating Title VII class actions, the claims of each putative class member are analyzed for timeliness vis-a-vis the EEOC charges on which they are attempting to piggyback.

(3) Rule 23(a) Defenses and Strategies

Plaintiffs in employment class actions often have difficulty satisfying the Rule 23(a) requirements of commonality, typicality, and adequacy of representation when employees with different claims of discrimination, different job functions, or from different organizational or geographic areas, seek certification of a class.

Many courts have held that current employees cannot represent rejected applicants for employment because factual differences between their claims defeat commonality.[21] In addition, a current employee might not be an adequate representative for a class of applicants who were denied employment because "conflicts might arise, for example, between employees and applicants who were denied employment and who will, if granted relief, compete with active employees for fringe benefits or seniority."[22] Certification has been denied for a class consisting of both hourly and salaried employees,[23] as well as a class of supervisory/managerial employees and nonsupervisory/nonmanagerial employees, due to inherent conflicts.[24] Courts have also denied class certification for employees who work at different positions with the employer.[25] Plaintiffs seeking certification of a class including both unionized and nonunionized workers may face a similar problem in demonstrating commonality.[26]

When putative class members work in different organizational units or geographic facilities, the critical inquiry is whether the employment decisions that are being challenged as discriminatory were made at a centralized or local level. Courts have rejected state-wide class certification because of lack of evidence of centralized decision making.[27] Similarly, a court has held that a class consisting of an entire university was

20. *See* Williams v. Owens–Illinois, Inc., 665 F.2d 918, 923–24 (9th Cir.1982). Under § 706 of Title VII, charges must be filed with the EEOC within 180 days of the alleged discrimination, unless there is a state or local civil rights agency with jurisdiction, in which case the limitations period is extended to 300 days. *See id.* at 923 n.2.

21. *See, e.g.,* General Telephone Co. v. Falcon, 457 U.S. 147, 158–59, 102 S.Ct. 2364, 2371–72, 72 L.Ed.2d 740 (1982). *Cf.* Richardson v. Byrd, 709 F.2d 1016, 1020 (5th Cir.1983) (allowing active employee to represent unsuccessful applicants because discriminatory policies affected both groups in the same way).

22. General Telephone Co. v. EEOC, 446 U.S. 318, 331, 100 S.Ct. 1698, 1707, 64 L.Ed.2d 319 (1980).

23. *See* Wakefield v. Monsanto Co., 120 F.R.D. 112, 116–17 (E.D.Mo.1988).

24. *See, e.g.,* Wagner v. Taylor, 836 F.2d 578, 595 (D.C.Cir.1987).

25. *See* Appleton v. Deloitte & Touche L.L.P., 168 F.R.D. 221, 229–31, 233 (M.D.Tenn.1996).

26. *See, e.g.,* Gramby v. Westinghouse Elec. Corp., 84 F.R.D. 655, 660 (E.D.Pa. 1979). *But see* Petty v. Peoples Gas Light & Coke Co., 86 F.R.D. 336, 341 (N.D.Ill.1979) (allowing nonunion members to represent union members when discrimination affected all equally.)

27. *See, e.g.,* Stastny v. Southern Bell Tel. & Tel. Co., 628 F.2d 267, 279–80 (4th Cir.1980).

inappropriate because the alleged discriminatory practice occurred only at the departmental level.[28]

Plaintiffs seeking class certification of employees working at multiple plants of a single employer often attempt to show a discriminatory practice or policy common to all such facilities or organizational units. A court has certified a class of employment applicants who had been rejected at multiple locations of the employer where evidence showed that their applications had been processed through one central location.[29]

Certain claims under Title VII, such as sexual harassment and retaliation, are often highly individualistic and fact-specific, and therefore less susceptible to class treatment under Rule 23(a).[30] Employees seeking certification of a class premised on alleged violations of the ADA face an especially difficult task in satisfying typicality. Allegations of an employer's failure to reasonably accommodate an employee necessarily focus on that person's particular disability. In *Lintemuth v. Saturn Corp.*, the court explained that "the highly personal nature of each representative's disability also subjects [his] claim[] to unique defenses under the ADA which are significant enough to destroy typicality."[31]

Plaintiffs often have difficulty satisfying the commonality and typicality requirements of Rule 23(a) when they bring claims of employment discrimination based on a theory of disparate treatment. Under a disparate treatment theory, plaintiffs attempt to show that they were treated less favorably than similarly situated employees of a different race or sex.[32] Disparate treatment claims usually focus on an employer's conduct towards specific persons. Because these claims generally are fact-specific and individualized, it is difficult to establish that the named plaintiff's claim is common and typical of all other claims. Plaintiffs seeking certification attempt to overcome this problem by demonstrating that the class member's claim was the result of a common pattern of discrimination by the employer. To advance this argument, it is necessary for the plaintiff to show that the alleged discrimination was "the standard operating procedure—the regular rather than the unusual practice."[33]

In contrast, adverse impact claims by their very nature appear to be more appropriate as "class claims." An adverse impact claim challenges employment practices that are "facially neutral in their treatment of different groups but ... in fact fall more harshly on one group than another and cannot be justified by business necessity."[34] For example, if

28. *See* Rosenberg v. University of Cincinnati, 118 F.R.D. 591, 594–95 (S.D.Ohio 1987).

29. *See* Kilgo v. Bowman Transp., Inc., 789 F.2d 859, 877–78 (11th Cir.1986).

30. *See* International Union, UAW v. LTV Aerospace, 136 F.R.D. 113, 130 (N.D.Tex.1991) (denial of class alleging sexual harassment); Hartman v. Wick, 600 F.Supp. 361, 366 (D.D.C.1984) (denial of class alleging retaliation).

31. 3 Am. Disabilities Cas. (BNA) 1490, 1493 (M.D. Tenn. 1994).

32. *See* International Brotherhood of Teamsters v. United States, 431 U.S. 324, 335 n. 15, 97 S.Ct. 1843, 1854 n. 15, 52 L.Ed.2d 396 (1977).

33. *Id.* at 336, 97 S.Ct. at 1855.

34. *Id.* at 336 n.15, 97 S.Ct. at 1855 n.15.

an employer institutes a policy requiring a college degree as a prerequisite for a clerical position, and that policy has a disproportionate adverse impact on black applicants, all black applicants without a college degree who were denied clerical positions would have a strong argument for class certification because they all would have common claims of discrimination.

(4) Statistics

The use of statistics in employment class actions presents additional strategic considerations. Plaintiffs often attempt to use statistics to advance employment class action claims under either a disparate treatment or disparate impact theory because evidence of statistically significant adverse treatment of protected groups can create an inference of discrimination, which is especially important in the absence of direct proof of discrimination.

Courts have become more sophisticated in their analysis of statistical data and more demanding of those who proffer such evidence. For example, plaintiffs often attempt to aggregate statistical data about all those adversely affected by certain employment decisions, regardless of position or organizational unit. To increase the probability that such data will be accepted as probative, plaintiffs' counsel may wish to focus specifically on the decision maker relevant to the proposed class or, if there is more than one such decision maker because the proposed class involves more than one organizational unit, to present the data broken down by unit and possibly to suggest the use of subclasses. Failure to follow such an approach can be problematical. In one case, for example, where the decisions at issue had been made at the departmental level, the court rejected the plaintiffs' proffered statistical analyses, stating that "[g]ross statistics are thus meaningless absent a departmental breakdown."[35] Where "[p]laintiffs' statistics grouped all employees together regardless of specialty or skill and failed to take into account nondiscriminatory reasons for the numerical disparities," another court rejected the analysis as seriously flawed.[36] As the Fifth Circuit has stated, "[t]he probative value of statistical evidence ultimately depends on all the surrounding facts, circumstances, and other evidence of discrimination."[37]

(5) Impact of the Civil Rights Act of 1991

Certification of race and sex discrimination class actions generally has been sought under Rule 23(b)(2). Certification of a class under Rule 23(b)(2) is appropriate only when plaintiffs seek final injunctive relief, and not in situations where the final relief consists exclusively or predominantly of money damages.[38] Following enactment of the Civil

---

35. Zahorik v. Cornell Univ., 729 F.2d 85, 95 (2d Cir.1984).

36. Furr v. Seagate Technology, Inc., 82 F.3d 980, 986–87 (10th Cir.1996).

37. *See* EEOC v. Texas Instruments, Inc., 100 F.3d 1173, 1184–86 (5th Cir.1996)

(citing Teamsters, 431 U.S. at 340, 97 S.Ct. at 1857).

38. *See* FRCP 23(b)(2), Advisory Committee Note, 1996 amendment.

Rights Act of 1991, which permits prevailing plaintiffs to recover compensatory and punitive damages, there has been an increase in employment class actions making demands for substantial monetary sums. In such cases, certification under Rule 23(b)(2) has become a topic of intense debate.

Some courts have stated that certification under Rule 23(b)(2) is permitted when the demand for money damages is merely incidental to the demand for injunctive relief.[39] The Supreme Court, however, has not yet ruled on this issue, but has stated in dicta that there is a "substantial possibility" that classes with monetary claims can only be certified under Rule 23(b)(3).[40] In employment class actions, where demands for monetary and injunctive relief are combined, some courts provide potential class members with the same opt-out rights that accompany certification under Rule 23(b)(3).[41] These cases are known as "hybrid class actions."

In addition, courts sometimes bifurcate a class action into two stages when there is a substantial monetary demand.[42] Stage one deals with the issues of liability and injunctive relief and is certified under Rule 23(b)(2). If liability is established, the court will then consider certifying the damages stage under Rule 23(b)(3), granting opt-out rights to employees with monetary claims to ensure due process. The decision to bifurcate employment class actions has become more controversial since passage of the Civil Rights Act of 1991, which provides for jury trials in Title VII actions. Because one jury often cannot sit for both stages of a lengthy bifurcated employment trial, the second jury, in the damages phase, may need to reconsider liability issues decided by the first jury. This problem undermines the utility of bifurcating many employment class actions involving a jury trial, because the trial on damages may need to encompass much, if not all, of what a single trial of the entire action would have contained.

(b) Opt–In Collective Actions

The second major type of employment class action is known as a "collective action." This special type of class action is authorized under the ADEA, the FLSA, and the Equal Pay Act, and is governed by the requirements of Section 216(b) of the FLSA.[43]

(1) Differences Between Collective Actions and Rule 23 Class Actions

The primary difference between collective actions and Rule 23 class actions is that Rule 23 actions have an opt-out procedure (under Rule

---

39. See, e.g., Edmondson v. Simon, 86 F.R.D. 375, 383 (N.D.Ill.1980). See also supra § 15.4.

40. See Ticor Title Ins. Co. v. Brown, 511 U.S. 117, 114 S.Ct. 1359, 128 L.Ed.2d 33 (1994) (per curiam).

41. See, e.g., Eubanks v. Billington, 110 F.3d 87, 94–95 (D.C.Cir.1997).

42. See Morgan v. UPS, 169 F.R.D. 349, 358 (E.D.Mo.1996).

43. 29 U.S.C.A. § 216(b) (West 1994).

23(b)(3)) and collective actions have an opt-in procedure. In a Rule 23 class action, each class member is bound by the judgment unless the person elects to opt-out of the class. In contrast, potential class members in a collective action are not bound by the result unless they have opted-in by filing a written consent with the court.[44]

Class actions and collective actions also differ in the criteria that plaintiffs must satisfy to meet the definition of a class. Unlike the Rule 23 prerequisites of numerosity, typicality, and the requirement that common questions of law and fact predominate, class members of a collective action must simply be "similarly situated."[45] Most courts have found that the Rule 23 class action criteria are inapplicable to collective actions.[46] Some courts, however, consider Rule 23 class action criteria as a guide in determining whether or not collective action plaintiffs have met the "similarly situated" test.[47]

(2) Two–Step Certification Process

Since the Supreme Court's 1989 decision in *Hoffmann–La Roche, Inc. v. Sperling*,[48] which made it clear that courts have discretion to authorize notice to potential class members in a collective action, courts have taken a two-step approach towards collective action certification.[49] The first step is conditional certification and notice to the putative class, and the second step is final certification or decertification.

Typically in collective actions, a representative plaintiff files suit (for ADEA claims, after filing a charge with the EEOC and receiving a notice of right to sue) and shortly thereafter (either before or after some preliminary discovery) files a motion asking the court to conditionally certify the class and authorize notice to potential class members. Alternatively, the employer may file a motion to strike the class. If the court conditionally certifies the class, a court-authorized notice is sent to potential class members. Among other things, the court may limit the geographic scope of the notice,[50] restrict the job positions included in the putative class, determine the contents of the notice,[51] and place a time limit after which plaintiffs will not be permitted to opt into the suit.[52]

---

44. *See id.*; Anderson v. Montgomery Ward & Co., 852 F.2d 1008, 1016 (7th Cir. 1988).

45. 29 U.S.C.A. § 216(b).

46. *See, e.g.*, Church v. Consolidated Freightways, Inc., 137 F.R.D. 294, 306 (N.D.Cal.1991); Owens v. Bethlehem Mines Corp., 108 F.R.D. 207, 209 (S.D.W.Va.1985).

47. *See* 7B Charles Alan Wright, Arthur R. Miller & Mary Kay Kane, Federal Practice and Procedure § 1752 (2d ed. 1986). *See also* Shushan v. University of Colorado, 132 F.R.D. 263, 268 (D.Colo.1990).

48. 493 U.S. 165, 169, 110 S.Ct. 482, 485, 107 L.Ed.2d 480 (1989).

49. *See, e.g.*, Mooney v. Aramco Servs. Co., 54 F.3d 1207, 1214 (5th Cir.1995).

Courts have discretionary authority to authorize notice but due process considerations do not require notice as they do in Rule 23 class actions, because the suit will not affect those plaintiffs who do not opt-in. *See, e.g.*, Allen v. Marshall Field & Co., 93 F.R.D. 438, 441–42 (N.D.Ill.1982).

50. *See, e.g.*, Pines v. State Farm General Ins. Co., 58 Fair Emp. Prac. Cas. (BNA) 387, 396 (C.D. Cal. 1992).

51. *See, e.g.*, Sperling v. Hoffman–La Roche, Inc., 118 F.R.D. 392, 404 (D.N.J. 1988).

52. *See, e.g.*, Pines, 58 Fair Emp. Prac. Cas. (BNA) at 397.

Once discovery is complete, the defendant typically will file a motion for decertification, and the court will either confirm certification or decertify the class.

(3) The "Similarly Situated" Requirement

In interpreting the "similarly situated" requirement of Section 216(b), the one issue on which courts agree is that the statute itself gives no guidance.[53] Courts tend to take an ad hoc approach, relying on the plain meaning of "similarly situated" and make the determination on a case-by-case, fact-specific basis. Although courts consider whether the plaintiffs are similarly situated in terms of their jobs, locations, and alleged harms, these factors appear unlikely to prove decisive if there are other issues that make it desirable to certify a class. The courts emphasize issues such as centralized decision making, the presence of a pattern or plan that connects the plaintiffs, and the variety and number of available defenses. Ultimately, courts appear to weigh the factors together, and will certify a class where a pattern or practice emerges, or where judicial economy suggest that the claims could best be handled in a collective action.

Some courts have stated that the standard for conditional certification is minimal, requiring only that plaintiffs allege the basis for a collective action in their complaint.[54] Other courts require "substantial allegations" that the proposed class members meet the requirement.[55] Many courts, while recognizing that conditional certification does not demand as strenuous a standard as final certification, demand at least some factual basis for the class allegations.[56]

After notice is sent, opt-ins are received, and discovery is completed, the court makes a final determination on certification, usually after the employer files a motion to decertify. The court may decide that the evidence is not enough to sustain the class certification, that the class is not sustainable under the "similarly situated" standard, or that the statute of limitations or other defenses bar some of the claims. For example, in *Lusardi v. Xerox*, the court decertified the class at the second stage, based in part on the disparate employment settings of the plaintiffs and the fact that the company's defenses differed for each plaintiff.[57]

---

53. *See* Lusardi v. Xerox Corp., 118 F.R.D. 351, 359 (D.N.J.1987) (citation omitted), *aff'd*, 975 F.2d 964 (3d Cir.1992); Garner v. G.D. Searle Pharmaceuticals & Co., 802 F.Supp. 418, 421 (M.D.Ala.1991) (citation omitted).

54. *See* Behr v. Drake Hotel, 586 F.Supp. 427, 431 (N.D.Ill.1984).

55. *See, e.g.,* Church v. Consolidated Freightways, Inc., 137 F.R.D. 294, 303–04 (N.D.Cal.1991).

56. *See, e.g.,* Severtson v. Phillips Beverage Co., 137 F.R.D. 264, 267 (D.Minn.

1991). *See also* D'Anna v. M/A–COM, Inc., 903 F.Supp. 889, 893–94 (D.Md.1995), in which the court recognized that the standard for determining if plaintiffs are "similarly situated" is lower for authorizing notice than for final certification, but demanded at least some factual support.

57. 118 F.R.D. at 359. *See also* Bayles v. American Medical Response, 950 F.Supp. 1053, 1067 (D.Colo.1996) (decertifying the class in an FLSA case).

(4) Strategies in Litigating Collective Actions

Plaintiffs in collective actions often strive to satisfy the "similarly situated" test by showing that there is a pattern, practice or plan of discrimination affecting the entire class.[58] For example, in *Pines v. State Farm General Ins. Co.*, the court granted conditional certification based on overtly age-based hiring recommendations contained in training manuals used throughout the company.[59] The court viewed the manuals as evidence of a corporate-wide discriminatory plan.[60]

One critical factor in collective actions is whether the employment decisions being challenged (such as layoffs due to a reduction-in-force) were made by a few high-level officials in a centralized office, or whether they were made by different supervisors at the division or departmental level.[61] Plaintiffs attempt to show that they are similarly situated by pointing to an employer's centralized decision making process, which affects the entire class. Defendants generally develop a line of attack to highlight the absence of similarities among the plaintiffs themselves as well as the potential class members.

Defendants sometimes attempt to limit or defeat certification if the decisions under scrutiny were made by different decision makers in separate departments or divisions, based on individualized facts and circumstances.[62] For example, in *Mooney v. Aramco Services Co.*, the Fifth Circuit upheld the district court's decertification of a class where a gradual downsizing of employees was executed in a decentralized manner by local supervisors, without a single, company-wide reduction-in-force.[63]

Plaintiffs often seek corporate-wide discovery to develop evidence of a common plan, pattern or practice of discrimination. The ability of an employer to preclude corporate-wide discovery is critical in defeating or limiting the scope of a collective action. Case law supports the position that in a proposed collective action, discovery often will be limited to those organizational or work units that made the decisions that are being challenged in the complaint of discrimination.[64]

As in Rule 23 employment class actions, the use of statistics and statistical experts is a frequent battleground in collective actions.[65] For example, when employers plan reductions-in-force, they generally conduct a statistical analysis of the impact that their actions will have on

58. *See, e.g.,* Frank v. Capital Cities Communications, Inc., 48 Fair Emp. Prac. Cas. (BNA) 551, 552–53 (S.D.N.Y. 1983).

59. *See* 58 Fair Emp. Prac. Cas. (BNA) at 397.

60. *See id.*

61. *See, e.g.,* Church v. Consolidated Freightways, Inc., 137 F.R.D. 294, 307–08 (N.D.Cal.1991); Lusardi, 118 F.R.D. at 359–61.

62. *See, e.g.,* Schwed v. General Elec. Co., 159 F.R.D. 373, 376–77 (N.D.N.Y. 1995).

63. 54 F.3d 1207, 1214–16 (5th Cir. 1995).

64. *See In re* Western Dist. Xerox Litigation, 140 F.R.D. 264, 269–71 (W.D.N.Y. 1991); Earley v. Champion Int'l Corp., 907 F.2d 1077, 1084–85 (11th Cir.1990).

65. *See, e.g.,* Garner v. G.D. Searle Pharmaceuticals & Co., 802 F.Supp. 418, 423 (M.D.Ala.1991).

protected groups, such as minorities, employees over the age of 40, and females. Plaintiffs attempt to obtain the employer's statistical analysis in discovery, and to the extent the employer's analysis shows an adverse impact on a particular group, plaintiffs argue that this establishes a pattern or practice of discrimination warranting class certification.

To preclude a litigation opponent from obtaining access to an employer's internal statistical analysis, employers often attempt to show that the analysis is privileged. If the statistical analysis was done in-house or by outside experts at the direction of counsel, it generally is protected by the attorney-client privilege. If it was prepared in anticipation of litigation, it is protected by the attorney work-product doctrine. Some employers argue that even if the statistical analysis was not prepared at the behest of counsel, it can still be withheld under the "critical self-analysis privilege." Although recognized by some courts, this latter theory does not have widespread support in employment litigation.[66]

Library References:

West's Key No. Digests, Federal Civil Procedure ☞184.
Wright, Miller & Kane, Federal Practice and Procedure: Civil 2d § 1752.

§ 15.29   Practice Checklist

(a) Seeking and Opposing Class Certification

(1) Whether a party should seek class certification is an important strategic decision in any litigation. While there are advantages in proceeding on behalf of a certified class, there are also many additional considerations that come into play when class certification is sought; the pros and cons of class certification should be weighed carefully by both the party seeking class certification and the opposing party. (*See* § 15.2)

(2) A plaintiff intending to seek class certification should address in the class action complaint all requirements for class certification under Rule 23(a) and the requirements of at least one subpart of Rule 23(b). Rule 23(a) requires the party seeking class certification to establish that the class is sufficiently numerous that joinder of class members is impracticable, that there are questions of law or fact common to all class members' claims, that the claim of the representative party is typical of the claims of class members, and that the representative and its counsel will adequately represent the class. Rule 23(b) has four subparts, which generally speaking allow class certification where the party opposing the class may face conflicting duties, where the disposition of one class member's claim may as a practical matter impact the ability of other class members to pursue their claims, where the party opposing the class has acted on grounds generally applicable to the class for purposes of equitable relief, or where common questions predominate class members' claims and a class action would be superior to other methods of litigation. (*See* FRCP 23(a) & (b); §§ 15.3–15.5)

---

66. *See* Etienne v. Mitre Corp., 146   F.R.D. 145, 146–48 (E.D.Va.1993).

(3) A motion for class certification should be filed as soon as practicable; local rules may require submission of such motions within defined time periods. Discovery may be appropriate in connection with the class motion and the court may elect to conduct an evidentiary hearing. (*See* FRCP 23(c)(1); § 15.7)

(4) A party seeking class certification must be prepared to address basic due process concerns and, in some cases, issues of subject matter jurisdiction. When an action is not based on federal question jurisdiction, it may be necessary in some circumstances for each class member in federal court to establish that its individual claim meets the jurisdictional minimum, or that its claim shares a common nucleus of operative fact with another claim properly before the court. Some state courts also may have limits on subject matter jurisdiction. (*See* §§ 15.6 and 15.9)

(5) Where a national class is sought (based on substantive state law), the jurisdiction in which the action is filed may have important repercussions with respect to, for example, statute of limitations issues. (*See* § 15.19(b))

(6) A party opposing class certification, in addition to responding to arguments raised by the moving party, should in the appropriate case explore management problems presented by choice of law considerations. (*See* FRCP 23(b)(3); § 15.19)

(b) The Class Certification Determination

(1) Although statutes of limitation on the claims of class members may be tolled pending a decision on class certification, such statutes typically begin to run again if and when class certification is denied, or when a putative class member excludes itself from the class. However, a class action may not operate to toll statutes of limitations in a subsequent class action. (*See* § 15.11)

(2) Standing and mootness considerations take on particular importance in class actions. Such considerations continue to be important through appellate review. Under current law, determinations regarding class certification in federal court are not appealable as of right; where appeal ultimately is taken as to class issues, there may be limits as to class members' standing to pursue the appeal. (*See* §§ 15.2(d), 15.10)

(3) If a class is certified, notice may be necessary or advisable. Also, counsel's ability to communicate with class members after class certification may be subject to considerations different from those that obtained prior to class certification. (*See* FRCP 23(c)(2) and (d)(2); §§ 15.8, 15.21(a)–(c))

(4) The method of notice to class members should be the best practicable under the circumstances, and the notice must fairly apprise class members of their rights and responsibilities. It is particularly in the interest of the party opposing the class that notice be fully adequate, to ensure a binding judgment. (*See* FRCP 23(c)(2); § 15.8)

(5) Class action certification may be limited to certain issues, or may involve subclasses. Parties opposing class certification, in particular,

should be alert to the possibility that the class for which certification is sought may be overly broad. (*See* FRCP 23(c)(4); § 15.12)

(c) Judgments and Settlements in Class Actions

(1) Judgments in class actions are intended to bind absent class members; a judgment in an action certified under FRCP 23(b)(3) is limited to those to whom notice was directed, who have not excluded themselves, and who the court finds to be members of the class. As with any action, the validity of a judgment in a class action is dependent on subject matter jurisdiction and personal jurisdiction over the defendant. Class actions, however, present additional issues as to adequacy of representation, adequacy of notice, and personal jurisdiction over absent plaintiff class members. (*See* FRCP 23(c)(2) and (3); §§ 15.6, 15.15)

(2) Settlements of class actions in federal court requires court approval under FRCP 23(e). Federal procedure allows settlement classes, but even where classes are certified for settlement purposes only the substantive requirements of Rule 23(a) and (b) should be considered. Parties wishing to fashion settlement classes must be particularly attuned to notice and adequacy issues, and to the possibility of conflicts among actual or potential class members if the class is overly broad. (*See* FRCP 23(e); § 15.16)

(3) Specific procedures have developed concerning settlement classes, involving preliminary approvals, opportunities to object, and final approval hearings. A court is not expected in passing on a proposed settlement to resolve the merits of the claims; rather, the court is expected to determine whether the proposed settlement is within a zone of reasonableness, from the standpoint of absent class members' interests. (*See* § 15.17)

(4) Attorneys' fees are often awarded on a "common fund" basis in class actions. Different courts take different approaches to computing fee awards; moreover, claims that allow for statutory fee awards may present different considerations. (*See* §§ 15.20, 15.21(g))

(d) Miscellaneous Points to Remember

(1) Rule 23 also allows for defendant class actions. (*See* § 15.13)

(2) Claims have been certified for class treatment in a wide variety of substantive areas, including antitrust, securities, mass torts, consumer fraud, patent actions, copyright and trademark actions, and employment litigation. (*See* §§ 15.22–15.28)

§ 15.30　Forms

(a) Form of Complaint Including Class Action Allegations in Federal Court 🖫

IN THE UNITED STATES DISTRICT COURT
FOR THE _____ DISTRICT OF _____

	)	CIVIL ACTION NO.
	)	
	)	
Plaintiffs,	)	COMPLAINT
	)	
v.	)	
	)	
Defendants.	)	CLASS ACTION
	)	
	)	
	)	JURY TRIAL DEMANDED

COMPLAINT

Parties

1. Plaintiffs are [allegations of identity and capacity that indicate standing].

2. Defendants are [allegations of identity and capacity in relation to plaintiffs].

Jurisdiction and Venue

3. This Court has jurisdiction over the subject matter of this action pursuant to [statutory bases for jurisdiction] because [allegations of diversity of citizenship, amount in controversy, federal questions and/or other bases for jurisdiction].

4. Venue is proper in this Court because [statutory and/or other bases for venue].

Definition Section

5. [If necessary].

Class Action Allegations

6. Plaintiffs bring this action as a class action pursuant to Federal Rule of Civil Procedure 23, on behalf of themselves and a class of persons similarly situated.

7. The class is defined herein, as follows: [describe characteristics common to all class members].

8. The class is sufficiently numerous that joinder of all members is impracticable insofar as, upon information and belief, the class is comprised of approximately [number of class members].

9.   There are questions of law and fact common to the class. These questions include, among others, [identify common questions and make factual allegations in support thereof].

10.   The claims of the representative parties are typical of the claims of the class. [Factual allegations supporting typicality].

11.   Plaintiffs will fairly and adequately protect the interests of the class. The interests of plaintiffs are representative and coincident with, not antagonistic to, those of the remainder of the class. [Factual allegations supporting adequacy of named plaintiffs]. In addition, plaintiffs are represented by experienced and able counsel [factual allegations supporting adequacy of class counsel].

12.   In addition, the prosecution of separate actions by individual members of the class would create a risk of

[(i) inconsistent or varying adjudications with respect to individual members of the class that would establish incompatible standards of conduct for defendants,] [and/or]

[(ii) adjudications with respect to individual members of the class that would as a practical matter be dispositive of the interests of the other members not parties to the adjudications or substantially impair or impede their ability to obtain compensatory or equitable relief,] [and/or]

[(iii) defendants have acted or refused to act on grounds generally applicable to the class, thereby making appropriate final injunctive relief or corresponding declaratory relief with respect to the class as a whole,] [and/or]

[(iv) (a) the questions of law and fact common to the members of the class predominate over any questions affecting individual members, and

(b) class treatment is a superior method for the fair and efficient adjudication of the issues in dispute because it permits a large number of injured parties, joinder of whom is impracticable, to prosecute their common claims in a single forum simultaneously, efficiently and without the duplication of effort and expense that numerous individual actions would engender. There are no difficulties likely to be encountered in the management of this class action that would preclude its maintenance as such, and no superior alternative exists whereby the relative rights of plaintiffs, class members and defendants can be fairly managed.

[(c) class members have no interest in individually controlling the prosecution of separate actions, and no other litigation has been commenced by or against any class member concerning the controversy]. [Note that if class is certified on basis of allegations of this & 12 (iv) (a-c) notice to all class members is required.]

[Factual allegations supporting 12 (b) basis for class claim].

Substantive Allegations

13.   [Factual allegations giving rise to claims].

COUNT I:

14.   Plaintiffs hereby incorporate by reference paragraphs 1—__, inclusive, as if fully set forth herein.

15.   [Allegations of elements of cause of action].

COUNT II:

16.   Plaintiffs hereby incorporate by reference paragraphs 1—__, inclusive, as if fully set forth herein.

17.   [Allegations of elements of cause of action].

Jury Trial Demanded

18.   Plaintiffs demand a trial by jury of all issues so triable in this case.

Prayer for Relief

WHEREFORE, plaintiffs pray that:

A.   The Court determine that this action may be maintained as a class action under Federal Rule of Civil Procedure 23, that plaintiffs are proper class representatives and that the best practicable notice of this action be given to the members of the class represented by plaintiffs;

B.   Plaintiffs and other members of the class recover the general and special compensatory damages determined to have been sustained by each of them respectively, including, but not limited to, [allegations regarding nature of damages] and that judgment therefore be entered herein against defendants in an amount to be determined;

[C. The Court issue an order requiring defendants to perform [description of remedial relief sought] for the benefit of plaintiffs,]

[D. In the alternative, the Court order the creation of monetary funds to be funded entirely by defendants, the purpose of which will be to enable plaintiffs to provide [description of remedial relief sought];]

E.   The Court grant such other, further or different relief as may be deemed just and proper.

DATED:

_____

[Signature, attorney and firm
name and address]

(b) Form of Answer Including Response to Class Action Allegations ▣

IN THE UNITED STATES DISTRICT COURT
FOR THE _____ DISTRICT OF _____

```
                                      )
IN RE: _____                        )
LITIGATION                            )
                                      )   MASTER FILE NO. _____
_____)
                                      )
This Document Relates to:             )
                                      )
CIVIL ACTION NO. _____              )
[Name of Plaintiff]                   )
_____)
```

ANSWER OF DEFENDANT _____

TO THE COMPLAINT OF _____

Defendant _____ answers the Complaint of plaintiffs _____ (collectively "Plaintiffs") in accordance with its numbered paragraphs as follows:

1. _____ lacks knowledge or information sufficient to form a belief as to the truth of the allegations contained in paragraph 1 and therefore denies them.

2. _____ admits the allegations contained in paragraph 2 that [describe facts admitted]. _____ denies the remaining allegations contained in paragraph 2; it lacks knowledge or information sufficient to form a belief as to the truth of the allegations regarding [ ] and therefore denies them.

3. _____ lacks knowledge or information sufficient to form a belief as to the truth of the allegations regarding the plaintiffs, the other defendants or this Court's subject matter jurisdiction pursuant to _____, and therefore denies them.

4. [_____ lacks knowledge or information sufficient to form a belief as to the truth of the averments of paragraph 4 and therefore denies them] [if appropriate].

5. _____ admits that plaintiffs define [_____] as set forth in paragraph 5. _____ denies that paragraph 5 embodies a correct definition of the word [_____].

6. _____ admits that plaintiffs allegedly bring this action on behalf of themselves and a class of persons similarly situated. _____ denies that this can proceed as a class action pursuant to Fed.R.Civ.P. 23.

7–12. The allegations of paragraphs 7–12 are allegations as to representation of absent persons. _____ [has moved to require the elimination of such allegations, and] denies that this action may proceed as a class action under Fed.R.Civ.P. 23 [insert appropriate subsections]. By way of further answer, the allegations of paragraphs 7–12 constitute conclusions of law to which no further response is required.

13–18. [Admit, deny or otherwise, as appropriate].

First Affirmative Defense

[Defenses specific to the claims].

WHEREFORE, _____ prays that plaintiffs' claims be dismissed, that judgement be entered in its favor, that it be awarded its costs and attorneys' fees and that the Court award such further relief as is just.

DATED:

_____

[Signature, attorney and firm name and address]

(c) Notice of Certification of Litigation Class and Exclusion Form 🖫

IN THE UNITED STATES DISTRICT COURT
FOR THE _____ DISTRICT OF _____

IN RE: _____   )   MASTER FILE NO. _____
LITIGATION   )
)
_____)
)
THIS DOCUMENT RELATES TO:)
ALL ACTIONS   )
_____)

NOTICE OF CLASS ACTION LITIGATION RELATING
TO _____ CLAIMS

This Notice is being sent to you pursuant to an Order of the United States District Court for the _____ District of _____ and Rule 23(c)(2) of the Federal Rules of Civil Procedure. The purpose of this Notice is to inform you of the pendency of a class action in which you are a member of a class. You are being informed of these matters so that you may make appropriate decisions as to what steps you may wish to take in relation to this litigation.

PLEASE READ THIS NOTICE CAREFULLY AND IN ITS ENTIRETY. THIS IS THE FIRST COURT NOTICE YOU HAVE RECEIVED OF THIS ACTION, REGARDLESS OF WHAT OTHER NOTICES YOU MAY HAVE RECEIVED IN THE PAST CONCERNING [NATURE OF THE ACTION] OR ANY OTHER LEGAL PROCEEDING.

1. There are now pending in the United States District Court for the _____ District of _____ claims brought by the following: [list plaintiffs]. These plaintiffs have brought suit on behalf of themselves, and all [others similarly situated/others (description)].

The complaint alleges that [brief description of factual basis for claims]. The complaint seeks [compensatory damages, punitive damages, and equitable relief,] and alleges that defendants should bear the cost of [remedial action, if applicable]. Plaintiffs' theories of liability include [list types of causes of action alleged, _e.g._, negligence, intentional tort, etc.].

2. The defendants are as follows: [list full name of each defendant].

Defendants deny that they are liable for any claim asserted by plaintiffs and they intend to pursue numerous affirmative defenses to plaintiffs' claims.

3. The court has not passed upon any of the contentions of the parties. The sending of this Notice is not to be construed as an expression of any opinion by the court about the merits of any claims or defenses. The foregoing is only a summary of the contentions of plaintiffs and defendants. The pleadings and other records of this litigation more fully reflect the respective contentions of the parties. You or your counsel may review the pleadings and other papers filed at the Office of the Clerk, United States District Court, [address].

4. On _____, 19__, this court certified a class action in this proceeding under Rule 23(b)(3) of the Federal Rules of Civil Procedure. The plaintiff class consists of all [general description of plaintiffs], more particularly defined as follows:

[Repeat verbatim class description included in class certification order]. This class certification does not imply a conclusion that any person or entity within the class was injured as a result of [alleged cause of harm]. This class applies to all claims for compensatory damages and equitable relief and participation in the class is voluntary. You are automatically a member of the class unless you exclude yourself, as more fully described in paragraph 7.

WHAT YOU MUST DO TO PROTECT YOUR RIGHTS:

5. If you fall within the definition of the class as set forth above, you are automatically a member of the class. [If applicable: The Court has determined that the class will be further defined to include the following subclasses: (1) class members who [circumstances particular to a sub-group of class members], (2) class members with [circumstances particular to a sub-group of class members] and (3) class members who have [other circumstances] (not specified in (1) or (2) above). A given class member may have only [circumstances in (1), circumstances in (2), circumstances in (3),] or any combination thereof.]

If you wish to exclude yourself from the class, for whatever reasons, you may elect to do so and you may opt-out.

6. If you exclude yourself from the class, you will not be bound by any determination in the class. You will be free to initiate your own independent law suit, but you will not share in any recovery on behalf of the class or any other benefit that may result from the class action litigation.

7. You may exclude yourself from the class only if you request exclusion in writing by signing and mailing the enclosed Exclusion Request to the Clerk, United States District Court for the _____ District of _____, P. O. Box _____, City, State, Zip Code, no later than midnight, _____, 19__. The filing of a law suit on your own behalf does not constitute a request for exclusion from the class. Failure to mail such request may preclude you from later being excluded.

8. If you do not exclude yourself by _____, 19__, from the class, you will be bound by any class judgment, whether or not favorable, and you may, but need not, enter an appearance in this action through counsel of your choosing. If you choose to enter an appearance through your own legal counsel, you will be liable for the legal fees of your personal counsel. Otherwise, the named plaintiffs and their counsel will represent your interests as a member of the class. Class members will not have to personally pay any of the attorneys' fees or cost of counsel whose services benefit this class litigation. To the extent that any monetary recovery is ultimately obtained on behalf of the class, your share of any recovery will be assessed, along with all others, on a pro rata or other fair and equitable basis prior to distribution, for the costs and expenses of this action, including such counsel fees as may be awarded by the court. A list of class counsel is available from the Clerk of Court at the address listed on the Notice of Exclusion.

9. If you wish to remain a member of the class for all purposes, you need do nothing at this stage of the proceedings.

10. Requests for changes of address, and inquiries regarding this Notice should be sent to:

Clerk, United States District Court for
the _____ District of _____
[In re: _____ Litigation,
Master file No. _____]
P.O. Box _____
_____ Street—Room _____

City, State Zip Code

_____
[Name]
Clerk of Court
U. S. District Court for the
_____ District of _____

Dated: _____, 19__

IN THE UNITED STATES DISTRICT COURT
FOR THE _____ DISTRICT OF _____

```
                                )
IN RE: _____                 )   MASTER FILE NO. _____
LITIGATION                      )
_____   )
                                )
THIS DOCUMENT RELATES TO:)
ALL ACTIONS                     )
_____   )
```

REQUEST FOR EXCLUSION FROM LITIGATION CLASS

TO: [Name]
    Clerk of Court
    P.O. Box _____
    City, State Zip Code

      DO NOT COMPLETE THIS FORM IF YOU WISH TO
      REMAIN A MEMBER OF THE LITIGATION CLASS

PLEASE TAKE NOTICE THAT _____

_____
               (Print name of person

_____
         or other entity requesting exclusion)

_____
                 (Print address)
hereby requests to be excluded from the Litigation Class.

_____   _____
(Date)   (Signature)

                     _____
                     (Print Name of Signator and
                     relationship of Signator to party
                     requesting Exclusion)

(THE DEADLINE FOR MAILING THIS COMPLETED FORM IS _____, 19__.)